GARNER'S
MODERN
ENGLISH
USAGE

Other Books Written or Edited by Bryan A. Garner

Black's Law Dictionary
(Thomson Reuters, 10th ed. 2014)

The Chicago Guide to Grammar, Usage, and Punctuation
(Univ. of Chicago Press, 2016)

The Chicago Manual of Style, ch. 5, "Grammar and Usage"
(Univ. of Chicago Press, 16th ed. 2010)

Garner on Language and Writing
with foreword by Justice Ruth Bader Ginsburg (ABA, 2009)

HBR Guide to Better Business Writing
(Harvard Business Review Press, 2013)

Quack This Way: David Foster Wallace and Bryan A. Garner Talk Language and Writing
(RosePen, 2013)

Garner's Dictionary of Legal Usage
with foreword by Judge Thomas M. Reavley (Oxford Univ. Press, 3d ed. 2011)

The Oxford Dictionary of American Usage & Style
(Oxford Univ. Press, 2000)

Reading Law: The Interpretation of Legal Texts
with Justice Antonin Scalia (Thomson/West, 2012)

Making Your Case: The Art of Persuading Judges
with Justice Antonin Scalia (Thomson/West, 2008)

The Redbook: A Manual on Legal Style
(West, 3d ed. 2013)

Legal Writing in Plain English
(Univ. of Chicago Press, 2d ed. 2013)

The Winning Brief
(Oxford Univ. Press, 3d ed. 2014)

The Elements of Legal Style
with foreword by Charles Alan Wright (Oxford Univ. Press, 2d ed. 2002)

Guidelines for Drafting and Editing Legislation
with foreword by Judge Harriet Lansing (RosePen, 2016)

Ethical Communications for Lawyers
(LawProse, 2009)

The Winning Oral Argument
(West, 2009)

The Rules of Golf in Plain English
with Jeffrey Kuhn (Univ. of Chicago Press, 4th ed. 2016)

A New Miscellany-at-Law
by Sir Robert Megarry (Hart, 2005)

Texas, Our Texas: Remembrances of the University
(Eakin Press, 1984)

Securities Disclosure in Plain English
(CCH, 1999)

Basic Law Terms
(West Group, 1999)

Criminal Law Terms
(West Group, 2000)

Family Law Terms
(West Group, 2001)

Business Law Terms
(West Group, 1999)

GARNER'S MODERN ENGLISH USAGE

FOURTH EDITION

Bryan A. Garner

OXFORD
UNIVERSITY PRESS
2016

OXFORD

UNIVERSITY PRESS

This book is a successor to three editions (1998, 2003, 2009) of *Garner's Modern American Usage*.

Oxford University Press is a department of the University of Oxford.
It furthers the University's objective of excellence in research,
scholarship, and education by publishing worldwide.

Oxford New York

Auckland Cape Town Dar es Salaam Hong Kong Karachi
Kuala Lumpur Madrid Melbourne Mexico City Nairobi
New Delhi Shanghai Taipei Toronto

With offices in

Argentina Austria Brazil Chile Czech Republic France Greece
Guatemala Hungary Italy Japan Poland Portugal Singapore
South Korea Switzerland Thailand Turkey Ukraine Vietnam

Oxford is a registered trade mark of Oxford University Press
in the UK and certain other countries.

Published in the United States of America by
Oxford University Press
198 Madison Avenue, New York, NY 10016
www.oup.com

Library of Congress Cataloguing-in-Publication Data is available upon request.

978-0-19-049148-2

3 5 7 9 8 6 4

Printed in the United States of America
on acid-free paper

To my beloved brothers,

Bradley Alan Garner
Cincinnati Conservatory of Music
Cincinnati, Ohio

Blair Arthur Garner
America's Morning Show
Nashville, Tennessee

and

**In memory of my late friends and mentors,
all of whom I dearly miss**

Professor Sheridan Baker (1918–2000)
The University of Michigan Department of English
Ann Arbor, Michigan

Dr. Robert W. Burchfield (1923–2004)
Editor in Chief, The Oxford English Dictionary Department
The University of Oxford

Hon. Thomas Gibbs Gee (1925–1994)
United States Court of Appeals for the Fifth Circuit
Houston, Texas

Professor Alan M.F. Gunn (1906–1989)
Texas Tech University Department of English
Lubbock, Texas

Tex Lezar, Esq. (1948–2004)
Former colleague at Carrington, Coleman, Sloman & Blumenthal
Dallas, Texas

Rt. Hon. Sir Robert Megarry (1910–2006)
Vice-Chancellor of the Supreme Court (U.K.)
Lincoln's Inn, London

Professor Roy M. Mersky (1925–2008)
Tarlton Law Library, The University of Texas
Austin, Texas

Justice Antonin Scalia
Supreme Court of the United States
Washington, D.C.

Professor Pat Sullivan (1924–2008)
West Texas A&M Department of English
Canyon, Texas

Professor John W. Velz (1930–2008)
The University of Texas Department of English
Austin, Texas

David Foster Wallace (1962–2008)
Pomona College Department of English
Claremont, California

Professor Charles Alan Wright (1927–2000)
The University of Texas School of Law
Austin, Texas

"Usage . . . is the surest pilot in speaking, and we should treat language as currency minted with the public stamp. But in all cases we have need of a critical judgment."
—Quintilian, ca. A.D. 88

"Modern faults of usage have two causes: indifference or rebellious recklessness, spurning rules; and half study, which finds specious justification for forms that are not really sound."
—Edward N. Teall, 1940

"To treat the sick, you must have a good knowledge of the healthy. But it is even better to know something about the disease. If the writer means to fight for the best possible use of language, he must be forever on his guard against the ailments that words are prone to."
—Konstantin Fedin, ca. 1950

"Presumably a youngster should be able to distinguish between *good* and *well*, between *done* and *did*, and if youngsters do not learn this naturally, as those in literate homes do, they must be taught the usage in school. There is at least as much reason to teach them to say, 'He invited Mary and me' as there is to teach them how to brush their teeth, to shift gears, or to ride in an airplane."
—Charlton Laird, 1970

"Language must take its place alongside diet, traffic safety, and the cost of living as something that everyone thinks about and talks about."
—Dwight Bolinger, 1980

"Standard American English—the English of our dictionaries and grammar books—is a great, messy deluge of words, some of which overlap in meaning, many of which have multiple meanings, and many of which can be used as various parts of speech. . . . Everyone who chooses to use Standard English must make an endless series of decisions about the language, and thereby has a say in how it develops."
—Barbara Wallraff, 2000

Contents

Preface to the Fourth Edition

With this new edition, Oxford University Press has decided to rename the book *Garner's Modern English Usage*—using *English* instead of *American*. That change restores what had been the idea behind the first edition. The implied global emphasis of *English* makes more sense today than ever before, given the book's broadly inclusive approach to World English, not just to American English and British English.

Through the Internet, we have access to the largest database for corpus linguistics ever compiled: the Google database of English-language books printed throughout the world. The use of big data in these pages doubtless makes *GMEU* the most thoroughly empirical work of its kind. I am grateful to the legal department of Google for arranging for me to be the first author explicitly licensed to reproduce results from the Google Ngram Viewer, which shows graphs depicting the relative frequency of specified sequences of words within the corpus of English-language books as compared with other sequences. From this big-data resource, it has become possible to calculate ratios on word frequency and phrase frequency in World English and in the two major subtypes: American English and British English. These ratios, found at the end of many entries, provide some fascinating data: the frequency of one form (the prevalent one) as contrasted with another (a variant).

Of course, the ngram data can hardly be viewed as infallible. There may be a false sense of precision in a ratio such as 4,376:1 (the idea that one word appears in print precisely 4,376 times for every one time that its variant appears). It may well be that the most current ratios available—for the year 2008—aren't as fully reliable as those for earlier years because the books having been scanned are a smaller proportion of the whole universe of candidates. (Still, the corpus includes 206,272 books just for 2008.) There may be other shortcomings. Nevertheless, on balance it seemed better to provide the data than not to, on the stipulation that readers mustn't view the ratios as immutable truth. Instead, these snapshots of the language, especially when viewed in their relationship to usage over time, can provide a sound basis for understanding linguistic developments and usage trends.

To arrive at accurate numbers, I used Google ngrams with contextualized searches within the 2012 Google corpus. The power of these ngrams would have astonished earlier lexicographers—just as it astonished me at first. They take much of the guesswork out of linguistic assessments of Standard Written English. Their reliability was confirmed to me time and again when I compared the results against other major corpora. We can now determine that the phrasal verb *to home in on* arose in English print about 1932. (The original metaphor related to homing pigeons.) We're also able to know that the variant form *to hone in on* emerged about seven years later and has never been as frequent a choice in published books. It now trails by a nearly 1.7-to-1 ratio.

That's in printed books throughout the English-speaking world. In British books, it's a 4-to-1 ratio. In American books, the ratio is 1.6 to 1. So in American English the variant has gained more ground. Anyone who attentively listens to American speech will notice that most people (perhaps 80%?) say *to hone in on*. Who are they? Mostly ordinary people. And who says *to home in on*? Mostly well-read people—subscribers to *The New York Review of Books*, *The New Yorker*, *The Atlantic Monthly*, or the like. That's supportable only by anecdotal evidence—one observer having tested this hypothesis on thousands of audiences over a 20-year period. Yes, the question fascinates me, and I've had the good fortune of being able to administer quizzes containing this issue to over 50,000 people on three continents. The evidence isn't entirely anecdotal, except that I've had to take people at their word about their reading habits.

The phrasing *to hone in on* began as a simple error—an example of WORD-SWAPPING, in which a term gets replaced by its near-homophone. Professional editors tend to stick to the original formulation, but in this instance the speech habits of English speakers, especially American ones, are increasingly at odds with what appears in well-edited English. At some point the editorial preference for the original phrasing (*to home in on*) will probably shift. But we're not yet to that point.

Ascertaining the facts about usage with ngrams is trickier than it might seem: you can't just search *home in* vs. *hone in*. You'd get many false positives for every reference in English-language books to a *home in Malibu*, etc., with hundreds of thousands of misleading results, if not millions. So I contextualized the searches, usually by inflecting a verb: *homed in on* vs. *honed in on*. (Google ngrams allow you to use up to five consecutive words for the purpose of contextualizing.) In that search, we've inflected the verb and included a terminal preposition to achieve precise results. A little ingenuity was required to arrive at many of the ratios displayed throughout the text.

With some phrases, big-data research is exceedingly difficult. With *as such*, for example, its rightness depends entirely on what has been said in the preceding sentence: what is the antecedent of *such*? A Google ngram can't tell you that. So with some words and phrases for which useful ngram data couldn't be gathered, no comparative information could be supplied. Either the ratios wouldn't be meaningful (as with *shapable* [AmE] vs. *shapeable* [BrE], or *supervisorial* [one sense] and *supervisory* [different sense]), or else no suitable search could be framed (as with the adverbial forms *supplely* vs. *supply* [the latter, of course, being much more frequent as a noun or verb], or *solon* [as contrasted with what?]). A fair amount of thought went into these decisions throughout. Where ratios do appear, it should be clear to you what is being compared against what (prevalent form vs. variant)—for which you may need to read the words within the entry just above. Where desirable, the search terms are supplied within parentheses, as when a reader might have reasonable doubts about what's being compared.

One of the advantages of big data is that outlier instances become trivial. In saying that *Christmas bazaar* is standard and **Christmas bizarre* a solecism (marked here by the asterisk), it matters not that a certain writer might have written, "I thought Christmas bizarre that year." In the larger scheme of big data, that odd instance becomes unimportant as against the others in which writers have mistakenly used the noun phrase **Christmas bizarre* in place of the standard phrase to refer to a seasonal marketplace.

A pessimist might well wonder why it's useful to record a 25,000-to-1 ratio (a few such huge discrepancies in usage are noted). The answer is one that you could hardly appreciate until you're suddenly in an argument with someone who insists that the outlier usage is correct. One of the virtues of a reliable usage guide is to settle debates between language aficionados, or between editor and author. The empirical evidence here marshaled reduces the degree of opinion involved in such matters.

How you think about the ratios is central to decisions about good usage. The ngrams give you diachronic evidence of usage (over, let's say, the past 300 years). They also allow you to calculate ratios for any given year within the span, up to the year 2008. That's the most recent time for which reliable statistics are available. Hence all my mentions of the "current ratio" refer to materials published in 2008. The ratios show a snapshot of usage as it existed in that year.

For those wishing to replicate my research results, the "smoothing" for the ngrams was set at 3, the database was English worldwide, and the year was 2008 (unless specified otherwise). Simply use the Google search engine to find "Ngram Viewer," and you'll soon discover the many delights that ngrams have to offer.

Let me illustrate the lexicographic utility of big data by citing what is in itself a point of only slight importance. When did the standard *hark back* start morphing into **hearken back*? (Again, the asterisk marks a nonrecommended variant.) According to

Webster's Dictionary of English Usage (1989)—and repeated in its update of 2002—the variant just doesn't appear in BrE: "We have no evidence that *hearken back* is establishing itself in British use, though it has occasional use in the U.S." That statement is an extrapolation based on the impressive Merriam-Webster lexicographic files compiled over the years through its reading program.

But with a few seconds of research using ngrams, it's possible to see that the variant **hearken back* first appeared in published British books in 1860 and occurred in other British writing throughout the 20th century. It didn't appear in American books with any appreciable frequency until 1887. In both varieties of English it began increasing significantly about 1960. In 1989, when *Webster's Dictionary of English Usage* was first published, the phrase *hark back* outranged **hearken back* in AmE by a 10-to-1 ratio, and in BrE by a 28-to-1 ratio. So the inroads have indeed been greater on the American side. It's also possible now to see that **harken back* occurred more frequently in print than **hearken back* from 1965 to 2000 in AmE, and from 1985 to 2000 in BrE—but only during those periods. In any event, both **hearken back* and **harken back* are variant phrases that have never seriously rivaled the standard phrase (*hark back*) in Standard Written English.

So the earlier usage commentators cited negatively by Merriam-Webster—Theodore Bernstein (1970) and Roy Copperud (1980)—were actually correct in their editorial recommendations against the variants. "They think it must be a mistake," intones the Merriam-Webster book. Well, yes. A variant newcomer that's just a by-form of an established term is going to be viewed as an editorial mistake. When Bernstein and Copperud were writing, it was probably a Stage 1 misusage, possibly Stage 2. The fact that Merriam-Webster's files contained a few instances of the linguistic interlopers hardly confirmed their full acceptability. In fairness, though, the Merriam-Webster editors were trying to extrapolate from the relatively sparse evidence they had.

Let's consider another simple yet even more obscure example: is the word for a wheelbarrow or dumpcart designed for farm use spelled *tumbrel* or *tumbril*? The word dates from the 14th century in English. The *OED* and most other dictionaries record the primary entry under *tumbrel*, and that was indeed the predominant spelling through the 18th century. But beginning about 1800, the spelling *tumbril* began to dominate. By 1830, its prevalence as the leading form in print sources was unquestioned, and the *-el* spelling has never again seriously rivaled the *-il* spelling. We know this from Google ngrams. Yet the dictionaries would lead you to conclude otherwise. This is an infinitesimal microcosm of the valuable information now available to us all.

It's interesting to speculate about why the change from *tumbrel* to *tumbril* occurred when it did, at the beginning of the 19th century. The fourth edition of a dictionary called *The Complete Farmer*, published in the 1790s, lists only the spelling *tumbrel* and defines it as "a dung-cart." There must be clues elsewhere.

The 1938 edition of the *Funk & Wagnalls New Standard Dictionary of the English Language* lists as one meaning of *tumbrel*: "A type of cart in which victims were carried to the guillotine during the first French Revolution [1787]: an erroneous use." *Webster's Second New International Dictionary* (1934) contains a similar definition (it's missing from the *OED*). Mentions of the word *tumbrel* spiked in the late 1780s and 1790s. The switch to the spelling *tumbril* occurred in 1800 in AmE and in the early 1820s in BrE. Could it be that farmers, especially those who wrote about farm-related subjects, wished to avoid, in their ordinary mentions of dumpcarts, associations with the bloody guillotines of revolutionary France and therefore chose the other spelling? That's just speculation. But such little discoveries hold the possibility of many new avenues of research.

Hark back and *tumbril* are just two tiny instances. Multiply those by 5,000 (for a usage guide)—or, ultimately, by a million (for a truly unabridged English dictionary). The degree of ascertainable knowledge about the language is greater than ever before.

In the past, lexicographers (including me) were playing a guessing game: presented with seven instances, four of them going one way and three another, the dictionary-writer would have to make an educated guess about what forms predominated in print. Their evidence was scanty and often unrepresentative. Now lots of guesswork has been eliminated by the powerful tool of big data; lexicography is being revolutionized. Certainly this book has been revolutionized. Every page has been reworked or confirmed by using the extraordinary help of big data.

Mind you, from its very inception in the late 1990s, this book has made copious use of many linguistic corpora. It's just that the corpus now available is incomparably more vast than what was available when the previous editions were written.

Have my editorial recommendations changed because of big data? Yes—a few of them. But on the whole, ngrams have borne out the overwhelming majority of judgments expressed in my earlier usage books. Used carefully, with sophistication, the ngrams allow much greater certainty about usage: dates, changes over time during the full period of Modern English, relative frequencies, and geographic limitations. These possibilities make it an exciting time to be a lexicographer.

One recurrent finding bears note. All varieties of English are powerfully influenced by American English. When my late friend Robert W. Burchfield was editor in chief of the *Oxford English Dictionary Supplement* in the 1970s, he noted that the center of gravity for the English language had shifted to North America. He was right. Again and again, one sees British English and World English following the lead of American usage, often with a lag time of 10 to 50 years. You'll see this trend noted in many entries throughout the book—but of course it's hardly a universal rule.

In this new edition, I've used the same basic techniques and sensibilities that I've always used: given the evidence that I have before me, what judgments would such eminent predecessors such as H.W. Fowler and Theodore Bernstein have made? That's what guides me. But you can read more about that in the rest of the front matter, if you care to—and as I'd encourage you to.

Bryan A. Garner
Dallas, Texas
15 November 2015

Preface to the First Edition

Not long ago, while I was standing at a rental-car counter in Austin, a young clerk told me that a free upgrade to a Cadillac might be available. She would have to see whether any Cadillacs were on the lot just then.

Two minutes passed as she typed, got on the telephone, twirled her hair around her index finger, and then typed some more. Finally, I said, "Can I get the upgrade?"

"You mean, 'May I get the upgrade,'" she responded.

I thought I had imagined it. "What?"

"You said, '*Can* I get the upgrade.' What you mean is, '*May* I get the upgrade.'"

As it happens, I had been working on the manuscript for this book only minutes before, so I couldn't help thinking how surreal the experience was. I felt a twinge of indignation on the one hand—the kind that almost anyone feels when corrected. But I also thought that her remark was charming in a way. She was doing her best to uphold good English.

But she was wrong, and I gently told her so: "I'm not asking for your permission. I want to know whether you have a Cadillac on the lot. I want to know whether it's physically possible for me to drive one of them. So: '*Can* I get the upgrade.'"

"Oh, I guess you're right," she said with resignation.

Experiences like that one give me hope: they show that some people still care about what happens to our language, however misplaced their concern might occasionally be.

The State of the Language

Do I contend that the language is decaying? That it was once in a pristine state and has been sliding ever since? That the glory days are over?

No, I don't. In many ways, writing today is better than ever. Our best journalists today are as talented a group as has ever worked in the language.

But a great deal of mediocre writing appears in print nowadays, and both written and oral assaults on the language do seem to come at high velocities. The speed comes from mass communications. Turn on the TV and listen to commentators on football, tennis, or golf, and you'll be treated to the heights of inarticulacy. Then imagine all the millions of viewers whose linguistic perceptions are affected by this blather.

There are good, clarifying forces at work on the language. There are also bad, obscuring forces at work. One language, many realities.

The reality I care about most is that some people still want to use the language well. They want to write effectively; they want to speak effectively. They want their language to be graceful at times and powerful at times. They want to understand how to use words well, how to manipulate sentences, and how to move about in the language without seeming to flail. They want good grammar, but they want more: they want rhetoric in the traditional sense. That is, they want to use language deftly so that it's fit for their purposes.

This book is for them.

First Principles

Before going any further, I should explain my approach. That's an unusual thing for the author of a usage dictionary to do—unprecedented, as far as I know. But a guide to good writing is only as good as the principles on which it's based. And users should naturally be interested in those principles. So, in the interests of full disclosure, here are the ten critical points that, after years of working on usage problems, I've settled on:

1. **Purpose.** The purpose of a usage dictionary is to help writers, editors, and speakers use the language effectively: to help them sound grammatical but relaxed, refined but natural, correct but unpedantic.
2. **Realism.** To guide users helpfully, recommendations on usage must be genuinely plausible. They must recognize the language as it currently stands, encourage reasonable approaches to editorial problems, and avoid refighting battles that were long ago lost.
3. **Linguistic Simplicity.** If the same idea can be expressed in a simple way or in a complex way, the simple way is better—and, paradoxically, it will typically lead readers to conclude that the writer is smarter.
4. **Readers' Reactions.** Generally, writing is good if readers find it easy to follow; writing is bad if readers find it hard to follow.
5. **Tightness.** Omitting needless words is important. As long as it's accurate, the briefest way of phrasing an idea is usually best because the brevity enhances speed, clarity, and impact.
6. **Word-Judging.** A word or phrase is somewhat undesirable if it has any one of the following characteristics, and is worse if it has two or more:
   (a) it sounds newfangled;
   (b) it defies logic;
   (c) it threatens to displace an established expression (but hasn't yet done so);
   (d) it originated in a misunderstanding of a word or its etymology;
   (e) it blurs a useful distinction.
7. **Differentiation.** If related words—especially those differing only in the suffix—begin to take on different senses, it's wise to encourage the latent distinctions when they're first emerging and then to follow them once they're established.
8. **Needless Variants.** Having two or more variant forms of a word is undesirable unless each one signals a distinct meaning.
9. **Conservatism.** If two constructions are current, and one of them has been widely condemned by authorities whose values are in line with those outlined in #6, the other construction is better.
10. **Actual Usage.** In the end, the actual usage of educated speakers and writers is the overarching criterion for correctness. But while actual usage can trump the other factors, it isn't the only consideration.

Reasonable though these points may seem to the professional writer or editor, they're likely to induce hissy fits among modern linguists, for whom #10 is the only valid concern (and only after deleting the word *educated*). The problem for professional writers and editors is that they can't wait idly to see what direction the language takes. Writers and editors, in fact, influence that direction: they must make decisions.

And a good usage dictionary should help in those decisions. H.W. Fowler's groundbreaking *Dictionary of Modern English Usage* did that in 1926 and for generations after; Theodore M. Bernstein's book *The Careful Writer* did it in 1965; and Wilson Follett's *Modern American Usage* did it in 1966. That has traditionally been the job of the usage dictionary: to help writers and editors solve editorial predicaments.

The State of the Genre

Somewhere along the line, though, usage dictionaries got hijacked by the descriptive linguists, who observe language scientifically. For the pure descriptivist, it's impermissible to say that one form of language is any better than another: as long as a native speaker says it, it's okay—and anyone who takes a contrary stand is a dunderhead. That has become something of a dogma among professional linguists.

Essentially, descriptivists and prescriptivists are approaching different problems. Descriptivists want to record language as it's actually used, and they perform a useful function—though their audience is generally limited to those willing to pore through vast tomes of dry-as-dust research. Prescriptivists—not all of them, perhaps, but enlightened ones—want to figure out the most effective uses of language, both grammatically and rhetorically. Their editorial advice should accord with the predominant practices of the best writers and editors.

For the pure descriptivist, it's silly to say that *infer* shouldn't be "misused" for *imply*. Presumably, it's also silly to say that *Hobson's choice* is the correct phrase and that *Hobbesian choice* is an ignorant error, because much evidence can be found for the latter. Likewise, we shouldn't prohibit any other example of what is here called WORD-SWAPPING. The extreme view is that even spell-checkers are a bad force because they ensure uniformity and stifle linguistic experimentation in spelling.[1]

Although there's little new to be said about this debate, this book does something quite new: it gathers reams of current linguistic evidence to show the many confusions into which writers fall. And they're constantly falling into them. As Joseph Epstein, the longtime editor of *The American Scholar*, has observed, "The English language is one vast San Andreas fault, where things are slipping and sliding every moment."[2] English usage is so challenging that even experienced writers need guidance now and then.

Quotations and Citations

This book contains thousands of quotations from published sources. Most are from newspapers, but many are from books and scholarly journals. These quotations came to my hand in various ways.

First, they came from my own reading. For many years, I've traveled a good deal, and whenever I go somewhere I make a point of reading and marking at least one local newspaper, usually more. When I return, I enter those sentences into my database.

Second, I have dozens of allies—members of the H.W. Fowler Society, an informal organization I founded—who send me clippings from newspapers. These Fowlerians, who are spread throughout the English-speaking world, have contributed enormously to the book with hundreds of examples.

Third, I've supplemented entries with examples gleaned from two online databases: NEXIS and WESTLAW. For two decades, they have provided full-text searchability for millions of published documents—a luxury that earlier lexicographers never enjoyed.

But before delving further into online sources, I should address a question that many readers will wonder about. Should I really name names? Should I give full citations in the way that I do? Won't it mortify a journalist to find some badly written sentence frozen in a reference book for all the world to see?

Well, I hope it isn't mortifying, and for me it's nothing new. I used the technique in the second edition of my *Dictionary of Modern Legal Usage* (1995). The citations appear for three reasons. First, they show that the examples are real, not fabricated. Second, they show the great variety of evidence on which the judgments in this book are based. And third, they're lexicographically noteworthy: they reflect how the language is being used in our culture in our time.

I have tried to be dispassionate in choosing examples. More of them come from my favorite newspaper, *The New York Times*, than from any other source: nearly 400 of the some 5,600 illustrative quotations. But a glance at the text will show that they're from all over the country. And many are British.

---

[1] See Sidney Landau, "Of Lexicography, Computers, and Norms," 64 *Am. Speech* 162, 163 (1989) ("I detest even the idea of spelling-correction programs. If they do not serve any heuristic purpose, they are pernicious by artificially limiting the range of spelling choices . . . . We thus artificially limit language change . . . and push all our students toward a common center of officially endorsed usages.").

[2] Joseph Epstein, "Mr. Fowler, He Live," *Weekly Standard*, 20 Jan. 1997, at 29.

Why should British quotations be included, given that this is a dictionary of *American* usage? Most often the reason is that it seems useful to record differences and similarities between British and American English. It's sometimes surprising to learn that a given error occurs much more frequently in British English (see, for example, **hark back (b)**).

Yet the book is American, both in its scope and in its point of view. During the mid-20th century, the English language's center of gravity shifted from England to the United States. And with that shift comes a certain responsibility on the part of those who speak and write American English.

Lexicographic Methods

It's fair to say that the guidance given here is based on a greater corpus of current published writings than any usage guide ever before published. For contemporary usage, the files of our greatest dictionary makers pale in comparison with the full-text search capabilities now provided by NEXIS and WESTLAW. So the prescriptive approach here is leavened by a thorough canvassing of actual usage in modern edited prose.

When I say, then, that *ethicist* is 400 times more common than *ethician*, I have searched vast databases of newspapers and journals to arrive at this round figure. As for those particular terms, the NEXIS databases (as of December 1997) contain 10,138 published documents in which *ethicist* appears, but only 25 documents in which *ethician* appears. (The ratio in WESTLAW's "allnews" database is 7,400 to 6.) So much for the dictionaries that give the main listing under *ethician*. They're out of step: the compilers might have 5 or 10 citation slips in their files, but that's a paltry number when compared with mountains of evidence that the searching of reliable databases can unearth. [Fourth-edition update: Google's ngrams show that the ratio in English-language books as of 2008 was 148 to 1.]

And when I say that *self-deprecating* (traditionally viewed as incorrect) is 50 times as common as *self-depreciating* (traditionally viewed as correct), I have searched those same databases to give this conservative figure. From 1980 to 1997, *self-deprecating* appeared in 16,040 NEXIS sources, and *self-depreciating* in only 353. (The ratio in WESTLAW is 9,860 to 159.) So much for the usage books that continue to recommend *self-depreciating*: that battle is lost. [Fourth-edition update: Google's ngrams show that the ratio in English-language books as of 2008 was 24 to 1.]

In this respect—the consideration of voluminous linguistic evidence to back up judgment calls—this book represents a radical departure from most other usage dictionaries.

Value Judgments

As you might already suspect, I don't shy away from making judgments. I can't imagine that most readers would want me to. Linguists don't like it, of course, because judgment involves subjectivity. It isn't scientific. But rhetoric and usage, in the view of most professional writers, aren't scientific endeavors. You don't want dispassionate descriptions; you want sound guidance. And that requires judgment.

Essentially, the ideal usage commentator needs to be both a scholar and a critic. The poet Robert Bridges knew that, when it comes to language, value judgments are crucial:

> Scientific philologists will often argue that phonetic decay is a natural process, which has always been at work, and has actually produced the very forms of speech that we value most highly; and that it is therefore a squeamish pedantry to quarrel with it at any particular stage, or to wish to interfere with it, or even to speak of decay or corruption of language, for that these very terms beg the question, and are only the particular prejudice of particular persons at a particular

time. But this scientific reasoning is aesthetic nonsense. It is absurd to pretend that no results of natural laws should be disapproved of because it is possible to show that they obey the same laws as the processes of which we approve. The filthiest things in nature are as natural as the loveliest: and in art also the worst is as natural as the best: while the good needs not only effort but sympathetic intelligence to attain and preserve it. It is an aesthetic and not a scientific question.[3]

At the same time, though, aesthetic judgments aren't enough. Bridges overstated the case: when we analyze language, scientific concerns should certainly enter the equation. But he was right, in this little-known passage, to skewer the doctrine on which descriptivism is largely based:

> [I]t is no fancy to see a beauty in human speech, and to prefer one [form of] language to another on account of such beauty, and to distinguish the qualities that make the beauty. Learning that forbids such an attitude is contemptible.[4]

Yet this willingness to judge should be tempered by scholarship. H.W. Fowler best embodied the qualities of the scholar-critic. He was a lexicographer, true, but he was also a literary critic. He wasn't exclusively one or the other. His interests were those of the professional editor more than those of the professional linguist. He shared that quality with Theodore Bernstein and Wilson Follett, but he knew more about linguistics than either of those writers. That knowledge was something he had in common with Bergen Evans, but he had better literary and editorial judgment than Evans, and he was confident in exercising that judgment. No one else has quite matched Fowler's blend of interests and talents: though not infallible, he was the most formidable prescriptive grammarian of the 20th century.

The touchstone for commenting on usage, then, is a mixture of scholarship and criticism. Whether I've reached it or not, that has been my goal.

An Autobiographical Note

What possesses someone to write a dictionary of usage? People frequently ask me that question about my *Dictionary of Modern Legal Usage*. I'll try to give an answer.

I realized early—at the age of 15—that my primary intellectual interest was the use of the English language. The interest might be partly genetic. My grandfather, Frank Garner of Amarillo, had more than a passing interest in language. This was magnified three or four times in my father, Gary T. Garner of Canyon, a true language aficionado. And then, as my father tells it, his interest seemed to be magnified a hundredfold in me. It became an all-consuming passion.

This passion has taken various forms at different times in my life. When I was 15 it consisted primarily in building my vocabulary. Then I discovered general semantics—the works of S.I. Hayakawa, Wendell Johnson, Stuart Chase, and Alfred Korzybski. Because I grew up in a university town—small though it was—these and other books were readily accessible. I read everything I could find on the subject.

Then, on a wintry evening while visiting New Mexico at the age of 16, I discovered Eric Partridge's *Usage and Abusage*. I was enthralled. Never had I held a more exciting book. I spent hours reading his advice on the effective use of words and his essays on everything from Johnsonese to précis writing. He kept mentioning another author, by the name of Fowler, so when I got back to Texas I sought out Fowler's *Modern English Usage*. And that book turned out to be even better.

Suffice it to say that by the time I was 18, I had committed to memory most of Fowler, Partridge, and their successors: the Evanses, Bernstein, Follett, and Copperud.

---

[3]Robert Bridges, *A Tract on the Present State of English Pronunciation* 15–16 (1913).

[4]*Id.* at 16.

I knew where they differed, and I came to form opinions about whose positions were soundest on all sorts of questions. I knew the work of those writers then better than I do today.

Yet my linguistic influences weren't just in books. Dr. Pat Sullivan of the English Department at West Texas A&M encouraged me from a very early age; from him I learned both transformational and traditional grammar. And my brother's godfather, Professor Alan M.F. Gunn of the English Department at Texas Tech University, nurtured my literary interests during his twice-yearly visits with our family.

College presented a wealth of opportunities. While at the University of Texas, I studied the history of the English language (in the English Department) and the Latin and Greek element in English (in the Classics Department), as well as Latin and French. Though I never mastered Old English, I acquired a passing knowledge of the Middle English of Chaucer and Gower. Two summers at Oxford University—where I studied Chaucer and T.S. Eliot—deepened my appreciation of how language and literature intersect. It was at Oxford that I first got to know Robert W. Burchfield, the editor of the *Supplement to the Oxford English Dictionary* (then underway), and Christopher Ricks, one of the great modern literary critics.

While at Texas and Oxford, I attended many lectures by noted linguists (who, not being positive influences, shouldn't be named). The second most bothersome thing, in my view at the time, was that they were dogmatically descriptive in their approach. The most bothersome thing was that they didn't write well: their offerings were dreary gruel. If you doubt this, go pick up any journal of linguistics. Ask yourself whether the articles are well written. If you haven't looked at one in a while, you'll be shocked.

At any rate, I gravitated away from the Linguistics Department and toward English and Classics. I ended up writing a thesis on the Latin influences in Shakespeare's language, excerpts from which made their way into learned journals. My mentors were John W. Velz, a Shakespearean of the first rank, and Thomas Cable, whose history of the English language (with Albert Baugh) is a classic.

Velz made many suggestions about what to publish, and where. As a 22-year-old budding scholar, I was honored to have an article published alongside one by Velz himself in an issue of *Shakespeare Studies*. Unfortunately, that very article of mine contains a linguistic gaffe that has found its way into the pages of this book: see **bequest.**

In any event, by the time I was an undergraduate—emboldened by Professor Velz's assurances that my work was worthy of publication—I knew that I would one day write a book in my favorite genre: a dictionary of usage.

This one is my second. The first, *Modern Legal Usage*, I wrote between 1981 and 1986; the first edition was published by Oxford University Press in 1987. In 1991, Oxford asked me to undertake this book, and I finished it at the beginning of 1998.

It is the product of a warped sense of fun: the idea that there's nothing more delightful than passing the hours chasing down linguistic problems in dictionaries and other reference books.

You know my approach. You know my influences. Discount the advice as you think advisable. No usage critic is infallible—certainly not I. But be assured that I have tried to know the literature in the field, to examine great quantities of linguistic evidence, and to use my best judgment as a professional writer and editor.

Acknowledgments

As with each previous edition of this book, I've been fortunate to have help from many quarters. At LawProse, Inc., my colleagues Karolyne H.C. Garner, Jeff Newman, Tiger Jackson, Becky R. McDaniel, Ryden McComas Anderson, and John S. Adams have provided invaluable help in suggesting and researching entries, finding illustrative examples, calculating and verifying ratios of frequency, and proofreading the manuscript. Others who performed valuable tasks were my project assistants, Mia Taylor and Esther Lee, and the Garner Law Scholars at two law schools: at Southern Methodist University School of Law, Jessica L. Kirk and William K. Knisley; and at Texas Tech University School of Law, Elizabeth Nanez.

At Oxford University Press, Casper Grathwohl, Damon Zucca, and Maxwell Sinsheimer provided valuable insights at many steps in the evolution of this new edition. At the composition house in Cleveland, Jeff Lachina and his staff produced beautifully set, accurate page proofs that made the final product clean and readable. Special thanks go to Chris Black, who managed the prepress operation with remarkable deftness.

I've had excellent suggestions along the way from any number of readers—thousands of them, in fact. Among the most prolific contributors were the late Sheridan Baker, Robert Ballou, Isabel Barzun, Charles Harrington Elster, Alexandra B. Garner, Caroline B. Garner, Gary T. Garner, Shmuel Gerber, Mark Halpern, Joseph Kimble, Karen Larsen, Nicholas Lemann, Thomas B. Lemann, Karen Magnuson, Jonathan McCall, John E. McIntyre, Brian Melendez, Alison Parker, Sir Christopher Ricks, the late Justice Antonin Scalia, Merrie Spaeth, Randall Tietjen, John R. Trimble, the late John W. Velz, Edward T. Wahl, Richard S. Walinski, Barbara Wallraff, Jeffrey S. Westbrook, and the late Charles Alan Wright. At Google, Jon Orwant (the deviser of Google's ngrams) and Darryl Chiang (of the legal department) proved enormously helpful.

It has been gratifying over the years to hear from so many people who are interested in English usage. This new edition has benefited from their support and enthusiasm.

B.A.G.

List of Essay Entries

This book contains essentially two types of entries: (1) word entries, which discuss a particular word or set of words; and (2) essay entries, which address larger questions of usage and style. For ease of reference, the essay entries—which appear throughout the book in small capitals—are listed below.

ABBREVIATIONS
- A. Acronyms and Initialisms
- B. Resulting Redundancies
- C. Initialese
- D. Plurals

-ABLE
- A. Choice of -able or -ible
- B. Attaching -able to Nouns
- C. Attaching -able to Intransitive Verbs
- D. Converting -ate Verbs into -able Adjectives
- E. Dropping or Retaining the Medial -e-

ABSOLUTE CONSTRUCTIONS

ABSTRACTITIS

ADJECTIVES
- A. Definition
- B. Noncomparable Adjectives
- C. Coordinate Adjectives
- D. Proper Names as Adjectives
- E. Adjectives vs. Adverbs
- F. Past-Participial Adjectives
- G. Phrasal or Compound Adjectives
- H. Modification of Adjectives Ending in -ed
- I. Adjectives Ending in -ly
- J. Adjectives That Follow the Noun
- K. Dates as Adjectives
- L. Comparative and Superlative Adjectives
- M. Animal Adjectives
- N. Adjectives as Nouns
- O. Adjectives as Verbs
- P. Nouns as Adjectives
- Q. Adjectives–Noun Disagreement

ADVERBS
- A. Placement of Adverbs
- B. Awkward Adverbs
- C. Double Adverbs
- D. Adverbs vs. Adjectives

AE

-AGOG(UE)

-AHOLIC; -AHOLISM

AIRLINESE

ALLITERATION
- A. Pleasant Examples
- B. Unpleasant Examples

AMERICANISMS AND BRITICISMS
- A. Generally
- B. Americanisms Invading BrE
- C. Briticisms Invading AmE
- D. Related Entries

ANACHRONYMS

ANIMAL ADJECTIVES

ANTE-; ANTI-

ANTICIPATORY REFERENCE

APPOSITIVES

ARCHAISMS
- A. Generally
- B. Mistakes Caused by Archaism

-ATABLE

-ATHLON

BACK-FORMATIONS

BE-VERBS
- A. Wrongly Omitted in Nonfinite Uses
- B. Circumlocutions with Be-Verbs
- C. For say
- D. Reduplicative Copula: is is

BI-; SEMI-

BUREAUCRATESE

-C-; -CK-

CANNIBALISM

CAPITALIZATION
- A. Generally
- B. Overcapitalizing
- C. Titles
- D. Up-Style Headings
- E. All Capitals
- F. Small Caps
- G. After Colon
- H. Names

-CAST

CASUALISMS
- A. Generally
- B. Changes over Time
- C. Shortened Forms
- D. Proliferation

-CE; -CY

CENTURY DESCRIPTIONS

CHRONOLOGY

-CIDE

CLASS DISTINCTIONS

CLICHÉS

CO-
- A. Hyphenation with
- B. Attaching to Noun Phrase
- C. When Unnecessary

COLLECTIVE NOUNS
- A. Number
- B. BrE vs. AmE

COMMERCIALESE

COMPARATIVES AND SUPERLATIVES
- A. Choice Between Comparative and Superlative
- B. Which to Use—Suffixes or more and most?
- C. Be-Verbs Repeated After Comparatives
- D. The Double Comparative

List of Abbreviations

adj. = adjective

adv. = adverb

AHD = *The American Heritage Dictionary of the English Language* (5th ed. 2011)

Am. = American

AmE = American English

arch. = archaic

A.S. = Anglo-Saxon

Aus. = Australian

BBBM = Charles Harrington Elster, *The Big Book of Beastly Mispronunciations* (2d ed. 2005)

Br. = British

BrE = British English

c. = century

ca. = (*circa*) around

Can. = Canadian

cap. = capitalized

cf. = (*confer*) compare with

COD = *The Concise Oxford Dictionary of Current English* (8th ed. 1990)

colloq. = colloquial

conj. = conjunction

DAEU = Margaret Nicholson, *A Dictionary of American-English Usage* (1957)

DARE = *Dictionary of American Regional English*

DCAU = Bergen Evans & Cornelia Evans, *A Dictionary of Contemporary American Usage* (1957)

ed. = edition; editor

e.g. = (*exempli gratia*) for example

Eng. = English

esp. = especially

ex. = example

fig. = figuratively

FMEU1 = H.W. Fowler, *A Dictionary of Modern English Usage* (1926)

FMEU2 = H.W. Fowler, *A Dictionary of Modern English Usage* (Ernest Gowers ed., 2d ed. 1965)

FMEU3 = R.W. Burchfield, *The New Fowler's Modern English Usage* (1996)

fr. = from; derived from; found in

Fr. = French

G.B. = Great Britain (i.e., England, Scotland, and Wales)

Ger. = German

Gk. = Greek

ibid. = (*ibidem*) in the same source

i.e. = (*id est*) that is

Irl. = Ireland

Ital. = Italian

Jap. = Japanese

L. = Latin

l.c. = lowercase

lit. = literally

L.J. = Law Journal

L. Rev. = Law Review

MAU = Wilson Follett, *Modern American Usage: A Guide* (1966)

ME = Middle English

MWDEU = *Merriam-Webster's Dictionary of English Usage* (1989)

n. = noun

no. = number

NOAD = *The New Oxford American Dictionary* (3d ed. 2010)

Norw. = Norwegian

obs. = obsolete

OE = Old English

OED = *The Oxford English Dictionary* (2d ed. 1989)

OED Supp. = *A Supplement to the Oxford English Dictionary* (4 vols., 1972–1986)

OF = Old French

OGEU = *The Oxford Guide to English Usage* (1983)

orig.	=	originally	s.v.	=	(*sub verbo*) under the word
p.	=	page	trans.	=	translator
phr.	=	phrase	U&A	=	Eric Partridge, *Usage &*
pl.	=	plural			*Abusage* (1942)
pmbl.	=	preamble	U.K.	=	United Kingdom (i.e., Great
pp.	=	pages			Britain and—since 1922—
p.pl.	=	past participle			Northern Ireland)
prep.	=	preposition	U.S.	=	United States
pron.	=	pronoun	USGPO	=	United States Government
pr.pl.	=	present participle			Printing Office, *A Manual*
pt.	=	part			*of Style* (rev. ed. 1986)
quot.	=	quotation	usu.	=	usually
repr.	=	reprinted	vb.	=	verb
rev.	=	revised by; revision	v.i.	=	intransitive verb
RH2	=	*The Random House Diction-*	v.t.	=	transitive verb
		ary of the English Language	W2	=	*Webster's New International*
		(2d ed. 1987)			*Dictionary of the English*
Russ.	=	Russian			*Language* (2d ed. 1934)
Scot.	=	Scottish	W3	=	*Webster's Third New Inter-*
sing.	=	singular			*national Dictionary of the*
SOED	=	*The New Shorter Oxford*			*English Language* (1961)
		English Dictionary (1993)	W11	=	*Merriam-Webster's Colle-*
Sp.	=	Spanish			*giate Dictionary* (11th
specif.	=	specifically			ed. 2003)
			WNWCD	=	*Webster's New World College*
					Dictionary (5th ed. 2014)

Pronunciation Guide

ə	*for all the vowel sounds in* amok, burger, but		n	*as in* note, clown
a	*as in* fact, vat		ñ	*the nasalized French* n *as in* contretemps, Saint-Saëns
ah	*as in* calm, father		ng	*as in* long, plank
ahr	*as in* bar, start		o	*as in* hot, posh
air	*as in* flare, lair		oh	*as in* loan, home
aw	*as in* tall, law		oi	*as in* join, ploy
ay	*as in* page, same		oo	*as in* rule, tomb
b	*as in* balk, job		oor	*as in* poor, lure
ch	*as in* chief, bench		or	*as in* board, court
d	*as in* deck, red		ow	*as in* plow, loud
e	*as in* leg, ferry		p	*as in* poem, drop
ee	*as in* flea, tidy		r	*as in* rank, hear
eer	*as in* mere, tier		s	*as in* cite, seek, pass
f	*as in* fence, off		sh	*as in* sharp, trash
g	*as in* go, mug		t	*as in* time, boot
h	*as in* harp, hold		th	*as in* thin, math
hw	*as in* which, while		<u>th</u>	*as in* there, bathe
i	*as in* rib, akin		uu	*as in* took, pull
ɪ	*as in* time, eye		v	*as in* vague, shiver
j	*as in* jump, magic		w	*as in* witch, away, suede
k	*as in* calm, keep, quit, school		y	*as in* year, union
l	*as in* lever, pill		z	*as in* zone, please
m	*as in* muck, drum		zh	*as in* measure, vision

Key to the Language-Change Index

Stage 1: A new form emerges as an innovation (or a dialectal form persists) among a small minority of the language community, perhaps displacing a traditional usage.

Stage 2: The form spreads to a significant fraction of the language community but remains unacceptable in standard usage.

Stage 3: The form becomes commonplace even among many well-educated people but is still avoided in careful usage.

Stage 4: The form becomes virtually universal but is opposed on cogent grounds by a few linguistic stalwarts (die-hard snoots). See the entry for **snoot**, p. 840.

Stage 5: The form is universally accepted (not counting pseudo-snoot eccentrics).

Expressions that are invariably poor usage are marked with an asterisk (*). For a more expansive explanation of the index, see pp. l–li.

If the index were not measuring change, but instead were expressing static linguistic phenomena, many serviceable analogies would come to mind. I list ten of them here simply to help readers envision the levels of acceptability intended to be conveyed by the idea of stages. We begin with the notation that appears at the bottom of each right-hand page, and then have the ten analogies.

Literal Shorthand References
Stage 1: Rejected
Stage 2: Widely shunned
Stage 3: Widespread but . . .
Stage 4: Ubiquitous but . . .
Stage 5: Fully accepted

School-Grade Analogy
Stage 1: F
Stage 2: D
Stage 3: C
Stage 4: B
Stage 5: A

Golf Analogy
Stage 1: Quadruple bogey
Stage 2: Triple bogey
Stage 3: Double bogey
Stage 4: Bogey
Stage 5: Par

Olfaction Analogy
Stage 1: Foul
Stage 2: Malodorous
Stage 3: Smelly
Stage 4: Vaguely odorous
Stage 5: Neutral

Skill-Level Analogy
Stage 1: Bungler
Stage 2: Hack
Stage 3: Rank amateur
Stage 4: Amateur
Stage 5: Professional

Military-Discharge Analogy
Stage 1: Dishonorable discharge
Stage 2: Bad-conduct discharge
Stage 3: Discharge for the good of the service
Stage 4: General discharge
Stage 5: Honorable discharge

Etiquette Analogy
Stage 1: Audible flatulence
Stage 2: Audible belching
Stage 3: Overloud talking
Stage 4: Elbows on table
Stage 5: Refined

Traffic-Penalty Analogy
Stage 1: $500 fine and jail time
Stage 2: $300 fine
Stage 3: $100 fine
Stage 4: Warning ticket
Stage 5: No stop

School-Discipline Analogy
Stage 1: Expulsion
Stage 2: 2-month suspension
Stage 3: 2-week suspension
Stage 4: 1-hour detention
Stage 5: No disciplinary action

Moral Analogy
Stage 1: Mortal sin
Stage 2: Capital sin
Stage 3: Venial sin
Stage 4: Peccadillo
Stage 5: Virtue

Parliamentary-Discipline Analogy
Stage 1: Expulsion
Stage 2: Censure
Stage 3: Reprimand
Stage 4: Warning
Stage 5: No action

Making Peace in the Language Wars

Bryan A. Garner

"This battle between linguistic radicals and
linguistic conservatives continues unabated."
—Robert W. Burchfield

Shortly after the first edition of my *Modern American Usage* appeared in 1998, a British reviewer—the noted linguist Tom McArthur—remarked about it: "Henry Watson Fowler, it would appear, is alive and well and living in Texas."[1] This might have seemed like the highest praise possible. After all, in the American press in the 1980s and 1990s, Fowler had been hailed as "immortal" (*Fortune*), "urbane" (*Boston Globe*), and even "saintly" (*L.A. Times*). Meanwhile, his 1926 *Dictionary of Modern English Usage* had been called "classic" (*New York Times*) and "indispensable" (*Christian Science Monitor*)—"one of the great works in and of the language" (*L.A. Times*).

But McArthur didn't intend much, if any, praise in his comment. Fowler, you see, was a prescriptivist: he issued judgments about linguistic choices.[2] McArthur, like almost every other linguist, is a descriptivist: he mostly disclaims making judgments about linguistic choices.[3] And the describers and the prescribers (if I may call them that) haven't been on speaking terms for a very long time.

The Wars

Prescribers seek to guide users of a language—including native speakers—on how to handle words as effectively as possible. Describers seek to discover the facts of how native speakers actually use their language. An outsider might think that these are complementary goals. In fact, though, insiders typically view them as incompatible. And the battles have been unpleasant, despite being mostly invisible (or irrelevant) outside academic linguistic circles. Hence David Foster Wallace's apt query: "Did you know that probing the seamy underbelly of U.S. lexicography reveals ideological strife and controversy and intrigue and nastiness and fervor on a nearly hanging-chad scale?"[4]

Prescribers like to lambaste their adversaries for their amoral permissiveness:

- **1952:** "Some of the vigilantes who used to waylay your themes to flog each dangling participle and lynch every run-on sentence now seem to be looking for a chance to lay the language on your doorstep like a foundling and run like hell before you can catch them and ask them how to rear the brat. They're convinced that it's healthy, that it will grow up very well-adjusted provided it's never spanked or threatened or fussed over. They're perfectly willing to furnish you with its past history, and even help you keep records on its day-to-day development, but they'll only tell you what it has done, not what it should or should not do. The English grammar textbook of

---

[1] ". . . That Is Forever Fowler," 15 *English Today* 59 (1999).

[2] See H.W. Fowler & F.G. Fowler, *The King's English* (1906); H.W. Fowler, *A Dictionary of Modern English Usage* (1926). For a solid biography of H.W. Fowler, see Jenny McMorris, *The Warden of English* (2001).

[3] See "Descriptive and Prescriptive Grammar," in *The Oxford Companion to the English Language* 286 (Tom McArthur ed., 1992) ("A *descriptive grammar* is an account of a language that seeks to describe how it is used objectively, accurately, systematically, and comprehensively.").

[4] David Foster Wallace, "Tense Present: Democracy, English, and the Wars over Usage," *Harper's Magazine*, Apr. 2001, at 39, 40.

the future may approach its subject in the same spirit in which the Kinsey report tackled sex."[5]

- **1965:** "The ideal philologist regards the 'misuse' of language as a psychiatrist regards murder: just one more phenomenon of human behaviour."[6]

- **1967:** "The linguisticists . . . are urgently, even fanatically, storming the classroom in order to persuade the old-fashioned grammar teacher that she, too, should be dispassionate in her attitude toward language so that the attitude of linguisticism can prevail: let her just accept the view that there are merely 'different' levels of usage—*not* 'good' and 'bad,' 'acceptable' and 'unacceptable'—and all will be well."[7]

- **2000:** "Modern-day linguists who insist on a 'nonjudgmental' approach to language like to belittle Fowler. They are fools."[8]

Describers, meanwhile, like to denounce prescribers as priggish, often ignorant, authoritarians prepared to fight to the death over nonissues such as split infinitives and terminal prepositions:

- **1960:** "Should one say 'None of them is ready' or 'None of them are ready'?
  "The prescriptive grammarians are emphatic that it should be singular. The Latinists point out that *nemo*, the Latin equivalent, is singular. The logicians triumphantly point out that *none* can't be more than one and hence can't be plural.
  "The linguist knows that he hears 'None of them are ready' every day, from people of all social positions, geographical areas, and degrees of education."[9]

- **1970:** "Those who fancy themselves preservers of standards in language, most of whom would hotly deny the appellation 'purist,' believe quite sincerely that their stand is highly traditional and regard as dangerous subversives those scholars who devote themselves to the objective description of their first-hand observations. Many who righteously maintain that split infinitives and terminal prepositions are cardinal sins regard themselves as forward-looking men of liberal temperament . . . ."[10]

- **1982:** "The eighteenth-century grammars, and more importantly the views of language and class which underpinned them, continue to terrorize English speech."[11]

- **1999:** "There is hardly any other area in life in which people so badly informed can actually be proud of their ignorance while still proclaiming themselves to be guardians of truth and saviors of others from error."[12]

At least one describer, Edward Finegan, has conceded that "linguists have not afforded the guardians [i.e., prescribers] a fair hearing," adding that "this imbalance is exacerbated by the bad press the guardians have in turn inflicted on linguists, a bad press that has bruised the credibility of the linguistics profession."[13] Indeed, the Lin-

---

[5]Louis B. Salomon, "Whose Good English?" 38 *Am. Ass'n Univ. Profs. Bull.* 441, 442 (Fall 1952) (as quoted in *The Ordeal of American English* 160, 161 (C. Merton Babcock ed., 1961)).

[6]Gary Jennings, *Personalities of Language* 8 (1965).

[7]Bertrand Evans, "Grammar and Writing," in *A Linguistics Reader* 111, 112 (Graham Wilson ed., 1967).

[8]Erich Eichmann, *Wall Street Journal*, 7 Jan. 2000, at W11.

[9]Bergen Evans, "Grammar for Today," 205 *Atlantic Monthly* 80, 81 (Mar. 1960) (as quoted in *The Ordeal of American English* 157, 158 (C. Merton Babcock ed., 1961)).

[10]Thomas Pyles & John Algeo, *English: An Introduction to Language* 29 (1970).

[11]Colin MacCabe, *The Listener*, 12 Aug. 1982, at 13–14.

[12]Ronald Wardhaugh, *Proper English: Myths and Misunderstandings About Language* 172 (1999).

[13]Edward Finegan, "On the Linguistic Forms of Prestige," in *The Legacy of Language: A Tribute to Charlton Laird* 146, 148 (Phillip C. Boardman ed., 1987).

guistic Society of America long ago conceded what remains true today: "a fair portion of highly educated laymen see in linguistics the great enemy of all they hold dear."[14]

In short, there's long been bad blood between the two camps. It continues to this day. Even when contemporary describers propose a rapprochement, it typically consists simply in having prescribers concede the error of their ways. For example, in their new *Cambridge Grammar of the English Language* (2002), Rodney Huddleston and Geoffrey K. Pullum airily note that "although descriptive grammars and prescriptive usage manuals differ in the range of topics they treat, there is no reason in principle why they should not agree on what they say about the topics they both treat."[15] That might seem like a promising statement, but in fact it's disingenuous—rather like a warring spouse who quarrelsomely proposes a "reconciliation" by insisting that all the fault lies with the other side. For in the very next sentence, we find our two conciliators claiming that prescribers (1) overrely on personal taste; (2) confuse informality with ungrammaticality; and (3) appeal to "certain invalid arguments"[16] (unspecified). That's it. In their view, it's all the fault of prescribers.

But the fault lies at least equally at the feet of the describers, many of whom (1) insist that their methods are the only valid ones; (2) disclaim any interest in promoting the careful use of language, often denouncing anyone who seeks to do so; and (3) believe that native speakers of English can't make a mistake and that usage guides are therefore superfluous.

You may think that's just hyperbole. Sadly, it isn't. True enough, there may not be such a thing as a "pure describer," since every commentator has at least some predilections about usage, however covert. But many describers also dogmatically oppose value judgments about language. That in itself is a value judgment—and a very odd one, in the eyes of ordinary people. Here's a sampling of what "pure describers" have said in the literature:

Lakoff: "For change that comes spontaneously from below, or within, our policy should be, Let your language alone, and leave its speakers alone!"[17]

McWhorter: "*Descriptive* grammar . . . has nothing to do with the rather surreal notion of telling people what they *should* say. The other grammar, which is about counterintuitive, party-pooping bizarrerie, . . . is called *prescriptive* grammar and is neither taught to nor discussed by linguists, except as the persistent little scourge that seems to have gotten hold of the Anglophone world."[18]

Trudgill: "Language change cannot be halted. Nor should the worriers feel obliged to try to halt it. Languages are self-regulating systems which can be left to take care of themselves."[19]

These writers see language as if it were merely a series of events to be duly recorded. They don't see it—or don't want to see it—as the product of human conduct and human decision, or its use as a skill that can either be left rudimentary or be honed.

Meanwhile, describers themselves write exclusively in Standard English. If it's really a matter of complete indifference to them, why don't they occasionally *flout* (or should that be *flaunt*?) the rules of grammar and usage? Their writing could *militate* (or is it

---

[14]Linguistic Society of America, *Report of the Commission on the Humanities* 156 (1964).

[15]*Cambridge Grammar of the English Language* 6 (2002).

[16]*Id.* at 6–7.

[17]Robin Tolmach Lakoff, *Talking Power: The Politics of Language* 298 (1990).

[18]John McWhorter, *The Word on the Street: Fact and Fable About American English* 62 (1998).

[19]Peter Trudgill, "The Meanings of Words Should Not Be Allowed to Vary or Change," in *Language Myths* 8 (Laurie Bauer & Peter Trudgill eds., 1999).

mitigate?) in favor of linguistic mutations if they would allow themselves to be *unconscious* (*unconscionable*?) in their *use* (*usage*?) of words, as they seemingly want everyone else to be. But they don't do this. They write by all the rules that they tell everyone else not to worry about. Despite their protestations, their own words show that correctness is valued in the real world.

Why should linguists believe—as many certainly do—that language, of all human tools, is uniquely incapable of being misused or abused? Why should language alone be immune to ignorant or careless handling? It's hard to imagine professionals in any other field of human endeavor making an analogous argument.

One surprising aspect of descriptivist doctrine is that it's essentially anti-education: teaching people about good usage, the argument goes, interferes with the natural, unconscious forces of language, so leave speakers alone. This doctrine relieves English teachers of the responsibility to teach standard English. And it dooms us all to the dialect of the households in which we've grown up. One result is rigidified social strata. After all, you're unlikely to gain any responsible position—such as that of a linguistics professor—if you can't speak and write standard English. So much for egalitarianism.

I'm mostly in the prescriptive camp (although, as I'll explain in a moment, I'm a kind of descriptive prescriber). The prescriptive camp explicitly values linguistic decisions and informed standards of correctness. It's a Fowlerian sensibility that Sir Ernest Gowers summed up as having five bases: "first the careful choice of precise words, second the avoidance of all affectations, third the orderly and coherent arrangement of words, fourth the strict observance of what is for the time being established idiom, and fifth the systematization of spelling and pronunciation."[20] Gowers and I are hardly alone among Fowler's successors:

Pei: "Don't be afraid to exercise your power of choice. If you prefer 'telephone' to 'phone,' or 'greatly' to 'very much,' don't be afraid to use them. It's your language as much as anyone else's. At the same time, try to have a good reason for your choice, because language is one of the finest products of man's intelligence, and should be intelligently employed and intelligently changed."[21]

Safire: "Some of the interest in the world of words comes from people who like to put less-educated people down—Language Snobs, who give good usage a bad name. Others enjoy letting off steam in a form of mock-anger, treating their peeves as pets. But most of the interest, I think, comes from a search for standards and values. We resent fogginess; we resist manipulation by spokesmen who use loaded words and catch phrases; we wonder if, in language, we can find a few of the old moorings. We are not groping for the bygone, we are reaching for a firm foothold in fundamentals."[22]

Marenbon: "It is far easier to destroy a standard language than to create one. A standard language requires a body of speakers who have been trained to distinguish correct constructions from incorrect ones, usual forms from those which are unusual and carry with them special implications. Such training is neither short nor easy; and it is unrealistic to expect that English teachers can give it to their pupils if, along with teaching standard English (as one form of the language, appropriate for certain occasions), they are expected to encourage speech and

---

[20]Sir Ernest Gowers, "H.W. Fowler: The Man and His Teaching," Presidential Address to the English Association, July 1957, at 14.

[21]Mario Pei, *All About Language* 9 (1954).

[22]William Safire, *On Language* xv (1980).

writing in dialect and to attend to the multiplicity of other tasks with which modern educationalists have burdened them. By devaluing standard English, the new orthodoxy is destroying it."[23]

Prescribers want to evaluate linguistic change as it occurs. They endorse the changes they consider fortunate and resist the ones they consider unfortunate—often with little success in the long run.

Explaining the Rift

The opposing views aren't easily reconciled. Prescribers like established forms in grammar and word choice. They encourage precision and discourage letting one word usurp another's meaning (*infer–imply, lay–lie, like–as*). They dislike the indiscriminate use of two forms, especially opposed forms, for one meaning (*categorically-uncategorically, couldn't care less–could care less, regardless–irregardless*). They value consistency and historical continuity (preferring *home in* over *hone in, just deserts* over *just desserts*, and *slough off* over *sluff off*).

Describers, meanwhile, remind us that linguistic change is a fact of life—and conclude that it's therefore not worth opposing. As one has asked: "If language is going to keep changing anyway—and it is—what is the use of posting the little rules and making people uncomfortable only to see them eventually blown away by the wind?"[24] Another prominent describer has even seemed to tout mass heedlessness: "The inert ignorance of the uneducated about their language . . . indeed has had a profound and on the whole a progressive effect on language, manifesting itself in an almost miraculously intricate and regular operation of known laws of linguistic behavior."[25] Perhaps because that view involves a value judgment (ignorance is progressive), some describers disclaim it in favor of a value-neutral and all but valueless position, such as this: "The most sensible view about any language is that it changes. It neither regresses nor progresses."[26]

In one of the most mind-blowing descriptivist passages ever penned, Donald J. Lloyd talked about linguistic change by allusively adopting a notoriously invidious view of rape: "There is no point in tiresome carping about usage; the best thing is to relax and enjoy it."[27]

Yet not all describers endorse fatalistic or optimistic views of change. Dwight L. Bolinger, a describer with impeccable credentials, has staked a position that most prescribers would find satisfactory: "If rules are to be broken, it is better done from knowledge than from ignorance, even when ignorance ultimately decides the issue."[28] Another, the Oxford professor Jean Aitchison, concedes that "language change . . . may, in certain circumstances, be socially undesirable."[29]

---

[23]John Marenbon, *Proper English?* 252–53 (Tony Crowley ed., 1991).

[24]John McWhorter, *The Word on the Street* 85 (1998). But see Peter Farb, *Word Play* 84 (1974) ("One justification sometimes heard for freedom in breaking the rules of the language game is that languages change with time anyway. But that argument is beside the point. Even though the rules may change tomorrow, they are still binding while they are in force today.").

[25]John S. Kenyon, "Ignorance Builds Language" (1938), in *A Language Reader for Writers* 175, 176 (James R. Gaskin & Jack Suberman eds., 1966).

[26]Ronald Wardhaugh, *Proper English: Myths and Misunderstandings About Language* 42 (1999).

[27]Donald J. Lloyd, "Snobs, Slobs and the English Language," in *A Linguistics Reader* 99, 102 (Graham Wilson ed., 1967).

[28]Dwight L. Bolinger, *Language: The Loaded Weapon* 55 (1980). Cf. Louis Foley, *Beneath the Crust of Words* 83 (1928) ("Ignorance has had considerable effect in the development of language. Many changes which have been made in the forms, uses, and meanings of words would certainly not have occurred if the language had been used only by those who knew it thoroughly.").

[29]Jean Aitchison, *Language Change: Progess or Decay?* 260 (3d ed. 2001).

One major difference between the prescriber and the describer, and their views toward change, has to do with the relative immediacy of linguistic perspective. The prescriber cares about how language is used here and now. The describer views language more distantly, observing that linguistic change is inevitable. After all, Latin evolved into French, Italian, and other Romance languages—and the French, Italians, and others haven't been adversely affected by linguistic evolution. This is like a geographer arguing that seismic disruptions along the San Andreas Fault hardly matter in the larger scheme of things, since continents and seas will come and go: in the history of the earth, an earthquake in Los Angeles doesn't amount geographically to a blip on the big screen. But of course earthquakes do matter to the people who experience them. And how language is used today—here and now—does matter to people who speak it, hear it, write it, and read it. Invoking the inevitability of linguistic drift doesn't help someone who is unsure about how to say *irrevocable*, what preposition to use after *oblivious*, or whether the verb after *a number of people* should be singular or plural. The linguistic choice that a speaker or writer makes will affect how others react. Linguists may take the long view, but good usage depends on the here and now.

Because usage constantly evolves, so must judgments about usage. Much of what Theodore Bernstein, an eminent *New York Times* editor, said in 1965 about the careful writer[30] endures to this day; some of it doesn't. That's the way usage is. The test of good usage has little to do with what endures, although good usage is fairly stable and tends to endure. It has more to do with what works for today's readership, distracting as few readers as possible. It's a test of credibility among contemporaries. Good usage reflects how a careful writer of today approaches linguistic questions.

One common tack of describers is to question all the assumptions about what is meant by "careful writers,"[31] "the best writers,"[32] or "respected people"[33]—the abstractions that prescribers postulate for establishing a standard of good usage. When it's impossible to identify exactly who these people are, describers claim victory by concluding that no such standard exists.[34]

But this idea that "careful writers" (etc.) are unidentifiable is a fallacious position for two reasons.

First, we say that usage is judged good not because the *best writers* employ it, but because it helps writers use words successfully.[35] Likewise, we say that apples are healthful not because wise people eat them, but because of their observable effects on the human body. The fact that we eat apples doesn't make them "good food."

---

[30]See Theodore M. Bernstein, *The Careful Writer* (1965).

[31]William Strunk Jr. & E.B. White, *The Elements of Style* 59 (3d ed. 1979) ("The careful writer, watchful for small conveniences, goes *which*-hunting, removes the defining *whiches*, and by so doing improves his work."); Maxine Hairston, *Successful Writing* 118 (2d ed. 1986) ("Although the verb *to be* in all its forms (*is, am, was, were, will be, have been*, and so on) remains the central verb in our language, careful writers use it sparingly.").

[32]William Strunk Jr. & E.B. White, *The Elements of Style* 72 (3d ed. 1979) ("It is no sign of weakness or defeat that your manuscript ends up in need of major surgery. This is a common occurrence in all writing, and among the best writers."); Thomas R. Lounsbury, *The Standard of Usage in English* vi (1908) ("The best, and indeed the only proper, usage is the usage of the best."); John F. Genung, *Outlines of Rhetoric* 9 (1893) ("A most valuable habit to cultivate . . . is the habit of observing words, especially as seen in the pages of the best writers; of tracing fine shades of meaning, and noting how suggestive, or felicitous, or accurately chosen they are. It is by keeping their sense for words alert and refined that good writers constantly enlarge and enrich their vocabulary."); Brainerd Kellogg, *A Text-Book on Rhetoric* 17 (1881) ("Rhetoric . . . has only *usage* as authority for what it teaches—the usage of the best writers and speakers. And this is variable, changing from generation to generation.").

[33]Bergen Evans & Cornelia Evans, *A Dictionary of Contemporary American Usage* v (1957) ("Respectable English . . . means the kind of English that is used by the most respected people, the sort of English that will make readers or listeners regard you as an educated person.").

[34]For a splendid example of this specious approach, see John Algeo, "What Makes Good English Good?" in *The Legacy of Language: A Tribute to Charlton Laird* 122–23 (Phillip C. Boardman ed., 1987).

[35]I owe this argument to I.A. Richards, *The Philosophy of Rhetoric* 52 (1936).

Second, the *careful writer* may exist for the language in the same sense as the *reasonable person* exists for law, or (in other fields) the *average voter* or the *typical consumer*: it's a pragmatic construct that allows for assessing and predicting behavior. The careful writer is essentially good usage anthropomorphized. It's irrelevant that you can't point to a particular person as a "careful writer," just as it's irrelevant to the law that no one is on every occasion a "reasonable person." This doesn't mean that a real standard doesn't exist. Even Richard W. Bailey of Michigan, a thoroughgoing describer, acknowledges that the linguistic standard exists: "Linguists who pretend that there is no consensus about the elite forms of English confuse their egalitarian ideals with the social reality that surrounds them."[36]

Still another difference between the camps is that describers want comprehensive descriptions of languages, while prescribers unapologetically treat only a selective set of linguistic problems. Describers have been known to criticize prescribers for this selectivity: "The normative tradition focuses on just a few dots in the vast and complex universe of the English language."[37] Because describers are "scientists" who seek to record and catalogue all the observable linguistic phenomena they can, they will go into great detail about matters that have minimal interest to everyone else—for example, why in English we don't say *House brick built is*. Prescribers, by contrast, who write for a wide audience, deal mostly with issues that can taunt even seasoned writers—to take examples from just one small span of entries from this book, the difference between *hearty* and *hardy*; whether the correct form is *harebrained* or *hairbrained*; or whether the predominant phrase is *hark back*, *harken back*, or *hearken back* (perhaps *harp back*?). So prescribers tend to assume that their readers already have some competence with the language.

Yet another major difference has to do with the use of evidence. Describers have always tried to amass linguistic evidence—the more the better. Prescribers are often content to issue their opinions ex cathedra. In fact, inadequate consideration of linguistic evidence has traditionally been the prescribers' greatest vulnerability. But the better prescribers, such as H.W. Fowler and Eric Partridge, have closely considered the facts underpinning their judgments. In this book, I've taken the descriptivist tack of citing voluminous evidence—perhaps more than some readers might think necessary. But those readers should consider how useful it is to see the contextual use of words, not in made-up examples but in published passages.[38]

While prescribers view language as involving a multitude of decisions, describers often discuss language as if its use were all a matter of instinct. "To a linguist or psycholinguist," writes Steven Pinker of MIT, "language is like the song of the humpback whale."[39] He tenaciously pursues this odd comparison, ridiculing prescribers as if they were essentially the same as naturalists claiming that "chickadees' nests are incorrectly constructed, pandas hold bamboo in the wrong paw, the song of the humpback whale contains several well-known errors, and monkeys' cries have been in a state of chaos

---

[36]Richard W. Bailey, "Whose Usage? Fred Newton Scott and the Standard of Speech," in *Centennial Usage Studies* 1 (Greta D. Little & Michael Montgomery eds., 1994).

[37]Sidney Greenbaum, "Current Usage and the Experimenter," 51 *Am. Speech* 163, 163 (1976). See also Sidney Greenbaum, *Good English and the Grammarian* 33 (1988) ("From a descriptive stance, normative rules seem trivial in that they affect relatively little of the language"). Cf. John Algeo, "Grammatical Usage: Modern Shibboleths," in *James B. McMillan: Essays in Linguistics by His Friends and Colleagues* 53, 61 (James C. Raymond & I. Willis Russell eds., 1977) (stating that usage books "address themselves mainly to an inherited list of problems rather than to real issues in contemporary English").

[38]Cf. Samuel Johnson, Preface, *A Dictionary of the English Language* (1755) ("Authorities will sometimes seem to have been accumulated without necessity or use, and perhaps some will be found, which might, without loss, have been omitted. But a work of this kind is not hastily to be charged with superfluities: those quotations, which to careless or unskilful perusers appear only to repeat the same sense, will often exhibit, to a more accurate examiner, diversities of signification, or, at least, afford different shades of the same meaning.").

[39]Steven Pinker, *The Language Instinct* 370 (1994).

and degeneration for hundreds of years."[40] He caps it off with this: "Isn't the song of the humpback whale whatever the humpback whale decides to sing?"[41]

The analogy is deeply fallacious in all sorts of ways. First, although the capacity for language may indeed be instinctive—and Pinker makes a good case for this in his book—the specifics of any given language (for example, why we call one object a *hat* and another a *table*) aren't instinctive at all. Words are arbitrary symbols that are learned, and there are lots of nuances. Second, human beings must make myriad decisions when forming sentences and paragraphs, whereas other animals aren't known to make the same kinds of decisions in following their instincts. Third, Pinker's line of reasoning would eliminate any means for judging the effectiveness of human expression. Yet we all know—and Pinker knows very well—that some human beings communicate more effectively than others.

So much for the describers' misplaced scientism: it can lead to astounding instances of muddled thought.

Reconciling the Camps

A greater sense of balance and impartiality—of where the truth lies—could end the age-old debate between describers and prescribers, if only both sides would acknowledge certain principles. More about these in a moment.

First, I should declare that I am a prescriber who uses descriptivist methods—in effect, a descriptive prescriber. I don't doubt the value of descriptive linguistics—up to the point at which describers dogmatically refuse to acknowledge the value of prescriptivism. Each side in this age-old debate should acknowledge the value of the other.

Before stating three principles that might allow for this reconciliation, I should draw attention to the danger of acknowledging my prescriptive tendencies. I may be playing into describers' hands by adopting this inflammatory label. Maybe I should instead take a lesson from D.J. Enright: "Many people without the benefit (as they see it) of a decent education still *want* to know how to use words. And since prescriptivism is the only brake we have on the accelerating spread of chaos, let's find some other name for it, one less reminiscent of the National Health Service."[42] Yet no new label readily suggests itself. Besides, changing the label probably won't change the reality.

Now to the fundamental principles.

1. *Linguistically, both speech and writing matter.*

When modern linguists focus exclusively on speech, they're overreacting to their predecessors' preoccupation with writing. Describers have a bias toward studying speech; prescribers have a bias toward studying writing.

Both are important. In any language, speech precedes writing. It accounts for the overwhelming majority of linguistic events. Yet writing is a form of language worth studying in its own right. For some reason, though, many linguists refuse to recognize this. As Roy Harris, the Oxford linguist, put it some years ago: "One of the sophistries of modern linguistics is to treat scriptism, which has probably dominated the concept of a language in literate societies for at least several millennia, as some kind of theoretical heresy."[43]

---

[40]*Id.*

[41]*Id.*

[42]D.J. Enright, *Fields of Vision* 224 (1990).

[43]Roy Harris, *The Language Makers* 7 (1980).

Writing endures and therefore helps stabilize the language. Universal literacy helps temper linguistic entropy. As more and more people become literate, the written and spoken forms of language influence each other—even while remaining distinct.

For the readers of this essay, a stable language is doubtless a desirable thing. Otherwise, the English language wouldn't be worth much as a lingua franca. Samuel Johnson rejected the idea of embalming the language,[44] and no one seriously wants to halt all change in a living language. "It is not a question of banning all linguistic changes," as F.L. Lucas put it. "Since language cannot stand still, the main thing for the public interest is that alterations in vocabulary and idiom should not become too rapid, reckless, and wanton . . . ."[45]

The study of writing—like the very fact that writing exists—serves as a conservative, moderating influence. Our literary heritage has helped form our culture. The means by which we record words on paper has an enormous influence on readers and on the culture as a whole.

One aspect of the writing-vs.-speech distinction is what linguists call "register": a user's style of language according to the subject, the audience, and the occasion. No one writes a job-application letter in the same style as a love letter; and no one speaks to an interviewer in the same way as to a pet. Most of us have five basic registers: (1) intimate, for conversations between family members and close friends; (2) casual, for everyday conversations; (3) consultative, for communicating with colleagues and strangers in conducting everyday business; (4) formal, for published essays and serious lectures; and (5) frozen, for religious and legal rituals.[46] Those who study oral communication (describers) incline toward 1–2 (occasionally 3); those who study written communication (prescribers) incline toward 3–4 (occasionally 2, sometimes 5). If describers and prescribers alike were more overt about the registers they're dealing with, many of their squabbles might wither away.

2. *Writing well is a hard-won skill that involves learning conventions.*

To educate people about the conventions of writing is good for them. Why? Because writing well requires disciplined thinking. Learning to write is a part of anyone's education.

What are the conventions that aspiring writers need to learn? Among other things, those who write expository prose must learn cognitive skills—how to:

- Summarize complicated matter.
- Maintain a cohesive train of thought.
- Support ideas with adequate evidence.

To communicate the material, the writer must also learn mechanical skills—how to:

- Vary sentence structure.
- Vary sentence length.
- Vary paragraph length.
- Connect ideas from sentence to sentence, and paragraph to paragraph.

Finally, to make certain that the communication is clear to the reader and free of distractions, the writer must learn stylistic skills—how to:

- Adopt a relaxed, natural tone.
- Omit unnecessary words.

---

[44]See the Preface to his *Dictionary of the English Language* (1755).

[45]F.L. Lucas, *Style* 43 (1955; repr. 1962).

[46]See generally Martin Joos, *The Five Clocks* (1962).

- Observe recognized grammatical niceties (subject–verb agreement, parallel constructions, logically placed modifiers, and so on).
- Distinguish between similar words that are easily confused, such as *affect* and *effect*, *principle* and *principal*, and the like.

Only the last three, for some reason, seem to trouble most describers, who overstate their objections. They like to caricature prescribers as insisting on such fripperies as *It's I* and *none is*, and as prohibiting all split infinitives, all prepositions as sentence-enders, and all conjunctions as sentence-starters.[47] The truth is that informed prescribers didn't take any of those positions at any time in the 20th century—and certainly not in the 21st. In fact, prescribers have been just as severe as describers in ridiculing such superstitions.[48]

Back to the main point: writing is a learned activity, no different in that regard from hitting a golf ball or playing the piano. Yes, some people naturally do it better than others. But apart from a few atypical autodidacts (who exist in all disciplines), there's no practical way to learn to write, hit a golf ball, or play the piano without guidance on many points, large and small. And everyone, even the autodidact, requires considerable effort and practice in learning the norms. The norms are important even to those who ultimately break them to good effect.

3. *It's possible to formulate practical advice on grammar and usage.*

Although 18th- and 19th-century grammarians' work was too often corrupted by whimsy and guesswork, their basic instincts were sound: we can indeed help writers on critical questions of grammar and usage.

Usage and style operate differently in writing and in speech. In oral communication, inflection and body language and interaction help convey meaning. And a speaker can perceive cues that invite immediate clarifications. But in writing, these aids to communication are absent: you rely exclusively on marks on a page (words and punctuation). A writer rarely gets a second chance to communicate effectively, so clear writing requires much more forethought. It's no wonder that publishers have produced thousands of books designed to teach people how to improve their writing.

Authorities on the written word echo each other in stressing how difficult good writing is: "Writing is hard work. A clear sentence is no accident. Very few sentences come out right the first time, or even the third time. Remember this in moments of despair. If you find that writing is hard, it's because it *is* hard."[49] Writers must learn to have a point, to deliver it efficiently, to cut the extra words that inevitably appear in any first draft, and to maintain a clean narrative line, among many other skills. These things trouble even professionals.

Prescriptive usage guides deal with many of the small points that writers grapple with. These manuals are pedagogical books intended to be browsed in as much as consulted. In this book, for example, many entries deal with emerging confusions in diction that

---

[47]See the quotations accompanying notes 9, 10; see also Steven Pinker, *The Language Instinct* 373–74 (1994) ("Most of the hobgoblins of contemporary prescriptive grammar (don't split infinitives, don't end a sentence with a preposition) can be traced back to . . . eighteenth-century fads.").

[48]See, e.g., H.W. Fowler, *A Dictionary of Modern English Usage* 586–87 (1926) (s.v. "Superstitions"); Eric Partridge, *Usage and Abusage* 159–60 [*it is me*], 204–05 [*none*], 296 [split infinitive], 245 [terminal preposition] (1940); Wilson Follett, *Modern American Usage: A Guide* 227 [*none*], 313 [split infinitive], 64 [*and, but*] (1966); Theodore M. Bernstein, *Miss Thistlebottom's Hobgoblins: The Careful Writer's Guide to the Taboos, Bugbears, and Outmoded Rules of English Usage* (1971) (passim).

[49]William Zinsser, *On Writing Well* 12 (6th ed. 1998). Cf. Alexei Tolstoy, "Advice to the Young Writer" (1939), in *Maxim Gorky, Vladimir Mayakovsky, Alexei Tolstoy, and Konstantin Fedin on the Art and Craft of Writing* 231, 231–32 (Alex Miller trans., 1972) ("Nobody has ever found that writing comes easy, that it 'flowed' from the pen. Writing is always difficult, and the more difficult it is, the better it turns out in the end.").

threaten to spread: *disburse* for *disperse, expatriot* for *expatriate, fruit melody* for *fruit medley, heart-rendering* for *heart-rending, marshal arts* for *martial arts, presumptious* for *presumptuous, reign in* for *rein in.* Other entries deal with plural forms that, for now, most careful writers want to maintain in plural senses, such as *criteria, paparazzi,* and *phenomena.* Still other entries urge wider acceptance of disputed usages, such as the singular *media.*

The focus is on the particular: these are the words and phrases that writers and editors must make considered choices about daily. There aren't just a few dozen trouble spots in the language, or even a few hundred. There are several thousand of them. Given the critical acumen of many readers, for a writer to remain unconscious of these pitfalls and write whatever sounds close enough will inevitably lead to a loss of credibility. Vague intelligibility isn't the touchstone; precision is.

As a field of study, usage doesn't hold much interest for modern linguists, who are drifting more and more toward quantitative psychology and theory. Their leading theorist, Noam Chomsky of MIT, has acknowledged, with no apparent regret, the pedagogical irrelevance of modern linguistics: "I am, frankly, rather skeptical about the significance, for the teaching of languages, of such insights and understanding as have been attained in linguistics and psychology."[50] An equally august prescriptivist, F.W. Bateson of Oxford, said just a few years later: "The professional linguist has very little to contribute to style considered as the *best* words in the *best* order."[51] If you want to learn how to use the English language skillfully and gracefully, books on linguistics won't help you at all.

Yet people *want* normative rules of language. Linguistic relativism, though valuable on some levels, has its limitations. True, it's probably helpful for students to hear insights such as this from Charlton Laird: "Nothing in language is essentially vulgar or genteel, barbarous or elegant, right or wrong, except as the users of the language want to feel that the locutions have those qualities."[52] But of course most writers believe that words and phrases can have right and wrong qualities. In a given social setting, those widely shared views matter enormously. And Laird—a sensible describer—recognized this:

> We must have standards. After all, who makes the language? You and I and everybody make the language. And what does this hydra-headed language-manufacturer want in his product? Obviously, he wants a number of things; he wants flexibility and versatility, but he also wants standards. He may not know just what standards he wants, nor how rigidly he wants them applied, but he does want them in spelling, in punctuation, in diction, in usage, in all aspects of language, and on the whole he relies on people of our sort [English teachers] to inform him which are the best standards and what he should do about them. We had better be prepared to tell him, and to know what we are talking about when we do so.[53]

Despite the describers' decades-old campaign to convince us that no uses of language are inherently better than others, literate people continue to yearn for guidance on linguistic questions. With great acuity half a century ago, an English teacher—Louis Salomon—characterized what remains the current state of affairs:

> The public may not care whether English teachers eat or not, but if there is any sentiment in favor of feeding them I'm willing to bet that the idea is to keep them

[50]Noam Chomsky, "Linguistic Theory," in *Northeast Conference on the Teaching of Foreign Languages* 43 (1966) (as quoted in J.B. Pride, *The Social Meaning of Language* 80 (1971)). Cf. Linguistic Society of America, *Report of the Commission on the Humanities* 155–56 (1964) ("The impact which the recent advances in linguistics have upon the general public [is] essentially zero.").

[51]F.W. Bateson, *The Scholar-Critic* 100 (1972).

[52]Charlton Laird, *And Gladly Teche* 47 (1970).

[53]*Id.* at 47–48.

alive as English teachers, that is, as a kind of traffic cop to tell the average person when to stop and when to move on, where he may park and where he may not. If English teachers don't want to be traffic cops—if they just want to stand on the corner and count the cars that try to beat the red light—then they might as well turn in their badges. Because sooner or later the taxpayers will (a) begin to wonder why the accident rate keeps going up, and (b) discover that a machine with an electric eye can do the counting more cheaply and more efficiently.[54]

Yet several linguists assert, essentially, that there is no right and wrong in language. Consider what one well-known linguist, Robert A. Hall Jr., famously said: "There is no such thing as good and bad (or correct and incorrect, grammatical and ungrammatical, right and wrong) in language. . . . A dictionary or grammar is not as good an authority for your speech as the way you yourself speak."[55] Some of the better theorists in the mid-20th century rejected this extremism. Here, for example, is how Max Black responded:

> This extreme position . . . involves a confusion between investigating rules (or standards, norms) and prescribing or laying down such rules. Let us grant that a linguist, qua theoretical and dispassionate scientist, is not in the business of telling people how to talk; it by no means follows that the speakers he is studying are free from rules which ought to be recorded in any faithful and accurate report of their practices. A student of law is not a legislator; but it would be a gross fallacy to argue that therefore there can be no right or wrong in legal matters.[56]

One might have thought that this no-right-and-no-wrong fallacy had long since been laid to rest. But it's very much with us, at least in academia. Through the latter half of the 20th century and still today, there has been an academic assault on linguistic standards. Today the remark "That's not good English" would likely be met with the rejoinder, "Says who?" This is because people are increasingly hearing the dogma that no use of language is better than any other.

Today the teaching of standard English is being labeled discriminatory. An essay published in 1998 by a University of Michigan linguist, James Milroy, says this: "In an age when discrimination in terms of race, color, religion, or gender is not publicly acceptable, the last bastion of overt social discrimination will continue to be a person's use of language."[57]

In other words, the spirit of the day demands that you not think critically—or at least not think ill—of anyone else's use of language. If you believe in good grammar and linguistic sensitivity, *you're* the problem. And there is a large, powerful contingent in higher education today—larger and more powerful than ever before—trying to eradicate any thoughts about good and bad grammar, correct and incorrect word choices, effective and ineffective style.

Terms of the Truce

Prescribers should be free to advocate a realistic level of linguistic tidiness—without being molested for it—even as the describers are free to describe the mess all around them. If the prescribers have moderate success, then the describers should simply describe those successes. Education entailing normative values has always been a part of literate society. Why should it suddenly stop merely because describers see this kind of education as meddling with natural forces?

---

[54]Louis B. Salomon, "Whose Good English?" 38 *Am. Ass'n Univ. Profs. Bull.* 441, 448 (Fall 1952) (as quoted in *The Ordeal of American English* 160, 163 (C. Merton Babcock ed., 1961)).

[55]Robert A. Hall Jr., *Leave Your Language Alone!* 6 (1950).

[56]Max Black, *The Labyrinth of Language* 70 (1968).

[57]James Milroy, "Children Can't Speak or Write Properly Any More," in *Language Myths* 64–65 (Laurie Bauer & Peter Trudgill eds., 1998).

Meanwhile, prescribers need to be realistic. They can't expect perfection or permanence, and they must bow to universal usage. But when an expression is in transition—when only part of the population has adopted a new usage that seems genuinely undesirable—prescribers should be allowed, within reason, to stigmatize it. There's no reason to tolerate *wreckless driving* in place of *reckless driving*. Or *wasteband* in place of *waistband*. Or *corollary* when misused for *correlation*. Multiply these things by 10,000, and you have an idea of what we're dealing with. There are legitimate objections to the slippage based not just on widespread confusion but also on imprecision of thought, on the spread of linguistic uncertainty, on the etymological disembodiment of words, and on decaying standards generally.

As Roy Harris has remarked: "There is no reason why prescriptive linguistics should not be 'scientific,' just as there is no reason why prescriptive medicine should not be."[58] Harris went even further, denouncing the antiprescriptive doctrine as resulting from naiveté:

> Twentieth-century linguists, anxious to claim "scientific" status for their new synchronic discipline, were glad enough to retain the old nineteenth-century whipping-boy of prescriptivism, in order thereby to distinguish their own concerns as "descriptive," not "prescriptive." When the history of twentieth-century linguistics comes to be written, a naive, unquestioning faith in the validity of this distinction will doubtless be seen as one of the main factors in the academic sociology of the subject.[59]

Elsewhere Harris has referred to "the anti-prescriptivist witch-hunt in modern linguistics."[60]

Other linguists have explained the blind spot that misleads so many of their colleagues. In 1959, C.A. Ferguson suggested that linguists too often take a blinkered look at the language, ignoring its social import: "[Describers] in their understandable zeal to describe the internal structure of the language they are studying often fail to provide even the most elementary data about the socio-cultural setting in which the language functions."[61]

Maybe this, in turn, is because linguistic investigations tend to be highly theoretical—and divorced from most people's immediate interests in language. Barbara Wallraff, an *Atlantic* editor who is a prescriber with acute judgment, puts it in a self-deprecating[62] way: "I am not an academic linguist or an etymologist. Linguistics and what I do stand in something like the relation between anthropology and cooking ethnic food, or between the history of art and art restoration."[63] Other analogies might be equally apt, such as musicologists vis-à-vis musicians, or sociologists vis-à-vis ethicists.

To my knowledge, anthropologists don't denounce ethnic food, and art historians don't denounce art restorers—especially not when the cooks and the artisans know a thing or two about the material they're dealing with. Musicologists don't censure musicians who teach others how to produce a vibrato. Sociologists don't look askance at ethicists who aim to guide human behavior. Those who study language could learn something from these other fields—something about balance, civility, and peaceful coexistence.

---

[58]Roy Harris, *The Language Makers* 151 (1980).

[59]*Id.* at 151–52.

[60]Roy Harris, *The Language Machine* 128 (1987).

[61]C.A. Ferguson, "Principles of Teaching Languages with Diglossia," in *Monograph Series on Languages and Linguistics* 437 (1959).

[62]I use this phrase advisedly. See p. 265 of this book.

[63]Barbara Wallraff, *Word Court* 2 (2000).

The Ongoing Tumult in English Usage

Bryan A. Garner

"Research from the New Literacy examines literacy practices, and literacy events, and many researchers have used it's [*sic*] perspective to look at what people do with literacy."
—Kate Pahl & Jennifer Rowsell[1]

A Solecistic Summary

The truce that I once proposed[2] between descriptivists and prescriptivists having been only conditionally excepted by a single linguist,[3] the embattlements must continue.

Linguistic history bares out the fact that since English has spreaded throughout the world, people who hue to traditional idioms can avoid the maelstorm of indivious solecisms that await for the unwary. Although the language is continually evolving, and insipient changes become widespreadly disbursed and then take route so that words become distant from their entomologies, the mileau in which these changes occur remains fairly constant. To ask whether all change can be quelched is a mute point—a serious misnomer. The language is a self-regulating system of disambiguation, without any official body of persons in high dungeon, at our beckon call, exerting a right to meet out punishment to a would-be literati who has a heyday abusing it—punishment that might amount not just to a mild annoyment but to caricature assassination.

For all intensive purposes, some linguistic shifts may past mustard, even those that don't harp back to Middle English or Early Modern English. People with an overweening interest in oversighting English sometimes, as a kind of guttural reaction, take all this for granite. There will never be paralyzation of a living language, nor even hiati in its evolution. And it may give piece of mind to know that linguistic change isn't something to be measured in decades, much less per anum. Improprietous words and phrases that may once have been considered abdominable, slightly course, or otherwise beyond the pail may, over time, become fully acceptable and no longer peak anyone's interest. But even if there are many a person whom misuse particular words and are allowed to do so with impugnity—and all tolled, English contains a heterogenous mother load of almost infinite potential errors—their credulity is likely to be strained in the minds of listeners and readers. The more populace the language community, the greater the wrecklessness with which some speakers and writers can reek havoc on the language itself. These phenomenon become their mode of operandi; for them, perhaps we might say they could not of known better, even if they had ought to. But in the end, close analyzation

---

Adapted from *Forum: A Publication of the Association of Literary Scholars and Critics* (Spring 2009).
[1]*Literacy and Education* 11 (2005).
[2]"Making Peace in the Language Wars," the preceding essay in this book (pp. xxxiii–xlv).
[3]See Peter Tiersma, "Language Wars Truce Accepted (with Conditions)," 8 *Green Bag 2d* 281–90 (2005).

> *should demonstrate that correct English usage should be brandishment*
> *enough—it's own reword.*

This fictitious summary of this essay contains no fewer than 63 more or less prevalent misusages (some of them quite popular) that represent potential shifts in English usage—that is, each of them can be readily documented in modern print sources. (For a key to this gallimaufry of bad usage, see the end of this essay.) When solecisms arise today, they can spread as never before—like linguistic infections. There are thousands of outbreaks throughout the English-speaking world at any one time.

The viral nature of linguistic change has assumed new dimensions with the advent of mass communications. Consider three examples. (1) On 31 August 1997, immediately after Princess Diana died in a car crash while being chased by tabloid photographers, reporters throughout the world that evening proclaimed that she'd been hounded by "paparazzis." Millions of viewers at once were exposed to the new double-plural. (2) In 1995, Mazda introduced America to its new luxury sedan, the *Millenia*, having trademarked the car name by changing the standard spelling of a word and dropping an -*n*-. With the ad campaigns that followed, millions of people were exposed to the single-*n* spelling and to the idea of having a single *Millenia*. In 2000, Mazda offered a special luxury sedan: the "Mazda Millenia Millennium Edition"—doubtless prompting in consumers everywhere even further linguistic befuddlement. (3) The new popularity of e-banking has made it commonplace for many of us to pay bills online. One bank now sends hundreds of thousands of e-mail acknowledgments every day, each beginning with an individualized salutation: "Dear Bryan A. Garner; A payment has been made . . . ." When an exasperated bank customer wrote to protest the repeatedly misused semicolon after the many salutations he receives daily, a bank representative coolly responded: "The semicolons are embedded in our computer systems, and there's no easy way to change the code. Besides, several of us here at the bank think the semicolons are correct." The customer's punctuational credentials matter not. When it comes to language, people with meager knowledge like to think of themselves as experts.

With each of these mass-communication "linguistic events" or "speech acts"—and my three examples could be multiplied a thousandfold—people not surprisingly come to view *paparazzis*, *Millenia*, and semicolons after salutations as normal. And their own usage soon reflects that view.

On the whole, teachers of English can do only so much to improve the situation—little but help inculcate a lively interest in words, grammar, punctuation, and the like. Even that much has seemed impossible to many. Certainly it's a great challenge to make those subjects lively and engaging. Yet the best teachers do.

But academia has promoted some nefarious ideas that have undermined those efforts, and the ideas have made headway among the teaching ranks. That is, some teachers now validate the demotic idea that no native speaker of any language can ever make a "mistake"—that there *are* no mistakes (just "different" ways of approaching speech acts). Even if they do believe that mistakes are possible in a native speaker's use of language, they may think that it would be discriminatory and politically unacceptable even to mention the errors. Some teachers think that their mission should be to focus on the appreciation of literature—that linguistic matters, especially those relating to usage, are beneath them. Or they may believe in the "new literacy," the idea that perpetuating standard English is a hopeless, thankless task because linguistic change is inevitable. Some teachers don't want to interrupt the "natural" process of linguistic change. Just go with the flow: as long as their students are intelligible to others, they are "literate" and engaging in "appropriate speech acts."

It's true, of course, that children learn to write better if they spend lots of time writing, as opposed to diagramming sentences and going through rote drills. Teachers generally now accept that truth. Yet it's almost as if the education system starts but never even tries to finish teaching children how to write.

Approaching a finish would mean recognizing that intelligibility is only part of the goal—perhaps the first part, but only a part. Another part is *credibility*. If students are to profit from their education, they need to acquire knowledge. For as the truism goes, knowledge is power. But power depends on having credibility with others.

Students don't need to have their own faddish or unthinking linguistic habits merely validated at school. They need to have their communication skills sharpened and elevated, lest they enter the adult speech-world handicapped by sounding ill-educated. This upgrading involves their acquiring, among other things, word-consciousness, which tends to retard linguistic change rooted in misunderstandings. This brings us back to usage, and to the viral outbreaks that sometimes become epidemics, even pandemics.

Descriptive linguists hardly resist change—of any sort. They certainly don't see degenerative change as a sign of "disease." Rather, they largely embrace change. As Mark Halpern observes, "Linguists' insatiable appetite for change in language is undoubtedly another phenomenon for which there is a mixture of reasons, but among them one is surely fundamental: without change, an important group of linguists would have little fresh material to study."[4] So if descriptive linguists welcome dialectal varieties and resist the teaching of a standard language because a standard language makes their linguistic laboratory less *interesting*,[5] they're like epidemiologists who get excited about the spread of new viruses.

But perhaps the disease metaphor isn't as apt as another biological metaphor—evolution. The forces of natural selection are every bit as much at work in living languages as they are in the rest of the natural world. Over time, words and phrases mutate both in form and in meaning, sometimes through useful innovation and sometimes through unconscious drift and pervasive error. Usually the mutations don't survive, but occasionally a change proves meritorious and ends up becoming a part of the standard language. That happens only if it's fit enough to survive—as a part of the natural selection that takes place in every language.

Sometimes the source of a mutation can be hard to pinpoint. Take, for example, the word *nimrod*. That word has always denoted a hunter. It derives from a name in Genesis: Nimrod, a descendant of Ham, was a mighty huntsman and king of Shinar. Most modern dictionaries even capitalize the English word, unlike similar eponymic words such as *mentor* (= a guide or teacher, from the name of a character in Homer's *Odyssey*) and *solon* (= a legislator, from the name of an ancient Athenian lawmaker, statesman, and poet).

But few people today capitalize *Nimrod*, and fewer still use it to mean "great hunter." The word has depreciated in meaning: it's now pejorative, denoting a simpleton, a goofy person, a dummy.

Believe it or not, we can blame this change on Bugs Bunny, the cartoon character created in the 1940s. He is so popular that *TV Guide* in 2002 named him the "greatest cartoon character of all time." Bugs is best known for his catchphrase "What's Up, Doc?" But for one of his chief antagonists, the inept hunter Elmer Fudd, Bugs would chide, "What a moron! [pronounced like *maroon*] What a nimrod! [pronounced with a pause like two words, *nim rod*]." So for an entire generation raised on these cartoons, the word took on the sense of ineptitude—and therefore what was originally a good joke got ruined.

Ask any American born after 1950 what *nimrod* means and you're likely to hear the answer "idiot." Ask anyone born before 1950 what it means—especially if the person is culturally literate—and you're likely to hear "hunter." The upshot is that the traditional sense is becoming scarcer with each passing year.

---

[4] Mark Halpern, *Language and Human Nature* 20 (2009).

[5] See, e.g., Ang Yiying, "Linguists Speak Up for Singlish," *Straits Times* (Singapore), 9 Dec. 2008 (quoting sociolinguist Anthea Fraser Gupta, who opposes the Speak Good English Movement in Singapore on the grounds that Singlish [a dialect of Singaporean English] should be allowed to flourish, and not be displaced by standard English, because from a linguist's perspective, the dialect makes Singapore "the equivalent of a really well-equipped laboratory for a chemist").

This little example illustrates the huge changes that words can and do undergo all the time. Sometimes the changes aren't semantic—changes in meaning—but instead involve word-formation. Take, for example, *bridegroom* or *groom*. In Middle English (ca. 1200–1500), the original term was *goom* (= man). The extra -*r*- was added centuries ago by false association with someone who works in a stable to care for horses. America's greatest lexicographer, Noah Webster, fought in vain in the early 19th century to make a man on his wedding day the *bridegoom* and all his attendants the *goomsmen*. But the English-speaking people would have none of it—they wanted their extra -*r*-, and they got it. The harmless mutation survived, and today we're wedded to it.

It's one thing to hear about past changes. We already know the outcomes and feel comfortable with them. But it's quite another to consider current word-struggles. Most people feel justified in taking a position on the current standing of a word or phrase. After all, the language belongs to all of us, and we all have a say.

So let's consider the major stages of verbal change. They were first suggested in a 1967 article by Louis G. Heller and James Macris in the journal *American Speech*. I've adapted their four stages into five. (Each nonstandard form below is preceded by an asterisk.)

Stage 1: A new form emerges as an innovation (or some dialectal usage persists) among a small minority of the language community, perhaps displacing a traditional usage. Examples include the misspelling *bellweather* for *bellwether*; the misbegotten *harp back* for *hark back*; the double negative *unrelentlessly* for the correct *relentlessly* or *unrelentingly*; and the dialectal *brung* for *brought*. People normally consider innovations at this stage outright mistakes. Most people who are aware of them hope they won't spread.

Stage 2: The form spreads to a significant portion of the language community, but it remains unacceptable in standard usage. Terms at this stage include using *alumni* and *criteria* as if they were singulars (*alumnus*, *alumna*, or even *alum* being correct, and *criterion* being the singular form); misspelling *baited breath* for *bated breath*; misspelling and mispronouncing *sherbet* as if it were *sherbert* (with an extra -*r*-); misusing *infer* for *imply*; using *peruse* to mean "scan hastily" rather than "read carefully"; and using a nominative pronoun in compound objects such as *between you and I* rather than *between you and me*. Terms in stage 2 often get recorded in dictionaries as variant forms, but this fact alone is hardly a recommendation for their use.

Stage 3: The form becomes commonplace even among many well-educated people, but it's still avoided in careful usage. Examples include *gladiolas* for *gladioluses* (or simply *glads*); *hone in* for *home in* (traditionally it's what homing pigeons do); *miniscule* for the correct spelling *minuscule*; misspelling *straitlaced* as if it were *straightlaced*; and the supposed contraction *'til* for the good old word *till* (as in *We'll be here till noon*).

Stage 4: The form becomes virtually universal but is opposed on cogent grounds by a few linguistic stalwarts (the traditionalists that David Foster Wallace dubbed "snoots": syntax nudniks of our time). Examples are pronouncing *flaccid* as /**flas**-id/ instead of the traditional /**flak**-sid/ (like *access* [/**ak**-ses/] and *accident* [/**ak**-sə-dent/]); using *kudos* as a plural noun; using *unbeknownst* for *unbeknown*; and saying or writing *the reason is because* instead of *the reason is that*.

Stage 5: The form is universally adopted except by a few eccentrics. It's a linguistic fait accompli: what was once merely *de facto* has become accepted as *de jure*. There's no going back here. Examples include *contact* as a verb (as in *I'll contact you next week*); the verb *finalize* (*Let's finalize our plans*); the adjective *interpretive* instead of the traditional *interpretative*; *pompom* in reference to cheerleaders' ornamental balls or tufts, instead of *pompon*; the adjective *self-deprecating* instead of the original *self-depreciating* (which the British still sometimes insist on); and saying *You can't have your cake and eat it too* (as opposed to the original and more logical sequence, from centuries ago: *You can't eat your cake and have it too*).

Many mutations never progress beyond stage 1. They stay in the shadows of the language, emerging now and again, mostly to the annoyance of educated people. Arguments frequently erupt about words and phrases in stages 2 and 3. But if a mutation makes its way to stage 4, its long-term progression to stage 5 is all but assured: it's just a question of the passing of time, whether decades or mere days.

As words go through their long lives, they swell and shrink, grow bright or dull, become loud or soft. To some degree they're always changing—most of them glacially, but some of them precipitately (or precipitously [stage 4]). Anyone who aspires to true proficiency with the language should cultivate the habit of assessing words.

I've tried to further that educational effort in my various writings, most notably in the book that you're now holding. For the third edition, I developed a "Language-Change Index," as just outlined. Of the nearly 11,000 usage entries in the book, I assigned rankings (stages 1 to 5) to more than 2,000 usages. The purpose is to measure how widely accepted various linguistic innovations have become. In their 1967 article, Heller and Macris rightly noted (in their characteristically odd phrasing) that "usage specialists can make a clear-cut demarcation of phrases in the evolutionary process relevant to the inception and development of alternative terms."[6]

A reference to the key to my five-stage ranking system appears at the bottom of each right-hand page. Once again, briefly, stage 1 represents usages that are widely rejected; stage 2, usages that have spread but are rejected by better-educated speakers and writers; stage 3, usages that have spread even to well-educated speakers and writers but are rejected by the most careful ones; stage 4, usages that are almost universal, being rejected only by the most conservative linguistic stalwarts; and stage 5, usages that, perhaps once condemned, are now universal even among the best-educated, most fastidious speakers and writers. That is, stage-5 usages are accepted by everyone except linguistic oddballs.

The rankings were arrived at by a variety of methods.

First, I had the benefit of many studies carried out and reported over the years. These were especially useful for the "canonical" usage problems—the ones that every serious usage guide treats. Most notable among these is Margaret M. Bryant's *Current American Usage* (1957), based on more than 900 specific surveys conducted by English teachers in the 1950s. But other surveys were also useful, including those of (1) the *American Heritage Dictionary* usage panels over the years (reported in various forums since the early 1970s), (2) William and Mary Morris's usage panel assembled for both editions of *Harper's Dictionary of Contemporary English Usage* (1975 and 1985), and (3) the findings reported in *Merriam-Webster's Dictionary of English Usage* (1989; concise ed. 2002). These surveys, of course, had to be weighted according to their dates and the predispositions of the survey participants (easily fathomable).

Second, I made extensive use of computer databases, including Google Books, WESTLAW, NEXIS, and the Oxford English Corpus. The findings here had to be weighted according to word frequencies of newer as compared with older usages. In this new edition of the book, I had the unprecedented advantage of Google's ngrams, which give a diachronic view of usage based on big data. This tool became the single most important determinant—but hardly to the exclusion of others.

Third, I have relied—unabashedly—on my own sense, based on a lifetime of serious linguistic study, of where a given usage falls on the spectrum of acceptability in Standard English. Part of this sense I have developed through attentive observation and part through daily correspondence with English-language aficionados throughout the world. Fortunately, my daily usage e-mails, known as Garner's Usage Tip of

---

[6]Louis G. Heller & James Macris, "English Usage and Modern Linguistic Theory," 42 *Am. Speech* 131, 132 (May 1967).

the Day,[7] have brought me into contact with thousands of language-lovers who have written to me about their linguistic views over the past several years. Additionally, I frequently discuss linguistic matters with acknowledged experts such as Charles Harrington Elster, Mark Halpern, Richard Lederer, Wendalyn Nichols, Christopher Ricks, John Simon, and Barbara Wallraff. These discussions have proved particularly helpful in differentiating stage-4 usages from stage-5 usages.

Finally, I had the benefit of preliminary rankings by more than 100 members of my industrious panel of critical readers, assembled for the purpose of preparing the third edition. They proved most helpful in conducting independent research into the prevalence of specific usages.

My thought was that assigning these rankings to various usages is much more helpful than what one finds in existing usage guides. On the one hand are traditionally stern naysaying handbooks that mostly just tell readers not to indulge in certain usages. On the other hand are permissive guides such as the *Merriam-Webster Concise Dictionary of English Usage*, in which the writers typically come out with milquetoast pronouncements. For example, the anonymous authors of that particular book won't call *could of* a mistake. The entry reads in full: "This is a transcription of *could've*, the contracted form of *could have*. Sometimes it is used intentionally—for instance, by Ring Lardner in his fiction. Most of you will want *could have* or *could've*." That's the full measure of its guidance. Then sometimes there's virtually no guidance at all: on the question whether the distinction between *infer* and *imply* is worth preserving, the *Merriam-Webster* authors give five reasons why it's not. Bizarrely, along the way they say that "the words are not and never have been confused."[8]

These sweeping statements, and hundreds of others like them in *Merriam-Webster*, simply don't comport with reality.[9] And they blur important distinctions in the gradations of usage. So the Language-Change Index helps the user understand something about answering the questions, Who uses a particular expression? Everybody? Highly literate people? Only moderately literate people? Only those whose language is pretty slipshod? And what does the use of a given expression say about its user?

The Language-Change Index rejects, naturally enough, the bizarre dogma that I touched on above—a dogma that many linguists have accepted since the mid-20th century—that a native speaker of English cannot make a mistake.[10] The belief is that anything a native speaker says is ipso facto linguistically correct. The dogma was first espoused by the linguist–lexicographer Allen Walker Read and soon came to be accepted within the ivory tower.[11] Increasingly, though, that view has fallen into disrepute for three reasons: (1) common experience refutes it (see the "solecistic summary" at the outset of this essay);[12] (2) native speakers reject it, as witness the fact that

---

[7]Anyone can sign up at www.lawprose.org.

[8]*Merriam-Webster's Concise Dictionary of English Usage* 421 (2002).

[9]Warnings against the perennial confusion of misusing *infer* for *imply* are legion in English handbooks. But if citations of actual misusages are needed, see the entry in the middle of this book (p. 464), where I note: "Don't be swayed by apologetic notes in some dictionaries that sanction the use of *infer* as a substitute for *imply*. Stylists agree that the important distinction between these words deserves to be maintained."

[10]See William E. Rutherford, *Language Universals and Second Language Acquisition* 164 (1987) ("During the period of American structuralism a myth became well established that a native speaker cannot make a mistake.").

[11]See, e.g., Bergen Evans, "Grammar for Today," 205 *Atlantic Monthly* 80, 80 (Mar. 1960) ("Scholars . . . do not believe that any language can become 'corrupted' by the linguistic habits of those who speak it. They do not believe that anyone who is a native speaker of a standard language will get into any linguistic trouble unless he is misled by snobbishness or timidity or vanity.").

[12]See Jefferson D. Bates, *Writing with Precision* 5–6 (rev. ed. 1985) ("'A native speaker of a language cannot make a mistake.' That statement is one I've encountered many times; possibly you've heard it too. No wonder we're confused. Either the statement is ridiculous, or there is no such thing as 'correct usage' anymore.").

they often admit errors in their speech and correct them;[13] and (3) the dogma sweeps away any analytical insights into differences between educated and uneducated speech, or even the different strata within standard English—and the relative statuses of certain words.[14] Besides, if a native speaker cannot make a mistake, then Mrs. Malaprop becomes unfunny in her verbal bungles, as when she refers not to *alligators* but to *allegories on the banks of the Nile*.

There is, however, a school of linguists who persist in adhering to a version of the no-mistake-is-possible dogma. Even today, they are curiously reluctant to allow the notion that if one wants to sound educated, one must avoid certain syntactic constructions and word choices. Many of these linguists cavalierly dismiss any effort to advance prescriptive notions about effective language. Consider John McWhorter, a prolific linguist, in his 2008 book *Our Magnificent Bastard Tongue*: "All attention paid to [linguistic prescriptions] is like medievals hanging garlic in their doorways to ward off evil spirits. In an ideal world, the time English speakers devote to steeling themselves against, and complaining about, things like *Billy and me* [as subject], singular *they*, and *impact* as a verb would be better spent attending to genuine matters of graceful oral and written expression."[15] So: *My friend said they might come over by themself this afternoon. I need to know the time, because it will impact when Billy and me will go to the store.* How can such a statement be consistent with "graceful oral and written expression"?

What I have here called a "solecism" McWhorter calls a "new way of putting things." And he says: "the conception that new ways of putting things are mistakes is an illusion."[16] Much more tendentiously, Steven Pinker argues that linguistic prescriptions "survive by the same dynamic that perpetuates ritual genital mutilations,"[17] and he refers to "the kind of terror that has driven the prescriptive grammar market in the United States during the past century."[18]

Many linguists, indeed, would argue the position to which McWhorter gives voice: "the notion that people are always 'slipping up' in using their native English is fiction."[19] Further still: "One must revel in disorder."[20] And the climax: "In our time, pedants are engaged in a quest to keep English's pronouns in their cages instead of *me* being used as a subject after *and* and *they* being used in the singular. Whether that fashion will pass I cannot say, but we do know that it is nothing but one more fashion."[21]

And what of the point that McWhorter and Pinker, like all other self-respecting linguists, use standard English themselves? This has been a conundrum that linguists have lived with for years. I noted the issue in the preceding essay:

---

[13]See Patricia Demers, *The Creating Word* 13 (1986) ("Professor Read's maxim, that a native speaker cannot make a mistake, is refuted by the evidence of common practice. Native speakers do not believe him, for they frequently correct themselves and sometimes each other: they are conscious of having made a mistake.").

[14]Cf. Mark Halpern, *Language and Human Nature* 122 (2009) ("At what point is a solecism committed by a single person transformed into a change in language that it is futile to resist?"); T.W.H. Holland, *The Nature of English* 136 (1967) ("Clearly we have not to accept as right any usage that any native speaker happens to adopt, nor even that large numbers happen to adopt. We shall not find ourselves accepting *them as don't like it* as sound usage, but why not? I suppose the only good reply is that people who use the language in a way we think good do not say it. This may be middle-class or upper-class snobbery, but it is also the defence of those who care about the clear and agreeable use of language, who value the power of making distinctions [that] are necessary or helpful.").

[15]John McWhorter, *Our Magnificent Bastard Tongue* 68–69 (2008).

[16]*Id.* at 72.

[17]Steven Pinker, *The Language Instinct* 374 (1994).

[18]*Id.* at 375.

[19]McWhorter at 70. Cf. Steven Pinker, *The Language Instinct* 371 (1994) ("The pervasive belief that people do not know their own language is a nuisance.").

[20]McWhorter at 77.

[21]*Id.* at 85.

[Linguists] themselves write exclusively in Standard English. If it's really a matter of complete indifference to them, why don't they occasionally *flout* (or should that be *flaunt*?) the rules of grammar and usage? Their writing could *militate* (or is it *mitigate*?) in favor of linguistic mutations if they would allow themselves to be *unconscious* (*unconscionable*?) in their *use* (*usage*?) of words, as they seemingly want everyone else to be. But they don't do this. They write by all the rules that they tell everyone else not to worry about. Despite their protestations, their own words show that correctness is valued in the real world.[22]

In a similar vein, a reviewer of David Crystal's *The Stories of English* called Crystal's consistent use of standard English while glorifying dialects "a major contradiction in the whole work," noting that "while it celebrates diversity [of usage] in every possible way, it is written throughout in flawless Standard English .... This is in a sense inevitable—the book wouldn't get printed otherwise—but one may also feel that the author is only theoretically sympathetic to nonstandards."[23] And the redoubtable Mark Halpern puts the point even more emphatically: "It is typical of the descriptivists to pat the uneducated on their heads and assure them that some poor usage is just fine, even if they would never dream of employing such usages in their own work. On this basis they plume themselves on being 'democratic,' and charge their prescriptivist opponents with elitism."[24]

As for McWhorter's own English, he has his lapses. For example, he is addicted to *as such* in the sense of "therefore."[25] Two examples of this wretched new misusage:

- "You learned what subjects and objects are, you learned your Parts of Speech. As such, you don't like someone coming along and deeming your effort and vigilance worthless."[26]
- "There are, believe it or not, languages where pronouns vary only for person but not number, such that *I* and *we* are the same word, *he*, *she*, and *they* are the same word, and as such, singular and plural *you* are the same word."[27]

And then there are the seeming attempts at youthful hipness by using multiple (often quadruple) exclamation marks and question marks, this in a book representing itself as a work of scholarship:

- "They do not specify for us that they are *in the process of eating the apples at this very instant!!!!*"[28]
- "[M]any grammarians considered the following words and expressions extremely déclassé: *all the time* (quality folks were to says *always*), *born in* (don't you know it's *born at*????), *lit* (What did I tell you, darling? It's *lighted*), *washtub* (I don't know why people can't say *washing tub* as they should!)."[29]

These are only a few examples.

To the extent that linguists do use standard English, it's sometimes under protest. McWhorter purports to answer "the question we [linguists] often get as to why we do not use [nonstandard] constructions ... in our own writing if we are so okay with them." The answer: "I was required to knuckle under."[30] And he adds: "At best I can wangle an

---

[22]Pp. xxxv–xxxvi.

[23]Tom Shippey, "We're Still at It," *Times Literary Supplement*, 20 Aug. 2004, at 11.

[24]Mark Halpern, *Language and Human Nature* 24 (2009).

[25]See p. 78 of this book.

[26]John McWhorter, *Our Magnificent Bastard Tongue* 68 (2008).

[27]*Id.* at 81.

[28]*Id.* at 72.

[29]*Id.* at 74.

[30]*Id.* at 66.

exception and get in a singular *they* or *their* once or twice a book. (I must note that the copy editor for this book, upon reading this section, actually allowed me to use singular *they* throughout the book. Here's to *them* in awed gratitude.)"[31] One wonders why copyediting might ever be necessary.

Descriptive linguists have long looked askance at anyone who purports to recommend certain uses of language over others, or to condemn isolated changes in language. In an otherwise superb history of the English language, Albert C. Baugh and Thomas Cable express pity for standard-bearing prescriptivists:

> Conservatives in matters of language, as in politics, are hardy perennials. We have seen many examples of the type . . . . They flourished especially during the eighteenth century, but their descendants are fairly numerous in the nineteenth and scarcely less common today. They generally look upon change with suspicion and are inclined to view all changes in language as corruptions. In retrospect they seem often melancholy figures, fighting a losing fight, many times living to see the usages against which they fought so valiantly become universally accepted. . . . If we might venture a moral, it would be to point out the danger and futility of trying to prevent the natural development of language.[32]

Their book, of course, is written in flawless STANDARD ENGLISH—and appears to have been fastidiously copyedited.

Outside the grove of academe, the garlic-hangers—the "conservatives in matters of language"—continue to hold sway. Not all of us are melancholy at all. I, for one, have come to delight in each new stage-1 misusage, each new solecism that I'm able to document and write about. It can be thrilling to discover for the first time someone misusing *corollary* for *correlation*; or *as such* without an antecedent, as if it were equivalent to *therefore*;[33] or one of a thousand other bungles. It's entertainingly outré to be able to write a couple of paragraphs like the "summary" at the outset of this essay (see the key on page lvi). It's sad, of course, to know that many teachers have given up the idea that they should teach good English.[34] But the proliferation of error can definitely be the source of a perverse joy. Let there be no doubt about that. Or about the fact that not everyone is incorrigible.

---

[31]*Id.*

[32]Albert C. Baugh & Thomas Cable, *A History of the English Language* 336 (5th ed. 2002).

[33]I was, as far as I know, the first critic to note this misusage: see *A Dictionary of Modern American Usage* 59–60 (1st ed. 1998).

[34]Consider this telling admonition from decades ago: "With the triumph of the doctrine of usage, amplified into 'the native speaker can do no wrong,' what does an English teacher have to teach his pupils that the pupils don't already know? After all, 'anyone who is not deaf or idiotic has fully mastered his native language by the end of his fifth year.' Teachers of English who listen to the siren song of the structuralists should perhaps begin to show some concern over the continuance of their own jobs, if not over anything else." Mario Pei, "*Webster's Third* in the Classroom," in *Words, Words, Words About Dictionaries* 110, 111 (Jack C. Gray ed., 1963).

Key to the Solecistic Summary

The truce that I once proposed between descriptivists and prescriptivists having been only conditionally *excepted* [accepted] by a single linguist, the *embattlements* [battles] must continue.

Linguistic history *bares* [bears] out the fact that since English has *spreaded* [spread] throughout the world, people who *hue* [hew] to traditional idioms can avoid the *maelstorm* [maelstrom] of *indivious* [invidious] solecisms that *await for* [await] the unwary. Although the language is continually evolving, and *insipient* [incipient] changes become *widespreadly* [widely] *disbursed* [dispersed] and then take *route* [root] so that words become distant from their *entomologies* [etymologies], the *mileau* [milieu] in which these changes occur remains fairly constant. To ask whether all change can be *quelched* [squelched] is a *mute* [moot] point—a serious *misnomer* [misconception]. The language is a self-regulating system of disambiguation, without any official body of persons in *high dungeon* [high dudgeon], at our *beckon call* [beck and call], *exerting* [asserting] a right to *meet* [mete] out punishment to a would-be *literati* [littérateur] who has a *heyday* [field day] abusing it—punishment that might amount not just to a mild *annoyment* [annoyance] but to *caricature* [character] assassination.

For all intensive purposes [For all intents and purposes], some linguistic shifts may *past* [pass] *mustard* [muster], even those that don't *harp back* [hark back] to Middle English or Early Modern English. People with an *overweening* [overwhelming] interest in *oversighting* [overseeing] English sometimes, as a kind of *guttural* [gut] reaction, take all this for *granite* [granted]. There will never be *paralyzation* [paralysis] of a living language, nor even *hiati* [hiatuses] in its evolution. And it may give *piece* [peace] of mind to know that linguistic change isn't something to be measured in decades, much less *per anum* [per annum]. *Improprietous* [Improper] words and phrases that may once have been considered *abdominable* [abominable], slightly *course* [coarse], or otherwise beyond the *pail* [pale] may, over time, become fully acceptable and no longer *peak* [pique] anyone's interest. But even if there *are* [is] many a person *whom* [who] *misuse* [misuses] particular words and *are* [is] allowed to do so with *impugnity* [impunity]—and *all tolled* [all told], English contains a *heterogenous* [heterogeneous] *mother load* [mother lode] of *almost infinite* [countless] potential errors—their *credulity* [credibility] is likely to be strained in the minds of listeners and readers. The more *populace* [populous] the language community, the greater the *wrecklessness* [recklessness] with which some speakers and writers can *reek* [wreak] havoc on the language itself. These *phenomenon* [phenomena] become their *mode of operandi* [modus operandi]; for them, perhaps we might say they could not *of* [have] known better, even if they *had ought* [ought] to. But in the end, close *analyzation* [analysis] should demonstrate that correct English usage should be *brandishment* [blandishment] enough—*it's* [its] own *reword* [reward].

A

a. A. Choice Between *a* and *an*. The indefinite article *a* is used before words beginning with a consonant sound, including /y/ and /w/ sounds. The other form, *an*, is used before words beginning with a vowel sound. Since the sound rather than the letter controls, it's not unusual to find *a* before a vowel or *an* before a consonant. Hence *a eulogy, a European country, a one-year term, a Ouija board, a uniform, an FBI agent, an MBA degree, an SEC filing.*

The distinction between *a* and *an* was not solidified until the 19th century. Up to that time, *an* preceded most words beginning with a vowel, regardless of how the first syllable sounded. The U.S. Constitution, for example, reads: "The Congress shall have Power . . . [t]o establish *an uniform* Rule of Naturalization." U.S. Const. art. I, § 8. But that's no excuse for a modern writer—e.g.:

- "The revisions include . . . [f]iling legislation to create *an uniform* [read *a uniform*] inspection code." Doris Sue Wong, "Revisions to Title 5 Unveiled," *Boston Globe*, 2 Aug. 1995, at 25.
- "How many men can claim to have been at the center of such *an wild* [read *a wild*] and sensual tableau?" Steven Saylor, "The House of the Vestals" (1993), in *The House of the Vestals* 225, 240 (1997) (perhaps a typo).
- "When touring Fontainebleu in 1677, John Locke noted that the back stairs leading to the apartments of the King's brother smelt like *an urinal* [read *a urinal*]." Anne Somerset, *The Affair of the Poisons* 47 (2003).

People worry about whether the correct article is *a* or *an* with *historian, historic,* and a few other words. Most authorities have supported *a* over *an*. The traditional rule is that if the *h-* is sounded, then *a* is the proper form. So people who aspirate their *h*'s and follow that rule would say *a historian* and *a historic*—e.g.:

- "Because this argument isn't so much *a historical* analogy as *a historical* desecration." Paul Greenberg, "'They All Do It'—Even the Founding Fathers?" *Wall Street J.*, 12 Oct. 1998, at A18.
- "The treatment of crime in Britain shows *a historic* shift away from the protection of life and property toward the pursuit of ideological ends." Paul Johnson, "Britain: A Thieves' Paradise," *Forbes*, 17 Feb. 2003, at 35.

This is not a new "rule." Even the venerated language authority H.W. Fowler, in the England of 1926, advocated *a* before *historic(al)* and *humble* (*FMEU1* at 1).

The theory behind using *an* in such a context is that the *h-* is weak when the accent is on the second rather than the first syllable (giving rise, by analogy, to **an habitual offender,* **an hallucinatory image,* and **an hysterical crowd*). Hence no authority countenances **an history,* though a few older ones prefer *an historian and *an historical.

Today, however, such wordings as **an hypothesis,* **an hereditary title,* and *an historic era are likely to strike readers and listeners as affectations in need of editing—e.g.:

- "If we value the information [that] they provide us, then the cognitive movement is reinforced and comes to be habitual: *an habitual* [read *a habitual*] pattern or pathway between neurons in the brain, *an habitual* [read *a habitual*] association of ideas in the mind." Nigel Rapport, "Context as an Act of Personal Externalisation," in *The Problem of Context* 194 (Roy Dilley ed., 1999).
- "[A]n agreement could be found among the members of the Security Council that they had the legitimate authority to start *an humanitarian* [read *a humanitarian*] intervention." Bruno Coppieters, "Legitimate Authority," in *Moral Constraints on War* 41, 50 (Bruno Coppieters et al. eds., 2002).
- "[She] laughed aloud, *an hysterical* [read *a hysterical*] sort of giggle, quickly stifled." Katharine Kerr, *Snare: A Novel of the Far Future* 591 (2003).

As Mark Twain once wrote, referring to *humble, heroic,* and *historical*: "Correct writers of the American language do not put *an* before those words." *The Stolen White Elephant* 220 (1882). Nearly a century later, the linguist Dwight Bolinger harshly condemned those who write *an historical* as being guilty of "a Cockneyed, cockeyed, and half-cocked ignorance and self-importance, that knoweth not where it aspirateth." Dwight Bolinger, "Are You a Sincere *H*-Dropper?" 50 *Am. Speech* 313, 315 (1975).

Anyone who sounds the *h-* in words of the type here discussed should avoid pretense and use *a*. *An* humanitarian is, judged even by the most tolerant standards, a pretentious humanitarian. See **herb** & **humble.**

LANGUAGE-CHANGE INDEX
1. **an historic(al)* for *a historic(al)*: Stage 3
Current ratio (*a historical* vs. *an historical): 3:1
2. *an habitual for *a habitual*: Stage 3
Current ratio (*a habitual* vs. *an habitual): 1.4:1

B. In Distributive Senses. *A*, in the distributive sense <ten hours a day>, has traditionally been considered preferable to *per*, which originated in COMMERCIALESE and LEGALESE. But *per* has muscled its way into idiomatic English in phrases such as *60 miles per hour, one golf cart per couple,* and *five books per student*. Although *an* could be substituted for *per* in the first of those phrases, *a* wouldn't work well in the second or third.

When the construction requires a PHRASAL ADJECTIVE, *per* is the only idiomatic word—e.g.: "Our *per-unit* cost is less than $1,000."/"The *$50-per-parent* fee seems unreasonably high."

C. Pronunciation. The indefinite article is ordinarily pronounced /ə/—not /ay/. The latter pronunciation

LANGUAGE-CHANGE INDEX (For the full key, see front matter pp. xxxi, l–li.)
Stage 1: Rejected. **Stage 2:** Widely shunned. **Stage 3:** Widespread but . . . **Stage 4:** Ubiquitous but . . . **Stage 5:** Fully accepted.
Invariably inferior forms marked by asterisk (*). • Ratios represent frequency of prevalent forms vs. variants in current books.

is appropriate only in cases of emphasis <I didn't say "clubs"; I said "*a club*">. But /ay/ is nearly ubiquitous among broadcasters, "who have been taught—and for good reason—to avoid filling pauses in their speech with *uh* or *um*. Thus, if they happen to pause on the article *a* when pronouncing it UH, they will appear to have committed this cardinal sin." *BBBM* at 2.

aback. See **taken aback.**

abalone (= an edible mollusk known for its mother-of-pearl shell lining) is pronounced /a-bə-**loh**-nee/. Cf. **calzone.**

abandon, vb. See **desert.**

abandonment; abandon, n. In most contexts, *aban-donment* (= the permanent relinquishment of any right or interest in a thing) is the noun that answers to the verb *abandon*. But in one particular idiom, *abandon* is the required noun: *wild abandon* or *reck-less abandon* (= unrestrained impulsiveness). The *SOED* dates the noun *abandon* (= surrender to natu-ral impulses; freedom from constraint or convention) back to the early 19th century. And it records *aban-donment* as sharing this sense from the mid-19th cen-tury. Still, *abandon* is so preponderant in this idiom that the two terms ought to be distinguished. In the following sentences, *abandon* better accords with modern usage:

- "Like a ventriloquist, the President put these words in the mouth of Dr. King: '. . . I did not fight for the right of black people to murder other black people with reck-less *abandonment* [read *abandon*].'" H. Bruce Franklin, "What King Really Would Have Said," *Phil. Inquirer*, 7 Dec. 1993, at A17.
- "But that reverb-drenched, Crazy-Horse-meets-Allman-Brothers-Band jamming, as precise as it is full of wild *aban-donment* [read *abandon*], is one great machine at work." Jeff Spevak, "My Morning Jacket One Great Machine," *Roches-ter Democrat & Chron.*, 16 Sept. 2002, at C2.
- "He walks straight into his boss's office, quits his job, goes on a pension and dives into a life of wild *abandon-ment* [read *abandon*], partying, drinking, taking drugs." David Wroe, "'I Chose to Be a Victim,'" *The Age*, 30 Nov. 2002, at 10.

LANGUAGE-CHANGE INDEX
abandonment misused for *abandon*: Stage 2
Current ratio: 7:1

abbreviable. So formed—not **abbreviatable*. See -ABLE (D) & -ATABLE.

ABBREVIATIONS. A. Acronyms and Initialisms.
Six points merit attention here. First, be aware of the technical difference between the two types of abbre-viated names. An *acronym* is made from the first letters or parts of a compound term. It's read or spo-ken as a single word, not letter by letter (e.g., *awol* = absent without official leave, *radar* = radio detection and ranging, and *scuba* = self-contained underwater breathing apparatus). An *initialism* is also made from the first letters or parts of a compound term, but it's

sounded letter by letter, not as one word (e.g., *r.p.m.* = revolutions per minute).

Second, the question often arises whether to place a period after each letter in an acronym or initialism. Searching for consistency on this point is futile. The trend nowadays is to omit the periods. Including them is the more conservative and traditional approach. Yet because an acronym is spoken as a single word (e.g., *UNESCO*), periods are meaningless. If an initialism is made up of lowercase letters, periods are often prefer-able: *rpm* looks odd as compared with *r.p.m.*, and *am* (as opposed to *a.m.*) looks like the verb. But with ini-tialisms made of uppercase letters, the unpunctuated forms are likely to prevail (as in *ABC, ATM, HIV, IRA, SUV, URL*, etc.).

Third, the best practice is to give the reader some warning of an uncommon acronym or initialism by spelling out the words and enclosing the acronym in parentheses when the term is first used. A reference to *CARPE Rules* may confuse a reader who does not at first realize that three or four lines above this acro-nym the writer made reference to a Committee on Academic Rights, Privileges, and Ethics. On the other hand, well-known abbreviations don't need this kind of special treatment—there's no need to announce a "Parent Teacher Association (PTA) meeting."

Fourth, capitalization raises various questions. In AmE there is a tendency to print initialisms in all capitals (e.g., FMLA, NJDEP) and acronyms in small capitals (e.g., GAAP, MADD, NASA). Some publications, however, use all capitals for both kinds. But in BrE the tendency is to uppercase only the first letter, as with *Ifor* and *Isa* for *Implementation Force* and *individual savings account*. An influential British commenta-tor once suggested (with little success on his side of the Atlantic) that the lowercasing be avoided: "From the full name to the simplified label three stages can be detected. For instance, the Society [for Checking the Abuse of Public Advertising] . . . becomes first *S.C.A.P.A.*, then *SCAPA*, and finally *Scapa*. In the inter-ests of clarity this last stage might well be discouraged, since thereby the reference is made unnecessarily cryp-tic." Simeon Potter, *Our Language* 177 (rev. ed. 1966). American writers have generally agreed with this view.

Fifth, don't use abbreviations that have already been taken. Although it's understandable how a writer in 1959 might have used *PMS* for *primary message sys-tems*, this would be worse than ill-advised today, since *premenstrual syndrome* is more commonly referred to by its initials than by its name. E.g.: "There are ten separate kinds of human activity which I have labeled Primary Message Systems (PMS). Only the first PMS involves language. All the other *PMS* [read *PMSes*] are nonlinguistic forms of the communication process." Edward T. Hall, *The Silent Language* 45 (1959). The language doesn't easily embrace dual-meaning acro-nyms. One exception is *IRA*, which has long referred to the Irish Republican Army but in the 1980s came to denote also an individual retirement account. Other examples exist, but all are generally to be avoided.

Once everyone thinks of the *FAA* as the Federal Aviation Administration, it's unwise to use that initialism in reference to the Federal Arbitration Act.

Sixth, when an indefinite article is needed before an abbreviation, the choice between *a* and *an* depends simply on how the first syllable is sounded. A vowel sound takes *an*, a consonant sound *a*—hence *an MGM film, an SOS, a DVD player, a UFO.* See **a (A)**.

B. Resulting Redundancies. Some acronyms and initialisms often appear as part of a two-word phrase in which the second word is what one of the short form's letters stands for. So a bank customer withdraws cash from an *ATM machine,* using a *PIN number* as a password. A supermarket clerk searches a milk carton for its *UPC code.* High-school seniors study hard for the *SAT test* (though the SAT owners now insist that the *T* does not stand for *test*—see **SAT**). Economists monitor the *CPI Index.* American and Russian diplomats sit down to negotiate at the *SALT talks* as their military counterparts consider whether to launch *ABM missiles.* Websites may display pages in *PDF format.* And scientists try to unlock the mysteries of the deadly *HIV virus.*

The problem with these phrases, of course, is that they are technically redundant (*automated-teller machine machine, personal-identification number number, Universal Product Code code, Scholastic Aptitude Test test, Consumer Price Index Index, Strategic Arms Limitation Talks talks, anti-ballistic missile missile, portable document format format,* and *human-immunodeficiency virus virus*). And although the redundancies may be passable in speech—especially with unfamiliar acronyms—they should be avoided in edited writing.

A slightly different type of redundancy arises if you define *ATC* as the *air-traffic control system* (the hyphen is preferable for the PHRASAL ADJECTIVE) but later write *ATC system,* as here: "The third factor I mentioned is the air traffic control system (ATC). The United States ATC is the finest system [delete *system*] in the world, and on a good weather day, with runways and navigation facilities working, things operate smoothly. However, sometimes the *ATC system* [read *ATC*] must slow the arrivals at a particular airport." Don Carty, "Why Was My Flight Canceled?" *Am. Way,* 1 May 2001, at 10. Perhaps the better solution in that passage would be to leave *system* out of the definition—e.g.: *The third factor I mentioned is the air-traffic control (ATC) system. The United States ATC system is the finest in the world, and in good weather, with runways and navigation facilities working, things operate smoothly. But sometimes the ATC system must slow the arrivals at a particular airport.*

See REDUNDANCY.

C. Initialese. One of the most irritating types of pedantry in modern writing is the overuse of abbreviations, especially abbreviated names. Originally, to be sure, abbreviations were intended to serve the convenience of the reader by shortening names so that cumbersome phrases would not have to be repeated in their entirety. The purported simplifications actually simplified. But many writers—especially technical writers—seem to have lost sight of this goal: they allow abbreviated terms to proliferate, and their prose quickly becomes a hybrid-English system of hieroglyphs requiring the reader to refer constantly to the original uses of terms to grasp the meaning. This kind of writing might be thought more scholarly than ordinary, straightforward prose. It isn't. Rather, it's tiresome and inconsiderate writing; it betrays the writer's thoughtlessness toward the reader and a puerile fascination with the insubstantial trappings of scholarship.

Three examples suffice to illustrate the malady:

- "As a comparison to these item-level indices, the factor-level indices IFS and C_ANR [*sic*] were both computed for the maximum likelihood factors. . . . Compression of the factor space tends to decrease both IFS and C_ANR, while excessive expansion is likely to also decrease the C_ANR, while the IFS might be expected to be reasonably stable. Thus, four rotation solutions were computed based upon Matthews & Stanton's (1994) extraction of 21 factors, the Velicer MAP test indicator of 26 (PCA) and 28 (image) factors, and Autoscree indicators of 17 and 21 factors for PCA and image respectively. From these solutions, it was hypothesized that a full 31 factor rotation might provide the optimal C_ANR parameters for the OPQ scales. Further, as a by-product of the use of MLFA, it is possible to compute a test." P. Barrett et al., "An Evaluation of the Psychometric Properties of the Concept 5.2 Occupational Personality Questionnaire," 69 *J. Occupational & Organizational Psychology* 1, 12 (1996).

- "For the initial model, the significant variable TRANS is only significantly correlated with SUBNO. SUBCTY is correlated with NI, with SUBNO, and with FSALEPER. NI, however, is significantly correlated with: (1) DOMVIN; (2) METH1; and (3) METH3. In the reduced model, these intercorrelations with NI are not an area for concern." Karen S. Cravens & Winston T. Shearon Jr., "An Outcome-Based Assessment of International Transfer Pricing Policy," 31 *Int'l J. Accounting* 419, 436 (1996) (parentheticals omitted).

- "SLIP, like VALP and ECC, is a defeasible constraint that is obeyed by all the types of head-nexus phrase considered thus far. It guarantees that (except in SLASH-binding contexts that we turn to in a moment) the SLASH value of a phrase is the SLASH value of its head-daughter." Ivan A. Sag, "English Relative Clause Constructions," 33 *J. Linguistics* 431, 446 (1997).

And so it goes throughout each article. See OBSCURITY.

When naming something new, one sometimes finds the task hopeless: consider the *ALI–ABA CLE Review,* as opposed to calling it the *American Law Institute–American Bar Association Continuing Legal Education Review.* You can't choose either one enthusiastically. Both sponsors must have their due (in part so that they can have their dues), and the initialisms might gradually become familiar to readers. But they aren't ideal because they give bad first impressions.

LANGUAGE-CHANGE INDEX (For the full key, see front matter pp. xxxi, l–li.)
Stage 1: Rejected. **Stage 2:** Widely shunned. **Stage 3:** Widespread but . . . **Stage 4:** Ubiquitous but . . . **Stage 5:** Fully accepted.
Invariably inferior forms marked by asterisk (*). • Ratios represent frequency of prevalent forms vs. variants in current books.

Remember that effective communication takes *two*—the writer and the reader. Arthur Quiller-Couch reminded writers never to forget the audience:

> [T]he obligation of courtesy rests first with the author, who invites the seance, and commonly charges for it. What follows, but that in speaking or writing we have an obligation to put ourselves into the hearer's or reader's place? It is *his* comfort, *his* convenience, we have to consult. To *express* ourselves is a very small part of the business: very small and unimportant as compared with *impressing* ourselves: the aim of the whole process being to persuade.
> Quiller-Couch, *On the Art of Writing* 291–92 (2d ed. 1943).

Abbreviations are often conveniences for writers but inconveniences for readers. Whenever that is so, the abbreviations should vanish.

Robert Burchfield warned that the proliferation of initialisms could profoundly affect the language as a whole: "As formations they are often ingenious—for example KWIC (*Key Word in Context*) and CARE (*Cooperative for American Relief Everywhere*, a federation of U.S. charities)—but they are barren, in that they cannot generate anything except themselves, and etymologically rootless. Each one that is formed takes the language fractionally away from its Germanic, and ultimately its Indo-European, origins." Robert W. Burchfield, *Unlocking the English Language* 65 (1989).

D. Plurals. See PLURALS (I).

abdomen is most commonly pronounced /**ab**-də-mən/, though some people continue to use the old-fashioned /ab-**doh**-mən/.

abdominal (= pertaining to the abdomen or belly) is so spelled. Perhaps under the influence of *abominable*, it is sometimes wrongly made **abdominable*—e.g.:

- "Colchicine, 0.5 or 0.6 mg every hour until relief or intolerable side effects (*abdominable* [read *abdominal*] cramping or diarrhea) occur . . . ." "Treatment of Gout," *Am. Fam. Physician*, 15 Mar. 1999, at 1624.
- "The uncertainty of Cox's status—he has not been able to practice for weeks because of an *abdominable* [read *abdominal*] strain, and he says he no longer wants to take painkillers—is only a small reflection of the uncertainty over the team's future." Gerald Eskenazi, "Add Cox to List of Jets' Troubles," *N.Y. Times*, 10 Dec. 1999, at D5.
- "Alfonso Soriano, diagnosed with tendinitis in his right shoulder, sat out Yankees' exhibition game vs. Twins yesterday in Fort Myers, as did Jason Giambi, who's battling strained *abdominable* [read *abdominal*] muscle." *N.Y. Post* (graphic), 8 Mar. 2003, Metro §, at 56.

Sometimes the substitution isn't an error but a pun, as in this headline: "Arnaldo Magnani *Abdominable* Snowman: Hefty tenor Luciano Pavarotti packs another white meteorite to hurl at girlfriend Nicoletta Mantovani after Saturday's Elton John AIDS fundraiser." "A Test of Albright's Domestic Policy," *Daily News* (N.Y.), 11 Feb. 1997, Gossip §, at 14.

LANGUAGE-CHANGE INDEX
*abdominable for *abdominal*: Stage 1
Current ratio (*abdominal* vs. **abdominable*): 44,048:1

*aberrance; *aberrancy. See **aberration**.

aberrant, adj.; **aberrational; aberrative.** These terms appear in order of descending frequency. *Aberrant* /**ab**-ər-ənt *or* ə-**ber**-int/ = deviating from behavioral or social norms. *Aberrational* /a-bə-**ray**-shə-nəl/ = of, relating to, or involving an aberration. *Aberrative* /ə-**ber**-ə-tiv/ = tending toward aberration. For *aberrant* as a noun, see **aberration**.

aberration; aberrant, n.; ***aberrance; *aberrancy.** *Aberration* = (1) a deviation or departure from what is normal or correct; or (2) a mental derangement. *Aberrant*, which is almost always used in reference to people, means "a deviant; one deviating from an established norm." **Aberrance* and **aberrancy* are NEEDLESS VARIANTS of *aberration*—enough so to be labeled linguistic aberrations themselves. See SPELLING (A).

aberrational; aberrative. See **aberrant,** adj.

abettor; *abetter. In both AmE and BrE, *abettor* is the more usual spelling. It was otherwise from about 1640 to 1750, but since then *abettor* has predominated. See -ER (A). Cf. **bettor.**

Current ratio: 2:1

abhor (= to detest, esp. on grounds of morality or ethics) is pronounced /ab-**hor**/ or /əb-**hor**/—not /ə-**bor**/. For an example of *adjure* misused for *abhor*, see **abjure** (C).

abide = (1) to stay, dwell <the right of entering and abiding in any state in the Union>; (2) to tolerate, withstand <we won't abide that type of misconduct>; (3) to obey (construed with *by*) <we abided by the rules>; (4) to await <our decision must abide the outcome of this struggle>; or (5) to perform or execute (in reference to court orders or judgments) <the lower courts must abide the judgments of the Supreme Court>. In sense 1, *abode* is the preferred past tense, and either *abode* or *abided* is the past participle. In all other senses, *abided* is the preferred past tense and past participle.

ability; capacity. The traditional distinction is that while *ability* is qualitative, *capacity* is quantitative. Hence, *ability* refers to a person's power of body or mind <a writer of great ability>; *capacity*, meaning literally "roomy, spacious," refers figuratively to a person's physical or mental power to receive <her memory has an extraordinary capacity for details>.

For the distinction between *capacity* and *capability*, see **capacity.**

abjection; abjectness. Both words refer to a state of being cast aside, abased, and humiliated. The subtle difference between the two is that *abjection* refers to the physical condition—e.g.: "*Abjection* was a way of surviving Stalin: you gave him something of your blood, without wavering." "Other Comments," *Forbes*, 3 Feb. 2003, at 26. *Abjectness* refers to the state of mind—e.g.: "But were he to continue in office, at least judging by the *abjectness* of his apology, MADD might just have found a national poster boy." Jim Coyle, "We've Come a Long Way in Public Attitudes," *Toronto Star*, 14 Jan. 2003, at B2. *Abjection* is used more frequently today by a 12-to-1 ratio.

abjure; adjure. A. Senses Distinguished. *Abjure*, the more frequently used of these words, may mean either (1) "to renounce" <Germany abjured the use of force>, or (2) "to avoid" <her evaluation abjured excessive praise>. In bygone days, people were sometimes required to "abjure the realm," i.e., go abroad. *Adjure* means "to charge or entreat solemnly; to urge earnestly" <Reagan adjured the Soviets to join him in this noble goal>.
B. Cognate Forms. The noun forms are *abjuration* (or **abjurement*—now defunct) and *adjuration*. The adjectival forms end in *-tory*. The agent nouns are *abjurer* and *adjurer*.
C. *Adjure* Misused. *Adjure* is sometimes misused for two other words, *abhor* and *require*. The first of these is hard to explain but easy to illustrate—e.g.: "Most of us don't dislike lawyers individually; we *adjure* [read *abhor*?] them as a group." "Our Legal System's Put Us in a Box," *Chicago Trib.*, 23 Aug. 1988, at C19.

The other error, *adjure* for *require* or *command*, occurs often in legal writing but elsewhere as well—e.g.:

- "Arizona law *adjures* [read *requires*] that statutes should be construed to effect their objects." *Knapp v. Cardwell*, 667 F.2d 1253, 1261 (9th Cir. 1982).
- "Assaying the quality of defendant's acts and omissions . . . *adjures* [read *requires*] just such a judgment call." *Swift v. U.S.*, 866 F.2d 507, 511 (1st Cir. 1989).
- "'Use Absolut,' he *adjures* [read *commands*] a waiter at the restaurant where he, Iris, Kate and Daniel have an uncomfortable dinner. 'I'll know if the bartender uses a house brand.'" Amanda Vaill, "A Story of Reckless Passion and Race," *Chicago Trib.*, 25 May 2003, Books §, at 3.

Fortunately, most writers use *adjure* correctly—e.g.: "Some talked of open schism last week, when she *adjured* him to 'rule' if he wanted to save home rule, and he replied that she had failed him in his moment of need." Michael Powell & Hamil R. Harris, "Norton's Exercise in Flexibility," *Wash. Post*, 7 Aug. 1997, at J1.
LANGUAGE-CHANGE INDEX
1. *adjure* misused for *abhor*: Stage 1
2. *adjure* misused for *require*: Stage 1

abjurer; *abjuror. The *-er* spelling, which has always predominated, is preferred. See -ER (A).
Current ratio: 5:1

-ABLE. A. Choice of *-able* or *-ible*. Many adjectives have competing forms ending in *-able* and *-ible*. Some of these have undergone DIFFERENTIATION in meaning; the less commonly used forms in some pairs are merely NEEDLESS VARIANTS of the predominant forms. The lists that follow contain the most troublesome words of this class.

Unlike *-ible*, *-able* is a living suffix that may be added to virtually any verb without an established suffix in either *-able* or *-ible*. Following are only some of the hundreds of adjectives preferably spelled *-able*:

actionable	contestable	lapsable
addable	contractable	lovable
admittable	conversable	mixable
advisable	convictable	movable
affectable	correctable	noticeable
allegeable	definable	offendable
analyzable	detectable	patentable
annexable	diagnosable	persuadable
arrestable	discussable	preventable
ascendable	endorsable	processable
assertable	enforceable	protectable
assessable	evadable	ratable
averageable	excisable	redressable
avertable	excludable	referable
bailable	expandable	retractable
blamable	extendable	revisable
changeable	extractable	rinsable
chargeable	ignitable	salable
circumscribable	immovable	suspendable
commensurable	improvable	tractable
committable	inferable	transferable
condensable	inventable	transmittable
connectable	investable	willable

Although *-ible* is now dead as a combining form in English, the words in the following list retain that suffix:

accessible	divisible	perceptible
adducible	edible	perfectible
admissible	educible	permissible
audible	eligible	plausible
collapsible	erodible	possible
collectible	exhaustible	producible
combustible	expressible	reducible
compactible	extensible	remissible
compatible	fallible	reprehensible
comprehensible	feasible	repressible
compressible	flexible	*rescissible
concussible	forcible	resistible
conductible	fusible	responsible
contemptible	gullible	reversible
controvertible	horrible	revertible
convertible	impressible	risible
corrodible	includible	seducible
corruptible	incorrigible	sensible
credible	indelible	submersible (*or*
deducible	intelligible	submergible)
deductible	interfusible	suggestible
defeasible	invincible	suppressible
defectible	irascible	susceptible
defensible	irrepressible	terrible
descendible	irresistible	transmissible
destructible	legible	uncollectible
diffusible	negligible	vendible
digestible	omissible	visible
discernible	oppressible	
dismissible	ostensible	

LANGUAGE-CHANGE INDEX (For the full key, see front matter pp. xxxi, l–li.)
Stage 1: Rejected. **Stage 2:** Widely shunned. **Stage 3:** Widespread but . . . **Stage 4:** Ubiquitous but . . . **Stage 5:** Fully accepted.
Invariably inferior forms marked by asterisk (*). • Ratios represent frequency of prevalent forms vs. variants in current books.

Some adjectives with the variant suffixes have different meanings. Thus *impassable* means "closed, incapable of being traversed"; its twin, *impassible*, means "unable to feel pain" or, less distinctively, "impassive, emotionless." *Passable* and *passible* have correspondingly positive meanings. (These pairs are formed from different Latin roots, L. *passus* "having suffered" and L. *passare* "to step.") Similarly, *impartible* means "not subject to partition" and *impartable* "capable of being imparted." *Conversable* means "oral," while *conversible* is a NEEDLESS VARIANT of *convertible*. *Forcible* means either "done by means of force" <forcible entry> or "characterized by force" <forcible behavior>; *forceable*, much less frequently encountered, means "capable of being overcome by force"; it would be the better term to describe a door that is "capable of being forced open." (See **forcible**.) For the similar difference between *educible* and *educable*, see **educable (A)**.

Other variant adjectives, though, are merely duplicative. Typical examples are *extendable*, *extendible*, and *extensible*. The first of these is now prevalent in AmE (though labeled obsolete in the *OED*). *Extensible* was, through the mid-20th century, the most common form, but today it trails *extendable* by a substantial margin, while *extendible* continues to appear infrequently. Writers and editors ought to settle on the most firmly established form—*extendable*, which is as well formed as the variants—and trouble their minds with weightier matters. See DIFFERENTIATION & MUTE E.

B. Attaching -able to Nouns. This passive suffix is usually attached to verbs, as in *avoidable*, *forgettable*, and *reproachable*. But sometimes it's attached to nouns, as in *marriageable*, *objectionable*, and *salable*. These do not mean "able to be married," "able to be objectioned," and so on. Although *marryable* and *objectable* would have been the more logical forms, time, idiom, and usage have made these and several other forms both ineradicable and unobjectionable.

C. Attaching -able to Intransitive Verbs. A few words formerly upset purists: *dependable* (*depend-on-able*), *indispensable* (*in-dispense-with-able*), *laughable* (*laugh-at-able*), *listenable* (*listen-to-able*), *reliable* (*rely-on-able*), and *unaccountable* (*un-account-for-able*). They're indispensable to the modern writer—not at all laughable. See **reliable.**

D. Converting -ate Verbs into -able Adjectives. When *-able* is added to a transitive polysyllabic verb ending in the suffix *-ate*, that suffix is dropped. Hence *accumulable*, *calculable*, *regulable*, etc. (See -ATABLE.) Exceptions, however, occur with two-syllable words, such as *rebatable* and *debatable*.

E. Dropping or Retaining the Medial -e-. This question arises in words such as *irreconcilable*, *microwavable*, *movable*, *resumable*, and *salable*. Although writers formerly put an *-e-* before *-able*, both AmE and BrE generally drop such a medial *-e-*, except in words with a soft *-c-* (*traceable*) or a soft *-g-* (*chargeable*). See MUTE E.

F. Compounds. English has a remarkable ability to accept unlikely forms such as *come-at-able* (1687) <the come-at-able facts of the case>, *get-at-able* (1799)

<the source of the leak may not be get-at-able>, and *unputdownable* (1947) <an unputdownable book>. These have been fashioned by adding *-able* to PHRASAL VERBS. In both AmE and BrE, the first two tend to be hyphenated (*come-at-able*, etc.). Yet *unputdownable* is universally solid, perhaps because none of the internal syllable breaks except *-able* begins with a vowel.

able to be [+ past participle]. This construction is rare—and rightly so. A sentence such as *That speech is able to be delivered by anyone* can always be advantageously revised: *Anyone can* [or *could*] *deliver that speech*. See PASSIVE VOICE.

ablution (= washing), which appears most commonly in the plural form, should generally be reserved for washing or rinsing as part of a religious rite. E.g.: "Before every prayer, Muslims perform *ablution*— washing their hands and face, rinsing their mouth and nose, and even washing their feet." Dr. Shagufta Hasan, "Age-Old Rituals Source of Health for Body, Mind," *Oregonian* (Portland), 18 July 2002, at 13. And the word may belong in exotic contexts—e.g.: "Early bathers were already making their morning *ablutions* [in the Ganges River]." Glenn Leichman, "Season's Greetings—on the Ganges," *Seattle Times*, 22 Dec. 1996, at K1. But the word is pretentious, or else facetious, when the reference is to the ordinary act of washing one's face and hands—e.g.: "By morning the water was usually frozen, calling for a trip to the kitchen to thaw it out before morning *ablutions*." Oliver Andresen, "Old-Time Winters Have a Biting Story to Tell," *Daily Herald* (Chicago), 24 Jan. 2003, at 3.

aboard. Usually restricted to ships or planes in BrE, this word is applied broadly in AmE to any public conveyance—e.g.: "The bus had about 35 pupils *aboard* from Varina and Mehfoud Elementary schools." Mark Bowes, "It Was Close to a 'Catastrophe,'" *Richmond Times-Dispatch*, 18 Jan. 1997, at B1. More recently, it has come to be applied to organizations as well—e.g.: "Longtime in-house attorney Thomas 'Tad' Decker was brought *aboard* in 2000 to become managing partner." Jeff Blumenthal, "New Year Brings Firm Leadership," *Legal Intelligencer*, 2 Jan. 2002, at 1.

abode. For the past tense of *abide*, see **abide.**

abode, place of. This phrase is a pretentious way of referring to someone's *home* or *house*. It's also redundant, since an *abode* is a place. See REDUNDANCY.

abolition; *abolishment. The latter is a NEEDLESS VARIANT. Cf. **admonition (B).**

Current ratio: 28:1

abominable (= [1] detestable, odious; or [2] extremely disagreeable) derives from the Latin adjective *abominabilis* "ill-omened" (seriously unlucky). During the Middle Ages, however, English writers mistook the ETYMOLOGY and believed—through a kind of "learned" folk etymology—that the word was *abhominable*, from *ab homine* (meaning "away from man; repulsive to mankind"). This usage persisted through the 17th century, and Shakespeare himself had a character in *The Tempest* (1611) refer to Caliban as "an abhominable Monster" (2.2.158). Indeed, Shakespeare's first folio includes 18 instances of the misspelled version. In what is probably Shakespeare's first play (*Love's Labour's Lost* [1588]), the laughable pedant Holofernes derides the "rackers of ortography" (5.1.24–25) who were starting to use the etymologically correct spelling of *abominable*. In fact, the rackers of orthography had done their work 300 years before the name Holofernes was ever dreamt up, when they started inserting the -*h*- into the Latin word: "The connection with *homo*, 'man,' is a very old error and antedates the adoption of the word into English." James Bradstreet Greenough & George Lyman Kittredge, *Words and Their Ways in English Speech* 342 (1901). Today usage has settled on the spelling *abominable* (things were set aright in the 18th century). The modern meaning of the word, however, derives from the erroneous etymology of medieval times.

aborigine, as a singular noun, is a BACK-FORMATION from the plural *aborigines* (L. *ab origine* "from the beginning"). Traditionally, the word *aboriginal* was considered the proper singular, but today *aborigine* is STANDARD ENGLISH as a singular noun. It predominates in print sources by a 2-to-1 ratio. (*Aboriginal* is still current in adjectival uses.)

The spelling *Aborigine*, with the initial capital, is traditional when referring to the indigenous peoples of Australia.

LANGUAGE-CHANGE INDEX
aborigine as a singular: Stage 5

abort = (1) (of a pregnancy, project, or mission) to end prematurely; (2) (of a fetus) to cause to be expelled before full development; or (3) (of a pregnant female) to cause to have an abortion. Senses 1 and 2 are more usual than sense 3, which, as an example of HYPALLAGE, strikes many readers as odd. E.g.: "In a case of 1949, the trial judge sentenced a husband who had tried to *abort* his wife and killed her to five years' penal servitude." Glanville Williams, *The Sanctity of Life and the Criminal Law* 155 (1957).

abortifacient. See **contraceptive.**

abortive; aborted. *Abortive* means "unsuccessful because cut short." It takes on the figurative sense of *aborted* (= cut short), as *an abortive attempt*, i.e., one cut short. (Note that -*ive*, an active suffix, here has a passive sense.) E.g.: "In the 50 years after the 1916 rising, an *abortive* anti-British rebellion, nationalists incorporated the tragedy into their vision of 'a heroic struggle against seven centuries of British oppression.' " "Famine, Politics Intertwined," *USA Today*, 15 Jan. 1997, at D2. *Abortive* is archaic in reference to abortions of fetuses, except in the sense "causing an abortion."

about. A. And *approximately*. When possible, use *about* instead of *approximately*, a FORMAL WORD often intended to lend a scientific air to prose. But it sounds pseudoscientific and pretentious when it appears in ordinary contexts.

B. And *around*. When there is a choice between *about* and *around*—as in *beat around* (or *about*) *the bush*, *strewn around* (or *about*) *the garden*, or *all around* (or *about*) *the city*—the word *around* greatly predominates in AmE. In those phrases, *about* sounds schoolmarmish.

C. *About the head*. Theodore M. Bernstein called this phrase "police-blotter lingo" (*The Careful Writer* at 5) when used in the sense "on" <the victim was pounded several times about the head>. The phrase might still be common in police blotters, but in published print sources it appears only occasionally—e.g.: "A Malaysian companion, 15, suffered a punctured eardrum from the interrogator's blows *about the head*." William Safire, "Singapore Adds Insult to Injury," *Star Trib.* (Minneapolis), 24 May 1994, at A15.

D. *At about*. This phrase is sometimes criticized as a REDUNDANCY, the argument being that *about* can often do the work by itself. It often can, but in many contexts, especially those involving expressions of time, the phrase *at about* is common, idiomatic, and unimpeachable <we'll arrive at about 9:00 tonight>.

above. A. Meaning "more than" or "longer than." Although *over* has come to be accepted in these senses, *above* should be restricted to informal contexts. It's a CASUALISM when used before a plural noun—e.g.:

- "Now, the RBI has allowed only the incentive of one percent for one-year deposits, 1.5 percent for two-year deposits and two percent for deposits *above two years* [read *of two years or more* or *of longer than two years*]." "NBFCs Allowed to Reimburse Part of Broker's Expenses," *Econ. Times*, 3 Oct. 1996, at 8. Cf. **over (A).**
- "A recent survey of New York City restaurants showed that only 12 percent had seating capacity *above* [read *for more than*] 200 people." Terry Fiedler, "Restaurants," *Star Trib.* (Minneapolis), 22 Apr. 1998, at D1.
- "The data shows the vast majority of users in Wales were men with *above* nine out of ten users being men in nearly every town." "Almost 3,000 Joined Adultery Website," *S. Wales Evening Post*, 24 Aug. 2015, at 2. (A possible revision: *The data show that over 90% of Welsh users were men.*)

LANGUAGE-CHANGE INDEX
above meaning "more than": Stage 4

B. For *above-mentioned*. *Above* is an acceptable ellipsis for *above-mentioned*, and it is much less inelegant <the above statements are his last recorded ones>. It was long thought that *above* could not properly act as an adjective. But the word was used in this way throughout the 20th century, even by the best writers. The *OED* records this use from 1873 and says that *above* "stands attributively," through ellipsis, for *above-said*, *above-written*, *above-mentioned*, or some other phrase.

LANGUAGE-CHANGE INDEX (For the full key, see front matter pp. xxxi, l–li.)
Stage 1: Rejected. **Stage 2:** Widely shunned. **Stage 3:** Widespread but . . . **Stage 4:** Ubiquitous but . . . **Stage 5:** Fully accepted.
Invariably inferior forms marked by asterisk (*). • Ratios represent frequency of prevalent forms vs. variants in current books.

Some critics have suggested that *above* in this sense should refer only to something mentioned previously on the same page, but this restriction seems unduly narrow. Still, it's often better to make the reference exact by giving a page or paragraph number, rather than the vague reference made possible by *above*. Idiom will not, however, allow *above* to modify all nouns: **above vehicle* is unidiomatic for *vehicle mentioned above*. (If you must say *mentioned*, put *above* after that word.) Better yet, simply write *the vehicle* if readers will know from the context which one you're talking about.

Less common than the adjectival *above* is the noun use <the above is entirely accurate>. Pooley's assessment still stands: "Any writer may feel free at any time to use 'the *above* statement,' and with only slightly less assurance, 'the *above* will prove.' In either case, he has the authority of scholars and standard literature." Robert C. Pooley, *Teaching English Usage* 130 (1946).

LANGUAGE-CHANGE INDEX
1. *above* as an adjective (as in *the above data*): Stage 5
2. *above* as a noun (as in *all of the above*): Stage 5

abridgable. So spelled—not **abridgeable*. See MUTE E.
Current ratio: 3:1

abridgment; abridgement. The first spelling is AmE; the second is BrE. Cf. **acknowledgment** & **judgment** (A). See MUTE E.

abrogable. So formed—not **abrogatable*. See -ABLE (D) & -ATABLE.

abrogate; arrogate. These words are sometimes confounded. *Abrogate*, the more common term, means "to abolish (a law or custom) by authoritative or formal action; annul; repeal." E.g.:

- "In 1964, heavy fighting began on Cyprus after Cypriot Archbishop Makarios *abrogated* a 1960 treaty signed by Cyprus, Greece and Turkey." "Almanac," *Chicago Trib.*, 4 Apr. 1997, Metro §, at 10.
- "Last month, the NYSE raised its fees to as much as $350 a branch from $250, but the SEC can *abrogate* the increase within 60 days, a period that ends in mid-March." Cheryl Winokur Munk, "SEC Is Reviewing Higher NYSE Fees on Branch Offices," *Wall Street J.*, 10 Feb. 2003, at C9.

Arrogate, meanwhile, means "to usurp"—e.g.:

- "And if [the justices of the U.S. Supreme Court] rule in favor of the McDougall panel, they have even more dramatically *arrogated* to themselves the role of super legislators." "Resolving Judicial Malpractice," *Detroit News*, 9 Apr. 1997, at A6.
- "Two dangerous impulses of government are at work: First is the desire to *arrogate* more power to the executive branch by refusing to acknowledge Congress' oversight role." Editorial, "Government's Path of Secrecy," *St. Petersburg Times*, 16 Jan. 2003, at A12.

The most common mistake between these words is to misuse *abrogate* for *arrogate*—e.g.:

- "Some of them have *abrogated* [read *arrogated*] to themselves the functions of faith, making claims that history will probably refuse them." Anthony Winterbourne, *Speaking to Our Condition: Moral Frameworks in Wagner's Ring of the Nibelung* 31 (2000).

- "Elizabeth *abrogated* [read *arrogated*] to herself the coen-esthetic realm of sensuous play, investing the state (and her own person) with the subject's primary affect, undercutting the Catholic cult of images." David Brett, *Rethinking Decoration: Pleasure and Ideology in the Visual Arts* 162 (2005). (Note the highfalutin tone, in which it's especially galling to see a word directly misapplied.)

See **arrogate.**

LANGUAGE-CHANGE INDEX
abrogate misused for *arrogate*: Stage 1
Current ratio (*arrogate to itself* vs.
*abrogate to itself): 84:1

abscess (= a small mass of pus collected in a hollow where tissue has decayed) is sometimes misspelled **absess* or **abcess*—e.g.: "Though the jokes start out low (tooth *absesses* [read *abscesses*], fake body casts), the sassin' siblings eventually show their true, warm, brotherly colors." "Fall Previews," *Newsday* (N.Y.), 8 Sept. 1996, at 4.

LANGUAGE-CHANGE INDEX
abscess misspelled **abcess* or **absess*: Stage 1
Current ratio: 3,257:16:1

abscond, vb., is both transitive ("to conceal [something]") and intransitive ("to depart secretly or suddenly; to hide oneself"). The intransitive uses are more common—e.g.:

- "She *absconded* in early December and eluded police for a month." Brian Maffly, "Rape-Shield Law Shielding an Injustice?" *Salt Lake Trib.*, 3 Oct. 1997, at D1.
- "When two girls *absconded* with a car from their parents' driveway for a joyride, they blamed Jenny's stolen car escapade for giving them the idea." Julia Prodis, "Life After Suicide Pact No Joy Ride," *Tulsa Trib. & Tulsa World*, 30 Nov. 1997, at A5.

While *abscond* is often followed by *with* to indicate a taking, and especially a theft, the word itself has no such meaning. Yet it is sometimes misused alone as a transitive with that sense—e.g.:

- "Do you . . . *abscond* [read *steal*] juicy thoughts, clever notions, oddball trivia and take it home to hang on the fridge or set under a paperweight?" Ina Hughes, "Even God Lost on Information Superhighway," *Knoxville News-Sentinel*, 27 Aug. 2001, at A2.
- "The biggest problem is the Chinese government is going to *abscond* [read *take*] about 97 percent of his paycheck, meaning the Houston Rockets are going to buy Beijing a couple of ICBMs in the next three years." David Whitley, "Projecting Boys into Men Won't Be Easy Tonight," *Orlando Sentinel*, 26 June 2002, at D1.

LANGUAGE-CHANGE INDEX
abscond misused for *steal*: Stage 1

abscondence; **abscondment*; **absc+sion*. The second and third are NEEDLESS VARIANTS rarely found. *Abscondence* is the preferred and most common noun corresponding to the verb *abscond*. E.g.: "Apart from these *abscondences*, the only clue to emotional turmoil was a struggle with his weight." Andrew Billen, "Playing the Shrink," *Observer*, 15 Sept. 1996, at 12. **Abscondance* is an infrequent misspelling.
Current ratio (in order of headwords): 2:1.5:1

absent, used as a preposition meaning "in the absence of" or "without," is commonly used in LEGALESE but is simply unnecessary JARGON. The better choices are *without* and *in the absence of*—e.g.:

- "*Absent* [read *Unless our city has*] these [qualities], the good citizens will choose to live *outside this environment* [read *elsewhere*?]." Robert J. Fauls Jr., "Let's Have Some Police Guidance," *Atlanta J.-Const.*, 21 Mar. 1996, at A17. (As it stood in the original sentence, *absent* was a kind of DANGLER, appearing to modify *citizens* instead of the city mentioned in the preceding sentence [not supplied here].)
- "That is, *absent* [read *without* or *in the absence of*] justification, anything goes." Jonathan Rauch, "For Better or Worse?" *New Republic*, 6 May 1996, at 18.
- "*Absent* a military solution, then, and *absent* a political one, the refugee crisis is unlikely to subside." "Cameron Responds to the Refugee Crisis with Spin," *Independent*, 8 Sept. 2015, at 2. (A possible revision: *Without a military or political solution, the refugee crisis is unlikely to subside.*)

Although Merriam-Webster has dated this usage from 1945, in fact it appeared in a law case 26 years earlier: "The *Dean* decision is a reminder . . . that fraud in the transferor is enough under 67e, *absent* good faith in and a fair consideration on the part of the transferee." *Richardson v. Germania Bank of New York*, 263 F. 320, 324 (2d Cir. 1919). For an interesting discussion of how this American legalism has spread into nonlegal contexts, see two pieces by Alan R. Slotkin, "Absent 'Without': Adjective, Participle, or Preposition," 60 *Am. Speech* 222 (1985); "Prepositional *Absent*: An Afterword," 64 *Am. Speech* 167 (1989).

LANGUAGE-CHANGE INDEX
absent for *without*: Stage 3

absentee, used as an adverb, is a useful linguistic development. E.g.: "Almost 9 percent of the voters voted *absentee*." Barbara Schlichtman, "Phillips, Chaney Apparently," *Sunday Advocate* (Baton Rouge), 6 Apr. 1997, at B4. It would be cumbersome in that context to have to write *voted as absentees*. Although some dictionaries record *absentee* only as a noun, the adverbial usage is increasingly widespread. The word may also function as an adjective <absentee ballot> <absentee landlord>.

LANGUAGE-CHANGE INDEX
absentee as an adverb: Stage 4

absentia, in. See **in absentia.**

absinthe; *absinth. The word derives from *artemisa absinthium*, the botanical name for common wormwood, a bitter herb used in folk medicines and drink flavors. In reference to the herb, *absinth was the predominant spelling in the 18th century. In the mid-19th century, a Swiss physician created a green medicinal alcoholic spirit with wormwood, green anise, and sweet fennel; he called it *absinthe*, and that has been the predominant spelling ever since, for both the herb and the drink. Both spellings occasionally appear in studies of the effects of wormwood mixed with alcohol, none of which have concluded that absinthe makes the heart grow fonder.

Current ratio (in order of headwords): 23:1

absolute. See ADJECTIVES (B).

ABSOLUTE CONSTRUCTIONS. Increasingly rare in modern prose, absolute constructions have traditionally allowed writers to vary their syntax while concisely subordinating incidental matter. The absolute phrase doesn't bear an ordinary grammatical relation to the rest of the sentence, since the noun or noun phrase does not perform any function (subject, object, apposition, etc.) that ordinarily attaches a noun grammatically to other words in the sentence. Yet the whole absolute phrase adverbially modifies some verb. For example: *The court adjourning, we left the courtroom.* This is equivalent to *When the court adjourned, we left the courtroom.*

This construction often has an antique literary flavor, and it gets creakier year by year. Few modern writers would use the nominative absolute in the way Herman Melville did: "A drumhead court was summarily convened, *he electing the individuals composing it* . . . ." *Billy Budd* 63 (1891; repr. [Signet ed.] 1979). In that sentence, the pronoun *he* is modified by the participle *electing; the individuals composing it* is the object of *electing*. The whole italicized phrase is a nominative absolute, since it has no grammatical function in the statement *A drumhead court was summarily convened.*

One does encounter more modern examples—e.g.:

- "Mike would not soon forget the frantic drive back to civilization, *the four-wheel-drive Land Rover slipping and sliding* up the muddy track into the hills." Michael Crichton, *Jurassic Park* 16 (1990).
- "When I visit the cemetery, I wonder what kind of life Mrs. Peter Anderson had, *she having been* pregnant and/or caring for children throughout much of her existence." L.T. Anderson, "Lessons on Home Schooling," *Charleston Gaz. & Daily Mail*, 15 June 1999, at C1.
- "He speaks in a voice that seems to emerge from a shadow. Perhaps it does, *he having been* conceived in the dark days of Europe following the last world war, and *he having been* nurtured under the repression of the ensuing Iron Curtain." James Keeran, "Andrei Codrescu: Man of Letters . . . and Radio," *Pantagraph* (Bloomington, Ill.), 28 Jan. 2000, at D1.

Yet as nominative absolutes become rarer, fewer and fewer writers understand how to handle them. Three problems arise.

First, many writers insert *with* at the beginning of the phrase (making it something like an "objective absolute") <With Jacobson being absent, the party was a bore>. E.g.:

- "In other local elections in France, the results were mixed, *with* [delete *with*] the right doing a bit better

LANGUAGE-CHANGE INDEX (For the full key, see front matter pp. xxxi, l–li.)
Stage 1: Rejected. **Stage 2:** Widely shunned. **Stage 3:** Widespread but . . . **Stage 4:** Ubiquitous but . . . **Stage 5:** Fully accepted.
Invariably inferior forms marked by asterisk (*). • Ratios represent frequency of prevalent forms vs. variants in current books.

than expected." "Balkan Dangers," *Economist*, 24 Mar. 2001, at 33.

- "*With her* [read *She*] having mastered all these skills, it was time . . . to get her to face up to the biggest challenge yet." Amy Edelstein, "It's Jessie the Messy," *Newsday* (N.Y.), 5 Mar. 2002, at B17. (A better revision: *Once she mastered all these skills, it was time . . . .*)

Second, some writers mistakenly make an absolute construction—what should be a "nominative" absolute—possessive. E.g.: "*His* [read *He*] having won an astonishing thirteen major golf events, including the 1930 Grand Slam (the British Open, the British Amateur, the U.S. Amateur, and the U.S. Open Championship), it's hard to fathom that Bobby Jones was little more than a part-time player." William Kissel, "Great Golf Shops," *Celebrated Living*, Mar. 2002, at 39–40.

Third, writers sometimes incorrectly separate the noun and the participle with a comma—e.g.: "President Clinton, having forcefully called attention to the atrocities in Bosnia, the U.N. decided to act." (Read: *President Clinton having forcefully called attention to the atrocities in Bosnia, the U.N. decided to act.*) See PUNCTUATION (D).

All in all, it's hard to quibble with the Fowler brothers' judgment that the absolute construction is "not much to be recommended." H.W. Fowler & F.G. Fowler, *The King's English* 124 (3d ed. 1931). Or with Lester King's later assessment: "The absolute construction is not wrong, merely stilted and clumsy. In my own editing, I always delete it and make some appropriate substitution." Lester S. King, *Why Not Say It Clearly* 33 (1978).

For a modern remnant of an absolute construction, see **provided.**

absolutely, in the sense "really" or "very much," is often a meaningless intensifier. *You should be absolutely ashamed of yourself* is the sort of thing a parent might say when scolding a child, but in polished writing the word *absolutely* adds nothing of value to that sentence.

absolve. Depending on the context, *absolve* takes either *of* or *from.* One is *absolved of* financial liability and *absolved from* wrongdoing—assuming that the authorities treat one kindly. *Absolve from* is the more frequent phrasing.

absorb; adsorb; *sorb. *Absorb* is the common term meaning "to soak up"; *adsorb* is a scientific term that refers to the collecting of condensed gas (or similar substance) on a surface. (Just try writing that without so much sibilance: it will stump even the most sedulous scribe.) **Sorb* is a relatively obscure term that embraces both of its prefixed siblings.

abstracter. See **abstractor.**

ABSTRACTITIS. "How vile a thing . . . is the abstract noun! It wraps a man's thoughts round like cotton wool." Arthur Quiller-Couch, *On the Art of Writing* 109 (2d ed. 1943). *Abstractitis* is Ernest Gowers's term for writing that is so abstract and obtuse

(hence abstruse) that the writer does not even know what he or she is trying to say (*FMEU2* at 5). Far be it from the reader, then, to find coherent meaning in such writing.

One sympathizes with a keen judge who wrestled with the Internal Revenue Code: "The words . . . dance before my eyes in a meaningless procession: cross-reference to cross-reference, exception upon exception—couched in abstract terms that offer no handle to seize hold of—leave in my mind only a confused sense of some vitally important, but successfully concealed, purport, which it is my duty to extract, but which is within my power, if at all, only after the most inordinate expenditure of time." Learned Hand, "Thomas Walter Swan," 57 *Yale L.J.* 167, 169 (1947).

Perhaps the best antidote to this malady—which in some degree afflicts most sophisticated writers—is an active empathy for one's readers. Rigorous thought about concrete meaning, together with careful revision, can eliminate abstractitis.

An example from political science illustrates the affliction:

> Rosenau defines linkage as "any recurrent sequence of behavior that originates in one system and is reacted to in another." While there remains little doubt that such linkages exist, it has nevertheless been convenient for scholars of comparative and international politics to disregard or, to use the more contemporary term, to hold constant, factors in the other sphere. Thus, for the student of international politics, the nation functions in the international environment on the basis of the givens of that system, unrestrained by any domestic considerations. Differences existing between national systems are not considered crucial to an understanding of a nation's international behavior. This approach to international politics has been referred to as the "realist" school, and among its leading proponents is Hans J. Morgenthau. From the other perspective, the student of comparative politics feels that the international system is virtually irrelevant for purposes of explaining domestic political events. In both cases, this has led to a rather stultified approach. Situations arose in which the actions of a nation appeared to be "irrational," in that they could not be explained adequately on the basis of the conceptual tools of either of the two approaches.
>
> It is to these types of problems that the emerging linkage politics approach addresses itself. The purpose of studying linkage politics is to gain a more complete understanding of events by taking account of a large number of variables that have a bearing on the ultimate behavior of a nation, whether this behavior be manifested in the domestic or international spheres. The adoption of such an approach does not imply that all previously unexplained phenomena now come within our grasp. It merely adds a new dimension to those phenomena already accounted for.
>
> Jonathan Wilkenfeld, Introduction, *Conflict Behavior & Linkage Politics* 1 (1973).

This passage doesn't give any examples of the principles it discusses. It combines PASSIVE VOICE with JARGON. And it has many of the archetypal abstract words known as ZOMBIE NOUNS—that is, words ending with these suffixes: *-tion, -sion, -ment, -ity, -ence, -ance.* Writers are well advised to take these longish nouns and turn them back into verbs or participles if possible—that is, write *adopting*, not *the adoption of*, and so on.

The Fowler brothers quote the following sentence—laden with zombie nouns—in *The King's English* (1906): "One of the most important reforms mentioned in the rescript is the unification of the organization of judicial institutions and the guarantee for all the tribunals of the independence necessary for securing to all classes of the community equality before the law" [42 words]. Arthur Quiller-Couch's revision eliminates the ZOMBIE NOUNS: "One of the most important reforms is that of the courts, which need to be independent within a uniform structure. In this way only can people be assured that all are equal before the law" [35 words]. *On the Art of Writing* 109–10 (2d ed. 1943). But the following revision is even better: "Among the most important reforms is to unify the courts so as to guarantee their independence and the equality of all people before the law" [25 words].

By some accounts, abstractitis leads to far worse things. "If concepts are not clear," wrote Confucius, "words do not fit." And consequences follow: "If words do not fit, the day's work cannot be accomplished, morals and art do not flourish. If morals and art do not flourish, punishments are not just. If punishments are not just, the people do not know where to put hand or foot." Confucius, *Analects* 13.3. When we descend into abstractitis, more than just our language is afflicted.

Fred Rodell, a Yale law professor, realist, and semanticist who frequently criticized lawyers' language, issued his own inimitable warning against abstractitis: "Dealing in words is a dangerous business, and it cannot be too often stressed that what The Law deals in is words. Dealing in long, vague, fuzzy-meaning words is even more dangerous business, and most of the words The Law deals in are long and vague and fuzzy. Making a habit of applying long, vague, fuzzy, general words to specific things and facts is perhaps the most dangerous of all, and The Law does that, too." Fred Rodell, *Woe Unto You, Lawyers!* 39 (1939; repr. 1980). See OBSCURITY.

ABSTRACT NOUNS, PLURALS OF. See PLURALS (J).

abstractor; *abstracter. The *OED* notes that *-or* is "analogically the more regular form." Since the early 1960s, it has been the more usual as well. See -ER (A).
Current ratio: 2:1

abstruse; obtuse. *Abstruse* = (of a subject matter, piece of writing, etc.) difficult to understand; recondite. *Obtuse* = (1) not pointed or sharp; or (2) dull in intellect, not perceptive.

abysm(al); abyss(al). Both nouns signify "a bottomless gulf." *Abyss* is in more widespread use and is therefore to be preferred. Though *abysm* is obsolescent, *abysmal* thrives (indeed, in some phrases it has become trite) as a figurative term for "immeasurably bad" <abysmal ignorance> <abysmal weather>. *Abyssal* is a technical oceanographic term <the geology of the abyssal deep>.

academically. So spelled—not **academicly*. E.g.: "The goal of the strategic plan is to keep the university competitive economically and *academicly* [read *academically*] through the year 2005, the release states." Frank Mastin Jr., "84 Employees Lose Their Jobs at Tuskegee University," *Montgomery Advertiser*, 2 Oct. 1997, at C2. See -IC.

LANGUAGE-CHANGE INDEX
academically misspelled **academicly*: Stage 1
Current ratio: 18:1

academy; academia; academe. An *academy* (/ə-**kad**-ə-mee/) is (1) a school, especially one to prepare for further education, usu. at the postsecondary level <college-prep academy>; (2) a school that provides specialized career training <police academy>; or (3) an organization of distinguished scholars, artists, scientists, or the like who aim to develop, promote, and maintain standards in a field <the National Academy of Sciences>. The term derives from *academia* (/ak-ə-**dee**-mee-ə/), which commonly refers to the academic community at large, or the society of university scholars <authorities from the worlds of business and academia>. Capitalized, it refers to Plato's school of philosophy in ancient Greece, which morphed into *Academe*. *Academe* (/**ak**-ə-deem/) is the oldest English-language term for a school or an academic community; today it's used almost exclusively to refer to an institution of higher education <halls of academe>, often in the SET PHRASE *groves of academe*.

a cappella (= [of singing] not accompanied by instrumental music) is sometimes misspelled **a capella*—e.g.: "Sarah Waltman and Lenore Lopez, both of Blue Island, were in the audience at Cafe Luna on the night when Yaseen made her *a capella* [read *a cappella*] debut." Annemarie Mannion, "Instant Stardom," *Chicago Trib.*, 17 Aug. 1997, Tempo Southwest §, at 1. Occasionally, it is misspelled with an apostrophe—e.g.: "A performance by the acclaimed Rust College *A'Cappella* [read *A Cappella*] Choir." "SLU," *Times-Picayune* (New Orleans), 1 Feb. 2001, Mandeville §, at 7. It's also wrong to spell the term as one word.

Though borrowed from the Italian for "chapel," the phrase has been thoroughly anglicized and should not be set in italic.

LANGUAGE-CHANGE INDEX
a cappella misspelled **a capella*: Stage 1
Current ratio: 4:1

accede; exceed. *Accede*, v.i., = (1) "to agree or consent"; (2) "to come into office or a position of stature"; or (3) "to enter a treaty or accord." It takes the preposition *to*. *Exceed*, v.t., means (1) "to surpass," or (2) "to go beyond the proper limits." The first syllable

LANGUAGE-CHANGE INDEX (For the full key, see front matter pp. xxxi, l–li.)
Stage 1: Rejected. **Stage 2:** Widely shunned. **Stage 3:** Widespread but . . . **Stage 4:** Ubiquitous but . . . **Stage 5:** Fully accepted.
Invariably inferior forms marked by asterisk (*). • Ratios represent frequency of prevalent forms vs. variants in current books.

of *accede* should be pronounced with a short *a-* to differentiate its sound from *exceed*.

Occasionally *exceed* is misused for *accede* (sense 1)—e.g.: "Eighty potential jurors filed into the Santa Clara County superior court chambers of Judge Charles Hastings after he, *exceeding* [read *acceding*] to the wishes of Davis' attorneys, instructed Joel and B.J. Klaas, the slain girl's grandparents, to remove the memorial buttons from their lapels." Michael Dougan, "Judge Orders Removal of Polly Klaas Buttons," *S.F. Examiner*, 14 Feb. 1996, at A2.

LANGUAGE-CHANGE INDEX
exceed misused for *accede*: Stage 1

accelerate (= to speed up), in STANDARD ENGLISH, is pronounced /ak-**sel**-ə-rayt/—not /ə-**sel**-ə-rayt/.

accent, v.t.; **accentuate.** These synonyms have a good latent distinction. H.W. Fowler noted that *accent* is more common in literal senses, *accentuate* in figurative senses (*FMEU1* at 7). Hence one properly *accents* the second syllable of the word *insurance*, but *accentuates* the advantages of buying life insurance from a reputable company.

ACCENT MARKS. See DIACRITICAL MARKS.

accentuate. See **accent.**

accept, in STANDARD ENGLISH, is pronounced /ak-**sept**/—not /ə-**sept**/, /ə-**sep**/, or /ak-**sep**/. See **except,** vb.

acceptance; **acceptancy;* **acceptation;** **accepition.* *Acceptance* expresses the active sense of the verb (to accept), and *acceptation* expresses the passive sense (to be accepted). The other two are NEEDLESS VARIANTS.

Acceptance, the broadest term, means (1) "the act of accepting" <Williams's acceptance of the award was delayed>, or (2) "the state of being accepted" <widespread acceptance of the theory>. Although *acceptation* can bear sense 2 of *acceptance* (in which it's really a NEEDLESS VARIANT), today its primary meaning is "a generally accepted meaning (of a word, phrase, or document)"—e.g.: "The Constitution's 'commerce clause,' . . . in its original *acceptation*, had merely granted Congress limited authority over the regulation of interstate commerce." Wilfred M. McClay, "A More Perfect Union? Toward a New Federalism," *Commentary*, Sept. 1995, at 28.

access, n. **A. Confused with** *excess. Access,* n., most commonly means (1) "the right or ability to enter or get near," (2) "a means of approaching," or (3) "retrievability of electronic information by computer." *Excess* = (1) an overabundance, superfluity; or (2) the amount by which one thing exceeds another. Sometimes *access* is misused for *excess*—e.g.:

- "[I]t has been noted that samples of this kind may be difficult to amplify with primers that give a product in *access* [read *excess*] of 400–500 bp." Finbarr E. Cotter, *Molecular Diagnosis of Cancer* 117 (1996).
- "The event starts at 6:15 p.m., and carries a record purse in *access* [read *excess*] of $2.5 million." Will Parrish,

"May Month of Speed and Money," *Herald* (Rock Hill, S.C.), 27 Apr. 1999, at B3.

LANGUAGE-CHANGE INDEX
access misused for *excess*: Stage 1

B. Meaning "outburst." This sense, though somewhat archaic, is unimpeachable. Still, the usage is likely to give most readers pause—e.g.:

- "In an *access* [better: *outburst*] of unbridled enthusiasm, he hangs by his heels from a Calder sculpture while crooning 'La donna e mobile.'" Donal Henahan, "A New Wave Director Goes to Work on 'Rigoletto,'" *N.Y. Times*, 8 Sept. 1985, § 2, at 31.
- "His 90-year-old wife, Ellen, battered by years of strokes, knocked him down in a sudden *access* [better: *fit*] of wild rage, and wandered out of the house in her nightgown." Pearl K. Bell, "The Other Side," *New Republic*, 18 Dec. 1989, at 39.
- "Chris Denning . . . was fired, Peel recalls, for remarking on air that he awoke that morning in such *an access of* [better: delete *an access of*] high spirits that he felt like a 15 year-old boy, but that sadly there were no 15 year-old boys available at four o'clock in the morning." D.J. Taylor, "The God of Adolescence," *Sunday Independent*, 29 Aug. 2004, at 6.

access, vb. **A. Generally.** As a verb, *access* has its origins in COMPUTERESE. Like a number of other nouns turned into verbs (e.g., *contact*), it now seems increasingly well ensconced in the language. As Ernest Gowers said about *contact*, it is an ancient and valuable right of English-speaking peoples to turn their nouns into verbs when they are so minded (*FMEU2* at 108). *Gain access to* or some other such equivalent is admittedly ungainly alongside *access*.

But outside computing and electronic contexts, using *access* as a verb still jars sensitive ears. Avoid the verb if there's a ready substitute—e.g.:

- "The residents had bypassed utility meters and were *accessing* [read *getting*] free gas, water, electricity and cable television, deputies said." "Man, Mom Arrested in Child Endangering Case," *Press-Enterprise* (Riverside, Cal.), 4 Dec. 1996, at B3.
- "There are now over 130 miles of converted trails in New York, all easily *accessed* [read *accessible*] by, what else, train." "Best of the Net," *Village Voice*, 21 Jan. 1997, at 25.

LANGUAGE-CHANGE INDEX
access as a verb outside computing contexts
<accessing the books>: Stage 4

B. For *assess.* Sometimes *access* is misused for *assess* (= to evaluate)—e.g.: "They track hundreds of trends, looking for connections and *accessing* [read *assessing*] the implications of major socio-economic and political events." Siona Carpenter, "Turning Point," *Times-Picayune* (New Orleans), 14 Jan. 1997, at F1.

LANGUAGE-CHANGE INDEX
access misused for *assess*: Stage 1

*accessary. See **accessory (A).**

accessible. So spelled—not **accessable*. The word is pronounced /ak-**ses**-i-bəl/. See -ABLE (A).

Current ratio: 2,404:1

accession = (1) a coming into possession of an office or right; (2) acquisition of (something connected to one's property) by growth, labor, or the like; or (3) a secondary or subordinate thing that is connected with another thing. The word is pronounced /ak-**se**-shən/, not /ə-**se**-shən/.

accessory, n. **A. And** **accessary,* n. *Accessory* now predominates in AmE and BrE in meaning both "abettor" and "a thing of lesser importance." Although H.W. Fowler championed a distinction between *accessory* and **accessary* (the first applying primarily to things, the second to people [*FMEU1* at 8]), **accessary* is now merely a NEEDLESS VARIANT and should be avoided.

Current ratio (*accessories* vs. **accessaries*): 275:1

B. Pronunciation. *Accessory* should be pronounced with the first *-c-* as a hard *-k-*: /ak-**ses**-ə-ree/. A common mispronunciation is /ə-**ses**-ə-ree/. Cf. **accession, flaccid** & **succinct.**

accidentally. So spelled. **Accidently* is a solecism— e.g.: "Big mistake—I *accidently* [read *accidentally*] turned on a full blast of icy water, [and] Debbie let out a bone-chilling yowl." Bob Puhala, "Kohler's 'Club' Cool Spot for Winter Whirl," *Chicago Sun-Times,* 15 Jan. 1995, Travel §, at 4. Big mistake indeed. The confusion arises partly from the popular pronunciation and partly from seemingly analogous terms such as *evidently* and *inadvertently.* Cf. **incidentally.**

LANGUAGE-CHANGE INDEX
accidentally misspelled **accidently*: Stage 1
Current ratio: 59:1

accident working. See **working.**

acclimate; acclimatize. Although the *-ize* form is preferred by H.W. Fowler and other BrE authorities, the shorter form—which actually predates the longer—is now standard AmE. Some American dictionaries put the primary definition under *acclimatize* /ə-**klı**-mə-tız/, but few Americans use this term; the main term is *acclimate* /**ak**-lə-mayt/. The corresponding nouns are *acclimation* /ak-lə-**may**-shən/ in AmE and *acclimatization* /ə-klı-mə-ti-**zay**-shən/ in BrE. See -IZE.

LANGUAGE-CHANGE INDEX
acclimate, vb., and *acclimation,* n.: Stage 5
Current ratio (*acclimate* vs. *acclimatize*): 3:1

accommodable. So formed—not **accommodatable,* as it is sometimes erroneously written. E.g.: "Ford [cites as the company's values] persistence, understanding business etiquette, and a demand in the industry to know the client's needs and deliver them in a concise, *accommodatable* [read *accommodable*] manner." Andrea Akins, "New Agency's Successes on the Fast Track So Far," *Nashville Bus. J.,* 21 June 1993,

at 35. But *accommodating* is far more common and familiar to readers. See -ABLE (D) & -ATABLE.

LANGUAGE-CHANGE INDEX
*accommodatable for *accommodable*: Stage 1
Current ratio (*accommodable* vs.
*accommodatable): 2:1

accommodate is one of the most frequently misspelled words in the language. See SPELLING (A).

accompanied. Since the 19th century, idiom has required *accompanied by,* not **accompanied with*—e.g.:

• "The book, inspired by his No. 1 song 'Butterfly Kisses,' features pictures of various fathers and daughters *accompanied with* [read *accompanied by*] short essays on growing up together." "Features, Books, Religious Bestsellers," *Christian Science Monitor,* 24 Dec. 1997, at 15.

• "Acupuncture has gained acceptance because more and more people seek therapy without the undesirable side effects often *accompanied with* [read *accompanying*] pharmaceutical drug treatments." "The Acupuncture Clinic," *Times Record News* (Wichita Falls, Tex.), 1 Sept. 2015, at A6.

Accompanied by, like *together with* and *along with,* does not make a singular subject into a plural one because it merely introduces a prepositional phrase. See SUBJECT–VERB AGREEMENT (E).

LANGUAGE-CHANGE INDEX
*accompanied with for *accompanied by*: Stage 2
Current ratio (*accompanied by* vs.
*accompanied with): 18:1

accompaniment is so spelled—not **accompanyment.* E.g.: "Ending his set with a shimmering 12-string guitar *accompanyment* [read *accompaniment*] to his first hit 'Part of the Plan,' Fogelberg returned for a one-song encore." Jack Leaver, "Fogelberg Revisits Good Years, to Hearers' Delight," *Grand Rapids Press,* 22 June 1997, at B7.

LANGUAGE-CHANGE INDEX
accompaniment misspelled **accompanyment*: Stage 1
Current ratio: 2,623:1

accompanist /ə-**kəm**-pə-nist/ is the standard form, not **accompanyist*—e.g.: "Paxton was in wonderful form, and *accompanyist* [read *accompanist*] Eric Weissberg added just enough instrumental firepower on guitar and dobro to lend the songs some spark." Greg Haymes, "Tom Paxton Shows He's Still at Top of His Songwriting Game," *Times Union* (Albany), 28 Mar. 1994, at C4.

LANGUAGE-CHANGE INDEX
accompanist misspelled **accompanyist*: Stage 1
Current ratio: 174:1

accord, n.; **accordance.** To be *in accord* is to be in agreement. E.g.: "The church agrees that Mary's message at those places is *in accord* with Catholic teaching and devotion." Steve Gushee, "For Many, Seeing Is Believing," *Palm Beach Post,* 17 Jan. 1997, at F1.

LANGUAGE-CHANGE INDEX (For the full key, see front matter pp. xxxi, l–li.)
Stage 1: Rejected. **Stage 2:** Widely shunned. **Stage 3:** Widespread but . . . **Stage 4:** Ubiquitous but . . . **Stage 5:** Fully accepted.
Invariably inferior forms marked by asterisk (∗). • Ratios represent frequency of prevalent forms vs. variants in current books.

To be *in accordance* is to be in conformity or compliance. Though sometimes cumbersome, the phrase is indisputably useful—e.g.: "Supporters of comprehensive sex ed are preparing to bring the battle to the states, compiling information detailing the least harmful way to design programs *in accordance* with the newly laid out federal standards." Clare Saliba, "Just Say No," *Village Voice*, 21 Jan. 1997, at 2. Certainly that wording is preferable to the legalistic phrase *pursuant to*. (See **pursuant to**.) But much depends on the precise phrase. For example, *in accordance with your request* is always stilted. Instead, write *as you requested* or some similar phrase.

Accord is sometimes wrongly used for *accordance*—e.g.:

- "Justice Marcos Aburto of the Supreme Court felt compelled to say that a decision would be made *in accord* [read *in accordance*] with the law and would not be influenced by outside pressure." Calvin Sims, "Case of '76 U.S. Assassination Reaching Final Stage in Chile," *N.Y. Times*, 15 May 1995, at A9.
- "An outside auditor [will] determine whether . . . the payments were disbursed *in accord with* [read *in accordance with* or *according to*] state law and local policy." "Hasty No-Bid Decision on Snap Just One Troubling Aspect of Deal," *Sun-Sentinel* (Ft. Lauderdale), 21 Dec. 1996, at A14.
- "The transaction went down *in accord* [read *in accordance*] with general plans outlined seven and a half months ago, except shareholders made a little more money than expected." Jeff Sturgeon, "Purchase of Valley Bank Complete," *Roanoke Times*, 2 July 2015, at A6.

LANGUAGE-CHANGE INDEX
in accord with misused for *in accordance with*: Stage 1

accord, v.t. **A. And** *afford.* These words share the meaning "to furnish or grant" <accorded (or afforded) all the respect due him>. Yet some DIFFERENTIATION is possible: *accord* has the nuance of granting something because it is suitable or proper <some 269 charter schools in 25 states have been accorded the freedom to do what is in their students' best interests>. *Afford*, in contrast, is the more general term meaning "to furnish (something) out of kindness, goodwill, or competitive strategy" <the airline afforded free upgrades to its most frequent fliers>.

B. Construing with Prepositions. When used intransitively, *accord* takes the preposition *in*, *to*, or *with*, depending on the context <we accord in our opinions> <we accord to plaintiff his due> <this accords with the prevailing view>.

accordance. See **accord,** n.

according. A. *According to.* This phrase means (1) "depending on"; (2) "as explained or reported by (a person)"; or (3) "in accordance with." In sense 2, the phrase is a weak form of attribution <according to Barbara Tuchman, . . .>; a text sprinkled with *according to*'s gives the appearance of having little originality. Use the phrase sparingly.

B. *According as.* This phrase, which has an antique literary flavor, means "in a manner corresponding to the way in which; just as." The phrase appears throughout the King James Version of the Bible—e.g.:

"And, behold, I come quickly; and my reward is with me, to give every man *according as* his work shall be." Revelation 22:12. In modern prose it carries a hint of ARCHAISM—e.g.: "Indiana schoolchildren will or will not learn to read and to write *according as* [read *depending on whether*] they are taught by their teachers and prodded by their parents." William F. Buckley, "What Has Caused the Gender Gap at the Polls?" *Las Vegas Rev.-J.*, 5 Nov. 1996, at B11.

C. As a Dangler. For *according* as an acceptable dangling modifier, see DANGLERS (E).

accordingly = (1) consequently, therefore <they were caught red-handed; accordingly, they were summarily fired>; or (2) in a corresponding or appropriate manner <they'll be dealt with accordingly>. See SENTENCE ADVERBS. The word is a heavy connector often replaceable to good advantage by *so*. Cf. **consequently.**

accost (= to approach and usu. to speak to in an abrupt or challenging manner) has historically had no connotations of physical contact. Hence it would traditionally be considered inappropriate in cases of physical violence—e.g.: "The victim, who was *accosted* [read *assaulted*] as he left the bar with three women, suffered scrapes and bruises." "Police Beat," *Capital* (Annapolis), 24 Aug. 1996, at A11. *Accost* simply isn't a strong enough word for that context. Cf. **altercation** & **assault.**

Also, *accost* isn't the right verb for what a threatening animal does, no matter how noisy it becomes—e.g.: "Two months later, a trio of yelping pit bull puppies *accosted* [read *attacked*] Waters in the basement of an apartment building." William Gaines & Laurie Cohen, "Workers' Comp Puts City on Injured List," *Chicago Trib.*, 12 Jan. 1997, at C1.

LANGUAGE-CHANGE INDEX
accost used in reference to a physical assault: Stage 3

accounting. See **bookkeeping** & **generally accepted accounting principles.**

accoutrement (= a supplementary item of dress or equipment; accessory) is predominantly so spelled in AmE and BrE alike, and always has been. Though given preference in several American dictionaries, **accouterment* has never prevailed in print. Likewise, the prevailing verb is *accoutre* in both AmE (by a 4-to-1 ratio) and BrE (by an 8-to-1 ratio).

Having been fully naturalized in the 16th century, the word is pronounced /ə-**koo**-tər-mənt/. It shouldn't be given a Frenchified pronunciation, as it sometimes is.

Current ratio (World English): 7:1
(AmE): 6:1

accredit (= [1] to establish as credible, or [2] to issue credentials to) is the verb corresponding to the noun *accreditation*. But **accreditate*, a BACK-FORMATION from *accreditation*, has arisen as a NEEDLESS VARIANT—e.g.: "The laboratory, on the second floor of the sheriff's Wheaton office, is one of 77 *accreditated* [read *accredited*] facilities in the country." Art Barnum, "Du Page Crime Lab Wins National

Accreditation," *Chicago Trib.*, 13 Mar. 1991, at D9. Although the longer form finds citations in the *OED* from the mid-17th century, these provide no basis for using it in contemporary prose. Besides, the *OED* labels the word obsolete.

Occasionally *accredit* is loosely used in place of *credit* or *attribute*—e.g.:

- "It would be reasonable to assume that at least some of Rusedski's astonishing recent improvement could be *accredited* [read *credited*] to his coach, Tony Pickard." Rosie DiManno, "More than Meets the Eye in Rusedski Affair," *Toronto Star*, 29 June 1998, at D6.
- "He was also an inventor and had several patents *accredited* [read *credited*] to his name." "John Steven" (obit.), *S. Bend Trib.*, 2 July 1999, at D5.
- "She *accredits* [read *attributes*] to her father, the retired Rev Hugh Dermot McMorran, one of the tenets of her policing 'beliefs.'" Alan Murray, "Force for the Future," *Belfast Telegraph*, 17 Dec. 2011, at 22.

The *OED* cites two examples, from 1876 and 1900, and labels this use an Americanism. But it doesn't represent the best in American usage.

LANGUAGE-CHANGE INDEX
1. **accreditate* for *accredit*: Stage 1
Current ratio: 336:1
2. *accredit* in the sense "credit" or "attribute": Stage 2

accreditation (= official approval given to someone or something by reason of having reached an acceptable standard) is pronounced /ə-kred-i-**tay**-shən/—not /ə-kred-i-**day**-shən/.

accrual; *accruement. The latter is a NEEDLESS VARIANT.
Current ratio: 528:1

accumulable. So formed—not **accumulatable*. See -ABLE (D) & -ATABLE.
Current ratio: 10:1

accumulate; accumulative; *cumulate; cumulative. *Accumulate* is far more common than **cumulate* as the transitive verb meaning "to pile up, collect." **Cumulate* should be avoided as a NEEDLESS VARIANT. *Accumulate* has the additional intransitive sense "to increase."

The adjectives demonstrate more palpable DIFFERENTIATION. In one sense they are synonymous: "increasing by successive addition," in which meaning *cumulative* is the usual and therefore the preferred term. *Accumulative* = acquisitive; inclined to amass. It would be salutary to strengthen this distinction.

accurate (= correct in every detail) is pronounced /**ak**-yə-rit/—not /**ak**-ə-rit/ or /**ak**-rit/. It's a matter of precision.

accusatory; accusatorial; accusative. *Accusatory* (= accusing; of the nature of an accusation) is occasionally confused with *accusatorial* (= of, relating to, or involving a criminal-law system in which the prosecution and the defense put forward their claims before an independent decision-maker). E.g.: "Before she could utter an *accusatorial* [read *accusatory*] word, Stella said, 'I know what you're thinking and the answer is no.'" Max Haines, "A Bitter Pill to Swallow," *Toronto Sun*, 31 Dec. 1995, at 42. To contrast *accusatorial* with *inquisitorial*, see **inquisitive.**

Accusative should be restricted to its grammatical sense, i.e., the case that marks the direct object of a verb or the object of certain prepositions. But it's sometimes used incorrectly in place of *accusatory*—e.g.: "Adopting an *accusative* [read *accusatory*] tabloid-TV style, the ad shows the Washington apartment of a lobbying firm where Kerry stayed intermittently over a period of months in 1989." Frank Phillips, "Weld Calls a Truce on Attack Ads," *Boston Globe*, 26 Oct. 1996, at A1.

LANGUAGE-CHANGE INDEX
accusative misused for *accusatory*: Stage 1

accuse; charge. One is *accused of*, then *charged with*, a crime. Perhaps under the influence of *charged with*, the verb *accused* is sometimes unidiomatically paired with *with*—e.g.: "Ross and Vince Fera, Local 57's recording secretary and a member of its executive board, were *accused with* [read *accused of*] violating the union's code of ethics." Jim McKay, "Monitor Accuses Union of Crime Ties," *Pitt. Post-Gaz.*, 25 Nov. 1997, at F1. (The headline writer got it right.) See **charge (A).**

LANGUAGE-CHANGE INDEX
*accused with for *accused of*: Stage 1
Current ratio: 131:1

*accusee is a NEEDLESS VARIANT of the noun *accused* (= a person accused of wrongdoing). E.g.:

- "Later, [Judge Oren R. Lewis] turned to James S. Augus, the senior Justice Department trial lawyer, and accused him of 'shifting the burden of proof' from the accuser [the Justice Department] to the *accusee* [read *accused*]." Robert Meyers, "Courtroom Becomes Classroom," *Wash. Post*, 17 Mar. 1979, at C3.
- "This would, of course, suggest Nicholas Daniloff, U.S. News' Moscow correspondent, as the actual *accusee* [read *accused*]." Rance Crain, "Spying Inside the Inside Story," *Advertising Age*, 29 Sept. 1986, at 46.
- "Blocking is often inspired; especially inspired is an indiscretion with the *accusee* [read *accused*] defending himself with back to desk, side by side with the accuser." Geoff Gehman, "Theatre Outlet Pulls All the Stops in Magical 'Moonshine,'" *Morning Call* (Allentown, Pa.), 10 Mar. 2001, at A60.

Occasionally **accusee* is erroneously used for *accuser*—e.g.: "If these accusations are grounded on truth, then surely the *accusee* [read *accuser*] has a lot less to fear than the accused." Letter of Brody Stewart, "Readers' Views," *St. Cloud Times* (Minn.), 12 Mar. 2002, at B5. See -EE.

LANGUAGE-CHANGE INDEX
1. **accusee* for the attributive noun *accused*: Stage 1
Current ratio: 164:1
2. **accusee* misused for *accuser*: Stage 1

---

accuser; *accusor. The *-er* form is standard. It has always predominated. See -ER (A).

Current ratio: 869:1

accustomed. Formerly, the idiom was *accustomed to do*, *accustomed to think*, etc. But in the mid-20th century the phrasing shifted to *accustomed to doing*, *accustomed to thinking*. Today the older usage sounds strange to many ears, but some traditionalists stick to it, especially in BrE—e.g.: "Both stem from the age profile of a profession in which nearly two thirds of teachers are over 40 and *accustomed to think* of early retirement as the norm." John Carvel, "Questioning Professionalism of Teachers Can Be Harmful," *Guardian*, 14 Jan. 1997, at 2.

Current ratio (*accustomed to being* vs. *accustomed to be*): 2:1

acerbic, in AmE, is sometimes said to be inferior to *acerb* because it is a syllable longer. But *acerb* is so rare and *acerbic* so common—much more common than its sibling in modern print sources—that the criticism is misplaced. *Acerbic* is also standard in BrE, in which *acerb* is now virtually unknown. (Predominant in the 18th century, *acerb* rapidly declined in the 19th.) The noun is *acerbity*.

Current ratio (*acerbic* vs. *acerb*): 59:1

achieve, v.t., implies successful effort at something more than merely surviving to a given age. Thus **achieving manhood* and **achieving womanhood* are ludicrous phrases, but they and others like them are fairly common EUPHEMISMS—e.g.: "Others remember the excitement of seeing the world and the satisfaction of *achieving* [read *reaching*] adulthood in such difficult times." Robert Preer, "Fifty Years Later, Pain of War Still Throbs," *Boston Globe*, 29 May 1994, South Weekly §, at 1.

Achilles' heel; Achilles tendon. Since the early 19th century, *Achilles' heel* has predominantly sported the possessive apostrophe—though the competition between the with-apostrophe and without-apostrophe forms has been keen since before 1900. Meanwhile, though, the attributive form *Achilles tendon* (no apostrophe) has been vastly predominant since the mid-19th century. Hence many (perhaps most) dictionaries justifiably list the terms as they are recorded at the head of this entry.

Current ratio (*Achilles' heel* vs. *Achilles heel*): 1.2:1
Current ratio (*Achilles tendon* vs. *Achilles' tendon*): 22:1

acknowledge. The phrasing *This acknowledges your letter of January 15* is pure COMMERCIALESE. Instead, try for a more relaxed tone: *Thank you for your January 15 letter*.

acknowledgment; acknowledgement. As with *judgment* and *abridgment*, the spelling without the medial *-e-* has always predominated in AmE. But in BrE the medial *-e-* is standard (but only since about 1970). See MUTE E.

*acquaintanceship, a NEEDLESS VARIANT of *acquaintance*, adds nothing to the language except another syllable, which we scarcely need. E.g.:

- "Mexicans, having been distanced from Jews for centuries, brought a mixed background to the new *acquaintanceship*

[read *acquaintance*]." Adina Cimet, *Ashkenazi Jews in Mexico* 3 (1997).
- "We eat, pay bills, maneuver through the social pleasantries of an average set of *acquaintanceships* [read *acquaintances*], and try to maintain the cock of whatever hat we have chosen to wear through the terrain of an entire life." Edward Hoagland, "Sex and the River Styx," *Harper's Mag.*, Jan. 2003, at 49, 59.

LANGUAGE-CHANGE INDEX
*acquaintanceship for *acquaintance*: Stage 2
Current ratio (*acquaintance* vs.
*acquaintanceship): 59:1

acquiesce (/ak-wee-**es**/) takes either *in* or *to*—e.g.:

- "We have a strong desire to work with President-elect Bush when our ideas and values intersect, but also a duty not to *acquiesce in* actions with which we fundamentally disagree." Evan Bayh, "The Wrong Man," *Wash. Post*, 19 Jan. 2001, at A37.
- "The question for Bush is whether to simply *acquiesce to* the demands of these industries that provided millions for Republican campaigns." "Bush Pick Signals Big Changes for Western Lands," *USA Today*, 16 Jan. 2001, at A14.

Acquiesce in is the more traditional choice; it has always been more common than *acquiesce to*.

A slight DIFFERENTIATION seems to be emerging. Though one may acquiesce *in* events (especially unfortunate ones), one acquiesces *to* proposals and requests, or the people who propose them—e.g.:

- "Our president . . . will go down in history as having *acquiesced in* our nation's moral decline." Richard Rorty, "I Don't Need Money from Social Security," *Seattle Post-Intelligencer*, 9 Mar. 2000, at A21.
- "Burleigh paints a depressing picture of a society that *acquiesced in* the establishment of a brutal dictatorship and facilitated the unfolding of its increasingly murderous policies." Omer Bartov, "Hitler's Willing Believers," *New Republic*, 20 Nov. 2000, at 29.
- "Attorney General Thomas F. Reilly . . . has blasted the DTE for *acquiescing to* utilities without investigating their claims of higher costs." Peter J. Howe, "Agency Approves Electricity Rate Hike," *Boston Globe*, 12 Dec. 2000, at C1.
- "Bush might *acquiesce to* smaller changes made by Congress in annual spending bills." Jim Barnett & Jeff Mapes, "Bush May Bring Rural America into White House," *Oregonian* (Portland), 14 Dec. 2000, at A15.

acquiescence. See **permission.**

acquirement; acquisition. Here's the difference: traditionally, *acquirement* denotes the power or faculty of acquiring, *acquisition* the thing acquired. But both may also mean "the act of acquiring"; *acquisition* is more usual in that sense.

acquirer. So spelled—not *acquiror.

Current ratio: 9:1

acquisition. See **acquirement.**

acquit. This verb once took either *of* or *from*, but since the early 18th century the preferred and vastly predominant preposition has been *of*. E.g.: "In the end James was induced to withdraw a letter resigning from the Society, after the Council had passed a resolution *acquitting* him *from* [read *of*] any unfairness."

K.M. Elisabeth Murray, *Caught in the Web of Words* 286 (1977).

LANGUAGE-CHANGE INDEX
acquit from for *acquit of*: Stage 1
Current ratio (*acquit of* vs. *acquit from*): 4:1

acquittal; acquittance; *acquitment.* *Acquittal* is the usual term, meaning (1) "the legal certification, usu. by a jury's verdict, that an accused person is not guilty of a charge"; or (2) "the discharge of a debt or other liability." **Acquitment*, a NEEDLESS VARIANT, is obsolete. *Acquittance* is obsolete in all senses except "a written release showing that a debtor has been discharged of an obligation." It would be advantageous to allow *acquittance* this commercial meaning and leave *acquittal* to the criminal law.

acre measures area, not length. To put it differently, *acre* is a square, not a linear, measure. But the word is sometimes misused as if it referred to length—e.g.: "There were about 1,500 people buried at the Hardin Cemetery, once a pristine landscape *nine acres across* [read *of nine acres*] and now a muddy lake where minnows and snapping turtles live alongside broken headstones and toppled graves." Isabel Wilkerson, "Cruel Flood: It Tore at Graves, and at Hearts," *N.Y. Times*, 26 Aug. 1993, at A1.

ACRONYMS. See ABBREVIATIONS.

across, in STANDARD ENGLISH, is pronounced /ə-**kraws**/—not /ə-**krawst**/.

act; action. Distinguishing between these overlapping words is no mean task. Generally, *act* is the more concrete word <an act of Congress>, *action* the more abstract <spring into action>. *Act* typically denotes the thing done, *action* the doing of it. *Act* is unitary, while *action* suggests a process—the many discrete events that make up a bit of behavior.

activate. See **actuate.**

ACTIVE VOICE. See PASSIVE VOICE.

actual fact, in. See **fact** (c).

actuality. See **in actuality.**

actuate; activate. The Evanses wrote that *actuate* means "to move (mechanical things) to action" and that *activate* means "to make active" (*DCAU* at 10). The distinction is a fine one not generally recognized by dictionaries.

The less common term, *actuate*, often appears as a fancy substitute for *motivate* in a variety of contexts. (Likewise, *actuation* sometimes displaces *motivation*.) This usage should generally be avoided on stylistic grounds, but it is not strictly incorrect—e.g.: "What we are talking about is harassment by a small but determined group of photographers *actuated* [better: *motivated*] by greed to the point that they have lost all

sense of humanity." David Mellor, "The People's Princess," *Daily Mail*, 1 Sept. 1997, at 12.

acumen (= shrewd perception) is traditionally pronounced /ə-**kyoo**-men/, but in recent decades the variant /**ak**-yə-men/ has become dominant. Charles Harrington Elster, who writes on pronunciation matters, thinks "that AK-yuh-men was the innovation of younger (not well-enough-) educated speakers who think nothing of shifting an accent here and there in an effort to sound more urbane or savvy. . . . Like most pseudosophisticated innovations, AK-yuh-men soon became a follow-the-leader pronunciation with two quite different ways of saying *acumen* countenanced by the dictionaries where one, in my opinion, would do just fine." *BBBM* at 8.

LANGUAGE-CHANGE INDEX
acumen accented on first syllable: Stage 3

ACUTE ACCENT. See DIACRITICAL MARKS.

A.D. See **B.C.**

ad, short for *advertisement*, is acceptable in all but the most formal contexts.

adage (= a familiar saying that had its origins in antiquity) often appears in the venially redundant phrase *old adage*. The phrase is especially inappropriate when the saying is a recent one—e.g.: "Like all mathematical models, the *old adage* [read *adage*] of garbage in-garbage out holds true." Lauren Rudd, "Intel's Dismal Numbers Mask Earnings Growth," *Orlando Sentinel*, 25 July 2001, at B6.

adamant (= unrelenting, unyielding) has no corresponding noun at the ready. *Adamantness* is awkward at best. There's a gap in the language, and to fill it some writers have begun using *adamance*, on the analogy of *brilliant–brilliance, preponderant–preponderance, protuberant–protuberance,* and the like. Although the NEOLOGISM is quite understandable, conservative writers would probably insist (adamantly, one supposes) on *adamant stand, adamant attitude,* or *insistence* in sentences such as these:

- "Some San Fernando Valley business groups are wary of LABA because it won't relent in its *adamance* [read *adamant stand*] toward neighborhood councils." Jim Newton, "A Look Ahead," *L.A. Times*, 14 Sept. 1998, at B1.
- "Clarke was taken aback by Neilson's *adamance on being* [read *determination to be*] back for the second round." "Flyers Coach Anxious to Return from Cancer," *Ariz. Republic*, 11 Apr. 2000, at C8.
- "The peace process marked by the Good Friday agreement of 1998 had been endangered by the IRA's *adamance* [read *resistance*] against giving up its guns and explosives in any manner that might suggest defeat in its guerrilla war for Irish unification." "Breakthrough on IRA Arms," *S.F. Examiner*, 10 May 2000, at A22.
- "The *opposition's adamance* [read *strength of the opposition*] stunned the commission and its staff." Bryan

LANGUAGE-CHANGE INDEX (For the full key, see front matter pp. xxxi, l–li.)
Stage 1: Rejected. **Stage 2:** Widely shunned. **Stage 3:** Widespread but . . . **Stage 4:** Ubiquitous but . . . **Stage 5:** Fully accepted.
Invariably inferior forms marked by asterisk (✳). • Ratios represent frequency of prevalent forms vs. variants in current books.

Hendricks, "AGFC Cancels Crown Lake Ramp Plans," *Ark. Democrat-Gaz.*, 16 Apr. 2015, at 25.

The *OED* traces *adamance* back to 1954, with additional examples from 1961 and 1979. In fact, though, the word appeared in print sources as early as 1931.

LANGUAGE-CHANGE INDEX
adamance: Stage 3

adapt; adopt. These two are occasionally confounded. To *adapt* something is to modify it for one's own purposes; to *adopt* something is to accept it wholesale and use it.

adaptation; *adaption; *adaptative; adaptive. The longer form is standard in the noun (*adaptation*), the shorter in the adjective (*adaptive*).

Current ratio (*adaptation* vs. **adaption*): 95:1
Current ratio (*adaptive* vs. **adaptative*): 288:1

addable. So spelled—not **addible*. See -ABLE (A).

Current ratio: 4:1

added to. See SUBJECT–VERB AGREEMENT (E).

addendum (= an addition or supplement) forms the plural *addenda*. It's sloppy to use *addenda* as a singular—e.g.:

- "It is a new, revised and enlarged edition with an *addenda* [read *addendum*] by Robert H. Kelby." Damon Veach, "Continental Army Officers, 1775–1783 Updated," *Advocate* (Baton Rouge) (Mag.), 16 Feb. 1997, at 28.
- "Two Cape Cod gunning shorebird decoys that arrived too late for catalogue listing and so were included in an *addenda* [read *addendum*] are thought to be early carvings done by Crowell in the late 1800s." Virginia Bohlin, "Decoys Gain Prestige, Patina of Folk Art," *Boston Globe*, 24 July 2005, at G26.
- "As the new caterer at the Van Wezel, he'll be creating some pre- and post-events as *an addenda* [delete *an*] to the performances." Deborah Seeber, "Party Time," *Sarasota Herald Trib.*, 1 Oct. 2006, at L78.

See PLURALS (B).

LANGUAGE-CHANGE INDEX
addenda used for the singular *addendum*: Stage 2
Current ratio (*an addendum* vs. **an addenda*): 3:1

addicted; dependent. Regarding people's reactions to drugs, the distinction between these terms can be important. Someone who is *addicted* to a habit-forming drug has an intense physiological need for it. Someone who is *dependent* on a drug has a strong psychological reliance on it after having used it for some time. *Addiction*, then, is primarily physical, whereas *dependency* (also known as *habituation*) is primarily psychological.

address, n. & vb. In several of its verb senses, this is a FORMAL WORD: (1) "to speak to" <Jones addressed the managers in a manner that they considered insubordinate>; (2) "to direct (a statement, question, etc.) to" <Walters addressed the question to Fawcett, not to Majors>; (3) "to call attention to" <the report addressed four issues>; (4) "to deal with" <it's time to address these problems>.

Whether as a verb or as a noun, *address* is preferably accented on the second syllable: /ə-**dres**/. But for a residence or business, /**ad**-dres/ is fully acceptable.

addressee. See -EE.

adduce; educe; deduce. All three are useful when discussing the evidence marshaled in support of an argument. To *adduce* is to put forward for consideration something such as evidence or arguments. E.g.: "What I saw were individuals who voted to cripple the education process on the basis of rumors they freely attributed to one or two unnamed sources rather than properly *adduced* evidence." "How to Reform Our National Intelligence," *Baltimore Sun*, 30 Nov. 1996, at A13.

To *educe* is to draw out, evoke, or elicit. This term is the rarest of the three, but it occasionally appears in the popular press—e.g.: "Hitherto, how [Thurber] fitted into the screwball reputation of that magazine has had to be *educed* from his 'The Years with Ross' (1959)." John McAleer, "The Thurber Spirit," *Chicago Trib.*, 17 Dec. 1995, at C1. Sometimes, however, *educe* is misused for *adduce*—e.g.: "But the only evidence *educed* [read *adduced*] in support of this theory is a passing and rather inconclusive comment made by the Bronte family cook." Terry Castle, "Hush Hush, Sweet Charlotte," *New Republic*, 22 Jan. 1996, at 32. For still more complications involving this word, see **educe.**

To *deduce* is to draw an inference. E.g.: "As it happens, scientists have *deduced* the nature of an evolutionary path that a primitive blood-clotting mechanism could have followed to evolve into the more complex cascade." Boyce Rensberger, "How Science Responds When Creationists Criticize Evolution," *Wash. Post*, 8 Jan. 1997, at H1. See **deduce.**

LANGUAGE-CHANGE INDEX
educe misused for *adduce*: Stage 1

adducible. So spelled—not **adduceable*. See -ABLE (A).
Current ratio: 13:1

adequate. A. And *sufficient*. Though both words were originally used in reference to quantity, *adequate* now tends toward the qualitative and *sufficient* toward the quantitative. Hence *adequate* means "suitable to the occasion or circumstances," and *sufficient* means "enough for a particular need or purpose." For more on *sufficient*, see **enough,** adj.

B. *Adequate enough. This phrase is redundant. Either word suffices alone—e.g.:

- "While Tyrol doesn't have a particularly large or sophisticated snowmaking system, it is *adequate enough* [read *adequate*] to cover 100 percent of the slopes." Mike Ivey, "Snowboarders Aid in Revival of Tyrol Basin," *Capital Times* (Madison), 22 Dec. 1995, at C1.
- "The question [is] whether a translation is *adequate enough* [read *adequate*] considering not only different legal terminology but also changes from the L1 legal system into the L2 legal system." Marie J. Myers, "Bilingualism and the Use of Voice Dictation Software for Personal Computers," in *Language for Special Purposes* 140, 144 (Felix Mayer ed., 2001).
- "The commander of the garrison was dead. Veranius had been an *adequate enough* [read *able*] officer—*adequate enough* [read *able enough*] to be spared for this command—but the Second Legion could ill afford to send another

centurion from the campaign being waged against the hill-forts." Simon Scarrow, *The Eagle and the Wolves* 23 (2004).

See ADJECTIVES (B).

adherence; adhesion. Both words derive from the verb *adhere*, but *adhesion* is generally literal and *adherence* generally figurative. One should write about *adherence* to tenets or beliefs, and about *adhesion* of bubble gum to the sole of one's shoe. The word more frequently called on is *adherence*—e.g.: "Clinton's slavish *adherence* to a corporate agenda cannot be understated." Adolph Reed Jr., "A Slave to Finance," *Village Voice*, 21 Jan. 1997, at 27. (The writer seems to have misused *understated* for *overstated*.)

Occasionally *adhesion* appears wrongly for *adherence*—e.g.:

- "The strong *adhesion* [read *adherence*] to technocratic rules would block self-initiative and encourage resignation." M.K. Welge, "A Comparison of Managerial Structures in German Subsidiaries in France, India, and the United States," *Mgmt. Int'l Rev.*, Jan. 1994, at 33.
- "Certainly they vaunted their *adhesion* [read *adherence*] to the belief in the 'great blessings . . . .'" David S. Forsyth, "Scots and the Union," *Herald* (Glasgow), 23 Sept. 1995, at 19.

LANGUAGE-CHANGE INDEX
adhesion misused for *adherence*: Stage 1

ad hoc, adv. & adj., is a widespread and useful term meaning "for this specific purpose." Some have questioned its justification in English (e.g., Vigilans [Eric Partridge], *Chamber of Horrors* 26 [1952]). But it is firmly established and serves the language well when used correctly <ad hoc committee>.

By extension—some would say SLIPSHOD EXTENSION—the term has come to mean "without any underlying principle that can be consistently applied"—e.g.: "The D.C. Council, for example, undermines the work of the commission by approving tax changes *on an ad hoc basis* [read *haphazardly*] in response to the whims of business groups." Rudolph A. Pyatt Jr., "One Bold Plan Deserves Another," *Wash. Post*, 16 Jan. 1997, at E3.

Generally speaking, the phrases *on an ad hoc basis* and *in an ad hoc way* are verbose for the adverb *ad hoc*. (See **basis (A).**) Likewise, *ad hoc* should rarely if ever be qualified by *very* or *fairly*. Finally, attempts to condense the phrase into one word (e.g., **adhocking*) have failed and should be forgotten, and there is no need to hyphenate it. See PHRASAL ADJECTIVES (H).

ad hominem [L. "to the person"] is shortened from the LATINISM *argumentum ad hominem* (= an argument directed not to the merits of an opponent's argument but to the personality or character of the opponent). Occasionally the full phrase appears—e.g.: "'But supposing it had come to something?' demanded Miss Barton, pinning the *argumentum ad hominem* with a kind of relish." Dorothy L. Sayers, *Gaudy Night* 371 (1936; repr. 1995).

The more usual shortened form is sometimes misspelled **ad hominum*—e.g.:

- "He is not without sin; Limbaugh himself has made *ad hominum* [read *ad hominem*] attacks on some with whom he disagrees." Debra J. Saunders, "Rush and the Juice," *S.F. Chron.*, 8 July 1994, at A23.
- "I don't believe that they'll get into a lot of *ad hominum personal* [read *ad hominem*] attacks." Andy Sher, "Quayle Predicting Different Approach by Gore This Time," *Nashville Banner*, 9 Oct. 1996, at A1.
- "I think most Americans are getting a bellyful of *ad-hominum* [read *ad hominem*] attacks and character assassinations." "A Character of Conservation," *Wash. Times*, 4 Mar. 2001, at B5.

LANGUAGE-CHANGE INDEX
ad hominem misspelled **ad hominum*: Stage 1
Current ratio: 87:1

adieu /ə-**dyoo**/ (= farewell) for *ado* /ə-**doo**/ (= fuss, trouble) is a surprisingly common error—e.g.:

- "So without further *adieu* [read *ado*], presenting the best of the 1994 NCAA Tournament field: . . . ." Jim Thomas, "Committee Digests Upsets: Extra Hours Bring About Little Change," *St. Louis Post-Dispatch*, 14 Mar. 1994, at C1.
- "If Teevens' 1992 and 1993 Green Wave teams, which tilted and rolled to a cumulative 5–18 record, are the only measuring stick, then it's much *adieu* [read *ado*] about nothing." Dave Lagarde, "Bigger and Stronger, But Is Wave Better?" *Times-Picayune* (New Orleans), 18 Aug. 1994, at D1.
- "So without further *adieu* [read *ado*], here's an early-week primer for this 60th annual event." John Lindsay, "The Road to San Antonio," *Cincinnati Post*, 11 Mar. 1998, at D8.

Sometimes a pun is clearly intended—e.g.: "And then there's Whitewater, which has taken on a miserable life of its own. If it ever ends, it'll be much *adieu* about nothing." Herb Caen, "Time of Our Lives," *S.F. Chron.*, 30 Mar. 1994, at C1. The opposite error—*ado* for *adieu*—is exceedingly rare.

LANGUAGE-CHANGE INDEX
adieu misused for *ado*: Stage 1
Current ratio (*without further ado* vs.
*without further adieu): 53:1

ad infinitum (= continuing without end) is pronounced /ad in-fi-**nI**-təm/—not /ad in-**fin**-i-təm/ or /ad in-fi-**nee**-təm/.

adjective (= a word that describes a noun or pronoun) is pronounced /**aj**-ik-tiv/—preferably not /**aj**-ə-tiv/.

ADJECTIVES. A. Definition. An adjective is a word that modifies a noun. The word is sometimes used sloppily as if it meant "noun"—e.g.:

- "'Excellence' is *an adjective* [read *a noun*] that describes something which is of the highest quality." "Their Work Stands Out," *Barrister*, Summer 1989, at 5. (In that sentence, *describes* should probably be *denotes*, and *which is* should be deleted.)

LANGUAGE-CHANGE INDEX (For the full key, see front matter pp. xxxi, l–li.)
Stage 1: Rejected. **Stage 2:** Widely shunned. **Stage 3:** Widespread but . . . **Stage 4:** Ubiquitous but . . . **Stage 5:** Fully accepted.
Invariably inferior forms marked by asterisk (*). • Ratios represent frequency of prevalent forms vs. variants in current books.

- "Indeed, greatness is *an adjective* [read *a word*] befitting this Irish-bred 5-year-old son of 1990 Breeders' Cup Turf champion In The Wings." Jay Richards, "Singspiel More Versatile than Superhorse Cigar," *Las Vegas Rev.-J.*, 4 Apr. 1997, at C6.

Of course, *excellence* and *greatness* are nouns; their corresponding adjectives are *excellent* and *great*.

B. Noncomparable Adjectives. Many adjectives describe absolute states or conditions and cannot take *most* or *more*, *less* or *least*, or intensives such as *very*, *quite*, or *largely*. The ILLOGIC of such combinations is illustrated in this sentence: "It is possible that this idea too has outlived its usefulness and soon will be *largely discarded*." The literal meaning of *discard* impinges on the METAPHOR here: it is hard to imagine a single idea being halfway discarded, though certainly it could be halfway discredited. Deleting *largely* clears the meaning.

The best-known noncomparable (/non-**kom**-pər-ə-bəl/) adjective is *unique* (= being one of a kind). Because something is either unique or not unique, there can be no degrees of uniqueness. Hence *more unique and *very unique are incorrect. Yet something may be *almost unique* or *not quite unique*—if, for example, there were two such things extant. (See **unique**.) The Hope Diamond is unique; a Gutenberg Bible is almost unique. The diamond is not "more unique," though. This writer of distinction got the distinction right: "I've got a Dante, and a Caxton folio that is *practically unique*, at Sir Ralph Brocklebury's sale." Dorothy L. Sayers, *Whose Body?* 16 (1923; repr. 1995) (several variants of the folio are known to exist, but none are identical).

Many other words belong to this class, such as *preferable*: "Stoll said the city also plans dozens of hearings with groups, showing different scenarios of how growth could be handled and getting feedback on what is *most preferable* [read *preferable*]." Jack Money, "Technology Useful in City Planning," *Sunday Oklahoman*, 27 Apr. 1997, at 2. Cf. COMPARATIVES AND SUPERLATIVES (D).

Among the more common noncomparable adjectives are these:

absolute	inevitable	singular
adequate	infinite	stationary
chief	irrevocable	sufficient
complete	main	unanimous
devoid	manifest	unavoidable
entire	only	unbroken
false	paramount	uniform
fatal	perfect	unique
favorite	perpetual	universal
final	possible	void
ideal	preferable	whole
impossible	principal	

For example, the phrase *more possible should typically be *more feasible* or *more practicable*, since something is either possible or impossible. E.g.: "The VA medical centers, which have a long history of hospitalizing patients, have been stepping up outpatient services as they become more and more *possible* [read *compatible*] with emerging technology." Mary McGrath, "Debate Over VA Center Comes Home," *Omaha World-Herald*, 16 Feb. 1997, at B1.

This general prohibition against using these words in comparative senses (e.g., "absolutely impossible") should be tempered with reason. It has exceptions. Good writers occasionally depart from the rule, but knowingly and purposefully. For example, the phrase *more perfect* appears in the U.S. Constitution: "We the People of the United States, in order to form a *more perfect* Union, establish Justice, insure domestic Tranquility, provide for the common defence, promote the general Welfare, and secure the Blessings of Liberty to ourselves and our Posterity, do ordain and establish this Constitution for the United States of America." U.S. Const. pmbl. One writer criticizes this phrase and suggests that it "should read 'to form a *more nearly perfect* Union.'" George J. Miller, "On Legal Style," 43 *Ky. L.J.* 235, 246 (1955). Although the Constitution is not without stylistic blemishes, this probably isn't one of them, and the suggested edit seems pedantic. See **more perfect.**

A few adjectives, such as *harmless*, are wrongly thought of as noncomparable. It's hopelessly donnish to insist that something is either *harmful* or *harmless* and that you can't write *more harmful*, *more harmless*, or *relatively harmless*. The same is true of many other words.

C. Coordinate Adjectives. When two adjectives modifying the same noun are related in sense, they should be separated by a comma (or else *and*). So we say *a big, sprawling house* and *a poignant, uplifting film*. But when the consecutive adjectives are unrelated, there shouldn't be a comma—hence *a big white house* and *a poignant foreign film*.

Some consecutive adjectives present close questions—e.g.: "The *brief, unsigned Supreme Court opinion* said that the lawyers for Ms. Benten had failed to show a substantial likelihood that the case would be won if it were argued before the United States Court of Appeals for the Second Circuit." Phillip J. Hilts, "Justices Refuse to Order Return of Abortion Pill," *N.Y. Times*, 18 July 1992, at 1. Is the fact that the opinion is brief related to the fact that it is unsigned? If so, the comma is proper; if not, the comma is improper. Because signed opinions tend to be longer than unsigned opinions, the comma is probably justified. But the string of adjectives is awkward and might be improved: *The brief Supreme Court opinion, which was unsigned, said . . . .*

For more on the punctuation of successive adjectives, see PUNCTUATION (D).

D. Proper Names as Adjectives. When a proper name is used attributively as an adjective, the writer should capitalize only that portion used in attribution <a University of Florida student> <a John Birch Society member>.

The practice of using as adjectives PLACE NAMES having two or more words should generally be resisted. But it is increasingly common. Although *California home* and *Austin jury* are perfectly acceptable, *Sacramento, California home* and *Austin, Texas jury* are not. To make matters worse, some writers place a second comma after the state (on the theory that the state is an APPOSITIVE). Hence, using a city plus the state as an adjective disrupts the flow of the sentence—e.g.: "Farmland's president, Marc Goldman, sent out sleuths who traced the missing containers to an *Elizabeth, N.J., warehouse* he says is filled with discarded bottles of designer water." Edward Felsenthal, "Nobody's Crying Yet, but There Must Be Spilled Milk Somewhere," *Wall Street J.*, 20 June 1990, at B1. Such constructions contribute to NOUN PLAGUE, lessen readability, and bother literate readers. For more on this phenomenon, see FUNCTIONAL SHIFT (B).

E. Adjectives vs. Adverbs. English contains a number of linking verbs (or copulas) apart from *to be*—e.g., *appear, become, feel, look, seem, smell, taste*. These verbs connect a descriptive word with the subject; hence the descriptive word following the linking verb describes the subject and not the verb. We say *He turned professional*, not **He turned professionally*. Writers frequently fall into error when they use linking verbs. One must analyze the sentence rather than memorize a list of common linking verbs, much as this may help. Often unexpected candidates serve as linking verbs—e.g.:

- "The rule sweeps too *broadly* [read *broad*]." (The writer intends not to describe a manner of sweeping, but to say that the rule is broad.)
- "Before the vote, the senator stood *uncertainly* [read *uncertain*] for several days.) (The word describes not the manner of standing, but the man himself.)

A similar issue arises with an object complement, in which the sequence is [subject + verb + object + complement]—e.g.:

- "Chop the onions *finely* [read *fine*]." (The sentence does not describe the manner of chopping, but the things chopped. The onions are to become fine [= reduced to small particles].)
- "Slice the meat *thinly* [read *thin*]." (As above.)

An elliptical form of this construction appears in the dentists' much-beloved expression, *Open wide* (= open your mouth wide). Cf. **badly** (A).

F. Past-Participial Adjectives. In certain phrases, there is a decided tendency for past-participial adjectives to lose their participial endings. Hence *iced cream* has become *ice cream*, *creamed cheese* has become *cream cheese*, *high-backed chair* has become *high-back chair*, and *skimmed milk* has become *skim milk*. Meanwhile, *chartered plane* threatens to become *charter plane*. Yet *iced tea* stubbornly retains the participial inflection in most print sources. Although purists battle this trend, its inevitability seems clear. Purists, of course, are free to continue using the past participles for the phrases in transition, but they may not get what they were expecting if they order "iced cream."

G. Phrasal or Compound Adjectives. See PHRASAL ADJECTIVES.

H. Modification of Adjectives Ending in -*ed*. See **very** (B).

I. Adjectives Ending in -*ly*. See ADVERBS (B).

J. Adjectives That Follow the Noun. See POSTPOSITIVE ADJECTIVES.

K. Dates as Adjectives. See DATES (C).

L. Comparative and Superlative Adjectives. See COMPARATIVES AND SUPERLATIVES.

M. Animal Adjectives. See ANIMAL ADJECTIVES.

N. Adjectives as Nouns. See FUNCTIONAL SHIFT (C).

O. Adjectives as Verbs. See FUNCTIONAL SHIFT (E).

P. Nouns as Adjectives. See FUNCTIONAL SHIFT (B).

Q. Adjective–Noun Disagreement. See CONCORD (E).

adjournment = (1) the act of suspending proceedings to another time or place; or (2) an adjourned meeting, i.e., a meeting "scheduled for a particular time (and place, if it is not otherwise established) by the assembly's 'adjourning to' or 'adjourning until' that time and place." *Robert's Rules of Order Newly Revised* § 9, at 90 (10th ed. 2000). As *Robert's* points out, because sense 2 is susceptible to confusion with sense 1, the phrase *adjourned meeting* is preferable to *adjournment* in sense 2. Reserve *adjournment* for its ordinary meaning: sense 1.

adjudicable. So formed—not **adjudicatable*. See -ATABLE.

adjudicative; *adjudicatory; *judicative. The first is standard; the second and third are NEEDLESS VARIANTS.

Current ratio: 19:12:1

adjure. See **abjure.**

adjurer; *adjuror. The -*er* spelling is standard. See -ER (A).

Current ratio: 3:1

adjuster; *adjustor. *Adjuster* (= one whose job is to determine the amount of loss suffered when an insurance claim is submitted and to try to settle the claim) is the preferred spelling—the one that has vastly predominated since the words came into common use in the 18th century. See -ER (A).

Current ratio: 19:1

administer, v.t.; **minister,** v.i. *Administer*, which suffices in most contexts, has four meanings: (1) "to give" <administer treatment> <administer the oath of office>; (2) "to dispense" <administer frontier justice>; (3) "to manage" <administer the state health department>; and (4) "to manage and dispose of" <administer the movie mogul's estate>. The verb *minister*, now exclusively intransitive, shares all but the second sense, though only rarely. *Minister* is most commonly used in the sense of attending to others' needs or, in religious

LANGUAGE-CHANGE INDEX (For the full key, see front matter pp. xxxi, l–li.)
Stage 1: Rejected. **Stage 2:** Widely shunned. **Stage 3:** Widespread but . . . **Stage 4:** Ubiquitous but . . . **Stage 5:** Fully accepted.
Invariably inferior forms marked by asterisk (*). • Ratios represent frequency of prevalent forms vs. variants in current books.

contexts, of administering sacraments. And people in need are *ministered to*. Cf. *administrate.

*administerable. See administrable.

*administerial. See administrative.

administrable; *administerable; *administratable. The first is the correct form. The other two are NEEDLESS VARIANTS, the last one being an abomination to boot. See -ABLE (D) & -ATABLE.

Current ratio: 75:3:1

*administrate is an objectionable BACK-FORMATION from *administration*. Avoid it as a NEEDLESS VARIANT of *administer*—e.g.:

- "Inevitably, his unenlightened attempts to teach and *administrate* [read *administer*] were doomed to failure." Roger Braun, "Remember the Bad, Old Administrator-Less," *Wis. State J.*, 31 Dec. 1994, at A9.
- "The only people who would have known just how [much trouble] Jeremy was in were the people involved in *administrating* [read *administering*] the wages deal." Christopher Brookmyre, *Quite Ugly One Morning* 108 (1996).
- "This musical comedy features adults playing prepubescent teens and the grownups who *administrate* [read *administer*] the contest." "Is It the Weekend Yet?" *Hartford Courant*, 17 Aug. 2015, at B8.

LANGUAGE-CHANGE INDEX
administrate for *administer*: Stage 1
Current ratio (*administer* vs. *administrate*): 86:1

administrative; *administrational; *administerial. *Administrative* is the general, all-purpose term meaning "of, relating to, or involving administration or an administration." The other two are NEEDLESS VARIANTS.

Current ratio: 42,983:18:1

admirable (= having good qualities worthy of respect) is pronounced /ad-mi-rə-bəl/—not /ad-**mir**-ə-bəl/.

admissible; *admissable; *admittable. *Admissible* (the standard word) = (1) allowable; or (2) worthy of admittance (i.e., gaining entry). The other two are NEEDLESS VARIANTS. See -ABLE (A).

Current ratio: 2,754:10:1

admission. A. And *admittance*. The distinction between these terms is old and useful, but it has a history of being ignored. *Admittance* is purely physical, as in signs that read "No admittance." E.g.: "Temple Israel in Boston, one of the largest congregations in the area, has told members that tickets will be required for *admittance*, ushers will be vigilant about security, and bags might be searched." Michael S. Rosenwald, "Synagogues Add Security for High Holy Days," *Boston Globe*, 6 Sept. 2002, at B8.

Admission is used in figurative and nonphysical senses: "His *admission* to the bar in 1948 began a career that would be long and noteworthy." *Admission* is also used, however, in physical senses when rights or privileges are attached to gaining entry: "He supervised 200 people involved in . . . the *admission* of immigrants at Newark International Airport and the

detention of illegal immigrants at Federal detention centers." Ronald Smothers, "Ex-Official at Office for Aliens Is Sentenced," *N.Y. Times*, 22 Apr. 1997, at B4.

Sometimes *admittance* is misused for *admission*, as when the subject is being accepted for enrollment in a school—e.g.:

- "Your recent story on Texas Woman's University students' reaction to their board of regents' decision to allow men *admittance* [read *admission*] made me wonder." Letter of Robert L. Hazelwood, "The Other Side Now," *Houston Post*, 30 Dec. 1994, at A26.
- "To the extent that some private colleges may not require B averages to gain *admittance* [read *admission*], it could be tougher to win a state scholarship." "All Students Receiving Aid Should Have a B Average," *Atlanta J.-Const.*, 20 Jan. 1995, at A10.

LANGUAGE-CHANGE INDEX
admittance misused for *admission*: Stage 2

B. And *confession*. In criminal law, a distinction has traditionally existed between these words: an *admission* is a concession that an allegation or factual assertion is true without any acknowledgment of guilt with respect to the criminal charges, whereas a *confession* involves an acknowledgment of guilt as well as of the truth of factual allegations.

admit. In the sense "to acknowledge (something negative) as true or valid," the phrase *admit to* is invariably inferior to *admit*—e.g.: "But now it turns out they did not completely *admit to* [delete *to*] their losses, thanks to an accounting gambit that is breathtaking in its audacity." Floyd Norris, "Cooking Books: How Hurricane Losses Vanished," *N.Y. Times*, 5 Sept. 1993, § 3, at 1. Cf. confess (A).

*admittable. See admissible.

admittance. See admission (A).

admittedly. See SENTENCE ADVERBS.

admonition. A. And *monition*. Both terms mean "a warning; caution." *Admonition* is the more common, less technical term—e.g.: "Then Jack Kemp chimes in with an *admonition* to listeners to beg Congress to ban the procedure in question 'before one more life is lost.'" Nell Bernstein, "Abortion Wars: A Smaller Sequel," *Newsday* (N.Y.), 9 Mar. 1997, at G5. This word has the additional sense "a mild reprimand"—e.g.: "Righter could face sanctions ranging from an official *admonition* to being stripped of his priesthood and rank as a bishop." Mark O'Keefe, "Bishop's Heresy Trial May Split Pro- and Anti-Gay Episcopal Factions," *San Diego Union-Trib.*, 29 Sept. 1995, at E4.

Monition, a specialized term, means either (1) "a summons to appear and answer in court as a defendant or to contempt charges"; or (2) "a formal notice from a bishop mandating that an offense within the clergy be corrected."

B. And *admonishment*. Strictly speaking, *admonishment* is the act of admonishing, while *admonition* is the warning or reproof itself. Whenever *admonishment* can be replaced with *admonition*, it should be.

admonitory; *admonitorial; monitory; *monitorial. The -ory forms predominate.

ad nauseam is frequently misspelled *ad nauseum—e.g.:

- "More frustrating than the targeted, test-marketed media coverage . . . is the intellectual echo chamber that diagnoses *ad nauseum* [read *ad nauseam*] with nary a cure." Letter of Dan Sullivan, "Audible Sigh," *Harper's Mag.*, Jan. 2003, at 5.
- "Notice that Mark Geragos mentions . . . innuendo and references *ad nauseum* [read *ad nauseam*] to the satanic cult theory perpetrated for the last two months." Loretta Dillon, *Stone Cold Guilty: The People v. Scott Lee Peterson* 56 (2005).

LANGUAGE-CHANGE INDEX
ad nauseam misspelled *ad nauseum*: Stage 2
Current ratio: 4:1

adolescent. See teenager.

adopt. See adapt.

adoptive; adopted. *Adoptive* = (1) related by adoption <adoptive parents>; or (2) tending to adopt <first he took an adoptive posture toward the proposal, but then he rejected it>. The phrase *adopted father* is an example of HYPALLAGE, to be avoided in favor of *adoptive father*. The Latin sourceword, *adoptivus*, applied both to the adopting parent and to the adopted child. But today *adoptive* is almost always used to refer to the adults rather than the children. This has been true, however, only since about 1940. In the 19th century, *adopted father* predominated. But it has fallen off greatly since the mid-20th century.

Another way of looking at it is to say that *adoptive* is the active form: an adoptive parent is one who has adopted a child. *Adopted* is the passive form: an adopted child is one who has been adopted by a parent. So what happens in extended senses?

In reference to a city or country, *adopted* is the better, more logical, and much more common choice—e.g.: "[Elton] John had faith in his *adopted* city, or at least in Agassi and Sampras." Todd Holcomb, "Agassi, Sampras Show Knack for Court Comedy," *Atlanta J.-Const.*, 15 Dec. 2000, at D5. Although *adoptive* sometimes appears in such contexts, it is comparatively uncommon and usually less metaphorically accurate (since people can typically choose where to live)—e.g.: "My grandparents . . . were very proud of their native land [Italy]. However, their *adoptive* [read *adopted*] country was first and foremost in their minds and hearts." James Cimino, "Why Give Cubans Preferential Treatment?" *USA Today*, 10 Apr. 2000, at A26.

LANGUAGE-CHANGE INDEX
1. *adopted mother* for *adoptive mother*: Stage 3
Current ratio (*adoptive mother* vs. *adopted mother*): 3:1
2. *adoptive country* for *adopted country*: Stage 1
Current ratio (*adopted country* vs. *adoptive country*): 20:1

adsorb. See absorb.

adult is pronounced either /ə-**dəlt**/ or /**ad**-əlt/ as a noun <adults only>, but only /ə-**dəlt**/ as an adjective <adult supervision>.

*adulter. See adulterer.

adulterable (= capable of being adulterated) is so formed—not *adulteratable. See -ABLE (D) & -ATABLE.

adulterant, adj.; *adulterate, adj.; adulterated; adulterine. See adulterous.

*adulteratable. See adulterable.

adulteration. See adultery (B).

adulterer; *adulter; adulteress; adultera; adulterator. *Adulterer* is the usual agent noun meaning "someone who commits adultery." But the usage issue doesn't stop there because that definition raises the question: Which participant is it, precisely, who commits adultery? The law gives three possible answers:

- Under the canon-law rule, a married participant is an adulterer and an unmarried one is a fornicator. The sex of the married participant doesn't matter.
- Under the common-law rule, both participants commit adultery if the married participant is a woman. But if the woman is the unmarried one, both participants are fornicators, not adulterers. This rule is premised on whether there is a possibility of "adulterating" the blood within a family. (Any offspring from an adulterous union were called *adulterini*.)
- Under modern statutory law, some courts hold that the unmarried participant isn't guilty of adultery (that only the married participant is), but others hold that both participants are adulterers.

The other forms occur much less frequently. *Adulter* is an obsolete variant of *adulterer*; it also had the meaning of *adulterator* (= counterfeiter). *Adulteress* is the feminine form, now disfavored because of the growing awareness of SEXISM—likewise with *adultera*, the term from the civil law. *Adulterator*, as suggested above, derives from the noun *adulteration*, and not from *adultery*.

Today all these terms—and their legal meanings—are somewhat obscure because the legal doctrines themselves have long been somnolent (not to say sleeping around).

adulterous; *adulterate, adj.; adulterant, adj.; adulterated; adulterine. *Adulterous* and *adulterate* both mean "of, characterized by, or pertaining to adultery," the former term being the more common. E.g.: "There are revelations about *adulterous* wrinkles in his generally happy fourth marriage to Lauren Bacall—an affair with a makeup artist for him and an affair with Frank Sinatra for her." L.S. Klepp, "Play It Again, Sam, and Again," *Entertainment Weekly*, 11 Apr. 1997, at 78. *Adulterate*, adj., more common in Shakespeare's

LANGUAGE-CHANGE INDEX (For the full key, see front matter pp. xxxi, l–li.)
Stage 1: Rejected. **Stage 2:** Widely shunned. **Stage 3:** Widespread but . . . **Stage 4:** Ubiquitous but . . . **Stage 5:** Fully accepted.
Invariably inferior forms marked by asterisk (*). • Ratios represent frequency of prevalent forms vs. variants in current books.

day than in ours, has been relegated to the status of a NEEDLESS VARIANT.

Adulterant = tending to adulterate <adulterant chemicals in the mixture>. *Adulterated* = (1) corrupted or debased <an adulterated culture>; or (2) corrupted by an impure addition; made spurious <the vintage wine was thoroughly adulterated once the water was added>. *Adulterine* = (1) spurious; (2) illegal; or (3) born of adultery <adulterine bastard>.

adultery. A. And *fornication*; *cohabitation*. *Adultery* = sexual intercourse engaged in voluntarily by a married person with a person who is not the lawful spouse. Generally today, it doesn't matter whether the other participant is married. (But see **adulterer**.) *Fornication* often implies that neither party is married, but it may also refer to the act of an unmarried person who has sex with a married person. *Cohabitation* is "the fact, state, or condition of living together, esp. as partners in life, usu. with the suggestion of sexual relations" (*Black's Law Dictionary* 316 [10th ed. 2014]). It's often a EUPHEMISM for an unmarried couple's living together—but unlike *adultery* or *fornication*, it now carries little suggestion of wrongdoing.

B. And *adulteration*. *Adulteration* = (1) the act of debasing, corrupting, or making impure; (2) a corrupted or debased state; or (3) something corrupted or debased. The Latin verb *adulterare*, from which both *adultery* and *adulteration* derive, encompasses all these senses.

adumbrate (= [1] to foreshadow, or [2] to outline) is a FORMAL WORD that has been called an affectation. For example, two influential writers said in 1901 that the word is "so high-sounding as hardly to be allowable even in elaborate writing." James Bradstreet Greenough & George Lyman Kittredge, *Words and Their Ways in English Speech* 7 (1901). But contemporary writers (especially critics and English professors) sometimes find it serviceable in formal literary contexts—e.g.: "Auden was already of the view that 'all genuine poetry is in a sense the formation of private spheres out of public chaos,' a claim that *adumbrates* his more developed sense of literature as making a secondary world, to be set against the primary world over which otherwise we have little or no control." Denis Donoghue, "W.H. Auden," *Wash. Times*, 9 Feb. 1997, Books §, at B8.

Traditionally pronounced /ə-**dəm**-brayt/, it is today more often pronounced /**ad**-əm-brayt/.

advance; advancement. Generally, *advance* refers to steady progress; *advancement* refers to progression (1) beyond what is normal or ordinary, and (2) involving an outside agent or force. Hence the *advancement* of science suggests a bigger step forward than the *advance* of science. And although someone might get an occupational *advancement*, we speak of the *advance* of civilization. In senses suggesting the action of moving up or bringing forth, *advancement* is the proper word <National Association for the Advancement of Colored People>.

The distinction gets fuzzier in financial contexts. Although we speak (properly) of *cash advances* and *advances on royalties*, in law *advancement* commonly refers to a parent's expenditure made for a child with the idea that it's to be deducted from the child's inheritance.

The phrases *advance notice, *advance plans, *advance warning, and the like are redundant.

advanced, adj., = (1) having progressed beyond most others <an advanced way of thinking>; (2) being beyond an elementary level <advanced studies> <advanced students>; (3) sophisticated <advanced weaponry>; or (4) toward the end of a span of time or distance <people who are advanced in age>. Though it has these several meanings, *advanced* does not mean "in advance"—a meaning for which *advance*, adj., suffices. Yet writers increasingly misuse *advanced* for this sense—e.g.:

- "With this law, your landlord must give you two days' *advanced* warning before entering your apartment." Ed Sacks, "New Tenant Wants to Get Out of Nightmarish Apartment," *Chicago Sun-Times*, 19 Jan. 1997, Housing §, at 7.
- "These are the parents who rarely give schools *advanced* notice of planned trips and who let their children stay home from school for minor problems." Tamara Henry, "Skipping School for Travel," *USA Today*, 27 Mar. 1997, at D10.

In both examples, *advance* is the intended word—yet it should be deleted as a REDUNDANCY. Cf. **advance guard**.

*advancee** is an 18th-century creation meaning either (1) "someone who advances," or (2) "someone who receives an advance payment." The word seems both unattractive and unnecessary—e.g.:

- "[I]f the *advancee* [read *recipient of the advance*] predeceases the intestate, no other person is affected or burdened . . . ." Lawrence Newman & Richard V. Wellman, *Comparative Law Studies* 389 (1976).
- "The division's biggest *advancee* [read *gainer*?] should be the Phoenix Cardinals (4–12), particularly if Joe Bugel's offensive line finds a comfort zone with young talent." John Hawkins, "Speed Reigns in NFL's Best Division," *Wash. Times*, 5 Sept. 1993, at G20. (A possible revision: *The Phoenix Cardinals (4–12) stand to gain the most in the division, particularly . . . .*)
- "There were 12 teams and 74 individuals that made their way out of a sectional tournament this past school year . . . . And most of those *advancees* [read *advancing to regionals*] come from the Ohio area." Bryan Walters, "Regional Runs," *Point Pleasant Register* (W. Va.), 25 June 2013, Sports §, at 6.

See -EE (A).

advance guard (= a military contingent sent before the main troops) is sometimes written *advanced guard*, a spelling that was dominant for most of the 19th century. The standard spelling today is *advance guard*, but the variant still often occurs—e.g.: "On the afternoon of April 1, after skirmishing all morning, Gen. Wilson's *advanced guard* [read *advance guard*] ran into Gen. Forrest's line of battle." William Rambo,

"Re-Enactor Recounts Fight," *Montgomery Advertiser*, 21 Apr. 1996, at C7.

The variant also occurs in figurative uses, in which the true meaning might be *avant garde*—e.g.: "Schwarzkogler, who died in 1969 either after accidentally falling from a window or defenestrating himself, was a young, emotionally fragile member of the controversial Viennese artistic *advanced guard* [read *avant garde*] of the 1960s." Robert W. Duffy, "Art as Revelation," *St. Louis Post-Dispatch*, 28 Jan. 1996, Everyday Mag. §, at C4. See **advanced**.

LANGUAGE-CHANGE INDEX
advanced guard for *advance guard*: Stage 4
Current ratio (*advance guard* vs.
advanced guard): 2:1

advancement. See **advance**.

ADVERBS. A. Placement of Adverbs. Many writers fall into awkward, unidiomatic sentences when they misguidedly avoid splitting up verb phrases. Although most authorities squarely say that the best place for the adverb is in the midst of the verb phrase, many writers nevertheless harbor a misplaced aversion, probably because they confuse a split verb phrase with the SPLIT INFINITIVE. H.W. Fowler explained long ago what writers still have problems understanding: "When an adverb is to be used with [a compound] verb, its normal place is between the auxiliary (or sometimes the first auxiliary if there are two or more) and the rest. Not only is there no objection to thus splitting a compound verb . . . , but any other position for the adverb requires special justification" (*FMEU1* at 448). Other authorities agree and have long done so, as the following sampling shows—e.g.:

- "[The adverb] frequently stands between the auxiliary and the verb, as 'He . . . *was attentively heard* by the whole audience.' " Robert Lowth, *A Short Introduction to English Grammar* 135 (rev. ed. 1782).
- "Those [adverbs] . . . which belong to compound verbs, are commonly placed after the first auxiliary." Goold Brown, *The Institutes of English Grammar* 167 (rev. ed. 1852).
- "When the tense of a transitive verb is compound, the adverb follows the first auxiliary if the verb is in the active voice [e.g., *the boy has always obeyed his father*], and immediately precedes the principal verb if the verb is in the passive voice [e.g., *the house can be quickly built*]." Josephine Turck Baker, *Correct English: Complete Grammar and Drill Book* 180 (1938).
- "When there is a compound verb form, it is usual to put the adverb between the auxiliary and the main verb. 'I have always wanted to do so.' 'He has rarely failed us.'" W.P. Jowett, *Chatting About English* 184 (1945).
- "Barring the infinitive, verb groups should be split . . . . In verb groups formed by parts of the verbs 'be,' 'have,' 'do,' 'can,' 'may,' and 'must,' adverbs are best placed immediately before the main verb." R.G. Ralph, *Put It Plainly* 60 (1952).
- "The truth is that more often than not the proper and natural place for an adverb is between the parts of a compound verb." Theodore M. Bernstein, *The Careful Writer* 26 (1965).
- "There is a frequent need to link an adverb with a compound verb ('I *have always been*'), and the regular place for the modifier is shown in the example." Jacques Barzun, *Simple & Direct* 63 (1975).

But confusion on this point is all but ubiquitous. The result is an unidiomatic, unnatural style—e.g.:

- "Circuit judges *currently are elected* [read *are currently elected*] in countywide races." Michael R. Zahn, "Two Veteran Judges Favor District System to Elect More Minority Judges," *Milwaukee J. Sentinel*, 18 Oct. 1994, at A1.
- "Capitalistic economies *easily can adjust* [read *can easily adjust*] to more unequal distributions of purchasing power." Lester C. Thurow, "Inequalities in Wealth a Political, Not Economic Problem," *USA Today*, 23 Nov. 1999, at A19 (also asserting that "policies . . . *easily could be designed* [read either *could easily be designed* or *could be easily designed*]").

In the following example, the first adverb is awkwardly placed and the second is right: "If you're doing serious research, possibly for a college course, then you *already have* [read *have already*] begun (or will *soon* begin to involve yourself in) Internet research." H. Eric Branscomb, *Casting Your Net* 1 (2000). For more on this point of splitting verb phrases, see SUPERSTITIONS (C).

A few general adverbs of time occur between subject and verb—"I *usually* play golf on Saturday," "We *never* do much in that room," "He *always* takes the credit for himself." Yet adverbs of place don't appear between subject and verb, and people never say, "I *there* saw her standing," "We *here* will stake our claim," "She *anywhere* loves to travel." The linguist W.F. Twaddell first noticed this point about adverbs of time as opposed to adverbs of place. He calls it "a rather complicated rule of English grammar," adding that "speakers of English are largely unaware of it, but the English they speak is consistent in conforming to it." W.F. Twaddell, "Meanings, Habits and Rules," in *A Linguistics Reader* 10, 11 (Graham Wilson ed., 1967).

B. Awkward Adverbs. Adjectives ending in *-ly* and *-le* often make cumbersome adverbs, e.g., *chillily, friendlily, ghastlily, holily, jollily, juvenilely, lovelily, sillily, statelily, supplely, surlily, uglily, wilily*, and so on. You needn't be timid in writing or pronouncing such adverbs when they're genuinely needed—e.g.: "During the year's cold months, when the abundant fenestration of her home office kept the room chilly, [the therapist] wore a pelisse of hand-tanned Native American buckskin that formed a somewhat *ghastlily* moist-looking flesh-colored background for the enclosing shapes her hands formed in her lap." David Foster Wallace, "The Depressed Person," *Harper's Mag.*, 1 Jan. 1998, at 57. But if they seem unnatural, you can easily rephrase the sentence, e.g., *in a silly*

LANGUAGE-CHANGE INDEX (For the full key, see front matter pp. xxxi, l–li.)
Stage 1: Rejected. **Stage 2:** Widely shunned. **Stage 3:** Widespread but . . . **Stage 4:** Ubiquitous but . . . **Stage 5:** Fully accepted.
Invariably inferior forms marked by asterisk (∗). • Ratios represent frequency of prevalent forms vs. variants in current books.

manner. A few words, however, act as both adjectives and adverbs; examples are *daily, early, hourly, kindly, stately,* and *timely.*

The same is true, to a lesser extent, of many adverbs derived from adjectives that end in *-y,* such as *funny* (making *funnily*). But they have a more widespread acceptance—e.g.: "His long play about the Civil War is obviously and *unfunnily* bad, but a hundred pages are devoted to reproducing the manuscript and another fifty to endless jawing about its relation to art, justice, and order." Jonathan Franzen, "Mr. Difficult," *New Yorker,* 30 Sept. 2002, at 100, 111.

If you do use unusual adverbs, use them sparingly. Some writers display an unfortunate fondness for them, as by using such forms as *consideredly, corollarily,* and the spurious **widespreadly.* Cf. -EDLY.

C. Double Adverbs. Several adverbs not ending in *-ly*—especially *doubtless, fast, ill, much, seldom, thus*—have NONWORD counterparts ending in *-ly.* Using **doubtlessly, *fastly,* etc. is poor style. The terms with the superfluous *-ly* reveal an ignorance of idiom.

D. Adverbs vs. Adjectives. See ADJECTIVES (E).

adversary, adj.; **adversarial.** *Adversary,* which can act as both noun and adjective, appears in phrases such as *adversary relationship* and *adversary system*—e.g.: "Granted, it is the job of an opposing political chairman working in the *adversary system* of American politics to try to make the worst case against the elected leader of the opposition party." Bill Hall, "The Premature Failure of Gary Locke's First Year," *Lewiston Morning Trib.* (Idaho), 26 Feb. 1997, at A10.

Though it has only recently made its way into dictionaries, *adversarial* has become fairly common in place of the adjective *adversary*—e.g.: "Our *adversarial,* court-based system of collecting child support creates hate and misunderstanding." Robin Miller, "Day in Court No Solace for Deadbeat Dad," *Baltimore Sun,* 10 Mar. 1995, at A13. This shift in usage occurred mostly during the 1980s. *Adversarial* often connotes animosity <adversarial conferences>, whereas *adversary* is more neutral and even clinical.

Current ratio (*adversarial relationship* vs. *adversary relationship*): 14:1

adverse; averse. To be *adverse to* something is to be turned in opposition against it <Thailand was adverse to Japan during most of World War II>. The phrase usually refers to things, not people. To be *averse to* something is to have feelings against it <averse to risk>. The phrase usually describes a person's attitude. Both words may take the preposition *to,* but *averse* also takes *from.*

Each word is occasionally misused for the other—e.g.:

- "Alistair Boyle's narrator Gil Yates is certainly not *adverse* [read *averse*] to a money-making scheme, however dubious." Jeremy C. Shea, "Everyone's a Con," *St. Louis Post-Dispatch* (Everyday Mag.), 4 May 1996, at D4.
- "He and Kasner say many investors are *adverse* [read *averse*] to risk and unlikely to substitute risky company

shares for conservative muni bond investments." John G. Edwards, "Cost of Interest Could Increase," *Las Vegas Rev.-J.,* 9 Jan. 2003, at D1.

- "People with chronic liver problems can lead normal lives until an *averse* [read *adverse*] reaction to something such as a viral infection or a fatty diet pushes them over the edge into liver failure." Linda Marsa, "An Artificial Liver May Bridge a Gap," *L.A. Times,* 20 Jan. 2003, at F3.

LANGUAGE-CHANGE INDEX
1. *adverse* misused for *averse*: Stage 2
2. *averse* misused for *adverse*: Stage 1

advert; avert. To *advert* to something is to refer to it, to bring it up in speech or writing, or to turn attention to it. In AmE the word is best reserved for formal contexts, especially legal writing—e.g.:

- "Brandeis frequently *adverted* to 'manhood' and 'manliness' in rallying his supporters in reform ventures." Clyde Spillenger, "Elusive Advocate," 105 *Yale L.J.* 1445, 1453 n.23 (1996). See **allude (A).**
- "He sometimes *adverted* to that distinction and thought that it was an obstacle to his being appreciated by English readers such as Ruskin." Denis Donoghue, "Of 'Song of Myself,'" *Hudson Rev.,* 1 July 2012, at 247 (referring to Walt Whitman).

To *avert* is to turn away or avoid, or to ward off—e.g.:

- "Clinton said even '5 million police officers' could not *avert* this kind of tragedy if children are not taught the difference between right and wrong." "Clinton Cites Need for Role Models," *Chicago Sun-Times,* 18 Oct. 1994, at 3.
- "Tuning in on the radio is like listening to the couple in the apartment next to you scream at each other. You just can't *avert* your ears." Bill Torpy, "How Awful Are the Braves? Just Listen," *Atlanta J.-Const.,* 10 Sept. 2015, at B1.

Occasionally, *advert* is misused for *avert*—e.g.: "Although five persons were injured, a real tragedy was *adverted* [read *averted*] because of the way firefighters and quick-acting neighbors in the area worked together." Stephen Byrd, "Smoking Blamed in Independence Fire," *Kansas City Star,* 20 May 1996, at B1. See MALAPROPISMS.

LANGUAGE-CHANGE INDEX
advert misused for *avert*: Stage 1

advertise. So spelled. But the erroneous form **advertize* occasionally occurs—e.g.: "A GOP consultant . . . was forced to quit Bob Dole's campaign yesterday after two tabloids reported he *advertizes* [read *advertises*] for group sex partners." Helen Kennedy, "Sex Flap Hits GOPer," *Daily News* (N.Y.), 13 Sept. 1996, at 21.

LANGUAGE-CHANGE INDEX
advertise misspelled **advertize*: Stage 1
Current ratio: 222:1

advertisement is chiefly pronounced /**ad**-vər-tīz-mənt/ or /ad-vər-**tīz**-mənt/ in AmE and /ad-**vər**-tiz-mənt/ in BrE.

advice; advise. *Advice* /ad-**vīs**/ (= counsel that one person gives another) is a noun. *Advise* /ad-**vīz**/ (= to counsel; try to help by guiding) is a verb. The spellings are sometimes confounded—e.g.: "All the programs take pains to inform you with large disclaimers that they are no substitute for real medical professionals (good *advise* [read *advice*]) and as such cannot be responsible if you use them improperly." Bob Bielk, "Dr. Disc," *Asbury Park Press* (Neptune, N.J.), 10 June 1997, at D1. See **advise.**

> LANGUAGE-CHANGE INDEX
> *advise* misused for *advice*: Stage 1
> Current ratio (*good advice* vs. **good advise*): 278:1

*advisatory. See **advisory.**

advise for *tell, say, explain, inform,* or *warn* is a pomposity to be avoided—e.g.:

- "The judge *advised* [read *told* or *warned*] Smith that he would not have the benefit of a skilled attorney who could identify legal issues or problems with the state's evidence." Kathryn Kranhold, "Mother's Plea Fails to Sway Suspect," *Hartford Courant*, 19 Oct. 1995, at A1.
- "Police *advised* [read *informed*] him of his rights before handcuffing him and transporting him to a nearby police station for booking." Don Babwin, "Chicago Police Arrest R. Kelly on Child-Porn Charges," *Phil. Inquirer*, 8 June 2002, at A4.

For examples confounding *advise* with *advice*, see **advice.**

adviser has been the standard spelling since the early 17th century. *Advisor* is a variant that became common in the 20th century but remains marginally less frequent. Note, however, that the adjectival form is *advisory*. See -ER (A).

> Current ratio (*adviser* vs. *advisor*): 1.1:1

advisory; *advisatory. The latter is a NEEDLESS VARIANT.

> Current ratio: 27,552:1

advocate; *advocator. The latter is a NEEDLESS VARIANT.

> Current ratio: 1,828:1

AE. In many words, *ae* is a remnant of the Latin digraph, formerly ligatured (æ), appearing in words of Latin and Greek origin. In many words in which this digraph once appeared, the first vowel has been dropped, esp. in AmE. One sees this tendency at work in *(a)eon, (a)estivate, (a)ether, (a)etiology, encyclop(a)edia, et c(a)etera,* and *f(a)eces.* But in some words, the *ae-* forms are established—for example, *aegis, aeolian, aerial, aerobic, aerosol, aerospace, aesthetic, diaeresis, paean,* and *praetor.*

Some words in BrE retain digraphs (e.g., *anaesthetic* and *foetus*) that AmE has shortened (e.g., *anesthetic* and *fetus*). Note that the preferred AmE forms are *aesthetic* but *anesthetic.* A definitive across-the-board statement about -ae- isn't possible—just as it isn't about most other usage matters.

aegis /ee-jis/ (= auspices, sponsorship) was originally a mythological term meaning "protective shield" or "defensive armor." The word is now used exclusively in figurative senses, usually in the phrase *under the aegis* (not *with the aegis*)—e.g.: "And they appreciate that for creditors, there are some benefits to having companies either liquidated or reorganized under the *aegis* of the bankruptcy code." Kim Strosnider, "Involuntary Bankruptcy?" *Portland Press Herald*, 15 Oct. 1996, at C5. The phrase is often equivalent to *under the auspices.* See **auspices.**

Be careful not to confuse *aegis* with leadership in general—e.g.: "*Under Waxman's aegis* [read *With Waxman directing* or *With Waxman as director*], [Neil Simon's *Lost in*] *Yonkers* fails to achieve the razor-sharp pacing and the superb characterizations that marked its Royal Alex engagement a few years ago." John Coulbourn, "Simon's Finest Found with 'Lost in Yonkers,'" *Toronto Sun*, 6 Feb. 1997, at 56.

The variant spelling **egis* is all but defunct.

> Current ratio (*aegis* vs. **egis*): 181:1

aeolian; *eolian (= carried, deposited, or affected by the wind) derives from the name of the Greek wind god Æolus. The word retains its *æ* digraph in English (decoupled), unlike so many other Greek derivatives that drop the *a,* such as *estuary.* Although *W11* lists **eolian* as the predominant spelling, that form is today less frequent than *aeolian* in AmE print sources and is little known in BrE. The word is pronounced /ee-**oh**-lee-ən/.

> Current ratio: 2:1

*aeon. See **eon.**

aerie. See **eyrie.**

Aesop (the Greek fabulist) is pronounced /**ee**-sop/ or /**ee**-səp/—not /**ay**-sop/.

aesthetic; *esthetic. Although some dictionaries have long recorded **esthetic* as the primary form in AmE, the form *aesthetic* remains much more common in AmE and BrE alike. See AE.

> Current ratio (World English): 23:1

*aestivate. See **estivate.**

aetiology. See **etiology.**

affect; effect. In ordinary usage, *affect* is always a verb; it means "to influence; to have an effect on." *Effect,* as suggested by its use in that definition, is primarily a noun meaning "result" or "consequence." To *affect* something is to have an *effect* on it. But as a verb, *effect* means "to bring about; produce."

Perhaps the most common error with these words is misusing *effect* for *affect*—here illustrated plentifully: "Katrina *effected* [read *affected*] everyone in the state of Mississippi in some way .... As the recovery from Hurricane Katrina began, thousands of *effected* [read *affected*] homeowners on the Coast began getting the bad news. ... Even before the power had been restored in some *effected* [read *affected*] areas,

---

LANGUAGE-CHANGE INDEX (For the full key, see front matter pp. xxxi, l–li.)
Stage 1: Rejected. **Stage 2:** Widely shunned. **Stage 3:** Widespread but . . . **Stage 4:** Ubiquitous but . . . **Stage 5:** Fully accepted.
Invariably inferior forms marked by asterisk (*). • Ratios represent frequency of prevalent forms vs. variants in current books.

Gulf Coast residents were looking for relief . . . . [T]he Scruggs Katrina Group . . . would be dedicated to representing homeowners *effected* [read *affected*] by the storms." Alan Lange & Tom Dawson, *Kings of Tort* 96, 97, 98, 100 (2009).

Using *affect* (= to influence) for *effect* (= to bring about) is also an old error that looks as if it will be increasingly difficult to stamp out. The mistake is especially common in the phrase *to effect change(s)*—e.g.:

- "Throughout the book her winning personality *affects* [read *effects*] changes in the drab and pitiful 'sad' people she encounters . . . ." Philip Martin, "Rags, Riches," *Ark. Democrat-Gaz.*, 17 Dec. 1995, at E1.
- "[It is] a good example of environmentalists working with corporations to *affect* [read *effect*] change." John Holusha, "Companies Vow to Consider Environment in Buying Paper," *N.Y. Times*, 20 Dec. 1995, at D5.

H.W. Fowler treated only the verb forms of these words, apparently because they didn't seem susceptible to confusion as nouns. But today even the confusion of nouns is fairly common—e.g.:

- "She doubted the majority flip would have a huge *affect* [read *effect*] on the council." Rona Kobell, "Republicans Ride Ehrlich Wave," *Baltimore Sun*, 6 Nov. 2002, at B8.
- "Most players, though, did not think it will have a lasting *affect* [read *effect*]." Ed Bouchette, "Looking Ahead," *Pitt. Post-Gaz.*, 14 Nov. 2002, at C6.
- "The Challenger accident had a large and lasting *affect* [read *effect*] on the Michoud plant." Gordon Russell & Keith Darce, "Once More, Attention Is Focused on Michoud," *Times-Picayune* (New Orleans), 2 Feb. 2003, Nat'l §, at 1.

Likewise, *effect* is sometimes misused for *affect*. See **effect (B)**. Cf. **impact**.

Affect may also mean "to pretend, feign, or assume (a characteristic) artificially"—e.g.: "One wonders at her choice to have all the actors *affect* Russian accents." Marshall Fine, "K-19," *J. News* (Westchester Co., N.Y.), 18 July 2002, at G5.

Although *affect* is almost always a verb, it does have a rare, somewhat vague noun sense in the fields of psychology and psychiatry: "In general, [*affect*] is characterized as a state brought about by actions almost wholly devoid of intentional control in accordance with moral and objective viewpoints. The term is also found in the literature as practically synonymous with 'emotion' in certain senses." 1 *Encyclopedia of Psychology* 28 (H.J. Eysenck et al. eds., 1972). Other definitions seem no clearer. One text defines *affect* as "the feeling-tone accompaniment of an idea or mental representation." Leland E. Hinsie & Robert Jean Campbell, *Psychiatric Dictionary* 18 (4th ed. 1970). The term certainly doesn't belong outside highly specialized contexts. And it seems questionable whether it justifiably belongs within them.

LANGUAGE-CHANGE INDEX
1. *affect* misused for *effect*, n. & vb.: Stage 1
Current ratio (*the bad effects* vs. **the bad affects*): 1,001:1
2. *effect* misused for *affect*, vb.: Stage 2
Current ratio (*affect our lives* vs. **effect our lives*): 55:1

affectable. So spelled—not **affectible*. See -ABLE (A).
Current ratio: 6:1

affectation. See **affection**.

affected, adj.; affective; affectional; affectionate. *Affected*, adj., = artificially assumed; pretended <a highly affected accent>. *Affective* = emotional <bipolar affective disorder>. *Affectional* = pertaining to affection <affectional displays>. *Affectionate* = loving, fond <affectionate children>.

Just as *affect* is sometimes misused for *effect*, so *affective* sometimes wrongly displaces *effective*—e.g.: "Physicians are also finding some non-opiate medications used to treat disease are *affective* [read *effective*] in controlling pain, Lingam said." Candace L. Preston, "Doctors Offer Balm of Nepenthe," *Bus. First* (Columbus), 27 June 1997, at 15. See **affect**.

LANGUAGE-CHANGE INDEX
affective misused for *effective*: Stage 1

affection; affectation. The first means "love, fondness"; the second means "pretentious, artificial behavior." In Elizabethan English, these words were used more or less interchangeably, but now each has acquired its own distinct sense—which is good for the language.

affectional; affectionate; affective. See **affected**.

affianced. See **affined**.

affidavit (= a voluntary declaration of facts written down and sworn to by the declarant before an officer authorized to administer oaths) sometimes appears in the REDUNDANCY **sworn affidavit*—e.g.:

- "[The] defendant gave no evidence whatsoever, but put in *a sworn affidavit* [read *an affidavit*], pleading in extenuation of her offence the treacherous conduct of the Fitzgeralds." Daphne du Maurier, *Mary Anne: A Novel* 333 (1972).
- "And he released three *sworn affidavits* [read *affidavits*] from former detectives who said they were forced to resign." Jacqueline Soteropoulos, "New Port Richey," *Tampa Trib.*, 7 Oct. 1995, at 1.
- "In *a sworn affidavit* [read *an affidavit*], the Mexican champion said he never received any insurance money . . . ." Greg Logan, "King Trial Starts Today," *Newsday* (N.Y.), Nassau & Suffolk ed., 10 Oct. 1995, at A44.

affiliable. So formed—not **affiliatable*. See -ABLE (D) & -ATABLE.

affined; affianced. *Affined* = closely related; connected. *Affianced* = engaged, betrothed.

affirm (= [1] to declare emphatically, or [2] [of an appellate court] to uphold a lower court's judgment) is sometimes misused for *vindicate* (= to justify by outcome): "The results tonight *affirmed* [read *vindicated*] Mr. McCain's decision to skip the Iowa caucuses." Richard L. Berke, "McCain Romps in First Primary," *N.Y. Times*, 2 Feb. 2000, at A1. Although one definition of *affirm* is "to validate or confirm," here *vindicated* or even *justified* would have been a better choice.

affirmation; affirmance. These terms, unfortunately, overlap somewhat. Yet sorting out usage isn't difficult: *affirmation* is preferable in every context but one—when an appellate court affirms a lower court's judgment <the Supreme Court's affirmance of the judgment came as a surprise>.

affirmative, in the; in the negative. These phrases have been criticized as jargonistic and pompous. (See, e.g., Quiller-Couch's statement quoted under JARGON.) They appear frequently in legal and pseudolegal writing. They can usually be improved—e.g.:

- "All the other questions were answered *in the affirmative* [read *yes*], including a query on whether the evidence showed that Mr. Simpson had acted with malice." Paul Pringle, "Jury Holds Simpson Liable in Slayings," *Dallas Morning News*, 5 Feb. 1997, at A1.
- "But the council did *vote in the affirmative on* [read *grant*] a request from the Contributory Retirement Board to accept a state law that indemnifies board members if civil actions are brought against them." David T. Turcotte, "Plan to Buy Goose Dog Advances in Gardner," *Telegram & Gaz.* (Worcester), 4 Mar. 1997, at B4.
- "The more I thought about these questions, the more it seemed to me that they had to be answered *in the negative* [read *no*]." Jonathan Schell, "American Democracy Defines Itself," *Newsday* (N.Y.), 1 Dec. 1996, at A34.

Cf. **yes** & **no.**

afflatus; *afflation; *inflatus. For the sense "inspiration" or "supernatural impulse," *afflatus* is the standard—though rare—term. E.g.: "Richard Brookhiser, the author and editor, reminded us that it is generally alien to Dole's temperament to act as the advocate, charged with disseminating his *afflatus*—he is more a technician." William F. Buckley, "Are the Conservatives Mutinous?" *Buffalo News*, 10 Apr. 1996, at B3. *Afflation and *inflatus are NEEDLESS VARIANTS.

The plural of *afflatus* is *afflatuses*, not *afflati. See HYPERCORRECTION (A) & PLURALS (B).

afflict. See **inflict.**

affluence; affluent. These words are preferably accented on the first syllable (/**af**-loo-ən[t]s/, /**af**-loo-ənt/), not the second (/ə-**floo**-ən[t]s/, /ə-**floo**-ənt/). See PRONUNCIATION (B).

afford. See **accord (A).**

affront. See **effrontery (A).**

*affrontery. See **effrontery (B).**

Afghan; Afghani. A person from Afghanistan is an *Afghan*. A thing from Afghanistan is an *Afghan* thing. It's a common error to make the noun or adjective *Afghani*, which correctly refers only to the basic monetary unit of the country and is not capitalized—e.g.:

- "In 1997, the organization launched a campaign to aid *Afghani* [read *Afghan*] women." Michelle Millhollon,

"Sisters Fast for Ramadan," *Advocate* (Baton Rouge), 28 Nov. 2002, at A1.
- "The civil affairs unit is helping *Afghanis* [read *Afghans*] rebuild their nation, Parsons said." Gary McLendon, "Citizen-Soldier Gives Afghanistan Lesson," *Rochester Democrat & Chron.*, 18 Dec. 2002, at F1.
- "Simple, serene place for approachable *Afghani* [read *Afghan*] food including good kebabs, fried eggplant and cardamom-scented milk pudding." "Critic's Choice: Restaurants Serving Ginger Desserts," *S.F. Chron.*, 20 Dec. 2002, at D17.

See DENIZEN LABELS.

Afghan is also (1) an alternative term for the Pashto language, (2) a short form of *Afghan hound*, and (3) (not capitalized) a crocheted or knitted blanket or shawl.

LANGUAGE-CHANGE INDEX
Afghani misused for *Afghan*: Stage 2

aficionado is often misspelled *afficionado—e.g.:

- "Orson St. John and Roswell Perkins, Manhattan-based attorneys by winter, Little Compton *afficionados* [read *aficionados*] by summer, became officers and legal advisers who could start tackling the call for a light." David Arnold, "Time to Shine: 40-Year Lighthouse Effort Ends in a Flash," *Boston Globe*, 9 Mar. 1997, at A1.
- "You will be shocked at the wealth of information in those tomes if you are not already an almanac *afficionado* [read *aficionado*]." David Hass, *Is Your Life Out of Whack?* 40 (2002).

LANGUAGE-CHANGE INDEX
aficionado misspelled *afficionado: Stage 1
Current ratio: 39:1

à fond; au fond. These GALLICISMS have different meanings. While *à fond* means "to the bottom," *au fond* means "at bottom." The terms also carry different figurative senses: *à fond* (/ah-fon/) means "fully, thoroughly" <she knows the subject of mineralogy *à fond*>; *au fond* (/oh-fon/) means "basically, fundamentally" <every good proofreader is, *au fond*, attentive to detail>. You're surely better off sticking to English phrases.

a fortiori (/**ah** for-shee-**or**-ee/ or /**ay** for-shee-**or**-I/), a term most commonly used in logic and argumentation, is an adverb meaning "by even greater force of logic; so much the more." The phrase is sometimes effective, but only if the intended readers are sure to get it—e.g.:

- "Federal judges already have pointed out that the constitutional right to abortion, that is, to destroy a life, *a fortiori* implies a right to assisted suicide, the right to destroy one's own life." Leon J. Podles, "The 'Big Tent' Case Against Abortion," *Wash. Times*, 22 Apr. 1996, at 28. (The argument is by greater force of logic, according to this writer, because if a person can take another life, surely one can take one's own.)
- "Indeed, human bloodshed even by an animal must be avenged, and, *a fortiori*, bloodshed by a man's own

LANGUAGE-CHANGE INDEX (For the full key, see front matter pp. xxxi, l–li.)
Stage 1: Rejected. **Stage 2:** Widely shunned. **Stage 3:** Widespread but . . . **Stage 4:** Ubiquitous but . . . **Stage 5:** Fully accepted.
Invariably inferior forms marked by asterisk (*). • Ratios represent frequency of prevalent forms vs. variants in current books.

brother—a clear reference to Cain and Abel." Leon R. Kass, "A Genealogy of Justice," *Commentary*, July 1996, at 44. (The argument is by greater force of logic because human bloodshed by a brother is more reprehensible.)

The phrase is used illogically when the proposition following *a fortiori* is no stronger than the one preceding it—e.g.:

- "The argument for 'mixing' the Jewish studies program at Queens College, of course, applies *a fortiori* to many other studies programs that have sprung up in recent years." "PC Absurdity at Queens," *Times Union* (Albany), 19 July 1996, at A14. (Why is the argument even stronger for non-Jewish programs? Because the sentence is reasoning from the particular to the general, a proficient editor would probably substitute *equally* for *a fortiori*.)
- "[The book] *Leakage* is an extraordinary achievement—a careful, probing, empirical analysis of the American macro-economy and, *a fortiori*, [of] any free-market economy in the world." George P. Brockway, "The Bleeding of the American Economy," *New Leader*, 4 Nov. 1996, at 12. (If the book *Leakage* is a good analysis of the American economy, why would it more surely be a good analysis of *any free-market economy in the world*? For *a fortiori*, substitute *even* without commas.)

Writers sometimes use *a fortiori* as an adjective, a usage to be resisted—e.g.: "Clearly, if laws depend so heavily on public acquiescence, the case of conventions is an *a fortiori* [read *even more compelling*] one." P.S. Atiyah, *Law and Modern Society* 59 (1983).

Afrikaner; *Afrikaaner; *Afrikander; Africander; *Africaander. These terms, frankly, are a mess. But let's sort through them. The first is the standard term for a South African of European, especially Dutch, descent. The second and third are variants of that word: *Afrikaaner reflects the spelling of the language Afrikaans, just as the end of *Afrikander (the predominant form until World War II) reflects the end of *Hollander*. The word *Africander*, meanwhile, denotes a breed of tall, red, humpbacked cattle prominent in South Africa; but it is also an obsolescent term for *Afrikaner*, and *Afrikaner* is an acceptable variant of *Africander*. *Africaander is a variant spelling of the name of the cattle breed. All clear now? See DENIZEN LABELS.

Afrikaner is pronounced /af-ri-**kah**-nər/; *Africander* and *Afrikander are pronounced /af-ri-**kan**-dər/.

aftereffect. One word.

*after having [+ past participle]. This construction is ordinarily incorrect for *after* [+ present participle]. That is, although either *having gone on for ten years* or *after going on for ten years* makes sense, coupling *after* with *having* [+ past participle] makes a REDUNDANCY—e.g.:

- "*After having had* [read *After having*] my fill of looking and wanting and wishing, I walked along the docks back to where I had parked my car." Jay Reed, "Imagination Can Run Wild at Racine Boat Show," *Milwaukee J. Sentinel*, 16 Aug. 1997, at 4.
- "The nearest [precedent] is to be found in the sad tale of Queen Caroline, the estranged consort of George IV, who died at Hammersmith in 1821, three weeks *after having*

been [read *after being*] excluded from the Coronation in Westminster Abbey." Kenneth Rose, "Precedent, Protocol and the Stately Ceremonial of Death," *Sunday Telegraph*, 7 Sept. 1997, at 29. (On the ambiguous *who* in that sentence, see REMOTE RELATIVES (A).)

- "Religion was the topic that finally got the teenager talking . . . while he was being interrogated by the Montreal police and RCMP *after having robbed* [read *after robbing*] a convenience store in Lachine earlier that month." Paul Cherry, "Debating Religion Got Teen Talking During Interrogation," *Montreal Gaz.*, 10 Sept. 2015, at A2.

LANGUAGE-CHANGE INDEX
*after having been for after being: Stage 3
Current ratio (*after being* vs. *after having been): 6:1

afterward; afterword. *Afterward* (= later) is preferred over *afterwards* by American editors, though in popular usage the two forms are used interchangeably. *Afterword* is a noun meaning "epilogue." Cf. **foreword.**

For more on *afterward(s)*, see DIRECTIONAL WORDS (A).

again, like *against*, is preferably pronounced in AmE with an /e/ in the second syllable—hence /ə-**gen**/ and /ə-**genst**/. The pronunciations /ə-**gayn**/ and /ə-**gaynst**/ are chiefly BrE variants—though *DARE* records that these pronunciations may be found in AmE in Atlantic States, adding that they "may be considered affected" (1 *DARE* at 19). The pronunciations /ə-**gin**/ and /ə-**ginst**/ are frequent among less educated speakers (*ibid.*).

agape. There are two words so spelled, with unrelated senses, different pronunciations, and even different syllabification. As a noun, *agape* (/ə-**gah**-pay/) comes from a Greek word for "brotherly love" and denotes (1) "spiritual love in contrast to earthly or sensual love," or (2) "a love feast." As an adverb, *agape* (/ə-**gayp**/) means "with mouth wide open, esp. in awe, surprise, or fear."

aged. A. Pronunciation. As an adjective, the word may be either one syllable (/ayjd/) <aged cheese> or two (/**ay**-jəd/) <an aged mentor>, depending on its sense. In the first of those uses, the word means "having been allowed to age"; in the second, it means "elderly." As an attributive noun similar to *elderly* <the sick, the weak, and the aged>, the word has two syllables (/**ay**-jəd/).

B. Used Adverbially in BrE. British publications have adopted a shorthand adverbial used of *aged*, found most commonly in obituaries. Essentially, BrE uses *aged* where AmE would use the phrase *at the age of*—e.g.:

- "Later in the week, I met a man who had gone to Oxford *aged* 17 to read English and by the age of 22 had become a don." Sarah Hervey-Bathurst, "The Spectator," *Country Life*, 17 June 1999, at 136.
- "Professor John Lawlor, scholar of medieval English, died on May 31 *aged* 81." "Professor John Lawlor" (obit.), *Times* (London), 7 July 1999, at 23.
- "James Farmer, who has died *aged* 79, was one of America's four leading civil rights leaders during the 1960s." "James Farmer" (obit.), *Guardian*, 13 July 1999, at 20.

- "Patrick Saul, who has died *aged* 85, was the founder of the National Sound Archive, the aural counterpart to the British Library." "Patrick Saul" (obit.), *Daily Telegraph*, 16 July 1999, at 31.

Though once in use in the U.S. (mostly before the mid-20th century), this adverbial use of *aged* is now little known in AmE.

C. **Aged . . . years old.* To say that someone is **aged 75 years old* is redundant—e.g.: "The average pension paid the average retiree, *aged 71.4 years old* [read *age 71.4* or *71.4 years old*], was $11,448 a year." "State Employee Pensions to Cost $4.7 Million More," *Providence J.-Bull.*, 18 Apr. 1995, at C5.

ageing; ageism. See **aging.**

agenda is (1) the plural form of *agendum*, which means "something to be done" (another, less proper plural of *agendum* being *agendums*); and, more commonly, (2) a singular noun meaning "a list of things to be done" or "a program." The plural of *agenda* in sense 2 is *agendas* (certainly not **agendae*). Decrying *agendas* as a double plural is bootless.

In fact, sense 1 of *agenda* is archaic today and sounds pedantic—e.g.: "Place your notes, thoughts, quotations, queries, and *lists of agenda* [read *agenda items*], divided according to topics, in envelopes." Lester S. King, *Why Not Say It Clearly* 74 (1978).

LANGUAGE-CHANGE INDEX
agenda as a singular noun: Stage 5
Current ratio (singular vs. plural): 9:1

*agendize, an ugly bureaucratic NEOLOGISM meaning "to put on an agenda," originated in the late 1980s and has spread—e.g.:

- " 'Mr. Eliot did not make a decision on his own,' he [Robert Bacon] said. 'We made an error and did not *agendize* that item.' " Craig Quintana, "West Covina Renewal Deals to Get Closer Look," *L.A. Times*, 28 Apr. 1988, San Gabriel Valley §, at 1.
- "William R. Ferris . . . thought that starting a tradition of presidential lecturers would raise the visibility of the annual Jefferson series and set up a nice chance for presidents to speak away from their usual *agendized* forums." Tom Peepen, "Presidency Becomes a Casualty," *Times Union* (Albany), 29 Sept. 1999, at A9.
- "Twice the Tustin school board has *agendized*, then tabled, the matter." George Stewart, "Red Tape Slows After-School Program Series," *Orange County Register*, 27 Sept. 2001, Tustin §, at 1.

The word remains JARGON and should be voted down.

agent provocateur. The predominant plural in English has always taken the French form: *agents provocateurs*, not **agent provocateurs*. See GALLICISMS & PLURALS (B).

Current ratio: 5:1

aggrandize (= [1] to increase the power or influence of, or [2] to exaggerate the reputation of)

is pronounced /ə-**gran**-dɪz/—or, archaically, /**ag**-rən-dɪz/.

aggravate; aggravation. Though documented as existing since the 1600s and today an engrained CASUALISM, *aggravate* for *annoy* or *irritate* has never gained the approval of stylists and should be avoided in formal writing. Strictly speaking, *aggravate* means "to make worse; exacerbate" <writing a second apology might just aggravate the problem>.

Even Oliver Wendell Holmes Jr. nodded once, using *aggravate* for *irritate* in one of his letters to Sir Frederick Pollock in 1895: "Our two countries *aggravate* each other from time to time." 1 *Holmes–Pollock Letters* 66 (1941). The lapse is common in modern writing—e.g.: "It has *aggravated* [read *irritated*] me when I have seen billboards that contained misspelled words, punctuation errors and other things that are fundamental to the English language." Letter of Shael Morgan, "Newspaper Critic Should Watch TV," *Fla. Today*, 31 Jan. 1998, at A12.

In some contexts, it's genuinely difficult to tell whether the word *aggravating* is an adjective or a present participle—e.g.: "The City of Washington is notorious for aggravating allergies, and Mr. Clinton said he expected his to be more severe there than in Arkansas." Lawrence K. Altman, "Clinton, in Detailed Interview, Calls His Health 'Very Good,' " *N.Y. Times*, 14 Oct. 1996, at A1, A14. The second half of that compound sentence suggests that the writer is using *aggravating* correctly. But taken alone, the phrase in the first half of the sentence (*Washington is notorious for aggravating allergies*) could refer to either (1) making allergies worse (preferred), or (2) allergies that are irritating or frustrating.

The confusion also occurs between the noun forms—e.g.:

- "Washington Coach Jim Lambright's insistence that his Huskies deserve to go to the Cotton Bowl instead of Oregon, and that the Ducks are overrated and lucky, has been met with bemusement and *aggravation* [read *irritation*] in Eugene." "Cotton Bowl Flap," *Austin Am.-Statesman*, 16 Nov. 1995, at C4.
- "Rush Limbaugh, still the industry giant, has an extra tone of *aggravation* [read *irritation*] as he denounces the unyielding poll leads of 'the Schlickmeister' and 'noted hetero fun-seeker,' President Clinton." Francis X. Clines, "Cool to Dole's Campaigning, Talk Radio Tries to Start Fire," *N.Y. Times*, 25 Sept. 1996, at A12.

Often when one word is commonly misused for a second word, part of the blame can go to a third word that sounds like the first but means something close to the second. Perhaps *exasperate* contributes to the misuse of *aggravate* (which sounds a bit like *exasperate*) in the sense of *irritate* (which is close in meaning to *exasperate*). Also, when *aggravate* is used in this sense, it often implies something more intense than merely *irritate*. It is closer in meaning to *exasperate*.

LANGUAGE-CHANGE INDEX
aggravate for *annoy* or *irritate*: Stage 4

LANGUAGE-CHANGE INDEX (For the full key, see front matter pp. xxxi, l–li.)
Stage 1: Rejected. **Stage 2:** Widely shunned. **Stage 3:** Widespread but . . . **Stage 4:** Ubiquitous but . . . **Stage 5:** Fully accepted.
Invariably inferior forms marked by asterisk (*). • Ratios represent frequency of prevalent forms vs. variants in current books.

aggregable; aggregatable. The first has long been the standard adjective. But in the mid-1990s, *aggregatable* overtook its shorter sibling in frequency of use—and it shows no signs of declining. The word became popular in Internet terminology, especially in the phrase *aggregatable global unicast address*. See -ABLE (D) & -ATABLE.

aggregate, n.; aggregation. Both may mean "a mass of discrete things or individuals taken as a whole," *aggregate* being the more usual term. *Aggregate* /**ag**-rə-git/ stresses the notion "taken as a whole" (as in the phrase *in the aggregate*), and *aggregation* /ag-rə-**gay**-shən/ is more nearly "a mass of discrete things." For "the act of aggregating," only *aggregation* will suffice.

aggregate, vb. A. Sense. *Aggregate* (/**ag**-rə-gayt/) = to bring together a mass of discrete things or individuals into a whole. The verb is sometimes misused for *total* in reference to sums—e.g.: "Trade between China and Taiwan has grown steadily in the past decade, *aggregating* [read *totaling*] almost $21 billion." V.H. Krulak, "China's Weapon Against Taiwan," *San Diego Union-Trib.*, 9 Mar. 1996, at B8.

   B. *Aggregate together*. This phrase is redundant—e.g.: "Terrestrial dust is mostly tiny fragments abraded from larger things; some of it may be even smaller things *aggregating together* [read *aggregating* or *clumping together*] to form motes of dust." C. Claiborne Ray, "Q&A," *N.Y. Times*, 13 Feb. 1996, at C5.

aggregation. See **aggregate,** n.

aggress. See BACK-FORMATIONS.

*aggrievance. See **grievance**.

agilely, adv., is occasionally misspelled **agiley*—e.g.: "But it's pointless to bemoan the status quo; what we need to do is work as *agiley* [read *agilely*] and cannily as we can with the situation as given to get across the many exciting and provocative and challenging works that continue to be written—and widely read." "Will Publishing Survive?" *L.A. Times*, 25 Feb. 2001, Book Rev. §, at 6. Cf. **futilely** & **solely**. See ADVERBS (B).

LANGUAGE-CHANGE INDEX
agilely misspelled **agiley*: Stage 1

aging; ageism. *Aging* is the standard spelling for the present participle for *age*, vb. *Ageing* is a chiefly BrE variant. (See MUTE E.) Yet *ageism* (= discriminatory feelings or practices toward a particular age group, esp. the elderly) has become standard probably because, as a fairly recent coinage (1969), it more readily suggests its meaning (and pronunciation) than **agism*.

agitable. So formed—not **agitatable*. See -ABLE (D) & -ATABLE.

agnostic. See **atheist**.

-AGOG(UE). This suffix derives from the Greek word meaning "to lead; drive." Traditionalists prefer retaining the *-ue*—hence *demagogue* (lit., "a leader of

people") and *pedagogue* (lit., "a leader of children"). Among other advantages, these spellings prevent any possible confusion with the adjective and adverb *agog* (= intensely excited) <all agog over the Christmas presents>.

   William Safire has predicted the demise of *-ue* forms: "Note the lack of a *u* in . . . [what] most of us would until recently *spell* [read *have spelled*] as *demagoguing*. But we live in a non-U world; just as *catalogue* and *dialogue* have been dropping their *ue* endings, so too will *demagogue* soon enough be spelled *demagog*, with its gerund *demagoging*." William Safire, "On Language," *N.Y. Times*, 21 May 2000, § 6, at 28, 30. For now, the traditionalist will continue to use the *-ue* forms—and their disappearance, if Safire is right, will be gradual enough that no one will get all agog over it. Cf. **demagogue**.

agree. A. Preposition *with*. *Agree with* means "to be in accord with (another)"; *agree to* means "to acquiesce in (usu. the performance or specifications of something)." One agrees *with* someone *on* or *about* a certain settlement <I agree with you about the color>. *Agree on* refers to the subject of the agreement <we agree on the color>.

   B. Transitive or Intransitive. In BrE, *agree* is coming to be used as a transitive verb <they agreed the change> where AmE would make it intransitive <they agreed to the change>. The usage may appear to be a typo when you first see it, but notice that it appears in the title as well as the first line of this: "The German cabinet yesterday *agreed* sweeping changes to unemployment benefits, aimed at making savings of DM17bn ($11bn) by 2000." Judy Dempsey, "Bonn Agrees Heavy Cut in Jobless Costs," *Fin. Times*, 13 June 1996, at 2.

AGREEMENT, GRAMMATICAL. See CONCORD & SUBJECT–VERB AGREEMENT.

agriculturist; agriculturalist. The shorter form (*agriculturist*) has traditionally been considered preferable, but the longer form is now nearly as common in AmE. Actually, *farmer* is even better if it applies.

Current ratio (in order of headwords): 2:1

ague (= a fever accompanied by chills) is pronounced /**ay**-gyoo/.

ahold. This noun is an American CASUALISM equivalent to *hold*. It ordinarily follows the verb *get*. Though omitted from most British dictionaries, it appears in most American dictionaries and surfaces fairly often in informal contexts—e.g.:

- "Brand, the Clay juvenile officer, said she isn't surprised the kids were able to get *ahold* of fireworks." Julianna Gittler & Cammi Clark, "Illegal, Dangerous, and Always Around," *Post-Standard* (Syracuse), 2 July 1998, at 13.
- "It's not as easy to get *ahold* of Hennepin County Sheriff Pat McGowan as recent news has led us to believe." Doug Grow, "Would Others Get Grams Treatment?" *Star Trib.* (Minneapolis), 13 Dec. 1999, at B2.
- "He got *ahold* of Theodore while clenching his teeth and saying, 'We'll see about this,' forcing the boy into his shoes." Jan Faull, "Parenting," *Seattle Times*, 3 Feb. 2001, at F1.

Even so, *get hold of* is much more frequent than *get ahold of* in AmE and BrE alike.

The dialectal variant **aholt* is quite uncommon even in recorded speech, and is much more provincial-sounding—e.g.: "'The Lord's going to get *aholt* of people,' she smiles." Bo Emerson, "Joyful Noise," *Atlanta J.-Const.*, 29 June 1997, Dixie Living §, at 1.

LANGUAGE-CHANGE INDEX
1. *ahold* for *hold*: Stage 2
Current ratio (*get hold* vs. *get ahold*): 18:1
2. **aholt* for *ahold*: Stage 1
Current ratio (*ahold* vs. **aholt*): 50:1

-AHOLIC; -AHOLISM. These newfangled "suffixes" derive from *alcoholic* and *alcoholism*, which were extended to *workaholic* and *workaholism*, and from there to other words indicating various addictions or obsessions. Each new term is automatically a MOR-PHOLOGICAL DEFORMITY. Most examples, though, are nonce-words (e.g., *beefaholic, footballaholic, spend-aholic, wordaholic*).

aide; aid, n. Both terms are used in reference to a person whose responsibility is to provide help to another <a physician's aide> <a teacher's aide>. The spelling *aide* is preferable—and it's much more common, probably because *aid* also has the sense of "practical help or support, such as money or food."

Current ratio (*teacher's aide* vs. **teacher's aid*): 8:1

aide-de-camp (= military aide) is so spelled—not **aid-de-camp*. Borrowed from French, the phrase should retain the French spelling—*aide*—especially considering that *aide* is itself now an English word (meaning "a staff member under one's authority"). The plural is *aides-de-camp*. See PLURALS (B).

Current ratio (*aide-de-camp* vs. **aid-de-camp*): 8:1

aim to [+ vb.]; **aim at** [+ vb. + -ing]. The idiom *aim to (do)* has long been typical of AmE—e.g.: "Rhetoric . . . aims to make us artists." Brainerd Kellogg, *A Text-Book on Rhetoric* 18 (1881). Although some British commentators have expressed a preference for *aim at (doing)*, that form is not prevalent today even in BrE.

*ain't. Is this word used orally in most parts of the country by cultivated speakers? In 1961, *W3* said it was, provoking a firestorm of protests from journalists and academics. See Herbert C. Morton, *The Story of Webster's Third* 153–70 (1994). *W3*'s assessment was quite a change from that of *W2* (1934), which had given it a tag: "*Dial. or Illit.*" The editor of *W3*, Philip Gove, explained the change by conceding that he had no large files of empirical evidence: "Knowledge of some kind of language behavior comes through contact with its observers and is not always documented because there seems to be no reason to collect additional evidence" (*ibid.* at 262). If that's the method,

then one can confidently say that *W3*'s treatment of *ain't* was flawed in its incompleteness.

In 1962, the year after *W3* was published, an apt cartoon appeared in *The New Yorker*. A man stands in the reception area of G. & C. Merriam Dictionary Division, as the receptionist says to him, "Sorry. Dr. Gove ain't in."

Yes, **ain't* is used by cultivated speakers, but almost always for either of two reasons: (1) to be tongue-in-cheek; and (2) to flaunt their reverse snobbery. For most people, it remains an emblem of poor usage—a NONWORD. All in all, the 1934 tag has either remained accurate or been bolstered.

LANGUAGE-CHANGE INDEX
*ain't used with a straight face: Stage 1

AIRLINESE. The JARGON of the airline business is notable in several ways. First, it has an odd vocabulary, in which *equipment* refers to the airplane you wish you were boarding ("The flight has been delayed because we don't have any *equipment*—it's in Pittsburgh"). Second, it relies heavily on DOUBLESPEAK, with a heavy dose of ZOMBIE NOUNS; *seat cushions may be used as flotation devices* means "if we crash in water, use your seat cushion to float"; *in the event of a loss in cabin pressure* means "if we lose cabin pressure so that no one can breathe"; *please use the trash dispenser for anything other than bathroom tissue* means "don't try to flush paper towels or anything other than bathroom tissue down the commode." (For still another example, see **only (B).**) Third, it is often stilted and redundant—e.g.: "It is a federal requirement to comply with all safety regulations." Fourth, it has borrowed many nautical terms, both directly (*aft, bulkhead, crew, fleet, galley, hold, stowage*) and by analogy (*airworthy, flight deck*). Finally, it contains many NEOLOGISMS, some formed by combining nouns (*cross-check, ground personnel*), some by affixation (*inflight*, adj.), and some by changing parts of speech (e.g., *overnight*, vb., as in "We'll have to overnight you"). Among other recent coinages are these:

- *enplane*: "PFCs are $1 to $3 fees that airports can tack on to the ticket price paid by each *enplaned* passenger, in order to finance the expansion of airfields and terminals." Jon McKenna, "Trends in the Region," *Bond Buyer*, 5 Sept. 1996, at 29.
- *enplanement*: "Though it recorded more than 600,000 *enplanements* in the mid-'70s, the state is now struggling to board about 350,000 passengers a year." Rick Steelhammer, "Airport Group Seeking Increased Federal Role," *Charleston Gaz.*, 14 Aug. 1996, at C1.
- *hub-and-spoke*: "The industry's *hub-and-spoke* system of operating, in which short flights feed customers into big airports, where they board longer flights, has also increased demand for regional jets," "Airline to Pay $1.4 Billion for 67 Jets," *N.Y. Times*, 18 June 1997, at C4.
- *interline*: "Southwest does not *interline* with other carriers, in part because it is simply unwilling to spend the extra time and money on the ground, waiting to board

LANGUAGE-CHANGE INDEX (For the full key, see front matter pp. xxxi, l–li.)
Stage 1: Rejected. **Stage 2:** Widely shunned. **Stage 3:** Widespread but . . . **Stage 4:** Ubiquitous but . . . **Stage 5:** Fully accepted.
Invariably inferior forms marked by asterisk (*). • Ratios represent frequency of prevalent forms vs. variants in current books.

passengers from connecting flights that are often delayed." Kevin Freiberg & Jackie Freiberg, *Nuts! Southwest Airlines' Crazy Recipe for Business and Personal Success* 52 (1996).

- *load factor*: "Instead of raising fares when *load factors* (ratio of passenger capacity to tickets sold) are up, Southwest increases the number of flights and expands the market." *Ibid.* at 53.
- *pushback*: "[The] ramp agent unhooks the *pushback* from the aircraft and the plane taxis toward the runway." *Ibid.* at 59.

Although these neologisms serve a genuine purpose, airlinese otherwise typifies some of the worst qualities of modern AmE (e.g., "We'll be on the ground *momentarily*"—see **momentarily**). And it has a debilitating effect because so many people are so frequently exposed to it. Small wonder that some of them feel tempted to dash for an emergency exit. See OBSCURITY.

airworthy, used in reference to aircraft, means "fit for flying." The word, surprisingly enough first used in 1829, was analogized from *seaworthy*. See AIRLINESE & **seaworthy.**

ait (BrE for "a small island") is predominantly so spelled—not **eyot*, a variant that was never common.
                                            Current ratio: 7:1

*aitiology. See **etiology.**

a la; à la. This GALLICISM, meaning "in the manner or style of," was borrowed into English in the late 16th century. It appears in such well-known phrases as *à la carte* (= according to the menu's individual pricing for an item) and *à la mode* (= [1] fashionable, stylish, or [2] topped with ice cream). The phrase often serves a comparative function <he's bound to be a record-breaking baseball player a la Hank Aaron> <a recipe for economic instability a la the 1930s>. Generally, it is written without the DIACRITICAL MARK and without italics <he chipped in a la Tom Watson>, unless it appears as part of a larger French phrase <steak *à la grecque*> <pommes *à la duchesse*>.

Alabamian; *Alabaman. The first, pronounced /al-ə-**bay**-mee-ən/ or /al-ə-**bam**-ee-ən/, is standard; the second is a variant form that occurs much less often in print. See DENIZEN LABELS.
                                            Current ratio: 2:1

alas; alack. *Alas*, a mild exclamation, expresses woe caused by a lamentable state of affairs. E.g.: "The creatures keep Susan alive (inexplicable unless she is meant to be mated with the king bug), and they stop evolving into humans (so we never, *alas*, see the final stage of a really uggy bug-man)." Richard Corliss, "Really Bugged: In *Mimic*, Giant Roaches Invade New York City," *Time*, 25 Aug. 1997, at 70.

Alack, a synonymous exclamation, is archaic. *Alas and alack* is a tiresome CLICHÉ. Because the words are so old-fashioned, virtually all uses have a touch of humorous irony.

See ARCHAISMS.

Albanian. This term may refer to someone from either Albania (in which case it's pronounced /al-**bay**-nee-ən/) or Albany, New York (in which case it's pronounced /**ahl**-bə-nee-ən/). See DENIZEN LABELS.

albeit. Though Eric Partridge pronounced this conjunction archaic (*U&A* at 41), it thrives in written AmE. Labeled "literary" in the *COD*, the word *albeit* means "though." The predominant modern use for *albeit* is to introduce concessive phrases—e.g.:

- "How did one of the most respected engineering schools in the country, *albeit* the smallest, reach such a low point?" Gord Henderson & Ted Shaw, "Controversy Turns Dreams to Turmoil," *Windsor Star*, 26 Oct. 1996, at A1.
- "There may be another way, *albeit* unconfirmed, to increase your odds." Shelly Branch, "Tax Audits Aren't Nice," *Fortune*, 17 Mar. 1997, at 188.
- "The fair has been an annual event, *albeit* one far removed from the thrill rides and demolition derby that have become popular attractions for modern fairgoers." Tammy Garrett, "White County Fair to Celebrate 80-Year Anniversary," *Ark. Democrat-Gaz.*, 10 Sept. 2015, at 68.

Albeit may also begin a subordinate clause, albeit *though* or *although* is more natural and more common with this type of construction—e.g.: "The state will let the free market do it, *albeit* the effects may accrue more unevenly and, perhaps, more brutally." Lucette Lagnado, "Sick Wards: New York's Hospitals Merge, Cut and Fret as Deregulation Nears," *Wall Street J.*, 25 Oct. 1996, at A1. Cf. **howbeit.**

The first syllable of *albeit* is pronounced like *all*, not like your friend *Al*.

albino. Pl. *albinos*. See PLURALS (D).

album /**al**-bəm/ is sometimes mispronounced with an intrusive *-l-*, as if it were /**al**-bləm/. See PRONUNCIATION (B), (C).

Albuquerque; Alburquerque. The accepted spelling of the city in New Mexico is *Albuquerque*. But the original spelling—used in the title of Rudolfo Anaya's novel by that name (published in 1992)—was *Alburquerque*. The place name is frequently misspelled **Alberquerque* or **Albequerque*.
        Current ratio (*Albuquerque* vs. *Alburquerque* vs.
        *Albequerque vs. **Alberquerque*): 1,149:25:1:1

Albuquerquean; *Albuquerquian. The first is standard; the second is an uncommon variant. See DENIZEN LABELS.

aleatory; fortuitous; stochastic. These words have similar but distinct meanings. The first two are especially close, meaning "depending wholly on chance." *Aleatory* derives from the Latin word for the game of dice: *alea jacta est* (= the die is cast). *Fortuitous*, meanwhile, carries the suggestion of an accident, usually but not always a happy one. (See **fortuitous.**) As it happens, *aleatory* usually refers to present descriptions or future events <the aleatory process of flipping a coin seems much too capricious for settling

a dispute>, *fortuitous* to past events <how fortuitous that we met here, and on this day>. *Stochastic*, the most rarefied of these words, means "random"; it is fairly common in the writing of economic analysts and statisticians.

Alfred, Lord Tennyson. See **Tennyson.**

algae; *algee. The plural word for the mostly aquatic, plantlike organisms capable of photosynthesis is *algae* (/**al**-jee/). No other spelling has been recorded in dictionaries, yet the phonetic misspelling **algee* occasionally and surprisingly appears in edited scholarship—e.g.: "Typha latifolia, Typha augustifolia, Phragmites australis, Scirpus sp., and different *algee* [read *algae*] were the prevalent plant species in the wetland." V.S.T. Ciminelli, "Biohydrometallurgy," in 11 *Process Metallurgy Series* 583 (2001).

The (rare) singular *alga* is pronounced /**al**-gə/.

alias is both adverb (= otherwise [called or named]), as an elliptical form of *alias dictus*, and noun (= an assumed name), today usually the latter. *Alias* refers only to names and should not be used synonymously with *guise* (= assumed appearance, pretense). See **pseudonym.**

alibi. A. As a Noun for *excuse*. Strictly speaking, the words are not synonymous, although the confusion of their meanings is understandable. *Alibi* is a specific legal term referring to the defense of having been at a place other than the scene of a crime. By SLIP-SHOD EXTENSION it came to be used (beginning in the 1920s) for an excuse or explanation for misconduct, usually one that shifts blame to someone else. This broader meaning has its defenders—e.g.: "Cynicism and the common man's distrust of the law have tinged *alibi* with a suggestion of improbability and even of dishonesty. Purists insist that it should be restricted to its legal meaning, and those who wish to be formally correct will so restrict it. In so doing, however, they will lose the connotation of cunning and dishonesty which distinguishes it from *excuse*." DCAU at 24. Their point is well taken, but *alibi* to denote a cunning excuse remains at best a CASUALISM.

LANGUAGE-CHANGE INDEX
alibi for *excuse*: Stage 3
Current ratio (*an excuse for not* vs.
an alibi for not): 63:1

B. As an Adverb. In recent years *alibi* has been used as an adverb (meaning "elsewhere" <he proved himself alibi>), but this usage should be avoided. Although "elsewhere" is the original Latin meaning of *alibi* (originally a locative of L. *alius* "other"), in English it has long served only as a noun, and harking back to the classical sense is an affectation.

LANGUAGE-CHANGE INDEX
alibi as an adverb: Stage 1

C. As a Verb. Nor should *alibi* be used as a verb, as it occasionally has been since the early 20th century. The examples below are doubly bad, since the misbegotten verb (meaning *excuse*) is based on the misused noun:

- " 'He looked very heavy-armed warming up,' Apodaca said. 'I'm not *alibiying* [read *making excuses*] for him, but I was very worried about him because of that start in Chicago.' " Rafael Hermoso, "Reynoso Feeling 'Lucky,' " *Record* (N.J.), 18 June 1997, at S1 (quoted speech).
- "Tyson *alibied* [read *said* or *tried to excuse himself by saying*] that he 'snapped' when he bit Holyfield—twice." Jeff Schultz, "Tyson's Main Event: Avoid Trouble," *Atlanta J.-Const.*, 11 July 1997, at F10.
- "I'd say there's a danger and plain lousy taste in distorting a current president's words to zip up a movie. 'It's fantasy, entertainment,' Zemeckis *alibied* [read *rationalized*]. 'It adds verisimilitude.' " Sandy Grady, "When Hollywood Distorts Reality for Big Bucks," *Milwaukee J. & Sentinel*, 23 July 1997, at 12.

LANGUAGE-CHANGE INDEX
alibi as a verb: Stage 1

alien, adj., takes the preposition *to* or, less commonly, *from*. For purposes of DIFFERENTIATION, H.W. Fowler noted, "there is perhaps a slight preference for *from* where mere difference or separation is meant (*We are entangling ourselves in matters alien from our subject*), and for *to* when repugnance is suggested (*cruelty is alien to his nature*)" (*FMEU1* at 15).

Current ratio (*alien to* vs. *alien from*): 13:1

alienable (= transferable to another) is so formed—not **alienatable*. See -ABLE (D) & -ATABLE.

aliquot, adj.; **aliquant,** adj. *Aliquot* = contained in a larger whole an exact number of times <4 is an aliquot part of 16>. *Aliquant* = contained in a larger number or quantity but not an exact number of times <4 is an aliquant part of 15>.

all. A. *All (of)*. The better construction is to omit *of* and write, when possible, "*All* the attempts failed." Since the beginnings of Modern English, the phrasing *all the* (+ plural noun) has vastly predominated over *all of* (+ plural noun): the *of*-variant was essentially nonexistent till the turn of the 20th century, and even now it is not nearly as frequent in print sources, whether in AmE or BrE. E.g.: "With the end to fighting, the group was disbanded, and *all* its members were ordered to burn their identity papers and go into hiding." P.H. Ferguson, "End of War Gave Life to Would-Be Kamikazes," *Austin Am.-Statesman*, 3 Sept. 1995, at A20. Although *all of* is more common in AmE than in BrE, it should generally be avoided in all formal writing. See **of (A).**

In two circumstances, though, *all of* is the better choice. The first occurs when a pronoun follows <all of them>, unless the pronoun is serving as an

LANGUAGE-CHANGE INDEX (For the full key, see front matter pp. xxxi, l–li.)
Stage 1: Rejected. **Stage 2:** Widely shunned. **Stage 3:** Widespread but . . . **Stage 4:** Ubiquitous but . . . **Stage 5:** Fully accepted.
Invariably inferior forms marked by asterisk (*). • Ratios represent frequency of prevalent forms vs. variants in current books.

adjective, either possessive <all my belongings> or demonstrative <all that jazz>. The second occurs when a possessive noun follows—e.g.: "Beyond *all of* Jones' ego-stroking maneuvers and incessant need for attention, this is what he is talking about." Paul Daugherty, "Cowboys Owner Smarter than Average Bear," *Cincinnati Enquirer*, 8 Sept. 1995, at B1.

Current ratio (*all the* vs. *all of the*): 8:1

B. With Negatives. *Not all*—as opposed to **all . . . not*—is usually the appropriate sequence in negative constructions. E.g.:

- "*All* literary sentences are *not* elaborate." George P. Krapp, *The Knowledge of English* 72 (1927). (A possible revision: *Not all literary sentences are elaborate.*)
- "*All* people do *not* possess *Life*'s intuitive perception that the word is so 'monstrous' that even to list it as a dialect variation is to merit scorn." Bergen Evans, "But What's a Dictionary For?" in *The Ways of Language* 77, 81 (Raymond J. Pflug ed., 1967). (A possible revision: *Not all people possess* Life's *intuitive perception . . . .*)
- "Students rightfully protest; and while *all of their complaints do not* [read *not all their complaints*] have merit, they too should be heard." William O. Douglas, *Points of Rebellion* 14 (1970).
- "When he screened Foster's office files two days after his death, Nussbaum decided that *all* of the papers were *not* relevant to the suicide inquiry." "Cops: White House Aide Foiled Probe," *Chicago Trib.*, 4 Feb. 1994, at N14. (Two possible revisions to remedy the ambiguity of the original: *Nussbaum decided that none of the papers were relevant./Nussbaum decided that some of the papers were not relevant.*)
- "Since *all teachers do not* [read *not all teachers*] teach the FSA subjects, other tests, like end-of-course exams, must be used." Sue Legg, "Testing—When Is Enough, Enough?," *Gainesville Sun*, 6 Sept. 2015, Opinion §.

See **not (A).** Cf. ***everyone . . . not.**

LANGUAGE-CHANGE INDEX
**all . . . not* for *not all*: Stage 3
Current ratio (*not all of them are* vs.
**all of them are not*): 10:1

C. As Subject. *All*, as subject, may take either a singular or a plural verb. When a plural noun is implied after *all*, the verb should be plural <all were present>—e.g.: "Until this morning, *all were* official residents of the three Dadaab refugee camps near the Kenya–Somalia border." David Finkel, "African Refugees Start Journey to Homes in Distant U.S.," *Miami Herald*, 25 Aug. 2002, at A16. But when *all* denotes a collective abstraction (as a mass noun), it should take a singular verb <all is well>—e.g.: "*All* she wants *is* people to be touched by the gifts she believes God has given her." Johanna D. Wilson, "Back Roads," *Sun-News* (Myrtle Beach, S.C.), 19 Aug. 2002, at C1.

Writers sometimes err, especially when a collective *all* has a plural complement in the predicate—e.g.: "All she needs *are* [read *is*] the open-house listings in the Sunday Real Estate section." Elliott Rebhun, "Checking Out the Scenery in Apt. 3C," *N.Y. Times*, 26 May 2001, at A11. The Christmas song "All I Want for Christmas Is My Two Front Teeth" gets it right.

D. And *any*. *All* follows a superlative adjective <the best of all>; *any* follows a comparative adjective <more than any other>. Constructions such as **more than . . . all* are illogical. See **best of all** & COMPARATIVES AND SUPERLATIVES.

All-American, n.; **All-America,** adj. As the headwords suggest, *All-American* is predominantly a noun <Jones is an All-American>. In the athletic sense, the preferred adjective has long been *All-America* <three Nebraska linemen were selected for the All-America team>, though usage is almost equally divided. In the more general sense, however, *all-American boy* or *all-American girl* is the only idiomatic phrasing.

Current ratio (*All-America team* vs.
All-American team): 1:1
Current ratio (*all-American kid* vs. *all-America kid):
[none possible because the latter
phrasing does not appear]

all-around, adj.; **all-round.** The first is the standard AmE form, the second the BrE form. In fact, though, *all-round* predominated in AmE till about 1950, when the slightly longer form overtook it in frequency of use. In both varieties of English, the other form is a variant. When Americans use *all-round*, they have traditionally felt the need to show the elision of *a* with an apostrophe: "The apostrophe is needed to indicate that the word is a shortening of 'around,' not the adjective 'round.' 'An all round man' would mean one who is completely curved, of globular construction." Edward N. Teall, *Putting Words to Work* 216 (1940). See **around.**

***allegator.** See **alleger.**

allege; contend. To *allege* is to formally state a matter of fact as being true or provable, without yet having proved it. The word once denoted stating under oath, but this meaning no longer applies. To *contend* is to strive against—or, in the advocate's sense, to state one's position in a polemical way.

Allege should not be used as a synonym of *assert, maintain, declare,* or *claim. Allege* has peculiarly accusatory connotations. One need not allege only the commission of crimes; but certainly the acts alleged must concern bad conduct or negligence. Of course, journalists commonly use the word when speaking about things that a suspect is thought to have done <the witnesses alleged that he stole the car from the Joneses' garage>—and they do it to avoid legal trouble.

alleged, adj. If the thing that is *alleged* has already been verified, then *alleged* is the wrong word. So the word is inappropriate when describing something that is known to have occurred. If the police believe that some particular person has committed a crime, that person is a genuine suspect, not an *alleged* one—e.g.: "The story goes that Pierce had a verbal beef a year ago with one of the three *alleged suspects* [read *suspects*], and, by chance, they crossed paths again." Will McDonough, "Cops and Players II," *Boston Globe*, 30 Sept. 2000, at G1.

Alleged is pronounced with two syllables (/ə-**lejd**/), not three.

allegedly (/ə-**lej**-id-lee/) does not mean "in an alleged manner," as it would if the adverb had been formed as English adverbs generally are. Wilson Follett considered adverbs like this one ugly and unjustified—especially *reportedly* (*MAU* at 279). Yet *allegedly* is a convenient space- and time-saver for *it is alleged that* or *according to the allegations*. Though not logically formed, *allegedly* is well established and, if used in moderation, unobjectionable. See -EDLY. Cf. **shamefacedly.**

LANGUAGE-CHANGE INDEX
allegedly: Stage 5

alleger; *allegator. The latter is a miserable excuse for a NEEDLESS VARIANT.

allegro. Pl. *allegros*, preferably not the Italian *allegri*. But some writers use the pedantic foreign plural—e.g.: "His delicate touch made the andante movements glisten like an expanse of water, his 3rd movement *allegri* [read *allegros*] skip deliriously." Rick Jones, "Rhythm, Religion and Gowns of Green for Television," *Evening Standard*, 29 July 1996, at 7. See PLURALS (D).

Current ratio: 3:1

allergen-friendly. See **-friendly.**

alleviable. So formed—not *alleviatable. See -ABLE (D) & -ATABLE.

ALLITERATION. A. Pleasant Examples. How language affects the ear should be a critical concern of every writer. Writers frequently harness sounds for any of several effects. When they repeat sounds in nearby words, the result is called *alliteration* (which has two subsets: *assonance* for vowels <reverie in poetry>, *consonance* for consonants <put pen to paper>).

Sometimes alliteration reinforces sarcasm, as when Vice President Spiro Agnew referred to the *nattering nabobs of negativism* or when Fred Rodell, a Yale professor, referred to due process as *that lovely limpid legalism*. Rodell, in fact, relished sarcastic alliteration, once referring to "the *tweedledum-tweedledee twaddle* of much that passes for *learned legal* argument." Fred Rodell, *Nine Men* 331 (1955).

At other times alliteration merely creates memorable phrasing—e.g.:

- "Only active measures, *promptly* applied, can *provide* this *poor, pusillanimous poop* with the *proper pep*." P.G. Wodehouse, *Right Ho, Jeeves* 129 (1934; repr. 1986) (consonance).
- "Nothing *sounds* more *studied* than a repeated *spontaneity*." Tom Stoppard, *Lord Malquist and Mr. Moon* pt. 2, at 1 (1966) (consonance).
- "She had a *sneaky, sly, shy, squamous* personality." Ursula K. Le Guin, *The Lathe of Heaven* 92 (1971) (consonance).

- "Music is unique among the *fine* arts in that it calls *for* a response not only *from* the *head* and the *heart* but also, *frequently, from* one or more of the *feet*." Frank Muir, *An Irreverent and Thoroughly Incomplete Social History of Almost Everything* 1 (1976) (consonance).
- "A moment later, the banister gave way, and the *pair* on the *stair* were in the *air*." Roger Zelazny, *A Night in the Lonesome October* 200 (1993) (assonance).

Sometimes alliteration is risky. If it leads you into SESQUIPEDALITY just for the sake of sound, it will probably annoy some readers—e.g.: "Lukacs has an *eagle eye* for the *etiology* of *error* and the seductions of false logic." Ron Rosenbaum, "Springtime for Hitler," *L.A. Times*, 23 Nov. 1997, at 12. If that writer hadn't been lured by alliteration, he almost certainly would have used *cause* rather than *etiology* there. See **etiology.**

B. Unpleasant Examples. The unconscious repetition of sounds, especially excessive sibilance (too many /s/ sounds, as in the phrase *especially excessive sibilance*), can easily distract readers: "When used by accident it falls on the ear very disagreeably." W. Somerset Maugham, "Lucidity, Simplicity, Euphony," in *The Summing Up* 321, 325 (1938). E.g.: "Everybody with a stake in solving the problem will have to *bear their fair share* of the costs involved." Robert Ebel, "Personal View: Soviet Reactors Need a Western Focus," *Fin. Times*, 13 July 1995, at 11. (A possible revision, which also solves the *everybody . . . their* problem: *Everybody with a stake in solving the problem will have to bear some of the costs.*)

The best way to avoid the infelicity of undue alliteration is to read one's prose aloud when editing. See SOUND OF PROSE.

Yet sometimes unpleasant alliteration isn't merely a matter of whether it's conscious or unconscious. That is to say, a writer may use it quite consciously but also quite unpleasantly, through poor literary judgment—e.g.: "The necessarily contextual, contested, and contingent character of substantive liberal principles necessarily prevents them, qua principles, from effectively inhibiting human brutality." Lief H. Carter, "Law and Politics as Play," 83 *Chicago-Kent L. Rev.* 1333, 1333 (2008).

*all . . . not. See **all** (B).

allocable. So formed—not *allocatable. See -ABLE (D) & -ATABLE.

Current ratio: 45:1

allocution. See **elocution.**

all of. See **all** (A).

all of a sudden. This is the idiomatic phrase, not *all of the sudden—e.g.:

- "I wasn't thinking of anything, but *all of the sudden* [read *all of a sudden*] I was no longer tired." Sam Brumbaugh, *Goodbye, Goodness: A Novel* 108 (2005).

- "*All of the sudden* [read *All of a sudden*] there was a huge flash and explosion." Ray A. Jones, *110 Questions and Answers on Electrical Safety* 4 (2011).
- "She came, saw and conquered, and *all of the sudden* [read *all of a sudden*], every second A-list pop star wanted a residency on the strip." Brendan Kelly, "'Crazy' Gamble Pays Off in Vegas," *Edmonton J.*, 29 Aug. 2015, at D1 (referring to Celine Dion).

Language-Change Index
*all of the sudden for *all of a sudden*: Stage 1
Current ratio (*all of a sudden* vs.
*all of the sudden): 48:1

allow; permit. These words have an important connotative difference. *Allow* suggests merely the absence of opposition, or refraining from a proscription. *Permit*, in contrast, suggests affirmative sanction or approval.

all ready. See **already**.

all right; *alright. **Alright* for *all right* has never been accepted as standard. Gertrude Stein used the shorter form, but that is not much of a recommendation: "The question mark is *alright* [read *all right*] when it is all alone." Gertrude Stein, "Poetry and Grammar" (1935), in *Perspectives on Style* 44, 48 (Frederick Candelaria ed., 1968). This short version may be gaining a shadowy acceptance—e.g.:

- "They are obviously thoroughly British and so are *alright* and should be reintroduced if possible." Richard Ryder, "Hands Off Our Ruddy Ducks," *Independent*, 30 June 1995, at 20.
- "There are to be 'tough new criminal penalties', including a doubling of the maximum sentence for fraud; *alright*, everyone can understand that, but a financial crisis SWAT team?" Bronwen Maddox, "Devil in the Detail Weakens President's Fervour," *Times* (London), 10 July 2002, at 14.

Still, the combined version cannot yet be considered good usage—or even colloquially all right.

Language-Change Index
*alright for *all right*: Stage 2
Current ratio (*all right* vs. **alright*): 8:1

all-round. See **all-around**.

all that. In negative statements, conditions, and questions, *all that* frequently means "to the expected degree"—essentially as an equivalent of *so very* <not all that exciting>. The expression is a CASUALISM dating back to the 17th century. E.g.:

- Negative statement: "Sure, we may smile ruefully at the memories of these past missteps, but they'll never really be *all that* funny." Ken Potts, "Remembering Mistakes Helps You Learn from Them," *Daily Herald* (Chicago), 13 Jan. 2001, at 4.
- Condition: "If these bogus graduates are *all that* smart and computer-savvy, why don't they design their own phony diplomas instead of paying 'thousands of dollars' to someone else?" "Furthermore," *Omaha World-Herald*, 28 Dec. 2000, at 12.
- Question: "As dysfunctional as the Los Angeles Lakers seem at the moment, is it really *all that* strange that notorious malcontent Isaiah Rider would actually sound

like the team's voice of reason?" David Leon Moore, "O'Neal–Bryant Flap Has L.A. Teammates Scratching Heads," *USA Today*, 12 Jan. 2001, at C8.

See **that (E)**.

all the; all these. See **all (A)**.

all the time. Margaret Nicholson criticizes this expression when used in a context that doesn't indicate a definite period (*DAEU* at 17). Hence she labels the following usage "slang": "Actors act while they are on stage, but he acts *all the time*."

This may have been one of Nicholson's pet peeves, since no other usage commentator has objected to the phrase. Though slightly informal, *all the time* in the nonliteral sense is acceptable English.

All the time is more polished phrasing than the unidiomatic **all of the time*. See **all (A)**.

all together. See **altogether**.

all told. One archaic meaning of *tell* is "to count." Hence the idiom is *all told* <all told, there were 14 casualties>, which dates from the mid-19th century. Some people write **all tolled*, perhaps because *toll* can mean "to announce with a bell or other signal." But this is an error—e.g.:

- "*All tolled* [read *All told*], perhaps half the people eligible to participate will do so." "Getting Out the Vote," *Columbian* (Vancouver, Wash.), 17 Oct. 2002, at C6.
- "In 1999–2000, each of the eight Ivy League colleges received at least 10,000 applications; *all tolled* [read *all told*], the Ivy League colleges received 121,948 applications that year and admitted only 23,532, fewer than one in five." Christopher Avery, Andrew Fairbanks & Richard Zeckhauser, *The Early Admissions Game: Joining the Elite* 7 (2003).

Language-Change Index
*all tolled for *all told*: Stage 1
Current ratio (*all told* vs. **all tolled*): 300:1

allude. A. And *advert* & *refer*. To *allude* is to refer to (something) indirectly or by suggestion only. To *advert* or *refer* is to bring up directly, *advert* being the more FORMAL WORD. (See **advert**.) *Allude* is misused for *refer* when the indirect nature of a comment or suggestion is missing—e.g.:

- "The generous wrath which had caused her to *allude* [read *refer*] to her betrothed as a pig in human shape had vanished completely." P.G. Wodehouse, *The Return of Jeeves* 37 (1954) (the angry fiancée had just said, "You're simply a pig in human shape!").
- "Calling on President Clinton to enter the debate forcefully, Jackson *alluded to* [read *referred to* or *quoted*] the words spoken by King on Aug. 28, 1963: 'I have a dream that this nation will rise up . . . .'" Chuck Finnie, "Jackson: Proposition 209 Equals 'Ethnic Cleansing,'" *S.F. Examiner*, 25 Aug. 1997, at A1.

In the following sentence, the writer creates an OXYMORON because an allusion can't be explicit: "The images in the grid *alluded explicitly to homosexuality* [read *depicted homosexuality explicitly*], since all showed male couples, most in sexual positions." Maud Lavin, "Robert Flynt at Witkin," *Art in America*, Feb. 1993, at 111.

LANGUAGE-CHANGE INDEX
allude used for a specific reference: Stage 3

B. And *illude* & *elude*. To *illude* (a rare verb) is to deceive with an illusion; to *elude* (a common verb) is to avoid or escape. Both words are sometimes misused for *allude*—e.g.:

- "He later added that 'It's more difficult than just having the money,' *illuding* [read *alluding*] to the politics that is played in owning a major professional sports team." Charles L. Griggs, "Black Athletes Lost in Sports Power Struggle," *Jacksonville Free Press*, 12 Mar. 1997, at 5. (For the use of the singular *is* with *politics*, see **politics**.)
- "But they draw the line at *eluding* [read *alluding*] to world events." Breuse Hickman, "Halloween Happenings Mean Pleasant Screams for Fright Fans," *Fla. Today*, 4 Oct. 2002, at 16.

The reverse error—*allude* for *elude*—is somewhat less common. E.g.: "Glenn said Derogatis also was charged with aggravated assault, possession of cocaine and *alluding* [read *eluding*] police." "Law & Order," *Star-Ledger* (Newark), 19 Dec. 2002, Essex §, at 39.

LANGUAGE-CHANGE INDEX
1. *illude* misused for *allude*: Stage 1
Current ratio (*allude to* vs. **illude to*): 56,182:1
2. *elude* misused for *allude*: Stage 1
Current ratio (*allude to* vs. **elude to*): 513:1
3. *allude* misused for *elude*: Stage 1
Current ratio (*eluded him* vs. **alluded him*): 254:1

C. For *suggest*. This is an attenuated use of *allude* to be avoided—e.g.: "As Johnson *alluded* [read *suggested*], who among us has no sin?" Letter of Karen M. Piet, "Jesus Forgave Sins of Those Who Repented and Told Them to Sin No More," *Rocky Mountain News* (Denver), 3 Sept. 1997, at A40.

LANGUAGE-CHANGE INDEX
allude misused for *suggest*: Stage 1

allusion. A. And *illusion*. While an *allusion* is an indirect reference <literary allusion>, an *illusion* is a deception <optical illusion>. But some writers bungle the two—e.g.:

- "Full of jokes, literary *illusions* [read *allusions*], fractured Shakespeare and physical comedy, it's a show that appeals to young and old." Nadine Goff, "'Buck Mulligan' Has Something for Everyone," *Wis. State J.*, 18 Sept. 1995, at C5.
- "'I try not to be too annoying,' he said, admitting that Councilwoman Ramona Martinez once asked if she could get 'extra credit' for enduring his literary *illusions* [read *allusions*]." Susan Greene, "Stalwart Pursues New Role," *Denver Post*, 9 Apr. 2003, at A19.

For the difference between *illusion* and *delusion*, see **illusion**. See MALAPROPISMS.

LANGUAGE-CHANGE INDEX
illusion misused for *allusion*: Stage 1
Current ratio (*literary allusions* vs.
*literary illusions): 84:1

B. And *reference*. See **allude** (A).

ALLUSION. See LITERARY ALLUSION.

allusive; **allusory*. The latter is a NEEDLESS VARIANT. See **elusive**.

Current ratio: 192:1

ally. As a noun, the accent is on the first syllable: /**al**-ı/. As a verb, the accent is on the second: /ə-**lı**/.

almond is preferably pronounced /**ah**-mənd/—not /**ahl**-mənd/ or (worse) /**al**-mənd/. The pronunciation /**am**-ənd/ is also sometimes heard. See PRONUNCIATION (B).

almost. A. Placement. This word is sometimes misplaced in a sentence—e.g.: "There is *almost a childlike simplicity* [read *an almost childlike simplicity*] in their straightforward depictions." Myra Yellin Outwater, "Early American 'Naive' Art a Surprise for Sophisticates," *Morning Call* (Allentown, Pa.), 10 Mar. 1996, at F1. Like *only*, the word *almost* should be placed immediately before the word it modifies. See **only** (A).

B. **Almost quite*. H.W. Fowler branded this phrasing an "illiteracy," and so it remains today—e.g.:

- "'They're feeding at the door,' a competing bookseller says jealously, and *almost quite* [read *almost*] literally." Raphael Sagalyn, "Bookstore Wars," *Wash. Post* (Mag.), 11 Mar. 1979, at 28.
- "Treacle tart and cream was terrific, with enough lemon cutting the syrup to make it feel *almost quite* [read *almost* or *quite*] health-giving." Fay Maschler, "How to Keep Cool on a Tightrope," *Evening Standard*, 4 July 1995, at 23.
- "'A Density of Souls' runs straight as a string until the last third, when all hell breaks loose (*almost quite literally*) [delete the entire parenthetical] and Rice's carefully constructed melodrama goes up like a transformer in a hurricane." Kevin Allman, "Grand Guignol 90210," *Times-Picayune* (New Orleans), 3 Sept. 2000, Travel §, at 6.

Oddly, however, this phrasing wasn't uncommon in the 17th and 18th centuries. It trailed off in the 19th century and was stigmatized in the 20th. See **quite**.

LANGUAGE-CHANGE INDEX
*almost quite: Stage 1

alms (= money or food given to the poor) is pronounced with the *-l-* silent: /ahmz/—not /ahlmz/ or /amz/.

alone. See **lone**.

LANGUAGE-CHANGE INDEX (For the full key, see front matter pp. xxxi, l–li.)
Stage 1: Rejected. **Stage 2:** Widely shunned. **Stage 3:** Widespread but . . . **Stage 4:** Ubiquitous but . . . **Stage 5:** Fully accepted.
Invariably inferior forms marked by asterisk (*). • Ratios represent frequency of prevalent forms vs. variants in current books.

alongside, prep., = at the side of. Hence one car is parked *alongside* another and logs are stacked *alongside* one another. It is unnecessary—and poor style—to write **alongside of**. See **of** (A).

LANGUAGE-CHANGE INDEX
**alongside of* for *alongside*: Stage 3
Current ratio (*alongside the* vs.
**alongside of the*): 25:1

along with. Like *together with*, this connective phrase does not affect the grammatical number of the sentence. E.g.: "He admitted that he, *along with* other board members, *are* [read *is*] no longer sure about anything concerning the [controversy]." Elizabeth W. Crowley, "Salem Dispute Drags On," *Patriot Ledger* (Quincy, Mass.), 7 Aug. 2002, at 1. See SUBJECT–VERB AGREEMENT (E).

When the sense is necessarily plural, use *and* instead of *along with*—e.g.: "He *along with* [read *and*] his wife, Edith, *were* the owners of the Snug Club until they sold it in 1997." "Thomas E. McDonald Sr." (obit.), *Daily Oklahoman*, 8 Aug. 2002, at C8.

a lot (= many) is the standard spelling. **Alot* has always been considered nonstandard—e.g.:

- "*Alot* [read *A lot*] of people have noticed that the two teams playing in the World Series have one very important thing in common." Charles A. Jaffe, "Investors Can Learn a Thing from Baseball," *Boston Globe*, 22 Oct. 2000, at F10.
- "*Alot* [read *A lot*] of kids found out yesterday that the easiest thing to do on ice skates is fall down." Eve Rubenstein, "Skating Stars, Past and Future," *S.F. Chron.*, 22 Nov. 2000, at A27.
- "Dalmatians are active and require *alot* [read *a lot*] of exercise and attention." "Dalmatian Alert," *Sarasota Herald-Trib.*, 2 Dec. 2000, at B7.

Cf. **all right.**

LANGUAGE-CHANGE INDEX
**alot* for *a lot*: Stage 2
Current ratio (*a lot* vs. **alot*): 659:1

aloud; out loud. The latter is colloquial when used in place of the former in expressions such as *read out loud*. Because of this—and because *read aloud* is 12 times as common as *read out loud* in modern print sources—*read aloud* should be preferred in edited prose. E.g.:

- "McGuffey's fifth and sixth readers had an abundance of the kind of poetry that demands to be read *out loud* [read *aloud*], like 'The Raven' by Edgar Allan Poe." Diane Ravitch, "Children's Books," *N.Y. Times*, 17 May 1987, § 7, at 46.
- "Oprah loves writing that begs to be read *out loud* [read *aloud*]." Marilyn Johnson, "Oprah Winfrey: A Life in Books," *Life*, Sept. 1997, at 44.

al Qaeda is preferably pronounced /al **kɪ**-də/, a fair Anglophone approximation of the Arabic pronunciation—not /al **kay**-də/. As one authority says, "When faced with two anglicizations of a foreign name, it is generally better (and more politic) to choose the one closer to the original, [and] al-KY-duh is closer to the Arabic than al-KAY-duh, which probably arose merely because *Qae-* suggested -KAY- to many speakers." *BBBM* at 22 (with a full five-paragraph discussion of the issue). See HOBSON-JOBSONISM.

already; all ready. *Already* has to do with time <finished already>, *all ready* with preparation <we are all ready>. The terms are occasionally misused—e.g.: "The Bahhumbug with lack of tact / Now called attention to the fact, / Which made it feel to Edmund Gravel / He was *already* [read *all ready*] to unravel." Edward Gorey, *The Headless Bust* 4 (1997).

LANGUAGE-CHANGE INDEX
already misused for *all ready*: Stage 1

alright. See **all right.**

also. This word is a close synonym of *too* (= as well), but its syntactic flexibility is greater <she was also there> <she also was there> <she was there, also>. Avoid treating the word as if it were a conjunction—e.g.: "The dishes were dirty, *also* [read *and*] several of them were broken." This poor use of *also* creates a RUN-ON SENTENCE.

For more on *also*, see **too** (A).

LANGUAGE-CHANGE INDEX
also as a conjunction: Stage 2

also not. This phrasing, which ordinarily follows a negative statement, is usually inferior to *nor*—e.g.:

- "*Race should also not* [read *Nor should race*] be a matter in law enforcement, prosecution or sentencing, but it is." Letter of Stanley S. White, "Unavoidable Reality," *Atlanta J.-Const.*, 23 Jan. 1997, at I5.
- "*He was also not* [read *Nor was he*] told until later, he says, about the allegations of military doctor Maj. Barry Armstrong that one of the Somali men may have been killed execution-style." David Pugliese, "Criminal Probe Delayed, Top Officer Tells Inquiry," *Windsor Star*, 28 Jan. 1997, at A8.
- "*Tosco is also not* [read *Nor is Tosco*] afraid to duke it out with the unions." Arthur Goldgaber, "Tosco's Gusher," *Fin. World*, 18 Mar. 1997, at 38.

See **nor** (A).

But when a contraction precedes the phrase and the tone is intentionally conversational, *also not* seems the more natural wording—e.g.:

- "They're *also not* as dangerous as other animals around the compound." Chris Vaughn, "Teen Goes Whole Hog for Hobby," *Ft. Worth Star-Telegram*, 27 Jan. 1997, at 4.

alter; altar. *Alter* (= to change) is a verb; *altar* (= the table or structure used for sacramental purposes) is a noun. But writers have sometimes confused the two—e.g.:

- "Civil liberties have been sacrificed on the *alter* [read *altar*] of zero tolerance." Jeff A. Schnepper, "Mandated Morality Leads to Legalized Theft," *USA Today* (Mag.), Mar. 1994, at 35.
- "We are learning that privacy and truth have been sacrificed on the *alter* [read *altar*] of greed, power, safety and

security." H. Roy Kaplan, "Striking a Balance of Freedom, Control," *Tampa Bay Times*, 4 July 2013, at A9.

LANGUAGE-CHANGE INDEX
alter misused for *altar*: Stage 1
Current ratio (*at the altar* vs. *at the alter): 46:1

alterative; alterant. Each word may act as both noun and adjective. As adjectives, they both mean "causing alteration." As nouns, however, the meanings diverge. An *alterant* is anything that alters or modifies. *Alterative* appears in medical contexts—though rarely now by physicians—in reference to a medicine that gradually changes unhealthy bodily conditions into healthy ones.

altercation. The traditional view is that this word refers to "a noisy brawl or dispute," not rising to the seriousness of physical violence. For authority limiting the term to the sense "wordy strife," see the *OED, W2, W3,* and Eric Partridge's *U&A.* But since about 1980 in AmE and BrE alike, the word has often denoted some type of scuffling or fighting, especially in police JARGON—e.g.:

- "A 29-year-old drugstore manager who was punched in the chest last month during an *altercation* has died of his injuries, Suffolk police reported yesterday." Olivia Winslow, "Man Punched in Chest During Store Spat Dies," *Newsday* (N.Y.), 12 Sept. 1997, at A32.
- "He was involved in a fight with Cincinnati's Bob Wren, who was cut during the *altercation*." Pete Dougherty, "Kinnear Will Miss One Game," *Times Union* (Albany), 17 Oct. 1997, at C1.
- "Fitzpatrick ascended to the starting position when Geno Smith suffered a broken jaw in a locker-room *altercation*." J.P. Pelzman, "Gang Green Quarterback Enjoying Ride," *Herald News* (West Paterson, N.J.), 10 Sept. 2015, at C1.

Some will lament this development as SLIPSHOD EXTENSION, but the purely nonphysical sense seems beyond recall. The real battle now is to limit *altercation* to light roughhousing. That is, it's wrong to say that someone is killed during an altercation. But police (and the reporters who interview them) tend to talk this way—e.g.:

- "Jonny E. Gammage died during an *altercation* [read *a struggle*?] with white suburban police officers after a traffic stop." Aliah D. Wright, "Veon Wants Race Relations Panel," *Pitt. Post-Gaz.*, 10 Sept. 1997, at B2.
- "The fatal *altercation* [read *confrontation* or *fight*] between Taylor and Mancuso had been brewing for a long time." Bill Poehler, "Death at Raceway Was Unfortunate, Preventable," *Statesman J.* (Salem, Ore.), 18 July 2015, at C1.
- "Samuel Harrell . . . was killed on April 21 during an *altercation* with several corrections officers." Amanda J. Prucell, "Legal Action Filed for Harrell," *Poughkeepsie J.*, 9 Sept. 2015, at A1.

Cf. **accost.**

LANGUAGE-CHANGE INDEX
altercation referring to physical violence: Stage 3

alter ego (lit., "other I") = a second self. Generally, it means "a kindred spirit" or "a constant companion." E.g.: "Stump Connolly is the *alter ego* of Scott Jacobs, a political reporter turned video producer." Bob Minzesheimer, " 'Trail Fever' and 'Stump' Split Vote on How to Pillory Politics," *USA Today*, 14 Aug. 1997, at D6. The phrase should not be hyphenated (except possibly as a PHRASAL ADJECTIVE).

alternate; alternative. A. As Nouns. *Alternative* is needed far more often than *alternate*. An *alternative* is a choice or option—usually one of two choices, but not necessarily. Etymological purists have argued that the word (fr. L. *alter* "the other of two") should be confined to contexts involving but two choices. Ernest Gowers termed this contention a fetish (*FMEU2* at 196), and it has little or no support among other stylistic experts or in actual usage. E.g.: "The county has *three alternatives* on how to meet the region's needs before its treatment plants reach capacity in 2010." "Officials Oppose Plan Expansion," *Seattle Times*, 26 Aug. 1997, at B2.

Indeed, *alternative* carries with it two nuances absent from *choice*. First, *alternative* may suggest adequacy for some purpose <an alternative to driving>; and second, it may suggest compulsion to choose <the alternatives are liberty and death>.

Alternate = (1) something that proceeds by turns with another; or (2) one that substitutes for another.

LANGUAGE-CHANGE INDEX
three or more *alternatives*: Stage 5

B. As Adjectives. *Alternative* = providing a choice between two or more things; available in place of another. E.g.: "Herman would not oppose the light without offering an *alternative* solution, he said." Mary Gail Hare, "Herman Opposes Traffic Signal at Springfield Ave.," *Baltimore Sun*, 29 Aug. 1997, at B1.

Alternate = (1) coming each after one of the other kind, every second one <the divorced parents had agreed on visits in alternate months>; or (2) substitute <although he didn't make the first team, he was named the first alternate player>.

Alternate is often misused for *alternative*, an understandable mistake given how close sense 2 of *alternate* is—e.g.: "Patton responded to the Atlanta Preservation Center's proposal for an *alternate* [read *alternative*] site for the classroom building." Christina Cheakalos, "Building a Better GSU in Six Years," *Atlanta J.-Const.*, 7 Sept. 1997, at G5.

LANGUAGE-CHANGE INDEX
alternate misused for the adjective
alternative: Stage 2
Current ratio (*alternative solution* vs.
**alternate solution*): 10:1

LANGUAGE-CHANGE INDEX (For the full key, see front matter pp. xxxi, l–li.)
Stage 1: Rejected. **Stage 2:** Widely shunned. **Stage 3:** Widespread but . . . **Stage 4:** Ubiquitous but . . . **Stage 5:** Fully accepted.
Invariably inferior forms marked by asterisk (*). • Ratios represent frequency of prevalent forms vs. variants in current books.

although; though. As conjunctions, the words are virtually interchangeable. The only distinction is that *although* is more formal and dignified. In print sources from the 16th century to the present day, *though* has occurred more frequently. *Though* serves also as an adverb <he stated as much, though>. Cf. **while.**

*Altho and **tho* are old-fashioned truncated spellings that were at one time very common, but failed to become standard. They should be avoided.

although . . . yet was formerly a common construction. The two words were considered CORRELATIVE CONJUNCTIONS—e.g.: "Wrote a 6th century Chinese master: '*Although* they dwell in seven jeweled palaces, and have fine objects, smells, tastes, and sensations, *yet* they do not regard this as pleasure . . . [and] seek only to leave that place.'" Howard Chuaeoan, "Other Faiths, Other Visions," *Time*, 24 Mar. 1997, at 78. Today the construction is seen only in the most formal contexts. Generally, either conjunction will suffice to give the same meaning, but with a more modern tone.

altogether; all together. *Altogether* = completely; wholly <the charges were altogether unfounded>. *All together* = at one place or at the same time <the board members were all together at that meeting>.

alum. See **alumnus (A).**

aluminum; aluminium. *Aluminum* is the standard spelling in AmE; *aluminium* is standard in BrE. In the first decade of the 19th century, the metallic element was named *aluminum* by the English chemist Sir Humphrey Davy. In 1813, *aluminium* was offered as being more "classical" in sound, since the *-ium* suffix harmonizes better with the names of other elements such as sodium, potassium, and magnesium. In his 1828 unabridged American dictionary, Noah Webster recorded the word as *aluminum*; his British counterparts, who admitted the word somewhat later, recorded it as *aluminium*. The AmE–BrE difference has existed ever since. It became most strongly pronounced beginning about 1900.

Aluminum /ə-**loo**-mi-nəm/ is sometimes, in AmE, mispronounced /ə-**lim**-i-nəm/. The BrE word *aluminium* is pronounced /al-yoo-**min**-ee-əm/ or /a-loo-**min**-ee-əm/.

alumnus; alumna. A. Plurals: *alumni; alumnae; alums; *alumns. Alumni* (/ə-**ləm**-nɪ/) refers either to male graduates or to males and females collectively; the singular form, which is masculine, is *alumnus*. *Alumnae* (/ə-**ləm**-nee/) refers to female graduates and not, traditionally, to mixed groups; the singular is *alumna*.

A more common mistake than confusing the gender of these words is confusing their number, as by using *alumni* or *alumnae* as a singular—e.g.: "He was an *alumni* [read *alumnus*] of Massachusetts Institute of Technology (MIT) and UCLA." "Abraham James Kennison" (obit.), *News Trib.* (Tacoma), 7 Jan. 1998, at B4. See PLURALS (B).

Alum is a clipped form that dodges the gender issue. This slangy CASUALISM appears often in chatty discussions about high-school and college sports—e.g.:

- "A group of former Kentucky residents and Wildcat *alums*—mostly female—gather to cheer on their team." Ethan Machado, "Team Spirits," *Oregonian* (Portland), 27 Mar. 1998, at 4.
- "He still has the support of influential *alums*, but it may be too late." Dick Weiss, "Penders on Ropes in Texas," *Daily News* (N.Y.), 29 Mar. 1998, at 93.

Alum is a better and more frequent spelling than **alumn*—e.g.:

- "Four Lancaster-Lebanon League *alumns* [read *alums*] are members of the 24th-ranked Penn State team." "Sports Digest," *Lancaster New Era*, 27 Sept. 1996, at C5.
- "I've been doing nothing all day but spouting bullshit: to the press, to trustees, to parents, to *alumns* [read *alums*]." Joanne Dobson, *Quieter than Sleep* 136 (1997).

B. **Former alumnus, alumna.* Just as a graduate is always a graduate, an *alumnus* or *alumna* is ever thus. Yet the strange REDUNDANCY **former alumnus* is fairly common—e.g.:

- "Gregory Bellamy, a friend of Sean Taylor's, speaks at a memorial service at Gulliver Preparatory School for the slain *former alumnus* [delete *former*] and NFL safety." Shandel Richardson & Joel Marino, "Rolle: Taylor Was a Target," *Sun-Sentinel* (Ft. Lauderdale), 29 Nov. 2007, at C1 (photo caption).
- "Many team principals are interviewed ([John] Wooden lovers all), as are entertaining *former alumni* [delete *former*] for extra juice." Mike Clark, "New on DVD: The UCLA Dynasty," *USA Today*, 14 Mar. 2008, at E9.

LANGUAGE-CHANGE INDEX
1. *alumni* as a singular: Stage 2
Current ratio (*an alumnus of* vs. **an alumni of*): 16:1
2. *alumnae* as a singular: Stage 1
Current ratio (*an alumna of* vs. **an alumnae of*): 36:1
3. *alum* as a clipped form: Stage 5
4. **alumn* as the spelling for the clipped form: Stage 1
Current ratio (*alums* vs. **alumns*): 160:1
5. **former alumni* for *alumni*: Stage 1
Current ratio (*the alumni* vs. **the former alumni*): 1,715:1

Alzheimer's (the brain disease) is pronounced /**ahlts**-hɪ-mərz/ (rhyming with *malts* in the first syllable) in AmE and /**alts**-hɪ-mərz/ in BrE. With either version, the first syllable ends with an /s/ sound, not a /z/ sound.

a.m.; AM; p.m.; PM. A. Generally. Whether you use small capitals or lowercase, keep your document consistent throughout. The lowercase letters are now more common, and with lowercase the periods are standard. But many editors prefer the look of AM.

These abbreviations stand for the Latin phrases *ante meridiem* ("before noon") and *post meridiem* ("after noon"). But some writers, when using the full phrases, mistake *meridiem* for *meridian*—e.g.: "Twelve noon is neither *ante meridian* [read *ante meridiem*] (before midday) nor *post meridian* [read *post meridiem*] (after midday)." Jim Cowley, "Notes and Queries," *Guardian*, 2 Oct. 1996, at T17.

B. Redundant Use. Because AM and PM are well understood to designate "morning" and "night" (or "afternoon" or "evening"), it is not necessary to use both designations—e.g.:

- "It was 11:45 *a.m.* Saturday *morning* [delete *a.m.* or *morning*] in Bangkok, Thailand." M.A.J. McKenna, "Disease Spreads Fear," *Atlanta J.-Const.*, 2 Apr. 2003, at A1.
- "As of 8 *p.m.* Tuesday *night* [delete *p.m.* or *night*], Fresno recorded 0.16 of an inch." "Cold Weather Returns to Valley for Weeklong Stay," *Fresno Bee*, 2 Apr. 2003, at B5.

C. And *noon*; *midnight*. Is *noon* 12 AM or 12 PM? What about *midnight*?

Logically—at least in theory and leaving aside the complications of time zones—neither is either. Neither one comes before (*ante*) or after (*post*) the moment when the sun is on the meridian (*meridiem*), that imaginary circle in the sky that includes the point directly overhead and both poles. Rather, *noon* is the moment from which other times are labeled AM or PM. To refer to *noon* as either 12 AM or 12 PM is not just logically and astronomically wrong, but ambiguous as well. The context may clear things up—few people eat lunch at *midnight*—but to say that lunch will be served at "12 AM" is sloppy writing that reflects sloppy thinking.

Idiom compounds the conundrum because, by convention, *midnight* is considered the end of the previous day, not the start of the following day. That would seem to recommend 12 PM *midnight*, but how can 12:00 PM be followed by 12:00:01 AM?

The simple solution is to shun both AM and PM and stick with the unambiguous words *noon* <registration starts at noon> and *midnight* <the deadline for filing taxes is April 15 at midnight>. The numeral 12 is superfluous with either word.

LANGUAGE-CHANGE INDEX
12 AM or 12 PM for noon or midnight: Stage 2

amalgam; amalgamation. Some DIFFERENTIATION is possible. *Amalgam*, the older term, means "a combination" <the restaurant serves an amalgam of regional cuisines>. *Amalgamation* means primarily "the act of combining or uniting; consolidation" <Snobelen announced the *amalgamation* of Metro's seven public-school boards into a single board>.

Avoid *amalgamation* whenever *amalgam* will suffice—e.g.: "This woozy *amalgamation* [read *amalgam*] of rock, funk, jazz and blues obviously tugs ardently at Connick's heart." Melissa Ruggieri, "For Connick, It's About Funk," *Richmond Times-Dispatch*, 28 Oct. 1996, at E7.

amass, vb. This is traditionally a transitive verb meaning "to accumulate (something) systematically over time" <the investigators amassed evidence against the suspect>. That is, someone amasses something; the things don't simply "amass." Although the *OED* records two intransitive uses (separated by some 300 years), it also labels those uses obsolete or archaic. Instances such as the following one violate idiom, *accumulate* being the better word: "Because Mattes lacked health insurance, and the malaria left her both physically exhausted and financially drained, the medical bills that *amassed* [read *accumulated* or *piled up*] during the illness completely wiped out her life savings." Denny Guge, "Clearing Hurdles," *America West Airlines Mag.*, Aug. 1999, at 128.

LANGUAGE-CHANGE INDEX
amass used in an intransitive sense: Stage 1

amateur. In best usage, an amateur (/**am**-ə-chər *or* am-ə-tər/) is a hobbyist, one who engages in an activity out of love and enthusiasm rather than for profit. This is still the meaning in phrases such as *amateur astronomer* and *amateur golfer*. In some uses it has long had a negative connotation of undeveloped skills <rank amateur> <an amateurish job>.

In recent years, it has come to be used as a synonym for *beginner*. A good alternative would be *novice* or *neophyte* (both usually neutral in connotation) or even *tyro* (with connotations of a bumbler).

Amateur has also become a genre of low-budget pornography (an odd usage, since it apparently involves "paid" amateurs).

The word is sometimes misspelled **amature*—e.g.: "Thanks to travel sites, Web cams and the ego of *amature* [read *amateur*] photographers, you can get your fill of colorful leaves by letting your fingers do the peeping." Stephanie Schorow, "Net Life," *Boston Herald*, 4 Oct. 2000, at 59.

LANGUAGE-CHANGE INDEX
amateur misspelled **amature*: Stage 1
Current ratio: 2,250:1

amatory; *amative. See **amorous.**

ambassador; *embassador. The first is the preferred spelling. See **embassy.**

Current ratio: 176:1

ambiance. See **ambience.**

ambidextrous. While *dexterous* is preferably spelled with two *e*'s, *ambidextrous* has only one. Of the *OED*'s nine citations for this word, only one has the two-*e* spelling; in modern print sources, the ratio is 43 to 1 in favor of *ambidextrous*. This inconsistency between *dexterous* and *ambidextrous* is something of a mystery. Cf. **dexterous.**

ambience; ambiance. These words denote the atmosphere of a place. *Ambience* (/**am**-bee-ən[t]s/) is an anglicized form that entered the language in the late

LANGUAGE-CHANGE INDEX (For the full key, see front matter pp. xxxi, l–li.)
Stage 1: Rejected. **Stage 2:** Widely shunned. **Stage 3:** Widespread but . . . **Stage 4:** Ubiquitous but . . . **Stage 5:** Fully accepted.
Invariably inferior forms marked by asterisk (*). • Ratios represent frequency of prevalent forms vs. variants in current books.

19th century. It's preferable to *ambiance* (/**ahm**-bee-ahn[t]s/), a Frenchified affectation that, since its proliferation in the mid-20th century, has become a VOGUE WORD.

In modern print sources, *ambience* is used more than twice as often as *ambiance*. Though the *New York Times* style manual specifies *ambience*, its editors (like all other editors) have occasionally stumbled—e.g.: "Ratings reflect the reviewer's reaction to food, *ambiance* [read *ambience*] and service with price taken into consideration." "What Lies Beneath: Serious Mexican Food," *N.Y. Times*, 11 Sept. 2002, at F6.

LANGUAGE-CHANGE INDEX
ambiance for *ambience*: Stage 4
Current ratio (*ambience* vs. *ambiance*): 2.3:1

ambulance /**am**-byə-lən[t]s/ is often mispronounced /**am**-byoo-lan[t]s/.

*ameba. See **amoeba.**

ameliorable. So formed—not **amelioratable.* See -ABLE (D) & -ATABLE.

ameliorate; *meliorate. *Ameliorate* is the standard term meaning "to make or become better." E.g.: "If injustices abound in that region—as they do almost everywhere—they will not be *ameliorated* by heaping invective on parties to the conflict." Letter of John B. Aycrigg, *Denver Post*, 23 Apr. 1997, at B6. **Meliorate* is a NEEDLESS VARIANT.

Ameliorate does not mean "to lessen"—e.g.: "It would also allow a return to more normal inventory management by *ameliorating* [read *lessening* or *reducing*] the likelihood of stumbling into the four pitfalls described earlier." Peter A. Meyer, "No One Is Laughing at Good News vs. Bad News in Corn Processing," *Milling & Baking News*, 18 Feb. 1997, at 19. Cf. **vitiate.**

LANGUAGE-CHANGE INDEX
ameliorate misused for *lessen*: Stage 1

amen (the conclusion to a prayer) may be pronounced either /**ah**-men/ or /**ay**-men/.

amenability. See **amenity.**

amenable (= [1] suitable for a particular type of treatment, or [2] willing to accept something without argument) is preferably pronounced /ə-**meen**-ə-bəl/—not /ə-**men**-ə-bəl/.

amend; emend. Both derive from the Latin verb *emendare* (= to free from fault). *Amend* = (1) to put right, change; or (2) to add to, supplement. This is the general word. The other is more specialized. *Emend* = to correct (as a text). The corresponding nouns are *amendment* and *emendation.*

amenity; amenability. These words, of unrelated origin, are occasionally confused. *Amenity* = (1) agreeableness <as a host, he showed great amenity to his guest's demands>; (2) something that is comfortable or convenient <the many amenities at the hotel make

guests quite happy>; or (3) a basic social convention <it's not just that he burps aloud—he seems to be unaware of most gustatory amenities>. *Amenability* = (1) willingness to approve, act, or yield <the bank's amenability to make the loan>; (2) legal responsibility; answerability <the corporation's amenability to suit in New York>; or (3) capability of being treated or tested <the victim's amenability to psychiatric treatment>.

The words are pronounced /ə-**men**-i-tee/ and /ə-meen-ə-**bil**-i-tee/.

American. As an adjective limited in application to the United States, this word has long been known to be anomalous. All North Americans and South Americans have claim to being called *Americans*, and yet the language has never quite recognized this fact: "In strict logic such a use is not justifiable, but common practice and understanding have long since put the word beyond the jurisdiction of logic." 1 George Philip Krapp, *The English Language in America* xiii (1925). Perhaps one reason for the firmly established usage is the lack of any reasonable alternative (*United Statesian*?).

American government. This phrase is acceptable when you're talking about the way the United States is governed, as opposed to "the government" as an entity—e.g.:

• "This seminar, dealing with congressional policies and *American government*, is presented by the Washington Workshops Foundation and will be attended by high school leaders from across the country." "School News," *Portland Press Herald*, 20 Dec. 1995, at B7.
• "The liberal welfare-state model of *American government* has run its course . . . ." John F. Stacks, "Good Newt, Bad Newt," *Time*, 25 Dec. 1995, at 90.

When you're speaking of the governing powers, though, the proper phrase is *U.S. government*—e.g.:

• "But such a situation also means that while the Chinese deal harshly with pro-democracy forces, the *American government* [read *U.S. government*] has very little leverage with which to pressure Beijing to alter its behavior." "Again, What About China?" *Wash. Times*, 23 Dec. 1995, at C2.
• "The man said he was a retired military officer from Syria, which the *American* [read *U.S.*] government deems a sponsor of terrorists." Diana Jean Schemo, "Diploma Mill Concerns Extend Beyond Fraud," *N.Y. Times*, 29 June 2008, at A14.

When *American government* is used with *an* or *any*, the reference is to the presidential administration at any particular time. *An* or *any American government* is the appropriate hypothetical phrase—e.g.:

• "Would *any American government* take similar risks with U.S. security, including delivering strategically important support in Congress?" Yossi Ben Aharon, "Momentum Madness," *Jerusalem Post*, 20 Dec. 1995, at 6.
• "At any rate, *an American government* can serve best by putting immediate American interests above almost everything." "Case for Bosnia Move Not Just U.S. Interests," *Dayton Daily News*, 20 Dec. 1995, at A14.

AMERICANISMS AND BRITICISMS. A. Generally. Although this book points out many differences between AmE and BrE, that is not its primary purpose. For guidance on distinctions not covered here, see Norman W. Schur, *British English A to Zed* (1987); Norman Moss, *British/American Language Dictionary* (1984); and Martin S. Allwood, *American and British* (1964). For differences in editorial style, compare *The Chicago Manual of Style* (16th ed. 2009) with Caroline Drake & Maureen Leach, *Butcher's Copy-Editing: The Cambridge Handbook for Editors, Copy-Editors, and Proofreaders* (4th ed. 2006).

B. Americanisms Invading BrE. During the 20th century, the English language's center of gravity gradually shifted from England to the United States. As a result, the most influential linguistic innovations occur in AmE, as a further result of which BrE speakers frequently bemoan American encroachments. For example, on 7 February 1995, Steve Ward of Bristol said in a letter published in *The Times*: "Sir, I am disappointed to see that even *The Times's* leader columns are succumbing to the relentless invasion of American English. In your leader of January 28, on the National Lottery, you state that 'stores which sell tickets for the draw have lottery-only lines on a Saturday.' Do you mean: '*Shops* . . . have lottery-only *queues*'?"

C. Briticisms Invading AmE. To some extent, transatlantic linguistic influences are reciprocal. In the late 20th century, it became common in AmE to use the Briticism *take a decision* (as opposed to the usual AmE *make a decision*). And many Americans have begun using *amongst* and *whilst*. (See **among (A)** & **whilst**.) On the whole, though, BrE's influences on AmE are so slight that few people take any notice.

D. Related Entries. For several other differences between the two major strains of English, see -ER (B), -OR & SPELLING (B).

amicable; amiable. The first came directly from Latin, the second from French, but the two forms are at base the same word. Yet they have undergone DIFFERENTIATION. *Amiable* applies to people <an amiable chap>, *amicable* to relations between people <an amicable resolution>.

Amicable is pronounced /**am**-i-kə-bəl/—not /ə-**mik**-ə-bəl/. *Amiable* is pronounced /**ay**-mee-ə-bəl/.

amicus curiae; friend of the court. These phrases refer to "someone who is not a party to a lawsuit but who petitions the court or is requested by the court to file a brief in the action because that person has a strong interest in the subject matter." *Black's Law Dictionary* 102 (10th ed. 2014). Lawyers write *amicus curiae*; journalists often write *friend of the court*. See LEGALESE.

The Latin phrase is variously pronounced. The singular is /ə-**mee**-kəs **kyoor**-ee-ɪ/ or /ə-**mɪ**-kəs **kyoor**-i-ee/

and the plural (*amici curiae*) is /ə-**mee**-kee **kyoor**-ee-ɪ/ or /ə-**mee**-see/ or /ə-**mɪ**-kee/ or /ə-**mɪ**-see/. Another acceptable pronunciation of the first word—a common pronunciation in AmE—is /**am**-ə-kəs/.

Current ratio (amicus curiae vs.
friend of the court): 5:1

amid. A. And *among*. *Amid* usually connotes position—e.g.: "*Amid* the public tributes, the one from Felix Frankfurter stood out." Barry Siegel, *Claim of Privilege* 186 (2008). *Among* often connotes a mingling—e.g.: "To see the true [Tom] Coughlin, watch him *among* friends and family, away from football." John Branch, "Coughlin's Playful Side Has Deep Roots in Florida," *N.Y. Times*, 6 May 2008, at D1.

B. And *amidst*; *in the midst of*; *mid*; *'mid*. *Amid* and *amidst* are slightly quaint words, especially the latter. Often the word *in* or *among* serves better. (But see **among (B)**.) Since the mid-19th century, *amid* has predominated in AmE and BrE alike. Today it is about 20 times as common as *amidst*.

In the midst of, a wordy equivalent, has always been more common than *amid*. It often lends a better cadence, as in these titles:

- David Freeman Hawke, *In the Midst of a Revolution* (1961).
- Louis Breger, *Freud: Darkness in the Midst of Vision* (2000).
- Geoffrey Warner, *In the Midst of Events: The Foreign Office Diaries and Papers of Kenneth Younger* (2005).

The preposition *mid* is poetic in all uses except the traditional compounds (e.g., *midnight*, *midstream*) or scientific uses; if the word is appropriate, however, *mid* is better than *'mid*.

*amn't I? See **aren't I?**

amoeba; *ameba. Since the mid-19th century, *amoeba* has been the standard spelling in all varieties of English. During the 1920s, AmE seemed close to adopting *ameba as standard, but that spelling has long since receded.

Current ratio: 11:1

amok; amuck. *Amok* is now the standard spelling. Usage authorities once held firmly to the idea that *amuck* is preferable to *amok*—solely on the mistaken notion that *amuck* is older in English and *amok* (though a better transliteration of the Malaysian word) was a late-coming "didacticism." In fact, both forms date from the 17th century. And in any event, *amok* became predominant in BrE about 1905 and in AmE about 1955. It is three times as common as *amuck* in print sources today—e.g.: "But by 2005, federal banking regulators were beginning to worry that mortgage lenders were running *amok* with exotic and often inscrutable new products." Edmund L. Andrews, "Fed Shrugged as Subprime Crisis Spread," *N.Y. Times*, 18 Dec. 2007, at

---

LANGUAGE-CHANGE INDEX (For the full key, see front matter pp. xxxi, l–li.)
Stage 1: Rejected. **Stage 2:** Widely shunned. **Stage 3:** Widespread but . . . **Stage 4:** Ubiquitous but . . . **Stage 5:** Fully accepted.
Invariably inferior forms marked by asterisk (∗). • Ratios represent frequency of prevalent forms vs. variants in current books.

A1. But some publications fight the trend—e.g.: "One symptom of lobbying run *amuck* is the proliferation of earmarks—spending placed in legislation without public review, for specific projects." Mike Allen & Perry Bacon Jr., "Can This Elephant Be Cleared Up?" *Time*, 15 Jan. 2006, at 22.

The long-term effect of the prevalent spelling may be that it will be mispronounced, as happens when the spelling doesn't match the sound. People may well come to say /ə-**mahk**/ instead of the correct /ə-**mək**/, just as so many mispronounce *buttock* as /bət-tahk/ instead of the correct /**bət**-ək/.

LANGUAGE-CHANGE INDEX
amok for *amuck*: Stage 5
Current ratio (*amok* vs. *amuck*): 3:1

among. A. And *amongst.* Most forms ending in *-st,* such as *whilst* and *amidst,* are ARCHAISMS in AmE. *Amongst* is no exception: in AmE it is pretentious at best. E.g.: "Imagine a city where the electricity and water companies are owned by the local authorities and, thanks to progressive planning and construction, prices are *amongst* [read *among*] the lowest in the country." Michael Dibdin, "Seattle Is the America Thatcher Ignored," *Seattle Times*, 17 Jan. 1997, at B5.

Amongst is more common and more tolerable in BrE, where it doesn't suggest affectation—e.g.:

- "With the deft wit of a real technician, Marber sets up the relationships *amongst* the employees." Michael Billington, "A Dab Hand," *Guardian*, 11 Feb. 1995, at 28.
- "But imagine the in-take of breath (muted) *amongst* the grey old heads bending over their Tupperware lunchboxes." Sue Mott, "Champion of British Sport," *Daily Telegraph*, 9 Dec. 1996, at 10.

Cf. **amid (B); whilst.**

Current ratio (AmE): 17:1
Current ratio (BrE): 8:1

B. With Mass Nouns. Generally, *among* is used with plural nouns and *amid* with mass nouns. Hence one is *among* friends but *amid* a crowd. (See COUNT NOUNS AND MASS NOUNS & **amid.**) *Among* is frequently misused for other prepositions—e.g.:

- "Incompetence in writing English is widespread *among* [read *in* or *within*] the legal profession." Robert W. Benson, "The End of Legalese," 13 *N.Y.U. Rev. L. & Soc. Change* 519, 570 (1984–1985).
- "*Among* [read *With*] the president's contingent are Mr. Robert Mosbacher, commerce secretary, and around 20 top U.S. executives." Stefan Wagstyl, "Japan Promises to Boost U.S. Imports," *Fin. Times*, 8 Jan. 1992, at 1.
- "*Among* [read *Contributing to*] last year's toll was a gas blast that leveled part of a New York City block, killing eight people and injuring 48 more." Nick Penzenstadler, "Scientists: Gas-Pipe Upgrades Paying Off in Cities," *Greenville News* (S.C.), 10 Sept. 2015, at B3.

LANGUAGE-CHANGE INDEX
among used with a mass noun: Stage 2

C. And *between.* See **between (A).**

amoral. See **immoral.**

amorous; amatory; **amative. Amorous* = (1) strongly moved by love and sex; (2) enamored; or (3) indicative of love. *Amatory* = of, relating to, or involving sexual love. **Amative* is a NEEDLESS VARIANT, not of *amatory* but of *amorous.*

*amortise. See **amortize.**

amortization; *amortizement. The latter is a NEEDLESS VARIANT.

Current ratio: 3,570:1

amortize; *amortise. The *-ize* form is standard in both AmE and BrE.

Current ratio: 16:1

*amortizement. See **amortization.**

amount; number. The first is used with mass nouns, the second with count nouns. Hence we say "an increase in the *amount* of litigation" but "an increase in the *number* of lawsuits." But writers frequently bungle the distinction—e.g.:

- "The *amount* [read *number*] of ex-players who talked shows that the authors did their homework." John Maher, "If Notre Dame Has to Cheat, Who Can Win Fairly?" *Austin Am.-Statesman*, 20 Sept. 1993, at D1, D9.
- "But they seldom mention the great *amount* [read *number*] of people who have been lifted out of poverty over the last few hundred years." Bjorn Lomborg, *The Skeptical Environmentalist* iv (2001).
- "Concerning fashion, artistic education at schools, children and youth literature, we can connect the high *amount* [read *number*] of women in these fields with their gender role model." Elisabeth Mayerhofer, "Exchange, Deception, and Disillusionment," in *Exchange and Deception: A Feminist Perspective* 133, 140 (Caroline Gerschlager & Monika Mokre eds., 2002).

See COUNT NOUNS AND MASS NOUNS.

LANGUAGE-CHANGE INDEX
amount misused for *number*: Stage 2
Current ratio (*number of people* vs.
*amount of people): 84:1

amount of, in the. See **check (B).**

amphibology; amphiboly. The form *amphibology* (= a quibble; ambiguous wording) predominates in AmE, *amphiboly* in BrE. E.g.: "*Amphibology* [occurs] when a phrase or sentence has two often-contrary meanings." Stephen Wilbers, "Can't Say Too Many Good Things About Clarity," *Orange County Register*, 15 May 1995, at D10.

The corresponding adjectives are *amphibological* and *amphibolous.*

ample (= abundant; plenty of), according to H.W. Fowler, should refer to abstract things <ample goodwill> but never to substances of indefinite quantity <ample foliage> (*FMEU1* at 19). Fowler's view appears to follow the *OED*'s principal definition, which reads: "Of things immaterial: Large in extent or amount, extensive, abundant, excellent." Some writers use it in that sense, to good effect—e.g.: "One advantage of the midwinter darkness is the *ample* opportunity it (in theory) provides for gazing at the colorful northern ignis." Wayne Curtis, "In Hot Water," *Atlantic*, Dec. 2006, at 155. But the distinction between immaterial and material things is hard to sustain in actual usage and leads to idle hairsplitting. Today the word frequently and naturally applies to material substances—e.g.:

- "The bread that came with it was tasty, with *ample* butter included." Rick Gershman, "At the Greenery, Dinner Take-out Is a Cut Above," *St. Petersburg Times*, 11 Jan. 1996, at D3.
- "Mortar must be cleaned up with *ample* water before it starts to harden." John O'Dell, "Bigger and Boulder," *L.A. Times*, 25 Jan. 1997, Home Design §, at 1.
- "China's tree-planting campaign has successfully reforested areas with *ample* rain, says Luo." Dennis Normile, "Ecology: Getting at the Roots of Killer Dust Storms," *Science*, 20 July 2007, at 317.

amuck. See **amok.**

amuse. See **bemuse.**

an. See **a** (A).

*anachronic. See **anachronistic.**

anachronism; *parachronism; prochronism; archaism. All these words indicate that, in some respect, the time is out of joint. An *anachronism* is any error in chronology, or something that is chronologically out of place <the Western movie contained several anachronisms, including a jet's vapor trail visible in the opening scene>. **Parachronism* is a NEEDLESS VARIANT of *anachronism*. A *prochronism* is a reference to a person, thing, or event at a date earlier than it existed <Shakespeare's notorious prochronism of putting a striking clock in *Julius Caesar*>. An *archaism* is something archaic, outmoded, or old-fashioned <the Senate's creaky archaisms, such as the two snuffboxes filled constantly with fresh snuff, can be endearing>. See ARCHAISMS.

anachronistic; *anachronic; *anachronous. The first is the standard adjective. The second and third are NEEDLESS VARIANTS.

Current ratio: 148:1:1

ANACHRONYMS. If you don't have broadband Internet service, you may still connect by *dial-up* service. If you phone someone but get a busy signal, you may try again by punching the button on your phone that is labeled *redial*. But try to buy a telephone that actually has a dial on it and you'll come home empty-handed. The *dial* in *dial-up* and *redial* is an anachronym: a word that lives on in a figurative sense even though technology or culture or history has rendered its literal sense absurd.

Anachronyms live on longer than might be expected when there is no ready replacement (say *dial* and people immediately think *telephone*). So we still "tune in" to a radio or television program even though there is no conventional tuner in digital sets, because how else are we going to select a station or channel?

But anachronyms live on by sheer force of habit as well. We still say *tin can* even though the cans are made of steel these days. It's still common to hear *tinfoil*, even though the technically correct *aluminum foil* is prevalent. When we send an e-mail, we may still include a *carbon copy* addressed to a third party. A few old fogeys still keep their beverages cool in the *icebox*. Cf. RETRONYMS.

anacoluthon (= an instance of syntactic incoherence or grammatical inconsistency within a sentence) predominantly makes the Greek form of the plural (*anacolutha*) in AmE and BrE alike—not **anacoluthons*.

Current ratio: 4:1

anaemia. See **anemia.**

anaesthetic. See **anesthetic** & AE.

analects; analecta. The English plural *analects* predominates over the Latin plural *analecta*. See PLURALS (B).

Current ratio: 1.4:1

analog. See **analogue.**

analogism. See **analogy.**

analogous; analogical. These words mean different things. *Analogous* /ə-**nal**-ə-gəs/ = parallel in certain respects. The word should be avoided where *similar* suffices, but the two are not perfectly synonymous. What is *analogous* serves as an analogy for guidance, while *similar* carries no such connotation.

Analogical /an-ə-**loj**-i-kəl/ = of, by, or expressing an analogy. E.g.: "Much of constitutional law is a tradition of 'common law' development, as judges specify and alter constitutional meaning through *analogical* reasoning in the course of deciding individual disputes." Cass R. Sunstein, "Making Amends," *New Republic*, 3 Mar. 1997, at 38.

analogue; analog. An *analogue* is a thing that is analogous to something else—e.g.: "Apparently, the planned conformity of Levittown and its *analogues*, coupled with the close proximity of the world's media capital, makes it the perfect crucible for ambient celebrities." G. Beato, "Long Island's New Breed of Low-Wattage Celebs," *Newsday* (N.Y.), 7 Sept. 1997, at G6. The spelling *analog* should be confined to technical contexts involving physics or computers. For a comment on the decline of the *-ue* form, see -AGOG(UE).

analogy; analogism. An *analogy* is a corresponding similarity or likeness. In logic, *analogy* means "an inference that, if two or more things are similar in some respects, they must be alike in others."

LANGUAGE-CHANGE INDEX (For the full key, see front matter pp. xxxi, l–li.)
Stage 1: Rejected. Stage 2: Widely shunned. Stage 3: Widespread but . . . Stage 4: Ubiquitous but . . . Stage 5: Fully accepted.
Invariably inferior forms marked by asterisk (*). • Ratios represent frequency of prevalent forms vs. variants in current books.

Analogism is a fairly rare term meaning "reasoning by analogy" <analogism is not the most rigorous form of reasoning>.

analyse. See **analyze.**

analysis; *analyzation. The first, of course, is the standard word. **Analyzation*, a pseudo-learned variant of *analysis*, is a NONWORD—e.g.:

- "Dr. David L. Carnes Jr. . . . will be heading the computer *analyzation* [read *analysis*] project." Paul H. Carr, "Dentists Drill into Big Market with Root Tool," *San Antonio Bus. J.*, 27 June 1988, at 1.
- "The module assists in the computerized design and performance *analyzation* [read *analysis*] of wooden pallets and skids." "Company Connections," *Buffalo News*, 28 Dec. 1996, at C14.
- "The younger Dylan has grown tired of such *over-analyzation* [read *overanalysis*]." Aaron Wherry, "Generation Gap: The Wallflowers Have a New Album," *Nat'l Post*, 3 Dec. 2002, at B4.

Cf. *****paralyzation.**

LANGUAGE-CHANGE INDEX
analyzation for *analysis*: Stage 1
Current ratio (*analysis* vs. *analyzation*): 21,501:1

analyst; analyzer; *analyzist. The first is standard in reference to a person who analyzes. The second is a NEOLOGISM for software that examines data for patterns, relationships, etc. The third is a NEEDLESS VARIANT.

analytical; analytic. No DIFFERENTIATION has surfaced between the two. In modern print sources, the long form is twice as common as the short, perhaps because it is perceived as being generally more euphonious. This being so, *analytic* could justifiably be labeled a NEEDLESS VARIANT—except in the few SET PHRASES denoting disciplines or schools of thought, such as *analytic geometry* and *analytic philosophy*.

Current ratio: 2:1

*****analyzation.** See **analysis.**

analyze; analyse. The first is AmE, the second BrE.

*****analyzer; *analyzist.** See **analyst.**

ananym. See **anonym.**

anarchy; anarchism. *Anarchy* is a state of lawlessness or disorder in society. *Anarchism* is a political theory antithetical to any form of government. The preferred adjectival forms are *anarchic* and *anarchistic*.

Anchorageite; *Anchoragite. The first spelling is standard. See DENIZEN LABELS.

anchor baby, a term dating from the mid-1990s, didn't come to widespread public attention until the 2016 U.S. presidential campaign. The phrase refers to a child born in the United States of a mother who has illegally crossed the border or overstayed her visa specifically to benefit from the Birthright Citizenship Clause of the U.S. Constitution, which makes every person born on U.S. soil a citizen of the country. Although the extent of the anchor-baby "problem" is a matter of debate, its existence is not. It is not clear whether opponents of the term object to the term itself or to the public highlighting of the existence of the issue. When asked to suggest an alternative term, opponents often cite *baby*—which, of course, is a vague hypernym that obscures the denotative fact that *anchor baby* is intended to convey. Arguments about the term and what it denotes will play out in coming years. Some will argue that it's a snarl-phrase, and others will insist that it's a straightforward descriptor uttered without malice or enmity. Any proposed synonym that doesn't approach DOUBLESPEAK is likely to inflame the debate—which suggests that the difficulty is not merely with the words themselves.

anchorite; *anchoret. This word, meaning "hermit," is predominantly spelled *anchorite*. In AmE, the preference is overwhelming.

Current ratio: 18:1

*****anchorperson.** See SEXISM (C).

anchors aweigh; anchors away. The linguistic history here is murky. The original phrase, in the 19th century, was indeed *anchors away*—and that form is about as common today in BrE as *anchors aweigh*. But in AmE, *anchors aweigh* has been the predominant form, thoroughly established, since the 1920s.

Sometimes—in especially poor usage—*aweigh* is corrupted into *way*, often as part of a lame pun. E.g.: "Anchors *way* [read *aweigh*?]: Former Chicago news anchors Larry Mendte and Giselle Fernandez . . . manage not to bump into each other." Marla Hart, "Psssst!" *Chicago Trib.*, 10 Dec. 1996, at C1.

For a related blunder—*under weigh* for *underway*—see **underway.**

Current ratio (World English): 2:1

anchovy (the small salty fish) is pronounced /**an**-choh-vee/ in AmE—not /an-**choh**-vee/. In BrE, the second syllable commonly has a schwa sound: /**an**-chǝ-vee/.

ancillary (= connected with or supporting something else) is preferably pronounced /**an**-si-ler-ee/ in AmE but /an-**sil**-ǝ-ree/ in BrE.

and. A. Beginning Sentences with. It is rank superstition that this coordinating conjunction cannot properly begin a sentence:

- "[T]he idea that a sentence should *never* begin with [*and*] is absurd. It would be quite as sensible to and worthy of consideration to insist that a sentence should never begin with *but* or *nor*." S.W.W., "'And' at the Beginning of a Sentence," 19 *N.Y. Teacher & Am. Educ. Monthly* 204, 205 (May 1870).
- "Objection is sometimes taken to employment of *but* or *and* at the beginning of a sentence; but for this there is much good usage." Adams Sherman Hill, *The Principles of Rhetoric* 88 (rev. ed. 1896).

- "Another stumbling-block to a certain type of academic mind is the conjunction *and*. It is often laid down as a rigid rule that a sentence should never begin with *and*. This was a point on which my own schoolmaster was inflexible. And quite recently a training college student whom I asked to comment on a passage from Malory condemned him for using 'the objectionable conjunction *and*.' And printers have an ugly trick of emasculating my meaning by turning my periods into commas because they happen to be followed by *and*. Taking down my Bible and opening it at random, I find that the eighth chapter of Exodus contains thirty-two sentences, twenty-five of which begin with *and*." Philip Boswood Ballard, *Teaching and Testing English* 26 (1939).
- "In medieval prose . . . *and* is a dominant word, especially at the beginning of the sentence. One sentence follows on another in simple succession, with a conjunction as head-word representing a link in a chain, or (to jump to another metaphor) a single step in the chronological development of the narrative. The pattern, as has already been pointed out, is familiar to us in the Authorized Version." G.H. Vallins, *The Pattern of English* 83 (1956).
- "That it is a solecism to begin a sentence with *and* is a faintly lingering superstition. The *OED* gives examples ranging from the 10th to the 19th c.; the Bible is full of them." Ernest Gowers, *FMEU2* at 29.
- "A prejudice lingers from the days of schoolmarmish rhetoric that a sentence should not begin with *and*. The supposed rule is without foundation in grammar, logic, or art. *And* can join separate sentences and their meanings just as well as *but* can both join sentences and disjoin meanings." Wilson Follett, *MAU* at 64.
- "Many years ago schoolteachers insisted that it was improper to begin a sentence with *and*, but this convention is now outmoded. Innumerable respected writers use *and* at the beginning of a sentence." William Morris & Mary Morris, *Harper Dictionary of Contemporary Usage* 37 (2d ed. 1985).
- "*And* the idea that *and* must not begin a sentence, or even a paragraph, is an empty superstition. The same goes for *but*. Indeed either word can give unimprovably early warning of the sort of thing that is to follow." Kingsley Amis, *The King's English* 14 (1997).

Schoolteachers may have laid down a prohibition against the initial *and* to counteract elementary-school students' tendency to begin every sentence with *and*. As Follett and Amis point out, the same superstition has plagued *but*. See **but** (A) & SUPERSTITIONS (D).

The very best writers find occasion to begin sentences with *and*—e.g.:

- "*And* the technique of the approach to poetry has not received half so much serious systematic study as the technique of pole-jumping." I.A. Richards, "An Experiment in Criticism" (1929), in *Richards on Rhetoric* 25, 31 (Ann E. Berthoff ed., 1991).
- "*And* the thought of being engaged to a girl who talked openly of fairies being born because stars blew their noses, or whatever it was, frankly appalled me." P.G. Wodehouse, *Right Ho, Jeeves* 95 (1934; repr. 1986).

- "Mr Rossiter quotes the observation of a B.B.C. official that his talks were 'too much the spoken word for *The Listener*.' And that in itself is significant. It means that in the medium of print, the long established syntax of the sentence, with its complex relationships, still holds its own. But what will happen in the future it is too early, as yet, to prophesy." G.H. Vallins, *The Pattern of English* 94 (1956; repr. 1957).
- "A dictionary is good only insofar as it is a comprehensive and accurate description of current usage. *And* to be comprehensive it must include some indication of social and regional associations." Bergen Evans, "But What's a Dictionary For?" in *The Ways of Language* 77, 79 (Raymond J. Pflug ed., 1967).
- "If we view the paragraph as a *discursive development of a proposition*, we can predict that the topic sentence of the paragraph in question will generate a development based on objectives. *And* this is exactly what we do find." W. Ross Winterowd, *Rhetoric: A Synthesis* 147 (1968).
- "*And* one had better make use of whatever beauty, elegance, riches the translator's language possesses, and hope that something emotionally, intellectually, aesthetically equivalent will emerge." John Simon, *The Sheep from the Goats* 397 (1989).
- "*And* there is, come to think of it, that unsounded *b*, to keep alive some small doubt." Christopher Ricks, *Beckett's Dying Words* 51 (1993).

B. For *or*. Oddly, *and* is frequently misused for *or* where a singular noun, or one of two nouns, is called for—e.g.: "While third-party candidates have mounted serious challenges for senator *and* [read *or*] governor in almost two dozen states this year, building an effective third-party apparatus is rare." Jonathan Rabinovitz, "Weicker's Victory: Lasting Legacy?" *N.Y. Times*, 5 Oct. 1994, at A13. (The phrase should be *senator or governor*; as written, the sentence says that in each of almost 24 states third-party candidates were running for both senator and governor—an idea belied by the context of the article.)

C. In Enumerations. Some writers have a tendency, especially in long enumerations, to omit *and* before the final element. To do so is often infelicitous: the reader is jarred by the abrupt period ending the sentence and may even wonder whether something has been omitted. One may occasionally omit *and* before the final element in an enumeration with a particular nuance in mind. Without *and*, the implication is that the series is incomplete—rhetoricians call this construction "asyndeton." With *and*, the implication is that the series is complete. This shade in meaning is increasingly subtle in modern prose.

D. Serial Comma Before *and* in Enumerations. On the question of punctuating enumerations, the better practice is to place a comma before the *and* introducing the final element. See ENUMERATIONS (B) & PUNCTUATION (D).

E. *But* misused for *and*. See **but** (C).

LANGUAGE-CHANGE INDEX (For the full key, see front matter pp. xxxi, l–li.)
Stage 1: Rejected. **Stage 2:** Widely shunned. **Stage 3:** Widespread but . . . **Stage 4:** Ubiquitous but . . . **Stage 5:** Fully accepted.
Invariably inferior forms marked by asterisk (✱). • Ratios represent frequency of prevalent forms vs. variants in current books.

*and etc. See etc. (B).

and/or. A legal and business expression dating from the mid-19th century, *and/or* has been vilified for most of its life—and rightly so. To avoid ambiguity, don't use it. Many writers—especially lawyers—would be surprised at how easy and workable this solution is.

Or alone usually suffices. If you are offered coffee or tea, you may pick either (or, in this case, neither), or you may for whatever reason order both. This is the ordinary sense of the word, understood by everyone and universally accommodated by the simple *or*.

But in two situations this ordinary sense of *or* does not accomplish everything we need. Both involve the level of exclusivity between the elements on either side of *or*. One comes up in the standard statement of punishment, "a $1,000 fine or a year in jail *or both*." The other comes up when the choices are mutually exclusive. If that exclusivity is important to point out—if the judge must choose between a fine and jail, for instance—the writer may substitute *but not both* for *or both* in the previous example. But these situations generally arise only when linguistic rigor is imperative, as in legal drafting.

and particularly. See particularly.

androcracy. See GOVERNMENTAL FORMS.

and which. See which (D).

*anecdotalist. See anecdotist.

anecdote. A. Adjective Forms: *anecdotal*; *anecdotic*; *anecdotical*. The form *anecdotal* is standard; the other forms are NEEDLESS VARIANTS. In reference to evidence, *anecdotal* refers not to anecdotes, but to personal experiences reported by one or more people.
Current ratio (the adjectives): 371:3:1

B. And *antidote*. *Anecdote* (= a brief story, usu. true and intended to amuse) is sometimes confused with *antidote* (= something that counteracts poison), resulting in a MALAPROPISM—e.g.:

- "One dog was poisoned but we found the *anecdote* [read *antidote*]." Dennis Pollock, "Home Alone Is Not This Guy's Choice During Holidays," *Fresno Bee*, 5 Dec. 1994, at F2.
- "The Oilers were 6–6 and staggering and looking for an *anecdote* [read *antidote*] to whatever was poisoning their system." John McClain, "On the Road Again," *Houston Chron.*, 22 Dec. 1996, Sports §, at 4.
- "He went to the hospital quickly but still died because there is no *anecdote* [read *antidote*] for glory lily poisoning." Katherine Snow Smith, "Know What to Do if Your Child Eats a Toxic Plant," *St. Petersburg Times*, 7 Apr. 2002, Neighborhood Times §, at 12.

The opposite error is less common, but it does occur—e.g.:

- "Laughter could be heard. It was the apparent jovial reunion following a successful hunt, no doubt accompanied by a few amusing *antidotes* [read *anecdotes*] of Spade's undress." John M. Bishop, *Casting Shadows with Shamans* 21 (2003).
- "Amanda delighted the two women by playing the consummate hostess, serving tea and cookies to their guest, telling funny *antidotes* [read *anecdotes*] about the cats,

and describing the dolls in remarkable detail." R.C. Morris, *Tender Prey* 162 (2005).

LANGUAGE-CHANGE INDEX
1. *anecdote* misused for *antidote*: Stage 1
2. *antidote* misused for *anecdote*: Stage 1
Current ratio (*amusing anecdote* vs.
amusing antidote): 190:1

anecdotist; *anecdotalist. The first is standard; the second is a NEEDLESS VARIANT that flourished for a time in the late 20th century.

anemia; anaemia. Denoting a medical condition in which one's blood has too few red blood cells, *anemia* has been the standard spelling in AmE only since about 1915. From the time when the word was first used in English in the 1820s, the BrE spelling has predominantly been *anaemia*. But the two spellings have been locked in close competition in BrE since about 1980.

anemone /ə-**nem**-ə-nee/ (= [1] a flower of the buttercup family; or [2] a flowerlike sea polyp) is so spelled—not *anenome*. But the misspelling (like the mispronunciation /ə-**nen**-ə-mee/) is common—e.g.:

- "On the right rear tail brilliantly colored clown fish have made their home in a sea *anenome* [read *anemone*], waving in the warm water like a happy baseball crowd." Bob Howarth, "Guadalcanal's Ironbottom Sound: A Terrible Beauty," *Indianapolis Star*, 6 Aug. 1995, at K1.
- "Two further points, illustrated by the *anenome* [read *anemone*] fish, are worth highlighting." Michael Begon, Colin R. Townsend & John L. Harper, *Ecology: From Individuals to Ecosystems* 555 (2006) (word misspelled five times on page).

The phrase *any money* can be a helpful mnemonic device for spelling, *an M on E* for pronunciation. See METATHESIS.

LANGUAGE-CHANGE INDEX
anemone misspelled *anenome*: Stage 1
Current ratio: 119:1

anent. Theodore M. Bernstein writes, "Except in legal usage, *anent* [= about] is archaic and semiprecious." *More Language That Needs Watching* 24 (1962). He could have omitted *except in legal usage* and *semi*. Perhaps the best statement is that *anent* "is a pompous word and nearly always entirely useless." Percy Marks, *The Craft of Writing* 47 (1932). Common in the 17th century, it has been in retreat ever since. See ARCHAISMS.

anesthesia. See anesthetic.

anesthesiologist. See anesthetist.

anesthetic, n.; anesthesia. An *anesthetic* (e.g., ether) causes *anesthesia* (= loss of sensation). Writers often administer the wrong term—e.g.: "Coroner's investigators said Jackie was 'very nervous' and was given *anesthesia* [read *an anesthetic*] by dentist Thien Luong, who was extracting a molar." John Asbury, "Death of Girl Who Choked on Tooth Ruled Accidental," *Press Enterprise* (Riverside, Cal.), 27 Aug. 2008, at C1.

AmE prefers the spellings above; the BrE spellings are *anaesthetic* and *anaesthesia*. See AE.

LANGUAGE-CHANGE INDEX
anesthesia misused for *anesthetic*: Stage 2
Current ratio: 6:1

anesthetist; anesthesiologist. Generally, *anesthetist* will serve for "someone who administers an anesthetic." The term dates from the late 19th century. *Anesthesiologist*, of World War II vintage, refers specifically to a physician specializing in anesthesia and anesthetics.

aneurysm (= a bulged blood vessel caused by disease) is the standard spelling. **Aneurism*, an etymologically inferior spelling that was common in the 19th century, is best avoided.

Current ratio: 24:1

Angeleno; *Los Angelean. The first is the standard term for someone who hails from or lives in Los Angeles. The second is a fairly uncommon equivalent. See DENIZEN LABELS.

Current ratio: 45:1

angina pectoris (= a medical condition that causes chest pains because of a weak heart) is pronounced /an-**jI**-nə **pek**-tə-ris/. It is typically shortened to *angina*.

angst (= strong anxiety and intense unhappiness brought on by worries) is traditionally pronounced in the German way (/ahngkst/), but today /ayngkst/ or /angkst/ predominates in AmE and BrE alike. See GERMANICISMS.

anilingus; *anilinctus. The term denotes a nonstandard thing, of course, but the standard form is *anilingus*. **Anilinctus* is a NEEDLESS VARIANT that many dictionaries record but that almost never appears in print. The term dates from the mid-20th century.

Because of its etymological association with *anal*, writers frequently, by false analogy (ahem) with that word, use a deviant spelling—e.g.:

- "The list contained 20 words for sexual acts that spanned the alphabet, from *analingus* [read *anilingus*] to zooerasty." Teresa Burney, "Sex Definitions Perplex Council," *St. Petersburg Times*, 9 Sept. 1993, Pasco Times §, at 1.
- "It was Carrie and chums who persuaded a couple of my friends to experiment with *analingus* [read *anilingus*]." "Learn to Love," *Guardian*, 4 Feb. 2003, at P20.

Cf. **cunnilingus.**

LANGUAGE-CHANGE INDEX
anilingus misspelled **analingus*: Stage 4
Current ratio (a shocker): 1:1.5

ANIMAL ADJECTIVES. If you have an English–Latin dictionary, look up any animal to find the corresponding Latin term. Then look up that term in an unabridged English-language dictionary and you're likely to find an English adjective—perhaps rare, but there nevertheless—ending in *-ine*. Some of these, of course, are well known:

asinine	=	of, relating to, or like an ass (donkey)
bovine	=	of, relating to, or like a cow
canine	=	of, relating to, or like a dog
elephantine	=	of, relating to, or like an elephant
equine	=	of, relating to, or like a horse
feline	=	of, relating to, or like a cat
serpentine	=	of, relating to, or like a snake

Others are somewhat less well known. Aficionados of Sherlock Holmes know that Sir Arthur Conan Doyle described Holmes more than once as having an *aquiline* nose. (That means "eagle-like.") Others that are middlingly well known appear from time to time—e.g.:

- "Jagger [acted as if he were] in the midst of a shopping spree, and the lean, *leonine* singer was a pounding, preening song-and-dance man—a kindlier version of the 'Clockwork Orange' rounder he played in the '70s." Greg Kot, "Stones Are Risk-Free, but Rockers in the End," *Chicago Trib.*, 25 Sept. 1997, at 2. (*Leonine* = of, relating to, or like a lion.)
- "'You have to treat the bear like a loaded, fully explosive-laden gasoline tanker,' Tamahori said. The *ursine* star came with his longtime trainers, who oversaw him in 'The Bear.'" Steve Murray, "Call of the Wild Put 'Edge' Director into His Element," *Atlanta J.-Const.*, 5 Oct. 1997, at L2. (*Ursine* = of, relating to, or like a bear.)
- "Jonathan Heale's colored woodcuts perfectly suit the two *porcine* heroes." Michael Dirda, "Children's Books," *Wash. Post*, 5 Oct. 1997, Book World §, at 11. (*Porcine* = of, relating to, or like a pig.)

For those who dabble in SESQUIPEDALITY, the less familiar ones are equally appealing, if the sense fits:

accipitrine	*corresponds to*	hawk
anserine		goose
avine		bird
cancrine		crab
caprine, hircine		goat
cervine, damine		deer
corvine		crow; raven
crocodiline		crocodile
crotaline		rattlesnake
falconine		falcon
ferine		any wild animal
hippopotamine		hippopotamus
hirundine		swallow
hystricine, porcupine		porcupine
lacertine		lizard
larine, laridine		gull
leporine		hare
lumbricine		earthworm
lupine		wolf
murine		mouse
ovine		sheep
pardine		leopard; panther
passerine		sparrow
pavonine		peacock

picine	woodpecker
piscine	fish
psittacine	parrot
ranine	frog
scolopendrine	centipede
soricine	shrew
struthionine	ostrich
suilline	swine
taurine	bull; ox
tigrine	tiger
vespine	wasp
viperine	viper
vituline	calf; veal
viverrine	mongoose
vulpine	fox
vulturine	vulture
zebrine	zebra
zibeline	sable

In each of these words, the last syllable is most commonly pronounced /-in/, but /-ın/ is also acceptable. Avoid /-een/, except in *elephantine* and *serpentine*. For more on the pronunciation of words ending in *-ine*, see -ILE.

For more on animal words, see Darryl Lyman, *Dictionary of Animal Words and Phrases* (1994); Stephen Potter & Laurens Sargent, *Pedigree: The Origins of Words from Nature* (1974).

animalculum (lit., "little animal") forms the plural *animalcula*, not **animalculae*—e.g.: "John Crawford, a reputable Baltimore physician and an early promoter of contagion theory in America, lost both his reputation and his practice for maintaining, in 1806/7, that disease was spread by microscopic insects or *animal-culae* [read *animalcula*]." Ronald Rees, "Under the Weather: Climate and Disease, 1700–1900," 46 *History Today* 35 (1996). But the more common term is *animalcule* (pl. *animalcules*). See DIMINUTIVES (B).

LANGUAGE-CHANGE INDEX
*animalculae for *animalcula*: Stage 2

animus is double-edged. At times the word is neutral, meaning "intention; disposition"—especially in legal texts. But more often in AmE *animus* denotes ill will, as if it were synonymous with *animosity*—e.g.:

- "Thomas won [the Senate's] approval by 52–48 and said it was 'a time for healing, not a time for anger or for *animus* or animosity.'" Aaron Epstein, "Bush Nominee Carries Closest Vote Since 1888," *Phil. Inquirer*, 16 Oct. 1991, at A1.
- "He . . . spent his whole life strung out between need of, and *animus* toward, his mother." Colin Walters, "The Life and Loves of Lord Byron," *Wash. Times*, 18 May 1997, at B6.
- "There's no *animus*, at least outwardly, between the one-year-and-done offensive coordinator and a Ravens franchise that he helped to franchise-record offensive numbers." Jon Meoli, "Over to the Other Side," *Baltimore Sun*, 10 Sept. 2015, at D1.

anise (= a plant with seeds strongly tasting of licorice) is pronounced /**an**-is/, rhyming with *Janice*.

annex, n.; **annexation;** ***annexment;** ***annexion.** *Annex* = something attached, as an appendix or a wing of a building. (**Annexe* is a chiefly BrE variant.) *Annexation* = (1) the act of attaching or incorporating (as territory within a municipality or nation); or (2) the state of having been attached or incorporated. **Annexment* and **annexion* are NEEDLESS VARIANTS of *annexation*.

annexable. So spelled—not **annexible*. See -ABLE (A).

annexation; *annexment; *annexion. See **annex,** n.

annihilable. So formed—not **annihilatable*. See -ABLE (D) & -ATABLE.

anniversary (= the day of the year on which an event occurred in a previous year) is today used informally to denote a milestone in months or even weeks. That usage has become increasingly common, perhaps because there is no convenient equivalent for terms shorter than a year (*milestone* is close, but it doesn't connote observance and recurrence the way *anniversary* does). Given the word's tight association with "year," however, this loose usage is subject to criticism and should be avoided if possible—e.g.:

- "So, how's he doing *at the one-month anniversary of his arrival* [read *a month after arriving*] in Richmond?" Margaret Edds, "Shucet Steers Troubled Roads Department on a Straight Course," *Virginian-Pilot* (Norfolk), 19 May 2002, at J5.
- "The only other week in 2002 when terrorism was the top evening news story came during the six-month *anniversary* [read *remembrance*] of the New York and Washington attacks." Mark Jurkowitz, "News Media Try to Give Public Fair Warnings," *Boston Globe*, 30 May 2002, at D6.

LANGUAGE-CHANGE INDEX
anniversary denoting any milestone: Stage 2

announce; annunciate; *enounce; enunciate. *Announce*, the best-known of these terms, may mean (1) "to proclaim" <she announced her independence>; (2) "to give notice of" <he announced that he would leave within the hour>; or (3) "to serve as announcer of" <Henry Longhurst announced the tournament>.

Annunciate is generally a NEEDLESS VARIANT of *announce*, except that it sometimes appears in religious contexts to lend a weighty effect. It has no place in other contexts—e.g.: "Mr. Clinton has made it difficult for union workers to receive a refund for dues used for political purposes, a right *annunciated* [read *announced* or, perhaps, *enunciated*] by the Supreme Court in a ruling known as the Beck decision." Greg Pierce, "Inside Politics," *Wash. Times*, 11 Feb. 1997, at A5.

Enunciate = (1) to formulate systematically; (2) to announce, proclaim; or (3) to articulate clearly. **Enounce* is a NEEDLESS VARIANT in sense 1 of *enunciate*. Sometimes writers misuse **annunciate* for *enunciate* (sense 3)—e.g.: "While her voice was clear and solid, she *annunciated* [read *enunciated*] just a little too much." Maureen Johnson, "'Grease!' Rocks, Despite a Few Slips," *Charleston Daily Mail*, 12 May 1997, at A10.

LANGUAGE-CHANGE INDEX
*annunciate misused for *enunciate*: Stage 1

annoy. See **aggravate.**

annoyance; *annoyment. The first has always been the standard term in Modern English. The second, when used with a straight face, is worse than a NEEDLESS VARIANT—it's a NONWORD that is itself what it denotes. E.g.: "Even into July, Howe had not stirred. Nor had Washington been active, to Adams's considerable *annoyment* [read *annoyance*]." John E. Ferling, *John Adams: A Life* 178–79 (1996). Occasionally it appears as a jocular antonym that echoes *enjoyment*—e.g.: "So here, for your *enjoyment/annoyment*: What new director found his preteen daughter's pot stash moments before his big film's premiere party, and what critic took the rap for it?" Michael Musto, "La Dolce Musto," *Village Voice*, 4 Feb. 1997, at 30.

> LANGUAGE-CHANGE INDEX
> *annoyment* for *annoyance*: Stage 1
> Current ratio (*annoyance* vs. *annoyment*): 4,360:1

annulment. So spelled—not *annullment* (a common misspelling). See **divorce (A).**

> Current ratio: 355:1

annunciate. See **announce.**

anoint is sometimes misspelled *annoint*—e.g.:

- "The piece did everything except *annoint* [read *anoint*] Gov. William Weld." Jon Klarfeld, "With These Friends, Who Needs Enemies?" *Boston Herald*, 16 Sept. 1994, at 27.
- "A few hundred years ago, doctors treating a wound with ointment also made sure to *annoint* [read *anoint*] the weapon that inflicted it." Scott McLemee, "Better Living Through Science," *Newsday* (N.Y.), 12 May 2002, at D33.

> LANGUAGE-CHANGE INDEX
> *anoint* misspelled *annoint*: Stage 1
> Current ratio: 97:1

anomalous; anomalistic. Something that is an anomaly is *anomalous*. That is, *anomalous* is the general adjective corresponding to the noun *anomaly*. But for astronomical anomalies, the adjective is *anomalistic*. Sometimes, though, this much narrower adjective erroneously displaces the broader one—e.g.:

- "Whether the conflicting findings between the levels of analysis are *anomalistic* [read *anomalous*] is unclear." David W. Romero, "Requiem for the Lightweight," *Presidential Studies Q.*, 1 Sept. 2001, at 454.
- "It fails to mention the *anomalistic* [read *anomalous*] 1981–83 digression of Gov. Frank White." Michael Storey, "Paper Trails: Has Hillary Forgotten Us?" *Ark. Democrat-Gaz.*, 26 Jan. 2003, at 53.

> LANGUAGE-CHANGE INDEX
> *anomalistic* misused for *anomalous*: Stage 1

anomie /a-nə-mee/ (= cultural anarchy and social instability) is the standard spelling. *Anomy* is a variant. The adjective is *anomic* (/ə-**nom**-ik/).

> Current ratio (*anomie* vs. *anomy*): 31:1

anonym; anonyme; ananym. An *anonym* (preferably spelled without the *-e*) is an anonymous person. (See **pseudonym.**) An *ananym* is a pseudonym arrived at by spelling the author's name backward (as, hypothetically, *Renrag* for *Garner*).

anorectic; anorexic. *Anorectic* (= suffering from a loss of appetite) is the general term, *anorexic* (= suffering from *anorexia nervosa*) the term specific to the medical condition characterized by self-starvation. As an adjective and also as a noun, both may refer to people with *anorexia nervosa*, but *anorexic* is far more common. *Anorectic* is mostly confined to the medical and scientific communities, while *anorexic* predominates in general writing.

As an adjective, *anorectic* has the additional meaning of "causing a loss of appetite" and is used to refer to drugs such as amphetamines and to their physical effects.

another has a schwa in the first syllable (/ə-**nəth**-ər/)—not /ay-/.

another think coming; *another thing coming. The traditional idiom is "If you think X, you've got another think coming." That phrasing has predominated since the expression became popular in the early 20th century. It may not be funny anymore, but it makes sense: X is wrong, so eventually you're going to think Y instead. But a surprising number of writers substitute *thing* for *think*, which is grammatical but not even vaguely clever. E.g.:

- "If Osama bin Laden imagined, in releasing a threatening new videotape days before the presidential election, that he could sway the votes of Kerry supporters like David and Jan Hill and Bush supporters like Paul Christene, he has *another thing coming* [read *another think coming*]." Kirk Johnson, "Voters, Their Minds Made Up, Say bin Laden Changes Nothing," *N.Y. Times*, 31 Oct. 2004, § 1, at 1.
- "If the leaders of the Democratic Party hope that they can fool the holy people by buying themselves white leatherette-bound Bibles and pink plastic Jesuses and turning up to give testimony at church, they've got *another thing coming* [read *another think coming*]." Nicholas von Hoffman, "Democrats Should Oppose Empowering the Pious," *N.Y. Observer*, 29 Nov. 2004, at 4.
- "If anyone is expecting Francona to gloat, they've got *another thing coming* [read *another think coming*]." Jeff Horrigan, "Unwelcome Mat: Not Much Brotherly Love in Philly for Francona," *Boston Herald*, 24 June 2005, at 123.

The *OED* lists *think* as a dialectal or colloquial noun, with several citations from the 19th century. It shows

LANGUAGE-CHANGE INDEX (For the full key, see front matter pp. xxxi, l–li.)
Stage 1: Rejected. **Stage 2:** Widely shunned. **Stage 3:** Widespread but . . . **Stage 4:** Ubiquitous but . . . **Stage 5:** Fully accepted.
Invariably inferior forms marked by asterisk (*). • Ratios represent frequency of prevalent forms vs. variants in current books.

the phrase *to have another think coming* first used in print in a 1937 article in *American Speech* reporting on the already-established use of that and similar phrases to mean "to be greatly mistaken."

The heavy-metal band Judas Priest may share some blame for the widespread acceptance of the variant wording; its most commercially successful song was "You've Got Another Thing Coming," first recorded in 1982.

LANGUAGE-CHANGE INDEX
another thing coming for *another think coming*: Stage 4
Current ratio (*another think coming* vs. *another thing coming*): 1.6:1

answer back is a common REDUNDANCY, especially in BrE—e.g.: "Hilary and Piers du Pre seem determined to wreak the ultimate revenge on their sister by discrediting her while she lies—unable to *answer back* [read *answer*]—in her grave." Julian Lloyd Webber, "An Insult to Jackie's Memory," *Daily Telegraph*, 4 Jan. 1999, at 15.

In AmE, the phrase is fairly common in sportswriting in the sense "to equal an opponent's recent scoring effort"—e.g.:

- "Jake Armstrong quickly *answered back* for the Knights, but the two-goal cushion was short-lived." Joe Connor, "La Jolla, Bishop's Tie One On in Wester," *San Diego Union-Trib.*, 16 Dec. 1998, at D6.
- "Wimberley would *answer back* with senior wide-out Matt Stroman hauling in a 22-yard TD pass from sophomore quarterback JoJo Weeks to knot the game up at 7–all late in the first quarter." Mark Rico, "More Than a Game," *San Marcos Daily Record* (Tex.), 9 Sept. 2015, Sports §, at 5.

Some writers have used the sports phrase metaphorically—e.g.: "The last time somebody tried to impose prohibition on Chicago, the city *answered back* with Al Capone." Peter Annin, "Prohibition Revisited?" *Newsweek*, 7 Dec. 1998, at 68. Despite the currency of this usage, *answer* can carry the entire load by itself.

LANGUAGE-CHANGE INDEX
answer back for *answer* (outside sports): Stage 3

antagonist. See **protagonist (C).**

Antarctica is frequently misspelled and mispronounced **Antartica*—e.g.: "Kroc expanded the golden-arches empire to every continent on the globe (except *Antartica* [read *Antarctica*])." Bob Ivry, "A Zillion Burgers Later—Perfection," *Record* (N.J.), 13 Sept. 1997, Your Time §, at 1. In fact, this misspelling occurs in about 3% of the modern journalistic sources containing the word. See **Arctic.**

LANGUAGE-CHANGE INDEX
Antarctica misspelled **Antartica*: Stage 1
Current ratio: 101:1

ANTE-; ANTI-. The prefix *ante-* means "before," and *anti-* "against." Thus *antecedent* (= something that goes before) and *antipathy* (= feelings against, dislike). In a few words *ante-* has been changed to *anti-*, as in *anticipate* (= to consider or use before the due or natural time) and *antipasto* (= an Italian appetizer,

usu. consisting of an assortment of cheeses, vegetables, meats, and olives).

In some compound words, the prefix *anti-* may cause ambiguities. See **antinuclear protester.**

antebellum. One word.

ANTECEDENTS, AGREEMENT OF NOUNS WITH. See CONCORD.

ANTECEDENTS, REMOTE. See MISCUES (C) & REMOTE RELATIVES.

antedate; predate. Both words are so common that it would be presumptuous to label either a NEEDLESS VARIANT. One sees a tendency to use *antedate* in reference to documentary materials, and *predate* in reference to physical things and historical facts. The DIFFERENTIATION is worth encouraging. Although *antedate* has historically been the more common of the two, *predate* has occurred more frequently in print sources since the late 1970s—in 2008 by a 4-to-1 margin.

For another sense of *predate*, see **predate.**

antenna. When the reference is to insects, *antennae* /an-**ten**-ee/ is the usual plural. But when the reference is to televisions and electronic transmitters, *antennas* is better. See PLURALS (B).

Current ratio (*insect antennae* vs. *insect antennas*): 17:1
Current ratio (*TV antennas* vs. *TV antennae*): 4:1

antenuptial. See **prenuptial.**

antepenultimate (= the next to the next-to-last) is sometimes misspelled **antipenultimate*—e.g.: "The two versions of the *antipenultimate* [read *antepenultimate*] poem on the Houghton manuscript offer an even stronger indication." Ashby Bland Crowder, "Attribution or Misattribution: New Poems by Robert Browning?" 43 *Philological Q.* 443 (2012). The corresponding noun *antepenult* is pronounced either /an-tee-**pee**-nəlt/ or /an-tee-pi-**nəlt**/.

anthropocentric; homocentric. Both words may denote a philosophy or worldview that puts human beings at the center of the universe or views them as the reason for creation. While *anthropocentric* is older and always correct in this sense, *homocentric* takes this sense only by SLIPSHOD EXTENSION. *Homocentric* is primarily a scientific term describing (1) a path that is round and concentric rather than oblique, esp. the path of a planet; or (2) the spreading rays of light from an apparent focal point, esp. rays of sunlight. So *anthropocentric* is always the better choice—e.g.:

- " 'I'm not *homocentric* [read *anthropocentric*]. I don't think people are the most important thing on the planet. We are part of the community of life.' " "Earth Lovers Battle Green Alien," *Baltimore Sun*, 11 June 2000, at A2 (quoting Mary Burks).
- "If the astonishing complexity of the double helix argues against a random emergence and argues in favor of intelligent design, and since no evidence of life elsewhere exists, then, though our location is not geocentric, the universe

might very well be *homocentric* [read *anthropocentric*]." Jeffrey Hart, "The Once and Future Life of Zoos," *Wash. Times*, 17 June 2001, Books §, at B7.

- "Some scientists say it is *anthropocentric* hubris to think people understand the living planet well enough to know how to manage it." Andrew C. Revkin, "Managing Planet Earth," *N.Y. Times*, 20 Aug. 2002, at F1.

Homocentric is inferior for another reason: to many people today the *homo-* prefix suggests primarily sexual orientation, not the species. And *homocentric* is now sometimes used in a homosexual sense— e.g.: "The introduction by the late Martin Taylor is a model of explication that discusses the strong homo-erotic element of much of the poetry without ever becoming a tedious, *homocentric* [read *gay-pride?*] rant." Scott Eyman, "Soldiers' Letters Give Civil War a Human Face," *Palm Beach Post*, 10 Nov. 2002, at J4.

LANGUAGE-CHANGE INDEX
1. *homocentric* for *anthropocentric*: Stage 1
Current ratio (*anthropocentric view* vs. *homocentric view*): 37:1
2. *homocentric* in the sense "homosexually oriented": Stage 1

anti- (= opposed to, against) is most traditionally pronounced /**an**-tee/ in AmE and BrE alike, but /**an**-tɪ/ is perfectly acceptable in AmE and tends to predominate among speakers born after about 1980. See ANTE-.

*an't I? See aren't I?

antiaircraft. See VOWEL CLUSTERS.

anticipate = (1) to sense beforehand; (2) to take care of beforehand; to preclude by prior action; forestall <they anticipated the problem by filing for bankruptcy>; (3) to await eagerly <this much-anticipated film is a great disappointment>; or (4) to expect <we anticipate that 40 people will attend>. Senses 3 and 4 have long been considered the result of SLIPSHOD EXTENSION. Sense 3 no doubt resulted from the unfortunate tendency for people to choose longer words. Generally, avoid *anticipate* when it's merely equivalent to *expect*. See **expect.**

The poor usage is now seemingly ubiquitous—e.g.: "It is *anticipated* [read *expected* or *estimated*] that the 70-team, invitation-only tourney will realize about $15,000 for the clubs." Bubbles Greer, "Fish Tales Part of Bass Tourney Preparations," *Sarasota Herald-Trib.*, 10 Sept. 1997, at B2. Indeed, sometimes this usage leads to near-ambiguities. In the following example, *anticipate* means "expect," but it suggests "forestall"— e.g.: "The foreboding of traffic snarls, towing and overall melee in connection with last night's Ohio State University football game may have prevented the problems officials had *anticipated*." Dean Narciso,

"Fears of Football-Related Traffic Frenzy Fizzle Out," *Columbus Dispatch*, 29 Aug. 1997, at D2.

LANGUAGE-CHANGE INDEX
anticipate for *expect*: Stage 4

anticipatory; *anticipative. The first is standard; the second is a NEEDLESS VARIANT.

Current ratio: 33:1

ANTICIPATORY REFERENCE (known also as *cataphora*) here denotes the vice of referring to something that is yet to be mentioned. A sentence will be leading up to the all-important predicate but before reaching it will refer to what is contained in the predicate. Or the reference may not even be explained until a later sentence. The reader is temporarily mystified. E.g.: "Conflict of laws is the study of whether or not, *and if so, in what way,* the answer to a legal problem will be affected because the elements of the problem have contacts with more than one jurisdiction." (A possible revision: *Conflict of laws is the study of whether the answer to a legal problem will be affected because the elements of the problem have contacts with more than one jurisdiction—and, if so, what the effect will be.*)

Only rarely can anticipatory reference be used in a way that doesn't bother the reader—e.g.: "We think it's clear—*and nobody has disputed this point*—that Carla has the first choice in deciding whether to take the furniture." Innocuous examples tend to involve personal pronouns <his most recent biographer called Lindley Murray a blockbuster author>.

Vexatious examples occur in a variety of forms. First, they're frequent with *do*-constructions—e.g.:

- "New Mexico, as *do* most states, invests a great deal of money in its highways." (Either put *as most states do* at the end of the sentence or change *as do* to *like*.)
- "English professors, as *do* [read *like*] novelists and journalists, produce a body of writing that can be analyzed to discern their underlying philosophies."

See **like.**

Second, sometimes *have* appears too early in the sentence—e.g.: "The president, as *have* [read *like*] many others, has tried to understand the dynamics of this dispute between the company and its workers."

Third, problems frequently crop up with pronoun references that anticipate the appearance of the noun itself—e.g.: "Mr. Hytner is a director who knows how to keep the pot on the boil; whether you agree with *them* [read *his points*] or not, he makes *his points* [read *them*] with boldness and panache." John Gross, "A Badly Brought-Up Bunch of Girls," *Sunday Telegraph*, 15 July 1990, at ix. (Another possible revision: *whether you agree with him or not, he makes his points . . . .*)

The best antidote to this problem is to become a stickler for orderly presentation and to develop an abiding empathy for the reader.

LANGUAGE-CHANGE INDEX (For the full key, see front matter pp. xxxi, l–li.)
Stage 1: Rejected. **Stage 2:** Widely shunned. **Stage 3:** Widespread but . . . **Stage 4:** Ubiquitous but . . . **Stage 5:** Fully accepted.
Invariably inferior forms marked by asterisk (*). • Ratios represent frequency of prevalent forms vs. variants in current books.

ANTICIPATORY SUBJECTS. See EXPLETIVES.

anticlimactic /an-tee-klɪ-**mak**-tik/ is the correct form. *_Anticlimatic_ is a solecism (referring seemingly to climate) that somehow became fairly widespread in the 20th century—e.g.: "The _anticlimatic_ [read _anticlimactic_] character of this encounter between St. Preux and Julie, in which writing seems to replace or displace person and event, recalls the almost comically _anticlimatic_ [read _anticlimactic_] moment of the consummation of their affair in the first part of the novel." David Marshall, _The Frame of Art: Fictions of Aesthetic Experience_ 121 (2005). But the erroneous form has never seriously rivaled the standard form in print sources. See **climactic.**

> LANGUAGE-CHANGE INDEX
> _anticlimactic_ misspelled *_anticlimatic_: Stage 1
> Current ratio: 28:1

antidote. See **anecdote** (B).

antinomy; antimony. These words are not to be confused. _Antinomy_ = a contradiction in law or logic; a conflict of authority. _Antimony_ = a brittle silvery-white nonmetallic chemical element common in alloys.

antinuclear protester is technically ambiguous, though everyone should know what is intended. For the literal-minded, however, it might suggest "a protester _denouncing_ the antinuclear cause," instead of "a protester _espousing_ the antinuclear position." So it might be preferable to write _nuclear-energy_ (or -_weapon_) _protester_ or _antinuclear advocate._ The same might be said of antiwar, anti-abortion, and antiglobalization protesters.

antipathy (= strong aversion; intense dislike) is sometimes misused for _antithesis_ (= opposite; contrast)—e.g.: "Jiang can wear tri-cornered hats and tour Independence Hall, but his regime represents the _antipathy_ [read _antithesis_] of America's democratic values." "Jiang's Smiles Are a Thin Mask," _Wis. State J.,_ 30 Oct. 1997, at A13.

Antipathy usually takes the preposition _toward_ or _against_ <they feel strong antipathy toward each other> <antipathy against the lame-duck mayor is palpable>. Also, it sometimes takes _to_ or _for_ <in the late 1990s, antipathy to tobacco manufacturers reached an all-time high> <society has always had an antipathy for child abuse>.

The adjectival form is _antipathetic._

> LANGUAGE-CHANGE INDEX
> _antipathy_ misused for _antithesis_: Stage 1

antipodes /an-**tip**-ə-deez/. This noun, meaning "the exact opposite or contrary things," is used most often in the plural form—sometimes even when the sense is singular <greed is the antipodes of charity>.

But the singular _antipode_ /**an**-ti-pohd/ is also quite frequent—e.g.: "Still, the black mood about the group seems the _antipode_ of those heady days over two years ago." Vito J. Racanelli, "Will Vodafone Be a Bellwether of the Bottom?" _Barron's,_ 6 May 2002, at MW6. This singular form might be worth encouraging when the meaning is singular because it promotes DIFFERENTIATION and makes intuitive sense. Yet the synonym _antithesis_ is better understood by most readers.

The capitalized plural—_Antipodes_—refers to Australia, New Zealand, and nearby islands (being on the opposite side of the planet from Europe). E.g.: "He toured the role in the _Antipodes_ a few years ago, but this is Soul's first shot at the West End." Jasper Rees, "From Here to Fraternity (or Whatever Happened to David Soul?)," _Independent,_ 30 Jan. 1997, Arts §, at 8.

antisocial, n. See **psychopath.**

antisocial personality. See **psychopath.**

antiterrorism; counterterrorism. The military distinguishes between these terms. _Antiterrorism_ is defensive, involving measures to protect against vulnerability to a terrorist attack. It is also sometimes called "hardening the target." _Counterterrorism,_ the more frequent term, "includes the full range of offensive measures to prevent, deter, and respond to terrorism." _U.S. Army Field Manual_ FM-78 (1992).

But the distinction is lost outside the military, where the words are used interchangeably. In each of the following examples, they illustrate the vice of INELEGANT VARIATION:

- "The Department of Defense is pouring billions of dollars into upgrading security and protection for U.S. forces, as well as funding private research and development of _antiterrorism_ technology. . . . For Idaho Technology and the handful of other obscure entrepreneurs that provide highly specialized _counterterrorism_ products and services, business is booming." Tony Pugh, "In a Changed World, Security Sells," _Phil. Inquirer,_ 13 Oct. 2001, at C1.
- "Despite President Bush's promise that his _antiterrorism_ chief will have Cabinet-level status and undefined control over 46 agencies and $11 billion in _counterterrorism_ spending, the betting is that the czar won't get far unless he can give orders and control purse strings." Lorraine Woellert, "Can Tom Ridge Take On the Terrorists? It's Up to Bush," _Bus. Week,_ 15 Oct. 2001, at 57.
- "The FBI is designated the leading agency for _counterterrorism,_ but receives only 1 percent of the government's _antiterrorism_ budget." George Will, "The New Investigators," _Tulsa World,_ 16 Oct. 2001, at 10.

antithesis. For a misuse of this word, see **antipathy.**

antithetical; *antithetic. _Antithetical_ (= exhibiting direct opposition) has become established in the phrase _antithetical to_ and in most other contexts. The shorter form should be avoided as a NEEDLESS VARIANT.

The phrase _directly antithetical_ verges on REDUNDANCY—e.g.: "The question is simple: Will Americans be forced to finance teachings _directly antithetical_ [read _antithetical_] to their best interests?" Leonce Gaiter, "School Vouchers Spit in the Eye of Our Democratic Principles," _L.A. Times,_ 4 Feb. 1996, at M5.

> LANGUAGE-CHANGE INDEX
> *_antithetic_ for _antithetical_: Stage 2
> Current ratio (_antithetical_ vs. *_antithetic_): 11:1

antitrust. So written—without a hyphen.

antivenin (= an antitoxin for venom, esp. from snakes) is often mistakenly written *antivenom*. The word *venin* refers to a toxic constituent of venom, and the name of the counteracting agent is formed from this word, not *venom*. But even though no general English-language dictionary recognizes the incorrect form, it now appears in print somewhat more often than the correct form—e.g.:

- "A new approach may lead to better snake *antivenoms* [read *antivenins*] than have been possible so far." Stephen Reucroft & John Swain, "Better *Antivenoms* [read *Antivenins*]," *Boston Globe*, 26 Sept. 2000, at D6.
- "He was fine after receiving *antivenom* [read *antivenin*]." Evan Henerson, "Preparing for the Hazards of the Season," *Rocky Mountain News* (Denver), 5 June 2001, at D3.
- "The bites of venomous snakes are indeed dangerous, but not always as deadly as many people think. In fact, the *antivenom* [read *antivenin*] is about as bad as the venom." Michael Dongilli, "He's Out to Shed Snake's Image," *Pitt. Post-Gaz.*, 25 July 2001, at N9.

LANGUAGE-CHANGE INDEX
antivenom for *antivenin*: Stage 4
Current ratio (*antivenins* vs. *antivenoms*): 1:1.2

a number of. See **number of (A).**

anxious. This word has a range of meaning. As the adjective corresponding to *anxiety*, it has long meant "uneasy, disquieted." In the most unimpeachable uses, the word stays close to that association—e.g.: "The latest holdup is the EPA's final approval of the companies' plans to test for lead at the 150 homes . . . . Some residents are getting *anxious*." Stacy Shelton, "Toxic Investigation," *Atlanta J.-Const.*, 13 Sept. 2002, at D1.

Today the word typically encompasses both worry and anticipation—e.g.: "Creator and anchorman Brian Lamb, the prince of un-chic, tirelessly fields the remarks of obnoxious callers, preening journalists, and *anxious* authors." "Spanning the Spectrum," *Nat'l Rev.*, 24 Mar. 1997, at 16. The word carries a sense of expectation. Here, for example, it seems appropriately used as the author discusses a major life change: "I was *anxious* to leave for Boston . . . . I was looking forward to a change." Elizabeth Morgan, *The Making of a Woman Surgeon* 219 (1980).

But when no sense of uneasiness is attached to the situation, *anxious* isn't the best word. In those instances, it displaces a word that might traditionally have been considered its opposite—namely, *eager*. E.g.: "Three years ago, the Latin music industry was caught up in crossover mania, *anxious* [read *eager*] to ride the popularity of singers such as Ricky Martin and Enrique Iglesias by selling their English-language albums to the American mainstream." David Cazares,

"Songstresses from Peru, Mexico to Grace Stages," *Sun-Sentinel* (Ft. Lauderdale), 13 Sept. 2002, at 30.

LANGUAGE-CHANGE INDEX
anxious for *eager*: Stage 4

any. A. Uses and Meanings. As an adjective, *any* has essentially six uses. (1) The most common occurrence is in conditional, hypothetical, and interrogative sentences, where *any* means "a (no matter which)" or "some" <if you have any salt, I'd like to borrow some> <if any problem were to arise, what would it likely be?> <is there any evidence of the crime?>. (2) In negative assertions, it creates an emphatic negative, meaning "not at all" or "not even one" <it was not in any way improper> <she did not know any member who was at the event>. (3) In affirmative sentences, it means "every" or "all" <any attempt to flout the law will be punished> <you are required to produce any documents relating to the issue>. (4) In a sentence implying that a selection or discretionary act will follow, it may mean "one or more (unspecified things or people); whichever; whatever" <any student may seek a tutorial> <pick any books you like> <a good buy at any price>. (5) In a declarative sentence or imperative involving a qualitative judgment, it means "of whatever kind" <you'll have to take any action you consider appropriate>. In this sense, there is sometimes the implication that the quality may be poor <any argument is better than no argument>. (6) In a declarative sentence involving a quantitative judgment, it means "unlimited in amount or extent; to whatever extent necessary" <this computer can process any quantity of numbers simultaneously>. In a related colloquial sense, it may mean "of great size or considerable extent" when following a negative <we won't be able to make any real headway this week>.

As an adverb, *any* is used before a comparative adjective or adverb in questions and in negative sentences <is he any better?> <they can't walk any faster>. Cf. **all (D).** See COMPARATIVES AND SUPERLATIVES.

B. Singular or Plural. *Any* may take either a singular or a plural verb. The singular use is fairly rare—e.g.:

- "He and Didi prop Sissy up in front of an Elvis mural to see if *any* of them *is* tall enough to ride the Rock 'n' Rollercoaster." Sandy Smith, "Sharing a Good Time," *Tennessean*, 18 July 1996, at D1.
- "If *any* of them *is* successful, it would be the first time an Asian American would serve on the council." Sarah Kershaw, "Chen Bumped Off Ballot in Flushing Race for Council Seat," *Newsday* (N.Y.), 15 Aug. 1997, at A6.
- "Many of the other professors have Washington strings to pull, and Tal isn't sure which side *any* of them *is* on." Laurie Muchnick, "A Debut Novel of Suspense and Social Observation," *Chicago Trib.*, July 7, 2002, Books §, at 7.

In such contexts, *any* is elliptical for *any one*; the sentence often reads better if *one* is retained. See **anyone (A).**

LANGUAGE-CHANGE INDEX (For the full key, see front matter pp. xxxi, l–li.)
Stage 1: Rejected. **Stage 2:** Widely shunned. **Stage 3:** Widespread but . . . **Stage 4:** Ubiquitous but . . . **Stage 5:** Fully accepted.
Invariably inferior forms marked by asterisk (✳). • Ratios represent frequency of prevalent forms vs. variants in current books.

C. Illogical Use. Avoid such ambiguities as this: "She was the best *of any* senior in the class." (Read: *She was the best senior in the class.* Or: *She was the best of all the seniors in the class.*) See **all** (D) & **best of all.**

LANGUAGE-CHANGE INDEX
*of any for *of all*: Stage 3

anybody. See **anyone** (B) & PRONOUNS (D).

anybody else's. See **else's** & POSSESSIVES (I).

anyhow (= in any way; in any manner) is a folksy CASUALISM for *anyway* or *nevertheless.* E.g.: "I'm not sure they would *anyhow* [read *anyway*]." John Ed Pearce, "Old Age: Not for the Unwary," *Courier-J.* (Louisville), 8 Jan. 1995, at D3.

LANGUAGE-CHANGE INDEX
anyhow for *anyway*: Stage 3
Current ratio: 8:1

anymore. A. Meaning "now." In the sense "now," "nowadays," or "still," the word *anymore* fits in three contexts: (1) negative declaratives <you don't bring me flowers anymore>, (2) yes/no questions <do you go there anymore?>, and (3) hypothetical clauses introduced by *whether* or *if* <I wonder whether they go there anymore>. In sense 1, the meaning is "now" or "nowadays"; in senses 2 and 3, the meaning is "still." When *anymore* is used in some other type of positive statement (not in sense 2 or 3), it is dialectal—e.g.: "The price of housing is outrageous *anymore* [read *these days* or *nowadays*]." In a linguistic study of Missourians, informants considered this dialectal usage "well established, though controversial." See Gilbert Youmans, "Any More on *Anymore*," 61 *Am. Speech* 61, 61 (1986). That means that the informants were all familiar with it, but many didn't like it. The findings would probably hold throughout most of the United States. See DIALECT.

LANGUAGE-CHANGE INDEX
anymore misused for *nowadays*: Stage 1
Current ratio (*Nowadays* vs. *Anymore* as first word in sentence): 14:1

B. And *any more*. While *anymore* conveys a temporal sense, *any more* conveys a sense of comparing quantities <I don't want any more tea, thank you> or degrees <I don't like it any more than you do>. Sometimes even careful writers muddle this distinction—e.g.:

- "*Peruse* . . . is not a word we use very often *any more* [read *anymore*]." *Merriam-Webster's Concise Dictionary of English Usage* 584 (2002).
- "By Fowler's time it apparently was not so rare *any more* [read *anymore*], and it is not at all rare today." *Ibid.* at 630.

LANGUAGE-CHANGE INDEX
any more misused for *anymore*: Stage 1

anyone. A. And *any one*. For the indefinite pronoun, the one-word spelling is required <anyone could do that>. Though formerly written as two words, the unification of the phrase is now complete. *Any one* = any single person or thing (of a number). E.g.: "When he

died, none of us could remember *any one* thing he'd said." Richard Hoffer, "The Player," *Sports Illustrated*, 30 Sept. 1996, at 13.

B. And *anybody*. The two terms are interchangeable, so euphony governs the choice in any given context. In practice, *anyone* appears in print about three times as often as *anybody.* Cf. **everyone** (C); **somebody.**

C. *Anyone . . . they*. In all types of writing, sentences like this one are on the rise: "If *anyone* thought Diana would be chastened, *they* were wrong." Jerry Adler & Daniel Pedersen, "Diana's Battle Royal," *Newsweek*, 11 Mar. 1996, at 20. Americans who care about good writing tend to disapprove—and strongly. But the tide against them is great, primarily because the construction is ubiquitous (and so handy) in speech. For more on this subject, see SEXISM (B) & PRONOUNS (D).

LANGUAGE-CHANGE INDEX
anyone . . . they: Stage 4

D. **Anyone . . . are*. Although *anyone . . . they* might arguably be acceptable, **anyone . . . are* isn't— e.g.: "Indeed, *anyone* who thought he or she could solve *their* immigration problems by getting hitched *are* in for a shock." Julie Tilsner, "Guardians of the Green Cards," *N.Y. Times*, 12 Apr. 1997, at 19. (A possible revision: *Indeed, those who thought they could solve their immigration problems by getting hitched are in for a shock.*)

E. *Anyone else's*. See **else's** & POSSESSIVES (I).

*anyplace for *anywhere* has appreciably crept into print sources only since the early 1960s. It remains nonstandard—e.g.: "The old [athletic director] hasn't gone *anyplace* [read *anywhere*], though." Ron Bush, "Green Replaces Smith at CSTCC," *Chattanooga Free Press*, 31 Jan. 1997, at H5. When the meaning is "any location," *any place* should always be two words <at any place>. E.g.: "Readers out there are looking for . . . *anyplace* [read *any place* or *a place*] that serves a good Italian beef sub, like the ones Cousins used to sell." Jeremy Iggers, "Celebrate Asian New Year in French," *Star Trib.* (Minneapolis), 7 Feb. 1997, at E15. Cf. ***noplace** & **someplace.**

LANGUAGE-CHANGE INDEX
*anyplace for *anywhere*: Stage 1
Current ratio (*anywhere* vs. **anyplace*): 64:1

anything; any thing. *Anything* is the far more general word, meaning "whatever thing." *Any thing*, for practical purposes, is limited to plural constructions <do you have any things to donate?> and to contrasts with *any person* <is there any thing or person that might be of help?>.

anytime, adv., = at any time; whenever. E.g.: "*Anytime* a seller rents back from a buyer, an interim occupancy agreement should be completed." Dian Hymer, "Seller Rent-Back Can Benefit Both Sides," *S.F. Examiner*, 25 Oct. 1992, at F1. Some writers consider this term a CASUALISM, but it is highly convenient and has—for whatever reason—gained more widespread acceptance than *anymore* (in positive contexts) and **anyplace*. Cf. **anymore** & ***anyplace.**

LANGUAGE-CHANGE INDEX
anytime for *whenever*: Stage 5

*anyways. This dialectal variant of *anyway* is very much on the rise in AmE speech—although its use is negligible in print sources (outside dialogue). It usually falls at the beginning or end of a sentence, to mean "in any event" or "just the same"—e.g.: "'Anytime a kid plays, it's learning *anyways* [read *anyway*].'" Peggy Hager, "Real-Life Playing," *Daily News* (L.A.), 17 Sept. 2002, News §, at AV4 (quoting Danielle Rothe).

At the beginning of a sentence, it often means "as I was saying before" or "be that as it may" (*anyhow* would be a better choice)—e.g.: "*Anyways* [read *Anyhow*], the Times sent a feller name-a Mark Stein out Phoenix way to report on where East Coast businessmen should hang their feedbags and sack out if they finds theyselves stranded in the desert." E.J. Montini, "Load Yer Guns, Boys, It's Time to Hunt Yankees," *Ariz. Republic*, 28 July 2002, at B3. See DIALECT.

LANGUAGE-CHANGE INDEX
*anyways for *anyway*: Stage 2
Current ratio (*anyway* vs. **anyways*): 76:1

anywhere; *anywheres. The first is standard. The second is dialectal. Cf. **nowhere.**

LANGUAGE-CHANGE INDEX
*anywheres for *anywhere*: Stage 1
Current ratio (*anywhere* vs. **anywheres*): 417:1

apart from. See **aside (B).**

apartheid. The traditional and preferred pronunciation of this Afrikaans term is /ə-**pahrt**-hayt/, the last syllable appropriately mimicking the word *hate*. But it is so commonly pronounced /ə-**pahr**-tit/ (like *tight*) that the variant is widely accepted. Not accepted are pronunciations that meld the *-t-* and *-h-* into a digraph.

apex forms the plurals *apexes* and *apices*. The latter has greatly predominated since the 17th century. See PLURALS (B).

Current ratio: 5:1

aphrodisiac (= a food, drink, or drug that strengthens the sex drive) is pronounced /af-rə-**diz**-ee-ak/—not /af-rə-**deezh**-ee-ak/.

apiary. See **aviary.**

aplomb (= self-assurance and poise) is pronounced either /ə-**plom**/ or /ə-**pləm**/.

*apolog. See **apologue.**

apologia. See **apology.**

apologue (= an allegorical story) is the standard spelling. **Apolog* is a variant. (Cf. **analogue, catalog(ue)** & **epilogue.**) For a comment on the decline of the *-ue* form, see -AGOG(UE).

apology; apologia. *Apology*, in its general sense, applies to an expression of regret for a mistake, usually with the implication of guilt. It may also refer to a defense of one's position, a sense shared with *apologia* /ə-pə-**loh**-jee-ə/. But *apologia* should preempt this meaning for purposes of DIFFERENTIATION.

apophthegm. See **apothegm.**

apostasy; *apostacy. The latter spelling is inferior, the original Greek word being *apostasia*. E.g.: "The church has had its share of negative publicity, most recently stemming from its September 1993 purge of writers and thinkers it accused of *apostacy* [read *apostasy*] for publishing work the church said preached false doctrine." Lisa Carricaburu, "Media-Wise Men Charting PR Path for LDS Church," *Salt Lake Trib.*, 23 Aug. 1997, at B1.

LANGUAGE-CHANGE INDEX
apostasy misspelled **apostacy*: Stage 1
Current ratio: 10:1

APOSTROPHES. See PUNCTUATION (A).

apothegm; apophthegm. These are variant synonyms for *aphorism*, *maxim*, or *epigram*. Although the longer spelling matches the Greek etymon, the shorter *apothegm* is now universally accepted. It's also easier to spell and seemingly to say (/**ap**-ə-them/)—though in fact the longer spelling is pronounced identically, with a silent *-ph-*. In his famous dictionary of 1755, Samuel Johnson gave the longer form a boost by listing both terms (two pages apart) but declaring the longer one to be "proper." It predominated till about 1850—not long after Noah Webster gave preference to the shorter form. In AmE there is a decided preference for *apothegm*; in BrE the two forms vie, but *apophthegm* is slightly more common. Doubtless these trends are traceable in large measure to the two great national lexicographers—Johnson (BrE) and Webster (AmE).

Silent in the noun, the hard *-g-* sound is pronounced in the adjective *apothegmatic* (/ap-ə-theg-**mat**-ik/). The word should not be confused with *apothem*, a term in geometry for a line connecting the center of a regular polygon with the center of any of its sides. See PRONUNCIATION (D).

Current ratio (*apothegm* vs. *apophthegm* in World English): 2:1

appall; appal. For this verb meaning "to shock and upset," the standard spelling in BrE was *appall* until

---

LANGUAGE-CHANGE INDEX (For the full key, see front matter pp. xxxi, l–li.)
Stage 1: Rejected. **Stage 2:** Widely shunned. **Stage 3:** Widespread but . . . **Stage 4:** Ubiquitous but . . . **Stage 5:** Fully accepted.
Invariably inferior forms marked by asterisk (*). • Ratios represent frequency of prevalent forms vs. variants in current books.

shortly after Samuel Johnson listed the word as *appal* in his 1755 *Dictionary of English Language*. Since the mid-1780s, *appal* has predominated in BrE. That spelling predominated also in AmE until the 1860s, when *appall* became preeminent. The dichotomy has remained: *appall* is AmE, *appal* BrE.

apparatus has the plural forms *apparatus* (the Latin form) and *apparatuses* (the native English form). Because the word has been thoroughly naturalized, *apparatuses* is standard—e.g.: "This . . . is meant to mean an incapacity, uncured by education, to know what our vocal *apparatuses*, along with our brains, are doing when sounds are uttered." Anthony Burgess, *A Mouthful of Air* 6 (1992). But the Latin plural does still appear occasionally—e.g.: "Two men were sitting there: one in an armchair, the other at a table where a curious selection of *apparatus* was laid out: mahogany boxes with brass terminals, copper-bound induction coils, and an instrument like a piano keyboard, the keys each marked with a letter of the alphabet." Phillip Pullman, *The Tin Princess* 173–74 (1994). See PLURALS (B).

Apparati is not a correct plural, even in Latin. It's an example of HYPERCORRECTION—e.g.:

- "Even out of competition, exercycles, ab crunchers, and personal-trainers-as-therapists are the *apparati* [read *apparatuses*] of life in the 90's." Marjorie Rosen, "Fat Chance," *N.Y. Times*, 4 Aug. 1994, § 6, at 37.
- "Who serves in the *apparati* [read *apparatuses*] of violence? . . . Are the rank and file in the *apparati* [read *apparatuses*] of violence likely to follow the orders of the top authorities?" Thomas S. Szayna, *Identifying Potential Ethnic Conflict* 318 (2000) (the solecism appears eight times on this one page).
- "Interestingly, an evolutionary epistemology that draws insights from the evolution of sensory *apparati* [read *apparatuses*] of living organisms provides a very Deweyan critique of spectator theory without any apparent awareness of Dewey's thought (Bartley 1987)." James L. Webb, "Dewey: Back to the Future," *J. Econ. Issues*, 1 Dec. 2002, at 981.

Cf. **nexus** & **prospectus**.

LANGUAGE-CHANGE INDEX
apparati for *apparatuses*: Stage 1
Current ratio (*apparatuses* vs. *apparati*): 21:1

apparel, vb., makes *appareled* and *appareling* in AmE, *apparelled* and *apparelling* in BrE. See SPELLING (B).

apparent = (1) seeming <the apparent motion of the planets>; or (2) obvious <the problems are quite apparent>. Sense 2 is usual after a BE-VERB.

In sense 1, the word is frequently misused in reference to fatalities. What happens is that the adverb *apparently* gets morphed into an adjective and paired with the wrong word (a noun) when logically it should modify a verb. For example, a person may die "*apparently* of a heart attack," but one doesn't die "of an *apparent* heart attack." Yet variations on this ILLOGIC are legion—e.g.:

- "Less than a month after basking in the Thanksgiving glow of release from North Korea, where he was held as a spy and threatened with execution, Evan C. Hunziker was found this morning in a rundown hotel here with a bullet in his head—dead of an *apparent suicide*." Timothy Egan, "Man Once Held as a Spy in North Korea Is a Suicide," *N.Y. Times*, 19 Dec. 1996, at A12. (A possible revision: . . . *Evan C. Hunziker was found this morning in a rundown hotel here with a bullet in his head, dead apparently by suicide.*)
- "Buster Auton will take over for the popular Elmo Langley, who died *of an apparent heart attack* in Japan in November." Mark Znidar, "Changes Abound as Another Season Nears Starting Line," *Columbus Dispatch*, 11 Feb. 1997, at F3. (A possible revision: *Buster Auton will take over for the popular Elmo Langley, who died in Japan in November, apparently of a heart attack.*)
- "Davenport, who died June 1 of *apparent 'natural causes,'* was exchanging texts with a convicted prostitute at the time of the crash." Lydia X. McCoy, "Families Sue Over Bush Crash," *Knoxville News-Sentinel*, 21 July 2015, at 5A. (A possible revision: *Davenport, who died June 1 (apparently of unrelated natural causes), was texting with a convicted prostitute when the crash occurred.*)

LANGUAGE-CHANGE INDEX
apparent heart attack, etc.: Stage 3

appear. The phrase *it would appear* is invariably inferior to *it appears* or *it seems*—e.g.: "*It would appear* [read *It appears*] that more than a few of us are desperate for an easy dinner." Ruth Fantasia, "Desperate Times Require Desperate Measures," *Virginian-Pilot & Ledger Star* (Norfolk), 7 Jan. 1998, at F1. See **would** & SUBJUNCTIVES.

On the sequence of tenses in phrases such as *appeared to enjoy* (as opposed to *appeared to have enjoyed*), see TENSES (B).

appellant. This word is ordinarily a noun meaning "a litigant who appeals against an adverse decision." Although dictionaries may provide some historical support for using *appellant* as an adjective corresponding to the noun *appeal*, this usage violates modern legal idiom, which reserves *appellate* for this purpose. E.g.: "The ruling must be reviewed by an *appellant* [read *appellate* or *appeals*] court before a new test can be scheduled." "Rifle, Bullet Should Be Retested, Judge Rules in King Case," *Columbia Daily Trib.*, 21 Feb. 1997, at A10.

LANGUAGE-CHANGE INDEX
appellant misused for *appellate*: Stage 1

appendant (= attached, associated) is the standard spelling. *Appendent* is a variant.

Current ratio: 28:1

appendectomy; appendicectomy. The first is standard in AmE. The second was long standard in BrE—e.g.: "We early called the process of *appendicectomy* 'hanger-on-cutting-out.'" Basil Cottle, *The Plight of English* 15 (1975). The longer form was long considered etymologically preferable—and perhaps it still is, in some quarters, since the appendix and not the "append" is removed (*-ectomy*)—but today the syncopated form *appendectomy* is the undisputed favorite in World English. The AmE preference for the shorter term was established by 1900; not until the mid-1970s did the shorter form become predominant in BrE.

Current ratio: 8:1

*appendent. See appendant.

appendixes; appendices. Both are correct plural forms for *appendix*, but *appendixes* has long been considered preferable outside scientific contexts—e.g.:

- "The authors of 'The Bell Curve' tell readers that they may limit their perusal to the summaries that precede each chapter, and that they may skip the main text. Still, 'The Bell Curve' is 845 pages long, and a reader who skips even the *appendixes* will miss many of the points the authors are at pains to make." Malcolm W. Browne, "What Is Intelligence, and Who Has It?" *N.Y. Times*, 16 Oct. 1994, § 7, at 3.
- "The book's three *appendixes* . . . will be helpful to newcomers to church traditions." "Beyond Smells and Bells: The Wonder and Power of Christian Liturgy," *Publishers Weekly Reviews*, 11 Feb. 2008, at 66.

Nevertheless, the nonnative plural is more frequent by a 3-to-1 margin. See PLURALS (B). Cf. index (A).

appertain; pertain. Some DIFFERENTIATION is possible. Both take the preposition *to*, but *appertain* usually means "to belong to rightfully" <the privileges appertaining to this degree>, whereas *pertain* usually means "to relate to; concern" <the meeting pertains to the headmaster's continued employment>.

applause. A. Singular or Plural. This word, derived from the Latin verbal noun *applausus*, means (1) "loudly expressed approval," or (2) "marked commendation." In English, the word traditionally appears in such a way that its number (singular or plural) is disguised <we could hear the applause> <he gained our applause>. But the *OED* gives only singular definitions, and when *applause* is the subject of a verb it takes a singular verb—e.g.: "The biggest *applause* comes after his nod to party loyalty." Paul Demko, "Here We Go A-Caucusing," *City Pages* (Minneapolis), 25 Apr. 2001, at 6.

Yet because the end of the word sounds much like a plural ending in *-s*, some writers (who deserve some hoots) erroneously use the word as if it were plural—e.g.:

- "Big *applause are* [read *applause is*] in order for the entire cast." Don Thomas, " 'Ragtime': Broadway's Got a New Hit Musical," *N.Y. Beacon*, 25 Feb. 1998, at 26.
- "The largest *applause were* [read *applause was*] reserved for the favourite oldies including 'Come Home,' 'She's a Star,' and an excellent performance of 'Tomorrow.' " Graham Young, "Shania Twain Special," *Evening Mail* (London), 8 Dec. 1999, at 27.
- "Talley . . . falls just once and is back on his feet before his family's teasing *applause die* [read *applause dies*] out." Nora K. Froeschle Jenks, "Speed Skater Qualifies for Winter Games in Alaska," *Tulsa World*, 13 Dec. 2000, at 4.

LANGUAGE-CHANGE INDEX
applause misused as a plural: Stage 2
Current ratio (*the applause was* vs.
the applause were): 75:1

B. Narrowing of Meaning. As suggested in (A), the word has never referred merely to clapping. Huzzahs would count as applause. But today the word is increasingly thought to be interchangeable with clapping—e.g.:

- "Several of the legislators burst into *applause*—and the loudest *clapping* seemed to come from the men." Yolanda Jones, "In Brief," *Memphis Comm. Appeal*, 15 Feb. 2008, at 1.
- "His answer was met with hearty *applause* from those in the audience, to which Clemens jokingly replied, 'Are you *clapping* because you want me not to be on city council?' " Marquita Brown, "Salem Residents Hear from Candidates," *Roanoke Times*, 23 Apr. 2008, at B10.
- "At Chelsea Cinema on Saturday there were close on 700 people (mainly women, all ages, and a smattering of homosexual men), whooping, *clapping* (Samantha, with the best lines, gets the most *applause*) and crying (look out for Charlotte saying 'no')." Glenda Cooper, "Carrie and Co. Beat Indy in Battle of Films," *Daily Telegraph*, 2 June 2008, at 5.

apple cider. Strictly speaking, this phrase is a REDUNDANCY because *cider* has traditionally referred to a drink made from apple juice. But for many decades now, beverage manufacturers have marketed other types of "ciders," from the juice of peaches, raspberries, and the like. So if *apple cider* is redundant, it is also sometimes necessary for clarity. Cf. tuna fish.

LANGUAGE-CHANGE INDEX
apple cider for *cider*: Stage 5

*appliable. See applicable (A).

applicable. A. And *appliable; *applyable. These two variants are incorrect. *Applicable*, the correct form, is properly accented on the first syllable (/**ap**-li-kə-bəl/), not on the second. See PRONUNCIATION (B).

Current ratio: 30,347:5:1

B. And *applicative; *applicatory. These forms are NEEDLESS VARIANTS of *applicable*. *Applicative* is also a needless variant of *applied*, as in the phrase *applicative psychology*.

Current ratio: 4,732:35:1

C. Be applicable. This construction is almost always inferior to the simple verb *apply*—e.g.:

- "Not all of these ideas, of course, *are really applicable* [read *really apply*] to my house or my life." Monty S. Leitch, "Home Improvement Via the Satellite Dish," *Roanoke Times*, 1 Sept. 1997, at A7.
- "Because no new lands will be added until the year 2000, the current brochure will *be applicable* [read *apply*] for the next three seasons." Charlie Meyers, "Public Hunting Access Getting a Shot in the Arm," *Denver Post*, 12 Sept. 1997, at D3.
- "They call Heath Miller 'Big Money,' but 'Big Country' would *be just as applicable for* [read *apply just as well to* or *be just as apt for*] the veteran tight end." Dan Gigler, "Pairing Steelers and Food," *Pitt. Post-Gaz.*, 9 Sept. 2015, at C1.

See BE-VERBS.

LANGUAGE-CHANGE INDEX (For the full key, see front matter pp. xxxi, l–li.)
Stage 1: Rejected. **Stage 2:** Widely shunned. **Stage 3:** Widespread but . . . **Stage 4:** Ubiquitous but . . . **Stage 5:** Fully accepted.
Invariably inferior forms marked by asterisk (*). • Ratios represent frequency of prevalent forms vs. variants in current books.

applicant; applicator; *applier. An *applicant* is "someone who applies for something (as a position in a firm)." *Applicator* = (1) a device for applying a substance, or (2) someone who applies a substance. *Applier is a NEEDLESS VARIANT of *applicator*.

Current ratio (*applicator* vs. *applier): 17:1

*applicative; *applicatory. See **applicable** (B).

*applier. See **applicant.**

*applyable. See **applicable** (A).

apposite. See **apt** (A).

apposition (= the grammatical relation between two words or phrases that stand for the same idea) is sometimes misused for *opposition*—an odd MALA-PROPISM. E.g.: "Their accounts were in stark *apposition* [read *opposition*] at several other points, too." Maureen Dowd, "Testimony Conflicts at Military Hearing on Abuse by Fliers," *N.Y. Times*, 18 Aug. 1993, at A1.

LANGUAGE-CHANGE INDEX
apposition misused for *opposition*: Stage 1

APPOSITIVES. An appositive points out the same person or thing by a different name, usually in the form of an explanatory phrase that narrows an earlier, more general phrase. So in the sentence "My brother Brad is a musician," *Brad* is the appositive of *brother*. Typically, in phrases less succinct than *my brother Brad* (in which *Brad* is restrictive), the appositive is set off by commas or parentheses:

- " 'Gotta watch what I do,' joked the dark-haired 18-year-old, the youngest child of Councilwoman Domenique Thornton and her husband, *Richard Thornton*." "In the Running for First Daughter," *Hartford Courant*, 11 Sept. 1997, at B7. (*Richard Thornton* is an appositive of *her husband*. And the entire phrase *the youngest child . . . Thornton* is an appositive of *18-year-old*.)
- "In that community, individual farming compounds were spaced between the complex of the community leader, *the caddi*, and the complex of *the xinesi*, the paramount religious authority." Timothy K. Perttula, *Southwest Hist. Q.* (Book Rev.), Apr. 2001, at 616. (*The caddi* is an appositive of *the community leader*, and *the paramount religious authority* is an appositive of *the xinesi*.)

Generally, a pair of commas (or, less frequently, parentheses or dashes) must frame an appositive unless the appositive is restrictive. So a person might write *my brother Blair* to distinguish Blair from another brother (say, Brad). But if Blair were the only brother, the reference should be to *my brother, Blair*. This is not a hard-and-fast rule, and many publications ignore commas with a name as a short appositive of relationship, for two reasons. The first is stylistic: the written comma <my husband, Bob> does not reflect any audible pause in the spoken sentence <"my husband Bob">. The second is practical: enforcing the rule would require finding out how many brothers the subject has before deciding between *his brother Blair* or *his brother, Blair*, and that can be a lot of effort for a small payoff.

One telltale signal that an appositive is restrictive is the definite article *the* preceding the noun—e.g.: *The*

grammarian Henry Sweet provided Shaw a model for Henry Higgins. (But reverse the order and it comes out differently: *Henry Sweet, the grammarian, provided Shaw a model for Henry Higgins.*) The signal is not infallible, however. Consider: *My favorite restaurant is Abacus. The chef, Kent Rathbun, trained at . . . .* Here, *the chef* is the main information and the name adds to it but could be omitted. In the previous example, though, *the grammarian* could not stand alone.

Emphatic appositives (also termed "intensive pronouns") are never set off by commas—e.g.: "*He himself* flunked the test." See PRONOUNS (E).

Some writers erroneously omit the comma that should follow an appositive introduced with a comma—e.g.:

- "In the lawsuit, Douglas Hartman, an Illinois air traffic controller[,] says he was forced to walk through a Tailhook-style gantlet during a workshop designed by Eberhardt to combat sexual harassment." Jean Marbella, "Daring Tailhook-Style Gantlet Stirs Up Debate," *Detroit News*, 12 Oct. 1994, at A12.
- "Barry Popik, an etymologist[,] has found the earliest use so far in a Dec. 1, 1883, Washington weekly called The Hatchet." William Safire, "On Language," *N.Y. Times*, 15 Dec. 2002, at 48, 49 (assuredly a copyediting error—as inside information has confirmed).

As a matter of CONCORD, an appositive should match its noun in part of speech and number. For example, it's wrong to use a noun appositive after a possessive—e.g.: "Merton W. Starnes's (Starnes) claim arrived in this office after the deadline had passed." The better strategy would be to avoid the shorthand definition altogether; on a second reference, *Merton W. Starnes* becomes *Starnes*—and no reasonable person would be confused. Likewise, it's wrong to use a singular noun with a plural appositive—e.g.: "The *spelling* 'kinda' and 'coupla' probably reflects* [read *spellings* 'kinda' and 'coupla' probably reflect*] the writer's feeling about the special status of these 'words.' " Dwight Bolinger, "*Couple*: An English Dual," in *Studies in English Linguistics* 30, 40 n.5 (Sidney Greenbaum et al. eds., 1979).

For the problem of the "disjointed" appositive, see ILLOGIC (D).

appraisal; appraisement. Although some dictionaries treat these as variants, the *OED* definitions suggest some divergence in meaning. Both may mean "the act of appraising, the setting of a price, valuation." But *appraisement*, when connoting the acts of an official appraiser, is the term usually used in reference to valuation of estates.

The more broadly applicable and more frequent term is *appraisal* in both literal and figurative senses—e.g.:

- "The plaintiffs cannot touch the money allotted them under a court-ordered *appraisal* of the market value of their properties." Laura Mansnerus, "The Mail's Expanding—and You're Evicted," *U.S. News & World Rep.*, 15 Sept. 1997, at 43.
- "Clinton should bring with him an honest *appraisal* of the situation." "Clinton's Indefinite Commitment to Bosnia," *S.F. Chron.*, 19 Dec. 1997, at A30.

Strange to say, H.W. Fowler classified *appraisal* among those words "that have failed to become really familiar and remained in the stage in which the average man cannot say with confidence off-hand that they exist" (*FMEU1* at 14). Yet *appraisal* has become the standard term in BrE as well as in AmE, largely from the American influence.

Current ratio (*appraisal* vs. *appraisement*): 70:1

appraisal valuation, though fairly common in financial and insurance contexts, is illogical and redundant—e.g.:

- "Clarifications are expected to be issued on performance measurement, accounting policies and *appraisal valuations* [read *appraisals*], according to Richard Carlson." "Task Force Sets Vote on Industry Reporting Standards," *Real Estate Fin. & Investment*, 4 Nov. 1996, at 2.
- "In reality, most home *appraisal valuations* [read *appraisals*] are based on recent, nearby comparable home sales prices." Robert J. Bruss, "Your Place: A Judgment Call How to Get a Fair Appraisal of Your Home," *Chicago Trib.*, 28 Jan. 2000, at 26.

appraise; apprise; *apprize. To *appraise* is to put a value on or set a price for (a thing). To *apprise* is to inform or notify (someone). Writers often misuse *appraise* when they mean *apprise*—e.g.:

- " 'Other employees also are kept *appraised* [read *apprised*] of developments within the company,' Highsmith said." Elena Bianco, "New Dimensions in Lumber," *Lewiston Morning Trib.* (Idaho), 4 Nov. 1990, at E1.
- "The elder Hugh called up the Charlotte Bank and *appraised* [read *apprised*] them of the situation." Katherine Burton et al., "NationsBank's $8.7 Billion Acquisition Matches CEO's Drive," *Commercial Appeal* (Memphis), 1 Sept. 1996, at C1.
- "Bandidos could be *appraised* [read *apprised*] of potential customers through Morse code." Larry Habegger & Natanya Pearlman, *Central America: True Stories* 130 (2002).

Occasionally, the opposite mistake occurs—e.g.: "The maximum loan-to-value is the percentage of the *apprised* [read *appraised*] value of the house the lender will finance." "Fall Mortgage News," *Seattle Times*, 20 Oct. 1996, at G1.

The NEEDLESS VARIANT **apprize* (rare) is synonymous with *appraise*, although it is sometimes erroneously used as an equivalent of *apprise*—e.g.: "You, in turn, for a fee, would be *apprized* [read *apprised*] of the date the city was notified of the potholes' existence." Bruce Williams, "Cities, States Limit Own Liability for Damage," *Cincinnati Post*, 5 Mar. 2002, at B12.

LANGUAGE-CHANGE INDEX
1. *appraise* misused for *apprise*: Stage 1
Current ratio (*apprised of* vs. **appraised of*): 16:1
2. *apprise* misused for *appraise*: Stage 1
Current ratio (*appraised at* vs. **apprised at*): 40:1
3. **apprize* misused for *apprise*: Stage 1
Current ratio (*apprised of* vs. **apprized of*): 8:1

appraisement. See **appraisal.**

appreciable. So formed—not **appreciatable*. E.g.: "It is most unlikely that it has been in the river where it was recently discovered for any *appreciatable* [read *appreciable*] length of time, the report said." "Cockroach Gives Cat an Alibi in Slayings," *Times-Picayune* (New Orleans), 8 Aug. 1995, at A4. See -ABLE (D) & -ATABLE.

LANGUAGE-CHANGE INDEX
*appreciatable for *appreciable*: Stage 1
Current ratio (*appreciable* vs. **appreciatable*): 10,516:1

appreciate = (1) to fully understand; (2) to perceive or detect; (3) to increase in value; or (4) to be grateful for. Sense 4 originated through SLIPSHOD EXTENSION but is now firmly established.

Sense 4 is often part of a wordy construction: "I would *appreciate it if you would send* [read *appreciate your sending*] me an application." Better yet: "Please send me an application."

LANGUAGE-CHANGE INDEX
appreciate in the sense "to be grateful for": Stage 5

apprise; *apprize. See **appraise.**

approbation; approval. There is no generally accepted distinction between these two words, except that the first is more unusual and dignified. Wilson Follett suggests that we restrict *approbation* to a favorable response on a particular occasion and use *approval* for a more general favorable attitude (*MAU* at 72).

As for the corresponding verbs, rarely does *approbate* justifiably supersede *approve*—e.g.: "Now the timid North Atlantic Treaty Organization 'expansion,' by practically *approbating* [read *approving*] the Hitler-Stalin Pact of 1939, invites the always-hungry Russian empire again to expand into Baltic States." "A Date to Remember," *Orlando Sentinel*, 8 May 1997, at A26. See **disapprobation.**

approbatory; *approbative. In modern print sources, *approbatory* is somewhat more common than **approbative*, a NEEDLESS VARIANT.

Current ratio: 1.4:1

appropriable—not **appropriatable*—is the adjective corresponding to *appropriate*, v.t. See -ABLE (D) & -ATABLE.

Current ratio: 38:1

appropriate, v.t. **A. And *misappropriate.*** *Appropriate* = (1) to set apart for a particular person or organization for a specific purpose <government-appropriated funds>; or (2) to take from a particular person or organization for a specific purpose <by appropriating her valuables and locking them away, her stepmother in effect stole them>. Sense 1 is the more usual in AmE, perhaps because it is better to give than to receive.

LANGUAGE-CHANGE INDEX (For the full key, see front matter pp. xxxi, l–li.)
Stage 1: Rejected. **Stage 2:** Widely shunned. **Stage 3:** Widespread but . . . **Stage 4:** Ubiquitous but . . . **Stage 5:** Fully accepted.
Invariably inferior forms marked by asterisk (*). • Ratios represent frequency of prevalent forms vs. variants in current books.

Sense 2 is gradually fading. *Misappropriate* = to apply (as another's money) dishonestly to one's own use. *Appropriate* has a more neutral, nonaccusatory connotation. Still, in meaning "to take from a particular person or organization for a particular purpose," it is tinged with some of the negative connotations made explicit in *misappropriate*. See **embezzle.**

B. And *expropriate*. *Expropriate* = (1) to exercise eminent domain over; to take, by legal action, private land for public use; or (2) to transfer title to another's property to oneself. Sense 1 is more usual—e.g.: "The government had every legal right to *expropriate* the land." Sheryl WuDunn, "Farmers Holding Out Against Japan Airport," *Dallas Morning News*, 7 Sept. 1997, at A26. Although sense 2 of *appropriate* seems generally consonant with sense 1 of *expropriate*, the latter is the better, more concrete term whenever it fits.

C. As a Contronym. See CONTRONYMS.

approval. See **approbation.**

approve. A. *Approve (of).* One may either *approve* something or *approve of* something. Usually, *approve* suggests formal sanction <the council approved the stadium plans>, whereas *approve of* suggests favorable sentiments <she approved of her mother's remarrying>. As a matter of linguistic frequency, the collocation *approve the* appears in print sources about four times as often as *approve of the*. Cf. **disapprove (of).**

B. And *endorse*. The two should be distinguished. To *endorse* is to support actively and explicitly. The word connotes action as well as attitude. To *approve*, apart from the sense of giving official sanction, is to consider right or to have a favorable attitude toward. The verb conveys an attitude or thought. In both senses, *approve* is more passive than *endorse* <she approved his stand on most issues but never endorsed his candidacy>.

C. And *approbate*. See **approbation.**

approximate; approximal; proximate. *Approximate* = (1) closely resembling; (2) nearly accurate; or (3) close together. *Approximal* = contiguous. *Proximate* = (1) very near; or (2) directly related. Sense 3 of *approximate* should usually yield to either *approximal* (if the two things are touching) or *proximate* (if the two things are close). See **proximate.**

*approximately about is a REDUNDANCY. See **about (A).**

apricot (the fruit) is pronounced /**ay**-pri-kot/ throughout the English-speaking world—/**ap**-ri-kot/ being a chiefly AmE variant.

April Fool's Day; *April Fools' Day. The singular-possessive form has been consistently more common since the term became popular in the mid-19th century.

Current ratio: 2:1

apropos (of). Both the long form (*apropos of*) and the short form (*apropos*) are generally unnecessary, though they might prove serviceable in informal letters. *Apropos of* (suggested by the French phrase *à propos de*)—meaning "with respect to"—is well established in English. Yet the GALLICISM *apropos* may be used as a preposition to mean "concerning, apropos of" <apropos your plans, let me tell you about our schedule>. Hence *of* can usually be included or omitted, as the writer desires. E.g.:

- "Then, *apropos of* nothing, he proclaims: 'I'm 105 years old!'" Anne Rochell, "The Goat Man Lives," *Atlanta J.-Const.*, 10 Sept. 1997, at D1.
- "As Leo Varadkar . . . put it last week *apropos* Greece, 'It seems like the student union has taken over the government.'" Ruth Dudley Edwards, "Sinn Fein Is Panicking as Its Brothers Wreak Havoc in Greece," *Sunday Independent*, 5 July 2015, at 23.

As for comparative frequency in print sources, *apropos of* has predominated over the rival form ever since they emerged in English in the early 19th century.

The word is sometimes misused for *appropriate*, adj., a mistake often signaled by the use of *to*—e.g.: "Just three years ago, Sears, Roebuck and Co.'s finance department built a data warehouse [that] the retailer, *apropos to* its business, calls a data mall." Leslie Goff, "Beitler Sees the Data Side of Sears," *Computerworld*, 15 Sept. 1997, at 79. (A possible revision: *Just three years ago, Sears, Roebuck and Co.'s finance department built a data warehouse called (appropriately) a data mall.*)

LANGUAGE-CHANGE INDEX
apropos misused for *appropriate*: Stage 1
Current ratio (*it is appropriate that* vs.
*it is apropos that): 270:1

apt. A. And *apposite*. Both words mean "fit, suitable." Whereas *apt* is the ordinary term, *apposite* is a FORMAL WORD.

B. And *likely*. Although some critics have objected to *apt* in a sense similar to *likely*, this usage has long been considered perfectly acceptable: "Even the dictionary justifies 'apt' in the sense of 'habitually likely,' thus graciously acknowledging the custom of many high-grade writers and the crowd." Edward N. Teall, *Putting Words to Work* 279 (1940). As Ernest Gowers explains, however, "in British usage *apt* always implies a general tendency; for a probability arising from particular circumstances *likely* is the word" (*FMEU2* at 34).

The same distinction between *apt* and *likely* applies in the best American usage. In the following sentences, *apt* is correctly used of general or habitual tendencies, rather than a likelihood in a particular instance—e.g.:

- "But be aware: seedling foliage looks like grass, and it is *apt* to be treated as such by meticulous gardeners." Nell Lewis, "Freeze Lays Fall Colors to Rest," *News & Record* (Greensboro), 10 Dec. 1997, at R4.
- "Fund managers . . . are more *apt* than most to dislike sick people and babies." Brian O'Reilly, "Does Your Fund Manager Play the Piano?" *Fortune*, 29 Dec. 1997, at 139.

LANGUAGE-CHANGE INDEX
1. *apt* for "habitually likely": Stage 5
2. *apt* for a particular instance: Stage 4

aquaculture (= the cultivation of marine life) is now the standard spelling. *Aquiculture—once given as the main headword in several American dictionaries—is now a variant.

Current ratio: 342:1

aquarium. The anglicized plural *aquariums* has been predominant in AmE and World English since the 1980s. In BrE, the predominant plural is still *aquaria*, though now by a very slender margin. See PLURALS (B).

Current ratio (World English): 2:1

aquatic (= involving water) is pronounced either /ə-**kwah**-tik/ or /ə-**kwat**-ik/.

*aquiculture. See **aquaculture**.

Arab; Arabic; Arabian. As an adjective, *Arab* has predominated in all varieties of English since the 1920s and has the broadest applicability. The longer terms tend to have specific applications. *Arabic* usually describes language, art, script, and numerals. *Arabian* refers to the cultures and geography of the regions where Arab peoples reside or to animals native to the Arabian peninsula.

Now for the nouns. *Arab* typically refers to any person of Arabic descent or an Arabic-speaking inhabitant of the Middle East or northern Africa. *Arabic* refers to the language. *Arabian* should be reserved for the breed of horse. See **Saudi**.

arbiter. See **arbitrator**.

arbitrable; arbitrability. Although these are the established forms, some writers use the NEEDLESS VARIANTS **arbitratable* and **arbitratability*, which have an extra syllable—e.g.: "Courts have held that an arbitration clause is to be construed so as to favor *arbitratability* [read *arbitrability*]." W. Dudley McCarter, "Arbitration Agreements Binding in Missouri," *Springfield Bus. J.*, 25 Apr. 1994, at 7. See -ABLE (D) & -ATABLE.

LANGUAGE-CHANGE INDEX
*arbitratability for *arbitrability*: Stage 1

arbitrage. See **arbitration** (A).

arbitrageur; *arbitrager. English-language dictionaries have traditionally preferred the Frenchified *arbitrageur* (= someone who simultaneously buys and sells different securities, commodities, currency, and the like to profit on price differences). Some journalists and courts have preferred the naturalized form, **arbitrager* (with the main accent on the first syllable: /**ahr**-bi-trah-jər/)—e.g.:

- "The *arbitragers* who were indicted yesterday were D. Ronald Yogada [and others] . . . ." Kurt Eichenwald, "Two Firms Are Charged as Insiders," *N.Y. Times*, 3 Nov. 1988, at 29.
- "Robert Freeman, 46, of Goldman, Sachs & Co., was one of the country's most powerful takeover-stock speculators, or *arbitragers*." Steve Swartz & James B. Stewart, "Kidder's

Mr. Wigton, Charged as 'Insider,' Ends His Long Ordeal," *Wall Street J.*, 21 Aug. 1989, at 1.

But by a 7-to-1 ratio, usage is now firmly set in favor of the GALLICISM *arbitrageur* (with the main accent on the last syllable: /ahr-bi-trah-**zhoor**/)—e.g.:

- "In a world adhering to the purities of the rational-markets faith, *arbitrageurs* should have instantly eliminated this discrepancy by simultaneously buying 3Com and selling Palm short, making themselves a mint." Holman W. Jenkins Jr., "Business World: Short Sellers Are People, Too!" *Wall Street J.*, 29 Jan. 2003, at A19.
- "The *arbitrageur* simultaneously buys the lower-priced asset and shorts the higher-priced version based on the certainty that the prices will eventually converge, at which point he will liquidate the position and collect a guaranteed profit." Mark Anderson, "How to Invest Like the Pros: A Cheat Sheet on the Leading Market Strategies That Have Made Some Investors Famously Rich," *Nat'l Post Bus. Mag.*, 1 Feb. 2003, at 56.

*Arbitrager ought to be considered a NEEDLESS VARIANT.

LANGUAGE-CHANGE INDEX
Current ratio: 7:1

*arbitratable. See **arbitrable**.

arbitration. A. And *arbitrage*. *Arbitration* = the process of submitting a dispute to a neutral third party whose decision is binding on the participants. *Arbitrage* = the simultaneous buying and selling of currencies or securities at different values in order to profit by price discrepancies.

Writers occasionally err by substituting *arbitrage* for *arbitration*—e.g.:

- "In a terse statement on Wednesday, Sir Leon said the EU 'will carefully study both the *arbitrator's* report and the two panel reports, and of course meanwhile reserve our right of appeal.' . . . In a parallel ruling, an *arbitrage* [read *arbitration*] panel decided the U.S. retaliation is legal but excessive." Elizabeth de Bony, *J. of Commerce*, 8 Apr. 1999, at A1.
- "What's more, in a hotly contested move, a state *arbitrage* [read *arbitration*] panel granted the Florida Windstorm Underwriting Association, a state pool of insurers, an average increase of 96 percent statewide, with rates climbing nearly 300 percent for homeowners in South Florida." Sharon Harvey Rosenberg, "Wind Damage Is Down This Hurricane Season, but Not Insurance Rates," *Miami Daily Bus. Rev.*, 26 Oct. 2000, at A1.

The opposite error is rare but not unknown—e.g.: "Futures and options based on the Russell 1000 provides *arbitrage* opportunities for investors . . . . The degree to which such *arbitrations take* [read *arbitrage takes*] place is likely to determine the pace at which the Russell 1000 overtakes the S&P 500." C. Michael Carty, "Favored Large-Cap Barometer Will Change," *Pensions & Investments*, 1 Nov. 1999, at 36.

In the Russian Federation, courts that settle commercial disputes are popularly called *arbitrage*

LANGUAGE-CHANGE INDEX (For the full key, see front matter pp. xxxi, l–li.)
Stage 1: Rejected. **Stage 2:** Widely shunned. **Stage 3:** Widespread but . . . **Stage 4:** Ubiquitous but . . . **Stage 5:** Fully accepted.
Invariably inferior forms marked by asterisk (*). • Ratios represent frequency of prevalent forms vs. variants in current books.

courts (reflecting the Russian pronunciation /ahr-bi-**trazh**/)—e.g.: "Here, she is outside the Federal *Arbitrage* Court in Kazan in front of a mural of Lenin." "Judge Discovers Striking Differences in the Way Russian Society Views Women," *Albuquerque J.*, 4 June 1999, at 14 (photo caption). The federation's highest such court, however, calls itself the "Supreme Arbitration Court" to avoid confusion with the term of speculation.

   B. And *mediation*. Both terms refer to resolving disputes through a neutral third party. Traditionally, the results of *arbitration* are binding—that is, the parties to the arbitrator's decision are bound by it. Because that aspect of the proceedings is not universally understood, the REDUNDANCY *binding arbitration* is unassailable in most contexts. In *mediation*, to the contrary, the mediator merely tries to help two disputing parties reach an agreeable solution; the parties are not, however, bound by a mediator's decisions.

   This distinction is muddied somewhat by the emergence of *nonbinding arbitration* in the U.S. and Canada. But nonbinding arbitration generally addresses just one aspect of the dispute, and the decision (there is no award) serves merely to help the parties reach a settlement. The arbitrator, unlike a mediator, does not actively negotiate toward a settlement.

arbitrator; arbiter. An *arbitrator* is a person chosen to settle differences between two parties. *Arbiter*, by contrast, is more general, meaning "anyone with power to decide disputes, such as a referee, judge, or commissioner." The terms overlap considerably, and they cause confusion on both sides of the Atlantic. When referring to legal arbitration, the term should be *arbitrator*. When legal disputes aren't at issue, the better term is *arbiter*.

   Hence in the popular phrase *final* or *ultimate arbiter*, the word *arbitrator* is inferior—e.g.: "Foreign attention enhances Assad's image as the *ultimate arbitrator* [read *ultimate arbiter*] in the region." John Walsh, "Accord: Diplomacy Ends Mideast Border Attacks," *Montgomery Advertiser*, 4 May 1996, at A8.

   *Arbitor is a frequent misspelling—e.g.:

- "Under the owners' proposal, they would have the right to reject an *arbitor's* [read *arbiter's*] ruling and declare the player a free agent." Dave Fay, "Union Says League Is Holding Up Agreement," *Wash. Times*, 30 Nov. 1994, at B2.
- "Ever since the 1954 Supreme Court desegregation decision, judges, not legislators, have been the *arbitors* [read *arbiters*] of social policy." Paul Craig Roberts, "Victory Trail from the New Majority Corral," *Wash. Times*, 11 Aug. 2000, at A17.

LANGUAGE-CHANGE INDEX
1. *arbitrator* for *arbiter*: Stage 1
2. *arbiter* misspelled **arbitor*: Stage 1
Current ratio (*arbiter* vs. **arbitor*): 1,538:1

arboretum. The predominant plural is *arboretums* (AmE) or *arboreta* (BrE). See PLURALS (B).

arc, vb., now uniformly makes *arced* and *arcing*, no longer **arcked* and **arcking*. See -C-.
   Current ratio (*arcing* vs. **arcking*): 4,915:1

archaeology (= the study of the remains of ancient peoples and their cultures) is the standard spelling in both AmE and BrE. **Archeology* is a variant spelling. (See AE.) The word is pronounced /ahr-kee-**ol**-ə-jee/, preferably not /ahr-kay-/.
   Current ratio: 13:1

archaic; obsolete; obsolescent. *Archaic* = old-fashioned; antiquated; characteristic of an earlier time and rarely used today. *Obsolete* = no longer in general use; out-of-date. *Obsolescent* = passing out of use; becoming obsolete. The phrase **totally obsolescent* or **completely obsolescent* is an OXYMORON—e.g.: "Widespread acceptance of that work would render his own much more conventional, delicately Impressionist poetry *completely obsolescent* [read *obsolete*]." Christopher Hampton, "The Long Brief Encounter," *Sunday Telegraph*, 6 Apr. 1997, at 9.

archaism. See **anachronism.**

ARCHAISMS. A. Generally. Many writers indulge in antiquated phrasings known primarily through the King James Version of the Bible or through Shakespeare. Avoid them, unless you're being jocular. Among the ones to be especially wary of are these:

alack	haply	shew (for *show*)
anent	howbeit	spake
anon	in sooth	to wit
begat	maugre	verily
belike	meseems	whilom
betimes	methinks	withal
divers	nigh	wot
durst	peradventure	ye
fain	perchance	yea
forsooth	saith	

One writer aptly says of a similar list: "These are easily avoided by anyone of the least literary sensibility." Herbert Read, *English Prose Style* 9 (1952).
   B. Mistakes Caused by Archaism. Archaism can be faulted in itself. But a still more embarrassing problem arises when the indulger doesn't understand how the phrasings work. In Early Modern English, the following singular forms frequently appeared:

Second Person	*Third Person*
thou goest	he (or she) goeth

Up to the 17th century, the *-eth* suffix was merely an alternative third-person singular inflection for an English verb. Used primarily in southern England, it had, by the end of that century, become obsolete. *She calls* and *he answers* took the place of *she calleth* and *he answereth*. Some writers, straining for an archaic literary touch, use this suffix with no regard to whether the subject is singular or plural. The following title illustrates this tendency: Bill Rogers, "The Bowls *Overfloweth* [read *Overflow*]," *Canyon News*, 25 Dec. 1994, at 9 (referring to the football bowls). This use of *-eth* with a plural subject has become lamentably common—e.g.:

- William F. Powers, "The Friendly Faces *Giveth*, the Fine Print *Taketh* Away," *Wash. Post*, 13 July 1993, at D1 (the singular use of *taketh* with *print* is correct here).
- "They *giveth* legroom, and they *taketh* away." Barbara Ann Curcio, "Worldwise," *Wash. Post*, 5 June 1994, at E3.
- "What the travel Gods *taketh* away, they sometimes *giveth* back." Alan Reinhart, "Taking Advantage of Life on the Road," *Nat'l Dragster*, 28 Aug. 2015, at 22.

Sometimes the second-person *-est* appears in the third person or even the first person—e.g.:

- "Whither *goest* the sport of boxing these days?" Bill Dwyre, "Arum's Next Big Promotion Definitely Goes the Distance," *L.A. Times*, 10 Aug. 2013, Sports §, at 2.
- "These silver linings provided balm to some, while the editorial writers and columnists—as always—worried aloud: Whither we *goest* into this nuclear night?" Bob Hill, "A Glimpse of News and Views at the Dawn of the Atomic Age of World War II," *Courier-J.* (Louisville), 3 Aug. 1995, at B1.

Sometimes an error creeps in from the mangling of a SET PHRASE. A famous quotation from Shakespeare's *Hamlet*, for example, is that "the lady doth protest too much" (3.2.230). Translate this to the first person and you have: "Perhaps *I doth* protest too much; it's just that the players' timing could have been better managed, methinks." Stephen Foster, "Case of Awkward Timing?" *Roanoke Times*, 8 Aug. 1995, NRV §, at 2. That's equivalent to saying *I does*.

A similar example appears in the phrase *the ice man cometh*, from Eugene O'Neill's play by that name. Refer instead to *men*—or to some other plural noun—and you make a hash of the phrase or at best an inept allusion:

- "The tax men *cometh*." Mary Ann Galante, "More Tax Audits Due as FBI Adds to County Force," *L.A. Times* (Orange County ed.), 21 May 1987, § 4, at 1.
- "Tickets are hot in Denver now that they know the ice men [i.e., hockey players] *cometh*." "Icy Reception May Await in Nashville," *Boston Globe*, 25 June 1995, at 94.
- "Cometh the hour, *cometh* the brothers." Adam Lusher, "Jeremy Corbyn Wants to Run the Country. His Brother Wants to Control the Weather," *Independent*, 29 Aug. 2015, at 8 (the use of *cometh* with *hour* is correct here).

Even when the writer gets the grammar right, it's not very heartening because the archaism makes the sentence ring false—e.g.:

- "But *doth* Nippon see through the wooden masks of a Noh drama—slow, plotless, and mistily symbolic?" James W. Scott, "Ad 1995," *Kansas City Star*, 1 July 1995, at C6.
- "As an example, what *doth* one think would happen in Washington if it was discovered that the chief guy in charge of the nation's finances had made his fortune in part by avoiding American taxes by way of putting his operations under flags of convenience?" Allan Fotheringham, "Columnists Need to Step into Fields Where Politicians Fear to Tread," *Fin. Post*, 12 Aug. 1995, § 1, at 19. (This passage is particularly inept because a redundant CASUALISM [*chief guy in charge*] is mixed with a pseudo-biblical style.)

- "When he goes to bed at night, the taxpayer pays for the pillow upon which Walker *doth* rest his weary head." Thomas L. Knapp, "Election 2016: Scott Walker vs. Government Dependence," *Jackson Star News* (Ravenswood, W. Va.), 23 July 2015, at A3.

And even in jocular contexts, the jocularity is typically lame:

- "Yet it's fitting that a comic rockumentary, Spinal Tap, has come closest to portraying the ridiculous truth of life as it *doth* rock and thence roll." David Belcher, "Source of the Sound That Goes with the Flow," *Herald* (Glasgow), 10 Aug. 1995, at 12.
- "So 'all the world's a stage', says Shakes, but *doth* the world need another staging of Hamlet, say I?" Shannon Harvey, "Bell Rings Up an Accessible Hamlet," *West Australian*, 5 Aug. 2015, at 6.
- "The Denver star receiver *doth* protest too much, methinks." Mark Kiszla, "D.T. Isn't Catching a Lot of Respect," *Denver Post*, 28 Aug. 2015, at B1.

Finally, even when the intent is to be humorous, one shouldn't betray an utter ignorance of how a given form was once used. In the mid-1990s, British Airways ran a commercial in which an Englishman strikes up a mock-Shakespearean dialogue that ends, "'Tis the way we make you feeleth." This construction is doubly bad because *feel*, in that sentence, is actually an infinitive in an elliptical construction: "'Tis the way we make you [to] feel[eth]." How awful. Maybe an ad agency was to blame.

*archeology. See **archaeology.**

archetype; prototype. These words are close in meaning, but a distinction between them should be encouraged. As commonly used, *archetype* means "an ideal, a standard or typical example," and most often applies to living things, especially human characteristics <Mother Teresa was an archetype of benevolence>. *Prototype*, by contrast, means "the original type that has served as a model for successors"; it most often refers to a physical model of a mechanical invention <the investors may want to see a prototype>.

Inconsistently enough, the corresponding adjectives are *archetypal* and *prototypical*. The several by-forms (**archetypic, *archetypical, *prototypal,* and **prototypic*) are NEEDLESS VARIANTS.

archipelago (= a group of small islands) is pronounced /ahr-ki-**pel**-i-goh/, not /ahr-chi-/. Pl. *archipelagoes* or (now more frequently) *archipelagos*. See PLURALS (D).

Current ratio (*-os* vs. *-oes*): 2:1

architectural; architectonic. *Architectural* is usually the literal, and *architectonic* the figurative, term. Whereas *architectural* relates to the design of physical structures, *architectonic* relates to rational organization or to the abstract structure of a thing or idea.

LANGUAGE-CHANGE INDEX (For the full key, see front matter pp. xxxi, l–li.)
Stage 1: Rejected. **Stage 2:** Widely shunned. **Stage 3:** Widespread but . . . **Stage 4:** Ubiquitous but . . . **Stage 5:** Fully accepted.
Invariably inferior forms marked by asterisk (*). • Ratios represent frequency of prevalent forms vs. variants in current books.

Although *architectonic* is sometimes used like *architectural*, it should be confined to figurative or abstract senses to make the DIFFERENTIATION complete.

-ARCHY. See GOVERNMENTAL FORMS.

*****arcked; *****arcking.** See arc.

Arctic; Antarctic. Always spelled (and best pronounced) with the first -*c*-: /**ark**-tik/, /ant-**ark**-tik/. See **Antarctica.**

ardor; ardour. The first is AmE, the second BrE. The BrE spelling was the predominant AmE spelling until the 1840s. See -OR; -OUR.

area, an abstract word, is sometimes used almost as a space-filler: *a problem in the area of domestic policy* should be *a problem in domestic policy*. E.g.: "Madeline Andrews, a third-grade teacher from the North School, in Londonderry, . . . has developed activities using computers for each theme and *subject matter area* [read *subject*]." "Celebrating All Aspects of Education in NH," *Union Leader* (Manchester, N.H.), 10 June 1996, at A8. Cf. **field.**

aren't I?; *****amn't I?; *****an't I? *Aren't I*, though illogical, is the standard contraction corresponding to *am I not*. **Amn't*, a dialectal form, is found mostly in Scotland and Ireland. See *****ain't.**

In the 1930s, Frank Vizetelly denounced *aren't I* as a "hopelessly ungrammatical . . . representation of '*an't I*,'" and declared **an't* (pronounced /ahnt/) to be "correct" and preferable to *aren't* if used with a singular pronoun. Vizetelly, *How to Use English* 83 (1932). Even though he acknowledged that there was no support for his position and that the term was archaic and heard only in London dialect, he insisted that educated people use **an't I* so that the verb would agree with its subject. (*Ibid.* at 71, 89–90.) Still, however, **an't* occurs only in DIALECT. And it is not limited to the first-person singular. E.g.:

- First-person singular: "Much earlier in the novel, Bone adamantly tells Granny that she '*an't* no fool and *an't* no bastard' ([page] 144); but, as the years progress, Bone has a harder time rejecting the horrible names that are given to her." Vincent King, "Hopeful Grief: The Prospect of a Postmodernist Feminism in Allison's *Bastard*," *Southern Literary J.*, 1 Oct. 2000, at 128.
- First-person plural: "'We don't never talk, do we?' Dede asks her mother near the end of *Cavedweller*. Delia shakes her head: 'We *an't* the type.'" Dorothy Allison, "Book Review: *Cavedweller*," *Boston Globe*, 15 Mar. 1998, at F1.
- Third-person singular: "'I say,' said Haley, and leaning back in his chair and gesturing impressively, 'I'll say this now, I al'ays meant to drive my trade so as to make money on't, fust and foremost, as much as any man; but then, trade *an't* everything, and money *an't* everything, 'cause we's all got souls.'" Editorial, "A Bill with the Devil," *St. Louis Post-Dispatch*, 18 Sept. 1998, at B6.

LANGUAGE-CHANGE INDEX
aren't I? for *am I not?*: Stage 5
Current ratio (*aren't I* vs. **amn't I*): 71:1

areola; aureole; aureola. *Areola* /air-ee-**oh**-lə/ = a circular pigmented area of skin, esp. that surrounding a nipple. Pl. *areolas* (or, in medical contexts, *areolae*). *Aureole* = a corona around the sun or moon. *Aureola* is the short name for *Hakonechloa macra Aureola*, an ornamental Japanese forest grass. But it is also a variant spelling of *aureole* and a common misspelling of *areola*—e.g.:

- "When it is still too difficult for the baby to latch on, it is sometimes necessary to use soft silastic nipple shields [that] cover the *aureola* [read *areola*] and nipple and give the baby a papilla that can be utilized." Fima Lifshitz, *Childhood Nutrition* 26 (1995).
- "The *aureola* [read *areola*] surrounds the nipple; it's darker than the rest of the breast." Felice Newman, *The Whole Lesbian Sex Book* 25 (1999).
- "She is naked, with one marionette-like arm upraised. Her *aureolas* [read *areolas*] are surrounded by concentric circles so that her breasts resemble marksmanship targets." Edward Guthmann, "Still in the Shadows, an Artist in His Own Right," *S.F. Chron.*, 3 Oct. 2006, at E1.

LANGUAGE-CHANGE INDEX
aureola misused for *areola*: Stage 2

Argentine; *****Argentinian. These terms are essentially interchangeable in practice, but *Argentine* is the vastly predominant form as both noun and adjective. The disparity in use is great enough to label **Argentinian* a NEEDLESS VARIANT. See DENIZEN LABELS.
Current ratio: 10:1

ARGOT. See JARGON.

arguably. See SENTENCE ADVERBS.

argument, n.; **argumentation.** *Argumentation* refers to the act or process of arguing, or the art of persuading. *Argument* should be reserved for all other contexts.

argumentative; *****argumentive. The longer form is the preferred adjective corresponding to *argumentation*.
Current ratio: 231:1

arise; rise. Although these words are sometimes interchangeable, there is a distinct tendency to make *arise* metaphorical <doubts arise> and *rise* literal <I rise about 6 AM each day>.

Arizonan; *****Arizonian. The first is standard; the second is a variant form that, although predominant in the 19th century, now occurs much less often in print. See DENIZEN LABELS.
Current ratio: 2:1

Arkansan; Arkie; *****Arkansawyer. The first is standard. Some Arkansas denizens don't like it because of the *Kansan* it contains and therefore prefer the fairly common CASUALISM *Arkie*. **Arkansawyer* is an infrequent variant. See DENIZEN LABELS.
Current ratio (in order of headwords): 25:13:1

Arkansas /**ahr**-kən-saw/. But the Arkansas River—which flows from Colorado through Kansas, Oklahoma, and Arkansas into the Mississippi River—is pronounced /ar-**kan**-zəs/ in the Kansas part of its run.

A 19th-century Arkansas statute ineptly prescribes the "only true" pronunciation of the state name: "Be it therefore resolved by both houses of the General Assembly, that the only true pronunciation of the name of the state, in the opinion of this body, is that received by the French from the native Indians and committed to writing in the French word representing the sound. It should be pronounced in three (3) syllables, with the final 's' silent, the 'a' in each syllable with the Italian sound, and the accent on the first and last syllables. The pronunciation with the accent on the second syllable with the sound of 'a' in 'man' and the sounding of the terminal 's' is an innovation to be discouraged." Ark. Code § 1-4-105 (1881). One can only imagine what happens when American speakers try to mimic an "Italian sound." One also wonders how many orthoepists testified before the legislative committee on this statute or were consulted about how the statute should be worded. In any event, no litigation has ever ensued over its interpretation.

***Arkansawyer; Arkie.** See **Arkansan.**

armadillo. Pl. *armadillos*—not **armadilloes*. Cf. **peccadillo.**

armful. Pl. *armfuls*—not **armsful*. See PLURALS (G).

Armistice Day. See **Veterans Day.**

arm's-length; *arms-length. In phrases such as *arm's-length transaction*, the correct form is to make *arm* possessive; the phrase is usually and best hyphenated when it appears before the noun it modifies <arm's-length negotiations>, but not otherwise <negotiate at arm's length>. Even when two people are dickering, the figurative distance between them is still a single *arm's length*. If the word becomes popular enough, it may one day become solid, like *beeswax* and *oneself*. But that day is not yet.
> Current ratio (*at arm's length* vs. **at arms length* vs. **at arms' length*): 19:2:1
> Current ratio (*arm's-length transaction* vs. **arms-length transaction*): 7:1

around; round. AmE prefers *around* <they walked around the gardens>, while BrE prefers *round* <they walked round the gardens>. See **all-around.** Cf. **about (B).**

arouse; rouse. In modern usage, *arouse* tends to be metaphorical <the speech aroused much interest>, and *rouse* tends to be literal <the alarm clock roused everyone in the cabin>.

arraignment; indictment. The meanings of these terms vary, depending on the jurisdiction. An *indictment* is almost universally the instrument charging a person with a felony; it also loosely refers to the act of charging someone with a crime. An *arraignment* is the reading of the indictment to the defendant or informing the defendant of the substance of the charge and calling for a plea to the charge. For more on *indictment*, see **indictment.**

arrant. See **errant.**

arrear(s). The most common use of either of the terms is the phrase *in arrears* (= behind in the discharge of a debt or other obligation). Current AmE and BrE idiom calls predominantly for this plural form, though in the late 18th and 19th centuries **in arrear* predominated. **In arrearages* is obsolete.
> Current ratio (*in arrears* vs. **in arrear* vs. **in arrearages*): 435:86:1

arrivee. See -EE.

arriviste. See **nouveau riche (B).**

arrogate (= to claim or seize without legal justification) shouldn't be used reflexively. Although it's possible to *arrogate* something to oneself, one cannot *arrogate* oneself something—e.g.:

- "The Court of Appeal stated that if such an injunction were granted, the English court would be *arrogating itself* [read *arrogating to itself*] the power to resolve the precise dispute between the parties." Aviva Golden, "Digest of Cases Reported in the Hilary Term," *Fin. Times*, 13 Apr. 1988, at I-20.
- "The hinges were being oiled to open the door for Lewis shamelessly to *arrogate himself onto* [read *to shamelessly arrogate to himself a place on*] the sprint relay team to win his unprecedented 10th gold medal." Steve Jacobsen, "Atlanta Olympics," *Newsday* (N.Y.), 2 Aug. 1996, at A89.
- "Robert Lowell and Richard Wilbur wrote poetry as a civic instrument, but few today seem willing to *arrogate themselves* [read *arrogate to themselves*] such an audience." Dave Lucas, "Masters of Verse Pinsky, Boland and Simic Provide Rhyme and Reason," *Plain Dealer* (Cleveland), 20 Apr. 2008, at G4.

Without the edits, those sentences illustrate the vice described at OBJECT-SHUFFLING.

For the distinction between *arrogate* and *abrogate*, see **abrogate.**

> LANGUAGE-CHANGE INDEX
> **arrogate oneself* for *arrogate to oneself*: Stage 1
> Current ratio (*arrogated to himself* vs. **arrogated himself*): 66:1

arse; ass. *Arse* is the spelling of the BrE SLANG term—in the anatomical sense, that is, not in the horse sense. In AmE, *ass* is the spelling for both meanings.

There's a story behind this. Today *ass* means both (1) "donkey," and (2) "a person's bottom." Sense 1 is the historical one; sense 2 originated in the mid-18th century as the result of a phonological change, as *arse* and *ass* became homophones. By the early 19th century, it was possible to engage in wordplay between the words—as in the 1802 cartoon in which one female rider says to another, "I'll show my Ass against any

LANGUAGE-CHANGE INDEX (For the full key, see front matter pp. xxxi, l–li.)
Stage 1: Rejected. **Stage 2:** Widely shunned. **Stage 3:** Widespread but . . . **Stage 4:** Ubiquitous but . . . **Stage 5:** Fully accepted.
Invariably inferior forms marked by asterisk (*). • Ratios represent frequency of prevalent forms vs. variants in current books.

Lady's at Wells" ("Neddy Paces at Tunbridge Wells," Kent). See Tony Fairman, "How the Ass Became a Donkey," 10 *English Today* 29–35 (1994).

LANGUAGE-CHANGE INDEX
ass meaning "derriere" (for *arse*): Stage 5

arsenious; *arsenous; arsonous. *Arsenious* /ahr-**sen**-ee-əs/ (= of, relating to, or involving arsenic) should not be confused as being an adjectival form of *arson* (*arsonous*). As for the arsenic-related adjective, the spelling with the *-i-* is standard; the other form is a NEEDLESS VARIANT.

Current ratio (*arsenious* vs. **arsenous*): 9:1

artefact. See **artifact.**

*artesan. See **artist (B).**

arthritis (the disease in joints) has three syllables: /ahr-**thrɪ**-tis/. Avoid adding the epenthetic schwa that makes it sound like *Arthur-itis.*

arthroscopic; orthoscopic. *Arthroscopic* (= of, relating to, or involving surgery performed with a viewing instrument inserted at a joint in the body) derives from *arthro-* "joint" + *-scopic* "viewing." The word is pronounced /ahr-thrə-**skah**-pik/. Yet many people confuse the beginning of this word with the many terms beginning *ortho-* "straight, correct" (such as *orthodontist, orthopedist,* and *orthotic*). So they mistakenly refer to **orthoscopic surgery*—e.g.:

- "*Orthoscopic* [read *Arthroscopic*] surgery, physical therapy and rehabilitation followed." Chris Antonacci, "Davis Feeling Good Again, Reaching New Highs," *Newsday* (N.Y., Nassau ed.), 19 Nov. 2004, at A76.
- "At the time, Isaac, as he was called by friends and family, had recently had *orthoscopic* [read *arthroscopic*] surgery on his knee and was using crutches to get around." Elizabeth Fitzsimons, "Death Becomes Lifesaving Cause," *San Diego Union-Trib.*, 2 May 2005, at B1.

Just to confuse matters, though, *orthoscopic* is in fact a word that means "rendering a proportionate image" or "giving a flat, undistorted image" <modern TVs give an orthoscopic view>.

LANGUAGE-CHANGE INDEX
orthoscopic misused for *arthroscopic*: Stage 1

articulable, not **articulatable,* is the correct form— e.g.: "The salient conclusion is, therefore, to scratch such invidious issues from one's *articulatable* [read *articulable*] political concerns." Letter of John R. Blake, "Modern Anti-Liberal Logic Sometimes Difficult to Grasp," *Seattle Times*, 7 Dec. 1991, at A21. See -ABLE (D) & -ATABLE.

LANGUAGE-CHANGE INDEX
*articulatable for *articulable*: Stage 1
Current ratio (*articulable* vs. **articulatable*): 36:1

artifact (= an object made or used by humans in an earlier era) is the standard spelling in AmE. *Artefact* is a chiefly BrE variant, and the predominant form there, though the *-i-* spelling is almost as frequent in BrE.

artifice is sometimes misspelled **artiface*—e.g.: "There are subtle lines between art and *artiface* [read *artifice*], between performance and reality." Jerry O'Brien, "No More Cocktail Dresses," *Providence J.-Bull.*, 10 Nov. 1995, at C1.

LANGUAGE-CHANGE INDEX
artifice misspelled **artiface*: Stage 1
Current ratio: 2,263:1

artist. A. And *artiste*. *Artist* (/**ahr**-tist/) is the general word for someone who creates works of aesthetic value, especially in the fine arts. *Artiste* (/ahr-**teest**/), a GALLICISM, is a more specialized word denoting (1) a public performer or entertainer, especially in song and dance; or (2) an affected, often flamboyant fop with artistic pretensions. Sense 2, the pejorative one, is now more common—e.g.:

- "Goodwin's Leontes, in long hair and greatcoat, has been conceived as a pathological *artiste*; we see him at a piano, lighted by a candelabrum and moodily fingering the keys." Peter Marks, "The Banked Fire of 'Winter's Tale,'" *Wash. Post*, 4 Sept. 2002, at C1.
- "It is the voice of Pearl Jam's Eddie Vedder, Creed's Scott Stapp and all the other sulking, groaning *artistes* who have labored over the past decade to rid rock 'n' roll of its unpretentious joy." Elysa Gardner et al., "Lifehouse Not Up to Code," *USA Today*, 17 Sept. 2002, at D4.
- "From the realm of show biz . . . came musical comedy veteran Leigh Scarritt in three roles—Babe the supermarket checker, Roberta the hooker and Dolores the waitressing *artiste*." Anne Marie Welsh, "'Working' Is Getting a Bit Tired," *San Diego Union-Trib.*, 23 Sept. 2002, at D1.

B. And *artisan*. Although these terms were once synonymous, they have undergone DIFFERENTIATION: an *artist* is someone skilled in any of the fine arts (such as painting), while an *artisan* is a crafter or one skilled at a trade. (**Artesan* and **artizan* are variant spellings.) Yet *artist* has degenerated to the point where many people use it in reference to anyone with a talent—e.g.:

- "'Burlesque is back!' bubbles Dixie Evans, the legendary 1950s-era striptease *artist*." "Bare-All Reunion," *L.A. Times*, 23 May 2002, § 6, at 37.
- "Here is where Rothan comes alive as a natural slapstick *artist*, her slim frame bending and whipping into frantic shapes as she flies into a panic at the fear of forgetting the signals, blowing the act and getting them both thrown into the clink." Elaine Liner, "Love You to Death," *Dallas Observer*, 18 July 2002, at 55.
- "Story follows a phobic con *artist* (Cage) and his protege (Rockwell), who are on the verge of pulling off a lucrative swindle when Cage's teenage daughter (Lohman) arrives unexpectedly." Dana Harris, "Lohman Joins 'Matchstick,'" *Daily Variety*, 29 July 2002, at 12.

Current ratio (*artisan* vs. **artizan* vs. **artesan*): 1,808:36:1

artless has opposing connotations. On the one hand, it is favorable when contrasted with the idea denoted by *artificial*—e.g.: "Generally, Ms. Benedis's works seem as *artless* as nature itself." Patricia Malarcher, "Show Features Artwork Formed from Cuttings and Branches," *N.Y. Times*, 9 Feb. 1997, at WC13. But it's often unfavorable when contrasted with *artful*—e.g.: "In an age of *artless* novels, here was an artful book." Richard Dyer, "Sibling Reveries," *Boston Globe*, 22 May 1994, at B15.

as. A. Causal Words: *as*; *because*; *since*; *for*. In the causal sense, *as* should generally be avoided because (not *as*!) it may be misunderstood as having its more usual meaning "while," especially when it is placed anywhere but at the beginning of the sentence. H.W. Fowler states: "To causal or explanatory *as*-clauses, if they are placed before the main sentence . . . there is no objection" (*FMEU1* at 31). This is most common in BrE—e.g.: "*As* she didn't get the original money, could she please have the larger sum?" Martin Waller, "Mail Shot," *Times* (London), 30 May 1997, at 29.

As Fowler suggested, however, the reverse order is infelicitous unless the reader necessarily knows what is to be introduced by the *as*-clause. So don't use it in midsentence—e.g.: "Indeed, some jurors confirmed later that they wished they had been given the manslaughter option *as* [read *because*] they didn't believe the au pair intended to harm the baby." Kimberly Mills, "'Au Pair' Decision Does Injustice to the Lone Innocent," *Seattle Post-Intelligencer*, 14 Nov. 1997, at A15.

Given the syntactic restrictions on *as*, we are left with three general-purpose causal conjunctions. *Because* is the strongest and most logically oriented of these. *Since* is less demonstratively causal and frequently has temporal connotations. But using *since* without reference to time is not, despite the popular canard, incorrect. (See SUPERSTITIONS (G).) *For*, the most subjective of the three, is the least used. If *because* points out a direct cause-and-effect relationship, *for* signals a less direct relationship, adding independent explanation or substantiation. Moreover, *for* is a coordinating conjunction and not, like *because* and *since*, a subordinating conjunction; hence it can properly begin a sentence—that is, one consisting only of an independent clause <I want to go home now. For I am tired>.

B. And *like*. See **like.**

as against = as compared with. E.g.: "The last Wednesday before the change, the newscast drew a 7.9 rating and 23 percent audience share in its first quarter hour, *as against* an 8.7 rating and 25 share for Channel 4." Gail Pennington, "St. Louis Daytime TV Gets New Shows, New Times," *St. Louis Post-Dispatch*, 4 Sept. 1997, at G6. The phrase is most common in Indian English, quite common in BrE, and somewhat uncommon in AmE.

The phrase is sometimes misused for *against*, especially in American law—e.g.: "Accordingly, for the foregoing reasons, petitioner is awarded summary judgment *as against* [read *against*] respondent."

"Harmit Realities LLC v. Phillips Educational Servs.," *N.Y.L.J.*, 9 July 1997, at 27.

Speakers of AmE sometimes use the phrase in completely different ways that can give rise to MISCUES. First, it's occasionally a shorthand for *as being against*—e.g.: "'I wouldn't classify our campaign *as against* [read *as being against*] Wisconsin,' CMAB official Nancy Fletcher said." "Cheese Wars," *Wis. State J.*, 12 Sept. 1997, at C1. And sometimes it's part of an *as . . . as* construction—e.g.: "Often the law enforcement agencies and the drug czar seem to spend as much time fighting among themselves *as against* [read *as they do against*] the drug lords." Gordon Witkin, "The Troubled Reign of the Nation's Drug Czar," *U.S. News & World Rep.*, 8 Sept. 1997, at 26.

LANGUAGE-CHANGE INDEX
as against misused for *against*: Stage 1

as . . . as. A. And *so . . . as*. In positive statements, the *as . . . as* construction is customary—e.g.: "The corn, which should be *as* tall *as* I am at this time of year, is barely half my height." Eason Jordan, "A Visit to the Land of the Vanishing Lake," *Time*, 25 Aug. 1997, at 52.

In the mid-20th century it was commonly held that *so . . . as* is preferable to *as . . . as* in negative statements—e.g.: "The Republican governor said he might support future efforts to raise the ballot bar on nonmajor party candidates, but *not so* high *as* Senate Bill 200 tried to set." Mario F. Cattabiani, "Ridge Vetoes Bill on Ballot Access," *Morning Call* (Allentown, Pa.), 26 June 1997, at A1. But *as . . . as* generally serves equally well in such negative statements, and examples abound in good literature.

LANGUAGE-CHANGE INDEX
as . . . as for *so . . . as* in negative statements: Stage 5

B. First *as* Omitted. It is fairly common to see this phrase with the first *as* left off <they were thick as thieves>. The construction is a CASUALISM that is often employed with CLICHÉS. It is unobjectionable in informal speech and writing, but avoid it in formal contexts.

C. Repetition of Verb After. Often, when the second *as* in this construction is far removed from the first *as*—or when there's otherwise an opportunity for ambiguity—the verb is repeated for clarity. E.g.: "Owner Ray Haynie—tall, slim and baritone-voiced—is *as* likely to be cleaning tables *as is* any employee." Ruth Fantasia, "Not Just Any Port in a Storm Sting," *Richmond Times-Dispatch*, 3 Dec. 1995, at H5. (If we deleted the *is*, employees might bring sexual-harassment claims against Ray.) But if the second verb isn't needed, omit it—e.g.: "Montreal is *as* likely to survive *as is* [read *as*] common civility." Mike Celizic, "Baseball Players Making Nice," *Record* (N.J.), 9 Apr. 1995, Sports §, at 3.

D. *As* [+ adj.] *a* [+ n.] *as.* In AmE, writers sometimes err by inserting *of* after the adjective. But good usage rejects this—e.g.: "From the sidelines, Nunez became nearly *as good of a cheerleader* [read *as good a cheerleader*] as he was a running back." Jaime Aron, "Westlake's Nunez Leads AP Honor Roll," *Austin Am.-Statesman*, 26 Oct. 1994, at C3. See **of (B).**

LANGUAGE-CHANGE INDEX
*not as good of a for *not as good a*: Stage 2
Current ratio (*not as good a* vs.
*not as good of a): 25:1

E. *As . . . than.* *Than* is sometimes misused for the second *as*—e.g.: "A Roper Starch poll says that 24 percent of consumers—twice *as* many *than* [read *as*] in 1987—say they never go to malls." Allison Lucas, "The Fall of the Mall," *Sales & Marketing Mgmt.*, 1 Apr. 1996, at 13. (But it would be *twice more than*.) See SWAPPING HORSES.

LANGUAGE-CHANGE INDEX
*as . . . than misused for *as . . . as*: Stage 1

as at (= as of) is characteristic chiefly of BrE financial JARGON—e.g.:

- "This book reflects the law *as at* August 1986." Stanley Berwin, *The Economist Pocket Lawyer* i (1986).
- "The restructuring was needed, the group said, after a cumulative loss of GBP 75.4m *as at* December 31, 1996." "Seafield Plans Restructuring," *Fin. Times*, 27 Nov. 1996, at 22.

It's a construction best avoided.

as a whole. See **in whole.**

as best; *as best as. The traditional idiom is *as best she can*, meaning "in the best way that she can." The *as* isn't part of a comparative *as . . . as* construction, which takes the positive form of the adjective (*as good as*), not the superlative (*best*). So adding a second *as* is poor form—e.g.:

- "But in the meantime, Michelle combed his coat *as best as she* [read *as best she*] could and adorned him yesterday with a pink ribbon and a yellow bandanna around his neck." Celeste Tarricone, "Lost Six Weeks, Sebastian Is Back in the Family Fold," *Providence J.-Bull.*, 10 June 1998, at C1.
- "Good dog owners try to discipline their dogs *as best as they* [read *as best they*] know how, but I don't think people give us a chance." D. Andrich, "Dog Bias," *Chicago Trib.*, 26 Sept. 1998, at 20.
- "He raised himself *as best as he* [read *as best he*] could on his hands and knees and crawled out of the store." Bruce Von Deylen, "Store Owner Felt Remorse, Fear After Shooting," *South Bend Trib.*, 31 Jan. 1999, at A1.

LANGUAGE-CHANGE INDEX
*as best as he can for *as best he can*: Stage 1
Current ratio (*as best he can* vs.
*as best as he can): 15:1

asbestos (the gray mineral once used in buildings and in protective clothing) is preferably pronounced /as-**bes**-təs/—not /as-**bes**-tohs/ (a mispronunciation based on the spelling).

as between. See **between (E).**

ascendable. So spelled—not **ascendible* (though, surprisingly, the *-i-* spelling predominated for a brief period around 1800). For an anomaly in spelling, see **descendible.** See -ABLE (A).

Current ratio: 13:1

ascendancy (= a position of dominant control; supremacy) is the standard term. **Ascendance* is a NEEDLESS VARIANT.

*Ascendency and **ascendence* are variant spellings not recommended.

Current ratio (*ascendancy* vs. **ascendency* vs.
*ascendance vs. **ascendence*): 207:53:31:1

ascendant, in the. Derived from astrology and denoting the part of the zodiac that is rising above the eastern horizon at a particular time, this phrase is sometimes mistakenly written **in the ascendancy*—e.g.:

- "A slower pace of reform, as advocated by Prime Minister Viktor S. Chernomyrdin, whose star is in the *ascendancy* [read *ascendant*] here, will only delay the dawn of recovery." R.W. Apple Jr., "Clinton in Europe: A Russian Tightrope," *N.Y. Times*, 15 Jan. 1994, § 1, at 6.
- "No such justification is available to support affirmative action for conservatives, who have never been excluded, and in fact were once greatly in the *ascendancy* [read *ascendant*], and who are no longer in the *ascendancy* [read *ascendant*] in some disciplines because they have chosen to go into others." Stanley Fish, "Postmodern Warfare," *Harper's Mag.*, 1 July 2002, at 33.

Avoid the variant spelling **ascendent*.

LANGUAGE-CHANGE INDEX
*in the ascendancy for *in the ascendant*: Stage 2
Current ratio (*in the ascendant* vs.
*in the ascendancy): 3:1

ascent. A. And *ascension.* Both *ascent* and *ascension* mean "the act of ascending." *Ascent*, however, has these additional senses: (1) "the act of rising in station or rank, or in natural chronological succession" <the ascent of man>; (2) "a method of ascending" <an unorthodox ascent>; and (3) "the degree of slope or acclivity" <a steep ascent>. And *ascension* also denotes (1) in Christianity, the ascent of Jesus Christ to heaven 40 days after his resurrection; and (2) in the astronomical term *right ascension*, the measure of the position of a celestial body along an equator as an arc from the first degree of Aries.

B. And *assent.* *Assent* (= agreement) is surprisingly often misused for *ascent*—e.g.:

- "Weihenmayer and several other climbers from throughout the United States have begun their *assent* [read *ascent*] to Mount Everest's summit with a lofty goal." Robert Sanchez, "Blind Climber Heads for Peak of Everest," *Rocky Mountain News* (Denver), 4 May 2001, at A24.
- "Mehrunnisa is calculating even as a child; by the age of 8, she tells everyone around her that she intends to marry Prince Salim (who is called Jahangir upon his *assent* [read *ascent*] to the throne)." Carmela Ciuraru, " 'Twentieth Wife' Opens the Door on Palace Life," *USA Today*, 14 Mar. 2002, at D4.

- "Analysts welcomed Zafirovski's *assent* [read *ascent*] to the position of Motorola president and chief operating officer." Rob Kaiser, "Motorola's No. 2 a Turnaround Vet," *Chicago Trib.*, 27 July 2002, Bus. §, at 1.

For the difference between *assent* and *consent*, see **assent**.

LANGUAGE-CHANGE INDEX
assent misused for *ascent*: Stage 1

as concerns. See **as regards.**

ascribe (= to attribute to a specified cause) is sometimes misused for *subscribe* in the sense "to think of favorably." Although the mistake was once thought to be found only among the semiliterate, today it appears in print with some frequency. Perhaps there is some influence from *aspire*, as the first and second examples suggest—e.g.:

- "Within the field of family and couple counseling, models are not generally *ascribing* [read *subscribing*] to the view of normality as process." Ray Woolfe & Windy Dryden, *Handbook of Counseling Psychology* 424 (1996).
- "Maybe there are enough readers in the publishing industry who *ascribe* [read *subscribe*] to Oscar Wilde's aphorism—'There is only one thing in the world worse than being talked about, and that is not being talked about.'" Janice D'Arcy, "'Happiness' Sadly Weak as Satire," *Hartford Courant*, 23 June 2002, at G3.
- "During opening arguments yesterday, prosecutor James Willett told the jury Powell 'happens to be a racist of the highest order' who *ascribes* [read *subscribes*] to the beliefs of the Ku Klux Klan and Adolf Hitler." Matthew Barakat, "Death-Penalty Trial Set in Motion by Letter Starts," *Richmond Times-Dispatch*, 14 Jan. 2003, at B2.

Still, *ascribe* is far more commonly used correctly—e.g.: "Van Gogh's accelerating cycles of mental disturbance will probably never be fully diagnosed, but they continue to be variously *ascribed* to epilepsy, manic-depressive illness and alcohol." Jo Ann Lewis, "Trove of Van Goghs to Visit Washington," *Wash. Post*, 13 Jan. 1998, at A1.

LANGUAGE-CHANGE INDEX
ascribe misused for *subscribe*: Stage 2
Current ratio (*don't subscribe to that* vs.
*don't ascribe to that): 43:1

as do. See ANTICIPATORY REFERENCE.

as equally. See **equally as.**

as far as. In its figurative uses, this phrase must be followed by some complement such as *that's concerned*, *that goes*, or *I know*—e.g.: "*As far as* they're concerned, January 1, 2000, will bring enough of a hangover." Neil Randall, "Welcome to the Millennium," *PC Mag.*, 23 Sept. 1997, at 229.

When the complement is omitted, idiom is severely violated. This seems to happen most often in reported speech—e.g.: "'*As far as* Ron Lynn [insert *is concerned*], I have no idea what the inner workings of [his]

team are.'" Lee Shappell, "Miracle Win over Redskins Revived Cardinals in '96," *Ariz. Republic*, 12 Sept. 1997, at C1 (quoting Vince Tobin, a coach). Having first been noted by Robert L. Chapman in "Trouble with the Pointing Phrase," 44 *Am. Speech* 305 (1969), this error is becoming fairly widespread in spoken English.

Idiom aside, however, *as far as* usually signals verbosity. So instead of *As far as he is concerned*, it's possible to save half the words by writing *As for him*, ... See **insofar as.**

LANGUAGE-CHANGE INDEX
as far as without a subject and verb
following: Stage 2

as follows; *as follow. *As follows* is always the correct form, even for an enumeration of many things. The expression is elliptical for *as it follows*—not *as they follow*.

Although the plural **as follow* sometimes appeared in 19th-century and earlier texts, today it is unidiomatic. In fact, the 19th-century grammarian Lindley Murray disfavored **as follow* long ago: "The phrases *as follow*, *as appears*, form what are called impersonal verbs, and should, therefore, be confined to the singular number: the construction being, 'as it follows,' 'as it appears.'" 1 Lindley Murray, *An English Grammar* 222 (5th ed. 1824) (adding that "analogy and usage favour this mode of expression" [*as follows*]).

Current ratio: 128:1

as good as or better than; *as good or better than. The second *as* is obligatory—e.g.: "It follows . . . that the dialogue will be either *as good as or better than* an exposition along the same lines." George Rudebusch, "Plato's Aporetic Style," in *Plato: Critical Assessments* 350, 351 (Nicholas D. Smith ed., 1998). Another, less creaky way of putting the idea is this: *It follows that the dialogue will be as good as an exposition along the same lines, or even better.*

Many writers, however, mangle their grammar by omitting the second *as* without rearranging the syntax as suggested above—e.g.: "A locally made cheese can be *as good or better than* [read *as good as or better than*] an imported, well-known variety." Jennifer Darling, *New Cook Book* 276 (2003). [An alternative wording: *A locally made cheese can be as good as an imported, well-known variety—or even better.*] Cf. **as much as or more than; as well as or better than.**

LANGUAGE-CHANGE INDEX
*as good or better than for
as good as or better than: Stage 3

ashen; ashy. A useful DIFFERENTIATION has emerged here. *Ashen* means "resembling the color of ashes" or, by extension, "pale" <her face became ashen when she heard the news>. *Ashy* more broadly means "of, relating to, or involving ashes" <an ashy residue>. The following examples track this distinction:

LANGUAGE-CHANGE INDEX (For the full key, see front matter pp. xxxi, l–li.)
Stage 1: Rejected. **Stage 2:** Widely shunned. **Stage 3:** Widespread but . . . **Stage 4:** Ubiquitous but . . . **Stage 5:** Fully accepted.
Invariably inferior forms marked by asterisk (*). • Ratios represent frequency of prevalent forms vs. variants in current books.

- "Seeing her husband *ashen*, with sunken eyes and a stooped look, Mickie had had enough. 'You're going to the doctor,' she said." Alexander Wolff, "Back in Action," *Sports Illustrated*, 23 Oct. 1995, at 94.
- "Panicked, he had turned pale, almost *ashen*." Laura Yee, "The View from the Flower Shop," *Plain Dealer* (Cleveland), 14 Feb. 1997, at F1.
- "It takes more than a frumpy wardrobe, constricted hairdo, overtly *ashy* makeup and cane to convert France's venerable, radiant diva of the big screen, Catherine Deneuve, into the glum, bisexual philosophy professor." Roger Hurlburt, "No Honor Among Bungling 'Thieves,'" *Sun-Sentinel* (Ft. Lauderdale), 31 Jan. 1997, at 7.
- "Winter's frigid temperatures, lower humidity and icy winds leave skin dry, *ashy* and scaly." "Spring Forward: Skin Care for a More Beautiful You," *Ebony*, Mar. 1997, at 28.

Asian; Asiatic. *Asian* is the predominant adjective for people or things from or related to Asia. Until the 1950s, *Asiatic* was 8 to 12 times as common in print as *Asian*. But after WWII, *Asian* rapidly became preferred and now predominates by a 14-to-1 ratio. Today, *Asiatic* is limited to academic uses such as *Asiatic style* (florid rhetoric), *Asiatic mode of production* (Marxist economic theory), and *Asiatic lion* (zoology).

aside. A. Mistakenly Meaning "on each side." *Aside*, adv., properly means "to one side, on one side" <she lay the book aside and fell asleep>. But it's sometimes used wrongly in the sense "on each side, per side"—e.g.:

- "For the lawyers, and there are three *aside* [read *for each side*] in this case, [jury selection] is vitally important." Christie Blatchford, "The End of the Beginning," *Toronto Sun*, 15 Nov. 1995, at 5.
- "Bill Guerin scored a controversial goal with the teams skating five *aside* [read *a side*] with 6:31 left in the second to gain a brief 3–2 lead." Kisha Ciabattari, "Richter Nets Two Goals as Canadiens and Devils Tie," *Asbury Park Press* (Neptune, N.J.), 15 Dec. 1996, at H3.
- "With teams locked 0–0 after regulation time, McCambridge used her pace to exploit the additional space afforded her as both sides dropped to nine *aside* [read *a side*] then seven *aside* [read *a side*]." Adam Clifford, "Extra Time Counts as Ships Shoot to Defend Title," *Mercury* (Hobart, Aus.), 6 Sept. 2015, at 61.

This usage occurs most commonly in sports contexts—and particularly (though not exclusively) outside the United States, where games with different team-size variants are more popular. Soccer, for instance, is usually played with 11 on each team, but seven-a-side and five-a-side variants are also common. While *aside* is used adverbially in the examples above, when such phrases are used as adjectives or nouns, they should properly take two hyphens—e.g.:

- "The sporting world splits into two camps over whether McIlroy was reckless in playing *five-aside* [read *five-a-side*] football so close to The Open or simply living his life." Derek Lawrenson, "There Is Life in G-Mac Yet," *Scottish Daily Mail*, 10 July 2015, at 82.
- "The winning team after *seven-asides* [read *seven-a-sides*] would be rewarded with Mars bars, the losers sent off on a punishing run." Lee Clayton, "Mars Bars and Brandy Prove Perfect Ingredients for the 'Lunatic' Who Goes His Own Way," *Daily Mail*, 5 Aug. 2006, at 100.

LANGUAGE-CHANGE INDEX
aside misused for *on each side*: Stage 1

B. *Aside from* vs. *apart from*. Though once considered inferior to *apart from*, *aside from* has become standard in AmE and BrE alike. But *apart from* appears far more frequently in print sources from both sides of the Atlantic. Cf. **outside.**

Current ratio (*apart from* vs. *aside from*): 6:1

as if; as though. Attempts to distinguish between these idioms have proved futile. Euphony should govern the choice of phrase. As a matter of word frequency, *as if* has always been the more common phrase in Modern English. Eric Partridge suggested that *as if* is usually preceded by a comma and that *as though* rarely is (*U&A* at 47).

A better distinction is that *as if* often suggests the more hypothetical proposition when cast in the subjunctive <as if he were a god>. E.g.: "As he came closer to it he felt a great strength flow into him from the west, *as if* Silence had taken him by the hand after all." Ursula K. Le Guin, *Tales from Earthsea* 161 (2001). By contrast, *as though* suggests a more plausible suggestion <it looks as though it might rain>.

asinine. So spelled. See SPELLING (A) & ANIMAL ADJECTIVES.

as is; as was. "He bought the company 'as is.'" Although a martinet of logic might insist on *as was* in the preceding sentence, that phrase is jarringly unidiomatic. *As is*, in the context of that sentence, is really an elliptical form of *as it is* or *on an "as is" basis* and is infinitely better than those paraphrases. The purpose of the phrase *as is*, of course, is for a seller to disclaim warranties and representations.

as it were. The *OED* defines this phrase as meaning "as if it were so, if one might so put it, in some sort," and describes it as "a parenthetic phrase used to indicate that a word or statement is perhaps not formally exact though practically right." It is a highly self-conscious phrase typically found in highly self-conscious writing. Each of the following examples would probably be improved by its deletion:

- "His unit gone ahead without him, Melander accepted an invitation, *as it were*, to become a runner for a company commander, Lt. Al Ungerlichter." Ed Lowe, "Unlocking Memories of Liberation," *Newsday* (N.Y.), 16 May 1997, at A8.
- "They first assembled during humid two-a-days at the pool of the Collegiate Village Inn, where many players are housed, to walk—or wade, *as it were*—through their playbook." Brian Schmitz, "Knights Prepared for Quixotic Quest," *Orlando Sentinel*, 13 Sept. 1997, at B1.
- "There was the slight inconvenience of 'training in a vacuum' in that first week, preparing for a match, *as it were*, without knowing who Kerry would be playing in that match." Paul Brennan, "Draw Keeps Kerry in a Vacuum for Another Week," *Kerryman* (Irl.), 2 Sept. 2015, at 66.

Cf. **if you will.**

asked /askt/ is sometimes mispronounced /ast/ or, through METATHESIS, /akst/. See PRONUNCIATION (B).

as much as or more than. The second *as* must appear in this phrase—e.g.: "In our sample, 31.5% of the wives earned *as much as or more than* their husbands." Diane F. Halpern & Susan E. Murphy, *From Work–Family Balance to Work–Family Interaction* 164 (2005).

A common blemish is to write **as much or more than*—e.g.: "Suppositional Departures lead to just *as much* bitterness, and even *more* subjunctives, *than* Actual Departures." James Thurber, "Ladies' and Gentlemen's Guide to Modern English Usage," in *The Ways of Language* 142, 146 (Raymond J. Pflug ed., 1967). [A suggested revision: *Suppositional Departures lead to just as much bitterness as, and even more subjunctives than, Actual Departures.*] Cf. **as good as or better than; as well as or better than.** See CANNIBALISM & ILLOGIC (B).

as of. A. Generally. *As of* should be used with caution. Originally an Americanism, the phrase frequently signifies the effective date of a document, as when the document is backdated, postdated, or signed by various people at different times <this contract is effective as of July 1>. When such a nuance is not intended, *as of* is the wrong phrase. Often it is inferior to *on*—e.g.: "Barnaby's employment with New Jersey Public Service ended *as of* [read *on*] September 30." Cf. **as at.**

B. *As of now.* This phrase, along with *as of* itself, has been criticized as downright uncivilized. Lord Conesford wrote: "An illiteracy is introduced when the words *as of* precede not a date, but the adverb *now. As of now* is a barbarism which only a love of illiteracy for its own sake can explain. What is generally meant is *at present.*" Lord Conesford, "You Americans Are Murdering the Language," in *Advanced Composition* 374, 383 (J.E. Warriner et al. eds., 1968).

But *as of now* does not mean "at present"; rather, it means "up to the present time." Wilson Follett also disapproved of the phrase—recommending instead *up to now* or *for the present* (*MAU* at 76)—but *as of now* is today unobjectionable in AmE.

LANGUAGE-CHANGE INDEX
as of now meaning "up to now": Stage 5

*as of yet. See ***as yet.**

*as per is commonly understood to mean "in accordance with." But writing texts have long condemned the phrase—e.g.:

- "As Per. This hybrid is inexcusable. Instead of 'as per your request' say 'in accordance with your request,' or 'in compliance with your request.'" Maurice H. Weseen, *Crowell's Dictionary of English Grammar* 55 (1928).

- "as per, 'in accordance with,' is such horrible commercialese that even merchant princes are less than riotously happy when their secretaries wish it on them." Eric Partridge, *U&A* at 47.

- "When used to mean 'according to' (*per* your request, *per* your order), the expression [*per*] is business jargon at its worst and should be avoided. Equally annoying is the phrase *as per.*" Charles T. Brusaw et al., *The Business Writer's Handbook* 478 (3d ed. 1987).

Originating in 18th-century COMMERCIALESE, **as per* is redundant for *per*. Yet even *per* is a LATINISM in place of which any one of several everyday equivalents would be better (*as, according to, in accordance with,* etc.)—e.g.:

- "*As per her request* [read *At her request* or *As she had requested*], her family scattered her ashes Saturday at the summit of Mt. Washington in New Hampshire, said her husband, James Gardner." Joe Haberstroh, "Irene S. Gardner, Retired Nurse" (obit.), *Newsday* (N.Y.), 10 Sept. 1997, at A49.

- "So *as per our predictions* [read *as we predicted*], we'll have to give Foss' date at South Sound Stadium with River Ridge on Oct. 24 the nod as the key game." Gary Brooks, "Key Games," *News Trib.* (Tacoma), 12 Sept. 1997, at C2.

- "*As per usual* [read *As usual*], Trump blew the little uber lefty punk out of the water with his reply." Roddy D. Riggs, "Game Plan," *Belleville News-Democrat* (Ill.), 10 Sept. 2015, at 242.

The phrase **as per usual*, which emerged in the late 19th century and became suddenly popular in the early 21st, is an embarrassing barbarism.

LANGUAGE-CHANGE INDEX
1. **as per* for *per* or *in accordance with*: Stage 3
2. **as per usual* for *as usual*: Stage 1
Current ratio (*as usual* vs. **as per usual*): 349:1

aspersions, to cast is a prolix CLICHÉ for *asperse* (= to disparage; criticize harshly), a little-known but useful verb—e.g.:

- "Fazio et al. should cast their barbs at ordained character assassins . . . rather than *aspersing* the American majority that claims to be both Christian and conservative." "An Undeserved Whacking," *Rocky Mountain News* (Denver), 14 July 1994, at A48.

- "And so to *asperse* her performance in this shabby way is to report irresponsibly and to forsake a goodly measure of any newspaper's goal of fairness." "Ford's Husband Denounces Use of Unnamed Critics," *Times-Picayune* (New Orleans), 10 Dec. 1999, at B6.

asphyxia; asphyxiation. The first refers to the condition of having insufficient oxygen resulting in suffocation. The second is the action of producing suffocation. Hence: "*Asphyxiation* [/as-fik-see-**ay**-shən/], also known as suffocation, is any interruption of breathing resulting in *asphyxia.*" Ann Ehrlich & Carol L. Schroeder, *Medical Terminology for Health Professions* 201 (2004).

LANGUAGE-CHANGE INDEX (For the full key, see front matter pp. xxxi, l–li.)
Stage 1: Rejected. **Stage 2:** Widely shunned. **Stage 3:** Widespread but . . . **Stage 4:** Ubiquitous but . . . **Stage 5:** Fully accepted.
Invariably inferior forms marked by asterisk (*). • Ratios represent frequency of prevalent forms vs. variants in current books.

as regards, a much-maligned phrase, is sometimes called a solecism. Actually, it's a traditional, perfectly good literary idiom more common in BrE than in AmE—e.g.:

- "The superiority *as regards* directness of association is not invariably on the side of gesture-language." Henry Sweet, *The History of Language* 4 (1900).
- "We might expect . . . a more wary approach *as regards* some of the dangers of the test." I.A. Richards, *Practical Criticism* 5 (1929; repr. 1964).
- "Southeast Asia's troubles could magnify what has already been a difficult summer for many U.S. multinational companies, at least *as regards* their ability to meet earnings growth targets." Tom Petruno, "Wall Street, California," *L.A. Times*, 2 Sept. 1997, at D1.
- "*As regards* the use of troops, Clinton's apparent stratagem is to deploy troops by executive action." James Gardner, "Exactly Which U.S. 'Values' Are Right for Bosnia?" *News & Record* (Greensboro), 7 Sept. 1997, at F3.

Though *as regards* is no more objectionable than *with regard to*, the whole lot of such phrases is suspect: "Train your suspicions to bristle up whenever you come upon *as regards, with regard to, in respect of, in connection with, according as to whether*, and the like. They are all dodges of jargon, circumlocutions for evading this or that simple statement." Arthur Quiller-Couch, *On the Art of Writing* 114 (2d ed. 1943). They are especially lame when used to start a sentence. See **regard (A).**

ass. See **arse.**

assassin; assassinator. Generally speaking, the latter can be regarded as a NEEDLESS VARIANT—e.g.: "Dr. Samuel Mudd was imprisoned there for setting the broken leg of Lincoln *assassinator* [read *assassin*] John Wilkes Booth." Morgan Stinemetz, "Lost in Time," *Tampa Trib.*, Sports §, 22 June 2001, at 8.

Yet *assassinator* has a rarefied mathematical sense. If you must know, it's the unique associated prime of a uniform right module over a right noetherian ring (and please don't ask for further elucidation of this bit of arcana). E.g.:

- "The set of all associated primes of M is denoted by Ass(M) (the '*assassinator*' of M)." Paul Moritz Cohn, *Basic Algebra: Groups, Rings, and Fields* 380 (2003).
- "If U is a uniform right module over a right noetherian ring, the unique associated prime of U is called the *assassinator* of U." K.R. Goodearl, *An Introduction to Noncommutative Noetherian Rings* 102 (2004).

Got that?

LANGUAGE-CHANGE INDEX
assassinator as an equivalent of *assassin*: Stage 1

assassination. When does a murder become an assassination? If a political figure is murdered—but not for political reasons or for hire—is it an assassination? The following passage rightly suggests that it is not: "An Egyptian diplomat was shot to death in the parking garage of his Geneva apartment building, authorities said yesterday. The victim was Alaa el-Din Nazmi, the commercial counselor in the Egyptian mission to the United Nations and other international organizations based in Geneva. Police said Nazmi was hit by six bullets. Prosecutors said they were treating the slaying as a *possible assassination*." "Egyptian Diplomat Shot to Death in Geneva," *S.F. Chron.*, 15 Nov. 1995, at C1.

Today, the word's meaning has been broadened beyond political killing. Here's a good modern definition of *assassination*: "the act of murdering someone (esp. a public figure) by surprise attack, usu. for hire or for political reasons." The word also appears figuratively in the sense "malicious ruining or destruction" in the SET PHRASE *character assassination*.

assassinator. See **assassin.**

assault; battery. In popular usage, these two are virtually synonymous. Most people use *assault* in referring to an incident that might begin with a threat and end with hitting and kicking. In fact, most people wouldn't say that someone had been *assaulted* unless the incident included physical contact. So in the popular mind, *assault* is essentially the same as *battery* (a rarer term).

But in law these terms have precise meanings. Essentially, an *assault* is the use or threat of force that causes the person to whom the force is directed to have a well-founded fear of physical injury or offensive touching. A *battery* is the use of force or violence on another (in the criminal sense), or any repugnant intentional contact with another (in the noncriminal, tort sense).

Shooting a gun just to the side of someone, if that person reasonably feared physical injury, or shooting a blank gun directly at someone, would be an *assault*. Hitting someone with a bullet would make the act a *battery*, even if the shooter never knew about the hit. And in the tort sense, an uninvited kiss by a stranger is considered a *battery*. Cf. **accost.**

assay; essay, v.t. These words, related etymologically, have distinct meanings. *Assay* = to test, to analyze. E.g.: " 'They all but stuck pure *HIV virus* [read *HIV*] in the mosquitoes. They *assayed* a huge variety of mosquitoes at various times in the first few days and found that the virus had been entirely digested.' " Donna Jacobs, "Pests & Pestilence: Why Can't a Mosquito Transmit AIDS?" *Ottawa Citizen*, 9 Mar. 1997, at C4 (quoting Dr. Paul Grimstad).

Essay (as a verb), though sometimes used synonymously with *assay*, most frequently takes on the meaning "to attempt; to try to accomplish." In this sense it is a FORMAL WORD—e.g.: "Caesar, a Durham native, played a church singer in the original production, but she has *essayed* the role of the meddling Mother Winters in the subsequent productions." Bill Morrison, "Blessed Assurance: Caesar Shines," *News & Observer* (Raleigh), 2 Mar. 1997, at G1. This usage is really an ARCHAISM; *attempt* or *try* serves better in ordinary contexts. Cf. **endeavor.**

assemblage; assembly. An *assemblage* is an unorganized group of people or things. An *assembly* is a group of people organized and united for some common purpose.

assent; consent. The traditional distinction is that *assent* denotes agreement with an opinion, while *consent* denotes permission to let something happen. *Assent* contains a touch more enthusiasm and support than *consent*, which suggests mere acquiescence. Today *assent* is becoming less and less common; it survives mostly in formal uses <with the override vote, the bill became law without the President's assent>.

For the confusion of *assent* with *ascent*, see **ascent (B).**

assert; exert. Writers sometimes confuse these quite different words. *Assert* = (1) to state with force and confidence <they asserted that the world is flat>; (2) to exercise or demonstrate (authority, a right, a privilege, etc.) <the committee never fully asserted its authority>; or (3) to behave or speak forcefully <instead of backing down, assert yourself in the debate>. *Exert* = (1) to put forth or apply (energy, force, strength, etc.) to something <the team members exerted all their strength and won the tug-of-war>; or (2) to make a physical or mental effort <you can't possibly write well without exerting yourself>.

When it comes to asserting authority or asserting a right—that is, sense 2 of *assert*—some writers mistakenly use *exert*. This seems to be the main context in which WORD-SWAPPING occurs between the words—e.g.:

- "Engine builders will *exert* [read *assert*] executive privilege, making sure the session is nothing more than a light workout." Don Coble, "One-Engine Rule Faces Test," *Augusta Chron.*, 25 May 2002, at C3.
- "The Ojibwe [tribe members] were simply *exerting* [read *asserting*] their rights under a treaty between the nation and the United States government." Steve Arney, "Ojibwe Indian Spreads Culture, Tradition," *Pantagraph* (Bloomington, Ill.), 8 Feb. 2003, at D1.
- "U.S. forces arrested . . . an [Iraqi] exile who named himself Baghdad's mayor. U.S. Central Command accused him of *exerting* [read *asserting*] authority he didn't have." "Baghdad 'Mayor' Held," *Chicago Trib.*, 28 Apr. 2003, at 3.

LANGUAGE-CHANGE INDEX
exert misused for *assert*: Stage 1

assertable. So spelled in ordinary contexts—not *assertible* (except in philosophy). See -ABLE (A).

assertedly. See -EDLY.

assertor, not **asserter*, is the usual agent noun corresponding to the verb *assert*. See -ER (A).

Current ratio: 1.2:1

assess. See **access,** vb. (B).

asseverate. See **aver (A).**

assignation. See **assignment.**

*assigner. See **assignor.**

assignment; assignation. *Assignment* = (1) a task or job; (2) the transfer of property; (3) the property so transferred; or (4) the legal document that brings about the transfer.

Assignation = (1) an assignment; (2) a tryst; or (3) an assignee (meaning "one to whom property rights or powers are transferred"). Because *assignation* is a NEEDLESS VARIANT of *assignment* in sense 1 and of *assignee* in sense 3, it should be confined to sense 2, in which it is truly useful <despite precautions, a pregnancy resulted from their middle-of-the-night assignation>. The word is pronounced /a-sig-**nay**-shən/—not /ə-sɪn-**ay**-shən/.

assignor; *assigner. The second has long been said to be the general term, and the first to be the legal spelling (as the correlative of *assignee*). In fact, though, the *-or* spelling has always predominated in all varieties of English. See -ER (A).

assimilable. So spelled—not **assimilatable*. See -ATABLE.

Current ratio: 127:1

assist, n., has come into the language through basketball and ice-hockey lingo <with an assist from her editors>. For now, it remains a CASUALISM.

assist, v.t., is genuinely useful in a few phrases in which *help* simply wouldn't do <assisted reproductive technology> <physician-assisted suicide>. But when *help* suffices, it's the better choice—e.g.:

- "The Trumbull officer . . . could have stopped the chase and *assisted* [read *helped*] the innocent victims of the crash, he said." Michael Remez, "Police Chases," *Hartford Courant*, 9 Dec. 1997, at A1.
- "Arvedson . . . slumped to the ice, where he stayed for about three minutes before being *assisted* [read *helped*] to the locker room." "Salo Makes a Point for Islanders," *Star-Ledger* (Newark), 17 Dec. 1997, Sports §, at 7.

Assist is even worse when it's buried in a phrase such as *be of assistance to* or *provide assistance to*. Once again, try *help* instead—e.g.: "Phone lines opened early this year to *provide assistance to* [read *help*] people in need." Mary Sansom, "Director Seeks Support to Open Tri-County Mission," *Charleston Gaz.*, 18 Jan. 1995, Metro West Kanawha §, at 5. See ZOMBIE NOUNS.

assisted suicide. See **euthanasia (B).**

*associate together is a REDUNDANCY. **Associate together in groups* is even worse. Cf. ***congregate together.**

LANGUAGE-CHANGE INDEX (For the full key, see front matter pp. xxxi, l–li.)
Stage 1: Rejected. **Stage 2:** Widely shunned. **Stage 3:** Widespread but . . . **Stage 4:** Ubiquitous but . . . **Stage 5:** Fully accepted.
Invariably inferior forms marked by asterisk (*). • Ratios represent frequency of prevalent forms vs. variants in current books.

associational; associative. These words are virtual synonyms ("of, relating to, or characterized by association"). *Associative* is now somewhat more common, especially in contexts involving psychology and mathematics <associative memory>. But *associational* also appears with some frequency, especially in legal contexts <associational rights>.

ASSONANCE. See ALLITERATION.

assuage (= to make less painful or severe) is pronounced /ə-**swayj**/—not /ə-**swayzh**/ or (worse) /ə-**swahzh**/.

as such. In this phrase, *such* is a pronoun requiring an antecedent—e.g.:

- "There has been an abundance of English slang from at least the sixteenth century to the present time, but it has always been recognized *as such* [i.e., as slang], and has at no time been supposed to be anything but a minor part of the English language." Sir William Craigie, "Our American English Marches Onward," *N.Y. Times*, 18 Aug. 1935, § 7, at 15.
- "I saw in this a threat to the British way of life, but I saw also that my seeing it *as such* [i.e., as a threat] was nonsense." Anthony Burgess, *A Mouthful of Air* 20 (1992).
- "Jake Coker was the starter even if Saban didn't anoint him *as such*." "Tide Buzz," *Huntsville Times*, 11 Sept. 2015, at B6. (*Starter* is the antecedent of *such*.)
- "We recognize that parents are the ultimate arbiters of their children's education, and *as such*, should be permitted to pull their children out of certain lessons in the curriculum." "Pulling Out Is Not the Answer," *Nat'l Post* (Can.), 11 Sept. 2015, at A8. (*Arbiters* is the antecedent of *such*.)

Sometimes the phrase causes an ambiguity when the referent isn't clear. When that is so, substituting *in principle* or some like phrase is recommended—e.g.: "There could, accordingly, be no grounded objection to the existence of images *as such*." Arthur C. Danto, "Likeness and Presence," *New Republic*, 7 Nov. 1994, at 43. (A possible revision: *There could, accordingly, be no objection in principle to the existence of images*.)

Also, some writers faddishly use *as such* as if it meant "thus" or "therefore"—e.g.: "These efforts represent a fundamental change in the way responsibility is spread throughout the organization, what practices and behaviors are nurtured and rewarded, and how care will be provided in the future. *As such,* [delete phrase] the change will not occur immediately nor easily." Kenneth W. Kizer et al., "The Veterans Healthcare System," *Hosp. & Health Servs. Admin.*, 22 Sept. 1997, at 283. This misuse is perhaps a SLIPSHOD EXTENSION from correct sentences such as the following, in which *icon* is the antecedent of *such*, but the sentence could be misread in such a way that *as such* would mean "therefore": "She will become an icon; *as such*, she will be a role model for years to come." Letter of Ruth W. Junk, "It Can Be OK to Imitate, but Not Deify, Good People," *Pantagraph* (Bloomington, Ill.), 11 Sept. 1997, at A12.

Obviously, this phrase requires much care.

LANGUAGE-CHANGE INDEX
as such for *therefore*: Stage 2

assume; presume. *Assume* means (1) to take upon oneself; to take over duties and responsibilities; or (2) to take for granted or without proof. *Presume* means (1) to take for granted or without proof; or (2) to undertake without permission. So one may *assume* a rank or office or authority by right, but another may *presume* to exercise the privileges of a rank, office, or authority despite a lack of right. *Presume* often carries a sense of arrogance, of going too far in acting without justification—hence the adjective *presumptuous.*

assuming. For *assuming* as an acceptable dangling modifier, see DANGLERS (E).

assumption; presumption. The connotative distinction between these words is that *presumptions* are more strongly inferential and more probably authoritative than mere *assumptions*, which are usually more hypothetical. *Presumptions* may lead to decisions, while *assumptions* typically don't.

Assumptive is pretentious for either *assumed* <assumptive beliefs> or *assuming* or *presumptuous* <an assumptive character>.

As for adverbs, always use the common forms derived from *presume*—that is, *presumably* (= I presume, it is to be presumed) or *presumptively* (= there is a presumption that). Stay away from *assumedly and **assumptively.*

assurance. See **insurance (A).**

assure; ensure; insure. A. *Assure* **for** *ensure.* A person *assures* (makes promises to, convinces) other people <our hosts assured us that we would have comfortable rooms>; a person *ensures* (makes certain) that things occur or that events take place <our hosts ensured that we had comfortable rooms>. To put it a little technically, if the verb is in the active voice, a predicate beginning with *that* should be introduced by the verb *ensure.*

Assure takes a personal object—e.g.: "Davis *assured* residents they can help decide which trees are to be cut." Bruce Schultz, "Cajundome Neighbors Air Problems," *Advocate* (Baton Rouge), 12 Sept. 1997, at B3.

In word frequency since 1900 (when the phrases came into common use), *ensure that* greatly outstrips *assure that. But the discommended usage crops up in other locutions as well—e.g.: "That would defeat the entire purpose of the legislation, which is to *assure* [read *ensure*] public perception of total independence." William Safire, "See-Nothing Congress," *N.Y. Times*, 23 June 1994, at A15. Theodore Bernstein doesn't discuss this point in *The Careful Writer*, but here's a less-than-careful usage: "What good writing can do . . . is to *assure* [read *ensure*] that the writer is really in communication with the reader, that he is delivering his message unmistakably and, perhaps, excellently. When that happens, the reader takes satisfaction in the reading and the writer takes joy in the writing." Theodore M. Bernstein, *The Careful Writer* vii (1965).

The following sentences illustrate the correct use of *ensure*:

- "There used to be an Eastern Idaho Sailing Association with more than 100 people, but the members' independent-minded personalities eventually *ensured* its demise." Paul Menser, "Wadsworth Set Sail into Yachting Business in 1940," *Idaho Falls Post Register*, 24 Mar. 1997, at A9.
- "The suspension of talks until midmorning *ensured* another gridlocked rush-hour throughout the San Francisco Bay area." "Transit Talks Called Off After Marathon Session," *Buffalo News*, 11 Sept. 1997, at A11.
- "The volcano's shieldlike shape *ensures* that the air at the summit is . . . cool and clear." "Hawaii: Under the Volcano," *Economist*, 12 Sept. 2015, at 70.

LANGUAGE-CHANGE INDEX
assure for *ensure*: Stage 3
Current ratio (*to ensure that* vs. **to assure that*): 22:1

B. Insure and ensure. *Insure* is best restricted to financial contexts involving indemnification; it should refer to what insurance companies do. *Ensure* should be used in all other senses of the word. Intransitively, *insure* is commonly followed by the preposition *against* <insure against loss>; it may also be used transitively <insure one's valuables>. Following is a commonplace peccadillo: "'He has an agenda, but with Clinton, he's reached the top and is going to *insure* [read *ensure*] that he serves his master,' says an observer." "The Young Master of the White House," *Time*, 4 Apr. 1994, at 25.

LANGUAGE-CHANGE INDEX
insure for *ensure*: Stage 3
Current ratio (*ensure that* vs. *insure that*): 37:1

C. Corresponding Nouns. See **insurance (A).**

assurer; *assuror.* The *-er* spelling, which has predominated since the late 19th century, is standard. See -ER (A).

Current ratio: 90:1

-ASTER. See DIMINUTIVES (A).

asterisk /**as**-tə-risk/. The mispronunciation of this word, as if it had no second *-s-*, is well known. (See PRONUNCIATION (B).) Not so well known are the resulting misspellings of the word. The most common one is **asterick*—e.g.:

- "Speaking of Khannouchi, when he and Belgian Eddy Hellebuyck become U.S. citizens this fall, will the critics of American distance running put *astericks* [read *asterisks*] next to their performances . . . ?" Steve Nearman, "Chicago, New York Battle for Top Marathon Runners," *Wash. Times*, 9 Aug. 1998, at C8.
- "Entries marked with the *asterick* [read *asterisk*] (*) did not run in the Sebastian River edition." "Crimewatch," *Fla. Today*, 4 May 1999, at B4.

- "*Astericks* [read *Asterisks*] appear for schools that are new and did not have test results from last year." "Reading the Charts," *San Diego Union-Trib.*, 28 July 1999, at A20.

Another misspelling, **asterik*, is nearly as common— e.g.: "The most memorable score in the 80-year history of the NFL—Chicago 73, Washington 0 in the 1940 championship game—always has deserved an exclamation point. Now it has got an *asterik* [read *asterisk*]." Bob Broeg, "59 Years Later, Baugh Casts Doubt on Bears' Rout," *St. Louis Post-Dispatch*, 5 Dec. 1999, at D1.

LANGUAGE-CHANGE INDEX
1. **asterick* for *asterisk*: Stage 1
Current ratio (*asterisk* vs. **asterick*): 1,347:1
2. *asterisk* pronounced like **asterick*: Stage 2

as . . . than. See **as . . . as (E).**

as the case may be. See **case (A).**

asthma /**az**-mə/. The *-th-* is silent.

as though. See **as if.**

astigmatism (= an uneven curvature of the cornea; a defect in a lens) is often incorrectly written (and pronounced) *stigmatism*—which, according to the *OED*, is actually a rare antonym of *astigmatism*. Sometimes the word is mistaken for a singular count noun (**a stigmatism* instead of *astigmatism*), as in the second and third examples below—e.g.:

- "Singh, the 1983 and 1995 Buick winner, had laser eye surgery last week to correct slight *stigmatism* [read *astigmatism*] and nearsightedness." John Nicholson, "Major Preparation Makes Tiger Woods Pass on Buick Open," *Nat'l Post*, 8 June 2000, at B15.
- "He has tried contacts, too, but that didn't work out, primarily due to *a stigmatism* [read *astigmatism*] on his right eye." Tim Buckley, "Polynice Eyes Better Shooting," *Deseret News* (Salt Lake City), 5 Oct. 2000, at D1.
- "One son was in special education classes, the mom was suffering from *a stigmatism* [read *astigmatism*], another son was juggling college and work to help support the family." Piper Nichole, *The For Sale by Owner Handbook* 223 (2005).

For further misuse of *stigmatism*, see **stigma (B).**

LANGUAGE-CHANGE INDEX
**a stigmatism* for *astigmatism*: Stage 1

as to. A. Defensible Uses. First, it must be said that *as to* is an all-purpose preposition to be avoided whenever a more specific preposition will do. But *as to* isn't always indefensible. The phrase is most justifiable when introducing something previously mentioned only cursorily: "*As to* concerns the fair might lose on-track business if it offered its signal to the OTBs, [Dun said]: 'I figured we were going to lose the handle either way.'" Jay Burns, "Farmington Takes Step Forward, Using OTB for New Revenue," *Portland Press Herald*, 7 Sept. 1997, at D8. In beginning sentences this way, *as to* is equivalent to the more colloquial *as for*. In effect,

LANGUAGE-CHANGE INDEX (For the full key, see front matter pp. xxxi, l–li.)
Stage 1: Rejected. **Stage 2:** Widely shunned. **Stage 3:** Widespread but . . . **Stage 4:** Ubiquitous but . . . **Stage 5:** Fully accepted.
Invariably inferior forms marked by asterisk (*). • Ratios represent frequency of prevalent forms vs. variants in current books.

the phrase is a passable shorthand form of *regarding, with regard to,* or *on the question of.*

The phrase is also (minimally) defensible when used for *about,* but that word is stylistically preferable in most contexts. *As to* smells of JARGON—e.g.:

- "The bill carries no presumptions *as to* [read *about*] the effect of incorporation." "Citizens and Swift Creek," *News & Observer* (Raleigh), 17 Mar. 1997, at A9.
- "Reasonable people may disagree *as to* [read *about*] the importance of the school system's efforts to prevent and detect thefts in the schools." Roy D. Nichols Jr., "Searches at Granby Are 'Reasonable,'" *Virginian-Pilot & Ledger Star* (Norfolk), 6 Sept. 1997, at B8.

B. Poor Uses. The main problem with *as to* is that it doesn't clearly establish syntactic or conceptual relationships, so it can hamper comprehensibility. In each of the following examples, another preposition would more directly and forcefully express the thought:

- For *about*: "There's no rule *as to* [read *about*] how long you have to wait before you can enjoy your creation." Dan Macdonald, "At-Home Winemaking," *Fla. Times-Union,* 14 Aug. 1997, at E6.
- For *on*: "It is always possible that your neighbor is not aware of how disturbing his or her behavior is and that he or she can be more sensitive to your concerns, or you can agree *as to* [read *on*] certain time *parameters* [read *limits*] or (if music is the culprit) what is an acceptable volume level." Robert Griswold et al., "What to Do When Noise Becomes Intolerable," *San Diego Union-Trib.,* 24 Aug. 1997, at H6. (On the use of *parameters* in the second example, see **parameters.**)
- For *of*: "The same is true *as to* [read *of*] other cases finding for leaders by applying the regulation." Robert P. Simons, "Environmental Lender Liability Rule Vacated," *Bankr. Ct. Decisions,* 24 Mar. 1994, at 11.
- For *for*: "There is no change in the prior IRA rules with regard to an individual's participation in other qualifying retirement plans. *As such* [read *Therefore*], the rules remain the same *as to* [read *for*] the maximum amount of adjusted gross income a taxpayer can have before the IRA deduction begins to phase out." George W. Smith III, "New Law Offers Businesses, Workers Retirement Options," *Gaz. Telegraph* (Colo. Springs), 12 Mar. 1997, at D1. (On the use of *as such* in that sentence, see **as such.**)
- For *by* or *at*: "Some people are a little surprised *as to* [read *by* or *at*] how quickly Veniard has gotten to his present level." Peter Zellen, "Bolles Grad Proves He Can Pitch in Pros," *Fla. Times-Union,* 28 June 1997, at 9.
- For *into*: "During a trip to the Mars Pathfinder Mission Control Center in Pasadena this summer, House Aeronautics and Space Subcommittee member Sheila Jackson-Lee, D-Texas, inquired *as to* [read *into*] whether the Pathfinder Mission had taken pictures of the American flag planted by Neil Armstrong in 1969." Leah Garchik, "Getting There," *S.F. Chron.,* 15 Sept. 1997, at E10. (Another wording, *asked whether,* would work even better in that sentence.)
- Superfluous: "Another equally important question is *as to* [delete *as to*] whether technical efficiency improvements due to economic reforms for each province over the periods were statistically important." K.P. Kalirajan Shiji Zhao, "Did the Technical Efficiency of State Enterprises Improve with the Same Speed in All Provinces of China?" *Applied Econ.,* 1 Mar. 1997, at 269. / "With the season down to a dozen games, it's an open question *as to* [delete

as to] whether Sele would have been placed at risk if he'd been asked to throw a couple of dozen more pitches." Gordon Edes, "Red Sox Called Out," *Boston Globe,* 17 Sept. 1997, at D3. See **question whether** & **whether (B).**

as was. See **as is.**

as well. When used at the beginning of a sentence, this phrase has traditionally been considered poor usage. But in Canada it's standard as an equivalent of *Also, . . .* or *In addition, ...* Each of the following examples comes from a Canadian publication. In AmE they would be edited as shown in the brackets:

- "*As well,* [read *And*] people would have to work longer to qualify for UI [unemployment insurance]." Derek Ferguson, "'Attack' on Jobless Riles Labor Chief," *Toronto Star,* 16 Apr. 1996, at A5.
- "*As well* [read *Also*], people can place a sticker announcing their donor consent on their driver's license at the time of renewal or on their Care Card." Pamela Fayerman, "$250,000 TV Ad Blitz Aims to Get More People Donating Organs," *Vancouver Sun,* 22 Apr. 1997, at B4.
- "*As well,* [read *And*] many of today's workers are stashing money in RRSPs, an estimated $6.5 billion this year alone." Mary Janigan, "Making the Middle Class Pay," *Maclean's,* 29 Sept. 1997, at 42.

LANGUAGE-CHANGE INDEX
as well as a sentence-starter (outside Canada): Stage 2
Current ratio (capitalized *Also* vs.
capitalized *As well*): 15:1

as well as. See SUBJECT–VERB AGREEMENT (E).

as well as or better than; *as well or better than. Some writers—a slight majority even, judging from the evidence of big data—illogically leave out *as* after *well*—e.g.:

- "Women would write in detail why they were working *as well or better than* [read *as well as or better than*] their male counterparts." Simon Hoggart, "All Present and Incorrect," *Observer Sunday,* 15 Dec. 1991, at 37, 38.
- "The second worry is whether Tennes can do *as well or better than* [read *as well as or better than*] the model." Robert Barker, "A New Fund Rides the Big Mo," *Bus. Week,* 1 July 2002, at 134.

Cf. **as good as or better than** & **as much as or more than.** See CANNIBALISM & ILLOGIC (B).

LANGUAGE-CHANGE INDEX
*as well or better than for
as well as or better than: Stage 3

*as yet; *as of yet. These are both invariably inferior to *yet* alone, *still, thus far,* or some other equivalent—e.g.:

- "Seven years ago, a woman, *not as yet* [read *not yet*] identified, died in a stream in Monroe, Clarion County." "Probe of 1990 Death Goes On," *Pitt. Post-Gaz.,* 25 July 1997, at B3.
- "From the American point of view, at least, there are *as yet* [read *still,* or simply delete *as yet*] relatively few signs that a worrisome deflation cycle is dawning." Tom Petruno, "Could Deflation Be the Next Bogeyman to Threaten the U.S. Economy?" *Buffalo News,* 25 Aug. 1997, at C2.
- "There are no plans *as yet* [read *yet*] to develop major Java products." Richard Evans, "Going Soft?" *Barron's,* 15 Sept. 1997, at 33.

As of yet is a vulgarism. Cf. **as of** (B) & ***but yet.***

LANGUAGE-CHANGE INDEX
1. **As yet* for *yet*: Stage 3
Current ratio (*not yet* vs. **not as yet*): 38:1
2. **as of yet* for *yet*: Stage 2
Current ratio (*not yet* vs. **not as of yet*): 5,415:1

-**ATABLE** does not generally appear other than in *-able* adjectives derived from two-syllable verbs (e.g., *create, vacate*). It does so in those cases because the *-able* adjectives would be unrecognizable. H.W. Fowler notes some long exceptions to the general rule (*inculcatable, inculpatable, incubatable*), and states his standard: "The practice should be to use *-atable* where the shorter form is felt to be out of the question" (*FMEU1* at 36). Other examples with which the shorter form is impracticable are *anticipatable, translatable,* and *infiltratable* (so that *infiltrable* not be thought to be derived from *infilter* [= to sift or filter in] rather than from *infiltrate*).

The following words, which occur with some frequency, are better than the *-atable* forms:

abbreviable	confiscable	manipulable
abdicable	corroborable	medicable
abrogable	cultivable	navigable
accommodable	delegable	obligable
accumulable	delineable	obviable
activable	demonstrable	operable
administrable	detonable	originable
adulterable	differentiable	participable
affiliable	eradicable	penetrable
aggregable	evacuable	perpetrable
agitable	evaluable	perpetuable
alienable	expropriable	predicable
alleviable	generable	propagable
allocable	indicable	regulable
ameliorable	inebriable	replicable
annihilable	inextirpable	repudiable
appreciable	inextricable	segregable
appropriable	infatuable	separable
arbitrable	infuriable	subjugable
articulable	invalidable	terminable
calculable	investigable	vindicable
communicable	isolable	violable
compensable	litigable	vitiable

At least one pair distinguished by the two suffixes has undergone DIFFERENTIATION. *Estimable* = worthy of esteem; *estimatable* = capable of being estimated.

at about. See **about** (D).

at all events. See **in any event.**

at arm's length. See **arm's-length.**

at fault; in fault. Today, *at fault* is commonly used in the sense "responsible for a wrong committed; blameworthy" <in a divorce, it's of little value to try to determine which spouse is more at fault>. An American critic once wrote that "hunting dogs [that] lose the scent are said to be *at fault*. Hence the phrase means perplexed, puzzled." He added that *in fault* means "in error, mistaken," with this example: "No certified public accountant should be *in fault*." Clarence Stratton, *Handbook of English* 24, 158 (1940). The phrase is virtually never used for *perplexed* or *puzzled* anymore. The phrase *at fault* is seven times as common in modern print sources as *in fault*.

atheist; agnostic; unbeliever; nonbeliever; freethinker. These terms denote different levels of religious skepticism. An *atheist* denies the existence of God altogether. An *agnostic* thinks a person cannot know for sure—in other words, God's existence cannot be proved or disproved. An *unbeliever* or *nonbeliever* might believe in God but not in a particular religion. Finally, a *freethinker* might belong to a particular religion but refuse to accept that religion's dogmas as incompatible with reason. See **disbelief.**

athlete has two syllables (/**ath**-leet/), not three (/**ath**-ə-leet/). See PRONUNCIATION (B). Cf. -ATHLON.

LANGUAGE-CHANGE INDEX
athlete pronounced with three syllables: Stage 2

-**ATHLON.** This suffix, from the Greek word for "contest," has two syllables. Avoid adding an *-a-* when spelling it and slipping in an epenthetic schwa when pronouncing it. For example, *triathlon* (an athletic contest featuring swimming, running, and bicycle races) is pronounced /trɪ-**ath**-lahn/, not /trɪ-**ath**-ə-lahn/. Likewise with *pentathlon* (swimming, running, steeplechase, fencing, and shooting) and *decathlon* (three races of varying distances plus high hurdles and six field events). See PRONUNCIATION (B). Cf. **athlete.**

ATM machine. For this redundant initialism, see ABBREVIATIONS (B).

atomic; atom, adj. These words should generally be confined to their natural parts of speech: *atomic* as an adjective and *atom* as a noun. But *atom* is sometimes used adjectivally, especially in the phrase *atom bomb.*

Current ratio (*atomic bomb* vs. *atom bomb*): 5:1

at present. See **at the present time.**

atrium. Pl. *atria* (predominant in World English) or *atriums* (which has made slight inroads since the mid-1970s). See PLURALS (B).

Current ratio: 17:1

*****attached hereto.** This phrase, symptomatic of COMMERCIALESE and LEGALESE, is normally redundant. Delete *hereto.*

attain; obtain. These two—both FORMAL WORDS—are sometimes confused. *Attain* = to achieve, accomplish

LANGUAGE-CHANGE INDEX (For the full key, see front matter pp. xxxi, l–li.)
Stage 1: Rejected. **Stage 2:** Widely shunned. **Stage 3:** Widespread but . . . **Stage 4:** Ubiquitous but . . . **Stage 5:** Fully accepted.
Invariably inferior forms marked by asterisk (*). • Ratios represent frequency of prevalent forms vs. variants in current books.

<she put extraordinary effort into attaining that goal>. *Obtain* = (1) to get, acquire <obtain a license>; or (2) to apply; be prevalent <several unusual customs obtain in that village>.

Attain, in another sense, is also a FORMAL WORD for "to reach (an age)." It's often simplifiable—e.g.: "Under prior law, if neither you nor your wife had *attained* [read *reached*] the age of 55 before you sold your house, the amount by which the adjusted sale price of your old house exceeded the purchase price of your new house would have been subject to the federal income tax." Walter Bithell, "New Tax Laws Will Help Parents Afford High Costs of College," *Idaho Statesman*, 31 Aug. 1997, at E4.

Occasionally—as a MALAPROPISM—*obtain* is misused for *attain*. E.g.: "The same exception . . . applies if U.S. residency or citizenship is renounced before *obtaining* [read *attaining*] age 18." Don W. Llewellyn, "Income and Transfer Tax Planning for Nonresident Aliens Holding or Disposing of U.S. Investment Assets," *Tax Mgmt. Int'l J.*, 11 Oct. 1996, at 643.

LANGUAGE-CHANGE INDEX
obtain misused for *attain*: Stage 1
Current ratio (*attaining the age of* vs.
obtaining the age of): 228:1

attempt. For phrasing such as *was attempted to be done*, see PASSIVE VOICE (B).

attend. See **tend.**

*****attendee.** See -EE.

at the back of. See **back of.**

at the present time; at this moment in time; at this time; at present. These are inferior to *now, nowadays, today*, or *currently*. On the poor use of *presently* in this sense, see **presently.** See also **at this time.**

at the time (that); at the time (when). These phrases are almost invariably verbose for *when*. An exception occurs when another *when*-clause is nearby <at the time it happened, when the moon had not yet risen, nobody was on the beach>.

at this juncture. See **juncture.**

at this moment in time. See **at the present time.**

at this time. This phrase often smacks of waffling OFFICIALESE, especially when the phrase comes at a SENTENCE END—e.g.: " 'We don't have any comments *at this time*,' said Disney spokesman Ken Green. . . . 'Our revenues and profits are record-setting *at this time*,' Mr. Green said." Christine Wicker, "Giant Against Giant," *Dallas Morning News*, 14 June 1997, at G1. The more natural wording would be something like this: *We don't have any comments right now. Our revenues and profits are currently setting records.* Worse, of course, is *at this point in time*. See **at the present time.**

attorney. See **lawyer.**

attorney general. Pl. *attorneys general* (both AmE and BrE)—though *attorney-generals* occurs also in BrE. See PLURALS (G) & POSTPOSITIVE ADJECTIVES.

Current ratio: 58:1

attribute, n.; **attribution.** An *attribution* (/a-trə-**byoo**-shən/) is the act or an instance of ascribing a characteristic, quality, or source. An *attribute* (/a-trə-byoot/) is a characteristic or quality so ascribed.

attribute, v.t. (= to credit [something] as resulting from a specified cause; to ascribe), is sometimes confused with *contribute* (= to play a significant part in producing something). The blunder is especially common among sportswriters—e.g.:

- "The Buccaneers made 22 percent of their shots in the first half and had 17 turnovers at halftime. Most of that can be *contributed* [read *attributed*] to Kansas' defense." Shannon Rose, "Kansas Freshman Pierce Scores 30 Points in Rout," *Kansas City Star*, 5 Jan. 1996, at D1.
- "Most of the Broncos' troubles this year can be *contributed* [read *attributed*] to their defense." Bert Sahlberg, "Flush with Inspiration," *Lewiston Morning Trib.* (Idaho), 23 Nov. 1996, at B1.

See MALAPROPISMS. For a brief comment on the misuse of *accredit* for *attribute*, see **accredit.**

The verb is pronounced /ə-**tri**-byoot/.

LANGUAGE-CHANGE INDEX
contribute misused for *attribute*: Stage 1

attribution. See **attribute,** n.

attributive is the standard term. *Attributory* is a variant form.

Current ratio: 461:1

at which time is a phrase that can almost always be improved, either by substituting *when* or by reworking the sentence—e.g.:

- "The letter says patients reported the incidents on April 16, *at which time* Luster was placed on administrative leave from his psychiatric technician position before he was fired [the next month]." Tammie Smith, "Mental Health Workers Fired After Sex Claims," *Tennessean*, 7 Aug. 1997, at B1. (A possible revision: *The letter says that when patients reported the incidents on April 16, Luster was placed on administrative leave from his position as psychiatric technician. The following month, he was fired.*)
- "Lester operated the company until he was 84 years old, *at which time* [read *when*], on January 1, 1979, he sold the business to Space Center, Inc. of St. Paul." "Robert R. Lester" (obit.), *Kansas City Star*, 14 Sept. 1997, at B9.
- "The lasers trained on the sails help push it to a transition point, *at which time* the craft essentially coasts all the way to the next star." Nick Wilson, "Cal Poly Professor Gets Grant to Build Interstellar Spacecraft," *Trib.* (San Luis Obispo, Cal.), 11 Sept. 2015, Local News §. (A possible revision: *The lasers trained on the sails help push it to a transition point; from there the craft essentially coasts all the way to the next star.*)

atypical; *untypical. *Atypical* has been the standard term since the late 19th century. (Before that time, neither term was common.) *Untypical* is a variant form.

Current ratio: 18:1

*auctorial. See authorial.

auditorium. Pl. *auditoriums*—preferably not *auditoria. See PLURALS (B).

Current ratio: 4:1

au fond. See *à fond*.

auger. See augur (A).

aught. A. Generally. *Aught* (= [1] anything; or [2] all) is an ARCHAISM in rapid decline. Today it is generally restricted to BrE—e.g.: "For *aught* I see they adjust themselves to their stations with all proper humility." Fintan O'Toole, "Race Issue Reflects Shameful Double Standards," *Irish Times*, 30 May 1997, at 14. In legal contexts, however, the term sometimes surfaces in the phrase *for aught that appears*.

B. For *nought*. By error, *a nought* (= a zero) was widely misconstrued as *an aught*. Thus, *aught* has come—mistakenly—to bear the sense "zero." One explanation from folk etymology (see ETYMOLOGY (D)) is that, among graduating seniors in 1900, the class of *nought-nought* sounded too negative; the class of *oh-oh* sounded too accident-prone; and the class of *zero-zero* sounded like a bunch of losers. So it became *aught-aught*. E.g.:

- "At the grass roots, a new organization, the National Alumni Forum, is urging its troops to withhold checks from alma mater until she bends her intellectual agenda to terms more favorable to the class of *aught* nine." Rick Perlstein, "Professional Correctness: Literary Studies and Political Change," *Nation*, 18 Dec. 1995, at 792.
- "Some old-timers say at the turn of the century, high school graduates were the class of double '*aught*.'" Rebecca Simmons, "The Class of '00 or 2000: What's It Going to Be?" *Knoxville News-Sentinel*, 10 Nov. 1996, at E1.
- "Twenty *aught* six . . . isn't that how they said it a century ago?" Jeff Metcalfe, "Class of '86," *Ariz. Republic*, 29 Dec. 1996, at F1.

These uses, to the American ear, sound either self-consciously old-fashioned or very British. The American way of saying 2006 is not "twenty aught six" but "twenty oh six" or "two thousand six." For more on *nought*, see **naught**.

LANGUAGE-CHANGE INDEX
aught in the sense of *nought*: Stage 5

C. Misused for *ought*. Occasionally, *aught* displaces *ought* (= should)—e.g.: "Maradona and Cantona *aught* [read *ought*] to show humility for their failure to live up to superstardom." Rob Hughes, "Maradona's Union," *Int'l Herald Trib.*, 20 Sept. 1995, at 21. Cf. **naught**.

LANGUAGE-CHANGE INDEX
aught misused for *ought*: Stage 1

au gratin (= sprinkled with breadcrumbs or grated cheese before being browned) is pronounced /oh **graht**-ən/ or /oh **grat**-ən/ in AmE. Avoid /aw/ in the first syllable. In BrE, the quasi-French pronunciation /oh grə-**tan**/ is common.

augur, n. & vb. A. And *auger*, n. & vb. These are very different words with similar spellings. They are pronounced identically: /**aw**-gər/. The more common one is *augur*. As a noun, it refers to a soothsayer or fortune-teller—e.g.: "[In ancient Rome], a man called an *augur* was said to be able to tell the future by observing the flight of birds." "No Ducks, No Glory," *Wash. Post*, 18 Jan. 2001, at C13. The word appears in Deuteronomy (18:10–12, NRSV): "one who practices divination, or is a soothsayer, or an *augur*, or a sorcerer, or one who casts spells." As a verb, *augur* means to forebode or presage—most commonly in phrases similar to those in which *bode* appears <augurs well> <augurs ill>. E.g.: "No theatrical spectacle could have been more majestic. It was poignant, it was glorious. And it *augured* war." Carolly Erickson, *Alexandra: The Last Tsarina* 219 (2001).

Auger refers to a tool with a center shaft and a helical flange, used for boring holes or for moving loose material—e.g.: "His machine roughs up the ice with an *auger*, squirts warm water over the ice and then squeegees that water to leave a smooth-as-glass surface behind the Zamboni." Nancy Lofholm, "Tres Slick: Zamboni in No-Rink Town," *Denver Post*, 2 Feb. 2001, at A1. The word also refers to a drill-like tool that rotates to gradually release particles of material such as animal feed—e.g.: "A computer-controlled system monitors temperatures and an *auger* feeds pellets into the furnace as needed." John Spears, "Put Another Blade of Grass on the Fire, Dear," *Toronto Star*, 7 Jan. 2001, at WB5. As a verb, it means to use such a tool. E.g.: "Durst . . . steered his six-rowhead Case 2166 combine through the fields and *augered* corn into a wagon driven by his father." Clare Howard, "Watching His Harvest," *Peoria J. Star*, 30 Sept. 2000, at A1.

Not surprisingly, some writers confuse the two words. Most commonly, *auger* is misused for *augur*—e.g.:

- "The highly partisan vote to begin open-ended impeachment proceedings against President Bill Clinton *augers* [read *augurs*] ill for the United States and for the world that depends upon its stability and leadership." "Partisan Impeachment Vote," *Ariz. Daily Star*, 10 Oct. 1998, at A18.
- "The dearth of rainfall that pervades virtually all of the Midlands *augered* [read *augured*] against pheasants and other game birds in several deadly ways." Charlie Meyers, "Tough Times Are Ahead for Pheasant Hunters," *Denver Post*, 23 July 2000, at C3. (Note also the clashing words in *dearth of rainfall that pervades*.)
- "Sens. John McCain (R-Ariz.) and Russell D. Feingold (D-Wis.) said that the skyrocketing election spending and new Senate allies *auger* [read *augur*] well for at least a ban on soft money." Alan C. Miller & T. Christian Miller, "America Waits," *L.A. Times*, 8 Dec. 2000, at A1.

LANGUAGE-CHANGE INDEX (For the full key, see front matter pp. xxxi, l–li.)
Stage 1: Rejected. **Stage 2:** Widely shunned. **Stage 3:** Widespread but . . . **Stage 4:** Ubiquitous but . . . **Stage 5:** Fully accepted.
Invariably inferior forms marked by asterisk (*). • Ratios represent frequency of prevalent forms vs. variants in current books.

And the reverse error sometimes occurs, especially with the noun (*augur* being misused for *auger*)—e.g.: "Chesapeake Fire Chief R. Stephen Best said most of the barrels recovered were found in one location, near the spot where an *augur* [read *auger*] drilled into a buried drum last fall during excavations." Robert McCabe, "Officials Find More Waste on City Land," *Virginian-Pilot* (Norfolk), 31 Jan. 2001, at B1.

LANGUAGE-CHANGE INDEX
1. *auger* misused for *augur*: Stage 1
2. *augur* misused for *auger*: Stage 1

B. And *augury*, n. An *augury* is an omen, portent, or indication of the future; or it can refer to the art of reading omens and the like. *Augur* is to *augury* as *soothsayer* is to *omen*—e.g.:

- "The results were invigorating and fearless, an exciting *augury* for the performances still to come." Joshua Kosman, "S.F. Symphony Gets Stravinsky 'Rite,'" *S.F. Chron.*, 14 June 1999, at E1.
- "Unfortunately for Bush, the *auguries* are disquieting: A recession and a fall in the stock market are both overdue." John O'Sullivan, "Profiting from Recession," *Chicago Sun-Times*, 26 Dec. 2000, at 33.

The word appears much more commonly in BrE than in AmE. But writers commonly misuse *augur* for *augury*—e.g.:

- "In what may be an *augur* [read *augury*] of coming events, soon after the ECAR meeting closed Enron Power Marketing pulled its offers to sell power." "The Heat Is On," *Retail Servs. Rep.*, 31 Mar. 2000, at 17.
- "This time the blood stayed dry, and many interpreted it as an *augur* [read *augury*] of misfortune." John L. Allen Jr., "Cardinal's Acquittal Met with Cynicism," *Nat'l Catholic Rptr.*, 5 Jan. 2001, at 28.

LANGUAGE-CHANGE INDEX
augur misused for *augury*: Stage 1

au jus. This phrase—in French, "with the juice"—is traditionally a POSTPOSITIVE ADJECTIVE meaning "(of a meat) served with its natural juice" <steak au jus>. But it has gradually been corrupted into a noun form <served with au jus> and then an attributive adjective <au jus sauce>—e.g.:

- "We had to ask the waitress to take the plate back, and to return it with horseradish sauce instead of the *au jus*." Robert Tolf, "Chuck's Still Cookin' After All These Years," *Sun-Sentinel* (Ft. Lauderdale), 27 Sept. 1996, Showtime §, at 39.
- "Evans uses beer in everything from *au jus sauce* to dessert." "Hops, Grains, and Earthy Flavors to Food," *Bulletin* (Bend, Or.), 17 Dec. 1996, at E1.

These uses are so well ensconced in culinary talk that there seems little hope of ousting them.

To make matters worse, the phrase is typically pronounced /oh **zhoos**/ or even /oh **joos**/ instead of the more nearly correct /oh **zhoo**/.

LANGUAGE-CHANGE INDEX
1. *au jus* as a noun: Stage 4
2. *au jus sauce*: Stage 3
3. *au jus* mispronounced /oh-**joos**/ or /oh-**zhoos**/: Stage 3

aunt (= the sister of one's mother or father) is predominantly pronounced /ant/ in AmE, though the BrE pronunciation /ahnt/ is also common in New England and Virginia.

aural; oral. *Aural* = of, relating to, or involving the ears or hearing. *Oral* = of, relating to, or involving the mouth or speaking. The words present little problem in their written form; they're most confusing when given orally and received aurally.

In the early 1960s, when "the pill" was introduced as the first oral contraceptive, some women reportedly mistook *oral* for *aural* and stuffed pills into their ears. See Jacki Wullschlager, "When Family Planning Met the Joy of Sex," *Fin. Times*, 2–3 June 2001, FT Weekend §, at v.

aureole; aureola. See **areola.**

auspices. *Under the auspices* /**aw**-spi-siz/ means "with the sponsorship or support of"—e.g.: "Hugo Boss has developed an art library *under the auspices* of the Guggenheim." Carol Vogel, "Inside Art," *N.Y. Times*, 7 Feb. 1997, at C28. But the phrase is frequently misconstrued as meaning "in accordance with" or "by means of"—e.g.:

- "A red light still burns outside the building as a reminder of its past, and each guest is furnished with a copy of Madame Bailey's city license issued in 1857 *under the auspices of* [read *in accordance with* or *under*] the 'ordinance concerning lewd and abandoned women.'" Jack Biesterfeld, "French Quarter a Rich Gumbo in Itself," *Record* (N.J.), 29 May 1994, Travel §, at T9.
- "*Under the auspices of* [read *With the help of*] new telemarketing rules, the Federal Trade Commission is cracking down on deceptive credit repair services for misleading advertising." "Today's News," *Am. Banker*, 29 Mar. 1996, at 1.
- "Quickly, it was moved and seconded that a name change be ordered *under the auspices of* [read *in accordance with*] Robert's Rules." Ron Schara, "Swamp Hunters Convene for Another Season of Grouse," *Star Trib.* (Minneapolis), 20 Oct. 1996, at C18.

See **aegis.**

LANGUAGE-CHANGE INDEX
under the auspices of misused for *in accordance with*: Stage 1

autarchy; autarky. Although some dictionaries treat these words as variants, they stem from different roots and should be distinguished. *Autarchy* = absolute rule or sovereignty; autocracy. *Autarky* = national economic self-sufficiency; isolationism. In the mid-1960s, *autarky* overtook *autarchy* in frequency of use.

authentic; genuine. Today the words are interchangeable in most sentences, but a couple of distinctions do exist. First, *authentic* is off-target when the sense is "substantial"—e.g.: "No cinema owner has ever lacked for customers with a Woody Allen film. Allen enjoys demi-god status with the intelligentsia but his films are also *authentic* [read *real* or *genuine*] crowd-pleasers, with many first-run titles playing for the better part of a year." Lisa Nesselson, "Obscure Helmers Have Gaul," *Variety*, 26 Aug. 2002, Deauville Film Fest. Supp., at 26. Second, *authentic* is an awkward choice when the sense is "sincere"—e.g.: ". . . the stirring color photographs of women and children in liberated Afghanistan, those huge, *authentic* [read *sincere* or *genuine*] smiles from human beings who have been rescued from misogynous thugs." George Vecsey, "Knicks Face One Rivalry at a Time," *N.Y. Times*, 16 Nov. 2001, at S1. Cf. **bona fide.**

The *OED* notes that late-18th-century theologians tried to differentiate the words, arguing that a book is *authentic* if its content is accurate, and *genuine* if it is correctly attributed to the writer. The point, weak as it was to begin with, has been preserved in some later usage guides.

authentication, so spelled, is occasionally misrendered **authentification*—e.g.:

- "Data encryption, one-time password generators, 'firewalls' and a user-*authentification* [read -*authentication*] system called Kerberos are all cited as effective ways to decrease the risk of password theft." Peter H. Lewis, "How to Keep Bandits from 'Snarfing' Your Passwords," *N.Y. Times*, 13 Feb. 1994, § 3, at 9.
- "Open Market software allows businesses to process Internet orders made with credit cards, conduct on-line customer service, order management, *authentification* [read *authentication*] and record keeping." Jon Auerbach, "Open Market Reportedly Wins Pack with AT&T," *Boston Globe*, 5 Oct. 1996, at F1.
- "When it comes to *authentification* [read *authentication*] of a high-five, there are two frequently cited sources." Jeff Strickler, "Give Her a Hand," *Star Trib.* (Minneapolis), 21 Apr. 2015, at E1.

LANGUAGE-CHANGE INDEX
*authentification for *authentication*: Stage 1
Current ratio: 394:1

author, n. On the use of this word in place of *I*, see FIRST PERSON.

author, v.t. **A. Status.** Since the mid-20th century, *author* has been rapidly becoming standard as a verb, though many writers still avoid it when they can. Generally it's a mildly turgid substitute for *write*, *compose*, or *create*—e.g.:

- "Dougherty now represents some of the country's top archery firms, serves as a consultant, and also stays very busy *authoring* [read *writing*] books and articles about bowhunting." Sam Powell, "Tulsa's Dougherty Is Due Induction into National Archery Hall of Fame," *Tulsa Trib. & Tulsa World*, 22 Dec. 1996, at B15.
- "She has lectured throughout the world, and *authored* [read *written*] articles in the press and in scholarly journals." "Chemistry Expert to Address Meeting," *Peoria J. Star*, 6 Feb. 1997, at B5.
- "'Humanized' stems from the work of [Aza] Raskin's late father, Jef Raskin, who created the vision for the Macintosh computer and *authored* [read *wrote*] the book 'The

Humane Interface.'" Ann Meyer, "A Simpler Approach to Computers," *Chicago Trib.*, 12 Feb. 2007, Bus. §, at 3.

Some journalists and lawmakers have taken to using *author* in reference to a politician who sponsors legislation. This seems irresponsible, given that few legislators today actually write the bills they promote. E.g.:

- "Abzug co-founded the National Women's Political Caucus in 1971, and *authored* [read *sponsored*] numerous bills intended to prevent sex discrimination." Stephanie Balzer, "Days of Speaking Softly Past, Says Abzug," *Bus. J.—Phoenix*, 28 Feb. 1997.
- "He also *authored* [read *sponsored*] the state's adoption law." Tracy Jordan, "Politician Will End His 17-Year Hiatus," *Morning Call* (Allentown, Pa.), 11 Mar. 1997, at B1.
- "Some did so out of solidarity over a procedural dispute with their partisan colleagues in the Senate—despite the fact that the resolution was *authored* [read *sponsored*] by John Warner, a Republican." Steve Kornacki, "Republican Senators Deepen a Hole for 2008," *N.Y. Observer*, 12 Feb. 2007, Opinions §, at 5.

Coauthor has been considered more acceptable as a verb, perhaps because *cowrite* seems deadpan. Yet *cowrite* and *cowriter* are often used in scriptwriting circles. See FUNCTIONAL SHIFT (D).

LANGUAGE-CHANGE INDEX
1. *author* for *write*: Stage 3
2. *coauthor* for *cowrite*: Stage 5

B. Origin. H.L. Mencken explained the origin of the modern usage in this way: "*To author* . . . arose on the movie lots to designate the preparation of a script. To say that a given author *writes* a given script may be inaccurate, for a great deal goes into it besides the mere writing of its text, and sometimes the text is the least part of it. So *to author* was born—and now, as new verbs have a way of doing, it has begun to displace *to write* in situations where *to write* would be quite as accurate and a great deal less slobbergomptious." H.L. Mencken, "The Birth of New Verbs," in *Aspects of American English* 92, 96 (Elizabeth M. Kerr & Ralph M. Aderman eds., 1963). The *OED*'s treatment of the verb suggests that this account is accurate. It is true, however, that there was an earlier period (ca. 1575–1650) when the verb was used in the sense "to cause" or "to declare."

authoress. See SEXISM (D).

authorial; *auctorial. The latter is a stuffy NEEDLESS VARIANT of the former.

Current ratio: 149:1

authority. For an interesting misusage, see **autonomy.**

autocracy. See GOVERNMENTAL FORMS.

autoeroticism; *autoerotism. Although most American dictionaries list the shorter form first, *autoeroticism* is four times as common as **autoerotism*. The shift in preference had occurred by the mid-1960s in

AmE and by the mid-1990s in BrE. The longer form ought to be accepted as standard.

Current ratio: 4:1

automaton (= [1] a humanoid robot that moves without visible outside control, or [2] someone who seems emotionless and unreflective) has predominantly formed the plural *automata* since the early 18th century. Although AmE seriously flirted with *automatons* from about 1915 to the early 1950s, that plural has been much in decline ever since.

Current ratio: 6:1

autonomy (= self-rule) is sometimes misused for *authority*—e.g.: "But Dave Checketts, president of Madison Square Garden, insisted that the 50-year-old Riley wanted part ownership and complete *autonomy of* [read *authority over*] the team, and that his heart was no longer in the job when those requests were denied." Clifton Brown, "Riley Quits over Difference with Management," *N.Y. Times*, 16 June 1995, at B14. This sentence suggests that Coach Pat Riley wanted the team to be entirely self-governing, but the context shows that he wanted authority for himself.

LANGUAGE-CHANGE INDEX
autonomy misused for *authority*: Stage 1

autopsy; postmortem. These equivalents are each current in AmE and BrE. *Autopsy* is slightly more common in both AmE and BrE. *Postmortem* now tends to be used figuratively <Let's do a postmortem on our performance>.

As a verb, *autopsy* dates back to the late 19th century but wasn't recorded in the dictionaries until much later. It means "to perform a postmortem examination on." E.g.:

- "Rhoda Walston, veterinary pathologist at the lab, *autopsied* the carcass and traced a trajectory showing the bear had been shot from the side, not the front." Kim Murphy, "Shielded Species Get High-Tech Lab Help," *L.A. Times*, 29 Dec. 1996, at A1.
- "All but 15 bodies have been recovered and *autopsied*." "Flight 800 Autopsy Reports Released," *Wash. Post*, 4 Jan. 1997, at A12.

auxiliary. So spelled, this word is best pronounced /awg-**zil**-yə-ree/. Perhaps through confusion with *ancillary*, it is often misspelled **auxillary* (and mispronounced /awg-**zil**-ə-ree/)—e.g.:

- "In the past week, the company has moved operations to its *auxillary* [read *auxiliary*] warehouse." Jeff Richgels, "Rising from the Ashes," *Capital Times* (Madison), 10 Aug. 1996, at C1.
- "She was a member of the Ladies *Auxillary* [read *Auxiliary*] of Gerald O'Neill Post #1683 American Legion." "Helen G. Featherstone" (obit.), *Times Union* (Albany), 14 Jan. 1997, at B6.

LANGUAGE-CHANGE INDEX
auxiliary misspelled **auxillary*: Stage 1
Current ratio: 805:1

avail. A. As a Verb. *Avail* = (1) to get the benefit of, make use of <to avail oneself of the opportunity>; or

(2) to be of advantage or utility <the attempts to rectify the problem availed no one>.

In sense 1, which is always reflexive, it's an error to use the PASSIVE VOICE—e.g.: "Where the special lump-sum averaging rule *is availed of*, there is no $20,000 exclusion allowed." Marshall L. Fineman, "New York State and City Income Tax Consequences of IRA and Pension Distributions," *CPA J.*, 1 June 1995, at 72. (A possible revision: *If the taxpayer uses the lump-sum averaging rule, no $20,000 exclusion is allowed.*)

In AmE, some jargonistic writers use the passive *be availed* in various incorrect senses. For example, some think it means "to be made available," a usage without any sanction—e.g.: "The court acknowledged . . . that . . . it was the inherent duty of government to ensure that equitable educational opportunity *was availed* [read *be made available* or *is made available*] to all of its citizenry." Chet Whye Jr., "40 Years After *Brown* Decision, Education Chances Slipping Again," *Denver Post*, 17 May 1994, at B7. Others seem to think *be availed* means "to be allowed"—e.g.: "On the other hand, in single-income families, only the working spouse *is availed* [read *is allowed*] the graduated tax rates." "The Taxman's Dual-Income Bias," *Fin. Post*, 9 Apr. 1994, at 16.

In Ireland, oddly, it is quite common to omit the reflexive object and to use *avail of* in the sense "to take advantage of"—e.g.:

- "Drapier also believes he has a duty to tell his readers that, yes, his wife *availed of* [read *took advantage of*] the Dunnes Stores 'Saucepans for Stamps' promotion." "Parties Try to Outdo Each Other in Their Race to the High Moral Ground," *Irish Times*, 14 Dec. 1996, at 14.
- "Galway United increased their lead on the hour when they *availed of* [read *took advantage of*] a poor clearance by Noel Hartigan." "First Blood to Galway in Final," *Irish Times*, 18 Dec. 1996, at 21. (The *they* in reference to a sports team is typical of BrE. See COLLECTIVE NOUNS.)

Irish examples of this usage are legion.

Often this verb, when used transitively (sense 2), could be replaced by a simpler word such as *help*, *profit*, or *benefit*—e.g.:

- "The sedate slopes averted mildew—death for grapes—and *availed* [read *helped*] Evans in his quest for developing a sweet purple grape." Bart Ripp, "Maritime Memento," *News Trib.* (Tacoma), 15 Oct. 1995, Soundlife §, at 10.
- "The Tide blitzed Danny Wuerffel, knocked him down, made him hurry. This was the formula plied by FSU, but it *availed Alabama not at all* [read *didn't help Alabama at all*]." Mark Bradley, "Florida 45, Alabama 30," *Atlanta J.-Const.*, 8 Dec. 1996, at E4.

Often simpler words also better express sense 1—e.g.: "Festival-goers *availed* [read *helped*] themselves to a buffet and a bellyful of ragtime, jazz standards and vaudeville classics." Michael Kuelker, "Ragtime Fest Opens with 6-Hour Session," *St. Louis Post-Dispatch*, 2 Sept. 1995, at D7. In that sentence, *avail* was also mistakenly matched with *to* rather than *of*.

LANGUAGE-CHANGE INDEX
*to be availed misused for *to make available*: Stage 1

B. As a Noun. *Avail* is frequently a noun having the sense "beneficial effect, advantage," especially in the phrase *to no avail*, meaning "without success"—e.g.:

- "We tried to get them to sing carols with us, but *to no avail*." Joe A. Ashley, "The Christmas Train," *Anchorage Daily News*, 24 Dec. 1996, at E1.
- "Wren got a shot off, but he even got his stick on an in-close rebound, *to no avail*." Phil Jackman, "Bandits Lose Lead in Third, Salvage 4–4 Tie with Blades," *Baltimore Sun*, 7 Feb. 1997, at D6.
- "Sometimes she'd cross her legs tightly, trying to make it all stop—to *no avail*." Andrea K. McDaniels, "Treatment for Parkinson's Could Replace Surgery," *Baltimore Sun*, 8 Sept. 2015, at A1.

avenge. A. And *revenge*, vb. & n. To *avenge* is to visit fitting retribution on a wrongdoer by reason of (a specified wrong). *Avenge* and *vengeance* have to do with justice, and often with the legal process—e.g.:

- "He longs to see his friends' deaths *avenged*, to get a date with Beth Penrose, and to keep her from the amorous advances of the FBI liaison working on the case." Susan Marx, "A Fruitful Mix of Mystery and Romance," *Orange County Register*, 27 July 1997, at F24.
- "Unable to control his combustible emotions, a man goes to prison for *avenging* an attack on his wife." "Freeze Frames," *Christian Science Monitor*, 12 Sept. 1997, at 13.

But the justice may also be taken upon oneself—e.g.:

- "In its statement, the Islamic Jihad said it carried out the attack to *avenge* the deaths of more than 30 Palestinian civilians during Israeli army raids in the Gaza Strip this month." Peter Mermann, "Car Bomb Kills at Least 16 in Northern Israel," *Baltimore Sun*, 22 Oct. 2002, at A16.
- "Petrucelli aspired to become a made man in the Luchese crime family, and stabbed Cicero to *avenge* the shooting of fellow Tanglewood Boys member Darin Mazzarella, Assistant U.S. Attorney David Raskin said." John Lehmann, "Mob Boss to Squeal at Slay Trial," *N.Y. Post*, 23 Oct. 2002, at 21.

Quite often, however, *avenge* has nothing to do with real justice, but only with evening a score, especially in sports and politics—e.g.:

- "Many present came holding tortured Rally Monkeys and a sense of inevitability the Giants would *avenge* Sunday's ugly 11–10 Game 2 loss." Joe Strauss, "Angels Pound Giants to Take Lead in Series," *St. Louis Post-Dispatch*, 23 Oct. 2002, at B1.
- "The goal is not only to *avenge* Al Gore's failure to capture the state in 2000, but also to set the stage for a Democratic presidential candidate in 2004." Katharine Q. Seelye, "McAuliffe Describes Jeb Bush as the Democrats' Top Target," *N.Y. Times*, 24 Oct. 2002, at A31.

To *revenge* is to inflict suffering or harm upon another out of personal resentment. *Revenge* has to do with getting even—e.g.: "In 1996, with Leslie at the lead, the Americans *revenged* that defeat." John Erardi, "Past Forward," *Cincinnati Enquirer*, 28 Mar. 1997, at F2. Actually, though, sportswriters use the two verbs almost interchangeably. If they're looking for hype, the word should be *revenge*.

Often, too, *revenge* is a reflexive verb—e.g.:

- "Solon, for example, opposed waiting until the dissatisfied class *revenged* itself with revolution and confiscation." William D. Snider, "A Three-Week Greek Sailing Cruise Turns into a Voyage Back in Time," *News & Record* (Greensboro), 30 June 1996, at F3.
- "Never having been able to afford the real thing as a young woman, she *revenged* herself by designing gigantic ropes of pearls and huge crystals." Patricia McLaughlin, "Fake Fur: Glamour Without Guilt," *St. Louis Post-Dispatch*, 3 Oct. 1996, Style West §, at 7.

Moreover, *revenge* can (and usually does) function as a noun, whereas *avenge* cannot.

B. *Avenge* for *get revenge*. Although the *OED* supports the notion that *avenge* may also mean "to take vengeance on (a wrongdoer)," this sense is labeled obsolete and the few examples are from the mid-17th century. Today this sense is fairly rare and not at all idiomatic—e.g.: "Not only did they *avenge* [read *get revenge on*] the schoolyard bullies and nasty teachers, but they're also famous for it, because they got their faces all over the news." Jack Levin & James Alan Fox, "Making Celebrities of Serial Killers Elevates Threat," *USA Today*, 23 Oct. 2002, at A13.

LANGUAGE-CHANGE INDEX
avenge in the sense "to get revenge on": Stage 2
Current ratio (*avenge his* vs. **avenge him*): 4:1

aver. A. And *asseverate*. These are FORMAL WORDS for *say* or *state*. *Aver* has its place in solemn contexts <Allen averred that he would somehow make things right>. *Asseverate*, a rarer and weightier word, is seldom justified. Both refer to affirmations of fact, usually with no implication that an oath has been taken.

B. Corresponding Noun: *averment* or **averral*. *Averment* is the preferred noun corresponding to *aver* in both AmE and BrE—e.g.: "Gingrich personally and his Contract [with America] are endlessly hammered for 'ms'-ness, as in columnist Robert L. Steinbeck's *averment* in the Tampa Tribune." Daniel Seligman, "Our Spirited Republicans, the Great Coed Bathroom Caper," *Fortune*, 25 Dec. 1995, at 231 (*"ms"-ness* referring to "mean-spiritedness"). **Averral* is a NEEDLESS VARIANT, perhaps coined with *avowal* in mind.

Current ratio: 36:1

average is a word that assumes a broad sample of subjects. As a verb, it does not mix well with *each*: "Each Boston member *averages* ten years of experience." (Read: *Members in Boston have an average of ten years' experience.* Or: *The Boston members average ten years' experience.*) See **each.**

averageable. So spelled.

averment; **averral*. See **aver (B).**

averse. See **adverse.**

avert. See **advert.**

LANGUAGE-CHANGE INDEX (For the full key, see front matter pp. xxxi, l–li.)
Stage 1: Rejected. **Stage 2:** Widely shunned. **Stage 3:** Widespread but . . . **Stage 4:** Ubiquitous but . . . **Stage 5:** Fully accepted.
Invariably inferior forms marked by asterisk (∗). • Ratios represent frequency of prevalent forms vs. variants in current books.

avertable. So spelled—no longer **avertible*. Though the *-i-* spelling was once standard, the *-a-* spelling became predominant in the 1980s and remains so. See -ABLE (A).

Current ratio: 5:1

aviary; apiary. An *aviary* is a place for captive birds; an *apiary* is a place for bees and beehives. The words derive from the Latin terms *avis* (= bird) and *apis* (= bee). *Aviary* has been the victim of SLIPSHOD EXTENSION in the sense *insectarium* (= a place for keeping and breeding insects)—e.g.:

- "Renaker is donating land and building materials to construct an *aviary* [read *insectarium*] where the insects will be bred and studied." Terry Rodgers, "Beauties and the Base," *San Diego Union-Trib.*, 12 Dec. 1991, at A1 (referring to butterflies).
- "The Insectarium features thousands of living and mounted insects from all over the world, a *butterfly aviary* [read, perhaps, *lepidoptarium* or *butterfly tent*], a working hive of bees and hands-on games." Allen Bradford, "Montreal Spices Birthday Fest with Charm and French Flavor," *Wash. Times*, 4 Oct. 1992, at E1.
- "Salopek said the bees would be taken to his house, where he has an *aviary* [read *apiary*] he uses for bees." Jorge Milian, "Buzz Quieted in Wellington," *Palm Beach Post*, 22 Aug. 2015, at B1.

LANGUAGE-CHANGE INDEX
aviary misused for *insectarium*, etc.: Stage 1

avocado. Pl. *avocados*—not **avocadoes*. See PLURALS (D).

Current ratio: 19:1

avocation; vocation. Although these words are quite different, many writers misuse *avocation* for *vocation*. The first means "hobby," whereas the second means "calling or profession." Here is the common mistake, worsened by REDUNDANCY: "My one life—my *professional avocation* [read *vocation*]—is to help prevent animal suffering." Michael Fox, "Animal Doctor," *St. Louis Post-Dispatch*, 28 Feb. 1996, Everyday Mag. §, at E2.

LANGUAGE-CHANGE INDEX
avocation misused for *vocation*: Stage 1

*avouch. See **vouch.**

await. A. And ***wait for.*** Because *await* is transitive, it doesn't take a preposition such as *for*. Essentially, *await* means the same thing as *wait for*: you can *await* someone's arrival or *wait for* the person to arrive. But **await for* isn't good English. Although it appears mostly in the writings of nonnative speakers of English (especially in foreign journals), it does surface in homegrown writing as well—e.g.:

- "He was being held by customs officials at Kennedy Airport, who captured him *while awaiting for* [read *while he awaited* or *while he waited for*] a Pakistan International Airline flight." "Suspect Held in NYC for 4 Ohio Deaths," *Cincinnati Enquirer*, 13 Sept. 1999, at B2.
- "Collectors eagerly *awaited for* [read *awaited* or *waited for*] each new card in the series." Anne Gilbert, "Ad Trade Cards Have Long History," *Chicago Sun-Times*, 25 June 2000, Sunday Homelife §, at 8.

- "Microsoft and Nintendo bide their time in their corners anxiously *awaiting for* [read *waiting for*] the bell to ring." Marc Saltzman, "The Console Game Wars Should Dominate in 2001," *Toronto Star*, 4 Jan. 2001, at FF3.

If no object is supplied (or clearly implied), *wait* is the proper term. That is, if the verb ends the clause, it shouldn't be *await*—e.g.:

- "The crew returned Saturday evening to Ellington Field in Houston where friends and family *awaited* [read *waited*]." Stephanie Asin, "Columbia Crew Sets New Mark," *Houston Chron.*, 24 July 1994, at A6.
- "The plane headed back to the gate, where airport police *awaited* [read *waited*], ATA spokeswoman Angela Thomas said." Katherine Shaver, "Puzzling Note to Pilot Delays Flight at National," *Wash. Post*, 7 Feb. 2003, at A2.
- "The blue-green water sparkled, and a pristine white-sand beach *awaited* [read *waited*], though it was already heavily dotted with visitors." Karin Esterhammer, "Destination: Thailand," *L.A. Times*, 9 Feb. 2003, at L10.

LANGUAGE-CHANGE INDEX
*awaiting for for *awaiting* or *waiting for*: Stage 1
Current ratio (*awaiting her* vs.
*awaiting for her): 454:1

B. And ***wait on.*** A waiter *waits on* tables. But a dinner partner does not *wait on* you to arrive. That is the distinction that critics made for more than a century: they objected to *wait on* in the sense of *await* or *wait for*—e.g.: "They *waited on* [read *waited for*] the jury's verdict." Even if this is not the best phrasing, however, *wait on* is now so common as a CASUALISM that it can't be labeled incorrect.

LANGUAGE-CHANGE INDEX
wait on in the sense "to wait for": Stage 5

awake(n). See **wake.**

away; aweigh. See **anchors aweigh.**

aweless; *awless. Since the mid-19th century, *aweless* has been the predominant spelling. But today **awless* competes closely with it, doubtless on the analogy of *awful*.

awesome, in the 1980s and 1990s, became a ubiquitous VOGUE WORD <That movie was totally awesome!>. For the time being, the word has been spoiled by overuse.

LANGUAGE-CHANGE INDEX
awesome for *excellent* or *stupendously good*: Stage 4

awful; awfully. The word *awful* has undergone several transformations. Originally, it referred to people and meant "filled with awe"; later it referred to things and meant "inspiring people with awe." Its meaning then degenerated to "horrible, terrible" <what an awful accident>. And *awfully*, meanwhile, became an equivalent of *very*, but with greater intensity <Joe was awfully sorry about the mix-up>. Nobody objects to these uses in speech, and few would in writing. But some begin to object when *awfully* intensifies adjectives with positive connotations <they're awfully good people> <Tiger played awfully well>. Although these uses have been called humorously illogical, they're actually quite close to the original sense.

Occasionally, of course, *awfully* can be ambiguous—e.g.: "He is *awfully* educated." But in sentences in which that ambiguity doesn't appear, the intensive *awfully* must be accepted as standard.

To use *awful* adverbially typifies dialectal usage—e.g.: "He's an *awful* [read *awfully*] good fellow."

> LANGUAGE-CHANGE INDEX
> 1. *awful* in the sense "very bad" <what an awful performance>, "shocking" <the casualties were just awful>, or "very great" <we did an awful lot of work>: Stage 5
> 2. *awful* as an adverb <she's awful nice>: Stage 1
> Current ratio (*awfully good* vs. **awful good*): 5:1
> 3. *awfully* for *very* with positive adjectives <an awfully pleasant evening>: Stage 4

awhile; a while. As a noun element, spell it as two words <he rested for a while> <it took quite a while to learn this>. As an adverb, spell it as one <he rested awhile>. Misuses are common—e.g.:

- "We lay back and rested *a while* [read *awhile*] in the warm breeze." Henry Miller, *Sexus* 58 (1949; repr. 1965).
- "She looked up at the sky *for awhile* [read *awhile* or *for a while*], remembering her father's astronomy lessons." Deborah Ellis, *Parvana's Journey* 54 (2004).

When the choice is between *for a while* and *awhile*, prefer the latter. And don't write **for awhile*.

> LANGUAGE-CHANGE INDEX
> 1. *a while* used adverbially for *awhile*: Stage 4
> Current ratio (*rested awhile* vs. **rested a while*): 1.4:1
> 2. *awhile* misused for *a while*: Stage 1
> Current ratio (*for a while* vs. **for awhile*): 11:1

awing. The present participle of *awe*, vb., is so spelled—not **aweing*. See MUTE E.

*awless. See **aweless.**

awoke(n). See **wake.**

awry (= [1] amiss, [2] askew) is pronounced /ə-**rı**/.

ax; axe. According to the *OED*, the spelling *ax* is "better on every ground of etymology, phonology, and analogy." But *axe* is standard in AmE and BrE. Despite what American desktop dictionaries have long said, the form ending in *-e* has predominated in print sources.

Compound words follow the same course—hence *pickaxe* and *poleaxe*.

> Current ratio (*axe* vs. *ax*): 2:1

axel; axle. The first is a figure-skating maneuver; the second is a rod or pin connecting two wheels. But *axle* sometimes wrongly displaces *axel*—e.g.:

- "An Olympic silver medal, a million-dollar professional skating gig and Saturday's marriage to her agent, Jerry Solomon, have put her a few leaps, bounds and triple *axles* [read *axels*] ahead of former rival Tonya Harding." "For Kerrigan, It's Happily Ever After," *Sacramento Bee*, 10 Sept. 1995, at A2.
- "Gale Tanger has just completed the triple *axle* [read *axel*], triple toe jump of figure skating judging." Gary Rummler, "Figure Skating Judge Worked Years to Reach Her Goal," *Milwaukee J. Sentinel*, 26 Sept. 1996, Neighbors §, at 5.
- "She was grudgingly admired as a superb sportswoman and the first skater in America, and the second woman ever, to achieve a *triple axle* [read *triple-axel*] jump." Barbara McMahon, "The Ice Princess and Me," *People* (U.K.), 19 Jan. 2014, at 26.

> LANGUAGE-CHANGE INDEX
> *axle* misused for *axel*: Stage 1

axes is the plural of both *axis* (pl. pron. /**ak**-seez/) and *ax* (pl. pron. /**ak**-səz/).

aye (= yes) is the standard spelling of this word, most commonly used in the parliamentary procedure of voting. The word is pronounced /ı/. **Ay* is a variant form.

> Current ratio (*ayes have* vs. **ays have*): 16:1

B

babysit > babysat > babysat. So inflected. The erroneous **babysitted* sometimes appears—e.g.:

- "Let us leave alone the fact that the pro-tem, non-elected prime minister of the land is being run and *babysitted* [read *babysat*] by a collection of coiffed lobbyists." Allan Fotheringham, "Salinger: From Flack to Hack and Back Again," *Fin. Post*, 9 Sept. 1993, at 13.
- "Dykeman frequently *babysitted* [read *babysat*] the child." "Teen Pleads Guilty to Kidnapping," *Peoria J. Star*, 25 Apr. 2001, at A1 (photo caption).

Cf. **sit.**

> LANGUAGE-CHANGE INDEX
> **babysitted* for *babysat*: Stage 1
> Current ratio (*babysat* vs. **babysitted*): 179:1

baccalaureate /bak-ə-**lor**-ee-ət/ = (1) a bachelor's degree conferred by a college (such as a *bachelor of arts* or *bachelor of science*); (2) a commencement address (esp. a religious one) given at a college graduation; or (3) a religious service held in connection with commencement events. In sense 1, it is redundant to refer to a **baccalaureate degree*. In sense 2, the word is a shortened form of the phrase *baccalaureate address* or *baccalaureate sermon*. In sense 3, it's a shortened form of *baccalaureate service*.

baccarat /bahk-ə-**rah**/ (the card game) is the standard spelling. **Baccara* is a variant.

> Current ratio: 62:1

LANGUAGE-CHANGE INDEX (For the full key, see front matter pp. xxxi, l–li.)
Stage 1: Rejected. **Stage 2:** Widely shunned. **Stage 3:** Widespread but . . . **Stage 4:** Ubiquitous but . . . **Stage 5:** Fully accepted.
Invariably inferior forms marked by asterisk (*). • Ratios represent frequency of prevalent forms vs. variants in current books.

bacchant, n. & adj.; **bacchante.** Traditionally, the language has distinguished between men and women who worshipped Bacchus, the Greek god of wine and revelry. By extension, a drunken carouser who is male is known as a *bacchant* (/**bak**-ənt/ or /bə-**kant**/), whereas one who is female is known as a *bacchante* (/bə-**kant**/ or /bə-**kahnt**/ or /bə-**kant**-ee/). Curiously, the feminine *bacchante* has occurred about twice as often in print sources as *bacchant* from 1800 to the present day—in both singular and plural uses. See SEXISM (D).

The word *bacchant* is also an adjective and in that role may refer to both men and women <during those months, she led a bacchant life>.

bachelor's degree. So written.

bacillus (= a rod-shaped bacterium) forms the plural *bacilli*. The words are pronounced /bə-**sil**-əs/ and /bə-**sil**-ɪ/. See PLURALS (B).

*backadation. See **backwardation.**

BACK-FORMATIONS are words formed by removing suffixes from longer words that are mistakenly assumed to be derivatives. Most commonly, a *-tion* noun is shortened to make a verb ending in *-te*—e.g., from *emotion* comes *emote*.

Such back-formations are objectionable when they are merely NEEDLESS VARIANTS of already existing verbs:

Back-Formed Verb	Ordinary Verb
*administrate	administer
*cohabitate	cohabit
*delimitate	delimit
*interpretate	interpret
*orientate	orient
registrate	register
remediate	remedy
*revocate	revoke
*revolute	revolt
*solicitate	solicit

Many back-formations never gain real legitimacy (e.g., *elocute, *enthuse), some are aborted early in their existence (e.g., *ebullit, *evolute), and still others are of questionable vigor (e.g., *aggress, attrit, effulge, evanesce, frivol*). *Burgle* (back-formed from *burglar*) continues to have a jocular effect (in AmE), as do *effuse, emote, laze,* and the learned word *metamorphose.* See **burglarize.**

Still, many examples have survived respectably, among them *collide, diagnose, donate, edit, elide, grovel, orate, peeve, resurrect,* and *sculpt.* *Enthuse may one day be among these respectable words; although it first appeared in the early 19th century, it still struggles for approval. Many other back-formations have filled gaps in the language and won acceptance through sheer utility.

The best rule of thumb is to avoid newborn back-formations that appear newfangled, but not better-established ones that, being only faintly recognizable as back-formations, are genuinely useful. Only philologists today recognize (much less condemn) as

back-formations *beg* (from *beggar*), *jell* (from *jelly*), *peddle* (from *peddler*), and *type* (from *typewriter*).

For specific discussions elsewhere in the dictionary, see **liaise, registrate, remediate** & **surveil.**

back of; in back of. In the sense "behind," these Americanisms strike a casual tone. Although *back of* was long considered a better form than *in back of*, the latter is now almost as common. (No one, after all, questions *in front of*.) Still, good editors tend to replace either phrase with *behind*—e.g.:

- "They are thinking of building an addition *in back of* [read *behind*] their offices and warehouse, which survived the fire." Monica von Dobeneck, "Burned Mill Bouncing Back," *Patriot & Evening News* (Harrisburg), 7 Oct. 1997, at B1.
- "Deer are starting to move now, and I have been seeing indications of that in the woods *in back of* [read *behind*] our house." Randy Julius, "Kids Get First Shot," *Enterprise* (Brockton, Mass.), 6 Sept. 2015, at 33.

Back of dates from late-18th-century AmE; it was adopted in BrE by the 1820s. *In back of* didn't become common until the 1930s in AmE and a decade later in BrE.

LANGUAGE-CHANGE INDEX
1. *back of* for *behind*: Stage 5
2. *in back of* for *behind*: Stage 4

backwardation; *backadation. This term—meaning "a fee paid by the seller of securities to allow for delivery after the delivery date originally agreed to" (*Black's Law Dictionary* 166 [10th ed. 2014])—is preferably spelled *backwardation.* H.W. Fowler included the term in his "ill-favored list" of hybrid derivatives (*FMEU1* at 241), but it has become standard. See HYBRIDS. It originated in BrE in the early 19th century.

backward(s). See DIRECTIONAL WORDS (A).

bacteria, the plural form of *bacterium*, takes a plural verb. From the mid-19th century, the term has predominantly been treated as a plural—e.g.:

- "Scientists reported today a sharp increase in antibiotic-resistant strains of the *bacteria* that *cause* pneumonia, meningitis and other diseases." "Sharp Rise Found in Resistance of Pneumonia Bacteria to Drugs," *N.Y. Times,* 25 Aug. 1995, at A18.
- "Some *bacteria* are pathogenic (disease causing) but many are beneficial, even essential to our health." Richard T. Bosshardt, "If Yogurt Doesn't Help, Probiotics May Be Solution," *Orlando Sentinel,* 1 Sept. 2002, Lake §, at K12.

See PLURALS (B).

Yet since the late 19th century, some writers have ignored the plural form and erroneously treated *bacteria* as singular—e.g.:

- "A second youth remained in the hospital yesterday suffering with the *bacteria* that *causes* [read *cause*] meningitis." Gail Hulbert, "High School Returning to Normal Following Meningitis Scare," *Providence J.-Bull.,* 25 Sept. 1996, at C5.
- "And so the *bacteria spreads* [read *spread*]." Angela Allen, "Hidden Threat: Food-Borne Illness," *San Diego Union-Trib.,* 5 Oct. 1997, at A1.
- "In all, 178 people were stricken with salmonella—*a common bacteria* [read *the common bacteria*] that *causes*

[read *cause*] food poisoning—and 22 were hospitalized with diarrhea, cramps, fever, nausea and other symptoms." Jerry W. Jackson, "Bad Luck Takes a Seat at Darden's Table," *Orlando Sentinel*, 2 Sept. 2002, CFB §, at 16.

The singular usage shows no signs of gaining ground in frequency of use.

LANGUAGE-CHANGE INDEX
bacteria as a singular: Stage 2
Current ratio (*a bacterium was* vs.
**a bacteria was*): 7:1

bad. See **badly** (A).

bade. See **bid** (A).

bad(-)faith. *Bad faith* is the noun phrase <in bad faith>, *bad-faith* the adjectival phrase <bad-faith promises>. Cf. **bona fide** & *bona fides.* See PHRASAL ADJECTIVES.

badly. A. And *bad*. With a linking verb such as *is, feels, seems,* or *tastes,* the predicate adjective *bad* is required, not the adverbial complement *badly*—e.g.:

- "But the punishment hardly seems to fit the 'crime' as presented, and both teacher and students come off looking *badly* [read *bad*]." Eric Ries, "Rip-Snortin' Romp," *Techniques*, 1 Feb. 2000, at 76.
- "A good rule of thumb is: If a mushroom looks, smells, or tastes *badly* [read *bad*], do not eat it." Art Judd, "Mushroom Madness," *Santa Fe New Mexican*, 21 June 2001, at C1.

See **feel** (B).

LANGUAGE-CHANGE INDEX
badly after a linking verb <**feel badly*> <**looked badly* after the loss>: Stage 2
Current ratio (*felt bad* vs. **felt badly*): 6:1

B. In the Sense "very greatly" or "very much." This use, as in *badly in need*, was formerly criticized. Having become established in the early 20th century, it is perfectly idiomatic in AmE—e.g.: "Democrats demanded concessions in a bill tightening immigration laws, another measure Republicans want *badly*." Dave Skidmore, "Congress Fights Budget Demons," *Chattanooga Times*, 28 Sept. 1996, at A4. But cf. **awful.**

Stick to *badly* (not *bad*) in this adverbial sense. One might expect a professional athlete to say, for example, " 'We need him *bad*, we need him real *bad*.' " Joe Donnelly, "Ecstasy, Agony," *Newsday* (N.Y.), 17 Dec. 1993, at 247 (quoting Herb Williams, a basketball player). But an announcement about a local symphony function should probably be more literate: "If you can meet these criteria, then the people who put on the Symphony Style Show need you *bad* [read *badly*]." Douglas Imbrogno, "In Search of a Fashionable Dog," *Charleston Gaz.*, 8 Sept. 1994, at D1. See ADVERBS (D).

LANGUAGE-CHANGE INDEX
1. *badly* for *very much* <badly in need>: Stage 5
2. *bad* for *badly* <we need some paper bad>: Stage 2
Current ratio (*need it badly* vs. **need it bad*): 2:1

badminton (the tennis-like game played with a shuttlecock) is pronounced /**bad**-min-tən/, with the medial *n*—preferably not /**bad**-mit-ən/.

Bagehot. The name of Walter Bagehot (1826–1877)—the economist and journalist—is frequently encountered in literary works. But few people know how to pronounce it: /**baj**-ət/.

bagful. Pl. *bagfuls*—not **bagsful.* See PLURALS (G).

Current ratio: 6:1

baggage; luggage. Signs in U.S. airports direct travelers to the *baggage claim* where they wait while *baggage handlers* unload the aircraft. In the U.K., travelers, especially in railroad stations, are accustomed to seeing signs for *left luggage* and *luggage vans* into which suitcases and packages are loaded. Although *baggage* predominated in AmE until the 1980s and is still favored, *luggage* has become almost equally common. In BrE, *luggage* is dominant.

In AmE and BrE alike, *baggage* has negative extended senses, some pejorative. For instance, one refers to metaphorically carrying *psychological baggage* or *political baggage*. In BrE slang, disliked women are referred to as *bags* or *baggage*. These may be factors for sometimes preferring *luggage*.

Bahamian (= a resident of the Bahamas) is pronounced /bə-**hay**-mee-ən/. See DENIZEN LABELS.

bail; bale. You *bail* water out of a boat but *bale* hay. In this particular sense, *bail* means "to dip out (water, etc.) with a bucket." But some writers mistakenly use *bale* in this sense, a confusion that has existed since the mid-19th century—e.g.:

- "The yacht started spinning in circles as the crew furiously *baled* [read *bailed*] water." "Cup Yacht Ends in a Spin," *Evening Standard*, 6 Jan. 1992, at 46.
- "The scenario was replayed up and down Village Road as homeowners, who were evacuated by boat Friday night, were back yesterday *baling* [read *bailing*] out water." Christine Schiavo, "Flood Waters Hit Home 18th Time in 30 Years," *Morning Call* (Allentown, Pa.), 23 Jan. 1996, at B1.
- "Some residents were forced to *bale* [read *bail*] water from their pools in a bucket brigade to drench flames as they neared homes." "Fire Destroys at Least 43 Homes in Florida," *L.A. Times*, 17 Apr. 1999, at A10.

To *bale* hay or cotton is to put it into a large bundle, usually compressed and wrapped. But a few writers (not many) mistakenly use *bail* in this sense—e.g.:

- "I helped our neighbor *bail* [read *bale*] hay or clean the barn." Wayde I. Goodall, *The Fruit of the Spirit* 37 (2000).
- "But a few days later, when Jahns drove to Lee to record Romney *bailing* [read *baling*] hay on one of his campaign 'work days,' she was politely turned away." Joanna Weiss, "Video Puts Campaigns on Record," *Boston Globe*, 20 Aug. 2002, Metro/Region §, at A1.

LANGUAGE-CHANGE INDEX (For the full key, see front matter pp. xxxi, l–li.)
Stage 1: Rejected. **Stage 2:** Widely shunned. **Stage 3:** Widespread but . . . **Stage 4:** Ubiquitous but . . . **Stage 5:** Fully accepted.
Invariably inferior forms marked by asterisk (✳). • Ratios represent frequency of prevalent forms vs. variants in current books.

In a related sense, of course, *bale* is also a noun: the product of *baling hay* is a *bale of hay*. But once again writers occasionally err—e.g.:

- "I can remember when we opened a *bail* [read *bale*] of hay that Dad would save." Carl Allen, "We Had to Save Everything," *Ledger* (Lakeland, Fla.), 13 Mar. 1995, at C6.
- "Sparks from a 14-acre controlled field burn near Star ignited two one-ton *bails* [read *bales*] of hay Thursday afternoon." "Briefs," *Idaho Statesman*, 2 Aug. 2002, Local §, at 1.
- "Matt threw the last *bail* [read *bale*] of hay inside the fence." Steve Galley, *Nicky's Time* 77 (2005).

LANGUAGE-CHANGE INDEX
1. *baling water* for *bailing water*: Stage 2
Current ratio (*bailing water* vs. *baling water*): 4:1
2. *bailing hay* for *baling hay*: Stage 2
Current ratio (*baling hay* vs. *bailing hay*): 5:1
3. *bail of hay* for *bale of hay*: Stage 1
Current ratio (*bale of hay* vs. *bail of hay*): 24:1

*baited breath. See **bated breath.**

bakeable. See MUTE E.

bald-faced; barefaced; boldface(d). What is *bald-faced* is unobscured by facial hair <bald-faced pirate>, trees <bald-faced mountain>, or other features <bald-faced hornet>—or, oddly enough in a specialized bovine sense, has white hair covering the entire face <bald-faced heifer>. Figuratively, and more commonly as an Americanism dating from the early 20th century, it describes something that is obvious, brazen, and shameless. Most often the term appears in the catchphrase *bald-faced lie*, but it goes as easily with other shameful acts—e.g.: "[H]ere the configuration reeks of *bald-faced* contrivance." Dan Craft, "Despite 'Signs,' It's Not About Them," *Pantagraph* (Bloomington, Ill.), 8 Aug. 2002, at D2.

The past-participial form (*bald-faced*) is grammatically correct and is preferred by those with finer-tuned ears over *bald-face*, which is also correct. The second form is far from rare—e.g.: "The chief U.S. negotiator, Dennis Ross, calls that a *bald-face* lie." Editorial, "Media Shows Its Bias for Palestinian Cause," *News & Record* (Greensboro), 30 May 2002, at A8.

What is *barefaced* is unobscured either by facial hair <a barefaced friar among all the bearded ones> or by a mask <though most of the robbers were masked, at least one was barefaced>. From the 18th century on, especially in BrE, the word has meant "unscrupulous" <barefaced warmongering>. Unlike the other terms in this entry, it makes an *-ly* adverb: *barefacedly* (/bair-**fay**-səd-lee/).

Occasionally a writer will mistakenly substitute *boldfaced* for one of the other words, thereby savaging the essence of the phrase—e.g.: "Getting my father to move to the nursing home was quite a feat, and I needed the help of my wife, my father's best friend, and a *boldfaced* [read *bald-faced*] lie." Kenneth A. McClane, "Driving; Family; Alzheimer's Disease Patients," *Antioch Rev.*, 22 Sept. 2006, at 604.

What is *boldface* is lettered in a thick typeface <boldface headline>—e.g.: "[H]ospital officials backed out after the proposal trumpeted in *boldface* type that no money would change hands." Andy Staples, "Pasco Picks Safety over Bureaucracy," *Tampa Trib.*, 21 Aug. 2002, Pasco §, at 5. Figuratively, what is *boldface* is emphasized or especially important—e.g.: "Over the years, those friends have included virtually every *boldface* name to set foot on the East End." Blair Golson, "Goose Creek Guest House Sells for $5.2 Million," *N.Y. Observer*, 19 Aug. 2002, Fin. §, at 11.

Boldface is the preferred and most common spelling, but also common are *bold-faced*, *bold-face*, and *boldfaced*—e.g.: "To add flava to his new hip-hop comedy, 'Death of a Dynasty,' director Damon Dash is giving cameos to a galaxy of *bold-faced* New Yorkers." "The Wide World of Harvey W," *N.Y. Post*, 31 July 2002, at 10.

The general sense of both *bald-faced* and *barefaced* is that something is shameless; the gist of *boldface* is that something is emphasized. But the distinction is not always observed. In general use, and especially in the catchphrase about shameless lying, the three are often used interchangeably. *Barefaced lie*, the most traditional term, predominates in BrE; *bald-faced lie* has predominated in AmE since the 1980s; and *boldface(d)* lie is simply an outlier (perhaps a slander against printers).

Because of the "shameful" connotation of *bald-faced*, it is occasionally used to describe a shameful truth, leading to a twist on the expression *bald-faced lie*—e.g.: "It is a *bald-faced* truth that men are attached to their hair, physically and emotionally." Dick Feagler, "Hair Today," *Plain Dealer* (Cleveland), 4 Aug. 2002, at B1.

LANGUAGE-CHANGE INDEX
boldface lie or *boldfaced lie* for *bald-faced lie*: Stage 1
Current ratio (*bald-faced lie* vs. *boldfaced lie* vs. *boldface lie*): 21:2:1

balding (= becoming bald), having emerged as a NEOLOGISM in the early 20th century, was once objected to because there was thought to be no corresponding verb *to bald*. In fact, though, the verb dates from the early 17th century and still occasionally appears <he's starting to bald>. There is no sound reason for objecting to *balding* (the word, that is, though many regret the reality it denotes).

LANGUAGE-CHANGE INDEX
balding: Stage 5

bale. See **bail.**

baleful; baneful. These words share the basic sense "evil," but their connotations are different. *Baleful* = threatening evil; ominous; menacing <a baleful look>. *Baneful* = causing evil; ruinous; destructive <the baneful excesses of modern society>. To help distinguish the words, consider that *bale* denotes evil, while *bane* denotes something highly repellent (formerly something that causes death).

balk, vb. (= [1] to obstruct or block; [2] to refuse to act; or [3] [of a baseball pitcher] to make an illegal motion before or during a pitch), is the standard spelling in AmE and BrE alike. *Baulk* is a chiefly BrE variant. The word is traditionally pronounced /bawk/.

Current ratio (*balking* vs. **baulking*): 7:1

*ball out. See **bawl out.**

balm (= [1] something that comforts, or [2] ointment for the skin) has a silent -*l*- (/bahm/).

balmy. See **barmy.**

baloney; bologna. For the word meaning "nonsense," *baloney* is the spelling (dating from the early 20th century)—e.g.: "Much of what the world thinks it knows about this dish (or dishes, for they are myriad) is a bunch of *baloney* (from Bologna, the north-central Italian town that is alleged to have invented this rather inferior meat)." Dora Jane Hamblin, "For the Gourmet and Gourmand, Bounty from Italy," *Smithsonian*, May 1991, at 84.

For the sausage, *bologna* (pronounced like *baloney*) is the spelling—e.g.: "After $12,000 in plumbing repairs through Aug. 30, jail officials said they stopped giving out the 6 p.m. *bologna*, lunchmeat or peanut butter sandwiches wrapped in plastic." Bartholomew Sullivan, "Beef or Baloney? Forty Fastidious Arkansas Inmates Turn Up Noses at Jail Sandwiches," *Commercial Appeal* (Memphis), 26 Sept. 1996, at A1.

But this clear, widely followed DIFFERENTIATION is sometimes muddled. Most often this occurs when the spelling *bologna* is used in reference to nonsense—e.g.:

- "'The idea that just a little pollution won't hurt anything is a bunch of *bologna* [read *baloney*],' said Jack Stephens, a soft-spoken veteran of World War II and the Korean War." Bob Hill, "Pipes and Map of Pipeline Diffuser/Location," *Courier-J. Mag.* (Louisville), 13 May 1990, at M4.
- "'There was no political motivation; that's a bunch of *bologna* [read *baloney*].'" Marv Cermak, "Duci Angry TV Show Failed to Include Fyvie," *Times Union* (Albany), 17 Aug. 1995, at B7 (quoting Richard Howland).
- "Regina Busse, 84, also recalls the broadcast and equated it to lunch meat. 'It was a bunch of *bologna* [read *baloney*],' she says." Brandon Morley, "Remembering the First 'Invasion,'" *J.-Gaz.* (Ft. Wayne, Ind.), 26 June 2005, at E1 (referring to Orson Welles's 1938 "War of the Worlds" broadcast). (The writer here has conflated the two words, mistaking *baloney* for a metaphor.)

Sometimes, too, the spelling *baloney* is pressed into service where *bologna* belongs—e.g.:

- "I remember . . . [t]he special deliciousness of a lunch made by a mother who cared enough about me to cut the crusts off a *baloney* [read *bologna*] sandwich or pack a freshly baked chocolate cookie." Susan Cheever, "Mothering," *Newsday* (N.Y.), 11 Nov. 1995, pt. II, at B2.
- "She would make fried chicken or *baloney* [read *bologna*] sandwiches." Steve Morse, "The Spirit and Song of LaVern Baker," *Boston Globe*, 30 Oct. 1996, at F3.
- "Don't say 'Hey, let's have a picnic,' then bury your nose in the Sunday sports section while Mom makes *baloney* [read *bologna*] sandwiches." Ralph Berrier Jr., "Giving

Gifts That Make Mom's Day," *Roanoke Times*, 4 May 2015, at E1.

In what appears to be an amalgam of the two words, *baloney* is sometimes misspelled **boloney*—e.g.: "I got some bad publicity during the trial with Jackie [Onassis] in 1972. . . . All this is *boloney* [read *baloney*]. I don't jump out of bushes. I hide behind bushes to get pictures." Patricia Sheridan, "Ron Galella," *Pitt. Post-Gaz.*, 24 June 2002, at D2. This error was at its peak in the mid-20th century but has since tapered off.

LANGUAGE-CHANGE INDEX
1. *bologna* misused for *baloney* in reference to nonsense: Stage 1
Current ratio (*bunch of baloney* vs. **bunch of bologna*): 14:1
2. *baloney* misused for *bologna* in reference to meat: Stage 3
Current ratio (*bologna sandwich* vs. **baloney sandwich*): 3:1
3. **boloney* for *baloney*: Stage 1
Current ratio (*baloney* vs. **boloney*): 40:1

baluster; balustrade; banister. A *baluster* /bal-ə-stər/ is a round, vertical support, as for a wineglass, a chair, or the rail on a stairway—e.g.: "The two-story house, which has a massive open porch with vase-shaped *balusters*, was renovated over seven years by Ms. Sarver and her ex-husband, Bob." Gretchen McKay, "Coming Up Roses," *Pitt. Post-Gaz.*, 1 Oct. 2006, Business §, at G1.

A *balustrade* /bal-ə-strayd/ is a set of balusters along with the rail they are supporting, as for a stairway or a barrier—e.g.: "Mr. Diamond's future penthouse has a 1,350-square-foot wrap terrace, though pesky *balustrades* interrupt the panorama from indoors." Max Abelson, "Park Slope Celebrity Tour!" *N.Y. Observer*, 2 Oct. 2006, Finance §, at 11.

Banister /ban-i-stər/ is the more common term for *balustrade*, but it typically denotes the handrail alone—e.g.: "Izzy Stone devoured newspapers. . . . His wife Esther recalled how Stone would slide down the *banister* of their Washington home to get the newspapers." John C. Ensslin, "The Stone Age," *Rocky Mountain News* (Denver), 29 Sept. 2006, Spotlight §, at D28.

Bamar. See **Burmese.**

bambino (Ital. "child, baby") forms the plural *bambinos*. The Italian plural, *bambini*, is ordinarily an affectation—e.g.: "Cynthia Hart's Victoriana Calendar (Workman, $9.95) gives you all kinds of commercial illustrations of fetching *bambini* [read *bambinos*] with more ringlets than are actually found in nature, and pinker cheeks and frillier dresses, too." Jeff Simon, "Counting the Days," *Buffalo News*, 13 Dec. 1995, at D1. See PLURALS (B).

But *bambini* seems less affected when it appears in a description of Italy, where *bambinos* might seem out

---

LANGUAGE-CHANGE INDEX (For the full key, see front matter pp. xxxi, l–li.)
Stage 1: Rejected. **Stage 2:** Widely shunned. **Stage 3:** Widespread but . . . **Stage 4:** Ubiquitous but . . . **Stage 5:** Fully accepted.
Invariably inferior forms marked by asterisk (*). • Ratios represent frequency of prevalent forms vs. variants in current books.

of place—e.g.: "Sounds of a street fair drew us toward the Piazza Santa Maria, where tented booths offered free tastes of organic honey and vegetables, and two mimes entertained the local *bambini* at the base of the fountain." Letter of Marcia Wood, "When in Rome," *N.Y. Times*, 17 Dec. 1995, § 5, at 15.

"The Bambino" was also a nickname for Babe Ruth.

banal (= pedestrian and uninteresting for lack of new ideas) is pronounced /bə-**nahl**/, /bə-**nal**/, or /**bay**-nəl/. It's "a word of many pronunciations, each of which has its outspoken and often intractable proponents." *BBBM* at 55.

bandanna (= a large, colorful handkerchief) is an 18th-century borrowing from Hindi. In AmE, the spelling *bandanna* has always been standard. In BrE, that spelling contended with *bandana* from the 18th century to the 20th. Only in the 1990s did *bandanna* establish itself as the predominant form in BrE.

bandeau (= [1] a hairband, or [2] a tube-top wrap that functions like a brassiere) has predominantly formed the plural *bandeaux* since the 1840s—before that *bandeaus* having been prevalent. Today the homegrown *bandeaus* is an infrequent variant in English-language print sources.

Current ratio (*bandeaux* vs. *bandeaus*): 7:1

bandit has two plural forms, *bandits* and *banditti*. The native-English form (*bandits*) is standard. (See PLURALS (B).) The Italian plural is usually tongue-in-cheek: "It can be a tough call if your dad takes a European vacation and gets kidnapped. Refuse to ransom the old geezer and he is entitled, under Louisiana's forced-heirship law, to disinherit you. You can always take a chance, though, figuring that he might have a tough time contacting his lawyer before the *banditti* slice him up." James Gill, "The Forced-Heirship Question," *Times-Picayune* (New Orleans), 9 Aug. 1995, at B7.

Current ratio (*bandits* vs. *banditti*): 8:1

baneful. See **baleful.**

banister (= the handrail on a staircase) is the standard spelling. **Bannister* is a variant. For more, see **baluster.**

bank holiday. See **legal holiday.**

bankrupt. A. And *bankrout. The spelling **bankrout* is obsolete. In the English Renaissance, scholars respelled French borrowings such as **bankrout* on the Latin model—hence *bankrupt.* Many of these respellings did not survive (e.g., **accompt* for *account*); *bankrupt* is one of the few that did. Cf. **comptroller.**

B. As a Noun. Although in popular speech and writing it is common to refer to a person as a *bankrupt*—a common usage since at least the early 16th century—modern bankruptcy statutes use the term *debtor* instead. In general usage, though, almost all of us are *debtors*; only the insolvent among us are *bankrupts.*

bankruptcy [fr. L. *bancus* "table" + *ruptus* "broken"] is sometimes misspelled **bankruptsy*—e.g.: "John Canney, *bankruptsy* [read *bankruptcy*] trustee for Ascutney, [called] Plausteiners' $1.1 million purchase 'the bargain of the year, maybe of the decade.'" Tony Chamberlain, "Plausteiners Bid to Revive Ascutney," *Boston Globe*, 16 Dec. 1993, Sports §, at 99.

LANGUAGE-CHANGE INDEX
bankruptcy misspelled **bankruptsy*: Stage 1
Current ratio: 44,571:1

*bannister. See **banister.**

banns (= the public announcement of a wedding, usu. posted in a church) is the standard spelling. *Bans* is a variant.

banquet; banquette. *Banquet* (/**bang**-kwit/) = an elaborate feast or ceremonial meal. E.g.: "The winners will be announced at a June 24 black-tie *banquet* at the Omni Richmond Hotel." Maria Osborn Howard, "Finalists Chosen for Entrepreneur Awards," *Richmond Times-Dispatch*, 1 June 1997, at 16.

Banquette (/bang-**ket**/) = a bench or sofa placed against or attached to a wall. E.g.: "Newspapers spilled across a red leather *banquette.*" Bob Spits, "The Long and Winding Road," *St. Louis Post-Dispatch*, 25 May 1997, at C3.

bans. See **banns.**

banshee (= in Gaelic folklore, a female spirit who, by wailing, warns a family that some family member will soon die) is the standard spelling. **Banshie* is a variant.

Current ratio: 873:1

Baptist is preferably pronounced /**bap**-tist/—not /**bab**-tist/, a pronunciation common especially in the Southern United States.

bar; debar; disbar. The first two have closely related meanings. *Bar* means "to prevent (often by legal obstacle)"—e.g.:

- "The agreement *barred* Hennessy from testifying against Soulsby during his confirmation hearing in October and guaranteed Hennessy better work assignments." Robert E. Pierre, "Another Critic of Chief Soulsby Disciplined," *Wash. Post*, 24 July 1996, at F3.
- "But this year, in response to Principal James D. McConnell's concerns that students were roaming the building unsupervised, students were *barred* from entering the building before 7:15 a.m., five minutes after staff members arrive." Jean Mikle, "District, Students Settle School Opening Dispute," *Asbury Park Press* (Neptune, N.J.), 19 Oct. 1996, at A3.
- "Lohmar is *barred* by judicial rules from talking about the Conard-King matter, which started Nov. 29." Nordeka English, "Controversial Cases Stir Lohmar-Cundiff Contest for Judge," *St. Louis Post-Dispatch*, 30 Oct. 1996, at 1.

In a corresponding sense, *bar* serves as a noun as well <a bar to all claims>.

Debar, a somewhat archaic FORMAL WORD, means "to preclude from having or doing (a thing), or entering (a realm of activity)." It is more common in BrE than in AmE—e.g.:

- "His enemies . . . had accused him of being a greengrocer by trade, something to be ashamed of, they had implied, which *debarred* him from public life." Richard Lambert, "The Goldsmith File," *Fin. Times*, 19 Oct. 1996, at 7.
- "A criminal conviction of the firm could bring licensing problems in some states and might result in efforts to *debar* Anderson from government work." David S. Hilzenrath & Susan Schmidt, "Anderson Seeking Quick Settlement," *Wash. Post*, 28 Feb. 2002, at A1.

The corresponding noun is *debarment*, a rather infrequent word.

Disbar means "to expel from the legal profession"—e.g.:

- "Despite a Bel Air lawyer's glowing references from several distinguished former and current judges, the Court of Appeals ruled Friday to *disbar* him from the practice of law." Mary E. Medland, "Testimonials, Blaming the Accountant Fail to Save Tax Evader's Law License," *Daily Record* (Baltimore), 20 May 1996, at 21. (Note the venial REDUNDANCY in *disbar from the practice of law*.)
- "The bar can reprimand or *disbar* an attorney." Alan Abrahamson & Chuck Philips, "State May Take Control of Rap Mogul's Case," *L.A. Times*, 26 Oct. 1996, at A1.
- "The state associations should enforce their codes of ethics—and *disbar* lawyers who do not comply with the law." Letter of Theodore J. Sheskin, "Of Corporate Lawyers and Accountability," *N.Y. Times*, 18 Aug. 2002, § 3, at 10.

The corresponding noun is *disbarment*—a word not in common use until about 1900.

barbaric; barbarous. These words share the basic sense "primitive, uncivilized." *Barbaric*, which is four times as common as *barbarous* in modern print sources, typically describes a lack of culture that ranges from trivialities to anything less than heinous destruction of human life—e.g.:

- "The *barbaric* American tradition of splitting the check is still unknown here." Scott Baldauf, "Dim Sum: A Celebration in Itself," *Christian Science Monitor*, 15 Feb. 1996, Food §, at 14.
- "The stories must have sounded *barbaric* to the teenager sitting wide-eyed among adults at the breakfast table. Thirty-three swats with a wooden paddle for violating the dress code by wearing cuffed pants (a possible hiding place for cigarettes) in junior high school." Sandy Banks, "Ban of the Paddle Left a Void in Discipline," *L.A. Times*, 3 Sept. 2002, So. Cal. Living §, pt. 5, at 1.
- "That changed, Adewale remembers, once they heard he could earn a college scholarship. America's *barbaric* sport then became something to stomach right up to the time he tore up his left knee during his senior season at Indiana." Dave Hyde, "Ogunleye a Royal Find for Dolphins," *Orlando Sentinel*, 4 Sept. 2002, at D8.

Occasionally, though, *barbaric* actions are shocking—e.g.:

- "California Department of Corrections chief James Gomez has much to answer for in response to shocking reports that Corcoran State Prison guards have staged *barbaric* gladiator battles among inmates and have shot more than 50 convicts—seven fatally—when they failed to quit fighting when ordered." "State Prison Barbarism," *S.F. Chron.*, 30 Oct. 1996, at A20.
- "Justice by the government was swift and *barbaric* by Western norms. The four were beheaded." Loganathan Naidoo, "Saudis, U.S. Patch Things Up," *Green Bay Press-Gaz.*, 31 Aug. 2002, at A6.

The word *barbarous* is reserved for contexts involving savage cruelty—e.g.:

- "Calling the rape of an Okinawan schoolgirl a premeditated and *barbarous* act, prosecutors yesterday demanded 10-year prison terms with hard labor for three accused U.S. servicemen." Willis Witter, "Okinawa Case Pressed in Court," *Wash. Times*, 30 Jan. 1996, at A15.
- "Dray's graphic descriptions of *barbarous* lynchings provide the most compelling passages; his narratives are not for the squeamish." Marilyn K. Howard, "Shameful Legacy of Hatred Exposed," *Columbus Dispatch*, 28 July 2002, at E7.

barbarism; barbarity. Both denote a lack of civilization. *Barbarism* refers either to tastelessness or to incorrect language. *Barbarity* refers to savagery and brutality. Although misuses can run either way, *barbarity* for *barbarism* is the more frequent problem—e.g.: "It hangs on even in rather sophisticated styles, long after the writer has ceased to commit such *barbarities* [read *barbarisms*] as dangling modifiers, agreement errors, reference errors, and case-form errors." Bertrand Evans, "Grammar and Writing," in *A Linguistics Reader* 111, 122 (Graham Wilson ed., 1967). Both words have declined in frequency since the mid-19th century.

> LANGUAGE-CHANGE INDEX
> *barbarity* misused for *barbarism*: Stage 1

barbarous. See **barbaric.**

barbecue; *barbeque; *bar-b-cue; *bar-b-que; *BBQ. The first form is the predominant spelling. It is also the preferred one since it most clearly resembles its Spanish parent, *barbacoa*, meaning "a wooden framework for supporting meat over a fire." The other forms—as well as variants such as *Bar-B-Q and *B-B-Q—are common in advertising but should be avoided in carefully edited prose.

> LANGUAGE-CHANGE INDEX
> Current ratio (*barbecue* vs.
> all six variants combined): 3:1

barbed wire (= strands of twisted wire with sharp projections that impede passage when the wire is used in a fence) is two words as a noun phrase <the fence is made of barbed wire> but should be hyphenated as a PHRASAL ADJECTIVE <barbed-wire fence>. The form *barbwire (though economical) is a NEEDLESS VARIANT, and *bob wire is either an attempt at being folksy or a silly blunder—e.g.:

LANGUAGE-CHANGE INDEX (For the full key, see front matter pp. xxxi, l–li.)
Stage 1: Rejected. **Stage 2:** Widely shunned. **Stage 3:** Widespread but . . . **Stage 4:** Ubiquitous but . . . **Stage 5:** Fully accepted.
Invariably inferior forms marked by asterisk (*). • Ratios represent frequency of prevalent forms vs. variants in current books.

- "A neighboring congressman has climbed over the *bob wire* [read *barbed-wire*] fence." William Murchison, "Armey Talks Horse Sense on Agriculture," *Dallas Morning News*, 3 Mar. 1990, at A31.
- "And they patched our pants after we snagged them crawling under a *bob wire* [read *barbed-wire*] fence." Guy Friddell, "Readers Share Depression Memories," *Virginian-Pilot & Ledger Star* (Norfolk), 12 Mar. 2001, at B1.

LANGUAGE-CHANGE INDEX
bob wire for *barbed wire*: Stage 1
Current ratio (*barbed wire* vs. *bob wire*): 1,129:1

*barbeque. See **barbecue.**

barbiturate is pronounced either /bar-**bich**-ər-it/ or (less good) /bar-bi-**t[y]oor**-ət/. The pronunciation /bar-**bich**-ə-wət/, though increasingly common, is best avoided. Of course, if you've taken one before trying to say the word, your listeners will probably make allowances.

*bar-b-que. See **barbecue.**

*barbwire. See **barbed wire.**

bare, v.t. (= to uncover), is sometimes confused with *bear* (= [1] to carry; or [2] to endure)—e.g.: "They've invited women to *bear* [read *bare*] their breasts on 'Whip 'em out Wednesday.'" Larry Bonko, "Meet Charles DeFoore, Your Local Man in the Fight Against Vulgar TV," *Virginian-Pilot* (Norfolk), 1 Sept. 2002, at E2.
   The verb is inflected *bare* > *bared* > *bared*. For the opposite error, see **bear out.**

LANGUAGE-CHANGE INDEX
bear misused for the verb *bare*: Stage 1
Current ratio (*bare your soul* vs. *bear your soul*): 14:1

barefaced. See **bald-faced.**

baritone; *barytone. Since 1850 or so, the first has been standard in both AmE and BrE. Before that, BrE used the form *barytone.*

Current ratio: 29:1

bar mitzvah; bat mitzvah; bas mitzvah. These terms are sex-specific. *Bar mitzvah* = (1) the ceremony celebrating a Jewish boy's reaching religious adulthood at the age of 13; or (2) a Jewish boy who has turned 13 and thus attained religious adulthood. *Bat mitzvah* (or its variant, *bas mitzvah*) has the same meanings for a Jewish girl, though her age can vary from 12 to 13.
   While these terms were once compounded into single words, or joined by hyphens, today they are written as two-word phrases.

Current ratio (*bat mitzvah* vs. *bas mitzvah*): 42:1

barmy; balmy. In the sense "crazy, slightly mad," *barmy* is the original term and the usual one in BrE, where the word most often appears <she's gone barmy on us>. In AmE, *balmy* is more common— but neither term is often encountered with this sense in AmE.

Each word has additional, unrelated meanings. *Barmy* = foamy, frothy <barmy malt liquor>. *Balmy* = pleasant, mild <balmy weather>.

barrel, vb., makes *barreled* and *barreling* in AmE, *barrelled* and *barrelling* in BrE. See SPELLING (B).

barring. For *barring* as an acceptable dangling modifier, see DANGLERS (E).

*bar sinister. See **bend sinister.**

*barytone. See **baritone.**

basal (= forming or belonging to a bottom or normative layer) is pronounced /**bay**-səl/—not /**bay**-zəl/.

basalt (the dark green-black rock) is pronounced /bə-**sawlt**/ or /**bay**-sawlt/.

base, misused for *bass*, is scandalously poor usage—e.g.:

- "'Three Days' was an exercise in carnality, propelled by the sinuous *base* [read *bass*] guitar of Flea." Michael Saunders, "Jane's Addiction: This Set Didn't Satisfy," *Boston Globe*, 8 Nov. 1997, at C3.
- "Made up of four sopranos, four altos, three tenors and three *bases* [read *basses*], the student singers have been sharing their voices with audiences in Algonquin." "Neighbor," *Daily Herald* (Chicago), 16 Nov. 2000, at 1.

LANGUAGE-CHANGE INDEX
base misused for *bass*: Stage 1
Current ratio (*bass guitar* vs. *base guitar*): 74:1

based on. This phrase has two good and two bad uses. First, the phrase may carry a verbal force (*base* being a transitive verb)—e.g.:

- "She said she *based* her ruling *on* Xiong's allegations." Len Armstrong et al., "Cops and Confessions," *Chicago Trib.*, 16 Dec. 2001, at 1.
- "Dr. Douglas Richman . . . *based* his findings *on* blood samples taken from 1,908 men and women." "New Drug May Make Hay Fever Less Painful," *St. Petersburg Times*, 19 Dec. 2001, at A5.
- "Senior Pakistani intelligence officials . . . said they *based* their estimates *on* immigration records." Molly Moore & Peter Barker, "Inside Al Qaeda's Secret World," *Wash. Post*, 23 Dec. 2001, at A1.

Second, in a passive sense, it may carry an adjectival force (*based* being read as a past-participial adjective)—e.g.:

- "A quick calculation *based on* U.S. data indicates a requirement of $13 billion a year for Afghanistan." Letter of Randal Haithcock, *BusinessWeek*, 24 Dec. 2001, at 18. [*Based on* is an adjectival phrase modifying *calculation*.]
- "There is no handicapping formula *based on* urgency." Paul Zimmerman, "Dr. Z's Forecast," *Sports Illustrated*, 24 Dec. 2001, at 80. [*Based on* modifies *formula*.]
- "Last year, advance publicity *based on* laboratory results said Craig's detector would be able to find mines as the operator walked at a normal pace." Charles W. Petit, "Risky Ground," *U.S. News & World Rep.*, 24 Dec. 2001, at 54. [*Based on* modifies *publicity*.]

But traditionally speaking, *based on* should have neither adverbial nor prepositional force. Here it's an adverb:

- "American officials said they attacked the convoy *based on* intelligence reports." Larry Kaplow & Don Melvin, "A Tricky Time in Afghanistan," *Atlanta J.-Const.*, 22 Dec. 2001, at A1. [*Based on* improperly modifies *attacked*. Try *because of* or *owing to* instead.]
- "He encourages his students to listen to the candidates and vote *based on* the issues, not *based on* their clan." Lornet Turnbull, "Local Election Set for Somali Civic Leadership," *Columbus Dispatch*, 22 Dec. 2001, at A1. [*Based on* improperly modifies *vote*. Try *according to* instead.]
- "Executives were compensated *based on* a market valuation formula." Bethany McLean, "Why Enron Went Bust," *Fortune*, 24 Dec. 2001, at 58. [*Based on* improperly modifies *compensated*. Try *according to* instead.]

And here it's a preposition (a DANGLER, to be exact):

- "*Based on* those conversations, Riley said he doubts Graham will play." "Graham's Father Killed," *Deseret News* (Salt Lake City), 22 Dec. 2001, at D4. [A suggested revision: *Riley said that because of those conversations, he doubts . . . .*]
- "*Based on* a survey of manufacturers' and retailers' orders for shrink-wrapped gift paper rolls, Appert estimates that overall Christmas season retail sales will be relatively flat." Jeffrey Hirsch, "It's Wrapping Up to Be a Poor Season for Gift Paper Services," *L.A. Times*, 22 Dec. 2001, at C1. [A suggested revision: *A survey . . . led Appert to estimate . . . .*]

LANGUAGE-CHANGE INDEX
based on used adverbially in place of *because* or *because of*: Stage 4

basically. So spelled—not **basicly*.

Current ratio: 6,002:1

basil (the strong-tasting herb used in cooking) is pronounced either /**baz**-il/ (the most traditional pronunciation) or /**bay**-zil/. The ordinary pronunciation of the proper name *Basil* is /**baz**-il/ in BrE but sometimes /**bay**-zil/ in AmE.

basilisk (= an imaginary snakelike animal in ancient stories, legendarily capable of killing people by looking at them) is pronounced either /**baz**-i-lisk/ or /**bas**-i-lisk/.

basis. A. In Wordy Constructions. The word *basis* often signals verbosity in adverbial constructions such as *on a daily basis* and *on a regular basis*, where a simple adverb would serve better—e.g.:

- "Each one is tremendously important to me *on a personal and professional basis* [read *both personally and professionally*]." Zig Ziglar, *Ziglar on Selling* 15 (1991).
- "Fain has refused to release the material because some of it, such as employee surveys, was collected *on a confidential basis* [read *confidentially*]." "Fired Town Manager to Request Hearing," *Hartford Courant*, 7 Sept. 1996, at B3.
- "The IOC must decide whether beach volleyball and women's softball, which were introduced *on a provisional basis* [read *provisionally*], should be retained for Sydney." "Sports Flashes," *Toronto Sun*, 12 Oct. 1996, at S18.

See FLOTSAM PHRASES. For *on a pro rata basis*, see **pro rata.**

B. Plural Form. The plural of *basis*, as well as of *base*, is *bases*. The pronunciations differ, however: for *basis*, the plural is pronounced /**bay**-seez/; for *base*, /**bays**-iz/.

basketful. Pl. *basketfuls*—not **basketsful*. See PLURALS (G).

Current ratio: 4:1

bas mitzvah. See **bar mitzvah.**

bas relief (= a style of art in which stone or wood is cut so that it has raised shapes) is pronounced with a silent *-s-* (/bah ri-**leef**/).

bass. See **base.**

bassinet (= a hooded basket used as a baby's cradle) is so spelled—not **bassinette*. The word probably derives from a modified form of the French word *barcelonnette*. But the mock-French form **bassinette* doesn't exist in French and shouldn't exist in English—e.g.: "You had the nursery all set up [with] matching quilts, crib bumpers, diaper bag and a *lacey* [read *lacy*] *bassinette* [read *bassinet*] or cradle just inches from the marital bed." Margery Eagan, "There's Double the Wisdom by the Time No. 3 Arrives," *Boston Herald*, 15 Mar. 1994, at 8. See GALLICISMS.

LANGUAGE-CHANGE INDEX
bassinet misspelled **bassinette*: Stage 2
Current ratio: 7:1

bastard. See **dastard (A)**, EUPHEMISMS & **illegitimate child.**

bastille; *bastile. Apart from historical references to the *Bastille*—the Paris prison stormed in 1789 during the French Revolution—the term is occasionally used as a dressy equivalent of *prison* or *jail*. Although the Middle English spelling was **bastile*, today the settled spelling is *bastille*, after the French.

Current ratio: 2:1

bated breath is the phrase from Shakespeare's *Merchant of Venice*: "Or shall I bend low and in a bondman's key, with *bated breath* and whisp'ring humbleness, say this: . . ." (1.3.122–25). The idea is that breath is *abated*, or stopped. **Baited breath* is a bungle that was not an appreciable issue in the language until about 1950. Today it is more common than ever, though the correct spelling remains far more frequent in modern print sources—e.g.:

- "During its 'Creature Feature' blowout, the aquarium wants kids and adults alike to celebrate the holiday with *baited breath* [read *bated breath*]." Bob Herguth, "Six Galleries of Aquatic Horror!" *Chicago Sun-Times*, 27 Oct. 1995, WKP §, at 3.
- "Start by replacing the outfield walls with stalks of corn. Give the corn a little bit of water, sunshine and just enough love to let it grow. Then wait with *baited breath* [read *bated breath*] for the ghosts of the Brewers' past to

LANGUAGE-CHANGE INDEX (For the full key, see front matter pp. xxxi, l–li.)
Stage 1: Rejected. **Stage 2:** Widely shunned. **Stage 3:** Widespread but . . . **Stage 4:** Ubiquitous but . . . **Stage 5:** Fully accepted.
Invariably inferior forms marked by asterisk (*). • Ratios represent frequency of prevalent forms vs. variants in current books.

come walking out!" Peter Kevechich, "Save the Brewers," *Milwaukee J. Sentinel*, 11 June 2002, at C2.

LANGUAGE-CHANGE INDEX
*baited breath for bated breath: Stage 2
Current ratio (bated breath vs. *baited breath): 9:1

bathe; bath, vb. In AmE, someone who takes a bath *bathes*; in BrE, one *baths*. In BrE, *bathe* suggests either swimming (especially in the sea) <to bathe in the North Sea> or dousing with a liquid <to bathe the wound in alcohol>.

bathetic, not *bathotic*, is the adjective corresponding to *bathos*. (See **bathos.**) The analogy is to *pathos* and *pathetic*. But some writers ill-advisedly write *bathotic*, which isn't recognized in modern dictionaries—e.g.:

- "Puffin's latest religious offering, *The Young Puffin Book of Bible Stories*, is so desperate to make these millennia-old stories 'relevant' that it frequently descends into *bathotic* [read *bathetic*] purple prose, often missing the point in the process." Nicola Tyrer, "The Day Noah Dropped the Olive Branch," *Daily Telegraph*, 29 Mar. 1989, at 17.
- "To that end Glimcher simply, unnecessarily, distilled much of the Cuban flavor right out of the movie, reducing the disjointed film to an uneven *bathotic* [read *bathetic*] telenovella that sloppily airbrushes over the mambo era." John Lannert, "Latin Notas," *Billboard*, 22 Feb. 1992, at 35.
- "This set of variations for cello and orchestra is not the typical overblown *bathotic* [read *bathetic*] Tchaikovsky work, but one full of grace and lightness." Robert C. Fuller, "Young Cellist's Symphony Performance Is Stunning," *Des Moines Register*, 22 Nov. 2005, at E3.

LANGUAGE-CHANGE INDEX
*bathotic for bathetic: Stage 1
Current ratio (bathetic vs. *bathotic): 24:1

bathos; pathos. These two words sometimes cause confusion. *Bathos* (/**bay**-thahs/) means "a sudden descent from the exalted to the trite, or from the sublime to the ridiculous." *Pathos* (/**pay**-thahs/) means "sympathetic pity," and is useful, for example, in reference to juries and theater audiences. Cf. **ethos.**

*bathotic. See **bathetic.**

bat mitzvah. See **bar mitzvah.**

*baton sinister. See **bend sinister.**

battery. See **assault.**

battle royal (= [1] a violent struggle among several contenders; or [2] a major dispute) forms the plural *battles royal*—not *battle royals*. See PLURALS (G) & POSTPOSITIVE ADJECTIVES.

LANGUAGE-CHANGE INDEX
Current ratio (battles royal vs. *battle royals): 1.5:1

*baulk. See **balk.**

bawl out (= to excoriate) is the phrase, not *ball out*. But because the mistake is possible, it sometimes occurs—e.g.:

- "Although Hallinan issued his memo reiterating his support of Salomon, he also reportedly 'balled out' [read

bawled out] his chief deputy for letting the situation deteriorate." Dennis J. Opatrny, "Hallinan Says Salomon Has His Backing," *Recorder* (S.F.), 9 May 2000, at 1.
- "'I got *balled out* [read *bawled out*] quite a bit.'" David Holmstrom, "Fred 'Demon' Marsh Has Reached 100 Years Young, and Still Believes in Forward Motion," *Christian Science Monitor*, 7 June 2000, at 14.
- "Ferris didn't have anything against or know Cowan personally, but became incensed when people told her that some commissioners had '*balled out*' [read *bawled out*] a news reporter over an article she had written about possible illegalities in his campaign report." Stephen L. Goldstein, "The Political Soap Opera," *Sun-Sentinel* (Ft. Lauderdale), 12 July 2000, at A23.

LANGUAGE-CHANGE INDEX
*ball out for bawl out: Stage 1
Current ratio (bawled him out vs.
*balled him out): 36:1

bay. See **gulf.**

bayonet. Both noun and verb are preferably pronounced /**bay**-ə-net/. The verb is inflected *bayoneted* and *bayoneting*.

bazaar. See **bizarre.**

*BBQ. See **barbecue.**

B.C.; A.D.; B.C.E.; C.E. The abbreviation B.C. (= before Christ) is usually so printed—in small capitals. By convention, B.C. follows the year <Julius Caesar died in 44 B.C.>. But A.D. (= *Anno Domini* "in the year of our Lord") properly precedes the year <Hadrian's wall was completed in A.D. 126>, unless the abbreviation is paired with a time frame expressed in words <the second century A.D.>.

Some scholars condemn B.C. and A.D. as undesirably sectarian. What about non-Christians? they ask. Why should non-Christians have to measure their calendar from the birth of Christ? A trend has therefore emerged to use B.C.E. (= before the common era) and C.E. (= common era)—the traditional Jewish designations—in place of the Christian labels. Unlike A.D., the abbreviation B.C.E. or C.E. never precedes the year. E.g.:

- "The Greeks were much interested in language just as they were interested in any number of things, and in the fifth and fourth centuries BCE they debated many linguistic issues." Ronald Wardhaugh, *Proper English: Myths and Misunderstandings About Language* 107 (1999).
- "70 CE: The Gospel of Mark is written, scholars believe. It contains the 'Little Apocalypse' (Mark 13), which includes Christ's words to his disciples, 'This generation shall not pass till all these things be fulfilled.'" Elizabeth Trever Buchinger, "The End? Again!?!" *Pensacola News J.*, 1 Jan. 2000, at B1.
- "In the year 167 BCE (Before the Common Era), Judea was a province under the control of the Syrian-Greek Empire." "Hanukkah, the Jewish Festival of Lights," *Orlando Sentinel*, 9 Dec. 2001, at G2. (Note that the use of B.C.E. and C.E. is uncommon enough that this editor felt a need to explain it to the readers.)

Whether this trend will catch on outside academic writing is still uncertain. There has already been much wrangling on the point, and there is sure to be more. Unless you feel strongly averse to them, the traditional tags are the better choice because they are clear to more readers.

By the way, many people mistakenly believe that A.D. means "after death." By that erroneous measure, about 33 years of history (Jesus' lifetime) would be lost.

be. See BE-VERBS.

bear > bore > borne. See **born.** See also **bare.**

bear out (= to support or confirm as evidence) is sometimes wrongly made **bare out*—e.g.:

- "These are just a few of the many numbers [that] *bare* [read *bear*] out the fact that Texas and Randall County are caught up in a wave of juvenile crimes." Bradley Harrington, "Living in Confinement," *Canyon News*, 31 Mar. 1996, at 1.
- "A luncheon date with his offensive line next week *bares* [read *bears*] that out." Gary Voet, "Edmonds Scores High as SCC's Quarterback," *Sacramento Bee*, 22 Nov. 1996, at E1.

For the opposite error, see **bare.**

The past-participial form of *bear out* is *borne out.* For *borne* vs. *born,* see **born.**

LANGUAGE-CHANGE INDEX
*bare out for *bear out*: Stage 1
Current ratio (*bear out* vs. **bare out*): 186:1

beat > beat > beaten. So inflected. The archaic past participle *beat* persists only in the CASUALISMS *I'm beat* (= I'm exhausted) and *can't be beat* (= is superb), and (vestigially) in the word *deadbeat.*

In DIALECT, *beat* frequently gets used as a past participle, and it sometimes creeps into otherwise highbrow prose—e.g.: "He gives other reasons for questioning the idea that Kennedy could have *beat* [read *beaten*] Richard Nixon in 1968." Garry Wills, "Waiting for Bobby," *N.Y. Rev. of Books*, 10 Feb. 2000, at 18.

But if that usage (*could have beat*) is nonstandard, the form **beated* is distinctly substandard, whether as a past tense or as a past participle—e.g.:

- "That win was even more gritty, since Disponzio had *beated* [read *beaten*] Golnar twice during the regular season." John Valenti & Joe Krupinski, "Vogts Doesn't Miss a Beat," *Newsday* (N.Y.), 9 Nov. 1995, at A86.
- "Daniels never left. Not after Rev. James Reeb, a Unitarian minister from Boston, was *beated* [read *beaten*] to death by four segregationists in Selma the next day." Bob Hohler, "Seminary Student Honors '65 Sacrifice," *Boston Globe*, 24 Aug. 1997, at A1.
- "Third-seeded Alberto Berasategui of Spain *beated* [read *beat*] unseeded countryman Joaquin Munoz 6–4, 6–4 in the first round." Paul Newberry, "Pro Tennis—Courier Saves U.S. Hopes," *Dayton Daily News*, 7 Apr. 1998, at C1.

See IRREGULAR VERBS.

LANGUAGE-CHANGE INDEX
1. *beat* misused for past-participial *beaten*: Stage 2
Current ratio (*had beaten* vs. *had beat*): 8:1
2. **beated* for simple-past *beat*: Stage 1
Current ratio (*beat me* vs. **beated me*): 6,176:1
3. **beated* for past-participial *beaten*: Stage 1
Current ratio (*was beaten* vs. **was beated*): 3,352:1

Beatrice and Benedick. See **Benedick.**

beau forms the plurals *beaus* and *beaux*, the second of which is predominant in both AmE and BrE. See PLURALS (B). Perhaps because of its quaintness, the word has been very much on the wane since about 1950.

beaucoup (= many or much) is pronounced /boh-**koo**/ or /**boh**-koo/—preferably not /**boo**-koo/ (usually a facetious illiteracy).

beau geste (= [1] a generous or magnanimous gesture, or [2] a transparently empty gesture meant to seem generous or magnanimous) suffers from an unfortunate ambiguity. Is the term laudatory or damning? In any event, its plural is *beaux gestes* (pronounced, like the singular, /boh **zhest**/)—not **beaus gestes.*

beau ideal (= [1] ideal beauty, or [2] the perfect example of a thing) has, since the early 19th century, predominantly formed the English plural *beau ideals*— not *beaux ideals* (the French plural) or **beaux ideal.* Sense 2 is attributable to a misunderstanding of the French phrase. Although *beau* is the noun and *ideal* the adjective in French, many mistakenly think that *beau* is the adjective and *ideal* the noun. Sense 1 is the strictly correct translation.

Current ratio (*beau ideals* vs. *beaux ideals* vs. **beaux ideal*): 27:2:1

beauteous. Though H.W. Fowler labeled this word a "poeticism" equivalent to *beautiful*, the process of DIFFERENTIATION has created a distinction between the two words. Today, *beauteous* typically means not just "beautiful" but "beautiful and sexy," when it refers to women (as it most commonly does)—e.g.:

- "It might be called 'Leaving Long Island,' except that no *beauteous* hooker gives Buscemi's lonesome loser-boozer a seraphic farewell." Malcolm Johnson, "One Sad Life Melts Away in 'Trees Lounge,'" *Hartford Courant*, 1 Nov. 1996, at E5.
- "The campaign to draw in listeners approaches hysteria. One *beauteous* young violinist displays herself sawing away while wearing a wet T-shirt." Bernard Holland, "The Decline and Fall of the Classical Empire?" *N.Y. Times*, 10 Nov. 1996, § 2, at 11.
- "Four *beauteous* Staten Islanders have reigned as Miss New York." Carol Ann Benanti, "The Tiara Through the Years," *Staten Island Advance*, 5 June 2015, Entertainment §, at 8.

One can understand why writers sometimes wish to avoid the commonplace *beautiful.* As one professional

LANGUAGE-CHANGE INDEX (For the full key, see front matter pp. xxxi, l–li.)
Stage 1: Rejected. **Stage 2:** Widely shunned. **Stage 3:** Widespread but . . . **Stage 4:** Ubiquitous but . . . **Stage 5:** Fully accepted.
Invariably inferior forms marked by asterisk (*). • Ratios represent frequency of prevalent forms vs. variants in current books.

editor put it, "*Beautiful* is an adjective so hackneyed that it has lost all force and really indicates little more than mild to moderate approval." Lester S. King, *Why Not Say It Clearly* 54 (1978).

because. A. Senses. The conjunction *because* ordinarily begins a dependent clause that expresses reason, cause, or motive for whatever idea appears in the main clause. It has a well-known sense ("for the reason that" or "by reason of") and, in expressions that amount to CASUALISMS, some senses that most dictionaries don't record. The most common of the seldom-recorded meanings is "and the evidence is that" <it must be snowing in Chicago because the airport has been shut down for "weather-related reasons">. This usage contains an ellipsis: "(I deduce) p because q." E.g.:

- "It must be genetic *because* it takes a certain amount of determination to want to take on the rigours of coaching the Canadian junior hockey team for a second year in a row." Donna Spencer, "Junior Coach Inspired by Daughter," *Globe & Mail* (Toronto), 20 Dec. 2001, at S5.
- "Someone out there must be sitting pretty—*because* the toilet seat is gone." Phillip Matier, "Drug-Sniffing Pooch Patrol Lands BART in the Doghouse," *S.F. Chron.*, 23 Dec. 2001, at A25.
- "The people who go to Times Square must be out-of-towners, *because* I never met a New Yorker who wanted to be anywhere near there when the clock struck midnight." Steve Lopez, "Doing Fine Without MSNBC or NFL," *L.A. Times*, 28 Dec. 2001, at B1.

Sometimes *because* occurs in a question in the sense "given the fact that" or "in view of the fact that" <Why are you wearing an overcoat, because it's 85 degrees out here!>. Here the ellipsis is "(I'm asking) p because q."

B. Punctuation with. The word *because* usually shouldn't follow a comma: when a dependent clause (the *because*-clause) follows the main independent clause of the sentence, no break is needed between the two. E.g.:

- "Apparently, I answered right *because* Barbara Hendra then did something that I have marveled at for nearly two decades." William Parkhurst, "Champagne Corks and Mafia Killers," in *My First Year in Book Publishing* 127, 130 (Lisa Healy ed., 1994).
- "Some writers objected to the loan words *because* of their obscurity." Sidney Greenbaum, *The Oxford English Grammar* 406 (1996).
- "Eliot knew she wanted him sitting beside her *because* she was afraid." Jhumpa Lahiri, *Interpreter of Maladies* 119 (1999).
- "Throughout, I've allowed more of me to appear, which is good only *because* it lets me point up how writers are entitled to their own tastes and crotchets." John Trimble, *Writing with Style* viii (2d ed. 2000).

Yet a comma may be all but necessary when the sentence is long or complex—e.g.: "I begged him to try to find some way of getting me out of this frightful situation in which I was enmeshed—assuring him that I would not blame him if he failed to do so, *because* it seemed to me, after some days of reviewing the matter, that I was beyond human aid." P.G. Wodehouse, *The Code of the Woosters* 56 (1938; repr. 1976). And

when an adverb such as *perhaps* or *possibly* precedes *because*, a comma usually precedes the adverb—e.g.: "I have not taught or examined in the Faculty in thirteen years, though I gather it is now at peace with itself, possibly *because* most of the professors are now women, possibly *because* the depredations of government have forced them into alliances against an external enemy, possibly *because* there is now not thought to be anything worth fighting for." Frank Kermode, *Not Entitled* 258 (1995).

C. Causing Ambiguity. Putting a purpose clause or phrase after a negative often causes ambiguities, attested by a priest's unintentionally humorous statement: "I wear no clothes to distinguish myself from the congregation." Sometimes the ambiguity is technical only—e.g.: "A proposition is not false *because* it is a truism darkly expressed." W.W. Buckland, *Some Reflections on Jurisprudence* 109 (1945). Does this mean that the proposition is not false for that reason but for some other? Or does it mean that the proposition isn't necessarily false at all? The latter, Buckland intended to say. Other examples:

- "Patricia Buthmann and Tim Tyroler on Tuesday lost their effort to block being evicted from the Casa Carranza apartments, 1803 N. Country Club Drive, Mesa, *because* they allowed a woman to stay with them who possessed two syringes suspected to be drug paraphernalia." Kris Mayes, "Renters Run Afoul of Eviction Law," *Phoenix Gaz.*, 29 Sept. 1994, at B1. (What trouble did the unwelcome person cause? Did the tenants get an eviction notice because of the syringe-bearing woman, or did they lose their attempt at blocking the eviction because of her?)
- "By most writers on Elgar the sketches have been underrated, held of small account. For two reasons. First, because they recycle some earlier material . . . . (But Bach's Mass in B minor, Handel's Messiah, Beethoven's Fidelio, Verdi's Requiem are *not* contemned *because* they use ideas from earlier compositions.)" Andrew Porter, "Classical: Elgar's Unfinished Business," *Observer*, 26 Mar. 1995, at 12. (To eliminate the ambiguity, change *because they use* to *for using*.)
- "Waters was *not* there *because* she had dismissed the CIA director's visit as meaningless." John L. Mitchell, "Undeterred, Waters Crusades for Answers Politics," *L.A. Times*, 4 Mar. 1997, at A3. (If not for that reason, then why *was* she there? A possible revision: *Waters was not there: she had dismissed the CIA director's visit as meaningless.*)

D. Wordy Substitutes for. *Because* is often needlessly replaced by a verbose phrase such as *for the reason that*, *due to the fact that*, or *on the grounds that*—e.g.:

- "The motion for setoff could also have been denied *for the reason that* [read *because*] Patterson had failed to raise the contribution claim in a timely fashion during the original proceeding." Theodore Postel, "Arbitration Award: Setoff," *Chicago Daily Law Bull.*, 3 June 1994, at 1.
- "In 1991, Bridgeport, Connecticut, sought Chapter 9 protection but a judge denied it *on the grounds that* [read *because*] the city was solvent." Tony Jackson, "Orange County Hit by Wall St. Selling," *Fin. Times*, 8 Dec. 1994, at 6. (*On the grounds that* suggests—wrongly, here—that the reason isn't really a good one.)
- "That led one local analyst, who asked not to be named *due to the fact that* [read *because*] he had not yet seen the

filing, to speculate that the company was burning through cash and needed more to fuel its growth." M. Sharon Baker, "RealNetworks Finally Jumps into IPO Whirl," *Puget Sound Bus. J.*, 3 Oct. 1997, at 4.

E. Beginning a Sentence with. There's an odd myth that it's poor grammar to begin a sentence with *because*. It seems to have resulted from grade-school teachers who were trying to prevent fragments such as this: "We came in from recess after 15 minutes. Because everyone was tired." (See INCOMPLETE SENTENCES.) One way to prevent third-graders from committing this error is to outlaw putting *because* at the head of a sentence. But as with so many other third-grade rules, it sweeps too broad. It would prevent a writer's putting the cause before the effect: "Because everyone was tired, we came in from recess after 15 minutes."

In any event, the "rule" has never had any basis in grammar, and good writers often have occasion to put the cause before the effect (completing the subordinate clause beginning with *because* in a main clause that follows a comma)—e.g.:

- "*Because* a psychologist working in this field is characteristically concerned with people who are in difficulties or suffering from mental ill-health, he meets them (typically) as patients in a psychiatric and therefore medical context." B.A. Farrell, "Abnormal Psychology," in *The New Fontana Dictionary of Modern Thought* 2 (Alan Bullock & Stephen Trombley eds., 2d ed. 1988).
- "*Because* of difficulty traversing rough terrain, Eugene was late in arriving at the battlefield." Paul K. Davis, *100 Decisive Battles from Ancient Times to the Present* 229 (1999).

See SUPERSTITIONS (F).

F. *Because*-Clause as Subject. Although using a *because*-clause as the subject of a sentence—as if *because* meant "the mere fact that"—is common in speech, it is not standard written English. A typical example: "*Because a golfer might not be an athlete doesn't mean he or she won't be a top competitor.*" Harvey Penick, *Harvey Penick's Little Red Book* 114 (1992). [A possible revision: *A golfer's not being an athlete doesn't mean he or she won't be a top competitor. Or: Even a golfer who isn't an athlete may well be a top competitor.*] The problem with making a subordinate clause into the subject, as in the original, is that a MISCUE is created: the reader expects a different syntactic outcome in the sentence and is surprised, even with a short sentence such as the Penick original, to find that the *because*-clause governs a finite verb.

G. Fragment Beginning with. See INCOMPLETE SENTENCES (B).

H. Coupled with *reason*. See *reason is because.
I. As a Causal Word Generally. See as (A).
J. And *by reason of*. See by reason of.
K. And *since*. See since & SUPERSTITIONS (G).
L. *Just because*. See just because . . . doesn't mean.

beck and call is the idiom—e.g.: "We want men who would hang on every word we uttered, laugh at every joke, however lame. They would attempt to buy our love with little tokens, gifts, poetry. They would be at our *beck and call*." L. Wayne Moss & Donna and Eve Shavatt, "The Daydream and Nightmare of Reality TV," *Pitt. Post-Gaz.*, 26 Jan. 2003, at W2. A *beck* is a summoning gesture. The word arose in Middle English and is related to both *beckon* and *beacon*.

Sometimes the phrase *beck and call* comes out as a MONDEGREEN: *beckon call. E.g.:

- "Eleven years ago, McMahon was king of Super Bowl XX, with his own podium and an audience at his *beckon call* [read *beck and call*]." Danny Wells, "Backup Draws a Crowd," *Charleston Gaz.*, 23 Jan. 1997, at C1.
- "Rather, the collars, which are actually called 'electronic trainers,' are intended to be used when training dogs to obey an owner's *beckon call* [read *beck and call*]." Stephanie A. Stanley, "Electronic Dog Collars Create Clash Between Jogger, Parish," *Times-Picayune* (New Orleans) (St. Tammany ed.), 12 Sept. 2000, at 1.
- "Don't forget the personal trainer, personal swing doctor, and personal sports psychologist at his *beckon call* [read *beck and call*]." George Willis, "Drive Time for Ty," *N.Y. Post*, 20 Jan. 2002, at 92.

*Beckon call is an understandable guess at the phrase, since one would naturally call out to *beckon* someone. And *beckon* (= to summon) is a more familiar term than its shorter sibling *beck*. But *beck and call* is the historical and still the greatly predominant phrase.

LANGUAGE-CHANGE INDEX
*beckon call for *beck and call*: Stage 1
Current ratio (*beck and call* vs. *beckon call): 71:1

beckon, vb., may be either transitive <she beckoned the child> or intransitive <she beckoned to the child>. The more economical usage is the transitive one. As an intransitive verb, *beckon* sometimes takes *to*, sometimes *at*, and sometimes *for*; the most traditionally correct preposition is *to*. But you can forestall that problem by making the verb transitive—e.g.: "A coaching lieutenant named Mike Martz . . . *beckoned for* [read *beckoned*] Green to join him and Vermeil in St. Louis in 1999." Jerry Magee, "There's No Separating Chiefs QB from NFL Change," *San Diego Union-Trib.*, 1 Oct. 2002, at D6.

beef. This word has two plurals: in reference to types of meat or to complaints, the plural is *beefs*; but in reference to fattened cattle, the preferred plural is *beeves*. See PLURALS (C). *Beeves* is more common by a 4-to-1 ratio.

beg. For the phrase *beg the question*, see **beg the question.**

beget. A. Sense. *Beget* = (1) to sire; to father (a child); or (2) to produce (a result). The metaphorical meaning (sense 2) is an understandable extension of the

LANGUAGE-CHANGE INDEX (For the full key, see front matter pp. xxxi, l–li.)
Stage 1: Rejected. **Stage 2:** Widely shunned. **Stage 3:** Widespread but . . . **Stage 4:** Ubiquitous but . . . **Stage 5:** Fully accepted.
Invariably inferior forms marked by asterisk (*). • Ratios represent frequency of prevalent forms vs. variants in current books.

biological meaning (sense 1). But whenever the context is biological, it's worth remembering that this word isn't gender-neutral—e.g.: "She laughed. 'One does not object to the desires of one's king! Of course, if *I beget* [read *I give birth to*] a child, that will put an end to it.'" Carolyn Meyer, *Doomed Queen Anne* 14 (2002) (quoting the character Queen Anne).

B. Inflection: *beget* > *begot* > *begotten*. Because **begat* is an archaic past-tense form, it should typically be replaced by *begot* (and sometimes *begotten*). It appears most commonly when a writer strives for a humorous echo of all the *begat*s in the King James Version of Genesis. But the humor often fails, as in the following misbegotten examples:

- "Entire generations of Cubs and Sox fans have been born, raised, *begat* [read *begotten*] new generations of frustrated fans and died since our last winner." Dennis Byrne, "'Mistake by the Lake' Moves West," *Chicago Sun-Times*, 10 Oct. 1995, at 27. (The sentence has a nonparallel construction that could be advantageously recast: *Entire generations of Cubs and Sox fans have been born and raised, have begotten new generations of frustrated fans, and have died since our last winner.* See PARALLELISM.)
- "He and his wife had three children, who later *begat* [read *begot*] eight grandchildren and 10 great-grandchildren." John Keilman, "A Man of Indomitable Spirit Is Cited," *Capital* (Annapolis), 25 Sept. 1996, at A10.
- "The shootings of Ronald Reagan and Press Secretary James Brady eventually *begat* [read *begot* or (better) *led to*] the Brady Law, which requires a waiting period for handgun purchases." Gordon Witkin, "A Very Different Gun Culture," *U.S. News & World Rep.*, 28 Oct. 1996, at 44.

See ARCHAISMS & IRREGULAR VERBS.

Because the past tense **begat* is so common in allusion to the Old Testament, writers sometimes misuse it for the present tense—e.g.: "'Jesse the Body [Ventura] *begats* [read *begets*] Jerry Springer.'" B. Drummond Ayres Jr., "Political Briefing: A Run for the Senate or a Brawl for It," *N.Y. Times*, 22 July 1999, at A14 (quoting the Democratic Party chairman of Hamilton County, Ohio). The speaker has a vague memory of the **begat* passage from Genesis, but no sense of how the verb is conjugated.

LANGUAGE-CHANGE INDEX
1. **begat* for *begot* or *begotten*: Stage 1
2. **begat* for present-tense *beget*: Stage 1

beggar description. To *beggar description* is to be indescribable or beyond description. The phrase originated in Shakespeare's reference to Cleopatra: "For her own person, / It beggar'd all description" (*Antony and Cleopatra*, 2.2.197–98). What the phrase says, in essence, is that something is so incredible as to make a beggar of anyone's powers of description—e.g.:

- "Recently, New Yorkers have been up in arms over something so grievous, so blasphemous, that it *beggars description*. I'll give it a shot, though. Mayor Bill de Blasio was caught eating pizza with a knife and fork." Jim Sullivan, "'Pizzagate' in Big Apple," *Boston Herald*, 15 Jan. 2014, at 17.

- "The camera takes us into the house, and what we see *beggars description*." Joan Acocella, "Let It Go," *New Yorker*, 15 Dec. 2014, at 69.

Writers can get it wrong in many ways. And so they do. In the following example, the correct idiom wouldn't work because it wouldn't match the sense. And although the writer's **begs description* approaches the literal sense, his echo of the related idiom seems like a MALAPROPISM: "Ask Jim Adkins what is his area of specialty and he simply says he 'deals with the human figure.' It's an answer that *begs description* [read *demands elaboration*?]. See his works and no elaboration is necessary." Mike Boslet, "An Artist's Intentions Bared," *Wash. Post*, 4 July 1996, at M8.

LANGUAGE-CHANGE INDEX
*beg description for *beggar description*: Stage 1
Current ratio (*beggar description* vs.
*beg description): 32:1

begging the question. See **beg the question.**

begin. A. *To begin.* As an introductory phrase used to enumerate reasons, the idiomatic phrase is *to begin with*, not *to begin*. In the following sentence, the lack of the preposition *with* makes *to begin* sound narrowly chronological, as if Aaron actually began something and then, at some indeterminate point, stopped: "*To begin* [add *with*], Aaron played a substantial role in negotiating both agreements."

B. And *commence* & *start*. *Begin* is the usual word. *Commence* is a FORMAL WORD; ceremonies and exercises are likely to *commence*, as are official proceedings. *Start* usually refers to an activity <to start running> <I started thinking>; *begin* is also acceptable in this sense. Both *begin* and *start* may be followed by an infinitive (*to* + verb), but *commence* may not. See **institute** & **commence.**

C. Past Tense and Past Participle. *Begin*, of course, makes *began* in the past tense and *begun* in the past participle. But writers occasionally misuse *began* as a past participle—e.g.:

- "Rivera was competing for a spot in the back end of the Orioles' rotation, but probably would *have began* [read *have begun*] the season at Rochester." Roch Kubatko, "O's Rivera May Be Out for Season," *Baltimore Sun*, 24 Feb. 2001, at C1.
- "The deal, which values Carlyle at nearly $20 billion, strengthens the buyout firm's ties to the Middle East, which *has began* [read *has begun*] to use the profits from higher oil prices to go on a buying spree." Andrew Ross Sorkin, "Carlyle to Sell Stake to a Mideast Government," *N.Y. Times*, 21 Sept. 2007, at C1.
- "What *had began* [read *had begun*] as an overnight hike in rugged Denali National Park had turned into a five-day drama marked by rollercoaster reports and emotions." Mary Lynn Smith, "2 Hikers Rescued After a Call from the Alaska Wilderness," *Star Trib.* (Minneapolis), 19 June 2008, at A1.

These misuses are nothing new. Vallins noted them in 1951: "'He has *began*' is still common in careless speech, and sometimes crops up in even more careless writing." G.H. Vallins, *Good English: How to Write It* 30 (1951). See IRREGULAR VERBS.

LANGUAGE-CHANGE INDEX
began for past-participial *begun*: Stage 1

begrudge. See **resent (A)** & **grudging.**

beg the question. This phrase has not traditionally meant "to invite an obvious follow-up question," as some mistakenly believe. The strict meaning of *beg the question* is "to base a conclusion on an assumption that is as much in need of proof or demonstration as the conclusion itself." The formal name for this logical fallacy is *petitio principii*. Following are two classic examples and a third from a book review:

- "Reasonable people are those who think and reason intelligently." (This statement begs the question, What does it mean to think and reason intelligently?)
- "Life begins at conception, which is defined as the beginning of life." (This comment is patently circular.)
- "These premises and conclusions are no longer controversial among qualified students of language, including the best lexicographers." Sumner Ives, "A Review of *Webster's Third New International Dictionary*" (1961), in *A Language Reader for Writers* 44, 47 (James R. Gaskin & Jack Suberman eds., 1966). (This statement begs the question, Who is a "qualified student of language"?)

In the following sentence, the writer mangled the SET PHRASE *beg the question* and misapprehended its meaning (by using *begs* for *ignores* and *issue* for *question* or *problem*): "Blaming Congress and the Democrats for 'criminalizing of policy differences with the executive branch' *begs* a much larger *issue* here: Should members of the executive branch be allowed to withhold vital information from those members of Congress charged by law to monitor specific actions of the president?" Letter of John M. Burns, *Wall Street J.*, 16 May 1990, at A17.

All that having been said, the use of *beg the question* to mean *raise another question* is so ubiquitous that the new sense has been recognized by most dictionaries and sanctioned by descriptive observers of language. Still, though it is true that the new sense may be understood by most people, many will consider it slipshod.

LANGUAGE-CHANGE INDEX
1. *beg the question* for *evade the issue*: Stage 3
2. *beg the question* for *invite the follow-up question*: Stage 4

behalf. The phrases *in behalf of* and *on behalf of* have traditionally signified different things. *In behalf of* means "in the interest or for the benefit of" <he fought in behalf of a just man's reputation>; *on behalf of* means "as the agent or representative of" <on behalf of the garden club, I would like to thank our luncheon speaker> <she appeared on behalf of her client>. In current usage, the distinction is seldom followed; *on behalf of* is much more common in both senses. But stalwart stylists continue to distinguish the two.

In the following passages, one phrase has been switched for the other:

- "'There's a certain irony in the movie role,' the prosecutor said. 'In 1980, our man kills an Iranian dissident *in behalf of* [read *on behalf of*] an oppressive government. Now he's in a movie critical of oppression.'" Francis X. Clines, "An Actor's Film Wins Raves, His Identity Attracts Scrutiny," *N.Y. Times*, 3 Jan. 2002, at A14 (quoting State's Attorney Douglas F. Gansler).
- "Both agents testified *on Barboza's behalf* [read *in Barboza's behalf*] at the 1971 Clayton Wilson murder trial." Jim Lawrence, "Hub Fed Judge Must Testify on Mob Hit," *Boston Herald*, 5 Jan. 2002, News §, at 2. (They didn't testify as Barboza's representatives, but they gave testimony helpful to his case.)

Upon behalf of is now considered much inferior to *on behalf of*. See **upon.**

behemoth (= a huge, powerful animal) is pronounced /bə-**hee**-məth/. The word is sometimes misspelled (and presumably mispronounced) **behometh*—e.g.: "The other quarterfinals feature Lleyton Hewitt against Tommy Haas during the day today and Sweden's Joachim Johansson against Andy Roddick in a battle of big-serving, ace-loving *behemeths* [read *behemoths*] at night, weather permitting." Marc Berman, "Rain Men—Federer Leads Agassi by Set," *N.Y. Post*, 9 Sept. 2004, at 84.

LANGUAGE-CHANGE INDEX
behemoth misspelled **behometh*: Stage 1

behest (bi-**hest**), a stronger word than *request*, means (1) "a command," or (2) "a strong urging." *Bequest* (= a gift by will) is sometimes misused for *behest*, perhaps because of its phonic similarity to *request*—e.g.:

- "Growing up in Harlem, he was inspired by his creative uncles and his 'religious' mother, at whose *bequest* [read *behest*], he says with a sheepish smile, he joined a Trappist monastery in Massachusetts." Dennis Grogan, "Elbow Room for Creativity," *Atlanta J.-Const.*, 20 June 1996, at K1.
- "The Guardian Angel Personal Alcohol Test strips are being handed out at the *bequest* [read *behest* or, more likely, *request*] of the Colorado State Patrol at two of Lower Downtown's bustling bars this weekend." Allison Sherry, "Test a New Party Guest," *Denver Post*, 1 Sept. 2002, at B3.
- "One sends Jimmy [Hopkins] on a panty raid at the *bequest* [read *behest*] of his gym teacher, and another involves stealing the school mascot uniform." "High School Was Never This Entertaining," *Wash. Post*, 8 Dec. 2006, at T41.

This error is a MALAPROPISM. See **bequest,** n.

LANGUAGE-CHANGE INDEX
bequest misused for *behest*: Stage 1
Current ratio (*at his behest* vs. **at his bequest*): 45:1

behold > beheld > beheld. The word *beholden* is an archaic past participle, now used only as an adjective meaning "indebted" and attached to a *to*-phrase—e.g.:

LANGUAGE-CHANGE INDEX (For the full key, see front matter pp. xxxi, l–li.)
Stage 1: Rejected. **Stage 2:** Widely shunned. **Stage 3:** Widespread but . . . **Stage 4:** Ubiquitous but . . . **Stage 5:** Fully accepted.
Invariably inferior forms marked by asterisk (*). • Ratios represent frequency of prevalent forms vs. variants in current books.

- "Ryan implies that Eckels will be *beholden* to the contractors underwriting a large part of his campaign." Alan Bernstein, "County Judge Race Pits Opposing Styles," *Houston Chron.*, 9 Oct. 1994, at A1.
- "The elder Mr. [Duncan D.] Hunter said each of the earmarked projects stands up to scrutiny and rejected the notion that accepting campaign funds from defense contractors made him *beholden* to them." Matthew Cella, "Hunter's Earmarks Benefit His Son," *Wash. Times*, 13 Oct. 2008, at A1.

See IRREGULAR VERBS.

behoove (= to be necessary or proper) is so spelled in AmE <it behooves you to bite your tongue in such circumstances>. In BrE, the spelling is *behove*. The word has an archaic flavor, and its noun form, *behoof*, is all but obsolete.

Historically, the verb in BrE was pronounced, as reflected in the AmE spelling, to rhyme with *move* and *prove*. In BrE today "it is generally made to rime with *rove*, *grove*, by those who know it only in books" (*OED*). In AmE it is pronounced /bi-**hoov**/.

Beijing; Peking. The traditional form, *Peking*, resulted from a system of transliteration called Wade–Giles Romanization, introduced by two 19th-century English scholars. (*Peiching* was a variant.) In 1979, the Chinese government settled on a system called Pinyin Romanization (also called the Chinese phonetic alphabet) to convert Chinese sounds into roman letters; it is thought to be a closer approximation of Chinese pronunciation in the Mandarin dialect (/bay-**jing**/, not /-**zhing**/ or /-**shing**/). The Pinyin system resulted in *Beijing*, and most American media have now adopted this name for the capital of China. Despite the success of Pinyin, Taiwan still adheres to Wade–Giles spellings—and so do some Western scholars on China.

being that. A. Meaning "because" or "since." Instead of using this awkward phrase in the sense of *because* or *since*, use one of those straightforward words—e.g.:

- "And working with the Big Eye network made sense, *being that* [read *because*] the show comes from David Letterman's Worldwide Pants productions, whose other shows . . . are all on CBS." Scott Pierce, "'Ed' Perseveres," *Deseret News* (Salt Lake City), 17 Nov. 2000, at C8. (Delete the comma before the newly inserted *because*.)
- "*Being that* [read *Since*] it's installed in the front where the driver can see, its main purpose should be for navigation." Lynne Harrison, "Entertain the Kids on That Long Road Trip," *Winnipeg Free Press*, 29 Dec. 2000, at E1.
- "Bill Duffy, a native son of Chicago and longtime resident of the city of St. Francis, deserves our accolades, *being that* [read *since*] he has done all that he could to save a part of the town's history for probably another century." Ken Garcia, "Gold Rush Era Anchored in Saloon," *S.F. Chron.*, 21 Dec. 2001, S.F. Today §, at 1.

Sometimes the best replacement is *given that* or *in that*—e.g.: "I guess they finally understand Bush has many supporters in Kentucky, *being that* [read *given that* or *in that*] he won the state by a sizable margin." Letter of Greg Schuler, "The C-J Headline," *Courier-J.* (Louisville), 19 Dec. 2000, at A6.

B. In an Absolute Construction. This phrase frequently appears in what grammarians call a "nominative absolute"—e.g.:

- "Berglund . . . said the company has learned a lot since the company entered the market four years ago, the biggest surprise *being that* shoppers actually like grocery shopping." Patricia Wen, "Old Ways Run Deep," *Boston Globe*, 17 Nov. 2000, at A1.
- "Harris has declared her intention to certify the statewide results after overseas absentee ballots have been counted, the expectation *being that* those votes will add to Bush's current 300-vote lead." Thomas B. Evans Jr., "Count Them All Again," *Wash. Post*, 18 Nov. 2000, at A23.
- "When someone describes a film of today as a ''70s picture,' . . . it's invariably meant as a backhanded compliment, the implication *being that* the film is so edgy, gloomy or contemplative that it has no hope of reaching a wide audience." Patrick Goldstein, "The Dubious Anniversary of Cimino's 'Heaven's Gate,' " *L.A. Times*, 12 Dec. 2000, at F1.

See ABSOLUTE CONSTRUCTIONS.

But this type of absolute construction often appears ill-advisedly in a separate sentence as a fragment. (See INCOMPLETE SENTENCES.) The best solution is to use an ordinary finite verb (*is* or *are*)—e.g.:

- "Over the years I've adopted a policy of excluding from my annual Top 10 list any picture that has not opened in the Tacoma area by the end of the calendar year. The reason *being* [read *is*] that it seems unfair to salute movies that the vast majority of *News Tribune* readers wouldn't have had the opportunity to see by the time the list is published." Soren Andersen, "Marvels and Mistakes," *News Trib.* (Tacoma), 29 Dec. 2000, at SL1. (As this example shows, the construction is sometimes nothing more than throat-clearing. The second sentence would be stronger if it started with *it*, omitting everything that came before that.)
- "Most duck hunts are the kind that begin somewhere in the cold and darkened hours when no one but the owls and night herons are about. The theory *being* [read *is*] that one must be waiting in ambush when the ducks wake up." Bob Simpson, "This Wintry Hunt Produces Duck, Mistletoe," *News & Observer* (Raleigh), 31 Dec. 2000, at C15.

The next best solution would be to combine the two sentences into one.

But take care not to create an unwieldy sentence—as would happen if the two sentences here were combined: "[George] Will details the faults of Gore, but ignores those of Bush, who has made as many exaggerations as Al Gore, usually pronouncing them incorrectly in the process. One of the most egregious exaggerations *being* [read *is*] that he championed this and that legislation regarding health care and education, when in fact it was the Texas Legislature that did most, if not all, of the work." Bill Amborn, "Will's Diatribe," *Press Democrat* (Santa Rosa), 17 Nov. 2000, at B6.

belabor; labor, v.t. Modern dictionaries suggest that the words are interchangeable. But in the early 20th century, *belabor* (= to attack physically) was not much used figuratively in phrases such as *to belabor* *an argument*, the preferred expression being *to labor an argument*—e.g.: "I need not *labor* the point that the four elements of the positivist creed just outlined are interdependent." Lon L. Fuller, *The Morality of Law* 193 (rev. ed. 1969).

The popular grammarian Edwin Newman once chided a Justice of the U.S. Supreme Court for writing "to say more would belabor the obvious," stating: "To *belabor* the obvious is to hit it, which hardly seems judicial conduct." Edwin Newman, Foreword to Morton S. Freeman, *A Treasury for Word Lovers* viii (1983).

In fact, though, the figurative sense of *belabor* has vastly predominated over the literal one since about 1950. It is standard—e.g.:

- "The embalmed, *belabored* fussiness of the filmmaker's style, laden with a sentimentality at once maudlin and coy, makes one wonder if the Belfast-born wunderkind hasn't gone slightly batty." David Baron, "Tired 'Tale' Likely to Leave You Cold," *Times-Picayune* (New Orleans), 5 Apr. 1996, at L22.
- "There's no need to *belabor* here the ingenious forms of folly that led the 'smart guys' on Wall Street to believe they could eliminate risk by making it invisible." Tim Rutten, "A Crisis of Trust Too," *L.A. Times*, 11 Oct. 2008, at A19.
- "[Author Ian] O'Connor *belabors* the rivalry a bit, describing how [Jack] Nicklaus and [Arnold] Palmer competed passionately for endorsements (Palmer was the clear winner) and contracts to design new golf courses (Nicklaus dominated)." Chuck Leddy, "Sizing Up Golf's Legendary Rivalry," *Boston Globe*, 13 Oct. 2008, Sidekick §, at 8.

LANGUAGE-CHANGE INDEX
belabor an argument for *labor an argument*: Stage 5
Current ratio (*belabor* vs. *labor a point*): 4:1

Belarusian; *Belarusan. For a citizen of Belarus, the first is the standard term. The second is a NEEDLESS VARIANT. See DENIZEN LABELS.

Current ratio: 17:1

belie = (1) to disguise, give a false idea of; (2) to contradict or prove the falsity of; or (3) to leave unfulfilled. Senses 1 and 2 are the most common—e.g.:

- "One of the newspaper articles boldly suggested that Rodman's popularity had possibly eclipsed Jordan's among the local citizenry—a wholly preposterous thought that was *belied* [i.e., proved false] by the cheers from the sellout crowd of 24,394 the moment Jordan was introduced before the contest." Anthony Cotton, "Bulls Get Jump on Knicks, 91–84," *Wash. Post*, 6 May 1996, at C8.
- "But Israel's image as a modern, progressive state is *belied* [i.e., contradicted] by laws that still intertwine synagogue and state." Israel Herziliya, "Wedlocked: Jewish Law Impedes Divorce for Some," *Dallas Morning News*, 30 Oct. 1996, at C5.
- "Campbell's quiet, restrained delivery *belies* [i.e., disguises] a fearlessness that's well beyond her 26 years." Tim Chan, "Shooting Stars," *Globe & Mail* (Toronto), 11 Sept. 2015, at 30.

The word does not mean "to disclose or reveal," as is sometimes thought. That is, some writers wrongly think of it in a sense almost antithetical to sense 1—e.g.: "It was a high for the professional from Opelika, Ala., whose soft drawl *belied* [read *betrayed* or *revealed*] his Southern roots." Becky Paull, "Boise Open's First Winner Hopes to Regain Glory," *Idaho Statesman*, 17 Sept. 1995, at C1.

belligerence; belligerency. *Belligerence* refers to a person's truculent attitude. *Belligerency* has traditionally been the preferred term in international law when referring to the status of a state that is at war—e.g.: "Other states are within their rights in declaring themselves neutral in the struggle, and since there can be no neutrals unless there are two belligerents, such a declaration is equivalent to a recognition of the *belligerency* of both parties." J.L. Brierly, *The Law of Nations* 134 (5th ed. 1955). Although *belligerency* was more common in print from 1860 to 1980, *belligerence* has predominated since then—in 2008 by a 2-to-1 ratio.

bellwether (= someone who takes the lead or initiative; a trendsetter) is sometimes mistakenly written *bellweather, perhaps because, like a weathervane, it shows which way the wind blows—e.g.:

- "The sheriff conducted me to one of the two vacant jury rooms, then the jury, *bell-weathered* [read *bellwethered*] by Callahan, the court officer, filed out and retired into the other directly opposite." Ephraim Tutt, *Yankee Lawyer* 226 (1943). (The verbal use illustrated in the quoted sentence is unusual—see FUNCTIONAL SHIFT (D).)
- "The annual Vermont Open, a *bellweather* [read *bellwether*] of the New England Pro state championships, will be played on Monday through Wednesday, June 10–12, at Lake Morey Country Club in Fairlee, Vt." John R. Hussey, "Abenaqui Pro Sheerin Earns Spot at Senior PGA Event," *Union Leader* (Manchester, N.H.), 7 June 2002, at C2.
- "The success of either or both of these events could be a *bellweather* [read *bellwether*] for another high-profile MMA promotion taking place July 26." Tim Lemke, "A Promotion Commotion," *Wash. Times*, 16 July 2008, at C2.

Less common but no less whimsical is the misspelling *bellwhether—e.g.: "Intel Corp. advanced to $22.08. The semiconductor *bellwhether* [read *bellwether*] was raised to 'buy' from 'neutral' by Bank of America, which said the stock was likely to climb significantly." "Market Movers," *Chicago Trib.*, 11 Apr. 2008, at C5.

LANGUAGE-CHANGE INDEX
1. *bellwether* misspelled *bellweather: Stage 1
Current ratio: 43:1
2. *bellwether* misspelled *bellwhether: Stage 1

beloved. This word can be spoken with two syllables /bi-ləvd/ or three /bi-ləv-id/. The two-syllable form is somewhat old-fashioned and is usually reserved for the past participle <the queen was beloved by her subjects>. The three-syllable form is used for the

LANGUAGE-CHANGE INDEX (For the full key, see front matter pp. xxxi, l–li.)
Stage 1: Rejected. **Stage 2:** Widely shunned. **Stage 3:** Widespread but . . . **Stage 4:** Ubiquitous but . . . **Stage 5:** Fully accepted.
Invariably inferior forms marked by asterisk (*). • Ratios represent frequency of prevalent forms vs. variants in current books.

adjective <my beloved wife> or the attributive noun <dearly beloved, we are gathered here . . .>. Justice Sonia Sotomayor uses the three-syllable version in referring to her best-selling autobiography *My Beloved World* (2013).

bemean. See **demean.**

bemuse; amuse. The meanings of these two words differ significantly. *Bemuse* = (1) to make confused or muddled; bewilder <the jury was bemused by all the technical evidence>; or (2) to plunge into thought; preoccupy <the math student was bemused with the concept of infinity>. *Amuse*, of course, means "to entertain" or "to cause laughter in" <the speaker amused the audience with various anecdotes>.

Yet many writers mistakenly use *bemuse* as a synonym for *amuse*—e.g.:

- "The show also has a quirky humor that will *bemuse* [read *amuse*] jaded adults and even manages to touch some deeper chords without descending to the saccharine." Lawrence Johnson, "Nutcracker: A Classic Musical," *Chicago Trib.*, 12 Dec. 1996, Tempo §, at 2.
- "Led by Costas' ability to *bemuse* [read *amuse*] viewers and make them care about the athletes, NBC's Sydney squad was at least the tops since ABC's 1980s heyday. 'I appreciate the kind comments,' Costas said." Rudy Martzke, "Ratings Don't Dent NBC's Stellar Effort," *USA Today*, 2 Oct. 2000, Bonus §, at E4.

benchmark (= a point of reference from which to make measurements) is best spelled as one word.

bend > bent > bent. So inflected (although *on bended knee* is a SET PHRASE). Occasionally the verb gets bent out of shape—e.g.:

- "A teammate dummied a run over the ball, and then Mikacenic hit a right-footed shot—Lakeside's first of the game—that *bended* [read *bent*] up and around Mount Rainier's four-player wall and into the far-post side netting." Melanie Brennan, "Girls Soccer: Lakeside Ousts Mount Rainier," *Seattle Times*, 22 Nov. 1997, at B7.
- "He rolled and *bended* [read *bent*] the wrist to prove its mobility and strength." Paul Grondahl, "Racing Form," *Times Union* (Albany), 26 July 1998, at T2.
- "Lest anyone accuse my little one of being partisan, she might well have copied Hillary Clinton's Democratic National Convention address if we had *bended* [read *bent*] the bedtime rule to allow her to stay up to watch it." Jennifer Wheary, "Copying the 'Can-Do' Sarah Palin," *Newsday* (N.Y.), 8 Sept. 2008, at A29.

But in soccer, *bended* is the accepted past-tense and part-participial form of *bend* (= to kick a ball with enough spin to make it curve)—e.g.: "[Keenan] Seguancia *bended* his free kick to the edge of the 6-yard box and [Leslie] Nwapa got past the defense and knocked it in." Kyle Sakamoto, "Roosevelt 2, Àiea 1," *Honolulu Advertiser*, 25 Jan. 2008, at D2. See IRREGULAR VERBS.

bend sinister; *baton sinister; *bar sinister. In heraldry, the *bend sinister* is a diagonal band on a shield, extending (from the viewer's vantage point) between the upper right and the lower left corners; it denotes bastardy in the family line—e.g.: "To the 99.9% of people in Britain and beyond who feel their identity to be defined adequately without the aid of impalements and *bends sinister* or a family tree going back to John of Gaunt, the vocation of Garter King of Arms must seem as fantastical as that of the Lion King or King Kong." "Anthony Wagner," *Economist*, 3 June 1995, at 95. As in that quotation, the plural form is *bends sinister*. See POSTPOSITIVE ADJECTIVES.

*Baton sinister is a variant form seldom encountered.

*Bar sinister, though perhaps the most common of the three, is strictly incorrect because a bar is a horizontal stripe. Unlike a diagonal band, a bar can't have a distinct left (sinister) aspect. And because **bar sinister* is hardly less arcane for most readers than *bend sinister*, it might as well be corrected to that form—e.g.: "Finland thinks of itself as 'The daughter of the Baltic,' although she is not clear on her parentage. No *bar sinister* [read *bend sinister*], implying illegitimacy, it's just that Finns are forever running through the birch bark and pines looking for a national identity." Kevin Keating, "Laplander Lullabies," *Int'l Travel News*, Mar. 1996, at 153.

In the 1990s, the phrase was probably best known as part of the name of a rock group, Simon and the Bar Sinisters—but most of the fans were probably unaware of the allusion, and the band wisely avoided the correct plural form: *bars sinister*. Before that, Simon Bar Sinister was one of the villains in the *Underdog* cartoon series (1964–1973).

Benedick; Benedict. Both names were once traditional for a recently married man, especially one who was previously considered a confirmed bachelor. The *-ick* spelling is more common in BrE, the *-ict* spelling in AmE.

The character in Shakespeare's *Much Ado About Nothing* is Benedick, but writers occasionally get the name wrong—e.g.:

- "This provides the central story, but the 'merry war' of sub-plot characters Beatrice and *Benedict* [read *Benedick*] is what distinguishes 'Much Ado,' and long ago became its most recognizable component." Richard Dodds, "Festival Opens with 'Much Ado,'" *Times-Picayune* (New Orleans), 24 June 1994, at L23.
- "The comedy is about mature, unwilling lovers, Beatrice and *Benedict* [read *Benedick*]—prototypes for later squabbling lovers like Spencer Tracy and Katharine Hepburn." Christopher Rawson, "Pittsburgh Public Theater Looks to the Familiar, Classic," *Pitt. Post-Gaz.*, 24 Feb. 2002, at E3.
- "Dan Snook will be *Benedict* [read *Benedick*], opposite Karen Ziemba as Beatrice." Frank Rizzo, "Will 'Our Town' Be New York City by Year's End?" *Hartford Courant*, 8 Aug. 2002, Cal. §, at 16.

Several dictionaries list *benedict* as a common noun for a newly married man who was formerly considered a confirmed bachelor. Among these are *AHD*, *W2*, *W11*, and *WNWCD*. This usage appears to have resulted from a Shakespearean allusion, but the spelling was changed from *-ick* to the more common *-ict*. (The *SOED*, by contrast, puts the main entry under *Benedick* and labels *-ict* a variant.) The usage is fairly uncommon today.

beneficent; benevolent; *benefic; beneficial. The etymological difference between *beneficent* and *benevolent* is that between deeds and sentiments. *Beneficent* = doing good; charitable (*benefic now being merely a NEEDLESS VARIANT). The word is pronounced /bə-**nef**-i-sənt/. *Benevolent* = well-wishing, supportive, (emotionally) charitable. Aside from the idiom *benevolent society*, the distinction should be cultivated: we should reserve *beneficent* for "doing good" and *benevolent* for "inclined or disposed to do good." *Beneficial* has the general meaning "favorable, producing benefits." Cf. **malevolent.**

beneficiary is pronounced /ben-ə-**fish**-ee-er-ee/ or /ben-ə-**fish**-ə-ree/—not /ben-ə-**fish**-ə-rer-ee/. Cf. **judiciary.**

benefit. A. Inflections of Verb. *Benefit* makes *benefited* and *benefiting* in AmE, *benefitted* and *benefitting* in BrE. See SPELLING (B).

B. Improving Wordy Constructions. As a verb, *benefit* typically functions more economically and smoothly in the active voice than in the passive—e.g.:

- "The launch of the Multia MI, which now complements the Alpha-based Multia, will *be significantly benefited by* [read *benefit significantly from*] the Digital/Microsoft alliance." Stephen Lawton, "Digital Adds Intel-Based Multia Client," *Digital News & Rev.*, 6 Nov. 1995, at 1.
- "Just as the public *is benefited by* [read *benefits from*] licensure, individual states also have a stake in establishing licensure legislation." Ronni Chernoff, "Licensure—Perseverance in a Good Cause," *J. Am. Dietetic Ass'n*, Aug. 1996, at 805.

See PASSIVE VOICE.

As a noun in the phrase *be of benefit to* or *be a benefit to*, the word (once again) can often perform better as an active-voice verb—e.g.:

- "Newmark said the structure would *be a benefit to* [read *benefit*] an area town planners had said needed redevelopment." Nancy Degutis, "Morristown Approves 6-Story Condo Building," *Star-Ledger* (Newark), 22 Aug. 2002, at 18.
- "In terms of [read *As to*] health, feng shui can not only help with issues [read *problems*] such as weight gain and weight loss, but it can also *be of benefit to* [read *benefit*] people with muscular sclerosis and chronic health problems." Catherine Murrell, "Feng Shui Principles Can Improve Home Life," *Chicago Sun-Times*, 20 Sept. 2002, at C16. (For more on the unparallel *not only . . . but also* construction in this sentence, see **not only . . . but also** & PARALLELISM.)

See BE-VERBS (B).

benefit of clergy = (1) at common law (12th c.–19th c.), the right of a clergyman not to be tried for a felony in the King's Court; or (2) by SLIPSHOD EXTENSION, religious approval as solemnized in a church ritual. By invoking the benefit of clergy—usually by reading the so-called *neck verse* (a biblical passage recited in Latin)—one accused of a felony could have the case transferred from the King's Court (which imposed the death penalty for a felony) to the Ecclesiastical Court (which did not).

In sense 2, the phrase is a popularized legal technicality, appearing most often in reference to children born out of wedlock—e.g.:

- "With her, and *without benefit of clergy*, he had five children, and it was his boast that, as each arrived, he dispatched it promptly to a foundling home." René A. Wormser, *The Story of the Law* 215 (1962).
- "Wakefield's generation, twenty years on, didn't just engage in sex *without benefit of clergy*, they talked about it." Rhoda Koenig, "Talkin' 'bout Their Generation," *New York*, 1 June 1992, at 57.
- "We weren't permitted to live together and have children in those days *without benefit of clergy*." Leo Haber, "Bobby," *Midstream*, Fall 2012, at 36.

benevolent. See **beneficent.**

benign; *benignant. The latter is a NEEDLESS VARIANT. The antonym of *benign*, however, is *malignant*.
        Current ratio (*benign* vs. *benignant): 28:1

bequeath = (1) to give (an estate or effect) to a person by will <she bequeathed the diadem to her daughter>; or (2) to give (a person) an estate or effect by will <she bequeathed her daughter the diadem>. Using the word as a fancy equivalent of *give* or *present* is an ignorant pretension—e.g.:

- "Apparently Mayor Annette Strauss plans to *bequeath* [read *present*] the gift personally to Her Majesty—something rarely done, according to protocol experts. Usually, a gift is *bequeathed* [read *presented*] to the queen's secretary, who then *bequeaths* [read *gives*] it to the queen." Helen Bryant, "Names & Faces," *Dallas Times Herald*, 5 Apr. 1991, at A2.
- "In addition to featuring a strong lineup of regional performers, . . . the festival *bequeaths* [read *awards*] its Golden Umbrella Award to a jazz artist—Seattle's beloved first lady of song, Ernestine Anderson." Paul de Barros, "Bumbershoot's Light Shines on Ernestine Anderson," *Seattle Times*, 30 Aug. 2002, at H6.

The word is pronounced /bi-**kweeth**/, with a soft *th*.
        LANGUAGE-CHANGE INDEX
        bequeath for *present* or *give*: Stage 1

bequest, n.; *bequeathal; *bequeathment. *Bequest* = (1) the act of bequeathing; or (2) personal property (usu. other than money) disposed of in a will. *Bequest* is sometimes confused with *behest*. See **behest.**

*Bequeathal and *bequeathment are NEEDLESS VARIANTS of sense 1 of *bequest*—e.g.:

- "What is known about Lillian Thomas Pratt is that she changed the face of the Virginia Museum, with a *bequeathal* [read *bequest*] that placed the commonwealth on the artistic map of the world." Sibella C. Giorello, "Egg Money: Lillian Thomas Pratt Gathered Some of the Finest Fabergé Pieces," *Richmond Times-Dispatch*, 18 Aug. 1996, at J1.

LANGUAGE-CHANGE INDEX (For the full key, see front matter pp. xxxi, l–li.)
Stage 1: Rejected. **Stage 2:** Widely shunned. **Stage 3:** Widespread but . . . **Stage 4:** Ubiquitous but . . . **Stage 5:** Fully accepted.
Invariably inferior forms marked by asterisk (*). • Ratios represent frequency of prevalent forms vs. variants in current books.

- "Martha [Boyle] receives this *bequeathment* [read *bequest*] as her family prepares to leave for its annual trip to Cape Cod—and one of the oceans that Olive never saw." Claire Martin, "Realizing How Many Lives One Person Can Touch," *Denver Post*, 19 Oct. 2003, Books §, at EE2.
- "Last updated in 1993, before the U.S. political lexicon had acquired 'soccer moms' (1996), 'fuzzy math' (2000) and 'Swift Boat spot' (2004), the book's newest version includes rich linguistic *bequeathals* [read *bequests*] from both the Clinton and second Bush White Houses." Katie Baker, "How to Sound Presidential," *Newsweek*, 24 Mar. 2008, at 17.

LANGUAGE-CHANGE INDEX
1. **bequeathment* for *bequest*: Stage 1
Current ratio (*bequest* vs. **bequeathment*): 381:1
2. **bequeathal* for *bequest*: Stage 1
Current ratio (*bequest* vs. **bequeathal*): 182:1

bequest, v.t., is obsolete in place of *bequeath*. Today it amounts to no more than a silly error that has appeared in a would-be Shakespearean scholar's writing: "And by so felicitously using the words newly *bequested* [read *bequeathed*] to English, [Shakespeare], more than any other writer of the English Renaissance, validated the efforts of earlier and contemporary neologists." Bryan A. Garner, "Shakespeare's Latinate Neologisms," 15 *Shakespeare Studies* 149, 151 (1982).

LANGUAGE-CHANGE INDEX
bequest misused for the verb *bequeath*: Stage 1
Current ratio (*bequeathed* vs. **bequested*): 411:1

bereave, v.t., yields as past-tense forms *bereft* and *bereaved*, and the same forms as past participles. *Bereaved* is used in reference to loss of relatives by death. *Bereft* is used in reference to loss of immaterial possessions or qualities.

As Bill Bryson observes, to be *bereft of* something is not merely to lack it but to have been dispossessed of it (*Dictionary of Troublesome Words* 26 [1984]). Hence the following uses are off target:

- "There may be more than six degrees of separation, but American Presidential candidates with ties to royalty have a distinct advantage over those *bereft of* [read *lacking*] noble connections." Nadine Brozan, "Chronicle," *N.Y. Times*, 28 Oct. 1996, at B12.
- "On the other hand, [the Third Symphony] is largely *bereft of* [read *lacking in* or *barren of*] engaging ideas and, in a word, boring." Bernard Holland, "From Penderecki, a Mob That Howls or Whispers," *N.Y. Times*, 28 Oct. 1996, at C15.
- "At the vegan restaurant Angelica Kitchen, in the East Village, there's a Reuben sandwich *bereft of* [read *without*] corned beef and Swiss cheese, which sort of makes you wonder why it doesn't just take a different name, like an Irving or a Bernard." Frank Bruni, "Not Missing the Meat (Mostly)," *N.Y. Times*, 15 Oct. 2008, at D10.

LANGUAGE-CHANGE INDEX
bereft of used without a sense of loss: Stage 3

berth (= a spot or position) is occasionally misspelled *birth*, sometimes (as in the first example below) with hilarious results—e.g.:

- "The Academy finished second behind Tufts University in the four-division regatta. Two Navy women earned *births*

[read *berths*] in the nationals last weekend." Jeff Nelson, "Race Wrapup," *Capital* (Annapolis), 19 Oct. 1995, at D6.
- "The Washington Wizards . . . are beginning to think about a playoff *birth* [read *berth*]." Justin Brown, "NBA's New York Story," *Christian Science Monitor*, 21 Dec. 2001, at 10.
- "The Tigers clinched an Empire 8 playoff *birth* [read *berth*], while improving their record 6–2, 6–1." "Andres, Vegy Help Spark MCC Shutout," *Rochester Democrat & Chron.*, 24 Sept. 2008, at D5.

LANGUAGE-CHANGE INDEX
birth misused for *berth*: Stage 1
Current ratio (*secure a berth* vs. **secure a birth*): 31:1

beseech > besought > besought; beseech > *beseeched > *beseeched. The traditional past tense and past participle is *besought*. The simple past is the more common usage—e.g.:

- "She tried to comfort me, *besought* me to come to breakfast." Lincoln Steffens, "Even Santa Claus Can't Put a Pony into a Stocking," *Star Trib.* (Minneapolis), 25 Dec. 1997, at E1.
- "'Let history treat me kindly,' California Democrat Maxine Waters, a deep-seated opponent of impeachment, *besought* shortly after the first article was approved." Craig Gilbert, "Historic Votes Send House 3 Articles of Impeachment," *Milwaukee J. Sentinel*, 12 Dec. 1998, at 1.
- "One evening, my sister *besought* a blessing on Jimmie Morton, the red-headed boy in the corner house who had a brown puppy and chewed bubble gum." John Gould, "Praying for Mother to Stay," *Christian Science Monitor*, 15 Jan. 1999, at 23.

The form *besought* will surprise some readers, who might have thought the past form to be **beseeched*, which the *OED* labels "now regarded as incorrect." It is a fairly common solecism—e.g.:

- "The presiding officer *beseeched* [read *besought*] speakers to avoid 'personally abusive' comments about the president of the United States." David M. Shribman, "Debate Shows the Roundup of Resentments," *Boston Globe*, 19 Dec. 1998, at A12.
- "McClelland frequently *beseeched* [read *besought*] the society to accept the design that he obsessively continued to modify." Mary Kay Ricks, "Washington Monuments That Never Quite Made It," *Wash. Post*, 13 Jan. 1999, at H3.
- "Coats had a powerful backer in former U.S. Rep. Louis Stokes, who *beseeched* [read *besought*] the Democratic Party to open countywide offices to black politicians." James Ewinger & Joe Hallett, "Mason's Biggest Foe in Prosecutor Bid May Be Memories," *Plain Dealer* (Cleveland), 15 Jan. 1999, at B1.

See IRREGULAR VERBS.

LANGUAGE-CHANGE INDEX
Current ratio (*besought* vs. **beseeched*): 5:1

beside (= [1] alongside; or [2] in comparison with) is surprisingly often misused for *besides* (= [1] other than, except; or [2] in addition). While the two words were once used interchangeably, *beside* has been reserved as the preposition and *besides* as the adverb since the late 18th century. But they are still confounded—e.g.:

- "When we speak of a unilateral contract, we mean a promise in exchange for which an act or something *beside* [read *besides*] another promise has been given as consideration." Clarence D. Ashley, "What Is a Promise in Law?" 16 *Harv. L. Rev.* 319, 319 (1903).

- "Hill is the only man *beside* [read *besides*] Trevino to win on the Senior Tour this year." Jaime Diaz, "At Tradition, Duel Falls Short of Hope," *N.Y. Times*, 31 Mar. 1990, at 30.
- "*Beside* [read *Besides*] pleading guilty to the murder, . . . Spradley also pleaded guilty to intimidating a key witness." Kent Faulk, "Once on Death Row, Man Walks Free After Reduced Sentence," *Birmingham News* (Ala.), 11 Sept. 2015, at A4.

Likewise, *besides* is sometimes misused for *beside*—e.g.: "Whether or not the city sets an attendance record is somewhat *besides* [read *beside*] the point, tournament organizers say." Gargi Chakrabarty & Michael Pointer, "Sales of Tickets Disappointing," *Indianapolis Star*, 28 Aug. 2002, at A1.

Language-Change Index
1. *beside* misused for *besides*: Stage 1
Current ratio (*Besides doing* vs. **Beside doing*): 24:1
2. *besides* misused for *beside*: Stage 1
Current ratio (*beside the point* vs. **besides the point*): 36:1

bestial (= behaving like an animal, esp. a cruel one) is pronounced /**bes**-chuul/ or /**best**-yuul/—not /**bees**-/.

bestir (= to stir [oneself] to action), in the modern idiom, is preferably confined to reflexive uses—e.g.:

- "This page agrees that the Dole tax-cut plan is misguided, but even we have to admit that it is possible to make a better argument for it than Mr. Dole could *bestir* himself to offer on Sunday." "The Missing Sermon on Taxes," *N.Y. Times*, 8 Oct. 1996, at A24.
- "What kind of people will not *bestir* themselves to exercise their franchise if doing so requires them to get off their couches and visit neighborhood polling places?" George Will, "Farewell, Election Day," *Newsweek*, 6 Oct. 2008, at 64.

It has long been regarded as unidiomatic to use *bestir* as an ordinary transitive verb—e.g.:

- "He sought to *bestir* [read *stir*] action at both the local and state levels." Rebecca Conrad, "The State Park Movement," *Des Moines Register*, 6 Oct. 1996, Opinion §, at 1.
- "How else can filmmakers and exhibitors hope to *bestir* [read *rouse*] audiences out of their high-definition, surround-sound home-theater cocoons?" Scott Galup, "New Dimensions in Film," *Wash. Times*, 18 Apr. 2008, at D1.
- "'Dr. Arbuthnot, the cliché expert,' created in the 1930s by *The New Yorker*'s Frank Sullivan, would have had a field day with the way red meat is racing through the political commentariat deploring anybody else's severe criticism that *bestirs* [read *stirs up* or *excites*] partisan crowds." William Safire, "Hot's Not Cool," *N.Y. Times*, 21 Sept. 2008, Mag. §, at 38.

Language-Change Index
bestir used as a transitive verb: Stage 1
Current ratio (*stirs the* vs. **bestirs the*): 341:1

best of all [+ pl. n.] is more logical than *best of any* [+ sing. n.]. Why? Because the all-encompassing plurality of *all* isn't as well conveyed by *any*—e.g.:

- "New York's clincher grabbed a 22.2 rating and 37 share, *the best of any Series game* [read *the best of all Series games* or *better than any other Series game*] this year." Steve Rosenbloom, "Good Morning," *Chicago Trib.*, 29 Oct. 1996, Sports §, at 1.
- "But last Friday, Hopewell's Steve Day had the *best* game *of any WPIAL running back* [read *of all WPIAL running backs*] this season." Mike White, "Graham Rethinks PSU Choice," *Pitt. Post-Gaz.*, 7 Nov. 1996, at E3.
- "That help was rewarded this year—labor unions fared *the best of any special interest group* [read *the best of all special-interest groups* or *better than any other special-interest group*]." Mark Martin, "Davis Signs Bills with Eye on Votes," *S.F. Chron.*, 2 Oct. 2002, at A4.

Cf. **better than any (other)** & ILLOGIC (B).

But when the sense is "one (no matter which)," and the noun that follows *must* be singular, the word *any* fills the bill—e.g.: "The *best* part of *any* Rush show isn't hearing the new songs done live, but experiencing the onstage chemistry." J.D. Considine, "It's a Rush," *Baltimore Sun*, 7 Nov. 1996, Md. Live §, at 8. See **any** (A).

Language-Change Index
best of any misused to mean *best of all*: Stage 4

bestowal; ***bestowment**. The latter is a NEEDLESS VARIANT.

Current ratio: 12:1

bet > bet > bet. *Bet*, not **betted*, is the preferred (and far more frequent) past tense and past participle. Still, the form **betted* occasionally appears, especially in BrE—e.g.:

- "Afternoon race cards from minor meetings in Britain are *betted* [read *bet*] on in Sri Lanka, Malaysia and India." "Galloping Globe-Trotters," *Economist*, 10 June 1995, at 82.
- "This could spell bad news for all those who *betted* [read *bet*] on Ekran." Lee Han Shih, "Ekran Chief Suffered Mild Stroke," *Bus. Times*, 1 Oct. 1996, at 1.
- "Oil prices recently touched the $135-a-barrel mark for the first time in history, as investors *betted* [read *bet*] that the price of crude will remain high for some time." Edmund Conway, "Don't Cut Fuel Tax, Urges OECD Head," *Daily Telegraph*, 4 June 2008, City §, at 5.

See IRREGULAR VERBS.

Language-Change Index
*betted for past-tense *bet*: Stage 1
Current ratio (*bet* vs. **betted*): 17:1

bête noire; ***bête noir**. The spelling *bête noire* /bet **nwahr**/—the only one with any standing in the dictionaries—is about four times as common in modern print sources as **bête noir* (in which, by the way, the gender of the adjective does not agree with that of the noun). The French term literally means "black beast," but in English it is used figuratively to mean "a person or thing that is strongly disliked or that should be avoided"—e.g.:

LANGUAGE-CHANGE INDEX (For the full key, see front matter pp. xxxi, l–li.)
Stage 1: Rejected. **Stage 2:** Widely shunned. **Stage 3:** Widespread but . . . **Stage 4:** Ubiquitous but . . . **Stage 5:** Fully accepted.
Invariably inferior forms marked by asterisk (*). • Ratios represent frequency of prevalent forms vs. variants in current books.

- "Dole tried to put President Clinton on the defensive last night by saying that Sen. Edward M. Kennedy, the *bête noire* of conservatives, was his friend." Chris Black, "The Friend of My Enemy Is . . . ," *Boston Globe*, 7 Oct. 1996, at A11.
- "As senator, Gore was the cable industry's *bête noire*, declaring it to be, following a spate of rate increases, 'a monopoly that's out of control.'" William Bradley, "A Reality Check on Gore," *Times Union* (Albany), 14 Oct. 1996, at A7.
- "With a quick nod to the troops, Mr. McCain, characteristically, hijacked the question and skipped to pork-barrel spending, his favorite *bête noire*." Katharine Q. Seelye, "A Scrappy Fighter, with a Debating Style Honed in and out of Politics," *N.Y. Times*, 23 Sept. 2008, at A25.

The plural form remains the French *bêtes noires*, as opposed to the more fully anglicized *bête noires—e.g.:

- "Parisian motorists' particular *bêtes noires* are the women police auxiliaries in bright blue uniforms who slap instant fines on illegally parked cars." "Copstyle: Parisian Meter Maids Go High Fashion," *St. Louis Post-Dispatch*, 2 Oct. 1994, at 2.
- "It simply requires the state board of education, if asked by local school districts, to help create an environment that promotes 'critical thinking' and 'objective discussion' not only about evolution and the origins of life but also about global warming and human cloning, two other *bêtes noires* of the right." "Louisiana's Latest Assault on Darwin," *N.Y. Times*, 21 June 2008, at A18.

Given that the circumflex remains over the first -*e*-, it is hardly surprising that the word has retained its foreign plural. See PLURALS (B).

betrothal; *betrothment. The latter is a NEEDLESS VARIANT.

Current ratio: 66:1

better. A. For *had better*. Dropping the *had* in expressions such as *You (had) better be going now* is acceptable only in informal speech or recorded dialogue. Even in the compressed space of a headline, the ellipsis is inadvisable—e.g.: "Perspective—The FCC *Better* [read *Had Better*] Shape Up Those Monopolies," *Communications Week*, 15 Apr. 1996, at 49. The phrasing is a low CASUALISM—e.g.:

- "If the Flyers are going to make an offer, they *better* [read *had better*] do it in a hurry." "Lightning Time Line," *St. Petersburg Times*, 16 Aug. 1997, at C10.
- "But with [Clinton's] animal magnetism running so strong, perhaps *I better* [read *I'd better*] steer clear of the White House." John F. Cogan, "President Irresistible," *N.Y. Times*, 18 Feb. 1998, at A25.

STANDARD ENGLISH still requires *you had better, I had better, she had better*, etc. Cf. **get** (C) [last ¶].

Sometimes *best* replaces *better*, as in *We had best be on our way*. This phrasing—*had best* rather than *had better*—is quite casual, but not low.

LANGUAGE-CHANGE INDEX
1. *better* for *had better*: Stage 3
Current ratio (*you had better go* vs. *you better go): 2:1
2. *had best* for *had better* in casual use: Stage 5
Current ratio (*you had better* vs. *you had best*): 14:1

B. And *bettor*. See **bettor.**

better . . . rather than. In this phrasing, the word *rather* is usually unnecessary, since *than* completes the comparison begun by *better*—e.g.:

- "When will the administration learn that it is *better* to disclose such arrangements up front *rather than waiting* [read *than to wait*] until the university has been sued?" Letter of Gordon J. Johnson, "Secrecy Suggests Something's Amiss," *Rocky Mountain News* (Denver), 3 July 1999, at A51.
- "It's *better* to remove weeds by the roots *rather than chopping* [read *than to chop*] them up with a tiller or cultivator, Akre says; many can re-sprout from the chopped-up bits." Beth Botts, "Success in the Vegetable Patch," *Chicago Trib.*, 15 June 2008, Home & Garden §, at 2.
- "Last year, Curlin appeared *better* when he raced outside other horses *rather than being hemmed in* [read *than when he was hemmed in*], which some believe cost him the Belmont." Jennie Rees, "It's Churchill Down, Fun to Go for Curlin," *Courier-J.* (Louisville), 15 June 2008, at C1.

The exception occurs when the phrase following *better* is rather long—e.g.: "The next two years could be *better* spent looking for new ways to accomplish this goal *rather than* simply trying to wring more money out of taxpayers' pockets." Jack Roberts, "Culprit Is Distribution Formula, Not Tax Structure," *Oregonian* (Portland), 6 Aug. 1999, at E11. Cf. **more . . . than.**

better than any (other). Ordinarily, *better than any other* is more logical than *better than any*, because the thing being proclaimed best is also one of the things being considered—e.g.: "Hooley, 63, knows this landscape and its residents *better than any other* elected official." Editorial, "Return Hooley to Congress," *Oregonian* (Portland), 4 Oct. 2002, at C6.

Writers who omit the word *other* fall into logical lapses—e.g.:

- "If there's been a down moment or a traumatic flashback in Monica Seles' 1996, then she's a *better actor than any* [read *better actor than any other*] athlete I've ever met." Michael Gee, "Seles Still Serves Up a Smile," *Boston Herald*, 7 Sept. 1996, Sports §, at 36.
- "Tommy Oravetz grew up in the FSU family and appreciated maybe *better than any player* [read *better than any other player*], even his fellow Tallahasseeans, what going to Omaha means." Steve Ellis, "Former 'Noles Players Play Supportive, Not Jealous, Role," *Tallahassee Democrat*, 13 June 2008, at C2.
- "Fitzgerald's defense played freer and faster, tackling *better than any* [read *better than any other*] Northwestern team in memory." David Haugh, "School's in Session for Turner," *Chicago Trib.*, 8 Sept. 2015, Sports §, at 1.

Cf. **best of all** & ILLOGIC (B).

Sometimes, though, the thing being touted is excepted, and then the *other* becomes unnecessary. For example, two different types of things are often compared, such as the two sexes in the first example or German versus British products in the second:

- "Her jump was not only tops for her division, but it was also *better than any* boy's jump in the same division." Joni Averill, "Capehart Is Part of New Generation," *Bangor Daily News*, 18 Aug. 1994, at PDA. (On the lack of PARALLELISM in that sentence, see **not only . . . but also.**)

- "Marks & Spencer confirmed last night that it sells only German fishfingers, claiming the quality is *better than any* British product." Justin Dunn, "Germans Scupper Captain Birds Eye," *Daily Mirror*, 18 Aug. 1994, at 1.

LANGUAGE-CHANGE INDEX
better than any for *better than any other*: Stage 3

bettor is the standard spelling for "someone who bets or wagers." *Better* has also been used in this sense, but it is liable to be confused with the comparative form of *good* or as a singular form of *betters* in the sense "people of higher skill or status." E.g.: "Each week the din coming from the Coliseum is tremendous—not from the birds crowing their heads off as they go about slaughtering each other but from the *betters* [read *bettors*] yelling out wagers until another is willing to accept the odds." Uli Schmetzer, "Philippines Erupt with Fowl Play," *Chicago Trib.*, 17 Sept. 1996, at 10. (The headline should have read "Philippines Erupts" or "Filipinos Erupt.") Cf. **abettor.**

LANGUAGE-CHANGE INDEX
better misused for *bettor*: Stage 1
Current ratio (*a heavy bettor* vs.
*a heavy better): 3:1

between. A. And *among.* *Between* is commonly said to be proper with two things, and *among* with more than two. Ernest Gowers calls this a "superstition" and quotes the *OED*: "In all senses *between* has been, from its earliest appearance, extended to more than two. . . . It is still the only word available to express the relation of a thing to many surrounding things severally and individually; *among* expresses a relation to them collectively and vaguely: we should not say *the space lying among the three points* or *a treaty among three Powers*" (*FMEU2* at 57). Another critic agrees: "A man may halt between *three* as well as *two* opinions." G.H. Vallins, *Better English* 68 (4th ed. 1957).

In terms of frequency, the collocation *between three* has outstripped *among three*—by a significant margin—in all periods of English since 1500. The same is true of *between four* vs. *among four*.

The rule as generally enunciated, then, is simplistic. Although it is an accurate guide for the verb *divide* (*between* with two objects, *among* with more than two), the only ironclad distinction is that stated by the *OED*: *between* expresses one-to-one relations of many things, and *among* expresses collective and undefined relations.

In fact, good writers commonly use *between* with more than two elements, in AmE and BrE alike—e.g.:

- "Sunday morning in Denmark Hill is for the six Huxtable daughters (the difference *between whom*, as Granville Barker puts it in his stage directions, 'is to the casual eye the difference between one lead pencil and another') a time of nursery scurryings and silences under the unwavering eye of their mother." J.K.L. Walker, "Edwardian Underwear," *TLS*, 11 Sept. 1992, at 19.

- "Part of the journey has been to discover the appropriate balance *between family, solitude and community*." Terry Waite, "A Long, Long Way to Travel," *Times* (London), 27 Aug. 1994, at 15.
- "'So I said, "Why don't you go build a fort in the woods?" I had no idea it would turn out to be this monstrosity' bolted *between* four treetops in the corner of her front yard." Elizabeth Maker, "Family Trees," *N.Y. Times*, 29 Sept. 2002, 14CN §, at 1.

Sometimes, however, the sense is anything but reciprocal or mutual. Without a one-to-one relation, *among* is the better word—e.g.:

- "The five dancing grandmothers have 25 grandchildren *between* [read *among*] them." "Dancing Grandmothers," *Austin Am.-Statesman*, 13 Sept. 1993, at B1 (photo caption).
- "In a recent interview, Mr. Weitzner explained the relationships *between* [read *among*] the various entities at 741 Alexander." Brett Pulley, "At One Office, Intricate Links in New Jersey's G.O.P. Funds," *N.Y. Times*, 8 July 1996, at A1, A9. (*Among* is correct here because the multitude of interlocking political organizations is being stressed.)

See SUPERSTITIONS (H).

B. *Between you and me*; **between you and I.* Because the pronouns following *between* are objects of the preposition, the correct phrase is *between you and me*. Yet the phrasing **between you and I* is appallingly common—"a grammatical error of unsurpassable grossness," as one commentator puts it. Interestingly, this grammatical error is committed almost exclusively by educated speakers trying a little too hard to sound refined but stumbling badly. It's almost surely an ingrained instance of hypercorrection based on childhood admonitions not to use *you and me* (or similar compounds) as the subject of the sentence—and, far more confusing to most people, as a predicate nominative in sentences such as *it is I*. See PRONOUNS (B) & HYPERCORRECTION (B).

Still, descriptive linguists—linguistic liberals—are fond of quoting early writers, who worked at a time when the language was not so fully developed, in support of poor usage. Back in 1892, Henry Sweet was quite right to say that in Early Modern English, "the usage was more unsettled than now, the nominative being as freely substituted for the objective as vice-versa, as in such constructions as *'tween you and I. You and I* were so frequently joined together as nominatives—*you and I will go together*, etc.—that the three words formed a sort of group-compound, whose last element became invariable." 1 Sweet, *A New English Grammar, Logical and Historical* 340–41 (1892).

Here is the characteristic view of modern descriptive linguists: "The meaning is clear; 'I' is no less, or more, euphonious than 'me'; if the usage offends, it does so because the hearer (occasionally) or the reader (more frequently) is in the habit of expecting 'me.' Why is such a habit worth fighting about?"

Ellsworth Barnard, *English for Everybody* 25 (1979). This view ignores the reality and the importance of the thousands of settled views of English usage. *I*, as an object of a preposition or a verb, has long been stigmatized. Using it in the objective case simply creates doubts about the speaker's ability to handle the language.

Randolph Quirk—a leading English grammarian of the late 20th century—puts all this in perspective: "I would not go along with making 'I' and 'me' interchangeable. It is true that Shakespeare used both, but that did not make it any more correct. There are permanent pressures on language, and the fact that they are resisted shows that people recognise the value of correct usage." As quoted in John O'Leary, "Language Police at Odds over Misuse of Pronouns," *Times* (London), 2 Oct. 1995, Home News §.

Among the better-considered views on the question are these:

- "If the ditch-digger's child said 'between you and me,' it would probably be ridiculed into using the environmentally more favored 'between you and I.' Thus the penalties provided for nonconformity nourish and perpetuate ungrammatical usage, and the folk speech is rooted deep in the life of the masses." Edward N. Teall, *Putting Words to Work* 4 (1940).
- "The nation is divided in its use of 'between you and me' and 'between you and I.' Let me begin by declaring that the only admissible construction of the two in standard use in the twentieth century is 'between you and me.' . . . *I, he*, and other pronouns were frequently used in the sixteenth and seventeenth centuries in ways now regarded as ungrammatical. Grammatical assumptions were different then." Robert W. Burchfield, *Points of View* 117 (1992).
- "English now recognizes only two inflections for all pronouns—the subjective (or nominative) 'I,' 'you,' 'he,' 'she,' 'they,' and the objective (or accusative) 'me,' 'you,' 'him,' 'her,' 'them.' The possessives, as in 'his face' or 'her hair' or 'their cheek,' are adjectival. The objective form is used after transitive verbs like 'hit,' 'kick,' 'love,' and also after prepositions like 'after,' 'for,' 'between.' It is because 'you' has become an invariable form—in number as well as in case—that the solecisms 'Between you and I' and 'Let you and I talk' are committed." Anthony Burgess, *A Mouthful of Air* 59 (1992).

In print sources, the STANDARD ENGLISH expression is in less danger today than it was in the 18th century: *between you and me* occurs with much, much greater frequency. In fact, the erroneous form represents barely a blip on the screen.

LANGUAGE-CHANGE INDEX
between you and I for *between you and me*: Stage 2
Current ratio (*between you and me* vs.
between you and I): 16:1

C. *Between* and Numbers. This usage causes problems if the things being counted are discrete units and the numbers at both ends of the spectrum are intended to be included. E.g.:

- "Saleh met with several other defendants in a Queens garage *between June 23 and June 24* [read (depending on the meaning) *from June 23 to June 24* or *on June 23 or 24*] to discuss getting cars for the conspiracy." Peg Tyre &

Kevin McCoy, "Busted at Beach," *Newsday* (N.Y.), 24 July 1993, at 3. (There is no time between June 23 and June 24.)
- "They had the option of booking *between one and three* [read *from one to three*] days." "Window on Tomorrow's World," *Birmingham Post*, 23 Aug. 2002, at 13. (Two is the only whole number between one and three.)

When you intend to refer to a range of possibilities from a low point to a high point, *from . . . to*, *between . . . and*, or *to* alone is the correct form, not **between . . . to.* E.g.:

- "Businesses estimate they lose *between $25 billion to $30 billion* [read *between $25 billion and $30 billion*] a year nationwide in lost productivity, errors and accidents attributable to poor literacy." William Celis III, "Study Says Half of Adults in U.S. Can't Read or Handle Arithmetic," *N.Y. Times*, 9 Sept. 1993, at A1, A16.
- "The large pressure difference between the low and a high over the southern Plains will generate winds *between* [read *from*] 18 to 36 m.p.h. in the wake of a sharp cold front." "High Winds Whip Upper Midwest," *Chicago Trib.*, 10 Sept. 1993, at 10.
- "*Between 500 to 1,000* [read *Between 500 and 1,000*] students a year are served by the district's Homeless Education Program." Richard Obert, "Homeless to Hopeful," *Ariz. Republic*, 11 Sept. 2015, at C1.

Of the first of those immediately preceding examples, supplied by the late Professor John W. Velz of the University of Texas, Velz commented: "It's a sad irony to find a subliterate idiom in an article about subliteracy. It's like a physicist's making a simple mistake in arithmetic."

LANGUAGE-CHANGE INDEX
1. *between* [date 1] *and* [date 2] for *from* [date 1] *to* [date 2]: Stage 2
2. **between* [date 1] *to* [date 2] for *between* [date 1] *and* [date 2]: Stage 2

D. *Choose between*. This construction (with various verbs of selection) takes *and*, not *or*. The misuse probably results from confusion between *between . . . and* and *either . . . or*—e.g.:

- "Guests can choose *between* 'Eve of the Eve Classic,' a smaller, more elegant affair with dinner and open bar, *or* [read *and*] the general 'Eve of the Eve' party, which accommodates more than 2,000 revelers." Audarshia Townsend, "Parties for the Celebratory Mood," *Chicago Trib.*, 21 Dec. 2001, at 31.
- "Russia . . . will face, in some instances, the choice *between* isolation *or* [read *and*] union with the rest of Europe." Eugene Rumer & Jeffrey Simon, "NATO: Russia Should Have a Seat at the Table," *L.A. Times*, 23 Dec. 2001, at M2.

E. *Between; as between*. Sometimes *as between* (= comparing; in comparison of) is misused for the straightforward preposition. E.g.: "The contractual provisions *as between* [read *between*] the parties are as follows." Cf. **as against.**

F. **Between each* and Other Constructions with Fewer than Two Objects. This phrasing is a peculiar brand of ILLOGIC, as in **between each house* and **between each speech* (instead of, properly, *between every two houses* and *between speeches*). Although it is possible to think of *_between each house_ as being an ellipsis for _between each house and the next_, native speakers of English don't consciously think of the phrase in this way. And the resulting expression is literally nonsensical—e.g.:

- "Customers can use the same dial tone to make multiple calls by pressing the pound sign _between each call_ [read _between calls_]." Carol Smith, "Options to Keep the Costs Down When Phoning from Abroad," _L.A. Times_, 2 Oct. 1996, at D4.
- "_Between each pitch_ [read _Between pitches_], the camera will dart between batter, Angel manager, Twin manager, a fan with her hands in front of her face, the Rally Monkey jumping up, the pitcher's eyes, some guy in the dugout biting his nails, the Rally Monkey landing, a fan with a Christmas tree on her head, a kid screaming." T.J. Simers, "The Inside Track," _L.A. Times_, 13 Oct. 2002, at D2.
- "The bells were traditionally rung at 6 a.m., noon and 6 p.m. in three groups of three chimes with a pause _in between each group_ [read _in between groups_], followed by nine consecutive strokes." Marilyn Salzl Brinkman, "Bells Will Toll for St. Joseph Again," _St. Cloud Times_ (Minn.), 14 June 2008, at C5.

LANGUAGE-CHANGE INDEX
*_between each period_ for _between periods_: Stage 2
Current ratio (_between periods_ vs.
*_between each period_): 67:1

between Scylla and Charybdis. See **Scylla and Charybdis.**

***between you and I.** See **between (B).**

betwixt is an ARCHAISM. On the few occasions when it appears, it's usually in the CLICHÉ _betwixt and between_ (meaning "in a middle position; neither one nor the other"). But sometimes it pops up on its own when the writer tries to affect quaintness—e.g.:

- "_Betwixt_ the owls and the frogs, the familiar sound [of the woodcock] comes from an old field not far from the house." "The Woodcock Dance Is Thrilling Rite of Spring," _Pitt. Post-Gaz._, 10 Mar. 1996, at D13. (A possible revision: _While the owls and the frogs sing, the familiar sound comes from an old field not far from the house._)
- "If you have $100 to burn, you could be living _betwixt_ the aspens and the firs." Brandon Loomis, "Chances Sold on $35,000 Lot," _Idaho Falls Post Register_, 3 Sept. 1996, at A10. (A possible revision: replace _betwixt_ with _among._)
- "So there is no contradiction, no cornering, no rock and a hard place for Bryant to be placed _betwixt_, she said." John Brummett, "Bryant Still Up a Tree," _Ark. Democrat-Gaz._, 15 Oct. 1996, at B7. (A possible revision: replace _betwixt_ with _between._)

bevel, vb., makes _beveled_ and _beveling_ in AmE, _bevelled_ and _bevelling_ in BrE. See SPELLING (B).

BE-VERBS. A. Wrongly Omitted in Nonfinite Uses. _Be_-verbs, usually in the infinitive or participial form, are often omitted from sentences in which they would add clarity. One explanation is that they are intended to be "understood." (See UNDERSTOOD WORDS.) But this explanation does not excuse the ambiguity and awkwardness often caused by such omissions. The bracketed verbs in the following sentences were omitted in the original sources.

- "These devices can be used to intercept a wire or oral communication; specifically designated as not [_being_] such devices are telephone or telegraph equipment furnished to a user and used in the ordinary course of business, and hearing aids."
- "If the Western film offer were found [_to be_] different from the musical film offer, then it might be more appealing."

B. Circumlocutions with _Be_-Verbs. Verb phrases containing _be_-verbs are often merely roundabout ways of saying something better said with a simple verb. Thus _be determinative of_ for _determine_ is verbose. But _be determinative_ is all right without an object <this factor may be determinative in a given situation>.

The following circumlocutory uses of _be_-verbs are common in stuffy writing. The simple verb is usually better:

be abusive of (abuse)
be applicable to (apply to)
be benefited by (benefit from)
be derived from (derive from)
be desirous of (desire or want)
be determinative of (determine)
be in agreement (agree)
be in attendance (attend)
be indicative of (indicate)
be in error (err)
be in existence (exist)
be influential on (influence)
be in possession of (possess)
be in receipt of (have received)
be in violation of (violate)
be operative (operate)
be productive of (produce)
be promotive of (promote)
be supportive of (support)

Many such wordy constructions are more naturally phrased in the present-tense singular: _is able to_ (can), _is authorized to_ (may), _is binding upon_ (binds), _is empowered to_ (may), _is unable to_ (cannot).

C. For _say._ In a contraction with a personal pronoun, and especially when accompanied by _like_, _be_-verbs used in the sense of "say" have become a common verbal tic among the younger generations—e.g.: "I'm like, 'What do you think?' And she's like, 'I don't know.' And I'm all, 'Well, I think . . . .'" Whether the tic seems to be determined more by emotional development than by age alone is a question for sociolinguists to determine. But it is poor usage. Cf. **go (B)** & **like (E).**

D. Reduplicative Copula: _is is._ See **is is.**

beyond a reasonable doubt. See **not guilty (B).**

beyond the pale. See **pale, beyond the.**

LANGUAGE-CHANGE INDEX (For the full key, see front matter pp. xxxi, l–li.)
Stage 1: Rejected. **Stage 2:** Widely shunned. **Stage 3:** Widespread but . . . **Stage 4:** Ubiquitous but . . . **Stage 5:** Fully accepted.
Invariably inferior forms marked by asterisk (*). • Ratios represent frequency of prevalent forms vs. variants in current books.

BI-; SEMI-. One can remember the proper prefix in a given context by noting that *bi-* means "two" <bifocals>, and *semi-* "half" <semicircle>. Hence *bimonthly* = every two months (not "twice a month") and *semimonthly* = every half-month, or twice a month. *Biweekly* and *semiweekly* work similarly.

Still, *bi-* has been used to mean "occurring twice in a (specified span of time)" so often (and legitimately, e.g., in *biannual*) that, for the sake of clarity, you might do well to avoid the prefix altogether when possible. See **biannual.**

LANGUAGE-CHANGE INDEX
bimonthly as a synonym of *semimonthly*: Stage 2

biannual; biennial; semiannual. *Biannual* and *semiannual* both mean "occurring twice a year." *Biennial* means "occurring once every two years." The distinction becomes important, for example, when contractual language provides for "*biannual* increases" or "*biannual* meetings." The best advice is not to rely on words like *biannual* and *biennial* if confusion might cause problems. For absolute clarity, use *semiannual* or *once every two years*. See BI- & **biennial;** see also NUMERICAL PREFIXES.

bias, vb., makes *biased* and *biasing* in AmE, *biassed* and *biassing* in BrE. See SPELLING (B).

Bible; bible. As a proper noun referring to the holy book, *Bible* is capitalized <Which book of the Bible are you referring to?>. As a common noun denoting any definitive text, it should be lowercase <that cookbook is the chef's bible>. The adjective *biblical* is always lowercase, even when it refers to the Bible <the biblical account of the flood>.

bicentennial; bicentenary. See **centennial.**

bicep; biceps. Despite its appearance, *biceps* is traditionally a singular noun. H.W. Fowler preferred the plural *bicepses*, which is rare, and mentioned also the technical form *bicipites*, also rare. He called *biceps*, as a plural, "a mere blunder" (*FMEU1* at 51).

His objection was pedantic: *bicepses* has hardly ever been used, whereas the plural *biceps* has been fairly common since the late 19th century. It is now standard—e.g.:

- "The heroines of 'Aliens' and 'Terminator 2,' however, developed their *biceps* between movies." Caryn James, "The Woman in 'True Lies,'" *N.Y. Times*, 17 July 1994, § 2, at 13.
- "The sculpted *biceps* reflect the constant work that's made him an attraction for Division I schools." Kevin Lonnquist, "Making a Name," *Dallas Morning News*, 25 Oct. 1996, at B4.
- "He's one of the team's hardest workers in the weight room, and his *biceps* look like tree trunks." Robert Gagliardi, "Gentry's Play Positive from Last Week, but UW Needs to Build from There," *Laramie Boomerang*, 10 Sept. 2015, at B1.

Naturally, the back-formed singular *bicep* has also caught on and in nontechnical contexts is the usual form—e.g.: "Lincoln Kennedy will be sidelined two weeks by a torn left *bicep*." "Slaughter Gets Deal with Jets," *Chattanooga Times*, 24 July 1996, at F5. But that

usage isn't uniform, even within a single publication in a single month: "Appier (8–7), sidelined since July 3 because of inflammation in his right *biceps*, allowed one run and three hits." "Padres Stop Rockies' Streak," *Chattanooga Times*, 19 July 1996, at E2. See BACK-FORMATIONS.

Today, to refer to a person's right *biceps* and to both *bicepses* or *bicipites* seems pedantic. (In 1939, one commentator said that he had "never met anyone with sufficient hardihood to use [*bicepses*]." William Freeman, *Plain English* 84 [Blanche C. Williams ed., Am. ed. 1939].) Although the ETYMOLOGY suggests that those forms are superior, the standard terms are now *bicep* as the singular and *biceps* as the plural. The same will probably someday be true for *triceps* and *quadriceps*. Cf. **pecs, quadriceps** & **triceps.**

Current ratio (*a torn biceps* vs. *a torn bicep*): 1.3:1

bid. A. Standard Past-Tense Forms. *Bid* (= to offer a bid) forms *bid* in the past tense—e.g.: "Williams also *bid* more than the state initially budgeted for that project." Jeffrey Brainard, "New Life for Zephyrhills Depot," *St. Petersburg Times*, 25 Oct. 1996, Pasco Times §, at 1.

When the thing offered is a greeting or a farewell, the past tense is *bade*, rhyming with *glad* (not *glade*)—e.g.:

- "Thousands of people, many of them police officers from throughout the West, *bid* [read *bade*] farewell to slain Pierce County sheriff's Deputy John Bananola yesterday in a funeral that had the toughest cops weeping with grief." Larry Lange, "Thousands Honor Slain Deputy at Funeral," *Seattle Post-Intelligencer*, 25 Oct. 1995, at A1.
- "Many shed tears or hugged each other as they *bade farewell* to waiters and waitresses they had befriended long ago." Henry K. Lee, "Oakland Patrons Bid a Sad Adieu to JJ's Diner," *S.F. Chron.*, 28 Oct. 1996, at A13.
- "With tears and her signature smile, Katie Couric *bade farewell* to the 'Today' show yesterday in a three-hour lovefest packed with celebrity guests and the regular folks who woke up with her for 15 years." Brittany Karford, "A Katie Lovefest," *Daily News* (N.Y.), 1 June 2006, News §, at 2.

See **forbid (A).**

So which past tense is correct in the phrase *to bid fair* (= to seem likely)—is it *bid fair* or *bade fair*? Although writers have used both, the *OED* records only *bade fair*, the better form—e.g.:

- "This fiasco *bid fair* [read *bade fair*] to destroy the fund of goodwill among the citizens of Europe." Patrick Minford, "Monetary Calm Threatened on Two Fronts," *Daily Telegraph*, 26 June 1995, at 22.
- "And paired as it was with a second congressional sleuthing effort, into the Whitewater affair, it *bade fair* to generate what passed for some agreeable theater, if not actual news." Brian Duffy, "Just Sniffing," *U.S. News & World Rep.*, 14 Aug. 1995, at 8.

LANGUAGE-CHANGE INDEX
1. *bid farewell* misused for the past-tense *bade farewell*: Stage 2
Current ratio (*he bade farewell* vs. *he bid farewell*): 5:1
2. *bid fair* misused for the past-tense *bade fair*: Stage 3
Current ratio (*he bade fair to* vs. *he bid fair to*): 2:1

B. *Bidded as a Solecism. The nonstandard past form *bidded isn't nearly as scarce as it should be—e.g.:

- "But for years, because of the way prison posts are bidded [read bid] for and filled by seniority, administrators have had little choice but to spend millions of dollars each year in overtime to fill vacant positions." Tom Mooney, "State Bows to ACI Union, Drops Privatization Idea," *Providence J.-Bull.*, 21 Oct. 1998, at B1.
- "As described by officials this week—a specific design has yet to be solicited, bidded [read bid], submitted and selected—the new bridge will feature a scaled-down, striking cable-stayed design and carry four lanes of traffic at a total project cost of $640 million." Editorial, "Spanning a River—and a Civic Gulf," *St. Louis Post-Dispatch*, 2 Mar. 2008, at B2.
- "Magee board chairman Fred D'Angelo top-bidded [read won the bidding for] a basketball ($1,200) signed by sports figures who attended . . . ." Michael Klein, "Inqlings: 'Happy Tears' Cast a Visible Lot," *Phil. Inquirer*, 13 May 2008, at E2.

See IRREGULAR VERBS.

LANGUAGE-CHANGE INDEX
*bidded for past-tense bid: Stage 1
Current ratio (bid vs. *bidded): 3,295:1

C. Past Participle. In the sense "to make a bid," the past participle is bid—e.g.: "NTL and France Telecom are each believed to have bid more than £200m." Mathew Horsman, "France Added to BBC Bid List," *Independent*, 29 Oct. 1996, at 17. Otherwise, the past-participial form is usually bidden—e.g.: " 'Good morning, Signor Mach,' one of them said as the fugitive Italian financier ventured from an apartment on the Boulevard St.-Germain in Paris on Sunday to buy the Italian newspapers from a corner kiosk, only to find himself arrested by the Italian plainclothes policeman who had just bid [read bidden] him good day." Alan Cowell, "Rich Italian Fugitive Finally Caught in Paris," *N.Y. Times*, 1 Nov. 1994, at A4. See IRREGULAR VERBS (A).

The simple past bade is sometimes misused for bidden, a mistake that should be universally forbidden—e.g.:

- "This historic spot (where Flora MacDonald is said to have bade [read bidden] farewell to Bonnie Prince Charlie after the Jacobite rebellion) is reasonably priced and sports a lively bar." Mary Gillespie, "If You Go," *Chicago Sun-Times*, 8 Mar. 1998, at 4.
- "With an Olympic flag hanging behind the casket, Florence Griffith Joyner was bade [read bidden] farewell in a two-hour funeral at Saddleback Community Church." "Morning Briefing," *Pitt. Post-Gaz.*, 27 Sept. 1998, at D2.
- "So when the Blackhawks offered Doug Gilmour a three-year deal for $18 million, . . . he was bade [read bidden] goodbye." Jay Greenberg, "Lamoriello's Way Is NHL's Best Way," *N.Y. Post*, 17 Dec. 1998, at 92.

LANGUAGE-CHANGE INDEX
1. bid misused for past-participial bidden: Stage 3
Current ratio (had bidden her vs. *had bid her): 3:1
2. bade misused for past-participial bidden: Stage 1
Current ratio (was bidden vs. *was bade): 23:1

bidden. See **bid** (C).

bid fair. See **bid** (A).

biennial = occurring every two years. If we climb the numerical ladder, we have triennial (3), quadrennial (4), quinquennial (5), sexennial (6), septennial (7), octennial (8), novennial (9), decennial (10), vicennial (20), centennial (100), millennial (1,000). See NUMERICAL PREFIXES; see also BI- & **biannual.**

bigamy; polygamy; deuterogamy; *digamy. Bigamy = the act of marrying one person while being married to another. It may be committed knowingly or unknowingly; if committed knowingly, bigamy is a criminal offense.

Polygamy is the generic term for multiple marriages and encompasses bigamy. The word is much used by anthropologists, describing both polygyny (/pə-**lij**-ə-nee/—the practice of having several wives) and polyandry (/**pahl**-ee-an-dree/—the practice of having several husbands).

Deuterogamy (/d[y]oo-tər-**ahg**-ə-mee/) and *digamy (/**dig**-ə-mee/) both mean "a legal second marriage, such as one occurring after a divorce or after the death of the first spouse." Deuterogamy is the more common term (to the extent that either might be called common!) and is not, like *digamy, liable to confusion with bigamy. Hence *digamy should be considered a NEEDLESS VARIANT. Of course, the term second marriage is more common—and more readily understood—than either of the other words.

Big Island. See **Hawaii** (A).

*big of. See **of** (B).

BIG WORDS. See SESQUIPEDALITY.

billfold. See **wallet.**

billiard. See **billion.**

billion. In most English-speaking countries, billion denotes a thousand millions (a 1 followed by nine 0's). In most of continental Europe and other German-, French-, and Spanish-speaking countries, it means a million millions (a 1 followed by twelve 0's)—a thousand millions being dubbed a milliard. Today, the two large-number systems are called the short scale and the long scale.

In the not-so-distant past, the scales were referred to as the American and British systems. But in 1974, by statute, the U.K. adopted the short scale.

The short system is based on thousands, so that a million is a thousand thousands, a billion is a thousand millions, a trillion is a thousand billions, and so forth. But the older long scale is based on millions, so that a billion is a million millions, the equivalent of a trillion in the short scale. Just as the long scale calls a thousand millions a milliard, it calls a thousand of its

LANGUAGE-CHANGE INDEX (For the full key, see front matter pp. xxxi, l–li.)
Stage 1: Rejected. **Stage 2:** Widely shunned. **Stage 3:** Widespread but . . . **Stage 4:** Ubiquitous but . . . **Stage 5:** Fully accepted.
Invariably inferior forms marked by asterisk (*). • Ratios represent frequency of prevalent forms vs. variants in current books.

billions a *billiard*. But that's another game. Cf. **trillion.** See NUMERALS.

Biloxi (the city in Mississippi) is pronounced /bi-**lǝk**-see/—not /bi-**lok**-see/.

bimonthly; semimonthly. See BI-.

bind > bound > bound. It was bound to happen: some writers have erroneously introduced a weak past-tense form (**binded*). The word suggests what punishment might be inflicted at their wrists (though no one says **binded and gagged*)—e.g.:

- "ABL players cannot play for the WNBA this season because they are *binded* [read *bound*] by their exclusive contracts until Aug. 31." Jason Quick, "ABL's Success Has to Be Seen," *Oregonian* (Portland), 17 Feb. 1997, at B1.
- "Russell had the cover laminated and *binded* [read *bound*] the book." Ellena Fortner, "Students' Book Generates Memories and Self-Discovery," *Ft. Worth Star-Telegram*, 9 Dec. 1997, at 1.
- "He'd sell in a minute if he could find a local buyer *binded* [read *bound*] to keeping the franchise here." Nick Horvath Jr., "Senators Still in a Midstate Hit," *Sunday Patriot-News* (Harrisburg), 12 Apr. 1998, at C1.

Occasionally, an even worse past form, *bounded*, appears, especially in reported speech—e.g.:

- "Members of a club are *bounded* [read *bound*] by a long-term contract only insofar as the arrangement makes it easier to attain each one's independent goals." Elias L. Khalil, "Two Kinds of Order: Thoughts on the Theory of the Firm," *Socio-Economics*, 1 Mar. 1999, at 157.
- "When asked if he was disappointed, [Jerry] Silverstein said, 'I don't know about disappointed. We're *bounded* by a contract.'" Dave Lance, "Miami to Play Cardinals After TCU Says No," *Dayton Daily News*, 2 Dec. 2003, at C1.

Bounded is correct, of course, for the past tense of the verb *bound* <they bounded up the hill>.

LANGUAGE-CHANGE INDEX
1. **binded* for past-tense *bound*: Stage 1
Current ratio (*is bound* vs. **is binded*): 7,363:1
2. *bounded* misused for past-tense *bound*: Stage 1
Current ratio (*bound by the contract* vs.
*bounded by the contract): 75:1

biographee. This seeming NEOLOGISM actually dates from 1841, but still it's a relative newcomer compared to *biographer* (1702). Of course, many English words ending in *-graphy*, such as *biography*, *calligraphy*, and *cartography*, have agent nouns ending in *-er* even though there is no corresponding verb. But the *-ee* noun *biographee* is anomalous. (See -EE (A).) Still, the word can be useful, especially in book reviews—e.g.:

- "The *biographees*' years of birth and death, places of birth, parentage and/or Welsh ancestors are indeed valuable genealogical data." Lloyd Bockstruck, "The Raisin: More than a Shriveled Grape," *Dallas Morning News*, 21 Oct. 1995, at C10.
- "But it's clear that the roles of biographer and *biographee* have been correctly assigned." Desson Howe, " 'Basquiat': Spray-Painted Valentine," *Wash. Post*, 16 Aug. 1996, at N31.
- "There is none of that grotesque gap between style of biographer and style of *biographee* that can plague the form."

Nicholas Lezard, "Sifting Fact and Fiction in Updike's Life and Work," *Evening Standard*, 24 Apr. 2014, at 44.

biopic (= a film that tells the story of someone's life), a PORTMANTEAU WORD from *biographical picture*, is pronounced /**bɪ**-oh-pik/. It doesn't rhyme with *myopic*, which has its accent on the second syllable.

bipolar disorder. See **manic depression.**

birth was used with some frequency in the Middle Ages as a verb. It fell into disuse, however, and has only recently been revived in standard AmE <she birthed four babies>. It often appears as a participial adjective <birthing room>. Some dictionaries label it dialectal. But given its usefulness and its long standing in the language, it should be accepted as standard.

LANGUAGE-CHANGE INDEX
birth as a verb: Stage 5

bishopric; diocese; see. These theological terms are closely related, even overlapping, but they can be treated as distinct. A *bishopric* is the position or rank of a bishop (or the district that the bishop is in charge of). A *diocese* is the district that a bishop is in charge of—in other words, identical with the alternative sense of *bishopric*. A *see* is a bishop's seat of authority or jurisdictional headquarters. See **diocese.**

bitcoin. Lowercase.

bite > bit > bitten. While *bit*, the past-tense form, is recognized in most dictionaries as an alternative past participle, since 1825 or so it has been far less common than the standard *bitten*. Although the *OED* labels it archaic, the participial *bit* lives on in some SET PHRASES—e.g.:

- "Carolina Hurricanes general manager Jim Rutherford has *bit his lip* since the former Hartford Whalers moved south five seasons ago." David Droschak, "Postseason Perks Up Canes Fans," *Chattanooga Times/Chattanooga Free Press*, 9 June 2002, at C9.
- "Even Maher's most ardent defender would probably agree, however, that Maher should have *bit his tongue* on the 'cowardly' comment. His timing was terrible." Tom Dorsey, " 'Politically Incorrect' Skewers Its Last Tonight," *Courier-J.* (Louisville), 28 June 2002, at E2.
- "Jacobson's has *bit the dust.*" Mary Kramer, "Who Will Ever Take Jacobson's Place?" *Crain's Detroit Business*, 19 Aug. 2002, at 9.

In most contexts, though, *bitten* is the preferred form—e.g.:

- "That probably would have happened by now had Barnes not been *bit* [read *bitten*] by a spider in Florida in May 1995." Phil Richards, "A Few Sobering Thoughts," *Indianapolis Star*, 19 Sept. 1996, at C1.
- "Neither Jensen nor Ashenbrenner has ever been *bit* [read *bitten*], which strikes me as somewhat amazing." Doug Clark, "Shake, Rattle and Head for the Hills," *Spokesman-Rev.* (Spokane), 1 May 1997, at B1.

See IRREGULAR VERBS.

LANGUAGE-CHANGE INDEX
bit misused as a past participle for *bitten*: Stage 2
Current ratio (*had bitten* vs. **had bit*): 6:1

bitter cold. This is an age-old SET PHRASE in which *bitter* functions adverbially. (See ADVERBS.) It appears, for example, at the outset of Shakespeare's *Hamlet* (1602), where Francisco says: "'Tis *bitter cold*, and I am sick at heart" (1.1.6–7). The phrase *bitterly cold* is an example of HYPERCORRECTION.

bivouac. A. As a Noun. This word is primarily a noun denoting a short-term encampment, especially one with little or no shelter. E.g.:

- "With their plastic hard hats and sun-burnished skin, the migrant laborers and their construction-site *bivouacs* did not fit with the image of a modern city that China's leaders wanted to project." Edward Cody, "During Games, a Forced Vacation for Beijing's Migrant Workers," *Wash. Post*, 21 Aug. 2008, at A8.
- "His living room has the poised-for-departure air of a boho *bivouac*." Gerri Hirshey, "Sharing a Taste of Honey, on an International Scale," *N.Y. Times*, 30 Nov. 2008, CT §, at 1.

Phrases such as *temporary bivouac, bivouac camp*, and the like create redundancies. See REDUNDANCY.

And *bivouac* is misused when the context suggests a long-term settlement—e.g.: "A president who believes government is the answer to everything quite naturally looks to government for a solution to the Michigan Militia, the Montana Maniacs, the Kansas Kooks, the Idaho Idiots and whatever other nut cases might be out there on permanent fantasy *bivouacs* [read *maneuvers*]." Kevin O'Brien, "Anti-Terrorism Laws to Solve the Wrong Problems," *Plain Dealer* (Cleveland), 30 Apr. 1995, at C1.

B. As a Verb. As a verb meaning "to temporarily make camp or take shelter" or "to provide with temporary shelter," *bivouac* makes the past tense *bivouacked* and the present participle *bivouacking*.

biweekly; semiweekly. See BI-.

bizarre; bazaar. *Bizarre* (= startlingly odd) is occasionally misused for *bazaar* (= a market, esp. a collection of small shops or vendors offering a wide variety of goods). The tricky spelling of the second word, which comes from Persian by way of Hindi and Turkish, may lead some writers into this error—e.g.:

- "The thought of yet another library bake sale or classroom Christmas *bizarre* [read *bazaar*] makes Polly Mire cringe." Andrea Vogt, "Obscure Tax Law Could Aid Schools," *Spokesman-Rev.* (Spokane) (Idaho ed.), 24 Dec. 1997, at B1.
- "The Holiday *Bizarre* [read *Bazaar*] in December, Singing Valentines in February, selling entertainment books and candy, were some of the fund-raisers this year." Michelle McGrier, "Lake Zurich High Choir Visits New York," *Daily Herald* (Chicago), 21 Mar. 2002, Neighbor §, at 3.
- "Verona United Methodist Church, 798 Herron Ave., will hold its 16th annual Christmas and Homespun *Bizarre*

[read *Bazaar*] beginning at 9:30 a.m. Saturday." "Valley Notes," *Pitt. Post-Gaz.*, 9 Oct. 2002, at E4.

See WORD-SWAPPING.

LANGUAGE-CHANGE INDEX
bizarre misused for *bazaar*: Stage 1

black, vb.; **blacken.** Both verbs mean "to make or become black," but *black* is confined to the narrow, physical sense of using black polish <Frank blacked his boots>, whereas *blacken* is used in all other physical senses <the sky blackened> as well as in figurative senses <the candidate's mood blackened when the indictment was unsealed>.

But the most common figurative sense—in which *blacken* means something like "to vilify, defame"—is widely avoided because of its invidious association with race.

blackmail referred initially to rent payable in cattle, labor, or coin other than silver (i.e., *white money*). Originating in Scotland from Old Norse *mal* (meaning "lawsuit"), it came to denote a kind of protection money: payment that robbers extorted from landowners for exemption from their raids. Today the word applies to any menacing demand made without justification—i.e., extortion generally.

Since at least the late 19th century, the word has been a verb as well as a noun—e.g.: "Watergater E. Howard Hunt *blackmailed* the White House into paying him hush money." "Stone's 'Nixon' Film Rocks with Conspiracies," *Boston Herald*, 13 Mar. 1995, at 17.

blamable. See **blameworthy (B)**.

*****blamableness.** See **blameworthiness**.

blame, v.t. In the best usage, one *blames* a person; one does not, properly, *blame* a thing *on* a person—e.g.: "I *blame* him *for* the fires." (Not: **I blame the fires on him*.) The collocation *blame it on* had no appreciable presence in the language till about 1900. Since then it has steadily become more common, especially in BrE. Blame it on Britons.

LANGUAGE-CHANGE INDEX
blame [the act or outcome] *on* [the actor or cause]
for *blame* [the actor or cause] *for* [the act or outcome]: Stage 3
Current ratio (*blamed him for it* vs. *blamed it on him*): 4:1

blameful. See **blameworthy (B)**.

blameworthiness; *blamableness. The latter is a NEEDLESS VARIANT.

Current ratio: 413:1

blameworthy. A. And *culpable*. Though the two words are etymologically equivalent, in 20th- and

---

LANGUAGE-CHANGE INDEX (For the full key, see front matter pp. xxxi, l–li.)
Stage 1: Rejected. **Stage 2:** Widely shunned. **Stage 3:** Widespread but . . . **Stage 4:** Ubiquitous but . . . **Stage 5:** Fully accepted.
Invariably inferior forms marked by asterisk (*). • Ratios represent frequency of prevalent forms vs. variants in current books.

21st-century usage the Anglo-Saxon *blameworthy* has tended to be used in noncriminal contexts, the Latinate *culpable* in criminal contexts. E.g.:

- "Are any of them *culpable* and at risk of indictment?" Andrew E. Serwer, "The Fall of a Buffett Wannabe," *Fortune*, 28 Oct. 1996, at 30.
- "A federal judge in Kansas City levied $15 million in punitive damages against R.J. Reynolds Tobacco . . . . [He] wrote in his decision that 'Reynolds' conduct was highly *blameworthy* and deserving of significant punishment.'" Gordon Fairclough, "Reynolds Ordered to Pay $15 Million," *Wall Street J.*, 24 June 2002, at A6.

In all phases of Modern English, the Latinate *culpable* has always appeared more frequently than the Anglo-Saxon *blameworthy*.

B. And *blamable*; *blameful*. *Blameworthy* is the usual word meaning "deserving blame." *Blamable* (so spelled—not *blameable) is a NEEDLESS VARIANT.

Blameful = imputing blame; blaming. E.g.: "The Sacramento City Teachers Association points a *blameful* finger at the district." Deborah Anderluh, "City District, Teachers Still at Loggerheads," *Sacramento Bee*, 8 Mar. 1996, at B1. The word is occasionally misused for *blameworthy*—e.g.:

- "Gambling is not in itself a *blameful* [read *blameworthy*] activity." David Spanier, "Poker," *Independent*, 28 Oct. 1994, at 24.
- "Rosenblum also finds the unions *blameful* [read *blameworthy*] . . . . They failed to communicate with their members and the community about what was truly at stake." Stephen Franklin, "Book Reveals Agony Behind Copper Strike," *Phoenix Gaz.*, 7 Feb. 1995, at D1.
- "'I voted for it. I'm as *blameful* [read *blameworthy*] as everyone else,' said Supervisor Roger Quindel." Steve Schultze, "Million Dollar Pensions Attacked," *Milwaukee J. Sentinel*, 6 Jan. 2002, at A1.

LANGUAGE-CHANGE INDEX
blameful misused for *blameworthy*: Stage 1

blanch; blench, v.i. The French word *blanc* (= white) is the root of both verbs, which long ago underwent DIFFERENTIATION. To *blanch* is to make (something) white. To *blench* is to become pale or white as blood withdraws from the surface of the skin—typically as a reaction to an emotional shock or stress. Despite the different meanings, AmE speakers long ago made *blanch* do the work of both words and never wholeheartedly embraced *blench*. In BrE, *blench* is rapidly losing ground to *blanch*, which now predominates in print sources by a 4-to-1 ratio.

Because *blench* has a second, older meaning ("to flinch; to shy away"), it can be ambiguous, as in this soliloquy:

I'll have these players
Play something like the murder of my father
Before mine uncle. I'll observe his looks.
I'll tent him to the quick. If he do *blench*,
I know my course.

(*Hamlet* 2.2.557–61.) Did Hamlet expect his uncle to turn pale or to recoil? Either meaning works, but recoiling has more dramatic effect than simply blanching.

In AmE, *blanch* is pronounced /blanch/ or /blahnch/; only the latter pronunciation is used in BrE.

blandish; brandish. *Blandish* = to cajole; to persuade by flattery or coaxing. E.g.: "They were pounced on by the [congressional] whips and relentlessly *blandished* with promises of favors and political support." Michael Wines, "The Budget Struggle," *N.Y. Times*, 6 Aug. 1993, at A1.

Brandish = to wave or shake in a menacing or threatening way. E.g.: "One [raider] *brandished* a gun and the other a knife." "Shop Raid Terror," *Daily Record* (Baltimore), 13 Mar. 1995, at 9.

Misusages occur most frequently with the corresponding nouns, especially *brandishment* for *blandishment*—e.g.: "Bargaining with the touts was almost as difficult as staying civil with them; but neither was as difficult as resisting their *brandishments* [read *blandishments*] toward our sweet little thing." David O. Seal, "Traveling by the Seat of Your Pants," *News Trib.* (Tacoma), 16 Feb. 1994, Food/Family §, at 3.

LANGUAGE-CHANGE INDEX
brandishment misused for *blandishment*: Stage 1

blasphemous (= seriously insulting to people's religious beliefs) is pronounced /**blas**-fə-məs/—not /blas-**fee**-məs/. Yet the verb *blaspheme* is pronounced /blas-**feem**/.

blatant; flagrant. Despite a fairly well-defined distinction, each word is misused for the other. What is *blatant* stands out glaringly or repugnantly; what is *flagrant* is deplorable and shocking, connoting outrage. A perjurer might tell *blatant* lies to the grand jury to cover up his *flagrant* breach of trust. Egregious criminal acts are *flagrant* <flagrant arson>, not *blatant*—e.g.: "No self-respecting country can permit the *blatant* [read *flagrant*] murder of four of its citizens to go unpunished." "Cuban Jets vs. Unarmed Cessnas," *Baltimore Sun*, 27 Feb. 1996, at A12.

Likewise, *flagrant* is sometimes misused for *blatant*—e.g.: "But all the singing performances were strong—Mary Westbrook-Geha as a *flagrantly* [read *blatantly*] unrepentant penitent." Richard Dyer, "A Compelling 'Balcony,'" *Boston Globe*, 15 June 1990, at 33. For the MALAPROPISM of misusing *fragrant* for *flagrant*, see **flagrant.**

The phrase **blatantly obvious* is a REDUNDANCY— e.g.: "That brought to mind—my mind, anyhow—a past convention when network in-house bias was so *blatantly obvious* [read *blatant*] that the GOP brass lodged a formal complaint about it." Jim Wright, "Your Humble Swami Does It Again! (Applause)," *Dallas Morning News*, 22 Sept. 1996, at J7.

LANGUAGE-CHANGE INDEX
1. *blatant* for *flagrant*: Stage 2
2. *flagrant* for *blatant*: Stage 2

bleary-eyed (= having tired, watery, bloodshot eyes) is the standard spelling. *Blear-eyed and *bleareyed are variants that, once common, have been in decline since the mid-20th century.

Current ratio (*bleary-eyed* vs. **blear-eyed* vs. **bleareyed*): 41:12:1

bleed > bled > bled. So inflected, even in figurative baseball uses—e.g.:

- "Rather than hitting those two-hop grounders to short-stop, I've *bleeded* [read *bled*] a couple through the infield lately." Rich Rupprecht, "Baseball Spawns Its Own Language," *Press Democrat* (Santa Rosa), 14 Mar. 1997, at C1.
- "Jeff Cirillo lined a double to left and scored when Matheny *bleeded* [read *bled*] a single to right." Vic Feuerherd, "Brewers Squander Chance," *Wis. State J.*, 31 Aug. 1997, at D5.

See IRREGULAR VERBS.

LANGUAGE-CHANGE INDEX
*bleeded for *bled*: Stage 1

BLENDS. See PORTMANTEAU WORDS.

blindman's buff (= a game in which a blindfolded player tries to catch and identify any one of several other players) is the traditional term; it dates from about 1600. But *blindman's bluff*, a 20th-century variant, is now common and almost equally acceptable.

Current ratio: 3:1

blintz; blintze. American dictionaries are about equally divided between these two spellings for the name of a rolled pancake stuffed with cottage cheese or another filling. But the predominant spelling today is *blintz*, which appears about ten times as often as the original Yiddish *blintze* in modern print sources.

bloc; block. Political groups or alignments are *blocs*, especially when the affiliates vote in lockstep fashion. *Block* serves in all other senses.

blond; blonde. A. As an Adjective. In French, the *-e* is a feminine tag, the spelling without the *-e* being the masculine. This distinction has generally carried over to BrE, so that *blonde* more often refers to women and *blond* more often refers to men. In AmE, though, there is a tendency to use *blond* in all senses—e.g.: "Currently there's an 'Absolut Dallas' ad that pictures a *blond woman's* tiara-adorned bouffant hairdo in the shape of a bottle." Melanie Wells, "Absolut's Eye-Catching Ads Command Teens' Attention," *USA Today*, 31 Jan. 1997, at B5.

Sometimes *blonde* is ill-advisedly applied to a man—e.g.: "It looks like these beautiful people are going to ride off into Madison Avenue bliss. But wait. The *blonde man* is kissing someone else. And that someone else is another man." Cristina Rouvalis, "Ad Fanatics Will Revel in Best-of-Fest Commercials," *Pitt. Post-Gaz.*, 27 June 1996, at D4.

When the word describes an inanimate object, the *-e* is invariably dropped <blond wooden chairs> <a honey-blond microbrewed beer>.

B. As a Noun. Though we may from time to time see *blond men* and *blond women* in print, when we see a reference to *a blonde* (or *a blond*) we almost always assume it's a woman. To avoid appearing sexist, it's best to refrain altogether from using this word as a noun. In fact, some readers will find even the adjective to be sexist when it modifies *woman* and not *hair*. Cf. **brunet(te).** See SEXISM (D).

blow > blew > blown. So inflected. See IRREGULAR VERBS.

bluish. So spelled—not **blueish*.

Current ratio: 41:1

boast, vb. In the sense "to have (something desirable)," this word is objectionable primarily on grounds of being a CLICHÉ <the town now boasts 300 retail merchants>. It has been STANDARD ENGLISH since the early 19th century.

LANGUAGE-CHANGE INDEX
boast as a transitive verb <Albuquerque boasts the largest airport in New Mexico>: Stage 5

boatswain (= a ship's officer in charge of the hull) is pronounced /**boh**-sən/. **Bosun, *bo's'n, *bos'n,* and **bo'sun* are variant forms.

bobby socks. So spelled—preferably not **bobby sox*.

*bob wire. See **barbed wire.**

bogey; *bogie; *bogy. *Bogey* = (1) an evil spirit, or (2) a score of one over par on a golf hole. **Bogy* and **bogie* are variant spellings.

Current ratio (in order of headwords): 9:3:1

*boldface lie. See **bald-faced.**

bologna. See **baloney.**

*boloney. See **baloney.**

bombastic is sometimes misconstrued to mean "strident" or "violent." Properly, *bombastic* (lit., "full of stuffing or padding") means "pompous, highfalutin, overblown." But the misunderstanding is all too common, perhaps because of the sound association with *bomb*—e.g.:

- "He is Action Man with a human outline, unlike the *bombastic* [read *barbarous*?] brutes incarnated in *Sly* or *Arnie*. As Hollywood is now committed to violent epics of convulsive crisis, unlike the old consensual social dramas the studios used to give us, Reeves is the man to have around." Alexander Walker, "Kinetic Reeves on a White-Knuckle Ride," *Evening Standard*, 29 Sept. 1994, at 32.

LANGUAGE-CHANGE INDEX (For the full key, see front matter pp. xxxi, l–li.)
Stage 1: Rejected. **Stage 2:** Widely shunned. **Stage 3:** Widespread but . . . **Stage 4:** Ubiquitous but . . . **Stage 5:** Fully accepted.
Invariably inferior forms marked by asterisk (*). • Ratios represent frequency of prevalent forms vs. variants in current books.

- "Only a plane crash. As if we have pushed these *bombastic* [read *dreadful*?] disasters down our hierarchy of fear, well below a new entry: terrorist attacks." Editorial, "Again, Smoke Blackens the Sky," *Chicago Trib.*, 13 Nov. 2001, at 18.
- "But the idea that the only legitimate response to that terrible day is to become as blind, bloodthirsty and *bombastic* [read *strident* or *violent*] as the terrorists themselves—the essence of Keith's song—is insulting." Julia Keller, "Toby Keith Out of Tune with Reality," *Chicago Trib.*, 21 July 2002, Arts & Entertainment §, at 2.

LANGUAGE-CHANGE INDEX
bombastic misused in a violent sense: Stage 2

bona fide. A. Meaning. This Latin phrase, meaning "good-faith," has been used as a legal term for "without fraud or deceit" (*Black's Law Dictionary* 210 [10th ed. 2014]) since at least the 16th century. Outside legal contexts, its meaning has been subject to SLIPSHOD EXTENSION—from "guileless" to "genuine," and later to "sincere" and even "very." The steps are subtle. Most often, for example, "guileless" and "genuine" overlap: a genuine effort is one that is done in good faith. At other times, though, what is genuine (in the sense "authentic") shows anything but good faith—e.g.:

- "Police said they are treating the incident as a *bona fide* [read *true*] assault." Jonathan D. Silver, "Former Prosecutor in 2nd Knife Attack," *Pitt. Post-Gaz.*, 4 Oct. 2002, at A1.
- "2000 Syrah. $18. . . . A *bona fide* [read *real*] steal." Paul Gregutt, "Cry Wolfe," *Seattle Times*, 6 Oct. 2002, Pacific NW §, at 12.

In best usage, *bona fide* should always denote honesty—e.g.: "Consumers can also help further stigmatize the bad guys by supporting *bona fide* Internet marketers." Robert Schroeder, "How Can We Halt the Spam Onslaught?" *Tulsa World*, 6 Oct. 2002, at G3.

As the extended uses of *bona fide* stray further from this classic sense and into the various meanings of "genuine," the attachment to "honesty" likewise fades. It may mean "genuine" in the sense of "qualified"—e.g.: "What can a *bona fide* [read *qualified*] cruise expert tell you?" Judi Dash, "Get Your Bearings," *News & Observer* (Raleigh), 6 Oct. 2002, at H1. Or it may mean "formally recognized"—e.g.: "Only in 1984 was SAD established as a *bona fide* [read *recognized*] medical condition." Lyn Cockburn, "Fighting Winter Blues," *Toronto Sun*, 31 Dec. 1995, Lifestyle §, at 46. Or it may just mean "real"—e.g.: "When there is a *bona fide* [read *real*] emergency, a medivac crew must respond faster than an ER doc." J.B. Orenstein, "From Thin Air," *Wash Post.*, 8 Oct. 2002, at F1.

In the nether reaches of these extended uses, *bona fide* becomes an amorphous and ornamental replacement for "real," often with a jocular flavor of "true blue" or lending dignity to the mundane—e.g.:

- "Those who were there now have a *bona fide* [read *classic*] Angels moment about which to tell their children and grandkids." Bob Keiser, "A Game Fans Will Remember," *Daily News* (L.A.), 5 Oct. 2002, at S8.
- "As a *bona fide* Jersey Girl . . . I'm here to say that New Jersey has it going on, and then some." Trish Boppert, "Hey New Jerseyans, Did You Hear the One About . . . ," *Record* (N.J.), 6 Oct. 2002, at O5.

B. Adjective or Adverb. *Bona fide* was originally adverbial, meaning "in good faith" <the suit was brought bona fide>. Today it is more commonly used as an adjective <it was a bona fide lawsuit>. The phrase is sometimes hyphenated when functioning as a PHRASAL ADJECTIVE, but it shouldn't be.

**C. Misspelled ***bonified*. During the late 20th century, the spurious form *bonified* emerged—e.g.:

- "Calvin Klein's unisex fragrance . . . is more like refreshing citrus water than a *bonified* [read *bona fide* or, better, *genuine*] perfume." Michelle Trappen, "You Nose How It Is," *Oregonian* (Portland), 29 Nov. 1995, at D4.
- "Much of the filming was done in a hospital setting, provided by Medstar, complete with a *bonified* [read *bona fide* or, better, *genuine*] nurse on the set to make sure everything was safe and authentic." John Drybred, "A Meaty TV Role Has Him Passing Up the Hamburgers," *Lancaster New Era*, 27 Dec. 1996, at 3.

On the reason for preferring *genuine* in those edits, see (A).

LANGUAGE-CHANGE INDEX
bona fide misspelled *bonified*: Stage 1
Current ratio: 676:1

D. Pronunciation. The phrase is pronounced /**boh**-nə fīd/ or, less often, /**bon**-ə fīd/. The pronunciation /**boh**-nə **fī**-dee/ is pedantic outside the law and precious even in legal contexts.

bona fides, n. **A. And *good faith; bonne foi*.** Though the adjective *bona fide* has been fully anglicized, the noun phrase *bona fides* has lost much ground—especially in AmE—to *good faith*. The trend should be encouraged. Perhaps the comparative infrequency of *bona fides* results from its pronunciation (/**boh**-nə **fī**-deez/), which sounds foreign and bombastic in comparison with *good faith*. The GALLICISM *bonne foi*, a variant, sounds still more so; fortunately, it is rare.

B. Meanings. The term *bona fides* has essentially three meanings: (1) "good faith" <he proved his *bona fides* through long dedication>; (2) "authenticity; the fact of actually being what one claims or seems to be" <the diploma proved her *bona fides* as a graduate of Princeton>; and (3) "proof of authenticity; credentials" <she could produce no *bona fides* showing that she was a graduate of the university>.

Sense 1, the traditional use, is now rare.

Sense 2, the product of SLIPSHOD EXTENSION, is fairly common. It can easily be improved with slight editing—e.g.:

- "Zinman long ago established his *bona fides as a conductor willing* [read *willingness as a conductor*] to do almost anything to help a soloist achieve his or her best." Stephen Wigler, "Ambidextrous Fleisher Joins BSO for an Off-the-Wall Party," *Baltimore Sun*, 8 Feb. 1996, at E4.
- "In Deloria's view, Custer established *his bona fides* [read *himself*] as a psychopath by his frenzied assault on Jeb Stuart's Confederates during the Battle of Gettysburg." Patricia Ward Biederman, "Symposium Will Take a Closer Look at Custer," *L.A. Times* (Valley ed.), 8 Aug. 1996, Calendar §, at B1.

And sense 3 follows hard upon sense 2, extending the slipshod extension still further—e.g.: "Having finished a course of study, like a medieval apprentice he would need to produce something that established his *bona fides* [read *credentials*] in the craft." "The Drag of Loss, the Flight of Youth," *Portland Press Herald*, 14 Jan. 1996, at E6.

LANGUAGE-CHANGE INDEX
1. *bona fides* in the sense "authenticity": Stage 4
2. *bona fides* in the sense "credentials": Stage 2

C. Number. If the variable meanings of *bona fides*, together with its air of affectation, weren't enough to make it a SKUNKED TERM, the grammatical dilemma it presents certainly is. Technically, of course, the noun phrase *bona fides* is singular: *this bona fides is*, not **these bona fides are*. Making *bona fides* singular sounds pedantic; making it plural is likely to offend those who have a smattering of Latin. Interestingly, this problem seems to occur only in senses 2 and 3 mentioned in (B)—e.g.:

- "Once the hero's *bona fides are* [read *credentials are* or *authenticity is*] established, Clancy's convoluted plot lumbers along like a runaway freight train." Gene Lyons, "Jack in Action," *Entertainment Weekly*, 23/30 Aug. 1996, at 115.
- "His campaign turf extends from the Republican hard right, where Dole's conservative *bona fides are* [read *credentials are*] sometimes questioned." Karen Hosler, "Kemp Makes Case for Diverse GOP," *Baltimore Sun*, 14 Sept. 1996, at A1.
- "No matter how Republican the president may sound, Ickes' liberal *bona fides are* [read *credentials are* or *commitment is*] questioned by none." Michael Rust, "Dick Morris Leaves a Vacuum," *Wash. Times*, 30 Sept. 1996, at 14.

Unfortunately, only a few careful writers will consciously avoid this usage. Most writers would never think to use the phrase at all, but the semi-educated—eager to impress—are likely to perpetuate the error.

boned; deboned; boneless. *Boned* describes something with bones either in <big-boned> or out <boned chicken>. In another sense, it is synonymous with *deboned* (which looks deceptively like an antonym) and *boneless*. Any one of these three terms might suffice in each of these sentences:

- "Do your *boneless* chicken breasts come out dry on the grill?" Dale Curry, "What's New in BBQ?" *Times-Picayune* (New Orleans), 28 June 2001, Food §, at 1.
- "Prudhomme said he created the turducken by layering *deboned* chicken, duck, and turkey with stuffing *between each layer* [read *between the layers*]." Crystal Bolner, "The Stuff of Legends," *Times-Picayune* (New Orleans), 23 Dec. 2001, Money §, at 1. See **between (F).**
- "Dave's is the place to pick up *boned* chickens stuffed with crawfish or shrimp or eggplant or sausage." Mary Tutwiler, "Real Food," *Times-Picayune* (New Orleans), 28 Apr. 2002, Travel §, at 1.

Today *boneless chicken* is by far the most frequent collocation, followed distantly by *boned chicken* and even more distantly by *deboned chicken*. No bones about it.

boneless. See **boned.**

*bonified. See **bona fide (C).**

bon mot /bohn **moh**/ = a well-turned phrase, witticism. The plural is traditionally formed in the French way—*bons mots* (pronounced /bohn **mohz**/). E.g.:

- "The ambassadorial corps, while justly renowned for *bons mots* and clever embassy patter, was even more brilliant." Kevin Chaffee, "An Exotic Night in 'Morocco,'" *Wash. Times*, 11 Dec. 1996, at C12.
- "Miss Piggy weighs in with *bons mots*." "Picks & Pans," *People*, 18 Aug. 1997, at 31 (photo caption).

But more commonly, the plural actually used is *bon mots*. This anglicized plural ought to be accepted on the same footing as *cul-de-sacs*—e.g.:

- "And people who imagine him eating canapes, sipping champagne and swapping *bon mots* with movie stars at Cannes and London have it all wrong, Jarvis said." Thomas R. O'Donnell, "Film Office Director Skips Glitz on Trips," *Des Moines Register*, 23 Mar. 1997, at 1.
- "The Duchess's *bon mots* festooned each window, serving as an understated backdrop to some rather gaudy frocks and baubles." Tunku Varadarajan, "New York Gasps at Wallis and Edward Show," *Times* (London), 11 Aug. 1997, at 5.

Current ratio (*bon mots* vs. *bons mots*): 1.2:1

See PLURALS (B).

bonne foi. See **bona fides, n. (A).**

bon vivant (/bohn vee-**vahn**/). **A. And *bon viveur** (/bohn vee-**vuur**/). Both mean "a person who lives well, esp. the companionable type who enjoys good wine and fine food." *Bon vivant* is standard in AmE and BrE.

*Bon viveur, a form virtually unknown in AmE, is a BrE variant—but little-known even there. The *OED* labels it a "pseudo-French" substitute for *bon vivant*—e.g.: "A *bon viveur* [read *bon vivant*] who enjoys good wine, he is widely read and has broad interests in the arts and music." "Hail to the Chief," *Sunday Telegraph*, 13 Oct. 1996, at 36. *Bon vivant* vastly predominates in all varieties of English.

Current ratio (*bon vivant* vs. **bon viveur*): 6:1

B. Plural Form. The traditional view is that the plural form is preferably the French *bons vivants*—e.g.: "Texas' problems against Baylor today don't end with the conclusion of the champagne brunch investigation and the eligibility of its *bons vivants*." Jonathan Feigen, "Concerns Aplenty Remain for UT vs. Baylor," *Houston Chron.*, 2 Nov. 1996, Sports §, at 4.

But the phrase is often considered anglicized enough to use the English plural *bon vivants*. Indeed, the English form is far more common—e.g.:

- "When '60 Minutes' reported this so-called 'French Paradox' several years ago, vin rouge sales surged as *bon vivants* hoped for some undiscovered antioxidant or a 'miracle' nutrient in the vin ordinaire drunk so copiously by the French with their high-fat diets." Fran Price, "Variety Balances Fatty Diet," *Richmond Times-Dispatch*, 16 Oct. 1996, at F3.

- "Passengers who have sailed on Marco Polo have described themselves as feeling like *bon vivants* aboard." Arline Bleecker, "Exotic Cruise Could Become Fashionable," *Orlando Sentinel*, 27 Oct. 1996, at L4.
- "There were the *bon vivants* who remained anchored to their bar stools, hoisting just one more brew in honor of the Yankees." Frank Bruni, "World Champs: The Fans," *N.Y. Times*, 28 Oct. 1996, at C6.

See PLURALS (B).

LANGUAGE-CHANGE INDEX
bon vivants as a plural: Stage 5
Current ratio (*bon vivants* vs. *bons vivants*): 2:1

bookkeeping; accounting. *Bookkeeping* (so spelled, it and *bookkeeper* being the only words in the English language with three consecutive pairs of doubled letters) is the uncritical recording of debts and credits or summarizing of financial information, usually about a business enterprise. *Accounting* differs from bookkeeping because it is not mechanical: it requires judgment about such issues as when a specified type of transaction should be recorded, how the amount of the transaction should be calculated, and how a balance sheet and income statement should be presented.

borborygmus (= intestinal rumbling caused by a gassy stomach) makes the standard plural *borborygmi* /bor-bə-**rig**-mɪ/—not **borborygmuses* (a rare variant). Cf. **flatulence.**

born; borne. Both are past participles of *bear*—*borne* for general purposes <she has borne a child> <the burden he has borne> and *born* only as an adjective or as a part of the fixed passive verb *to be born* <she was born in 1987>. *Bear in mind* yields *borne in mind*—e.g.:

- "The trial judge, Justice Tucker, said that the Crown had *born* [read *borne*] in mind that a trial of Mr. Turner before that of Asil Nadir . . . would be 'lengthy and costly.'" Frank Kane, "Analysts Cast Adrift by Code of Silence," *Guardian*, 2 Oct. 1993, at 33.
- "That point should be *born* [read *borne*] in mind today as Colorado voters review a long list of important primary elections in races for the U.S. Senate." *Denver Post*, 13 Aug. 1996, at B6.

This misuse provides evidence of the great difficulty that modern writers have with homophones. Inevitably, the more common form—through confusion—assimilates to the less common form. Hence, although *born* is virtually never mistakenly made *borne*, the opposite error is common—e.g.:

- "They combed student records for anyone who might have *born* [read *borne*] a personal grudge against the academics who received the packages." Ian Katz, "Death in the Post," *Guardian*, 15 May 1995, at T2.
- "It is clearly unfair that the bulk of the burden should be *born* [read *borne*] by the owners of existing homes and businesses in the city." "Phoenix Should Make Developments Pay Their Own Way," *Ariz. Republic*, 25 May 1995, at B6.
- "Human service agencies that have seen their funding stop have *born* [read *borne*] the brunt of the standoff thus

far." Karen Langley & Kate Giammarise, "Plan to Override Budget Fails," *Pitt. Post-Gaz.*, 26 Aug. 2015, at A1.

LANGUAGE-CHANGE INDEX
born misused for *borne*: Stage 1
Current ratio (*borne by him* vs. **born by him*): 31:1

bosk; *boscage; *boskage. All three mean "a thicket." The first is the standard term. The second and third are NEEDLESS VARIANTS. But if the choice were between **boscage* and **boskage*, the former would be considered the better spelling.

Current ratio (*bosk* vs. **boscage* vs. **boskage*): 4:3:1

both. A. *Both . . . and.* These CORRELATIVE CONJUNCTIONS must frame matching sentence parts—e.g.:

- "He was trying *both* to establish himself in his new league *and* to justify the contract extension he was given through 2002." Phil Rogers, "Indians' Grissom Showing He's Big-Time Player," *Chicago Sun-Times*, 11 Oct. 1997, at 3. (The conjunctions frame two infinitives.)
- "Gunshot residue was observed on Mr. Foster's right hand, consistent *both* with the test firings of the gun *and* with the gun's cylinder gap." Jerry Seper, "Starr Probe Finds Foster Killed Himself," *Wash. Times*, 11 Oct. 1997, at A1. (The conjunctions frame two prepositional phrases beginning with *with*.)
- "Immunocompromise presents unique challenges *both* to the pet lover *and* to the veterinarian involved." Robin Downing, "Illness Doesn't Mean Separation," *Denver Post*, 12 Oct. 1997, at D8. (The conjunctions frame two prepositional phrases beginning with *to*.)

See PARALLELISM.

B. **Both . . . as well as.* This construction is both unidiomatic and verbose for *both . . . and.* E.g.:

- "But I think it should be obvious—*both* to the characters *as well as* [read *and*] to the reader." Denise Gess, "Susan Lucci's Next Movie of the Week," *News & Observer* (Raleigh), 14 Sept. 1997, at G4.
- "The bank operations there will include *both* branch business *as well as* [read *and*] the bank's commercial-vault business." Mark Mensheha, "First National Bank Plans to Open Branch on North Side," *San Antonio Bus. J.*, 10 Oct. 1997, at 6.

LANGUAGE-CHANGE INDEX
*both . . . as well as for *both . . . and*: Stage 2

C. Redundancies with. Several wordings with *both* cause redundancies. One is **both . . . each other*—e.g.:

- "Earlier, *both sides had blamed each other* [read *each side had blamed the other*] for the error that saw tax revenues collected when they shouldn't have been." Jerry Graff, "Edinburgh Treasurer Wants Full Tax Report," *Indianapolis News*, 31 July 1995, at D8.
- "*Both men knew each other* [read *The men knew each other*] and lived in the same general area, authorities said." "Man, 19, Arrested in Fatal Shooting," *San Diego Union-Trib.*, 25 May 1996, at B2.
- "Brown said negotiations could produce a good substitute for Proposition L if *both sides treated each other* [read *each side treated the other* or *the two sides treated each other*] with respect, something notably absent in the campaign." David R. Baker & Edward Epstein, "Brown Suggests Compromise on S.F. Growth Policy," *S.F. Chron.*, 15 Nov. 2000, at A17.

Another is *both alike—e.g.: "This makes treating *both alike* [read *the two alike*] difficult." Daniel F. Akerson, "Let the Innovators Innovate," *Investor's Bus. Daily*, 8 Apr. 1996, at A2. Still another is *both . . . similar—e.g.: "In other words, the mission of *both* [read *the two*] state agencies is *similar*." Garvey Winegar, "Money Source of Friction Between Outdoor Agencies," *Richmond Times-Dispatch*, 17 Jan. 2001, at E2. See REDUNDANCY.

   D. Both (of) the. Though the idiom is falling into disuse, *both the* (or *both these*) has a fine pedigree and continues in formal English—e.g.:

- "*Both these* movements are thus defined by Euclid." James Odell, *An Essay on the Elements, Accents, and Prosody of the English Language* 60 (1806).
- "The hazard, in *both these* respects, could only be avoided, if at all, by rendering that tribunal more numerous." *The Federalist*, No. 65, at 398 (Alexander Hamilton) (Clinton Rossiter ed., 1961).

The alternative phrasing, *both of the* (or *both of these*), is somewhat more common in AmE.

   E. *Both (of) the last; *both (of) the last two. These phrases are unidiomatic and unnecessarily wordy for *the last two*—e.g.:

- "One aspect of the game the Vikings need to work on is breaking the full-court press, which plagued them in *both of* [delete *both of*] the last two losses." Jeff Zeigler, "ECSU Hopes to Rebound After Taking Short Break," *Virginian-Pilot* (Norfolk), 18 Dec. 1994, at 19.
- "The fact that so many municipalities changed hands in *both of the last* [read *the last two*] municipal contests suggests that Paraguayan politics is getting more sophisticated than old stereotypes suggest." "Burt Wins in a Polarised Capital," *Latin Am. Weekly Rep.*, 28 Nov. 1996, at 549.
- "Huddersfield have conceded late goals in *both of* [delete *both of*] their last two Championship matches." "Big Match Guide," *South Wales Echo*, 11 Sept. 2015, at 54.

*boughten.** See **buy** (A).

bouillon. See **bullion.**

bountiful; bounteous. *Bounteous* is poetic or literary for *bountiful*, which is generally the preferable and the more frequently occurring term.

   Current ratio (*bountiful* vs. *bounteous*): 4:1

bouquet (= [1] a flower arrangement meant to be carried; nosegay; [2] a compliment; or [3] the aroma of a particular wine) is preferably pronounced /boo-**kay**/—not /boh-/.

bourgeois; *burgeois. This term, pronounced /boor-**zhwah**/, means "a member of the middle class" (which is called, collectively, *bourgeoisie* /boor-zhwah-**zee**/). The first spelling (with the -*ou*-) is standard; the second is a variant form. Often the term, which is almost always disparaging, is used attributively as an adjective <a philistine petty bourgeois existence>.

The mass noun *bourgeoisie*, by the way, takes a singular verb when it functions as subject <the bourgeoisie is disillusioned>. A loanword from French, *bourgeoisie* (= citizenry) expanded in meaning after the Industrial Revolution to refer to either (1) the middle class or (2) in Marxian theory, the economically supreme class that owns capital, property, and the means of production. The erroneous spelling *bourgeousie* is surprisingly common:

- "Her examples, drawn from mid-twentieth century Britain, include some of the very, very rich (allowed to spend excessively, have flamboyant divorces, look down on the *bourgeousie* [read *bourgeoisie*]." Sara Meadows, *The Child as Social Person* (2009).
- "After the hurly-burly and the social animation of Père Lachaise, where many local families go to picnic, we found the Cimetière Montparnasse in the 14th, the burial place of Beckett and his wife, Suzanne, austere and clinical, close to where they had lived, very much the resting place of the haute *bourgeousie* [read *bourgeoisie*]." Hugh Oram, "An Irishman's Diary," *Irish Times*, 25 Apr. 2011, Opinion §, at 15.
- "What the *bourgeousie* [read *bourgeoisie*] engendered was a Creole industrial enterprise centred on sugar." G. Roger Knight, *Sugar, Steam and Steel: The Industrial Project in Colonial Java, 1830–1885* 204 (2014).

boutique (= [1] a small shop that sells fashionable items, or [2] a firm that specializes in a narrow array of services) is preferably pronounced /boo-**teek**/—not /boh-/.

bowdlerize (= to remove all the passages in a book, play, etc. containing offensive and esp. sexual references) is preferably pronounced /**bowd**-lə-rīz/— not /**bohd**-/. The term derives from the name of Thomas Bowdler (1754–1825), who expunged all the sexual and scatological references from his edition of Shakespeare's plays (1818).

boycott; embargo. While both terms refer to the suspension of trade with a certain person, company, state, or nation, the difference is how the suspension is imposed. Historically, a *boycott* is an organized popular protest (the word comes from Capt. C.C. Boycott, an English landlord who was stigmatized by his Irish tenants for raising rents in 1880), while an *embargo* is imposed by a government (or, in the case of a *news embargo*, by the originator of the story). So even if the U.S. government were to lift its trade *embargo* against Cuba, the exile community in Miami might still *boycott* Cuba as long as it remained communist.

boyish. See **girlie.**

BRACKETS. See PUNCTUATION (P).

braggadocio (= excessively proud talk) is preferably pronounced /brag-ə-**do**-shee-oh/—not /brag-ə-**do**-see-oh/.

LANGUAGE-CHANGE INDEX (For the full key, see front matter pp. xxxi, l–li.)
Stage 1: Rejected. **Stage 2:** Widely shunned. **Stage 3:** Widespread but . . . **Stage 4:** Ubiquitous but . . . **Stage 5:** Fully accepted.
Invariably inferior forms marked by asterisk (∗). • Ratios represent frequency of prevalent forms vs. variants in current books.

Brahmin; Brahman; Brahma. For people, the spelling *Brahmin* (or *Brahman*) denotes (1) the highest caste or a member of that caste in classical Indian society; or (2) a member of upper-class New England society. *Brahmin*, the older spelling, is preferred <a Brahmin holy man> <a Boston Brahmin>. The popular breed of cattle originating in India are *Brahman* or *Brahma* cattle. But in reference to a specific sex, the males are almost always *Brahma bulls*, whereas the females may be *Brahma* or *Brahman cows*.

brake; break. A *brake* is a device that slows something, esp. to a halt. *Break* is a multisense word, the most common meanings being (1) a sudden separation into pieces, (2) a snapping off or detachment, and (3) a penetration through the surface of (something).

Sometimes the two are erroneously interchanged, especially in reference to the brakes on a vehicle—e.g.:

- "Police said the truck, driven by LeRoy Anthony Gaul, 59, was approaching an intersection when its *breaks* [read *brakes*] failed." "Murder Suspect Nabbed in Mason City," *Des Moines Register*, 14 Oct. 1998, at 3.
- "Survivors told how they shouted at the driver to slow down just before he lost control—he told police on the scene that his *breaks* [read *brakes*] failed." "Relatives Fly Out as South Africa Crash Probe Launched," *Evening News* (Scotland), 28 Sept. 1999, at 3.

The words also function, of course, as verbs: a person may *brake* a car (apply the brakes) or *break* a bowl (drop it and watch it smash into pieces). But what does one do to a fall? The traditional idiom is to *break* (i.e., interrupt) a fall. The *OED* cites two 19th-century examples, the earlier being by Thomas Babington Macaulay. Some modern writers, however, have misunderstood the idiom and replaced *break* with *brake* (= to slow down). Though perhaps understandable, the error is an error nonetheless—e.g.:

- "You had no way to *brake* [read *break*] your fall, and spent the post-apex part of the journey screaming in terror as the pavement rushed up." James Lileks, "I Can't Warm Up to Work When It's So Nice Outside," *Star Trib.* (Minneapolis), 2 May 1999, at B3.
- "That wasn't enough to *brake* [read *break*] the fall from grace." Steve Hummer, "Is This Fall Slump Becoming Normal?" *Atlanta J.-Const.*, 27 Oct. 1999, at D1.

Modern technology, here as elsewhere, has complicated this usage. Consider this sentence: "It must then pop a parachute and power on retro-rockets to *brake* [read *break*?] its fall." Kathy Sawyer, "NASA Goes for a Martian Pole in One," *Wash. Post*, 3 Dec. 1999, at A3. Since the retrorocket is indeed a kind of *brake*, the sentence straddles two idioms.

LANGUAGE-CHANGE INDEX
1. *break* misused for *brake*: Stage 1
Current ratio (*brake pedal* vs. **break pedal*): 89:1
2. **brake a fall* for *break a fall*: Stage 1
Current ratio (*break their fast* vs. **brake their fast*): 47:1

brandish. See **blandish.**

brand-new, adj. So spelled (and hyphenated)—preferably not **bran-new*. The phrase is sometimes written

bran'-new to show that the *-d* is usually dropped when the word is pronounced. Although sounding the *-d* in speech is more than a little pretentious, the contracted written form is unnecessary.

Current ratio: 80:1

brassiere (the women's undergarment) is, oddly enough, sometimes confused with *brazier* (= [1] someone who works in brass; or [2] a pan used for holding burning coals), which is pronounced /**bray**-zhər/. In the 1950s, an Oklahoma legislator questioned the president of the University of Oklahoma, George Lynn Cross, about why the taxpayers' hard-earned money had been spent on women's undergarments. Cross calmly explained that the Egyptian brazier (in sense 2), along with some burial jewelry, had been acquired for a university museum. Randy Krehbiel, "George Cross: The Inimitable OU President," *Tulsa Trib. & Tulsa World*, 24 Apr. 1994, at N1.

Although the French pronunciation of *brassiere* is /brah-si-**er**/, the standard American pronunciation is /brə-**zeer**/. In BrE, it's /**braz**-yə/.

breach, n.; **broach; breech.** *Breach* (= [1] n., an opening or gap; or [2] vb., to break open) can be a troublesome word. In general usage, it is confused with two other words: *breech,* n. (= [1] buttocks; or [2] the lower or back part [of something, as a gun]), and *broach,* v.t. (= [1] to make a hole in [something] to let out liquid; or [2] to bring up for discussion). The confusion of *breach* with *breech* occurs most often when writers mistakenly use the latter where *breach* belongs—e.g.:

- "To fill the *breech* [read *breach*], factor in how much income your investments might spin off." "How to Put a Price Tag on the Retirement You Want," *Tampa Trib.*, 5 Nov. 1996, Bus. & Fin. §, at 7.
- "She had ordered them all to sit, a *breech* [read *breach*] of protocol, but she wanted them to realize only their tasks of discovery mattered now." Karen Harper, *The Queene's Cure* 238 (2002).

But *breech birth* (= the delivery of a baby buttocks-first or feet-first) is sometimes wrongly made **breach birth*, an error that has been on the rise since 1950—e.g.:

- "The AMA wanted the bill altered to allow doctors to perform the procedure if they became afraid for the mother's life in a *breach* [read *breech*] birth." Nancy E. Roman, "AMA Backs Bill to Ban Partial-Birth Abortion," *Wash. Times*, 20 May 1997, at A1.
- "Called Danzante carvings, the panels show a woman writhing during a *breach* [read *breech*] birth." "Christmas in Oaxaca—Tradition with a Twist," *Milwaukee J. Sentinel*, 23 Nov. 1997, Travel §, at 1.

For *breeches* (= pants), see **breeches.**

The lapse with *broach* occurs when someone mistakenly writes of **breaching a topic* or *subject*—e.g.:

- "When Faldo *breached* [read *broached*] that subject to his wife of nine years, Gill wasn't exactly overjoyed." Steve Hershey, "Changes in Life Agree with Faldo," *USA Today*, 16 Apr. 1996, at C2.
- "When rumors regarding Kordell Stewart first surfaced, many talk-show callers attempted to *breach* [read *broach*]

the topic." James M. Rossini Wilkins, "Get the Facts Straight," *Pitt. Post-Gaz.*, 12 Jan. 2002, at D3.

The meanings of *breach* and *broach* are similar only in reference to dikes or levees or walls (*breach* = to break open; *broach* = to make a hole in). E.g.: "Less than three months ago—in the immediate aftermath of the *breaching* of the Berlin Wall—the Chancellor's closest aides were predicting that five to eight years might still be needed before unity became a reality." David Marsh, "Kohl Takes the Burden of Unity on His Shoulders," *Fin. Times*, 22 Feb. 1990, at 3.

It's awkward to broach this subject, but sometimes a writer seems thoroughly befuddled. After a well-publicized tiger escape, a journalist led his account with this sentence: "The San Francisco Zoo was closed to visitors Wednesday as investigators tried to figure out how Tatiana *broached* 20-foot-high walls and a 15-foot-wide moat and attacked three men before being shot and killed by police." Dan Chapman, "Eye on the Tiger," *Atlanta J.-Const.*, 27 Dec. 2007, at D1. Tatiana got out, to be sure, but not by making a hole in the wall. And how, pray tell, does one "broach a moat"? Tatiana seems to have scaled the wall and crossed the moat.

LANGUAGE-CHANGE INDEX
1. *breech* for *breach*: Stage 1
Current ratio (*breach of protocol* vs. **breech of protocol*): 21:1
2. **breach birth* for *breech birth*: Stage 1
Current ratio (*breech birth* vs. **breach birth*): 9:1
3. *breach* for *broach*: Stage 1
Current ratio (*broached the subject* vs. **breached the subject*): 310:1

breach, v.t. Despite a rumor that some crotchety law professors have been spreading, one can *breach*—not just *break*—a contract, a promise, or the peace. Using *breach* in figurative senses is a very modest extension of the old literal sense "to make a breach in (a wall, boundary, etc.)." Indeed, the *OED*'s first citation for the verb is this one from Boorde in 1547: "[Obliviousness] may come to young men and women when their mind is *breached*" (spelling updated).

And the figurative meaning appears routinely in well-edited writing—e.g.:

- "In August, a jury found the diocese had *breached* its duty to parishioners when it failed to probe claims of sexual abuse." "News from Every State: Connecticut," *USA Today*, 8 Sept. 1997, at A16.
- "The lawsuit filed in Washington state court claims that US Airways *breached* its contract with Boeing." "Briefly," *L.A. Times*, 13 Sept. 1997, at D2.

breach, more honored in the. Strictly speaking, this phrase refers to an unjust rule that is better broken than obeyed. Hence in Shakespeare's *Hamlet*, where the phrase originated, Hamlet says that the Danes' riotous drinking "is a custom / More honored in the breach than in the observance" (1.4.17–18). But writers frequently misapply the phrase to a just rule that, in practice, is often broken—e.g.:

- "It is an American custom (perhaps *more honored in the breach* [read *more often breached than observed*]) as well as a Chinese one to show respect for one's elders." Judith Martin, "Ingenuity Can Overcome This Language Barrier," *Chicago Trib.*, 8 Oct. 1989, at C6.
- "Fireworks laws, like speeding laws—and increasingly, banking and accounting laws—are 'customs *more honored in the breach* than in the observance,' as Hamlet might have put it." Editorial, "Observing the Breach," *St. Louis Post-Dispatch*, 3 July 2002, at B6. (The quotation is inapt: the writer couldn't possibly be encouraging the violation of these laws.)
- "The 1917 Constitution affirmed labor rights, and those rights, though *more honored in the breach than the observance* [read *more often breached than observed*], could be upheld by the state at the expense of capitalists." Colin Danby, "Firms in a Neoliberal Transition: The Case of Mexico 1990–1994," *J. Econ. Issues*, 1 Sept. 2002, at 581.

LANGUAGE-CHANGE INDEX
more honored in the breach in reference to an often-broken rule: Stage 4

bread and butter. This construction is most commonly considered a COLLECTIVE NOUN phrase calling for a singular verb—e.g.:

- "An editor must never forget where his *bread and butter* (or cake) *comes* from." William Targ, "What Is an Editor?" in *Editors on Editing* 4, 27 (Gerald Gross ed., rev. ed. 1985).
- "WestJet's *bread and butter is* still short-haul flights in the West." Brent Jang, "Ottawa Must Open the Skies in One-Sided Airline Game," *Globe & Mail* (Toronto), 4 May 2001, at B9.
- "While most major casino companies base their biggest operations in Las Vegas, Harrah's *bread and butter is* locals-oriented casinos spread all over the country." Christina Brinkley & Joseph T. Hallinan, "Riverboat Casinos Are Flush Despite Soft Economy," *Wall Street J.*, 23 May 2001, at A2.

A plural verb (which appears in print sources only a quarter as often) tends to seem pedantic—e.g.: "Nation didn't quite throw in the towel on live music . . . , but its *bread and butter are* [read *is*] the dance parties that fill the place Wednesday through Saturday." Eric Brace, "Some Things That Went Bump in the Nightwatch," *Wash. Post*, 29 Dec. 2000, at T5. See SUBJECT–VERB AGREEMENT (D).

break. See **brake.**

breakdown = (1) failure <the breakdown of the bus didn't delay them long>; or (2) subdivision <the breakdown on the financial statement showed which subsidiaries owed the most in taxes>. Sense 1 is much older (ca. 1832) and has long been established. Sense 2 was once considered OFFICIALESE, especially after it first appeared in the mid-20th century, but today is generally viewed as natural and useful.

break-in, n. So hyphenated.

breath; breathe. The first is the noun, the second the verb. But *breath* (/breth/) is often mistaken for *breathe* (/bree<u>th</u>/)—e.g.:

- "It was as if the questioner could not fathom the fact that the carrier of two X chromosomes would be able to *breath* [read *breathe*] the same rarefied air as men." Kitty Kelley, "Washington's New Wimp Factor," *N.Y. Times*, 28 Nov. 1992, at 13.
- "After all, to stretch, you have to slow down, *breath* [read *breathe*] deeply, relax." Theresa McCourt, "Injuries Sometimes Start in the Head," *Sacramento Bee*, 16 Oct. 1996, at F5.
- "Owen says his daughter's throat was so swollen she could hardly *breath* [read *breathe*]." Camilla Mortensen, "Kids: Don't Drink the Toxic Water," *Eugene Weekly*, 26 May 2011, at N1.

LANGUAGE-CHANGE INDEX
breath misused for *breathe*: Stage 1

breathable. So spelled—not **breatheable*. See MUTE E.
Current ratio: 205:1

breathe. See **breath**.

breech. See **breach**, n.

breeches; britches. The word *breeches* (= pants, esp. short ones) dates from before the 12th century. *Britches*, an altered form of *breeches*, dates from the early 19th century. Both are pronounced /**brich**-iz/, and both are used today—e.g.:

- "*Breeches* and jodhpurs are her usual attire." Catharine Schaidle, "Dunlap Woman Is Fully Trained in Shoeing Horses," *Peoria J. Star*, 19 Nov. 2000, at B5.
- "Kors' fox-hunt basics included slim, stretchy *britches* and jodhpurs." Libby Callaway, "Lauren and Kors Are Hot to Trot," *N.Y. Post*, 15 Feb. 2001, at 18.

Interestingly, *breeches* is almost a FORMAL WORD, while *britches* verges on DIALECT.

The expression *too big for your britches/breeches* can be read literally to mean that you no longer fit into your pants or, more commonly, that you are overconfident or cocky—e.g.: "One thing we don't cotton to in Arkansas is getting *too big for your britches*. I'd say 'breeches,' but that would be getting too big for them." Anon., "Newly Slim Governor's Pants Too Tight," *Arkansas Times*, 13 Oct. 2005, at 18. In this SET PHRASE, the spelling is invariably *britches*, not *breeches*.

breed > bred > bred. So inflected. Yet the ill-bred form **breeded* (common in the 18th century but not since then) still sometimes appears. Note that in the following examples, the first two instances are literal, the last two figurative. Either way, the past tenses should be *bred*—e.g.:

- "She also *breeded* [read *bred*] and exhibited Afghan hounds." "Mary Thompson, Pilot, Engineer, Autism Activist," *Boston Herald*, 10 May 1998, at 79.
- "They have been bullied and *breeded* [read *bred*] out of existence by cousin trout species." Mike Taugher, "Recasting Conservation," *Albuquerque J.*, 23 Aug. 1998, at B1.
- "As confusion about how much reimbursement the township expected *breeded* [read *bred*] new misunderstandings Thursday, McKarski confirmed that township fees are about $25,000." Matt Assad, "City Officials Fear Demands Could Doom a Landfill Deal," *Morning Call* (Allentown, Pa.), 20 Feb. 1998, at B1.

- "Phil *breeded* [read *bred*] controversy." Jay Mariotti, "Jackson Gets the Last Word—and It's 'No,'" *Chicago Sun-Times*, 22 June 1998, at 82.

See IRREGULAR VERBS.

LANGUAGE-CHANGE INDEX
*breeded for past-tense *bred*: Stage 1
Current ratio (*bred* vs. **breeded*): 3,289:1

brethren. The plural form *brethren* has survived most prominently in contexts involving religious, legal, and fraternal organizations—almost always in reference to people who aren't brothers by birth.

Sometimes, though, *brethren* is used literally or figuratively in the context of tribes, allies, and even colleagues—e.g.:

- "He just wishes more Public League schools would mimic their suburban *brethren* by prominently displaying their trophies the way those institutions do." Barry Temkin, "New Lift for Old Rivalry," *Chicago Trib.*, 6 Sept. 1996, Sports §, at 12.
- "They saw their Tutsi *brethren* massacred by the hundreds of thousands in Rwanda in 1994." "World & Nation Briefs," *Columbian* (Vancouver, Wash.), 25 Oct. 1996, at A4.
- "The warlord's superior military might is the main reason the Taliban is prepared to negotiate with him, despite the supposedly intolerable support he almost certainly receives from Russia and his *brethren* in Uzbekistan." Alex Spillius, "An Opponent the Taliban Would Love to Subdue," *Daily Telegraph*, 25 Oct. 1996, at 20.
- "These days things have leveled out for the musical *brethren* of Campagna and Carter—both of whom sadly personified the concept of 'Live fast, die young.'" Hunter Hauk, "And the Punk Band Will Play On," *Dallas Morning News*, 13 Aug. 2015, at E1.

Is *brethren* male-specific? Although courts have considered the word generic in some contexts, most readers are unlikely to see it as gender-neutral. The word is unlikely to flourish in AmE because of its perceived SEXISM. Nor does *brethren and sistren* seem likely to catch on, *sistren* being the analogous archaic plural of *sister*. Unlike its male sibling, *sistren* is now chiefly dialectal.

Breton. See **Briton (B).**

BREVE. See DIACRITICAL MARKS.

bribery. See **extortion**.

bridal; bridle. These two are sometimes the victims of WORD-SWAPPING. *Bridal*, adj., = of, for, or relating to a bride or wedding. *Bridle*, n., = part of a horse's harness. But instances do occur in which writers misuse *bridal* for *bridle*—e.g.: "A horse *bridal* [read *bridle*] hangs around her neck like a necklace or dog leash." Lynn Pyne, "Don't Chicken Out: See Photos Seized by Cops," *Phoenix Gaz.*, 28 May 1994, at D3.

The opposite error also occurs—e.g.: "It is also supposed to be symbolic of the canopy once held over the *bridle* [read *bridal*] couple to protect them from the 'evil eye.'" Monie Heath, "Wedding Customs Have Roots in History," *Herald-Sun* (Durham, N.C.), 27 Mar. 1994, at G5. But sometimes, as one might expect, the writer isn't erring at all but is having fun—e.g.: "It was a wedding with a true *bridle* party. Dillon arrived in a pony-drawn carriage." Tracey Thomas, "Wedding Captures the Spirit," *Hartford Courant*, 4 July 1995, at C6.

LANGUAGE-CHANGE INDEX
1. *bridal* misused for *bridle*: Stage 1
2. *bridle* misused for *bridal*: Stage 1
Current ratio (*bridle path* vs. **bridal path*): 20:1

bride-elect. See **bride-to-be.**

bridegroom. See **groom.**

brideprice; dowry. *Brideprice* = in marriage customs of some cultures (mostly in Asia), the money or goods that pass from the prospective groom or his family to the bride or her family. *Dowry* = money or goods passing from the bride's side to the groom's. Neglected by many dictionaries (though not by *W3* or *RH2*), the term *brideprice* is established among anthropologists. It is an unfortunate label because it helps perpetuate the myth that in some cultures families sell their daughters into marriage. Some scholars have suggested *bridewealth* and *bridecost* as alternatives, but the misleading label appears, for the time being, to be entrenched. See generally Jack Goody, *The Oriental, the Ancient and the Primitive* (1990). For more on *dowry*, see **dower.**

bride-to-be; *bride-elect. The first form, which outnumbers the second by a 9-to-1 ratio in newspaper wedding announcements, is standard. The second is a preposterous form, no election having taken place— e.g.: "The *bride-elect* [read *bride-to-be*], a graduate of Handels Academy, Wolfsberg, Austria, . . . is chief physical therapist in Kinderspital Zurich-University Children's Hospital." "Andrew Nash to Wed in Austria," *Buffalo News*, 15 Apr. 2001, at E4. Surprisingly, though, **bride-elect* emerged as long ago as the early 19th century and was even more common than *bride-to-be* until about 1915.

LANGUAGE-CHANGE INDEX
**bride-elect* for *bride-to-be*: Stage 2
Current ratio (*bride-to-be* vs. **bride-elect*): 9:1

bridge the gap. This is the established idiom, dating from the 17th century. Through mistaken sound association, some writers use **breach the gap* in place of *bridge the gap*. The result is worse than a broken idiom: it's a logical absurdity. To *breach* something is to create a gap in it, not to close the gap. As nouns, *gap* and *breach* are synonymous. Still, the error is fairly common—e.g.:

- "His power existed in the gap between the two parties . . . and in the electric anticipation that he might seek to *breach* [read *bridge*] it." David M. Shribman, "Upheaval in Halls of Power: One Man's Shift Changes All the Rules of Politics," *Boston Globe*, 25 May 2001, at A1.
- "He says that his group has reached out to African Americans, but says more could be done to *breach* [read *bridge*] the gaps within the American Muslim community." Mary Rourke, "One Faith, Two Minds," *L.A. Times*, 30 Jan. 2002, § 5, at 1.

- "The council's program is one of several attempts to *breach* [read *bridge*] the widening gap between what children are taught about personal finance and what they need to know." Julie Tripp, "Econ 101 at Any Age," *Sunday Oregonian* (Portland), 31 Mar. 2002, at F8.

LANGUAGE-CHANGE INDEX
**breach the gap* for *bridge the gap*: Stage 1
Current ratio (*bridge the gap* vs.
**breach the gap*): 285:1

bridle. See **bridal.**

brilliance; brilliancy. *Brilliance* is now standard in describing a quality or state. *Brilliancy*, not quite a NEEDLESS VARIANT, means "something brilliant" <the brilliancies in Edmund Wilson's writings> and is generally useful only in the plural.

brimful, adj. So spelled—not **brimfull.*

Current ratio: 34:1

bring. A. Inflected Forms: *bring* > *brought* > *brought*. The form **brung*, a dialectal word that came to prominence in the 19th century, is not in good use except in variations of the jocular phrase *dance with the one that brung ya*. For example, one politician told a crowd, " 'The voters of the 25th District are the ones who *brung* me, and they are the ones I want to dance with.' " Catherine Candisky, "2 Vying for House Say They Get Things Done," *Columbus Dispatch*, 25 Sept. 1996, at B6 (quoting Republican Jim Mason of Ohio). See IRREGULAR VERBS.

LANGUAGE-CHANGE INDEX
**brung* for *brought*: Stage 1
Current ratio (*brought* vs. **brung*): 1,642:1

B. And *take*. *Bring* suggests motion toward the writer or reader <please bring me a soda>. *Take* suggests motion in the opposite direction <just after you put the soda down, he took it from me>. Cf. **come (B).**

The distinction might seem to be too elementary for elaboration here, but misuses do occur—e.g.: "If the gentleman wishes to *bring* [read *take*] you somewhere, he should say to the hosts, 'I have been seeing a great deal of someone whom I would like you to meet,' and then give them your name so that they can issue you a proper invitation." Judith Martin, " 'And Guest' Invitation Irks This Companion," *Chicago Trib.*, 6 Apr. 1997, at 4.

The rule becomes complicated when the movement has nothing to do with the speaker—e.g.: "When my dad was courting my mom, a single mother of two, he used to *take* her a bag of groceries instead of flowers." In such a situation, the choice of *bring* or *take* depends on motion toward or away from whatever is being discussed. So in the previous example, *bring* would work as well if the point of view was that of the mother rather than the father.

And despite the direction of the movement, *bring* is the only choice in idioms such as "bring to the table."

LANGUAGE-CHANGE INDEX
bring misused for *take*: Stage 3

LANGUAGE-CHANGE INDEX (For the full key, see front matter pp. xxxi, l–li.)
Stage 1: Rejected. **Stage 2:** Widely shunned. **Stage 3:** Widespread but . . . **Stage 4:** Ubiquitous but . . . **Stage 5:** Fully accepted.
Invariably inferior forms marked by asterisk (∗). • Ratios represent frequency of prevalent forms vs. variants in current books.

bring (an) action against is verbose for *sue*—e.g.: "He said Washington law also allows store and club owners to *bring action against* [read *sue*] juveniles who fake their credentials." Richard Grimes, "Underage Proposal a Really Good Idea," *Charleston Daily Mail*, 24 Oct. 1996, at B1. Similar wordiness appears in the kindred phrases *bring legal proceedings against* and *institute legal proceedings against*. *Take action against* is broader, encompassing physical as well as legal action.

brinkmanship (= a method of gaining a negotiating advantage by suggesting a willingness to do something very dangerous or destructive) is written with no *-s-* after *brink*, though many people mistakenly add it on the analogy of *gamesmanship*. In the mid-20th century, the humorist Stephen Potter invented many facetious formations with *-manship*, including *gamesmanship*, *golfmanship*, and *one-upmanship*. Although he didn't himself originate *brinkmanship*, he embraced the word and used it in print in 1958.

In modern print sources, *brinkmanship* predominates over **brinksmanship* by a 4-to-1 ratio.

briquette (= a small, compacted block, as of charcoal) is the standard spelling. **Briquet* is a variant.

Current ratio: 4:1

Brit, a colloquial shortening of *Briton* or **Britisher*, is recorded in the *OED* from 1901. As an adjective, it describes anything that is British. Unlike many other national and ethnic CASUALISMS, it is not pejorative—perhaps because it was homegrown. See **Briton (A).**

Britain. See **Great Britain.**

britches. See **breeches.**

Briticism; Britishism. We have long needed a word to denote any custom or quality associated with British people. Although *Briticism* was prevalent in the 19th century, the two forms have been close contenders in print sources since about 1910. H.W. Fowler preferred *Britishism* on scholarly grounds (*FMEU1* at 57), but it has been mostly the nonscholarly writers who have followed his preference—e.g.:

- "Mr. Bryson writes in snappy, novelistic prose that's seasoned with little-old-lady *Britishisms*." Michiko Kakutani, "A Land of Civilities, Achievements and 'Chumley,' " *N.Y. Times*, 16 Aug. 1996, at C30.
- "Shakespeare & Company stresses native accents, not faux *Britishisms*." Ed Siegel, "Full-Bawdied 'Measure' Comes East," *Boston Globe*, 12 Sept. 1996, at E2.
- "In this quaint *Britishism*, my identity presented itself." Mark Harding, "A Kid-Canuck's Call to the Front," *Globe & Mail* (Toronto), 14 Oct. 2014, at L8.

Most American desktop dictionaries nevertheless list *Briticism* as the main term. Since about 1980, the two forms have closely vied for predominance in general English-language print sources. Cf. **Scotticism.**

Current ratio: 1.05:1

BRITICISMS. See AMERICANISMS AND BRITICISMS.

*Britisher. See **Briton (A).**

Briton. A. And **Britisher*. The word *Briton*—the word that Britons themselves recognize—is about seven times as common in print sources as **Britisher*, an Americanism. For that reason, and because Britons often consider **Britisher* a vague insult, *Briton* should be preferred—e.g.: "It would not be a good idea to ask the famously crabby *Britisher* [read *Briton*] if this rush of Stateside success makes the prospect of working in Hollywood, with a decent-sized budget, attractive." Rod Dreher, "The Secret's Out," *Sun-Sentinel* (Ft. Lauderdale), 13 Oct. 1996, at F1. See **Brit.**

LANGUAGE-CHANGE INDEX
*Britisher for *Briton*: Stage 2
Current ratio: 7:1

B. And *Breton*. A *Briton* /**brit**-ən/ is a British subject—that is, a native or citizen of Great Britain. A *Breton* /**bret**-ən/ is a native or citizen of the region in northwestern France called Brittany (Fr. *Bretagne*).

broach. See **breach,** n.

broadcast > broadcast > broadcast. So inflected. In his book *Words and Rules* (2000), Steven Pinker condemns Theodore Bernstein, the estimable author of *The Careful Writer*, for his 1965 preference for the past-tense *broadcast* over **broadcasted*. Pinker says that this preference "had long been a losing battle," and quotes H.L. Mencken in support of **broadcasted*. Back in 1936, Mencken said that **broadcasted* "is what one commonly hears." Yet with only five minutes' work on the WESTLAW database, it was possible in 2000 to show that in modern print, the ratio staggeringly favors *broadcast* (19,805 sources) and not *broadcasted* (86) as a past form. (More recently, Google ngrams show the ratio in World English to be still quite overwhelming.) Bernstein was right in 1965, and Pinker should have known better than to rely on a 1936 quotation as his sole evidence against Bernstein—a *New York Times* editor with his ear firmly to the ground—whom he snidely accuses of "hectoring people into sticking with the irregular." See -CAST & IRREGULAR VERBS.

LANGUAGE-CHANGE INDEX
*broadcasted for *broadcast*: Stage 1
Current ratio (*had broadcast* vs. **had broadcasted*): 25:1

brokerage; brokage. *Brokerage* = (1) the business or office of a broker <real-estate brokerage is a profession requiring knowledge and experience>; or (2) a broker's fee <brokerage differs from an underwriting commission>.

The archaic *brokage* (or, alternatively, *brocage*) means "the corrupt jobbing of offices; the bribe unlawfully paid for any office" (*OED*). It's also a NEEDLESS VARIANT of *brokerage*.

bronco; bronc; broncho. The standard form is *bronco* (= a wild, unbroken horse). *Bronc* is a colloquial clipping. *Broncho* is a variant spelling used for some sports teams; for example, the University of Central Oklahoma calls its players the *Bronchos*, and a few high-school teams use the same spelling. But the spelling *bronco* has predominated since the 1950s. Oddly, before that time, *broncho* was the predominant form, but it fell mysteriously into decline in the mid-20th century.

Pl. *broncos.* See PLURALS (D).

brooch; broach, n. The first denotes a type of pinned jewelry. The second is a tool for tapping a cask (or, as a verb, to break through something, such as a barrel's bung or the surface of water). *Brooch* is best pronounced, like *broach*, to rhyme with *coach.* It may also be pronounced to rhyme with *mooch*, although this *-ooch* pronunciation is less common and falling more and more out of favor.

Perhaps because of its dominant pronunciation, *brooch* is sometimes misspelled *broach*—e.g.:

• "Here one can find white gold bracelets for $1,250 or diamond *broaches* [read *brooches*] for $520,000." Ginia Bellafante, "With Tribal Chic, Chunky Jewelry Is Back," *N.Y. Times,* 4 June 2002, at B11.
• "She was wearing an evening gown of pink chiffon joined at one shoulder with a big *broach* [read *brooch*] sparkling with diamonds." Charlaine Harris, *All Together Dead* 172 (2007).

LANGUAGE-CHANGE INDEX
broach misused for *brooch*: Stage 1
Current ratio (*diamond brooch* vs.
*diamond broach): 18:1

brother. See **brethren.**

brother-in-law. Pl. *brothers-in-law.* See PLURALS (G).

brunette; brunet. Unlike its counterpart *blond(e)*, this word is seldom applied to males, even though the form *brunet* is the masculine in French. Some have suggested that *brunet* appears most often as a noun, while *brunette* is reserved for the adjective. But in fact *brunette* commonly serves both functions, and in frequency it greatly outnumbers the rival form—e.g.:

• Adjective: "Other Folsom friends rooting for the *brunette* pianist are 1st District Police Juror Bernie Willie and his wife, Sharla." Melissa Bienvenu, "Miss La. Is Familiar Face for Folsom," *Times-Picayune* (New Orleans), 14 Sept. 1996, at B1.
• Adjective: "The syndicated 'Real TV' will include footage of a *brunette* Angie Dickinson from a 1958 appearance on 'The Bob Cummings Show.'" "Oprah Snares the Mother of All Interviews: Madonna," *Daily News* (N.Y.), 9 Dec. 1996, at 68.
• Noun: "Miss Lamour played the exotic *brunette* who fell in league with the playboy with the ski-jump nose and his smooth-voiced pal who vied for her attentions." Annie Shooman, "'Road' Movies Actress Dorothy Lamour Dies," *Chattanooga Free Press,* 23 Sept. 1996, at A7.
• Noun: "Most recently, however, Basinger asked to be made into a *brunette*." Jeryl Brunner, "French Toast," *In Style,* Dec. 1996, at 84.

Cf. **blond.** See SEXISM (D).

*brung. See **bring** (A).

bruschetta, referring to a Tuscan appetizer of grilled bread topped with garlic, olive oil, herbs, and often tomatoes, grew to prominence in the English vocabulary only as recently as the 1980s. The term is preferably pronounced /broo-**sket**-ə/, as in Italian. But in AmE /broo-**shet**-ə/ is disappointingly ubiquitous. Most culinary authorities agree on the recommended pronunciation. Cookbooks by all the following authors admonish their readers to use the /k/ pronunciation, not the /sh/: Jack Bishop, Al Getz, Edward Giobbi, Federico Moramarco, Peggy J. Parks, Judy Pochini, David Rosengarten, Andrew Schloss, and Clifford A. Wright. One writer plumps for the anomalous /broosh-**ket**-ə/. See Mary C. Baker, *Fresh from Dover Canyon* 8 (2003). But that pronunciation is best eschewed /es-**chood**/.

The pronunciation of *bruschetta* has made cameo appearances in more than one novel, most notably here: "I pronounced it *brushetta*, as I had always heard people in restaurants do. She shook her head in pain. '*Brusketta*, dear, *brusketta*. Ch in Italian is hard,' she murmured." Barry McCrea, *The First Verse* 16 (2005).

brusque; *brusk. The first spelling is standard. In AmE, the term is pronounced /brəsk/; in BrE, it's /broosk/.

Current ratio: 60:1

Brussels sprout (= a small, edible bud akin to cabbage) is so spelled and capitalized—not *brussels sprout* and especially neither *Brussel sprout nor **brussel sprout.*

bucketful. Pl. *bucketfuls*—not **bucketsful.* See PLURALS (G).

Current ratio: 3:1

buck naked; *butt naked. Both forms mean "completely undressed." The original and standard expression, dating from the 1920s, is *buck naked*—e.g.:

• "With Lucille Ball flair she torches houses and locks herself out of the house *buck naked*." Tom Cunneff et al., "My Favorite Housewife," *People,* 24 Jan. 2005, at 38.
• "The current centerfolds, *buck naked* though they may be, communicate almost no suggestion of anything. In Playboy pinups, one is not looking for the note of the divine that one finds in the Venuses of ancient statuary, let alone for the pathos of Rembrandt's nudes." Joan Acocella, "The Girls Next Door," *New Yorker,* 20 Mar. 2006, at 144.

The origin of *buck naked* is a matter of speculation, and many theories are just folk etymology. (See ETYMOLOGY (D).) The most prevalent guess is that *buck* derives from Old English terms for male deer, goats, and some other animals. The skin of bare buttocks, presumably, is considered pale and smooth like buckskin. Another theory is that *buck* refers to the racist term for a male African-American—especially in reference to slaves, who were stripped naked for potential buyers to inspect them before an auction. The real answer is probably lost to time.

The form *buck naked* has traditionally been much more common in edited publications than *butt

LANGUAGE-CHANGE INDEX (For the full key, see front matter pp. xxxi, l–li.)
Stage 1: Rejected. **Stage 2:** Widely shunned. **Stage 3:** Widespread but . . . **Stage 4:** Ubiquitous but . . . **Stage 5:** Fully accepted.
Invariably inferior forms marked by asterisk (*). • Ratios represent frequency of prevalent forms vs. variants in current books.

naked. The more graphic version does appear, usually in reported quotations but sometimes not—e.g.:

- " 'Yo, he belongs in the zoo,' said Wu-Tang Clan's de facto leader, referring to Jackass' Steve-O, who paid tribute to ODB by taking the stage with the rapper's mother, stripping down *butt naked* [read *buck naked*] and performing what he called 'dirty back flips'—just picture The Silence of the Lambs' Buffalo Bill strutting his stuff." Ben Quinones, "Wu-Tang Clan—and a Cast of Thousands," *L.A. Times*, 7 Aug. 2006, Cal. §, at E3.
- "Burnett and CBS aren't stupid. They needed people to start buzzing about Survivor again, as they did when some fat guy named Richard Hatch won $1 million after walking around *butt-naked* [read *buck-naked*] for most of the show." Kevin D. Thompson, " 'Survivor' to Play a Sensitive Game," *Palm Beach Post*, 10 Sept. 2006, TV Post §, at 3.

Outside edited publications, though, the more graphic **butt naked* has outranged the standard phrase in popular usage, judging by hits on Internet search engines.

LANGUAGE-CHANGE INDEX
*butt naked for *buck naked*: Stage 4
Current ratio (*buck naked* vs. **butt naked*): 1.6:1

budgerigar (= Australian parakeet) is a transliteration of an Aboriginal word common in BrE but rare in AmE, enough so that it is often accompanied by an explanation—e.g.: "[O]ver the years, I've seen performing pooches, *Budgerigars* (a small parrot) and any number of other tricked-up critters." Chris Jones, "Feline Follies," *Chicago Trib.*, 8 Dec. 2006, On the Town §, at 1.

More familiar to American ears is the shortened form, *budgie*—e.g.: "The English *budgerigar*, also known as a *budgie*, is a larger cousin of the common parakeet." Greg Okuhara, "Breeder Works to Take Birds to New Heights," *Houston Chron.*, 2 Apr. 2006, at B3.

As a transliterated term, the word is susceptible to variants in spelling and pronunciation. *W2*, for example, lists it as **budgereegah* and **budgerygah*—both with the primary accent on the final syllable. Today, the standard spelling is *budgerigar* and the preferred pronunciation stresses the first syllable: /**bəj**-ə-ree-gahr/.

budget, vb., forms *budgeted* and *budgeting* in AmE and BrE alike. See SPELLING (B).

budget-making is best hyphenated. See **decision-making.**

buffet. When speaking of the serve-yourself meal, say either /bə-**fay**/ or /boo-**fay**/. When speaking of the pummeling blow, say /**bəf**-it/. But in BrE, the pronunciation /**bəf**-it/ is common for both senses.

bulk, n., sometimes causes writers to doubt which form of a verb to use, singular or plural—e.g.: "Although nearly a third of blacks have moved into the middle class, the *bulk* of blacks *fall* [*falls*?] into a troubled underclass, as Andrew Hacker's *Two Nations* so cogently proves." Edward T. Chase, "The Trouble with Friendship," *Nation*, 17 June 1996, at 33. Most writers—who might find support in the principle of SYNESIS—would write *fall* in that sentence. And they have the better position: when the phrase *bulk of the* is followed by a plural count noun, the verb should be plural <the

bulk of the criticisms are valid>. But when it's followed by a singular mass noun, the verb should be singular <the bulk of the criticism is valid>. The form is attested from the early 19th century in historical dictionaries. See COUNT NOUNS AND MASS NOUNS & SYNESIS.

bulk large, an equivalent of *loom large*, is a SET PHRASE (perhaps even something of a CLICHÉ). To use the unidiomatic adverb *largely* is an example of HYPERCORRECTION—e.g.: "The first point I would make is that certain matters which *bulk largely* [read *bulk large*] in 'incidental' grammar teaching are not fundamental questions of grammar at all." Hunter Diack, "A Re-Examination of Grammar," in *A Linguistics Reader* 152, 154 (Graham Wilson ed., 1967).

LANGUAGE-CHANGE INDEX
*bulk largely for *bulk large*: Stage 2
Current ratio (*bulk large* vs. **bulk largely*): 4:1

BULLETS. See PUNCTUATION (B).

bullion; bouillon. The first term, referring to an ingot of precious metal, is rarely misspelled. The second, referring to a broth, is often misspelled like the first—e.g.:

- "But some things haven't changed: rooms with large balconies that overlook the beach, the periwinkle blue-and-white color scheme, bullshots on the beach (*bullion* [read *bouillon*] and vodka) and, upon checkout, a hand-written bill rather than a computer printout." David Swanson, "Picture Yourself . . . You Can Really Afford It," *Columbus Dispatch*, 27 May 2001, at F1.
- "She also revealed a recipe secret: adding chicken *bullion* [read *bouillon*] to the dish pumps up the flavor." Leanne Libby, "Red Delicious," *Corpus Christi Caller-Times*, 24 Oct. 2001, at B6.

Bullion is pronounced /**buul**-yən/. *Bouillon* is pronounced /**buul**-yən/, /**buul**-yon/, or sometimes /boo-**yawn**/.

LANGUAGE-CHANGE INDEX
bullion misused for *bouillon*: Stage 1

bulrush, denoting a type of marsh plant, is sometimes misspelled **bullrush*—e.g.: "With *bullrushes* [read *bulrushes*] springing up in the bay where pickleweed once grew, and pressure mounting to do something to help endangered saltwater species, it was only a matter of time before cities like San Jose came to view their sewage as an enticing supply of freshwater, Ritchie said." Jill Leovy, "Reclaimed Waste Water May Ease State's Thirst," *L.A. Times*, 17 Aug. 1997, at A1. The word derives from the Middle English *bulryshe*, from *bol* (= stem). It's unconnected with *bull*.

LANGUAGE-CHANGE INDEX
bulrush misspelled **bullrush*: Stage 1
Current ratio: 14:1

bumptious (= unpleasantly and loudly arrogant, conceited, and presumptuous) is sometimes misspelled **bumptuous*—e.g.:

- "He is too *bumptuous* [read *bumptious*], pushy and vulgar for claims to full brotherhood." Murray Kempton, "D'Amato's Hopes Rest on Senate's Tender Mercies," *Newsday* (N.Y.), 7 Mar. 1991, at 11.

- "A *bumptuous* [read *bumptious*] feudal lord, Zardari was accused by political foes of amassing not millions but hundreds of millions through corruption." Tim McGirk, "Bhutto, Asif Baba and the 40 Thieves," *Sacramento Bee*, 10 Nov. 1996, at F2.
- "At her funeral, her friend Rupert Everett described her as 'a one-off . . . your own creation in a world of copycats' and that *bumptuous* [read *bumptious*] originality shines through here." Jess Cartner-Morley, "A Head for Fashion," *Guardian*, 20 Nov. 2013, at 12 (referring to fashion designer Isabella Blow).

Cf. **scrumptious.**

LANGUAGE-CHANGE INDEX

bumptious misspelled **bumptuous*: Stage 1
Current ratio: 600:1

buncombe. See **bunkum.**

bungee; *bungy; bungie. When the fad (later sport) of jumping from high places with elastic ropes attached to one's body or ankles became popular in the 1980s, *bungee* became twice as common in every use <bungee cords> <bungee ropes> as **bungy*, and it is now 20 times as common. It's the only accepted spelling for *bungee jumping*. The now-rare spelling *bungie* was the 19th-century name for rubber from India and products made from it.

bunkum; buncombe. This term refers to political talk that is empty or insincere. It derives from an early-19th-century speech made by a U.S. congressman representing Buncombe County, North Carolina. He felt compelled, despite other pressing business, to "make a speech for Buncombe" during a session of Congress.

Buncombe long remained the standard spelling, and some writers prefer it as recalling the interesting origin of the word. E.g.: "Or would we dig deeply into our stories of neighborliness and *buncombe* and cobble together something almost great?" Thomas Hine, "Don't Blame Mrs. O'Leary," *N.Y. Times*, 15 July 1990, § 7, at 13. But beginning in the early 1970s, the spelling *bunkum* overtook the traditional spelling in frequency of occurrence in printed books. It is now the standard form.

The shortened CASUALISM is spelled *bunk* (= nonsense) <that's all bunk!>. A clipped form of *bunkum*, it dates from the early 20th century. Henry Ford immortalized the word when he said, "History is more or less bunk."

Current ratio: 2:1

buoy (= a floating object that marks an area in a sea, lake, etc.) is preferably pronounced /**boo**-ee/ in AmE, or /boy/ in BrE.

bureau. The better plural form is *bureaus*, which has consistently predominated since the 16th century. The Frenchified plural, **bureaux*, is pretentious. See PLURALS (B).

Current ratio: 21:1

bureaucracy. See GOVERNMENTAL FORMS.

bureaucrat (= an official of a bureaucracy), a word tinged with pejorative overtones, is sometimes misunderstood and misspelled **beaurocrat* (as if it derived from *beau*, instead of *bureau*)—e.g.: "With smooth, almost dapper features and an unassuming air, one could almost dismiss Jerry Nicely as simply a pleasant run-of-the-mill *beaurocrat* [read *bureaucrat*]." Renee Elder, "Nothing Run of the Mill About Nicely," *Tennessean*, 9 June 1996, at E1.

LANGUAGE-CHANGE INDEX

bureaucrat misspelled **beaurocrat*: Stage 1
Current ratio: 1,761:1

BUREAUCRATESE (/byuu-rahk-rə-**teez**/), the JARGON of bureaucrats, is a type of writing characterized by ZOMBIE NOUNS, PASSIVE VOICE, overlong sentences, and loose grammar. Add to that an overlay of DOUBLE-SPEAK and OFFICIALESE, and you end up with bureaucratese at its finest. Here's an example drawn from a classic work:

> Where particulars of a partnership are disclosed to the Executive Council the remuneration of the individual partner for superannuation purposes will be deemed to be such proportion of the total remuneration of such practitioners as the proportion of his share in partnership profits bears to the total proportion of the shares of such practitioner in those profits.
>
> Quoted in Ernest Gowers, *The Complete Plain Words* 2 (Sidney Greenbaum & Janet Whitcut eds., 3d ed. 1988).

Cf. OBSCURITY & OFFICIALESE.

*burgeois. See **bourgeois.**

burgeon literally means "to put forth buds; sprout." Although some usage experts have considered the word objectionable in the sense "to flourish, grow," no good reason exists to avoid it in this figurative sense <the burgeoning middle class>. But the word preferably refers to growth at early stages, not to full-blown expansion.

LANGUAGE-CHANGE INDEX

burgeon in the sense "to mushroom": Stage 4

burglarize; burgle. An American coinage from the late 19th century, *burglarize* is defined awkwardly and circuitously by the *OED* as "to rob burglariously." A better definition is "to go into (a building) with the purpose of stealing something" (*Black's Law Dictionary* 238 [10th ed. 2014]. The word is still largely confined to AmE.

Burgle, a BACK-FORMATION of comparable vintage, has the same meaning. Although *burgle* is usually facetious or jocular in AmE, it's standard and colorless in BrE—e.g.: "'Do NOT give your address, as burglars often read these and then *burgle* the house when the watch dog is all too clearly absent.'" Miles Kington, "Don't Let That Budgie Destroy Your Life," *Independent*, 24 Oct. 1996, at 22 (quoting J. Millington Smythe).

LANGUAGE-CHANGE INDEX (For the full key, see front matter pp. xxxi, l–li.)
Stage 1: Rejected. **Stage 2:** Widely shunned. **Stage 3:** Widespread but . . . **Stage 4:** Ubiquitous but . . . **Stage 5:** Fully accepted.
Invariably inferior forms marked by asterisk (*). • Ratios represent frequency of prevalent forms vs. variants in current books.

In AmE, *burglarize* appears about twice as often as *burgle*—e.g.:

- "A man who dressed in women's clothing and pretended he was injured so he could enter and *burglarize* homes has pleaded guilty in Hennepin County District Court." Margaret Zack, "Man Pleads Guilty to Burglary," *Star Trib.* (Minneapolis), 6 Oct. 1995, at B2.
- "The suspects are not the first to use public transportation to come to the area and *burglarize* homes." Carl Allen, "Sharp-Eyed Neighbor Leads to Arrests," *Buffalo News*, 29 Oct. 1996, at B5.
- "Tercero was convicted of fatally shooting Robert Berger, 38, who was in a Houston dry-cleaners shop in March 1997 when Tercero came in to *burglarize* it." "Texas Court Halts Execution After Defense Says a Witness Lied," *Wash. Post*, 26 Aug. 2015, at A3.

Current ratio (*burglarized* vs. *burgled* in AmE): 2:1
Current ratio (*burgled* vs. *burglarized* in BrE): 10:1
Current ratio (World English): 1:1

burglary; robbery; theft; larceny. The exact definitions of these terms may vary from jurisdiction to jurisdiction. But it is universal that people and institutions are the objects of *robbery*; places are the objects of *burglary*; and things are the objects of *larceny* and *theft*. The four terms overlap to a degree, but no two are perfectly synonymous.

Burglary = (1) (in the classic common-law sense) the act of breaking and entering another's dwelling at night with intent to commit a felony (e.g., murder) or—in jurisdictions with statutes making petit larceny a misdemeanor—possibly petit larceny as well; or (2) (in the modern AmE sense) the act of breaking and entering a building with the intent to commit a felony (dropping the requirements that it be [a] a dwelling, and [b] at night).

The other three are less complicated. *Robbery* = the felonious taking of personal property by force or threat of force from the immediate presence of the victim. *Theft* is a statutory wrong that is broader than *robbery*, although nonlawyers often consider the words synonymous. *Theft* means "the taking of personal property without the owner's consent, and with the intent to deprive the owner of its value." *Theft* is also broader than *larceny* (= the felonious stealing of personal property; the fraudulent taking and carrying away of a thing without claim of right) because it includes the lawful acquisition and later appropriation of the personal property.

burgle. See **burglarize.**

BURIED VERBS. See ZOMBIE NOUNS.

Burmese; Bamar; Burman; Myanmarese; Myanmaran. For any inhabitant of Myanmar (Burma), or for more than one, the label *Burmese* is standard. *Bamar* and *Burman* denote a member of the country's dominant ethnic group, with *Bamar* being the preferred term. *Burman* has become an outdated variant for *Burmese*—e.g.: "The *Burmans* [read *Burmese*], when they are addressing a superior, introduce a special particle, *taunin* or something similar, into

the verb." Otto Jespersen, *Mankind, Nation, and Individual from a Linguistic Point of View* 130 (1946).

The variant *Myanmarese* appears in BrE sources, especially in Asia. *Myanmaran* is very rare but not unknown. See DENIZEN LABELS.

burn > burned > burned. So inflected—increasingly even in BrE. As a verb, *burnt* is chiefly a BrE form, usually the past participle but sometimes the past tense. In AmE, *burnt* is almost exclusively an adjective <burnt orange> <burnt rubber>. But as a CASUALISM, *burned out* (= physically or emotionally exhausted) is preferable to **burnt out.*

burqa; burka; *burkha. *Burqa* (= a loose garment that covers the whole head and body, with an open or veiled slit for vision, usu. worn by Muslim women) is the predominant spelling in all varieties of English. *Burka* is a less common but acceptable variant. **Burkha* is a NEEDLESS VARIANT.

Current ratio (in order of headwords): 9:5:1

bursar (= the person at a school or college who deals with accounts and office work) is preferably pronounced /**bər**-sər/—not /**bər**-sahr/—in AmE. In BrE, it's /**bə**-sə/. AmE is rhotic, so that a final -*r* is enunciated, whereas in BrE it's silent.

burst > burst > burst. So inflected. As a past-tense or past-participial form, **bursted* is a mistake—e.g.:

- "Among emergencies that agencies and managers name are such things as a *bursted* [read *burst*] water pipe." Betty Lonngren, "Rental Rapport," *Chicago Trib.*, 13 Oct. 1995, at D28.
- "Teaster's swollen, purple arm *bursted* [read *burst*], and he began to improve." "World Converged on Mountain Town to Witness Albert Teaster's Act of Faith," *Asheville Citizen-Times* (N.C.), 16 Aug. 1996, at B1.

See IRREGULAR VERBS.

The dialectal form *busted* carries an air of jocularity. In STANDARD ENGLISH, the word is *burst*—e.g.: "McCarthy's interception was negated by a roughing-the-passer penalty and nine plays later Mark O'Brien *busted* [read *burst*] in from 2 yards." Cory Nightingale, "Warriors Thwart Upset Bid," *Boston Globe*, 28 Nov. 1997, at D16.

As a CASUALISM, *busted* has many possible meanings: (1) "arrested" <the cops busted him>; (2) "caught" (and usu. punished) <busted for cheating on an exam>; (3) "broken" <a busted arm>; (4) "rendered insolvent" <busted by rising expenses>; (5) "demoted" <busted to private>; and (6) "physically struck" <busted in the face>. Examples of each sense follow:

- Sense 1: "The feds *busted* 11 Bonanno crime-family members and associates yesterday, including the reputed acting underboss, Richard Cantarella." Denise Buffa, "Bonanno No-No's," *N.Y. Post*, 3 Oct. 2002, at 29.
- Sense 2: "Washington assistant Cameron Dollar is the latest college hoops coach to get *busted* for overly aggressive recruiting tactics." Jon Saraceno, "Jones Can Play the Heavy vs. Ruiz," *USA Today*, 4 Oct. 2002, at C3.

- Sense 3: "Callers will stay on hold as long as it takes, just to share the latest bits of news from home: a *busted* water pipe, a sick relative, a bad day at work." Kris Axtman, "Texas 'Prison Show' Links Familiar Voices Worlds Away," *Christian Science Monitor*, 4 Oct. 2002, at 1.
- Sense 4: "The only art class I ever took nearly *busted* me. We were instructed to buy 2 cubic feet of Styrofoam, some dowels, an electric motor, 100 square feet of variously colored tissue paper and 75 feet of string. Do you have any idea how many bowls of chili at the student center that translates into?" Jake Vest, "Keep the Degree—I'll Just Have Lunch," *Orlando Sentinel*, 28 Sept. 2002, at H1.
- Sense 5: "On Thursday morning . . . it dwindled from an intense, 145-mph Category 4 hurricane to a more manageable, if still dangerous, Category 2 storm. . . . By Thursday evening, it was *busted* to a tropical storm, with 50-mph wind." Andrea Elliott & Martin Merzer, "Weakened Hurricane Lili Tears Through Louisiana," *Miami Herald*, 4 Oct. 2002, at A1.
- Sense 6: "Latrell Sprewell did punch someone. He *busted* Don Chaney right in the chops." Mitch Lawrence, "Star Player & Fractured Franchise Both Blow It," *Daily News* (N.Y.), 3 Oct. 2002, at 89.

As might be expected with a jocular casualism, *busted* plays a role in some colorful idioms—e.g.: " 'It takes our graduates six to eight months to land their first real job,' she said. 'This happens if they *busted* their butts during art school.' " Karen Cotton, "So You Wanna Be an Artist?" *Wyoming Trib.-Eagle*, 4 Oct. 2002, at B1 (quoting a perky interviewee).

LANGUAGE-CHANGE INDEX
**bursted* for *burst*: Stage 1
Current ratio: 689:1

bus, n. & v.t. The plural form of the noun (meaning "a large vehicle that holds many passengers") is *buses*. The verb (meaning "to transport by bus") is inflected *bus* > *bused* > *bused*; the present participle is *busing*. When the *-s-* is doubled, the sense is different: *bussed* means "kissed," and *bussing* means "kissing." Cf. **gases.** See SPELLING (B).

The verb *bus*, as a BACK-FORMATION from *busboy*, has the additional meanings "to work as a busboy or busgirl" and "to clear dishes from (a table)." Here, too, the better-inflected forms are *bused* and *busing* <he helped pay his way through college by busing tables>.

business is universally two syllables in STANDARD ENGLISH: /**biz**-nəs/. In AmE, the pronunciation /**bid**-nəs/ is sometimes heard, especially in the South and Southwest; it is dialectal.

busted. See **burst.**

but. A. Beginning Sentences with. It is a gross canard that beginning a sentence with *but* is stylistically slipshod. In fact, doing so is highly desirable in any number of contexts, as countless stylebooks have said (many correctly pointing out that *but* is more effective than *however* at the beginning of a sentence)—e.g.:

- "The group of Adversative conjunctions represented by BUT (called Arrestive) very often fulfil the office of relating consecutive sentences. . . . An entire paragraph is not unfrequently devoted to arresting or preventing a seeming inference from one preceding, and is therefore appropriately opened by But, Still, Nevertheless, &c." Alexander Bain, *English Composition and Rhetoric* 110 (4th ed. 1877).
- "Objection is sometimes taken to employment of *but* or *and* at the beginning of a sentence; but for this there is much good usage." Adams Sherman Hill, *The Principles of Rhetoric* 88 (rev. ed. 1896).
- "Not long ago I had a long and labored letter from an old proofreader who was all worked up over the 'buts' and 'ands' in a story in the *Saturday Evening Post* . . . . [H]e was ready, actually, to fight for his ideas . . . and they were false, ill-founded ideas. They were not good ideas. They represented old, dead styles . . . and style is an affair of the living. Style is life. That proofreader was in a backwater; the eddies moved about him but made no progress; he was going about in circles—moving, but getting nowhere. He was all out of step with the times into which he had lived. He had linguistic arteriosclerosis." Edward N. Teall, *Putting Words to Work* 28–29 (1940).
- "*But* (not followed by a comma) always heads its turning sentence; *Nevertheless* usually does (followed by a comma). I am sure, however, that *however* is always better buried in the sentence between commas; *But* is for the quick turn; the inlaid *however* for the more elegant sweep." Sheridan Baker, *The Practical Stylist* 16–17 (1962).
- "Of the many myths concerning 'correct' English, one of the most persistent is the belief that it is somehow improper to begin a sentence with [*and, but, for, or,* or *nor*]. The construction is, of course, widely used today and has been widely used for generations, for the very good reason that it is an effective means of achieving coherence between sentences and between larger units of discourse, such as paragraphs." R.W. Pence & D.W. Emery, *A Grammar of Present-Day English* 106 n.15 (2d ed. 1963).
- "A student writer will almost invariably give *however* first position in a sentence . . . . In any case, *however* works best if it is inside the sentence. Just exactly why this position is best is one of those stylistic mysteries that can't really be explained. It simply sounds better that way. And the importance of sound can't be dismissed, even in silent reading.

. . .

"Occasionally you will find yourself with a *however* that simply refuses to be tucked into a sentence comfortably. In that case, change it to *but* and put it in first position." Lucile Vaughan Payne, *The Lively Art of Writing* 85–86 (1965).
- "If you begin a sentence with *and* or *but* (and you should occasionally), don't put a comma after it. You want to speed up your prose with those words, and the comma would simply cancel out any gain. The comma is necessary only if a parenthetical clause immediately follows that first word—e.g., 'But, from all the evidence, that proves to be a sound conclusion.' " John R. Trimble, *Writing with Style* 81 (1975).
- "*But* works especially well as the opening word of a paragraph." Maxine Hairston, *Successful Writing* 97 (2d ed. 1986).

- "The widespread public belief that *but* should not be used at the beginning of a sentence has no foundation but is seemingly unshakeable." Robert W. Burchfield, *Points of View* 119 (1992).
- "I can't overstate how much easier it is for readers to process a sentence if you start with 'but' when you're shifting direction." William Zinsser, *On Writing Well* 74 (6th ed. 1998).
- "If you want to begin a sentence by contradicting the last, use *but* instead of *however*." Christopher Lasch, *Plain Style* 101 (Stewart Weaver ed., 2002).

For examples of successive sentences starting with *and* and *but*, see **and** (A). See also SUPERSTITIONS (D).

Good writers often begin sentences with *but* and have always done so. Samples from 20th- and 21st-century writers follow:

- "*But* in such a story as *Lispeth*, for example, he succeeds in giving you the tragedy for what it is worth." Edmund Wilson, "Things I Consider Overrated" (1920), in *From the Uncollected Edmund Wilson* 127, 136 (1995).
- "*But* reading his speeches in cold blood offers a curious experience." H.L. Mencken, "The Archangel Woodrow" (1921), in *The Vintage Mencken* 116, 119 (1955).
- "*But* the arts of business, too, call all the while for closer application to the work in hand." Thorstein Veblen, "The Captain of Industry" (1923), in *The Portable Veblen* 377, 384 (1948; repr. 1969).
- "*But* such simplicity of instinct is scarcely possible for human beings." Bertrand Russell, *Education and the Good Life* 192 (1926).
- "*But* it must not be assumed that intelligent thinking can play no part in the formation of the goal and of ethical judgments." Albert Einstein, "Science and Religion" (1939), in *Ideas and Opinions* 41, 42 (1954).
- "*But* Joyce manages to do something even more subtle than that." Vladimir Nabokov, "Ulysses" (ca. 1955), in *Lectures on Literature* 285, 346 (Fredson Bowers ed., 1980).
- "*But* it is a careful, angry, honest film, and nothing it says is less apposite now than it would have been ten years ago, or twenty." James Agee, *Agee on Film* 206 (1958).
- "*But* it does not follow from this that Betjeman's work is foolish." John Wain, "John Betjeman," in *Essays on Literature and Ideas* 168, 171 (1963).
- "*But* perhaps the more valuable achievement to come out of France for the novel has been a whole body of criticism inspired by the new novelists." Susan Sontag, *Against Interpretation* 104 (1966).
- "*But* the misdirection of effort remains uncorrected." I.A. Richards, *So Much Nearer* 69 (1968).
- "*But* if I were asked something easier—to name a good book that we don't read and that the people of the future will read—I'd be less at a loss." Randall Jarrell, "An Unread Book," in *The Third Book of Criticism* 3, 50 (1969).
- "*But* the virtues of the film are many and considerable." John Simon, *Movies into Film* 78 (1971).
- "*But* the modesty is usually false." William Safire, *What's the Good Word?* 44 (1982).
- "*But* he had got used to that and it did not disquiet him." Ursula K. Le Guin, *The Other Wind* 143 (2001).

These are not good writers on bad days. No: they were having good days. And the list could be expanded a thousandfold.

Some years ago, a researcher found that 8.75% of the sentences in the work of first-rate writers—including H.L. Mencken, Lionel Trilling, and Edmund Wilson—began with coordinating conjunctions (i.e., *And* and *But*). Francis Christensen, "Notes Toward a New Rhetoric," 25 *College English* 9 (1963). In a recent survey of *The New York Times* and *U.S. News & World Report*, the figure is about the same. To the professional rhetorician, these figures aren't at all surprising.

All this enthusiasm for the construction, though, must be tempered to this extent: don't start consecutive sentences with *But*. E.g.: "It is not now, and I trust it never will become, my purpose to argue that grammatical knowledge is not a *good* in itself. *But*, then, I believe that *any* knowledge is good. *But* [read *Even so,*] I suggest that grammatical knowledge taught as an end in itself, taught without a calculated, relentless focus on its applicability to problems that occur in writing, will have no appreciable value to a student in his writing." Bertrand Evans, "Grammar and Writing," in *A Linguistics Reader* 111, 116 (Graham Wilson ed., 1967). Cf. **yet** (A).

B. More than One in a Sentence. Putting this subordinating conjunction twice in one sentence invariably makes the sentence unwieldy and less easy to read. E.g.: "*But* this opening misleads because the focus dissipates as the play progresses and the scattershot climax drips with sentiment *but* is ultimately unsatisfying." A. Levine, "Barely Afloat 'Raft of Medusa,'" *Pitt. Post-Gaz.*, 10 Oct. 1997, at 34. (A possible revision: *But this opening misleads because the focus dissipates as the play progresses. Although the scattershot climax drips with sentiment, it's ultimately unsatisfying.*)

C. For *and*. This lapse is surprisingly common. The misuse of *but* for *and* often betrays the writer's idiosyncratic prejudice. That is, if you write that someone is *attractive but smart*, you're suggesting that this combination of characteristics is atypical. E.g.:

- "There [was] . . . a *wealthy but nice-looking* [read *wealthy, nice-looking*] family." Helen Fielding, "Eating Out: A Posher Sort of Poppadom," *Independent*, 3 Dec. 1995, at 66. (Are wealthy people typically not nice-looking? On the reason for the comma between the adjectives in the revision, see PUNCTUATION (D).)
- "Billy's father, Dr. Istvan Jonas, . . . is a man of sterling rectitude, *poor but honest* [read *poor and honest*], determined to pass his upcoming naturalization exams." Michael Wilmington, "'Telling Lies in America' Lets Bacon Sizzle," *Chicago Trib.*, 24 Oct. 1997, at C1. (Is the writer really suggesting that poor people are typically dishonest?)
- "He's gruff and sensitive, *talented but hard-working* [read *talented and hard working*], plain-speaking but as smart as anyone." Tom E. Curran, "Andruzzi Has More than Paid His Dues," *Providence J.-Bull.*, 3 Oct. 2003, at 14. (Are talented people typically lazy? The writer has also made the converse lapse in the first pairing: *gruff* and *sensitive* are more often viewed as opposites than complements, so *but* would be more appropriate than *and* between them.)

D. Preposition or Conjunction. The use of *but* in a negative sense after a pronoun has long caused confusion: is it *No one but she* or *No one but her*? When *but* is a preposition (meaning "except"), the objective *her* (or *him*) follows. But when *but* is a conjunction, the nominative *she* (or *he*) has traditionally been considered proper.

The correct form depends on the structure of the sentence. If the verb precedes the *but*-phrase, the objective case should be used—e.g.: "None of the defendants were convicted *but him*." But if the *but*-phrase precedes the verb, the nominative case is proper: "None of the defendants *but he* were convicted." That sentence is considered equivalent to "None of the defendants were convicted, *but he was convicted*." (Although that rewording doesn't seem to make literal sense—given that he was one of the defendants—it serves to show the grammar of the sentence excepting him from the absolute word *none*.) *But* thus acts as a conjunction when it precedes the verb in a sentence, as in this one from Thomas Jefferson: "Nobody *but we* of the craft *can understand* the diction, and find out what [the statute] means." Here the subject of *can understand* is *nobody*, and the *but* heads the understood clause: *nobody can understand, but we can understand*.

That's the common explanation. But Edward Teall has filed a dissenting opinion. Although it seems never to have caught on, Teall's logic seems impeccable: "Here . . . are three examples of 'but' and its mischievous pranks: 'No one but you and I know what is on these notice boards'; 'And who but he had urged letting Devinish in'; 'No one but he knew what this had cost him.' The pronouns after 'but' should be in the objective case, being governed by 'but.' The defense frequently offered for these wrong nominatives is that the sentence really means 'No one knew, but you and I knew'—which is silly, because if no one knows, you and I don't know. 'Who but he' and 'No one but he' are just dumb errors." Edward N. Teall, *Putting Words to Work* 165 (1940).

LANGUAGE-CHANGE INDEX
No one but me was there: Stage 5

*but nevertheless. This REDUNDANCY has been fairly common in the language since the late 17th century. But it is a redundancy nevertheless. Usually you can drop either word. *Nevertheless* is typically the one to drop—e.g.: "Val Kilmer probably agrees, *but nevertheless* [read *but*] he's committed to an attempt to regain control." Stephen Hunter, "Stars Reveal a Normal Side," *Baltimore Sun*, 4 Apr. 1997, at E1.

If special emphasis is needed, either *but . . . still* or a construction with *though* or *although* is the better choice—e.g.: "In Hanover, conditions are not as bad *but are nevertheless* [read *but are still*] considered taxing." Alexander Reid, "Wanted: New Police Stations," *Boston Globe*, 2 Apr. 1995, South Weekly §, at 1. Cf. ***but yet.**

but that; but what. These peculiar idioms, used in expressions of doubt, may strike the modern reader as quaint or affected. *But that*, the more literary of the two, is used today most commonly in negative constructions—e.g.: "I do not doubt *but that* you are disappointed." Most readers would find the *but* in that sentence to be superfluous and would translate the sentence to read, "I do not doubt *that* you are disappointed." *But what* is used in the same way, but it's rarer and more colloquial—e.g.: "I don't know *but what* it might be the best thing for my own special interest, which is bicycling." Don Harvey, "A Changing Cycle in Traffic Patterns," *L.A. Times*, 18 Aug. 1996, at B6.

*butt naked. See **buck naked.**

buttock. Pronounced /bət-ək/, not /bət-tahk/. See PRONUNCIATION (B).

but which. See **which (D).**

*but yet is a REDUNDANCY for *but* or *yet*. Common in the 16th century, this collocation has been falling in use fairly steadily since 1700. Try dropping either word—e.g.:

- "So Close, *But Yet* [read *Yet*] So Far: K.C. Finds Ways to Be Best in West." Headline, *Denver Post*, 23 Sept. 1996, at D1.
- "She said the fact that Novy voted against raising the property-tax rate *but yet* [read *but* or *yet*] approved a larger budget does not represent a consistent stand." Lisa Buie, "Novy, Challenger Are Trading Taunts," *St. Petersburg Times*, 29 Oct. 1996, at 1.

Sometimes *but* and *yet* fall together in a way that creates not a contrast but a MISCUE. In the sentence that follows, *yet* means *still*, but the sentence is easily misread: "Rider, gifted *but yet to decide* [read *but still undecided*] whether he wants to play in the NBA, promptly went into his act, missing this, showing up for that, and was suspended for the season opener." Mark Heisler, "NBA Preview," *L.A. Times*, 31 Oct. 1996, at C6. Cf. **as yet.**

buy. A. Inflected Forms: *buy > bought > bought*. The form **boughten* (= store-bought as opposed to homemade) is an archaic past-participial adjective formed on the analogy of words such as *broken, driven*, and *frozen*. In the sense "store-bought," **boughten* still occurs in dialectal AmE. E.g.:

- "In those days any *boughten* [read *store-bought*] cookie we would see in Maine was made by the Loose-Wiles Biscuit Company, which had a huge brick factory near the railroad tracks in Boston's North End." John Gould, "Father Wasn't the Suing Kind," *Christian Science Monitor*, 9 Feb. 1990, at 17.
- "Up until [the 1920s], the costs for *boughten* [read *store-bought*] goods always ended in zeros." Pearl Swiggum, "A Penny Saved Can Mean a Lot," *Wis. State J.*, 2 Aug. 1993, at D2.
- "The old man hated waste and preferred the Tampa Tribune to store-*boughten* [read *-bought*] toilet paper." Jeff Klinkenberg, "Cracker Cattle Comeback," *St. Petersburg Times* (Fla.), 6 July 2002, at D1.

See IRREGULAR VERBS.

LANGUAGE-CHANGE INDEX
*boughten: Stage 1
Current ratio (*bought* vs. **boughten*): 2,510:1

B. And *purchase*. As a verb, *buy* is the ordinary word, *purchase* the more FORMAL WORD. Generally,

LANGUAGE-CHANGE INDEX (For the full key, see front matter pp. xxxi, l–li.)
Stage 1: Rejected. **Stage 2:** Widely shunned. **Stage 3:** Widespread but . . . **Stage 4:** Ubiquitous but . . . **Stage 5:** Fully accepted.
Invariably inferior forms marked by asterisk (*). • Ratios represent frequency of prevalent forms vs. variants in current books.

buy is the better stylistic choice. As one commentator says, "Only a very pompous person indeed would say he was going to *purchase* an ice-cream cone or a bar of candy." Robert Hendrickson, *Business Talk* 61 (1984). Traditionally, however, *purchase* has been the preferred word for real estate.

Purchase may also act as a noun; *buy* is informal and colloquial as a noun <a good buy>.

buyout, n. One word.

bye-bye. The informal valediction is so spelled—not **by-by.*

Current ratio: 12:1

byelaw. See **bylaw.**

by-election is the preferred spelling. **Bye-election* is a variant.

Current ratio: 17:1

*bye the bye. See **by the by.**

bylaw; byelaw. Both the spelling and the sense differ on the two sides of the Atlantic. In AmE, *bylaws* are most commonly a corporation's administrative provisions that are either attached to the articles of incorporation or kept privately. In BrE, *byelaws* are regulations made by a local authority or corporation, such as a town or a railway.

The spelling without the *-e-* is standard in AmE. Though etymologically inferior, *byelaw* (sometimes hyphenated) is common in BrE. Increasingly, though, the spelling *bylaw* is appearing in BrE just as commonly as the longer form.

Current ratio (World English): 10:1

by means of is usually verbose for *by* or *with*—e.g.:

- "Vasectomy is surgical sterilization of a man *by means of* [read *by*] cutting or removing a section of the vas deferens, the tube that carries sperm from the testicle to the urethra." "Living with Cancer," *Daily News* (L.A.), 13 Feb. 1994, at L16.
- "The Pithlochaskotee Chapter of the Daughters of the American Revolution is introducing the 2002–2003 American History and Junior American Citizens Programs *by means of* [read *with*] three separate contests." "Contest, Scholarship Opportunities Are Plentiful," *St. Petersburg Times*, 2 Oct. 2002, at 3.

byproduct usually appears as a single word in modern print sources, many of which follow the Associated Press and *New York Times* styles. But it also frequently appears in its hyphenated form (*by-product*), sometimes even in the same publication—e.g.:

- "The growing distaste for cheap eateries is a *byproduct* of a larger shift in habits." Noel C. Paul, "As Tastes Shift, Fast-Food Giants Swallow Hard," *Christian Science Monitor*, 2 Oct. 2002, at 1.
- "Thus another significant prospective *by-product* [read *byproduct*] of military action against Mr. Hussein could be the liberation of 22 million Iraqis from their stultifying economic and political bondage." John Hughes, "Do Iraqis Want Invasion?" *Christian Science Monitor*, 2 Oct. 2002, at 9.

by reason of is usually an artificial way of saying *because of*. Although *not guilty by reason of insanity* is a SET PHRASE, in other phrases the words *by reason of* can usually be improved—e.g.: "Joudrie was sent there after being found not criminally responsible *by reason of* [read *because of*] a mental disorder." Kevin Martin, "Dorothy Joudrie Punched in Face," *Toronto Sun*, 16 July 1996, at 23.

Sometimes the unidiomatic **by reason that* appears—e.g.: "Respondent's contention is untenable *by reason that* [read *because*] FCA § 1118 does not make the application of the CPLR automatic." "FCA Not CPLR Applies Precluding Appeal," *N.Y.L.J.*, 18 July 1996, at 21 (reporting a judicial opinion).

by the by (= incidentally) has been the standard spelling since the 17th century. **By the bye* (archaic) and **bye the bye* are variants. The phrase in any form is appearing nowadays with less and less frequency.

Current ratio (*by the by* vs. **by the bye* vs. **bye the bye*): 96:65:1

by virtue of. See **virtue of.**

byword (= [1] a proverb or saying; or [2] someone or something representing a specific quality) is best spelled as one word and not hyphenated.

- Sense 1: "In the upper echelons of fashion, personalisation has become the new *byword* for luxury." Katie Wright, "Fashion Gets Personal," *Newcastle J.* (U.K.), 18 Aug. 2015, at 21.
- Sense 2: "One of the major internal tasks facing the pope has been the reform of the Vatican Bank, which had become a *byword* for scandal and dysfunction." Paul Vallely, "The Bipartisan Pontiff," *N.Y. Mag.*, 9 Sept. 2015, at 1.

C

-c-; -ck-. When adding a suffix to a word ending in *-c*, how do you keep the hard sound (/k/) from becoming soft (/s/)? With native suffixes (*-ed, -er, -ing, -y*), you generally do it by inserting a *-k-*. Hence *mimic* becomes *mimicked*, *traffic* becomes *trafficker*, *frolic* becomes *frolicking*, and *panic* becomes *panicky*. An exception exists in both AmE and BrE for the verb *to talc*, which anomalously makes *talced* and *talcing*—still pronounced with a hard *-c-*.

But classical suffixes (*-ian, -ism, -ist, -ity, -ize*) don't take the *-k-* and therefore become soft: *politician, cynicism, publicist,* and *criticize*.

cabala; cabbala; *cabalah; *cabbalah; *kabala; *kabbala; *kabbalah. Meaning "an esoteric or secret doctrine"—and pronounced /kə-**bah**-lə/ or /**kab**-ə-lə/—this word is preferably spelled *cabala* in AmE, *cabbala* in BrE. The others are variant forms.

cablecast > cablecast > cablecast. Dating from the mid-1960s, this verb is so inflected. The weak past form **cablecasted* is poor usage—e.g.:

- "The release of 'Flaming Pie' was delayed a week to allow the publicity express to rev up on VH-1 (which *cablecasted* [read *cablecast*] a week of McCartney promotions) and the Internet (which featured an online McCartney chat and live audio and video)." "Entertainment Briefs," *Chicago Sun-Times*, 21 May 1997, at 51.
- "Opening night highlights and an artist's talk were featured last month on 'Spotlight on Northbrook Arts,' a program *cablecasted* [read *cablecast*] on Northbrook's government channel, NCTV Channel 17." Karie Angell, "Artist Creates Ketubah for Second Generation of Patrons," *Northbrook Star* (Ill.), 8 Nov. 2010, News §.

See -CAST & IRREGULAR VERBS.

LANGUAGE-CHANGE INDEX
*cablecasted for past-tense *cablecast*: Stage 1

*cabob. See **kebab.**

cacao. See **cocoa.**

cache, n.; **cachet,** n. *Cache* /kash/ = (1) a hiding place for money, goods, etc.; (2) a hidden stash of money, goods, etc.; or (3) a type of high-speed computer memory (also, in this sense, termed *cache memory*). Although sense 3 is quite common in computing contexts, sense 2 is the most frequent nonspecialist sense—e.g.: "Schechter was brought to New York from Cambridge, England, where he had established his credentials by rediscovering a *cache* of invaluable literary fragments that had lain for centuries in a Cairo genizah, or storage closet." Clifford E. Librach, "Does Conservative Judaism Have a Future?" *Commentary*, 1 Sept. 1998, at 28.

Cachet /ka-**shay**/, borrowed from French in the 18th century and now thoroughly anglicized (except in its pronunciation), originally meant "stamp" or "distinguishing mark." Today it generally means "popular prestige" or "high commercial or political status"— e.g.: "With their *cachet* and cash, tech executives are in high demand on Capitol Hill." Jeffrey H. Birnbaum, "Getting to Know the Hill," *Time*, 14 Aug. 2000, at B12. It also has three other meanings: (1) an official seal, esp. one denoting approval; (2) a commemorative postal design; and (3) a waferlike capsule used to dispense bad-tasting medicine.

As might be expected—given the prevalence of WORD-SWAPPING—*cache* is sometimes misused for *cachet*, presumably by writers who mistakenly think that the French word is *caché*. The error has become fairly common and betrays an utter lack of understanding of what the word is intended to denote—e.g.:

- "If Michael Jordan, the new Wizards' president, wants to use his *cache* [read *cachet*] to attract free agents, he will need cap room." Selena Roberts, "Howard for Ewing? The Rumor Is Out," *N.Y. Times*, 2 Feb. 2000, at A25.
- "He maintained his home in the Elderwoods. This alone was enough to give him a certain *cache* [read *cachet*], for

the Elderwoods was considered a sorcerous place, where creatures of myth were known to gallivant about." Peter David, *Sir Apropos of Nothing* 88 (2001).

- "Once upon a time, there was a certain *cache* [read *cachet*] that went along with being the heavyweight champion of the world, an intrigue, a certain fighting prestige." Steve Simmons, "Round Peg in Squared Circle," *Toronto Sun*, 6 June 2002, at S4.

LANGUAGE-CHANGE INDEX
cache misused for *cachet*: Stage 1
Current ratio (*a certain cachet* vs.
*a certain cache): 12:1

cacophony. So spelled. See SPELLING (A).

cactus. Pl. *cacti* or *cactuses*. Although *cactuses* is more common in ordinary usage, *cacti* predominates in modern print sources, especially in botanical contexts. See PLURALS (B).

Current ratio: 7:1

caddie; caddy. *Caddie* = someone who carries a golf bag for a player, esp. for hire. *Caddy* = a box or other container. Occasionally *caddy* is mistakenly rendered *caddie*—e.g.: "In addition to such touches as a bookshelf with travel books and a globe, and a wheeled tea *caddie* [read *caddy*], there must have been upward of 100 pieces of silver plate." Stephen Harriman, "A Day at the Races," *Virginian-Pilot* (Norfolk), 20 May 1996, at E1. (For more on *upward* in that example, see **upward(s).**)

LANGUAGE-CHANGE INDEX
caddie misused for *caddy*: Stage 1
Current ratio (*tea caddy* vs. **tea caddie*): 24:1

cadre (/**kad**-ree/ or /**kah**-dray/), meaning "a tightly knit group," usually takes a plural verb despite being grammatically singular. E.g.: "He intimidates many who work for him, yet a *cadre* of loyal executives has [read *have*?] followed him from company to company." Betsy Morris, "Big Blue," *Fortune*, 14 Apr. 1997, at 68, 70. (See SYNESIS.) This sentence presents a close call because the writer might have used the singular verb to emphasize the oneness of the group.

In China, a *cadre* (singular noun) is a low-level Communist Party official in charge of a local community or military organization. In the former Soviet Union, a *cadre* was a local cell actively promoting the party line, or a member of such a cell (a sense now moribund).

Caesarean; *Caesarian. See **cesarean section.**

cafe; café. Originally a loanword from French, *cafe* without the DIACRITICAL MARK is three times as common as *café*. Pronounced /ka-**fay**/, it's sometimes jocularly pronounced in BrE as /kaf/.

caftan (= a usu. lightweight, loose robe or tunic of Arabic origin) has predominated over *kaftan* in AmE

LANGUAGE-CHANGE INDEX (For the full key, see front matter pp. xxxi, l–li.)
Stage 1: Rejected. **Stage 2:** Widely shunned. **Stage 3:** Widespread but . . . **Stage 4:** Ubiquitous but . . . **Stage 5:** Fully accepted.
Invariably inferior forms marked by asterisk (*). • Ratios represent frequency of prevalent forms vs. variants in current books.

and World English since the 1920s. But in the last few years, *kaftan* and *caftan* have been used almost equally in BrE, *kaftan* being slightly more common.

Current ratio (World English): 2:1

cagey (= sly, cunning) is the standard spelling. **Cagy* is a variant.

Current ratio: 26:1

cake, having and eating. See **you can't eat your cake and have it too.**

calculable. So formed—not **calculatable.* See -ABLE (D) & -ATABLE.

Current ratio: 419:1

calculated = (1) deliberately taken or made <a calculated risk>; or (2) likely <the weather is calculated to slow play in the Masters today>. Sense 2 represents a debasement in meaning that damages the utility of the word in sense 1.

calculate out, a popular phrasing from about 1880 to 1940, is typically verbose for *calculate*—e.g.:

- "Besides trying to *calculate out* [read *calculate*] how much money to count on from SuperMall sales taxes, city budget writers are also trying to figure out how much money they're going to lose from a new tax break." Patti Epler, "Auburn Budget Swims in a Sea of Unknowns," *News Trib.* (Tacoma), 17 Oct. 1995, at B1.
- "Once we have identified the relevant coalitions, we then have to *calculate out* [read *calculate*] the power index formula for each one." Steffen Eckmann & Adrian Widdowson, "Calculating Shareholder Influence," *Accountancy,* Feb. 1996, at 108.

See PHRASAL VERBS.

Sometimes, though, the phrase means "to amount to a total figure," as a business-jargon equivalent of the intransitive use of *work out* (which is better). In that use of the phrase, the word *out* is necessary—e.g.: "That *calculates out* [read *works out*] to about the price of a margarita a day." Scott Burns, "Have You Been Missing Those Margaritas?" *Dallas Morning News,* 21 July 1996, at H1.

*caldron. See **cauldron.**

calendar; calender. These are separate words. *Calendar,* of course, is the common term, meaning "a register of the days of the year" or "a schedule." *Calender* means either "a rolling machine used in glazing paper or smoothing cloth" or "a mendicant dervish," most often the former—e.g.: "Shurtape is one of the nation's top three manufacturers of duct tape, which is produced through a heat and pressurization process on a machine called a *calender.*" J. Thomas Grady, "A Sticky Story: The Uses of Duct Tape Just Seem to Keep Growing," *Sunday Star-News* (Wilmington, N.C.), 16 Mar. 2003, at E5.

But the ordinary term *calendar* is often misspelled *calender*—e.g.:

- "K.D. Schmidt, an *Austin Daily Statesman* Linotype operator with a stiff mustache and flexible fingers, looks at the *calender* [read *calendar*] to remind himself exactly what

day it is." Michele Stanush, "1896 News of the Day," *Austin Am.-Statesman,* 26 Oct. 1996, at C1.
- "A newcomer to the festival scene has stormed its way into the North East *calender* [read *calendar*] announcing that it has completely sold out in only its third year." Hugh MacKnight, "Hardwick Live Hits Right Note with Sell-Out," *Newcastle J.* (U.K.), 22 Aug. 2015, News §, at 28.

LANGUAGE-CHANGE INDEX
calendar misspelled *calender*: Stage 1
Current ratio (*calendar year* vs.
*calender year): 333:1

calf has a silent *-l-*: /kaf/. Pl. *calves* /kavz/. See PLURALS (C).

caliber; caliper. *Caliber* = (1) the diameter of a cylinder, esp. the bore of a gun <a .44-caliber pistol>; or (2) degree of worth or competence; quality <the Wharton School of Business turns out CEOs of the highest caliber>. (The BrE spelling is *calibre.* See -ER (B).) *Caliper* = (1) (usu. pl.) a tool used for measuring thickness or diameter; (2) thickness, as of paper or cardboard; (3) a part of a disc-brake system; or (4) a metal leg brace. **Calliper* is a variant BrE spelling.

Current ratio (*caliper* vs. **calliper*): 15:1

caliphate (= [1] an Islamic theocracy, or [2] a period of Islamic theocratic rule) is pronounced /**kal**-i-fayt/ or /**kal**-i-fət/. Through METATHESIS, the term is sometimes mispronounced by bungling news announcers as if it were /**kaf**-i-layt/.

calisthenics; callisthenics. In all forms of English, the one *-l-* spelling predominates by a 16-to-1 ratio.

calk. See **caulk.**

callous; callus. The first is the adjective ("hardened, unfeeling"), the second the noun ("hardened skin"). Unfortunately, during the early 1990s Dr. Scholl's—the company specializing in foot products—mistakenly advertised **callous removers* instead of *callus removers,* encouraging further confusion.

The plural of *callus* is *calluses,* preferably not **calli*—which, surprisingly enough, predominated until the mid-20th century. See PLURALS (B).

Current ratio (*calluses* vs. **calli*): 3:1

calvary; cavalry. Despite having wholly unrelated meanings, these words are often confused. *Calvary* = (1) (cap.) the place near Jerusalem where Jesus was crucified; (2) (sometimes cap.) a depiction or representation of Jesus' crucifixion; or (3) (l.c.) an experience of intense suffering; an ordeal. *Cavalry* = (1) a military unit mounted on horseback; or (2) a motorized military unit.

The reason for the confusion, of course, is the similarity in sound and spelling—the two words contain the same seven letters. When spoken, the sounds in the word *cavalry* (/**ka**-vəl-ree/) are sometimes transposed (a process known as METATHESIS), resulting in a mispronunciation of the word as /**kal**-və-ree/. And because it is misspoken, it is also misused in print—e.g.:

- "Raina feeds him chocolate and when he feels safe enough to talk, he calls the Bulgarian leader of the *calvary* [read *cavalry*] charge 'an operatic tenor.'" Anne Marie Welsh, "A Wry, Wise Look at the Classics," *San Diego Union-Trib.*, 8 June 1996, at E5.
- "The third annual Civil War encampment of the Lafayette Artillery Company served up field demonstrations of infantry marches and *calvary* [read *cavalry*] charges, complete with an unexpected horse fall." Paul Clifton-Waite, "Slice of Civil Strife," *Union Leader* (Manchester, N.H.), 25 Aug. 1996, at B1.
- "After the second mile into the race, the Franklin Park environ resembled a *calvary* [read *cavalry*] charge with 40 runners near the front." John Connolly, "In the Long Run, Villanova Too Tough," *Boston Herald*, 17 Nov. 1996, at B17.

Civilians seem to have to relearn this every time a new war breaks out—e.g.:

- "'Oh yeah, he's ready to deploy,' shouted a hoarse Pfc. Tim Rose, 26, who works on an anti-aircraft battery for the 3rd Armored *Calvary* [read *Cavalry*] Regiment." Jim Hughes, "Fort Carson Soldiers Enthusiastic as They Watch War Begin," *Denver Post*, 20 Mar. 2003, at A4.
- "While U.S. Marines and British forces seized the southern port city of Umm Qasr, the Army's 3rd Infantry Division, 7th *Calvary* [read *Cavalry*] Division and elements of the 101st Airborne Division moved northwest along the Euphrates River." Thomas Caywood, "Air Attacks Upped as Ground Forces Advance," *Boston Herald*, 22 Mar. 2003, News §, at 10.

Cf. **irrelevant** & **regiment**.

LANGUAGE-CHANGE INDEX
calvary misused for *cavalry*: Stage 1

calyx /**kay**-liks/ (= the green whorl on a flower that protects it before it opens) predominantly makes the plural *calyces* in all varieties of English. Although the anglicized plural *calyxes* enjoyed predominance in English-language print sources from about 1790 to 1820, it has seriously receded since then.

Current ratio (*calyces* vs. *calyxes*): 4:1

calzone (= a baked or fried turnover made of pizza dough filled with meat, cheese, and sauce) is preferably pronounced /kal-**zohn**/, as in Italian. But the most common pronunciation in AmE is /kal-**zohn**-ee/. Cf. **abalone**.

*camarade. See **comrade**.

camaraderie is routinely misspelled **camraderie, *comraderie,* and even **comradery* because of a mistaken association with *comrade*—e.g.:

- "Ah, yes, the *camraderie* [read *camaraderie*]." Anthony Flint, "A Return to the Sweatshops," *Boston Globe*, 21 Feb. 1995, Metro §, at 1.
- "But the *comraderie* [read *camaraderie*] hasn't spread to the assembly line." Micheline Maynard, "Strike Stalls GM," *USA Today*, 29 Sept. 1994, at B1.
- "In a show of *comradery* [read *camaraderie*], McNealy cut his own salary . . . in 1993 after Sun's stock had dropped

dramatically." David Einstein, "High Tech Turnover," *S.F. Chron.*, 13 Jan. 1995, at F1.

Although the words *camaraderie* and *comrade* are etymologically related—both derive from the French *camarade*—the English spellings are well enough established that each of the variant spellings is an error. Of course, careful speakers probably won't misspell *camaraderie*—it has five syllables: /kah-mə-**rah**-də-ree/.

LANGUAGE-CHANGE INDEX
camaraderie misspelled **comraderie,
camraderie, or **comradery*: Stage 1
Current ratio (*camaraderie* vs. **comradery* vs.
*comraderie vs. **camraderie*): 1,167:26:7:1

camelopard (= giraffe) is an old-fashioned word still used in Europe. In English-speaking contexts, it is sometimes misspelled through association with *leopard*—e.g.:

- "Some, like Mark Twain's travelling actor who painted himself with rings and stripes to look like a *cameleopard* [read *camelopard*], have all of a sudden painted themselves like the Russian tricolor flag." Yevgeny Yevtushenko, "Please, Don't Panic: Capitalism in Russia," *New Perspectives Q.*, 22 Mar. 1996, at 8.
- "Jog around our reservoir of dreams, Jackie, diamonds dripping from your eyes as a load of *cameleopards* [read *camelopards*] trot past the Texas Book *Suppository* [read *Depository*] to what remains of Camelot." Benjamin Ivry, "At the Jackie Onassis Auction," *Paris Rev.*, 1 Jan. 2000, at 47.

The word is pronounced /kə-**mel**-ə-pahrd/.

LANGUAGE-CHANGE INDEX
camelopard misspelled **cameleopard*: Stage 1
Current ratio: 2:1

came near [+ **present participle**], in the sense "almost," is a CASUALISM that can usually be replaced by *almost* [+ past-tense verb]—e.g.: "Armed with might and mystique, the Cowboys *came near losing* [read *almost lost*] to the NFL's Tinker Toy team Sunday in Cincinnati." Frank Luksa, "Looking into the Whys of Cowboys 23, Bengals 20," *Dallas Morning News*, 1 Nov. 1994, at B2. The phrasing was especially common from about 1850 to about 1950.

campanile (= a high bell tower that is usu. separate from any other building) is preferably pronounced /kam-pə-**nee**-lee/—not /**kam**-pə-neel/.

can. A. And *may.* The distinction between these words has been much discussed over the years, beginning with Samuel Johnson's *Dictionary of the English Language* (1755). Generally, *can* expresses physical or mental ability <He can lift 500 pounds>; *may* expresses permission or authorization <The guests may now enter>, and sometimes possibility <The trial may end on Friday>. Although only an insufferable precisian would insist on observing the distinction

LANGUAGE-CHANGE INDEX (For the full key, see front matter pp. xxxi, l–li.)
Stage 1: Rejected. **Stage 2:** Widely shunned. **Stage 3:** Widespread but . . . **Stage 4:** Ubiquitous but . . . **Stage 5:** Fully accepted.
Invariably inferior forms marked by asterisk (*). • Ratios represent frequency of prevalent forms vs. variants in current books.

in informal speech or writing (especially in questions such as "Can I wait until August?"), it's often advisable to distinguish between these words.

But three caveats are necessary. First, educated people typically say *can't I* as opposed to the stilted forms *mayn't I* and *may I not*. The same is true of other pronouns <Why can't she go?> <Can't you wait until Saturday?>. Second, *you can't* and *you cannot* are much more common denials of permission than *you may not* <No, you can't play with any more than 14 clubs in your bag>. Third, because *may* is a more polite way of asking for permission, a fussy insistence on using it can give the writing a prissy tone.

> LANGUAGE-CHANGE INDEX
> *can* for *may*: Stage 4

B. And *could.* These words express essentially the same idea, but there is a slight difference. In the phrase *We can supply you with 5 tons of caliche*, the meaning is simply that we are able to. But in the phrase *We could supply you with 5 tons of caliche if you'd send us a $5,000 deposit*, the *could* is right because of the condition tacked onto the end; that is, there is some stronger sense of doubt with *could*. See SUBJUNCTIVES.

And in interrogatives, *could* indicates willingness: *Could you meet me at 7:00 PM?* This asks not just whether you're able, but also whether you're willing.

In still another circumstance—in the subordinate clause of a complex sentence—the choice between *can* and *could* depends on the sequence of tenses, as does the choice between any other present- and past-tense verb. If the verb in the main clause expresses a past event, *could* appears in the subordinate clause <she asked me to go so that I could meet my great-aunt>. But if the verb in the main clause expresses a present or future event, *can* appears in the main clause <she is asking me to go so that I can meet my great-aunt> <she will ask me to go so that I can meet my great-aunt>. See TENSES (B).

canal, vb. (= to build a canal), is pronounced /kə-**nal**/ and makes *canalled* and *canalling*—not **canaled* and **canaling*. See SPELLING (B).

cancel, vb., makes *canceled* and *canceling* in AmE, *cancelled* and *cancelling* in BrE. Note, however, that in *cancellation* the *-l-* is doubled (*-ll-*) because the accent falls on the third syllable. See SPELLING (B).

cancel (out). See PHRASAL VERBS.

candelabrum (= a branched candlestick with several candles, or a branched lamp with several lights) forms the plural *candelabra*, which appears far more often. Even so, the singular form remains quite common—e.g.:

- "The actor is speaking of his role as Lumiere, a life-size, fully functional *candelabrum*, in the national touring production of 'Beauty and the Beast,' which kicked off a four-month stint at the Kennedy Center." Nicole Arthur, "All for 'The Beast,'" *Wash. Post*, 9 June 1996, at G1.
- "There is a lustrous warmth to the light that gives forth from the candles on a menorah—the nine-branched

candelabrum used during Hanukkah." John Nichols, "Festival of Lights," *Capital Times* (Madison), 7 Dec. 1996, at A11.
- "A footman from the Silver Pantry is adjusting the top of a mid-17th-century 4ft *candelabrum*." Jessica Salter, "The Queen Awaits," *Daily Telegraph*, 25 July 2015, at 20.

Three problems arise with this word.

First, some writers use *candelabra* as a singular—e.g.: "The holiday centered on lighting the eight-branch *candelabra* [read *candelabrum*] called the menorah." Jan M. Brahms, "Alas, Hanukkah Is 'Jewish Christmas,'" *Capital Times* (Madison), 7 Dec. 1996, at A9.

Second, as a result of the false singular just mentioned, writers are tempted to use the double plural **candelabras* (an error dating from the late 19th century)—e.g.: "The dignity is leavened by some whimsical touches, such as chandeliers and *candelabras* [read *candelabra*] entwined with iron flowers and a giant piggy bank behind the small bar." B. Samantha Stenzel, "Neighborhood Restaurant Offers Innovative Cuisine," *Chicago Sun-Times*, 21 Nov. 1997, at 36.

Third, and least seriously, some writers stick to the native-English plural even though the foreign plural has been thoroughly established—e.g.: "But this Hanukkah season, which runs through Dec. 13, Mickey is appearing on menorahs—seven-branch *candelabrums* [read *candelabra*]—and dreidels—spinning toy tops." Carl Schoettler, "Pan-Cultural Mickey Mouse Makes a Plug for Hanukkah," *Chicago Sun-Times*, 8 Dec. 1996, at 35. See PLURALS (B).

The word may be pronounced /kan-də-**lah**-brəm/ or /kan-də-**lay**-brəm/.

> LANGUAGE-CHANGE INDEX
> 1. *candelabra* for *candelabrum* as a singular: Stage 4
> Current ratio (*a candelabrum* vs.
> **a candelabra*): 1.04:1
> 2. **candelabras* for *candelabra* as a plural: Stage 3
> Current ratio (*two candelabra* vs.
> **two candelabras*): 3:1
> 3. **candelabrums* for *candelabra*: Stage 1
> Current ratio (*candelabra* vs. **candelabrums*): 177:1

candidacy; candidature. The first is the standard term in AmE, the second traditionally in BrE. But since the late 1970s, *candidacy* has become the predominant form in British print sources.

> Current ratio: 5:1

can hardly; *can't hardly. The first is STANDARD ENGLISH; the second is DIALECT. E.g.: "We *can't hardly* [read *can hardly*] blame all those fine doctors for leaving." Rob Ross, "If We Were Handing Out Awards," *Pitt. Post-Gaz.*, 4 Mar. 2002, at C2.

There is some debate about **can't hardly*, only half of which need be taken seriously. Traditionalists call it a double negative—*not* and *hardly* both being negatives—and condemn the phrase on that ground. Descriptive linguists counter (unpersuasively) that *hardly* is not really a negative at all and say that **can't hardly* is perfectly acceptable.

But regardless of whether it's a double negative, **can't hardly* is not STANDARD ENGLISH. And the phrase can always be replaced by a more logical and more direct phrase in one of two ways. If a strong negative is intended, use *can't* (or *cannot*). If a soft negative is intended, use *can hardly* (or, more typically, *could hardly*).

LANGUAGE-CHANGE INDEX
*can't hardly for *can hardly*: Stage 1
Current ratio (*can hardly* vs. **cannot hardly*): 98:1

canister (= a small container) is the standard spelling. **Cannister* is a variant. Inconsistently enough, though, *cannikin* (= a small can) is the established form in preference to the variant forms **canikin* and **canakin*.

Current ratio (*canister* vs. **cannister*): 39:1

*can might. See DOUBLE MODALS.

CANNIBALISM. This is H.W. Fowler's term for constructions in which certain words "devour their own kind" (*FMEU1* at 64). Words that commonly fall prey are *as*, *to*, and *that*. E.g.:

- "But the playwright's the thing, and he comes across *as* fascinating, mercurial and doomed *as* any of his fictional creations." Matt Roush, "Hepburn's Holiday Gift," *USA Today*, 19 Dec. 1994, at D3. (The *as* in the phrase *comes across as* has swallowed the first *as* in the phrase *as fascinating, mercurial and doomed as*. A possible revision: *But the playwright's the thing, and he comes across as being as fascinating, mercurial, and doomed as any of his fictional creations*.)
- "Most impressively, however, he power cleans a whopping 485 pounds—more than 100 pounds *than* [read *more than*] the 367-pound Davis." Olin Buchanan, "The Numbers Game," *Austin Am.-Statesman*, 21 Oct. 2000, at F5. (If either [*more*] *than* is changed to *over* [= more than], then the incompleteness of the phrasing becomes apparent—two *more thans* having been called for in the original sentence. Because that phrasing would be gawky, the sentence needs editing. A possible revision: *Most impressively, however, he power-cleans a whopping 485 pounds—over 100 pounds more than the 367-pound Davis*.)

There are two similar blunders. The first results from omitting *as* after *regard*, *treat*, *accept*, *acknowledge*, and other verbs that are unidiomatic without it (such as the PHRASAL VERB *come across*). E.g.: "We *regard* him *as* holy as a saint." Although the strictly correct phrasing would be *regard him as* [*being*] *as holy as a saint*, the better course is to use another word: "We *consider* him as holy as a saint." Or: "*We believe* [or *To us*] he is as holy as a saint." The second blunder occurs with incomplete comparisons—e.g.: **as bad or worse than*, **as much or more than*. These phrases should be *as bad as or worse than* and *as much as or more than*. E.g.:

- "They compromised at 8 feet, but in many spots the competition among walkers, dog walkers and runners has worn paths *as wide or wider than* [read *as wide as or wider than*] planners sought." Steve Brandt, "Which Path Will Lake Harriet Take?" *Star Trib.* (Minneapolis), 24 Jan. 1996, at B1.

- "Your caladiums should have produced tubers that are *as big or bigger than* [read *as big as or bigger than*] the ones you planted." Dan Gill, "Caladium Conundrum," *Times-Picayune* (New Orleans), 26 Sept. 1997, at E1.

See **as . . . as (E)** & ILLOGIC (B).

Problems of this kind are most readily spotted by reading aloud. The ear tends to hear them even if the eye doesn't see them. See SOUND OF PROSE.

cannikin. See **canister.**

cannon. Pl. *cannons* or (especially in military jargon) *cannon*. See **canon.**

cannot should not appear as two words, except in the rare instances when the *not* is part of another construction (such as *not only . . . but also*)—e.g.: "His is among very few voices that *can not only* get away with numbers like 'You Are So Beautiful to Me' and a reggae/salsa remake of 'Summer in the City,' but actually make them moving." Jamie Kastner, "Joe Cocker Proves He Can Still Rock 'n' Roll," *Toronto Sun*, 8 Mar. 1995, at 64. *Cannot* is preferable to *can't* in formal writing. See CONTRACTIONS.

cannot help but; cannot help ——ing; cannot but. In formal contexts, the last two phrases have traditionally been preferred—e.g.:

- "Engaged in these activities, the critic *cannot but* formulate value judgments." John Simon, *The Sheep from the Goats* xix (1989).
- "When I put this on the list, I *can't help feeling* a little puffed up." V. Diane Woodbrown, "Why Women Need to Speak Up Against Gender Imbalance," *S.F. Examiner*, 8 Jan. 1997, at A15.

Still, because *cannot help being* and (especially) *cannot but be* are increasingly rare in AmE and BrE alike, they strike many readers as stilted.

Cannot help but, which took root during the 20th century, is becoming an accepted idiom <I cannot help but think you did that on purpose>. A less awkward construction is *cannot help ——ing* <I cannot help thinking you did that on purpose>. But the first construction should no longer be stigmatized on either side of the Atlantic—e.g.:

- "Experts say Thomas' court performance *cannot help but* be affected by the traumatic Senate confirmation hearings." Aaron Epstein, "Thomas Survives Controversy, Wins Senate Confirmation, 52–48," *Phil. Inquirer*, 16 Oct. 1991, at A1.
- "Texas *cannot help but* consider what its victory over Tech will mean." Jonathan Feigen, "UT Regains Control of Its Fate," *Houston Chron.*, 11 Nov. 1996, Sports §, at 13.
- "One *cannot help but* wonder what producer, geared up to supply supermarkets, got dumped to make way for all those North American berries." Emily Green, "A Load of Coq," *Independent*, 14 Nov. 1996, Features §, at 2.

Occasionally writers twist the phrase not just unidiomatically, but illogically—e.g.: "I *cannot help from*

LANGUAGE-CHANGE INDEX (For the full key, see front matter pp. xxxi, l–li.)
Stage 1: Rejected. **Stage 2:** Widely shunned. **Stage 3:** Widespread but . . . **Stage 4:** Ubiquitous but . . . **Stage 5:** Fully accepted.
Invariably inferior forms marked by asterisk (*). • Ratios represent frequency of prevalent forms vs. variants in current books.

refraining myself to comment [read *cannot refrain from commenting*] on Ms. Gabor's flagrant disrespect of the law." Letter of Joel Rosen, "Zsa Zsa's Encounter with Police," *L.A. Times*, 24 June 1989, § 2, at 9. If the writer couldn't help refraining, then the letter wouldn't have been written! On the misuse of *refrain* as a reflexive verb, see **restrain**.

LANGUAGE-CHANGE INDEX
1. *cannot help but* for *cannot but*: Stage 5
Current ratio (*cannot but* vs. *cannot help but*): 1.3:1
2. *cannot help from* for *cannot but*: Stage 1
Current ratio (*cannot but* vs.
cannot help from): 658:1

canon; cannon. *Canon* = (1) a corpus of writings <the Western canon>; (2) an accepted notion or principle <canons of ethics>; (3) a rule of ecclesiastical law (either of the Roman Catholic canon law or of the Anglican Church); or (4) a cathedral dignitary.

Cannon = (1) a big gun; or (2) the ear of a bell, by which the bell hangs. *Cannon* incorrectly displaces *canon* surprisingly often—e.g.:

- "The state Criminal Justice Commission said yesterday in Wallingford that there was no evidence that Litchfield County State's Attorney Frank Maco violated the *cannon* [read *canon*] of ethics for lawyers by his remarks." "Allen Filing Rejected," *Newsday* (N.Y.), 4 Nov. 1993, at 18.
- "White's friends say her fledgling campaign for retention is hampered by the judicial *cannon* [read *canon* or, more likely, *canons*] of ethics, which *restricts* [or, with *canons*, *restrict*] her ability to defend herself." Andy Sher, "Crime Fears, Death Penalty Debate Stirring Furor over Judge Election," *Nashville Banner*, 22 July 1996, at A1.

LANGUAGE-CHANGE INDEX
cannon misused for *canon*: Stage 1

cantaloupe; cantaloup. The first is AmE /**kan**-tə-lohp/; the second is BrE /**kan**-tə-loop/.

*can't hardly. See **can hardly.**

can't have your cake and eat it too. See **you can't have your cake and eat it too.**

can't help but. See **cannot help but.**

can't seem. Although this phrase is technically illogical (e.g., "I can't seem to find my coat" is more logically rendered "I seem to be unable to find my coat"), it is also undoubtedly idiomatic. Idiom tends to prefer succinctness over logic, and here the logical construction is verbose. Linguists use the term "raising" to describe the process of moving a negative from a subordinate clause to a main clause. So "I think I will not go" becomes "I don't think I will go." (See **don't think.**) The phrase *can't seem* is one of the more popular instances of raising. It became established in the late 19th century and grew rapidly in popularity during the 20th.

Regardless of its label, this process is quite common, especially in speech. But it also occurs in writing—e.g.:

- "Shaq's mother *can't seem* to remember to give him the pill each morning, so Clifton got a doctor's permission to do

it himself." Mary Jane Fine, "When Hugs Aren't Enough," *Palm Beach Post*, 7 Nov. 1994, at A1.
- "But all the lawsuits in the world *can't seem* to slow down tobacco profits." Dan Beucke, "Week in Business," *Newsday* (N.Y.), 6 Oct. 1996, at F2.
- "The notional premise of this foray into meta-comedy is that the outwardly earnest duo *can't seem* to write a skit they like." Mark Monahan, "Comedy," *Daily Telegraph*, 22 Aug. 2015, at 19.

LANGUAGE-CHANGE INDEX
can't seem: Stage 5

canvas; canvass. *Canvas*, almost always a noun, is the heavy cloth. In its rare verbal sense, it means "to cover with such a cloth."

Canvass, v.t., = (1) to examine (as votes) in detail; (2) to take stock of opinions, esp. those of individuals; (3) to solicit orders or political support; or (4) to discuss or debate. The term is fairly common in all four senses—e.g.:

- Sense 1: "Town cops got a complaint about swastikas and phrases painted on a stately home on Carriage House Lane, and when they *canvassed* the neighborhood, they found anti-Semitic graffiti on three other houses and on a wooden shelter on the golf course, 50 feet away." Patrice O'Shaughnessy, "Marred by Hate," *Daily News* (N.Y.), 17 Nov. 1996, News §, at 6.
- Sense 2: "Before driving east on an unclogged U.S. 50, I *canvassed* people for suggestions of things to do." Jeannette Belliveau, "Beach, with Blanket," *Wash. Post*, 8 Mar. 1995, at B9.
- Sense 3: "Solicitations to the volunteers bring in nearly $700,000 a year, while the volunteers' door-to-door *canvassing* takes in close to $300,000 a year." Larry Riggs, "Big Names, Big Changes," *Direct*, 1 Sept. 1996, at 1.
- Sense 4: "Mr. Bolger's soothing New Year comments also *canvassed* the potentially divisive issue of republicanism." "Calm Before Political Storm," *Evening Post* (Wellington), 9 Jan. 1995, at 4.

As a noun, the word *canvass* means "the act of canvassing."

capable. The phrase *is capable of* [verb + -ing] can be (not *is capable of being*) put more simply—typically by writing either *can* [+ verb] or *is able to* [+ verb]. This bit of verbosity is especially common in sportswriting—e.g.:

- "Talk to him for a while and you come to the conclusion that either he *is capable of being* [read *can be*] very calm in difficult circumstances or he's a very good actor." Kent Youngblood, "Two Men, One Opportunity," *Star Trib.* (Minneapolis), 27 Sept. 2001, at C10.
- "Duhon said he thinks that Dunleavy *is capable of being* [read *can be*] an outstanding rebounder." Bill Cole, "Two Goals, Williams, Duke," *Winston-Salem J.*, 15 Nov. 2001, at F1.
- "Quarterback Quincy Carter needs to continue to improve and prove he *is capable of being* [read *can be*] a starter in the NFL." Richard Justice, "Restoring Glory," *Houston Chron.*, 16 Dec. 2001, Sports §, at 1.

capacity; capability. These words overlap, but each has its nuances. *Capacity* = the power or ability to receive, hold, or contain <the jar was filled to

capacity>. Figuratively, it refers to mental faculties in the sense "the power to take in knowledge" <mental capacity>. In law, it is frequently used in the sense "legal competency or qualification" <capacity to enter into a contract>. *Capability* = (1) power or ability in general, whether physical or mental <he has the capability to play first-rate golf>; or (2) the quality of being able to use or be used in a specified way <nuclear capabilities>. See **ability** & **incapacitation.**

capital, n.; **capitol.** The first is a city, the seat of government; the second is a building in which the state or national legislature meets (fr. L. *capitoleum*, the Roman temple of Jupiter). Until October 1698, when the Virginia governor specified that *Capitol* would be the name of the planned statehouse in a village then known as Middle Plantation, the word *capitol* had been used only as the name of the great Roman temple at Rome. See Mitford M. Mathews, *American Words* 62–63 (1959; repr. 1976).

Capital, whether as noun or as adjective, is called on far more frequently than *capitol.*

Capitol Hill is where the U.S. *Capitol* (the building) is located in Washington, D.C., the nation's *capital.*

capitalist; capitalistic. *Capitalist* is the general adjective <capitalist enterprises>; the *-istic* form, a favorite of Marxists, is typically pejorative <for much of the 20th century, Hong Kong was the world's most capitalistic city>.

CAPITALIZATION. A. Generally. The decision whether to capitalize a word seems simple at first. There are really just three rules: capitalize the first word of a sentence, the pronoun *I*, and proper names. What could be easier?

Then the "yeah-but" bug bites. You're writing a business letter and you notice that everyone capitalizes *Company* when it refers to your company, even when it's not used with the company's name. Isn't that a common noun that should be lowercase? You read the newspaper and notice that *President* is capitalized when referring to the U.S. president, but not when referring to a foreign president or the president of a corporation. You notice that the newspaper's headline is capitalized just as in a regular sentence, but a newsletter you receive capitalizes the first letter of every word in its headlines—and the supermarket tabloids you sneak a peek at while waiting in line capitalize every bigger-than-life letter in their screaming headlines.

So what are the standards? For writing that goes into print, the standards—in capitalization more than in most other aspects of written English—lie in house styles. That means that how you capitalize will usually be decided by someone else, not you (unless you're a publisher, or maybe a poet). Yet some general conventions offer helpful guidance. The most important is the modern trend away from capitalization, resulting in a minimalist rule: unless there's a good reason to capitalize, don't.

But don't think that this simple rule can answer all your questions. Despite the three simple rules above, there are many other arcane capitalization rules, and you'll never learn every one any more than you will ever learn how to spell every word in the English language. You'll always need a dictionary to look up spellings you're not sure about, and you'll find a comprehensive resource such as *The Chicago Manual of Style* indispensable for explaining the minutiae and conventions of capitalizing. Other excellent manuals are *The Associated Press Stylebook and Briefing on Media Law* and the venerable but aging *Words into Type.*

There is simply no way to reason out why *Stone Age* is capitalized but *space age* is usually not, why *October* is capitalized but *autumn* is not, why in scientific names the genus is capitalized but the species is not—even when the species name is derived from a proper name <*Rhinolophus philippinesis*>.

Despite all those paradoxes, and many others, the following conventions may prove useful when deciding whether to capitalize:

- Capitalize the first word of a sentence even if the word standing alone would be an exception to the rule to capitalize proper nouns, such as *eBay* <EBay reported higher earnings Tuesday>.
- Capitalize the first word of a complete sentence within a sentence, such as a direct quotation <I said, "Do you want to dance?">.
- When a common noun is part of a proper name, capitalize it when the entire name appears <Mississippi River>, but not when it is separated from the proper name <the Mississippi and Missouri rivers>. See NAMES (A).
- Capitalize the adjectival form of a noun that is always proper <Keynesian economics> but not one from a noun that can also be common <congressional investigation> or that has lost any connection with the thing described by the combined term <french fries>.
- Usually capitalize all letters of an acronym or initialism (and avoid periods) <NCAA>, but follow the preferred style if it is different <Nasdaq> and any style established by long usage <U.S.> <mpg> <AM> <A.D.>. (See ABBREVIATIONS (A).) This is another area in which a style manual is essential.
- Capitalize compass directions when they refer to identifiable places <the American West>, but not when they are just general directions <go west, young man>.
- Capitalize days of the week <Monday>, months of the year <June>, and holidays <Fourth of July>, but not seasons <fall>, even if used attributively <spring 2004 semester>.
- Capitalize historic eras <the Roaring Twenties>, but not general labels that could apply to many eras <the golden age of radio>.
- Capitalize sparingly to show personification <it's not nice to fool Mother Nature> or that something is being elevated from the commonplace for some rhetorical purpose <still waiting for that One Big Deal>.

LANGUAGE-CHANGE INDEX (For the full key, see front matter pp. xxxi, l–lii.)
Stage 1: Rejected. **Stage 2:** Widely shunned. **Stage 3:** Widespread but . . . **Stage 4:** Ubiquitous but . . . **Stage 5:** Fully accepted.
Invariably inferior forms marked by asterisk (✳). • Ratios represent frequency of prevalent forms vs. variants in current books.

B. Overcapitalizing. Inexperienced writers—and overzealous house stylists—often tend to capitalize common nouns inappropriately. As mentioned above, a house style may insist that certain common nouns (e.g., *Company, University, City*) be capitalized when referring to its own institution. But even this holdout against the modern trend is weakening—the University of Colorado at Boulder recently declared that its internal style is to always make *university* lowercase when it stands alone. A few nouns that are arguably common in form are always capitalized, such as *House* (for House of Representatives) and *Crown* for the British monarchy. But that's not an excuse to capitalize *federal* or *government*. Again, a style manual is invaluable for handling the exceptions to the rule.

It isn't always inexperience that leads to overcapitalizing. Sometimes it's propaganda. As one modern grammarian notes, propagandists "invariably capitalize the name of their philosophy, the title of their leader, the term for the group's adherents, and so on." Barbara Wallraff, *Word Court* 80 (2000).

C. Titles. Titles also give writers some trouble. In general, an actual title is capitalized when it comes before a name <Chairman Mao>, but not when it follows a name <Colin Powell, former chairman of the Joint Chiefs of Staff>. Labels that are not titles are never capitalized <physicist Niels Bohr> (but see TITULAR TOMFOOLERY). A well-known nickname may rise to the level of a proper noun and require capitalization <Old Blue Eyes>. A trademark is a proper name akin to a title and should always be capitalized <Dr Pepper> unless the trademark is designated as lowercase <iPod>. Titles of works of art and publications are capitalized like up-style headings (see (D)) <*Gone with the Wind*> <*Journal of the American Medical Association*>.

Styles differ over whether to capitalize an article at the beginning of a name or title. In general, always capitalize an article when it is part of the title of a book, play, or other literary or artistic work <*A Clockwork Orange*> <*The Color Purple*>, but leave it lowercase if it is not part of the title <the Bible>. Do not capitalize *the* at the beginning of a company's or university's name <the Chubb Group> <the Heritage Foundation> <the University of Washington>. Rules for articles at the beginning of newspaper and magazine names are not as well settled. Associated Press style is to capitalize *the* when it is a formal part of the name <*The Nation*> <*The New York Times*>, and to leave it lowercase when it is not <the *National Review*> <the *Los Angeles Times*>. While that advice is sensible, it can be burdensome as well. How do you know the formal name of a publication? The World Wide Web makes that task easier and less expensive than the AP's instruction to buy *Editor & Publisher's International Year Book*. Finally, *the* is lowercase when referring to many countries and geographic entities <the Marshall Islands> <the Philippines>, but capitalized in the names of some cities <The Pas, Manitoba> <The Dalles, Oregon>. And as *The New York Times Manual of Style and Usage* points out, the capital of the Netherlands is The Hague.

D. Up-Style Headings. Avoid them. An up-style heading is one in which most words are capitalized. As far as readability is concerned, a block of text set up-style is just slightly easier to read than a block of all-caps text (see (E)).

But the up-style has its place, as in the taglines in this and most other manuals. It also has advantages in marking the hierarchy of headings. This is especially so if the output is straight from a word processor, as most writing in business and academia is. Typesetting for publications gives a lot more flexibility for signaling the structure of a document by layout devices. In a business or academic report, the writer is likely to use just one or two typefaces and sizes. So a bold, centered, up-style heading might signal, for example, that this division in the document is at a lower level than the bold, centered, all-caps heading above, but at a higher level than the down-style, flush-left headings that follow.

When using up-style headings, capitalize the first and last words and all other words except for articles, conjunctions, and short prepositions (usually fewer than five letters). Consider the *to* in an infinitive a preposition or particle and leave it lowercase, too. But don't fail to capitalize a noun, pronoun, verb, adjective, or adverb just because it is short <It Is Too Easy to Forget>. And remember: many words that are common as prepositions can also serve as adverbs <Stand Out in a Crowd> <Walk out the Door>. In these examples, *out* is an adverb in the first, a preposition in the second.

Two final things. First, always capitalize *that* in up-style headings, whether it is serving as a relative pronoun, demonstrative adjective, or conjunction. This carves out an exception to the usual rules, but it's simple, handy, and consistent. Second, consider using another exception to the rule by capitalizing the short preposition *with* if it appears close to or parallel with the longer preposition *without*. Otherwise, the result is awkward and confusing, perhaps even misleading by implying significance where none is intended.

E. All Capitals. Avoid them. A block of all caps is hard to read, and the longer the block, the harder it is to read. We learn to recognize words by the shape of the letters, even if we're not conscious of it. The ascenders and descenders give words their distinctive shapes. Words set in all caps lose those signals.

That said, the all-caps style does have its place, especially in major headings, set in boldface type and never running over one line. Even in this use, however, the style is best confined to simple tags such as **CONCLUSION**. The combination of caps and boldface can help when setting up a hierarchy of heading styles (see (D)).

F. Small Caps. The use of small caps is uncommon in general writing, but for some uses the style is appropriate, and more writers ought to consider adopting it. Specifically, small caps are helpful where large caps would be unnecessarily obtrusive. For example, 56 B.C. just looks tidier than 56 B.C. Similarly, if the style you must follow requires caps rather than lowercase letters for *a.m.* and *p.m.*, 5:37 PM looks a bit more restrained than 5:37 PM. When you're listing academic degrees, small caps can help prevent the string of abbreviations from overpowering the person's name <Don Hill, B.S., M.B.A., ED.D., J.D., LL.M.>. And in other places where tags and abbreviations are standard, small caps can help lower the volume somewhat <DATE:>. Small caps are also used in citations for specialized writing in certain fields, such as law. For more guidance on using small caps, see *The Chicago Manual of Style*.

  G. **After Colon.** See PUNCTUATION (C).

  H. **Names.** See NAMES (A).

capitol. See **capital.**

Capitol Hill. See **capital.**

capitulatory; *capitulative. The standard adjective corresponding to *capitulation* is *capitulatory* /kə-**pich**-ə-lə-tor-ee/. The form *capitulative*, which is much less common, is a NEEDLESS VARIANT—e.g.: "Solidarity activists and many independent economists maintain that authorities save their most effective weapon of the price campaign for last: *capitulative* [read *capitulatory*] wage hikes above the level of prices for any factory considered a potential trouble spot." Jackson Diehl, "Poles Await Yearly Rise in Prices," *Wash. Post*, 25 Jan. 1988, at A15.

Current ratio: 30:1

cappuccino (= Italian-style coffee with steamed milk) has always been so spelled with two doubled consonants. *Capuccino* and *cappucino* are NEEDLESS VARIANTS.

Current ratio (*cappuccino* vs. *cappucino* vs. *capuccino*): 185:2:1

capricious (= [1] changing quickly and suddenly, or [2] likely to change one's mind suddenly and to behave unexpectedly) is preferably pronounced /kə-**prish**-əs/—not /kə-**preesh**-əs/. Yet the corresponding noun is *caprice* /kə-**prees**/.

capsize has always been so spelled. Yet the misspelling *capsise* occasionally appears in BrE and World English. E.g.: "Ships at sea are cracked like straws, curraghs and rafts in the lough *capsise* [read *capsize*]." Carolyn White, *A History of Irish Fairies* 92 (2005).

Current ratio: 797:1

captor; *capturer. The latter is a NEEDLESS VARIANT.

caramel (= [1] burnt sugar used to color or sweeten food; or [2] a smooth, chewy, caramel-flavored candy) is the standard spelling. The word is pronounced /**kar**-ə-məl/ (best), /**kar**-ə-mel/ (second best), or /**kahr**-məl/ (worst). *Carmel* is a misspelling that results from the third pronunciation—e.g.:

- "Another offering is the Cow Pie, which is made of chocolate, pecans and *carmel* [read *caramel*]." Anna Driver, "Kids Sweet on Slimy Gum, Candy Rats," *Commercial Appeal* (Memphis), 14 June 1997, at B7.
- "The shops in Oak Glen and Yucaipa still offer *carmel* [read *caramel*] apples, peanut brittle, chocolates and salt water taffy." Gail Wesson, "Carl Granlund, Assemblyman's Father" (obit.), *Press-Enterprise* (Riverside, Cal.), 21 Oct. 1997, at B6A.

Another slight influence leading to this error might be a place name: Carmel, California (which is pronounced /kahr-**mel**/).

LANGUAGE-CHANGE INDEX
caramel misspelled *carmel*: Stage 1

carat; karat; caret. These homophones have distinct meanings. *Carat* = a unit of weight for gemstones, equal to 200 milligrams <a 2-carat diamond>. *Karat* = a unit of fineness for gold <a 24-karat gold bracelet>. *Caret* = a typographic mark (^) used to indicate an insertion <a heavily edited page filled with cross-outs and carets>.

Not surprisingly, the first two words are the most frequently confused—so much so that dictionaries list *carat* as a variant spelling of *karat* (in addition to defining *carat*'s ordinary sense). But the DIFFERENTIATION ought to be encouraged.

The less common error is to misuse *caret* for the unrelated word *carat* or *karat*—e.g.: "Boaters often liked to have the names of their yachts painted in *24-caret* [read *24-karat*] gold leaf, as well." Shannon Oboye, "James Tribbett, Expert at Gold-Leaf Lettering," *Sun-Sentinel* (Ft. Lauderdale), 15 Mar. 2001, at B15.

LANGUAGE-CHANGE INDEX
caret misused for *karat*: Stage 1

caravanserai (= in eastern countries, an inn with a large open central area where groups of travelers with animals can stay) has been predominantly so spelled since the 18th century. The most common variants are *caravansary* (predominant in AmE in the late 19th century) and *caravansery*. *Caravanserai* is pronounced /kar-ə-**van**[t]-sə-rı/.

Current ratio (*caravanserai* vs. *caravansary* vs. *caravansery*): 56:22:1

carburetor; carburettor. The first is AmE (pronounced /**kahr**-bə-ray-tər/ [formally /**kahr**-byə-ray-tər/]); the second is BrE (pronounced kah-byə-ray-tə/ [*OED*] or /kah-byə-**ret**-ə/ [Jones]).

carcass (= the dead body of an animal or, less often, a human) is the standard spelling. *Carcase* is a variant (still occasionally seen in BrE, but not recommended in AmE or any other form of STANDARD ENGLISH).

Current ratio: 6:1

LANGUAGE-CHANGE INDEX (For the full key, see front matter pp. xxxi, l-li.)
Stage 1: Rejected. **Stage 2:** Widely shunned. **Stage 3:** Widespread but . . . **Stage 4:** Ubiquitous but . . . **Stage 5:** Fully accepted.
Invariably inferior forms marked by asterisk (*). • Ratios represent frequency of prevalent forms vs. variants in current books.

cardinal numbers; ordinal numbers. Cardinal numbers signify quantity (*one, two, three,* etc.); ordinal numbers signify position (*first, second, third,* etc.). To keep the terms straight, associate *ordinal* with *order*. See NUMERALS (F).

card shark; cardsharp. The traditional distinction is that a *card shark* is a skillful player, while a *cardsharp* (usually a closed compound) is a cheat. Here, the terms are used in these senses:

- "He matches the ivied education with a stint working at Christie's in London, which makes him right for the antiquities game: half tweedy professor, half Texas Hold 'Em *card shark*." Bo Emerson, "A Herculean Try for Goddess," *Atlanta J.-Const.*, 2 Jan. 2007, at A1.
- "Pretty soon Eddie's been beat up, there's a dead showgirl in a swimming pool, and the pit boss has given up chasing *cardsharps* in favor of chasing hoods." Kevin Allman, "Get Out of the Way, Gender Benders," *Wash. Post*, 17 Dec. 2006, Book World §, at T13.

But occasionally a writer will use *card shark* where the sense is that the player cheats. A useful distinction gets obliterated in the shuffle—e.g.:

- "Mr. Kahn took an expansive view of . . . coded communications, from the solution of hieroglyphics and cuneiform writing to hobo chalk markings and the signals used by *card sharks* [read *cardsharps*] to cheat unwitting opponents." Martin Edlund, "David Kahn Talks About His Life in Code," *N.Y. Sun*, 30 Mar. 2004, Arts & Letters §, at 16.
- "Supposedly based on the teachings of *card shark* [read *cardsharp*] 'Dickie Richard,' the book offers genuine tips for cheating along with a humorously amoral philosophy." Will Pfeifer, "Know When to Hold 'Em," *Rockford Register Star* (Ill.), 23 Jan. 2006, at C1.

LANGUAGE-CHANGE INDEX
card shark misused for *cardsharp*: Stage 1

careen; career, vb. *Careen* = (1) v.i., to tip or tilt <the sailboat careened and then sank>; or (2) v.t., to cause to tip or tilt <they careened the ship on the beach to scrape the barnacles and caulk the seams>. *Career* = to move wildly at high speed. E.g.: "His car overturned yesterday after *careering* out of control across three lanes of the motorway." "M4 Driver Drowns," *Sunday Telegraph*, 11 Feb. 1990, at 2.

Since the early 20th century, AmE has made *careen* do the job of *career*, as by saying that a car *careened* down the street. On September 7, 1992, in a campaign speech in Wisconsin, President George H.W. Bush said that "product liability has *careened* out of control." Likewise: "Imagine yourself as Ridge Racer, *careening* in a rocket-powered car through an ever-changing, three-dimensional landscape." "Fight to the Finish," *Newsweek*, 12 Dec. 1994, at 56. In frequency of use in AmE, phrases such as *careened off the road* and *careened out of control* have no close rivals with *careering* counterparts. *Careening off course* is now standard.

Concededly, though, a few writers reserve *career* for such uses—e.g.:

- "Monday night, while he [Silvio Berlusconi] reaffirmed his promise to deliver a 'new Italian miracle,' supporters

careered through the streets of Rome blasting their car horns and crying 'Silvio! Silvio!'" Kevin Fedarko, "Knight of the New Right," *Time*, 11 Apr. 1994, at 59.
- "A hot rod *careered* out of control during a drag race and flew into the grandstand Sunday." "Out-of-Control Car Kills Woman at Race," *Chicago Trib.*, 11 Nov. 1996, at 12.
- "A car *careered* out of control last evening and crashed into a knot of people on the sidewalk." Daniel J. Wagin, "Metro Briefing: Fatal Car Crash," *N.Y. Times*, 20 July 2001, at B6.

It's understandable why most people aren't comfortable with this verbal usage of *career*. The word derived from a Latin term for *road* or *path*, and later denoted a racetrack, but today people think of it only as a noun: the path of a life's work.

The new use of *careen* may also have been influenced by the word *carom* (= to rebound after colliding)—e.g.: "Among those comforted were seven students, ages 10 to 15, who were riding their bicycles Sunday with Dale Tutkowski when two cars collided and one car *caromed* into the teacher." Joe Williams & Lisa Sink, "Pupils Who Saw Teacher Hurt Seek Comfort," *Milwaukee Sentinel*, 18 Oct. 1994, at A1.

LANGUAGE-CHANGE INDEX
careen in the sense "to move swervingly or lurchingly": Stage 5

caret. See **carat.**

cargo. Pl. *cargoes.* See PLURALS (D).

Caribbean is sometimes misspelled **Caribean* or **Carriban*. The pronunciation /kar-i-**bee**-ən/ is preferred because of its derivation from *Carib* /**kar**-ib/, the name of the native inhabitants of the islands that Christopher Columbus landed on and explored in 1493 (the Lesser Antilles) and of the northern coast of South America. The pronunciation /kə-**rib**-ee-ən/ is common, however, especially in BrE.

*caricature assassination. See **character assassination.**

*carmel. See **caramel.**

carnal knowledge. This is an old legal EUPHEMISM for sexual intercourse—dating back at least to the 17th century. The phrase is often paired, in references to rape, with *ravish*, a word that will strike some readers as romanticizing a horrible criminal act. (See **ravish**.) Except in quotations and historical references, the phrase *carnal knowledge* can be advantageously replaced by *sexual intercourse*.

carnivore, n. Pl. *carnivores* or (less commonly) *carnivora*. Believe it or not, the latter was predominant in print sources up to 1925. See PLURALS (B).

Current ratio (*carnivores* vs. *carnivora*): 13:1

carom. See **careen.**

carousel; carousal. A *carousel* (/**ka**-rə-sel/) is a carnival merry-go-round or, by extension, another machine that turns in a circle, such as a baggage carousel at an airport or the film-holder on a slide projector.

(*Carrousel is a variant spelling.) A carousal (/kə-**row**-zəl/) is a drunken spree.

The two spellings are occasionally confounded, almost always in the direction of -el's being erroneously changed to -al—e.g.:

- "While rocking horses and carousals [read carousels] abound in a second guestroom, they are outnumbered by dozens of toy mice peeking behind candlesticks and hanging from clocks throughout the house." Julie Landry, "Busy Fingers Decorate for Tour," Times-Picayune (New Orleans), 3 Dec. 1995, at G1.
- "Today they will dismantle the 40 horses, benches and other items that make up the carousal [read carousel]." David Connerty, "Nostalgia Loses," Portland Press Herald, 25 Mar. 1997, at B1.

LANGUAGE-CHANGE INDEX
carousal misused for carousel: Stage 1

carte blanche; *carta blanca. The French form, carte blanche (= free permission), is usual—not the Italian *carta blanca, which is a NEEDLESS VARIANT. The phrase, meaning literally "a white card," does not take an article—e.g.: "The team's owner gave the coach carte blanche to trade or waive players." It is pronounced /kahrt **blahnsh**/ or /**blahnch**/. The plural is cartes blanches (/kahrt(s) **blahnsh**/ or /**blahnch**/).

*carven, adj., is inferior to carved because it is a nontraditional revival of a Renaissance form and because it remains rare. E.g.: "Each feature was fine, attenuated, carven [read carved], the eyelids solemn and the mouth curved and cut like a fruit." Helen Simpson, "The Bed," Cosmopolitan, Jan. 1993, at 210.

LANGUAGE-CHANGE INDEX
*carven for carved: Stage 1
Current ratio: 32:1

caryatid (= a pillar in the shape of a female figure) is preferably pronounced /kar-ee-**at**-id/—not /**kar**-ee-ə-tid/, /kə-**rɪ**-ə-tid/, or /kar-ee-**ay**-tid/.

case. A. Generally. H.W. Fowler wrote of case: "There is perhaps no single word so freely resorted to as a trouble-saver, and consequently responsible for so much flabby writing" (FMEU1 at 65). Arthur Quiller-Couch condemned it as "jargon's dearest child." On the Art of Writing 106 (1916).

The offending phrases include in case (better made if), in cases in which (usually verbose for if, when, or whenever), in the case of (usually best deleted or reduced to in), and in every case (better made always, if possible). The word case especially leads to flabbiness when given different senses in the same passage—e.g.: "The popular image of a divorce case has long been that of a private detective skulking through the bushes outside a window with a telephoto lens, seeking a candid snapshot of the wife in flagrante delicto with a lover. Such is not exactly the case." Joseph C. Goulden, The Million Dollar Lawyers 41 (1978).

B. Meaning "argument." This meaning is commonplace and is no more objectionable than any other use of the word—e.g.:

- "Lincoln repeated his case from town to town in the seven debates with Douglas." Alfred Kazin, "A Forever Amazing Writer," N.Y. Times, 10 Dec. 1989, § 7, at 3.
- "With Tenet sitting behind him in the Security Council chamber last week, Powell made his case in a 77-minute speech interspersed with satellite photographs and recordings of intercepted communications." Kevin Whitelaw, "Prosecutor Powell," U.S. News & World Rep., 17 Feb. 2003, at 26.

This is the meaning of case in the title of the book (Making Your Case: The Art of Persuading Judges [2008]) by Justice Antonin Scalia together with me.

C. Grammatical Case. See PRONOUNS (B) & POSSESSIVES.

D. Meaning "lawsuit." In legal contexts, the word case can be especially slippery. When the word is simply equivalent to lawsuit, legal stylists tend to replace the word to avoid potential ambiguity. For example, in the sentence "In this case, the argument in favor of comparative negligence is at its strongest," does the writer mean (strictly) "in this lawsuit" or (more broadly) "in this type of circumstance"? Context may supply the answer, but if the first meaning is intended, it's best to eliminate the ambiguity by using lawsuit instead.

*cash money is a 19th-century REDUNDANCY that peaked in frequency of use during World War II and has persisted despite a sharp post-War decline—e.g.:

- "The deal also makes Wirtz cough up a pile of valuable cash money [read cash] (more valuable than oxygen) this year AND next year, making it nearly impossible to trade Roenick." Steve Rosenbloom, "Views from Out of Bounds," Chicago Trib., 9 Aug. 1996, Sports §, at 2.
- "He has decided to let Sotheby's turn [the bones] into cash money [read cash]." Don Singleton, "T-Rex New Kid on the Block," Daily News (N.Y.), 17 Nov. 1996, at 18.
- "If Jim McElwain is any example, should Mike Bobo bolt for greener (cash money [read cash]) pastures as soon as he has a 10-win season at CSU?" Benjamin Hochman & Mark Kiszla, "Who Has the Better Head Coaching Job?" Denver Post, 9 Aug. 2015, at C2.

-CAST. On the analogy of broadcast, many 20th-century NEOLOGISMS arose, such as cablecast (1975), podcast (2004), radiocast (1931), simulcast (1948), and telecast (1937). They are IRREGULAR VERBS (like cast itself) that don't change in the past tense. Adding -ed, though fairly common, is incorrect. For individual treatments, see **broadcast, cablecast, radiocast & telecast.**

cast > cast > cast. So inflected. *Casted is incorrect as a past-tense or past-participial form—e.g.:

- "For a week, the three men swapped fish tales, told ghost stories, baited hooks, casted [read cast] both fishing and song lines." John Harper, "Top Talent Creates 'Songs and

LANGUAGE-CHANGE INDEX (For the full key, see front matter pp. xxxi, l–li.)
Stage 1: Rejected. **Stage 2:** Widely shunned. **Stage 3:** Widespread but . . . **Stage 4:** Ubiquitous but . . . **Stage 5:** Fully accepted.
Invariably inferior forms marked by asterisk (*). • Ratios represent frequency of prevalent forms vs. variants in current books.

Legends' Recording," *Virginian-Pilot* (Norfolk), 2 June 1996, Carolina Coast §, at 22.
- "After 3½ weeks of pain and all kinds of diagnostic tests, the fracture was finally found and the foot *casted* [read *cast*] in plaster up to the knee." Regina Wachter, "Mom's Sprain Strains Family," *Newsday* (N.Y.), 21 Oct. 1996, at B14.

See -CAST & IRREGULAR VERBS.

There does seem to be a tendency to use **casted* when *cast* means "to supply with a lineup of actors," but this should be resisted—e.g.:
- "Hollywood honcho Frederick Golchan, the executive producer of the Richard Gere–Sharon Stone flick 'Intersection,' was in town the other day scouting locations for 'Kimberly.' Golchan's latest not-yet-*casted* [read *-cast*] project is about a woman coxswain who joins a men's rowing team." Gayle Fee & Laura Raposa, "Kerry's Lovelife a People-Pleaser," *Boston Herald*, 4 June 1996, at 19.
- "Klepper recently *casted* [read *cast*] the feature film 'Thinner,' based on Stephen King's book." "Casting Director Holds Workshops at Capital Rep," *Times Union* (Albany), 24 Oct. 1996, at B11.

LANGUAGE-CHANGE INDEX
*casted for *cast* as a past-tense form: Stage 1
Current ratio (*had cast* vs. **had casted*): 1,484:1

caster; castor. Several terms are represented by these spellings. What follows are the senses recommended for each spelling. *Caster* = (1) someone who casts something; (2) a small wheel fixed on the leg of a piece of furniture so that it may be pushed or pulled in any direction; or (3) a shaker for sprinkling sugar, salt, pepper, etc. *Castor* = (1) an oil made from castor beans (an Old World herb); (2) the herbivorous rodent normally termed *beaver*; (3) a beaver hat; or (4) the perfume ingredient gathered from dried beaver glands.

casual. See **causal (B).**

CASUALISMS. A. Generally. Some expressions characteristic of speech (but appearing also in writing) declare either freedom from inhibition or an utter lack of solemnity. They may add a relaxed freshness, or they may seem inappropriately unbuttoned. Although they overlap to some degree with SLANG, they can't always be so labeled. They make up the least formal type of STANDARD ENGLISH, and they're standard only in informal contexts. All the expressions that make up this peculiar subset of English are here termed *casualisms.*

Some of these are on the high side of informality because of their durability. Examples are using *if* to mean *whether* <getting the Boxster depends on if Daddy can afford the insurance> and using terms such as *junkie* (= a drug addict), *poppycock* (= nonsense), *Saturday night special* (= a small pistol), and *washout* (= a fiasco). One might find any of these expressions in informal contexts.

Expressions on the low side of informality often blend into slang, perhaps because the references tend to be uncivil or unpleasant, or to sound adolescent. Examples are referring to a person as a *wuss*, *dork* (or

dorkus maximus), or *poohead*, and referring to the act of vomiting as *hurling, blowing chunks, snapping your cookies, tossing your lunch,* or *talking on the great white telephone.*

Still other expressions are in the middle, such as *cave* for *cave in* <the child pleaded for 30 minutes for the doll, and finally her parents caved>, *futz around* (= to waste time), *gabfest* (= an event where people talk garrulously), *iffy* (= uncertain), *like* as a conjunction <like I said>, *put-up job* (= a deception), *way* used as a synonym for *totally* <way cool!>, *you guys* (a plural for *you*), and *zit* (= pimple).

B. Changes over Time. Like any other expressions, casualisms can undergo appreciation and depreciation. Because casualisms start at the low end of the linguistic spectrum, they typically appreciate in meaning if they move at all. Two words—*flu* and *butt*—illustrate this phenomenon. *Flu* began as an informal shortening of *influenza*, but gradually it took over as the main word to denote the disease. *Influenza* is now considered a hyperformal word; *flu* has become the ordinary word (no longer a true casualism).

Butt presents a different story. In reference to a person's posterior, it was considered rude, even slightly profane, in the mid-20th century. By the 1990s, when the baby boomers had come of age and had children of their own, many were shocked to find that PE teachers were having their children do "butt-lifts" (so called). A dictionary published in 2000 has a label that reads (quite accurately): "potentially offensive, although heard almost everywhere." Richard A. Spears, *NTC's Dictionary of American Slang and Colloquial Expressions* 61 (2000). So *butt* no longer gives offense? What a bummer.

This shifting of register is a recurrent phenomenon, as a linguist noted in the 1960s: "We know that colloquial usage is customarily twenty or thirty years ahead of formal usage and that the border marauders of today may well be the solid grammatical citizens of tomorrow." Dora Jean Ashe, "One Can Use an Indefinite 'You' Occasionally, Can't You?" in *A Linguistics Reader* 63, 65 (Graham Wilson ed., 1967).

C. Shortened Forms. *Butt*, of course, is a shortened form of *buttocks* (/bət-əks/). In fact, many casualisms are truncated words. Among the established terms in this category are *auto* (automobile), *bike* (bicycle), *bra* (brassiere), *deli* (delicatessen), *phone* (telephone), *plane* (airplane), *pub* (public house), *temp* (temporary employee), *tux* (tuxedo), and *zoo* (zoological gardens). All of these are high casualisms, being old and established.

Newer truncated forms tend to fall in the middle to low range. Examples abound:

bro (brother)
burbs (suburbs)
carb (carbohydrate)
carb (carburetor)
combo (combination)
cred (credibility)
cuke (cucumber)

fridge (refrigerator)
hood (neighborhood)
limo (limousine)
natch (naturally)
nuke (nuclear)
perp (perpetrator)
phenom (phenomenon)
rents (parents)
TV (television)
Vegas (Las Vegas)
veggies (vegetables)

More than ever before, shortenings take the form of acronyms and initialisms. They're also properly classifiable as casualisms, even when formally introduced the first time, as in "chief executive officer (CEO)." Once again, examples abound:

CFO (chief financial officer)
CIO (chief information officer)
COO (chief operating officer)
ER (emergency room)
HMO (health-maintenance organization)
HOV (high-occupancy vehicle)
ICU (intensive-care unit)
IME (independent medical examination)
IV (intravenous [tube])
OR (operating room)
PC (personal computer *or* political correctness)
SUV (sport-utility vehicle)
VIP (very important person)
VP (vice president)

See ABBREVIATIONS (A).

D. Proliferation. What accounts for the proliferation of casualisms in modern prose? There seem to be two main causes. First, casualisms reflect the ever-greater sense of speed in modern society. Clipped speech is faster speech. Second, manners have long been moving away from stiff formality, as the Evanses noted:

> Forty years ago it was considered courteous to use formal English in speaking to strangers, implying that they were solemn and important people. Today it is considered more flattering to address strangers as if they were one's intimate friends. This is a polite lie, of course; but it is today's good manners. Modern usage encourages informality wherever possible and reserves formality for very few occasions. [*DCAU* at vii]

Each generation seems a little less formal than the previous one. The Evanses themselves might have been shocked at the habit that today's receptionists and telephone solicitors have of immediately calling people by their first names. When the baby boomers are gone, people might marvel that this was ever considered unduly familiar.

The originator of the term *casualism*, by the way, was the estimable Theodore M. Bernstein, author of *The Careful Writer* (1965). Here's how he summed up his entry on the subject: "The designation *casualism* does not imply that the expression is necessarily unsuitable for serious writing. It is not a red light; it is an orange light" (p. 95).

casualty; *casuality. *Casuality is an obsolete NEEDLESS VARIANT of *casualty* (= [1] a person killed or hurt in a war or an accident; [2] a chance occurrence, esp. an unfortunate one; [3] the state of being casual; or [4] an incidental charge or source of income). Sometimes the British press seems to use both forms for INELEGANT VARIATION—e.g.: "Observers warned that *casualty* reports were unreliable because both sides tend to exaggerate the other's *casualities* [read *casualties*] while understating their own losses." "Turkish Troops Kill 72 Rebels," *Fin. Times*, 13 June 1996, at 2. In modern prose, *casuality is either a peculiarly common typographical error or else an affectation by those who erroneously believe Briticisms to be their "speciality." (See AMERICANISMS AND BRITICISMS.) The word itself is a kind of casualty—e.g.:

- "We suffered 49,151 *casualities* [read *casualties*] and 12,520 dead, the heaviest toll of the war in the Pacific." Letter of Mike Fancher, "The Atomic Bomb," *Atlanta J.-Const.*, 14 Aug. 2000, at A10.
- "One *casuality* [read *casualty*] is longtime Council Member Michael G. McGuire. Not only did he lose his seat on the Amherst Democratic Committee, but he also lost his place as a delegate to the state committee." Lisa Haarlander, "Infighting Leaves Democrats Scrambling to Regroup," *Buffalo News*, 14 Sept. 2000, at B3.
- "Howard Griffith is the latest *casuality* [read *casualty*], as he's out with a knee injury." Dan Caesar, "Rams Report," *St. Louis Post-Dispatch*, 15 Oct. 2000, at C8.

LANGUAGE-CHANGE INDEX
*casuality for *casualty*: Stage 1

cataclysm; cataclasm. The meanings of these words are fairly close, especially in figurative senses. A *cataclysm* is a tremendous flood or violent disaster. A *cataclasm* is a tearing down or disruption.

catalogue; catalog. Though librarians have come to use *catalog* with regularity, *catalogue* is still the better and the more frequent form in World English. *Cataloging* makes about as much sense as *plaging*. "If the professionals decline to restore the -*u*- to the inflected forms," wrote Wilson Follett in 1966, "let them simply double the -*g*-" (*MAU* at 97). But Follett's advice has largely fallen on deaf ears, and in AmE *catalog* and *cataloging* are now prevalent and seemingly unstoppable—e.g.: "There are eighty million boxes down there, all crammed full of paper and *uncataloged* [read *uncatalogued* or, in Follett's view, *uncatalogged*] gifts." Julie Kenner, *Carpe Demon* 241 (2005). Cf. **analog, apologue** & **epilogue**. For a comment on the decline of the -*ue* form, see -AGOG(UE).

catastrophe forms the plural *catastrophes*—not *catastrophies.

Current ratio: 71:1

catch fire; *catch on fire. The phrase *catch fire*, dating back to the 17th century, is about six times as common in print sources as *catch on fire, a late-19th-century

LANGUAGE-CHANGE INDEX (For the full key, see front matter pp. xxxi, l–li.)
Stage 1: Rejected. **Stage 2:** Widely shunned. **Stage 3:** Widespread but . . . **Stage 4:** Ubiquitous but . . . **Stage 5:** Fully accepted.
Invariably inferior forms marked by asterisk (*). • Ratios represent frequency of prevalent forms vs. variants in current books.

innovation that has hardly spread like wildfire. The word *on* is a needless particle—e.g.:

- "Tuesday night's lightning storms temporarily diverted attention for Piedmont when two power poles *caught on fire* [read *caught fire*] after lightning strikes." Duncan Murrell, "Power Crews See Light at End of Fran Outage," *Chapel Hill Herald*, 12 Sept. 1996, at 1.
- "Investigators believe Flight 592 *caught on fire* [read *caught fire*] after SabreTech, a ValuJet maintenance contractor, improperly packed and labeled some 150 oxygen generators." Elizabeth A. Marchak, "ValuJet Victims' Kin Fault Probe of Hazardous Cargo," *Plain Dealer* (Cleveland), 21 Nov. 1996, at A22.
- "We need to . . . keep[] water clean and healthy for humans and animals, and definitely not allow it to *catch on fire* [read *catch fire*] again." Ellen McNulty & Steve Filipek, "In Our Best Interest," *Ark. Democrat-Gaz.*, 21 Aug. 2015, at 17.

See PHRASAL VERBS.

LANGUAGE-CHANGE INDEX
catch on fire for *catch fire*: Stage 3
Current ratio: 6:1

catch-22; Hobson's choice. Not the same in good usage. *Catch-22* = an insoluble problem in which one must do something to do a second thing, which must be done before one can do the first thing. *Hobson's choice* = (1) a situation in which one is presented with only one "choice," and hence no choice at all; or (2) a situation in which either of one's two choices is bad. See **Hobson's choice.**

Catch-22 derives from the title of Joseph Heller's 1961 novel, in which by rule, you can't fly missions if you're crazy, but if you don't want to fly missions you're not crazy. Today the phrase is not treated as a proper noun, so the standard form is lowercase.

catchup. See **ketchup.**

categorically = without qualification. E.g.: "Sells, a half-Serb, *categorically* condemns the behavior of the Serbian political, military and literary elite." Istvan Deak, "With God on Their Sides," *New Republic*, 25 Nov. 1996, at 31.

For a MALAPROPISM involving this word, see ***uncategorically.**

category. So spelled. See SPELLING (A).

cater-corner(ed). See **catty-corner(ed).**

catholically; *catholicly. Both may mean either "with wide sympathies" or (when capitalized) "in a manner inclined toward Catholicism." No DIFFERENTIATION has emerged, but *catholically* (pronounced /kə-**thol**-ik-lee/) is about ten times as common as **catholicly*, which can now be branded a NEEDLESS VARIANT. That form, however, was predominant through the mid-19th century.

catsup. See **ketchup.**

catty-corner(ed); kitty-corner(ed); cater-corner(ed). These terms all mean "located at a diagonal." The original phrase, in Middle English, was *catre-cornered*

(lit., "four-cornered")—*catre* deriving from the Latin *quattuor*. Today the forms arrived at through folk etymology, *catty-corner* and *kitty-corner*, are by far the most common. (See ETYMOLOGY (D).) The form *cater-corner*, the preferred form in most dictionaries, is less common but not at all rare. Its past-participial forms are infrequent enough not to be recommended.

Current ratio (*kitty-corner* vs. *catty-corner* vs. *cater-corner*): 29:27:1
Current ratio (*catty-corner* vs. *catty-cornered*): 5:1

caucus, vb., makes *caucused* and *caucusing* in AmE and BrE alike. (See SPELLING (B).) The term is an Americanism.

cauldron; *caldron. The first is the preferred spelling in AmE and BrE alike—and has been so since about 1900. *Cauldron* outnumbers **caldron* by a 5-to-1 ratio in AmE print sources—e.g.:

- "Lebanon, under the rule of a despotic regime . . . , will continue to be a *cauldron* of unrest, criminality, terrorism and war." Daniel Nassif, "Syria's Control of Lebanon Is a Danger to All," *Wash. Times*, 15 Aug. 1996, at A19.
- "Chefs have been working for days, preparing *cauldrons* of a new dish called 'Boliche Suey,' to mark the occasion." Steve Otto, "Big Guava Taken by China!" *Tampa Trib.*, 1 July 1997, Metro §, at 1.
- "He remained in that competitive *cauldron* for 11 years." Stephen Seplow & Jonathan Storm, "Brandon Tartikoff, TV Wunderkind, Dead at 48," *Record* (N.J.), 28 Aug. 1997, at L9.

caulk; calk. *Caulk* = (1) vb., to fill (cracks or seams) in order to make airtight or watertight; or (2) n., the pastelike material used for this purpose (also known as *caulking*). *Calk* = (1) n., a piece fitted to a shoe (esp. a horseshoe) to prevent slipping; (2) vb., to fit with calks; or (3) vb., to injure with a calk. Both words are pronounced /kawk/ or /kok/.

Though *calk* is sometimes used for *caulk*, the words have undergone DIFFERENTIATION, so that the spellings should be distinguished according to the definitions above.

causal. A. And *causative*. These words, though unfortunately muddled by some writers, should be kept distinct. *Causal* = (1) of, relating to, or involving causes; entailing causation <they could find no causal connection between a missile and the crash>; or (2) arising from a cause <three causal conditions>. So in sense 1, the phrases *causal connection*, *causal link*, and *causal relationship* are SET PHRASES—e.g.:

- "The actual research now shows that the percentage of women with immune system-related diseases (such as lupus and scleroderma) is the same within the general population as within the breast implant population. In other words, there's no *causal connection*." Sandy Finestone, "Breast Implant Scare Has Lessons for Juries, Journalists," *Sacramento Bee*, 2 Sept. 1996, at B7.
- "The standard argument was that no scientifically accepted *causal link* between smoking and disease had been demonstrated." Ron Haybron, "Checking Studies to Make Sure They Are Needed," *Plain Dealer* (Cleveland), 30 Nov. 1997, at J10.

Causative = (1) operating as a cause; effective as a cause <various causative agents can result in the disease>; or (2) expressing a cause <causative phrase>. Hence one speaks of *causative agents, causative factors,* and *causative roles*—e.g.: "Wertheimer drove the streets of greater Denver searching for possible *causative* agents of childhood cancer." Gary Taubes, "Fields of Fear," *Atlantic Monthly,* Nov. 1994, at 94.

Causal is occasionally misused for *causative*—e.g.: "While apathy and fear of change allow the system to continue, two *causal* [read *causative*] agents are money and power." David Lassie, "Public School System Is a Liability," *Times* (Shreveport), 13 Aug. 2002, at A7.

The opposite mistake likewise appears—e.g.:

- "But Finn Posner, operations engineer with the state DOT's Bureau of Railroads, said there appeared to be no *causative* [read *causal*] link between the two occurrences." Peg Warner, "2 Hurt in Train–Truck Wreck," *Union Leader* (Manchester, N.H.), 2 Oct. 1996, at A1.
- "That means that underwriters would have to show a *causative* [read *causal*] connection between any failure to follow the code and a claimed loss." "Owner-Friendly Terms Herald a Sophisticated Insurance Market," *Bus. Times,* 20 Nov. 1996, at 1.

LANGUAGE-CHANGE INDEX
causative misused for *causal*: Stage 1
Current ratio (*causal link* vs. **causative link*): 35:1

B. And *casual*. What is *casual* is informal or relaxed <casual dress>, occasional <casual work>, or unstructured <a casual meeting>. The word has nothing to do with causation. It is a common typographical error to transpose the two middle letters in *causal* and *casual,* whichever one is being used—e.g.:

- "If your supervisor can show he gave other employees scheduling flexibility because they earned it with tenure and quality work, you need to prove a *casual* [read *causal*] relationship between voicing your concerns and his denial." Lynne Curry, "Workers Reporting Fraud Are Protected," *Anchorage Daily News,* 5 Aug. 2002, at E1.
- "Make sure employees know the difference between an appropriate *causal* [read *casual*] look and one that is inappropriate." Sarah Hale, "Groom Yourself for Success," *Orlando Sentinel,* 9 Sept. 2002, C.B. §, at 20.

Since the late 1970s, many books have mistakenly referred to **causal sex.* Was that a typographical error, or did it cause something (in which event it should be *causative*)? See METATHESIS.

LANGUAGE-CHANGE INDEX
casual misused for *causal*: Stage 1

causal determinism. See **fatalism.**

causality; causation. These words have a fine distinction. *Causality* = the principle of causal relationship; the relation of cause and effect <causality is a very large subject in philosophy>. *Causation* = (1) the causing or producing of an effect <multiple causation complicates the analysis>; or (2) the relation of cause and effect <the principles of causation weren't even considered>. True, sense 2 of *causation* overlaps with the meaning of *causality.* But generally that sense is best left to *causality.*

Causation should not be used for *cause*—e.g.: "Similarly, if affirmative action was the *causation* [read *cause*] of White male labor displacement, the unemployment statistics would reflect such displacement." Byron A. Ellis, "The Displacement Myth," *Baltimore Afro-Am.,* 5 Aug. 1995, at A5.

LANGUAGE-CHANGE INDEX
causation misused for *cause*: Stage 1
Current ratio (*was the cause of* vs.
*was the causation of): 7,800:1

causative. See **causal.**

cause célèbre (/kawz sə-**leb**/ or /kohz say-**leb**-rə/) does not mean "a famous cause or ideal," as it is sometimes used—e.g.:

- "This brief overview just scratches the surface of a tangle of rules and regulations that have accumulated since education reform became the *cause célèbre* [read *principal cause*] in politics 10 years ago." Ann Melvin, "School Reform Will Focus on Local Control," *Dallas Morning News,* 26 Nov. 1994, at A33.
- "To some fervent left-wingers, if you're not with them and their *cause célèbre* [read *cause*], you're against them." Richard A. Fisher, "We Must 'Reinvent Citizenship' by Using Non-Partisan Values," *Palm Beach Post,* 1 Dec. 1994, at A19.
- "While the drive to allow women members at Augusta National has become a national *cause célèbre* [read *cause*] in some quarters, there are more fundamental issues facing women golfers in Rhode Island." Paul Kenyon, "2 R.I. Women's Golf Groups Should Link Up," *Providence J.-Bull.,* 11 Sept. 2002, at D1.

The primary meaning has long been "a trial or decision in which the subject matter or the characters are unusual or sensational" (*Black's Law Dictionary* 266 [10th ed. 2014]). The term has been legitimately extended from the strict legal sense to mean "a famous or notorious person, thing, or event"—e.g.:

- "Her run-in with the law has made Blake a *cause célèbre* in the ranch country near Peyton, a tiny hamlet on old U.S. 24 northeast of Colorado Springs." Andy Van De Voorde, "Helicopter 54, Where Are You?" *Denver Westword,* 7 Dec. 1994, at 8.
- "As the first clear-cut case of a genetic difference in taste, this phenomenon became a sort of scientific *cause célèbre* in the 1930's and 1940's." John Willoughby, "Taste? Bud to Bud, Tongues May Differ," *N.Y. Times,* 7 Dec. 1994, at C1.
- "A few years ago, it would have been unimaginable that a shaken-baby case involving a British teenager, a family none of us had heard of before, and murky medical evidence would have become an international *cause célèbre.*" Eric Black, "The Gigastory and Its Lack of Greater Meaning," *Star Trib.* (Minneapolis), 13 Nov. 1997, at A24.

LANGUAGE-CHANGE INDEX
cause célèbre misused to mean
"famous cause": Stage 1

*cause . . . is due to. This phrasing is redundant—e.g.: "*The cause of crime is largely due to* [read *Crime results largely from* or *Crime is largely due to*] the loss of individual character." Cal Thomas, "Morals, Not Money, Cure Crime," *Cincinnati Enquirer*, 9 Aug. 1994, at A6. See **due to** & REDUNDANCY.

cautionary; cautious. *Cautionary* = encouraging or advising caution <cautionary signs>. *Cautious* = exercising caution <cautious drivers>.

cavalry. See **calvary.**

caveat (L. "let him beware") means, in ordinary speech and writing, merely "a warning"—e.g.:

- "One *caveat*: Don't keep topiaries out of a sunny spot for too long." Martha Stewart, "Make an Ornamental Statement—Shape a Topiary," *Dayton Daily News*, 17 Oct. 1996, Homelife §, at 7.
- "This reportedly would help about 10 percent of women. However, there are a few *caveats*. No drinking. And there's a risk of low blood pressure and fainting." Ann McFeatters, "Your Government at Work," *Ark. Democrat-Gaz.*, 22 Aug. 2015, at 16.

The word derives from the Latin phrase *caveat emptor* (= let the buyer beware), which is widely used—e.g.: "The old home-buying legal rule used to be '*caveat emptor!*' (let the buyer beware). But in 1984 a California Court of Appeal was the first to hold a home seller and real estate broker liable for damages to the buyer for failure to disclose unstable soils [that] caused severe home damage." Robert Bruss, "Disclosure, Insurance Help Sellers Avoid 'Bad-House' Lawsuits," *Chicago Trib.*, 7 Dec. 1996, New Homes §, at 2.

The traditional pronunciation of the word (/**kay**-vee-aht/) is far less common today than /**kav**-ee-aht/.

caviar (= the preserved roe of large fish, served as a delicacy) had become the standard spelling in AmE by 1915, and in BrE by 1965. Before that, *caviare* was standard in both those varieties of English.

Current ratio: 8:1

cavil, vb. (= to complain over a small point; carp), makes *caviled* and *caviling* in AmE, *cavilled* and *cavilling* in BrE. See SPELLING (B).

Caymanian; Cayman Islander. The first, pronounced /kay-**may**-nee-ən/, is standard; the second is a common variant. See DENIZEN LABELS.

Current ratio: 20:1

-CE; -CY. Choosing between these two endings can be tricky. Many nouns, of course, have comfortably settled into one form (*avoidance, coincidence, forbearance, intelligence*) or the other (*agency, constancy, decency, vacancy*). But some words can have both endings—and when they do, they often bear quite different meanings: *dependence, dependency; emergence, emergency; excellence, excellency.* When they don't (as in *buoyancy, buoyance*), one variant usually dominates (here, *buoyancy*). See DIFFERENTIATION.

Unfortunately, no general principles can be accurately deduced from the available specimens. The best advice is to stay alert to possible distinctions between spellings and to consult a good dictionary.

C.E. See **B.C.**

cease, a FORMAL WORD, can often be replaced by *stop* or *end*—e.g.:

- "The noises *ceased* [read *stopped*] after three or four nights, and we have not seen any raccoons for a week or so." Alan Lupo, "After Raccoon Revelry Comes the Cleanup," *Boston Globe*, 11 May 1995, at A1.
- "All the more reason Congress must *cease* [read *stop* or *end*] its partisan bickering and unambiguously back the president." "Saddam's Enablers," *N.Y. Post*, 18 Sept. 2002, at 28.

ceasefire, n. One word in both AmE and BrE.

cede; secede; concede. *Cede* = to give up, grant, admit, or surrender <by treaty, the tribe ceded about 20 million acres of aboriginal land>. *Secede* = to withdraw formally from membership or participation in <South Carolina was the first to secede from the United States>. *Concede* = (1) to admit to be true <I concede your point>; (2) to grant (as a right or a privilege) <in settlement, the landowner conceded a right-of-way to his neighbor>; or (3) to admit defeat (as in an election) <Dole conceded to Clinton in a gracious, moving way>.

CEDILLA. See DIACRITICAL MARKS.

ceiling, used in the sense of "maximum," is in itself unobjectionable but can sometimes lead to unfortunate mangled metaphors. E.g.: "The task force recommended *increasing* the *ceilings*." One *raises* a ceiling rather than *increases* it.

An English writer on usage quotes a preposterous example about "a ceiling price on carpets." In using words figuratively, of course, one must keep in mind their literal meanings. See METAPHORS.

celebrant. A. And *celebrator*. *Celebrant* best refers to a participant in a religious rite <the celebrant at the baptism>. *Celebrator* is the better word for someone who celebrates—e.g.: "Never let it be said that we last-minute *celebrators* have to be satisfied with the leftovers, the discards, the old and the ugly." Warren Berry, "Our Favorite Things," *Newsday* (N.Y.), 16 Dec. 2001, at H5.

Often, however, *celebrant* appears where *celebrator* would be the better word—e.g.: "Enzo & Lucia's Restaurant . . . will be open Wednesday just in time for New Year's Eve *celebrants* [read *celebrators*]." "The Briefs," *Daily Herald* (Chicago), 21 Dec. 2001, at 1. Cf. **confirmand.**

LANGUAGE-CHANGE INDEX
celebrant for "a participant in a celebration": Stage 3

B. *Funeral celebrants*. Although *celebrant* simply means "someone who performs a religious rite" and doesn't necessarily have anything to do with jubilation, its sound association makes it unfit for funeral contexts. Why invite tasteless jokes? That's the effect of saying that this or that religious figure will be the chief *celebrant* at a funeral—e.g.:

- "The Rev. Stephen Karani will *be the Celebrant of* [read *conduct*] Fanny's Funeral Mass." Virginia G. Canfield, "Fanny A. Fusco" (obit.), *Star-Gaz.* (Elmira, N.Y.), 11 Sept. 2002, at C4.
- "His Eminence Bernard Cardinal Law will *be the Principal Celebrant* [read *officiate*] in a funeral Mass at 11 a.m. tomorrow." "Rev. Robert Flagg of Brighton, Seminary Dean, at 63" (obit.), *Boston Herald*, 29 Sept. 2002, at 71.

So when a rite is for a sad occasion, it's better to avoid the word, even though one might say that the mourners are celebrating a life. Some reasonable people will consider *celebrant* in such a context offensive.

celebrator. See **celebrant (A).**

celibate. See **chaste (B).**

cello. This word is an 18th-century clipping of *violoncello*; until the late 20th century, it was often printed *'cello*. Today the form *cello*, without the apostrophe, is standard. See **violoncello.**

Since 1880, the standard English plural has been *cellos*, not **celli*.

> Current ratio (*cello* vs. *'cello*): 11:1
> Current ratio (*cellos* vs. **celli*): 13:1

cellphone, a shortened and telescoped form of *cellular telephone*, is increasingly so spelled. There is no good reason to retain the two-word version (*cell phone*), which necessitates hyphenating as a PHRASAL ADJECTIVE (e.g., *cell-phone use* as opposed to *cellphone use*). See CASUALISMS (C).

Celt; Celtic; *Kelt; *Keltic. The Boston *Celtics* will always be /**sel**-tiks/, but increasingly the early Britons (*Celts*) are called /kelts/, and the things relating to them are *Celtic* /**kel**-tik/. Historians generally prefer the /k/ sound. **Kelt* and **Keltic* are variant spellings.

> Current ratio (*Celts* vs. **Kelts*): 20:1
> Current ratio (*Celtic* vs. **Keltic*): 68:1

cement; concrete. These terms are not technically interchangeable because *cement* is a bonding agent that may be used to join discrete components such as bricks or the aggregate of water, sand, and other elements comprised in *concrete*. *Cement* is pronounced /sə-**ment**/—not /**see**-ment/. See PRONUNCIATION (B).

censor, n.; censer; sensor. The first of these homophones is someone who suppresses; the second is either the vessel in which incense is burned or the person who carries that vessel; the third is something that detects. To compare the nouns *censor* and *censure*, see **censor; censure (B).**

censor; censure. A. As Verbs. To *censor* (/**sen**-sər/) is to scrutinize and revise, to suppress or edit selectively. E.g.: "The news is severely *censored* by the Pentagon and the Arab information agency." Lucille Povero, "Local Newspaper Is the Best Hope of Getting the Truth," *St. Petersburg Times*, 11 Jan. 1991, City Times §, at 2.

To *censure* (/**sen**-shər/) is to criticize severely, to castigate. E.g.:

- "Acting on Steele's advice, majority members threatened to impeach Keefer, which they could not legally do, but settled for *censuring* her for betraying board confidences and lawyer-client communications." Roger Stuart, "School Board Censure Has Familiar Ring," *Pitt. Post-Gaz.*, 21 Nov. 1994, at B1.
- "Hyde was *censured* by the council two months ago after he admitted to violating the city ethics code." Wayne Snow, "Council to Consider Removing Planning Panel Member," *Atlanta J.-Const.*, 21 Nov. 1996, Extra §, at M6.
- "Among the tenured professor's supporters is the American Association of University Professors, a Washington-based academic group that has threatened to *censure* the university if Al-Adrian is dismissed." Courtenay Edelhart, "Prof Defends Expression of His Beliefs," *Indianapolis Star*, 12 Sept. 2002, at A34.

The word *censure* was widely mispronounced like *censor* in Congress during the impeachment proceedings against President Clinton (Dec. 1998–Jan. 1999), when *censure* was much discussed as a lesser measure against the President. The resulting misuse in print, common especially in the verb form, merits censure—e.g.:

- "House Ethics Chairman Jim Hansen . . . used his senior standing to nudge colleagues further toward impeachment and away from *censoring* [read *censuring*] the president." John Heilprin, "Utah Delegation Backs Airstrikes, Questions Timing," *Salt Lake Trib.*, 17 Dec. 1998, at A1.
- "Meanwhile, House Republicans may pay dearly for their magnificent obsession with William Jefferson Clinton. Once *censored* [read *censured*] or exonerated by the Senate, the president may extend an olive branch to the House." "We Can Wait," *News & Observer* (Raleigh), 29 Dec. 1998, at A10.

Sometimes the writer's intent becomes unclear—e.g.: "A production about her Bavarian adventure was so scandalous that the Lord Chamberlain, who *censured* [read *censored*, probably] plays, banned it." Michael Alpert, *London 1849: A Victorian Murder Story* 36 (2004). The reader can't be certain whether the lord routinely banned or panned plays.

> LANGUAGE-CHANGE INDEX
> *censor* misused for *censure*: Stage 2

B. As Nouns. *Censor*, n., = someone who inspects publications, films, and the like before they are released to ensure that they contain nothing heretical, libelous, or offensive to the government. Although it would be nice to pronounce this use of the term obsolete, censors remain prominent in some places. E.g.:

- "A movie made to finesse Chinese *censors* can easily slip through the grasp of Western audiences." Georgia Brown, "A Time to Live and a Time to Die," *Village Voice*, 22 Nov. 1994, at 64.
- "A recent American film, *Dangerous Game*, which stars Madonna and Harvey Keitel, has been banned by the film *censor*, Mr. Sheamus Smith." Michael Dwyer, "Madonna Film Is Banned by the Censor," *Irish Times*, 23 Nov. 1994, at 1.

LANGUAGE-CHANGE INDEX (For the full key, see front matter pp. xxxi, l–li.)
Stage 1: Rejected. **Stage 2:** Widely shunned. **Stage 3:** Widespread but . . . **Stage 4:** Ubiquitous but . . . **Stage 5:** Fully accepted.
Invariably inferior forms marked by asterisk (*). • Ratios represent frequency of prevalent forms vs. variants in current books.

- "Pentagon *censors* scrub TroopTube videos of sensitive footage, profanity, and other content that would be 'inappropriate for families,' [Lt. Col. Les] Melnyk says." Dan Ephron, "A Few Good Viral Videos," *Newsweek*, 24 Nov. 2008, at 10.

Censure, n., = (1) a judgment of condemnation; or (2) a serious reprimand. Sense 1: "There have long been calls to deny new livers to alcoholics as a form of moral *censure*." Froma Harrop, "Organ Transplants Raise the Issue of Medical Rationing," *Sacramento Bee*, 21 Nov. 1996, at B9. Sense 2: "Mack and O'Dell voted against *censure*, which Tobolski said applies to the one incident and can be repeated if legislators do not like Mack's comments." Donna Snyder, "Legislator Censured for Calling Leadership Corrupt," *Buffalo News*, 9 Jan. 1997, at C5.

censorious; censorial. *Censorious* (= severely critical) is the adjective corresponding to the verb *censure*, not *censor*. E.g.: "Ah well, it was no business of Cadfael's, nor had he any intention of getting involved. He did not feel particularly *censorious*." Ellis Peters, "The Price of Light," in *A Rare Benedictine* 45, 59 (1988). *Censorial* describes the work or attitude of a censor. The two words are occasionally confounded—e.g.: "'I suspect,' William added, 'that this was Shakespeare's [expurgated] copy for the Master of the Revels. He wished to be free of the Master's *censorious* [read *censorial*] pen.'" Peter Ackroyd, *The Lambs of London* 100 (2006).

LANGUAGE-CHANGE INDEX
censorious misused for *censorial*: Stage 1

censorship (= the practice or institution of suppressing the expression of ideas thought to be uncongenial to those in power) is a word whose mention in AmE immediately brings up the First Amendment. It is one of those politically charged VOGUE WORDS that people use irresponsibly. It shouldn't mean simply the denial of governmental largesse; that is, an artist who is denied federal subsidies is not the object of censorship. The word should refer to active suppression, not merely lack of support.

censure. See **censor.**

centennial; centenary. In all the anniversary designations (*bi-*, *sesqui-*, etc.), whether used as adjectives or as nouns, the *-ial* forms are preferred in AmE, the *-ary* forms in BrE.

center; centre. The first is the AmE spelling, the second the BrE. See -ER (B).

***center around.** Something can *center on* (avoid *upon*) or *revolve around* something else, but it cannot **center around* because the center is technically a single point. The solecism, which began spreading in the early 19th century, is now common—e.g.:

- "They said the debate now *centers around* [read *centers on* or *revolves around*] what price Sandoval should pay for her mistake." Annie Hill, "Young Mother Sobs as Trial Begins in Tot's Suffocation," *Denver Post*, 5 Nov. 1996, at B3.
- "The title story, which concludes the section, *centers around* [read *centers on* or *revolves around*] another strong

male narrator." Annette Sanford, "Gusher Days," *Dallas Morning News*, 12 Jan. 1997, at J8.
- "It *centers around* [read *centers on* or *revolves around*] the story of an attorney, Atticus Finch, appointed to defend a black man named Tom Robinson, who is accused of raping a white woman." Frances Hubbard, "Actress Discusses 'To Kill a Mockingbird' Role," *Daily Press* (Newport News, Va.), 22 Aug. 2015, at A5.

LANGUAGE-CHANGE INDEX
center around for *center on* or *revolve around*: Stage 3
Current ratio (*centering on* vs.
centering around): 4:1

centi-. See **hecto-.**

centimeter (/**sen**-ti-mee-tər/) is sometimes, in medical JARGON, given a precious pronunciation: /**son**-ti-mee-tər/. Avoid this.

centre. See **center.**

centripetal; centrifugal. The key to sorting out these science-related adjectives can be found in the Latin roots added to *centri-* (= center). *Petere* (= to go toward; to seek) survives in words such as *impetus* and *compete*. *Fugere* (= to go away from; to flee) survives in words such as *fugitive* and *refuge*. Hence, *centripetal force* attracts something toward the center (think of a falling object pulled by gravity), while *centrifugal force* repels something away from the center (think of riders on a merry-go-round).

Here, the words are used in their traditional, literal senses:

- "There is nothing you can shoot on a satellite that will 'cut the string' and it will fall out of the sky. The 'string' is *centripetal* force, that balances the gravity pulling down with the satellite's own speed of motion." Patrick J. O'Connor, "China Missile Adds to Space Junk, Risks," *Chicago Sun-Times*, 29 Jan. 2007, Editorial §, at 34.
- "When uranium, in the form of uranium hexafluoride gas, is fed into the cylinder, *centrifugal* forces push it outward against the spinning wall." Dan Charles, "U.S. Centrifuge Work Revived in Updated Form," *Wash. Post*, 23 Apr. 2007, at A6.

The words can also bear figurative senses, to mean "tending to unite" (*centripetal*) and "tending to pull apart" (*centrifugal*)—e.g.:

- "[Wal-Mart] is *centripetal* in the lives of millions who shop there, work there, manufacture goods sold there or who formerly worked for—or owned—the competition." Donna Marchetti, "What Made Us a Nation of Wall-to-Wall Wal-Marts?" *Plain Dealer* (Cleveland), 31 Jan. 2007, at E2.
- "Over the long term, governments usually find it in their interest to bridge the *centrifugal* forces of diversity rather than to exploit them, if only to promote stability." Eduardo Porter, "The Divisions That Tighten the Purse Strings," *N.Y. Times*, 29 Apr. 2007, § 3, at 4.

Yet because *centripetal* is a more obscure term than *centrifugal*, using a replacement word would clarify the meaning. The Wal-Mart example above might have benefited from substituting *central* for the highfalutin *centripetal*.

Writers sometimes misuse *centripetal* for *centrifugal*—e.g.:

- "[Niall] Ferguson observes that many nation-states that emerged out of the wreckage of the Ottoman Empire, from Yugoslavia to Iraq, were able to contain those conflicts by ruthless repression. *Centripetal* [read *Centrifugal* or, better, *Factious*] energies often exploded once the dictator died or was toppled." James Traub, "The Way We Live Now," *N.Y. Times*, 10 Dec. 2006, Mag. §, at 19.
- "Cleverly, subtly, [Colm] Toibin explores the tensions of this expanding world through the relationship between mothers and sons. The *centripetal* [read *centrifugal* or, better, *divisive*] force of prosperity peels and tears at them." John Freeman, "A Credit to a Grand Tradition," *Hartford Courant*, 28 Jan. 2007, at G4.

See WORD-SWAPPING.

LANGUAGE-CHANGE INDEX
centripetal misused for *centrifugal*: Stage 1

CENTURY DESCRIPTIONS. Some of us, apparently, forget from time to time that *19th century* describes the 1800s, that *18th century* describes the 1700s, and so on. Take, for example, R.B. Collins's article titled "Can an Indian Tribe Recover Land Illegally Taken in the Seventeenth Century?" 1984–1985 *Preview of United States Supreme Court Cases* no. 8, p. 179 (18 Jan. 1985), which discusses land acquired by New York from the Oneida Indians in 1795. The title should refer to the 18th century, not the 17th.

What particular years make up the course of a century has also caused confusion. Strictly speaking, since the first century ran from A.D. 1 through 100, every century begins with a year ending in the digits 01. The last year of a century ends in 00. But the popular mind has moved everything back a year, in the belief that 2000 marked the beginning of the 21st century. This confusion is unfortunate but seemingly ineradicable.

One other point merits our attention. As compound adjectives, the phrases denoting centuries are hyphenated; but they are not hyphenated as nouns. Hence, "The 12th-century records were discovered in the 19th century." See PHRASAL ADJECTIVES (A) & (G).

cerebral. In AmE this word is pronounced /sə-**ree**-brəl/ in all contexts except one—the phrase *cerebral palsy*, which is most often pronounced /**ser**-ə-brəl **pahl**-zee/. This exception derives from an old pronunciation of *cerebral*: in the early 1900s, the preference was for the first syllable to be accented.

ceremonial; ceremonious. The DIFFERENTIATION between these words lies more in application than in meaning; both suggest a punctilio in following the customs and trappings of ceremony. *Ceremonial* is the general word relating to all manner of ceremonies, but is used only in reference to things—e.g.:

- "Don Larsen, who pitched the only perfect game in World Series history, threw out the *ceremonial* first pitch." Don

Bostrom, "'Big Daddy' Is the Big Bopper for Yanks in Post-Season," *Morning Call* (Allentown, Pa.), 22 Oct. 1996, at C7.
- "A Catholic priest's *ceremonial* robe apparently protected him from harm Friday when a woman shot him three times in the chest with a pellet gun." "Priest Shot with Pellet Gun as He Gives Communion," *Orlando Sentinel*, 23 Nov. 1996, at A20.

Ceremonious, a less common and mildly disparaging word, suggests an overdone formality. It is used in reference both to people and to things—e.g.:

- "Never sentimental or *ceremonious*, [Bernard] Witkin wrote a $10,000 check a couple of years ago to Rod Duncan, an Alameda County judge facing a recall campaign." Claire Cooper, "Witkin Left Legacy in Law, Philanthropy," *Sacramento Bee*, 29 Dec. 1995, at A3.
- "Walking the plank would have been too *ceremonious* for the real pirates, who much preferred slicing their victims up in redblooded swordplay." Donna Marchetti, "Real Pirates Were Not Swashbuckling," *Plain Dealer* (Cleveland), 27 Oct. 1996, at I11.

The word is more often seen in its negative adverbial form, *unceremoniously*, where it means "without fanfare"—e.g.: "He has always been a fan favorite and has *unceremoniously* given plenty back to the community." David Dupree, "'Glove' Fits Better Now than Ever," *USA Today*, 5 Apr. 2002, at C3. It typically connotes abruptness and disrespect—e.g.: "That's how he learned he'd been *unceremoniously* cut from the preseason roster of a team with one of the strangest nicknames he'd ever heard—the Piranhas." Carlton Stowers, "Desperate Measures," *Dallas Observer*, 4 Apr. 2002, at 21.

certainty; certitude. *Certainty* = (1) an undoubted fact; or (2) absolute conviction. Sense 2 is very close to that reserved for *certitude*, which means "the quality of feeling certain or convinced." E.g.:

- "The decision that thrust the world into the nuclear age and cast doubt on the moral *certitude* of the United States still has the power to incite bitter and contentious debate." Andrea Ston, "Dissecting a Decision That Shook the World," *USA Today*, 27 July 1995, at A4.
- "Walter Winchell felt an unambiguous *certitude* in his words and wanted them published in the *Washington Times Herald*, where President Franklin D. Roosevelt and other national leaders could learn from them." A.E.P. Wall, "Library's Failure to Provide Pornography Is Not Censorship," *Orlando Sentinel*, 11 Mar. 1997, at A11.

Justice Oliver Wendell Holmes stated, rather memorably, "*Certitude* is not the test of *certainty*. We have been cock-sure of many things that were not so." "Natural Law," in *Collected Legal Papers* 311 (1920). Other writers sometimes echo this aphorism—e.g.: "He was the sort of thinker for whom (to borrow a phrase of Oliver Wendell Holmes) *certitude* was the only proof that *certainty* required." Louis Menand, "James Family Values," *New Republic*, 18 Dec. 1995, at 29.

---

cesarean section; caesarean section. The first is the standard spelling in AmE for the term denoting the surgical procedure for delivering a baby—with a lowercase *c*-. In BrE the spelling *caesarean section* has predominated since the early 1990s. Apart from surgical birthing, *Caesarean* is the adjective meaning "of, relating to, or involving Caesar"; **Caesarian*, **Cesarean*, and **Cesarian* are variant spellings of *Caesarean*.

cession. See **session.**

ceteris paribus (= other things being equal or the same) is, for the most part, an unnecessary LATINISM. Other things being equal, the common English phrase is better—e.g.:

- "The revenues from the charges can be used either to reduce other taxes or to increase government expenditures on desirable activities without, *ceteris paribus* [read *assuming no other changes*], any further increase in taxes." Wilfred Beckerman, "Beware Rules and Regulations," *New Statesman & Soc'y*, 22 Mar. 1996, at 29.
- "Moreover, even if current growth rates are maintained, Argentina is simply not going to develop its way out of the problem, *ceteris paribus* [delete the phrase, which comes as a WEASEL WORD at the end]." Roger Fontaine, "Argentina's Winter of Discontentment," *Wash. Times*, 28 Aug. 1996, at A19.
- "These forecasts are *ceteris paribus*—'other things held constant.'" Michael R. King, "The BoC's Oil Price Strategy," *Globe & Mail* (Toronto), 25 May 2015, at B4. (A possible revision: *These forecasts assume that other factors will remain constant.*)

In English the phrase is pronounced /**set**-ə-ris **pa**-ri-bəs/. Cf. *mutatis mutandis.* See SESQUIPEDALITY.

Ceylonese. See **Sri Lankan.**

chad. As the world came to know in the protracted aftermath of the 2000 U.S. presidential election, *chad* is the debris left behind when computer data cards are punched. After emerging in the 1950s, the word was always a mass noun: a pile of thousands of them was just called the *chad* (similar to *chaff*)—e.g.: "The problem with punch cards is hanging *chad*, or little bits of paper that cling to the ballot after being punched out, Clem said." Michael Kaiser, "Canvassing Board to Consider Recount Request," *Press J.* (Vero Beach, Fla.), 7 Oct. 2000, at A5. See COUNT NOUNS AND MASS NOUNS.

Until the Florida re-count controversy that followed the 2000 election, there was no need to address the tiny remnants individually. But when the little pieces of paper were individually examined, sometimes with magnifying glasses, *chad* suddenly became a singular count noun with a plural form (*chads*)—e.g.: "Dade elections supervisor David Leahy said a likely reason for the newly found votes were 'hanging *chads*'—the little paper squares that voters punch through to cast a vote." Steve Bousquet, Phil Long & Lesley Clark, "As Florida Recounts, Bush Lead Shrinks to Less than 1,000 Votes," *Miami Herald*, 9 Nov. 2000, at A1. (Note the subject–verb agreement problem in *reason . . . were.* A suggested revision: *David Leahy said the newly found votes probably resulted from "hanging chads"* (etc.). See SUBJECT–VERB AGREEMENT (B).)

chagrin, vb. See SPELLING (B).

chairman; chairwoman; *chairperson; chair. Sensitivity to SEXISM impels many writers to use *chair* rather than *chairman*, on the theory that doing so avoids gender bias. E.g.: "Jeanie Austin [is the] former national *co-chair* of the RNC." Dan Balz, "Race for Top GOP Post Has Real Campaign Feel," *Wash. Post*, 16 Jan. 1997, at A4. Certainly *chair* is better than **chairperson*, which is widely considered an ugly and trendy word.

Many readers and writers continue to believe, however, that there is nothing incongruous in having a female *chairman*, since *-man* has historically been sexually colorless. Hence in 1967, *chairman* was paired with *he or she*: "The Lord Chancellor, following up his proposals about the retiring age for justices, has announced that no one may be elected *chairman* after he or she has reached the age of 70, though existing *chairmen* may continue." R.M. Jackson, *The Machinery of Justice in England* 187 (5th ed. 1967).

In journalistic sources in the 1990s, *chairman* outnumbered **chairperson* by a 100-to-1 margin. Even so, the consciously nonsexist forms are gaining ground and may well prevail within the next couple of decades. If we're to have a substitute wording, we ought to ensure that *chair* and not **chairperson* becomes the standard term—e.g.: "Mrs. Berman was instrumental in founding the Rhode Island State Nurses Association, District One, and served as *chairperson* [read *chair*] for the Tucks Scholarship Fund." "Sara Ruth Berman" (obit.), *Providence J.-Bull.*, 15 Jan. 1997, at C6. Some criticize this usage of *chair* as both ugly and absurd, arguing that a *chair* is a piece of furniture. In fact, though, *chair* is not a recent coinage, but a parliamentary term that dates to the mid-17th century.

One caveat: if we adopt a term such as *chair*, it must be used in reference to males and females alike. In recent years, there has been a lamentable tendency to have female *chairs* (or **chairpersons*) and male *chairmen*. That is no better than having *chairwomen* and *chairmen*. After all, in most circumstances in which people lead committees, the sex of the leader is irrelevant. See SEXISM (C).

LANGUAGE-CHANGE INDEX
1. **chairperson* as a gender-neutral term: Stage 2
Current ratio (*chairman* vs. **chairperson*): 13:1
2. *chair* as a gender-neutral term: Stage 5
Current ratio (*chair of the committee* vs. **chairperson of the committee*): 4:1

chaise longue (/shayz **long**/ or /**lawng**/), meaning "a couchlike chair," forms the anglicized plural *chaise longues*—no longer **chaises longues*. That has been true since the 1930s. See PLURALS (B).

Many people commit the embarrassing error of saying or writing **chaise lounge*—e.g.: "Resin manufacturers are now trying to shatter their low-rent stereotype with ambitious new designs like folding deck chairs and *chaise lounges* [read *chaise longues*] in designer colors like hunter green." Andrew Page, "More than Just Monoblock, Resin Furniture Moves Upmarket," *Nat'l Home Center News*, 7 Aug. 1995, at LG32. The problem is that *lounge*, when put after *chaise*, looks distinctly low-rent. See METATHESIS.

LANGUAGE-CHANGE INDEX
chaise lounge for *chaise longue*: Stage 3
Current ratio (*chaise longue* vs. *chaise lounge*): 1.4:1

challenged. On the use of this adjective to mean "disabled" or "handicapped" <physically challenged>, see EUPHEMISMS.

chamois. When referring to the leather, this word is pronounced /**sham**-ee/. (It has the variant spellings **chammy*, **shammy*, **shamois*, and **shamoy*.) But when referring to the goatlike antelope, the word may be pronounced either that way or /sham-**wah**/.

chamomile (= a fragrant plant whose flowers are used for making tea) is the standard spelling. **Camomile* is a variant. Whatever the spelling, the word is pronounced either /**kam**-ə-mıl/ or /**kam**-ə-meel/.

Current ratio (*chamomile* vs. **camomile*): 4:1

champ; chomp. The original term for what horses do to their bits is *champ*. *Chomp* is an American variant.

The idiom *champing at the bit* evokes the image of an impatient horse, especially one eager for a race to start. In contemporary print sources, *champing at the bit* predominates only in BrE; since the mid-1990s, *chomping at the bit* has become preeminent in AmE. Either phrase, though, must suggest a kind of friskiness that is absent in the following example: "Visitors tie their horses and the animals peacefully *champ* [read *chew*?] their bits." "Forging a Career Around Horses," *Tulsa World*, 30 May 1999, Bus. §, at 1.

Otherwise, the two verbs have undergone some degree of DIFFERENTIATION. What one *champs* is not actually eaten, but just bitten or gnawed, nervously. But to *chomp* something is to take a bite out of it and usually to consume it: in DIALECT, *chomp* is colloquially accompanied by the adverb *down* <chompin' down catfish>.

LANGUAGE-CHANGE INDEX
chomping at the bit for *champing at the bit*: Stage 5
Current ratio (*chomping* vs. *champing at the bit*): 15:1

channel, vb.; **channelize.* Because no real DIFFERENTIATION has developed between these terms, **channelize* ought to be branded a NEEDLESS VARIANT. *Channel*, the usual term, means (1) "to form channels in, to groove"; (2) "to guide"; or (3) "to act as a medium through whom the dead (or absent) supposedly speak." It makes *channeled* and *channeling* in AmE, *channelled* and *channelling* in BrE. See SPELLING (B).

Current ratio (*channeled* vs. **channelized*): 15:1

Chanukah. See **Hanukkah.**

chaotic. See **inchoate.**

chaperon (= a person, esp. an elder, who accompanies others, esp. youngsters, to ensure good conduct) was the standard spelling from the 18th century to about 1950—after the French etymon of the same spelling. *Chaperone* began as a variant form apparently misspelled as a result of the (correct) long *-o-* in the final syllable. That is, because the word is pronounced /**shap**-ə-rohn/ or /shap-ə-**rohn**/, some writers mistakenly added the final vowel, and by 1970 that form was predominant in both AmE and BrE print sources. Although most dictionaries still list *chaperone* as only a secondary variant, it is unquestionably now standard—e.g.:

- "When the Mall of America in Bloomington, Minn., . . . announced a curfew and *chaperone* [read *chaperon*] policy for adolescents in September, teenagers seemed well on their way to becoming pariahs." Ann Hulbert, "Politicians, Like, Really on Teens' Case," *USA Today*, 21 Nov. 1996, at A15.
- "A *chaperone* [read *chaperon*] (the word baby sitter was discreetly avoided) was hired to look after the children on tour." Ted Lambert, "Back to Experimental Theater and Back to Ancient Troy," *N.Y. Times*, 8 Dec. 1996, § 2, at 5.

In 2003, the lexicographers at Merriam-Webster reversed the positions of *chaperon* and *chaperone*, for the first time giving the variant form primacy in their *W11*. The editors of *NOAD* soon followed suit. And so what had once been a misspelling became the established norm, aided and abetted by the not entirely somnifacient Broadway musical *The Drowsy Chaperone* (2001).

LANGUAGE-CHANGE INDEX
chaperon spelled as *chaperone*: Stage 5
Current ratio (*chaperone* vs. *chaperon*): 3:1

chaplaincy; **chaplainship.* Though common in the 18th century, the latter is now a NEEDLESS VARIANT.
Current ratio: 72:1

character; reputation. Very simply, the semantic distinction is that *character* is what one is, whereas *reputation* is what one is thought by others to be.

character assassination (= defamation, esp. to create public distrust), a phrase that gained prominence in the mid-20th century, is sometimes rendered **caricature assassination*, usually for comic effect—e.g.: "I limited my comments to what I objected to the most—the line drawing, which I referred to as '*caricature assassination.*'" Laurence H. Meyer (quoted by Keith J. Kelly in "After Self-Assessment, Conde Springs for Redesign," *N.Y. Post*, 7 July 2004, at 32).

At other times, though, the phrase is mangled into a MONDEGREEN—e.g.: "[Tom] DeLay spokesman Jonathan Grella released a statement that accused Democrats of '*caricature assassination*' [read

LANGUAGE-CHANGE INDEX (For the full key, see front matter pp. xxxi, l–li.)
Stage 1: Rejected. **Stage 2:** Widely shunned. **Stage 3:** Widespread but . . . **Stage 4:** Ubiquitous but . . . **Stage 5:** Fully accepted.
Invariably inferior forms marked by asterisk (*). • Ratios represent frequency of prevalent forms vs. variants in current books.

'character assassination']." Hans Nichols & Jonathan E. Kaplan, "We Could Have Nixed It, Say Dems," *The Hill*, 15 June 2004, at 1.

LANGUAGE-CHANGE INDEX
*caricature assassination for *character assassination*: Stage 1

charge, n. & v.t. **A. In the Sense "accusation."** To write that someone has been *accused* of a *charge* is a REDUNDANCY. E.g.: "On May 1, Jackson, the former captain of the women's track team, and the other women went to the Navy Yard in Washington to testify at an Article 32 hearing, the military's version of a grand jury. That night, *she was accused of a charge of her own* [read *she herself was accused* or *she herself was charged with an offense*]." JoAnna Daemmrich, "Mid Charged with Lying," *Baltimore Sun*, 3 June 1996, at B1. See **accuse.**

B. Active and Passive Use. *In charge of* can have either an active or a passive sense—e.g.:

- "The farmhand was left *in charge of* the livestock."
- "The livestock were left *in charge of* the farmhand."

But the usual passive wording is *in the charge of*, which prevents any possible ambiguities. E.g.: "The truck was *in charge of* [read *in the charge of*] Mack Free, who was instructed not to permit any person to ride upon or drive it." To one not accustomed to *in charge of* in the passive construction, the subject and object appear to have been confused—the sentence seems to say that the truck had authority over Mack Free. One more example: "It had been the practice in Texas to assign a Pullman conductor to trains with two or more sleeping cars, while in trains with only one sleeping car that car was *in charge of* [read *in the charge of*] a porter."

chargeable. So spelled—not **chargable*. See MUTE E.

Current ratio: 309:1

chargé d'affaires. Pl. *chargés d'affaires.* See PLURALS (B).

charivari; *shivaree; *chivaree; *charivaree. It's not customary now for friends and family to serenade a wedding couple with a boisterous clanging of kettles and blowing of horns. But when it does happen, the standard term for it is *charivari* (from French, deriving from medieval Latin *caribaria* "headache"). The others are variant forms. In English, the term is conventionally pronounced /shiv-ə-**ree**/.

Current ratio (for first three headwords): 21:3:1

charted. For the mistake of writing **unchartered territory* instead of *uncharted territory*, see **uncharted.**

chartered plane, not **charter plane*, is the traditional form. One specially hires an airplane, ship, bus, or the like by a contract known as a *charter*. Once the contract is in place, the means of conveyance has been *chartered*. During the 20th century, speakers and writers increasingly dropped the *-ed*, but this is neither the best nor the most frequent usage—e.g.: "Scott McInnis, a Colorado representative whose home district is larger than Florida, rides tiny *charter* [read *chartered*]

planes between several far-flung stops." "Sallying Fourth," *N.Y. Times*, 29 June 1997, § 6, at 13.

LANGUAGE-CHANGE INDEX
*charter plane for *chartered plane*: Stage 4
Current ratio (*a chartered plane* vs.
*a charter plane): 2:1

chary (= cautious) is a FORMAL WORD close in meaning to *wary* (and rhyming with it)—e.g.: "Indonesia, once *chary* of foreign investment, is now worried about losing out to China, Vietnam and other countries." Andrew Pollack, "Companies Rediscovering Indonesia," *N.Y. Times*, 6 Dec. 1994, at D1. The word sometimes implies "sparing, ungenerous" <chary of praise>.

chasm is pronounced /**kaz**-əm/.

chassis. Pl. *chassis*—preferably not **chassises.*

chaste. A. And Gender. *Chaste* (= untainted by unlawful sexual intercourse; virtuous; sexually continent) is a word that applies to males and females alike. E.g.: "As a young and *chaste* boy, Yava said, he would often be called on to help construct the sand painting, lending the power of his purity." Barbara Yost, "Navajos Seek Answer with Help of Old Ways," *Phoenix Gaz.*, 4 June 1993, at A2.

Unfortunately, however, a bias pervades the word's usual applications so that it typically refers to women and girls. E.g.:

- "One view is that a fallen woman who has fully reformed is *chaste*, while another is that chastity before marriage means physical virginity—a woman can be seduced only once. There is nothing unchaste about marital intercourse and hence, under either view, a widow or divorcee may be an unmarried female of previously *chaste* character." Rollin M. Perkins & Ronald N. Boyce, *Criminal Law* 463–64 (3d ed. 1982).
- "President Jackson told the Cabinet that Peggy was '*chaste* as a virgin,' to which Mr. Clay replied, 'Age cannot wither nor time stale her *infinite* virginity!'" "Speakers and Spleen," *Courier-J.* (Louisville), 7 Dec. 1994, at A10.

B. And *celibate*. There is also some confusion about the sense of *chaste*, as opposed to *celibate*. A person who is *chaste* is innocent of unlawful sex—that is, does not engage in sex with anyone other than the person's spouse. So in both secular law and church law, a person who frequently has sex, but only with his or her spouse, is chaste. By contrast, a person who is *celibate* (in the word's original sense and still the only definition in the *OED*) abstains from marrying—and sex, too, but only as a consequence of the choice not to marry. The times have passed that meaning by, and today this traditional sense is obsolescent at best. It may remain current with the vow of celibacy that Catholic priests make (i.e., a promise not to marry). But it is almost universally understood, even in that context, to mean "abstaining from sex"—e.g.: "His case underscores the growing debate within the church over whether there is a place in the priesthood for gay men, even *celibate* ones." Sacha Pfeiffer, "Crisis in the Church," *Boston Globe*, 25 Nov. 2002, at A1.

And while many word extensions result in the loss of a useful and unique term, here the shift in meaning of *celibate* has resulted in the creation of a term that has no good substitute—especially since *chaste* sounds archaic, carries outdated connotations about sex, and has drifted toward becoming gender-specific. It would be difficult, for example, to replace *celibate* in the example above gracefully.

chasten; chastise. These words are close in meaning, but distinct. *Chasten* = to discipline, restrain, punish, subdue. *Chastise* = (1) to punish, thrash; or (2) to castigate, criticize.

Chastise is so spelled; **chastize* is incorrect but not uncommon. See -IZE.

Current ratio (*chastise* vs. **chastize*): 66:1

chauvinism. A. Generally. Traditionally, *chauvinism* (/**shoh**-və-niz-əm/) refers to fanatical patriotism. The word's eponym is Nicolas Chauvin, a French soldier who was ridiculed for being excessively devoted to Napoleon.

By metaphorical extension, the word has been broadened to denote exaggerated belief in the superiority of any group, class, or cause. Today *male chauvinism*, which (as a phrase, not a phenomenon) dates back to the late 1960s, is something of a CLICHÉ, being the word's most frequent application—e.g.: "In 1999, the socialist-feminist magazine *Mother Jones*, hardly a bastion of *male chauvinism*, reported that 'women report using violence in their relationships more often than men' and 'wives hit their husbands at least as often as husbands hit their wives.'" Stephen Baskerville, "A Tool Kit to Destroy Families," *Wash. Times*, 9 Dec. 2001, at B5.

Indeed, some writers have come to use *chauvinism* as if it were synonymous with *male chauvinism*—e.g.:

- "But a year later, as feminism reached even West Peoria, women began complaining about *chauvinism*." Phil Luciano, "Mike's Bar Stands Test of the Times," *Peoria J. Star*, 31 Oct. 2001, at B1.
- "Madonna says that her husband doesn't like her wearing see-through tops and tells her not to look like a slapper. Instead of being affronted, she's clearly delighted by his *chauvinism*." Lynda Lee-Potter, "Brash, Brave and a Boost for the Feisty Over-Forties," *Daily Mail*, 28 Nov. 2001, at 13.
- "*Chauvinism* remains in abundant supply in racing, but those who feel in their bones that a man will always outride a woman had a blow struck against their beliefs at the Shergar Cup here on Saturday when female riders beat three other teams composed of male stars from around the world." Chris Cook, "Sammy Jo Bell Wins Two Shergar Cup Races and Lifts Ascot's Silver Saddle," *Observer*, 8 Aug. 2015, Sport §.

To the linguistic traditionalist, these uses (or misuses) are arrant nonsense. But others view the term as a handy, more pejorative alternative to *sexism*.

LANGUAGE-CHANGE INDEX
chauvinism for *male chauvinism*: Stage 3

B. And *jingoism*. The void left by the shift in the meaning of *chauvinism* from national pride to supposed sexual superiority has been filled by *jingoism*. Essentially synonymous with *chauvinism* in its traditional sense, *jingoism* has the added layer of xenophobic and aggressive attitudes toward foreign policy—e.g.: "Gilmour goes overboard in trying to rationalize and justify Kipling's racism and *jingoism*. He argues, for example, that 'white' in *The White Man's Burden* does not refer to skin color but rather to 'civilization and character' and that Kipling's imperialistic beliefs were essentially humane and benevolent rather than based on greed, paternalism and self-interest." Earl L. Dachslager, "The Kipling Paradox," *Houston Chron.*, 23 June 2002, Zest §, at 19.

Sometimes the word takes on an even softer sense, suggesting a provincialism or regionalism that is broader than national sovereignty—e.g.: "The prime minister's evident glee that the BA order had gone to a 'European' company is mere *jingoism* at bottom." "New Labour, Old Corporatism," *Wall Street J. Europe*, 27 Aug. 1998, at 6.

check. A. And *cheque*. Both denote a written order directing a bank to pay money to a specified person. The first, much older spelling is standard AmE. The second has been used by the British since the early 19th century. Still, the second spelling turns up occasionally in AmE.

B. *Check in the amount of*. Instead of this wordy phrasing <enclosed is a check in the amount of $75>, use *check for* <enclosed is a check for $75>.

cheroot /shə-**root**/ (= a cigar with square ends) is the standard spelling. **Sheroot* is a little-used AmE variant.

cherub /**cher**-əb/. This word has two plurals—*cherubs* and *cherubim*—that have undergone DIFFERENTIATION. *Cherubs*, which is six times as common in modern print sources, applies when the reference is either to winged child-angels or to children with chubby red faces. *Cherubim* (a Hebrew plural) applies when the reference is to an entire order of angels. Cf. **seraph.** See PLURALS (B).

The double plural **cherubims* is erroneous—e.g.: "Among the items inside the tabernacle are reproductions of the golden lampstand . . . and the Ark of the Covenant topped by *cherubims* [read *cherubim* or *cherubs*]." Lori Van Ingen, "Mennonite Center's Tabernacle Hasn't Moved Since 1975," *Intelligencer-J.* (Lancaster, Pa.), 13 July 2002, at B4.

LANGUAGE-CHANGE INDEX
*cherubims for the plural *cherubim* or
cherubs: Stage 1

chest of drawers, an old-fashioned equivalent of *dresser* or *bureau*, is sometimes mistakenly morphed

LANGUAGE-CHANGE INDEX (For the full key, see front matter pp. xxxi, l–li.)
Stage 1: Rejected. **Stage 2:** Widely shunned. **Stage 3:** Widespread but . . . **Stage 4:** Ubiquitous but . . . **Stage 5:** Fully accepted.
Invariably inferior forms marked by asterisk (*). • Ratios represent frequency of prevalent forms vs. variants in current books.

into *chester drawers—e.g.: "[The following items were stolen:] snow blower, lawn mower, weed eater, table, chester [read chest of] drawers, three racks, love seat, couch, bike, value over $3,800, reported Monday." "The Record," *Omaha World-Herald*, 28 May 1993, at 12. This error has been characterized as "orthographically represent[ing] a common pronunciation of chest of drawers." Allison Burkette, "The Story of Chester Drawers," 76 *Am. Speech* 139, 141 (2001).

In a similar vein, *Chip and Dale furniture can sometimes be found in classified ads.

LANGUAGE-CHANGE INDEX
*chester drawers for chest of drawers: Stage 1
Current ratio (chest of drawers vs.
*chester drawers): 595:1

chicanery; chicane, n. In contexts other than those involving horse racing, auto racing, and card games, the noun *chicane* is a NEEDLESS VARIANT of *chicanery* (= trickery). In modern publications, *chicanery* outnumbers *chicane* by a 3-to-1 margin—e.g.: "[T]he fake fireworks, fake singing, allegations of child labor in gymnastics, tape delays and whatever other *chicanery*, artificial ingredients and editing that have shaped impressions of the first week of the Made in China Games did not dent the ratings." Phil Rosenthal, "Conventions Need Olympic-Style Splash," *Chicago Trib.*, 17 Aug. 2008, Bus. §, at 2.

As a verb, *chicane* can be useful (though it's comparatively rare)—e.g.: "Ironically, this is also the age when children desire to belong to organizations whose primary function is to solicit, wheedle and *chicane*." Tom Miller, "Don't Kid Yourself—It's the Attack of the Fund-Raising Urchins," *Seattle Times*, 4 Dec. 1994, Sunday Punch §, at 6.

Chicanery is pronounced with a /sh/: (/shi-**kay**-nə-ree/)—not a /ch/.

Chicano; Chicana. See **Hispanic.**

chide > chided > chided. These are the preferred inflections today in AmE and BrE alike. *Chid* is a variant past tense and past participle that was standard until the early 20th century. Like the variant past participle *chidden, it should be avoided.

The gerund *chiding* acts as the noun <perhaps this chiding will have some effect>. With *chidance, Fred Rodell was surely punning on *guidance*: "But the thirty-year story of the Court under Holmes's *chidance* can best be told neither in strict chronological sequence nor in the specific records of specific Justices (other than Holmes)." *Nine Men* 191 (1955). See IRREGULAR VERBS (D).

Current ratio (chided vs. *chid): 7:1
Current ratio (had chided vs. *had chidden): 21:1

chief. In AmE, the comparative *chiefer* and the superlative *chiefest* are archaic—the word *chief* being considered a noncomparable adjective. See ADJECTIVES (B).

But the superlative form still occasionally appears in BrE—e.g.:

- "*Chiefest* of the blue-nose pubs is the Rosevale, partly owned by Rangers manager Walter Smith and run by Paul Burns." Tom Shields, "Musical Walkers Take Refuge with Old Firm Rivals," *Herald* (Glasgow), 7 July 1995, at 17.
- "It is doggedness, unglamorous persevering doggedness, which is the *chiefest* quality in winning county championships." "Cricket: Kent Take Positive Option," *Sunday Telegraph*, 18 Aug. 1996, at 8.
- "His principal targets are the clergy, and he is not afraid of the *chiefest* among them." Anthony Cronin, "The Sunday Poem," *Sunday Independent*, 22 Mar. 2015, at 22 (referring to the 16th-century poet John Skelton).

Chief Justice of the United States. Though usage has varied over time, this is now the generally preferred title—not *Chief Justice of the United States Supreme Court or *Chief Justice of the Supreme Court of the United States.

chiffonier (= a tall chest of drawers) is the standard spelling. *Chiffonnier is a variant. The word is pronounced /shif-ə-**neer**/.

Current ratio: 4:1

childlike; childish. *Childlike* connotes simplicity, innocence, and truthfulness <childlike faith>. *Childish* connotes puerility, peevishness, and silliness <childish sulking>.

Sometimes *childish* (the negative term) wrongly displaces *childlike* (the positive term)—e.g.:

- "The text rang out with honesty and simplicity, whether voicing Anne's *childish* [read *childlike*] innocence or her tragic sense of weariness." Marc Shulgold, "Aspen Music Festival Builds to a Big Finale," *Rocky Mountain News* (Denver), 21 Aug. 1995, at A42.
- "Some drawings have a delightful, almost *childish* [read *childlike*] simplicity." Jacqueline Hall, "Sketches Show How Architects Develop Ideas," *Columbus Dispatch*, 15 Sept. 2002, at G8.

LANGUAGE-CHANGE INDEX
childish misused for childlike: Stage 2
Current ratio (childlike innocence vs.
*childish innocence): 3:1

children, the plural of *child*, makes the possessive form *children's*. The form *childrens' is erroneous—e.g.: "Clad in water-repellent gear, carrying umbrellas and pulling their *childrens'* [read *children's*] wagons, they streamed into the park." Rob Kasper, "Spit Out Those Seeds of Doubt and Plant Watermelon Again," *Baltimore Sun*, 2 June 2001, at D1. See POSSESSIVES (B).

LANGUAGE-CHANGE INDEX
*childrens' for children's: Stage 1
Current ratio (children's vs.
*childrens'): 334:1

child-slaying. For the 19th-century adverb, see **infanticide.**

chili (= [1] a hot pepper; or [2] a spicy beef stew that, when prepared north of Texas's Red River, often contains beans) is so spelled in AmE—*chilli* in BrE. Avoid *chile*, which is Spanish, not English.

chiliad; chiliast. See **millenarian.**

chillily. For this 19th-century adverb, see ADVERBS (B).

chimera. A. Spelling and Pronunciation. The form *chimera* is now standard, **chimaera* rarely appearing. The word is pronounced /kɪ-**meer**-ə/.

> Current ratio: 7:1

B. Plural. The better plural is *chimeras*. The form *chimerae* is an affectation—e.g.: "Similarly grotesque creatures can be found in French furniture of the Francis I period (1483–1547), when *chimerae* [read *chimeras*], draped human figures, and stylized scrolls were popular motifs." Page Talbott, "Allen and Brother, Philadelphia Furniture Makers," *Mag. Antiques*, May 1996, at 716. See PLURALS (B).

> Current ratio (*chimeras* vs. *chimerae*): 38:1

chimpanzee may be pronounced /chim-pan-**zee**/ or /chim-**pan**-zee/. The first of those pronunciations now predominates.

*chinchy. See **chintzy.**

Chinese, n. Although everyone feels comfortable using *Chinese* as an adjective <Chinese restaurants> and as a COLLECTIVE NOUN <the Chinese have rich cultural traditions>, a sense of awkwardness arises when using it as a singular noun <he's a Chinese>. There is a tendency to prefer it as an adjective <he's Chinese>. The same tendency may be seen in other nationalities denoted with the *-ese* suffix (e.g., Burmese, Sudanese, Vietnamese).

Most dictionaries, however, define *Chinese* as a singular noun meaning "a native of China" or "a citizen of China." And certainly the need occasionally arises to refer to a person from China, as we use *an American* to refer to a person from the United States (see **American**) or *a Russian* to refer to a person from Russia. And while everyone with any sense knows that *Chinaman* has long been considered derogatory, *Chinese* is not so considered and fills the need—e.g.:

- "As *a Chinese* who grew up in a Chinese society, I shouldn't feel ashamed if my opinions don't align with those of most American minorities." Shu Shin Luh, "A Minority View," *Wash. Post*, 8 Aug. 1999, at B1.
- "An official—*a Chinese* who would give only his surname, Huo—says construction stalled because Beijing delayed the final batch of funding, worth $600,000." Charles Hutzler, "China Fears Melding of Islam, Separatism," *Houston Chron.*, 27 Aug. 2000, at 34.
- "The only two who failed to vote 'yea' were Vitaly Smirnov, a Russian with the good sense to abstain, and He Zhenliang, *a Chinese* who voted against the measure." Mike Vaccaro, "Golden Ruling for Canadian Pair," *Star-Ledger* (Newark), 16 Feb. 2002, at 1.

chink (= a fissure or slit, as in armor) derives from the Middle English word *chine*, meaning "crack." The SET PHRASE is *chink in the armor*—often elaborated to *chink in* [someone's] *armor*. But because the word *Chink* is also a racial slur against the Chinese (dating from the late 19th century), some have begun erroneously writing **kink in the armor*, the word *kink* suggesting an irregularity or imperfection. This unetymological shift in usage may gain acceptance in the end because of racial sensitivities, but it is not yet even close to being standard. E.g.:

- "Two games into the season, Atholton's softball team has shown no *kinks* [read *chinks*] in its armor." Stan Rappaport, "Atholton Keeps the Competition Scoreless Again," *Baltimore Sun*, 25 Mar. 2001, at E17.
- "For the most part, Paragon lives up to its name, with a few minor *kinks* [read *chinks*] in its aspiring armor." Meridith Ford, "Dining Out," *Providence J.-Bull.*, 29 Nov. 2001, at L15.
- "Likewise any *kinks* [read *chinks*] in the armor should be taken care of now rather than discovering them out on the water." Dan Radel, "Cabin Fever? Five Fishing Activities to Avoid It," *Asbury Park Press*, 12 Feb. 2015, at A7.

But sensitivities understandably run high. On 30 August 2015, *The Wall Street Journal* tweeted a headline: "A Chink in His Armor? Xi Jinping Looks Vulnerable for the First Time." Within moments it had been untweeted, yet indignant readers had preserved and retweeted it—furiously questioning the *WSJ*'s judgment. People wanted to know whether it was clueless or purposeful. Either conclusion is damning.

> LANGUAGE-CHANGE INDEX
> *kink* misused for *chink*: Stage 2

chintz; *chints. *Chintz* is the preferred spelling for fabric originally imported to Great Britain from India, featuring large patterns of flowers or birds. The original spelling, **chints*, is now obsolete.

> Current ratio: 107:1

chintzy (= cheap, gaudy) is the standard spelling. **Chinchy* is a variant.

> Current ratio: 72:1

chipotle (= a smoked jalapeño pepper used in cooking various dishes, esp. Mexican food) dates in English from the 1950s. Today it is often, through METATHESIS, misspelled **chipolte* (and mispronounced that way as well)—e.g.: "The smoky three sisters soup ($7.50) was chock full of cannellini beans, squash and fresh corn and spiked with *chipolte* [read *chipotle*] and ginger." Kathleen Allen, "A More Elegant Presidio," *Ariz. Daily Star*, 11 May 2001, at F9. The word is also occasionally spelled *chilpotle*, which is the etymological spelling of the Nahuatl word (meaning "smoked chili"). But the established spelling in English is *chipotle*. The word is pronounced /chee-**poht**-lay/ or /chi-/.

> LANGUAGE-CHANGE INDEX
> *chipotle* misspelled **chipolte*: Stage 1
> Current ratio: 155:1

LANGUAGE-CHANGE INDEX (For the full key, see front matter pp. xxxi, l–li.)
Stage 1: Rejected. **Stage 2:** Widely shunned. **Stage 3:** Widespread but . . . **Stage 4:** Ubiquitous but . . . **Stage 5:** Fully accepted.
Invariably inferior forms marked by asterisk (*). • Ratios represent frequency of prevalent forms vs. variants in current books.

*chiropody; *chiropodist. The first syllable of these words is preferably pronounced /ki/, not /chi/. But /shi/ is common and (barely) acceptable. The words are labeled "factitious" by the *OED*; are less common than their synonyms, *podiatry* and *podiatrist*; and ought to be avoided in most contexts.

chisel, vb., makes *chiseled* and *chiseling* in AmE, *chiselled* and *chiselling* in BrE. See SPELLING (B).

chitterlings (= cooked pig intestines) is the standard term. Despite its spelling, it's pronounced /**chit**-linz/. As an almost inevitable result, the variant spellings **chitlings* and **chitlins* have emerged. Cf. **victuals.**
                Current ratio (*chitterlings* vs. **chitlins* vs.
                                            *chitlings): 32:20:1

chivalrous; chivalric. *Chivalrous*, always the more popular term, best applies to a person, *chivalric* to a quality or thing.
    Chivalrous is the older term, dating from the 14th century. It describes a valiant knight or, later, a gracious man—e.g.: "At least Kutcher is a *chivalrous* hiking partner. He carries the tape recorder. He offers to carry my bag." Rachel Abramowitz, "A Career Buff-Up," *L.A. Times*, 24 Sept. 2006, Cal. §, at E1.
    Chivalric dates from shortly before 1800. It best means "of, relating to, or involving chivalry"—e.g.: "[H]e can discourse knowledgeably about rare editions and Old Master prints, work with a fine sensibility at his photographic studies, succor those less fortunate and comport himself with an almost *chivalric* courtesy." Michael Dirda, "Trust No One in This Accomplished Victorian Suspense Novel," *Wash. Post*, 1 Oct. 2006, Book §, at T15.

*chivaree; *charivaree. See **charivari.**

chlorophyll (the green pigment in plants) has been the standard spelling since the word became widespread in the early 20th century. **Chlorophyl* is a variant.
                                            Current ratio: 97:1

choate. See **inchoate.**

chocoholic (= someone who craves chocolate), a slang term dating from the late 1960s, is predominantly so spelled in all varieties of World English—not **chocaholic.*
                                            Current ratio: 19:1

chocolate (the sweet brown delicacy) is preferably pronounced /**chawk**-lit/ or /**chawk**-ə-lit/. The two-syllable pronunciation (somewhat preferred) is the result of syncope, by which an internal syllable is collapsed.

chocolaty. So spelled in AmE, but *chocolatey* in BrE.

chomp. See **champ.**

choose between. See **between** (D).

choosy. So spelled—not **choosey.*

chord; cord. *Cord* (= [1] string, rope; [2] a measure of wood equaling 128 cubic feet; [3] an electrical cable; or [4] a ribbed fabric) is different from *chord*, which is reserved for musical and geometric senses. When the reference is to the voice-producing organs—in which the anatomical part resembles a string or rope—*cord* is the correct word. But writers frequently err—e.g.:

- "I'm crusading for alternatives to the current-traditional paradigm and will continue to do so until either my vocal *chords* [read *cords*], or my pen, or both, give out." Donald C. Stewart, "Composition Textbooks and the Assault on Tradition," in *The Writing Teacher's Sourcebook* 180, 186 (Gary Tate & Edward P.J. Corbett eds., 1981).
- "Miss Anderson still likes to exercise her vocal *chords* [read *cords*] on Irish folk songs." "Acting Jobs Best at Home," *Omaha World-Herald*, 25 Feb. 1996, at E1.
- "In the coming months, you will stretch your muscles and vocal *chords* [read *cords*], study the origin of mankind and learn more about yourself." Tad Bartimus, "A Warm Welcome, Students and Parents, to the Beginning of a Beautiful Friendship," *Seattle Times*, 15 Sept. 2002, at L2.

And sometimes *cord* displaces *chord* in references to music—e.g.:

- "The sound of the dulcimer reaches lightly to the soul. It strikes a resonant and responsive *cord* [read *chord*] in most people." Suzanne Stenzel, "In the Heart of Harmony," *Pitt. Post-Gaz.*, 11 Feb. 1996, at VN1.
- "These statements struck a harsh *cord* [read *chord*] with me." Al Hohl Evergreen, "Ratings Don't Reflect a Radio Station's Impact," *Rocky Mountain News* (Denver), 14 Mar. 1996, at A47.
- "Though her first song was inspired by poetry that just came to her, Emma said most of the time she's inspired by *cords* [read *chords*] or a melody." Linda Murphy, "Westport Junior Composes Original Song for Contest," *Herald News* (Fall River, Mass.), 14 Sept. 2014, at D1.

LANGUAGE-CHANGE INDEX
1. *chord* misused for *cord*: Stage 3
Current ratio (*vocal cords* vs. **vocal chords*): 4:1
2. *cord* misused for *chord*: Stage 1
Current ratio (*strike a chord* vs. **strike a cord*): 25:1

choreograph, like *orchestrate*, has become a CLICHÉ when used figuratively. In the most jejune modern language, careers are *choreographed* and events are *orchestrated*. See **orchestrate** & VOGUE WORDS.

chrestomathy. This word, denoting an anthology of literary passages (especially those from one author), is best pronounced /kre-**stom**-ə-thee/.

Christian, n., appears unfortunately in contexts in which it seems to be used synonymously with *fundamentalist right-winger*. A letter to the editor in *The New York Times* quite rightly objects: "I was disappointed to read a headline that began 'As Christians Pull the G.O.P. to the Right' (news article, June 27). Such broad-brush characterizations [are misleading]. . . . Liberals proud to be Christian include Eugene McCarthy, George McGovern, the Browns of California, Jimmy Carter, Mario Cuomo and the Rev. Jesse Jackson. Of course, it is also true that certain other Christians have heard their religious beliefs calling them to more conservative causes. But treating this one point on the spectrum as if it stood for a Christian monolith is as offensive as it is misleading." Letter of A.G. Fortunato, "Don't Use 'Christian' as a Synonym for the Right-Wing Fringe," *N.Y. Times,* 10 July 1994, at E18.

Christian name. For the meaning of this term, see the discussion at **surname.**

christie (= a high-speed turn in skiing) is the standard spelling. ******Christy* is a variant. The word is a shortened form of *Christiana swing,* the place name *Christiana* being an archaic name for Oslo, Norway.

Christmas. See **Xmas.**

chronic is best reserved to describe diseases and physical conditions that persist over time <a chronic backache>. But it is sometimes loosely and unwisely used for *habitual* or *inveterate*—e.g.:

- "High school football coaches are *chronic* [read *habitual*] exaggerators." Jim Browitt, "Timberline, Lapwai in Crucial CIL Game," *Lewiston Morning Trib.* (Idaho), 1 Oct. 1993, at B4.
- "Albert's lawyer, Roy Black, . . . [claimed] that Albert's accuser had a pattern of threatening past boyfriends, was a *chronic* [read *habitual*] liar and was mentally unstable." "Albert Pleads Guilty in Sex Case," *Sacramento Bee,* 26 Sept. 1997, at A1.

The corresponding adverb is *chronically*—not **chronicly.*

At one time, **chronical* was the predominant adjective, but it has been in decline since the 1760s and is now a NEEDLESS VARIANT.

LANGUAGE-CHANGE INDEX
chronic misused for *habitual* or *inveterate*: Stage 3
Current ratio (*habitual* or *inveterate drinker* vs. **chronic drinker*): 4:1
Current ratio (*chronically* vs. **chronicly*): 9,939:1
Current ratio (*chronic diseases* vs. **chronical diseases*): 412:1

chronicle, n. & vb., is frequently misspelled **chronical*—e.g.:

- "Frame your interests with photographs that *chronical* [read *chronicle*] your life and are cherished keepsakes." Frances Ingraham Heins, "Framed!" *Times Union* (Albany), 23 Jan. 2000, at H1.
- "Her book, 'God, Dr. Buzzard and the Bolito Man,' is a detailed, readable *chronical* [read *chronicle*] of Saltwater Geechee heritage on the island." Steve Hendrix, "Sweet Georgia Coast," *Wash. Post,* 19 May 2002, at E1.

In its one near-legitimate use, **chronical* is a NEEDLESS VARIANT of the adjective *chronic.*

LANGUAGE-CHANGE INDEX
chronicle misspelled **chronical*: Stage 1
Current ratio: 5,322:1

CHRONOLOGY. Many writing problems—though described in various other ways—result primarily from disruptions in chronological order. In narrative presentations, of course, chronology is the essential organizer. The brain can more easily process the information when it's presented in that order. So generally, the writer should try to work out the sequence of events and use sentences and paragraphs to let the story unfold.

Even at the sentence level, disruptions can occur. The following example comes from a handbook for band directors: "Improved intonation often results when students take up their instruments after singing their parts aloud once the director realizes that there are intonation problems." This is in reverse chronological order. But the sentence can easily be recast: *A director who detects intonation problems should try having the students put their instruments down and sing their parts aloud. Often, when they play again, their intonation will be improved.*

Another elementary example: "Eight people died after being taken to a hospital, and 26 were killed instantaneously, the radio said." "Crash Kills 34 from Aid Flight," *Las Vegas Rev.-J.,* 19 July 1995, at A10. (A possible revision: *The radio report said that 26 were killed instantaneously and that 8 others died after being taken to the hospital.*)

But consider the more subtle problem presented by a legal issue phrased (as lawyers generally do it) in one sentence:

> Is an employee who makes a contract claim on the basis that her demotion and reduction in salary violate her alleged employment contract, and who makes a timely demand under the Attorney's Fees in Wage Actions Act, disqualified from pursuing attorney's fees under this statute without the court's addressing the merits of her claim?

Now let's date the items mentioned in that statement:

> Is an employee [hired in Oct. 1997] who makes a contract claim [in Sept. 1998] on the basis that her demotion and reduction in salary [in June 1998] violate her alleged employment contract [dated Sept. 1997], and who makes a timely demand [in Aug. 1998] under the Attorney's Fees in Wage Actions Act, disqualified from pursuing attorney's fees under this statute without the court's addressing [in May 1999] the merits of her claim?

The dates (which no one would ever actually want in the sentence) show that the sentence is hopelessly out of order. We improve the story line by highlighting the chronology—and we make the issue instantly more understandable:

> Lora Blanchard was hired by Kendall Co. as a senior analyst in October 1997. She worked in that position for eight months, but in June 1998 Kendall demoted her to the position of researcher. Two months later, she sued for breach of her employment contract and sought attorney's fees. Is she entitled to those fees under the Attorney's Fees in Wage Actions Act?

Of course, part of the improved story line comes from the enhanced concreteness that results from naming

LANGUAGE-CHANGE INDEX (For the full key, see front matter pp. xxxi, l–lii.)
Stage 1: Rejected. **Stage 2:** Widely shunned. **Stage 3:** Widespread but . . . **Stage 4:** Ubiquitous but . . . **Stage 5:** Fully accepted.
Invariably inferior forms marked by asterisk (*). • Ratios represent frequency of prevalent forms vs. variants in current books.

the parties. But the main improvement is finding the story line.

Remember: chronology is the basis of all narrative.

chrysalis. Pl. *chrysalises* or *chrysalides*. Of these two, -*ses* is better because it retains the singular's spelling within it, and the pronunciation likewise reflects that of the uninflected noun. (*Chrysalides* is pronounced /kri-**sal**-i-deez/.) A third plural, *chrysalids, should be avoided because it is formed from the noun *chrysalid, a NEEDLESS VARIANT of *chrysalis*. See PLURALS (B).

chute. See **shoot.**

chutzpah /**huut**-spə/, a Yiddishism dating from the late 19th century, did not gain widespread use until the 1960s and 1970s. It is a curious word, having both negative and positive connotations in AmE. On the one hand, some consider it unfavorable—e.g.: "Alan Dershowitz, the white knight of religious correctness, should have been a tad more judicious in his choice of a title for his book *Chutzpah*. Leo Rosten's book *Hooray for Yiddish!* defines *chutzpah* as 'ultra-brazenness, shamelessness, hard-to-believe effrontery, presumption or gall'—traits that many Jews and Gentiles would hardly classify as desirable." Letter of Chloë Ross, *New York*, 16 Dec. 1991, at 6.

On the other hand (and perhaps this says something about American culture), many consider *chutzpah* desirable—e.g.: "Team president Matt Millen approached Detroit management late in the week in hopes of landing coach Marty Mornhinweg a contract extension after the Lions went 2–14 last season. . . . Not only didn't Millen get what he came for, he was told that both he and Mornhinweg would have their positions evaluated at season's end. Ouch. But we do admire Millen's *chutzpah*." Sean Brennan, "Going Deep," *Daily News* (N.Y.), 9 Sept. 2002, at 12. *W11* defines it first as "supreme self-confidence" but then unnerves us with "nerve, gall." The word sits uneasily on the fence that divides praise and scorn.

Variant spellings include *chutzpa, *hutzpah, and *hutzpa—all best avoided.

Current ratio (*chutzpah* vs. variants in preceding paragraph): 463:24:5:1

cicatrix (= a scar in tissue where a wound has healed) makes the plural *cicatrices*—not *cicatrixes. The BACK-FORMATION of the variant plural—the supposed singular *cicatrice—is to be avoided in AmE and BrE alike.

Current ratio (*cicatrices* vs. *cicatrixes): 213:1

-CIDE. This suffix denotes either the act of slaying [fr. L. -*cīdium* "cutting, killing"] or someone who slays [fr. L. -*cīda* "cutter, killer"]. Hence *fratricide* is either the killing of one's brother or someone who kills his or her brother. Some common words ending in this suffix are these:

homicide	= the act of killing a person
	= the killer of another person
infanticide	= the act of killing a baby
	= one who kills a baby
matricide	= the act of killing one's mother
	= the killer of one's own mother
parricide	= the act of killing one's father
	= the killer of one's own father
patricide	See **parricide.**
regicide	= the act of killing the king or queen
	= the killer of the king or queen
suicide	= the act of killing oneself
	= one who kills oneself

Though a few others, such as *fratricide* and *sororicide*, are generally known, we also have many less common words ending in -*cide*. For example, *famicide* (= the destroyer of someone's reputation) was once used as a synonym for *slanderer*. *Prolicide* (= the act of killing offspring either before or soon after birth) is broad enough to subsume both *feticide* and *infanticide*.

The coinages with this suffix, naturally, are no more sex-neutral than words in any other corner of the language. The *OED* records *uxoricide* (= the slayer of one's wife) but not *mariticide* (= the slayer of one's husband), which can be deduced only from the adjective *mariticidal* (= of, relating to, or involving someone who murders her husband).

Scientists have developed *algicides*, *fungicides*, *germicides*, and *insecticides* (known also as *pesticides*, though this word can be used more broadly than *insecticides*). And to disinfect their combs and other utensils, American barbers commonly use a trade-marked product ominously called "Barbicide." Hence this suffix, like -EE, is perhaps losing its literal force.

Naturally, wags have seized on this suffix for jocular purposes to make such words as *suitorcidal* (= fatal to suitors) and *prenticecide* (= the killing of an apprentice). The poet Oliver Wendell Holmes invented a word that some dictionaries label jocular. Perhaps, however, this word ought to be taken seriously: *verbicide*—"That is violent treatment of a word with fatal results to its legitimate meaning, which is its life. . . . Homicide and *verbicide* . . . are alike forbidden." Oliver W. Holmes [Sr.], *Autocrat of the Breakfast Table* i (1858). One mission of this dictionary is to prevent verbicide.

For entries related to this one, see **homicide, parricide** & **suicide.**

cider. See **apple cider.**

cigarette; *cigaret. The latter is a NEEDLESS VARIANT.

Current ratio: 493:1

cinematographic; *cinemagraphic. In modern print sources, *cinematographic*, the traditionally correct form, is about 130 times as common as *cinemagraphic, the etymologically inferior form. The latter arose through the linguistic process known as syncope—the loss of an unstressed syllable in the middle of a word. Though increasingly common even among filmmakers, *cinemagraphic is not yet recorded in general dictionaries and ought to be avoided—e.g.:

- "But 'Dragonheart' is a beautiful piece of *cinemagraphic* [read *cinematographic*] work." Joseph Szadkowski, "Big Talent, Miniature Art," *Wash. Times*, 8 June 1996, at B4.

- "Young as they are, the Wachowskis already have developed a fine sense of *cinemagraphic* [read *cinematographic*] brinkmanship." Gene Wyatt, "'Bound' Not a Film for All," *Tennessean*, 25 Oct. 1996, at D7.

Cinematographic is pronounced /sin-ə-mat-ə-**graf**-ik/.

LANGUAGE-CHANGE INDEX
*cinemagraphic for *cinematographic*: Stage 1
Current ratio (*cinematographic* vs.
*cinemagraphic): 130:1

cipher (= [1] a nonentity; or [2] a coded message) is the standard spelling. *Cypher is a primarily BrE variant.

Current ratio: 7:1

circuitous; circuity. See **circumlocution (A).**

circularize began as a mid-19th-century NEOLOGISM meaning "to send circulars to" <all the local business owners were circularized>. By extension, it came to mean "to publicize" <the play's premiere was circularized throughout the city>. In these senses, the word is still considered jargonistic. See -IZE.

In the late 20th century, however, the word took on a new meaning in space-flight contexts—a meaning closer to what the word parts suggest: "to make circular." E.g.:

- "The platform's orbit will later be *circularized* at about 310 miles for a two- to three-year mission measuring ozone levels throughout the depth of the atmosphere." "TOMS Launched on Pegasus XL, One Year Late," *Aerospace Daily*, 3 July 1996, at 22.
- "As Odyssey uses the [Martian] atmosphere to *circularize* its orbit, it has encountered sort of a jet stream disturbance over the north pole." Ann Schrader, "Mars Probe Adjusts to Shift in Atmosphere," *Denver Post*, 17 Dec. 2001, at A10.

This sense—though absent from most dictionaries— is clearly useful.

CIRCUMFLEX. See DIACRITICAL MARKS.

circumlocution. A. Generally. Circumlocution is roundabout speech or language, or else the use of many words where a few would suffice. People who use circumlocutions are generally not admired for doing so, as the following quotations attest:

- "Robb, a genius at *circumlocution*, did his best to avoid offending anybody, at the expense of taking a definable stand on any issue." Stuart Klawans, "Ollie's Army," *Nation*, 8 July 1996, at 35.
- "It's really grown tiresome, hearing so many versions of the same excuse, so many *circumlocutions* around the truth." Anita Creamer, " 'Experimenting' with the Truth," *Sacramento Bee*, 19 Aug. 1996, at C1.
- "Perhaps that's because the Prime Minister, with his weird *circumlocutions*—'a not inconsiderable degree of'—does not come across as a silver-tongued smoothie." Ann Leslie, "Why Women Find This Man So Smarmy," *Daily Mail*, 11 Oct. 1996, at 8.

One of the most famous government departments in all literature is Charles Dickens's "Circumlocution Office" in *Little Dorrit* (1857–1858).

B. And *circuity*. Circumlocution is not the noun form corresponding to *circuitous*, which means "winding, tortuous, anfractuous"—the noun for *circuitous* being *circuity*. E.g.: "I bring this up because only now do I recognize the vast *circumlocution* [read *circuity*] of the route [that] I've been cheerfully driving for the past year, a path [that] was anything but a straight line, horizontally or vertically." Jay Bailey, "Riding on the Disneyland Bypass Road," *Jerusalem Post*, 6 Sept. 1996, at 10.

LANGUAGE-CHANGE INDEX
circumlocution misused for *circuity*: Stage 1

C. Adjectival Forms. If the noun corresponding to *circuitous* is seldom used, so is the adjective corresponding to *circumlocution*: *circumlocutory*. E.g.: "He's impatient with compliments, *circumlocutory* in his answers and cheerfully forthcoming with amusing stories that, on reflection, tell you almost nothing about him." Ken Ringle, "Fighting Words," *Wash. Post*, 21 Aug. 1996, at D1.

Avoid the synonymous variants *circumlocutionary and *circumlocutious—e.g.:

- "The *circumlocutionary* [read *circumlocutory*] comic has just returned from a stint at Bally's Casino in Las Vegas." Michael Blowen, "Carlin Is Cable Ready," *Boston Globe*, 15 Apr. 1992, at 90.
- "It's my contention that's in no small part because Tonks, for all his *circumlocutionary* [read *circumlocutory*] council and committee speeches and media scrums, simply cannot get Metro's message across." Dick Chapman, "Metro's Communications Gap," *Toronto Sun*, 5 Nov. 1995, at C4.
- "In my *circumlocutious* [read *circumlocutory*] way, I've given the impression that the column will be about baseball. No, it's about redundancy." Art Trujillo, "Work of Art—A Cheeseburger Con Queso," *Las Vegas Opt*, 27 Aug. 2013, columns p.

LANGUAGE-CHANGE INDEX
1. *circumlocutionary for *circumlocutory*: Stage 1
Current ratio (*circumlocutory* vs.
*circumlocutionary): 15:1
2. *circumlocutious for *circumlocutory*: Stage 1
Current ratio (*circumlocutory* vs.
*circumlocutious): 10:1

CIRCUMLOCUTION. See BE-VERBS (B) & PERIPHRASIS.

circumnavigate; circumvent. *Circumnavigate* (= to go completely around [something], esp. to sail around the earth) is occasionally displaced by *circumvent* (= [1] to get around [an obstacle or obligation], esp. by creative means; or [2] to encircle)—e.g.:

- "[Gus] McCloud is now attempting to *circumvent* [read *circumnavigate*] the world from pole to pole, [Albert] Rutherford said." Damiane Ricks, "Pilot Hopes to

LANGUAGE-CHANGE INDEX (For the full key, see front matter pp. xxxi, l–li.)
Stage 1: Rejected. **Stage 2:** Widely shunned. **Stage 3:** Widespread but . . . **Stage 4:** Ubiquitous but . . . **Stage 5:** Fully accepted.
Invariably inferior forms marked by asterisk (*). • Ratios represent frequency of prevalent forms vs. variants in current books.

Encourage Others to Fly," *Advocate* (Baton Rouge), 15 Nov. 2004, at B1.

- "These two 50-somethings from Albuquerque were doing this section of the river as a prerequisite to their lifetime goal: to *circumvent* [read *circumnavigate*] the southern part of North America on water." Dave Menicucci, "Come Hell or High Water," *Albuquerque J.*, 21 Aug. 2008, at C1. (An even better edit would be to change *circumvent* to *sail around* and omit *on water*.)

Circumnavigate implies active travel. When no act is involved, *circumvent* (in sense 2) is the better choice— e.g.: "Twenty billion [bottles] . . . . If all of them were laid end to end, they would *circumvent* the Earth's equator 76 times." Michele Jacklin, "Add Bottled Water to the List of Redeemables," *Hartford Courant*, 23 Mar. 2005, at A9. Both words involve a way to get around an obstacle. But the obstacle one *circumnavigates* is always physical, while the obstacle one *circumvents* is usually legal or social. See **circumvent**.

LANGUAGE-CHANGE INDEX
circumvent misused for *circumnavigate*: Stage 1
Current ratio (*circumnavigate the globe* vs.
**circumvent the globe*): 62:1

circumscribable; *circumscriptable; *circumscriptible. The first form is standard. Until about 1950, the standard term was *circumscriptible—but the reversal in word frequency has been so pronounced since then that the older form has become a NEEDLESS VARIANT. See -ABLE (A).

circumstances. A. *In* or *under the circumstances.* Some writers prefer *in the circumstances* to *under the circumstances*. The latter is unobjectionable, however, and since 1830 or so has been much more common. E.g.: "*Under the circumstances*, we think that the board made the right decision."

In 1926, H.W. Fowler wrote that the insistence on *in the circumstances* as the only right form is "puerile" (*FMEU1* at 77). In the mid-20th century, G.H. Vallins agreed: " '*Under* the circumstances' has established itself in English idiom; '*in* the circumstances' is merely a proud variant of those who remember their 'grammar' not wisely but too well." G.H. Vallins, *Better English* 61–62 (4th ed. 1957). But Theodore M. Bernstein found a slight DIFFERENTIATION between the two: "*In the circumstances* refers merely to existing conditions, and implies a continuing state of affairs . . . . *Under the circumstances* refers to conditions that impel or inhibit action, and implies a transient situation, long or short." Theodore M. Bernstein, *The Careful Writer* 101 (1965).

LANGUAGE-CHANGE INDEX
under the circumstances: Stage 5

B. *Surrounding circumstances. This phrase, which is about as common in BrE as it is in AmE, has been stigmatized as a REDUNDANCY on etymological grounds. The *OED* confirms this, noting that *circumstance* derives from the Latin *circumstantia* "standing around, surrounding condition." In AmE, it appears most commonly in legal contexts, though not exclusively so. It shows no signs of disappearing—e.g.:

- "The emotional and physical shock of giving birth, as well as other *surrounding circumstances* [read *circumstances*], led doctors to believe that Kraft was not responsible for stabbing her child." Heather Wiese, "From 'Attempted Murder' to Misdemeanor," *Des Moines Register*, 17 Oct. 1996, Metro Iowa §, at 4.

- "We try to distinguish saves by *surrounding circumstances* [read *all the circumstances*]. We include the size of the score, the length of time pitched, and the presumed difficulty of the situation." Leonard Koppett, "Call the 'Pen, Baseball, to Salvage Saves," *Seattle Post-Intelligencer*, 2 Aug. 2002, at C5.

C. *In some circumstances.* This phrase is wordy for *sometimes*. First popular in the 17th century, it waned in the 19th and then surged in the 20th—in both AmE and BrE. But that's no recommendation of it.

circumvent; undermine. *Circumvent* = (1) to get around or escape from (a requirement) through means that are unusual but defensible; or (2) to hem in; circumscribe. Today sense 1 is more common—e.g.:

- "By calling them sober houses they *circumvent* zoning regulations." Carole Paquette, "Reining in Rentals of 'Sober Houses,' " *N.Y. Times*, 8 Dec. 1996, Long Island §, at 1.

- "Senator Mark C. Montigny of New Bedford, who has fought against laws that allow public universities to *circumvent* the public bidding process, said the projects must be subject to strict oversight." Peter Schworm, "Work on Dorm Goes On Despite AG Ruling," *Boston Globe*, 20 Aug. 2008, at B3.

Circumvent is more neutral than *undermine*, which means "to impair or weaken, esp. by insidious or stealthy means" <the mole successfully undermined the political campaign>. Cf. **obviate**.

For the misuse of *circumvent* to mean *circumnavigate*, see **circumnavigate**.

cirrus (= [1] a light cloud shaped like feathers, or [2] a flexible appendage or tendril) makes the plural *cirri*— not *cirruses. See PLURALS (B).

citable. So spelled—not *citeable. See MUTE E.

Current ratio: 40:1

cite, n. A. As a Casualism for *citation.* Using *cite* as a noun—in place of *citation*—is a CASUALISM. E.g.: "Check and double-check your *cites*. . . . We are constantly trying to make sense out of erroneous *cites*." Christopher P. Hamilton, "Trial Management," *Mass. Lawyer*, 16 Dec. 1996, at B5. The longer form looks more dignified and is much more common in print sources—e.g.: " 'Women in Archaeology' is professionally produced, with a single bibliography and an index, in distinct contrast to 'Equity Issues,' which has multiple (and repetitive) reference lists, no index, and many typographical errors, misspellings (Virginia Wolf!), and incorrect *citations*." Tracey Cullen, "Equity Issues for Women in Archeology," *Antiquity*, 1 Dec. 1995, at 1042. Cf. **quote**.

LANGUAGE-CHANGE INDEX
cite as a noun in place of *citation*: Stage 3

B. For *site.* *Cite* shouldn't be confused with *site* (= a location or place)—e.g.:

- "The city is looking at several *cites* [read *sites*] for a new business center." John Gallant, "A Magic Beginning for Center," *Las Vegas Rev.-J.*, 6 Jan. 1994, at B1.
- "The reunion is set for Sept. 26–28 at several *cites* [read *sites*] in Baton Rouge and West Baton Rouge Parish." "Reunion Group Planning Meeting," *Advocate* (Baton Rouge), 12 July 1997, at B4.

The opposite error—*site* for *cite*—is rarely seen outside legal writing (and almost always involves verbs). E.g.:

- "Nevertheless, the existence of mefloquine-resistant/3, berghei and the two *sited* [read *cited*] cases of P. falciparum with decreased susceptibility are cause for genuine concern about the future deployment of this new drug." John M. Mansfield, *Parasitic Diseases* 41 (1984).
- "More materially, the majority *sites* [read *cites*] no authority for its position that a decent law abiding citizen of this State can be criminally convicted based solely on one wobbly inference toddling upon another." *Frost v. State*, 2 S.W.3d 625, 635 n.7 (Tex. App. 1999).
- "Plaintiff *sites* [read *cites*] no authority supporting a claimed right to prevent the Town from purchasing land abutting his, whether in a buildable lot or a ten-foot strip." *Welch v. Paicos*, 66 F.Supp.2d 138, 166 (D. Mass. 1999).

LANGUAGE-CHANGE INDEX
1. *cite* misused for *site*: Stage 1
Current ratio (*building site* vs. *building cite*): 1,285:1
2. *site* misused for *cite*: Stage 2
Current ratio (*citing authority* vs. *siting authority*): 5:1

cite, v.t. **A. General Senses and Use.** *Cite,* v.t., = (1) to commend <the mayor cited him for his charitable giving>; (2) to adduce as authority <in arguing the point, he cited the 11th edition of *Encyclopaedia Britannica*>; or (3) to summon before a court of law <he was cited for contempt>.

In sense 2, the object of *cite* should be the authority cited, not the person to whom it is cited. The following loose usage is not uncommon in AmE: "Plaintiff is unable to *cite the court to any Connecticut cases which* [read *cite any Connecticut cases that*] answer this question." "Property," *Conn. Law Trib.*, 1 Apr. 1996, at 374 (reporting a law case). See OBJECT-SHUFFLING.

A related problem is using *cite* as an intransitive rather than as a transitive verb—that is, saying that the writer is *citing to a case* rather than *citing a case*. This looseness, common especially among lawyers, results perhaps from the noun form *citation to*—e.g.: "In addition, Thomson will make available to any interested party standardized licenses for a West service called Star Pagination, which is a widely accepted method for *citing to* [read *citing*] Federal and state case law." "Thomson Acquisition of West Approved," *Information Today*, 17 July 1996, at 3.

In sense 3, some people have recently begun writing that a person is *cited to* court. In this CASUALISM, *cite* is shorthand for "to summon with a citation" and is surely inferior to *summon*—e.g.:

- "He claimed the hunters knew that their activities were illegal because almost 40 other hunters left before TWRA officers could *cite* [read *summon*] them to court." Lance Coleman & Dan Cook, "Baited-Field Bust Bags 40+ Area Dove Hunters," *Chattanooga Free Press*, 4 Sept. 1996, at B2.
- "A sheriff's deputy charged a South Point woman and a Fort Gay, W.Va., man with possession of drugs (marijuana) and drug paraphernalia in Fayette Township and *cited* [read *summoned*] them into court last week." "Man Reports Computer, iPod, DVDs, More Stolen," *Herald-Dispatch* (Huntington, W. Va.), 31 Mar. 2012, at 1.

B. And *quote*. These words are usefully differentiated. To *cite* an authority is to give its substance and to indicate where it can be found. To *quote* is to repeat someone else's exact words and to enclose them in quotation marks or block-quotation form. In scholarly writing, citations routinely follow quotations. See **quote**.

citizen. A. And *resident*. With U.S. citizens, the terms *citizen* and *resident* are generally viewed as being interchangeable in reference to state residency or citizenship. But the words are not interchangeable when other political entities (e.g., cities) are the frame of reference: *citizen* implies political allegiance and a corresponding protection by the state, whereas *resident* denotes merely that one lives in a certain place. It is possible to be a U.S. *citizen* while being neither a *citizen* nor a *resident* of any particular state. (That is, American citizens can reside abroad.) See **citizenship**.

B. And *subject*. Subject (= a person subject to political rule; any member of a state other than the sovereign) is not merely the BrE equivalent of the AmE *citizen*. A *citizen* is a person from a country in which sovereignty is believed or supposed to belong to the collective body of the people, whereas a *subject* is someone who owes allegiance to a sovereign monarch.

citizenry; citizens. Both are acceptable plurals of *citizen*, but *citizens* is the more general term that is far more prevalent. Two aspects of *citizenry* distinguish it: first, it is a COLLECTIVE NOUN (although it frequently takes a plural verb), emphasizing the mass or body of citizens; and second, it is, as *W2* notes, frequently used by way of contrast to soldiery, officialdom, or the intelligentsia. Here it is opposed to one part of officialdom (some might say *intelligentsia*): "The written Constitution lies at the core of American 'civil religion'; not only judges but also the *citizenry* at large habitually invoke the Constitution."

citizenship; residence; domicile. The distinctions between these related terms are important. *Citizenship* = the status of being a citizen, with its attendant rights and privileges. *Residence* = (1) the act or fact of living in a particular place for a time <a one-year residence requirement for in-state tuition>; (2) the locale in which one actually or officially lives <he has recently

made Nevada his residence>; or (3) a house or home <a two-story residence>. (*Residency* is a NEEDLESS VARIANT of *residence* in senses 1 and 2.) In some legal contexts, the more specific word *domicile* is frequently used in place of the broad sense 2 of *residence*. *Domicile* = a person's fixed, permanent, and principal home for legal purposes.

cityward has always been the standard term in AmE—not *citywards* (which was standard in BrE only through the early 20th century—but no longer). See DIRECTIONAL WORDS (A).

Current ratio: 3:1

civic rights. See **civil rights.**

civilian clothes; street clothes. The first should be reserved for military or paramilitary (e.g., police) contexts. When contrasting with sports uniforms or theater costumes, *street clothes* is better—e.g.:

• "On game days, [Steve] Bono is usually found on the sideline, dressed in *civilian clothes* [read *street clothes*] with clipboard in hand." Jim Jenkins, "Bono Passes This Screen Test: 49ers' Third-String Quarterback Aids Defense," *Sacramento Bee*, 27 Oct. 1990, at D4.
• "Three of the Sharks' better players were in *civilian clothes* [read *street clothes*] and sat in the press box." Ron Bergman, "Injury-Plagued Sharks No Match for Flames," *San Jose Mercury News*, 24 Feb. 1993, at C1.
• "Village police Chief Hugh Flanigan told The Star-Beacon in nearby Ashtabula that the unarmed man in *civilian clothes* [read *street clothes*] repeatedly tried to convince the Youngstown officer that he was a real lawman, but eventually drove away." "Fake Officer Tries to Pull Over Policeman," *Charleston Gaz.* (W. Va.), 5 Aug. 2015, at A6.

LANGUAGE-CHANGE INDEX
civilian clothes used in nonmilitary contexts: Stage 2

civil rights; civil liberties; civic rights. Commonly viewed as an Americanism, *civil rights* actually dates back to 16th-century BrE. After two centuries of sporadic use, it gained popularity again by 1750 in BrE and then sprang to worldwide attention in AmE in the 1770s. But the phrase reached its zenith in frequency of occurrence in the late 20th century, beginning in the 1960s. In AmE, the phrase refers generally to the individual rights guaranteed by the Bill of Rights and by the 13th, 14th, 15th, and 19th Amendments, as well as by legislation such as the Voting Rights Act. These rights include freedom of speech and religion; the right to vote; freedom from involuntary servitude; the enjoyment of life, liberty, and property; the right to privacy; due process; and equal protection of the law. Some of these rights, such as the right to vote, are restricted to citizens; others, such as due process and equal protection, apply equally to anyone within the state's jurisdiction.

The phrase *civil liberties*, a less frequent term, refers generally to the liberties guaranteed to everyone by law or custom against undue governmental interference. *Civil rights* is also sometimes used in this broader sense: "The subject was '*civil rights*,' that is, the liberties of man as man and not primarily as an economic animal." Robert G. McCloskey, *American Supreme Court* 170 (1960).

Civic rights is a much less common phrase. It sounds at once less weighty than the other two phrases and less idiomatic. When it appears, it often verges on being a NEEDLESS VARIANT of *civil rights*—e.g.:

• "Lincoln [was] unwilling to alienate a public opinion that everywhere in the North was implacably, savagely opposed to giving slaves movement or *civic rights* [read *civil rights*]." Alfred Kazin, "A Forever Amazing Writer," *N.Y. Times*, 10 Dec. 1989, § 7, at 3.
• "The peace deal signed on Aug. 13 by the Macedonian and ethnic Albanian parties in Macedonia's government grants ethnic Albanians many of the greater *civic rights* [read *civil rights*] the rebels say they have sought." Ian Fisher, "Report Says Macedonians Killed Civilians in Revenge," *N.Y. Times*, 5 Sept. 2001, at A1.
• "The walk started June 1 with O'Neal, *civic rights* [read *civil-rights*] legend Bob Zellner, college and graduate students from out of state, and other civil activists." "Thomasville Pastor Walks to D.C. to Support Rural Hospitals," *News & Record* (Greensboro), 4 July 2015, News §.

-ck-. See **-c-.**

clamor (= to cry out loudly; raise an uproar) is now sometimes, through WORD-SWAPPING, misused for *clamber* (= to climb, usu. with great effort)—e.g.:

• "As they left the road to descend into Junior's bottomland, a three-legged, patch-haired dog of the terrier kind *clamored* [read *clambered*] out from under the porch and ran low to the ground and completely soundless on a trajectory straight to Inman, who had learned to heed a silent dog more than a barking dog." Charles Frazier, *Cold Mountain* 202 (1997). (The error is especially salient in this sentence because the dog is "soundless.")
• "When we returned to the house, we opened the large windows, let the ocean breeze roll in, and *clamored* [read *clambered*] up the oak staircases to bed." Melissa A. Trainer, "Mobile Guide: Camping in Comfort," *Wall Street J.*, 2 Sept. 1997, at A16.
• "Venus [Williams] then *clamored* [read *clambered*] up into the stands to briefly join the fun." Charles Bricker, "Venus at Her Brightest," *Sun-Sentinel* (Ft. Lauderdale), 9 July 2000, at C1.

What's the best way to stop this spreading error? Whenever you see or hear it, clamber up on a soapbox and clamor about it. By the way, the two words aren't homophones: *clamber* is pronounced /klam-bər/.

LANGUAGE-CHANGE INDEX
clamor misused for *clamber*: Stage 1

clandestine is best pronounced /klan-**des**-tin/ or /-tən/, not /klan-**des**-tɪn/ or /**klan**-də-stɪn/.

clangor (= a loud sound that continues for a long time) is the AmE spelling, *clangour* the BrE. (See -OR; -OUR.) The word is preferably pronounced /**klang**-ər/—not /**klang**-gər/.

clapboard (= a long, narrow board that is thicker at the bottom so that it may be used for siding) is pronounced /**klab**-ərd/.

claret (= a red wine from the Bordeaux region, or a similar wine from elsewhere) is pronounced /**klar**-ət/.

It's an English word that was borrowed from French and anglicized in Middle English. Some people today mistakenly give it a Frenchified pronunciation (/kla-ret/ or, worse, /kla-**ray**/). Cf. **Meritage.**

clarinetist. So spelled in AmE, *clarinettist* being standard in BrE.

class is not interchangeable with *kind* or *type*. We may have a type or kind of *thing*, but a class of *things*. E.g.:

• "His work . . . [on] ionic crystals extended considerably our understanding of *this class of material* [read either *this class of materials* or *this type of material*]." Harvey Flower, "Professor Peter Pratt," *Independent*, 17 Mar. 1995, at 20.
• "Traditionally, this *criteria* [read *criterion*] has revolved around the *class* [read *type*] of vehicle (e.g., sports car vs. family sedan; 8 cylinder vs. 4 cylinder), driver behavior (e.g., number of speeding tickets, the expected annual miles to be driven), and driver characteristics (e.g., age, gender)." " 'System and Method for Insurance Underwriting and Rating' in Patent Application Approval Process," *Insurance Business Weekly*, 23 Aug. 2015, at 170. (See **criterion.**)

The second example just above illustrates travel JARGON, in which *class* refers to the level of luxury.

class act. See **classy.**

CLASS DISTINCTIONS. Many linguistic phenomena discussed in this book—especially those involving vocabulary and pronunciation—are explainable partly under the heading of "class." That is, many linguistic pratfalls can be seen as class indicators—even in a so-called classless society such as the United States. Several books and essays address the subject, including (most famously) Alan S.C. Ross's essay "U and Non-U," in *Noblesse Oblige* (Nancy Mitford ed., 1956; repr. 1974); Charles C. Fries's *American English Grammar* (1940); T.H. Pear's *English Social Differences* (1955); Richard Buckle's *U and Non-U Revisited* (1978); Thomas Pyles's "The Auditory Mass Media and U," in Pyles, *Selected Essays on English Usage* 103 (John Algeo ed., 1979); and Paul Fussell's *Class* (1983).

Professor Ross's influential essay divided traits in England into U (upper-class) and non-U (not upper-class—meaning "vulgar" or sometimes "typical of social climbers who put on airs"). Among the linguistic markers he listed were the following:

U	Non-U
black tie	tuxedo, tux
civilized (of a person)	cultivated, cultured
lunch	dinner (midday meal)
dinner, supper	evening meal
sick	ill
have a bath	bathe, take a bath
How do you do?	Pleased to meet you!
jam	preserves
vegetables	greens
rich	wealthy
She's a nice woman	She's a nice lady
He's a nice man	He's a nice gentleman

Ross listed these items as an anthropologist might—not to prescribe what people should do but to describe the way in which speech and writing were class indicators in the England of the 1950s.

American etiquette books have contained similar lists, but with a prescriptive purpose. Emily Post's *Etiquette: The Blue Book of Social Usage* contained such a list for Americans (the headings having been supplied here merely for convenience):

U	Non-U
I would like to buy	I desire to purchase
I suppose	I presume
big house	mansion
good food, delicious food	lovely food
beautiful house	elegant home
formal clothes	formals
curtains	drapes, draperies
flowers	corsage

Other writers have other lists, and other lines of demarcation. The American writer Paul Fussell, for example, puts "proles" on the bottom rung of the ladder: they unselfconsciously engage in poor usage such as double negatives (*I don't have no butter*) and subject–verb disagreements (*he don't have no butter*). Ross and Post are pretty well unconcerned about proles. In the middle, according to Fussell, is the insecure middle class, whose language is often inflated (see OFFICIALESE & BUREAUCRATESE) and pretentious (see EUPHEMISMS, FORMAL WORDS & HYPERCORRECTION). At the top are the upper-middle and upper classes, whose language is typically relaxed and straightforward—a plainspoken style.

There is perhaps greater fluidity between classes with AmE speakers than with BrE speakers. But T.H. Pear's observations about the process of changing classes in England apply equally to the United States: "As soon as members of the lower classes rise socially, they tend to adopt, and when 'middle-middles' become 'upper-middles' they, in their turn, drop, middle-class euphemisms; for unless they do, they may find their ascent of the social ladder hindered by people at both ends of it." *English Social Differences* 90 (1955). Part of the rise, of course, depends on educational level, and to that degree the word *prole* corresponds with *lowbrow*; *middle-class* corresponds with *middlebrow*; and *upper-middle-class* and *upper-class* correspond with *highbrow*.

But taste as well as education enters the assessment, as Fussell observes, and speech is the telltale sign:

[T]here is a tight system of social class in this country, [and] linguistic class lines are crossed only rarely and with great difficulty. A virtually bottomless social gulf opens between those who say "Have a nice day" and those who say, on the other hand, "Goodbye," those who when introduced say "Pleased to meet you" and those who say "How do you do?" There may be some passing intimacy between those who think *momentarily* means *in a moment* (airline captain over loudspeaker: "We'll be

LANGUAGE-CHANGE INDEX (For the full key, see front matter pp. xxxi, l–li.)
Stage 1: Rejected. **Stage 2:** Widely shunned. **Stage 3:** Widespread but . . . **Stage 4:** Ubiquitous but . . . **Stage 5:** Fully accepted.
Invariably inferior forms marked by asterisk (*). • Ratios represent frequency of prevalent forms vs. variants in current books.

taking off momentarily, folks") and those who know it means *for a moment*, but it won't survive much strain. It's like the tenuous relation between people who conceive that *type* is an adjective ("She's a very classy type person") and people who know it's only a noun or verb. The sad thing is that by the time one's an adult, these stigmata are virtually unalterable and ineffaceable.

Paul Fussell, Class 198 (1983).

That conclusion—that class indicators are "unalterable and ineffaceable"—offers little hope for those who believe in education. The critical phrase, though, is *by the time one's an adult.* Somebody who has shown no interest in language through early adulthood is unlikely to acquire the habit later. And to the extent that language reflects class, one's class is pretty well set in early adulthood. But there is surely some hope even beyond that point.

Most usage guides are silent on the subject of class. If they serve as useful guides, they typically reflect upper-middle-class preferences, as this book generally does. For that is the class into which most even modestly intellectual achievers fall, and the class to which the ambitious members of the middle class most aspire. The following charts list some of the obvious markers.

Vocabulary Markers in AmE

U	Non-U
before	*prior to
between you and me	*between you and I
a criterion	*a criteria
died	passed away, passed on
drinks	beverages
driver	chauffeur
feel bad	*feel badly
fewer items	*less items
if I had	*if I would have (or would've)
if I hadn't been there	*if I hadn't have been there
in regard to, with regard to	*in regards to, *with regards to
John saw my brother and me	*John saw my brother and I
later	subsequently
lie down	lay down
May I help you?	How may I assist you? May I be of assistance?
more fun, most fun	*funner, *funnest
my partner and I *or* my partner and me	my partner and myself
not too big a box	*not too big of a box
a phenomenon	*a phenomena
pregnant	expecting
regardless	*irregardless
send Sally and me a copy	*send Sally and I a copy
themselves	*theirselves
this is she (in answering a telephone caller's question)	*this is her
use, n. & vb.	utilization, utilize
what kind of bird	*what kind of a bird

you and I are through [nothing]	*me and you are through real classy, class act, high-class

Pronunciation Markers in AmE

Word	U	Non-U
accurate	**ak**-yə-rit	**ak**-ə-rit
adult	ə-**dəlt**	**ad**-əlt
applicable	**ap**-li-kə-bəl	ə-**plik**-ə-bəl
asterisk	**as**-tə-risk	**as**-tə-rik
beneficiary	ben-ə-**fish**-ee-er-ee	ben-ə-**fish**-ə-rer-ee
comparable	**com**-pər-ə-bəl	kəm-**par**-ə-bəl
coupon	**koo**-pahn	**kyoo**-pahn
descent	di-**sent**	**dee**-sent
deteriorate	di-**tir**-ee-ə-rayt	**dee**-tir-ee-ayt, di-**tir**-ə-rayt
escalate	**es**-kə-layt	**es**-kyə-layt
escape	es-**kayp**	ek-**skayp**
especially	es-**spesh**-ə-lee	ek-**spesh**-ə-lee
etc.	et **set**-ə-rə	ek **set**-ə-rə
exquisite	**ek**-skwiz-it	ek-**skwiz**-it
fiancé(e)	fee-ahn-**say**	fee-**ahn**-say
grievous	**gree**-vəs	**gree**-vee-əs
height	hɪt	hɪtth
heinous	**hay**-nəs	**hee**-nəs, **hee**-nee-əs
homage	**hom**-ij	**ah**-mij
intellectual	in-tə-**lek**-chuu-[w]əl	in-ə-**lek**-shəl
interesting	**in**-trə-sting	**in**-ə-res-ting
library	**lɪ**-brer-ee	**li**-ber-ee
mischievous	**mis**-chə-vəs	mis-**chee**-vee-əs
nuclear	**n(y)oo**-klee-ər	**noo**-kyə-lər
often	**of**-ən	**of**-tən
police	pə-**lees**	**poh**-lees
preferable	**pref**-ər-ə-bəl	pri-**fər**-ə-bəl
probably	**pro**-bə-blee	**prol**-ee
secretary	**se**-krə-ter-ee	**se**-kə-ter-ee
subsidiary	səb-**sid**-ee-er-ee	səb-**sid**-ə-rer-ee, səb-**sid**-ə-ree
toward	tord	twahrd, tə-**word**, tword
wash	wahsh	wahrsh

For still more mispronunciations, see PRONUNCIATION (B).

classic; classical. *Classical* refers to anything relating to "the classics" (whether in Greek or Latin literature, English literature, or music); *classic* may also serve in this sense, although not in phrases such as *classical education* and *classical allusion. Classic,* an overused word, has the additional sense "outstandingly authoritative or important."

The adverb *classically* can be ambiguous because it answers to both *classic* and *classical.*

classy; class act. These terms are distinctly *déclassé:* "I . . . instantly dismiss anyone who tells me that some other person 'has class,' 'is classy,' or 'is a class act,' the last of these being the most arrogant. What these speakers are telling you is that since they are among the few people who recognize class, it is their obligation to point it out to sorry-ass folks like you." George Carlin, *Brain Droppings* 142 (1997).

claustral. See **cloistral.**

clean, v.t.; **cleanse.** *Clean* is literal, *cleanse* usually figurative. Hence *cleanse* is often used in religious or moral contexts—e.g.:

- "Subsequently, a traditional Navajo medicine man and a Hopi spiritual leader conducted a *cleansing* ceremony that returned the spirit of the student's mother to its resting place." Norine Dresser, "Remaining Safe from the Remains," *L.A. Times*, 20 Apr. 1996, at B7.
- "Wetli has also delved into such exotic religions as voodoo and Santeria, even attending ceremonies where he was rubbed with chickens to *cleanse* him of evil spirits." Mark Mooney, "Medical Examiner Steps into a Harsh Limelight," *Daily News* (N.Y.), 22 July 1996, at 4.
- "Online, meanwhile, authorities struggled to *cleanse* a raging conversation that attacked the official response and the system that had allowed such a disaster to happen." Nathan Vanderklippe, "Rage Against Leaders Builds in Wake of Tianjin Blast," *Globe & Mail* (Toronto), 17 Aug. 2015, at A1.

Marketers and advertisers no doubt understand the subtle distinction between *clean* and *pure* in promising shampoo that "cleanses your hair" and in naming toilet-bowl cleaners *cleansers*. So do propagandists in euphemizing mass slaughter and banishment as "ethnic cleansing."

cleanliness; cleanness. *Cleanliness* (the more frequently used word) refers to people and their habits, *cleanness* to things and places.

cleanly. This word can be either an adverb or an adjective. Most commonly, it functions as an adverb meaning "in a clean manner"—e.g.:

- "Even when it hits off-center (as it does this month) instead of *cleanly*, the moon manages a total eclipse." Bob Beman, "Earthly Shadows," *Discover*, Sept. 1996, at 35.
- "I like the taut lines of the A8's *cleanly* styled body." Richard Truett, "1997 Audi A8," *Orlando Sentinel*, 21 Nov. 1996, at F1.
- "No one could accuse Ritchie of not then striking the ball *cleanly*." Jason Burt, "Benteke Earns Rebuilt Liverpool a Flawed Victory," *Daily Telegraph*, 18 Aug. 2015, at 2.

In this sense, the word is pronounced /**kleen**-lee/.

But sometimes *cleanly* functions as an adjective—and is pronounced /**klen**-lee/—in a sense corresponding to the noun *cleanliness*. It means either (1) "(of a person) habitually clean"; or (2) "(of a place) habitually kept clean." In sense 2, a simple *clean* is surely preferable. In the first and second examples that follow, sense 1 applies. In the third, sense 2 applies:

- "'Owing to the leaning and handling of dirty persons, tobacco-spitting, the deposit of broken fruit and waste of all sorts of eatables, and other filthy practices voluntary or otherwise, the summer houses, seats, balustrades, balconies of the bridges are frequently forbidding to *cleanly* persons, who are thus deprived of what they deem their rights upon the Park.'" Elizabeth Barlow, "Rebuilding the Olmsted," *N.Y. Times*, 9 May 1981, § 1, at 23 (quoting Frederick Law Olmsted, one of Central Park's designers and its original administrator, from a writing dated 1860).
- "'The people who park here are very *cleanly* people. They don't leave any cans or bottles,' he said." Estela Villanueva, "Fair Neighborhood Fares Well," *Des Moines Register*, 28 Aug. 1996, ATE §, at 1 (quoting Bob Wilcox).
- "'Our whole approach to quality assurance is not cracking the whip but to point out why things like dusting the pictures, a *cleanly* [read *clean*] room, are important,' [Ray] Sawyer said." Timothy N. Troy, "Budget Host Cultivates Quality," *Hotel & Motel Mgmt.*, 15 Aug. 1994, at 3.

Note that the first example is antique and that the second and third examples occur in reported speech. Today *cleanly* is more common in speech than in writing.

cleanness. See **cleanliness.**

cleanse. See **clean.**

clearly. Exaggerators like this word, along with its cousins (*obviously, undeniably, undoubtedly*, and the like). Often a statement prefaced with one of these words is conclusory, and sometimes even exceedingly dubious. As a result—though some readers don't consciously realize it—*clearly* and its ilk are WEASEL WORDS. Just how much *clearly* can weaken a statement is evident in the following example, in which the author uses the word to buttress a claim about his own state of mind: "*Clearly*, I am not to be convinced that this is a small matter." Stephen White, *The Written Word* 3 (1984). See OVERSTATEMENT, SENTENCE ADVERBS & **very.** Cf. **obviously.**

cleave, v.t., = (1) to divide or separate, split; or (2) to adhere to firmly. In other words, it has opposite meanings. (See CONTRONYMS.) In sense 1, *cleave* yields the past tense *cleft* (or, less good, *clove*) and the past participle *cleft* (or, again less good, *cleaved*). The past-participial adjective is *cloven*. Hence: "He cleft the Devil's cloven hoof with a cleaver." In sense 2, the verb is inflected *cleave > cleaved > cleaved*. Hence: "Antoinette's tongue *cleaved* to the roof of her mouth, and she said nothing." Wayne Thomas Batson, *The Final Storm* 279 (2006).

The COD sanctions, for BrE usage, *cleave > clove > cloven* for all senses, though *cleft* is used adjectivally in SET PHRASES such as *cleft palate* and *cleft stick*. Luckily, the term is literary, so that generally only literary scholars must trouble themselves with these inflections. See IRREGULAR VERBS.

The past form **clefted* is an infrequent solecism—e.g.:

- "*Clefted* [read *Cleft*] sandstone floors, hand-troweled walls, rough-hewn beams and distressed wood furnishings add to the western feel, says Wood." Sherri Vasquez, "Scale and Natural Materials Define the Mode That's Known as Western," *Rocky Mountain News* (Denver), 31 Mar. 1996, at D19.
- "He doesn't quite nail the subtleties of Ian's inner conflicts, but he's got a fascinating-looking face, with a hugely

---

LANGUAGE-CHANGE INDEX (For the full key, see front matter pp. xxxi, l–li.)
Stage 1: Rejected. **Stage 2:** Widely shunned. **Stage 3:** Widespread but . . . **Stage 4:** Ubiquitous but . . . **Stage 5:** Fully accepted.
Invariably inferior forms marked by asterisk (*). • Ratios represent frequency of prevalent forms vs. variants in current books.

clefted [read *cleft*] chin and an aspect that seems radically different when shot from different angles." Matthew Gilbert, " 'Saint' Saved from Soap by Small Touches," *Boston Globe*, 21 Nov. 1998, at C1.

- "Adding to the confusion is the fact that the valleys in this deeply *clefted* [read *cleft*] buffer zone between Austria and the rest of Italy seem to function as discrete cultural entities." Ben Ross, "Italy's Adventure Centre," *Independent*, 14 Apr. 2012, at 4.

See IRREGULAR VERBS.

LANGUAGE-CHANGE INDEX
*clefted misused for *cleft*: Stage 1
Current ratio (*cleft* vs. *clefted): 151:1

clematis (= a flowering plant that attaches itself to trees, buildings, or fences as it grows) functions as both singular and plural—*clematises and *clemati being rare variants, the latter of which is downright wrong.

Current ratio (*clematis are* vs. *clematises are): 21:1

clench. See **clinch.**

clerk. The AmE pronunciation is /klərk/. The BrE is /klahrk/.

clew. See **clue.**

cliché, n. & adj.; **clichéd,** adj. As a noun, *cliché* was borrowed from French in the mid-19th century to denote a printer's stereotype block (= a metal printing plate that is stamped or cast from a mold). The process was used to send ads, illustrations, and other matter to be printed, especially in multiple publications. By the end of the 1800s, *cliché* and *stereotype* were both being used figuratively, the first for a saying grown trite from overuse, the second for an oversimplified generalization.

Clichéd and *cliché* are both used as adjectives corresponding to *cliché* and meaning "trite" or "stale." Both are 20th-century coinages: the *OED* dates *clichéd* from 1928, *cliché* from 1959. And both have their detractors.

Clichéd is spelled like a regular English verb's past participle, although it does not correspond to any such verb. But probably because past participles often serve as adjectives, *clichéd* sounds comfortable to English ears.

In French, *cliché* is participial in form (analogous to *distingué*, *outré*, and *passé*), answering to the verb *clicher* (= to click). So while *clichéd* sounds like an English participial adjective but traditionally isn't one, *cliché* is a participle in fact—just not in English. And *clichéd* might be called a double past participle.

Yet both forms are well established in English as adjectives. And the *cliché* spelling is becoming more popular all the time.

LANGUAGE-CHANGE INDEX
1. *cliché* as an adjective: Stage 5
2. *clichéd* as an adjective: Stage 3
Current ratio (*clichéd image* vs. *cliché image*): 4:1

CLICHÉS. Writing pundits frequently warn against clichés:

- "The purpose with which these phrases are introduced is for the most part that of giving a fillip to a passage that might be humdrum without them; they do serve this purpose with some readers—the less discerning—though with the other kind they more effectually disserve it." H.W. Fowler, *FMEU1* at 224.

- "Modern writing at its worst does not consist in picking out words for the sake of their meaning and inventing images in order to make the meaning clearer. It consists in gumming together long strips of words [that] have already been set in order by someone else, and making the results presentable by sheer humbug." George Orwell, "Politics and the English Language," in *Modern Essays on Writing and Style* 98, 103–04 (Paul C. Wermuth ed., 1964).

- "Don't use [clichés] unwittingly. But they can be effective. There are two kinds: (1) the rhetorical—*tried and true, the not too distant future, sadder but wiser, in the style to which she had become accustomed*; (2) the proverbial—*apple of his eye, skin of your teeth, sharp as a tack, quick as a flash, twinkling of an eye*. The rhetorical ones are clinched by sound alone; the proverbial are metaphors caught in the popular fancy. Proverbial clichés can lighten a dull passage. You may even revitalize them because they are frequently dead metaphors . . . . Avoid the rhetorical clichés unless you turn them to your advantage: *tried and untrue, gladder and wiser, a future not too distant*." Sheridan Baker, *The Practical Stylist* 243–44 (8th ed. 1998).

As Baker suggests, you'll sometimes need clichés. They're occasionally just the ticket, but only when no other phrase fills the bill. Despite that standard, you'll find more clichés in modern writing than you can shake a stick at. Some common ones are these:

at the end of the day
blissful ignorance
but that's another story
comparing apples and oranges
conspicuous by its absence
crystal clear
far be it from me
fast and loose
get with the program
his own worst enemy
if you catch my drift
innocent bystander
moment of truth
more in sorrow than in anger
more sinned against than sinning
my better half
nip in the bud
on the same page
pulled no punches
sea change
six of one, half a dozen of the other
throw the baby out with the bathwater
viable alternative

In deciding whether to use a cliché, consider the following approaches.

First, you might occasionally pun with the final word of a cliché to arrive at a new kind of memorable truth: a drink might be *conspicuous by its absinthe*; a dirt-talking disc jockey might be *his own worst enema*; a farmer might tend to his *better calf*; bankruptcy is sometimes *a fate worse than debt*. But if you're going to play with a cliché, it should usually be with a pun: don't simply change one word to arrive at the same meaning. That is, don't write *more in sorrow than in outrage* or *comparing apples and pomegranates*. And don't twist the cliché out of shape or extend it and think it becomes fresh again, as one newscaster read from her script about an official's resignation: *It was the ultimate straw that broke the conscience of everyone's back.*

Second, when a cliché suggests itself, you would do well to follow these guidelines: use it only if (1) you work to replace it but can't find a good substitute, and (2) it doesn't strike your ear as being stale. Cf. SET PHRASES.

For more on the subject, see Robert Hartwell Fiske, *The Dimwit's Dictionary: 5,000 Overused Words and Phrases and Alternatives to Them* (2002); Christine Ammer, *Have a Nice Day—No Problem!* (1992); Walter Redfern, *Clichés and Coinages* (1989); Peggy Rosenthal & George Dardess, *Every Cliché in the Book* (1987); Eric Partridge, *A Dictionary of Clichés* (1940; repr. 1963).

client. A. And *customer*. By definition, a *client* is someone who engages the services of a professional, whereas a *customer* gives custom or trade to a business, often with regularity. An accountant or a lawyer has *clients*; a grocery store or telephone company has *customers*.

Yet the line of demarcation between these two words has shifted considerably in recent years. By the 1980s, Massachusetts bureaucrats had begun calling welfare recipients their "clients." See Jon Keller, "Massachusetts's Strange Protest Vote," *Wall Street J.*, 20 Sept. 1990, at A14. By the 1990s, things had gotten worse. For example, the *Sunday Times* writes of two prostitutes: "Both women took *clients* to their flats." John Davison & Michael Durham, "Prostitutes Go in Fear of London 'Ripper,'" *Sunday Times* (London), 18 Aug. 1991, § 1, at 5.

The bad trend continues—e.g.:

- "Many years ago, in a small-claims court in Los Angeles, there was a suit brought by a bookmaker—in an illegal profession—against a *client* [read *customer*] who owed him several thousand dollars." Bill Christine, "Bettors Having Trouble Getting Out of the Gate," *L.A. Times*, 17 Feb. 2002, Sports §, at 8.
- "Yesterday's manslaughter conviction marks the first time in Norfolk County history that a drug dealer has been held accountable for contributing to a *client's* [read *customer's*] death." Dave Wedge, "Man Jailed for Supplying Fatal Drug Dose," *Boston Herald*, 28 June 2002, News §, at 28.
- "Police examined documents belonging to prostitutes and their *clients* [read *customers*] on a road near Naples in Southern Italy in July." "Some Are Fearful as Italy Weighs Legalizing Brothels," *Boston Globe*, 15 Sept. 2002, at A6 (photo caption).

B. Plural Form: *clients*; *clientele*; *clientage; *clientelage; *clientry. *Clients* is the best choice because

it is the least pretentious and by far the most common. *Clientele* has degenerated somewhat in meaning, having been widely used in nonprofessional contexts. E.g.: "Ella B. Sunshine operated a thriving business as a custom dressmaker for an exclusive *clientele* in Greater Cleveland for 25 years." "Ella B. Sunshine, 99, Custom Dressmaker" (obit.), *Plain Dealer* (Cleveland), 27 Jan. 1995, at B11. Indeed, the profession for which *clientele* is perhaps most often used today is the oldest one—e.g.: "Police said the alleged sex-for-sale operation used Asian prostitutes and served an exclusively Asian *clientele*." Peyton Whitely, "Global Links Sought in Alleged Sex Ring," *Seattle Times*, 1 Feb. 1995, at B3.

*Clientage, **clientelage*, and **clientry* are NEEDLESS VARIANTS of *clientele*.

Current ratio (in order of headwords in (B)): 230,399:11,202:398:4:1

climactic; climacteric; climatic. Until the mid-20th century, *climactic* (/klī-**mak**-tik/) was thought to be inferior to *climacteric* (/klī-**mak**-tə-rik/). But by the early 1950s, the shorter word had eclipsed the longer variant as the adjective corresponding to *climax*—e.g.:

- "As the band breaks at the climax, out of the sudden silence Curtis Fowlkes bursts into a solo even more *climactic*." Robert Bourne, "Goin' to 'Kansas City,'" *DownBeat*, Mar. 1996, at 22.
- "In the *climactic* trial, Roxie beats the rap, only to be abandoned by reporters rushing on to the next case." Richard Zoglin, "That Old Razzle-Dazzle," *Time*, 25 Nov. 1996, at 102.

Having fallen into disuse as a NEEDLESS VARIANT of *climactic*, *climacteric* is now to be avoided in this sense. It lives on as a rare scientific term: a *climacteric* fruit is one that can be picked unripe and then induced to ripen in the presence of a hormone-bearing ethylene gas that the fruit itself produces. Apples are *climacteric* fruits and can be forced to ripen (or even spoil) in a paper bag.

But *climacteric* also has legitimate uses as a noun: (1) "an epochal event or critical turning point"; (2) "menopause, or the male phase corresponding to menopause"; or (3) "years of human life marked by multiplying by 7 the odd numbers 3, 5, 7, and 9, the resulting periods occurring at ages 21, 35, 49, 63— some add 81." In sense 3, the ages 63 and 81 are both called the *grand climacteric*.

Climatic (/klī-**mat**-ik/) is the adjective corresponding to *climate*—e.g.: "Long-term weather forecasts, which have been feeding the corn price frenzy, are seen by some as ominous because they include certain *climatic* events associated with droughts in the recent past." John Schnittker, "Thought for Food," *Wash. Post*, 1 May 1996, at A19.

Occasionally, though, *climatic* becomes a MALAPROPISM for *climactic*. This error became widespread in print sources only in the late 20th century—e.g.:

- "In a *climatic* [read *climactic*] finish to more than four hours of questioning, prosecutor Chris Darden asked Lopez if she had told her friend Sylvia Guerra that she was going to be paid $5,000 for her testimony." William Carlsen, "Prosecutor Raises Possibility of Bribe in Alibi for O.J.," *S.F. Chron.*, 3 Mar. 1995, at A1.
- "It became *anticlimatic* [read *anticlimactic*] less than a lap later, however, when Mike Wallace's engine let go, dumping oil on the track." Tom McCollister, "Jarrett Adds Brickyard to 1996 Trophy Case," *Atlanta J.-Const.*, 4 Aug. 1996, at C1.
- "But others are like rocks . . . that plop into the narrative so loudly that subsequent revelations become *anti-climatic* [read *anticlimactic*]." Nancy Pate, "Quindlen Delivers Some Pleasures," *Orlando Sentinel*, 17 Sept. 2002, at E1.

See **anticlimactic.**

LANGUAGE-CHANGE INDEX
1. *climactic* as an equivalent of *climacteric*: Stage 5
2. *climatic* misused for *climactic*: Stage 1
Current ratio (*anticlimactic* vs. **anticlimatic*): 28:1

climb. A. Declension: *climb > climbed > climbed*. The past-tense **clumb* or **clomb* and the past-participial **clumb* are dialectal. They sometimes occur in reported speech, especially **clumb*—e.g.:

- "In 'The Busher Pulls a Mays,' Keefe writes to 'Friend Al' that 'the way we been going you would think we *clumb* in to 1st.'" Jerry Klinkowitz, "Let the Games Begin," *Chicago Trib.*, 23 Apr. 1995, at C1.
- "Mr. Wimberly, who's 73, says he hasn't '*clumb* a tree' and used a cane pole since his 40s." Nancy Kruh, "The Path to Pecan Pie," *Dallas Morning News*, 23 Nov. 1995, at C1.
- "Like Lt. Zebulon Pike said when he discovered it in 1806, 'I seen it and I *clumb* it,' we *clumb* it too, and thrilled to a midsummer snowball fight." Larry Alexander, "'Little Monsters' Head West," *Intelligencer J.* (Lancaster, Pa.), 25 July 2001, at 1.

See IRREGULAR VERBS (D).

LANGUAGE-CHANGE INDEX
*clumb for *climbed*: Stage 1
Current ratio (*climbed* vs. **clumb*): 2,969:1

B. *Climb down*. Although some purists have branded this phrasing illogical, in fact it is perfectly idiomatic—and certainly more natural-sounding than *descend*. E.g.: "When he [Esteban Toledo] was 8, he used to hide in the trees on the golf course in Mexicali. He would *climb down*, fish golf balls out of a pond with his toes, then clean the balls and sell them back to the golfers at the country club." Thomas Bonk, "Behind the Ball," *L.A. Times*, 7 Dec. 1996, at C1. This phrasing became widespread beginning about 1850.

LANGUAGE-CHANGE INDEX
climb down: Stage 5

clinch; clench. These words are historically identical: one word with two spellings. But by 1900 they had undergone DIFFERENTIATION, and they are now distinct words. *Clinch* is figurative, and *clench* physical. Hence you *clinch* an argument, case, or debate, but you *clench* your jaw, or your teeth, or your fists—e.g.:

- "But one claim . . . would really *clinch* the argument." Stephen Jay Gould, "Planet of the Bacteria," *Wash. Post*, 13 Nov. 1996, at H1.

- "Janet *clenched* her teeth together, the way she did when Lynnanne was being snide, and took a step forward." Patricia C. Wrede, "The Lorelei," in *Book of Enchantments* 128, 143 (1996).
- "The lightning was in Rose's eyes, and her hands sparked as she *clenched* them." Ursula K. Le Guin, *Tales from Earthsea* 129 (2001).

Although *clench* is traditionally transitive, it is occasionally used in intransitive constructions to good effect—e.g.: "Her stomach *clenched* in fear." Kathy Lynn Emerson, *Face Down Under the Wych Elm* 8 (2000).

The exceptions to the *clinch–clench* distinction occur in boxing, carpentry, and metalworking: clutching one's opponent in boxing is *clinching*, and fastening something with a screw or a rivet is likewise *clinching*. Apart from these specialized meanings, *clinch* should be reserved for nonphysical contexts. Here it is used ill-advisedly: "After their speeches, Mr. Bentsen and Mr. Clinton *clinched* [read *clenched*] hands together with Gov. Ann Richards on the stage of the party's state convention as 'Deep in the Heart of Texas' played over the loudspeakers." Sam Attlesey & Wayne Slater, "Bentsen Strongly Endorses Clinton," *Dallas Morning News*, 6 June 1992, at A1.

LANGUAGE-CHANGE INDEX
clinch misused for *clench*: Stage 1
Current ratio (*clenched fists* vs. **clinched fists*): 16:1

cling > clung > clung. So inflected—as it has been since the verb first appeared in Old English more than a thousand years ago. Cling to the strong past forms, despite the pitiable shift toward weakening them. It doesn't matter whether the usage is literal or (as in the first and third examples below) metaphorical—e.g.:

- "They were characterized by maudlin string arrangements and the cries of pedal steel guitars that *clinged* [read *clung*] to the pain in her voice." Dave Hoekstra, "Country's Queen: Wynette's Voice Carried Pain, Soul," *Chicago Sun-Times*, 8 Apr. 1998, at 52.
- "A young woman *clinged* [read *clung*] to his arm for support." Jonathan D. Rockoff, "A Peaceful Life Cut Short by Violence," *Providence J.-Bull.*, 28 Sept. 2001, at B1.
- "Central *clinged* [read *clung*] to a 14–13 lead." Jeffrey Reinhart, "'Manheim Magic' Strikes Again," *Lancaster New Era*, 6 Oct. 2001, at B1.
- "With the blaze escalating, Francesca—crying and coughing—climbed onto the window ledge and *clinged* [read *clung*] to the roof to avoid being burned." Bill Hoffman, "In the Line of Fire," *N.Y. Post*, 27 Dec. 2001, at 9.

See IRREGULAR VERBS.

LANGUAGE-CHANGE INDEX
*clinged for *clung* as a past tense: Stage 1
Current ratio (*he clung* vs. **he clinged*): 19,030:1

clique (= a small group of people who keep to themselves and treat others as outsiders) is pronounced either /kleek/ or /klik/ (the former being the preference of most cultivated speakers). The corresponding adjective is *cliquish* (/**kleek**-ish/ or /**klik**-ish/), meaning "snobbishly confining one's interests to a small in-group." E.g.: "Jews and homosexuals appear in the hater's mind as small, *cliquish* and very powerful groups, antipathetic to majority values." Andrew Sullivan, "When Plagues End," *N.Y. Times*, 10 Nov. 1996, § 6, at 52. **Cliquey* (sometimes also spelled **cliquy*) is a NEEDLESS VARIANT.

> Current ratio (*cliquish* vs. **cliquey* vs. **cliquy*): 131:78:1

clitoridectomy; *clitorectomy. *Clitoridectomy* is the traditional and predominant spelling of the term denoting the surgical removal of part or all of the clitoris. It appears more than ten times as often as **clitorectomy*, which was virtually unknown before the mid-20th century.

clitoris is traditionally and preferably pronounced /**klit**-ə-ris/, though /kli-**tor**-is/ is listed as an alternative pronunciation in most current dictionaries. The corresponding adjective is *clitoral* (/**klit**-ə-rəl/)—preferably not **clitoric*.

> Current ratio (*clitoral* vs. **clitoric*): 1,238:1

cloistral; claustral. *Cloistral* is the preferred adjective answering to the noun *cloister* in the literal sense. That is, *cloistral* typically refers to spatial confines—e.g.:

- "From this *cloistral* complex, with its neo-Gothic clock tower, grassy quadrangles and vaulting archways painted primrose yellow, Maharishi, speakerphone at hand, is supervising what he believes to be the salvation of the human race." David Friend, "The Return of Mister Bliss," *Life*, Nov. 1990, at 82.
- "Another home, Casa Prieto López, is larger than the architect's own house, more monumental, and is set amid *cloistral* walled gardens for which enchanted is no empty adjective." Guy Trebay, "Elaborate, Multicolored Altars of Mexico City," *Int'l N.Y. Times*, 14 June 2014, at 23.

Claustral is a Latinate equivalent that is best confined to the metaphorical sense "isolated from the world"—e.g.: "Bosworth's account does have its share of booze, pills, closeted homosexuality and suicide, but instead of a dark and *claustral* world of furtive incest, hers is a story told against the broad landscape of mid-20th-century American politics." *L.A. Times*, 11 May 1997, Book Rev. §, at 9.

*clomb. See **climb (A).**

closable. So spelled (traditionally) in AmE and BrE alike—not **closeable* (a spelling that has inexplicably surged in recent years). See MUTE E.

> Current ratio: 1:1

close proximity is a REDUNDANCY that sprang to popularity in the late 19th century and has not receded.

closure; cloture. The general noun corresponding to the verb *close* is *closure*. E.g.: "Don't expect *closure*—an end to the argument over whodunit—if O.J. Simpson's first feverishly hyped day on the witness stand Friday means anything." Bill Boyarsky, "The Spin: More

Ambiguity than Answers," *L.A. Times*, 23 Nov. 1996, at A21.

In AmE, *cloture* is standard in but one narrow sense: "the procedure of ending debate in a legislative body and calling for an immediate vote." E.g.: "In one Congress in which he was Senate majority leader, the minority leader, Robert Byrd, tried eight times to win *cloture* and break a Republican filibuster on campaign finance reform." "A Promise of Reform," *Wash. Post*, 22 Oct. 1996, at A18. *Closure* is usual in BrE in this parliamentary sense.

clothes is pronounced /klohz/. To pronounce the *-th-* is to engage in HYPERCORRECTION.

cloture. See **closure.**

clove; cloven. See **cleave.**

clubbable (= fit for membership in a club) is the standard spelling. **Clubable* is a variant that vied for supremacy throughout the 19th century and early 20th but had clearly lost by 1950.

> Current ratio: 4:1

clue; clew. *Clue* is the only current spelling for the sense "a hint; a bit of evidence." The spelling *clew* survives as a nautical term ("the lower corner of a sail") and in some literal and mythological references to thread and the like ("a ball of thread").

Clue is construed with *to* or *about*, not *as to*—e.g.:

- "Documents handed over to defense attorneys for Robert Tulloch, 17, and his best friend, James Parker, 16, contain no *clues as to* [read *clues to* or *clues about*] why the pair would kill Half and Susanne Zantop." Franci Richardson & Jack Sullivan, "Link for Suspects, Victims Lacking in Dartmouth Case," *Boston Herald*, 14 Mar. 2001, at 14.
- "She dislikes talking about her playing career and is guarded about giving many *clues as to* [read *clues to*] how good she might have been." Alan Hart, "A Sports Star Still Shines in Schuylerville," *Times Union* (Albany), 27 Mar. 2001, at F7.

See **as to.**

> Current ratio (*no clues* vs. *no clews*): 8:1

cluing. So spelled (traditionally) in AmE and BrE alike—not **clueing* (which, like **closeable*, has mysteriously swelled in popularity since about 1980). See MUTE E.

*clumb. See **climb (A).**

c/o. This abbreviation for *in care of* has legitimate uses and odd misuses. If Vicki Jackson of Los Angeles is visiting Bob Lindsay, one of her bankers in Dallas, and someone has sent a package to her in Dallas for midday delivery, then the address should probably read: "To Vicki Jackson, c/o Bob Lindsay, InterSecure Bank." That way, if the receptionist doesn't know who

LANGUAGE-CHANGE INDEX (For the full key, see front matter pp. xxxi, l–li.)
Stage 1: Rejected. **Stage 2:** Widely shunned. **Stage 3:** Widespread but . . . **Stage 4:** Ubiquitous but . . . **Stage 5:** Fully accepted.
Invariably inferior forms marked by asterisk (*). • Ratios represent frequency of prevalent forms vs. variants in current books.

Vicki Jackson is, at least the package will be drawn to Bob Lindsay's attention.

But there are also nonsensical uses. For example, a letter to Bob Lindsay shouldn't be addressed to "InterSecure Bank, c/o Bob Lindsay." The address should be simply to "Bob Lindsay, InterSecure Bank."

co-. A. Hyphenation with. Generally, this prefix—which means "together with" or "joint"—does not take a hyphen (e.g., *coauthor, cohost, cosponsor*). The hyphen should appear only when the unhyphenated form might lead the reader to mistake the syllables (e.g., *co-occurrence, co-organizer*) or when the writer thinks that a word is a new form or NEOLOGISM (e.g., *co-golfer, co-secretary*). See PUNCTUATION (J).

B. Attaching to Noun Phrase. This creates an awkward construction but is sometimes almost inevitable, as in *copersonal trainer*. Some writers and editors would make this *co-personal trainer*, which is hardly an improvement. Yet the hyphen is necessary because *co-* modifies the two-word phrase *personal trainer*, not just *personal*. The best solution is simply to avoid the choice altogether, as by writing *fellow personal trainer*.

C. When Unnecessary. The *co-* prefix can be distracting (some people find it impossible to read *coworker* without thinking *cow*, for example), and it's usually best to leave it off when it adds nothing to the meaning of the sentence. It is always redundant in some words <copartner> and often redundant in others <co-conspirator>. And when the meaning is plain from the context, the *co-* prefix is unnecessary and prime for editing—e.g.: "For seven years, the restaurant operated in Belmont—until a recent hefty rent increase chased its *coowners* [read *owners*], Susan Alper and Lauren Speisman, out of that location." "Small Bites," *Boston Globe*, 4 July 2002, Globe West §, at 5.

coarse, adj. The word *coarse* (= [1] inferior in quality, or [2] unrefined, rude, and vulgar) is sometimes misspelled *course* (through confusion with the noun, of course). It's a vulgar, unrefined instance of WORD-SWAPPING—e.g.:

- "Never use *course* [read *coarse*] sandpaper! The grit imbeds itself in the contact metal." Vaughn D. Martin, "Troubleshooting for Boaters," *Electronics Now*, 1 June 1996, at 41.
- "Allow to cool, peel skin off and grate potato with *course* [read *coarse*] grater." "Chef's Choice," *Newcastle Herald*, 14 Apr. 1999, at 32.
- "Since it was developed last spring, 'Action' has raised eyebrows among insiders for its *course* [read *coarse*] language and references to sex." Richard Huff, "'Action' Up for Tough Rating," *Daily News* (N.Y.), 22 July 1999, at 104.

Originally, it is true, *coarse* and *course* were the same word. But the difference in spelling and in meaning emerged in the 18th century, and the words have long since gone their separate ways.

LANGUAGE-CHANGE INDEX
course misused for *coarse*: Stage 1

coauthor, vb. See **author,** v.t. (A).

coaxial (= sharing an axis) <coaxial cable> is the standard spelling. **Coaxal* is a variant.

Current ratio: 194:1

cockscomb; coxcomb. A *cockscomb* is the fleshy red growth on a rooster's head. A *coxcomb* is either a hat resembling a cockscomb (formerly worn by jesters) or a foolishly conceited dandy or fop. Both terms are pronounced /**koks**-kohm/. The figurative *coxcomb* has always been the more frequently used term in Modern English. Its corresponding noun, *coxcombry*, means "foppery."

cockswain. See **coxswain.**

cocoa; cacao. *Cocoa* is a brown chocolate powder or a drink made from this powder. *Cacao* is the tree or the seeds that are the source of cocoa powder. *Cocoa butter* and *cacao bean* are the standard terms—not **cacao butter* and **cocoa bean.*

co-conspirator. See **conspirator** & CO-.

coconut is sometimes spelled **cocoanut* (which was actually the standard spelling up to about 1920)—e.g.: "The bar offers . . . appetizers, salads, sandwiches and pizza, including spicy *cocoanut* [read *coconut*] calamari and sashimi." Susan F. Yim, "Maui, Hawaii," *Star Trib.* (Minneapolis), 16 Feb. 1997, at G8. Unless you're writing a historical novel, stick to *coconut.*

Current ratio: 7:1

code (= [1] a collection of rules <penal code>; [2] a system of symbolic communication <Morse code>; [3] a system of encryption <*The Da Vinci Code*>; or [4] computer programming <machine code>) can be a mass or a count noun. A mass mailing, for example, might target specific ZIP *codes*—there, *code* is a plural count noun. But in sense 4, *code* is preferably a mass noun referring to the entire set of instruction lines in a piece of software, and it's singular in form. E.g.: "[M]any game developers now accept product placements for milk, DVDs and other wares, embedding them deep into the game's software *codes* [read *code*]." Rachel Konrad, "Like Product Placement in Movies, Companies Are Hiding Brands in Secret Code in Video Games," *Houston Chron.*, 16 Jan. 2007, Bus. §, at 4. See COUNT NOUNS AND MASS NOUNS.

codex. Although the more easily understandable plural of this noun—meaning "a bound sheaf of manuscript leaves, esp. of an ancient or classic work or of the Scriptures"—might be *codexes*, the form *codices* is standard: it greatly predominates in print sources. See PLURALS (B).

Current ratio (*codices* vs. *codexes*): 60:1

codify is best pronounced /**kod**-ə-fɪ/, not /**koh**-də-fɪ/. This word, like *codification*, was one of the philosopher Jeremy Bentham's NEOLOGISMS; it dates from around 1800.

coed. This word (which has been traced back to 1875) is quite acceptable as an adjective <coed dormitory>, but not as a noun <a 23-year-old coed>. Why? Two reasons: (1) the noun use almost invariably denotes a female student in a way that strikes many as sexist (men are just called *students*), and (2) the usage dates back to the time when female college students were relatively rare. See SEXISM (E).

*coemployee is a NEEDLESS VARIANT of *coworker*.

coequal, n. & adj., often means nothing that *equal* does not also mean; it should be rejected in those contexts. And while styles vary, it is best spelled without a hyphen (see CO-). E.g.:

- "The Founders of this country were wise enough to know that by establishing three *co-equal* [read *equal*] branches of government, they were also creating an inherent tension." "Courts for the Future," *Baltimore Sun*, 6 Oct. 1996, at F2.
- "Make [actress Meagan] Good more prominent, or at least *coequal with* [read *equal to*] the lead." Verne Gay, "Just Cut 'Mr. Robinson's' Class," *Newsday* (N.Y.), 5 Aug. 2015, at B20.

Yet this word, in frequent use from the 17th century on, can be useful in implying the standard of comparison. For example, in "the co-eternal and co-equal Son," a snippet quoted in the *OED*, if only *equal* had been used the reader would wonder, Equal to what? *Coequal* implies the second and third divinities with which the Son is said to be equal. That type of comparison should always be implicit with this word, even when used as a noun—e.g.: "My company is a large, liberal-minded institution that thrives on convivial collegial consensus among persons who . . . are complete *coequals* right up to the time an actual disagreement occurs. At this point, the rules change slightly. We go from Candy Land to rock–paper–scissors. Editors are rock. Writers are those gaily colored wussy plastic paper clips." Gene Weingarten, "Below the Beltway," *Wash. Post*, 12 May 2002, Mag. §, at W3. This nuance is fairly rare, however; for most purposes, *equal* suffices. Still, it is simplistic to say, as William Safire does, that "today's usage frowns on *co-equal* as redundant." "Send in Sovereign for Socialist," *N.Y. Times*, 6 Jan. 1991, § 6, at 8, 10. Cf. *copartner.

Although *equal* usually takes the preposition *to*, *coequal* takes *with*.

coercible. So spelled—not *coerceable. See -ABLE (A).

coercion, though originally applicable only to physical force, is now commonly used to describe moral and economic pressures. E.g.: "[People are debating] whether 'economically disadvantaged' volunteers can fairly weigh the health risks of tests, or whether the lure of being paid $85 a day, plus room and meals, amounts to economic *coercion*." Chris O'Malley, "NIH Takes Look at Lilly's Drug Tests," *Indianapolis Star*, 24 Nov. 1996, at E1. Such uses are a natural extension of

the original sense ("the control by force of a voluntary agent or action").

coffee klatch. *Kaffeeklatsch,* a German loanword borrowed in the late 19th century, means "a coffee-drinking group that engages in leisurely conversation." It has been anglicized to *coffee klatch,* which since the 1960s has been standard in AmE and BrE alike. In English-speaking contexts, *kaffeeklatsch (despite its being the etymon) is a mere variant, as is *coffee klatsch.

Current ratio (*coffee klatch* vs. *kaffeeklatsch* vs. *coffee klatsch*): 7:2:1

cognition; cognation. *Cognition* = thinking; use of the intellect. *Cognation* = a cognate relationship.

cognitive; *cognitional. *Cognitive* (= of, relating to, or involving cognition, or to the action or process of knowing) is the standard term. *Cognitional is a NEEDLESS VARIANT.

Current ratio: 801:1

cognizant; *cognisant. The *-z-* spelling is standard in AmE and in BrE. Not until the 1940s did BrE begin shedding the *-s-* spelling.

Current ratio: 8:1

cognoscente; cognoscenti. This word, almost always used in the plural (*-ti*), is often spelled incorrectly. The misspellings are varied—e.g.:

- "You'll also find a *cognoscenti's* [read *cognoscente's*] lexicon of ferret lingo." Dan Kincaid, "Magazines," *Ariz. Republic*, 25 Aug. 2002, at E4.
- " 'He was never a favorite of design *cognoscente* [read *cognoscenti*], museum curators and theorists of design.' " Gary Mullinax, "Raymond Loewy," *News J.* (Wilmington, Del.), 25 Aug. 2002, at H10 (quoting a museum director).
- "When the preseason polls come out, don't be surprised if a fair number among the hockey *cognescenti* [read *cognoscenti*] figure that the Bruins won't make the playoffs." Kevin Paul DuPont, "I Love a Parade but Stanley Cup Party for Bruins Is Only a Dream," *Boston Globe*, 13 Sept. 2002, at D1.

Generally, *experts* or *authorities* will suffice, either one being easier to spell—not to mention to pronounce: /kon-yə-**shen**-tee/, /kohn-yə-**shen**-tee/, or /kog-nə-**shent**-ee/.

cohabit, the verb for *cohabitation*, is analogous to *inhabit*—e.g.: "To cohabit is to dwell together," says one treatise, "so that matrimonial cohabitation is the living together of a man and woman ostensibly as husband and wife." Joel P. Bishop, *Marriage, Divorce, and Separation* § 1669, at 694 (1891).

*Cohabitate is a misbegotten BACK-FORMATION that has never seriously competed with *cohabit* in print sources. It appears only sporadically in edited English—e.g.: "There's little evidence that tax rates are pushing people to *cohabitate* [read *cohabit*] rather than marry (most *cohabitating* [read *cohabiting*]

LANGUAGE-CHANGE INDEX (For the full key, see front matter pp. xxxi, l–li.)
Stage 1: Rejected. **Stage 2:** Widely shunned. **Stage 3:** Widespread but . . . **Stage 4:** Ubiquitous but . . . **Stage 5:** Fully accepted.
Invariably inferior forms marked by asterisk (∗). • Ratios represent frequency of prevalent forms vs. variants in current books.

relationships end within two years)." Maggie Galla-gher, "Too Much Talk," *Wash. Post*, 5 Oct. 1997, at C3.

LANGUAGE-CHANGE INDEX
cohabitate for *cohabit*: Stage 2
Current ratio (*cohabiting* vs. *cohabitating*): 8:1

cohabitant; *cohabitee; *cohabitor. **Cohabitee*, though increasingly common (especially in BrE) for a person living with another as if married, is etymo-logically the poorest form. (See -EE.) It ought to be avoided in favor of *cohabitant*, which is more frequent anyway and has long been so—e.g.: "From July, mar-ried people who file for divorce will have a legal right to claim part of their ex-spouse's pension; but *cohabi-tees* [read *cohabitants*] will still have no such right, irrespective of how long their relationship lasted." Jean Eaglesham, "Plan Ahead for an Even Break," *Independent*, 5 May 1996, at 16. Not only is *cohabi-tant* etymologically preferable because it is derived from the present participle of the Latin verb, it is also much more common, especially in AmE. **Cohabitor* is a NEEDLESS VARIANT that seldom occurs.

LANGUAGE-CHANGE INDEX
cohabitee for *cohabitant*: Stage 2
Current ratio (in order of headwords): 38:10:1

*cohabitate. See **cohabit.**

cohabitation. See **adultery** (A).

cohabitative; *cohabitive. The first, long the prevail-ing form, is morphologically superior. The general rule is that in Latinate nouns of this type, the adjectival form derives from the noun form. Hence *cohabitative* follows from the noun *cohabitation*. Cf. **interpretative.**
Current ratio: 3:1

*cohabitee. See **cohabitant.**

*cohabitive. See **cohabitative.**

*cohabitor. See **cohabitant.**

coherent (= [1] clear and reasonable, or [2] connected or united by common goals or beliefs) is preferably pronounced /koh-**heer**-ənt/—not /koh-**hair**-ənt/.

cohort(s). Most traditionally, *cohort* has been a mass noun denoting "a band of warriors." It was extended to nonmilitary uses <the baby-boom cohort>. Some crit-ics, such as Wilson Follett, can accept that extension but regard anything further as a SLIPSHOD EXTENSION:

> [I]f the word is to retain its force it should observe two requirements: (1) it should designate members, too numerous to be conveniently counted, of some sort of united group, and (2) it should imply some sort of strug-gle or contest. *No one of the candidates succeeded in com-pletely marshaling his cohorts before the first ballot* / *To the legion of the lost ones, to the cohort of the damned*—in such uses the sense of the word is preserved.
> *MAU* at 99.

This is a very conservative view of the word, espe-cially given that the sense of a singular "colleague, associate, companion" dates from the 18th century

and has been by far the more common meaning since the mid-20th. E.g.: "Senator Biden and his *cohorts* didn't hear, but it appears that thousands of others did." "Mr. Bork's Book," *Wall Street J.*, 8 Dec. 1989, at A10. Still, this newer meaning has remained a rather informal one for this respectable word, which in for-mal writing often retains its older sense.

Follett's sense 1 is common in phrases such as *birth cohort*, which is defined as a "group, born in the same year, selected for study as the individuals march through time so that researchers can assess the nature and influence of factors affecting their behavior." Der-mot Walsh & Adrian Poole, *A Dictionary of Criminol-ogy* 22 (1983).

LANGUAGE-CHANGE INDEX
cohort in reference to an individual: Stage 5

coiffeur; coiffure. A *coiffeur* is a male hairdresser; the word is pronounced /kwah-**fər**/. (A female hairdresser is a *coiffeuse* /kwah-**fyuuz**/.) A *coiffure*—sometimes shortened to *coif*—is a hairstyle; the word is pronounced /kwah-**fyuur**/.

coin a phrase. To *coin* is to mint afresh, to invent, or to make current—e.g.: "Whoever said money can't buy happiness sure knew how to *coin a phrase*." Tom Weber, "U.S. Mint Causing Two-Bit Ire," *Bangor Daily News*, 20 Aug. 2002, at B1. The phrase doesn't mean "to use," as some writers have mistakenly thought since the mid-20th century—e.g.:

- "To *coin a phrase* [read *borrow a phrase*] from the movie, 'Rudy,' he's six-foot nothing and a hundred and noth-ing." Roger McAfee, "Maturing Merricks Gives Bulldogs Boost," *Intelligencer J.* (Lancaster, Pa.), 28 Feb. 2002, at C1.
- "Rocker kicks it up a notch, *to coin a phrase* [read *as they say*]." Tom Walter, "Who Is This Helen West?" *Commercial Appeal* (Memphis), 8 June 2002, at E1.
- "To *coin a phrase* [read *use a cliché*], 'Knowledge is power.'" Joseph R. Cernuto III, "Port St. Lucie City Council Dis-trict 3," *Stuart News/Port St. Lucie News* (Stuart, Fla.), 1 Sept. 2002, Martin County §, at V36.

You can't coin an old phrase. See WORD PATRONAGE.

Here something is truly (though clumsily) coined: "It will be the age of, to *coin* a rather clumsy neolo-gism, countrycules." Edwin M. Yoder Jr., "Strange New World: The Rise of the Modern Micro-State," *Wash. Post*, 24 June 1990, at C2. (On the use of *-cule* in coun-trycules, see DIMINUTIVES (B).) But technically, to *coin a neologism* is redundant. See NEOLOGISMS.

Although it is typically the writer who is doing the coining when this phrase is used, it may well be some-one else instead—e.g.: "Nearly two years before Neil Armstrong would *coin the phrase* as he stepped onto the lunar surface, the first Saturn V flight—AS-501, in NASA parlance—was truly a 'giant leap' in America's race to the moon." Timothy R. Gaffney, "Saturn V a 'Giant Leap,'" *Dayton Daily News*, 4 Nov. 2002, at B1.

LANGUAGE-CHANGE INDEX
coin a phrase misused to mean
"borrow a phrase": Stage 3

coitus (= the act of having sex) is pronounced /**koh**-i-təs/—not /koh-ɪ-təs/ or /**koy**-təs/.

colander (= a bowl having holes in the bottom and sides for removing liquid, esp. water, from food) has been predominantly so spelled since about 1850. Before that, **cullender* was a frequent variant.

Current ratio: 30:1

coleslaw. So spelled—not **coldslaw*. Yet the mistake isn't uncommon—e.g.:

- "A mound of French fries and a big bowl of creamy *cold-slaw* [read *coleslaw*] arrived." Robert Lindsey, "Correspondent's Choice," *N.Y. Times*, 30 Oct. 1983, § 10, at 10.
- "When Tyler's Place burned earlier this year, Orange Mounders lost more than a place to go for great and delicious hamburgers and hot dogs with Glover's famous secret *coldslaw* [read *coleslaw*] recipe." Whitt A. Sengstacke Jr., "Tyler's Place, Orange Mound Landmark, Rising from Ashes to Former Beauty," *Tri-State Defender* (Memphis), 20 May 1998, at B8.
- "This week, Jamie Oliver sets out to make enough fried chicken, *coldslaw* [read *coleslaw*], sticky potato wedges and charred corn to feed a family of four—for just £10." "Best Documentary," *Irish Independent* (Belfast), 28 June 2014, at 46.

The error derives from folk etymology, the mistaken notion being that the term refers to the temperature at which the dish is ordinarily served. The true etymology is that *coleslaw* comes from the Dutch *koolsla* [*kool* "cabbage" + *sla* "salad"]. See ETYMOLOGY (D).

LANGUAGE-CHANGE INDEX
coleslaw misspelled **coldslaw*: Stage 1
Current ratio: 438:1

coliseum; colosseum; Colosseum. For the amphitheater of Vespasian in Rome, *Colosseum* is the proper name. For any other large building or assembly hall, the word is traditionally *coliseum* (AmE) or *colosseum* (BrE). But since 1970 or so, BrE has tracked AmE on this point, so that *coliseum* is preferred in both the primary varieties of English.

collaborate. For the confusion of this word with *corroborate*, see **corroborate (C).**

collaborator. The phrase **fellow collaborator* is a REDUNDANCY—e.g.: "According to longtime set designer and *fellow collaborator* [read *collaborator*] Catherine Martin, Luhrmann succeeds in leaving his mark on a film whose title insists only on the mark that 'William Shakespeare' has left on the Romeo and Juliet legend." Courtney Lehmann, *Shakespeare Remains* 145 (2002).

collage is pronounced /kə-**lahzh**/.

collapsible. So spelled—not **collapsable*. See -ABLE (A).

Current ratio: 184:1

collate (= [1] to compare critically; [2] to assemble in order; or [3] to verify the order of) is best pronounced /**kol**-ayt/ or /kə-**layt**/, not /**koh**-layt/.

collect is a verb sometimes loosely used in the press. As any lawyer will confirm, being awarded damages is quite a different thing from collecting them: "Under Thursday's ruling, plaintiffs could *collect* [read *seek* or *receive*] damages from local governments only if they proved that discrimination resulted not from the act of an individual but from an official policy." William Choyke, "High Court Backs DISD in Rights Suit," *Dallas Morning News*, 23 June 1989, at A1. Perhaps most local governments would be good for most judgments, but to use *collect* in this way is sloppy thinking about the law. *Receive*, which sounds akin to *collect*, is actually quite different because it connotes a giver (the jury).

collectible; collectable. First, the adjectival uses. The *-ible* spelling, long the predominant form, is much more common than the *-able* spelling in AmE. But in BrE, *collectable* has prevailed in print sources since about 1935. See -ABLE (A).

With the noun uses, especially as a plural, the story is different. The spelling *collectibles* is predominant in both BrE and AmE—more strongly so in AmE. That has been so since the noun use came to prominence in the 1970s.

Current ratio (*highly collectible* vs.
highly collectable): 2:1
Current ratio (*collectibles* vs. **collectables*): 13:1

COLLECTIVE NOUNS. A. Number. A collective noun names an aggregate of individuals or things with a singular form. For example, *ensemble*, *group*, and *team* refer to several people, but each word is singular.

The main consideration in skillfully handling collective nouns is consistency in the use of a singular or plural verb. If, in the beginning of an essay, the phrasing is *the faculty was*, then every reference to *faculty* as a noun should be singular throughout the whole. On the other hand, a writer who wishes to emphasize the individual members more than the body of people may decide to write *the faculty were*, though *members of the faculty were* is preferable because it's more accurate.

But switching back and forth between a singular and a plural verb is lamentably common: "Mark Pattison's *Memoirs* is not strictly speaking an autobiography . . . . His *Memoirs* do not so much tell the story of his life . . . . Mark's father, as the *Memoirs* make plain, dominated his son's early years . . . . The *Memoirs* describes clearly. . . ." V.H.H. Green, Introduction, Mark Pattison, *Memoirs of an Oxford Don* 1, 6 (1988). Here, the problem seems to arise because the writer can't decide on a consistent use of the common

LANGUAGE-CHANGE INDEX (For the full key, see front matter pp. xxxi, l–li.)
Stage 1: Rejected. **Stage 2:** Widely shunned. **Stage 3:** Widespread but . . . **Stage 4:** Ubiquitous but . . . **Stage 5:** Fully accepted.
Invariably inferior forms marked by asterisk (*). • Ratios represent frequency of prevalent forms vs. variants in current books.

noun *memoirs*, which may be used as a plural noun but should not be capitalized, and the proper noun *Memoirs*, which is the singular title of a book.

Apart from the desire for consistency, there is little "right" and "wrong" on this subject: collective nouns sometimes take a singular verb and sometimes a plural one. The trend in AmE is to regard the collective noun as expressing a unit; hence, the singular is the usual form. When the individuals in the collection or group receive the emphasis, the plural verb is acceptable <that deconstructionist school were not wholly in error>. But generally in AmE, collective nouns take singular verbs, as in *the jury finds, the panel is, the committee believes, the board has decided*, etc.

B. BrE vs. AmE. Just the opposite habit generally obtains in BrE, where collective nouns tend to take plural verbs. The British tend to write, e.g., "The *board have* considered the views of the shareholders." BrE has gone so far in some contexts that many Americans would suspect a typographical error: "Oxford were the winners of the 136th University Boat Race, but many will say that Cambridge were the heroes." Richard Burnell, "Oxford Hold Off Brave Light Blues," *Sunday Times* (London), 1 Apr. 1990, at B1. See CONCORD (A).

In the days after the American Revolution, not surprisingly, American practice was closer to the prevailing British practice. E.g.: "The House of Representatives shall chuse *their* [modernly, *its*] Speaker and other Officers; and shall have the sole Power of Impeachment." U.S. Const. art. I, § 2.

The reversal in practice has become so firmly established in AmE that it is hardly wrong to say that with certain collective nouns, singular verbs are preferred. But you can't be doctrinaire on this point of usage. The dilemma frequently occurs with nouns such as *couple, faculty, majority,* and *press*—e.g.:

- "The French press *have* [read, in AmE, *has*] said he is too expansion-minded." Judi Bevan, "Lafarge's Conquering Hero," *Daily Telegraph*, 30 Nov. 1997, at 3.
- "And *faculty are* [or *the faculty is*] committed to improving curriculum based on information from a variety of sources." Sarah A. Derks, "State Nursing Panel OK's Shelby State," *Commercial Appeal* (Memphis), 4 Dec. 1997, at A19.

These are questions more of local idiom than of correct or incorrect grammar. See COUNT NOUNS AND MASS NOUNS.

collectivize (= to confiscate private property, esp. means of production and arable land, for government use) has long had strongly negative connotations. E.g.: "The history of the Ukrainian famine—in which Moscow's requisitioning of the Ukrainian harvest, along with its orders to *collectivize* agriculture, caused the starvation of millions of people—was long caught in the disinformation and silence imposed by Stalin." Felicity Barringer, "A City of Memorials Finds Itself Filling Up," *N.Y. Times*, 20 Dec. 2006, at A12.

But lately the term has been acquiring senses more positive—e.g.: "Group shows can be lacking in cohesion, but they can also *collectivize* a definite vibe, a current in art or society." Rosemary Ponnekanti, "Quilts, Nativity House Artists Reflect Societal Contrasts," *News Trib.* (Tacoma), 5 Nov. 2006, at E5. Given the word's history, however, a substitute such as *generate* would serve better in such a sentence.

collegial; collegiate. It would serve the purposes of DIFFERENTIATION and would accord with educated usage to reserve *collegial* as the adjective for *colleague,* and *collegiate* as the adjective for *college*—e.g.:

- "By forging a *collegial* triumvirate with Senate President Stanley Rosenberg and Speaker of the House Robert DeLeo, Baker and his legislative colleagues created budgetary solutions under dire circumstances." "Baker Continues to Earn Our Endorsement," *Enterprise* (Brockton, Mass.), 16 Aug. 2015, at 6.
- "A 2014 study of youth joblessness . . . found roughly 8.5 percent of college graduates between the ages of 21 and 24 were unemployed. . . . It tells us that the post-*collegiate* job market, just like the rest of the labor market, certainly isn't nearly back to normal." "Another Education Subsidy," *Courier* (Findlay, Ohio), 19 Aug. 2015, at 4.

Both words are pronounced with a soft -g- sound (like -j-). *Collegiate* usually doesn't present a problem, since *college* also takes a soft -g- sound. (Note, though, that the three-syllable pronunciation /kə-**lee**-jət/ is preferred over the four-syllable /kə-**lee**-jee-ət/.) But sometimes *collegial* is mispronounced with a hard -g-, probably on the influence of *colleague*. Resist that sort of peer pressure.

collide is construed with *with* or *against*. Although *with* is more common today, the *OED* provides historical evidence of *against*, and that usage still sometimes appears—e.g.: "In the eighth he collided *against* the outfield wall while chasing a drive by Missouri designated hitter Jake Epstein." Rick Cantu, "Aspito's 3-Run Homer Saves Longhorns," *Austin Am.-Statesman*, 20 Feb. 1999, at C3.

Current ratio (*collide with* vs. *collide against*): 86:1

collodion; *collodium. *Collodion* /kə-**loh**-dee-ən/ (= an alcohol–ether solution used as a coating for wounds or photographic film) is the standard term. **Collodium* is a NEEDLESS VARIANT.

Current ratio: 67:1

colloque; *collogue. Both are informal and relatively rare words meaning "to confer (with another) in private." One usage authority labeled **collogue* "colloquial for *talk confidentially.*" George P. Krapp, *A Comprehensive Guide to Good English* 152 (1927). Either would be useful as a verb corresponding to the noun *colloquy*. Because it is already more common, *colloque* is more likely to gain wide acceptance—e.g.: "That won't and shouldn't prevent members who share interests from *colloguing* [read *colloquing*], but it will make at least a small dent in the House budget." "A Tall Wall for the Deficit Cutters," *L.A.*

Times, 12 Dec. 1994, at B6. *Colloque* is pronounced /kə-**lohk**/. See **colloquy.**

Current ratio: 23:1

colloquial. A good deal of confusion has surrounded this word. Traditionally, lexicographers used it to denote that a word so labeled is typical of cultivated conversation or informal speech, as opposed to the most formal style of written prose. E.g.: "The sensible man *speaks* colloquially most of the time. When he wants to be formal or unusually impressive he tries to speak as he thinks he writes. But on these occasions he often makes a pompous ass of himself." Bergen Evans, "Your Speech Is Changing" (1959), in *Readings in the Language Arts* 4, 8 (Verna Dieckman Anderson et al. eds., 1964).

But many dictionary users mistook the label as indicating a departure from high grammatical standards—even though the dictionary writers who used the label had no such intention. Hence *colloquial,* and especially the corresponding noun *colloquialism,* gradually took on negative connotations. In the second half of the 20th century, most lexicographers dropped the labels. At the same time, mediocre writers strove for hyperformal stiffness, as another authority noted: "Most of us, when we write, have a fear of dropping into colloquialism, and so go to almost any lengths of stilted periphrasis to avoid it." G.H. Vallins, *Good English: How to Write It* 145 (1951).

Things have gradually changed, partly as a result of the electronic age: modern communications are increasingly informal. We have come closer to developing a style of speakable writing—one that is natural, idiomatic, and comfortable. Perhaps, after a period of degenerate connotations, *colloquial* will become a term of praise. See CASUALISMS.

colloquy; colloquium. *Colloquy* (/**kahl**-ə-kwee/) means "a formal discussion," as between diplomats or between a judge and counsel. E.g.: "His curious *colloquy* with a 17-year-old boy on sentencing day in a marijuana case got more than the boy's attention." David Doege, "Crawford at Center Court," *Milwaukee J. Sentinel,* 24 Nov. 1996, at 1. Pl. *colloquies.* For the verb corresponding to *colloquy,* see **colloque.**

Colloquium (/kə-**loh**-kwee-əm/)—meaning "an academic conference or seminar"—is frequently misspelled **colloquim.* Most American dictionaries prefer the plural *colloquiums,* but *colloquia* has always been predominant in both AmE and BrE. See PLURALS (B).

Current ratio (*colloquia* vs. *colloquiums*): 10:1

collusion (= an agreement between two or more people to trick or defraud another) always has the flavor of deceit. Occasionally the word is misunderstood to mean "collaboration," as opposed to "collaboration in wrongdoing"—e.g.:

- "Golding's style has the effect of exposing the person of the novelist, as if writer and reader were *working in collusion on* [read *collaborating in*] a tricky moral quest." Jonathan Raban, "The Paper Men," *Atlantic Monthly,* Apr. 1984, at 142.
- "What Mr Boyle calls disappointment (and incentive to renunciation) many readers will surely see as an appetite for more and more, an appetite whetted in a man like Goethe by poetry and real experience, *working in collusion* [read *collaborating*] till the point of death." "A Man of Girth," *Economist,* 11 Mar. 2000.

Is it possible to defraud yourself? No, although writers occasionally try this trick—e.g.: "By working until midnight, you enable your boss to give you assignments late without consequences. No one can take advantage of you without your *collusion* [read *acquiescence*]." Lynne Curry, "Rein in Chaotic Manager," *Anchorage Daily News,* 16 Sept. 2002, at D1.

LANGUAGE-CHANGE INDEX
collusion misused for *collaboration:* Stage 1

collusive (= involving a secret agreement for illegal, esp. fraudulent, purposes) is the preferred form. **Collusory* is a NEEDLESS VARIANT.

Current ratio: 1,251:1

Colombian, adj.; **Columbian.** *Colombian* = of, relating to, or involving the South American country of Colombia. *Columbian* = of, relating to, or involving America or Christopher Columbus.

The adjective *pre-Columbian* (= of, relating to, or involving America before Columbus's arrival) should be so written—not **precolumbian.*

COLONS. See PUNCTUATION (C).

Coloradan; Coloradoan. These two names vie closely for predominance. *Coloradan* has had the slight edge since the 1860s, but there have been periodic reversals in frequency of use in print sources. *Coloradan* is the safest editorial choice for now, even though *Coloradoan* has recently shown signs of resurgence. See DENIZEN LABELS.

Current ratio (*Coloradans* vs. *Coloradoans*): 3:1

colosseum. See **coliseum.**

Columbia; Colombia. Both proper nouns honor Christopher Columbus. The difference in spelling depends on whether the noun derives from Latin or Italian. In North America, the Latin *Columbus* is the basis of *Columbia,* as in the District of Columbia and Columbia University. In South America, the Italian form (*Colombo*) prevails as the name of the nation—Colombia.

Columbian. See **Colombian** & DENIZEN LABELS.

Columbusite. See DENIZEN LABELS.

LANGUAGE-CHANGE INDEX (For the full key, see front matter pp. xxxi, l–li.)
Stage 1: Rejected. **Stage 2:** Widely shunned. **Stage 3:** Widespread but . . . **Stage 4:** Ubiquitous but . . . **Stage 5:** Fully accepted.
Invariably inferior forms marked by asterisk (*). • Ratios represent frequency of prevalent forms vs. variants in current books.

columnist. In pronouncing this word, be sure to sound the *-n-*: /kol-əm-nist/.

comatose. Although the pronunciation /**kom**-ə-tohs/ was once thought preferable, the word is almost universally /**koh**-mə-tohs/ in AmE today. It got that way by analogy with *coma.*

combat is pronounced /**kom**-bat/ as a noun, /kəm-**bat**/ as a verb. Although some authorities accept the inflected forms *combating* and *combated*, those spellings suggest the pronunciations /kəm-**bay**-ting/ and /kəm-**bay**-təd/. *Combatting* and *combatted* are more in keeping with general principles of English word formation: the stress is on the /**bat**/ syllable before and after the suffix is added. See SPELLING (B). Admittedly, however, the spellings *combated* and *combating* predominate in actual usage—perhaps coinciding with a tendency to stress the first syllable. See PRONUNCIATION (C).

Current ratio (*combating* vs. *combatting*): 22:1

combustible. So spelled—not **combustable.* (See -ABLE (A).) **Combustible engine* is a mistake for *combustion engine.* In fact, it erroneously suggests that the engine is flammable (or, as we used to say, *inflammable*—see **flammable**). E.g.:

- "Terrill said the use of *combustible* [read *combustion*] engines, such as those running chain saws, lawnmowers and weedeaters, should be curtailed, as should campfires." Larry D. Hatfield, "Hot Winds Fan New Fire Fears," *S.F. Examiner,* 13 Oct. 1995, at A1.
- "Can El Nino explain this hot winter? La Nina? Or is it our *combustible* [read *combustion*] engines, our coolants, our C.F.C.'s?" D.T. Max, "Ominous Clouds," *N.Y. Times Mag.,* 13 Mar. 2002, § 6, at 19.
- "The international summit on energy and environmental issues is taking place in the city that made its name and fortune from the *combustible* [read *combustion*] engine." Alejandro Bodipo-Memba & Suzette Hackney, "Energy Leaders to Meet in Detroit," *Detroit Free Press,* 1 May 2002, Domestic News §, at 1.

LANGUAGE-CHANGE INDEX
Current ratio (*combustible* vs. **combustable*): 736:1
*combustible engine for *combustion engine*: Stage 1
Current ratio (*combustion engine* vs. **combustible engine*): 303:1

come. A. *Come > came > come.* So inflected. Nonstandard past forms <he come here yesterday> <she hasn't came yet> typify DIALECT. For a good discussion, see Sali Tagliamonte, "*Come/Came* Variation in English Dialects," 76 *Am. Speech* 42, 42–43 (2001).

B. And *go*. Usually, *come* denotes movement toward the speaker's current location <come here, Fido>, while *go* is the opposite <you should go now>. But as with *take* and *bring*, there is room for nuance in using these words. For example, *I'll come over at 8 tonight* is far more idiomatic than *I'll go over at 8 tonight.* One who hears the first sentence knows exactly where the speaker is going, but one who hears the second sentence doesn't. So especially in conversation, it is

point of view that determines word choice rather than notions of movement.

For an analogous problem with *bring* and *take*, see **bring (B).** See also **immigrate.**

C. In Subjunctive Uses. In the phrases *come what may* and *I'll be ready come Friday,* the word *come* exemplifies a persistent use of the SUBJUNCTIVE mood.

D. For *cum*. See *cum.*

comedian; comedienne. In AmE, the word *comedian* is generally used in reference to comic actors or entertainers of either sex—e.g.:

- "The *comedian* fears she has caught herself saying the wrong thing in discussing her one-woman show." Margot Ebling, "Intimate Exposure," *Village Voice,* 26 Nov. 1996, at 86.
- "*Comedian* Amy Schumer wrote and stars in this funny vehicle as a selfish, rude jerk whose pro-pleasure, anti-romance outlook is tested when she meets a nice sports doctor." "Now Showing," *Long Beach Press-Telegram,* 19 Aug. 2015, at 3.

But *comedienne,* despite its sex-specific nature, remains quite common—e.g.: "Clad in a sweater set and black slacks, the five-foot-nothing Deirdre Flint looks more like a kindergarten teacher than a rabble-rousing musical *comedienne.*" Lisa Suhay, "Strudel Is This Comic Singer's Muse," *Christian Science Monitor,* 4 Apr. 2003, Features §, at 16. See SEXISM (D).

comedic. See **comic.**

comedienne. See **comedian.**

come off it. This colloquial idiom is as old as Chaucer. For some reason, a few writers who use it feel inclined to make it **come off of it,* which is unidiomatic—e.g.:

- "There are some presenters who, without ever knowing it, prompt their audiences to think, 'Oh, *come off of it* [read *come off it*].'" Ron Hoff, *"I Can See You Naked"* 97 (1992).
- "Now, we have people who are saying we shouldn't attack these people due to the fact we will accidentally kill civilians. *Come off of it* [read *Come off it*], people; wars and soldiers do not try to pick the civilians as targets, they end up that way." Letter of William Reinhart, *Chattanooga Times/Chattanooga Free Press,* 10 Oct. 2001, at B8.
- "He also rejected the notion that passing a farm bill would guarantee civilian and military food security. 'Let's come *off of it* [read *come off it*],' Lugar demanded. 'To imply somehow we need a farm bill in order to feed our troops, to defend our nation, is ridiculous.'" Deroy Murdock, Pork-Barrel Spending Cuts into War Dollars," *Deseret News* (Salt Lake City), 14 Oct. 2001, at AA7.

See **off of.*

LANGUAGE-CHANGE INDEX
*come off of it for *come off it*: Stage 2
Current ratio (*come off it* vs. **come off of it*): 36:1

comeuppance (= a just rebuke or minor retaliation) is the standard spelling of this Victorian coinage. **Comeupance* is a rare variant.

Current ratio: 761:1

comfort. See **solace.**

comic; comical; comedic. These words are confusingly similar. *Comic* and *comical* both mean "funny" or "humorous." *Comic* is generally used, however, for what is intentionally funny, and *comical* for what is unintentionally funny. Hence the latter term may mean "laughable" in a derisive sense—e.g.: "Kaelin, a struggling actor who was a shaggy-haired, *comical* figure at Simpson's criminal trial, appeared with his hair cut and neatly combed, wearing a white shirt, green tie and dark green sport coat." Linda Deutsch, "Kaelin: Simpson Brooded About Ex-Wife's Sex Life," *Austin Am.-Statesman*, 20 Nov. 1996, at A5.

Comedic = of, relating to, or involving the form or nature of a dramatic comedy—i.e., a play that ends as the audience would wish (as the opposite of *tragic*). E.g.:

- "Director Paula Welter compares the W. Randolph Gavin play to the *comedic* style of television's 'Mad About You.'" Thomas Becnel, "'Heavenly Body' Opens Artspace Theatre Season," *Sarasota Herald-Trib.*, 30 Aug. 1996, at T18.
- "His enormous *comedic* talents were known throughout the industry." Valerie Burgher, "Color Bind," *Village Voice*, 26 Nov. 1996, at 82.

Sometimes *comedic* is misused for *comical*—e.g.: "Their first attempts to navigate the creek were *comedic* [read *comical*]—an aquatic, slapstick skit of unintended rammings and beachings." Paul McHugh, "Canoeists Discover Bay Secrets," *S.F. Chron.*, 18 Dec. 1997, at D7.

LANGUAGE-CHANGE INDEX
comedic misused for *comical*: Stage 1

*comingle. See **commingle.**

comity = a practice among political entities (as countries, states, or courts of different jurisdictions), involving esp. mutual recognition of legislative, executive, and judicial acts (*Black's Law Dictionary* 324 [10th ed. 2014]). E.g.: "The appeals court also held that *comity* prohibited the State judge from conducting an independent hearing on the same factual questions considered by the federal judge." Jennifer P. Heimmel, "State Conviction Reversed After Finding That It Was Obtained by Federal Plea Agreement Breach," *N.J.L.J.*, 18 Mar. 1996, at 29.

The word is sometimes (especially in BrE) mistaken as meaning "league" or "federation," especially in the phrase *comity of nations*. That use typifies SLIPSHOD EXTENSION and involves euphemizing: the vagueness of the phrase seems better to the writer than the directness of a substitute such as *community of nations* or *the family of civilized nations*, which begs the question, Which nations are civilized? Examples of this loose sense follow:

- "It is globally important to bring China into full partnership in the *comity of nations* [read *community of nations*], in spite of recent saber-rattling." "Shocking Position," *Baltimore Sun*, 7 Sept. 1995, at A15.

- "But those settlements did succeed in bringing France and Germany into the *comity* [read *family*] of European nations, despite the suspicions left by decades of conflict." Rodric Braithwaite, "The West Has a Russia Problem It Isn't Facing," *Int'l Herald Trib.*, 3 Dec. 1996, at 8.

Very occasionally, the phrase *comity of nations* appears in a correct sense ("courtesy afforded by countries to one another's political entities")—e.g.: "Furthermore, he said, under the concept of *comity of nations*, or a mutual respect for other countries' laws, a successful overseas liability claim could be subsequently brought against the company in a U.S. court." Judy Greenwald, "Exports Create Unique Exposures," *Bus. Ins.*, 2 Dec. 1996, at 2.

LANGUAGE-CHANGE INDEX
comity of nations for *community of nations*: Stage 1

commander-in-chief. Pl. *commanders-in-chief*—not **commander-in-chiefs*. See PLURALS (G).

Current ratio: 15:1

commando. Pl. *commandos*, the variant *commandoes* having been superseded long ago (by 1900). See PLURALS (D).

Current ratio: 18:1

COMMAS. See PUNCTUATION (D).

COMMA SPLICES. See RUN-ON SENTENCES.

commemorative; *commemoratory. The first has been standard since the 16th century; the second is a NEEDLESS VARIANT.

Current ratio: 724:1

commence; begin; start. Except in describing formal ceremonies or exercises, or legal actions, *commence* is usually unnecessarily stilted for *begin*, with which it is denotatively equivalent. The *OED* notes that "*begin* is preferred in ordinary use; *commence* has more formal associations with law and procedure, combat, divine service, and ceremon[y]." Often *commence* appears where *begin* would be better—e.g.: "Scungio was told that if she hoped to build a house before the town *commenced* [read *began*] work on the road . . . , she should propose what sort of gravel thoroughfare she could pay for." Barbara C. Potter, "Planning Board Approves Hartford Pike Rezoning," *Providence J.-Bull.*, 6 Mar. 1997, at D6. See **begin (B).**

Stylists have long condemned *commence* if it introduces an infinitive, *begin* being preferable—e.g.: "She trekked into the wilds of Africa and *commenced to live among and study* [read *began to live among and to study* or *began living among and studying*] mankind's closest relations." Michael Kilian, "Grunt Work," *Chicago Trib.*, 3 Sept. 1995, at C1.

Definite nuances exist with *start* as opposed to *begin* or *commence*. Usually used of physical movement, *start* suggests an abruptness not present in the

LANGUAGE-CHANGE INDEX (For the full key, see front matter pp. xxxi, l–li.)
Stage 1: Rejected. **Stage 2:** Widely shunned. **Stage 3:** Widespread but . . . **Stage 4:** Ubiquitous but . . . **Stage 5:** Fully accepted.
Invariably inferior forms marked by asterisk (*). • Ratios represent frequency of prevalent forms vs. variants in current books.

other two words <gentlemen, start your engines>. See **institute**.

commendable; commendatory. The former means "praiseworthy, laudable" <a commendable achievement>, and the latter means "expressing commendation, laudatory" <a commendatory letter of appreciation>. Like other differentiated pairs ending in *-able* and *-atory*, these words are sometimes confused. Most commonly, *commendatory* erroneously displaces *commendable*—e.g.:

- "It is reprehensible . . . to write a brief primarily to express an uncomplimentary opinion of one's adversary; it is *commendatory* [read *commendable*] to write a brief for the purpose of advising the court; it is neither reprehensible nor *commendatory* [read *commendable*] to write a brief because the client insists—merely good business." Mortimer Levitan, "Confidential Chat on the Art of Briefing," 1957 *Wis. L. Rev.* 59, 60.
- "Responses of American business to disaster have included some *commendatory* [read *commendable*] actions." James Russell, "Kind Acts Abundant in Wake of Storm," *Miami Herald*, 17 Sept. 1992, at C3.
- " 'It is very *commendatory* [read *commendable*] that Dr. [Philip] Conn has put the interests of the university ahead of his own interests,' [J. Wade] Gilley said." "Martin Chancellor Requests Reassignment," *Chattanooga Times/Chattanooga Free Press*, 19 Sept. 2000, at B5.

LANGUAGE-CHANGE INDEX
commendatory misused for *commendable*: Stage 1
Current ratio (*commendable* vs.
commendatory): 12:1

commensurate. A. And *commensurable*. In all but mathematical contexts, *commensurable* is a NEEDLESS VARIANT of *commensurate*. *Commensurable* legitimately means "having, or reducible to, a common measure; divisible without remainder by the same quantity" (*OED*). *Commensurate* (/kə-**men**-shuur-ət/) means (1) "coextensive"; or (2) "proportionate."

B. Confounded with *commiserate*. Through WORD-SWAPPING, writers sometimes confuse *commensurate* with *commiserate* (kə-**mi**-zə-rayt), which is properly a verb meaning "to sympathize with." E.g.:

- "For the first time, the Daytona 500 purse is *commiserate* [read *commensurate*] with the race's stature as one of America's premier sporting events." Tony Fabrizio, "Underpaid Drivers Finally Get Due," *Fla. Times-Union*, 12 Feb. 1998, at C5.
- "No major labor implications, though pay *commiserate* [read *commensurate*] with additional responsibilities could be an issue for the Seattle Police Management Association." Kimberly A.C. Wilson, "Schell, Stamper Outline Police 'Action Plan,'" *Seattle Post-Intelligencer*, 21 Sept. 1999, at A1.
- "Lauren LePage, 22, will serve as assistant to the governor's chief of staff, John McGough—a position that administration officials describe as entry-level and is *commiserate* [read *commensurate*] with her experience, work history and education." Kevin Miller, "LePage Gives Staff Position to Daughter," *Bangor Daily News*, 23 Dec. 2010, at 1.

LANGUAGE-CHANGE INDEX
commiserate misused for *commensurate*: Stage 1
Current ratio (*is commensurate with* vs.
*is commiserate with): 459:1

comment; commentate. The longer form is a BACK-FORMATION from *commentator*, but an established one dating from the late 18th century. If *commentate* were only a NEEDLESS VARIANT of *comment*, its existence would be unjustified. But it enjoys the DIFFERENTIATION of meaning "to give a commentary on" or "to expound persuasively or interpretatively." Meanwhile, *comment* implies brevity. Hence scholarly commentators typically *commentate* rather than *comment* when expounding their disciplines. The word is, of course, grandiose when used of television journalists and, more so, sportscasters. Still, it is too late to object to their being called *commentators*.

Both verbs are traditionally intransitive <she commented favorably on the book> <he commentated for ABC Sports during the U.S. Open>. *Commentate* is now sometimes used as a transitive verb <he commentated the U.S. Open>, but the newfangled usage is not recommended.

LANGUAGE-CHANGE INDEX
1. *commentate* as a verb: Stage 5
2. *commentate* as a transitive verb (e.g., *He commentated the Masters*): Stage 1

COMMERCIALESE. This is the peculiar JARGON of business, typified by words and phrases such as these (from correspondence):

> acknowledging yours of
> beg to advise
> enclosed herewith
> enclosed please find
> further to yours of [date]
> in regard to
> inst.
> in the amount of
> of even date
> pending receipt of
> please be advised that
> please return same
> pleasure of a reply
> prox.
> pursuant to your request
> regarding the matter
> regret to inform
> thanking you in advance
> the undersigned
> this acknowledges your letter
> ult.
> we are pleased to note
> with regard to
> your favor has come to hand
> yours of even date

Books on business writing have long admonished writers to avoid these mind-numbing wads of verbiage—e.g.: "All stereotyped words [that] are not used in talking should be avoided in letter writing. There is an idea that a certain peculiar commercial jargon is appropriate in business letters. The fact is, nothing injures business more than this system of words found only in business letters. The test of a word or phrase or method of expression should be, 'Is it what I would say to my customer if I were talking to him instead of writing to him?'" Sherwin Cody, *How to Do Business by Letter* 20 (19th ed. 1908). Cf. OBSCURITY.

For more on the subject, see the following books:

- L.E. Frailey, *Handbook for Business Letters* (2d ed. 1965).
- Maryann V. Piotrowski, *Effective Business Writing* (1989).
- Gary Blake & Robert W. Bly, *The Elements of Business Writing* (1991).
- Charles T. Brusaw et al., *The Business Writer's Handbook* (4th ed. 1993).
- Bryan A. Garner, *HBR Guide to Better Business Writing* (2013).

comminate; comminute. The first means "to denounce," the second "to pulverize." Which verb is more frequently used? *Comminute*—from the 18th century on.

commingle; *comingle. *Commingle* (= to mingle together) has been the accepted spelling since the 18th century. In contemporary print sources, it is about 17 times as common as *comingle, which, though slightly older, has failed to become standard. E.g.: "Humor and pathos *comingle* [read *commingle*] evenly." "Rich, Relevant 'Raisin,'" *Seattle Times*, 28 Oct. 1994, at H25. When *comingle does appear, it's often unnecessarily hyphenated—e.g.: "Sexuality and violence *co-mingle* [read *commingle*] here, so this is not for the squeamish." Kim Morgan, "'Fudoh' Highlights Mike's Intoxicating Violence and Humor," *Oregonian* (Portland), 18 Oct. 2002, Arts & Living §, at 20.

There are two diametrical tendencies: (1) the growing prevalence of the spelling *commingle*; and (2) the shift in popular pronunciation away from the preferred /kə-**ming**-gəl/ and toward /**koh**/ for the first syllable. These two tendencies are at odds with each other; they seem certain to keep usage unsettled.

Although *mingle* has also been used in reference to combining funds, *commingle* is the more usual term—e.g.: "You do not want to *mingle* [read *commingle*] these funds with other IRA accounts." Carla Lazzareschi, "How Co-ops Differ from Condos," *L.A. Times*, 8 May 1994, at D4.

LANGUAGE-CHANGE INDEX
*comingle for *commingle*: Stage 1
Current ratio (*commingle* vs. *comingle): 17:1

comminute. See **comminate.**

commiserate. See **commensurate (B).**

*commissible. See **committable.**

commitment; commission; committal. *Commitment* = (1) dedication; devotion to a special task or purpose <the company's unwavering commitment to the black community>; (2) an engagement to fill a future obligation <she has several commitments this month>; or (3) the action of committing an insane or mentally retarded person to the charge of another <his mental illness led to commitment to an asylum>.

Commission = (1) the authority to perform a task or function <this action exceeded the delegate's commission>; (2) a group of people entrusted with this authority, usu. by appointment <the health commission's meeting lasted all day>; (3) a military appointment <the cadet received his commission on the eve of battle>; (4) a payment made to an agent or broker, usu. as a percentage of a sale <Joyner received a 4% commission>; or (5) the action of doing or perpetrating (a crime, etc.) <the commission of a felony>.

Committal is a NEEDLESS VARIANT of the other two terms in all but two senses. First, it bears the sense "the action of burying a body in a grave"—e.g.: "*Committal* services and burial will take place at a later date in Cold Spring Cemetery, Cape May." "Gretchen Neubrand" (obit.), *Stuart News/Port St. Lucie News* (Stuart, Fla.), 20 Mar. 1997, at B4. Second, in BrE *committal* refers to the imprisoning of a debtor as a way of enforcing a court's judgment.

committable; *commissible; *committible. The first has been the established form since the early 18th century. E.g.: "That leaves Mata, who has had many psychological evaluations since being extradited to Minnesota, in limbo. He is neither competent nor *committable*." Margaret Zack, "Man Is Incompetent to Stand Trial, but Also Uncommittable," *Star Trib.* (Minneapolis), 22 July 1997, at B1. The other forms are NEEDLESS VARIANTS. See -ABLE (A).

Current ratio (*committable* vs. *commissible): 14:1

committal. See **commitment.**

committee. So spelled. See SPELLING (A).

*committible. See **committable.**

common. See **mutual (A).**

commonality; commonness; commonalty; commonage; *commonty. The common character of these words may cause confusion. The ordinary words are *commonality* and *commonness*. Although historically the two have overlapped, they are best kept separate in accordance with the following definitions. *Commonness*, the general noun corresponding to *common*, may mean: (1) "the state or quality of being common" <the commonness of cable television>; (2) "the quality of being public or generally used" <the commonness of the thoroughfare>; (3) "the state of being run-of-the-mill" <the commonness of his writing>; or (4) "vulgarity" <the commonness of a sot>. *Commonality* = the possession of an attribute in common with another <stressing commonality rather than divisiveness>.

The remaining words are more easily distinguished. *Commonalty* = (1) commoners; the general body of the community (excluding nobility); (2) a municipal corporation (a sense to be avoided with this word

LANGUAGE-CHANGE INDEX (For the full key, see front matter pp. xxxi, l–li.)
Stage 1: Rejected. **Stage 2:** Widely shunned. **Stage 3:** Widespread but . . . **Stage 4:** Ubiquitous but . . . **Stage 5:** Fully accepted.
Invariably inferior forms marked by asterisk (*). • Ratios represent frequency of prevalent forms vs. variants in current books.

because *corporation* is the ordinary term); or (3) a general group or body. In the following sentence, the writer may be using *commonalty* in sense 3—in which case it's a REDUNDANCY—or may have intended *commonality*: "The Alabama code stood as a statement of the rules of the game that a family of professionals . . . adhered to in recognition of their *commonalty* [read *commonality*?] and because it might, by forcing an affiliation, help keep them out of trouble." Jethro K. Lieberman, *Crisis at the Bar* 56 (1978). But *commonalty* probably displaces *commonality* as often as it does because it is a typo that spell-checkers can't catch and that proofreaders easily miss—e.g.: "The two candidates—incumbent Leon Young and challenger Walter Lanier—also say they want to create more programs tailored to the youths in the area, but that's where the *commonalties* [read *commonalities* or, better, *similarities*] between the two end." Felicia Thomas-Lynn, "Battling Democrats Agree on Profiling," *Milwaukee J. Sentinel*, 4 Sept. 2002, at B5.

Commonage = (1) the right to pasture animals on common land; (2) the condition of land held in common; or (3) an estate or property held in common. **Commonty*, in its existing uses, is a NEEDLESS VARIANT of *commonage*.

LANGUAGE-CHANGE INDEX
commonalty misused for *commonality*: Stage 1

common-law marriage has one meaning in AmE and another in BrE. In American law, the phrase generally denotes an agreement to be married, followed by cohabitation and a public recognition of the marriage. Common-law marriages are valid in many states, such as Texas, though others have abolished the institution, as New York did in 1932.

In England, *common-law marriage* now refers only to a marriage celebrated according to a common-law form in a place where the local forms of marriage cannot be used (e.g., a desert island) or are morally unacceptable to the parties (e.g., because of religious differences), or where no cleric is available. Additionally—and more commonly in BrE—the phrase refers to an illicit union of some duration. As Sir Robert Megarry writes, "The so-called *common-law marriage*, little known in England save as a polite verbal cloak for fornication or adultery of the less ephemeral type, has a respectable ancestry in America." *A Second Miscellany-at-Law* 210 (1973).

commonness. See **commonality.**

common noun. See **proper noun.**

commonsense, adj. **A. And *commonsensical*; **commonsensible*.** The adjective *commonsense* (always solid as this part of speech) dates from the mid-17th century and vastly predominates over the other two, both of which date from the mid- to late 19th century. *Commonsense* should generally be preferred over *commonsensical* or **commonsensible* <a commonsense approach>—though *commonsense* may cause a MIS-CUE if it does not immediately precede the noun it

modifies <an approach that is commonsense>. That is, it may be read as a noun when it functions as a predicate adjective.

As between *commonsensical* and **commonsensible*, one might suspect that *-ible* would be the more usual: the dictionaries have traditionally listed it first, and it's modeled on the existing word *sensible*. (*Sensical* is rare.) In fact, though, *commonsensical* predominates in print sources by a more than 120-to-1 ratio—e.g.: "But Kim argued that his actions regarding Flores's artwork were simply practical and *commonsensical*." Celeste Katz, "Culture Clash," *Providence J.-Bull.*, 6 Nov. 1997, at D1. But again, *commonsensical* should be confined to uses—as in the example just quoted—in which a noun doesn't immediately follow.

Current ratio (*commonsense reasons* vs.
commonsensical reasons): 7:1
Current ratio (*commonsensical* vs.
*commonsensible): 122:1

B. And *common sense*, n. Although the adjective is one word, the noun is two: *common sense*.

*commonty. See **commonality.**

commonweal; commonwealth. *Commonweal* = the general welfare or common good. E.g.: "It has become shorter than a Chicago spring, this post-election respite when politicians have some small latitude to do what is necessary for the *commonweal* rather than what is necessary to get re-elected." John McCarron, "Buckling Down to Work," *Chicago Trib.*, 4 Nov. 1996, at 21.

Commonwealth = a nation, state, or other political unit <the British Commonwealth>. E.g.: "While no one in the police department or the *commonwealth*'s attorney's office could remember a case in which a convicted criminal actually harmed a witness, the threats have intimidated witnesses into retracting testimony or disappearing." Gordon Hickey, "Witness's Safe Houses Sought," *Richmond Times-Dispatch*, 26 Nov. 1996, at B3. Among the 50 states, four are traditionally known as *commonwealths*: Kentucky, Massachusetts, Pennsylvania, and Virginia. See **territory.**

communicative; *communicatory. The latter has been a NEEDLESS VARIANT since the 17th century.

Current ratio: 633:1

commute. A. And *commutate*. The latter is a technical term meaning "to regulate the direction of (an electric current)." *Commute* = (1) to travel back and forth regularly, esp. over a significant distance and esp. to one's job; (2) to exchange (a punishment or penalty) for one of less severity; or (3) to change (one kind of payment) into or for another.

B. And *pardon*. In sense 2, to *commute* a punishment or penalty is to reduce it, or to substitute in its place a milder punishment or penalty. To *pardon* someone who has been convicted or punished is to excuse the person without exacting any further penalty.

compact, n., adj. & v.t. The noun is accented on the first syllable, the verb on the second. The adjective is rendered both ways, preferably /kəm-**pakt**/ except in reference to a midsize car.

compactible; compactable. Since the mid-20th century, the first has been predominant in AmE, the second in BrE. See -ABLE (A).

comparable; comparative. *Comparable* is stressed on the first syllable (/**kom**-pə-rə-bəl/); *comparative* is stressed on the second syllable (/kəm-**par**-ə-tiv/ or /-**pair**-/). *Comparable* = capable of being compared; worthy of comparison <comparable salaries>. *Comparative* = (1) of, relating to, or involving comparison <a comparative discourse on economics>; (2) involving comparison <the field of comparative religion>; or (3) estimated by comparison <comparative distances>.

Occasionally *comparative* is used where *comparable* is called for—e.g.: "This industry, from the capital standpoint, is quite *comparative with* [read *comparable to*] the banking industry." John M. Boyle, "The Role of Capital in the Banking Industry," *Am. Banker*, 2 Dec. 1980, at 4. Though the *OED* documents this use of *comparative* with four examples ranging from the early 17th to the early 19th century, it labels the usage obsolete.

For a common mispronunciation of *comparable*, see PRONUNCIATION (B).

LANGUAGE-CHANGE INDEX
comparative misused for comparable: Stage 1

COMPARATIVES AND SUPERLATIVES. A. Choice Between Comparative and Superlative. When two items are being compared, a comparative adjective is needed <the greater of the two>; when more than two are being compared, the superlative is needed <the greatest of the three>. The blunder of using the superlative adjective when only two items are being compared is increasingly common, especially in AmE—e.g.:

- "The *tallest* [read *taller*] of the two pyramids is nearly 500 feet." Alan Byrd, "Pyramids? Not in My Backyard, Foes Say," *Orlando Bus. J.*, 30 Sept. 1994, at 1.
- "He has raced in *worst* [read *worse*] conditions, of course, and often won." Samuel Abt, "Rain Plagues Tour de France," *Austin Am.-Statesman*, 2 July 1995, at C8.
- "With the first half of the game over, the *most* [read *more*] important half is yet to be played—this time on the voter's turf." Dan Luzadder & Lynn Bartels, "Broncos Score Upset on Political Field," *Rocky Mountain News* (Denver), 12 May 1996, at A5.
- "The *youngest* [read *younger*] of Jean's two children from a previous marriage, a 16-year-old boy, lived with the couple until about a year ago." Nancy Lewis, "Crafts a Lucrative Outlet for Legally Blind Woman," *Virginian-Pilot* (Norfolk), 10 Oct. 1996, at 15.

One idiomatic exception occurs when we put our *best foot* forward, since (of course) we have only two.

LANGUAGE-CHANGE INDEX
Superlative with two objects <best of the pair>: Stage 4

B. Which to Use—Suffixes or *more* and *most*? Apart from irregular forms such as *good > better > best*, comparatives and superlatives are formed by either (1) adding the suffixes -*er* and -*est* (e.g., *broader, broadest*), typically when the adjective is one or two syllables; or (2) using the additional words *more* and *most* (e.g., *more critical, most critical*), a form required with words having three or more syllables and typical with two-syllable words. It was once possible to write *interestinger* and *honestest*, but no longer. Several words have a choice of forms (e.g., *commoner, -est* or *more, most common; tranquil(l)er, -est* or *more, most tranquil; stupider, -est* or *more, most stupid; naiver, -est* or *more, most naive*). The terminational forms are usually older, and some of them are becoming obsolete.

Still, if a word ordinarily takes either the -*er* or the -*est* suffix—and that formation sounds more natural—it's poor style to use the two-word form with *more* or *most*. E.g.:

- "Few things in this world short of yard work are *more dull* [read *duller*] than watching animated characters play basketball." Daniel Neman, "Double Drivel," *Richmond Times-Dispatch*, 15 Nov. 1996, at C1.
- "The answers we sought proved *more simple* [read *simpler*] than we imagined." Mike Swift & Deborah Petersen Swift, "The Road Opened Our Hearts," *Hartford Courant*, 7 Jan. 1997, at A1.

C. *Be*-Verbs Repeated After Comparatives. It usually isn't necessary to repeat the verb *to be* before the second element of the comparison—e.g.: "Thus, full-scale intervention is much *less likely than is* [read *less likely than*] subversion or other covert activities in such cases." Richard K. Herrmann & Michael P. Fischerkeller, "Beyond the Enemy Image and Spiral Model," *Int'l Organization*, 22 June 1995. And if the *be*-verb is repeated, it usually shouldn't go immediately after *than*. The preceding example, then, might read: *Thus, full-scale intervention is much less likely than subversion or other covert activities are in such cases.* See INVERSION & **than** (A).

D. The Double Comparative. Among literate speakers and writers, the double comparative is fairly uncommon. But it does occasionally appear in print—e.g.: "Does it mean that change will be a bit *more slower* [read *slower*], a bit more careful, a bit more reasoned than totally revamping the health care system? Yes." Leonard Marcus, "New Approach Needed to Restore System's Balance," *Am. Medical News*, 2 Dec. 1996, at 45. (If the writer of that sentence wanted the PARALLELISM of three *mores*, then the first phrase should have been *more slow*.)

LANGUAGE-CHANGE INDEX
*more slower for slower, etc.: Stage 1

For an example of the double superlative, see *****least worst.**

LANGUAGE-CHANGE INDEX (For the full key, see front matter pp. xxxi, l–li.)
Stage 1: Rejected. **Stage 2:** Widely shunned. **Stage 3:** Widespread but . . . **Stage 4:** Ubiquitous but . . . **Stage 5:** Fully accepted.
Invariably inferior forms marked by asterisk (*). • Ratios represent frequency of prevalent forms vs. variants in current books.

E. *Greater of A (or) (and) B.* Logic loses to idiom when deciding whether to use the conjunctive *and* or the disjunctive *or* in phrases such as *the greater of A [and? or?] B.* Logic would seem to demand *and* to include all the options in the comparison before one is singled out as being the *lesser, biggest, oldest, latter,* etc. But in fact, since the early 20th century *or* has been about ten times as common in print as *and* with this type of phrasing.

F. Absolute Adjectives. See ADJECTIVES (B).

compare and contrast. See **contrast (B).**

compare with; compare to. The usual phrase has for centuries been *compare with,* which means "to place side by side, noting differences and similarities between" <let us compare his goals with his actual accomplishments>. *Compare to* = to observe or point only to likenesses between <he compared her eyes to limpid pools>. Cf. **contrast (A).**

Compare and contrast is an English teacher's tautology, for in comparing two things (one thing *with* another) one notes both similarities and differences.

COMPARISONS, FALSE. See ILLOGIC (B).

compatible. So spelled—not *compatable. See -ABLE (A).

Current ratio: 2,714:1

compel; impel. *Compel* is the stronger word, connoting force or coercion, with little or no volition on the part of the one compelled. *Impel* connotes persuasive urging, with some degree of volition on the part of the one impelled—e.g.: "He moved like a sleepwalker, like one *impelled.*" Ursula K. Le Guin, *The Lathe of Heaven* 88 (1971).

compendious means "abridged, succinct," not "voluminous," as writers often mistakenly believe—e.g.:

- "In an archive at Harvard he found a *compendious* [read *bulky*?], multivolume, handwritten journal entitled 'Amos Webber Thermometer Record and Diary.'" Jonathan Yardley, "His Place in Time," *Wash. Post,* 4 Feb. 1996, Book World §, at 3.
- "She has a *compendious* [read *comprehensive*?] knowledge of the novels of Jane Austen." Bill Workman, "A Woman of Means," *S.F. Chron.,* 20 Sept. 1996, Peninsula Friday §, at P1.
- "Even if you knew nothing of Mencken, coming to him by way of this fresh new collection, 'H.L. Mencken on American Literature,' you would hardly be surprised to learn that in mid-career he published an enormous linguistic study, 'The American Language,' whose ever-expanding revisions and *compendious* [read *extensive*] supplements preoccupied him nearly to the end of his long life." Brad Leithauser, "Mencken's World of Words," *L.A. Times,* 16 June 2002, Book Rev. §, at 6. (Notice the REDUNDANCY of *fresh new,* either one of which suffices.)

Perhaps the error stems from the idea that a compendium is, at best, a fairly comprehensive abridgment. But properly speaking, the emphasis falls on *abridgment,* not on *comprehensive.* And some would say that the word does not at all suggest

comprehensiveness: "'The Penguin Book of Irish Fiction' doesn't carry a guarantee of mauling you if you read it. But thanks to Colin Toibin, who should have been included (one understands why he wasn't) in the anthology as well, we have the best *compendium* of Irish fiction since 'The Field Day Anthology of Irish Writing,' a *more comprehensive* work published in 1991." Mike Lanagan, "In Toibin's Compendium, the Luck of the Irish," *Buffalo News,* 12 Mar. 2000, at F5.

LANGUAGE-CHANGE INDEX
compendious misused for *comprehensive:* Stage 3

compendium forms either of two plurals: *compendiums* or *compendia.* The native-grown plural was prevalent from the 17th century to the mid-20th. Since about 1950, the Latinate plural has enjoyed a resurgence. But many sensible editors haven't enjoyed it—e.g.:

- "Far too many of these books are *compendia* [read *compendiums*] of facts designed to provide tidbits for cocktail-party chatter." Martin Morse Wooster, "The Special Problems with Special Education," *Wash. Times,* 11 Sept. 1994, at B6.
- "One of the chief shortcomings of *compendiums* like this is finding what you want quickly." Ranny Green, "Need a Gift Idea for That Cat Owner? Then Read On," *Seattle Times,* 20 Nov. 1994, at H6.

See PLURALS (B). For the sense of the word, see **compendious.**

Current ratio (*compendia* vs. *compendiums*): 3:1

compensable; *compensatable; *compensible. The adjective *compensable* correlates to the noun *compensation.* *Compensible is a fairly common misspelling. No major dictionary records the NEEDLESS VARIANT *compensatable, which since 1913 has infrequently displaced *compensable.* See -ABLE (A); -ATABLE.

Current ratio (in order of headwords): 418:16:1

compensate. A. Transitive or Intransitive. *Compensate* may or may not take *for,* and either way means "to make up for, to counterbalance (a loss)." The modern tendency is to omit *for,* but the sound of a sentence may outweigh the interests of concision. E.g.:

- "The International Commission of Jurists . . . concluded that the women's physical and emotional suffering both during the war and afterwards must be *compensated for* by the Japanese government." "Slave Compensation," *Atlanta J.-Const.,* 23 Nov. 1994, at A8.
- "The Army Corps does address mitigation, but not all wetland and wildlife losses can be *compensated.*" "Isle of Wight Coal Storage," *Virginian-Pilot* (Norfolk), 24 Nov. 1994, Suffolk Sun §, at 6.

B. And *recompense.* These verbs are almost precisely synonymous <to recompense a victim for injuries>, but *recompense* is a FORMAL WORD less commonly used. Until about 1750, though, the two were about equal in frequency of use. See **recompense.**

compensatory; *compensative. The latter has been a NEEDLESS VARIANT since the 17th century.

Current ratio: 269:1

competence; competency. Though H.W. Fowler considered *competency* a NEEDLESS VARIANT, since the late 19th century these terms have come to exhibit a DIFFERENTIATION that should be encouraged. *Competence* usually bears the general sense "a basic or minimal ability to do something." E.g.: "Inman got his reputation in the first place. Was it based on the ability of Washington insiders to judge the character and *competence* of public officials?" Jeff Greenfield, "Inman Exit Shows Insiders Can Err," *Chicago Sun-Times*, 24 Jan. 1994, at 23.

Today *competency* is unnecessary in all but its legal sense: "the ability to understand problems and make decisions; the ability to stand trial." A severely mentally retarded person, an incompetent, is said to have legal *incompetency*. The usual phrase is *competency to stand trial*. See **incompetence.**

Avoid INELEGANT VARIATION with these two terms—e.g.: "But the primary suggestion is that counselor *competency* [read *competence*] is a matter of personal *competence* and independence, relying on counselor abilities and sensibility to boundaries of loyalty." Ralph D. Barney & Jay Black, "Ethics and Professional Persuasive Communications," *Public Relations Rev.*, 22 Sept. 1994, at 233. (This incompetent sentence, of course, does not quite contain a comprehensible thought—as, perhaps, the variation strives unsuccessfully to disguise.)

complacency; *complacence. *Complacency*, the preferred form, occurs in print sources 21 times as often as *complacence, a NEEDLESS VARIANT since the 17th century.

Current ratio: 21:1

complacent; complaisant. *Complacent* (/kəm-**play**-sənt/) means "self-satisfied; smug." E.g.: "One thing for sure about the calm response: It does not mean that Dayton is *complacent* about its place in the world." Martin Gottlieb, "Dayton Remains Calm," *Dayton Daily News*, 17 Nov. 1996, at B13. See ***self-complacent.**

Complaisant (/kəm-**play**-zənt/) means "obliging; tending to go along with others." E.g.: "The moans and groans out of Wall Street are echoed by a *complaisant* financial press that monitors and blows out of proportion (or often misinterprets) every economic indicator or statistic." Hobart Rowen, "Fed's Anti-Inflation Mindset Could Spell Trouble for the Economy," *Wash. Post*, 9 Oct. 1994, at H2. Today it is a rare word. But until about 1830 it was more common than *complacent*.

compleat is an archaic variant of *complete* with no place in modern contexts, unless facetiousness is intended. Even so, it is a one-word CLICHÉ.

*complected. See **complexioned.**

complement. See **compliment** & **supplement.**

complementary. See **complimentary.**

complete. See ADJECTIVES (B).

completely, an intensive adverb, is often superfluous, as in the phrase *completely superfluous* (made doubly superfluous by further REDUNDANCY in the sentence that follows): "There's a *completely superfluous* [read *superfluous*] lemon-basil sauce on and around the fish *that's really not necessary* [delete phrase], but sopping it up with bread is nice." Nicki Pendleton, "Caffe Milano," *Nashville Banner*, 19 June 1996, at C3.

Indeed, the word *completely* creates redundancies when coupled with myriad adjectives—e.g.:

- "For 12 long minutes the board was *completely silent* [read *silent*], seemingly stunned by this news." Joseph Nocera, "Investing in a Fool's Paradise," *Fortune*, 15 Apr. 1996, at 86.
- "Naturally, the software industry wants to see this change happen, because no software is ever *completely perfect* [read *perfect*]." Ed Foster, "The Gripe Line," *InfoWorld*, 28 Oct. 1996, at 60.
- "No gallery of pictures can ever show the true breadth of Christmas because it is celebrated in a *completely unique* [read *unique*] and original manner within the heart of each person who treasures it." Charles Hirshberg, "Christmas Around the World," *Life*, Dec. 1996, at 24.

See ADJECTIVES (B).

*completely obsolescent. For this phrase, see **archaic.**

complexioned; *complected. The first has been standard since the 17th century; the second, a 19th-century Americanism, has been a NEEDLESS VARIANT since it first appeared. Today, *complexioned* is about four times as common in print sources—e.g.:

- "I had hoped to tease some comments from our big-boned, ruddy-*complexioned* tour guide, who stood in the middle of the gardens as if he were fixed to that dry landscape like a stubborn cactus." Chris Card Fuller, "Sailing into New Waters," *L.A. Times*, 24 Nov. 1996, at L8.
- "Her daughter caught a glimpse of the salesman, who was described at the time as a dark-*complexioned* man in his mid-20s, wearing beige slacks and a dress shirt and tie." Josh Dulaney, "Gunned Down at Her Front Door," *Long Beach Press-Telegram*, 26 July 2015, at 8.

Still, an editor could make a good case for dropping *complexioned* altogether in those two sentences and instead using *dark* and *ruddy*. And one wonders whether *dark-complexioned* is merely a roundabout wording for *black* or *African-American*.

But the word **complected*—an irregularly formed word, since the noun is *complexion* and not *complection*—still occasionally appears. It should be edited—e.g.: "What is it about this rosy-*complected* [read -*complexioned* or, better, -*faced*] man that sends CEOs into rages?" Julie Schmit, "Lerach: Silicon Valley's Nightmare," *USA Today*, 23 Oct. 1996, at B1.

LANGUAGE-CHANGE INDEX
*complected for *complexioned*: Stage 2
Current ratio (*complexioned* vs. **complected*): 4:1

LANGUAGE-CHANGE INDEX (For the full key, see front matter pp. xxxi, l–li.)
Stage 1: Rejected. **Stage 2:** Widely shunned. **Stage 3:** Widespread but . . . **Stage 4:** Ubiquitous but . . . **Stage 5:** Fully accepted.
Invariably inferior forms marked by asterisk (∗). • Ratios represent frequency of prevalent forms vs. variants in current books.

complicit; *complicitous. Neither term was much used until the late 1960s. Although *complicitous is the older term (dating from the mid-19th century), it appears only rarely in comparison to complicit, which is a BACK-FORMATION made on the analogy of implicit. It dates from about 1950. Though most dictionaries don't include the word, it has become quite common—e.g.:

- "The murders have come mostly from the right, but from the left, as well, and it is widely felt that the government has been at least complicit in the deaths of several liberals." Nicholas Lemann, "How Realpolitik Undid One Diplomat," Wash. Post, 6 July 1980, at A1.
- "Far from attacking racism at its root, Mr. Freedman charges, Finch was complicit in it." David Margolick, "Chipping at Atticus Finch's Pedestal," N.Y. Times, 28 Feb. 1992, at B1.
- " 'Shanghai Knights,' like 'Shanghai Noon,' was written by Alfred Gough and Miles Millar, and opens once again in the Forbidden City, where a pretender to the British throne becomes complicit in a dastardly deed." Joe Morgenstern, "In 'Shanghai Knights,' Chan Plays It for Kicks," Wall Street J., 7 Feb. 2003, at W1.

Because it is at least as well formed as its alternative and has now established itself as the more common form, complicit should be accepted as standard. *Complicitous, despite its promising beginnings, should now be regarded as a NEEDLESS VARIANT.

Current ratio: 14:1

compliment; complement. Both as verbs and as nouns, these words are often confounded. Compliment = (1) vb., to praise <she complimented the book lavishly>; or (2) n., a laudatory remark <her generous compliments emboldened the young author>. Complement = (1) vb., to supplement appropriately or adequately <special Thai desserts complemented the curries nicely>; or (2) n., an adequate supplement <the flowering plants are a splendid complement to the trees offered at the nursery>.

Compliment sometimes displaces complement, especially in the phrase full complement (= a complete set)—e.g.:

- "The Contract Appeals Board has never had a full compliment [read complement] of five administrative judges, the task force said, noting that the agency 'at times has had difficulty achieving a quorum because of understaffing.' " Vernon Loeb, "Task Force Assails D.C. Procurement System," Wash. Post, 15 Feb. 1996, at B3.
- "The West Brookfield Police Department now has a full compliment [read complement] of six full-time police officers." J.P. Ellery, "2 Full-Time Officers Appointed," Telegram & Gaz. (Worcester), 13 Nov. 1996, at B2.
- "Effective July 2008, this new law provides for the full compliment [read complement] of APNs, regardless of specialty, to credential with the Colorado Medicaid Services and open new channels to health care access." Tay Kopanos, "Government Affairs and Public Policy Committee," Colorado Nurse, 1 Dec. 2008, at 13.

The reverse error, complement for compliment, is rare but does occur—e.g.: "The letter from Tiger complemented [read complimented] Laddie Boy for sticking

by his master despite the hard times and accusations." Stanley Coren, The Pawprints of History 269 (2002).

LANGUAGE-CHANGE INDEX
1. *full compliment for full complement: Stage 1
Current ratio (full complement vs.
*full compliment): 14:1
2. complement misused for the verb
compliment: Stage 1
Current ratio (complimented her on vs.
*complemented her on): 32:1

complimentary; complementary. This pair of adjectives is even more susceptible to confusion than the corresponding nouns. When a mistake occurs, complementary usually displaces complimentary—e.g.:

- "[William M.] Finkelstein knows his parents can handle it—and then some. 'If they catch wind of somebody saying some less than complementary [read complimentary] remarks about the show, they hunt them down,' he said, laughing." Deborah Seibel, "Creator Draws on His Past to Conduct 'Civil Wars,' " Chicago Trib., 15 Mar. 1992, TV Week §, at 3.
- "His teacher thought he was quite intriguing and original, and sent the manuscript to Faber in London, who published it, sent him the customary ten copies, complementary [read complimentary] author's copies, while he proceeded to get out on the street and try to sell." William Gaddis, The Rush for Second Place 127 (2002).
- "During their stays, guests will be given complementary [read complimentary] access to the Queen City Racquet and Fitness Center." Jenny Callison, "Business Notes," Cincinnati Enquirer, 13 Apr. 2003, at D3.
- "Casino host Sam Boyd, son of Boyd Gaming Chairman Bill Boyd, keeps the players comfortable with complementary [read complimentary] rooms and other amenities as the game stretches from hours into days." Jeff Simpson, "Big Games Bring In Big Money, Big Names," Las Vegas Rev.-J., 13 Apr. 2003, at E1.

LANGUAGE-CHANGE INDEX
complementary misused for complimentary: Stage 1

comply. A. Preposition with. Since the 17th century, comply has taken the preposition with, not to—e.g.:

- "Vickers already complies to [read complies with] U.S. Department of Defense standards." Kelly Russell, "U.S. Companies Fall in Line with Europe to Guarantee Product Quality," Miss. Bus. J., 9 Jan. 1995, at 1.
- "In this case its power is further weakened because the Postal Service is not an actual federal agency and complies to [read complies with] the preservation act voluntarily." Tom Angleberger, "Post Office Closing Won't Be Delayed," Roanoke Times, 8 Aug. 1997, at NRV1.

LANGUAGE-CHANGE INDEX
*comply to for comply with: Stage 1
Current ratio (comply with vs. *comply to): 185:1

B. For follow. Comply suggests a hierarchy of authority: an inferior complies with an order from a superior. That's certainly not the case when the Arizona Supreme Court decides not to follow a recommendation of the Arizona Commission on Judicial Conduct: "In its 23-year history, the commission has only once recommended that a judge be removed from office. The Supreme Court did not comply with [read *follow*] that recommendation." Joe Salkowski, "Jett Shouldn't Be Removed, Panel Is Told," *Ariz. Daily Star*, 15 Jan. 1994, at A1, A2.

compose. See **comprise (A).**

compound, v.t., has been the victim of a SLIPSHOD EXTENSION arising from its primarily legal sense. The word has four basic meanings: (1) "to let a fund grow by adding interest earned to the principal, thereby earning more interest"; (2) "to put together, combine, construct, compose" <to compound sand and gravel>; (3) "to settle (any matter) by a money payment, in lieu of other liability" <to compound a debt>; and (4) "to forbear from prosecuting in exchange for a bribe, or to cause (a prosecutor) so to forbear" <to compound a felony>. For senses 3 and 4—the legal senses—the noun corresponding to this verb is *composition*.

The word has been sloppily extended because "non-lawyers have misapprehended the meaning of *to compound* a felony. . . . [The word] is now widely abused to mean: to make worse, aggravate, multiply, increase." Philip Howard, *New Words for Old* 19 (1977). No doubt the interpretation follows an analogy with savings growing as the interest compounds. Examples of this usage now abound—e.g.:

- "The Sandbridge shoreline has been retreating throughout all recorded history, and buying a little more time while gambling on federal support only *compounds* [read *worsens*] the city's problems." Letter of H. Pritchard-Rudnick, "Sandbridge Sticker Shock," *Virginian-Pilot* (Norfolk), 17 Dec. 1996, at A18.
- "To *compound* [read *aggravate*] the problems for the Tar Heels, Vince Carter, who suffered a hip pointer in the loss to Wake Forest, is doubtful for Saturday's matchup with Virginia." Carter Strickland, "Around the Atlantic Coast Conference," *Morning Star* (Wilmington, N.C.), 10 Jan. 1997, at C3.
- "The daftness was *compounded* [read *worsened*] by the caption, which treated this legendary archetype on the same level as a colour photograph of Kinnear." Guy Keleny, "Lies, Damn Lies and Pork Pies Might Damage Your Health," *Independent*, 22 Aug. 2015, at 39.

Most American lawyers probably don't understand the phrase *to compound a felony* when they see it in older lawbooks. It is not quite true, then—at least in the United States—that "to write 'he *compounded* the offence' (when what is meant is that he did something to aggravate the offence) is to vex every lawyer who reads the sentence, and to provoke numbers of them to litigious correspondence in defence of their jargon." Howard, *New Words for Old* at 20.

LANGUAGE-CHANGE INDEX
compounding a felony used in the sense "aggravating a felony": Stage 4

COMPOUND ADJECTIVES. See PHRASAL ADJECTIVES.

COMPOUND SENTENCES. See SUBORDINATION AND COORDINATION.

comprehensible. So spelled—not **comprehensable*. See -ABLE (A).

Current ratio: 6,135:1

compressible. So spelled—not **compressable*. See -ABLE (A).

Current ratio: 2,447:1

comprise. A. And *compose*. Correct use of these words is simple, but increasingly rare. The parts *compose* the whole; the whole *comprises* the parts. The whole is *composed* of the parts; the parts are *comprised* in the whole. *Comprise*, the more troublesome word in this pair, means "to contain; to consist of"—e.g.:

- "It will be seen that this little book *comprises* three sections not unusual in a college handbook." John Crowe Ransom, *A College Primer of Writing* iii (1943).
- "In 1989 the second edition of the *OED comprised* twenty large volumes." Anthony Burgess, *A Mouthful of Air* 343 (1992).
- "Summit Hall Farm *comprises* several hundred acres on the exterior portion of the original settlement of the Gaither family." Lana White Austin, "History and High Tech in Montgomery," *Wash. Times*, 30 May 1997, at F41.

B. Erroneous Use of **is comprised of*. The phrase **is comprised of* is increasingly common but has long been considered poor usage. It was not a frequent collocation until about 1950. Replace it with some other, more accurate phrase—e.g.:

- "The Rhode Island Wind Ensemble *is comprised of* [read *comprises* or *has*] 50 professional and amateur musicians, ranging in age from 15 to 82." "At the Colleges: Brown University," *Providence J.-Bull.*, 14 Sept. 1997, at H3.
- "This group *is comprised of* [read *comprises* or *is made up of*] the 160,000 uninsured residents of Nassau County and an estimated equivalent number of under-insured." Letter of Rosemarie C. Guercia, "Providing Health Care," *Newsday* (N.Y.), 6 Oct. 1997, at A33.
- "Moreover, the crowd in the mysterious room *was comprised of* [read *comprised* or *was composed of*] adults, and Harry knew there were not nearly that many teachers at Hogwarts." J.K. Rowling, *Harry Potter and the Goblet of Fire* 584 (2000).

LANGUAGE-CHANGE INDEX
*is comprised of for *comprises*: Stage 4
Current ratio (*comprises* vs. **is comprised of*): 6:1

C. *Comprise* for *make up* or *constitute*. If the whole comprises the parts, the reverse can't be true—e.g.:

- "Of the 50 stocks that *comprise* [read *make up*] the index, 40 had gains, 8 had losses and 2 were unchanged." "Market Finishes Monster Week," *Fla. Today*, 15 June 1997, at E2.
- "The 18 countries that *comprise* [read *constitute* or *make up*] APEC represent some of the fastest growing economies in the world." "U.S. Ties to Asia: Why Should We Care?" *Daily News* (L.A.), 25 Nov. 1997, at B1.

LANGUAGE-CHANGE INDEX
comprise misused for *are comprised in* or *constitute*: Stage 3

LANGUAGE-CHANGE INDEX (For the full key, see front matter pp. xxxi, l–li.)
Stage 1: Rejected. **Stage 2:** Widely shunned. **Stage 3:** Widespread but . . . **Stage 4:** Ubiquitous but . . . **Stage 5:** Fully accepted.
Invariably inferior forms marked by asterisk (*). • Ratios represent frequency of prevalent forms vs. variants in current books.

D. *Comprise* for *are*. This is an odd error based on a misunderstanding of the meaning of *comprise*. E.g.: "They *comprise* [read *are*] three of the top four names in the batting order of the 30 most influential sports people in B.C. for 1997." Mike Beamish, "B.C.'s Top Guns," *Vancouver Sun*, 22 Feb. 1997, at G1.

E. Misspelled **comprize*. This is an infrequent error—e.g.: "Hence, if a sample *were comprized of* [read *comprised*] a wide diversity of organizations, drawn from several industries, an accounting firm classified as having an 'elite' culture in this study may be classified as having a 'collegial' culture compared to other organizations included in another study." Scott Holmes & Stephen Marsden, "An Exploration of the Espoused Organizational Cultures of Public Accounting Firms," *Accounting Horizons*, Sept. 1996, at 26.

LANGUAGE-CHANGE INDEX
comprise misspelled **comprize*: Stage 1
Current ratio (*comprised* vs. **comprized*): 683:1

F. *Compromise* for *comprise*. See DOUBLE BOBBLES.

comptroller (= a government official in charge of finance, audits, and the like) is really the same word as *controller* (the spelling used for the equivalent person in private business). The word is pronounced /kən-**troh**-lər/—the same as *controller*. Sounding the *-p-* has traditionally been viewed as semiliterate. (See PRONUNCIATION (B).) *Comptroller* is more common in AmE than in BrE, where it is archaic.

The strange spelling of *comptroller* originated in the zeal of 15th-century Latinists who sought to respell medieval French loanwords on the "purer" Latin model. Hence *account* became *accompt*, and *count* became *compt*. *Comptroller* is one of the few survivals among such respellings, and it is also one of the bungles perpetrated by those ardent Latinists: the *con-* in *controller* was mistakenly associated with the word *count*, when in fact it is merely the Latin prefix. So the respelling (which was never supposed to affect the pronunciation) should never have been. But we are several centuries too late to correct it, the result being that many people have difficulty pronouncing the word.

LANGUAGE-CHANGE INDEX
comptroller mispronounced /**komp**-troh-lər/: Stage 4

compute; **computate*. The first is standard. The second is a back-formed NEEDLESS VARIANT—e.g.: "The OSRAP gives logisticians the ability to vary the parameters used in *computating* [read *computing*] requirements." John R. Millard, "Computing Requirements for a Changing Army," 33 *Army Logistician*, Mar. 2001, at 21. See BACK-FORMATIONS.

LANGUAGE-CHANGE INDEX
*computate for *compute*: Stage 1
Current ratio (*compute* vs. **computate*): 18,445:1

COMPUTERESE, the JARGON of computer wizards, is making inroads into STANDARD ENGLISH. Thus *access* and *format* and *sequence* have become verbs, *input* has enjoyed widespread use as both noun and verb,

and *online* and *user-friendly* have begun to be used as models for NEOLOGISMS (e.g., *on-stream* used of an oil well, *reader-friendly* used of well-written documents). No one can rightly object, of course, to computerese in computing contexts, where it is undeniably useful. But many computer terms have acquired figurative senses, thereby invading the general language. Careful users of language are wary of adopting any of these trendy locutions. Although some of the terms may remain and become standard, many others will keep their jargonistic stigma. Still others will thrive for a time and then fall into disuse. Such are the vagaries of the English vocabulary. See OBSCURITY.

computerize. See -IZE.

comrade; **camarade*. The latter, an archaic GALLICISM, is a NEEDLESS VARIANT. See **camaraderie**.
Current ratio: 12,486:1

comstockery (often cap.) refers to prudish censorship, or attempted censorship, of supposed immorality in art or literature. In 1873, Congress passed the so-called Comstock Law—a federal statute to control obscenity, pornography, abortion, and the use of contraceptives—pushed through by one Anthony Comstock (1844–1915), who was a leader of the New York Society for the Suppression of Vice. George Bernard Shaw invented the word *comstockery*, pejorative from the first, when he wrote in *The New York Times* in 1905: "*Comstockery* is the world's standing joke at the expense of the United States."

concede. See **cede**.

concededly. See -EDLY & SENTENCE ADVERBS.

*concensus. See **consensus**.

concept; conception. Both may mean "an abstract idea." *Conception* also means "the act of forming abstract ideas." H.W. Fowler wrote that *conception* is the ordinary term, *concept* the philosophical term (*FMEU1* at 88). But the words have undergone a reversal since he was writing in 1926, and today *concept* is the ordinary term.

True, *concept* is sometimes just a high-flown equivalent of *design, program, thought,* or *idea*—e.g.:

- "Like everyone else familiar with 'Star Trek,' Frakes has his own thoughts about the longevity of the *concept* [read *program* or *idea*], which debuted on television 30 years ago this fall." Ron Weiskind, "Frakes to Helm Next 'Trek' Film—Behind the Camera," *Chicago Sun-Times*, 12 Apr. 1996, Weekend Plus §, at 58. (On the use of *helm* as a verb, see **helm**.)
- "That is good news for [Senator] Kerry, who was dragged kicking and screaming to the *concept* [read *idea*] of a long series of debates that began in April." Geeta Anand et al., "Defying Assumptions, Poll Shows Debates Helped Kerry with Voters," *Boston Globe*, 8 Sept. 1996, at B7.
- "The basic *concept* [read *idea*] is to activate a string while lightly touching one of its nodes—a point where the string divides into fractional lengths." Muriel Anderson, "Sweeping Palm Harmonics," *Guitar Player*, Dec. 1996, at 146.

But the word is becoming so commonplace that it has lost most of the original distinction.

When the reference is to a way of conceiving or a manner of thought, as opposed to some straightforward idea, *conception* is the right word—e.g.:

- "Economists are often too narrow or mechanical in their *conception* of risk, viewing it simply as the variance or standard deviation of the expected return." Charles Cathcart, "Broader Implications of the Information Age," *Global Investor*, Feb. 1996, at 42.
- "The wider audience attracted to 'Going Publick' on Friday had the advantage of comparing very different *conceptions* of dance." "A 'Publick' Service," *Wash. Post*, 19 Nov. 1996, at D9.
- "In addition, he returns to Murger's *conception* of the central character of Mimi, giving her a sexy, tempestuous, flirtatious character as well as making her a heroin addict." Ellen Pfeifer, "'Boheme,' Callas Get Worked Over," *Boston Herald*, 24 Nov. 1996, at 43.

conception, immaculate. See **immaculate conception.**

conceptual; conceptualistic; conceptional; conceptive. These words are very close. *Conceptual* and *conceptional* both mean "of, relating to, or involving a conception or idea"—*conceptual* being the usual term. E.g.: "The *conceptual* design work, funded by the Transportation Trust Fund, is scheduled for completion next summer." Pat R. Gilbert, "Bergen to Get Rte. 4 Project, Light-Rail Study," *Record* (N.J.), 7 Nov. 2002, at A3.

When not simply a NEEDLESS VARIANT of *conceptual*, the word *conceptional* serves as the adjective corresponding to a different kind of conception, namely, the fertilization of an egg—e.g.:

- "It is not easy to reconcile this attitude with the papal concession of some kinds of anti-*conceptional* measures." Glanville Williams, *The Sanctity of Life and the Criminal Law* 69 (1957; repr. 1972).
- "Retardation of neuronal maturation in premature infants was compared with term infants of the same post-*conceptional* age." Naomi Breslau et al., "Psychiatric Sequelae of Low Birth Weight at 6 Years of Age," 24 *J. Abnormal Child Psychology* 385 (1996).

Conceptualistic = (1) of, relating to, or involving philosophical or psychological doctrine of conceptualism; or (2) employing or based on conceptions. In sense 2, *conceptualistic* bears a pejorative sense—e.g.: "This highly *conceptualistic* reasoning is not only difficult to square with the language of section 2(c); it also impedes efforts to interpret that provision." Arthur H. Travers, "Commercial Bribery and the Antitrust Laws," 40 *Antitrust Bull.* 779 (1995).

Conceptive = of, relating to, or involving the process of mental conception (i.e., forming thoughts and ideas). E.g.: "Contemporary genetic research continues to reveal how profoundly other more 'spiritual' traits of the person, such as intelligence and emotive temperament, are molded by one's *conceptive* history."

John J. Conley, "Narcissus Cloned," *America*, 12 Feb. 1994, at 15. Sometimes, though, *conceptive* appears in contexts in which *conceptional* would be better—e.g.: "Early methods of *preconceptive* [read *preconceptional*] sex selection—which, in contrast to *post-conceptive* [read *postconceptional*] selection, seem to afford greater latitude to human ingenuity—may be roughly sorted into biologic and symbolic techniques." Owen D. Jones, "Bringing the Child of Your Choice into the Future," *Recorder* (S.F.), 31 Aug. 1993, at 8.

conceptualize, a 19th-century coinage, is often a bloated word that can be replaced by *conceive, envision, think, understand,* or *visualize*—e.g.:

- "Like Veblen, Innis *conceptualizes* [read *conceives of* or, better, *sees*] the price system as an active social force." Fletcher Baragar, "The Influence of Thorstein Veblen on the Economics of Harold Innis," 30 *J. Econ. Issues* 667 (1996).
- "His ability to *conceptualize* [read *conceive* or, possibly, *understand* or *see*] and demarcate diverse legal systems opened the world of comparative law to generations of students." Wolfgang Saxon, "Rudolf Schlesinger, 87, Expert on the World's Legal Systems," *N.Y. Times*, 22 Nov. 1996, at D19.
- "Class 29 is seeking an artist or landscape architect to *conceptualize* [read *design*] and fabricate the monument." Amanda Purser, "Local Briefs," *Pensacola News J.*, 14 Aug. 2015, at A4.

concern, n., merits editorial attention when used in either of two ways. First, it is sometimes used in the sense of "company," "firm," or "business." In this use, the word smacks of old-fashioned BUREAUCRATESE and should usually yield to a more precise word—e.g.:

- "He [Erskine Boyce Bowles] has long been the President's first choice to succeed Mr. Panetta, but he had to be persuaded, having just last January started a merchant banking *concern* [read *firm*] that specializes in buying mid-sized companies on behalf of investors." Todd S. Purdum, "After the Election: The Players," *N.Y. Times*, 9 Nov. 1996, § 1, at 1.
- "Other researchers charged that the Nazis sold leather from Jewish factories to the Swiss shoe *concern* [read *company*] Bally." Nomi Morris, "Nazis, Gold—and Justice," *Maclean's*, 11 Nov. 1996, at 32.

The word is more defensible when it refers to more than just businesses, as in this example where *concerns* might also include interests such as land or mineral rights that are leased to the businesses: "Of West Virginia's 34 senators, . . . [4] have interests in oil, gas and timber *concerns.*" Scott Finn, "Legislators' Conflicts Can Cut Both Ways," *Sunday Gaz. Mail* (Charleston, W. Va.), 28 May 2000, at A1.

Second, the word is sometimes otiose—e.g.: "This has become one of the most troubling aspects of the Clinton tenure, its across-the-board willingness to subvert national agencies charged with law enforcement and security *concerns* [delete *concerns*]." "Integrity of the Institutions," *Wall Street J.*, 20 Mar. 1997, at A16, A20. The word adds nothing to that sentence.

LANGUAGE-CHANGE INDEX (For the full key, see front matter pp. xxxi, l–li.)
Stage 1: Rejected. **Stage 2:** Widely shunned. **Stage 3:** Widespread but . . . **Stage 4:** Ubiquitous but . . . **Stage 5:** Fully accepted.
Invariably inferior forms marked by asterisk (✲). • Ratios represent frequency of prevalent forms vs. variants in current books.

concerning. For this word as an acceptable dangling modifier, see DANGLERS (E).

concerto (= a musical composition for orchestra and a solo instrument) has two plurals: *concertos* (preferable) and *concerti* (pretentious). The anglicized plural has greatly predominated since the 18th century. Both *Grove's Dictionary of Music and Musicians* (Eric Blom ed., 5th ed. 1954—as well as later editions) and the *Harvard Dictionary of Music* (Willi Apel ed., 1972) use the plural form *concertos*. But in foreign phrases where the Italian plural is unavoidable, it is quite proper: *concerti grossi, concerti ecclesiastici*, etc. See PLURALS (B).

Occasionally the incorrect form **concertoes* appears—e.g.: "When I work on Mozart *concertoes* [read *concertos*], for example, there has to be a minimum of time expended—long periods." Jeff Simon, "Keith Jarrett: A Rare Interview," *Buffalo News*, 25 Aug. 1996, at F1 (attributing the statement to Keith Jarrett).

LANGUAGE-CHANGE INDEX
1. *concertos* as a plural (as opposed to *concerti*): Stage 5
Current ratio: 9:1
2. *concertos* misspelled **concertoes*: Stage 1
Current ratio: 25,893:1

concessionaire (= the owner or manager of a refreshment stand at a recreational facility) is the standard term. **Concessioner* and *concessionary* are NEEDLESS VARIANTS.

concessive; concessionary; concessional. *Concessive* = (1) tending to concede <a concessive stance in negotiating>; or (2) expressing the idea of concession <*whereas* is commonly a concessive word>. *Concessionary* = of, relating to, or involving concession or concessions <concessionary companies— e.g., food vendors at the fairgrounds>. *Concessional* is the usual word in financial contexts when the reference is to a concessional loan, one offered on favorable terms—e.g.: "Generous *concessional* treatment of debt-burdened African economies is essential if the continent's development crisis is to end." "Aid and Reform in Nigeria," *Fin. Times*, 6 Jan. 1992, at 10.

LANGUAGE-CHANGE INDEX
*concessional for *concessive*: Stage 1

conch (= the spiral shell of a large mollusk) is pronounced either /konk/ (preferred) or /konch/. The plural form depends on which pronunciation is used. Those who say /konk/ make the plural *conchs*; those who say /konch/ make the plural *conches*. Historically, *conchs* has been the usual plural in both AmE and BrE, but *conches* has recently surged ahead, especially in BrE.
Current ratio (*conches* vs. *conchs*): 1.5:1

concierge /kon-see-**airzh**/ is frequently mispronounced /kon-see-**air**/ by those affecting a French pronunciation. In French, though, the *-g-* is pronounced /zh/ because the vowel *-e* follows it. So the word is not like many other French words—*lait* and *rendezvous*, for example—in which the final consonant is silent.

Still, an informal survey at hotels in major American cities suggests that about half of all hotel employees use the incorrect pronunciation. See PRONUNCIATION (B) & HYPERCORRECTION (K).

LANGUAGE-CHANGE INDEX
concierge mispronounced /kon-see-**air**/: Stage 2

conciliatory; *conciliative. *Conciliatory* = (1) tending to conciliate; or (2) of, relating to, or involving conciliation or mediation. **Conciliative* has been a NEEDLESS VARIANT for centuries.
Current ratio: 1,394:1

concision; conciseness. Drawing a fine distinction, H.W. Fowler wrote: "*Concision* means the process of cutting down, and *conciseness* the cut-down state" (*FMEU1* at 295). In fact, though, the two are generally used as synonyms for the cut-down state—e.g.:

• "Pagels' footnotes are a model of erudition and *conciseness*." Shalom Goldman, "Elaine Pagels Traces the Religious Roots of the Tendency to Demonize the Other," *Newsday* (N.Y.), 4 June 1995, at 29.
• "The type is undoubtedly familiar to Kennedy, a former newspaperman who has successfully transferred the virtues of clarity and *concision* to fiction." R.Z. Sheppard, "Living with the Ashes," *Time*, 13 May 1996, at 92.
• "The second of the pair seems to me one of the finest things Knussen has ever done, a miracle of *conciseness* and profundity that is all over in less than three minutes." Andrew Clements, "Classical CD of the Week," *Guardian*, 22 Nov. 1996, at T20.
• "Tempchin's best songs, whether vintage or on his lovingly crafted new album, are marvels of *concision*." George Varga, "Parts of Tempchin's Past Re-Emerge as New Path Opens," *San Diego Union-Trib.*, 9 Aug. 2015, at E7.

Both words are common today, *conciseness* a little more so in both BrE and AmE. When *concision* appears, it is typically used in a sense that Fowler implicitly disapproved. This frequency might reflect the influence of *precision*, by analogy.

What ruling, then? If any DIFFERENTIATION is now possible, the word *conciseness*—like other *-ness* words—emphasizes a quality, whereas *concision* emphasizes a static condition. This is a fine distinction indeed, and one that not all writers will be able to apply. When the distinction is hard to make, let euphony govern. But it would be a mistake (and a bootless one) to brand either word a NEEDLESS VARIANT.

conclusive; conclusory; *conclusionary; *conclusional. *Conclusive* (the common word) = authoritative; decisive. *Conclusory* (a common legal term) = expressing a factual inference without stating the facts or reasoning on which the inference is based <conclusory allegations>. The other two words are NEEDLESS VARIANTS of *conclusory*.
Current ratio (*conclusory* vs. **conclusionary* vs. **conclusional*): 108:7:1

concomitance; *concomitancy. Though neither is common, *concomitance* is standard. **Concomitancy* is a NEEDLESS VARIANT.
Current ratio: 27:1

CONCORD = grammatical agreement of one word with another to which it relates. Concord embraces number, person, case, and gender. It applies most often to (1) a subject and its verb; (2) a noun and its pronoun; (3) a subject and its complement; (4) a noun and its appositive; (5) a relative pronoun and its antecedent; and (6) an adjective and its noun. Errors in concord for (1), (2), and (3) are examined at (A), (B), and (C) below; for (4), see APPOSITIVES; for (5), see (D) below and REMOTE RELATIVES; for (6), see (E) below.

A. Subject–Verb Disagreement. Errors in SUBJECT–VERB AGREEMENT are, unfortunately, legion in AmE, especially in speech—e.g.:

- "Every one of us *have* [read *has*] a role to play . . . ." President Bill Clinton, State of the Union Address, 23 Jan. 1996, at 8:49 PM CST.
- In reference to Haiti: "The flow of desperate refugees to our shores *have* [read *has*] subsided." President Bill Clinton, State of the Union Address, 23 Jan. 1996, at 8:56 PM CST.
- "The price of sports tickets *are* [read *is*] rising." Barbara Kingsley, "Soaring Ticket Prices Test Fans' Loyalty," *Seattle Times*, 19 Jan. 1997, at D6.
- "When one of us *suffer* [read *suffers*], all of us *suffers* [read *suffer*]." President George W. Bush, speech to the Victory 2002 Luncheon, Charleston, S.C., 29 July 2002.

But the error does occasionally find its way into edited publications, too—e.g.:

- "Because words *is* [read *are*] my business, I knew most of the examples on the Web page, though I had to look up 'oubliette.'" Mel White, "Words Qua Words," in *Active Years*, Nov. 2004, at 64.
- "Obviously, gryphon and human *wasn't* [read *weren't*] the only *thing* [read *things*] in its mix." Keri Arthur, *Full Moon Rising* 217 (2006).

The most common error occurs with the EXPLETIVE *there*, and especially when it's contracted with the verb *is* (e.g., *There's two ways we can go* instead of *There are two ways we can go*). This error also occurs with the adverbs *here* (e.g., *Here's your menu and wine list* instead of *Here are your menu and wine list*) and *where* (e.g., *Where's my wallet and keys?* instead of *Where are my wallet and keys?*). The grammarian Ed Good, who trains technical writers, calls this "[t]he biggest grammar mistake in the United States." C. Edward Good, *A Grammar Book for You and I . . . Oops, Me!* 301 (2002). For more on this error, see **there is (B).**

The agreement mistake can also come up in relative clauses—e.g.: "'We must not be silent,' said German Chancellor Angela Merkel at a memorial ceremony in Berlin's renovated Rykestrasse synagogue, one of the few that *was* [read *were*] not burned down that night by the Nazis . . . ." Bret Stephens, "'Tolerance' Is Not the Lesson of Kristallnacht," *Wall Street J.*, 11 Nov. 2008, at A15. (The antecedent of the relative pronoun *that* is *few*, not *one*, so the pronoun takes on the number of its antecedent.) See **one of the [+ pl. n.] who (*or* that).**

Are these merely symptoms of the decay of modern English? Consider: "The adequate narration may take up a term less brief, especially if explanation or comment here and there *seem* [read *seems*] requisite to the better understanding of such incidents." Herman Melville, *Billy Budd* 73 (1891; repr. [Signet ed.] 1979).

Quoting Melville is not to excuse lapses of this kind: every generation can be more vigilant about its subjects and verbs. But we shouldn't consider these problems to have been unthinkable two or three generations ago. Slips of the pen can be found in the works of writers from Shakespeare to the present.

The British—oddly to American eyes and ears—consider organizations, especially sports teams, plural—e.g.:

- "On the field, England *were* going through their ritual reincarnation . . . . England *are* beset by similar urges." Kevin Mitchell, "Terrace Provides a Few Horse Laughs," *Observer*, 25 July 1997, Sport §, at 2.
- "When the rain arrived yesterday, Australia *were* 201 runs ahead." Graham Otway, "Aussies Turn the Screw," *Sunday Times* (London), 27 July 1997, § 2, at 1.

Kingsley Amis defends this construction: "Anybody with a tittle of wit knows that country-plus-plural refers to a sporting event or something similar. This is precisely what the verb is doing in the plural. It shows that a number of individuals, a team, is referred to, not one thing, a country." Kingsley Amis, *The King's English* 59–60 (1997). But Americans are no more accustomed to saying *England are* than they are to writing *anybody with a tittle of wit*. It's pure BrE, and *England are* surely isn't BrE at its best.

B. Noun–Pronoun Disagreement. Depending on how you look at it, this is either one of the most frequent blunders in modern writing or a godsend that allows us to avoid sexism. Where noun–pronoun disagreement can be avoided, avoid it. Where it can't be avoided, resort to it cautiously because some people may doubt your literacy—e.g.: "You can only teach a person something if that person can comprehend and use what is being taught *to them* [delete *to them*]." J.M. Balkin, "Turandot's Victory," 2 *Yale J. Law & Humanities* 299, 302 (1990).

This type of disagreement in number is especially common in BrE—e.g.:

- "Under new rules to be announced tomorrow, it will be illegal for *anyone* to donate an organ to *their wife*." Aileen Ballantyne, "Transplant Jury to Vet Live Donors," *Sunday Times* (London), 25 Mar. 1990, at A3.
- "Anyone can set *themselves* up as an acupuncturist." Sarah Lonsdale, "Sharp Practice Pricks Reputation of Acupuncture," *Observer Sunday*, 15 Dec. 1991, at 4.
- "A starting point could be to give more support to the company secretary. *They are*, or should be, privy to the confidential deliberations and secrets of the board and

LANGUAGE-CHANGE INDEX (For the full key, see front matter pp. xxxi, l–li.)
Stage 1: Rejected. **Stage 2:** Widely shunned. **Stage 3:** Widespread but . . . **Stage 4:** Ubiquitous but . . . **Stage 5:** Fully accepted.
Invariably inferior forms marked by asterisk (*). • Ratios represent frequency of prevalent forms vs. variants in current books.

the company." Ronald Severn, "Protecting the Secretary Bird," *Fin. Times*, 6 Jan. 1992, at 8.

As this seeming sloppiness mounts—and invades edited AmE—the complaints mount as well. For example: "Columnist James Brady . . . noted on page 38 that Richard F. Shepard was grammatically incorrect when he wrote, 'Nobody remembers a journalist for *their* writing.' Perhaps it was Mr. Shepard who wrote the headline for the AT&T ad that appeared on Page 37 of the same issue: 'This florist wilted because of *their* 800 service.'" Letter of Jerry Galvin, *Advertising Age*, 4 Nov. 1991, at 26.

Why is this usage becoming so common? It is the most convenient solution to the single biggest problem in sexist language—the generic masculine pronoun. A recent advertisement says, "Every student can have *their* own computer," so as to avoid saying *his own computer*—a phrasing that would probably alienate many consumers. *The Macmillan Dictionary of Business and Management* (1988) defines *cognitive dissonance* as "a concept in psychology [that] describes the condition in which *a person's* attitudes conflict with *their* behavior" (p. 38). In his 1991 State of the Union address, President George Bush said: "If *anyone* tells you that America's best days are behind her, then *they're* looking the wrong way." And one of the best-edited American papers allows this: "If the newspaper can't fire him for an ethical breach surely *they* [read *it*] can fire him for being stupid." Michael Gartner, "U.S. Law Says We Have to Kill Saddam Hussein the Hard Way," *Wall Street J.*, 31 Jan. 1991, at A15. In all varieties of World English, resistance to the singular *they* is fast receding.

For related discussions, see **each (A)**, PRONOUNS (D) & SEXISM (B).

C. Subject–Complement Disagreement: Mismatched Number in Cause and Effect. Another common mistake, in AmE and BrE alike, is to attribute one result to two separate subjects, when logically a separate result necessarily occurred with each subject—e.g.:

- "In school, seats are not assigned, yet students tend to sit in the same seats or nearly the same each time, and sometimes feel vaguely resentful if *someone else gets* [read *others get*] there first and *takes 'their' seat* [read *take 'their' seats*]." Robin T. Lakoff, *Talking Power: The Politics of Language in Our Lives* 121 (1990). (This might be broken into two sentences, the second of which would read: *They sometimes feel vaguely resentful if "their" regular seats are taken by others.*)
- "Designated hitter Jason Layne, already sporting a black eye, was hit by *a pitch* [read *pitches*] twice." Rick Cantu, "Texas Baseball Team Thumps Favorite Tech," *Austin Am.-Statesman*, 15 Mar. 1996, at C1, C9. (The grammar here misleadingly suggests that the batter was hit twice by the same pitch.)

A related problem occurs in the following sentence, in which *both* is followed by a singular complement (*candidate*): "Today, both camps were enthusiastic about how *their candidate* fared." Richard L. Berke, "Rival Camps in Final Debate Faced Subtle and Basic Aims," *N.Y. Times*, 18 Oct. 1996, at A1, C21. The error

could have been corrected by saying *each camp was . . . its candidate* or *both camps were . . . their candidates*.

This is not an infallible rule, however. When the complement is not a concrete noun, the singular is usually required <the compromise let both adversaries retain their dignity>. The singular is also needed with mass nouns, of course <both cities get their water from the same reservoir>. And sometimes neither the singular nor the plural can prevent ambiguity. As one authority pointed out, in *Both men rely heavily on their wives*, the men may or may not be bigamists; but if the sentence is written *Both men rely heavily on their wife*, then she most certainly is one. Barbara Wallraff, *Word Court* 127–28 (2000).

D. Relative Pronoun–Antecedent Disagreement. This problem doesn't often arise, but a relative pronoun is supposed to agree with its antecedent in both number and person. So it's correct to say *It is I who am here*, not **It is I who is here*. Because *I* is first-person singular, *who* must also be first-person singular, and the verb—it naturally follows—must be *am*. Strictly speaking, the following forms are correct:

- *I who have made*;
- *one who has*;
- *they who have*; and
- *I who am*.

E.g.:

- "I have said ugly things about gay people, and I've laughed at gay jokes. I, *who am* female and black, and *who know* firsthand the sting of contempt." Betty Winston Bayé, "Facing One's Own Anti-Gay Bias," *Courier-J.* (Louisville), 10 Apr. 1997, at A11.
- "In fact, it is *they who have* been let down." Randy Harvey, "Robinson Proved Only That He Should Move On," *L.A. Times*, 24 Nov. 1997, at C2.

E. Adjective–Noun Disagreement. Some agreement problems arise between an adjective and the noun or nouns it modifies—e.g.: "In an outpouring of grief such as is seldom seen, the 'beloved community' of Martin Luther King's dream, Tony Brown's 'Team America' came to say good-bye to Barbara [Jordan]. People of *all races*, social *class* [read *classes*], national *origin* [read *origins*] and sexual *orientation* [read *orientations*] joined in mourning her death." Rosemary Simmons, "Barbara Jordan's Example Inspires Texas," *Daily Texan*, 21 Feb. 1996, at 4. But that sentence might read better if *all* were replaced by the "singular" adjective *every* and if each of the nouns were made singular: *People of every race, social class, national origin, and sexual orientation . . . .*

F. Possessive Noun as Antecedent. See POSSESSIVES (K).

concrete. See **cement.**

concupiscence (= inordinate lust; extreme sexual desire) is pronounced /kən-**kyoo**-pi-sən[t]s/.

concussion; contusion. *Concussion* = (1) violent shaking; (2) shock caused by a sudden impact; or (3) injury to the brain caused by a heavy blow.

Contusion = a bruise; an injury resulting from a blow that does not break the skin.

condemn; contemn. To *condemn*, in one sense, is to render judgment against (a person or thing) <the court condemned the accused to life in prison>. The word has passed from legal into general usage mostly in the figurative sense "to disapprove forcefully; to declare reprehensible"—e.g.: "Spiritual rites and modern development clashed when members of a Native American tribe *condemned* the way the Irvine Co. on Wednesday reburied ancient artifacts unearthed in 1994 during the building of a Newport Beach housing development." Tina Nguyen, "Chief Unhappy with Reburial of Tribal Artifacts," *L.A. Times*, 28 Nov. 1996, at B1.

In AmE, *condemn* has the additional legal sense "to pronounce judicially (land, etc.) as converted or convertible to public use, subject to reasonable compensation." E.g.:

- "In *condemning* the structure, city inspectors said large sections of the roof and walls had collapsed." Will Tracy, "Council Approves Spending to Raze State Theater," *Hartford Courant*, 26 Apr. 1994, at B3.
- "They fear a massive Everglades restoration project—which includes plans to *condemn* property and raise the water table—will drive them from their land." "Property Rights: Quiet Revolt," *Fla. Times-Union* (Georgia ed.), 16 Sept. 2002, at B4.
- "Government should *condemn* property only as a last resort. It should *condemn* only to acquire property it cannot otherwise get that is necessary, not merely desirable, for the public good." Editorial, *Salt Lake Trib.*, 19 Sept. 2002, at A18.

Contemn = to hold in contempt; to disregard; esp., to treat (as laws or court orders) with contemptuous disregard. The *OED* notes that it is "chiefly a literary word"—e.g.:

- "Rooted as he was in the idiom of Shakespeare and Donne, he *contemned* such trendy ploys." "Richard Burton, RIP," *Nat'l Rev.*, 7 Sept. 1984, at 17.
- "From Henry James through John O'Hara, the Irish, once much *contemned* in American life, were sensitively attuned to the horrors of snobbery and stimulated by the delights of social attainment." Joseph Epstein, *Commentary* (Book Rev.), Nov. 1994, at 52.
- "The best regime would recognize the duty to evaluate all human beings on an equal basis, regardless of nationality, and to respect or to *contemn* persons strictly in accordance with their virtue." Thomas L. Pangle, "Justice Among Nations in Platonic and Aristotelian Political Philosophy," *Am. J. Political Science*, 1 Apr. 1998, at 377.

In legal contexts, the corresponding agent noun *contemnor* is common. But see **contemner.**

condemned, n. As a matter of FUNCTIONAL SHIFT, the past-participial adjective *condemned* is often used as a noun <the condemned were given one last wish>. Occasionally writers erroneously use the word *condemn* in this sense—e.g.: "The drop from the gallows was designed to break the *condemn's* [read

condemned's] neck (ensuring near instant death)." Rhett Morgan, "Gallows at Fort Smith Still Attracting Attention," *Tulsa World*, 28 June 2001, at 9.

LANGUAGE-CHANGE INDEX
condemn misused for the attributive noun *condemned*: Stage 1

condemner; condemnor. The *-er* spelling (/kən-dem-ər/) is preferred in the general sense "one that disapproves." But in AmE, *condemnor* (/kon-dem-nor/) or /kən-dem-nər/) predominates in the sense "a public or semipublic entity that expropriates private property for public use." See -ER (A).

condensable. So spelled—not **condensible.* See -ABLE (A).

Current ratio: 7:1

condole, v.i.; **console,** v.t. To *condole* is to express sympathy; one *condoles with* another *on* a loss. The verb is intransitive. Although the corresponding plural noun, *condolences*, is quite common, the verb form is rare, especially in AmE. E.g.:

- "Our king could devote himself to *condoling* with flood victims and boosting American products abroad." Stephen Budiansky, "Putting Monarch Envy in Its Rightful Place," *U.S. News & World Rep.*, 27 May 1991, at 12.
- "Thompson, though *condoling* with Ned on his father's death, hopes that Ned might be persuaded to host a reception for the organisation." "Guinness Peer Wants to Ban Bomb," *Evening Standard*, 22 June 1992, at 8.

To *console* is to comfort (another), especially in grief or depression. E.g.:

- "Clinton—who *consoled* victims' families earlier in the day—ordered that more baggage be screened or hand-searched and that aircraft making international flights be fully inspected." "Experts Key In on Brief Noise in Cockpit Voice Recorder," *Detroit News*, 26 July 1996, at A1.
- "Fisher *consoled* the parents at the home and later met with them at All Children's Hospital in St. Petersburg, where the child was taken." Phuong Nguyen, "Agency for Victims Seeking Volunteers," *Sarasota Herald-Trib.*, 29 Nov. 1996, at B1.

Occasionally, *condole* is misused for *console*—e.g.: "And as always, countrymen everywhere can continue *condoling* [read *consoling*] the forlorn Cubs, from sea to shining sea." Thomas Stinson, "Baseball '94: It's a Brand New Ballgame!" *Atlanta J.-Const.*, 1 Apr. 1994, at E21.

LANGUAGE-CHANGE INDEX
condole misused for *console*: Stage 1
Current ratio (*consoling the* vs. **condoling the*): 33:1

condominium. Pl. *condominiums.* See PLURALS (B).

condonation; **condonance; condonement. *Condonation* = (1) the pardoning of a fault or misdeed, esp. when the pardon is merely implicit, as when a person who has been wronged acts toward the offender as if the offense is forgotten; or (2) in law, the complete

---

LANGUAGE-CHANGE INDEX (For the full key, see front matter pp. xxxi, l–li.)
Stage 1: Rejected. **Stage 2:** Widely shunned. **Stage 3:** Widespread but . . . **Stage 4:** Ubiquitous but . . . **Stage 5:** Fully accepted.
Invariably inferior forms marked by asterisk (∗). • Ratios represent frequency of prevalent forms vs. variants in current books.

forgiveness and wiping out of a marital offense, esp. adultery. Today, in both AmE and BrE, the word is fairly rare—smacking of SESQUIPEDALITY—and in law is usually confined to discussions of matrimonial offenses.

Condonance is a NEEDLESS VARIANT. *Condonement* is a technical term in certain card games.

Current ratio (*condonation* vs. **condonance*): 389:1

conduce to, though slightly bookish, is often a better and always a shorter way of saying *be conducive to* (something desirable)—e.g.: " 'Writing,' Mamet says in his book, 'is a magnificently solitary occupation. One works by oneself all day long, wondering, dreaming, supposing. All attitudes to which Vermont *conduces*.' " Tim Rutten, "National Geographic Travels on Literary Paths," *L.A. Times* (Home ed.), 19 July 2002, Living §, at 1. See BE-VERBS (B).

When the result referred to is undesirable, *lead* or *contribute* is typically a better word choice—e.g.:

- "Finally, the scheme might well *conduce to* [read *lead to*] the creation of separatist schools that reject the American civic culture even more forcefully than conventional public schools, under the spell of multiculturalism, are already doing." Chester E. Finn Jr., "Can the Schools Be Saved?" *Commentary*, Sept. 1996, at 41, 44.
- "[A conditional sentence is] weak, and nothing *conduces* [read *contributes*] more certainly to giving the impression that one is a windbag." Reid Buckley, "The 10 Commandments of Public Speaking," *Forbes*, 18 Nov. 1996, at 61.
- "This disorientation—or spiritual anomie—stems from strategic loss in history. It *conduces to* [read *leads to*] an insufficiency of self-belief and self-confidence." Irvin Studin, "Coequal Status for Aboriginals Vital to Our Future," *Toronto Star*, 28 Dec. 2014, at A11.

conductive; conducive. *Conductive* describes a thing's ability to conduct energy <conductive wire> <heat-conductive>. *Conducive* describes the quality of promoting, contributing to, or helping to bring about some outcome <conducive to success> <conducive to growth>. *Conductive* is sometimes misused for *conducive*—e.g.:

- "The [University of Michigan's] witnesses emphasized repeatedly that . . . a diversity of viewpoints, experiences, interests, perspectives and backgrounds . . . creates an atmosphere most *conductive* [read *conducive*] to learning." Ward Connerly, "Q: Does Diversity in Higher Education Justify Racial Preferences?" *Insight*, 14 May 2001, at 40.
- "Ever the competitor, Tiger Woods said he would not bet on himself to win the 2001 U.S. Open, but that's only because the short odds are not *conductive* [read *conducive*] to a big payday." Damon Hack, "Transcending the Sport," *Newsday* (N.Y.), 13 June 2001, at A70.
- " 'State parks have the type of terrain that's not necessarily *conductive* [read *conducive*] to cell phones,' said Tim O'Neill, a Delavan police captain and emergency medical technician." Anita Clark, "Pay Phones Going Back in at Parks by July 4," *Wis. State J.*, 1 July 2001, at A1.

LANGUAGE-CHANGE INDEX
conductive misused for *conducive*: Stage 1
Current ratio (*conducive to health* vs.
*conductive to health): 77:1

conduit is pronounced /**kon**-doo-it/ in AmE, /**kon**-dit/ or /kən-dit/ in BrE.

confectionary; confectionery. Despite some overlap, these terms are usefully distinguished. *Confectionary*, an adjective, means (1) "of, relating to, or resembling a confection"; or (2) "of, relating to, or involving confectioners." *Confectionery*, always a noun, means (1) "confections collectively; candy"; or (2) "a confectioner's business or place of business; candy store." The latter is the more frequently used term.

confederation; federation. The distinction between these two words is subtle, but it's crucial to understanding the nature and history of American political power.

A *confederation* is a league of states, each of which retains its sovereignty. The states may delegate some rights and powers to a central authority—but they do not delegate supremacy over their internal affairs, including the right to withdraw from the confederation. A *federation* is a union of states with a strong central authority and no true regional sovereignty. In the United States, we speak of the *sovereign states*, and they do retain extensive rights and powers of their own. But they are always subject to the U.S. Constitution (the fundamental law of the land) and to the powers it gives to the national government.

William Safire has observed that in 1789 the United States changed, in Northerners' minds, from a confederation to a federation. But to Southerners, the country retained the characteristics of a confederation. Later, of course, in 1860, Southerners thought that the union could be dissolved. When the Southern states seceded, they chose the word *confederation* to describe their own grouping—although they did not put a right to secede in their own constitution, an inconsistency noted in the North. See William Safire, "Confederacy Rises Again," *N.Y. Times*, 29 Sept. 1991, § 6, at 18.

confer. In Latin, *confer* means "to compare," whence the present English meaning of the abbreviated form of *compare*, namely, *cf.* The unabbreviated form *confer* no longer has this meaning; today it means (intransitively) "to come together to take counsel and exchange views" or (transitively) "to bestow, usu. from a position of authority."

In this latter (transitive) sense, one *confers* something *on*, not *in*, another. E.g.:

- "Web-surfing most likely will not *confer* jurisdiction *in* [read *on*] that service's home state." Dale M. Cendali & James D. Arbogast, "Net Use Raises Issues of Jurisdiction," *Nat'l L.J.*, 28 Oct. 1996, at C7.
- "He said lower interest costs will *confer* benefits *on* all borrowers." Barry Flynn, "Fed Slashes Rates by Hefty Half Point," *Orlando Sentinel*, 7 Nov. 2002, at A1.

LANGUAGE-CHANGE INDEX
*confer in for *confer on*: Stage 1

conferee = (1) a member of or participant in a conference; or (2) one on whom something is conferred. Although this word has the look of a NEOLOGISM, it predates the Declaration of Independence. Sense 1 is now usual—e.g.:

- "Multipoint communication that supports up to eight *conferees* is essential for videoconferencing to be accepted, he said." Justin Hibbard, "NetMeeting Gets Videoconferencing," *ComputerWorld*, 9 Dec. 1996, at 8.
- "In July, Republican House and Senate *conferees* quickly discarded a similar $3 billion fund designed to help states do exactly that." Jeffrey L. Katz, "Small Change," *New Republic*, 9 Dec. 1996, at 14.
- "Attractions like golf—a second course is planned— a beach club built around a man-made lake and beach and the nearby plantations would entice the *conferees* to bring families and stay longer." Chris Fink, "State Money OK'd for Resort Complex," *State-Times/Morning Advocate* (Baton Rouge) (Metro ed.), 21 Sept. 2002, at A1.

*Conferree is a variant form best avoided.

conferencing. Although the *OED* records *conference* as a (rare) verb from 1846, the *SOED* and *W3* omit it. Increasingly common in AmE, *conferencing* is often a bloated NEEDLESS VARIANT of *conferring*. The word has also become rather widespread in the forms *teleconferencing* and *videoconferencing*, favorite activities in American business. The word is likely to survive in those forms.

LANGUAGE-CHANGE INDEX
1. *conference* as a verb: Stage 4
Current ratio (*conferring* vs. *conferencing*): 2:1
2. *conference* in the compounds *teleconferencing* and *videoconferencing*: Stage 5

conferment. See **conferral.**

conferrable. So spelled. It is pronounced with the stress on the second syllable: /kən-**fər**-ə-bəl/. Throughout the 19th century, the spelling **conferrible* was common—but that was superseded by 1900. Cf. **referable.**

Current ratio: 16:1

conferral; conferment. The question is a straightforward one: are we to model the noun after *referral* or *deferment*? Most linguistic questions like this were settled centuries ago, but *confer* is one of those verbs for which English speakers have less frequently needed a corresponding noun.

Dictionaries suggest that *conferral* is a NEEDLESS VARIANT of *conferment* and that it ought to be treated as such. But American sources suggest otherwise. In denoting the act of conferring, *conferral* appears in hundreds of federal-law cases (more than 20 times as often as *conferment*) and in hundreds of state cases (almost 6 times as often). Judicial usage, then, inclines dramatically toward *conferral*. E.g.: "A distinct feature of our Nation's system of governance has been the *conferral* of political power upon public and municipal corporations for the management of matters of local concern." *Owen v. City of Independence*, 445 U.S. 622, 638 (1980).

In the popular press, likewise, *conferral* appears today nearly twice as often as *conferment*, which predominated for most of the 20th century.

If a distinction between the terms is possible, it is that *conferral* refers to the awarding of an honor or title <the evening concluded with the conferral of an honorary degree on the graduation speaker>, while *conferment* refers to the event where a *conferral* takes place <the annual conferment dinner will be held on June 16>. This DIFFERENTIATION seems worth encouraging.

confess. A. *Confess to* for *confess*. Traditionally, people *confess* crimes, guilt, weaknesses, faults, and the like. Less traditionally—though at least since the 18th century—people have *confessed to* these things. Euphony should govern the phrasing. In the following three examples, *confess to* sounds better than *confess* alone would have:

- "Did ever anybody seriously *confess to* envy?" Herman Melville, *Billy Budd* 39 (1891; repr. [Signet ed.] 1979).
- "I *confess to* never having attended a tractor pull." William Safire, "Virile Women Target Tobacco Men," *N.Y. Times*, 11 Mar. 1990, § 6, at 18.
- "But worse, he was convicted even after the lead witness against him, Ivan F. Boesky, *confessed to* keeping millions of dollars in ill-gotten profits." "Adding Insult to Injury," *N.Y. Times*, 15 July 1990, at F2.
- "In this episode, the recipient of the coveted single date, who *confesses* to being a bit 'high-maintenance,' gets to don a bikini and go stand-up paddleboarding." Sue Yeap, "Remote Patrol," *West Australian*, 19 Aug. 2015, at 5.

Cf. **admit.**

Current ratio (*confessed guilt* vs. **confessed to guilt*): 10:1

B. **Confess innocence* for *profess innocence*. This misusage is nothing short of a MALAPROPISM (probably influenced by the similar-sounding *confess ignorance*)—e.g.:

- "Kathleen Turner . . . *confesses* [read *professes*] innocence when two neighbors . . . confront her." Philip Wuntch, "Serial Mom," *Dallas Morning News*, 15 Apr. 1994, at C1.
- "Exactly six months ago, Daniel Strader stood before 2,000 members of his father's congregation and *confessed* [read *professed*] his innocence." Thomas Roe Oldt, "Strader Took Investors' Trust to the Bank, Then to Big House," *Ledger* (Lakeland, Fla.), 30 July 1995, at F5.

LANGUAGE-CHANGE INDEX
*confess innocence for *profess innocence*: Stage 1

confessedly = (1) by general admission or acknowledgment; or (2) by personal confession (*OED*). Wilson Follett too narrowly declared that "the test of legitimacy for an adverb made from an adjective is that it fit the formula *in [x] manner*" (*MAU* at 279), a formula that *confessedly* does not fit. Follett's primary objection was to *reportedly*, the earliest recorded use of which was in 1901. *Confessedly* has been used since

LANGUAGE-CHANGE INDEX (For the full key, see front matter pp. xxxi, l–li.)
Stage 1: Rejected. **Stage 2:** Widely shunned. **Stage 3:** Widespread but . . . **Stage 4:** Ubiquitous but . . . **Stage 5:** Fully accepted.
Invariably inferior forms marked by asterisk (*). • Ratios represent frequency of prevalent forms vs. variants in current books.

at least 1640, however, and is undeniably (or perhaps confessedly) useful. Still, adverbs ending in -edly can assuredly be overworked.

Following are two typical—and unobjectionable—uses of confessedly:

- "Ask the confessedly road-weary singer that question as she sits in a Minneapolis hotel room, and another one presents itself." Mike Boehm, "O.C. Pop Beat: Kirsty MacColl on Her Own Terms," L.A. Times, 6 Apr. 1995, at F1.
- "Biographies may become more like portraits, he says, less academic, more confessedly subjective." Jerome Weeks, "The Bio Boom," Dallas Morning News, 14 Jan. 1996, at C1.

See -EDLY.

*confess innocence. See confess (B).

confession. See admission (B).

confidant; confidante; confident, n. The forms confidant and confidante have an interesting history. Until 1700 or so, the English word was confident (= a trusty friend or adherent), the correct French forms being confident and confidente. But early in the 18th century, English writers began substituting an -a- for the -e- in the final syllable, perhaps because of the French nasal pronunciation of -ent and -ente.

Today the forms confidant and confidante predominate in both AmE and BrE, though confidante is falling into disuse because of what is increasingly thought to be a needless distinction between males and females. Despite the poor ETYMOLOGY, one can be confident in using confidant (/**kon**-fi-dahnt/) for either sex, as it is predominantly used in American writing—e.g.:

- "In softer profile, [Hillary] Clinton comes across as a well-organized working mother and her husband's closest confidant." Kenneth L. Woodward, "Methodist Influence on Hillary Clinton," Plain Dealer (Cleveland), 29 Nov. 1994, at E1.
- "Her admiration for Richard Nixon, whom she served as adviser and confidant for the last four years of his life, led her to believe that revealing the words he spoke in their private conversations would help restore his reputation." Myron A. Marty & Dale Singer, "Politics," St. Louis Post-Dispatch, 28 Nov. 1996, at 13.

See SEXISM (D).

In any event, it's wrong to make confidante refer to a male—e.g.:

- "The executive producer job went to Jeff Zucker, a Katie Couric confidante [read confidant], but someone who is hardly a favorite of Gumbel's." "Fox TV Reported Seeking 'Today' Host Bryant Gumbel," Plain Dealer (Cleveland), 30 Nov. 1994, at E10.
- "He was the confidante [read confidant] of five U.S. presidents, from Woodrow Wilson to Franklin Roosevelt." "Humorist-Performer Rogers Remembered," Tampa Trib., 30 Nov. 1994, Baylife §, at 4.
- "The leadership he applied to the process, the attention to contrary stratagems, was evident even earlier to another confidante [read confidant] who found himself suddenly consulted by Mr. Powell about the political art of a strategic retreat." Francis X. Clines, "Variation on a War Game: How Powell Arrived at No," N.Y. Times, 12 Nov. 1995, at 1, 12.

LANGUAGE-CHANGE INDEX
1. confidant for either sex: Stage 5
2. confidante for a male: Stage 3

confide in; confide to. Confide in (= to trust or have faith in) is the more common phrase in general usage—e.g.: "While she didn't confide in Dallek, she did write a paper on Morris' twenty-year friendship with Clinton." "Morris the Catch," Texas Monthly, Dec. 1996, at 21.

Confide to = (1) to communicate (something) in confidence to; (2) to entrust (an object of care or a task) to. Except in legal contexts <responsibilities confided to the legislature>, the phrase occurs most commonly today in sense 1—e.g.:

- "He does some cooking, he said, and confides his thoughts and fears to compassionate staff members." Cynthia Hubert, "New AIDS Retreat Enables Resident to Savor Life," Sacramento Bee, 23 Apr. 1995, at B1.
- "In '90s fashion, he confides to another that he's now a vegetarian." Jennifer Phelps, "Heartburn Hotel," Des Moines Register, 14 Aug. 1996, Today §, at 3.

confinable. So spelled—not *confineable. See MUTE E.
Current ratio: 24:1

confirmand (/kon-fər-**mand**/) = a person confirmed or to be confirmed in a religious rite supplemental to baptism. E.g.:

- "Her church's group of 12 included members of the confirmation class. Several of the other 13 participating churches had confirmands participating." Steve Snyder, "Bumper Crop Walk Held," Harrisburg Patriot, 21 Oct. 2002, at B16.
- "At church, Jonathan, Steffanie and Michael are in the second year of a two-year confirmation program, and all confirmands are required to do a . . . service project." Clare House & Diane M. Bitting, "A Gift of Reading," Lancaster New Era, 19 Dec. 2002, Teen Weekend §, at 5.

The word is analogous to *honorand (= a person to be honored), a word now generally displaced by honoree. See honoree.

Perhaps because the Latinate suffix -and (meaning "about to be") is rather unusual in English, many writers misspell confirmand as if it had a different suffix: *confirmant. This mistaken form isn't recorded as a word in the OED or most other dictionaries. Hence it's a NONWORD—e.g.:

- "Among those gathered at the church was the family of Arlova Vorm, whose grandson, Dustin Vorm, is a sixth-generation confirmant [read confirmand] of the church." Terry Turner, "Re-created Circuit Ride Celebrates Origins of Church," South Bend Trib., 27 Sept. 2001, Local §, at 1.
- "The Bishop is at Grace Church this weekend to confirm and receive new members into the church. He will meet with the confirmants [read confirmands] and their mentors following dinner." "Religion in the Twin Tiers," Star-Gaz. (Elmira, N.Y.), 9 Nov. 2002, at C4.

If *confirmant were appropriate at all, it would refer to the priest or minister performing the rite (the celebrant)—not to the person being confirmed. Cf. celebrant.

LANGUAGE-CHANGE INDEX
*confirmant for confirmand: Stage 1
Current ratio (the confirmands vs.
*the confirmants): 23:1

confirmation; conformation. Confirmation (= verification) is occasionally displaced by conformation

(= [1] correspondence with norms; or [2] compliance with regulations)—e.g.:

- "For multiple orders, indicate the name of each recipient, telephone number and include a stamped, self-addressed envelope for *conformation* [read *confirmation*] ticket and number." "My Communities," *Honolulu Advertiser*, 8 Dec. 2008, at B3.
- "The university had not received a *conformation* [read *confirmation*] from [Loy] Vaught, and The Press was unable to contact him." "Hughes to Join Celebration," *Grand Rapids Press*, 17 Jan. 2009, at D3.

Conformation is most commonly found in sense 1, especially denoting the match between an animal and the ideal attributes of its breed—e.g.: "The amateur competition continues at 8 a.m. today in the Coliseum, with the horses doing a reining pattern and then working a cow before they are judged on their *conformation*." Ann Schrader, "Horses Show Ranch Skills for a Bit of Glory," *Denver Post*, 15 Jan. 2009, at B5. Sense 2 verges on OFFICIALESE—e.g.: "[County planning director Brian] Clifton said the county doesn't usually require a bond in issuing a location *conformation* permit, but SME offered to post it." Karl Puckett, "MEIC Asks Judge to Void Plant Zoning," *Grand Falls Trib.*, 28 Oct. 2008, at M1.

confirmatory; *confirmative. The latter is a NEEDLESS VARIANT.

Current ratio: 31:1

confiscable. So formed—not **confiscatable*. See -ABLE (D) & -ATABLE.

Current ratio: 25:1

confiscatory (/kən-**fis**-kə-tor-ee/) is the adjective corresponding to the verb *confiscate*. It means "of, relating to, or involving confiscation; tending to confiscate." And it most often crops up in the context of taxes—e.g.:

- "But the party, with a long history of *confiscatory* taxation and state intervention, is still not trusted on the economy." "Labor Party Shifts Its Economic Approach," *Rocky Mountain News* (Denver), 28 Sept. 1994, at A31.
- "Economic reform means eliminating hyperinflation and revising a totally capricious tax system that does not work domestically and is *confiscatory* on firms owned abroad." Christopher Ogden, "Back in the Fray," *Time* (Int'l ed.), 18 Nov. 1996, at 28.

Colloquially, the word bears the sense "stealing with legal authority" <confiscatory landlords>.

confit; confiture. Both derive from the French verb *confire*, meaning "to prepare." A *confit* (/kahn-**fee**/) is a preparation of meat or poultry stewed in its own fat with seasonings and then congealed. The retained French pronunciation reflects the fact that the word *confit* did not enter the English language until the mid-20th century. A *confiture* (/**kahn**-fi-chuur/) is a confection of candied fruit—a preserve or jam. The pronunciation was anglicized shortly after the word entered English in the early 19th century.

conflicted, adj.; **conflictual.** *Conflicted* means "affected by conflicting emotions, allegiances, duties, or the like." The word dates back only to the late 1960s. By the 1990s, it had become a VOGUE WORD—e.g.:

- "Many Asian Americans—who see all too few nonstereotypical images of Asian Americans in popular media—are *conflicted* over Liu's character." Annie Nakao, "She's No Madame Butterfly," *Record* (Northern N.J.), 29 Mar. 1999, at L7.
- "Even Arkansans *are conflicted* about Clinton and his legacy, much like other Americans." Bill Nichols, "Ark. Caps Clinton's Sentimental Journey," *USA Today*, 18 Jan. 2001, at A8.
- "When the teams split a doubleheader two weeks ago in Winona, Minn., Tschida expected to feel *conflicted* and maybe even slightly uncomfortable, but he had no such emotions." Jason Wolf, "Coach Makes Smooth Move," *Star Trib.* (Minneapolis), 17 Apr. 2001, at C5.

Conflictual, a much rarer term, means "of, relating to, or characterized by conflict." The word is documented in the *OED* from 1961—e.g.:

- "The conflict in Kashmir was renewed just as the Berlin Wall fell, and both countries continued their *conflictual* habits without reference to the wider world." Paula Newberg, "India vs. Pakistan," *San Diego Union-Trib.*, 22 May 1994, at G4.
- "Whether a marriage is openly *conflictual* or relentlessly harmonious, a marriage that is unable to adapt to changes like births, economic ups and downs, departures of children and retirement will become stressed." Hugh Leavell, "Don't Avoid Conflict—Manage It," *Palm Beach Post*, 22 Nov. 1996, at F3.

The more popular of these words, *conflicted*, should be avoided in watered-down senses. For example, if the simple word *disagree* will work, then use it—e.g.: "Analysts *are conflicted about* [read *disagree*] whether the economic slowdown will help or hurt club growth." Mark Albright, "Expanding the Club," *St. Petersburg Times*, 4 June 2001, at E8.

conflict of interest. Today the phrase "ranges from being a euphemism for the result of outright bribery to describing a situation in which one subject to a duty takes a position inconsistent with that duty." John T. Noonan Jr., *Bribes* 446 (1984).

conform takes the preposition *to* or *with*. H.W. Fowler objected to *conform with*, but most authorities find it quite acceptable. E.g.: "Libya said the investigations *conformed with* international law and did not violate its sovereignty." Paul Lewis, "Libya Offers Some Cooperation in Plane Bombings," *N.Y. Times*, 15 Feb. 1992, at A5. Even so, *conform to* is the far more frequent collocation in all phases of Modern English.

Current ratio (*conforms to* vs. *conforms with*): 11:1

conformation. See **confirmation.**

conformity; conformance. *Conformity* has always been the usual term, *conformance* being confined

LANGUAGE-CHANGE INDEX (For the full key, see front matter pp. xxxi, l–li.)
Stage 1: Rejected. **Stage 2:** Widely shunned. **Stage 3:** Widespread but . . . **Stage 4:** Ubiquitous but . . . **Stage 5:** Fully accepted.
Invariably inferior forms marked by asterisk (*). • Ratios represent frequency of prevalent forms vs. variants in current books.

largely to senses regarding technical compliance—e.g.: "Dan Korus, division manager, said that the registration by Underwriters' Laboratories is . . . part of an overall plan to bring all major facilities of Vishay Electronic Components into *conformance* with ISO 9000 quality guidelines." Bernard Levine & Fred Guinther, "Vishay's Dale Electronics, Inc.," *Electronic News*, 15 Apr. 1996, at 32. In a related use, *conformance* often functions as an adjective in phrases such as *conformance testing*—e.g.: "We're urging the FCC to issue strong regulations governing the areas of network interconnection, unbundling, portability, mutual traffic exchange, pricing standards and *conformance* standards." Heather Gold, "Perspective—The FCC Better Shape Up Those Monopolies," *Communications Week*, 15 Apr. 1996, at 49.

In other uses, *conformance* might justifiably be labeled a NEEDLESS VARIANT. E.g.: "Antista . . . [added] that the fish and game commission, when permitting new wildlife refuges and rescue services, routinely requires applicants to show *conformance* [read *conformity*] with local zoning codes." "Wildlife in the City," *Sarasota Herald-Trib.*, 25 Nov. 1996, at A8.

Like its corresponding verb, *conformity* takes either *to* or *with*—the latter being more common since the 1820s. E.g.:

- "They attempted to reform the church to be in greater *conformity with* the Bible that—they believed—forbade such things as wedding rings, Sabbath sports and Christmas celebrations." Diana Butler, " 'Holy Day' Isn't Just for Puritans," *Plain Dealer* (Cleveland), 28 Nov. 1996, at B7.
- "It *harkens* [read *harks*] back to years before the mid-2000s when people could eat food without having to consider whether their choices were in *conformity with* their chosen subculture." Andrew Edwards, "Contemplating the Cultural Cachet of Curious Chips," *Long Beach Press-Telegram*, 8 Aug. 2015, News §, at 3. (See **hark back**.)

confusable. So spelled—not **confusible*. See -ABLE (A).
Current ratio: 11:1

confute. See **refute**.

congé; congee. *Congé* (/kon-**zhay**/ or /**kon**-jay/) = (1) formal permission to leave; (2) a formal bow signaling goodbye; or (3) a farewell. E.g.: "It seems that between 1991, when Mr. Clark signed up, and 1996 when he was given his *congé*, age withered his prospects." "Ageism Pays," *Fin. Times*, 17 Oct. 1996, at 19. The word is a GALLICISM that some private American schools use in an annual alumni party called *all-school congé*, which doesn't necessarily coincide with graduation. **Congée* is a variant spelling.

Congee (/**kon**-jee/) = a rice porridge characteristic of some Asian cuisines. E.g.:

- "A teacher once beat him with a ruler for eating *congee* with dried shrimp for breakfast instead of more traditional American fare." Michael O'Regan, "Chinese-American Hero Makes History," *South China Morning Post*, 7 Nov. 1996, at 4.
- "Hope Key . . . offers an irresistibly wide variety of serious seafood dishes (including frog and snail dishes) as

well as comfort foods such as chow foons (thick noodle dishes), hot pots and *congees* (rice porridge)." Eve Zibart, "A Clarion Call for Clarendon," *Wash. Post*, 22 Nov. 1996, Weekend §, at 25.

congenial; genial. A subtle difference exists and should be promoted. *Congenial* = (1) having similar tastes; compatible; kindred <a congenial married couple>; or (2) to one's liking; suitable; pleasant <a congenial workplace>. *Genial* = affable; friendly; cordial <her usual genial disposition>. Hence *genial* applies to individuals, while *congenial* is generally reserved for people collectively or for environments.

The DIFFERENTIATION is less pronounced with the noun forms, the word *congeniality* often doing the work for both adjectives—hence "Miss Congeniality" (not "Miss Geniality"). But *geniality* remains current, and there is no reason why beauty-pageant usage—though well established—should control what careful writers do. *Congeniality*, then, might usefully be reserved for groups of people and environments, *geniality* for individuals.

congeries (= a collection; aggregation) is ordinarily a singular noun—e.g.:

- "Multiculturalism, by contrast, casts the world as a *congeries* of particularisms; and it regards the idea of an all-embracing humanity with suspicion." Sean Wilentz, "Sense and Sensitivity," *New Republic*, 31 Oct. 1994, at 43.
- "The microchip is a formidable accomplishment, too—one that is also a *congeries* of some of the most advanced technologies and talents of this age." Owen Edwards, "The Basilica Chip," *Forbes*, 7 Oct. 1996, at 140.

As both examples show, the word frequently has a slightly pejorative cast, suggesting "a perplexing bunch of things."

The form **congerie* (sometimes spelled **congery*) is a false-singular noun recorded by the *OED* and *W3*, a kind of BACK-FORMATION made on the mistaken assumption that *congeries* is the plural of such a noun. E.g.:

- "The greatest effect of the closing will be what happens to the land under the century-old *congerie* [read *congeries*] of industrial buildings." Anthony DePalma, "Town Quandary: 20 Acres, RIV VU," *N.Y. Times*, 20 Feb. 1983, § 8, at 1.
- "When a *congerie* [read *congeries*] of women's organizations announced that this was the 'Year of the Woman' and that they were going to do their utmost to get more women into Congress, the media instantly took up the cry." Richard Grenier, "Yearning to Look Down on Someone," *Wash. Times*, 18 July 1992, at C3.
- "It is already a *congery* [read *congeries*] of standard practices that constitutes assisted suicide or euthanasia in disguise." William Joseph Buckley et al., "Ethics of Palliative Sedation and Medical Disasters," 28 *Ethics & Medicine* no. 1, 1 Apr. 2012, at 35. (On the relative pronoun *that* in this example, see REMOTE RELATIVES.)

In fact, although the singular *congeries* is most frequent, the word can also be a plural—e.g.: "I learned [economic theory] all as *congeries* of interrelated propositions." H.W. Arndt, *A Course Through Life: Memoirs of an Australian Economist* 3 (1985).

The word is pronounced /**kon**-jə-reez/ or /kən-**jir**-eez/ or /kon-jə-**reez**/ in AmE; and /kən-**jeer**-eez/ or /kən-**jeer**-i-eez/ in BrE.

LANGUAGE-CHANGE INDEX

congery or **congerie* as false singular
of *congeries*: Stage 1
Current ratio (*a congeries* vs. **congerie* vs.
*congery): 90:3:1

congratulate. The traditional idiom is to *congratulate* a person *on* or *for* something. The verb shouldn't be construed with a *that*-clause—e.g.:

- "Keno should be *congratulated that he was* [read *congratulated on being*] able to keep the donation down to $35,000." Jim Driskill, "Facts on Candidate Hawker Weren't All on Table," *Ariz. Republic*, 14 Mar. 2000, at 4.
- "Board members should be *congratulated that they realize* [read *congratulated for realizing*] this need." "Workers as Administrators," *Salt Lake Trib.*, 24 Oct. 2000, at A12.
- "Catherine Zeta Jones is to be *congratulated that she now bears* [read *congratulated for now bearing* or *congratulated now that she bears*] the name of one of Scotland's famous families." R. Morton Douglas, "Flemish Factor," *Daily Telegraph*, 24 Nov. 2000.

This verb is sometimes also the victim of OBJECT-SHUFFLING. You're supposed to congratulate people for their virtues, not congratulate the virtues themselves. This error occurs in BrE more often than in AmE—e.g.:

- "As one who was in the Forum when the bomb arrived, he *congratulated the vigilance of staff* [read *congratulated the staff for their vigilance*]." Gerry Moriarty, "Army Defuses 'Crude but Viable' Parcel Bomb Sent to UK Unionist Party Leader," *Irish Times*, 25 July 1997, at 6.
- "People grasped him by the hand, *congratulated his courage* [read *congratulated him for his courage*], skill and foresight." Sue Denham, "The Things People Will Do for a Union Card," *Sunday Times* (London), 21 Mar. 1999, at 21.

The word should be pronounced /kən-**grach**-ə-layt/, not /-**graj**-/.

LANGUAGE-CHANGE INDEX

1. *congratulate* construed with a *that*-clause: Stage 3
2. *congratulate* with an inanimate object: Stage 2

congratulatory; *congratulant; *congratulative. *Congratulatory* is the usual word. The other forms are NEEDLESS VARIANTS.

Current ratio (in order of headwords): 4,514:3:1

*congregate together is a REDUNDANCY that was common in the mid-19th century but has since retreated. Cf. ***associate together.**

Congress does not require an article, except in references to a specific session <the 104th Congress>. Although some congressional insiders use the phrase, **the Congress* is a quirk to be avoided in polished prose. The possessive form is preferably *Congress's*—e.g.: "Ms. Rosen said it is *Congress's* responsibility because it gave

regulators the framework for RESPA." "HUD Supports RESPA Review," *Nat'l Mortgage News*, 4 Nov. 1996, at 16. See POSSESSIVES (A). Cf. **Parliament.**

congressional, like *constitutional*, should be written with a lowercase *c-*, even though the noun corresponding to the adjective is capitalized.

*Congressperson is an unnecessary substitute for *representative, congressional representative, member of Congress, Congressman*, or *Congresswoman.* E.g.: "Be sure to check out the upcoming vote on the amendment just to see if your *congressperson* [read *representative*] has the guts to vote against something enormously popular and incredibly dumb." Molly Ivins, "Budget Amendment Is Popular—and Dumb," *Idaho Statesman*, 20 Nov. 1996, at A11. See SEXISM (C).

LANGUAGE-CHANGE INDEX

*Congressperson: Stage 2
Current ratio (*Congressman/-woman* vs.
*Congressperson): 34:1

congruent; congruous. Although these words are largely synonymous—meaning "in agreement or harmony; appropriate"—interesting distinctions have arisen. *Congruous* (/**kong**-groo-əs/)—once thought to be the more widely used term—is actually quite infrequent in the sense "appropriate, fitting; marked by harmonious agreement." But it does occasionally occur—e.g.: "She made it her first priority to create an interior that would be *congruous* with the exterior, giving the house a more authentically Mediterranean feel." Glynis Costin, "A House of Her Own," *Town & Country*, July 1996, at 68. The negative form *incongruous* ("not in harmony; unfitting") is far more common. See **incongruous.**

And oddly enough, the word *congruent* (/**kong**-groo-ənt/ or /kən-**groo**-ənt/) has largely taken over as the antonym of *incongruous.* True, it has always had legitimate uses in math and physics, and has long been prevalent in the sense "coinciding throughout; in accordance with." But today it is also the usual term in the broadest senses—e.g.:

- "Such idiosyncratic experiments in style were hardly *congruent* with official pressure to honor the ascent of socialism through prescriptive prose about the beauty of collective farming." Cynthia Ozick, "The Year of Writing Dangerously," *New Republic*, 8 May 1995, at 31.
- "His pro-choice and pro-death penalty provisions are *congruent* with majority opinion in California." Patrick Reddy, "Slim Pickings for Dole in California," *Sacramento Bee*, 15 Sept. 1996, at F1.
- "Like the *congruent* decor in our homes or the finely trimmed shrubs dotting our manicured lawns, many of us severely limit the range of our feelings." Philip Chard, "Embracing Chaos of Life Is Difficult for Most of Us," *Milwaukee J. Sentinel*, 3 Dec. 1996, Good Morning §, at 1.

LANGUAGE-CHANGE INDEX (For the full key, see front matter pp. xxxi, l–li.)
Stage 1: Rejected. **Stage 2:** Widely shunned. **Stage 3:** Widespread but . . . **Stage 4:** Ubiquitous but . . . **Stage 5:** Fully accepted.
Invariably inferior forms marked by asterisk (*). • Ratios represent frequency of prevalent forms vs. variants in current books.

The corresponding nouns are *congruence* and *congruity*. **Congruency* is a NEEDLESS VARIANT.

conjoin generally provides no nuance not included in *join* or *combine*—e.g.:

- "In consequence, homosexuality and secrecy were *conjoined* [read *joined*] inseparably in a place that became known as the closet." "A Love That Dares Speak Its Name," *Economist*, 15 July 1995, at 68.
- "Those events, *conjoined* [read *combined*] with the current DSO season's unremarkable programing and the orchestra's inconsistent music-making through the season's first half, might lead one to wonder where the maestro's head really is." Lawrence B. Johnson, "Notes of Caution," *Detroit News*, 30 Nov. 1996, Accent §, at C1.
- "Lewis required that Paramount bust down the walls of two adjacent soundstages so he could *conjoin* [read *combine*] them to build his massive, all-inclusive set for his second work." Robert Koehler, "Revered or Reviled, Lewis Made a Mint for Par," *Variety*, 15 July 2002, "Paramount at 90" Supp., at 56. (For more on the use of *bust*, see **burst**.)

W11 defines *conjoin* as "to join together (as separate entities) for a common purpose." *Join together* is, of course, a venial REDUNDANCY, just as *conjoin* is something of a one-word redundancy. But these phrases do slightly shade *join*. Perhaps on those rare occasions when you want the precise nuance suggested by *W11*'s definition—combining for a common purpose—*conjoin* is the proper word.

Further, the phrase *conjoined twins* has emerged as a nonethnic substitute for *Siamese twins*. And in this literal sense, the word seems appropriate—e.g.:

- "*Conjoined twins* occur when a single fertilized egg fails to divide completely to form identical twins." Dick Stanley, "St. David's Physicians to Separate Joined Twins," *Austin Am.-Statesman*, 6 July 1995, at A1.
- "*Conjoined twins* less than a week old took their first airplane ride yesterday." Sandra Dibble, "Conjoined Twins Are Flown to Mexico City," *San Diego Union-Trib.*, 2 Aug. 1996, at 7.

CONJUNCTIONS. A. Starting Sentences with. Wilson Follett called the notion that sentences shouldn't start with conjunctions a "prejudice [that] lingers from a bygone time . . . . The supposed rule is without foundation in grammar, logic, or art" (*MAU* at 64). Good writers have long made use of the clear signals that short conjunctions give to the reader—e.g.: "Tell her you love her. *And* you couldn't resist telling her what you'd like to do with or without custard. *But* tell her that you're married to Matey and any hint of scandal would seriously damage the Chambers image. *So* you'll both just have to be extraordinarily brave about it. That way you won't come out as an idiot who can't manage his e-mail and she'll still feel loved." John Mortimer, "Rumpole and the New Year's Resolutions," in *Rumpole and the Primrose Path* 38, 57 (2003). See **and, but, for** & **so.**

B. Correlative Conjunctions. See CORRELATIVE CONJUNCTIONS.

C. As Prepositions. See FUNCTIONAL SHIFT (G).

D. Subordination and Coordination. See SUBORDINATION AND COORDINATION.

conjure. In its usual sense ("to play the sorcerer"), the first syllable of this verb is stressed: /**kon**-jər/. In its rare sense ("to supplicate, beseech"), the stress is on the second syllable: /kən-**joor**/.

By idiom, the word most often appears with the particle *up*—e.g.: "The process uses gamma rays, electrons or X-rays to kill pathogens such as E. coli and salmonella. But to some, the process and the word *conjures up* images of radioactive food that has been zapped with nuclear energy." Cindy Skrzycki, "Zapping a New Label on Irradiation?" *Wash. Post*, 5 Nov. 2002, at E1. But it can also stand alone—e.g.: "Mead. The very word *conjures* carousing Vikings around a leaping fire, or cryptic Celts melting into the shadows of an ancient forest." James P. DeWan, "The Buzz of Bees," *Chicago Trib.*, 6 Nov. 2002, Good Eating §, at 3.

conjurer; *conjuror; *conjurator. *Conjurer*—not **conjuror*—is the preferred spelling for the word meaning "magician; juggler." E.g.: "Though once considered the domain of alchemists and other soul-bargaining *conjurers* . . . , glasshouses, or greenhouses, soon became proof of a homeowner's modernity and wealth." Mitchell Owens, "At Home with Books," *N.Y. Times*, 5 Dec. 1996, at C1. **Conjurator* is an obsolete word meaning "one joined with others by an oath; a co-conspirator."

Current ratio (in order of headwords): 5,231:2,657:1

connectable; *connectible. The first is standard in both AmE and BrE. It's much more common than the second in modern print sources. See -ABLE (A).

Current ratio: 9:1

Connecticut is pronounced /kə-**net**-i-kət/. The medial -*c*- is silent.

Connecticuter. See **Nutmegger.**

connection; *connexion; connexity. The spelling -*tion* is standard in AmE; -*xion* is an almost obsolete spelling formerly preferred in BrE. Up to 1967, the Oxford dictionaries used the spelling **connexion*, with an -*x*-; in that year, the switch was made to *connection*. (This despite the predominance of *connection* in BrE by 1850!) The word means basically (1) "the act of connecting" <the connection of loose ends>; (2) "the state of being connected" <the connection of these events>; or (3) "a connecting part" <the bridge's connection with the land>.

Some writers use *connexity* in a distinct way, synonymously with *connectedness* (= the quality of being connected). E.g.: "John's storytelling has the virtues of economy, *connexity*, and depth." Thomas D'Evelyn, "Looking at the Bible as Literature," *Christian Science Monitor*, 21 Oct. 1987, at 19. British writers use it much more often than American writers—e.g.:

- "Here's a group of small green landscapes. Here are some monumental bodies. Here are two still-lives, both with fruit and a vessel. Here are some seated nudes. Now compare and contrast, note likenesses and differences. This unrelenting *connexity* can be a bit nagging, and the connections are sometimes slight." Tom

Lubbock, "Two of a Kind?" *Independent*, 17 May 2002, at 9.

- "In the same decade of the 1990s that gave the US the strength and size of Behemoth and the rapidity and *connexity* of Ariel, we tried once more to develop an international rule of law; a rule of law that would cover the benign superpower as well." John Lloyd, "America, with Relish, Spits on Britain," *New Statesman*, 8 July 2002, at 18.

At times, though, *connexity* acts as a NEEDLESS VARIANT of *connection*—e.g.: "There should be some *connexity* [read *connection*] between this defendant and this crime." Huey L. Golden, "Knowledge, Intent, System, and Motive," 55 *La. L. Rev.* 179, 207 (1994).

Connexity also had a brief—very brief—life as a label for the intent of the new young generation (aka Gen Y) on remaining "wired" at all times. A 1999 study by the ad agency Saatchi & Saatchi tried to coin two new terms, in fact, in the title of its report on "The *Connexity* Generation: America's New Digital *Prosumers*." But in pop language, those who coin phrases often see them fall through the boardwalk.

Current ratio (*connection* vs. **connexion*): 29:1

connection with, in. See **in connection with.**

*connect together is a REDUNDANCY that was common especially in the 18th and 19th centuries. If the intended sense is "to connect with one another," *connect* or *interconnect* is usually the better choice—e.g.:

- "All of the individual elements are *connected together* [read *connected* or *interconnected*] to perform one function." Byron Miller, "Fuzzy Logic," *Electronics Now*, May 1996, at 29.
- "Check the markings of your electrical decorations to determine the maximum number of decorative lights (light strings) and decorations that may be *connected together* [read *strung together*]." Phil Mulkins, "Underwriters Laboratories Sheds Light on Lighting," *Tulsa World*, 20 Nov. 1996, at A2.
- "Technology problems like Wednesday's that temporarily knock out vital services and conveniences of modern life are likely to become more common as computers and other electronic devices increasingly *connect together* [read *interconnect*] over the Internet." Michael Liedtke & Steve Rothwell, "Tech World Takes a Tumble," *Times Union* (Albany), 9 July 2015, at A1.

Why isn't *interconnect* a one-word redundancy? Because it connotes several things, as in the first example, where *interconnected* gives a better picture than *connected* (which has a one-to-one implication) would. See **together.**

connect up. In this phrase, which is common especially in computing contexts, the word *up* is usually unnecessary—e.g.: "Paths and steps link the various levels of our landscapes and *connect up* [read *connect*] our gardens and houses." Susan Heeger, "The Hard Stuff," *L.A. Times* (Mag.), 23 Oct. 1994, at 32. See PHRASAL VERBS.

*connexion; connexity. See **connection.**

conniption. So spelled. See SPELLING (A).

connivance (fr. L. *connīvēre* "to wink at") is not, as popularly supposed, "conspiracy to act together for an illegal end," although it is a form of collusion. *Connivance* is passively allowing another to act illegally or immorally, especially when one has a duty to stop or report the action—silence and neglect when one should be vocal and monitory. E.g.: "Already the Bosnians are smuggling in heavy weaponry with the *connivance* of Turkey and Iran." Jacob Heilbrunn, "Flirting with Disaster," *New Republic*, 2 Dec. 1996, at 28.

connive = (1) (with *at*) to avoid noticing something that one should report, oppose, or condemn; to passively cooperate (esp. in wrongdoing) by closing one's eyes as it happens; or (2) (with *with*) to cooperate secretly.

Sense 1 is traditional—e.g.: "Most of the money being wasted on these nostrums comes from the pockets of people who have *connived* at their own fleecing." Katherine A. Powers, "The Honest Truth About Hokum," *Boston Globe*, 2 Dec. 2001, at E3. This construction is more common in BrE than AmE—e.g.: "Edward Heath railroaded Britain's entry into Europe through Parliament, courtesy of revolting Labour Europhile MPs who cheerfully *connived at* the deception Heath was perpetrating upon British voters." Melanie Phillips, "Europe Is a Poisoned Chalice," *Observer*, 2 June 1996, at 6.

In sense 2, the connotation is usually milder than *conspire*, more venial and less blameworthy. Because it is a SLIPSHOD EXTENSION, it can usually be improved on—e.g.:

- "A shipment of Norton McNaughton shirts and jackets still bore their original tags and enough unscrupulous shoppers *connived* [read *managed*] to get 'refunds' at department stores that some of Pittsburgh's better department stores called to complain." Patty Tascarella, "Gabriel's Expands No-Frills Discount Clothing Chain," *Pitt. Bus. Times & J.*, 12 June 1995, at 4.
- "Navarrette remembers how he and Bustamente, who would one day become his college roommate, *connived* [read *contrived*] to get into a class that West Hills Community College didn't offer." Phoebe Wall Howard, "Bustamente Ushers In a New Era," *Fresno Bee*, 17 Nov. 1996, at A1.
- "Public-choice theory taught that bureaucrats *connived* [read *conspired*] to expand their pomp and powers by spending ever more." "Kenneth Clarke's Triumph," *Economist*, 23 Nov. 1996, at 63.

Perhaps because of the suffix and the word's unsavory, even criminal connotations, *connive* is sometimes used to mean something like *con*, a SLIPSHOD EXTENSION that should be discouraged—e.g.:

LANGUAGE-CHANGE INDEX (For the full key, see front matter pp. xxxi, l–li.)
Stage 1: Rejected. **Stage 2:** Widely shunned. **Stage 3:** Widespread but . . . **Stage 4:** Ubiquitous but . . . **Stage 5:** Fully accepted.
Invariably inferior forms marked by asterisk (*). • Ratios represent frequency of prevalent forms vs. variants in current books.

- "Facing bankruptcy and eviction, and discovering that Etheline is being courted by her longtime accountant (Danny Glover), Royal *connives* [read *plots*] to move back into the family brownstone." Dan Webster, "Anderson and Wilson Take Viewers to *Alternate* [read *Alternative*] Reality," *Spokesman-Rev.* (Spokane), 12 July 2002, Weekend §, at 7. See **alternate (B).**
- "Protected but not coddled by a loving mom (Helen Mirren), the crippled, odd-looking and hence 'unemployable' Bill Porter ingenuously *connives* [read *works*] his way into people's hearts—and eventually their homes—through dogged persistence." Mike McDaniel, "Macy Sells Story," *Houston Chron.*, 14 July 2002, Television §, at 2.
- "Set in Florida, it tells the story of a white developer who tries to *connive* [read *con*] the predominantly black beach community of Plantation Island into selling a strip of ocean-front land on which he plans to build condominiums." John Petkovic, "The Characters Are Tasty, but the Plot Isn't Done," *Plain Dealer* (Cleveland), 2 Aug. 2002, Friday Mag. §, at 46.

LANGUAGE-CHANGE INDEX
1. *connive* misused for *conspire* or *contrive*: Stage 4
2. *connive* misused for *plot* or *con*: Stage 2

connoisseur (= an authority, esp. on matters of taste) is best pronounced in three syllables (/kahn-ə-**sər**/) to rhyme with *sir*. As pronunciation connoisseur Charles Harrington Elster puts it, "there is no *sewer* in *connoisseur*." *BBBM* at 105. Although traditionally a noun <a wine connoisseur> <a connoisseur of Flemish art>, it is often used attributively (that is, as an adjective)—e.g.: "By the time a marathon of bidding ended early Saturday morning, a record $755,185 had been paid for *connoisseur* [or *fine*] wines, trips to exotic destinations, banquet meals to be cooked by star chefs and a broad selection of what were grouped as 'luxury items.'" William Rice, "A Rich Toast to Lyric," *Chicago Trib.*, 26 Feb. 2003, Good Eating §, at 2.

connote. A. And *denote*. *Connote* (/kə-**noht**/) = to imply something in addition to the literal meaning, esp. some emotional response such as tone, flavor, or association. *Denote* (/di-**noht**/) = to convey literal meaning. The nouns are *connotation* and *denotation*. *Denote* is rarely if ever misused. *Connote*, however, is becoming rarer by the day in its traditional sense, illustrated here: "In careful usage, 'notoriety' carries a *connotation* of wickedness, evil, or gravely bad conduct." James J. Kilpatrick, "A Little Refresher Course," *Tulsa World*, 25 Nov. 1996, at A8.

How are *connote* and *connotation* misused? They are frequently confused with *denote* and *denotation*, just as *literally* is often misused for *figuratively*. E.g.:

- "Webster's Dictionary gives 'din' the negative *connotation* [read *definition* or *denotation* or *sense*] of 'a welter of confused or discordant sounds.'" Geoffrey Himes, "Chris Whitley's Shift Reflects His Concept of the Blues," *Dallas Morning News*, 22 Mar. 1995, at C4.
- "Surfing (an overused term) *connotes* [read *denotes*] unstructured Net browsing for fun or profit." Gabriel Goldberg, "Surfing the Internet and Other Sources of

Enterprise Information," *Enterprise Systems J.*, July 1996, at 44.

See **literally.**

Moreover, only words and other symbols can *connote*, not acts. *Connote* isn't a general-purpose equivalent of *suggest* or *associate*, nor is *connotation* a replacement for *overtone* or *implication*—e.g.:

- "I believe that Sayles did a good job with his flashbacks. Most of them *connoted* [read *suggested*] feelings of tension and empathy." "A Salute to 'Lone Star' Movie," *Times-Picayune* (New Orleans), 28 July 1996, at B6.
- "Morrison says when belly dance originated in the Middle East, sexual *connotations* [read *overtones*] were never the intention." Jeff Commings, "Dancers Belly Up to World Festival," *Albuquerque Trib.*, 20 Sept. 2002, at C2.
- "Clawson said he thinks someone from the skeet shooting party, several of whom did not know Hatfill, told the FBI about the joke, which took on far more sinister *connotations* [read *implications*] as agents desperately searched for the anthrax killer." Wayne Washington, "Fighting Terror Global Impact; Anthrax Probe Raises Doubts on FBI," *Boston Globe*, 23 Sept. 2002, at A1.

B. And **connotate*. **Connotate* is a NEEDLESS VARIANT of *connote*—e.g.:

- "Other factions wanted to eliminate 'National' from NCTE's name because it *connotated* [read *connoted*] 'nationalism.'" Carol Innerst, "Language Groups Call All English Dialects Valid," *Wash. Times*, 12 Mar. 1996, at A3.
- "As with the PT Cruiser and New Beetle, two other popular, low-priced, four-cylinder offerings introduced during the past five years, Mini styling is best described as retrospective, or heritage, or whatever word *connotates* [read *connotes*] a bygone era." Dave Boe, "Two Vehicles Earn Journalistic Honors at Detroit Show," *Daily Herald* (Chicago), 20 Jan. 2003, Auto Plus §, at 1.

See BACK-FORMATIONS.

LANGUAGE-CHANGE INDEX
*connotate for *connote*: Stage 1

consanguineous; consanguine; *consanguineal; consanguinean. The general adjective corresponding to *consanguinity* is *consanguineous* (= related by common ancestry). E.g.: "The boy suffered from a rare form of dwarfism called pyknodysostosis, which is more common in children of *consanguineous* parents than of others." Robert Wernick, "A Little Man Who Brought a Parisian Era to Vivid Life," *Smithsonian*, Nov. 1985, at 64.

By HYPALLAGE, the phrase *consanguineous marriage* denotes a marriage between blood relations (cousins and other close relatives). E.g.: "These marriages, called *consanguineous*, are now prohibited in 30 states—although not in California—and carry heavy criminal penalties in nine." Thomas H. Maugh II, "More Kissing Cousins Are Marrying, New Studies Find," *L.A. Times*, 15 Feb. 1993, at A10.

If *consanguineous* is relatively rare—confined mostly to those who engage in SESQUIPEDALITY—the other terms are even rarer. *Consanguine* and **consanguineal* have been taken up by anthropologists and linguists and differentiated from the primary adjective. *Consanguine* = based on an extended group of blood relations esp. of unilinear descent and constituting the functional familial unit in a society (*W3*). **Consanguineal* shares this sense and is a NEEDLESS VARIANT. *Consanguinean* is a Roman-law term meaning "having the same father." It is opposed to *uterine* (= having the same mother).

For related words (true blood relations), see **sanguine.**

conscience' sake; conscience's sake. The traditional and overwhelmingly predominant form is *conscience' sake,* which is parallel to *goodness' sake.* Many writers, though, have made it *conscience's sake,* which is hard to speak—e.g.: "She knows it won't make a difference, but she has to go through the motions for *conscience's sake* [read *conscience' sake*]." Nelson Pressley, "Emotional Jackpot Eludes 'Boomtown,'" *Wash. Times,* 10 Nov. 1994, at C16. See POSSESSIVES (N).

Current ratio: 6:1

conscionable is not a mere NEEDLESS VARIANT of *conscientious* in its sense of "being guided by one's conscience," though some dictionaries so suggest. And indeed, it sometimes performs that unnecessary role—e.g.: "Otherwise *conscionable* [read *conscientious*] members of a different party hint that ethics and morality have little, if any, bearing on one's appropriateness and aptitude for elected leadership." Donna Madden, "People, Not Parties, Define Values," *Chicago Trib.,* 31 Oct. 1996, at 26.

As a positive correlative of *unconscionable,* the word *conscionable* means "agreeable to a good conscience; just and reasonable" and refers to things as opposed to people <a conscionable bargain>. E.g.:

- "If any politician from a non-tobacco state is going to come to the aid of the country's least *conscionable* industry, it stands to reason that it would be America's least honorable governor." Steve Wilson, "Symington's Call to Snuff Tobacco Suit Defies Explanation," *Ariz. Republic,* 20 Oct. 1996, at A2.
- "It is no more *conscionable* to indulge in monetary bondage for laborers today than it was to accept human bondage in the past." "A Little Humility Recommended," *Tulsa World,* 24 Nov. 1996, at G2.
- "In another time, though, the business on the bend was even less *conscionable*—for decades, it was the site of the city's slave pens and auction blocks." Nicholas Mancusi, "Review: 'Murder, D.C.' by Neely Tucker," *Miami Herald,* 3 July 2015, at 680.

For a mistake involving the negative form, see **unconscionably.**

consensual; consentaneous; consentient. *Consensual,* by far the most common of these terms, means "having or expressing or made with consent." *Consentaneous* and *consentient* are both used in that sense, as well as in two others: (1) "unanimous"; and (2) "agreeing." When used for *consensual,* either of the other two words is a NEEDLESS VARIANT. And when used in either of the other two senses, each is easily simplified—as the defining words above suggest. Gorham Munson said as much in the mid-20th century: "Take the word 'consentaneous' . . . . [I]t is a good word in a rich prose pageant. But in a simple style among workaday companions 'consentaneous' is as out of setting as a man in evening dress would be in the bleachers at an afternoon baseball game." Gorham Munson, *The Written Word* 93 (rev. ed. 1949).

Current ratio (in order of headwords): 149:1:1:1

consensus = a majority opinion or generally accepted view. Hence two common phrases, **consensus of opinion* and **general consensus,* are prolix. E.g.: "It's not a surprise that the possibility of war with Iraq has been the hot topic among these veterans lately, and after a few minutes of conversation, it's easy to understand the *general consensus* [omit *general*] at Sweeney Post." Katharine McQuaid, "Local Sweeney Post Veterans Support American Military Action Against Iraq," *Union Leader* (Manchester, N.H.), 20 Sept. 2002, at A18. In the following sentence, we're accosted by a double REDUNDANCY: "While there is no way of knowing for sure, it appears the *general consensus of opinion* [omit *general* and *of opinion*] is that hunting accidents have been reduced by requiring hunter education in a majority of states before hunters can purchase that first license." Warren Cloninger, "Were Good Ol' Days That Good?" *Lewiston Morning Trib.* (Idaho), 28 Sept. 1995, at C2.

Because a *consensus* is the collective unanimous opinion of several people, there should be more than two sides agreeing. Strictly speaking, a consensus of two is impossible—e.g.:

- "Oxygen reimbursement cuts have been one of the few areas where the two sides have *reached consensus* [read *agreed* or *reached an agreement*]." "Clinton Administration to Cut Home-Oxygen Payments," *Orange County Register,* 20 Jan. 1996, at C2.
- "In the days before the talks broke down, both sides had *reached consensus* [read *agreed*] on water rights, new housing permits and several other issues." "Walking Away from Peace," *St. Petersburg Times,* 4 Nov. 1996, at A10.

Consensus is unrelated to *census,* but that word nevertheless frequently causes the misspelling **concensus*—e.g.: "The emphasis on developing leadership capacity in all students, he says, is reflected in corporations where *concensus building* [read *consensus-building*] and working in teams have replaced the old style of centralized authority." Nina McCain, "Striving

LANGUAGE-CHANGE INDEX (For the full key, see front matter pp. xxxi, l–li.)
Stage 1: Rejected. **Stage 2:** Widely shunned. **Stage 3:** Widespread but . . . **Stage 4:** Ubiquitous but . . . **Stage 5:** Fully accepted.
Invariably inferior forms marked by asterisk (*). • Ratios represent frequency of prevalent forms vs. variants in current books.

to Change the System," *Boston Globe*, 27 Oct. 1996, at B12. See SPELLING (A).

LANGUAGE-CHANGE INDEX
1. **general consensus of opinion*: Stage 2
Current ratio (*consensus was* vs. **general consensus of opinion was*): 25:1
2. **general consensus*: Stage 4
Current ratio (*the consensus was* vs. **the general consensus was*): 3:1
3. **consensus of opinion*: Stage 4
Current ratio (*the consensus was* vs. **the consensus of opinion was*): 13:1
4. *consensus* misspelled **concensus*: Stage 1
Current ratio: 501:1

consent. See **assent.**

consentaneous; consentient. See **consensual.**

consequent; consequential; subsequent. *Consequent* means "following as a direct result" <consequent injuries>. *Consequential* (a rarer term) means "following as an indirect or secondary result" <consequential costs>. In its other proper sense, *consequential* may serve as an opposite of *inconsequential*, thus meaning "important" (or, occasionally, "self-important"). In the following sentences it means "important, of consequence," a sense prematurely labeled obsolete by the *OED*:

- "Bob Dole promised a campaign 'about *consequential* things, things that are real,' but he's giving us one based on that ephemeral question, 'What does your soul look like?'" Maureen Dowd, "Liberties: Fillet of Soul," *N.Y. Times*, 26 May 1996, § 4, at 11.
- "Looking back on it now, I see clearly that it was the single most *consequential* thing that ever happened to me professionally." Pete Dexter, "Decision 20 Years Ago Made All the Difference," *Sacramento Bee*, 18 Nov. 1996, at C2. (On the use of *single most* in that sentence, see **single most.**)
- "A contemporary said of Chief Justice John Marshall—the most *consequential* American never to be president—that 'he hit the Constitution much as the Lord hit the chaos, at a time when everything needed creating.'" George Will, "Stuck to the U.N. Tar Baby," *Wash. Post*, 19 Sept. 2002, at A27.

In all other senses, *consequent* is the correct term where the choice is between the shorter and longer forms. Usually, *consequent* is just a fancy equivalent of *resulting*—e.g.:

- "South Barrington . . . has five major state highways passing through the village and a *consequent* high volume of truck traffic." Joseph Sjostrom, "Trucks Take Heat for Flying Debris," *Chicago Trib.*, 5 Sept. 1996, at D1.
- "The other 20 percent arise from broken blood vessels and *consequent* hemorrhaging into brain tissue." Paul Donohue, "First Step for Stroke," *St. Louis Post-Dispatch*, 11 Dec. 1996, Everyday Mag. §, at E2.

Consequent is frequently misused for *subsequent*, perhaps partly because of the logical fallacy *post hoc, ergo propter hoc* ("after this, therefore because of this")—a trap for those who equate sequence with causation, thinking that if one event occurred after another, the first event must have caused the second. The word *consequent* expresses a causal relation and

usually a temporal relation as well <she couldn't contain the scandal and couldn't prevent her consequent demotion>; *subsequent* is solely temporal <this all came after her elevation to the Senate and subsequent reputation as a coalition-builder>. See **subsequently.**

consequently. This heavy connector is often best replaced by *so.* See SENTENCE ADVERBS. Cf. **accordingly.**

conservational; conservative; conservatory, adj. These words are to be distinguished. *Conservational* = of, relating to, or involving conservation. *Conservative* = characterized by a tendency to preserve or keep intact or unchanged; believing in the maintenance of existing political and social institutions. *Conservatory* (rarely used as an adjective) = preservative. For an error with *conservative*, see **conservative.**

conservatism (= the political philosophy that favors preserving what has been firmly established and opposes changes in orthodoxy) is the standard term. **Conservativism* is a NEEDLESS VARIANT.

Current ratio: 62:1

conservative is surprisingly often, through a kind of visual METATHESIS, printed **conversative*—e.g.: "The Hoover Institution, a *conversative* [read *conservative*] California-based think tank at Stanford University, also found that the hijackers were eligible to vote in state and federal elections." Katrice Franklin, "Immigrants Trapped by DMV Requirements," *Virginian-Pilot & Ledger Star* (Norfolk), 23 July 2002, at B1. For the meaning of *conservative*, see **conservational.**

LANGUAGE-CHANGE INDEX
conservative misspelled **conversative*: Stage 1
Current ratio: 22,906:1

conservatory. See **conservational.**

consider, when used alone, most often means "to think of as being" <she considered him rude>. The phrasing *consider as* is usually redundant. It has only one legitimate use, when meaning "to treat as for certain purposes" <this Dylan song, when considered as poetry, is a masterpiece>. It's usually desirable to drop *as* from *consider as*—e.g.:

- "In resigning as board chairman, David Ambrose cited what he *considered as* [read *considered*] unethical business practices." Mary McGrath, "Finance Chief Resigns," *Omaha World-Herald*, 8 Aug. 1995, at 16.
- "Historically, pain has not been *considered as* [read *considered*] a symptom unto itself that requires treatment." Richard J. Leth, "New Pain Treatments," *Des Moines Register*, 11 Oct. 1997, at 8.
- "The drug Depo Provera inhibits the sex drive and has been *considered as* [read *considered*] a kind of 'chemical castration' for chronic offenders." M.W. Guzy, "Can We Isolate Sexual Predators?" *St. Louis Post-Dispatch*, 27 Mar. 1998, at B7.

considerable, used adverbially, is dialectal—e.g.:

- "The 5th Street Deli actually has *considerable* [read *considerably*] more aesthetic charm than its predecessor." Lisa Kingsley, "Deli Delivering Delightful Dressings, Savory Salads," *Des Moines Register*, 15 Aug. 1996, at 19.

- "Guys such as Gwynn admitt[ed] that Montreal's defeat at Atlanta on the scoreboard was of *considerable* [read *considerably*] more interest than the Chargers' score updates against the Raiders." Mike Downey, "The Padres Are Hardly *Shaking* [read *Quaking*] in Their Boots," *L.A. Times*, 23 Sept. 1996, at C1.

LANGUAGE-CHANGE INDEX
considerable misused adverbially
for *considerably*: Stage 1
Current ratio (*considerably more* vs.
considerable more): 95:1

considering. For this word as an acceptable dangling modifier, see DANGLERS (E).

consignee (= one to whom goods are consigned) is pronounced /kon-si-**nee**/ or /kon-si-**nee**/. Cf. **consignor.**

consignor; consigner. *Consignor* is the technical—and *consigner* the nontechnical—correlative of *consignee*. A *consignor* (or *consigner*) dispatches goods to another on *consignment*. Perhaps because the very nature of this relationship is legal and technical, the *-or* spelling has been much more pervasive since the terms came into common use about 1800. The two words are often pronounced differently: *consignor* /kon-si-**nor**/ or /kən-**si**-nor/; *consigner* /kən-**si**-nər/. Cf. **consignee.**

Current ratio (in order of headwords): 28:1

consistency; *consistence. The former has been standard since about 1800, before which time the two words tussled for preeminence. The latter is now a NEEDLESS VARIANT—e.g.:

- "Though Natrone Means was unable to run with his usual *consistence* [read *consistency*], Ronnie Harmon was often effective in the backfield and Eric Bieniemy contributed one stirring sortie." Welton Jones, "Bowled Over, Could a Sequel Be Super?" *San Diego Union-Trib.*, 31 Jan. 1995, at E1.
- "The award was given to developers who exhibited *consistence* [read *consistency*] in excellence and quality." Leon M. Tucker & Chris Tisch, "Builder Accused of Lying to Buyers," *St. Petersburg Times*, 1 Feb. 2002, N. Pinellas Times §, at 1.

Cf. **inconsistency.**

LANGUAGE-CHANGE INDEX
*consistence for *consistency*: Stage 1
Current ratio (*consistency* vs. **consistence*): 58:1

consist of; consist in. American writers often ignore the distinction. *Consist of* is used in reference to materials; it precedes the physical elements that compose a tangible thing. The well-worn example is that concrete *consists of* sand, gravel, cement, and water.

Consist in (= to have as its essence) refers to abstract elements or qualities, or intangible things. Hence a good moral character *consists in* integrity, decency, fairness, and compassion. This construction is literary in tone and is not often seen today in general writing. Sad to say, it may now seem creaky to most readers.

The following sentences demonstrate the traditional use of *consist in*:

- "He hailed the new 'trans-Atlantic relationship' as *consisting in* 'certain Enlightenment ideals of universal applicability.'" Samuel Francis, "Loyalties Tilting Closer to Home," *Wash. Times*, 19 Nov. 1991, at F1. (On the spelling of *transatlantic*, see **transatlantic.**)
- "Received wisdom has it that nationhood *consists in* a kind of quasi-mystical union between a people, their culture and their land." James Geary Oxford, "Making History: Norman Davies' New Europe," *Time* (Int'l ed.), 16 Dec. 1996, at 54.
- "E.M. Forster had published three novels before he had any clear idea of what the sex act *consisted in*." Louis Menand, "The Women Come and Go," *New Yorker*, 30 Sept. 2002, at 126, 127.

By traditional standards, *consist of* wrongly displaces *consist in* here: "The beginning of wisdom *consists of* [read *consists in*] recognizing that a balance needs to be struck." Henry Kissinger, "How to Achieve the New World Order," *Time*, 14 Mar. 1994, at 73, 74.

The opposite error—using *consist in* for *consist of*—is rare but does occur: "Typically [the bill of complaint in equity] *consisted in* [read *consisted of*] three parts: the narrative, the charging, and the interrogative parts." Fleming James, *Civil Procedure* § 2.4, at 64 (1965).

LANGUAGE-CHANGE INDEX
1. *consist of* misused for *consist in*: Stage 4
2. *consist in* misused for *consist of*: Stage 1

console. See **condole.**

CONSONANCE. See ALLITERATION.

consort is pronounced /**kon**-sort/ as a noun and /kən-**sort**/ as a verb.

consortium is pronounced /kən-**sor**-sh[ee]-əm/ and now also, in BrE, /kən-**sor**-tee-əm/. The plural *consortia* has been standard since the 18th century. The plural *consortiums* didn't come into common use until the late 20th century, and it is still far less frequent than *consortia*. See PLURALS (B).

Current ratio (*consortia* vs. *consortiums*): 7:1

conspectus; prospectus. These terms are not synonymous. A *conspectus* is a comprehensive survey, summary, or synopsis. (The plural is *conspectuses*.) A *prospectus* is a document describing the chief features of something that is forthcoming. (The plural is *prospectuses*.) See **prospectus.**

Avoid the hypercorrect plural **conspecti*—attested from the early 19th century. The etymon is a fourth-declension Latin noun whose plural doesn't change form: *one conspectus, two conspectus*. So **conspecti* is false Latin and ridiculous English. Make it *conspectuses*. See PLURALS (B) & HYPERCORRECTION.

conspicuousness; *conspicuity. The latter is a NEEDLESS VARIANT that occasionally appears. Typically,

LANGUAGE-CHANGE INDEX (For the full key, see front matter pp. xxxi, l–li.)
Stage 1: Rejected. **Stage 2:** Widely shunned. **Stage 3:** Widespread but . . . **Stage 4:** Ubiquitous but . . . **Stage 5:** Fully accepted.
Invariably inferior forms marked by asterisk (*). • Ratios represent frequency of prevalent forms vs. variants in current books.

the sentence can be advantageously reworded—e.g.: "Experts claim that, because daytime running lights do *increase the conspicuity of motor vehicles* [read *make motor vehicles more conspicuous*], they must also be increasing safety on the road." "Daytime Running Lights Are Standard on Some New Cars," *Times Union* (Albany), 1 Feb. 1996, at T2.

Current ratio: 1.2:1

*conspirational. See **conspiratorial.**

*conspirative. See **conspiratorial.**

conspirator; *conspiratorialist; coconspirator. *Conspirator* (= one engaged in a conspiracy) finds a NEEDLESS VARIANT in **conspiratorialist*—e.g.: "He ordered Christic and its chief *conspiratorialist* [read *conspirator*], Daniel Sheehan, to pay $1 million toward the defendants' legal bills." L. Gordon Crovitz, "Lawyers Make Frivolous Arguments at Their Own Risk," *Wall Street J.*, 20 June 1990, at A17.

The term *coconspirator* (unlike *copartner) is not always redundant. When speaking or writing of conspirator A and referring to conspirator B, it is far easier to use *coconspirator* than, say, *fellow conspirator*.

LANGUAGE-CHANGE INDEX
1. **conspiratorialist* for *conspirator*: Stage 1
Current ratio (*conspirator* vs.
**conspiratorialist*): 919:1
2. *coconspirator* meaning "fellow conspirator":
Stage 5

conspiratorial; *conspiratory; *conspirational; *conspirative. The first is standard; the others are NEEDLESS VARIANTS.

Current ratio (in order of headwords): 189:2:1.5:1

*conspiratorialist. See **conspirator.**

*conspiratory. See **conspiratorial.**

conspire together is almost always redundant—e.g.:

• "That kind of dramatic, sensory evidence could help prosecutors move their case beyond one of focusing largely on circumstantial clues that suggest that McVeigh and Nichols *conspired together* [read *conspired*] to plan and carry out the attack." Richard A. Serrano & Ronald J. Ostrow, "Government Builds Its Oklahoma Bombing Case with Video, Audiotape," *Fresno Bee*, 31 Dec. 1995, at A8.
• "The two agents, by Washam's own account, did not *conspire together* [read *conspire*], however." Jamie Satterfield, "Washam Wrote Explanation of Troubles," *Knoxville News-Sentinel*, 18 Aug. 2015, at A1.

See **together.**

Sometimes, though, a word such as *together* seems necessary to complete the thought or to create PARALLELISM with another idea in the sentence—e.g.:

• "[Those accused] have denied *conspiring together* and with four others to defraud the Department of Social Security." "Immigrants in Benefit Fraud Trial," *Daily Telegraph*, 27 Oct. 1994, at 6 (*and with four others* completes the thought).
• "Federal prosecutors oppose severance, arguing that McVeigh and Nichols *conspired together* and should be tried together on charges of blowing up the federal building in Oklahoma City on April 19, 1995." Gaylord Shaw, "Bomb Suspects at Odds," *Newsday* (N.Y.), 2 Oct. 1996, at A4 (*conspired together* is parallel with *tried together*).

constitute. See **comprise (c).**

constitutional should not generally be capitalized, though *Constitution* (in reference to the U.S. Constitution) should be. The adjective has two meanings: (1) "of, relating to, or involving the Constitution" <constitutional rights>; and (2) "proper under the Constitution" <constitutional actions by the police>. Thus sense 1: "The diversion of a job to a competitor is not an invasion of a *constitutional* right." And sense 2: "The Wisconsin statute, which is similar to the Norris-LaGuardia Act, has also been held *constitutional*." The opposite of *constitutional* in sense 1 is *nonconstitutional*, and in sense 2 *unconstitutional*. See **nonconstitutional.**

constitutionalist; *constitutionist. The standard form of the term is *constitutionalist* (= [1] someone who studies or writes on the Constitution; or [2] a supporter of constitutional principles). The form *constitutionist is a NEEDLESS VARIANT. E.g.: "Constitutionists [read *Constitutionalists*] could manage to gain a strong enough foothold in Congress to back a president who would use his legitimate veto power to curtail spending." "Perils of the Line Item Veto," *Wash. Times*, 29 Sept. 1996, at B5.

LANGUAGE-CHANGE INDEX
*constitutionist for *constitutionalist*: Stage 1

construct (= to build) for *construe* (= to interpret) occurs fairly frequently because the word *construction* serves as the noun for both verbs. (See **construction.**) As a result, writers sometimes use *construct* as a kind of BACK-FORMATION—e.g.:

• "In his historical interpretation of the Supreme Court's role in *constructing* [read *construing*] the United States Constitution, the late Robert G. McCloskey divided constitutional law into three periods." Barbara H. Craig, *Chadha* vii–viii (1988).
• "Conservative judges do not make law. . . . Rather they *construct* [read *construe*] the laws and Constitution in accordance with the intent of the Founders and Framers, resisting the temptation to graft their own philosophy into the law." Commentary, "Senatorial Cherry Picking," *Wash. Times*, 18 Nov. 2001, at B5.

LANGUAGE-CHANGE INDEX
construct misused for *construe*: Stage 1

construction is the noun corresponding to both *construct* and *construe*. In law, *construction* usually corresponds to *construe*. One might think that the *construction of statutes* is the business of legislatures, since lawmakers *construct* (i.e., build) statutes. But *construction* in that phrase means "the process of construing," which is the business of the courts. For an extended discussion of confusion wrought by the fact that *construction* answers to both *construe* and *construct*, see Antonin Scalia & Bryan A. Garner, *Reading Law: The Interpretation of Legal Texts* 13–15 (2012).

constructive; constructional. These terms are not to be confused. *Constructive* = (1) of, relating to, or involving the creation of something <the painstaking constructive process that resulted in the opera>; (2) designed to promote improvement <constructive criticism>; or (3) (of an act, statement, or other fact) having a given effect in law—because a court so declares—though the effect may not exist in fact <constructive fraud> <constructive trust>.

Constructional = (1) of or relating to building or the construction business; or (2) of, relating to, or involving the act or process of construing. Sense 1: "He retired as a *constructional* inspector from the Naval Base and was an Army veteran of World War II." "Nelson B. Clark" (obit.), *Virginian-Pilot* (Norfolk), 16 Sept. 1996, at B4. Sense 2: "This court is aware of the general *constructional* preference in favor of a surviving spouse." "Estate of Marvin P. Middlemark," *N.Y.L.J.*, 1 Oct. 1996, at 26.

construe, vb. For the meaning, see **construct.** For the noun form, see **construction.**

consul; counsel; council. *Consul* (/**kon**-səl/) = a governmental representative living in a foreign country to oversee commercial matters. *Counsel* (/**kown**-səl/) = a legal adviser or group of legal advisers. (See **counsel** & **lawyer.**) *Council* (/**kown**-səl/) = a body of representatives. (See **council.**)

consulate; consulship. *Consulate* = the office, term of office, jurisdiction, or residence of a consul. *Consulship* = the office or term of office of a consul. *Consulate* is the more common and (therefore) the broader term. *Consulship* may be useful in conveying one's meaning precisely.

Because *consulate* most often means "the office or official premises of a consul," the phrase **office of the consulate* is a REDUNDANCY—e.g.: "Starting Tuesday, people wishing to pay their respects may sign the book in the *offices of the consulate* [read *consulate* or *offices of the consul*], on the 13th floor of the south tower of the building, at 400 N. Michigan." Brenda Warner Rotzoll, "Chicago Bids Farewell," *Chicago Sun-Times*, 1 Sept. 1997, at 3.

LANGUAGE-CHANGE INDEX
*office of the consulate for *consulate*: Stage 1

consul general. Pl. *consuls general.* See PLURALS (G) & POSTPOSITIVE ADJECTIVES.

consulship. See **consulate.**

consult, as an intransitive verb, takes the preposition *with* (another person), or *on* or *about* (a matter). The verb may also be used transitively <to consult the document itself>. As with *invite* (for *invitation*), avoid the casual use of the verb to mean "consultation."

For a brief mention of *consult* as a noun in place of *consultation,* see **disconnect.** Cf. **invite.**

consultation. The English writer Philip Howard has stated that in BrE, *consultation*

> can mean a conference at which the parties, for example, lawyers or doctors, *consult* or deliberate. Modern legal usage confines this sense to meetings with more than one counsel present. You can have a *consultation* with your doctor on your own. But you must be able to afford the fees of at least two lawyers simultaneously before you can properly describe your meeting with them as a *consultation.*
> Philip Howard, *Weasel Words* 57 (1979).

So in BrE, *consultation* refers to a meeting of two or more counsel and the solicitor who instructs them by leading the discussion and giving advice on their findings.

No such restrictive meaning is given the term in AmE. If you consult with your lawyer on a certain matter, that act is *consultation.*

consultative; *consultive; *consultatory; *consultory. Both *consultative* and **consultive* are old: the former is recorded from 1583, the latter from 1616. But *consultative* is preferable because it matches the stem of its related noun, *consultation.* Though *consultative* is also over 200 times as common as **consultive,* the latter does occasionally appear in print—e.g.: "Her intention is to get council members involved in coordinating and *consultive* [read *consultative*] roles with the citizens drafting the 37 neighborhood plans." "A Workable Connection for Neighbors, City Hall," *Seattle Times,* 17 Feb. 1996, at A15. Like **consultive,* the forms ending in *-ory* are NEEDLESS VARIANTS.

Current ratio (in order of headwords): 5,541:24:2:1

consummate as an adjective is pronounced /kən-**sum**-it/, and as a verb /**kon**-sə-mayt/. To pronounce the word /**kon**-sə-mət/ as an adjective is acceptable, but that pronunciation has long been considered an inferior one.

Consummate is sometimes misspelled **consumate*—e.g.: "Widely regarded as a *consumate* [read *consummate*] professional and bridge builder with a reputation for mediating potentially explosive disputes, Scott, 59, said yesterday he is leaving to spend more time with his family." William K. Rashbaum, "No. 2 City Cop Plans to Retire in December," *Newsday* (N.Y.), 27 Oct. 1994, at A62.

LANGUAGE-CHANGE INDEX
consummate misspelled **consumate*: Stage 1
Current ratio: 210:1

contact, v.t. Many language authorities vehemently objected to this verb in the first half of the 20th century, as H.L. Mencken observed: "When *to contact* dawned in the early '20s a howl went up from the

---

LANGUAGE-CHANGE INDEX (For the full key, see front matter pp. xxxi, l–li.)
Stage 1: Rejected. **Stage 2:** Widely shunned. **Stage 3:** Widespread but . . . **Stage 4:** Ubiquitous but . . . **Stage 5:** Fully accepted.
Invariably inferior forms marked by asterisk (*). • Ratios represent frequency of prevalent forms vs. variants in current books.

American Holoferneses, and presently it was echoed *fortissimo* in England, and to this day it reverberates from crag to crag of the precipices of Athene. I must confess at once that I share this priggish loathing, and never use the word myself, just as I never use *alright*, but the plain fact remains that there is plenty of excuse for it in the genius of the English language, and that many other verbs in daily use are no more legitimate." H.L. Mencken, "The Birth of New Verbs," in *Aspects of American English* 92, 93 (Elizabeth M. Kerr & Ralph M. Aderman eds., 1963). As Mencken suggested, *contact* is now firmly ensconced as a verb. Brevity recommends it over *get in touch with* or *communicate with*; it should not be considered stylistically infelicitous even in formal contexts. E.g.:

- "One former Palatine village official *contacted* during the investigation called the BGA report a 'sleazy witch hunt.'" John Carpenter & Becky Beaupre, "Panel Slams Palatine Probe," *Chicago Sun-Times*, 21 Nov. 1997, at 6.
- "The Goodmans *contacted* Searle and presented him with a detailed record of their claim to the painting." Adam Zagorin, "Saving the Spoils of War," *Time*, 1 Dec. 1997, at 87.

If, however, the meaning is clearly either *call* or *write*, the specific verb is preferable.

LANGUAGE-CHANGE INDEX
contact as a verb meaning "to get in touch with": Stage 5

contagious; infectious. These words are misused even by educated writers and speakers when discussing diseases. Germs and viruses that cause *contagious* diseases, such as influenza and head colds, are easily transmitted from person to person (or animal to animal, as with foot-and-mouth disease). Those that cause *infectious* diseases, such as cholera and typhoid, are usually spread through the environment (e.g., contaminated food or water). Some infectious diseases, such as sexually transmitted ones, can be passed from person to person through certain types of direct contact, but not through indirect or casual contact. See **infectious.**

contemn. See **condemn.**

contemner; contemnor. Most dictionaries list the spelling ending in *-er* as predominant; it was overwhelmingly so in 19th-century BrE and AmE, but is less so today. The *-or* spelling now predominates by a slight margin. See -ER (A).
Current ratio (*contemnor* vs. *contemner*): 1.1:1

contemplative is preferably accented on the second syllable: /kən-**tem**-plə-tiv/.

contemporary; contemporaneous. Both refer to coinciding periods of time. *Contemporaneous* usually refers to either actions or things, *contemporary* to people. But *contemporary* also commonly refers to things in the sense "current"—a sense to be avoided in contexts referring to past times, lest the word give rise to a MISCUE or outright ambiguity—e.g.:

- "He believes Italy is the best place to sample the major styles of Western architecture, from ancient Greek and Roman temples to medieval, Renaissance and *contemporary* [read *current*] styles." Thomas W. Gerdel, "Relationships with His Clients Inspire Architect's Designs," *Plain Dealer* (Cleveland), 13 June 1995, at C4. (*Contemporary* could be momentarily misread as referring to styles flourishing in medieval and Renaissance times.)
- "Fantasy fiction . . . is medieval in atmosphere, 19th-century in its concerns, *contemporary* [read *current*] in its manners." Edward Rothstein, "Flaming Swords and Wizards' Orbs," *N.Y. Times*, 8 Dec. 1996, § 7, at 60. (*Contemporary* might be read as referring to the 19th century.)
- "Italian art, too, has enjoyed a renaissance—in appreciation for the old masters and for *contemporary* [read *today's*] artists." Helen Forsberg, "It's Italian," *Salt Lake Trib.*, 8 Dec. 1996, at J8. (*Contemporary* might be read as referring to lesser artists working at the same time as the old masters.)

When no other time frame is mentioned, then we may infer "contemporary with us" to denote current rather than historical contexts.

Contemporaneous does not precisely mean "simultaneous"; rather, it means "belonging to the same time or period; occurring at about the same time." Hence the following sentences are correct:

- "Replete with notes and chronologies of both Dos Passos' life and of the world events *contemporaneous* with the action of the novels, its edition of 'U.S.A.' is one to savor." Roger Miller, "A Grand Sweep of America, in 1,288 Pages," *Milwaukee J. Sentinel*, 6 Oct. 1996, Cue §, at 9.
- "Thus, if Paula Jones's case ever came to trial, a jury would have to decide if they believe her—and her six *contemporaneous* witnesses—or Bill Clinton and his state trooper." Carl M. Cannon, "Days of Reckoning," *New Republic*, 2 Dec. 1996, at 34.
- "An attempt by the Star to match known fatal confrontations with *contemporaneous* media reports left too many gaps." Rosie DiManno, "Thorny History of Race Statistics," *Toronto Star*, 18 Aug. 2015, at A2.

*Cotemporaneous is a NEEDLESS VARIANT of *contemporaneous*; likewise, **cotemporary* is a NEEDLESS VARIANT of *contemporary*.

contempt; contemptibility; contemptuousness; contumacy. These words are quite distinct. *Contempt* = (1) (generally) the act or state of despising; the condition of being despised; (2) (in law) action interfering with the administration of justice. *Contemptibility* = the quality or fact of being worthy of scorn. *Contemptuousness* = the quality of being scornful or disdainful. *Contumacy* = willful contempt of court (**contumacity* being a NEEDLESS VARIANT). For more, see **contumacy.**

contemptuous. A. And *contemptible*. *Contemptuous* = expressing contempt. *Contemptible* = worthy of contempt or scorn. See -ABLE (A).

B. And *contumacious*. These words are often interchangeable, but while *contumacious* may connote scorn, it strictly denotes only willful disobedience. *Contemptuous* is much more common in print—e.g.: "Mr. Milosevic appears *contemptuous* of the judges and prosecutors, reserving his interest and civility for those senior politicians, diplomats and generals from the West who have testified. To them he sometimes even seems ingratiating." Marise Simons, "Reviving Memories of Yet Another Evil," *N.Y. Times*, 22 Sept. 2002, § 4, at 3.

In the sense "recalcitrant," *contumacious* is chiefly a literary word—e.g.: "The children are unattractive characters, brimming with the misguided assurances of youth. They are proud, naively optimistic, *contumacious*, disagreeable." Bill Eichenberger, "Small-Scale Life Looms Larger in *Visitors*," *Columbus Dispatch*, 1 Feb. 1998, at H7.

contemptuousness. See **contempt.**

contend. See **allege** & **contest,** v.t.

content, adj.; **contented,** adj. These two words are essentially synonyms, though *content* is somewhat more common as a predicate adjective <I'm feeling quite content>, and *contented* somewhat more common as an adjective preceding a noun <contented workers>.

content, n. **A. And *contents*.** When referring to written matter or oral presentation, *content* refers to the ideas or thoughts contained (in words) as opposed to the method of presentation. Wilson Follett disapproved of the modern tendency to use *content* as well as *contents* for "what is contained" (*MAU* at 107), but the usage is old and is now common. It got a boost with the growth of the World Wide Web, being commonly used to refer to the material on websites. And the DIFFERENTIATION it represents—as explained below—is genuinely helpful.

Whereas *content* invariably refers to nonmaterial things, *contents* refers most commonly to material ingredients—e.g.: "Birthdays, holidays and special occasions, Forman is usually greeted with that flat skinny box that makes no secret of its *contents*." "Sticking Their Necks Out," *Times-Picayune* (New Orleans), 13 Aug. 1996, at F1. But sometimes it refers to nonmaterial ingredients, especially when the suggestion is that many items are being considered—e.g.: "Kirkland police improperly kept secret the *contents* of a crime report on Northeast District Judge Rosemary Bordlemay and were ordered by a court to release the document." Kevin Ebi, "City Loses Suit, Bid to Shield Jurist," *Seattle Times*, 29 Dec. 1995, at B1.

B. And *contentment*. In the sense "the fact or condition of being fully satisfied (i.e., contented)," the word *contentment* is now standard. *Content* is reserved for a single idiom: *to (one's) heart's content*. But as an adjective it is frequently seen—e.g.: "She was *content* with her arrangement." See **content,** adj.

contentious. See **tendentious (c).**

conterminous; coterminous; *coterminant; *coterminate; *coterminal. *Conterminous*, the oldest and until 1900 the most prevalent of these words, means "having or enclosed within a common boundary." E.g.: "One district is *conterminous* with Cook County, and three justices are elected at-large from there." Doug Finke, "Redrawing of Court Boundaries Shaky," *State J.-Register* (Springfield, Ill.), 6 Dec. 1996, at 13. Cf. **contiguous.**

Coterminous, now the most frequently used of these words, is an altered form of the original *conterminous*. It, too, means "coextensive in extent or duration." For the sake of DIFFERENTIATION, *coterminous* should be confined to this figurative or metaphorical sense, and *conterminous* reserved for physical and tangible senses—e.g.:

- "What should trouble Democrats most is the prospect of an avalanche of defections polarizing Southern politics along racial lines, so that being Republican and white and Democrat and black become *conterminous* [read *coterminous*]." Ross K. Baker, "A Dixie Democrat Bails Out," *Sacramento Bee*, 19 Apr. 1995, at B9. (The word's meaning is creaky at best in that sentence.)
- "Forests blanket the reservation and follow its and the county's *coterminous* [read *conterminous*] boundaries so tightly that American astronauts once spotted it from space and asked what they were seeing." Michael Hirsley, "Native American Stereotypes Live On in Sports Logos, Rituals," *Chicago Trib.*, 24 Oct. 1995, at 1.

*Coterminant, **coterminate*, and **coterminal* are NEEDLESS VARIANTS.

contest, v.t. **A. And *contend*.** In the sense "to fight," *contest* is almost always transitive <to contest an election>, and *contend* is intransitive <to contend against an opponent>. *Contend* may be transitive when it means "to maintain, assert" and is followed by a *that*-phrase <the striking workers contend that the pension fund is inadequate>.

B. Pronunciation. The noun is pronounced /**kon**-test/; the verb is pronounced /kən-**test**/.

contested election, in AmE, means either (1) "an election the validity of which has been challenged," or (2) "a political race with more than one candidate." Sense 2 is the sole meaning in BrE.

context of, in the; in a . . . context. These phrases are often used superfluously. "During the seventh century B.C., Egypt was repeatedly though always briefly occupied by Assyrian armies and *later infiltrated by Greek and other Aegean elements in a military and subsequently a commercial context* [read *later infiltrated militarily and then commercially by Greek and other Aegean elements*]."

contextual, not *contextural*, is the adjective corresponding to *context*. But the intrusive *-r-* often appears—e.g.:

- "For choreographers, *contextural* [read *contextual*] issues are at risk. In a bar setting, the cultural context calls for humor; anything else seems out of place." Gia Kourlas, "A New Stage for Modernists: the Nightclub," *N.Y. Times*, 30 Sept. 2001, § 2, at 33.

- "Buildings have been limited to 35 feet in height or three stories since the 1970's, but now there is talk of *contextural* [read *contextual*] zoning, which would honor the local character." Nancy Beth Jackson, "City Island; Close-Knit Waterfront Enclave in Bronx," *N.Y. Times*, 14 Apr. 2002, § 11, at 5.

For similar mistakes, see **contractual** & **pretextual**. For more on the intrusive -*r*-, see PRONUNCIATION (C).

It is true, however, that *contextural* is a bona fide adjective formed from *contexture* (a close synonym of *texture* meaning "a weaving together of elements into a whole"). It's pretty rare, but it does sometimes occur—e.g.: "As for the rating, the ensemble concept, the *contextural* solos, and the subtle variety add a star." Owen Cordle, "Blue Motion: Sound Recording Reviews," *Down Beat*, June 1994, at 38.

LANGUAGE-CHANGE INDEX
contextual misspelled *contextural*: Stage 1
Current ratio (*contextual information* vs.
**contextural information*): 2,742:1

contiguous means not merely "close to" or "near," but "abutting; sharing a boundary." It is commonly misused in the phrase *the 48 contiguous states*, which is illogical because only a few states can be *contiguous* to one another. (And *neighboring* is surely better than *contiguous*—it's more down-to-earth.) The counterargument might be that the *lower 48* (another illogical idiom since they are not as "low" in this sense as Hawaii) are the only ones that are *contiguous* with *any* other state. But that's a stretch. Even *the continental United States* is incorrect (though common) because as it is understood it does not include Alaska, a sizable state on the northwest corner of the North American continent. Technically speaking, the proper way to put the idea would be *the 48 conterminous states* (see **conterminous**). But there's not much chance of that phrase catching on, so we're stuck with the illogical idioms. And of those, *contiguous states* and *continental United States* are about equally common. See ILLOGIC.

Contiguous to for *next to* is sometimes a pomposity. *Contiguous* should always be construed with *to*—not *with*.

contingency; *contingence. The latter is a NEEDLESS VARIANT.

Current ratio: 166:1

continual; continuous. *Continual* = frequently recurring; intermittent. E.g.: "And [the police are] removing [the homeless]—by police rides to the edge of town, by *continual* issuing of citations for camping, by mass towing of vehicles and by routine discarding of people's belongings." Paul Boden, "Where Can Homeless Go?" *USA Today*, 3 Dec. 1997, at A24. *Continuous* = occurring without interruption; unceasing. E.g.: "Crow Canyon archaeologists want to study the 12th- and 13th-century village to determine exactly when it was inhabited and whether it was occupied

continuously or intermittently." Nancy Plevin, "Dirt, Sweat and Blisters," *Santa Fe New Mexican*, 8 Sept. 1996, at E1. A good mnemonic device is to think of the -*ous* ending as being short for "one uninterrupted sequence."

The two words are frequently confused, usually because *continuous* horns in where *continual* belongs—e.g.:

- "Minutes after the arrest, Wayne Forrest, a Deputy Attorney General helping prosecute the case, told the presiding judge, Charles R. DiGisi, that the sheriff's office had been engaged in a '*continuous* [read *continual*] course of misconduct' in the Spath case." Robert Hanley, "Courthouse Arrest Roils Trial of Officer in Teaneck Killing," *N.Y. Times*, 18 Jan. 1992, at 9.
- "The variety of tactics included *continuous* [read *continual*] nagging, crying, screaming, embarrassing parents in public, sulking and emotional blackmail." Maggie Brown, "Children 'Put Pressure on Adult Buying,'" *Independent*, 30 Apr. 1992, Home News §, at 3.
- "*Continuous* [read *Continual*] interruptions are frustrating because *it often means* [read *they often mean*] you have to warm up all over again or don't get a complete workout." Nick Lackeos, "Getting into Shape," *Montgomery Advertiser*, 1 Jan. 1996, at B1.

The phrase **almost continuous* indicates that *continual* is the right word—e.g.: "The antidepressant Prozac has been in the news *almost continuously* [read *continually*] since it was introduced in Belgium in 1986." Jennifer Barrs, "Prozac on the Front Page," *Tampa Trib.*, 24 Nov. 1996, at 8.

A related mistake is to use *continuous* for something that happens at regular (e.g., annual) intervals—e.g.: "The White House tree-lighting ceremony has been held *continuously* [read *annually*] since 1923." "Lighting the National Christmas Tree," *Herald-Sun* (Durham, N.C.), 6 Dec. 1996, at A1.

LANGUAGE-CHANGE INDEX
continuous misused for *continual*: Stage 3

continuance. A. Opposed Senses. *Continuance* has conflicting senses in lay and legal usage. Generally, it means (1) "keeping up, going on with, maintaining, or prolonging"; or (2) "duration; time of continuing." E.g.: "Every citizen also wants lower taxes and a *continuance* of any and all federal spending programs that directly have some positive impact on each one's lives." Larry A. Smith, "Future Shock: It's Entitlements, Stupid," *Fresno Bee*, 16 Nov. 1996, at B7. (For more on *each one's lives* in that sentence, see CONCORD (B).)

But in American law, *continuance* means "postponement; the adjournment or deferring of a trial or other proceeding until a future date" <motion for continuance>. E.g.: "Her trial is scheduled for late next month but a *continuance* is expected." Anne Koch, "Teen Says She Didn't Kill Pickup Driver," *Seattle Times*, 17 July 1996, at B3.

B. And ***continuation; continuity.*** *Continuation* is the general word meaning "continued maintenance; carrying on or resumption of (an action, etc.); that by which a thing is continued" (*COD*). E.g.:

- "By putting more money in the public schools each year, the state has allowed the *continuation* of 'a bureaucratic system that seems incapable of improving itself.'" "GOP Expected to Push for School-Choice Bills," *Herald-Sun* (Durham, N.C.), 2 Dec. 1994, at C14.
- "The budget proposed by Pierce contains no new employees and a *continuation* of programs and infrastructure projects." Hal Dardick, "Attempt Will Be Made to Cut Mayor's Levy Hike," *Chicago Trib.*, 2 Dec. 1996, at D3.

Continuity = connectedness; unbrokenness; uninterruptedness. E.g.: "The transition is as seamless as possible, and the retirement causes little or no interruption of service to the customers. Such *continuity* is vital in order for companies to maintain a good reputation and a competitive edge." James E. Challenger, "Wanted: A Better Way to Retire," *Houston Chron.*, 1 Dec. 1996, Outlook §, at 1.

*continue on** is a minor but bothersome REDUNDANCY—e.g.:

- "We *continued on* [read *continued* or *went on*] and found that the wolf stayed with the marked path." Chris Welsch, "Making Tracks," *Star Trib.* (Minneapolis), 4 Dec. 1994, at G1.
- "As he *continued on and on* [read *went on and on* or *continued*], uninterrupted by me, he proceeded to answer his own objections." "To Manage Employees Better, Manage to Listen," *Indianapolis Bus. J.*, 8 July 1996, at 68.
- "Big drops were soon followed by big gains and the market would *continue on* [read *continue*] its six-year run." "Stocks Plunge over China Slowdown," *Detroit News*, 22 Aug. 2015, at A5.

See PHRASAL VERBS.

LANGUAGE-CHANGE INDEX
continue on: Stage 3

continuity. See **continuance (B)**.

continuous. See **continual**.

continuum. Pl. *continua* or *continuums*. The former has always predominated in print sources—and continues to today. See PLURALS (B).

Current ratio (*continua* vs. *continuums*): 6:1

contracept, v.i., is a BACK-FORMATION that rose to prominence in the late 20th century but is not yet included in most dictionaries. It is a jargonistic word popular among social activists. E.g.:

- "Feminist rights include feminist responsibilities; the right to obtain an abortion brings with it the responsibility to *contracept*." Naomi Wolf, "Our Bodies, Our Souls," *New Republic*, 16 Oct. 1995, at 26.
- "Put starkly, Buchanan argues in his new book, 'The Death of the West,' that white people are too rich, selfish, godless and guilt-ridden to have children, and so are *contracepting* themselves out of existence." "Godless and Childless," *Wash. Times*, 25 Jan. 2002, at A2.

contraceptionist. See **contraceptor**.

contraceptive, n.; **abortifacient,** n. A *contraceptive* is a device or drug designed to prevent conception. An *abortifacient* is a device or drug intended to produce a miscarriage. Neither term should be used to include the other.

contraceptor; contraceptionist. What is the agent noun corresponding to *contraception*? William Safire preferred *contraceptionist* ("On Language," *N.Y. Times*, 30 Dec. 1990, § 6, at 6). But *contraceptor* is five times as common in modern print sources, and usage suggests a worthwhile distinction: a *contraceptor* is someone who uses contraception, while a *contraceptionist* is someone who advocates its use.

CONTRACTIONS. A. Generally. Many writers, especially those who write in formal situations, feel uncomfortable with contractions. And perhaps contractions don't generally belong in solemn contexts.

But why shouldn't writers use them in most types of writing? Some excellent writers use contractions to good effect, even in books—e.g.:

- "I *won't* offer an analysis of the passage and its working; some of the main points are fairly obvious." F.R. Leavis, *The Common Pursuit* 102 (1952).
- "The ideal book reviewer['s] . . . own literary quality should be obvious in his prose. If he is an academic, he *shouldn't* allow this to show through." Joseph Epstein, "Reviewing and Being Reviewed," in *Plausible Prejudices: Essays on American Writing* 44, 56 (1985).
- "If I *hadn't* [paid Billy a compliment], I doubt *we'd* ever have become friends. In fact, if I *hadn't*, he might just have shot me." Larry McMurtry, *Anything for Billy* 14 (1988).
- "*It's* no longer the sheepish effusions that score for Byron, but his goatish satires and letters." John Simon, *The Sheep from the Goats: Selected Literary Essays* xviii (1989).
- "Did sloths make a chirping sound? Tina *didn't* think so, but she *wasn't* sure." Michael Crichton, *Jurassic Park* 14 (1990).
- "Deep-seated conflict in the North was another story—it *wasn't* supposed to exist." Nicholas Lemann, *The Promised Land* 117 (1991).
- "I felt almost wonderful. If it *hadn't* been for the other occupant of my publisher's waiting room, *there'd* have been no 'almost.'" Phyllis A. Whitney, *Woman Without a Past* 1 (1991).
- "Victims *don't* occupy a higher moral plane. *They've* just suffered more." Jonathan Rosen, "The Trivialization of Tragedy," in *Dumbing Down: Essays on the Strip Mining of American Culture* 270, 280 (Katharine Washburn & John F. Thornton eds., 1996).
- "Weinstein *doesn't* doubt that the Hollywood establishment wishes him ill, but he *doesn't* think *it's* personal." Ken Auletta, "Beauty and the Beast," *New Yorker*, 16 Dec. 2002, at 81.

The common fear is that using contractions can make the writing seem breezy. For most of us, though, that risk is nil. What you gain should be a relaxed sincerity—not breeziness. Among the wisest words on the subject are these:

LANGUAGE-CHANGE INDEX (For the full key, see front matter pp. xxxi, l–li.)
Stage 1: Rejected. **Stage 2:** Widely shunned. **Stage 3:** Widespread but . . . **Stage 4:** Ubiquitous but . . . **Stage 5:** Fully accepted.
Invariably inferior forms marked by asterisk (*). • Ratios represent frequency of prevalent forms vs. variants in current books.

- "*I don't* and *you don't* and *we don't* are easy and proper, except where high dignity is required." Edward N. Teall, *Putting Words to Work* 32 (1940).
- "Don't start using . . . contractions . . . at every single opportunity from here on. It's not as simple as that. Contractions have to be used with care. Sometimes they fit, sometimes they don't. It depends on whether you would use the contraction in speaking *that particular sentence* (e.g. in this sentence I would say *you would* and not *you'd*). It also depends on whether the contraction would help or hinder the rhythm that would suit your sentence for proper emphasis. So don't try to be consistent about this; it doesn't work. You have to go by feel, not by rule." Rudolf Flesch, *The Art of Readable Writing* 97 (1949; repr. 1967).
- "Such common contractions as *it's, that's, they're,* and *she'll* are correct in almost all written communications in business and the professions. Whether or not you choose to use them is a matter of personal preference." David W. Ewing, *Writing for Results in Business, Government, and the Professions* 358 (1974).
- "Use occasional contractions. They'll keep you from taking yourself too seriously, tell your reader that you're not a prude, and help you achieve a more natural, conversational rhythm in your style." John R. Trimble, *Writing with Style* 78 (1975).
- "Your style will be warmer and truer to your own personality if you use contractions like *won't* and *can't* when they fit comfortably into what you're writing." William Zinsser, *On Writing Well* 75 (6th ed. 1998).

B. Ill-Advised Forms. While you can use contractions such as *can't, don't,* and *you'll* to good advantage, you may stumble if you contract recklessly. A few contractions that occur in speech don't translate well into writing because they're not instantly readable—the mind's tongue trips over them, however briefly. Examples of ones generally to avoid (except perhaps in quoted speech) include **I'd've, *it'd, *she'd've, *there're,* and **who're.* Two in particular—*should've* and *would've*—are common CASUALISMS that can't be strongly condemned.

Two mistakes commonly occur with such contractions. First, the reduced *have* in several of these forms is sometimes mistaken for an *of.* (See **of (D).**) Second, the conditional past perfect (*if I'd* [= I had] *known*) is sometimes mistakenly given a superfluous *-'ve* (**if I'd've known*)—e.g.: "If *I'd've* [read *I'd*] passed up on the date *he'd've* [read, perhaps, *he'd have*] been in like Flynn." Will Self, "A Novella in Several Live Performances," *Independent,* 7 June 2000, at 7. See ***had have** & TENSES (A).

One last point. The form **who're* is particularly ugly because of its visual resemblance to *whore*: "How is it that many people *who're* [read *who are*] convinced that Oliver Stone's *JFK* was a documentary about a right-wing plot to get Jack Kennedy are satisfied that Vincent Foster's peculiar death in Fort Marcy Park was an open-and-shut case of suicide?" William P. Cheshire, "You Don't Have to Be Oliver Stone to Wonder About Foster's Death," *Ariz. Republic,* 29 Sept. 1994, at B6.

C. Miscue with Contracted *is*. Be careful about contracting *is* with a noun (*the President's going back to Washington*) as opposed to a pronoun (*he's going*

back *to Washington*). A MISCUE commonly results because it reads at first as if it's a possessive: "If *Baker's spitting* [read *Baker is spitting*] into the wind anyhow, he might as well have a little fun. . . . But *Baker's anything* [read *Baker is anything*] but a quietist." David Gates, "Paper Chase," *N.Y. Times* (Book Rev.), 15 Apr. 2001, § 7, at 8, 9.

D. Mispronounced Contractions. See PRONUNCIATION (B).

contractual is sometimes erroneously written (or pronounced) **contractural,* with an intrusive *-r-.* E.g.: "KCTS refused to release the budget figures, citing *contractural* [read *contractual*] obligations." Chuck Taylor, "KCTS Confronts Its Future," *Seattle Times,* 17 Nov. 1996, at M1. For similar mistakes, see **contextual** & **pretextual.**

LANGUAGE-CHANGE INDEX
contractual misspelled **contractural*: Stage 1
Current ratio: 663:1

contradict. See **gainsay.**

contradictory; *contradictive; *contradictional; contradictious. *Contradictory* = opposite, contrary. **Contradictive* and **contradictional* are NEEDLESS VARIANTS of *contradictory.*

Contradictious = inclined to contradict or quarrel. The word is applied to people—e.g.: "But General Gordon had always been a *contradictious* person—even a little off his head, perhaps, though a hero; and besides he was no longer there to contradict." Carol Brightman, "Character in Biography," *Nation,* 13 Feb. 1995, at 206.

contraindicate is medical JARGON meaning "to make (a treatment, practice, etc.) inadvisable." In nonspecialist contexts, though, a simpler, more straightforward term is better—e.g.:

- "Researchers concluded that prophylactic pseudoephedrine is useful for preventing barotrauma, but since the medication is *contraindicated in* [read *inadvisable for*] patients with many medical conditions . . . , a consultation with your own doctor is recommended." Allan Bruckheim, "Health Line," *Chicago Trib.,* 28 Mar. 1995, at C7.
- "Although medical professionals stress the health benefits of breast-feeding, there are instances in which it is *contraindicated* [read *inadvisable* or *not recommended*]." Melanie Choukas-Bradley, "Babes in Arms Get a Hand," *Wash. Post,* 1 Oct. 1996, at D5.

Cf. **indicated, to be.**

And when the subject does not relate directly to health, the word is often a MALAPROPISM—e.g.:

- "At this time we find nothing in our investigation at this point to *contraindicate* [read *contradict*] the medical examiner's report." Tommy Perkins, "Autopsy Shows S.C. Man Drowned," *Morning Star* (Wilmington, N.C.), 23 June 2000, at B2. (Note the REDUNDANCY in *at this time* and *at this point,* which are symptoms of OFFICIALESE.)
- "'What I have been told is that we generally take our lead from the regional office (of the Department of Public Welfare), and the regional office had come out with nothing to *contraindicate* [read *warn against*] sending

children there,' Stoffa said." David Slade, "Foster Mom/ Dad Probe Widens," *Morning Call* (Allentown, Pa.), 24 Sept. 2000, at A1 (quoting John Stoffa, county director of human services).

contralto. Pl. *contraltos*, preferably not **contralti* (an affectation). From 1850 to the present day, *contraltos* has seriously outranged the Italianate plural in frequency of use in print sources. See PLURALS (B).

Current ratio: 21:1

contrary. A. *Contrary to* or **contrary from*. *Contrary* takes the preposition *to*. **Contrary from* has never been standard. E.g.:

- "The facts of a cynical European political elite, defending Mr. Arafat, are *contrary to* the facts on the ground." Amos Perlmutter, "Distress Signals . . . Amid Mideast Turbulence," *Wash. Times*, 1 Oct. 1996, at A15.
- "*Contrary to* two breathless reports in a local weekly newspaper, 'Mars Attacks!' was not filmed in Richmond." Daniel Neman, "Execution of 'Mars' Less Great than Idea," *Richmond Times-Dispatch*, 13 Dec. 1996, at C5.

B. *On the contrary; to the contrary; quite the contrary*. *On the contrary* marks a contrast with a statement or even an entire argument just made. It has always been the most usual phrasing—e.g.:

- "I hold neither of those views. *On the contrary*, I argue that biochemical systems—as well as other complex systems— were designed by an intelligent agent." Letter of Michael J. Behe, " 'And God Saw That It Was Good,' " *Newsweek*, 7 Oct. 1996, at 24.
- "Yet it has no real conclusion. *On the contrary*, several narrative threads are conspicuously left dangling." Madison Smartt Bell, "Southern Shadows," *Chicago Trib.*, 10 Nov. 2002, Books §, at 1.

To the contrary marks a contrast with a specific noun or noun phrase just mentioned. E.g.: "The answer is not a mystery. It is, *to the contrary*, quite simple and can be given quite simply." Bob Dole, "Bob Dole's Acceptance Speech," *Wash. Monthly*, Oct. 1996, at 20. (The contrast is with the noun *mystery*.)

Quite the contrary can do the job of either of the other two phrases. The phrase is usually either a verbless sentence or a verbless clause followed by a semicolon—e.g.:

- "Don't think that if you have been had once, your luck has to change. *Quite the contrary*; you probably have gotten yourself on a list with others who have been defrauded and are now a prime target." Jonathan N. Axelrod, "Get Poor Quick," *Pitt. Post-Gaz.*, 7 Oct. 1996, at B7.
- "This is not to suggest that Peres sought to provoke a Lebanon crisis during March and April, though. *Quite the contrary*. All the evidence indicates that . . . Peres was trying to maintain calm." Jonathan Marcus, "Toward a Fragmented Policy?" *Wash. Q.*, Autumn 1996, at 19.

contrast. A. Prepositions with. One *contrasts* something *with*—not *to*—something else. But it's permissible to write either *in contrast to* or *in contrast with*. Cf. **compare with.**

B. *Compare and contrast*. This is an English teacher's REDUNDANCY.

C. Pronunciation. As a noun, *contrast* is accented on the first syllable: /**kon**-trast/. As a verb, it's accented on the second syllable: /kən-**trast**/.

contravene. A. And *violate*. *Contravene* = (1) (of people) to transgress, infringe (as a law); to defy; or (2) (of things) to be contrary to, come in conflict with. E.g.: "While the matter has been in the courts, the U.S. Department of Transportation issued a letter saying the airport's regulation *contravenes* federal law and policy." Howard Pankratz, "Centennial Injunction Voided," *Denver Post*, 13 Dec. 1996, at A24. The word can usually be advantageously replaced by the simpler word *violate*.

In AmE, *contravene* is less usual than *violate*, but in BrE just the opposite is true. Whereas Americans think of *contravene* as a fancy equivalent of *violate*, to Britons it (like its corresponding noun, *contravention*) is more an everyday word—e.g.:

- "The origins of the dispute lie in the leakage to the market of Russian diamonds, *contravening* Russia's agreement with De Beers." Kenneth Gooding, "Diamond Cartel Cuts Up Rough," *Fin. Times*, 24 Aug. 1995, at 17.
- "Its action is a blatant *contravention* of the 1951 refugee convention, whose signatories are bound not to repatriate refugees by force." "Border Trouble," *Fin. Times*, 24 Aug. 1995, at 11. (In this latter example, note the unpleasant ring of *contravention/convention*.)

In AmE, a simpler, more direct writing style favors *violate* over *contravene*.

B. And *controvert*. *Contravene* shouldn't be confused with *controvert* (= to dispute or contest; to debate; to contend against or oppose in argument). Although *controvert* is mostly confined to legal contexts, it does appear elsewhere—e.g.:

- "In the Information Culture we flip from one momentous medical theory to another the next day. The second absolutely *controverts* the first, and it all seems normal because our heads are spinning with data." Jim Klobuchar, "Screaming, Hissing and Moaning Over Election Campaign," *Star Trib.* (Minneapolis), 27 Oct. 1994, at B3.
- "Perry is an expert at producing numbers persuasive to his case. They are not easy to *controvert*." Greg Heberlein, "Fearing the Worst? Relax, It Won't Be That Bad," *Seattle Times*, 29 Oct. 1995, at F1.
- "At one point in the tour of Sprague, prisoners hollered about the facility's dismal conditions. Jail officers did not *controvert* them." Christopher Collins, "County Jail System Needs Reform," *Times Record News* (Wichita Falls, Tex.), 5 July 2015, at A1.

C. And **controvene*. This error, dating from the late 19th century, results from confusion of *contravene* with *controvert*. E.g.: "The State's use of a jailhouse informant to elicit inculpatory information from Wilson *controvened* [read *contravened*] his right to counsel." *Wilson v. Henderson*, 742 F.2d 741, 748 (2d Cir. 1984). The same problem occurs in the noun form: "The Long Island Bank is seeking a court order declaring that the Comptroller acted 'in *controvention* [read *contravention*] of the law' and that his approval is 'null and void.'" "Citibank Branch Target of Suit," *Am. Banker*, 6 July 1979, at 3.

LANGUAGE-CHANGE INDEX
contravene misspelled **controvene*: Stage 1
Current ratio: 1,619:1

D. And *contravent. This form is a misbegotten BACK-FORMATION used by writers who, reaching for the verb corresponding to *contravention*, forget that *contravene* is the correct form—e.g.:

- "You should say that it is clear from the letter that it expects your current code to produce an overpayment, and that consequently it *contravents* [read *contravenes*] regulation 7(e)." "New Tax Code for Widow," *Fin. Times*, 28 Dec. 1985, at vi.
- "[The] decision appears to *contravent* [read *contravene*] the clear legislative intent of IEEPA." Jules Lobel, "Emergency Power and the Decline of Liberalism," 98 *Yale L.J.* 1385, 1417 n.175 (1989).

LANGUAGE-CHANGE INDEX
*contravent for *contravene*: Stage 1
Current ratio (*contravene* vs. **contravent*): 4,946:1

contribute. For the MALAPROPISM in which this word is confused with *attribute*, vb., see **attribute.**

contributory; *contributary; contributive; contributorial; contributional. *Contributory* = (1) making contribution; contributing to a common fund <contributory donations>; or (2) bearing a share toward a purpose or result <contributory negligence>. **Contributary* is a NEEDLESS VARIANT of *contributory*. *Contributive* = having the power of contributing; conducive <exercise is contributive to health>. *Contributorial* = of, relating to, or involving a contributor <contributorial recognition>. *Contributional* (a rare word, rarely necessary) = of, relating to, or involving a contribution <contributional achievements>.

Current ratio (*contributory* vs. **contributary*): 319:1

controller. See **comptroller.**

CONTRONYMS. A surprising number of words can bear contradictory senses. They're known as "contronyms," or "autantonyms." Typically, context eliminates any real possibility of ambiguity. A truly recondite contronym is *anabasis* (/ə-**nab**-ə-səs/), which (according to *W11*) can mean either a military advance or a military retreat. Xenophon (ca. 431–352 B.C.) used the word in reference to Cyrus the Younger's attack on his brother, Artaxerxes, in 401 B.C. (The Cyrus army advanced and the Artaxerxes army retreated: it's all a matter of perspective.) The word has been recorded in English from 1706, mostly in reference to advances. Following are some less erudite examples:

- *Appropriate* = (1) to take exclusive possession of <appropriate land for a public school>; or (2) to give over to

another person or group for its own use <appropriate funds for the biology department>.
- *Cleave* = (1) to stick together <Shall a man cleave unto his wife?—Genesis 2>; or (2) to split apart <cleave the logs with a hatchet>.
- *Dispose of* = (1) to get rid of; or (2) to have the use of.
- *Draw* = (1) to open <please draw the curtains>; or (2) to close <please draw the curtains>.
- *Drift* = the general direction of an argument. But when an argument *drifts*, it has no general direction.
- *Dust* = (1) to sprinkle powder over <dust the pastries with powdered sugar>; or (2) to remove the dust from <you haven't dusted the shelves yet>.
- *Fast* = (1) in rapid motion <she ran fast>; or (2) motionless <the ship is tied fast to the dock>.
- *Let* = (1) to allow or permit <let our guests see the painting>; or (2) (archaically) to prevent or hinder <the sheriff's pursuit was let by the suspect's accomplice>.
- *Oversight* = (1) an obligation to supervise <the committee has oversight over the project>; or (2) failure to be vigilant <it was an oversight—just a silly oversight>.
- *Ravel* = (1) to disentangle <ravel a tall tale>; or (2) to entangle <become raveled in a fraud>.
- *Sanction* = (1) to express approval <the league sanctioned a new tournament>; or (2) to express disapproval <the city council sanctioned the city manager for the unauthorized expenditures>.
- *Scan* = (1) to read hastily <just scan the street signs>; or (2) to examine carefully <scan the map and plot our course>.
- *Torsibility* = (1) capability of being twisted; or (2) resistance to being twisted.
- *Trim* = (1) to add to the edges of <she trimmed the dress with lace>; or (2) to cut off the edges or tips <trim your hair>.

controversial is preferably pronounced /kon-trə-**vər**-shəl/, not the affected /kon-trə-**vər**-see-əl/.

controversy is pronounced /**kon**-trə-vər-see/ in AmE and BrE, but sometimes also /kən-**trah**-və[r]-see/ in BrE. The word appears surprisingly often in the mangled form **controversary*. One example suffices: "It is only fitting that we delve into Irish history to relate a tale fraught with *controversary* [read *controversy*] for lo these past 144 years." Max Haines, "A Scream from the Past," *Toronto Sun*, 17 Mar. 1996, at 5.

LANGUAGE-CHANGE INDEX
controversy misspelled **controversary*: Stage 1
Current ratio: 18,339:1

controvert. So spelled—not **contravert*, a misspelling that litters much legal writing. See **contravene (B).**

Current ratio: 90:1

controvertible. So spelled—not **controvertable*. See -ABLE (A).

Current ratio: 313:1

contumacious. See **contemptuous (B).**

contumacy; *contumacity; contumely. Of the two forms of the noun corresponding to *contumacious*, *contumacy* (/**kon**-tyuu-mə-see/) is the usual term, meaning (1) "rebellion against authority"; or (2) "willful contempt of court." Sense 1 is the nonlegal sense—e.g.:

"But he was a backslider, and finally was removed from the rolls [of the church] in 1880 for *contumacy*." Perre Magness, "Church Celebrates a Colorful 150 Years," *Commercial Appeal* (Memphis), 21 Apr. 1994, Neighbors §, at ME2. **Contumacity* is a NEEDLESS VARIANT. For the corresponding adjective, see **contemptuous (B).**

Contumely (/kon-**tyoo**-mə-lee/), easily confused with *contumacy*, is a literary word meaning "rude and haughty language." Shakespeare wrote, in *Hamlet*, of "the proud man's *contumely*" (3.1.70). More recent examples are not common, but the word does still appear—e.g.:

- "With considerable vituperation, *contumely* and plain old harrumphing, members of the General Assembly finally passed a couple of ethics bills affecting public officials." "All's Quiet . . . ," *Columbus Dispatch*, 2 Feb. 1994, at A10.
- "Targets for *contumely* include the Labour MP Russell Kerr ('a drunken boor'), the journalist John Junor ('an unamiable . . . old swine'), and his fellow Tory MP Robin Maxwell-Hyslop (whom he describes variously as 'an unpleasant . . . eccentric,' 'a nasty bit of work,' and 'always . . . a man to avoid')." Gerald Kaufman, "Elegy to a Political Career," *Sunday Telegraph*, 2 Oct. 1994, Books §, at 11.

Contumely can properly refer not just to scornful language but to scorn itself—e.g.:

- "And congressional concern over subsidized art calculated to arouse *contumely* or hatred of racial, ethnic, gender, religious, or other groups or values reflects a legitimate goal." Bruce Fein, "Dollars for Depravity?" *Wash. Times*, 19 Nov. 1996, at A14.
- "But the point to be examined isn't whether Mr. Gingrich suffers the *contumely* of much of the public." William F. Buckley, "GOP Future Needs Aye of Newt," *Cincinnati Enquirer*, 22 Nov. 1996, at A10.

Current ratio (*contumacy* vs. **contumacity*): 100:1

contusion. See **concussion.**

conundrum. Pl. *conundrums*. The mistaken form **conunda* sometimes appears—e.g.: "The rhythms of baseball, unlike those of more hectic games, often induce in the spectator long thoughts and provide ample opportunity to tackle *conunda* [read *conundrums*] that have long stumped philosophers for millennia." George W. Hunt, "What Are Hyenas Laughing at Anyway?" *America*, 13 Apr. 1996, at 2. (If the author was trying to make **conunda* parallel to *millennia*, the echo hardly works.) See PLURALS (B).

LANGUAGE-CHANGE INDEX
*conunda for *conundrums*: Stage 1
Current ratio (*conundrums* vs. **conunda*): 38:1

convener; **convenor.* *Convener* has been standard for centuries. Although the *-or* spelling inexplicably surged in the 1990s, it remains a NEEDLESS VARIANT. See -ER (A).

Current ratio: 1.3:1

convention(e)r. Today the usual term for one attending a convention is *conventioneer*. It has been standard since the 1930s.
Current ratio (*conventioneer* vs. **conventioner*): 132:1

conversable; **convertible; convertible.* *Conversable* = easy to talk with; enjoyable as a conversationalist. E.g.: "Friends say Ethel Kropf was as likable as they come—kind, thoughtful, *conversable*, quick with a compliment and full of stories." Alex Tizon, "Ethel Kropf, 97, Was Full of Stories," *Seattle Times*, 20 June 1995, at B6.

*Conversible is a NEEDLESS VARIANT of *convertible* (= capable of being converted). E.g.: "As well as Comcast's deal, an issue for The Limited, the U.S. women's clothing chain, also had a success with a \$50m *conversible* [read *convertible* issue] paying a 6¾ per cent coupon with a put option to give a 9.48 per cent yield after five years." Maggie Urry, "Low-Cost Borrowing Via a Convertible," *Fin. Times*, 2 Sept. 1985, § II, at 20. See -ABLE (A).

conversant in; conversant with. Although at times these phrasings have been interchangeable, a DIFFERENTIATION appears to be emerging. *Conversant in* suggests "thoroughly versed in" and connotes a good deal of expertise—e.g.:

- "The MSI show is a means for any user—nonusers, too—to become more fluent with the 'techie' concepts and terms used by people more *conversant in* the computer revolution." Mike Conklin, "Networld Shows the Way," *Chicago Trib.*, 3 Apr. 2001, at 3.
- "Sophisticated, savvy and stylish, fluent in French and *conversant in* history, Jacqueline Kennedy may not have been the greatest first lady—a title historians tend to bestow on Eleanor Roosevelt." Lisa Anderson, "Museum Exhibit Explores Jackie Kennedy's Impact," *Seattle Times*, 24 Apr. 2001, at A9.
- "The cosmopolitan Negroponte—London-born, Greek American, Yale-educated, *conversant in* five languages—should placate U.N. members who sense a rise in American jingoism." Jay Branegan, "With Friends Like These Can a New Envoy Bring the U.S. and U.N. Together?" *Time* (Int'l ed.), 21 May 2001, at 25.

Conversant with (since 1800 the more usual phrasing) tends to suggest somewhat less expertise—that is, a general familiarity with something. E.g.:

- "From an early age he [John Adams] read and relished Greek and Latin, was *conversant with* Thucydides and Tacitus, as avaricious a bookman as his immortal correspondent Thomas Jefferson." Edwin M. Yoder Jr., "The Amiable Classicist," *Wash. Post*, 27 May 2001, Book World §, at T3.
- "The company ultimately benefits from an education system that has better teachers who are *conversant with* the area's dominant business." Mark Simon, "Win-Win Program Needs More Sponsors," *S.F. Chron.*, 29 May 2001, at A13.
- "Chafee said Mr. Bush, plainly *conversant with* the political challenges ahead, pointed out that although the GOP must

---

LANGUAGE-CHANGE INDEX (For the full key, see front matter pp. xxxi, l–li.)
Stage 1: Rejected. **Stage 2:** Widely shunned. **Stage 3:** Widespread but . . . **Stage 4:** Ubiquitous but . . . **Stage 5:** Fully accepted.
Invariably inferior forms marked by asterisk (*). • Ratios represent frequency of prevalent forms vs. variants in current books.

defend more seats in 2002, there are several vulnerable Democrats running for reelection in states that he carried last year." John E. Mulligan, "Chafee Foresees Stalemate for Senate, Bush," *Providence J.-Bull.*, 8 June 2001, at A1.

conversationalist; *conversationist. The standard term is *conversationalist*. Older authorities preferred **conversationist*, but that obsolescent word (predominant till about 1850) is now almost never used.

Current ratio: 43:1

converse, n.; **obverse,** n.; **inverse,** n.; **reverse,** n. In logic, these words denote various types of opposition. *Converse* = a statement derived from another statement by transposing the terms on each side of an antithesis <honor without courage; courage without honor>. *Obverse* = an equivalent statement made by negative inference <no person is immortal; all people are mortal>. *Inverse* = a statement made by inference from an original negative proposition by changing the subject but keeping the predicate the same <no comedy is drama; some noncomedies are drama>. *Reverse*, the broadest of these terms, means simply "the contrary"—and embraces the other three.

converse, vb.; ***conversate; *conversationalize.** *Converse* (/kən-**vərs**/) is the standard verb corresponding to the noun *conversation* <she converses with ease in several languages>.

The dialectal variant **conversate*, a BACK-FORMATION, is sometimes heard, as reported here: "The Westerfield case had its cast of characters whose testimony made them local celebrities—the friends of the van Dams', the bartender at Dad's Cafe who kept using the word '*conversate*' on the witness stand." Alex Roth, "Guilty on All Counts," *San Diego Union-Trib.*, 22 Aug. 2002, at A1. During the trial referred to in that quotation, the bartender received an anonymous hate letter over his use of this word; the writer expressed "outrage that he [the bartender] hadn't spoken proper English." Alex Roth, "Westerfield Trial: Dad's Uneasy with Notoriety," *San Diego Union-Trib.*, 21 July 2002, at A1. (A serious breach of decorum: proponents of good English should always remain civil. Hate mail isn't the way.)

In print, this NONWORD almost always appears in reported speech—e.g.:

- "Sometimes, Charles admits, he misses the old life. Or certain things that came with the old life. 'I miss just walking around. I like *conversating* with people.'" Bill Marvel, "Cast into the Darkness," *Dallas Morning News*, 28 Jan. 2001, at F1.
- "'Since I'm traveling a lot, we *conversate* via e-mail.'" Mike McGraw, "Rose to Honor Father," *Daily Herald* (Chicago), 16 Apr. 2002, at 7 (quoting Jalen Rose).
- "During a College World Series game, she heard a sportscaster say the coach was '*conversating*' with the pitcher." "Smiley Anders," *Advocate* (Baton Rouge), 24 June 2002, at B1.

Meanwhile, **conversationalize* (along with cognates such as **conversationalization*) is a piece of bureaucratic mumbo jumbo—e.g.: "'[C]onversationalization'

. . . [occurs when] the presenter is constructed as an ordinary bloke talking to ordinary people, sharing with them . . . a commonsense world of ordinary experience." Norman Fairclough, *Media Discourse* 10 (1995). No ordinary bloke would use the word. See -IZE & BUREAUCRATESE.

Current ratio (*converse*, vb., vs. **conversate*): 498:1

*conversible. See **conversable.**

convertible. So spelled—not **convertable*. See -ABLE (A) & **conversable.**

Current ratio: 1,745:1

conveyance, n. **A. Meaning "vehicle."** *Conveyance* is sometimes used as a FORMAL WORD for *car* or *vehicle*—a pomposity to be avoided. E.g.: "Parents of bused students who are unhappy with the county's transportation arrangements always have the option of getting their children to school in *private conveyances* [read *their own cars*]." "Children Are Parents' Responsibility," *Sun-Sentinel* (Ft. Lauderdale), 21 Sept. 1995, at A18.

B. And *conveyal. *Conveyance* is the better noun corresponding to the verb *convey*. **Conveyal* is a NEEDLESS VARIANT.

conveyer is the general spelling for "a person or thing that conveys." In mechanical uses, however, as in *conveyor belt*, the *-or* spelling is standard.

convict, v.t. A person is *convicted of* a crime, *for* the act of committing a crime, or *on* a particular count. But a person is not **convicted in a crime*: "A Palestinian suspected in the bombing of Pan Am Flight 103 was *convicted* today along with three co-defendants *in* [read *for*] a series of attacks in northern Europe four years ago." "Pan Am Bombing Suspect Convicted *in* [read *for*] Other Attacks," *N.Y. Times*, 22 Dec. 1989, at 3.

convictable. So spelled in AmE and BrE alike—not **convictible*. See -ABLE (A).

convince. See **persuade.**

convolvulus (= a morning glory having funnel-shaped flowers and triangular leaves) predominantly forms the plural *convolvuli* (/kon-**vol**-vyə-lɪ/) in all varieties of English. The plural *convolvuluses* is a variant.

Current ratio: 2:1

coolly. So spelled—not **cooly*. E.g.: "It's a nicely restrained, *cooly* [read *coolly*] observant effort." Lloyd Sachs, "'Boys Life' Even Better the Second Time Around," *Chicago Sun-Times*, 15 Aug. 1997, at 30.

LANGUAGE-CHANGE INDEX
coolly misspelled **cooly*: Stage 1
Current ratio: 40:1

co-op. The shortened form of *cooperative* (= an organization owned by and run for the benefit of those who use its services), *co-op* is hyphenated even though the longer form isn't. Without the hyphen, it looks like the word for a chicken pen.

cooperate; *co-operate. AmE did away with the hyphen about 1910; BrE took till about 1980. The word is solid.

Current ratio: 6:1

co-opt. This word, from the Latin *cooptare* "to choose or elect," has an obligatory hyphen because without it a MISCUE almost certainly takes place. *Coöpt* is an old-fashioned variant. The word means (1) "to recruit (someone) as a member," (2) "to gain the allegiance of (an opponent or potential opponent)," or (3) "to absorb or assimilate; to make use of."

Co-opt is sometimes wrongly written *co-op* (which is properly only a shortening of *cooperative*): " 'The danger here is clear—people trying to *co-op* [read *co-opt*] the campaign finance reform issue and pass off fake reforms as real.' " Alison Mitchell, "McCain Returns to an Uneasy Senate," *N.Y. Times*, 20 Mar. 2000, at A19 (quoting Fred Wertheimer). See **co-op.**

LANGUAGE-CHANGE INDEX
co-op misused for *co-opt*: Stage 1
Current ratio (*to co-opt the* vs. *to co-op the*): 193:1

COORDINATE ADJECTIVES. See ADJECTIVES (C).

coowner. Because the general AmE practice is not to hyphenate prefixes, some writers prefer *coowner*. For example, the American Law Institute has used the term *coownership* in the title of one of its restatements of the law. The question whether the better form is *coowner* or *co-owner* is largely one of familiarity. To some writers—particularly lawyers—*coowner* and *coownership* are everyday words. But other writers think that the solid versions are visually jarring, so they write *co-owner* and *co-ownership*. See CO- & PUNCTUATION (J).

copacetic; *copasetic; *copesetic; *copesettic. The first is the standard spelling for this tongue-in-cheek term meaning "first-rate; quite satisfactory." The word is slangy and jocular. Its ETYMOLOGY—variously attributed to Italian, Creole French, and Hebrew—is unknown. The second, third, and fourth spellings are variant forms (the last one especially rare). See SLANG.

Current ratio (first three headwords): 33:21:1

*copartner need not exist alongside *partner*. The joint relationship (i.e., that the existence of one partner implies the existence of one or more other partners) is clear to all native speakers of English. Because *copartner* adds nothing to the language, it should be avoided as a NEEDLESS VARIANT. E.g.: "In her firm, which she shares with Amy Newman, Rakinic feels it's a plus having a woman as a *copartner* [read *partner*]." Leslie M. Clouden, "Suburbs Are a Welcome Home for Women Out on Their Own," *Legal Intelligencer*, 10 July 1996, at S1. Cf. **coequal.**

LANGUAGE-CHANGE INDEX
*copartner for *partner*: Stage 1
Current ratio (*partner* vs. *copartner*): 2,052:1

*copartnership is a NEEDLESS VARIANT of *partnership*—e.g.: "Beyond the despotism and repression at home, China's foreign policy isn't worthy of the expanded *copartnership* [read *partnership*] with the United States that Mr. Glickman advocates." "Too Soon for MFN Status," *Wash. Times*, 14 Nov. 1993, at B5.

LANGUAGE-CHANGE INDEX
*copartnership for *partnership*: Stage 1
Current ratio (*partnership* vs. *copartnership*): 377:1

*copasetic; *copesetic; *copesettic. See copacetic.

copse; coppice. In the mid-18th century, Samuel Johnson defined *coppice* as "low woods cut at stated times for fuel; a place overrun with brushwood." (*A Dictionary of the English Language* [1755].) In the etymological note, he added: "It is often written *copse*." In other words, *coppice* (a Latinized spelling) and *copse* (an anglicized phonetic spelling arrived at through the linguistic process known as syncope) are the same word. Both spellings date from the 16th century, and modern desktop dictionaries define the term as "a thicket, grove, or growth of small trees" (*W11*) or "a thicket of small trees or shrubs" (*WNWCD*).

But the two leading desktop dictionaries disagree about which spelling predominates: *W11* puts the main entry under *coppice*, while *WNWCD* puts it under *copse*—each with a cross-reference to the alternative spelling. So which lexicographic team has it right? Merriam-Webster or Webster's New World? The latter. *Copse* outnumbers *coppice* in modern print sources by a 2-to-1 ratio. And so we debouch from the linguistic thicket.

Finally, a tip for scatologically minded word-lovers: many of the most weirdly cognate and thoroughly obscene, cloacal, and stercoraceous words in the English language appear in unabridged dictionaries between *coppice* and *copse*.

Current ratio (*copse* vs. *coppice*): 2:1

copula; cupola. *Copula* = (1) a linking verb, such as *be, feel*, or *seem*, that expresses a state of being rather than action; or (2) a link or connection in general—e.g.: "This is the age of parsing, a word that once referred to the grammatical analysis of sentences. Now it means playing games with words, as Bill Clinton did with the *copula* 'is' in worming his way out of charges of illicit copulation." Rob Morse, "Outlawing Cock and Bull Stories," *S.F. Chron.*, 31 Aug. 2001, at A2. *Cupola* = an arched or domed roof, as on an astronomical observatory.

Through an odd sort of METATHESIS, *copula* wrongly displaces *cupola* fairly often, probably by writers not versed in architecture—e.g.:

- "Each has its own *copula* [read *cupola*], Boston Gables, as well as numerous peaks with windows galore, all topped by a metal roof." Karl Kell, "Abita Man Wakes Up Every

LANGUAGE-CHANGE INDEX (For the full key, see front matter pp. xxxi, l–li.)
Stage 1: Rejected. Stage 2: Widely shunned. Stage 3: Widespread but . . . Stage 4: Ubiquitous but . . . Stage 5: Fully accepted.
Invariably inferior forms marked by asterisk (*). • Ratios represent frequency of prevalent forms vs. variants in current books.

Day in the House of His Dreams," *Times-Picayune* (New Orleans), 30 Sept. 2001, Slidell §, at 4.

- "The home . . . features six bedrooms, six full baths and two half baths, a three-story porch and an octagonal *copula* [read *cupola*]." Brennan Kearney, "For a Family, a House with History and Walls That Seem to Speak," *N.Y. Times*, 17 May 2002, at F7.
- "Naming opportunities remain. . . . [Y]ou could donate $40,000 to name the Garden Café *Copula* [read *cupola*]." Maryalice Koehne, "Donations Campaign Takes Root," *Milwaukee J. Sentinel*, 26 May 2002, at N8. (Since the cupola hasn't been named yet, there's no need to capitalize *cupola* in that sentence as a proper noun.)

LANGUAGE-CHANGE INDEX
copula misused for *cupola*: Stage 1

COPULAS, ADVERBS OR ADJECTIVES AFTER. See ADJECTIVES (E).

copy, v.t., in the sense "to send a copy to" <he copied me on the letter>, is a voguish CASUALISM to be avoided in formal contexts—e.g.: "It is therefore legitimate to *copy* [read *send a copy to*] the recipient's boss." Mark H. McCormack, *What They Don't Teach You at Harvard Business School* 138 (1984).

LANGUAGE-CHANGE INDEX
copy as a verb meaning "to send a copy to": Stage 4

copyeditor; copyediting; copyedit, vb. Each is now preferably a single unhyphenated word—e.g.:

- " 'Copyediting' is one of those made-up words that somehow needed to be written that way. I—and many others before me—made the term one word, even though *Webster's* says that 'copy editor' is two. With 'proofreading' indisputably one word, it seems appropriate that 'copyediting' should be also. And 'copyeditor.' As we shall see, a copyeditor *copyedits* copy. Throughout this book, then, 'copyeditor' and 'copyediting' will be one word." Karen Judd, *Copyediting: A Practical Guide* 1 (1982).
- Elsie M. Stainton, *The Fine Art of Copyediting* (1991).
- "A *copyeditor* found the following ubiquitous error." Mary Newton Bruder, *The Grammar Lady* 126–27 (2000).

copyright, n. & vb., is so spelled. ***Copywrite* is a not infrequent mistake for the verb—e.g.:

- "You said you didn't know the author's name. Well, she's Portia Nelson, and her piece was *copywritten* [read *copyrighted*] in 1985." Jeffrey Zaslow, "Woman Wants to Marry but Boyfriend Says 'No,'" *Chicago Sun-Times*, 1 Dec. 1992, § 2, at 36.
- "Most of the really vicious stuff said, sung and written these days is the work of professional scumbags, syndicated, *copywrited* [read *copyrighted*], mass-marketed and protected by free-speech guarantees." Jack Kisling, "No Joke—It'll Make You Want to Kill," *Denver Post*, 24 Nov. 1996, at H3.
- "Companies also must have formal business plans that outline their potential for increasing jobs and capital investment in the state, and must feature intellectual properties that are patented, *copywritten* [read *are copyrighted*] or are pending for either process." Deborah M. Todd, "House Bill Proposes Tax Break for Angel Investors," *Pitt. Post-Gaz.*, 4 Nov. 2011, at A1.

Still another mistake is ***copywright*—e.g.:

- "Barsky is a partner in Sonnenschein Nath & Rosenthal, where he practices and specializes in intellectual property, trademark and *copywright* [read *copyright*] matters." Jerry

Berger, "Shaping Up at City Hall Won't Be by Jenny Craig," *St. Louis Post-Dispatch*, 8 May 1996, at E1.

- "Raptors forward Walt (The Wizard) Williams was asked if he had the foresight to *copywright* [read *copyright*] the moniker." Bill Harris, "Raptors Watch," *Toronto Sun*, 8 Dec. 1996, Sports §, at 14.

For a similar error, see **playwriting.** For *copyright* as an adjective, see **copyrighted.**

LANGUAGE-CHANGE INDEX
1. **copywrite* for *copyright*: Stage 1
Current ratio (*copyright* vs. **copywrite*): 12,146:1
2. **copywright* for *copyright*: Stage 1
Current ratio (*copyright* vs. **copywright*): 35,979:1

copyrighted; copyright, adj. For the sense "secured or protected by copyright," *copyrighted* is the better and by far the more usual form. As an adjective, the form *copyright* is uncommon enough that it does not sufficiently announce what part of speech it is playing—e.g.: "Thanks and appreciation for the use of *copyright* [read *copyrighted*] material." Jefferson D. Bates, *Writing with Precision* xviii (rev. ed. 1985; repr. 1988).

copyrighter. See **copywriter.**

copywriter; copyrighter. A *copywriter* is a person who writes copy, especially for advertisements and public relations. A *copyrighter* is a person who obtains or owns the copyright to an expressive creation. In that correct sense, the word is a shorter but obscure variant of *copyright owner* or *copyright holder*. It is frequently, however, misused for *copywriter*—e.g.: "About a dozen people turned out. One of them was Robert Montecalvo, a 63-year-old advertising *copyrighter* [read *copywriter*]." Richard Salit, "North Providence Republicans Looking to Get Back in Race," *Providence J.-Bull.*, 28 Feb. 2001, at C1.

LANGUAGE-CHANGE INDEX
copyrighter misused for *copywriter*: Stage 1

coquette /koh-**ket**/ (= a flirtatious girl or woman) is the standard spelling. *Coquet*, a variant, is uncommon—no doubt because, in English, this term has historically been sex-specific. See SEXISM (D).

But *coquet* is perfectly good as a verb meaning either (1) "to behave as a coquette," or (2) "to consider (something) jestingly but not as a serious possibility." Sense 2 isn't sex-specific, but sense 1 usually is—e.g.: "The band is tight. Sharon's rich, sensuous voice *coquets* above the piano, the drums, the bass." Arthur Allen, "When It Comes to Twins, Sometimes It's Hard to Tell the Two Apart," *Wash. Post*, 11 Jan. 1998, Mag. §, at W6. The verb is inflected *coquetted* and *coquetting*.

cord. See **chord.**

cornet; coronet. *Cornet* (/kor-**net**/) = a brass wind instrument somewhat smaller than a trumpet. *Coronet* (/kor-ə-**net**/) = (1) a crown; (2) the joint of skin and horn at the top of a horse's hoof; or (3) (cap.) any of various brands of products, such as Dodge cars or paper towels. The second term is sometimes misused for the first—e.g.: "He played *coronet* [read *cornet*] in the Modern

Woodman's Band and the Browningsville Band." "Garner W. Duvall Sr." (obit.), *Wash. Post*, 31 Aug. 2002, at B9.

LANGUAGE-CHANGE INDEX
coronet misused for *cornet*: Stage 1
Current ratio (*cornet player* vs. **coronet player*): 32:1

cornetist (= a cornet player) has been the standard spelling since the word was first used in the 19th century. **Cornettist* is a variant.

Current ratio: 14:1

cornucopia (= a horn-shaped container filled with fruit and flowers, intended to represent a time of bounty and prosperity) has always (from the 18th century) formed the plural *cornucopias* in AmE. In the late 19th century, the Latinate plural *cornucopiae* became predominant in BrE; that preference has persisted in BrE up to this day. The AmE plural is pronounced /korn-yə-**koh**-pee-əz/, the BrE plural /korn-yə-**koh**-pi-ee/.

corollary; correlation. A *corollary* is a subsidiary proposition inferred from a main proposition—or, by extension, a practical consequence or result. E.g.: "Remember the axiom that says that the bureaucracy expands to use the money available to it? And the *corollary* . . . that if money is not expended, then next year's budget will be trimmed to meet the lesser needs?" James R. Stone, "Use It or Lose It," *Fresno Bee*, 12 Apr. 1999, at B6. A *correlation*, by contrast, is an interdependence between existing phenomena. E.g.: "There doesn't seem to be a proven *correlation* between the rise of baby-proofing and the decline of injury." Mark Stewart, "Locking In Safety," *Wash. Times*, 13 Apr. 1999, at E1.

In recent years, unfortunately, *corollary* has come to be misused for *correlation* (the word far more frequently needed)—e.g.:

- "Rizzo . . . does not see a logical *corollary* [read *correlation*] between accidents, injuries, and a total ban on fireworks sales." Richard Duckett, "Firefighters on Guard for the Fourth," *Telegram & Gaz.* (Worcester), 5 July 1996, at A1.
- "Researchers have found a direct *corollary* [read *correlation*] between the number of hours children watch TV and the number of pounds they weigh." "Not Just Vanity: Obesity Is a Health Problem," *Syracuse Herald-J.*, 2 Nov. 1998, at A6.
- "While there are a lot of *corollaries* [read *correlations*] between where Hardee's is now and where Carl's was four or five years ago, there's one profound difference: Hardee's is a significant player in the breakfast business—something Carl's never was." Greg Johnson, "The Persuaders," *L.A. Times*, 21 Jan. 1999, at C6.

A corollary to the second bulleted example above: there might be a correlation between the number of hours that someone watches TV and that person's tendency to misuse *corollary* for *correlation*.

LANGUAGE-CHANGE INDEX
corollary misused for *correlation*: Stage 1
Current ratio (*a correlation between* vs.
**a corollary between*): 474:1

coronet. See **cornet.**

corpora. See **corpus.**

corporal; corporeal. These terms have undergone DIFFERENTIATION. *Corporal* (/**kor**-pə-rəl/) = of or affecting the body <corporal punishment>. *Corporeal* (/kor-**por**-ee-əl/) = having a physical material body; substantial. E.g.: "Actual people aren't images, but substantial, physical, *corporeal* beings with souls." Larry Woiwode, "Television: The Cyclops That Eats Books," *USA Today* (Mag.), Mar. 1993, at 84.

Corporeal sometimes wrongly displaces *corporal*—e.g.:

- "*Corporeal* [read *Corporal*] punishment is cruel only if it is applied arbitrarily." Edward C. Lanfranco, "A Little Humility and Public Exposure for Taggers Would Be Justified," *Fresno Bee*, 30 Apr. 1994, at B7.
- "The Chapel Hill-Carrboro City Schools is one of about 30 N.C. school systems that have banned *corporeal* [read *corporal*] punishment." Merri Petrovits, "Spanking Issue Continues to Generate Heat," *Chapel Hill Herald*, 3 Jan. 1996, at 6.

LANGUAGE-CHANGE INDEX
**corporeal punishment* for *corporal punishment*: Stage 1
Current ratio (*corporal punishment* vs.
**corporeal punishment*): 47:1

corporeality; corporeity. A distinction is possible. *Corporeality* (/kor-por-ee-**al**-i-tee/) = bodily existence. *Corporeity* (/kor-pə-**ray**-i-tee/) = materiality itself; substantiality; the quality of having substance.

corps. The singular *corps* is pronounced like *core*. The plural form—also spelled *corps*—is pronounced like *cores*. President Barack Obama created a minor furor in February 2010 when he referred to Navy *corpsmen* as /**korps**-mən/ instead of /**kor**-mən/.

corpulence; *corpulency. The predominant literary synonym for *obesity* was **corpulency* in the 18th century. But in the 19th century *corpulence* gradually became the standard term in print sources—first in BrE (about 1850) and then in AmE (about 1870).

Current ratio: 3:1

corpus (= body, either literally or figuratively) traditionally forms the plural form *corpora*. This is the usual plural found in linguistic, legal, medical, and other technical contexts—e.g.:

- "Structural linguists had confined themselves, at least in theory, to describing the sentences found in *corpora*." Graham Wilson, Foreword, *A Linguistics Reader* xxiv (Graham Wilson ed., 1967).
- "There is surely no legal impediment to the distant heirs of that Mongolian potentate adding to the *corpora* of whatever trusts may strike their fancy." David B. Young, "The Pro Tanto Invalidity of Protective Trusts," 78 *Marq. L. Rev.* 807, 835 (1995).

LANGUAGE-CHANGE INDEX (For the full key, see front matter pp. xxxi, l–li.)
Stage 1: Rejected. **Stage 2:** Widely shunned. **Stage 3:** Widespread but . . . **Stage 4:** Ubiquitous but . . . **Stage 5:** Fully accepted.
Invariably inferior forms marked by asterisk (*). • Ratios represent frequency of prevalent forms vs. variants in current books.

- "Inside the penis are two long expandable chambers, filled with spongy tissue, called the *corpora cavernosa*." Steve Sternberg, "Impotence Treatment Keeps Urologists Busy," *Wash. Post*, 5 Nov. 1996, Health §, at 8.

Occasionally the form **corpuses* appears. It might be more immediately recognizable to most people, but it's still rare. See PLURALS (B).

Current ratio (*corpora* vs. **corpuses*): 69:1

corpus delicti—meaning "the body of a crime" and emphatically not "dead body"—is generally outmoded in law, but it still occasionally appears there and elsewhere. In cases of felonious homicide, the *corpus delicti* is usually evidence of a death and of a criminal agency as its cause. This *corpus delicti* is usually established by proof of the dead body and evidence that the death didn't result from natural causes. But the dead body isn't necessary to establish a *corpus delicti*.

Both in and outside law, the phrase is sometimes misspelled **corpus delecti*, a sort of macabre etymological double entendre (Latin *delecti* means "of delight"). E.g.: "The medical examiner will no longer examine the *corpus delecti* [read *corpus delicti*]." Dominic J. Baranello, "E Pluribus Unum? (Or Something)," *N.Y. Times*, 15 Sept. 1996, Long Island §, at 19.

LANGUAGE-CHANGE INDEX
*corpus delecti for *corpus delicti*: Stage 1
Current ratio (*corpus delicti* vs. **corpus delecti*): 14:1

corral, vb. *Corralled* and *corralling* are so spelled—not **corraled* and **corraling*. See SPELLING (B).

correctable. So spelled—not **correctible*. See -ABLE (A).

Current ratio: 17:1

correctional; corrective. *Correctional* = of, relating to, or involving correction, usu. penal correction <correctional officer>. E.g.: "Jack L. Webb, 59, of Haymarket, Va., and Jeffress A. Wells, 60, of Fuquay-Varina, N.C., were fined $2,500 and sentenced to 30 days in a community *correctional* facility and two years' supervised probation." Ruth Larson, "2 Ex-Agriculture Aides Get Jail Time for Clinton Fund Raising," *Wash. Times*, 14 Dec. 1996, at A2. The phrases *correctional facility* and *correctional institution* are really just EUPHEMISMS for *jail* or *prison*.

Corrective = tending to correct <corrective measures>. E.g.:

- "Among its charges, he said, are identifying regulations that should be streamlined or eliminated and developing *corrective* legislation." Raymond W. Vodicka, "Sen. Bond Seeking to Help Businesses," *St. Louis Post-Dispatch*, 15 Dec. 1994, at 1.
- "[There was a] woman with one leg longer than the other, which caused her to walk sideways. The elves arranged for *corrective* surgery." Stacy Downs, "Elves Set to Work This Year's Miracles," *Kansas City Star*, Olathe §, 14 Dec. 1996, at 1.

correctness; correctitude. *Correctness* is the standard noun corresponding to the adjective *correct* in most senses—e.g.:

- "I cannot come to any conclusion as to the *correctness* of one term over another—'hot dog' or 'frank.'" Paul Donohue, "Hope, Skepticism on Arthritis Diets," *St. Louis Post-Dispatch*, 24 Aug. 1995, at G5.
- "But the U.S. believes there is an inherent *correctness* and conviction in its positions with which the rest of the world invariably should agree." Adonis Hoffman, "Increasingly, U.S. Finds Itself Whistling Alone," *Christian Science Monitor*, 13 Dec. 1996, at 18.

Correctitude is a PORTMANTEAU WORD—a blend of *correct* and *rectitude*. It refers to what is proper in conduct or behavior, and it has moralistic overtones, especially in BrE. E.g.:

- "The local political allies of the west tend to be unrepresentative, dissolute or repressive rulers.... Against them Islam seems to provide certainty of belief and *correctitude* of behaviour." Godfrey Jansen, "The Soldiers of Allah," *Economist*, 27 Jan. 1979, at 45 (but since *correctitude* refers to behavior, the last phrase is redundant).
- "It is to Henry VIII that Prince Charles owes the monarchy's anomalous position as supreme head of the Church, Defender of the Faith, by which was meant, at the time, the Catholic faith, in all its Catholic *correctitudes*." Brian Sewell, "Charles and the Rich Royal Legacy of Lust," *Evening Standard*, 3 Sept. 1996, at 11.

In AmE, *correctitude* often has the connotation of too much rectitude—e.g.: "This is period instrument playing of the dour, forbidding sort, all grainy sonorities and joyless *correctitude*." Joshua Kosman, "An Early 'Silla' in Time for Mozart Fest," *S.F. Chron.*, 17 Mar. 1991, Datebook §, at 45.

Since the early '90s, *correctitude* has also sometimes been the choice to form the noun corresponding to *politically correct*. Perhaps the *rectitude* root connotes the elevation of political views to the level of religious fervor—e.g.:

- "One response to PC has been the National Association of Scholars, or NAS, which aims to counter what it sees as the excesses of political *correctitude* with a devotion to what it sees as traditional scholarly values." "'Multiculturalism' Leads to Multifactionalism as Tradition and Change Battle on America's Campuses," *Boston Globe* (City ed.), 7 Apr. 1991, at A23.
- "Political *correctitude* just isn't a worthy goal for any thinking person. And to seek political *correctness* in art is to see art through a distorted prism." Mick LaSalle, "Unreleased Movie on AFI List," *S.F. Chron.*, 4 Jan. 2015, at M26.

Still, *political correctness* remains the usual and preferred phrase. See POLITICAL CORRECTNESS.

correlation (= a proportional correspondence between things) is the standard spelling. **Corelation* is a variant.

For the misuse of *corollary* for *correlation*, see **corollary.**

Current ratio (*correlation* vs. **corelation*): 3,726:1

CORRELATIVE CONJUNCTIONS, or conjunctions used in pairs, should join structurally identical sentence parts, sometimes called "matching parts." Simple nouns never cause problems <neither fish nor fowl>. When we use constructions with phrases and clauses, however, PARALLELISM may become a problem. Following are examples with some of the more common correlative conjunctions:

- **Both . . . and:** "As with the 1983 news coverage, it is through this sort of presentation that horror video watching becomes *both symptomatic* [read *a symptom*] of sickness *and* the precursor of despicable forms of behavior." Peter Fraser, "Nasty . . . But Naughty," *Guardian*, 9 May 1992, at 26. See **both (A).**
- **Either . . . or:** "But here's where the obscenity surfaces: Whenever a black is hired to run anything in professional sports, the inference is always there that he was hired *either* because of affirmative action *or* because of a fluke." Terence Moore, "See Green's Résumé, Not His Color," *Atlanta J.-Const.*, 15 Jan. 1992, at D2. See **either (c).**
- **Neither . . . nor:** "There is little reason to hold manufacturers strictly liable for injuries caused by the misuse of firearms that are *neither* negligently produced *nor* defective in design." Bruce Kobayashi, "Gun-Liability Lawsuits Aim at the Wrong Targets," *San Diego Union-Trib.*, 5 July 1996, at B7. See **neither . . . nor.**

Some of the other common correlatives in English are:

- *although . . . nevertheless;*
- *although . . . yet;*
- *as . . . as;*
- *as . . . so;*
- *if . . . then;*
- *just as . . . so (also);*
- *not only . . . but also;*
- *notwithstanding . . . yet;*
- *since . . . therefore;*
- *so . . . that;*
- *when . . . then;*
- *where . . . there;* and
- *whether . . . or.*

correspondent; co(-)respondent. A *correspondent* is a person who communicates regularly in writing with another person or a (usu. professional) person who makes reports or sends dispatches from a place where something significant is taking or has taken place. In American law, a *corespondent* (so spelled, without a hyphen) is (1) a coparty who responds to a petition; (2) (only in some states) a coparty who responds to an appeal; or (3) in a divorce case, a paramour who is named or sued by the injured spouse. Only sense 3 of *co-respondent* (so spelled) applies in BrE.

corrigendum; erratum. These words are used synonymously to denote a printing error discovered only after the work has gone to press. *Corrigendum* (lit., "a thing to be corrected") is perhaps technically more accurate (since a correction is being made). But *erratum* (lit., "error") is older in English and more common. The plurals are *corrigenda* and *errata*—and they occur more frequently than the singulars. See **errata.**

corroborate. A. Senses and Uses. *Corroborate* = (1) to support (a statement, argument, etc.) with evidence that is consistent; to confirm; or (2) to confirm formally (a law, etc.). Sense 1 is more common—e.g.: "Experts said a major issue when recovered-memory cases go to court is the lack of *corroborating* evidence, often because the allegations date so far back." Jeremy Olson, "Repressed Memories a Gray Area," *Omaha World-Herald* (Midlands ed.), 25 Sept. 2002, at A1.

In either sense, this verb is transitive <the last witness corroborated the testimony of other witnesses>. Hence **corroborate with* is inferior to *corroborate*. In the PASSIVE VOICE, the phrasing *corroborated by* is usual—e.g.: "The novelists Gaskell and Disraeli and Hardy were not so naive, and their realism is *corroborated by* this book." "Compassionate Curiosity," *Economist*, 25 Jan. 1975, at 96. See -ABLE (D), -ATABLE & SPELLING (A).

B. Pronunciation. In October 1991, during Justice Clarence Thomas's confirmation hearings, Senator Joseph Biden and other members of the Senate Judiciary Committee consistently mispronounced this word as if it were *cooberate*—like *cooperate* with a *-b-* instead of a *-p-*. The correct pronunciation is /kə-**rob**-ə-rayt/.

C. And *collaborate*. The word *corroborate* is occasionally used where *collaborate* (= to work jointly with [another] in producing) belongs—e.g.: "The family *corroborated* [read *collaborated*] on a project to replicate a 1705 microscope." Edythe Jensen, "Family Turns Hobbies into Businesses," *Ariz. Republic/Phoenix Gaz.*, 5 Nov. 1994, Tempe §, at 1.

The opposite error (*collaborate* for *corroborate*) is also all too frequent—e.g.: "[Suicide expert Frank] Campbell said it was insulting that the board discounted the woman's testimony that was *collaborated* [read *corroborated*] by an outside licensed professional counselor." Amy Wold, "Suicide Agency Official Appeals Decision on Violations," *Advocate* (Baton Rouge), 31 Aug. 2001, at A14.

LANGUAGE-CHANGE INDEX
1. *corroborate* misused for *collaborate*: Stage 1
Current ratio (*collaborated on* vs.
**corroborated on*): 78:1
2. *collaborate* misused for *corroborate*: Stage 1
Current ratio (*was corroborated by* vs.
**was collaborated by*): 158:1

corroborative; *corroboratory*. The first is standard; the second is a NEEDLESS VARIANT. Despite the supremacy of *corroborative*, the phrase *corroborating evidence* is now much more common than *corroborative evidence*.

Current ratio (*corroborative* vs. **corroboratory*): 28:1

corrodible (= susceptible to corrosion) is so spelled—not **corrodable*. Another variant form, **corrosible*, is less than desirable because it doesn't readily suggest the underlying verb, *corrode*; it is also less common. See -ABLE (A).

LANGUAGE-CHANGE INDEX (For the full key, see front matter pp. xxxi, l–li.)
Stage 1: Rejected. **Stage 2:** Widely shunned. **Stage 3:** Widespread but . . . **Stage 4:** Ubiquitous but . . . **Stage 5:** Fully accepted.
Invariably inferior forms marked by asterisk (*). • Ratios represent frequency of prevalent forms vs. variants in current books.

corrupter; **corruptor.* The *-er* spelling has always predominated and is therefore preferred. See -ER (A).

Current ratio: 4:1

corruptible. So spelled—not **corruptable.* See -ABLE (A).

Current ratio: 689:1

cortex (= the outer layer of a bodily organ, esp. the brain) has predominantly formed the plural *cortices* since the 17th century. *Cortexes* is a latecoming variant. In print sources today, *cortices* predominates. The corresponding adjective is *cortical* /**kor**-ti-kəl/.

Current ratio: 30:1

*cosey; *cosie. See **cozy.**

cosset. *Cosseted* and *cosseting* are so spelled—not **cossetted* and **cossetting.* See SPELLING (B).

cost > cost > cost. This is the normal way to inflect this verb. But when the sense is "to determine the cost of," the past tense and past participle both become *costed*— e.g.: "Its plan to rebuild the Royal Shakespeare Theatre at Stratford, originally *costed* at £80 million, is also one of three Lottery projects still earmarked for Arts Council support." Penny Layden, "£50m Lifeline for Arts Gives New Hope to 'Ailing' RSC," *Evening Standard,* 5 Jan. 1999, at 9. This usage is especially common in BrE; in AmE the common choice is *estimated.*

The past-participial adjective likewise appears frequently—e.g.: "Birmingham's National Exhibition Centre put in a full *costed* bid for a green-field site on the edge of the city." Chris Gray, "Charles Falconer," *Birmingham Post,* 8 Jan. 1999, at 13. See IRREGULAR VERBS.

cost-effective; cost-efficient. These are the current jargonistic adjectival phrases for *economical. Cost-effective* is about 12 times as common in modern print sources as *cost-efficient.* See VOGUE WORDS.

*cosy. See **cozy.**

*cotemporary; *cotemporaneous. See **contemporary.**

cotenant. In AmE, no hyphen appears: *cotenant,* not *co-tenant.* In BrE, the hyphenated form predominates.

coterminous; *coterminant; *coterminate; *coterminal. See **conterminous.**

could. See **can** (B).

*could care less. See **couldn't care less.**

*could might. See DOUBLE MODALS.

could not help but. See **cannot help but.**

couldn't care less is the correct and logical phrasing, not **could care less*—e.g.: "The American people *could care less* [read *couldn't care less*] who's White House Chief of Staff." George Will, on *This Week with David Brinkley,* 3 July 1994. If you *could* care less, you're

saying that you do care *some.* Invariably, though, writers and speakers who use the phrase mean that they don't care at all.

In modern AmE print sources, *couldn't* (or *could not) care less* predominates over **could care less* by a 2-to-1 margin. And the erroneous version is even rarer in published BrE.

Although some apologists argue that **could care less* is meant to be sarcastic and not to be taken literally, a more plausible explanation is that the *-n't* of *couldn't* has been garbled in sloppy speech and sloppy writing. As a linguist explains: "A listener has not heard the whole phrase; he has heard a slurred form. *Couldn't care* has two dental stops practically together, *dnt.* This is heard only as *d* and slurring results. The outcome is *I c'd care less.*" Atcheson L. Hench, "Could(n't) Care Less," 48 *Am. Speech* 159, 159 (1973). For a careful seven-step explication of the loss of this alveolar closure, see James Sledd, "[kŭt] [kŭt] Be [kŭt], [kŭt] It?" 68 *Am. Speech* 218–19 (1993). See ILLOGIC (A) & **underestimate.**

LANGUAGE-CHANGE INDEX
*could care less for *couldn't care less:* Stage 4
Current ratio *(couldn't care less* vs.
*could care less): 2:1

*could of. See **of** (D).

council; counsel. *Council* (= a deliberative assembly) is primarily a noun. *Counsel* (= to advise) is primarily a verb, but in legal writing it's commonly used as a noun meaning "a legal adviser or group of legal advisers" <counsel for the corporation>. See **counsel** & **consul.**

councillor; counselor. A *councillor* is a member of a council. (**Councilor* is a variant spelling.) A *counselor* is either someone who gives advice (such as personal advice) or a lawyer. (In BrE, it's spelled *counsellor.*) See **lawyer.** Cf. **counselor.**

councilmanic, a 19th-century AmE coinage, is the unfortunate—and the only—adjective corresponding to *councilman.* E.g.: "Bill Cirocco was appointed at that time to fill her vacant *councilmanic* seat." Nancy Gish, "Murdoch Sworn In to First Full Term," *Buffalo News,* 2 Jan. 1997, at B5. Of course, *council seat* or *seat on the council* would be much better in that sentence. See SEXISM (C).

council member. Two words for now, but there is a trend to join them into one.

counsel. A. Scope of Term. In BrE, *counsel* is used only of barristers (litigators), whereas in AmE it is frequently used of office practitioners (e.g., *general counsel*) as well as of litigators. See **lawyer, consul** & **council.**

B. Number. *Counsel* may be either singular or plural. In practice it is usually indeterminate <right to counsel> or plural <all counsel were present>—e.g.:

- "'I'm always hesitant to interfere with cases, especially where you have two *counsel* present.'" "A Conversation with Judge H. Terry Grimes," *Pa. Law Weekly,* 5 Dec. 1994, at 7.

- "Dickstein, Shapiro & Morin, one of Washington's largest law firms, said yesterday that it has hired 13 partners and three *counsel* and made offers to more than 20 associate attorneys from Anderson Kill Olick & Oshinsky." David Segal, "New York Insurance Law Specialists Defect to Dickstein, Shapiro & Morin," *Wash. Post*, 13 June 1996, at D11.

But examples of the singular are common enough—e.g.:

- "There is no excuse for a *counsel* who has obtained a thorough understanding of the case at bar . . . presenting to the court a statement [that] has no definite plan, [that] mingles material and immaterial facts, and [that] is verbose and discursive." William M. Lile et al., *Brief Making and the Use of Law Books* 370 (3d ed. 1914).
- "*Counsel* arguing a case is permitted to assert that a precedent has had unhappy consequences." Michael Zander, *The Law-Making Process* 239 (2d ed. 1985).
- "Bondi submitted a response to a motion last month to the appeals court that claims opposing *counsel* is not 'entitled to appellate attorney's fees' because she dropped her appeal after the U.S. Supreme Court legalized same-sex marriage." "Bondi's Bills for Crusade Coming Due," *Tampa Bay Times*, 9 Sept. 2015, at A8.

Counsels is sometimes mistakenly used as a plural of *counsel*—especially when nonlawyers are writing about the law. Part of this tendency comes from the popularization of the phrases *independent counsel* and *general counsel*. At the federal level, there are occasionally calls for *an independent counsel* to be appointed. And if two are needed, the tendency is to say *two independent counsels*. That makes the third example below understandable—even acceptable—but it doesn't excuse the first two:

- "This might seem a strange approach for *counsels* [read *counsel*] responsible for representing not just Valeo and Henshaw but the interests of their employers, the U.S. House and Senate, as well." Barbara H. Craig, *Chadha: The Story of an Epic Constitutional Struggle* 73 (1988).
- "Four lawyers were named Nov. 25 to serve as legal *counsels* [read *counsel*] for the transition." "Clinton's Justice Review Team Named," *Nat'l L.J.*, 7 Dec. 1992, at 2.
- "Independent *counsels* were created under a 1978 law that Congress allowed to expire in 1992." Tony Mauro, "The Investigators: 2 Types of *Counsels*," *USA Today*, 13 Jan. 1994, at A5.

counsel of perfection = (1) orig., advice of Jesus on ways to strive for perfection, given in Matthew 19; (2) consequently, the virtues of obedience, chastity, and charity appearing in the vows of monastic orders; or (3) a noble but unattainable ideal.

While the phrase itself is uncommon in general use, the allusive sense 3 comes up occasionally—e.g.: "A professor at my seminary, Jacob Rader Marcus, once said, 'It may well be that we cannot love our neighbor as we love ourselves—that is a *counsel of perfection*—but the least we can do is to tolerate him and his differences.'" James A. Gibson, "Muslims Grievously Offended by Caricatures of Mohammed Are Justified," *Pitt. Post-Gaz.*, 12 Feb. 2006, at J1.

The phrase is furthest from perfection when it merely denotes casual advice—e.g.: "In Cantonese Roasted Duck ($14.95), the skin had been rendered almost free of fat, while remaining richly flavored. In a *counsel of perfection*, some of the meat was a little dry but tender and revealing solid depth of flavor." John Batchelor, "This Experience Is Worth the Wait," *News & Record* (Greensboro), 17 Aug. 2006, at GT27. One wonders at the writer's intention there.

counselor, counsellor; counseled, counselled; counseling, counselling; counselable, counsellable. The preferred spellings are *counselor, counseled, counseling*, and *counselable* in AmE, and *counsellor, counselled, counselling*, and *counsellable* in BrE. See SPELLING (B). For the sense in which *counselor* means "lawyer," see **lawyer.** Cf. **councillor.**

counterfeit; imitation; forgery. These words overlap to some degree. Although something *counterfeit* is always an *imitation*, an *imitation* may not be *counterfeit*. A *counterfeit* article is an imitation produced in violation of a law. For example, if the law requires a license to reproduce or copy something or forbids representing a reproduction or copy as genuine, or altogether forbids an item's reproduction, then an item made or sold in violation of the law is *counterfeit* <the flea-market seller said the counterfeit "Gucci" handbags from China were discounted factory seconds from Italy>.

An *imitation* is an exact copy, or a thing made to resemble something else. It is usually identified as a copy <the label says "imitation leather">.

A *forgery* is a document made or altered in a way that harms another's rights. Before the advent of paper money, the distinction between *forgery* and *counterfeiting* was clear because *counterfeiting* referred only to the making of false metallic coins. Once money began to grow on trees, however, criminals looked for ways to copy it—and this activity also came to be known as *counterfeiting*. Today, the usual expressions are *counterfeit a $20 bill* and *forge a check*.

counterterrorism. See **antiterrorism.**

countless applies only to count nouns. So you might refer to *countless bags* but not to **countless baggage*. See COUNT NOUNS AND MASS NOUNS.

COUNT NOUNS AND MASS NOUNS. Count nouns are those that denote enumerable things and that are capable of forming plurals (e.g., *cranes, parties, minivans, oxen*); mass (noncount) nouns are often abstract nouns—they cannot be enumerated (e.g., *insurance, courage, mud*). Many nouns can be both count <he gave several talks> and mass <talk is cheap>, depending on the sense. These are few, however, in

LANGUAGE-CHANGE INDEX (For the full key, see front matter pp. xxxi, l–li.)
Stage 1: Rejected. **Stage 2:** Widely shunned. **Stage 3:** Widespread but . . . **Stage 4:** Ubiquitous but . . . **Stage 5:** Fully accepted.
Invariably inferior forms marked by asterisk (*). • Ratios represent frequency of prevalent forms vs. variants in current books.

comparison to the nouns that are exclusively either count or mass. Use of these two types of nouns may introduce problems with number, especially when the use of count nouns strays into a use of mass nouns or vice versa. See PLURALS (J).

coup de grâce /koo də **grahs**/ means "a blow of mercy," a compassionate act that puts a mortally wounded person or animal out of misery. The phrase is sometimes mispronounced /koo də **grah**/, as if the last word were spelled *gras* (as in *pâté de foie gras*). But worse than that, the phrase is sometimes mistakenly written **coup de gras*—e.g.:

- "Lady Thatcher may not be indestructible, but her memoirs show that anyone seeking to apply the *coup de gras* [read *coup de grâce*] will have to pay highly for the privilege." Philip Ziegler, "Thatcher Memoirs," *Daily Telegraph*, 18 Oct. 1993, at 4.
- "Keith pulled up and hit a wide-open Chris Federico for the *coup de gras* [read *coup de grâce*] and a 19–7 lead with 6:50 remaining in the game." John Devlin, "A League Title on the Horizon," *Denver Post*, 22 Oct. 1994, at D4.
- "Lori's win was the *coup de gras* [read *coup de grâce*] of Troy's 13–5 victory over Sunny Hills, which had won 20 straight league championships until this year." Craig Outhier, "The Judds: Mother-Daughter Tennis Duo Help Propel Troy into Playoffs," *Orange County Register*, 14 Nov. 1996, at 18.

Even the sense is sometimes mangled. To make *coup de grâce* cruel, bloody, and painful is to torture the phrase—e.g.: "I saw a fox being torn to pieces by a pack of hounds. It was the final act, *the coup de gras* [delete erroneous phrase] in what we call a country sport." Michael Herd, "This Land of No Hope and Gory Pursuit," *Evening Standard*, 30 Dec. 1993, at 46.

LANGUAGE-CHANGE INDEX
1. *coup de grâce* mispronounced
/koo də **grah**/: Stage 2
2. **coup de gras* for *coup de grâce*: Stage 1
Current ratio (*coup de grâce* vs. **coup de gras*): 75:1

couple. A. Number. *Couple* (= pair) is a COLLECTIVE NOUN like *team*, *company*, or *faculty*. As a rule, a collective noun in AmE takes a singular verb unless the action is clearly that of the individual participants rather than collective. When two people form a couple, they may act as individuals <the couple plan to take jobs in Philadelphia> or as a single entity <the couple is buying a house>. But unlike other collective nouns, *couple* should take a plural verb far more often than a singular one. The plural construction is also far more convenient because it eliminates the need to find a suitable pronoun.

Other collective nouns don't present this problem. When the noun is, say, *team*, we have no trouble referring to *its* win–loss record. But the neuter pronoun *it* feels too impersonal to use with as intimate a word as *couple*. So we sometimes see a sentence with *couple* as a subject, a singular verb, and a plural pronoun—e.g.: "In the pilot, one *couple is* having a sexual 'dry spell' in *their* marriage." "Looking for Laughs This TV Season?

Keep Flipping," *Austin Am.-Statesman*, 15 Sept. 2002, Show World §, at 4. There is no graceful fix in these situations—the grammatically correct one, changing *is* to *are*, is especially jarring here because *one couple* seems to demand *is*. It is possible, however, to rewrite: *In the pilot, one of the married couples is having a sexual "dry spell."* See PREVENTIVE GRAMMAR.

B. For *a few*. As a noun, *couple* has traditionally denoted a pair. (As a verb, it always denotes the joining of two things.) But in some uses, the precise number is vague. Essentially, it's equivalent to *a few* or *several*. In informal contexts this usage is quite common and unexceptionable—e.g.:

- "This slick, cozy shop, which underwent a makeover a *couple of years* back, is a hybrid of takeout and restaurant." A.C. Stevens, "Why Cook Tonight?" *Boston Herald*, 15 Sept. 2002, Food §, at 65.
- "Those most anxious should practice at least once in front of a *couple of people* to be comfortable with an audience." Molly Williamson, "Unlocking the Power of Public Speaking," *Milwaukee J. Sentinel*, 15 Sept. 2002, at L12.

C. With or Without *of*. The traditional use of *couple* has been as a noun, usually meaning "two" (but see (B)). As a noun, it requires the preposition *of* to link it to another noun <a couple of dollars>. Using *couple* as an adjective directly before the noun has been very much on the rise since the late 20th century <a couple dollars>. This innovation strikes many readers as unidiomatic and awkward—or perhaps downright wrong. But the change will doubtless continue. That is, the age-old expression *a couple of people* will become **a couple people*. For now, the traditional phrasing is still eight times as common as the adjectival use in modern print sources—e.g.:

- "Philip Walker's press clippings singing the bluesman's praises take *a couple of people* to lift." Dan Nailen & Jesus Lopez Jr., "Out & About," *Salt Lake Trib.*, 21 June 2002, at E12.
- "I was blocking the view of *a couple of people* in the rows behind me." Judith Martin, "Taking the Other Root," *Wash. Post*, 14 Aug. 2002, at C11.

But the clipped phrasing, a low CASUALISM, does surface in print—e.g.: "I mentioned to *a couple people* [read *a couple of people*] that the golf courses get paid whether people play or not." Bob Bestler, "Fair Weather Finds a Way During Event," *Sun-News* (Myrtle Beach, S.C.), 29 Aug. 2002, at B1.

When the phrasing is changed, the relative frequency in usage changes. The phrase *couple of things* is about eight times as common in print sources as **couple things*—e.g.: "We will always be able to look back and say a *couple of things*." Joe Logan, "Andrade Holds On," *Phil. Inquirer*, 15 Sept. 2002, at D1. But *couple of hundred things* is not even twice as common as *couple hundred things*. When a numerical term follows *couple*, many writers delete the idiomatic *of*. Examples can be found of both types (the *of* versions consistently appearing 30–40% more often than the *of*-less versions)—e.g.:

- "De Bizemont sells only to interior designers and other members of the trade, at wholesale prices ranging from a *couple of hundred* dollars to several thousand." Kim Boatman, "For a Warm, Homey and Colorful Touch, Try Fabric," *Chicago Trib.*, 8 Sept. 2002, at 10.
- "Every Wednesday and Friday a *couple of dozen* members turn out for boozy money games." Alan Shipnuck, "Life of the Party," *Sports Illustrated*, 9 Sept. 2002, at 52.
- "A *couple of thousand* fans were in the stands." Paul Meyer, "Notebook," *Pitt. Post-Gaz.*, 12 Sept. 2002, at D3.

In each of those sentences, some writers wouldn't use the *of* after *couple*.

This shift in usage may be fully acceptable someday. Perhaps everyone will come to use *couple* as an adjective. (See FUNCTIONAL SHIFT (B).) Words can and often do change their parts of speech. After all, the word *couple* is firmly established in one adverbial use (see (D)). But idiom has not yet admitted this casual expression as standard.

For the foreseeable future, editors will be justified in editing sentences such as the following:

- "A *couple things* [read *couple of things*] need to be mentioned." Mark Knudson, "Items That Need Sorting," *Ft. Collins Coloradoan*, 8 Sept. 2002, at D2.
- "Auto makers offer GPS in their new cars as an upgrade, for a *couple thousand* [read *couple of thousand*] dollars." Elliot Spagat, "Hand-Held Homing Devices," *Wall Street J.*, 11 Sept. 2002, at D2.
- "Only a *couple dozen* [read *couple of dozen*] members signed up." Bruce Mohl, "War Fears Put Pressure on Heating Oil Prices," *Boston Globe*, 15 Sept. 2002, at C3.

For just the opposite tendency—the intrusive *of*—see **of** (B). Cf. **type of**.

LANGUAGE-CHANGE INDEX
couple things for *couple of things*: Stage 2
Current ratio (*couple of things* vs. **couple things*): 8:1

D. With Words of Comparison. When *couple* is used with comparison words such as *more*, *fewer*, and *too many*, the *of* is omitted <have a couple more shrimp>. In the predicate of the previous example, *shrimp* is the direct object. It is modified by the adjective *more*, which in turn is modified by the adverbial phrase *a couple*. There is no place in the example for *of* (neither **a couple of more shrimp* nor **a couple more of shrimp* makes sense). But if the informal sentence structure can be slightly inverted, the *of* becomes idiomatic again <I'll have a couple of shrimp more>. E.g.:

- "The way Padraig Harrington sees it, he played nothing but good shots at the par-5 13th hole, just a *couple too many*." Phil Richards, "Palmer's Final Round Not Quite Finished," *Indianapolis Star*, 13 Apr. 2002, at D8.
- "He launched a *couple more* ringers from his black-gloved hands before calling it a day just after 1 p.m. Saturday." Justin Kmitch, "Last Day for Last Fling," *Daily Herald* (Chicago), 2 Sept. 2002, Neighbor §, at 1.

coupled with, like *together with* and *accompanied by*, is used with a singular and not a plural verb when the first of the two nouns is singular <a cup of coffee, coupled with two eggs over easy, makes up her morning ritual>. See SUBJECT–VERB AGREEMENT (E).

couple (of) dozen, hundred, etc. See **couple** (C).

coupon should be pronounced /**koo**-pon/, not /**kyoo**-pon/. The mispronunciation betrays an ignorance of French and the finer points of English. Imagine *coup d'etat* pronounced with /kyoo/ as the first syllable. See PRONUNCIATION (B).

LANGUAGE-CHANGE INDEX
coupon pronounced /kyoo/ instead of /koo/: Stage 4

courtesan (= a prostitute who caters to rich customers) is the standard spelling. **Courtezan* is a variant. It is pronounced /**kor**-tə-zən/.

Current ratio: 32:1

courthouse. One word.

court judgment. See **judgment** (C).

court-martial. A. Generally. *Court-martial* (= an ad hoc military court convened to try and to punish those accused of violating military law) is hyphenated both as noun and as verb. The *OED* lists the verb as colloquial, an observation now antiquated. As to spelling, in AmE the final *-l* is not doubled in *court-martialed* and *court-martialing*, although in BrE it is. (See SPELLING (B).)

The plural of the noun is *courts-martial*. See PLURALS (G) & POSTPOSITIVE ADJECTIVES.

B. And *court marshal*. One meaning of *marshal* is "a judicial officer who provides court security, executes process, and performs other tasks for the court" (*Black's Law Dictionary* 1121 [10th ed. 2014]). It's therefore not surprising that *court marshal* has become a frequent phrase—e.g.:

- "He became *court marshal* in 1989 and would start each court session by calling, 'Oyez, oyez.' " "Cancer Kills High Court Marshal," *Charleston Gaz.*, 7 July 1995, at C2.
- "Mr. Moskowitz and the construction workers refused to leave until last week's visit by *court marshals*." Mark Francis Cohen, "At Former Synagogue, Proper Burial an End to Seamy Chapter," *N.Y. Times*, 26 Jan. 1997, § 13, at 7.

Not surprisingly, therefore, the phrase *court-martial* is now often mistakenly written **court marshal*—e.g.:

- "A lieutenant gave him a summary *court marshal* [read *court-martial*], fined him $25 and booted him out of headquarters." Tom Bell, " 'I Was Patton's Barber,' " *Anchorage Daily News*, 27 July 1995, at E1.
- "A veritable platoon of foot soldiers from both sides have been whistled off on enforced leave, whether by official *court marshal* [read *court-martial*] or injury in action." Mike Davidson, "Calling Time on This Unhealthy Obsession," *Daily Mail*, 3 Mar. 1997, at 61.

LANGUAGE-CHANGE INDEX (For the full key, see front matter pp. xxxi, l–li.)
Stage 1: Rejected. **Stage 2:** Widely shunned. **Stage 3:** Widespread but . . . **Stage 4:** Ubiquitous but . . . **Stage 5:** Fully accepted.
Invariably inferior forms marked by asterisk (*). • Ratios represent frequency of prevalent forms vs. variants in current books.

- "The Civil War re-enactment will include demonstrations of battles, house-to-house skirmishes, a *court marshal* [read *court-martial*] and an execution." Barri Bronston, "Parents and Children," *Times-Picayune* (New Orleans), 3 Mar. 1997, at C3.

See **marshal**.

LANGUAGE-CHANGE INDEX
court marshal for *court-martial*: Stage 1
Current ratio (*court-martialed* vs. *court-marshaled* vs. *court-marshalled*): 78:1:1

court of appeals; court of appeal. Both forms occur in AmE, but *court of appeals* is more common. (*Court of appeal*, though, is the only form in BrE.) The correct form is the one that is statutorily prescribed or customary in a given jurisdiction. For example, although most appellate courts in the United States are individually called a *court of appeals*, the term in California and Louisiana is *court of appeal*.

The plural forms are *courts of appeals* and *courts of appeal*. The singular possessive forms are *court of appeals'* and *court of appeal's*; the plural possessives are *courts of appeals'* and *courts of appeal's*.

Court of St. James's = the British royal court. Although one sometimes encounters **Court of St. James*, even in BrE, the better and more traditional form is *Court of St. James's*. E.g.: "In 1938, Mrs. Kennedy accompanied her husband to the Court of St. *James* [read *James's*] and was formally welcomed by King George VI." Robert D. McFadden, "Rose Kennedy, Political Matriarch, Dies at 104," *N.Y. Times*, 23 Jan. 1995, at A1, B7. Despite appearing to be a redundant double possessive, *Court of St. James's* is historically accurate because the former seat of the British court in London is St. James's Palace. So in *Court of St. James's*, the term *Palace* has historically been an UNDERSTOOD WORD at the end. Cf. POSSESSIVES (D).

LANGUAGE-CHANGE INDEX
Court of St. James for Court of St. James's: Stage 4

courtroom. So spelled—without a space or a hyphen.

cousinhood; cousinage. *Cousinage* has the disadvantage of possible confusion with an unsavory homophone, *cozenage* (= fraud). So *cousinhood* might therefore be considered preferable. In any event, *cousinhood* greatly predominates in modern print sources.

*couth, a BACK-FORMATION from *uncouth*, has long been disapproved by usage authorities. The *OED* records the word as a Scotticism meaning "kind, affable, agreeable, pleasant," from the 14th century. But its new incarnation (in the sense "cultured, civilized") first appeared in the late 19th century as a direct antonym of *uncouth*. In short, some people consider **couth* an uncouth word. Its popularity ebbed over the course of the 20th century.

LANGUAGE-CHANGE INDEX
couth as an antonym of uncouth: Stage 4

coverage. This word has traditionally been used in the singular as a mass noun, but in modern insurance parlance it has increasingly come to be used in the plural as a count noun. This example shows both uses—e.g.: "Today, 24-hour *coverage* is generally the centralized, and, in some cases, integrated management and administration of the separate insurance *coverages* that are packaged as a product." Edward Zutler, "Agents, Brokers Must Respond to 24-Hour Challenge," *Nat'l Underwriter*, 23 Sept. 1996, at 19. Here, *coverage* is a mass noun like *protection*, but *coverages* is a count noun like *policies*. (Also, in the quoted sentence the phrase *and, in some cases, integrated* should be placed in parentheses or set off by em-dashes—without the comma before *and*.) See COUNT NOUNS AND MASS NOUNS & PLURALS (J).

covert was traditionally pronounced like *covered*, except with a *-t* at the end: /kəv-ərt/. Still, /koh-vərt/, nearly rhyming with *overt* (but for the stress), is the more common pronunciation in AmE nowadays.

covetous /kəv-ə-təs/ is so spelled—not **coveteous*.

coworker. So spelled—without a hyphen. Cf. CO- & **coowner.**

cowrie (= [1] a gastropod that inhabits warm seas and produces a brightly colored shell, or [2] the shell of this creature, esp. as once used as a medium of exchange in parts of Africa and Asia) has been predominantly so spelled since the 1920s. **Cowry* is a variant spelling.

cowrite. See **author**, v.t. (A).

coxcomb. See **cockscomb**.

coxswain; *cockswain. Both spellings are pronounced /kok-sən/. The word denotes a sailor who steers the ship and is in charge of the crew. Most dictionaries, American and British, correctly list *coxswain* as the main headword. It has greatly predominated since the 18th century.

Current ratio: 7:1

coyote. In standard American speech, this word is pronounced /kı-yoh-tee/. But in the western United States, the pronunciation /kı-oht/ is often heard.

According to Charles Harrington Elster, both pronunciations have been acceptable since the word was first recorded in dictionaries in the late 19th century. The two-syllable version dominated until the 1960s, when "the weight of authority . . . shifted" to the latter, with the two-syllable version "heard chiefly in the western United States." *BBBM* at 113. Unsurprisingly, the mascot of the University of South Dakota is pronounced /kı-oht/.

cozen /kəz-ən/ is a literary and archaic word meaning "to cheat"—e.g.:

- "We're being had, you know. *Cozened*, gulled, bamboozled, and led up the garden path by the usual suspects." Walter Stewart, "At the Mercy of Money Traders," *Toronto Sun*, 30 Jan. 1995, at 11.

- "Street-smart prisoners may think they are clever enough to outsmart any cop, but they can often be *cozened* by detectives who know their culture, as it were." Nat Hentoff, "Yes, Officer, I Want to Confess," *Village Voice*, 26 Mar. 1996, at 9.
- "Contrived complexity is at the heart of almost all white-collar fraud. Corporate *cozeners* are praying that the public will soon tire of legal polysyllabics, and go looking for activity that can be capsulized in four-letter words." Don Bauder, "Bored by Boardrooms, Bedazzled by Bedrooms," *San Diego Union-Trib.*, 14 July 2002, at H2.

But some writers, engaging in a recent misusage, have apparently misinterpreted the word as if it meant "coddled" or "pampered"—e.g.:

- "These plants will acquire strength and size until they are ready to be sent into the fields to continue their new life. They will be *cozened* [read *coddled* or *nurtured*?] just as a new child in the family would be flattered and protected." "Truckpatch Remembered," *Wash. Post*, 1 Mar. 1995, Food §, at E1.
- "Today's car is designed to soothe and placate victims of road angst; it is a place where naked id is cuddled, coddled and *cozened* [read *cozied*?]." Bob Wiemer, "Dump Car Phones, but Keep the Fuzzy Dice," *Newsday* (N.Y.), 12 Feb. 1996, at A26.
- "Strictly for women, it *hearkens* [read *harks*] back to the days when very rich, very *cozened* [read *pampered*?] women arrived by chauffeured limo with Louis Vuitton trunks stuffed with cocktail dresses for dinner." Cynthia Robbins, "Guilty Pleasures," *S.F. Examiner* (Mag.), 14 July 1996, at M15. (For the reason for changing *hearkens* in that sentence, see **hark back (A).**)
- "Coupled with Matamoros' gift for stillness, it all creates a *cozening* [read *comfortable* or *cozy*?] bed of sound in which memories blossom and occasionally burst into flame in ways we've rarely seen before." John Coulbourn, "A New Moon Rising," *Toronto Sun*, 1 Nov. 1996, at 7.

Other writers seem to want the word to mean "summon"—e.g.:

- "Barkers *cozened* [read *hailed*?] her as she passed—'Step right up! Step right up and have a go!'" Annette Curtis Klause, "The Hoppins," in *Short Circuits* 183, 186 (Donald R. Gallo ed., 1992).
- "She stood staring at her own ring finger, remembering as if *cozening* [read *summoning*?] back a dream . . . ." Nancy Springer, "Mariposa," in *Firebirds* 107, 120 (Sharyn November ed., 2003).

LANGUAGE-CHANGE INDEX
1. *cozen* misused for *coddle*: Stage 1
2. *cozen* misused to mean "summon": Stage 1

cozy (= warm and comfortable) is the standard spelling. (The covering for a teapot is a *tea cozy*.) *Cosy*, *cosey*, *cosie*, *cozie*, and *cozey* are variant forms.
Current ratio (in order of spellings within entry):
4,057:1,903:186:9:4:1

-CRACY. See GOVERNMENTAL FORMS.

craft brewery. See **microbrewery.**

cramp one's style. This is the SET PHRASE meaning "(of an outside influence) to interfere with one's freedom to act"—e.g.: "Producers say the minimum requirements *cramp* artistic style and lead to the unnecessary hiring of additional musicians." Tania Padgett, "Broadway Musician Walkout Looming," *Newsday* (N.Y.), 2 Mar. 2003, at A16.

Some writers change *cramp* to *crimp* (= to make pinched or bent), perhaps because the phrase *put a crimp in* has a similar meaning: "to hurt (something's) chances." But it isn't idiomatic to say that something *crimps someone's style*, much as the writers may complain that this stricture is cramping their style—e.g.:

- "Bush . . . seems determined to avoid letting new fears for his safety *crimp* [read *cramp*] his style." Mike Allen, "In Wyo., Bush Opts Not to Catch Their Drift," *Wash. Post*, 10 Feb. 2002, at A5.
- "Health-conscious Americans might suspect the new rules are an effort to shield non-smokers from second-hand smoke, or to *crimp* [read *cramp*] the style of smokers." James Brooke, "Tokyo Blows Smoke Indoors to Keep Streets Tidy," *Chicago Trib.*, 11 Dec. 2002, News §, at 35.
- "Wealthy people and business owners aren't going to let a little recession *crimp* [read *cramp*] their style." James McNair, "Charter Jet Company Flies in Face of Weak Economy," *Cincinnati Enquirer*, 2 Mar. 2003, at D1.

LANGUAGE-CHANGE INDEX
crimping one's style for *cramping one's style*: Stage 1
Current ratio (*cramp your style* vs. *crimp your style*): 26:1

crane, v.t., = (1) to lift as if by a machine made for the purpose; or (2) to stretch (one's neck) for the purpose of seeing better. The word is sometimes wrongly written *crain*, which is a NONWORD—e.g.:

- "Restrained by yellow ropes and signs that read, 'Please Look, Don't Touch,' spectators *crained* [read *craned*] necks to get a few glimpses of the car's spotless interior." Susan Howard, "A Love Affair with Cars of Their Youth," *Newsday* (N.Y.), 12 Sept. 1988, at 21.
- "Hundreds of people stood three and four deep along the rail, and hundreds more *crained* [read *craned*] from upper levels of the shopping mall as the Zamboni machine finished smoothing the ice surface for Harding's solo practice." Michael Janofsky, "Always Tonya: Cool as Ice, but Troubled in Her Quest," *N.Y. Times*, 7 Feb. 1994, at B5, B6.

This blunder obscures the METAPHOR in the phrase *to crane one's neck*, as the long-necked bird does when reaching out.

LANGUAGE-CHANGE INDEX
crain for *crane*: Stage 1

cranium. Pl. *craniums* or *crania*—the latter being especially common in medical texts. See PLURALS (B).

crape. See **crepe.**

crape myrtle (= a colorful East Indian shrub commonly grown in the southern and southwestern U.S.)

LANGUAGE-CHANGE INDEX (For the full key, see front matter pp. xxxi, l–li.)
Stage 1: Rejected. **Stage 2:** Widely shunned. **Stage 3:** Widespread but . . . **Stage 4:** Ubiquitous but . . . **Stage 5:** Fully accepted.
Invariably inferior forms marked by asterisk (*). • Ratios represent frequency of prevalent forms vs. variants in current books.

is often misspelled **crepe myrtle*, perhaps by those who mistakenly relate the word to the French delicacy *crepe* (/krep/). *Crape* (= a band made of thin twill fabric and worn on the upper arm as a sign of mourning) is a 17th-century anglicized spelling of the French word; it's pronounced /krayp/. E.g.:

- "You can grow a *crepe* [read *crape*] myrtle—lilac of the South—in DeWitt, but only if it's sheltered by other trees or structures." Jim Reilly, "Tree Search," *Syracuse Herald Am.*, 4 Oct. 1998, at AA1.
- "Tree-huggers were chaining themselves to *crepe* [read *crape*] myrtles." "Mass Transit," *Fla. Times-Union*, 19 Nov. 1998, at B4.
- "The gardens are sprinkled with red, yellow and purple blooms adding an array of color to the scene. Flowering plants include black-eye susans, impatiens and *crepe* [read *crape*] myrtles." "Magnolia Forest Garden Club's 'Garden of the Month,'" *Times-Picayune* (New Orleans), 16 Aug. 2015, at H1.

See **crepe.**

LANGUAGE-CHANGE INDEX
*crepe myrtle for *crape myrtle*: Stage 4
Current ratio (*crape myrtle* vs. **crepe myrtle*): 1.04:1

crappie (= a freshwater sunfish found in the central and eastern United States) is the standard spelling. **Croppie*, a variant, is closer to a phonetic spelling. Both words are pronounced /krop-ee/, though some dictionaries list *crappie* as /krap-ee/.

Current ratio: 66:1

crashworthy. See -WORTHY.

crawfish; crayfish. Although *crayfish* has traditionally been considered standard AmE—and *crawfish* a dialectal variant—things have changed. With the rise in popularity of Cajun cuisine in the 1980s came a general awareness of such dishes as *crawfish étouffée*. And today, most people who buy the freshwater crustaceans for cooking call them *crawfish*. But in other contexts—for example, among zoologists—*crayfish* remains standard. *Crawdad*, another dialectal variant, is still current in parts of the South.

LANGUAGE-CHANGE INDEX
1. *crawfish* for *crayfish*: Stage 5
Current ratio (*crayfish* vs. *crawfish*): 2:1
2. *crawdad* for *crayfish*: Stage 2
Current ratio (*crayfish* vs. *crawdad*): 20:1

cream cheese; *creamed cheese. Although **creamed cheese* was the original phrase, *cream cheese* has been standard since the 18th century. See ADJECTIVES (F).
Current ratio: 522:1

crèche (= [1] a scene representing the birth of Jesus, [2] a foundling hospital, or [3] a daycare center) is so spelled with a grave accent—not a circumflex (**crêche*). Sense 3 applies almost exclusively in BrE, where the accent is typically dropped. See DIACRITICAL MARKS.

credal. See **creedal.**

credible; credulous; creditable. *Credible* = believable; *credulous* = gullible, tending to believe; *creditable* = worthy of credit, laudable. See **incredible.**

credit, v.t. See **accredit.**

credo (= a formal statement of a person's or group's basic beliefs) is pronounced either /**kray**-doh/ or /**kree**-doh/.

credulity (= gullibility) should not be confused with *credibility* (= believability), as it is in the phrase **it strains credulity*—e.g.:

- "Several aspects of the play strain *credulity* [read *credibility*], particularly the ease with which total strangers gain admittance to the beleaguered heroine's basement apartment." Everett Evans, "Wait, Wait, Wait," *Houston Chron.*, 25 July 1994, Houston §, at 1.
- "And in all honesty, the story veers into an over-the-top territory that strains *credulity* [read *credibility*]." Deirdre Donahue, "Kellerman's 'Web' Mystery Weaves Trouble into Paradise," *USA Today*, 18 Jan. 1996, at D4.

Credulity did originally mean "belief," but that sense has long been obsolete.

credulous. See **credible.**

creedal; credal. In AmE, *creedal* is the standard spelling of the adjective corresponding to *creed*. In BrE, it's *credal*.

creep > crept > crept. So inflected. Yet the weak form ending in *-ed* has been creeping along as a variant form, especially in nonstandard usage, since the 18th century. Avoid it. E.g.:

- "Furber acknowledged that their grocery store prices have *creeped* [read *crept*] up." Patricia Wen & Bruce Mohl, "Grocery-Shopping Services in Tough Battle for Limited Clientele," *Boston Globe*, 18 Oct. 1998, at B2.
- "As their car *creeped* [read *crept*] home, the couple noticed dim lights glowing near their house." David Templeton, "Dondora's Doomsday Message," *Pitt. Post-Gaz.*, 29 Oct. 1998, at F1.
- "Hints of the old Wrexham *creeped* [read *crept*] in during the second half at Kidderminster." "Why N.Wales Is Rediscovering Its Love for Dragons," *Daily Post* (Liverpool), 21 Aug. 2015, at 21.

See IRREGULAR VERBS.

Although *crept* is the standard form, the slang PHRASAL VERB *creep out* (= to frighten or disgust) forms *creeped out*—e.g.: "Completely *creeped out* by the events, acting commissioner Bud Selig put a halt to the winter meetings." Larry Stone, "Trades: The Talk at Winter Meeting," *Seattle Times*, 11 Dec. 1998, at D1. See SLANG.

LANGUAGE-CHANGE INDEX
creeped misused for *crept*: Stage 1
Current ratio (*crept in* vs. **creeped in*): 345:1

crepe; crape. A *crepe* (/krep/ or /krayp/) is either a thin, French-style pancake or a type of thin crinkled fabric. In the pancake sense, the word often appears with the circumflex: *crêpe*. (See DIACRITICAL MARKS.) A *crape* /krayp/ is a band made of that fabric and worn around the arm as a sign of mourning. See **crape myrtle.**

crept. See **creep.**

crescendo, n., refers to a gradual increase in the volume of sound, not to a blast or even to a peak. To say that something *reaches a crescendo is woolly-minded—e.g.: "The tension reached a crescendo [read peak or climax] last January, when, in a move to restore peace, Nicastro did not reappoint one of the new board members, Denise Murphy, and replaced her with the Rev. William Barnes." Loretta Waldman, "Library Board Member Announces Resignation," *Hartford Courant*, 11 Jan. 2001, at B1. Pl. *crescendos*. See PLURALS (D).

The plural is *crescendos*—preferably not the Italianate **crescendi*.

LANGUAGE-CHANGE INDEX

1. *crescendo* in reference to a climax or peak: Stage 4
2. **crescendi* as a plural: Stage 2
Current ratio (*crescendos* vs. **crescendi*): 10:1

crevice; crevasse. These two words are often confused. A *crevice* is a narrow crack or break, as in the ground, a sidewalk, or a wall. E.g.: "They are curious animals, nosing into cracks and *crevices* with their pointy snouts." Nancy J. Smeltzer, "Hedgehogs Curling Up in More Homes," *Columbus Dispatch*, 15 Dec. 1994, at C1.

A *crevasse* is a large split or rupture, as in a levee, glacier, or embankment. E.g.: "The 48-year-old climber would rappel down the deepest *crevasse*, haul himself up the deepest slope and slide into a sleeping bag to warm a victim of hypothermia." Mike Tharp, "Traveler's Death Still a Mystery," *Rocky Mountain News* (Denver), 5 Dec. 1994, at A26.

Crevice is pronounced /**krev**-is/; *crevasse* is pronounced /krə-**vas**/.

*criminate. See **incriminate.**

crimp. See **cramp one's style.**

crisis forms the plural *crises*, not **crisises*—e.g.:

- "To be sure, a good case can be made that this restricting legacy of the Gulf of Tonkin resolution may not be in the nation's best interest in terms of a swift resolution of *crisises* [read *crises*]." Thomas V. DiBacco, "Anguished Legacy of Tonkin Resolution," *Orlando Sentinel*, 7 Aug. 1994, at G3.
- "Earlier this year, the Organization of African Unity (OAU) discussed setting up a rapid intervention force for such *crisises* [read *crises*] but shelved the idea." Judith Matloff, "Crisis in the Heart of Africa," *Christian Science Monitor*, 30 Oct. 1996, Int'l §, at 7.
- "Teens act out because their hormones have gone crazy. I can only wonder if someone is getting big money to discover that the same thing happens to women with PMS, and men having mid-life *crisises* [read *crises*]." Linda Stasi, "What Are Those Kids Thinking?" *N.Y. Post*, 30 Jan. 2002, at 63.

LANGUAGE-CHANGE INDEX

*crisises for *crises*: Stage 1
Current ratio (*crises* vs. **crisises*): 4,477:1

criterion. A. And the Plural Form *criteria*. *Criteria* is the plural, *criterion* the (originally Greek) singular. A Ph.D. in linguistics once defended *criteria*

as a singular because "not everyone knows that the singular is *criterium*"! (Indeed.) (See (C).) The plural **criterions* is occasionally seen, but it has failed to become standard. Infrequently, though not infrequently enough, one even sees **criterias*. Here are the correct forms:

- "The commission . . . has published its *criteria* for eligibility. Its central, repeated *criterion* for participation in the debates: 'the realistic chance of being elected.' " William Safire, "Three's a Crowd at the Debates," *Cincinnati Enquirer*, 6 Sept. 1996, at A18.
- "Melissa Knierim wants an opera house in the Poconos, and if determination and hard work are the *criteria* for getting one, order your tickets now." Gail Scudder, "There's an Opera in the Air," *Morning Call* (Allentown, Pa.), 19 Dec. 1996, at N1.

But especially since 1950 or so, writers have sometimes wanted to make *criteria* a singular—e.g.:

- "Grade your business from 'A' to 'F' on each *criteria* [read *criterion*]." Scott Clark, "Self-Test Helps Tell If Your Firm Meets Media's Grade," *Ariz. Bus. Gaz.*, 2 Feb. 1995, at 23.
- "As Beebe met *every criteria* [read *every criterion* or *all the criteria*] for such a designation—scenic views, mature trees, stone walls, crossings over waterways, a width of less than 20 feet and a dirt surface—the request was granted last October by the planning and zoning commission." Claudia Van Nes, "Saving the Roads Less Traveled," *Hartford Courant*, 17 Nov. 1996, at B1.
- "The *criteria* [read *criterion*] is fatalities per driver." Jim Sullivan, "Artful Viewing," *Boston Globe*, 10 Oct. 2001, at C4.

Cf. **media** & **phenomenon.** See PLURALS (B).

LANGUAGE-CHANGE INDEX

criteria as a false singular for *criterion*: Stage 2
Current ratio (*a criterion* vs. **a criteria*): 14:1

B. *Criterion* Misused as a Plural. Oddly, perhaps because *criteria* is so often wrongly thought to be singular, the correct singular and plural forms have—in some writers' minds—done something of a role reversal. So *criterion* is sometimes incorrectly used as the plural form—e.g.:

- "A state law adopted in 1959 outlines many *criterion* [read *criteria*] for consolidation, but no communities have ever met all the *criterion* [read *criteria*]." Kimberly Garcia, "Town, Village Cooperate for a Change," *Wis. State J.*, 31 Oct. 1994, at B1.
- "State law lists several *criterion* [read *criteria*] for what defines residency." Stacie Oulton, "Kane Offers Residency Proof," *Denver Post*, 20 July 1996, at B2.

LANGUAGE-CHANGE INDEX

criterion as a false plural for *criteria*: Stage 1
Current ratio (*several criteria* vs. **several criterion*): 134:1

C. And *criterium*. Since about 1970, *criterium* has denoted "a bicycle race of a specified number of laps on a closed course over public roads closed to normal traffic" (*W11*). The word was borrowed from the French, in which *critérium* means "competition." E.g.:

LANGUAGE-CHANGE INDEX (For the full key, see front matter pp. xxxi, l–li.)
Stage 1: Rejected. **Stage 2:** Widely shunned. **Stage 3:** Widespread but . . . **Stage 4:** Ubiquitous but . . . **Stage 5:** Fully accepted.
Invariably inferior forms marked by asterisk (*). • Ratios represent frequency of prevalent forms vs. variants in current books.

- "Jonathan [Page], 17, won the 72-mile road race and placed fourth and fifth, respectively, in the *criterium* and the time trials in the 17- and 18-year-old division at the national junior cycling championships." "Faces in the Crowd," *Sports Illustrated*, 24 Oct. 1994, at 26.
- "He also races in dirt *criteriums*, road races, road *criteriums* and road time trials." James Ensign, "Rider of Year's Wheels Keep Turning," *Des Moines Register*, 18 Dec. 1996, at 8.

As the second example illustrates, the plural of *criterium* in the sense just given is *criteriums*, not *criteria*.

Occasionally, writers confuse *criterium* with *criterion*—e.g.:

- "In that case, a major *criterium* [read *criterion*] for breaking ties would be conference records, and the Cardinals would have one of the worst in the group." Kent Somers, "Playoff Chances Too Tough to Call," *Ariz. Republic*, 13 Dec. 1994, at C1.
- "My sole *criterium* [read *criterion*] was this: Did he make a difference?" Rick Ryan, "Wuerffel Whiffs on One Man's Heisman's Ballot," *Charleston Gaz.*, 14 Dec. 1996, at C5.

LANGUAGE-CHANGE INDEX
criterium misused for *criterion*: Stage 1

critique, n. & v.t. Until recently, this word was almost always a noun. But in the late 20th century (beginning especially in the 1980s), the verb became quite common as a neutral equivalent to the word *criticize*, which had by then acquired negative connotations. In fact, though, the verb *critique* dates from the mid-18th century.

The verb is conjugated *critiqued* and *critiquing*. Some writers mistakenly write **critiqing* (perhaps from the poor influence of *cataloging* [see **catalog(ue)**])—e.g.:

- "The sometimes animated *critiqing* [read *critiquing*] . . . is intended only to help a 24-year-old quarterback get better." "Holmgren: Favre Not Perfect," *Capital Times* (Madison), 25 Oct. 1993, at B3.
- "While lacking any sexually graphic details, Ruth gets downright dirty while describing, and unavoidably *critiqing* [read *critiquing*], her meals with Andrews." Braden Keil, "Terminal Gets Some Dim Sum," *N.Y. Post*, 11 Apr. 2001, at 39.

LANGUAGE-CHANGE INDEX
critique as a verb: Stage 5

crocus (= a spring-blooming flower of the iris family, usu. in purple, yellow, or white) has predominantly formed the plural *crocuses* since the early 19th century—not the Latinate **croci*.

Current ratio: 5:1

*crosier. See **crozier.**

croupier. So spelled. See SPELLING (A).

crow, v.i. A cock *crows*. But if you want to describe what a cock has already done, do you say *crowed* or *crew*? The modern preference is for *crowed*—e.g.:

- "Above the din of car horns, a cock *crowed*." David Arnold, "Cooped Up in the Suburbs," *Boston Globe*, 15 Dec. 1994, at 1.
- "Early-bird discounts encouraged shoppers to splash through crowded parking lots to save a few bucks before

the cock *crowed*." Becky Tiernan, "Stores Lure Big Crowds," *Tulsa World*, 30 Nov. 1996, at A1.

But until about 1920, published instances of the collocation *cocks crew* were more common than those of *cocks crowed*; in BrE, the two collocations were about equal. In the 1920s, that changed in both varieties of English, and *crowed* came to predominate as the past-tense form.

Occasionally today, *crew* pops up in allusion to the King James Version—e.g.: "And immediately the cock *crew*." Matthew 26:74. Or sometimes the writer needs a rhyme, as in the following title: "When the Cock *Crew*, the Neighbors Started to Sue," *Smithsonian*, Aug. 1988, at 113.

Current ratio (*cocks crowed* vs. *cocks crew*): 3:1

crozier; *crosier. Although *crozier* (= a bishop's ornate staff resembling a shepherd's crook) has been the predominant spelling since the early 20th century in all varieties of World English, some American dictionaries have been slow to recognize its preeminence and continue listing the word under the variant spelling **crosier*.

Current ratio: 5:1

crudité. The raw vegetables served with a dip or dips are called *crudités*. Calling them *crudities* (= things that are rough and unrefined) is shockingly unrefined:

- "The Blythswood Square menu offers an excellent range of afternoon teas, including . . . the Tea Tox Afternoon Tea, consisting of delicious healthy options such as vegetable *crudities* [read *crudités*] and a detox salad." Sophie Hughes, "Britain's Best Teas," *Daily Telegraph*, 13 Aug. 2014, Lifestyle §.
- "I also liked this hybrid between hummus and guacamole for a new dip to serve with fresh vegetable *crudities* [read *crudités*], crackers, or tortilla chips." Nancy Lindahl, "'Tis Now the Season of Pointy Green Things," *Marin Independent J.* (Cal.), 28 Apr. 2015, Features §.

cruel, adj., makes *crueler* and *cruelest* in AmE, *crueller* and *cruellest* in BrE.

crummy; crumby. When the meaning is "worthless" or "inferior," the spelling is *crummy*. When the meaning is "consisting of or giving off crumbs," the spelling is *crumby*. But some writers err by using *crumby* when they mean *crummy*—e.g.:

- "You . . . are on the highway unsuccessfully trying to get [the tire] off with the *crumby* [read *crummy*] wrench that came with your car." Tom Incantalupo, "New Car, New Year," *Newsday* (N.Y.), 1 Jan. 1996, § II, at B30.
- "Perhaps he was one of the new generation of get-rich-quick entrepreneurs—you know the sort of thing—set up a *crumby* [read *crummy*] little chain of theme restaurants or pubs, float it on the stock market, then as the idea begins to pale and lose its appeal, sell to the highest bidder." Jeremy Warner, "Ten Years After the Big Bang, Little Has Changed," *Independent*, 26 Oct. 1996, at 23.

LANGUAGE-CHANGE INDEX
crumby misused for *crummy*: Stage 1

crystallize. So spelled—not **crystalize.*

cubiclize. See -IZE.

cuckoo (= silly, crazy) is sometimes misspelled
coocoo—e.g.: "I assumed Mr. Nelson's prolonged
isolation had brought on that endemic Maine malady known sometimes as *cabin-coocoo* [read *cabin-
cuckoo*] and sometimes as woods-nutty." John Gould,
"From Rosy Bower to Pulpit Pond," *Christian Science Monitor*, 23 May 1980, at 20. Likewise, the correct form is *cuckoo clock*—e.g.: "The new girl found
orphanage life like living in a *coocoo* [read *cuckoo*]
clock." R.H. Growald, "Girls Didn't [Care] About
Orphanage Director," *San Diego Union-Trib.*, 18 Apr.
1991, at B2.

LANGUAGE-CHANGE INDEX
cuckoo misspelled *coocoo*: Stage 1
Current ratio: 345:1

cudgel, vb., makes *cudgeled* and *cudgeling* in AmE,
cudgelled and *cudgelling* in BrE. See SPELLING (B).

cue; queue. A. As Nouns. Though pronounced the
same, these words have different meanings. *Cue* =
(1) a signal to begin; a hint; or (2) a stick used in
billiards, pool, or shuffleboard. *Queue* = (1) a line of
people or things waiting their turn; or (2) a hanging
braid of hair. See (C).

Not surprisingly, the two are sometimes
confused—e.g.:

- "Like most birds, teal don't start their migration based
  on air temperatures, but take their *queue* [read *cue*] to
  head south from the shortening hours of daylight." Bob
  Marshall, "Teal Season Starts Perfectly," *Times-Picayune*
  (New Orleans), 25 Sept. 1994, at C16.
- "People were forced to stand in long *cues* [read *queues*]
  at five emergency water stations in Amagasaki." "Kansai
  Striving to Recover from Effects of Devastation," *Daily
  Yomiuri* (Japan), 19 Jan. 1995, at 3.

LANGUAGE-CHANGE INDEX
1. *queue* misused for *cue*: Stage 1
2. *cue* misused for *queue*: Stage 1
Current ratio (*long queues* vs. *long cues*): 86:1

B. *Cue up*; *queue up*. To *cue up* a videotape, an
audiotape, a compact disc, or a DVD is to have it ready
for playing at a particular point. E.g.:

- "His brother *cued up* the tape, the rousing theme song from
  'Rocky.'" Mark Pazniokas, "Out of Prison, Santopietro Welcomed Home," *Hartford Courant*, 17 Sept. 1996, at A3.
- "You can bet your remote control clicker that every network has already *cued up* video of the glowering Dole,
  eyes flitting, hanging that warmonger tag on an astonished Mondale." David Nyhan, "Should Dole Go for the
  Jugular?" *Boston Globe*, 4 Oct. 1996, at A19.

To *queue up* is to line up—e.g.:

- "On my way to a week's cruise in the Galapagos on the
  Albatros, a luxurious 80-foot dive boat, I *queued up* in
  the airport in Quito, Ecuador." Karen Misuraca, "Where
  the Wild Things Are," *S.F. Examiner*, 4 Dec. 1994, at T5.

- "Florida State students *queued up* for probably the most
  prized ticket they would ever use." Tim Layden, "No. 1 vs.
  No. 2," *Sports Illustrated*, 2 Dec. 1996, at 36.

C. In Pigtails. The braid of hair is spelled *queue*,
not *cue*. E.g.: "Instructed by French dancing masters
in the stately steps and deep curtsies of the minuet,
the young men had indeed to mind their pieds (feet)
and *queues* (pigtails) to keep from losing their balance or their huge wigs." Laurie Lucas, "Anniversa-
ries," *Press-Enterprise* (Riverside, Cal.), 15 Nov. 1995,
at D4.

But of course, some writers get it wrong—e.g.: "The
pigtail or '*cue*' [read '*queue*']—as cultivated by sailors—
was hair twisted or plaited, commonly prettied up by
a binding of spun yarn and the whole applied with a
dose of Stockholm tar which gave its gravity-defying
look." Letter of William Wood, "Tarred Pigtail," *Daily
Telegraph*, 9 July 1992, at 16.

LANGUAGE-CHANGE INDEX
queue (= pigtail) misspelled *cue*: Stage 1

cueing. So spelled—not *cuing*. See MUTE E.
Current ratio: 3:1

cuisine is pronounced /kwi-**zeen**/ or /kwee-**zeen**/—
not /kyoo-**zeen**/.

cul-de-sac. Pl. *cul-de-sacs*—not *culs-de-sac* (a common variant until about 1940). See PLURALS (B).
Current ratio: 4:1

-(C)ULE. See DIMINUTIVES (B).

culinary is pronounced /**kyoo**-lə-ner-ee/ or (less
good) /kəl-ə-ner-ee/.

culpable; *inculpable*; *culpatory*; *culpose*. *Culpable* (= guilty, blameworthy) is the ordinary word
among this group. E.g.:

- "Merritt said yesterday that Christian conservatives were
  not *culpable* in North's defeat." Kent Jenkins Jr., "Uncertainties Arise on Morning After GOP Triumph," *Wash.
  Post*, 10 Nov. 1994, at C1.
- "Roberts' husband, who is not being held *culpable*, was at
  sea on a Norfolk, Va.-based ship at the time of the baby's
  death." Dennis O'Brien & Stephania H. Davis, "Mom at
  Base Is Held in Baby's Death," *Chicago Trib.*, 15 Nov. 1996,
  Metro Lake §, at 1.

See **blameworthy (A).**

Inculpable is ambiguous. Avoid it as a CONTRONYM.
It may mean (1) "(of a person) able to be inculpated
[i.e., guilty]"; (2) "(of a statement or action) pointing
toward guilt"; or (3) "(of a person) not culpable [i.e.,
innocent]." The word has traditionally borne sense 3,
but in fact it is used in all three ways—e.g.:

- "On the other hand, it's nice to know I can join the ranks
  of those who have excuses that render them *inculpable*
  [i.e., guiltless] for their behavior." Tami Plyler, "Excuses,
  Excuses, Excuses," *Union Leader* (Manchester, N.H.),
  7 Mar. 1995, at A5.

LANGUAGE-CHANGE INDEX (For the full key, see front matter pp. xxxi, l–li.)
Stage 1: Rejected. **Stage 2:** Widely shunned. **Stage 3:** Widespread but . . . **Stage 4:** Ubiquitous but . . . **Stage 5:** Fully accepted.
Invariably inferior forms marked by asterisk (*). • Ratios represent frequency of prevalent forms vs. variants in current books.

- "During the period of custodial questioning, the defendant made numerous *inculpable* [i.e., guilt-pointing] as well as potentially exculpable statements." "*People v. James Biggs*," *N.Y.L.J.*, 7 Nov. 1995, at 25.

See **inculpatable.**

The other two terms are rare. *Culpatory*, meaning "expressing blame," is a NEEDLESS VARIANT of *inculpatory*. (See **inculpatory.**) *Culpose*, the rarest of all, means "characterized by criminal negligence." Neither has anything to recommend it.

*culs-de-sac. See **cul-de-sac.**

cultivable; *cultivatable. The first (pronounced /kəl-tə-və-bəl/) predominates in AmE usage, being eight times as common in print as *cultivatable*, which has become a NEEDLESS VARIANT—e.g.: "Kenneth Hobbie, president and CEO of the U.S. Feed Grains Council in Washington, said that by 2050, Asia will have nine times more people than the Western Hemisphere per *cultivatable* [read *cultivable*] acre." Ann Toner, "Exports Only Part of Ag Success Story, Official Says," *Omaha World-Herald*, 9 Nov. 1996, at 34. See -ABLE (D) & -ATABLE.

LANGUAGE-CHANGE INDEX
cultivatable for *cultivable*: Stage 2
Current ratio (*cultivable* vs. *cultivatable*
in World English): 12:1

cultivated. See **cultured.**

cultural diversity = (1) diversity within a culture; pluralism; or (2) diversity among cultures. The phrase often masks this ambiguity. Sense 1 is more common—e.g.: "The United States Air Force Band of Liberty [will play] songs highlighting America's musical and *cultural diversity*." "Live This Weekend," *Providence J.-Bull.*, 7 June 2001, at L28.

Some have unconvincingly argued that sense 1 represents a self-contradiction. An English professor, for example, argues that a culture is based on shared values and beliefs. That is, *culture* is what brings us together and makes us one, while diversity is what separates us from one another. So people who share values and beliefs, the reasoning goes, are not diverse, and a culture made up of unshared values and beliefs is not a culture. See David Pichaske, "There Is No Such Thing as 'Cultural Diversity,'" *Monitor* (Minn. State Univ. Student Ass'n), Feb. 1995, at 9. Regardless of the merits of the argument, *cultural diversity* is a useful term in a melting-pot society, and if it falls by the wayside it won't be because it is illogical.

As practiced on college campuses, *cultural diversity* often takes on sense 2. That is, in the name of cultural diversity, curricula today often emphasize works from outside the Western tradition.

cultured; cultivated. Correctly, the former is used in reference to people and pearls, the latter in reference to the mind, tastes, speech, or behavior. A *cultured* person has refined tastes; a *cultivated* mind is well trained and highly developed.

-CULUS. See DIMINUTIVES (B).

cum (/kəm/ or /koom/) is a Latin preposition meaning "with." In English, it bears that same sense, or sometimes "along with being; and." It's usually hyphenated before and after—e.g.:

- "Such changes have done nothing to tame the fundamental irreverence, particularly among the young, for the high Confucian-*cum*-communist culture of the mainland." Andrew Higgins, "Shuffling the Cards of Identity," *Guardian*, 28 June 1996, at 14.
- "The hit television show 'The Simpsons' sporadically highlights the dull-normal antics of Cletus and his stripper wife, Brandine, a '90s version of the hillbilly-*cum*-trailer trash archetype." Richard Morin, "Unconventional Wisdom," *Dallas Morning News*, 26 May 1997, at C10.
- "Or splurge and join the Explorers Club for a conference-*cum*-cruise on the last weekend of May." J.A. Lobbia, "Summer in the City," *Village Voice*, 3 June 1997, at 2.

But some writers confuse this word with *come*, as Fritz Spiegl notes: "A film critic in the *Sunday Times* recently described the character of Thomas Jefferson in a new film as 'a sort of founding father *come* speak-your-weight machine.' Twice: once in the body of the text, and again in the caption to the picture." Spiegl, "Usage and Abusage," *Daily Telegraph*, 8 July 1995, at 32.

*cumbrance. See **encumbrance.**

cumin; *cummin. *Cumin* (= a carrot-like herb whose seeds are used as a spice esp. in Mexican and Indian cooking) became the predominant spelling in AmE about 1930 and in BrE a few years later. Pronounced /**kyoo**-min/, *cumin* has universally replaced the older spelling *cummin* (pronounced /kəm-in/).

Current ratio: 13:1

cummerbund (= a wide waistband worn with tuxedos and other formal dress) is the standard spelling. *Kummerbund* is a variant. *Cummerbun*, *cumberbun*, and *cumberbund* are simply errors—e.g.:

- "Long, elegant dresses, bow ties, *cummerbuns* [read *cummerbunds*] and corsages." Kai Fawn Miller, "The Real Deal on Wheels," *Times & Eagle* (Reading, Pa.), 16 May 1996, at 14.
- "A man dressed in a black tuxedo jacket, red dress shirt, purple and pink *cumberbun* [read *cummerbund*] and black pants asked the employee at the Edwards Theater if he could buy some popcorn." "Costa Mesa Police Blotter," *Orange County Register*, 8 Aug. 1996, at 5.
- "'Sometimes,' [Josh] Penn said shortly after midnight, drink in hand and *cumberbund* [read *cummerbund*] pressed firmly against the Monty bar, 'the show has to follow the script.'" Mike Scott, "'Beasts of the Southern Wild' Makers Look to the Future After Shutout," *Times-Picayune* (New Orleans), 27 Feb. 2013, Living §, at C1.

The pronunciation is /kəm-ər-bənd/.

LANGUAGE-CHANGE INDEX
cummerbund misspelled **cummerbun*,
*cumberbun, or **cumberbund*: Stage 1
Current ratio (*cummerbund* vs. **cumberbund* vs.
*kummerbund): 69:1.2:1

*cummin. See cumin.

Cummings, E.E. The poet Edward Estlin Cummings (1894–1962), a shy man, early in his career used the lowercase *i* for the first-person singular pronoun. (This habit, now commonplace in Internet exchanges, was highly unusual.) Cummings's critics then began referring to him sarcastically in print as *e.e. cummings*. The practice stuck, and that was how his name appeared on book covers. Does this mean we should all use lowercase letters in spelling his name? Those most familiar with the man think not, and they use ordinary CAPITALIZATION. Norman Friedman, the founder and then president of the E.E. Cummings Society, summed up the poet's "philosophy of typography" this way: "that *he* could use caps and lowercase as he wished, but that when others referred to him by name they ought to use caps." *Spring: The Journal of the E.E. Cummings Society*, 1992, at 114–21. Nor is it true that Cummings legally changed his name to lowercase letters. After that story appeared in the preface to a biography about Cummings, his widow angrily denied it. See NAMES (A).

*cumquat. See kumquat.

*cumulate; cumulative. See accumulate.

cumulus. Pl. *cumuli.* (See PLURALS (B).) Although the corresponding adjective is *cumulous*—and although the noun *cumulus* itself means "cloud"—the standard phrasing is *cumulus cloud.* E.g.:

- "The type of clouds that cross Wisconsin changes seasonally, and you find more *cumulus clouds* this time of the year." John Malan, "Today Is Likely to Be More Typical of a Day in June," *Milwaukee J. Sentinel*, 5 June 1996, Sports §, at 8.
- "Above, a ceiling fan turns lazily, barely disturbing the *cumulus clouds* of smoke." Linda Federman, "Music for Folks at an Irish Pub," *Wash. Times*, 14 Dec. 1996, at B1.

The phrase *cumulous clouds*, though not strictly wrong, is certainly unusual—e.g.: "South of town, puffy white *cumulous* [read, preferably, *cumulus*] clouds began to explode upwards." Rob Schneider, "Some Students Do All Their Studies in the Classroom," *Indianapolis Star*, 16 June 1996, at A1.

Current ratio (*cumulus clouds* vs. *cumulous clouds*): 15:1

cuneiform (= [1] wedge-shaped; [2] written in wedge-shaped characters; or [3] the wedge-shaped characters themselves) is pronounced in four distinct syllables (/kyoo-nee-ə-form/ or /kyoo-**nee**-ə-form/), not in three (/**kyoo**-nə-form/). Probably because of the mispronunciation, the word is occasionally misspelled *cuniform*—e.g.: "His price: Reportedly between $4.5 million and $7 million, depending on how the Sumerian *cuniform* [read *cuneiform*] in the contract translates into English."

Jim Slotek, "Ace Ventura: Stinking Rich," *Toronto Sun*, 22 Mar. 1994, at 42.

LANGUAGE-CHANGE INDEX
cuneiform misspelled and mispronounced
**cuniform*: Stage 1
Current ratio: 308:1

cunnilingus; *cunnilinctus. The standard spelling of this term, dating from the late 19th century, is *cunnilingus.* *Cunnilinctus*, a variant form that appears in some dictionaries, almost rivaled the standard form in print sources of the 1930s, but it ebbed and is rarely used today. Cf. **anilingus.**

Current ratio: 26:1

cupful. Pl. *cupfuls*—not *cupsful.* See PLURALS (G).
Current ratio: 33:1

cupola (= a round structure on the top of a building, usu. shaped like an upside-down bowl) is pronounced /kyoo-pə-lə/—not /kyoo-pə-loh/ or /koo-pə-lə/. It has universally formed the plural *cupolas* since the 18th century—not *cupolae.* The inflected form is *cupolaed* <a cupolaed building>. For a mistake sometimes made with this word, see **copula.**

curative; *curatory; curatorial. For the meaning "of, relating to, or involving the cure of diseases," *curative* is preferred over *curatory*, which is a NEEDLESS VARIANT. *Curatorial* = of, relating to, or involving a curator. E.g.: "The entries by the museum *curatorial* staff are brief but intelligent." David Bonetti, "The Pick of the Art Books," *S.F. Examiner*, 10 Dec. 1996, at D1.

curb; kerb. *Curb* is the AmE spelling; *kerb* is a BrE variant. And BrE makes an interesting distinction: the physical sense of a raised stone or concrete edge for a road or path is a *kerb*, while anything that metaphorically halts or checks is a *curb*—e.g.:

- "The chances are you would stumble before even stepping off the *kerb*." "Computers That Run Themselves," *Economist*, 21 Sept. 2002, Tech. Q. §, at 26.
- "In Germany, the government wants to encourage more part-time working and remove *curbs* on self-employment." Tony Major, "Germany Drags Europe Down," *Fin. Times*, 27 Feb. 2002, at 4.

AmE uses *curb* in all senses.

cure; heal. Both words are commonly used in medical senses. To *cure* is to successfully treat or remove (an illness, disease, or disorder), especially with medicine <an antibiotic will cure that infection>. It is often used as a passive-voice verb meaning "to get well again" <I'm cured!>. *Cure* is invariably transitive.

Heal may be either transitive or intransitive. As a transitive verb, it is essentially synonymous with *cure* but is used less frequently. As an intransitive verb, it generally denotes recovery from wounds or injuries <that cut needs time to heal> <broken bones heal

LANGUAGE-CHANGE INDEX (For the full key, see front matter pp. xxxi, l–li.)
Stage 1: Rejected. **Stage 2:** Widely shunned. **Stage 3:** Widespread but . . . **Stage 4:** Ubiquitous but . . . **Stage 5:** Fully accepted.
Invariably inferior forms marked by asterisk (*). • Ratios represent frequency of prevalent forms vs. variants in current books.

slowly>. *Heal* is the word more often used in figurative senses <time heals all wounds>, but at law one *cures* a title defect, delivery of nonconforming goods, and other legal problems.

curio. Pl. *curios.* See PLURALS (D).

curiously. See SENTENCE ADVERBS.

current, n.; **currant.** A *current* is (1) a steady flow of a fluid element, such as water, air, or electricity, in a definite direction <wind currents>, or (2) metaphorically, the movement of something intangible <the current of time> <the current of conversation>. A *currant* is a fruit, either (1) a very small raisin produced from a Mediterranean variety of seedless grapes, or (2) the dried, edible berry of a Eurasian shrub. As homophones, the words are occasionally confounded—e.g.:

- "Some [fruits] to consider include apples, apricots, banana chips, blueberries, cranberries, *currents* [read *currants*], figs, ginger, mango, pears, peaches, plums, raisins, and strawberries." Maurie Markman et al., *Cancer Nutrition and Recipes for Dummies* 248 (2013).
- "They had nothing to do but stare at ocean *currants* [read *currents*]." D.L. Faughn & S.D. Schakel, *Below Gravity III: The Resurrection* 56 (2015).

currently. See **at the present time** & **presently.**

curriculum. Pl. *curricula* or *curriculums.* The Latin plural remains much more common. E.g.:

- "These *curricula* don't 'radically change the way students learn how to add, subtract, multiply and divide.'" "Bethlehem's Math Program Gives Students an Edge," *Morning Call* (Allentown, Pa.), 24 Sept. 2002, at A12.
- "Even as many other colleges and universities have abandoned their core *curriculums,* Columbia University has held fast." Karen W. Arenson, "Science May Soon Join Core Courses at Columbia," *N.Y. Times,* 26 Sept. 2002, at B3.

See PLURALS (B).
　　Current ratio (*curricula* vs. *curriculums*): 19:1

curriculum vitae. See **vita.**

CURSING. See PROFANITY.

cursory; cursorial. *Cursory* = perfunctory, superficial. E.g.:

- "Fire investigator Charles D. Chamberlain of the State Fire Marshal's Office said [that] he would be looking for a cause but [that] nothing appeared suspicious on a *cursory* view." "Fire Destroys Bar Outside Meredith," *Union Leader* (Manchester, N.H.), 20 July 1996, at A5.
- "Building inspector Chuck Vincent told the board that owner Michael Kilpatrick has made *cursory* repairs to the house and failed to meet the Oct. 9 fix-it-up deadline set by the board during the summer." Ruth Laney, "Board Tries to Quiet Noise Fight," *Advocate* (Baton Rouge), 14 Nov. 1996, at B4.

Cursorial = (1) of, relating to, or involving running; or (2) (of an animal) adapted for running. E.g.:

- "Challenging this is the 'ground up,' or *cursorial* theory, which maintains that small, running dinosaurs developed wings and flight to control themselves while leaping off the ground to snag prey or escape from predators." David F. Salisbury, "Searching for Key to Bird Flight Amid Tree-Dwelling Dinosaurs," *Christian Science Monitor,* 15 June 1984, at 3.
- "On this basis, Archaeopteryx appears to have been a perching bird, not a *cursorial* predator." Alan Feduccia, "Evidence from Claw Geometry Indicating Arboreal Habits of Archaeopteryx," *Science,* 5 Feb. 1993, at 790.

curtail means "to cut back," not "to stop completely." Therefore, the phrases **completely curtailed,* **totally curtailed,* and similar others are misuses—e.g.:

- "Their halcyon days of wine and roses, if not *totally curtailed* [read, perhaps, *totally over*], certainly would be cramped beyond recognition." "Commission Needs More Catalysts to Change," *St. Petersburg Times,* 22 Aug. 1990, at 2.
- "But fans will be glad to hear he hasn't *completely curtailed* [read *completely stopped*] performing." Beth Wood, "His Tendinitis Is Nothing to Fret About," *San Diego Union-Trib.,* 28 Dec. 1995, Night & Day §, at 12.
- "The weather has greatly reduced the fishing and seems to have *completely curtailed* [read, depending on the sense, *curtailed* or *stopped*] the fish stories." Dennis Chapman, "Fishing Report," *Palm Beach Post,* 6 Feb. 1996, at C9.

But *curtail* is the right word when there is only a scaling back—e.g.:

- "Banking and government offices will be closed or services *curtailed* in the following countries and their dependencies this week because of national and religious holidays." "This Week's Holidays," *L.A. Times,* 27 Nov. 1994, at L3.
- "A number of court decisions *curtailed* such blatant bias in the public schools by the 1970s." Stephanie Spellers, "Faith Enters the Classroom," *Knoxville News-Sentinel,* 23 Nov. 1996, at B1.

CURTAILED WORDS. See BACK-FORMATIONS.

curtsy. So spelled—preferably not **curtsey.*
　　Interestingly, the *OED* records *courtesy* as an obsolete form of *curtsy.* Yet it's not quite obsolete. It occurs many times in a 21st-century book, in each instance as a NEEDLESS VARIANT of *curtsy*—e.g.:

- "She was making her *courtesy* [read *curtsy*] to him. He bowed to her. They both straightened up and stood in silence." Ursula K. Le Guin, *The Other Wind* 162 (2001).
- "Lebannen bowed. 'Your presence honors us, Princess.' She performed a deep, straight-backed *courtesy* [read *curtsy*] and said, 'Thank you.'" *Ibid.* at 201.

LANGUAGE-CHANGE INDEX
courtesy misused for *curtsy:* Stage 1

curvaceous. So spelled—not **curvacious.*
　　Current ratio: 110:1

CUSSING. See PROFANITY.

customer. See **client (A).**

cut > cut > cut. So inflected. The past form *cutted is erroneous. See IRREGULAR VERBS.

cut-and-dried, the age-old PHRASAL ADJECTIVE, is sometimes wrongly written *cut-and-dry—e.g.: "The gift dilemma is further complicated currently by companies' increased activity in international markets, where the ethical questions tend to be much less *cut-and-dry* [read *cut-and-dried*]." Diane Trommer, "Supply Chain Model Poses New Ethical Challenges," *Electronic Buyers' News*, 4 Aug. 1997, at E26. (For more on the word choice in that sentence, see **dilemma.**)

LANGUAGE-CHANGE INDEX
cut-and-dry for *cut-and-dried*: Stage 2
Current ratio (*cut-and-dried* vs. *cut-and-dry*): 8:1

cut in half is the idiom except in cooking, where *cut into halves* emphasizes the two parts of something, both of which are to be dealt with—e.g.:

- "*Cut* the cantaloupes *into halves*, scoop out the seeds and turn them upside down to drain." "What's Under the Rind Makes Terrific Soup and Salsa," *Fresno Bee*, 31 July 1996, Food & Life §, at 5.
- "To assemble: *Cut* the cake *into halves* lengthwise." Sarah Fritschner, "Romanian Connection Brings Exotic to Church Fair," *Courier-J.* (Louisville), 11 Dec. 1996, at D1.
- "Peel and devein the shrimp; *cut in halves*." "Make Short Order of Dinner with This Shrimp Linguine," *Times-Picayune* (New Orleans), 12 Dec. 1996, at F2.

Perhaps because *cut in half* is synonymous with *halve*, some writers fall into the error of writing **cut in halve*—e.g.: "If a recipe calls for seeded tomatoes, *cut them in halve* [read *halve them* or *cut them in half*] crosswise and squeeze each tomato half gently to force out the seeds." Martha Stewart, "Vine-Ripened Tomatoes Beg for Picking, Devouring," *Dayton Daily News*, 8 Aug. 1996, at 8. (Stewart was not victimized by a local editor; the syndicated piece appeared throughout the nation in this form.)

LANGUAGE-CHANGE INDEX
*cut in halve for *cut in half*: Stage 1

-CY. See **-CE.**

cyclone. See **hurricane.**

cyclopean; *cyclopian. This word—meaning (1) "of or like a cyclops"; or (2) "huge, gargantuan"—is now almost uniformly spelled *cyclopean* or *Cyclopean*. The spelling **cyclopian* is a variant.

The word has two acceptable but very different pronunciations: /sɪ-klə-**pee**-ən/ and /sɪ-**kloh**-pee-ən/. The former predominates and is preferred. See **cyclops.**

Current ratio (*cyclopean* vs. **cyclopian*): 34:1

*cyclopedia; *cyclopedic. During the 20th century, these forms were superseded by *encyclopedia* and *encyclopedic*. The words **cyclopedia* and **cyclopedic* are now NEEDLESS VARIANTS.

In BrE the tendency has been to spell all forms of these words *-paed-* or *-pæd-*, but today the *-ped-* spellings are very much on the rise because of the AmE influence. See AE.

*cyclopian. See **cyclopean.**

cyclops. Pl. *cyclopes* /sɪ-**kloh**-peez/ or *cyclopses* /sɪ-**klop**-səz/. The classically formed plural, *cyclopes*, still predominates in AmE and BrE alike—e.g.:

- "Post-apocalyptic *cyclopes* line the wall of a sewer like bats in black leather, and Siamese-twin sisters who suggest taloned ravens cackle over sinister purposes." Jay Carr, "Dungeonlike 'City' Casts Eerie Spell," *Boston Globe*, 9 Sept. 1995, at 65.
- "Coverage of the Champions League final was more one-eyed than a *Cyclopes'* convention for which only Polyphemus has bothered turning up." Robin Scott-Elliot, "Holding's Honeyed Growl Drowned Out by Sky's Chelsea Cheerleaders," *Independent*, 21 May 2012, at 20.

Although most dictionaries don't list the plural *cyclopses*, it is becoming common. Indeed, *cyclopses* ought to be fully accepted as standard—e.g.:

- "We are bombarded with vainglorious descriptions and fantastic illustrations of dragons, giants, *cyclopses*, griffins (lashed to a flying machine), the anthropophagi and men whose heads grow beneath their shoulders." "Still Questing for the Holy Grail," *Fin. Times*, 20 July 1996, at 16.
- "Meanwhile, soldiers with unpronounceable names challenge creatures that look like *cyclopses*, furry whatchamacallits (dubbed furballs) or crosses between vultures and alligators." Charan Levitan, "Cool Fights with a Scummy Sorcerer," *Sun-Sentinel* (Ft. Lauderdale), 1 Nov. 1996, Showtime §, at 12.

See PLURALS (A).

It's wrong, by the way, to make *cyclops* itself into a plural—e.g.: "Other highlights I remember: Sinbad battling a baby croc and its gigantic mother, several *cyclops* [read *cyclopses* or *cyclopes*] and a fire-breathing dragon." Jim Bawden, "Movie Previews," *Toronto Star*, 3 Mar. 1997, Starweek §, at 8.

LANGUAGE-CHANGE INDEX
cyclops as a false plural for *cyclopses* or *cyclopes*: Stage 2

*cypher. See **cipher.**

cypress (= a cone-bearing tree) shouldn't be confused with *Cyprus* (= the Mediterranean island nation south of Turkey). Yet it sometimes is—e.g.:

- "On the way home, past olive groves, Romanesque bell towers and rows of lovely *cyprus* [read *cypress*] trees that jut from the landscape like giant swaying plumes, I see light glowing." Pamela Gerhardt, "In the Hills of Tuscany, a Family Discovers That Living like a Local Can Be a Joy," *Wash. Post*, 10 Mar. 2002, at E1.
- "A pilot who walked away from a helicopter crash and later slammed his plane into a *cyprus* [read *cypress*] swamp was legally intoxicated at the time of his death, officials said Monday." "Pilot Crashes Twice," *Cincinnati Post*, 18 June 2002, at A2.

And the errors go both ways—e.g.:

- "Last year Wright played for a club team, Apoel, on the island of *Cypress* [read *Cyprus*], Greece." Mark Rosner, "Joey the Greek," *Austin Am.-Statesman*, 20 July 1994, at C1.

LANGUAGE-CHANGE INDEX (For the full key, see front matter pp. xxxi, l–li.)
Stage 1: Rejected. **Stage 2:** Widely shunned. **Stage 3:** Widespread but . . . **Stage 4:** Ubiquitous but . . . **Stage 5:** Fully accepted.
Invariably inferior forms marked by asterisk (*). • Ratios represent frequency of prevalent forms vs. variants in current books.

- "Best of all, Saga does not charge a single supplement on many of its tours to places such as Greece and the Greek Islands, Malta, Majorca, Spain, Portugal, Sicily, *Cypress* [read *Cyprus*], Turkey, Nicaragua, Great Britain, Ireland, depending on departure date." Gene & Adele Malott, "Savvy Solo Seniors Can Avoid Supplement Fees," *Grand Rapids Press*, 1 Mar. 1998, at K6.

Consider the challenges that travel writers face: Los Angeles has a suburb named *Cypress*, and *cypress* trees grow both there and on *Cyprus*.

LANGUAGE-CHANGE INDEX
1. **cyprus tree* for *cypress tree*: Stage 1
Current ratio (*cypress tree* vs. **cyprus tree*): 50:1
2. **Cypress* for *Cyprus*: Stage 1

czar; tsar. Outside academic circles, the spelling *czar* is overwhelmingly predominant in AmE and always has been. *Tsar*, which is closer to the Russian form, is the preferred form in BrE and in academia. It is also the form traditionally used with Russian emperors and monarchs <Tsar Nicholas II>. Americans' colloquial use of *czar* to denote a person of great power or authority (often with a suggestion of tyranny) is hardly new—it dates back to the mid-19th century. And even the specialized sense of a person appointed to steer policy and enforcement in a certain field <drug czar> <energy czar> <car czar> goes back at least to the early 1930s.

D

-'**D.** See -ED.

dachshund is pronounced /**dahk**-sənd/ or /**daks**-huunt/. It's occasionally mispronounced /**dash**-ənd/, and it's occasionally misspelled **daschund* or **dachsund*.

Current ratio (*dachshund* vs. **daschund* vs. **dachsund*): 256:2:1

daemon; demon. Both are pronounced /**dee**-mən/. The spelling *daemon* distinguishes the Greek-mythology senses of supernatural being, indwelling spirit, etc. from the modern sense of devil's helper (*demon*). E.g.: "The *daemon* in him played the game just as it wrote the poems." Jeffrey Meyers, "Poets and Tennis—Drop Shots and Tender Egos," *N.Y. Times*, 2 June 1985, § 7, at 24. *Daemon* is also a term of art in the field of information technology, referring to a background process or thread (primarily in UNIX).

dais is generally pronounced /**day**-is/ (preferably not /**dɪ**-is/)—but it may be pronounced, especially in BrE, to rhyme with *pace*.

Dalmatian. So spelled (and capitalized)—not **dalmatian* or (worse yet) **dalmation*. E.g.: "Large, muscular and energetic, *dalmations* [read *Dalmatians*] typically require a lot of open space to rove and frolic." Clint Thomas, "*Dalmation* [read *Dalmatian*] Owners Urged to Provide Proper Environment," *Charleston Gaz.*, 12 Feb. 1997, at 15 (misspelled throughout article). As with many other dog breeds, such as German shepherds and French poodles, the name reflects a place of origin: Dalmatia, now a region of northern Croatia.

LANGUAGE-CHANGE INDEX
Dalmatian misspelled **Dalmation*: Stage 1
Current ratio: 46:1

damage(s), n. The singular *damage* refers to loss or injury to person or property; the plural *damages* refers to monetary compensation for such a loss or injury.

damn, adj. & adv., for *damned*—as in *that damn cat*—though attested from the 18th century, remains something of a CASUALISM. Yet it occurs with great frequency—e.g.:

- "Let the student choose [subjects] himself, and make *damn* [read *damned*] sure he says something *about* the subject—rather than merely turning in a description or summary or noncommittal analysis of it." Martin Russ, *Showdown Semester: Advice from a Writing Professor* 31 (1980).
- "It was very *damn* [read *damned*] dark in the mid-1930s when I was born and biology was destiny with a vengeance." Jill Tweedie, "Strange Places," in *On Gender and Writing* 112, 112 (Michelene Wandor ed., 1983).
- "It's not easy to single out what has made so perennially fascinating the whole Boomer Heaven mix of self-righteous anger, hormonal overdrive, orange bean bags and *damn* [read *damned*] good music." Katherine Knorr, "Live, Loud, in Your Face: Welcome to the '60s," *Int'l Herald Trib.*, 23 Mar. 2001, at 24.

The wretchedly misspelled form *dam*, too, sometimes appears—e.g.: "It seems every year we need a plumber because the house sewer system has an inadequate one-way relay instead of two, and the *dam* [read *damned*] thing gets overloaded." Carole Hall, "Multiple Sclerosis: Keeping Your Perspective," 3 *Real Living with Multiple Sclerosis* 6 (May 1996). If this is intended as a EUPHEMISM, it is a particularly ineffective one. Cf. **goddamned.**

LANGUAGE-CHANGE INDEX
1. *damn* for *damned*: Stage 5
Current ratio (*damn thing* vs. *damned thing*): 3:1
2. *dam* for *damned*: Stage 1
Current ratio (*damned thing* vs. **dam thing*): 58:1

damned, adj. & adv. See **damn.**

damnedest is so spelled—preferably not **damndest*.

Current ratio: 4:1

damp, v.t.; **dampen.** Both may mean "to make damp, moisten," but each word carries at least one additional sense. *Damp* = (1) to stifle or extinguish <damp the

furnace>; or (2) to deaden the vibration of (a piano string). *Dampen* = to check, diminish, or depress <the news of Mr. Ratliff's illness dampened our spirits>. Although the words sometimes overlap in these additional senses, they are best kept distinct.

dandruff is sometimes misspelled **dandriff*—which was actually a variant spelling in the early 19th century, but it had been sloughed off by 1900.

Current ratio: 156:1

danger. A. *In danger of life*; *in danger of death*. Curiously, these phrases are synonymous. *Life* is the only exception to the idiom requiring *in danger of* to be followed by the peril and not by what is exposed to it. Thus, we say *in danger of losing his honor, in danger of being thrown from the bridge*, etc.

B. **Running the danger*. Idiomatically speaking, one runs a *risk*, not a *danger*—e.g.:

- "If you parody your bland role model with utter brilliance, then you *run the danger* [read *run the risk*] of being too clever for your own good." Barry Walters, " 'Brady' Sequel Is Like One Long Episode," *S.F. Examiner*, 23 Aug. 1996, at D3.
- "I *run the danger* [read *run the risk*] myself of oversimplifying." James M. Klurfeld, "Politicians' Economic Plans Simplistic," *Fresno Bee*, 25 Aug. 1996, at B7.
- "Begin the shot, but it is not until the club is fully drawn that you can set the downward swing to begin. Get any of this wrong and you *run the danger* [read *run the risk*] of your shot falling short, heading into a hazard or massively overshooting your target." Cheryl Mullin, "Rory's First Game on Par with Tiger," *Birmingham Mail* (U.K.), 18 July 2015, at 10. (On *shot falling short* for *shot's falling short*, see FUSED PARTICIPLES.)

LANGUAGE-CHANGE INDEX
*run the danger for *run the risk*: Stage 1
Current ratio (*run the risk* vs. **run the danger*): 40:1

DANGLERS. A. Generally. So-called danglers are ordinarily unattached participles—either present participles (ending in *-ing*) or past participles (ending usually in *-ed*)—that do not relate syntactically to the nouns they are supposed to modify. That is, when the antecedent of a participle doesn't appear where it logically should, the participle is said to "dangle"—e.g.: "*Watching* from the ground below, the birds flew ever higher until they disappeared." In effect, the participle tries to sever its relationship with its noun or pronoun and thus to become functionally a preposition. Gerunds may also dangle precariously—e.g.: "By *watching* closely, the birds became visible." (See (D).) Usually, recasting the sentence will remedy the ambiguity, ILLOGIC, or incoherence: "Watching from the ground below, we saw the birds fly higher until they disappeared." / "By watching closely, we were able to see the birds."

Most danglers are ungrammatical. In the normal word order, a participial phrase beginning a sentence ("Walking down the street,") should be directly followed by the noun acting as subject in the main clause ("I saw the house"). When that word order is changed, as by changing the verb in the main clause to the PASSIVE VOICE, the sentence becomes illogical or misleading: "Walking down the street, the house was seen." It was not the house that was walking, but the speaker.

Some danglers, though, are acceptable because of long-standing usage. Examples are easy to come by: "*Considering* the current atmosphere in the legislature, the bill probably won't pass." But avoiding the dangler would often improve the style: "With the current atmosphere in the legislature, the bill probably won't pass." Several other examples are discussed below in (E).

Despite the sloppiness of danglers in general, they have been exceedingly common even among grammarians. For example, a biographical entry on Lindley Murray (1745–1826), the best-selling grammarian of the early 19th century, condemned his participial habits: "[In] spite of his proverbial credit as an authority, his own style was by no means a model of excellence; it was not impeccable even on grammatical grounds, the 'misallied participle' being only too frequent." 3 *Chambers's Cyclopaedia of English Literature* 740 (1903). The same habit can be found in other grammarians of repute—e.g.:

- "*By habituating* themselves to the practice of pointing, their attention will naturally be directed to clearness of thought." John Wilson, *A Treatise on Punctuation* 3 (23d ed. 1871).
- "*Never having been* taught as a system in any school, but only as a division of some other branch, no special importance was ever attached to [punctuation]." Edmund Shaftesbury, *One Hundred Lessons in Punctuation* 5 (1893).
- "*In answering* the questions, it has always been my aim to present opinion and state facts in the most workably helpful way." Edward N. Teall, *Putting Words to Work* viii (1940).
- "*Being a lexicographer* rather than a philologist—if indeed the name of lexicographer may be extended to include those who make compilations from the dictionaries of others—my interest has been more especially aroused by two aspects of linguistic study which lie somewhat outside the scope of the strict philologist." Logan Pearsall Smith, *Words and Idioms* vi–vii (5th ed. 1943).
- "*In speaking* to a child or about a child, it is usual to add the ordinary diminutive suffix." Otto Jespersen, *Mankind, Nation, and Individual from a Linguistic Point of View* 131 (1946).
- "Even *admitting* that a really compelling style is the result of years of cultivation, much scholarly writing is certainly worse than it needs to be." Donald J. Lloyd, "Our National Mania for Correctness," in *A Linguistics Reader* 57, 57 (Graham Wilson ed., 1967).

Likewise, danglers have appeared in the work of reputable fiction writers. For example, Herman Melville's famous short story "Bartleby the Scrivener" (1856) contains seven danglers. See Leedice Kissane, "Dangling Constructions in Melville's 'Bartleby,'" 36 *Am. Speech* 195 (1961).

All this has led one commentator to suggest that danglers are mere peccadilloes: "The loosely related participle phrase occurs pretty frequently in modern usage. Though grammar, insisting on the pure adjectival relationship, is against it, tradition is on its side; and, provided the result is not patently incongruous, it is not too lightly to be condemned." G.H. Vallins, *The Pattern of English* 56–57 (1956; repr. 1957). Other commentators are less forgiving:

- "In my daily work [as an editor], the presence of a participle at the portals of a statement is as ominous as the buzzing of a rattlesnake in my path." Eugene S. McCartney, *Recurrent Maladies in Scholarly Writing* 59 (1953).
- "Failures to look ahead and consider the grammatical compatibility of the following clause are exceedingly common, especially in unscripted speech." Robert W. Burchfield, *Points of View* 93 (1992).

B. Present-Participial Danglers. In the sentences that follow, mispositioned words have caused grammatical blunders. The classic example occurs when the wrong noun begins the main clause—that is, a noun other than the one expected by the reader after digesting the introductory participial phrase. E.g.: "The newspaper said that *before being treated* for their injuries, *General Mladic* forced them to visit the wards of wounded at the Pale hospital, telling them, 'here's what you have done' and 'you have also killed children.'" Marlise Simons, "Report Says Serbs Tormented 2 French Pilots," *N.Y. Times*, 29 Dec. 1995, at A5. That wording has General Mladic being treated for others' injuries. Hence danglers reflect a type of bad thinking. See ILLOGIC (c).

Another manifestation of this error is to begin the main clause with an EXPLETIVE (e.g., *it* or *there*) after an introductory participial phrase:

- "*Applying* those principles to the present situation, *it* is clear that the company must reimburse its employee." (A possible revision: *If we apply these principles to the present situation, it becomes clear that . . . .* Or better: *Given those principles, the company must . . . .*)
- "*Turning* to England, *it* ought to be noted first that that country, though late in doing so, participated fully in the medieval development sketched above." Grant Gilmore & Charles L. Black Jr., *The Law of Admiralty* 8 (2d ed. 1975). (A possible revision: *Although England was late in doing so, it participated fully in the medieval development sketched above.*)
- "*After reviewing* the aforementioned strategies, *it* becomes clear that there is no conclusive evidence regarding their success." Bernard J. Putz, "Productivity Improvement," *SAM Advanced Mgmt. J.*, 22 Sept. 1991, at 9. (A possible revision: *Even a detailed review of those strategies provides no conclusive evidence about how successful they are.*)

As in that last example, danglers occurring after an introductory word are just as bad as others but are harder for the untrained eye to spot—e.g.: "I have always found John Redwood thoughtful, intelligent and rather convivial. I sincerely hope that we can remain friends after the dust has settled. He has conducted a skilled campaign. Yet, *being* a thoughtful man, I suspect that in his heart of hearts he wishes some of his supporters . . . would just disappear." Jerry Hayes, "A White-Knuckle Ride I Cannot Join," *Independent*, 30 June 1995, at 21. (The writer here seems to attest to his own thoughtfulness. A possible revision: *Yet because he is a thoughtful man, I suspect that in his heart of hearts he wishes . . . .* Or: *Yet I suspect that, because he is a thoughtful man, in his heart of hearts he wishes . . . .*)

C. Past-Participial Danglers. These are especially common when the main clause begins with a possessive—e.g.: "*Born* on March 12, 1944, in Dalton, Georgia, Larry Lee Simms's qualifications . . . ." Barbara H. Craig, *Chadha: The Story of an Epic Constitutional Struggle* 79 (1988). (Simms's qualifications were not born on March 12—*he* was. A possible revision: *Born on March 12, 1944, in Dalton, Georgia, Larry Lee Simms had qualifications that . . . .*)

D. Dangling Gerunds. These are close allies to dangling participles, but here the participle acts as a noun rather than as an adjective when it is the object of a preposition:

- "*By instead examining* the multigenerational ethnic group, *it* becomes clear that the Irish had fully adjusted to American society by the time of the First World War." Michael Cottrell, Book Rev., *Canadian Hist. Rev.*, Sept. 1994, at 453. (A possible revision: *By instead examining the multigenerational ethnic group, we see that the Irish . . . .*)
- "*Without belaboring* the point, *the central premise* of this article is that the average pharmacist, preparing myriad prescriptions each day, does not have the time to provide CPS." Matthew M. Murawski, "Introduction to Personnel Management," *Drug Topics*, 10 June 1996, at 170. (A possible revision: *In brief, the central premise of this article . . . .*)

E. Acceptable Danglers, or Disguised Conjunctions. Any number of present participles have been used as conjunctions or prepositions for so long that they have lost the participial duty of modifying specific nouns. In effect, the clauses they introduce are adverbial, standing apart from and commenting on the content of the sentence. Among the commonest of these are *according, assuming, barring, concerning, considering, given, judging, owing to, regarding, respecting, speaking, taking* (usu. *account of, into account*). Thus:

- "Horticulturally *speaking*, the best way to prune the tree is probably to remove some of the lowest branches by cutting them off at the trunk." Mary Robson, "Pine Needles Won't Harm," *Seattle Times*, 14 Aug. 1994, at G3.
- "*Assuming* everyone shows up who's supposed to (not a given in this sport of last-minute scratches), this could be the finest assemblage of talent for a Long Island road race in a decade." John Hanc, "Cow Harbor Still Attracts Big Names," *Newsday* (N.Y.), 18 Sept. 1997, at A94.
- "*Considering* how hated Belichick was in Cleveland, it's incredible that another owner would want him as a head coach." John McClain, "John McClain's NFL Report," *Houston Chron.*, 7 Dec. 1997, at 24.

For an arguable example, see **except (B)**.

F. Ending Sentences with Danglers. Traditionally, grammarians frowned on *all* danglers, but during the 20th century they generally loosened the strictures for a participial construction at the end of a sentence. Some early-20th-century grammarians might have disapproved of the following sentences, but such sentences have long been considered acceptable:

- "Sarah stepped to the door, looking for her friend."
- "Tom's arm hung useless, broken by the blow."

Usually, as in the first example, the end-of-the-sentence dangler is introduced by a so-called coordinating participle: *looking* is equivalent to *and looked*. Similarly:

- "Vexed by these frequent demands on her time, she finally called upon her friend, *imploring* him to come to her aid." (*Imploring* = *and implored*.)
- "The New Orleans–bound steamer rammed and sank the freighter ten miles from her destination, *sending* her to the bottom in ten minutes." (*Sending* = *and sent*.)
- "She died before her brother, *leaving* a husband and two children." (*Leaving* = *and left*.)

A few editors would consider each of those participles misattached, but in fact they are acceptable as coordinating participles. As for the few who object, what would they do with the following sentence: "The boy ran out of the house *crying*"?

danse macabre; dance macabre. An art form meant to remind people of their mortality and of death as a social equalizer, *danse macabre* is more than ten times as common as *dance macabre*, an upstart spelling from the 19th century. Because macabre is a POSTPOSITIVE ADJECTIVE, the plural is *danses macabre* or *dances macabre*. See PLURALS (G).

dare. A. Generally. It's been called "one of the subtlest and most variegated verbs in the language" (Robert W. Burchfield, *Points of View* 123 [1992]) and also "one of the trickiest" (William Safire, "Love That Dare," *N.Y. Times*, 17 May 1987, § 6, at 10). The subtleties arise because *dare* is both an ordinary verb <he dares you to pick up the snake> and a modal verb <he dare not do it himself>. And the form it takes (*dares* vs. *dare* in those examples) changes with that grammatical function.

B. As a Full Verb. When *dare* is used as a full verb, it behaves just like most other verbs: it takes an *-s* with a third-person-singular subject <Robert always speaks his mind bluntly and *dares* anyone to disagree>. The form is identifiable by the presence of an explicit infinitive (with *to*) after *dare* (here, *to disagree*).

C. As a Modal. *Dare* was an Old English modal. When it is used as an auxiliary verb (like the modern modals *will*, *must*, and, more closely, *ought*), the infinitive either is missing its *to* <*Dare* he disagree with Robert?> or is missing altogether but understood <He *dare* not!>. This occurs chiefly, but not only, in interrogative or negative sentences. In those sentences, the form *dares*—although sometimes used mistakenly in striving for correctness—would be unidiomatic, because *dare* in this usage behaves like other uninflected modals <*Will* he disagree with Robert?> <he *must* not>.

D. Past Forms. As a modal verb, *dare* raises an interesting question of tense: in reference to past time, should one write (1) *Although challenged to do it, he dare not*, or (2) *Although challenged to do it, he dared not*? The *OED* endorses the first and calls the second "careless," but that advice was written when that part of the great dictionary was published in 1894 (and the dandy but now archaic *durst* was still available—see (E)). More recent grammarians are more lenient—e.g.:

- " 'Dare' in the sense of 'challenge' has formed a new past tense *dared* . . . as 'He *dared* not go.' " J.C. Nesfield, *English Grammar Past and Present* 355 (rev. ed. 1924; repr. 1948).
- "We may say *I do not dare* and *do you dare?*, or we may use the older forms and say *I dare not* and *dare you?* Some grammarians feel that this is license enough and object when the new forms are used in the old construction, that is, without the *to* of the infinitive, as in *he dares go*, *he dared go*, *I don't dare go*. . . . But the best writers and speakers have not agreed with them." *DCAU* at 126.
- "As a modal, *dare* exhibits abnormal time reference in that it can be used, without inflection, for past as well as present time: 'The king was so hot-tempered that no one *dare* tell him the bad news.' The main verb form *dared (to)* might also occur here." Randolph Quirk et al., *A Comprehensive Grammar of the English Language* § 3.42, at 138 (1985).
- "The marginal modal auxiliary *dare* has a past form *dared* <esp. BrE>." Ibid. § 10.68, at 797 n.(b).

These more modern grammarians' analyses are borne out by actual usage—e.g.:

- "A male screener wanded the woman's breasts—twice, even though a female screener was hanging around just steps away; the angry husband said he *dared not* complain lest they miss their flight." Edwin Black, "Travel Security," *Chicago Trib.*, 2 Dec. 2001, at 1.
- "Mayo said he *dared not* declare it a little blue heron without confirmation from others." Steve Grant, "Bird Count Turns Up a Few Surprises," *Hartford Courant*, 23 Dec. 2001, at B1.
- "Another of their quirks is a proclivity for skinny-dipping—something they *dared not* attempt at the beaches around Flinders." David Wroe, "Fridge Magnet Car Attracts the Curious," *The Age*, 31 Dec. 2001, at 4.

It is odd, however, to see the past-tense form in the SET PHRASE *how dare you*—e.g.: " 'How *dared* you!' Jon shouted, waving his arms for emphasis. 'That dish was ours, the property of the entire Order! How *dared* you even *think* to appropriate it for your own uses!' " Patricia C. Wrede, *Mairelon the Magician* 91 (1991). Most writers and editors would insist on making those phrases *How dare you!* See (F).

E. And *durst*. The form *durst*, which is a past indicative and past SUBJUNCTIVE along with *dared*, is

---

LANGUAGE-CHANGE INDEX (For the full key, see front matter pp. xxxi, l–li.)
Stage 1: Rejected. **Stage 2:** Widely shunned. **Stage 3:** Widespread but . . . **Stage 4:** Ubiquitous but . . . **Stage 5:** Fully accepted.
Invariably inferior forms marked by asterisk (✻). • Ratios represent frequency of prevalent forms vs. variants in current books.

obsolete in AmE. In BrE, it still occurs rarely, always in a negative sentence or conditional clause in which there is an infinitive either understood or having no *to* <none *durst* answer him>. In AmE (and almost always in BrE), *dared* would substitute: *durst* today is strictly jocular—e.g.: "How 'bout giving Puffy a ring? With these haggard elders on board, none *durst* judge the wily ol' plagiarist's heart." Keith Harris, "Souled Out," *Village Voice*, 25 June 2002, at 65. See ARCHAISMS.

F. *How dare.* This exclamatory construction involves an INVERSION: *How dare he do that!* is an idiomatic phrasing of the interrogative *How (does/did he) dare (to) do that?* The subject–actor (*he*) appears after the verb (*dare*) and is always in the nominative case—e.g.: "How dare *she* tell taxpayers to take on more responsibility to help neighborhood kids. How dare *she* be right!" Denise Smith Amos, "It's Up to Us to Ensure Kids Are OK," *Cincinnati Enquirer*, 18 Aug. 2002, at 2. Some people mistakenly think that a pronoun following *dare* must be in the objective case, apparently misconstruing it as an object of the verb *dare*—e.g.: " '[I]n a state that has predictable and documented needs, how dare *us* [read *we*] claim that the responsible public policy was handing out $30 here and $300 there to families that have desperate needs for not the dollars but the services?' " Gwyneth K. Shaw, "Improving Children's Well-Being," *Orlando Sentinel*, 22 May 2001, at A1. On the use of the past-tense *dared* in this phrase, see (D).

LANGUAGE-CHANGE INDEX
*how dare us (or *how dare him) for how dare we (or how dare he): Stage 1

daredevilry; daredeviltry. The latter has become a NEEDLESS VARIANT—though it was predominant in AmE print sources from 1900 until the 1990s. Perhaps AmE was influenced by BrE, in which *daredevilry* has always been standard. See **deviltry.**

Current ratio: 3:1

daresay; dare say. Four points merit attention. First, the term (meaning "to venture or presume to say") is now generally spelled as one word in AmE, two in BrE. Second, the term is now confined to first-person uses <I daresay she'll be late>. Third, the term is increasingly rare and formal-sounding. Fourth, *daresay* should not ordinarily be followed by the conjunction *that*—e.g.:

- "Further, without imagination, I *daresay* there would be no knowledge or civilization for inventions, and education itself depends upon an open and active mind." Kellye Dubard, "Gwinnett Ideas: The Meaning of Santa Claus," *Atlanta J.-Const.*, 25 Dec. 1994, at J9.
- "Sounds as if they're selling anything that's not tied down. Any chance I could pick up one of those antique phones? I *daresay that* [read *daresay*] in some houses in rural America you could still find them." Michael Balhoff & Matthew Boyle, "Qwest Passes His Test," *Fortune*, 30 Sept. 2002, at 178.

Of course, as a demonstrative pronoun or adjective, *that* after *daresay* is unobjectionable <I daresay that's right> <I daresay that plan is doomed>.

DASHES. See PUNCTUATION (G), (H).

dastard. A. Confusion with *bastard.* *Dastard* (= coward) is commonly muddled because of the sound association with its harsher rhyme, *bastard.* Although H.W. Fowler insisted that *dastard* should be reserved for someone who avoids all personal risk (*FMEU1* at 103), modern writers tend to use it as a printable EUPHEMISM for the more widely objectionable epithet—e.g.:

- "Samuel Ramey is the *dastard* of the piece, the treacherous, lecherous, murderous Assur." Herbert Glass, "On the Record: Cheryl Studer Scores as Semiramide," *L.A. Times*, 22 May 1994, at 51.
- "Along with heroes, villains have changed, too. My guys' enemy was always a scheming *dastard* so obsessed with the bottom line that in a modern adventure film he would be the hero." Jack Kisling, "Remakes I'd Rather Not See," *Denver Post*, 26 July 1994, at B7.
- "We hate seeing our friends and countrymen beheaded by a bunch of thugs and hate the fact that our reaction to those ugly pictures is that we want to kill those *dastards*, no matter what the cost. But we also hate the idea of sending our brave men and women to war again so soon after the last one got so mucked up." Brian Greenspun, "Our Nation's Role in Striving for Goodwill Toward All Men," *Las Vegas Sun*, 14 Dec. 2014, at 1.

British writers, on the other hand, have remained truer to the word's original sense—e.g.: "Last week I moved house from London to Brighton but like a genuine spineless *dastard* I flatly denied its implications on personal relationships to the last." Lynne Truss, "Au Revoir Is So Much Easier than Saying an Irrevocable Goodbye," *Times* (London), 8 Feb. 1994, Features §.

Recent American dictionaries record one meaning of *dastard* as being "a person who acts treacherously or underhandedly." So the new meaning should probably now be considered standard.

LANGUAGE-CHANGE INDEX
dastard in the broad sense "a despicable person": Stage 5

B. Corresponding Adjective: *dastardly.* Like the noun form, the adjective *dastardly* has been subjected to SLIPSHOD EXTENSION. Although most dictionaries define it merely as "cowardly," it is now often used as if it meant "sneaky and underhanded; treacherous"—e.g.:

- "Like her aunts and a long line of female relatives before her, she's a witch. A white one, which means that no matter how much havoc Sabrina may create until she gets a handle on her powers, she's not likely to use them for anything more *dastardly* than cute boy-trappage." Claire Bickley, "Sabrina Simply Enchanting," *Toronto Sun*, 26 Sept. 1996, at 65.
- "He's b-a-a-a-c-k. *Dastardly* J.R. Ewing and his oft-manipulated clan rise from TV dustdom to air three times a day on TNN, Cable Channel 37, beginning Monday." Rita Sherrow, "Weekend TV Highlights," *Tulsa World*, 27 Sept. 1996, at 20.
- "Of course that project would now have to be put on hold for the time being. Another grievance against the

dastardly intruder." Fred Saberhagen, *A Coldness in the Blood* 209 (2002).

data (/**dat**-ə-/ or /**day**-tə/) is a SKUNKED TERM: whether you write *data are* or *data is*, you're likely to make some readers raise their eyebrows. Technically a plural, *data* has, since the 1940s, been increasingly treated as a mass noun taking a singular verb. But in more or less formal contexts it is preferably treated as a plural—e.g.:

- "While recent U.S. Census *data show* that the average working woman's pay has declined in the '90s, highly educated, high-paid women keep gaining ground." Jeanhee Kim, "The New Way to Get Rich? Get Married!" *Money*, Oct. 1996, at 141.
- "The *data are* derived from tests performed on expectant mothers." "The Plague," *Economist*, 24 Mar. 2001, at 53.

Many writers use it as a singular, however, risking their credibility with a small minority of readers—e.g.:

- "There *isn't* any *data*." Graham Wilson, Foreword, *A Linguistics Reader* ix (Graham Wilson ed., 1967).
- "No *data is* offered to suggest that women are being adversely hit by the dearth of articles." "A Woman's Place Is in the Law," *Globe & Mail* (Toronto), 24 Aug. 1993, at A14.
- "But now NRG, hit by charges that its *data isn't* reliable, has some competition." "Gallup Goes to Hollywood," *Newsweek*, 28 Mar. 1994, at 43.
- "Browsing the World Wide Web these days is less like surfing than like crawling: *data drips* like molasses onto your computer screen, sometimes taking several minutes to create a single page of text." Michael Krantz, "Wired for Speed," *Time*, 23 Sept. 1996, at 54.

One context in which the singular use of *data* might be allowed is in computing and allied disciplines. See COMPUTERESE.

In one particular use, *data* is rarely treated as a singular: when it begins a clause and is not preceded by the definite article. E.g.: "*Data* over the last two years *suggest* that the rate at which gay men get AIDS has finally begun to flatten out." Lawrence K. Altman, "Who's Stricken and How: AIDS Pattern Is Shifting," *N.Y. Times*, 5 Feb. 1989, at 1.

Datum, the "true" singular, is sometimes used when a single piece of information is referred to—e.g.:

- "We accept the law as a necessary *datum*, but that is not to say that we are required to accept it in abeyance of our critical faculties." F.R. Leavis, *The Common Pursuit* 166–67 (1952).
- "The inclination of the orbital plane to our line of sight is another desirable *datum*." Philip A. Charles & R. Mark Wagner, "Black Holes in Binary Stars," *Sky & Telescope*, May 1996, at 38.
- "Confident that my brain—assuming it had any blood left in it—would react hysterically to any syllables remotely sounding like 'eject,' I took comfort in this *datum*." Christopher Buckley, "How I Went Nine Gs in an F-16 and Only Threw Up Five Times," *Forbes*, 23 Sept. 1996, at 116.

Still, in nonscientific contexts, *datum* is likely to sound pretentious.

Because *data* can be either a plural count noun or a singular mass noun, both *many data* and *much data* are correct—e.g.:

- "Numerous expert and representative interests are consulted, and *many data* assembled, often over a long period." Carleton K. Allen, *Law in the Making* 433 (7th ed. 1964). (The verb *are* is understood after *data*. See UNDERSTOOD WORDS.)
- "But *much* of the *data* in present personnel files *is* highly subjective." William O. Douglas, *Points of Rebellion* 21 (1970).
- "Finding out exactly how *much* digital *data makes* its way from smartphone apps or an Internet-connected PC to data brokers and digital advertisers is an uphill battle." Deborah Todd & Chris Potter, "Privacy Takes a Hit While Digital *Data Is* Scooped Up, Passed Around," *Pitt. Post-Gaz.*, 6 Sept. 2015, at A1.
- "The transfer of soil data to digital format has allowed a wide range of interpretations, but *many data are* still not freely available as *they* are held by a number of different bodies." "Reports on General Science Findings from University of Ft. Hare Provide New Insights," *Science Letter*, 21 Aug. 2015, at 534.

See COUNT NOUNS AND MASS NOUNS.

As a historian of the English language once put it, "A student with one year of Latin [knows] that *data* and *phenomena* are plural." Albert C. Baugh, "The Gift of Style," 34 *Pa. Bar Ass'n* 101, 105–06 (1962). And that's what makes the term skunked: few people use it as a plural, yet many know that it is technically a plural. Whatever you do, if you use *data* in a context in which its number becomes known, you'll bother some of your readers. Perhaps 50 years from now—maybe sooner, maybe later—the term will no longer be skunked: everybody will accept it as a collective. But not yet. See PLURALS (B).

LANGUAGE-CHANGE INDEX

data as a mass noun: Stage 4

Current ratio (*The data are* vs. *The data is*): 2:1

database. One word. See SPELLING (D).

datable (/**dayt**-ə-bəl/). So spelled in AmE and BrE alike—not **dateable*. See MUTE E.

Current ratio: 11:1

data processing. Two words.

DATES. A. Order. One may unimpeachably write either *May 26, 2009*, or *26 May 2009*. The latter—the BrE method, which is also used in the American military—is often better in prose, for it takes no commas. It appears in dates throughout this book.

Of the usual AmE method—*May 26, 2009*—the first editor of the *OED* said: "This is not logical: 19 May 1862 is. *Begin* at day, *ascend* to month, *ascend* to year; not *begin* at month, *descend* to day, then *ascend* to year." James A.H. Murray, as quoted in *Hart's Rules for Compositors and Readers at the OUP* 18 n.1 (39th ed. 1983).

LANGUAGE-CHANGE INDEX (For the full key, see front matter pp. xxxi, l–li.)
Stage 1: Rejected. **Stage 2:** Widely shunned. **Stage 3:** Widespread but . . . **Stage 4:** Ubiquitous but . . . **Stage 5:** Fully accepted.
Invariably inferior forms marked by asterisk (*). • Ratios represent frequency of prevalent forms vs. variants in current books.

B. Month and Year. *February 2010* is better than *February of 2010*. Stylebooks have long agreed that no comma should appear between the month and the year. Among the mountains of evidence that might be amassed are these sources: *The Washington Post Deskbook on Style* 127 (1978); Kate L. Turabian, *A Manual for Writers of Term Papers, Theses, and Dissertations* 30 (5th ed. 1987); *The Chicago Manual of Style* 176 (15th ed. 2003); *Publication Manual of the American Psychological Association* 63 (4th ed. 1994); *Scientific Style and Format* 227 (6th ed. 1994); Joseph Gibaldi, *MLA Handbook for Writers of Research Papers* 70 (1999); Allan M. Siegal & William G. Connolly, *The New York Times Manual of Style and Usage* 101 (1999); *Webster's New World English Grammar Handbook* 161 (2001).

It may therefore seem strange to encounter an article in *The New Yorker*, one of our best-edited literary magazines, in which *January, 2000* and *March, 2000* appear on the first page, and then five similar references appear throughout the piece. (See Scott Turow, "To Kill or Not to Kill," *New Yorker*, 6 Jan. 2003, at 40–47.) This seems anomalous: almost every professional editor would immediately delete the superfluous commas. Yet seasoned readers of *The New Yorker* know that these little bacilli in month–year references are one of the unfortunate conventions of the magazine's house style.

C. As Adjectives. Modern writers have taken to making adjectives out of dates, just as they do out of place names—e.g.: "His July 1998 book contract resulted in a record advance." The more traditional rendering of the sentence would be: "In his book contract of July 1998, he received a record advance." Although occasionally using dates adjectivally is a space-saver, the device should not be overworked: it gives prose a breezy look.

And the practice is particularly clumsy when the day as well as the month is given—e.g.: "The court reconsidered its July 12, 2001 privilege order." Stylists who use this phrasing typically omit the comma after the year, and justifiably so: in the midst of an adjective phrase (i.e., the date), it impedes the flow of the writing too much. Still, that second comma sometimes surfaces—e.g.: "Harvey is accused of murder, robbery and burglary in the *June 16, 1985,* [read *June 16, 1985*] slaying of Irene Schnaps, 37, who suffered 15 blows to the head with a hatchet in her Hunters Glen apartment." Jim O'Neill, "12 Potential Jurors Get Boot at Murder Trial," *Star-Ledger* (Newark), 29 Oct. 1994, at 19.

The idea of the comma after the year, as it has commonly been taught, is that the year is in apposition, so the second comma is required. But if that year is an appositive, it's unlike other APPOSITIVES; it certainly isn't interchangeable with the noun (the date) that precedes it. The more plausible argument—supporting the absence of the comma after the year—has two parts. First, the comma is really just separating the two numerals, so if a second comma isn't syntactically required, then it doesn't belong <a November 17, 2001 meeting>. Second, the comma after the date marks a nonexistent pause: when a full date is used adjectivally, a knowledgeable speaker of the phrase marches toward the noun instead of pausing after the year. An adjective represents a surge forward, while a comma represents a backward-looking pause. It makes little sense to punctuate a forward-looking adjective with a pause at the end of it.

Most usage books that call uniformly for a comma after the year in a full date, by the way, don't address the question raised just above. They show the comma without illustrating what happens when the date functions as an adjective. In other words, they illustrate the easy cases, not the more difficult ones. That's probably because the date-as-adjective phenomenon didn't really come into full flower until the late 20th century. Even after the shift was well underway, most usage guides ignored the problem.

D. 2010s vs. 2010's. When referring to decades, most professional writers today omit the apostrophe: hence, *2010s* instead of *2010's*. That's the dominant style (although *The New York Times* uses the apostrophe). See PLURALS (K) & PUNCTUATION (A). On whether a decade is singular or plural, see SUBJECT–VERB AGREEMENT (L).

Current ratio (*1990s* vs. *1990's*): 65:1

E. Spans. Although a span of time may be denoted with an en-dash (*1997–2002*), the dash should not appear if the word *from* introduces the numbers: *from 1997 to 2002* (not **from 1997–2002*).

datum. See **data.**

daylight-saving(s) time. Although the singular form *daylight-saving time* is the original one, dating from the early 20th century—and is preferred by most usage critics—the plural form is now extremely common in AmE. E.g.: "When *daylight savings time* kicks in, a guard will be posted from 5 to 10 p.m." Christine Bordelon, "Kenner Post Office Getting Update," *Times-Picayune* (New Orleans), 15 Sept. 1996, at D1.

The rise of the plural form (*daylight-savings time*) appears to have resulted from the avoidance of a MISCUE: when *saving* is used, readers might momentarily puzzle over whether *saving* is a gerund (the saving of daylight) or a participle (the time for saving). Also, of course, we commonly speak of how to "save time" (of saving time), and this compounds the possible confusion. Using *savings* as the adjective—as in *savings account* or *savings bond*—makes perfect sense. But in print sources, the singular form still appears twice as often as the plural. Cf. **saving(s).**

Saving is commonly omitted when used with the names of time zones <Pacific Daylight Time>, and when used as a general term to distinguish from standard time <2 PM daylight time>.

Regardless of whether you use the plural or the singular, you can prevent most miscues by hyphenating the PHRASAL ADJECTIVE: *daylight-saving time* or *daylight-savings time.*

LANGUAGE-CHANGE INDEX
daylight-savings time for *daylight-saving time*: Stage 5
Current ratio (*daylight-saving time* vs.
daylight-savings time): 2:1

D-Day; *D-day. Originally (from about 1918) a military codeword denoting any operation, the term is most famously associated with 6 June 1944, when during World War II the Allies landed in France to begin the spread of their forces throughout Europe under the command of General Dwight D. Eisenhower. By metaphorical extension, the term is sometimes used to refer to any day when an important event is to take place.

The initial *D* in *D-Day* is simply an abbreviated form of *day*. The term was already in somewhat popular use before 1944—from about 1941—in BrE and AmE alike. From the beginning, it has predominantly been written with both *D*'s capitalized: *D-Day*, not *D-day.
Current ratio: 6:1

de. See NAMES (D).

*deaccelerate. See **decelerate.**

deadline is one word; formerly it was hyphenated. The term comes from the American Civil War era, when it denoted a line outside a prison beyond which inmates could be shot as escapees.

deadly; deathly. *Deadly* = able to cause death <deadly venom>. *Deathly* = like death <deathly ill>. The phrase *deadly dull* has vastly predominated over *deathly dull* since the 18th century—e.g.: "Any critical biography with the words 'the Rise of Modern Criticism' as part of its title had better be comprehensible if it is to escape being *deadly* dull." James E. Person Jr., "Glimpses of Brooks' Life Are Still Revealing," *Virginian-Pilot* (Norfolk), 15 Sept. 1996, at J2.
Current ratio (*deadly dull* vs. *deathly dull*): 18:1

deal. A. Past Tense and Past Participle. *Deal* makes *dealt*, not *dealed*, but the erroneous form sometimes occurs—e.g.: "Recently, Salerno *dealed* [read *dealt*] in secret to get an arena for the Florida Panthers built in the city just south of Oakland Park Boulevard and the Sawgrass Expressway." Rafael Lorente, "Sunrise Slashes Rates in Trash Contract," *Sun-Sentinel* (Ft. Lauderdale), 21 Aug. 1996, at 3. The only context in which *dealed* is standard is in the rhyming SET PHRASE *wheeled and dealed*—e.g.: "Big as a linebacker and sometimes brusque as a bully, he *wheeled and dealed* and wined and dined with a swagger." Bob Secter, "New Lifestyle to Begin for Rostenkowski," *Chicago Trib.*, 22 July 1996, at N1. See IRREGULAR VERBS (D).
Current ratio (*has dealt* vs. *has dealed): 23,595:1

B. Deal with; deal in. People in business *deal in* what they buy and sell <he deals in stocks and bonds>, but they *deal with* other people (but see below). *Deal* should not be used transitively where *deal in* is intended.

Yet in one context *deal* is transitive, in a phrase originating in the language of the underworld. We say that a person *deals drugs*, not *deals in drugs—e.g.:

- "Two Barnesville brothers have been charged with growing marijuana in their yard and *dealing drugs* from their home in Vulcan Village, state police at Frackville said." "Two Brothers Charged by Police Drug Raiders," *Morning Call* (Allentown, Pa.), 6 Sept. 1996, at B3.
- "A husband had been arrested for *dealing drugs*, which meant the lady's tips went straight to his lawyer and she couldn't leave town before trial." Edward Hoagland, "Sex and the River Styx," *Harper's Mag.*, Jan. 2003, at 49, 53–54.

Perhaps this exception exists because *dealing drugs* is reprehensible; to say that one *deals in* contraband would sanitize it, as if it were an alternative to dealing in cosmetics or foodstuffs. Or perhaps the phrasing is a metaphorical extension: *dealing drugs* as one might *deal cards*.

Deal with is a vague PHRASAL VERB for which there is almost always a better, more specific substitute—e.g.: "If called [in a civil case], defendants are required to testify under oath, and can be *dealt with* [read *treated*] severely by judges if they refuse." "Son of Simpson Trial Is No Rerun," *Baltimore Sun*, 20 Sept. 1996, at A2.

But when *deal with* is roughly equivalent to *handle*, it is unobjectionable: "He pointed out that since Singapore was SIA's home base, the office *dealt with* a wide range of routes and services." Rahita Elias, "SIA Expects Outbound Sales to Grow 10%," *Bus. Times*, 20 Sept. 1996, at 18.

dearly (= deeply, fondly) presents no problem when it modifies a verb <she dearly loved music>. As a modifier of an attributive past participle, it is familiar in the SET PHRASE *dearly beloved*. Acting on that model, though, writers sometimes paint themselves into an unidiomatic corner—e.g.: "Zulu, owner of Zulu Tattoo in Los Angeles, says tattoos have become like lockets, those tiny trinkets of gold or silver hung from thin necklaces that held a portrait or a lock of hair of the *dearly* [read *dear*] departed." DeNeen L. Brown, "Indelible Link: Lives Lost to Tragedy Linger in the Flesh of Those Left Behind," *Wash. Post*, 31 Aug. 2008, at M1. (Really, the whole phrase should be rewritten, perhaps by making it *a lock of hair of a departed loved one*.)

dearth = scarcity <there was a dearth of Americans at the festival>. But the word is commonly misunderstood as meaning a complete lack or absence of something. This misunderstanding is revealed especially in the nonsensical phrase *complete dearth, which has lurked in the linguistic shadows since the early 19th century. E.g.:

- "Approximate number of calls logged by the 'O.J. Hotline' before it was disconnected due to *a complete dearth* [read *the lack* or *the absence*] of concrete leads pointing to other suspects: 250,000." Richard Roeper, "The O.J. Trial . . . Again: This Time by Numbers," *Chicago Sun-Times*, 4 June 1995, Show §, at 2.

LANGUAGE-CHANGE INDEX (For the full key, see front matter pp. xxxi, l–li.)
Stage 1: Rejected. **Stage 2:** Widely shunned. **Stage 3:** Widespread but . . . **Stage 4:** Ubiquitous but . . . **Stage 5:** Fully accepted.
Invariably inferior forms marked by asterisk (*). • Ratios represent frequency of prevalent forms vs. variants in current books.

- "But the pile of circumstantial evidence against Jewell is in stark contrast to the *complete dearth* [read *absence* or *lack*] of direct incriminating evidence that has surfaced so far." Ralph Ranalli, "Guilty or Not, Bomb Suspect Lives a Nightmare," *Boston Herald*, 4 Aug. 1996, at 1.
- "In many parts of the country, there *was a complete dearth of* [read *were no*] sales and little construction activity during the downturn." Cynthia M. Fraser, "True Value?" *Nat'l Real Estate Investor*, 1 Nov. 2014, at 44.

LANGUAGE-CHANGE INDEX
*complete dearth for *absence* or *lack*: Stage 1

death; demise; decease, n.; surcease. *Death* is the common word, the other three being FORMAL WORDS (in order of increasing formality) that act almost as EUPHEMISMS. There is nothing wrong with the word *death*, although it has inherently unpleasant connotations. But that is the nature of the subject, and writing *decease* or *surcease* is only a little less ridiculous than writing *going to meet his Maker*.

Deceased, adj., is quite acceptable, having been established by usage and not striking most readers as circumlocutory. For an odd misusage, see **diseased**.

deathly. See **deadly**.

debacle is pronounced /di-**bahk**-əl/ or (less good) /di-**bak**-əl/—not /**deb**-i-kəl/.

debar. See **bar**.

*debarcation. See **debarkation**.

*debark. See **disembark**.

debarkation; *debarcation. The former has always been the standard spelling in AmE and BrE alike: it means "getting off the ship (the bark, or barque)."
Current ratio: 36:1

debauch; debouch. These words are liable to confusion. *Debauch* /di-**bawch**/, the more prevalent word, means "to defile; to seduce away from virtue; to corrupt." E.g.: "More pervert than poet, this character *debauches* the cycle boy's sister, forcing her into sadomasochistic acts with paying clients, some merely disgusting, others so arcane I couldn't tell what was behind them." Alexander Walker, "Confusion Reigns on a Ride to Trouble," *Evening Standard*, 21 Mar. 1996, at 26. The corresponding noun is *debauchery*.

Debouch /di-**boosh**/ = to emerge or cause to emerge; to come out into open ground—e.g.:

- "A group of humpback whales began routinely to feed near the bay's mouth in 1991—as many as 19 in a winter—in the food-rich plume of water *debouching* from the bay, fed by runoff from the bay watershed." "Whales in Delmarva Area," *Baltimore Sun*, 22 Sept. 1996, at B12.
- "We *debouched* from the carriage and instructed the hackman to return to the village and return for us in the morning." Richard A. Lupoff, "The Incident of the Impecunious Chevalier," in *My Sherlock Holmes* 3, 13 (Michael Kurland ed., 2003).

The word, which has a military origin, shouldn't refer to going *into* a place—e.g.: "We *debouched into* [read

went into] the hotel dining room and suddenly there was a surge in Sharpe's popularity." Tom Sharpe, "A Blot in My Life," *Daily Telegraph*, 9 Sept. 1995, at 1. The corresponding noun is *debouchment*.

debility; debilitation. *Debility* = weakness; feebleness. *Debilitation* = the act of making weak or feeble. It is a fairly common error to misuse *debilitation* for *debility*—e.g.: "Although [Fidel Castro] could yet reappear in the halls of power in Havana, the evidence of his physical *debilitation* [read *debility*] and cognitive inconsistencies suggests that if he does return, it will be in an emeritus capacity." Brian Latell, "Raul Castro: Confronting Fidel's Legacy in Cuba," *Wash. Q.*, Summer 2007, at 53.

LANGUAGE-CHANGE INDEX
debilitation misused for *debility*: Stage 1

debonair (= suave, urbane) is the standard spelling. It's pronounced /deb-ə-**nair**/. **Debonaire* is a variant spelling.
Current ratio: 23:1

deboned. See **boned**.

debouch. See **debauch**.

debridement (= [1] the operation of cutting away dead or contaminated tissue, or [2] the enlargement of a passage for pus to flow from an abscess) is a GALLICISM used chiefly by surgeons and dentists. It is pronounced /di-**breed**-mənt/—not /di-**brɪd**-mənt/.

debris (= [1] pieces of waste material, or [2] the pieces of something left after the thing has been destroyed in an accident, explosion, etc.) is pronounced /də-**bree**/ in AmE and /**deb**-ree/ or /**day**-bree/ in BrE. The acute accent is now normally omitted from the *-e-*.

debtor. See **bankrupt** (B).

decathlon. See **-athlon**.

decease, n. See **death**.

decease, v.i., = to die. "He *deceased* without children." This verbal use of *decease* is even more pompous than the noun use. The straightforward *die* is usually better. See **diseased**. Cf. **death**.

deceased. See **diseased**.

deceive; defraud. To *deceive* is to induce someone to believe in a falsehood. The deceiver may know the statement to be false or may make it recklessly. To *defraud* is to cause some kind of injury or loss by deceit. *Defrauding* leads a person to take action, whereas *deceiving* merely leads a person into a state of mind.

decelerate is sometimes erroneously remade into **deaccelerate*, especially in speech.
Current ratio: 357:1

deceptive; deceitful. Although both words connote "misleading," *deceptive* does not necessarily indicate dishonesty. A person or thing may mislead another with bad intent <deceptive business practice> <deceptive answer> or with no bad intent <appearances can be deceptive>. But someone or something *deceitful* always has an underlying intent to lie, cheat, or defraud by misleading <deceitful story> <deceitful game>.

deceptively (= misleadingly) can itself be a deceptive word: it is inherently ambiguous and should therefore be avoided entirely as a SKUNKED TERM. When it modifies an adjective, it might indicate that something is not what it appears to be, but the nature of that discrepancy is not immediately clear. For example, what is *deceptively smooth* might be either (1) rough in appearance but actually smooth, or (2) smooth in appearance but actually rough—e.g.: "At a *deceptively smooth* spot I let off the brakes and attempted to catch up. Instantaneously, my front tire hit a huge leaf-covered rock, nearly bringing me to a standstill." Jeb Tilly, "Wild Today, Gone Tomorrow?" *Wash. Post*, 16 Nov. 2001, at T64.

Many writers use *deceptively* as if to enhance the adjective, but the resulting phrases can be even more ambiguous—e.g.:

- "So sure, we need to goad our reluctant governor and state agencies and state Legislature to take the *deceptively dangerous* issue of waste tires more seriously." Fred Lebrun, "A Smoking Mound of Problems," *Times Union* (Albany), 12 Mar. 2002, at B1. (Is something here dangerous or not? And is it the issue or the tires?)
- "The building is *deceptively large*—12,000 square feet of potential office space—and it has an advantage that many older businesses, designed for a different time, do not: ample parking." Roger Williams, "Where We Live: Census Tract 10," *News-Press* (Ft. Myers, Fla.), 1 Sept. 2002, at G1. (Is the building larger or smaller than it looks?)
- "Until that changes, even a new interest-rate cut by the Fed could fail to stop the *deceptively serious* downturn." David Leonhardt, "Downturn Lasts as Fed Meets," *Chattanooga Times*, 24 Sept. 2002, at C1. (Is the economic downturn worse than it appears or really nothing to worry about?)

Sometimes context can clarify what *deceptively* means—e.g.:

- " 'Lowhead dams are *deceptively dangerous* and can range from a drop-off of six inches to as much as 25 feet,' said John Wisse of ODNR." "State Issues Boating Advisory for Rivers, Streams," *Dayton Daily News*, 16 May 2002, at D7. (The dams can be more dangerous than they look.)
- "The creek, though narrow, is *deceptively deep*. Sailing ships brought supplies and goods to a landing here, making it a thriving port." Molly Murray, "Discovering Delaware," *News J.* (Wilmington, Del.), 23 Sept. 2002, at A1. (It's deeper than it looks.)

The word often signals verbosity, introducing a phrase that might be distilled to a single word—e.g.:

- "It's Charlie Brown country—*a deceptively easy* [read *an enjoyable*?] place to spend a couple of hours." Evan Henerson, "Comic Genius; Schulz's Immortal Characters

Captured in 'Charlie Brown,'" *Daily News* (L.A.), 16 Aug. 2002, at U19. (The sentence appeared at the end of a glowing review.)
- "The river looks *deceptively well-watered* [read *full*?] as it makes its way through Albuquerque, its appearance at odds with the reality of New Mexico's long-term drought." "Keeping the Rio Alive," *Albuquerque Trib.*, 21 Sept. 2002, at A1 (photo caption).

Sometimes simply omitting the word improves the sentence—e.g.: "I like to think I have a good sense of humor, but what is considered funny is so *deceptively subjective* [read *subjective*]." Ramsey Campbell, "Humor Is in the Mind of the Beholder, Despite British Study," *Orlando Sentinel*, 13 Oct. 2002, at K10.

decimate. Originally this word meant "to kill one in every ten," but this etymological sense, because it's so uncommon, has been abandoned except in historical contexts. Now *decimate* generally means "to cause great loss of life; to destroy a large part of." Even allowing that extension in meaning, the word is commonly misused in two ways.

First, the word is sometimes mistakenly applied to an obliteration or utter defeat—e.g.:

- "When he did reach Preston Flats the town looked not only uninhabited but deserted, as if plague had swept through and *decimated it* [read *destroyed it* or, perhaps, *killed everybody*]." Cormac McCarthy, *Outer Dark* 131 (1968).
- "Incidentally, this particular cyclamen is one of the species that had been nearly *totally decimated* [read *obliterated*] in its native Mediterranean lands by mindless digging for commercial gain." Joan Lee Faust, "Caution: Ants at Work (Watch Your Step)," *N.Y. Times*, 3 Jan. 1993, N.J. §, at 6.
- "If you've watched American Hoggers you know boars are known to be vicious and territorial animals that breed like crazy and *decimate* [read *destroy*] land." "Wishful Thinking for Animal Lovers," *Caledon Enterprise* (Can.), 19 Aug. 2015, Opinion §, at 1.

Second, the word is misused when it is used lightly of any defeat or setback, however trivial or temporary, especially when applied to inanimate things—e.g.:

- "With her slingshot she even *decimates* [read *breaks*?] their searchlight." Jerry Tallmer, "Wartime France Turned Deadly Cute," *Record* (N.J.), 30 Aug. 1996, Lifestyle §, at 39.
- "The Steelers may be *decimated* [read *hampered* or *plagued*] by injuries, but they possess great depth on defense." "The Bettor's Edge," *Boston Herald*, 6 Sept. 1996, at 76.
- "House Republicans have eagerly attacked and, as of last year, effectively *decimated* [read *wiped out*] family-planning funds." Sara Engram, "Preserving the World's Families," *Plain Dealer* (Cleveland), 7 Sept. 1996, at B11.

And sometimes the METAPHOR is simply inappropriate—e.g.: "He said he had watched lung cancer *decimate* [read *emaciate* or *ravage*] his sister's body." Phoebe Wall Howard, "Gore: Ticket Is 'Bridge to the Future,'" *Fresno Bee*, 30 Aug. 1996, at A1.

In fact, though, the word might justifiably be considered a SKUNKED TERM. Whether you stick to the

LANGUAGE-CHANGE INDEX (For the full key, see front matter pp. xxxi, l–li.)
Stage 1: Rejected. **Stage 2:** Widely shunned. **Stage 3:** Widespread but . . . **Stage 4:** Ubiquitous but . . . **Stage 5:** Fully accepted.
Invariably inferior forms marked by asterisk (*). • Ratios represent frequency of prevalent forms vs. variants in current books.

original one-in-ten meaning or use the extended sense, the word is infected with ambiguity. And some of your readers will probably be puzzled or bothered.

LANGUAGE-CHANGE INDEX
1. *decimate* for large-scale destruction: Stage 5
2. *decimate* for complete destruction: Stage 3
3. *decimate* for the figurative destruction of a single thing or person <she was decimated by the news>: Stage 4
4. *decimate* for *hamper* or *plague*: Stage 3

decision, take a. See AMERICANISMS AND BRITICISMS (C).

decisioning for *deciding* or *decision-making* is symptomatic of JARGON in two fields—banking and boxing. The term gained prominence beginning in the latter half of the 20th century. In banking, *decisioning* is the term for deciding whether to extend credit—e.g.:

- "Officials said the system has an 'expert *decisioning*' capability, which automatically obtains access to relevant returned check data and makes the pay/no-pay decision." Steven Marjanovic, "Mellon to Test Return Item Processing Plan," *Am. Banker*, 8 June 1995, at 13.
- "On-line credit verification and evaluation systems quickly and accurately assess creditworthiness without the drawbacks of manual *decisioning*." Philip N. Burgess Jr., "Instantaneous Credit Reporting Offers Economical Gains to Credit," *Business Credit*, Feb. 1996, at 25.
- "Banks can incorporate new data sources and analytics into their *decisioning* processes over time, achieving continual performance improvements and incremental cost savings and revenue gains." Roger Ahern, "Originations: Where Cost, Risk, and Profit Start," *Collections & Credit Risk*, 3 Jan. 2005, at 42.

In boxing cant, the verb *decision* means "to defeat (an opponent) not by knockout but by a decision of the judges." Sportswriters are much enamored of the word—e.g.:

- "David Diaz (139) became an Olympian by *decisioning* Zabdiel Judah." Michael Holley, "Mesi Win a Stunner: Hartford's Clay-Bey Upset at US Boxoffs," *Boston Globe*, 20 Apr. 1996, at 82.
- "Germany's Ralf Rocchigiani (39–7–7) successfully defended his WBO cruiserweight title for the fourth time, *decisioning* Nigeria's Bashiru Ali (41–14) in Essen, Germany." "U.S. Tops Japan for 2–0 Lead in Federation Cup," *Palm Beach Post*, 14 July 1996, at C2.
- "Hector Camacho looked so bad in *decisioning* Arturo Nina the other night, it makes it a lock that Sugar Ray Leonard will come back." Barry Horn, "From Overstated Media Guides to Overweight Boxers," *Dallas Morning News*, 24 Aug. 1996, at B2.

decision-making, n., is a generic term for *deciding* and, though useful in some contexts, is much overworked in modern prose—especially in the redundant BUREAUCRATESE *decision-making process*. The word smacks of business JARGON and is often merely a grandiloquent way of saying *deciding*: after all, when one makes decisions, one decides.

It is now frequently spelled as one word, even by the U.S. Supreme Court. One sees the same one-wordism tendency at work in the terms **budgetmaking* and

*policymaking. These compounds are too bulky to look like anything but jargonistic English; a simple hyphen does a lot.

declaim; disclaim. To *declaim* is to speak formally in public (hence the adjective *declamatory*). To *disclaim* is to disavow, deny, or renounce (as a manufacturer sometimes does in its warranties). Both words can be transitive, but what one declaims is one's opinion or message, not what one is denouncing. In that context the preposition *against* is needed—e.g.: "Though some, including the National PTA, *declaim* [read *declaim against* or *denounce*] the use of children as fund-raisers, most parents recognize that the profits support necessary programs and defray costs such as travel and uniforms." Stephanie Dunnewind, "Beyond Bake Sales," *Seattle Times*, 31 Aug. 2002, at E1.

LANGUAGE-CHANGE INDEX
declaim misused for *denounce*: Stage 1

declarative; declaratory; declamatory. Both *declarative* and *declaratory* mean "having the function of declaring, setting forth, or explaining"; their DIFFERENTIATION lies in established uses, not in meaning. We speak of *declarative* sentences in grammar, but *declaratory* judgments in law.

Declamatory, which is sometimes confused with *declaratory*, means "haranguing; of, relating to, or involving declaiming oratorically." Here it's correctly used: "By contrast, the *declamatory* rhetoric of 'War Scenes'—a 1969 setting of excerpts from Walt Whitman's diaries—felt rather hectoring, marked by ungainly leaps in the vocal line and a striving after effect." Joshua Kosman, "Rorem in the Afternoon Offers Few Challenges," *S.F. Chron.*, 26 Sept. 1994, at E3.

declination; *declinature; declension. All three words are used in denoting the act of courteously refusing, but *declination* now far outstrips the other two in frequency of use. In referring to the act of declining, **declinature* and *declension* ought to be considered NEEDLESS VARIANTS of *declination*.

But even *declination* is open to ambiguity because it also means (1) "a downward bend or slope"; (2) "a deterioration; falling off"; or (3) "a deviation." *Declension* has the same problem because it may mean "a downhill slope"; (2) "a decline or decrease"; or (3) "a grammatical inflection or class of words."

Current ratio (*declination* vs. **declinature*): 120:1

decline, v.i. & v.t. This verb has two distinct senses and yields two noun forms. *Declination* derives from *decline* in the sense "to refuse." *Decline*, n., derives from *decline* in the sense "to go downhill."

décolletage, n.; **décolleté,** adj. *Décolletage* = (1) the top edge of a woman's dress cut very low to show cleavage and shoulders; or (2) the full dress itself, so cut. *Décolleté* = (1) (of a woman) wearing a strapless or low-cut dress; or (2) (of a dress) having a low-cut neckline. Both words are normally not italicized but retain their DIACRITICAL MARKS.

The etymologically related verb *decollate* (= to behead) dates from the 15th century—but it is rarely associated with these GALLICISMS. *Décolleté* was popular in the late 18th century, but mostly in phrases such as *décolleté gowns*, *décolleté women*, etc. The noun *décolletage* came into the language in the late 19th century in such phrases as *deep décolletage*, *modest décolletage*, *daring décolletage*, and *extreme décolletage*.

Both words are pronounced in a French way: for *décolletage*, either /day-kol-ə-**tahzh**/ or /day-kol-**tahzh**/; for *décolleté*, either /day-kol-ə-**tay**/ or /day-kol-**tay**/.

deconstruction (= a method of reading by which one finds the subtext beneath the text and inverts their importance) for *destruction* is an odd error—e.g.: "Fire is an extremely fast and effective means of *deconstruction* [read *destruction*]. All urban fires are in some sense man-made." Thomas Hine, "Don't Blame Mrs. O'Leary," *N.Y. Times*, 15 July 1990, § 7, at 13.

LANGUAGE-CHANGE INDEX
deconstruction misused for *destruction*: Stage 1

decorous (= proper; in good taste) is pronounced with the primary accent on the first syllable: /**dek**-ə-rəs/.

decry; descry. *Decry* = to denounce or disparage. E.g.: "Party fund-raisers, while *decrying* the amounts spent this year, say both parties are caught in a financial version of an arms race." Leslie Wayne, "Campaigns Exploiting Financial Loopholes," *Austin Am.-Statesman*, 8 Sept.v 1996, at A1.

Descry = to see in the distance; discern with the eye. Today it is most often used figuratively—e.g.:

- "From the nine peaks of this series, we can *descry* and yearn to climb other pinnacles." David Elliott, "'Middleman' Delivers the Diamond," *San Diego Union-Trib.*, 4 Apr. 1994, Night & Day §, at 24.
- "I was wondering if you might conceivably *descry* significance in the fact that it happened soon after those comets started banging into my favorite planet, Jupiter." Daniel Seligman, "Ask Mr. Statistics," *Fortune*, 5 Sept. 1994, at 113.
- "So anxious are boomers about their careers that some experts *descry* a whole new genre of midlife crisis." Ronald Henkoff, "So, You Want to Change Your Job," *Fortune*, 15 Jan. 1996, at 52.

Occasionally writers misuse *descry* for *decry*—e.g.: "As much as we *descry* [read *decry* or *condemn*] such acts, we should come to grips with some fundamental truths." Terry Plumb, "What Did He Look Like?" *Herald* (Rock Hill, S.C.), 12 Feb. 2006, at E1. And in some sentences, the word *descry* is barely intelligible, a fancy trinket dragged in to dress up the sentence—e.g.:

- "On Friday, she sported a sign *descrying* [read *proclaiming*?] 'Fur Is Dead' along with her mistress, whose sandwich board carried a gruesome message." John Ure, "'Fur Free Friday' Brings 100 to Protest at Two S.L. Malls," *Salt Lake Trib.*, 26 Nov. 1994, at B2.

- "Hugh Burns asked rhetorically if Williams' portrayal of Abu-Jamal as a highly intelligent and articulate individual made him less *descrying* [read *critical*?] of the death penalty than an average man who committed murder." Samuel B. Fineman, "Abu-Jamal Hearings Conclude," *Legal Intelligencer*, 12 Sept. 1995, at 1.

LANGUAGE-CHANGE INDEX
1. *descry* misused for *decry*: Stage 1
2. *descry* misused for *proclaim*: Stage 1

dedicatory; *dedicative; *dedicatorial. The first form is standard; the other two are NEEDLESS VARIANTS.
Current ratio: 857:5:1

deduce. A. And *deduct*. The former means "to infer," the latter "to subtract." *Deduct* is sometimes misused for *deduce*—e.g.: "Ideal methods in thought and research, logically observed and *deducted* [read *deduced*] for possible changes in light of different circumstances were foreign to him." Letter of George E. Hayney, "What's Ahead for the U.S. Supreme Court?" *St. Petersburg Times*, 14 July 1991, at D3. See **adduce** & **deducible**.

LANGUAGE-CHANGE INDEX
deduct misused for *deduce*: Stage 1

B. And *induce*. To *deduce* is to reason from a general principle to a specific conclusion. To *induce* is either (1) to reason from many specific observations to a general principle or (2) to cause (a result)—sense 1 being the one at issue in discussions of logic. As it happens, although reasoning by *induction* is as commonly referred to as reasoning by *deduction*, the verb *induce* is much less common than *deduce*. The following examples, though, show how the two verbs are sometimes contrasted:

- "The research logic is predictive; future manifestations of a phenomenon are *deduced* from theoretical laws and axioms or *induced* from historical antecedents." Craig L. Thompson et al., "Putting Consumer Experience Back into Consumer Research," 16 *J. Consumer Research* 133 (1989).
- "A success theory of value will ultimately be *induced* from the world of facts instead of *deduced* from a set of [general] premises." Diane Swanson, "A Critical Evaluation of Etzioni's Socioeconomic Theory," 11 *J. Bus. Ethics* 545 (1992).
- "The answers to these questions will be *induced* from the level of class and national consciousness expressed through direct political intervention, not *deduced* from abstract economic formulas about the 'Crises of World Capitalism.'" James Petras, "U.S. Empire-Building," *Canadian Dimension*, Mar. 2003, at 9.

deducible; deductible. The former means "inferable." E.g.: "Attorneys can make statements in opening and closing arguments that are reasonably *deducible* from allowed evidence . . . ." "Alabama," *USA Today*, 15 Oct. 1992, at A8. The word is sometimes misspelled **deduceable*. See -ABLE (A).

Deductible, a favorite word during the tax season, means "capable of being (usu. lawfully) subtracted"—

LANGUAGE-CHANGE INDEX (For the full key, see front matter pp. xxxi, l–li.)
Stage 1: Rejected. **Stage 2:** Widely shunned. **Stage 3:** Widespread but . . . **Stage 4:** Ubiquitous but . . . **Stage 5:** Fully accepted.
Invariably inferior forms marked by asterisk (*). • Ratios represent frequency of prevalent forms vs. variants in current books.

e.g.: "On Wednesday, for example, [Michael J. Coles] held a news conference to encourage Mr. Gingrich to call for the release of a draft report about claims that the Speaker improperly used tax-*deductible* donations to finance a college course he taught in 1993." Kevin Sack, "Entrepreneur Sets His Sights on Gingrich," *N.Y. Times*, 18 Sept. 1996, at A19. The word is sometimes misspelled **deductable*.

deduct. See **deduce** (A).

deduction; induction. See **deduce** (B).

deem is a FORMAL WORD that imparts the flavor of ARCHAISM. It frequently displaces a more down-to-earth term such as *consider, think,* or *judge*—e.g.:

- "*Deeming* [read *Finding*] them 'fatally flawed,' the Howard County School Boundary Line Committee put two elementary school redistricting plans out of their misery last night during its final meeting." Tricia Bishop, "Boundary Panel Puts End to 2 Elementary Redistricting Plans," *Baltimore Sun* (Howard ed.), 11 Oct. 2002, at B3.
- "The authorities have in several cases used rape charges to imprison religious leaders *deemed* [read *thought*] to be a menace." Rik Eckholm, "3 Church Leaders in China Are Sent to Prison for Life," *N.Y. Times*, 11 Oct. 2002, at A10.

de-emphasize. This word is traditionally hyphenated, since the reader may at first see *deem*. See PUNCTUATION (J).

Current ratio (*de-emphasize* vs. *deemphasize*): 1.1:1

deep-freeze > deep-froze > deep-frozen. **Deep-freezed* should be deep-sixed—e.g.: "[One] time Jordan, hot-shot rookie, was *deep-freezed* [read *deep-frozen*] by jealous teammates." Ian O'Connor, "The Star's Fever Rages," *Daily News* (N.Y.), 8 Feb. 1998, at 58. See IRREGULAR VERBS (E). Cf. **freeze.**

LANGUAGE-CHANGE INDEX
*deep-freezed for *deep-frozen*: Stage 1
Current ratio (*deep-frozen* vs. **deep-freezed*): 583:1

deep-seated. So spelled. **Deep-seeded* is a misbegotten METAPHOR, a MALAPROPISM, especially because something truly **deep-seeded* probably wouldn't be able to grow. The true metaphor derives from horseback riding (deep in the seat), not from planting seeds deeply—e.g.:

- "The small-town tradition has built a fierce sense of community and a *deep-seeded* [read *deep-seated*] suspicion of outsiders, social historians say." Marcelino Rodriguez, "Vigilante Justice on Rise in Mexican State," *Dallas Morning News*, 5 July 1994, at A5.
- "The 6-year-old superhorse can't do anything to solve racetracks' *deep-seeded* [read *deep-seated*] problems." Ed Gray, "Keeping Track: Travers Gets Top 3-some," *Boston Herald*, 18 Aug. 1996, at B24.
- "At the Green Valley Library in Henderson, 'the wall' is a place where people go to post messages about *deep-seeded* [read *deep-seated*] secrets, loneliness, worries, aspirations and dreams." "Library Offers a Different Kind of Wall Post," *Las Vegas Sun*, 11 Apr. 2012, at 8.

LANGUAGE-CHANGE INDEX
*deep-seeded for *deep-seated*: Stage 1
Current ratio (*deep-seated* vs. **deep-seeded*): 144:1

defalcate. A. And *peculate*; *embezzle*. These words are broadly synonymous, all three meaning "to misappropriate money in one's charge." *Defalcate* and *peculate*, the latter being slightly more common today in referring to public moneys, are FORMAL WORDS that describe a bad action about as neutrally as possible. *Embezzle* is the popular word, more highly charged with negative connotations. See **defalcation.**

B. Pronunciation. Several pronunciation guides suggest that the first syllable may be stressed: /**def**-al-kayt/ or /**def**-əl-kayt/. See, e.g., John B. Opdycke, *Don't Say It: A Cyclopedia of English Use and Abuse* 236 (1939). Others suggest that the corresponding noun is pronounced /def-al-**kay**-shən/. See, e.g., William H. Phyfe, *20,000 Words Often Mispronounced* 244 (1937).

But these pronunciations have a problem. Anyone who hears them is likely to think of *defecate* and *defecation*. Therefore, if one must utter these words at all, the safest course is to use the following pronunciations, which all pronunciation guides accept as standard: *defalcate* /dee-**fal**-kayt/ or /di-**fal**-kayt/; *defalcation* /dee-fal-**kay**-shən/. Pronouncing the second syllable /fawl/ is not standard.

defalcation may refer either to the act of embezzling or to the money embezzled, usually the former—e.g.: "The suspect's name is not being released by First Commercial, nor are many details of the alleged *defalcation* [i.e., the act]." Mark Anderson, "First Commercial Bank Hit with Alleged Embezzlement," *Bus. J.—Sacramento*, 12 Sept. 1994, § 1, at 2. See **defalcate.**

By SLIPSHOD EXTENSION, some writers have misused *defalcation* when referring merely to a nonfraudulent default. To be a *defalcation*, a deficiency in money matters must be fraudulent and must be the fault of someone put in trust of the money. To speak of a *loan defalcation* is to fall into ambiguity—e.g.: "Fairfield First Bank submitted a report to the Federal Deposit Insurance Corp. and the state Department of Banking (DOB), detailing the alleged losses caused by White's 'loan *defalcations*,' according to David Tedeschi, a spokesman for the DOB." Don Dzikowski, "Bank Sues Insurers to Recoup Lost Funds," *Fairfield County Bus. J.*, 12 June 1995, at 1. That sentence does not reveal just how serious the alleged wrongdoing was: it was either a criminal act or a noncriminal failure to pay on time.

defamation; libel; slander. These three terms are distinguished in law. *Defamation* = an attack on the reputation of another. It encompasses both *libel* (in permanent form, especially in writing) and *slander* (in transitory form, especially by spoken words). See **libel.**

defamatory; **defamative*. *Defamatory* is the standard term; **defamative* is a NEEDLESS VARIANT.

default, n. & vb. A *default* is a failure to act when an action is required, especially the failure to pay a debt—either interest or principal—as it becomes due <the account is in default>.

A default is also something that will happen unless something prevents it. It is a common term in

COMPUTERESE, referring to a preference setting that will be used unless a different setting is specified; in this sense it is usually attributive and serves as an adjective <C is the default drive>. But this usage predates computers: in law, for example, a defendant who does not contest a claim may face a *default* judgment.

As a verb, *default* is ordinarily intransitive. And when used intransitively, the verb idiomatically requires the preposition *on* <she defaulted on the loan>. Occasionally, though, writers fall into the unidiomatic—e.g.: "Financed by Credit Lyonnais, Parretti soon *defaulted to* [read *defaulted on*] his loans." Daniel R. Marcus, "Big Deals: Tracinda et al./MGM," *Am. Lawyer*, Sept. 1996, at 116.

But transitive uses sometimes crop up <she defaulted the loan>. That usage may have arisen from the common adjectival use of *defaulted*, especially in computer JARGON—e.g.:

- "College officials said they didn't know the dollar amount of *defaulted* loans." Deborah C. Whitten, "Penn Valley Plans Loan Program Appeal," *Kansas City Star*, 3 Sept. 1994, at C4.
- "The company forgave about $10.5 million in *defaulted* loans by former customers." Marc Davis, "Court Revives Suit Against Transouth in Used-Car Fraud Case," *Virginian-Pilot* (Norfolk), 14 Sept. 1996, at D1.
- "Servicing a *defaulted* loan cost an estimated $2,357 in 2014 compared with just $134 for a performing loan." Kate Berry, "Six Takeaways from Big Banks' Strong 2Q Mortgage Results," *Nat'l Mortgage News*, 3 Aug. 2015, at 1.

defeasance; *defeasement. *Defeasance* (= an annulment or abrogation), the standard form, is much more common than *defeasement in modern print sources. E.g.:

- "He said he intended to negotiate a restructuring of FFr3bn in loans from banks to support its FFr13bn off-balance sheet '*defeasance*' of non-performing loans hived off as part of a restructuring earlier this year." Andrew Jack, "GAN to Prepare for Sell-Off with FFr9bn Sale," *Fin. Times*, 15 Dec. 1995, at 22.
- "The county is working with bond counsel, Hassenbalg said, to determine what their options and obligations are with respect to that debt and its possible *defeasance*." Katherine M. Reynolds, "N.J. County Debates Bid to Sell Hospital," *Bond Buyer*, 18 Dec. 1995, at 6.
- "To sell the facilities, the city would first have to put $1.3 million into a bond *defeasance* escrow account to repay those who purchased the tax-free revenue bonds issued seven years ago to finance arena improvements." Judith Davidoff, "Panel Urges Sale of Two Ice Arenas," *Capital Times* (Madison), 27 Aug. 2002, at A3.

Still, *defeasement—a NEEDLESS VARIANT—sometimes appears. E.g.: "'Defeasing' bonds is a highly technical financial maneuver, Puig said, which is necessary in this case because the bonds have a provision that prohibits prepayment for 10 years. In a *defeasement* [read *defeasance*], the county would put the sale money in a special fund that would eventually pay off the bonds." "Keep Knick, Coyne Writes," *Times Union* (Albany), 7 June 1995, at B1.

And with all this use of the nouns, it is hardly surprising that writers have felt the need for a corresponding verb: *defease*. It's a 19th-century BACK-FORMATION from *defeasance*—e.g.:

- "The not-for-profit hospital . . . is being sold to an investor-owned chain in a deal that involved *defeasing*, or replacing the collateral of, the hospital's tax-exempt bonds." Sandy Lutz, "IRS Hikes Cost of Buying Tax-Exempts," *Modern Healthcare*, 3 July 1995, at 18.
- "Last year, the city chose J.P. Morgan Securities Inc. as adviser on the hotel sale, which would involve *defeasing* about $28 million of outstanding debt issued by the United Nations Development Corp. to finance the hotel." Christina Pretto, "Mayor Tells How UN Helps N.Y.C.," Mum on Hotel Sale," *Bond Buyer*, 25 Aug. 1995, at 5.
- "Even better, if the dollar turned around, as the Treasury was saying it would, then the U.S. government could score a profit by '*defeasing*' the bonds—a method of calling in the debt." James K. Glassman, "Why Buy High When Lows Are Out There?" *Wash. Post*, 24 Sept. 1995, at H1.

LANGUAGE-CHANGE INDEX
*defeasement for defeasance: Stage 1
Current ratio (*defeasance* vs. *defeasement): 530:1

defeasible. So spelled—not *defeasable. See -ABLE (A).

defect, *n.* In the best usage, one refers to the *defects in* things and the *defects of* people. For the distinction between a *defect* and a *deficiency*, see **defective.**

defective; deficient; defectible. The primary difference to be noted is between *defective* (= faulty; imperfect; subnormal) and *deficient* (= insufficient; lacking in quantity). The same basic distinction holds for the nouns *defect* and *deficiency*. In the following sentence, *deficiency* is misused for *defect*: "A devastating steam explosion and fuel-core meltdown in Unit 4 was caused by operator errors and reactor design *deficiencies* [read *defects*]." William F. Miller, "Effects of Chernobyl Are Still Felt in Ukraine," *Plain Dealer* (Cleveland), 20 July 1996, at B4.

Defectible, an extremely rare word, means "likely to fail or become defective."

LANGUAGE-CHANGE INDEX
deficiency misused for defect: Stage 1

defence. See **defense.**

defenestrate (= to throw out a window [lit. or fig.]) is a mid-20th-century BACK-FORMATION from the noun *defenestration*, which dates from the early 17th century. The noun is far more common than the verb.

defense. A. Spelling. *Defense* is AmE; *defence* is BrE (or very antiquated AmE). Modern American writers who use the British spelling are likely to seem affected.

B. Pronunciation. The standard pronunciation has long been with the accent on the second syllable: /di-**fen**[t]s/. But primarily as a result of sports talk, some have shifted the accent to the first syllable: /**dee**-fen[t]s/.

LANGUAGE-CHANGE INDEX (For the full key, see front matter pp. xxxi, l–li.)
Stage 1: Rejected. **Stage 2:** Widely shunned. **Stage 3:** Widespread but . . . **Stage 4:** Ubiquitous but . . . **Stage 5:** Fully accepted.
Invariably inferior forms marked by asterisk (*). • Ratios represent frequency of prevalent forms vs. variants in current books.

If you want to sound like a general or a lawyer, use the first of these pronunciations; if you want to sound like a sports announcer or a cheerleader, use the second. Cf. **offense.**

LANGUAGE-CHANGE INDEX
defense pronounced with accent on first syllable:
Stage 4

C. As a Verb. In the mid-20th century, *defense* came into use as a sports CASUALISM in the sense "to defend against (a play, etc.) effectively." Because the meaning is sometimes vague and a better word or phrase is available, careful speakers and writers are likely to avoid this usage (which is inarguably more economical and may well become standard)—e.g.:

- "The 49ers also can't be encouraged by the way they've *defensed* [read *defended against*] the pass all season." Jeffri Chadiha, "49ers Set Sights on Freeman," *S.F. Examiner*, 3 Jan. 1999, at C5.
- "In addition, Thomas Whitelaw successfully *defensed* [read *defeated* or *defended against*] all of Kyphon's counterclaims against Pabban for $17 million." "Thomas Whitelaw Wins $15.4M Verdict for Pabban Development," *J. of Engineering*, 4 June 2014, at 1778.
- "He totaled 63 tackles, seven sacks, three passes *defensed* [read *deflected*], four forced fumbles and one interception." Mary Kay Cabot, "LB, DB Added to Aid Hamstrung Roster," *Plain Dealer* (Cleveland), 17 Aug. 2015, at B2.

LANGUAGE-CHANGE INDEX
defense as a verb: Stage 2

defensible. So spelled—not **defensable*. See -ABLE (A).

defer; defer to. *Defer* (= to postpone) yields the nouns *deferral* and *deferment*. (See **deferral.**) *Defer to* (= to give way to) yields the noun *deference.*

deferment. See **deferral.**

deferrable /di-fər-ə-bəl/ is so spelled—not **deferable*. Cf. **inferable** & **transferable.**

Current ratio: 33:1

deferral; deferment. Although *deferment* is the term traditionally listed in dictionaries—and is nearly 300 years older—*deferral* (dating from the late 19th century) is now much more common in print sources from all varieties of English. It ought to be considered standard as the generic noun corresponding to *defer*—e.g.:

- "Under Clinton's proposal, tax *deferral* would be eliminated." Gary Klott, "Parts of Clinton Tax-Cut Plan Go Further than Dole's," *Houston Chron.*, 16 Sept. 1996, Bus. §, at 2.
- "While many companies use *deferral* in their accounting, it's the size of AOL's figure that has made it controversial." David S. Hilzenrath, "AOL Fights to Retain Subscribers," *Wash. Post*, 16 Sept. 1996, at A1.
- "The decision on the export licence will be deferred until November 18, and the *deferral* could be extended until February 18 if a serious intention to raise funds to buy the watercolour at the recommended price emerges." Emily Beament, "UK Buyer Sought for First Picture of Niagara Falls," *Herald* (Glasgow), 20 Aug. 2015, at 9.

In this particular use, *deferment* is now a NEEDLESS VARIANT.

But *deferment* does have one special use, in the sense "an official postponement of military service." This use was common when the military draft was in effect, but it has since atrophied.

Current ratio (*deferral* vs. *deferment*): 4:1

defer to. See **defer.**

deficient; deficiency. See **defective.**

definite. A. And *definitive*. These words are increasingly confused. *Definite* = fixed, exact, explicit. *Definitive* = authoritative; conclusive; exhaustive; providing a binding answer.

The most frequent error is misuse of *definitive* for *definite*—e.g.: "He has some very *definitive* [read *definite*] views on golf-course architecture, and it's hard not to like what he says." Michael Mayo, "New Honda Home on Solid Ground with McCumber," *Sun-Sentinel* (Ft. Lauderdale), 13 Mar. 1994, at C19.

LANGUAGE-CHANGE INDEX
definitive misused for *definite*: Stage 1

B. As Misspelled. The word is often misspelled **definate*. See SPELLING (A).

Current ratio: 6,218:1

definitely. So spelled. See SPELLING (A).

deflection (= the act of making something go to one side) is the standard spelling. **Deflexion* is an archaic BrE variant.

Current ratio: 99:1

deforest; disafforest; **disforest*. For the act of cutting down trees, especially clear-cutting, *deforest* has predominated in AmE since the 1860s and in World English since the 1920s. *Disafforest* dominated in BrE until the mid 1980s, when *deforest* inexplicably overtook it to become much more common. The more practical **disforest* was strong in the 19th century but declined as *deforest* rose. It is now a NEEDLESS VARIANT.

Current ratio (in order of headwords): 49:3:1

defraud. See **deceive.**

defraudation; **defraudment*. Writers seldom need to use a noun formed from the verb *defraud*, perhaps because the noun *fraud* itself usually suffices. When they find the occasion, however, the word is *defraudation*—e.g.: "The sad reality is that the apathy you encountered when you called county officials undoubtedly would have continued after your *defraudation*, unless your loss towered above the county's in-house limit, which might be as high as $150,000." Fay Faron, "Retiree Was Too Wary for Scam Artist," *Dallas Morning News*, 13 Sept. 1996, at C8. **Defraudment* is a NEEDLESS VARIANT.

Current ratio: 3:1

*defraudulent is a NEEDLESS VARIANT of *fraudulent*. See **fraudulent.**

defunct, in a ghastly blunder, is sometimes written **defunk*—e.g.:

- "Several segments of the *defunk* [read *defunct*] 'Hotel' were filmed at the Fairmont." "Another of Nation's Landmark Hotels on Auction Block," *San Diego Union-Trib.*, 3 Mar. 1989, Bus. §, at 1.
- "The hearings had virtually nothing to do with the murky financial dealings of a *defunk* [read *defunct*] Arkansas savings bank and its ties with Bill and Hillary Clinton." "School for Scandal," *Houston Chron.*, 7 Aug. 1994, at 2.
- "The lion's share of the budget: $930,000 will go toward accelerating business and industry recruitment . . . and not for the development of the *defunk* [read *defunct*] Commerce Center project." "Business Roundup: Destination Rutherford Not Old Plan," *Daily News J.* (Murfreesboro, Tenn.), 2 Mar. 2003, at 10.

The accent is on the second syllable: /di-**fəngkt**/.

LANGUAGE-CHANGE INDEX
defunk for *defunct*: Stage 1

defuse (= [1] to remove the detonating device from [a bomb, etc.]; or [2] to render less volatile) is the standard spelling. *Defuze* is a variant. For a similar variation in spelling, see **fuse.** For confusion of *defuse* with *diffuse*, see **diffuse.**

degenerative; **degeneratory.* The latter is a NEEDLESS VARIANT.

Current ratio: 18,683:1

degree. See **diploma.**

degrees. See **180-degree turnaround.**

deictic (/**dɪk**-tik/) is a literary term meaning "proving or showing by direct demonstration." Even in scholarly works, writers feel obliged to explain the term— e.g.: "If we accept [Marcel] Duchamp's part objects as signifiers in this sense, they appear as '*deictic*,' that is to say, as directly pointing to—as demonstrative of— the subject." Erika Naginski, "Eros-en-Valise," *Art J.*, 22 Sept. 2007, at 122. For a discussion of deictic terms from a grammatical point of view, see POINTING WORDS.

deign (/dayn/), properly speaking, means "to condescend (to do something) in a way that reveals a perceived affront to one's dignity." E.g.: "Before his election as Prime Minister of Israel, Benjamin Netanyahu had sworn he would never *deign* to meet Yasser Arafat, a man he considered little more than a terrorist." Lisa Beyer, "Netanyahu Meets with Arafat—But That's All," *Time*, 16 Sept. 1996, at 54.

When used in the sense "to decide, see fit," the word has fallen victim to SLIPSHOD EXTENSION—e.g.: "On some nights, during two hours of prime-time coverage, the networks *deigned* [read *decided* or *saw fit*] to show less than half an hour from the podium." "Conventional Wisdom," *Christian Science Monitor*, 6 Sept. 1996, at 20.

LANGUAGE-CHANGE INDEX
deign misused for *decide* or *see fit*: Stage 2

deism. See **theism.**

deity /**dee**-i-tee/ is sometimes misspelled **diety*— e.g.: "Historically, women from the Mithila region of northern India painted images of Hindu *dieties* [read *deities*] on the walls to make their homes safe from the dangers of the outside world." Elizabeth Barr, "Buying Opportunity," *Buffalo News*, 2 Jan. 2004, at G24.

LANGUAGE-CHANGE INDEX
deity misspelled **diety*: Stage 1
Current ratio: 303:1

déjà vu is preferably so written—with two accents (but no longer in italics). Originally, this was a technical psychological term referring to the illusion that one has already experienced something that is happening for the first time. In the 1950s and 1960s, the term became popular and the sense of illusion was weakened. That is, *déjà vu* began to apply to situations in which the person knows full well that the precise experience isn't a repeat of an earlier one, merely that it is similar. That sense is dominant and standard today—e.g.: "As a lifelong Republican, I watched the Republican National Convention with a dismaying sense of *déjà vu*." Clyde W. Prestowitz Jr., "How Tax Cuts Can Hurt U.S. Abroad," *Sacramento Bee*, 7 Sept. 1996, at B7. See DIACRITICAL MARKS.

In AmE the phrase is pronounced /day-zhah **voo**/.

*delapidation. See **dilapidation.**

delectable. So spelled. But it is sometimes misspelled **delectible*—e.g.: "All three feature menus of the most *delectible* [read *delectable*] seafood to be found on the 200-mile-long estuary." Kenneth R. Clark, "Virginian Solitude," *Chicago Trib.*, 19 June 1994, Travel §, at C5. See -ABLE (A).

LANGUAGE-CHANGE INDEX
delectable misspelled **delectible*: Stage 1
Current ratio: 3,787:1

delegable is the word, not **delegatable*. But many writers mistakenly use the latter form—e.g.: "The reality is that oversight simply is not *delegatable* [read *delegable*]." Warren F. McFarlan & Richard L. Nolan, "How to Manage an IT Outsourcing Alliance," *Sloan Mgmt. Rev.*, Jan. 1995, at 9. See -ABLE (D) & -ATABLE.

LANGUAGE-CHANGE INDEX
*delegatable for *delegable*: Stage 1
Current ratio (*delegable* vs. **delegatable*): 11:1

delegate. See **relegate.**

deliberate, adj.; **deliberative.** These words should be differentiated. *Deliberate* = (1) intentional, fully considered; or (2) unimpulsive, slow in deciding. *Deliberative* = of, or appointed for the purpose of, deliberation or debate (*COD*).

LANGUAGE-CHANGE INDEX (For the full key, see front matter pp. xxxi, l–li.)
Stage 1: Rejected. **Stage 2:** Widely shunned. **Stage 3:** Widespread but . . . **Stage 4:** Ubiquitous but . . . **Stage 5:** Fully accepted.
Invariably inferior forms marked by asterisk (*). • Ratios represent frequency of prevalent forms vs. variants in current books.

Deliberative is sometimes misused for *deliberate* in both sense 1 and sense 2. Misuse for sense 1: "War thus will be a *deliberative* [read *deliberate*] act, not a reflex." "More than 'Consult,'" *Christian Science Monitor*, 22 Oct. 1990, at 20. Misuse for sense 2: "DeLauro came to this decision in a *deliberative* [read *deliberate*], uncharacteristically subdued way for someone known for overly aggressive ways of making her points." David Lightman, "DeLauro's View: Don't Go It Alone," *Hartford Courant*, 9 Oct. 2002, at A4.

LANGUAGE-CHANGE INDEX
deliberative misused for *deliberate*: Stage 1

delimit; *delimitate. *Delimit*, the preferred form, is not merely a fancy variation of *limit*, as many seem to believe. The word means "to define; determine the boundaries of"—e.g.: "Having declared an EEZ, China will now have to *delimit* its disputed sea boundaries with its maritime neighbors—South Korea, Japan and Vietnam." Mark J. Valencia, "China, and the Law of the Sea Convention," *Bus. Times*, 29 June 1996, Special §, at 4.

The long form **delimitate*, a BACK-FORMATION from the noun *delimitation*, is a NEEDLESS VARIANT. E.g.: "Each of these areas is further *delimitated* [read *delimited*] by instructive and informative segments." Paul W. Kittle, "Collision: Theory vs. Reality in Expert Systems," *Library Software Rev.*, Mar. 1991, at 162.

LANGUAGE-CHANGE INDEX
*delimitate for *delimit*: Stage 1
Current ratio (*delimit* vs. **delimitate*): 62:1

delineate (lit., "to draw or sketch") means figuratively "to represent in words; to describe." It is sometimes misused for *differentiate* (an error on the rise since the 1950s)—e.g.:

- "But considering the individuals involved, it's difficult to *delineate* [read *differentiate*] between fact and fiction." Dave Luecking, "Bowman, Keenan 2-Man Head of Bureau of Minds," *St. Louis Post-Dispatch*, 5 May 1996, at F1.
- "While it's not always easy to *delineate* [read *differentiate*] between legitimate communication to constituents and distribution of political material, taxpayers certainly have a right to be suspicious when material is distributed shortly before or during a political campaign season." "Identify Material Publicly Funded," *State-Times/Morning Advocate* (Baton Rouge), 24 Aug. 1996, at B6.
- "In Burlington's testimony on Monday, he said he only brought up that comment to *delineate* [read *differentiate*] between the N-word being targeted at someone and the word being discussed in a 'journalistic context.'" Dan Spinelli, "N-Word Lawsuit Intensifies as Colleague Testifies," *Phil. Daily News*, 10 June 2015, Local §, at 3.

LANGUAGE-CHANGE INDEX
delineate misused for *differentiate*: Stage 1

delinquent, in AmE, can apply to either things or people <delinquent taxes> <delinquent youth>. In BrE, it applies only to people.

delirium tremens. This phrase—often abbreviated as *d.t.'s* or *D.T.'s*—should not be used, as it sometimes is,

to describe frenzied drunkenness. In fact, it denotes a mental disease characterized by violent mania, with tremors and hallucinations, usually induced by sudden abstinence from alcohol or another drug after excessive use over a prolonged period. A synonymous phrase is *mania à potu*.

delivery. A. And *deliverance*. *Delivery*, the more usual word, is used in reference to (1) a transfer or conveyance (of something); (2) an utterance <a stammering delivery of the speech>; or (3) a giving of birth <premature delivery>. *Deliverance* is a legal and religious term usually meaning "rescue, release," although at one time it overlapped with *delivery* in almost every sense.

B. Cant Uses. It has become voguish in some circles to use *delivery of* where *providing* or *provision for* would normally appear, especially in reference to services. Like any other trendy expression, it ought to be avoided. E.g.: "It is irrational to equate the cost of total confinement with the alleged harm resulting from a change in method of *the delivery of* [read *providing*] dental services." See VOGUE WORDS.

Delphi, not **Delphos*, is the place name for the location of the oracle (or shrine) belonging to the Greek god Apollo. The usual phrase is *oracle of Delphi*, *oracle at Delphi*, or *Delphic oracle*. But some writers get it wrong—e.g.: "Even when the all-seeing oracle of *Delphos* [read *Delphi*] pronounces her innocent, the king will not listen." Peter Haugen, "A Play-by-Play Look at the Season," *Sacramento Bee*, 3 Mar. 1996, Encore §, at 16. *Delphos* is the name of cities in Kansas and Ohio.

Delphic, adj., = (1) oracular; or (2) ambiguous; cryptic.

LANGUAGE-CHANGE INDEX
*oracle of Delphos for *oracle of Delphi*: Stage 1
Current ratio (*oracle of Delphi* vs.
*oracle of Delphos): 16:1

delphinium. Although the plural **delphinia* was somewhat common before 1900, the standard plural has been *delphiniums* ever since then.

Current ratio (*delphiniums* vs. **delphinia*): 644:1

deluge (= [1] an overwhelming flood, or [2] a large amount of something that one receives at the same time) is preferably pronounced /del-**yooj**/. The same is true of the verb <they deluged her with Twitter messages>.

delusion. See **hallucination** & **illusion.**

delusive; delusional; *delusory. *Delusive* = (1) tending to delude, deceptive; or (2) of the nature of a delusion. Usually sense 1 applies. *Delusional* is the more usual term for sense 2—e.g.: "Florence acted under a completely *delusional* perception of reality." **Delusory* is a NEEDLESS VARIANT of the other two.

deluxe. Although this adjective was originally (from the early 19th century) written as two words—*de luxe*—it became predominantly solidified in AmE print sources by 1965, in World English by 1970, and in BrE by the late 1980s. Of course, the word means "outstandingly luxurious and high-quality." The word has undergone some downgrading in sense because of hyperbolic uses—most notably in the description of some very ordinary hotel rooms as "deluxe rooms." It is preferably pronounced /di-**ləks**/—not /di-**looks**/, /di-**luuks**/, or /**dee**-ləks/.

> Current ratio (*deluxe* vs. *de luxe): 5:1

demagogue is predominantly a noun meaning "a leader who maintains power through appeals to the mob." *Demagog is a variant form, but today it is seen in print much less frequently than the longer form—e.g.: "Most of those whom political *demagogs* [read *demagogues*] call 'the rich' are simply people in the top 10 or 20 percent of the income distribution." Thomas Sowell, "Revealing the Secret Identity of the So-Called 'Rich,'" *Detroit News*, 17 Apr. 1995, at A10. See -AGOG(UE).

When the word has been used as a verb, it has historically been intransitive, not transitive. That is, one may *demagogue* (= play the demagogue), or one may *demagogue on* an issue (= appeal to the mob on an issue), but one doesn't *demagogue* an issue. Some writers try to make the verb transitive—e.g.: "Similarly, Rep. Rod Chandler, the Republican candidate for U.S. Senate, has *demagogued* [read *demagogued on*] the issue." "Unsoeld's Sound Approach," *Seattle Times*, 29 Sept. 1992, at A6.

> LANGUAGE-CHANGE INDEX
> *demagogue* as a transitive verb: Stage 4

demagoguery; *demagogy. *Demagoguery* (= the practices of a political agitator who appeals to mob instincts) is more than twice as common in print as *demagogy, which (in the absence of any useful DIF-FERENTIATION) ought to be labeled a NEEDLESS VARI-ANT. E.g.: "Such *demagogy* [read *demagoguery*] aside, there are good grounds to object to this particular venture." "Skate and Hate," *Baltimore Sun*, 26 Aug. 1994, at A16. That was not always true: *demagogy was the usual term in AmE till the early 1950s and in BrE till about 2000.

> Current ratio: 2:1

demarcation (= the act of marking limits) is the standard spelling and has been since about 1780. *Demarkation is a variant.

> Current ratio: 75:1

demean; bemean. Formerly, authorities on usage disapproved of *demean* in the sense "to lower, degrade," holding that instead it really means "to conduct (oneself)." For example, an early-20th-century usage critic wrote that "*demean* signifies 'to behave' and does not mean *debase* or *degrade*." Frank H. Vizetelly, *A Desk-Book of Errors in English* 62 (1909). The meaning "to behave," now archaic, is infrequently used in

legal contexts—e.g.: "The oath of office now generally administered in all the states requires the lawyer to uphold the law; to *demean* himself, as an officer of the court, uprightly; to be faithful to his trust." In this sense, of course, the verb corresponds to the noun *demeanor*. It is this sense that also shows up in *misdemeanor*.

Yet the other sense, which has been with us since at least 1601, is now dominant—e.g.:

- "He was not blessed with a sense of humour, and believed his wife *demeaned* herself when she played the clown." "Woman of the People and Anarchist of Sorts," *Daily Telegraph*, 29 July 1995, Books §, at 7.
- "School district officials fired Maria de la Rosa last year after Latino students complained that the Philippines native *demeaned* and verbally abused them with ethnic slurs." Paul Elias, "Judge Refuses to Reinstate Teacher," *L.A. Times*, 10 Nov. 1995, at B2.
- "For the Government of Ontario, in turn, to make this about particular individuals (the Prime Minister or Finance Minister, for example) *demeans* the seriousness of the issue." Lorne Sossin, "Federal–Provincial Sniping over Ontario Pension Plan Has to Stop," *Globe & Mail* (Toronto), 10 Aug. 2015, at B4.

Meanwhile, the word with which *demean* was confused in arriving at its popular meaning—*bemean* (= to debase)—has become obsolescent.

> LANGUAGE-CHANGE INDEX
> *demean* for *debase* or *degrade* (oneself): Stage 5

demesne (= at common law, a lord's land held as his absolute property and not as feudal property through a superior) is pronounced either /di-**meen**/ or /di-**mayn**/. Today in AmE, unless the word appears in a historical context, it is usually either figurative (as in the first two examples) or jocular (as in the third)—e.g.:

- "Describing Heaney as 'the greatest Irish poet since Yeats,' critic and Harvard professor Helen Vendler said, 'It is entirely fitting that Seamus should be in the *demesne* of Homer when this news arrives. He writes with equal attention to the poetic and human law.'" Patti Hartigan, "Irish Poet, Harvard Teacher Seamus Heaney Wins Nobel," *Boston Globe*, 6 Oct. 1995, at 1. (Vendler echoes Keats's "On First Looking into Chapman's Homer," which refers to a poetic realm of gold "that deep-browed Homer ruled as his demesne.")
- "On one side of the drape is the *demesne* of Western medicine . . . . On the other side of the drape, another pair of hands are at work." George Howe Colt, "See Me, Feel Me, Touch Me, Heal Me," *Life*, Sept. 1996, at 34.
- "I plan to go out somewhere in the *demesne* in which I live soon and plant it." Roz Young, "Raising Trees Isn't Easy in Apartment," *Dayton Daily News*, 11 May 1996, at A13.

But in BrE, the word retains its literal sense, especially in reference to land within a large estate—e.g.:

- "For sheer pathos there is nothing to equal Wanda Ryan Smolin's article on that exquisite rural *demesne* Killua Castle in Westmeath, the onetime home of the Chapmans of Lawrence of Arabia fame." "A Splendid Ruin Brought to Life," *Irish Times*, 20 Jan. 1996, at 15.

LANGUAGE-CHANGE INDEX (For the full key, see front matter pp. xxxi, l–li.)
Stage 1: Rejected. **Stage 2:** Widely shunned. **Stage 3:** Widespread but . . . **Stage 4:** Ubiquitous but . . . **Stage 5:** Fully accepted.
Invariably inferior forms marked by asterisk (*). • Ratios represent frequency of prevalent forms vs. variants in current books.

- "Lavinia, Dowager Marchioness of Cholmondeley, at whose *demesne* the sorry incident occurred, is understood to be mortified." Walter Ellis, "Windsor Watch," *Sunday Times* (London), 30 June 1996, Features §.
- "With its vast *demesne* and the modern Robert Trent Jones Senior-designed golf course, Adare Manor also has a die-hard following of well-to-do weekend breakers from Dublin, Cork, Limerick and Galway cities." Mark Keenan, "Walking on Adare Glass," *Irish Independent*, 19 June 2015, at 10.

demi-. This prefix indicates that a thing is (1) half the size or quality of another (e.g., *demitasse* = a small cup for coffee), or (2) of inferior or less than full rank, size, or status (e.g., *demigod* = a less-important deity). It's occasionally used pejoratively to belittle someone or something—e.g.: "On and on, painting Stalin a little taller, a bit more substantial, without a withered arm and never, ever with another Party leader, those fatuous *demi-tyrants* who sooner or later were erased from pictures and marched to a cell." Martin Cruz Smith, *Tatiana* 20 (2013).

demise. See **death.**

democracy. This term, meaning literally "government by the people," is often employed loosely, sometimes tendentiously and sometimes disingenuously (as when the post–World War II Soviet Union was referred to as a "democracy"). Originally a Greek term, *democracy* was understood by the Greeks very differently from the way we understand it today: Greek democracy was an institution limited to male clan members who were citizens; a huge population of slaves and other subordinated classes were disenfranchised. The same, of course, might be said of the United States before the abolition of slavery and before women gained the right to vote. Notions of democracy change with changing notions of who "the people" are. Throughout history, the term has gradually come to be more and more inclusive. See GOVERNMENTAL FORMS.

Democrat. A. And *democrat*. The capital *D* distinguishes the sense "a member of the Democratic Party" from the broader sense, which is denoted by a lower-case *d*.

B. *Democrat(ic)*, adj. During much of the late 20th century, Republicans were fairly successful in denigrating the noun *Democrat*, which often appeared in such phrases as *tax-and-spend Democrats* and *big-spending Democrats*. Interestingly, though, the adjective *Democratic* didn't undergo this depreciation in meaning. In the 1980s and 1990s, therefore, some Republicans preferred to refer to the **Democrat Convention* as opposed to the *Democratic Convention*. The former suggests something like a drunken party, whereas the latter suggests dignified proceedings.

The usage has continued, with typical reference to the **Democrat Party* from its GOP opponents, and occasionally in the press—e.g.:

- "Shelby County *Democrat* [read *Democratic*] Party Chairman Linda Montgomery rose to Zerr's defense." Jerry Graff, "GOP Contest for Mayor Set," *Indianapolis Star*, 5 Dec. 2002, at S1.

- "While Democrats outnumber Republicans 52–46 in the state House of Representatives, it will be up to McMorris to offer alternatives to *Democrat* [read *Democratic*] proposals and make sure the minority voice is heard on budget and other issues." Editorial, "Our Views," *Olympian* (Olympia, Wash.), 7 Dec. 2002, at A7.

In politics, of course, this type of semantic jockeying is a practice without end, as this columnist well knows: "Talk radio is rewriting the political language. . . . Environmentalists are wackos. The Democratic Party is the *Democrat* Party. Taxation is theft." Tom Teepen, "Talk Radio Isn't Just Talk," *Chattanooga Times/Chattanooga Free Press*, 29 Nov. 2002, at B8. And if *Republic* could somehow be loaded with pejorative connotations, you can be sure the Democrats wouldn't hesitate to do so.

LANGUAGE-CHANGE INDEX
*Democrat Party for *Democratic Party*: Stage 2
Current ratio (*Democratic Party* vs.
*Democrat Party): 31:1

demon. See **daemon.**

demonic; demoniac; *demoniacal. The two primary words are fiendishly close in meaning. *Demonic* /di-**mon**-ik/ = (1) of, relating to, or involving a demon <demonic beings>; (2) savagely wild and cruel <demonic cackling over the bloodshed>. *Demoniac* /dem-ə-**nɪ**-ik/ = as if possessed by or influenced by a demon; uncontrolled and evil <now confesses to a more or less demoniac adolescence>. In some of its uses, *demoniac* verges on the senses of *demonic*, which has grown dramatically in frequency of use since the 1930s. Before that time, *demoniac* was the most frequent of all the terms. **Demoniacal* is a NEEDLESS VARIANT of *demoniac*; as between these two, the shorter *demoniac* has predominated in World English since the 18th century.

demonstrable /di-**mon**-strə-bəl/ is the word, not **demonstratable*, a NEEDLESS VARIANT—e.g.:

- "On the issue of funding, there is a very strong, statistically *demonstratable* [read *demonstrable*] correlation between the quality of a public university and the extent to which it is supported by the state." G.A. Clark, "Low Pay for Professors Devastates State Schools," *Ariz. Republic/Phoenix Gaz.*, 29 Mar. 1995, Tempe Community §, at 4.
- "Banks still want a solid track record of experience in the business field and, preferably, a *demonstratable* [read *demonstrable*] ability to turn a profit." Neil Orman, "Improved Lending Still Rides on Prospects for Big Returns," *Austin Bus. J.*, 13 Oct. 1995, § 1, at 18.
- "In some cases, she said, she gives herself a challenge. For example, can she come up with a skill-and-action game that's fast-paced and *demonstratable* [read *demonstrable*] on TV?" Don Dodson, "Woman Creates Children's Games," *Courier* (Lincoln, Ill.), 25 May 2012, at 6.

See -ABLE (D) & -ATABLE.

LANGUAGE-CHANGE INDEX
*demonstratable for *demonstrable*: Stage 1
Current ratio (*demonstrable* vs.
*demonstratable): 341:1

demur; demure. *Demur,* v.i., = (1) to object; take exception; or (2) to hesitate or decline because of doubts. Although sense 2 is labeled archaic in *W11* and the *COD,* it appears with great frequency in AmE—e.g.:

- "When offered payment for this essential service, Waterhouse *demurred,* suggesting instead the payment be used to fund an underprivileged child's attendance at Collier Services' summer camp." "Stepping Out," *Asbury Park Press* (Neptune, N.J.), 1 Sept. 1996, at D6.
- "Clarke lobbied the USTA for a 90-and-over group, and when the organization *demurred* he organized his own annual round-robin event." Dyke Hendrickson, "Maine Seniors Flock to Games," *Portland Press Herald,* 1 Sept. 1996, at D11.
- "Johnson *demurred* when asked whether his vision for a new president could be taken as a criticism of Tomlinson." Jan Herman & Mike Boehm, "Orange County Arts Center Celebrates and Looks Ahead," *L.A. Times,* 3 Sept. 1996, at F1.

Demure is the adjective meaning (1) "reserved, modest"; or (2) "coy in an affected way." Sense 1 is somewhat more usual—e.g.:

- "A luminous beauty, both sensuous and *demure,* she [Ingrid Bergman] was a star for more than 40 years." Jane Sumner, "Jane Sumner's Picks & Pans," *Dallas Morning News,* 25 Aug. 1996, Television §, at 43.
- "The photograph is of a *demure* girl wearing a dark blouse and a light, frilly collar, giving the camera a smile that is at once humble and mischievous." Duncan Murrell, "Family's Roots Tied I-85 Victim to Area," *Chapel Hill Herald,* 28 Aug. 1996, at 1.
- "As a *demure* secretary in 'The V.I.P.s,' she stole scenes from Richard Burton." Roger Lewis, "Is Downton Dowager Really Kenneth Williams in Drag?" *Daily Mail,* 21 Aug. 2015, at 50 (referring to Maggie Smith).

The words are also confused in speech, when *demure* /di-**myuur**/ is said instead of *demur* /di-**mər**/.

DENIZEN LABELS. What do you call someone from ——? Often that's not an easy question to answer, whether it's a city, state, province, or country. Anyone who lives in Columbus, Ohio—or the other Columbuses in Georgia, Indiana, and Nebraska—is called a *Columbusite.* But someone from the small town of Columbus, Mississippi, is called a *Columbian.* Those inconsistencies can be a little confusing, but at least they're undisputed within a given locale.

Sometimes the authorities can't agree about a single locale. Someone from Michigan is (formerly by statute) called a *Michiganian*—but many Michiganians prefer to be called *Michiganders.* Almost no Michiganians want to be called **Michiganites,* but the United States Government Printing Office (which puts out a style manual) specifies **Michiganite.* Best for Michiganians and others to follow the law or local preference—not what some stylesheet-writer in Washington says.

Loose guidelines exist for naming denizens. George R. Stewart, a historian and onomastician, developed seven main guidelines—what H.L. Mencken called "Stewart's Laws of Municipal Onomastics"—that were cited in the best up-to-date work on this subject, Paul Dickson's *Labels for Locals* (1997). Here they are: (1) If the place name ends in *-a* or *-ia,* add *-n* <Alaska, Alaskan> <California, Californian>. (2) If the name ends in *-i* or a sounded *-e,* add *-an* <Hawaii, Hawaiian> <Albuquerque, Albuquerquean>. (3) If the name ends in *-on,* add *-ian* <Oregon, Oregonian>. (4) If the name ends in *-y,* change the *-y* to an *-i* and add *-an* <Albany, Albanian>. (5) If the name ends in *-o,* add *-an* <Chicago, Chicagoan>. (6) If the name ends in a consonant or a silent *-e,* add either *-ite* or *-er,* depending on euphony <Maine, Mainer> <New Hampshire, New Hampshirite>. (7) If the name ends in *-polis,* change that to *-politan* <Minneapolis, Minneapolitan>.

What follows are some of the less obvious denizen labels, also known as "demonyms," in places overriding Dickson's preferences because additional research showed this to be necessary.

States

Alabama	Alabamian, *Alabaman
Alaska	Alaskan
Arizona	Arizonan, *Arizonian
Arkansas	Arkansan, Arkie, *Arkansawyer
California	Californian
Colorado	Coloradan, Coloradoan
Connecticut	Nutmegger, Connecticuter (USGPO)
Delaware	Delawarean
Florida	Floridian
Georgia	Georgian
Hawaii	Hawaiian
Idaho	Idahoan
Illinois	Illinoisan /il-ə-**noy**-ən/ (pref. not *Illinoisian*)
Indiana	Hoosier, Indianan, *Indianian
Iowa	Iowan, *Iowegian
Kansas	Kansan
Kentucky	Kentuckian
Louisiana	Louisianian, *Louisianan
Maine	Mainer
Maryland	Marylander
Massachusetts	Bay Stater (by state law), Massachusettsan (USGPO)
Michigan	Michigander (by popular consensus), Michiganian (official), *Michiganite (rare, but recommended by USGPO)
Minnesota	Minnesotan
Mississippi	Mississippian
Missouri	Missourian
Montana	Montanan
Nebraska	Nebraskan
Nevada	Nevadan
New Hampshire	New Hampshirite

New Jersey	New Jerseyan, New Jerseyite (USGPO)
New Mexico	New Mexican
New York	New Yorker
North Carolina	North Carolinian, Tarheel
North Dakota	North Dakotan
Ohio	Ohioan
Oklahoma	Oklahoman, Sooner, Okie
Oregon	Oregonian
Pennsylvania	Pennsylvanian
Rhode Island	Rhode Islander
South Carolina	South Carolinian
South Dakota	South Dakotan
Tennessee	Tennessean, *Tennesseean
Texas	Texan
Utah	Utahn (preferred), Utahan
Vermont	Vermonter
Virginia	Virginian
Washington	Washingtonian
West Virginia	West Virginian
Wisconsin	Wisconsinite
Wyoming	Wyomingite

U.S. Cities

Akron	Akronite
Albany	Albanian
Albuquerque	Albuquerquean, *Albuquerquian
Anchorage	Anchorageite, *Anchoragite
Annapolis	Annapolitan
Austin	Austinite
Baltimore	Baltimorean
Bellingham, Wash.	Bellinghamster
Boston	Bostonian
Buffalo	Buffalonian
Cambridge	Cantabrigian
Canton, Ohio	Cantonian
Chicago	Chicagoan
Cincinnati	Cincinnatian
Cleveland	Clevelander
Columbus (Ga., Ind., Neb., Ohio)	Columbusite
Columbus (Miss.)	Columbian
Corpus Christi	Corpus Christian (/**kris**-tee-ən/)
Detroit	Detroiter
District of Columbia	Washingtonian
Dodge City	Dodge Citian
El Paso	El Pasoan
Fairbanks	Fairbanksan, Fairbanksian
Fort Worth	Fort Worthian, *Fort Worther
Grand Rapids	Grand Rapidian
Greensboro, N.C.	Greensburgher
Hanover, Pa.	Hanoverian
Harrisburg	Harrisburger
Honolulu	Honolulan
Houston	Houstonian
Independence, Mo.	Independent
Indianapolis	Indianapolitan
Jackson	Jacksonian
Jersey City	Jersey Cityite
Kansas City	Kansas Citian
Knoxville	Knoxvillian
Las Cruces	Crucen (/**kroo**-sən/)
Las Vegas	Las Vegan
Lawrence, Kan.	Lawrentian (/lə-**ren**-shən/)
Lawrence, Mass.	Lawrencian (/lə-**ren**-shən/)
Lebanon, Pa.	Lebanonian
Los Angeles	Angeleno, *Los Angelean
Louisville	Louisvillian
Madison	Madisonian
Manhattan (N.Y. or Kan.)	Manhattanite
Maui	Mauian
Memphis	Memphian
Miami	Miamian
Milwaukee	Milwaukeean
Minneapolis	Minneapolitan
Nashville	Nashvillian
Newark	Newarker
New Orleans	New Orleanian, *New Orleansian
New York City	New Yorker
Oklahoma City	Oklahoma Citian, *Oklahoma Cityan
Omaha	Omahan
Palm Beach	Palm Beacher
Pensacola	Pensacolian
Philadelphia	Philadelphian
Phoenix	Phoenician
Pittsburgh	Pittsburgher, *Pittsburger
Pontiac	Pontiacker
Portland	Portlander
Princeton	Princetonian
Providence	Providentian
Sacramento	Sacramentan
Saginaw	Saginawian
Salt Lake City	Salt Laker
San Antonio	San Antonian
San Diego	San Diegan
San Francisco	San Franciscan
San Jose	San Josean
San Marino	San Marinan, *San Marinoite
Santa Fe	Santa Fean
Saratoga Springs	Saratogian
Saugus	Saugonian
Sault Sainte Marie	Sooite
Savannah	Savannahian
Schenectady	Schenectadian
Seattle	Seattleite, *Seattlite
Shreveport	Shreveporter
Spokane	Spokanite
St. Louis	St. Louisan
St. Paul	St. Paulite
Tallahassee	Tallahasseean
Tampa	Tampan
Taos	Taoseno
Troy	Trojan
Tucson	Tucsonan, *Tucsonian, *Tucsonite
Twin Cities	Twin Citian
Wilkes-Barre	Wilkes-Barrean
Williamsport	Williamsporter

Countries

Afghanistan	Afghan
Argentina	Argentine, *Argentinian
Azerbaijan	Azerbaijani
Bahamas	Bahamian
Belarus	Belarusian, *Belarusan
Belgium	Belgian
Cayman Islands	Caymanian, Cayman Islander
China	Chinese

Colombia	Colombian	Paraguay	Paraguayan
Czech Republic	Czech	Peru	Peruvian
Denmark	Dane	Philippines	Filipino
Egypt	Egyptian	Poland	Pole
El Salvador	Salvadoran, *Salvadorean, *Salvadorian	Portugal	Portuguese
		Puerto Rico	Puerto Rican
England	English	Qatar	Qatari
Finland	Finn, Finnish, *Finlander	Romania	Romanian
France	French	Russia	Russian
Germany	German	Rwanda	Rwandan
Great Britain	Briton	San Marino	Sammarinese, *San Marinese
Greece	Greek	Saudi Arabia	Saudi, *Saudi Arabian
Greenland	Greenlander	Scotland	Scot
Grenada	Grenadian, *Grenadan	Senegal	Senegalese
Guam	Guamanian	Seychelles	Seychellois
Guyana	Guyanese	Singapore	Singaporean
Haiti	Haitian	Slovakia	Slovak
Honduras	Honduran	Slovenia	Slovene
Hungary	Hungarian	Somalia	Somali
Indonesia	Indonesian	South Africa	South African
Iran	Iranian	Spain	Spaniard
Iraq	Iraqi	Sri Lanka	Sri Lankan, *Ceylonese
Ireland	Irish	Sudan	Sudanese
Israel	Israeli	Sumatra	Sumatran
Italy	Italian	Suriname	Surinamese, *Surinamer
Jamaica	Jamaican	Swaziland	Swazi
Japan	Japanese	Sweden	Swede
Jordan	Jordanian	Switzerland	Swiss
Kazakhstan	Kazakh	Syria	Syrian
Kenya	Kenyan	Tahiti	Tahitian
Korea	Korean	Taiwan	Taiwanese
Kuwait	Kuwaiti	Tajikistan	Tajik
Laos	Lao, Laotian	Thailand	Thai
Lebanon	Lebanese	Tobago	Tobagonian
Libya	Libyan	Togo	Togolese
Liechtenstein	Liechtensteiner	Tonga	Tongan
Luxembourg	Luxembourger	Trinidad	Trinidadian
Macedonia	Macedonian	Tunisia	Tunisian
Madagascar	Malagasy	Turkey	Turk
Malaysia	Malaysian	Turkmenistan	Turkmen (pl. Turkmens)
Maldova	Maldovan	Uganda	Ugandan
Mali	Malian	Ukraine	Ukrainian
Malta	Maltese	United States	American
Martinique	Martiniquais	Uruguay	Uruguayan
Mexico	Mexican	Uzbekistan	Uzbek
Micronesia	Micronesian	Vanuatu	Ni-Vanuatu
Monaco	Monacan, Monegasque	Venezuela	Venezuelan
Mongolia	Mongolian	Vietnam	Vietnamese
Morocco	Moroccan	Virgin Islands	Virgin Islander
Myanmar	Burmese, Myanmarese	Wales	Welsh
Nepal	Nepalese	Zambia	Zambian
The Netherlands	Hollander, Netherlander, *Netherlandian	Zimbabwe	Zimbabwean

Foreign Cities and Regions

New Zealand	New Zealander
Nicaragua	Nicaraguan
Niger	Nigerien (/nɪ-jir-ee-**en**/)
Nigeria	Nigerian (/nɪ-**jir**-ee-ən/)
Norway	Norwegian
Oman	Omani
Pakistan	Pakistani
Palau	Palauan
Panama	Panamanian

Alberta, Canada	Albertan
Amsterdam, the Netherlands	Amsterdammer
Athens, Greece	Athenian
Baghdad, Iraq	Baghdadi
Bangkok, Thailand	Bangkokian
Béarn, France	Béarnais (not *Béarnaise*)
Beijing, China	Beijinger

LANGUAGE-CHANGE INDEX (For the full key, see front matter pp. xxxi, l–li.)
Stage 1: Rejected. **Stage 2:** Widely shunned. **Stage 3:** Widespread but . . . **Stage 4:** Ubiquitous but . . . **Stage 5:** Fully accepted.
Invariably inferior forms marked by asterisk (*). • Ratios represent frequency of prevalent forms vs. variants in current books.

Belgrade, Yugoslavia	Belgrader
Berlin, Germany	Berliner
Bern, Switzerland	Bernese
Birmingham, England	Brummie
Bogotá, Colombia	Bogotano
Bologna, Italy	Bolognese
Bordeaux, France	Bordelais
British Columbia, Canada	British Columbian
Brussels, Belgium	Bruxellois
Budapest, Hungary	Budapesti
Buenos Aires, Argentina	Porteño
Cairo, Egypt	Cairene
Cambridge, England	Cantabrigian
Canton, China	Cantonese
Cheshire, England	Cestrian
Copenhagen, Denmark	Copenhagener
Cork, Ireland	Corkonian
Cornwall, England	Cornish
Devonshire, England	Devonian
Dijon, France	Dijonese, Dijonnais
Dublin, Ireland	Dubliner
Dundee, Scotland	Dundonian
Edinburgh, Scotland	Edinburgher
Exeter, England	Exonian
Flanders, Belgium	Flemish
Florence, Italy	Florentine
Fontainebleau, France	Bellifontain
Geneva, Switzerland	Genevan, Genevese
Genoa, Italy	Genovese, Genoan
Glasgow, Scotland	Glaswegian
The Hague, Netherlands	Hagenaar
Halifax, Nova Scotia	Haligonian
Hamburg, Germany	Hamburger
Hampshire, England	Hantsian
Hanover, Germany	Hanoverian
Havana, Cuba	Havanan
Helsinki, Finland	Helsinkian
Hong Kong, China	Hong Konger, *Hong Kongite, *Hong Kongian
Isle of Man, England	Manx
Isle of Wight, England	Vectian
Istanbul, Turkey	Istanbulite, Istanbullu
Jerusalem, Israel	Jerusalemite
Johannesburg, S. Africa	Johannesburger
Lima, Peru	Limeño
Lisbon, Portugal	Lisboan
Liverpool, England	Liverpudlian
London, England	Londoner
Lyons, France	Lyonnais
Madrid, Spain	Madrileno
Majorca, Spain	Majorcan
Manchester, England	Mancunian
Manila, Philippines	Manilite
Manitoba, Canada	Manitoban
Melbourne, Australia	Melburnian
Metz, France	Messin
Mexico City, Mexico	Chilango
Milan, Italy	Milanese
Montenegro, Yugoslavia	Montenegrin
Moscow, Russia	Muscovite
Naples, Italy	Neapolitan
Nazareth, Israel	Nazarene
New Brunswick, Canada	New Brunswicker
Newcastle, Australia	Novocastrian
Newcastle, England	Geordie

Newfoundland, Canada	Newfoundlander, Newfie
New South Wales, Australia	New South Welshman
Nice, France	Niçois
Norfolk, England	North Anglian
Northumberland, England	Northumbrian
Nova Scotia, Canada	Nova Scotian
Ontario, Canada	Ontarian
Oxford, England	Oxonian
Paris, France	Parisian
Prague, Czech Republic	Praguer
Prince Edward Island, Canada	Prince Edward Islander
Quebec, Canada	Quebecer
Quito, Ecuador	Quiteño
Rio de Janeiro, Brazil	Carioca
Rome, Italy	Roman
Saint-Cloud, France	Clodoaldien
Salzburg, Austria	Salzburger
San Juan, Puerto Rico	San Juanero
Santiago, Chile	Santiaguino
Sao Paulo, Brazil	Paulista
Saskatchewan, Canada	Saskatchewanian
Serbia, Yugoslavia	Serb
Shanghai, China	Shanghailander
Shropshire, England	Salopian
St. Croix, U.S. Virgin Islands	Cruzan
Stockholm, Sweden	Stockholmer
St. Petersburg, Russia	St. Petersburger
Stratford-on-Avon, England	Stratfordian
Sydney, Australia	Sydneysider
Tangier, Morocco	Tangerine
Tasmania, Australia	Tasmanian
Tehran, Iran	Tehrani
Tel Aviv, Israel	Tel Avivian
Tokyo, Japan	Tokyoite
Toronto, Canada	Torontonian
Tripoli, Libya	Tripolitan
Trois-Rivières, Canada	Trifluvien
Vancouver, Canada	Vancouverite
Venice, Italy	Venetian
Verona, Italy	Veronese
Vienna, Austria	Viennese
Winnipeg, Canada	Winnipegger

denote (= to indicate) for *denominate* (= to assign a name) is a common error—e.g.: "Teenagers whose parents are home at what the researchers *denoted* [read *denominated* or *called*] 'key times'—in the morning, after school, at dinner and at bedtime—are less likely to smoke, to drink or to use marijuana." "What Teenagers Need, Etc.," *Wash. Times*, 14 Sept. 1997, at B2.

For the difference between *denote* and *connote*, see **connote.**

LANGUAGE-CHANGE INDEX

denote misused for *denominate*: Stage 1

denounce; renounce. *Denounce* = (1) to condemn openly or publicly; (2) to accuse formally; or (3) to formally announce the termination of (a treaty or pact). Sense 1 is most common—e.g.:

- "Jack Kemp and I will use the White House as a bully pulpit to *denounce* both drug use and the pushers who sell the poison." Bob Dole, "One-on-One with the Candidates," *USA Today*, 23 Sept. 1996, at A10.
- "Alas, a new study (which Mr. Pa *denounces*) suggests that the vaccine is useless." "Drug Firms; Limited Imagination," *Economist*, 28 Sept. 1996, at 80.

Renounce = (1) to give up or relinquish, esp. by formal announcement; or (2) to reject or disown. Both senses of this word are common.

- Sense 1: "The burgeoning 'patriot movement' [has followers contending that] the federal government holds no power over them once they *renounce* citizenship." Steve Ryfle, "Broderick Deceived Followers, Jurors Told," *L.A. Times*, 28 Sept. 1996, at B1.
- Sense 2: "The danger now is that Palestinians will *renounce* Arafat and Netanyahu both." "Arab and Jew: A Clash That Could Have Been Avoided," *Star Trib.* (Minneapolis), 27 Sept. 1996, at A20.

Some writers use *denounce* when they mean *renounce*—e.g.:

- "Supreme Court Justice David Souter administered the oath to people who *denounced* [read *renounced*] their Russian, Guyanan and even Bosnian citizenships, among others, to become Americans." Randy Weston, "375th Anniversary, Growth Issues Mark Event-Filled Year," *Patriot Ledger* (Quincy, Mass.), 26 Dec. 1995, at 13.
- "They have *denounced* [read *renounced*] their U.S. citizenship and set up their own racist, sexist, frontier society." Deborah Mathis, "We Deserve Freedom from Montana Freemen," *Houston Chron.*, 12 May 1996, Outlook §, at 6.

LANGUAGE-CHANGE INDEX
denounce misused for *renounce*: Stage 2

*denouncement. See **denunciation.**

dentifrice (an old-fashioned, rather fancy word for "toothpaste") is so spelled—not (through METATHESIS) **dentrifice.* E.g.: "In children, this condition [fluorosis] has been associated with fluoride supplements, formulas containing fluoride, and fluoride *dentrifices* [read *dentifrices*]." Olga M. Sanchez, "Anticipatory Guidance in Infant Oral Health," *Am. Family Physician*, 1 Jan. 2000, at 115. The word is rarely used outside medical and dental contexts.

LANGUAGE-CHANGE INDEX
dentifrice misspelled **dentrifice*: Stage 1
Current ratio: 21:1

denunciation; *denouncement. The latter has been a NEEDLESS VARIANT since the 16th century.

deny (= to declare untrue; repudiate; refuse to recognize or acknowledge) is sometimes misused for *refuse* or *decline*. These words are synonymous in certain constructions, such as *He was denied* (or *refused*) *this*. But in modern usage *refuse* or *decline* properly precedes an infinitive, whereas with *deny* this construction is an ARCHAISM—e.g.: "Zimmerman moved that Harmon dismiss herself. She *denied* [read *declined*]

to do so stating, among other things, that the motion should have been filed much earlier." Deborah Tedford, "Judge Contests 'Impropriety' Finding of Appellate Court," *Houston Chron.*, 18 Apr. 1995, at 12.

LANGUAGE-CHANGE INDEX
deny misused for *decline*: Stage 1

depart. This is a FORMAL WORD typical of AIRLINESE and OFFICIALESE. In traditional idiom, one *departs from* a place. But today many writers ill-advisedly drop the *from*. That is, *depart* has become an ERGATIVE VERB: though the word has traditionally been intransitive, writers are now making it transitive. The *OED* calls this usage "rare" except in the phrase *depart this life*. The resurgence may have begun among headline writers—e.g.: "Lane Departs City Hall," *Oregonian* (Portland), 16 Oct. 2000, at E3. But it is spreading into usage more generally, especially in reference to local government—e.g.:

- "I'm wondering what 7.5 million New Yorkers will do when this strange man *departs* City Hall." Joseph Dolman, "False Peace in City Hall Isn't Good for City," *Newsday* (N.Y.), 20 Sept. 2000, at A42.
- "His take-charge actions in these lame-duck days have inspired many to wonder what comes next after he *departs* City Hall." Liz Trotta, "Giuliani Defines Strength, Leadership in N.Y. Crisis," *Wash. Times*, 14 Sept. 2001, at A4.
- "Term limits may force them out of the City Council, but not all the members—or their staffs—will be *departing* city government." Frankie Edozien, "Councilors Get New Lease on Political Life," *N.Y. Post*, 20 Dec. 2001, at 20.

depend. This word typically takes *on* (or, less good, *upon*—see **upon**). When a clausal complement follows the verb, to omit the *on* is a CASUALISM—e.g.:

- "It all *depends when* [read *depends on when*] the hardware gets delivered." "Comcast to Offer Cable Modems," *Bus. J.* (Sacramento), 26 May 2000, at 2.
- "So what is this place called? *Depends what* [read *Depends on what*] night you're there." Tyler Gray, "By Any Name, Creativity Is Welcome," *Orlando Sentinel*, 17 Nov. 2000, at 58.
- "It all *depends who's* [read *depends on who's*] in the kitchen." Michael Bauer, "Lovely Grand Cafe Craves Stability," *S.F. Chron.*, 12 Jan. 2001, at C14.

In English-language print sources, the collocation *depends on what* is much more common than **depends what*—and has steadily been more frequent since the early 18th century.

The truncated phrase *that depends*, without a complement, is often heard in conversation.

LANGUAGE-CHANGE INDEX
depend for *depend on*: Stage 2
Current ratio (*depends on what* vs.
*depends what): 16:1

dependant. See **dependent,** n.

dependence; dependency. These variants have undergone DIFFERENTIATION. *Dependence*, more common

LANGUAGE-CHANGE INDEX (For the full key, see front matter pp. xxxi, l–li.)
Stage 1: Rejected. **Stage 2:** Widely shunned. **Stage 3:** Widespread but . . . **Stage 4:** Ubiquitous but . . . **Stage 5:** Fully accepted.
Invariably inferior forms marked by asterisk (*). • Ratios represent frequency of prevalent forms vs. variants in current books.

since the 16th century, is the general word meaning (1) "the quality or state of being dependent"; or (2) "reliance." *Dependency* is a geopolitical term meaning "a territory under the jurisdiction of, but not formally annexed by, a nation." (See **territory**.) These words are commonly misspelled *dependance and **dependancy.*

Sometimes *dependency* is misused for *dependence*—e.g.: "Citing the Army's *dependency* [read *dependence*] on reservists, Mr. Cohen last month postponed a planned reduction of 25,000 Guard and Reservist positions, a 4 percent cut that would have saved $900 million over the next five years." Steven Lee Myers, "New Role of Guard Transforming Military," *N.Y. Times,* 24 Jan. 2000, at A1, A22.

Unfortunately, the distinction is not complete: *dependency* is the term for drug habituation as well. See **addicted.**

LANGUAGE-CHANGE INDEX
dependency misused for *dependence*: Stage 2

dependent, adj. See **addicted.**

dependent, n.; **dependant.** For the noun, the older spelling is *dependant.* The *OED* notes: "from the 18th c. (like the adj.) spelt *dependent,* after L.; but the spelling -*ant* still predominates in the [noun]." *W11* countenances -*ent* over -*ant.* The *COD* continues the Oxonian preference for -*ant,* noting that -*ent* is chiefly American. Certainly the British DIFFERENTIATION in spelling between the adjective and the noun is a useful one, but it remains tenuous in BrE. The AmE preference for -*ent* for both noun and adjective has been strong since 1950.

deplane. This word, like *enplane* and *reinplane,* is characteristic of AIRLINESE, a relatively new brand of JARGON dating from the latter half of the 20th century. Careful writers and speakers stick to such time-honored expressions as *get off, get on,* and *get on again.*

LANGUAGE-CHANGE INDEX
deplane for *get off* (an airplane): Stage 4

deport; disport. *Deport* = (1) to behave (oneself); or (2) to banish, remove. *Disport* is a reflexive verb meaning (1) "to amuse (oneself)"; or (2) "to display (oneself) sportively." The two are sometimes confounded—e.g.: "It is hard to believe that the same ensemble and conductor who *disported* [read *deported* or, better, *comported*] themselves in so perfunctory a fashion in a showcase tour are the personnel of this expansive, supple, disciplined and engrossing Sixth Symphony." Lawrence B. Johnson, "Classical Briefs," *N.Y. Times,* 22 Sept. 1996, § 2, at 40.

LANGUAGE-CHANGE INDEX
disport misused for *deport* or *comport*: Stage 1

deportation; deportment. Both derive ultimately from L. *deportare* (= to carry off, convey away), but to say that these words have undergone DIFFERENTIA-TION is a great understatement. *Deportation* = the act of removing a person to another country; the expulsion

of an alien from a country <Baraca's deportation took only two months to process>. *Deportment* = the bearing, demeanor, or manners of a person <his deportment hardly suggests his regal lineage>.

Yet *deportment* is sometimes misused for *deportation*—e.g.: "Thurman supported measures that would . . . [m]ake it easier to deport criminal aliens after they serve their sentences and expand the number of crimes for which aliens risk *deportment* [read *deportation*]." Jim Ross, "Thurman Kept Contract with Her Constituents," *St. Petersburg Times,* 10 Apr. 1995, Hernando Times §, at 1.

LANGUAGE-CHANGE INDEX
deportment misused for *deportation*: Stage 1

depositary; depository; *depositee. Most authorities have agreed through the years that *depositary* is the better term in reference to people with whom one leaves valuables or money for safekeeping and that *depository* is standard in reference to places. True, lawyers often refer to a *depositary bank,* and this phrase has become common in legal parlance. But *depository* has continued to be used consistently for places—e.g.: "Cragg recounted how the central *depository* for stocks in India was recently robbed at gunpoint." Barry Strudwick & Chris Grant, "Investing Without Geographic Limits Leads Fund Manager to Odd Places," *Daily Record,* 19 Sept. 1996, at 7. Cf. **repository.**

**Depositee,* a NEEDLESS VARIANT of *depositary,* was popular for a time in the mid-19th century. E.g.: "Only Murrieta, at 22.7 percent, showed strong growth in bank deposits . . . . Big Bear Lake was the top *depositee* [read *depositary*] in San Bernardino County at $23,160." Andy McCue, "Latest Stats Reveal Facts About Region," *Press-Enterprise* (Riverside, Cal.), 3 Sept. 2000, Bus. §, at I1.

LANGUAGE-CHANGE INDEX
*depositee for *depositary*: Stage 1
Current ratio (*depositaries* vs. *depositees): 83:1

depot (= [1] a railway or bus station, [2] a place where buses are kept and repaired, or [3] a place where goods are stored until needed) is pronounced /**dee**-poh/ in AmE and /**dep**-oh/ in BrE.

depravity; depravation. *Depravity* is the condition of being corrupt or perverted—e.g.: "For much of the outside world, Barry's transition from prison inmate to Democratic mayoral nominee is fresh evidence of the *depravities* of life in the nation's capital." Howard Kurtz, "At the Post-Mortem, Media Examine Their Wounds," *Wash. Post,* 15 Sept. 1994, at C1.

The much rarer word *depravation* denotes the act or process of depraving or corrupting—e.g.: "In the candlelight of evening, the dirge-like chant of the book of Lamentations fills our sanctuaries, as we hear the horrors and *depravations* of humanity against humanity." Linda Joseph, "Tisha B'Av Recalls Calamity," *Sun-Sentinel* (Ft. Lauderdale) (Boca Raton ed.), 12 July 2002, at 3. Cf. **deprivation.**

Depravation is fairly often misused where *deprivation* (= want; destitution) was intended—e.g.: "The painter, fond of all sorts of geometric shapes, used ladders repeatedly to represent hope and escape from social injustice and economic *depravation* [read *deprivation*]." Ann Hicks, "Over the Line," *Greenville News* (S.C.), 11 Aug. 2002, at E1. Both words denote hardships, but of a different sort.

LANGUAGE-CHANGE INDEX
depravation misused for *deprivation*: Stage 1

deprecate; depreciate. The first word has increasingly encroached on the figurative senses of the second, while the second has retreated into financial contexts. *Deprecate* means "to disapprove earnestly"—e.g.:

- " 'Well,' he admitted, *deprecatingly*, 'one can't suppress one's natural instincts altogether; even if one's reason and self-interest are all the other way.' " Dorothy L. Sayers, *Gaudy Night* 351 (1936; repr. 1995).
- " 'Ah, that was thirty-five years ago! Long before you were born, my dear.' Herr Landauer shook his head *deprecatingly*, his boot-button eyes twinkling with benevolence: 'Now I have not the time for such studies.' " Christopher Isherwood, *The Berlin Stories* 150 (1963).
- "There must be a proper balance between urban and rural, industrial and agricultural development. And a spirit of excessive tolerance is to be *deprecated*." Jonathan Romney, "Apollo 13," *New Statesman & Society*, 22 Sept. 1995, at 29.

Depreciate, transitively, means "to belittle, disparage"; and, intransitively, "to fall in value" (used in reference to assets or investments). The phrase *self-deprecating* is, literally speaking, a virtual impossibility, except perhaps for those suffering from extreme neuroses. Hence *self-depreciating*, with *depreciate* in its transitive sense, has historically been viewed as the correct phrase—e.g.:

- "You seem to take some special pleasure in making yourself the butt of your own peculiar sense of humor. . . . All day long the same thing. In some little way or other, everything is ironical, or *self-depreciating*." Philip Roth, *Portnoy's Complaint* 264 (1969).
- "Sadly, Grizzard did not have the *self-depreciating* humor of a Jeff Foxworthy, the self-proclaimed redneck comedian." Bill McClellan, "If Southern Writer Were Judging the Games, What Would His Verdict Be?" *St. Louis Post-Dispatch*, 25 July 1996, at B1.
- "In a characteristically *self-depreciating* moment, Romano says, 'I was so nervous about my acting that I was surprised at how—I've got to phrase this just right—at how non-disappointed I was when I saw the pilot.' " James Endrst, " 'Everybody' Loves Romano," *Austin Am.-Statesman*, 15 Sept. 1996, at 4.

Unfortunately, the form *self-deprecating*—despite its mistaken origins—is now nearly 25 times as common in print as *self-depreciating*. Speakers of AmE and BrE routinely use *self-deprecating*. However grudgingly, we must accord to it the status of STANDARD ENGLISH—e.g.:

- "He's smart, articulate, funny, alternately *self-deprecating* and proud of his success." John Clark, "Call Him Mr. Nice Guy," *L.A. Times*, 1 Sept. 1996, Calendar §, at 3 (portrait of Howard Stern).
- "Milken doesn't drive himself much anymore, but he has a *self-deprecating* explanation for why that's the case: He says he used to do so many things while driving that he kept having collisions." Jeanie Russell Kasindorf, "What to Make of Mike," *Fortune*, 30 Sept. 1996, at 86.
- "She arrives in Doc Marten boots and a black playsuit, refreshingly unfiltered, straight-talking and *self-deprecating* from the start. 'I feel like I've gained new sweat pores. I'm sweating in places I've never sweated before,' she laments." Jane Mulkerrins, "Innocent Abroad," *Daily Telegraph*, 22 Aug. 2015, at 30.

LANGUAGE-CHANGE INDEX
self-deprecating for *self-depreciating*: Stage 5
Current ratio: 24:1

depreciatory; *depreciative. Both mean either "declining in value" or "disparaging." In both AmE and BrE, *depreciatory* is the predominant term—e.g.: "Try to find out what you mean—what you would go to the stake for—and put it down without frills or *depreciatory* gestures." Jacques Barzun & Henry F. Graff, "Clear Sentences: Right Emphasis and Right Rhythm" (1957), in *Perspectives on Style* 3, 19 (Frederick Candelaria ed., 1968). *Depreciative might reasonably be labeled a NEEDLESS VARIANT.

Current ratio: 3:1

deprivation; privation; *deprival. All three words mean "the action of depriving or taking away." The words share that general sense as well as specific senses relating to the depriving of an office, position, or benefice. *Deprivation* is the usual word. *Privation* is the more literary word; its primary sense is "the lack of life's ordinary amenities."

*Deprival (noted in the *OED* in four 17th- and 19th-century examples) is merely a NEEDLESS VARIANT of *deprivation*. E.g.: "Confinement of investigation to physically based suffering does not . . . exclude measures such as starvation or *deprival* [read *deprivation*] of sleep." James Heath, *Torture and English Law* 5 (1982).

For the confusingly similar *depravation*, see **depravity**.

LANGUAGE-CHANGE INDEX
*deprival for *deprivation*: Stage 1
Current ratio (*deprivation* vs. *deprival): 329:1

depute, v.t.; deputize. To *depute* is to delegate <these responsibilities she deputed to her agent>. To *deputize* is to make (another) one's deputy <the sheriff then deputized four men who had offered to help in the search>.

De Quincey, Thomas (1785–1859). Although the *Dictionary of National Biography* (1917) states that "De Quincey himself wrote his name 'de Quincey' and

LANGUAGE-CHANGE INDEX (For the full key, see front matter pp. xxxi, l–li.)
Stage 1: Rejected. **Stage 2:** Widely shunned. **Stage 3:** Widespread but . . . **Stage 4:** Ubiquitous but . . . **Stage 5:** Fully accepted.
Invariably inferior forms marked by asterisk (*). • Ratios represent frequency of prevalent forms vs. variants in current books.

would have catalogued it among the Q's" (vol. 5, at 835), the long-established practice was to write *De Quincey* and to catalogue it in the D's. But when the revised edition was published in 2004 as the *Oxford Dictionary of National Biography*, the entry appeared under Q (vol. 45, at 700) without so much as a cross-reference at the appropriate place in D. The rewritten entry appears under "Quincey, Thomas Penson De," and the name throughout is written *De Quincey*.

de rigueur (= proper; required by custom or etiquette) is sometimes misspelled **de rigeur* or **de riguer*—e.g.:

- "If such affirmation of a transcendent order via the assertion of human dignity is *de rigeur* [read *de rigueur*] for tragedy, *Timon* does not qualify." Rolf Soellner, *Timon of Athens* 22 (1979).
- "I was tired of absorbing abuse while paying premium prices and receiving less service and courtesy than are *de riguer* [read *de rigueur*] in most small towns." Susan D. Haas, "Surly Hosts Want Traveling Wallets, Not Real Visitors," *Morning Call* (Allentown, Pa.), 31 Aug. 1996, at A35.

The phrase is pronounced /də ri-gər/.

LANGUAGE-CHANGE INDEX
de rigueur misspelled **de rigeur* or **de riguer*: Stage 2
Current ratio (*de rigueur* vs. **de rigeur*): 7:1

derisive; derisory; *derisible. *Derisive* = scoffing; expressing derision. *Derisory* = worthy of derision or of being scoffed at. Although *derisive* and *derisory* at one time overlapped and were frequently synonymous, the DIFFERENTIATION is now complete, and using the two interchangeably is a mistake. **Derisible*—an uncommon word appearing more often in BrE than in AmE—is a NEEDLESS VARIANT of *derisory*.

derogatory; *derogative. The first is standard. The second has been a NEEDLESS VARIANT in all phases of Modern English.

Current ratio: 66:1

derring-do (= daring action) derives, according to the *OED*, from a "chain of misunderstandings and errors." Originally, the term was *dorryng do*, a verb phrase meaning "daring to do." A 16th-century misprint in the poetry of John Lydgate (ca. 1370–1450) made it *derrynge do*, which Spenser (1579) misunderstood and used as a noun phrase meaning "manhood, chivalry." Then Sir Walter Scott popularized the phrase in *Ivanhoe* (1820) with the spelling *derring-do*, and this has been the settled spelling ever since. But because of its historical and modern associations with *daring*, writers often use the erroneous spelling **daring-do*—e.g.:

- "A glimpse at Waters' 1972 'Pink Flamingos' is a surprising reminder that for all their scatological *daring-do* [read *derring-do*], the Farrelly brothers are mainstream by comparison." Sid Smith, "As Shock Cinema, 'Mary' Is No 'Flamingo,'" *Chicago Trib.*, 19 July 1998, at 2.
- "Instead, it is also called 'Flower Flange' and has more to do with flowers than fighting and *daring-do* [read *derring-do*]." Joe L. Rosson, "'Dewey' Glass Water Pitcher Patriotic," *Knoxville News-Sentinel*, 25 Sept. 1998, at D2.
- "They spent hours regaling themselves with their motorized *daring-do* [read *derring-do*] while lakefront residents had to close windows and doors." Mark McGarrity,

"Driven to Distraction," *Star-Ledger* (Newark), 11 Oct. 1998, at 7.

LANGUAGE-CHANGE INDEX
derring-do misspelled **daring-do*: Stage 1
Current ratio: 16:1

derringer (= a small pistol) is so spelled even though the person for whom it was named was Henry Deringer (1786–1868), with only one -*r*-. Today **deringer* (sorry, Henry) is only a variant spelling, and neither form is capitalized.

desalination; salinization. *Desalination* is the beneficial process of removing salt from seawater (or occasionally other salty water), rendering it potable. *Salinization* (or occasionally *salinisation* in BrE) is the harmful impact that concentrations of mineral salts in groundwater have on arable land, potentially rendering it barren. Oddly enough, **desalinization* and **salination* are NEEDLESS VARIANTS of the two terms. Perhaps the anomalous differences in preferred forms are attributable to the fact that the terms developed in different fields of study (water science vs. agriculture). For whatever reason, *desalination* is nine times as common in modern print sources as its variants, while *salinization* is six times as common as its variants—including the first-recorded form of that term, **salinification*, which has all but disappeared.

Current ratio (*desalination* vs. **desalinization*): 9:1
Current ratio (*salinization* vs. **salination*): 6:1

descendant; *descendent. A majority of American desktop dictionaries list *descendant* as the predominant spelling for the noun <a generation of descendants> and **descendent* as the corresponding adjective <a descendent line on the map from northwest to southeast>. In fact, though, the spelling **descendent* is quite rare in comparison with -*ant*—even in adjectival uses—whether in AmE or in BrE. It is therefore properly classifiable as a NEEDLESS VARIANT.

Descendant is sometimes misspelled by omitting the -*s*-, perhaps from confusion with *decedent*—e.g.: "I could also recall the fact that after all Frau Brockhaus was a *decendant* [read *descendant*] of Richard Wagner's." Dietrich Fischer-Dieskau, *Reverberations* 360 (Ruth Hein trans., 1989).

LANGUAGE-CHANGE INDEX
descendant misspelled **decendant*: Stage 2
Current ratio (*descendant* vs. **descendent*): 8:1

descendible. Traditionally so spelled—not **descendable*. (See -ABLE (A).) But this creates something of an anomaly because *ascendable* has long been preferred over **ascendible*. Such are the vagaries of our language.

Current ratio (*descendible* vs. **descendable*): 13:1

descent /di-sent/ is often mispronounced /**dee**-sent/. See PRONUNCIATION (B).

descry. See **decry.**

desegregation; integration. Although no distinction between a requirement of *integration* and a requirement of *desegregation* is ordinarily observed in legal usage, the distinction may be important in understanding the constitutional law of race and the schools. Certainly it would be useful, in reference to public schools in the United States, if we distinguished between court-ordered *desegregation* (= the abrogation of policies that segregate races into different institutions and facilities) and court-ordered *integration* (= the incorporation of different races into existing institutions for the purpose of achieving a racial balance).

desert, vb.; **abandon,** vb. You can either desert or abandon a place or a person, but only *abandon* works for plans or efforts. E.g.: "Attempts were also made to use the shredded currency as insulation, mattress filling, and 'drilling mud' for oil exploration, but again the material was not suitable and those efforts were *deserted* [read *abandoned*]." Calvin Sims, "In Recycling of Greenbacks, New Meaning for Old Money," *N.Y. Times*, 22 May 1994, at 1, 12.

Language-Change Index
desert misused for abandon: Stage 1

deserts. See **just deserts.**

deshabille. See **dishabille.**

desiccate. So spelled. See SPELLING (A).

desiderata (= things wanted or needed) is the plural form of *desideratum*—e.g.:

- "'Honesty,' 'sensitivity,' 'a sense of humor' are among the current *desiderata*." Merle Rubin, "'Evelina' Gives Enlightening Look at 18th Century," *Wash. Times*, 9 Apr. 1995, at B7.
- "At its best his work amply fulfils these *desiderata*." Vernon Scannell, "Poignant Bawd," *Daily Telegraph*, 13 July 1996, Books §, at 14.

Although the plural is more common, the singular has many appropriate uses—e.g.:

- "In our time, empirical evidence has become the *desideratum* for belief." David K. Hart, "The Moral Sense," *Society*, Mar. 1995, at A75.
- "However it is done, efficiency often leads to loss of another *desideratum*—the personal touch." Pat Guiteras, "Health Care Changes Mean Few Doctors Do Duty at Office and Hospital," *Chapel Hill Herald*, 18 Sept. 1996, at 5.

Some writers misuse *desiderata* as a singular—e.g.: "The British were keen to secure a *desiderata* [read, perhaps, *desideratum*—or reword] in Arabia in view of Britain's 'special political interests' in the region." Clive Schofield, "Eritrea and Yemen at Odds in the Red Sea," *Jane's Intelligence Rev.*, 1 June 1996, at 264.

The pronunciation is /də-sid-ə-ray-tə/ or /də-sid-ə-rah-tə/.

Language-Change Index
desiderata misused as a singular: Stage 1
Current ratio (a desideratum vs. *a desiderata): 93:1

designer. *Designer*, an agent noun dating from the mid-17th century, has three primary senses: (1) someone who designs or plans; an originator of a plan; (2) (archaic) a plotter against Christ; and (3) someone who makes an artistic plan or design for construction—and, by extension, someone who invents and markets fashionable clothing. Sense 3 gave rise, beginning in the 1960s, to attributive uses: *designer scarves, designer labels, designer jeans.* And soon, even things other than garments were tagged with this label: *designer cars, designer houses,* even *designer water.* In this voguish use, the term is simply intended to connote status and expense. But as the former editor of the *OED* said a couple of decades after *designer* this and that became all the rage, the attributive use looks as if it will be "staying around for a while." Robert W. Burchfield, *Points of View* 126 (1992).

desirable; desirous. *Desirable* is used in reference to things or people that are desired. *Desirous* is used in reference to the desirer's emotions. What is *desirable* is attractive and worth seeking; a *desirous* person is impelled by desire.

Occasionally, *desirous* is misused for *desirable*—e.g.: "John Ortego said telephone marketing and sales jobs created in Erie County at Ingram Micro and Softbank Services Group fit the description of *desirous* [read *desirable*] service-sector positions." James M. Odato, "State's Business Leaders Urged to Help Spur Economy," *Buffalo News*, 13 Sept. 1996, at A13.

But even when *desirous* is correct, it usually appears in the wordy phrase *(be) desirous of*, which can be shortened to *desire* or *want*—e.g.:

- "The coaches *are desirous of building* [read *want to build*] a winning tradition in each of their sports." Kevin Lonnquist, "Pantego Increases Staff Size," *Dallas Morning News*, 12 Aug. 1996, at B1.
- "But the competition should heat up as banks, eager to find a new source of loan earnings and *desirous of* [read *desiring* or *wanting*] improved Community Reinvestment Act ratings, plunge into this area." James B. Arndorfer, "Banks Extending Reach to Compete with Nonbanks," *Am. Banker*, 26 Aug. 1996, at 10.
- "Obama is gambling that the dynamics of Iranian domestic politics—a young population more *desirous of* [read *interested in*] enjoying the fruits of modernity than in pursuing a revolutionary Islamist agenda—will result in Iran choosing ultimately to play a responsible and stabilizing role rather than an irresponsible and destabilizing one." Andrew J. Bacevich, "A Deal to Reboot Mideast Policy?" *L.A. Times*, 7 Aug. 2015, at 15. (On *Iran choosing* vs. *Iran's choosing*, see FUSED PARTICIPLES.)

Language-Change Index
desirous misused for desirable: Stage 1

desist, a FORMAL WORD for *stop* or *leave off*, is usually followed by the preposition *from* or (less commonly) *in*—e.g.: "Clinton told congressional leaders that he has sent a written warning to Saddam through the Iraqi mission at the United Nations in New York to *desist from* all threatening moves against U.S. pilots—or face devastating consequences." Leo Rennert, "U.S. Force Ordered to Kuwait," *Fresno Bee*, 18 Sept. 1996, at A1.

desistance—not **desistence*—is the noun corresponding to *desist*, vb.

Current ratio: 16:1

Des Moines (the city in Iowa) is pronounced /də-**moyn**/—and no other way.

despair, v.i., takes the preposition *of* <she despairs of his inability to drive>.

*despatch. See **dispatch.**

desperado (= a violent criminal not afraid of danger) predominantly forms the plural *desperadoes*—not **desperados*. See PLURALS (D).

Current ratio: 5:1

despite; in spite of. The two are almost always interchangeable. The compactness of *despite* recommends it, and it has greatly predominated in AmE and BrE print sources since the early 1950s.

Current ratio (*despite the fact that* vs. *in spite of the fact that*): 4:1

despoliation; *despoilment. See **spoliation.**

despot (= a cruel and unfair ruler) is pronounced /**des**-pət/—preferably not /**des**-pot/.

destination. This word commonly appears in two supposed redundancies—*final destination* and *ultimate destination*. But neither phrase is necessarily redundant. If a shipment has a series of stops or transfers—i.e., a series of "immediate destinations"—it may have a *final* or *ultimate destination*. You might be on your way to Hong Kong, with a stopover in Tokyo. If someone in the airport asked about your destination, you might characterize Tokyo as the *immediate destination* (i.e., the destination of that particular flight) and Hong Kong as the *ultimate destination* (the destination of the entire trip). See REDUNDANCY.

   Yet the phrase *final destination* or *ultimate destination* should not be used (as it commonly is) in contexts in which such specificity is not called for—e.g.: "Huard might have been born to be a quarterback. He might have been raised to be a quarterback. He might have dreamed of being an NFL quarterback. But it is Holmgren who can push him to that *final, ultimate destination* [read *destination* or, better, *goal*]." Laura Vecsey, "Huard's Future in Talented Hands," *Seattle Post-Intelligencer*, 19 Apr. 1999, at E1. Cf. **final outcome.**

*destroyable. See **destructible.**

destruct, vb., originated in the 17th century as a NEEDLESS VARIANT of *destroy*. By the early 20th century, it had largely fallen into disuse. In the 1950s, however, the word arose once again—this time as a high-tech espionage term arrived at as a BACK-FORMATION from

the noun *destruction*. Today, it is confined mostly to the phrase *self-destruct*.

destructible. So spelled in AmE and BrE alike—not **destructable*. See -ABLE (A). **Destroyable* is a NEEDLESS VARIANT.

Current ratio: 270:1

desuetude (= a state of long-term disuse) is preferably pronounced /**des**-wi-tyood/—not /di-s[y]oo-i-tood/.

desultory (= done without plan or purpose) is preferably pronounced /**des**-əl-tor-ee/ or /**dez**-əl-tor-ee/—not /di-**səl**-tə-ree/.

*detainment; *detainal. See **detention.**

detectable. So spelled in AmE and BrE alike—not **detectible*. See -ABLE (A).

Current ratio: 103:1

detector; *detecter. The former spelling is standard in AmE and BrE alike. See -ER (A).

Current ratio: 3,945:1

détente /day-**tahnt**/ (= a period in which two countries with strained relations relax the tensions between them) is typically so written, with the acute accent but in roman type (not italic). See DIACRITICAL MARKS.

detention; *detainment; *detainal. *Detention* = holding in custody; confinement; compulsory delay. **Detainment* and **detainal* are NEEDLESS VARIANTS.

Current ratio (*detention* vs. **detainment*): 88:1

determent. See **deterrent.**

determinable = (1) capable of being ascertained; or (2) liable to be cut short. The first is the general sense; the second is a term of art in law.

determinacy (= the quality of having fixed rules or being definitely settled), the correct form, is sometimes incorrectly rendered **determinancy,* perhaps under the influence of such words as *permanency*—e.g.: "Economic *determinancy* [read *determinacy*] . . . is a simplistic and reductionist approach to explaining international relations." Burdin H. Hickock, "Foreign Policy," *Policy Rev.*, Winter 1982, at 3.

LANGUAGE-CHANGE INDEX
determinacy misspelled **determinancy*: Stage 1
Current ratio: 63:1

determinant. See **determiner.**

determinately; determinedly. *Determinately* (= conclusively, definitively) is sometimes misused for *determinedly* (= with firm resolve or strong willpower)—e.g.:

- "Amid the bloody civil war, with Luanda beleaguered by the Popular Movement's enemies to the north and the south, Neto *determinately* [read *determinedly*] took the oath of office as president of the first independent government of Angola in a stuffy second-floor room of Luanda's city hall." Caryle Murphy, "Rebel Poet-Doctor," *Wash. Post*, 12 Sept. 1979, at A22.

- "[Jay] Leno, a nightclub veteran, appeared *determinately* [read *determinedly*] unruffled by the negative remarks he read." Daniel Cerone, " 'Tonight'—Familiar Growing Pains," *L.A. Times*, 4 June 1992, at F1.

Sometimes, of course, *determinately* is just the right word—e.g.: "Did not Werner Heisenberg in 1927 convincingly argue that the physical universe cannot be measured *determinately* and thus may just be chaotic and without structure?" Simon Oswitch, "Digging Cage," *L.A. Times*, 29 Mar. 1987, Calendar §, at 95.

LANGUAGE-CHANGE INDEX
determinately for *determinedly*: Stage 1

determination of whether. Although the preposition *of* is unnecessary, it has commonly appeared in this phrase since the mid-20th century. Many skilled editors prefer to remove it. See **whether (c).**

determinedly. See **determinately.**

***determine if.** See **determine whether.**

determiner; determinant. Both mean "that which determines," but only *determiner* denotes a person who determines. In the general sense, preference might be given to the native-English suffix *-er*, but one could not be faulted for using either term: euphony should be the determiner. And *determinant* often simply sounds better—e.g.: "The use of the traditional business concept of value as the *determinant* of choices would set the environmental debate back decades." "The Challenge of Going Green," *Harvard Bus. Rev.*, July–Aug. 1994, at 37.

determine whether; *determine if. Although **determine if* has historically been used by reputable writers, it has never been as common as *determine whether* in edited prose. The *whether* form is considered better because *if* erroneously suggests a conditional statement as opposed to a neutral hypothetical. E.g.:

- "Tests were being done to *determine if* [read *determine whether*] the bees were of the Africanized variety." "Man, 85, Survives More than 300 Bee Stings," *Record* (N.J.), 20 Sept. 1996, at L6.
- "Without a clear, consistent method of evaluating the performances of the chief attorney and county administrator, it's difficult, if not impossible, for the commissioners and the public to *determine if* [read *determine whether*] these two top employees are meeting their goals and objectives." "Value of Evaluations," *Sarasota Herald-Trib.*, 20 Sept. 1996, at A14.
- "A seasoned duck hunter and cook can always *determine if* [read *determine whether*] a fowl is taken east or west of I-35." "Editorial," *Abilene Reporter-News* (Tex.), 23 Aug. 2015, at G12.

For a similar problem with **doubt if* for *doubt whether*, see **doubt (a).**

LANGUAGE-CHANGE INDEX
**determine if* for *determine whether*: Stage 4
Current ratio (*determine whether* vs. **determine if*): 2:1

determinism. See **fatalism.**

deterrent, n.; **deterrence; determent.** A *deterrent* is something that deters. *Deterrence* is the act of deterring, especially in criminal-law and military contexts. It is more abstract than *determent*, which likewise denotes the act (or fact) of deterring, but usually with the connotation of preventing something on a particular occasion.

dethrone; *disenthrone. The latter has been a NEEDLESS VARIANT of infrequent occurrence since the 16th century.

Current ratio: 249:1

de Tocqueville. See NAMES (D).

detoxify; *detoxicate. Since the mid-20th century, *detoxify* has prevailed in AmE and BrE alike. **Detoxicate* is a NEEDLESS VARIANT.

Current ratio: 125:1

detract; distract. Although *detract* can be transitive (meaning "to divert") as well as intransitive (meaning "to take something away"), the transitive use—by far less common—encroaches on territory better served by *distract*. So instead of using the phrase **detract attention from*, careful writers say *distract attention from*.

detractive; *detractory. Although neither is common, the latter is a NEEDLESS VARIANT. *Detractive* = tending to detract; defamatory.

Current ratio: 4:1

detriment. The correct idiom is *to the detriment of*. But occasionally it's mangled—e.g.: "One of the issues about which Justice complained was that Microsoft would bundle its own applications into Windows *at the detriment of* [read *to the detriment of*] competing applications." David Radin, "Microsoft Puts Java Back into the Mix," *Pitt. Post-Gaz.*, 12 Sept. 2002, at E12. The writer has conflated *to the detriment of* with *at the expense of*—to the detriment of good usage.

LANGUAGE-CHANGE INDEX
**at the detriment of* for *to the detriment of*: Stage 1
Current ratio (*to* vs. **at the detriment of*): 101:1

Detroit /di-**troyt**/ is frequently mispronounced /**dee**-troyt/. See PRONUNCIATION (B).

deuterogamy. See **bigamy.**

deviance; *deviancy. See **deviation.**

deviant; deviate. A. As Adjectives. *Deviant* is normal. The first edition of the *OED* (1933) labeled both these adjectives "obsolete" and "rare." The *OED Supp.* (1972) deleted the tag on *deviant* and cited many examples in the sense "deviating from normal social standards or behavior." The word is common—e.g.:

- "He wasn't a young rebel, *deviant*, troubled or neurotic, didn't die early and wasn't weirdly erotic." James Warren, "America's Love, and Need, for the Duke," *Chicago Trib.*, 16 Aug. 1996, Tempo §, at 3.

LANGUAGE-CHANGE INDEX (For the full key, see front matter pp. xxxi, l–li.)
Stage 1: Rejected. **Stage 2:** Widely shunned. **Stage 3:** Widespread but . . . **Stage 4:** Ubiquitous but . . . **Stage 5:** Fully accepted.
Invariably inferior forms marked by asterisk (✳). • Ratios represent frequency of prevalent forms vs. variants in current books.

- "However, [the drug] does not change an abuser's proclivity toward *deviant* sex, experts say." Ellen Hale, "Value of Chemical Castration Doubted," *Courier-J.* (Louisville), 28 Aug. 1996, at A4.
- "Only the faintest electronic hum, audible to dogs and superhumans, suggested his *deviant* handiwork." Jeff Turrentine, "The Hotel Dick," *Forbes*, 23 Sept. 1996, at 41.

Although *deviant* is the predominant adjective, it has had to compete—unfortunately—with *deviate*. The latter, a NEEDLESS VARIANT of *deviant*, is common in AmE—e.g.: "Nora Mae Roberts is charged with one count of first-degree violation of a minor, involving alleged intercourse or *deviate* [read *deviant*] sex with a 17-year-old boy." Mike Rodman, "Ex-Girls' Basketball Coach Pleads Guilty to Sexually Violating 3 Players," *Ark. Democrat-Gaz.*, 15 Feb. 1995, at B1.

LANGUAGE-CHANGE INDEX
deviate used as an adjective in place of *deviant*: Stage 1
Current ratio (*deviant behavior* vs. **deviate behavior*): 185:1

B. As Nouns. Both *deviate* and *deviant* are used as (generally pejorative) nouns meaning "a person who, or thing which, deviates, esp. from normal social standards or behavior; specif., a sexual pervert" (*OED*). Although the two forms are both common, the noun *deviant*, as in *sexual deviant*, has predominated as a matter of word frequency since about 1970. *Deviant* has the advantage of deriving from the preferred adjective. (See FUNCTIONAL SHIFT.) All in all, *deviate* is best reserved for its verb function.

A few writers use **deviationist*, but that word is uncommon and ungainly enough to be labeled a NEEDLESS VARIANT.

Current ratio (*sexual deviant* vs. **sexual deviate*): 5:1

deviation; deviance; *deviancy. The general term for "an act or instance of deviating" is *deviation* <a ship's deviation from its voyage route> <deviation from orthodox religion>. *Deviation* is more neutral in connotation than *deviance*, which means "the quality or state of deviating from established norms, esp. in social customs." **Deviancy* is a NEEDLESS VARIANT.

Current ratio (*deviance* vs. **deviancy*): 10:1

device; devise. *Device*, n., = (1) something devised; or (2) a mechanical or electronic invention. *Devise* is predominantly a verb meaning "to invent or innovate."

Often, though, *devise* is used when *device* is the intended word—e.g.: "Jeremiah Wood, 6, was hurt Friday evening when he fell off the fender of a tractor driven by a relative and was struck by a brush hog, a mechanical *devise* [read *device*] used for chopping weeds." Judith VandeWater, "Two Boys Are Injured in Separate Accidents over Weekend While Visiting," *St. Louis Post-Dispatch*, 4 June 1996, at 1.

As a legal term, *devise* is sometimes used as a noun meaning "a gift of property by will."

LANGUAGE-CHANGE INDEX
devise misused for *device*: Stage 1
Current ratio (*ingenious device* vs. **ingenious devise*): 749:1

deviltry; devilry. Since the early 1800s, *deviltry* has predominated in AmE, *devilry* in BrE. But both words commonly appear in both varieties. One possible distinction between the two forms is that *deviltry* seems to denote a less serious type of mischief—e.g.: "When it debuted during the grim depths of the war, Coward's comedy of death and spiritualist *deviltry* drew some criticism as inappropriately morbid for the tough times." Joan Bunke, "At the Guthrie," *Des Moines Register*, 28 Sept. 1997, at 5. In the interests of DIFFERENTIATION, the distinction ought to be encouraged. But see **daredevilry.**

devisability; divisibility. The former means specifically "the capability of being given in a will"; the latter, much more common, means "the capability of being divided."

devise. See **device.**

deviser; devisor; divisor. A *deviser* is someone who invents or contrives. A *devisor* is someone who disposes of property (usually land) by will. *Divisor* is a mathematical term referring to the number by which another number is divided. All three are pronounced /di-**VI**-zər/.

devoid, a variant of *void*, adj., is current only in the idiom *devoid of*—e.g.:

- "If voters opt for the elected board, which was drenched in politics and *devoid of* educational inspiration, many of Payzant's reforms could come undone." "Class in Session," *Boston Globe*, 29 Aug. 1996, at A24.
- "Architecturally, a cathedral on this site would remain a free-standing, self-referencing monument, *devoid of* urban context." Kevin Starr, "Where to Put Cathedral, Recreate L.A.," *L.A. Times*, 8 Sept. 1996, at M1.

Because this phrase is a favorite of hyperbolists, it should be used cautiously.

To couple this adjective with the adverb *totally* or *completely* is to produce an extremely common REDUNDANCY, since *devoid* is an absolute adjective. (See ADJECTIVES (B).) E.g.:

- "Bursting with excess pride, and *totally devoid* [read *devoid*] of taste or restraint, Mother Ginger harbors a legion of future narcissists who will spend their lives seeking the appreciative applause so reliably delivered by 'Nutcracker' audiences." Barbara Gilford, "At the Heart of 'The Nutcracker,'" *N.Y. Times*, 4 Dec. 1994, at 22.
- "Despite the fact that Reese writes pretentiously in his column about 'perspective' on the Arab-Israeli conflict, in reality his column is *completely devoid* [read *devoid*] of objectivity and balance." Ted Lapkin, "Reese's Mideast Views Lack Context," *Orlando Sentinel*, 18 Nov. 1996, at A11.

devotee. See -EE.

dexterous; *dextrous; dextral. *Dexterous*, the preferred spelling in both AmE and BrE, means "clever, adept, skillful, artful." The spelling **dextrous* predominated in BrE through the late 18th century but has waned drastically in print sources since about

1800. *Dextral* means "on the right; right-handed." See **ambidextrous.**

    Current ratio (*dexterous* vs. *dextrous): 6:1

diabetes is pronounced either /dɪ-ə-**bee**-teez/ or /dɪ-ə-**bee**-tis/.

diachronic; synchronic. A *diachronic* study is concerned with changes during a (usually specified) period of time. A *synchronic* study is concerned with the state of a subject at a given time, without reference to its historical antecedents.

DIACRITICAL MARKS, also known as "diacritics," are orthographical marks that indicate a special phonetic quality for a given character. They occur mostly in foreign languages. But in English a fair number of imported terms have diacritical marks. Sometimes they survive indefinitely, but often they fall into disuse as terms are fully naturalized. (See GARNER'S LAW.) Nobody today, for example, writes *hôtel* or *rôle*. Although those spellings can be found in some 19th-century publications, they were falling out of fashion even then. To the extent that modern readers encounter diacritical marks, the main ones are as follows:

- **acute accent** (´): /ə-**kyoot**/. This mark generally indicates a stressed syllable or rising inflection. It sometimes appears in imported words to show that a final syllable is not silent, especially in words imported from French (as in *flambé* and *résumé*). It also appears over vowels in Spanish either to mark the syllable that has the highest degree of stress or to distinguish words otherwise identical in form but of different meaning.
- **breve** (˘): /breev/ or /brev/. This mark, used most commonly in pronunciations, indicates that a vowel is short or unstressed. That is, /bĕt/ in some pronunciation guides signifies the same thing as /bet/ does in this book.
- **cedilla** (¸): /sə-**dil**-ə/. This mark appears under the French and Portuguese *c* when the letter is to be pronounced as an *s* rather than as a *k* (as in *façade*). Generally the cedilla is quickly dropped in English-language contexts—so today *facade* doesn't usually have one. See **facade.**
- **circumflex** (^): /**sər**-kəm-fleks/. This mark was used over vowels in ancient Greek to indicate a rising–falling tone. Today it appears most commonly over French vowels after which an *-s-* was once elided (as in *côte* [our *coast*] and *fête* [our *feast*]).
- **diaeresis [umlaut]** (¨): /dɪ-**er**-ə-sis/ and /**uum**-lowt/. The diaeresis sometimes appears in English over the second of two adjacent vowels to indicate that the vowel is treated as a second syllable (as in *Chloë* or, archaically, *coöperate*, and *naïve*—but see below on the practice at *The New Yorker*). It appears in several Indo-European languages but is generally associated with German (in which it is termed an *umlaut*). See **umlaut.**
- **grave accent** (`): /grayv/. In ancient Greek, this mark signaled a lower inflection, in contrast to the higher inflection called for by the acute accent. In English, the grave is rarer than the acute accent, but it does appear on occasion to indicate a falling inflection or that a final syllable is to

be pronounced separately (as in *blessèd* or *learnèd*). E.g.: "She must retrieve her horse and leave this *cursèd* place." Candace Robb, *The Riddle of St. Leonard's* 197 (large-print ed. 1997). The grave accent is sometimes used in French over the vowels *a*, *e*, and *u*, and is also used in Italian.

- **háček** (ˇ): /**hach**-ek/. In Slavic and certain other languages, this mark is placed over a letter to show modification of the sound.
- **macron** (¯): /**may**-kron/ or /**mak**-ron/. This mark, used most commonly in pronunciations, indicates that a vowel is long. That is, in some pronunciation guides, /bōt/ signifies the same thing as /boht/ does in this book.
- **okina** (ʻ): /oh-**kee**-nə/. This character (also called a *hamzah*) appears mostly in the Arabic and Hawaiian languages. It marks the glottal stop in the Hawaiian language and is sometimes carried over into English contexts. It is similar to the grave accent but does not appear above a letter. See **Hawaii (B).**
- **tilde** (˜): /**til**-də/. This mark appears over the Spanish *n* to indicate the palatalized sound apparent in *señor*.

One well-known publication, *The New Yorker*, has the notable idiosyncrasy of using diacritical marks that most publications have abandoned, especially the diaeresis in place of old-fashioned hyphens (or nothing at all). While most American dictionaries recommend *cooperate*, *The New Yorker* insists on *coöperate*—e.g.: "I think if people are open and *coöperate* you get there faster." Ken Auletta, "Beauty and the Beast," *New Yorker*, 16 Dec. 2002, at 65, 70. Other examples of the diaeresis emerge frequently in that magazine—e.g.:

- "The postmodern enterprise was even more radical: to resist absorption or *coöptation* by an all-absorbing, all-*coöpting* System." Jonathan Franzen, "Mr. Difficult," *New Yorker*, 30 Sept. 2002, at 100, 108.
- "This was when vodka acquired its long-term *doppelgänger*—home brew." Victor Erofeyev, "The Russian God," *New Yorker*, 16 Dec. 2002, at 56, 58.
- "Optimistic but never *naïve*, she was tough and comforting at the same time." Roger Angell, "Anna Hamburger," *New Yorker*, 16 Dec. 2002, at 40.
- "Forget superheroes, or the *reëmergence* of wizards with beards down to their belts." Anthony Lane, "Looking Back," *New Yorker*, 16 Dec. 2002, at 106.
- "He has *reëstablished* his bona fides with the heart of the Party." Jeffrey Toobin, "Candide," *New Yorker*, 16 Dec. 2002, at 42, 43.

This house style is out of step with general American usage.

After fretting over when and how often to use diacritical marks, one can sympathize with the mid-20th-century views of Simeon Potter: "By great good fortune English spelling has escaped those tiresome diacritical marks placed above, beneath, before or after the letter, or inserted within it, which in a greater or less degree disfigure French, German, Italian, Spanish, Czech (solely the work of Jan Hus), Polish, Norwegian, Danish, Swedish, and even modern Turkish (unadvisedly introduced by Kemal Atatürk)." *Our Language* 73 (rev. ed. 1966).

LANGUAGE-CHANGE INDEX (For the full key, see front matter pp. xxxi, l–li.)
Stage 1: Rejected. **Stage 2:** Widely shunned. **Stage 3:** Widespread but . . . **Stage 4:** Ubiquitous but . . . **Stage 5:** Fully accepted.
Invariably inferior forms marked by asterisk (*). • Ratios represent frequency of prevalent forms vs. variants in current books.

diaeresis; *dieresis. Although American dictionaries can be found supporting both spellings, occurrences of *diaeresis* in print outnumber the competing form by a wide margin. See AE, DIACRITICAL MARKS & **umlaut.**

Current ratio: 4:1

diagnose = to identify, esp. a disease or problem. Strictly speaking, it is the disease or problem that is diagnosed, e.g.: "Eichelman went to the doctor, who didn't *diagnose* the broken bone and told the swimmer he would be back in the pool in a few days." Jason L. Young, "Senior Is Eager to Make Up for Lost Season," *Indianapolis Star*, 7 Dec. 2002, at S4.

Through OBJECT-SHUFFLING, the object of this verb sometimes becomes the patient rather than the disease—e.g.: "She helped with his story to raise awareness about Chiari, especially so doctors could *diagnose its victims* [read *diagnose it* earlier." Jennifer Berry Hawes, "Enduring Together," *Post & Courier* (Charleston, S.C.), 1 Dec. 2002, at G1. It is much more common to see the passive construction followed by a *with*-phrase—e.g.: "It took a full two weeks before Epps *was diagnosed with* West Nile Virus." Charity Vogel, "When a Virus Kills," *Buffalo News*, 2 Oct. 2002, at B1. This idiomatic syntax is too common to be called erroneous, though a careful writer will still avoid it in formal writing. It also acquits itself of logical fault by lending rhetorical punch, since the name of the disease falls at the end of the sentence. See SENTENCE ENDS.

For more on the formation of this verb from the noun *diagnosis*, see BACK-FORMATIONS.

diagnosis; prognosis. There is an important distinction between these words. A *diagnosis* is an analysis of one's present bodily condition with reference to disease or disorder. A *prognosis* is the projected future course of a present disease, disorder, or other disadvantageous situation. E.g.: "Mr. Yeltsin did not specify his *diagnosis* or the type of procedure he will undergo, making it difficult to comment about his *prognosis*, the American doctors said." Lawrence K. Altman, "Russia's Top-Flight Cardiology Hospital," *N.Y. Times*, 6 Sept. 1996, at A6. See **prognosis.**

The plurals are *diagnoses* and *prognoses*.

DIAGONAL. See PUNCTUATION (Q).

diagram(m)er; diagram(m)ing. See **program(m)er** & SPELLING (B).

dial, vb., makes *dialed* and *dialing* in AmE, *dialled* and *dialling* in BrE. See SPELLING (B).

DIALECT. A. Definition. The term *dialect* has two main senses: (1) in the popular sense, it refers to any linguistic variety other than the standard language; (2) in the linguist's sense, it refers to any linguistic variety that is shared by a group of speakers, including the standard variety. Sense 1 tends to be a depreciatory label, since it applies chiefly to nonprestigious varieties; sense 2 tends to be neutral, since it applies to all varieties. To those who adhere to sense 1, *standard*

dialect is an OXYMORON; to those who adhere to sense 2, the phrase makes perfect sense.

Granting the utility of the dialectologist's sense 2, we have nonetheless adopted the popular sense for purposes of this book—though without denigrating the many nonstandard varieties that enrich the English language and its literature.

B. The Nature of Dialect. Dialects are mainly of two types: *regional dialects* and *class dialects*. Regional dialects result from geographic dispersion and settlement patterns. For the United States, the regional types have been carefully catalogued and charted in Frederic G. Cassidy and Joan Houston Hall's *Dictionary of American Regional English*. Class dialects can indicate upbringing or educational level, sometimes both. Over time, class dialects have eclipsed regional dialects in importance: "In the course of the history of the English language regional dialects have become less important as more and more speakers have learned to speak standard English, but class dialects have, for good or ill, become more important." G.L. Brook, *A History of the English Language* 14 (1958).

Because education typically entails the inculcation of standard language (as a result of both classroom learning and peer pressure, often more strongly the latter), what results is often a type of bidialectalism. As Otto Jespersen, one of the great linguists, put it: "People whose minds are awake and developed cannot be confined to a dialect." *Mankind, Nation, and Individual from a Linguistic Point of View* 71 (1946). So a person who grows up speaking dialect may later acquire STANDARD ENGLISH and be able to move comfortably into and out of the two linguistic varieties. This is known to linguists as "dialect-switching" or "code-switching."

No dialect is perfectly homogeneous, and it is difficult to separate regional from class dialects. Although regional variations exist in every social class (see CLASS DISTINCTIONS), these variations become less and less pronounced over the country as a whole toward the top of the social scale, where almost everyone speaks and writes a form of Standard English.

Dialectologists have arrived at two especially important conclusions. First, dialectal differences "arise not from mental or moral inferiority but from differences in cultural experience, and . . . the most divergent dialect, however ill-suited for middle-class conversation, has a dignity and beauty of its own." Raven I. McDavid Jr., "Dialect Differences and Social Differences," in *Varieties of American English* 34, 47 (Anwar S. Dil ed., 1980). Second, "anyone who cannot use the language habits in which the major affairs of the country are conducted, the language habits of the socially acceptable of most of our communities, would have a serious handicap." Charles Carpenter Fries, *American English Grammar* 13 (1940).

This book, of course, is principally about Standard English. So when the text says that a given usage is "erroneous" or "incorrect" or "not preferred," the judgment is expressed from the point of view of Standard

English. Dialectologists often point out that multiple negation ("I didn't do nothin'") and similar departures from Standard English are perfectly appropriate to the dialects that are being spoken. That is true enough, but it is not particularly helpful to one who strives to learn and use Standard English. That this standard may have no intrinsic superiority to dialect is beside the point: it is the national standard and the international lingua franca. As Fries put it in 1940, with what some might today consider offensive indelicacy, it is the language used by the "socially acceptable."

Although some people regret the demise of dialects with the spread of Standard English, others are inclined to believe that this is a good thing. Otto Jespersen was among the latter: "If we think out logically and bravely what is for the good of society, our view of language will lead us to the conclusion that it is our duty to work in the direction which natural evolution has already taken, i.e. towards the diffusion of the common language at the cost of local dialects." Otto Jespersen, *Mankind, Nation, and Individual from a Linguistic Point of View* 72 (1946). On the other hand, dialects are surprisingly hardy and perennial, as other linguists have noted: "With monotonous regularity writers on dialect say that dialects are passing out of use and that it will soon be too late to record them, but if dialects are dying they are, like King Charles II, taking an unconscionable time about it." G.L. Brook, *A History of the English Language* 199 (1958).

C. Dialect Exemplified. There are several salient characteristics of dialect: mistakes with irregular verbs (see IRREGULAR VERBS), subject–verb disagreement (see SUBJECT–VERB AGREEMENT), misused pronouns (see PRONOUNS), double negatives, nonstandard word choices, and stigmatized pronunciations (see PRONUNCIATION). The following examples, which can occur in the uneducated speech of virtually all ethnic groups, are a few of the many speech markers that typify dialect. Many of them are not strictly limited by geography within the United States; to determine geographic dispersion, one would have to consult any of the many linguistic atlases that pinpoint the degree of distribution.

Mistakes with Irregular Verbs
- DIALECT: We haven't drank any water yet. STANDARD: We haven't drunk any water yet.
- DIALECT: She drug it all the way around the barn. STANDARD: She dragged it all the way around the barn.
- DIALECT: I done it. But I shouldn't have [or *of*] did it. STANDARD: I did it. But I shouldn't have done it.
- DIALECT: If I'd have [or *I'd've* or *I'd of*] been there, I'd have seen her. STANDARD: If I had been there, I'd have seen her.
- DIALECT: I haven't tooken anything that didn't belong to me! STANDARD: I haven't taken anything that didn't belong to me!
- DIALECT: I haven't went there yet. STANDARD: I haven't gone there yet.

Subject–Verb Disagreement
- DIALECT: They was there because they was going home together. STANDARD: They were there because they were going home together.
- DIALECT: She don't know. STANDARD: She doesn't know.
- DIALECT: You wasn't even there. STANDARD: You weren't even there.

Misused Pronouns
- DIALECT: Me and John are going now. STANDARD: John and I are going now.
- DIALECT: It's hisn. No, it's ourn. It ain't hern. STANDARD: It's his. No, it's ours. It isn't hers.
- DIALECT: Them books are good. STANDARD: Those books are good.

Multiple Negation
- DIALECT: We don't have no apples. STANDARD: We don't have any apples.
- DIALECT: He hadn't done nothing wrong. STANDARD: He hasn't done anything wrong.
- DIALECT: It don't make no never-mind. STANDARD: It doesn't make any difference.

Word Choice
- DIALECT: This here chili is too hot. STANDARD: This chili is too hot.
- DIALECT: Where's it at? STANDARD: Where is it?
- DIALECT: My teacher learned me how to add. STANDARD: My teacher taught me how to add.
- DIALECT: Seein' as how we're fixin' to leave, we better eat up. STANDARD: Since we're getting ready to go, we'd better finish eating.
- DIALECT: He was hollerin' up a storm. STANDARD: He was yelling quite loudly.
- DIALECT: Lessin you wanna stay here, I'd like you to go with me. STANDARD: Unless you want to stay here, I'd like you to go with me.
- DIALECT: I like to got ran over. STANDARD: I almost got run over.
- DIALECT: I seen him run over yonder. STANDARD: I saw him run over there.

Pronunciations

	STANDARD	DIALECTAL
asked	/askt/	/ast/ or /akst/
can't	/kant/	/kaynt/ or /kent/
car	/kahr/	/kah/
cement	/sə-**ment**/	/**see**-mint/
Detroit	/di-**troyt**/	/**dee**-troyt/
entire	/en-**tɪr**/	/**in**-tɪr/
I	/ɪ/	/ah/
there	/t͟hehr/	/t͟hahr/
these	/t͟heez/	/deez/
umbrella	/əm-**brel**-ə/	/əm-brel-ə/
wash	/wahsh/	/wahrsh/
window	/**win**-doh/	/**win**-dər/
wrestling	/**res**-ling/	/**ras**-lin/
yellow	/**yel**-oh/	/yel-ə/ or /**yel**-ər/

D. Bibliography. There is a rich body of literature on American, English, and other dialects. The following books make for a good starting point:

- G.L. Brook, *Varieties of English* (1973).
- Craig M. Carver, *American Regional Dialects* (1987).

- Frederic G. Cassidy & Joan Houston Hall eds., *Dictionary of American Regional English* (1985–2012).
- Timothy Shopen & Joseph M. Williams eds., *Standards and Dialects in English* (1980).
- Peter Trudgill, *On Dialect: Social and Geographic Perspectives* (1983).
- Harold Wentworth, *American Dialect Dictionary* (1944).
- Walt Wolfram & Natalie Schilling-Estes, *American English* (1998).

dialectal; dialectical; dialectic. These words are frequently confused. The adjective for *dialect* (= a regional variety of language) is *dialectal* (/dı-ə-**lek**-təl/). The adjective for *dialectics* (= the art of argument) is *dialectical* (/dı-ə-**lek**-ti-kəl/). Broadly speaking, *dialectical* means "of, relating to, or involving logical argument, historical development, or the resolution of contradictory ideas." The term is usually confined to philosophical contexts.

The term *dialectical* is often misused for *dialectal*—e.g.:

- "Among the dozens of Russian-English dictionaries in her library, none specifically addressed idiom, that expressive, *dialectical* [read *dialectal*] language unique to a community or class of people." Paul Grondahl, "No Rushin' the Russian," *Times Union* (Albany), 5 June 1995, at C1.
- " 'Waiting on' is a *dialectical* [read *dialectal*] locution on the rise and splitting its meaning." William Safire, "On Language," *N.Y. Times*, 12 Nov. 1995, § 6, at 18.
- " 'Cretin' is normally thought to come from the Swiss French *dialectical* [read *dialectal*] term *crestin*, usually thought to be the local word for Christian." Letter of Donald F. McCabe, " 'Cretin' from 'Christian,' " *Wash. Post*, 9 May 1996, at A22.

Dialectic—a noun denoting the art of rigorously logical argumentation—is, when used as an adjective, a NEEDLESS VARIANT of *dialectical*.

LANGUAGE-CHANGE INDEX
dialectical misused for *dialectal*: Stage 1

dialogue; dialog; duologue. *Dialogue* = (1) a conversation between two or more people; or (2) the exchange of ideas. The longer spelling is preferred. Despite the common misunderstanding, the prefix is *dia-* (across), not *di-* (two). For a comment on the potential decline of the *-ue* form, see -AGOG(UE). Cf. **catalog(ue).**

Duologue, most commonly a theatrical term, means "a conversation between two people only." It is often contrasted with *monologue*—e.g.:

- "Schnittke and his librettist Jurgen Kochel reduce the tale to a series of monologues and *duologues* involving Faust, Mephistopheles and the latter's female half, Mephistophela." Andrew Clark, "Schnittke's 'Faust' Premiered—Hamburg Opera," *Fin. Times*, 29 June 1995, at 13.
- "Originally a virtuoso *duologue*, the material here is divided among eight splendid comediennes under Laura Marchant's efficient direction." David C. Nichols, "Fertile Feminist Insight Enlivens 'Parallel Lives,' " *L.A. Times*, 9 Aug. 2002, at F32.

When used as a verb, *dialogue* is a particularly grating VOGUE WORD that has risen greatly in popularity since 1960—e.g.:

- "[Karl Ludvig Reichelt] *dialogued* [read *spoke*] with the monks, studied their practices, and participated in their rituals and meditations, always eager to learn." Notto R. Thelle, "Changed by the East," *Int'l Bull. of Missionary Research*, 1 July 2006, at 115.
- "The United States *dialogued* [read *spoke*] with the Soviet Union, even during the most dangerous phases of the Cold War, and the USSR was a far greater threat to world peace than Iran will ever be." Pierre Atlas, "Cease Fire. Now!" *Chicago Sun-Times*, 6 Aug. 2006, at B2.
- "Together these aspects of engagement help us to better understand the climate of engagement within which this particular online group *dialogued together about* [read *discussed*] their life histories." Mary Ziegler et al., "Creating a Climate of Engagement in a Blended Learning Environment," *J. of Interactive Learning Research*, 22 Sept. 2006, at 295.

LANGUAGE-CHANGE INDEX
dialogue as a verb, or *dialoguing as a gerund: Stage 2

diarrhea; diarrhoea. The term denoting the physical symptom of abnormally frequent bowel movements consisting of watery stools is predominantly spelled *diarrhea* in AmE and *diarrhoea* in BrE. The British spelling was usual from the 18th century through the early 20th, but in AmE *diarrhea* became the predominant spelling about 1915, and that spelling has become predominant today in World English.

Current ratio: 3:1

dice. In formal usage, the numbered cube used in games of chance is called a *die*, and two or more are *dice*. But the word *dice* is often used sloppily as a singular—e.g.:

- "Risks are calculable and can be insured against—for instance, the chance of a normal single *dice* [read *die*] throwing a six is one in six." Samuel Brittan, "Some Ruminations on Risk," *Fin. Times*, 11 Apr. 1996, at 12.
- "You win the fight by rolling one *dice* [read *die*] two times." Dean Weesner, "By Jove Rates an A," *Wis. State J.*, 23 Apr. 1996, at C2.

Julius Caesar's *the die is cast* (i.e., one of the pair of dice is thrown) is sometimes mistakenly thought to mean that a machinist's cutting or stamping device has been cast in the foundry.

LANGUAGE-CHANGE INDEX
dice as a false singular: Stage 2

dicey (= risky; unpredictable) has been so spelled in all varieties of English since the word was coined by mid-20th-century aviators. But the misspelling *dicy has begun to appear in 21st-century print sources.

Current ratio: 46:1

dicta. See **dictum.**

diction = (1) enunciation; distinctness of pronunciation; or (2) word choice. Often sense 2 is overlooked. This book, in large measure, addresses problems of diction in that sense.

dictum. A. Generally. *Dictum* = (1) an authoritative pronouncement; (2) a statement in a court decision that is of lesser authority than law because it is not part of the court's legal ruling; or (3) a customary saying. The word can carry different connotations, as the varied senses indicate.

In sense 1, *dictum* denotes a statement that carries the weight of a rule—e.g.: "William Morris, the 19th-century British designer, offers one of the best ideals for creating a satisfying home: 'Have nothing in your house that you do not know to be useful or believe to be beautiful.' . . . Morris's *dictum* is constantly reflected in the pages of glossy shelter magazines, where serene, uncluttered rooms have been arranged to perfection by a small army of decorators and stylists and captured on paper by artful photographers." Marilyn Gardner, "As Trees Shed Leaves, People Shed 'Stuff,'" *Christian Science Monitor*, 9 Oct. 2002, at 14.

In sense 2, *dictum* is a shortened form of *obiter dictum* (L. "said in passing") and denotes part of a court ruling that contains discussion and comments that are not a necessary part of the court's ruling. In this sense, dictum is less than a rule: it may be persuasive as an argument, but it is not binding legal precedent—e.g.: "Access Now also cites a 1999 opinion by Richard Posner, the chief judge for the 7th U.S. Circuit Court of Appeals in Chicago. An influential conservative, Posner said in a nonbinding *dictum* that the ADA applies to Web sites." Matthew Haggman, "South Florida Advocacy Group for Disabled Tests Bounds of ADA with Suits Against Airlines over Web Sites," *Broward Daily Bus. Rev.*, 2 Oct. 2002, at A1.

In sense 3, the word denotes a truism—e.g.: "The more fastidious response is expressed in the traditional *dictum* 'Two wrongs don't make a right.'" Randy Cohen, "Everyday Ethics," *Chicago Trib.*, 3 Oct. 2002, Tempo §, at 2. (Given this sense of *dictum*, the word *traditional* is redundant in that sentence.)

B. Singular and Plural. The plural of *dictum* is *dicta*. *Dictums is an uncommon variant that barely sprouted in the latter half of the 20th century. (See PLURALS (B).) *Dicta* is sometimes misused as a singular noun—e.g.: "However, the court's *dicta*, while reporting its case research in the Farley decision, *places* [read *place*—or else *dictum . . . places*] Montana in support of a belief held by approximately 16 states that common minerals mined as construction materials . . . are not minerals for the purposes of conveyance in deeded mineral rights." R. Lee Aston, "Assays from the Legal Vein," *Engineering & Mining J.*, July 1996, at N16.

Able writers generally have no difficulty getting the number correct—e.g.:

- "Of course, [Governor George] Allen is a public figure, and his public *dicta* are there for all to hear on television and radio." Jeff E. Schapiro, "Paramilitary Group Seeks Respectability by Association," *Richmond Times-Dispatch*, 11 Aug. 1996, at F2.
- "All of this is delivered in a memorably laconic manner, grandfatherly *dicta* and pedantic film-buff citations sitting cheek by jowl." Iain Bamforth, "Cinema Verities," *N.Y. Times*, 1 Sept. 1996, § 7, at 11.

LANGUAGE-CHANGE INDEX
dicta misused as a singular in place of *dictum*: Stage 1

***didn't ought to** is nonstandard for *shouldn't*—e.g.:

- "The cumbersome procedures will be a very reasonable price to pay for stopping people from doing what they *didn't ought to* [read *shouldn't*]." Karl Dallas, "Gupta Technologies Inc.'s Data Base Management System," *PC User*, 3 July 1991, at 61.
- "Council chairman Peter Randle says Kings has never been King's, and it *didn't ought to* [read *shouldn't*] start now with this apostrophe nonsense." David Newnham, "Diary: Dotty Tale of the Dot with a Curved Tail," *Guardian*, 19 Oct. 1994, at 22 (perhaps a facetious example).

Oddly, this expression reached its zenith in frequency of occurrence during the 1920s. It has since subsided. See DOUBLE MODALS.

LANGUAGE-CHANGE INDEX
**didn't ought to* for *shouldn't*: Stage 1
Current ratio (*shouldn't* vs. **didn't ought to*): 4,889:1

didn't used to. See **used to (B)**.

die, n. See **dice**.

die, v.i. **A. Preposition with.** *Die of* (= to die as a result of [a disease or ailment]) is the standard idiom. *Die from* is also common, especially when the death results from physical trauma <died from injuries received in a traffic accident>. *Die with* is nonstandard—e.g.: "And I felt them two years ago, holding me up and keeping me strong at the memorial service after his dad *died with* [read *died of*] cancer." Sharon Randall, "Memories," *Topeka Capital-J.*, 19 Sept. 2000, at C1.

Even so, *die with AIDS* is not uncommon: one doesn't die of it. AIDS weakens the immune system so much that you die of something else. Yet *died of AIDS* is far more common in print than *died with AIDS*.

LANGUAGE-CHANGE INDEX
die with misused for *die of*: Stage 2
Current ratio (*died of* vs. *died with*): 7:1

B. And *dye*, v.t. The verb *dye* (= tint or treat with a coloring agent) is sometimes mistakenly written *die*—e.g.:

- "Berwyn's Martinez (29–2), who *died* [read *dyed*] his hair bright green before the bout, scored his 16th knockout." Larry Hamel, "Martinez Beats Nunez in TKO," *Chicago Sun-Times*, 15 Nov. 1998, Sports §, at 14.
- "But the slippery editor *died* [read *dyed*] his hair and managed to blend in with fleeing refugees to arrive safely in Macedonia and take up his old post in exile." Philip Smucker, "Exiled Kosovars Regain Leading Press Voice," *Pitt. Post-Gaz.*, 27 Apr. 1999, at A4.
- "He *died* [read *dyed*] his hair blond and has used the remarkable resemblance to get in audition doors." Rick Bentley, "Star Potential," *Fresno Bee*, 21 Sept. 1999, at E1.

See **dying**.

LANGUAGE-CHANGE INDEX
die misused for *dye*: Stage 1

C. *Die off*. See PHRASAL VERBS.

die is cast. See **dice** & **aleatory**.

LANGUAGE-CHANGE INDEX (For the full key, see front matter pp. xxxi, l–li.)
Stage 1: Rejected. **Stage 2:** Widely shunned. **Stage 3:** Widespread but . . . **Stage 4:** Ubiquitous but . . . **Stage 5:** Fully accepted.
Invariably inferior forms marked by asterisk (*). • Ratios represent frequency of prevalent forms vs. variants in current books.

die off. See PHRASAL VERBS.

*dieresis. See **diaeresis.**

dietitian (= an expert in how foods affect health) is the standard spelling in all major varieties of English. **Dietician* is a variant.

Current ratio: 3:1

differ. When it comes to one's approach to a subject, to differ *from* a person is merely to be unlike the other. But to differ *with* a person is to take issue explicitly with the other. In the following passage, the meaning is a little obscure. Queenie Leavis, F.R. Leavis's wife, seems less justifiably upset if *differ from* is correctly used: "The trust [the F.R. Leavis Lectureship Trust] appointed a lecturer who ventured to *differ from* Leavis on literary matters, and whose private income aroused Queenie's envy (apparently Leavis did not dare to tell her of the appointment, which made it worse when she found out)." John Carey, "The Prose and Cons," *Sunday Times* (London), 6 Aug. 1995, § 7, at 3. If the lecturer had *differed with* Leavis, then Queenie's upset might be more understandable.

The phrasing *differ from* typically appears whenever two things are unalike—e.g.: "Assisted suicide *differs from* euthanasia, in which the doctor may take an active role in the death, such as by administering lethal injection." Bob Groves, "Doctor-Assisted Suicide Called an Obligation," *Record* (N.J.), 20 Sept. 1996, at A5.

difference; discrepancy; disparity. A difference—not really a discrepancy or a disparity—exists between these words, but it's largely one of connotation. *Difference* is the most general of the three, meaning "the quality or state of being unalike or dissimilar" <a difference of less than $20> <a difference of opinion>. *Discrepancy* suggests that the difference is between things that should be consistent <a discrepancy in the bank statements>. *Disparity* usually implies that the difference is inequitable or unfair <a disparity in the treatment of men and women>. See **differential (A).**

different. A. *Different from; different than; different to.* *Different than* is often considered inferior to *different from.* The problem is that *than* should follow a comparative adjective (*larger than, sooner than,* etc.), and *different* is not comparative—though, to be sure, it is a word of contrast. *Than* implies a comparison, i.e., a matter of degree; but differences are ordinarily qualitative, not quantitative, and the adjective *different* is not strictly comparative. Hence writers should generally prefer *different from*—e.g.: "He performed to everything from jazz to the bossa nova to Brahms and Scarlatti, establishing a style very *different from* that of Bill (Bojangles) Robinson, Fred Astaire and the Nicholas Brothers." "Paul Draper," *Dayton Daily News*, 21 Sept. 1996, at B3.

Still, it is indisputable that *different than* is sometimes idiomatic, and even useful, since *different from* often cannot be substituted for it—e.g.: "This designer's fashions are typically quite *different* for men *than* for women."

Also, *different than* may sometimes usefully begin clauses if attempting to use *different from* would be so awkward as to require another construction—e.g.:

- "Life for Swann, who held out to sign a two-year, $7 million contract in August, is a lot *different than* it was for him in Lynn." Steve Conroy, "Ugly Duckling Becomes Swann," *Boston Herald*, 13 Sept. 1996, at 104.
- "'But the Pac-10 and Big Ten might have a *different* goal *than* we do.'" Don Borst, "Big 12 Joins Fold for Super Alliance," *News Trib.* (Tacoma), 21 Sept. 1996, at C8 (quoting Bill Byrne).

When *from* nicely fills the slot of *than,* however, that is the idiom to be preferred—e.g.:

- "The spell checker it invokes is completely *different than* [read *different from*] that which the others share." Paul Bonner, "On Windows," *Computer Shopper*, Oct. 1996, at 564.
- "One could argue that . . . Russia is no *different than* [read *different from*] other nations." Max Jakobson, "Finland: A Nation That Dwells Alone," 19 *Wash. Q.* 37 (1996).
- "The selection of the federal jury in Puerto Rico following the state trial would be no *different than* [read *different from*] selecting a second jury for Tsarnaev after his initial death sentence had been publicized." Milton J. Valencia, "Killer's Appeal Could Guide Tsarnaev's Plan," *Boston Globe*, 23 Aug. 2015, at A1.

Different to is common and unobjectionable BrE— e.g.: "The trouble is that attending to the parts is quite *different to* surveying the whole." Rob Cowan, "Classical Review," *Independent*, 5 Dec. 1997, at 22.

LANGUAGE-CHANGE INDEX
different than for *different from*: Stage 3
Current ratio (*different from* vs. *different than*): 11:1

B. *Than* with Adverbial Forms. With the adverb *differently,* the word *than* often follows—a usage common since the 17th century. This usage is especially common in speech, but it also appears in print—e.g.:

- "In the future, however, HARP will be handling things *differently than* it did in the Quick case." Marion Gammill, "Remodel Morass Has Client Seeing Red," *Fresno Bee*, 1 Sept. 1996, at B1.
- "But he will be going at things a bit *differently than* in past years." Steve Carlson, "Virginia Tech Touts Cornell Brown as Its Best Player Since Bruce Smith," *Virginian-Pilot* (Norfolk), 6 Sept. 1996, at C1.

When no independent clause immediately follows *differently,* though, *from* works well and is preferable—e.g.:

- "Why should artists be treated any *differently than* [read *differently from*] scientists?" Roche Schulfer, "Defending NEA," *Chicago Trib.*, 21 Sept. 1996, at 23.
- "We found that businesspeople who have been dressing casually for five years react to salespeople's dress *different than* [read *differently from*] those who recently have gone casual." John T. Molloy, "Car Dealer Not Sold on Adopting Clients' Casual Style," *Houston Chron.*, 26 Sept. 1996, Fashion §, at 6.

In terms of word frequency in modern print sources, *differently from* is more common than *differently than.* The difference is less stark with the adjective *different* (which more than six times as commonly takes *from* as opposed to *than*).

LANGUAGE-CHANGE INDEX
1. *differently than* preceding an independent clause: Stage 5
Current ratio (*differently than they did* vs. *differently from how they did*): 21:1
2. *differently than* not preceding an independent clause: Stage 2
Current ratio (*differently from him* vs. **differently than him*): 10:1

C. *Three different*, etc. When following a number, *different* is sometimes a superfluity <Bennett backed Forbes as a candidate for five different reasons>. Sometimes, however, the word *different* adds a desirable emphasis <scientists examined the problem using three different methods>. The word is emphatic in the same way as *distinct*. In fact, if you wouldn't feel comfortable replacing *different* with *distinct*, you shouldn't be using *different*.

D. And *differing*. The difference between the adjective *different* and the participle *differing* is the difference between the verb phrases *differ from* and *differ with*. The first describes unlike things <Chevys are different from Fords>. The second describes unlike thinking <Democrats and Republicans have differing opinions>. According to the *OED*, the use of *differing* in the sense of "different" was "very common in the 17th and early 18th" centuries but is now rare or obsolete. That assessment, suggesting a marked DIF-FERENTIATION between the words, is unduly sanguine. In fact, the imprudent use of *differing* for *different* is not rare at all in modern print sources—e.g.:

- "Bridge Builders is a program started by Mystrom that brings families from *differing* [read *different*] ethnic backgrounds together in social settings." Don Hunter, "Forceful Personality Creates Fans and Foes," *Anchorage Daily News*, 25 Mar. 2003, at B1.
- "The quarter-horses . . . all leave the starting gate with *differing* [read *different*] sizes and styles." Darren Hunt, "Springing into Action," *El Paso Times*, 26 Mar. 2003, at C1.
- "He objected to the *differing* [read *different*] wage requirements for rural and urban areas, saying it sends a message that rural workers are worth less than urban workers." Leslie Reed, "Measure to Alter Tax Breaks Advances," *Omaha World-Herald*, 26 Mar. 2003, at B1.

differentia (= a distinguishing characteristic), a technical term dating from the 16th century, has predominantly made the plural *differentiae* (/dif-ə-**rent**-shi-ee/) since the mid-19th century—though *differentias* was in frequent use before that time. See PLURALS (B).

Current ratio (*differentiae* vs. *differentias*): 8:1

differentiable. So formed—not **differentiatable*. See -ABLE (D) & -ATABLE.

Current ratio: 971:1

differential. A. And *difference*. Traditionally, the noun *differential* had only specialized mathematical, biological, and mechanical senses. As a popularized technicality, it was extended to mean "a difference in wages or prices" <a port differential between tariff rates>. E.g.: "Drivers receive only straight time for the extra day, with no pay *differential*." Michael Davis, "Ryder, Union Still Troubled," *Tennessean*, 15 Jan. 1998, at E1.

But the word's intrusion into the domain of *difference* should stop there. The following use of *differential* was ill-advised: " 'Julie's Unicorn' is still another story that deserves whatever time you spend on it. I'd like to hear this one read aloud, and hang the *time differential* [read *time difference* or *difference in time*]." Jim Hopper, "Eccentric Orbits," *San Diego Union-Trib.*, 14 Dec. 1997, Books §, at 7.

B. And *different*. *Differential*, adj., = (1) of, exhibiting, or depending on a difference; or (2) constituting a specific difference. The adjective is less often misused than the noun. Sense 1 is more usual—e.g.: "Town Council President Paul Ash, who lived in Burbank—where residents get preferential treatment in their own city programs—said while he supported the *differential* treatment there, he doesn't agree with it in Stevenson Ranch." Naush Boghossian, "Is There Fair Play in Parks?" *Daily News* (L.A.), 8 Dec. 2002, at C1.

DIFFERENTIATION is the linguistic process by which similar words, usually those having a common ETYMOLOGY, gradually diverge in meaning, each one taking on a distinct sense or senses. The pair *beside* and *besides* provide a good example. They're etymologically identical (fr. OE *be sīdan* "by the side of"). *Beside* has kept the original sense. But *besides*—once interchangeable with *beside*—is now restricted to the sense (1) "other than; in addition to" <we have much more besides books> or (2) "beyond; apart from" <I don't need anything besides this>. Another example: *human* and *humane* were used indiscriminately up to the 18th century. During the 1700s, *humane* took on the sense "merciful," while *human* became the general adjective to describe Homo sapiens.

Differentiation may result from differently suffixed forms that develop distinct meanings, as with *derisive* and *derisory*. Or it may result from differently prefixed forms, as with *heritable* and *inheritable*. Many examples involve PHRASAL VERBS that come to mean something different from the base verbs; for example, *die off* is distinguished from *die*; *face up to* from *face*; *lose out* from *lose*; and *pay up* from *pay*. Still others involve a distinction based on the choice of preposition after a verb, as with *acquiesce in* vs. *acquiesce to* (see **acquiesce**).

Although many by-forms undergo differentiation, many others don't. *Investigative* and *investigatory*, for example, have never been semantically marked off from each other. Nor have *analytical* and *analytic*, *channel* (vb.) and *channelize*, or *demagoguery* and *demagogy*. When no distinction emerges, the less common form can be labeled a NEEDLESS VARIANT.

The true stylist necessarily appreciates why differentiation enriches the language. This appreciation can lead to a continual disenchantment with the forces—such as SLIPSHOD EXTENSION and WORD-SWAPPING—that are constantly being exerted on language. Richard Grant White, a 19th-century usage critic, extolled differentiation and condemned muddlement (in the heavy prose typical of the time): "The desynonymizing tendency of language enriches it by producing words adapted to the expression of various delicate shades of meaning. But the promiscuous use of two words each of which has a meaning peculiar to itself, by confounding distinctions impoverishes language, and deprives it at once of range and of power." *Words and Their Uses, Past and Present* 161 (2d ed. 1872).

What follows is a list of words that, having undergone some degree of differentiation, are discussed in their appropriate places in this book. The entries can be found at the word in the left-hand column:

acquiesce in	acquiesce to
alien from	alien to
amalgam	amalgamation
amicable	amiable
apology	apologia
appertain	pertain
architectural	architectonic
artist	artisan
ashen	ashy
beauteous	beautiful
carat	karat
caulk	calk
ceremonial	ceremonious
champ	chomp
cherubs	cherubim
clinch	clench
collegial	collegiate
comment	commentate
competence	competency
concision	conciseness
congenial	genial
content (n.)	contents
conterminous	coterminous
conversant in	conversant with
corporal (adj.)	corporeal
declarative	declaratory
dependence	dependency
deportation	deportment
derisive	derisory
deviltry	devilry
disorganized	unorganized
dissatisfied	unsatisfied
divestiture	divestment
dower	dowry
earthen	earthly	earthy
effect (vb.)	effectuate
elliptic	elliptical
emigrant	émigré
enormity	enormousness
envision	envisage

envoi	envoy	
estimable	estimatable	
expectancy	expectation	
farther	further	
fatal	fateful	
feign	feint	
fictitious	fictive	fictional
financer	financier	
gabardine	gaberdine	
heritable	inheritable	
homely	homey	
inadvertence	inadvertency	
incident to	incidental to	
incredible	incredulous	
individualize	individuate	
insurgence	insurgency	
junta	junto	
legitimate (vb.)	legitimize	
lineage	linage	
luxurious	luxuriant	
mandatory	mandatary	
manikin	mannequin	
mayhem	maim	
monotonous	monotonic	
mustache	mustachio	
objectify	objectivize	
observance	observation	
paean	paeon	
peaceable	peaceful	
periodic	periodical	
pommel	pummel	
possessive	possessory	
prize (vb.)	prise	
prohibitive	prohibitory	
refractory	refractive	
reparable	repairable	
repetitive	repetitious	
retaliatory	retaliative	
rhyme	rime	
sarcophagus	sarcophagous	
seise	seize	
sensual	sensuous	
sergeant	serjeant	
spurt	spirt	
sublimate	sublime (vb.)	
suppositious	supposititious	

differently. See **different** (B).

differently abled. See EUPHEMISMS.

different than. See **different** (A).

differing. See **different** (D).

***diffusable.** See **diffusible**.

diffuse; defuse, *vb*. To *diffuse* something is to disperse it from a single source. To *defuse* is to make something threatening safe, especially a dangerous situation or a bomb (by deactivating it).

Diffuse can have very different connotations, depending on its context, because of how dispersal can work. When dye is dropped into water, as it *diffuses* it both increases (in apparent size) and decreases (in concentration). Similarly, light that is *diffused*, as through a window shade, is made softer. But when the thing being *diffused* is not diminished by being spread—literacy or religion, for example—it grows in both size and strength. So we find a connotation of building rather than weakening in the Carnegie Foundation's mission of promoting "the advancement and *diffusion* of knowledge and understanding."

The notion that something *diffused* is softened like filtered light may explain why some writers misuse *diffuse* for the similar-sounding *defuse*—e.g.:

- "Leaders were hopeful last week that the agreement would *diffuse* [read *defuse*] the possibility of violence at today's march." Joe Hallett, "Cincinnati: Has Anything Changed?" *Columbus Dispatch*, 7 Apr. 2002, at A1.
- "With almost 1 million troops stationed on both sides of the India–Pakistan border and with Pakistan having recently test-fired another round of missiles, Deputy Secretary of State Richard Armitage and Defense Secretary Donald Rumsfeld were sent to the region for emergency exercises in diplomacy to try to *diffuse* [read *defuse*] tensions." "The India–Pakistan War Machine," *Wash. Times*, 5 June 2002, at A16.
- "Now the three-person squad has a bomb suit, X-ray systems and other sophisticated tools to *diffuse* [read *defuse*] bombs and check suspicious packages." Michelle Sutherlin, "Officer Trains for Bomb Team," *Daily Oklahoman*, 13 June 2002, Norman Today §, at 1.

LANGUAGE-CHANGE INDEX
diffuse misused for *defuse*: Stage 1

diffusible (= capable of being readily scattered or spread) has been so spelled since the 18th century—not **diffusable*.

Current ratio: 21:1

dig > dug > dug. The inflections weren't always so. A verse in the King James Version of the Bible reads: "And Isaac *digged* again the wells of water, which they had *digged* in the days of Abraham his father." Genesis 26:18. And another: "He is like a man which built a house and *digged* deep, and laid the foundation on a rock." Luke 6:48. Altogether, 35 biblical verses use *digged*. Today, however, *digged* is dialectal. See IRREGULAR VERBS.

*digamy. See **bigamy.**

digestible /di-jes-ti-bəl/ is so spelled—not **digestable*. See -ABLE (A).

Current ratio: 145:1

digestion (= [1] the body's transformation of food into useful substances, or [2] the ability of one's body to make food undergo this transformation) is preferably pronounced /di-**jes**-chən/—not /**dı**-jes-chən/. And the pain known as *indigestion* is preferably /in-di-**jes**-chən/—not /in-dı-**jes**-chən/.

The corresponding verb *digest* is preferably /di-**jest**/ and the adjective *digestive* /di-**jes**-tiv/.

Yet the noun *digest* (= an abstract or synopsis of a book, report, etc.) is pronounced /**dı**-jest/.

digitize; digitalize. *Digitize* has led two lives. In its first, it meant "to point at" or "to manipulate with the fingers." That sense is rare today, but the computer age has found a new use for the word: "to convert into a binary string of data." The connection with the root word *digit* is that the binary on and off signals are represented by zeros and ones in the resulting code.

Digitalize, a medical term dating from the 1920s, means "to give digitalis to," referring to the drug derived from the digitalis plant and used in treating heart conditions. Since the reincarnation of *digitize*, however, *digitalize* has been invading its territory as a variant—e.g.:

- "[Mayor Michael Bloomberg] said the high-tech scheme, which would *digitalize* [read *digitize*] patient records, would save 'hundreds of millions of dollars.'" Stephanie Gaskell & Carl Campanile, "Mike Has $100M Rx for Healthcare," *N.Y. Post*, 25 Oct. 2005, at 24.
- "The upgrade also included a project to *digitize* [read *digitize*] the station's archives and uploading broadcast town meetings to the Internet for on-demand viewer access." Derrick Perkins, "Salem Community TV Director Outlines Future Upgrades," *Union Leader* (Manchester, N.H.), 24 June 2008, at B2. (In that sentence, *uploading* should be *to upload* for reasons of PARALLELISM.)

There are two problems with having the two words bear the same meaning. First, because *digitalize* has a distinct (if specialized) sense of its own, keeping the words separate serves DIFFERENTIATION. Second, *digitize* is used more than ten times as often as *digitalize* in the binary-code sense, making the latter a NEEDLESS VARIANT.

LANGUAGE-CHANGE INDEX
digitalize misused for *digitize*: Stage 1
Current ratio (*digitized data* vs.
*digitalized data): 17:1

dignity. *Dignity* is a quality one possesses. It is not a synonym for *respect*, so it's mangled in the phrase **treat with dignity*—e.g.:

- "Whatever the parent's limitations, Grathwol encourages caregivers to treat him or her with *dignity* [read *respect*]." Gail Rosenblum, "Losing Her Sight, but Not Her Vision," *Star Trib.* (Minneapolis), 3 June 2006, at E3.
- "[T]hose with legitimate needs would like the pleasure of dealing with officials who treat them with *dignity and respect* [read *respect*]." Jarvis DeBerry, "When Did Every Victim Become a Criminal?" *Times-Picayune* (New Orleans), 15 Aug. 2006, Metro §, at 7.

The undignified phrase is spreading in American print sources.

LANGUAGE-CHANGE INDEX
*treat with dignity for *treat with respect*: Stage 1
Current ratio (*treat with respect* vs.
*treat with dignity): 10:1

digraph. See **diphthong (B).**

LANGUAGE-CHANGE INDEX (For the full key, see front matter pp. xxxi, l–li.)
Stage 1: Rejected. **Stage 2:** Widely shunned. **Stage 3:** Widespread but . . . **Stage 4:** Ubiquitous but . . . **Stage 5:** Fully accepted.
Invariably inferior forms marked by asterisk (*). • Ratios represent frequency of prevalent forms vs. variants in current books.

dike; dyke. *Dike* (= [1] a wall or bank to keep back water and prevent flooding, or [2] a protective barrier or obstacle) is so spelled in AmE—though it is *dyke* in BrE. On this point as on so many others, though, BrE is moving toward the AmE spelling: *finger in the dike* (= a small action to prevent a catastrophe) is the vastly preponderant spelling both in AmE and in World English, and it threatens to become so in BrE.

In AmE, *dyke* is a DYSPHEMISM for *lesbian*. It is best abstained from if one seeks to avoid giving offense.

dilapidation. So spelled. **Delapidation* is a common misspelling.

Current ratio: 68:1

dilation; dilatation. Both forms may mean: (1) "expansion"; (2) "in medical practice, the enlargement of a body part (as a limb, cavity, or vessel)"; or (3) "speaking or writing at length." Although *dilatation* might be considered etymologically superior, *dilation* is more common today in every sense in most varieties of English, especially AmE. E.g.:

- "A sudden *dilation* of facial blood vessels causes a blush." Paul Donohue, "Diet May Affect Blushing," *Sun-Sentinel* (Ft. Lauderdale), 17 July 1994, at E2.
- "Some of those responses are *dilation* of pupils, heart rate increase, contraction of muscles and filling the lungs with air." "A Collectible Well Worth Saving," *Fresno Bee*, 5 Sept. 1994, at A2.

Still, *dilatation* often occurs, especially in BrE and in names of medical conditions—e.g.:

- "There were several areas where points that could have been made simply in a couple of sentences seemed to have suffered toxic *dilatation* into whole paragraphs." Ian Forgacs, "Inflammatory Bowel Disease: From Bench to Bedside," *Lancet*, 25 June 1994, at 1623.
- "Dog bloat.—The technical term is gastric *dilatation* volvulus, and it's common in large dogs." "Dog-Eat-Dog World Breeds Emergencies," *Rocky Mountain News* (Denver), 29 July 1994, at D2.

Despite its frequency, this longer form might conveniently be labeled a NEEDLESS VARIANT, if it weren't for its prevalence in medical usage.

Strangely, a misconception is afoot that *dilation of the eyes* means "constriction or narrowing of the pupils," when in fact just the opposite is meant. To *dilate* on a subject is to expand on it, and for one's pupils to *dilate* (e.g., from being in the dark or from the use of certain drugs) is likewise for them to expand.

The words are pronounced /dɪ-**lay**-shən/ and /dil-ə-**tay**-shən/.

Current ratio (*dilation* vs. *dilatation*): 1.2:1

dilatory (= [1] tending to delay, or [2] tending to cause dilation) is now occasionally misused for *deleterious* (= harmful)—e.g.:

- "Anti-takeover measures often have a *dilatory* [read *deleterious*] effect on a company's stock." Heather Harreld, "Stock Dips, Takeover Guard on Deck," *Triangle Bus. J.*, 21 Apr. 1995, at 1.

- "Pregnant substance-abusing women and their children have been vulnerable, not only because of the potential *dilatory* [read *deleterious*] effects of the drugs on them . . . but especially because of the blameful public attitude toward these women." David Lewis, "Pregnant Substance Abusers Need Our Help," *Brown Univ. Dig. of Addiction Theory and Application*, 1 Jan. 1998, at 12.

The pronunciation is /**dil**-ə-tor-ee/.

LANGUAGE-CHANGE INDEX
dilatory misused for *deleterious*: Stage 1

dilemma = a choice between two unpleasant or difficult alternatives. This word should not be used by SLIPSHOD EXTENSION for *plight* or *predicament*. Originally a Greek word meaning "a double assumption," the word often appears in the colorful CLICHÉ *horns of a dilemma*—e.g.: "News media moguls find themselves on the *horns of a dilemma*. They all feel they must have a presence on the Internet, but none has yet figured out how to make money there." T.R. Reid & Brit Hume, "All the News That's Fit to Pay For," *Buffalo News*, 20 Aug. 1996, at E8. (That situation leaves them with two bad options: be unavailable on the Internet or lose money.)

The adjective is *dilemmatic*—e.g.: "Naturally, working with an interior designer can get you off the *dilemmatic* hook—just drop a few buzzwords like 'palazzo,' 'knotty pine,' and 'Regency.'" Victoria Lautman, "Spinning the Style Dial," *Chicago Trib.*, 22 Sept. 1996, Home Design Mag. §, at 8.

LANGUAGE-CHANGE INDEX
dilemma in reference to a problem or predicament not involving a clear choice between alternative courses of action: Stage 4

dilettante (= someone who just dabbles in a subject or skill and never masters it), an Italian loanword dating from 1748, primarily made the Italian plural *dilettanti* through the mid-20th century. By 1940 the anglicized plural *dilettantes* had become predominant in AmE, and by 1975 in BrE. It has been standard in World English since the mid-1950s.

Current ratio (*dilettantes* vs. *dilettanti*): 2:1

diminish (= to reduce in size, importance, etc.) may be either transitive or intransitive: something or someone diminishes something else, or the thing that gets smaller simply diminishes. But it's not idiomatic English to say that something or someone **diminishes from* something else: the *from* is superfluous. This error in idiom may result from confusion with *detract from* (= to diminish the desirability of)—e.g.:

- "Army's first five opponents have a combined record of 7–21. . . . That doesn't *diminish from* [read *diminish* or *detract from*] the accomplishment of being 5–0." Charles Bennett, "Cadets Running Over Opponents," *Times-Picayune* (New Orleans), 18 Oct. 1996, at D6.
- "Most of the 10 miles of trail that run through Hill Forest aren't traditional footpaths but rather old roads . . . . But that doesn't *diminish from* [read *diminish* or *detract from*] the experience of hiking them." Joe Miller, "Escape Along the Flat River," *News & Observer* (Raleigh), 25 Oct. 1996, at 14.

• "For the past two weeks, amid the NBA free-agency frenzy, the Heat mostly have been on mute. But that doesn't *diminish from* [read *diminish* or *detract from*] the reality of again being a team back in the mix." Ira Winderman, "A Quiet Summer, but Loud Expectations for Retooling Heat," *Naples Daily News* (Fla.), 12 July 2015, at C3.

LANGUAGE-CHANGE INDEX
*diminish from for *detract from*: Stage 1

diminishment. See **diminution.**

diminuendo (= a musical direction to become gradually quieter), an Italian loanword dating from 1775, has predominantly made the plural *diminuendos* from 1850 on. The Italianate plural *diminuendi is pure pretension today. See PLURALS (B).

  Current ratio (*diminuendos* vs. *diminuendi): 5:1

diminution; *diminishment. The latter is a NEEDLESS VARIANT. *Diminution* /dim-ə-**nyoo**-shən/ or /-**noo**-shən/ is often mispronounced /dim-yoo-**nish**-ən/, by METATHESIS. And it is sometimes erroneously spelled *dimunition—e.g.: "Dilution of talent rarely translates into *dimunition* [read *diminution*] of interest." Bob Verdi, "World Cup Is Great, but the Earth Didn't Move or Angels Sing," *Chicago Trib.*, 6 July 1994, Sports §, at 1.

LANGUAGE-CHANGE INDEX
diminution misspelled *dimunition: Stage 1
Current ratio: 250:1

diminutive, meaning "small," is pronounced /di-**min**-yə-tiv/—not /di-**min**-ə-tiv/.

DIMINUTIVES. Many English words have suffixes (such as *-elle*, *-ette*, and *-let*) showing that the words connote small, petty, or inferior things. Often these things are smaller or younger than the referents of unsuffixed words: a *piglet*, for example, is a young *pig*. So-called diminutive suffixes sometimes lead double lives. For example, *-ette* may denote a feminine form <bachelorette> or show that something is an imitation <leatherette>. And a diminutive suffix may appear in a word that is not a diminutive of anything (e.g., a *jerkin* is a sleeveless jacket, not a small *jerk*). The most common diminutive suffixes are discussed below.

  A. *-aster.* In Latin and Romance languages, this suffix expresses a resemblance. In English it is usually—though not always—used pejoratively to connote that something is inferior or petty. It first appeared in this sense in the late 16th century and became common in the 17th century. It is relatively rare today.

  criticaster (= an inferior or minor critic)
  grammaticaster (= an inferior grammarian)
  medicaster (= a quack; a medical charlatan)
  philologaster (= an incompetent philologist)
  poetaster (= a poet who writes trash)
  politicaster (= a contemptible politician)

Despite the temptation to think so when a new reality show airs, the pejorative *-aster* is unrelated to the *-caster* in *broadcaster*.

  B. *-(c)ule; -culus.* The first of these came into English from Latin by way of French; the second came directly from Latin. Both suffixes connote something small. The first appeared in the late 16th century, but both became common during the 17th century. Many scientific and medical words have these endings.

  animalcule (= a microscopic animal; a bacterium)
  calculus (= lit., a small pebble on an abacus)
  canalicule; canaliculus (= a small duct or canal)
  capsule (= a small cylindrical container)
  corpuscule (= a minute particle of matter)
  flocculus (= a small egg-shaped lobe of the cerebellum)
  globule (= a small round particle; a drop)
  granule (= a small grain; a pellet)
  homunculus (= a small person or humanoid being)
  molecule (= the smallest fundamental unit for a chemical reaction)
  nodule (= a small swelling in the body)
  sacculus (= the smaller of two fluid-filled sacs in the inner ear)

  C. *-el.* This French suffix traditionally denotes something small or of no great importance. It first appeared in the 13th century.

  bowel (= small intestine)
  chapel (= a small building for religious worship)
  hovel (= a wretched dwelling)
  pimpernel (= a small flower of the primrose family)
  roundel (= a small disk)
  tunnel (= a narrow tube or pipe)

  D. *-elle; -ella.* The first, older suffix is French; it appeared in the 15th century. The second is Italian, introduced into English in the 18th century. Each connotes something short, small, or insignificant.

  bagatelle (= a trifle)
  boccarella (= a small opening to either side of a glass furnace's main opening)
  brocatelle (= imitation brocade)
  camerelle (= a small chamber)
  chlorella (= a single-celled alga)
  novella (= a short novel)
  vaccinella (= a secondary eruption after vaccination)

  E. *-en.* This Saxon ending became part of the English language before the Norman Conquest. Attached to nouns it connotes either "made of" <wooden> or, especially with a living thing, youth.

  chicken (= the offspring of fowl)
  kitten (= a very young cat)
  maiden (= a girl, esp. one too young for marriage)

  F. *-et; -ette.* In Old French, *-ette* was feminine and corresponded to the masculine *-et*. English made no clear distinction, which is why *bassinet* is sometimes spelled *bassinette (a spelling that doesn't exist in French—see **bassinet**). In the 17th century, *-ette* began to predominate in forming English diminutives.

LANGUAGE-CHANGE INDEX (For the full key, see front matter pp. xxxi, l–li.)
Stage 1: Rejected. **Stage 2:** Widely shunned. **Stage 3:** Widespread but . . . **Stage 4:** Ubiquitous but . . . **Stage 5:** Fully accepted.
Invariably inferior forms marked by asterisk (*). • Ratios represent frequency of prevalent forms vs. variants in current books.

ballonet (= a small gas-filled compartment in an airship)

baronet (= the lowest inheritable English title, denoting a gentleman commoner rather than a nobleman)

cellaret (= a cabinet for storing wines)

cigarette (= a slim, short, tobacco-filled cylinder, smaller than a cigar)

kitchenette (= a very small kitchen)

nymphet (= a sexually mature girl, esp. one near the age of consent)

pipette (= a slender pipe used by chemists to measure small quantities of liquid)

statuette (= a statue or figurine that is smaller than life-size)

G. -ie; -y. These Scottish suffixes began appearing in English in the 16th century and became common during the 17th century. They were used to form diminutives of common nouns and proper names. Except in modern Scottish spellings, both are now restricted mostly to nouns and to some diminutive proper names.

birdie (= a little bird)

Charlie; Charley (= Charles; Charlene)

doggy; doggie (= a puppy or small dog)

Jeanie (= Jean, Jeanette, etc.)

kitty (= a young cat)

Kitty (= Catharine, Kathryn, etc.)

mousie; mousy (= a mouse, esp. a young or very small one)

pussy (= a cat)

Sally; Sallie (= Sarah)

sonny (= a boy or a young man, esp. one of inferior standing)

Willie; Willy (= William)

See **veggie**.

H. -ing. Because this Old English suffix has many modern uses, spotting it in its diminutive function is tricky. It mostly appears in words that denote something fractional or something that is part of a larger thing.

farthing (= a quarter-penny)

riding (= an administrative or political subdivision)

tithing (= a tenth part)

I. -kin. Although commonly seen in modern English, -kin rarely connotes a diminutive anymore. It was derived from Dutch and German, but unlike those languages, English at first used the suffix only for (usually male) diminutive proper names. It survives today in surnames such as *Watkins* (from Walter:Wat), *Dickens* (Richard:Dick), and *Perkinson* (Peter:Perkin). Beginning in the 16th century, the suffix was attached to nouns to form diminutives.

babykins (= an infant)

cannikin (= lit., a small can; a canister)

catkin (= derived fr. the Dutch for "kitten": *katteken*)

lambkin (= lit., a small or young lamb; used affectionately of young children)

manikin (= a very small person or a human figure used by an artist)

J. -let. This suffix, borrowed from the French -elet, may denote a diminutive when appended to an ordinary noun <booklet, ringlet>. But when it is appended to the name of a body part <arm, neck>, it may refer to an ornament <armlet, necklet>. Yet in the oldest English words ending in -let (e.g.,

bracelet, chaplet, gauntlet, hamlet), the suffix is neither a diminutive nor an ornament. Although a few diminutives with -let appeared in the 16th century, -let wasn't used much until the 18th and 19th centuries. Today it is the most commonly used diminutive suffix for nonce-words.

factlet (= trivia)

leaflet (= an informative writing on a single piece of paper)

murrelet (= a small North Pacific auk)

piglet (= a baby pig)

rivulet (= a very small stream)

roundlet (= a small circle or circular thing)

streamlet (= a narrow river)

K. -ling. Derived from Norse, -ling is relatively rare as a diminutive suffix in modern use. When attached to a noun, it may connote (1) ownership by or affiliation with something, usu. a superior thing or person <hireling, underling>, (2) youth <codling, duckling>, or (3) contempt <princeling, godling, moonling>. Apart from sense 2, -ling has rarely been used to connote physical smallness.

atheling (= a prince; the eldest son of a Saxon king)

fosterling (= a foster or adopted child, esp. one treated as inferior to other children)

foundling (= an abandoned infant who is taken in and cared for, esp. out of charity)

gosling (= a baby goose)

lordling (= a petty, insignificant lord)

sapling (= a small, very young tree)

L. -ock. The origins of this Old English suffix are unknown. The suffix is occasionally used to form diminutive nouns, but not every noun ending in -ock is or was a diminutive. Words such as *bullock* (= a castrated bull; a steer) and *hillock* (= a small hill) are clearly diminutives. Some words, especially animal names such as *haddock* (= a species of north Atlantic fish) and *ruddock* (= a robin), may have originated as diminutives. But for other words, such as *mattock* (= a pickaxe-shaped agricultural tool) and *warlock* (= a sorcerer), the suffix may have a different origin.

paddock (= a small pasture or enclosure for animals)

tussock (= a small bunch or tuft, as of grass or hair)

diocese = a jurisdictional subdivision, esp. of (1) a bishop or (2) a province under control of the Roman Empire after Constantine. Today the word is best pronounced /dɪ-ə-sees/ or /-sis/, not /-seez/. The second pronunciation is dominant in BrE and is preferred by some AmE authorities. The third is recorded in *W3* but, in the words of one commentator, "has little authority." Charles Harrington Elster, *BBBM* at 150.

The plural is regular in form (*dioceses*) and is pronounced with four syllables: /dɪ-ə-sees-iz/ or /dɪ-ə-sis-iz/. But some speakers (most notably newscasters) mistakenly use the three-syllable variant /dɪ-ə-seez/ as a plural.

The adjectival form is *diocesan*, pronounced /dɪ-**ahs**-i-sin/ or /-zən/.

For more on the term *diocese*, see **bishopric**.

diphtheria is properly pronounced /dif-**theer**-ee-ə/, not /dip-**theer**-ee-ə/. See PRONUNCIATION (D).

LANGUAGE-CHANGE INDEX
1. *diphtheria* mispronounced /dip-**thir**-ee-ə/: Stage 4
2. *diphtheria* misspelled **diptheria*: Stage 1
Current ratio: 50:1

diphthong. A. Spelling and Pronunciation. It's *diphthong* (/**dif**-thong/), not **dipthong* (/**dip**-thong/). The word is often misspelled (and mispronounced)—e.g.: "He [Sir Alec Guinness] didn't frighten Americans and colonials with cavernous and well-rounded *dipthongs* [read *diphthongs*], as John Gielgud did." Ray Conlogue, "A Master of Wit and Subtlety," *Globe & Mail* (Toronto), 8 Aug. 2000, at R10. See PRONUNCIATION (D).

LANGUAGE-CHANGE INDEX
1. *diphthong* mispronounced /**dip**-thong/ (instead of /**dif**-thong/): Stage 4
2. *diphthong* misspelled **dipthong*: Stage 1
Current ratio: 37:1

B. And *digraph*. Strictly speaking, *diphthong* is a phonetic term denoting a gliding vowel sound from one simple vowel sound to another within the same syllable, as in *down* or *join*. Some people use the term loosely to denote a digraph (two letters representing a single sound, such as *ph* in *phone* or *ea* in *lean*) or ligature (two or more letters written together, such as *æ* or *œ*)—e.g.: "Use *e* instead of the *diphthongs* [read *digraph*] *ae* or *oe* when the spellings are coequal: *archeology* (but *subpoena*)." Robert A. Webb, *The Washington Post Desk-Book on Style* 146 (1978). [Note that Webb's plural was incorrect: the *or* between *ae* and *oe* makes the object of *use* properly singular.]

diploma; degree. The traditional distinction is worth preserving. Secondary schools award *diplomas* to graduates. Colleges and universities award *degrees* to successful candidates. It's a common hyperbole for writers to overstate the achievement of high-school grads—e.g.:

• "Victor Manuel Bautista Lopez, the mayor, says they hope to launch a high school *degree* [read *diploma*] program for all cops this year, and the town is talking to local universities about a college program." Sara Miller Llana, "Backstory: The Book 'Em Club," *Christian Science Monitor*, 1 Feb. 2007, Features §, at 20.
• "For many workers with only a high school *degree* [read *diploma*], the pay can be transformative." Johnny Dwyer, "This Hammer for Hire," *N.Y. Times*, 4 Feb. 2007, § 14, at 1.
• "Evidence of the dramatic link between education and income is seen in the 75 percent gap between the average wages of college graduates and high school graduates and the 42 percent gap between those with high school *degrees* [read *diplomas*] and those without them, he said." Patrice Hill, "Bernanke Suggests Job Skills to Combat Inequality," *Wash. Times*, 7 Feb. 2007, Bus. §, at C8.

LANGUAGE-CHANGE INDEX
degree misused for *diploma*: Stage 3

diplomat; **diplomatist*. Although the longer form predominated in 19th-century usage, the shorter form had established itself as standard by 1910 in AmE and by 1930 in BrE. Hence **diplomatist* is now a NEEDLESS VARIANT. But it still occasionally appears—e.g.:

• "That's why they wanted to bump off a man who had once ruled his native land with the iron hand of a communist leader, who had the rank of a general in the interior ministry police, who went on to be a respected *diplomatist* [read *diplomat*]." "Shevardnadze's Sad Land," *Baltimore Sun*, 11 Sept. 1995, at A8.
• "While Kennan needs no introduction to foreign-policy thinkers, *diplomatists* [read *diplomats*] and historians . . . , he is less well known to the public." S.J. Hamrick, Book Rev., *Chicago Trib.*, 14 Apr. 1996, at C6.
• "John's widowed mother Hilda—daughter of the *diplomatist* [read *diplomat*] Sir Maurice de Bunsen—went on to marry Major General Sir Guy Salisbury-Jones, marshal of the diplomatic corps." "John Yerburgh" (obit.), *Daily Telegraph*, 9 July 2014, at 29.

Current ratio: 8:1

DIRECTIONAL WORDS. A. The Suffix *-ward(s)*. In AmE, the preferred practice is to use the *-ward* form of directional words, as in *toward*, *forward*, and *westward*. Words ending in *-ward* may be either adjectives or adverbs, whereas words ending in *-wards*, common in BrE, may be adverbs only. These are typical preferred AmE forms:

cityward	shoreward
coastward	sideward
downward	skyward
outward	sunward
rearward	toward
seaward	upward

All these are also predominant today in BrE—except, that is, for *towards*. See **toward** (A).

A slight exception in AmE is the adverb *backwards*, which is frequently used (though still much less often than *backward*). (It's anomalous that many people who say *forward* also say *backwards*.) When *backward* and *forward* combine in a phrase (either word coming first), be consistent about using the *-s*; by far the more common AmE usage is to leave it off both words. As an adjective, only *backward* is accepted <a backward move>. See TOWARD (A). Cf. **afterward**.

B. Capitalization. The words *north*, *south*, *east*, and *west* (and compounds such as *southeast*) should not be capitalized when used to express directions <we went north>. They are properly capitalized when used as proper nouns denoting regions of the world or of a country <the Far East> <the Pacific Northwest>.

But when a directional word appears as an adjective before a geographic proper name, it is lowercase <eastern United States> <southern Italy> <south Florida>. If, however, the adjective is part of the proper name, it should be capitalized <North Dakota> <East Anglia>.

C. Verbose Constructions. To use such words as *easterly* in phrases like *in an easterly direction* is prolix. In fact, the simple word for the direction (*east*) usually suffices in place of the word ending in either *-erly* or *-wardly*. E.g.: "In Portsmouth, when you're going north on U.S. 17 on High Street, you're traveling *in a westwardly direction* [read *west*]." Ida Kay Jordan, "Hurricane Escape Plan May Lead Some Down the Road to Confusion," *Virginian-Pilot* (Norfolk), 5 June 1994, Portsmouth Currents §, at 2.

The one useful distinctive sense that forms such as *southward* and *southerly* convey is that the movement is more or less in the direction indicated—but not in a straight line. E.g.: "Many of the bees escaped from his lab and have moved steadily *northward* ever since." "Bee Not Afraid?" *Fresno Bee*, 22 Sept. 1994, at B6.

D. An Infrequent Error: *northernly for northerly, etc. Occasionally writers err by making the directional words ending in *-erly* into words ending in *-ernly*—e.g.:

- "The districts of Downstate Democratic Reps. Richard Durbin of Springfield and Lane Evans of Rock Island would move clockwise in *westernly* [read *westerly*] and *northernly* [read *northerly*] directions under the GOP proposal." Thomas Hardy, "Hispanic District, Fewer Democrats in GOP Map," *Chicago Trib.*, 30 July 1991, News §, at 3.
- "The models showed that the cloud of nerve gas initially traveled in a *southernly* [read *southerly*] direction from the blast site." Philip Shenon, "Study Sharply Raises Estimate of Troops Exposed to Nerve Gas," *N.Y. Times*, 24 July 1997, at A18.

Though the *-ernly* words are recorded in the *OED*, they're noted as being rare or obsolete. Cf. **nor'easter.**

LANGUAGE-CHANGE INDEX
*northernly, *southernly, etc. for northerly, southerly, etc.: Stage 1
Current ratio (*westerly direction* vs. **westerly direction*): 293:1

directly; direct, adv. *Directly* = (1) in a straight line; without interruption <we flew directly from Dallas to Frankfurt>; (2) immediately <they left directly after the decision>; (3) with no intervening agent <she was directly responsible>; (4) totally <directly on point>; (5) soon <they'll be going directly>; or (6) as soon as <directly we saw him, we cheered to express our appreciation>. In sense 1, *direct* is interchangeable as an adverb, especially in mid-20th-century BrE <we flew direct from Dallas to Frankfurt>. Sense 5 is typical of southern AmE. Sense 6 is exclusively BrE.
Current ratio (*flew directly to* vs. *flew direct to*): 6:1

directly antithetical. See **antithetical.**

directorial (in five syllables), not **directoral*, is the adjective corresponding to *director*—e.g.:

- "Mr. Wuhl makes his *directoral* [read *directorial*] debut in the film, which opens on Friday." Michaelin McDermott, "Channel Surfing," *N.Y. Times*, 5 May 1996, § 2, at 26.
- "One of the most significant *directoral* [read *directorial*] differences between this film and Zwick's other epics is

that he lets the story tell itself and relies less on musical cues." Deborah Peterson, "Courage Behind the Camera," *St. Louis Post-Dispatch*, 12 July 1996, at E1.
- "It is his first *directoral* [read *directorial*] effort since his Oscar-winning debut with 1989's 'Dances with Wolves.'" Frank Rizzo, "Dances with Mail," *Hartford Courant*, 1 Sept. 1996, at G9.

LANGUAGE-CHANGE INDEX
*directoral for *directorial*: Stage 1
Current ratio (*directorial* vs. **directoral*): 87:1

DIRECT QUESTIONS. See QUESTIONS, DIRECT AND INDIRECT.

dis, v.t.; **diss.** *Dis*—also spelled *diss*—is a clipped form of *disrespect*, vb. (or, less likely, *dismiss* or *disparage*). This SLANG term came into existence in the early 1980s and into vogue in the early 1990s—e.g.:

- "In the 'other body,' where four GOP members are running for president, Gingrich would like senators to ponder the theoretical possibility of a President Newt before they *dis* the bills he sends them." Howard Fineman, "President Newt?" *Newsweek*, 19 June 1995, at 34.
- "Thou shalt not *diss* [read *dis*], unless you can afford a Dream Team of morally disengaged attorneys." Edward P. Moser, "Words to Live By," *Wall Street J.*, 25 Mar. 1997, at A18.

Of course, the inflected forms are *dissed* and *dissing*—e.g.:

- "The contemporary street sensitivity to being *dissed* immediately emerges in these memories of office humiliation." Philippe Bourgois, "Workaday World, Crack Economy," *Nation*, 4 Dec. 1995, at 706.
- "Pucker up: actress Helen Mirren is *dissing* the kissing of Harrison Ford—recently named one of Playgirl's '10 Sexiest Men of 1997.'" Jeanne Beach Eigner, "Public Eye," *San Diego Union-Trib.*, 4 Dec. 1997, at E2.
- "The Lions receiver *dissed* the victorious Alouettes in a radio interview after the game." Lowell Ullrich, "Speeches as Stale as the Offence," *Vancouver Province*, 23 Aug. 2015, at A68.

By 2008 it had already come to feel dated by most people who had earlier used it enthusiastically.

One outcome of the *dis* fad is that the transitive verb *disrespect*, which had fallen into disuse, has been called out of retirement—doubtless by writers (or their editors) who really wanted to use *dis* but just couldn't bring themselves to do it. E.g.: "Hovan apparently felt *disrespected* by Favre, and their war of words heated up to where Favre was caught on camera giving Hovan a one-finger salute." Rick Braun, "Several May Get Fines for Post-Game Melee," *Milwaukee J.*, 12 Dec. 2002, Packer Plus §, at 12.

LANGUAGE-CHANGE INDEX
dis as a verb: Stage 4
Current ratio (*to dis him* vs. *to diss him*): 1:1

disability. A. And inability; liability. These words overlap only slightly but are frequently confounded; they are best keenly distinguished. *Disability* = (1) the condition of being disabled <his disability began after the accident in March 2002>; (2) a disabling injury, illness, or handicap <she has a disability>; (3) legal incapacity <Ralph's disability disqualifies him from entering into contracts>; or (4) a restriction or disadvantage <not having a car would be a real disability>. *Inability* = the absence of ability; the lack of power or means <our inability to get there on time>. *Liability* = (1) a monetary obligation <some credits and some liabilities>; (2) a drawback <one liability in this plan is that it would have to be approved by a supermajority of shareholders>; (3) a duty or burden <liability for military service>; or (4) probability <What is the liability of having that happen?>.

B. And *disablement*. *Disablement* = (1) the act of disabling; the condition of being disabled; or (2) the imposition of a legal disability. Sense 1 is more usual—e.g.: "With that, the team has seen 13 players make 16 trips to the DL, surpassing the previous franchise mark of 15 *disablements*." Nancy Gay, "Giants Deal Leiter to Expos, Lose to Cubs," *S.F. Chron.*, 31 July 1996, at D1. See (A) for the senses of *disability*.

BrE sometimes uses *disablement* <disablement insurance> in contexts in which AmE would use *disability* <disability insurance>.

disafforest. See **deforest.**

disapprobation, mostly BrE, is a FORMAL WORD meaning "disapproval"—e.g.: "Ever since her [the Queen's] offspring reached maturity—about the time the media regressed fully into immaturity—the family that was supposed to be a model for the British nation, indeed the Commonwealth, has been exposed to ridicule and *disapprobation*." Elisabeth Ribbans, "London Observer," *Star Trib.* (Minneapolis), 28 Aug. 1996, at A17. In ordinary prose, this noun—like so many other ZOMBIE NOUNS ending in *-tion*—leads to top-heaviness: "The oohs and aahs of *disapprobation* [read *disapproval* or *scorn*] must add to the umpires' burdens and tax their objectivity." Mike Brearley, "Why Must We Play It Again on Screen?" *Observer*, 25 Aug. 1996, at 11. See **approbation.**

disapprove (of). Like *approve*, *disapprove* may be both transitive (without *of*) <The council disapproved the plan> and intransitive (with *of*) <Many readers disapproved of the editorial>. Usually, the transitive *disapprove* suggests formal rejection, while *disapprove of* suggests unfavorable sentiments. Also, *disapprove* alone tends to appear in formal, official contexts; *disapprove of* is the everyday phrasing—appearing about four times as often in print sources as the prepositionless version. Cf. **approve (A).**

disassemble. See **dissemble.**

*disassociate. See **dissociate.**

disastrous is so spelled—not **disasterous*, a fairly common misspelling.

Current ratio: 497:1

disbar. See **bar.**

*disbark. See **disembark.**

disbelief; unbelief; nonbelief; misbelief. *Disbelief* = (1) shocked incredulity; or (2) the mental rejection of something after considering its plausibility. In sense 2, *disbelief* results from active, conscious decision. *Unbelief* denotes the state of doubt, of not having made up one's mind. Thus, while an atheist's state of mind is *disbelief* (sense 2), an agnostic's state of mind is *unbelief* or *nonbelief*. (See **atheist.**) *Nonbelief*, which answers well to *nonbeliever*, might be a NEEDLESS VARIANT were it not so very common as to be uncancelable. A *misbelief* (the rarest of these words) is an erroneous or false belief.

disbursal. See **disburse.**

disburse; disperse. *Disburse*, from the Latin *bursa* "purse," is used chiefly in reference to distribution of money <the directors disbursed dividends to the stockholders>. *Disperse* is used in reference to distribution of all other things, such as crowds or diseases. In cultivated speech, these words are not homophones. The failure to distinguish them in common speech may have contributed to their confusion in print. *Disburse* sometimes appears erroneously in place of *disperse*—e.g.:

- "A crowd on the campus of Kent State University in Kent, Ohio, is *disbursed* [read *dispersed*] with tear gas on May 4, 1970." "Fraternity Reunion Offers Insight into Kent State," *Dallas Morning News*, 13 Nov. 1994, at A12 (photo caption).
- "Sure enough, the car drew a crowd. When they *disbursed* [read *dispersed*], it took me a good 15 minutes to figure out how to remove [the top]." Matt Nauman, "You Might Never Even See One of These Cars!" *Times Union* (Albany), 3 Aug. 1995, at T8.
- "Late in the evening of 5 October, the Vojvodina leaders appealed to the collective federal presidency to order the military to *disburse* [read *disperse*] the crowd." Louis Sell, *Slobodan Milosevic and the Destruction of Yugoslavia* 59 (2003).

The corresponding nouns—*disbursement* and *dispersal*—are subject to the same confusion. It is quite proper to refer to the *disbursement* (i.e., paying out) of money, but not to the **disbursal* of cards or the "disbursement" of crowds. E.g.:

- "A pilot within the purchasing department would precede a potential *disbursal* [read *dispersal*] of thousands of cards." Colleen Entenman, "Are You Ready for the Purchasing Card?" *Bus. Credit*, Nov. 1995, at 29.
- "Although they were quick to say that no problems are anticipated, authorities said as many as 60 deputies will undergo an eight-hour training course Thursday—learning crowd control and *disbursement* [read *dispersal*] techniques." Adam Folk, "Officers Gear Up with Riot Training," *Augusta Chron.* (Ga.), 28 Oct. 2008, at A3.

Nor is it correct to use the NONWORD **dispersement* when *dispersal* is intended—e.g.: "What concerns Fresno State coach Jerry Tarkanian is the Bulldogs'

LANGUAGE-CHANGE INDEX (For the full key, see front matter pp. xxxi, l–li.)
Stage 1: Rejected. **Stage 2:** Widely shunned. **Stage 3:** Widespread but . . . **Stage 4:** Ubiquitous but . . . **Stage 5:** Fully accepted.
Invariably inferior forms marked by asterisk (*). • Ratios represent frequency of prevalent forms vs. variants in current books.

potential to be off-balance defensively, at least in the *dispersement* [read *dispersal*] of players on the floor." Andy Katz, "'Dogs Will Be Going to Work on Mistakes," *Fresno Bee*, 13 Nov. 1996, at D4.

Nor, finally, is it right to use that same nonword when *disbursement* is the intended word—e.g.:

- "Other than the change of venue, the other major question facing the Presidents Cup will be the *dispersement* [read *disbursement*] of funds." Barker Davis, "Where Does the Presidents Cup Go from Here?" *Wash. Times*, 11 Sept. 1996, at B1.
- "Completion of the plan was slowed by disagreements among day-care providers over money *dispersement* [read *disbursement*]." Doris Sue Wong, "Day-Care Centers Say Subsidy Hikes Promised in June Still Haven't Arrived," *Boston Globe*, 23 Oct. 1996, at D9.
- "[Jay] Goldstone pointed out that the impact on the city's general fund was negligible, because the single *dispersement* [read *disbursement*]—$914,000 in police and firefighter overtime—was largely reimbursed." Eleanor Yang Su & Brent Schrotenboer, "Counting the Cost of Staging U.S. Open," *San Diego Union-Trib.*, 24 Nov. 2008, at A1.

LANGUAGE-CHANGE INDEX
1. *disburse* misused for *disperse*: Stage 1
Current ratio (*disperse the crowd* vs.
**disburse the crowd*): 107:1
2. *dispersement for *dispersal*: Stage 1
Current ratio (*dispersal* vs. *dispersement): 407:1
3. *dispersement for *disbursement*: Stage 1

disc. See **disk** (A).

discard, vb. More frequently than might be imagined, this verb is erroneously made *disgard, perhaps because the *-c-* is often pronounced as if it were *-g-*, and perhaps also from the influence of *disregard*. Of course, *discard* began as a card-playing term, but now it appears more often in figurative senses—e.g.:

- "Only 10 percent answered correctly that [the amount of] motor oil *disgarded* [read *discarded*] in the United States is 10 times greater than the amount of oil spilled in Alaska." Casey Bukro, "Americans Fail Quiz on Pollution," *Chicago Trib.*, 8 Nov. 1991, at C12.
- "Because the economy is now in recession, however, some housing experts are questioning the wisdom of *disgarding* [read *discarding*] the old 28/36 rule of thumb." Marilyn Kennedy Melia, "How Much of a Stretch Will You Make for a Mortgage?" *Chicago Trib.*, 9 Dec. 2001, Real Est. §, at 2.
- "If you're wondering what became of El Guapo's *disgarded* [read *discarded*], tent-like duds, be advised they have all been put to good use. Harrison took the bags to the nearest Goodwill Industries outlet." Steve Buckley, "Red Sox Hurler Rich Garces Has Been Growing Along Nicely," *Boston Herald*, 3 Mar. 2002, at B20.

The error appears to be as common in British as in American publications—e.g.: "For every new chart-buster, there are bound to be a million half-finished fragments which are *disgarded* [read *discarded*] after a few chords." "Root," *Times* (London), 10 Oct. 1998, at 4.

LANGUAGE-CHANGE INDEX
*disgard for *discard*: Stage 1

discernible. So spelled—not *discernable. See -ABLE (A).

disciplinary; ***disciplinatory.** *Disciplinary* = (1) related to discipline <disciplinary rules>; or (2) carrying out punishment <disciplinary measures>. *Disciplinatory has long been a NEEDLESS VARIANT.

Current ratio: 36,968:1

disc jockey has been the standard spelling since the phrase emerged in the mid-20th century. *Disk jockey is a variant.

Current ratio: 6:1

disclaim. See **declaim.**

discomfit, vb. **A. Meanings and Inflection.** *Discomfit* = (1) to thwart or frustrate, or (2) to disconcert; to put into a state of unease and embarrassment. Sense 2 is relatively new, a result of confusion of *discomfit* and *discomfort* (see C). Once considered a usage error, this extension is now the most common usage and is accepted as standard.

Discomfit makes the past tense *discomfited*, not *discomfitted—e.g.: "Matilde Dembowski . . . obviously had no intention of admitting him to intimacy and . . . was in some ways *discomfitted* [read *discomfited*] by his attentions." Robert Alter, *A Lion for Love* 146 (1979) (biography of Stendhal).

B. And *discomfiture*. The preferred noun is *discomfiture*. Ill-trained writers use phrases such as **much to his discomfit*, in which either *discomfort* or *discomfiture* is intended.

C. And *discomfort*. *Discomfort* is preferably a noun, not a verb. Writers sometimes use it when they seem really to mean *discomfit* in its newer sense (to disconcert)—e.g.:

- "Not only has it embraced what amounts to a social crusade—something that some journalists find *discomforting* [read *discomfiting*]—but it has set a goal it almost certainly will not meet." Ellis Cose, "A City Room of Many Colors," *Newsweek*, 4 Oct. 1993, at 82.
- "These melanist notions and other extremes of Afrocentrism are *discomforting* [read *discomfiting*] to many black educators." Leon Jaroff, "Teaching Reverse Racism," *Time*, 4 Apr. 1994, at 75.
- "Sometimes his access was *discomforting* [read *discomfiting*] to the men at the top." Seymour M. Hersh, "The Wild East," *Atlantic Monthly*, June 1994, at 61, 62.

LANGUAGE-CHANGE INDEX
discomfort misused for *discomfit*: Stage 2
Current ratio (*discomfited* vs. *discomforted): 7:1

D. **Discomforture. *Discomforture is a NONWORD for either *discomfort* or *discomfiture*—e.g.: "The stubbornness of the owners in repeating their rhetoric in the past made it even harder to believe that they aren't on their way to re-experiencing their *discomfortures in* [read *discomfort of* or *discomfitures of*] the past." Murray Kempton, "Schott Tries Patience of the Owners," *Newsday* (N.Y.), 15 Sept. 1994, at 8.

LANGUAGE-CHANGE INDEX
*discomforture for *discomfort* or *discomfiture*: Stage 1

discommend is the opposite of *recommend*, not of *commend*. E.g.: "I read in Wednesday morning's edition of *The Press-Enterprise* that they still *discommend* eating bacon." Letter of F.D. Richardson, "Riverside Bring on the Eggs," *Press-Enterprise* (Riverside, Cal.), 17 Nov. 1995, at A10. The verb was much more widely used in the 18th century than it is today.

disconcertion; *disconcertment; *disconcertation. The first is the preferred noun corresponding to the verb *disconcert*. The others are NEEDLESS VARIANTS.

Current ratio: 27:17:1

disconnect, n., (= disconnection) is a VOGUE WORD that arose in the 1980s and became seemingly ubiquitous after about 1995. It is primarily used to label (1) a clash between what is expected and what happens <a disconnect between our mission statement and our admissions policy>; or (2) more mundanely, the failure of a connection such as the Internet, telephone, or utility <I didn't hang up—we just had a disconnect>.

Disconnect typifies a popular trend in CASUALISMS, by which an established noun is truncated to form a new noun that looks the same as the corresponding verb but differs in pronunciation. The new noun has the accent on the first syllable (/**dis**-kə-nekt/), while the verb has the accent on the last (/dis-kə-**nekt**/). This pronunciation scheme follows the pattern of many standard verb–noun pairs, such as *contest* and *progress*.

Other vogue words that have gone through the same process include *consult* and *invite*. The new forms are generally inappropriate in formal writing.

discontinuance; discontinuation; discontinuity. See **continuance.**

discount, vb., meaning "to make a deduction; reduce," is sometimes used as if it meant "to disregard entirely," especially in the hyperbolist's phrase **wholly discount* <the board wholly discounted her version of events>. But this makes a hash of the word's fundamental sense. The wording is stronger without the WEASEL WORD *wholly*—e.g.:

- "He had *wholly discounted* [read *discounted* or *minimized*] his wife's genius." Stefan Kanfer, "Anecdotes from Scheherazade," *Time*, 15 Nov. 1982, at 90. (In a less malevolent reading, the phrase in that sentence might mean "never noticed.")
- "But that doesn't mean that he doesn't ask many of the right questions, or that the answers he suggests can be *wholly discounted* [read *disregarded*]." John Gross, "Blunt's Treason: How, How Much, How Long?" *N.Y. Times,* 21 Oct. 1988, § C, at 33.
- "[Gary] Posner . . . *wholly discounts* [read *denies* or, perhaps, *scoffs at*] the 'powers' of those who claim to possess some psychic ability." "Mind Games," *Dallas Observer,* 7 June 2001, at 8.

discover; invent. To *discover* is (1) to recognize for the first time something that exists, such as electricity or a law of nature, or has come into existence, such as a new species, or (2) to devise a new use for or application of something already known, such as synthetic silk. To *invent* is usually to consciously create something that did not previously exist and that has not been thought of by anyone else. For example, in creating a new chemical compound, a person may *invent* it by planning its creation (studying the properties of various chemicals and their known interactions and deducing how they will work together). On the other hand, one may accidentally combine chemicals in an unintended amount or manner, and then notice an interesting product, thus *discovering* a new compound.

discrepancy. For the distinctions between *discrepancy, difference,* and *disparity,* see **difference.**

discrete; discreet. Although the two words ultimately have the same Latin origin, the spelling *discreet* came into English through French. Today the two spellings are treated as different words. *Discrete* means "separate, distinct" <three discrete land masses>; *discreet* means "cautious, judicious" <a discreet confidant>. *Discreet* is most commonly used in reference to behavior, especially speaking or writing. Until about 1950, *discreet* was the more common word, but today instances of *discrete* outnumber those of *discreet* by a 4-to-1 margin.

The usual error is to misuse *discreet* for *discrete*—e.g.:

- "He is clearly not at home with strategic views, but prefers handling *discreet* [read *discrete*] issues rather than sweeping ideas." Bernard Gwertzman, "Working Profile: George P. Shultz," *N.Y. Times,* 17 May 1985, at A16.
- "Having control over a *discreet* [read *discrete*] section of the line fosters a sense of autonomy and pride among workers." Karen Lowry Miller, "The Factory Guru Tinkering with Toyota," *BusinessWeek,* 17 May 1993, at 95.
- "It was decided to break down the system into more *discreet* [read *discrete*] sections, as dictated by conditions on the pipeline." Philip J. Dusek, "Pipeline Integrity Program Helps Optimize Resources," *Pipeline & Gas J.,* Mar. 1994, at 36.

Sometimes, though, the opposite blunder appears—e.g.:

- "Mr. Bradshaw said almost everything the group did locally was *discrete* [read *discreet*]." Peter Applebome, "Bloody Sunday's Roots in Deep Religious Soil," *N.Y. Times,* 2 Mar. 1993, at A8.
- "The selections are tasteful with visceral mayhem, profanity, and sex almost nonexistent, or *discretely* [read *discreetly*] handled." Jim Bencivenga, "Tales That Sift Fact from Fable," *Christian Science Monitor,* 25 July 1996, at 21.

See **indiscreet.**

LANGUAGE-CHANGE INDEX
1. *discreet* misused for *discrete*: Stage 1
Current ratio (*discrete units* vs. **discreet units*): 43:1
2. *discrete* misused for *discreet*: Stage 2
Current ratio (*discreet distance* vs. **discrete distance*): 8:1

LANGUAGE-CHANGE INDEX (For the full key, see front matter pp. xxxi, l–li.)
Stage 1: Rejected. **Stage 2:** Widely shunned. **Stage 3:** Widespread but . . . **Stage 4:** Ubiquitous but . . . **Stage 5:** Fully accepted.
Invariably inferior forms marked by asterisk (*). • Ratios represent frequency of prevalent forms vs. variants in current books.

discretion, at your. Although *in your discretion* was more common through most of the 19th century, *at your discretion* became the top choice in the 20th century. Since about 1950 it has predominated, and it's about four times as common today. Remember, though, that in the choice of preposition, you have full discretion.

*discriminant, adj. See **discriminatory.**

discriminate, v.i., = (1) to make a clear distinction; or (2) to make an unfavorable or unfair distinction. In sense 1, the preposition *between* is quite common—e.g.: "Plosser and others warned that interest rate cuts are blunt instruments that do not discriminate *between* investment and consumption." Peter G. Gosselin, "Fed Trims Rates in Bold Move to Avoid Recession Economy," *L.A. Times*, 19 Apr. 2001, at A1. In sense 2, the verb takes the preposition *against*—e.g.:

- "Sheehan thinks female athletes are being *discriminated against*." "Mullins Kept His Spirits Up," *Times-Picayune* (New Orleans), 10 July 1994, at C2.
- "In their suit, the condo residents claim they are being *discriminated against* because single family homes receive curbside pickup." Theresa Walton, "Goffstown and Condo Owners Ironing Out Compromise on Suit," *Union Leader* (Manchester, N.H.), 6 Aug. 1994, at 12.

In sense 2, it cannot properly be used transitively—e.g.:

- " 'Men are not being *discriminated* [read *discriminated against*] at the University of Illinois, the swimmers are,' said Ellen Vargyas, senior counsel for the Women's Law Center." Mike Dame, "Men Fight Backlash of Title IX," *Orlando Sentinel*, 21 Aug. 1994, at C6.
- "Some believe even that the only one being *discriminated* [read *discriminated against*] today is the white male, and that a return to 'equality' (i.e. status quo) is in order." "Race Relations Solutions Offered," *Press-Enterprise* (Riverside, Cal.), 2 Sept. 1996, at B6.

The same error, by implication, crops up in the past-participial adjective <an illegally discriminated employee>. In this loose usage, which dates from the mid-20th century, *discriminated* is equivalent to *downtrodden, oppressed,* or *persecuted*—e.g.:

- "Long after they have left their status as *discriminated minority* [read *oppressed minority*], Jews alone among American immigrant groups retain a loyalty to political liberalism, to governments of compassion and justice." Marlene A. Marks, "Government Need Not Be the Enemy," *Sun-Sentinel* (Ft. Lauderdale), 7 Feb. 1995, at A16.
- "Mr. Say was born in Japan of a father who was Korean, a much *discriminated minority* [read *oppressed minority*] in the country, and a Japanese mother who was born in San Francisco." James Sterngold, "No Place Like Home, Sometimes," *N.Y. Times*, 22 Nov. 2000, at E1.

LANGUAGE-CHANGE INDEX
discriminate misused for *discriminate against*: Stage 1

discriminated, adj. See **discriminate.**

discriminating. See **discriminatory.**

discrimination. See **discriminatory** (2d paragraph).

discriminatory; *discriminative; discriminating; *discriminant, adj. Of these, only **discriminative* is ambiguous; it is a NEEDLESS VARIANT of both *discriminatory* (= applying discrimination in treatment, esp. on ethnic grounds) and *discriminating* (= keen, discerning, judicious). **Discriminant* is a NEEDLESS VARIANT of *discriminating.*

Because *discriminatory* has extremely negative connotations and *discriminating* (traditionally) quite positive connotations, the noun *discrimination* has suffered from a split personality <discrimination is rampant within the company> <our selections are the result of the finest discrimination in taste>. But the negative sense has largely driven out the positive. At least one usage critic urges that we combat this negative view of *discrimination*: "*Discrimination* can be a very good thing—even the world's most discriminating people practice it. You don't tolerate discrimination? Then I guess you'll be fighting for the rights of the world's child-molesting day-care workers and nose-picking sandwich makers." Bill Walsh, *Lapsing Into a Comma* 119 (2000). But the word has undergone seemingly irreversible pejoration.

Current ratio (*discriminatory* vs. **discriminative*): 9:1

discus (= a heavy flat circular object that in sport is thrown as far as possible), a Latin loanword dating from the mid-17th century, makes the plural *discuses*—not **disci.*

discussable. So spelled—not **discussible.* See -ABLE (A).

Current ratio: 3:1

diseased; deceased. The first describes a body that is racked with illness, usually a bacterial or viral infection. The second describes a person or thing that has died. Although a *diseased* person may become *deceased*, it is surprising that either word would ever be misused for the other. It does happen, however, perhaps as a result of computer spelling-checkers—e.g.:

- "It is the only charity golf tournament that raises money for treatment of a *decease* [read *disease*] that affects African Americans." Charles L. Griggs, "Sickle Cell Tourney Got Me Involved," *Jacksonville Free Press*, 27 May 1998, at 5.
- "But hypocrisy is a contagious *decease* [read *disease*], especially in the Clinton White House, and why should Richardson be immune?" Miguel Perez, "Opinion: Clinton's Appointees," *Record* (N.J.), 19 June 1998, at L11.

LANGUAGE-CHANGE INDEX
decease misused for *disease*: Stage 1

disembark; *debark; *disbark. *Disembark*, the preferred term since the late 18th century, is over ten times as common in modern print sources as the other two forms combined. **Debark* and **disbark* are NEEDLESS VARIANTS.

Current ratio: 3,028:218:1

disembodied; dismembered. *Disembodied* = separated from the physical body, esp. as a spirit. The word is stretched too far when used to describe a body part severed from the torso—e.g.: "Having said all that, did we really need to see the *disembodied* [read *severed*] heads? In a word: yuck. We got the idea with the hacksaw and the meat cleaver, thanks." Bill Goodykoontz, "Heading for a Shock," *Ariz. Republic*, 21 Nov. 2002, at E6.

Dismembered = (1) (of bodily limbs) cut from the torso; or (2) (of a torso) characterized by limbs' having been cut off. This term does not work well with heads—e.g.: "In a flurry of recent TV appearances promoting his new book on families, the former vice president has been seen . . . floating as a *dismembered* [read *detached*] head in a jar on the Fox cartoon show 'Futurama,' where he's dubbed 'the inventor of the environment.'" Liz Marlantes, "A 'New' Al Gore Returns," *Christian Science Monitor*, 19 Nov. 2002, at 1.

disenfranchise; disfranchise. Though *disfranchise* was long favored—from the 18th century to the mid-20th—*disenfranchise* is now much more common in print. It's the standard term meaning "to deprive of the right to exercise a franchise or privilege, esp. to vote." E.g.: "Part of this holding back was the result of white men, the persons in power, being unwilling or unable to reach out and bring in persons who traditionally had been *disenfranchised*." Jai Ghorpade, "California Civil Rights Initiative," *San Diego Union-Trib.*, 22 Sept. 1996, at G3.

LANGUAGE-CHANGE INDEX
disenfranchise for *disfranchise*: Stage 5
Current ratio (*disenfranchised* vs. *disfranchised*): 5:1

***disenthrone.** See **dethrone.**

***disforest.** See **deforest.**

disfranchise. See **disenfranchise.**

***disfunctional.** See **dysfunctional.**

dishabille /dis-ə-**beel**/ (= a state of careless or partial dress) is so spelled in AmE—though beginning in 20th-century BrE the usual spelling has been *deshabille*. The word was anglicized in the 17th century and in fairly widespread use through the late 19th century. There was little cause for reverting to the GALLICISM *déshabillé* in the 20th century, even toward the end of that period when more and more people were dressing in a casual and even careless way. To keep things tidy, *dishabille* should be printed in roman type (not italic) and without DIACRITICAL MARKS.

Current ratio (*dishabille* vs. *deshabille*): 1.2:1

disincentive; nonincentive. The former provides an incentive not to do something; the latter is no incentive at all.

***disincentivize** is JARGON for *discourage* or *deter*. It became popular in the mid-1980s and remains so—e.g.: "'We're competing with Los Angeles and New York firms for talent,' Bochner said. 'We don't want to *disincentivize* people from coming here because there are huge gaps in salary.'" Jessica Guynn, "Wilson Sonsini Opens Its Purse for Associates: $5,000 Raises," *S.F. Daily J.*, 12 Oct. 1995, at 2. See ***incentivize.**

disinformation; misinformation. These words are not synonyms. *Disinformation* = deliberately false information <Soviet disinformation>. *Misinformation* = incorrect information <widespread misinformation about HIV and how it is transmitted>. Sometimes the more pejorative word (*disinformation*) is misused for the less pejorative—e.g.: "Not surprisingly, the low level of scrutiny she was thought to deserve accounts for a significant amount of *disinformation* [read *misinformation*] in reference works." Susan Staves, "Traces of a Lost Woman," *Profession*, 1995, at 36 (in an article charging not deliberate lies but oversights).

LANGUAGE-CHANGE INDEX
disinformation misused for *misinformation*: Stage 1

disingenuous. See **ingenious.**

disintegrative; *disintegratory. The latter is a NEEDLESS VARIANT.

Current ratio: 193:1

disinterest; uninterest. *Disinterest* = (1) impartiality or freedom from bias or from chance of financial benefit <the judge showed disinterest in the way that every judge should>; or (2) lack of concern or attention <the team members suffered from the disinterest of their traditional supporters>. Leading writers and editors almost unanimously reject sense 2, in which *uninterest* (recorded fr. 1890) is the better term because it is unambiguous—e.g.:

- "He may empathize with modern American theater, but his *uninterest* in American opera is resounding." Ned Rorem, "Of Zeffirelli and Carmen: Memories and Reacquaintances," *N.Y. Times*, 8 Sept. 1996, § 2, at 61.
- "A couple of years back, the Toronto-based alternative folk-pop group Moxy Fruvous released its U.S. major-label debut, 'Bargainville,' to overwhelming critical and commercial *uninterest*." Stephen Thompson, "2 Release Parties on Tap," *Wis. State J.*, 19 Sept. 1996, at 9.
- "Canadian converts to Islam risk social and religious isolation because of rejection by their families and *uninterest* from inhospitable mosque communities, a new groundbreaking study is revealing." Chris Cobb, "Islamic Converts Face Rough Road, New Study Says," *Ottawa Citizen*, 27 July 2015, at A5.

But *disinterest* still predominates in this sense—e.g.: "Nancy Aldera, a Precinct 39 poll worker who had little to do in last Tuesday's school board election because only 24 people voted, said she doesn't know why there is so much *disinterest* in voting." Jonathan

Roos, "You Can Lead Them to the Polls," *Des Moines Register*, 15 Sept. 1996, at 1. Reserving *uninterest* for this use would be tidier, but because *uninterest* remains comparatively rare, DIFFERENTIATION seems unlikely to take hold on a broad scale.

disinterested; uninterested. Given the overlapping nouns (see **disinterest**), writers have found it difficult to keep the past-participial adjectives entirely separate, and many have given up the fight to preserve the distinction between them.

But the distinction is still best recognized and followed because *disinterested* captures a nuance that no other word quite does. Many influential writers have urged the preservation of its traditional sense. The typically understated A.R. Orage rhapsodized over the word: "No word in the English language is more difficult [than *disinterestedness*] to define or better worth attempting to define. Somewhere or other in its capacious folds it contains all the ideas of ethics and even, I should say, of religion . . . . I venture to say that whoever has understood the meaning of 'disinterestedness' is not far off understanding the goal of human culture." *Readers and Writers (1917–1921)* 29 (1922; repr. 1969).

A *disinterested* observer is not merely "impartial" but has nothing to gain from taking a stand on the issue in question. The illustrative quotations that follow deal with journalists' disinterest:

- "In the film, Wexler's directorial debut, a cameraman portrayed by Robert Forster must wrestle with being a *disinterested* observer or becoming emotionally involved with what he sees through his lens." Donald Liebenson, "Finally Coming In from the 'Cool,'" *L.A. Times*, 26 Aug. 1996, at F1.
- "Decisions like the court's 4–1 ruling in a Twin Falls case put everyone on notice that cameras carried by journalists might as well be carried by police. And that erodes the position of *disinterested* neutrality that enables news organizations to cover breaking events without becoming part of them." Jim Fisher, "Public Loses When Journalists Become Arms of Police," *Lewiston Morning Trib.* (Idaho), 2 Sept. 1996, at A8.

Yet *disinterested* is frequently used (or, in traditionalists' eyes, misused) for *uninterested*—e.g.:

- "On a day when seeded players fell by the wayside like overripe tomatoes, Agassi looked sickly and almost *disinterested* [read *uninterested*]." George Gross, "Mighty Have Fallen," *Toronto Sun*, 25 June 1996, at 67.
- "He wants an alternative program that will help disruptive and *disinterested* [read *uninterested*] students." Barbara Behrendt, "Candidates Line Up for School Board Seats," *St. Petersburg Times*, 25 Aug. 1996, at 1.
- "Sales at many chains will look good because they were so poor last year because of the unusually hot weather and *disinterested* [read *uninterested*] shoppers." "Back-to-School Shopping Gets Good Grades," *Tampa Trib.*, 3 Sept. 1996, Bus. & Fin. §, at 6.

LANGUAGE-CHANGE INDEX
disinterested misused for *uninterested*: Stage 4
Current ratio (*uninterested children* vs.
*disinterested children): 1:1

disinvestment = (1) consumption of capital; or (2) the withdrawal of investments, esp. for political reasons. Although sense 1 is the traditional one, sense 2 is more common today—e.g.:

- "About half of the 200 American companies in Kenya have *disinvested* and unemployment is growing." Andrew Hogg, "Frightened Moi Vows He Will Cull Democratic 'Rats,'" *Sunday Times* (London), 8 July 1990, at I20.
- "The implications would be significant if it could be shown, empirically, that every new office park, mall and subdivision built 'out there' [in the suburbs] caused *disinvestment* 'back here' [downtown]." "Measuring the Costs of Sprawl," *Chicago Trib.*, 20 Sept. 1996, at 22.
- "We chose to *disinvest* in the health of our center city and mis-invest in the wealth of what was at that time woodlands." Kaya Herron & David Koon, "Bangin': An Oral History of the Little Rock Gang Wars," *Ark. Times*, 16 July 2015, at 12.

For a word similar in meaning—*divestment*—see **divestiture.**

disk. A. And *disc. Disk* is the more usual spelling. *Disc* is the spelling used in four senses: (1) a phonograph record; (2) an optical disk (as an audio compact disc or videodisc); (3) a tool making up part of a plow; and (4) a component of a brake system. Otherwise, *disk* is the preferred spelling for general reference to thin circular objects, intervertebral disks, celestial bodies, and computer disks.

B. And *diskette.* Both *diskette* and *disk* may refer to computer-data storage media. *Disk* may mean (1) the computer's permanently installed hard drive, (2) a compact disc that contains a program, data, or music (though this is better known as a CD), or (3) the small, flat, portable magnetic medium. *Diskette* always bears this last sense, and unsurprisingly it has been on the wane since about 1990: thumb drives and wireless technology have superseded diskettes. (The synonym *floppy disk* is also rapidly declining in use—probably because the cases that held disks were floppy only for a short period in the 1980s.) *Disk* is commoner and shorter, but neither form can be fairly criticized.

***disk jockey. See **disc jockey.**

dislodgment; dislodgement. The first spelling predominates in AmE (and historically in English generally, from about 1800); the second has predominated in BrE since about 1950.

dismembered. See **disembodied.**

dismissal; *dismission. The much older word **dismission* (1547) has given way almost completely to the upstart *dismissal* (1778), considered a mere variant in the early 19th century. Today, **dismission* is the NEEDLESS VARIANT.

Current ratio: 66:1

dismissible. So spelled—preferably not **dismissable.* See -ABLE (A).

Current ratio: 3:1

*dismission. See **dismissal.**

disorganized; unorganized. The first, the more frequently used term today, means "in confusion or disarray; broken up." The second means "not having been organized," but in a less pejorative sense.

disorient; *disorientate. The longer form is a NEEDLESS VARIANT of the shorter—e.g.: "There, upset and *disorientated* [read *disoriented*], Berkelbaugh drew the attention of a security guard." Johnna A. Pro, "Tunnel Vision," *Pitt. Post-Gaz.*, 2 Feb. 1997, at A1. See **orient**.

> LANGUAGE-CHANGE INDEX
> *disorientate* for *disorient*: Stage 2
> Current ratio: 8:1

disparaging (= slighting, insulting) for *disconcerting* or *discouraging* is a MALAPROPISM. E.g.: "The report found several *disparaging* [read *discouraging*] statistics for the revitalization area, which includes privately owned homes from Ninth to Fourteenth avenues S, and 23rd to 28th streets. [For example, 66% of the residents] live below the poverty level." Sabrina Miller, "Neighborhood Shapes Its Future," *St. Petersburg Times*, 9 Aug. 1995, City Times §, at 1.

> LANGUAGE-CHANGE INDEX
> *disparaging* misused for *disconcerting* or
> *discouraging*: Stage 1
> Current ratio (*discouraging circumstances* vs.
> *disparaging circumstances*): 79:1

disparate /**dis**-pə-rit/ = (1) markedly different <an expert in such disparate fields as economics and literary criticism>; or (2) unequal <before *Brown v. Board of Education*, blacks were subjected to radically disparate treatment in American schools>.

disparity. See **difference**.

dispassionate. See **impassionate**.

dispatch; *despatch. Although these two remain in a tight linguistic race, the former spelling is editorially preferred in both AmE and BrE.

> Current ratio: 2:1

dispel. So spelled—not *dispell. Cf. **excel, expel** & **extol**.

> Current ratio: 186:1

disperse; dispersal. See **disburse**.

disport. See **deport**.

disposal; disposition. Both mean generally "a getting rid of," but *disposal* more often has to do with trash or inconsequential items, whereas *disposition* is used in reference to things that are arranged, settled, or otherwise managed. *Disposition* connotes a preconceived plan and an orderly arrangement. *Disposal*, by contrast, bears negative connotations—more so in AmE than in BrE.

Disposition also—and primarily—means "mood; temperament; inclination."

dispose for *dispose of* is jargonistic phrasing among waste-handlers—e.g.:

- "One goal for residential recycling is to achieve 5 percent per capita reduction in total waste *disposed* [read *disposed of*], McClain said." Eleni Chamis, "Solid Waste Authority Votes to Join Marketing Co-op," *Knoxville News-Sentinel*, 18 Aug. 1994, at B6.
- "But Ms. Graves says the numbers are a little skewed because the figures include all the waste *disposed* [read *disposed of*] by a county." Jeff Selingo, "Lawmakers Relax Rules on Cutting Landfill Trash," *Morning Star* (Wilmington, N.C.), 21 June 1996, at B1.

For the use of this verb in diametrically opposed senses, see CONTRONYMS.

> LANGUAGE-CHANGE INDEX
> *dispose* misused for *dispose of*: Stage 1

disposition. See **disposal**.

disproportionate; disproportional. See **proportional**.

disprove > disproved > disproved. So inflected consistently since the 18th century. *Disproven* is a variant past participle that has never been standard in any variety of English. See **proved**.
Current ratio (*had disproved* vs. *had disproven*): 18:1

dispute; disputation. These words should be differentiated. *Dispute* = controversy <goods in dispute>; *disputation* = formal argument or debate <effective disputation involves debunking the major counterarguments>.

disqualified; unqualified. These words have quite different senses. *Disqualified* = disabled; debarred. *Unqualified* = not meeting the requirements. An *unqualified* applicant doesn't have the skills or training that the job requires. A *disqualified* applicant, even one with the skills and training, can't be considered because of some rule, such as a policy against nepotism.

disquiet; *disquieten. The standard verb is *disquiet* (= to bother or disturb). The form *disquieten—not recorded in many dictionaries—is a NEEDLESS VARIANT. It is somewhat more common in BrE than in AmE—e.g.: "What will Europe consist of, and who will decide about the future shape and destiny of that suddenly and dramatically *disquietened* [read *disquieted*] continent?" George Weidenfeld, "What Europe Can Do, What Europe Must Do," *Independent*, 8 July 1991, at 19.

> LANGUAGE-CHANGE INDEX
> *disquieten* for *disquiet*: Stage 1
> Current ratio (*disquieted* vs. *disquietened*): 444:1

*disremember (= to forget), dating from 1815 in the *OED*, has long been considered a dialectal term. See DIALECT. Cf. **misremember**.

LANGUAGE-CHANGE INDEX (For the full key, see front matter pp. xxxi, l–li.)
Stage 1: Rejected. **Stage 2**: Widely shunned. **Stage 3**: Widespread but . . . **Stage 4**: Ubiquitous but . . . **Stage 5**: Fully accepted.
Invariably inferior forms marked by asterisk (*). • Ratios represent frequency of prevalent forms vs. variants in current books.

disrespect, vb. See **dis.**

***diss,** v.t. See **dis.**

dissatisfied; unsatisfied. Some DIFFERENTIATION exists between these words. To be *dissatisfied* is to be positively bothered by the lack of satisfaction, whereas to be *unsatisfied* is to be less than completely satisfied. So a person whose accounts are in arrears has debts that are *unsatisfied*—and creditors who are *dissatisfied*.

dissemble; disassemble. *Dissemble*, meaning "to present a false appearance; to conceal the truth," was a fairly common word through about 1900. It has since become rare, but it does still appear—e.g.:

- "The boy answered [my questions] simply, directly and honestly, unlike most adults, who *dissemble*, ramble or tell you everything but the answer to the question." Judith S. Johnessee, "The Day a Boy Lost His Cat and Became a Man," *Plain Dealer* (Cleveland), 15 Dec. 1994, at E9.
- "The problem is that the Pentagon's credibility is shot. And as it has *dissembled*, it has only increased the confusion and suffering for those who fought the war." "As Vets Suffer, Pentagon Blows Gulf Investigation," *USA Today*, 13 Dec. 1996, at A14.

By contrast, the word *disassemble* (= to take apart) didn't flourish until the mid-20th century. Yet it is now the more frequent word—e.g.:

- "The Edgewood trainees . . . [learn] along the way how to assemble, *disassemble* and repair [the computers]." Neal R. Peirce, "Cyberspace Experiments—in the 'Hood," *Baltimore Sun*, 24 July 1995, at A9.
- "On New Year's Day, the neighbors get together to take the decorations down, *disassemble* the arches and store them for the year." Leslie Sowers, "City Sidewalks, Pretty Sidewalks," *Houston Chron.*, 24 Dec. 1996, at 1.

Unfortunately, some writers use *dissemble* when they mean *disassemble*—e.g.:

- "Rushakoff said that he had to spend a lot of money learning how to use the right tools and the right procedures to *dissemble* [read *disassemble*] computers." Myra Pinkham, "Obsolete Machines Yield New Fortunes," *Am. Metal Market*, 24 Jan. 1996, at 5.
- "Today, Green ships out . . . tables, computer desks, beds, bookcases, and sofas that can be assembled and *dissembled* [read *disassembled*] in a matter of minutes." Suzi Parker, "Furniture You Put Together in a Snap," *Christian Science Monitor*, 19 July 2000, at 19.
- "In the Sikorsky case, the 148-Mbyte assembly was *dissembled* [read *disassembled*] into its 250 component files, which were translated independently and then reassembled." "Comanche Helicopter Blends CAD Models from 14 Suppliers," *Design News*, 3 Sept. 2001, at 31.

LANGUAGE-CHANGE INDEX
dissemble misused for *disassemble*: Stage 2

disseminate. So spelled—not **dissiminate*.
Current ratio: 6,482:1

dissent, n.; dissension; *dissention. *Dissent* refers to a difference of opinion, whether it is citizens dissenting from the decision of a governmental body or a judge dissenting from a majority opinion. A *dissent*, as opposed to *dissent* as a mass noun, refers to a

dissenting judicial opinion—e.g.: "Judge Dennis wrote a brazenly activist *dissent*." Thomas L. Jipping, "President Clinton's Judicial Legacy," *Wash. Times*, 17 Sept. 1996, at A19.

Dissension refers to contentious or partisan arguing—e.g.: "Dr. Mazzullo, who declined to comment about the *dissension* surrounding his contract renewal, has been a lightning rod for some residents' discontent." Merri Rosenberg, "Greenburgh Passes School Budget," *N.Y. Times*, 22 Sept. 1996, § 13, at 4.

**Dissention* is a mistaken form of *dissension*—e.g.: "Their prime-time speeches . . . could help forge the unity that propels the first black man into the presidency. Or they could highlight the splits and *dissention* [read *dissension*] that provide John McCain the opening he needs to win the White House." Christy Hoppe, "On Obama Ticket, Biden Fills In Blanks," *Dallas Morning News*, 24 Aug. 2008, at A1.

LANGUAGE-CHANGE INDEX
**dissention* for *dissension*: Stage 1
Current ratio (*dissension* vs. **dissention*): 11:1

dissent, v.i. Idiomatically, this verb takes *from* or (much less commonly) *against*, preferably not *to* or *with*—e.g.:

- "The court also ordered the county to pay White's legal expenses, although Justice Paul E. Pfeifer *dissented from* that part of the ruling." James Bradshaw, "Counties Told to Keep Full Records," *Columbus Dispatch*, 22 Aug. 1996, at D1.
- "Three justices who *dissented from* the majority opinion in the Kiryas Joel case said they would uphold the initial legislation." "New Law, New Hope in Kiryas Joel Battle," *N.Y. Times*, 7 Sept. 1996, § 1, at 20.
- "She *dissented against* seven of eight Federal Open Market Committee decisions last year and will vote again on policy in 2016." Jeff Kearns, "Fed Heads Hint Again of Looming Rate Hike," *Nat'l Post* (Can.), 22 Aug. 2014, at 3.

dissenter; dissentient, n. *Dissenter* is standard in AmE for "someone who withholds assent, or does not approve or agree." E.g.: "Reports suggest that one of the three *dissenters* [on the jury] was 'scared to death' of precisely the kind of retaliation that put Nee in his grave." Peter Gelzinis, "Townies Know What Judge's Bias Refuses to Let Her See," *Boston Herald*, 8 Sept. 1996, at 10.

Dissentient is somewhat more frequent in BrE, probably because the term *dissenter* (usually with an initial capital) has a special religious and social meaning in British history (i.e., someone who dissents from or refuses to conform—specifically, from the 17th century on—to the tenets and practices of the Church of England).

dissenting; dissentient, adj.; **dissentious.** *Dissentient* is sometimes used in BrE where *dissenting* would ordinarily appear in AmE. E.g.:

- "One and all admire that I had got hold of a good thing. Not a *dissentient* voice." P.G. Wodehouse, *Right Ho, Jeeves* 28 (1934; repr. 1986).

- "The issue of foreign policy decision making may also be tackled because the Community will remain ineffective in this area unless the present unanimity rule is modified somewhat even if only to the extent of permitting decisions on foreign policy to be taken despite one *dissentient* [read, in AmE, *dissenting*] voice." Garret Fitzgerald, "Presidency Offers Chance to Keep Goodwill of EU States," *Irish Times*, 4 May 1996, at 12.

One ambiguity in *dissentient* is that readers might interpret it as a derogatory opposite of *sentient*; the true opposite of *sentient* (= feeling), however, is *insentient*. *Dissentious* (= given to dissension; quarrelsome) is a word that rarely appears.

*dissention. See **dissent,** n.

dissentious. See **dissenting.**

dissimilar has always preferably taken the preposition *to*, not *from*. E.g.: "In the '60s, the blue-collar neighborhoods were dominated by gangs of youths not at all *dissimilar from* [read *dissimilar to*] the warring clans of 'Braveheart' and 'Rob Roy,'" Gary Dretzka, "'Small Faces' Is Another Grim Picture of Scottish Life," *Chicago Trib.*, 3 Sept. 1996, at C3.

> LANGUAGE-CHANGE INDEX
> *dissimilar from for *dissimilar to*: Stage 2
> Current ratio (*dissimilar to* vs. *dissimilar from): 3:1

dissociate; *disassociate. *Dissociate* is the preferred term; *disassociate is a NEEDLESS VARIANT. *Dissociate* takes the preposition *from*. E.g.:

- "To *dissociate* himself *from* such impairments, Dole released the medical summary of his exam last month." "What's Really Up, Doc?" *Plain Dealer* (Cleveland), 26 July 1996, at B10.
- "It is worse to see supposed liberals, such as President Boris Yeltsin's chief of staff Anatoly Chubais, *dissociating* themselves *from* the deal." "Beyond Chechnya's Cease-Fire," *Wash. Post*, 5 Sept. 1996, at A22.

> LANGUAGE-CHANGE INDEX
> *disassociate for *dissociate*: Stage 3
> Current ratio: 3:1

dissolution of marriage. See **divorce (B).**

dissolvable; dissoluble. The word meaning "capable of being dissolved" was traditionally *dissoluble* (dating from the early 16th century). But since the late 1980s in AmE and the late 1990s in BrE, *dissolvable* has become the predominant form. It seems here to stay.

> Current ratio: 1.2:1

dissyllable (= a word of two syllables) has been predominantly so spelled in all varieties of English since the 18th century. Beginning in the 1970s, there was a concerted effort among philologists to use *disyllable*—"the better spelling," according to Robert W. Burchfield (*FMEU3* at 221)—but the

GALLICISM-like spelling with the -*ss*- has persisted and predominated.

> Current ratio: 2:1

distensible (= capable of being distended) has been the standard form since the 18th century—*distendable and *distendible being NEEDLESS VARIANTS.

> Current ratio (*distensible* vs. *distendable vs. *distendible): 201:3:1

distention; distension. For the noun corresponding to the verb *distend* (= to become swollen and fully extended), these spellings are close competitors throughout the English-speaking world. AmE tends to prefer *distention*, BrE *distension*.

distill; distil. The spelling *distill* is standard in AmE, *distil* in BrE.

distinct; distinctive; distinguished. The first means "well defined, discernibly separate" <distinct speech>, and the second means "serving to distinguish, set off by appearance" <a distinctive red bow tie>. *Distinct* speech is well enunciated, whereas *distinctive* speech is idiosyncratically accented, different from that of surrounding speakers. *Distinctive* is sometimes misused for *distinguished* (= notable; famous)—e.g.: "Festivities begin Friday night at a Commonwealth Club/Inforum event, where a *distinctive* [read *distinguished*] group of authors will discuss the question 'Dystopia/Utopia? Can the Bay Area Uphold a New Generation of Writers?'" Heidi Benson, "Litquake a Big One for S.F.," *S.F. Chron.*, 10 Oct. 2002, at D1.

> LANGUAGE-CHANGE INDEX
> *distinctive* misused for *distinguished*: Stage 1

distract. See **detract.**

distrait; *distraite; distraught. *Distrait*, a word borrowed from French and pronounced /di-**stray**/, means "distracted or preoccupied, esp. because of anxiety." Although the word typically refers to a person, it sometimes refers to personified things—e.g.: "As it looks to the start of the 21st century and the end of 14 years under Socialist President Francois Mitterrand, the world's fifth largest military power and fourth biggest economy is *distrait* and irresolute." Thomas Sancton, "If at First You Don't Succeed," *Time*, 24 Apr. 1995, at 46.

*Distraite (pronounced /di-**strayt**/) is the feminine version of *distrait*. For English-language purposes, it is a NEEDLESS VARIANT not listed in most dictionaries, and it might be considered objectionable partly on grounds of SEXISM—e.g.:

- "In New Zealand, my father's first posting as a young first secretary, there was the delightfully *distraite* [read *distrait*] Lady Cumming-Bruce." Katie Hickman, "The Dutiful and the Damned," *Sunday Telegraph*, 9 Oct. 1994, at 1.

LANGUAGE-CHANGE INDEX (For the full key, see front matter pp. xxxi, l–li.)
Stage 1: Rejected. **Stage 2:** Widely shunned. **Stage 3:** Widespread but . . . **Stage 4:** Ubiquitous but . . . **Stage 5:** Fully accepted.
Invariably inferior forms marked by asterisk (*). • Ratios represent frequency of prevalent forms vs. variants in current books.

- "She is slightly *distraite* [read *distrait*] in manner, drily amused by life, not easily impressed, and unnervingly sexy." "Small, Pure and Sexy," *Sunday Telegraph*, 14 July 1996, at 9.
- "Even Lady Ditherby-Stoat appeared a trifle *distraite* [read *distrait*] as she discussed the novels of Lord Beaconsfield with Mr. Hellespont." Charlotte MacLeod, "The Mysterious Affair of the Beaird-Wynnington Dirigible Airship" (1986), in *It Was an Awful Shame and Other Stories* 178, 187 (2002).

Both words, though, can typically be replaced by an ordinary term such as *distracted, preoccupied*, or *absent-minded*—or, if the anxiety level is high enough, by *distraught*, which means either "deeply agitated" or "insane." E.g.: "Lucy had still been all but bedridden when her neighbor died. And she'd been *distraught* when the news was brought to her that he was dead." Kathy Lynn Emerson, *Face Down Under the Wych Elm* 8 (2000).

LANGUAGE-CHANGE INDEX
distraite for *distrait*: Stage 2
Current ratio (*distrait* vs. *distraite*): 6:1

distrustful; mistrustful. The difference here is subtle because both terms mean "having or showing doubt; lacking confidence." But *distrustful* implies suspicion or wariness based on an informed judgment, whereas *mistrustful* suggests uncertainty or uneasiness. So one might be *distrustful* of a used-car dealer's puffing, yet *mistrustful* of a stranger's advice. Note that both adjectives take the preposition *of*.

disyllable. See **dissyllable.**

dive > dived > dived; dive > dove > dived. Although *dove* is fairly common in AmE (on the analogy of *drove*), *dived* has long been considered the preferable past-tense form. But times are changing: since 1986, the frequency of *he dove into* in AmE has surpassed that of *he dived into* (not true of BrE). So it is time to declare *dive > dove > dived* standard AmE alongside the older forms. E.g.:

- "A 23-year-old Severna Park man was in critical condition at Maryland Shock Trauma Center in Baltimore yesterday after he *dove* into a pool and suffered a cervical fracture to his neck, Anne Arundel County fire officials reported." "Man Is Critically Injured in Dive into Pool During Bachelor Party," *Baltimore Sun*, 16 July 2001, at B5.
- "Facing Vladimir Nunez, Shinjo lined a ball to the right-center gap, where centerfielder Eric Owens *dove* for the ball but came up empty." Jason Butler, "Shinjo's Double Ends Crazy Game," *Newsday* (N.Y.), 19 July 2001, at A80.
- "After intermission, the four musicians *dove* into Ravel's only contribution to the quartet repertoire." Edward Reichel, "Something Old, Something New, Played Masterfully," *Deseret News* (Salt Lake City), 9 Oct. 2002, at C9. (On the use of *masterfully* in the title of that article, see **masterful.**)

LANGUAGE-CHANGE INDEX
dove for *dived* as a past tense: Stage 5
Current ratio (*she dove* vs. *she dived*): 1.2:1

divergence; *divergency. The latter is a NEEDLESS VARIANT.

Current ratio: 172:1

diverse; divers. *Diverse* implies difference, whereas *divers* implies severalty. *Diverse* /di-**vərs**/ means "differing widely; unlike; varied"—e.g.:

- "As Chicago's religious community becomes even more *diverse*—recent surveys show that there are more Muslims in the Chicago area than Jews, more Thai Buddhists than Episcopalians—the potential for strife increases." Cathleen Falsani, "2 Suburbs, 12 Faiths Under One Umbrella," *Chicago Trib.*, 13 Sept. 1996, at 12.
- "Liberia, a nation smaller than New York State, has more than 30 linguistic groups and myriad *diverse* folkways." Harold McNeil, "Blacks Told of Strategies in Tracing Roots," *Buffalo News*, 20 Sept. 1996, at B5.

Divers (= various, sundry)—pronounced /**dɪ**-vərz/—remains a part of AmE only as a curiosity. Formerly it meant not only "various," but "several" as well. For example, in *The Merchant of Venice*, Shakespeare referred to "divers [i.e., 'several'] of Antonio's creditors" (3.1.113); in *As You Like It*, he wrote that "time travels in divers [i.e., 'various'] paces with divers [again, 'various'] persons" (3.2.308–09).

Today *divers* is an ARCHAISM, and its only accepted meaning is "various," as in the following examples:

- "The possible perils are precluded by the filing of the notice of pendency which thereafter binds anyone subsequently obtaining an interest in the property, be they fee owners, mortgagees, grantees, tenants or *divers* others." Bruce J. Bergman, "Who's Hiding in the House," *N.Y.L.J.*, 25 Jan. 1995, at 5.
- "[The] literature section . . . is sprinkled with works featuring Yeats, Orpen, Synge and *divers* others of Irish interest." "O'Connor Leads Impressive List of Works in de Veres Auction," *Irish Times*, 2 Dec. 1995, at 24.
- "Lee cries four times, Jackson cries twice, and *divers* others Blue and Gray chew up the scenery." John Stark Bellamy II, "Shaara's Civil War Prequel Pretty Impressive," *Plain Dealer* (Cleveland), 18 Aug. 1996, at J11.

divestiture; *divesture; divestment. The standard noun corresponding to the verb *divest* is *divestiture*. E.g.:

- "*Divestiture* of owned production facilities is common in electronics business here—Apple, Hewlett-Packard, IBM and National Semiconductor recently sold facilities with contracts to become their major customers." "Philips Plans Sale of U.S. TV Plant," *Consumer Electronics*, 2 Sept. 1996, at 9.
- "Completing *divestitures* already under way and those announced Friday will all but conclude Thomson's reorganizing process." "Takeover Target Loewen to Buy Cemetery Company," *Orlando Sentinel*, 21 Sept. 1996, at C10.
- "The forecast improvement over last year is primarily due to *divestiture* of the crop insurance business and growth in the average credit portfolio." Jennifer DeWitt, "Deere by Division," *Quad-City Times* (Davenport, Iowa), 22 Aug. 2015, at 8.

Divesture is a NEEDLESS VARIANT—e.g.: "Without the *divesture* [read *divestiture*], Otten would have controlled eight of the largest ski resorts serving skiers in eastern New England." Penny Parker, "Gillett Returns to Skiing," *Denver Post*, 11 Sept. 1996, at D1.

Divestment, not at all uncommon, might seem to be another NEEDLESS VARIANT. Yet it appears in a number of legal phrases, such as *vested interest subject to divestment*. And it appears in many other contexts, usually involving the release of assets—e.g.: "In a few cases, the losers are Japanese companies, part of a multibillion-dollar *divestment* of their American assets." Verne G. Kopytoff, "Asian Investment Is on the Rise in Los Angeles," *N.Y. Times*, 22 Sept. 1996, § 9, at 7. To the extent that *divestment* deals more particularly with assets than *divestiture* (a more general word), using it in these contexts serves the cause of DIFFERENTIATION. At this stage, though, the difference is incipient only. Cf. **disinvestment**.

> LANGUAGE-CHANGE INDEX
> **divesture* for *divestiture*: Stage 1
> Current ratio (*divestiture* vs. **divesture*): 49:1

*dividable. See **divisible**.

divide up. See PHRASAL VERBS.

divisibility. See **devisability**.

divisible /di-**viz**-ə-bəl/ is so spelled—not **divisable*. (See -ABLE (A).) **Dividable* is a NEEDLESS VARIANT.

> Current ratio: 1,165:1

divisive (= causing a lot of disagreement between people) is preferably pronounced /di-**vIh**-siv/, not /di-**vis**-iv/.

divisor. See **deviser**.

divorce. A. And *annulment*. A *divorce* recognizes the existence of a valid marriage, whereas an *annulment* treats the marriage as if it had never existed. Even so, in most jurisdictions the "nonexistence" of the marriage is not considered absolute: any children conceived before the annulment are considered legitimate.

B. And *dissolution of marriage*. In the 1970s, the word *divorce* was struck from many statutes and replaced by the EUPHEMISM *dissolution of marriage*.

C. And *legal separation*. A *legal separation* is "an arrangement whereby a husband and wife live apart from each other while remaining married, either by mutual consent (often in a written agreement) or by judicial decree" (*Black's Law Dictionary* 1572 [10th ed. 2014]).

divorcée; divorcé. The usual word—*divorcée*—properly refers only to a woman. The masculine form is *divorcé*, which has been AmE usage since the late 19th century. But some writers have tried to create male *divorcées*—e.g.:

- "Parents were lulled into security by Martin's plausible manner and his implied message that, as an ex-police officer, he was a man to be trusted. Gregarious *divorcée* [read *divorcé*] Martin was a familiar figure in Manchester in his open-top sports cars." "Ex-Policeman Brainwashed Schoolgirls with Drugs," *Herald* (Glasgow), 13 Sept. 1996, at 3. (On the use of *gregarious divorcée* as a "title" in that sentence, see TITULAR TOMFOOLERY.)
- "She has two men in her life: wealthy *divorcée* [read *divorcé*] Ray Porter (Martin) and struggling musician Jeremy." "Danes Tries Her Hand in a Counter Culture," *San Diego Union-Trib.*, 27 Oct. 2002, at F10.

Both words are pronounced /di-vor-**say**/ or /-**see**/.

> LANGUAGE-CHANGE INDEX
> *divorcée* misused for *divorcé*: Stage 2

divorcement is now obsolete for *divorce* in the sense "the dissolution of the marriage tie," although it persisted in this sense up to the mid-20th century. For example, David O. Selznick directed Katharine Hepburn and John Barrymore in the 1932 film *A Bill of Divorcement*. But even with the legal term, *bill of divorce* has been standard since the 18th century.

Divorcement survives in the general figurative sense "the severance or complete separation of any close relation, esp. a business relation"—e.g.: "1941–42 . . . Justice Dept. pursues *divorcement* of theaters from studios." Keithe Collins, "Reeling in the Years," *Daily Variety*, 8 Mar. 2001, Special §, at 6.

> Current ratio (*a divorce* vs. *a divorcement*): 1,183:1

divulge, v.t., = to make known (esp. something secret); reveal. E.g.: "Yet Mattel executives wouldn't *divulge* any details of the coming job cuts." David Robinson, "Mattel Puts Profits Before Morale During Holidays," *Buffalo News*, 25 Dec. 1994, at 11. The verb should not be used where *say* or *tell* would suffice—e.g.: "What Dunton, a portly man who was dressed in jeans and a striped shirt Wednesday, *divulged* [read *said*] to investigators is unclear." Matt Krasnowski, "Witness Takes Jail over Talking in Cowlings' Case," *State J.-Register* (Springfield, Ill.), 8 Sept. 1994, at 2. The accent is on the second syllable: /di-**vəlj**/.

divulgence; *divulgation; *divulgement. Though the latter two date from the early 17th century, *divulgence*, which dates from the early 19th century, is now the preferred noun corresponding to the verb *divulge*.

> Current ratio: 15:11:1

*djinni. See **genie**.

do, as. See **like** & ANTICIPATORY REFERENCE (A).

do; doh. In the "sol-fa syllables" made famous in *The Sound of Music* (1965)—do, re, mi, fa, sol, la, ti, do—the AmE spelling of the first and last syllable is *do* /doh/. The BrE spelling is said to be *doh* (FMEU3 at 224)—but the linguistic evidence in BrE print sources points to *do*. See **so; sol**.

LANGUAGE-CHANGE INDEX (For the full key, see front matter pp. xxxi, l–li.)
Stage 1: Rejected. **Stage 2:** Widely shunned. **Stage 3:** Widespread but . . . **Stage 4:** Ubiquitous but . . . **Stage 5:** Fully accepted.
Invariably inferior forms marked by asterisk (*). • Ratios represent frequency of prevalent forms vs. variants in current books.

dock, n. Since the late 19th century, usage commentators have occasionally criticized the landlubber's use of *dock* for *wharf* or *pier*. But this sense has been common since that time. In fact, nautically speaking, *dock* has two senses: (1) "a large structure or excavated basin for receiving ships, equipped with gates to keep water in or out"; and (2) "a landing pier; wharf" (*WNWCD*). Although Theodore Bernstein and Wilson Follett both disapproved of sense 2, most commentators today accept it. It should be considered standard.

doctoral. So spelled—not **doctorial.* E.g.:

- " 'In World War II, the USO served as a transforming organization, helping create and develop a shared national American culture,' says Teri Tynes of Austin, Texas, whose *doctorial* [read *doctoral*] dissertation at the University of Texas, 'A Theater Worth Fighting For,' examined the group." Tom Squitieri, "USO Observes an Active 50th with War in Gulf," *USA Today*, 4 Feb. 1991, at A7.
- "[There will be a] screening of 'Viktor und Viktoria' (1933), introduced by UC Berkeley *doctorial* [read *doctoral*] candidate Sanjay Hukku, at 9 p.m. Fri." Reyhan Harmanci, "Gender Bender," *S.F. Chron.*, 20 Sept. 2007, at G36.

The pronunciation is /**dok**-tə-rəl/, not /dok-**tor**-əl/ or /dok-**tor**-ee-əl/.

Language-Change Index
*doctorial for *doctoral*: Stage 1
Current ratio (*doctoral* vs. **doctorial*): 461:1

doctrinal; doctrinaire; *doctrinary. *Doctrinal* (/**dok**-trə-nəl/ or /dok-**tri**-nəl/) is the neutral term, meaning "of, relating to, or involving a doctrine." E.g.: "To both Protestants and Catholics, Moon is guilty of grievous *doctrinal* heresies—by preaching, as he does, that Christ's mother, Mary, was not a virgin, and by arguing that he and his wife, the 'True Parents,' are on earth to finish the job Jesus failed to do." Michael S. Serrill, "Moon Beams into Brazil," *Time*, 23 Sept. 1996, at 31.

Doctrinaire (/dok-trə-**nair**/) = slavishly or impractically adhering to dogma; highly dogmatic. "Sad to say, these selections will be made not by the police officers' benefactor but by a *doctrinaire* liberal whose largest campaign contributions from a professional group come from (for God's sake!) trial lawyers." Don Feder, "Crimefighter Bill Much Overrated," *Boston Herald*, 25 Sept. 1996, at 31. **Doctrinary* is a NEEDLESS VARIANT of *doctrinaire*.

Doctrinaire is sometimes misspelled **doctrinnaire*, on the apparent analogy of *questionnaire*—e.g.:

- "It does indicate a willingness on the part of the House leadership to negotiate along less conservative *doctrinnaire* [read *doctrinaire*] lines." " 'Endangered' Moderates," *Times & Eagle* (Reading, Pa.), 4 Nov. 1995, at A6.
- "In *doctrinnaire* [read *doctrinaire*] terms the decree stated the fundamentals of the Communist doctrine." Malbone W. Graham, *New Governments of Central Europe* 229 (2007).

Cf. **millionaire** & **questionnaire**.

Language-Change Index
doctrinaire misspelled **doctrinnaire*: Stage 1
Current ratio: 1,568:1

documentary; *documental. The latter is a NEEDLESS VARIANT.

Current ratio: 117:1

DOCUMENT DESIGN. Traditionally, writers have been relatively unconcerned with the look of their documents. This lack of concern didn't have many horrible consequences in the days of typewriters, when the primary design choices were the width of the margins and the amount of underlining and capitals.

But with the advent of word processing, document design has become much more important as writers are presented with all kinds of new formatting and printing options. Failing to knowledgeably use these options puts the writer at a disadvantage because most readers have become accustomed to well-designed documents. In short, it has become essential to know something about typography and design.

In this space, of course, it's impossible to offer any more than the simplest primer on the subject. But a few particularly important points deserve mention.

A. Readable Typeface. For text, a readable typeface probably means a serif typeface, such as the one used throughout this book, as opposed to a sans-serif (/sanz-**ser**-if/) typeface made up of only straight lines. Serifs are short strokes that project from the ends of the main strokes that make up a character.

> This is a serif typeface: Times New Roman.
> This is a sans-serif typeface: Univers.

Although sans-serif typefaces often work well in headings and the like, they can be difficult to read in text. Among the better serif typefaces are Bookman, Caslon, Garamond, Palatino, and Times New Roman. One typeface long predominated in American business: Courier. Avoid it at all costs. `Courier is an eyesore.`

B. White Space. Ample white space makes a page more inviting. The primary ways to create white space on the page are to use generous margins (for example, margins greater than one inch for letters and other business documents), to supply headings and subheadings, and to enumerate items in separate paragraphs, subparagraphs, or bulleted lists.

C. Headings and Subheadings. Artfully employed, headings and subheadings make a document much easier to follow. Not only do they serve as navigational aids for readers, they also help writers organize thoughts more logically than they might otherwise. See **widow.**

D. Avoiding All Caps. See CAPITALIZATION (E).

E. Avoiding Underlines. Generally, italicizing is preferable to underlining, which was traditionally (on a typewriter) nothing more than a poor substitute for italics. The effect of underlining is to take up white space between lines, thereby making the lines harder to read.

F. Listing. Enumerate items by breaking down lists into paragraphs and subparagraphs. Using a tabulated list allows the writer not only to display the points better but also to improve the sentence structure. Make sure that the list falls at the end of the sentence—not at the beginning or in the middle. See ENUMERATIONS.

G. Bullets. On this extremely useful device, see PUNCTUATION (B).

H. Hanging Indents. In most text, when you indent an item to be listed—whether it's a bulleted item or an entire paragraph—don't begin the second line of the item at the left margin. Instead, begin it just below the first line, with the enumerating signal hanging to the left. Examples appear throughout this book in bulleted lists.

I. Ragged Right Margin. Many readability specialists insist that unjustified right margins make text more readable than justified ones do. In letters, contracts, and the like, an unjustified right margin is often desirable.

J. Citations in Footnotes. Citations tend to clutter the text; you can easily minimize this cluttering by moving citations to footnotes (and avoiding footnotes for discussion purposes). See FOOTNOTES.

K. Characters per Line. Ideally, a line of type should accommodate 45 to 70 characters, but the "fine print" that characterizes so many legal documents often spans 150 characters to the line. In text of that kind, the reader's eye tends to get lost in midline or in moving from the end of one line to the beginning of the next. One way to improve a document with a large block of text—and, typically, small margins on each side—is to use a double-column format. That design can be extremely helpful, for example, in consumer contracts such as residential leases.

L. Select Bibliography. For more on this subject, see Philip Brady, *Using Type Right* (1988); Robert Bringhurst, *The Elements of Typographic Style* (1992); and *Words into Type* (3d ed. 1974).

dogged. As a past-tense or past-participial verb, *dogged* is pronounced /dawgd/ or /dogd/ <they were dogged by problems>. But as an adjective, the word is pronounced /**dawg**-id/ or /**dog**-id/ <golfers are the dogged victims of an inexorable fate>.

doggerel (= bad, often silly poetry) is the standard spelling. It is pronounced with three syllables (/**dawg**-ər-əl/). **Doggrel* is a variant form that predominated in BrE until about 1880. It has since become nonstandard.

Current ratio: 12:1

doggy; doggie. Oddly, AmE prefers *doggy* in all uses except the phrase *doggie bag* (attested from 1958). BrE is consistent with *doggy* for all uses of the word.

dogma. Pl. *dogmas* (/**dawg**-məz/) or **dogmata* (/**dawg**-mə-tə/). The simple plural is preferred over the Greek **dogmata*—e.g.:

- "If The Union doesn't subscribe to the unisex *dogmata* [read *dogmas*] of our frumpy homogenizers—and I sometimes wonder—such distinctions should be borne in mind." Letter of R.R. Dalling, "Valley Center Churlish Caricature," *San Diego Union-Trib.*, 17 Apr. 1985, at B7.

- "Neither of them sat through the gobbledygook that passes for education courses, nor absorbed the *dogmas* of the day that pass for thinking." Thomas Sowell, "Hardly the Last Word on Education 'Reform,'" *Tampa Trib.*, 20 Sept. 1996, at 17. (The mispaired *Neither . . . nor* in that sentence will cause a MISCUE for many readers. See **neither . . . nor (C)**.)

See PLURALS (B).

Current ratio: 45:1

doldrums, always plural, denotes a state of low energy, boredom, depression, or lifelessness—e.g.: "The annual Spring Flower Show chases away the winter *doldrums* from 9 a.m. until 5 p.m. daily until May 10." "3 Things We Love About Lincoln Park," *Chicago Sun-Times*, 9 Feb. 2009, News §, at 3. The word is thought to derive from the Old English *dol* (= dull) and is related to the word *dolt*. The suffix appears to have been influenced by *tantrum*, and it has nothing to do with the percussion instrument. Hence anyone who thinks the word alludes to "dull drums" is engaging in folk etymology. (See ETYMOLOGY (D).)

Substituting *dull* for *dol* makes for a natural if overused pun—e.g.: "Hope for Summer Movie *Dulldrums*." Headline, *L.A. Times*, 1 May 2008, at E1. But sometimes it's clear error—e.g.:

- "In their continuing effort to snap Shawn Green out of his *duldrums* [read *doldrums*] at the plate, the Dodgers batted their cleanup hitter second vs. the Brewers." "Baseball Log," *Pitt. Post-Gaz.*, 26 May 2004, at B5.
- "Marlow also pulled Weston out of its *duldrums* [read *doldrums*] after Dracut (12–8–2) took the initial lead." Bruce Lerch, "Savio Shakes Off Rust, Tips Salem," *Boston Herald*, 6 Mar. 2007, Sports §, at 50.

When capitalized, the term denotes an equatorial zone of light winds where sailing ships are prone to becalming—e.g.: "Days blend into one another. We cross the *Doldrums*, the vast belt of low pressure and light wind that girdles the equator." Matthew Power, "Sailing Toward Paradise," *N.Y. Times*, 23 Dec. 2007, Travel §, at 1. The *OED* speculates that this sense comes from a misunderstanding of the idiom *in the doldrums* as referring to a physical location.

dollars. When the dollar sign appears with a numeral, using the word *dollars* is redundant—e.g.: "By October this year, Mr. Bradley had raised nearly *$20 million dollars* [read *$20 million*]." James Dao, "Seeking Upset, Bradley Enlists Unlikely Model," *N.Y. Times*, 27 Dec. 1999, at A1, A12. See REDUNDANCY.

dollhouse; doll's house; **dolls' house.* The BrE preference today is for the oldest form, dating from the 18th century: *doll's house*. The strong AmE preference (since about 1970) is for the 19th-century solid form *dollhouse*. The plural possessive **dolls' house* is a variant that has predominance nowhere in World English.

LANGUAGE-CHANGE INDEX (For the full key, see front matter pp. xxxi, l–li.)
Stage 1: Rejected. **Stage 2:** Widely shunned. **Stage 3:** Widespread but . . . **Stage 4:** Ubiquitous but . . . **Stage 5:** Fully accepted.
Invariably inferior forms marked by asterisk (*). • Ratios represent frequency of prevalent forms vs. variants in current books.

dolma. Pl. *dolmas* or (somewhat pretentiously in English-language contexts) *dolmades*.

Current ratio: 1:1

dolor (= sorrow, distress) is sometimes said to be the AmE spelling, *dolour* the BrE spelling. In fact, though, *dolor* has predominated in all varieties of English print sources since the 17th century. See -OR; -OUR.

Current ratio: 11:1

Domesday Book (= the record of a 1086 survey made under William the Conqueror to catalogue English lands and landholdings) has been predominantly so spelled in all varieties of English since 1800. Before that, the variant *Doomsday Book* was prevalent. That term, however, is subject to serious misinterpretation today. The name is said to derive from the idea that the survey judged all people without bias, just as the Last Judgment is supposed to do.

Current ratio: 13:1

domestic; domesticated. A *domestic* animal is a pet, such as a cat or dog, that lives with the family. A *domesticated* animal is a formerly wild animal that has long been bred for human use (common examples being cattle, pigs, and sheep).

domesticate. See **domiciliate.**

domesticated. See **domestic.**

*domesticize. See **domiciliate.**

domicile; *domicil. *Domicile* /dom-ə-sil/ is spelled both with and without the final -*e*, but the better and more common spelling today is with it. The incomplete-looking **domicil* predominated in AmE for most of the 18th century. See **citizenship.**

Current ratio: 18:1

domiciliate; domesticate; *domesticize. *Domiciliate* = to establish a domicile or home. *Domesticate* = (1) to make domestic; (2) to make a member of the household; or (3) to tame (wild animals) or cultivate (wild plants) for human use. **Domesticize* is a NEEDLESS VARIANT of *domesticate*. See -IZE.
 Current ratio (*domesticated* vs. **domesticized*): 806:1

dominance; domination. *Dominance* = the fact or position of being dominant. *Domination* = the act of dominating; the exercise of ruling power.

dominant, adj. Just as *predominant* is sometimes ill-advisedly written *predominate* (preferably a verb, not an adjective), so *dominant* is sometimes wrongly written *dominate* (as if it were pronounced /**dom**-i-nit/ or /-nət/)—e.g.:

- "Thirty-seven respondents reporting information about rental agreements said 50/50 share leases and basic cash rent arrangements remain the *dominate* [read *dominant*] types." Chris Anderson, "Farmland Pricetags Increase," *Pantagraph* (Bloomington, Ill.), 9 June 2001, at A12.
- "Jeff Moore divides aloes into three categories based on their *dominate* [read *dominant*] characteristic—form, flowers or foliage." Mary Hellman James, "Favorites Grouped by Form, Flowers, Foliage," *San Diego Union-Trib.*, 20 Jan. 2002, at I25.
- "They will encourage the silent members and try to hold back the verbose, *dominate* [read *dominant*] members." Charles Lessard & Joseph Lessard, *Project Management for Engineering* 3 (2007).

Dominate (/**dom**-ə-nayt/) is a verb, not an adjective—or at least no dictionaries have yet recorded an adjectival use.

LANGUAGE-CHANGE INDEX
dominate misused as an adjective in place of *dominant*: Stage 1
Current ratio (*dominant role* vs. **dominate role*): 312:1

dominate. See **predominate,** vb.

domination. See **dominance.**

dominatrix. Although most dictionaries record *dominatrices* as the plural, *dominatrixes* is more common in print and should be accepted as standard. See SEXISM (D).

Current ratio: 1.3:1

domino. A. Plural Form. Since the mid-19th century, the standard form has been *dominoes*, not **dominos*. See PLURALS (D).

Current ratio: 4:1

 B. *Dominoes is.* When referring to the game—not to the individual pieces used in the game—the word *dominoes* takes a singular verb <dominoes is a game with long-lasting appeal>.
 C. *Dominoes are.* When referring to costumes—hooded robes with eye masks, or the masks themselves—*dominoes are* is correct <the dominoes that most revelers wear with their Venetian carnival costumes are now unavailable in local stores>.

donate, a BACK-FORMATION from *donation*, was once considered a vulgar substitute for *give*. Today, however, it is a slightly FORMAL WORD that is unexceptionable.

done (= finished), when used as an adjective, is sometimes criticized, but the word has been so used since the 15th century <call me when you're done>. Many stylists prefer *through* <call me when you're through>.

don't. See CONTRACTIONS.

don't think. This phrasing has sometimes been criticized as illogical. After all, you *do* think: you simply think something negative. But the phrasing is perfectly idiomatic and centuries old—e.g.:

- "I'd always wondered where I'd be when we found the aliens, but I *don't think* I ever imagined I'd see them on my computer screen." Wayne Rash Jr., "Rash's Judgment," *Communications Week*, 12 Aug. 1996, at 82.
- "I *don't think* he's spent much time in New York or San Francisco, but I got his drift." Christopher Buckley, "How I Went Nine Gs in an F-16 and Only Threw Up Five Times," *Forbes*, 23 Sept. 1996, at 116.
- "There are a number of countries that are friends and allies of the United States. With our power and friends,

I *don't think* anyone would want to chance our retaliation." Sid Gordon, "Try to Keep the Peace Throughout the World," *Times Union* (Albany), 23 Aug. 2015, at D3.

For more on this phenomenon, which linguists call "raising," see **can't seem.**

donut. See **doughnut.**

Doomsday Book. See **Domesday Book.**

doorjamb. For the confusion of *jamb* with *jam*, see **jam.**

dos and don'ts. This is the logical form—not **do's and don'ts*—because the plural of *do* needs no apostrophe (just as the plural of *don't* needs no apostrophe). See PLURALS (L) & PUNCTUATION (A).

dotage. See **dote.**

dotcom. This word from the computer age refers to a company that does its primary business on the Internet, or provides goods or services to other companies that do. It is written as one word. E.g.: "It seems like only yesterday that *dotcoms* were hotter than hot." Rem Reider, "At the Crossroads," *Am. Journalism Rev.*, Mar. 2001, at 6. It once connoted a company that was raking in investors yet never making a profit, and after the tech bubble burst in 2000 the word was often replaced by *dot bomb.*

dote, vb.; **dotage,** n. These terms apply both to uncritical (and sometimes foolish) affection (such as "puppy love") and to mental impairment (such as senility). But the modern trend is to use the verb *dote* only in the former sense <dote on one's children>, and the noun *dotage* only in the latter sense <the debilities of dotage>.

DOUBLE ADVERBS. See ADVERBS (C).

DOUBLE BOBBLES. A double bobble occurs when somebody reaches for a word—in fact, the *wrong* word—and then mistakes another word for that wrong word. It's a word twice removed from its correct use. Two ready examples are **Hobbesian choice* (when misused for a difficult choice) and *compromise* (when misused for *comprise*).

A *Hobson's choice* is really a take-it-or-leave-it choice. (See **Hobson's choice (A).**) By SLIPSHOD EXTENSION, though, the phrase came to refer to any difficult choice. And to compound the problem, some writers reach for the extended sense and miss entirely: they confuse Thomas Hobson, a relatively obscure man, with his famous contemporary Thomas Hobbes (1588–1679). The resulting MALAPROPISM is amazingly common—e.g.: "There was a *Hobbesian choice* [read *Hobson's choice*] to be made: To get an hour-long 'Letterman,' ABC also would have to kill 'Nightline.' " Verne Gay, "Letterman's One-Night Stand," *Newsday* (N.Y.), 8 July 2002, § II, at B23. See **Hobson's choice (C).**

A similar error occurs when *compromise* is confused with *comprise*, which itself is often misused for *compose* or *constitute*. In strict usage, the parts compose the whole; the whole comprises the parts; the whole is composed of the parts; the parts are comprised in the whole. Hence the phrase **is comprised of* is always poor and should be replaced by *is composed of*, *is made up of*, or *comprises*. See **comprise (A).**

Sometimes, however, the writer wanting the incorrect *comprise* seizes upon a doubly incorrect word, *compromise*—e.g.:

- "The nation's 1.1 million secular Jews, those born Jewish but practicing no religion, *compromise* [read *make up*] 20 percent of the core Jewish population." "A Portrait of Jews in America," *Numbers News* (Am. Demographics, Inc.), Jan. 1994, at 4.
- "Women *compromise* [read *make up*] 60 percent of the 400,000 California adults estimated to have been seriously mentally ill in 1989." Nancy Weaver, "Mentally Ill Women Bear Brunt of State Cuts in Care, Report Says," *Sacramento Bee*, 8 Mar. 1995, at A1.
- "Thomas C. Stevens, managing partner, said David L. Parham will replace Hooker as chair of the litigation practice area, which *compromises* [read *constitutes*] a third of the firm's 335 lawyers." "Business Briefs," *Plain Dealer* (Cleveland), 8 July 1995, at C2.

One more example. There's a difference between the words *forebear* (= an ancestor) and *forbear* (= to refrain). To choose the latter in place of the former, in a noun sense, would be a single bobble. But to morph the word into **forbearer* is a double bobble:

- "We have inherited the animal characteristics of our *forbearers* [read *forebears*]. They in turn inherited the animal characteristics of their *forbearers* [read *forebears*], who also inherited the animal characteristics of their *forbearers* [read *forebears*]." Richard Townsend, *The Evolution of the Mind* 41 (2003).
- "When we academics honor our greatest intellectual *forbearers* [read *forebears*], we presumably carry the highest obligation of fidelity to their ideas." Lief H. Carter, *Law and Politics as Play*, 83 Chi.-Kent L. Rev. 1333, 1334 (2008).

All the misuses discussed here are so spectacularly wrong that they merit their own special name: hence "double bobbles." For other examples, see **euphuism, *had have & reek.**

DOUBLE COMPARISONS. See COMPARATIVES AND SUPERLATIVES (D).

double entendre; *double entente. The English phrase—sometimes thought to be pseudo-French, but actually 17th-century French—is *double entendre*. The modern French form, **double entente*, is an affectation—e.g.:

- "Martin Booth writes the scripts, funny in a conventional way, with rather more *double entente* [read *double entendres*] than I expected." B.A. Young, "The Man Within," *Fin. Times*, 11 July 1987, at xvii.

LANGUAGE-CHANGE INDEX (For the full key, see front matter pp. xxxi, l–li.)
Stage 1: Rejected. **Stage 2:** Widely shunned. **Stage 3:** Widespread but . . . **Stage 4:** Ubiquitous but . . . **Stage 5:** Fully accepted.
Invariably inferior forms marked by asterisk (*). • Ratios represent frequency of prevalent forms vs. variants in current books.

- "If the Elizabethan herbal *doubles ententes* [read *double entendres*] were still in vogue, Ophelia's mad scene would provoke even more blushes." Stan Kelly-Bootle, "Let No Man Steal Your Time," *Computer Language*, June 1989, at 83.
- "The *double entente* [read *double entendre*]—the prison image and baseball—makes the name beautiful in the eyes of team management." "Joliet Slammers: The Coming of a New Franchise," *Herald News* (Joliet, Ill.), 17 Feb. 2011, Sports §, at 38.

Double entendre originally referred to any ambiguity (usually a pun) giving rise to more than one meaning, but now connotes that one of those meanings is indecent or risqué—e.g.:

- "Sex in an upscale cabaret is never explicit, but *double entendre* is always a welcome visitor." Michael Barnes, "It's Cabaret in Austin, Darling!" *Austin Am.-Statesman*, 15 July 1996, at E1.
- "The company has an owl logo, but it 'acknowledges that its name is considered a slang term for a portion of the female anatomy,' according to company literature, and the six businessmen who founded Hooters were aware of the *double entendre* when they chose the name." William Conroy, "A Hooters Near You," *Asbury Park Press* (Neptune, N.J.), 18 July 1996, at C1.
- "The male/female question leads to all kinds of *double entendres*. Jokes about males on top of females. And females on top of males." Alona Wartofsky, "He Sells Hard Shells," *Wash. Post*, 7 Sept. 1996, at C1.

The best pronunciation is /**dəb**-əl ahn-**tahn**-drə/.

LANGUAGE-CHANGE INDEX
double entente for *double entendre*: Stage 1
Current ratio (*double entendre* vs.
double entente): 45:1

DOUBLE GENITIVES. See POSSESSIVES (D).

DOUBLE MODALS. In grammar, a *modal* (short for *modal auxiliary*) is a verb such as *can, could, may, might, must, ought, shall, should, used, will,* or *would.* A modal is used with another verb to express grammatical mood—that is, to indicate the speaker's attitude toward the factuality or likelihood of what is being said: (1) the indicative expresses objective fact <Sam can play the piano>; (2) the imperative expresses a command or request <play it again, Sam>; and (3) the subjunctive expresses something hypothetical or contrary to fact <if Sam were up to it, he would play>. (See SUBJUNCTIVES.)

Modal auxiliaries are distinguished from the primary auxiliaries: *am, are, is, was, were, be, being, been, do, does, did, have, has, had.* Primary auxiliaries often team up to indicate tense in a verb phrase <are being stubborn> <have been patient>. Sometimes they team up with modal auxiliaries for the same purpose <will have arrived>.

But in STANDARD ENGLISH, only one modal appears in a verb phrase. A double modal, as the name implies, is a combination of two modals in such nonstandard expressions as these:

*can might	*might had better
*could might	*might ought
*had ought	*might should
*may can	*might supposed to
*may could	*might've used to
*may should	*might would
*may supposed to	*must could have
*may used to	*ought to could
*may will	*shouldn't ought to
*might can	*should ought
*might could	*used to could

These phrases are not uncommon in regional DIALECT—especially in the South—but they do not belong in STANDARD ENGLISH and rarely appear in print. E.g.: "Although I have only spent one day on the water at Lay Lake, and interviewed perhaps 20 percent of the field, I still believe I *might can* [read *might*] get pretty close." Steve Bowman, "Expect the Unexpected When Classic Title on Line," *Ark. Democrat-Gaz.*, 8 Aug. 1996, at C4.

The problem with most double modals, of course, is that only one of the verbs is needed. In the most common double modal, **might could*, the word *might* can usually be dropped without a change in meaning. So unless you're recording dialect or creating fictional dialogue—or mimicking regional speech for comic effect—don't use double modals. Cf. ***might should have.**

DOUBLE NEGATIVES. See NEGATIVES (B).

DOUBLE PASSIVES. See PASSIVE VOICE (B).

DOUBLE POSSESSIVES. See POSSESSIVES (D).

DOUBLESPEAK, the language of disinformation, is a subset of EUPHEMISM. In the words of a leading text on the subject:

> Doublespeak is language that pretends to communicate but really doesn't. It is language that makes the bad seem good, the negative appear positive, the unpleasant appear attractive or at least tolerable. Doublespeak is language that avoids or shifts responsibility, language that is at variance with its real or purported meaning. It is language that conceals or prevents thought; rather than extending thought, doublespeak limits it.
>
> William Lutz, *Doublespeak* 1 (1989).

In the language of doublespeak, poor people are *fiscal underachievers*; hobos or "street people" are *non-goal-oriented members of society*; prostitutes are *sexual workers* or *sexual service providers*; graffiti sprayers are *wall artists*; and students whose grades are borderline are *emerging students*.

Although *doublespeak* is commonly associated with George Orwell's *1984*, the term he used in that book was *Newspeak*. But the idea is the same.

Apart from a few words and phrases that have become very common—for example, *exceptional* used in reference to children with severe learning disabilities or subnormal intelligence (see **exceptional (B)**) and *only* purposely misplaced (see **only (B)**)—doublespeak is not generally the subject of this book. For good treatments, see Lutz's work cited above and several earlier works: Mario Pei, *Words in*

Sheep's Clothing (1969); Mario Pei, *Double-Speak in America* (1973); Mario Pei, *Weasel Words: The Art of Saying What You Don't Mean* (1978); William Lambdin, *Doublespeak Dictionary* (1979); and Hugh Rawson, *A Dictionary of Euphemisms & Other Doubletalk* (1981).

DOUBLE SUBJECTS. Linguists term it "pronominal apposition"—the use of a dependent pronoun in a sentence such as *My brother he's the president.* Of course, the *he* is unnecessary there, and its use marks the speaker as a speaker of DIALECT.

Interestingly, though, the difference between this substandard usage and standard usage is slight—though quite perceptible. William Labov explains the kinship between the double subject in standard and in nonstandard speech:

> [I]t is not always realized that the "nonstandard" aspect is merely a slight difference in intonation. A standard speaker frequently says the same thing, with a slight break after the subject: *My oldest sister—she works at the bank, and she finds it very profitable.* There are many ways in which a greater awareness of the standard colloquial forms would help teachers interpret nonstandard forms. Not only do standard speakers use pronominal apposition with the break noted above, but in casual speech they can also bring object noun phrases to the front, "foregrounding" them. For example, one can say
>
> My oldest sister—she worked at the Citizens Bank in Passaic last year.
>
> The Citizens Bank, in Passaic—my oldest sister worked there last year.
>
> Passaic—my oldest sister worked at the Citizens Bank there last year.
>
> Note that if the foregrounded noun phrase represents a locative—the "place where"—then its position is held by *there*, just as the persons are represented by pronouns. If we are dealing with a time element, it can be foregrounded without replacement in any dialect: *Last year, my oldest sister worked at the Citizens Bank in Passaic.*
>
> William Labov, "The Study of Nonstandard English," in *Language: Introductory Readings* 543, 547–48 (Virginia P. Clark et al. eds., 4th ed. 1985).

Labov's final examples—with the "foregrounding"—are quite informal, even if they are standard. Some journalists habitually use that type of sentence.

There is, of course, the more formal, oratorical type of double subject, as in *We the people of the United States . . . .* See APPOSITIVES.

DOUBLING OF FINAL CONSONANTS. See SPELLING (B).

doubt. A. *Doubt that; doubt whether; *doubt if.* The phrasing *doubt that* (the most common of the three) is used primarily in negative sentences, statements of skepticism, and questions—e.g.:

- "McPherson also *doubted that* the council would want to change the job description from secretary to manager." Jim Hosek, "Kuchta Retires," *Pitt. Post-Gaz.*, 4 Sept. 1996, at S1.
- "Consider Ronald Reagan: he was widely considered an amiable, affable fellow—but no one *doubted that* he could be aggressive if he needed to be." William F. Allman, "The Serotonin Candidate," *Forbes*, 23 Sept. 1996, at 134.

Doubt whether is used primarily in affirmative statements (again, though, of skepticism)—e.g.:

- "But even if the rules can survive legal challenge, they *doubted whether* David Kessler, the Food and Drug Administration's chief, can reach his goal of cutting youth smoking in half within seven years." "White House Expected to Attempt to Regulate Tobacco as Drug," *Tampa Trib.*, 22 Aug. 1996, at 11.
- "[David] Cone went on the disabled list after doctors removed an aneurysm from the right-hander's pitching shoulder, and the Yankee front office *doubted whether* he could return before next spring." "Big-League Recoveries," *Record* (N.J.), 4 Sept. 1996, at N6.

*Doubt if is less sound because it suggests a conditional statement. The phrase *doubt that* will usually replace **doubt if*—e.g.: "Dr. Hughes *doubted if* [read *doubted that*] it would be used to screen all women as the test was not 100 per cent accurate." Bryan Christie, "Premature Births Targeted by New Test," *Scotsman*, 3 Sept. 1996, at 3. This usage appears most commonly in BrE. Cf. **I'm not sure that** & **determine whether.**

LANGUAGE-CHANGE INDEX
*doubt if for *doubt that*: Stage 3
Current ratio (*doubt that* vs. **doubt if*): 11:1

B. Followed by a Negative. *Doubt* can be confusing when followed by a negative—e.g.: "I *doubt* whether the company *will not* take the further step when necessary." This sentence merely states that the writer thinks the company *will* take the further step.

C. And **misdoubt*. See **misdoubt*.

*doubt if. See **doubt (A).**

*doubtlessly is a NONWORD for *doubtless* (a mild expression of certainty), *no doubt* (a stronger expression of certainty), or *undoubtedly* (the strongest of these three expressions of certainty). The word *doubtless* is itself an adverb <the Framers doubtless feared the executive's assertion of an independent military authority unchecked by the people>. The form **doubtlessly* is therefore unnecessary—e.g.:

- "Lebed, who has made no secret of his longing to be Russia's defense minister, *doubtlessly will* [read *will doubtless*] take great personal satisfaction *from* [read *in*] being courted by Yeltsin." James P. Gallagher, "Russians Lift Yeltsin into Runoff," *Chicago Trib.*, 17 June 1996, at N1. (On the position of the adverb within the verb phrase, see ADVERBS (A).)
- "[Brett Favre's] protracted divorce from the Packers *doubtlessly* [read *undoubtedly*] has him determined to prove they should have welcomed him back." Bob DiCesare,

LANGUAGE-CHANGE INDEX (For the full key, see front matter pp. xxxi, l–li.)
Stage 1: Rejected. **Stage 2:** Widely shunned. **Stage 3:** Widespread but . . . **Stage 4:** Ubiquitous but . . . **Stage 5:** Fully accepted.
Invariably inferior forms marked by asterisk (*). • Ratios represent frequency of prevalent forms vs. variants in current books.

"Favre Saga Has Parallels to Montana," *Buffalo News*, 8 Aug. 2008, at B1.

- "The laws of supply and demand suggest that some people would pay for spots at jammed lots . . . . Other riders are *doubtlessly* [read *no doubt*] at a tipping point on the cost of riding the train vs. driving to work." Editorial, "Keep Parking Free," *Dallas Morning News*, 19 Aug. 2008, at A12.

Cf. **clearly.** For other adverbs with a superfluous -*ly*, see ADVERBS (C).

LANGUAGE-CHANGE INDEX
*doubtlessly for *doubtless*: Stage 1
Current ratio (*doubtless* vs. **doubtlessly*): 41:1

doubt that; doubt whether. See **doubt** (A).

doughnut; donut. The first spelling, which is more common, is preferred because it retains the name of the main ingredient (though on this rationale it might be aptly renamed *sugarnut* or *oilnut*). *Donut*—or, worse, *do-nut*—should be reserved for eatery names and advertising.

Current ratio: 1.5:1

dour, in the best speech, rhymes with *lure*. But many people say it as if it rhymed with *sour*.

douse; dowse. These words are best kept separate. To *douse* (/dows/) is to soak with liquid, as by immersing or drenching <she immediately doused the flame with water>. To *dowse* (/dowz/) is to try to find something underground by "divining" for it, as with a divining rod that is supposed to help in locating water, oil, or buried treasure <with nothing more than a twig, they went dowsing for gold>.

Douse is sometimes misused for *dowse*—e.g.: "She walks over to a tree that stands at the edge of one circle of stones, picks up a stick that lies nearby, holds it out toward the circle like a *dousing* [read *dowsing*] rod." Rick Wilber, "Scotland's Ancient Stones Teach Students," *Tampa Trib.*, 17 Mar. 1996, Travel §, at 1.

But the opposite error, *dowse* for *douse*, is more common—e.g.:

- "[T]he next year quickly *dowsed* [read *doused*] his spirits." John Harold Plumb, *Sir Robert Walpole* 131 (1956).
- "So firefighters use tankers to shuttle water to portable tanks, which are filled with water that firefighters draw on to *dowse* [read *douse*] fires." John C. Keuhner, "Pond Solves Firefighting Problem," *Plain Dealer* (Cleveland), 25 Oct. 1995, at B1.
- "Derry firefighters, assisted by departments from four towns, *dowsed* [read *doused*] five or six burning cars with foam last night at the same junkyard where more than 100 vehicles burned five months ago." "Correction: Stacked Cars Burn," *N.H. Sunday News*, 25 Nov. 2001, at A4.

LANGUAGE-CHANGE INDEX
1. *douse* misused for *dowse*: Stage 1
Current ratio (*dowsing rod* vs. **dousing rod*): 13:1
2. *dowse* misused for *douse*: Stage 1
Current ratio (*dousing the fire* vs. **dowsing the fire*): 14:1

dove. See **dive.**

dovecote (= a small house for pigeons) is the standard spelling. **Dovecot* is a variant. The word is pronounced /**dəv**-koht/ when spelled -*cote* or /**dəv**-kot/ when spelled -*cot*.

Current ratio: 2:1

dower; dowry. These waning terms are related etymologically (fr. L. *dot-*, *dos* "gift, marriage portion") but are best kept distinct in modern usage. *Dower* = the widow's legal share during her lifetime of the real estate owned by her deceased husband. E.g.: "Even though [a wife] wasn't recorded as an owner, the fact that she was married to the owner would give her an interest in the property upon his death. It's known as the '*dower*.'" Joe Blundo, "A Question (or Several) of Title," *Columbus Dispatch*, 6 Nov. 1994, at J1.

Dowry is occasionally used as a synonym of *dower*, but doing so muddles the DIFFERENTIATION between the words. In the best usage, *dowry* denotes the money, goods, or real estate that a woman brings to her husband in marriage. E.g.:

- "The bishop would sneak into the nobleman's home at night and leave little bags of gold for the girls' *dowries*." Nancy Marlowe, "Why Does Santa Claus Come Down the Chimney?" *Asheville Citizen-Times*, 24 Dec. 1995, at C3.
- "And these Catholic nuns provide *dowries* so these girls can have Hindu weddings to Hindu husbands." Patrick Soran, "Kind Encounters," *Denver Post*, 22 Dec. 1996, Travel §, at T1.
- "The *dowry* Raylyn brought to her marriage was her mom and dad, the best mother-in-law and father-in-law a guy could ever hope to have." "Raylyn Lucille Stadler" (obit.), *Siskiyou Daily News* (Yreka, Cal.), 19 Aug. 2015, at 5.

Because the cultural practice of giving dowries is obsolescent in the West, the word itself took on an archaic flavor in the second half of the 20th century. For more on this term, see **brideprice.**

down payment. Two words, not one.

Current ratio: 18:1

downplay (= to de-emphasize), dating from the 1950s, became a VOGUE WORD after about 1985 and remains so. If a CASUALISM is desired, the PHRASAL VERB *play down* generally suffices—e.g.: "Theiss also *downplayed* [read *played down*] the importance of police groups altogether, saying many of them are 'vintage labor unions' that typically back Democrats." Marc Lacey, "Sherman Endorsed by Police Groups," *L.A. Times*, 21 Sept. 1996, at B2. Both expressions are casualisms.

LANGUAGE-CHANGE INDEX
downplay for *play down*: Stage 4
Current ratio: 3:1

downstairs, adj., as in *downstairs bathroom*, is sometimes wrongly made either **downstair* or **downstair's*. Cf. **upstairs.**

Current ratio (*downstairs rooms* vs. **downstair rooms*): 51:1

Down syndrome, named after the British physician J.R.H. Down (1828–1896), has been predominantly so written in AmE since the late 1980s and in BrE since the late 1990s. Before that, the usual form was *Down's syndrome* (the second word is never capitalized in any standard format). From 1900 to the early 1970s, *mongolism* was the standard term, but that term came increasingly to be seen as highly offensive because it named a chromosomal disorder after a race of Asian people thought to resemble those afflicted with the disease. In 1868, Down wrote the essay "The Ethnic Classification of Idiots," in which he likened various congenital conditions to ethnicities. In the end, it would take more than a century to dislodge *mongoloid, mongolism,* and *Mongolian idiocy* from the vocabulary of intellectual disabilities. In 1961, four scientists wrote to the British medical journal *The Lancet* objecting to the *M*-terms and proposing four alternatives. The editor selected *Down syndrome* (well, the possessive form of it, originally), and the rest is history.

> Current ratio (*Down syndrome* vs. *Down's syndrome*): 3:1

downward(s). See DIRECTIONAL WORDS (A).

dowry. See **dower.**

dowse. See **douse.**

doyen; doyenne. *Doyen* (/doi-**yen**/ or /**doi**-yən/) = (1) a knowledgeable person with vast experience; the senior member of a group; or (2) one of the oldest examples of something in a given category. Sense 1: "The prose style of John Kenneth Galbraith, *doyen* of the American left, is instantly recognisable both for its idiosyncratic construction, crying to be read aloud in its author's basso profundo, and for its sweeping compression of facts and ideas." Martin Vander Weyer, "The Apostle of Welfare," *Sunday Telegraph,* 22 Sept. 1996, Books §, at 13. Sense 2 often looks as if it's merely personification—e.g.: "Morgan Guaranty, the *doyen* of U.S. banks since J.P. Morgan Jr. wore short pants, remains a triple-A credit in the estimation of Standard & Poor's Corp." John W. Milligan, "How Moody's and S&P Play the Bank Rating Game," *U.S. Banker,* Aug. 1996, at 55.

Doyenne /doi-**yen**/, the feminine counterpart, occurs almost as frequently, but only in sense 1:

- "Maida Heatter—*doyenne* of desserts, queen of cookies, sultana of sweets—seems to feel that everyone, deep down, shares her passionate conviction." Suzanne Hamlin, "A Passion for Baking and Recipes That Really Deliver," *N.Y. Times,* 1 Nov. 1995, at C3.
- "Soon after the move to Twin Falls, Ben was put in touch with [Beverly] Hackney, one of the *doyennes* of Idaho's small ballet community, who hired him to teach classes in her studio." Jim Hopkins, "The Tragedy Ahead," *Idaho Statesman,* 11 Aug. 1996, at A1.

See SEXISM (D).

dozen makes two plural forms: *dozens* and *dozen.* The first is used when the number is inexact or unspecified

<dozens of geese>, the second when the count is precise <three dozen doughnuts>.

draconian; draconic. *Draconian* (the usual form) is derived from the name *Draco,* a Greek legislator of the 7th century B.C. who drafted a code of severe laws that included the death penalty for anyone caught stealing a cabbage. As the *Century Dictionary* put it, "he prescribed the penalty of death for nearly all crimes—for lesser crimes because they merited it, and for greater crimes because he knew of no penalty more severe." Today, *draconian* (sometimes but not usually capitalized) refers to any cruel or excessively severe rule or punishment, not only legislation.

Sometimes the word is the victim of SLIPSHOD EXTENSION, when applied to any rule or policy that is viewed as harsh though not really cruel—e.g.: "Phil Seelig, president of the Correction Officers Benevolent Association, said his organization would appeal the decision to the State Court of Appeals on the ground that random drug testing was unnecessarily *draconian* [read *harsh* or *burdensome*] and violated constitutional protection against unlawful searches." "Court Upholds Drug Testing of Correction Officers," *N.Y. Times,* 13 Oct. 1989, at 10.

In one of its senses, *draconic* is a NEEDLESS VARIANT of *draconian*—e.g.: "Knowing, as he must, of the unforgiving and *draconic* [read *draconian*] rules of Islamic law, he still sold this material for publication." "Did Clinton Commit Faux Pas in Meeting with Rushdie?" *San Diego Union-Trib.,* 2 Dec. 1993, at B13. But in another sense, *draconic* means "of, relating to, or like a dragon" <the child protagonist is rescued by a friendly dragon and raised with its own draconic brood>.

> LANGUAGE-CHANGE INDEX
> 1. *draconian* meaning "harsh" but without a sense of cruelty: Stage 3
> 2. *draconic* misused for *draconian*: Stage 1
> Current ratio (*draconian measures* vs. **draconic measures*): 79:1

draft; draught. Since the late 19th century, *draft* has been standard AmE in all meanings of the word. In BrE, *draught* is the usual spelling in all but the following three senses: (1) "a bank's payment order"; (2) "the compulsory enlistment of people into military service"; and (3) "an initial or preliminary version." American writers who use *draught* are likely to seem pretentious or pedantic.

The BrE form is susceptible to a strange misspelling—e.g.: "Sharee took a quick *drought* [read *draught*] of the water, using it sparingly since we had no idea how long we would be making our way underground, or how long the water supplies we found along the way would hold out." Peter David, *The Woad to Wuin* 112 (2002). (The error is not a typo—it appears repeatedly in the book.)

*draftsperson. See SEXISM (C).

LANGUAGE-CHANGE INDEX (For the full key, see front matter pp. xxxi, l–li.)
Stage 1: Rejected. **Stage 2:** Widely shunned. **Stage 3:** Widespread but . . . **Stage 4:** Ubiquitous but . . . **Stage 5:** Fully accepted.
Invariably inferior forms marked by asterisk (*). • Ratios represent frequency of prevalent forms vs. variants in current books.

drag > dragged > dragged. The past-tense and past-participial *drug* is a dialectal form common in the southern United States—e.g.: "Mazur said his father lipped the fish and *drug* it well back up on the bank so it couldn't get away." Mike Leggett, "1 Fish, 2 Fish, Red Fish, Big Fish," *Austin Am.-Statesman*, 16 Jan. 1994, at D12.

The linguistic authorities have had some negative things to say. *W2* (1934), the last of the great prescriptive dictionaries, called *drug* "dialectal" and "illiterate." More recent dictionaries, such as *RH2*, call it, more chastely, "nonstandard." The *OED* calls it obsolete except in DIALECT.

A Southerner named Charles Allen Lloyd, the well-informed author of an interesting book called *We Who Speak English* (1938), might be expected to defend the expression. But he doesn't:

> Mistakes in the formation of the past tense of irregular verbs have already been discussed, but not mentioned at that time was the fairly common use of "drug" for "dragged," for which I can find no shadow of an authority even in those dictionaries that record "dove" as a colloquial possibility for the past tense of "dive." Yet I recall a young man who had been an instructor of English in a small college narrate his experiences in the World War and tell how he "drug" a wounded foot for a mile to the dressing-station. The foot, I am glad to say, had made an excellent recovery, but his English seemed to be still suffering.
> *Ibid.* at 182.

A word now about the nature of this issue. The question, to a traditional grammarian, is whether *drag* is a regular or an irregular verb. (See IRREGULAR VERBS.) No existing grammars list *drag* among the irregular verbs.

Even the *Dictionary of American Regional English* (1991), in volume 2, lists the form *dragged* as "usual," adding that *drug* is "also frequent." One of the chief resources for that dictionary—*Dialect Notes*, a publication of the American Dialect Society—provides rich information on how the form is distributed. One writer listed *drug* as a "frequent" past tense in Nebraska, and also Massachusetts, Pennsylvania, North Carolina, Illinois, Kansas, and Tennessee. See Louise Pound, "Word-List from Nebraska (III)," 4 *Dialect Notes* 271, 274 (1913–1917). It was said to be "very common" in East Alabama and common in Kentucky, Louisiana, New Jersey, and—surprisingly—New Brunswick, Nova Scotia, and Newfoundland. Not so surprisingly, it was said to be "rare" in New York City. See B.S. Monroe & Clark S. Northup, "Some Lumber and Other Words," 2 *Dialect Notes* 394, 396 (1900–1904).

As a matter of distribution, perhaps the best summing-up is that of E. Bagby Atwood, the Texas linguist, in 1953: "*Dragged* . . . predominates among cultured informants everywhere, but it predominates among the other types only in N.Y., n. Pa., e. Va., S.C., and Ga. Elsewhere in these [noncultured] types it is more or less narrowly limited by the competing form *drug*." *Survey of Verb Forms* 9 (1953) (as quoted in the *Dictionary of American Regional English*). Whether President Bill Clinton would rank as a "cultured informant" might be a disputable point, but when he was debating Bob Dole on 16 Oct. 1996, he said: " 'Then we took

comments as we always do. And there were tens of thousands of comments about how we ought to do it. That's what *drug* [read *dragged*] it out.' " "Transcript of Second Televised Debate Between Clinton and Dole," *N.Y. Times*, 17 Oct. 1996, at B10.

> LANGUAGE-CHANGE INDEX
> *drug* as past tense and past participle of *drag*:
> Stage 1
> Current ratio (*dragged it out* vs. **drug it out*): 33:1

dragoman (= an interpreter or guide in the Near East or Middle East) has formed the standard plural *dragomans* since the mid-19th century—not **dragomen*.

> Current ratio: 3:1

dramatic; drastic. Each word is sometimes misused for the other. *Dramatic* = (1) of or like a drama; or (2) filled with action or emotion. *Drastic* = extreme in effect; severe; harsh. Sense 2 of *dramatic*, of course, is allied with the sense of *drastic*, but the two words work idiomatically with different types of subjects. Measures that a person takes—or things that a person does to remedy a serious problem—are *drastic*. If those measures work, and especially if they work well, the results may be *dramatic*.

Dramatic sometimes displaces *drastic*, especially in reference to a person's doing something dramatic to correct a bad situation—e.g.:

- "And have college administrators do one more smart thing. Let them do something *dramatic* [read *drastic*] to level the playing field so that all schools can cope with the emancipation, to wit: spread the windfalls and bonanzas around." John Underwood, "Reading, Writing and Remuneration," *N.Y. Times*, 11 Sept. 1994, § 8, at 13.
- "According to Ricardo Diaz, executive director of the city Housing Authority, something *dramatic* [read *drastic*] needed to be done." Mike Nichols, "Hitting Home: Renovation Project Transforming Hillside," *Milwaukee J. Sentinel*, 24 Aug. 1996, News §, at 1.
- "Embattled late night host Stephen Colbert went to much more *dramatic* [read *drastic*] measures to blow up the Twitter account that sparked last week's #CancelColbert social media movement." "Forget Simply Pressing Delete," *Pitt. Post-Gaz.*, 2 Apr. 2014, at C7.

Drastic, likewise, displaces *dramatic* when the reference is to *drastic results*—e.g.:

- "Each of those scenarios has been played out in California, with sometimes *drastic* [read *dramatic*] results." Douglas P. Shuit, "Federal Health Care Fight to Have Major Impact on State," *L.A. Times*, 11 Dec. 1995, at A1.
- "Obviously many Democrats had feared more *drastic* [read *dramatic*] results and heaved a sigh of relief that no greater losses had occurred." L. Douglas Wilder, "Politics in '96 Will Be a Roller-Coaster Ride," *Richmond Times-Dispatch*, 4 Feb. 1996, at F1.

See WORD-SWAPPING.

> LANGUAGE-CHANGE INDEX
> 1. *dramatic* misused for *drastic*: Stage 1
> Current ratio (*drastic measures* vs.
> **dramatic measures*): 33:1
> 2. *drastic* misused for *dramatic*: Stage 1
> Current ratio (*dramatic improvement* vs.
> **drastic improvement*): 10:1

dramaturge; dramaturg; *dramaturgist. *Dramaturge* (= [1] a playwright; or [2] a theatrical adviser) is the traditional term, the others being NEEDLESS VARIANTS. Although *dramaturge* is sometimes exactly the word needed, it's fustian when used merely as the name for an avid reader of plays. And even in sense 2, it's a EUPHEMISM that makes the position sound more grandiose—e.g.: "A *dramaturg* [read *dramaturge*] deals with the literary side of the theater by reading plays, researching their background and communicating their meaning to artists and audiences. Though the tradition developed in Europe, it has become increasingly fashionable for theaters in the United States to hire a staff *dramaturg* [read *dramaturge*]." Lawson Taitte, "What's a *Dramaturg* [read *Dramaturge*]?" *Dallas Morning News*, 25 Apr. 1993, at C1.

The spelling is that of the French etymon: *dramaturge*. Since about 1980, the *e*-less spelling *dramaturg* (also, oddly, pronounced /**drah**-mə-tərj/) has been in the ascendant. Though for the time being its frequency is greatest, it can't be recommended as the preferable spelling.

draperies; drapes. Usage critics and etiquette mavens have long preferred *draperies* over *drapes*, but both have been stamped as a lowbrow usage. The term *curtains* is perhaps the best choice. Since 1980 or so, *drapes* has appeared more frequently in print sources than *draperies*. See CLASS DISTINCTIONS.

Current ratio (*curtains* vs. *drapes* vs. *draperies*): 8:1.4:1

drastic. See **dramatic**.

draught. See **draft**.

draw. For the use of this verb in diametrically opposed senses, see CONTRONYMS.

draw on. See PHRASAL VERBS.

dreadnought (= [1] a thick wool coat; or [2] a heavily armored battleship) is the standard spelling. *Dreadnaught* is a variant. See **naught**.

Current ratio: 5:1

dream has the past-tense and past-participial forms *dreamed* and *dreamt*. For both past forms, *dreamed* is more common in AmE and BrE alike.

Current ratio: 4:1

dreck (= worthless filth) is preferably so spelled. The form *drek*, though closer to the original Yiddish spelling, is a mere variant in AmE.

Current ratio: 4:1

drier; dryer. *Drier* is the adjective meaning "more dry." *Dryer* is the appliance that dries things. The error works both ways—e.g.:

- "He also talks about killing mimes, clothes-*drier* [read *dryer*] lint and falling asleep in satellite dishes." Warren

Rhodes, "Comic Wright Thinks Deeply of Tiny Things," *Anchorage Daily News*, 4 Oct. 2002, at H5.
- " 'It wasn't any *dryer* [read *drier*] for them,' said Venia, who refused to use the weather as an excuse." Rick Jakacki, "Second-Half Struggles Cost Vikings, Again," *Times Herald* (Port Huron, Mich.), 5 Oct. 2002, at C1.

See **dry**.

LANGUAGE-CHANGE INDEX
1. *dryer* misused as a comparative adjective (for *drier*): Stage 2
Current ratio (*drier climate* vs. *dryer climate*): 9:1
2. *drier* misused for the noun *dryer*: Stage 3
Current ratio (*clothes-dryer* vs. *clothes-drier*): 4:1

drift. For the use of this word in opposite senses, see CONTRONYMS.

drink > drank > drunk. So inflected. The past participle surprises some people <have you drunk your milk?> because they associate *drunk* with "inebriated." And for this reason, no doubt, *drank* has encroached on the past-participial *drunk*—e.g.:

- "Jabil Circuit offered free cab rides home to any of its employees who might have *drank* [read *drunk*] too many toasts." Teresa Burney, "Spoils of the Holiday Season," *St. Petersburg Times*, 21 Dec. 1997, at H1.
- "The rest of the beer was *drank* [read *drunk*] by construction workers the day after the crash-landing." Yoji Cole & Judd Slivka, "Swayze Rescuers May Face Charges," *Ariz. Republic*, 14 June 2000, at A1.
- "On Good Friday the popular nightclub's image was scarred as Luther Casteel of Elgin, who had *drank* [read *drunk*] at the bar earlier wearing a suit, returned sporting a mohawk, wearing camouflage and toting four guns, according to the police." Terri Tabor, "JB's Owner Pledges to Reopen," *Daily Herald* (Chicago), 21 Apr. 2001, at 9.

See IRREGULAR VERBS & DIALECT.

LANGUAGE-CHANGE INDEX
1. *drank* as past participle of *drink*: Stage 2
Current ratio (*has drunk* vs. *has drank*): 12:1
2. *drunk* as simple past of *drink*: Stage 1
Current ratio (*he drank* vs. *he drunk*): 32:1

drink-driving. See **drunk driving**.

drive. A. Inflected Forms: *drive > drove > driven*. *Drived* (for *drove*) seems to have become standard in some sports terms. In baseball, PHRASAL VERBS made from nouns that are in turn derived from strong verbs are often weakened to -*ed* forms, as when *fly out* becomes *flied out*—the only instance in which *flied* (instead of *flew*) is correctly used as a past tense. And the same thing has happened with *line-drive* (which has invaded the lingo of other sports). For many writers and editors, some other phrasing is usually preferable—e.g.:

- "Skates crunched across the ThunderDome ice. Pucks *line-drived* [read *ricocheted*] off the fence." Hubert Mizell, "Strike Looms but Passion to Play Burns," *St. Petersburg Times*, 22 Sept. 1994, at C1.

- "After three incompletions, Harmon *line-drived his attempt* [read *kicked a line drive*] wide left." Elliot Tannenbaum, "Kutztown Avoids Tie on Missed Field Goal," *Reading Eagle* (Pa.), 2 Oct. 1994, at D10.
- "A second remained when Zendejas *line-drived it* [read *kicked a line drive*] at Spellman, who came up the middle and didn't even need to jump." "Bits 'n' Pieces," *Press-Enterprise* (Riverside, Cal.), 19 Dec. 1994, at D6.

Though uncommon, the word *drived* as an ordinary past-tense verb—a mistake for *drove*—is not unheard of: "Only Chaffin, who also *drived* [read *drove*] a 1995 Ford Thunderbird, and Buford, have won the Late Model events in the fifth week of running." Charles Searcy, "Buford Wins in His Return," *Tennessean*, 30 Apr. 1995, at C3.

More common is the erroneous **drived* as a past participle displacing *driven*—e.g.:

- "He threw away the baton and then jumped in a getaway car *drived* [read *driven*] by Smith." John Painter & Bill MacKenzie, "Affidavit Says Stant Stalked Kerrigan," *Oregonian* (Portland), 20 Jan. 1994, at A1.
- "At the Fallowfield Road intersection the van hit the vehicle *drived* [read *driven*] by Joshua's grandmother, moments after it narrowly avoided colliding with another vehicle which was forced off the road." Mark Richardson, "Teen Pleads Guilty in Boy's Crash Death," *Ottawa Citizen*, 5 Oct. 1994, at B1.
- "There are reports of a single-electrode microfluidic electrochemical sensor *drived* [read *driven*] by capillary force." "Patent Application Titled 'Integrated Type Microfluidic Electrochemical Biosensor System and Method for Rapid Biochemical Analysis' Published Online," *Biotech Week*, 24 June 2015, at 1249.

LANGUAGE-CHANGE INDEX
1. **drived* for the simple-past *drove*: Stage 1
Current ratio (*drove a* vs. **drived a*): 21,809:1
2. **drived* for the past-participial *driven*: Stage 1
Current ratio (*driven by* vs. **drived by*): 15,905:1

B. Dialectal Variants. There are two dialectal past-tense forms—**driv* (surviving in the southern U.S. and New England) and **druv* (occurring mostly in Kentucky). It would surely be no loss if they were driven into extinction.

drivel, vb., makes *driveled* and *driveling* in AmE, *drivelled* and *drivelling* in BrE. See SPELLING (B).

driver's license. So written (or *driver's licence* in BrE)—not **drivers license*, **drivers' license*, or **driver license*, no matter what the card in your wallet may tell you. The predominant plural is *driver's licenses*, not **drivers' licenses*.

droll (= amusing; humorous; whimsical) is so spelled, even though the French word it comes from is *drôle*. That spelling better matched the word's pronunciation (/drohl/, not to rhyme with *doll*), but the word has been spelled *droll* in English since the early 17th century. Today **drole* (in English) can be regarded only as a misspelling. E.g.: "Finally, Gail Collins's *drole* [read *droll*] prediction about the same contest: 'It looks now as if the race will be won by the candidate with the largest immediate family.'" Richard Goldstein, "Primary Rib," *Village Voice*, 20 Sept. 1994, at 9.

The word always means "funny" in one sense or another. Most commonly, it means "witty, esp. in an offbeat way"—e.g.: "A diminutive Southerner with *droll* wit and a childlike voice, Capote was the toast of the New York society party circuit in the 1960s even while becoming one of America's most famous writers." Eric Harrison, "'Infamous,' Indeed," *Houston Chron.*, 15 Oct. 2006, Zest §, at 14.

Far less often, it's used to mean unintentionally funny, even ludicrous—e.g.: "How *droll* and obtuse that conservatives think the Constitution should remain anchored against the tides of change while those currents bring with them torrents of newfangled iPods and ever-changing gusts of news; one day about Britney Spears, the next day Paris Hilton." Jonah Goldberg, "Living Constitution's Double Standard," *Chicago Trib.*, 25 Aug. 2006, Commentary §, at 27.

Perhaps because the words look and sound a bit similar, *droll* is sometimes misused as a synonym for *dull*. The result is a startling MALAPROPISM—e.g.: "The local recruiting firm Accounting One created the stand-up comedy contest last year to try to show a lighter side to the profession saddled with a *droll* [read *dull*] image." Mike Tierney, "Bottom Line: It's OK to Laugh at Accountants," *Atlanta J.-Const.*, 15 Oct. 2006, Bus. §, at C3.

LANGUAGE-CHANGE INDEX
droll misused for *dull*: Stage 1

drone; drudge. *Drone* = (1) a male bee; (2) an idler living off others' work; (3) an unmanned aircraft or watercraft; or (4) a monotonous tone or buzzing. *Drudge* = (1) one whose work is menial or boring; or (2) drudgery. Surprisingly (since a drone bee does no work), *drone* is increasingly used as a synonym of *drudge*—e.g.: "The first act chronicles dystopian rebel Winston Smith's witheringly dull life as a *drone* [read *drudge*] in a government records office, where the drudgery involves creating a historical reality based on the whims of the ruling party." Peter Marks, "1984," *Wash. Post*, 5 Sept. 2008, Weekend §, at WE41. This trend is worth resisting because it may create a CONTRONYM—that is, this use of *drone* is a near-antonym of the traditional sense 2.

LANGUAGE-CHANGE INDEX
drone in the sense "drudge": Stage 2

drought; **drouth*; **drout*. *Drought* has been the predominant, standard form of the word in all phases of Modern English. **Drouth* is archaic in BrE but still occasionally appears in AmE texts. Even so, *drought* (pronounced /drowt/, not /drowth/ or /drawt/) is the preferred form in both linguistic communities. The simplified spelling **drout*, though toyed with in the mid-20th century, never took hold.

Misusing *drought* for *flood* is perhaps just an odd mental glitch triggered by *drown*—e.g.: "Spring is a time of heightened concern about *drought* [read *flooding*]. In a typical year, melting snowpacks can conspire with increased rainfall to send rivers over their banks. Sometimes in northern areas, ice jams exacerbate the floods on swollen rivers. This year, spring flooding is less likely than normal." "Weather Report," *N.Y. Times*, 15 Mar. 1995, at A9. For another misuse—*drought* for the BrE *draught*—see **draft.**

LANGUAGE-CHANGE INDEX
drought misused for *flooding*: Stage 1
Current ratio (*drought* vs. *drouth vs. *drout): 7,423:112:1

drove, vb. See **drive.**

drown. A. *Drowned* and *drownded. The past-tense form is *drowned*, not *drownded—the latter being dialectal. E.g.: "True, [the flooding] helped duck and geese populations, but it also *drownded* [read *drowned*] millions of other living creatures who weren't favored targets." "Hunters Are Not Really a Tool of Nature," *Buffalo News*, 14 Feb. 1993, at 8. (See IRREGULAR VERBS (D).) The dialectal form appears in the speech of uneducated characters in the works of Dickens, Kipling, and Twain.

Sometimes the correct form is made to establish a more severe, unsympathetic character, as here: "The Drownded Uncles, the children called them. 'Drowned,' Marion corrected. Marion was forever improving anyone who could be improved. 'The Drownded Uncles of Skipper Sid,' the kids would say anyway. 'The Drownded Brothers of Skipper Sid,' Marion would correct them again. Drowned, she meant, not drownded. They were mixing her up." Dawn Rae Downton, *Seldom: A Memoir* 132 (2002).

LANGUAGE-CHANGE INDEX
*drownded as past tense of *drown*: Stage 1
Current ratio (*drowned* vs. *drownded): 106:1

B. *Drowned*; *was drowned*. In the best usage, if somebody *drowned* it was an accident, but if somebody *was drowned* foul play was involved.

drudge. See **drone.**

drug, vb. See **drag.**

drunk, adj.; **drunken.** Traditionally, *drunk* has been an adjective appearing in the predicate <they were drunk>, whereas *drunken* has preceded the noun <a drunken sailor>. Today, the words mostly bear distinct senses. *Drunk* = intoxicated, inebriated. *Drunken* = given to drink; morbidly alcoholic.

So *drunken* usually denotes a habitual state—e.g.: "Molly Ringwald stars as a waitress with a *drunken* buffoon of a father and a churchgoing mother she calls 'Ma.'" Ginia Bellafante, "New (and Not) for '96," *Time*, 23 Sept. 1996, at 70. This nuance is slightly counterintuitive, given that *a drunk* refers to someone who is habitually drunk. Although *drunken* sometimes means merely "exhibiting intoxication,"

the better term for this meaning is *drunk*—e.g.: "A confidential computer disk containing the names of 4,000 AIDS patients was mailed anonymously to a newspaper after a *drunken* [read *drunk*] public health worker showed it to friends and dropped it outside a bar." "Briefly," *Commercial Appeal* (Memphis), 20 Sept. 1996, at A2.

Drunken also frequently describes not a person or group of people, but their *brawl*, *orgy*, or *party*, through HYPALLAGE—e.g.: "She agreed not to speak ill of Astra, which has been embroiled in a scandal since tawdry tales of *drunken* company parties and fraternity-party behavior were made public earlier this year." Beth Healy, "Judge Deals Setback to Ex-Astra Worker," *Boston Herald*, 21 Sept. 1996, at 15.

drunk driving; *drunken driving; drink-driving. The first is the predominant phrase in both AmE and BrE. The second was the usual phrase from the 1920s to about 1980; it fell out of use perhaps primarily because *drunken* connotes a greater level of intoxication than *drunk*, and by the 1980s methods were being developed to determine with greater precision a person's blood alcohol content. The standard term today—*drunk driving*—exemplifies HYPALLAGE because it is the driver, not the driving, that is drunk. To American eyes, though, the BrE variant, *drink-driving*, looks extremely odd—e.g.: "A London public health watchdog yesterday demanded a cut in the *drink-driving* limit as they revealed the £20bn a year cost of accidents in the capital." James Meikle, "Drink-Drive Limit 'Must Be Cut,'" *Guardian*, 11 Oct. 2002, at 14.

The phrase *driving drunk* is a convenient and universal equivalent, in which *drunk* functions as an adverb (in place of whatever adverbial phrase the local statutes use, e.g., *driving while intoxicated* or *driving under the influence*). When the verb *drive* becomes a gerund <he was arrested for driving drunk> and therefore requires an adjective rather than an adverb, *drunk driving* provides a neat shorthand.

Current ratio (in order of headwords): 7:2:1

drunken. See **drunk.**

dry, adj., makes *drier* and *driest*—not *dryer and *dryest. Oddly, however, *dryly* is preferred over *drily. See **drier.**

Current ratio (*driest* vs. *dryest): 12:1
Current ratio (*dryly* vs. *drily): 3:1

dryer. See **drier.**

d.t.'s. See **delirium tremens.**

dual (= double; twofold) is sometimes misspelled *duel*—e.g.:

- "The refinements . . . include a modified cam and carburetor, higher compression ratio, larger valves and *duel*

LANGUAGE-CHANGE INDEX (For the full key, see front matter pp. xxxi, l–li.)
Stage 1: Rejected. **Stage 2:** Widely shunned. **Stage 3:** Widespread but . . . **Stage 4:** Ubiquitous but . . . **Stage 5:** Fully accepted.
Invariably inferior forms marked by asterisk (*). • Ratios represent frequency of prevalent forms vs. variants in current books.

[read *dual*] exhausts to trumpet the sound and strength." Marshall Schuon, "About Cars: A New Model That Can Put the Fun Back in Driving," *N.Y. Times*, 28 Dec. 1980, § 5, at 11.

- "Having satisfied the *duel* [read *dual*] purposes of his marriage, siring a legitimate heir and settling his debts, George announced to Caroline a formal separation." Michael Farquhar, "Love Stinks: Some Matches Are Made in Heaven. Some, in Hell," *Wash. Post*, 11 Feb. 1996, at F1.

Of course, *duel* is a noun that originally meant "a formal combat between two people, fought with weapons, under an accepted code of procedure, and in the presence of witnesses." Today, however, because the practice that it denotes has fallen into disuse, the term *duel* has extended its sense to refer to any contest between two opponents.

LANGUAGE-CHANGE INDEX
duel misused for *dual*: Stage 1
Current ratio (*dual nature* vs. *duel nature): 259:1

dubious = (1) causing uncertainty <his credentials were dubious>; or (2) doubting <we are dubious about whether we'll be able to attend>. Although sense 2 has occasionally been criticized, it is now in good use.

dubious distinction has the dubious distinction of being one of our most overworked expressions.

Dubya. The quintessentially Texas pronunciation of the letter *W* took on national and international significance in 2001, when the son of the 41st U.S. president took the oath of office as the 43rd. The problem was that both men's names are confusingly similar: George Herbert Walker Bush, the father, and George Walker Bush, the son. Since their names are not identical, they are not technically Sr. and Jr. (see NAMES (B).) *Elder* and *younger* has precedent (the two Plinys and the two U.S. Supreme Court Justices Harlan), but it's awkward. Within their family, father and son have been known to go by *41* and *43*. Popularly, and in the press, they came to be distinguished as George Bush and George W. Bush.

That convention had a historical antecedent: the country's second president was John Adams and its sixth was Adams's son, John Quincy Adams. The latter was always distinguished from the former by his middle name.

In the end, though, it was a nickname based on the son's middle initial that served to distinguish the son. That was appropriate, since the affable George W. had a knack for giving other people nicknames. So he became *Dubya*. Both the idiosyncratic pronunciation and the spelling became standard quickly. Not only was it a convenient way to distinguish the two presidents, but it was also acceptable to Dubya's friends and foes alike. To supporters it connoted Bush's down-home personality; to opponents it ridiculed his Texas roots and (through its association with DIALECT) a perceived lack of intelligence.

The term has always been favored more by Bush's opponents than by his supporters. For example, it appears in the title of the left-wing British satire *The Madness of George Dubya* (2003), taking off, of course, on the title of the play *The Madness of George III*. And there was the unflattering 2008 movie *Dubya*.

Dictionaries vary greatly about what pronunciations of the letter *W* they sanction. *W2* and the *NOAD*, for example, give only one: /dəb-əl-yoo/ (like *double you*). *W3* also recognizes /dəb-lyə/ and, "in rapid speech," /də-b[ə]yə/ or even /də-byee/. *Dubya* is mostly Southern dialect and is especially common in Bush's home state of Texas.

duct tape. So spelled—not *duck tape, whether that was its original name or not.

On 10 February 2003, the U.S. Department of Homeland Security declared a "level-orange" terrorism alert and advised people to stock up on plastic sheeting and duct tape. Soon after, William Safire of *The New York Times* firmly declared that *duck tape was the original form, dating from World War II when Johnson & Johnson developed the material for the U.S. Army to waterproof ammunition cases. He cited two wartime ads, one for Venetian blinds "in cream with cream tape or white with *duck tape*," and another for surplus "cotton *duck tape*."

Phooey! fired back Jan Freeman of *The Boston Globe* the following week. First, who uses duct tape on Venetian blinds? Second, cotton duck tape is more likely cotton duck fabric in tape form. Third, why hasn't Paul Dickson, author of *War Slang*, ever heard soldiers mention *duck tape? For that matter, why do Tim Nyberg and Jim Berg—who have written five books on the tape's many uses and have been promoting the Army *duck tape story for years—call themselves "the Duct Tape Guys"?

The fact is that *duct tape* is over 60 times as common in print as *duck tape, and that is unquestionably the standard spelling.

One writer explains the origin of the misuse: "Duct tape is so seldom used on heating ducts that most people mispronounce it 'duck tape' as they use it to mend parkas and sheath short cables. I came close to using it on a duct once." Ed Quillen, "It Even Works for Hanging Pipes," *Denver Post*, 20 Feb. 1994, at E3. But the fact that people don't really associate the tape with ducts does not explain the error (after all, who associates the tape with ducks, either?). Instead, it is the side-by-side *t* sounds that are to blame: it's unnatural to separate them in speech, and it's a natural error to spell the phrase as it sounds. And the misuse is common—e.g.:

- "Their tactic is then to put the metal back in place with *duck tape* [read *duct tape*], and disguise the cut with paint." John Dillin, "Two U.S. Approaches to Mexico?" *Christian Science Monitor*, 18 Oct. 1993, at 4.
- "They brought insect repellent, wore head nets and, following the sage advice of yours truly, sealed their cuffs, leg bottoms and waist with *duck tape* [read *duct tape*]." Dick Nelson, "Oh, Those Pesky Black Flies," *Times Union* (Albany), 19 June 1994, at D13.

• "With all the technology available these days in motorsports, rubber hammers and *duck tape* [read *duct tape*] did as much as anything to piece Gordon's car back together." David Scott, "Jeff Gordon Suffers His Worst Day at Indy," *Charlotte Observer*, 26 July 2015, at 347.

One company, Henkel Consumer Adhesives, owns the trademark on "Duck Tape," and that brand name surely aggravates the confusion. As Safire pointed out, the *Times* article reporting the Homeland Security alert was accompanied by a picture of two rolls of "Duck Tape." The difference is that *duct tape* is the generic name for the material—a common noun that is always lowercase. *Duck Tape* is a mildly fanciful brand name—a proper noun that is always capitalized and properly used only as an adjective, as in "Duck Tape brand duct tape" (or, more likely, "Duck Tape brand adhesive"). Keeping the terms distinct is vital to maintaining trademark protection, so even on the company's website one will find the accepted generic spelling: "Tell us your duct tape Real Story!" <www.ducktapeclub.com>.

LANGUAGE-CHANGE INDEX
duck tape for *duct tape*: Stage 2
Current ratio (*duct tape* vs. **duck tape*): 66:1

dudgeon (= anger, resentment, indignation) is sometimes confused with *dungeon*—e.g.:

• "Lately the voyeurs and Phil Donohue viewers are in high *dungeon* [read *dudgeon*] about revelations about Bruce Benson's personal life." Letter of Brian Wareing, "Benson's Personal Problems Pale in Comparison to Romer's Impersonal Misdeeds," *Rocky Mountain News* (Denver), 18 Oct. 1994, at A31.
• "Assaulting Clinton's 'character' with the rhetoric of dishonesty and immorality is reminiscent of the high *dungeon* [read *dudgeon*] inspired among socially right people by the 'treachery' of Franklin D. Roosevelt and John F. Kennedy." Scott Aiken, "Rhetoric Aside, Bob and Bill Are Alike," *Cincinnati Bus. Courier*, 28 Oct. 1996.

Although the term appears most often after the adjective *high*, it does sometimes appear without it—e.g.:

• "Because they are nursing their *dudgeon* and savouring their victories rather than thinking with care, antismokers believe themselves to be upholding liberal social principles when in fact they are traducing them." "Blowing Smoke," *Economist*, 20 Dec. 1997, at 59.
• "From the media's spluttering *dudgeon*, an innocent bystander would have thought Blumenthal was the reincarnation of William Allen White." Jeff Jacoby, "Sid Blumenthal, the Reporter's Friend?" *Boston Globe*, 3 Mar. 1998, at A11.

LANGUAGE-CHANGE INDEX
*high dungeon for *high dudgeon*: Stage 1
Current ratio (*high dudgeon* vs. **high dungeon*): 81:1

duel, vb., makes *dueled* and *dueling* in AmE, *duelled* and *duelling* in BrE. Likewise *duelist* predominates in AmE, *duellist* in BrE. See SPELLING (B) & **dual.**

due to. The traditional view is that *due to* should be restricted to adjectival uses in the sense "attributable to," usually following the verb *to be* (sometimes understood in context). But the stylist may wish to avoid even correct uses of the phrase, which one writer calls a "graceless phrase, even when used correctly," adding, "Avoid it altogether." Lucile V. Payne, *The Lively Art of Writing* 148 (1965). Under that view, *due to* is a SKUNKED TERM.

Despite the traditional view that the adjectival use is best (*due* being equivalent to *attributable*), the phrase is commonly used as a preposition or conjunctive adverb meaning *because of, owing to, caused by,* or *on grounds of*—e.g.:

• "*Due to* [read *Because of*] a mistake in Lincoln-Mercury's press material, which we didn't notice until we read Nissan's press material, the maximum cargo room listed for the Villager in our 1992 review was incorrect." Tom Incantalupo, "Road Test: Nissan Quest," *Newsday* (N.Y.), 16 Sept. 1994, at A63.
• "Viewers were supposed to care about characters they knew little about and, *due to* [read *owing to*] expense and logistics, the adventures were limited to gimmicks and dialogue on the sub's bridge." Paul Lomartire, "'Seaquest' Charts Course to Florida," *Palm Beach Post*, 17 Sept. 1994, at D1. See **owing to.**
• "Color fading is when pigments degrade *due to* [read *because of*] ultraviolet ray exposure." Rosie Romero, "Why Arizona Houses Aren't Like Houses Anywhere Else," *Ariz. Republic*, 22 Aug. 2015, at H1.

Two studies reported in 1962 found that as a matter of word frequency in edited text, *because of* appeared 62% of the time, *due to* 30%, and *owing to* 8%. See Margaret M. Bryant, *Current English Usage* 81 (1962).

Sometimes the examples of *due to* are somewhat comical—e.g.: "Only the likes of Trigger and C'Lock can expect to compete with the big boys *due to* superior graphical interfaces and good quality, unique content." "Your Friendly Global Medium," *New Media Age*, 19 Sept. 1996, at 6. We all know what babies are due to. But what are big boys due to? The reader might momentarily wonder. New media age indeed!

In the following examples, the phrase is used in the traditionally preferred way. But as Payne notes, the sentences might be improved by eliminating it—e.g.:

• "Trend reports show that pants are expected to be at the core of women's fall wardrobes. This shift is *due to* increasingly casual office dress codes." "A Leg Up," *Sunday Advocate* (Baton Rouge), 11 Sept. 1994, People §, at 4. (A possible revision: *This shift has resulted from increasingly casual office dress codes. Or: Why? Office dress codes have become increasingly casual.*)
• "The widening of the gap was *due* largely *to* the increase in black-female-headed families." "Black Families Now Earn Even Less than Whites, Census Says," *Virginian-Pilot* (Norfolk), 16 Sept. 1994, at A12. (A possible revision: *The gap has widened largely because of the increase in the number of families headed by black females.*)

LANGUAGE-CHANGE INDEX (For the full key, see front matter pp. xxxi, l–li.)
Stage 1: Rejected. **Stage 2:** Widely shunned. **Stage 3:** Widespread but . . . **Stage 4:** Ubiquitous but . . . **Stage 5:** Fully accepted.
Invariably inferior forms marked by asterisk (*). • Ratios represent frequency of prevalent forms vs. variants in current books.

- "One key reason that rigs are still running at all in the United States is *due to* the resilience of the service sector." Don Briggs, "Current Downturn May Be New Normal," *Alexandria Daily Town Talk* (La.), 22 Aug. 2015, at A4. (A possible revision: *The U.S. rigs' continued operation is due in large part to the resilience of the service sector. Or: The service sector's resilience is partly responsible for U.S. rigs' continued operation.*)

Due followed by an infinitive is not a form of the phrase *due to,* although it looks deceptively similar. E.g.:

- "Polk commissioners are *due to reconvene* this morning to narrow the field of eight finalists who were interviewed Wednesday and Thursday." Jerry Fallstrom, "Wahl Waits for Word from Polk," *Orlando Sentinel,* 16 Sept. 1994, at 1.
- "A last-ditch round of the so-called 'framework' talks is *due to open* in Washington later today." Jonathan Annells, "Hurd Rallies Japan to Free Trade Cause," *Evening Standard,* 19 Sept. 1994, at 37.
- "The 49-year-old was *due to marry* his fiancée Hana Chochrunova on March 9 this year." Joanne Sweeney, "The Co Antrim Man Walking 900 Miles in 30 Days in Memory of the Beloved Uncle He Lost to Cancer," *Belfast Telegraph,* 22 Aug. 2015, at 17.

LANGUAGE-CHANGE INDEX
due to misused for *because of* or *owing to*: Stage 4

due to the fact that, common in speech, can almost always be boiled down to *because*—e.g.:

- "They don't work, in no small part *due to the fact that* [read *because*] Sara appears to have abandoned acting and is content merely to look pretty." John Scalzi, "Van Damme's New Film Kicks," *Fresno Bee,* 16 Sept. 1994, at F3.
- "Even if theory and data were perfect, there might be less than a perfect correlation *due to the fact that* [read *because*] exogenous variables can always intervene." Llewellyn D. Howell & Brad Chaddick, "Models of Political Risk for Foreign Investment and Trade," 29 *Columbia J. World Bus.* 70 (1994).
- "Some exhibitors are not increasing the size of their booths, *due partly to the fact that* [read *partly because*] several other regional and international travel markets are being held between next month and November." Agnes Wee, "Interactive Kiosks for Asia Travel Market," *Bus. Times,* 30 Aug. 1996, at 4.

For more about this phrase, see **because (D).**

duffel, the preferred spelling for the bag, is an eponymous term deriving from the city of Duffel, Belgium. But because the *-el* spelling departs from analogous terms spelled *-le*—such as *muffle, scuffle, shuffle,* and also those such as *baffle, hassle, tussle*—the word is frequently misspelled **duffle.* (Mussels, the crustaceans, are exceptional.)

From the 1930s (when the bag first became popular) to the 1970s, the two spellings vied closely for predominance. Not until about 1980 was *duffel bag* unquestionably standard. The less usual spelling, which is about 20% as common as *duffel* in modern print sources, still occurs in some well-edited newspapers—e.g.:

- "Across the street from Gypsy Me is Cedar Key Canvas, with a large seaman's *duffle* [read *duffel*] bag for $57." Dale Koppel, "Old-Timey Cedar Key: Easy Street," *Sun-Sentinel* (Ft. Lauderdale), 22 Oct. 1995, at J6.
- "The drugs were found tightly bound and wrapped in 187 kilo-sized bundles, stuffed in six *duffle* [read *duffel*] bags." "Troopers Stop Cars and Find *Duffle* [read *Duffel*] Bags Full of Cocaine," *N.Y. Times,* 26 Oct. 1995, at B4.

LANGUAGE-CHANGE INDEX
duffel misspelled **duffle*: Stage 3
Current ratio: 3:1

du jour (= of the day) is a GALLICISM that has been used with menu items since the late 1960s <soup du jour>. Now it has become voguish in the sense "voguish." It is the phrase du jour—e.g.:

- "Drugs will always be a problem, city vice squad boss John McCormick said in the 1970s, when smack was the scourge *du jour* [read *of the day*]." Bill Foley, "Drug War Proves to Be No Walkover," *Fla. Times-Union,* 11 Nov. 1996, at A5.
- "Into this category fall the other *stories du jour* [read *trendy stories*] that command our attention and disdain simultaneously, and in equal measure: Paula Jones, Kelly Flynn, Whitewater, campaign finance and, as ever, anything about the Kennedys." Asta Bowen, "As Consumers of Information, We'd Rather Be Titillated than Satisfied," *Seattle Post-Intelligencer,* 17 July 1997, at A13.
- "Yesterday's top news may disappear into a black hole as the media spotlight rushes to the next *topic du jour* [read *hot topic*]." "Loyalty and Realpolitik," *Christian Science Monitor,* 30 Mar. 1998, at 12.

Even if those uses are borderline, there can be no doubt that coupling *du jour* with *today* is over the line—e.g.: "The issue *du jour today* [read *of the day*] was welfare, which meant that Mr. Alexander added a few paragraphs on the subject to his standard speech." David E. Rosenbaum, "New England Finds G.O.P. Trying Out New Tactics," *N.Y. Times,* 15 Feb. 1996, at B15. This redundant phrasing seems to have begun in American restaurants, where it is not uncommon to hear servers say, "Our soup *du jour today* [or even *our soup du jour of the day!*] is chicken noodle." See REDUNDANCY.

The phrase is often mistakenly written **de jour*—e.g.:

- "But she passed it up, along with the soup *de jour* [read *du jour*] and other sandwich and salad selections." Karen Hayes, "Catered Approach to Town Meetings," *Boston Globe,* 22 Mar. 1998, South Weekly §, at 1.
- "The soup *de jour* [read *du jour*] features such varieties as collard green or garbanzo bean." Carol Jeffares Hedman, "Easter Meals Served Up with a View," *Tampa Trib.,* 20 Apr. 2000, Fla. §, at 8.
- "The Bengals are the team *de jour* [read *du jour*] in the NFL." Mark Curnutte, "Rushing Defense a Concern," *Cincinnati Enquirer,* 20 Sept. 2005, at C1.

*De jour could become the great misspelling of our day.

In French, by the way, *du* is a sort of contraction for *de le* in the same way that *au* is for *á le. Du* and *au* are used only with masculine nouns such as *jour.* So although it's possible that the mistaken **de jour* results from rusty knowledge of French grammar, more likely it results from Americans' general ignorance of foreign tongues.

LANGUAGE-CHANGE INDEX
du jour misspelled *de jour: Stage 2
Current ratio: 6:1

dullness; *dulness. Although *dulness predominated in print (both AmE and BrE) from the 18th century through the early 20th, *dullness* experienced an exciting surge in the first two decades of the 20th century and had established itself as the standard form by the 1920s.

Current ratio: 2:1

duly authorized. Because *authorize* denotes the giving of actual or official power, *duly* (i.e., "properly") is usually unnecessary in the expression *duly authorized*. Likewise, *duly* is almost always redundant in phrases such as *duly signed*.

dumb = (1) unable to speak; or (2) stupid. Although sense 1, the traditional usage, has long been considered preferable <deaf and dumb>, sense 2 has predominated in such a way as to make the term a disparaging one. Today, *mute* is the generally preferred term for someone who cannot speak. The origin of using *dumb* to mean "stupid" is invidious. In law, a person who was mute (and usually deaf, too) was automatically deemed an idiot (not my word—it can be found in scholarly texts). The usage is centuries old.

dumbfounded is the standard spelling. *Dumfounded is a variant that enjoyed some popularity in AmE about 1890 to 1910, but it has waned.

Current ratio: 8:1

duodenum is pronounced either /doo-oh-**dee**-nəm/ or /doo-**wod**-ə-nəm/.

duologue. See **dialogue.**

duplex (= a house divided into two parts so that it has two separate homes in it) forms the plural *duplexes*.

duplicate, adj.; **duplicative; *duplicatory; duplicitous.** *Duplicate* = (1) being identical to another ; or (2) existing in identical or corresponding parts or versions . *Duplicative* = unnecessarily doubled or repeated. (*Duplicatory is a NEEDLESS VARIANT of *duplicative*.) *Duplicitous* (= marked by duplicity) is a late-19th-century coinage generally understood to denote the two-faced taking of inconsistent positions, and therefore carries the meaning "deceitful."

American and British legal writers have latched onto the word *duplicitous* in the sense of doubleness, from the old legal meaning of *duplicity* (= double pleading). A nonlawyer might be confused by the following uses of the word—as suggested, in the last two examples, by quotation marks around *duplicitous* (mistranslated in the next-to-last example):

- "An information charging a conspiracy to commit burglary is not *duplicitous* because it alleges that the conspiracy was to commit two or more different burglaries." *Hamilton v. People*, 51 P. 425, 425 syl. 4 (Colo. 1897). (The specimen just quoted antedates the earliest known use [1928] given in *W11*.)
- "The allegation in a single count of a conspiracy to commit several crimes is not *duplicitous*." *Braverman v. U.S.*, 317 U.S. 49, 54 (1942).
- "The State Court of Appeals ruled that the indictment used to obtain his 1986 conviction was '*duplicitous*,' or not specific enough." "Prosecutor Won't Seek New Abuse Charges," *N.Y. Times*, 21 Sept. 1989, at B11.
- "Attorney Michael McDermott, who is representing Officer Gregory Haffensteiner, contends the official misconduct count in the indictment is '*duplicitous*' because it lumps the charges against the men together instead of charging the officers individually." Paul Nelson, "Schenectady Cops Seek Dismissal of Charges," *Times Union* (Albany), 12 Nov. 2008, at D6.

Current ratio (*duplicative* vs. *duplicatory): 162:1

during such time as is verbose for *while*. The phrase typifies LEGALESE.

during the course of is almost always verbose for *during*.

durst. See **dare** (E).

dust. For the use of this verb in opposite senses, see CONTRONYMS.

Dutch. See **Netherlands** (A).

dutiful; *duteous. The usual term is *dutiful*. Although formerly in good use, *duteous is an archaic NEEDLESS VARIANT.

Current ratio: 31:1

DVD. When this advancement in optical-disc technology hit the market in 1997, the letters stood for *digital video disc* as surely as CD stood for *compact disc*. It was originally called that because the discs were primarily used for playing movies. But the medium soon proved to have so many other uses—such as games, computer software, and data storage—that the industry soon retrofitted the *DVD* abbreviation with a new name, *digital versatile disc*. That was so obviously contrived that today industry insiders agree that the letters stand for nothing. The public, on the other hand, still clings to the original name as well as its contorted offspring—e.g.:

- "Using DVDs for personal use is tricky because the powers-that-be are battling to make their versions of the *digital versatile disc* the universal standard." Chris Seper, "Picking the Best: DVD Format," *Plain Dealer* (Cleveland), 9 Dec. 2002, at E2.
- "Agents on Monday seized 35,000 compact discs, 10,000 digital video discs (DVDs) and 156 CD burners with the capacity to copy compact discs 40 times faster than the standard CD burners available on personal computers."

William Glanz, "Seizure in Music Piracy Is Largest," *Wash. Times*, 12 Dec. 2002, at C7.

As in those two examples, the plural doesn't need an apostrophe. See PLURALS (I). See also **videodisc**.

The letters can easily stand alone because they are almost universally recognizable: the DVD boom has been the most successful consumer-electronics start-up in history. *DVD* is used far more often than either full phrase. But *digital video* now exists as a consumer-electronics field of its own, so the original term for the medium will probably persist.

DVD isn't the only well-known abbreviation that has been declared a mere assemblage of letters, and this isn't the first time the public has ignored the declaration and gone merrily on its way with the old usage. See **SAT**; see also **GOP**.

dwarf. Pl. *dwarfs.* The form **dwarves,* a variant form, occasionally appears—e.g.:

- "The sculptors of Benin long have made their finest objects—their regal heads and life-size *dwarves* [read *dwarfs*], their animals and birds and ceremonial swords—out of molten brass." Joseph McLellan et al., "Here & Now," *Wash. Post*, 25 Sept. 1994, at G3.
- "In this case, Alvio Renzini, of the European Southern Observatory, and a team of eight colleagues have investigated white *dwarves* [read *dwarfs*] (old stars in which nuclear fusion is at an end) in a globular cluster of stars." John Gribbin, "The Universe's Age Will Have Us Seeing Stars," *Guardian*, 1 Aug. 1996, at 8.

When he released his famous movie in 1938, Walt Disney got it right: *Snow White and the Seven Dwarfs.* See PLURALS (C). Cf. **wharf.**

LANGUAGE-CHANGE INDEX
*dwarves for *dwarfs*: Stage 3
Current ratio (*dwarfs* vs. **dwarves*): 3:1

dwell has two past-tense forms, *dwelt* and *dwelled.* The former has always appeared more frequently in print sources from the 17th century on—e.g.:

- "Written in her childhood voice, it is a laugh-out-loud peek into the lives of those who *dwelt* there [Mooreland, Indiana] in the 1960s and '70s." Beverly Beyette, "World View, Direct from Rural Indiana," *Chicago Trib.*, 2 Oct. 2002, Tempo §, at 6.
- "At both funerals, their pastor, First Methodist's R.A. Nussel, *dwelt* upon that love." John Hamner, "Hand in Hand, Life Was Sweet," *Sarasota Herald-Trib.*, 13 Oct. 2002, at F2.

The two forms may be undergoing DIFFERENTIATION: *dwelled* tends to refer to the physical act, while *dwelt (upon)* takes as its object an idea or other abstract concept.
Current ratio (*dwelt upon* vs. *dwelled upon*): 21:1

dyarchy. See GOVERNMENTAL FORMS.

dybbuk (= a dead person's wandering soul that comes to inhabit the body of a living person) is the standard spelling. **Dibbuk* is a variant. The word is pronounced /**dib**-ək/. Pl. *dybbuks* or (less good) **dybbukim.*
Current ratio (*dybbuk* vs. **dibbuk*): 16:1

dying; dyeing. *Dying* corresponds to the verb *die* (= to expire), *dyeing* to the verb *dye* (= to color with a dye).

Dyeing is often mistakenly written *dying*—e.g.:

- "From Fountain Valley, the water could be distributed by the Orange County Water District to golf courses, a *carpet-dying* [read *carpet-dyeing*] firm and other reclaimed-water users." Jonathan Volzke, "Another Plan for Treated Sewage?" *Orange County Register*, 14 July 1996, at B1.
- "One lead has resulted in a cooperative agreement with a *carpet-dying* [read *carpet-dyeing*] business." Mary Judice, "Fast Track to Success," *Times-Picayune* (New Orleans), 2 Feb. 1997, at F1.

See **die (B).**

LANGUAGE-CHANGE INDEX
dying misused for *dyeing*: Stage 1

dyke. See **dike.**

dynamic, as a noun, is a VOGUE WORD that sprang to currency in the latter half of the 20th century. E.g.: "In the first case, a mediation is stipulated. In the second, the *dynamic* leads almost inevitably in that direction." (A possible revision: *In the second, it is almost inevitable.*) But *dynamics* does have some good uses in expressions such as *group dynamics* and *interpersonal dynamics.*

dynamo (= [1] a power generator, or [2] an inexhaustibly energetic and forceful person) forms the plural *dynamos*—not **dynamoes.* The metaphorical extension from sense 1 to sense 2 occurred in the late 1940s. See PLURALS (D).
Current ratio (*dynamos* vs. **dynamoes*): 320:1

dysfunctional (= functioning abnormally) is occasionally misspelled **disfunctional*—e.g.:

- "Some of the conservative leaders who were demanding less government jumped all over the Illinois Department of Children and Family Services for not preventing the murder and abuse of babies born into *disfunctional* [read *dysfunctional*] families." John McCarron, "Doctor, I'm Confused," *Chicago Trib.*, 24 July 1995, at 9.
- "Have these intellectual irrationals who have broken up yet another family come from *disfunctional* [read *dysfunctional*] homes where morality and discipline are unknowns?" "Applauding Responsible Parenting," *Virginian-Pilot* (Norfolk), 30 July 1996, at A14.
- "Part and parcel of the Marine Fisheries Commission was the *disfunctional* [read *dysfunctional*] law enforcement agency known as the Florida Marine Patrol." Zach Zacharias, "Red Snapper Open Season Is Too Short," *Sarasota Herald-Trib.* (Fla.), 7 May 2015, at C6.

LANGUAGE-CHANGE INDEX
dysfunctional misspelled **disfunctional*: Stage 1
Current ratio: 456:1

DYSPHEMISM (/**dis**-fə-miz-əm/) = (1) the substitution of a disagreeable word or phrase for a neutral or even positive one; or (2) a word or phrase so substituted. Dysphemism is the opposite of EUPHEMISM. Examples usually fall into the realm of SLANG—e.g.:

Ordinary Term	Dysphemism
accountant	bean-counter
athlete	(dumb) jock

baker	dough roller
cadaver, corpse	stiff
carpenter	termite
Christian fundamentalist	Bible-thumper, Bible-beater
civil servant	paper-shuffler, paper-pusher
conservative	reactionary
crawfish	mudbug
detective	dick, gumshoe
doctor	pill-pusher, quack
environmentalist	tree-hugger
executive	fatcat
fashion model	clothes-peg
fraternity member	frat rat, frat boy
intellectual	egghead, nerd, bookworm
investigative journalist	snoop, scoop
jailer	screw
lawyer	mouthpiece, shyster, pettifogger
liberal	bleeding heart, granola head, pinko
Marine	jarhead, grunt
mason	mud dauber
mechanic	grease monkey

newscaster	talking head
newspaper editor	inkstained wretch
office worker	pencil-pusher
pilot	flyboy
plumber	turd herder
police officer	fuzz, pig
printer	ink dauber
psychiatrist	shrink, spook, wig picker
referee	zebra
rural resident	bumpkin, hick, yokel, rube, redneck
sorority member	sore whore, bowhead
surgeon	sawbones, cutter
urbanite	city slicker
urologist	plumber

Many dysphemisms, of course, are hardly printable, as when the word *man* or *woman* is reduced in reference to the low word for a sexual organ. Most racist terms likewise illustrate the phenomenon of dysphemism.

Although they frequently appear in dialogue, dysphemisms rarely find a place in well-edited prose that is not intended to be jocular or to replicate casual speech.

E

each. A. Number. The word *each* raises problems of number. Does it take a singular or plural verb, regardless of the construction? Must a pronoun referring to it be singular, or is *they* acceptable?

As for the first question, *each* traditionally takes a singular verb, and the best practice is to write *each . . . is* regardless of whether a plural noun intervenes (*each of the members is*)—e.g.:

- "*Each* of the main senses of the word *are* [read *is*] then further subdivided semantically." Reinhard Hartmann, "Handy, if Slightly Heavy," 10 *English Today* 53, 53 (1994).
- "Sapienza knows that *each* of the players *are* [read *is*] very gifted." J. Mikel Ellcessor, "One of the Guys," *Pitt. Post-Gaz.*, 25 July 1997, at 16.
- "*Each* of the finalists *have* [read *has*] already been guaranteed $5,000 for the nonprofit of their choice." Linda Charlton, "There's a Lot Going on at B B Brown's Gardens," *Daily Commercial* (Leesburg, Fla.), 27 Aug. 2015, at N23. (On the use of *their* in that sentence, see CONCORD (B).)

The exception occurs when *each* acts in apposition to a plural subject but does not constitute the subject itself <they each have a dollar>. When that is so, *each* functions adverbially and the verb should be plural—e.g.:

- "JR's four Tokyo commuter lines *each has* its own color." Peter McGill, *The American Express Pocket Guide to Tokyo* 13 (1988). (Two possible revisions: [1] *JR's four Tokyo commuter lines each have their own color.* [2] *Each of JR's four Tokyo commuter lines has its own color.*)
- "The athletes *each are* seeking more than $50,000 in compensation and Carver and Miller are seeking reinstatement

and damages in excess of $1 million." Lisa Magenheimer, "Interim Coach Hopes to Overcome Instability," *Tampa Trib.*, 7 Mar. 1996, Pasco §, at 6. See APPOSITIVES.

As for the second question, pronouns having *each* as an antecedent are traditionally (and most formally) singular. E.g.: "Each of them got into *their* [read *his* or *her*, depending on context] car and drove off." But the word *they* has come to take on a singular sense in informal constructions of this type, as the generic masculine pronoun continues to decline in use. (See SEXISM (B).) The better practice, though, is to change the reference to a plural: "*Both of them* got into *their* cars." Or: "*All of them* got into *their* cars."

LANGUAGE-CHANGE INDEX
1. *each* with a plural verb <each have chores to do>: Stage 2
Current ratio (*each of them is* vs. *each of them are): 12:1
2. *each* followed by a plural *their* or *they* <each did their share>: Stage 4
3. *they each have*: Stage 5

B. **Each . . . apiece.*** This construction is a REDUNDANCY—e.g.:

- "The 33 largest American plantations *each* receive more than $1 million *apiece* [delete *apiece*] in higher sales prices." Stephen Moore, "Corporate Welfare for Select Few Hurting Others," *Houston Chron.*, 6 Apr. 1995, at A33.
- "Ben Tanner and Kirk Gammill *each* added a goal *apiece* [delete *apiece*]." Derek Samson, "Volleyball Tourney Pits Best of A-1, A-2," *Idaho Statesman*, 4 Oct. 1996, at C2.

C. *Between each.* See **between** (F).

LANGUAGE-CHANGE INDEX (For the full key, see front matter pp. xxxi, l–li.)
Stage 1: Rejected. **Stage 2:** Widely shunned. **Stage 3:** Widespread but . . . **Stage 4:** Ubiquitous but . . . **Stage 5:** Fully accepted.
Invariably inferior forms marked by asterisk (*). • Ratios represent frequency of prevalent forms vs. variants in current books.

each and every. This emphatic (and trite) phrase, like *each* or *every* alone, requires a singular verb—e.g.: "Each and every one of them *are* [read *is*] devoted." Robert D. Signoracci, "Outgoing Mayor Thanks Cohoes," *Times Union* (Albany), 26 Dec. 1999, at B4.

LANGUAGE-CHANGE INDEX
**each and every one are* for
each and every one is: Stage 1
Current ratio: 14:1

each other. A. And *one another*. Usage authorities have traditionally suggested that *each other* should refer to two people or entities <John and Bob helped each other>, *one another* to more than two <all of them loved one another>. Yet this 19th-century rule has often been undermined in the literature on usage—e.g.:

- "A distinction is set up in the schools between *each other* and *one another*, according as the reference is to two or to more than two persons; and yet scarcely a good author can be found who does not use the two forms interchangeably." Adams Sherman Hill, *Our English* 33 (1888).
- "It has been maintained that *each other* should be used where only two are concerned, and *one another* where there are more than two; but the distinction is not necessary. The expressions are interchangeable." John F. Genung, *Outlines of Rhetoric* 311–12 (1893).
- "Failure to observe the distinction [between *each other* and *one another*] may be a technical fault, but it is not a serious offence." Edward N. Teall, *Putting Words to Work* 283 (1940).
- "Purists make a distinction between them, using *each other* for two things or persons only, and *one another* for more than two things or persons. In spite of Fowler's rather perverse repudiation of it, this distinction is a convenient one, though so often ignored as not to have any real validity." G.H. Vallins, *Better English* 48 (4th ed. 1957).

Careful writers and editors will doubtless continue to observe the distinction, but no one else will notice.

LANGUAGE-CHANGE INDEX
each other for *one another* (i.e., for more than two items): Stage 4

B. Possessive Forms: *each other's* and *one another's*. The possessive forms are *each other's* and *one another's*. The noun that follows is typically plural <each other's cars> <they praised each other's presentations>, but the more logical construction is singular <each other's car> <they praised each other's presentation>. Whether the phrase is *each other's* or *one another's*, it's fairly common to see the apostrophe drift waywardly (and mistakenly) to the end of the phrase, perhaps because the idea of reciprocity gets overshadowed by the sense of plurality—e.g.:

- "They can look back in time to see the field being planted, view closeups of insect damage to the corn, or read *one anothers'* [read *one another's*] comments." Laurent Belsie, "More Fun than Watching Paint Dry," *Christian Science Monitor*, 26 July 2001, at 1.
- "We keep up on *each others'* [read *each other's*] lives [read *life*] in a casual sort of way." Glenn Harlan Reynolds, "Community by the Book," *Wall Street J.*, 28 Dec. 2001, at A16.

- "A 2-year-old program . . . trains space explorers how to stay on *each others'* [read *each other's*] good *sides* [read *side*]." Elisabeth A. Wright, "NASA Focusing on Personal Space Training," *L.A. Times*, 30 Dec. 2001, at B5.

LANGUAGE-CHANGE INDEX
1. **each others'* for *each other's*: Stage 1
Current ratio (*each other's* vs. **each others'*): 15:1
2. **one anothers'* for *one another's*: Stage 1
Current ratio (*one another's* vs. **one anothers'*): 190:1

**early beginnings* is a REDUNDANCY that was especially common during the mid-20th century. By the 1990s it had fallen in frequency but still occurred—e.g.: "One of the nation's most skilled neurosurgeons, Dr. Carson candidly recalls his *early beginnings* [read *beginnings* or *early days*] in poverty." Joy Bennett Kinnon, "10 Who Beat Welfare," *Ebony*, Nov. 1996, at 166.

early on (= at an early stage) is not the odious locution that some people think. Slightly informal, it has long been perfectly idiomatic in both AmE and BrE. E.g.: "A chemistry professor who later turned to computer science as a profession, he learned *early on* to love the pleasures of long, solitary treks." Patrick Rogers & Ron Arias, "Kidnapped! Bird-Watcher John Heidma's Vacation Trip to Ecuador Goes Terribly Wrong in the Rain Forest," *People*, 7 Oct. 1996, at 121. For *later on*, see **later (B).**

LANGUAGE-CHANGE INDEX
early on in the sense "at an early stage": Stage 5

earnesty. This word, as a synonym of *earnestness*, is listed in the *OED* with only two citations—from 1572 and 1591. One might have thought it to be long obsolete, but it still sometimes appears. Since it doesn't really fill any gap in the language, writers and editors would be wise to stick to the established *earnestness*—e.g.:

- "Born three years after the civil war, he carries an image of the new post-Franco generation, of youthful *earnesty* [read *earnestness*], of modernness tempered with mature moderation." Ana Martinez-Soler, "Spain and Socialism," *Christian Science Monitor*, 21 Oct. 1982, at 12.
- "She spoke often and extemporaneously about winning, losing, overcoming, focusing and so forth with a matter-of-fact *earnesty* [read *earnestness*] that suggested she believed it all fervently." Sara Corbett, *Venus to the Hoop* 52 (1997).
- "If all Semisonic has going for it is *earnesty* [read *earnestness*] and poignancy, well, that's a lot more than most other bands." Malcolm Mayhew, "Semisonic Concert at Deep Ellum Strangely Irresistible," *Ft. Worth Star-Telegram*, 31 Jan. 1999, at 14.

LANGUAGE-CHANGE INDEX
**earnesty* for *earnestness*: Stage 1
Current ratio (*earnestness* vs. **earnesty*): 6,412:1

earth. In reference to the planet we live on, *earth* is usually preceded by *the* and is not capitalized. *The sun* and *the moon* are treated the same way <a full moon occurs when the sun and moon are on opposite sides of the earth>. But the proper names of those celestial bodies (*Sol* and *Luna*), though used rarely, are capitalized with no article preceding them. Likewise, when *Earth* is referred to as a proper noun, it is capitalized and usually stands alone—e.g.: "They've named it Quaoar, pronounced KWA-oh-war, after a California Indian creation deity. It's about one-tenth the size of *Earth* and orbits *the sun* every 288 years." Faye Flam, "'Quaoar's Discovery Puts Pluto on Edge of Demotion," *Advocate* (Baton Rouge), 8 Oct. 2002, at A2.

In reference to the stuff that the planet is made of, Roy Copperud states that lowercase "*earth* without *the* means soil" <the excavation left a large pile of earth> (*American Usage and Style: The Consensus* 117 [1980]).

earthen; earthly; earthy. Although these terms have historically overlapped, some degree of DIFFERENTIATION has emerged. *Earthen* = made from earth (as soil or clay) <earthen pottery>. (The word can be pronounced /ər-thən/ or /ər-thən/.) *Earthly* = of, relating to, or involving the earth as opposed to the heavens; terrestrial <earthly delights>. The word distinguishes not only the temporal from the heavenly, but also the mortal <earthly remains> from an afterlife. *Earthy* = (1) simple; plain; practical <earthy farm folk>; or (2) coarse; gross; unrefined <earthy sense of humor>.

easier is the comparative form both of the adjective *easy* and of the adverb *easily*. In the latter use, it's a CASUALISM equivalent to *more easily*—e.g.:

- "Although most people are still taking the postal route to employment, finding professional work is now being accomplished *much quicker and easier* [read, perhaps, *much more quickly and easily*] thanks to personal computers, modems and the Internet." Dean Golemis, "Making Connections," *Chicago Trib.*, 26 Jan. 1996, at C1.
- "They'll cook faster and the middles will get done *easier* [or *more easily*]." "Hamburger Helper," *Palm Beach Post*, 15 Aug. 1996, Food §, at 1.

In modern print sources, the collocation *done more easily* is much more common than *done easier*. See **easy.**

LANGUAGE-CHANGE INDEX
easier used adverbially for *more easily*: Stage 4
Current ratio (*done more easily* vs. *done easier*): 4:1

easily. See **easy.**

east; easterly; eastward(s). See DIRECTIONAL WORDS.

Easter Sunday. Though technically redundant, this phrase is unobjectionable. In fact, the REDUNDANCY is understandable: in many contexts, *Easter* refers to the holiday period beginning late Friday and ending Sunday—e.g.: "We're going to New York for Easter weekend." That example can be shortened, with no change in meaning, to "We're going to New York for Easter." So *Easter Sunday* is more specific than *Easter* as popularly used. Historically, in fact, *Easter* could apply to the whole week that begins with Easter

Sunday. The phrase *Easter Sunday* has been common in print sources since the 18th century.

eastwardly. See DIRECTIONAL WORDS (C).

eastward(s). See DIRECTIONAL WORDS.

easy; easily. The word *easy*, generally an adjective, functions arguably as an adverb in some SET PHRASES: *go easy* (*on me*, etc.), *easy does it*, and *take it easy*. But because the verbs can be understood as elliptical linking verbs, the word *easy* can quite appropriately be considered an adjective. Wherever an adverb is needed, of course, *easily* is the right word. See **easier.**

eat > ate > eaten. The dialectal past-tense forms *et* and *eat* occur mostly in uneducated speech in New England and along the Atlantic Coast, as well as in the Midwest. The pronunciation /et/ for *ate* is traditional in BrE but fading.

eatable. See **edible.**

eat your cake and have it too. See **you can't eat your cake and have it too.**

eaves. This noun, meaning "the overhanging lower edge of a roof," is—despite its appearance—historically singular. But since the 19th century, *eaves* has been misinterpreted as a plural form, and so the misbegotten singular *eave* was born (as a BACK-FORMATION). Today it can hardly be criticized as nonstandard—e.g.:

- "Paper wasps . . . build those familiar, often large papery nests either suspended from a branch or *eave*, or fitted inside an abandoned animal burrow." Allen M. Young, "In Praise of Wasps," *Chicago Trib.* (Mag.), 25 Aug. 1996, at 32.
- "Snow hangs ominously over the *eave* of her home in Lake View as Diana Szczutkowski clears a path." "Weather Woes Deepen by a Foot or More," *Buffalo News*, 13 Jan. 1997, at A1 (photo caption).
- "A row of rooms and a small office with a crisp US flag fluttering from an *eave* faced a narrow, too-steep beach." John Connor, "Hidalgo of Cuba Then, Part I," *Guns Mag.*, Sept. 2015, at 78.

ebullient (/i-**buul**-yənt/ or /-**bəl**-/) is frequently mispronounced /**eb**-yə-lənt/. See PRONUNCIATION (B). The corresponding noun is either *ebullience* (/i-**buul**-yənts/) or—more traditionally—*ebullition* (/eb-ə-**lish**-ən/).

ebullit. See BACK-FORMATIONS.

echo. Pl. *echoes*—not *echos. See PLURALS (D).

ecological; ecologic. See -IC.

ecology. When it originated in the late 19th century, this word referred to the biological study of living organisms and their environment <comparative ecology>. By natural extension during the mid-20th century, the word came to refer to the interaction itself, as opposed to its study <the ecology of Church Street>. By still

LANGUAGE-CHANGE INDEX (For the full key, see front matter pp. xxxi, l–li.)
Stage 1: Rejected. **Stage 2:** Widely shunned. **Stage 3:** Widespread but . . . **Stage 4:** Ubiquitous but . . . **Stage 5:** Fully accepted.
Invariably inferior forms marked by asterisk (*). • Ratios represent frequency of prevalent forms vs. variants in current books.

further extension—a SLIPSHOD EXTENSION—the word sometimes takes on the sense of the environment itself. When that is true, *environment* is a better word—e.g.:

- "Hundreds of Puerto Ricans demanded an end to bombing exercises that they say are harming the island's *ecology* [read *environment*] and its residents' health." Andrew Jacobs, "Protests Intensify in Puerto Rico as Navy Resumes Bombing Drills," *N.Y. Times*, 28 Apr. 2001, at A1.
- "Winning scant mention during Saturday's ceremonies was the concern that foreign organisms that attached to the bottom of the new dry dock during its journey from China could damage Maine's coastal *ecology* [read *environment*]." Ted Cohen, "BIW Unveils Its New, $240 Million Dry Dock," *Maine Sunday Telegram*, 6 May 2001, at B1.

Ecology was formerly spelled with a digraph: *œcology* (so listed in the first edition of the *OED*).

LANGUAGE-CHANGE INDEX
ecology misused for *environment*: Stage 1

economic. A. And *economical*. *Economical* means "thrifty" or, in the current JARGON, "cost-effective" <it's not economical to have so many workers with duplicative responsibilities>. *Economic* should be used for every other meaning possible for the words, almost always in reference to the study of economics <economic growth>. Hence we have *economic studies* and *economic interest* but *economical shopping*. See -IC. Cf. **uneconomical**.

B. And *financial*. *Economic* is increasingly often misused for *financial*. When the reference is to pecuniary affairs of a household or business, the word should be *financial*, not *economic* (which refers to larger-scale finances). There is an irony in the usage, since *economic* comes from a Greek word meaning "management of the household." E.g.: "The firm financed a string of big-budget movies that perpetually left it on the brink of *economic* [read *financial*] ruin but managed to come up with a big hit often enough to stay afloat." Steve Pond, "Beating the Financial Terminator?" *Wash. Post*, 17 Oct. 1995, at C7.

But the phrase *economic ruin* is acceptable when the reference is to a geographic area (such as a town) or a country—e.g.:

- "The news these days is filled with dire predictions about the *economic ruin* awaiting our increasingly long-lived nation." Vern Bengston, "Grandparenting Styles Differ," *Charleston Daily Mail*, 10 Oct. 1995, at A8.
- "The American exit threatened his town with *economic ruin*, and his family, a long-standing local dynasty, with the loss of its power base." "How to Convert a Military Power Base—Filipino Style," *Sacramento Bee*, 15 Oct. 1995, at F3.

LANGUAGE-CHANGE INDEX
economic misused for *financial*: Stage 3

ecstasy. So spelled, not **ecstacy*—e.g.: "Sometime in late January or early February the Seahawks will provide something permanent. It will inspire either a euphoria approaching religious *ecstacy* [read *ecstasy*] or a groundswell of frustrated hopelessness." Ted Miller, "Leap of Faith or Fall from Grace?" *Seattle Post-Intelligencer*, 9 Dec. 2006, Sports §, at D1.

When the word denotes the drug MDMA, the spelling remains the same but the term is usually capitalized—e.g.: "In Oklahoma, sad to say, studies show that while the use of drugs such as marijuana, cocaine and *ecstacy* [read *Ecstasy*] by young people has declined, the average percentage of kids in grades eight, 10 and 12 who say they've tried those substances is above the national average." Editorial, "High Rise; Teen Drug Use Numbers Sobering," *Oklahoman* (Oklahoma City), 6 Jan. 2007, at A10.

Occasionally the word is also misspelled with an *-x-* displacing the *-c-*. Here, the doubly mangled spelling got past the copy desk: "What begins with sitcom-style infighting turns to touchy-feely reconciliation when the family stoner drops a tab of *Extacy* [read *Ecstasy*] in patriarch Ira's drink." Peter Debruge, "When Do We Eat?" *Daily Variety*, 13 Apr. 2006, at 20. See SPELLING (A).

LANGUAGE-CHANGE INDEX
ecstasy misspelled **ecstacy* or **extacy*: Stage 1
Current ratio (*ecstasy* vs. **ecstacy* vs.
*extacy): 312:11:1

ecstatic (/ek-**stat**-ik/ or /-**stad**-/) is frequently mispronounced /e-**stad**-ik/. See PRONUNCIATION (B).

ecumenical /ek-yoo-**men**-i-kel/ (= supporting the idea of greater cooperation and unity between different branches of Christianity) has been predominantly so spelled since the 1920s in AmE and the 1950s in BrE—the earlier spelling having been **oecumenical* or **œcumenical*. The corresponding noun is *ecumenism* /e-**kyoo**-mi-niz-əm/—a variant being **ecumenicism*.

Curious thing about this word: some have tried to extend its reach beyond Christianity to promote better understanding among people of all religious faiths. That certainly reflects the spirit of the word, and yet it may well damage or at least dilute its central meaning.
Current ratio (*ecumenism* vs. **ecumenicism*): 25:1

-ED; -'D. Although R.W. Burchfield says that the BrE preference is for past-participial adjectives such as *cupola'd arch, mustachio'd, shanghai'd sailor*, and *subpoena'd witness* (*FMEU3* at 237), the strong preference in AmE is for *cupolaed arch, mustachioed, shanghaied sailor*, and *subpoenaed witness*—and even *stockinged feet* (although people tend to say *stocking feet*). The past-tense *OK'd* is an exception (though the spelled-out *okayed* eliminates the issue—see **okay**). The forms *cc'd* and *bcc'd* are universally preferred.

edema /e-**deem**-ə/ (= a swelling in a body part caused by an abnormal accumulation of fluid in cells or in a body cavity) has been the predominant spelling in AmE since 1910 and in BrE since the late 1970s. The variant spelling **oedema* or **œdema* is universally falling into disuse.
Current ratio (*edema* vs. **oedema*): 5:1

edgewise; edgeways. Both words are mostly restricted to versions of the phrase *couldn't get a word in* *edgewise*. In AmE, it's always *edgewise*; in BrE, it's typically *edgeways*.

edible; eatable. These adjectives are broadly synonymous, but they can be differentiated. What is *edible* is capable of being eaten without danger, or fit for consumption <edible plants>. E.g.:

- "The autumn olive, which many conservationists viewed until recent years as ideal, is appealing because its berries are *edible* by deer and birds, and the plants grow quickly and hold back erosion." Anne Paine, "Autumn Olive Deemed Too Invasive," *Tennessean*, 1 Oct. 1996, at B1.
- "With any type of *edible* wild mushrooms, it is very important that you always cook them thoroughly." Kathy Casey, "Wild Mushrooms," *Seattle Times*, 2 Oct. 1996, at F1.

What is *eatable* is at least minimally enjoyable or palatable <the food at that restaurant isn't even eatable>. E.g.: "Along the way, they've maintained a live-and-let-live attitude with the gawkers who show up to watch as they paw through the garbage and recycle the *eatable* morsels." George Snyder, "Dump Bears May Pose Menace," *S.F. Chron.*, 29 July 1995, at A13.

Eatable is often used as an attributive noun, usually in the plural—e.g.:

- "These people produce *eatables* most of us enjoy." Letter of Robert E. Smith Jr., "Hog Producers Get Bad Rap," *Morning Star* (Wilmington, N.C.), 10 June 1996, at A6.
- "We can assume that such concentrations of rich *eatables* made them natural synonyms, as time went on, for something politically desirable." George Hebert, "Real Pork in Real Barrels," *Virginian-Pilot* (Norfolk), 15 July 1996, at A7.
- "One of those vehicles tows a trailer personally designed by the Duke of Edinburgh—full of drawers, recesses, cubby-holes and compartments from which in short order all *eatables*, dishes and utensils are retrieved." John MacLeod, "A Picnic in Scotland?" *Scottish Daily Mail*, 18 June 2015, at 17.

edification. In the phrase *for your edification* (= for your moral or intellectual instruction), the word *edification* is sometimes misused (usually but not always for jocular effect) to mean "for your enjoyment" or the like—e.g.:

- "Dennis has come to the Tishomingo Lodge and Casino to perform daredevil dives for the *edification* [read *thrill*] of the casino guests." Elmore Leonard, "The Best Kind of 'Blues,'" *Rocky Mountain News* (Denver), 15 Feb. 2002, at D28.
- "Everyone says vaguely snotty things about each other and hidden cameras record, for our *edification* [read *titillation*], sundry couples' first kisses." David Kronke, "Time to Break the Ice," *Daily News* (L.A.), 2 June 2002, at U10.
- "They danced, they tossed their wild hair, they bounded athletically for the *edification* [read *entertainment*] of the assembled crowd along the street's edge." Kage Baker, *The Anvil of the World* 173–74 (2003).
- "Does [NFL Commissioner Roger] Goodell plan to have owners, team presidents and head coaches sign an annual noncheating pledge at the league meeting every March? One suspects that the real purpose of even committing

such ideas to paper is simply theater for the *edification* [read *appeasement*?] of the public." Bill Ordine, "Spy Reply," *Baltimore Sun*, 8 Mar. 2008, Sports §, at 15.

LANGUAGE-CHANGE INDEX
edification misused in the sense
of "thrill, titillation": Stage 1

Edinburgh (the capital of Scotland) is pronounced /**ed**-in-bər-ə/ in four syllables—not /**ed**-in-bərg/. The latter, though, is the correct pronunciation of Edinburg, Texas, the seat of Hidalgo County. In BrE, some speakers syncopate the pronunciation of the Scottish city to /**ed**-in-brə/.

-EDLY. With words ending in *-edly*, the classic adverbial formula *in an X manner* does not always work. Although *amazedly* means "in an amazed manner," *allegedly* does not mean "in an alleged manner" and *purportedly* does not mean "in a purported manner." Nor does *admittedly* mean "in an admitted manner." Rather, the unorthodox formula for these words is *it is . . . -ed that*; i.e., *allegedly* means "it is alleged that," and so on. Instead of bewailing the unorthodoxy of these words ending in *-edly*, we should welcome the conciseness they promote and should continue to use the forms that have made their way into common usage. We have many of them:

admittedly	deservedly
advisedly	designedly
allegedly	markedly
assertedly	reportedly
assuredly	resignedly
avowedly	supposedly
concededly	unadvisedly
confessedly	undoubtedly

See **allegedly** & **confessedly**.

Even so, any new or unusual form ending in *-edly* ought to be avoided if a ready substitute exists, whether or not the *in an X manner* formula works—e.g.:

- "There is a certain appearance of arrogance in the readiness of men to stand up in front of others and preach a sermon or deliver an address, as though their thoughts were *recognizedly* superior to those of the audience." Edward N. Teall, *Putting Words to Work* 11 (1940). (Here the thoughtful reader is likely to pause and wonder why the writer didn't use the more recognizable word: *recognizably*. If there's a real nuance here, it probably isn't worth achieving.)
- " 'I'm as awkward an interviewee as you're likely to get,' he says, laughing *embarrassedly*." Clive Anderson, "Mr. Funny: Peculiar Interview," *Sunday Telegraph*, 29 Sept. 1996, Features §, at 3. (Here the more natural wording would be to replace *embarrassedly* with the phrase *with embarrassment*.)

See **qualifiedly**.

educable. A. And *educible*. *Educable* = capable of being educated. *Educible* = capable of being elicited (i.e., educed). See **educational** & **educe**.

LANGUAGE-CHANGE INDEX (For the full key, see front matter pp. xxxi, l–li.)
Stage 1: Rejected. **Stage 2:** Widely shunned. **Stage 3:** Widespread but . . . **Stage 4:** Ubiquitous but . . . **Stage 5:** Fully accepted.
Invariably inferior forms marked by asterisk (*). • Ratios represent frequency of prevalent forms vs. variants in current books.

B. And **educatable.* Although the shorter form is standard, the longer variant sometimes crops up—e.g.: "Sooner or later, we have to go back to the realization that the only education the *educatable* [read *educable*] can ever get that will keep them from going to prison has to come from their parents." "Parental Responsibility," *Phoenix Gaz.,* 23 Mar. 1995, at B8. See -ATABLE.

> LANGUAGE-CHANGE INDEX
> **educatable* for *educable*: Stage 1
> Current ratio (*educable* vs. **educatable*): 66:1

educate the public, to. Typically, this phrase simply means "to seek to change public opinion." Whether the means is through disseminating information or propaganda is often in the eye of the beholder. But the only desired result is typically to have masses of people think differently about some issue—e.g.:

- "Phillips said county history shows that land-acquisition measures require two or three elections to fully *educate the public.*" Susan Byrnes & David Schaefer, "Failed Park Measures Still Have a Chance, Bond Supporters Say," *Seattle Times,* 19 Sept. 1996, at B5.
- "The AFL-CIO ads are intended to *educate the public* about Hoke's congressional voting record on such issues as Medicare, education and pension rights, the AFL-CIO said." Evelyn Theiss, "Labor Unions' Money Targets Hoke-Kucinich Race," *Plain Dealer* (Cleveland), 10 Oct. 1996, at A1.
- "An unprecedented coalition of record companies, artists, and music organizations led by the Recording Industry Assn. of America (RIAA) announced Sept. 26 the launch of an aggressive multimedia campaign designed to *educate the public* that unauthorized downloading of digital music is illegal." Bill Holland, "Coalition Sets Anti-Piracy Ad Campaign," *Billboard,* 5 Oct. 2002, Upfront §, at 4.

Of course, the "educators" almost always have a vested interest in all the free "education" they dispense. But that's not always the connotation—e.g.:

- "Through nearly three decades of organized protests and attempts to *educate the public* and corporate-owned utilities *to* [read *about* or *on*] the virtues of alternative sources of energy and conservation, Crocker has generated an emotional electricity of his own." Paul Levy, "Still Active After All These Years," *Star Trib.* (Minneapolis), 27 Sept. 1994, at E1.
- "[Kevin] McGowan is one of only a handful of ornithologists studying crows, and his research in Ithaca has given scientists a vivid picture of how crow communities work. He tries to *educate the public,* too, with a Web site chock full of crow facts and trivia." Nell Boyce, "Feathered Friends," *U.S. News & World Rep.,* 14 Oct. 2002, at 68.

educational; educative; *educatory. *Educational* = (1) having to do with education <educational issues>; or (2) serving to further education <educational films>. (In sense 1, *education* is often used attributively, to prevent a MISCUE that sense 2 was intended <education issues>: an *educational issue* is not an issue that is educational.) *Educative* = tending to educate; instructive <educative lectures>. **Educatory* is a NEEDLESS VARIANT of *educative.*

For a related word, see **educable.**

> Current ratio (*educational* vs. *educative* vs. **educatory*): 28,905:374:1

educator; educationist; *educationalist. *Educator,* a 17th-century coinage that didn't become popular till the 19th century, is a FORMAL WORD for *teacher;* it dignifies the person described. E.g.: "Tomorrow, she will receive the Outstanding Teacher Award during Alumni Day at Lehigh University. Five other *educators* also will be honored." Denise Reaman, "Freemansburg Teacher to Get Award for English Instruction," *Morning Call* (Allentown, Pa.), 4 Oct. 1996, at B1.

Educationist, by contrast, is a DYSPHEMISM suggesting a puffed-up teacher who cloaks commonplace ideas in abstract, theoretical language or else turns common sense on its head—e.g.:

- "The educator John Keats noted a fundamental divide between the progressive *educationist,* for whom 'the individual has only a functional significance in society,' and the traditionalist, to whom 'society is merely a function of individuals.' " John R. Dunlap, "Dumb and Dumber: Does Choice Matter?" *Am. Spectator,* Sept. 1996.
- "*Educationists* love the humane-sounding idea of self-esteem. It gives them cover for low standards and low effort both on their part and that of students." Walter Williams, "Girl Who Received Top Marks in School Couldn't Read Street Signs," *Chattanooga Free Press,* 15 Sept. 1996, at B7. (At the end of the sentence, PARALLELISM could be maintained by changing *both on their part and that of students* to *both on their part and on the part of students.*)
- "Not surprisingly, *educationists* love a system where brand-new schools are built to their liking, while they retain control." "The Business of Schooling," *Richmond Times-Dispatch,* 27 Sept. 1996, at A16.

In World English, *educator* appears in print more frequently than *educationist* by a ratio of 34 to 1, and than **educationalist* by a ratio of 42 to 1.

In BrE, *educationist* is sometimes used in the sense that *educator* bears in AmE—e.g.: "The current project involving *educationists,* churchmen and others, in an effort to strengthen the teaching of morality in the national school curriculum, has now reached substantial agreement on the way forward—about everything except sex." Clifford Longley, "Sacred and Profane," *Daily Telegraph,* 30 Aug. 1996, at 23.

*Educationalist is essentially a NEEDLESS VARIANT of *educationist.* And like that term, it is sometimes used in BrE without negative connotations—e.g.: "Peter Chambers, *educationalist* [read *educationist* or *educator*], born November 27, 1933; died September 19, 1996." Martin Wainwright, "Peter Chambers" (obit.), *Guardian,* 5 Oct. 1996, at 18. **Educationalist* is somewhat more common in BrE than in AmE.

> LANGUAGE-CHANGE INDEX
> **educationalist* for *educationist*: Stage 4
> Current ratio (*educationist* vs. **educationalist*): 1.2:1

*educatory. See **educational.**

educe, vb. (= to elicit; evoke), should be distinguished from the verb *adduce* (= to bring forward for analysis) and from the noun *educt* (= something educed). The word is so rare—and its meaning so easily captured in more direct ways—that it is seldom serviceable. E.g.:

"The first few hearings have *educed* [read *elicited* or *brought out*] several interesting comments by several interested parties." John Javetski, "House Takes a Broader View of Restructuring," *Electrical World*, Dec. 1995, at 5.

Sometimes the word appears where *deduce* or *infer* or even *glean* would be better—e.g.: "Hitherto, how he fitted into the screwball reputation of that magazine has had to be *educed* [read *deduced* or *gleaned*] from his 'The Years with Ross' (1959)." John McAleer, "The Thurber Spirit," *Chicago Trib.*, 17 Dec. 1995, at C1. See **adduce**.

LANGUAGE-CHANGE INDEX
1. *educe* misused for *elicit*: Stage 1
2. *educe* misused for *deduce*: Stage 1

educible. So spelled—not *educeable. See -ABLE (A) & **educable** (A).

-EE. A. General Principles. This suffix (from the French past-participial -*é*) originally denoted "someone who is acted upon"; the sense is inherently passive. It's an especially active suffix; that is, people are continually creating NEOLOGISMS with it. Some of these look fairly ridiculous (e.g., *civilizee*), but some readily become quite familiar (e.g., *honoree*, dating from the early 1950s). Although there are exceptions (e.g., *biographee*), words ending in -*ee* are almost always made from verbs in the PASSIVE VOICE—e.g.:

> *acquittee* = one who is acquitted
> *arrestee* = one who is arrested
> *conscriptee* = one who is conscripted
> *detainee* = one who is detained
> *educatee* = one who is educated (by an educator)
> *expellee* = one who is expelled
> *inauguree* = one who is inaugurated
> *indictee* = one who is indicted
> *invitee* = one who is invited
> *liberee* = one who is liberated
> *permittee* = one who is permitted
> *returnee* = one who is returned
> *selectee* = one who is selected
> *separatee* = one who is separated
> *shelteree* = one who is sheltered
> *smugglee* = one who is smuggled
> *telephonee* = one who is telephoned

The suffix also has a dative sense, in which it acts as the passive agent noun for the indirect object. This is the sense in which the suffix is most commonly used in peculiarly legal terminology:

> *abandonee* = one to whom property rights are relinquished
> *advancee* = one to whom money is advanced
> *consignee* = one to whom something is consigned
> *disclosee* = one to whom something is disclosed
> *grantee* = one to whom property is granted
> *lessee* = one to whom property is leased
> *patentee* = one to whom a patent is or has been issued
> *trustee* = one to whom something is entrusted
> *vendee* = one to whom something is sold

At least one word ending in -*ee* has both a normal passive sense and a dative sense. *Appointee* = (1) one who is appointed; or (2) one to whom an estate is appointed. Sense 2, of course, is primarily legal.

The suffix -*ee*, then, is correlative to -*or*, the active agent-noun suffix: some words ending in -*ee* are formed as passive analogues to -*or* agent nouns, and not from any verb stem: *indemnitee* (= one who is indemnified; analogue to *indemnitor*); *preceptee* (= student; analogue to *preceptor*).

These are the traditional uses of the suffix. There is a tendency today, however, to make -*ee* a general agent-noun suffix without regard to its passive sense or the limitations within which it may take on passive senses. Hence the suffix has been extended to PHRASAL VERBS, even though only the first word in the phrase appears in the -*ee* word. So *discriminatee* (= one who is discriminated against) and *tippee* (= one who is tipped off). Then other prepositional phrases have gradually come into the wide embrace of -*ee*: *abortee* (= a woman upon whom an abortion is performed); *confiscatee* (= one from whom goods have been confiscated).

Some -*ee* words contain implicit possessives: *amputee* (= one whose limb has been removed); *breachee* (= one whose contract is breached); *condemnee* (= one whose property has been condemned). In still other words, -*ee* does not even have its primary passive sense—e.g.:

> *arrivee* = one who arrives
> *asylee* = one who seeks asylum
> *attendee = one who attends
> *benefitee* = one who benefits (or, possibly, "is benefited")
> *escapee* = one who escapes
> *signee* = one who signs
> *standee = one who stands

Finally, the suffix is sometimes used to coin jocular words such as *cheatee* (= one who is cheated).

The upshot of this discussion is that -*ee* is subject to abuse and that writers must be careful about the forms they use. For active senses we have -*er*, -*or*, and -*ist* at our service; we should be wary of adopting any new active forms ending in -*ee* and do our best to see that *attendee and *standee—or *signee* in an active sense (see **signee**)—together with similar forms, come to an eternal rest. Otherwise, we risk wasting any sense to be found in this suffix. For example, "the unskilled workers used to 'dilute' skilled workers in time of war should have been called *diluters* instead of *dilutees*; the skilled were the dilutees" (*FMEU2* at 146).

B. Word Formation. The principles applying to words ending in -ATABLE apply also to agent nouns ending in -*ee*. Thus we have *inauguree*, not *inauguratee; *subrogee*, not *subrogatee (though the latter is infrequently used mistakenly for the former).

C. Stylistic Use of. Stylists know that -*ee* agent nouns are often inferior to more descriptive terms.

LANGUAGE-CHANGE INDEX (For the full key, see front matter pp. xxxi, l–li.)
Stage 1: Rejected. **Stage 2:** Widely shunned. **Stage 3:** Widespread but . . . **Stage 4:** Ubiquitous but . . . **Stage 5:** Fully accepted.
Invariably inferior forms marked by asterisk (*). • Ratios represent frequency of prevalent forms vs. variants in current books.

They sometimes objectify the people they describe, although the writer may intend no callousness—e.g.: "[Catherine] Ojok and another *abductee* [read *abducted woman*] ran away when [Gen. Raska] Lukwiya told them they would become 'his wives' as soon as they had their first menstrual period." Ben de la Cruz, "Moving Past Life as a Rebel Slave," *Wash. Post,* 29 July 2008, at A11.

E.E. Cummings. See **Cummings.**

eerie (= fear-inducing; strange; weird) has always been the predominant spelling. The variant spelling **eery* appeared sometimes in BrE until the mid-19th century. Although it is becoming frightfully common again, **eery* is best considered a NEEDLESS VARIANT.
                                                    Current ratio: 61:1

effect, v.t. **A. Generally.** This verb—meaning "to bring about, make happen"—is increasingly rare in English. Besides sounding pretentious, it often spawns wordiness. The verb tends to occur alongside ZOMBIE NOUNS such as *improvement*—e.g.:

- "But just as some transactions were about *to be effected* [read *to take effect* or *to be concluded*], the settlement plans were delayed indefinitely following a meeting of bankers at the central bank." Victor Mallet, "Kuwait Delays Interbank Plan," *Fin. Times,* 4 July 1991, at I4.
- "It meditates instead on the despoliations and interferences *effected* [read *wrought*?] by science, technology and industry—or on nature's response to these human disturbances." Alice Thorson, "Canvases Writhe with Life in Organic Abstraction Exhibit," *Kansas City Star,* 7 Oct. 1994, at H19.
- "For some schools in the state, the present system of oversight has not *effected improvement* [read *improved things* or *improved anything* or *brought about improvement*]." "School Reform Plan Deserves Passing Grade," *News & Record* (Greensboro), 2 May 1995, at A6. (Another possible revision: *The present system of supervision has failed to improve many schools in this state.* [On the use of *oversight* in the original sentence, see **oversight (A).**])

B. And *affect*. *Effect* (= to bring about) is often misused for *affect* (= to influence, have an effect on). The blunder is widespread—e.g.:

- "Opponents say it would *effect* [read *affect*] only a small number of people—in New York an estimated 300 criminals a year—and would have little effect on the causes of crime." Ian Fisher, "Why '3-Strike' Sentencing Is a Solid Hit This Year," *N.Y. Times,* 25 Jan. 1994, at A16.
- "It would also *effect* [read *affect*] pensions tied to the rate of inflation and union contracts with automatic adjustments based on inflation." Adam Clymer, "As Parties Skirmish over Budget, Greenspan Offers a Painless Cure," *N.Y. Times,* 11 Jan. 1995, at A1.
- "So far, 63 buildings in downtown Boston and the suburbs have been *effected* [read *affected*] this week by the strike." Dina Gerdman, "Janitors' Strike Spreads into Quincy," *Patriot Ledger* (Quincy, Mass.), 3 Oct. 2002, News §, at 1.
- "The fallout has *effected* [read *affected*] young men already worried about keeping their college football dreams alive." David Wharton, "Hitting the Books," *L.A. Times,* 11 Oct. 2002, Sports §, pt. 4, at 16.

It could be that the widespread misuse of *impact* is partly an attempt to sidestep the problem of how to spell *affect.* See **affect** & **impact.**

                    LANGUAGE-CHANGE INDEX
                effect misused for *affect*: Stage 2

C. And *effectuate*. Most dictionaries define these words identically, but their DIFFERENTIATION should be encouraged. Although both mean "to accomplish, bring about, or cause to happen," stylists have generally considered *effect* the preferable word, *effectuate* a NEEDLESS VARIANT.

No longer need this be so. The growing distinction—common especially in law—is that *effect* means "to cause to happen, to bring about" <effect a coup>, while *effectuate* means "to give practical effect to (some underlying goal)" <effectuating the purpose of the statute>. As a matter of word frequency, *effect* (as a verb) is much more common than *effectuate.*

effective; efficacious; efficient; effectual. All these words mean generally "having effect," but they have distinctive applications. *Effective* = (1) having a high degree of effect (used of a thing done or of the doer) <more effective study habits>; or (2) coming into effect <effective June 3, 1994>. *Efficacious* = certain to have the desired effect (used of things) <efficacious drugs>. *Efficient* = competent to perform a task; capable of bringing about a desired effect (used of agents or their actions or instruments) <an efficient organization>. *Efficient* increasingly has economic connotations.

Effectual, the rarest and perhaps the most troublesome of these words, means "achieving the complete effect aimed at"—e.g.:

- "The power over the purse may in fact be regarded as the most complete and *effectual* weapon with which any Constitution can arm the immediate representatives of the people." Letter of William Hall, "Gingrich and Founding Fathers," *Advocate* (Baton Rouge), 22 Jan. 1996, at B6 (paraphrasing *The Federalist* No. 58).
- "Not only is the rabies vaccine completely *effectual* for dogs and cats, but more states are requiring proof of a rabies vaccine to obtain a license for a dog." Ann L. Huntington, "Vaccine Has Not Eliminated Rabies Threat," *Hartford Courant,* 26 Mar. 1996, at E5. (In that sentence, *completely* is redundant with *effectual.* See **completely.**)
- "George Washington [remarked] in his first annual message to Congress in 1790 that to be prepared for war is one of the most *effectual* ways of preserving peace." Merrick Carey & Loren Thompson, "Misplaced Priorities on Preserving the Peace," *Wash. Times,* 29 May 1996, at A17.

Why the most troublesome? Because *effectual* is often stretched to describe a person instead of a person's action or some other thing—e.g.:

- "Jenkins . . . became a not wholly *effectual* [read *effective*] President of the Commission." "A Grand Old Chancer: Profile of Roy Jenkins," *Sunday Telegraph,* 7 Jan. 1996, at 25.
- "They seem to shy away from any moves to render the society more responsive and council members more

effectual [read *effective*]." "An Open Letter to the Profession," *Lawyer*, 13 Feb. 1996, at 14.

- "Staffing of the role with *effectual* [read *effective*] individuals is crucial for maximizing an asset's effects." Hugh McFadden, "Common Sense: Improving the Efficacy of Wide Area Surveillance," *Air & Space Power J.*, Mar.–Apr. 2015, at 74.

This stretch is all the more understandable because the negative form—*ineffectual*—usually does describe a person <an ineffectual manager>. But the history of *effectual* has not been parallel: most often, it doesn't refer to people.

On the use of *effectually* for *effectively*, see **effectively.**

LANGUAGE-CHANGE INDEX

effectual misused for *effective*: Stage 3

effectively; effectually. *Effectively* = (1) in an effective manner; well <to speak effectively>; (2) in effect, actually <she has effectively become his mother-surrogate>; or (3) completely; almost completely <that resource is now effectively gone>. All three senses are common.

Effectually (= completely achieving the desired result) often wrongly displaces *effectively* in senses 2 and 3—e.g.:

- "Schools [that] had once been mixed were now *effectually* [read *effectively*] segregated." Nik Cohn, "Aftershock: The Bradford Riots Came as a Surprise to Outsiders," *Guardian*, 15 July 1995, at T20.
- "And introduction of government assistance dictated secularization of the programs, he said, *effectually* [read *effectively*] cutting out the very heart that made it successful." Maureen Boyce, "Group Says Religion Key to Helping Homeless," *Sun-Sentinel* (Ft. Lauderdale), 10 July 1996, City Plus §, at 6.

Curiously, the adverb *effectually* was significantly more common than *effectively* until just after 1900, when the word-frequency poles were suddenly reversed. Why that is so remains a minor linguistic mystery. See **effective.**

LANGUAGE-CHANGE INDEX

effectually misused for *effectively*: Stage 2

effectual. See **effective.**

effectually. See **effectively.**

effectuate. See **effect (c).**

effeminate. See **female.**

effete, now a SKUNKED TERM, has traditionally meant "worn out, barren, exhausted"—e.g.:

- "In contrast, many of the new album's icily elegant, minor-chord-driven tunes sound uninspired, *effete*, even cynical—older indeed, but not necessarily in ways that one associates with creative growth." Elysa Gardner, "Record Rack," *L.A. Times*, 12 May 1996, Calendar §, at 69.

- "Since a population tends to be mirrored by its elected representatives, this has resulted in an *effete* city council generally devoid of original ideas." Letter of Gene Bunnting, "Move on Annexation," *Houston Chron.*, 21 May 1996, at A23.

But today—owing in large measure to Vice President Spiro Agnew, who used the phrase *effete corps of impudent snobs*—writers have made it the victim of SLIPSHOD EXTENSION, often using it to mean "sophisticated and snobbish." This development might show the influence of the rhyme with *elite*. In any event, the usage predates Agnew's famous phrase by several decades, having arisen in the 1920s. It was quite common by the latter half of the 20th century—e.g.:

- " 'He was cooing to her like a turtle dove. After her money, of course. All the same, these *effete* [read *decadent*] aristocrats of the old country. Make a noise like a rich widow anywhere in England, and out come all the Dukes and Earls and Viscounts, howling like wolves.' " P.G. Wodehouse, *The Return of Jeeves* 111 (1954).
- "True Chicagoans know that South Siders—salt-of-the-earth, blue-collar beer drinkers—are Sox fans, while *effete*, [read *stuffy* (no comma)] North Side yuppies are Cubs fans." Sara Paretsky, "Baptism in the Bungalow Belt," *Chicago Trib.*, 29 Aug. 1996, at N3.
- "Now, lest I be branded *an effete* [read *a sophisticated*] lunchroom snob, my second-favorite lunch was Campbell's Chicken Gumbo soup in one of those smelly old-fashioned thermoses." Maureen Clancy, "Lunch Box Memories," *San Diego Union-Trib.*, 5 Sept. 1996, Food §, at 5.

Still others use it as a genteelism denoting weakness or (surely because the words look similar) effeminacy—e.g.:

- "I had already done what I could to protect him, insisting he be given a normal-sounding, non-French, regular-kind-of-guy name, and extracting a solemn promise from my wife that there would be no prissy haircuts or other *effete* [read *frilly* or *effeminate*] embellishments." Joe Dirck, "Poodle?! He's a Peruvian Pit Bull," *Plain Dealer* (Cleveland), 28 Apr. 1996, at B1.
- "From the 1940s on, American film saw the rise of a snide, supercilious and vaguely gay villain, starting with the manipulative Clifton Webb in the detective noir film *Laura*. That tradition of the *effete* [read *effeminate*], aristocratic villain has lived on." Ana Swanson, "The Love That Dare Not Speak?" *Toronto Star*, 2 Aug. 2015, Insight §, at 2.
- "But Buckley's *effete* [read *refined* or *genteel*] mannerisms were also in Vidal's cross hairs. 'They're both gay-baiting each other,' Neville notes." John Anderson, "The Birth of TV News Discourse," *Wash. Post*, 6 Aug. 2015, at C1 (referring to William F. Buckley and Gore Vidal).

As with other skunked terms, the thing to do is simply to avoid using it.

LANGUAGE-CHANGE INDEX

1. *effete* to mean "sophisticated, snobbish": Stage 4
2. *effete* to mean "effeminate": Stage 3

LANGUAGE-CHANGE INDEX (For the full key, see front matter pp. xxxi, l–li.)
Stage 1: Rejected. **Stage 2:** Widely shunned. **Stage 3:** Widespread but . . . **Stage 4:** Ubiquitous but . . . **Stage 5:** Fully accepted.
Invariably inferior forms marked by asterisk (∗). • Ratios represent frequency of prevalent forms vs. variants in current books.

efficacious. See **effective.**

efficacy; efficiency. *Efficacy* = the capacity for producing a desired effect; effectiveness <the drugs had greater efficacy when administered at bedtime>. *Efficiency* = the ability to accomplish something with minimum time or effort <the managers worked on improving plant efficiency>. So *efficacy* exists when you can do something at all, while *efficiency* exists when you can do something quickly and well.

efficient. See **effective.**

effluence (= something that flows out) has come into use as a EUPHEMISM for various bodily excretions—e.g.:

- "To those who are sweating, hurting and knocking the *effluence* out of one another in the humidity-soaked, 90-plus heat, this amounts to a free ride." Gene Seymour, "Haircut, Rookie Year Over for Sauerbrun," *State J.-Register* (Springfield, Ill.), 20 July 1996, Sports §, at 9.
- "An ugly naked man does painful, bloody damage to himself (he pares his fingernails with a knife down to the bone, for example), eats his nose *effluence* and hammers his teeth." Barbara Schulgasser, "Spike and Mike's Animated Shorts Long to Be Tasteless," *S.F. Examiner*, 20 Sept. 1996, at C5.
- "European travelers arriving in the Indian state of Goa in 1990 were met at the airport by animal *effluence* and epithets." Crocker Snow Jr., "Tourism Destroys Tourism," *WorldPaper*, Sept. 1996, at 3.

If this trend continues, the word will degenerate so that it will no longer be possible to write about *effluence* with positive connotations, as here: "The magic scent is not some romantic elixir but the aromatic *effluence* of our immune system." F. Bryant Furlow, "The Smell of Love: How Women Rate the Sexiness and Pleasantness of a Man's Body Odor Hinges on How Much of Their Genetic Profile Is Shared," *Psychology Today*, Mar. 1996, at 38.

The word is pronounced /**ef**-loo-ən[t]s/. Cf. **affluence.**

effluvium. A. Plural Form. *Effluvium* (= [1] a smelly emanation or stench; or [2] industrial waste) forms the plurals *effluvia* and *effluviums*. The former has long predominated and is established as standard. See PLURALS (B).

Current ratio (*effluvia* vs. *effluviums*): 97:1

B. Singular Form. By noxious contamination, the plural form *effluvia* has invaded the territory of the singular. It ought to be rebuffed, usually not by changing to *effluvium* but by making the verb plural—e.g.: "What distinguishes this brisk and eminently readable book from the business-related *effluvia* that *crosses* [read *cross*] our desks is Adler's almost canine attention to the real story." Gil Schwartz, "This Hole Was the Pits," *Fortune*, 14 June 1993, at 140. Why not *effluvium crosses*? Because the plural form *effluvia* has taken on figurative senses for which the singular is largely considered inappropriate or unavailable—as in that sentence. It appears likely that *effluvium* will go

the way of *datum*: the plural form is relatively common (and struggling to stay plural), while the singular form is disappearing. See **data.**

LANGUAGE-CHANGE INDEX
effluvia misused as a singular: Stage 1

effrontery. A. For *affront*. *Effrontery* (= shameless insolence), when misused for *affront* (= an open insult), is a MALAPROPISM. E.g.:

- "This is the ultimate *effrontery* [read *affront*] to the people who support the team—the fans." "Don't Tread on Me," *St. Louis Post-Dispatch*, 15 Sept. 1989, at C2.
- "The novel carries with it the noble lesson that a premature verdict based on supposition is an *effrontery* [read *affront*] to justice if the dignity of even one person is abridged or disregarded." Bruce Simon, "Mob Action Has Tragic Aftermath," *Richmond Times-Dispatch*, 19 Nov. 1995, at G4.

LANGUAGE-CHANGE INDEX
effrontery misused for *affront*: Stage 1
Current ratio (*an affront to* vs. *an effrontery to): 252:1

B. Misspelled *affrontery.** This MALAPROPISM has occurred with some frequency since the late 18th century. It remains fairly common today—e.g.:

- "His fiery Spanish nature refused to allow him to accept such *affrontery* [read *effrontery*]." Furman Bisher, "Alvarez Puts 'W' Back in Wisconsin," *Atlanta J.-Const.*, 4 Mar. 1994, at E1.
- "Sweet the vista was, until a barman had the *affrontery* [read *effrontery*] to rattle through the aisle with a cart bearing cans of Dortmunder Union." Cal Fussman, "Tilting at Beer Kegs," *Esquire*, Feb. 1998, at 96.
- "But beware, the august Augusta acres don't take too kindly toward such *affrontery* [read *effrontery*]. This battleground of Richmond County is littered with the great expectations of players who have led the Masters after the first round." Furman Bisher, "History Against DiMarco," *Atlanta J.-Const.*, 6 Apr. 2001, at D10.

The correct form *effrontery* derives from the French *effronté* (lit., "shameless"). The erroneous form *affrontery has no real pedigree because it isn't a legitimate word: the *OED* calls it an obsolete mistake for *effrontery*, and the permissive *W3* doesn't even record it. In fact, the error results from confusion with *affront*, which derives from the French *affronter* (lit., "to confront" or "to strike on the head"). See NONWORDS.

LANGUAGE-CHANGE INDEX
*affrontery for *effrontery*: Stage 1
Current ratio (*effrontery* vs. *affrontery): 141:1

effulge. See BACK-FORMATIONS.

-EFY. See -FY.

e.g. A. Generally. This abbreviation, short for *exempli gratia* (/ek-**sem**-plee **grah**-tee-ə/) [L. "for example"], introduces representative examples. In AmE, it is preferably followed by a comma (or, depending on the construction, a colon) and unitalicized. In BrE, curiously enough, the periods are sometimes omitted—e.g.: "The problem with seeking a legislative cure for the ethical disease is that most of the perceived outrages are either already illegal (*eg*, Pentagon officials taking bribes) or beyond the reach of the law (politicians' sexual adventures)." "Washington on an Ethics Kick," *Economist*, 28 Jan.–3 Feb. 1989, at 19. To American eyes, *eg* looks like *egg* misspelled.

B. Style and Usage. As with other familiar abbreviations of Latin phrases—such as *etc.*, *et al.*, and *i.e.* (and despite the way they appear in this sentence)—*e.g.* is not italicized <serve with a favorite fruit, e.g., peaches or apricots>. And like the others, it is best confined to lists, parenthetical matter, and citations rather than in text, where some substitute such as *for example* is more natural <it goes well with fruit, such as peaches or apricots>.

C. With *etc*. Using the abbreviation *etc.* after an enumeration following *e.g.* is superfluous because one expects nothing more than a representative sample of possibilities. But *etc.* might be required after *i.e.* (L. *id est* "that is") to show the incompleteness of the list.

D. Clear Reference. One should clearly indicate what the signal refers to: "Out-of-pocket losses include medical expenses, lost earnings, and the cost of any labor required to do things that the plaintiff can no longer do himself (e.g., a housekeeper)." But "things that the plaintiff can no longer do himself" are not exemplified by *a housekeeper*. (Or does the writer mean *housekeeping* or *be a housekeeper*?) In any event, wherever readers encounter an *e.g.*, they rightly expect a sampling of appropriate items—not an ambiguous or all-inclusive listing. In the given example, it might be: *e.g., keep house, drive a car, tend the garden.* See **i.e.**

*egality is the anglicized form of the French *égalité* (= equality). The *OED* pronounces the GALLICISM obsolete, and so it should be, in deference to *equality*. E.g.:

- "Is this a sign of greater *egality* [read *equality*], inverted snobbery, or simple confusion?" Robert Harris, "The Way We Were," *Sunday Times* (London), 22 July 1990, Books §, at 8-1.
- "But one of the wealthier families, acting out of a sense of *egality* [read *equality*] and good fellowship, would insist that all members of the class be included in their children's guest lists." Charlton Heston, "Heston on Heston," *Chicago Trib.*, 3 Sept. 1995, Sunday Mag. §, at 13.
- "Thus Marx lives on, masquerading as social justice, *egality* [read *equality*] and fairness—all the while punishing people for being productive and successful." Editorial, "Wealth Distribution Bias," *Saratoga Herald-Trib.*, 5 July 2000, at A12.

*egis. See **aegis.**

egotism; egoism; egocentrism; egocentricity; egomania. *Egotism* = an exaggerated sense of self-importance; self-praise; arrogance. *Egoism* is a philosophical term meaning "a doctrine that self-betterment is the guiding method of existence, or that self-interest is the primary motive in all one's

actions." The use of *egoism* in the sense "selfishness" is a SLIPSHOD EXTENSION—e.g.:

- "Minnesotans esteem honest intellectual pursuit, practiced without *egoism* [read *egotism*] or puffery." *Star Trib.* (Minneapolis), 22 June 2002, at A20.
- "Unlike his peers—Lawrence J. Ellison of Oracle, Steven P. Jobs of Apple Computer or Bill Gates of Microsoft—he is not only not a technologist, he is also not known for overt *egoism* [read *egotism*], or for ruffling feathers." Matt Richtel, "A Cheerleader, for a Company in a Midlife Funk," *N.Y. Times*, 23 June 2002, § 3, at 1. (Notice how the four negatives in one sentence fatigue the reader, and the unparallel construction deepens the mire.)
- "Finally, we'd look for a healthy combination of humility (to prevent obstructive *egoism* [read *egotism*]), intelligence and creativity." Editorial, "Help Wanted: Supervisor," *Roanoke Times*, 8 Oct. 2002, at A12.

The other three words are closely related. *Egocentrism* and *egocentricity* are synonymous, with perhaps a slight degree of difference. *Egocentrism* = the quality of being self-centered and selfish; looking only to one's own feelings and needs. *Egocentricity* = the quality of being egocentric, individualistic, or self-centered. *Egomania* is extreme *egocentrism*.

> LANGUAGE-CHANGE INDEX
> *egoism* misused for *egotism*: Stage 2

egregious /i-**gree**-jəs/ formerly meant "outstanding," but has been specialized in a pejorative sense so that it now means "outstandingly bad." E.g.:

- "Without their coaches' guidance, thousands of children will walk away from major-league ballparks and Little League fields believing that gifted athletes can get away with *egregious* behavior." Adrienne T. Washington, "Orioles Strike Out by Supporting Alomar," *Wash. Times*, 4 Oct. 1996, at C2.
- "I should be a most *egregious* host to expose my guests to the tender mercies of the servants in the Pope's Little House." Chelsea Quinn Yarbro, *Communion Blood* 75 (1999) (the Pope's Little House being the starting point of an inquisitorial condemnation).
- "The subject fires up people on all sides of liability disputes: the ones who've been harmed; the budget hawks; and the lawmakers who scuffle year after year over special relief bills to get cash for victims of *egregious* acts that left people injured for life." Steve Patterson, "Golf Course Owner Fuming Over Cost to Fix Bulldozer Damage Caused by State," *St. Augustine Record* (Fla.), 26 Aug. 2015, News §.

> LANGUAGE-CHANGE INDEX
> *egregious* in the sense "very bad": Stage 5

egress. See **ingress.**

eisegesis. See **exegesis.**

either. A. Pronunciation. The preferred pronunciation is /**ee**-thər/, not /**ɪ**-thər/. This has long been so. A 19th-century linguist criticized the *eye* pronunciation, calling the *ee* pronunciation "better-supported and more analogical." William Dwight Whitney,

LANGUAGE-CHANGE INDEX (For the full key, see front matter pp. xxxi, l–li.)
Stage 1: Rejected. **Stage 2:** Widely shunned. **Stage 3:** Widespread but . . . **Stage 4:** Ubiquitous but . . . **Stage 5:** Fully accepted.
Invariably inferior forms marked by asterisk (*). • Ratios represent frequency of prevalent forms vs. variants in current books.

Language and the Study of Language 43 (5th ed. 1874). Still, /ɪ-thər/ is the dominant pronunciation in BrE, and it remains common (though arguably pretentious) in AmE. Cf. **neither (A)**.

B. Number of Elements. Most properly, *either . . . or* can frame only two alternatives, and no more: "Now Mr. Arafat has failed for a year to keep the promise without which he never would have seen *either* the White House, its lawn, Mr. Clinton *or* Mr. Rabin [omit *either*]." A.M. Rosenthal, "Yasir Arafat's Promise," *Wall Street J.*, 9 Sept. 1994, at A15.

It is understandable that writers would want to be able to say *any of the following* in fewer than seven syllables—and those who like *either* for this purpose may succeed in the long run. But the better practice, for the time being, is to rely on the disjunctive *or* for a list of many—not *either . . . or*. Cf. **neither.**

LANGUAGE-CHANGE INDEX
either . . . or with more than two items: Stage 3

C. Faulty Parallelism with *either . . . or*. This is a common problem: "New Hampshire Right to Life sends its newsletter to about 10,000 abortion opponents that Mrs. Hagan said *either contributed money or time* [read *contributed either money or time*] to the cause." Gustav Niebuhr, "G.O.P. Race Jumps to Where Fundamentalists Are Few and Far Between," *N.Y. Times*, 19 Feb. 1996, at A9. See PARALLELISM.

D. Singular or Plural. As the subject of a clause, *either* takes a singular verb—e.g.:

- "The law [is] . . . supposed to be 'family friendly,' but we suggest you keep the kids away from Mom or Dad next April when *either* of them *are* [read *is*] bouncing off the walls with the complex instructions for filing claims." "Getting Taxes on Track," *Wall Street J.*, 2 Oct. 1997, at A22.
- "Reimer did not say whether *either* of them *is* a job candidate." "McKinney Stripped of Army Title in Sex Case," *Sun-Sentinel* (Ft. Lauderdale), 10 Oct. 1997, at A5.

Nouns framed by *either . . . or* take a singular verb when the noun closest to the verb is singular, but a plural verb when that noun is plural—e.g.:

- "What happens when grown children continue to pull on mom's apron strings or play on her 'mom guilt' for longer than *either they or she needs*?" Ruth Walsh, "Magazine's 'Mover and Shaper' to Speak," *St. Petersburg Times*, 5 Jan. 1994, at D2.
- "He gives every sign of not stopping until *either he or they are* thoroughly defeated." Marianne Means, "Investigators Waiting in the Wings," *Rocky Mountain News* (Denver), 3 Nov. 1996, at A81.

LANGUAGE-CHANGE INDEX
either . . . or construction followed by a verb not agreeing with second member: Stage 3

E. *Not . . . either*. This phrasing should typically be a *neither . . . nor* construction—e.g.: "They are cynical shams that *do not require either* the council *or* the mayor to abide the weak processes they establish." "Flouting the Public's Will," *Times-Picayune* (New Orleans), 15 Mar. 1996, at B6. (A possible revision: *They are cynical shams that require neither the council nor the mayor even to abide the weak processes they establish.*)

F. *Either or both*. This phrase denotes the meaning generally assigned to *and/or*. Generally speaking, though, neither phrase finds a place in good writing. E.g.: "*Either or both* [read *Both*] parties may expect increasing voter disinterest if they accept newly elected members running as members of the other party." Letter of Charles P. Hughes, "Whatta Deal?" *Chattanooga Times*, 13 Apr. 1995, at A6. (On the use of *disinterest* in that sentence, see **disinterest**.) See **and/or.**

G. Meaning "each of two" or "both." *Either* in this sense <houses on either side of the street> is less common than *each* (or *both*). But it is perfectly idiomatic—e.g.: "The framed lists—there is one on *either* side of the chapel—are rolls of all the Dominican sisters from the Springfield Roman Catholic diocese." Steven Spearie, "Sisters in Spirit," *State J.-Register* (Springfield, Ill.), 28 Nov. 1997, at A7.

For more on *either . . . or*, see CORRELATIVE CONJUNCTIONS & PARALLELISM.

ejaculate. Though one of Henry James's favorites, this verb can no longer be used in sober writing as a synonym for "exclaim." Today it inevitably carries sexual overtones, even when the exclamatory meaning is the primary one. E.g.: "An enormous kerfuffle erupted nearby, followed by a shriek of maniacal laughter. 'Crumbs!' *ejaculated* [read *exclaimed*] William. 'What was that?'" David Aaronovitch, "Violet Voter Finds Just the Job for William," *Independent*, 9 Oct. 1997, at 6.

ejectee. See -EE.

eke out, a PHRASAL VERB, has traditionally meant "to supplement with great effort or bit by bit; to add to (something); to make (something) go further or last longer." Today, this traditional usage is rare, but it still sometimes appears—e.g.:

- "John Andre, their martyred co-conspirator, received a memorial in the Poets Corner of Westminster Abbey—something of an irony since he *eked out* his income by writing doggerel and was unpopular with his fellow officers who patronized him as an opportunist." Robert Taylor, "Benedict Arnold Lost Gamble on Warfare," *Commercial Appeal* (Memphis), 2 Sept. 1990, at G4.
- "The deal promises to be the first in a series of part current, part advance refundings as the fiscally strapped state . . . *ekes out* as much debt service savings as possible." Martin Z. Braun, "N.J. Eyes $450M GO Refunding," *Bond Buyer*, 16 Oct. 2002, at 1.
- "Look up, look down, to attic and basement, for usable space, as we do on Page 5. Look at a handful of clever ideas about where else to *eke out* space, on Pages 4 and 8." "In Our Houses, Something Real," *Wash. Post*, 16 Oct. 2002, at T2.

Instead, the phrase is most commonly used nowadays in the sense "to succeed in obtaining or sustaining (a thing) with great difficulty"—e.g.:

- "In Tokyo, stocks *eked out* small gains by the end of Friday's session after a three-day winning streak." "Stocks Languish in Flat Session," *S.F. Examiner*, 27 Sept. 1996, at B1.
- "Dick Chrysler . . . *eked out* a narrow victory in 1994." Matthew Rees, "The Mini-Clintons," *Weekly Standard*, 14 Oct. 1996, at 8.

Although this usage began by SLIPSHOD EXTENSION, it is now firmly entrenched as standard.

Unfortunately, by still further extension, sportswriters have come to use *eke* without its inseparable companion *out*, as if it meant something like *squeak*—e.g.: "Actually, you surely noticed that Northwestern *eked* [read *squeaked*? *fought*?] back into the Top 25 to take the last rung on the strength of whipping the mighty Ohio U. Bobcats." Larry Guest, "Why Are the Pollsters Against Northwestern?" *Orlando Sentinel*, 25 Sept. 1996, at D1.

LANGUAGE-CHANGE INDEX
1. *eke out* in the sense "to get by with great difficulty": Stage 5
2. *eke* misused for *squeak* or *fight*: Stage 3

-EL. See DIMINUTIVES (c).

elaborate, vb., may be either transitive <to elaborate a point> or (more commonly) intransitive <to elaborate on a point>. Although both *to elaborate* and *to elaborate on* may mean "to work out in detail," the former suggests "to produce by labor," and the latter suggests "to explain at greater length." Knowing this nuance allows you to choose the apter phrasing.

elapse once had two uses, as a noun and as a verb. Today, however, the noun is an ARCHAISM—*lapse* being the noun corresponding to the verb *elapse*. E.g.:

- "Thus, only those emigrating permanently will escape the charge and only then after the *elapse* [read *lapse*] of three years and in relation to non-UK assets." Donald Elkin, "Finance & the Family (Expatriates)," *Fin. Times*, 14 July 1990, at vi.
- "But the *elapse* [read *lapse*] of 21 years had weakened much of the evidence, and the district attorney refused to prosecute the case." Kevin Johnson, "Cold Cases: The Heat's on Now," *USA Today*, 19 Sept. 1995, at A3.
- "Many of the faces repeat with an *elapse* [read *a lapse*] of years, turning giggly, sparrowlike girls in middy blouses into graceful young women or pensive boys into jocular young adults." Carolyn Jack, "Prints from Glass Plates Depict Life of River Town," *Plain Dealer* (Cleveland), 29 Mar. 2002, at E1.

LANGUAGE-CHANGE INDEX
elapse used for *lapse*: Stage 1

elder; eldest. These are variants of *older* and *oldest*, with restricted uses such as *elder statesman*, *elder in the church* (or *church elder*), or *elder brother* (or *sister*). If *older* or *oldest* works in context, it's probably the better choice.

elderly. This adjective began as a EUPHEMISM for *aged* or *old*, but even *elderly* has now acquired negative connotations. Perhaps *senior*, the newest euphemism, will one day have to be replaced as our youth-dominated popular culture continually denigrates anything associated with old people.

As an adjective, *elderly* has traditionally been applied most often to people <an elderly aunt>, but it may apply to other living things <an elderly dog> or, rarely, something personified <an elderly ship>.

As a noun, *the elderly* has undergone pejoration and is now generally disused in favor of *senior citizens*. Deciding at what age people become *the elderly* must be left to your own good judgment. That's one advantage of *senior citizen*: American culture has loosely established that you become a senior citizen at 60 to 65. There's no quarrel about that range as being the standard; at 65, only the facts can then be disputed, as some people embark on a post-30 quest to misrepresent their age.

eldritch (= weird, eerie) is sometimes misspelled **eldrich*—e.g.: "June is the month of the summer solstice, and of Midsummer's Eve—when, according to *eldrich* [read *eldritch*] lore, witches, fairies, spirits of the dead and supernatural folk of all sorts are abroad and active." Jim Wise, "Midsummer Past Is Brought Home on a Whiff of Magnolia," *Herald-Sun* (Durham, N.C.), 19 June 2000, at B1.

LANGUAGE-CHANGE INDEX
eldritch misspelled **eldrich*: Stage 1
Current ratio: 30:1

-elect is uniformly hyphenated as a combining form—hence *president-elect*, *chair-elect*, etc. See POSTPOSITIVE ADJECTIVES. See also **bride-to-be.**

elector = (1) esp. in BrE, a legally qualified voter; or (2) in AmE, a member of the electoral college chosen by the states to elect the president and vice president. Sense 1 appears occasionally in AmE, especially in older works—e.g.: "The first view to be taken of this part of the government relates to the qualifications of the *electors* and the elected." *The Federalist* No. 52, at 325 (James Madison) (Clinton Rossiter ed., 1961). Sense 2 is more usual in modern AmE—e.g.: "The President held office for four years and then had to be given—or denied—a second term by *electors* picked by the people." Fred Rodell, *Nine Men* 44 (1955).

electoral (= of, relating to, or involving electors) is so spelled. But **electorial* is a common misspelling—e.g.:

- "Their analyses of Liberal bills on *electorial* [read *electoral*] redistribution, settling Pearson airport contracts, and Yukon Indian settlements were thorough." Douglas Fisher, "Media Prejudice Traps Reformers," *Toronto Sun*, 22 July 1994, at 11.
- "Both camps agreed that today's Supreme Court hearing will be the defining moment in a five-week battle over who is the winner of Florida's 25 *electorial* [read *electoral*] votes, which either candidate would need to reach the 270 *electorial* [read *electoral*] votes required to win the White House." William Douglas, "Supreme Court to Hear Arguments Today That Could Finally Settle Battle for White House," *Newsday* (N.Y.), 11 Dec. 2000, at A4. (The

LANGUAGE-CHANGE INDEX (For the full key, see front matter pp. xxxi, l–li.)
Stage 1: Rejected. **Stage 2:** Widely shunned. **Stage 3:** Widespread but . . . **Stage 4:** Ubiquitous but . . . **Stage 5:** Fully accepted.
Invariably inferior forms marked by asterisk (*). • Ratios represent frequency of prevalent forms vs. variants in current books.

both . . . *agree* construction is redundant in that sentence: see **both** (**c**).)

- " 'The proliferation of these marriage-definition ballot measures in a quarter of the states during the same election cycle shows how easily journeyman political organizers, whether conservative or liberal, can manipulate the *electorial* [read *electoral*] debate with hot-button issues,' said Executive Director Edwin Bender." Julie Carr Smyth, "Funds Flowed to Ohio for Gay-Marriage Vote," *Plain Dealer* (Cleveland), 25 Jan. 2006, at B2.

The word is preferably pronounced /i-**lek**-tə-rəl/, not /ee-lek-**tor**-əl/.

LANGUAGE-CHANGE INDEX
electoral misspelled **electorial*: Stage 1
Current ratio: 5,203:1

electric; electrical; electronic. *Electric* = (1) of, relating to, or operated by electricity <electric train> <electric chair>; or (2) thrilling; emotionally charged <a musician's electric performance>. *Electrical* overlaps with sense 1 of *electric*—that is, it commonly means "concerned with electricity" <electrical engineering> <electrical outlet>. The choice between the two seems to be governed largely by euphony: although *electric* is more usual, *electrical* occurs in a few SET PHRASES beginning with vowels.

Electronic = (1) of, relating to, or involving electrons; or (2) of, relating to, or involving the branch of physics known as electronics, or to systems or devices developed through this science. Sense 2 is far more common—e.g.: "Toyota treats a blueprint for a change on an engineer's desk (or its *electronic* equivalent) the way it would an unfinished component." Alex Taylor III, "How Toyota Defies Gravity," *Fortune*, 8 Dec. 1997, at 100.

eleemosynary /el-ə-**mos**-ə-ner-ee/, related etymologically to the word *alms*, is a FORMAL WORD for *charitable*. E.g.:

- "It requires an effort considerably more sustained than the bursts of *eleemosynary* fervor witnessed at holiday time." Clyde Haberman, "Giving Thanks at St. Bartholomew's," *N.Y. Times*, 22 Nov. 1995, at B7.
- "In fact, Roper is an *eleemosynary* institution, and the Medical Society of South Carolina acts only in the capacity of trustees, not owners." "Tradition Powerful," *Post & Courier* (Charleston, S.C.), 10 Aug. 1996, at A14.

elegance; elegancy. A distinction has emerged. *Elegance* is the quality or state of being elegant. *Elegancy* is a thing that is thought to be elegant. Concededly, though, the history of these words is a messy one. Since 1750, *elegance* has eclipsed *elegancy* in frequency of occurrence.

Current ratio: 180:1

ELEGANT VARIATION. See INELEGANT VARIATION.

elegy; eulogy. An *elegy* is a mournful song or poem, whereas a *eulogy* is a funeral oration or, by extension, a laudatory speech. Writers occasionally misuse *elegy* for *eulogy*—e.g.:

- "Speaking in precise, well-crafted paragraphs, Poland's most popular political figure delivered an

extemporaneous *elegy* [read *eulogy*] to the movement that had spawned him." Adam Karatnycky, "The Age of Solidarity: Testing Poland's Patience," *New Republic*, 11 June 1990, at 20, 21.
- "Thirteen bright student orators delivered formal *elegies* [read *eulogies*] to education and shared personal stories of fear, striving and laughter." Dan Carpenter, "Parting Words," *Indianapolis Star*, 11 June 1995, at A1.
- "After the players were introduced, Knight gave a moving *elegy* [read *eulogy*] for his old coach and friend." "Just One Minute: College Basketball," *Indianapolis Star*, 1 Feb. 2010, at B1.

LANGUAGE-CHANGE INDEX
elegy misused for *eulogy*: Stage 1

elemental; elementary. *Elemental* is the more specific term, meaning (1) "of, relating to, or involving the elements of something; essential" <an elemental component of the machine>; or (2) "of, relating to, or involving a force of nature, or something like it" <elemental rage>. E.g.: "From the ringing words of his first inaugural—'the only thing we have to fear is fear itself'—Roosevelt's presidency was about taking charge and *elemental* fairness." David Warsh, "Hollywood vs. History Books," *Boston Globe*, 24 Dec. 1995, at 69.

Elementary means "introductory; simple; fundamental." E.g.: "Ms. Handler [noted] that the company's real goal was to realize Mr. Hillis's dream of building computers that could 'learn' and perform more than *elementary* reasoning." David E. Sanger, "A Computer Full of Surprises," *N.Y. Times*, 8 May 1987, at D1.

elephantine (= slow, heavy, and awkward, like an elephant) is pronounced /el-i-**fan**-tin/, /el-i-**fan**-teen/, or /el-i-**fan**-tin/—always with the accent on the third syllable, not the first or last. See ANIMAL ADJECTIVES.

elf. Pl. *elves*. See PLURALS (**c**).

elfin; elfish; elvish. The distinction is slight. *Elfin* = (1) of, relating to, or resembling an elf; or (2) having the magical qualities of an elf. *Elfish* = having the mischievous, prankish qualities of an elf. *Elvish* is a NEEDLESS VARIANT of *elfin*, but it's also a language in J.R.R. Tolkien's *Rings* trilogy (a capitalized proper noun in this sense).

elicit. See **illicit** & **solicit** (**A**).

eligible may be equally well construed with either *for* or *to* (an office). *Eligible for* is more common today—e.g.: "Vicki Johnson, formerly of Parkway Place, whose history as a good tenant made her and her two children *eligible for* relocation, summed up our sentiments exactly." "Scattered-Site Housing," *Courier-J.* (Louisville), 3 Oct. 1996, at A10.

But *eligible to*, though archaic-sounding today, has unimpeachable credentials—e.g.:

- "No person except a natural born citizen . . . shall be *eligible to* the office of president." U.S. Const. art. II, § 1.
- "No judge of any court . . . shall during the term for which he is elected or appointed, be *eligible to* the legislature." Tex. Const. art. III, § 19.

Current ratio (*eligible for the* vs. *eligible to the*): 11:1

eliminate, strictly speaking, means to get rid of something that already exists <we downsized to eliminate several layers of bureaucracy that had built up>. The verb should not be misused for *prevent* or *avoid*; that is, it shouldn't refer to something that doesn't yet exist. E.g.:

- "Two readers who experienced debilitating crashes with Power Mac 8500 systems were able to *eliminate* [read *prevent*] crashes by moving DRAM DIMMS away from the vicinity of the cache." Ric Ford, "Coming Clean: Apple Has a New Set of PCI Updates," *MacWEEK*, 4 Dec. 1995, at 52.
- "You will save wear and tear on your back and *eliminate* [read *prevent*] future back problems with this simple precaution." "*Quality* [read *High-Quality*] Tools Will Make Garden Work Easier," *State J.-Register* (Springfield, Ill.), 27 Dec. 2002, Mag. §, at A11. (For more on the use of *quality* here, see **quality.**)

LANGUAGE-CHANGE INDEX
eliminate misused for *prevent*: Stage 2

-ELLE; -ELLA. See DIMINUTIVES (D).

ELLIPSES. See PUNCTUATION (F) & QUOTATIONS (E).

elliptic; elliptical. There is much overlap. The adjective *elliptic* most strongly corresponds to the noun *ellipse*, the geometric term—e.g.: "Mars is fourth from the sun, having an *elliptic* orbit ranging from 129 to 156 million miles distant from it, compared to our average 93 million miles." Mina Walther, "Far from Humble, There May Be No Place Like Home: Earth," *Sarasota Herald-Trib.*, 8 Sept. 1996, at F6.

The adjective *elliptical* traditionally corresponds most strongly to *ellipsis*, the grammatical and rhetorical term for an omission—e.g.: " 'Goodbye South, Goodbye' tells its difficult-to-follow story in a fractured *elliptical* style that mirrors the characters' rootless, jumpy lives." Stephen Holden, "Wheeling and Dealing in Taiwan's Backwaters," *N.Y. Times*, 1 Oct. 1996, at C13. See -IC.

The four-syllable *elliptical* occurs more than twice as often in print as *elliptic*, and the DIFFERENTIATION suggested above may not hold firm—given the rise in the 1990s of "ellipticals" as training equipment (also known as "elliptical machines"). These machines have the user's feet travel in an ellipse. What may happen in the long term is that *elliptic* will be the scientific term answering to *ellipse* and that *elliptical* will be the popular term for all senses.

elocute, meaning "to speak in a grand, affected manner," is a usually facetious BACK-FORMATION from *elocution*—e.g.: "Simon Russell Beale plays Oswald, the afflicted Alving son. He's an actor who *elocutes* so well that talk no longer reveals character but effectively conceals it." Vincent Canby, "A Crowd Under the National's Umbrella," *N.Y. Times*, 12 June 1994, § 2, at 5.

elocution; locution; allocution. *Elocution* = style in speaking; the art of speaking persuasively. *Locution* = a word or phrase. *Allocution* = (1) a formal address; (2) a judge's formal address asking a criminal defendant to speak in mitigation of the sentence to be imposed; or (3) loosely, a criminal defendant's speech in mitigation of the sentence to be imposed.

elope. The *OED* and many other dictionaries define this term as if it had historically been a sexist one in law: "**a.** *Law.* Of a wife: To run away from her husband in the company of a paramour. **b.** In popular language also (and more frequently) said of a woman running away from home with a lover for the purpose of being married" (*OED*). These definitions suggest that only women can elope, but even legal writers have long made men as well as women elopers—e.g.:

- "If evidence was admitted to show that House had armed himself, and was hunting for Steadman, under the impression that the latter had *eloped* with his wife, and was secreting himself in that vicinity, it is difficult to see upon what principle his threats in that connection were excluded." *Alexander v. United States*, 138 U.S. 353, 356 (1891).
- "James Campbell had *eloped* with the wife of one Ludlow." *Adger v. Ackerman*, 115 F. 124, 130 (8th Cir. 1902).

Today the word does not ordinarily apply exclusively to women. It may, of course, as here: "After an idyllic childhood, Anderson impulsively *eloped* at 18 and endured a wedding night that she called 'one of the great disasters in the history of sex on this planet.' " Dana Kennedy, "The Anderson Tapes," *Entertainment Weekly*, 27 Oct. 1995, at 82. But more typically the word applies to the couple—e.g.: "He and his bride-to-be decided to *elope* to Canada." Marty Meitus, "Apples of Our Eye," *Rocky Mountain News* (Denver), 9 Oct. 1996, at D3.

*else but; *else than. Instead of either of these ungainly phrases, use a simple *but* or the more idiomatic *other than*—e.g.: "This has nothing to do with some supposed slacker mentality that strikes 20-somethings deaf and dumb to anything *else but* [read *but* or *other than*] the boob tube." Helen Ubinas, "What?! This Place Doesn't Have Cable?!" *Hartford Courant*, 1 Aug. 1997, at E1.

else's. Possessive constructions such as *anyone else's* and *everyone else's* are preferred to the obsolete constructions **anyone's else* and **everyone's else*. Although *whose else* is technically correct, modern usage prefers *who else's* by analogy to the forms made with *anyone* and *everyone*. *Who else's* has predominated over *whose else* in AmE since the 1960s and in BrE since the 1990s. See POSSESSIVES (I).

Current ratio (*anyone else's* vs. **anyone's else*): 168:1
Current ratio (*who else's* vs. *whose else*): 2:1

*else than. See ***else but.**

LANGUAGE-CHANGE INDEX (For the full key, see front matter pp. xxxi, l–li.)
Stage 1: Rejected. **Stage 2:** Widely shunned. **Stage 3:** Widespread but . . . **Stage 4:** Ubiquitous but . . . **Stage 5:** Fully accepted.
Invariably inferior forms marked by asterisk (*). • Ratios represent frequency of prevalent forms vs. variants in current books.

elude. See **allude** (B).

elusive; *elusory; illusory; *illusive; allusive. *Elusive* (rather than *elusory) is the usual adjective related to *elude*; *illusory* (rather than *illusive) is the usual adjective related to *illusion*. In short, *elusory and *illusive are NEEDLESS VARIANTS.

More than that, however, the multiple forms can lead to confusion between them. Most commonly, *illusive is misused for *elusive*—e.g.:

- "This unlikely pair manages to outflank the stolid legal bureaucracy, chase down an *illusive* [read *elusive*] serial killer and still find time to savor Gotham's more exotic attractions." "Crime in the Big Apple," *St. Louis Post-Dispatch*, 14 June 1992, Everyday Mag. §, at C5.
- "One firm . . . specializes in helping students enrolled in prep schools, colleges or universities find the often-*illusive* [read *elusive*] student discount fares offered by most major U.S. airlines." James T. Yenckel, "Discount Fares for Students on the Wing," *Wash. Post*, 27 Mar. 1994, at E1.
- "Pats found the *illusive* [read *elusive*] third goal with just six minutes left on the clock." Jessica Farry, "Pats Wallop Three Goals Past Rovers," *Sligo Champion* (Ireland), 28 July 2015, Sport §, at 38.

Allusive (= containing an allusion or characterized by use of allusion) is also occasionally misused where *elusive* is the intended meaning—e.g.: "Toyota brought Scion, its small car intended to catch the eye of *allusive* [read *elusive*] Gen Y." Jay Binneweg, "A Whimper, Not a Bang," *Santa Fe New Mexican*, 11 Jan. 2003, at E1.

LANGUAGE-CHANGE INDEX
1. *illusive misused for *elusive*: Stage 1
Current ratio (*elusive concept* vs.
*illusive concept): 24:1
2. *allusive* misused for *elusive*: Stage 1

*elvish. See **elfin.**

EM-; IM-. See **EN-.**

e-mail; E-mail; email. Since the 1990s, *e-mail* has remained the prevalent form in print sources. The letter *e*—short for *electronic*—is sometimes capitalized, but the trend is to make it lowercase. The unhyphenated *email* is unsightly, but it might prevail in the end. In print sources, *e-mail* is almost twice as common as *email*. Ultimately, the hyphen may well disappear—since that is what midword hyphens tend to do—but for the time being it is more than holding its own. (The same is true of *e-commerce* and other forms prefixed by *e-*.)

Some bootless objections remain. A few writers have objected to *e-mail* as a shortened form of *e-mail message* <send me an e-mail>—and also to using it as a COUNT NOUN <I had three e-mails>. Both of these uses are now standard. Others have questioned whether *e-mail* should function as a verb <please e-mail me with the answer>, but that question has long since been answered affirmatively.

LANGUAGE-CHANGE INDEX
email for *e-mail*: Stage 4
Current ratio (*e-mail* vs. *email*): 2:1

e-mail list; Listserv. An *e-mail list* is a subscription service through which participants discuss topics relevant to the forum through e-mails. *Listserv* is software that runs *e-mail lists*. Although it is common to see *listserv* used to refer to *e-mail lists* generically, that use should be avoided—e.g.: "For about three years I subscribed to an Internet '*listserv*' [read *e-mail list*] that gave charter enthusiasts across America an opportunity to chat." Marion Brady, "Charter Schools: Incubators of Innovation?" *Orlando Sentinel*, 13 Nov. 2002, at A17. *Listserv* is a registered trademark of L-Soft International, Inc. and should always be capitalized. There is no -*e* on the end of the name because the software was originally written to run on university IBM mainframe computers, whose filenames were limited to eight characters. And so, for example, the name of a list set up to discuss the works of Shakespeare is *Shakspar*.

emanate (= to flow forth, issue, originate from) has diverse uses. Sometimes the word refers to something physical—e.g.: "Inside, the hardwood floors gleamed and delicious aromas *emanated* from the kitchen." Jamie Marshall, "Charm on the Farm," *Town & Country Monthly*, Sept. 1996, at 49. At other times, though, the movement is figurative—e.g.: "All the more ironic was the fact that this fatuous rhetoric *emanated* from Chicago, of all places." "Educators or Lobbyists?" *Wash. Times*, 1 Sept. 1996, at B2.

*embarcation. See **embarkation.**

embargo. Pl. *embargoes*—not *embargos. See PLURALS (D). For more on the word, see **boycott.**
Current ratio: 8:1

embarkation; *embarcation; *embarkment. *Embarkation* = (1) the act of going on board a means of transportation; or (2) the act of starting a mission or enterprise. The second and third forms have been NEEDLESS VARIANTS since the 18th century.
Current ratio (in order of headwords): 64:2:1

embarrass. See SPELLING (A).

embarrassedly. See -EDLY.

*embassador. See **ambassador.**

embassy; legation. Often assumed to be synonymous in diplomatic contexts, these words should be distinguished. An *embassy* is under an ambassador, and a *legation* is under a minister, envoy, chargé d'affaires, or other diplomatic agent not having the titular rank of ambassador.

embattled, adj. This word has traditionally meant "ready for battle," usually in reference to an aggressor whose troops and weapons are ready for fighting. Only since the mid-20th century has the word taken on a sense similar to *beleaguered* (perhaps through sound association with *battered*) and been applied instead to the victim of aggression. Today this derived sense threatens to vanquish the original sense (which might, sadly, be said to be "embattled")—e.g.:

- "The House overwhelmingly agreed to abolish the *embattled* Immigration and Naturalization Service on Thursday and create two new agencies to handle enforcement and immigration services." "National Briefs," *Charleston Gaz.*, 26 Apr. 2002, at A7.
- "This year, NetWorld faces two hurdles: the date and the fact that it serves the *embattled* telecommunications industry." Caroline Wilbert & Russell Grantham, "The Approach of Sept. 11," *Atlanta J.-Const.*, 4 Aug. 2002, at C1.
- "But it may be hard for the SEC and its *embattled* head, Harvey Pitt, to ignore the evidence Congress has unearthed." Samantha Levine et al., "The Trickledown Dow," *U.S. News & World Rep.*, 5 Aug. 2002, at 17.

embezzle; misappropriate; steal. *Embezzle* (= to fraudulently convert personal property that one has been entrusted with) is now always used in reference to fiduciaries. *Misappropriate* means "to take for oneself wrongfully" and may be used of anyone—fiduciary or not. *Steal*, like *misappropriate*, is a broader term than *embezzle*; it has the same meaning as *misappropriate*, but much stronger negative connotations. See **defalcate** (A) & **appropriate** (A).

emblazon; *emblaze; *imblaze. The first is the standard spelling. The second and third are NEEDLESS VARIANTS. See EN-.

Current ratio (in order of headwords): 763:83:1

embryo. Pl. *embryos*, not *embryoes. See PLURALS (D).

Current ratio: 8,143:1

EM-DASHES. See PUNCTUATION (G).

emend. See **amend.**

emery board (= a file used as a manicuring implement) is sometimes misspelled *emory board, as if it had some connection with the Georgia university—e.g.: "With the egg suspended on straws inside the tube of paper taped to a platform of *emory* [read *emery*] boards, Farnhof dropped the device onto a target." Lisa Teachey, "Fun: Learning the Formula for Rice Science Olympiad," *Houston Chron.*, 27 Jan. 1997, at A13. *Emery* is the anglicized version of the French word *émeri* (ultimately of Greek derivation), denoting a coarse, granular mineral used for grinding or polishing.

LANGUAGE-CHANGE INDEX
emery board misspelled *emory board: Stage 1
Current ratio: 57:1

emigrant; émigré. There is a latent DIFFERENTIATION between these words. An *emigrant* is someone who leaves a country to settle in another. *Émigré* has the same sense, but applies especially to one in political exile. The first acute accent is often omitted (*emigré*) in AmE. As for frequency of occurrence in English-language contexts, *emigrant* has greatly predominated over *émigré*.

emigrate. See **immigrate.**

émigré. See **emigrant.**

eminent. See **imminent.**

eminently (= notably, conspicuously) is frequently used, in mild HYPERBOLE, to mean "very" <eminently qualified>. For some common misuses, see **imminent** & **infinitely** (A).

Emmy (= the statuette given as a television award) forms the plural *Emmys*—not *Emmies. See PLURALS (E).

Current ratio: 27:1

emote. See BACK-FORMATIONS.

emotional; emotive. Although both words can mean "of, relating to, or involving emotion or the emotions," *emotional* is the usual term in this sense. Otherwise, the two are differentiated. *Emotional* = affected by emotion; showing strong emotion <the victims were highly emotional about the incident even several years later>. *Emotive* = arousing emotion <emotive words>.

*empale. See **impale.**

empanel; impanel. *Empanel* (= to put on a panel; esp., to swear [a jury] to try an issue or case) is now the preferred spelling in both AmE and BrE. E.g.: "It isn't clear how long final questioning will last or when a jury can be *empaneled* for opening statements." "102 Make the Cut for Simpson Jury Pool," *Times-Picayune* (New Orleans), 10 Oct. 1996, at A2. *Impanel*, though once the predominant form, might now be regarded as a NEEDLESS VARIANT. Yet it occurs just about as frequently.

Current ratio: 1:1

empathic; empathetic. *Empathic* (= of, relating to, displaying, or eliciting empathy) has long been the usual form. But *empathetic* is frequently encountered, doubtless because of the close analogy to *sympathetic*—e.g.:

- "Five years ago, Harvard psychologist Carol Gilligan published 'Meeting at the Crossroads,' a luminously *empathetic* study of adolescents at an all-girls private school in Cleveland." Susie Linfield, "Desperately Seeking Perfection," *L.A. Times*, 7 Sept. 1997, Book Rev. §, at 8.
- "In the end, it probably takes someone with Zellweger's *empathetic* openness to isolate the most unifying aspect of the 'Rubies' controversy." Bob Strauss, "The Unsinkable Renee Zellweger," *Boston Globe*, 29 Mar. 1998, at N9.

For now, the term *empathic* is standard in print sources. But a terminological shift may be at work.

Current ratio: 1.4:1

empathy; sympathy. *Empathy* is the ability to imagine oneself in another person's position and to experience all the sensations connected with it. *Sympathy* is compassion for or commiseration with another.

LANGUAGE-CHANGE INDEX (For the full key, see front matter pp. xxxi, l–li.)
Stage 1: Rejected. **Stage 2:** Widely shunned. **Stage 3:** Widespread but . . . **Stage 4:** Ubiquitous but . . . **Stage 5:** Fully accepted.
Invariably inferior forms marked by asterisk (*). • Ratios represent frequency of prevalent forms vs. variants in current books.

emphatic; *emphatical. Since about 1820, *emphatic* has been the standard term—eclipsing the previously popular *emphatical. See -ic.

Current ratio: 98:1

empirical; empiric, adj. *Empirical* is the word generally used, and *empiric* might easily be labeled a NEEDLESS VARIANT. But medical writers, surprisingly enough, often use *empiric*—e.g.:

- "We recognize that there was more *empiric* therapy used in nonclinic patients by the primary care physicians without recourse to bronchoscopy." R. Andrew McIvor et al., "An Effectiveness Community-Based Clinical Trial of Respirgard II [etc.]," 110 *Chest*, July 1996, at 141.
- "*Empiric* treatment with cefotaxime and dexamethasone was begun." J.D. Colmenero et al., "Complications with Brucella Melitensis Infection," 75 *Medicine*, July 1996, at 195.

Still, medical writers use *empirical therapy* and *empirical treatment* about as often as they put *empiric* in those phrases, and it would doubtless be a good thing if their usage mirrored general usage.

Current ratio: 72:1

employ is a FORMAL WORD for *use*—and is inferior whenever *use* might suffice.

employe(e). Although *employé*, the French form, might logically be thought to be better as a generic term, *employée* (which in French denotes the feminine gender) is so widespread—minus the accent mark—that it is not likely to be uprooted. Although *The Wall Street Journal* and *U.S. News and World Report* were longtime holdouts for *employe*, the form *employee* is standard. See **independent contractor.**

Current ratio (*employees* vs. *employes*): 169:1

emporium (= a large shop) predominantly made the plural *emporiums* in all varieties of English from about 1830. Around 1940, BrE predominantly adopted the Latinate *emporia*, and within a decade World English followed suit. But by 1960, the homegrown plural *emporiums* once again firmly established itself in AmE. So today it's *emporiums* in AmE and *emporia* in much of the rest of the world. See PLURALS (B).

Current ratio (World English): 1.2:1

empower; *impower. The second is an obsolete spelling that rapidly declined after about 1780. For the popular use of *empower*, see VOGUE WORDS. See also EN-.

Current ratio: 503:1

emulable, not *emulatable, is the traditional form of the adjective meaning "capable of being emulated." E.g.: "All I'm asking is that we take a look at the examples of behavior exhibited by Columbus and ask ourselves if they are justifiable and *emulatable* [read *emulable*]." Scott Lafee, "Take That Columbus!" *San Diego Union-Trib.*, 6 Oct. 1991, at D1 (misusing the word as if it meant "worthy of emulation"). The form *emulatable has been on the rise since about 1960. See -ATABLE.

LANGUAGE-CHANGE INDEX
*emulatable for emulable: Stage 4
Current ratio (*emulable* vs. *emulatable): 1:1

emulate. *Emulate* = to strive to equal or rival; to copy or imitate with the object of equaling. A person may emulate another person, but not a habit or a style. The word is frequently misused for *adopt*—e.g.:

- "Culture research is now being published in the leading organizational journals, but (ironically) only by *emulating* [read *adopting*] the same positivist research model that culture researchers originally deplored." Daniel R. Denison, "What Is the Difference Between Organizational Culture and Organizational Climate?" 21 *Academy Mgmt. Rev.* 619, 644 (1996).
- "For his second directing job (after 1994's black-comic 'Killing Zoe'), Avary *emulates* [read *adopts*] a novelist's style, retracing narrative steps to depict multiple points of view." Bob Ross, "Love Is in the Air," *Tampa Trib.*, 11 Oct. 2002, Friday Extra §, at 25.

For a word with which *emulate* is occasionally confused, see **immolate.**

LANGUAGE-CHANGE INDEX
emulate misused for *adopt*: Stage 1

-EN. See DIMINUTIVES (E).

EN-; IN-. No consistent rule exists for determining which form of the prefix to use before a given word. But it's fair to say that the French form *en-* is more a living prefix than *in-*. That is, *en-* has won most of the battles in which it contended against *in-*.

The following lists show the preferred form at left and the variant on the right. Of course, when the root word begins with a -*b-*, -*m-*, or -*p-*, the prefixes typically become *em-* and *im-*.

Preferred Form	Variant Form
embalm	*imbalm
embark	*imbark
embed	*imbed
embitter	*imbitter
embody	*imbody
embolden	*imbolden
embosom	*imbosom
embower	*imbower
embrown	*imbrown
empower	*impower
encage	*incage
encapsulate	*incapsulate
encase	*incase
enclasp	*inclasp
enclose	*inclose
enclosure	*inclosure
encrust	*incrust
encryption	*incryption
encumber	*incumber
encumbrance	*incumbrance
endow	*indow
endowment	*indowment
endue	*indue
enfold	*infold
engraft	*ingraft
engulf	*ingulf
enlace	*inlace
enmesh	*inmesh
ensheathe	*insheathe
enshrine	*inshrine
ensnare	*insnare

ensoul	*insoul
ensphere	*insphere
ensue	*insue
enthrall	*inthrall
enthrone	*inthrone
entice	*intice
entitle	*intitle
entomb	*intomb
entreat	*intreat
entrench	*intrench
entrust	*intrust
entwine	*intwine
entwist	*intwist
enwind	*inwind
enwrap	*inwrap
enwreathe	*inwreathe
imbrue	*embrue
impale	*empale
impoverish	*empoverish
inflame	*enflame
ingrain	*engrain
inquire	*enquire
inquiry	*enquiry
inure	*enure

Especially troublesome to writers are word pairs with varying prefixes according to inflection: *enjoin* but *injunction*, *encrust* but *incrustation*, etc.

enamel, vb., makes *enameled* and *enameling* in AmE, *enamelled* and *enamelling* in BrE. See SPELLING (B).

enamor; enamour. The first is AmE, the second BrE. Though each spelling can be found in both varieties, *enamor* has made greater inroads into BrE than *enamour* has into AmE. World English is tending toward the AmE spelling. See -OR; -OUR.

enamored takes the preposition *of*, not *with* or *by*—e.g.:

- "There are also the areas we are becoming *enamored with* [read *enamored of*]: for example, health insurance, security companies." "South Africa Invites U.S. Biz Back," *Crain's Detroit Bus.*, 30 Sept. 1996, at 45.
- "Hines loves the home. He's *enamored of* Aspen and the Rocky Mountains." Steve Raabe, "High Gear," *Denver Post*, 13 Oct. 1996, at 14.

LANGUAGE-CHANGE INDEX
enamored with for *enamored of*: Stage 4
Current ratio (*enamored of* vs. *with* vs. *by*): 11:6:1

encase; *incase. The first is the standard spelling. See EN-.

enclave (= a small, distinct area or district where an insular group of people live), a 19th-century French loanword, long received the anglicized pronunciation /**en**-klayv/. In recent years, however, a gallicized pronunciation /**on**-klayv/ has become commonplace in AmE. See GALLICISMS.

enclose; *inclose. The former spelling is now preferred in all senses. E.g.: "While parents are off

shopping, children ages 3 to 8 can play in the *glassed-inclosed* [read *glass-enclosed* or *glassed, enclosed*] child-care center." Gregory J. Gilligan, "Kids Quarters," *Richmond Times-Dispatch*, 26 July 1993, Bus. §, at 1. See EN-.

Current ratio: 9:1

*enclosed please find; *please find enclosed; *enclosed herewith; *enclosed herein. These phrases—common in commercial and legal correspondence since the mid-19th century—are archaic deadwood for *here are, enclosed is, I've enclosed*, or the like. Interestingly, business-writing texts have consistently condemned the phrases since the late 19th century:

- "[*Please find enclosed:*] A more ridiculous use of words, it seems to me, there could not be." Richard Grant White, *Every-Day English* 492 (1880).
- "*Inclosed herewith please find. Inclosed* and *herewith* mean the same thing. How foolish to tell your reader twice exactly where the check is, and then to suggest that he look around to see if he can find it anywhere. Say, 'We are inclosing our check for $25.50.'" Wallace E. Bartholomew & Floyd Hurlbut, *The Business Man's English* 153 (1924). (If that sentence had been written recently, *inclose* would have been *enclose*.)
- "*Please Find Enclosed.* This worn-out formula is not in good use in letters, either business or personal." Maurice H. Weseen, *Crowell's Dictionary of English Grammar* 470 (1928).
- "When you read a letter that sounds as if it were a compendium of pat expressions from some musty old letter book of the goose-quill period, do you feel that you are communing with the writer's mind? On the contrary, if you have a discerning mind, you know that you are merely getting a reflex from one who lacks taste and good mental digestion. . . . [W]hen you compose letters, beware these bromides: . . . *inclosed please find.*" H. Cramp, *Letter Writing: Business and Social* 22–23 (1930).
- "Business words and expressions borrowed from an earlier generation can make your writing sound artificial and pedantic. Every letter will read like a form letter, and you will sound bored or, even worse, boring. Thinking up substitute phrases is easy if you put your mind to it. Consider some of these revisions: . . . *Enclosed please find* [becomes] *I am enclosing.*" Maryann V. Piotrowski, *Effective Business Writing* 53 (1989).

Current ratio (*enclosed is the* vs. **enclosed please find*): 16:1

enclosure; *inclosure. The first spelling is standard in all senses. See EN-.

encomium (= warm praise) forms the plural *encomiums* or *encomia*. The native-English plural has been predominant since the 18th century and is still standard—e.g.:

- "Even worse is Ms. Noonan's sunny valentine to Ronald Reagan, which is less an essay than a toastmaster's collection of *encomiums*." Michiko Kakutani, "Looking to Presidents for Signs of Character," *N.Y. Times*, 9 Apr. 1996, at C18.

LANGUAGE-CHANGE INDEX (For the full key, see front matter pp. xxxi, l–li.)
Stage 1: Rejected. **Stage 2:** Widely shunned. **Stage 3:** Widespread but . . . **Stage 4:** Ubiquitous but . . . **Stage 5:** Fully accepted.
Invariably inferior forms marked by asterisk (*). • Ratios represent frequency of prevalent forms vs. variants in current books.

- "It was a night of film clips, *encomiums* and inside jokes." Burl Stiff, "His Mission: To Live Up to Night in His Honor," *San Diego Union-Trib.*, 29 Sept. 1996, at D4.
- "The eulogies and *encomiums* have centred exclusively upon the departing Tom Watson." Oliver Brown, "Thomson Endorsement Inspires Scott to Purge His Open Nightmares," *Sunday Telegraph*, 19 July 2015, Sport §, at 3.

See PLURALS (B).

Current ratio: 4:1

encounter, vb., = (1) to come across; meet with <she had never encountered the word>; (2) to confront (an adversary); engage in conflict with <he finally encountered his nemesis at the entrance to the factory>; or (3) to run into (a difficulty or complication) <we've never encountered that problem>. Although sense 1 is occasionally criticized, it dates from the 14th century and has an unimpeachable lineage.

encrust; incrust. *Encrust* is the standard spelling; **incrust* is a rare variant. See EN-.

Current ratio: 4:1

*encrustation. See incrustation.

encryption (= the act of encoding or enciphering) is so spelled—not **encription* or **incryption*.

encumbrance; *incumbrance; *cumbrance. The preferred spelling of this word, meaning "a claim or liability that is attached to property and that may lessen its value," is *encumbrance* in both AmE and BrE. **Cumbrance* is a NEEDLESS VARIANT. See EN-.

Current ratio (in order of headwords): 146:44:1

encyclopedia; *encyclopaedia. The *-ae-* was predominantly shortened to *-e-* in AmE by 1905 and in BrE by 1970. **Encyclopaedia* is an archaic spelling throughout the English-speaking world. See AE.

Current ratio: 5:1

EN-DASHES. See PUNCTUATION (H).

endear, v.t., is properly a reflexive verb. President John F. Kennedy endeared himself to the press. Wanglers endear themselves to the people they'd like to manipulate. But in the following sentence, *endear* is used incorrectly as a regular transitive verb—as a near-synonym of *charm*—instead of as a reflexive: "Roberts, whose Columbo-like, disheveled personality has *endeared* [read *endeared him to* or *charmed*] reporters for decades—he once set his desk on fire with a cigarette—is likely to help morale." Larry Reibstein, "It's Back to the Future," *Newsweek*, 18 Apr. 1994, at 41.
LANGUAGE-CHANGE INDEX
endear misused for *charm*: Stage 1

endeavor, vb., is a FORMAL WORD for *attempt* or *try*—either of which is preferable in everyday contexts. But *endeavor* suggests more of a challenge and more of a sustained effort—e.g.:

- "If you are trying to prove that your ancestor arrived in Texas before the closing days of the Republic in the 1840s or if you are *endeavoring* to learn how, when and where your foreign-born Texas ancestors were naturalized, the

voter registration lists will reveal these facts." Lloyd Bockstruck, "Confederate Lists Can Aid Genealogists," *Dallas Morning News*, 31 Aug. 1996, at C11.
- "A quartet of representatives *endeavoring* to bring commercial air cargo business to the Inland Port will market the Moreno Valley-area airport at the International Air Cargo Forum and Exposition 2002 in Hong Kong, Sept. 17–20." Darla Martin Tucker, "March Hopes to Drum Up Cargo Carriers in China," *Bus. Press/California*, 16 Sept. 2002, at 1.

Much the same is true of *endeavor,* n., which means "an undertaking; earnest effort." E.g.: "From that standpoint, [the march] has the makings of a worthy *endeavor*—one designed to promote pride in Latinos, a diverse group of ethnicities, as well as push political awareness." "A March for Civil Rights," *Press-Enterprise* (Riverside, Cal.), 9 Oct. 1996, at A14.

ended, p.pl.; **ending,** pr.pl. In phrases such as *the year ending 31 December 1997*, some fiscal writers have pedantically insisted that *ending* should be *ended* if the year has already passed. The present participle, it is argued, should be used for future periods <the week ending 7 March 2026>, but not past ones. In those circumstances, the argument runs, the past participle is more accurate <the week ended 14 September 1996>.

But the correlative term *beginning* is used in analogous senses <the week beginning 12 January 1992>, and there is no valid objection to *ending*, whether the reference is to a future or past period.

endemic. See epidemic.

end(ing), n. *End*, not *ending*, corresponds most idiomatically to the noun *beginning*. E.g.: "The turnover of the Sinai is a beginning, not an *ending* [read *end*]." In print sources since 1700, the phrase *beginning and end* has consistently appeared more frequently than *beginning and ending*—today by an almost 3-to-1 ratio. See PARALLELISM.

endive. The traditional pronunciation is /**en**-dɪv/. The Frenchified /**on**-deev/ is an affectation.

ENDNOTES. See FOOTNOTES (B).

endorse; indorse. The usual spelling is *endorse*, and that is the only acceptable spelling when the word is used figuratively to mean "to express approval of publicly; to support." E.g.: "The IRS, of course, doesn't sanction or *endorse* specific investments." Karen Cheney, "Don't Be Taken In by the Phony Investing Pitches," *Money*, Mar. 1997, at A1. For more on the meaning of *endorse*, see **approve (B).**

In legal discussions relating to checks and other negotiable instruments, *indorse* predominates in AmE. But popularly, *endorse* is the more frequent spelling in all contexts—and most checks have "Endorse here" printed on the back. **Endorse on the back* is a REDUNDANCY: *en-* means "on" and the root *dors-* means "back."

endorsee. See -EE.

endow; *__indow.__ The first is the standard spelling. The second is a variant spelling. See EN-.

Current ratio: 68:1

end product is usually a REDUNDANCY for *product.*

end result, a REDUNDANCY for *result,* rose to prominence over the course of the 20th century. Safire called it "redundant, tautological and unnecessarily repetitive, not to mention prolix and wordy." William Safire, "Peace-ese," *N.Y. Times,* 17 Nov. 1991, § 6, at 22. The only exception occurs when the writer needs to refer to *intermediate results* as well as *end results.* Cf. **final outcome.**

endue; *__indue.__ Both mean (1) "to provide with a quality or trait"; or (2) "to put on (a piece of clothing)" (*AHD*). Although neither form is common, the spelling *endue* predominates. *__Indue__ is a NEEDLESS VARIANT. See EN-.

Current ratio: 2:1

energy-saving, adj., is so hyphenated. See PHRASAL ADJECTIVES.

enervate; innervate. *Enervate* (/ˈen-ər-vayt/) means "to drain the vigor out of"—e.g.: "It is a great and *enervating* mistake for young writers not to see all the hazards that stand between them and successful communication." Gorham Munson, *The Written Word* 32 (rev. ed. 1949). Probably because the word sounds a bit like *energize,* it is sometimes used where that word would convey the intended meaning—e.g.:

- "Gutsy performances by 'Deep Impact' in 29 territories and a three-day weekend in parts of Europe gave exhibs some cheer last week, but not enough to *enervate* [read *energize*] overall business that was characterized as flat in France, quiet in the U.K. and indifferent in Spain." Don Groves, "'Godzilla' Storms Malaysian B.O.," *Variety,* 14 June 1998, Film §, at 14.
- "The intent of cliché makers is to color up and *enervate* [read *innervate* or *enliven*] language so as to make it easier to comprehend. Alarmingly, it does not always work that way." Edward S. Spector, "Seeking Some Closure on Those Tired Clichés," *Buffalo News,* 4 May 2001, at B18.

Innervate (/i-ˈnər-vayt/) means "to supply with energy" or "to supply (a muscle) with nerves." It is most often found in medical writing—e.g.: "The doctor severs a few of the nerves that *innervate* the vocal muscles so they don't keep the cords slammed shut." Dr. Paul Donohue, "Surgery May Be Solution for Vocal Muscles," *Grand Rapids Press,* 30 Mar. 2007, at C7.

LANGUAGE-CHANGE INDEX
enervate misused for *energize:* Stage 1

*__enflame.__ See **inflame.**

enforce; *__inforce. A. Spelling.__ The latter is an archaic spelling whose only vestige appears in *reinforce.* See EN-.

Current ratio: 325:1

B. "Enforcing" a Contract. Lawyers continually speak of *enforcing* contracts, but this term is not apt unless one is seeking specific performance. Usually, the law merely specifies a remedy for breach of contract—damages—and does not compel performance.

enforceable; *__enforcible.__ Since the mid-19th century, *enforceable* has been the preferred spelling in both AmE and BrE. E.g.: "A contract is *enforcible* [read *enforceable*] even though it does not specify the type of deed to be given." Robert Kratovil, *Real Estate Law* 83 (1946). Cf. **forcible.**

LANGUAGE-CHANGE INDEX
enforceable misspelled *__enforcible:__ Stage 1
Current ratio: 238:1

England. See **Great Britain.**

English, vb. This useful verb, dating from the 14th century and meaning either "to render in English" or "to translate into English," occurs frequently in linguistic texts but often surprises those unfamiliar with such texts—e.g.: "A number of words that only a few years ago were still thought of as lifted from the Latin have now become so completely *Englished* that they take the *-er* ending instead of *-or.*" Edward N. Teall, *Putting Words to Work* 99 (1940). Of course, *anglicize* is the more common and less jarring alternative.

engraft; *__ingraft.__ Since the 1790s, the standard spelling has been *engraft.* See EN-.

Current ratio: 6:1

engrave > engraved > engraved. The past-participial form *__engraven__ is an ARCHAISM—e.g.:

- "Despite the computerisation and increased sophistication of the Treasury model, it still seems to have *engraven* [read *engraved*] in its heart: 'Improvement means disaster.'" Samuel Brittan, "A New Look at Productivity," *Fin. Times,* 25 Feb. 1982, § I, at 21.
- "While at this place we had the opportunity and pleasure of examining some remarkably fine toned portraits from the brush of H. Bundy, a backwoods Vermont artist, and, unless we much mistake, his name will yet be *engraven* [read *engraved*] high on the pinnacle of fame." Lauren B. Hewes, "Horace Bundy: Itinerant Portraitist," *Mag. Antiques,* Oct. 1994, at 486.
- "My own role was to accompany him now and then to the village cenotaph, no doubt to see if the names *engraven* [read *engraved*] thereon had changed." Paul West, "My Father Weightless: Reflections on the Gravity of War," *Harper's Bazaar,* Dec. 2002, at 67.

See IRREGULAR VERBS (B).

The adjectival use of *engraved* predominates—e.g.: "An *engraved* silver urn, one of his old prizes, held a dozen felt-tipped pens, one of which he now took in hand." Arthur Miller, "The Bare Manuscript," *New Yorker,* 16 Dec. 2002, at 82, 91.

LANGUAGE-CHANGE INDEX
engraven for the past-participial *engraved:* Stage 1
Current ratio (*had engraved* vs. *__had engraven__): 12:1

enhance (= to heighten, intensify, or improve) should refer to a quality or condition, not to people. So while you can enhance people's education or experience or even salaries, you can't really enhance people themselves. But some writers fall into error—e.g.: "If all workers do what they are supposed to do together,... everyone will be *enhanced from* [read *improved by*] working together." Sheila Storm, "Knowlton Focuses on Details," *Successful Bus.*, 27 Sept. 1993, at 1.

Similarly, because *enhance* has long had positive connotations, it is a mistake to use it in reference to something bad, such as injuries—e.g.: "Papiano says that the intubation *enhanced* [read *aggravated*] the injury." William Nack, "From Fame to Shame," *Sports Illustrated*, 19 Apr. 1993, at 70. Unfortunately, lawyers have developed what they call the *enhanced-injury doctrine*, which allows an injury victim to seek damages from a deep-pocket company even if the company didn't directly cause the injury; under that rule, a person seriously injured by a drunk driver in a car crash could sue not only the driver but also the car manufacturer for not making the victim's car safe enough for such a crash. The use of *enhance*, though not a good choice, is understandable: to a plaintiff's lawyer who stands to gain a percentage of any recovery, an injury can be "enhanced" if the potential damages are greater. By this logic, though, an excruciating death would be the most "enhanced" situation. This is pure torture to the English language.

enigma. Pl. *enigmas*—preferably not **enigmata*. See PLURALS (B).

Current ratio: 99:1

enjambment (= in poetry, the continuation of a line, couplet, or verse from one to the next without a noticeable pause) is the standard spelling—e.g.: "Traditional forms are reanimated through syncopated rhythms and line *enjambment*." Rita Dove, "Poet's Choice," *Wash. Post*, 2 Sept. 2001, at T12. **Enjambement* is a variant spelling common in the late 19th century but now archaic.

*enjeopard. See **jeopardize.**

enjoinder; injunction; enjoinment. The words of the Fowler brothers are as apt today as they were when first written:

> As *rejoin rejoinder*, so *enjoin enjoinder*. The word is not given in the [first edition of the *OED*], from which it seems likely that Dickens ["Merely nodding his head as an *enjoinder* to be careful."] invented it, consciously or unconsciously. The only objection to such a word is that its having had to wait so long, in spite of its obviousness, before being made is a strong argument against the necessity of it. We may regret that *injunction* holds the field, having a much less English appearance; but it does; and in language the old-established that can still do the work is not to be turned out for the new-fangled that might do it a shade better, but must first get itself known and accepted.
>
> H.W. Fowler & F.G. Fowler, *The King's English* 53 (3d ed. 1931).

The *OED* contains two illustrative examples of *enjoinder*, but *injunction* still generally "holds the field" in both positive and negative senses of *enjoin*.

Yet *enjoinder* has become more common than it was in the Fowlers' day in the sense "a command, esp. one that prohibits." E.g.: "Never go to bed mad. For generations, wise old long-marrieds have offered this advice to spatting couples—an *enjoinder* endorsed by many of their modern professional congeners, marriage counselors." Michael Segell, "Make Love and War," *Esquire*, Aug. 1997, at 128.

Enjoinment, missing from *W2* and labeled archaic in *W3*, is recorded in the *OED* from the 17th century in the sense "the action of enjoining." Today this word is fairly common in legal contexts <the court's enjoinment of their picketing was fully warranted>. It has been fairly steadily used in print sources from the early 19th century to the present day.

enjoy myself. See **I enjoyed myself.**

*enlargen, which is recorded in neither the *OED* nor *W3*, is a NEEDLESS VARIANT of *enlarge*, vb. It has appeared sporadically since the early 19th century and remains surprisingly common—e.g.:

- "A reddened spot appears on the skin, *enlargens* [read *enlarges*], and becomes raised, like a pimple." Amy J. Vellucci, "Rash of Lake Itch Complaints May Be Just the Beginning," *N.H. Sunday News*, 10 July 1994, at A1.
- "Four years later, the U.S. Army Corps of Engineers, while *enlargening* [read *enlarging*] the Intracoastal Waterway, dumped dredge material at the island's northeastern corner." Tao Woolfe, "Glancing Back," *Sun-Sentinel* (Ft. Lauderdale), 22 Mar. 1996, Palm Beach Plus §, at 3.
- "He started stealing his wife's birth control pills in an attempt to *enlargen* [*enlarge*] his breasts, had plastic surgery on his face and underwent his own procedures to remove body hair." Dave Wedge, "Deadly Docs," *Boston Herald*, 23 July 2000, at 1.

LANGUAGE-CHANGE INDEX
*enlargen for the verb *enlarge*: Stage 1
Current ratio (*enlarge* vs. **enlargen*): 6,573:1

enliven; liven; liven up. *Enliven* has long been considered preferable to *liven*, but *liven up* is a common PHRASAL VERB in informal contexts and is the only idiomatic choice in an intransitive construction—e.g.:

- "After a couple of dull weeks, things *liven up* a bit Saturday." Michael C. Lewis & Joe Baird, "Kiwi Bowl Game Just Might Share Fate of the Dodo," *Salt Lake Trib.*, 16 Oct. 1996, at D2.
- "To *liven* the board *up* for the 6-year-old, the engineering students painted it bright yellow and added pink bows to the fanciful lion-shaped paper clip at the top." Sandra Barbier, "Tulane Students Design Desk for Paralyzed Kindergartner," *Times-Picayune* (New Orleans), 24 Mar. 1997, at B1.
- "Voight *livens up* the proceedings with a performance that out-hams even the porcine star of 'Babe.'" Russell Evansen, "Voight Puts Slithery 'Anaconda' over the Top," *Wis. State J.*, 16 Apr. 1997, at C3.

But except in that CASUALISM, *liven* alone is really just a NEEDLESS VARIANT of *enliven*—e.g.: "The

Rockets essentially gutted their team to bring in forward Charles Barkley, whose presence should *liven* [read *enliven*] and inspire the Rockets to make one more run at an NBA title." George Diaz, "Rockets Coming of Age," *Orlando Sentinel*, 1 Nov. 1996, at G21.

LANGUAGE-CHANGE INDEX
liven up meaning "to enliven": Stage 5

en masse. Pronounced /en **mas**/ or /ahn **mas**/.

enology (= the knowledge or study of wines and winemaking), a word introduced in the early 19th century, is predominantly so spelled in AmE—*oenology* in BrE. Oddly, however, *oenophile* (= a lover of wines) is the standard spelling in both AmE and BrE. Whoever decided this point of AmE usage must have been tippling unduly.

Current ratio (*enology* vs. *oenology* in World English): 2:1

enormity; enormousness. The historical DIFFEREN-TIATION between these words should not be muddled. *Enormousness* = hugeness, vastness. *Enormity* = outrageousness, ghastliness, hideousness. For example, Alan Dershowitz once said that Noam Chomsky "trivializes the *enormity* of the Chinese massacre [at Tiananmen Square on 4 June 1989]." Letter of Alan Dershowitz, "Left's Response to Beijing Massacre," *L.A. Times*, 13 July 1989, § 2, at 6. But President George Bush was less fastidious when referring to a different event: on 10 July 1989, he said he was buoyed and cheered by "the enormity of this moment," a historic challenge to reform the Polish economy.

The following examples typify the careful writer's usage—e.g.:

- "The last question invites comparison of the mere misfortunes of the defendant with the *enormity* of the killing." Thomas Raup, "Today's Death Penalties," *Baltimore Sun*, 21 July 1996, at F1.
- " 'A limited encounter with the Devil,' his clansmen now try to explain, even as they realize the *enormity* of his sin." William Safire, "Be Nobody's Puppet," *N.Y. Times*, 5 Sept. 1996, at A23.
- "And the Orwellianly named Truth and Reconciliation Commission continues to hold hearings that air grim stories of what apartheid regimes did—albeit with rather less energy to air the equally grim stories of past *enormities* by the now-in-power African National Congress." Ross Mackenzie, "Overseas Items That Should Be Campaign Topics, but Oddly Aren't," *Richmond Times-Dispatch*, 26 Sept. 1996, at A15.

The *OED* notes that "recent examples [of *enormity* for *enormousness*] might perh. be found, but the use is now regarded as incorrect." Its evidence certainly shows a historical trend to make the word mean "monstrous wickedness," but the secondary meaning never really disappeared—e.g.:

- "To appreciate the befuddling *enormity* [read *vastness*] of these Olympics you need to wrestle with the following.

In Atlanta this weekend there are 42,000 volunteer workers, 30,000 police and soldiers, 15,000 media personnel and 10,788 athletes." Paul Hayward, "Business Opens for Olympics," *Daily Telegraph*, 20 July 1996, at 30.
- "A biographical sketch prepared by the university shows the *enormity* [read *magnitude*] of his energy and output." Martha Jackson, "Portraits of an Artist," *Charleston Daily Mail*, 5 Sept. 1996, at D1.
- "Titanic's numbers raised Fox's confidence in the *enormity* [read *enormousness*] of the women's market." David Ansen, "The Court of King Jim," *Newsweek*, 13 Apr. 1998, at 70.
- "The *enormity* [read *enormousness*] of Mr. Gore's triumph allows him to move more quickly to patch up relations with Mr. Bradley's backers." Richard L. Berke, "A Sweep by Gore *Assures* [read *Ensures*] Nomination," *N.Y. Times*, 8 Mar. 2000, at A1, A16. (For more on *assure* and *ensure*, see **assure**.)

Some sentences teeter on an ambiguity: is the word used correctly (and something horrific is afoot) or incorrectly (so that sheer size is at issue)? E.g.: "Americans are well aware of the *enormity* of the long-term-care problem that is facing the country." Karen McNally Bensing, "Insurance Can Defray Cost of Long-Term Care," *Plain Dealer* (Cleveland), 21 July 1996, at F6. How you read that sentence depends on your political inclinations: either something sinister is at work or else a big problem looms. The ambiguity might be considered splendid; yet it might also lead one to conclude that this is a SKUNKED TERM.

Again, is the writer of the following sentence partisan? And if so, is the writer a Republican or a Democrat? "Pick a superlative, any superlative. Chances are it doesn't come close to portraying the *enormity* of the Republican victory Tuesday." "Big Win," *Amarillo Globe-Times*, 10 Nov. 1994, at A4.

LANGUAGE-CHANGE INDEX
enormity misused for *immensity*: Stage 4

enough, adj.; **sufficient.** Although *enough* modifies either count nouns <enough books> or mass nouns <enough stamina>, *sufficient* should modify only mass nouns <sufficient oxygen>. (See COUNT NOUNS AND MASS NOUNS.) And while the usage problem can be solved by making it *sufficient numbers of*, the single word *enough* does the job better—e.g.: "The Pacific Maritime Assn., which represents shipping lines and terminal operators, claims the union has been deliberately slowing the work pace by failing to dispatch *sufficient numbers of* [read *enough*] skilled workers to job sites." Nancy Cleeland & David Streitfeld, "Logjam at Ports Continues as Sides Blame Each Other," *L.A. Times*, 17 Oct. 2002, Bus. §, pt. 3, at 2.

There are, of course, exceptions to the general rule: *sufficient* (or more often *insufficient*) *funds* is a common phrase. But the following examples misuse *sufficient* for *enough* or *adequate*:

- "President Rosemary Brester reports she's encountering substantial problems finding *sufficient* [read *enough*]

LANGUAGE-CHANGE INDEX (For the full key, see front matter pp. xxxi, l–li.)
Stage 1: Rejected. **Stage 2:** Widely shunned. **Stage 3:** Widespread but . . . **Stage 4:** Ubiquitous but . . . **Stage 5:** Fully accepted.
Invariably inferior forms marked by asterisk (∗). • Ratios represent frequency of prevalent forms vs. variants in current books.

people to meet her expanding order book." Steve Wilhelm, "Boeing Buildup Drains Work Force," *Puget Sound Bus. J.,* 26 July 1996, at 1.

- "The architectural firm did not provide *sufficient* [read *adequate*] specifications to lay the Masonite properly." Daniel P. Jones, "Town OK's $50,000 to Fix Warped High School Stage," *Hartford Courant,* 7 Oct. 2002, at B5.
- "That would have been the 'easy answer,'" said Jack Grobe, head of the committee in charge of deciding . . . when First-Energy has made *sufficient* [read *enough*] changes to the plant's management so it can be trusted to operate safely." John Funk, "NRC Praises Davis-Besse for Handling of New Issue," *Plain Dealer* (Cleveland), 17 Oct. 2002, at C4.

For more on *sufficient,* see **adequate (A).**

LANGUAGE-CHANGE INDEX
sufficient used with a count noun: Stage 3

enough, adv.; **sufficiently.** The same rule of thumb that applies to the adjectives applies to the adverbs as well—though because of the strictures of grammar, errors with this pair are less likely to occur.

*enounce.** See **announce.**

enplane. See AIRLINESE.

*enquire.** See **inquire.**

enquiry. See **inquiry (B).**

enroll; enrol. *Enroll* is the standard spelling in AmE, *enrol* in BrE.

enrollee. See -EE.

enrollment; enrolment. This word is spelled *-ll-* in AmE and *-l-* in BrE.

en route; *enroute. The standard form is *en route.* In modern print sources (mostly American), the closed-up *enroute* appears occasionally; although the *OED* suggests that this one-word version is exclusively North American (the earliest example being 1967), it occurs also in BrE.

The phrase is pronounced /en root/ or /on root/. Avoid /in/. Although /rowt/ is accepted for the word *route* by itself, in this phrase the pronunciation should invariably be /root/. For more, see **route.**
Current ratio: 17:1

ensue; *insue. The first is the standard spelling.
Current ratio: 2,347:1

*ensurance.** See **insurance (A).**

ensure; insure. See **assure.**

*enswathe** is a NEEDLESS VARIANT of *swathe,* vb. See **swathe.**
Current ratio (*to swathe* vs. *to enswathe*): 65:1

enter. A. For *enter into*. Idiomatically speaking, one *enters into a contract* with another; one does not merely *enter a contract.* E.g.: "At the time the contract is *entered* [read *entered into*], the agreed-upon payment must be a reasonable forecast of just compensation for the harm that would be caused by a breach." Even so, *to enter into a contract with* is usually prolix for *to contract with.*

LANGUAGE-CHANGE INDEX
enter a contract for *enter into a contract*: Stage 1

B. The Phrase *enter in*. Although to the modern ear this phrase is a REDUNDANCY, it occurs frequently in poems, in hymns, and especially in the Bible (KJV). It does not belong in mundane passages.

enterprise is often misspelled *enterprize*—e.g.: "The study is part of an effort to figure out what to do with programs like the *enterprize* [read *enterprise*] zones." Aldo Svaldi, "Bidders Seek Chance to Guide State's Hand," *Denver Bus. J.,* 23 Aug. 1996, at A4. The spelling *H.M.S. Enterprize* can be seen in the opening credits of the *Star Trek* series *Enterprise.* There, the spelling reflects the correct name of an 18th-century ship.

LANGUAGE-CHANGE INDEX
enterprise misspelled *enterprize*: Stage 1
Current ratio: 238:1

enthrall; enthral; *inthrall; *inthral. The spelling *enthrall* is standard in AmE, *enthral* in BrE. The *in-* spellings are to be avoided. See EN-.

*enthuse,** vb., is a widely criticized BACK-FORMATION avoided by writers and speakers who care about their language. The verb can be either transitive or intransitive. As a transitive verb, it was originally confined to passive-voice uses <I am enthused by the game>, but by the mid-1990s the word had taken on active uses <she enthused me about the game>. E.g.:

- Transitive: "They *enthused* [read *inspired*] student volunteers with their ideas." "The First Glint of a New Japan," *Economist,* 24 July 1993, at 33.
- Transitive: "'After discovering that the bags were no longer being imported into the U.S., I tracked down the company in Denmark, and, well,' he *enthuses* [read *gushes*], 'here we are!'" Lynell George, "Once Feared Lost, This Relationship Is in the Bag Again," *L.A. Times,* 15 Oct. 2002, Calendar §, pt. 5, at 12.
- Intransitive: "Avon Editor in Chief Bob Mecoy *enthuses* [read *raves* or *rhapsodizes*] about the graphic-novel form." Peter Plagens, "Drawing on the Dark Side," *Newsweek,* 5 Sept. 1994, at 70.

Although the adjective *enthused* is virtually always inferior to *enthusiastic,* it is increasingly common—e.g.:

- "Wall Street was *enthused* [read *enthusiastic*], bidding up CBS stock $50 in one day to $313." Larry Reibstein, "Barry Diller's Greatest Hit?" *Newsweek,* 11 July 1994, at 46.
- "With reviews like that, Detroit is so *enthused* [read *enthusiastic*] about its prospects that it is positioning the new class of compacts as the centerpiece of an old-fashioned, '50s- and '60s-style all-out autumn advertising blitz." Janice Castro, "Small Cars, High Hopes," *Time,* 12 Sept. 1994, at 58.
- "The coming project he sounds most *enthused* [read *enthusiastic*] about is 'The Foreigner,' an English-language

drama to be directed by Martin Campbell." Julie Makinen, "East Meets West," *Chicago Trib.*, 26 Aug. 2015, Arts & Entertainment §, at 4.

LANGUAGE-CHANGE INDEX
1. **enthuse* for *gush*: Stage 2
2. **enthused* for *enthusiastic*: Stage 3
Current ratio (*highly enthusiastic* vs. **highly enthused*): 20:1

entice; *intice. The latter is an obsolete spelling of *entice* (= to lure, attract). **Inticement* is also obsolete for the corresponding noun *enticement*. Both *i-* spellings are therefore NEEDLESS VARIANTS, but they occasionally appear in modern sources—e.g.:

• "The decline of the International Motor Sports Association, among other diversions, has *inticed* [read *enticed*] the biggest names in road racing to SCCA Trans-Am racing." Jeff Olson, "Trans-Am Stars to Be Out in Full Force at Grand Prix," *Des Moines Register*, 2 July 1994, Sports §, at 1.
• "Hindu fringe groups have accused missionaries of using money and other means to convert poor and illiterate Indians. Christian groups deny using such *inticements* [read *enticements*], which *is* [read *are*] illegal in Indian law." *St. Louis Post-Dispatch*, 24 Jan. 1999, at B7. (On the misuse of *is* for *are* in that sentence, see REMOTE RELATIVES.)

Current ratio: 413:1

entire is accented on the second syllable: /en-**tir**/, not /**en**-tir/. On this word as a noncomparable adjective, see ADJECTIVES (B).

entitle; title, v.t. The word *entitle* has two meanings: (1) "to provide with a right or title to something" <entitled to a discount>; and (2) "to give a title to" <a book entitled *Woe Unto You, Lawyers!*>. Sense 1 is more common. And sense 2, in the best usage, is confined to the past-participial adjective (as in the illustration with the book title).

As a transitive verb, *title* is preferred over *entitle*. Hence *What are you going to title your article?*, not **What are you going to entitle your article?*

The *Associated Press Stylebook* and several other newspaper guides reserve *entitled* to mean having a right to do or have something. But sense 2 actually predates sense 1, and both senses are well established.

entomology; etymology. *Entomology* is the study of insects. *Etymology* is the study of word origins or, more usually, the derivation of a given word. The two words are occasionally confounded—e.g.:

• "Fly fishermen must also study *the etymology of insects* [read *entomology*], what *they* [read *insects*] look like, how they move, so they can mimic them." Marianne Costantinou, "Reel-Life Story with a Cast of Thousands," *S.F. Examiner*, 31 May 1999, at A12. (Besides the usage error, this buggy sentence also contains a latent REDUNDANCY [*entomology of insects*] and an ambiguity [*they* with two possible antecedents].)

• "To begin, one should go to the *root entomology* [read *etymology*] of the words." Michael Storey, "Otus the Head Cat," *Ark. Democrat-Gaz.*, 14 Oct. 2000, at E3. (*Root etymology* is redundant.)

See ETYMOLOGY.

Entomology is sometimes, in its spelling, confusingly influenced by the spelling of *etymology*—e.g.: "It is no accident that Musil was trained as an engineer, that Ernst Jünger and Nabokov should be serious *entymologists* [read *entomologists*], that Broch and Canetti are writers schooled in the exact and mathematical sciences." George Steiner, *In Bluebeard's Castle* 130 (1971).

LANGUAGE-CHANGE INDEX
1. *etymology* misused for *entomology*: Stage 1
2. *entomology* misused for *etymology*: Stage 1
3. *entomology* misspelled **entymology*: Stage 1

entrance; entry; entranceway; entryway. Both *entrance* and *entry* may refer to the act of entering. In reference to structures, *entrance* connotes a single opening, such as a door, while *entranceway, entryway,* and *entry* suggest a longer means of access, such as a corridor or vestibule.

entrust, not **intrust*, is now the usual and preferred spelling. See EN-.

Current ratio: 7:1

enumerable; innumerable. Though close in pronunciation, these words have opposite meanings. *Enumerable* = countable; capable of being listed. *Innumerable* = unable to be counted. The words should be pronounced distinctly so that listeners won't misunderstand.

In writing, the most common error with these words is to misuse *enumerable* for *innumerable*—e.g.:

• "From 9 to 5, Hornbuckle runs Community Preschool in Newport Beach, where piles of paperwork, incessant telephone calls and *enumerable* [read *innumerable*] split-second decisions conspire to challenge her characteristic composure." Zan Dubin, "Mommies' Dearest Wishes," *L.A. Times*, 9 May 1991, OC Live §, at 3.
• "[The Constitution] is about 15 pages in size and much of the language is brief and concise. It cannot be expected to cover the *enumerable* [read *innumerable*] experiences of human existence over the many years." Bernard H. Siegan, "Judging Thomas," *San Diego Union-Trib.*, 22 Sept. 1991, at C1.
• "In one of his *enumerable* [read *innumerable*] and lackluster comeback attempts, he had a new comic book and a comic book store in Santa Rosa." Marc D. Allan, "Swing, Dive with Bands from Chicago and Berkeley," *Indianapolis Star*, 21 Feb. 1996, at E5.

Both terms are sometimes misspelled **inumerable*. Most frequently the term misspelled is *innumerable*—e.g.: "He had to rescue *inumerable* [read *innumerable*] wounded soldiers on Omaha Beach

LANGUAGE-CHANGE INDEX (For the full key, see front matter pp. xxxi, l–li.)
Stage 1: Rejected. **Stage 2:** Widely shunned. **Stage 3:** Widespread but . . . **Stage 4:** Ubiquitous but . . . **Stage 5:** Fully accepted.
Invariably inferior forms marked by asterisk (*). • Ratios represent frequency of prevalent forms vs. variants in current books.

while under constant fire." Greg Seigle, "Saving the Wounded," *Wash. Times*, 6 June 1994, at E10.

The word *number* is redundant when used with either term. See REDUNDANCY.

ENUMERATIONS. A. *First(ly), second(ly), third(ly); one, two, three.* The best method of enumerating items is the straightforward *first*, *second*, and *third*. The forms *firstly*, *secondly*, and *thirdly* sound stuffy and have an unnecessary syllable, and *one*, *two*, and *three* sound especially informal. E.g.: "This leaves but two possible effects of the service mark's continued use: *One* [read *First*], no one will know what CONAN means. *Two* [read *Second*], those who are familiar with the plaintiff's property will continue to associate CONAN with THE BARBARIAN." *Conan Props. v. Conan Pizza*, 752 F.2d 145, 156 (5th Cir. 1985) (Clark, J., dissenting). See **firstly.**

B. Comma Before the Last Element. The question whether to use the serial comma—or, as it's sometimes called, the "Harvard" comma or "Oxford" comma—is more vehemently argued than any other punctuation issue. Fashions in public-school textbooks and journalists' manuals come and go, but only one method is ironclad in avoiding unnecessary ambiguities: inserting a comma before the final element. Hence *a, b, and c* rather than *a, b and c*. Problems arise, for example, with elements containing two or more items, as *a and b, c and d, e and f, and g and h*. The last two elements are muddled if the comma is omitted.

Consider this sentence, an example of how using the serial comma can prevent a syntactical train wreck: "Like almost any modern player, most of the $80 models play DVDs, music CDs, video CDs, MP3 music disks you've created on your computer and so on." On your computer and what? The classic example of ambiguity is the apocryphal book dedication, "To my parents, Ayn Rand and God."

This sort of thing creeps into print more often than journalists might expect—e.g.: "The university's chemistry, biology, physics and marine and environmental-science departments, which are now scattered around campus, will be housed in the center with its 73 laboratories." Chris Moran, "USD Given $10 Million for Science, Tech Center," *San Diego Union-Trib.*, 14 June 2002, at B2. Still, the trend among journalists is to omit the serial comma. Hence the rule as stated by a leading authority in punctuation: "Three or more elements in a series are separated by commas. When the last two elements (words, phrases, or clauses) in a series are joined by a conjunction, a comma comes before the conjunction—unless you're a journalist." Karen Elizabeth Gordon, *The New Well-Tempered Sentence* 46 (rev. ed. 1993). See PUNCTUATION (D).

C. Within a Single Sentence. To keep the sentence short, enumerate items with parenthetical numbers: *(1), (2), (3)*, etc. Of course, if the sentence becomes overlong anyway, you're better off dividing it up.

D. *And* **Before the Last Element.** See **and** (c).

E. Bullets. See PUNCTUATION (B).

enunciate /i-nən-see-ayt/. Ironically, the word is sometimes mispronounced /shee/ in the third syllable. For the sense, see **announce.**

enunciation. See PRONUNCIATION (F).

***enure.** See **inure.**

envelop is the verb ("to wrap or cover"), *envelope* the noun ("wrapper, covering"). The verb is pronounced /en-**vel**-əp/; the noun is pronounced either /**en**-və-lohp/ or /**on**-və-lohp/.

enviable; envious. That which is *enviable* arouses envy or is at least worthy of it. A person who is *envious* feels or is struck by envy. *Envious* usually takes the preposition *of* <envious of her sister's success>, but historically has also taken *against* or *at*. See **jealousy.**

The pair is in the unenviable position of being susceptible to WORD-SWAPPING—e.g.:

- "Mr. Strauss's financial disclosure statement . . . details what is already widely known: the 72-year-old lawyer is a power broker of abundant wealth and *envious* [read *enviable*] political and corporate connections." Stephen Labaton, "Strauss to Forgo $4 Million in Pay to Take Moscow Post," *N.Y. Times*, 13 July 1991, at 3.
- "Northwestern has an *envious* [read *enviable*] record in producing outstanding performers." "Kup's Column," *Chicago Sun-Times*, 17 Sept. 1997, at 70.
- "Teleglobe, with its trans-oceanic and satellite links, is in the *envious* [read *enviable*] position of being able to bridge U.S. Internet content with an information-hungry world." Barrie McKenna, "D.C.'s Internet Success Runs Deep," *Globe & Mail* (Toronto), 27 Dec. 1999, at B7.

LANGUAGE-CHANGE INDEX
envious misused for *enviable*: Stage 1
Current ratio (*enviable reputation* vs.
**envious reputation*): 91:1

envision; envisage. Although *envisage* is more than a century older—having been used since the early 19th century—*envision* is now much more common in AmE. Today, *envisage* is a literary word in AmE, but the ordinary word in BrE. Not until the mid-1970s, however, did *envision* supplant *envisage* as the more usual term in AmE.

Both words mean "to visualize," but there is perhaps an incipient DIFFERENTIATION underway—one that should be encouraged. As suggested by *W11*, *envision* means "to picture to oneself" <I don't envision winning the tournament>, while *envisage* means "to contemplate or view in a certain way" <she envisages the building as being in a state of severe decline>.

In fact, though, American speakers and writers tend to use *envision* in both ways, to the exclusion of *envisage*—e.g.:

- "Wilk said she could even *envision* someone turning the house into a bed-and-breakfast with a horror theme." "Killer Deal: 'The Silence of the Lambs' House Up for Sale," *Daily Telegram* (Adrian, Mich.), 20 Aug. 2015, at B5.
- "Champions of the coming age of autonomous vehicles *envision* a time when car accidents do indeed become

a regrettable horror of the past, in the same league as smallpox and bloodletting." Kristine Owram, "What Will Insurers Do Without Drivers?," *Edmonton J.*, 22 Aug. 2015, at C8.

- "Weiss *envisions* it as a Wall of Fame, with scores of artists." David Menconi, "UNC's Own Rock and Roll Hall of Fame," *News & Observer* (Raleigh), 22 Aug. 2015, Entertainment §.

Still, *envisage* is hardly unknown in AmE—e.g.: "President Clinton's advisers . . . earnestly hope that the fragile arrangement *envisaged* in the Dayton peace plan will somehow hang together." Mike O'Connor, "Stray Cable from Bosnia Creates Stir in Capital," *N.Y. Times*, 10 Oct. 1996, at 29.

*en vogue. See **in vogue**.

envoi; envoy. For the sense "a postscript to a poem or essay," both spellings are used. Major American dictionaries are divided on the point—some listing *envoi* first and others *envoy* first. In that sense, though, *envoi* is the more usual spelling by a 6-to-1 ratio in print sources.

That development makes for useful DIFFERENTIATION because *envoy* is now used almost exclusively in diplomatic contexts. Both words are preferably pronounced /**en**-voi/, not /**on**-voi/.

envy. See **jealousy** & **enviable**.

*eolian. See **aeolian**.

eon (= an indefinitely big era) is the standard spelling in AmE and BrE alike. *Aeon is an obsolescent variant. See AE.

epaulette; epaulet. In the 1780s, English borrowed this word from French, in which the word is spelled *epaulette*. Through 1880, that was the predominant spelling in English as well, but from 1900 or so the feminine suffix was frequently dropped: *epaulet* vied with *epaulette* for about a century, during which time most American dictionaries gave priority to *epaulet*. Today, however, *epaulette* remains the more frequent spelling in AmE and BrE alike. *Epaulette* is accented on the last syllable, *epaulet* on the first.
Current ratio (*epaulette* vs. *epaulet*): 1.5:1

épée (= a fencing sword, narrow with a sharp point) is normally so spelled, with its two accents, and pronounced either /e-**pay**/ or /**ep**-ay/. See DIACRITICAL MARKS.

epenthetic (= of, relating to, or consisting of the insertion of a superfluous syllable or sound into the middle of a word) is the standard adjective—*epenthetical being a NEEDLESS VARIANT. Several mispronunciations contain *epenthetic* schwas, such as /**ath**-ə-leet/ for what should be a two-syllable *athlete* and /**reel**-ə-tər/

for what should be a two-syllable *realtor*. See **athlete** & **realtor**. See also PRONUNCIATION (B).
Current ratio: 668:1

epexegesis. See **exegesis**.

epic, adj.; ***epical.** See **epochal** (A).

epicenter (BrE *epicentre*). This is a scientific term meaning "the point on the surface of the earth just above the underground focal point of an earthquake." It shouldn't be used thoughtlessly as a synonym for *center*—e.g.:

- "Jan-Wolter Wabeke, 52, has been at the *epicenter* [read *center*] of the debate over the Netherlands' social legislation both at home and abroad." Christopher Dickey & Friso Endt, "Playing by Dutch Rules," *Newsweek Int'l*, 4 June 2001, at 18.
- "Ramsey, who is elusive about his home life, is the only one of the five who lives in public housing, which was at the *epicenter* [read *center*] of the summer's gang warfare." Alex Kotlowitz, "Proving Ground," *Chicago Trib.*, 10 June 2001, Mag. §, at 12.
- "Clearly, urban areas are at the *epicenter* [read *center*] of welfare reform." Bruce Katz & Katherine Allen, "Cities Matter," *Brookings Rev.*, 1 July 2001, at 30.

One of William Safire's correspondents, a geophysicist named Joseph D. Sides, attributes this type of misusage to "spurious erudition on the part of writers combined with scientific illiteracy on the part of copy editors." (As quoted in Safire, "On Language," *N.Y. Times*, 6 May 2001, § 6, at 22.) But maybe these types of misusage are just metaphorical descriptions of focal points of unstable and potentially destructive environments.

LANGUAGE-CHANGE INDEX
epicenter misused for *center*: Stage 1

epicure. See **gourmet**.

epicurean. So spelled—preferably not *epicurian. E.g.:

- "If people know how to taste [chocolate] properly, they may view it like that other great *epicurian* [read *epicurean*] matchmaker." Jay Cridlin, "Can Cocoa Bring People Together?" *St. Petersburg Times*, 6 June 2008, at 51.
- "Asian cuisine is nothing if not adventurous, and the Munchers were ready to push the *epicurian* [read *epicurean*] envelope." Peter Genovese, "Currying Flavor," *Star-Ledger* (Newark), 13 June 2008, Today §, at 61.

The same recipe spoils other cognates of *epicure* as well—e.g.: "One would end up no doubt oscillating madly between *epicurianism* [read *epicureanism*] and stoicism." Joseph Brodsky, *On Grief and Reason* 331 (1995).

LANGUAGE-CHANGE INDEX
epicurean misspelled *epicurian: Stage 1
Current ratio: 151:1

---

epidemic; endemic. A disease is an *epidemic* when it breaks out and rages in a community, only to subside afterward. A disease is an *endemic* when it constantly exists within a certain population or region. The latter term, which also applies to plants, is comparatively rare.

The words are sometimes used as adjectives. *Epidemic* = extremely prevalent; widespread. *Endemic* = native to a particular region or group. Cf. **pandemic.**

epigram; epigraph. Because these similar-sounding terms are similar in meaning, they are therefore often subject to WORD-SWAPPING. *Epigram* = (1) a short, witty poem; or (2) a concise, pointed, and usu. clever saying. (Cf. **apothegm.**) *Epigraph* = (1) an inscription, esp. on a building or statue; or (2) a thematic quotation at the beginning of a book, chapter, etc. So although an *epigram* can constitute an *epigraph*, the reverse does not hold true.

epilogue (= a parting word at the end of a written or spoken presentation) is so spelled—not **epilog*. Cf. **analogue, catalog(ue)** & **dialogue.** For a comment on the potential decline of the *-ue* form, see -AGOG(UE).

Episcopal Church; *Episcopalian Church. Strictly, one refers to the *Episcopal Church* and to an *Episcopal minister*. The word *Episcopalian* is most commonly a noun, as in *I'm an Episcopalian*. Yet many writers have started using *Episcopalian* as an adjective—e.g.:

- "The Liberal Catholic Church . . . is independent of the Roman Catholic and *Episcopalian* [read *Episcopal*] Church." Luisa Yanez, "Church Dissolves Cultural Barriers," *Sun-Sentinel* (Ft. Lauderdale), 30 May 1988, at B3. (Note the CONCORD problem here.)
- "Chauncey, descended from clergymen (his father was an *Episcopalian* [read *Episcopal*] minister, his ancestors Puritans), went to church, and afterward he added to the day's diary entry." Nicholas Lemann, "The Structure of Success in America," *Atlantic Monthly*, Aug. 1995, at 41, 42.

LANGUAGE-CHANGE INDEX
*Episcopalian Church for *Episcopal Church*: Stage 1
Current ratio (*Episcopal Church* vs.
*Episcopalian Church): 64:1

epistolary (= of, relating to, or based on letters) is sometimes wrongly made **epistolatory*—e.g.:

- "Both were hypochondriacs—an important *epistolatory* [read *epistolary*] bond—Jefferson suffering from headaches, Madison from bowel trouble." Paul Johnson, "Founding Fathers," *Daily Telegraph*, 23 Apr. 1995, at 9.
- "The author has transformed the historical Pacienza into the protagonist of her remarkably interesting novel *The Secret Book of Grazia Dei Rossi*, an *epistolatory* [read *epistolary*] tale of an Italian Jewish proto-feminist torn between duty and love." Sharon Gibson, "Love, Duty Drive Renaissance Novel," *Houston Chron.*, 21 Sept. 1997, Zest §, at 27.

A cognate of *epistle* (letter), the word is pronounced /i-**pis**-tə-ler-ee/.

LANGUAGE-CHANGE INDEX
*epistolatory for *epistolary*: Stage 1
Current ratio (*epistolary* vs. **epistolatory*): 155:1

epitaph. See **epithet** (B).

epithet. A. Meanings. *Epithet* = (1) an esp. apt description or label, whether the quality denoted is favorable or unfavorable; or (2) a slur or an abusive term. Sense 2 is quickly driving out sense 1.

LANGUAGE-CHANGE INDEX
epithet for *slur* or *term of abuse*: Stage 5

B. And *epitaph*. *Epitaph* (= a gravestone inscription) is sometimes misused for *epithet* in the sense of "a derogatory name." Today the blooper is irksomely common—e.g.:

- "Santiago, of the 3400 block of Lituanica, beat the mailman with a pool cue and shouted racial *epitaphs* [read *epithets*], Burnett said." "2 Convicted in Racial Attack on Postman," *Chicago Sun-Times*, 12 Mar. 1994, at 38.
- "Then like a tornado he withdrew again to the inside dorm balcony, screaming profane *epitaphs* [read *epithets*] at the cringing Andrew." George T. Eidson Jr., "Notes from the Inside," *Orlando Sentinel*, 10 Sept. 1995, Florida §, at 7.
- "He is a man taken to belittling his staff and his wife, using racial *epitaphs* [read *epithets*] when speaking with men he knows to be bigots and bragging of extramarital affairs." Stephen Watson, "A *Masterful* [read *Masterly*] Saga of LBJ's Senate Years," *Buffalo News*, 12 May 2002, at F5. (See **masterful.**)

In Canada, this error has provoked the ire of a letter-writer: "Art Hanger, the Calgary Reform MP, last week accused Liberal Mary Clancy of 'hurling epitaphs' when she attacked Reform immigration policy. [¶] Clancy replied mockingly that 'marble epitaphs' are rather too heavy to hurl, and chided Hanger for his misuse of language. [¶] Actually, they're both wrong—but who expects politicians to understand English? [¶] An epitaph is not a headstone: it's a funeral oration or a memorial inscription written on a tomb." Sydney Sharpe, "Calgary Schools Benefit from Companies' Castoffs," *Calgary Herald*, 22 Jan. 1995, at A2.

LANGUAGE-CHANGE INDEX
epitaph misused for *epithet*: Stage 1
Current ratio (*contemptuous epithet* vs.
*contemptuous epitaph): 45:1

C. And *expletive*. These words overlap somewhat, since a shouted *epithet* is also an *expletive* in the sense of "an exclamation, esp. a profane or scatological exclamation." But *expletive* is also a term in grammar, referring to a word that serves no real purpose in a sentence but merely fills a syntactic space (most commonly *it* or *there*, as in *it is raining* or *there is something we need to talk about*). See EXPLETIVES.

epitome /i-**pit**-ə-mee *or* ee-**pit**-ə-mee/ = (1) an ideal representation of a class of things; or (2) a summary, abstract. E.g. (sense 1): "In short, he is the *epitome* of all that many liberals find evil in the boardrooms of America." Ted Bunker, "No Place for Liberals at This CEO's Table," *Boston Herald*, 7 Oct. 1996, at 26.

The word does not mean "pinnacle" or "climax"—e.g.:

- "ESPN reached the *epitome* [read *pinnacle* or *zenith*] of boredom during its marathon coverage of the NFL draft."

Bruce Jenkins, "They're Everywhere," *S.F. Chron.*, 27 Apr. 1996, at D2.

- "Jordan's masterstroke was choosing Liam Neeson, whose penchant for deeply emotional yet disturbingly complex men reached its *epitome* [read *pinnacle* or *zenith*] in *Schindler's List*." Bruce Kirkland, "Michael Collins a Powerful, Tragic Portrait," *Toronto Sun*, 11 Oct. 1996, at 77.
- "Strained pranks and smutty jokes reach their *epitome* [read *pinnacle* or, more appropriately here, *low point*] in the show's big inspiration: having a dog fall in love with Harris's leg." Tom Shales, "Primal-Time Programming," *Wash. Post*, 19 Sept. 1999, at G1.

LANGUAGE-CHANGE INDEX
epitome misused for *pinnacle*: Stage 1
Current ratio (*reach the pinnacle* vs.
**reach the epitome*): 46:1

epoch (/**ep**-ək/) = (1) a date of an occurrence that starts things going under new conditions; or (2) a period of history. Some stylists object to sense 2 as an example of SLIPSHOD EXTENSION—an unnecessary word since *era* fills the role nicely. But the extension occurred in the 17th century, and good writers today use the word in that sense—e.g.: "Scientists at the Smithsonian Institution . . . have challenged . . . the notion that our early ancestors were prodded into existence in response to abrupt environmental changes during the Pliocene *epoch*." Curt Suplee, "Team Challenges Theory Linking Climate Change, Evolutionary Surge," *Wash. Post*, 28 Nov. 1997, at A4.

In the taxonomy of geological time, an epoch is a division of a period, which in turn is a division of an era. For example, today we are in the Holocene Epoch of the Quaternary Period of the Cenozoic Era.

epochal. A. And *epic*, adj.; *epical. Epochal (/**ep**-ə-kəl/) = marking an epoch, or a new period in chronology. The word should not be used lightly. "Five devastating *epochal* floods have visited the valley since the establishment of the commission." (Only if the writer intended to convey that five epochs had passed since the establishment of the commission—an unlikely meaning—would *epochal* have been correct.)

Epic = (1) of, relating to, or involving an epic (i.e., a long heroic narrative); or (2) surpassing what is ordinary or usual. *Epical is a NEEDLESS VARIANT.

Current ratio (*epic poem* vs. *epical poem): 615:1

B. And *epoch-making*. The phrase *epoch-making*—a near-equivalent of *epochal*—is sometimes mistakenly written *epic-making. E.g.: "We are at the end of only the second decade of the revolutions in microelectronics and telecommunications, and the lesson of other *epic-making* [read *epoch-making*] innovations, such as electricity, is that productivity gains . . . will likely continue." Peter Morici, "Export Our Way to Prosperity," *Foreign Policy*, 22 Dec. 1995, at 3.

LANGUAGE-CHANGE INDEX
*epic-making for *epoch-making*: Stage 1

eponym; eponymous. *Eponym* (= a person, place, or thing that gives its name to someone or something else) is sometimes misused to denote the bearer of the borrowed name—e.g.: "Nouns derived from proper names of people or places, such as sandwich, are called *eponyms* [read *namesakes*]." Howard Wolinsky, "Click Here: Our Favorite Places on the Net," *Chicago Sun-Times*, 24 Oct. 2006, Financial §, at 54.

Likewise, the adjective *eponymous* (= characteristic of a person, place, or thing that gives its name to someone or something else) is traditionally used with the source of the name—e.g.: "Made from gamay grapes grown in the *eponymous* region of France, Beaujolais Nouveau is a red wine produced very quickly through a process known as carbonic maceration." Allison Knab, "A Little Beau Peek," *Chicago Trib.*, 15 Nov. 2006, at 34.

But today, *eponymous* is commonly (and sloppily) used with the derived name rather than the eponym itself—e.g.: "His *eponymous* London restaurant earned three stars in the latest Michelin guide, so achievement of that goal rests on his New York venture." Jennifer Leuzzi, "Gordon Ramsay Lands in New York," *N.Y. Sun*, 15 Nov. 2006, Food & Drink §, at 11. (A possible revision: *His London restaurant, which bears the owner's name, earned three stars . . . .*) Sticking with the traditional usage would clear up ambiguities such as this example from the same source: "Other Warhols on offer at Christie's include 'Sixteen Jackies' (estimate upon request), and his *eponymous* four-panel portrait of the novelist Judith Green (estimate $2 million–$3 million)." João Rivas, "Another Record Week?" *N.Y. Sun*, 13 Nov. 2006, Arts & Letters §, at 13. Is that portrait named after Green or Warhol? Or is the reader to take *eponymous* literally and conclude that Green was named after the portrait?

LANGUAGE-CHANGE INDEX
eponym for *namesake*: Stage 2

equable. See **equitable.**

equal, n. & adj. See **coequal.**

equal, vb., makes *equaled* and *equaling* in AmE, *equalled* and *equalling* in BrE. See SPELLING (B).

equal if not better. This phrase works if the thing being compared has already been mentioned and doesn't need further mention in a sentence—e.g.: "The Pac-10 has *equal, if not better,* drawing power, but as a shaper of college athletics, its best days have passed." Percy Allen, "Pac-10 Plays Waiting Game as Stakes Rise," *Seattle Times*, 28 Aug. 1996, at F13 (comparing the Pac-10 with the Big Eight athletic conference, mentioned in the previous paragraph). But if the point of comparison is yet to be made and a *than*-phrase follows *better*, the construction is illogical because you cannot say that something is *equal than* something

LANGUAGE-CHANGE INDEX (For the full key, see front matter pp. xxxi, l–li.)
Stage 1: Rejected. **Stage 2:** Widely shunned. **Stage 3:** Widespread but . . . **Stage 4:** Ubiquitous but . . . **Stage 5:** Fully accepted.
Invariably inferior forms marked by asterisk (*). • Ratios represent frequency of prevalent forms vs. variants in current books.

else. You have to make it *equal to* in order to parallel *better than*—e.g.:

- "Under Columbia's tutelage, the quality of care is *equal, if not better than,* [read *equal to, if not better than, the quality of care*] before." Frank Cerne, "Corporate Takeover? Healthcare Consolidation Could Improve Financial Stability," *Hospitals & Health Networks,* 20 Mar. 1995, at 44.
- "We should make their salaries *equal (if not better than)* [read *equal to (if not better than)*] those of the administrators." Gwen Diaz, "A 10-Point Parent Proposal," *Ledger* (Lakeland, Fla.), 17 Oct. 1995, at B6.
- "Humphreys in his pomp for Ireland *was at least the equal if not better than* his nemesis Ronan O'Gara." Tony Ward, "Sexton Is Now a Man Under Severe Pressure," *Belfast Telegraph,* 12 May 2015, Sport §, at 49. (Here, *equal,* preceded by *the,* functions as a noun, making the construction even more illogical by creating a false parallel with the adjective *better.* A possible revision: *Humphreys's pomp for Ireland at least equaled—if not surpassed—that of his nemesis, Ronan O'Gara.*)

See ILLOGIC (B). Cf. CANNIBALISM & PARALLELISM.

Of course, the mistake is far less frequent than the correct phrasing in edited English—e.g.: "Harrington says the Red Sox must have a stadium that is *equal to, if not better than,* the new ones in Cleveland, Baltimore and Toronto." Will McDonough, "Harrington Expounds on Ballpark, Figures," *Boston Globe,* 6 Mar. 1996, at 61.

If *equal* and *better* are used as verbs, of course, no prepositions are needed. The usage becomes less tricky—e.g.: "Banks' investment performance has at least *equaled if not bettered* that of their non-bank competitors." "You Don't Have to Be Big," *ABA Banking J.,* Nov. 1988, at 57.

LANGUAGE-CHANGE INDEX
equal if not better than for
equal to if not better than: Stage 4
Current ratio (*equal to if not better than* vs.
equal if not better than): 2:1

equally as. The particle in this phrase is almost always unnecessary and faulty—e.g.:

- "The sauce would work *equally as* [read *equally*] well on chicken, fish, onions, or any food that's good cooked on the grill or in the broiler." Patricia Mack, "No Cooking Tonight," *Record* (N.J.), 25 Sept. 1996, at F1.
- "Senior Darnell Morgan (5-9, 171) leads the way with 466 yards. Chapman plays defense *equally as* [read *equally*] well." "Game Day," *L.A. Times,* 12 Oct. 1996, at C15.
- "While the hosts of late-night talk shows set the tone and the guests pull in the viewers, the bands are *equally as* [read *equally*] important." Leo Pusateri, "Developing Value Culture Means New Ideas," *Bus. First* (Buffalo), 19 Jan. 1998, at 27.

The variant phrase *as equally* is just as (i.e., equally) poor—e.g.:

- "Johnson, who had 37 points in the victory over MTSU, was *as equally* [read *equally*] unstoppable in the opening half." Phil Stukenborg, "Tigers Tandem Gets 55 to Beat Blazers," *Commercial Appeal* (Memphis), 18 Dec. 1997, at D1.
- "Grayhawk placed both of its courses on the top 25 list, but the clubhouse is *as equally* [read *equally*] impressive." "Public Courses: The Top 25," *Ariz. Republic,* 9 Jan. 1998, at 10.

Not every use, though, is incorrect: if the words *equally as* simply appear together but are really parts of other constructions, all may be well <I love you equally as a nephew and as a friend>.

LANGUAGE-CHANGE INDEX
equally as for *equally*: Stage 2
Current ratio (*equally important* vs.
**equally as important*): 29:1

equal to none is a confusion of two other idioms, namely, *second to none* and *equal to the best*—e.g.:

- "Charles Mosley . . . [was] strangely described by the publisher as possessing a knowledge of the subject and attention to detail '*equal to none.*'" Hugh Massingberd, "Proving the Jeremiahs Wrong," *Spectator,* 28 Aug. 1999, at 34. (The whole sentence would have to be rewritten, of course, if the phrase were changed to *second to none*—which would no longer be strange.)
- "She had a head for business *equal to none* [read *second to none*] and never let her pursuit of Euterpe . . . get in the way of the practical agenda." Hilary Masters, "Harriet Munro: The Untold Story," *Va. Q. Rev.,* 1 Oct. 2001, at 680.

LANGUAGE-CHANGE INDEX
**equal to none* for *second to none*: Stage 2
Current ratio (*second to none* vs.
**equal to none*): 122:1

equanimity (= evenness of mind, esp. under pressure) often appears in the redundant phrase **equanimity of mind*—e.g.:

- "After compiling these other successes, she entered the next bar exam with *equanimity of mind* [read *equanimity*], and passed." Vivian Dempsey, "A State of Mind for a Second Try," *Recorder* (S.F.), 24 Nov. 1992, at 7.
- "A mature person of mellow temperament, retaining *an equanimity of mind* [read *equanimity*] under all circumstances, with a complete understanding not only of himself or herself but of his or her relations, is a person of true character." Fan Xing, "The Chinese Cultural System," *SAM Advanced Mgmt. J.,* Jan. 1995, at 14, 18.

The pronunciation is /ee-kwə-**nim**-ə-tee/ or /e-/.

equilibrium. Few dictionaries record a plural form. Although *W11* and *AHD* give precedence to *equilibriums* over *equilibria,* the latter remains much more common in print sources. A survey of writers in the early 2000s found that writers under 45 were more likely to prefer *equilibriums,* which has remained little used but stable.

Current ratio (*equilibria* vs. *equilibriums*): 25:1

equine. See ANIMAL ADJECTIVES.

equinoctial; *equinoxial. The former has been standard since the early 18th century. The latter is a NEEDLESS VARIANT.

Current ratio: 59:1

equitable; equable. *Equitable* (/**ek**-wi-tə-bəl/), deriving from *equity,* has associations of justice and fairness, or that which can be sustained in a court of equity. To nonlawyers it generally means "fair," whereas to lawyers it may also mean "fair" but just as often means "in equity" <equitable jurisdiction> <equitable remedies>. *Equable* (/**ek**-wə-bəl/) = even; tranquil; level.

Each word is sometimes misused for the other—e.g.:

- "Certainly Henman's realistic approach and his *equitable* [read *equable*] temperament make him better equipped than most to overcome what has basically been a sudden lack of confidence." John Parsons, "Henman Hoping to End His Slump," *Daily Telegraph*, 18 Feb. 1998, at 39.
- "The objectives include . . . [establishing] an *equable* [read *equitable*] allocation of district capital funds for facility construction." Eva Jo Goins, "Board Sets Objectives for Fixing Schools," *Santa Fe New Mexican*, 18 Oct. 2000, at P1.

LANGUAGE-CHANGE INDEX
equable misused for *equitable*: Stage 1
Current ratio (*equitable distribution* vs.
*equable distribution): 63:1

equivalence; equivalency. In most contexts, *equivalency* is a NEEDLESS VARIANT of *equivalence*. But the *-cy* form is standard in the term *high-school equivalency exam*. See -CE.

equivalent. A. Prepositions with. As an adjective, *equivalent* preferably takes the preposition *to*, not *with*—e.g.: "The $20 million is more than any other NFL coach will receive and approximately *equivalent with* [read *equivalent to*] the $3 million a year that Pat Riley and John Calipari earn in the NBA." "Sports Digest: Jets," *Baltimore Sun*, 8 Feb. 1997, at C2. As a noun, it almost always takes the preposition *of* <this Australian wine is an equivalent of a good, robust Burgundy>.

LANGUAGE-CHANGE INDEX
*equivalent with for *equivalent to*: Stage 1
Current ratio (*equivalent to* vs.
*equivalent with): 112:1

B. A Malapropism: **equivocal with*. Misusing *equivocal* for *equivalent* is a surprising MALAPROPISM, committed here by the chair of a college biology department: "Though physical sexual identity is not *equivocal with* [read *equivalent to*] sexual orientation, the point I am trying to make is that not all things are as black and white as some homophobes might like them to be." Joseph Adam Pearson, "Homophobia a Useless Passion That Destroys Lives on Both Sides," *Ariz. Republic*, 28 Sept. 1994, at B6.

LANGUAGE-CHANGE INDEX
equivocal misused for *equivalent*: Stage 1

equivocal. See **unequivocal.**

equivoque (= [1] an ambiguous term; or [2] a punning word) is the standard spelling. **Equivoke* is a variant. The word is pronounced /**ek**-wə-vohk/.

Current ratio: 8:1

-ER. A. And -or. These agent-noun suffixes can be especially vexatious. Many words that were once considered Latin borrowings have become so thoroughly naturalized that they take *-er* instead of *-or* (e.g., *adviser, prohibiter, promoter, propeller*). But not *impostor* (which does not refer to someone who *imposts*). The historical tendency has been to make the Latinate *-or* the correlative of *-ee* (especially in legal writing), hence *donee/donor, indemnitee/indemnitor, obligee/obligor, offeree/offeror, transferee/transferor, vendee/vendor*. See -EE.

Attempts to confine *-er* to words of Anglo-Saxon origin and *-or* to those of Latin origin are fruitless because so many exceptions exist on both sides of the aisle. Nevertheless, Latinate words tend to take *-or*, though there are many exceptions—a few of which appear below in the *-er* column:

-er	*-or*
adapter	abductor
conjurer	collector
corrupter	distributor
digester	impostor
dispenser	infiltrator
endorser	investor
eraser	manipulator
idolater	offeror
profferer	persecutor
promoter	purveyor
requester	surveyor

B. And -re. Words borrowed from French generally arrived in English with the *-re* spelling. Most such words have gradually made the transition to *-er*. A few words may be spelled only *-re*, such as *acre, chancre, massacre*, and *mediocre*, because of the preceding *-c-*. Still others—the great majority—have variant spellings, the *-er* ending usually being more common in AmE and the *-re* ending in BrE. The following words have this distinction: *caliber, -re; center, -re; goiter, -re; liter, -re; louver, -re; luster, -re; meager, -re; meter, -re; miter, -re; niter, -re; reconnoiter, -re; scepter, -re; sepulcher, -re; somber, -re; specter, -re; theater, -re*. Likewise *maneuver, manoeuvre*. An odd exception is *accoutre* (both AmE and BrE)—the putative AmE spelling **accouter* never having caught on.

Occasionally, heated debates break out over how to spell such words. In the late 1970s and early 1980s, the Government Printing Office was accused of upsetting the balance of trade by recommending *liter* over *litre*. The pro-*litre* forces argued that other nations would be more likely to import American goods if those goods bore the *litre* spelling. But when the GPO conducted a worldwide survey, it found that more people spell it *liter* than *litre*. (That was true in World English beginning about 1900.) And so *liter* it remained in official American publications. See Lee Lescaze, "The Style Board: Telling Government Where to Put Its Hyphens," *Wash. Post*, 18 Oct. 1980, at A3.

Some American companies have started using the *-re* spellings to distinguish themselves and perhaps to try to bring some cachet to their projects. Many major cities, for example, have downtown buildings called *Such-and-Such Centre.* Next door might be the *Such-and-Such Theatre.* People who go into such centers and theaters should be on their best behavior—no, make that *behaviour.*

C. And -est. See COMPARATIVES AND SUPERLATIVES.

era (= a period in history known for a particular event or for specific characteristics) is legitimately pronounced either /eer-ə/ or /air-ə/—the former being traditional.

eradicable. So formed—not **eradicatable.* See -ABLE (D) & -ATABLE.

ERGATIVE VERBS. A. Generally. In the mid-20th century, grammarians devised the term *ergative* ("working") to describe a verb that can be used (1) in the active voice with a normal subject (actor) and object (the thing acted on) <I broke the window>; (2) in the PASSIVE VOICE, with the recipient of the verb's action as the subject of the sentence (and most often the actor's becoming the object of a *by*-phrase <the window was broken by me>; or (3) in what one textbook called "the third way," as an intransitive verb (without a direct object) <the window broke>. Ergative verbs show remarkable versatility. For example, you might say that *he is running the machine* or *the machine is running, she spun the top* or *the top spun, the crew decided to split the rail* or *the rail splits at that point.*

Not all verbs can be ergative: you couldn't, for instance, change *I cleaned the window* to **The window cleaned.* And verbs that are ergative with some nouns are not ergative with others, so you couldn't change *I broke a bad habit* into **A bad habit broke.*

The unfamiliar term *ergative* isn't especially helpful to most people trying to understand these verbs and the idiomatic way they function. But in general, ergative verbs tend to communicate a change of state <Geller bent the spoon> <the spoon bent>, and we may think of that change as "working." The change may also be a change of position instead of a change of state <spin the bottle> <the bottle spins>, or it may be a change of movement <may I drive your car?> <your car drives nicely>. It may also be a change brought about by cooking <steam the rice> <the rice is steaming>, an activity that seems conducive to ergative verbs.

B. Uses. Because the ergative verb eliminates the actor altogether, sentences that use it suggest some action that takes place spontaneously. Why? It may be because of a rule <hunting season starts in November> or a natural process <when the leaves drop> that makes the actor irrelevant. It may be a device to hide the actor <the rumor spread quickly throughout the office> or even to create mystery <the door slammed shut behind them>.

C. Misuses. Sometimes writers ill-advisedly give transitive verbs intransitive uses as if the verbs were ergative—e.g.: "Even the Infamous Could Redeem Were Jesus Here, Book Says," *Austin Am.-Statesman,* 30 July 1994, at A20. This headline writer showed enough sophistication to use the SUBJUNCTIVE *were* (for a condition contrary to fact) but confused the passive *to be redeemed* with the active *to redeem.* Likewise, in STANDARD ENGLISH the verb *pique* is transitive only—hence possibly passive—but the writer of the following sentence tried to make it ergative (perhaps to avoid the passive voice): "Anderson was impressed with Weiskopf's attitude. And when others also called to sing the praises of Loch Lomond, Anderson's interest *piqued* [read *was piqued*]." Bill Huffman, "Course of 'Compelling' Beauty," *Ariz. Republic,* 29 Sept. 1994, at D6. (This misuse of *pique* might also result from confusion with *peak.* See **pique.**)

Ergative verbs take some getting used to, so new coinages are likely to sound as jarring as nouns suddenly made into verbs <grow the business> (see FUNCTIONAL SHIFT). They can give prose a voguish, trendy tone <that jacket wears nicely on you> or else a tone of COMMERCIALESE <the books shipped yesterday> <sorry, your flight canceled>.

ergatocracy. See GOVERNMENTAL FORMS.

ergo [L. "therefore"] is a slightly archaic equivalent of *therefore* or *hence.* Its traditional use is in logic, where it introduces the conclusion to a syllogism. But outside logic, *ergo* tends toward light irony, while *therefore* and *hence* tend toward seriousness. Today *ergo* often has a tongue-in-cheek effect—e.g.:

- "Too much or too powerful baking powder can give your cake an artificial high, which cannot be maintained after it comes out of the oven. *Ergo,* you might want to cut back on the amount called for." Gail Perrin, "The Q & A Corner," *Boston Globe,* 8 Oct. 1997, at E3.
- "Greek physicians such as Galen (130–201 A.D.) believed . . . that treatment of disease and injury was based on keeping each humor in proper equilibrium. *Ergo,* fevers, allegedly caused by an excess of blood, were treated by bleeding." Thomas V. DiBacco, "Burn Treatment: Way Cool!" *Wash. Post,* 4 Nov. 1997, at Z10.
- "Oslo was only the last among several sensible European cities . . . to withdraw their bids to host the 2022 Winter Games in the face of public resistance and IOC arrogance. *Ergo* Beijing, again. Neither cost nor public opinion *matter* [read *matters*] in what has become the natural territory of the modern Olympic Games." John Barber, "Toronto, Please Don't Make an Olympic Bid for 2024," *Toronto Star,* 26 Aug. 2015, at A13. (On the *neither . . . nor* problem of grammatical number, see **neither . . . nor (A).**)

The word is pronounced /air-goh/ in Latin, but /ər-goh/ in English.

eristic, adj.; ***eristical.** *Eristic* has always been the predominant and therefore standard form of this word, which means "of, relating to, or involving controversy or disputation." See -IC.

Current ratio: 24:1

erodible; *erodable; *erosible. The standard form—almost ten times as common in print as the other forms combined—is *erodible*. See -ABLE (A).

Current ratio: 566:84:1

erotica (= print or photographic materials intended to appeal to prurient interests) is a plural form, and it is appropriately used in the plural when clearly referring to more than one object—e.g.: "A set of Roman erotic frescoes *were* [read *was*] unveiled in Pompeii yesterday. . . . The discovery of the *erotica*, some of which *are* humourous or bawdy, has led to a theory that the baths also contained a lupanar, or brothel." Bruce Johnston, "Erotic Pompeii Frescoes Unveiled," *Daily Telegraph*, 15 Nov. 2001, at 20. But that convention is far from universally observed in World English, as a parallel example shows: "A collection of 800 figures decorates the walls both inside and out. The *erotica is* especially energetic and provocative. Then again, living in the middle of nowhere 1000 years ago, there must have been plenty of time for yoga and much, much more." Brian Johnston, "India's Ancient Erotica Site," *Southland Times* (N.Z.), 12 Dec. 2001, Travel §, at 17.

In fact, today *erotica* is almost always used as a singular noun, in reference to the genre itself—e.g.:

- "The future Lord Cobbold, sometimes nicknamed the Blue Baron, . . . has been criticised by those who do not believe that *erotica is* a suitable way to make a living for an Eton-educated blueblood." Hamida Ghafour, "Blue Baron Launches Red-Blooded Sex Book," *Daily Telegraph*, 26 Nov. 2001, at 7.
- "Brief explanatory titles note [that] this early century *erotica was* shown mostly in the waiting rooms of French brothels as a sort of appetizer, and that 'uncles' often brought teenage nephews to such fare after mass on Sundays 'to start their initiation into manhood.'" Todd McCarthy, "The Good Old Naughty Days," *Variety*, 10–16 June 2002, at 31.
- "The Justice Department must convince the Supreme Court that same policy should cover the explicit *erotica* that *permeates* various Web sites." Editorial, "Public Libraries Are No Place for Porn," *Indianapolis Star*, 29 July 2002, at A16.

eroticism; *erotism. The latter has been a NEEDLESS VARIANT since it first emerged in the late 19th century. Cf. **autoeroticism.**

Current ratio: 22:1

err. Traditionalists rhyme this word with *fur*; others tend to make it rhyme with *bear*. Each side is likely to think the other errs.

Pronunciation authorities have long preferred /ər/ over /air/. Among the overwhelming number are these: Richard Soule & Loomis J. Campbell, *Pronouncing Handbook of Words Often Mispronounced* 30 (1873); E.B. Warman, *Warman's Practical Orthoepy and Critique* 196 (1887); John H. Bechtel, *Hand-Book of Pronunciation and Phonetic Analysis* 50 (1900); Thorleif Larsen & Francis C. Walker, *Pronunciation: A Practical Guide to American Standards* 68 (1930); Charles B. Anderson, *A Guide to Good Pronunciation* 51 (1931); Daniel Jones, *An English Pronouncing Dictionary* 148 (7th ed. 1946); Estelle B. Hunter, *A Short-Cut to Correct Pronunciation* 26 (1946); Morriss H. Needleman, *A Manual of Pronunciation* 111 (1949); Ruth Gleeson & James Colvin, *Words Often Misspelled and Mispronounced* 75 (1963).

A few authorities have gone beyond just listing /ər/ and have discussed the issue—e.g.:

- "*Err.* Rhymes with *her*. In spite of *error* and *errant*, don't say 'We have *aired* and strayed from thy ways like lost sheep.' Let the thought of *deterring* deter you from a mispronunciation of *erring*." Alfred H. Holt, *You Don't Say!* 57 (1937).
- "*Err* must be pronounced to rime with *were*, not with *ware* . . . . The imperfect tense *erred* rimes with *herd*, and the present participle *erring* rimes with *purring*." John Baker Opdycke, *Don't Say It* 303 (1943). (On his spelling of *rhyme*, see **rhyme.**)
- "Some argue that *err* is etymologically connected to the words *error* and *errant*, and so should be pronounced similarly. This does not cut the mustard, because to draw such a parallel now, after UR has been the only recognized pronunciation since time immemorial, is pedantic and sophistical, a feeble attempt to find a legitimate reason for a mistake . . . . AIR did not appear in a dictionary until the 1960s, and despite its rapid rise to popularity, most current authorities still prefer UR." Charles Harrington Elster, *There Is No Zoo in Zoology* 51 (1988).

At least one language commentator did an about-face in the mid-20th century. In 1931, Frank Colby said: "Properly pronounced, *err* rhymes with *fur, her, purr.*" *Your Speech and How to Improve It* 114 (1931). By 1950, he had changed his mind: "It must be that dictionary makers are under oath not to listen to people talk. Why else would the dictionaries, without exception, refuse to recognize the Standard American pronunciation ehr for *err*? They insist on 'urr,' to rhyme with *burr*. . . . The truth is that *err* and *erring* are so closely associated with *error* (both are from the Latin *errare*, 'to err'), that ehr and EHR-ing are the natural and most logical pronunciations. They most assuredly prevail at all levels of American speech." Frank O. Colby, *The American Pronouncing Dictionary of Troublesome Words* 147 (1950).

The ranks of the traditionalists are shrinking, and the counterintuitive nature of the old pronunciation (given the sound of *error* and *errant*) seems to have doomed it. But those who care about our linguistic heritage and use the language with flair avoid the snare of /air/ and boldly say /ər/.

LANGUAGE-CHANGE INDEX
err pronounced /air/: Stage 4

LANGUAGE-CHANGE INDEX (For the full key, see front matter pp. xxxi, l–li.)
Stage 1: Rejected. **Stage 2:** Widely shunned. **Stage 3:** Widespread but . . . **Stage 4:** Ubiquitous but . . . **Stage 5:** Fully accepted.
Invariably inferior forms marked by asterisk (*). • Ratios represent frequency of prevalent forms vs. variants in current books.

errant; arrant. *Errant* = (1) traveling; itinerant <knight errant>; or (2) fallible, straying from what is proper. Sense 2 overwhelmingly predominates—e.g.:

- "On other holes, strategically placed bunkers keep *errant* shots from going too far astray." Chris Dortch, "Challenges Fly Wild at New Eagle Bluff Course," *Chattanooga Times*, 26 Oct. 1995, at C6.
- "He's been sent to the Italian coast by a wealthy San Francisco industrialist to bring back the man's *errant*, decadent son, Philipe (Maurice Ronet)." Stephen Hunter, "Scorcese Rescues Evil Chiller from Kinder, Gentler Time," *Fla. Times-Union*, 4 Oct. 1996, at D3.

Generally used in reference to people or their actions, *errant* is not synonymous with *erroneous*—e.g.: "He piles so many *errant* [read *erroneous*] conclusions atop skewed observations atop false premises that you hardly know where to start." Gregory Stanford, " 'Color Bar' Will Die Once Talent Matters More than Race," *Milwaukee J. Sentinel*, 4 Aug. 1996, Crossroads §, at 3.

Arrant began as an alteration of *errant* and originally had the same sense ("wandering"), but now usually appears as a term of contempt, as in *arrant knave* or *arrant nonsense*. It has two meanings: (1) "utter; extreme"; and (2) "egregious; outstandingly bad." Often those two senses seem to converge—e.g.: "Because of the majority's *arrant* abuse of the filibuster, 60 Senate votes will be required this morning to move the issue." "Down to the Wire on Ethics," *Boston Globe*, 30 Sept. 1994, at 18.

Sometimes *errant* is misused for *arrant* where there is no sense of wandering or straying—e.g.: "Applying this logic, my living room may be considered an uplands gateway to the uplands. Such *errant* [read *arrant*] nonsense could be extended ad infinitum." Marvin Petal, "Oxnard Needs PVP Plant," *Ventura County Star*, 26 Sept. 2002, at B7. *Arrant nonsense* has been a SET PHRASE since the mid-18th century.

LANGUAGE-CHANGE INDEX
1. *errant* misused for *erroneous*: Stage 2
2. *errant* misused for *arrant*: Stage 2
Current ratio (*arrant nonsense* vs.
errant nonsense): 9:1
3. *arrant* misused in what should be *knight errant*:
Stage 1
Current ratio (*knight errant* vs. *knight arrant*): 666:1

errata. Like *addenda* and *corrigenda*, the plural form *errata* (= errors; corrections to be made) should be used only when listing more than one item. E.g.: "It is important to clarify some of its abundant *errata*." Letter of Mark A. Caldwell, "Flat Wrong," *Chattanooga Times*, 29 July 1995, at A4. See PLURALS (B).

If there is only one mistake, the singular *erratum* is called for—e.g.: "Professor Esmond Wright, doyen of British Americanists and former holder of the chair of modern history at Glasgow University, insists his 'embarrassing *erratum*' was totally unintentional." Rob Brown, "Apology as History Repeats Itself," *Scotland on Sunday*, 16 June 1996, at 3. The English plural *erratums* is not used. See **corrigendum.**

The pronunciation is /i-**rah**-tə/ or /i-**ray**-tə/—not /i-**rat**-ə/.

erroneous is sometimes erroneously spelled *erronious.*

Current ratio: 1,361:1

ersatz (= serving as an artificial and inferior substitute), a 19th-century German loanword, is pronounced either /**air**-sahts/ or /**air**-zahts/.

erstwhile; quondam; whilom; sometime. Each of these terms means "onetime, former, at a former time," and those simpler alternatives are almost always better. By far the most common in AmE and BrE is *erstwhile* (/**ərst**-w[h]ıl/), which is called a "literary" word in the *OED*. The least common are *quondam* (/**kwon**-dəm/) and, even rarer, *whilom* (/**hwı**-ləm/). (See **quondam** & ARCHAISMS.) The word *sometime*, an invitation to a MISCUE, is often misused as if it meant "occasional, from time to time." See **sometime (B).**

We need one of these words in the language—probably *erstwhile*—because *former* and *onetime* do not always suffice. Our embarrassment of riches, with four synonyms for one sense, is exceeded only by most writers' embarrassment at having to use any one of them in addressing a less-than-learned audience. Following are examples of each, from the least common to the most:

- "Gerald Asher, the *whilom* wine merchant and distinguished wine writer, was in town recently to talk about . . . Chardonnay clones." Frank J. Prial, "Wine Talk," *N.Y. Times*, 25 Apr. 1990, at C11.
- "Remember Bernie? He was the *quondam* CIA hireling from Miami who attained notoriety as one of the Watergate burglars." Harry Rosenfeld, "Money Continues to Talk in Politics," *Times Union* (Albany), 4 Sept. 1994, at B5. (*Quondam* is much more common in BrE than in AmE.)
- "This is Playmate of the Year, 1972, *sometime* lover of Hefner and wife of former right-hand man Victor Lownes." Anton Antonowicz, "22 Years Older and She's Still Every Playboy's Dream," *Daily Mirror*, 29 Sept. 1994, Features §, at 1.
- "Not so bad if you don't mind being served by an *erstwhile* barista who's now required to know just as much about chorizo and goat cheese as macchiatos and frappuccinos." "It's More than Average, Joe," *Sun-Sentinel* (Ft. Lauderdale), 20 Aug. 2015, at A1.

For more on *onetime* (as opposed to *one-time*), see **one-time.**

eruption; irruption. *Eruption* = the act or process of bursting or breaking out <a volcanic eruption>. *Irruption* = the act or process of rushing or breaking in; violent entry or invasion <an irruption of water through a breach in the dam and into the spillway>. *Irruption* also carries the specialized sense of "an abrupt increase in the local population of an animal"—e.g.: "Ornithologists call these erratic southern movements 'invasions' or 'irruptions' and refer to these species as 'irruptive migrants.' " Scott Shalaway, "The Wild Side," *Gaz. & Daily Mail* (Charleston, W. Va.), 16 Feb. 1996, at D1.

escalate is pronounced /**es**-kə-layt/, not /**es**-kyə-layt/. See CLASS DISTINCTIONS.

escape. As an intransitive verb, with *from* or *out of,* *escape* means "to gain one's liberty by fleeing; to get free from detention or control" <he escaped from prison>. As a transitive verb, with a direct object, it means either (1) "to succeed in avoiding (something unwelcome)" <they escaped suspicion>, or (2) "to elude (observation, search, etc.)" <its significance had previously escaped me>.

The word is pronounced /es-**kayp**/—not /ek-**skayp**/. See PRONUNCIATION (B).

escapee (= someone who escapes) should more logically be *escaper* or *escapist.* (See -EE.) But the life of our language has not followed logic. In all varieties of English, writers now choose *escapee* much more often than *escaper.* That's too bad: *escapee* uses the passive *-ee* suffix to denote an activity that usually involves great ingenuity and exertion—more, say, than *attendee.*

Escapist suggests Houdini, i.e., someone who makes a living putting on "escapes" from difficult predicaments (also known as an *escapologist*). *Escapist* also has irrelevant figurative uses, as in *escapist fiction* (i.e., as the adjective corresponding to *escapism*).

One writer defines *escapee* as "one who has been caught after escaping, or while preparing to escape." Paul Tempest, *Lag's Lexicon* 75 (1950). Perhaps that is how a *lag* (= a convict sentenced to penal servitude) understands the term. But most writers and speakers would find nothing amiss in saying, "The *escapees* were never caught," and would object only to their not being caught.

LANGUAGE-CHANGE INDEX
escapee for "one who escapes": Stage 5

eschew, v.t.; **eschewal,** n. The second syllable of both words is pronounced just as the word *chew* is pronounced: /es-**choo**/. Many seem to think that the *esch-* sequence is pronounced /esh/. It is not. The /esh/ sound makes the word resemble a sneeze.

esophageal, the adjective corresponding to the noun *esophagus* /i-**sof**-ə-gəs/, is a word typically pronounced only by doctors. And most American doctors say /i-sof-ə-**jee**-əl/; but the traditional pronunciation (reflected, for example, in *W2*) is /ee-soh-**faj**-ee-əl/.

esophagus (= the tube through which food and drink pass from the pharynx to the stomach) has been the standard AmE spelling since about 1915. *Oesophagus,* the traditional spelling dating back to the 18th century, has long been standard in BrE, but since 1980 *esophagus* has continually threatened to overtake it in frequency within British print sources. In World English, *esophagus* predominates.

Current ratio: 4:1

esoterics is, strictly speaking, incorrect for *esoterica,* and most dictionaries do not yet recognize it. But it

predominated in published texts throughout the 19th century and is now almost as common in AmE as *esoterica.* In some plainspoken contexts, *esoterics* sounds natural where *esoterica* would seem precious—e.g.: "The same easy strength is there, and the same earthy approach to the *esoterics* of law." Fred Rodell, *Nine Men* 331 (1955). Both forms should be considered plural. Cf. **erotica.**

Current ratio (*esoterica* vs. *esoterics*): 3:1

especial; special. The line is muddy to nonexistent. One might defensibly read the historical evidence to suggest that traditionally, *especial* (= distinctive, significant, peculiar) is the opposite of *ordinary* <the public press is entitled to peculiar indulgence and has *especial* rights and privileges>—and that *special* (= specific, particular) is the opposite of *general* <this community has special concerns>. Increasingly, though, *special* is driving out *especial* in all senses—and has steadily been doing so since the mid-19th century.

Especial is so rarely used in AmE today—even in learned journals—that some might term it obsolescent. But it does occasionally appear, most often when modifying a noun whose corresponding adjective would naturally take the adverb *especially.* That is, a writer who might otherwise refer to something that is *especially powerful* would refer to its *especial power*—e.g.: "I found myself wishing the NSO had packed a show-stopper—an American work of *especial* power and virtuosity." Tim Page, "NSO Visits the Cradle of Classical," *Wash. Post,* 26 Oct. 1997, at G1. The phrase *special power* might have connoted something like a superhuman or otherworldly power—surely not the intended sense. On the whole, though, *especial* might confidently be categorized as an ARCHAISM.

especially (= much more than usual; to a particularly high degree) is pronounced /e-**spesh**-ə-lee/—not /ek-/. See *****most especially.**

espresso (= a specially prepared coffee through which steam is forced under high pressure) is so spelled—not *****expresso.** But writers frequently use the erroneous form—e.g.:

• "I selected a chocolate box with caramel and *expresso* [read *espresso*] cream." Dora Ann Reaves, "Fantasy Comes True," *Post & Courier* (Charleston, S.C.), 10 Oct. 1996, Summerville §, at 2.
• "It is the color of chocolate truffles, the *expresso* [read *espresso*] that gets you through the morning and the dirt in your flower garden. Brown." Jackie White, "Shades of Brown," *Tulsa World,* 10 Dec. 2002, at D6.

For the proper and common mispronunciations, see PRONUNCIATION (B).

LANGUAGE-CHANGE INDEX
espresso misspelled *****expresso:* Stage 1
Current ratio: 47:1

LANGUAGE-CHANGE INDEX (For the full key, see front matter pp. xxxi, l–li.)
Stage 1: Rejected. **Stage 2:** Widely shunned. **Stage 3:** Widespread but . . . **Stage 4:** Ubiquitous but . . . **Stage 5:** Fully accepted.
Invariably inferior forms marked by asterisk (*). • Ratios represent frequency of prevalent forms vs. variants in current books.

Esq., in AmE, typically signifies that the person whose name it follows is a lawyer. The mild honorific is used nowadays with the names of men and women alike; it is incorrect, however, if it appears with any other title, such as *Mr.* or *Ms.* In BrE, of course, *esquire* is used of any man thought to have the status of a gentleman.

One law review has devoted several pages to an article on whether women attorneys should use *esquire*. Richard B. Eaton, "An Historical View of the Term *Esquire* as Used by Modern Women Attorneys," 80 *W. Va. L. Rev.* 209 (1978). As to the title and purpose of that article, however, it is worth noting that "*Esq.* is . . . not used on oneself, e.g. neither on a card (which bears *Mr.*) nor on a stamped-and-addressed envelope enclosed for a reply." Alan S.C. Ross, "U and Non-U: An Essay in Sociological Linguistics," in *Noblesse Oblige* (Nancy Mitford ed., 1956). But somehow, the idea has gotten out that *Esq.* is something you put after your own name—e.g.: "These [lawyers] assembled here are not ordinary litigators. Instead of appending a mere 'Esq.' after their names, they are 'Factl'—Fellows of the American College of Trial Lawyers." David Margolick, "At the Bar," *N.Y. Times*, 10 Mar. 1989, at 23. In fact, it is quite non-U for a lawyer to put *Esq.* on cards, stationery, and self-addressed envelopes. See CLASS DISTINCTIONS.

The real question, therefore, is not whether women should append *Esq.* to their own names but whether others should append it to women attorneys' names. The answer: if you're going to use *Esq.* with attorneys' names, do it for both sexes. If precisionists are bothered by this practice, they should pretend that *Esq.*, when used after a woman's name, stands for *esquiress* (recorded in the *OED* from 1596). See SEXISM (D).

-ESQUE. This suffix—meaning "like, resembling"—almost always creates a solid word, as in *romanesque*, *Rubenesque*, *statuesque*. E.g.: "One could almost see the *Clintonesque* curling and biting of the lip for dramatic effect." "New Democrats and New Laborites," *Omaha World-Herald*, 20 Nov. 1997, at 28. Of course, given the suffix's meaning, it's wrong to add *-like* to the end of such a word—e.g.: "A man painted in white stands on a pedestal striking various *statuesque-like* [read *statue-like* or *statuesque*] poses." Alan Byrd, "Will the Real Key West Please Stand Up?" *Orlando Bus. J.*, 23 May 1997, at 1.

-ESS. See SEXISM (D).

essay, v.t. See **assay.**

-EST. For antique verb forms such as *goest* and *sayest*, see ARCHAISMS (B). For superlative adjectives such as *strongest* and *finest*, see COMPARATIVES AND SUPERLATIVES.

estate agent. See **realtor.**

***esthetic.** See **aesthetic.**

estimable; estimatable. These terms have undergone DIFFERENTIATION. *Estimable* once meant "capable of being estimated," but now exclusively bears the meaning "meriting high esteem; deserving respect; admirable." E.g.:

- "The *estimable* Janet McTeer takes on Elizabeth, a role that is to actresses what the triple axel is to female skaters." Lyn Gardner, "Vivat! Vivat Regina!" *Guardian*, 25 Oct. 1995, at T15.
- "And the *estimable* Dr. Snyder surely understands that he has enjoyed good press. I've practically put him on Rushmore." John Brummett, "Updating the Conventional Wisdom," *Ark. Democrat-Gaz.*, 3 Oct. 1996, at B7.

Estimatable, the less common term, means "capable of being estimated." E.g.:

- "They prefer programs that offer a projected rate of return for an *estimatable* degree of risk." Arthur R. Carlson, "How to Find and Work with Outside Investors," *Oil & Gas J.*, 27 Oct. 1986, at 56.
- "John Eisele of Deloitte & Touche said accounting rules require a company to set aside reserves when losses are 'probable and *estimatable*.'" David Phelps & Tony Kennedy, "Citi Equity Group Placed in Involuntary Bankruptcy," *Star Trib.* (Minneapolis), 19 May 1994, at D1.
- "Mr. Kelly said a judgment or a settlement would have to be 'likely and *estimatable*' to take a reserve for any litigation." Matt Ackerman, "BNY Mellon CEO: Cycle's Still Building," *Am. Banker*, 23 June 2008, at 1.

See -ATABLE.

Oddly, *inestimable* (= [1] priceless; [2] incalculable) has not undergone the DIFFERENTIATION of *estimable*.

estimate, n.; **estimation.** A distinction should be observed. *Estimate* = an approximate calculation or judgment. *Estimation* = (1) the process of approximately calculating or judging; or (2) judgment of worth.

estivate (/**es**-tə-vayt/), v.i., from L. *aestas* "summer," is the opposite of *hibernate* (= to sleep through the winter). It usually moderates to something like "to spend a lazy summer"—e.g.:

- "Of course as you get older, your taste for roaring around France one night per town fades considerably, and you lean toward one spot where you *estivate* indefinitely." Henry Mitchell, "Reveries from the Chateau Circuit," *Wash. Post*, 18 July 1986, at D2.
- "Wining, dining and *estivating* with such clients, Feigen comports himself as their social equal." Grace Glueck, "Old Masters, New Tycoons," *N.Y. Times*, 29 Nov. 1987, § 6, at 2.
- "I live in Summerland, California, where the Ojai crowd and other world travelers come for respite to *estivate* and walk the shores in Zen meditation." Letter of T.R. Napton, "A View from Paradise," *Fortune*, 30 Sept. 1996, at 20.

In zoology, the word bears a technical sense correlative to *hibernate*—e.g.: "As the weather heats up this month, they should retreat to their burrows to *estivate*, the summer equivalent of hibernation." Gail Wesson, "Rodent-Buster Gets Call in Squirrel Crisis," *Press-Enterprise* (Riverside, Cal.), 14 July 1996, at B3.

***Aestivate** is a variant spelling. See AE.

estrogen (= a female hormone produced in the ovaries) is predominantly so spelled both in AmE and in World English. In BrE, ***oestrogen** predominated in the mid-20th century, but since the mid-1970s the simplified spelling without the digraph has become predominant even there. Cf. **estrus.**

Current ratio: 8:1

estrous cycle (= the reproductive cycle of female mammals) is so spelled—not **estrus cycle.* For a similar difference in spelling between adjective and noun, see *mucous membrane* under **mucus.** See also **estrus.**

Current ratio: 5:1

estrus (= the periodic sexual excitability of a female placental mammal) has been predominantly so spelled in AmE since the 1930s and in World English since the 1960s. In BrE, the spelling *oestrus* (or, with a digraph, *œstrus*) has been consistently preferred since the 18th century. See **estrous cycle.** Cf. **estrogen.**

Current ratio: 2:1

-ET. See DIMINUTIVES (F).

et al. A. Generally. *Et al.* is the abbreviated form of the Latin phrase *et alii* (= and others), which is used only in reference to people, whereas *etc.* is used in reference to things. Since *alii* is abbreviated, it always takes a period. But American writers commonly mispunctuate it **et al, *et. al.,* or **et. al*—all wrong.

B. Style and Usage. As with other familiar abbreviations of Latin phrases such as *etc., i.e.,* and *e.g.* (and despite their appearance here), *et al.* is not italicized <Jefferson, Madison, et al.>. And like the others, *et al.* is best confined to lists, parenthetical matter, and citations. Avoid it in text, where a substitute such as *and (the) others* is more natural <as conceived by Jefferson, Madison, and the others>.

C. With Possessives. *Et al.* does not fit comfortably alongside possessives: "Clifford T. Honicker's chilling account of Louis Slotin's, S. Allan Kline's *et al.* encounter with the Nuclear Age is as horrific as it is emblematic." Letter of Glenn Alcalay, *N.Y. Times,* 10 Dec. 1989, § 6, at 14. (Read: *Clifford T. Honicker's chilling account of Louis Slotin's, S. Allan Kline's, and others' encounter . . . .*)

D. For *etc.* For the misuse of *etc.* for *et al.,* see **etc.** (C).

etc. A. Generally. More than 400 years ago, John Florio wrote: "The heaviest thing that is, is one *Etcetera.*" It is heaviest because it implies a number too extensive to mention. Following are some of the most sensible words ever written on *etc.*:

> Every writer should be on his guard against the excessive use of *etc.* Instead of finishing a thought completely, it is easy to end with an *etc.,* throwing the burden of finishing the thought upon the reader. If the thought is adequately expressed, *etc.* is not needed. If the thought is not adequately expressed, *etc.* will not take the place of that which has not been said. The use of *etc.* tends to become a slovenly

habit, the corrective for which is to refrain from using *etc.* except in the driest and most documentary kind of writing.
> George P. Krapp, *A Comprehensive Guide to Good English* 229 (1927).

Writers should generally try to be as specific as possible rather than make use of this term. Still, it would be foolish to prohibit *etc.* outright because often one simply *cannot* practicably list all that should be listed in a given context. Hence, rather than convey to the reader that a list is seemingly complete when it is not, the writer might justifiably use *etc.* (always the abbreviation). In text, a substitute such as *and others* is usually a better choice.

B. **And etc.* This is an ignorant REDUNDANCY, *et* being the Latin *and.* The error may be partly a holdover from the now-obsolete abbreviation of the phrase using an ampersand and *-c: &c.* That form should rest in peace.

C. For *et al.* The term *etc.* should be reserved for things, not for people; *et al.* serves when people are being mentioned. But liberal ideologues might think the following usage quite appropriate: "The presidential heavyweight hopefuls—Dole, Sen. Phil Gramm, ex-Tennessee Gov. Lamar Alexander, etc. [read *et al.*]—were present and accounted for at the GOP Midwest leadership conference in Green Bay over the weekend." "Lake Jump," *Chicago Trib.,* 22 May 1995, § 1, at 12. See **et al.**

LANGUAGE-CHANGE INDEX
etc. misused for *et al.*: Stage 3

D. Misspelled and Mispronounced. When spelled out, the Latin words should be separate <et cetera>. When pronounced, the term should not be shortened to three syllables—so /et **set**-ə-rə/, not /et **set**-rə/. The abbreviation is surprisingly often misspelled **ect.,* perhaps because the *-t-* in the first syllable of *etc.* is often mispronounced as a *-k-* or *-x-* (as if it were *ex cetera*). See PRONUNCIATION (B).

E. Punctuating. Punctuate around this phrase just as if the words *and others* were substituted in its place. For example, don't put a comma after *etc.* if it's the tail end of a subject <side dishes of carrots, potatoes, broccoli, etc. are also available>. The *Chicago Manual of Style* sits on the fence about this point, recommending the extra-comma approach but allowing the no-comma approach. But because it's more logical—and consistent with other phrases in a series—the more fastidious approach is to omit the comma.

F. Style and Usage. As with other familiar abbreviations of Latin phrases such as *et al., i.e.,* and *e.g.* (and despite their appearance here), *etc.* is not italicized <lions, tigers, bears, etc.>. And like the others, *etc.* is best confined to lists and parenthetical matter. Avoid it in text, where some substitute such as *and the like* is far more natural <lions, tigers, bears, and other wild animals>.

G. Repeating. It's possible to repeat *etc.* to denote a great multiplicity—e.g.: "For every tone of voice, there is a corresponding literary style. So many tones of voice—hearty, earnest, pensive, shrill, rebuking, strident, whispering, *etc., etc.,* so many styles are there. When you ask yourself in advance of writing something, what style shall be adopted, you are really asking, in what tone shall this piece be written." Gorham Munson, *The Written Word* 72 (rev. ed. 1949). In *The English Governess at the Siamese Court* (1870), Anna Leonowens quoted the King of Siam as saying *et cetera* twice; it became thrice in the musical *The King and I* (1951) for comic effect.

H. Using with *e.g.* or *i.e.* See **e.g.**

-ETH. See ARCHAISMS (B).

ethical, like *grammatical* and *legal,* carries a double meaning: "conforming to ethics" and "relating to ethics." Here the meaning is not entirely clear (though the latter is probably the sense): "Her independence from the White House was uncertain as she faced a tough decision over the future of the F.B.I., which was in turmoil over the *ethical* problems of its director, William S. Sessions." David Johnston, "Oddly, Reno's Profile Rises from the Ashes of Disaster," *N.Y. Times,* 1 May 1993, at 1.

ethicist; *ethician.* *Ethician* is more than two centuries older (dating from the early 17th century) and is therefore given precedence in most dictionaries. But *ethicist* overwhelmingly predominates in modern usage—being about 150 times as common in print—so *ethician* is now a NEEDLESS VARIANT. E.g.: "George Annas, a Boston University medical *ethicist,* opposes the legislation and predicted it will never pass in Massachusetts." Liz Kowalczyk, "Curren Case Shows Need for Regulations," *Patriot Ledger* (Quincy, Mass.), 24 Aug. 1996, at 1. The matter was settled even more soundly when Randy Cohen's popular column, "The Ethicist," was established in *The New York Times Magazine* in February 1999.

LANGUAGE-CHANGE INDEX
ethicist for one who specializes in ethics: Stage 5
Current ratio (*ethicist* vs. *ethician*): 148:1

ethics. A. And *ethos.* Although the distinction escapes many writers, it is plain. *Ethics* = the field of moral science. Bentham defined *ethics* as "the art of directing men's actions to the production of the greatest possible quantity of happiness, on the part of those whose interest is in view." Jeremy Bentham, *An Introduction to the Principles of Morals and Legislation* 310 (1823; repr. 1948). The singular form *ethic* means "a set of moral principles."

Ethos /ee-thahs *or* ee-thohs/ = the characteristic spirit and beliefs of a community, people, or group. E.g.: "Part of the appeal of Zisquit's work is its juxtaposition of a minimalist approach to poetic language . . . with an *ethos* and sense of place that is filled with echoes and refiguration of the Old Testament and the ancient world." R.D. Pohl, "A Minimalist Whose Work

Embraces the Ancient World," *Buffalo News,* 7 Dec. 1997, at G5. See **ethos.**

The term *ethos* sometimes appears where *atmosphere* would be more appropriate—e.g.: "But he has his place in athletics history as one of the four members of the British team which ran to a marvellous victory in the 4 x 400 metres relay in the highly-charged *ethos* [read *atmosphere*] of the Berlin Olympics of 1936." "Godfrey Brown" (obit.), *Times* (London), 7 Feb. 1995, Features §. Despite Jesse Owens's great feats in 1936—performed while Hitler watched—an event such as the Olympics is too fleeting to give rise to an ethos.

B. And *morals.* H.W. Fowler concisely states a distinction: "*ethics* is the science of morals, and *morals* are the practice of ethics" (*FMEU1* at 152). Although such a distinction might be observed in Philosophy 101, the terms overlap in common usage, both bearing the sense "principles or habits regarding right and wrong." Cf. **morale.**

ethos (= a set of ideas and moral attitudes that typify a particular group) is preferably pronounced /**ee**-thahs/, though /**ee**-thohs/ is commonly heard. Cf. **bathos.**

etiology. Outside the field of medicine (and arguably within it), *etiology* is unnecessary and pompous for *cause.* E.g.: "The author traveled to Sinedu's home in Addis Ababa, seeking insights into her life and the *etiology* [read *cause*] of her bloody act." Peggy Deans Earle, "Behind a Bloody Crime at Harvard," *Virginian Pilot & Ledger Star* (Norfolk), 29 Oct. 1997, at E4. This use apparently stems from medical JARGON—e.g.: "Many HMOs would have you believe that looking at the *etiology* of [health] problems is nonessential." Joyce Thieman, "Lack of Choice Hurting Mental Health Patients," *Cincinnati Bus. Courier,* 24 Oct. 1997, at 34.

Aetiology is a common BrE variant. *Aitiology* is a variant spelling to be avoided.

Current ratio (*etiology* vs. *aetiology* vs. *aitiology*):
7,107:1,451:1

-ETTE. See DIMINUTIVES (F) & SEXISM (D).

etymology. See **entomology.**

ETYMOLOGY. A. English Etymology Generally. Etymology is the study of word derivations. Understanding etymology often leads to a greater appreciation of linguistic nuances. For example, knowing the history of words such as the following can open up vistas:

- *abominable,* L. *ab-* "off, away from" + *ominarie* "to prophesy, forebode"—hence "being an evil omen."
- *exorbitant,* L. *ex-* "out of, away from" + *orbita* "wheel track"—hence "off track" or "out of line."
- *inoculate,* L. *in-* "into" + *oculus* "eye (i.e., 'bud,' as in eye of a potato)"—hence to graft a bud from one plant to another, where it will continue to grow. The sense of implanting germs to produce immunity from a disease dates from the early 18th century.
- *symposium,* Gk. *syn-* "together" + *posis* "a drink." The term was extended from "a drinking party" to "a convivial meeting for intellectual stimulation," and then was

extended further to "a collection of articles published together on a given topic."

Learning the classical roots and prefixes of English words—as by studying Donald M. Ayers's *English Words from Latin and Greek Elements* (Thomas D. Worthen ed., 2d ed. 1986)—will certainly repay the effort.

But while the study can help considerably, making a fetish of it can lead to many linguistic fallacies. For many words, modern usage is pretty well divorced from etymology. For example, in distinguishing *assiduous* from *sedulous*, it doesn't particularly help to say that *assiduous* is "sitting to" a thing and that *sedulous* is "without trickery." It would be more helpful to note that although the words are close synonyms, *assiduous* is much more common (by a 6-to-1 ratio in print). And although the etymology of *assiduous* suggests greater intensity, the rarity of *sedulous* betokens a special intensity.

Another fallacy arises when pedants object inflexibly to HYBRIDS or MORPHOLOGICAL DEFORMITIES. Some, for example, insist that *homophobe*, in Greek, would refer to a self-hater. But in English, of course, *homo* is simply a SLANG shortening of *homosexual*, and *homophobe*—though at variance with classical word formation—is perfectly understandable to any reasonable speaker of AmE. The etymological "error" is no error at all. See **homophobe**.

So learn all you can about etymology, but temper that knowledge with other types of linguistic facts. Then you'll be in a position to choose words prudently. And you'll be better equipped to answer questions such as these: Must *alternatives* be limited to two? Must a *decimation* involve the destruction of only 10% of a group of things? Is the better spelling *lachrymose* or **lacrimose*? Must a *magistrate* be the supreme judge in a given jurisdiction? Which spelling is right: *idiosyncrasy* or **idiosyncracy*? Does *inflammable* mean that something will ignite, or won't? For views on those questions, see the appropriate entries.

B. Native vs. Classical Elements. The English language has undoubtedly benefited from its diverse sources. This diversity springs mostly from the English Renaissance, when writers decided to supplement what they considered a meager vocabulary by importing words.

They borrowed freely from foreign languages—mostly Latin, French, and Greek—when adding to the English word-stock. William Caxton, who introduced printing into England in 1477, is credited in the *OED* with the first use of *abjure, admiration, apparition, calumnious, capacity, desperate, factor, ingenious, inhuman, nuptial, seduce,* and *sumptuous*, among many other words. It might be hard for modern readers to imagine a time when those words seemed foreign or absurd. But many of Caxton's other borrowings haven't fared so well: for example, *excidion* (= a rooting out), *exercite* (= army), *magistration* (= a command). Another early word-borrower, Thomas Elyot, wrote in the early 16th century. Like Caxton, Elyot had his word-coining successes (*animate, attraction, education, excrement, exterior, frugality, irritate, persist*) and his failures (*allective, applicate, assentatour*). In that respect, these writers are typical of the age.

Some coinages from that period seem to have arisen not from any felt need but from a particular writer's penchant for the far-fetched. Our historical dictionaries are brimming with strange and ridiculous formations, such as *celeripedian* (= a swift footman) and *latrocination* (= highway robbery). Many such terms, which appeared only once or twice in the recorded history of the language, were coined by fervent neologists who had little or no sense of linguistic necessity. See NEOLOGISMS.

The result of all this word-coining, though, is that English now has many sets of words formed from analogous etymological elements. Many of these words, having coexisted in English for many centuries, retain the same basic meanings:

Greek	Latin/French	Anglo-Saxon
enchiridion	manual	handbook
hypogeal	subterranean	underground
prolegomenon	prologue	foreword
prophesy	predict	foretell
sarcophagous	carnivorous	meat-eating

But others have undergone DIFFERENTIATION to varying degrees:

Greek	Latin/French	Anglo-Saxon
——	postpartum	afterbirth
prodrome	precursor	forerunner
prognosis	prescience	foreknowledge
sympathy	compassion	fellow feeling
thesis	position	placement

Those listings show that the Greek derivatives tend to be the most arcane, the Latin a little less so, and the Anglo-Saxon not at all. But this tendency has many exceptions. The Anglo-Saxon *gainsay* is certainly less common today than the Latin *contradict*, and the Anglo-Saxon *hapless* is out of luck in competition with the Latinate *unfortunate*. And the Greek is much more common than the Latin in the following pairs: *anonymous* (Gk.) and *innominate* (L.); *hypodermic* (Gk.) and *subcutaneous* (L.); *anthology* (Gk.) and *florilegium* (L.).

All in all, though, the generalization about Greek derivatives—when they have synonyms from Latin or Anglo-Saxon—holds true. Many Greek terms lie at the periphery of the English language—e.g.:

analphabetic (= illiterate [L.], unlettered [A.S.])
anamnesis (= reminiscence [L.])
chirography (= handwriting [A.S.])
exlex (= outlaw [A.S.])
peritomy (= circumcision [L.])

LANGUAGE-CHANGE INDEX (For the full key, see front matter pp. xxxi, l–li.)
Stage 1: Rejected. **Stage 2:** Widely shunned. **Stage 3:** Widespread but . . . **Stage 4:** Ubiquitous but . . . **Stage 5:** Fully accepted.
Invariably inferior forms marked by asterisk (*). • Ratios represent frequency of prevalent forms vs. variants in current books.

They therefore serve writers inclined toward SESQUI- PEDALITY, but they seem laughable to those inclined toward PLAIN LANGUAGE.

In specialized writing, a knowledge of classical languages is especially helpful: Latin in law, for example, or Greek and Latin both in medicine. But regardless of your career path, it's useful to enhance your awareness of Greek and Latin word roots. You'll gain a greater sensitivity to the English language and its origins and nuances.

C. Etymological Awareness. Through wide reading and a conscious sensitivity to words and their origins, good writers become aware of etymological associations that may escape others. Ignorance of etymologies can easily lead writers astray, as when a journalist gave the label *holocaust* (Gk. "burnt whole") to a flood. Following are sentences in which writers wandered into etymological bogs:

- "The right to exclude or to expel aliens in war or in peace is an inherent and *inalienable* right of every independent nation." (The root *alien-* causes problems when we say that a country has an *inalienable* right to exclude *aliens.*)
- "What we are concerned with here is the automobile and its *peripatetic* [= able to walk up and down, not just *itinerant*] character."
- "This is a result which, if at all possible *consonant* [lit., "sounding together"] with *sound* judicial policy, should be avoided."

In the first and third specimens, an incongruous repetition of the root sense occurs; in the second, the writer has insensitively abstracted and broadened a word still ineluctably tied to its root sense. Cf. SOUND OF PROSE & VERBAL AWARENESS.

D. Folk Etymology. Popular notions of etymology are often quite colorful—and quite wrong. Indeed, word origins are a common subject of conversation in English-speaking countries. But such discussions ought to be well grounded because linguistic resources are widely available to serve as guides.

That wasn't always so, and folk etymology has left its mark on the language. Take a few common examples. *Pea* is a false singular of *pease*, which was mistakenly taken as a plural. Likewise, *a newt* is a historical error for *an ewt*, *an adder* for *a nadder*, and *an apron* for *a napron*. *Titmouse* now makes the plural *titmice* even though the word has no real connection with *mouse* or *mice*. *Primrose* and *rosemary* were earlier *primerole* and *romarin*, neither of which has anything to do with roses, but they were respelled precisely on that mistaken assumption.

Historical examples may be interesting, but modern examples are still reparable. To cite but one example, many well-educated people believe that *posh* means "port outward, starboard home," and that the word refers to the most desirable positions in an ocean liner. In fact, though, professional etymologists haven't ascertained that etymology—indeed, they've pretty much rejected it. So under *posh*, most dictionaries say "origin unknown." Although the popular notion

would make it a colorful term, the facts unfortunately get in the way of a good story.

In fact, etymologists are immediately suspicious of any proffered word origin that involves an acronym. But that doesn't stop the stories from being told like the urban legends they usually are. No, *tip* does not mean "to insure promptness." (And in any event, *tep* would have been the better spelling if the word were an acronym, since *ensure* would be correct in this context, not *insure*. See **assure.**) In fact, the word goes back to the Middle English *tippe*, and from there probably further back to the Low German, but the precise origin isn't known. That's the kind of answer that can spawn silly ahistorical theories.

A typical example of folk etymology occurs in the following sentence, in which the writer apparently wants the base word *mean* to bear its ordinary English sense in the word *demean*: "By ridiculing the idea of vampires ('Vampires haunt Russian psyche,' 14 November), you *demean* yourself (literally, deprive yourself—and us—of meaning) and hold out a less-than-supporting hand to the northern Russians whose plight you depict." Letter of M.J. Platts, "They Say Vampires, We Have Phobias," *Independent*, 18 Nov. 1992, at 22. In fact, though, *demean* doesn't mean "to deprive of meaning"; rather, its sense is "to lower in quality or position."

For other examples of folk etymology treated in this book, see **coleslaw, helpmate, hiccup, parti-colored, rescission (A)** & **Welsh rabbit.** For a good study on the subject, see Hugh Rawson, *Devious Derivations* (1994). For a useful historical work, see A. Smythe Palmer, *The Folk and Their Word-Lore* (1904).

E. Bibliography on English Etymology. Those wishing to look further into etymology should consult the books listed in the Select Bibliography at the end of this book.

Euclidean (= of, relating to, or devised by Euclid, the Greek mathematician who lived about 300 B.C.) is the standard spelling. **Euclidian* is a variant. Cf. **Mephistophelean** & **Shakespearean.**

Current ratio: 13:1

eulogy takes *a*, not *an*—and has done so since the mid-19th century. (See **a (A).**) For the misuse of *elegy* for *eulogy*, see **elegy.**

EUPHEMISMS are supposedly soft or unobjectionable terms used in place of harsh or objectionable ones. The purpose is to soften; the means is usually indirection—saying one thing and meaning another. To discerning readers, of course, some euphemisms may seem unnecessarily mealy-mouthed—even silly.

We euphemize if we refer to someone not as *drunk*, but as *inebriated* or *intoxicated*; not as a *drug addict*, but (much more vaguely) as *impaired*; not as having *died*, but as having *passed away*; not as *mentally retarded*, but as *exceptional* or *special*; not as *disabled*, but as *differently abled* or even *challenged*; not as *malingering*, but as *suffering from a factitious disorder.*

In some contexts, to be sure, you might prefer a euphemism. If plain talk is going to provoke unnecessary controversy—if talk about *illegitimate children* or *sodomy* will divert attention from your point by offending people—then use an established euphemism.

Indeed, the phrase *illegitimate children* exemplifies the need sometimes to throw over old forms of expression. One legal publisher's system of indexing legal topics went from *Bastards* in the 1960s to *Illegitimate Children* in the 1970s to *Children Out-of-Wedlock* in the 1980s. Some writers use *nonmarital children* to convey the idea. The point is that we shouldn't scar innocent people with ugly epithets.

Other euphemisms, however, are roundabout and clumsy. Some writers use *rodent operative* or *extermination engineer* in place of *rat-catcher*. We see *pregnancy termination* rather than *abortion*; *sexually ambidextrous* rather than *bisexual*; *armed reconnaissance* rather than *search-and-destroy mission*; *permanent layoff* rather than *firing*. For every unpleasant or socially awkward subject, euphemisms are usually available.

Sometimes, though, euphemisms appear for words that might otherwise seem innocuous. In the workplace, for example, the terms *employee* and *worker* may be thought to have unpleasant associations with the division between management and labor. So in the 1990s, some companies promoted the terms *partner*, *teammate*, *crew member*, and the like to avoid what might be perceived as putting people down. As organizations become "flattened," traditional titles (such as *senior executive vice president*) and even generic terms (such as *manager*) fall by the wayside. Likewise, the lower spheres are upgraded as *secretaries* become *assistants* or even *administrative assistants*.

Still other euphemisms denote things that have historically caused serious discomfort. In law, *unnatural offense* (or *crime*) *against nature* is not uncommon in place of *sodomy*. Indeed, Arthur Leff gives *abominable and detestable crime against nature* as a "rather enthusiastic euphemism . . . found in many 19th-century (and some current) statutes, referring to a not fully specified range of sexual crimes." Arthur A. Leff, "The Leff Dictionary of Law," 94 *Yale L.J.* 1855, 1866 (1985).

Euphemisms are often subtle. *Incident* appears in place of *accident* in a U.S. statute limiting total liability to $200 million for a single "nuclear incident," presumably because *incident* is vaguer and sounds less alarming. Today *revenue enhancement* (= tax increase) and *investment* (= increased government spending) are commonly used by American politicians reluctant to call things by their more understandable names.

In the mock-heroic style that was popular in the 19th century, euphemisms were quite common. Among some writers, the style persisted well into the 20th century. In the following sentence, for example, a judge uses an elaborate euphemism for the hymen: "[The statute] further says to the libertine, who would rob a virtuous maiden, under the age of 18 years, of *the priceless and crowning jewel of maidenhood*, that he does so at his peril." *Bishop v. Liston*, 199 N.W. 825, 827 (Neb. 1924). Perhaps the judge didn't mean to be so literal as to think of the hymen, but the phrasing certainly suggests it.

Again, some subjects cry out for euphemisms or circumlocutions. Explicitness or directness would be undesirable to almost everyone here: "Five balloons containing marijuana were properly admitted [into evidence] since they derived from a source independent from an allegedly unconstitutional *digital rectal search* of the inmate, namely, from the *tip* of a reliable informant." *United States v. Caldwell*, 750 F.2d 341 syl. (5th Cir. 1984). Still, the final phrase could advantageously be changed because *tip* verges on losing its metaphorical quality in that particular context.

All in all, though, one can hardly disagree with the assessment that euphemisms are irrational and quaintly uncandid: "They are only intelligible when both parties are in on the secret, and their silly innocence masks a guilty complicity, which is why they almost invariably wear a knowing, naughty-postcard smirk. At the close of the taboo-breaking century, they ought to have become comically redundant." Neil Powell, "How to Put It Properly," *TLS*, 3 Sept. 1993, at 32. Even so, they thrive as much today as ever. Cf. DYSPHEMISM. See CLASS DISTINCTIONS.

In the end, too, they leave a linguistic garbage-heap in their wake. Once a euphemism becomes standard, it loses its euphemistic quality: "This is the usual destiny of euphemisms; in order to avoid the real name of what is thought indecent or improper people use some innocent word. But when that becomes habitual in this sense it becomes just as objectionable as the word it has ousted and now is rejected in its turn." Otto Jespersen, *Growth and Structure of the English Language* 230 (9th ed. 1952). Hence the vocabulary regarding unpleasant things remains in constant flux.

The only solution would be for people to be less squeamish in their use of language. And that's not likely to happen—not in AmE, at any rate—without a cultural upheaval.

Among the better treatments of the subject are John Ayto, *Euphemisms* (1993); Keith Allan & Kate Burridge, *Euphemism and Dysphemism* (1991); Judith S. Neaman & Carole G. Silver, *Kind Words: A Thesaurus of Euphemisms* (2d ed. 1990); R.W. Holder, *A Dictionary of American and British Euphemisms* (1987); D.J. Enright, *Fair of Speech: The Uses of Euphemism* (1985); Hugh Rawson, *A Dictionary of Euphemisms and Other Doubletalk* (1981).

LANGUAGE-CHANGE INDEX (For the full key, see front matter pp. xxxi, l–li.)
Stage 1: Rejected. **Stage 2:** Widely shunned. **Stage 3:** Widespread but . . . **Stage 4:** Ubiquitous but . . . **Stage 5:** Fully accepted.
Invariably inferior forms marked by asterisk (*). • Ratios represent frequency of prevalent forms vs. variants in current books.

euphemistic is sometimes subject to WORD-SWAPPING with *euphonious* (= involving a pleasant combination of sounds)—e.g.:

- "With many plans, you can either buy a high option or low option (*euphoniously* [read *euphemistically*] termed 'standard option'), depending on your view of your needs and your budget." Victor Cohn, "Asking Pertinent Questions About HMOs," *Wash. Post*, 3 Nov. 1987, Health §, at 16.
- "That date quickly became what is now *euphoniously* [read *euphemistically*] called a 'meaningful relationship.'" Dick Rosenberg, "Date That Ended Grandly," *Jerusalem Post*, 5 Aug. 1994, at 2.
- "In the *euphonious* [read *euphemistic*] language of pilots, the model made an uncontrolled landing, or, as an NAL spokesman said, 'The trial objectives were not achieved during flight.'" Winn L. Rosch, "High-Speed Planes May Take Off Soon," *Plain Dealer* (Cleveland), 18 July 2002, at C2.

For a similar error, see **euphuism.**

LANGUAGE-CHANGE INDEX
euphonious misused for *euphemistic*: Stage 1

euphonium (= a brass instrument similar to a baritone horn, being somewhat smaller than a tuba) forms the plural *euphoniums*, not *euphonia*. In music circles, the plural form *euphoniums* is commonplace, but some writers use the pretentious Latin plural—e.g.: "The performance edition used on this occasion did call for two Wagner tubas, a.k.a. *euphonia* [read *euphoniums*], or baritone horns, and they added to the general richness and resonance of sound." Donald Dierks, "Symphony Does Right by Talmi, Bruckner," *San Diego Union-Trib.*, 1 Dec. 1990, at E11. See PLURALS (B).

The word *euphonia*, though not recorded in most dictionaries, refers to a kind of bird found in North and South America (the plural being either *euphonias* or *euphonia*)—e.g.: "Rare hummingbirds, honeycreepers and singing *euphonia* . . . are endangered and seen only sporadically in Florida during annual migrations." Julie Kay, "Jewels of the Sky," *Miami Herald*, 30 Sept. 1995, at B2.

LANGUAGE-CHANGE INDEX
euphonia used for *euphoniums*: Stage 1

EUPHONY. See SOUND OF PROSE.

euphuism (/yoo-fyoo-iz-əm/) derives from John Lyly's play entitled *Euphues* (1578), in which the characters speak in an affected, highly ornate style. The term now denotes a convoluted, embellished prose style. But it's sometimes misused for *euphemism*—e.g.:

- "Twice, in 1987 and 1991, under duress to win at a more brisk clip, Brewer bought extra time by overhauling his staff—a time-honored *euphuism* [read *ruse*] for transferring blame." Jim Bailey, "Parker Doesn't See Red over Coaching Ups, Downs," *Ark. Democrat-Gaz.*, 16 July 1994, at C5. (Because the writer refers to a nonverbal evasion, *euphemism* wouldn't be a good replacement. See DOUBLE BOBBLES.)
- "Blowing smoke is *an euphuism* [read *a euphemism*] when associated with a person's braggadocio, but it is virtual reality

when second-hand tobacco fumes float around in the workplace." Robert A. Brown, "Second-Hand Smoke in the Workplace," *Heating, Piping, Air Conditioning*, Mar. 1995, at 36.
- "Like many old Southerners, Rucker prefers gentlemanly *euphuisms* [read *euphemisms*] to mask life's brutal confrontations." Jim Schlosser, "Raising a Rail Ruckus," *News & Record* (Greensboro), 14 Apr. 1996, at E1.

A close synonym is *gongorism* (/**gahng**-gə-riz-əm/), after the style of the Spanish poet Luis de Góngora y Argote (1561–1627). This word is only for those who dabble in SESQUIPEDALITY.

Unlike its corresponding noun, the adjective *euphuistic* is rarely misused. Here it appears correctly:

- "The virtuoso style mimics the sexual display, becoming a *euphuistic* romp through all the elaborate rhetorical tropes available to 16th-century prose—from alliteration, antithesis and anaphora to zeugma and chiasmus." Maureen Quilligan, "Glistening Torsos," *N.Y. Times*, 25 May 1986, § 7, at 16.
- "For some, the result is, in a word of Hardwick's Elizabethan time, *euphuistic*: elegant but given to symmetry, antithesis, alliteration, and other stylistic devices." Hugh Aldersey-Williams, "History Lesson," *Architectural Record*, Mar. 1996, at 92.

For a similar error, see **euphemistic.**

LANGUAGE-CHANGE INDEX
euphuism misused for *euphemism*: Stage 1

eurythmics (= the practice of moving the body to rhythms, esp. those of music, as a method of teaching or interpretation), a term dating from the 1920s, is traditionally so spelled. It takes a singular verb <eurythmics is helpful in reinforcing language acquisition>. Although the standard spelling of the word (ironically) has no internal *rhythm*—because the Greek term on which it is based is *eurythmos*—there is a variant spelling *eurhythmics (a spelling that surged to predominance in the late 1980s, alas). E.g.: "The workshop she attended Thursday focused on *eurhythmics* [read *eurythmics*]—using body movements to interpret music." Kendra Martinez, "Music Teachers Use Bodies at BSU Workshop," *Idaho Statesman*, 25 July 1997, at B2. (Cf. **rhythmic.**) The rock band popular in the 1980s got the name right: *Eurythmics.*

Eurythmy (developed by Rudolf Steiner and Marie von Silvers, also in the 1920s) is primarily about the movement as therapy, and may or may not involve music. It is likewise spelled with one *h* even though it is all about *rhythm*. Cf. **rhythmic.**

Current ratio (*eurythmics* vs. *eurhythmics): 1:2

euthanasia. A. And *mercy killing.* These synonyms are widespread, the former perhaps being more connotatively neutral. *Mercy killing* usually applies to people exclusively, while *euthanasia* applies equally to animals.

B. And *physician-assisted suicide.* In *euthanasia*, the doctor may take an active role in the death, as by administering a fatal dose of a drug. In *physician-assisted suicide* (sometimes shortened to *assisted suicide*), the doctor supplies the means of death, but the patient takes the decisive step.

euthanize; *euthanatize. These terms, meaning "to subject to euthanasia," are used most commonly in reference to pets. If we must have such a word, the longer version might seem the better candidate because it is properly formed, strictly speaking, and is older, dating in the *OED* from 1873. But in modern writing, *euthanize* greatly predominates and has become standard—e.g.:

- "Because the dog's vaccinations were not current, it was *euthanized.*" "Central Mass. Digest," *Telegram & Gaz.* (Worcester), 14 Sept. 1996, at A2.
- "Often, Rust said, shelter workers would be forced to *euthanize* injured or sick animals if a volunteer veterinarian couldn't be reached." Curtis Killman, "Animal Shelter to Contract with Private Veterinarian," *Tulsa World*, 14 Sept. 1996, at A9.
- "After witnessing a significant decline in his condition over the past few weeks, zoo officials decided to humanely *euthanize* him Tuesday morning." "Denver Zoo Mourns Death of Lion Rajah," *Denver Post*, 26 Aug. 2015, at A2. (On the split infinitive in this example, see SPLIT INFINITIVES.)

See -IZE.

Current ratio: 54:1

evacuable. So formed—not *evacuatable. See -ABLE (D) & -ATABLE.

Current ratio: 7:1

evacuee. See -EE & **refugee.**

evadable. So spelled—not *evadible. See -ABLE (A).

Current ratio: 13:1

evaluable. So formed—not *evaluatable. See -ABLE (D) &-ATABLE.

Current ratio: 80:1

evangelical; evangelistic. Today the older term *evangelical* (fr. ca. 1531) is so closely tied with fundamentalist, proselytizing Christians that it should not be applied more generally. *Evangelistic* (fr. ca. 1845), though also redolent of Christian associations, may be used more broadly to mean "militantly zealous."

evasion; evasiveness. *Evasion* (= [1] the deliberate avoidance of doing what one should, or [2] an instance of deliberately not answering a question or not talking about something) is always an act. *Evasiveness* (= the tendency not to answer questions directly or not to talk about things that need to be discussed) is always a quality.

even, adv., gives rise to syntactic problems similar to those arising from *only*. It should be placed directly before the word it modifies. Note, for example, the difference in meaning between *this summer is even hotter and wetter* and *this summer is hotter and even wetter*. See **only.**

evening. What period of a day is *evening*? According to most dictionaries, it is the later part of the day through the early part of the night or (not much more specifically) the period between sunset and bedtime or darkness. In many places, *evening* begins when the workday is over, around 5:00 PM. But in some regional dialects, *evening* can mean the entire time after 12:00 noon until dark.

event. The AmE phrase is usually *in the event that* [+ clause]—an equivalent of *if* <in the event that they fail>. The British generally write *in the event of* [+ noun phrase] (usually a ZOMBIE NOUN)—as Americans often do <in the event of failure>. Either phrase is typically inferior to *if*.

In BrE, *in the event* also means "in (the) result" or "in the end," a usage likely to result in a MISCUE for American readers—e.g.: "*In the event*, the Miami communiqué will be notably less Washington-centred than when it was first drafted." "High Hopes in Miami," *Economist*, 10 Dec. 1994, at 15.

eventuality is a needless pomposity for several everyday words, each of which is more specific: *event, possibility, outcome, contingency, consequences,* or *result*. E.g.:

- "Mindful of the fact that their chief executive will one day have to replace his battered old Mercedes with a new one, [the board has] made provision for that expensive *eventuality* [read *event* or *outcome*]." John Naughton, "In This Week's Supermarket Sweep, the Prize Is £621,000 a Year," *Guardian*, 25 Aug. 1996, at 2.
- "This is the way the world ends—with humans evolving into billions of electronic navel-gazers? Without navels, even? Ironically, the film cumulatively argues against such an *eventuality* [read *an outcome* or *a possibility*]." Arthur Salm, "Aaack! to the Future," *San Diego Union-Trib.*, 13 Sept. 1996, at E11.

The phrase **in the eventuality* is especially pretentious. E.g.: "Some speculate that building so close to the base—against the Air Force's recommendations—would threaten the base *in the eventuality of* [read *in the event of* or *if there are*] future military closures." Sybil Fix, "Air Crash Rift Widens over Mall," *Post & Courier* (Charleston, S.C.), 6 Aug. 1995, at A1. See **event.**

eventuate is "an elaborate journalistic word that can usually be replaced by a simpler word to advantage." George P. Krapp, *A Comprehensive Guide to Good English* 231 (1927). E.g.:

- "According to [John] McEuen, the new album is based on the thought-provoking premise that Nashville and country music had never *eventuated* [read *happened* or *developed*]." Jack Hurst, "King of the Ode," *Chicago Trib.*, 7 Sept. 1995, at B10.
- "The expected public resentment of Clinton—which Mari Will said would give Dole an easy time of it in the primaries—has not *eventuated* [read *occurred* or *materialized*]." Garry Wills, "Dole Is Part of Republican Collapse," *Times Union* (Albany), 13 Sept. 1996, at A14.

ever. A. Superfluous. For phrases in which *ever* is superfluous, see **rarely ever* & **seldom ever.**

LANGUAGE-CHANGE INDEX (For the full key, see front matter pp. xxxi, l–li.)
Stage 1: Rejected. **Stage 2:** Widely shunned. **Stage 3:** Widespread but . . . **Stage 4:** Ubiquitous but . . . **Stage 5:** Fully accepted.
Invariably inferior forms marked by asterisk (*). • Ratios represent frequency of prevalent forms vs. variants in current books.

B. *Ever* for *every*. Clipping *every* to *ever* is typical of DIALECT—e.g.:

- "Shaquille O'Neal needs a breather *ever* [read *every*] once in a while." Michael Murphy, "Look Out Below," *Houston Chron.*, 7 Nov. 2000, Sports §, at 1.
- "Reading a book and then *ever* [read *every*] so often glancing out the window is a magnificent experience and when combined with an occasional nap it is pure heaven." John Douglas, "Joy of Train Travel Not Fully Appreciated," *Grand Rapids Press*, 19 Dec. 2001, at A19.

In dialectal speech, *everybody* becomes **everbody*. So too in some writing, though one suspects that it's often a typographical error: "*Everbody* [read *Everybody*] knows what prolonged exposure to transponder rays does to a man." Linwood Barclay, "New Series 'Highway 407 Patrol' Takes Its Toll," *Toronto Star*, 17 Dec. 2001, at E1.

LANGUAGE-CHANGE INDEX
1. *ever* misused for *every*: Stage 1
2. **everbody* for *everybody*: Stage 1

Everglades, a place name thought to have been coined in 1823 from *glyde* or *glaed*, meaning "opening in the forest," predominantly takes a singular verb—e.g.:

- "The *Everglades is* in the early stages of a repair job that has become a major industry." Kevin Spear, "High-Stakes Fight Looms in 'Glades," *Orlando Sentinel*, 26 Dec. 2001, at A1.
- "The *Everglades is* a great place for canoeists and kayakers." Mark Chapman, "Beauty and the Beasts," *Boston Herald*, 21 Feb. 2002, at 44.
- "With so little else happening in the Legislature this year of redistricting, the *Everglades is* a priority." "Money for the 'Glades," *Palm Beach Post*, 4 Mar. 2002, at A16.

But some writers ill-advisedly make it plural—e.g.:

- "The *Everglades are* [read *is*] nearly topped off." Neil Santaniello, "Lake Outlook," *Sun-Sentinel* (Ft. Lauderdale), 19 July 2001, at A1.
- "Though the *Everglades are* [read *is*] unique, *they remain* [read *it remains*] a mystery." Randy Schultz, "A Watershed for Rescuing Everglades," *Palm Beach Post*, 19 Aug. 2001, at E1.
- "Widely viewed as useless swamp 50 years ago, the *Everglades are* [read *is*] now the focus of the largest ecosystem-restoration effort ever." Phyllis McIntosh, "Reviving the Everglades," *Nat'l Parks*, 1 Jan. 2002, at 30.

Likewise, the city of Port Everglades takes a singular verb—e.g.: "Port Everglades *is* working on a security plan." Steven Thomma et al., "Six Months After Terrors Struck the United States, Americans Are . . . ," *Miami Herald*, 10 Mar. 2002, at 1.

LANGUAGE-CHANGE INDEX
*Everglades are for *Everglades is*: Stage 3
Current ratio (*The Everglades is* vs.
*The Everglades are): 3:1

ever since. This is the standard phrase. **Every since* is DIALECT—e.g.: "Her mother . . . took her to Jazzercise classes in Los Alamos and she's been a devotee *every since* [read *ever since*]—except for her high-school years when taking Jazzercise 'wasn't cool.'" John Knoll,

"Popular Dance Class Returns to Pojoaque," *Santa Fe New Mexican*, 31 July 2002, Pojoaque §, at 4.

LANGUAGE-CHANGE INDEX
*every since for *ever since*: Stage 1
Current ratio (*ever since* vs. **every since*): 280:1

ever so often. See **every so often.**

every. A. Meaning "all." With an abstract noun—as opposed to a COUNT NOUN—the word *all* is more apt than *every*. E.g.: "Now both the law enforcement community and, apparently, the judiciary, are going to the opposite extreme by giving the Freemen *every leniency they can* [read *all the leniency they can*]." "Make the Freemen Obey the Law," *Times Union* (Albany), 12 Aug. 1996, at A6.

B. Meaning "complete" or "utmost." To say that you have *every confidence* in something isn't logical, but it's now an established CASUALISM—e.g.:

- "I *have every confidence* [or *am quite confident*] that our own attorneys . . . are perfectly capable of researching the applicable statutes and case law on this issue." Letter of Henry A. Pulkowski Jr., "Moon Director Questions ACLU in Lawsuit," *Pitt. Post-Gaz.*, 2 June 1994, at W2.
- "At yet another level, they are being told that you *have every confidence in* [or *are quite confident of*] their physical recovery." Lou Makarowski, "Hurt Athletes Need Support in Recovering," *Houston Chron.*, 29 Sept. 1996, at 21.

C. *Each and every*. See **each and every.**

everybody. See **everyone (A), (C)** & PRONOUNS (D).

everybody else's. See **else's** & POSSESSIVES (I).

everybody . . . they. See **everyone (A),** CONCORD (B), PRONOUNS (D) & SEXISM (B).

every day, adv.; **everyday,** adj. One tries to accomplish something *every day*; but an *everyday* feat would hardly be worth accomplishing. The two are often confused—e.g.:

- "But what of the phrase 'per stirpes,' symbolic here of the hundreds of Latin and law French words still used *everyday* [read *every day*] by fully modernized American lawyers whose penchant for foreign languages probably extends no further?" Richard Weisberg, *When Lawyers Write* 99 (1987).
- "We are confronted *everyday* [read *every day*] with having to decide exactly what they cover." Ronald Wardhaugh, *Proper English: Myths and Misunderstandings About Language* 21 (1999).

LANGUAGE-CHANGE INDEX
1. *everyday* misused for the two-word adverbial phrase *every day*: Stage 2
Current ratio (*happens every day* vs.
*happens everyday): 10:1
2. *every day* for the adjective *everyday*: Stage 1
Current ratio (*everyday experience* vs.
*every day experience): 55:1

everyone. A. Singular or Plural? Today it is standard BrE to use *everyone* and *everybody* with a singular verb but a plural pronoun—e.g.:

- "Almost *everybody* now seems to be a 'victim' of something—of society or *their* own weaknesses." Susan Crosland, "The Aftershock of Anger," *Sunday Times* (London), 22 Oct. 1989, at B2.
- "The compilation of the *OED* made it possible for *everyone* to have before *them* the historical shape and configuration of the language." R.W. Burchfield, *Unlocking the English Language* 169 (1989).
- "*Everyone* in the ground that day couldn't take *their* eyes off it." Keith Duggan, "If Tyrone Overturn Logic It Will Be Harte's Greatest Achievement," *Irish Times*, 22 Aug. 2015, Sport §, at 12.

Here's a statement of the BrE view: "Jane Austen wrote 'every body' as two words and considered the phrase as singular; we now write one word, 'everybody,' and consider it as plural, equivalent to 'all people.' Hence the entry in the *Dictionary* under 'agreement' gives 'Everybody knows this, don't they?' as an example of notional concord, obviously rightly: we would not accept 'Everybody knows this, doesn't he or she?' " Paul Dean, "More Grammatical than Thou," *TLS*, 22 Apr. 1994, at 8.

But many Americans continue to think of this usage as slipshod, *everybody* requiring a singular. After all, they reason, nobody—not even Paul Dean—would say *everybody know* instead of *everybody knows*. An early usage critic remarked insightfully (while disapproving): "The use of this word is made difficult by the lack of a singular pronoun of dual sex . . . . Nevertheless, this is no warrant for the conjunction of *every* and *them*." Richard Grant White, *Every-Day English* 420–21 (1884). A goodly number of Americans now take the same stand, thereby making a happy solution elusive.

So although *every student . . . they* would pass unnoticed in the British press, it still gets a *sic* from *Newsweek*: " 'The question is, how do we change education to give every student what they [sic] need to compete in a more complex . . . world?' " Joe Klein, "Michigan's Tuna Surprise," *Newsweek*, 6 Sept. 1993, at 21 (quoting Beverly Walkow, executive director of the Michigan Education Association). See CONCORD (B), PRONOUNS (C)–(D) & SEXISM (B).

B. And *every one*. This sentence should make the distinction evident: "*Every one* of the employees attended the company picnic, and *everyone* had a good time." If you're unsure about whether the single word *everyone* is right, mentally substitute the synonymous *everybody* to see whether the sentence still makes sense; if it does, *everyone* is the correct form.

C. And *everybody*. Because the terms are interchangeable, euphony governs the choice in any given context. In practice, *everyone* appears in print about twice as often as *everybody*, which is probably more common in speech. Cf. **anyone (B).**

everyone else's. See **else's** & POSSESSIVES (I).

everyone . . . not, in place of *not everyone*, is just as illogical as ***all . . . not**. E.g.: "But if richness needs gifts with which *everyone is not endowed* [read *not everyone is endowed*], simplicity by no means comes by nature." W. Somerset Maugham, "Lucidity, Simplicity, Euphony," in *The Summing Up* 321, 322 (1938). (Otherwise, the sense is that no one is endowed with gifts.) See ILLOGIC (B). Cf. **all (B).**

LANGUAGE-CHANGE INDEX
everyone . . . not for *not everyone*: Stage 2
Current ratio (*not everyone is* vs.
everyone is not): 6:1

everyone . . . they. See **everyone (A),** CONCORD (B), PRONOUNS (D) & SEXISM (B).

every other. A. Illogical Use. In sentences involving a comparison, *every other* is sometimes used illogically in place of *all others*; that is, **more than every other member collectively* is inferior to *more than all other members collectively*. When the sense is of taking things collectively, the plural is needed. Otherwise, the literal sense suggests undoing a dismemberment (especially in the second and third examples below, because the reference is to people)—e.g.:

- "More people fish, camp and hunt than just about *every other outdoor pursuit* [read *all other outdoor pursuits*] put together." Tom Stienstra, "Expert Advice: Sportsmen's Expo Worth It," *S.F. Examiner*, 5 Mar. 1995, at D9.
- "Amis got more attention in the States than any other literary novelist this year. It was more attention, you could argue, than *every other serious novelist* [read *all other serious novelists*] put together." David Streitfeld, "Book Report," *Wash. Post*, 30 July 1995, Book World §, at 15.
- "For recent readings by such literary stars as A.S. Byatt, Jamaica Kincaid, Graham Swift and Robert Coover, Comstock probably traveled farther than *every other member* [read *all other members*] of the audience put together." David Streitfeld, "One for the Books: Missouri Bibliophile Rolland Comstock Goes to Great Lengths to Indulge His Passion," *Wash. Post*, 19 Aug. 1996, at B1. (With apologies to Mr. Streitfeld for citing two in a row.)

See ILLOGIC (B).

A similar problem often arises with the phrasing *every other . . . except*—e.g.:

- "Wake [Forest] has beaten *every other ACC opponent* [read *every ACC opponent*] (except Florida State) at least twice since '83." Larry Keech, " 'Noles Rarin' to Go Against Pack," *News & Record* (Greensboro), 19 Sept. 1996, at C3.
- "Cuba has paid compensation to *every other country with claims there except the United States* [read *every country with claims there except the United States*]." James Rosen, "Tougher Embargo of Cuba Lamented," *Sacramento Bee*, 24 Feb. 1997, at A4.

LANGUAGE-CHANGE INDEX (For the full key, see front matter pp. xxxi, l–li.)
Stage 1: Rejected. **Stage 2:** Widely shunned. **Stage 3:** Widespread but . . . **Stage 4:** Ubiquitous but . . . **Stage 5:** Fully accepted.
Invariably inferior forms marked by asterisk (*). • Ratios represent frequency of prevalent forms vs. variants in current books.

For those sentences to make any sense, Wake Forest must be one of its own opponents, and Cuba must be a country with claims in Cuba.

LANGUAGE-CHANGE INDEX
every other misused for *all other*: Stage 3

B. Ambiguous Use. The phrase *every other* can give rise to an ambiguity: when you say *every other person you see*, does that mean all the people you see or half the people you see (every second person)? When there is a remote possibility of misunderstanding, or even of a MISCUE, the best practice is to rewrite—e.g.:

- "When I was a junior—even my first semester as a senior—I swore I wouldn't fall prey to the evils that seemed to hit *every other person* [read *everybody* or *half the students*] [during] their last semester of high school." Julia O'Malley, "Sliding into a Senior Slump," *Anchorage Daily News*, 8 Mar. 1996, at E1. (On the use of *every . . . person . . . their*, see **everyone (A).**)
- "If a user visits *Yahoo!*, the screen will be the same as it is for *every other person who reaches* [read *everybody else who reaches*] the site." Bob Cook, "Thunderstone Rolling Out," *Crain's Cleveland Bus.*, 3 June 1996, at 7.
- "Just as remarkable is the vivid sense she provides of *every other person* [read *everybody else*] in the room, from Miguel struggling to hold her up to her cheerful midwife and nonchalant doctor." Robert Hurwitt, "More than Ever, 'Family Secrets' Worth Sharing," *S.F. Examiner*, 3 Oct. 1996, at C5.

*everyplace; *anyplace; someplace. These forms are considered vulgarisms for *everywhere*, etc. An exception occurs when the words are separated (*every place, any place, some place*) to mean "each (any, some) location." See **someplace** & ***noplace**.

every so often; ever so often. The first, by far the more common idiom since the early 1900s, means "occasionally" <we go to Lockhart for barbecue every so often>. The second—a quaint phrasing in the manner of *ever so grateful*—means "with great frequency" <you're extremely thoughtful to call me ever so often>. On the dialectal use of *ever so often*, see **ever (B).**

every time. Two words. But many writers try to solidify the phrase—e.g.:

- "Then this past Saturday night against Fresno State, Cooper had the Tiger faithful perched on the edge of their seats *everytime* [read *every time*] he touched the ball." Hunt Archbold, "'Lizard' Slithers His Way into AU Playing Picture," *Montgomery Advertiser*, 11 Sept. 1996, at C1.
- "*Everytime* [read *Every time*] you cross the street, you take a risk." Steff Gelston, "Don't Let Fear of the Financial Unknown Be Harmful," *Boston Herald*, 13 Oct. 1996, at 43.
- "He may have been one of the most celebrated talents in football's greatest team, but *everytime* [read *every time*] he watches a re-run of the Golden Years video that was produced in their honour, he blushes a little." Michael Clifford, "Shooting Stars," *Irish Daily Mail*, 18 Aug. 2015, at 53.

LANGUAGE-CHANGE INDEX
everytime for *every time*: Stage 1
Current ratio (*every time* vs. *everytime*): 163:1

evidence. A. And *testimony*. These words overlap but are not always interchangeable. *Testimony* is a species of *evidence*; it refers only to evidence received through the medium of witnesses. *Evidence*, the broader term, includes all means by which a fact in issue is established or disproved; hence *evidence* may include documents and tangible objects. The word *evidence* has also long been used in the sense "the law of evidence," generally dealing with what is and is not admissible at trial.

B. And *proof*. Strictly speaking, the two words are not synonymous. Unlike *evidence*, the word *proof* applies to the effect of the evidence, not to the way in which truth is established.

C. As a Count Noun. *Evidence* is not generally taken to be a count noun; hence the plural form is unusual at best. E.g.: "Yet in spite of all these *evidences* of judicial humility in these areas, it would be an error to assume that the judiciary had lost self-confidence altogether as a result of its chastening experience in the 1930's." Robert G. McCloskey, *The American Supreme Court* 190 (1960). See COUNT NOUNS AND MASS NOUNS.

evidence, v.t.; evince. These words, favorites of lawyers, are often inferior to *show* or *express* or *indicate*. Properly, to *evidence* something is to serve as proof of its truth, existence, or occurrence. Justifiable uses of this verb are typically in the PASSIVE VOICE—e.g.: "The highway environs southbound are fairly litter-free. The inescapable conclusion, *evidenced* by the clutter of takeout coffee containers, is that sloppy folk on their way to work in the morning drain their cups, roll down the windows of their vehicles and heave out the empty containers." Peter M. Knapp, "Slobs Littering Route 3 Ought to Clean Up Their Act," *Patriot Ledger* (Quincy, Mass.), 28 Sept. 1996, at 19. And when these folks get to work, many of them start speaking and writing.

In other situations, a different verb would be preferable—e.g.:

- "A puppy was hit three days ago by a motorist who slowed down and then continued without *evidencing* [read *showing*] any further concern." Letter of Frances J. Jessup, "A Plea to Enforce Speed Limits," *Columbian* (Vancouver, Wash.), 18 July 1996, at B6.
- "The cakes are much in demand, as *evidenced* [read *demonstrated*] by the crowds at several local Asian markets last weekend." Gail Tirone Finley, "Mooncakes Ready for Big Chinese Fest," *Houston Chron.*, 26 Sept. 1996, City §, at 1.
- "Plus, *evidenced* by his popularity in NBA-sanctioned propaganda, Kemp could be on the verge of major marketing breakthroughs." Elliott Almond, "Sonic Training Camp—Kemp Won't Report, Cites Frustration," *Seattle Times*, 1 Oct. 1996, at C1. (Read: *And as his popularity in NBA-sanctioned propaganda shows, Kemp could be on the verge of major marketing breakthroughs.* In the original sentence, the absence of *as* before *evidenced* makes the sentence ungrammatical; also, coupling the informal *plus* with the formal *evidenced* is jarring.)

Evince properly means "to show, exhibit, make manifest," but has been objected to as "a bad word and unnecessary . . . a favourite with callow journalists" (*U&A* at 113). In fact, the word can usually be replaced to good advantage—e.g.:

- "Amazingly, we *evince more anger at* [read *get angrier over*] Bob Dole's simple mention of a clinically proven fact (i.e., that smoking isn't always addictive) about a legal but unhealthy product than we do *at* [read *over*] Mr. Clinton's confession to violating the drug laws (without, of course, ever taking a deep breath)." John Kolbe, "Lost: Our Moral Outrage," *Cincinnati Enquirer*, 25 July 1996, at A15.
- "Bad as things were, though, the crowd seemed quite content with the situation—which itself is testament to the kind of charisma Pearl Jam *evinces* [read *displays*] in concert." J.D. Considine, "Bad Gets Lost in a Crowd," *Baltimore Sun*, 26 Sept. 1996, at E1.
- "They suspended him for three more games for failing to *evince* [read *show*] enough contrition." Mark Bradley, "Falcons' Chaos Leaves George the Scapegoat," *Atlanta J.-Const.*, 1 Oct. 1996, at F1.

Sometimes, as H.W. Fowler noted, *evince* is misused for *evoke, get, receive,* or some other everyday term—e.g.: "Plans for NATO enlargement still receive majority support from the German public and elites. But a heightened German role, or the absorption of costs for an extension east, *evinces* [read *gets* or *receives*] less support." Daniel Nelson, "Germany Faces Dilemma," *Defense News*, 8 July 1996, at 21.

evidentially for *evidently* is a pretentious error—one that would not occur if the user weren't trying to inflate the term. E.g.: " 'Just tossing out that he [Jerry Jones] could hire anybody to coach this team to win the Super Bowl bothered me. It bothered my ego. I put together a team that won two Super Bowls. *Evidentially* [read *Evidently*], he doesn't appreciate that.' " Gary Myers, "Johnson Has Little to Sweat While Chilling in Florida's Sun," *Austin Am.-Statesman*, 27 July 1995, at C8 (quoting Jimmy Johnson, the football coach).

Although this error might seem analogous to using *partially* for *partly*, the word *evidentially* (the adverb corresponding to the adjective *evidential* and the noun *evidence*) has a technical legal sense that makes it an erroneous alternative to *evidently*—not a valid parallel to an existing term, as is the case with *partially*.

LANGUAGE-CHANGE INDEX
evidentially misused for *evidently*: Stage 1

evidentiary; evidential. What is the adjective corresponding to the noun *evidence*? In AmE, it's *evidentiary*—but in BrE it's predominantly *evidential*. For a possible technical DIFFERENTIATION, see *Garner's Dictionary of Legal Usage* 336 (3d ed. 2011).

Evidentiary is sometimes misspelled **evidenciary*—e.g.:

- "Allen contends he has solid evidence but had hoped not to present it until an *evidenciary* [read *evidentiary*] hearing." Mike Manzo, "Attorney Asks Judge to Reopen Drug Case," *Union Leader* (Manchester, N.H.), 31 Aug. 1994, at 5.

- "In the wake of the Bernardo conviction, Rosen's talk of an appeal has centred [on] trial judge Mr. Justice Patrick LeSage's comments to the jury prior to their deliberations and his rulings on *evidenciary* [read *evidentiary*] issues." Scott Burnside & Alan Cairns, "It's Over . . . or Is It?" *Toronto Sun*, 9 Sept. 1995, at 22.

LANGUAGE-CHANGE INDEX
evidentiary misspelled **evidenciary*: Stage 1
Current ratio: 1,563:1

evidently. The pronunciation /**ev**-i-dənt-lee/ is preferred over /ev-i-**dent**-lee/—the latter evidently occurring only in AmE. But when the word is said with emphasis, the accent naturally shifts to the penultimate syllable.

evince. See **evidence,** v.t.

evoke; invoke. The difference between these words is fairly subtle—and therefore is sometimes lost on even the most careful of writers. *Evoke* = (1) to call to mind or produce (memories, emotions, etc.) <the photographs evoked feelings of disgust>; or (2) to elicit or draw forth <the commencement address evoked laughter and applause>. *Invoke* = (1) to call on (a higher power) for blessing, guidance, or support <Homer invoked the Muse in each of his epics>; (2) to cite as an authority <the newspaper's reply invoked the First Amendment>; (3) to solicit; entreat <the rebels invoked the aid of the U.S. military>; (4) to summon by incantation; conjure <the wizard invoked a host of evil spirits>; or (5) to put into effect; implement <after the bombing, the governor invoked tighter security measures>.

The words' etymologies provide a useful way to remember their basic senses. *Evoke* is derived from the Latin *evocare*, meaning "to call out"; *invoke* is derived from the Latin *invocare*, meaning "to call on." Both words are used properly in this sentence: "The senator's speech, which invoked the names of statesmen ranging from Thomas Jefferson to Martin Luther King, evoked both hoorays and boos."

The most common mistake in using these words is substituting *evoke* for sense 1 or 2 of *invoke*. This error occurs especially in the phrase *evoke the name of*, but also in other phrases—e.g.:

- Sense 1: "Then Heard *evoked* [read *invoked*] the name of God in his next untruth wherein he accused the Zulu demonstrators of attempting to 'storm the ANC headquarters.' " Letter of Jerry McGlothlin, "South African Zulus," *L.A. Times*, 7 Apr. 1994, at B6.
- Sense 1: "At the Sunday worship of the Re-imagining conference, a liturgy *evoked* [read *invoked*] 'Creator God Sophia.' " Larry Witham, "Bishop Calls for Calm on 'Sophia' Issue," *Wash. Times*, 11 June 1994, at A5.
- Sense 1: "The leader of Turkey's Islamic party opened his first news conference as prime minister by *evoking* [read *invoking*] God's blessing." "Turkey's Islamic Leader Eyes Moderate Course," *Record* (N.J.), 30 June 1996, at A17.

LANGUAGE-CHANGE INDEX (For the full key, see front matter pp. xxxi, l–li.)
Stage 1: Rejected. Stage 2: Widely shunned. Stage 3: Widespread but . . . Stage 4: Ubiquitous but . . . Stage 5: Fully accepted.
Invariably inferior forms marked by asterisk (*). • Ratios represent frequency of prevalent forms vs. variants in current books.

- Sense 2: "As his fellow Democratic candidates have done across the country, Mr. Yates *evoked* [read *invoked*] the name of the Republican Speaker of the House, Newt Gingrich, to hang around his opponent's neck like a millstone." Don Terry, "Illinois Lawmaker Proves a Tough Target for G.O.P.," *N.Y. Times*, 24 Oct. 1996, at A10.

> LANGUAGE-CHANGE INDEX
> *evoke* misused for *invoke*: Stage 2

evolute, as a noun, bears a highly technical meaning in mathematics (denoting a type of curvature); and as an adjective, it bears a fairly technical meaning in botany ("turned back; unfolded").

But some writers have tried to make it a verb, as a BACK-FORMATION from *evolution*, thereby concocting a NEEDLESS VARIANT for *evolve*—e.g.:

- "Throughout, there is also a renewed emphasis on legs through above-the-knee skirts, Bermuda shorts and pants that fit second-skin tight. Shoulders, though still emphasized, are *evoluting* [read *evolving*]." Patricia McColl, "Messages from Milan," *N.Y. Times*, 6 Oct. 1985, § 6, at 77.
- "Young, the head of Cigna HealthCare of Mid-America, says this country is *evoluting to* [read *evolving into*] 'an integrated care management system focused on providing high-quality care.'" A.A. Soto, "HMOs Are So Large, They Have to Be Regulated," *St. Louis Post-Dispatch*, 17 Oct. 1998, Editorial §, at 3.

> LANGUAGE-CHANGE INDEX
> *evolute* for *evolve*: Stage 1
> Current ratio (*evolving* vs. *evoluting): 3,768:1

EX-, when meaning "former," should always be hyphenated: "A bitter *exemployee* [read *ex-employee*] can do great harm . . . . [W]hen people feel they have been fired 'fairly' . . . they will be reluctant to bad-mouth their *excompany* [read *ex-company*]." Mark H. McCormack, *What They Don't Teach You at Harvard Business School* 199 (1984).

A problem arises when using the prefix with a noun phrase. Is an *ex-brain surgeon* a former brain surgeon, one formerly having a brain, or a specialist in head-autopsies? Although a nitpicker might argue for either of the last two, most reasonable readers will understand that *ex-* applies to the entire phrase, not just to the attributive. By far the better approach is to use *former* rather than to prefix the first word of a phrase. Otherwise, where should the prefix go in the following examples?

- "Others say that *ex-corporate middle managers* [read *former corporate middle managers*] are prone to reproducing the world they knew." Kirk Johnson, "Franchise Shops Draw Downsized Managers," *Commercial Appeal* (Memphis), 26 June 1994, at C3.
- "The company, owned by two London marketing men who live in Dorset, and run by Mr. Paul Simmons, an *ex-corporate financier* [read *a former corporate financier*], produces 850 tons of lime annually." "Quarry Firm Buried by Bureaucracy," *Daily Telegraph*, 15 Aug. 1994, at 7.

For an illogical use of this prefix, see **ex-felon.*

Some copyeditors have learned to use an en-dash when a hyphenated combining form (such as *ex-*)

combines with a compound having a space: *ex–brain surgeon*, and the like. The compounds tend to read somewhat better this way. (See PUNCTUATION (H).) Still, it's always best to look for a solution that won't make the reader do a double take.

ex, n., is a CASUALISM in the sense "a former spouse or lover." The plural of *ex* is *exes*, and the possessive is *ex's*—but be aware that many readers will find these forms odd-looking.

exacerbate (= to make worse) seems to be following the course of its traditional synonym, *aggravate*. That is, writers sometimes use it as a fancy substitute for *irritate*, perhaps influenced by *exasperate*—e.g.: "Louis Lyons, former curator of the Nieman Foundation at Harvard, and James Boylan, editor of the Columbia Journalism Review, are *exacerbated* [read *irritated*] by *you know*—which both say they hear too often over radio and TV." Newsweek Editors, "Up Tight About Hang-Ups," in *Coming to Terms with Language: An Anthology* 68, 69 (Raymond D. Liedlich ed., 1973).

Meanwhile, the word *exasperate* (traditionally "to irritate thoroughly" but archaically "to make harsher") is often confounded with *exacerbate*. Yet the DIFFERENTIATION between the words has been complete for many generations. Using *exasperate* in its obsolete sense is now poor usage—e.g.:

- "In most cases, players want to do the right thing. And in 99.9 percent of each of those cases, you can find so-called 'friends' who *exasperate* [read *exacerbate*] the problem." George Robinson, "Pacman Needs to Get New Friends," *Leaf-Chron.* (Clarksville, Tenn.), 19 June 2007, at C1.
- "The meetings come as growth has packed Tecumseh South Elementary beyond its capacity with anticipated growth expected to *exasperate* [read *exacerbate*] the problem." Barbara Hollingsworth, "Boundary Talks Continue," *Topeka Capital-J.*, 15 Jan. 2008, Local §, at 2.
- "Of course our government would insist that they run any such projects, which would further *exasperate* [read *exacerbate*] the problem." Letter of Jim McClain, "Crisis Requires Visionary Leader," *Daily Record* (Morristown, N.J.), 22 May 2008, at 2.

> LANGUAGE-CHANGE INDEX
> 1. *exacerbate* misused for *irritate*: Stage 1
> 2. *exasperate* misused for *exacerbate*: Stage 1

exact same. This expression, which sprang into currency after 1950, is a lazy truncation of *exactly the same*. Although *the exact same* is acceptable in informal speech, it's not an expression for polished prose—e.g.:

- "There is not one briefcase, however. There are several; they're *the exact same* [read *exactly the same*] shade of pale aqua, and they all get swapped by characters skulking in and out of various dressing cubicles." David Richards, "All Roads Lead to Mother in a Game of Spy Versus Spy," *N.Y. Times*, 5 Dec. 1994, at C11.
- "He buys her the same clothes Madeleine wore, takes her to a beauty salon to have her hair and makeup done just like Madeleine's, even puts her in *the exact same* [read *the same* or *identical*] high heels." Joanna Connors,

"'Vertigoooooooo,'" *Plain Dealer* (Cleveland), 6 Dec. 1996, Friday §, at 5.

- "Whenever the goofer says something wrong, take the next available occasion to say the *exact same* [read *same*] thing yourself." Mary Newton Brudner, *The Grammar Lady* 60 (2000).

And because *exactly the same* is a phrase of pinpoint precision, to qualify the idea by saying **almost the exact same* is doubly bad—e.g.:

- "Yes, No. 4 Alabama (10–0) and No. 6 Auburn (9–0–1) play *almost the exact same* [read *almost the same* or *the same*] brand of football." J.A. Alande, "It's Showdown Time for Alabama, Auburn," *Wash. Post*, 19 Nov. 1994, at H6.
- "In a characteristically un-didactic history lesson, Thomas preceded the 1913 'Rite' with two works of *almost the exact same* [read *almost the same*] age: Webern's Six Pieces for Orchestra, Op. 6 (1909) and the Adagio from Mahler's uncompleted 10th Symphony (1910)." Joshua Kosman, "'Rite' Not Quite Right," *S.F. Chron.*, 27 Sept. 1996, at C1.

For a similar example involving *exact*, see **just exactly.**
LANGUAGE-CHANGE INDEX
the exact same for *exactly the same*: Stage 2
Current ratio (*exactly the same* vs. *the exact same*): 6:1

exalt; exult. To *exult* is to rejoice exceedingly. To *exalt* is to raise in rank, to place in a high position, or to extol.

Exalt is rather frequently misspelled **exhalt* or **exhault*—e.g.:

- "The serjeant might perform military duties rather less *exhalted* [read *exalted*] than those of a knight." Alan Harding, *A Social History of English Law* 32 (1966).
- "God would . . . make him an instrument to *exhalt* [read *exalt*] His mightiness and reach out to others." Mark Wangrin, "Ordained a Running Back as a Lad, Priest Holmes Has Never Wavered from His Calling," *Austin Am.-Statesman*, 10 Sept. 1994, at C1.

These errors seem to result from confusion with words such as *exhale, exhort,* and (even more strongly) *exhaust*. In the last two words, the -*h*- isn't pronounced, and the vowel in the second syllable of *exhaust* is generally sounded just as it is in *exalt*.
LANGUAGE-CHANGE INDEX
exalt misspelled **exhalt* or **exhault*: Stage 1
Current ratio: 3,999:5:1

example; exemplar; *exemplum; exemplification.
Example, of course, is the general term. *Exemplar* = an ideal or typical example. E.g.: "The artist [Carl von Marr], regarded as his era's foremost *exemplar* of German academic realism, was born to German immigrants in Milwaukee in 1858 and died in Munich in 1936." James Auer, "West Bend Gallery Buys Massive Oil," *Milwaukee J. Sentinel*, 30 Nov. 1995, at 8. The Latin **exemplum* is usually a NEEDLESS VARIANT of *example*—e.g.:

- "From Caesar's murder on, however, he is an *exemplum* [read *example*] both in compelling minor detail and in his sure awareness of the historic scale of the events he is helping to shape." Alistair Macaulay, "Julius Caesar—Theatre," *Fin. Times*, 6 July 1995, at 23.
- "Most of the town, and especially Byron, stand in awe of Maars, who is an *exemplum* [read *example*] of the community's most cherished values—generosity, tolerance, self-reliance and unflagging determination." David W. Madden, "A Farm Boy Returns as a Man," *S.F. Chron.*, 13 Aug. 1995, Sunday Rev. §, at 10.
- "The author finds his *exemplum* [read *example*] in an episode revealing the personal sensitivity, to injured blacks, of one of his children." Benjamin DeMott, "Put on a Happy Face: Masking the Differences Between Blacks and Whites," *Harper's Mag.*, Sept. 1995, at 31.

In the specialized literary sense "a moralizing tale or parable; an illustrative story" (*OED*), *exemplum* is justifiably used—e.g.: "Here is an *exemplum vérité* that the Franciscan nuns at Nativity grade school in Washington told my brothers when they were preparing to take their First Communion: 'There was a wicked little boy in the grip of the Devil. When he went to Communion, he did not swallow the Host, but deliberately concealed it in the corner of his mouth. He went to his hideout with his gang, put the Host on the ground and hammered a nail through it. The Host spurted blood. The boys ran back and confessed . . . .'" Maureen Dowd, "'The Moral of the Story Is . . . ,'" *N.Y. Times*, 24 Dec. 1995, § 4, at 9.

Exemplification = (1) the act or process of serving as an example <by way of exemplification>; (2) a case in point; an illustration <that exemplification is rather far-fetched>; or (3) (in law) an attested copy of a document with an official seal. In sense 2, the word is usually just a lofty synonym of *example*—e.g.: "A single episode may be noted as a fair *exemplification* [read *example*] of this." Herbert S. Gorman, "Hopeless in Chandrapore," *N.Y. Times*, 6 Oct. 1996, § 7, at 38.
LANGUAGE-CHANGE INDEX
exemplification misused for *example*: Stage 1

example where, long thought to be stylistically inferior to *example in which*, is now the predominant phrasing in AmE and BrE alike. Some editors mourn this linguistic fact. But it's a fact. See **where.**

exasperate. See **exacerbate.**

ex cathedra; ex officio; *ex officiis. *Ex cathedra* = (1) adv., from the chair or throne; with authority; (2) adj., authoritative. Following is a literal adverbial use: "A doctrine concerning faith or morals can be declared infallible by an ecumenical council of the church, consisting of all the bishops and the pope, or by the pope alone speaking officially from the papal throne (*ex cathedra*)." Dave Condren, "Pope's Stance on Women Fuels Debate," *Buffalo News*, 1 Dec. 1995,

LANGUAGE-CHANGE INDEX (For the full key, see front matter pp. xxxi, l–li.)
Stage 1: Rejected. Stage 2: Widely shunned. Stage 3: Widespread but . . . Stage 4: Ubiquitous but . . . Stage 5: Fully accepted.
Invariably inferior forms marked by asterisk (*). • Ratios represent frequency of prevalent forms vs. variants in current books.

at B1. Increasingly today, *ex cathedra* has connotations of a peremptory attitude—e.g.: "The Attorney General's letter asserts *ex cathedra* and without citation of a single authority that . . . ." Peter Shane & Harold Bruff, *The Law of Presidential Power* 205 (1988). The phrase is pronounced /eks kə-**thee**-drə/ or occasionally /eks **kath**-ə-drə/.

Ex officio (= by virtue of one's office) may likewise be both adjective and adverb <the chairman is an ex officio member of all standing committees> <the chairman became a member ex officio>. A widespread misconception has it that by definition, an ex officio member of a deliberative body may not vote. That isn't necessarily so; nothing forbids a body from allowing an ex officio member to vote. But it is a common parliamentary practice. *Ex officio* should be neither hyphenated nor spelled as one word. The phrase is pronounced /eks ə-**fish**-ee-oh/ or (rarely) /eks ə-**fik**-ee-oh/. **Ex officiis* is a NEEDLESS VARIANT.

Current ratio (ex officio vs. *ex officiis): 514:1

exceed. A. In the Phrase **exceed more than***.** This phrase is a common REDUNDANCY—e.g.:

- "The county attorney of Charles County, Md., said its losses *exceed more than* [read *exceed*] $1.3 million from derivatives trades." "Derivatives Put in Role of Fall Guy," *Ark. Democrat-Gaz.*, 10 Oct. 1994, at D1.
- "Volchkov will only begin to get his salary, which cannot *exceed more than* [read *exceed*] $875,000 a year under the NHL's cap, if he makes the club this season." Rachel Alexander, "First-Round Selection Volchkov Signs Contract," *Wash. Post*, 21 Sept. 1996, at H9.
- "What's considered affordable by experts is fluid, but it is typically defined as housing costs that do not *exceed more than* [read *exceed*] 30 percent of an individual's monthly income." Kirsten Crow, "City's Need for Housing Grows," *Corpus Christi Caller-Times*, 2 Aug. 2015, at A1.

LANGUAGE-CHANGE INDEX
exceed more than for *exceed*: Stage 1
Current ratio (*exceed 10* vs.
exceed more than 10): 169:1

B. And *accede*. See **accede**.

exceedingly. A. And *exceeding*, adv. *Exceedingly* (= extraordinarily) is often used as a mild hyperbole roughly equivalent to *quite* or *very*. It doesn't usually present any problems, but it does have an old-fashioned by-form, *exceeding* <exceeding kind>. Instead of this ARCHAISM, use *exceedingly*—e.g.:

- "The Jets have also rushed the ball *exceeding* [read *exceedingly*] well this season." Terry Price, "Jets," *Hartford Courant*, 3 Nov. 1991, at C11.
- "Abramson notes the firm has done *exceeding* [read *exceedingly*] well in marketing energy to other utilities." Wes Kendall, "Fran Jeffries Performance," *Courier-J.* (Louisville), 22 Dec. 1991, at E1.

B. And *excessively*. An antiquarian book dealer sends out a catalogue in which seven of the books are described as "excessively rare." He means *exceedingly*. While *excessively* imparts the idea of undesirable surplus, *exceedingly* takes the quality stated to its zenith.

excel. So spelled—not **excell*. Cf. **dispel, expel** & **extol**.

Current ratio: 90:1

excellence; excellency. The DIFFERENTIATION between these terms is essentially complete. *Excellence* = the quality of being excellent. *Excellency* has been so narrowed in meaning that it functions today almost exclusively as a title for a high dignitary in government or the church <Would you like another, Your Excellency?>. This narrowing in sense had largely been accomplished by 1900.

except, prep. & conj. **A. As Preposition and Conjunction.** When *except* begins a phrase (with no finite verb) rather than a clause, it is a simple preposition not followed by the relative pronoun *that* <all people except farmers owning more than 500 acres> <no one must leave the room except with permission>. But when *except* as a conjunction introduces a clause (with a finite verb), it should be followed by *that* <all vice presidents are to receive a 10% bonus in compensation, except that no bonus on previous bonuses is allowed>.

If a pronoun follows a prepositional *except*, the pronoun should be in the objective case, not the nominative—e.g.: "Everyone has been accounted for except *he* [read *him*]." If a pronoun follows a conjunctive *except* and serves as the subject of the clause's verb, it should be in the nominative case—e.g.: "He's generally easygoing, except that *he* doesn't tolerate laziness." See PRONOUNS (A), (B).

B. *Excepting*. Except in the phrase *not excepting*, this word should not be used as a substitute for *except for* or *aside from*—e.g.:

- "But rarely in the post World War II era, *excepting* [read *aside from* or *with the exceptions of*] the Netherlands during the '70s and England's championship team of 1966, do the outsiders make it past the semifinals." Javier Solano, "History Favors the Latin Teams," *Orlando Sentinel*, 15 June 1994, at D10. (The interruptive phrase in that sentence might be improved a little by enclosing it in em-dashes. See PUNCTUATION (G). But it needs more work than that: *the Netherlands* aren't an exception to *the post–World War II era*. The parts of the sentence are misassembled.)
- "That means they may spend all their time trying to figure out who else can command close to her top price of $350 (*excepting* [read *aside from*] the Las Vegas shows)." Robert Hilburn, "Streisand Tour Ends," *L.A. Times*, 26 July 1994, at F1.
- "But he remains unbeaten in 10 global championship sprint finals over the past seven years, *excepting* [read *not including*] the false start that ruled him out of the 100m final at the 2011 World Championships in Daegu." Martha Kelner, "Cheater Beater Bolt," *Daily Mail*, 24 Aug. 2015, Sport §, at 78.

It's true that *excepting* is one word, not two, and that it might be considered an acceptable dangling modifier (or "disguised conjunction"). (See DANGLERS (E).) But many knowledgeable readers will disapprove of it as a dangler. And in any event, it's less natural-sounding than the edited versions—which add one more word but no extra syllables.

except, vb., = (1) to exclude; omit <present company excepted>; or (2) = to object; take exception <I except to that statement>. Sometimes, in one of the grossest errors that a published writer can commit (or a copy-editor miss), *except* is misused for *accept*—e.g.:

- "Why would these industries offer government officials gifts, unless it is to influence decisions in their behalf? Why do we need a full-fledged investigation? They either *excepted* [read *accepted*] the gifts or they didn't!" "Officials Reap Profits of Their Influence," *Rocky Mountain News* (Denver), 7 Sept. 1994, at A38.
- "On Monday, the phone starts ringing with heart-breaking stories about a father and son or daughter who just wanted to get in on a good hunt and *excepted* [read *accepted*] an invitation from a host they thought they could trust." Steve Bowman, "Dove Hunting Season Aims to Start with a Bang," *Ark. Democrat-Gaz.*, 29 Aug. 1996, at C8.

LANGUAGE-CHANGE INDEX
except misused for *accept*: Stage 1
Current ratio (*well accepted* vs.
*well excepted): 1,438:1

excepting. See **except** (B).

exceptional. A. And *exceptionable*. *Exceptional* = out of the ordinary; uncommon; rare; superior. *Exceptionable* = open to exception; objectionable. E.g.: "It is the same ideological insularity that found nothing terribly *exceptionable*—until the firestorm—with the racial spoils system advocated by Lani Guinier." Charles Krauthammer, "Abortion Is Legal, Not Moral," *Cincinnati Enquirer*, 13 Feb. 1995, at A10.

Exceptionable, of course, is the much rarer term. And about 20% of the time it appears in print, it's misused for *exceptional*—e.g.:

- "Feemster, who died in a 1963 airplane accident, was a pushy Sammy Glick type much disliked by the *Journal's* editorial staff, but his *exceptionable* [read *exceptional*] business skill and hustle persuaded skeptical advertisers to support a newspaper that had no home town, no photographs, no sports, and a gray, unchanging front page." David Graulich, "Worldly Power: The Making of the *Wall Street Journal*," *Wash. Monthly*, Jan. 1987, at 58.
- "Meanwhile, Hamed has appealed to the British press for a better understanding of his *exceptionable* [read *exceptional*] talent following his remarkable victory over Steve Robinson." Steve Bunce, "Murray's Title Spur," *Daily Telegraph*, 13 Oct. 1995, at 34.
- "Indian food holds up remarkably well on a buffet table and Khyber Pass's table is *exceptionable* [read *exceptional*]—especially at the bargain price of $8.95 during the week (it is $9.95 on weekends and $5.95 for lunch)." Jean Marie Brownson, "Khyber Pass Takes Indian Cuisine to New Heights," *Chicago Trib.*, 17 Apr. 1996, Good Eating §, at 2.

LANGUAGE-CHANGE INDEX
exceptionable misused for *exceptional*: Stage 1
Current ratio (*exceptional circumstances* vs.
*exceptionable circumstances): 1,073:1

B. Meaning "physically or mentally handicapped." The problem with using the word as a EUPHEMISM in this way is that it can result in ambiguity: *exceptional* can mean either "having above-average intelligence" (i.e., gifted) or "having below-average intelligence" (i.e., retarded). In passages such as the following, *exceptional* is symptomatic of DOUBLESPEAK: "The Resource Directory also lists state and federal agencies that can assist parents with *exceptional* children." Patricia Galbreaith, "Hints for the Disabled," *Dallas Morning News*, 1 Aug. 1997, at C10.

LANGUAGE-CHANGE INDEX
exceptional as doublespeak for *handicapped*: Stage 3

exception proves the rule, the. This phrase is the popular rendering of what was originally a legal maxim, "The exception proves (or confirms) the rule in the cases not excepted" (*exceptio probat regulam in casibus non exceptis*). Originally, *exception* in this maxim meant "the action of excepting"—not, as is commonly supposed, "that which is excepted"—so the true sense of the maxim was that by specifying the cases excepted, one strengthens the hold of the rule over all cases not excepted.

At least two spurious explanations of *the exception proves the rule* exist. One is that because a rule does not hold in all instances (i.e., has exceptions), the rule must be valid. This misunderstanding of the phrase commonly manifests itself in the discourse of those who wish to argue that every rule must have exceptions. A more sophisticated, but equally false, explanation of the phrase is that *prove* here retains its Elizabethan sense (derived from the Latin) "to test," so that the sense of the phrase is that an exception to a rule "tests" the validity of the rule. This erroneous explanation appears, of all places, in Tom Burnam, *A Dictionary of Misinformation* 79 (1975).

By the way, the *FMEU1* entry on this phrase is perhaps the only one in which the great H.W. Fowler is all but incomprehensible.

excess. See **access**, n. (A).

****excess verbiage.** See **verbiage**.

EXCLAMATION POINTS. See PUNCTUATION (I).

excludable; *excludible; *exclusible. The standard form is *excludable*. See -ABLE (A). Cf. **includible**.

exculpate; exonerate. Whereas the former has the primary sense "to free from blame or accusation," the latter means literally "to free from a burden," and only by extension is it synonymous with the former. See **exonerate.**

exculpatory; *exculpative. The latter is a NEEDLESS VARIANT. Cf. **culpable** & **inculpatory**.
Current ratio: 547:1

LANGUAGE-CHANGE INDEX (For the full key, see front matter pp. xxxi, l–li.)
Stage 1: Rejected. **Stage 2:** Widely shunned. **Stage 3:** Widespread but . . . **Stage 4:** Ubiquitous but . . . **Stage 5:** Fully accepted.
Invariably inferior forms marked by asterisk (*). • Ratios represent frequency of prevalent forms vs. variants in current books.

excuse, n. See **alibi.**

excuse me; pardon me. Traditionally, *excuse me* was used for minor offenses such as bumping into someone; *pardon me* was reserved for more serious situations requiring a more explicit apology. Today, the terms are interchangeable, *excuse me* being slightly less formal. *Sorry* is even less so.

When the word *me* receives the stress, either *pardon me* or *excuse me* is used either as a mild challenge of someone else or as a polite waving off of someone else's apology. When the first word is stressed in either phrase and an interrogative inflection is given, the sense is typically "What did you say?"

executor (= someone who is appointed in a will to administer a deceased person's estate) is the standard spelling. *Executer is an obsolete variant. The word is pronounced with the accent on the second syllable: /ig-**zek**-yə-tər/. See **trustee (B).**

Current ratio (*executor* vs. *executer): 109:1

executrix. See SEXISM (D).

exegesis; epexegesis; eisegesis. *Exegesis* (/eks-ə-**jee**-sis/), the usual term, means "explanation or exposition (as of a word or sentence)." The other two are rare. *Epexegesis* = the addition of a word or words to convey more clearly the meaning implied, or the specific sense intended, in a preceding word or sentence (*OED*). *Eisegesis* (/ɪ-sə-**jee**-sis/) = the interpretation of a word or passage by reading into it one's own ideas (*OED*). But surely *reading into*—or some like phrase—is clearer.

Each of these terms forms the plural by changing the final syllable to *-es*; hence *exegeses, epexegeses,* and *eisegeses.*

exemplar. See **example.**

exemplary has two almost contradictory connotations: *exemplary damages* (better known as *punitive damages*) make an example out of a wrongdoer, whereas *exemplary behavior* is model behavior. *Exemplary* is sometimes misunderstood as meaning "severe" in phrases such as *exemplary punishment.* The meaning is always that the accompanying noun should set an example for others' behavior.

exemplification; *exemplum. See **example.**

exempli gratia. See **e.g.**

exert. See **assert.**

exeunt (/**ek**-see-ənt/) [L. "they leave"], an Elizabethan stage direction, means that two or more actors leave the stage. (The corresponding singular in Latin is *exit* "he or she leaves.") The phrase *exeunt omnes* means that all leave. Most people first see it in a Shakespeare play. And they often seem at once confused by it and tempted to use it—e.g.:

- "In the small American delegation, no one takes a Sweet Swan of Avon Cup. Robert Downey Jr. is hardly employed as Rivers, though he *exeunts* [read *exits*] terrifically,

gasping in interrupted sex." David Elliott, "Drunk on Violence," *San Diego Union-Trib.*, 18 Jan. 1996, Entertainment §, at 4.
- "*Exeunt* [read *Exit*] first Yankee (as Shakespeare might have directed this scene) never to be seen in this very select society again." Perry Young, "The Honorable Redneck," *Chapel Hill Herald*, 17 Aug. 1996, at 4.

Of course, Shakespeare would never have used the word for a single player.

One reason people mistakenly use *exeunt* for one person may be that, in Elizabethan texts, it sometimes appears as if one person leaves the stage. Although *Exeunt executioners* is clear at the beginning of Act 4, Scene 1 in *King John, Exeunt* alone—at the end of that scene—isn't. Hubert delivers a line to Arthur, and the direction *Exeunt* immediately appears. A reader who didn't understand what Hubert said, that Arthur was to stick close by, might think that only Hubert left the stage at that point. But then Arthur isn't in the next scene (he must have left!). Alas, readers don't tend to keep stage directions as much in mind as they do dialogue.

LANGUAGE-CHANGE INDEX
exeunt misused for *exit*: Stage 1

*ex-felon is an illogical expression—except, perhaps, in reference to a pardoned offender—because a convicted offender does not lose the status of felon merely by serving out a criminal sentence. Once a felon, always a felon. But *ex-convict* is quite all right, *convict* now being viewed as a close synonym of *prisoner.* The phrase *ex-felon was little used until the early 1960s.

LANGUAGE-CHANGE INDEX
*ex-felon in the sense "a felon who has completed a sentence": Stage 3

*exhalt; *exhault. Each is a misspelling of *exalt.* See **exalt.**

exhaustible. So spelled—not **exhaustable.* See -ABLE (A).

Current ratio: 299:1

exhibit a tendency is wordy for *tend.* The verbose phrase occurs sometimes in the singular, sometimes in the plural—e.g.:

- "Patients with the disorder *exhibit tendencies* [read *tend*] to attack their therapists or others who are trying to help them, McEvoy said." Warren Hastings, "Court Bars Discipline of Psychologist," *Union Leader* (Manchester, N.H.), 21 Mar. 1992, at 6.
- "Ruzimatov (now also deputy artistic director of the Kirov) still *exhibits the tendency to flaring nostrils and tiresome rodomontade* [read *tends to flare nostrils and engage in tiresome rodomontade*]." Sophie Constanti, "Kirov Ballet: London Coliseum," *Independent*, 12 July 1995, Reviews §, at 12.
- "With some, who *exhibit a tendency to* [read *tend toward*] risky behaviors, the questions get thornier and the lines more blurred." Craig Schneider & Ernie Suggs, "A Closer Look: Organ Transplant Policies," *Atlanta J.-Const.*, 5 Apr. 2015, at A1.

In the second example quoted, the suggested revision concededly uses as many words as the original, but the result achieves a more logical PARALLELISM by aligning the infinitives (*to flare* and *(to) engage*) rather than the nouns (*nostrils* and *rodomontade*). See BURIED VERBS.

exhilarate is so spelled—not **exhilirate*. Remember its etymological connection with *hilarious*.

Current ratio: 71:1

*exhorbitant. See **exorbitant.**

exigency; *exigence. The form ending in *-cy* is standard; the other is a NEEDLESS VARIANT.

Current ratio: 4:1

exigent; *exigeant. The first is the standard term meaning "requiring immediate action." **Exigeant* is a NEEDLESS VARIANT.

Current ratio: 14:1

existence—often misspelled **existance*—is commonly misused for *inception*, especially in the phrase **since its existence*. E.g.:

- " 'It was an evenly matched series. They just had a little more pitching depth than us,' said player/coach Jeff Thompson, a former Pitt catcher who has served that role for Canonsburg since its *existence* [read *beginnings*]." David Assad, "Canonsburg Hopes Pitching Can Lead It to a Championship," *Pitt. Post-Gaz.*, 11 June 1995, at W11.
- "Riyadh-based The Arab Investment Company (TAIC) has moved from a modest beginning to the pinnacle of its glory in 20 years since its *existence* [read *inception*]." Furqan Ahmed, "TAIC Moves On in Field of Investments," *Moneyclips*, 10 Aug. 1995.

LANGUAGE-CHANGE INDEX
*since its existence for *since its inception*: Stage 1
Current ratio (*since its inception* vs.
*since its existence): 70:1

exit has been an acceptable verb since the early 17th century <they exited from the building about 3:00 AM>. Those who object to it on grounds that one does not "entrance" a building have a misplaced prejudice.

But when used transitively, as opposed to intransitively with the preposition *from*, the verb typifies police talk—e.g.:

- "As traffic came to a standstill in both directions, these men *exited* their vehicles and became involved in a brief foot pursuit." Letter of Master Police Officer Robert W. Mathieson," *Virginian-Pilot* (Norfolk), 26 July 1996, at 7.
- "He then turned his car around again, *exited* the vehicle and revealed a knife." Gary Mays, "Joliet Man Charged with Robbing Women of Diamond Rings," *Chicago Trib.*, 29 Aug. 1996, at D5.

exodus means "a mass departure or emigration." Hence the common phrase **mass exodus* is a REDUNDANCY, perhaps a venial one influenced by *mass migration*—e.g.: "On the streets, buses lined the curb, waiting for the *mass exodus* [read *exodus*] of fans after the game." Kevin Mayhood, "Loyal Indians Fans Soak Up Playoff Atmosphere," *Columbus Dispatch*, 4 Oct. 1995, at B2. As a corollary to that point, one person's leaving does not make an *exodus*—e.g.: "Jones' *exodus* [read *exit*] has sparked a discussion among university staffers and the deaf community over what went wrong with the training program." Lynn O'Shaughnessy, "Student Concern Helped to Oust Leader at CSUN Center for Deaf," *L.A. Times*, 27 Oct. 1985, § 2, at 8.

LANGUAGE-CHANGE INDEX
*mass exodus for *exodus*: Stage 3

ex officio. See **ex cathedra.**

exonerate, in the sense "to free from responsibility or blame," takes a person as an object. E.g.:

- "The Rev. James McCloskey, who worked for three years to *exonerate* Baker, said Baker, 41, was 'in a state of shock and disbelief' after learning of his new trial." "New Trial Ordered for Man in Prison Nearly 24 Years," *Des Moines Register*, 28 Aug. 1997, at 6.
- " 'Young Sam' is 50 and has spent much of his life trying to *exonerate* his father." James Bradshaw, "Sheppard's Attorneys Barred from Testifying," *Columbus Dispatch*, 18 Nov. 1997, at C3.

The term is sometimes misused in either of two ways. First, it's sometimes applied to a thing as opposed to a person, in the sense "to rule out (something) as a cause"—e.g.: "The cruise control and the electronic fuel injection system were *exonerated* [read *ruled out as causes*] when a National Highway Traffic Safety Administration study concluded in 1989 that there was no defect." Helen Kahn, "Jury Clears 300ZX of Sudden Acceleration," *Automotive News*, 1 Oct. 1990, at 39. Second, it's sometimes misused for *condone* (= to overlook or disregard [an offense])—e.g.: "Included is a shocking segment in which Florida State football players essentially *exonerate* [read *condone*] Phillips' conduct." Milton Kent, "After Ratings Famine, Browns Have a Feast Against Steelers," *Baltimore Sun*, 30 Nov. 1995, at D2. Cf. **exculpate.**

LANGUAGE-CHANGE INDEX
1. *exonerate* misused to mean "to rule out": Stage 1
2. *exonerate* misused for *condone*: Stage 1

exorbitant (lit., "having departed or deviated from one's track [*orbit*] or rut") is sometimes mistakenly spelled **exhorbitant*—perhaps because it is confused with *exhort*. E.g.: "The developers and tenants, however, insist the costs are far from *exhorbitant* [read *exorbitant*]." Geeta Anand, "Mission Main Funds in Jeopardy," *Boston Globe*, 6 May 1997, at B1.

LANGUAGE-CHANGE INDEX
exorbitant misspelled **exhorbitant*: Stage 1
Current ratio: 87:1

exorcise (= to purge of something spiritually bad, esp. evil spirits) is so spelled in AmE. The preferred BrE

---

spelling is *exorcize*. These preferences are the oppo-site of the usual ones (see -IZE). The word is best pro-nounced /**ek**-sor-siz/ to distinguish it from *exercise*.

The MALAPROPISM of using *exercise* for *exorcise* conjures up an image of devils doing aerobics (or, if they are zombies, anaerobics)—e.g.:

- "Winning the team title also *exercised* [read *exorcised*] some demons for Morristown." Chris Kowalczyk, "Wil-son's Golden Showing Helps Morristown Dominate," *Star-Ledger* (Newark), 5 May 2002, Sports §, at 17.
- "The Barons *exercised* [read *exorcised*] the demons that have sometimes plagued them when they faced Edison's David Huff." Ted Apodaca, "Barons Ride into Sunset," *Orange County Register*, 9 May 2002, Sports §, at 1.

LANGUAGE-CHANGE INDEX
exercise misused for *exorcise*: Stage 1
Current ratio (*exorcise the evil* vs.
*exercise the evil): 38:1

exordium (= a formal introduction to a writing) forms the plurals *exordiums* and *exordia*. The former might be considered preferable, but the two still vie for preeminence. See PLURALS (B).

Current ratio (*exordia* vs. *exordiums*): 2:1

exoticism; *exotism. The latter is a NEEDLESS VARIANT.
Current ratio: 165:1

expandable; *expansible; *expandible. The first is the standard term. The second and third are NEED-LESS VARIANTS. See -ABLE (A).

Current ratio (in order of headwords): 227:16:1

expatiate; expatriate; *expatriot. *Expatiate* (/ek-**spay**-shee-ayt/) means (1) "to wander"; or (2) "to discourse on (a subject) at length." *Expatriate* (/eks-**pay**-tree-ayt/) means (1) "to leave one's home country to live elsewhere"; or (2) "to banish; exile."

Expatriate (/eks-**pay**-tree-it/) is also a noun mean-ing "a person who lives permanently in a foreign land." It is sometimes mistakenly spelled **expatriot*, a form based on a misunderstanding of the root word. In fact, *expatriate* (L. *ex-* "out of" + *patrie* "native land") is a fairly neutral word, but the mistaken form **expatriot* appears to attach some opprobrium—e.g.:

- "And Georgia *expatriots* [read *expatriates*] sometimes bring up burgers and hot dogs from the Varsity, a vintage '50s drive-in near Georgia Tech in Atlanta." Laura Outer-bridge, "Home Is Where the Tastebuds Are," *Wash. Times*, 3 Apr. 1995, at C10.
- "Saudi Arabia has a population of 17 million people, a third of them *expatriots* [read *expatriates*]." "Saudi King Hands Power to Half-Brother," *Austin Am.-Statesman*, 2 Jan. 1996, at A1.
- "As they sat around San Diego's Balboa Park, discussing the issue, the *expatriots* [read *expatriates*] realized that a large number of their town's population of 3,500 lived in and around San Diego County." Alfredo Corchado, "Importing Changes," *Dallas Morning News*, 23 Sept. 1996, at A1.

LANGUAGE-CHANGE INDEX
expatriate misspelled **expatriot*: Stage 1
Current ratio: 332:1

expect is informal or colloquial for *think* or *suppose*, as here: "I *expect* that it will take three weeks," instead of "I think it will take three weeks." Most properly, *expect* means "to look forward to and rely on." See **anticipate.**

expectancy; expectation. Despite an overlap in actual use, the DIFFERENTIATION is clear-cut. *Expectancy* = that which is anticipated or forecast; something expected <a life expectancy of 70 years>. *Expecta-tion* = the act or state of anticipating the occurrence of something <an expectation of high profits>. The most common error is to misuse *expectation* for *expec-tancy*—e.g.: "The impairment must adversely affect life *expectation* [read *expectancy*] and not just the qual-ity of life." "Cash in the Magnificent 70s," *Fin. Times*, 19 July 1997, at 21.

LANGUAGE-CHANGE INDEX
expectation misused for *expectancy*: Stage 1

expectorate is a genteelism for *spit*, convenient for the writer fond of INELEGANT VARIATION, as in the first and second examples below—e.g.:

- "Carrey . . . spits so copiously that he covers himself and two other characters with dripping mucus. Of course, it wouldn't be an Ace Ventura movie if he only *expectorated* [read *spat*]. First he has to snort long and loudly, in order to gather his mucus supply, which he seems to be drawing not only from the sinus area but from every inner bodily crevice." Roger Ebert, "Call of the Vile," *Chicago Sun-Times*, 10 Nov. 1995, at 43. (For more on the past tense of *spit*, see **spit.**)
- "Brad Ausmus, the Padres' leadoff man, adjusted his bat-ting helmet and *spit* [read *spat*]. Catcher Dan Wilson *expectorated* [read *then spat*] between the bars of his mask and rifled the ball back to the mound." David Casstevens, "Why, He's the Spitting Image of . . . ," *Ariz. Republic*, 1 Mar. 1996, at C1.
- "Last Friday night in Toronto, Alomar, called out on a third strike and then ejected from the game, *expectorated* [read *spat*] in the face of umpire John Hirschbeck." Woody Paige, "Umps Deserve the Right Call," *Denver Post*, 2 Oct. 1996, at D1.

Sometimes, though, it can be used for good comical effect—e.g.: "Well, there is the rule against spitting in public places, which has been *expectorated* from the governmental maw on the grounds that it was widely violated and might ruin spring training if applied vigorously to ballplayers." "Getting Rid of Ridiculous Rules," *Tampa Trib.*, 30 June 1996, at 2.

expediency. A. And *expedience. *Expediency* is usual; **expedience* is a NEEDLESS VARIANT.

Current ratio: 11:1

B. And expedition. *Expediency* (= consideration of what is politically convenient) is sometimes con-founded with *expedition* (= promptness, haste). (The corresponding adjectives *expedient* and *expeditious* are likewise misused. See **expeditious.**) Mark Olshaker completed his book on the Unabomber 13 days after the capture of the suspect (later convicted), Theodore Kaczynski. But because the book's coauthor was a former FBI agent, Olshaker had to submit the book to the FBI for a standard but prolonged review. On the subject of the delay in publishing caused by the FBI's review of the book, Olshaker was quoted: "'If this is the F.B.I.'s idea of *expediency* [read *expedition*], then I can see why it took them 18 years to catch the Unabomber.'" Doreen Carvajal, "The Long Unabom Manhunt Becomes a Paperback Sprint," *N.Y. Times*, 2 May 1996, at A1.

> LANGUAGE-CHANGE INDEX
> *expediency* misused for *expedition*: Stage 1

expedient. See **expeditious.**

*expediential. See **expeditious.**

expedite. See SPELLING (A).

expedition. See **expediency (B).**

expeditious; expedient, adj.; ***expediential.** *Expeditious* = quickly accomplished, prompt <an expeditious decision>. *Expedient* = (1) desirable, advantageous <a surprisingly expedient device for controlling a difficult problem>; or (2) based on self-interest <the regent's decision was politically expedient>. **Expediential* is a NEEDLESS VARIANT.

Expedient as a synonym for *expeditious* has long been considered obsolete. Oddly, though, it persists where *expeditious* would be better, probably in part because of the sound of *speed* in the middle of *expedient*. In the following examples, notice that *expedient* (= self-interested) suggests something rather different from *expeditious* (= prompt):

- "Ask them if they got what they ordered. Did the builder respond to their problems in an *expedient* [read *expeditious*] fashion? Were the repairs satisfactory?" Sharon L. Warzocha, "'Walk-Through' Is Buyer's Last, but Vital, Step," *L.A. Times*, 12 May 1991, at K1.
- "Clearly the government will have to act as *expediently* [read *expeditiously*] as possible to deliver on housing and jobs for blacks living in substandard conditions in the townships and squatters' camps." "A Peaceful Election Bodes Well for New Era," *Dallas Morning News*, 4 May 1994, at A32.
- "The people who work there are the friendliest and most *expedient* [read *expeditious*] humans in the world." Shannon Bryan, "Getting Outside in Augusta," *Portland Press Herald*, 20 Aug. 2015, at A1.

> LANGUAGE-CHANGE INDEX
> *expedient* misused for *expeditious*: Stage 1

expel. So spelled—not **expell*. Cf. **dispel, excel** & **extol.**

> Current ratio: 163:1

expend is a FORMAL WORD that often seems less appropriate than *spend*—e.g.:

- "It also provided procedures to document the threat and do something about it before businesses *expended* [read *spent*] time and money expanding and relocating." "Controlling Pollution," *Knoxville News-Sentinel*, 21 Mar. 1996, at A14.

- "Cosmic bowling is not the first time Brunswick has *expended* [read *spent*] time and energy giving bowling a face lift." David Young, "Brunswick Pins Down a Strategy," *Chicago Trib.*, 28 May 1996, at N1.
- "Accelerators and government chest-thumping about entrepreneurship *expend* [read *spend* or, in this case, perhaps *waste*] scarce tax dollars on public relations, notably fancy websites and social-media campaigns, to remind taxpayers how their money is being put to magnificent use in 'innovation hubs.'" Neil Seeman, "'Accidental' Entrepreneurs," *Globe & Mail* (Toronto), 22 Aug. 2015, at B5.

expense, v.t. In general use, this is an overblown substitute for *spend* and ought to be avoided. In accounting, though, it is a handy bit of JARGON, distinguishing a business operating cost whose benefit is immediate rather than long-range from a capital purchase whose benefit will continue over several years. E.g.:

- "If these products go into production, revenues could go off the chart because, unlike Hollywood, characters and concepts were *expensed* at the time of their creation and not amortized over time." Stephen Pounds, "Big Entertainment's Big Plans," *Palm Beach Post*, 30 June 1996, at E1.
- "Goodwill is an intangible or artificial asset that can be written off or *expensed* over a number of years." David Shook, "High Court Ruling on Thrifts May Cost Taxpayers $20 Billion," *Patriot Ledger* (Quincy, Mass.), 2 July 1996, at 30.
- "The company has now *expensed* $625 million to cover the cost of the Ignition Compensation Fund, which has found 124 deaths caused by the defect." Greg Gardner, "Color GM Greener, UAW More Hopeful," *Detroit Free Press*, 24 July 2015, at A1.

The word in this sense should be confined to accounting contexts—not used as an overblown synonym for *spend*. Cf. ***inexpense.**

expensive. Because the word means "high-priced," the phrase **expensive prices* is a REDUNDANCY—e.g.:

- "Some travelers report *expensive prices* [read *high prices*] in larger cities like Split and Zagreb where hotel rooms are booked by United Nations and NATO officials and journalists." Jim Simon, "Rebounding in War's Wake," *Austin Am.-Statesman*, 23 June 1996, at F6.
- "We settled for a reserve chardonnay at the *too expensive price* [read *unduly high price*] of $6.50 a glass." M.F. Onderdonk, "Winery Is Delicious Setting for a Meal at Williamsburg Tavern," *Virginian-Pilot* (Norfolk), 6 Oct. 1996, at F1.
- "Unsurprisingly, Manhattan soars with the *most expensive prices* [read *highest prices*] in the city." Amber Jamieson, "Realty $oar Points," *N.Y. Post*, 16 Aug. 2015, News §, at 2.

*experimentalize is a NEEDLESS VARIANT of *experiment on* or *experiment with*—e.g.: "The sometimes desperate attempt to *experimentalize* [read *experiment with*] social topics resulted in laboratory experiments that were sometimes rather poor caricatures of the social phenomena to be investigated." George

---

LANGUAGE-CHANGE INDEX (For the full key, see front matter pp. xxxi, l–li.)
Stage 1: Rejected. **Stage 2:** Widely shunned. **Stage 3:** Widespread but . . . **Stage 4:** Ubiquitous but . . . **Stage 5:** Fully accepted.
Invariably inferior forms marked by asterisk (*). • Ratios represent frequency of prevalent forms vs. variants in current books.

Mandler, "The Situation of Psychology," *Am. J. Psychology*, 22 Mar. 1996, at 1.

LANGUAGE-CHANGE INDEX
experimentalize for *experiment on* or *experiment with*: Stage 1
Current ratio (*experiment with* vs. *experimentalize*): 1,186:1

expertise (= special knowledge or skill in a particular subject, esp. when learned by training or long experience) is preferably pronounced /ek-spər-**teez**/—not /-**tees**/.

expiration; expiry. *Expiration* is the usual word for "termination" in all types of World English. *Expiry* is a chiefly BrE variant.

explain. See **explicate.**

explanatorily. See SENTENCE ADVERBS.

expletive. See **epithet** (C).

EXPLETIVES. In general usage, *expletives* are understood to be curse words or exclamations. This sense was fortified in AmE during the Watergate hearings in the early 1970s, when coarse language was replaced with *expletive deleted* in transcripts of the White House tapes. In grammar, however, an *expletive* is a word having no special meaning but standing (usually at the beginning of a clause) for a delayed subject. The two most common expletives are *it* and *there* at the beginnings of clauses or sentences. See **it** & **there is.**

explicable (= able to be easily explained and understood) is pronounced either /**ek**-spli-kə-bəl/ or (less traditionally) /ek-**splik**-ə-bəl/. See PRONUNCIATION (C). Cf. **inexplicable.**

explicate; explain. The terms are synonymous, but are used in different contexts. *Explain* is the ordinary term. *Explicate* (lit., "to open up pleats; to unfold") is more learned and connotes formal, orderly presentation or justification, often of a text. Oddly, the adjectives *explicable* (/**ek**-spli-kə-bəl/) and *inexplicable* occur more frequently in print than the verb *explicate*.

*explodable. See **explosible.**

exploitative; *exploitive; *exploitatory. The second and third forms are NEEDLESS VARIANTS. The adjective follows the noun; so *exploitation* yields *exploitative*, whereas *prevention* yields *preventive*. See **preventive.**
   Current ratio (in order of headwords): 5,007:767:1

explosible; *explodable. *Explosible* has been the standard adjective since the mid-19th century.
   Current ratio: 3:1

exponential. This word is not synonymous with *rapid*. Growth is *exponential* when the rate of growth increases over time. But a savings account with compound interest could be viewed as growing exponentially in a sense: the percentage growth of the balance over the original principal goes up every year, and at an ever-increasing rate. If the rate is 5% at simple interest, though, the balance will not increase rapidly. Yet writers frequently use *exponential* and *exponentially* as hyperbolic equivalents of *rapid* and *rapidly*—e.g.:

- "The *exponential* growth of spam also has spawned a number of software programs designed specifically to rid your inbox of junk mail." David Einstein, "There's No Sure Way to Eliminate Spam from Your Mailbox," *S.F. Chron.*, 13 Dec. 2001, at B4. (Note the REDUNDANCY in that sentence: all computer programs are software, and vice versa, so *software programs* is ill-advised.)
- "That seemingly premature pronouncement bodes an *exponential* increase in costs." "We Must Pay for Ridgway Case," *Seattle Post-Intelligencer*, 14 Dec. 2001, at B4.
- "Since 1999, when many mainstream consumers began shopping on the Internet, Web retailers have often seen *exponential* gains in sales." Chris Reidy, "Slump Seen in Holiday Sales," *Boston Globe*, 21 Dec. 2001, at C1.

exposé should have the acute accent on the final letter to prevent confusion with the verb *expose*. E.g.: "Investigative reports, following in the tradition of the muckrakers, are always looking for an *expose* [read *exposé*]." See DIACRITICAL MARKS & GARNER'S LAW.

ex post facto is slightly pompous but fairly common when used for *after the fact*. The phrase does have legitimate uses in the sense "retroactive" <ex post facto laws>. **Ex post* for *ex post facto* is an odd ellipsis without literary legitimacy—e.g.: "As a rule, therefore, courts will not engage in *ex post inquiries* [read *ex post facto inquiries*] regarding the substantive fairness of contract terms." Maureen B. Callahan, Note, "Post-Employment Restraint Agreements," 52 *U. Chi. L. Rev.* 703, 704 (1985). Yet another strange shortening omits the *ex*—e.g.: "Finally, her charge that after rejecting his overtures she then was discriminated against in her lower-level state job seems *a post facto* [read *an ex post facto* or *an after-the-fact*] concoction by her lawyers." Albert R. Hunt, "Politics & People: Jones v. Clinton," *Wall Street J.*, 29 May 1997, at A19.
   The phrase was formerly spelled **ex postfacto* on occasion, but this spelling is archaic. Some writers hyphenate the term when it functions as a PHRASAL ADJECTIVE <ex-post-facto reasoning>, but the hyphens are unnecessary in this SET PHRASE.
   In law, *ex post facto* and *retroactive* are distinguishable. Based on the historical usage of *ex post facto law*, the U.S. Supreme Court interprets the constitutional ban on them as applying specifically to crimes and punishments, not to civil statutes. That is, a person may not be convicted of an act that was not illegal when it was done. Nor may a person be sentenced to a harsher punishment than that which applied when the act was done. In some circumstances, though, a civil statute may apply retroactively.

LANGUAGE-CHANGE INDEX
1. **ex post* for *ex post facto*: Stage 1
2. **post facto* for *ex post facto*: Stage 1

expound; propound. *Expound* = to explain. *Propound* = to set forth; to put forward for consideration.

Both are best used transitively. In the best usage, one *expounds* an idea or doctrine—rather than *expounding on* it. Likewise, one *propounds* questions to a jury.

express, adj.; **expressed.** Both words are antonyms of *implied*, but as different parts of speech. As an adjective meaning "specific, definite, clear," the word should be *express*—e.g.:

- "She helped to write the Illinois Constitution, which includes an equal-rights clause and an *expressed* [read *express*] right of privacy." Steve Neal, "Netsch Could Be Toughest Edgar Rival," *Chicago Sun-Times*, 23 Mar. 1993, at 21.
- "The court found that although Criado was an at-will employee, ITT had created an *expressed* [read *express*] limitation on its right to fire any employee who followed the code of conduct." Lisa Jenner, "Employment-at-Will Liability," *HR Focus*, Mar. 1994, at 11.
- "The agency has an *expressed* [read *express*] duty under the act to protect the public health." "EPA's New Mandates Won't Come Cheaply," *Ariz. Republic*, 23 June 2015, at A12.

Express, then, is closely allied with *explicit*; *implied*, as the antonym, is closely allied with *implicit*. See **implied** & **implicit.**

As a verb, *expressed* is a past-tense or past-participial form of the verb *express*—e.g.: "Not only did he say good things, but he also said the right things and *expressed* the right concerns." "Valvano's Toughest Challenge," *St. Louis Post-Dispatch*, 29 Jan. 1989, at F3.

LANGUAGE-CHANGE INDEX
expressed misused for *express*: Stage 1
Current ratio (*an express provision* vs. **an expressed provision*): 227:1

expressible. So spelled—not **expressable*. See -ABLE (A).

Current ratio: 98:1

*expresso. See **espresso.**

expropriate. See **appropriate** (B).

expungement; expunction. The word *expungement*, unrecorded in many dictionaries, might be thought a NEEDLESS VARIANT. But because it is about four times as common in print as *expunction*, and has been since the mid-1960s, it ought to be considered standard—e.g.:

- "Any person required to register may be relieved of this duty upon the granting of a petition of *expungement* by the court upon demonstration of appropriate behavior." Daniel Feldman, "Does This Register?" *Newsday* (N.Y.), 21 Aug. 1994, at A40.
- "They also note that during the two decades between the conviction and the *expungement*, the file was open to the general public, which means countless copies could have been disseminated legally." Chris Ison, "Prescott Says St. Paul Police Cost Him His Job," *Star Trib.* (Minneapolis), 24 Aug. 1994, at B4.

- "*Expungement* is a way to erase a criminal scar." Stephen Hudak, "Wiping Slate Clean of a Criminal Past," *Plain Dealer* (Cleveland), 3 Sept. 1996, at B1.
- "The motion, which seeks *expungement* of his record and restoration of his privileges, said Mr. Nichols refused to stand during the counting of prisoners because he was not being furnished with whole wheat bread." Arnold Hamilton, "Prosecutors' Interview with FBI Scientist in Bombing Case Postponed," *Dallas Morning News*, 13 Sept. 1996, at A28.

exquisite. A. Pronunciation. The word is better pronounced with the first syllable accented (/**ek**-skwiz-it/); in AmE, however, stressing the second (/ek-**skwiz**-it/) is acceptable.

LANGUAGE-CHANGE INDEX
exquisite pronounced /ek-**skwiz**-it/ rather than /**ek**-skwiz-it/: Stage 5

B. Use. Although there is historical justification for using *exquisite* (= acute) in reference to pain, modern readers are likely to find this use macabre at best, for they generally understand the word as meaning "keenly discriminating" <exquisite taste> or "especially beautiful" <an exquisite vase>. For many readers, the obsolescent sense is merely a MISCUE—e.g.: "Steve R., a sign painter, suffered such *exquisite* [read *excruciating*] pain in his ankle that he could barely walk." Louise Continelli, "Learning to Control Chronic Pain," *Buffalo News*, 6 Sept. 1994, Lifestyles §, at 1.

*extacy. See **ecstasy.**

extant (= still existing) is preferably pronounced /**eks**-tənt/, not /ek-**stant**/—but the latter pronunciation is at least acceptable in AmE.

extemporaneous; extempore, adj.; ***extemporary; *extemporal.** The first is the usual form in AmE, the second in BrE (closing up, in English, the Latin phrase *ex tempore*). The others are NEEDLESS VARIANTS.

extemporaneously; extempore, adv. In AmE, the latter is the Latin-lover's (or Anglophile's) NEEDLESS VARIANT of the former. Like the adjective, the adverb *extempore* is usual in BrE.

extempore, adj.; ***extemporary.** See **extemporaneous.**

extemporize. See **temporize** (B).

extendable; extendible; extensible. Though dictionaries are split between *extendable* and *extendible*, the *-able* spelling is much more natural-looking and much more common. It ought to be preferred. *Extensible*, surprisingly enough, has been the most common of these three adjectives since about 1800. It is especially common in metaphorical uses <extensible markup> and technical ones <extensible membranes>. See -ABLE (A).

LANGUAGE-CHANGE INDEX (For the full key, see front matter pp. xxxi, l–li.)
Stage 1: Rejected. **Stage 2:** Widely shunned. **Stage 3:** Widespread but . . . **Stage 4:** Ubiquitous but . . . **Stage 5:** Fully accepted.
Invariably inferior forms marked by asterisk (*). • Ratios represent frequency of prevalent forms vs. variants in current books.

extension. So spelled—not **extention*. For a similar misspelling (**dissention* for *dissension*), see **dissent,** n.
    Current ratio (*extension* vs. **extention*): 997:1

extenuate (= to lessen the seriousness of [something bad] by partial excuse) should be used only of the fault that is minimized, not of the person who committed it. The *OED* cites improper uses (so labeled) such as "The pursuer's steward . . . *extenuated* himself calmly enough," in which the word is used as if it meant "to extenuate the guilt of; to plead partial excuses for" (*OED*).

extenuating circumstance (= a fact or situation that makes one's actions seem more understandable and less blameworthy) is sometimes confused with *attenuating circumstance* (= an intervening event, including the passage of time, that weakens the connection between two other events). Both are usually legal phrases.
    The first phrase is far more common than the second. In American legal contexts, an *extenuating circumstance* may reduce the severity of punishment. By extension, it denotes any situation that ameliorates some negative outcome that one expects or fears—e.g.: "Citing *extenuating circumstances*, officials said two players who do not technically meet Little League requirements as Harlem residents can play anyway." Stephanie Saul & Joshua Robin, "Harlem Squad Gets OK to Play," *Chicago Trib.*, 16 Aug. 2002, Sports §, at 1.
    In European courts, *attenuating circumstance* is used in the same sense that *extenuating circumstance* is used in U.S. courts—e.g.: "According to precedents from the Nuremberg war crimes trial, a defense of following orders from higher authorities can be considered an *attenuating circumstance* for crimes committed in wartime." Edward Cody, "French Court Asked to Sentence 'Torturer' Barbie to Life in Prison," *Wash. Post*, 1 July 1987, at C1.
    But in U.S. law, *attenuating circumstance* is used only when the prosecution is trying to get evidence admitted despite its connection with "tainted" evidence—material obtained by unconstitutional means. If the connection is direct, the second piece of evidence is suppressed. Yet if the connection is *attenuated* (weak or weakened), the second piece of evidence is admissible—e.g.: "In this case there were no *attenuating circumstances* to cure the lingering infirmity of the warrantless residential arrest." "Police Version of Events Disbelieved; Arrest in Home Is Deemed Unlawful," *N.Y.L.J.*, 28 May 1996, at 25.
    Because the terms sound similar, writers occasionally use *attenuating* where *extenuating* is the intended word. And here the problem seems even worse, *attenuating* being misused for *aggravating*: "The *attenuating* [read *aggravating*] circumstances that contributed to this staggering number of executions don't help soften the shocking fact that we're tops in our country and that we surpass, on a per capita basis, two nations that are notorious for their

disregard for human life." Raoul Carubelli, "Notorious Number," *Daily Oklahoman*, 2 Jan. 2002, at A6. See DOUBLE BOBBLES.

LANGUAGE-CHANGE INDEX
attenuate misused for *aggravate*: Stage 1

external. See **extraneous.**

extinguishment; extinction. Both words are nouns corresponding to the verb *extinguish*. *Extinguishment* usually refers to the process <extinguishment of the fire> and *extinction* to the resultant state <extinction of a species>. In financial contexts, it is common to refer to the *extinguishment of debt*.

extol (= to praise highly) is so spelled—e.g.: "Now [Justin] Raimondo runs a Web site called antiwar .com, in which he *extols* the good old days of the America First Movement." Ronald Radosh, "The Red and the Brown," *Boston Globe*, 13 Oct. 2002, at D1. The word is sometimes misspelled **extoll*. Cf. **dispel, excel** & **expel.**
    Occasionally the word is misused as if to mean "condemn highly"—e.g.:

- "Unfortunately, the American Academy of Pediatrics (AAP) is publishing a new book in December, *Guide to Your Child's Sleep*, that *extols* [read *warns about*] the dangers of the family bed. Fortunately, I know better, but I grieve for the new parents who will be sorely confused by this nonsense." Peggy O'Mara, "It's None of Their Business," *Mothering*, 1 Nov. 1999, at 6.
- "The lyric *extols* [read *decries*] some of the evils in the world, but [Scott] Krippayne adds that what he thinks probably grieves God most is if we 'grow numb to injustice.'" Deborah Evans Price, "Higher Ground," *Billboard*, 19 May 2001, at 51.
- "She says hello to everyone she passes, *extols* [read *condemns*] the evils of development to those who will listen and marvels over the great blue herons and egrets as if she's seeing them for the first time." Kimi Yoshino, "Victory Lap of Sorts for Supporters of Bolsa Chica Wetlands Restoration," *L.A. Times*, 19 Nov. 2001, Cal. §, pt. 2, at 4.

The word is pronounced /ik-**stohl**/.

LANGUAGE-CHANGE INDEX
extol misused for *condemn* or *decry*: Stage 1

*extorsive. See **extortionate.**

*extorter. See **extortionist.**

extortion; bribery. These terms are sometimes confounded. *Extortion* = (1) the corrupt obtaining of something of value by illegal means, such as force or coercion; or (2) the offense committed by a public official who illegally obtains something of value by using his or her office. *Bribery* = the giving or promising of something of value to an officer in return for corrupt behavior. If the briber takes the initiative, it is bribery; if the bribee takes the initiative, it is extortion.

extortionate; *extortionary; *extortive; *extorsive. *Extortionate* (= [1] given to or characterized by extortion; or [2] [of prices] exorbitant) has been the standard term since the late 18th century. The others are NEEDLESS VARIANTS. E.g.:

- "Phanor Arizabaleta, considered No. 5 in the [Cali] syndicate, was convicted and sentenced for *extorsive* [read *extortionate*] kidnapping Tuesday by a regional judge in Cali, the chief prosecutor's office said." "Datelines," *Deseret News* (Salt Lake City), 16 Apr. 1997, at A4.
- "The alleged misconduct includes mismanagement of funds, *extortive* [read *extortionate*] conduct and abuse of power." Richard Marosi, "Police Officer Files Whistle-Blower Lawsuit Against the LAPD," *L.A. Times*, 9 Oct. 2002 (Home ed.), Cal. Metro §, pt. 2, at 3.
- "But last Saturday, the first day the museum was open to the public, attendees paid an *extortionary* [read *extortionate*] fee for an experience that, for many, was probably not all that different from their first sexual encounter—lots of buildup, and just like that, it's over." Kevin Canfield, "That Empty Feeling After New York's MoSex," *Hartford Courant*, 10 Oct. 2002, at D1.

Current ratio (in order of headwords): 718:22:14:1

extortionist; *extortioner; *extorter. From 1750 until the 1960s, **extortioner* was standard and held the field. In 1968, *extortionist* surpassed it in AmE (in frequency of use in print sources, that is), and in 1990 the same thing happened in BrE. *Extortionist* is now standard. The others await their ransoms.

Current ratio (in order of headwords): 19:12:1

EXTRA- (= lying outside the province or scope of) is a prefix that, during the 20th century, has formed hundreds of new adjectives—mostly for learned or literary purposes. The prefix has been adopted by many writers to form NEOLOGISMS not yet found in unabridged dictionaries. These writers usually do no harm and, in fact, occasionally coin useful words. Following are four representative examples of 20th-century neologisms using this prefix—which, by the way, usually takes no hyphen:

- "This means that he studies telepathy, clairvoyance and other *extrasensory* phenomena, although, he explains, 'I don't have any parapsychological powers.'" Lynne Ames, "About Westchester," *N.Y. Times*, 4 Apr. 1982, § 11, at 2.
- "In a 1966 HBR article, Felix Kaufman implored general managers to think beyond their own organizational boundaries to the possibilities of *extracorporate* systems." James I. Cash Jr. & Benn R. Konsynski, "IS Redraws Competitive Boundaries," *Harv. Bus. Rev.*, Mar.–Apr. 1985, at 134.
- "And 'Surfiction,' in *Fever*, fashions a collage from a professor's *extratextual* meanderings and a post-structuralist dissection of a work by Charles Chestnut." Sven Birkets, Book Rev., *New Republic*, 13 July 1992, at 42.
- "Someday, some enterprising historian will have to do an investigation into the *extramusical* reasons that we were sold a bill of goods on a small group of then-young players around Isaac Stern—Zubin Mehta, Daniel Barenboim, Pinchas Zukerman and so on—and were somehow convinced they were the best and the brightest." Tim Page, "Mostly Mozart Is Its Own Best Argument," *Newsday* (N.Y.), 5 Aug. 1994, at B17.

extract. See **extricate.**

extradite = (1) to surrender or deliver (a fugitive) to another jurisdiction; or (2) to obtain the surrender of (a fugitive) from another jurisdiction (*Black's Law Dictionary* 704 [10th ed. 2014]). Embarrassingly enough, the word is often wrongly thought to be related to *indict*. In fact, though, the roots are entirely different: *extradite* derives from L. *ex-* "from" and *traditio* "the act of handing over," whereas *indict* derives from the Anglo-French *enditer* "to write down." See **indict.**

But instances of the mistaken **extradict* and **extradiction* are legion—e.g.:

- "Prosecutors argued that . . . he had jumped bail after a 1984 Federal mail-fraud conviction and disappeared for nine years until being found and *extradicted* [read *extradited*] from Europe last year. . . . She said he lived in Africa and Europe until being found in Amsterdam and *extradicted* [read *extradited*] to the United States in February 1993." Robert D. McFadden, "Big Spender Is Charged with Fraud on Welfare," *N.Y. Times*, 7 Oct. 1994, at B1.
- "He was *extradicted* [read *extradited*] from Ohio in May 1995 after being sentenced to death for the stomping and beating death of an elderly Toledo man." Carol Demare, "Defendant Tells Jury He's Already on Death Row," *Times Union* (Albany), 27 Sept. 1996, at B4.
- "EU arrest warrants, introduced in 2004, have been used with increasing regularity in a variety of cases and allow for quick *extradiction* [read *extradition*] of suspects to their home countries." Toby Helm & Jamie Doward, "Megan Case Sparks Row as Police Warn Cameron on Europe-Wide Crime Fight," *Observer*, 30 Sept. 2012, Home News §, at 3.

LANGUAGE-CHANGE INDEX
*extradict for *extradite*: Stage 1
Current ratio (*extradited* vs. **extradicted*): 225:1

extraneous; extrinsic; external. These words are closely related. *Extraneous* = (1) not essential or inherent <she used her discretion in adding some extraneous ingredients>; (2) not relevant <he talked at length about extraneous issues>; or (3) coming from outside <extraneous matter>.

Extrinsic, which shares senses 1 and 3 of *extraneous*, primarily means "not inherent"; it is the usual antonym of *intrinsic* (= belonging to the essential nature of something). E.g.: "[In] American culture, in [de Tocqueville's] view, . . . artistic standards would be determined not by the *intrinsic* quality of the art but by the *extrinsic* size of the audience." Robert Brustein, "The Decline of High Culture," *New Republic*, 3 Nov. 1997, at 29.

External means simply "outer, exterior." It's the usual antonym of *internal*—e.g.: "Just as controversy embroiled its birth, the state of Israel is again racked by *internal* divisions and *external* dilemmas with its 50th anniversary fast approaching." Storer H. Rowley, "Anniversary Prompts Soul-Searching," *Chicago Trib.*, 29 Nov. 1997, at 4.

extraordinary is preferably pronounced with five syllables (/ek-**stror**-di-ner-ee/), not six (/ek-strə-**or**-di-ner-ee/). See PRONUNCIATION (B).

extreme unction. See **last rites.**

extricate; extract. One *extracts* (= draws forth) something from a person or a thing. One *extricates* (= removes) a person (or, rarely, a thing) from a tangled encumbrance or situation.

extrinsic. See **extraneous.**

extrovert (= one whose interests are outwardly directed for the most part, often tending toward social activities) is now accepted as the standard spelling. *Extravert*, though modeled directly on the German etymon, has been nothing but a variant in English since the mid-1920s.

This is unfortunate because *extrovert* is a MORPHO-LOGICAL DEFORMITY, the *-o-* having come from a misguided attempt at paralleling *introvert*. (See **intro-vert.**) The Latin prefixes are *intro-* and *extra-*. But it's now too late: the forms are set in English.

exuberant. A. And *exorbitant*. *Exuberant* = (1) having extremely high spirits; gushingly enthusiastic; or (2) flamboyant; overelaborate. *Exorbitant* = exceeding a reasonable or appropriate amount. Although some dictionaries record an extra sense for *exuberant* (also "extreme" or "very great"), when the adjective refers to a monetary amount the correct word is *exorbitant*—e.g.:

- "Navarro . . . warns that some less-experienced Santeros have lost sight of the religion's significance and placed more emphasis on charging *exuberant* [read *exorbitant*] fees for their services." Ralph R. Ortega, "Followers Seek Respect for Santeria," *Asbury Park Press* (Neptune, N.J.), 20 Apr. 1997, at AA1.
- "Empty stands translate to fans saying we are not going to pay *exuberant* [read *exorbitant*] prices to watch whiny high-priced, watered-down talent." Gregg Ebbert, "Empty Seats Tell Story of Baseball," *Morning Call* (Allentown, Pa.), 8 May 1997, at B4.
- "Originally designed by Bernard Lipfert for the Ideal Novelty and Toy Company, these rare composition dolls command an *exuberant* [read *exorbitant*] price on the secondary market." Denise I. O'Neal, "Youthful Indulgences," *Chicago Sun-Times*, 16 May 1997, Weekend §, at 3.

B. Misspelled. *Exuberant* is fairly commonly misspelled *exhuberant*—e.g.:

- "The little Church of the Resurrection on the Catherine Canal, with its nine domes and its enamels, mosaics, and gilding in the *exhuberant* [read *exuberant*] Russian seventeenth-century style, strikes one as a curiosity imported from abroad." Clarence Brown, *Mandelstam* 10 (1973).
- "Unlike Washington Park's garden on the Downing Street side, famed for its large flower beds and *exhuberant* [read *exuberant*] colors, this garden is meant to be a place of tranquility and serenity." Joanne Ditmer, "Garden Will Honor Public Parks Donors," *Denver Post*, 5 Oct. 1996, at E1.

LANGUAGE-CHANGE INDEX
exuberant misspelled *exhuberant*: Stage 1
Current ratio: 449:1

exult makes the noun *exultation*. But there are two NEEDLESS VARIANTS: *exultance* and *exultancy*. E.g.:

- "There is a quality of complete technical proficiency, every movement controlled and finished, and an *exultance* [read *exultation*] in dance for its own sake—even before it is harnessed to the service of choreography." Mary Clarke, "The Gift of Graft," *Guardian*, 3 Mar. 1994, Features §, at 7.
- "There is no place like it, no place with an atom of its glory, pride, and *exultancy* [read *exultation*]." Alexander Wolff, "Last Spring, the Newly Unretired Michael Jordan Lit Up Manhattan," *Sports Illustrated*, 13 Nov. 1995, at 108.

For the difference between *exult* and *exalt*, see **exalt.**

eyeing; *eying*. The first is the preferred spelling.

eye of the storm. This allusion refers to the center of a tropical storm, which is remarkable for its calm winds and blue skies. Writers usually employ the phrase accurately to denote serenity in the midst of chaos—e.g.: "In *Eye of Storm*, [Tony] Dungy Calmly Sails to Victory." Headline, *Baltimore Sun*, 5 Feb. 2007, Sports §, at D1.

But often, the sense is just the opposite, denoting a state of chaos at the center of a raging controversy—e.g.: "Fast forward to the 2000 presidential election, with Harris in the *eye of the storm* [read *center of the controversy*]—vilified as a witch, praised as a hero, both of which were undeserved." Thomas Tryon, "Katherine Harris' Own Party Had a Key Role in Her Swift Descent," *Sarasota Herald-Trib.*, 12 Nov. 2006, at F1.

LANGUAGE-CHANGE INDEX
eye of the storm misused to mean "center of controversy": Stage 1

eyes peeled. The phrase is so spelled, though some erroneously make it *eyes pealed*—e.g.:

- "The mug can be lifted to the mouth, a necessity during the Super Bowl, when all eyes are *pealed* [read *peeled* or, better yet, *fixed*] on the television and not watching where soup may be dripping." Jo Northrop, "Filling Mugs with Meals," *Wash. Post*, 26 Jan. 1983, at E10. (*Fixed* is the better choice because the CLICHÉ [*eyes peeled*] means "watchful," not "focused.")
- "Fans should keep their eyes *pealed* [read *peeled*] for a sneaky glimpse of an American billionaire disguised beneath a Stetson." Mat Kendrick, "Five Ways to Beat the Finalday Monotony," *Birmingham Mail* (U.K.), 9 May 2015, Sport §, at 78.
- "They will keep your eyes *pealed* [read *peeled* or, better, *glued*] to the sky as they perform their formation flying routine." "Radio Control Flying Circus to Land at Butler County Airport," *Cincinnati Enquirer*, 2 July 2015, at S6.

LANGUAGE-CHANGE INDEX
eyes pealed for *eyes peeled*: Stage 1
Current ratio (*eyes peeled* vs. *eyes pealed*): 72:1

eyewitness is spelled as one word, not two. Avoid *eyeball witness*—e.g.: "*Eyeball witnesses* [read *Eyewitnesses*] can estimate the speed of a car in an accident or the value of the family home or other owned real estate. For the most part, however, the law confines people to testimony about what they actually saw or heard." Martin Paskind, "Courts Get New Rules on Expert Testimony," *Albuquerque J.*, 19 Jan. 1998, at 10.

Sometimes, of course, the folksy phrase can be humorous—e.g.: "A number of readers wrote to assure me that horned toads when threatened can indeed shoot blood from their eyes. The trick was seen by *eyeball witnesses*—early Spanish explorers to modern scientists." Kent Biffle, "Hunting the Toad?" *Dallas Morning News*, 29 Apr. 2001, Texas & SW §, at A45.

LANGUAGE-CHANGE INDEX
eyeball witness for *eyewitness*: Stage 1
Current ratio (*eyewitness* vs.
eyeball witness): 4,009:1

eyrie (= [1] the nest of a predatory bird, esp. one built on a crag or precipice, [2] the brood within such a nest, or [3] by extension, a human habitation, whether hovel or fortress, in a high place) has long been the standard spelling in all varieties of English. In the 18th century, the spelling was **aery*, or sometimes **eyry*. In the 19th and 20th centuries, *aerie* became fairly common, especially in AmE. Although *eyrie* has predominated almost universally since about 1850 in English-language print sources, American lexicographers have tended to list the main headword at *aerie*. But so does the OED, which notes that "the spelling *eyrie* seems to have been introduced by [Henry] Spelman" in a glossary of 1664 "to support his notion of its derivation from egg." Yet because no etymology for this word is certain—*W11* suggests a relation to the Vulgar Latin *agrum* "nest"—the lexicographers have avoided the *eyrie* spelling. As the *OED* remarks under E, this is "now the commonest spelling." Regardless of the spelling, the word is pronounced either /**air**-ee/ or /**eer**-ee/.

Current ratio (*eyrie* vs. *aerie* vs. **aery* vs.
*eyry): 10:5:3:1

F

facade is pronounced /fə-**sahd**/. Today the cedilla beneath the *-c-* (*façade*) is usually dropped. See DIACRITICAL MARKS.

facet, vb., makes *faceted* and *faceting* in AmE and BrE alike. *Facetted* and *facetting* are secondary variants. See SPELLING (B).

face up to. See PHRASAL VERBS.

facile /**fas**-əl/. Always meaning "easy" in one sense or another, this word may connote either proficiency or shallowness. The writer must achieve clarity through context. Sometimes the word connotes the ease that comes with artistic mastery—e.g.: "Nicolai Dobrev played the jester, a noble baritone with a *facile* instrument." Keith Powers, "Teatro Lirico Shines in Performance of Dark Verdi Comedy," *Boston Herald*, 30 Mar. 2002, Arts & Life §, at 26. More often, it connotes triteness or oversimplification—e.g.: "But most mental health experts say closure is no holy grail, only rendered so by people seeking *facile* solutions to complex problems." Samar Farah, "Lots of People Are Looking for It. But What Exactly Do They Hope to Find?" *Christian Science Monitor*, 28 Mar. 2002, Features §, at 13.

facilitate (= to aid, help, ease) is a FORMAL WORD to be used sparingly because it is often jargonistic. So is the agent noun *facilitator* (= helper; teacher; seminar leader), as the telltale quotation marks in the following examples suggest:

- "Everett Clark, chairman of the Education 2000 Task Force, mentioned the meeting after a presentation to council members from the group's new '*facilitator*,'

Andrea Tannenbaum. The council hired Tannenbaum for $10,000 through the end of the year to guide the task force." Lizabeth Hall, "Citizen Task Force, School Board Plan Talks in Bloomfield," *Hartford Courant*, 29 Oct. 1996, at B1.

- "Poking fun at a system that calls teachers '*facilitators*' and uses the euphemism 'extensions' for homework is just too easy." Mark Pino, "Celebration's a Spot for Fun in a Fishbowl," *Orlando Sentinel*, 20 Dec. 1996, Osceola §, at 1.

- "The seminar's two '*facilitators*'—doctors who are present only to nudge the deliberations in certain directions—ease the students through the various options, trying to get them to understand that it is not enough for a doctor to simply diagnose DKA caused by patient noncompliance." Jim Atkinson, "So Much to Learn, So Little Time," *Texas Monthly*, Jan. 1997, at 118.

As H.W. Fowler and others have noted, it's better to write that an *action* rather than the *actor* is facilitated (*FMEU1* at 164). Hence *The return of refugees must be facilitated by the international community*, not **Refugees must be facilitated in their return by the international community*. Of course, using active voice facilitates framing a better sentence: *The international community must facilitate the return of refugees*. See PASSIVE VOICE.

facilitator. See VOGUE WORDS.

facility. This word is surplusage in phrases such as *jail facility* and *museum facility*—e.g.: "Airports that aren't well-served by airline clubs or that don't have major *hotel facilities* [read *hotels*] nearby will put in conference rooms of their own, he predicted." Carol Smith, "Companies Meet Each Other at the Airport,"

LANGUAGE-CHANGE INDEX (For the full key, see front matter pp. xxxi, l–li.)
Stage 1: Rejected. **Stage 2:** Widely shunned. **Stage 3:** Widespread but . . . **Stage 4:** Ubiquitous but . . . **Stage 5:** Fully accepted.
Invariably inferior forms marked by asterisk (*). • Ratios represent frequency of prevalent forms vs. variants in current books.

L.A. Times, 20 July 1995, at D5. And sometimes the word is a EUPHEMISM for *building*—e.g.: "The Fort Lauderdale development firm that bought the rest of the mall complex 16 months ago—including the main mall *facility* [read *building*], a nearby strip shopping center and the former Sam's Wholesale Club building—is studying redevelopment plans." Catherine Crownover, "'Demalling' for Economic Survival," *Fla. Times-Union*, 28 Oct. 1996, at 10. On the variation between *facility* and *building* in that sentence, see INELEGANT VARIATION.

Not only is *facility* often unnecessary; it has also become virtually meaningless. The word is so abstract that it refers to just about anything, from an Olympic village to a toilet.

facsimile transmission. See **fax.**

fact, adj. See **factual.**

fact, n. **A. *Fact of the matter.*** This FLOTSAM PHRASE occasionally serves well in speech—to fill up space while the speaker thinks of what to say next—but generally has no justification in writing.

> Current ratio (*fact is that* vs. **fact of the matter is that*): 8:1

B. *Fact that.* It is imprudent to say, as some have, that this phrase should never be used. At times it cannot reasonably be avoided <they ignored the fact that all the elections had been against them>. One writer has suggested that *because* will usually suffice for *the fact that*. Vigilans [Eric Partridge], *Chamber of Horrors* 63 (1952). Yet rarely, if ever, is *because* a good substitute for that phrase (as opposed to the longer phrase *because of the fact that*)—e.g.: "*The fact that* singer-songwriters like Sarah McLachlan and Jewel have managed to break through the homogenized slop that record companies are distributing does not mean that music or women have been liberated." Letter of Elizabeth Van Rij, "The Gals Take Over," *Time*, 11 Aug. 1997, at 5.

When *the fact that* can easily be avoided, it should be—e.g.: "Aniston, who still admits a yen for Big Macs and mayo-on-white-bread sandwiches, objects to *the fact that* [read *the way*] 'Hollywood puts pressure on women to be thin.'" Samantha Miller & Craig Tomashoff, "Jennifer's Prime Time," *People*, 11 Aug. 1997, at 98. (See FLOTSAM PHRASES.) But sometimes it's all but inescapable—e.g.: "He has learned to laugh again at little ironies, such as *the fact that* he, unlike several of his rescuers, did not get poison ivy that day." Don Colburn, "Robert Griffith Lost One Leg in a Construction Accident on August 17th," *Wash. Post*, 23 Sept. 1997, at Z12.

C. *In actual fact.* Apart from being a moderate pomposity for *actually*, this phrase is a REDUNDANCY: all facts are actual, just as they are all true (see (E)). When one is uncertain of the truth of allegations, then there might be "alleged facts," as opposed to "actual facts." Aside from that situation, though, shun the phrase in formal prose. Teall's 1940 ruling still holds:

"Open to challenge in writing supposed to be done with skill and deliberation, the expression [*in actual fact*] is entirely pardonable in ordinary conversation or in familiar writing. It is used to emphasize the reality of the stated fact. The word 'fact' has become very weak." Edward N. Teall, *Putting Words to Work* 277 (1940).

D. *In point of fact.* This phrase is verbose for *in fact* or *actually*—e.g.: "*In point of fact* [read *In fact*], as Michael Waller notes on today's Op-ed page, Russian Prime Minister Victor Chernomyrdin specifically warned Vice President Gore in a letter against rushing the process with other countries before ratification by the two most important signatories, Russia and the United States." "Don't Rush the Chemical Weapons Treaty," *Wash. Times*, 4 Mar. 1997, at A20.

E. **True facts.*** This is a common REDUNDANCY, especially in legal writing—e.g.:

- "Two Sandwich teachers accused of showing a sexually explicit foreign film to a class of seventh-graders say they have done nothing wrong and are being fired from their jobs without the *true facts* [read *facts* or *truth*] of the incident being revealed." Tom Farmer, "2 Teachers Who Showed Racy Movie Crying Foul," *Boston Herald*, 20 Nov. 1997, at 18.
- "But it's a *true fact* [read *fact*] that my maternal grandmother was sent to her grave by the egg salad at a Methodist church picnic." C.W. Gusewelle, "Don't Try to Snuff Out Stuffing," *Kansas City Star*, 25 Nov. 1997, at B2.
- "Has he forgotten that Japanese schoolchildren are still not being taught the *true facts* [read *truth*] of what happened in the Far East during that dreadful period in history?" Campbell Thomson, "Japan Must Stop the Airbrushing of History If Progress Is to Be Made," *Herald* (Glasgow), 7 July 2015, at 15.

Writers debase the word when they qualify *facts* with an adjective like *true* or *incorrect*. We ought to be able to rely on the facts being facts, instead of having to wonder whether the writer failed to describe what kind of facts they are. Cf. (C) above.

LANGUAGE-CHANGE INDEX

*true facts for *facts*: Stage 2

Current ratio (*the facts* vs. *the true facts): 136:1

factional; factious; fractious. These words are confusingly similar. *Factional* = of, relating to, or involving a faction or factions. E.g.: "*Factional* fighting has dragged the people of Somalia's capital back to the darkest days of the civil war in 1992." Greg Barrow, "300 Killed in Somalia's Week of War," *Guardian*, 20 Dec. 1996, at 12. *Factious* = given to faction; acting for partisan purposes. E.g.: "Louisiana Democrats are *factious* as well. Their division is largely along racial lines." Jack Wardlaw, "GOP Renewal," *Times-Picayune* (New Orleans), 18 Aug. 1996, at B7. *Fractious* = refractory, unruly, fretful, peevish. E.g.: "Perhaps . . . [Jewish and Christian] cultures and traditions are not really that far apart. After all, we all get frayed and *fractious* at Christmas." "Let Children Sing Carols and Light the Menorah," *Independent*, 20 Dec. 1996, at 17.

factitious; fictitious. Both have the basic sense "artificial." *Factitious* = (1) produced artificially by human intervention; not natural; or (2) produced by contrivance; sham. Sense 1 tends to be confined to technical contexts—e.g.: "*Factitious* panniculitis, caused by self-injury, constitutes a real prospect when the patient appears to have undue secondary gain from the ailment." Henry Schneiderman, "Young Woman with Spots on Shins," *Consultant*, July 1996, at 1501. Sense 2 appears in nonspecialized writing—e.g.: "At first I thought the comment was *factitious*, but the anger and emotion on his face indicated otherwise." Jim Monaghan, " 'Last Man Standing' Campaign Tactic Is Killing Colorado Politics," *Denver Post*, 2 Nov. 1996, at B7.

Fictitious = imaginary; not real. For the difference between *fictitious* and its two close allies, *fictional* and *fictive*, see **fictional.**

factitious disorder. For this phrase as a euphemism for *malingering*, see EUPHEMISMS.

factlet. See **factoid** (B).

fact of the matter. See **fact** (A).

factoid. A. Contradictory Senses. *Factoid* = (1) an assertion that, although widely accepted as factual, is not or may not be true; or (2) an isolated, usu. surprising fact; an interesting bit of trivia. Sense 1 dates from the early 1970s. A decade later, sense 2 arose with the launch of *USA Today*. Some people object to this sense because the *-oid* suffix generally denotes a resemblance to something but not the thing itself (e.g., a humanoid isn't human; an asteroid isn't a star; an ovoid is shaped like—but isn't—an egg; etc.).

Norman Mailer seems to have coined the term in his 1973 biography *Marilyn* to mean "a fact that has no existence before appearing in a magazine, newspaper, or other mass-media outlet." It was this original sense that the speaker here quoted had in mind: " 'Washington at the moment is full of *factoids*, unsubstantiated statements repeated often enough that they take on the color of facts,' said Malcolm Wallop, a Wyoming Republican." Susan F. Rasky, "Decision on Tower as Elusive as Facts," *N.Y. Times*, 13 Feb. 1989, at B6.

But in the early 1980s the term was appropriated by *USA Today* for the kind of easy-to-digest news element that is the hallmark of that paper and later media such as *CNN Headline News*. The transformation in the public's perception of the word *factoid* was almost instantaneous, as this quotation—made a week after *USA Today* began publishing—attests:

> To read USA Today is to subject oneself to information overload. In charts, boxes, graphs, lists, roundups, maps, it subjects the reader to a bombardment of facts. That most of them are of absolutely no moment is not the point; USA Today understands that Americans love information, statistics, trivia—that they mistake data for knowledge, gossip for news—and it offers all in abundance. Reading it

is a numbing, exhausting experience, so relentless is the onslaught of *factoids*.
>
> Jonathan Yardley, "A Paper for a U.S.A. on the Go," *Wash. Post*, 20 Sept. 1982, at C1.

Today sense 2 is nearly universal and must be accepted as standard—e.g.:

- "It's filled with interesting *factoids*: 'Beadin' a Path to Buffalo' is covered with 75,000 glass beads; the 'Penny for Your Thoughts' used 20,300 pennies; and 'Chia Buffalo' drinks more water than a live buffalo ever would." Paula Voell, "Just Buffalo," *Buffalo News*, 21 Nov. 2000, at D1 (referring to various works of art).
- "*Factoid*: The number of tourists visiting metro Orlando rose 31 percent during the past five years." Richard Verrier, "Orlando Folks Run Nebraska Museum," *Orlando Sentinel*, 11 Dec. 2000, at 8.
- "*Factoid*: One part per million equates to one second in 11 1/2 days. One part per billion equates to one second in 32 years. And one part per trillion is the same as one second in 32,000 years." *San Diego Union-Trib.*, 13 Dec. 2000, at F2.

LANGUAGE-CHANGE INDEX
factoid in reference to an interesting fact: Stage 5

B. And *factlet*. The loss of *factoid* in sense 1 is unfortunate in another way, too: there is already a perfectly good term for a piece of trivia—*factlet*. While it is etymologically more correct (since *-let* is a diminutive suffix), it is far rarer today than *factoid*. But it does still appear, even (as the first example shows) in the source of *factoid*'s sense 2—e.g.:

- "All assessments of Gore's future seem to include the obligatory *factlet* that since Martin Van Buren, no sitting vice president other than George Bush has been directly elected president." Walter Shapiro, "Gore vs. Bradley: Get Ready to Rumble," *USA Today*, 9 June 1999, at A2.
- "The home page of the campaign's Web site, www.whatwouldjesusdrive.org, features a portrait of a prayerful Jesus with a caption that changes each time a visitor logs on with a new *factlet* about our wasteful driving habits." Tom Brazaitis, "Can Any Car Be Anointed a Holy Roller?" *Plain Dealer* (Cleveland), 17 Nov. 2002, at H3. (Does the visitor have to supply a *factlet* in order to log on, or does the website show a random *factlet* when the visitor logs on? See MISCUES (B).)

Current ratio (*factoids* vs. *factlets*): 123:1

factor, n., traditionally means "an agent or cause that contributes to a particular result." By SLIPSHOD EXTENSION, it has taken on the sense "a thing to be considered; an event or occurrence." It's often a symptom of verbosity—e.g.: "The index rates suppliers *according to factors including* [read *by their*] flexibility and their importance to the business." John Riley, "Top Suppliers Score Low in TIF User Poll," *Computer Weekly*, 20 May 1999.

factotum (= [1] a general servant with myriad duties, or [2] a jack-of-all-trades) forms the plural *factotums*,

LANGUAGE-CHANGE INDEX (For the full key, see front matter pp. xxxi, l–li.)
Stage 1: Rejected. **Stage 2:** Widely shunned. **Stage 3:** Widespread but . . . **Stage 4:** Ubiquitous but . . . **Stage 5:** Fully accepted.
Invariably inferior forms marked by asterisk (*). • Ratios represent frequency of prevalent forms vs. variants in current books.

not **factota*. (See PLURALS (B).) But some writers use the Latin plural as an affectation—e.g.:

- "The presence of the *factota* [read *factotums*] of the new world order on Egyptian soil will be seen as approval . . . of Cairo's indiscriminate war against its own Islamic extremists." "Sharm School," *New Republic*, 1 Apr. 1996, at 8.
- "*All of* [read *All*] the attempts were made by *factota* [read *factotums*] who didn't reveal they were working on a book for Sommers." Alex Beam, "Atlantic Piece Takes Swipe at Harvard Prof," *Boston Globe*, 19 May 2000, at D1.

The word is pronounced /fak-**toh**-təm/.

LANGUAGE-CHANGE INDEX
*factota for *factotums*: Stage 1
Current ratio (*factotums* vs. **factota*): 19:1

fact that. See fact (B).

factual; fact, adj. In phrases such as *fact(ual) question*, the longer form is preferable. The phrase *fact question* can be slightly jarring; more important, it can mislead readers. In the following sentence, for instance, the use of *factual* would have circumvented the reader's thinking either that *fact* is a noun or that *existence of fact* is an unhyphenated PHRASAL ADJECTIVE: "The court held that . . . the *existence of fact issues* [read *existence of factual issues*] made summary judgment inappropriate." "Individual Rights," *Conn. Law Trib.*, 23 Aug. 1993, at L9.

The sentences that follow illustrate the better usage:

- "The referee will hear the case, make *factual findings* and, depending on the outcome, recommend discipline." Jim Ross, "Former Judge Faces Bar Charges," *St. Petersburg Times*, 30 Dec. 1994, Citrus Times §, at 1.
- "High courts seldom second-guess lower courts on *factual findings*, Foley said." Susan Essoyan & Bettina Boxall, "Gay Marriages on Hold While Ruling Is Appealed," *L.A. Times*, 5 Dec. 1996, at A3.

Notably, *factual* has two meanings: (1) "of or involving facts" <factual issue>; and (2) "true" <a factual depiction>. Sense 1 is the one that appears in phrases such as *factual finding* and *factual question*. Sense 2 appears in phrases such as *factual account* and *factual narrative*—e.g.: "All in all, 'The Woman Behind the Myth' offers a good *factual* account of Evita's life—but no great insight." "A&E's 'Evita' Combines Woman with Myth," *Charleston Gaz.*, 19 Dec. 1996, at D8.

faecal. See fecal.

faerie = (1) fairyland; or (2) a fairy. Sense 1 is archaic, sense 2 unnecessary except as a fancy spelling. Because the word isn't generally needed, the variant spelling **faery* (to be avoided) merits only the barest mention.

faint, vb.; **feint,** vb. Both verbs are pronounced /faynt/. To *faint* is to lose consciousness suddenly after experiencing a temporary decrease of blood to the brain <he faints at the sight of blood>. To *feint* is to make a movement signaling one action before taking another <the boxer feinted with his left and then struck with his right>.

fair. A. And *fare*. Properly an adjective or noun, *fair* is sometimes misused for the verb *fare* (= [1] to experience good or bad fortune or treatment; or [2] to happen or turn out)—e.g.:

- "While [Tim] Couch didn't *fair* [read *fare*] too badly at Cleveland's recent mini-camp, the most impressive rookie was running back Madre Hill." Alex Marvez, "Enshrining Elway Will Have to Wait," *Rocky Mountain News* (Denver), 2 May 1999, at C24.
- "Is there any surprise NASA would *fair* [read *fare*] poorly?" Dave Weldon, "Flaws in NASA Poll," *Orlando Sentinel*, 16 Mar. 2002, at A25.
- "The Illini won six of their last eight games, defeated two NCAA Tournament teams in the process and *faired* [read *fared*] well in the Big Ten tournament." Patricia Babcock McGraw, "Illini Softball Left Out in the Cold Again," *Daily Herald* (Chicago), 18 May 2002, Sports §, at 1.

LANGUAGE-CHANGE INDEX
fair misused for *fare*: Stage 1
Current ratio (*fared well* vs. **faired well*): 23:1

B. *Bid fair*. For the past tense of this PHRASAL VERB, see bid (A).

Fairbanksan; Fairbanksian. The first is standard. The second is a variant form for the noun—but it is standard as an adjective <Fairbanksian weather>. See DENIZEN LABELS.

fait accompli (= something accomplished and not now changeable), from French, makes the plural *faits accomplis*. E.g.: "But in the view of the palace, by presenting her demands as *faits accomplis*, Diana was limiting Charles's room to bargain." Jerry Adler & Daniel Pedersen, "Diana's Battle Royal," *Newsweek*, 11 Mar. 1996, at 20. See PLURALS (B).

The singular and plural forms are pronounced identically: /**fayt** ə-kom-**plee**/ or /**fet** ə-kom-**plee**/.

faker; fakir. A *faker* (/**fay**-kər/) is a fraud. A *fakir* (/fə-**keer**/ or /**fay**-kər/) is a Muslim or Hindu religious ascetic who is supported by alms. The following example misapplies *fakir* to prophets in Buddhism, Christianity, and other religions. Undoubtedly the writer was sacrificing sense to sound, intending a cynical pun: "All the time and energy humans have wasted on trying to find religious solutions to suffering, then you come along and make Buddha and Jesus and the rest of them look like the *fakirs* they were." Ursula K. Le Guin, *The Lathe of Heaven* 126 (1971).

falcon. For many years, this word had two standard pronunciations, /**fawl**-kən/ and /**faw**-kən/. The latter is older and corresponds with the word's Old English root, *faucon*. But the former—with the *-l-* vocalized—long dominated.

In the 1960s, the pronunciation /**fal**-kən/ soared to prominence, probably because the Ford Motor Company used it in all the advertising for its newly developed compact car called the Falcon. (See John Greenway, "Henry Ford and the Pronunciation of 'Falcon,'" 35 *Am. Speech* 306, 306–07 [1960].) Since the Atlanta Falcons football team was established in

1965, those associated with that team have used the /fal/ pronunciation. And the /fawl/ version has largely fallen into disuse except by some fans of movies such as *The Maltese Falcon* and *Star Wars* (with Han Solo's *Millennium Falcon*).

*falderol. See **folderol.**

fall through the cracks. The *cracks* in this idiom are the openings between slats, as on a boardwalk. Things can *fall through the cracks*, but nothing can fall *between* them, because that's where the slats are. Yet the idiom is often mangled into the illogical **fall between the cracks*—e.g.:

- "But Mr. Ball argued that the program reaches a segment of the population that normally *falls between* [read *through*] *the cracks*." Sally Brady & Leslie Koren, "Jail Not Sole Option for Drunkards," *Wash. Times*, 21 Dec. 1998, at C7.
- "King said her priority is helping students in regular classes, who she said often *fall between* [read *through*] *the cracks*." "In Brief," *Wash. Post*, 27 Mar. 2002, at B3.
- "You look at this picture and wonder. How could someone so squared away *fall between* [read *through*] *the cracks*?" Peter Rowe, "Police, Family Search for Answer as Man Vanishes During Routine Walk," *San Diego Union-Trib.*, 14 July 2002, at E1.

LANGUAGE-CHANGE INDEX
*fall between the cracks for *fall through the cracks*: Stage 3
Current ratio (*fall through the cracks* vs. **fall between the cracks*): 3:1

false, in a phrase such as *false statement*, is potentially ambiguous, since the word may mean either "erroneous, incorrect" or "purposely deceptive."

On *false* as a noncomparable adjective, see ADJECTIVES (B).

FALSE COMPARISON. See ILLOGIC (B).

falsehood; falseness; falsity. *Falsehood* = (1) an untrue statement; a lie <many falsehoods were uttered during the campaign>; or (2) the act or practice of lying <truth and falsehood became difficult to distinguish>. *Falseness* = (1) the quality of being untrue <the speech carried an air of falseness>; or (2) tendency to lie; deceitfulness <falseness of character>. *Falsity* is synonymous with sense 1 of either word (although more commonly with *falseness*), but it appears too frequently to be labeled a NEEDLESS VARIANT.

fanatic; fanatical. *Fanatic* is either a noun or an adjective; *fanatical* is exclusively an adjective. For purposes of DIFFERENTIATION, it would be best to reserve *fanatic* for its noun sense. In actual usage, however, this distinction isn't always followed—e.g.:

- "The words zealot, assassin and thug all derive from historic *fanatic* [read *fanatical*] movements within, respectively, Judaism, Islam and Hinduism." Robin Wright,

"The Extremists," *L.A. Times*, 6 Nov. 1995, at A12. (In that sentence, *historic* should almost certainly be *historically*—that is, movements that have historically been fanatical—unless the sense is *historic movements that have been fanatical*, in which case the original is poorly worded.)

- "Frank Sinatra sang 'New York, New York' over the stadium speakers and the most *fanatic* [read *fanatical*] crowd on the continent sang along." Dan Moffett, "Yankees Capture Series," *Palm Beach Post*, 27 Oct. 1996, at A1.
- "If the people who are *fanatic* [read *fanatical*] about such things start passing laws and regulations that prevent the rest of us from pursuing our consumer preferences for less chic but also less expensive food, that's quite something else." William Watson, "The $2 Tomato," *Nat'l Post* (Can.), 18 Aug. 2015, at 11.

fandango (= [1] an energetic Spanish-style dance, or [2] a foolish act) forms the plural *fandangos*—not **fandangoes*. See PLURALS (D).

Current ratio: 3:1

*fantasm. See **phantasm.**

fantasy; *phantasy. The first has been the preferred spelling in both AmE and BrE since the late 19th century.

Current ratio: 20:1

far be it from . . . . Because *from* is a preposition, and the next word in the phrase is the object of that preposition, what follows must be in the objective case—e.g.: "Oh, far be it from *we* [read *us*] mere mortals to question a good thing." "Hello-ooo, Thanks for Giving Us Poolside," *Peoria J. Star*, 16 Nov. 2001, at A4. See PRONOUNS (B). See also SUBJUNCTIVES.

LANGUAGE-CHANGE INDEX
*far be it from we for *far be it from us*: Stage 1

*far distance is a REDUNDANCY. In most contexts, each word implies the other. A more idiomatic phrasing is always available—e.g.:

- "Unlike a methadone clinic where people travel *from far distances* [read *long distances*] for heroin-addiction treatment, the community health clinics would be regular doctors' offices." Meredith Carlson, "Clinics Will Be Tough Sell with New Britain Council," *Hartford Courant*, 2 Dec. 1994, at B1.
- "Down on the field, he could see Tampa Bay Coach Jon Gruden snarling as always with his mouth simple to read even from such a *far distance* [read *distance*]." Les Carpenter, "In New Orleans, a Reassuring Voice," *Wash. Post*, 25 Sept. 2006, at E11.
- "In Morocco, a goatherder gives a hunting rifle to his sons and, while practicing in the hills, one of the boys fires at a tourist bus winding down the road in the *far distance* [read *distance*]." David Ansen, "As the World Burns," *Newsweek*, 30 Oct. 2006, at 64.

LANGUAGE-CHANGE INDEX
*far distance for *long distance*: Stage 2
Current ratio (*long distance* vs. **far distance*): 6:1

LANGUAGE-CHANGE INDEX (For the full key, see front matter pp. xxxi, l–li.)
Stage 1: Rejected. **Stage 2:** Widely shunned. **Stage 3:** Widespread but . . . **Stage 4:** Ubiquitous but . . . **Stage 5:** Fully accepted.
Invariably inferior forms marked by asterisk (*). ● Ratios represent frequency of prevalent forms vs. variants in current books.

fare. A. As a Noun. Because this word, in one of its senses, means "food," the phrase **food fare* is a silly REDUNDANCY—e.g.:

- "Other *food fare* [read *fare*] includes jambalaya, oysters on the half shell, fried alligator and sausage, onion mums and Cajun pistols." Maria Giordano, "Orange Fest Looks 'A Peeling,'" *Times-Picayune* (New Orleans), 1 Dec. 1994, at F1.
- "It takes little effort to incorporate pears into your holiday and winter *food fare* [read *food* or *fare* or *cooking*]." Bob Longino, "A Pear for All Seasons," *Atlanta J.-Const.*, 13 Nov. 1997, at H1.
- "Adam Leu said the original idea was to have light *food fare* [read *fare*] for those using the play area." Jeff Barron, "More than a Restaurant," *Lancaster Eagle-Gaz.* (Ohio), 26 July 2015, at M2.

B. As a Verb. See **fair (A).**

LANGUAGE-CHANGE INDEX
*food fare for *fare*: Stage 1

far-flung; far-fetched. These adjectives are, literally speaking, etymological opposites—*far-flung* literally meaning "flung (i.e., cast) a long distance" and *far-fetched* meaning "fetched (i.e., retrieved) from afar." Of course, both terms are now used almost exclusively in their figurative senses. *Far-flung* means "widespread" or "remote"; *far-fetched* means "improbable" or "strained."

Some dictionaries make *far-fetched* a single word, without the hyphen. Although that may signal the future of this term, it isn't now the predominant form in any variety of literary English.

farrago (= a confused or jumbled mixture; hodgepodge) is pronounced /fə-**ray**-go/ or /fə-**rah**-go/ and makes either of two plurals: *farragoes, farragos*. Although *-oes* is the traditional plural, it has given way to *-os* in the 1950s in AmE and in the 1960s in BrE. See PLURALS (D).

Current ratio (*farragos* vs. *farragoes*): 2:1

far-reaching. One of our most overburdened adjectival phrases, this otiose METAPHOR should be used cautiously. The phrase should always be hyphenated—e.g.: "In a move with *far-reaching* significance in the battle over American military bases in Japan, the Supreme Court here ruled unanimously today that the central Government has the authority to seize private land so that it can be used by United States forces." Nicholas D. Kristoff, "Japanese Court Rules Government Can Seize Land for U.S. Bases," *N.Y. Times*, 29 Aug. 1996, at A17.

farther; further. Both are comparative degrees of *far. Further* is much more ubiquitous than *farther* in everyday speech and writing. But the two have undergone some degree of DIFFERENTIATION. In the most punctilious usage, *farther* is thought to refer only to physical distances, *further* only to figurative distances—e.g.:

- "After popping in to say hello to Sue's dad, we walked *further* [read *farther*] up Main Street to the Maritime

Museum." Elise Ford, "A Piece of the Rockwell," *Wash. Post*, 14 Dec. 1994, at C9.

- "Some [people] walk no *farther* than the synagogue on the Sabbath." Jo Sandin, "Hanukkah Is Time to Ask Questions of Identity," *Milwaukee J. Sentinel*, 5 Dec. 1996, at 1.
- "[Chad] Johnson has taken the florid displays of flanker ego even *further*, brashly predicting victories, à la his idol Muhammad Ali, and once sending Pepto Bismol to an opposing secondary before a game." Karl Taro Greenfeld, "It's Good to Be Chad," *Sports Illustrated*, 30 Oct. 2006, at 58.
- "That said, moms who've been *farther* [read *further*] down the road say, 'Just wait.' Just wait for preadolescent angst." Paula Spencer, "What's Your Favorite Parenting Stage?" *Parenting*, Nov. 2006, at 76.

In BrE, *further* is typically both physical and figurative, whereas *farther* is generally physical only. But some writers fail to observe the point—e.g.: "In a move [that] goes *farther* [read *further*] than anything the Conservatives have proposed, a Labour government will set up a new, independent watchdog, the General Teaching Council." Charles Reiss & Howard Smith, "Labour Will Sack the Bad Teachers Says Blair," *Evening Standard*, 26 July 1994, at 17.

The superlatives—*farthest* and *furthest*—follow the same patterns. *Furthermost* is a fairly rare equivalent of *farthest* (not *furthest*)—e.g.: "The National Park Service administers the monument located about 65 miles northwest of Gillette, in Wyoming's *furthermost* [better: *farthest*] corner of Crook County." Christopher Smith, "Tribes Say Devils Tower Is No Name for a Pious Peak," *Salt Lake Trib.*, 4 Sept. 1996, at A1. Sometimes it is used where it shouldn't be—e.g.: "That was the *furthermost* [read *furthest*] thing from [the company's] mind." Eli Setencich, "Co-op Is Reaping Fruits of Generosity," *Fresno Bee*, 30 Sept. 1996, at B1.

LANGUAGE-CHANGE INDEX
1. *further* for physical distances: Stage 4
Current ratio (*traveled farther* vs. *traveled further* in AmE): 2:1
2. *farther* for figurative distances: Stage 2
Current ratio (*read further* vs. **read farther*): 19:1

fascia (/**fash**-ee-ə/ or /**fash**-ə/ or /**faysh**-/) = (1) a flat strip or band, such as an architectural joint covering or a piece of molding around a doorway; (2) a distinct band of color, esp. in a multicolored spectrum; or (3) a thin layer of tissue that encases or connects muscles, organs, and bones. Pl. *fascias* or *fasciae*. The plural *fasciae* (/**fash**-i-ee/) is much more frequent in anatomy (sense 3), *fascias* in all other senses. See PLURALS (B).

Current ratio (*fasciae* vs. *fascias*): 5:1

fasciitis. See **plantar fasciitis.**

fast. For the use of this word in opposite senses, see CONTRONYMS. For the NEEDLESS VARIANT **fastly*, see **fastly.**

fasten, like *glisten, listen,* and *often,* has a silent *-t-*: /**fas**-ən/.

*fastly, an obsolete form, now exists only as a NON-WORD, since *fast* serves as both adverb and adjective.

Even so, writers occasionally perpetrate sentences with phrases such as *the fastly held rule* and *fastly becoming so*. In the first, *firmly* would serve better; in the second, *fast*. Journalists have gone quite far with this unnecessary adverb—e.g.:

- "The new owner said he is keeping the original building, even though it may have been less expensive to build a new one, in order to preserve one of the few remaining ties to the past in the *fastly changing* [read *fast-changing*] northwest suburbs." Jim Michalski, "Fan Helps Keep Pizza Parlor Alive," *Chicago Trib.*, 4 July 1989, at D2.
- "And thus, with election time *fastly* [read *fast*] approaching, it may have to pay the consequences of accepting Mao's forecast." James Hill, "Taiwan's Fate Belongs to Beijing," *Phoenix Gaz.*, 15 Mar. 1996, at B11.
- "But he doubted the Fleming Island hatchery would remain that for long, being a 'very prime' piece of real estate, he said, in a *fastly developing* [read *fast-developing*] area." Christopher Calnan & Gregory Richards, "1,000 Tyson, Humana Jobs Cut," *Fla. Times-Union*, 6 Dec. 2002, at A1.

Two of these examples involve PHRASAL ADJECTIVES—*fast-changing* and *fast-expanding*—but there is no more need for the *-ly* adverb in those phrases than anywhere else. For other adverbs with a superfluous *-ly*, see ADVERBS (C).

LANGUAGE-CHANGE INDEX
fastly for *fast*: Stage 1
Current ratio (*is fast becoming* vs. *is fastly becoming*): 859:1

fatal; fateful. Though both are etymologically tied to the noun *fate*, they have undergone DIFFERENTIATION. *Fatal* means "of, relating to, or involving death," while *fateful* means "producing grave consequences." The most common mistake is to use *fatal* for *fateful*, but sometimes one would be presumptuous to suggest any change, so close is the call: "Like Henry Kissinger and other modern scholars, Mr. Gelb considers the *fatal* turning point not Munich in 1938, but the failure by France and Britain to oppose German reoccupation of the Rhineland in 1936." John Lehman, "The 'Heroic' Retreat Was Really a Rout," *Wall Street J.*, 9 Oct. 1989, at A6.

But most times when no immediate death results, *fateful* is the better choice—e.g.:

- "McCarron made a *fatal* [read *fateful*] decision to try and putt out. His ball caught a tuft of kikuya and trickled to 8 feet above the hole—a brutal turn of events." Brian Murphy, "McCarron's Loss Mattiace's Gain," *S.F. Chron.*, 18 Feb. 2002, at C2 (losing a golf tournament may be brutal, but it's not the end of the world). (For more on *try and* in this quotation, see **try and**.)
- "To some Republicans, any tax increase would be a *fatal* [read *fateful*] decision for Democrats—a sin so great that voters would rush to McCallum, elect him by a wide margin and send Republican majorities to the Legislature." Matt Pommer, "A Cigarette Tax Hike Wouldn't Hurt Dems," *Capital Times* (Madison), 18 Mar. 2002, at A3.

- "In the United States, if we deny a sports team the chance to trounce its foe absolutely and unequivocally, we call for the head of the official who makes the *fatal* [read *fateful*] decision." Letter of William O. Beeman, *Providence J-Bull.*, 14 July 2002, at F9.

In some circumstances a writer using *fatal* must be careful not to create an absurdity—e.g.: "Monday's bombing was the first *fatal* suicide bombing in Israel since Oct. 10, when a 71-year-old woman was killed in an attack in Tel Aviv." Craig Nelson, "14 Perish After Suicide Bombers Turn Packed Bus into an Inferno," *Austin Am.-Statesman*, 22 Oct. 2002, at A1. (A possible revision: *Monday's explosion was the first suicide bombing in Israel that killed any bystander . . . .*)

On *fatal* as a noncomparable adjective, see ADJECTIVES (B).

LANGUAGE-CHANGE INDEX
fatal misused for *fateful*: Stage 1

fatalism; determinism; necessitarianism. *Fatalism* = (1) the philosophical view that the future is fixed regardless of human attempts to influence it; or (2) an attitude of submitting oneself to fate. Critics of this view—in either sense—complain that "it encourages ignorance, sloth, and vice." Thomas Mautner, *A Dictionary of Philosophy* 147 (1996).

Determinism = (1) the view that every fact in the universe is guided by the law of causation—i.e., that every effect derives from its causes; or (2) the idea that people do not exercise free will but are instead the product of their genetic, physical, and psychical conditions. In sense 2—the rarer sense—determinism is a type of fatalism. But sense 1, known also as *necessitarianism* or *causal determinism*, is distinct from *fatalism* because it "still leaves room for the possibility that human action may be causally effective in ensuring that this happens rather than that." Antony Flew, *A Dictionary of Philosophy* 119 (2d ed. 1984). Although determinists don't disavow free will, they deny the existence of chance: they concede merely that "our ignorance of the laws or all relevant antecedent conditions makes certain events unexpected and, therefore, apparently happen 'by chance.'" *The Cambridge Dictionary of Philosophy* 198 (Robert Audi ed., 1995). Cf. **free will.**

fateful. See **fatal.**

Father Christmas. See **Santa Claus.**

father-in-law. Pl. *fathers-in-law*—not *father-in-laws*. See PLURALS (G).

Current ratio: 7:1

fathom (= a six-foot length [1.83 meters] for measuring depth in water) predominantly forms the regular plural *fathoms* in all varieties of World English <five fathoms deep>. Through about 1830, *fathom* predominantly formed its own plural <five fathom deep>, but this usage has sunk.

LANGUAGE-CHANGE INDEX (For the full key, see front matter pp. xxxi, l–li.)
Stage 1: Rejected. **Stage 2:** Widely shunned. **Stage 3:** Widespread but . . . **Stage 4:** Ubiquitous but . . . **Stage 5:** Fully accepted.
Invariably inferior forms marked by asterisk (*). • Ratios represent frequency of prevalent forms vs. variants in current books.

fault, at; in fault. See **at fault.**

fauna, a singular word with a collective implication, refers to the animal life in a particular region. Hence *fauna* should take a singular verb, not a plural, and may be referred to as *a fauna*—e.g.: "At the Lascaux cave, lying to the west of this site but which had *a* similar *fauna* at the time, he said, the images were overwhelmingly of bison and horses, but here bears and rhinos—animals that man did not usually hunt or eat—predominated." Marlise Simons, "Prehistoric Art Treasure Is Found in French Cave," *N.Y. Times*, 19 Jan. 1995, at A1, A5.

The word most often appears in the phrase *flora and fauna*, roughly equivalent to "plants and animals," but writers sometimes mistake *fauna* for the "plants" element—e.g.: "Shortly before approaching the Blue Ridge Parkway, look for a forest area filled with natural growing *fauna* [read *flora*] and fern gardens with awesome hiking trails." Judy Ausley, "Take to the Hills, Enjoy the Ride," *Herald* (Rock Hill, S.C.), 11 Oct. 2002, at D1. Cf. **flora.**

LANGUAGE-CHANGE INDEX
fauna misused for *flora*: Stage 1

faux pas [Fr. "false step"] is both the singular and the plural spelling. But the singular is pronounced /foh **pah**/ or (less good) /**foh** pah/, and the plural is pronounced /foh **pahz**/ or (less good) /**foh** pahz/.

favor; favour. Until the 1840s, *favour* was the standard spelling in AmE and BrE alike. During that decade, *favor* became the predominant spelling in AmE— as did *favorable* and *favorite*. BrE still favors *favour*, *favourable*, and *favourite*. See -OR; -OUR.

fax, n. & vb. This term is now all but universal, in the face of which *facsimile transmission* is an instant ARCHAISM—and a trifle pompous at that. *Fax*, which is now perfectly appropriate even in formal contexts, first appeared in the mid-1970s—e.g.: "In the past two years, *fax* installations have more than doubled from fewer than 50,000 to more than 100,000 units." "The Office of the Future," *BusinessWeek*, 30 June 1975, at 48. The verb dates from the mid-1980s—e.g.: "The prints are then *faxed* from the regional centers." PJH, "Data Detectives Use a New Technique to Match Fingerprints," *Data Communications*, Feb. 1984, at 56.

The noun plural is *faxes*.

Some writers mistakenly put the word in all capitals, as if it were an acronym. It isn't. It's just a clipped form with a slight change in spelling: write *fax*, not **FAX*.

LANGUAGE-CHANGE INDEX
fax as n. & vb.: Stage 5

fay. See **fey.**

faze; phase. *Faze* = to disconcert; daunt. *Phase*, vb., = to carry out (a plan, program, etc.) in stages. *Phase* for *faze* is an increasingly common blunder—e.g.:

- "Maybe all Johnson really needs to do is watch how much fun Soriano is having. Nothing seems to *phase* [read *faze*]

this young Yankee." Bill Madden, "Johnson's Slump Stumping Yanks," *Daily News* (N.Y.), 15 May 2002, Sports §, at 56.
- "The activist is *unphased* [read *unfazed*] by the criticism. She comes from a family of feminist revolutionaries." Fariba Nawa, "US-Grown Feminist's Pace of Reform Riles Afghan Women," *Christian Science Monitor*, 31 July 2002, World §, at 7.
- "Her new horse, Emily, has never jumped in an arena like the Farm Show Complex, but Plunkett said her mare won't be *phased* [read *fazed*] by the big crowd and bright lights." Rebecca J. Ritzel, "Getting a Jump on the Competition," *Intelligencer J.* (Lancaster, Pa.), 18 Oct. 2002, at B1.
- "The Bath side were *unphased* [read *unfazed*], emerging comfortable six-wicket victors after the visitors were dismissed for only 138." "Cricket Munden and Ollis Give Brislington the Perfect Start," *Bristol Evening Post* (U.K.), 3 Aug. 2015, at 46.

The opposite error (*faze* for *phase*) also occurs, but more rarely—e.g.: "All that while shooting guard Art Mlotkowski, shadowed all over the court by Northport senior Rob Sanicola, was *fazed* [read *phased*] out of the offense." John Valenti, "Northport Beats Copiague," *Newsday* (N.Y.), 26 Feb. 1995, at 13.

LANGUAGE-CHANGE INDEX
1. *phase* misused for *faze*: Stage 2
Current ratio (*didn't faze him* vs.
**didn't phase him*): 8:1
2. *unphased* for *unfazed*: Stage 1
Current ratio (*unfazed by* vs. *unphased by): 36:1
3. *faze* misused for *phase*: Stage 1
Current ratio (*being phased out* vs.
*being fazed out): 422:1

fearful; fearsome. In a perfect world, there would be strict DIFFERENTIATION here: *fearful* would be confined to the sense "full of fear, afraid"; *fearsome* would be reserved for "causing fear, horrible." Alas, the world isn't quite so perfect, and there is considerable overlap.

feasible = (1) capable of being accomplished; (2) capable of being used or handled to good effect; or (3) reasonable, likely. Sense 3 is a classic example of SLIP-SHOD EXTENSION. The extended sense is ambiguous. Does someone who says that a cure for cancer is *feasible* mean that a cure can definitely be found (if we work hard enough to find it) or that a cure might one day be found (but not necessarily)?

To avoid this problem, it's best to reserve *feasible* for senses 1 and 2. When sense 3 is the intended meaning, *possible* or *probable* is the better choice. Cf. **viable.**

The word is sometimes misspelled **feasable*. See -ABLE (A).

feature. The classic book popularly known as "Strunk & White" cautioned against using this word, citing the following example: "A *feature* of the entertainment especially worthy of mention was the singing of Miss A." William Strunk Jr. & E.B. White, *The Elements of Style* 47 (3d ed. 1979). The authors advise: "Better use the same number of words to tell what Miss A. sang and how she sang it." This sound advice is disparaged in *MWDEU*, which states:

This advice [in Strunk & White] seems a bit naive; it is distinctly possible that the example is a minor masterpiece of tact. If Miss A. happens to have more friends than talent, it may be better not to tell what she sang and how she sang it. We may have the same politic avoidance of judgment in this example:

> A feature of the program was a panel discussion in which visitors from other institutions shared the benefits of their own, related experience—Calvin H. Plimpton, *Amherst College Bulletin*, November 1967

MWDEU at 436.

Of course, this is pure folderol. Almost any passage in need of editing can find an apologist for its original form, but Strunk and White were urging authors to sharpen their ideas. And even without sharpening, the final quotation cited in *MWDEU* could use a good edit—*During a panel discussion, visitors from other institutions shared the benefits of their experience*—which also trims the sentence from 23 words to 14.

February is still preferably pronounced /**feb**-roo-air-ee/ or, in BrE, /**feb**-roo-ə-ree/—preferably not /**feb**-yoo-air-ee/ or /**feb**-yə-ree/.

fecal; faecal. Meaning "of, relating to, or consisting of waste from the bowels," the word *fecal* is so spelled in AmE, *faecal* in BrE. Before 1800, *fecal* was the universal spelling, and in AmE it has persisted. It is also a frequent variant in BrE. Since 1900 or so, World English has tended toward *fecal*.

feces (BrE **faeces**). When it comes to SUBJECT–VERB AGREEMENT, this noun can be tricky. Though plural in form and labeled plural in dictionaries, the word *feces* is often treated as a mass noun and construed with a singular verb—e.g.:

- "In each of those instances, the pool had to be closed after *feces was* found in the water." Cory Haven, "Things May Be Looking Up for Plymouth Community Pool," *South Bend Trib.*, 9 July 2002, at D1.
- "Mr. Gorman said studies have shown that goose *feces contains* more than 100 types of bacteria, many of which are resistant to antibiotics." Linda Saslow, "Canada Geese: It's Love and Hate," *N.Y. Times*, 14 July 2002, 14LI §, at 3.
- "Overcash chose the class over self-study because at MUSC, students also learn the slang terms their future patients will be using. 'You can't ask a person how their baby's *feces is* if they don't know the word for *feces.*'" Wevonneda Minis, "Speaking the Language," *Post & Courier* (Charleston, S.C.), 5 Aug. 2002, at D1.

It makes some sense to equate *feces* with *excrement*.

When the stuff appears in discrete pieces, *feces* is used as a count noun and takes a plural verb. E.g.: "Before dogs were domesticated, they ate a much more varied diet, including the bones of their prey. Therefore, their *feces were* much harder and dry." Jill Bowen, "Problem Anal Glands Need Vet Treatment," *Roanoke Times*, 21 July 2002, at NRV18.

Some writers, however, use a plural verb for the mass-noun sense, probably on grounds that the word derives from a Latin plural (*faēces*). This usage has been somewhat more common than the singular applications from the late 18th century on, but only just. E.g.:

- "Colton said dog *feces have* [or *has*] been one of the worst sources of coliform bacteria contamination for at least two years." Lane Lambert, "Quincy May Ban Dogs from Parks," *Patriot Ledger* (Quincy, Mass.), 23 Apr. 1997, at 1.
- "Barnes said inspectors don't know how long the pigeon *feces have* [or *has*] been in the water holding tank." Justo Bautista & Michael Casey, "New Water Problems at Senior Complex," *Record* (N.J.), 1 July 1997, at A1.
- "Gull *feces contain* [or *contains*] high concentrations of the coliform bacteria." Tom Held, "Manitowoc Gets Federal Permit to Kill 100 Gulls," *Milwaukee J. Sentinel*, 9 Aug. 2002, at B3.

See COUNT NOUNS AND MASS NOUNS.

federal. See **national.**

federalism. In U.S. politics, this word is a double-edged sword. It is used by proponents of a strong central government to denote a system in which the national government has broad powers to compel states to conform to policies set by Congress (e.g., the Federalist Party of the Founders), and by opponents of a strong central government to denote a system in which the states are sovereign entities free to set their own policies subject only to strict construction of the U.S. Constitution (e.g., today's Federalist Society).

Nowadays the word is employed both by the left (e.g., in arguments against Department of Justice opposition of state laws sanctioning the medical use of marijuana) and by the right (e.g., against enforcement of statutory civil-rights actions on behalf of state employees). In polemical contexts (where it most often appears), the word has become fairly hazy and ambiguous.

federation. See **confederation.**

feed > fed > fed. So inflected. *Feeded* is a solecism—e.g.: "It was a friendly family environment that Brown needed and *feeded* [read *fed*] off." Robin Miller, "Today, Indy Says Goodbye to One of Its Favorite Friends," *Indianapolis Star*, 10 Mar. 1997, at C1. See IRREGULAR VERBS.

LANGUAGE-CHANGE INDEX
feeded as a past-tense form: Stage 1
Current ratio (*fed the* vs. *feeded the*): 9,542:1

feel. A. For *think*. *Feel* is a weak and informal substitute for *think, believe, maintain,* or *submit.* E.g.: "We *feel* [read *believe*] that the plan should be summarized in considerable detail." When the idea is phrased on an emotional rather than a cognitive level, the resulting sentence seems to minimize the thoughts being

LANGUAGE-CHANGE INDEX (For the full key, see front matter pp. xxxi, l–li.)
Stage 1: Rejected. **Stage 2:** Widely shunned. **Stage 3:** Widespread but . . . **Stage 4:** Ubiquitous but . . . **Stage 5:** Fully accepted.
Invariably inferior forms marked by asterisk (✳). • Ratios represent frequency of prevalent forms vs. variants in current books.

reported—e.g.: "She *feels* [read *thinks* or *believes*] that crime prevention must start with helping small children find their way out of poverty and neglect, and that society's resources should go toward better education and housing, not more jails." Bob Cohn & Eleanor Clift, "The Contrary Voice of Janet Reno," *Newsweek*, 11 Oct. 1993, at 30.

B. Feel bad; *feel badly*. When someone is sick or unhappy, that person feels *bad*—not *badly*. In this phrase, *feel* is a linking verb, which takes a predicate adjective instead of an adverb. In modern print sources, *feel bad* outnumbers *feel badly* by a 9-to-1 margin. Although most professional writers know this point of usage, a few get it wrong—e.g.:

- "Manager Dusty Baker's attention was divided. He felt *badly* [read *bad*] for Dunston and was depressed over a ninth-inning rally gone sour." Nick Peters, "Giants, Dunston Suffer a Blow," *Sacramento Bee*, 5 Aug. 1996, at D1.
- "He says he felt *badly* [read *bad*] for Jamie Brandon." Barry Temkin, "Ex-Mr. Basketball Makes His Past Work for His Future," *Chicago Trib.*, 20 Dec. 1996, Sports §, at 14.
- "Several of the teens said they also felt *badly* [read *bad*] that their problems caused their parents pain." Patricia Wen, "For Gay Teens, a Place to Call Home," *Boston Globe*, 22 Oct. 2002, at B1.

Not to excuse these errors, but they may result from the misplaced fear that *feel bad* somehow suggests wickedness or personal evil.

But the same error crops up even with adjectives other than *bad*. Here it's *miserable*: "Every couple of years, the American Bar Association's monthly magazine publishes an article detailing how *miserably* [read *miserable*] many lawyers feel." Judson Hand, "Writer Judson Hand Signs Off from Column," *Asbury Park Press* (Neptune, N.J.), 27 Nov. 1997, at A33. See ADVERBS (D) & HYPERCORRECTION. Cf. **badly (A).**

LANGUAGE-CHANGE INDEX
feel badly for *feel bad*: Stage 2
Current ratio (*feel bad* vs. *feel badly*): 9:1

C. Feel like. To avoid using *like* as a conjunction, writers usually need to change this phrase to *feel as if*. E.g.: "But on a combined income of $60,000, McDonald and his wife Cindy, who have five children, *feel like* [read *feel as if*] they're just scraping by." Marc Levinson, "Living on the Edge," *Newsweek*, 4 Nov. 1991, at 23. See **like (c).**

On the other hand, the familiar CASUALISM expressing a preference is perfectly grammatical <I feel like pizza tonight>. The object of the preposition *like* in this example is the understood gerund *eating* (which functions as a noun), and the object of that gerund is the noun *pizza*. So the expression, while a CASUALISM, is not at all substandard.

feet. See **foot.**

feign; feint. These words, though deriving from the same French verb (*feindre* "to touch or shape"), have undergone DIFFERENTIATION in English. To *feign* is

either to make up or fabricate <she feigned an excuse> or to make a false show of <he feigned illness>. To *feint* is to deliver a pretended blow or attack designed to confuse an opponent momentarily. *Feint* is also, in its older (but still current) sense, used as a noun meaning either a sham or a pretended blow or attack (i.e., the act of *feinting*).

feint. See **faint.**

feldspar (= a crystalline mineral found in igneous rocks) has been the standard spelling since about 1890. *Felspar*, a variant, predominated for most of the 19th century, but shortly before 1900 the etymologically superior spelling—closer to the German loanword *Feldspat*—replaced it.

fellatio (= oral sex performed on a male) is pronounced /fə-**lay**-shee-oh/—not /fə-**lah**-tee-oh/.

***fellow collaborator.** See **collaborator.**

felo-de-se. See **suicide (A).**

female, adj.; **feminine; woman(ly); womanlike; womanish; effeminate.** These adjectives all share the sense "of, relating to, or involving women." *Female* is a neutral term usually used to indicate the sex of a person (or an animal or plant), in contrast with *male* <a female cadet> <my female coworkers>. *Feminine* typically refers to what are traditionally considered a woman's favorable qualities <feminine grace>. *Womanly* often carries these positive connotations as well <womanly intuition>, but it's also used to distinguish an adult female from a girl <her womanly figure>. (*Woman* is sometimes used attributively where *female* would be more natural <a woman lawyer>.) *Womanlike* (the rarest of these words) is synonymous with *womanly*, though perhaps a bit more neutral <womanlike features>. Finally, *womanish* and *effeminate* are now almost always used in a derogatory way in referring to men who supposedly lack manly qualities <his womanish laugh> <his effeminate gestures>.

In this era of political correctness, the use of any of these terms can be offensive in certain contexts. See SEXISM. Cf. **girlie** & **male.**

FEMININE ENDINGS. See SEXISM (D).

FEMININE PRONOUNS USED GENERICALLY. See SEXISM (B).

femininity; *feminity*. Both terms date from the 14th century. But *femininity*, which matches the syllables in *masculinity*, has been standard for so long that the other may rightly be considered a simple misspelling.
Current ratio: 139:1

femur (= thigh bone) makes the Latinate plural *femora* in technical writing but the normal plural *femurs* in everyday contexts. Of course, it is rare to need the plural in everyday contexts. See PLURALS (B).
Current ratio (*femora* vs. *femurs*): 1.2:1

feral (= [1] of, relating to, or involving a wild beast; or [2] formerly domesticated but now having become wild) is traditionally pronounced /**feer**-əl/, but /**fer**-əl/ is now common in AmE and BrE alike.

ferment, n. & vb. To *ferment* /fər-**ment**/ something is to cause it to undergo a physical change in composition through enzymatic effervescence, especially as sugar is converted into alcohol (*fermentation*). As a noun, *ferment* /**fər**-mənt/ denotes (1) a yeast or enzyme that causes fermentation, or (2) a situation of great unrest, trouble, or excitement in a country or region, esp. caused by political change.

ferret, v.i., makes *ferreted* and *ferreting* in both AmE and BrE. See SPELLING (B).

fervent; fervid; perfervid. These adjectives describe three gradations of ardor or zeal (listed also in order of word frequency in print sources). To be *fervent* is either to show warm feelings or to be strongly devoted to something. To be *fervid* is to have those qualities in a stronger degree. And to be *perfervid* is to be fanatically zealous. The prefix *per-* is an intensifier here.

festive; festal. *Festive* = (1) of, relating to, or involving a feast or festival; or (2) joyful, merry <a festive mood>. *Festal,* a rarer word, shares only sense 1 of *festive* and is probably the better word in that sense. Today it is used primarily in connection with religious observances <festal vespers> <festal liturgy>, but not exclusively so—e.g.: "Six Degrees presents a ceremonial tapping of the Paulaner Oktoberfest *Festal* keg by Former Seattle Seahawk Blair Bush, Oct. 12, 7 p.m." "Food Notes," *Seattle Post-Intelligencer,* 11 Oct. 2000, at E2.

Festschrift (= a collection of writings forming a volume presented by the authors as a tribute to a [usu. senior] scholar), a German loanword, forms the plurals *Festschrifts* and *Festschriften.* The German plural predominates in English-language contexts, just as the German capitalization is retained. For the reasons given at PLURALS (B), it would be understandable if one preferred the anglicized *Festschrifts.*
     Current ratio (*Festschriften* vs. *Festschrifts*): 3:1

fetch (= to get and bring to) was once a fully respectable word. It appears, for example, in the King James Version of the Bible: "Fetch me, I pray thee, a little water in a vessel" (1 Kings 17:10). But in AmE (much more than in BrE), the word has undergone depreciation. One linguist who noted this trend in the 1960s posited two possible reasons: "Perhaps the command latent in it is resented as undemocratic. Or maybe its use in training dogs to retrieve has made some people feel that it is an undignified word to apply to human beings." Bergen Evans, "But What's a Dictionary For?" in *The Ways of Language* 77, 86 (Raymond J. Pflug ed., 1967). For whatever reason, the word now has

associations of hick talk, perhaps in part because it was commonly used in the 1960s television show *The Beverly Hillbillies.* It also rings of racism, a connotation dating at least from the vaudeville and film career of Lincoln Perry (1902–1985), better known by his stage and screen name of Stepin Fetchit.
     Oddly, though, when used in the monetary senses "sell for" and "bring in," the word carries no negative baggage—e.g.:
* "Miramax unspooled the Philip Glass-scored docu 'Naqoyqatsi' with exclu engagements in Gotham and L.A., *fetching* a fulsome $16,500." Carl DiOrio, "'The Ring' Goes Ka-ching," *Daily Variety,* 22 Oct. 2002, News §, at 1.
* "If Quintiles shares were *fetching* their all-time high of $56 plus, Gillings would have had to offer more than $6.6 billion to acquire the company." David Ranii, "Is Quintiles Going Up or Down?" *News & Observer* (Raleigh), 22 Oct. 2002, at D1.

Nor is the participial adjective *fetching* (= attractive, alluring) in any way stained by the connotations that its root word carries—e.g.: "She wrapped her unfaltering soprano around two of Sondheim's most *fetching* and wrenching ballads, 'In Buddy's Eyes' and 'Losing My Mind.'" Peter Marks, "Kennedy Center's Sondheim Treat to N.Y.," *Wash. Post,* 23 Oct. 2002, at C1.
     Because *fetch* means "to go get and bring back," the phrase **go fetch* is a REDUNDANCY—e.g.:
* "Next, the hijacker released a third man to *go fetch* [read *fetch*] the two escapees." Sonni Efron, "Raid Ends Moscow Hostage Drama," *L.A. Times,* 15 Oct. 1995, at A4.
* "Presley's manager, Col. Tom Parker, asked Green to *go fetch* [read *fetch*] Elvis at the Little Rock airport." Timothy Finn, "Music-Lover Suggestions for All 11th-Hour Santas," *Kansas City Star,* 20 Dec. 1996, at 23.

LANGUAGE-CHANGE INDEX
*go fetch for *fetch*: Stage 1

fete (= [1] an outdoor gala, or [2] a major celebration) is normally so written, without the traditional circumflex over the first -*e*- (see DIACRITICAL MARKS). The word is pronounced either /fayt/ or /fet/ (the latter being the French pronunciation).

fetid /**fet**-id/ (= emitting an offensive odor; stinky) is a FORMAL WORD <brown fetid water at the bottom of the creek>. The pronunciation /**feet**-id/ is a nonstandard variant. The obsolescent variant spelling **foetid* has not been predominant in BrE print sources since the late 17th century. It has always been a recessive spelling in World English. The corresponding noun is *fetor* /**fet**-ər/ (= stench).
     Current ratio (*fetid* vs. **foetid*): 7:1

fetus; *foetus. The first has been the standard spelling in AmE since 1910 and in BrE since 1970. **Foetus* is now but a variant spelling. Pl. *fetuses.* See PLURALS (B).
     Current ratio: 6:1

LANGUAGE-CHANGE INDEX (For the full key, see front matter pp. xxxi, l–li.)
Stage 1: Rejected. **Stage 2:** Widely shunned. **Stage 3:** Widespread but . . . **Stage 4:** Ubiquitous but . . . **Stage 5:** Fully accepted.
Invariably inferior forms marked by asterisk (*). • Ratios represent frequency of prevalent forms vs. variants in current books.

fever. See **temperature** (B).

feverish; **feverous.* The first is standard; the second is a NEEDLESS VARIANT.

Current ratio: 185:1

few. See **couple** (B).

fewer; less. *Fewer* emphasizes number, and *less* emphasizes degree or quantity. **Fewer number* and **fewest number* are illogical tautologies, since *fewer* means "of smaller number." E.g.: "The *fewest number* [read *smallest number*] of people use the library between 4:30 and 7:00 PM." (Or, better, read: *The fewest people use the library between 4:30 and 7:00 PM.*) See **less** (A) & (B).

*One fewer isn't much of an idiomatic possibility, while *one less* is <one less bell to answer>. Probably in an attempt to be refined, the writer here incorrectly avoids using the word *less*: "Texas Tech officials emerged from a second full day before the NCAA Committee on Infractions having to deal with *one fewer* [read *one less*] allegation, Chancellor John Montford said Saturday." Doug Hensley, "NCAA Drops One Allegation," *Amarillo Globe-Times*, 26 Apr. 1998, at C1.

LANGUAGE-CHANGE INDEX
1. **fewer* [or *fewest*] *number* for *smaller* [or *smallest*] *number*: Stage 3
Current ratio (*smallest number* vs. **fewest number*): 3:1
2. **one fewer* for *one less*: Stage 3
Current ratio (*one less* vs. **one fewer*): 12:1

*few in number is a common REDUNDANCY—e.g.: "They were once prized for their tasty bacon, but when new breeds came along that were cheaper to raise and produced more bacon, the Tamworths declined and they are now *few in number* [read *scarce* or *uncommon*]." Ray Moseley, "Duo Fleeing for Their Lives," *Chicago Trib.*, 16 Jan. 1998, at 6.

fey, adj.; **fay,** n. *Fey* derives from the Old English *fæge* ("doomed to die") and carries the related sense "in an unusually excited state (like one about to die)." By an old SLIPSHOD EXTENSION, the word came to mean "whimsical, otherworldly, enchanting, eccentric," perhaps from confusion with *fay* (see below). This shift in meaning was noticed as early as 1950: "Construed to mean 'elfin' by most literate people, [*fey*] is defined as 'fated to die'; its popular meaning has only recently crept into a single dictionary. Confronted with this lag, editors say that the citation slips have not yet shown sufficient evidence to justify the new sense." Felicia Lamport, "Dictionaries: Our Language Right or Wrong" (1950), in *Words, Words, Words About Dictionaries* 64, 65 (Jack C. Gray ed., 1963). Today the word's original meaning is all but forgotten. E.g.: "An upsurge of book sales in cyberspace could have dramatic effects on the fortunes of the already *fey* and contradictory world of book publishing." "Even Before Books," *Wash. Post*, 4 Aug. 1997, at A18.

Fay (= a fairy or elf) is always a noun—e.g.: "And a key mythological figure is Melusina, a *fay* from an ancient fairy tale who is half-woman, half-serpent." Norman Weinstein, Book Rev., *Parabola*, 22 Sept. 1995, at 116. One writer mistakenly says that *fay* is an adjective meaning "elfin" or "elflike." See Kenneth G. Wilson, *The Columbia Guide to Standard American English* 193 (1993). See **elfin**.

Adding to the confusion is the name of King Arthur's nemesis, Morgan Le Fey. Originally, *fey* referred to the fact that Morgan brought Arthur's doom by bearing him a son predestined to destroy his father. But as the legend changed and was embellished with time, Morgan became less human and more magical. Today her name is alternatively spelled *Fey* and *Fay*, and she is almost always portrayed as a sorceress: more a fairy than a human.

fez (= a brimless thimble-shaped hat) forms the plural *fezzes*—not **fezes*. See PLURALS (A).

Current ratio: 3:1

fiancé; fiancée. A *fiancé* is male, a *fiancée* female. The better pronunciation is /fee-ahn-**say**/ (approximating the French). The middlebrow AmE pronunciation is /fee-**ahn**-say/. (See CLASS DISTINCTIONS.) In AmE—unlike BrE—the accents are usually retained. See DIACRITICAL MARKS.

Fiancé is sometimes misused for *fiancée*—e.g.:

- "An undercover FBI agent posing as an immigrant looking for a wife was told he could be happily married to an American woman for $6,000. The agent had an appointment to meet his *fiancé* [read *fiancée*] and get a marriage license yesterday but he broke the date." Helen Peterson, "L.I. Matri-Money Ring Busted," *Daily News* (N.Y.), 11 Apr. 1997, at 10.
- "Howard has been dumped by the *fiancé* [read *fiancée*] he adored." Richard Corliss, "Caution: Male Fraud," *Time*, 18 Aug. 1997, at 61.

This error may result from an effort to avoid gender-specific endings. But to a traditionalist, this is one context in which a person's sex makes a difference. Calling a man's *fiancée* his *fiancé*, or calling a woman's *fiancé* her *fiancée*, raises a new issue in the reader's mind: is the writer referring to a same-sex marriage?

LANGUAGE-CHANGE INDEX
fiancée for *fiancé* (and vice versa): Stage 2

fiasco (= a complete failure) forms the plural *fiascos* or (less frequently) *fiascoes*. See PLURALS (D).

Current ratio: 2:1

fiber is the AmE spelling; *fibre* is BrE. See -ER (B).

fibroma (= a benign tumor made up of fibrous tissue) formerly made the classical plural *fibromata*, but the homegrown plural *fibromas* had become predominant in AmE by 1935 and in BrE by the late 1950s. See PLURALS (B).

Current ratio: 12:1

fibula (= the outer of the two bones between a vertebrate's knee and ankle), perhaps because it appears mostly in technical contexts, predominantly forms the Latinate plural *fibulae* /**fib**-yə-lee/ in AmE and BrE alike—*fibulas* being a variant. Cf. **tibia.** See PLURALS (B).

Current ratio: 8:1

fictional; fictitious; fictive; *fictionary. Although these forms overlap to a great degree, they have undergone some useful DIFFERENTIATION. *Fictional* = of, relating to, or having the characteristics of fiction. E.g.:

- "Despite widespread public criticism of the movie's [i.e., Oliver Stone's *JFK*'s] speculative and *fictional* nature, it sparked a furor in 1992 that led to the creation of the records review board." Mark Wrolstad, "Open to Debate," *Dallas Morning News*, 19 Nov. 1994, at A31.
- "It's not hard to understand the retro appeal of a *fictional* hero such as Dirk Pitt." Valerie Takahama, "When Sea Calls, Author Answers," *Orange County Register*, 17 Nov. 1996, at F35.

Fictitious = (1) false, counterfeit; or (2) imaginary. Sense 1: "His 1993 Nissan Sentra had a *fictitious* license plate, said Phillip Roland, a spokesman for the Las Vegas Metropolitan Police." Steve Newborn, "Fugitive Arrested in Vegas," *Tampa Trib.*, 13 Dec. 1996, Polk §, at 4. Sense 2: "Garrison Keillor, host of radio's 'A Prairie Home Companion,' touts duct tape as the 'old reliable' for everything from repairing Lamborghinis to performing heart surgery, in *fictitious* ads by the equally *fictitious* American Duct Tape Council." "Duct Tape Never Gets a Bad Wrap," *Chicago Trib.*, 21 Oct. 2002, Tempo §, at 1. See **factitious.**

Fictive = having the capacity of imaginative creation <*fictive* talent>. Apart from this narrow sense, *fictive* is a NEEDLESS VARIANT of both *fictional* and *fictitious*—e.g.:

- "But when an earthly reality hovers too near a *fictive* [read *fictional*] one, it sends a shadow onto the landscape that can dominate, even supersede the imagination." Gail Caldwell, "The Munro Doctrine," *Boston Globe*, 3 Nov. 1996, at D15.
- "When the real rocks are exhibited alongside the *fictive* [read *fictitious* or, better yet, *fake*] ones, it is impossible to tell them apart." Richard Dorment, "The Arts: Perfection in the Everyday," *Daily Telegraph*, 13 Nov. 1996, at 21.
- "Its interviewees were drawn largely from the Princeton area, near the *program's fictive epicenter* [read *fictional program's setting*]—and, consequently, included a high concentration of frightened listeners." Robert Nason, "When Earthlings Panic," *Weekly Standard*, 17 Aug. 2015, at 34 (referring to Orson Welles's 1938 "War of the Worlds" broadcast). (The italicized phrasing raises at least three issues solved by the rewording. See **epicenter.**)

*Fictionary is an unusual NEEDLESS VARIANT of *fictional*—e.g.: "A man who will occasionally paint other persons—even *fictionary* [read *fictional*] persons—as worse than they really are may not unnaturally be expected to depict himself as somewhat better than

he is." Grant M. Overton, *Why Authors Go Wrong and Other Explanations* 2 (1919).

LANGUAGE-CHANGE INDEX
fictive misused for *fictitious* or *fictional*: Stage 1

fiddle. It's often thought that *fiddles* are the instruments of country-and-western musicians, *violins* those of orchestral musicians. In fact, though, many great violinists refer to their *fiddles*, perhaps as a type of DYSPHEMISM.

fidget, v.i., makes *fidgeted* and *fidgeting* in both AmE and BrE. See SPELLING (B).

fiduciary, adj. & n.; **fiducial,** adj. For all ordinary purposes, use *fiduciary* as both adjective <fiduciary relationship> and noun <as trustees, they are fiduciaries>. *Fiducial* is mostly confined to physics and mathematics. A *fiducial line* or *point* is one used as a base—as a boiling point is in thermometry. A *fiducial edge* is the thin edge of a ruler or scale against which a line is drawn.

fief; fiefdom. *Fief* (/feef/) is the standard term to refer to a feudal estate. *Fiefdom* has traditionally been classifiable as a NEEDLESS VARIANT, but since the late 20th century it has been very much on the rise in figurative, extended senses <he treats the law library as if it's his own little fiefdom>.

field. The phrase *the field of* is vague and often unnecessary—e.g.:

- "Lindsey . . . accrued a 3.91 grade point average while studying *in the field of* [delete *in the field of*] communications." "Carter Gets Pharmacy Degree, Loyd Academic Honors," *Knoxville News-Sentinel*, 12 July 1994, at B2.
- "For O'Neill and Hajnal, the war solidified their desire to enter *the field of* [delete *the field of*] law enforcement." Andy Kravetz, "10 Years Ago Today, America and Its Allies Launched an Air Blitz Against Iraq," *Peoria J. Star*, 17 Jan. 2001, at A1.

Cf. **area.**

field day. See **heyday (B).**

15 minutes of fame (= a brief period of public exposure or recognition) paraphrases a 1968 Andy Warhol comment that "in the future, everyone will be world-famous for 15 minutes." Writers sometimes mar the allusion by shortening the promised time by 14 minutes and 45 seconds—e.g.:

- "There is more to [Kevin] Conrad than those *15 seconds of fame* [read *15 minutes of fame*]." Fred Pearce, "How to Save the Climate and the Forests Too," *New Scientist*, 22 Mar. 2008, at 36.
- "Jenny Frydryk worked hard for what could be her *15 seconds of fame* [read *15 minutes of fame*]." Brett Rowland, "15 Minutes of Fame," *The Reporter* (Fond du Lac, Wis.), 25 Apr. 2008, at A1. (The headline writer got it right.)

LANGUAGE-CHANGE INDEX (For the full key, see front matter pp. xxxi, l–li.)
Stage 1: Rejected. **Stage 2:** Widely shunned. **Stage 3:** Widespread but . . . **Stage 4:** Ubiquitous but . . . **Stage 5:** Fully accepted.
Invariably inferior forms marked by asterisk (*). • Ratios represent frequency of prevalent forms vs. variants in current books.

Occasionally, *15 seconds* is more literal and appropriate than the original witticism—e.g.: "Between innings, fans were featured on the JumboTron. . . . [E]veryone was getting face time. Well, not exactly face. One teenage boy was ready for his *15 seconds of fame* and mooned the in-house camera, his cheeky smile splattered above the scoreboard." Troy E. Renck, "I'm Just Moonstruck by It All," *Denver Post*, 20 Apr. 2008, at CC16.

LANGUAGE-CHANGE INDEX
15 seconds of fame for *15 minutes of fame*: Stage 1
Current ratio (*fifteen minutes of fame* vs.
fifteen seconds of fame): 25:1

fifth is pronounced /fifth/. Whether the version without the medial *-f-* (/fith/) is a mispronunciation, a hasty pronunciation, or a casual pronunciation is debatable. But one thing is certain: it's not as good. See PRONUNCIATION (B).

Fifth Amendment. The idiom is *take the Fifth*, not *plead the Fifth* (a solecism very much on the rise since about 1950)—e.g.:

• "He was advised to keep silent and *plead* [read *take*] the Fifth Amendment." Kevin Diaz, "$4 Million Award's a Start Toward a Clean Slate," *Star Trib.* (Minneapolis), 22 Oct. 1994, at A1.
• "[P]rosecutor Daniel Saunders announced to the court that he'd been notified by [Bertram] Fields' then attorney, famed trial maven John Keker, that Fields planned to *plead the Fifth* [read *take the Fifth*] if called as a witness." Rachel Abramowitz, "Can We Get a Witness?" *L.A. Times*, 21 Apr. 2008, at E1.

LANGUAGE-CHANGE INDEX
plead the Fifth for *take the Fifth*: Stage 3
Current ratio (*took the Fifth* vs. *pleaded the Fifth* vs.
pled the Fifth): 10:3:1

figure is pronounced /**fig**-yər/ in AmE and /**fig**-ə/ in BrE.

filet mignon. The plural of this phrase is *filet mignons* (or, more stuffily, *filets mignons*). (See PLURALS (B).) But when the second word is dropped, the plural is *filets*. While AmE uses the spelling *filet* /fi-**lay**/, BrE spells it *fillet* /**fil**-ət/.

filigree (= ornamentation consisting of a network of gold or silver wires, or other materials similarly intertwined) is sometimes misspelled *fillagree* or *filagree*—e.g.:

• "We've grown tired of the *filagree* [read *filigree*] that's on the window." Beth Sherman, "Buttoning Up a Collection Display," *Newsday* (N.Y.), 19 June 1997, at B27.
• "For his fancy dinnerware, he pairs coral-colored Limoges china with gold-*filagree* [read *filigree*] Romanian glassware—'provenance Pier 1.'" Karen Klages, "Chocolate Tasting, Open-Hearth Cooking Are February's Key Themes," *Chicago Trib.*, 2 Feb. 2003, Home & Garden §, at 3.

LANGUAGE-CHANGE INDEX
filigree misspelled *fillagree* or *filagree*: Stage 1
Current ratio (*filigree* vs. *filagree* vs.
fillagree): 110:6:1

Filipino. See **Philippine Islands.**

filter, vb.; *filtrate,* vb. The latter is a NEEDLESS VARIANT—e.g.:

• "We buy sprinkler systems instead and spray expensively *filtrated* [read *filtered*] drinking water all over the garden." Anna Pavord, "And Hummingbirds Flicker by Tall, White Foxgloves," *Independent*, 2 Mar. 1996, at 12.
• "And while the town must scrounge for rainwater, just 10 kilometers away, a Petroecuador water pump sends *filtrated* [read *filtered*] water to employees at the local refinery." Matthew Yeomans, "Fool's Gold," *Village Voice*, 4 Feb. 1997, at 46.

Of course, *filtrate* is perfectly proper as a noun meaning "a liquid that has been filtered"—e.g.: "It pumped untreated hog slurry into the system, where a chemical and separation process was to result in clear *filtrate* and biosolids—matter high in nutrients that could be used as garden or crop fertilizer." Anne Fitzgerald, "Odor Control: Smell of Money," *Des Moines Register*, 2 Feb. 1997, at 1.

LANGUAGE-CHANGE INDEX
filtrate misused for the verb *filter*: Stage 1
Current ratio (*filtered* vs. *filtrated*): 232:1

filterable. So spelled in AmE and BrE alike—preferably not *filtrable*.

Current ratio: 13:1

filtrate. See **filter.**

finable. So spelled in AmE and BrE alike—preferably not *fineable*. See MUTE E.

Current ratio: 4:1

final, adj. See ADJECTIVES (B).

final analysis, in the. See **in the final analysis.**

final destination. See **destination.**

finalize = (1) v.t., to complete; bring to an end; put in final form; or (2) v.i., to conclude. Coined in the mid-19th century, *finalize* flourished as a VOGUE WORD in the late 20th century, a favorite of jargonmongers. For that reason alone, many writers avoid it. But the word's advantage is that it has the compactness of a single word, as opposed to most of its equivalents: *make final, put into final form,* and *bring to an end.* Today few people object to it, and it is all but ubiquitous—e.g.:

• "The show was taped for future broadcast, but theater officials have yet to *finalize* an air date and network contract." Victoria Dawson, "First Lady of Ford's," *Wash. Post*, 22 June 1987, at B1.
• "Charles and Diana will *finalize* their divorce this spring." Linda Barnard, "Stargazing," *Toronto Sun*, 18 Dec. 1994, at 87.
• "HUD also contends that the county failed to *finalize* a contract for an administrator to oversee task-force operations." Mike Bucsko, "Anti-Bias Pact Not Observed, HUD Says," *Pitt. Post-Gaz.*, 20 Dec. 1996, at A1.

Still, *complete* is a better choice when it will suffice, as in the last example quoted above. See -IZE.

LANGUAGE-CHANGE INDEX
finalize: Stage 5

final outcome; final result; final upshot. Each of these is a common REDUNDANCY, since *outcome*, *result*, and *upshot* are all generally understood as final. It may be, however, that because modern technology—whether in instant replays on television or in computer calculations—allows us to view all sorts of preliminary results, some further qualification is considered desirable. But that's merely an excuse, not a sound rationale. And besides, writers often use the wordy phrases even when they don't mean them—e.g.:

- "The *final outcome* [read *outcome*] was a convincing 90–76 America East victory over the Northeastern Huskies." Andrew Neff, "Reed's Six 3-Pointers Help Bears Down Northeastern," *Bangor Daily News*, 16 Jan. 2003, at C9.
- "They both said the process won't be as important as the *final result* [read *result*]." Tom Bell, "State Lawmakers Differ on Need for Tax-Reform Panel," *Portland Press Herald*, 16 Jan. 2003, at B1.

Cf. **destination.**

Sometimes, however, *final result* or a similar phrase is needed to contrast something with preliminary estimates—e.g.: "Compuware now expects to earn 6 to 7 cents a share for the fiscal third quarter; analysts were expecting a profit of 9 cents a share. . . . Compuware will announce its *final results* for the quarter on Jan. 22." "Compuware Lowers Earnings Estimate," *N.Y. Times*, 10 Jan. 2003, at C3. Cf. **end result.**

Like its cousins, *final upshot* is a minor redundancy, since the word *upshot* implies finality—e.g.: "Just what the *final upshot* [read *upshot*] of the postgame outburst will be remains to be seen." "Rose Shoves Ump Again in Brawl," *San Diego Union-Trib.*, 16 Aug. 1989, at D2.

LANGUAGE-CHANGE INDEX
1. *final outcome* for *outcome*: Stage 2
2. *final results* for *results* (when not contrasted with preliminary results): Stage 2
3. *final upshot* for *upshot*: Stage 1

FINAL PREPOSITION. See PREPOSITIONS (B).

final result. See **final outcome.**

final upshot. See **final outcome.**

finance is pronounced either /fə-**nan**[t]s/ or /**fɪ**-nan[t]s/. The first is traditionally the better pronunciation.

financeable. So spelled. See -ABLE (E).

financial. See **economic** (B).

financier; financer. *Financier* = someone whose business is lending money. *Financer* = someone who finances a particular undertaking. The DIFFERENTIATION should be encouraged, but not everyone bothers with it—e.g.: "But the bank, which used to be a major *financer* [read *financier*] of Third World projects, finds

itself now a relatively minor factor in dollar terms." R.C. Longworth, "World Bank Looking to Overlooked Needs," *Chicago Trib.*, 1 Nov. 1996, Bus. §, at 2.

Many dictionaries, including the *OED* and *W2*, inaccurately list *financer* as obsolete. Others, such as *RH2* and *W3*, simply omit it. But it does appear with some frequency—e.g.:

- "The Saudi Arabian government has come under renewed pressure over its pursuit of terror *financers* in its midst." David Crawford, "German Terror Inquiry Hits Snag," *Wall Street J.*, 6 Dec. 2002, at A5.
- "The e-commerce company moved closer to its Austin *financers* and then closed last year as the demand for Internet services plummeted during the dot-com crash." "Knoxville Entrepreneur Tries New Austin-Based Business," *Knoxville News-Sentinel*, 9 Dec. 2002, at C1.
- "For years, R.J. Reynolds Co. was the largest private *financer* of tobacco-related research at NCSU." Catherine Clabby, "NCSU to Map Out Tobacco," *News & Observer* (Raleigh), 12 Dec. 2002, at A1.

Current ratio: 32:1

fine-toothed comb; fine-tooth comb. The latter spelling has long been more than twice as common as the former. Because *fine-toothed comb* better reflects the literal meaning—a comb with teeth set close together, rather than a comb with fine (very thin) teeth—that spelling might be thought preferable even in figurative senses <she went over the contract with a fine-toothed comb>. See ADJECTIVES (F). But print sources favor *fine-tooth comb*. Cf. **iced tea, skim milk** & **stained glass.**

LANGUAGE-CHANGE INDEX
fine-tooth comb for *fine-toothed comb*: Stage 5
Current ratio (*tooth* vs. *toothed*): 2:1

finicky is the preferred spelling—not **finnicky*. *Finical* is a pedantic variant that is seldom used today, though it was fairly common till about 1820. Anyone who uses it is likely to be thought of as being, well, finical.

Current ratio (*finicky* vs. *finical* vs. **finnicky*): 175:37:1

finis (= end, conclusion) is a 15th-century Latin loanword that was early anglicized as /**fin**-is/, and English-language dictionaries have long recorded this pronunciation. In the late 20th century, however, many people mistook the word for a GALLICISM of recent vintage and started saying /fee-**nee**/. Today this nouveau pronunciation threatens to drive out the traditional one.

*fiord. See **fjord.**

fir. The name of the evergreen tree is occasionally misspelled *fur*, creating an odd mental image—e.g.:

- "One of the most visible signs of the strong winds was the toppling of an almost 80-foot *fur* [read *fir*] tree near a Congress Street home in Fairfield." Greg Clarkin, "Scrambling

LANGUAGE-CHANGE INDEX (For the full key, see front matter pp. xxxi, l–li.)
Stage 1: Rejected. **Stage 2:** Widely shunned. **Stage 3:** Widespread but . . . **Stage 4:** Ubiquitous but . . . **Stage 5:** Fully accepted.
Invariably inferior forms marked by asterisk (*). • Ratios represent frequency of prevalent forms vs. variants in current books.

for Power After a One-Two Punch of Storms," *N.Y. Times*, 22 Jan. 2006, § 14CN, at 11.

- "Eileen Meert plants a canaan *fur* [read *fir*] tree Saturday as Josh Hickman, center, digs a hole and Domien Meert fertilizes the hole at Meert Tree Farm in Festus." "A Growing Knowledge of Trees," *St. Louis Post-Dispatch*, 12 Apr. 2006, Bus. §, at A12 (photo caption).

LANGUAGE-CHANGE INDEX
*fur tree for *fir tree*: Stage 1
Current ratio (*fir tree* vs. **fur tree*): 124:1

fire; terminate; let go; lay off. *Fire* has the sense of dismissing an employee for cause, such as for inadequate performance or moral turpitude. The word implies abruptness and forcibleness and is therefore viewed as being derogatory. A common EUPHEMISM is *terminate*; another is *let go*.

Lay off means "to dismiss (an employee), often temporarily, because of slow business or the seasonal nature of some work, such as agriculture." Because *fire* is shorter, headline writers are often tempted to substitute it (wrongly) for *lay off* or (BrE) *make redundant*—e.g.: Robert Naylor Jr., "Amtrak to Cut Routes, *Fire* [read *Lay Off*] 5,500 Workers," *Austin Am.-Statesman*, 15 Dec. 1994, at A13. Although *lay off* is a common euphemism for *fire*, the distinction is a useful one.

firefighter. See SEXISM (C).

firmament. The *firmament* is the sky, the canopy of stars (as people once envisioned it). It was "firm" because it was thought to be a fixed and immutable dome. Today the word is often used in a metaphorical sense to mean the constellation of "stars" (celebrities or key people) in a certain field. But sometimes writers seem misled by the "firm" portion of the word, using *firmament* as if it meant *ground* or *foundation*—e.g.:

- "The pair present an affecting love story against the racial *firmament* [read *climate*] Jack Johnson/Jefferson encountered during his reign that began in 1908 and ended seven years later." Jeff Rivers, "Films with Punch," *Sun-Sentinel* (Ft. Lauderdale), 27 Dec. 2001, at E3.
- "Miller-motivated dancers have feet that often seem to revel in light contact with the *firmament* [read *ground*]. They don't grind into the floor. They caress it." Terry Morris, "DCDC's New Work Playful, Quirky," *Dayton Daily News*, 2 Feb. 2002, at C4.
- "The rules turn out to be liberating, and those placid in-between moments act as the *firmament* [read *foundation*], making Ellie's wacky, always-going-wrong existence believable." Manuel Mendoza, "Perfect Timing for 'Ellie,'" *Dallas Morning News*, 26 Feb. 2002, at C1.

Perhaps the misuse is influenced also by confusion with *terra firma* (= solid ground).

LANGUAGE-CHANGE INDEX
firmament misused for *ground* or *foundation*: Stage 1

first and foremost should not merely displace *first*. The *OED* describes it as a "strengthened" phrase— i.e., an especially emphatic one—and dates it from the 16th century.

*first annual. This phrase expresses a promoter's wish, not a fact. An event that is held or occurs once a year is an annual event. But its first occurrence is not annual because it didn't happen the previous year. The *AP Stylebook* sensibly recommends mentioning that the organizers plan to hold the event annually.

first-come, first-served. As a PHRASAL ADJECTIVE, this term has obligatory hyphens. It sometimes appears with the comma (recommended), and sometimes without, as *first-come-first-served* (also acceptable). When a noun doesn't appear at the end, and the phrase is simply used as a statement, a comma comes between the two parts, which are unhyphenated: *first come, first served*.

The past-participial *served* is required in this phrase. The first people to come are the first who *are served* (not the ones who *serve*). But some writers erroneously use *serve*—e.g.:

- "The 3,000 to 5,000 division series tickets will be sold on a *first-come, first-serve* [read *first-come, first-served*] basis." John Shea, "Playoff Ticket Plan Announced," *S.F. Examiner*, 15 Sept. 2000, at D4.
- "Tickets to 111 different events will be available through the Salt Lake Organizing Committee's Web site, www.saltlake2002.com, on a *first-come, first-serve* [read *first-come, first-served*] basis." Lisa Riley Roche, "200,000 Games," *Deseret News* (Salt Lake City), 4 June 2001, at B4.
- "The five members picked to hear a specific case are selected on a *first-come, first-serve* [read *first-come, first-served*] basis." Jerry Lauzon, "Lawyer for Athletes Alleges Conflict of Interest," *Portland Press Herald*, 19 Oct. 2002, at A1.

LANGUAGE-CHANGE INDEX
*first-come, first-serve for *first-come, first-served*: Stage 3
Current ratio (*first come first served* vs. **first come first serve*): 3:1

first edition. This phrase is ambiguous: it means one thing to an author or publisher and quite another to a book collector or antiquarian bookseller. To an author or publisher, *first edition* refers to any printing of the first unrevised version of a book. In this sense, a first edition of H.W. Fowler's *Dictionary of Modern English Usage* could be any one of the several printings from 1926 to 1965 (when the second edition, as revised by Sir Ernest Gowers, was published). To a book collector or used-book seller, only the first printing (in the first year of publication) is a first edition.

*first iteration. See **reiterate.**

firstly, secondly, thirdly, etc. are today considered inferior to *first, second, third*, etc. Many stylists prefer *first* over *firstly* even when the remaining signposts are *secondly* and *thirdly*. See ENUMERATIONS (A).

first name. See NAMES (D).

FIRST PERSON. A. Generally. Immature writers use *I* and *me* at every turn. It's therefore a customary rite of passage for every grade-school student to write an essay without ever using first person. As a writing exercise, this is useful.

Yet it arguably does much harm as well. Many students come to believe that in writing, there's something inherently wrong with first person. So even later in life, they go to great lengths to avoid it, as by using phrases such as *the present writer, the author,* and so on. It leads them to PASSIVE VOICE and to ZOMBIE NOUNS. If you're the actor, the belief runs, omit the actor. It all leads to ABSTRACTITIS.

But graceless circumlocutions serve no real stylistic purpose and are inferior to the straightforward pronouns *I* and *me.* Late in his career as a writer, Jerome Frank confessed that he had long shunned the first-person pronoun, preferring *the writer* to *I* on the assumption that the indirect phrasing signified modesty. With age he became wiser and concluded: "To say *I* removes a false impression of a Jovian aloofness." *Courts on Trial* vii–viii (1950).

Of one common set of self-obscuring devices—*it is suggested that, it is proposed that,* and *it is submitted that*—Fred Rodell observed, "Whether the writers really suppose that such constructions clothe them in anonymity so that people cannot guess who is suggesting and who is proposing, I do not know." "Goodbye to Law Reviews—Revisited," 48 *Va. L. Rev.* 279, 280 (1962). We do know, however, that these phrases often make sentences read as if they had been "translated from the German by someone with a rather meager knowledge of English." *Ibid.*

None of this should suggest that every personal opinion should include the word *I.* Most opinions are transparently personal and need no direct mention of the writer—e.g.: "Though Einstein is routinely lionized as a great scientific mind, Newton was the most original thinker that science has ever produced." No moderately sophisticated reader would assume that this statement is anything more than an opinion. And it is much more convincingly stated without inserting the phrase *in my opinion.* See **I personally, myself** & SUPERSTITIONS (I).

B. Editorial *we.* "The editorial 'we' . . . is fitted only for expressing corporate policy." Walter Raleigh, *On Writing and Writers* 25 (George Gordon ed., 1926). That judgment remains sound.

It is certainly eccentric to see a solo writer using *we* and *our* when no one else is involved—e.g.: "*We* do not propose in this little volume to treat of these changes in their chronological sequence—to show, for instance, in what respects the English of Chaucer differs from that of Alfred, the English of Shakespere [*sic*] from that of Chaucer, and the English of the nineteenth century from that of the sixteenth. Information of this kind must be sought for in regular histories of the English language. *Our* purpose is merely to give some idea of the causes by which the more remarkable changes in the language were brought about." Henry Bradley, *The Making of English* 14 (1904; repr. 1951). The first-person *I* and *My* would surely sit more comfortably in those sentences—and probably would have even in 1904. See **they** (B).

fisc (= a governmental treasury; exchequer) has been predominantly so spelled in AmE and BrE alike since the 18th century. *Fisk is a variant spelling. The adjective form is *fiscal.*

Current ratio (*fisc* vs. *fisk): 4:1

fish; fishes. The Evanses wrote in 1957 that the plural *fish* is of recent vintage and opined that "the life expectancy of a new irregular plural, such as *fish,* is not very long." *DCAU* at 179. But the *OED* cites *fish* as the plural form as long ago as 1300. Today, *fish* is the firmly established plural. *Fishes* appears rarely, at least outside ichthyology. When it does appear, it usually refers to more than one species—e.g.:

- "While two Asian *fishes* have recently made news for their ability to survive in the wilds of America, the U.S. Fish and Wildlife Service said last week it plans to restrict the sale of one of their cousins, a carp used on Southern fish farms to eat disease-carrying snails." David Mercer, "Farmers Fret over Plans to Limit Carp," *Ark. Democrat-Gaz.,* 6 Aug. 2002, at D1.
- "A chapon, right, the first of five *fishes,* gets bouillabaisse under way at L'Epuisette." R.W. Apple Jr., "A Prime Kettle of Fish," *N.Y. Times,* 7 Aug. 2002, at F1 (referring to five species of fish).

Fish does take the regular *-es* ending to form the plural possessive—e.g.: "A Yozuri Crystal Minnow seems to be the *fishes'* preference." David Sikes, "Island Time," *Corpus Christi Caller-Times,* 4 Aug. 2002, at B14. And the plural form *fishes* persists in idioms such as *The Godfather*'s "Luca Brasi sleeps with the *fishes,*" as well as the biblical allusion "loaves and *fishes.*"

***fisk.** See **fisc.**

fission. The standard AmE pronunciation today is either /**fish**-ən/ or /**fizh**-ən/. The second now predominates (probably to parallel the sound of the correlative term *fusion* /**fyoo**-zhən/), even though the first corresponds to analogous words such as *mission.* Cf. **rescission** (B).

fist bump; fist pump. A *fist bump* is a greeting made by bumping knuckles. A *fist pump* is a celebratory gesture made by holding out a fist with the elbow

LANGUAGE-CHANGE INDEX (For the full key, see front matter pp. xxxi, I–Ii.)
Stage 1: Rejected. **Stage 2:** Widely shunned. **Stage 3:** Widespread but . . . **Stage 4:** Ubiquitous but . . . **Stage 5:** Fully accepted.
Invariably inferior forms marked by asterisk (*). • Ratios represent frequency of prevalent forms vs. variants in current books.

cocked and jerking down (or sometimes up or away from the body). Although the terms are sometimes confounded, this writer got both right: "She looked at the stands and saw the Wolf Pack and gave them a *fist pump.* Andrew came over to her and said, 'Crab legs with all the trimmings.' Micala smiled and gave her trainer a *fist bump.*" D.K. Barnes, *High Country Dreams* 104 (2005).

fisticuffs (= a fistfight), though singular in sense (a single fistfight being *fisticuffs*), is plural in form. Still, one refers to *fisticuffs,* not *a fisticuffs—e.g.: "The city's famously combative District Attorney, Terence Hallinan, who got into *a fisticuffs* [delete *a*] with a trade-union leader at Mr. Davis's last birthday celebration, said the party-givers' biggest error might have been to invite a pair of political columnists from The San Francisco Chronicle." Tim Golden, "Political 'Party' Goes So Far, Even San Francisco Is Aghast," *N.Y. Times,* 10 May 1997, at 1, 15. Often found in the idiom *to trade fisticuffs,* the word carries a quaint tone.

fist pump. See **fist bump.**

fistula (= an abnormal opening into a natural canal or hollow organ) has predominantly formed the plural *fistulas* in AmE since about 1940, but the Latinate plural *fistulae* /**fis**-chə-lee/ has been standard in BrE since the mid-19th century. See PLURALS (B).

Current ratio (*fistulas* vs. *fistulae* in World English): 2:1

fit > fitted > fitted (traditionally); **fit > fit > fit** (more modernly in AmE). Just since the mid-20th century, AmE has witnessed a shift in the past tense and past participle from *fitted* to *fit.* Traditionally, *fit* would have been considered incorrect, but it began appearing in journalism and even scholarly writing as early as the 1950s. David S. Berkeley, "The Past Tense of 'Fit,'" 30 *Am. Speech* 311 (1955).

This CASUALISM now appears even in what is generally considered well-edited American journalism, especially where the *fit* is not a physical attachment but a match—e.g.:

- "This 'modified Münchausen syndrome,' in FBI terminology, occurs in someone who wants to be a hero so badly that he creates emergencies so he can rescue people. Jewell, a police wannabe, *fit* this profile and also had the characteristics of people who use pipe bombs—white single men in their 30s or 40s with a martial bent." James Collins, "The Strange Saga of Richard Jewell," *Time,* 11 Nov. 1996, at 60, 62.
- "He [Steven Morrissey] never quite *fit* as a proper rock star." Ann Powers, "A Conflicted Champion of the Lonely and Losers," *N.Y. Times,* 28 Nov. 1997, at E1.
- "Collins *fit* the typical profile of a Menimo confidant." Scott S. Greenberger, "'Dr. No' Has Mayor's Ear," *Boston Globe,* 8 Apr. 2003, at B1.

And it appears in fine scholarly writing—e.g.: "English land tenure, and the English way of life among landed gentry, *fit* this social order more than was true in the North." Lawrence M. Friedman, *A History of American Law* 66 (2d ed. 1985).

The traditionally correct past tense still surfaces, especially in BrE, but in AmE it is becoming rarer (and stuffier) year by year—e.g.:

- "The Mermaid [an inn] *fitted* our plans perfectly." Edmund Antrobus, "Bloody Boo Time!" *Asbury Park Press* (Neptune, N.J.), 27 Oct. 1996, at F1.
- "Nothing else *fitted* the facts." Colin Edwards, *The Father of Forensics* 239 (2006).

Yet where the *fit* is a physical coupling, *fitted* is the natural choice—e.g.:

- "A most interesting item in my coin collection is a disk that *fitted* the pressure-spray nozzle on our apple-orchard pump some 50 years ago." John Gould, "Coins of the Heart, a Currency That Keeps," *Christian Science Monitor,* 27 Dec. 1996, at 21.
- "The 4-year-old colt underwent several procedures and was *fitted* with fiberglass casts." Mark Blaudschun, "Survival Struggle Ends for Champion Barbaro," *Boston Globe,* 30 Jan. 2007, Sports §, at A1.
- "Don't rent ski boots. Buy a good midpriced pair . . . . If they're properly *fitted,* you'll always be comfortable." Anne Z. Cooke & Steve Haggerty, "Strategies for Best Results on the Slopes," *St. Petersburg Times,* 30 Jan. 2007, SSP §, at 6.

And the traditional form remains with prefixed derivatives (e.g., *outfitted, retrofitted*). Although *fitted* may one day be extinct as a verb form, it will undoubtedly persist as an adjective <fitted sheets>.

Anthony Burgess considered the past *fit* to be one of the prime differentiators between BrE and AmE: "A British reader of American expository prose feels totally at home until he comes to 'fit' as a past tense ('This fit his theory') and the past participle 'gotten,' which has disappeared from Britain (except in dialectical forms, where it often appears as 'getten')." Anthony Burgess, *A Mouthful of Air* 280 (1992). See IRREGULAR VERBS. Cf. **knit.**

LANGUAGE-CHANGE INDEX
fit as a past-tense form: Stage 5

fjord; *fiord. In modern sources, *fjord*—the preferred spelling—greatly outnumbers **fiord.*

Current ratio: 3:1

flaccid. A. Pronunciation. *Flaccid* is preferably pronounced /**flak**-sid/, not /**flas**-id/. All the traditional pronunciation guides have said so—and they're right. The /ks/ pronunciation is common in words with a -*cc*- preceding an -*i,* -*e,* or -*ee,* such as *accession, accident, succeed,* and *vaccination.* As one authority explains: "When *cc*- precedes -*e* or -*i,* the first *c*- is pronounced *k*-, the second *s*-, as in *accede, accelerate, accept, accessible, flaccid, succinct,* etc." Norman Lewis, *Dictionary of Modern Pronunciation* 76 (1963). The one set of exceptions to that rule involves Italian words and names commonly used in English (the -*cc*- having a /ch/ sound): *cappuccino, carpaccio, Gucci, Puccini,* etc. Cf. **accessory (B)** & **succinct.**

Over a long period, many pronunciation authorities have listed only /**flak**-sid/, not even mentioning /**flas**-id/. See, e.g., John H. Bechtel, *Handbook of Pronunciation and Phonetic Analysis* 53 (1900); Andrew

J. Graham, *The Standard-Phonographic Dictionary* 154 (1908); Josephine Turck Baker, *Correct Standardized Pronunciation* 201 (1919); Charles B. Anderson, *A Guide to Good Pronunciation* 55 (1931); Alfred H. Holt, *You Don't Say!* 62 (1937); *NBC Handbook of Pronunciation* 142 (1940); Morriss H. Needleman, *A Manual of Pronunciation* 126 (1949); John S. Kenyon & Thomas A. Knott, *A Pronouncing Dictionary of American English* 167 (1953); Ruth Gleeson & James Colvin, *Words Most Often Misspelled and Mispronounced* 82 (1963); Daniel Jones, *Everyman's English Pronouncing Dictionary* 192 (A.C. Gimson ed., 14th ed. 1977); Samuel Noory, *Dictionary of Pronunciation* 116 (3d ed. 1979).

Since the 19th century, some authorities have explicitly disparaged the *k*-less pronunciation:

- "Flaccid—flak´sid, *not* flas´id." Richard Soule & Loomis J. Campbell, *Pronouncing Handbook of Words Often Mispronounced* 35 (1873). Identical phrasing appears in other books, such as Alfred Ayres, *The Orthoepist* 70 (1881); Julian W. Abernethy, *Correct Pronunciation* 50 (1912); and William Henry P. Phyfe, *20,000 Words Often Mispronounced* 317 (rev. ed. 1937).
- "*Flac´cid* means having little or no resistance, yielding easily to force or weight or pressure. It rhymes with *back slid*, that is, *flack´sid*. The noun *flaccidity* is pronounced *flak sid´ i t*. Don't say *flassid* to rhyme with *acid*." John Baker Opdycke, *Don't Say It* 343 (1943).
- "*Flaccid* should not rhyme with *placid*. . . . Note that *flaccid* is syllabified *flac-cid*. The *c* ending the first syllable is pronounced k; the second *c* is followed by *i* and is therefore pronounced s." Frank O. Colby, *The American Pronouncing Dictionary of Troublesome Words* 158 (1950).
- "Although FLAK-sid-sayers are now in the minority, there's no denying it's one heck of a respectable minority. A survey of sources published since the 1960s reveals that an overwhelming number of authorities prefer FLAK-sid." Charles Harrington Elster, *BBBM* at 203–04.

The limp, flabby pronunciation of the word—which some have tried to rationalize as a kind of sensory onomatopoeia (the logic being that *flaccid* denotes what is soft and should therefore have a soft *-c-* in the middle)—started gaining some (grudging) acceptance in the mid-20th century in *W3* (1961) and in other wordbooks—e.g.:

- "*Flaccid* is preferably pronounced /**flak**-sid/, but some people say /**flas**-id/, which is also acceptable." *Reader's Digest Success with Words* 240 (1983).
- "The older pronunciation is (flak´sid), but the variant (flas´id) has been recorded in dictionaries since about the middle of the 20th century." *The American Heritage Book of English Usage* 222 (1996).

It's recorded in *Webster's New World Dictionary* (1994), all right, but only as a secondary variant. *W10* (1993) obelizes /**flas**-id/ with the mark "÷" (suggesting that it's "considered by some to be unacceptable"), but then it labels /**flak**-sid/ as being "appreciably less common." Meanwhile, the second edition of the *OED* (1989) lists only /**flak**-sid/. *W11* (2003) removed the "÷" and, without comment, gave preference to /**flas**-id/.

In short, this word is a kind of SKUNKED TERM: pronounce it in the traditional way, and you'll take some flak for doing so; pronounce it in the new way, and the cognoscenti will probably infer that you couldn't spell or say *cognoscenti*, either. See PRONUNCIATION (B).

LANGUAGE-CHANGE INDEX
flaccid pronounced /**flas**-id/ instead of /**flak**-sid/:
Stage 4

B. Misspelling. As a result of the spreading mispronunciation, the misspelling **flacid* (on the analogy of *placid*) has arisen—e.g.:

- "Naomi, Toshiyuki and I unrolled the long, *flacid* [read *flaccid*] canopy while Richard positioned a huge electric fan at the mouth." Elliot Neal Hester, "The Sky's the Limit for Central Florida Vacations," *Boston Herald*, 16 May 1996, at 54.
- "The succulent shellfish practically melted on the tongue, but the tempura coating was oddly *flacid* [read *flaccid*]." Cynthia Kilian, "A Win, Win Situation," *N.Y. Post*, 12 May 2002, at 55.
- "We few, we unhappy few, grimace through the molasses-on-grits Southern accents, shake our heads at the historical revisionism and snort at the static dullness of this endless, *flacid* [read *flaccid*] adaptation of another historical novel about America's defining moment." Roger Moore, "This Civil War Epic Is God-Awful and Generally a Waste," *Orlando Sentinel*, 21 Feb. 2003, Cal. §, at 20.

LANGUAGE-CHANGE INDEX
flaccid misspelled **flacid*: Stage 1
Current ratio: 333:1

flack. See **flak.**

flagrancy; *flagrance. The first is standard; the latter is a NEEDLESS VARIANT. See -CE.

Current ratio: 4:1

flagrant (= glaring) is occasionally confused with *fragrant* (= nice-smelling)—e.g.:

- "The Inspector General examined the 45 businesses that were assessed penalties by OSHA in 1989 and 1990 for *fragrantly* [read *flagrantly*] violating safety laws." L.M. Sixel, "Big OSHA Fines Often Cut Down to a Pittance," *Houston Chron.*, 2 Apr. 1992, at A1.
- "U.S. Secretary of State Madeleine Albright and United Nations Ambassador Bill Richardson huff and puff in one breath that Iraq's Saddam Hussein will not get away with *fragrantly* [read *flagrantly*] violating the United Nations." "Oust Saddam!" *Augusta Chron.*, 14 Nov. 1997, at A4.
- "Ryan Volenberg, a conservation warden with the DNR, said the salmon run is very popular with sportsmen and women, but is also known for *fragrant* [read *flagrant*] violations." Neil Rhines, "Salmon Run: Poor So Far," *Herald Times Reporter* (Manitowoc, Wis.), 4 Oct. 2004, at A1.

See MALAPROPISMS.

LANGUAGE-CHANGE INDEX (For the full key, see front matter pp. xxxi, l–li.)
Stage 1: Rejected. **Stage 2:** Widely shunned. **Stage 3:** Widespread but . . . **Stage 4:** Ubiquitous but . . . **Stage 5:** Fully accepted.
Invariably inferior forms marked by asterisk (*). • Ratios represent frequency of prevalent forms vs. variants in current books.

For more on the use of *flagrant*, see **blatant**.

LANGUAGE-CHANGE INDEX
fragrant misused for *flagrant*: Stage 1

flail; flay. To *flail* is (1) to beat or thrash (something), or (2) to move in a thrashing motion, esp. to whip one's arms about wildly—e.g.: "He'd start off stiff, his body virtually twitching with nervous energy, and then gradually his arms would start to move, then *flail*, his movements becoming wilder until he seemed to be tearing open." Jonathan Hayes, "Joy Division: More Unknown Pleasures," *N.Y. Observer*, 10 Sept. 2001, Arts & Entertainment §, at 23.

To *flay* is (1) to rip the skin or hide off (something), or (2) to deprive (a person) of property by extortion or exaction—e.g.: "David Faber uses his take-no-prisoners approach to disembowel investment banking firms, expose methods of corporate deceit, *flay* the conspiring accounting firms, and generally lay bare how investor billions are made and lost (mostly lost) through greed and incompetence." Book Rev., "Best Stock Pickers Do Their Own Homework," *Pitt. Post-Gaz.*, 21 July 2002, at E2.

Flay is sometimes misused for *flail*—e.g.:

- "If you really and truly are that outdoorsy, spending many weekends *flaying* [read *flailing*] about in mud, water or over yonder dale, then the versatility of the Explorer is well worth the deficit in ride and handling." David Booth, "Pseudo-ute v. Sport-ute," *Nat'l Post*, 29 Sept. 2000, at E2.
- "He was nicknamed 'the human locomotive' because of his ungainly style—arms *flaying* [read *flailing*], head rolling, and his tongue hanging out." Larry Stewart, "The Irish Track," *L.A. Times*, 21 Dec. 2000, at D2.
- " 'Who knows where he is!' Trinidad said, *flaying* [read *flailing*] her arms into the air." Allistair Scrutton, "For Better or Worse," *Sun-Sentinel* (Ft. Lauderdale), 11 Feb. 2001, at A24.

LANGUAGE-CHANGE INDEX
flay misused for *flail*: Stage 1
Current ratio (*flailing his arms* vs.
*flaying his arms): 39:1

flair. See **flare.**

flak; flack. *Flak* (orig. referring to fragments of artillery shells, esp. those used for anti-aircraft guns, built to explode into destructive pieces) = annoying criticism or opposition. *Flack* = a press agent. The most common problem with these words is that *flack* is misused for *flak*—e.g.:

- "*Variety*'s Todd McCarthy says he received a good deal of *flack* [read *flak*] for his negative review." Georgia Brown, "Riviera of No Return," *Village Voice*, 7 June 1994, at 54.
- "The Corps of Engineers has taken a lot of *flack* [read *flak*] for the levee failures." Paul Purpura, "Q&A with the Military Community," *Times-Picayune* (New Orleans), 22 Oct. 2006, Nat'l §, at 10.
- "[W]e never bought Internet, dot-com or telecom stocks for our clients. Although we took a lot of *flack* [read *flak*] in 1998 and 1999 for this stand, . . . we were *proven* [read *proved*] right when the dot-com bubble burst in the early 2000s." Ric Edelman, "The Truth About Money," *Capital* (Annapolis), 17 Dec. 2006, Bus. §, at B2. (See **proved.**)

But the misuses go both ways. Occasionally *flak* ousts *flack* from its rightful place—e.g.:

- "To reporters, they are derisively known as '*flaks*' [read '*flacks*'], whose main duties consist of peddling press releases." Bryan Burrough & John Helyar, *Barbarians at the Gate* 293 (1990).
- "So how does the president feel about the Oscar Mayer wiener song being sung in Spanish? . . . I get transferred to the Media Office and reiterate my desire to talk to a press *flak* [read *flack*]." Melanie Conklin, "Wiener Wish in Spanish Is OK," *Wis. State J.*, 20 May 2006, at A1.
- "Public relations *flaks* [read *flacks*] started pushing 'Back To School 2006' supplies and stories the day before classes let out in June." Lauri Githens, "As Summer Rolls On, Don't Forget to Get Kids Ready for School," *Rochester Democrat & Chron.*, 26 July 2006, at H9.

During the 1960s, the noun *flack* was made into a verb. A person who *flacks* provides publicity. But *flak* has appeared in this context, too—not commonly, but often enough to warrant caution. E.g.: "Monday, I was all over Chicago *flakking* [read *flacking*] my new book *On the Line* (Harcourt Brace, $21.95), about last year's elections." Larry King, "Zipping by the Rest Stops on the Highway of Life," *USA Today*, 22 Nov. 1993, at D2.

LANGUAGE-CHANGE INDEX
1. *flack* misused for *flak*: Stage 3
Current ratio (*caught flak* vs. *caught flack): 3:1
2. *flak* misused for *flack*: Stage 2
Current ratio (*PR flacks* vs. *PR flaks): 6:1

flambeau (= a flaming torch) predominantly forms the plural *flambeaux* in AmE and BrE alike—not *flambeaus*.

Current ratio: 10:1

flamenco = (1) the Spanish music originally played by gypsies and characterized by stomping and clapping; or (2) the dance typically performed to this music. Occasionally writers confuse this word with *flamingo* (the long-necked pink bird)—e.g.:

- "You can hear not only aspects of Mexican folk dance but *flamingo* [read *flamenco*] dancing as well." Paul Cook, "Desenne," *Am. Record Guide*, Sept. 1995, at 134.
- "Other activities of this May Saturday include a *flamingo* [read *flamenco*] dancer and children's activities." Donna Larcen, "Dominick Dunne's Home Among Dozens Open for Touring This Year," *Hartford Courant*, 25 Apr. 1996, at G8.
- "Performers brought in to provide entertainment will include an Asian Lion dancer, a Celtic dance *troop* [read *troupe*], South American dancers and *flamingo* [read *flamenco*] dancers." "Hayes Elementary Hosts International Fest," *Houston Chron.*, 31 Jan. 2001, This Week §, at 10. (On the misuse of *troop* in that sentence, see **troop.**)

LANGUAGE-CHANGE INDEX
flamingo misused for *flamenco*: Stage 1

flamingo. Pl. *flamingos*. From 1820 to 1940, the alternative plural ending *-oes* predominated. See PLURALS (D).

Current ratio: 2:1

flammable; inflammable. The first is now accepted as standard in AmE and BrE alike. Though examples of its use date back to 1813, in the 1960s and more so later it became widespread as a substitute for *inflammable*, in which some people mistook the prefix *in-* to be negative rather than intensive—e.g.: "[T]heir fireplace is mounted in a black box built out of *an inflammable* [read *a nonflammable* or *a noninflammable*] material made of pressed paper." Michael Cannell, "A 180-Degrees View of a Hotbed of Housing Design," *N.Y. Times*, 4 Jan. 2007, at F7. Traditionally, the forms were *inflammable* and *noninflammable*; today they are *flammable* and *nonflammable*. By the early 1970s, purists had lost the fight to retain the older forms. See NEGATIVES (A).

Even staunch descriptivists endorsed the prescriptive shift from *inflammable* to *flammable*—e.g.: "A word is bad if it is ambiguous to such a degree that it leads to misunderstanding. For me, the perfect example of such a word is *inflammable*, if it is applied to substances. As most dictionaries now recognize, *inflammable* can be confused with *non-combustible*, and so lead to accidents." Archibald A. Hill, "Bad Words, Good Words, Misused Words," in *Studies in English Linguistics for Randolph Quirk* 250, 252 (1983). Cf. **inflammatory**.

LANGUAGE-CHANGE INDEX
flammable (= combustible): Stage 5
Current ratio (*flammable* vs. *inflammable*): 2:1

flare; flair. *Flare* = a sudden outburst of flame; an unsteady light. *Flair* = (1) outstanding skill or ability in some field; or (2) originality, stylishness. By far the most common confusion occurs when *flare* displaces *flair*—e.g.:

- "Today also is National Handwriting Day in honor of the birth of John Hancock. Hancock had a real *flare* [read *flair*] for writing—especially those insurance policies." Kathy Borlik, "Worth Waking Up For," *South Bend Trib.*, 12 Jan. 2002, at A2.
- "Just as disappointing is the failure of [John] Clancy to show the *flare* [read *flair*] he has demonstrated in previous Edinburgh visits with shows such as 'Americana Absurdum,' 'Horse Country' and 'Fatboy.'" Mark Fisher, "Midnight Cowboy," *Variety*, 14–20 Aug. 2006, at 34.
- "[Mark] Cuban would love to see [Sidney] Crosby or one of the sport's other young guns show some *flare* [read *flair*] and self-promotion on the ice." Brian Milner, "Marketing of NHL Misses Net," *Seattle Post-Intelligencer*, 24 Jan. 2007, at D1.

LANGUAGE-CHANGE INDEX
flare misused for *flair*: Stage 1
Current ratio (*natural flair* vs. **natural flare*): 10:1

flatulate, vb. In the 1960s and early 1970s, my grandfather, Texas Supreme Court Justice Meade F. Griffin (1894–1974), liked to tell his family the definition of a perfect host: "When your guest *flatulates*, so do you!" It never occurred to anyone in the family that *flatulate* wasn't a bona fide word. Yet it wasn't in the dictionaries, then or for the most part now, because

lexicographers have overlooked both *flatulate* and its cognate noun *flatulation*. They have been much kinder to the synonyms *crepitate* (recorded in the *OED* from 1623—and labeled obsolete) and *crepitation* (recorded, in the sense of liberating enteric airs, from 1822). Despite the paltry evidence given in the *OED* for both of those words, they have always been, as an empirical matter, more common than the words formed by analogy from *flatulence* and *flatulent*.

Flatulate and *flatulation* appear to have been mostly medical terms when they emerged in the 19th century. *Flatulated* was a past-participial adjective meaning "bloated," and *flatulation* was a fancy synonym for bloating—e.g.:

- "Complains now of palpitation (violent), hot flashes, cold feet, dizzy spells, menses irregular, indigestion; *flatulated* [i.e., *bloated*]; bowels irregular." Reynold W. Wilcox, "Cactus Grandiflorus: A Clinical Study," 7 *Post-graduate* 85, 91 (Feb. 1892).
- "Every . . . recurring *flatulation* and old-fashioned belly-ache, is traced to an inflamed or, in some manner or another, abnormal appendix." Otto Juettner, "The Slaughter of the Innocents," 37 *Toledo Medical and Surgical Reporter* 5, 6 (Jan. 1911).
- "A year ago he began to be troubled with gas, at first chiefly by night, later also by day; relieved by eructations and *flatulated*, but passing mostly by rectum." "Case 8063," 8 *Case Records of the Massachusetts General Hospital* 1 (7 Feb. 1922).

One of the earliest traceable uses of *flatulate* as a verb occurred in an unusually poignant passage in an 1883 issue of *Obstetric Gazette*: "What is there more absolutely provoking to the physician than to witness a patient of this character strain and groan and grunt and scream and defecate and micturate and *flatulate* and vomit and moan and lament and strain again, without accomplishing any advancement?" H.V. Sweringen, "Cases from Practice," 6 *Obstetric Gaz.* 169, 170 (Apr. 1883). The word didn't gain currency in nonmedical usage until the 1960s. Today it is fairly common—e.g.:

- "A student had *flatulated* quite loudly." David Romanelli, *Yeah Dave's Guide to Livin' in the Moment* 156 (2009).
- "The least '*flatulating*' legumes are said to be (in this order) lentils, split peas, adzuki beans, mung beans, black-eyed peas, and anasazi beans." Crescent Dragonwagon, *Bean by Bean* 7 (2012) (*flatulating* meaning "causing flatulence").
- "One day when we were out for a ride, I *flatulated* and then said, 'Excuse me.' Kristen asked why I said that, and I told her, 'Because of that noise I made,' and she responded, 'I can smell that sound you made!'" Don Brock, "Modesto-Area Dads on Being Dads," *Modesto Bee*, 14 June 2014.

There is certainly enough linguistic evidence to support the treatment of these words in individual dictionary entries. Hence *flatulate* isn't at all classifiable as a NONWORD.

flatulence; *flatulency. These words—meaning either (1) "having excessive intestinal gas," or (2) "pomposity and pretentiousness"—came into use in the late 17th

---

LANGUAGE-CHANGE INDEX (For the full key, see front matter pp. xxxi, l–li.)
Stage 1: Rejected. **Stage 2:** Widely shunned. **Stage 3:** Widespread but . . . **Stage 4:** Ubiquitous but . . . **Stage 5:** Fully accepted.
Invariably inferior forms marked by asterisk (*). • Ratios represent frequency of prevalent forms vs. variants in current books.

century. The older term, **flatulency*, gave way to *flatulence* by 1760 and is now a NEEDLESS VARIANT. Except for a brief period from 1790 to 1810, *flatulence* has been predominant throughout the English-speaking world. Cf. **borborygmus**.

Current ratio: 26:1

flaunt; flout. Confusion about these terms is so distressingly common that some dictionaries have thrown in the towel and now treat *flaunt* as a synonym of *flout*. But the words are best kept separate.

Flout has always meant "to contravene or disregard; to treat with contempt." The word almost never causes a problem. Here it's correctly used: "A record rider turnout, fueled by the mayor's earlier pledge to end the escort and crack down on cyclists *flouting* traffic laws, poured into the streets on an improvised route." Chuck Finnie & Rachel Gordon, "Critical Mass Reaches Another Fork in the Road," *S.F. Examiner*, 3 Aug. 1997, at B1. But the rare mistake of misusing *flout* for *flaunt* does sometimes occur—e.g.:

- "But he had hardly left Read's doorstep before anguish smote him at thus *flouting* [read *flaunting*] his wealth in the face of Read's poverty." Sarah Gertrude Liebson Millin, *The Burning Man* 280 (1952).
- "Mr. Talton was soon joined by almost two dozen other conservative Republicans who filed en masse into the clerk's office to *flout* [read *flaunt*] their disapproval for their colleague and fellow party member." Christy Hoppe, "GOP Shows Off Its Own Defection," *Dallas Morning News*, 25 May 2000, at A33, A35.

Flaunt predominantly means "to show off or parade (something) in an ostentatious manner" <if you've got it, flaunt it>. The word is most often used correctly—e.g.:

- "Most vivid among the gaggle of grandchildren are the trashy and very available Dori (Maria Mervis), complete with body-*flaunting* garb; [and others]." Christopher Rawson, "Putting the Fun in Funeral," *Pitt. Post-Gaz.*, 23 May 1997, at 30.
- "He donates millions to religious and charitable groups, yet *flaunts* his own wealth." Marc Gunther, "Will Uncle Bud Sell Hollywood?" *Fortune*, 18 Aug. 1997, at 185.

But the word is often incorrectly used for *flout*, perhaps because it is misunderstood as a telescoped version of *flout* and *taunt*—e.g.:

- "In Washington, the White House issued a statement that deplored the Nigerian Government's '*flaunting* [read *flouting*] of even the most basic international norms and universal standards of human rights.'" Howard W. French, "Nigeria Executes Critic of Regime; Nations Protest," *N.Y. Times*, 11 Nov. 1995, at A1.
- "This isn't just a problem in the pro and college ranks. . . . Players in recreation leagues and even third-grade soccer tyros have been known to *flaunt* [read *flout*] the rules." Editorial, "Tell Us How You'd Restore Discipline," *Cincinnati Enquirer*, 4 Jan. 2007, at C6.
- "We are supposed to be a nation of laws, and being able to cherry-pick which laws to follow is not supposed to be part of the process. If so, each American undoubtedly could find a law to *flaunt* [read *flout*]." Tom Knott, "Illegals for Diversity? The 'Logic' Is Ludicrous," *Wash. Times*, 25 Jan. 2007, Metro §, at B2.

One federal appellate judge who misused *flaunt* for *flout* in a published opinion—only to be *sic*'d and corrected by judges who later quoted him—appealed to *W3* and its editors, who, of course, accept as standard any usage that can be documented with any frequency at all. The judge then attempted to justify his error and pledged to persist in it. See William Safire, *I Stand Corrected* 158–59 (1984). Seeking refuge in a nonprescriptive dictionary, however, merely ignores the all-important distinction between formal contexts, in which strict standards of usage must apply, and informal contexts, in which venial faults of grammar or usage may, if we are lucky, go unnoticed (or unmentioned). Judges' written opinions fall into the first category.

LANGUAGE-CHANGE INDEX
flaunt misused for *flout*: Stage 3
Current ratio (*flouting the rules* vs.
*flaunting the rules): 5:1

flautist. See **flutist**.

flavor; flavour. The first is AmE, the second BrE. The same spellings hold in the derivatives ending in *-ful*, *-less*, *-some*, etc. The AmE spellings were solidly predominant in AmE print sources by 1850. See -OR; -OUR.

flay. See **flail**.

*flection. See **flexion**.

fledgling; *fledgeling. The first spelling is standard in AmE and BrE alike. The second is a variant spelling. See MUTE E.

Current ratio: 114:1

flee > fled > fled. So inflected. **Fleed* is a solecism—e.g.:

- "Lexington police say Wallace Charles Lanford *fleed* [read *fled*] the prison camp about 8 p.m." "Man Convicted of Murder Escapes from Davidson Jail," *News & Record* (Greensboro), 15 Nov. 1995, at BH2.
- "The Worcester Democrat pulled his ticket for the third time and *fleed* [read *fled*] the scene before the Ethics Commission SWAT team could surround him." Lee Hammel, "Kennedy, Harshbarger Have Experienced Help," *Telegram & Gaz.* (Worcester), 21 June 1997, at A3.
- "Shortly after, Skelly *fleed* [read *fled*] the island after being suspected of working for the CIA." Mimi Whitefield, "After Fleeing Fidel, Newsman Ready to Return to Cuba," *Miami Herald*, 9 June 2015, News §.

See IRREGULAR VERBS.

Readers may occasionally encounter **fleed* as an obsolete past participle not of *flee* but of *flay*—e.g.: "She *fleed* at him, and, to cut a long story short, he owned to having carried off five sack altogether, upon her promising not to persecute him." Thomas Hardy, *Far from the Madding Crowd* 76 (1905).

LANGUAGE-CHANGE INDEX
*fleed for *fled*: Stage 1
Current ratio (*he fled* vs. **he fleed*): 5,470:1

fleshly; fleshy. *Fleshly* = (1) bodily, corporeal <the soul's fleshly counterpart>; (2) carnal, sensual

<fleshly desires>; or (3) worldly, not spiritual <fleshly pleasures>—e.g.: "'We cannot fight a *fleshly* appetite by indulging in it.'" John Duke, "Addictions Vary, but All Find Help in Program," *Indianapolis Star*, 27 Jan. 2007, at 2.

Fleshy = (1) resembling flesh <a fleshy pink>; (2) plump <fleshy fingers>; or (3) pulpy, succulent <a fleshy grapefruit>—e.g.: "The scallops . . . were firm, *fleshy*, and bursting with flavor." Terra Walters, *Capital* (Annapolis), 26 Jan. 2007, Entertainment §, at 2.

Not surprisingly, these terms are susceptible to WORD-SWAPPING—e.g.:

* "Modotti's technique left her portrait subjects looking so *fleshly* [read *fleshy*] that the prints themselves seem to have skin." Kenneth Baker, "Southern Exposure," *S.F. Chron.*, 2 Sept. 2006, at E1.
* "Max Boot . . . does as much as any other writer of recent vintage to bring the *fleshy* [read *fleshly*] reality of warfare back into view." Paul McLeary, "Why It's Better to Be Smart than Strong," *Christian Science Monitor*, 23 Jan. 2007, Features §, at 17.

LANGUAGE-CHANGE INDEX
fleshly misused for *fleshy*: Stage 1

flesh out; flush out. To *flesh out* is to put flesh on bare bones—that is, to move beyond the merest rudiments and to elaborate; to add some nuance and detail. To *flush out* (probably a hunting metaphor) is to bring something into the open light for examination. *Flush out* is sometimes misused for *flesh out*—e.g.: "Both sides say their case was hampered by the disappearance of Anait Zakarian, whom they said they needed to help *flush out* [read *flesh out*] some of the details." Tina Daunt, "No Release for Victims," *L.A. Times*, 16 Oct. 1996, at B1.

LANGUAGE-CHANGE INDEX
flush out misused for *flesh out*: Stage 2

fleshy. See **fleshly.**

fleur-de-lis; *fleur-de-lys; *fleur-de-luce. The first has been standard in all varieties of World English since the 18th century. The second and third are variant spellings. The standard plural is *fleurs-de-lis*. Whether singular or plural, the standard pronunciation is /flər-də-**lee**/.

Current ratio (in order of headwords): 143:59:1

flexible. So spelled—not *flexable. See -ABLE (A).

flexion; *flection. *Flexion* = (1) the act of bending or flexing; esp., the bending of a joint with flexor muscles; or (2) a bend in something. *Flection* is a NEEDLESS VARIANT that has never been common in any sense. Among American desktop dictionaries, only *W11* and *NOAD* correctly list *flexion* as the main headword for all senses.

Current ratio: 135:1

flied out. See **fly.**

flier; flyer. *Flier* is the standard form in AmE, *flyer* in BrE.

flight attendant. See **stewardess.**

fling > flung > flung. So inflected. *Flinged* is a blunder—e.g.:

* "Ryan would have at least stomped his feet or *flinged* [read *flung*] a clipboard into the air, wouldn't he?" Bob McManaman, "Where Is Buddy Goat Gruff?" *Ariz. Republic*, 8 Oct. 1995, at E1.
* "Then, he snapped. He had a lackey fetch his diamond-encrusted G-Unit chain, a relic from his time in 50 Cent's posse. Then Game *flinged* [read *flung*] it out to the 50-yard line, where it fell into the hands of a fan." Dan Aquilante, "Game for a Fight," *N.Y. Post*, 7 June 2005, at 48.
* "[T]he sophomore *flinged* [read *flung*] the ball toward the basket and it climbed over the rim as the buzzer sounded." Robert Burns, "Lincoln Finishes Fourth, Glenwood Sixth at Collinsville," *State J.-Register* (Springfield, Ill.), 31 Dec. 2005, Sports §, at 9.

See IRREGULAR VERBS.

LANGUAGE-CHANGE INDEX
flinged for *flung*: Stage 1
Current ratio (*flung* vs. *flinged*): 5,881:1

flippant; flip, adj. *Flippant* = (1) inappropriately nonserious or disrespectful; pert; or (2) glib, talkative. Sense 2—the older one—has become archaic. *Flip*, a clipped form, is a CASUALISM that is gaining ground on the more traditional word. But as a matter of word frequency, the collocation *flippant remark* appears in modern print sources much more often than *flip remark*.

Current ratio (*flippant remark* vs. *flip remark*): 5:1

floatation. See **flotation.**

flock. Although this word has two plurals, *flocks* and *flock*, the first vastly predominates. E.g.: "Longshore has three *flocks* of hens and one flock of toms for people who want 30- to 40-pound birds." Mike Lafferty, "Turkeys Turn Tail on Cramped Pens," *Columbus Dispatch*, 24 Nov. 1996, at C1.

floes (= sheets of ice on a body of water [fr. Norw. "flo" = "flat layer"]) should not be confused with *flows*—e.g.:

* "By awarding Pittsburgh's sole casino license to the North Shore developer, the state's Gaming board did not put the Penguins on an ice *flow* [read *floe*] and kick them down river." Gene Collier, "Penguins Will Get What They Want," *Pitt. Post-Gaz.*, 21 Dec. 2006, at C1.
* "Lengthening and heightening the bridge will allow engineers to place the abutments outside of the normal high water mark, thereby increasing the water flow area and reducing the risk of damage from ice *flows* [read *floes*]." Kevin Miller, "State Panel Supports Replacement of Allagash Waterway Bridge," *Bangor Daily News*, 5 Jan. 2007, at B8.

LANGUAGE-CHANGE INDEX (For the full key, see front matter pp. xxxi, l–li.)
Stage 1: Rejected. **Stage 2:** Widely shunned. **Stage 3:** Widespread but . . . **Stage 4:** Ubiquitous but . . . **Stage 5:** Fully accepted.
Invariably inferior forms marked by asterisk (*). • Ratios represent frequency of prevalent forms vs. variants in current books.

- "His father used to take him down to the riverfront during the winter months, when the water was still flowing and completely jammed up with ice *flows* [read *floes*]." Mike Jackson, "One Man's Formula for Success Includes a Life Lesson for All of Us," *Daily Herald* (Chicago), 11 Jan. 2007, Sports §, at 9.

Of course, when ice actually does flow, as in a melting glacier, that movement is a *flow*—e.g.: "Very deep, beautiful lakes . . . may be the product of something rather ugly. They are a regular feature of ice sheets, but it is only in the last few years that scientists have linked them to the fact that ice *flow* within those sheets appears to be accelerating in response to climate change." "Greenland Blues," *New Scientist*, 7 Jan. 2006, at 39.

LANGUAGE-CHANGE INDEX
flows misused for *floes*: Stage 2
Current ratio (*ice floes* vs. **ice flows*): 7:1

flora, like *fauna*, is a singular word with a collective implication. It refers to the plant life in a particular region. The word has two plurals, both rarely used: *floras* and *florae*. The first is standard. See PLURALS (B). Cf. **fauna**.

florilegium (= an anthology) forms the plural *florilegia*—the homegrown **florilegiums* being essentially nonexistent in literary language. The singular is pronounced /flor-i-**lee**-jee-əm/.

floruit (L. "he or she flourished") is a learned word meaning "a period during which a person, idea, etc. flourishes." So rare is the word that it hasn't achieved its own floruit. Yet it does appear in scholars' prose—e.g.:

- "We may prefer to read about how things were or seemed to be in the days of our favorite author's *floruit*, rather than to see them as they are today." Robert Eisner, "The Lure of Literature," *N.Y. Times*, 27 Mar. 1994, § 5, at 31.
- "J.M. Edmonds, . . . the ultimate source for most modern versions of Sappho, was so fond of supplementing her fragmentary texts that one disgruntled colleague described him [Edmonds] as 'the only ancient lyric poet with a twentieth-century *floruit*.'" Peter Green, "Overdue Poetic Justice," *Wash. Times*, 17 Dec. 1995, at B8.
- "It is generally true, I would judge, that Olympia's *floruit* as a venue of athletic excellence is reckoned around the sixth to fourth centuries B.C., with the erection of the Temple of Zeus in c. 460 B.C. signaling an apex of Classical decorum." Nigel Spivey, "Olympia, Olympiads and Olympic Bronze," *Antiquity*, 1 Dec. 2005, at 956.

The phrase **floruit period* is a REDUNDANCY—e.g.: "The U.S., according to Valladao, is like ancient Rome in its *floruit period* [read *floruit*]." "Hail Mr. President," *Fin. Times*, 3 Dec. 1996, at 5.

Occasionally the word bears its original Latin sense, often in its abbreviated form (*fl.*)—e.g.:

- "The Greek philosopher Democritus (*floruit* c. 420 B.C.) gets a mention." "Melancholy Men," *Sunday Telegraph*, 3 Mar. 1996, Books §, at 14.
- "Euclid . . . *fl.* 300 B.C.; Gr. mathematician: author of a basic work in geometry." *WNWCD* at 468.

The word is pronounced /**flor**-yoo-it/.

LANGUAGE-CHANGE INDEX
*floruit period for *floruit*: Stage 1

flotation; *floatation. *Flotation*, the standard spelling, first appeared in the mid-19th century. According to *The Oxford Dictionary of English Etymology* (1966), "the sp. with *flot-* has been adopted to make the word conform to [*flotilla* and *flotsam*], and *rotation*" (p. 364). A more recent work gives a different ETYMOLOGY: "The current spelling appeared . . . probably by influence of French *flottaison*, which was used in technical terms translated into English, such as *ligne de flottaison* line of flotation." *The Barnhart Dictionary of Etymology* 393 (Robert K. Barnhart ed., 1988). **Floatation* is a variant.

Current ratio: 11:1

FLOTSAM PHRASES just take up space without adding to the meaning of a sentence. So there is usually no reason, when it is clear whose opinion is being expressed, to write *In my opinion* or *It seems to me that*. Other examples are *in terms of, on a . . . basis, my sense is that, in the first instance, the fact of the matter*, and *the fact that*. (Admittedly, some of these phrases may be useful in speech.) We have enough written words without these mere space-fillers. See **basis (A)** & **fact (A), (B)**.

flounder; founder. Both verbs signal failure, but the literal senses—and therefore the images conveyed metaphorically—differ. To *flounder* is to struggle and plunge as if in mud (not, in other words, to fail completely)—e.g.: "Sun Microsystems Inc. yesterday posted its fourth loss in five quarters . . . as the computer market *flounders*." Chris Gaither, "Sun Posts Loss," *Boston Globe*, 18 Oct. 2002, at D3. To *founder* is (of a person or animal) to go lame; (of a building) to fall down or give way; (of a horseback rider) to fall to the ground; (of livestock) to become sick from overeating; (of a ship) to fill with water and sink— e.g.: "The show picked up emotional steam in Act 2, when the parallel romances *founder* on the rocks of prejudice and racism." Harriet Brown, "'South Pacific' Takes Audience to Tropical Isle," *Capital Times* (Madison), 7 Oct. 2002, at D3.

flout. See **flaunt.**

flowed; flown. Surprisingly, these words are often confused. *Flowed* is the past tense and past participle of *flow* <the lava flowed to the sea>. *Flown* is the past participle of *fly* <I had just flown to Chicago>. See **fly** & **overflow.**

flows. See **floes.**

fluently; fluidly. Both adverbs derive from the same Latin root, *fluere* (= to flow), and both connote grace and elegance. When referring to one's mastery of a foreign language, *fluently* appears far more often than *fluidly*. The latter word might usefully imply a higher level of mastery than the former—e.g.: "My ability to speak Khmer *fluently* but not *fluidly* exposed my real identity." Putsata Reang, "A Search for Home," *Seattle Times*, 27 July 1999, at E1.

fluid; liquid; gas. Nonscientists often confuse these terms. A *fluid* is any substance that is capable of flowing and that changes shape under pressure; in other words, a fluid is not a solid. Fluids include both liquids and gases. A *liquid* is a fluid that has a fixed volume (such as water or oil). A *gas* is a fluid that can expand indefinitely (such as oxygen or steam). Although these words should be kept distinct in scientific contexts, *fluid* is sometimes used as a loose synonym of *liquid* in nontechnical writing <bodily fluids>.

fluky /**floo**-kee/ (= [1] uncannily lucky, or [2] constantly changing) has been predominantly so spelled in AmE and BrE alike since the late 19th century. **Flukey* is a variant spelling.

Current ratio: 4:1

fluoride; fluoridation; fluorescent. So spelled. Probably because of one pronunciation of the first syllable (/flohr/), these words are often misspelled with *-ou-* instead of *-uo-* in the first syllable—e.g.:

- "*Flouride* [read *Fluoride*] has been added to the town's water for the last few years." Eun Lee Koh, "Manganese Levels Will Be Examined," *Boston Globe*, 18 Nov. 2001, Globe West §, at 1.
- "House Bills 159 and 309 could disrupt the *flouridation* [read *fluoridation*] called for in the November 2000 referendums approved by voters in Salt Lake and Davis counties." Troy Goodman, "Fluoride Fear Baffles Experts, Spawns Bills," *Salt Lake Trib.*, 25 Feb. 2002, at C1.
- "A soft *flourescent* [read *fluorescent*] light burns constantly so Lindh's jailers can always check on him." Andrew Miga, "Taliban John's Life Behind Bars," *Boston Herald*, 24 Mar. 2002, at 1.

In any event, the preferred pronunciations start with /fluur-/.

Language-Change Index
fluorescent misspelled **flourescent*: Stage 1

flush out. See **flesh out.**

flutist; flautist; fluter. *Flutist* (/**floo**-tist/), the oldest word (dating from the early 17th century), is generally preferred by professional flute players in the United States. It also predominates in modern AmE print sources by a 2-to-1 ratio—and has always been the more prevalent term. The old joke within the profession is that only a second-rate flutist prefers to be called a *flautist* (/**flow**-tist/ or /**flaw**-tist/). *Fluter* is an unusual DYSPHEMISM.

But *flautist* predominates in BrE and has done so since about 1880, after British writers began revising the word to make it a GALLICISM.

Current ratio (in World English in order of headwords): 59:35:1

fly > flew > flown. Despite those irregular inflections, in baseball it is standard to say that a player who has hit a *fly ball* (i.e., one hit high into the air) has *flied*—e.g.:

- "After getting a good rip on a 2-and-1 fastball but fouling it off the catcher's chest protector, Fielder *flied* out to the rightfield warning track." Rob Parker, "World Series: Yankees vs. Braves," *Newsday* (N.Y.), 21 Oct. 1996, at A54.
- "Brian McFall led off with a double off third baseman Pope's glove and took third when John Whittleman *flied* out to right." Stacy Kaneshiro, "Sharks Squander Opportunities Before Beating Cane Fires, 4–2," *Honolulu Advertiser*, 20 Oct. 2006, Sports §, at D1.
- "With two out and a runner on second in the seventh, Casey missed a chance to extend the Tigers' lead when he *flied* to right against reliever Tyler Johnson." Tyler Kepner, "Cardinals Put Tigers on the Brink," *N.Y. Times*, 27 Oct. 2006, at D1.

Cf. **flowed.** See IRREGULAR VERBS.

flyer. See **flier.**

Flynn, in like. See **in like Flynn.**

fob off. See **foist** (B).

focus. A. As a Noun. Pl. *focuses* or *foci* (/**foh**-sɪ/). The plural *foci*—typical in medical and other technical texts—may strike readers as pretentious in ordinary prose. E.g.:

- "A story on teenage smoking had two primary *foci* [more accurately *messages* or *conclusions*], one of which is that white male teens smoke more than black male teens." "'Just Killing Time Now'—Does Anyone Disagree?" *Buffalo News*, 1 Sept. 1996, at M11.
- "[A]t the hotel in which Laure and the narrator stay, the hotelier becomes one of many shifting *foci* for our anti-hero's obsession . . . ." Edie Meidav, "French Lovers on a Road Trip Collide with Beckett's Novels," *S.F. Chron.*, 20 Nov. 2007, at E2.

See PLURALS (B). Even so, *foci* is much more common in print sources than the plural *focuses*.

Current ratio (*many foci* vs. *many focuses*): 5:1

B. As a Verb. *Focus* makes *focused* and *focusing* in AmE, *focussed* and *focussing* in BrE. See SPELLING (B).

*foetus. See **fetus.**

fogy; fogey. This word, a DYSPHEMISM for a more or less elderly person with hidebound ideas, is predominantly spelled *fogy* in AmE, *fogey* in BrE. The ETYMOLOGY of the word is unknown.

foist. A. Preposition with: *off* vs. *on*. Traditionally speaking, *foist* takes the preposition *on*—e.g.: "That network has *foisted* innumerable Virtual Celebrities *on* us." Richard Roeper, "'The Spot' Marks a New Batch of Virtual Celebrities," *Chicago Sun-Times*, 15 Dec. 1996, Upfront §, at 2.

LANGUAGE-CHANGE INDEX (For the full key, see front matter pp. xxxi, l–li.)
Stage 1: Rejected. **Stage 2:** Widely shunned. **Stage 3:** Widespread but . . . **Stage 4:** Ubiquitous but . . . **Stage 5:** Fully accepted.
Invariably inferior forms marked by asterisk (*). • Ratios represent frequency of prevalent forms vs. variants in current books.

When the phrase is as unidiomatic as *foist with, a different verb is in order: "An employer *is foisted with* [read *bears the*] responsibility to a third party if his employee commits a tort in the course of his employment." Stanley Berwin, *The Economist Pocket Lawyer* 231 (1986).

Foist off on is awkward and wordy (perhaps influenced by *fob off on*—see (B)). The *OED* quotes Charlotte Brontë as having written *foist off on* but calls the phrase "rare." It is fairly rare today. It ought to be rarer—e.g.: "We always seem ready to *foist off on* [read *foist on*] young people those things that we don't wish to do ourselves." Karen Love, "What's the Role of Prayer in Public Life?" *Denver Post*, 4 May 1996, at B7.

LANGUAGE-CHANGE INDEX
foist off on for *foist on*: Stage 1
Current ratio (*foisted on* vs. *foisted off on*): 24:1

B. And *fob off*. *Foist* shares one sense with *fob off*: "to offer or pass (something) to someone falsely or fraudulently" <lemons foisted on unsuspecting car buyers>. But it should not also take sense 2 of *fob off*: "to trick (someone) with something inferior." H.W. Fowler summed up the distinction well: "The public can be *fobbed off* with something, or the something can be *fobbed off* on the public; but *foist* has only the second construction" (*FMEU1* at 184). In fact, though, *fob off* is pretty much confined to BrE—e.g.: "Customers are sometimes *fobbed off* with a car [that] does not entirely meet their expectations." Haig Simonian, "FT Guide to: New Number Plates," *Fin. Times*, 4 Aug. 1997, at 8.

-FOLD. See **twofold.**

folderol; *falderol. In journalism and other print sources, *folderol*—the preferred spelling—greatly outnumbers *falderol. The word means either "nonsense" or "a useless trifle."

Current ratio: 138:1

foliage (= plant leaves collectively) is three syllables /**foh**-lee-ij/. Like *verbiage*, this word is subject to a syncopated mispronunciation: /**foh**-lij/. See **verbiage.**

folio. Pl. *folios.* See PLURALS (D).

FOLK ETYMOLOGY. See ETYMOLOGY (D).

folk(s). This CASUALISM has two plurals in STANDARD ENGLISH: *folk* <rural folk> and *folks* <folks say>. *Folks* is most commonly synonymous with *relatives, relations, kinfolks,* or *kinsmen.* Often it takes on a more restricted meaning, referring either to parents <my folks are both in a nursing home> or to one's immediate family (including siblings) to the exclusion of more distant relatives <Where do all your folks live?>. Context usually supplies some degree of clarity. The term can also refer to people more generally <good evening, folks!> <those folks over there>. Sometimes it is used as the plural of *you* <you folks>. Cf. **y'all.**

follow. See **comply (B).**

following (= after), when used to begin a sentence or clause, often results in a misplaced modifier and a MIS-CUE—e.g.: "*Following* [read *After*] lunch, the students came back to the high school and the art students took over." Sharon Henson Pope, "Teachers Urge Students to Try Art, Creativity," *St. Louis Post-Dispatch*, 12 Dec. 1994, at 1. The problem, of course, is that some readers might envision a line of hungry students trailing a caterer's truck.

But even when *following* doesn't begin the sentence, if it means "after" it can almost always be simplified—e.g.:

- "Javier Colon of Mission Hill and Ramon Peres of Roxbury, both 22, escaped after a 'routine trip' to the barber shop building on the grounds *following* [read *after*] breakfast." Jack Sullivan, "Two Escape Deer Island and Remain at Large," *Boston Globe*, 1 Jan. 1991, at 23.
- "Mr. Allen also said, in a conversation *following* [read *after*] his speech, that Delta would like to expand . . . when it has the resources." Lisa Biank Fasig, "Delta's Allen Defends Local Fare Structure," *Cincinnati Enquirer*, 16 Nov. 1996, at B16.
- "[Elon] Musk also looks down on holidays, having nearly died from malaria *following* [read *after*] a trip to Brazil and South Africa in 2000." Jeff Dyer, "Tesla's Secret Formula," *Forbes*, 7 Sept. 2015, at 40.

LANGUAGE-CHANGE INDEX
following for *after*: Stage 4

foment, vb., = to incite or rouse <the rebels fomented a revolution>. Although the word was once used as a noun—the *OED* records sparse uses from 1540 to 1892—the corresponding noun has long been *fomentation* (= incitement, instigation). But some writers want to revive *foment* as a noun—e.g.: "In the social *foment* [read *fomentation*] of the 1960s and 1970s, Donahue was a pioneer in discussing both personal and political issues with a largely female audience." Jane Hall, "At the End of a Long Run, Phil Donahue Looks Back," *L.A. Times*, 3 May 1996, at F2. Perhaps this poor usage arises from confusion with *ferment* (= agitation). Indeed, *ferment* might be the better edit in the sentence just cited. It certainly seems the better choice in these examples:

- "There hardly could be better circumstances to nurture political *foment* [read *ferment*]." Harry Austin, "Tinder for a Saudi Bomb," *Chattanooga Times*, 3 July 1996, at A6.
- "A less noble reason is that art has long been the victim of political *foment* [read *ferment*]: The French Revolution and, in particular, the Reign of Terror are appalling cases in point." Mario Naves, "Middle Age's Stony Features," *N.Y. Observer*, 25 Dec. 2006, Culture §, at 18.
- "As this year ends and a new one begins, the role of God among all nations must be acknowledged if there is to be any comprehension of why the world is in such *foment* [read *ferment*] and chaos." Victoria A. Brownworth, "Faith: Something Worth Fighting For," *Baltimore Sun*, 31 Dec. 2006, Ideas §, at F7.

Although *fomentation* doesn't appear frequently, it remains much more common in printed sources than the noun uses of *foment*—e.g.:

- "For decades, extremists on both sides spoiled any hope of Arab acceptance of the Jewish state of Israel with their *fomentation* of hatred and bloodshed." "Clinton's Mideast Trip," *USA Today*, 26 Oct. 1994, at A12.
- "Protest is too often confused by the mainstream with *fomentation* of outright revolution." Glenn Nelson, "Abdul-Rauf Controversy Showed Hypocrisy of NBA Standards," *Seattle Times*, 17 Mar. 1996, at D6.

Hence *foment*, as a noun, ought to be considered a NEEDLESS VARIANT.

Foment is invariably transitive. If it doesn't have an object, choose a different verb—e.g.: "And wherever the expatriates go, instability and civil war *foment* [read *follow, fester*, or the like]." "Iraqi Refugee Exodus Another Bush Bonus," *Palm Springs Post*, 4 Jan. 2007, at A23.

LANGUAGE-CHANGE INDEX
1. *foment* as a noun for *fomentation*: Stage 3
Current ratio (*the fomentation of* vs.
*the foment of: 2:1
2. *foment* for *ferment*: Stage 1
Current ratio (*political ferment* vs.
*political foment): 36:1

fondue (= a dish consisting of melted cheese or other hot liquid into which chunks of food are dipped) is the standard spelling. *Fondu is a variant.

Current ratio: 9:1

font. Technology has changed the meaning of this term. In the days of hot type, a font was one set of a typeface, in a single size (e.g., 9 point) and style (e.g., bold italic). The advent of phototypesetting allowed characters of different sizes to be made from a single master, as on a filmstrip, and later several styles of the same type family could be carried on the master as well. Computers, of course, can hold many typefaces and many variations of the same family. So today, rather than one size and style of a typeface, *font* most often denotes a whole family of styles that can be printed at almost any size.

fontanelle (= one of several soft spots in a baby's skull in which bone has not yet formed and hardened) has been the predominant spelling in both AmE and BrE since before 1800. Although some dictionaries (such as *W11*) list the variant spelling *fontanel as the main headword, it remains but a variant.

Current ratio: 2:1

***food fare.** See **fare (A).**

foolscap; fool's cap. *Foolscap* is a size of paper (around 13½ by 17 inches), so called because 17th-century papermakers used a *fool's cap* as their watermark. A *fool's cap* is either (1) the hat once worn by court jesters, with three peaks, each tipped with a bell; or (2) the conical hat formerly put on dull pupils or,

notably, on political dissidents in Maoist China. In sense 2, it's also called a *dunce cap* or *dunce's cap*.

foot; feet. When you use a number greater than one to denote a distance, use the plural *feet* <a fence ten feet high>, unless the distance is part of a PHRASAL ADJECTIVE <a ten-foot fence>.

foot-and-mouth disease. A. And *hoof-and-mouth disease*. Although some commentators have erroneously suggested otherwise, *foot-and-mouth disease* has long been the predominant phrase in AmE and BrE alike, as well as the accepted term in veterinary medicine. It is true, however, that *hoof-and-mouth disease* is an Americanism dating from the late 19th century. But this version, despite its stronger claim to logic (since hoofed animals aren't usually said to have "feet"), never progressed beyond its status as a CASUALISM and a secondary variant. There is also an unrelated childhood condition called "Hand, Foot, and Mouth Disease," characterized by ulcerated sores in the mouth and rashes on the extremities.

B. Whether to Hyphenate. During the devastating 2001 outbreak of the disease in Europe, five major newspapers and magazines over a two-day period hyphenated the PHRASAL ADJECTIVE, and one didn't:

- "The Irish Republic yesterday confirmed its first case of *foot-and-mouth disease* in the current outbreak." John Murray Brown et al., "Foot-and-Mouth in Irish Republic," *Fin. Times*, 23 Mar. 2001, at 1 (hyphenating in both text and headline).
- "Mr Blair . . . has been concentrating on the *foot and mouth epidemic*." Keith Harper, "Rail Plans Crippled by Cash Crisis," *Guardian*, 23 Mar. 2001, at 1.
- "Ministers were forced onto the defensive over their handling of the *foot-and-mouth epidemic* last night." Philip Webster et al., "Foot and Mouth Epidemic Will Rage Until August," *Times* (London), 23 Mar. 2001, at 1 (hyphenating throughout the text but not in the headline).
- "The spread of *foot-and-mouth disease* appears to be accelerating." Marc Champion, "The Grim Reaper: Epidemic Rips into Small U.K. Farmers," *Wall Street J. Europe*, 23–24 Mar. 2001, at 1.
- "Britain's *foot-and-mouth epidemic* took an ominous turn Friday." Tom Buerkle, "Foot-and-Mouth Is 'Out of Control' in Britain," *Int'l Herald Trib.*, 24 Mar. 2001, at 1 (in which the photo caption refers to the *hoof-and-mouth epidemic*).
- "The plague of *foot-and-mouth disease* that has descended on Britain's farms descended on Conservative Central Office like manna from heaven." "Pre-Election Fever," *Economist*, 24 Mar. 2001, at 48.

The *Financial Times* and *The Wall Street Journal Europe* both sensibly hyphenate the phrase in headline and text alike, whereas *The Times* loses nerve and omits the hyphens from its headlines. *The Guardian*, meanwhile, omits hyphens everywhere—even when *foot-and-mouth* appears as a noun phrase, without *disease* or *epidemic* or some other noun following

---

LANGUAGE-CHANGE INDEX (For the full key, see front matter pp. xxxi, l–li.)
Stage 1: Rejected. **Stage 2:** Widely shunned. **Stage 3:** Widespread but . . . **Stage 4:** Ubiquitous but . . . **Stage 5:** Fully accepted.
Invariably inferior forms marked by asterisk (*). • Ratios represent frequency of prevalent forms vs. variants in current books.

it—e.g.: "The first case of *foot and mouth* [read, preferably, *foot-and-mouth*] was confirmed yesterday in Co Louth, just south of the border in the [Irish] republic." Rosie Cowan, "Republic in Shock as Disease Arrives," *Guardian*, 23 Mar. 2001, at 4.

FOOTNOTES. A. The Good and the Bad. Footnotes are the mark of a scholar. Overabundant, overflowing footnotes are the mark of an insecure scholar—often someone who gets lost in the byways of analysis and who wants to show off. Underinclusive footnotes mark the scholar who (1) wants to write for a popular audience and fears that footnotes will be a turnoff; (2) doesn't really know the literature in his or her field very well; or (3) doesn't care to give credit where credit is due.

The difficult thing for any scholarly writer is to achieve a balance. Much depends on the subject matter, the intended audience, and the content of the writing. On the one hand, footnotes are "reminders that scholarship is an intrinsically communal enterprise—building on, revising or replacing the work of predecessors. History as we know it would not exist without source notes. Neither would philosophy, which even at its most original involves a dialogue with thinkers alive and dead." Kenneth L. Woodward, "In Praise of Footnotes," *Newsweek*, 9 Sept. 1996, at 75. On the other hand, footnotes can be "the horrid squeakings [that] arise when an author puts a brand new pair of shoes on his brain child. . . . Let all beware of too copious annotation, one of the deadly sins of literature." Fairfax Downey, "Literary Chiropody," in *The Modern Writer's Art* 98 (Theodore J. Gates & Robert E. Galbraith eds., 1936).

Footnotes are generally an excellent place for citations. But discursive footnotes—those that contain substantive discussion—ought generally to be kept to a minimum.

B. Versus Endnotes. Whereas footnotes appear at the foot of the page, endnotes appear at the end of an article, chapter, or book. (Endnotes are often mistakenly called footnotes.) In general, footnotes are easier on the reader than endnotes, which require flipping through pages to locate references. But scholarly journals and books increasingly use endnotes to simplify printing and unclutter pages.

FOR-; FORE-. As you'll observe in many of the following entries, these prefixes cause a great deal of confusion. You can usually arrive at the correct prefix for any given word by remembering that *fore-* always means "before" <forebears = ancestors>. *For-* may mean either "completely" <forfeit = to lose (something) completely> or "against" <forbear = to refrain (from some action) against one's inclination>.

for is one of several causal words in the English language, the most prominent others being the subordinating conjunctions *because, since,* and *as.* (See **as (A).**) And because *for* is roughly equivalent to those words, some grammarians have mislabeled it a subordinating conjunction. But unlike those words, *for* has always been proper at the beginning of an independent clause—e.g.:

- "Perhaps I should feel grateful for the hard work Ms. Smith has put in on my behalf. *For* she certainly has worked very hard indeed." Brandon Robson, "Shelf Life," *Independent*, 11 Jan. 1998, at 27.
- "Earlier, Parish had said he was proud and flattered to have his number retired. *For* he always had lived in Bird's long shadow." Bill Reynolds, "Green with Pride," *Providence J.-Bull.*, 19 Jan. 1998, at A1.
- "When placed in a New Zealand market context, the sportiness of the R3 isn't exactly unique either. *For* sitting in showrooms are a number of similarly focused models." "Yamaha's Bantamweight Champ," *Manawatu Standard* (N.Z.), 28 Aug. 2015, at 21.

The better grammatical view is this: "Because . . . *for* can stand at the beginning of an independent statement or even of a paragraph, it can be classed as a coordinating conjunction." R.W. Pence & D.W. Emery, *A Grammar of Present-Day English* 124 n.31 (2d ed. 1963).

*fora. See **forum.**

for all intents and purposes; to all intents and purposes; *for all intensive purposes. The original phrase, dating from the 17th century, is *to all intents and purposes.* The other phrase, with *for* at the outset, is a relative latecomer that cropped up in BrE in the late 19th century and spread to AmE in the mid-20th century. By the 1990s *for* was almost as common as *to* in AmE, whereas *to* retained predominance in BrE. Both forms are used today, *for* being more common in AmE and *to* in BrE—e.g.:

- "Vermeer's mainly domestic scenes . . . are also, *to all intents and purposes,* priceless." Nigel Reynolds, "The Drawing Power of Vermeer," *Daily Telegraph*, 10 June 1996, at 4.
- "It is only when life has, *for all intents and purposes,* already abandoned the patient that Dr. Kevorkian steps in." Kevin Theis, "Assisted 'Suicide,'" *Chicago Trib.*, 17 Dec. 1996, at 28.

Either form, though, often qualifies as a FLOTSAM PHRASE.

Because some people mishear the phrase, the MONDEGREEN **for all intensive purposes* has arisen—e.g.:

- "The basic numbers given above will not have changed much—bankers say that imports could be depressed a bit further—and with reserves that are *for all intensive purposes* [read *for all intents and purposes*] negligible there will be a clear payments lump." Terry Povey, "A Rosier Tint to the Financial Horizon," *Fin. Times*, 15 Oct. 1984, § III, at v.
- "*For all intensive purposes* [read *For all intents and purposes*], the electrically powered automobile is dead—and they are considered dinosaurs of the past." Arthus Abrom, "The Forgotten Art of Electric-Powered Automobiles," in *The Tesla Papers* 89 (David Hatcher Childress ed., 2000).
- "*For all intensive purposes* [read *For all intents and purposes*], the Titans' Super Bowl dreams ended right there." Aaron Wilson, "'Determined' Mitchell Broke Titan Hearts

with Return," *Leaf-Chronicle* (Clarksville, Tenn.), 8 Jan. 2001, at C4.

See MALAPROPISMS.

LANGUAGE-CHANGE INDEX
for all intensive purposes for *for all intents and purposes*: Stage 1
Current ratio (*all intents and purposes* vs. *all intensive purposes*): 191:1

foramen /fə-**ray**-mən/ (= a small opening or perforation, esp. in a bone or plant ovule) predominantly forms the classical plural *foramina*—not **foramens.* See PLURALS (B).

Current ratio: 49:1

for a period of. See **period of.**

forbade; *forbad. See **forbid.**

forbear /fohr-**bair**/, v.t.; **forebear** /fohr-bair/, n. Though unrelated, these words are confused in every conceivable way. *Forbear*—the verb meaning "to refrain from objecting to; to tolerate"—is inflected *forbear > forbore > forborne.* But because the inflected forms appear only infrequently, writers sometimes fall into error—e.g.: "A borrower who lives in the home five years after doing the work may have the loan *forebeared* [read *forborne*]." Gary Mayk, "Grants and Loans Available to Buyers," *Morning Call* (Allentown, Pa.), 28 May 1995, at G1. (See IRREGULAR VERBS.)

Forebear—always a noun—means "ancestor" (usually used in the plural). **Forebearer* is an incorrect form of this noun—e.g.: "Like his *forebearers* [read *forebears*], Joe is community minded and committed to public service." Marta Adams, "Barrett Has a Commitment to Cheyenne and Wyo.," *Wyo. Trib.-Eagle* (Cheyenne), 23 July 2002, at A8.

Forebear is occasionally misused for *forebear*—e.g.:

- "You should also be alert for literate members of society in the areas where your *forbears* [read *forebears*] resided." Lloyd Bockstruck, "Genealogists Owe Debt to South Carolina Record Keeper," *Dallas Morning News*, 17 Dec. 1994, at C13.
- "The founding fathers of cyberspace . . . , like their *forbears* [read *forebears*], were almost exclusively white, male, middle-aged and privileged." Peter H. Lewis, "Technology," *N.Y. Times*, 28 Aug. 1995, at D3.

The opposite error, though less common, also occurs—e.g.:

- "The governor scrupulously *forebore* [read *forbore*] to notice Mark Green in 1986 and could barely conceal his hostility to Robert Abrams in 1992." Murray Kempton, "Can D'Amato Save Cuomo?" *Newsday* (N.Y.), 26 Oct. 1994, at A16.
- "An agreement was made to *forebear* [read *forbear*] the interest and principal from August 2014 until June 30,

2015." Stanley Dunlap, "Macon-Bibb Officials Approve Blight Funding Split with a Last-Minute Change," *Macon Telegraph* (Ga.), 22 July 2015, at 580.

See WORD-SWAPPING.

LANGUAGE-CHANGE INDEX
1. *forbear* misused for *forebear*: Stage 2
Current ratio (*their forebears* vs. **their forbears*): 6:1
2. *forebear* misused for *forbear*: Stage 1
Current ratio (*must forbear* vs. **must forebear*): 38:1
3. **forebearer* for *forebear*: Stage 1
Current ratio (*our forebears* vs. **our forebearers*): 46:1

forbearance. So spelled—not **forebearance,* which is a NONWORD. But some writers blunder—e.g.:

- "But the 1903 National League pennant went to the Pittsburgh Pirates, whose owner, Barney Dreyfuss, greatly appreciated the American League's *forebearance* [read *forbearance*] in not putting a team in his city." J. Anthony Lukas, "The Year the World Series Was Canceled," *N.Y. Times*, 23 Oct. 1994, § 4, at 15.
- "[I]f you don't pause in the adjoining retail shop and practically fill a suitcase with all sorts of parcels and those familiar red tartan tins of shortcake . . . , you're showing far more *forebearance* [read *forbearance*] than yours truly." Joe Crea, "You're a Loch to Find Castles and Whisky, but a Monster Hunt Will Come Up Empty," *Plain Dealer* (Cleveland), 25 Feb. 2007, at K6.

LANGUAGE-CHANGE INDEX
*forebearance for *forbearance*: Stage 1
Current ratio (*forbearance* vs. **forebearance*): 74:1

forbid > forbade > forbidden. A. Standard Forms. The past tense is *forbade* (rhyming with *glad*)—e.g.: "[Locke] sharply distinguished the respective spheres of Church and State and *forbade* each from meddling in the other." Clifford Orwin, "Civility," 60 *Am. Scholar* 553, 557 (1991). *Forbid* is sometimes wrongly used as a past-tense form—e.g.:

- "Susan has dropped the restraining order that once *forbid* [read *forbade*] him [from making] any contact with her." Brian Biggane, "Fitzpatrick's Life Improving, but His Time in Goal Isn't," *Palm Beach Post*, 31 Mar. 1995, at C1.
- "He growled at people. He *forbid* [read *forbade*] his broadcasters from referring to the team as the 'Cubbies.'" Frederick C. Klein, "The Cubs Win? Sometimes Yes, Sometimes No," *Wall Street J.*, 9 May 1997, at B9.
- "Pythagoras swore off it entirely and *forbid* [read *forbade*] his followers to indulge." Emily Eakin, "If It's Funny, You Laugh, but Why?" *N.Y. Times*, 9 Dec. 2000, at A23.

In fact, the slack usage is so common that some dictionaries now list *forbid* as an alternative.

Some writers—no doubt those who pronounce *forbade* correctly—use the variant spelling **forbad.* It was common from about 1660 to 1800. Today it is an ARCHAISM. Avoid it—e.g.:

- "The 1967 Age Discrimination in Employment Act . . . *forbad* [read *forbade*] bias based on age." Judy Foreman, "Workplace Age Bias Rising, but Proving It Can Be a Job," *Boston Globe*, 31 Jan. 1994, at 25.
- "[Steve] Reina is a member of the Troy Interfaith Group, which held its own National Day of Prayer at Northminster Presbyterian Church after the Christian-only group *forbad* [read *forbade*] non-Christian involvement." Valerie Olander, "Prayer Day at Center of Council Race," *Detroit News*, 15 June 2005, at K8.
- "The Constitution *forbad* [read *forbade*] Congress from creating 'an establishment of religion,' but this was no mysterious concept known only to deep thinking legal scholars." Thomas Sowell, "Silly War on Symbols Can Be Prelude to Tragedy," *Sun-Sentinel* (Ft. Lauderdale), 23 Dec. 2005, at A19.

See IRREGULAR VERBS & **bid (A)**.

Meanwhile, the laughable form *forbidded occasionally appears—e.g.: "Gramola told Williams to remove the headphones, originally thinking a PIAA regulation *forbidded* [read *forbade*] Williams from taking them into a huddle." Kevin Freeman, "Williams, Novak to Meet, Hash Out Their Differences," *Lancaster New Era*, 28 Oct. 1997, at C1.

Finally, *forbade* is often misspelled *forebade, doubtless through an erroneous sense of ETYMOLOGY. In fact, the *for-* here means "against"; it has nothing to do with *fore-*, meaning "before." E.g.: "To make matters worse, experts said, PG&E and Edison couldn't protect themselves from the high prices by entering into long-term contracts because regulations set during deregulation *forebade* [read *forbade*] them." Mary Fricker, "Experts: Surge in Energy Cost Not Predictable," *Press Democrat* (Santa Rosa), 18 Jan. 2001, at E1.

LANGUAGE-CHANGE INDEX
1. *forbid* for the past-tense *forbade*: Stage 2
Current ratio (*he forbade it* vs. *he forbid it): 6:1
2. *forbade* mispronounced /fər-**bayd**/: Stage 4
3. *forbade* misspelled *forebade: Stage 1
Current ratio: 563:1

B. Preposition with. In formal contexts, *forbid* traditionally takes the preposition *to* or, less formally, *from*. H.W. Fowler stated that *forbid from doing* is unidiomatic (*FMEU1* at 186), but it is increasingly common. In fact, it is probably more common today than *forbid to do*, but both forms appear frequently—e.g.:

- "In exchange, the Government forbids newspaper vending machines, *forbids* small stores *from selling* papers and gives the union sole right to use the public sidewalks to sell newspapers." Anthony DePalma, "Despite Gains, Press Freedom in Mexico Is Still Limited," *N.Y. Times*, 20 Nov. 1994, § 1, at 3.
- "As a condition of bond, judges often *forbid* suspects *from contacting* victims." Janice Haidet Morse, "Official: Law Has Loopholes," *Dayton Daily News*, 13 Dec. 1996, at B2.
- "On a 9–0 vote, the court struck down laws in Rhode Island and 10 other states that *forbid* retailers *to advertise* their prices for beer, wine or liquor." David G. Savage, "Advertisers' Free-Speech Rights Bolstered," *L.A. Times*, 14 May 1996, at A1.

- "The rules expressly *forbid* drill sergeants *to have* intimate relationships with their recruits." Eric Schmitt, "Sex in the Ranks," *Sacramento Bee*, 24 Nov. 1996, at F1.

Cf. **prohibit**.

forbore; forborne. See **forbear**.

forceable. See **forcible**.

forceps. This is traditionally a singular noun <this forceps isn't big enough>. But on the mistaken assumption that the word is plural, the word is increasingly joined with a plural verb. The error is old—e.g.: "The *forceps are* [read *is*] compact, *they are* [read *it is*] easy to handle and *have* [read *has*] firm gripping power." *Surgery, Gynecology and Obstetrics* 662 (F.H. Martin ed., 1915).

The English plural is either *forceps* or *forcepses*. In *The Origin of Species*, Charles Darwin used *forcepses*. The Latin plural is *forcipes* /**for**-si-peez/, which was fairly common in technical books from 1800 to about 1975.

Since the early 19th century, the BACK-FORMATION *forcep has occasionally appeared—e.g.:

- "With a considered tug Mr. Shehata soon frees the organ from one of the small holes in the donor's stomach. He strides swiftly across the theatre, skirting trays of gleaming equipment, with it dangling from a *forcep* [read *forceps*]." "It's All a Bit More Stressful with a TV Audience," *Nottingham Evening Post* (U.K.), 25 Nov. 2006, at 12.
- "The resected polyps were retrieved by M-S technique, in which suction, regarded as the leading technique, was taken in combination with channel occlusion, trap, snare, and grasping *forcep* [read *forceps*]." "New Findings Reported from Zhejiang University Describe Advances in Polypectomy," *Med. Devices & Surgical Tech. Week*, 18 May 2008, at 333.

Cf. **biceps**.

LANGUAGE-CHANGE INDEX
*forcep for *forceps* as a singular: Stage 2
Current ratio (*a forceps* vs. *a forcep): 38:1

forcible; forceable; forceful. Oddly, we have the spellings *enforceable* but *forcible*. (See **enforceable**.) The usual form, *forcible* means "effected by force against resistance"—e.g.:

- "Driving the 4% dip in violent crime through June were drops in homicide, 2%; *forcible* rape, 6%." Robert Davis, "Random Killings Hit a High," *USA Today*, 5 Dec. 1994, at A1.
- "Steel insulated or solid core wood doors offer the most resistance to *forcible* entry, provided there are no sidelights." Linda Syron, "Helpful Ways to Keep Burglars at Bay," *Toronto Sun*, 15 Dec. 1996, at H10.

Forceable, though it might appear a NEEDLESS VARIANT, carries a passive sense: "capable of being forced" <she tried to coerce him, but he simply wasn't forceable>.

Because *forcible* properly refers only to physical force, it shouldn't be used where *forceful* is needed, the latter carrying figurative as well as literal meanings—e.g.: "A Washington Post–ABC News survey of U.S. voters taken Wednesday night confirmed the doubts *forcibly* [read *forcefully*] expressed by a dozen Illinois voters in a two-hour group interview in this Chicago suburb Monday." David S. Broder & Richard Morin, "Clinton, Bush Score Few Points in Sampling of Nation's Voters," *Houston Chron.*, 20 Mar. 1992, at A3.

LANGUAGE-CHANGE INDEX
forcibly misused for *forcefully*: Stage 3
Current ratio (*stated forcefully* vs. **stated forcibly*): 3:1

FORE-. See **FOR-**.

forebear. See **forbear**.

*forebearance. See **forbearance**.

forebode (= to predict [usu. something bad]; foretell) is sometimes misspelled **forbode*—e.g.:

- "If the personalities of the principals on both sides of the table don't mesh, it *forbodes* [read *forebodes*] what well could be a bad marriage between the firms." Ursula Miller, "Investment Banker Manages Mergers," *Cincinnati Enquirer*, 4 Mar. 1996, at D1. (On the odd syntax of that sentence, in which the unidiomatic phrase *well could be* appears in place of the more natural *could well be*, see ADVERBS (A).)
- "[T]he track is purportedly built atop an ancient Indian burial ground and the place seems to ooze a sense of morbid *forboding* [read *foreboding*]." Brant James, "In Junior's Words," *St. Petersburg Times*, 28 Apr. 2007, Sports §, at C12.

See **FOR-**.

LANGUAGE-CHANGE INDEX
forebode misspelled **forbode*: Stage 1
Current ratio: 44:1

forecast > forecast > forecast. So inflected. **Forecasted* is a solecism that spread during the 20th century and lingers still—e.g.:

- "In July 1996, Cohen *forecasted* [read *forecast*] that the Dow would pass 6000 by Dec. 31, and it did." Richard Wilner, "Goldman Offers 57 Partnerships," *N.Y. Post*, 21 Oct. 1998, at 39.
- "They *forecasted* [read *forecast*] a 14.3% increase in 1998." Shawn Tully, "Stocks May Be Surging Toward an Earnings Chasm," *Fortune Mag.*, 1 Feb. 1999, at 26.
- "Merger speculation and environmental issues aside, many in the industry believe that a *forecasted* [read *forecast*] supply/demand imbalance provides the basis for long-term optimism." Len Boselovic, "Big Coal Taking It on the Chin," *Pitt. Post-Gaz.*, 3 Aug. 2008, at D1.

See **-CAST** & **IRREGULAR VERBS**.

LANGUAGE-CHANGE INDEX
*forecasted for past-tense *forecast*: Stage 2
Current ratio (*forecast that* vs. **forecasted that*): 9:1

foreclose. A. Constructions with. Today, *foreclose* most commonly indicates one or more possibilities <his failure of the exam forecloses the possibility of a promotion>.

In the context of a real-estate foreclosure, the verb is generally intransitive: one *forecloses on* property

or a mortgage. E.g.: "William J. Hedebrand, a man the town took to court in 1984 over a house he built illegally in West Suffield, is now trying to persuade the town not to *foreclose on* his property." Mindy A. Antonio, "Man Offers to Settle Debt He Owes Suffield," *Hartford Courant*, 22 Dec. 1994, at B1.

But the verb was formerly often transitive, so that a sentence like that one would have read, "William J. Hedebrand . . . is now trying to persuade the town not to *foreclose* his property." This usage is infrequent but not unknown—e.g.: "On the following April 10 the Bank instituted an action to *foreclose* its mortgage." Grant Gilmore & Charles L. Black Jr., *The Law of Admiralty* 953 (2d ed. 1975).

Some writers even use **foreclose against*, but *on* is more idiomatic—e.g.: "You can't foreclose *against* [read *on*] my home if you didn't record the mortgage." Robert J. Bruss, "Failure to Record Realty Files Can Be Costly," *Chicago Trib.*, 21 July 1994, at C5.

Foreclose (a person) *from* (an action) is an archaic construction still occasionally used, but the instances are too convoluted to quote. That in itself should serve as adequate warning to avoid it.

B. Misspelled **forclose.* **Forclose* is an erroneous form that sometimes appears—e.g.:

- "And both the Norwest Bank and the Federal Land Bank have moved in court to *forclose* [read *foreclose*] on the farm." "Illicit Crop Almost Saved Farm," *N.Y. Times*, 7 Sept. 1988, at A24.
- "Town officials are taking steps to *forclose* [read *foreclose*] on the following property owners . . . ." Kim Martineau, "Town Pursues Property of Tax Scofflaws," *Hartford Courant*, 7 Nov. 2002, at B3.

See **FOR-**.

LANGUAGE-CHANGE INDEX
foreclose misspelled **forclose*: Stage 1
Current ratio: 716:1

forefathers; founding fathers. Both may denote the founders of the country, but the two shouldn't be combined—e.g.: "What would Washington, Jefferson, Madison and the other *founding forefathers* [read *founding fathers*] say about us today?" Charlie Rea, "The Moral Implications of Tax Cutting," *Roanoke Times*, 30 Jan. 2001, at A11. *Forefathers* is an old-fashioned synonym for *ancestors*; some writers avoid it because of its sexist overtones. (See SEXISM.) But *founding fathers* seems unobjectionable and historically accurate in reference to those who participated directly in establishing the U.S. Constitution and the American government. Meanwhile, the term *founders* (often capitalized) is common nowadays; it may denote the founders of anything, such as a town or a corporation.

LANGUAGE-CHANGE INDEX
*founding forefathers for *founding fathers*: Stage 1
Current ratio (*founding fathers* vs. **founding forefathers*): 507:1

LANGUAGE-CHANGE INDEX (For the full key, see front matter pp. xxxi, l–li.)
Stage 1: Rejected. **Stage 2:** Widely shunned. **Stage 3:** Widespread but . . . **Stage 4:** Ubiquitous but . . . **Stage 5:** Fully accepted.
Invariably inferior forms marked by asterisk (✱). • Ratios represent frequency of prevalent forms vs. variants in current books.

foregather; forgather. The latter (meaning "to meet in a group; assemble") has long been thought to be the standard spelling—as the listings in the *OED* and *W11* attest. In fact, though, in modern print sources, both AmE and BrE, the spelling *foregather* has enjoyed a significant preponderance. (See FOR-.) In any event, though, *gather* usually suffices—e.g.: "On the Greek isle of Skagathos, a gaggle of New Agers *forgather* [read *gather*], booked by Skagathos Holidays to enroll in such courses as Orgasmic Consciousness and Therapy of Fiction Writing." Nicholas Delbanco, "From D.M. Thomas, a Fine, Funny Novel of the Writing Life," *Chicago Trib.*, 9 June 1996, Books §, at 9. (On second thought, the quirky word might be appropriate in that particular context.)

forego; forgo. Although a few apologists argue that these words are interchangeable, there's a distinction worth preserving. True, for over a century (ca. 1800–1900), *forego* was used in all senses. But about 1900 some DIFFERENTIATION emerged—a nuance observed today by fastidious writers. *Forego*, as suggested by the prefix, means "to go before." *Forgo* means "to do without; pass up voluntarily; waive; renounce." Cf. **forswear.**

Using *forego* where *forgo* would be better is a persistent problem. Examples of the poor usage are legion—e.g.:

- "That realization not only helped Lavelle's brother but convinced her to *forego* [read *forgo*] a career as a social worker or psychologist and instead become a teacher." "Challenged Students Get Special Help," *L.A. Times*, 11 Apr. 1997, at B2.
- "[T]he beauty of the trees by night, and the rapture of lovers under the stars, these things we shall *forego* [read *forgo*]." Alan Paton, *Cry, the Beloved Country* 72 (2003).
- "But the eye-popping purchase price offered by an investment group called Clipper Equity understandably raises fears that to recoup its investment, Clipper would *forego* [read *forgo*] its subsidies and attempt to raise rents, eventually forcing out many of Starrett's 14,000 tenants." "Protecting Affordable Housing," *N.Y. Times*, 18 Feb. 2007, § 14, at 11.

The opposite mistake—misusing *forgo* for *forego*—is much less common. E.g.:

- "The *forgoing* [read *foregoing*] arguments largely concern comparison of higher taxa." Theodore H. Bullock, "Comparative Neuroscience Holds Promise for Quiet Revolutions," *Science*, 3 Aug. 1984, at 473.
- "All of the *forgoing* [read *foregoing*] are contributing factors to [Detroit Rescue Mission Ministries'] current shortfall." Donald F. DeVos, "Mission Downsizes as Donations Fall Off," *Detroit News*, 10 Apr. 2002, at S6.

Forwent and *forewent* are the past-tense forms. While *forewent* is hopelessly archaic <they forewent us to the theater>, *forwent* is occasionally useful—e.g.:

- "'I'm not going to say never to anything,' said Moulton Patterson, who *forwent* a bid for reelection." Debra Cano, "Moulton Patterson May Seek Council Seat," *L.A. Times*, 14 Dec. 1994, at B2.
- "Program director Gregg Roberts suspects the informants who *forwent* their rewards are serving time in prison."

Trevor Nelson, "Bad Guys Seldom Caught Through Offers of Cash," *Rocky Mountain News* (Denver), 23 May 1995, at A30.

Forgone and *foregone* are the past-participial forms. *Foregone* is correct in the phrase *foregone conclusion* because the idea is that the conclusion "went before" the question: everybody knew the answer before the question was posed. Naturally, though, blunders arise, even in the writings of those who should know better—e.g.: "[I]t was *forgone* [read *foregone*] that *disinterested* would lose its older sense once *uninterested* lost the sense of 'having a stake in,' which we retain only in the fixed phrase *interested party*." Geoffrey Nunberg, "The Decline of Grammar," *Atlantic Monthly*, Dec. 1983, at 44. (For more on the usage issue discussed in that sentence, see **disinterest** & **disinterested**.) Meanwhile, the past participle of *forgo* is *forgone*, without the medial *-e-*: "I would have given a lot for a few columns about what the Flynn years cost Boston in the way of *foregone* [read *forgone*] opportunities." David Warsh, "In Sight of Milton," *Boston Globe*, 26 Oct. 1993, at 37. See FOR-.

LANGUAGE-CHANGE INDEX
1. *forego* misused for *forgo*: Stage 4
Current ratio (*forgo the opportunity* vs.
*forego the opportunity): 1:1
2. *forgoing* misused for *foregoing*: Stage 1
Current ratio (*the foregoing* vs. **the forgoing*): 101:1

forehead traditionally rhymes with *horrid*, as in the nursery rhyme: "There was a little girl, who had a little curl / Right in the middle of her forehead; / When she was good, she was very, very good, / But when she was bad she was horrid." But in AmE, the word is commonly (and acceptably) pronounced /**for**-hed/.

foreign language; second language. There are connotative differences. A *foreign language* is learned mostly for the cultural insight it may provide. A *second language* is learned mostly for utilitarian purposes.

In technical usage, a *foreign language* is one you learn so that you can communicate with foreigners; a *second language* is one you learn so that you can communicate with people in the country where you live. People living in the U.S. who speak either English or Spanish may learn the other as a *second language*. But if the same people learned German or Urdu, for example, they would probably learn it as a *foreign language*.

forejudge. There are two words spelled this way. The first is a NEEDLESS VARIANT of *prejudge*. It's sometimes misspelled *forjudge*. See **prejudge**.

The second, deriving from Middle English *forjuggen* ("to judge outside"), is an unetymologically spelled variant of an ARCHAISM. It should be *forjudge* because it means "to expel or dispossess by judicial decree." But the *OED* shows that *forejudge*, with an *-e-*, has been used with this legal meaning since the late 16th century. In any event, the term is quite rare in this sense. When the word is needed, *forjudge* is the better spelling. See FOR-.

foreman. A. Generally. In the sense "a person in charge of a group of workers" <the foreman on the docks>, *foreman* dates from the 16th century. But pressure is afoot to find gender-neutral alternatives, and the words *supervisor*, *chief*, and *leader* seem to be the most likely candidates. See SEXISM (C).

B. Legal Sense. Of the three choices—*foreman*, *foreperson*, and *presiding juror*—the best is the last. E.g.: " 'We are working diligently,' the *presiding juror* concluded in the message." George Flynn, "Turner Jury Eyes Secret Service Probe," *Houston Chron.*, 11 Oct. 1996, at 33. The word *foreperson*, though one word, is less satisfactory because it uses the *-person* suffix. (See SEXISM (C).) Yet that form is, for the time being, ensconced in federal procedural rules and may be difficult to oust.

It's mildly surprising to see *foreman* and *foreperson* being used together for purposes of INELEGANT VARIATION—e.g.: "And since the *foreperson* is the single most influential person on a jury, lawyers will do anything to keep good *foreman* material off." Robin T. Lakoff, *Talking Power: The Politics of Language in Our Lives* 114–15 (1990). (On the use of *single most* in that sentence, see **single most.**)

Current ratio (*foreman of the jury* vs. *presiding juror*): 2:1

forename. For the meaning of this term, see the discussion at **surname.**

*foresake. See **forsake.**

foreseeable is occasionally misspelled **forseeable*—e.g.:

- "The rest of the county's working farmland is up-county, protected, for the *forseeable* [read *foreseeable*] future, by zoning that prohibits dense development." Frank Ahrens, "The Sun Sets on a Fertile Crescent," *Wash. Post*, 25 Nov. 1996, at C1.
- "The subprime mortgage market collapse just might give private-equity titan Cerberus a headache for the *forseeable* [read *foreseeable*] future." Roddy Boyd, "GMAC's Subprime State May Hurt Creditors," *N.Y. Post*, 5 Mar. 2007, at 31.

See FOR-.

LANGUAGE-CHANGE INDEX
foreseeable misspelled **forseeable*: Stage 1
Current ratio: 150:1

foreshorten (= to shorten lines for rendering three-dimensional perspective in two dimensions) dates from the Renaissance and is best left in the field of art—e.g.: "Even Titian does not *foreshorten* his boughs rightly." John Ruskin, *The Works of John Ruskin* 71 (1887). Otherwise, it adds nothing but a syllable to *shorten*—"But scrawled within [the genome] are clues about our future, which can be downright terrifying. Rather than expand our sense of possibilities, they *foreshorten* [read *shorten*] them. . . . From our genes,

we learn how we may die." Jennifer Senior, "Chronicle of a Death Foretold," *N.Y. Times*, 11 May 2008, Book Rev. §, at 28.

forestall; forestal(l)ment. Although the predominant verb is *forestall* in AmE and BrE alike, the standard noun is *forestallment* in AmE but *forestalment* in BrE.
Current ratio (*forestall* vs. **forestal*): 42:1

forever. One word. The *OED* suggests a distinction—the solid *forever* meaning "incessantly" <she's forever twirling her hair> and the two-word **for ever* meaning "for all future time" <we'll be together for ever>. But the solidified version has become standard in both AmE and BrE, and the two-word version is best described as archaic.

forewent. See **forego.**

foreword (= a book's introduction, esp. one written by someone other than the author) is often misspelled like its homophone, *forward*—e.g.:

- "In his *forward* [read *foreword*] to Delgado's book, Andrew Hacker defends the storytelling movement." Jeffrey Rosen, "The Bloods and the Crits," *New Republic*, 9 Dec. 1996, at 27.
- "In his *forward* [read *foreword*] to the book, Alexander Woollcott describes him as 'the most notable city editor of his time,' endlessly fascinated by 'the changeless and ever-changing Baghdad which is the territory of his staff.' " "Mythic City Editor Is Brought Back to Life," *N.Y. Times*, 18 Oct. 1999, at C18.
- "In the *forward* [read *foreword*] to his book, [José] Cisneros writes that the first Spanish horses were responsible for bringing civilization to our continent and that he considers it his mission to 'follow their hoofprints along and across the land . . . .' " Gary Cartwright, "Pasó por Aquí," *Texas Monthly*, Dec. 2006, at 182.

See FOR-. Cf. **preface.**

LANGUAGE-CHANGE INDEX
forward misused for *foreword*: Stage 2
Current ratio (*book's foreword* vs. **book's forward*): 10:1

forfeiture is naturally pronounced /**for**-fi-chər/. Pompous speakers are fond of pronouncing the final syllable /tyoor/.

for free. See **free.**

forgather. See **foregather.**

forgery. See **counterfeit.**

forgo. See **forego.**

formality; formalism. These words are quite distinct. *Formality* denotes (1) conformity to rules or customs; (2) strict precision in manners; or (3) an obligatory step in a process. *Formalism*, by contrast, denotes strict adherence to traditional or prescribed forms, especially without regard to substantive import. The

LANGUAGE-CHANGE INDEX (For the full key, see front matter pp. xxxi, l–li.)
Stage 1: Rejected. **Stage 2:** Widely shunned. **Stage 3:** Widespread but . . . **Stage 4:** Ubiquitous but . . . **Stage 5:** Fully accepted.
Invariably inferior forms marked by asterisk (*). • Ratios represent frequency of prevalent forms vs. variants in current books.

word is generally pejorative—e.g.: "[Cinematographer Wally] Pfister and director Christopher Nolan used an unfettered camera to help them defy the stuffy *formalism* associated with period pieces and suggest contemporary parallels to their tale of Victorian-era illusions." Sheigh Crabtree, "A Year of Some Dark Movie Magic," *L.A. Times*, 18 Feb. 2007, Sunday Cal. §, at E6. *Formalism* also refers to various schools of thought or style, as in mathematics, art, architecture, and literature.

The corresponding adjective, *formalistic*, carries perhaps even more strongly negative connotations than *formalism*—e.g.:

- "Her colleague Rose Rosengard Subotnik blames Schoenberg for the whole notion of contemporary music as an unpopular, *formalistic*, not to say academic, pursuit, removed from society and powerless to change it." David Schiff, "Schoenberg, Alive (Gasp!) and Well," *N.Y. Times*, 16 Jan. 1994, § 2, at 25.
- "He accuses the courts of a *formalistic*, almost ritualistic, application of rules." Earl E. Shamwell Jr., "In Pursuit of Justice," *Conn. Law Trib.*, 1 Apr. 1996, at 43.
- "Current law affords the able-bodied a right that is denied to some disabled people, namely the right to kill themselves, . . . based on a *formalistic* moral distinction, between killing yourself and someone else killing you on your behalf, that is meaningless in practical terms." Andrew Coyne, "If Euthanasia Is a Right, Why Not for All?," *Nat'l Post* (Can.), 18 Oct. 2014, at A4.

For other words susceptible to confusion with *formalistic*, see **formulaic.**

formally. See **formerly.**

FORMAL WORDS are those occupying an elevated level of diction. The English language has several levels of diction, and it frequently has synonyms existing on the different levels. So *residence* is formal, *house* is the ordinary word, and *digs* (or *pad* or *crib*) is SLANG. Likewise, *proceed* is formal, *go* is ordinary, and *head on over* is slang.

In written AmE, the unfortunate tendency has long been to reach for the formal word that is widely known. So writers steer away from SESQUIPEDALITY but choose pomposities that everyone recognizes. That's what leads people to write (or occasionally say) *be of assistance* instead of *help*, *attire* instead of *clothes*, *inebriated* instead of *drunk*. Early in the 19th century, the novelist James Fenimore Cooper worried that "the love of turgid expressions is gaining ground, and ought to be corrected." "On Language," in *The American Democrat* 117–24 (1838) (repr. in *A Language for Writers* 110, 113 [James R. Gaskin & Jack Suberman eds., 1966]). For stylists, that worry is perpetual, as each generation becomes enamored of its own brands of linguistic inflation: DOUBLESPEAK, OFFICIALESE, and the like.

The problem with formal words is that they are symptomatic of those stylistic disturbances. One way or another, they lead to stuffiness—the great fault in modern writing: "For most people . . . in most situations, in the writing of everyday serious expository prose, it is the Stuffy voice that gets in the way. The reason it gets in the way, I submit, is that the writer is scared. If this is an age of anxiety, one way we react to our anxiety is to withdraw into omniscient and multisyllabic detachment where nobody can get us." Walker Gibson, *Tough, Sweet & Stuffy* 107 (1966).

In the left-hand column below are some of the chief symptoms—not in every context, of course, but whenever the terms in the right-hand column would do:

Formal Word	Ordinary Word
accommodation(s)	room
accompany	go with
annex, vb.	attach
appear	look, seem
append	attach
approximately	about
arrive	come
attain	reach
attired	dressed
cast, vb.	throw
cease	stop
commence	begin, start
complete	finish
conceal	hide
continue	keep on
deem	consider, treat as
demise	death
depart	go
desist	stop
detain	hold
discover	find
donate	give
effectuate	carry out
emolument	pay
employ (an instrument)	use
endeavor	try
evince	show
expedite	hasten
expend	spend
expiration, expiry	end
extend	give
forthwith	immediately, now, soon, promptly
henceforth	from now on
imbibe	drink
inaugurate	begin
indicate	show
individual	person
initiate	begin
inquire	ask
institute	begin, start
interrogate	question
intimate, vb.	suggest
luncheon	lunch
manner	way
necessitate	require
obtain	get
occasion, vb.	cause
peruse	read
place, vb.	put
portion	part
possess	own, have
present, vb.	give
preserve	keep
prior	earlier
prior to	before

proceed	go (ahead)
purchase	buy
receive	get
relate	tell
remain	stay
remainder	rest
remove	take away, haul off
request, vb.	ask
retain	keep
secure	get
subsequently	later, afterward
subsequent to	after
sufficient	enough
summon	send for, call
terminate	end
utilize	use

format, v.t., makes *formatted* and *formatting* in both AmE and BrE. See SPELLING (B).

formative; formidable. *Formative* (= of, relating to, or involving development) is unrelated to *formidable* (= inspiring fear or awe; hard to overcome). Yet the second word is occasionally misused for the first in the phrase *formative years*—e.g.:

- "Do you really think a day-care center can do a better job of loving and caring for your children in their *formidable* [read *formative*] years?" Edward V. Golden, "U.S. Shouldn't Subsidize Child-Care Responsibilities," *Times Union* (Albany), 29 Jan. 1998, at A10.
- "Duncan's Spurs career, still in its *formidable* [read *formative*] years, is rich in background already." Brent Zwerneman, "Silver, Black Suit Duncan," *San Antonio Express-News*, 10 July 2000, at C10.
- "He became a member of James Brown's ultra-hip, ever funky J.B.'s back in 1964. . . . During the course of the conversation, Parker touched upon his *formidable* [read *formative*] years with Brown." Ian D'Giff, "Q&A Maceo Parker," *J. News* (Westchester Co., N.Y.), 6 June 2002, at G31.

See **formidable** & WORD-SWAPPING.

LANGUAGE-CHANGE INDEX
formidable misused for *formative*: Stage 1

former; latter. A. Application. If these terms are to be used at all (and it's often best to abstain), they should apply only to a series of two. The *former* is the first of two, the *latter* the second of two. In contexts with more than two elements, *first* should be used rather than *former*, *last* rather than *latter*.

Former and *latter* can bewilder the reader when coupled with numbers—e.g.: "The *former* are liberals first and Catholics second, the *latter* Catholics first, liberals second." David R. Carlin Jr., "A Liberal Catholic Taxonomy," *Commonweal*, 22 Sept. 1995, at 8. (A possible revision, based on the fuller text: *Catholic liberals are liberals first and Catholics second; liberal Catholics are Catholics first and liberals second.* There is, by the way, a certain irony in the revision: what is described as *first* is the second word, and what is described as *second* is actually the first. The point is

that the noun in each phrase [*Catholic liberal* vs. *liberal Catholic*] is the more important word.)

B. Misapplication. Sometimes otherwise brilliant writers get confused with *former* and *latter* and then misapply one term or the other—e.g.: "Thus, if for some special reason, X has contracted with Y to go on the *former's* [read *latter's*] own land, it is obvious that X has, as regards Y, both the privilege of entering and the duty of entering." Wesley Newcomb Hohfeld, *Fundamental Legal Conceptions* 39 (1919; repr. 1946).

LANGUAGE-CHANGE INDEX
former misused for *latter*: Stage 1

C. Latter without former. May one have a *latter* without an explicit *former*? Yes, as long as there are two identifiable elements. For a similar problem, see **on the other hand.**

*former alumnus, etc. See **alumnus (B).**

formerly; formally. *Formerly* (= once, at a time in the past) is sometimes confounded with *formally* (= [1] by authorized sanction; or [2] based on form rather than substance). Doubtless the blunder results from the similar pronunciations—e.g.:

- "Roger Westwell, *formally* [read *formerly*] chief accountant for Nadin Contracting, has now been promoted to financial controller of the company." "Mining People," *Mining Mag.*, Dec. 1989, at 543.
- "The Sheriff's Office *formally* [read *formerly*] had used for its rolling station a converted bread truck and a county hand-me-down bookmobile." "Playback," *Herald-Sun* (Durham, N.C.), 8 Sept. 2002, at C3.

LANGUAGE-CHANGE INDEX
formally misused for *formerly*: Stage 1
Current ratio (*was formerly the case* vs.
*was formally the case): 105:1

*former veteran. See **veteran.**

formidable is preferably pronounced /**for**-mə-də-bəl/, not /for-**mid**-ə-bəl/. See **formative.**

formula. Pl. *formulas* or *formulae* /**form**-yə-lee/. The native plural, ending in -*s*, predominates in all but scientific writing—e.g.: "Their appearances, after all, are mostly ceremonial, and they are expected to mouth empty and generally comforting *formulae* [read *formulas*]." Richard Mitchell, *Less than Words Can Say* 77 (1979). See PLURALS (B).

formulaic; formulistic; formalistic. *Formulaic* = of, relating to, following, or constituting a formula. *Formulistic* = fond of formulas. *Formalistic* = adhering unduly to form without regard to substance.

fornication. See **adultery (A).**

forsake > forsook > forsaken. So inflected. *Forsaked is a solecism that has never had currency—e.g.:

LANGUAGE-CHANGE INDEX (For the full key, see front matter pp. xxxi, l–li.)
Stage 1: Rejected. **Stage 2:** Widely shunned. **Stage 3:** Widespread but . . . **Stage 4:** Ubiquitous but . . . **Stage 5:** Fully accepted.
Invariably inferior forms marked by asterisk (*). • Ratios represent frequency of prevalent forms vs. variants in current books.

- "Lawrence . . . *forsaked* [read *forsook*] his love of classical piano for the wild blue yonder." James Hill, "1st Black Astronaut Added to Space Hero Roster," *Chicago Trib.*, 27 Oct. 1997, at 1.
- "Taking up the sport [soccer] at age 5, he frequently *forsaked* [read *forsook*] the pleasurable vices of most teenagers to work on his game." Michael Lewis, "Ford Drives UNCW," *Morning Star* (Wilmington, N.C.), 10 Nov. 1998, at C1.
- "Katz, a first-team all-Hillsborough County pick at Brandon High in 1997, *forsaked* [read *forsook*] a full scholarship at Southern Wesleyan to play close to home and friends at Tampa." Brant James, "Local Connection Is Paying Off for Tampa Series," *St. Petersburg Times*, 13 Apr. 2000, at C12.

Forsake is sometimes corrupted into **foresake*— e.g.: "It *foresakes* [read *forsakes*] the rounded look of the previous Camry for a crisper, squarer silhouette." James R. Healey, "Moving Target Toyota Aims at No. 1 Spot," *USA Today*, 25 Sept. 1996, at B1. See FOR- & IRREGULAR VERBS.

LANGUAGE-CHANGE INDEX
1. **forsaked* for *forsook*: Stage 1
Current ratio (*forsook* vs. **forsaked*): 1,434:1
2. **foresake* for *forsake*: Stage 1
Current ratio (*forsake* vs. **foresake*): 615:1

*forseeable. See **foreseeable.**

for sure (= certain, certainly) is a colloquial idiom that dates back to the 17th century and persists as a CASUALISM <Am I going? For sure.>. The phrase grew staggeringly in popularity during the 20th century.

forswear (= to renounce; pledge to give up) is sometimes misspelled **foreswear*—e.g.:

- "In threatening a trade war, the administration also undercut the fledgling World Trade Organization and the principles that nations *foreswear* [read *forswear*] tariffs as weapons and play by the same rules." John Talton, "It's Too Soon to Celebrate Trade Pact," *Cincinnati Enquirer*, 29 June 1995, at B11.
- "By the same token, Israel should be asked to *foreswear* [read *forswear*] future persecution of Lebanese civilians." "The Enemies of Lebanon's People," *Boston Globe*, 19 Apr. 1996, at 18.
- "He proposed a chivalrous code of conduct for outer space security that essentially asks all capable militaries to voluntarily *foreswear* [read *forswear*] making space a shooting gallery." John Siebert, "Outer Space Warfare and Metaphor Drag," *Ploughshares Monitor*, Summer 2015, at 14.

If **foreswear* were a proper word, it might mean "to swear before," since the prefix *fore-* denotes a previous time. See FOR-. Cf. **forego.**

LANGUAGE-CHANGE INDEX
forswear misspelled **foreswear*: Stage 2
Current ratio: 8:1

forte (= a person's strong point) has long been thought to be preferably pronounced with one syllable, like *fort.* That's because the word is originally French (in which *fort* means "strong," corruptly made with a feminine *-e* suffix) and is so pronounced. But most speakers of AmE use the two-syllable version (/**for**-tay/), probably under the influence of the Italian *forte,* a two-syllable word referring to a musical notation to play or sing loudly. Though it might have been nice to keep the two words separate in pronunciation, that hasn't happened—and the two-syllable version can no longer be condemned. What can be condemned is the pretentious pronunciation /for-**tay**/ and the occasional use of an acute accent on the *-e.*

LANGUAGE-CHANGE INDEX
forte (= strong point) as two syllables: Stage 5

for the duration of is reducible to *during* or *throughout*—e.g.:

- "For all practical purposes, Oscar-winning Walter Matthau became Albert Einstein *for the three-month duration of the filming* [read *during the three-month filming*] of 'I.Q.'" Joyce J. Persico, "The Eyes Had It for Matthau," *S.F. Examiner*, 24 Dec. 1994, at C1.
- "Treasury prices opened firmer Monday morning and remained in positive territory *for the duration of* [read *during* or *throughout*] the session." Niamh Ring, "Trading Grinds to a Near Halt as 'Bored' Players Ready for Holiday," *Bond Buyer*, 26 Dec. 1996, at 1.

for the purpose of [+ vb. + -ing]. This construction signals wordiness—e.g.:

- "Elections Board lawyer George Dunst said the board could agree with the group's argument that because it was created solely *for the purpose of boosting* [read *to boost*] voter turnout, what it does and who gives to it can remain secret." Steven Walters, "Court Race Defends Its Anonymity," *Milwaukee J. Sentinel*, 13 July 1997, at 5.
- "And if you're doing it only *for the purpose of selling* [read *to sell*] your house more quickly, yes, you should avoid overimproving." Ruth Hepner, "Pick Improvements to Make Home Nicer for You," *Wash. Times*, 1 Aug. 1997, at F2.

for the reason that. See **because (D)** & **reason why.**

fortitude refers to inner strength, willpower, and courage. Yet writers often seem to use it in reference to physical strength, stamina, or endurance—e.g.: "Talk-show host David Brudnoy showed off his physical *fortitude* [read *prowess*], bearhugging a reporter and lifting her off the floor." Susan Bickelhaupt, "Neely's New Shtick," *Boston Globe*, 20 Sept. 1996, at D2.

LANGUAGE-CHANGE INDEX
fortitude in the sense "physical strength": Stage 3

fortuitous, strictly speaking, means "occurring by chance," not "fortunate." The traditional sense remains fairly strong—e.g.:

- "Unless the victim dies, the law cannot assume that the transgressor really meant to kill—even though whether the victim lives or dies might be entirely *fortuitous*." Jerome H. Skolnick, "A Capital Offense Spared by Luck?" *L.A. Times*, 27 Aug. 1993, at B7.
- "He began his career with a *fortuitous* meeting and handshake with his brother, William C. Liedtke Jr., whom he encountered by chance on the South Pacific island of Saipan during the war. They decided that if they survived the war, they would start an independent oil and gas business." "J. Hugh Liedtke" (obit.), *Tulsa World*, 1 Apr. 2003, at A12.

See **aleatory**.

Meanwhile, of course, the word is commonly misused for *fortunate*, in itself a very unfortunate thing—e.g.:

- "My choice of Leeds University was quite *fortuitous* [read *lucky* or *fortunate*]. A few weeks before the university session was scheduled to begin, I was given a scholarship to study in England." Wole Soyinka, "Yoruban Astrophysics," *Wash. Post*, 9 Apr. 1995, at C3.
- "That Smoltz would be so *fortuitous* [read *fortunate* or *lucky*] is something of a good howl in itself, given all the cruel twists in his career." Tom Verducci, "Eye Opener," *Sports Illustrated*, 10 June 1996, at 46.
- "Keeping home and business under one roof is a constant challenge for Coover. Perhaps the *most fortuitous* [read *most fortunate* or *best*] feature of the house is a full-length staircase between the second and third floors, which physically separates the living and work areas." Alvin Rosenbaum, "The Balancing Act," *Home Office Computing*, Dec. 1996, at 62.

In the phrases **fortuitous accident* and **fortuitous coincidence*, the word *fortuitous* bears the right sense but is redundant: every accident or coincidence is fortuitous. Writers using those phrases, though, almost invariably mean "fortunate" or "lucky"—e.g.:

- "Without that *fortuitous accident* [read *lucky accident*] of layout, even Conran's space might have stayed empty." Claudia H. Deutsch, "The Shops at Citicorp Center," *N.Y. Times*, 16 June 1996, § 9, at 10.
- "By a *fortuitous coincidence* [read *fortunate coincidence*] that allows a unique movement-by-movement comparison, Pittsburgh Symphony's incoming music director, Mariss Jansons, has recorded a Sibelius disc released simultaneously with Maazel's completion of his third Sibelius cycle." Robert Croan, "Two Perspectives on Sibelius," *Pitt. Post-Gaz.*, 1 Sept. 1996, at F9.

Fortuity is the seldom-seen noun corresponding to *fortuitous* (usually in the strict sense)—e.g.: "Voters tend to be more straightforward, rewarding presidents who, whether by *fortuity* or by design, happen to be in office when the public's pocketful swells." John Liscio, "History, and Hard Numbers, Favor Bill Clinton," *Commercial Appeal* (Memphis), 18 Aug. 1996, at C1. *Fortuitousness*, which emphasizes the quality as opposed to the state of being fortuitous, is also rare.

LANGUAGE-CHANGE INDEX
fortuitous misused for *fortunate*: Stage 3

fortunately. See SENTENCE ADVERBS.

Fort Worthian; *Fort Worther. The first is the standard term for someone who hails from or lives in Fort Worth, Texas. The second is a fairly uncommon equivalent. See DENIZEN LABELS.

forum. The standard plural *forums* has predominated in AmE since the early 1930s and in BrE since the mid-1970s. Although **fora* was prevalent in earlier periods, it is now a pedantic ARCHAISM—e.g.:

- "Their various *forums* unite hobbyists." Tom Foremski, "Selecting Online Services," *Fin. Times*, 3 Dec. 1997, at 4.
- "Even so, the debate over bigness—and how big is too big for corporate entities—continues in many different *forums*." Tom Petruno, "Your Money," *L.A. Times*, 7 Dec. 1997, at D1.
- "His presence at conventions and other public *fora* [read *forums*] honors it still." David A. Mittell Jr., "Governors We Have Known," *Providence J.-Bull.*, 15 June 2006, at B5 (referring to former Massachusetts Governor Michael Dukakis).

But some writers, especially in political science and law, persist in using the Latinate plural. See PLURALS (B).

Current ratio (*forums* vs. **fora*): 4:1

forward; *forwards. *Forward* is the usual form in both AmE and BrE. See DIRECTIONAL WORDS (A).
Current ratio: 29:1

forwent. See **forego**.

founder. See **flounder** & **forefathers**.

founding fathers. See **forefathers**.

fourth estate (= the journalistic profession; the news media) was coined as a jocular extension of the three estates of the (English) Realm. These "estates" represented social classes that were traditionally considered to have specific and distinct political powers. The English estates were (1) Lords Spiritual, (2) Lords Temporal, and (3) the Commons. (In France, the three analogous estates were [1] the clergy, [2] the nobles, and [3] the commons.)

Today, of course, this system of classifying estates is obsolete, but the term *fourth estate* is still commonly used, especially to indicate the media's extraordinary influence on politics—e.g.:

- " 'But now journalists make more than the people they are covering, and the *fourth estate* has become a conservative elite.' " "Culture, Et Cetera," *Wash. Times*, 31 Dec. 1996, at A2 (quoting John F. Kennedy Jr.).
- "Don't stop reading. This isn't just another journalist spouting off about the public's right to know or the role of the *fourth estate*." Mickie Valente, "What This Verdict May Mean to You," *Tampa Trib.*, 23 Jan. 1997, Bus. & Fin. §, at 1.

foyer. The best pronunciation for this word is /foy-ər/, not the affected /foy-ay/ or the Frenchified and old-fashioned /fwah-yay/.

fracas (= a noisy fight; brawl) is pronounced /fray-kəs/ in AmE and /frak-ah/ in BrE. Pl. *fracases*.

fractious. See **factional**.

*fraenum. See **frenum**.

LANGUAGE-CHANGE INDEX (For the full key, see front matter pp. xxxi, l–li.)
Stage 1: Rejected. **Stage 2:** Widely shunned. **Stage 3:** Widespread but . . . **Stage 4:** Ubiquitous but . . . **Stage 5:** Fully accepted.
Invariably inferior forms marked by asterisk (*). • Ratios represent frequency of prevalent forms vs. variants in current books.

fragile; frangible; friable. *Fragile*, the most common term, means "delicate, brittle" <a fragile vase> <a fragile ego>. *Frangible* means "breakable" but doesn't necessarily imply inherent weakness <frangible bones>. *Friable* means "crumbly" <friable asbestos>. See **friable.**

FRAGMENTS, SENTENCE. See INCOMPLETE SENTENCES.

fragrant. For a humorous MALAPROPISM, see **flagrant.**

framable. So spelled—not **frameable.* See MUTE E.

frambesia; framboesia. The technical term for the tropical skin disease known also as *yaws* is *frambesia* in AmE, *framboesia* in BrE. Both are pronounced /fram-**bee**-zhee-ə/ or /fram-**bee**-zhə/.

franchisor; *franchiser. **Franchiser* was long the preferred form for the word denoting the holder of a franchise. It predates *franchisor* by about 120 years—the *-or* spelling dating only from the 1960s. But today the *-er* form is ambiguous: it may denote the granter of a franchise or the holder of one, as here: "Regulators also emphasize that before potential investors write any checks, they need to read and be sure they understand the disclosure documents—called Uniform Franchise Offering Circulars—that *franchisers* are required to file in certain states." Richard Gibson, "Have I Got a Franchise Opportunity for You!" *Chicago Trib.*, 22 May 2007, Small Bus. §, at 6.

Perhaps because of that ambiguity, *franchisor* is about ten times as common as **franchiser* in law, and about eight times as common in modern print sources. It has won the fight in our fast-food nation—and has won the franchise as the newly preferred spelling.

LANGUAGE-CHANGE INDEX
franchisor: Stage 5

frangible. See **fragile.**

frangipani /fran-ji-**pan**-ee/ (= [1] a tropical American shrub; [2] a perfume obtained from the shrub's flowers; or [3] an almond-flavored tart or custard) is the standard spelling. **Frangipane* and **frangipanni* are variants.

Current ratio (*frangipani* vs. **frangipane* vs. **frangipanni*): 30:4:1

Frankenstein. In Mary W. Shelley's novel *Frankenstein* (1818), Dr. Victor Frankenstein creates a gruesome creature that eventually kills the doctor's brother and sister-in-law, and tries but fails to kill the doctor before ending its own life. Strictly speaking, then, a *Frankenstein* (usually capitalized) is a creator of a monster or other destructive agency, while a *Frankenstein's monster* is either a monster that turns on its creator or a destructive agency that cannot be controlled.

But popular usage has created a monster of its own: *Frankenstein* has come to refer to the creature itself. Today this ubiquitous usage must be accepted as standard—e.g.:

- "A visit to 'Bordello of Blood' is like a date with *Frankenstein* on Prozac: It's a bloated, lumbering, bloody bore." Rick Holter, "'Bordello' Merely Rolls Over and Goes to Sleep," *Dallas Morning News*, 16 Aug. 1996, at C5.
- "'I freaked out in the hospital when I saw myself. I looked like *Frankenstein* . . . . They cut your legs and your chest.'" Tom Roland, "Truth and Consequences: K.T. Oslin Wouldn't Have It Any Other Way," *Tennessean*, 18 Jan. 1997, at D1 (quoting K.T. Oslin).

LANGUAGE-CHANGE INDEX
Frankenstein in reference to a monster: Stage 5

frantically—so spelled—is fairly often wrongly made **franticly*, probably because the *-al-* is not pronounced. E.g.:

- "U.S. Park Police said two officers spotted a man waving his arms *franticly* [read *frantically*] and pulled over, but the baby was born before they made it to the truck." "Baby Arrives on Parkway," *Wash. Post*, 13 May 1997, at B8.
- "'This is so much fun, and it's all about tradition and getting everyone out here together,' Leverton said moments before he began *franticly* [read *frantically*] dancing circles with a group of four children." Geoff Grammar, "Lighting the Menorah," *Santa Fe New Mexican*, 30 Nov. 2002, at B1.

See -IC.

LANGUAGE-CHANGE INDEX
frantically misspelled **franticly*: Stage 1
Current ratio: 94:1

fraternal. This word means "brotherly," with one exception: twins that develop from separate ova are *fraternal* regardless of their sex—e.g.:

- "Our daughter has 3-year-old *fraternal* twin girls." Letter to Dr. T. Berry Brazelton, "Adult Shares Memories of Ending a 'Babyish' Comfort," *Times Union* (Albany), 5 Sept. 2007, at E2.
- "Shavon [Miles], a *fraternal* twin, was born March 10, 1994. Within months, she and her brother were in the hospital, where doctors determined that the twins had internal injuries and were blind from being shaken." Ofelia Casillas, "Girl's Abuse Was Hinted Early On," *Chicago Trib.*, 17 Sept. 2007, News §, at 1.

fratricide (= [1] the killing of one's brother, or [2] someone who kills his or her own brother) has been conscripted by the military to denote (1) the accidental or intentional killing of one's brother- or sister-in-arms, also known as *friendly fire*; or (2) the detonation or disablement of one nuclear warhead by the explosion of another missile aimed at the same target. See -CIDE.

fraudulent; *fraudful; *defraudulent. The last two are NEEDLESS VARIANTS.

Current ratio (*fraudulent* vs. **fraudful*): 507:1

fraught. A. Generally. *Fraught* (= laden, equipped) typically takes *with* in an ominous statement <a statement fraught with doubt>. While in the original sense a ship might be *fraught* with riches or democracy *fraught* with blessings (to use two phrases quoted in the *OED*), today *fraught with* is invariably associated with danger or something else bad.

There is a new sense of *fraught*, too—"distressed" or "distressing"—dating from the mid-1960s. This new use (without a *with*) is now fairly common. Though much more frequent in BrE than in AmE, the sense does appear in American sources—e.g.:

- "He was an energetic campaigner and perhaps most important in such a politically *fraught* time, he was not a politician." Elizabeth Kolbert, "Abortion, Dole's Sword in '74, Returns to Confront Him in '96," *N.Y. Times*, 8 July 1996, at A1, A8.
- "The sail-off escape of Kevin Patterson proves more funny than *fraught* as he flees a broken heart and tries to put his army days behind him." Gilbert Lewthwaite, "H₂O: Life, Death, War," *Baltimore Sun*, 23 July 2000, at F11.
- "Podeswa's starting points are the five senses . . . through which he tells a tale of disconnected urbanites whose attempts at human connection are *fraught* and incomplete." Deborah Hornblow, "Intellectual Ambitions of 'Five Senses' Go Unrealized," *Hartford Courant*, 11 Aug. 2000, at D5.

LANGUAGE-CHANGE INDEX
fraught (without *with*): Stage 5

B. Fraught with and wrought with. *Wrought*, an archaic past participle of *work*, is frequently but erroneously substituted for *fraught* in the idiom *fraught with* (danger, peril, etc.)—e.g.:

- "Despite the joyous homecoming, the transition from a life that was *wrought* [read *fraught*] with danger and emotion won't be easy for the soldiers or their families, said Lt. Col. Mary Erickson, a Combat/Operational Stress Control Officer." Sharon Schmickle, "Home After Doing Their Job," *Star Trib.* (Minneapolis), 7 Apr. 2004, at B1.
- "LaValle admits that the Highway Department is *wrought* [read *fraught*] with problems. But he denies he is at their source." Anne Givens, "Highway Chief Jabs at LaValle," *Newsday* (N.Y.), 18 May 2004, at A24.
- "The Games will go on. But they will go on so *wrought* [read *fraught*] with problems and scandals that some athletes have decided not to attend." "Cancel Olympics: No One Really Cares," *Miami Herald*, 20 June 2004, at C15.

The confusion may be due in part to the similarity of another idiom, *wrought up* (= worked up; excited).

LANGUAGE-CHANGE INDEX
wrought with misused for *fraught with*: Stage 1

fräulein (the German word for an unmarried woman) is pronounced /**froy**-lɪn/—not /**frow**-lɪn/.

-FREE. Except with an indisputably established word such as *carefree*, this combining form always takes a hyphen, whether the resulting phrase appears before or after what it modifies <alcohol-free drinks> <drinks that are alcohol-free>.

free; for free. Because *free* by itself can function as an adverb in the sense "at no cost," some critics reject the phrase *for free*. A phrase such as *for nothing, at no cost*, or a similar substitute will often work better.

Yet while it's true that *for free* is a CASUALISM that is severely overworked in ads, the expression is far too common to be called an error. It dates from the early 20th century. Sometimes the syntax all but demands it—e.g.: "Soft-dollar arrangements . . . include various services like research and information that big institutional clients receive *for free* from brokers." Anita Raghavan, "Pension Fund Plans to Scrap Certain Deals," *Wall Street J.*, 26 Jan. 1995, at A5. That same writer, however, omitted the *for* when it wasn't needed: "That research is sent *free* to the client." *Ibid.*

For an early discussion of this usage, see John R. Krueger, "On Pleonastic 'For,'" 41 *Am. Speech* 79–80 (1966).

LANGUAGE-CHANGE INDEX
for free instead of *free*: Stage 4
Current ratio (*get it free* vs. **get it for free*): 1:1

freedom. A. And *liberty*. These synonyms have connotative distinctions. *Freedom* is the broader, all-encompassing term that carries strong positive connotations. *Liberty*, slightly less emotive, generally suggests the past removal of restraints on specific freedoms.

B. Freedom of vs. freedom from. Both are correct, the first denoting possession of a right and the second denoting protection from a wrong. Note the shift in forms: *freedom of speech* but *freedom from oppression, pestilence, coercion*, etc.

*free gift. This REDUNDANCY, the result of advertisers' attempted assurances that you'll really get something for nothing, isn't much used by careful writers. But that's not to say it's not used—e.g.:

- "Merchants offered special discount drawings, fashion shows, decorating tips and *free gifts* [read *gifts*]." Michelle Daniels, "Sani Family Event Benefits Hinds Hospice," *Fresno Bee*, 29 Dec. 1995, at B2. (The serial comma would clarify that sentence; that is, insert a comma before the *and*. See ENUMERATIONS (B) & PUNCTUATION (D).)
- "Volunteers at the 20th annual Tammi Tuck Wrap-a-thon distributed *free gifts* [read *gifts*] to the children in West Palm Beach." Natalie Hopkinson, "No Children Got Left Out at Annual Toy Giveaway," *Palm Beach Post*, 25 Dec. 1996, at B2.
- "He was also softened up with *free gifts* [read *gifts*] such as tablecloths and coasters." Andrew Levy, "Dementia Sufferer, 103, Swindled Out of £60,000," *Daily Mail*, 27 Aug. 2015, at 28.

BrE has the related tautology **free gratis* (or **free and gratis*), which is hardly ever seen in AmE—e.g.:

- "I am not demanding that the shares should be given out *free gratis* [read *free* or *gratis*]." Padraig Yeates, "Telecom Urged to Allocate Shares to Workers," *Irish Times*, 7 Feb. 1996, at 2.

LANGUAGE-CHANGE INDEX (For the full key, see front matter pp. xxxi, l–li.)
Stage 1: Rejected. **Stage 2:** Widely shunned. **Stage 3:** Widespread but . . . **Stage 4:** Ubiquitous but . . . **Stage 5:** Fully accepted.
Invariably inferior forms marked by asterisk (✳). • Ratios represent frequency of prevalent forms vs. variants in current books.

- "They know that they can leave *free gratis* [read *free* or *gratis*] and pocket all the transfer fee." Ian Paul, "Where Egos Are Part of the Game," *Herald* (Glasgow), 8 Oct. 1996, at 35.

A little history may surprise you. *Free gift is much older than you might have thought. In contexts discussing what is "freely given," the phrase dates back to the late 17th century. In 1684, Henry Abbut wrote a book with an inspired title: *A Free Gift, Freely Given of God to Henry Abbut*. A 1722 polemic pamphlet printed in London was titled *A Free Gift to the Clergy*. A year later, the same author (Thomas Woolston) produced *A Second Free-Gift to the Clergy*, and the same year a *Third*. They were all anti-clergy tracts containing allegations against "Ministers of Antichrist." So the phrase is old, even if the modern context in which it appears is much different. You might well be wary of using it.

Language-Change Index
1. *free gift for *gift*: Stage 4
2. *free gratis for *free*: Stage 2

free rein is the correct spelling of this phrase—not *free reign. The allusion is to horses, not to kings or queens. But some writers have apparently forgotten the allusion—e.g.:

- "Indianapolis deserves to be a healthy and livable city, not just a place where developers enjoy *free reign* [read *free rein*], routinely decimating our few remaining significant tree stands." Letter of Clarke Kahlo, "The Public's Interest in Tree Protection," *Indianapolis Star*, 19 Jan. 1997, at B4. (On the use of *decimating* in that example, see **decimate**.)
- "Holmgren was quoted in a New Orleans paper as saying his players have a fairly *free reign* [read *free rein*] to enjoy New Orleans during their stay there. However, he did warn them about talking to 'weird women.'" Danny Wells, "Backup Draws a Crowd: McMahon Still a Super Attraction," *Charleston Gaz.*, 23 Jan. 1997, at C1.
- "The forward was given *free reign* [read *free rein*] behind Clark by Warburton but the home players were not so accommodating." "Oduwa Repeatedly Hacked as Rangers Cruise Once Again," *Daily Telegraph*, 20 Aug. 2015, Sport §, at 6.

Full rein is a synonymous but less common expression. See **rein**.

Language-Change Index
*free reign for *free rein*: Stage 3
Current ratio (*free rein* vs. *free reign): 3:1

freethinker. See **atheist**.

free will, n.; **freewill,** n.; **freewill,** adj. Although some philosophers have begun using the one-word spelling for the noun, the standard form remains *free will* (= [1] the view that people have the power to make choices and are not predestined either by earlier causes or by divine will; or [2] voluntary choice). (Cf. **fatalism**.) But when the adjective is needed, *freewill* (= voluntary) is the predetermined choice <that was her freewill decision>.

freeze > froze > frozen. So inflected. Yet the barbarous *freezed isn't uncommon—e.g.:

- "When they say they *freezed* [read *froze*] taxes for three years, what they are really saying is, 'We have frozen your overtaxation for three years.'" John Springer, "Tax Rate Is an Issue in Bristol," *Hartford Courant*, 26 Oct. 1997, at B1.
- "To complete the procedure, he said, Karina's body needs to be *freezed* [read *frozen*] for 14 minutes at 68 degrees Fahrenheit to stop blood flow." Victor Manuel Ramos, "Retirees Open Home and Hearts to Sick Girl," *Newsday* (N.Y.), 31 July 1998, at A26.
- "In season through July, mulberries keep in the fridge only for a few days after picking but they can be *freezed* [read *frozen*] for later use." Gretchen McKay, "Purple Reigns with Mulberries Everywhere," *Pitt. Post-Gaz.*, 17 June 2015, at C1.

Cf. **deep-freeze**. See IRREGULAR VERBS.

Language-Change Index
*freezed for *froze*: Stage 1
Current ratio (*froze* vs. *freezed): 494:1

French Words. See GALLICISMS.

frenetic; *phrenetic; frenzy; *phrenzy; *phrensy. Although *phrenetic and *phrenzy are closer to the original Greek word (*phrenetikos* "having brain inflammation")—and predominated until about 1880—the *f-* spellings have long been standard in both AmE and BrE. Today, *phrenetic, *phrenzy, and variant spellings such as *phrensy are all oddball ARCHAISMS—e.g.:

- "Anyway, you can still make the best of a *phrenetic* [read *frenetic*] December." Peter C. Hotton, "Deck the Halls, Safely and Sanely," *Boston Globe*, 5 Dec. 1993, Home & Garden §, at A94.
- "And he understood . . . that the Senate was uniquely insulated against the *phrensy* [read *frenzy*] of public opinion." Robert A. Caro, *The Years of Lyndon Johnson: Master of the Senate* 373 (2002).

Language-Change Index
1. *phrenzy or *phrensy for *frenzy*: Stage 1
Current ratio (*frenzy* vs. *phrenzy vs. *phrensy): 113:1:1
2. *phrenetic for *frenetic*: Stage 1
Current ratio (*frenetic* vs. *phrenetic): 95:1

frenum; *fraenum. Since about 1900, *frenum* /free-nəm/ has been the standard spelling—in AmE and BrE alike—for the word denoting a connecting fold of skin or mucous membrane that supports or restrains the movement of an organ or body part <lingual frenum> <labial frenum>. The Latinate spelling *fraenum is now but a variant form. If the *frenum* is small, the DIMINUTIVE *frenulum* is used <clitoral frenulum>—*fraenulum being a variant.

Current ratio (*frenum* vs. *fraenum): 10:1

frenzy. See **frenetic**.

frequently. This adverb can be ambiguous when used with a plural subject and verb. Do individuals do something frequently (i.e., often), or is the characteristic true of a group that may do something only once (i.e., commonly)? Note the MISCUE here: "A study last year by Jack Hadley of the Georgetown University School of Medicine showed that uninsured patients arrived at the hospital sicker than those with health insurance, and died in the hospital more *frequently*." Jane Bryant Quinn, "Woe the Reformers," *Newsweek*, 19 Oct. 1992, at 55. If the final clause is changed to *and were more likely to die in the hospital*, the miscue disappears.

fresco. Pl. *frescoes*. See PLURALS (D).

friable; fryable. *Friable* = able to be crumbled into dust or powder <friable soil>. E.g.: "The ideal carrot soil is sandy loam, or at least something *friable* and well-draining." Sylvia Thompson, "Garden Fresh: Underground Royalty," *L.A. Times*, 3 Nov. 1994, at H18. *Fryable* = able to be fried <a fryable chicken>. E.g.: "It was a long time before I appreciated eggplant as anything other than a breadable, *fryable*, bakeable medium." Molly O'Neill, "Essential Eggplant," *N.Y. Times* (Mag.), 23 Aug. 1992, § 6, at 49. See **fragile**.

friar. See **fryer**.

fridge, a shortened form of *refrigerator*, is so spelled—not **frig*.

friend. This word has settled into some exceptional idioms: *a friend of mine*; *he is friends with me*; *she made friends with me*; *he has been a friend to me*. Handle them with care.

For more on *a friend of mine*, see POSSESSIVES (D).

friendlily. See ADVERBS (B).

-FRIENDLY. When used in a compound with another word, *-friendly* implies ease of use. Several such compounds have become VOGUE WORDS on their own, probably beginning with *user-friendly*. That term usually describes a device, software, or website that is easy to use—e.g.: "I use online resources nearly exclusively for researching your complaints and keeping up to date on consumer issues. . . . None of these sites requires a fee, and most of them are pretty *user-friendly*." Suzanne Palmer, "Consumers' Protection Is Information," *St. Petersburg Times*, 4 Feb. 2007, at E3. Many other analogous terms also exist, such as *customer-friendly*, *driver-friendly*, and *pet-friendly*.

These compounds are best hyphenated, since the construction puts a spin on the usual sense of *friendly*. The hyphen is occasionally omitted in such compounds—e.g.: "The future of newspapers is the Internet . . . . But the present is still in print. And part of the strategy is to make the print version more *reader friendly* [read *reader-friendly*]." Mike Littwin, "Where's Littwin? Way Back Here on News 38," *Rocky Mountain News* (Denver), 23 Jan. 2007, News §, at 38.

In all these terms, *-friendly* means that the thing being discussed is good for the user, customer, driver, pedestrian, or reader. But one recent marketing term turns that sense on its head—e.g.: " 'I think [the school

cafeteria] is also going to introduce more *allergen-friendly* choices. More and more kids, it seems, have peanut or milk allergies.' " Linda Bock, "School System Faces Gluten Allergies Head-On," *Telegram & Gaz.* (Worcester), 1 June 2006, at B1 (quoting Diane O. Mercier, a parent). Here, the meaning is not that the food is "friendly" or beneficial to allergens, but quite the opposite—that it contains no allergens. The twist may cause some readers to suffer an unpleasant gastrointestinal reaction.

friend of the court. See **amicus curiae**.

*frier. See **fryer**.

frijol /free-**hohl**/ (= a bean used in Mexican cuisine) forms the plural *frijoles* /free-**hoh**-leez/, which typically refers to refried beans. Because the plural is much more common than the singular, it's hardly surprising that the BACK-FORMATION **frijole* has emerged as a singular form. Avoid it.

LANGUAGE-CHANGE INDEX
*frijole as a false singular for *frijol*: Stage 3
Current ratio (*a frijol* vs. **a frijole*): 2:1

frisson (/free-**sohn**/) is a GALLICISM meaning "a shiver of excitement or emotion"—e.g.: " 'But I don't know what that is,' she answered, trying to persuade herself, as she spoke, that the touch of his hand was giving her a tremendous *frisson*." Aldous Huxley, *Brief Candles* 232 (1957).

frivol, vb. This word, meaning "to trifle; to fritter away time," is a lighthearted BACK-FORMATION from *frivolous* dating from the mid-19th century. Its peak in popularity came about 1920. It's inflected *frivoled*, *frivoling* in AmE, *frivolled*, *frivolling* in BrE. E.g.:

- " 'Be frivolous with me,' he begs Mr. Waterston, who—typical American or no typical American—has plainly never *frivoled* in his life." Walter Kerr, "Verbal Witchcraft Produces Magical Responses Out Front," *N.Y. Times*, 12 June 1988, § 2, at 5.
- "Ten percent of tax revenues devoted to deficit reduction is 10 percent that cannot be *frivoled* away on new spending." "The Cultural Elite in New York, the Republicans in Houston," *Wash. Times*, 23 Aug. 1992, at B2.
- "Not all our elected officials *frivol* their time away on trivial matters such as ethics." Dan Majors, "Thought for Food in U.S. House," *Pitt. Post-Gaz.*, 8 Jan. 2003, at B1.

frivolity; frivolousness. *Frivolity* (= [1] silliness, light-mindedness; or [2] a frivolous act or thing) isn't a general-purpose noun corresponding to the adjective *frivolous*. It is, of course, just the word for the child who is being silly or for the silly things that a child might do, but it doesn't work for the more negative connotations of *frivolous*. For example, when lawyers engage in frivolous conduct, courts take that as a serious offense and often fine the lawyers large

---

LANGUAGE-CHANGE INDEX (For the full key, see front matter pp. xxxi, l–li.)
Stage 1: Rejected. **Stage 2:** Widely shunned. **Stage 3:** Widespread but . . . **Stage 4:** Ubiquitous but . . . **Stage 5:** Fully accepted.
Invariably inferior forms marked by asterisk (*). • Ratios represent frequency of prevalent forms vs. variants in current books.

sums. To call an offending lawyer's conduct *frivolity* is to trivialize it—there's nothing lighthearted about a frivolous lawsuit. So in that context, the better noun is *frivolousness*—e.g.:

- "The seriousness of the issues and the preceding discussion of them belies the claims of *frivolity* [read *frivolousness*]. Sanctions are denied." "Court Decisions: Right to Litigate Is Deemed Waived in One of Two Consolidated Actions," *N.Y.L.J.*, 7 Apr. 1994, at 21.
- "In allowing sanctions against those whose *frivolity* [read *frivolousness*] was short-lived, and perhaps caused little harm, the new rule promotes deterrence." Jeffrey A. Parness, "How to Deter Frivolous Papers," *Legal Times*, 21 Nov. 1994, at S7.
- "As no check or witness's name was attached, the court denied the motion, with $50 costs, saying sanctions for *frivolity* [read *frivolousness*] should be permitted in small claims cases." "New Trial Is Denied, with $50 Costs," *N.Y.L.J.*, 8 Feb. 1995, at 25.

LANGUAGE-CHANGE INDEX
frivolity misused for *frivolousness*: Stage 1

frizz (= to make tight curls) is the standard spelling. ***Friz* is a variant.

Current ratio: 7:1

froe (= a chopping tool with the handle set at a right angle to the blade, traditionally used in splitting shingles) is the standard spelling. *Frow* is a variant.

Current ratio: 1.1:1

frog legs; frogs' legs; *frog's legs; *frogs legs. Although *frog legs* seems to be the most natural phrase, there is an amazing mélange of forms.

Some cookbook authors write *frog legs*. See, e.g., Irma S. Rombauer & Marion Rombauer Becker, *Joy of Cooking* 415 (1975); Jacqueline Killeen, *The Whole World Cookbook* 267 (1979); Fredy Girardet, *The Cuisine of Fredy Girardet* 44 (1982); Emeril Lagasse, *Louisiana Real & Rustic* 61 (1996).

But most writers on culinary matters write *frogs' legs*. See, e.g., Ruth R. Tyndall, *Eat Yourself Full* 66 (1967); Helen Corbitt, *Helen Corbitt Cooks for Company* 67 (1974); *Gourmet's France* 426 (1978); Howard Mitcham, *Creole Gumbo and All That Jazz* 242 (1978); Pierre Franey, *More 60-Minute Gourmet* 132–33 (1981); *France: A Culinary Journey* 46 (1992). This form appears to be a direct translation of the French *cuisses de grenouilles* (= legs of frogs, or frogs' legs).

The other forms are less defensible. At least one writer uses **frog's legs*, as if they were served always in pairs (and carefully matched up). See Jacques Pepin, *La Methode* 79 (1979). Some writers indecisively mix two or more forms. See Alan Davidson, *The Oxford Companion to Food* 321 (1999) (using both *frog legs* and *frogs' legs*).

Those citations don't quite reflect general usage in newspapers and journals. Of 1,600 examples checked in WESTLAW's ALLNEWS database in January 2002, the breakdown was as follows: *frog legs*—880 (55%); *frogs' legs*—450 (28%); **frog's legs*—194 (12%); and **frogs legs*—76 (5%). Likewise, informal surveys suggest

that most cultivated speakers who would order this item say *frog legs*. The cookbook writers' preference for *frogs' legs* seems a mite pedantic. In any event, the two forms to be avoided are **frog's legs* (unless you're talking about a particular frog) and **frogs legs* (unless you eat them without utensils or napkins)—e.g.:

- "They were out of *frog's legs* [read *frog legs* or *frogs' legs*] the night we ordered them, so we can't say whether we agree." Molli Yood & Andy Yood, "Food, Fun and Music Are the Order of the Day," *Wash. Post*, 8 Nov. 2001, So. Md. §, at T6.
- "Johnny's Bistro . . . offers . . . an appetizer list that includes country pork pate, *frogs legs* [read *frog legs* or *frogs' legs*] and other delicious treats." Ralph McGreevy, "Carve Out Time for Bite and a Belt," *Plain Dealer* (Cleveland), 14 Dec. 2001, at 26.
- "That top price . . . buys one of the stars of the menu, a dish of sweet, succulent little *frogs legs* [read *frog legs* or *frogs' legs*], one of the best renditions I've had in years." Marion Warhaft, "But Ask for Favourites, Anyway," *Winnipeg Free Press*, 21 Dec. 2001, at D4.

LANGUAGE-CHANGE INDEX
1. *frog legs*: Stage 5
2. *frogs' legs*: Stage 5
3. **frog's legs*: Stage 3
4. **frogs legs*: Stage 1
Current ratio (in order of headwords): 11:9:4:1

from hence; from thence. The words *hence* (= from this time, from this place) and *thence* (= from that time, from that place)—as well as *whence*—are sufficient without the preposition *from*. E.g.: "Collier, then 32, was an erudite intellectual who had gone to the best prep schools and *thence* to Yale." Matt Walsh, "Don't Buy Until You See the Whites of Their Eyes," *Forbes*, 19 Dec. 1994, at 76. Yet grammarians have never considered *from hence* and the like incorrect, and the word *from* may help orient readers who aren't very familiar with these increasingly creaky words. James Boswell, Samuel Johnson's biographer, used *from thence*: "Mr. Scott of University College, Oxford . . . accompanied [Johnson] *from thence* to Edinburgh." 5 *Life of Johnson* 16 (1791).

The two phrases *from hence* and *from thence* appeared frequently in printed books from about 1580 to 1800 but gradually fell into disuse. Today they hardly ever appear except in quotations or in purposeful attempts at an antique tone. See **hence, thence** & **whence**.

*from henceforth. See **henceforth (B)**.

from thence. See **from hence**.

from whence. See **from hence, thence** & **whence**.

frowsy (= unkempt, untidy, slovenly), the standard spelling, has predominated in World English since the 19th century. **Frowzy* and **frouzy* are variants.

Current ratio (*frowsy* vs. **frowzy* vs. **frouzy*): 20:9:1

frustrum (a geometric term referring to the remaining part of a cone or pyramid that has had its top cut

off by an intersecting plane parallel to the base) over-whelmingly forms the plural *frustra*—not **frustrums*.
Current ratio: 223:1

fryable. See **friable.**

fryer (= [1] someone who fries; [2] something intended for frying, esp. a small chicken; or [3] a large frying pan) has been predominantly so spelled since the late 1930s in AmE and the early 1960s in BrE. Today *fryer* appears in print sources more than ten times as often as **frier*, a NEEDLESS VARIANT. Of course, *fryer* shouldn't be confused with *friar* (= a member of a mendicant religious order).

fuchsia is so spelled—after the German botanist Leonhard Fuchs (1501–1566). The term denotes either (1) a decorative shrub with drooping reddish-purple or purplish-pink flowers, or (2) the color associated with those flowers. Although the botanist's name was pronounced /fuuks/ or /fooks/, the derivative word is /**fyoo**-shə/. Doubtless because of its standard pronunciation in English, the term is often misspelled **fuschia*.
Current ratio: 14:1

FUDGE WORDS. Phrases such as *it seems* and *it appears* will make your writing sound tentative—and sometimes that's no doubt how you want to sound. But if you use them frequently, readers' energy and attention will fly.

fuel, vb., makes *fueled* and *fueling* in AmE, *fuelled* and *fuelling* in BrE. See SPELLING (B).

fugitive, adj., is a FORMAL WORD in the sense "elusive, fleeting." E.g.:

- "The latter being dependent on the vagaries of light, it is *fugitive*, even evanescent." "The Picture of Excellent Photography," *Portland Press Herald*, 8 Oct. 1995, at E1.
- "Such books would now be priceless reminders of dancers lost and dances forgotten, monumental little mementos of the fleeting times of a *fugitive* art." Clive Barnes, "Jack Mitchell: Photographer to the Dance," *Dance Mag.*, Jan. 1996, at 64.
- "She moved every year of her childhood from school to school and her character itself is *fugitive*, preliminary." Sam Leith, "Review: The Rise and Fall of Great Powers," *Guardian*, 7 June 2014, at 10.

An even more learned equivalent is *fugacious*, which is a literary word as well as a botanical term describing plants that wither or drop their leaves early. On the use of this type of word, see SESQUIPEDALITY.

-FUL. See PLURALS (G).

fulcrum. Pl. *fulcrums*. Although the Latinate plural **fulcra* predominated in print sources from the early 18th century to the mid-20th, it has largely been superseded. See PLURALS (B).
Current ratio: 2:1

fulfill; fulfil. The first is the AmE spelling, the second the BrE spelling.

fulfillment; fulfilment. The word is spelled *-ll-* in AmE, *-l-* in BrE.

full complement. For the mistaken phrase **full compliment*, see **compliment.**

full-fledged is a SET PHRASE in AmE. But BrE writers often use *fully fledged*. See **fledgling.**

fullness is preferably so spelled—not **fulness*.

full-scale, a PHRASAL ADJECTIVE, should be hyphenated.

FULL STOP. See PUNCTUATION (L).

fully fledged. See **full-fledged.**

fulsome (= abundant to excess; offensive to normal tastes or sensibilities) is still best used in its traditional, disparaging sense—e.g.: " 'Superbad' . . . begins with pornography. The loud, large, and ribald Seth (Jonah Hill) calls his best friend . . . to discuss in *fulsome* detail a Web site called 'Vag-Tastic Voyage.' " Richard Brody, "The Biblical Sense," *New Yorker*, 17 Dec. 2007, at 20. But unfortunately, the loose usage to mean "very full" dominates today—e.g.:

- "Her energy is both warm and *fulsome* [read, perhaps, *vibrant*], and her big, deep laugh is always at the ready, especially when she is goofing on herself." Allison Glock, "Uma," *Redbook*, 1 Mar. 2008, at 114 (describing Uma Thurman).
- "Even for moviegoers who don't automatically gravitate to such fare, 'Prince Caspian' allows the [C.S.] Lewis book to spring to *fulsome* [read *full*], fantastic life." Barbara Vancheri, "Chronicles of Caspian," *Pitt. Post-Gaz.*, 16 May 2008, at D1.

The word might justifiably be treated as a SKUNKED TERM because the loose sense is so common, especially in the expression *fulsome praise*. Usually the intended sense of that expression is something like "lavish praise," as opposed to repulsive praise—e.g.: "Just before Mobutu was run out of his lair in Kinshasa, National Public Radio played some old audiotapes of the *fulsome* [read *lavish*] praise heaped on this corrupt blackguard by Presidents Reagan and Bush." David Nyhan, "Those Buddies of Uncle Sam We Didn't Know Were Soooo Baaad," *Boston Globe*, 25 May 1997, at D4. Cf. **noisome.**

LANGUAGE-CHANGE INDEX
fulsome in a flattering sense: Stage 4

fumitory (= a flowering plant of the genus *Fumaria*) is sometimes misspelled *fumatory*—e.g.: "Here's what's blooming this week: Basil Balm, Bee Balm, Butterfly Bush, Carolina Phlox, Fringe Loosestrife, *Fumatory* [read *Fumitory*]." "Botanical Gardens," *Asheville Citizen-Times* (N.C.), 5 July 1996, at C2.

LANGUAGE-CHANGE INDEX (For the full key, see front matter pp. xxxi, l–li.)
Stage 1: Rejected. **Stage 2:** Widely shunned. **Stage 3:** Widespread but . . . **Stage 4:** Ubiquitous but . . . **Stage 5:** Fully accepted.
Invariably inferior forms marked by asterisk (*). • Ratios represent frequency of prevalent forms vs. variants in current books.

Actually, *fumatory* is a rare word meaning "a smoking room or section."

LANGUAGE-CHANGE INDEX
fumatory misused for *fumitory*: Stage 1

fun, traditionally a noun, has come into vogue as an adjective—but only as a CASUALISM. Why has usage changed here? Two main reasons. (1) Unlike other nouns of emotion, *fun* hasn't had a corresponding adjective to mean "productive of fun." *Funny* long ago took on other senses, such as "risible" and "weird." Most other nouns of emotion have adjectives that mean "productive of" <excitement–exciting> <fear–fearful> <gloom–gloomy> <sadness–sad>. But not *fun*, which is among the most popular nouns of emotion. (2) Because *fun* is always a mass noun, it never appears with an indefinite article. So although we may say *This is a pleasure* or *a joy*, we cannot say **a fun*. Instead we say *This is fun*—and this predicate noun looks as if it might be a predicate adjective. There are other reasons that get more technical. For a detailed explanation, see Dwight Bolinger, " 'It's So Fun,' " 38 *Am. Speech* 236–40 (1963).

For speakers who consider *fun* in *This is fun* to be a predicate adjective, it's no significant change to say, instead, *This is a fun thing to do*—or *This is so fun* instead of *This is so much fun*. Still, the usage remains casual at best—e.g.: "To liven things up the last few weeks of the season, some resorts create *fun* events to entice customers." Susan McKee, "Ski Resorts Making Plans for Season-Ending Events," *Sacramento Bee*, 16 Apr. 1997, at C7.

R.W. Burchfield notes that "in serious writing, it (so far) lacks a comparative and a superlative" (*FMEU3* at 318). That may be true of serious writing, but not of spoken AmE (especially among those born after 1970 or so)—e.g.:

- " 'It's always *funner*,' says 13-year-old Jeff Oehrlein, 'to be where the parents aren't.' " Mary Battiata, "The Friday Night Ice Age," *Wash. Post*, 6 Dec. 1982, at B1.
- " 'You've got to be super-aggressive and ride just a hair over your head without blowing it,' agrees Mike Cotes, 42, a Spokane condominium maintenance man who won the Masters Amateur category last year. 'It's pretty intimidating to do it. Once you get comfortable with it, it's the "*funnest*" thing to do.' " Fiona Cohen, "Legendary Banked Slalom Preview," *Bellingham Herald* (Wash.), 6 Feb. 2003, at B1.
- " 'It definitely wasn't one of the *funner* games I have ever played in,' Duke freshman J.J. Redick said after making only three of 12 shots." Tim Peeler, "Duke Gets Ugly Win in 'Man's Game,' " *News & Record* (Greensboro), 10 Feb. 2003, at C1.

The *NOAD* records *funner* and *funnest* as informal. Some writers use them seriously—e.g.:

- "This year, he was the guy everybody but Bob Huggins wanted to replace with Chadd Moore, the faster, *funner* [read *more fun*] freshman." Lonnie Wheeler, "Barker Reason Bearcats Are 13–3," *Cincinnati Post*, 7 Jan. 2003, at C1.
- "This is the simplest, arguably *funnest* [read *most fun*], fondue of all—particularly for kids." "Do You Fondue?" *Wash. Post*, 12 Feb. 2003, Food §, at 4.

The linguist Steven Pinker has been quoted as saying that he "can tell whether people are under or over thirty years old by whether they're willing to accept *fun* as a full-fledged adjective. ['Boomers allow *fun* to have a few adjective privileges, and slackers allow it to have most or all of them, including modification by *so* and comparative *-er* and *-est* forms.']" Barbara Wallraff, *Word Court* 87 (2000).

To traditionalists, the adjectival *fun* and its comparative forms remain blemishes in both writing and speech.

LANGUAGE-CHANGE INDEX
1. *fun* as an adjective <a fun place>: Stage 4
2. *fun* as an inflectable adjective (hence *funner*, *funnest*): Stage 2
Current ratio (*more fun* vs. *funner*): 211:1

FUNCTIONAL SHIFT. A. Generally. Renaissance rhetoricians called it *enallage* (/i-**nal**-i-jee/), and some modern grammarians call it *transfer*: the ability of a word to shift from one grammatical function to another. A noun acts as an adjective (*candy store*); an adjective as a noun (*a collectible*); a noun as a verb (*housing the collection*); a verb as a noun (*apt quotes*); and so on. Many of these functional shifts lead to a compactness that Americans like: "We Americans will not use the more elaborate form when the simpler, more direct one is absolutely unambiguous and does the work without a hitch." Edward N. Teall, *Putting Words to Work* 25 (1940).

By itself, of course, a word has no part of speech. Only in context does a part-of-speech label make any sense. Still, many words appear usually as one or another part of speech, so that we tend to think of even an isolated word as being a noun, verb, adjective, etc. For example, most people see *umpire* as a noun, and to say that you are *umpiring* a baseball game sounds, to most speakers of English who might pause to consider the point, as if you are using a noun as a verb. This type of shift involves an age-old custom that was especially robust in the Elizabethan age. Although a functional shift sometimes upsets purists—indeed, a new shift (such as *officing* or *tasking*) often seems ugly at first—both colloquial usage and literary usage tend to defy them in the long run.

But this inevitably runs only to certain types of shifts: noun-to-adjective, noun-to-verb, verb-to-noun, and adjective-to-noun. Other shifts are generally much less acceptable in English. For example, adverb-to-conjunction shifts are thoroughly disapproved; hence it remains a solecism to use *however* or *also* as a conjunction to combine two independent clauses with no more punctuation than a comma. As another example, preposition-to-verb shifts are considered CASUALISMS (*upping* the ante, *downing* a bear, or *outing* an acquaintance).

B. Nouns as Adjectives. The transmutation of nouns into adjectives is one of the most frequent types of functional variation. Henry Bradley noted this linguistic feature in 1904:

One highly important feature of English grammar which has been developed since Old English days is what has been called the attributive use of the substantive, which may be exemplified by such expressions as "a silk hat," "the London County Council," "the Shakspere Tercentenary," "Church of England principles," "a House of Commons debate," "the Marriage Law Amendment Act," "the half-past-two train," "the London, Brighton, and South Coast Railway," "the High-street front of the Town Hall," "my lawyer cousin." No other European language has anything exactly parallel to this usage.

Henry Bradley, *The Making of English* 64 (1904).

Usually the semantic shift is unobjectionable, as in the first word in each of the following phrases: *body weight, insurance policy, telephone wires, home repairs, family problems.*

Occasionally, however, shifts of this kind give rise to ambiguities or play tricks on the reader. Perhaps the worst problems arise when an adjective used as a noun is then used as an adjective—a recipe for ambiguity. Examples are *poor relief* (relief for the poor), *editorial reply* (if the sense is a reply to an editorial, as opposed to an editorial that replies to something else), and *hypothetical discussion* (if the sense is the discussion of a hypothetical). And it would be unwise for one writing about a statute concerning invalids to call it an *invalid statute*. The problem increases as the phrases grow longer <explosive device detection equipment> (see PHRASAL ADJECTIVES).

To make a somewhat different point, the reader's expectations are thwarted when a noun is used adjectivally in place of the more usual adjective. E.g.: "Police would have access to the fingerprints for *investigation* [read *investigative*] purposes only after obtaining a court order." "Giving Fingerprints: Price of Security," *News Trib.* (Tacoma), 4 Mar. 1997, at A10. Often, of course, the sense conveyed is different when one uses the noun adjectivally as opposed to the adjective form. For example, *pornography commission* seems to mean something different from *pornographic commission* (which is somehow difficult to visualize). But at other times, the two ways of phrasing the idea are synonymous, as in *prostate cancer* vs. *prostatic cancer* or *pronoun problem* vs. *pronominal problem*. The main difference is that, in such pairs, the more usual phrasing uses the noun (*prostate cancer, pronoun problem*). Only specialists use adjectives such as *prostatic* and *pronominal*. Or, for that matter, *adjectival* (over *adjective*, adj.).

The adjective–noun relationship often becomes vague when nouns that would normally follow prepositions are adjectives placed before nouns, and the relation-bearing prepositions are omitted. Hence *victim awareness* is a vague phrase: does it mean *on the part of, by, of* ? E.g.: "*Victim awareness* gained momentum in the early 1980s, with the passage of the Victim and Witness Protection Act." We can deduce that the

intended sense is *awareness (on the part of the public) of victims and their rights*, but perhaps we should not ask our readers to have to make such deductions. The same sort of uncertainty infects *victim restitution* (= full restitution to the victim of a crime).

Almost every phrasal adjective involves a noun phrase used adjectivally—hence *birch tree* yields *birch-tree study, government department* yields *government-department brouhaha, space flight* yields *space-flight objectives*, and so on.

C. Adjectives as Nouns. Many English words that are ordinarily adjectives can function as nouns (*collectibles, edibles, receivables, rentals*). *Indigent* was originally an adjective (15th c.), but it came to be used as a noun (16th c.). The same process occurred with *editorial, hypothetical, postmortem, principal* (= [1] principal investment, or [2] principal administrator), *ignitables, potential, explosives*, and *recitative*. Among recent examples are *finals* (= final examinations) and *classifieds* (= classified advertisements). Other examples are not hard to come by:

my dearest
the accused
the condemned
the deceased
the elite
the homeless
the poor
the religious
the rich

Though words that have recently undergone semantic shift are typically unsuitable for formal contexts, we should resist the benighted temptation to condemn all such shifts in parts of speech if they help fill gaps in the language. But as one commentator notes, some shifts have little to recommend them: "Can't we at least use correct English? That would distinguish Richmond from those places where the likes of 'multicultural collaboratives' are springing up. *Collaborative*, of course, is not a noun; it is an adjective. There can no more be a *collaborative* for youth than there can be an *exhaustive* for marathoners or a *repressive* for dictators or a *suggestive* for exotic dancers." Robert Holland, "No Collaboration Without Elaboration," *Richmond Times-Dispatch*, 30 July 1997, at A13. As the headline says, the critic here would substitute the noun *collaboration*.

D. Nouns as Verbs. A type of semantic shift a little less common than the noun-to-adjective shift occurs when nouns function as verbs. There are scores of examples, such as *appeal, bias, deal, function* (as in the preceding sentence), *handle, people, perfume, reward, room, silence, survey*, and *weather*. Often these new usages are slangy—e.g.:

- " 'The Firm' . . . for a time even out-*box-officed* 'Jurassic Park.' " Joe Dirck, "Grisham's Latest Loses on Appeal," *Plain Dealer* (Cleveland), 22 May 1994, at K1.

LANGUAGE-CHANGE INDEX (For the full key, see front matter pp. xxxi, l–li.)
Stage 1: Rejected. **Stage 2:** Widely shunned. **Stage 3:** Widespread but . . . **Stage 4:** Ubiquitous but . . . **Stage 5:** Fully accepted.
Invariably inferior forms marked by asterisk (∗). • Ratios represent frequency of prevalent forms vs. variants in current books.

- "He'd be as busy *ambassadoring* in Rome as he's been *mayoring* in Boston." David Nyhan, "Bill's Dabble at Diplomacy," *Boston Globe*, 2 May 1997, at A23.
- "Samples were *air-expressed* to Atlanta for testing." Ken Kaye, "Asbestos Threat Delays Flights," *Sun-Sentinel* (Ft. Lauderdale), 3 Dec. 1997, at B3.
- "George will be *limoed* to the Vet and given great seats." "The Winners! When 'K' Means a Home Run," *Phil. Daily News*, 12 Sept. 2002, at 41.
- " 'Unless you can type, you're not going to make it,' she said. 'But they don't even call it typing anymore; anymore, it's called *keyboarding*.' " Chuck Stinnett, "E-Mail, PC Have Redefined the Field and the Job," *Evansville Courier & Press*, 15 Dec. 2002, at F1. (On the second use of *anymore* in that sentence, see **anymore**.)

Although some writers enjoy referring to *fast-tracking* budgets, *tasking* committees, and *mainstreaming* children, be wary of these VOGUE WORDS. They reek of JARGON.

Increasingly, too, people are turning noun phrases into awkward PHRASAL VERBS even when much simpler verbs are available. This phenomenon typically involves an evolution from the simple verb to the noun phrase and then to the phrasal verb. For example, hotel clerks frequently deal with customers who, when checking in, request a different room from their preassigned one—that is, they *change rooms*. The staffers then refer to this as a *room change*, and that phrase becomes so customary among those staffers that they begin using it as a verb. So in some hotels—especially in New York—it's not uncommon to hear someone at the front desk say, "Did you *room-change*?" Of course, the more natural question would be, "Did you change rooms?" The same phenomenon is apparent when gate agents (using AIRLINESE) say that a flight has been *gate-changed*, or when children ask whether they can go *bike-ride* or *ice-skate*.

Some brand names are susceptible of being used as verbs (e.g., *Xerox* for "copy a document," *FedEx* for "send a package," *Rollerblade* for "skate on inline skates"). E.g.: "But when her mother *Googled* her way onto the blog and learned her daughter was planning to adopt, she got upset and asked Friedman, 'When were you going to tell me this?' " Pamela Paul, "The New Family Album," *Time*, 12 Apr. 2004, at A1. This type of CASUALISM is often considered sloppy: among other things, it can result in a cease-and-desist letter from the trademark's owner. See (B).

For other examples of noun-to-verb shifts, see **author, autopsy, gift, honcho, impact, juxtaposition, mainstream, office, premier** (where *premiere* is discussed) & **reference.**

E. Adjectives as Verbs. Adjective-to-verb transformations have never been common in English. They usually have a jargonistic quality (as in the first and third examples below) or a trendy quality (as in the second). Careful writers tend to avoid them or, when quoting someone else, to distance themselves with telltale quotation marks (as in the first example):

- "The New York City Fire Commissioner directed that her cargo tanks be '*inerted*' through the introduction of carbon dioxide into the tanks." Grant Gilmore & Charles L. Black Jr., *The Law of Admiralty* 925 (2d ed. 1975).

- "Clinton would be well-advised to *low-key* the task force before it announces anything embarrassing." Joe Klein, "Time to Step Back," *Newsweek*, 17 May 1993, at 40.
- "If any industry can be described as cutthroat, disk drives fit the bill. The industry *obsoletes* its products every nine months." Brian Deagon, "Quantum Sells Division to Maxtor for $1.4 Billion," *Investor's Bus. Daily*, 30 Mar. 2001, at A6.

There are exceptions <greening rooftops>. And to copyeditors, it is natural to talk about *lowercasing* and *uppercasing* words. But to those not familiar with copyediting, references such as these smell of JARGON.

F. Prepositions as Adverbs or Particles. Many prepositions (such as *by, down, in, off, on,* and *up*) function also as particles in PHRASAL VERBS (some grammarians call them adverbs). The distinguishing feature is that the preposition invariably has an object <we walked by the park>, whereas a particle does not <they never came by>. When people bristle at the sight of a sentence-ending preposition, the preposition is often functioning as a particle <we'll try to work you in>. See PREPOSITIONS (B) & SUPERSTITIONS (A).

G. Conjunctions as Prepositions. Conjunctions such as *but* and *than* may serve as prepositions. Compare the prepositional *but* in *Everyone but you was there* (*but* meaning "except") with the conjunctive *but* in *She liked the design, but she didn't like the drawing.* See **but** (D) & **than** (C).

H. Any Other Part of Speech as an Interjection. Almost any word can serve as an interjection. You might call it an exclamatory noun or verb, or an exclamatory conjunction, but in fact it is probably functioning as an interjection: *great!* (adjective); *moron!* (noun); *look!* (verb); *fast!* (adverb); *you!* (pronoun); *if only!* (conjunction).

fundament = (1) basis; or (2) anus or buttocks. Sense 2 is more common in BrE than in AmE—e.g.: "There is even a 12-step group for people addicted to 12-step groups—which is very Fight Club, but surely only a small step away from one's head disappearing entirely up one's own *fundament*." Mimi Spencer, "Let's Talk About Me," *Sunday Times* (London), 19 Jan. 2003, Features §, at 12. But because sense 2 is current in AmE as well, it typically can't be used without creating a double entendre. One hardly knows what to think about sentences such as this: "This is the best of the best, and like it or not, it's the *fundament* of our private culture and public life." Kyrie O'Connor, " 'Great Books,' with a Classic Male Slant," *Hartford Courant*, 22 Sept. 1996, at G3. To avoid trouble, try *foundation*.

Sometimes the word is misused in the plural as an INELEGANT VARIATION of *fundamentals*—e.g.: "[Kyle] Korver is like a golfer, always tinkering, always looking for the perfect swing. He'll watch other players, work on his *fundaments* [read *fundamentals*], tweak his own shot." Tom Shatel, "Korver Puts in the Hours to Become Jays' Big Shot," *Omaha World-Herald*, 18 Jan. 2003, at C1. (He wouldn't get far by working on his fundament.)

funeral; funereal; funerary; *funebrial. *Funeral,* commonly a noun, serves as its own adjective <funeral expenses>. *Funereal,* adj., which is frequently confused with *funeral,* means "solemn, mournful, somber." *Funerary* = of, used for, or connected with burial. **Funebrial* is a NEEDLESS VARIANT of *funereal.* H.W. Fowler wrote that no one who can help it uses *funerary* or **funebrial* (*FMEU1* at 205).

funeral home. This Americanism dating from the 1920s is, in the incisive commentary of a mid-20th-century critic, "unquestionably one of the ultimates of verbal absurdity." J. Donald Adams, "Ugly Words," in *The Ways of Language* 2, 2 (Raymond J. Pflug ed., 1967). By the 1960s, the phrase was ubiquitous: "It now disfigures the streets of every American town and city." *Ibid.* It had also pervaded BrE by that time. The particular silliness of the phrase is that there is no such thing as a "home" for funerals.

So what did such a place used to be called? *The undertaker's* (itself a bygone EUPHEMISM). Centuries ago it was *the deadhouse.* Later *the morgue.* Then *the mortuary.* Then *the mortician's.* Then *the funeral parlor.* And finally a *funeral home,* where the bodies are kept in a *slumber room.*

funereal; funerary. See **funeral.**

fungus. Pl. *fungi:* /fən-jɪ/, not /fəng-gɪ/. See PLURALS (B). The noun *fungicide* likewise has a soft *-g-* /fən-ji-sɪd/.

funnel, vb., makes *funneled* and *funneling* in AmE, *funnelled* and *funnelling* in BrE. See SPELLING (B).

funnily. See ADVERBS (B).

fur. For an odd misusage, see **fir.**

furor; furore. *Furor* /fyuur-ər/ is the standard spelling in AmE, *furore* /fyuu-ror-ee/ in BrE. Why the difference? Although both AmE and BrE predominantly adopted the Latin spelling of the word (*furor*) in the 18th century, in the late 19th century BrE publications increasingly adopted the Italian spelling (*furore*), which became unquestionably predominant in BrE during the 1940s.

further. See **farther.**

*furtherest is a dialectal term not to be found in good writing—except in dialogue involving nonstandard speech. Dating from the early 19th century, this NONWORD mars a good many pieces—e.g.:

- "*Furtherest* [read *Furthest*] along is an investigation of the disclosure in life insurance policies." John F. Berry, "Insurance Industry Faces Federal Fire," *Wash. Post,* 18 July 1977, at D11.
- "Duke's only real hope is that the open primary system operates as it has many times in the past, selecting the candidate from the *furtherest* [read *furthest*] right and the

one from the *furtherest* [read *furthest*] left for the runoff, thereby pitting Duke against, say, Fields." Jack Wardlaw, "Some New, Interesting Developments in Senate Race," *Times-Picayune* (New Orleans), 25 Feb. 1996, at B7.
- "The plan targets aid on a sliding scale . . . . Those *furtherest* [read *furthest*] below average get the most; those highest on the scale get the least." Tom Fahey, "School Aid 'Losers' May Band Together," *Union Leader* (Manchester, N.H.), 10 Feb. 2005, at A1. On the choice between *furthest* and *farthest* in that sentence, see **farther.**

See DIALECT.

LANGUAGE-CHANGE INDEX
*furtherest for *furthest*: Stage 1

furthermore, adv. & conj. This word is quite proper, of course, but its heaviness can weigh down a passage. A quicker word—such as *also, and, besides, further,* or even *moreover*—usually serves better.

*further to your letter. This phrase, like **enclosed please find,* epitomizes business JARGON. If you want to write effective letters, don't use it.

*fuschia. See **fuchsia.**

fuse, n.; **fuze.** A *fuse* is a wick or other combustible cord for an old-fashioned explosive. A *fuze* is for more high-tech explosives: it's a mechanical or electronic device used for detonations.

In a different sense, *fuse* refers to a component that protects an electrical circuit by preventing it from overloading. The two CLICHÉS derive from the different senses of the word: *blow a fuse* from the electrical-component sense, and *have a short fuse* from the wick sense.

FUSED PARTICIPLES. H.W. Fowler gave the name "fused participle" to a participle that is (1) used as a noun (i.e., a gerund), and (2) preceded by a noun or pronoun not in the possessive case—thus *Me going home made her sad* rather than the preferred *My going home made her sad.* Or *Shareholders worried about the company reorganizing* rather than the preferred *Shareholders worried about the company's reorganizing.*

The fused participle is said to lack a proper grammatical relationship to the preceding noun or pronoun. Yet no one today doubts that Fowler overstated his case in calling fused participles "grammatically indefensible" and in never admitting an exception. The grammarians Otto Jespersen and George Curme have cited any number of historical examples and have illustrated the absolute necessity of the fused participle in some sentences (barring a complete rewrite)—e.g.: "The chance of that ever happening is slight."

But Fowler had a stylistic if not a grammatical point. Especially in formal prose, the possessive ought to be used whenever it is not unidiomatic or unnatural. In the following sentences, then, possessives would have been better used than the nouns and pronouns in the objective case:

- "If his patients asked, he would not object to *them trying* [read *their trying*] it." Elisabeth Tacey, "Doctor Puts Faith in Shark Cancer Cure," *S. China Morning Post*, 21 Apr. 1994, at 3.
- "The pattern of our life, which now involves *me spending* [read *my spending*] some days each week totally alone so as to write, proves to be creative and necessary for all of us." Terry Waite, "A Long, Long Way to Travel," *Times* (London), 27 Aug. 1994, at 15.
- "Now when 11-year-old Shelby Young rides the bus to Loudon Grade School, he doesn't worry *about the older kids soaking* [read *that the older kids will soak*] him with water guns." Carrie Sturrock, "Separate Buses, Better than Equal," *Concord Monitor*, 7 Sept. 1994, at B1. (The difference in meaning between *kids soaking* and *kids' soaking* is slight: as currently worded, *the older kids soaking him* seems elliptical for *the older kids who are soaking him* [in which case the original sentence is right]. But the writer probably meant *their soaking him*—hence *the older kids' soaking him*. The question is what he's not worrying about: the *kids* or the *soaking*. The revised version, with a new subordinate clause [*that the other kids will soak him*], is a good way to avoid the problem altogether.)

A modern rule might be formulated thus: when the *-ing* (present) participle has the force of a noun, it is preferably preceded by a possessive, especially in formal contexts. But when the *-ing* participle has the force of a verb, a nonpossessive word is acceptable, especially in informal contexts. When the participle falls in the predicate—as it usually does when case selection is a subtle question—another key is to analyze what the proper direct object should be. Consider this exchange: *Is John in the shower? / Yes, I heard him singing. / Is he talented? / Yes, I heard his singing.* The object of the first reply may be John himself (*him*), but the object of the second is clearly John's (hence, *his*) singing.

Yet there are other exceptions. For example, there's typically no choice of construction when you're using nonpersonal nouns <he was responsible for the luggage having been lost>, nonpersonal pronouns <she couldn't accept nothing being done about the problem>, and groups of pronouns <he regretted some of them being left out in the rain>. For a scholarly discussion of still other exceptions, see Thomas Nunnally, "The Possessive with Gerunds," 66 *Am. Speech* 359, 363–65 (1991).

If you can't get a handle on fused participles, then just remember the words of an influential grammarian: "It's a niggling point but one on which many people niggle." Paul Roberts, *Modern Grammar* 20 (1968).

LANGUAGE-CHANGE INDEX
Garden-variety fused participle <I can understand him not wanting to participate>: Stage 3

fusible. So spelled—not **fusable*. See -ABLE (A).

futilely, adv., is sometimes misspelled **futiley*—e.g.:

- "As she *futiley* [read *futilely*] tries to emotionally latch on to someone . . . , she becomes more unhinged." Paul Sherman, "Video View," *Boston Herald*, 2 July 1995, at 10.
- "But the bottom line is Starks got the calls and the Nuggets were left *futiley* [read *futilely*] pleading their case to referees." Dave Krieger, "Nuggets End East Trip 0–4," *Rocky Mountain News* (Denver), 15 Dec. 1996, at C12.
- "Whales traces his spiritual quest to write his life's magnum opus as he *futiley* [read *futilely*] rages against his condition." Charlotte Cripps, "Brainwaving but Drowning," *Independent* (U.K.), 2 June 2003, at 18.

Cf. **agilely** & **solely.** See ADVERBS (B).

LANGUAGE-CHANGE INDEX
futilely misspelled **futiley*: Stage 1

future, in the near. This phrase is unbearably wordy for either of the simple one-word equivalents: *soon* and *shortly*. See **in future.**

fuze. See **fuse.**

-FY. Most verbs ending in *-fy*—from the French *-fier* or Latin *-ficare* "to do or make"—are preceded by an *-i-* (e.g., *classify, mollify, mortify, pacify*). But a few of them aren't: *liquefy, putrefy, rarefy, stupefy.* The reason for the difference is merely that the corresponding infinitives in French and Latin are spelled with an *-e-* (*liquefier*, etc.), and the words were borrowed directly into English from those infinitives. In any event, it's a common error to misspell these words *-ify*. The same mistaken switch of *-e-* to *-i-* occurs in the corresponding nouns, which should be *liquefaction, putrefaction, rarefaction,* and *stupefaction.*

G

GAAP. See **generally accepted accounting principles** & ABBREVIATIONS (A).

gabardine; gaberdine. These variant spellings have undergone DIFFERENTIATION. *Gabardine* is the modern fabric having a hard finish and diagonal ribs. *Gaberdine* is the outer garment traditionally associated with Jews of the Middle Ages.

Gaelic; Gallic. *Gaelic* /**gay**-lik/ means "Scottish" or "Irish"; *Gallic* /**gal**-ik/ means "French."

As a noun, *Gaelic* denotes the language spoken by the Celts of the Scottish Highlands—or, more broadly, by the Celts of Ireland and the Isle of Man as well. *Gallic*, though formerly denoting a person from France, is not used as a noun in modern English.

gaffe; gaff, n. *Gaffe* = (1) a blunder in etiquette; faux pas; or (2) a blatant error. *Gaff* (a rarer word) = (1) a long pole with a metal hook used in fishing; (2) a metal spur; (3) a trick or swindle; (4) harsh treatment, abuse; or (5) (BrE) a cheap theater.

Gaffe is sometimes misspelled *gaff*—e.g.:

- "'His biggest risk,' Mr. Schoen said, 'is that something will happen and he will make another *gaff* [read *gaffe*] as he did in 1989.'" Catherine S. Manegold, "Giuliani Shows a Polished Image," *N.Y. Times*, 7 Sept. 1993, at A1.
- "The Webster episode is only Pitt's latest ethical *gaff* [read *gaffe*]." Steven Syre, "Money Men on Hot Seat," *Boston Globe*, 3 Nov. 2002, at E2.

LANGUAGE-CHANGE INDEX
gaff misused for *gaffe*: Stage 1

gainsay; contradict. Originally *gainsay* [ME "to say against"] was the popular word and *contradict* the erudite one. Today just the opposite is true: "This is an interesting example of the substitution of a learned word for a popular word. *Withsay* [or, later, *gainsay*] is pure Anglo-Saxon, and *contradict* is a 'learned' borrowing [from Latin]. Yet few words are now more popular than *contradict*." James B. Greenough & George L. Kittredge, *Words and Their Ways in English Speech* 215 (1902). *Gainsay* is today a FORMAL WORD somewhat more common in BrE than in AmE—e.g.: "He is nonetheless persuaded of a heroism in his subject that will not be *gainsaid*." Andrew Mcneillie, "Part Woolf, Part Lamb," *Guardian*, 13 Sept. 1994, at T13.

gait (= a manner of walking, trotting, etc.) is sometimes confused with *gate*—e.g.:

- "Eddie squinted at the ball through thick black-framed glasses, his spindly legs and stooped shoulders giving him an awkward *gate* [read *gait*]." Hilary Waldman, "They Were Family," *Hartford Courant*, 24 Nov. 1991, at 14.
- "He was moving with the feeble *gate* [read *gait*] of an old man." Greg Logan, "Hampton Jitney Running on Empty," *Newsday* (N.Y.), 9 Dec. 1994, Sports §, at A118.
- "American Creams, which were not recognized as a breed until 1950, are medium-size draft horses, weighing about 1,600 to 1,800 pounds.... Their *gate* [read *gait*] is smooth and easy, and their temperament is amiable and trustworthy." Suzanne Hively, "American Cream Is Featured Draft at Lake Farmpark Horse Show," *Plain Dealer* (Cleveland), 16 May 2002, at E3.

LANGUAGE-CHANGE INDEX
gate misused for *gait*: Stage 1

gala (= a huge party or public entertainment to celebrate a special occasion) is most traditionally pronounced /**gay**-lə/, but in recent years it has been largely displaced by /**gahl**-ə/ or /**gal**-ə/.

gallant. In all senses as an adjective, this word is best pronounced /**gal**-ənt/. (In the dated sense "polite and attentive to women," it may also be pronounced /gə-**lahnt**/ or /gə-**lant**/.) As a noun, however, the word is pronounced either /gə-**lahnt**/ or /gə-**lant**/. Today the noun is considered literary.

Gallic. See **Gaelic.**

GALLICISMS (/**gal**-ə-siz-əms/) appear frequently in modern prose—e.g., *blasé*, *coup de grâce*, *cul-de-sac*, *joie de vivre*, *mésalliance*, *succès d'estime*, *tête-a-tête*, and *tour de force*. None of these is unduly *recherché*, to use yet another. But foreignisms of any kind become affectations when used in place of perfectly good English terms—e.g., *peu à peu* for *little by little*, or *sans* for *without*. (See **sans**.)

One stylist of high repute cautions sternly against all but thoroughly anglicized Gallicisms: "Of *Gallicisms* . . . it is perhaps not necessary to say much: they are universally recognized as a sign of bad taste, especially if they presuppose the knowledge of a foreign language. A few foreign words, such as *cliché*, have no English equivalent and are in current use; and there may be others [that] are desirable. But except in technical works it will generally be found possible to avoid them." Herbert Read, *English Prose Style* 10 (1952).

On whether to italicize words borrowed from French and other languages, see ITALICS (B).

For a fascinating collection of loan translations from French, see A.A. Prins, *French Influence in English Phrasing* (1952). Cf. GERMANICISMS.

gallop makes *galloped* and *galloping* in both AmE and BrE. See SPELLING (B).

galosh (= an overshoe designed to keep shoes dry) is the standard spelling. **Galoshe* and **golosh* are variants. The pronunciation is /gə-**losh**/.

Current ratio (*galosh* vs. **golosh* vs.
*galoshe): 22:14:1

gambade; gambado. These synonymous doublets have come into English through French (*gambade*) and Spanish (*gambado*). They denote (1) the spring of a horse, (2) an antic-filled dance; a caper or gambol. *Gambade* /gam-**bayd**/ is slightly older in English and has always been slightly predominant in AmE and BrE alike. Although *gambado* /gam-**bay**-doh/ has shared the two senses listed above, it has undergone DIFFERENTIATION, so that in its primary sense today it denotes a horse rider's legging. The standard plural is *gambadoes*, not **gambados*. See PLURALS (D).

Current ratio (*gambadoes* vs. **gambados*): 5:1

gambit. A. General Uses. In chess, a *gambit* is a move, usually an opening move, likely to sacrifice a piece to gain a strategic advantage. In strictest usage, it is the sacrifice that makes a tactical move a *gambit*. The word lost some of its unique punch when writers began applying it loosely to any trick, tactical move, or ploy. But that shift in meaning was clear by the mid-20th century, especially in the popular satires of Stephen Potter, most notably *The Theory and Practice of Gamesmanship* (1947), *Some Notes on Lifemanship* (1950), *One-Upmanship* (1951), and *Golfmanship*

LANGUAGE-CHANGE INDEX (For the full key, see front matter pp. xxxi, l–li.)
Stage 1: Rejected. **Stage 2:** Widely shunned. **Stage 3:** Widespread but . . . **Stage 4:** Ubiquitous but . . . **Stage 5:** Fully accepted.
Invariably inferior forms marked by asterisk (*). • Ratios represent frequency of prevalent forms vs. variants in current books.

(1968). For example, in the last of these, Potter wrote: "History is a *gambit*. More precisely the writing of history is a double or treble *gambit*. It is a way of saying 'I think' and 'what about this' in a tone [that] is supposed, simply by adding the word 'History', to silence argument" (p. 3). Throughout his many satirical texts, Potter used and popularized *gambit* as a synonym for *psychological ploy*.

Today this use is relatively common—e.g.:

- "In general, their *gambits* [read *tactics*] are legal. The state laws on who's eligible for Medicaid conceal many weak points that let moneyed people onto the rolls." Jane Bryant Quinn, "Moneyed Freeloaders Put Pressure on Medicaid," *Pantagraph* (Bloomington, Ill.), 31 May 2001, at C3.
- "In addition to its other provocative narrative *gambits* [read *twists*], 'Six Feet Under' tweaks stereotypes by having its gay characters also the show's most devoutly religious, even though many faiths would blindly condemn them." David Kronke, "Killer Comedy," *Daily News* (L.A.), 1 June 2001, at L30.
- "The double-name *gambit* [read *trick*] isn't new to Chicago." Betsy Rothstein, "Coping with Burden of Being Jesse Jackson Jr.," *The Hill*, 10 Apr. 2002, at 36.

B. For *gamut*. *Gamut* = a full range or extent, literally of musical notes, but more often figuratively of anything <the gamut of available options>. Misusing *gambit* for *gamut* is an increasingly common MALAPROPISM—e.g.:

- "Participants run the *gambit* [read *gamut*] of age and experience from 14-year-old riders to men in their early 20s with very little exposure to the bulls." Donna Logan Wisdom, "Despite Risk, Amateur Bull Riders Chase Rodeo Dreams," *Times Union* (Albany), 28 May 1995, at G1.
- "[Valerie] Harper's performance is nothing short of amazing: not only does she pull off the acting equivalent of a marathon, but as [Golda] Meir she runs the emotional *gambit* [read *gamut*] from joy to devastation to frustration to reflection." Mat DeKinder, "Harper Shines as Golda Meir," *St. Louis Post-Dispatch*, 26 Apr. 2006, at C5.
- "So why do we mentor? Faculty motivations run the *gambit* [read *gamut*] from sheer altruism to a utilitarian interest in research assistance." W. Brad Johnson, *On Being a Mentor: A Guide for Higher Education Faculty* 17 (2006).

LANGUAGE-CHANGE INDEX
running the gambit for *running the gamut*: Stage 1
Current ratio (*running the gamut* vs.
running the gambit): 89:1

C. In the Sense "opening." Because the chess *gambit* is most often associated with openings, some criticize *opening gambit* as a REDUNDANCY. But strictly speaking, it's not: a *gambit* can come at any point in a chess game.

gambling. See **gaming**.

gambol (/**gam**-bəl/), vb., makes *gamboled* and *gamboling* in AmE, *gambolled* and *gambolling* in BrE. See SPELLING (B).

gaming; gambling. The first is a EUPHEMISM for the second, especially in law and casino advertising—e.g.: "State officialdom, when hoping to sound professional

and clinical, uses the term *gaming* as having an ameliorative sense. By contrast, . . . *gambling* has a pejorative connotation." Thomas L. Clark, "Gaming and/or Gambling: You Pays Your Money," 10 *Verbatim*, Spring 1984, at 20.

gamut. See **gambit** (B).

ganglion (= [1] an encapsulated group of nerve cells external to the brain and spinal cord, or [2] a cystic tumor on a tendon sheath) has predominantly formed the plural *ganglia* since the early 19th century—not *ganglions*.

Current ratio: 51:1

gantlet; gauntlet. Lexicographers and usage critics—especially American ones—have sought since the 19th century to make a distinction. One runs the *gantlet* (= a kind of ordeal or punishment) but throws down the *gauntlet* (= a glove). The trend, however, is to use *gauntlet* for all senses (a trend reinforced by the 1977 Clint Eastwood movie *The Gauntlet*). In fact, though, writers of English have never reserved *gantlet* for the ordeal. Instead, despite etymological faultiness in conflating two different words—*gauntlet* (glove) and *gantlope* (ordeal)—*gauntlet* has taken over both meanings. One is tempted to resist, as this book did in earlier editions, but empirical evidence now available shows that *run the gauntlet* outdistances *run the gantlet* by an 11-to-1 margin and has consistently done so since about 1800. The "battle" was lost before it began. Hence usages like this one are legion, and typical: "They tortured him last year, dragged him through a senseless frat-boy *gauntlet* that accomplished nothing." Jay Mariotti, "Sauerbrun Kicks Away Past at Last," *Chicago Sun-Times*, 4 Sept. 1996, § 1, at 10.

Many writers, however, have heeded all the editorial admonitions—e.g.:

- "In the lawsuit, Douglas Hartman, an Illinois air traffic controller[,] says he was forced to walk through a Tailhook-style *gantlet* during a workshop designed by Eberhardt to combat sexual harassment. Hartman says he became a victim himself when he was groped by his female co-workers, who then rated his sexual attributes." Jean Marbella, "Daring Tailhook-Style Gantlet Stirs Up Debate," *Detroit News*, 12 Oct. 1994, at A12.
- "The streetside culinary *gantlet* of hot grease and grills—stands selling everything from tacos to burgers to funnel cakes, pierogis and pizza—was shuttered, awaiting the evening rush." Brian E. Albrecht, "Year of Pig at Popular E. Side Fest," *Plain Dealer* (Cleveland), 3 Aug. 1996, at B2.
- "On opening day, the East Harlem school was a model of nostalgic decorum as the 50 young women . . . marched into their school through a *gantlet* of reporters and cameras." Liz Trotta, "School-Choice Ideas Gaining Ground in New York City," *Wash. Times*, 15 Sept. 1996, at A1.

The word *gauntlet* is uncontroversially used in the phrase *throwing down the gauntlet* (= issuing a challenge)—e.g.:

- "But now it is too late to throw down the *gauntlet* to the Americans." Emily Sheffield, "Jackdraw," *Guardian*, 18 July 1996, at 17.

- "Don Davis, who threw down the *gauntlet* through newspaper ads, figures his Corvette is the better car." "People," *Orange County Register,* 4 Sept. 1996, at A2.
- "Anyone who passes her has thrown down the *gauntlet.*" Patricia Volk, "Shotgun Weddings," *N.Y. Times,* 15 Sept. 1996, § 5, at 1.

The corresponding phrase is *pick up the gauntlet* (= accept a challenge)—e.g.:

- "It remains for the Palestinians to *pick up the gauntlet* and accept the challenge to adopt the path of nonviolent resistance." David R. Hunsicker Jr., "Do Palestinians Have Courage to Resist Nonviolently?" *Morning Call* (Allentown, Pa.), 30 July 2002, at A9.
- "The outcome depends on whether other big institutional investors *pick up the gauntlet* that has been thrown down by the Missouri Public School Retirement System." David Nicklaus, "Pension Fund May Get Ball Rolling for Startup Businesses," *St. Louis Post-Dispatch,* 21 Aug. 2002, at C1.

Occasionally the phrase invites a confused META-PHOR—e.g.: " 'It probably just took a person who was willing to *pick up the gauntlet* and run with it,' Burk said about Earle's leadership." Dean Geroulis, "High Schools Mark 100 Years of Progress," *Chicago Trib.* (Park Ridge ed.), 18 Sept. 2002, at 26 (Eddon Burk praising C.A. Earle).

LANGUAGE-CHANGE INDEX
gauntlet for *gantlet*: Stage 5
Current ratio (*running the gauntlet* vs. *running the gantlet*): 11:1

gaol. See **jail.**

garage is pronounced /gə-**rahzh**/ in AmE, /**gar**-ij/ in BrE.

garden path; primrose path. The two phrases have similar but not quite the same meanings.

Garden path, the phrase that appears in print more frequently, is usually literal—e.g.: "Ipe is also available in interlocking tiles that require no nails or finish. Using a jigsaw to cut rounded edges or odd corners, they can be placed on the surfaces of decks, courtyards, balconies, patios, porches, hot tub and pool surrounds, *garden paths,* garages and saunas." Stacy Downs, "Brazilian Walnut Hardwood Prized for Its Good Looks," *Chicago Trib.,* 29 Sept. 2006, Your Place §, at 16. But it may also be used figuratively to denote an intentional misleading—e.g.: "Blair has been under pressure at home from critics who contend that he let U.S. President Bush take him down the *garden path* in Iraq." Editorial, "Horror in London," *Tulsa World,* 8 July 2005, at A14.

Primose path, on the other hand, is almost always allusive. It traditionally denotes a profligate or debauched lifestyle destined for ruin—e.g.: " 'The man is said to be a well-to-do merchant of Memphis, but he followed the *primrose path* too far in Los Angeles,' the newspaper said." "Man on Bender Seeks to Go

Straight," *L.A. Times,* 24 Sept. 2006, News §, at A3. The phrase was used twice by Shakespeare, in *Hamlet* (1.3.45–51) and *Macbeth* (2.3.17–18).

It would be helpful to distinguish the two phrases. But unfortunately, *primrose path* is now being used more and more frequently the same way as *garden path,* to denote being misled, as here: "Regardless of form—oil, gas, coal or nuclear—the Green movement is blocking efforts to harness our accustomed energy sources while leading us down the *primrose path* [read *garden path*] of so-called 'renewable energy.' " Steven Milloy, "Color Energy Woes Green," *Wash. Times,* 7 June 2005, at A16.

*****garden snake.** See **garter snake.**

GARNER'S LAW OF LOANWORDS. The more arcane or technical a loanword (= a word borrowed from another language), the more likely it is to retain a foreign plural, diacritical marks, and italics; the more common it becomes, the more likely it is to lose them. Corollary: if the loanword becomes widespread, it typically loses italics first, diacritical marks second, and a foreign plural last.

garnish; garnishee, v.t. In AmE, the usual verb form is *garnish* (= to take property, usu. a portion of someone's wages, by legal authority). *Garnishee* is usually reserved for the noun sense "a person or institution, such as a bank, that is indebted to another whose property has been subjected to garnishment, esp. to satisfy the debt." The noun corresponding to *garnish* is *garnishment.*

In BrE, however, and in a few North American jurisdictions, *garnishee* as well as *garnish* is used as a verb. Although the *OED* gives passing notice to this usage and to the corresponding noun **garnisheement,* these forms are historically unwarranted and therefore ill-advised—e.g.:

- "Our caller felt certain that repayment had been fully made, and that the *garnisheement* [read *garnishment*] of his wages should end." "The Ombudsman," *Dayton Daily News,* 5 May 1996, at B5.
- "A Virginia court this year ordered the money *garnisheed* [read *garnished*] from six months of Brawley's wages as a nurse there." Michael Gartland, "Pay-Up Time for Brawley," *N.Y. Post,* 4 Aug. 2013, News §, at 6.
- "He said the senators who have yet to reimburse their expenses should either go to arbitration, or see their wages *garnisheed* [read *garnished*] (if they are still sitting) or face a lawsuit (if they are retired)." Daniel Leblanc & Gloria Galloway, "Senate Leaders Say Changes to Rein In Spending Have Already Been Made," *Globe & Mail* (Toronto), 10 June 2015, at A1.

Current ratio (*garnished his wages* vs. **garnisheed his wages*): 5:1

garrote, vb. (= to strangle with a cord or wire), is the standard spelling today in World English. *Garrotte,*

LANGUAGE-CHANGE INDEX (For the full key, see front matter pp. xxxi, l–li.)
Stage 1: Rejected. **Stage 2:** Widely shunned. **Stage 3:** Widespread but . . . **Stage 4:** Ubiquitous but . . . **Stage 5:** Fully accepted.
Invariably inferior forms marked by asterisk (*). • Ratios represent frequency of prevalent forms vs. variants in current books.

*garotte, and *garote are variants—the first of which was once the predominant BrE spelling.

The word is traditionally pronounced /gə-**roht**/, but /gə-**rot**/ now predominates and must be accepted as standard. With the first of these pronunciations, it's inflected *garroted* and *garroting* in AmE (to preserve the long -*o*-); with the second, it's *garrotted* and *garrotting* (with a short -*o*-). See SPELLING (B).

The word is also a noun meaning "a cord or wire for strangling."

Current ratio (*garroted him* vs. *garrotted him* vs. *garotted him*): 14:3:1

garter snake; *****garden snake.** A *garter snake* is a non-venomous North American snake having longitudinal stripes that resemble garters. A *garden snake* is an unknown variety—perhaps "a snake that can be found in a garden." But beginning about 1960, the herpetologically challenged have often referred to this unknown species—e.g.:

- "These were not those cute little *garden* [read *garter*] snakes, but rattlers and cobras." Kathleen Merryman, "Spine Shivering Stories," *News Trib.* (Tacoma), 29 Oct. 1997, Fam. §, at 1.
- "Midway through the three-week program, campers have already seen a *garden* [read *garter*] snake, dragonflies, frogs and lots of grasshoppers and crickets." Molly Kavanaugh, "Backyard Wonderland," *Plain Dealer* (Cleveland), 5 Aug. 1998, at B1.
- "In an extraordinary passage in which the boy describes catching and then killing a *garden* [read *garter*] snake, he seems to encapsulate all the contradictions of human behavior." Edith Milton, "A Tumult of Experience Through a Child's Eyes," *Boston Globe*, 29 Nov. 1998, at F3.

LANGUAGE-CHANGE INDEX
garden snake for *garter snake*: Stage 2
Current ratio (*garter snake* vs. *garden snake*): 8:1

gas. See **fluid.**

gases, not *gasses*, is the plural form of the noun *gas*. Still, for the verb *gas*, *gassed* is the accepted past tense and *gasses* is the third-person singular in the present tense. Cf. **bus.** See SPELLING (B).

Current ratio (*the gases* vs. *the gasses*): 42:1

gasoline; *****gasolene.** The first is standard in AmE and BrE alike; the second is a primarily BrE variant.

gateau (= a rich, elaborately decorated cake), an 18th-century French loanword, predominantly retained its original circumflex (*gâteau*) until the early 20th century. The standard plural is *gateaux* in all varieties of World English—not *gateaus*. Whether singular or plural, the word is pronounced /gah-**toh**/ in AmE and /ga-**toh**/ (or even /**gat**-oh/) in BrE.

Current ratio (*gateaux* vs. *gateaus*): 63:1

gaudy (= [1] ostentatious, showy; or [2] dazzlingly brilliant or extravagant) is the standard spelling. *Gawdy* is an archaic variant that still sometimes appears—e.g.: "Chris Warren carried nine times for 61 yards as Seattle averaged a *gawdy* [read *gaudy*] 6.1

yards per rush." Peter King, "Inside the NFL," *Sports Illustrated*, 22 Sept. 1997, at 56 (photo caption). In BrE, *gaudy* is also a noun denoting an annual festivity, especially at a college.

Current ratio (*gaudy* vs. *gawdy*): 181:1

gauge is often misspelled *guage*, perhaps because when *gauge* is spelled correctly it looks as if it might be pronounced the same as *gouge*, so the writer "corrects" it by transposing the first two vowels. The misspelling might also be influenced by *language*, despite the differences in pronunciation (/**lang**-gwij/ vs. /gayj/). The *OED* calls the misspelling "a mere blunder."

When *gauge* refers to the width of wire, needles, or shotgun barrels—or to the thickness of sheet metal—higher numbers indicate narrower thicknesses. So avoid words such as *small* and *large* in favor of less ambiguous terms such as *thick* and *thin*—e.g.: "The company reported that [the thief] frequented the business, bringing in *large-gauge* [read *heavy-gauge*] copper wiring to sell." "Wire Thief Faces 10 Years," *Huntsville Times* (Ala.), 4 Apr. 2008, at B1. When *gauge* refers to the width of railroad tracks, the best descriptors are *standard*, *broad*, and *narrow*.

gauntlet. See **gantlet.**

gavel, vb., makes *gaveled* and *gaveling* in AmE, *gavelled* and *gavelling* in BrE. See SPELLING (B).

gavotte (= [1] a lively dance that originated in 17th-century France; or [2] the music accompanying this dance, set in a brisk 4/4 time) is the standard spelling. *Gavot* is a variant.

Current ratio (*gavottes* vs. *gavots*): 12:1

gay. A. Generally. In 1980, a well-known language critic commented: "[The] special-interest use of *gay* undermines the correct use of a legitimate and needed English word. It now becomes ambiguous to call a cheerful person or thing gay; to wish someone a gay journey or holiday, for example, may have totally uncalled-for over- and undertones and, in conservative circles, may even be considered insulting. The insulting aspect we can eventually get rid of; the ambiguous, never. What do we do about it? If we energetically reject *gay* as a legitimate synonym for *homosexual*, it may not be too late to bury this linguistic abomination." John Simon, *Paradigms Lost* 27 (1980).

Hardly anyone today would dispute, though, that it's too late to contain the word. *Gay* is now all but universal in referring to homosexuals, both male and female, and has been embraced by the gay community. Its stronger associations are with men, so that we have the phrase *gay and lesbian affairs*, as if lesbians weren't gay. See (B).

The homosexual sense of *gay* first appeared in the mid-20th century; before that the word did, however, bear the derogatory senses "leading an immoral life" and "(of a woman) engaging in prostitution" (*SOED*). Those connotations have disappeared in recent years.

But is Simon's point about ambiguity a valid one? Consider the following passage, from a book published in 1993. Was Hoccleve homosexual?

> Hoccleve, Thomas (c.1369–c.1450) poet, began to work as a clerk/copyist in the Privy Seal in about 1378, and had his salary raised to £10 a year in 1399, and to £13 6s.8d in 1408. This, with his private means of £4 a year, should have been adequate, but his pay was often late and he lived a gay bachelor life—dressing fashionably, travelling to the office by boat, eating and dining in taverns, and entertaining pretty girls. All this we know from "La Mâle Règle," a poem which includes a plea to the Treasurer, asking for his back pay. A few years later, his long-awaited benefice having failed to materialize, he married, for love.
>
> Antony Kamm, *Collins Biographical Dictionary of English Literature* 216 (1993).

Readers are likely to believe, at first, that he was homosexual—because of the word *gay*. By the end of the passage, most readers will be convinced that Hoccleve was heterosexual and that the author has simply used *gay* in an old-fashioned way. A few might finish the passage thinking that Hoccleve was bisexual. But almost any observant reader will have spent some time considering Hoccleve's sexuality—to the detriment of the information that's actually being conveyed. The writer would have been well advised to avoid the traditional sense of *gay*; it's now all but obsolete. And that's just as well, since there are (and always have been) plenty of alternative choices that have no sexual connotations.

The new sense of *gay* is standard. Trying to reclaim the old sense is an exercise in futility. Meanwhile, there's much to be said for gays' having a more or less neutral term to describe themselves—something besides the familiar old DYSPHEMISMS.

LANGUAGE-CHANGE INDEX
gay meaning "homosexual": Stage 5

B. **Gay and lesbian.*** Though common, this phrasing is peculiarly redundant, since lesbians are gay women. So to say *gay and lesbian raises a genus–species problem akin to saying **human beings and women* (an insult to women). What is actually happening, no doubt, is that *gay* is undergoing what linguists call specialization—that is, in some of its senses the word is becoming sex-specific. In the end, *gay* may end up referring always to men. In the meantime, though, it's more logical to use *gay* as a solo adjective, as in the title of the *Handbook of Affirmative Psychotherapy with Lesbians and Gay Men* (2002). And when the use is attributive—a noun sense being desired—it's probably more clearly descriptive to refer to *gay men and women*, as in the title of Tom Cowan's *Gay Men and Women Who Enriched the World* (1997).

gazebo. Pl. *gazebos.* See PLURALS (D).

geisha (= a Japanese woman trained in the arts of dancing, singing, conversation, and other entertainment, esp. for men), an 1881 Japanese loanword, is preferably pronounced /**gay**-shə/—not /**gee**-shə/.

geminate. So spelled. See SPELLING (A).

gemology; gemmology. For "the study of gems," the first is AmE; the second, BrE.

gender has long been used as a grammatical distinction of a word according to the sex assigned (usually arbitrarily in the Romance languages) to a given noun. It has newly been established in the language of the law in phrases such as *gender discrimination*, a use disapproved as jargonistic by some authorities. In reformers' eyes, it eliminates the distracting word *sex* (which, of course, denotes coitus as well as physical characteristics that contribute to one's sense of self).

In recent years, *sex* in one of its senses has narrowed its meaning to designate a set of physical characteristics <sex change>, while *gender* (at least in academic circles) increasingly denotes the social and psychological distinctions between men and women <gender roles>. For example, most academics today would use *gender* in place of *sex* in the following sentence: "Given strong patriarchal traditions here, it is hardly surprising that the criticism is often put in ways that emphasize the two leaders' *sex*, even if Bangladesh has had plenty of reason in 22 years of nationhood scarred by military coups and assassinations to conclude that men in power are no less likely than women to be governed by the whims of personality and ambition." John F. Burns, "Two Women, at the Top and at Odds," *N.Y. Times*, 28 July 1994, at A7. As worded, the sentence might even contain a MISCUE for some readers; that is, one might expect the sentence to be completed differently—e.g.: "Given strong patriarchal traditions here, it is hardly surprising that the criticism is often put in ways that emphasize the two leaders' *sex*, which by all accounts is becoming more frequent."

There are, in short, legitimate reasons for preferring *gender* outside grammatical contexts. But polemicists sometimes argue that the reasons are entirely political—e.g.: "The ['gender equity'] industry prefers the word 'gender' to 'sex' because 'sex' suggests immutable differences, while 'gender' suggests differences that are 'socially constructed' and can be erased by sufficiently determined social engineers." George F. Will, "A Train Wreck Called Title IX," *Newsweek*, 27 May 2002, at 82.

gendered is a jargonistic VOGUE WORD (dating from the early 1970s) meaning "biased in favor of one sex." The term can seem preposterous at times. A correspondent who contributed the following example asked whether the suggestion is to remove all men and women from the military: "'There are now demands to change the culture of the military, to create an *ungendered* military as if that were the ultimate

LANGUAGE-CHANGE INDEX (For the full key, see front matter pp. xxxi, l–li.)
Stage 1: Rejected. **Stage 2:** Widely shunned. **Stage 3:** Widespread but . . . **Stage 4:** Ubiquitous but . . . **Stage 5:** Fully accepted.
Invariably inferior forms marked by asterisk (*). • Ratios represent frequency of prevalent forms vs. variants in current books.

solution to social problems having to do with sexuality.'" Elaine Donnelly, as quoted in "Experimental Army," *Wash. Times*, 29 Sept. 1997, at A2. Presumably, the sense is "a military free from sexual biases," but the language is badly stretched—at least, that is, the language as it stood in the early 2000s. See FUNCTIONAL SHIFT (B) & **unisex**.

gender-neutral. See **unisex**; see also SEXISM.

genealogy (= [1] the study of the history of a family, or [2] a description or depiction of how family members and their ancestors are related), an Anglo-French loanword from the 14th century, doesn't end (like so many other words) in *-ology*—but instead in *-alogy*. How is it pronounced, then? Traditionally /jee-nee-al-ə-jee/, as opposed to /-ahl-ə-jee/. Cf. **mineralogy**.

genera. See **genus**.

***general consensus.** See **consensus**.

generalissimo. Pl. *generalissimos*. See PLURALS (D).

generalized (= made general) sometimes appears in contexts where *general* would serve better—e.g.: "For what begins in many of the stories as rich subject matter with great possibilities for originality soon turns—because of the hurried, vague patches and *generalized* [read *general*] language—predictable or, worse, uninteresting." Mark Bautz, "'Golden Boys' Offers Gilded Promises, but Results Are Dull and Tarnished," *Wash. Times*, 6 Oct. 1991, at B8. The sentence surely does not intend to convey that the language was *made general* by the author, but that it *is general*.

LANGUAGE-CHANGE INDEX
generalized misused for *general*: Stage 1

generally has three basic meanings: (1) "disregarding insignificant exceptions" <the quality of the acting is generally very high>; (2) "in many ways" <he was the most generally qualified applicant>; and (3) "usually" <he generally leaves the office at five o'clock>. Sense 3 is the least effective in formal writing, although at times it merges with sense 1.

generally accepted accounting principles; generally accepted accountancy principles. The first is the usual phrase in AmE and BrE alike. The second is a variant. The phrase is often abbreviated *GAAP* /gap/—e.g.: "[Deferred Acquisition Cost] is the way insurers defer some of the costs of acquiring a customer and amortize them over a number of years under *generally accepted accounting principals* [read *principles*], or *GAAP*." Lee Ann Gjertsen, "Insurers' Annuity Moves Could Crimp Bank Profits," *Am. Banker*, 1 Nov. 2002, Ins./Inv. Prods. §, at 1. Because *GAAP* is an acronym, it should not have a period after each letter. See ABBREVIATIONS (A) & **principal (B)**.

***generally always; *usually always.** These are unconscious OXYMORONS that have occasionally appeared since the 19th century—e.g.:

- "There's *generally always* [read *generally*] a Harmon student on staff." Karen Hulenhuth, "That Neighborhood Intimacy," *Kansas City Star*, 24 Mar. 1996, Star Mag. §, at 6.
- "We *generally always* [read *generally*] know who is in the running for the largest companies." Matt Krantz, "Federal Signal Puts Being Tops at Top of List," *Investor's Bus. Daily*, 10 Dec. 1996, at A4.
- "It's always something. And it's *usually always* [read *usually*] something silly." C. Jemal Horton, "*Thomas'* [read *Thomas's*] Coaching Is Reason Pacers Are Talk of the League," *Indianapolis Star*, 29 Nov. 2002, at C3. (For more about forming the possessive of *Thomas*, see POSSESSIVES (A).)

LANGUAGE-CHANGE INDEX
1. **generally always*: Stage 1
2. **usually always*: Stage 1

generative; generational. The distinction is clear. *Generative* = procreative. *Generational* = pertaining to generations. The two words seem to have been correctly used in the following passage: "We also need to honor the *generative* obligation and claim our part in the transmission and upholding of life. We are the *generational* bridge to the future for the human community." Kenneth Vaux, "The Vatican's Cry of Protest," *Chicago Trib.*, 20 Mar. 1987, at C19.

genericness; *genericalness; genericism. *Genericness*, though odd-looking, is now the most widely used noun corresponding to the adjective *generic*—at least in AmE. It is recorded from 1939 in the *OED* and appears most commonly in reference to trademarks—e.g.: "Microsoft sued Windows for trademark infringement, but a judge found that Windows is generic. Microsoft says the findings were based on 'a fundamental misapprehension of the test for *genericness*.'" Cathy Keim, "Loose Change," *St. Petersburg Times*, 21 Apr. 2002, at H1. Despite its specialized currency, *genericness* retains an un-English appearance. Cf. ***prolificness** under **prolificacy**.

Genericalness, listed in the *OED* and *W2*, does not, like *genericness*, flout principles of English word formation. But perhaps because it derives from the archaic adjective *generical, it is exceedingly rare. It has no standing in the language.

Genericism /jə-**ner**-i-siz-əm/ has also appeared, sometimes in legal contexts and sometimes, well, generically—e.g.: "The Gateway/Dell 200 certainly gives new meaning to the expression 'PC clone.' But it's only the most blatant symptom of the PC industry's creeping *genericism*." Rob Pegoraro, "Latest from Gateway, Dell: Separated at Birth?" *Wash. Post*, 9 June 2002, at H7. Though labeled "rare" in the *OED*, it has been the prevalent term in BrE since the 1970s.

Current ratio (*genericness* vs. *genericism*): 2:1

Genevese; Genovese. The first denotes an inhabitant of Geneva, Switzerland; the second, an inhabitant of Genoa, Italy. But because the two words are so easily confused, many writers and editors prefer *Genevan* for the Swiss inhabitant and *Genoan* for the Italian one. See DENIZEN LABELS.

genial. See **congenial**.

genie; jinni; *djinni. Although these words overlap, *genie* (/**jee**-nee/) more commonly denotes the magic spirit that, when summoned, carries out its master's wishes (the best-known one living inside Aladdin's lamp). On the other hand, a *jinni* (/ji-**nee**/ or /**jin**-ee/) is a spirit or demon that, according to Muslim mythology, appears on Earth in human or animal form and exercises supernatural powers. **Djinni* is a variant spelling of *jinni*.

Both words have multiple plural forms. *Genie* forms *genies* or, less good, **genii*. (See PLURALS (B).) *Jinni* forms *jinn* (which itself sometimes wrongly appears as the singular) or *jinns* (corresponding to the incorrect singular *jinn*). The variations are so common that some dictionaries disagree about which spelling is standard. Cf. **genius**.

GENITIVES. See POSSESSIVES.

genius = (1) a person of high intellectual and inventive power; or (2) the prevailing character or spirit; characteristic method or procedure. Sense 2 often refers to language—e.g.:

- "What has been called 'the *genius* of the language' can't be resisted. If the new meaning attached to a word satisfies enough people, that use will stick." Allan Massie, "Minimising the Language Potential," *Scotsman*, 19 Sept. 1995, at 15.
- "We go to poetry to meditate, to feel, to experience our private lives through the outward *genius* and beauty of language." Donald Hall, "Poetry's Muchness and Manyness," *St. Louis Post-Dispatch*, 5 May 1996, Everyday Mag. §, at C1.
- "It was just by some miracle that the core notion of 'common sense'—of taking things sometimes towards the cliff, but not over—became instilled in the *genius* of our language, and possibly not in some other ones." David Warren, "Misjudging the People," *Ottawa Citizen*, 8 Nov. 2009, at A11.

In its oldest sense, *genius* means "a guardian spirit assigned to a newborn child"—e.g.: "All the souls had now chosen their lives, and they went in the order of their choice to Lachesis, who sent them with the *genius* whom they had severally chosen, to be the guardian of their lives and the fulfiller of the choice . . . ." Plato, 10 *The Republic*, in 1 *The Dialogues of Plato* 878 (Benjamin Jowett trans., 1937).

The plural *geniuses* is preferred over *genii* except in the sense of demons or spirits. E.g.: "These themes are an integral part of the book as she ventures into the realm of the *genii*, ghosts and spirits." Chris Reynolds, "Anne Rice Afraid of the Dark?" *Ark. Democrat-Gaz.*, 8 Sept. 1996, at J7. (See PLURALS (B).) The *genii* in that quotation, by the way, is different from *genies* (= magical servants). For more on *genie*, see **genie**.

Genovese. See **Genevese**.

gentleman. A. General Use. *Gentleman* should not be used indiscriminately as a genteelism for *man*, the

generic term. *Gentleman* should be reserved for reference to a cultured, refined man. It is a sign of the times that "no word could be, it seems, more thoroughly out of style than *gentleman*." John Mortimer, "Wooster Sauce," *Sunday Times* (London), 29 Sept. 1991, § 7, at 6. In 2001, a Phoenix resort specified that at one of its restaurants, "Jackets are required for *gentlemen*." Which leaves one to wonder what's required for all the other men.

In BrE, the word formerly referred to a man of independent means not working gainfully. No doubt because the word is a vestige of a class-conscious society, it often appears in ironic phrases, especially in BrE <gentleman of the road = highway robber> <gentleman who pays the rent = pig>.

B. Set Phrases. *Gentleman* appears in many SET PHRASES, such as the introductory "ladies and gentlemen" and auto racing's "gentlemen, start your engines." A *gentlemen's agreement* is an informal one that relies on the good faith of the parties rather than the legal obligations created by a contract. *Gentlemen* carries no class distinction as the sign on a public restroom, nor do its connotations of civility translate when it's used in the EUPHEMISM *gentlemen's club*.

C. And *gentleperson*. This word is occasionally used as a neutral term in salutations, especially in the plural, but it has never lost its look of jocularity. *The Second Barnhart Dictionary of New English* (1980) says this of *gentleperson*: "often used humorously or ironically." E.g.: "*Gentlepeople* don't read other *gentlepeople's* e-mail." James Coates, "Computer Privacy? It's Not a Given," *Chicago Trib.*, 23 May 1993, at C1. Jocularity aside, the plural is *gentlepersons*, not **gentlepeople*.

LANGUAGE-CHANGE INDEX
gentleperson for *gentleman*: Stage 1

genuflection; *genuflexion. The first is the standard spelling in both AmE and BrE; the second is a chiefly BrE variant.

Current ratio: 4:1

genuine. See **authentic**.

genus. The only plural form included in many dictionaries is *genera*, but both the *OED* and *RH2* include the variant *genuses*. That variant has become fairly common, and it is undeniably more comprehensible to more people—e.g.:

- "New kinds of dinosaurs are described every month. Peter Makovicky, curator of dinosaurs at the Field Museum in Chicago, estimates there are 900 valid *genuses*, at least double the figure from two decades ago." Jerry Adler, "Buried Treasure," *Newsweek*, 27 June 2005, at 44.
- "He created his own system of classification, his own set of *genuses* and species, under rubrics like 'Charity, Aged,' 'Charity, Children,' and 'Charity, Tuberculosis.'" Edward Rothstein, "Categorized, Compared and Displayed: Social

Ills as Museum Specimens," *N.Y. Times*, 22 Jan. 2007, at E3 (referring to Francis Greenwood Peabody, a professor of Christian morals at Harvard from 1886 to 1912).

- "One is enthroned upon a symbol-studded 'Tree of Life,' one kneels in apology to a sawed-off trunk with an all-seeing eye among its rings, and others are painted on slick slabs of wood—nymphs of different *genuses*." Leah Ollman, "No Need to Read Beyond the Book Title," *L.A. Times*, 6 Apr. 2007, at E27.

Still, somewhat surprisingly, *genera* overwhelmingly predominates in modern usage, whether AmE or BrE—e.g.:

- " 'In Search of Nature' amounts to a kind of précis of decades of work encapsulating his close study of ant *genera*." Edward Hoagland, "The Best Books of 1996," *L.A. Times*, 29 Dec. 1996, Books §, at 4.
- "The campanula genus, which comprises more than 300 annuals, perennials and biennials, has become one of the most popular and identifiable *genera* in the United States." Erle Nickel, "These Abundant Bells Are a Joy to Behold," *S.F. Chron.*, 17 Jan. 2007, at WB8.
- "[T]he boundaries between plant species are far more porous than they are in animals, and different species and even *genera* of plants cross-hybridize with each other surprisingly often." Natalie Angier, "Green, Life-Giving and Forever Young," *N.Y. Times*, 17 Apr. 2007, at F1.

See PLURALS (B). Cf. **species**.

LANGUAGE-CHANGE INDEX
genuses for *genera*: Stage 3
Current ratio (*genera* vs. *genuses*): 372:1

geographical; geographic. Since the early 18th century, *geographical* has been the standard adjective throughout the English-speaking world. In the late 19th century, *geographic* emerged as a serious competing form—bolstered no doubt by the 1888 founding of *National Geographic Magazine* (its original name). Only in the late 1980s did *geographic* surpass *geographical* in AmE in frequency of use in print sources. The two remain locked in a tight race—but only in AmE. In BrE, *geographical* is more than twice as common in print sources. See -IC.

Current ratio (*geographical area* vs.
geographic area): 1:1

geometric; *geometrical. *Geometric* has been the standard term in AmE since the 1950s and in BrE since the 1970s. Long the prevalent term, *geometrical is now a NEEDLESS VARIANT. See -IC.

Current ratio: 2:1

geriatric. This word is an adjective meaning either (1) "of, relating to, or involving the branch of medicine known as geriatrics" or (2) "of, relating to, or involving old age." (*Geriatrical is a NEEDLESS VARIANT.) An old person is no more a *geriatric* than a young one is a *pediatric*. Yet *geriatric* is becoming a pejorative VOGUE WORD in just that noun sense—e.g.: "To your left, you will find several *geriatrics* [read *old people* or *senior citizens* or (perhaps) *octogenarians*] trying to keep pace with Richard Simmons' invigorating workout video, 'Sweatin' to the Oldies.' " George Diaz, "Save

Your Pay-Per-View Money Until a Real Fight Comes Along," *Orlando Sentinel*, 21 Oct. 1994, at D3.

LANGUAGE-CHANGE INDEX
geriatric as a noun meaning "old person": Stage 2
Current ratio (*geriatric* vs. *geriatrical): 29,610:1

GERMANICISMS. Although the English language is known as a Germanic language (evolving from Anglo-Saxon) and has a basic Germanic syntax, it has not borrowed as heavily from the modern German vocabulary as it has from the Romance languages Latin and French. Even so, the German contribution has been significant. Among the more frequent Germanicisms in English are these, all of which can be found even in abridged English dictionaries:

allergen	hasenpfeffer	rucksack
angst	hinterlands	sauerkraut
anlage	histamine	schadenfreude
biergarten	katzenjammer	schnapps
blitz	kindergarten	schriftsprache
bratwurst	kitsch	schuss
bundt	kohlrabi	stein
delicatessen	lederhosen	strudel
diesel	leitmotif	sturm und drang
doppelgänger	neanderthal	tannenbaum
dummkopf	poltergeist	waltz
feldspar	pretzel	wanderlust
foosball	pumpernickel	weltanschauung
frankfurter	quartz	weltzschmerz
gesundheit	rathskeller	wunderkind
glockenspiel	realpolitik	zeitgeist
hamburger	rottweiler	zeppelin

Although in German the nouns are capitalized, loanwords tend to be lowercased as soon as they become common in English. See **gestalt**.

gerontocracy. See GOVERNMENTAL FORMS.

gerrymander, an early-19th-century satirical PORTMANTEAU WORD, combines the name of Elbridge Gerry (governor of Massachusetts from 1810 to 1812) with the ending of *salamander*. When Gerry's party redistricted Massachusetts in 1812 to favor the Anti-Federalists, Essex County was divided in a way that made one voting district look, in the eyes of Federalists, something like a salamander. A famous editorial cartoon in the *Boston Gazette* added a dragon's head, wings, and claws, and named the beast the *gerrymander*. Hence *gerrymandering* came to refer to the practice of arranging electoral divisions so as to give one political party an unfair advantage.

Gerry's name was pronounced with a hard -g-: /**ger**-ee/, and *gerrymander* was originally pronounced /**ger**-ee-man-dər/. Today /**jer**-ee-man-dər/ predominates, though both pronunciations are standard.

When extended beyond geographic senses, the word is subjected to what could only be described as SLIPSHOD EXTENSION: "In the last few years, the 30-second 'attack ad' and the 10-second television news 'sound bite' have become such prominent . . . features of political campaigns that members of Congress have introduced more than two dozen bills in an attempt to *gerrymander* them out of existence." Randall Rothenberg, "Politics on TV: Too Fast, Too Loose?" *N.Y. Times*, 15 July 1990, at E1. How the metaphor of gerrymandering fits that sentence is anyone's guess.

*gerry-rig. See **jury-rig.**

GERUNDS. Oddly, there is a widespread prejudice against nouns ending in *-ing*. It's largely unfounded. When it comes to reducing verbosity, one effective way is to use gerunds directly; so *administering the medicine* is better than *the administration of the medicine, presenting the proposal* is better than *the presentation of the proposal*, etc. See DANGLERS (D), FUSED PARTICIPLES & ZOMBIE NOUNS.

gestalt; *Gestalt.* Borrowed from German in the mid-19th century, this term denotes a shape, configuration, or structure that, as an object of perception, forms a specific whole or unity incapable of expression simply in terms of its parts. This VOGUE WORD was formerly capitalized and italicized because it was long treated as a German noun (hence the italics), and in German all nouns are capitalized. But today it is increasingly treated as a naturalized word—e.g.:

- "So Clinton becomes the consensus candidate, capitalizing on the latest *gestalt* of the electorate." Gloria Borger, "The Little Big Men," *U.S. News & World Rep.*, 28 Oct. 1996, at 37.
- "But at least give them credit for trying to break the destructive *gestalt* of our times—this absurd idea that the only way to deliver public services and bolster the economy is to keep on taxing and spending more." Lorrie Goldstein, "Kicking the Guilt over Tax Breaks," *Toronto Sun*, 12 Jan. 1997, at C3.

Even those who capitalize the term today don't usually italicize it. It is pronounced /gə-**shtahlt**/ or /gə-**stahlt**/. See ITALICS (B) & GERMANICISMS.

get. A. Generally. *Get* is good English. Yet many writers want to avoid it because they consider it too informal; they prefer *obtain* or *procure*, two FORMAL WORDS. The same tendency is at work here that leads some writers to shun *before* in favor of **prior to, later* in favor of **subsequent to*, and the like. But confident, relaxed writers use the word *get* quite naturally—e.g.:

- "It was until recently a civil offense, called 'alienation of affections,' for which either spouse could *get* damages." Max Radin, *The Law and You* 54 (1948).
- "Duke was obviously referring to some of the conference championship teams or playoff winners that either *got* lucky or hot during the playoffs or played an unimpressive schedule to win a conference title and gain an automatic berth." Gordon S. White Jr., "N.C.A.A. Tourney Snubs Syracuse," *N.Y. Times*, 9 Mar. 1981, at C1.
- "People have told the Amherst couple to *get* divorced." Miriam Hill, "The Costs of Caring," *Plain Dealer* (Cleveland), 3 Feb. 1997, at D1.

Although some pedants have contended that *get* must always mean "to obtain," any good dictionary will confirm that it has more than a dozen meanings, including "to become." So the second and third bulleted examples above are quite proper. And it's entirely acceptable to use such phrases as *get sick, get well, get rich*, and *get angry*.

Anthony Burgess has noted the enormous versatility of *get*: "Foreign learner and native speaker alike can get through a great part of the day with only one verb . . . 'get.' . . . I get up in the morning, get a bath and a shave, get dressed, get my breakfast, get into the car, get to the office, get down to work, get some coffee at eleven, get lunch at one, get back, get angry, get tired, get home, get into a fight with my wife, get to bed." *A Mouthful of Air* 60 (1992). And he speculates that people regard it as a vulgar word precisely because it makes life so easy.

B. Inflection: *get > got > gotten, got.* The past participle *gotten* predominates in AmE, *got* in BrE. As recently as the early 20th century, some British writers benightedly lambasted the American form. Consider this misbegotten advice: "America need not boast the use of 'gotten.' The termination, which suggests either wilful archaism or useless slang, adds nothing of sense or sound to the word. It is like a piece of dead wood in a tree, and is better lopped off." Charles Whibley, "The American Language," 183 *Blackwood's Mag.* 117, 118 (1908). Others, however, noted that *gotten* was the standard BrE form as late as the early 20th century. See G.H. Vallins, *Good English: How to Write It* 31 (1951). See IRREGULAR VERBS.

C. *Have got* for *have* or *must.* The phrase *have got*—often contracted (as in *I've got*)—has long been criticized as unnecessary for *have*. In fact, though, the phrasing with *got* adds emphasis and is perfectly idiomatic—e.g.:

- "Most pathetic lyrics: The dumbest lyrics *have got* to be 'Whose junkpile or Chevelle is this? You boys come here to race or just kiss?' from '455 Rocket.'" Kathy Mattea, "In Sync," *Richmond Times-Dispatch*, 21 Mar. 1997, at E11.
- "For this offense to work, *he's got* to be able to do more than dump the ball off desperately to his receivers." Michael Wilbon, "Latest Effort Leaves a Lot to Be Desired," *Wash. Post*, 6 Oct. 1997, at C1.
- "That's pretty cool, but as an Ohio boy, *I've got* to go with the Fighting Irish in this one." Michael Beaven, "Sports Sage Knows All and Sees All for Week 1," *Akron Beacon J.*, 27 Aug. 2015, at C1.

The *OED*, under *get* (24), has examples of *have got* from 1876 to 1889. Ruskin is cited. Jespersen adds Disraeli, Dickens, Eliot, Wilde, Shaw, Wells, Trollope. Although the *OED* calls it "colloquial or vulgar," Albert H. Marckwardt and Fred Walcott say (in light of the strong authorial evidence) that it's good literary English. *Facts About Current English Usage* 29 (1938).

LANGUAGE-CHANGE INDEX (For the full key, see front matter pp. xxxi, l–li.)
Stage 1: Rejected. **Stage 2:** Widely shunned. **Stage 3:** Widespread but . . . **Stage 4:** Ubiquitous but . . . **Stage 5:** Fully accepted.
Invariably inferior forms marked by asterisk (*). • Ratios represent frequency of prevalent forms vs. variants in current books.

The main error to watch out for is omitting *have* in either its full or its contracted form. That is, such expressions as **I gotta leave now* and **I got a $10 bill in my billfold* aren't in good use. But *I've got to leave now* and *I've got a $10 bill in my billfold* are good English. Cf. **better** (A).

D. **Passive Voice with** *get.* See PASSIVE VOICE (A).

get rid of. See PHRASAL VERBS.

get the best of; get the better of. Eric Partridge suggested a narrow distinction between these verb phrases: "Properly, the former applies to swindling and other trickery, whereas the latter has no offensive connotation and simply = to overcome, to defeat" (*U&A* at 135). But the *OED* records no such distinction, and today the phrases are used synonymously to mean "to gain the advantage over" or "to prevail against." The older phrase, *get the better of,* dates from the early 18th century and occurs with somewhat greater frequency in modern print sources. *Get the best of* emerged in the 19th century and appears most often in AmE. *Get the best of* is about three times as common in print as the other.

gewgaw /**gyoo**-gaw/ (= a gaudy trinket or flashy bauble) has been predominantly so spelled since the 16th century. The 20th-century variant *geegaw hardly qualifies as even a lexicographic gewgaw.

ghastlily. See ADVERBS (B).

ghetto forms the plural *ghettos,* not *ghettoes—and certainly not the pretentious **ghetti.* See PLURALS (B), (D).

Current ratio (*ghettos* vs. *ghettoes vs. *ghetti): 310:61:1

gibberish. So spelled—not *jibberish (a misspelling that arises from the pronunciation). E.g.: "At best they strove for remote, unrealizable ideals—insofar as their revolutionary *jibberish* [read *gibberish*] could be deciphered at all." Dietrich Fischer-Dieskau, *Reverberations* 326 (Ruth Hein trans., 1989).

LANGUAGE-CHANGE INDEX
gibberish misspelled *jibberish: Stage 1
Current ratio: 98:1

gibbet (= an upright post used to hang executed criminals; a gallows) is pronounced /**jib**-it/, with a soft *g*-.

gibbous (= [1] protuberant, convex, or [2] having or resembling a hump; humpbacked) is most traditionally pronounced /**gib**-əs/, but today the standard pronunciation is /**jib**-əs/.

gibe; jibe; gybe; jive. A. Meanings. This set of words can be hard to keep straight.

Gibe is both noun and verb. As a noun, it means "a caustic remark or taunt"—e.g.: "Irving Lewis . . . personified the faceless civil servants who, for all the *gibes* about pointy-headed bureaucrats, make government work." "The Lives They Lived," *N.Y. Times,* 29 Dec. 1996, § 6, at 13. As a verb, it means "to heckle, mock, or taunt."

Jibe is generally considered a verb only, meaning "to accord with, to be consistent with"—e.g.: "The sight just doesn't *jibe* with the image of her character." Jamie Schilling Fields, "Saintly Bernard," *Texas Monthly,* Jan. 1997, at 52.

Gybe, a sailing term meaning primarily "to shift a sail from one side of a vessel to the other while sailing before the wind," is so spelled in BrE but is usually spelled *jibe* in AmE.

Jive, like *gibe,* is both noun and verb. As a noun, it refers either to swing music or to the argot of hipsters. As a verb, it means "to dance to swing music" or "to tease"—e.g.: "Snipes and Harrelson previously *jived* and juked and ragged their way through 'White Men Can't Jump,' so they're old hands at this." Jeff Simon, "Right on Track," *Buffalo News,* 24 Nov. 1995, at G31.

B. **Jive for jibe.** Some writers misuse *jive* for *jibe*—e.g.:

- "If staying in a dorm doesn't *jive* [read *jibe*] with your requirements for ski accommodations, the Fireside still may suit you." David Gonzales, "Fireside: A Cozy Spot for the Budget Skier," *Dallas Morning News,* 13 Dec. 1992, at G3.
- "The new songs were clamorous and spacey, with distorted hooks and extended feedback that *jived* [read *jibed*] well with the futuristic stage lighting." Sandy Stahl, "Separate Accommodations Prevent Lollapalooza from Coming Together," *Morning Call* (Allentown, Pa.), 5 Aug. 1995, at A53.
- "Former deputy prosecutor Lawrence Taylor . . . believes the district attorney's media-driven loser image doesn't *jive* [read *jibe*] with reality." Bill Blum, "In Defense of the Prosecution," *L.A. Times,* 28 July 1996, Book Rev. §, at 1.

LANGUAGE-CHANGE INDEX
jive misused for *jibe*: Stage 2
Current ratio (*jibe well with* vs. *jive well with*): 9:1

C. **Jibe for gibe.** While *jibe* is a recognized variant spelling of *gibe,* it is not the preferred spelling. And since the words are confusing enough as it is, the alternative spelling should be avoided—e.g.:

- "Chat rooms on the hockey fan website Faceoff.com were filled with *jibes* [read *gibes*] from fans and detractors alike." Eric Beaudan, "Canadian Hockey Up Against the Financial Boards," *Christian Science Monitor,* 13 Jan. 2003, World §, at 5.
- "During football season, he hung a Purdue flag on the rectory that drew good-natured *jibes* [read *gibes*] from the parish's Michigan, Michigan State and Notre Dame alums." David Shepardson, "Parishes Hope Sex Crisis Over," *Detroit News,* 14 Jan. 2003, at C3.
- "Once the game started, players continued to exchange *jibes* [read *gibes*], but that was the extent through the first 20 minutes." Will Parrish, "Eagles Get Key Big South Victory Against Liberty," *Herald* (Rock Hill, S.C.), 17 Jan. 2003, at C1.

LANGUAGE-CHANGE INDEX
jibe misused for *gibe*: Stage 4
Current ratio (*bitter gibes* vs. *bitter jibes): 2:1

D. **Other Mistaken Uses.** While less frequent than the above misuses, other errors do occur. *Jibe* is sometimes mistaken for *jive*—e.g.: "Plug and play. It sounds so 'good to go.' . . . Yet the 'plug and pray' *jibe* [read *jive*], while admittedly tired, exists among engineers for a reason." Leslie Ellis, "Plug and Play: Easy, Right? Ha!" *Multichannel News*, 13 Jan. 2003, at 30. Even less frequent is the misuse of *gibe* for *jibe*, though this error also sometimes occurs—e.g.: " 'The Gift of the Magi' is played out in the broader-than-broad conventions of uninspired children's theater, which doesn't really *gibe* [read *jibe*] with the material." Roy Proctor, " 'Gifts' Appears Fashioned for Non-Existent Audience," *Richmond Times-Dispatch*, 9 Dec. 2002, at E5.

LANGUAGE-CHANGE INDEX
gibe misused for jibe: Stage 1

giblets (= the edible internal organs of a fowl) is preferably pronounced /**jib**-lits/, not /**gib**-lits/.

gift, vb. It may be surprising to learn that English speakers have been using *gift* as a verb since the 16th century. The traditional *gift* that is *gifted* is some innate talent (i.e., a gift from God) or a grant, especially of land, from a sovereign or a noble. That sense lives on, most often in the participial adjective <a gifted pianist> but also in participial phrases—e.g.: "*Gifted* with size, speed and a strong arm, his abilities were apparently lost on recruiters." Will Webber, "St. Pius Standout Headed to Air Force," *Albuquerque J.*, 8 Feb. 2007, Sports §, at 7. (Note that *gifted* is a dangling participle in that sentence: see DANGLERS (C).)

But now *gift* as a verb is on the rise in a more mundane realm—e.g.: "M&M's is looking to be a big presence at this year's Oscar fest. The candymaker already has *gifted* all the nominees in the top acting categories with boxes of personalized M&Ms." Lewis Lazare, "M&M, BBDO Score Oscar Winner," *Chicago Sun-Times*, 8 Feb. 2007, Fin. §, at 49. (Read: *The candymaker has already given all the nominees in the top acting categories boxes of personalized M&Ms.*)

Though old, the usage is not yet standard. Still, English speakers often transform nouns into verbs (see FUNCTIONAL SHIFT (D)) and sometimes revive moribund usages. A century ago, many stylists objected to using *contact* as a verb, though it had been used that way since the early 19th century; few writers feel uncomfortable with the verb today. *Gift* may end up in the same class.

A perceived difference, however, is that we already have a perfectly good verb (*give*) and even a secondary verb for formal contexts (*donate*). The objection to *contact* was only that it made people uncomfortable, but there was no existing equivalent—*get in touch with* being far more cumbersome. Cautious writers may prefer to restrict *gift* to its noun uses for now. We are accustomed to *gifted children*, but not *gifted stock*.

From *gift* as a verb, it was a natural step to *regift* (= to give an unwanted gift to someone else, under

the pretense that it was selected for that person)— e.g.: "Their child received an unwanted Webkinz for a recent birthday—and it's already rewrapped for Christmas *regifting*." Daniel McGinn, "Waving 'Bye to Webkinz?" *Newsweek*, 10 Dec. 2007, at 18.

LANGUAGE-CHANGE INDEX
1. <i>gift</i> for <i>give</i>: Stage 2
2. <i>regift</i>: Stage 4

gigolo. Pl. *gigolos*—neither *gigoloes nor *gigoli. See PLURALS (D).

gild. A. And *guild*. To *gild* a thing is to put a thin layer of gold on it. Misusing *guild* (= an association made up of people with similar occupations or interests) for the verb *gild* is a fairly common error—e.g.:

- "Inside, large parts of the *guilded* [read *gilded*] baroque monastery have been removed to reveal four stone chambers of the original Inca temple." Nathaniel C. Nash, "An Archeologist's Cry: Reclaim Site for Incas!" *N.Y. Times*, 31 Aug. 1993, at A6.
- "It did make perfect sense to have the 'Final Draw' at the Las Vegas convention center and have Dick Clark as the host. But Stevie Wonder? Isn't that *guilding* [read *gilding*] the lily just a bit?" Taylor Buckley, "Did the World Cup Draw Really Need the Vegas Glitz?" *USA Today*, 21 Dec. 1993, at C11.
- "No one is fooled by *guilding* [read *gilding*] the lily." Gene Amole, "A Pox on Shameless Public Radio's Ode to Ploy," *Rocky Mountain News* (Denver), 14 Feb. 2002, at A6.

LANGUAGE-CHANGE INDEX
guild misused for gild: Stage 1
Current ratio (<i>gilded</i> vs. *<i>guilded</i>): 162:1

B. *Gilding the lily*. The phrase *gilding the lily* misquotes its Shakespearean source, which reads, "To gild refined gold, to paint the lily" (*King John* 4.2.11). But because the phrase has become a CLICHÉ, criticizing the misquotation would be as fruitless as complaining about the inaccuracy of "Play it again, Sam" (which is never actually said in the film *Casablanca*—the line is "Play it, Sam").

gimme, a golf term shortened from "give me," refers to a short putt that needn't be holed—usually because playing partners concede that the player would sink it. The plural form, naturally, is *gimmes*. But occasionally the plural is mistakenly written *gimmies—even by those who spell the singular form correctly. This mistake occurs, for example, throughout the following book (even in the title): Jane Blalock & Dawn-Marie Driscoll, *Gimmies* [read *Gimmes*], *Bogeys and Business* (1996).

Gimme is also used outside golf contexts as an adjective for various types of free merchandise, especially baseball caps bearing advertising logos and messages <gimme cap>.

LANGUAGE-CHANGE INDEX
*<i>gimmies</i> for <i>gimmes</i>: Stage 3
Current ratio (<i>gimmes</i> vs. *<i>gimmies</i>): 4:1

LANGUAGE-CHANGE INDEX (For the full key, see front matter pp. xxxi, l–li.)
Stage 1: Rejected. **Stage 2:** Widely shunned. **Stage 3:** Widespread but . . . **Stage 4:** Ubiquitous but . . . **Stage 5:** Fully accepted.
Invariably inferior forms marked by asterisk (*). • Ratios represent frequency of prevalent forms vs. variants in current books.

gimmickry. So spelled—not **gimmickery*.

Current ratio: 69:1

ginkgo /**ging**-koh/ (= a gymnospermous tree indigenous to Asia, with tasty yellow fruit enclosed in a malodorous seed-bearing jacket) is the standard spelling. **Gingko* and **jingko* are variants.

gin out. See **gin up** (B).

gin up /jin əp/. **A. Generally.** *Gin up* (= [1] to rev up (as an engine); or [2] to concoct) is a late-19th-century Americanism that is barely mentioned in the *OED* and appears to have been missed by most American lexicographers (being omitted from most dictionaries). *Gin* here is derived from a clipping of *engine*. The PHRASAL VERB is increasingly common—e.g.:

- "So they *ginned up* a 'law and order' message suggesting that Democrats were soft on crime." David S. Broder, "Mudball Politics," *Wash. Post*, 4 Nov. 1990, at C7.
- "'This is a law enacted by Congress. This is not something we just *ginned up* out of whole cloth.'" Carl Ingram, "Debt-Reduction Bill Could Cost Community Colleges," *L.A. Times*, 21 Dec. 1990, at A3 (quoting Bill Moran, of the U.S. Department of Education).
- "The Phillies organization has been working hard to *gin up* a tide of nostalgia for the last season in 'The Vet,' but it's an impossible sell." "There's Nothing Like the Home Opener to Make Spring a Reality," *Morning Call* (Allentown, Pa.), 4 Apr. 2003, at A14.

B. And *gin out*. This related phrase means "to produce, esp. on a routine basis or in a hurry"—e.g.: "We'll call it the Courthouse Diet Plan, and I'll *gin out* a trade paperback so we can stay on the *New York Times* bestseller list for years and years." Tom Alleman, "Why Are Lawyers So Cranky? They Don't Eat Enough Ribs," *Fulton Co. Daily Rep.* (Ga.), 20 Sept. 2002, at 1. Occasionally, though, it loosely replaces *gin up* in sense 1—e.g.: "Those three hard-working, high-tech liters *gin out* [read *gin up*] 225 horses, good enough to sling you to 60 mph in 6.4 seconds, BMW tells us." Brooks Peterson, "330i Another BMW Winner," *Corpus Christi Caller-Times*, 25 May 2002, at E4.

LANGUAGE-CHANGE INDEX
gin out misused for *gin up*: Stage 1

*gipsy. See **gypsy.**

girl. This word is widely (and understandably) regarded as an affront when used in reference to an adult, just as *boy* is. But for a female minor, *girl* is the appropriate word; for an odd avoidance of the word in its proper context, see ***minor woman.**

girlie; girly; girlish. First having appeared in the late 19th century, *girlie* (= [1] of or like a girl, or [2] featuring naked or scantily clad women) has always been the predominant spelling in AmE and BrE alike. Since about 1990, however, *girly* has inexplicably surged in English-language print sources. Today it closely rivals *girlie*.

With either spelling, the term is likely to be considered a DYSPHEMISM. Those who in sense 1 refer to *girlie behavior, girlie girls,* or *girlie stuff* often do so with condescension—though admittedly, too, sometimes with approbation. Those who in sense 2 refer to *girlie magazines, girlie bars,* and *girlie shows* (the terms are hopelessly old-fashioned) almost invariably do so with disapproval.

Girlish (= of or like a girl) can often carry positive connotations of innocence and artlessness <girlish charm>—though it can also tend in the other direction <girlish emotions>. In this way, the term doesn't quite mirror *boyish*, which is almost invariably positive <boyish enthusiasm> <boyish grin>. This fact doubtless tells us something about cultural views; any discussion of it belongs in a book on sociology, not English usage.

Current ratio (*girlie* vs. *girly*): 1.1:1

gist (= the main point or essential part), pronounced /jist/, is so spelled. The word is sometimes misspelled **jist*—e.g.: "The *jist* [read *gist*] of the opening is: Does Junior's trade to Cincinnati mean Senior will be taking over for McKeon as manager?" John Fay, "Griffey's 1st Day Lasts for 3 Hours," *Cincinnati Enquirer*, 22 Feb. 2000, at D1.

LANGUAGE-CHANGE INDEX
*jist for *gist*: Stage 1
Current ratio (*the gist of* vs. **the jist of*): 357:1

give in to temptation. So written—not **give into temptation*. See PHRASAL VERBS.

Current ratio: 7:1

given. For this word as an acceptable dangling modifier, see DANGLERS (E).

given name. For the meaning of this term, see the discussion at **surname.**

given (that). At the head of a statement (most commonly), *given* is an age-old shorthand way of saying "assuming as a fact" or "with [the thing stated] supplied as a basis for reasoning." If what follows *given* is a mere phrase (without a verb), *given* appears alone—e.g.: "*Given* her high position, she does have opposition." Larry Whitham, "Episcopalians Brace for Divisive Sessions," *Wash. Times*, 13 July 1997, at A4. But if a clause follows (with a verb), a *that* should accompany *given*—e.g.: "*Given that* he was a medical student at Brown before turning to professional hockey, Bill McKay might be expected to be a quick study." Peter Barrouquere, "McKay Learns How to Wing It," *Times-Picayune* (New Orleans), 26 Nov. 1997, at C3. Cf. **provided.**

For more on wrongly omitted *that*s, see **that** (B).

giveth . . . taketh away. This phrasing alludes to the biblical sentence, "The Lord gave, and the Lord hath taken away." Job 1:21 (King James Version). Though variations on this phrase have become cliché, they have a resilient wittiness—e.g.: "For another thing what Subsection (1) *giveth*, Subsection (2) largely *taketh away*: the promise, even if made, will be 'binding' only within narrow limits." Grant Gilmore, *The Death of Contract* 74–75 (1974). Note that *giveth* is a form found 141 times in the King James Version, but not in the quoted verse. See ARCHAISMS.

gizmo (= a gadget) is the preferred spelling. *Gismo is a variant.

Current ratio: 34:1

gladiolus—/gla-dee-**oh**-ləs/ or (pretentiously) /glə-**dɪ**-ə-ləs/—is the singular form. The plural form is *gladioluses* or (predominantly) *gladioli*, the latter pronounced /gla-dee-**oh**-lee/ or /-lɪ/. See PLURALS (B).

But because *gladiolus* is sometimes wrongly taken to be a plural, especially in speech, the mistaken BACK-FORMATION *gladiola has emerged. It is an arrant mistake that should be stamped out. E.g.:

- "A *gladiola* [read *gladiolus*] among a patch of violets, her spirit shines all the more brightly against the backdrop of her restrictive society." Mary McCarty, "The Real Little Women," *Dayton Daily News*, 1 Jan. 1995, at C1.
- "Minutes later they crowd into Celsa Garcia's house, delivering their figures of Joseph and Mary to a makeshift corner altar that Ms. Garcia, 65, has draped with garlands of *gladiolas* [read *gladioli*] and pine." Sam Dillon, "Tehuixtla Journal," *N.Y. Times*, 25 Dec. 1996, at A4.
- "Anyone at the fair at 11 a.m. Thursday, Sept. 3, can join the new *gladiola* [read *gladiolus*] competition in the Horticulture Building. Fairgoers can try to make a *gladiola* [read *gladiolus*] arrangement in 10 minutes." Debra J. Groom, "State Fair Gears Up," *Advance-News* (Ogdensburg, N.Y.), 23 Aug. 2015, at 7.

LANGUAGE-CHANGE INDEX
1. *gladiola for *gladiolus* as a singular: Stage 2
Current ratio (*gladiolus* vs. *gladiola): 6:1
2. *gladiolas for *gladioli* as a plural: Stage 3
Current ratio (*gladioli* vs. *gladiolas vs. *gladioluses*): 31:10:1

glamour. So spelled, even in AmE. But the related words *glamorize* and *glamorous* change the *-our-* to *-or-*. See -OR. Cf. **squalor.**

glance; glimpse. The traditional idioms are that one *takes* or *gives a glance* but *gets a glimpse*. But these idioms are occasionally confounded—e.g.:

- "Members of a Polk County School Board steering committee *took a first glimpse Tuesday at* [read *got a first glimpse Tuesday of* or *took a first glance Tuesday at*] the report that could become the district's landmark school improvement plan." Janet Marshall, "School Improvement Plan Shown," *Ledger* (Lakeland, Fla.), 5 June 1996, at B1.
- "He shook his head as he *got his first glance at* [read *got his first glimpse of* or *took his first glance at*] the stat sheet." Mike DeCourcy, "Tigers Earn Sloppy Win," *Commercial Appeal* (Memphis), 3 Dec. 1996, at D1.

LANGUAGE-CHANGE INDEX
1. *glimpse* misused for *glance*: Stage 1
2. *glance* misused for *glimpse*: Stage 1

glassful. Pl. *glassfuls.* See PLURALS (D).

glean (= to gather [esp. information or, orig., crops left over after a harvest]) is occasionally confounded with *gleam* (= to shine)—e.g.: "A social worker visits new patients to *gleam* [read *glean*] information about their social and financial resources." Editorial, "The Graying of Texas," *Dallas Morning News*, 30 Dec. 1999, at A24.

LANGUAGE-CHANGE INDEX
gleam misused for *glean*: Stage 1

glimpse. See **glance.**

glitter; *glister; glisten. *Glitter*, dating from the 14th century, derives from the Middle English *gliteren*. It has four senses: (1) to sparkle; to reflect many small flashes of light <the sequins glittered>; (2) to flash positive emotions <when praised, the children glittered>; (3) to be spectacularly attractive <at the party, the couple glittered>; and (4) to be superficially attractive or exciting; to flash <those arguments may glitter, but there's little substance to them>.

*Glister is related to *glitter*, having arisen from the same root, with the same meaning, and at the same time. It is now an archaic or dialectal form of *glitter* (in sense 1) <all is not gold that glisters>.

Glisten is the oldest term; the OED cites its use in a poem written about 1000. To *glisten* is to "produce a lustrous shine or sparkle like light on water" <the wood's polish is so brilliant it glistens> <moonlight glistening on snow>. In modern usage, *glisten* most often occurs in allusions to moisture in some form <her eyes glistened with unshed tears>.

glue, vb., preferably makes *gluing*, not *glueing. E.g.: "Teams start out with easier actions such as painting graffiti, *glueing* [read *gluing*] locks and breaking windows." Rebecca Merritt & Steve Lundgren, "A Guerrilla War for Animal Rights," *Bulletin* (Bend, Or.), 3 Aug. 1997, at B1. See MUTE E.

Current ratio: 17:1

gnaw > gnawed > gnawed. The form *gnawn is an archaic past participle—e.g.: "In the end Kent scored 250, which, on a comfortable pitch, more or less guaranteed *gnawn* [read *gnawed*] umbrellas." Christopher Martin-Jenkins, "Benson and Hedges Cup," *Daily Telegraph*, 31 May 1995, at 34. See IRREGULAR VERBS (B).

LANGUAGE-CHANGE INDEX
gnawn used for the past participle *gnawed*: Stage 1
Current ratio (*had gnawed* vs. *had gnawn): 169:1

go. A. Inflection: *go > went > gone.* To use *went* as a straight-faced past participle is to engage in low DIALECT that isn't appropriate even for the sports pages—e.g.:

LANGUAGE-CHANGE INDEX (For the full key, see front matter pp. xxxi, l–li.)
Stage 1: Rejected. **Stage 2:** Widely shunned. **Stage 3:** Widespread but . . . **Stage 4:** Ubiquitous but . . . **Stage 5:** Fully accepted.
Invariably inferior forms marked by asterisk (*). • Ratios represent frequency of prevalent forms vs. variants in current books.

- "Larry Jackson has *went* [read *gone*] beyond expectations." Jerry Reigle, "Feature Winners' List Longer This Season," *Harrisburg Patriot*, 4 Apr. 1996, at D5.
- "Since last Saturday, he has *went* [read *gone*] 12-for-31 (.387) in nine games." "Clearing the Bases," *Wis. State J.*, 23 Aug. 1998, at D4.
- "The North Heincke Road First Church of God has *went* [read *gone*] through 5 pastors and 2 building expansions since it opened in 1923." Pam Dillon, "Miamisburg Church Celebrates 75 Years of Service," *Dayton Daily News*, 10 Oct. 1998, at C6.

See IRREGULAR VERBS.

LANGUAGE-CHANGE INDEX
went misused for *gone*: Stage 1
Current ratio (*had gone* vs. **had went*): 358:1

B. Meaning "say." The use of *go* as a synonym for *say* is seemingly part of every American teenager's vocabulary ("So I go, 'Whattaya mean?' and he goes, 'Whattaya mean by askin' that?'"). It occurs in the past tense also: "Then he *went*, like, 'No way!'" This is low-level SLANG. Cf. BE-VERBS (C) & **like** (E).

LANGUAGE-CHANGE INDEX
go in the sense "say": Stage 4

goatherd; *goatherder. *Goatherd* (= someone who tends goats) is the standard form, parallel in form to *shepherd*—e.g.: "Legend has it that the coffee bean was 'discovered' centuries ago when a *goatherd* in Abyssinia (modern-day Ethiopia) stumbled upon his animals cavorting in an unusually energetic manner." "The World (Coffee) Cup," *Wash. Post*, 28 Feb. 2003, at T31. The NEEDLESS VARIANT **goatherder*, though not recorded in most dictionaries, makes occasional stray appearances—e.g.: "Claude Campbell . . . takes readers into the Gaza strip, places us in a Palestinian *goatherder's* [read *goatherd's*] tent and makes it as believable a place as your neighbor's kitchen." Pat MacEnulty, "Jewish Angel Counsels a Palestinian," *Sun-Sentinel* (Ft. Lauderdale), 3 Mar. 2002, at D10.

LANGUAGE-CHANGE INDEX
*goatherder for *goatherd*: Stage 1
Current ratio (*goatherd* vs. **goatherder*): 34:1

gobbledygook; gobbledegook. Maury Maverick's original spelling was *gobbledygook*, and today that spelling outnumbers its variant form by a ratio of about 7 to 1 in AmE. Yet since the early 1990s, *gobbledegook* has been the predominant form in BrE print sources—but barely. Nevertheless, most American and British dictionaries list *gobbledygook* first.

The term refers to the obscure language characteristic of jargonmongering bureaucrats. Thus *iterative naturalistic inquiry methodology* supposedly refers to a series of interviews. Much technical writing is open to the criticism of being gobbledygook. One of the purposes of this book is to wage a battle against it. See ABSTRACTITIS, JARGON, LATINISMS, LEGALESE, OBSCURITY & PLAIN LANGUAGE.

goddamned; goddamn, adj.; **goddam.** Strictly speaking, the first form is the only correct one. Yet because

of the way this word is spoken—the final *-d* usually being silent—the latter two spellings commonly appear in print. In terms of word frequency in print, *goddamn* is by far the most common, followed by *goddamned*, and then *goddam*. The more loosely spelled forms make the expletive seem less literal, and therefore somewhat less offensive—e.g.:

- "'Hated those *goddam* meetings,' she says." Karen Schoemer et al., "Rockers, Models and the New Allure of Heroin," *Newsweek*, 26 Aug. 1996, at 50.
- "Rostenkowski said in a recent interview: 'Lyndon Johnson was in Texas, and he called me. "*Goddamn* you," he said. "Take that . . . get up there . . . tell Carl Albert." Oh, he was mad.'" John A. Farrell, "'68 Convention Unrest Boosted O'Neill's House Rise," *Boston Globe*, 1 Sept. 1996, at A15.
- "'He never misses a day,' said Robert Beaudoin. 'With that small boat, he'll be out no matter what the *goddam* weather is.'" Peter Pochna, "Lobsterman's Creed: Keep It Simple," *Portland Press Herald*, 2 Sept. 1996, at C1.
- "Then someone handed me a metal pole with a glowing jellyfish perched at the top. I was now the Jellyfish King. I danced around with the jellyfish and poked the air with it until my arms got tired and I scoured feverishly for someone to pass the jellyfish to. Will someone please take this *goddamn* jellyfish?" Andrew Magary, "My Morning Ravers," *GQ*, 1 Aug. 2015, at 48.

See **damn.**

godlily. See ADVERBS (B).

-goer. This combining form attaches to many nouns denoting places or events without the need of a hyphen, resulting in words such as *beachgoer, concertgoer, moviegoer, museumgoer, partygoer, seagoer*. The no-hyphen rule was adopted by the *AP Stylebook* in 2014.

goes without saying, it. This phrase isn't generally suitable for formal contexts, although it may be appropriate in speech or in informal prose. Often, an editor is justified in thinking that if it really goes without saying, then it need not be said.

Goethe /gə[r]-tə/. "Americans who pronounce Goethe's name 'Go-eeth' are not always poor, ignorant clodhoppers in need of pity." Edward N. Teall, *Putting Words to Work* 19 (1940). Oh, no?

*go fetch. See **fetch.**

golf. One may either *play golf* (the phrase dates from ca. 1575) or simply *golf* (ca. 1800)—that is, *golf* can be a verb as well as a noun. Most golfers use the older phrasing and say that they *play golf* <I'll be playing golf on Saturday>, whereas nowadays nongolfers tend to be the ones who use *golf* as a verb <she'll be golfing on Saturday>. In modern print sources, *played golf* is 20 times as common as *golfed*.

Writers on golf often disparage the verb *golf* as symptomatic of linguistic dufferdom—e.g.:

- One writer states: "If you call yourself a golfer, you never use *golf* as a verb. You never say 'We went *golfing*'. *Golf* to a golfer is a noun. A guy tells you he '*golfs*,' and you know he's clueless." David Burgin, "A True Olympian's Golden Review," *S.F. Examiner*, 14 June 1998, at D18.

- Another refers mockingly to "the unwashed who think the word *golf* and its derivatives can be used as verbs ('Hey, Ralph, ya wanna go *golfing* tomorrow?' 'Nah, Jim, I *golfed* yesterday')." David Climer, "Senior Tour Isn't Aging Very Nicely," *Tennessean*, 20 July 1999, at C1.
- A third says that "using *golf* as a verb [is] a linguistic gaffe akin to shortening San Francisco to Frisco." Bill Ott, "Blue Fairways," *Booklist*, 1 Sept. 1999, at 63.

See FUNCTIONAL SHIFT (D).

If you're serious about golf and writing, stick to the noun uses of *golf*. That will never tee off anyone.

The *-l-* is pronounced in this word, preferably: /gahlf/ or /gawlf/—not /gahf/ or /gawf/.

go missing (= to disappear, become lost) is a Briticism that has encountered an odd mix of resistance and acceptance in AmE. Still, it seems to be on an irreversible ascent—e.g.: "In Fort Worth last June, bronze memory urns disappeared from graveyards. The following month, at a high school football field in Washington, D.C., 750 pounds of aluminum bleachers *went missing*." Telis Demos, "The Dark Side of Metal Madness," *Forbes*, 9 July 2007, at 32.

The phrase, now recorded in *W11* and *NOAD*, chafes many Americans. Some object to the notion of voluntariness that *go* suggests (did the bleachers in the example above run away and hide?). They incorrectly assume that the idiom suggests voluntary absence and should therefore be restricted to uses such as desertion or going AWOL. Others believe it to be ungrammatical.

But many usage pros defend it—e.g.:

- "Why has this construction lasted so long and now blossomed? It does a semantic job that needs doing, that's why. No other term quite encapsulates 'to become lost inexplicably and unexpectedly,' which connotes suspicion of trouble. From the most serious loss (a person kidnapped, or a soldier unaccounted for or absent without leave) to an irritating minor loss (an object is mislaid), to *go missing*—always in the past tense, *went*, or past participle, *gone*—conveys a worried, nonspecific meaning that no other word or phrase quite does." William Safire, "Gone Missing," *N.Y. Times*, 27 June 2004, § 6, at 21.
- "People ask me over and over again about certain things. For instance, where did '*gone missing*' come from? England. Is it a blight on our language? I don't think so." Barbara Wallraff, "Get Original, Brief, Lively Comments in Print," *Times Union* (Albany), 27 Nov. 2005, at G2.
- "Why have Americans . . . shunned *gone missing*? It's neither unclear nor ungrammatical (if you can *go bankrupt*, why not *go missing*?), and action-verb boosters should be applauding it as stronger than *is missing*. Anti-British prejudice can't explain the animus; even people who don't know its pedigree heap scorn on *gone missing*." Jan Freeman, "Missing in Action," *Boston Globe*, 19 Nov. 2006, at E3.

Although the phrase has been traced to the late 19th century, it spread primarily in World War I with reports of British air and sea missions when planes or ships didn't return. It began its spike in AmE usage in the mid-1990s, especially in missing-persons reports—e.g.:

- "Authorities in Oregon are searching for a Garden Grove Jesuit priest and his traveling companion, who may have *gone missing* as long as two weeks ago during a tour of the Pacific Northwest." Christian Berthelsen, "Garden Grove Priest and Friend Reported Missing," *L.A. Times*, 22 June 2007, at B1.
- "One of the actor's friends has *gone missing*, and it seems an easy enough matter for her to look into. Of course, that's before people start dying, putting Wiggins herself in jeopardy." David J. Montgomery, "Mysteries," *Chicago Sun-Times*, 24 June 2007, Books §, at B9.
- "Melodie Rowe was a quiet 17-year-old when she *went missing* from her Syracuse, N.Y., home in September 1972." Richard Willing, "New Scientific Progress Makes Identifying Remains Easier," *USA Today*, 25 June 2007, at A2.

gondola (= a long narrow boat with a flat bottom and high points on each end, traditionally used in Venetian canals) is pronounced /**gon**-də-lə/—not /gon-**doh**-lə/.

good, adv. "You did good." "Yeah, I played good tonight. Practice is coming along real good."

These *good*s would once have been considered clearly nonstandard, even substandard. They're typical of DIALECT, the adverb being *well*—not *good*. But in a few SET PHRASES, the adverbial *good* cannot be replaced; among these are *did it but good* and *a good many more*.

Although adverbial uses appear frequently in print, they are almost always in reported speech—e.g.:

- "The coyote ran up and tried again to bite Hawthorne. 'I kicked him *good*,' and the animal ran back in the woods." Rex Springston, "New Kent Man Battles Coyote 'Tooth and Nail,'" *Richmond Times-Dispatch*, 28 Jan. 2003, at A1.
- "'We came out, threw the ball up the court *good*, passed *good*, looked for the open man,' [coach Wayne] Berry said." "Calais, MA Lynx in Split," *Bangor Daily News*, 29 Jan. 2003, at C4.
- "'[Larry] Dixon ran so *good* last year, it was unbelievable,' [Tony] Schumacher said." "May the Force Be Withered?" *Daily News* (L.A.), 6 Feb. 2003, at S9.

While the adverbial *good* is rare in edited prose, it has become almost universal in sports, even when the speaker obviously knows the right word—e.g.: "St. Joe's coach Mark Simon, who had to laugh a little and shook his head as he reviewed the Wolverines, [said]: 'They shot the ball very *good*, they passed the ball inside very *well*.'" Keith McShea, "Falls Crushes St. Joe's with Third-Quarter Blitz," *Buffalo News*, 29 Jan. 2003, at C3.

Of course, *real good* (a common dialectal phrase) may also occur in STANDARD ENGLISH if *good* is a noun, as here: "'I believe in what we do, especially in

LANGUAGE-CHANGE INDEX (For the full key, see front matter pp. xxxi, l–li.)
Stage 1: Rejected. **Stage 2:** Widely shunned. **Stage 3:** Widespread but . . . **Stage 4:** Ubiquitous but . . . **Stage 5:** Fully accepted.
Invariably inferior forms marked by asterisk (*). • Ratios represent frequency of prevalent forms vs. variants in current books.

civil affairs. No one is in a better position to do real *good*," [Sgt. Anna] Grogan said." Amy Joyner, "A Mission to Heal," *News & Record* (Greensboro), 10 Feb. 2003, at A1.

LANGUAGE-CHANGE INDEX
1. *good* for *well* (as an adverb) in reference to personal performance (as in **the team played good*): Stage 2
Current ratio (*played well* vs. **played good*): 11:1
2. *good* for *well* (as an adverb) in reference to the functioning of inanimate things (as in **the engine runs good*): Stage 3
Current ratio (*runs well* vs. **runs good*): 8:1

goodbye; good-bye; good-by; *goodby. Each of the first three is listed as the main headword in at least one major American dictionary. But *goodbye* is by far the most usual form, since the hyphen seems almost as archaic here as in **to-day* and **to-morrow*. And it has the advantage of resembling the related terms *bye* and *bye-bye*. The final headword—**goodby*—is merely a variant.

Current ratio (in order of headwords): 69:51:9:1

good(-)faith. *Good faith* is the noun phrase <in good faith>, *good-faith* the PHRASAL ADJECTIVE <good-faith efforts>. See **bona fide** & ***bona fides.***

goodness' sake. So written. See POSSESSIVES (N).

goodwill. Formerly two words, then hyphenated, the term has now become one word both as an adjective <a goodwill gesture> and as a noun <a symbol of our goodwill>.

Google. Because *Google* is a proper noun and trademark denoting the company that so successfully launched its Internet search engine in 1998, dictionaries don't generally list the noun. But within a few years of the company's founding, the verb *google* came to prominence in the sense "to look (something) up on the Internet using the Google search engine." The term has spun off such derivatives as *googleable* (= having a significant presence on the Internet) and *google-ganger* (= someone having the same name as oneself and therefore showing up in search results when one googles oneself). A variant term for the latter is *dopplegoogler*—which, like *googleganger*, is modeled on the German word *doppelgänger* (= someone who bears a striking resemblance to someone else).

Even the verb is more often capitalized than not.

goose bumps; gooseflesh; goose pimples; goose skin. All four terms refer to the skin condition brought on by fear, exhilaration, or cold, and marked by bumps located at hair follicles, especially on the forearms. *Goose bumps* (often written *goosebumps*) is the newest term, dating only from the 1930s. Yet today, in both AmE and BrE, it appears much more often in print sources than *goose pimples*, which dates from the late 19th century. In BrE, the older *gooseflesh* (early 19th century) and *goose skin* (mid-17th century) are still common as well. In medical circles, the condition is called *horripilation* (essentially, "hair standing on end") or, less commonly, *piloerection*.

Current ratio (in order of headwords): 126:33:15:1

goosey (= [1] of, relating to, or resembling a goose; [2] foolish; or [3] hypersensitive to being prodded or startled) is the standard spelling. **Goosy* is a variant. *Loosey-goosey* is a low CASUALISM meaning "relaxed" (as in "loose as a goose") or, in describing machinery, "rattletrap."

GOP. A. Generally. This abbreviation, short for *Grand Old Party* (= the Republican Party), may be doomed. In late 2002, the editors at *The Wall Street Journal* and at several other newspapers decided to drop it from all copy, including headlines, on grounds that not everyone knows what it stands for. See William Safire, "On Language," *N.Y. Times*, 15 Dec. 2002, at 48. Safire objected, pointing out that he knows what a DVD is but doesn't know what the letters stand for. *Ibid.* (See **DVD.**) Part of the problem, it seems, is that while *Republican Party* has the short form *GOP*, *Democratic Party* has no equivalent short form. (That's a quirk of language.) Also, some editors believe that abbreviations should be explained with the full phrase on first use, and they rebel at writing out "Grand Old Party" in each piece in which the phrase appears. If the abbreviation falls into disuse, it will dwindle very gradually. The 2002 editorial decision may ultimately be registered as a temporary blip in the history of the term, as editors retreat from a hasty decision because headlines and quotations make the abbreviation unavoidable. Then again, the decision may signal the onset of moribundity.

B. Redundancy. When coupled with *party*, *GOP* creates an odd REDUNDANCY. **GOP party* represents **Grand Old Party party*. Either drop *party* or change *GOP* to *Republican*—e.g.:

- " 'We're playing ball,' said *GOP party* [read *GOP*] chairman Richard S. Williamson." Lynn Sweet, "Bush Plans Major Illinois Ad Blitz," *Chicago Sun-Times*, 27 Oct. 2000, at 4.
- "In those cases, local Democrats are seeking to have tossed out thousands of absentee ballots because of alleged mishandling of the ballot applications by *GOP party* [read *GOP*] workers." Bob Davis & Phil Kuntz, "Gore Comments Unnerve Certain Democrats," *Wall Street J.*, 6 Dec. 2000, at A12.
- "The *GOP party* [read *GOP*] leaders . . . then learned how to apply for a job in the prospective Bush administration." Tyler Whitley, "Republicans Cheer Halt in Fla. Recount," *Richmond Times-Dispatch*, 10 Dec. 2000, at C1.

LANGUAGE-CHANGE INDEX
*GOP Party for *GOP*: Stage 2

*gormand. See **gourmet.**

gossip, vb., makes *gossiped* and *gossiping* in both AmE and BrE. See SPELLING (B).

got, p.pl.; **gotten.** See **get (B).**

gotten. See **get.**

gourmet; gourmand; epicure. As a noun, *gourmet* now means "a connoisseur of food and drink," although it originally referred more specifically to a connoisseur of wine. *Gourmet* (/goor-**may**/ or /**goor**-may/) shares with *gourmand* (/goor-**mahnd**/ or /**goor**-mahnd/) the basic sense "someone who loves good food and drink," but their connotations have come to be markedly different. A *gourmet* knows well and appreciates the finer points of food and drink. A *gourmand*, on the other hand, is commonly understood to be a glutton for food and drink. An *epicure* (/**ep**-i-kyoor/) is essentially the same as a gourmet, though perhaps with a touch of overrefinement. Epicureanism is a philosophy concerned with personal happiness and freedom from pain.

The pejorative sense for *gourmand* has been the source of some confusion because the corresponding GALLICISM, *gourmandise* (/goor-mən-**deez**/), means "gastronomic expertise; an appreciation of fine cuisine." The negative connotations of *gourmand* and the positive connotations of *gourmet* were once decried by those who want *gourmand* to correspond to *gourmandise*:

> The word [*gourmet*] first began to take on its improper sense in the last decade of the 18th century, a time when certain noble lords, not to mention the nouveaux riches (who are always with us), were quite ignorant of true gastronomy . . . . But it was not till well on in the 19th century that this word was applied to the *gastronome*, or connoisseur of the table. Then the stupid, pretentious, and ill-mannered new rich of the Second Empire (1851–1870) began to feel squeamish over the shameful word *gourmand*, and soon it was replaced, among these ridiculous snobs, by *gourmet* . . . . Let us not fear *gourmand*. It has only one meaning. *La gourmandise* is and always has been celebrated as a virtue among the kind of sensitive people who despise gluttony as they do drunkenness.
>
> M. des Ombiaux, as quoted in Donald Moffat, "Gourmet or Gourmand?" *Atlantic Monthly*, Apr. 1956, at 90, 91.

But the gourmand is no longer such a celebrated figure. The "ridiculous snobs" of the mid-19th century held sway, the curious result being that *gourmand* no longer corresponds to *gourmandise*. (*Gormand is a variant spelling formerly common.)

The word *gourmet* is also used—and perhaps overused—as an adjective meaning "of, involving, or serving fine or exotic food" <a trendy gourmet restaurant>. With *gourmet chocolates on the pillow* and *gourmet pasta and sauce sets*, the word has been devalued to the point that it merely describes food with pretensions.

governance. In 1926, H.W. Fowler pronounced *governance* an ARCHAISM for which either *government* or *control* suffices, allowing it only in "rhetorical or solemn contexts" (*FMEU1* at 220). The word was simply in a prolonged lull. In the 1960s, it was awakened in AmE and by the 1990s had become something

of a VOGUE WORD throughout the English-speaking world. In legal contexts, it frequently refers to running or governing a corporation—e.g.: "Pierre-Henri Leroy [is] founder of Proxinvest, which advises companies on French corporate *governance* issues." "French Drug Stocks Soar as Elf Proposes Alliance," *N.Y. Times*, 20 Dec. 1996, at D4.

governing (= regulating, controlling) is sometimes mistakenly written *governoring*—e.g.:

- "The regents, historically a coordinating board rather than *governoring* [read *governing*] board, were given the power to cut only funding, not actual programs." John Funk, "Regents' Cutbacks Hit Humanities," *Plain Dealer* (Cleveland), 10 June 1996, at B1.
- "Cigars have become a major concern as they are becoming a status symbol and need to have the same tight laws *governoring* [read *governing*] them as cigarettes, he said." Tom Ernst, "Clergyman Sees Place for Church in Anti-Smoking Campaign," *Buffalo News*, 5 Jan. 1997, at C6.
- "Glenda Kendrick, a spokeswoman for Justice's Office of Justice Programs, said each of the department's grant programs has different rules *governoring* [read *governing*] how states may use the money." Craig Whitlock & Lori Montgomery, "Md. Agency's Use of Grants Investigated," *Wash. Post*, 13 Aug. 2002, at B1.

Though rare, *governoring* does have its use in denoting an automotive device that limits a vehicle's speed (its *governor*)—e.g.: "The factory sets its top speed at 130 miles per hour and warns drivers to call if the *governoring* system breaks." Royal Ford, "2000 Audi TT: A Smooth, Sultry Scamperer," *Boston Globe*, 23 May 1999, at F1.

LANGUAGE-CHANGE INDEX
governoring misused for *governing*: Stage 1

government is preferably pronounced with the -*n*- distinctly in the second syllable: /**gǝv**-ǝrn-mǝnt/. According to the pronunciation expert Charles Harrington Elster, it is "one of a number of words that careful speakers are particularly diligent about pronouncing precisely. . . . How you say it is an indication of whether you are an average educated speaker or a cultivated one." *BBBM* at 229. Robert W. Burchfield, the *OED* chief editor and BBC consultant, said that *government* belongs "to a small group of words that [give] a maximum of offence to listeners if pronounced in a garbled manner, with the first *n* silent." *FMEU3* at 339.

governmental; government, adj. Increasingly today, the noun *government* is used attributively—that is, in an adjectival function <government rules and regulations>. In only a few phrases is *governmental* the more frequently encountered adjective, examples being *governmental authority* and *governmental organization*. On the whole, though, the longer form appears to be in retreat. The choice seems to do not with whether

LANGUAGE-CHANGE INDEX (For the full key, see front matter pp. xxxi, l–li.)
Stage 1: Rejected. **Stage 2:** Widely shunned. **Stage 3:** Widespread but . . . **Stage 4:** Ubiquitous but . . . **Stage 5:** Fully accepted.
Invariably inferior forms marked by asterisk (*). • Ratios represent frequency of prevalent forms vs. variants in current books.

a vowel follows the word, since *government agency* predominates over *governmental agency* in AmE and BrE alike, but rather with meter. Over time, the longer form may well look and sound more and more archaic.

GOVERNMENTAL FORMS. The English language abounds in words denoting almost every conceivable form of government, usually ending in either *-cracy* or *-archy*. What follows is only a sampling of the scores of familiar and arcane terms:

androcracy	=	government by men
autocracy	=	government by a single person
bureaucracy	=	government by administrative bureaus
democracy	=	government by the people
dyarchy	=	government by two rulers
ergatocracy	=	government by workers
gerontocracy	=	government by the elderly
gynecocracy	=	government by women
hagiocracy	=	government by saints
juvenocracy	=	government by youth
kakistocracy	=	government by a country's worst citizens
kleptocracy	=	government by thieves
meritocracy	=	government by those who have the most merit
monarchy	=	government by a king or queen
ochlocracy	=	government by the mob (also termed *mobocracy*, a HYBRID)
oligarchy	=	government by a small group of people
pantisocracy	=	government by all people equally (in a utopia)
plutocracy	=	government by the wealthy
polyarchy	=	government by many people
stratocracy	=	government by the military
technocracy	=	government by technicians
theocracy	=	government by religious leaders

Bureaucracy, of course, does not refer only to government by administrative bureaus. More commonly, it denotes inaccessible and inefficient government characterized by red tape. See BUREAUCRATESE.

governor-general (= a governor of high rank; esp., the chief representative of the British Crown in a Commonwealth country) has always predominantly formed the plural *governors-general*, not **governor-generals*.

Current ratio: 4:1

gracile (/gras-əl/) = slender, physically slight <gracile vines> <long, gracile fingers>. The word is sometimes misused for *graceful*—e.g.: "The Adagio has all the pretty, *gracile* [read *graceful*] wit you expect from Mozart." Stephen Brookes, "Music," *Wash. Post*, 11 May 2006, at C9. Sometimes the meaning is doubtful—e.g.: "The exhibition includes many works by well-known artists—a *gracile* [read *small*? *graceful*?] drawing of a dancer before a mirror by Henri Matisse." Margaret Moorman, "Best of a Decade and Whimsical Works," *Newsday* (N.Y.), 21 Dec. 1990, § II, at 85.

LANGUAGE-CHANGE INDEX
gracile misused for *graceful*: Stage 1

gracious (= kind and polite) is sometimes misused for *grateful* (= thankful). Common in speech (and reported speech), the error occurs less commonly in written work. But it does appear—e.g.:

- "He is *gracious* [read *grateful*] for all the newfound attention, even if it catches him a bit off-guard." Adam Mertz, "FitzRandolph Mulls," *Wis. State J.*, 20 Mar. 2002, at A1.
- "She was very *gracious* [read *grateful*] for the love and support of her family." "Marlyn R. Riffey" (obit.), *Patriot-News* (Harrisburg), 4 Aug. 2002, at B8.

President George W. Bush was quoted as making this gaffe in 2001: "I'm so thankful, and so *gracious*—I'm *gracious* [read *grateful* times two] that my brother Jeb is concerned about the hemisphere as well." As quoted in "Weather in Florida Can Play Tricks on Your Mind," *Chicago Sun-Times*, 14 June 2001, at 38. See **grateful.**

LANGUAGE-CHANGE INDEX
gracious misused for *grateful*: Stage 1

graduate, vb. The traditional idiom (dating from the 16th century) was that the school *graduated* the student or the student *was graduated* from the school. By extension (during the 19th century), a student was said to *graduate* from the school. (See ERGATIVE VERBS.) Those two uses of the verb are standard, as Teall explained in the mid-20th century: " 'Graduate' may be a transitive or an intransitive verb. To be graduated is to be admitted to a scholastic standing or an academic degree; to graduate is to pass the final examinations, be dismissed with honor, take the degree. Many teachers ride the 'was graduated' hobby, but common usage, good literary practice and dictionary sanction may all be lined up on the side of the active [intransitive] form, 'to graduate.' " Edward N. Teall, *Putting Words to Work* 280 (1940).

Today the old-fashioned *was graduated* is most common in wedding announcements and obituaries—e.g.:

- "Born and raised in Philadelphia, she *was graduated from* the University of Pennsylvania in 1974." Paul M. Rodriguez, "Thankless Task," *Insight Mag.*, 21 May 2001, at 10.
- "He *was graduated from* Moberly High School in 1949." "Wheeler, Ronald Eugene" (obit.), *Roanoke Times*, 24 May 2001, at B2.
- "The bride-elect . . . *was graduated from* Archmere Academy in Claymont, Del." "Elizardi/Gragg," *Times-Picayune* (New Orleans), 26 May 2001, at 3. (On the use of *bride-elect*, see **bride-to-be.**)

In the mid-20th century, usage began to shift further toward an even shorter transitive form: students were said to **graduate college* (omitting the *from* after *graduate*). This poor wording is increasingly common—e.g.:

- "Today three quarters of boys and half of girls have had sex by the time they *graduate* [read *graduate from*] high school." Michele Ingrassia, "Virgin Cool," *Newsweek*, 17 Oct. 1994, at 59, 60.
- "None of the brothers *graduated* [read *graduated from*] college." Bruce Upbin, "Scholars of Shelf Space," *Forbes*, 21 Oct. 1996, at 210.
- " 'I have a reading disorder,' Leschuk says, yet he struggles to think of any friends who *graduated* [read *graduated from*] college who are doing as well." Del Jones, "Diplomas Decline as Degrees of Separation in the Workforce," *USA Today*, 3 Jan. 1997, at B1.

You may be happy to learn, however, that the collocation *graduated from college* remains much more common in modern print sources than *graduated college*. That ratio is bound to shrink over time.

LANGUAGE-CHANGE INDEX
1. *graduate* as an intransitive verb (as in *he graduated from college*): Stage 5
2. *graduate* as a transitive verb (as in **he graduated college*): Stage 3
Current ratio (*he graduated from college* vs. **he graduated college* vs. *he was graduated from college*): 29:3:1

graffiti. *W11* notes that this plural, originally Italian, "is sometimes used with a singular verb as a mass noun <the *graffiti* is being covered with fresh paint . . .>." This shift has largely taken place since the late 1980s. (Cf. **data**.) Yet one still sees it being used as a plural— e.g.: "During the past year *graffiti* have begun to appear in cities." Lara Marlowe, "Revolutionary Disintegration," *Time*, 26 June 1995, at 42, 43. See PLURALS (J).

Sometimes one sees *graffito* when the sense is undeniably singular and the mass noun would be inappropriate—e.g.:

- "The young Indian submerged in the menacing urban emptiness of a London ghetto where the least offensive *graffito* says 'Go Home to Pakistan.'" Julian Symons, "The Three Faces of Ruth Rendell," *Wash. Post*, 18 Oct. 1987, Book World §, at 9.
- "Tommaso adds a peace symbol to his completed *graffito*." John McPhee, "Season on the Chalk," *New Yorker*, 12 Mar. 2007, at 58.
- "Troops in Qurah, Iraq, rest under a *graffito* left by insurgents." *Time*, 16 Apr. 2007, at 28 (photo caption).

See COUNT NOUNS AND MASS NOUNS.

LANGUAGE-CHANGE INDEX
graffiti as a singular mass noun: Stage 5
Current ratio (*the graffiti was* vs. *the graffiti were*): 3:1

*grainary; *grainery. See **granary**.

grammar is often misspelled **grammer*—e.g.: "Writing Center tutors go through extensive training before being assigned to students. They complete notebooks on how to tutor and meet weekly to role-play, hear guest lecturers, complete *grammer* [read *grammar*] exercises and look at their own writing." "Center Has the Write Stuff for Students," *Boston Herald*, 11 Aug. 2002, Mag. §, at M2. See SPELLING (A).

LANGUAGE-CHANGE INDEX
grammar misspelled **grammer*: Stage 1
Current ratio: 559:1

GRAMMATICAL AGREEMENT. See CONCORD & SUBJECT–VERB AGREEMENT.

grammatical error. Because *grammatical* may mean either (1) "relating to grammar" <grammatical subject> or (2) "consistent with grammar" <a grammatical sentence>, there is nothing wrong with the age-old phrase *grammatical error* (sense 1). It's as acceptable as the phrases *criminal lawyer* and *logical fallacy*. The phrase *grammatical error* dates from the 18th century.
Current ratio (*grammatical error* vs. *error in grammar*): 9:1

granary (= a place where grain is stored, esp. wheat) is most traditionally pronounced /**gran**-ə-ree/, though /**gray**-nə-ree/ is also acceptable. The spellings **grainary* and **grainery* are obsolete variants.
Current ratio (*granary* vs. **grainery* vs. **grainary*): 798:3:1

grandad. See **grandpa**.

granddad. See **grandpa**.

grandeur (= impressive beauty, power, or size) has long been preferably pronounced /**gran**-jər/ or /**gran**-juur/—not /**gran**-door/ or /**gran**-dyoor/ (two grandiose overpronunciations).

grandfather clause = a clause in the constitutions of some southern American states exempting from suffrage restrictions the descendants of men who voted before the Civil War. The *OED* misleadingly labels this phrase colloquial; it is the only available name for these statutes, and it appears in formal writing. E.g.: "A state law directly denying Negroes the right would be overthrown as a matter of course, and in 1915 the Court had invalidated a so-called *'grandfather clause'* [that] required literacy tests of those who were *not* descendants of those who could vote in 1867." Robert G. McCloskey, *The American Supreme Court* 212 (1960). Moreover, it has taken on an extended sense, referring to any statutory or regulatory clause exempting a class of people or transactions because of circumstances existing before the clause takes effect.

This phrase has given rise to the verb *grandfather*, meaning "to cover (a person) with the benefits of a grandfather clause." E.g.: "The council could, and should, have crafted language that *'grandfathered'* Mrs. Gary's job." "Nepotism Has No Place in Government," *Baltimore Sun*, 12 Jan. 1998, at A14. Sometimes, in passive uses, the phrase is *be grandfathered in*—e.g.: "There is one exception to the ban on new roads: Any project already on the drawing board can *be 'grandfathered' in*, or continued as scheduled because its planning occurred before the new restrictions were put in place." Christina Nifong, "Environmental Battle—New Roads vs. Clean Air," *Christian Science Monitor*, 14 Jan. 1998, at 3.

A few writers and speakers—sometimes in jest— have resorted to *grandparent clause* to avoid what might be perceived as SEXISM—e.g.: "Since she was ordained four years before the policy was issued,

Spahr was sure a *grandparent clause* [read *grandfather clause*] would protect her." Yonat Shimron, "Gay Presbyterians Fight for Ordination," *News & Observer* (Raleigh), 30 Mar. 1996, at A1. That neutering skews the historical sense and is likely to strike most readers and listeners as too politically correct or downright jocular. The phrase is appropriate, however, in other contexts, such as some parental-notification laws that let grandparents substitute for parents in giving permission for a minor to have an abortion.

LANGUAGE-CHANGE INDEX
grandparent clause for *grandfather clause*: Stage 1
Current ratio (*grandfather clause* vs.
grandparent clause): 660:1

grandfather clock; *grandfather's clock. The first is standard; the second is a variant form.

Current ratio: 10:1

grandma (= grandmother) is generally so spelled in AmE and BrE alike. The *-d-* being silent, both *granma* and *gramma* are infrequent variants.

grandpa; granddad; grandad. These are colloquial terms for *grandfather*. *Grandpa* (the most prevalent term) is sometimes shortened to *granpa*, *gramp*, *grampa*, or *gramps*, all of which are recognized as good colloquial English. As for the *-dad* terms, the standard spellings are *granddad* in AmE and *grandad* in BrE.

grandparenting. See **parenting.**

grateful; gratified. The distinction is well established. *Grateful* = appreciative, thankful <I'm grateful for your help>. *Gratified* = pleased, satisfied <we're gratified that you'll attend our party>. Cf. **gracious.**

gratis is pronounced /**grat**-is/ in AmE, traditionally /**gray**-tis/ in BrE. For a serious blunder involving this word, see **persona non grata.**

gratuitous; fortuitous. These two words are occasionally confounded. *Gratuitous* = (1) done or performed without obligation to do so <gratuitous promises>; or (2) done unnecessarily <gratuitous criticisms>. *Fortuitous* = occurring by chance <fortuitous circumstances>. See **fortuitous.**

gravamen (= the crux of a complaint or accusation) has predominantly formed the classical plural *gravamina* since the 18th century. The term appears primarily in legal writing. Although some have naturalized the plural to *gravamens*, that form remains a variant only.

The term is sometimes misspelled **gravaman* and is subject to uncertainty in pronunciation. The traditional pronunciation is /grə-**vay**-mən/, but many lawyers today say /**grah**-və-mən/.

Current ratio (*gravamina* vs. *gravamens*): 21:1

GRAVE ACCENT. See DIACRITICAL MARKS.

gravel, vb., makes *graveled* and *graveling* in AmE, *gravelled* and *gravelling* in BrE. See SPELLING (B).

gravitas. Not many LATINISMS spring into popular use. This one arose in English in the 1920s, mostly lay dormant until the early 1990s, and then became a VOGUE WORD. Meaning "personal stature, trustworthiness," it carried lots of weight during the 2000 U.S. presidential campaign. People used it to denote something once conveyed by the CLICHÉ *presidential timber*. The election year saw *gravitas* take off, appearing twice as often in U.S. print sources as it had in 1999, and almost three times as frequently as it had in 1998. It has since been sagging a bit under its own weight. But in its heyday it soared with literary eagles—e.g.:

- "What is troubling to Republicans who have plighted their troth to this man is not that they think he is a coarse or cruel man. Rather it is that Carlson's profile suggests an atmosphere of adolescence, a lack of *gravitas*—a carelessness, even a recklessness, perhaps born of things having gone a bit too easily so far." George F. Will, "Not Ready for Prime Time?" *N.Y. Post*, 12 Aug. 1999, at 35.
- "It is the biggest question of the primary season whether Mr. Bush will be rejected by the voters, on the grounds that he is lacking in such *gravitas* as is evident in John McCain and Steve Forbes." William F. Buckley Jr., "The Party Spoiler . . . and the Thug," *Wash. Times*, 10 Sept. 1999, at A18.
- " 'He has to show his *gravitas*,' said a top Bush aide, 'and he can't make any mistakes. If he pulls that off, he's probably unstoppable.' " Thomas M. DeFrank, "Bush Score in Debate a Primary Concern," *Daily News* (N.Y.), 2 Dec. 1999, News §, at 4.

gray; grey. The former spelling is more common in AmE, the latter in BrE; both are old, and neither is incorrect. The BrE preference had been established by 1715, the AmE preference by the mid-1820s. Note that *greyhound* is an invariable spelling.

Great Britain consists of England, Scotland, and Wales—all three on the island known to the Romans as *Britannia*. (Modern usage routinely shortens the name to *Britain*.) It differs from *United Kingdom*, which also includes Northern Ireland.

Some people wrongly think of *Great Britain* as a boastful name. But it's not: it's rooted in history. *Great Britain* was once contrasted with *Little Britain* (or simply *Brittany*), in France, where the Celtic Bretons lived. Although the *OED*'s last citation for *Little Britain* dates from 1622, the term *Great Britain* has persisted (though perhaps not without a sense of pride).

Grecian; Greek. As adjectives, these words both generally mean "of, relating to, or involving Greece or the Greeks." If a difference exists, it's that *Grecian* more often refers to ancient Greece—and in particular its art and architecture <Grecian urn>. An exception is *Greek mythology*. In general, though, *Greek* is the broader term <Greek salad>.

greenkeeper (= the person in charge of the upkeep of a golf course) is the standard term. **Greenskeeper* is a chiefly AmE variant.

Current ratio: 2:1

Grenadian; *Grenadan. The first is standard; the second is a NEEDLESS VARIANT. See DENIZEN LABELS.

Current ratio: 7:1

grey. See **gray.**

grievance; *aggrievance. The latter is a NEEDLESS VARIANT.

Current ratio: 2,997:1

grieve is most often an intransitive verb meaning "to feel grief." It is also, traditionally, a transitive verb meaning (1) "to cause distress to," or (2) "to suffer from the loss of." Sense 2 is now more common— e.g.: "After taking leave to *grieve* his wife, he returns to CTU in an unexpectedly violent temper." Matthew Gilbert, "Television Review: *24*," *Boston Globe*, 29 Oct. 2002, at C1.

But recently the verb has taken on a new meaning: "to bring a grievance for the purpose of protesting." The emergence of this sense is not entirely surprising because it is implied by the words *grievable* and *grievant*. It's most often used in employment contexts—e.g.:

- " 'Given the circumstances of what happened, I find it almost unbelievable that they would *grieve* this disciplinary action,' he said earlier this week." Tom Farmer, "2 More Firefighters Disciplined for Delay," *Boston Globe*, 25 Aug. 2005, NW §, at 3 (quoting John C. Curran, mayor of Boston).
- "[Sgt. Brett] Eisenlohr, who has worked for the department since July 1982, is *grieving* the discipline, which he has already served." Katie Melone, "3 Police Officers, Sergeant Suspended," *Hartford Courant*, 17 Apr. 2007, at B3.
- " 'There is too much deal-making,' [Special Counsel Merrick] Bobb wrote. 'An employee has everything to gain and nothing to lose by *grieving* discipline. The nearly inevitable result of the grievance will be an ultimate reduction in the discipline.' " Troy Anderson, "Discipline Flaw Lets Deputies Play System," *Daily News* (L.A.), 17 May 2007, Valley §, at N1.

Stylists are not likely to use the verb, but neither are they likely to be awarded relief.

LANGUAGE-CHANGE INDEX
grieve meaning "to bring a grievance": Stage 3

grievous (/**gree**-vəs/) is frequently misspelled **grievious* and mispronounced (/**gree**-vee-əs/), just as *mischievous* is frequently misspelled **mischievious* and similarly mispronounced. These are grievous and mischievous malformations. See **mischievous.**

Current ratio (*grievous* vs. **grievious*): 440:1

grill; grille. A *grill* is a cooking device, especially one with a gridiron over an open flame; as a verb, it means to cook something on a grill. By extension, a *grill* is also an informal restaurant serving a limited menu highlighting *grilled* (or often just fried) food. A *grille* is a protective metal latticework such as that in front of an automobile's radiator.

Grill is a recognized variant spelling for *grille*, but not vice versa—e.g.: "He hauls a huge *grille* [read *grill*], made from a split oil tank, to the park and cooks chickens by the dozen." Michael Sangiacomo, "Cook Finds Buyers for Homemade BBQ Sauce," *Plain Dealer* (Cleveland), 15 Oct. 2001, at B10. Still, *grille* is very popular in the pretentious names of restaurants, perhaps to suggest a pub-like atmosphere, as in *Ye Olde Bar & Grille*. In fact, the name has become so ubiquitous that the mere detail that a *grille* is not a *grill* is unlikely to make a difference.

LANGUAGE-CHANGE INDEX
grille misused for *grill*: Stage 2
Current ratio (*charcoal grill* vs.
**charcoal grille*): 333:1

grimace (= a facial expression of physical pain or mental disgust) is now almost universally pronounced /**grim**-əs/. But the word came into English from French in the 17th century as /gri-**mays**/ (rhyming with *face*), and as recently as the 1970s that pronunciation was still preferred. Charles Harrington Elster pinpoints the death of the traditional pronunciation: "Then came the inane McDonald's restaurant advertising campaign with Ronald McDonald the clown and his puppet sidekick GRIM-is, and poor old gri-MAYS swiftly became as strange as a square hamburger." *BBBM* at 233.

grind > ground > ground. So inflected. But the erroneous form *grinded* is gaining ground—e.g.:

- "The ancient constitutional process of impeachment *grinded* [read *ground*] into operation again yesterday for the first time in 24 years." David M. Shribman, "A Titanic Jousting Act," *Pitt. Post-Gaz.*, 20 Nov. 1998, at A17.
- "The Giants' return units have all but *grinded* [read *ground*] to a halt." Neil Best, "Giants vs. Broncos," *Newsday* (N.Y.), 13 Dec. 1998, at C12.
- "Masahiro Tanaka (9–6), coming off a complete-game victory last Saturday in Toronto, *grinded* [read *ground*] through six innings." Erik Boland, "Yanks Go Down Swinging to Tribe," *Newsday* (N.Y.), 22 Aug. 2015, at A34.

See IRREGULAR VERBS.

In one context, however, *grinded* is perfectly legitimate (though lamentable, in the eyes of high-school chaperons everywhere). There is now a style of dancing known as *grinding*, involving a female's pressing her buttocks against her partner's groin (through clothing), or sometimes a direct rubbing of groins or of her breasts, often with vigorous perfrication. (Call it part of the coarsening of our culture.) Someone who has engaged in such dancing would say that he or she *grinded*, not *ground*. *O tempora! O mores!*

LANGUAGE-CHANGE INDEX
grinded misused as a past tense
in a nondancing sense: Stage 1
Current ratio (*ground his teeth* vs.
**grinded his teeth*): 78:1

LANGUAGE-CHANGE INDEX (For the full key, see front matter pp. xxxi, l–li.)
Stage 1: Rejected. **Stage 2:** Widely shunned. **Stage 3:** Widespread but . . . **Stage 4:** Ubiquitous but . . . **Stage 5:** Fully accepted.
Invariably inferior forms marked by asterisk (*). • Ratios represent frequency of prevalent forms vs. variants in current books.

grisly; grizzly; gristly; grizzled. *Grisly* = ghastly, horrible <grisly murders>. *Grizzly* = (1) grayish; or (2) of, relating to, or involving the large brown bear that inhabits western North America. Each word is sometimes misused for the other. Most commonly, *grizzly* displaces *grisly* from its rightful position—e.g.: "That night the television news is full of the *grizzly* [read *grisly*] horror of it all." Myra MacPherson, "Songs for a Native Son," *Wash. Post*, 2 May 1980, at C1. But the opposite error also occurs—e.g.: "Dolphins, storks, cranes, pelicans, *grisly* [read *grizzly*] bears, an 8-foot map of Texas: Joe Kyte has stuffed them all." "Topiary Reindeer Harmless Grazers," *Pitt. Post-Gaz.*, 30 Nov. 1996, at D1.

Gristly = (of meat) containing an unappetizing amount of cartilage. The error is rare, but on occasion this word is also misused for *grisly*—e.g.: "In London, take in Jack the Ripper's walking tour that explores hidden courtyards and gaslit alleyways of London in the year 1888, when residents were shocked and frightened by a series of *gristly* [read *grisly*] murders." Jerry Morris, "Hunting Ghosts in Old England," *Boston Globe*, 27 Oct. 1996, at M2.

Grizzled is a synonym for *grizzly* in the sense of "grayish," most often describing hair streaked with gray—e.g.: "Jennet turned her attention to Davy Ingram, deep in conversation with Zachary Alday, a middle-aged man whose most distinguishing feature was a mole on one cheek. Ingram, younger but more *grizzled*, showed no outward trappings of newfound wealth." Kathy Lynn Emerson, *Face Down Across the Western Sea* 47 (2002). Because gray hair and beards are associated with old men, *grizzled* has also come, by extension, to describe any old-timer. In fact, this is its most common use today—e.g.: "Those, as *grizzled* fans here say while sipping a Hudepohl, were the days." Todd Jones, "Good Old Days Gone for Good for the Reds in Cincinnati?" *Columbus Dispatch*, 23 July 2002, at D1.

LANGUAGE-CHANGE INDEX
grisly misused for *grizzly*: Stage 1

grocery /grohs-[ə]-ree/ is often mispronounced /groh-shree/. See PRONUNCIATION (B).

groom = (1) someone who takes care of horses; or (2) a bridegroom. Both senses are standard. Some writers, however, have ill-advisedly objected to sense 2, which is first recorded in Shakespeare's *Othello* (1604): *like bride and groom* (2.3.173). But there's no sound basis for objecting to *groom* in sense 2.

The historical facts are these. The original term was *bridegoom*, not *bridegroom*, and the unetymological *-r-* got added in the early 16th century (probably from the influence of what has now become sense 1). In the early 17th century, Shakespeare (or perhaps predecessors or contemporaries) shortened *bridegroom* to *groom* through aphaeresis. In 1755, Samuel Johnson recorded both *bridegroom* and *groom* as standard.

In 1806, Noah Webster defined *bridegroom* as "the name of a new-married man." But 22 years later, in his big two-volume *American Dictionary of the English Language*, Webster decided to revive *bridegoom* without the *-r-*—which had lain dormant since the 14th century—to no avail. And he cut *groomsman* (which he had recorded in his 1806 *Compendious Dictionary of the English Language*) from the big dictionary of 1828, presumably because the prospect of touting *goomsman* made him uneasy. As for *bridegoom* (again without the *-r-*), Webster wrote that "[t]his word, by a mispronouncing of the last syllable, has been corrupted into *bridegroom*, which signifies a *bride's hostler* . . . . Such a gross corruption or blunder ought not to remain a reproach to philology." Yet it has remained.

Somehow, in the middle of the 19th century, a prejudice against *groom* as a shortened form of *bridegroom* arose, perhaps from the fallacious thought that a word can have only one correct meaning. But it makes no more sense than objecting to *plane* for *airplane* or *ball* for *baseball* <Play ball!>.

grotesquerie (= something grotesque; a grotesque quality) is the preferred spelling. **Grotesquery* is a variant—not exactly a grotesquerie, just a variant.

Current ratio: 3:1

grotto (= a small picturesque cave, whether natural or artificial) has predominantly formed the plural *grottoes* since the early 19th century in both AmE and BrE. **Grottos* is a variant form. See PLURALS (D).

Current ratio: 2:1

grounds, on the. See **because (D).**

groundwater. One word.

ground zero = (1) the site of a bomb explosion, esp. a nuclear bomb, or (2) the site of the destroyed World Trade Center. Sense 1 is typically literal—e.g.: "To the northeast, tunneled one mile below the surface of Cheyenne Mountain, is the NORAD facility—in all likelihood, *ground zero* during a nuclear attack." David Feela, "A Bull Market," *Denver Post*, 31 Dec. 2000, Perspective §, at K2. But it may also be figurative—e.g.: "The nation's jails and prisons are at *ground zero* of the war against AIDS." Scott Wyman, "Out of Jail and into the Arms of Angels," *Sun-Sentinel* (Ft. Lauderdale), 31 Dec. 2002, at B1.

As a reference to the site of the former World Trade Center, *ground zero* might seem to be a proper noun requiring capitalization. But a year after the terrorist attack, that usage had not become standardized: for example, *Newsday* and *Newsweek* capitalized it but *The New York Times* and *U.S. News & World Report* did not. And though some do not capitalize the phrase when referring to the New York site, others mistakenly capitalize it even when it's used generically—e.g.: "'Everybody's slate is wiped clean,' Lyons said. 'It does make it a little easier from the standpoint that everybody starts at *Ground Zero* [read *square one*].'" Rob Daniels, "Scholarship Rule Stirs Up Controversy," *News & Record* (Greensboro), 15 July 2002, at C1.

As in the example just quoted, it is common to hear and read phrases such as *start from ground zero* and *back to ground zero* where the meaning is *start from scratch* or *back to square one*. In these phrases, using *ground zero* is ill-advised because (1) a ready-made phrase is already at hand (either of the substitutes just mentioned), (2) the sense of destruction is wholly absent, and (3) the phrases seem to trivialize the 2001 devastation of lower Manhattan, with which the phrase is now so closely associated—e.g.:

- "Members of the Orchard Park Village Board held out hope Monday that planning for the Orchard Downs site at the village's heart might not be back *at ground zero* [read *to the drawing board*]." Elmer Ploetz, "Board Hopeful for Project at Four Corners Site," *Buffalo News*, 14 Aug. 2001, at C3.
- "It starts at *ground zero* [read *square one*] and helps you develop routines you can do on your own." Lowell E. Sunderland, "Fitness Is Not Just for Fanatics," *Baltimore Sun*, 7 Apr. 2002, at B3.
- "Baer knew he didn't have to start from *ground zero* [read *scratch*]." David Wooks, "Irish Defense Ahead of the Offense," *Indianapolis Star*, 29 Apr. 2002, at C6.

> LANGUAGE-CHANGE INDEX
> *ground zero* for *square one*: Stage 1

grovel, vb., makes *groveled* and *groveling* in AmE, *grovelled* and *grovelling* in BrE. See SPELLING (B). The word is pronounced either /**grah**-vəl/ or /**grə**-vəl/.

grow, v.t. Although this verb is typically intransitive <he grew two inches taller over the summer>, its transitive use has long been standard in phrases such as *grow crops* and *grow a beard*.

Recently, however, *grow* has blossomed as a transitive verb in nonfarming and nongrooming contexts. It is trendy in business JARGON: *growing the industry*, *growing your business*, *growing your investment*, and so on. But because many readers will stumble over these odd locutions, the trend should be avoided—e.g.:

- "The plan was to help each key industry develop an industry allocation, create a business plan, create a strategic plan and then implement the plans to *grow* [read *expand* or *develop*] the industry." John M. Grund, "Triage It, but Don't Kill It," *Oregon Bus.*, Jan. 1997, at 26.
- "To this common mix Quantum has added a clever way to keep the teams' collective vision focused on how to *grow* [read *expand* or *develop*] the business rather than just on how to cooperate inside." Thomas A. Stewart, "Another Fad Worth Killing," *Fortune*, 3 Feb. 1997, at 119.
- "Whether you are an existing landlord looking to *grow* [read *expand*] your portfolio or looking to become a first-time landlord, my thoughts are take advice from as many people as possible." "Are Homeowners Warming to the Idea of Renting?" *Canterbury Times* (U.K.), 19 Aug. 2015, at 33.

> LANGUAGE-CHANGE INDEX
> *grow* as a transitive verb in reference to nonliving things <growing the economy>: Stage 3

grudging (= reluctant; with grumbling) is the standard adjective in phrases such as *grudging acceptance*. Avoid the participial adjective **begrudging*—e.g.: "I have heard even some die-hard Hillary-haters express *begrudging* [read *grudging*] admiration for her determination, resourcefulness and fierce advocacy for her beliefs." Clarence Page, "Obama's Next Hurdles," *Chicago Trib.*, 14 May 2008, News §, at 27.

> LANGUAGE-CHANGE INDEX
> **begrudging* for *grudging*: Stage 2
> Current ratio (*a grudging respect* vs.
> **a begrudging respect*): 13:1

grueling; gruelling. Meaning "extremely tiring and demanding," *grueling* is the standard spelling in AmE, *gruelling* in BrE. The spellings diverged in the 1930s, before which time *gruelling* was standard in all varieties of World English.

gruesome is so spelled—not **grewsome*. E.g.: "Hughes's innkeeper obligingly applied his mouth to the 'Blawing Stwun,' producing 'a *grewsome* [read *gruesome*] sound between a moan and a roar.'" Christopher Somerville, "Back Again to Tom Brown's Vale Days," *Daily Telegraph*, 5 Feb. 1994, at 36. Let us hope that the next edition of this book does not have to report that, since the previous edition, this misusage grew some.

> LANGUAGE-CHANGE INDEX
> *gruesome* misspelled **grewsome*: Stage 1

guacamole (= a dip made with mashed avocados and a combination of lime or lemon, chiles, onions, tomato, and cilantro) is usually pronounced /gwah-kə-**moh**-lee/. In the Southwest, it is often pronounced /gwah-kə-**moh**-lay/, a bit closer to the Spanish pronunciation.

guarantee, n. & vb.; **guaranty,** n. These homophones are related in meaning as well as in sound, but they are not interchangeable. The broader term, *guarantee*, is more common and is used as a noun and a verb. To *guarantee* something is to assure someone that a promise will be kept <our company guarantees customer satisfaction>. As a noun, a *guarantee* is the promise itself <bring this written guarantee with your proof-of-purchase card if the television breaks down>.

The narrower term, *guaranty*, is a promise to pay money if someone else fails to do so <a mortgage guaranty company>. It is mostly used in banking and other financial contexts, and seldom appears outside legal writing.

A person who gives a *guaranty* is a *guarantor* <the guarantor must sign a guaranty for the car loan in case the borrower doesn't make the payments>.

guerrilla (Sp. for "raiding party") = a member of a small band of military fighters who, mostly through surprise raids, try to harass and undermine occupying

---

LANGUAGE-CHANGE INDEX (For the full key, see front matter pp. xxxi, l–li.)
Stage 1: Rejected. **Stage 2:** Widely shunned. **Stage 3:** Widespread but . . . **Stage 4:** Ubiquitous but . . . **Stage 5:** Fully accepted.
Invariably inferior forms marked by asterisk (*). • Ratios represent frequency of prevalent forms vs. variants in current books.

forces. The word is preferably so spelled—not **guerilla*. It's often used attributively <guerrilla warfare>.

The MALAPROPISM **gorilla forces* occasionally surfaces.

Current ratio (guerrilla warfare vs.
*gorilla warfare): 400:1

guess what. This is an imperative phrase, not an interrogative one. So it shouldn't end with a question mark. Hence the title of Mervin Bishop's *Guess What!* (1995) is preferable to the title of Mem Fox's *Guess What?* (1990), Beau Gardner's *Guess What?* (1985), and Taro Gomi's *Guess What?* (1992).

guild is often misused for *gild.* See **gild.**

guillotine (= a piece of equipment to behead people by slicing) entered English in the late 18th century and was almost immediately anglicized in pronunciation: /gil-ə-teen/. Only in the mid-20th century did AmE speakers begin re-Frenchifying the pronunciation to /gee-yə-teen/. See PRONUNCIATION (D).

guilty. See **not guilty.**

gulf; bay. In oceanographic contexts, these words share the basic sense "a portion of an ocean or sea surrounded by land; an indentation in a shoreline." The difference between the terms is this: a *gulf* is narrow at the mouth but deeply recessed; a *bay* is a wide, shallow inlet. But historically, the distinction hasn't been rigorously followed: consider the Gulf of Mexico with its vast mouth and the Hudson Bay with its narrow one.

gully (= a small ravine) is sometimes misspelled **gulley*—perhaps because of the similarity to *valley*. The correct plural is *gullies*. E.g.: "Its six small fields, severed by roads, *gulleys* [read *gullies*] and a river, made it awkward for modern machinery, and much of the land was unproductive." Larry Towell, "The World from My Front Porch," *Life*, Sept. 1997, at 62.

LANGUAGE-CHANGE INDEX
gully misspelled **gulley*: Stage 1
Current ratio: 14:1

*gunnel. See **gunwale.**

gunwale /gən-əl/ (= the upper edge of a boat's side) is the standard spelling. **Gunnel*—a phonetic spelling—is a variant.

Current ratio: 10:1

gustatory; *gustatorial. The latter is a NEEDLESS VARIANT.

Current ratio: 234:1

gut reaction. This phrase, meaning "an instinctive response," is sometimes malapropistically said (and written) **guttural reaction*, or, what is worse, **gutteral reaction*—e.g.:

- "And it's told in Mamet's poetry of the inarticulate dispossessed—a language of ellipses, crudities and *gutteral reactions* [read *gut reactions*]." Bob Hicks, "Ain't Misbehavin'," *Oregonian* (Portland), 18 Jan. 1991, at R21.

- "But there is a scene—one of the most revealing in the documentary series—when Carole Brennan, Menino's press spokesperson, tangles with Herald reporter David Guarino over a story he's reporting about the mayor's daughter and her *gutteral reaction* [read *gut reaction*] to angry firefighters picketing Menino." Monica Collins, "Where's the Hub, Bub? ABC's Documentary Series 'Boston 24/7' Presents a Harsh Dose of Reality," *Boston Herald*, 30 May 2002, at 59.

- "But it is emotion talking. It is the raw, *guttural reaction* [read *gut reaction*] to someone daring to suggest that Rice athletics be scaled back, played at a diminished level or even vaporized." John P. Lopez, "Rice Needs Our Help, Not Just Our Concerns," *Houston Chron.*, 7 May 2004, Sports §, at 1.

Occasionally, the redundant DOUBLE BOBBLE **guttural instinct* (for *instinct*) also appears—as does **gutteral* instinct (a triple bobble):

- "What's more, his vacuous screen presence—he gives the impression of a man with absolutely nothing on his mind—is actually a bonus in the role of a beleaguered jungle-dweller who drop kicks cops and swings from skyscrapers driven by *gutteral instinct* [read *instinct*] alone (and, anyway, I heard Robert De Niro was unavailable for the role)." Joel Rubinoff, "He May Not Be Arnold but Tarzan Gets It Done," *Hamilton Spectator* (Ont.), 11 Oct. 2003, at 19.

- "And it's weird enough with the Braves having a *guttural instinct* [read *the instinct*] to pull for the Mets the night Glavine is going for 300." Carroll Rogers, "Braves Blog," *Atlanta J.-Const.*, 2 Aug. 2007, Sports §.

See MALAPROPISMS & DOUBLE BOBBLES.

LANGUAGE-CHANGE INDEX
*guttural reaction for gut reaction: Stage 1

guttural. So spelled—not **gutteral*, which is a frequent misspelling. The confusion probably occurs because of a mistaken association with *gutter*, when in fact *guttural* derives from the Latin *guttur* ("throat"). E.g.: "I find myself gripping the handle and uttering a *gutteral* [read *guttural*] 'vroom! vroom!'" Ron Alexander, "Metropolitan Diary," *N.Y. Times*, 30 Oct. 1996, at C2. See **gut reaction.**

LANGUAGE-CHANGE INDEX
guttural misspelled **gutteral*: Stage 1
Current ratio: 32:1

guy; guys. The singular form is invariably masculine, and the plural often is, too <Dave Barry's Complete Guide to Guys>. But the plural is now often used inclusively to address a group that includes males and females, especially in the CASUALISM *you guys*. It can be seen as a handy term because the truly inclusive alternatives are more likely to offend ("guys and gals" or, worse, from the '50s musical, "guys and dolls").

gybe. See **gibe.**

gymnasium. Pl. *gymnasiums*—preferably not **gymnasia* (the standard plural till about 1900). See PLURALS (B).

Current ratio: 1.2:1

gynecocracy. So spelled—not **gyneocracy*. See GOVERNMENTAL FORMS.

Current ratio: 7:1

gypsy. In literal senses, denoting members of the tribes that migrated from northern India to Europe in the 14th or 15th century as well as their language, *Gypsy* is capitalized. (The term now preferred is *Roma*.) In figurative senses—as an adjective meaning "wanderer" or a verb meaning "to live like a Gypsy"—it is not. Nor is it capitalized in such phrases as *gypsy cab* and *gypsy moth*. The term comes from an erroneous belief that the people were from Egypt. Cf. **Romany.**

*Gipsy, the standard spelling for much of the 19th century (and in BrE, for much of the 20th as well), is an occasional variant.

Because *gypsy* is often used in a pejorative sense, some authorities recommend avoiding it in all contexts. But that advice seems unduly strict. A *gypsy cab* easily becomes an *unlicensed cab*, but there is no ready substitute for *gypsy moth*.

Current ratio (*gypsy* vs. **gipsy*): 3:1

gyrfalcon /jər-**fal**-kən/ (= a large falcon found in Arctic regions) is the standard spelling. **Gerfalcon* (standard through the early 20th century) is a variant.

Current ratio: 2:1

gyro. Two words are so spelled. A *gyro* (/**jɪ**-roh/) is a spinning (gyrating) device such as a gyroscope or a gyrocompass. *Gyro* (/**yee**-roh/ or /**zhir**-oh/) is a loaf of meat, typically lamb, but sometimes beef, pork, or a mixture, prepared by roasting the loaf on a rotating vertical spit. A *gyro* is also a sandwich made from the meat and served in folded or rolled-up pita bread.

The sandwich takes its name from the singular Greek noun *gyros*, meaning "a turning" (no doubt a reference to the spit that the meat is roasted on). The *-s* in *gyros* was erroneously taken to be plural, and the singular *gyro* was formed—e.g.: "We made do nicely with . . . a hearty double-fistful of beef shawarma, the Middle Eastern version of a *gyro*, sporting marinated meat, lettuce, tomato and tahini tucked into a warm pita." Nancy Leson, "Middle East Inspires a Middling Feast at Aladdin," *Seattle Times*, 25 Jan. 2002, at H3. See BACK-FORMATIONS.

Today *gyros* is typically a plural—e.g.: "Jose Bineda said he wants to make his *gyros* even better; he wants to buy a machine to roast lamb on a spit." Sue Kovach Shuman, "Hermanos Restaurant in Manassas Serves Up a Whole World of Flavors," *Wash. Post*, 23 Jan. 2002, Prince William Extra §, at T5.

Two final points. First, although *gyros* occasionally appears as a singular (like *kudos*), the plural form **gyroses* is essentially unknown as an English word. Second, the phrase *gyro sandwich*, like *pizza pie*, might be considered a venial REDUNDANCY, but perhaps it shouldn't be: the meat is also served on platters and as pizza toppings.

H

ha—the interjection that expresses surprise, triumph, discovery, anger, and various other states of mind—is so spelled. **Hah* is a variant spelling.

For laughter, *ha-ha* is the usual spelling.

habeas corpus (lit., "you shall have the body") = a writ ordering that a person be brought before a court, esp. to ensure that the person has not been illegally imprisoned. When used as a PHRASAL ADJECTIVE, the term is sometimes hyphenated—e.g.: "The Senate is scheduled to consider crime legislation, including *habeas-corpus* proposals, possibly as soon as next week." *Wall Street J.*, 16 May 1990, at B6. But with such a prima facie foreignism (like *prima facie* in that phrase), the hyphen is unnecessary to prevent MISCUES. See PHRASAL ADJECTIVES (H).

The traditional plural *habeas corpora* has gradually given way to *habeas corpuses*. See **corpus.**

Current ratio (*habeas corpuses* vs. *habeas corpora*): 2:1

habitability; **inhabitability*. Because of confusion over the prefix *in-*, which is intensive and not negative in **inhabitability* (or, e.g., in *inflammable*), today the positive form is *habitability* and the negative form *uninhabitability*. **Inhabitability* has never been much used—and whenever it is used it's ambiguous. See **flammable** & NEGATIVES (A).

Current ratio: 30:1

habituation. See **addicted.**

*habitude. As generally used today, this GALLICISM is a NEEDLESS VARIANT of *habit*, one that supplies a hint of ARCHAISM—e.g.: "Tocqueville spent nearly a year examining American *habitudes* [read *habits*] and mores." Richard Wolin, "Liberalism as a Vocation," *New Republic*, 2 Sept. 1996, at 34. (On the use of *Tocqueville*—without the particle *de*—in that sentence, see NAMES (D).)

LANGUAGE-CHANGE INDEX
*habitude for *habit*: Stage 1
Current ratio (*habit* vs. **habitude*): 241:1

habitué (= a frequent visitor to a particular place, or sometimes a resident) is printed in roman type but

LANGUAGE-CHANGE INDEX (For the full key, see front matter pp. xxxi, l–li.)
Stage 1: Rejected. **Stage 2:** Widely shunned. **Stage 3:** Widespread but . . . **Stage 4:** Ubiquitous but . . . **Stage 5:** Fully accepted.
Invariably inferior forms marked by asterisk (*). • Ratios represent frequency of prevalent forms vs. variants in current books.

predominantly retains the acute accent. If you aspirate the *h*, it should be *a habitué*; if not, it can permissibly be *an habitué*. Both forms appear with frequency in English-language print sources. BrE tends more toward *an* over *a*. See **a (A)**.

Although the French pronunciation is /hə-bich-ə-**way**/, English speakers often anglicize the pronunciation to /hə-**bich**-ə-way/. Avoid the misspelling **habituee*.

háček. See DIACRITICAL MARKS.

had better. See **better (A)**.

*had have; *had've; *had of. All these constructions are poor usage, the word *had* being sufficient by itself. *Had* is the auxiliary verb used in forming the past-perfect tense. It commonly expresses a past condition <if I had been there, I would have said something> or a wish <I wish I had been there>. (See TENSES (A).) A superfluous *have* after *had* is typical of DIALECT, and it sometimes makes its way into print—e.g.:

- "Lazutina said her success would not have happened if she *had have* [read *had*] stayed with Grushin." "Russia Earns Women's Cross-Country Sweep," *Salt Lake Trib.*, 20 Feb. 1998, at D4.
- "He also said that the fact he was arrested in Las Vegas also supports his innocence because *if he had have* [read *if he had*] been involved in the crime, he would have left town." Glenn Puit, "Victims of Quadruple Homicide Lost Lives for $240, Officials Say," *Las Vegas Rev.-J.*, 29 Aug. 1998, at A1.
- "If they *had have* [read *had*] been [asked to justify their actions], they might have come out of it subject to an idiot tax." Chris Young, "Tax Deal for Pros a Con Job," *Toronto Star*, 28 Nov. 1998, at C6.

Those inclined to make this mistake often collapse the erroneous phrase into the contraction **had've*—e.g.:

- "My friend Russ called. 'Read your article today. Well written, *wished you had've* [read *wish you had*] warned me what it was about.'" James A. Buist, "On Friendship and Not Wanting to Know," *Globe & Mail* (Toronto), 17 Nov. 1998, at A26.
- "'I wish there *had've* [read *had*] been something like this group then.'" Ed Marcum, "Support Group Shows Grieving Spouses How to Begin Living Again," *Knoxville News-Sentinel*, 12 July 2000, at W1 (quoting Sue Lane).
- "*Waistin'* would've been a slacker classic if it *had've* [read *had*] been written 10 years ago." Patrick Donovan, "More Light," *The Age*, 20 Oct. 2000, at 7.

Worst of all, the contracted *have* is sometimes mistakenly rendered *of*, resulting in a DOUBLE BOBBLE. Notice that two of the following three instances occur in quoted speech (in which **had've* would have been the better transcription of dialectal phrasing):

- "'If I *had of* [read *had*] known that, we would have been looking for those papers for all those years.'" Hayes Hickman, "Getting Flag for Veteran's Funeral Takes Some Planning," *Knoxville News-Sentinel*, 11 Nov. 1999, at A1 (quoting the daughter of a deceased veteran).
- "'If I *had of* [read *had*] dropped 20 spots I would have called myself a real dummy,' Doyle said." "Doyle Leads,"

Houston Chron., 5 Mar. 2000, at 11 (quoting Allen Doyle, the professional golfer).
- "If he *had of* [read *had*] been 10 years older he could have tried some of the water sports." Sue Mathias, "Time to Relax in a Dalmatian Idyll," *Daily Express* (London), 30 June 2001.

Sometimes this same error is rendered **I'd of* (where *I'd* alone would be correct).

For more on this type of error, see **of (D)**.

LANGUAGE-CHANGE INDEX
1. **had have* or **had've* for *had*: Stage 2
Current ratio (*had been* vs. **had have been*): 31,802:1
2. **had of* for *had*: Stage 1
Current ratio (*had been* vs. **had of been*): 84,741:1

*had ought. See **ought (C)** & DOUBLE MODALS.

had rather; would rather. Both phrases are idiomatic and old <he had rather play golf> <she would rather be fishing>. Today *would rather* is the predominant form. But both forms are fully established. The *OED*, under *rather* (9d), cites examples of *had rather* from 1450 to 1875. Otto Jespersen's *Modern English Grammar* (1948) cites writers such as Daniel Defoe (1660–1731), William Makepeace Thackeray (1811–1863), George Bernard Shaw (1856–1950), and H.G. Wells (1866–1946). For the similar phrase *had better*, see **better (A)**.

*had used to be is unidiomatic and awkward in place of *had been* or *had once been*—e.g.: "Still there came a time when I was anxious again. I was still in St. Louis but in another apartment, shared with the man who was later to be my husband. The house *had used to be* [read *had once been*] a butcher's shop." Abby Frucht, "Come in, Come in," *Seattle Times*, 21 May 1995, Pacific §, at 50. See **used to**.

LANGUAGE-CHANGE INDEX
*had used to be for *had once been*: Stage 1
Current ratio (*had once been* vs. **had used to be*): 235:1

*had've. See ***had have**.

haemoglobin. See **hemoglobin**.

haemorrhage. See **hemorrhage**.

hagiarchy; hagiography; hagiolatry. These words—meaning, respectively, "rule by saints," "biography of saints," and "idolatry of saints"—may be pronounced either with a hard -*g*- (as Fowler preferred) or with a soft -*j*- sound. The only disadvantage of the traditional pronunciation with the hard -*g*- (/**hag**-ee-ahr-kee/, etc.) is that it sounds more as if it denotes "rule by hags" than "rule by saints."

hagiocracy. See GOVERNMENTAL FORMS.

hagiography. See **hagiarchy**.

hagiolatry. See **hagiarchy**.

Hague, The. The definite article in this place name is always capitalized. See **Netherlands.**

Current ratio (*The Hague* vs. **the Hague*): 3:1

*hah. See **ha.**

hail, vb. See **hale.**

*hail and hardy. See **hale and hearty.**

*hairbrained. See **harebrained.**

*hairbreadth. See **hair's breadth.**

*hairlip. See **harelip.**

hair-raising, a near-equivalent of the Latin *horribilis* (= making to stand on end), is sometimes misrendered **hair-razing,* as in the headline for an item that began: "Jimmy Johnson's hair was messed up, and he couldn't have cared less because he had just seen his Dallas Cowboys mess up the Buffalo Bills even worse." Randy Riggs, "Beating Bills Was *Hair-Razing* [read *Hair-Raising*] Experience," *Austin Am.-Statesman,* 24 Jan. 1994, at C10. The error occurs also in BrE—e.g.: "Hail a taxi here and be prepared for a *hair-razing* [read *hair-raising*] journey spiced with general discomfort and rudeness from the driver." David Usborne, "New Rulebook Leaves Cabbies Speechless," *Independent,* 6 July 1996, at 13.

To *raze* is either to tear down or to cut close (as with a razor). See **raze.**

LANGUAGE-CHANGE INDEX
*hair-razing for *hair-raising:* Stage 1

hair's breadth; hair's-breadth; *hairbreadth; *hairsbreadth. Although most American dictionaries list **hairbreadth* first as both noun and adjective, that is one of the less common forms. The standard terms today are *hair's breadth* as a noun <victory by a hair's breadth> and *hair's-breadth* as an adjective <a hair's-breadth victory>. E.g.:

- "Eventually it will blunt conservatism's edge, leaving voters to see but a *hair's-breadth* difference between Republicans and Democrats." "Crisis of the Soul," *Daily Oklahoman,* 27 July 1997, at 12.
- "In 1972, we came within a *hair's breadth* of being arrested by Franco's Spanish police." Linda Matchan, "Can You Really Go Back?" *Boston Globe,* 17 Aug. 1997, at M1.

The other forms are NEEDLESS VARIANTS.

The phrase is sometimes wrongly written **hare's breath* or **hair's breath*—e.g.:

- "CBS won by a *hare's breath* [read *hair's breadth*], followed by ABC and NBC, in a close race." Kinney Littlefield, "Cable Viewers Get Their Kicks from Football," *Orange County Register,* 5 Dec. 1993, at F11.
- "The Harvest Moon Inn, a *hair's breath* [read *hair's breadth*] away from achieving four-star status in the mere

months of its existence, is clearly on the rise." "Discover Rising Food Star at the Harvest Moon Inn," *Asbury Park Press* (Neptune, N.J.), 31 Mar. 1996, at D5.

- "You don't come a *hare's breath* [read *hair's breadth*] away from making an Olympic team by taking part in a hobby." Bill Ward, "Hasbach Takes His 'Hobby' to New Heights," *Tampa Trib.,* 21 Apr. 2001, at 21.

LANGUAGE-CHANGE INDEX
1. **hare's breath* for *hair's breadth:* Stage 1
Current ratio (*hair's breadth* vs. **hare's breath*): 420:1
2. **hair's breath* for *hair's breadth:* Stage 1
Current ratio (*hair's breadth* vs. **hair's breath*): 27:1

hale, vb., = to compel to go. This is the correct verb in the idiom *hale into court*—e.g.: "Taney ordered that the general himself be *haled into court.*" Robert G. McCloskey, *The American Supreme Court* 98 (1960). Unfortunately, though, the verb is often mistakenly written *hail*—e.g.:

- "He grabbed the trespasser by the seat of the pants and the scruff of the neck and tossed him out—an outburst that got the diminutive mystic, much to his dismay, *hailed* [read *haled*] into court for sedition." Wilson Frank, "That Rare Thing: A Happy Man," *Des Moines Register,* 2 June 1996, at 5.
- "Although the court eventually recognized that the three officials were just doing their job, these agents and others similarly situated may, in the future, be less willing to do that job in the most effective manner, based on a reasonable fear that they could be *hailed* [read *haled*] into court and potentially subjected to personal civil liability as a result." Michelle Visser, "Sovereign Immunity and Informant Defectors: The United States' Refusal to Protect Its Protectors," 58 *Stanford L. Rev.* 663, 692 (2005).

LANGUAGE-CHANGE INDEX
hail misused for *hale:* Stage 2
Current ratio (*haled into court* vs.
*hailed into court): 9:1

hale and hearty is the SET PHRASE meaning "strong and healthy." But writers often get one or the other of the words wrong, and occasionally both—e.g.:

- "[S]tepping into the maelstrom that is today's health care environment . . . is a daunting prospect for even the most *hail and hardy* [read *hale and hearty*] executive." Kim Norris, "Hard Task Met with a Smile," *Detroit Free Press,* 23 Apr. 2003, at E1.
- "In two outings, biologists got 34 walleye ready to spawn, yielding 1.3 million eggs. Of those, 938,500 walleye fry emerged *hail and hearty* [read *hale and hearty*] and were released in South Bay at pre-selected sites, a phenomenal 71.5 percent survival rate." Fred LeBrun, "Turnaround for Walleye," *Times Union* (Albany), 27 Apr. 2006, at C7.
- "The reasons for the paradox are a matter of some debate. Some scholars attribute it to immigration, which may draw selectively from the ranks of the *hale and hardy* [read

LANGUAGE-CHANGE INDEX (For the full key, see front matter pp. xxxi, l–li.)
Stage 1: Rejected. **Stage 2:** Widely shunned. **Stage 3:** Widespread but . . . **Stage 4:** Ubiquitous but . . . **Stage 5:** Fully accepted.
Invariably inferior forms marked by asterisk (*). • Ratios represent frequency of prevalent forms vs. variants in current books.

hale and hearty]." Juliet Chung, "Healthier than You Might Expect," *L.A. Times*, 28 Aug. 2006, at B1.

Cf. **hardy.**

LANGUAGE-CHANGE INDEX
*hail and hardy (any variation) for *hale and hearty*: Stage 1
Current ratio (*hale and hearty* vs. **hale and hardy* vs. **hail and hearty*): 59:2:1

*Haley's Comet. See **Halley's Comet.**

half. A. *Half (of).* The preposition *of* is often unnecessary. Omit it when you can—e.g.: "Nearly *half of* [read *half*] the people in Cuba receive economic help from family and friends in the United States." "Family Pulls Painting from Auction," *Fresno Bee*, 28 Nov. 1997, at C2. Here the better form appears:

- "Everyone else can still write off only *half* the cost of that cinnamon roll." Nancy Gibbs, "A Conspiracy of Celebration," *Time*, 11 Aug. 1997, at 26.
- "About *half* the prisoners had been loaded on planes for Miami." Evan Thomas, *Robert Kennedy: His Life* 237 (2000).

Concededly, in modern print sources the collocation *half of the* has outnumbered *half the* since about 1900, today by a 2-to-1 ratio. The shorter form vastly predominated in the 18th and 19th centuries and remains perfectly idiomatic. Of course, when a pronoun follows, the *of* is typically needed <half of them are>.

B. Number. Although we say *half of it is*, we should say *half of them are*. When the noun or pronoun following *half of* is singular, then *half* is treated as singular; but when the noun or pronoun is plural, then *half* is treated as plural. For the principle underlying the latter phrase, see SYNESIS.

C. *Half a dozen* and *a half dozen.* For this noun phrase, either *half a dozen* or *a half dozen* is good form. The predominant form in print sources has always been *half a dozen*. Avoid **a half a dozen* and *half of a dozen*. When the phrase is used as an adjective, it becomes a PHRASAL ADJECTIVE that should be hyphenated <a half-dozen twirlers with the band>.

Current ratio (*half a dozen* vs. *a half dozen*): 5:1

D. **Two halves.* This phrase is often redundant—e.g.:

- "Die-cut into *two halves* [read *halves*], this coilbound book works both from a pictorial and alphabetical point of view." Gordon Morash, "Toy Box Books," *Edmonton J.*, 4 Dec. 1994, at B1.
- "Peel your own or buy peeled fresh squash cut into *two halves* [read *halves*]." Donna Lee, "Eating Lean and Liking It," *Providence J.-Bull.*, 5 Mar. 1997, at G1.

On the plural *halves*, see PLURALS (C).

Current ratio (*cut into halves* vs. **cut into two halves*): 3:1

half-staff; half-mast. As a memorial, most flags on land fly at *half-staff*. Strictly speaking, they fly at *half-mast* only on ships and at naval stations. (That's because only there does a flag hang from the part of a ship known as the mast.) This is a distinction that newspaper styles are usually careful to make, but that dictionaries and the general public mostly ignore—e.g.: "Friday night, the flags at Scarborough Downs were lowered to *half-mast* [read *half-staff*]." Steve Solloway, "Former Downs GM Dies," *Maine Sunday Telegram*, 11 Aug. 2002, at D9.

As a METAPHOR, either phrase will do. Writers usually choose *half-mast*, perhaps because it seems more colorful—e.g.:

- "[H]e was down on one creaky knee, one arm propped on the scorer's table for ballast, tie at *half-mast*, sweater long ago discarded, voice in that familiar, rasping, jackhammer syncopation, eyes ablaze like a blast furnace and sweeping the floor, seeing every sin." Bill Lyon, "Villanova–Temple Matchup a Contrast in Coaching Styles," *Phil. Inquirer*, 21 Mar. 2002, at E1.
- "He looks like a man in serious need of a double espresso, his eyelids dangerously close to *half-mast*." Gordon Edes, "A Lot to Like About Gordon," *Boston Globe*, 1 Apr. 2002, at D4.

But sometimes *half-mast* is undoubtedly chosen because of its phonic similarity to *half-assed*—e.g.: "We weren't too crazy about Bill Clinton's 'don't ask, don't tell' policy (although we adored Bill, and especially his charming wife Hillary) but we figured even a *half-mast* policy that would let gay soldiers serve their country was better than just tossing them out on their keisters because of their sexual orientation." Dennis Rogers, "Putting Liberals in a Quandary," *Dallas Morning News*, 16 Feb. 2002, at B1.

LANGUAGE-CHANGE INDEX
half-mast misused for *half-staff*: Stage 2

half-yearly. See **biannual.**

Halley's Comet, named after Edmund Halley /**hal**-ee/ (1656–1742), is often misspelled **Haley's Comet*. In print sources, the misspelling is almost 25% as common as the correct one—e.g.: "For Rita's own mother, there were brighter memories—watching *Haley's* [read *Halley's*] comet with her father." Marie Villari, "Heritage Retraced from a Thousand Cups of Tea," *Post-Standard* (Syracuse), 15 Feb. 2001, at 9. This probably results from the widespread mispronunciation /**hay**-leez/ for /**hal**-eez/. Even if the erroneous pronunciation can be called "standard," the spelling remains unchanged.

LANGUAGE-CHANGE INDEX
*Haley's Comet for *Halley's Comet*: Stage 1
Current ratio (*Halley's Comet* vs. **Haley's Comet*): 15:1

*halliard. See **halyard.**

Halloween, a contracted form of *All Hallow Even*, is so spelled. **Hallowe'en*, a variant spelling, is pedantic.

hallucination; delusion. A *hallucination* results from disturbed sensory perceptions, as when a person "hears voices" or sees ghosts. A *delusion* results from disturbed thinking, as when a person incorrectly imagines that he or she is being persecuted. Cf. **illusion.**

halo. Pl. *halos* (in AmE), *haloes* (traditionally in BrE). The American-style plural is making inroads into BrE. It predominates in World English. See PLURALS (D).

> Current ratio (*halos* vs. *haloes*): 3:1

halve (= to separate into two equal portions) is preferably pronounced like *have*. The pronunciation /hahv/ is less good—and worse still is /halv/.

For the plural noun *halves*, see **half (D)**.

halyard (= a rope device designed for raising or lowering something, as a flag or a ship's sail) is the standard spelling. *Halliard* and *haulyard* are variants.

> Current ratio (*halyard* vs. *halliard* vs. *haulyard*): 237:33:1

hamstring, vb. *Hamstrung* is the settled past-tense and past-participial form. Although this form has no etymological basis—that is, the verb comes from the noun *hamstring* and not from any form of the verb *string* (we don't "string the ham")—the past tense *hamstringed* hardly exists today and strikes most readers as pedantic. E.g.:

- "Anderson was in fine physical form, still striking all the characteristic moves of a *hamstringed* [read *hamstrung*], drunken marionette." Tom Phalen, " 'Jolly Jethros' Keep Crowd Involved," *Seattle Times*, 23 Oct. 1992, at 8.
- "Mr. Clinton . . . might investigate how President Lyndon Johnson's minute direction of operations *hamstringed* [read *hamstrung*] the military and prevented victory." "Political Warriors," *Orange County Register*, 13 Aug. 1993, at B10.
- "Wind was just one factor that *hamstringed* [read *hamstrung*] city and rural firefighters who teamed up to control and then extinguish the fire around 1:15 p.m." David Diehl, "Blaze Shows State Is at High Fire Risk," *Bismarck Trib.*, 21 May 2002, at A1.

> LANGUAGE-CHANGE INDEX
> *hamstringed* for *hamstrung*: Stage 1
> Current ratio (*hamstrung* vs. *hamstringed*): 135:1

hamzah. For a brief discussion of this DIACRITICAL MARK in Hawaiian English, see **Hawaii (B)**.

hand, on the other. See **on the other hand**.

handcraft. See **handicraft**.

hand down. See PHRASAL VERBS.

handful. A. Plural. The word is *handfuls*, not *handsful*. See PLURALS (G).

> Current ratio: 77:1

B. *Handful is* or *handful are*. When followed by the preposition *of* plus a plural noun, *handful* typically takes a plural verb—e.g.:

- "Today there *is* [read *are*] only a *handful* of residents in what is left of the white section of town." Peter Applebome, "Deep South and Down Home, but It's a Ghetto All the Same," *N.Y. Times*, 21 Aug. 1993, at 1, 6.

- " 'There *is* [read *are*] a *handful* of people around the Pebbled Sea who pay highly for magical curiosities,' replied Niko." Tamora Pierce, *Circle of Magic: Daja's Book* 119 (1998).
- "A *handful* of local teams *is* [read *are*] hitting the pool this fall to compete in the quickly emerging sport of water polo." Tom Ramstetter, "St. X Rises to Top in Water Polo," *Cincinnati Enquirer*, 26 Aug. 2015, at C2.

For the reason, see SYNESIS. In both AmE and BrE, the collocation *a handful are* has predominated over *a handful is* in print sources since about 1950; before that, the two usages were close contenders from about 1890 on.

> Current ratio (*a handful of them are* vs.
> *a handful of them is*): 13:1

handicapped. The phrases *handicapped-accessible* and *handicap-accessible* are illogical. Although *wheelchair-accessible* makes sense (accessible by wheelchair), *handicapped-accessible* does not—unless we do some contortions to suggest that it means "accessible to the handicapped."

Handicapped parking is a well-known example of HYPALLAGE.

handicraft (= [1] an art or avocation requiring manual skill; or [2] an article made by manual skill) is the standard noun. *Handcraft*, n., is a NEEDLESS VARIANT.

But the verb *handcraft* (= to fashion by hand) and the adjective *handcrafted* are perfectly good. In fact, sometimes *handicraft* is wrongly asked to do their work—e.g.: "Dress up a wooden container with a selection of *handicrafted* [read *handcrafted*] tiles." "Tile Looks Terrific Out in the Garden," *S.F. Chron.*, 25 June 1997, Home §, at 5 (photo caption).

> LANGUAGE-CHANGE INDEX
> *handicrafted* for *handcrafted*: Stage 1
> Current ratio (*handcrafted* vs. *handicrafted*): 670:1

handiwork, n. So spelled—not *handywork*.

> Current ratio: 99:1

handkerchief /**hang**-kər-chif/. Pl. *handkerchiefs*—not *handkerchieves*. See PLURALS (C).

> Current ratio: 392:1

hands and knees. The mental image of a person begging has the pleader on knees. Yet speakers often embellish that image unnecessarily—e.g.: "The Muncie City Council's finance committee last week made final recommendations on next year's municipal budget after listening to tax protesters do everything but beg on *hands and knees* [read *their knees*]." Larry Riley, "Muncie City Council Failed to Curtail Spending," *Star Press* (Muncie, Ind.), 23 Sept. 2007, at A7.

handsful. See **handful (A)**.

hand-wringing. See **wring (B)**.

LANGUAGE-CHANGE INDEX (For the full key, see front matter pp. xxxi, l–li.)
Stage 1: Rejected. **Stage 2:** Widely shunned. **Stage 3:** Widespread but . . . **Stage 4:** Ubiquitous but . . . **Stage 5:** Fully accepted.
Invariably inferior forms marked by asterisk (*). • Ratios represent frequency of prevalent forms vs. variants in current books.

*handywork. See **handiwork.**

hangar; hanger. The shelter for airplanes is spelled *hangar.* All other senses belong to the spelling *hanger.* But that spelling sometimes invades the domain of *hangar*—e.g.: "[They] convert[ed] scores of old warehouses into offices and production sites, and airplane *hangers* [read *hangars*] into sound stages." Joel Kotkin, "The Business of Entertainment," *L.A. Times,* 29 Dec. 1996, at M1.

> LANGUAGE-CHANGE INDEX
> *hanger* misused for *hangar:* Stage 3
> Current ratio (*aircraft hangar* vs.
> **aircraft hanger*): 4:1

hanged; hung. Coats and pictures are *hung,* and sometimes so are juries. But criminals found guilty of capital offenses are *hanged*—at least in some jurisdictions. To be *hanged* is to be suspended by the neck with a rope or cord for the purpose of causing death—e.g.:

- "The six officers were executed by a firing squad and the two civilians were *hanged,* the radio said." "Libya Hints at CIA Plot, Executes 8," *Chicago Trib.,* 3 Jan. 1997, at 5.
- "But while mere murderers were *hung* [read *hanged*], a quick thing if the hangman were skilled, women found guilty of poisoning their husbands were condemned to be burnt at the stake." Kathy Lynn Emerson, *Face Down Beneath the Eleanor Cross* 32 (2000).
- "Mr. Caskey, pushing fifty, had taken up with his secretary, whereupon his wife *hung* [read *hanged*] herself." Edward Hoagland, "Sex and the River Styx," *Harper's Mag.,* Jan. 2003, at 49, 50.

But the mere fact that a person is suspended doesn't mean that *hanged*—which implies an attempted killing or self-killing—is always the right word. If a person is suspended for amusement or through malice, and death isn't intended or likely, then *hung* is the proper word—e.g.: "He charges that authorities did little or nothing after he complained at various times of being attacked by dogs, shot at, beaten with a rake and tortured while being *hanged* [read *hung*] upside down." Jeffrey A. Roberts, "Despite Suit, Gilpin Retains Racial Epithet," *Denver Post,* 3 Jan. 1997, at B1. In Italy in 1944, Benito Mussolini and his mistress were executed and then their bodies *hung* upside down, but press reports often say incorrectly that they were *hanged*—e.g.: "Hitler decided to do so after hearing that Partisans had captured and shot Italian dictator Benito Mussolini, and *hanged him* [read *hung his body*] upside down in Milan plaza." "A Time of Remembrance," *Plain Dealer* (Cleveland), 8 May 1995, at B8. See IRREGULAR VERBS.

> LANGUAGE-CHANGE INDEX
> *hung* for *hanged* in reference to an execution: Stage 3
> Current ratio (*hanged by the neck* vs.
> **hung by the neck*): 3:1

hanger. See **hangar.**

hanger-on (= a sycophantic follower) forms the plural *hangers-on*—not **hanger-ons.* See PLURALS (G).

> Current ratio: 212:1

Hanukkah; Chanukah; Hanukah. The spelling of the Jewish Festival of Lights—an eight-day celebration that falls in November or December—has long been troublesome. Today, though, *Hanukkah* is much more common in AmE and BrE print sources than the next-most-common variants, *Chanukah* and *Hanukah.* It also generates almost three times as many hits on Internet search engines as *Chanukah,* and ten times as many as *Hanukah.* The festival's name has been spelled many other ways as well. It's a matter of tricky transliteration: how to represent some Hebrew sounds that do not correspond to any letter or combination of letters in the Latin alphabet.

The beginning sound is especially troublesome, being not quite an /h/ sound nor a /ch/ sound but what phoneticians call a *voiceless fricative.* (*Chutzpah* begins with the same sound.) The sound is represented in phonetics by a symbol resembling a connected *k* and *h.* The Yiddish linguist Max Weinreich (1894–1969) transliterated the word as *khanike,* but added that in English the spelling should be *Hanukkah.*

That spelling certainly predominates in AmE. It is also becoming more common in BrE, which has traditionally preferred the *Ch-* variant.

haply (= by chance, perhaps) is an ARCHAISM best avoided—e.g.: "One may rush out into the middle of Broadway in moving traffic observed by a large group of police officers *haply* [delete *haply*] grazing on doughnuts and not merit even a menacing belch." Scott Patterson, "The Truth About Jaywalking," *Virginian-Pilot* (Norfolk), 23 Dec. 1995, at A10. Many readers of that sentence would misread *haply* as a misprint for *happily;* they are to be sympathized with, not disapproved of.

happily means "fortunately," not "in a happy manner," when used as here:

- "*Happily,* the title sequence, which always gives me a delicious feeling of nervous apprehension, is unchanged." William Leith, "Television: Saturday 14 September," *Observer,* 8 Sept. 1996, at 58.
- "*Happily,* some things never change." Craig Smith, "Music Hall Madness Will Reign Again," *Santa Fe New Mexican,* 30 Nov. 1996, Feliz Navidad §, at 10.

See SENTENCE ADVERBS. Cf. **hopefully.**

hara-kiri (Jap. "belly-cutting") is often misspelled in various ways, including **hari kari, *hari-kari,* and **hiri kiri.* These misspellings may be especially tempting because they exemplify what linguists call "reduplicative" or rhyming syllables, whereas the actual phrase does not have reduplicative sounds. E.g.:

- "While Baltimoreans are certainly entitled to their disappointment—the fear here is the brass section of the Colts' Band will be found on their trombone slides, *hari kari* [read *hara-kiri*] style, any day now—the city has apparently learned nothing from Washingtonians' ritual whining about losing the Senators eons ago." Johnette Howard, "Baltimore Suffers NFL's Growing Pains," *Wash. Post,* 2 Dec. 1993, at B3.

- "'*Hiri kiri* [read *Hara-kiri*] squeeze!' I yelled. '*Hiri kiri* [read *Hara-kiri*] squeeze!' To which an Asian gentleman seated to my right turned, nodded and said, 'Very good, very good.'" Mike Downey, "Now It Seems Winning Is Also a Mania," *L.A. Times*, 26 June 1995, at C1.
- "I'm beginning to wonder when the instructor plans to pass out the *hari-kari* [read *hara-kiri*] swords and provide us with a more merciful end to offing ourselves." Tom Murawski, "The Pen May Be Mightier, but the Sword Is So Much More Cool," *Chapel Hill Herald*, 18 Sept. 2002, Editorial §, at 5.

Fortunately, the proper spelling is more than twice as common in print as any of the erroneous forms.

LANGUAGE-CHANGE INDEX
hara-kiri misspelled **hari-kari* or **hiri kiri*: Stage 2
Current ratio (*hara-kiri* vs. **hari-kari*): 6:1

harass; harassment. During the Senate's confirmation hearings on the appointment of Justice Clarence Thomas in October 1991, senators were divided over whether to say /**har**-is/ and /**har**-is-mənt/ on the one hand, or /hə-**ras**/ and /hə-**ras**-mənt/ on the other. (They were divided on other issues as well.) Because the proceedings were closely watched throughout the country, the correct pronunciation became a popular subject of discussion. Although in BrE first-syllable stress predominates—and many Americans (therefore?) consider it preferable—in AmE the second-syllable stress is standard.

The words are often misspelled *-rr-*. See SPELL-ING (A).

LANGUAGE-CHANGE INDEX
harass misspelled **harrass*: Stage 1
Current ratio: 64:1

harbor (= a shelter for vessels) has been predominantly so spelled in AmE since the early 1840s; *harbour* has been the established BrE spelling since Middle English. See -OR; -OUR.

hardly. In DIALECT, this word appears in at least three erroneous forms: **can't hardly* (for *can hardly*), **not hardly* (for *hardly*), and **without hardly* (for *almost without*). See **can hardly** & **not hardly*. Cf. **scarcely any.**

LANGUAGE-CHANGE INDEX
1. **can't hardly* for *can hardly*: Stage 1
Current ratio (*can hardly* vs. **cannot hardly*): 98:1
2. **not hardly* for *hardly*: Stage 1
Current ratio (*is hardly* vs. **is not hardly*): 282:1
3. **without hardly* for *without*: Stage 1
Current ratio (*without being* vs. **without hardly being*): 51,558:1

hard put. G.H. Vallins once insisted that it's wrong to say *the reader is hard put to know what is happening*, insisting instead on adding *to it* to the sentence: *the reader is hard put to it to know what is happening*. Vallins, *Better English* 73 (4th ed. 1957). Today, however, idiom doesn't even allow the *to it*, and virtually no one is hard put to know why—because hardly anyone even thinks of it.

hard sell = (1) strong pressure tactics used in selling; or (2) a difficult sales job resulting from reluctant buyers. So the phrase can be used in a negative sense (about the seller's actions) from the buyer's perspective (sense 1), or a negative sense (about the buyer's actions) from the seller's perspective (sense 2). Sense 1 is the more traditional one—e.g.:

- "When you start looking at builders' furnished models, don't avoid the sales agent because you fear the *hard sell*." Katherine Salant, "Browsers Welcome to New Home Models," *Chicago Trib.*, 28 Dec. 1996, New Homes §, at 3.
- "Don't fall for the *hard sell*. Some of the most dubious investments and 'bargains' around are sold with a now-or-never urgency befitting heart transplants." Ronald Campbell, "No Free Lunch," *Orange County Register*, 30 Dec. 1996, at D3.

Though sense 2 has become common, it is shared with the phrase *hard sale* (a more logical form). Indeed, whereas *sell* is usefully a noun in sense 1 because the phrase denotes the seller's actions, it isn't needed in sense 2, which denotes the buyer's actions. So the better, more logical phrasing for sense 2 is *hard sale*—e.g.:

- "The movie is going to be a *hard sell* [read *hard sale*] for most of today's audiences." Vincent Canby, "'Stanley and Iris': A World Not Seen," *N.Y. Times*, 9 Feb. 1990, at B4.
- "Adequate hand washing—which involves more than just a quick swipe under tepid water—remains a *hard sell* [read *hard sale*]." Kathleen Donnelly, "Keep Hands Clean, Germ-Free," *News & Record* (Greensboro), 3 Jan. 1997, at D1.
- "Hurricane Katrina created opportunities for Jindal to push public policy initiatives that might have been a *hard sell* [read *hard sale*] otherwise." Julia O'Donoghue, "After the Storm, a Political Shift," *Times-Picayune* (New Orleans), 30 Aug. 2015, at A2.

LANGUAGE-CHANGE INDEX
hard sell misused for *hard sale*: Stage 1

hardy; hearty. *Hardy* = bold, vigorous, robust. *Hearty* = (1) warm and enthusiastic <a hearty greeting>; (2) strong and healthy <a hearty rancher>; (3) (of food) nourishing, satisfying <a hearty meal>; or (4) (of an eater) needing or demanding plenty of food <a hearty appetite>. Although sense 2 of *hearty* overlaps somewhat with *hardy* (and is therefore avoided by some careful writers), the other senses don't. Still, some writers confuse the two words—e.g.:

- Sense 1: "A *hardy* [read *hearty*] welcome home to Cleo Parker Robinson and the 18 members of her dance troupe." Robert Jackson, "Cleo Parker Robinson Troupe a Hit in Kenya," *Rocky Mountain News* (Denver), 8 Feb. 1996, at D2.
- Sense 3: "Milwaukee Bucks center Alton Lister . . . settled in on the more secluded side of the counter for a *hardy*

LANGUAGE-CHANGE INDEX (For the full key, see front matter pp. xxxi, l–li.)
Stage 1: Rejected. **Stage 2:** Widely shunned. **Stage 3:** Widespread but . . . **Stage 4:** Ubiquitous but . . . **Stage 5:** Fully accepted.
Invariably inferior forms marked by asterisk (∗). • Ratios represent frequency of prevalent forms vs. variants in current books.

[read *hearty*] meal after a practice with the team." Edith Brin, "Lifelong Dream," *Milwaukee J. Sentinel*, 23 Nov. 1995, at 10.

- Sense 4: "It is an immensely popular spot that has been serving huge portions of gutsy food to enthusiastic *hardy* [read *hearty*, and delete *enthusiastic*] eaters for nearly three years." Richard Jay Scholem, "A La Carte," *N.Y. Times*, 31 Dec. 1995, Long Island §, at 10.

Cf. **hale and hearty.**

Sometimes, too, *hearty* is misused for *hardy*. We speak of *hardy* (not *hearty*) plants—e.g.:

- "At first, Thronson's customers were mostly public agencies seeking cheap, *hearty* [read *hardy*] plants to adorn highways and public buildings." Vince Kohler, "Growth Industry: The Nursery Business Is Going Strong in Oregon," *Oregonian* (Portland), 10 July 1994, at K1.
- "These are solid, *hearty* [read *hardy*] plants that can take a lot of neglect—a perfect choice for first-time gardeners." Tara Aronson, "May Gardening," *S.F. Chron.*, 3 May 1995, Home §, at 1.
- "Turnips, which also date back to ancient times, are *hearty* [read *hardy*] vegetables, able to survive long, cold winters stored underground." Amy Peterson, "Root Force: Let the Roots That Nourish Plants Nourish You," *Diabetes Forecast*, Aug. 1995, at 32.

LANGUAGE-CHANGE INDEX
1. *hardy* misused for *hearty*: Stage 1
Current ratio (*hearty laugh* vs. **hardy laugh*): 61:1
2. *hearty* misused for *hardy*: Stage 1
Current ratio (*hardy plants* vs. **hearty plants*): 78:1

harebrained is the correct form; **hairbrained* is the common blunder. The misspelling falls just short of being what it attempts to denote—e.g.:

- "But what makes the episode such a delight is that it takes us inside the goofy mind of Helms and his *hairbrained* [read *harebrained*] sidekick." David Zurawik, " 'Homicide' Goes Out with a Bang," *Baltimore Sun*, 5 May 1995, at D1.
- "[Lincoln] did argue that whites were superior to blacks in some ways (though not in having a right to freedom), and he did support some *hairbrained* [read *harebrained*] schemes to send blacks to Africa or Central America." Edward Achorn, "The Latest Lincoln Conspiracy Theory," *Providence J.-Bull.*, 23 Apr. 2002, at B5.
- "Mocked by its failure to find Osama bin Laden, the Bush Administration . . . exchanged the hard currency of our inherent idealism for the counterfeit coin of a *hair-brained* [read *harebrained*] cynicism." Lewis H. Lapham, "Cause for Dissent," *Harper's Mag.*, Apr. 2003, at 39.

LANGUAGE-CHANGE INDEX
*hairbrained for *harebrained*: Stage 1
Current ratio (*harebrained* vs. **hairbrained*): 11:1

harelip (= a congenital deformity in which the upper lip is cleft, like that of a hare) is sometimes erroneously spelled **hairlip*—e.g.:

- "The company president [in the novel is] a ranting little geek with wild, Hitler eyes and a pronounced *hairlip* [read *harelip*]." Bill DeYoung, "Crews Leaves Bottle, Returns to Writing," *Ledger* (Lakeland, Fla.), 15 Oct. 1995, at G4.
- "She says she was willing to overlook his *hairlip* [read *harelip*] and the resulting speech impediment." Alan Cairns, "Profile of a Pedophile," *Toronto Sun*, 31 Mar. 1996, at 26.

- "Gay said that over the years he has caught many deformed fish, especially brown bullhead catfish, known as hornputs, that had *hairlips* [read *harelips*], body lesions and festering sores." Richard Higgins, "Tracing Health of Assabet River State," *Boston Globe*, 12 Oct. 1997, at 1.

The term is considered offensive. *Cleft lip* has been the preferred term since the late 1950s.

LANGUAGE-CHANGE INDEX
*hairlip for *harelip*: Stage 1
Current ratio (*harelip* vs. **hairlip*): 43:1

*hare's breath. See **hair's breadth.**

hark back. A. And *hearken back; *harken back. The phrase *hark back* is now the preferred form throughout the English-speaking world. E.g.:

- "For an example of this sort of hazard, Biggs *harks back* to June 1950, when the Japanese market fell more than 50 percent in eight days as hostilities flared in Korea." Chet Currier, "Russia Mutual Fund May Require Leap of Faith," *News & Record* (Greensboro), 21 July 1996, at E2.
- "But the concept *harks back* to the first World's Fair in 1851 in London, for which Joseph Paxton designed the Crystal Palace." Herbert Muschamp, "Melding Past and Present in Portugal," *N.Y. Times*, 22 Nov. 1996, at C24.

*Hearken back and **harken back* are NEEDLESS VARIANTS that, taken together, are markedly less common than *hark back*.

B. Wrongly Written *harp back. This odd mistake seems not to have spread beyond BrE—e.g.:

- "It just encourages blokes to *harp* [read *hark*] back to a time when men were men and women were very pissed off." Julia Clarke, "Isn't It About Time That Rabbie Was Barred?" *Daily Record* (Glasgow), 24 Jan. 1996, at 28.
- "It makes interesting reading for those who *harp* [read *hark*] back to a golden age of *childish* [read *childlike*] innocence, and condemn the horrors and 'new sexuality' of modern children." Euan Ferguson, "Reclaiming the Streets: Full of Woe or Far to Go?" *Observer*, 9 June 1996, at 16. (See **childlike.**)
- "The coach is determined not to let his men *harp* [read *hark*] back to that September result in Limerick as a means of motivation." "Al: Don't Think About Last Time," *Daily Record* (Glasgow), 11 Apr. 2015, at 51.

Curiously, most British dictionaries say nothing about this error.

LANGUAGE-CHANGE INDEX
*harp back for *hark back*: Stage 1
Current ratio (*harked back* vs. **harped back*): 170:1

*harp back. See **hark back** (B).

harp on (= to talk or write about persistently and tediously) is frequently miswritten **hark on*, especially in BrE. Whereas *harp on* usually takes a direct object <kept harping on his foibles>, **hark on* often occurs in the collocation **hark on about* (as in the second and third examples below)—e.g.:

- "It's about stitching the club into the fabric of the community for years to come, rather than *harking on* [read *harping on*] times past." Michael Gannon, "The Dons of a New Era," *Daily Herald* (Glasgow), 18 Apr. 2013, at 30.

- "He's at a different club now and no one will move forward if they keep *harking on about* [read *harping on*] the past." Ian Rush, "Five Things Rodgers Must Do to Turn Season Around," *Irish Independent*, 13 Dec. 2014, at 75.
- "You're probably sick of hearing about them, to be fair. But Conor O'Brien is worth *harking on about* [read *harping on*]." "More from the Village Folk," *Daily Mirror*, 17 Apr. 2015, at 12.

HARVARD COMMA. See PUNCTUATION (D).

hashtag (#) is the quintessential VOGUE WORD of the early 21st century. Known also as the *pound sign* or *number symbol*, it took on a new life with the advent of Twitter and other social-media sites. People would post a message and then add, for example, "#goodmemories" or "#happilymarried"—always without internal spaces or punctuation. About 2008, the term even entered conversations as people would make a comment and then remark, "Hashtag annoyed" or "Hashtag HappyMothersDay." Often the term is invoked with more than a tinge of sarcasm: someone else will self-pityingly harp on personal disappointments, and another (perhaps a "frenemy") will say, "Hashtag Woeisme."

hassle (= [1] a squabble; or [2] a needlessly difficult situation) is sometimes misspelled **hassel*—e.g.: "Take the big *hassel* [read *hassle*] over the IMF contribution. Right off, this was interpreted in Congress as a bank-bailout operation." Joseph D. Hutnyan, "Beleaguered Banks Glad to Get the Easter Break," *Am. Banker*, 1 Apr. 1983, at 4.

LANGUAGE-CHANGE INDEX
hassle misspelled **hassel*: Stage 1
Current ratio: 958:1

has to do with; is to do with. The first predominates in AmE and BrE alike; the second is a chiefly BrE variant. E.g.: "The other measure *is to do with* [or, in AmE, *has to do with*] one's colleagues." Lucy Kellaway, "Yes, We Have No Free Bagels," *Fin. Times*, 15 Jan. 2001, at 10.

hateable. So spelled in both AmE and BrE—not **hatable*. See MUTE E.

Current ratio: 6:1

*haulyard. See **halyard.**

hauteur /hoh-**tuur**/ is a GALLICISM denoting haughtiness in manner—e.g.:
- "This gives her dancing a folkish, down-home, countrified cast, a bit of humor or even a moment of toughness in the midst of her conventional flamenco *hauteur*." Judith Green, "La Tania, Marin Move Past Gypsy Roots of Flamenco," *S.F. Examiner*, 12 Oct. 1996, at C1.
- "Robinson goes for a dry *hauteur* as Jacqueline, which she often achieves, anchoring the play in a certain feigned reality." Jan Herman, "French Farce," *L.A. Times*, 14 Jan. 1997, at F4.

- "[Brad] Smith is a polished, thoughtful, and credible advocate whom some have described as the face of the kinder, gentler, post-monopoly Microsoft. But that's not really an apt description of Smith; he projects intensity, determination, a hint of Ivy League *hauteur*, and ambition." Roger Parloff, "Microsoft Takes On the Free World," *Fortune*, 28 May 2007, at 76.

have. On the question of morphing *'ve* into *of*, see **of** (D).

have got. See **get** (C).

have your cake and eat it too. See **you can't eat your cake and have it too.**

having said that. This phrase, which hedges a previous assertion, is a frequent source of DANGLERS. The phrase is perfectly fine, of course, if *I* or a word for some other speaker follows the comma: "*Having said that*, I freely acknowledge that I have returned to work to catch up on my rest." Tom Jackson, "Snared in Pasco's Comfy Time Warp," *Tampa Trib.*, 20 July 1999, Pasco §, at 1. But the expression becomes a mid- to low CASUALISM when it's not anchored to a term for the speaker in the main clause—e.g.:

- "*Having said that*, after a while one gobsmacking building looks pretty much like another." Simon Hattenstone, "48 Hours in . . . Prague," *Guardian*, 27 June 1998, at 10.
- "*Having said that*, it's time to step out from behind the safety of third person to say goodbye." Frank LoMonte, "Georgia's Potential Untapped," *Fla. Times-Union*, 24 May 1999, at B1.
- "*Having said that*, some clubs are going to be more aggressive and growth-oriented." Hank Ezell, "Investment Club Strategy," *Atlanta J.-Const.*, 3 July 1999, at 32.
- "*Having said that*, there is no excuse ever for violence at a concert." Letter of Ed Levine, "Promoter Michael Lang Owes Region an Apology," *Post-Standard* (Syracuse), 12 Aug. 1999, at 20.

An easy solution is simply to delete the phrase, which doesn't say much anyway.

The variant *that said* does not create the same problems: it's an elliptical nominative absolute standing for *that having been said* <That said, some clubs are going to be more aggressive>.

havoc, vb., forms *havocked* and *havocking*. See -C-.

havoc, wreak. See **wreak** (C). See also **reek.**

Hawaii. A. Sense. To most people, the place name *Hawaii* is unambiguous. It refers to the 50th state of the U.S., comprising eight volcanic islands (and more than 120 islets), inhabited from the 5th century A.D. by Polynesians, annexed by the United States as a territory in 1900, and admitted as a state in 1959. The islands have individual names: Oahu, Maui, Kauai, Molokai, and so on. The biggest island, which is geologically the newest and still has active volcanoes, is called *Hawaii*.

LANGUAGE-CHANGE INDEX (For the full key, see front matter pp. xxxi, l–li.)
Stage 1: Rejected. **Stage 2:** Widely shunned. **Stage 3:** Widespread but . . . **Stage 4:** Ubiquitous but . . . **Stage 5:** Fully accepted.
Invariably inferior forms marked by asterisk (*). • Ratios represent frequency of prevalent forms vs. variants in current books.

Hence an ambiguity: when you say *Hawaii*, do you mean all the islands collectively (the 50th state) or just the biggest of the islands? To cure this ambiguity, the big island is usually called *the Big Island* (so capitalized). But officially it is known as *Hawaii*.

In New York, of course, a similar problem exists: the major city and the state bear the same name. But here the semantic hegemony goes the other way (from the smaller political unit to the larger): if you say you're going to New York, everyone assumes it's New York City—no one thinks of Albany or Rochester or Buffalo. But if you say you're going to Hawaii, most people would think of Oahu or Maui—few would assume that you're referring to the Big Island.

B. Spelled *Hawai'i*. Sometimes you'll see a DIA-CRITICAL MARK (called an *okina* [/oh-**kee**-nə/], *'u'ina* [same pronunciation], or *hamzah* [/**ham**-zə/ or /**hahm**-zə/] inserted in *Hawaii* and other Hawaiian names, usually between repeated vowels <Ni'ihau> but occasionally between vowels not repeated <O'ahu>. E.g.: "It looks like the rest of Hawai'i." Andrew Doughty & Harriett Friedman, *Maui Revealed* 141 (2001). It is typically printed as an inverted comma, not as an apostrophe. This accent marks a glottal stop—a sharp guttural break that prevents a diphthong.

The okina is part of the Hawaiian language. It didn't crop up much in English-language contexts until the late 20th century. For example, the *Honolulu Advertiser* began using the okina on all its pages in October 2000, and today its front-page motto contains an odd-looking possessive: *Hawai'i's Newspaper*. But usage isn't uniform: whereas the *Honolulu Advertiser* uses the okina throughout, names mentioned in the *Maui News* are free of it.

As a diacritical mark in an English context, the mark seems largely out of place and undesirable: (1) it smacks of a provincialism that resists linguistic assimilation to standard AmE; (2) it isn't much help to the nonnative speaker who seeks to pronounce Hawaiian names correctly (look at *'u'ina* itself—most speakers would be at a loss to know how to say it); (3) it leads to odd-looking phrases, such as the *Honolulu Advertiser's* motto; and (4) most Hawaiian names (such as *Hawaii* itself) have been assimilated into English without the mark—usage has long been settled, and the okina simply unsettles it.

A University of Hawaii professor opposed the needless diacritical mark in English contexts as early as 1973: "The use of diacritics is not only superfluous but also contrary to the facts of conventional HE [Hawaiian English] orthography and normal HE pronunciation . . . . The practice must therefore be regarded as sheer pedantry or as sheer folly if it is to be interpreted as a pitch for the preservation of the glottal stop and the like in HE loans." Stanley M. Tsuzaki, "Hawaiian English," 48 *Am. Speech* 117, 119 (1973).

C. Pronunciation. Most Americans say /hə-**wI**-ee/ or /hə-**wah**-ee/—the only pronunciations recognized by most English-language dictionaries. Most locals say /hə-**vI**-ee/, since in the Hawaiian language

a -*w*- preceded by a vowel is pronounced as a -*v*-. The -*v*- sound is an "insider" pronunciation, used only by denizens of Hawaii. Among residents interviewed in August 2002, most agreed that it would be pretentious for anyone but a longtime resident to adopt the pronunciation. If one moved to the state, there might well be social pressures after some time to adopt the -*v*-pronunciation. And the feeling among interviewees was that the pressures would be much weaker on the island of Oahu than on the other islands.

Hawaiian. Among residents of Hawaii, this term expresses ethnicity, not nativity or residency. Whereas most state labels refer to where you were born or now live (e.g., *Californian, Iowan, New Yorker*), *Hawaiian* is reserved only for those descended from indigenous Hawaiian Islanders. E.g.: "*Hawaiians* believe that all of life is part of a force they call ma'ana, and they believe ma'ana can be shared." Judith Kreiner, " 'Aloha' Speaks Volumes in Hawaii," *Wash. Times*, 7 Oct. 2000, at E1. Other residents of Hawaii, even those born there, are termed *locals* or *islanders*. The standards explained here are pretty well recognized in the press—e.g.:

- "The term '*Hawaiian*' refers to an ethnic group, a person who is of Polynesian descent. Unlike a term like Californian, Hawaiian should not be used for everyone living in Hawaii. The distinction is not trivial. Possible alternatives: islander, Hawaiian resident." "Ten Tips for Covering Asian American Issues," *Presstime*, June 2001, at 12.
- " '*Locals*' [is] a term that includes native Hawaiians and certain non-European ethnic groups, but generally not white people or the middle class of any colour." Christina Thompson, "Forked Tongue," *Australian*, 13 June 2001, at B19.
- " '*Hawaiian*' refers to the original inhabitants of the islands, the Polynesians, and their descendants." Vera Vida, "Island Cooking," *Patriot Ledger* (Quincy, Mass.), 24 Apr. 2002, Features §, at 27.

In the following example, *Hawaiians* is loosely used as meaning "all residents of Hawaii": "New Yorkers pay about 14 cents and *Hawaiians* [read *residents of Hawaii*] pay nearly 17 cents, according to the Department of Energy." John Woolfolk, "Regulators to Boost Power Bills by as Much as 36 Percent," *San Jose Mercury News*, 27 Mar. 2001, State & Regional News §, at 10.

See DENIZEN LABELS. On a related subject, see **Native American.**

***hayday.** See **heyday** (A).

He; Him. When referring to God, most professional writers and editors don't capitalize the pronouns—e.g.: "God is a spirit. I have had tremendous messages from *him*, which are from the Bible; it's not something I've dreamed up or had a vision of. It's important to study the Bible on a daily basis so *he* can speak to me." Billy Graham, as quoted in "Of Angels, Devils and Messages from God," *Time*, 15 Nov. 1993, at 74. Is *Time* bowing to secularism? No. As the 14th edition of *The Chicago Manual of Style* noted, "in few areas is an author more tempted to overcapitalize or an editor more loath to urge a lowercase style than in religion" (§ 7.74, at 265

[14th ed. 1993]). In the 16th edition, the hand-wringing is gone: "Pronouns referring to God or Jesus are not capitalized" (§ 8.94, at 427 [16th ed. 2010]).

Many versions of the Bible itself—including the King James Version, the Revised Standard Version, the New International Version, and the English Standard Version—don't capitalize *he* or *him* in reference to God. So while members of the clergy might capitalize these pronouns in letters to the congregation, other writers should make them lowercase.

*he/she. See **he or she (B).**

HEADLINESE. A. Headlines and Headings Generally. Headlines in journalism, like headings in other documents, are both the most important and least important parts of the writing. They are the most important because they are the most read and, if effectively written, most valuable to the reader. Their value comes in attracting the reader's attention and guiding the reader to where particular information might be found. Piquing the reader's interest is equivalent to a salesperson's getting a foot in the door. It's not the closing of the deal by any means. The text must deliver what the head promises or the deal's off. That's why the heading might also be said to be the least important part of the writing.

Besides capturing the reader's attention and generating interest, headlines (or, in documents, headings and subheadings) guide the reader through the content. Headlines show the reader where to find things of interest, both on a first reading and later, when the reader wants to refer to that information. In longer articles and essays—and certainly in documents—headings and subheadings are crucial finding tools.

The ability to write brief, accurate, and clear headlines and headings is an important skill, and a hard one to learn. As a University of Kansas journalism professor put it: "Many students find précis writing a hard art to master. A newspaper copy editor has to master not only the art of writing a précis but also the far more difficult art of writing a précis of a précis. He writes news headlines." John B. Bremner, *HTK* 1 (1972).

B. Peculiar Usage of. Space constraints are responsible for the odd, nonconversational way in which news headlines are often written. The "count" (loosely speaking, the number of lowercase letters that can fit in a column of type) is absolute and often small. So short words are the headline writer's friend. And since good heads are those that get attention, short, snappy words are especially close friends. So a basketball player becomes a *cager*, a school superintendent becomes a *chief*, and a symposium becomes a *confab*. The epitome of this style of headline writing remains the alliterative banner over a 1935 article in *Variety* about rural moviegoers' preference for stories of city life: "Sticks Nix Hick Pix." See ALLITERATION (A).

It's easy to see how that sort of writing becomes hackneyed pretty quickly, and in fact much of the old cant is falling or has fallen into disuse. Lawmakers are seldom called *solons* anymore, track-and-field athletes *thinclads*, or tickets *ducats*. But the short action verbs—such as *axe* (= fire), *balk* (= object; oppose), *hit* (= adversely affect), *inks* (= signs), *mull* (= consider), *nab* (= arrest), *nix* (= refuse; veto), *rap* (= criticize), *rout* (= defeat handily), and *slay* (= murder)—are still common. Likewise, short nouns remain useful—words such as *buzz* (= chatter), *cap* (= limit), *cut* (= reduction), *guru* (= expert), *probe* (= investigation), and *toll* (= number of casualties; extent of damage).

ABBREVIATIONS, acronyms, and initialisms naturally fit the need for short forms, and well-known ones get plenty of use <State St. CEO: No Need for Fresh Capital> <EPA Weighs TVA's Duty in Cleanup> <FCC Fines 9 Cable Providers>. But editors rightly discourage or even ban the use of obscure initialisms as too reader-unfriendly <Host Agrees: 'No Thanks' to Gutted ESG>.

Finally, the use of nouns as adjectives is fairly common in headlines <Massey Ltd. Seeks Canada Financial Aid> <Okinawa Case Pressed in Court>. In text, a writer would be better off using the adjectival forms *Canadian* and *Okinawan*. See FUNCTIONAL SHIFT.

C. Peculiar Grammar of. Another effect of space constraints in headlines is the adoption of punctuation and syntax constructions that are not found in general prose. They would sound strange indeed in conversation.

Commas and semicolons serve unique purposes in headlines, largely because periods usually appear only in abbreviations. Commas routinely stand in for the conjunction *and* <Obama, Biden Take Oaths>. Semicolons stand in for periods and join two sentences, sometimes sentences that would not easily fit together as independent clauses in a compound sentence <Israel Speeds Withdrawal from Gaza; Efforts to Buttress Ceasefire Continue>.

Colons show up often in headlines, serving one of two purposes. They may follow an introductory tag <GOP: On the Road to Recovery?>, an attribution <Cops: Real-Life Horror at Cinema>, or the equivalent of a dateline <Illinois: Legal Team Quits Impeachment Defense>. Or they may be used traditionally, linking a statement with some explanation, supporting information, resulting outcome, or other related matter <As Flight Went Down, He Got Ready to Help at Exit: 'I Thought, You Sat in This Seat, You Have to Figure This Out'>.

Single quotation marks replace the double marks used in AmE text <Fond Memories of 'Shoeshine Man'>.

Headlines also show several oddities of syntax, all of which are also aimed at saving space. The articles

LANGUAGE-CHANGE INDEX (For the full key, see front matter pp. xxxi, l–li.)
Stage 1: Rejected. **Stage 2:** Widely shunned. **Stage 3:** Widespread but . . . **Stage 4:** Ubiquitous but . . . **Stage 5:** Fully accepted.
Invariably inferior forms marked by asterisk (*). • Ratios represent frequency of prevalent forms vs. variants in current books.

a, *an*, and *the* are often omitted altogether, as are *be*-verbs <Coke-Fired Plant [Is a] Bad Idea>. Having the option of using or omitting these words gives headline writers some flexibility in making heads fit the space allowed.

Verb tenses also differ from the traditional rules of English grammar. The present tense often denotes recent past events <Rain Delays Game 2 of Series> <Fiat, Chrysler Form Alliance>. And the infinitive often denotes future tense <Sears to Keep Layaway Option> <New Chief to Face Budget Crunch>.

D. Peculiar Style of. Some final points. First, as a matter of style, the passive voice is far more common in headlines than in general prose, where its overuse is a well-known fault. The reason for its acceptance in headlines is that once a writer has reduced the gist of a story to a mere handful of words, the most important thing about the story turns out to be the recipient of the action (the object), not the actor (the subject). The natural word order, then, becomes passive <Recount Ordered in Mayoral Election> <Dads Locked Up Till They Pay Up>. See PASSIVE VOICE.

Second, line breaks should reflect logical and grammatical breaks as closely as possible. Sometimes a break can create a MISCUE. Consider the headline *Political / ads blitz / — — —*, for example. After reading the first two lines, the reader might think that's the subject, a three-word noun phrase, and expect a verb such as *planned* to follow. When the final line turns out to be *viewers*, the reader might hesitate and then look back before realizing that *blitz* is the verb. Even when no miscue is possible, it's best not to split a preposition from its object between lines, for example, or *to* from the verb in an infinitive.

In a similar vein, the importance of hyphenating PHRASAL ADJECTIVES becomes apparent in the close quarters of a headline. Consider this headline: "Wall Street Retreats as Bank Fears Crash Party," *Orlando Sentinel*, 21 Jan. 2009, at B7. Which bank is afraid of a crash party? That could have been *Bank-Fears Crash Party* or *Banks' Fears Crash Party*.

E. Guidance for Journalists. Over the years, newspaper editors and web designers have developed many pointers for effective headline writing. Among the principal ones are these:

- Capsulize the gist of the piece. Use words that apply so specifically to the story that they couldn't be used to headline another one <Pa. Race Won't Tip Superdelegates>.
- Make a definite statement with a concrete idea that can be easily grasped. Always prefer a tangible example over a general concept <50 Iraqis Die in Suicide Bombing> (as opposed to *Violence Continues in Middle East*).
- Ensure that the headline reflects the right tone for the publication and for the specific article, be it serious and sober or light and sensational <All 155 Aboard Safe as Crippled Jet Crash-Lands in Hudson (*N.Y. Times*)> <CRASH RESCUE A REAL SLAM DUNK / GEESE KO ENGINES (*N.Y. Post*)>.
- Include a verb <A Dash of Wit Salts Obama's Speech>, even if it's only implied <Scalia, Long Shy of News Media, Now More Open> (in which *Is* is implied after *Media*).

Hence every headline is a statement. If suppressed, the verb must be readily supplied by the reader's mind—its feeling remains <Air Trips Slowest in Past 20 Years>.

- Use the present tense, not past <Chaos Rules at Nevada Polygamist Hearing> (not *Chaos Ruled . . .*).
- Use an active verb if possible <Attacks Rooted in Religion Energize Faith in Many>. Avoid the word *was* <B.U. Ex-President Named as Man on Drifting Barge> (as opposed to *Man on Drifting Barge Was Ex-President of B.U.*).
- Don't repeat any important word in any part of the same headline <Businesses Absorb Oil Costs> (as opposed to *Business Costs Rise with Oil Costs*).
- Omit articles unless necessary for the sense <3 Charged with Arlington Heights Apartment Break-In>.
- Avoid ending lines with fizzle-words. Put the punch word at the end. <Icicles Can Hurt Roofs, Interiors of Homes, and, of Course, Passersby>.
- Avoid cramming in too much information <To Nest Best, Feather Together> (as opposed to *To Pamper Their Parrots, Cockatiels, and Macaws, Bird Lovers Are Creating a Whole New Species of Rooms*).
- Avoid a clutter of punctuation <School Woes Aren't Over Yet> (as opposed to *Political Animals of Public Schools; So the Amarillo Unified School Board Has Finally Been Assimilated by the Recall/Reform Movement: Problem Solved, Right? Nope!*).
- Don't use a comma as a substitute for any word except *and* <Pet Owners, Landlords Need Win–Win Strategy>.

F. Further Reading. For reliable treatments, see Robert E. Garst & Theodore M. Bernstein, *Headlines and Deadlines* (1933); John B. Bremner, *HTK* (1972); Barbara G. Ellis, *The Copy-Editing and Headline Handbook* (2001); Paula LaRocque, *Heads You Win: An Easy Guide to Better Headline and Caption Writing* (2003).

headlong. See **headstrong**.

headquarters. This noun commonly takes a plural verb, as in the first two examples listed below. But the singular predominates when the reference is to a building, as in the third example, or to authority (as opposed to a place), as in the fourth example:

- "Heather Cook [is the] manager of public relations for SurfControl, whose U.S. *headquarters are* in Scotts Valley, Calif." Morgan Lee, "General Services to Add Internet Filters," *Albuquerque J.*, 11 Dec. 2000, at 4.
- "The company's world *headquarters are* in Ramat-Gan, Israel." "Technology," *Atlanta J.-Const.*, 18 Jan. 2001, at C2.
- "The Louisiana Lottery Corp.'s new state *headquarters is* still on the drawing board, but it's already turning heads." Scott Dyer, "Lottery Building Bends with Downtown Decor," *Advocate* (Baton Rouge), 17 Dec. 2000, at B1.
- "Its *headquarters is* in Tide Point." Stacey Hirsh, "High-Techs Learn Some Old Rules," *Baltimore Sun*, 21 Jan. 2001, at P5.

Of course, if you're torn by this dilemma, you can usually recast the sentence <the company has its headquarters in St. Louis>.

headstrong, adj.; **headlong,** adv. *Headstrong* (= stubborn, obstinate) is sometimes misused for the adverb *headlong* (= [1] headfirst; or [2] in a blindly impetuous way)—e.g.:

- "While my parents' generation rushed *headstrong* [read *headlong*] into adulthood, mine has tried to postpone it as long as possible." Don McLeese, "Birth Rights or Wrongful Births?" *Austin Am.-Statesman*, 1 May 1997, at E1.
- "Mr. Chehabi wasn't exactly running *headstrong* [read *headlong*] into the great unknown." Cheryl Hall, "A Rock-Solid Reputation," *Dallas Morning News*, 18 Jan. 1998, at H1.
- "His underlying message was more subtle: Republicans should not rush *headstrong* [read *headlong*] this early into backing either of the two most popular contenders: Gov. George W. Bush of Texas or Elizabeth Dole." Richard L. Berke, "Lamar Alexander Declares Run for President in 2000," *N.Y. Times*, 10 Mar. 1999, at A15.

Sometimes the senses truly seem to merge, as *headstrong* takes on an adverbial quality more evocative than *headlong*—e.g.: "Creationists have run *headstrong* into teachers and scientists who have effectively lobbied their state and local school boards." Michael Janofsky, "New Mexico Rules Out Teaching Creationism," *Times-Picayune* (New Orleans), 10 Oct. 1999, at A13.

LANGUAGE-CHANGE INDEX
headstrong misused for *headlong*: Stage 1

head up, vb.; **heads-up,** n. & adj. **A.** *Head up,* vb. This PHRASAL VERB is voguish in business and academic JARGON—e.g.:

- "Nigel Wilson, a transit expert at the Massachusetts Institute of Technology, will *head up* the panel." Doug Hanchett, "MBTA on Board for Review of Silver Line Buses," *Boston Herald*, 22 Oct. 2000, at 9.
- "At Rocco, Ranelin will *head up* a superb band that includes greats John Heard on bass and Roy McCurdy on drums and rising pianist Danny Grissett." Zan Stewart, "Valley Life Ticket to Slide," *L.A. Times*, 8 Dec. 2000, at B5.
- "Reddy, of the school of computer science, *heads up* something called the Aura project." Steve Hamm, "Net Culture," *BusinessWeek*, 11 Dec. 2000, at 102.

B. *Heads-up,* n. & adj. As a noun, this CASUALISM is a voguish substitute for "warning"—e.g.: "[Louis W.] Uccellini said this new forecasting method should . . . give local governments a *heads-up* to get out their snow plows and call in their snow-removal crews." Scott Burke, "Better Forecasts in the Future?" *Capital* (Annapolis), 17 Nov. 2002, at A1. As a PHRASAL ADJECTIVE, it is informal for "alert"—e.g.: "Franco Wakhisi tied it at 1–1 in the 73rd minute with a *heads-up* play." Will Parrish, "Eagles Meet Coastal for BSC Title, NCAA Berth," *Herald* (Rock Hill, S.C.), 17 Nov. 2002, at D3.

heal. See **cure.**

healthcare; health care. In actual usage—especially among healthcare providers—the one-word version

is well on its way. It seems inevitable. The problem with *health care* as a noun phrase is that it requires a hyphen when used attributively, as a PHRASAL ADJECTIVE <health-care issues>—and few people seem to have patience for this nicety. And *healthcare* is different from *managed care* and *medical care* because it's a compound formed from two one-syllable words.

healthful; healthy. Strictly speaking, *healthy* refers to a person (or personified thing) in good health, *healthful* to whatever promotes good health. E.g.: "Low-fat dairy products . . . will keep us feeling *healthy* and good about ourselves, she says. A vegetarian, Barnes takes *healthful* dishes to parties." Pat Dooley, "Dreaming of a Lite Christmas," *Dayton Daily News*, 17 Dec. 1996, Metro §, at 1. In fact, though, many writers use *healthy* when they mean *healthful*, and *healthy* threatens to edge out its sibling altogether. Such a development would be unhealthful, since it would lead to a less healthy state of the language. Although the phrase *healthful recreation* was more common in print sources from 1770 to about 1960, since that time *healthy recreation* has become predominant in AmE and BrE alike.

LANGUAGE-CHANGE INDEX
healthy for *healthful*: Stage 4

hear. See **listen.**

***hearken back.** See **hark back (A).**

heart-rending is sometimes wrongly written **heart-rendering*—e.g.:

- "He's proudest, perhaps, of his non-musical work, including *heart-rendering* [read *heart-rending*] shots taken during the early '60s of the Appalachian poor and the civil-rights movement in the South." Craig Marine, "Wild at Heart," *S.F. Examiner*, 26 May 1996, at M6.
- "He returns to his regular style on a cover of Larry Graham's R&B classic, a *heart-rendering* [read *heart-rending*], emotional 'One in a Million You.'" Teresa Graham, "Record Reviews," *Times Union* (Albany), 24 July 1997, at 31.
- "What a humbling, rewarding, *heart-rendering* [read *heart-rending*] experience." Hugh McMillan, "Puget Sound Honor Flight Leaves Indelible Memory for WWII Vet," *News Trib.* (Tacoma, Wash.), 10 June 2015, at 1141.

Of course, the verb *rend* (= to split, tear) has nothing to do with the verb *render* (= to make, perform, provide). The errant phrase is particularly unpleasant because one definition of *render* is "to boil down (fat)." See **rend** & MALAPROPISMS.

LANGUAGE-CHANGE INDEX
**heart-rendering* for *heart-rending*: Stage 1
Current ratio (*heart-rending* vs.
**heart-rendering*): 72:1

hearty. See **hardy.**

heave > heaved > heaved. The past-tense *hove* is archaic in all uses except the nautical phrases *heave*

LANGUAGE-CHANGE INDEX (For the full key, see front matter pp. xxxi, l–li.)
Stage 1: Rejected. **Stage 2:** Widely shunned. **Stage 3:** Widespread but . . . **Stage 4:** Ubiquitous but . . . **Stage 5:** Fully accepted.
Invariably inferior forms marked by asterisk (*). • Ratios represent frequency of prevalent forms vs. variants in current books.

into view and *heave into sight*, both meaning "to become visible"—e.g.:

- "We were waiting for a table when Jerry Simpson *hove* into view, at the helm of a 23-foot fiberglass boat." Peter Rowe, "How Hot Is It?" *San Diego Union-Trib.*, 14 Nov. 1996, at E1.
- "Last time, when the University of Arkansas Marching Band *hove* into view, Brotman boomed, so he recalls, 'Mr. President, here comes the Arkansas band.'" Paul Hendrickson, "Pageantry: America's Answer to Royalty," *Wash. Post*, 20 Jan. 1997, at E17.

Some writers incorrectly understand the past-tense *hove* as a special present-tense verb. The error is most prevalent in BrE—e.g.:

- "But along with empathy there is wry humour too, particularly when England's cricket supremo, Ray Illingworth, *hoves* [read *heaves*] into view." Harry Pearson, "All Over Bar the Shouting," *Independent*, 9 Nov. 1996, Books §, at 8.
- "Not long after, the O2 Arena—completing the trinity of London's major tennis venues—*hoves* [read *heaves*] into view." Andy Murray & Mike Dickson, "I've Got to Make the Most of This Because It Won't Last Forever," *Daily Mail*, 27 June 2015, at 108.

LANGUAGE-CHANGE INDEX
hove misused for present-tense *heave*: Stage 1
Current ratio (*heaves* vs. *hoves*): 85:1

heaven's sake. So written—not (as often erroneously written) **heavens sake*, **heaven's sakes*, **heaven sakes*, or **heavens' sake*.
Current ratio (in order of terms in entry): 204:7:5:2:1

hecto-; centi-. *Hecto-* derives from the Greek *hekaton*, *centi-* from the Latin *centum* (both meaning "one hundred"). Whereas the root *hecto-* means "multiplied by 100," *centi-* means "divided by 100." Hence a *hectometer* is 100 meters; a *centimeter* is a hundredth of a meter.

he'd better; he better. See **better (A).**

hegemony /hi-**jem**-ə-nee/ is a fundamentally political term ("political dominance; the leadership or predominant authority of one state of a confederacy, union, or region over the others") that has been imported into commercial and nonpolitical contexts. E.g.:

- "Influential men began to expand the old-fashioned and physiologically specific definition of masculinity into an overwhelming concept implying social and (especially important at Harvard) intellectual *hegemony*." Susan Jacoby, "What Makes a Real Man?" *Newsday* (N.Y.), 15 Dec. 1996, at C36.
- "Clearly, the new peace process on all three tracks—Syrian, Palestinian and moderate Arab states—is shaping to play out as part of the wider struggle between Iran and the U.S. for regional *hegemony*." Leslie Susser, "An Ambush on the Way to Peace," *Jerusalem Rep.*, 20 Aug. 2007, at 14.

The term verges on being a VOGUE WORD.

The corresponding adjective is *hegemonic*—e.g.: "As history shows, *hegemonic* empires almost automatically elicit universal resistance, which is why all such aspirants eventually have exhausted themselves." Christopher Layne & Benjamin Schwarz, "U.S. Can Become Less of a Target," *Times Union* (Albany), 18 Nov. 2002, at A7.

hegira /hi-**ji**-rə/ (= a journey undertaken to escape a troublesome situation) is the standard spelling. **Hejira* is a variant (although the Arabic word for "emigration, flight" is *hijra*). When used in reference to Muhammad's flight from Mecca to Medina in A.D. 622, the word is capitalized: *Hegira*.

height has a distinct /t/ sound at the end. To pronounce or write this word as if it were **heighth* is less than fully literate—e.g.: "Second-seeded Syracuse had intermittent difficulties with No. 15 Coppin State's zone defenses, but Syracuse's *heighth* [read *height*] and strength won out." "Tourney Was Here in '90," *Richmond Times-Dispatch*, 15 Mar. 1996, at D3. The mistake may occur for any of several reasons: (1) other words conveying measurement end in *-th* (e.g., *depth*, *width*, *breadth*); (2) people might confuse its ending with that of *eighth*; or (3) **highth* is an archaic variant once used in southern England. See CLASS DISTINCTIONS & PRONUNCIATION (B).

LANGUAGE-CHANGE INDEX
height misspelled or mispronounced
*heighth: Stage 2
Current ratio: 1,652:1

heinous /**hay**-nəs/—rhyming with "pain us"—is one of our most commonly mispronounced words. It is also frequently misspelled **heinious*—e.g.: "[It was as if] Maris had committed some *heinious* [read *heinous*] crime in threatening Ruth's record." Sean McAdam, "All Ripken Wants Is to Play, Play and Play," *Providence J.-Bull.*, 11 Aug. 1995, at D1. See PRONUNCIATION (B).

For the misuse of *onerous* for *heinous*, see **onerous.**

LANGUAGE-CHANGE INDEX
1. *heinous* mispronounced /**hee**-nəs/ or
/**hee**-nee-əs/: Stage 4
2. *heinous* misspelled **heinious*: Stage 1
Current ratio: 3,123:1

heiress. Despite the feminine ending (see SEXISM (D)), this word shows no signs of obsolescence in denoting a woman who has inherited wealth—e.g.:

- "So far five young women have claimed to be the missing *heiress*." Mary Evertz, "Romance Writer Takes a Turn at Mystery and Intrigue," *St. Petersburg Times*, 23 July 1995, at D7.
- "Like so many of the repressed characters in the novels of Henry James, Isabel Archer, a young American *heiress* who has the notion that she will find happiness abroad, is a psychosexual tuning fork." Tom Gliatto et al., "Screen," *People*, 27 Jan. 1997, at 21.
- "'Mistress America' also harks back to an even earlier age, when madcap *heiresses* played by Claudette Colbert or Carole Lombard would traipse around Manhattan with louche abandon." Ann Hornaday, "'Mistress America' Celebrates Women, Screwball Comedies," *Denver Post*, 28 Aug. 2015, at 7C.

Although *heiress-apparent* is more strictly correct, *heiress* is also commonly used to denote a woman who stands to inherit—e.g.: "[Paris] Hilton stands to inherit $30 million of her family fortune, but in 2005 she made a reported $7 million on her own. The hotel *heiress's* name is emblazoned on everything from perfume to lip-enhancement serum." Meghan Keane, "She's with the Brand," *N.Y. Sun*, 21 Aug. 2006, at 16. Purists frown on that usage as loose.

*hejira. See **hegira**.

helix yields the plural *helices* or *helixes*. The classical plural *-ces* vastly predominates in modern print sources. Cf. **appendixes**. See PLURALS (B).

helm, vb. Originally a nautical term meaning "to steer," *helm* has been borrowed by the entertainment industry in the sense "to direct or produce (a film, play, album, etc.)." This extended sense, now entrenched in showbiz talk, is likely to strike many readers as newfangled and catchpenny—e.g.:

- "The multiple-director system works sometimes, as witness Zucker/Abrahams/Zucker *helming* the hits 'Airplane!' and 'Ruthless People.'" "The Movies: Blank Checks," *L.A. Times* (Mag.), 27 May 1990, at 22.
- "Shadowy friend Steve Albini will be *helming* Schneider's second solo effort, and has tentatively assembled bands to alternately back the quirky vocalist." Kieran Grant, "Shadowy Doings," *Toronto Sun*, 26 Aug. 1995, Entertainment §, at 38.
- "'La Promese,' a study of immigration *helmed* by brothers Luc and Jean-Pierre Dardenne, won the Golden Spike award for best film." John Holland, "Euro Indies Give Fest a Big Boost," *Variety*, 4–10 Nov. 1996, at 20.

help. See **assist,** v.t.

help but. See **cannot help but.**

helpmate; helpmeet. *Helpmeet*, now archaic, was the original form, yet folk etymology changed the spelling to *-mate*, which is now the prevalent form. (See ETYMOLOGY (D).) In fact, *helpmate* is now about twice as common as *helpmeet*.

Here's the story behind the development of the words. *Helpmeet* is a compound "absurdly formed" (as the *OED* puts it) from the two words *help* and *meet* in Genesis: "an help meet for him" (Genesis 2:18, 20), in which *meet* is really an adjective meaning "suitable." Some writers still use *helpmeet*—e.g.: "Naturally, I am a loyal and patient *helpmeet* whose only reward is a smile on the lips of my beloved—a smile, and ceaseless extravagant praise." Jon Carroll, "Movie at Our House," *S.F. Chron.*, 3 Sept. 1996, at D8. But *meet* was widely misunderstood as *mate*, and the form *helpmate* sprang up and has been predominant since the 18th century—e.g.: "She leads the choir, works with its youth and is her husband's steadfast and (usually) cheerful *helpmate*." Marie Rhodes, "These Real-Life 'Preacher's

Wives' Both Defy, Embody Stereotypes," *St. Petersburg Times*, 4 Jan. 1997, Seminole Times §, at 8.

Helpmate means "a companion or helper," and it need not refer to a spouse—e.g.: "We need to talk about the frustrations you face when you rely on a computer—Mac or IBM-compatible—as electronic *helpmate*." Bill Husted, "Mac–IBM Battle Hides Bigger Problem," *Palm Beach Post*, 13 Jan. 1997, at 7.

help to. In most contexts, the better practice is to use a bare infinitive after *help* (if the choice is between a fully expressed infinitive [with *to*] and a bare one [without *to*])—e.g.: "Critics called this a bookkeeping gimmick that *helps* disguise the true cost of the bill." Janet Hook, "Lawmakers Reach Deal on Tax Relief," *L.A. Times*, 26 May 2001, at A1. Notice how two writers, on the same day and in the same publication, handled the word:

- "The accord also *helps to* [read *helps*] avoid a destabilizing competition in northeast Asia among Communist-ruled North Korea and two of its immediate neighbors, Japan and China." "N. Korea, U.S. Near Nuclear Arms Ban," *Milwaukee J. Sentinel*, 18 Oct. 1994, at A1.
- "An accord with the United States that will open North Korea's nuclear program to inspection should *help* resolve nuclear tensions 'once and for all,' North Korea's top negotiator said Tuesday." "Accord Eases Tension with North Korea," *Milwaukee J. Sentinel*, 18 Oct. 1994, at A1.

The bare-infinitive form after *help* overtook the *to*-form in the late 1960s and remains more than twice as common with various verbs.

hemoglobin; haemoglobin. *Hemoglobin* (= the red protein that transports oxygen in the blood of vertebrates) has been the standard AmE spelling since about 1900. *Haemoglobin* was the established BrE spelling from the late 19th century, but the levels of *hemoglobin* in BrE print sources surged in the 1970s, and the two spellings have vied for supremacy ever since. So far, *haemoglobin* holds a slight lead in BrE.

In AmE and BrE alike, *a* (not *an*) precedes the word. See **a** (A).

Current ratio (World English): 4:1

hemorrhage; haemorrhage. *Hemorrhage* (= an escape of blood from a ruptured blood vessel) has been the established AmE spelling since about 1800, *haemorrhage* the established BrE spelling since about 1850. Since the late 1970s, however, BrE has increasingly tended toward *hemorrhage*: the two spellings are now locked in rivalry in BrE.

In AmE and BrE alike, *a* (not *an*) precedes the word. See **a** (A).

Current ratio (World English): 4:1

hence. This adverb has several meanings, listed here in decreasing order of frequency: (1) "for this reason; therefore" <your premise is flawed; hence, your

LANGUAGE-CHANGE INDEX (For the full key, see front matter pp. xxxi, l–li.)
Stage 1: Rejected. **Stage 2:** Widely shunned. **Stage 3:** Widespread but . . . **Stage 4:** Ubiquitous but . . . **Stage 5:** Fully accepted.
Invariably inferior forms marked by asterisk (*). • Ratios represent frequency of prevalent forms vs. variants in current books.

argument fails>; (2) "from this source" <she grew up in Colorado: hence her interest in mountain climbing>; (3) "from this time; from now" <our anniversary is just two weeks hence>; and (4) "from this place; away" <the park is three miles hence>.

From hence for *hence* (in senses 3 and 4) is an ARCHAISM. See **from hence.** Cf. **thence** & **whence.**

henceforth. A. And **henceforward.* The latter is a NEEDLESS VARIANT.

Current ratio: 8:1

B. **From henceforth.* This phrase is an ARCHAISM that the *OED* records as having last been current in the 17th century. Today the word *from* ought to be rooted out of the phrase—e.g.:

- "We are told that they have just remastered that disc, and all orders *from henceforth will be* [read *will henceforth be*] filled using the new one, not the one Mr. Bauman complains about." Editor's Note, *Am. Record Guide*, 1 Mar. 1994, at 190.
- "*From henceforth* [read *Henceforth*], Connerly suggested last week, applicants to the UC system no longer should petition by name." Peter H. King, "Under Every Rock, Agents of Diversity," *L.A. Times*, 16 Mar. 1997, at A3.
- "'IMPORTANT!!! We can no longer refer to the Freedom Fuel Initiative,' John Sullivan, a deputy assistant at the Energy Department wrote in a memo. '*From henceforth* [read *Henceforth*] it is to be referred to as "The President's Hydrogen Fuel Initiative."'" H. Josef Hebert, "U.S. Finds It Isn't Free to Use Zippy Phrase," *Chicago Trib.*, 15 Feb. 2003, News §, at 8.

LANGUAGE-CHANGE INDEX
*from henceforth for *henceforth*: Stage 3
Current ratio (*Henceforth* vs. **From henceforth*
at start of sentence): 38:1

C. Misused for *hence.* Whereas *henceforth* means "from this point on," *hence* can mean "after now." Idiomatically, one speaks of *two years hence*, not **two years henceforth*—e.g.: "But there are simply too many happy and successful quarterbacks who have been left in Fassel's wake to think that Brown won't be joining that list at some point *henceforth* [read *hence*]." Bob Glauber, "Brown Ultimate Test for Fassel," *Newsday* (N.Y.), 15 Jan. 1997, at A71. See **hence.**

LANGUAGE-CHANGE INDEX
henceforth misused for *hence*: Stage 1

D. For *thenceforth.* When you're discussing past or future events, and you mean "from that time forward"—and you don't mind sounding extremely formal—the word you want is *thenceforth*, not *henceforth*. E.g.: "The film sank without trace but Denholm's part in it lived on in the memories of casting directors. *Henceforth* [read *Thenceforth* or *After that*], he found his greatest success as a failure." Susan Elliott, "The Day Denholm Said He Wanted an Open Marriage," *Daily Mail*, 22 Aug. 1994, at 28. Even when *thenceforth* is accurate, a better wording is usually possible, such as *then, from that time, from then on, later,* or *after that*—e.g.: "The jewel in the crown of the museum this year will be the reopening in late

September of what will *thenceforth* [read, perhaps, *then*] be known as the Janet Annenberg Hooker Hall of Geology, Gems, and Minerals." Hank Burchard, "Coming Soon to a Museum Near You," *Wash. Post*, 3 Jan. 1997, at N26.

LANGUAGE-CHANGE INDEX
henceforth misused for *thenceforth*: Stage 1

he or she. A. Generally. The traditional view, now widely assailed as sexist, was that the masculine pronouns are generic, comprehending both male and female. One way to avoid the generic masculine *he, his,* and *him* is to use—not at every turn, but sparingly—*he or she, his or her,* and *him or her.* These expressions, in occasional use from the 17th century on, have been very much on the rise since the early 1970s. E.g.: "The notion that a business can teach a customer about *his or her* desires will reshape industries, he says." "Strategy with a Touch of Showbiz," *Fin. Times*, 7 Aug. 1997, at 14.

Another way to avoid the problem—not possible in all contexts—is to pluralize the antecedent of the pronoun. E.g.: "If *children* think *they* look different—because *they* feel a lot bigger or a lot smaller or a lot thinner than *their* peers—it calls extra attention to *them* and can make *them* uncomfortable." Nancy Anderson, "Parents' Network," *Boston Herald*, 3 Aug. 1997, at 51. The disadvantage of such a wording is that it often too strongly suggests a singleness of mind in the group, as opposed to the uniqueness of an individual mind. This despite, in the example given, an implication of unique differences.

He or she is by no means a newfangled concession to feminism. In 1837, the English Wills Act stated: "And be it further enacted, That every Will made by a Man or Woman shall be revoked by *his or her* Marriage (except a Will made in exercise of Appointment . . .)." See SEXISM (B).

LANGUAGE-CHANGE INDEX
he or she for *he*: Stage 5

B. **He/she.* One big problem with using this contrived device is that once you start you can't stop. Sometimes this gets quite out of hand. But it's rare to see such an exquisite example as this: "If a child is not corrected when he/she first misspells a word, by the time he/she is in eighth grade, the errors are so ingrained they are never even noticed. . . . I think it is a disservice to the child to let him/her go along for seven years and then tell him/her that the spelling is all wrong." Letter of M. Ann Davis, "Spelling Important," *Ariz. Republic/Phoenix Gaz.*, 9 Sept. 1995, at B8. What about letting him/her go seven years using **he/she* and **him/her*, when reasonable readers will otherwise think that he/she is off his/her rocker? See PUNCTUATION (Q).

LANGUAGE-CHANGE INDEX
*he/she for *he or she*: Stage 2

herb, n.; **herbal**, adj. Although *herb* is pronounced /ərb/, *herbal* has traditionally been pronounced /**hər**-bəl/. In BrE, a *herbal* has predominated in usage since 1890. In AmE, *a* and *an* vied closely until the early 1970s, when *an* decisively won. Today, /ər-bəl/ predominates in AmE. It therefore seems more natural to most American readers to sip *an herbal tea*, not *a herbal tea*. But *herbicide*, with an aspirated *h-*, should be preceded by *a*, not *an*. See **a (A)**. Cf. **homage** & **humble.**

In BrE, the aspirated *h* in *herb* has been restored since the early 19th century. It's a telltale distinction in pronunciation between AmE and BrE.

Herculean is pronounced either /hər-**kyoo**-lee-ən/ or /hər-kyə-**lee**-ən/. Although the first of these was traditionally considered the better pronunciation, today the second predominates.

hereabout(s), adv. This FORMAL WORD, meaning "in this vicinity," has been predominantly spelled with the final *-s* since the 17th century. The shorter form is a variant.

Current ratio: 5:1

hereditary. See **heritable.**

heretofore. See **hitherto** & **up to now.**

herewith. See ***enclosed please find.**

heritable; inheritable; hereditary. As between the first two—both meaning "capable of being inherited"—*heritable* has been standard since 1800. It is more than three times as common as *inheritable*. E.g.: "Robert Pilarski counsels and tests patients who may be at risk for *heritable* forms of cancer, considered to be 5 percent to 10 percent of all cancers." Betsy Witteman, "Genetic Testing, the Pluses and Minuses," *N.Y. Times,* 2 Nov. 1997, at CN14. Somewhat surprisingly, a DIFFERENTIATION seems to be emerging: *heritable* almost always refers to traits and genetic characteristics, and *inheritable* refers more commonly (though not exclusively) to wealth, titles, and goods. E.g.: "Memberships will be *inheritable* and will carry no annual fee for at least the club's first five years of operation." Jerry Dean, "Boathouse, Club to Anchor Waterfront," *Knoxville News-Sentinel,* 9 Nov. 1997, at D1. One notable exception is the Western Heritable Investment (a major landlord in the New York City diamond district). The negative forms are *nonheritable* and *uninheritable.*

Hereditary = (1) descending by inheritance from generation to generation <hereditary privileges customary in European societies>; or (2) transmitted genetically from parent to offspring <fat under the eyelids is hereditary>. Although ***an hereditary*** was once common, since the 1930s *a hereditary* has predominated in AmE and BrE alike. See **a (A).**

hers, an absolute possessive, is sometimes wrongly written ***her's*—e.g.:

- "One man, who had started the somewhat lengthy process of filling out his forms, stood up and said, 'I don't have time for this,' ripped up his form, took his wife's form out of her hand and tore *her's* [read *hers*] up, too." Natasha Korecki, "Workers Scramble to Correct Poll Glitches," *Daily Herald* (Chicago), 4 Apr. 2001, at 4.
- "Arthur is excited about planning his birthday, until he finds out his friend Muffy is planning *her's* [read *hers*] on the same day." Gretchen Marie-Goode, "Arthur's Celebration," *Hartford Courant,* 3 May 2001, at 24.
- "Let the mother remember that the daughter's mistakes are *her's* [read *hers*] to make." Barbara Donlon, "Wishes for a Daughter Who's Growing Every Minute," *Boston Herald,* 13 May 2001, at 55.

See POSSESSIVES (C).

LANGUAGE-CHANGE INDEX
**her's* for *hers:* Stage 1
Current ratio (*hers* vs. **her's*): 134:1

***herstory.** See SEXISM (C).

hesitancy; *hesitance; hesitation. Strictly speaking, *hesitancy* is a quality ("the state of being hesitant; reluctance"), while *hesitation* is an act ("the act of hesitating"). So the better usage is to say that you have *no hesitancy* about doing something, not to say that you have *no hesitation.* But *hesitation* may well drive *hesitancy* out of the language. In word frequency within modern print sources, it vastly predominates over *hesitancy.* Meanwhile, **hesitance* is a NEEDLESS VARIANT of *hesitancy.*

Current ratio (*hesitation* vs. *hesitancy* vs. **hesitance*): 87:8:1

heterogeneous; *heterogenous. The first is the correct spelling of the term meaning "diverse in some characteristic" <the university strives to achieve a culturally heterogeneous student body>. The preferred six-syllable pronunciation is a mouthful (/he-tə-rə-**jee**-nee-əs/). A less rigorous elided pronunciation (/he-tə-**rah**-jə-nəs/) corresponds to the second spelling, which the *OED* calls "less correct." Because *heterogeneous* has predominated since the 17th century and is about 28 times as common in modern print sources as **heterogenous,* the latter ought to be considered a NEEDLESS VARIANT. Still, it does appear with some regularity in otherwise well-edited publications—e.g.:

- "In District 5, he will represent the county's most *heterogenous* [read *heterogeneous*] neighborhoods . . . . One in five district residents is Latino, many of them recent immigrants." Michael H. Cottman, "Broad Support Powered Latino to Historic Win," *Wash. Post,* 10 Nov. 2002, at C1.
- "One line of research, for instance, shows that all students learn better in racially *heterogenous* [read *heterogeneous*] settings than in racially *homogenous* [read *homogeneous*] ones." "The Big One Hits the Court," *Atlanta J.-Const.,* 1 Apr. 2003, at A12.

LANGUAGE-CHANGE INDEX (For the full key, see front matter pp. xxxi, l–li.)
Stage 1: Rejected. **Stage 2:** Widely shunned. **Stage 3:** Widespread but . . . **Stage 4:** Ubiquitous but . . . **Stage 5:** Fully accepted.
Invariably inferior forms marked by asterisk (*). • Ratios represent frequency of prevalent forms vs. variants in current books.

Heterogenous is also an obsolete medical term describing foreign tissue. For the antonyms, see **homogeneous.**

LANGUAGE-CHANGE INDEX
heterogenous for *heterogeneous*: Stage 1
Current ratio (*heterogeneous* vs. *heterogenous*): 28:1

hew. A. And *hue*. *Hew*, vb., = (1) to chop, cut; or (2) to adhere or conform (to). Thus sense 1: "Other pieces in this amazing residence include functional tables, chairs and benches, typically *hewed* from a single piece of wood and incised with a variety of designs." Laura Pope, "Where Furniture, Sculpture Collide," *Union Leader* (Manchester, N.H.), 25 Aug. 1996, at E1. And sense 2: "So many actors pretend not to be seeking fame and fortune that Firth's protestations naturally arouse skepticism. But he has *hewed* to this line from the start." Bart Mills, "That Tortured Look," *Chicago Trib.*, 2 Jan. 1997, Tempo §, at 11.

There are actually two words spelled *hue*. One, deriving from Anglo-Saxon, means (1) "color" <a yellowish hue>, or (2) "appearance, complexion" <partisans of every hue>. The other derives from Old French and means "a loud shout made by someone pursuing a suspected felon" <they raised the hue and cry>—or, by extension, "an uproar." In any event, apart from its use as a past-participial adjective <multihued image>, the word is consistently a noun.

But some writers misuse the word for the verb *hew*—e.g.: "Mr. Major *hued* [read *hewed*] to a more middle-of-the-road strategy, arguing that a common currency would certainly not happen by the end of the century." John Darnton, "Major's Scorecard," *N.Y. Times*, 7 July 1995, at A2.

For the misuse of *hew* for *hue* in the SET PHRASE *hue and cry*, see **hue and cry.**

LANGUAGE-CHANGE INDEX
hued misused for *hewed*: Stage 1
Current ratio (*hewed to* vs. *hued to*): 20:1

B. Inflections. In sense 2, the preferred past participle is *hewn* in BrE and *hewed* in AmE. For an American publication, the following example gets the form wrong: "His campaigning this fall shows how closely he has *hewn* [read, in AmE, *hewed*] to that strategy." John F. Harris, "Out Loud, Clinton Puts Little Emphasis on His Party," *Wash. Post*, 24 Oct. 1996, at A17.

In sense 1, the exceptional form in AmE is the past-participial adjective *rough-hewn*. See IRREGULAR VERBS.

Current ratio (*has hewed to* vs. *has hewn to*): 6:1

heyday. A. Spelling. So spelled—not *heydey* or *hayday*. E.g.:

- "In its *heydey* [read *heyday*], Microsoft vs. Apple was computing's Coke vs. Pepsi, its Ali vs. Frazier." Kevin Maney, "Goliath Takes a Bite of Apple," *USA Today*, 7 Aug. 1997, at A1.
- "However, the children of those who played in the club's *hayday* [read *heyday*] are becoming old enough to play, and are bringing the club back to where it used to be."

Mike Allende, "Can-Am Summer 7s Rugby Tournament," *Bellingham Herald* (Wash.), 15 July 2001, at D1.

LANGUAGE-CHANGE INDEX
heyday misspelled *heydey* or *hayday*: Stage 1
Current ratio: 1,519:7:1

B. And *field day*. Each term most often appears in its distinct SET PHRASE: *in* (*its, his, her, their*) *heyday* (= in [its] prime) and *having a field day* (= having an extraordinarily good time). Dwight Bolinger was perhaps the first to note that when the terms are switched in these phrases, the result is a classic MALAPROPISM: "The columnist Peter Weaver wrote *Professional bill collectors are having a heyday*, confusing *heyday* with *field day*; the two are faintly related in the common notion of 'prosperity.' *Heyday* itself may have developed in a similar way from an exclamation *heyda* 'hey there!' used to express exaltation and later applied to a time of excitement, causing the *-da* part to be identified with *day*." *Language: The Loaded Weapon* 23 (1980).

The error isn't common, but *heyday* does sometimes displace *field day*—e.g.:

- "The play, an actors' *heyday* [read *field day*], is rich with memories of the sisters and their camaraderie." Janet Maslin, "5 Unmarried Sisters in Postcard Ireland," *N.Y. Times*, 13 Nov. 1998, at E1.
- "Critics had a *heyday* [read *field day*] with Sheffield last season when he didn't want to dive for balls on artificial turf because it causes rug burns." Joe Christensen, "Devo, Diving Don't Mix," *Press-Enterprise* (Riverside, Cal.), 4 May 2000, at E6.

The opposite error is quite rare.

LANGUAGE-CHANGE INDEX
heyday misused for *field day*: Stage 1
Current ratio (*had a field day* vs. *had a heyday*): 24:1

hiatus. The standard plural has been *hiatuses* since about 1800. The Latinate plural *hiatus* is not only rare but also liable to cause confusion. (See PLURALS (B).) *Hiati* is a malformed plural—e.g.: "They have offers from Columbia for four movies during their *hiati* [read *hiatuses*]." Army Archerd, "Just for Variety," *Daily Variety*, 10 Nov. 1992. See HYPERCORRECTION (A). Cf. **apparatus.**

LANGUAGE-CHANGE INDEX
hiati for *hiatuses*: Stage 1
Current ratio (*hiatuses* vs. *hiati*): 49:1

hiccup; *hiccough*. The first is the standard spelling; the second is a variant form arrived at through folk etymology. See ETYMOLOGY (D).

Hiccup, vb., traditionally makes *hiccuped* and *hiccuping* in AmE and BrE alike. See SPELLING (B).

Current ratio: 5:1

hie (= to hurry or hasten) makes the present participle *hieing*—e.g.: "Many of the 28,000 fleetfoots and plodders *hieing* the 26.2 miles of Sunday's New York City Marathon were at the starting line because of Dr. George Sheehan." Colman McCarthy, "Running on a Higher Plane," *Wash. Post*, 16 Nov. 1993, at B11. The verb is often reflexive—e.g.: "As they bustle about, sometimes *hieing* themselves off to unseen corners of their establishment, we meet their clientele." John Coulbourn, "Less Is More with Two," *Toronto Sun*, 27 Nov. 1996, Entertainment §, at 7.

hierarchical; *hierarchic. The latter is a NEEDLESS VARIANT that is not nearly as common as the standard term, *hierarchical*. See -IC.

Current ratio: 37:1

highfalutin (= pretentious, pompous) has been the standard spelling since the mid-19th century, as opposed to **highfaluting*, **highfalutin'*, or **hifalutin*. But the variants persist—e.g.: "Chief among these are the geo people—those apostles of geopolitics, geostrategies and all the *hifalutin'* [read *highfalutin*] rest—who argue against the 'sentimentality' of human rights and democratic concerns." Meg Greenfield, "No Hard Feelings?" *Newsweek*, 27 Sept. 1993, at 80. The *W11* spelling is *highfalutin*, without the apostrophe and with *high* spelled out. The *OED*, recording the word as an Americanism dating from the mid-19th century, has two spellings: *highfalutin* (first) and **highfalutin'*. The *Funk & Wagnalls New Standard Dictionary* (1942) records **hifalutin* (without the apostrophe) as a variant spelling; the main entry is under *highfalutin*. (Other variants listed there are **highfaluten* and **highfaluting*.) The best course is to do two things: spell the word *highfalutin*, and avoid being what it denotes.

*highjack. See **hijack.**

highlight > highlighted > highlighted. **Highlit* is a variant past-tense and past-participial form that occasionally surfaces—e.g.:

- "The story is read aloud at a speed suggesting a pre-literate user, [and] *highlit* [read *highlighted*] words are defined at a level appropriate for a smart 5th grader." "Says You," *Wash. Post*, 29 Mar. 1995, at R25.
- "It has an ingratiating, easy-to-navigate interface; users can click on icons, *highlit* [read *highlighted*] words or map points of Stratford-upon-Avon or London to explore." "Fast Forward Data Bank—What's in Gigastore?" *Wash. Post*, 27 Sept. 1995, at R25.
- "It is The Great Metaphysician, a figure some 10 feet tall, female, with elements of architecture and the instruments of architectural drawing, *highlit* [read *highlighted*] in gold, pressed into her dress of dark brown bronze." Brian Sewell, "Shadow Cast," *Evening Standard*, 30 Jan. 2014, at 40.

LANGUAGE-CHANGE INDEX
*highlit for *highlighted*: Stage 1
Current ratio (*highlighted* vs. **highlit*): 4,258:1

highly regarded. See **regard (B).**

high-tech. So written—not **hi-tech*.

*highth. See **height.**

hijack. Vehicles and airplanes are *hijacked*, not people. E.g.: "'It's horrifying, because it's like a kidnapping,' said Greg Britt, a 34-year-old language instructor from Atlanta who was *hijacked* [read *abducted* or *held up*] in a cab at knife point last year, then ordered to make 12 separate withdrawals from automatic-teller machines—six before midnight and six after the new day began, when he was able to withdraw more." Steve Fainaru, "Mexico's Risky Ride: The Hazards of Hailing a Cab in Capital," *Boston Globe*, 6 Feb. 1997, at A1. Cf. **skyjack.**

The word is often misspelled **highjack*—e.g.:

- "Buildings are bombed and planes are *highjacked* [read *hijacked*]." Anita G. Nicholls, "Jerry Falwell Isn't This Nation's Problem," *Richmond Times-Dispatch*, 28 May 1997, at A8.
- "The need for such work became clear to Karadja in December 1994, during the *highjacking* [read *hijacking*] of an airplane in which her daughter and sister were on board." Scott Peterson, "Amid Algeria's Massacres," *Christian Science Monitor*, 9 Jan. 1998, Int'l §, at 1.

LANGUAGE-CHANGE INDEX
*highjack for *hijack*: Stage 1
Current ratio (*hijack* vs. **highjack*): 30:1

Him. See **He.**

hindmost; *hindermost. The latter has long been a NEEDLESS VARIANT.

Current ratio: 6:1

hindrance (= [1] someone or something that makes the accomplishment of something difficult, or [2] the act of making something difficult for someone to do something) is two syllables: /**hin**-drin[t]s/. Avoid the epenthetic schwa between the two syllables: there is no *hinder* in *hindrance*.

Current ratio (*hindrance* vs. **hinderance*): 28:1

hippocampus (= [1] a mythological sea monster with the head and front legs of a horse and the tail of a dolphin or fish, or [2] a ridge along the lower section of each ventricle of the brain, where memory is stored) has predominantly formed the plural *hippocampi* since the 18th century—in AmE and BrE alike. **Hippocampuses* is a rare variant.

Hippocratic oath. So spelled, after the name of the Greek physician Hippocrates (known as the "Father of Medicine"). But the main word is often misspelled **Hypocratic*—e.g.:

- "Astaphan said he began prescribing performance-enhancing drugs for Canada's top athletes earlier in 1983 because he believed the *Hypocratic* [read *Hippocratic*] oath required him to do so." "Johnson on Steroids Since '81, Doctor Says," *L.A. Times*, 24 May 1989, at A8.
- "Chefler also wonders whether any physician who performs [a] surgical castration [as] provided for in Shurden's bill would be in violation of the *Hypocratic* [read *Hippocratic*] oath, which states a doctor's first priority is to

LANGUAGE-CHANGE INDEX (For the full key, see front matter pp. xxxi, l–li.)
Stage 1: Rejected. **Stage 2:** Widely shunned. **Stage 3:** Widespread but . . . **Stage 4:** Ubiquitous but . . . **Stage 5:** Fully accepted.
Invariably inferior forms marked by asterisk (*). • Ratios represent frequency of prevalent forms vs. variants in current books.

'do no harm.'" Chuck Ervin, "Sex Offender Bill Awaiting Action," *Tulsa World*, 1 June 2002, at 1.

- "And I want to reassure you that the *hypocratic* [read *Hippocratic*] oath taken by new physicians doesn't just apply to them." Donald E.L. Johnson, "Integrity Is Critical Issue for All Institutions," *Health Care Strategic Mgmt.*, 1 July 2002, at 2.

For those seeking to denigrate the medical profession, one of the most shopworn bromides is to say something to the effect that *Hippocratic* should be changed to *hypocritical.*

LANGUAGE-CHANGE INDEX
Hypocratic for *Hippocratic*: Stage 1
Current ratio (*Hippocratic oath* vs.
Hypocratic oath): 489:1

hippopotamus. Pl. *hippopotamuses* or *hippopotami.* The anglicized plural (*-muses*) appears almost four times as frequently as the other in journalistic publications. But when scientific sources are added to the mix of print sources, *hippopotami* has predominated since the late 18th century. See PLURALS (B).

Current ratio (*hippopotami* vs. *hippopotamuses*): 2:1

hirable. So spelled—not *hireable*. See MUTE E.
Current ratio: 2:1

hire, vb.; **rent,** vb. In AmE, one *hires* a person and *rents* a thing, whether personal or real property <hire a consultant> <rent furniture> <rent a studio>. In BrE, both people and personal property are *hired* <hire a driver> <hire a car>. For the BrE terms applicable to real property, see **rent,** vb.

hiri kiri. See **hara-kiri.**

Hiroshima is preferably pronounced /hi-roh-**shee**-mə/, a close approximation of the Japanese pronunciation; /hi-**roh**-shi-mə/, though common, is unsound.

his. A. *One . . . his.* See **one** (B).
B. *His or her.* See **he or she** & SEXISM (B).

Hispanic, n.; **Latino; Latina; Chicano; Chicana.** To denote someone of Spanish descent, the term *Hispanic* (gender-neutral in all its applications) was the commonest of all these terms from 1980 to 2000. Since that time, it has vied closely with *Latino* /la-**tee**-noh/ for predominance—the feminine form being *Latina* /la-**tee**-nə/. The first similar words to gain widespread use in AmE were the much more specific terms *Chicano* /chi-**kah**-noh/ (= a U.S. resident of Mexican extraction) and its feminine equivalent *Chicana* /chi-**kah**-nə/, which arose in the late 1960s and spread in the 1970s. (Note that the first syllable isn't /shi-/.) But a hypernym having been needed for the broader group, *Hispanic* and *Latino* have eclipsed the more specialized terms (including *Mexican-American*). Justice Sonia Sotomayor of the U.S. Supreme Court, of Puerto Rican descent, is more frequently identified in the press as a Latina than as Hispanic.

If a definite article is needed before *Hispanic,* it should be *a*, not *an*. See **a** (A).

hisself. See PRONOUNS (E).

historian. Although *an historian* was standard in the 18th century and the early 19th, *a historian* became predominant in AmE by 1890 and in BrE by 1960. See **a** (A).
Current ratio (*a historian* vs. *an historian*): 4:1

historical. A. And *historic. Historical,* meaning "of, relating to, or involving or occurring in history," is called on for use far more frequently. *Historic* means "historically significant" <the Alamo is a historic building>. An event that makes history is *historic; momentous* happenings or developments are *historic*—e.g.: "The Supreme Court's *historic* decision about whether mentally competent, dying patients and their doctors have the right to hasten death won't be known for months." "Voices: Should Doctors Be Able to Assist Terminally Ill Patients in Suicide?" *USA Today*, 10 Jan. 1997, at A12.

A documented fact, event, or development—perhaps having no great importance—is *historical.* E.g.: "Despite the *historical* data, some people just don't feel comfortable knowing their loan's rate can drift up 5 or 6 points." Ilyce R. Glink, "Refinancing Is Wise, Even in a Bouncy Market," *Chicago Sun-Times*, 24 Jan. 1997, at 8.

Examples of *historic* used incorrectly for *historical* could easily run for several pages—e.g.:

- "The Sunday Trading Act, which formally became law yesterday, removes *historic* [read *historical*] anomalies of the kind that allowed shopkeepers to sell pornographic magazines but not Bibles on the Sabbath, and instant but not ground coffee." Marianne Curphey, "M&S Gives Up Fight to Keep Stores Shut on Sundays," *Times* (London), 27 Aug. 1994, at 5.
- "The odds are now on a further easing of monetary policy and there is a good *historic* [read *historical*] correlation between falling interest rates and a rising stock market." "Indian Summer," *Fin. Times*, 13 June 1996, at 12.
- "Rape is also *an historic* [read *a historical*] soldiers' sport." Edward Hoagland, "Sex and the River Styx," *Harper's Mag.*, Jan. 2003, at 49, 62.

The far less common mistake is misusing *historical* for *historic*—e.g.: "Gary Pinkel didn't know what to expect after Toledo and Nevada found themselves going into a *historical* [read *historic*] overtime in the Las Vegas Bowl." "Vegas Bowl Passes OT Test," *Austin Am.-Statesman*, 16 Dec. 1995, at E5. See -IC.

LANGUAGE-CHANGE INDEX
1. *historic* for *historical*: Stage 3
Current ratio (*historical development* vs.
historic development): 23:1
2. *historical* for *historic*: Stage 3
Current ratio (*historic occasion* vs.
historical occasion): 3:1

B. A *historic(al)*; *an historic(al).* On the question whether to write *a* or *an historic(al)*, see **a** (A).

hi-tech. See **high-tech.**

hither; thither; whither. All three are ARCHAISMS in decline, *hither* (= here; to this place) being the most common. Except in the PHRASAL ADJECTIVE *come-hither* (= sexually appealing) or the quaint expression *hither and yon*, the word *hither* is best replaced with a more modern term—e.g.: "They are men who have come from Europe—German, Irish, French and Scandinavian—men that have come from Europe themselves, or whose ancestors have come *hither and settled here* [read *here and settled*], finding themselves our equals in all things." Andrew Delbanco, "The Universalist," *New Republic*, 20 Jan. 1997, at 26.

Thither (= there; to that place) is even more strikingly archaic, but it sometimes appears with *hither* for a pleasant touch of humor and euphony—e.g.: "We have forfeited this joy and peace for the tinsel and glitter, the rushing *hither and thither*." Kathy Hogan, "The True Meaning of Christmas," *Indianapolis News*, 11 Dec. 1996, at A13.

Whither (= where; to what place) is the most old-fashioned of all <at Chelsea Square, whither we had gone>. It has virtually no place in modern writing. For a misusage, see **wither.**

hitherto; thitherto. *Hitherto* = heretofore; up to this time. *Thitherto* = theretofore; up to that time. These ARCHAISMS are hardly worth using, since the terms just used in defining them—*heretofore* and *theretofore*—are perfectly equivalent and much more common. Cf. **up to now.**

HIV virus. For this redundant acronym, see ABBREVIATIONS (B).

hoard; horde. A *hoard* is a stash of something, usually hidden away. To *hoard* items is to accumulate them and stash them away. A *horde* is a throng or teeming crowd (originally a nomadic tribe). Like many other pairs of homophones, these give writers trouble. *Hoard* often displaces *horde*—e.g.:

- "Ice-cream melted in seconds, sweat beads trickled down faces and *hoards* [read *hordes*] of residents hurried to the beach to avoid the searing temperatures that scorched the county Saturday afternoon." Jody Kleinberg, "Heat Sizzles to 8-Year High," *Press Democrat* (Santa Rosa), 21 July 1996, at B1.
- "A dry winter wasn't enough to reduce the roving *hoards* [read *hordes*] of Africanized honey bees that have swarmed the region in recent years." Joyesha Chesnick, "Abuzz About Bees," *Tucson Citizen*, 7 Aug. 1999, at B1.
- "Thanks to the movie 'Titanic,' *hoards* [read *hordes*] of teenagers head to the railings to mimic the famous scene in the movie in which the ship's hero shouts, 'I'm king of the world.'" Anne Veigle, "Set Sail for Fascinating Journey Through Navy Museum," *Wash. Times*, 10 Aug. 1999, at E5.

Likewise, *horde* (exclusively a noun) sometimes displaces the verb *hoard*—e.g.:

- "They prefer to binge on points rather than *hording* [read *hoarding*] a stash." Ryan Ori, "Semifinal Victors Turn Foes Inside Out," *Peoria J. Star*, 14 Mar. 1999, at D16.

- "No ticket *hording* [read *hoarding*] allowed, though." "TGIF," *Fla. Today*, 23 July 1999, at G7.
- "The U.S. is poised for a spate of even more heightened deal-making after years of slow growth and *hording* [read *hoarding*] cash." Alexander Coolidge, "Merger Mania Hits Home with 2 Takeovers in 1 Week," *Cincinnati Enquirer*, 24 May 2015, at G1.

Finally, through a mistaken association of the two words, the misspelling **hoarde* often crops up—e.g.: "This has provoked *hoardes* [read *hordes*] of ethnic Albanian refugees to return to their homeland before it is safe." "Civilized Nations Should Never Resort to War," *Buffalo News*, 14 July 1999, at B3.

LANGUAGE-CHANGE INDEX
1. *hoard* misused for the noun *horde*: Stage 2
Current ratio (*hordes of* vs. **hoards of*): 6:1
2. *horde* misused for the verb *hoard*: Stage 1
Current ratio (*hoarding of* vs. **hording of*): 61:1
3. *horde* misspelled **hoarde*: Stage 1
Current ratio: 3,213:1

*hoarhound. See horehound.

hobo (= [1] a homeless, impecunious vagrant, or [2] a migratory worker), an Americanism dating from the late 19th century, has always predominantly formed the plural *hoboes*—not **hobos*. See PLURALS (D).
Current ratio (*hoboes* vs. **hobos*): 1.1:1

HOBSON-JOBSONISM. This term denotes the principle that with loanwords, foreign-sounding phonemes of the original language are modified to approximate the phonemes available in the borrowing language. Hence *Rodriguez*, pronounced in Spanish with two instances of the guttural *r*, is normally pronounced with the usual English *r* in English-speaking contexts—even when spoken by a Spanish speaker. An insistence that *Rodriguez* be enunciated just as it would be in Spanish—with the concomitant idea that an anglicized pronunciation is a "mispronunciation"—is perverse.

Most English speakers, for example, don't have trilled *r*'s or guttural *ch*'s—hence *terza rima* comes out /**tɑrt**-zə **reem**-ə/ and *Bach* comes out /bahk/. To insist that Johann Sebastian's last name must have a guttural aspiration at the end is sheer pedantry and pretension: *Johann* can naturally be said /**yoh**-hahn/, but *Bach* cannot naturally be said /bahkh/. I once watched a European music critic spend 15 minutes trying to teach an accomplished American music professor how to say the name *Leoš Janáček* authentically. In the end, /**lay**-ohs yah-**nah**-chek/ was as close as the available phonemes made it possible to come. Frustrated, the music critic ended up declaring his efforts unsuccessful. Cf. PRONUNCIATION (D).

The term got its name from *Hobson-Jobson*, an 1866 glossary of South Asian terms collected during the British rule of India, each term having been roughly transcribed into approximate English pronunciations.

LANGUAGE-CHANGE INDEX (For the full key, see front matter pp. xxxi, l–li.)
Stage 1: Rejected. **Stage 2:** Widely shunned. **Stage 3:** Widespread but . . . **Stage 4:** Ubiquitous but . . . **Stage 5:** Fully accepted.
Invariably inferior forms marked by asterisk (*). • Ratios represent frequency of prevalent forms vs. variants in current books.

The book was written by Henry Yule and A.C. Burnellin and updated in 1903. The title comes from an entry in the glossary denoting a ritual Muslim procession called *Ya Hasan, Ya Husain*. The authors' "transliteration" was widely considered pejorative.

Hobson's choice. A. Generally. This ever-spreading catchphrase has loosened its etymological tether. Tradition has it that Thomas Hobson (1549–1631), a hostler in Cambridge, England, always gave his customers only one choice among his horses: whichever one was closest to the door. Hence, in literary usage, a *Hobson's choice* came to denote no choice at all—either taking what is offered or taking nothing.

Though purists resist the change, the prevailing sense in AmE is not that of having no choice, but of having two bad choices—e.g.:

- "Meanwhile, the women—if we can believe them—had a *Hobson's choice*: Either lie and ruin men's careers and lives; or tell it like it was and learn to live with hell in this man's Army." Deborah Mathis, "Race Becomes Issue in Aberdeen Rape Cases," *Fla. Today*, 15 Mar. 1997, at A11.
- "Walking that thin line between trusting your customer and seeking protection from risk can be a *Hobson's choice*. Make the deal and risk not getting paid. Turn down the sale and you reduce the risk of being stiffed, but you won't stay in business long." David J. Wallace, "Draft Transactions Can Leap Trade Barriers," *Denver Bus. J.*, 6 June 1997, at A20.
- "The city then foists a *Hobson's choice* upon its electorate: Either vote to tax the city's property owners with a sizable bond issue, or just endure the increasingly unsafe streets and bridges." Lester Kleinberg, "Seattle's Crumbling Roads," *Seattle Times*, 26 June 1997, at B5.

In a sense, this usage isn't much of a SLIPSHOD EXTENSION. After all, the choice of either taking what is offered or taking nothing must often be two poor options.

B. Article with. Traditionally—and still in BrE—the phrase takes no article; that is, you are faced not with *a Hobson's choice* but with *Hobson's choice*. In AmE, though, the phrase usually takes either *a* or *the* (as in the preceding examples).

C. *Hobbesian choice. Amazingly, some writers have confused the obscure Thomas Hobson with his famous contemporary, the philosopher Thomas Hobbes (1588–1679). The resulting MALAPROPISM, while increasingly common since the early 1980s, is still beautifully grotesque:

- Henry A. Kissinger, "How to Live with a *Hobbesian Choice* [read *Hobson's Choice*]," *L.A. Times*, 11 June 1995, at M2. (Kissinger probably wasn't responsible for the headline.)
- "Governing is full of *Hobbesian choices* [read *Hobson's choices*] between clashing, sometimes irreconcilable ideas." Dana Milbank, "Is Negativity Good for Politics? Positively," *Wash Post*, 2 Apr. 2000, at B1.
- "If you have to shoot yourself in the foot, should it be the right or the left? Italian Prime Minister Silvio Berlusconi faced that *Hobbesian choice* [read *Hobson's choice*] last week." Malcolm Beith, "Decisions," *Newsweek*, 24 Dec. 2001, at 8.
- "But there was a *Hobbesian choice* [read *Hobson's choice*] to be made: To get an hour-long 'Letterman,' ABC also

would have to kill 'Nightline.'" Verne Gay, "Letterman's One-Night Stand," *Newsday* (N.Y.), 8 July 2002, at B23.

See DOUBLE BOBBLES.

LANGUAGE-CHANGE INDEX
Hobbesian choice for *Hobson's choice*: Stage 1
Current ratio (*Hobson's choice* vs.
Hobbesian choice): 41:1

hoe, vb., makes *hoeing* and *hoeable.* See **row to hoe.**

hoi polloi = the common people, the masses. Because *hoi* in Greek means "the (plural)," *the hoi polloi* is technically redundant. But the three-word phrase has spread since about 1850, has become common, and ought to be accepted.

What shouldn't be accepted, though, is the growing misuse of *hoi polloi* to refer to the elite. This might occur through a false association with *hoity-toity* (= arrogant, haughty) or *high and mighty*—e.g.: "You may shell out $75 or $80 per person, sans tax and tip, for the Tribute experience, but, trust me: This is money very well spent. Which is why Tribute has been drawing Detroit power brokers and the *upper-end hoi polloi* [read, perhaps, *upper crust*] since it opened in April." Jane Rayburn, "Restaurant Reviews," *Detroit News*, 3 July 1997, at F5.

LANGUAGE-CHANGE INDEX
1. *the hoi polloi* for *hoi polloi*: Stage 5
2. *hoi polloi* in the sense "elite": Stage 1

hoist(ed) with one's own petar(d). This Shakespearean phrase, meaning "ruined by one's own scheming against others," raises several editorial issues.

First, the actual line in *Hamlet* is *hoist with his own petar* (3.4.207). The form *petar* is an archaic variant of *petard*, meaning "an explosive device used in ancient warfare to blow open a gate or to breach a wall." So *hoist with one's own petard* literally means to blow oneself into the air with one's own bomb. In modern print sources, *petard* greatly outnumbers *petar*—in journalism by a 66-to-1 ratio. So almost every writer who uses the phrase updates Shakespeare by using *petard*. Or more likely, they're relying on editions of Shakespeare in which the spelling has been modernized.

Second, the verb is ordinarily inflected *hoist > hoisted > hoisted*. But Shakespeare used *hoist* as the past participle for the archaic verb *hoise* (= to raise aloft). Many writers update *hoist* and make it *hoisted*; that is the usual form by a 2-to-1 ratio in modern journalistic sources. E.g.: "In these areas, feminists are in danger of being *hoisted by their own petard*." Jean Bethke Elshtain, "Harassment and Politics Are Poor Bedfellows," *Newsday* (N.Y.), 19 Jan. 1997, at A46. But in published books *hoist* predominates by a 7-to-1 ratio and has done so since 1850. Book authors and publishers have tended to treat *hoist with his own petard* as a SET PHRASE.

Third, as illustrated in the quotation just above, there is a question about what preposition to use. Shakespeare's was *with*, not *by*, and that preference has consistently been reflected in book publishing since the early 19th century. But *by* now preponderates by a 4-to-1 ratio in journalism. Some writers mistakenly use *on*, possibly from the false notion that *petard* refers to a sword or lance. Whatever the reason for the mistake, *on* makes no literal sense—e.g.: "Mr. Family Values, the holier-than-thou little butterball, hoisted *on* [read *with* or *by*] his own petard." Margery Eagan, "Naughty Newtie Samples America's Moral Decay," *Boston Herald*, 10 Aug. 1995, at 4.

In sum, almost every contemporary writer who uses this popular phrase misquotes Shakespeare in some way—and it would be pedantic to insist on *hoist with his own petar*. The usual renderings are *hoist with his own petard* and *hoisted by his own petard*. Some preference might be given to the first of those. See LITERARY ALLUSION.

hold out. See PHRASAL VERBS.

hole in one. Pl. *holes in one*—not **hole in ones*. See PLURALS (G).

Current ratio: 70:1

holistic (= [1] of, relating to, or involving holism, i.e., the theory [esp. as applied in medicine] that organisms have an existence other than as the mere sum of their parts; or [2] relating to or concerned with complete systems rather than with their component parts) is so spelled. But the word is fairly often misspelled **wholistic*, a blunder that began spreading in AmE in the 1930s and in BrE in the 1950s. E.g.:

- "So Duke started the long journey toward recovery, sampling traditional veterinarian medicine, canine acupuncture, obedience techniques, *wholistic* [read *holistic*] medicine, and animal behavior modification." Michelle Dally Johnston, "Behavior Modification: Problem Dogs Can Be Helped, but It Takes Time," *Denver Post*, 18 Aug. 1997, at F1.
- "The Ursuline Sophia Center . . . provides local women with programs and services that foster *wholistic* [read *holistic*] growth and health in body, mind, heart and spirit." Marcus Gleisser, "Nun Named Spiritual Director of Sisters of Charity Hospitals," *Plain Dealer* (Cleveland), 2 Sept. 1997, at C2.
- "Barker is still highly motivated to lead her team to victories, but Barker has developed a much more *wholistic* [read *holistic*] approach to dealing with her players." Bob Buttitta, "Coaching Calling," *Ventura County Star*, 11 Feb. 2015, at C3.

LANGUAGE-CHANGE INDEX
holistic misspelled **wholistic*: Stage 1
Current ratio: 79:1

Holland. See **Netherlands.**

hollowware (= concave serving dishes that are traditionally fairly hollow) is the standard spelling. **Holloware* is a variant.

Current ratio: 4:1

holocaust (Gk. "burnt whole") is one of our most hyperbolic words, beloved of jargonmongers and second-rate journalists. The historical sense from World War II, of course, is beyond question. Figurative applications of the term, however, are often questionable. Here it is used to no avail in reference to a scandal: "He would soon be engulfed in a *holocaust* of painful controversy that would maim several lives, wound hundreds of other people, and jostle the foundations of the fashion industry." Inherent in the sense of the word, whether literal or figurative, is the idea of a complete burning; hence it may be used appropriately of fires, but not, for example, of floods.

Also, of course, it brings to most modern minds the Nazi campaign to exterminate European Jews during World War II. When referring to that ghastly series of atrocities, the word is capitalized. And because of its association with those acts of genocide, the word is generally seen as inappropriate when used in reference to deaths that are (1) not caused by malice and (2) not on a massive scale. E.g.: "History has a way of repeating itself, doesn't it? I consider what happened in Chicago this summer—the poor dying in their own apartment buildings [from the heat wave]—America's own *Holocaust* . . . . Who is responsible for this inhumane negligence?" Kathy Arthur, "Heat and Negligence Are Killers," *Roanoke Times*, 31 July 1995, at A4. (That terrible heat wave in Chicago caused nearly 200 deaths, but it shouldn't have been called a *holocaust*—especially not with a capital *H*.) See ETYMOLOGY (C).

LANGUAGE-CHANGE INDEX
holocaust in reference to death brought about by natural causes (e.g., *the holocaust caused by the African famine*): Stage 3

homage is best pronounced /**hom**-ij/. It is a silly (but quite common) pretension to omit the /h/ sound. Cf. **herb** & **humble.**

home. See **house.**

home in, not **hone in*, is the correct phrase. In the early 20th century, the METAPHOR referred to what homing pigeons do; by the early 20th century, it referred also to what aircraft and missiles do.

And by the late 20th century, some writers had begun mistaking the phrase by using the wrong verb, *hone* (= to sharpen) instead of *home*—e.g.:

- "While Mr. Bradley *honed* [read *homed*] in on healthcare, Mr. Gore scolded his opponent as lacking a comprehensive education plan and for supporting a school voucher program when he was in the Senate." Richard L. Berke, "Bradley, in Debate with Gore, Goes on the Attack," *N.Y. Times*, 18 Dec. 1999, at A12.
- "The knowledge gained from these conferences informs the intervention and helps the instructional team *hone* [read *home*] in on the specific strategies that will help the

LANGUAGE-CHANGE INDEX (For the full key, see front matter pp. xxxi, l–li.)
Stage 1: Rejected. **Stage 2:** Widely shunned. **Stage 3:** Widespread but . . . **Stage 4:** Ubiquitous but . . . **Stage 5:** Fully accepted.
Invariably inferior forms marked by asterisk (*). • Ratios represent frequency of prevalent forms vs. variants in current books.

students move forward." Carol Collier Kuhlthan et al., *Guided Inquiry: Learning in the 21st Century* 120 (2007).

- "British and American agents began to *hone in* [read *home in*] on his location and activities." Herbert von Feilitzsch, *The Secret War on the United States in 1915* 209 (2015).

In modern print sources—both AmE and BrE—the collocation *homing in on the* ~ predominates over **honing in on the* ~ by a 2-to-1 margin. For more on these competing phrases, see pp. ix–x.

Language-Change Index
*hone in for *home in*: Stage 4

homely; homey. These two words have undergone differentiation. *Homey* means "characteristic of a home; homelike." *Homely* originally shared this sense, but it was gradually extended to mean "simple, unpretentious." From there, the word was extended further to the sense that is prevalent in AmE (but not BrE) today: "unattractive in appearance; plain." R.W. Burchfield points out that if *homely* refers to a British woman, it means that she is "adept at housekeeping, warm and welcome" (*FMEU3* at 363). A *homely* American woman, however, is simply unattractive. *Homey* has been predominantly so spelled in AmE since about 1905 and in BrE since about 1915. Before that time, **homy* was the standard spelling.

homeopathy (= a therapeutic system, developed in the 18th century, premised on the idea that "like cures like," that infinitesimally small doses of medicine are best, and that only one medicine should be taken at a time) is pronounced /hoh-mee-**ah**-pə-thee/. The corresponding adjective is *homeopathic* /hoh-mee-ə-**path**-ik/.

homeowner. One word.

home page (the first page encountered by a website visitor) is predominantly spelled as two words in both AmE and BrE—though unification seems inevitable. Cf. **website** & **webpage.**

homestead, v.t. The past tense is *homesteaded*, not *homestead*. Someone who homesteads is a *homesteader*.

homey. See **homely.**

homicide refers not to a crime (as is commonly thought), but to the killing of a person, whether lawful or unlawful. The word is frequently misspelled **homocide*. See **murder** (A) & -cide.

Further, the word is preferably pronounced /**hom**-i-sɪd/—not /**hohm**-i-sɪd/.

*hommos. See **hummus.**

homocentric. See **anthropocentric.**

homogeneous; *homogenous. Although strictly speaking these words are distinct, they have become thoroughly conflated through confused misuse and mispronunciation. The more common term is *homogeneous* /hoh-mə-**jeen**-ee-əs/, which means "of

uniform characteristics" <Japan is a more homogeneous society than the United States>. **Homogenous* /hə-**mah**-jə-nəs/, meanwhile, is a slightly archaic biological term describing genetically related tissue or organs. The terms have a long history of causing trouble. In 1934, *W2* recorded *homogeneous* as a variant spelling of the technical term **homogenous*, but not vice versa. In 1961, *W3* recorded each spelling as a variant of the other.

To further complicate matters, *homogeneous* is routinely mispronounced in four syllables, like the medical term *homogenize* and its four-syllable confusion. Naturally, that only encourages the spelling confusion. Add to this the cognate four-syllable verb *homogenize* and its four-syllable participle that's familiar on milk products: *homogenized*. Actually, it's amazing that anyone uses the original spelling and pronunciation anymore.

Yet the two spellings appear in print with remarkable homogeneity: a March 2003 newspaper-database search found 774 instances of **homogenous* and 787 instances of *homogeneous* in the previous six months, including these from *The New York Times* during the same month:

- "The $425 million foundation . . . has financed such plans in Oregon and South Dakota, in communities that are smaller and more *homogenous* [read *homogeneous*]." Stephanie Strom, "A Withdrawn Aid Offer Leaves Yakima Bruised," *N.Y. Times*, 6 Mar. 2003, at A20.
- "'Beyond the Melting Pot' . . . scoffed at 'the notion that the intense and unprecedented mixture of ethnic and religious groups in American life was soon to be blended into a *homogeneous* end product.'" Adam Clymer, "Daniel Patrick Moynihan Is Dead," *N.Y. Times*, 27 Mar. 2003, at A1 (quoting Moynihan).

Writers are best advised to use *homogeneous*, and to pronounce all five syllables. It corresponds nicely to its antonym, *heterogeneous*. See **heterogeneous.**

The scientific community has moved on from the theft of its four-syllable term, **homogenous*, and today uses *homologous* instead.

Language-Change Index
1. **homogenous* for the traditional *homogeneous*:
Stage 3
Current ratio (*homogeneous* vs. **homogenous*): 5:1
2. *homogeneous* pronounced nontraditionally
with four syllables: Stage 4

homophobe, n. This word, together with its cognates *homophobia* and *homophobic*, dates from the mid-1960s but didn't become widespread until the 1980s. Some writers object to the words on etymological grounds—e.g.: "The gays' most recent coinage is 'homophobe,' their epithet for anyone they accuse of being against them. But that is an error, . . . since it would not translate as anti-homosexual but . . . as 'somebody fearing or disliking *himself*.'" Gary Jennings, *World of Words* 71 (1984). Jennings's analysis, of course, depends on translating from Greek, in which the noun *homos* means "same." If you instead interpret the prefix *homo* as an abbreviation for *homosexual*, then the term *homophobe* makes sense. Besides, it's surely better than *homosexualphobe*, and it appears quite often in print—e.g.:

- "There is no doubt that [Patrick Buchanan] is a dangerous *homophobe*; in more than one column, he argued that the people he calls the 'pederast proletariat' deserve to die of AIDS." Robert Scheer, "Why I Can't Stand Pat," *Playboy*, July 1992, at 47.
- "Now researchers armed with naughty movies and a device that measures male sexual arousal have collected evidence suggesting that many *homophobes* may be sexually aroused by men." Richard Morin, "New Facts and Hot Stats from the Social Sciences," *Wash. Post*, 8 Sept. 1996, at C5.
- "A passing driver shouted at him while driving through the lot, calling him a four-letter word and a *homophobe*." Craig Gilbert, "Protests Follow Walker," *Milwaukee J. Sentinel*, 17 Aug. 2015, at A1.

See ETYMOLOGY (A).

> LANGUAGE-CHANGE INDEX
> *homophobe*: Stage 5

*homy. See **homely; homey.**

honcho (= leader, chief, boss) is a SLANG term derived from the Japanese word *hancho* (lit., "squad leader"). The word typically appears in the SET PHRASE *head honcho*; although some consider that phrase redundant, it is thoroughly established.

Journalists have recently begun using the word as a verb, the effect being breezy and voguish-sounding—e.g.:

- "Party sources said that Bill Daley, who *honchoed* [read *championed*?] passage of the North American Free Trade Agreement for the Clinton administration, also supports the vice-president." Greg Hinz, "Forget 1996: Corporados Look to 2000," *Crain's Chicago Bus.*, 2 Sept. 1996, at 4.
- "I dealt with this treaty to ban chemical weapons for almost eight years, first as a U.N. Ambassador *honchoing* [read *championing*?] the issue there and then as U.S. arms control director for most of the Reagan years." Ken Adelman, "Fallout from a Failed CWC Treaty," *Wash. Times*, 18 Sept. 1996, at A17.
- "He *honchoed* [read *directed*] state probes that led to jailing Jerry Sandusky and dozens of state lawmakers and aides caught up in public corruption." John Baer, "The Philly Sting That Stung No One," *Phil. Daily News*, 17 Mar. 2014, at 4.

As in the last example quoted, this verbal use is so vague that one can claim to have "honchoed" without ever being accused of claiming too much credit. See FUNCTIONAL SHIFT (D).

> LANGUAGE-CHANGE INDEX
> *honcho* as a verb: Stage 2

*hone in. See **home in.**

honeyed, not **honied*, is the standard form in AmE and BrE alike—e.g.: "This is a mold that weakens the skins and allows the water to escape at the same time imparting an extraordinary *honied* [read *honeyed*]

flavor to the concentrated juice." Frank J. Prial, "Wine Talk," *N.Y. Times*, 24 July 1996, at C4. Cf. **moneyed.**

> LANGUAGE-CHANGE INDEX
> *honeyed* misspelled **honied*: Stage 1
> Current ratio: 9:1

Hong Kong; Hongkong. The spelling preferred by the major dictionaries and stylebooks is the two-word *Hong Kong*. A few publications, such as *The Economist*, use the one-word form.

> Current ratio: 48:1

Hong Konger; *Hong Kongite; *Hong Kongian. The first is standard throughout the English-speaking world. The others are NEEDLESS VARIANTS. See DENIZEN LABELS.

*honied. See **honeyed.**

*honorand. See **honoree.**

honorarium. Pl. *honoraria* or *honorariums*. Though the latter has much to commend itself as a homegrown plural—and is *The New York Times'* preferred plural—*honoraria* generally prevails in AmE and BrE alike. See PLURALS (B).

> Current ratio (*honoraria* vs. *honorariums*): 5:1

honoree; honorand. In the 19th century, these two forms sprang up, both denoting a person who receives an honor. Both words are acceptably formed. The *OED* records only *honorand*, which predominates in BrE but appears only occasionally in AmE—e.g.: "But as President Harry S. Truman's newly appointed secretary of state, Marshall was one of 12 *honorands* at the following year's Commencement." John T. Bethell, "The Ultimate Commencement Address," *Harvard Mag.*, May–June 1997, at 36. In AmE today, *honorand* is no better than a NEEDLESS VARIANT because *honoree* has taken the field—e.g.:

- "Among the *honorees* in 10 categories are Cambodian sculptor Chum Sambath, conductor David Wilson and Wade Hobgood, dean of the College of the Arts at Cal State Long Beach." Steven Linan, "Morning Report," *L.A. Times*, 14 Oct. 1997, at F2.
- "The evening, hosted by the Arkansas Game and Fish Foundation, began with the Governor's Reception for the *honorees* and their families." Cary Jenkins, "100 Years on Record," *Ark. Democrat-Gaz.*, 30 Aug. 2015, at 40.

hoof. This word, pronounced either /huuf/ or /hoof/, has undergone a curious change in its plural. From 1700 to about 1975, the predominant form in English-language print sources was *hoofs*, analogous to *roofs*. But in the early 20th century, *hooves* emerged as a competing plural and became predominant first in BrE (1960) and later in AmE (1975). In modern journalistic sources, *hooves* is now five times more common; in book publishing, the two forms are about

LANGUAGE-CHANGE INDEX (For the full key, see front matter pp. xxxi, l–li.)
Stage 1: Rejected. **Stage 2:** Widely shunned. **Stage 3:** Widespread but . . . **Stage 4:** Ubiquitous but . . . **Stage 5:** Fully accepted.
Invariably inferior forms marked by asterisk (*). • Ratios represent frequency of prevalent forms vs. variants in current books.

equally common. Traditionalists will stick to *hoofs*, just as they do to *roofs*. See **roof** & PLURALS (C).

Current ratio (*hooves* vs. *hoofs*): 1.1:1

hoof-and-mouth disease. See **foot-and-mouth disease.**

hoofed. So spelled—preferably not **hooved*. E.g.: "He's seen Powell load animals into a trailer—a place where most four-legged *hooved* [read *hoofed*] animals don't want to go." Lela Garlington, "A Gentler Way of Training," *Commercial Appeal* (Memphis), 3 Nov. 1996, at B1. Cf. **roofed.**

LANGUAGE-CHANGE INDEX
*hooved for *hoofed*: Stage 1
Current ratio (*hoofed* vs. **hooved*): 10:1

*hoop-de-do. See **whoop-de-do.**

Hoosier; Indianan; *Indianian. The first is the standard name for someone who hails from or lives in Indiana. The second and third forms are fairly rare variants (the second less rare than the third). See DENIZEN LABELS.

Current ratio: 63:1.3:1

*hooved. See **hoofed.**

hopeful, n. When used in the sense "a candidate," this word smacks of journalese. It came into vogue especially after World War II. E.g.:

- "Garcia and nine other City Council *hopefuls* [read *candidates*] are vying for an appointment that will fill the District 4 council seat left vacant after Cook was elected mayor on Nov. 7." Roberto Hernandez, "10 Seeking Colton Council Seat," *Press-Enterprise* (Riverside, Cal.), 15 Dec. 2000, at B3.
- "For our part, *The Sun* pledges to make public safety a central issue by which all the *gubernatorial hopefuls and legislative candidates* [read *gubernatorial and legislative candidates*] will be measured in the 2002 state elections." "Violent Crime Pays in a City of Soft Sentences," *Baltimore Sun*, 18 Dec. 2000, at A12.
- "When Fox turned over the very same Friday 10 p.m. hour to presidential *hopefuls* [read *candidates*] Al Gore and George W. Bush in October, only 2.9 million watched." Lisa de Moraes, "For NBC, Julie Andrews Brings the Sound of Memory," *Wash. Post*, 20 Dec. 2000, at C7.

LANGUAGE-CHANGE INDEX
hopeful for *candidate*: Stage 4

hopefully. A. Generally. Four points about this word. First, it was widely condemned from the 1960s to the 1980s. Briefly, the objections are that (1) *hopefully* properly means "in a hopeful manner" and shouldn't be used in the radically different sense "I hope" or "it is to be hoped"; (2) if the extended sense is accepted, the original sense will be forever lost; and (3) in constructions such as "Hopefully, it won't rain this afternoon," the writer illogically ascribes an emotion (*hopefulness*) to a nonperson. *Hopefully* isn't analogous to *curiously* (= it is a curious fact that), *fortunately* (= it is a fortunate thing that), or *sadly* (= it is a sad fact that). How so? Unlike all those other SENTENCE ADVERBS,

hopefully can't be resolved into any longer expression involving a corresponding adjective (*hopeful*)—but only the verb *hope* (e.g., *it is to be hoped that* or *I hope that*). See SLIPSHOD EXTENSION. Cf. **thankfully.**

Second, whatever the merits of those arguments, the battle is now over. The *AP Stylebook*, considered the bible of U.S. newspaper copy desks, controversially accepted the "it is hoped" or "let's hope" sense in its 2012 edition. *Hopefully* is now a part of AmE, and it has all but lost its traditional meaning—e.g.:

- "*Hopefully*, other guests will join in the ensuing brawl." Mike Royko, "Why Perot Sings Wedding Bell Blues," *Dallas Morning News*, 31 Oct. 1992, at A31.
- "That way, if one of them gets stuck in traffic on the way to the ceremony, the other will—*hopefully*—still make it there in time." Ed Brown, "The Most Glam Job in Accounting," *Fortune*, 31 Mar. 1997, at 30.
- "*Hopefully*, one day we will all grow older." Pamela DeCarlo, "Never Too Old for HIV Prevention," *San Diego Union-Trib.*, 26 Nov. 1997, at B7.

Sometimes the word is genuinely ambiguous (if the original meaning is considered still alive)—e.g.: "Dave Krieg will take the snaps and, *hopefully*, hand off to RB Garrison Hearst." Larry Weisman, "NFC East: Teams Aim at Dallas Dozen," *USA Today*, 1 Sept. 1995, at E14. (Is Krieg hoping for the best when Hearst runs? Or is the writer hoping that Krieg won't pass the football or hand off to another running back?) Indeed, the original meaning *is* alive, even if moribund—e.g.:

- "But if one can't very *hopefully* go about understanding the learning process, one can with more confidence try to figure out the thing learned, the grammar." Graham Wilson, Foreword, *A Linguistics Reader* xxiii (Graham Wilson ed., 1967).
- "Officials recently have pointed *hopefully* to signs of increased usage of the garage." John Laidler, "Low Usage Plagues Lynn MBTA Station," *Boston Globe*, 9 Oct. 1994, North Weekly §, at 1.
- "Joe Lieberman looks *hopefully* toward the White House." Jeffrey Toobin, "Candide," *New Yorker*, 16 Dec. 2002, at 42.
- "On the trip, Paul tentatively, *hopefully*, begins a flirtation with a young painter, Fern." Meryl Gordon, "Cinderella Story," *New York*, 13 Jan. 2003, at 24, 26.

Third, some stalwarts continue to condemn the word, so that anyone using it in the new sense is likely to have a credibility problem with some readers—e.g.:

- "Where we do not move forward, we regress. To be sure, it begins with slight lapses. Errors of usage—confusing 'disinterest' with 'uninterest,' using 'hopefully' for 'it is to be hoped.' And then, with astonishing swiftness, the rot sets in." Henry Louis Gates Jr., "Canon Confidential: A Sam Slade Caper," *N.Y. Times*, 25 Mar. 1990, § 7, at 1.
- "In the 1969 Usage Panel survey [*hopefully*] was acceptable to 44 percent of the Panel; in the most recent survey it was acceptable to only 27 percent." *AHD3* at 871.
- "Professor Michael Dummett, an Oxford logician, condemns the new usage of *hopefully* because only a person can be hopeful, and in many such cases there is nobody around in the sentence to be hopeful." "Christopher Howse's Grammar School Lesson XXVII," *Daily Telegraph*, 11 Dec. 1996, at 21.

- "Although various adverbs may be used to modify entire clauses, *hopefully* isn't among them—yet. I only hope I won't have to concede that it is until I'm an old, old woman." Barbara Wallraff, *Word Court* 120 (2000).

Fourth, though the controversy swirling around this word has subsided, it is now a SKUNKED TERM. Avoid it in all senses if you're concerned with your credibility: if you use it in the traditional way, many readers will think it odd; if you use it in the newish way, a few readers will tacitly tut-tut you.

LANGUAGE-CHANGE INDEX
hopefully as a sentence adverb: Stage 4
Current ratio (*I hope it won't* vs.
Hopefully it won't): 17:1

B. History. Throughout the late 20th century, the common wisdom was that the use of *hopefully* as a sentence adverb began sometime around the early 1930s. Then, in 1999, the lexicographic scholar Fred R. Shapiro, using computer-assisted research, traced it back to Cotton Mather's 1702 book, *Magnalia Christi Americana*, in this sentence: "Chronical diseases, which evidently threaten his Life, might *hopefully* be relieved by his removal" (p. 529). The evidence then skips to 1851, and then to the 1930s. See Fred R. Shapiro, "Earlier Computer-Assisted Evidence on the Emergence of *Hopefully* as a Sentence Adverb," 75 *Am. Speech* 439 (1999).

horde. See **hoard.**

horehound (= a minty herb sometimes used for medicinal purposes) has always been the standard spelling. **Hoarhound* is a variant.

Current ratio: 10:1

horns of a dilemma. See **dilemma.**

horrific; horrendous; horrible; horrid. The words are listed in decreasing degree of horror.

hors d'oeuvre. Although this noun serves as both the singular and the plural in French, the anglicized plural *hors d'oeuvres* became standard in English during the 20th century. See PLURALS (B) & SPELLING (A).

LANGUAGE-CHANGE INDEX
hors d'oeuvres as a plural of *hors d'oeuvre*: Stage 5

horsey; *horsy. For this adjective (as opposed to the diminutive noun *horsie*), the standard spelling has been *horsey* since the 18th century—in AmE and BrE alike. The *SOED* misgauges the historical evidence by listing **horsy* first.

Current ratio (*horsey face* vs. **horsy face*): 1.5:1

hospitable is traditionally pronounced /**hos**-pit-ə-bəl/, though /hah-**spit**-ə-bəl/ is now widespread and acceptable. Cf. **inhospitable.**

hostler; ostler. *Hostler* (= [1] someone who takes care of horses or mules, esp. at an inn or stable; or [2] someone who moves a railroad engine or a truck at the end of a trip) is so spelled in AmE—and has been, predominantly, since about 1850. The BrE spelling has always been *ostler*—representing the mute *h-* that has typified the word's pronunciation in BrE beginning in Middle English. Sense 2 does not apply in BrE.

house; home. In the best usage, the structure is always called a *house.* So it is not good form to speak of a recently built *home* that hasn't yet been sold. Nor should one point to the building and call it one's *home*: it's a *house* except in non-U speech. (See CLASS DISTINCTIONS.) The word *home* connotes familial ties.

The plural *houses* should be pronounced /**howz**-əz/, not /**hows**-əz/.

houseful. Pl. *housefuls.* See PLURALS (G).

hove. See **heave.**

hovel (= a small dirty habitation) is preferably pronounced /**həv**-əl/ to rhyme with *shovel*—not /**hoh**-vəl/ or /**hah**-vəl/. For a hovel in the mountains, see **eyrie.**

hover, vb., pronounced /**həv**-ər/, is surprisingly often mispronounced /**hoh**-vər/.

howbeit. This literary word, a true ARCHAISM, means "nevertheless" and begins principal clauses—e.g.: "Bryan suspects Megan of murder but is *loathe* [read *loath*] to arrest her; there are simply not enough facts. *Howbeit* there are rumors aplenty." Mary Starr, "*Historic* [read *Historical*] Tome Captures Your Attention," *Telegraph Herald* (Dubuque), 18 Feb. 2001, at E6. (For the reason for changing *loathe* to *loath*, see **loathe.** See also **historical (A).**) But it can always be replaced by some better, more modern word, such as *still* or *nevertheless.* And when it is used—almost always pretentiously—it's usually the wrong word. That is, modern writers who use it tend to put it into a subordinate clause and wrongly make it equivalent to *albeit, though,* or some other word—e.g.:

- "Everyone in Texas had come from somewhere else, *howbeit* [read *albeit* or *though*] several generations removed." Uldene Harrison McIntyre, "Demise of the Stairs of Bedias," *Houston Chron.*, 29 Mar. 1992, Tex. Mag. §, at 4.
- "This is a form of isolationism, *howbeit* [read *albeit* or *though*] selective." Robert A. Seiple, "Peace Is an Integral Part of the Fight Against Hunger," *Seattle Times*, 28 Nov. 1996, at B7.
- "That will create jobs, *howbeit* [read *albeit* or *though*] mainly minimum wage." "Positive Jobs Report Isn't All Great News," *London Community News* (Ontario, Can.), 14 Aug. 2014, Opinion §, at 1.

Cf. **albeit.**

LANGUAGE-CHANGE INDEX
howbeit for *though*: Stage 2

how come is a CASUALISM for *why.* Although it has an ancient lineage, avoid it in serious writing.

LANGUAGE-CHANGE INDEX (For the full key, see front matter pp. xxxi, l–li.)
Stage 1: Rejected. **Stage 2:** Widely shunned. **Stage 3:** Widespread but . . . **Stage 4:** Ubiquitous but . . . **Stage 5:** Fully accepted.
Invariably inferior forms marked by asterisk (*). • Ratios represent frequency of prevalent forms vs. variants in current books.

how dare. See **dare (F).**

however. A. Beginning Sentences with. It seems everyone has heard that sentences should not begin with this word—not, that is, when a contrast is intended. But doing so isn't a grammatical error; it's merely a stylistic lapse, the word *But* or *Yet* ordinarily being much preferable. (See **but (A).**) The reason is that *However*—three syllables followed by a comma—is a ponderous way of introducing a contrast, and it leads to unemphatic sentences. E.g.:

- "*However*, Gross forced third baseman Alan Andrews to pop up." Timothy Sullivan, "Dave Kolar, Manager of the Ambridge-Baden Economy," *Pitt. Post-Gaz.*, 8 July 1997, at D3. (Better: *But Gross forced third baseman Alan Andrews . . . .*)
- "*However*, Nets sources report, when Keith Van Horn got into a tussle with Utah's Karl Malone during a preseason game, Williams stepped in and defended the honor—and the game—of his rookie teammate." Jackie MacMullan, "No. 7 New Jersey Nets," *Sports Illustrated*, 10 Nov. 1997, at 126. (Better: *But Nets sources report that when Keith Van Horn . . . .*)
- "*However*, these small issues should not take away from what is a detailed, and intellectually stimulating collection." Ni Bhroimeil Una, "Identity and Governance," *Irish Lit. Supp.*, Fall 2015, at 9. (Better: *But these small issues . . . .*)

But when used in the sense "in whatever way" or "to whatever extent," *however* (not followed by a comma) is unimpeachable at the beginning of a sentence. E.g.: "*However* we manage to perform the feat of perceiving productive relationship, we may be thankful that we can." Max Black, *The Labyrinth of Language* 67 (1968).

1700 ratio (*But* vs. *However* as sentence-starter):	28:1
1800 ratio:	19:1
1900 ratio:	24:1
2008 ratio:	3:1

B. Emphasizing Certain Words. Assuming that *however* isn't put at the front of a sentence, the word has the effect of emphasizing whatever precedes it. If you say, "Jane, however, wasn't able to make the trip," you're presumably contrasting Jane with others who were able to go. But if the story is about Jane alone, and the fact that she had been hoping to make a trip, the sentence should be something like "Jane wasn't able, however, to make the trip." Some otherwise good writers don't seem to understand this straightforward point of rhetoric. Cf. **therefore (A).**

C. Undue Delay in the Sentence. Because of the point established in (B), it's quite unwise to put the *however* very far into a long sentence. The cure is an initial *But*—e.g.: "We use data only for individuals from the former West Germany in this study, *however*, and restrict our attention to data reported for the years prior to 1989, the year of reunification." Kenneth A. Couch & Thomas A. Dunn, "Intergenerational Correlations in Labor Market Status," *J. Hum. Resources* 210 (1997). (Read: *But we use data only for individuals from the former West Germany in this study. And we restrict our attention to the years before 1989, the year of reunification.*)

D. Playing a Role in Run-On Sentences. Like a few other adverbs—notably *therefore* and *otherwise*—*however* often plays a role in RUN-ON SENTENCES. These sentences don't appear nearly as often in print as they do in informal writing, student papers, and the like. They read something like this: "I wanted to go on the trip, however, there wasn't a slot available." One cure, of course, is a semicolon after *trip*. But the better cure is usually to give the sentence an initial *Although*-clause: "Although I wanted to go on the trip, there wasn't a slot available."

hub-and-spoke, adj. See AIRLINESE.

hue. See **hew (A).**

hue and cry = (1) formerly, a general call to citizens to chase down and capture a suspected criminal; or (2) commonly, a general clamor or uproar. *Hue* here is used in a sense (= an outcry) that is now obsolete except in this SET PHRASE.

The phrase is occasionally misrendered **hew and cry*—e.g.:

- "It would not be surprising to see airlines charge Coach passengers for checking their bags. Or at least trial balloon it. The *hew and cry* [read *hue and cry*] would be loud, but you can never tell what carriers will do." Alfred Borcover, "Is Checked Baggage Going the Way of the Free Lunch?" *Chicago Trib.*, 29 Apr. 2007, Travel §, at 2.
- "All of which makes the *hew and cry* [read *hue and cry*] from [James] Dobson's pro-life detractors so puzzling." Dan Gilgoff, "Dobson's Bit-by-Bit Strategy Has Worked," *Denver Post*, 10 June 2007, at E3.

LANGUAGE-CHANGE INDEX
*hew and cry for *hue and cry*: Stage 1
Current ratio (*hue and cry* vs. **hew and cry*): 253:1

human, n. Purists long objected to *human* as a shortened form of *human being*, but today it's so pervasive—even in formal writing—that it should be accepted as standard. References to *humans* as opposed to *human beings* became predominant in AmE about 1978 and in BrE about 1985.

LANGUAGE-CHANGE INDEX
human as a noun equivalent to *human being*: Stage 5

humankind; mankind. *Humankind*, a 17th-century creation, is unexceptionable, while *mankind* is, to many people, a sexist word. The prudent writer will therefore resort to *humankind*—e.g.: "They are so convinced of its authenticity and importance to *humankind* that they have created the Turin Shroud Center, a research facility that mixes hard science and deep faith." Dick Kreck, "105 Degrees West Longitude," *Denver Post*, 30 Nov. 1997, at 4. See SEXISM (C) & **womankind.**

Current ratio (*mankind* vs. *humankind*): 4:1

humanness. So spelled—not **humaness*. But the misspelling is fairly common—e.g.: "Humaness [read

Humanness] is overpowered by conformity and order, and beauty is rendered irrelevant." Margaret Hawkins, "Sculptures Pit Uniqueness vs. Uniformity," *Chicago Sun-Times*, 18 Mar. 1994, Weekend Plus §, at 27.

LANGUAGE-CHANGE INDEX
humanness misspelled *humaness: Stage 1
Current ratio: 457:1

humble is now preferably pronounced with the *h*-sounded: /**həm**-bəl/. But the pronunciation without an aspirated *h*- has long been common. In fact, *humble* was recognized as having a silent *h*- as early as the 17th century: "In *Latin* [letters] are to be pronounced as often as they are written: and in particular the letter *h*, as in *haeres, homo, humilis*, though it be not sounded in the English words, as in *heir, honour, humble*." Elisha Coles, *Syncrisis* 2 (1677).

In Humble, Texas (near Houston), the residents all say /əm-bəl/. That pronunciation has led local writers to use *an* before the proper name—e.g.: "West Brook got on the board early in the second quarter following *an* Humble fumble." Brian McTaggart, "Ambres, West Brook Stun No. 1 Humble," *Houston Chron.*, 16 Nov. 1997, at 19. Most out-of-town readers would probably find that phrase odd-looking. But locals know better—and proudly so. See **a (A)**. Cf. **herb** & **homage**.

hummus; *hommos. The standard spelling for this paste of ground chickpeas and tahini has long been *hummus*. It first appeared in 19th-century English as the anglicized Arabic word for chickpea. The alternative spelling, *hommos, was equally common until 1880, but *hummus* predominates today by a 549-to-1 ratio. There are at least 18 more variant spellings, but all are rare. The only one worth mentioning is *humus, which is the modern Turkish spelling.

Current ratio (in order of headwords): 549:1

hundred /**hən**-drid/ is sometimes mispronounced /**hən**-drit/ or /**hə**-nərd/. See PRONUNCIATION (B).

hung. See **hanged.**

hurdle. See **hurl.**

hurl; hurtle; hurdle, vb. To *hurl* (/hərl/) is (1) to throw or fling mightily <hurl a javelin>, (2) to speak (epithets, etc.) vehemently <hurl abuse>, or (3) to vomit <hurled three times last night>. Sense 3 is SLANG. To *hurtle* (/**hərt**-əl/) is to move or make something else move with great velocity, especially in a reckless or uncontrolled manner and often with a collision resulting <the car hurtled down the street, scraping vehicles parked on both sides> <the symphony had already begun as the usher hurtled us to our seats>. To *hurdle* (/**hərd**-əl/) is (1) to jump over (an obstacle) while running or jogging <he hurdled two suitcases on his way to the airline's gate>, or (2) to overcome (difficulties,

etc.) <with some deft politicking, she hurdled opposition to the proposal>. Of course, *hurdle* is also (and primarily) a noun denoting an obstacle or barrier.

The *OED* notes that *hurtle* is "sometimes confused with *hurl*," distinguishing the two in this way: "the essential notion in *hurtle* is that of forcible collision, in *hurl* that of forcible projection." A more appropriate distinction today is that *hurl* denotes a greater degree of separation between the propelling force and the thing propelled than *hurtle* does: you *hurl* a discus but *hurtle* down the hallway.

Although collision was an essential part of *hurtle*'s original meaning (dating from the 13th century), the word took on a collisionless sense in the early 16th century. Today the idea of violent impact depends largely on the preposition that follows the verb: *against, into*, or *together* denotes a collision <hurtled against [*or* into] a tree> <the knights hurtled their steeds together>, whereas *along, by, down, past*, and *up* tend to denote collisionless rushing <the car hurtled by [*or* past] the crowd> <the horse hurtled along [*or* down *or* up] the road> <the plane hurtled up into its flight pattern>.

The essential idea of *hurdle* is leaping over obstacles. Sometimes the word is misused for *hurtle*—e.g.:

- "You have people *hurdling* [read *hurtling*] down the road in machines that weigh several tons." Julie M. King, *Post-Standard* (Syracuse), 19 Dec. 2002, at 2.
- "What he'd seen were pieces of Columbia *hurdling* [read *hurtling*] toward earth." Nancy Bergeron, "Policeman Sickened by Sight of Shuttle," *News-Star*, 4 Feb. 2003, at A6.

The opposite error, *hurtle* for *hurdle*, is somewhat less common but does occur—e.g.:

- "It was awkward hearing the applause and congratulations, as if I had *hurtled* [read *hurdled*] a major obstacle." Mary Awosika, "Don't Cry Out Loud," *Sarasota Herald-Trib.*, 6 July 2001, at 12.
- "He watched three horses *hurtle* [read *hurdle*] a brush jump on the Great Meadow steeplechase course." Ian Shapira, "Bringing Ponies to the People," *Wash. Post*, 9 Oct. 2002, at B1.

LANGUAGE-CHANGE INDEX
1. *hurdle* misused for *hurtle*: Stage 2
2. *hurtle* misused for *hurdle*: Stage 1

hurricane; typhoon; cyclone. All three terms refer to massively destructive storms that form over oceans and generate high winds. *Hurricane* is the term used by meteorologists for North America, the Caribbean, Hawaii, and the northeastern Pacific Ocean. *Typhoon* is used for storms in Asia, from the northwestern Pacific down to the China Sea. *Cyclone* is the most common term used for storms in the South Pacific and the Indian Ocean.

hurt > hurt > hurt. The past form *hurted, which has been nonstandard from the 18th century, appears

LANGUAGE-CHANGE INDEX (For the full key, see front matter pp. xxxi, l–li.)
Stage 1: Rejected. **Stage 2:** Widely shunned. **Stage 3:** Widespread but . . . **Stage 4:** Ubiquitous but . . . **Stage 5:** Fully accepted.
Invariably inferior forms marked by asterisk (*). • Ratios represent frequency of prevalent forms vs. variants in current books.

most frequently in quotations from dialectal speakers—e.g.: "'She *hurted* me to the point where I just walked up to her and shanked her probably like six, seven times,' said Bell, then 24, who was charged with murder for the July 2000 stabbing of his mother, Netta." Ken Armstrong, Steve Mills & Maurice Possley, "Coercive and Illegal Tactics Torpedo Scores of Cook County Murder Cases," *Chicago Trib.*, 16 Dec. 2001, at C1. For more on nonstandard tense forms, see DIALECT.

Current ratio (*had hurt* vs. **had hurted*): 2,656:1

hurtle. See **hurl.**

*hutzpa(h). See **chutzpah.**

huzza, an exclamation of joy or approval for formal occasions, has been the predominant spelling since the late 1600s. **Huzzah* is a variant. Of course, *hurrah* and *hurray* are more common—and much less formal.

Current ratio (*huzza* vs. **huzzah*): 2:1

HYBRIDS, or words composed of morphemes from different languages (such as *teleprinter* [Gk. *tele-* + OF *preint*]), became quite common in the 20th century. In fact, they have existed for a very long time in English: *grandfather* (dating from the 15th century) has a French prefix and an English root; *bicycle* (dating from the mid-19th century) has a Latin prefix and a Greek root. One occasionally finds hybrids criticized in older literature—e.g.:

- "*Ize* and *ist* 'are Greek terminations, and cannot properly be added to Anglo-Saxon words. *Ist* is the substantive form, *ize* the verbal.' Jeopard*ize* is one of the monsters made by adding *ize* to an English verb. *Jeopard* means to put in peril—and jeopard*ize* could mean no more . . . . So, also, is the Anglo-Saxon *er* (sign of the doer of a thing) 'incorrectly affixed to such words as *photograph* and *telegraph*'; the proper termination is *ist*: *photographist, telegraphist*, the same as *paragraph–paragraphist*. *Geographer* and *biographer* are exceptions firmly fixed in the language." Ralcy Husted Bell, *The Worth of Words* 149–50 (1902).
- "*A-* (not) is Greek; *moral* is Latin. It is at least desirable that in making new words the two languages should not be mixed." H.W. Fowler & F.G. Fowler, *The King's English* 50 (3d ed. 1930).
- "Neologisms . . . should be formed with some regard to etymological decency; the marriage of a so very English word as *swim* with a so very Greek vocable *stad* strikes one as an unseemly misalliance." Eric Partridge, *U&A* at 202.

Today, though, only a few Classics professors object. As an American lexicographer once observed, "Not many people care whether a word has Greek and Latin elements mixed in it." Mitford Mathews, *American Words* 93 (1959). Perhaps this is because of our increasing ignorance of Classical tongues. Whatever the cause, though, modern neologists have little regard for the morphological integrity of the words they coin.

Virtually all the hybrids condemned by H.W. Fowler in *FMEU1* (e.g., *amoral, bureaucracy, cablegram, climactic, coastal, coloration, gullible, pacifist, racial, speedometer*) are now passed over without mention even by those who consider themselves purists.

Other hybrids that Fowler didn't mention also fall into this class:

antedate	meritocracy
antibody	merriment
aqualung	monorail
automobile	naturopathy
biocide	postwar
claustrophobia	retrofit
ecocide	riddance
epidural	semiyearly
likable	telegenic
lumpectomy	television
megaton	transship

We also have our own fringe hybrids: *botheration, raticide, scatteration,* and *monokini* (the last being a MORPHOLOGICAL DEFORMITY as well).

One rarely hears complaints about hybrids, though Mario Pei once called the legal term *venireman* a product of "the worst kind of hybridization (. . . half Latin, half Anglo-Saxon)." *Words in Sheep's Clothing* 83 (1969). The nonsexist *veniremember*, of course, solves that problem. See **venireman.**

Other hybrids are widely accepted. *Breathalyzer* (formerly *drunkometer*) has become standard, although in 1965 Ernest Gowers wrote that the term was "stillborn, it may be hoped" (*FMEU2* at 253). *Creedal* is a near-commonplace hybrid. And Fowler may not be resting in peace.

hygienic (= [1] of, relating to, or involving healthfulness or cleanliness; or [2] healthful) is often misspelled **hygenic*—e.g.: "But that, Mr. Deedrick subsequently told Ms. Clark, could stem from the different *hygenic* [read *hygienic*] conditions Mr. Simpson has encountered in jail, or even the different brand of shampoo he was using." David Margolick, "After 92 Days of Testimony, Simpson Prosecution Rests," *N.Y. Times*, 7 July 1995, at A1, A12.

LANGUAGE-CHANGE INDEX
hygienic misspelled **hygenic*: Stage 1

hymeneal; hymenal; hymenial. Though related etymologically, these words have taken on quite distinct senses. *Hymeneal* = of, relating to, or involving marriage. E.g.: "In the evening, the party streamed off to the medieval hilltop town of Asolo, . . . along whose streets groups of men spontaneously and undrunkenly came together to sing *hymeneal* numbers to the couple." Alex Hamilton, "Italy: The Wedding Procession," *Guardian*, 3 June 1995, at 56. *Hymenal* = of, relating to, or involving the hymen. E.g.: "If the pain is superficial, it might be caused by *hymenal* strands or lack of vaginal lubrication." Allan Bruckheim, "Health Line," *Chicago Trib.*, 23 Dec. 1996, at C7. *Hymenial* = of, relating to, or involving the superficial layer of spore-producing cells in fungi. See DIFFERENTIATION.

HYPALLAGE /hɪ-**pal**-ə-jee/, known also as the transferred epithet, is a figure of speech in which the proper subject is displaced by what would logically be the object (if it were named directly). Usually hypallage is a mere idiomatic curiosity. It has a distinguished lineage—a famous example being Shakespeare's line from *Julius Caesar*: "This was the most unkindest cut of all" (3.2.183). It was not the *cut* that was unkind, but rather the *cutter*. Hence the object has become the subject.

In any number of everyday phrases, an adjective logically modifies not the noun actually supplied, but an implied one—e.g.:

> angry fight
> black colleges
> cruel comments
> cynical view
> disgruntled complaints
> drunken parties
> elementary classroom
> English-speaking countries
> feminine napkin
> gay marriage
> Greek neighborhood
> handicapped parking
> hasty retreat
> healthy foods
> humble opinion
> nondrowsy cold medicine
> overhead projector
> permanent marker
> provincial attitude
> unfair criticisms
> vulnerable period
> well-educated home

Generally, this figure of speech is harmless, even convenient. Pedants who complain about almost any phrase like the ones listed ("But the marker itself isn't permanent, is it?") are simply parading their own pedantry. Perhaps the phrase that most commonly gives rise to spurious objections is *The book says . . .*—which is perfectly good English.

hyperbaric. See **hyperbolic** (B).

hyperbola /hɪ-**pər**-bə-lə/ (= in geometry, a curved line that moves so that the difference of its distances from two fixed points is constant) has formed the standard plural *hyperbolas* since the 18th century—the classical plural **hyperbolae* (/hɪ-**pər**-bə-lee/) being both a variant and an unfortunate homophone of *hyperbole*.
Current ratio (*hyperbolas* vs. **hyperbolae*): 5:1

HYPERBOLE. See **OVERSTATEMENT**.

hyperbolic. A. Two Meanings. It's no exaggeration to say that this word has two remarkably different meanings, one rooted in the abandon of rhetoric and another in the rigors of mathematics. In fact, though, it is essentially two separate adjectives. The more common by far answers to *hyperbole* (= the rhetorical device of deliberate overstatement)—e.g.: "He has written a book . . . that may never be confused with, say, 'War and Peace' or 'Wuthering Heights,' but it's

a book with a more provocative title—including a *hyperbolic* exclamation point—'Perfect I'm Not!'" Ira Berkow, "Colorful Pitcher, but Not a Stand-Up Guy," *N.Y. Times*, 3 Mar. 2003, at D3. The other one answers to *hyperbola* (= in geometry, a pair of open and infinite curves mirrored about their vertices)—e.g.: "Against notable losses in recent years, such as famed architect I.M. Pei's *hyperbolic* paraboloid when the Adam's Mark hotel expanded in 1997 and Currigan Hall, conference attendees were generally optimistic." J. Sebastian Sinisi, "State's Preservationists See Reasons for Optimism," *Denver Post*, 11 Feb. 2003, at F9.

B. And *hyperbaric*. *Hyperbolic* is sometimes mistakenly used in place of *hyperbaric* (= of, relating to, or involving a pressurized chamber used in scientific experiments and medical treatment)—an odd error: "*Hyperbolic* [read *Hyperbaric*] oxygen chambers have been used successfully by several National Hockey League clubs, and that has not gone unnoticed in the National Football League." Vinny DiTrani, "High-Tech Rush for Giants?" *Record* (N.J.), 12 June 1995, at S2.

LANGUAGE-CHANGE INDEX
hyperbolic misused for *hyperbaric*: Stage 1
Current ratio (*hyperbaric oxygen* vs.
*hyperbolic oxygen): 319:1

C. And **hyperbolical*. The standard adjective has been *hyperbolic* since the late 19th century—not **hyperbolical*.

HYPERCORRECTION. Sometimes people strive to abide by the strictest etiquette, but in the process behave inappropriately. The very motivations that result in this irony can play havoc with the language: a person will strive for a correct linguistic form but instead fall into error. Linguists call this phenomenon "hypercorrection"—a common shortcoming.

This foible can have several causes. Often, it results from an attempt to avoid what the writer wrongly supposes to be a grammatical error. (See **SUPERSTITIONS**.) At other times, it results from an incomplete grasp of a foreign grammar, coupled with an attempt to conform to that grammar. Yet again, it sometimes results from a misplaced sense of logic overriding a well-established idiom. A few of the most common manifestations are enumerated below.

A. False Latin Plurals. One with a smattering of Latin learns that, in that language, most nouns ending in *-us* have a plural ending in *-i*: *genius* forms *genii*, *nimbus* forms *nimbi*, *syllabus* forms *syllabi*, *terminus* forms *termini*, and so on. The trouble is that not all of them do end in *-i*, so traps abound for those trying to show off their sketchy knowledge of Latin:

Hypercorrect Plural	Latin Plural	English Plural
*apparati	apparatus	apparatuses
*fori	**fora*	forums
*ignorami	[A vb. in L.]	ignoramuses

LANGUAGE-CHANGE INDEX (For the full key, see front matter pp. xxxi, l–li.)
Stage 1: Rejected. **Stage 2:** Widely shunned. **Stage 3:** Widespread but . . . **Stage 4:** Ubiquitous but . . . **Stage 5:** Fully accepted.
Invariably inferior forms marked by asterisk (*). • Ratios represent frequency of prevalent forms vs. variants in current books.

*isthmi	[Gk. sing. n.: isthmos]	isthmuses
*mandami	[A vb. in L.]	mandamuses
*mittimi	[A vb. in L.]	mittimuses
*nexi	nexus	nexuses
*octopi	[Gk. pl. octopodes]	octopuses
*prospecti	prospectus	prospectuses
*stati	status	statuses

B. *Between you and I.* Some people learn a thing or two about pronoun cases, but little more. They learn, for example, that it is incorrect to say *It is me* or **Me and Jane are going to school now.* (See **it is I.**) But this knowledge puts them on tenterhooks: through the logical fallacy known as "hasty generalization," they come to fear that something is amiss with the word *me*—that perhaps it's safer to stick to *I.* They therefore start using *I* even when the objective case is called for: "She had the biggest surprise for Blair and *I* [read *me*]." / "Please won't you keep this between you and *I* [read *me*]." These are gross linguistic gaffes, but it is perennially surprising how many otherwise educated speakers commit them. See **between (B)** & PRONOUNS (B).

Many writers and speakers try to avoid the problem by resorting to *myself*, but that is hardly an improvement. See **myself.**

C. Number Problems. Sometimes, in the quest for correctness, writers let their sense of grammar override long-established idioms. They may write, for example, **A number of people was there*, when the correct form is *A number of people were there.* Or they will write, **A handful of problems arises from that approach*," instead of *A handful of problems arise from that approach.* For more on these correct but "antigrammatical" constructions, see SYNESIS & **number of.**

D. Redundantly Formed Adverbs. The forms *doubtless, much,* and *thus* are adverbs, yet some writers overcompensate by adding *-ly,* thereby forming barbarisms: **doubtlessly, *muchly,* and **thusly.* See ADVERBS (C).

E. *As* **for** *like.* When writers fear using *like* as a conjunction, they sometimes fail to use it when it would function appropriately as a preposition or adverb. Thus *She sings like a bird* becomes **She sings as a bird.* But the latter sentence sounds as if it is explaining the capacity in which she sings. The hypercorrection, then, results in a MISCUE. See **like (C).**

F. *Whom* **for** *who.* Perhaps writers should get points for trying, but those who don't know how to use *whom* should abstain in questionable contexts. That is, *against whom, for whom,* and the like may generally be instances in which the writer knows to choose *whom.* But things can get moderately tricky—e.g.: "In 'An Independent Woman,' Barbara is confronted by an African-American burglar, *whom* [read *who*] she realizes is well-educated but desperate." Jocelyn McClurg, "At 82, Fast Has Slowed but Hasn't Stopped as a Writer," *Fresno Bee,* 3 Aug. 1997, at G2. Although *whom* in that sentence may seem to be the object of *realizes,* in fact it is the subject of the verb *is.* See **who** & PRONOUNS (B).

G. Unsplit Infinitives Causing Miscues. Writers who have given in to the most widespread of SUPERSTITIONS—or who believe that most of the readers have done so—avoid all split infinitives. They should at least avoid introducing unclear modifiers into their prose. But many writers do introduce them, and the result is often a MISCUE or ambiguity—e.g.: "Each is *trying subtly to exert* his or her influence over the other." Mark H. McCormack, *What They Don't Teach You at Harvard Business School* 26 (1984). In that sentence, does *subtly* modify the participle *trying* or the infinitive *to exert*? Because we cannot tell, the sentence needs to be revised in any of the following ways: (1) *Each is subtly trying to exert his or her influence over the other,* (2) *Each is trying to exert his or her influence subtly over the other,* (3) *Each is trying to subtly exert his or her influence over the other,* or (4) *Each is trying to exert his or her subtle influence over the other.* See SPLIT INFINITIVES.

H. Unsplit Verb Phrases. A surprising number of writers believe that it's a mistake to put an adverb in the midst of a verb phrase. The surprise is on them: every language authority who addresses the question holds just the opposite view—that the adverb generally *belongs* in the midst of a verb phrase. (See ADVERBS (A).) The canard to the contrary frequently causes awkwardness and artificiality—e.g.: "I *soon will be calling* you." (Read: *I will soon be calling you.*) See SUPERSTITIONS (C).

I. Prepositions Moved from the Ends of Sentences. "That is the type of arrant pedantry up with which I shall not put," said Winston Churchill, mocking the priggishness that causes some writers and speakers to avoid ending with a preposition. See PREPOSITIONS (B) & SUPERSTITIONS (A).

J. Borrowed Articles for Borrowed Nouns. When a naturalized or quasi-naturalized foreignism appears, the surrounding words—with a few exceptions, such as *hoi polloi*—should be English. So one refers to *finding the mot juste,* preferably not **finding le mot juste.* But see **hoi polloi.**

K. Overrefined Pronunciation. Some foreignisms acquire anglicized pronunciations. For example, in AmE *lingerie* is pronounced in a way that the French would consider utterly barbarous: /lon-jə-**ray**/, as opposed to /la[n]-**zhree**/. (See **lingerie.**) But for a native speaker of AmE to use the latter pronunciation sounds foolish. Another French word that gives some AmE speakers trouble is *concierge*: it should be pronounced /kon-see-**erzh**/, not /kon-see-**er**/. See **concierge.**

Similarly, American and British printers refer to the typefaces without "feet" (small projections coming off the straight lines) as *sans serif* /sanz **ser**-if/, not /sahnz sə-**reef**/. The latter pronunciation may show a supposed familiarity with the French language (though *serif* is Dutch), but it betrays an unfamiliarity both with publishing and with the English language.

Even native-English words can cause problems. The word *often,* for example, preferably has a silent *-t-,* yet some speakers (unnaturally) pronounce it because of the spelling. The next logical step would be to pronounce *administration* /ad-min-i-**stray**-tee-on/, and all other words with the *-tion* suffix similarly. See PRONUNCIATION (A) & **often (A)**.

hypertension is medical JARGON for *high blood pressure*. Because of the confusing terminology, some writers confound *hypertension* with *nervous tension*, as those in medicine know: "Hypertension and 'nervous tension' are not the same thing. Some people can feel very tense and have normal blood pressure, and others can feel quite relaxed and have high blood pressure." "Hypertension," *HealthTips*, Dec. 1992, at 45.

hyphenate; hyphen, vb.; *****hyphenize.** *Hyphenate* had become the standard verb in AmE by 1900 and in BrE by 1940. In BrE, *hyphen* is a variant. **Hyphenize* is a NEEDLESS VARIANT in both AmE and BrE—except perhaps in the sense analogous to *hyphenization* described in the immediately following entry.
> Current ratio (*hyphenated* vs. *hyphened* vs.
> **hyphenized*): 1,446:33:1

hyphenation; hyphenization. *Hyphenation* is the standard form for the literal use of hyphens to separate words into syllables—e.g.: "Since the demise of typewriters and the universal use of computers in the newsroom, *hyphenization* [read *hyphenation*] is done automatically by the computer." Jean Otto, " 'Van' or 'Von'?" *Rocky Mountain News* (Denver), 1 Jan. 1995, at A106.

Although *hyphenization*, dating from the mid-19th century, has traditionally been just a NEEDLESS VARIANT of *hyphenation*, some degree of DIFFERENTIATION now appears to be emerging: increasingly, the word denotes the designation of ethnic origins by using compound forms such as *African-American, Asian-American, Mexican-American*, and the like. With its *-ize* infix, *hyphenization* carries negative connotations of divisiveness—e.g.:

- "While she sometimes describes herself as Indo-American, Mukherjee deplores the ghettos of ethnic *hyphenization*." John Habich, "Mukherjee Is Inspired by Struggles of Immigration," *Star Trib.* (Minneapolis), 24 Mar. 2002, at E1.
- "They sometimes face school boards or parents who worry that lessons that used to focus on a unified sense of 'America' are falling by the wayside in an era of *hyphenization*." Stacy A. Teicher, "Opening the Book on Race," *Christian Science Monitor*, 18 June 2002, Features §, at 14.

Inconsistently enough, though, we use the term *hyphenated Americans*, dating from the late 19th century—not **hyphenized Americans*.

hyphenize. See **hyphenate.**

HYPHENS. See PUNCTUATION (J) & PHRASAL ADJECTIVES.

hypnotism; hypnosis. These words aren't quite interchangeable. One might use either term to name the art of mesmerism, but one should never say, "He is under *hypnotism*." *Hypnotism*, the more popular word only in the late 19th century, refers only to the practice or art; *hypnosis* refers either to the practice or to the state of consciousness itself. But some writers mistakenly use **under hypnotism* when they mean the person was *under hypnosis*—e.g.: "*Under hypnotism* [read *Under hypnosis*] in the office of John C. 'Jack' Kasher, the woman described being taken into the saucer and seeing people four feet tall with large heads, wraparound eyes and four fingers on each hand." Michael Kelly, "Prof: UFOs 'Out There,' " *Omaha World-Herald*, 15 Feb. 2000, News §, at 13.

The two words are susceptible to INELEGANT VARIATION—e.g.: "In 1988, the Texas Court of Criminal Appeals ruled that testimony helped by *hypnotism* was admissible as evidence, providing certain procedural safeguards were followed. *Hypnosis*, often associated with stage shows that seem to transform spectators into clucking chickens, is easily misunderstood." Rachel Boehm, "Past Hints: Crime Fighters Glean Clues with Hypnosis," *Dallas Morning News*, 7 Mar. 1993, at A39. Either word, consistently used, might suffice in that passage. Probably the better choice would be the less restrictive one: *hypnosis*.

hypnotize is pronounced /**hip**-nə-tiz/. The erroneous /**hip**-mə-tiz/, with an /m/ sound, is all too common. See PRONUNCIATION (B).

> LANGUAGE-CHANGE INDEX
> *hypnotize* mispronounced /**hip**-mə-tiz/: Stage 2

*****Hypocratic.** See **Hippocratic.**

hypostatize /hi-**pos**-tə-tiz/ (= to make an idea into, or to regard it as, a self-existent substance or person) has been standard since the early 19th century. **Hypostasize* is a NEEDLESS VARIANT.
> Current ratio (*hypostatized* vs.
> **hypostasized*): 2:1

hypotenuse (= the longest side of a right triangle, lying opposite the 90° angle) is the standard spelling. **Hypothenuse* is a variant with a spelling that departs from that of the Greek etymon.
> Current ratio: 10:1

hypothecate is not, as some believe, a synonym of *hypothesize* (= to make a hypothesis, i.e., a proposition put forward for discussion). *Hypothecate* is a legal term meaning "to pledge (property) without delivery of title or possession."

President George H.W. Bush occasionally misused *hypothecate*—e.g.:

- " 'So I'm not going to speculate or *hypothecate* [read *hypothesize*] beyond that. I want to see them out of

LANGUAGE-CHANGE INDEX (For the full key, see front matter pp. xxxi, l–li.)
Stage 1: Rejected. **Stage 2:** Widely shunned. **Stage 3:** Widespread but . . . **Stage 4:** Ubiquitous but . . . **Stage 5:** Fully accepted.
Invariably inferior forms marked by asterisk (*). • Ratios represent frequency of prevalent forms vs. variants in current books.

there ...'" "Confrontation in the Gulf," *N.Y. Times*, 9 Aug. 1990, at A15 (quoting President Bush).

- "Our sitting president, George Bush, . . . said, 'Now is no time to speculate or *hypothecate* [read *hypothesize*], but rather a time for action . . . .'" Don Addis, "Wrapping Up Homelessness," *St. Petersburg Times*, 22 Mar. 1992, at D5.

LANGUAGE-CHANGE INDEX
hypothecate misused for *hypothesize*: Stage 1
Current ratio (*hypothesize that* vs.
*hypothecate that): 1,375:1

hypothesis. Pl. *hypotheses* /hɪ-**po**-thə-seez/. See PLU-RALS (B).

hypothetical; *hypothetic. The longer form is now standard.

Current ratio: 129:1

hysterical; *hysteric. The first has been the standard adjective since the early 19th century; the second is a NEEDLESS VARIANT.

Current ratio: 10:1

I

I; me. See FIRST PERSON, PRONOUNS (A), (B) & **it is I.**

ibid.; ib.; id.; op. cit.; loc. cit. *Ibid.* is an abbreviation of *ibidem* (L. "in the same place"); *ib.* is a variant abbreviation that, despite its greater compactness, fell into disuse about 1900 (before which time it had been standard for a century). *Id.* is an abbreviation of *idem* (L. "same"). Both *ibid.* and *id.* are commonly used in citations to denote that a reference is to a work cited immediately before. The first is the abbreviation more generally used; the second is typical of legal writing.

Op. cit. is an abbreviation of *opere citato* (L. "in the work cited"). *Loc. cit.* (or *l.c.*) is an abbreviation of *loco citato* (L. "in the place cited"). Either abbreviation was formerly used, along with the author's last name, as a short citation to an earlier-cited work. In modern bibliography, though, *op. cit.* and *loc. cit.* are disfavored. The trend is to use instead a shortened form of the work's title, such as *Modern English Usage* or *GMEU* for this book.

-IBLE. See -ABLE (A).

-IC; -ICAL. Adjective pairs ending in these two suffixes, which denote "of, like, or relating to," could easily fill up an entire page. Suffice it to say that you should keep a couple of good dictionaries nearby to help you decide which adjective to use. But keep in mind the two "desirable tendencies" cited by H.W. Fowler (*FMEU1* at 249): favoring DIFFERENTIATION where it exists (as with *economic* vs. *economical* and *historic* vs. *historical*) and rejecting NEEDLESS VARIANTS that are truly needless (such as **biologic* and **ecologic*).

Most adjectives ending in *-ic* form the adverb by adding *-ally* (e.g., *academically, frantically, plastically, prolifically,* and *rustically*). The most notable exceptions are *impoliticly* and *publicly*.

ice cream; *iced cream. Although **iced cream* was the original phrase, *ice cream* predominated in print sources by 1880 and is firmly entrenched as the standard form today. See ADJECTIVES (F).

iced tea; ice tea. The first is more logical and far more frequent in print. In speech, however, the /d/ sound in *iced* is usually slurred into the following /t/; hardly anyone asks a server for a glass of /ɪsd **tee**/. But despite this indistinct pronunciation, *iced tea* shows little evidence of following the progression of **iced cream* to *ice cream*. See ADJECTIVES (F). Cf. **fine-toothed comb, skim milk** & **stained glass.**

Current ratio: 8:1

-ICS. It can sometimes be difficult to decide whether to use a singular or plural verb with words such as *acoustics, athletics,* and *politics*. If a word is used as the name of an academic discipline, it is singular <linguistics is the study of human languages>. Otherwise, it is plural <this theater's acoustics are terrible>. A good clue that a plural verb is needed is the presence of a pronoun, article, or possessive before the *-ics* word <statistics guides decision-making> <your statistics are misleading>.

ID; I.D. The first is preferable for this shortened form of *identification*. In the second, the periods should indicate that the initials *I* and *D* each stand for something. But they don't: everybody knows that *I.D.* is simply shorthand. Given the illogic of the periods—and the trend in AmE away from periods in abbreviations—the form *ID* is better. See ABBREVIATIONS (A).

As an abbreviation with periods (*I.D.*), it can mean many different things to different people, such as "intradermal" to the dermatologist, "inside diameter" to the physiologist, "infective dose" to the bacteriologist—and those are just the medical senses.

id. See **ibid.**

I'd better; I better. See **better** (A).

ideal. See ADJECTIVES (B) & **idyll** (B).

*idealogy. See **ideology.**

identical takes either *with* or *to*. Historically, *with* has been considered better because one has *identity with* something or someone, not *to* it. *Identical to* was not widely used until the mid-20th century. The *OED*'s illustrative examples contain only the phrase *identical with*. But since the mid-1970s in AmE and the mid-1980s in BrE, *identical to* has been the predominant form in print sources.

The phrase *same identical*—more often heard than seen—is redundant. E.g.:

- "From dawn to darkness they [cult members] lived *the same, identical,* [read *identical*] controlled lives." "Death of a Salesman," *Seattle Times*, 1 Apr. 1997, at B4.
- "No one who has not traveled the *same identical* [read *same*] road could possibly know the mountains that were climbed, the blood, sweat and tears and the fear like punches in the gut constantly in a barrage that few professional fighters could or would tolerate." Patricia Tedesco, "Utica Community Was There When the Times Were Tough," *Observer-Dispatch* (Utica, N.Y.), 6 Aug. 2015, at A7.

LANGUAGE-CHANGE INDEX
identical to for *identical with*: Stage 5
Current ratio (*to* vs. *with*): 2:1

identify = (1) to treat as or consider identical <he identified his parents' interests with his own>; (2) to ascertain or demonstrate what something or who someone is <the building in the photograph has not yet been identified>; (3) to associate or affiliate with <she has never been identified with the impressionist school>; (4) to consider (oneself) as being associated or affiliated with <nevertheless, she identified herself with the impressionists>; or (5) to understand sympathetically or intuitively, esp. through experience. Sense 5 is often disapproved of because when used in that way, *identify* is a VOGUE WORD—more specifically, a pop-psychology CASUALISM—bearing a nontraditional sense. Sometimes it is followed by *with*, sometimes not—e.g.:

- *With*: "Let's face it, this is one governmental service that the people can *identify* closely *with*." "Superior Court to Soon Appear No Longer a Mirage," *Ariz. Republic*, 2 June 2001, at 2.
- *With*: "While many parents haven't suffered as many difficulties as Cheever has, most can *identify with* the 'accidental' manner in which she has gained some important insights." Rosemary Herbert, "Growing Pains," *Boston Herald*, 10 June 2001, at 51.
- *No with*: "Although Accorsi feels for Cleveland fans, he can't really *identify* as he could when the Colts moved." Don Pierson, "Ernie Accorsi Is the Giants' GM but Has Ties to Baltimore's Storied Football Past," *Chicago Trib.*, 19 Jan. 2001, at 1.
- *No with*: "'We've all experienced workplace politics . . . . It's duplicity and hardball. It's serious emotions. We can *identify*.'" Diana Lockwood, "Feeling Good," *Columbus Dispatch*, 6 June 2001, at F2 (quoting Mark Burnett, producer of the television series *Survivor*).

In each of those sentences, a more conservative writer (or, in the final example, a more conservative speaker) would probably have used the verb *understand* in place of *identify with* or *identify*.

Here the cant phrase is inappropriately used in reference to early-19th-century historical figures: "In the end, the difference was that Jefferson *identified with* Virginia while Marshall *identified with* the United States." J. Wade Gilley, "University's Namesake Was Great for Many Reasons," *Charleston Gaz.*, 3 Feb. 1997, at A5. Neither Jefferson nor Marshall would have identified with writing like that. Cf. **relate to.**

LANGUAGE-CHANGE INDEX
identify with (as in *I could identify with the main character*): Stage 4

ideology. So spelled. But many writers misunderstand its ETYMOLOGY, believing that the word is somehow derived from our modern word *idea*, and so misspell it **idealogy*. In fact, like several other words beginning with *ideo-* (e.g., *ideograph*), *ideology* passed into English through French (*idéologie*) and has been spelled *ideo-* in English since the 18th century. Although the bungled spelling has become common enough that it's listed in some dictionaries, that isn't a persuasive defense of its use. Cf. **minuscule.**

LANGUAGE-CHANGE INDEX
ideology misspelled **idealogy*: Stage 2
Current ratio: 3,781:1

id est. See **i.e.**

idiosyncrasy. So spelled, though often erroneously rendered **idiosyncracy* (as if the word denoted a form of government)—e.g.: "Their *idiosyncracies* [read *idiosyncrasies*] are patrician." David Margolick, "Similar Histories, and Views, for 2 Court Finalists," *N.Y. Times*, 30 May 1993, at 9. Fortunately, in modern print sources, the correct spelling outnumbers the erroneous one by a 12-to-1 ratio.

For the many words properly ending in *-cracy*, see GOVERNMENTAL FORMS.

LANGUAGE-CHANGE INDEX
idiosyncrasy misspelled **idiosyncracy*: Stage 2
Current ratio: 12:1

idolize; *idolatrize. The first has been standard since the 17th century. The second is a NEEDLESS VARIANT. E.g.: "We're free, free at last from the bombardment of the media for the Super Bowl and the *idolatrizing* [read *idolizing*] of the combatants." "Glad Football Idolatry Over," *Ariz. Republic*, 3 Feb. 1996, at B6.

LANGUAGE-CHANGE INDEX
*idolatrize for *idolize*: Stage 1
Current ratio (*idolize* vs. **idolatrize*): 247:1

I doubt that; I doubt whether; *I doubt if. See **doubt (A).**

idyll. A. Spelling and Pronunciation. *Idyll* (= [1] a poem or prose composition depicting rustic simplicity; or [2] a narrative, esp. in verse, resembling a brief epic) is the standard spelling. **Idyl* is a variant. Either way, the word is pronounced /ɪ-dəl/, like *idle*.

B. Adjective Misused. *Idyllic* = of, belonging to, or resembling an idyll; full of pastoral charm or rustic picturesqueness. E.g.: "But after a pretend visit to Antarctica, it's easy in Christchurch to decide to spend

LANGUAGE-CHANGE INDEX (For the full key, see front matter pp. xxxi, l–li.)
Stage 1: Rejected. **Stage 2:** Widely shunned. **Stage 3:** Widespread but . . . **Stage 4:** Ubiquitous but . . . **Stage 5:** Fully accepted.
Invariably inferior forms marked by asterisk (*). • Ratios represent frequency of prevalent forms vs. variants in current books.

most of your time outdoors, especially on an *idyllic* spring day in November." Millie Ball, "Take a Boat Ride to Christchurch, New Zealand," *Times-Picayune* (New Orleans), 26 Jan. 2003, Travel §, at 1. The word is often misused as if it meant *ideal*—e.g.:

- "The setting couldn't be more *idyllic* [read *ideal*] for Marcus Allen. It's Super Bowl week in his hometown of San Diego." Randy Covitz, "Allen Would Feel Right at Home if He Makes It into Hall of Fame," *Kansas City Star*, 25 Jan. 2003, Sports §, at 1.
- "[I]t would constitutionally mandate an almost *idyllic* [read *ideal*] situation in which 'every Michigan resident has affordable and comprehensive health care coverage through a fair and cost-effective financial system.'" Editorial, "No Health Plan," *Flint J.* (Mich.), 13 Jan. 2008, at A10.

To say that the governor of New York has an *idyllic* (= pastoral, countrified) life is preposterous. In fact, the meaning here seems to be "suggestive of a storybook; fairy-tale": "It's hard to say what role, if any, Mr. Spitzer's escalating disappointment in Albany played in his extraordinarily risky, self-destructive behavior, and it remains unclear when his once seemingly *idyllic* life went so awry." Danny Hakim & Michael Powell, "A Leader Recalled as Focused but Unable to Bend," *N.Y. Times*, 23 Mar. 2008, at 18.

LANGUAGE-CHANGE INDEX
idyllic misused for *ideal*: Stage 3

-IE. See DIMINUTIVES (G).

i.e. A. Generally. The abbreviation for *id est* (L. "that is") introduces explanatory phrases or clauses. Although the abbreviation is appropriate in some scholarly contexts, the phrase *that is* or the word *namely* is more comprehensible to the average reader.

B. And *e.g.* *I.e.* is frequently confounded with *e.g.* (short for *exempli gratia* [L. "for example"])—e.g.:

- "Our increased expectation is due to the company growing its presence in the $2 billion U.S. meal-replacement market through increased advertising in national magazines (*i.e.* [read *e.g.*,] People, Readers Digest, Parade) and newspapers (*i.e.* [read *e.g.*,] Globe and Enquirer)." Taglich Brothers, "How Analysts Size Up Companies," *Barrons*, 18 Nov. 2002, at 35 (that use of *i.e.* indicates that advertising will not be placed in other magazines and newspapers).
- "The production staff and Gateway reps huddle. They shoot a screen test of a fuller-figured blonde cast as an extra and decide that she—with some work (*i.e.* [read *e.g.*, unless that was all the work needed], ditch the suede pants)—looks more like a mom." Frank Ahrens, "Gateway Ditches Cow Motif for a Sleeker Image," *Miami Herald*, 18 Nov. 2002, at 27.
- "I have many electrical items that no longer work, *i.e.* [read *e.g.*]: cameras, video recorder, outlet strip, video rewinder, to name a few." Sandy Shelton, in question to "Post Your Problems," *Pitt. Post-Gaz.*, 19 Nov. 2002, at A14 (and since *e.g.* means "for example," *to name a few* is redundant).

See **e.g.**

LANGUAGE-CHANGE INDEX
i.e. misused for *e.g.*: Stage 2

C. Style and Usage. As with other familiar abbreviations of Latin phrases such as *etc.*, *et al.*, and *e.g.* (and

despite their appearance here, where they are being discussed as terms), *i.e.* is not italicized <the state capital, i.e., Jefferson City>. And like the others, *i.e.* is best confined to lists, parenthetical matter, footnotes, and citations rather than used in text, where some substitute such as *namely* is more natural <the state capital, which is Jefferson City>.

Formerly it was said that in speaking or reading, the abbreviation should be rendered *id est.* But this is never heard today, whereas the abbreviated letters *i.e.* are occasionally heard.

D. Punctuation. Generally, a comma follows *i.e.* in AmE (though not in BrE). E.g.:

- "The implicit assumption is that the fountains were designed for some wading—*i.e.*, 'interactive' participation." "Tempest in a Memorial Pool," *Wash. Post*, 3 Aug. 1997, at C8.
- "There was absolutely no need for any U.S. network to 'cover' (*i.e.*, 'interpret') the funeral." Letter of Mary L. Spencer, "Too Much Talk," *Indianapolis Star*, 2 Oct. 1997, at E7.

I enjoyed myself. Though literalistic pedants sometimes criticize this idiom as hopelessly illogical (which it is), it is standard—e.g.:

- "And *I enjoyed myself*, so it doesn't seem that I failed." Dan McGrath, "For Better or Worse, This Gig Was Fun," *Sacramento Bee*, 20 Aug. 1995, at A2.
- "In all, *I really enjoyed myself*, even if there was no yapping." Tony Kornheiser, "I May Not Know Opera, but I Know a Major Babe When I See One," *Rocky Mountain News* (Denver), 26 Jan. 1997, at B6.
- "*I enjoyed myself* and the children seemed to enjoy listening to me read." Frank Roberts, "Reading to Children Takes Real Talent," *Virginian-Pilot* (Norfolk), 17 Aug. 1997, Suffolk Sun §, at 7.

For some similar idioms, see ILLOGIC (A).

if. A. And *whether*. It's good editorial practice to distinguish between these words. Use *if* for a conditional idea, *whether* for an alternative or possibility. Hence *Let me know if you'll be coming* means that I want to hear from you only if you're coming. But *Let me know whether you'll be coming* means that I want to hear from you about your plans one way or the other.

B. If, and only if. Ordinarily, this adds nothing but unnecessary emphasis (and perhaps a rhetorical flourish) to *only if*. E.g.: "Such a 'homocentrist' position takes the human species to define the boundaries of the moral community: you are morally considerable *if, and only if,* [read *only if*] you are a member of the human species." Colin McGinn, "Beyond Prejudice," *New Republic*, 8 Apr. 1996, at 39. The variation *if, but only if*, which sometimes occurs in legal writing, is unnecessary and even nonsensical for *only if*.

Yet in math and logic, *if and only if* marks a relationship in which if either proposition is true (or false), both are true (or false).

C. For *though, even if,* or *and*. Some writers use *if* in an oddly precious way—to mean "though," "though perhaps," "even if," or even "and." Though several dictionaries record this use, it's not recommended because it typically carries a tone of affectedness—e.g.:

- "On one level of analysis these are unrelated 'accidents.' But on another they are concrete, *if* [read *though*] mainly unconscious and uncoordinated, responses to industry's need for concentrated and specialized learning." Richard Ohmann, *English in America* 289 (1976).
- "Their presentation is passionate; their prose hectic, *if* [read *and*] occasionally hectoring; their Darwin ambitious, angry and agitated." Roy Porter, "Devil's Chaplain," *Sunday Times* (London), 29 Sept. 1991, § 7, at 3.
- "Trump regularly puts his mouth in gear before his brain and the results are usually fascinating, *if* [read *even if*] sometimes offensive." Michael Putney, "Whatever Happened to the Summer Doldrums?" *Miami Herald*, 21 July 2015, Opinion §.

Cf. **if not.**

if and when. A. Generally. The single word *when* typically conveys everything this three-word phrase does. Although the full idiom does emphasize both conditionality and temporality, if a thing is done at a certain time it is *ipso facto* done. Still, the phrase helpfully sets up two conditions: (1) I won't perform my duty unless you perform yours, and (2) don't expect me to go first. As a popular idiom, *if and when* is not likely to disappear just for the sake of brevity.

LANGUAGE-CHANGE INDEX
if and when for *if*: Stage 4

B. And *when and if*. Perhaps in an attempt to get out of a rhetorical rut, some writers reverse these words and make it *when and if* with no change in nuance intended. But that construction loses any logical value that the original may have had—*when* the thing is done, there is no further question about *if* it will be done. Some other phrasing is usually advisable—e.g.:

- "Lawmakers should have a right to determine *when and if* [read *when*] such a tax should be considered." "Local Assessors Require Oversight," *Sunday Advocate* (Baton Rouge), 28 July 2002, at B8.
- "But with only a little bit of light from their dwindling lamps, miners could never tell *when or if* [read *whether*] the water was coming back at them." Guy Gugliotta, "In a Flooded Coal Mine, 3 Days of Waiting, Praying," *Wash. Post*, 29 July 2002, at A1.
- "*When and if* [read *If*] Gonzalez signs a new contract, Dunn is a backup again." Adam Teicher, "Chiefs Won't Ask Dunn to Be Another Gonzalez," *Kansas City Star*, 30 July 2002, at C1.

When and if can have a distinct nuance, however, by emphasizing that the event may never happen. Punctuation can help—e.g.: "The investment is usable, however, only *when—and if*—you take the profits out." Jane Bryant Quinn, "Home Sweet Piggy Bank?" *Newsweek*, 29 July 2002, at 58.

When *not* is substituted for *and*, the construction emphasizes the inevitability of the event at some point—e.g.: "And he's the only one making arguments from the perspective of the men and women who will run into those buildings *when (not if)* they catch fire." Terry Golway, "A Terrifying Vision of Towering Infernos," *N.Y. Observer*, 29 July 2002, Pol. & Op. §, at 5.

if ever there was; if ever there were. When posing a question beginning with one of these phrases, the writer or speaker almost invariably means to raise a question of historical fact—not to state something contrary to fact. So the past-indicative *was* is called for, not the subjunctive *were*. (See SUBJUNCTIVES.) If the subjunctive were in order (now, *that's* counterfactual!), it would be the past subjunctive: **if ever there had been*. But this wording is clearly erroneous and unidiomatic. In modern print sources, the correct phrasing (*if ever there was*) is more than four times as common as the incorrect one—e.g.: "A dark horse *if ever there was* one, Beaver was suddenly thrust into the limelight." Colin Eatock, "A Dark Horse on a Rescue Mission," *Globe & Mail* (Toronto), 7 Aug. 2002, at R3.

The phrasing also raises questions of verb tense. The ordinary sequence of tenses is to have a past-tense verb in the principal clause when the subordinate clause is in the past tense, as in *If ever there was an artistic genius, he was it.* Many published examples exhibit this sequence of tenses—e.g.:

- "That was followed by the terror of anthrax and by the threat in Afghanistan, an unlikely combination *if ever there was one*." Douglas Gould, "It's Been an Astonishing, Unpredictable Year," *Globe & Mail* (Toronto), 28 Dec. 2001, at 11.
- "*If ever there was* a gimme, this was it." Wright Thompson, "Risk and Reward," *Times-Picayune* (New Orleans), 30 Dec. 2001, Sports §, at 1.

Yet many others violate this grammatical sequence by having the principal verb in the present tense, as in *If ever there was an artistic genius, he is it.* Nearly a third of the examples in modern print sources have the main clause in the present tense—e.g.:

- "*If ever there was* a team in need of validation, *it's* Nebraska." Eric Olson, "Defensive Huskers Dig In," *Wash. Post*, 27 Dec. 2001, at D1.
- "*If ever there was* a character created for the modern world of media, Jimmy *seems* to be it." Eric Elkins, "Paving the Way for Gold," *Denver Post*, 30 Dec. 2001, at E1.
- "*If ever there was* a time to make your move, *it's* now." Trevor Delaney, "Five Tempting Sectors," *Wall Street J.*, 30 Dec. 2001, at 3.

To change any one of those last three examples to *If ever there has been . . .* might seem unnatural and pedantic, yet many fastidious writers do it to good effect. E.g.: "*If ever there has been* a franchise that had a hold on a region, *it's* the Leafs." Bill Griffith, "Turning Over All the Leafs in Toronto," *Boston Globe*, 24 Aug. 2001, at E10. The logic is certainly heightened with the more punctilious sequence. See TENSES (B).

LANGUAGE-CHANGE INDEX (For the full key, see front matter pp. xxxi, l–li.)
Stage 1: Rejected. **Stage 2:** Widely shunned. **Stage 3:** Widespread but . . . **Stage 4:** Ubiquitous but . . . **Stage 5:** Fully accepted.
Invariably inferior forms marked by asterisk (*). • Ratios represent frequency of prevalent forms vs. variants in current books.

By the way, a variation of the basic phrase without INVERSION of the usual word order—namely, *if there ever was*—is also quite common and is perfectly good English.

iffy (= uncertain) is a CASUALISM dating from the mid-20th century—e.g.:

- "Hair growth? It's *iffy*. Some say yes; others no. You would think that female hormones in the birth-control pills would reduce facial hair growth." Paul Donohue, "Immune System's Been in the News a Lot Lately," *St. Louis Post-Dispatch*, 15 Nov. 1996, Everyday Mag. §, at E2.
- "We also believe Michael Jordan can wheeze, struggle, brick, shoot air balls, be frozen by Allen Iverson and depend on *iffy* officiating calls to win games he normally devours like a chew toy." Jay Mariotti, "Next Heroics for MJ Involve Taking a Seat," *Chicago Sun-Times*, 20 Mar. 1997, at 118.
- "The two banks' fit had been *iffy* from the start." Peter Galuszka, "Will Keycorp Be Shark Bait?" *Business Week*, 7 Apr. 1997, at 121.

if it be. See SUBJUNCTIVES.

if need be. This phrase can lead to problems of tense-shifting. For example, in the sentence "We always did what we had to do, if need be," the tense abruptly switches from past (*did*) to present (*be*). Eric Partridge suggested *if need were* as a substitute (*U&A* at 150), but that phrase is both archaic and unidiomatic. The best course is often to rephrase with *if necessary*—though in the example above, the phrase is redundant and could be dropped without any loss of meaning. See TENSES.

if not is often an ambiguous phrase to be avoided. It may mean either (1) "but not; though not"; or (2) "maybe even." Sense 2 is exemplified in the following sentences, but in each one it's possible to misread the phrase as bearing sense 1:

- "If all this is true, the President [Reagan] should go down in history as one of the greatest, *if not* the greatest." William L. Jones, "The President, Iran, and the Boland Amendment," *San Diego Union-Trib.*, 20 Dec. 1986, at B11.
- "The greater Phoenix area is one of the fastest—*if not* the fastest—growth areas for call centers nationwide." Paul Giblin, "Accent-Neutral Phoenix Draws Calling Centers," *Dallas Morning News*, 8 Dec. 1996, at A45.
- "One of the best, *if not* the best, predictors of health care expenditure levels in a given geographic area or political jurisdiction is family or per-capita income." Lawrence D. Cohen, "Managed Care Can Right Its Own Ship," *Hartford Courant*, 16 Feb. 1997, at B3.

Sense 1 is confusing if, as is quite likely, the reader first thinks of the phrase in terms of the more common sense 2. It would be clearer to substitute *though* for *if*:

- "She gave proficient, *if not* [read *though not*] profound, readings." Josef Woodard, "Monroe Plays Mostly in a Classical Mode," *L.A. Times,* 12 Apr. 1996, at F14.
- "This is the story William Kleinknecht lays out competently *if not* [read *though not*] stirringly in 'The New Ethnic Mobs,' a useful primer on the shifting criminal threat." Ralph Blumenthal, "Books of the Times," *N.Y. Times*, 5 Sept. 1996, at C21.
- "Kwan's conservative short program, adequately *if not* [read *though not*] flawlessly executed, gave her the votes of all nine judges for first place." John Markon, "Kwan Takes the Safe Route to Lead in U.S. Skating Finals," *Richmond Times-Dispatch*, 15 Feb. 1997, at D5.

Generally speaking, when an understated term such as *adequate* or *competent* precedes *if not*, it has sense 1; when a more laudatory term precedes the phrase, sense 2 applies. Cf. **if.**

-IFY. See -FY.

if you will. This phrase typifies the language of those who engage in WORD PATRONAGE. An elliptical form of *if you will allow me to use the phrase*, the phrase is almost always best deleted. Cf. **as it were.**

ignis fatuus (= will o' the wisp; a delusive hope or desire) forms the plural *ignes fatui*. But even the few readers who understand the singular LATINISM are likely to puzzle over the plural.

ignitable. So spelled in AmE and BrE alike—not **ignitible*. See -ABLE (A).

Current ratio: 6:1

ignominy is accented on the first, not the second, syllable: /**ig**-nə-min-ee/.

ignoramus. Until 1934, if a grand jury in England considered the evidence of an alleged crime insufficient to prosecute, it would endorse the bill *ignoramus*, meaning literally "we do not know" or "we know nothing of this." Long before, though, the word *ignoramus* had come to mean, by extension, "an ignorant person." In 1615, George Ruggle wrote a play called *Ignoramus*, about a lawyer who knew nothing about the law; this fictional lawyer soon gave his name to all manner of know-nothings, whether lawyers or nonlawyers.

The modern nonlegal meaning appears most frequently—e.g.: "There's no surprise—or challenge—in watching a sycophantic, misogynistic *ignoramus* like Burdette win out over the self-effacing, truth-loving Hutchinson." Lawrence Bommer, "'Lip Service' Subtle as a Sledgehammer," *Chicago Trib.*, 5 Aug. 1997, at 2.

The plural is *ignoramuses*. The form **ignorami* is a pseudo-learned blunder, since in Latin *ignoramus* is a verb and not one of the Latin nouns ending in *-us*. This erroneous form reached the peak of its popularity in print (often in jocular contexts) in the 1920s but today is relatively infrequent. See PLURALS (B) & HYPERCORRECTION (A).

The word is preferably pronounced /ig-nə-**ray**-məs/—not /ig-nə-**ram**-əs/.

Current ratio (*ignoramuses* vs. **ignorami*): 32:1

ignorant; stupid. *Stupid* refers to a lack of innate ability, whereas *ignorant* refers merely to a lack of knowledge on a particular subject. Geniuses are *ignorant* of many facts, but that doesn't make them *stupid*. But *stupid* people can't grasp that they are *ignorant* of even the most basic facts.

LANGUAGE-CHANGE INDEX
ignorant for *stupid*: Stage 4

-ILE; -INE. Most words with these endings are best pronounced with the *-i-* short rather than long. Thus: *agile* /**aj**-əl/, not /**aj**-ɪl/; *genuine* /**jen**-yoo-in/, not /**jen**-yoo-ɪn/. But as with any other rule of pronunciation, there are many exceptions, among them *infantile* /**in**-fən-tɪl/, *magazine* /mag-ə-**zeen**/, and *turpentine* /**tər**-pən-tɪn/.

Also, the ANIMAL ADJECTIVES ending in *-ine* may go either way, but they tend to have the long *-i-*, as in *feline* and *asinine*.

ilex (= a holly or holm oak) has made the standard plural *ilexes* since the early 19th century—not **ilices.* See generally PLURALS (B).

Current ratio: 30:1

ilk. A. Meaning. Originally, this Scottish term meant "the same"; hence *of that ilk* meant "of that same [place, territory, or name]" <McGuffey of that ilk>. By extension during the 19th century—from a misunderstanding of the Scottish use—*ilk* came to mean "type" or "sort" <Joseph McCarthy and his ilk>. Because there is little call outside Scotland for the original sense, the extended use must now be accepted as standard—e.g.:

- "That those of the *ilk* who call themselves journalists succumb is something to be loudly denounced—and roundly rejected." Jane Ely, "Multiple-Choice Puzzle Circles Diana's End," *Houston Chron.,* 3 Sept. 1997, at A25.
- "Renji terms Pearlman and his *ilk* clever but dangerous." Maggie Farley, "Showdown at Global Warming Summit," *L.A. Times,* 7 Dec. 1997, at A8.
- "It's composed essentially like Nickelback and bands of the similar *ilk.*" B.J. Lisko, "Excellent Label Debut from Akron Rockers," *Repository* (Canton, Ohio), 27 Aug. 2015, at E14.

Still, one occasionally encounters puzzling uses that seem worthy of disapproval—e.g.: "It is also maddening to know there exists the human *ilk* that would, for whatever twisted motive, drag our young over the line." Gil Griffin, "Essayist Takes Race Relations Personally," *San Diego Union-Trib.,* 24 Nov. 1997, at E1. The sentence would surely be improved by changing *there exists the human ilk that* to *there exist people who.*

LANGUAGE-CHANGE INDEX
ilk for *type* or *sort*: Stage 5

B. Connotation. The word's accepted definition is hardly defamatory. But the word increasingly conveys derogatory connotations (perhaps from sound association with the expletive *ick*?)—e.g.: "The book wrestles with the excruciating ethical dilemmas facing America . . . in battling Osama bin Laden and his *ilk.*" Jean Bethke Elshtain, "Duty Bound," *Wash. Post* (Book Rev.), 6 Apr. 2003, at T4. It has been known to give offense—e.g.: "Larouche wrote her own letter to the editor . . . to attack me and my opinions personally, such as by calling me and my '*ilk*' (whoever they are) 'hypocrites in Birkenstocks.'" Letter of Hanna Bordas, *Boston Globe,* 6 Apr. 2003, Mag. §, at 3.

ill. The comparative form of this adjective is *worse,* the superlative *worst.* The adverb is *ill, *illy* being an illiterate NONWORD that is acceptable neither in formal writing nor in nondialectal informal writing. *Ill* itself acts as an adverb—e.g.: "There he had knocked a hole in the roof and poured in gasoline, a primitive technique *that illy fit* [read *ill-fitting* or *that ill fitted*] the Waldbaum evidence." Murry Kempton, "Standing by Convictions, Wrongly," *Newsday* (N.Y.), 19 Aug. 1994, at A8. For other adverbs with a superfluous *-ly,* see ADVERBS (C).

LANGUAGE-CHANGE INDEX
*illy for the adverb *ill*: Stage 1

illation (= the act of inferring or something inferred) is a learned term little used today, though a few philosophers are quite fond of it. (See SESQUIPEDALITY.) *Inference* serves just as well—and it's more understandable.

illegal; illicit; unlawful. These terms are fundamentally synonymous, although *illicit* carries moral overtones <illicit love affairs> in addition to the basic sense of all three: "not in accordance with or sanctioned by law." Since 1800 or so, *illegal* has been the most frequently used, followed by *unlawful* and then *illicit.* During most of the 18th century, *unlawful* appeared in print somewhat more frequently than *illegal.*

Illegal is not synonymous with *criminal,* though some writers mistakenly assume that it is. Anything against the law—even civil statutes—is, technically speaking, *illegal,* but only violations of criminal law are *criminal.* See **legal.**

For two MALAPROPISMS involving *illicit,* see **illicit.**

illegal immigrant; illegal alien; undocumented immigrant; undocumented alien. The terminology relating to those who come to live in another country without official permission is highly charged—increasingly so since about 1980. From 1930 on, *illegal immigrant* has been the usual phrase in BrE, but only from about 1945 to 1970 was it the predominant term in AmE.

About 1970, *illegal alien* surged into common use in AmE, and it remains predominant today. But some think it doubly tendentious: coupling the dysphemistic *alien* with the negatively charged *illegal* makes it easy, the argument goes, to dehumanize people who struggle to improve their lives without complying with bureaucratic requirements for entry. People who hold views something like this consider *illegal alien* a snarl-phrase and prefer instead a EUPHEMISM such as *undocumented immigrant* (or, even more euphemistically, *undocumented worker*).

Those who, on the other hand, prefer *illegal alien* note that *alien* is the age-old legal term for a noncitizen within a country—that there are *resident aliens* who have green cards that allow them to stay indefinitely. Those taking this position note that both unsanctioned

LANGUAGE-CHANGE INDEX (For the full key, see front matter pp. xxxi, l–li.)
Stage 1: Rejected. **Stage 2:** Widely shunned. **Stage 3:** Widespread but . . . **Stage 4:** Ubiquitous but . . . **Stage 5:** Fully accepted.
Invariably inferior forms marked by asterisk (*). • Ratios represent frequency of prevalent forms vs. variants in current books.

entry into the United States and overstaying one's visa are infractions—hence illegal. On this view, *illegal alien* is therefore a denotatively accurate phrase for someone who is present in a country in violation of the immigration laws. People with this view scorn *undocumented* as DOUBLESPEAK because the word ordinarily means "unaccounted for" but in this instance seems to bear the anodyne sense "not having the requisite documents to enter or stay in a country."

There are those who take the (very) long view that, anthropologically speaking, people have always migrated across land masses according to their needs. Notions of national sovereignty, they might say, are relatively recent constructs.

Although few might be thought to share this radical view, something like it has become fairly mainstream. On 7 March 2015, addressing the nation from Selma, Alabama, 50 years after Martin Luther King Jr.'s famous march, President Barack Obama said (as part of a long litany): "We are the people who swim across the Rio Grande in search of a better life." In his very next utterance (after completing the litany), he disclaimed the idea that "some of us are more American than others."

In such a climate, the phrase *illegal alien* is perceived as hostile—mostly by those on the left. *Undocumented immigrant* has gradually become preferable in their eyes. Yet that phrase is viewed as hopelessly evasive and misleading by those on the right.

So the terminology is shifting. Big data tell us that as of 2008, *illegal alien* remained prevalent in AmE print sources, followed closely by *illegal immigrant*, which itself was nearly three times as common as *undocumented immigrant*. Least common of all was *undocumented alien*. Meanwhile, in the Republican-primary presidential debates of 2015, the attributive noun *illegals* was used by moderators and candidates alike—which is rather like the 1920s habit of referring to people afflicted with tuberculosis as *tuberculars*.

The resolution of these political and terminological struggles is yet to be documented.

Current ratio (in order of headwords): 11:9:3:1

illegible; unreadable. *Illegible* = not plain or clear enough to be read (used of bad handwriting or defaced printing). *Unreadable* = too dull, obfuscatory, or nonsensical to be read (used of poor writing).

illegitimate child. Although the phrase is still often used, and although it's undeniably better than *bastard*, it's also undeniably insensitive. Since the mid-1970s, it has been falling in frequency of use. As a far-sighted judge once observed, "There are no illegitimate children, only illegitimate parents." *In re Estate of Woodward*, 40 Cal. Rptr. 781, 784 (Dist. Ct. App. 1964) (Yankwich, J.). Increasingly, the phrase *child out of wedlock* or *nonmarital child* is displacing *illegitimate child*. See EUPHEMISMS & **natural child.**

illicit. This adjective, meaning "illegal," appears in two MALAPROPISMS. First, it is sometimes used for *elicit* (= to bring out)—e.g.:

- "The NFL tempered Cincinnati's first free agent signing Wednesday when it raised the league's salary cap $500,000, making it $2.5 million higher than in 1994 and *illiciting* [read *eliciting*] more fears from Bengals General Manager Mike Brown for the future." Geoff Hobson, "Bengals Rocked by New, Expanded Salary Cap," *Cincinnati Enquirer*, 23 Mar. 1995, at D1.
- "The 43-point average of its star player *illicits* [read *elicits*] awe." Doug Bedell, "Home-schoolers Team Wins Amid Controversy," *Dallas Morning News*, 16 Jan 1998, at B2.
- "Few comments *illicit* [read *elicit*] more disbelief, disgust, and downright anger than suggestions that the economy has performed as well during George W. Bush's presidency as during Bill Clinton's." Bob Rayner, Editorial, "Horrors! Bush's Record Betters Clinton's," *Richmond Times-Dispatch*, 27 June 2007, at A11.

This misuse caught the attention of a famous linguist during the first half of the 20th century: "Illiterate spellers will often write *illicit* for *elicit*, *enumerable* for *innumerable*, etc." Otto Jespersen, *Growth and Structure of the English Language* 146 n.25 (9th ed. 1938).

Second, and perhaps more surprisingly, the word is sometimes misused for *solicit*—e.g.:

- "Pele was banned from the World Cup draw last December after accusing Texiera of *illiciting* [read *soliciting*] bribes for Brazilian television rights." Mike Mulligan, "Havelange Gets Sixth Term," *Chicago Sun-Times*, 17 June 1994, World Cup §, at 129.
- "Yet, it is those volunteers and the community-spirited donations they *illicit* [read *solicit*] that keep the doors open at nearly every food pantry you'll find." Jerry Nunn, "Hunger Pains," *Bay City Times* (Mich.), 30 Nov. 2007, at E1.

For more on the word, see **illegal.**

LANGUAGE-CHANGE INDEX
1. *illicit* for *elicit*: Stage 1
Current ratio (*elicited* vs. **illicited*): 2,853:1
2. *illicit* for *solicit*: Stage 1

Illinois is pronounced /il-ə-**noy**/—not /il-ə-**noyz**/. See PRONUNCIATION (B).

Illinoisan; *Illinoisian. The first, pronounced /il-ə-**noy**-ən/, is standard. The second is a NEEDLESS VARIANT. See DENIZEN LABELS.

Current ratio: 5:1

illiterate = (1) unable to read or write; or (2) unlettered. Sense 1 refers to the most minimal literacy, sense 2 to grander notions of literacy. Today sense 1 threatens to drive out sense 2.

ILLOGIC. A. Generally. The writer on language who would dare drag logic into the discussion must do so warily. For centuries, grammarians labored under the mistaken belief that grammar is nothing but applied logic and therefore tried to rid languages of everything illogical. But to paraphrase Justice Oliver Wendell Holmes, the life of the language has not been logic: it has been experience.

No serious student believes anymore that grammatical distinctions necessarily reflect logical ones. Our language is full of idioms that defy logic, many of them literary and many colloquial. We should not, for example, fret over the synonymy of *fat chance* and *slim chance*, *burn up* and *burn down*, or *miss* and *near miss*. We should instead smile at the playful genius of the language. Applying "linguistic logic" to established ways of saying things is a misconceived effort.

We see this misconception today when armchair grammarians insist that *grammatical error* is an Irish bull; that *I don't think so* is wrong in place of *I think not* (see **don't think**); that *the reason why* is wrong (no more so, certainly, than *place where* or *time when*); that *a number of people* must take a singular, not a plural, verb (see SYNESIS); that *none* must always take a singular verb; or that, in *Don't spend any more time than you can help*, the final words should be *can't help*. When logic is used for such purposes, it is worse than idle: it is harmful.

That does not mean, of course, that logic is of no concern to the writer. For rhetorical purposes, logic is essential. Some readers will seek out holes in the logic; but almost all readers will be distracted if they notice this type of problem. In evaluating our own writing, therefore, we should strictly follow idiom and usage, but otherwise apply logic.

The exercise will tighten your prose. Since idiom does not yet prefer *could care less*, much less require it, write *couldn't care less*. Logically speaking, if you say that you *could care less*, then you're admitting that you care to some extent. (See **couldn't care less.**) Logic will help you avoid saying *I was scared literally to death*, because you'll recognize the literal meaning of *literally*—and you're still alive to report how scared you were. Likewise, logic would have you banish thoughtless words such as *preplanned*.

Logic promotes clear thinking. To avoid the ills catalogued below, consider closely how your words and sentences relate to one another.

B. Illogical Comparison. This lapse occurs commonly in locutions such as *as large if not larger than*, which, when telescoped, becomes *as large than*; properly, one writes *as large as if not larger than*. (See CANNIBALISM.) Similar problems occur with classes of things. For example, when members of classes are being compared, a word such as *other* must be used to restrict the class: "Representative democracy is better than any [other] political system in the world."

Another problem of comparison occurs when the writer forgets the point of reference in the comparison:

- "Like the hard-hitting Dianne Feinstein, a candidate for California's governorship, *Silber's views are striking* [read *Silber strikes*] a chord among many Democrats tired of losing." Mike Graham, "Democrats' New Breed Upsets the Party Old Guard," *Sunday Times* (London), 15 Apr. 1990, at A23. The sentence compares a person to someone's views.
- "Like many others in Los Angeles, the quake helped Mr. Becker decide to leave." "Deciding to Escape Los Angeles," *N.Y. Times*, 18 Feb. 1994, at A10 (photo caption). This is a fine dangling modifier: the quake joined many others in L.A. in persuading Mr. Becker to leave.

- "But the bone marrow transplant Mr. Getty is to receive is different from the earlier *cases* [read *ones* or *transplants*] because the marrow is being processed so that it consists of only two types of cells." Lawrence K. Altman, "Hope in AIDS Case Is Put in Marrow from Baboon," *N.Y. Times*, 15 Dec. 1995, at A1, A16. You don't compare a *transplant* to a *case*, which in medicine comprises the whole situation—the patient, the doctors, the injection, and everything else relating to the patient's problem.
- "Significantly, although industrial relations is regarded as more important than when the survey was last conducted, in September, it does not rate in the top 10 most dominant issues." Michael Gordon, "Voters Swing Back to ALP on Issues," *Weekend Australian*, 20–21 Jan. 1996, at 1. Insert the word *now* after *important*. Otherwise, it seems as if you're comparing *industrial relations* to a given time. In fact, we're comparing the importance of the issue then and now.

For related issues, see **best of all, better than any (other), everyone . . . not, every other (A)** & **vice versa.**

C. Danglers and Misplaced Modifiers. Every dangler or misplaced modifier perverts logic to some degree, sometimes humorously—e.g.: "I saw the Statue of Liberty flying into Newark." To avoid these disruptions of thought, remember that a participle should relate to a noun that is truly capable of performing the participle's action. Another example: "The 1993 law, which was invalidated before it went into effect, required pregnant teen-agers or their doctors to notify a parent or guardian at least 48 hours before undergoing abortions." Aaron Epstein, "High Court Leaves Intact Abortion Rule," *Amarillo Daily News*, 30 Apr. 1996, at A1. Who is getting abortions? This sentence literally suggests that doctors are getting abortions, but that they must notify their parents first.

For a fuller discussion of these matters, see DANGLERS & MISCUES (B).

D. The Disjointed Appositive. Phrases intended to be in apposition shouldn't be separated—e.g.:

- "A respected English legal authority on the common law, the view of William Blackstone permeated much of the early thinking on freedom of expression." John Murray, *The Media Law Dictionary* 11 (1978). (Blackstone himself, not Blackstone's *view*, is the respected authority.)
- "As the editor of *Godey's Lady's Book* from 1837 to 1877—years in which this widely read magazine almost never mentioned the Civil War because war was not the business of ladies—Hale was regarded as one of America's most influential women." Mark Kurlansky, *Salt: A World History* 305 (2002). (The author's assertion for the years 1837 to 1860 is illogical—the Civil War didn't begin until 1861, so of course it wasn't mentioned before then.)

See APPOSITIVES.

E. Mistaken Subject of a Prepositional Phrase. This problem crops up usually when a word or phrase intervenes between the noun and the prepositional phrase referring to that noun. Often, as in the example below, the noun (*school bus*) functions as an

---

LANGUAGE-CHANGE INDEX (For the full key, see front matter pp. xxxi, l–li.)
Stage 1: Rejected. **Stage 2:** Widely shunned. **Stage 3:** Widespread but . . . **Stage 4:** Ubiquitous but . . . **Stage 5:** Fully accepted.
Invariably inferior forms marked by asterisk (*). • Ratios represent frequency of prevalent forms vs. variants in current books.

adjective: "*Wallin was the school bus driver in which* [read *Wallin was driving the school bus in which*] Hillman and Ellington and Kleven were passengers." Cf. REMOTE RELATIVES.

F. Poor Exposition of Sequence. Don't ask your readers to assume what is not logically possible by your very assumptions—e.g.: "The twin-engine turbo prop Merlin Fairchild 300 carrying driver Alan Kulwicki and three other men suddenly dropped off the radar screen and crashed *shortly before landing*." Karen Allen & Erik Brady, "Motor Sports," *USA Today*, 5 Apr. 1993, at C9. (The plane crashed before it would have landed, but as it happened the plane never did land in any normal sense of the word. And if you take the crash itself as a landing, the logic of the temporal sequence is absurd.)

G. **Times less than.*** Brand Y may cost twice as much as Brand X, but that doesn't mean Brand X is twice as cheap as Brand Y. Farburg may be two times as far away as Nearville, but that doesn't mean Nearville is two times closer than Farburg. Big Dog may be twice the size of Little Dog, but that doesn't mean Little Dog is two times smaller than Big Dog.

One time is 100% of the cost, distance, size, or any other measure. If you take away "one time" something, you've taken away all there is. If you walk toward me and cover all the distance, you can't get any closer—you can't be twice as close as you were before. If the price is discounted *one time* or 100%, the item is free. **Two times cheaper*, if it means anything, might imply that the store will pay *you* the full price of Brand Y if you will take Brand X home with you. That mangles the meaning of *cost*, and it surely isn't what the writer means.

What does the writer mean? Probably "half," but who can say for sure? Yet despite the illogic of the phrase, it is used all the time, even in scientific literature—e.g.:

- "It came within just 4,000 miles of the 10-mile-wide nucleus of the comet, *or about 10 times closer than* [read *much closer than*] any of the other four missions to Halley's Comet." Bernie Reim, "One Eye's on Planets, One's on Spring," *Portland Press Herald*, 28 Feb. 2001, at C3.
- "Virus levels in the one animal were intermittently higher but still *more than 100 times lower than* [read *less than 1% as much as*] those in four control animals that had not received the vaccine." "HIV Vaccines: New Prime-Boost Strategy Shows Promise in Monkeys," *Gene Therapy Weekly*, 22 Mar. 2001, at 9.
- "States were further required to limit soot from power plants, cars and other sources to 2.5 microns, or *28 times smaller than* [who can be sure what this means?] the width of a human hair." "EPA's Tougher Clean Air Rules Cloud the Michigan Economy," *Detroit News*, 5 Apr. 2001, at 2.

H. **Times more than.*** A problem similar to but far less egregious than the illogic of **times less than* comes up when we say that X is **two times more than* Y. The common understanding is that if Y is 1, then X is 2. But strictly speaking, one *time more* than Y could also be 2, because *more* implies that the result of 1-times-X is added to X to arrive at Y. The more

precise and unambiguous wording is "X is two times as much as Y."

I. Miscellaneous Other Examples. For various other brands of poor thinking, see ADJECTIVES (B), **all** (D), **between** (F), **contiguous**, **every other** (A), ***exfelon**, ***least worst**, **much less**, **much-needed**, **same** (C), **temperature** (B), ***these kind of**, **underestimate**, ***up to —— off** and **more**, **wean**, **within**, ***without scarcely** & **yet** (B).

illude. See **allude** (B).

illuminate; illumine; *illume. *Illuminate* is most common by far. *Illumine* is archaic except in poetry. **Illume* is obsolescent.

Current ratio (in order of headwords): 104:10:1

illusion; delusion. These words are used differently despite their similar meanings. An *illusion* exists in one's fancy or imagination. A *delusion* is an idea or thing that deceives or misleads a person. *Delusions* are dangerously wrong apprehensions; *illusions* are also wrong perceptions, but the connotation is far less dire. Cf. **hallucination.**

Sometimes *delusion* is misused as hyperbole for *illusion*—e.g.: "Houston Coach Kim Helton has no *delusions* [read *illusions*] about why the Cougars ended an 11-game losing streak by beating Southern Methodist 38–15." Mark Rosner, "Longhorns Had *Alternate* [read *Alternative*] Plan Ready," *Austin Am.-Statesman*, 23 Oct. 1995, at C3.

For a misuse of *illusion* for *allusion*, see **allusion.**

LANGUAGE-CHANGE INDEX
delusion misused for *illusion*: Stage 1

illusory; *illusive. The former has been the predominant form since about 1850. **Illusive* is a NEEDLESS VARIANT. See **elusive.**

Current ratio: 7:1

illustrate, in modern usage, means "to provide a good example of (something); to exemplify." In the following sentence it is used ambiguously: "Jennings's analysis *illustrates* the fallacy of accepting the theory too literally." The writer here wasn't claiming—as the sentence seems to do—that Jennings's analysis is itself a good example of "the fallacy of accepting the theory too literally." Rather, the sentence was intended to hold up Jennings's analysis as one that elucidates well the nature of this fallacy.

Illustrate is accented on the first syllable: /**il**-ə-strayt/.

illustrative. A. Pronunciation. The second syllable is accented: /i-**ləs**-trə-tiv/, not /i-ləs-tray-tiv/.

B. And *illustrious.* *Illustrative* means "providing a good illustration or portrayal; representative." *Illustrious* means "distinguished; acclaimed; renowned." Occasionally, through WORD-SWAPPING, *illustrative* displaces *illustrious*—e.g.:

- "Karloff received a great number of critical plaudits and many critics called the film a fine climax to a long and illustrative [read *illustrious*] film career." Michael R. Pitts, *Horror Film Stars* 85 (1991).

- "Both Howard and Eugene Odum continued basic research on the relation of energy to ecosystem structure and function into the new millennia in astonishingly long and *illustrative* [read *illustrious*] careers." 2 *Encyclopedia of Energy* 144 (Cutler J. Cleveland & Robert U. Ayers eds., 2004).

LANGUAGE-CHANGE INDEX
illustrative misused for *illustrious*: Stage 1

*illy. See **ill.**

IM-. See **EN-.**

imaginative; imaginary. *Imaginative* (= creative) is occasionally misused for *imaginary* (= unreal)—e.g.:

- "Robin, foraging in a deserted plantation house for wine for the wounded, finds a book that recounts 'an unheard-of prodigy [that] . . . occurred in England during the reign of King Stephen.' This story both sustains Robin as the war becomes more horrific, and helps him to escape brutality in his *imaginative* [read *imaginary*] world." Mary A. McCay, "The Blue and the Gray and the Green," *Times-Picayune* (New Orleans), 26 May 2002, Books §, at 5.
- "It's easy to forget the utterly *imaginative* [read *imaginary*] things that flourish as rumors and 'fact' when something untoward happens." Liz Smith, "An Instinct for Money," *Newsday* (N.Y.), 29 May 2002, at A15.

LANGUAGE-CHANGE INDEX
imaginative misused for *imaginary*: Stage 1

imbecile; imbecilic. The preferred adjectival form of *imbecile*, n., was once thought to be *imbecile*. But *imbecilic*, which emerged in the late 19th century, is now standard as well.

LANGUAGE-CHANGE INDEX
imbecilic: Stage 5
Current ratio (*imbecile grin* vs. *imbecilic grin*): 2:1

imbibe is a FORMAL WORD meaning "to drink"—e.g.: "She sees groups of women 'having some social interaction' over piping hot cups, but adds that men *imbibe* as well." Lisa Martin, "The New Brew," *Ark. Democrat-Gaz.*, 13 Feb. 1997, at E1. The word often occurs in figurative senses—e.g.:

- "And young existentialists can *imbibe* the heady atmosphere of Ze Left Bank." Joe Williams, "Name Your Poison," *St. Louis Post-Dispatch*, 6 Feb. 1997, at 29.
- "He personifies the new breed of musicians, South Asian in origin, who haven't forgotten their roots but have *imbibed* the culture they're placed in." Vivien Goldman, "Gimme Indi Pop!" *Village Voice*, 18 Feb. 1997, at 68.

The corresponding noun is *imbibition* /im-bə-**bish**-ən/, which is not so rare as one might suspect—e.g.: "Wanda Morehead, a captain from Newark and secretary of the charter group, could recall only one customer in nine years whose *imbibitions* dangerously compromised his inhibitions." Dave Golowenski, "Skippers Deal with All Types on Charter Boats,"

Columbus Dispatch, 14 Apr. 2002, at D15. The word **imbibement* is a NEEDLESS VARIANT—e.g.: "A 'made' mobster is formally inducted through a ritual that entails the commingling of blood, recitation of oaths and an *imbibement* [read *imbibition*] of wine." Scott Ladd, "Why the Tough Should Get Going," *Newsday* (N.Y.), 26 Nov. 1991, at 43.

*imblaze. See **emblazon.**

imbroglio. Pl. *imbroglios*. See PLURALS (D).

imbue (= [1] to inspire [a person, group of people, etc.] with; or [2] to saturate; soak or stain) is subject to OBJECT-SHUFFLING. Properly, a person is *imbued with* values; values aren't **imbued into* a person. In the latter phrase, *imbue* appears to have been misused for *instill*. The mistake is fairly common—e.g.:

- "In announcing the gifts, Jamail invoked the memory of his mother, Marie, and the values she *imbued* [read *instilled*] in him." Armando Villafranca, "Attorney Jamail, Wife Hand Out $17 Million," *Houston Chron.*, 5 Sept. 1996, at A1.
- "While the landscape at the Holt home might not be pristine, the sauciness she *imbues in it* [read *imbues it with*] more than makes up for the occasional weed." Susan Banks, "A Garden That's a Riff on Paintings," *Pitt. Post-Gaz.*, 14 June 2014, at B1.
- "His parents David and Naomi would *imbue* [read *instill*] in him a strong sense of right and wrong; of justice and social equality." "Jeremy Corbyn, the Boy to the Manor Born," *Sunday Telegraph*, 23 Aug. 2015, News §, at 13 (the title here being a pun: see **manner born, to the.**)

See **impart** & **instill.**

LANGUAGE-CHANGE INDEX
imbue misused for *instill*: Stage 1
Current ratio (*instilling in them* vs.
*imbuing in them): 77:1

I'm enjoying myself. See **I enjoyed myself.**

imitation. See **counterfeit.**

immaculate conception. Even among Catholics, it's a common misconception that this phrase refers either to the birth of Jesus (properly called the *virgin birth*) or to the impregnation of Mary. In fact, the doctrine of the *immaculate conception* refers to the conception of Mary herself, not Jesus. According to the doctrine, at the time Mary was conceived in her mother's womb, God sanctified her by removing "all stain of original sin." The phrase is often misapplied to refer to the conception that led to the "virgin birth" of Jesus, even by those who purport to be knowledgeable about church doctrine—e.g.:

- "Orthodox Christianity allows priests to marry; the Roman Catholic Church does not. And Orthodox Christians do not believe in the *immaculate conception of Jesus Christ* [read *immaculate conception of Mary*]." Lois M. Collins, "Patriarchal Pilgrimage," *Deseret News* (Salt Lake City), 4 Oct. 1997, at C1.

LANGUAGE-CHANGE INDEX (For the full key, see front matter pp. xxxi, l–li.)
Stage 1: Rejected. **Stage 2:** Widely shunned. **Stage 3:** Widespread but . . . **Stage 4:** Ubiquitous but . . . **Stage 5:** Fully accepted.
Invariably inferior forms marked by asterisk (*). • Ratios represent frequency of prevalent forms vs. variants in current books.

- "The last time a millennium turned in the parts of the world that date things from the *immaculate conception* [read *birth*] of Jesus Christ, no more than a hundred scholarly clerics supposed that it mattered." Michael Heywood, "Forget These Zeros, Bring on the Tukes," *Columbian* (Vancouver, Wash.), 31 Dec. 1999, at A9.
- "For decades, that pilgrimage was repeated each Dec. 8, which Catholics celebrate as the feast of Mary's *'immaculate conception'* of Jesus [omit *of Jesus*]." Carol Jeffares Hedman, "Shrines Provide Peace on Earth," *Tampa Trib.*, 11 July 2000, Pasco §, at 1.

One writer gamely corrected his error: "I implied that the birth of Jesus was the result of the *Immaculate Conception*. Uh-uh. The term doesn't refer to Mary conceiving the infant Jesus without sexual intercourse, but to Mary herself having been conceived without original sin in her soul. The friars back at St. Bonaventure must be so bummed with me." Mark McGuire, "Fox News Can Start from Scratch," *Times Union* (Albany), 15 Nov. 1999, at C1.

LANGUAGE-CHANGE INDEX
immaculate conception in reference to Jesus: Stage 2

immanent. See **imminent.**

immaterial; nonmaterial, adj. Although both may mean "not consisting of a material substance," *immaterial* tends to mean "of no substantial importance; inconsequential." *Nonmaterial*, by contrast, generally means "cultural, aesthetic" <the nonmaterial rewards of a career in theater>.

immediately, used as a conjunction in the sense "as soon as, promptly when," is obsolete in AmE but still occurs in BrE—e.g.: "He succeeded in persuading MPs to vote to restore the ban on benefits for all those who fail to claim asylum *immediately* they arrive in Britain." Paul Eastham, "MPs Slam Door on Bogus Refugees," *Daily Mail*, 16 July 1996, at 11. In AmE phrasing, the word *when* or *after* would be inserted after *immediately*.

immerse; *immerge. Both mean "to dip or plunge into liquid," but *immerse* is now the standard term. **Immerge*, which was infrequent in the 18th century and exceedingly rare today, is a NEEDLESS VARIANT—e.g.: "Fishing a bottle out of the pot, I carelessly *immerged* [read *immersed*] my fingers into the boiling hot water." Stacie L. Bezduch-Moore, " 'I Was Pregnant at 16,' " *Teen Mag.*, Mar. 1995, at 62.

Current ratio: 113:1

immigrate; emigrate. *Immigrate* = to migrate into or enter (a country). *Emigrate* = to migrate away from or exit (a country). In other words, *immigrate* considers the movement from the perspective of the destination; *emigrate* considers it from the perspective of the departure point. Perhaps it was indicative of the relative worth of the two forms of government that before the Soviet Union collapsed in the late 20th century, the United States was plagued by illegal *immigration* and the Soviet Union by attempts at illegal *emigration*.

Emigrate is to *immigrate* as *go* is to *come*, or as *take* is to *bring*. People *emigrate from* or *out of*, and

immigrate to or *into*. And just as those other two pairs are sometimes misused, *emigrate* and *immigrate* sometimes get reversed—e.g.:

- "The store is owned by Maria Guadalupe Flores, a native of Mexico who *emigrated* [read *immigrated*] into the U.S. at age 17." "Cinderella Story MN," *Pioneer Press* (St. Paul), 19 May 1996, at D6.
- "His most recent hire is a programmer he recruited and helped to *immigrate* [read *emigrate*] from Singapore." Lisa Biank Fasig, "Jetsoft Co. Scans Its Way to Innovation," *Cincinnati Enquirer*, 25 May 1997, at J3.

The terms can be almost interchangeable, with the help of the right preposition or adverb. In the first example, *emigrated to* rather than *into* would properly convey the same meaning as *immigrated into*. In the second, *immigrate here from Singapore* would correct the meaning as well as the recommended edit, *emigrate from Singapore*.

LANGUAGE-CHANGE INDEX
emigrate misused for *immigrate*: Stage 2

imminent; eminent; immanent. *Imminent* = certain and very near; impending <imminent danger>. *Eminent* = distinguished; unimpeachable <Moore is an eminent cardiac surgeon>. (See **eminently.**) *Immanent* (primarily a theological term) = inherent; pervading the material world <the immanent goodness of the divine will>.

These words are misused in more ways than one might suppose. *Imminent*, of course, ousts *eminent* from its rightful place (perhaps the most common misusage)—e.g.:

- "While making employees 'raise their hands to go to the bathroom,' may have a 19th century ring to it, such rules may be *imminently* [read *eminently*] sensible on assembly lines." "Their Unappointed Rounds the Issue: Postmaster to Relax Work Rules Following Massacres," *Rocky Mountain News* (Denver), 14 May 1993, at A62.
- "Fortunately, Peebles seems *imminently* [read *eminently*] qualified to build a 500-room Crowne Plaza Hotel on the 4.4-acre site." Jack Nease, "Convention Center Hotel Escaped Becoming Racial Crisis," *Sun-Sentinel* (Ft. Lauderdale), 27 Feb. 1997, at D3.
- "The *imminently* [read *eminently*] qualified Johnson associate Ed Tapscott (a good friend) should have a team to run, finally." Michael Wilbon, "Network Man Hits Nothing but Net," *Wash. Post*, 19 Dec. 2002, at D1.

But *eminent*, likewise, sometimes wrongly displaces *imminent*—e.g.: "[A] judge indicated on a court document that Cho [Seung-Hui] 'is mentally ill and in need of hospitalization, and presents an *eminent* [read *imminent*] danger to self or others as a result of mental illness . . . .' " Nancy Gibbs et al., "Darkness Falls," *Time*, 30 Apr. 2007, at 36.

Finally, *immanent* (= inherent) sometimes appears where *imminent* belongs—e.g.:

- "Had it been an A priority—signifying present or *immanent* [read *imminent*] danger to life—any police car in the city would have been ordered to the scene, he said." Ray Tessler, "S.F. Police Dispatcher's Role Questioned in the Death of Carlsbad Attorney's Son," *L.A. Times* (S.D. ed.), 12 Oct. 1990, at B2.

- "HB 2850 allows a driver to delay reporting an automobile accident involving over $500 damage if such driver is in fear of '*immanent* [read *imminent*] danger of bodily injury' by other individuals involved in the accident." Jan Pauls, "1994 Legislative Update: Transportation and Utilities," *J. Kansas Bar Ass'n*, Aug. 1994, at 40.

LANGUAGE-CHANGE INDEX
1. *imminent* for *eminent*: Stage 2
2. *eminent* for *imminent*: Stage 2
3. *immanent* for *imminent*: Stage 1

immolate = (1) to kill or destroy as a sacrifice, esp. by fire; or (2) to kill or destroy for any reason, esp. by burning. Sense 1 is the classic sense—e.g.: "Sati was the Hindu practice where widows would allow themselves to be *immolated* on the funeral pyres of their late husbands as the ultimate proof of their loyalty." Stephen Mansfield, "A City Caste in Royal Mold," *Daily Yomiuri* (Japan), 20 Jan. 1996, at 7.

Sense 2 is a product of SLIPSHOD EXTENSION; the word loses its traditional nuance of sacrificial destruction—e.g.: "She *immolates* a closetful of fine clothing, then holds a fire sale to get rid of the rest of her soon-to-be-ex's possessions." Michael Warren, "Bold, Determined, and Dangerous," *Des Moines Register*, 18 Jan. 1996, Today §, at 2. This sense sometimes appears for purposes of INELEGANT VARIATION—e.g.: "Fearing that he looked presumptuous, Williams has already burned roughly 100 of the cards and is searching for the last 400, which he also hopes to *immolate* [read *destroy* or *burn*]." Christian Stone, "The Rose Bowl Seemed Far Away After Northwestern," *Sports Illustrated*, 16 Sept. 1996, at 54.

Immolate is a transitive verb, not an intransitive one—nothing merely "immolates." Rather, an agent of some kind, usually a person, *immolates* something else. But some writers misunderstand this—e.g.: "If a can of nitrate stock *immolates* [read *catches fire* or *burns*], he said, a deluge sprinkler system would kick in." Steven Rea, "Preserving a Legacy in the Poconos," *Orange County Register*, 25 Aug. 1996, at F13.

immoral; unmoral; amoral. These three words have distinct meanings. *Immoral*, the opposite of *moral*, means "evil, depraved." The word is highly judgmental. *Unmoral* means merely "without moral sense, not moral," and is used, for example, of animals and inanimate objects. *Amoral*, perhaps the most commonly misused of these terms, means "not moral, outside the sphere of morality; being neither moral nor immoral." It is loosely applied to people in the sense "not having morals or scruples."

immovable. So spelled in AmE and BrE alike—not *immoveable. See MUTE E.

immune may take the preposition *to* or *from*, depending on nuance. What you're *immune from* can't touch you; what you're *immune to* may touch you but it has no effect. The collocation *immune to* is now the more common phrase.

To be *immune to* something is to be impervious to it—e.g.:

- "'Yesterday I made sales to people from Ireland, England, Sweden and Denmark, and that was before lunch,' he said. 'Presley is *immune to* the ups and downs of war and the economy.'" Doug Warren, "Presley Pilgrimage," *Boston Globe*, 14 Aug. 2002, at B1 (quoting Steve Templeton, an Elvis-memorabilia vendor).
- "Despite its considerable resources, Intel, which has $8 billion in cash, is not *immune to* market forces." Alex Pham, "Intel to Use Technology for Building Tinier Chips," *L.A. Times*, 14 Aug. 2002, Bus. §, pt. 3, at 1.

To be *immune from* something is to be free of some duty, liability, or restriction that others are subject to—e.g.:

- "The fact that Hale viewed husbands as *immune from* rape prosecution is not surprising." Susan Estrich, *Real Rape* 73 (1987).
- "Judges are *immune from* such lawsuits." William K. Slate II, "The Justice-at-a-Price Guys Take Aim at Arbitration," *L.A. Times*, 13 Aug. 2002, Cal. Metro §, pt. 2, at 13.
- "New York, California and North Carolina agreed last month to require that all investment houses . . . make stock analyst reports *immune from* influence by the investment banking side of their firms." David Cay Johnston, "Officials of 14 States Pledge Protection of Pension Assets," *N.Y. Times*, 13 Aug. 2002, at C7.

In this latter sense, the preposition *from* is preferable to *to*, but *to* is used so commonly that it can't be stigmatized as incorrect—e.g.: "Commission member John O. Wynne of Norfolk, a former publishing executive, noted that the largest sectors of the Virginia budget, including education and Medicaid, will be *immune to* [read, preferably, *immune from*] Wilder commission cuts." R.H. Melton, "Wilder Panel Adopts Guide for Va. Cuts," *Wash. Post*, 15 Aug. 2002, at B1.

Current ratio (*immune to* vs. *immune from*): 2:1

immunity; impunity. An *immunity* is any type of exemption from a liability, service, or duty—or (of course) a bodily resistance to an illness. *Impunity* is exemption from punishment; for a spreading misuse of this word, see **impunity.**

I'm not sure that; I'm not sure whether. The first phrase means "I doubt" <I'm not sure that we can make it in time>; the second means "I wonder if; I don't know if" <I'm not sure whether Shakespeare died in the 16th or the 17th century>. (He died in the 17th—in 1616.) Cf. **doubt (A).**

impact, v.i. & v.t. *Impact* was traditionally only a noun. In the mid-20th century, however, it underwent a semantic shift that allows it to act as a transitive or intransitive verb. So uses such as the following have

LANGUAGE-CHANGE INDEX (For the full key, see front matter pp. xxxi, l–li.)
Stage 1: Rejected. **Stage 2:** Widely shunned. **Stage 3:** Widespread but . . . **Stage 4:** Ubiquitous but . . . **Stage 5:** Fully accepted.
Invariably inferior forms marked by asterisk (*). • Ratios represent frequency of prevalent forms vs. variants in current books.

become widespread (and are also widely condemned by stylists):

- "The researchers concluded that this low level of intensity may have *impacted* [read *affected*] the results." Katherine Preble, "Forget Warming Up," *Tampa Trib.*, 17 July 1997, Baylife §, at 3.
- "Breast-feeding can be *impacted* [read *affected*] by visitation and custody decisions." Carol Brzozowski-Gardner, "Her Specialty: Lactation Advocacy," *Sun-Sentinel* (Ft. Lauderdale), 30 Nov. 1997, at E1.
- "Though the I-285/Georgia 400 interchange is squarely in the midst of our PCIDs, it *impacts* [read *affects*] traffic flow across metro Atlanta and the 29 counties included in our metro area." Yvonne Williams, "Opening Our Own Wallets to Help Speed Traffic Flow," *Atlanta J.-Const.*, 1 Sept. 2015, at A8.

These uses of the word would be perfectly acceptable if *impact* were performing any function not as ably performed by *affect* or *influence*. If *affect* as a verb is not sufficiently straightforward in context, then the careful writer might use *had an impact on*, which, though longer, is probably better than the jarring *impact* of *impacted*. Reserve *impact* for noun uses and *impacted* for wisdom teeth. See FUNCTIONAL SHIFT (D) & VOGUE WORDS.

Interestingly, *impact* as a verb might have arisen partly in response to widespread diffidence about the spelling of *affect*. In terms of word frequency, the verb use of *impact* skyrocketed after 1980. See **affect**.

LANGUAGE-CHANGE INDEX
1. *impact* as a transitive verb <this could impact our decision>: Stage 3
Current ratio (*might affect the* vs. *might impact the*): 12:1
2. *impact* as an intransitive verb <this could impact on our decision>: Stage 3
Current ratio (*might affect the* vs. *might impact on*): 11:1

*impactful, adj., is barbarous JARGON dating from the mid-1960s. Unlike other adjectives ending in *-ful*, it cannot be idiomatically rendered in the phrase *full of* [+ quality], as in *beautiful* (= full of beauty), *regretful* (= full of regret), *scornful* (= full of scorn), and *spiteful* (= full of spite). If *impact* truly denotes a quality, it does so only in its newfangled uses as a verb <it impacts us all> and as an adjective <the mechanic's tool known as an impact driver>.

Whatever its future may be, *impactful* is, for now, a word to be scorned. Among its established replacements are *influential* and *powerful*—e.g.:

- "If Labor Secretary John Dunlop can win labor and management support for such far-reaching changes . . . , he will have made an infinitely *impactful* contribution to the fight against inflation." M.S. Forbes Jr., "Help the City if It Helps Itself," *Forbes*, 15 Aug. 1975, at 15. (A possible—and less hyperbolic—revision: *If Labor Secretary John Dunlop can win labor and management support for such far-reaching changes . . . , he will have made a truly significant contribution to the fight against inflation.*)
- "After eight *impactful* [read *influential*] and sometimes tumultuous years, Lou Swift's term on the Colorado

Wildlife Commission expired earlier this month." Charlie Meyers, "Two Men's Contributions as Big as All Outdoors," *Denver Post*, 22 Mar. 1998, at C2.
- "Elise makes several short but *impactful* [read *memorable*] appearances as Laura, the production's assistant stage manager." Christine Dolen, "A 'Godot' Parody at Thinking Cap Finds the Laughs in Waiting to Go On," *Miami Herald*, 29 Aug. 2015, Entertainment §.

LANGUAGE-CHANGE INDEX
impactful for *influential* or *powerful*: Stage 2

impale (= to drive a stake or lance through [usu. a living body]) is the standard spelling, *empale* being a variant spelling. Sometimes the word is misspelled *impail*—e.g.:

- "Another pattern with a nautical basis is the 'Pineapple,' for returning sea captains *impailed* [read *impaled*] these fruits on their fenceposts as symbols of good luck." William Zimmer, "Cozy Household Items Show Top Quality Artistry," *N.Y. Times*, 30 Nov. 1986, § 11, at 38.
- "The billboards show a dog with a large fishhook *impaled* [read *impaled*] in its upper lip. The message reads: 'If you wouldn't do this to a dog, why do it to a fish?'" Bill Sargent, "PETA Wants Fishing Columns Deep-Sixed," *Fla. Today*, 3 Apr. 2005, Outdoors §, at 10.

LANGUAGE-CHANGE INDEX
1. *impale* misspelled *impail*: Stage 1
Current ratio (*impaled* vs. *impailed*): 1,068:1
2. *empale* for *impale*: Stage 1
Current ratio (*impaled* vs. *empaled*): 192:1

impanel. See **empanel.**

impart = (1) to give (information, a quality, etc.) <the sage imparted wisdom to dozens of followers daily>; or (2) to make known or explain <she imparted the details of her plan>. In good idiom, you impart something to a person (as opposed to imparting a person with something)—e.g.: "While in the hole, she meets some truly deep roots who *impart her with supernatural powers* [read *impart supernatural powers to her*]." "New Line Buys Rights to Novel," *Star-Ledger* (Newark), 2 Apr. 1997, at 27. (See OBJECT-SHUFFLING.) Sometimes this misusage could be corrected simply by changing *impart* to *imbue*—e.g.: "The Times declared that the Princess Royal's 'innate feelings of a benevolence of mind' *imparted* [read *imbued*] her with a beauty that went far beyond what the power of a dress could bestow." Marilyn Morris, "The Royal Family and Family Values in Late Eighteenth-Century England," *J. Family Hist.*, 1 Oct. 1996, at 519. See **imbue.**

LANGUAGE-CHANGE INDEX
1. *impart someone with something* for *impart something to someone*: Stage 1
2. *impart* misused for *imbue*: Stage 1
Current ratio (*imbued with* vs. *imparted with*): 124:1

impartable; impartible. These are two different words. *Impartable* = capable of being imparted (made known or bestowed). *Impartible* = indivisible. In the first, the prefix *im-* is intensive; in the second, it's negative. Historically, the word *impartible* has occurred with far greater frequency than *impartable*. See -ABLE (A).

impartially. See **partially** (B).

*__impass.__ See **impasse**.

impassable. See **impassible**.

impasse (= [1] a deadlock; or [2] a blind alley), a French loanword, is sometimes misspelled *__impass__—e.g.: "Finally Brearley broke the *impass* [read *impasse*], taking the puck around the back of the Renegades' net and scoring on a wraparound shot at 19:01." Katrina Waugh, "Roanoke Fights Back in 2nd," *Roanoke Times*, 6 Dec. 1997, at C1.

LANGUAGE-CHANGE INDEX
impasse misspelled *__impass__: Stage 1
Current ratio (*an impasse* vs. *__an impass__*): 699:1

impassible; impassable. These words have separate origins and meanings. *Impassible* = incapable of feeling or suffering. *Impassable* = not capable of being passed. Since the 18th century, *impassable* has occurred with far greater frequency. See -ABLE (A). Cf. **passable**.
   Occasionally, *impassible* wrongly displaces *impassable*—e.g.:

- "The recreation area's parking problem . . . leaves the park's main road nearly *impassible* [read *impassable*]." Shalmali Pal, "Pelican Park Gets Tough on Parking," *Times-Picayune* (New Orleans), 11 May 1996, at A1.
- "Interstate 35 has often seemed like an *impassible* [read *impassable*] barrier for promoters of African-American shows, gospel and otherwise." Michael Point, "Lift Every Voice and Sing," *Austin Am.-Statesman*, 31 Jan. 1997, at F1.

LANGUAGE-CHANGE INDEX
impassible misused for *impassable*: Stage 1
Current ratio (*impassable barrier* vs.
__impassible barrier__): 19:1

impassionate. Because this adjective can mean either "impassioned" or "dispassionate," it is best avoided in favor of one of those defining words. In short, it is a SKUNKED TERM. Despite its absence from American desk dictionaries, *impassionate* is still used by journalists in both senses—e.g.:

- "An intense, *impassionate* [read *impassioned*] personality, even when she was young, Bush began putting on variety shows at age 5, charging the neighbors 15 cents to attend." Joanne Kaufman, "Barbara Bush Rides Out the Pain of a Doomed Soap Opera Role," *People*, 1 Feb. 1988, at 56.
- "Thermometers are altogether *impassionate* [read *dispassionate*]." Ron Spomer, "If the Car Starts, You Can Shoot," *Lewiston Morning Trib.* (Idaho), 27 Dec. 1990, at E2.
- "But the National Rifle Association said crime has skyrocketed nationally and that *impassionate* [read *dispassionate*] statistics don't back up Griffin's stance." Barbara Carmen, "Gun Bill Opposed by Council," *Columbus Dispatch*, 13 June 1995, at C2.

- "Last year, Barack Obama stood before the General Assembly and delivered an *impassionate* [read *impassioned*] call for Palestinian statehood within a year." Robert Z. Nemeth, "Beware of Arab Spring," *Worcester Telegram & Gaz.*, 2 Oct. 2011, at A14.

impecunious (= poor; penniless) is sometimes misused in either of two ways. Some writers seem to think it means "unthrifty," as in *she was utterly impecunious with her earnings*. Other writers mistake the word as meaning "hapless, unfortunate," as in *the impecunious junior left to work on the assignment through the night*. For the antonym *pecunious*, see **pecuniary**.

impel. See **compel**.

impending. See **pending**.

impenitence (= the quality or state of not regretting something one has done and of having no intention of refraining in the future) has been the established form since the late 18th century. *__Impenitency__ is a NEEDLESS VARIANT.

Current ratio: 9:1

imperative. See **imperious** (B).

imperial. See **imperious** (A).

imperil, vb., makes *imperiled* and *imperiling* in AmE, *imperilled* and *imperilling* in BrE. See SPELLING (B).

imperious. A. And *imperial*. Deriving from the same root (L. *imper-* "power over a family, region, or state"), these words have been differentiated by their suffixes. *Imperial* = of or belonging to an emperor or empire. E.g.: "Hoagland notes that the *imperial* collection now on view at the National Gallery was removed from the Forbidden City, but he fails to point out that the transfer occurred in the 1930s to avoid capture by the Japanese, not the Communists, as he suggests." "Clues to China," *Wash. Post*, 22 Feb. 1997, at A21.
   Imperious = overbearing, supercilious, tyrannical. E.g.: "The man running this gold mine at Bear, Stearns is Richard Harriton, 61, an imposing and *imperious* man who came to the firm in 1979." Gretchen Morgenson, "Sleazy Doings on Wall Street," *Forbes*, 24 Feb. 1997, at 114.
   B. And *imperative*. An *imperative* (= commanding, obligatory) tone can come from anyone in a position of authority; an *imperious* tone comes from someone who, in that position, tries to wield power in a dictatorial way.

imperium = supreme authority. E.g.: "Silberman . . . has unmitigated scorn for the scholarly, predominantly Catholic '*imperium*' whose 'orthodox interpretation of the Dead Sea Scrolls [has] prevailed,' despite the conflicting testimony of the scrolls themselves." Alan Ireland, "Probing the Mysteries of the Dead Sea Scrolls," *Evening Standard*, 8 Feb. 1997, Books §, at 14.
   Pl. *imperia*. See PLURALS (B).

LANGUAGE-CHANGE INDEX (For the full key, see front matter pp. xxxi, l–li.)
Stage 1: Rejected. **Stage 2:** Widely shunned. **Stage 3:** Widespread but . . . **Stage 4:** Ubiquitous but . . . **Stage 5:** Fully accepted.
Invariably inferior forms marked by asterisk (*). • Ratios represent frequency of prevalent forms vs. variants in current books.

impermissible. So spelled. See -ABLE.

impersonation; *personation. The latter is a NEED-LESS VARIANT.

Current ratio: 10:1

impersuadable; *impersuasible. See **persuadable.**

impervious; *imperviable. *Impervious* = (1) not allowing something to pass through <the concrete in the basement is impervious to water>; or (2) not open to <some people are impervious to reason>. Sense 1, which is literal, most commonly (but not exclusively) refers to the soaking of water or some other liquid through a surface—e.g.:

- "Sunset Valley's subdivision regulations at the time allowed builders to cover as much as 70 percent of the land with *impervious* cover, such as parking lots or buildings that keep storm water from naturally filtering into the ground." Steven Kreytak, "Sunset Valley Puts Development on Hold," *Austin Am.-Statesman*, 2 Dec. 2002, at A1.
- "There is definitely a story—about Bolshevik resistance to the White Russians—and there is definitely a hero, the square-jawed, craggily handsome Timosh, who remains *impervious* to bullets when he bares his chest to attackers in the climactic scene." Philip Kennicott, "Ukraine's Dovzhenko, Auteur of the Proletariat," *Wash. Post*, 3 Dec. 2002, at C1.

Sense 2 is figurative ("thick skull" comes to mind)—e.g.: "To be biased is to be settled on an issue because of one's background, and to be *impervious* to reason and common sense." Jay Evensen, "It's Rocky Who Is Divisive on Plaza Issue," *Deseret News* (Salt Lake City), 24 Nov. 2002, at AA1.

Avoid using *impervious* in the watered-down sense "not affected by"—e.g.: "And he says he is untroubled by the criticism from Congress. Much of it, he says, is domestic politics, aimed at President Bush, whose recent electoral victories have made him *impervious* [read *immune*] to other political broadsides." Christopher Marquis, "Saudi Tries to Calm U.S. Opinion," *N.Y. Times*, 2 Dec. 2002, at A21.

*Imperviable is a NEEDLESS VARIANT that has seldom appeared in print.

Current ratio: 2,579:1

impetus. See **impotence (B).**

impinge; infringe. *Impinge* is intransitive only, followed by *on* or *upon*—e.g.: "He acknowledges that the line separating 'fine' art from craft is blurry in the present era. He even calls making such distinctions 'dangerous,' likely to *impinge* on the creative 'elbow room' of artists." Anna Webb, "Frame Job," *Idaho Statesman*, 5 Nov. 2002, Thrive §, at 28. *Infringe*, by contrast, may be either transitive or intransitive—e.g.:

- "Lilly, in a federal lawsuit filed Tuesday in its Indianapolis hometown, said the generic treatment would *infringe* four patents related to the drug." "Lilly Sues to Block Osteoporosis Generic," *L.A. Times*, 28 Nov. 2002, Bus. §, at 3 (transitive).
- "Washington, though populous and wealthy, would *infringe* on the Baltimore Orioles' market, setting up

potential legal opposition from that club." David A. Markiewicz, "Keeping It International," *Atlanta J.-Const.*, 1 Dec. 2002, at D3 (intransitive).

H.W. Fowler pointed out that *infringe* was historically transitive far more commonly than intransitive, "but 20th-century newspaper columns give a very different impression, viz that *infringe* can no longer stand at all without *upon*." Nowadays things aren't quite that bad, though: the two uses are split about evenly. The distinction is that patents and copyrights are typically *infringed*, while other rights are typically *infringed on*. As a matter of style, however, the transitive construction is almost always stronger.

Though *impinge* and *infringe* are often used as if they were interchangeable, we might keep in mind the following connotations from the literal senses: to *impinge* is to strike or dash *upon* something else; to *infringe* is to break in and thereby damage, violate, or weaken.

impious is pronounced /**im**-pee-əs/, not /im-**pɪ**-əs/.

implement = (1) to carry out or put into effect; to take practical steps toward the fulfillment of; or (2) to furnish with implements. In sense 1, which is more common, the word typifies BUREAUCRATESE but is sometimes undeniably useful. *Carry out* is often better and less vague.

implementer. Although the variant spelling *implementor predominated for much of the late 20th century, today *implementer* is considered standard.

Current ratio: 4:1

implication is the noun corresponding to both *implicate* and *imply*. Thus it means (1) "the action of implicating, or involving, entangling, or entwining" <Smith's implication of Jones in the crime>; (2) "the action of implying; the fact of being implied or involved" <by necessary implication>; or (3) "that which is implied or involved" <implications of wrongdoing>.

implicit (= implied) functions as a correlative of *explicit* (= express or expressed), just as *implied* is a correlative of *express* <no warranty, either express or implied>. H.W. Fowler called *implicit* "a shifty word" and suggested that the language would be better off without it. The problem, he pointed out, is that while *implied* and *express* are neat opposites, *implicit* and *explicit* seem to overlap when they mean "complete, unmitigated" <implicit trust> <explicit pornography>. In this sense, the words can sometimes become interchangeable—e.g.: "Gun enthusiasts, particularly those most active in the NRA, share no *implicit* [read *innate*] trust in a beneficent government. . . . *Explicit* faith is reserved for family and community." Michael Powell, "Call to Arms," *Wash. Post* (Mag.), 6 Aug. 2002, at W8. (For more on using different words to mean the same thing, as with *trust* and *faith* in that quotation, see INELEGANT VARIATION.)

The *OED* labels this usage both obsolete and erroneous. But in fact it shows no signs of disappearing, and "erroneous" may be a bit harsh. Noah Webster used the word in this disputed sense: "To men who have been accustomed to repose almost *implicit* confidence in the authors of our principal dictionaries and grammars, it may appear at first incredible, that such writers as Johnson and Lowth, should have mistaken many of the fundamental principles of the language." Noah Webster, *A Compendious Dictionary of the English Language* iii (1806). In that book, Webster defined *implicit* as "resting upon another, involved, real," and *implicitly* as "absolutely, by inference."

Logic is on the side of this usage: if one has *implicit* faith in something, no evidence or rationalization is needed to bolster that belief. The *Century Dictionary* recognized this sense of *implicit* in 1895: "involved in or resulting from perfect confidence in or deference to some authority or witness; hence, submissive, unquestioning, blind." And the phrase *implicit faith* does not carry any negative connotation the way *blind faith* may. So in certain SET PHRASES in religious contexts, the writer may have no choice. Even so, the Presbyterian Church USA muddied the waters a bit when it adopted a statement on faith in June 2002. That document contained the following implicit reference to non-Christians: "We neither restrict the grace of God to those who profess *explicit faith* in Christ nor assume that all people are saved regardless of faith."

Still, in most contexts the writer is well advised to seek an alternative wording—e.g.:

- "Such *implicit* [read *complete* or simply delete *implicit*] trust heralds a new dawn in married life—until we get the next sex poll, and spouses revert to normal." Nancy McIntyre, "Have Sexual Revolutionaries Surrendered?" *Ariz. Republic*, 18 Nov. 1994, at F20.
- "In an ideal situation, police, prosecutors and the medical examiner's office should have *implicit* [read *complete*] confidence in the skill and professionalism of each other if justice is to be adequately served." "Benz Should Make Graceful Retreat in Response to 'No Confidence' Vote," *Sun-Sentinel* (Ft. Lauderdale), 20 May 1996, at A8.

See **impliedly.**

LANGUAGE-CHANGE INDEX
implicit for *complete*: Stage 4

implicitly. See **impliedly.**

implied; express. These adjectives are correlative <there are no express or implied warranties>. *Expressed* is sometimes incorrectly contrasted with *implied.* See **express.**

impliedly; implicitly. Though neither form is strictly incorrect, *impliedly* (answering to *expressly*) is awkward and characteristic of LEGALESE. H.W. Fowler wrote merely that "*impliedly* is a bad form" (*FMEU1* at 260). Though unknown to most people, it is a favorite of lawyers. *Impliedly* is old, dating in the *OED* from ca. 1400. Still, *implicitly*—long the usual term—is normally an improvement. See **implicit.**

Current ratio: 25:1

imply. See **infer (B).**

impolitic, adj. (= not politic; injudicious; imprudent), forms the unusual adverb *impoliticly.* Some writers impoliticly make it **impolitically*—e.g.: "All these solicitations are protected speech and . . . the government may not discriminate among them—even when some of them are *impolitically* [read *impoliticly*] and counterproductively 'surly, bilious, [and] argumentative.'" Stuart Comstock-Gay, "The Panhandler's Message," *Baltimore Sun*, 22 Sept. 1994, at A13. See -IC. Cf. **politically.**

LANGUAGE-CHANGE INDEX
*impolitically for *impoliticly*: Stage 1

import, n.; **importation.** A product that comes into a country from abroad is an *import.* The process of bringing it in is *importation.*

importantly. This word is enjoying an odd vogue. Here, Meg Greenfield uses it puzzlingly: "But almost without exception, it seems, the thing [a politician's prospective embarrassment] comes back and *importantly* it looks worse and gets worse the second time around." Meg Greenfield, "We're Wallowing Again," *Newsweek*, 25 Apr. 1994, at 72. See **more important(ly)** & SENTENCE ADVERBS.

importation. See **import.**

*importunacy. See **importunity.**

importune is a verb meaning "to beg or beseech; entreat." It is also a NEEDLESS VARIANT of the adjective *importunate* (= troublesomely urgent) and an obsolete variant of *inopportune.* The intended meaning in the following sentence is not clear, but perhaps *inopportune* would have been the right word: "It is a minor comfort to learn that Soviet audiences in the 1950's and 60's coughed as *importunely* [read *inopportunely*] during concerts as their free-world counterparts." Bernard Holland, "Classical View: Horsepower in Place of History," *N.Y. Times*, 18 Feb. 1996, § 2, at 33.

LANGUAGE-CHANGE INDEX
importune misused for *inopportune*: Stage 1
Current ratio (*inopportune time* vs.
*importune time): 213:1

importunity; *importunacy. The second is a NEEDLESS VARIANT of the first, which means "irksome tenacity in soliciting something."

Current ratio: 77:1

impossible. See ADJECTIVES (B).

LANGUAGE-CHANGE INDEX (For the full key, see front matter pp. xxxi, l–li.)
Stage 1: Rejected. **Stage 2:** Widely shunned. **Stage 3:** Widespread but . . . **Stage 4:** Ubiquitous but . . . **Stage 5:** Fully accepted.
Invariably inferior forms marked by asterisk (*). • Ratios represent frequency of prevalent forms vs. variants in current books.

*impossible to underestimate. See **underestimate.**

impostor; *imposter; imposture. The *-or* spelling is preferred over *-er* for the actor. *Imposture*, a term now rarely seen (though common in Early Modern English), is the act of fraud itself or a spurious thing (and of course, the spurious thing could also be the actor). See -ER (A) & SPELLING (A).

    Current ratio (*impostor* vs. **imposter*): 3:1

impotence. A. And *sterility. Impotence* (/**im**-pə-tən[t]s/) refers to the inability of a male to copulate (esp. to achieve an erection), and *sterility* to anyone's inability to procreate. *Impotence* in the modern literal sense should be used only in reference to men. **Impotency* is a NEEDLESS VARIANT. See **potence.**

    Current ratio (*impotence* vs. **impotency*): 11:1

    B. And *impetus. Impotence* for *impetus* (= force, impulse) is a MALAPROPISM worthy of Mrs. Malaprop, Mistress Quickly, or Archie Bunker. E.g.: "The main *impotence* [read *impetus*] for recruiting people who have published is to ensure that they are used to long hours." This is a blunder that professional writers seldom make: most instances occur in unpublished documents.

    C. Pronunciation. The word *impotence* is pronounced /**im**-pə-tən[t]s/—not /im-**poh**-tən[t]s/. The corresponding adjective is /**im**-pə-tənt/—not /im-**poh**-tənt/.

                LANGUAGE-CHANGE INDEX
        impotence misused for *impetus*: Stage 1

*impower. See **empower.**

impracticability (= practical impossibility) is sometimes misspelled **impractibility*—e.g.: "The *impractibility* [read *impracticability*] of backing reservoir water back over Hanford reactor sites helped prevent construction of Ben Franklin Dam." Bill Dietrich, "Ecology—An Opportunity or Embarrassment?" *Seattle Times*, 9 Nov. 1992, at D1.

impractical. A. And *impracticable. Impractical* = not manifested in practice; incapable of being put to good use. *Impracticable* = not workable or accomplishable; infeasible. Although *impractical* is considered an ordinary word today and *impracticable* an unusual one, that was not always true: from the late 17th century until the mid-20th, *impracticable* appeared far more commonly in print than its shorter sibling. Cf. **practical.**

    B. And *unpractical.* H.W. Fowler had a point in believing that "the constant confusion between *practicable* and *practical* is a special reason for making use of *im-* and *un-* to add to the difference in the negatives" (*FMEU1* at 260). But *unpractical* has not been used much in AmE since about 1900, and it has been in decline in BrE since 1950. Even so, it occasionally appears (perhaps because of Fowler's influence)—e.g.: "The letter on behalf of Mr. Underwood's 'Ketchup-Only' bill is a spoof on the arguments being made for the English-only bill, an Underwood aide said, adding that the Guam Democrat is seeking to illustrate his point that making English the official language of the United States is *unpractical*." "Spoof Pours It On in 'Try to Nationalize Ketchup,'" *Toledo Blade*, 20 Oct. 1995. The word *unpractical* isn't included in *W11*, and even in the (British) *COD* the entry under *impractical* is longer than the one under *unpractical* (which is moribund). See **possible (A)** & **practical.**

    Current ratio (*impractical* vs. *unpractical*): 13:1

impregnable; impregnatable. Etymologically, these two words are unrelated—the *g* in *impregnable* having been added by Renaissance philologists who misunderstood the history of the Middle English *imprenable* (= not able to be taken). In any event, the meanings today are also quite distinct. *Impregnable* = not capable of subjugation by force; not subject to being taken by assault. *Impregnatable* = [1] capable of being made pregnant, or [2] capable of being permeated or saturated.

impresario. So spelled. See SPELLING (A).

impressive; impressible; impressionable. *Impressive* = likely to impress people <an impressive array of trophies>. *Impressible* (a fairly rare word) = easily impressed <if that doesn't impress you, you're not impressible>. *Impressionable* = easily influenced <impressionable children>.

    Impressible is misused for *impressive* especially in the adverbial form—e.g.:

- "There is no doubt that Gayle Martin, who performed *impressibly* [read *impressively*] on the piano at the National Gallery last night, has developed her own personal musical style." Joan Reinthaler, "Gayle Martin," *Wash. Post*, 23 June 1980, at C9.
- "And as for whether Reeves can act, he does *impressibly* [read *impressively*] rise a notch above his usual mediocre performances." Kris Dessen, "'Speed' Hits Perfect Pace," *News Trib.* (Tacoma), 11 June 1994, at H2.
- "It was Higgins' *impressibly* [read *impressively*] swinging, persistently groove-driven drumming—along with the sterling work of bassist Haden—that laid the foundation for the Coleman group's free-jazz flights of fancy." Jon Thurber, "Billy Higgins" (obit.), *L.A. Times*, 4 May 2001, Metro §, at 6.

    Impressible is the preferred spelling—not **impressable*. See -ABLE (A).

                LANGUAGE-CHANGE INDEX
    impressibly misused for *impressively*: Stage 1

imprimatur; *imprimatura; *imprimature. The normal form for ordinary purposes is *imprimatur* (pronounced /im-pri-**mah**-tər/ or /im-**prim**-ə-tər/), meaning literally "let it be printed," from the formula used in the Roman Catholic Church by an official licenser, approving a work to be printed. This term (now meaning "commendatory license or sanction; sponsorship") takes the preposition *on*—e.g.: "The announcement . . . puts Pena's *imprimatur on* a draft proposal that was announced two months ago." "Rocky Flats Cleanup May Speed Up," *Salt Lake Trib.*, 8 Aug. 1997, at A14. **Imprimatura* is a NEEDLESS VARIANT.

Imprimature (= a print, impression) is an obsolete term sometimes wrongly used for *imprimatur*—e.g.: "He produced the special under the *imprimature* [read *imprimatur*] of his Daddy's Krazee production company." Allan Johnson, "Standup Guy," *Chicago Trib.*, 26 Dec. 1991, at C15.

LANGUAGE-CHANGE INDEX
imprimature for *imprimatur*: Stage 1
Current ratio (in order of headwords): 368:11:1

*improper noun. See **proper noun.**

improprietous is a NONWORD that sometimes displaces *improper*—e.g.:

- "'We'll try to come to grips with the facts and see if there was any *improprietous* [read *improper*] activity.'" Michael Eastman, "Supply Purchases for Greenbelt Homes Questioned," *Wash. Post*, 29 Nov. 1979, Md. Weekly §, at 3 (quoting Joseph Jenkins).
- "'If somebody else feels it's *improprietous* [read *improper*] then they're just going to have to live with it.'" Colleen Heild, "Lottery Meeting Kept Quiet," *Albuquerque J.*, 4 May 1997, at A1 (quoting Bruce Wiggins).
- "Having seen and heard our president halfheartedly admit to an *improprietous* [read *improper*] relationship, I am now more convinced than ever that this man is a shrewd and pathological liar." Editorial, "Americans Right to Want Decency in White House," *Pantagraph* (Bloomington, Ill.), 22 Aug. 1998, at A12.

The word, a BACK-FORMATION from *impropriety*, is highly improper.

LANGUAGE-CHANGE INDEX
improprietous for *improper*: Stage 1
Current ratio (*improper* vs. *improprietous*): 11,972:1

improvise is sometimes misspelled *improvize*—e.g.: "Harrelson likes to gamble and *improvize* [read *improvise*] his way out of jams." Robert Denerstein, "Formula Derails This 'Money Train,'" *Rocky Mountain News* (Denver), 24 Nov. 1995, at D6.

LANGUAGE-CHANGE INDEX
improvise misspelled *improvize*: Stage 1
Current ratio: 235:1

improviser; *improvisator; *improvisor; improvisatore. The usual term for "someone who improvises" is *improviser*. (The *-or* spelling is not preferred.) *Improvisator* is an archaic FORMALISM. *Improvisatore* is an Italianate literary word meaning "someone who composes verse or drama extemporaneously."

Current ratio (*improviser* vs. *improvisator* vs. *improvisor*): 23:1.4:1

*improvize. See **improvise.**

imprudent; impudent. *Imprudent* = rash; indiscreet. *Impudent* = insolently disrespectful; shamelessly presumptuous.

impugn. A. And *oppugn; repugn. *Impugn* (= to challenge, call into question) has been the most usual of these three terms since the late 17th century. E.g.: "In a second ruling today, Judge Sweeney also appeared to *impugn* the church's handling of accused molesters who had been placed back in parishes after receiving therapy." Pam Belluck, "Judge Denies Church's Bid to Seal Records on Priests," *N.Y. Times*, 26 Nov. 2002, at A18.

Oppugn and *repugn* are less frequently encountered. *Oppugn* = to controvert or call into question; to fight against. *Repugn* is an ARCHAISM meaning "to offer opposition or strive against; to affect disagreeably or be repugnant to."

B. For *impute. This is a strange error, *impute* meaning "to ascribe or attribute." E.g.: "Overall, Kupetz rejected the notion that a court should simply ignore the actual intention of the parties and *impugn* [read *impute*] constructive intent in every instance." Irving D. Labovitz, "Countering Fraudulent Conveyance and Voidable Preference Concerns in LBOs," *J. Commercial Lending*, Mar. 1993, at 34. See **impute.**

LANGUAGE-CHANGE INDEX
impugn misused for *impute*: Stage 1

C. Corresponding Noun. *Impugnment* is the standard noun corresponding to *impugn*. *Impugnation* is an obsolete variant. For the mistaken form *impugnity* (for *impunity*), see **impunity (B).**

Current ratio (*impugnment* vs. *impugnation*): 2:1

impunity. A. Meaning and Use. This word means "free from punishment or other adverse consequences"; it typically appears in the idiom *with impunity* <she can fire her predecessor's staff with impunity>.

Sometimes this SET PHRASE, *with impunity*, gets mangled into *without impunity* (which seems to suggest that punishment or adverse consequences would follow, but that's never the intended sense). This error appears most frequently in sportswriting—e.g.:

- "Without Camby patrolling the middle, the Pacers drove to the hoop *without impunity* [read *with impunity*]." Marc Berman, "Knicks Say No Camby, No Excuses," *N.Y. Post*, 11 Nov. 2001, at 102.
- "I would have the NCAA . . . [a]llow athletes to transfer to another school *without impunity* [read *with impunity*], should their head coach leave for a job elsewhere." Kirk Bohls, "Some Prudent Suggestions for the NCAA," *Austin Am.-Statesman*, 27 Jan. 2002, at C1.
- "Reggie Miller is 36, still firing jumpers [i.e., jump shots] *without impunity* [read *with impunity*], still building his Hall of Fame resume at an age when most great two-guards have lost their legs, lost their desire, lost their passion and nerve and mental edge." Dave D'Alessandro, "Miller May Be Down to His Final Shot," *Star-Ledger* (Newark), 28 Apr. 2002, Sports §, at 7.

For more on this word, see **immunity.**

LANGUAGE-CHANGE INDEX
without impunity for *with impunity*: Stage 1
Current ratio (*with impunity* vs. *without impunity*): 235:1

LANGUAGE-CHANGE INDEX (For the full key, see front matter pp. xxxi, l–li.)
Stage 1: Rejected. **Stage 2:** Widely shunned. **Stage 3:** Widespread but . . . **Stage 4:** Ubiquitous but . . . **Stage 5:** Fully accepted.
Invariably inferior forms marked by asterisk (*). • Ratios represent frequency of prevalent forms vs. variants in current books.

B. *Impugnity*. Some writers apparently confuse the word *impunity* as having some association with *impugn* (= to assail the integrity of [a person, a person's motives, etc.])—e.g.:

- "Did they mean to threaten and compromise the security of the United States so as to pursue with *impugnity* [read *impunity*] their designs in Berlin and elsewhere?" Terence Ball, *Idioms of Inquiry* 105 (1987).
- "[T]he institutions of punishment and imprisonment have the responsibility to sustain the very lives that enter their domains precisely because they have the power, in the name of 'ethics,' to damage and destroy lives with *impugnity* [read *impunity*]." Judith Butler, *Giving an Account of Oneself: A Critique of Ethical Violence* 37 (2003).

LANGUAGE-CHANGE INDEX
impunity misspelled **impugnity*: Stage 1
Current ratio: 3,944:1

impute (= to ascribe; to regard [usu. something bad] as resulting from or being possessed by) takes *to*. There is a growing idiomatic bias in favor of *imputing* undesirable things or qualities—e.g.:

- "'That in no way reflected my being,' she said in an interview, *imputing* the nude photos *to* 'a few foolish days of being stupid.'" Louise Continelli, "Vanessa's Revenge," *Buffalo News*, 23 June 1996, at G1.
- "The State House is fertile ground for rumors and speculation that *impute* motive *to* every pronouncement and bit of posturing by the major players." Brian C. Mooney, "Finnernan Challenge," *Boston Globe*, 1 Feb. 1997, at B2.
- "Rambo seems reluctant to *impute* unsavory motives to either pastor, and there are no sex or accounting scandals in this church." Margaret Gray, "Competition in Clergy," *L.A. Times*, 24 Aug. 2015, Calendar §, at 3.

See **impugn** (B).

I myself. See **myself** & **I personally**.

IN-. See **EN-** & **NEGATIVES** (A).

in; into. These prepositions aren't ordinarily interchangeable, and care must be taken in choosing between them: *in* denotes position or location, and *into* denotes movement. So a person who swims *in* the ocean is already there, while a person who swims *into* the ocean is moving from, say, the mouth of a river. There are many exceptions, however, especially with popular idioms <go jump in a lake>.

inability. See **disability** (A).

in absentia (= not present), typically used in legal contexts, is sometimes misspelled **in abstentia*—e.g.: "Congress holds the key. It can permit courts to hold trials of defendants '*in abstentia* [read *in absentia*],' with the defendants not present." Dan Robinson, *Nuevo Laredo: A Prelude to War* 361 (2009).

in accord; in accordance. See **accord, n.**

in a . . . context. See **context of.**

in actual fact. See **fact** (C).

in actuality. This phrase, which became voguish during the 20th century, is virtually always inferior to *actually*.

inadmissible. So spelled. **Inadmissable* is a common misspelling. See -ABLE (A).

inadvertence; inadvertency. The DIFFERENTIATION between these terms should be carefully observed. *Inadvertence* = an inadvertent act; a fault of inattention. *Inadvertency* = the quality or state of being inadvertent <the inadvertency of the act is not disputed>. **Inadvertancy* is a common misspelling.

inadvisable; *unadvisable. The latter, though common in the 19th century, has become a NEEDLESS VARIANT.

inalienable; unalienable. The first is slightly better formed, with a Latinate prefix as well as suffix. And although Jefferson used *unalienable* in the Declaration of Independence ("unalienable rights")—that form predominated in the 18th century—*inalienable* is nearly five times as common as *unalienable* in modern print sources. Hence *inalienable* is preferable in all contexts except those where the Declaration of Independence is directly quoted or cited. But even then, *unalienable* is often displaced—e.g.: "The Declaration of Independence offered a remarkable mission statement, 'We hold these Truths to be self-evident, that all Men are created equal, that they are endowed by their Creator with certain *inalienable* [read *unalienable*] Rights.'" Tristram Hunt, "Can Obama Purge America's Original Sin?" *Times* (London), 30 Aug. 2008, Features §, at 17.

*inalterable. See **unalterable**.

in a —— manner. See **manner**.

inanity; inanition. As the noun corresponding to *inane*, *inanity* means "intellectual or spiritual emptiness or shallowness; vapidity." *Inanition*, by contrast, means "emptiness from lack of nourishment." *Inanition* sometimes gets misused for *inanity*—e.g.: "Elvis didn't have to appear in just 'Elvis movies,' those formulaic monuments to cinematic *inanition* [read *inanity*], full of females, fistfights, forgettable songs—and little else." Mark Feeney, "Elvis Movies," *Am. Scholar*, Winter 2001, at 53, 54.

LANGUAGE-CHANGE INDEX
inanition misused for *inanity*: Stage 1

in any event; at all events. These phrases are perfectly synonymous. The first is somewhat more common in AmE, the second in BrE. The BrE phrase is a loan translation of the French *à tous événements*.

inapposite (= inappropriate; irrelevant) is sometimes misspelled **inopposite*—e.g.: "Federal laws governing probate and land use can lead to results *inopposite* [read *inapposite*] to traditional laws for communal property." David S. Case & David A. Voluck, *Alaskan Natives and American Laws* 117 (3d ed. 2012).

Current ratio: 216:1

inapt; unapt; inept. Although these words overlap in meaning, they can be usefully distinguished. *Inapt* = not suitable, fitting, or appropriate <an inapt

quotation>. *Unapt* = not likely or inclined <she is unapt to tolerate laziness>. *Inept* = lacking aptitude; clumsy; incompetent; foolish <an inept basketball player who can't dribble, pass, or shoot>. Although *inept* can also mean "inappropriate," that sense is rare today. And because the word is usually intended as an insult, it's an inapt choice in other contexts.

in arrears. See **arrear(s).**

inartistic; unartistic. *Inartistic*, which refers to people, means "lacking in artistic taste; not appreciative of art" <a workaday, inartistic writer of pulp fiction>. *Unartistic*, which refers to things, means "not relating or conforming to art" <an unartistic photograph>.

inasmuch as; in as much as; insofar as; in so far as. In AmE, the standard spellings are *inasmuch as* and *insofar as*. In modern BrE, usage is split: *inasmuch as* is standard, and *in so far as* is preferred as four separate words.

However the phrase is spelled, though, *inasmuch as* is almost always inferior to *because* or *since*. In fact, as H.W. Fowler noted, "its only recommendation as compared with *since* is its pomposity" (*FMEU1* at 263). See **insofar as.** Cf. **insomuch.**

inaugural, n.; inauguration. The ceremony for a president entering office is the *inauguration*; the speech the president makes on this occasion is the *inaugural address*, sometimes shortened to *inaugural*. The word is correctly pronounced with the liquid *-u-* sound in the penultimate syllable: /i-**naw**-gyə-rəl/.

inaugurate is a FORMAL WORD (some might say pompous) for *begin* or *start*, being more formal even than *commence*. Little has changed since Richard Grant White wrote that *inaugurate* "is a word [that] might better be eschewed by all those who do not wish to talk high-flying nonsense." *Words and Their Uses, Past and Present* 128 (2d ed. 1872). Cf. **initiate.**

in back of. See **back of.**

in behalf of; on behalf of. See **behalf.**

Inc. Unless otherwise required by syntax, a comma need not follow this abbreviation—e.g.: "Pantheon, Inc. was founded in 1998." Nor does a comma have to precede it, although typically one does. Modern journalistic style is to omit both commas. For the comma before *Inc.*, though, it's best to follow the individual company's preference. Cf. NAMES (B).

incapable; unable. The words are basically synonymous, with perhaps a slight difference in connotation. *Incapable* suggests a permanent lack of ability <an incapable worker>, while *unable* often suggests a temporary lack of ability <I'm unable to accept your offer right now>. But these are hardly absolutes: if you're

unable to lift 500 pounds, there's no implication that you'll ever be able to.

incapacitation; incapacity. These words should be distinguished as follows: *incapacitation* = the action of incapacitating or rendering incapable; *incapacity* = lack of ability or qualification in some legal respect. See **capacity.**

in case; in cases in which. See **case** (A).

*****incase.** See **encase.**

*****incentivize; *incent,** vb. These NEOLOGISMS—dating from the mid-1970s—have become VOGUE WORDS, especially in American business JARGON. E.g.:

- "Together, the programs represent the most aggressive *incentivizing* to date by Honda." "Subaru, BMW Are Now Offering Consumer-Incentive Programs," *Atlanta J.-Const.*, 15 Mar. 1991, § S, at 6. (A possible revision: *Together, the programs provide the best incentives that Honda has ever offered.*)
- "And you know, we shouldn't *incent* [read *provide incentives for*] all the wrong behaviors. Right now, what we're doing is *incenting* [read *encouraging*] young girls to leave home, to not marry the person they're . . . having a child with because they won't get the welfare check if they're married." Jack Thomas, "Ann Romney's Sweetheart Deal," *Boston Globe*, 20 Oct. 1994, at 61.
- "Today it is management—usually *incentivized by stock options and the like* [read *having stock options and other incentives*]—that seeks to be recognized by institutional shareholders." Benjamin Mark Cole, "New Economic Pressures Force Banks to Cut Costs, Consolidate," *L.A. Bus. J.*, 24 Mar. 1997, at 29.

Incentivize, an -IZE barbarism, is much more common than *incent*, a BACK-FORMATION. There is no good incentive to use either one.

LANGUAGE-CHANGE INDEX
1. *incentivize*: Stage 3
2. *incent*: Stage 1
Current ratio (*to provide incentive* vs. *to incent*): 3:1

inception; incipiency. Both words mean "beginning, commencement, initiation." The difference is that *inception* refers to the action or process of beginning, while *incipiency* refers to the fact or state of having begun. *Inception* is far more often the appropriate word.

inchoate. A. Meaning and Pronunciation. *Inchoate*, pronounced /in-**koh**-it/ in AmE and /**in**-koh-ət/ in BrE (always three syllables), means "just begun; in the early stages of forming; not fully developed"—e.g.: "American understanding of Islamic terrorism then was still *inchoate*. Al-Qaida was barely on the screen." Terry McDermott et al., "Al-Qaida 'Engineer' Slips Dragnet," *Newsday* (N.Y.), 27 Dec. 2002, at A42.

B. And *choate*. The prefix is an intensive *in-*, not a negative or privative *in-*. So the BACK-FORMATION

LANGUAGE-CHANGE INDEX (For the full key, see front matter pp. xxxi, l–li.)
Stage 1: Rejected. **Stage 2:** Widely shunned. **Stage 3:** Widespread but . . . **Stage 4:** Ubiquitous but . . . **Stage 5:** Fully accepted.
Invariably inferior forms marked by asterisk (*). • Ratios represent frequency of prevalent forms vs. variants in current books.

choate (= complete)—premised, as it is, on the notion that *inchoate* is a negative—makes little sense. But it's now established in law <choate lien>.

C. And *chaotic*. Because what is undeveloped is usually also confused and incoherent, the context in which *inchoate* is used often suggests those errant senses. The resemblance of *-choate* to *chaotic* probably reinforces this misunderstanding. For whatever reason, *inchoate* is often misused to mean something more like *chaotic* than *aborning*—e.g.:

- "Valencius concludes that . . . American settlers 'transformed a landscape they experienced as wild and *inchoate* [read *alien*?] into the familiar and understood.'" Myron A. Marty, "Book Links Health of Missouri, Arkansas Pioneers to the Land," *St. Louis Post-Dispatch*, 22 Dec. 2001, at G10.
- "Surrounded by *an inchoate* [read *a chaotic*] household of prostitutes and riffraff, the good-hearted Lick survives a brutal correctional school, masters the steamy new music, rubs shoulders with Louis Armstrong and Kid Ory and pines for his high-yellow stepsister, Sylvie." Mark Rozzo. "First Fiction," *L.A. Times*, 24 Nov. 2002, Book Rev. §, at 14.
- "But when Thursday night came, Satre found the words, talking about how it is possible to fall in love with institutions—Stanford, in his case—and 'even something as *inchoate* [read *chaotic*?] as a company,' Harrah's." Thomas J. Walsh, "Phil Satre Stepping into Elder Statesman's Role," *Reno Gaz.-J.*, 12 Jan. 2003, at E1.

LANGUAGE-CHANGE INDEX
inchoate misused for *chaotic*: Stage 1

D. And *innate*. Harder to understand is the misuse of *inchoate* to mean "innate" or "inherent"—e.g.:

- "A bored and sophisticated American couple, Port and Kit Moresby, travel to North Africa, where the heat and light and estranging landscape, the incomprehensible languages and customs and *inchoate* [read *innate*?] sensuality unmoor them psychologically and emotionally." Fredric Koeppel, "Library of America Adds Staunch Exile to List," *Commercial Appeal* (Memphis), 2 Feb. 2003, at F1.
- "*Music Man* is not one of the most wise or even coherent products of American musical theater. . . . But, like Oklahoma, it can be mesmerizing in all its energy, optimism and certainty about the *inchoate* [read *inherent*?] goodness of the American character." David Zurawik, "Forecast: Warm Glow Moves In from River City, Iowa," *Baltimore Sun*, 16 Feb. 2003, at F14.

LANGUAGE-CHANGE INDEX
inchoate misused for *innate*: Stage 1

incident; incidence. A. Meanings. Although these words overlap, their primary senses are distinguishable. An *incident* is an occurrence or happening <several unfortunate incidents led to the curfew>. Though *incidence* sometimes bears this sense, it more often means "the rate of occurrence" <a high incidence of truancy>. In fact, whenever *incidence* appears where *incident* would fit, a switch is probably in order—e.g.:

- "In the last couple of years there have been several *incidences* [read *incidents*] of applause in the middle of movements." Richard Dyer, "No Encore of This Audience, Please," *Boston Globe*, 9 Oct. 1998, at D15.

- "There were several *incidences* [read *incidents*] of unruly behavior by fans, players, and LSU band members." Michael DiRocco, "Alabama Coach in Denial Mode," *Fla. Times-Union*, 7 Dec. 2001, at C4.
- "Police don't have simple answers for these unrelated *incidences* [read *incidents*], but they believe it could be a combination of drugs, gangs, population spurts, socioeconomics and heat-of-the moment exchanges." Javier Erik Olvera, "String of Homicides Stuns Tulare," *Fresno Bee*, 16 Mar. 2003, at A1.

This error is common in educated speech. Also, beware that *incidents* and *incidence* are homophones that may give listeners trouble.

LANGUAGE-CHANGE INDEX
incidence misused for *incident*: Stage 2

B. *Incident* Meaning "accident." See EUPHEMISMS.

incidentally. A. Generally. This SENTENCE ADVERB commonly introduces casual asides and minor digressions—e.g.:

- "The dictionary says a schmuck is a person who is 'clumsy or stupid; an oaf.' (*Incidentally*, there are four people named Oaf with phone listings.)" Mike Royko, "Downloading Some Lowdown Computer Statistics," *Houston Chron.*, 20 Jan. 1995, Houston §, at 2.
- "*Incidentally*, the best-tailored trousers have a cuff, from 1 1/4 to 1 1/2 inches wide." Lois Fenton, "'Flood Pants' Shrink Image," *Chicago Sun-Times*, 15 Feb. 1997, § 2, at 37.

H.W. Fowler's observation, though too harsh, still holds a kernel of truth: "those who find it most useful are not the best writers" (*FMEU1* at 264).

B. And *incidently*. *Incidentally* means "loosely, casually" or "by the way." *Incidently* (a rare word that the *OED* labels obsolete) means "so as to be incident to or resultant from; so as to depend on or appertain to something else." The most common mistake with these words is to misspell *incidentally*, no doubt because of the pronunciation—e.g.:

- "*Incidently* [read *Incidentally*], her openness is an indicator of the good quality of your relationship with her as well." Sylvia B. Rimmq, "Parents Sleeping Nude Shouldn't Bother Child," *Plain Dealer* (Cleveland), 18 Jan. 1997, at E2.
- "Its walls and windows can repel fire from .50-caliber guns—which, *incidently* [read *incidentally*], are on the prohibited equipment list, along with grenade launchers and weaponized aircraft." Callum Borchers, "Obama Order Spares Mass. Firm," *Boston Globe*, 21 May 2015, at A1.

Cf. **accidentally.**

LANGUAGE-CHANGE INDEX
incidently misused for *incidentally*: Stage 1

incident to; incidental to. Though to some extent interchangeable historically, these phrases have undergone a plain DIFFERENTIATION that has gained acceptance among stylists. *Incidental to* means "happening by chance and subordinate to some other thing; peripheral"—e.g.: "Inside a Niketown or the REI store in Seattle, shopping seems *incidental to* the spectacle of the store." Hugo Kugiya, "What's in Store?" *Seattle Times*, 19 Oct. 1997, at 16.

Incident to is a legalism meaning "closely related to; naturally appearing with"—e.g.: "The government argued that the search of the Cadillac's passenger compartment was permissible since it was *incident to* Adam's arrest." "Search & Seizure," *Chicago Daily Law Bull.*, 11 July 1994, at 1. Over the history of Modern English, *incident to* has appeared in print far more frequently than *incidental to*.

incipiency. See **inception.**

incipient; insipient. The former means "beginning, in an initial stage"; the latter is an obsolete word meaning "unwise, foolish." But *incipient* is often misspelled with an *-s-* —e.g.:

- "Mexico lost little time reasserting itself as a no-nonsense nation renowned for dealing in summary justice. *Insipient* [read *Incipient*] terrorism was brutally repressed for a couple of years, then burst forth between 1972 and 1975." Bill Waters, "Guatemalan President Cautious," *Ariz. Republic*, 4 May 1986, at C6.
- "Allen devised a program for factory workers at Bridgeport Machines to detect the signs and symptoms of angina pain and *insipient* [read *incipient*] heart attacks." James Lomuscio, "First a Checkup, Then to Baseball," *N.Y. Times*, 6 Aug. 1995, at CN13.
- "What's more, [Ralph Nader] has tapped into an *insipient* [read *incipient*] social movement that raised its voice even before his candidacy came along." Salim Muwakkil, "Gore: Our Defense Against a 3-Headed Beast," *Chicago Trib.*, 6 Nov. 2000, Commentary §, at 17.

Given the rarity of *insipient*, it's a little surprising to see it used correctly—e.g.:

- "But spare us the inevitable flood of self-satisfied, self-congratulatory interviews that will follow this *insipient* actor's [i.e., Michael Caine's] resurrection, rendering indigestible our morning coffee." Letter of Richard Harris, "A Sharp Kick from a Man Called Horse," *Sunday Times* (London), 6 Aug. 1995, § 3, at 8.
- "*Insipient* proposals to create and raise taxes are hardly what D.C. officials had in mind when they established the commission in 1996." Editorial, "Kill the Lawyers' Tax," *Wash. Times*, 4 May 1998, at A16.
- "Some legislators tried to change the constitution to allow (and therefore guarantee) unequal and ineffective public education in Texas. Fortunately, they failed to convince their less *insipient* colleagues and the public of the merits of their ambition." Editorial, "Texas Public School Finance Needs Efficiency Experts," *Houston Chron.*, 8 July 2001, Outlook §, at 2.

LANGUAGE-CHANGE INDEX
insipient misused for *incipient*: Stage 1

*incitation. See **incitement.**

inciteful; *incitive; *incitative; *incitatory; incitant. What is the adjective meaning "tending to incite"? Most American dictionaries don't list one, and the *OED* merely records sparse and ancient examples of **incitive*, **incitative*, and **incitatory*—all of which should today be considered NEEDLESS VARIANTS of *inciteful*. This word is a legal NEOLOGISM that first

appeared in mid-20th-century AmE. Today it is fairly common even outside law—e.g.:

- "He is not going to be dragged into any warfare with Reggie Miller, the undisputed king of the *inciteful* comment. But just because Latrell Sprewell won't engage in verbal jousting does not mean he will in any way back down." Paul Schwartz, "Spree–Reggie War Brewing," *N.Y. Post*, 25 May 2000, at 92.
- "Oslo was mortally wounded the day the Palestinian leader issued his first *inciteful* message to an Arabic-speaking crowd." Julian Schvindlerman, "Oslo's Collapse," *Wash. Times*, 21 Nov. 2000, at A17.
- "They [the essays] are almost always *inciteful*, occasionally insightful, witty, moving, revealing, and intelligent, and invariably universal." Curt Schleier, "Wasserstein Discovers Birth, Loss and Her WASP Roots," *Grand Rapids Press*, 20 May 2001, at J6.

The word has two unfortunate qualities. First, it is anomalously formed. Unlike most words ending in *-ful*, it doesn't consist of a [noun +] *-ful* construction (as with *beautiful, colorful, hurtful, merciful, pitiful*), but of [verb +] *-ful*. That's quite unusual. Second, the word is liable to confusion with its homophone, *insightful*—e.g.: "That may not be the most *inciteful* [read *insightful*] analysis of human nature. But under those circumstances it'll do." Janet Maslin, "Terrifying a Mass Killer with Pure Brain Power," *N.Y. Times*, 20 Dec. 2001, at E10. Where the word isn't clearly a mistake, as in that quotation, the reader (and the listener more so, with no spelling clue) may have to think twice to know whether you are condemning your subject's inflammatory comments or praising your subject's enlightening observations. So for *inciteful*, consider using an unambiguous alternative such as *antagonistic, incendiary,* or *provocative.*

Incitant is both a noun meaning "an activating agent" and an adjective meaning "activating." But that rare word pertains to physical rather than emotional causation: things that trigger disease or chemical reactions, for example.

LANGUAGE-CHANGE INDEX
inciteful misused for *insightful*: Stage 1

incitement; *incitation. The latter is a NEEDLESS VARIANT.

Current ratio: 26:1

inclement (= unmerciful, stormy) is increasingly replaced by the MALAPROPISM and NONWORD **inclimate*. Because *inclement weather* is such a common phrase—a SET PHRASE, really—many have come to hear the phrase as a redundant comment on the *climate* as well as the *weather*. Hence the erroneous **inclimate weather*—e.g.:

- "Because of the soggy turf and *inclimate* [read *inclement*] weather Thursday, the Bears practiced at South Park instead of behind their traditional Halas Hall facility."

LANGUAGE-CHANGE INDEX (For the full key, see front matter pp. xxxi, l–li.)
Stage 1: Rejected. **Stage 2:** Widely shunned. **Stage 3:** Widespread but . . . **Stage 4:** Ubiquitous but . . . **Stage 5:** Fully accepted.
Invariably inferior forms marked by asterisk (*). • Ratios represent frequency of prevalent forms vs. variants in current books.

Fred Mitchell, "Bits & Pieces on Chicago's Teams," *Chicago Trib.*, 20 Oct. 1989, at C11.

- "The Cotton Bowl Classic, always threatened by *inclimate* [read *inclement*] weather, had to live with IRS audits, internal squabbling and increased competition from other major bowls in the 1990s." "What Killed the SWC?" *Dallas Morning News*, 6 Aug. 1995, at B13.
- "Worcester State plays host to the Central Mass./Western Mass. Super Bowls Dec. 7, and in the event of *inclimate* [read *inclement*] weather, Belmont, Mansfield, and Catholic Memorial are possible backup sites for EMass games." Chris Forsberg, "MIAA Declares Two Sites Super," *Boston Globe*, 16 May 2002, at C10.

In pronouncing the word, stress the second syllable, not the first.

LANGUAGE-CHANGE INDEX
inclimate weather for *inclement weather*: Stage 1
Current ratio (*inclement weather* vs.
inclimate weather): 781:1

*inclose. See **enclose.**

*inclosure. See **enclosure.**

*includable. See **includible.**

include. A. Introducing Exhaustive or Nonexhaustive List. The word has traditionally introduced a non-exhaustive list but is now coming to be widely misused for *consists of*—e.g.: "The Department of Public Safety report detailing the reprimand was released to the AP . . . one day after the all-male, three-member Public Safety Commission cleared the Rangers of wrongdoing in a separate sexual harassment charge. [¶] The [three-member] commission—which *includes* [read *consists of*] Robert Holt of Midland, James Francis of Dallas and Ronald Krist of Houston—said it would continue to investigate whether any changes in policy are needed." Chip Brown, "Bush Defends Rangers Amid Allegations of Discrimination," *Austin Am.-Statesman*, 14 July 1995, at B1. Only three people are on the commission, and all are named.

Hence the age-old lawyers' phrase *including but not limited to* is, strictly speaking, a REDUNDANCY. See Antonin Scalia & Bryan A. Garner, *Reading Law: The Interpretation of Legal Texts* 132–33 (2012).

B. To include. Use of the phrase *to include* to mean "including" is a silly bit of OFFICIALESE. Unfortunately, it's much too common in military, healthcare, and legal writing—e.g.:

- "Mrs. Vieira consented to a search of the *home to include* [read *home, including*] their home computer." *U.S. v. Vieira*, 64 M.J. 524, 527 (A.F. Ct. Crim. App. 2006).
- "As an initial matter, this case demonstrates that a hospital can be held liable for the acts of the personnel working at the facility, *to include* [read *including*] doctors." Blake J. Delaney, "Improper Use of Forceps Results in Large Federal Tort Verdict," *Healthcare Risk Mgmt.*, 1 Feb. 2007.

includible. Predominantly so spelled in all varieties of English—not **includable*. Weirdly enough, its antonym is spelled *excludable*. See -ABLE (A).

Current ratio: 3:1

inclusive. This word is often helpful in expressing lengths of time. For example, the phrase *from November 1 to December 15 inclusive* makes it clear that both the starting date and the ending date are included; without the word *inclusive*, the meaning is debatable.

incognito (= [1] in disguise; or [2] under an assumed name) is sometimes misused for *incommunicado* (= unable, unwilling, or forbidden to communicate with others)—e.g.:

- "The crackdown, which began almost two weeks ago, has included the arrest and imprisonment of activists, some of whom are apparently being held *incognito* [read *incommunicado*] in Cuban jails." "Over Cuba: Castro Shows Again That He's Not to Be Trusted," *Houston Chron.*, 27 Feb. 1996, at A18.
- "The reporter for U.S.-funded Radio Liberty has yet to tell the full story of his arrest, his days held *incognito* [read *incommunicado*] by Russian troops and the weeks that followed the prisoner exchange." Jamie Dettmer, "Putin Revives Soviet-Style Media Curbs in Russia," *Wash. Times*, 27 Feb. 2000, at C12.
- "Warring with this nation's tradition of freedom, the Bush administration . . . [h]as rounded up hundreds of foreign nationals living in the United States and has held them *incognito* [read *incommunicado*]." Gregory Stanford, "Fight Against Terror Must Not Trample Rights," *Milwaukee J. Sentinel*, 8 Sept. 2002, Crossroads §, at J1.

Although the traditional pronunciation was /in-**kog**-ni-toh/, the standard today is /in-kog-**nee**-toh/.

LANGUAGE-CHANGE INDEX
incognito misused for *incommunicado*: Stage 1

incommensurate; incommensurable. See **commensurate.**

in common with occasionally displaces *like* from its rightful place—e.g.: "Houdini, however, wanted to be special. *In common with* [read *Like*] many other entertainers of the time (including Al Jolson and Irving Berlin), he was the son of a rabbi." Andrew Rosenheim, "Escapes of an Egotist," *TLS*, 5 Nov. 1993, at 24. See **like (c).**

*incommunicative. See **uncommunicative.**

incomparable; noncomparable; *uncomparable. *Incomparable* (= so good as to be beyond comparison) is the usual word; it has been in common use since the 15th century. *Noncomparable* (= not similar enough to something else to allow comparison) emerged in the early 20th century to rival its synonym, **uncomparable*. By 1940, *noncomparable* had been established as standard. **Uncomparable* remains a NEEDLESS VARIANT.

The words are pronounced /in-**kom**-pər-ə-bel/ and /non-**kom**-pər-ə-bel/. Don't stress the third syllable.

incompetence; incompetency. A growing distinction exists between these forms, especially in law. Reserve *incompetency* for contexts involving sanity or ability to stand trial or to testify; use *incompetence* when referring to unacceptable levels of performance. See **competence.**

INCOMPLETE SENTENCES. A. Fragments. Grammarians typically define *fragment* as a part of a sentence punctuated as if it were complete. Usually denoting an error—as opposed to literary license—the term *fragment* (or *frag.*) appears frequently in the marginal jottings of high-school and college English teachers. That is to say, some high-school and college students don't know how to write complete sentences. Hence elementary grammars warn against constructions such as the following one, in which a main clause and a subordinate clause are each written as a complete sentence:

> We usually go to the fair in the evening. Because everything is more glamorous under the lights.
> Ex. fr. Philip Gucker, *Essential English Grammar*
> 133 (1966).

The fragment might be corrected in any of several ways:

> We usually go to the fair in the evening because everything is more glamorous under the lights.
> We usually go to the fair in the evening; everything is more glamorous under the lights.
> We usually go to the fair in the evening. Everything is more glamorous under the lights.

This type of elementary problem rarely occurs in the writing of those who know enough about writing to be able to construct complete sentences. (The more frequent problem is RUN-ON SENTENCES, which occur when writers punctuate two sentences as if they were one.) Therefore, basic advice on avoiding fragments—"don't write a phrase or dependent clause as if it were a complete sentence"—is of limited utility to most writers. Further, for reasons discussed in (B), that advice might be misleading.

B. Incomplete Sentences in Informal Writing. Grammarians' definitions of the word *sentence* range widely. Here's a sampling:

- "A sentence is a group of words containing a subject and a predicate and expressing a complete thought." C. Rexford Davis, *Toward Correct English* 1 (1936).
- "A complete sentence says something about something." Robert M. Gorrell & Charlton Laird, *Modern English Handbook* 195 (2d ed. 1956).
- "Sentence [means] a group of words consisting of a finite verb and its subject as well as any complement that may be present and any modifiers that belong to the verb, to the subject, to the complement, or to the entire statement, the whole group of words constituting a grammatically complete statement, i.e., a statement that is clearly not part of a larger structure." Ralph M. Albaugh, *English: A Dictionary of Grammar and Structure* 170 (1964).
- "A sentence is a combination of words so connected as to express a complete thought: Man is mortal. Is man mortal? How mortal man is!" James C. Fernald, *English Grammar Simplified* 161 (Cedric Gale ed., 2d ed. 1979).

Given that the word *complete* appears in each of those definitions, one might surmise—as many writers believe—that it is impossible to write an *incomplete* sentence and still be within the bounds of good usage.

Yet the more sophisticated grammarians have long qualified the notion of "completeness." The great linguist Otto Jespersen defined *sentence* as "a (relatively) complete and independent unit of communication . . .—the completeness and independence being shown by its standing alone or its capability of standing alone, *i.e.* of being uttered by itself." *Essentials of English Grammar* 106 (1933; repr. 1964). Similarly but more specifically, C.T. Onions defined *sentence* as a group of words—or sometimes a single word—that makes a statement <I'm a tennis enthusiast>, a command <Open the window>, an expression of a wish <Let's go>, a question <How are you?>, or an exclamation <What a deal!>. *Modern English Syntax* 1 (B.D.H. Miller ed., 1971). More recently still, a dictionary of grammar states that a sentence "usually" has a subject and a predicate. Sylvia Chalker & Edmund Weiner, *The Oxford Dictionary of English Grammar* 358 (1994). And Sidney Greenbaum commented, "The traditional definition of a sentence states that a sentence expresses a complete thought. The trouble with this notional definition is that it requires us to know what a complete thought is." *The Oxford English Grammar* 308 (1996).

It appears possible, then, for a sentence to be "incomplete"—i.e., with a subject or verb that is at best implicit—without being "incorrect." Jespersen called one type "amorphous sentences," noting both that they are "more suitable for the emotional side of human nature" and that it would be impossible to say precisely what is "left out." *Essentials* at 105, 106. Examples are *Yes! / Goodbye! / Thanks! / Nonsense! / Of course! / Why all this fuss? / Hence his financial difficulties! Ibid.* at 105–06.

More modern authorities agree—e.g.:

- "Experienced writers know how to use fragments deliberately and effectively—noun phrases and verb phrases that add a detail without a full sentence and invariably call attention to themselves." Martha Kolln, *Rhetorical Grammar* 190 (3d ed. 1999).
- "Only the most tin-eared, fuddy-duddy excuses for copy editors routinely convert every single fragment they see into a complete sentence." Bill Walsh, *Lapsing into a Comma* 201 (2000).

More than a dozen types of verbless sentences occur in modern prose. As the examples below illustrate, the important quality in each type is that the sentence be short enough that the reader will recognize it as purposely incomplete:

- *Transitional:* "It will be worth our while to consider the loans from a few languages, as they have great cultural importance. First the Dutch." Otto Jespersen, *Growth and Structure of the English Language* 158 (9th ed. 1938).
- *Afterthought:* "I write entirely to find out what I'm thinking, what I'm looking at, what I see and what it means. What I want and what I fear." Joan Didion, "Why I Write" (1976), in *The Living Language* 397, 399 (Linda A. Morris

et al. eds., 1984). / "Although most Americans sense that they live within an extremely complicated system of social classes and suspect that much of what is thought and done here is prompted by consideration of status, the subject has remained murky. And always touchy." Paul Fussell, *Class* 1 (1983).

- **Emphatic:** "As a rough principle enjoining on the ordinary writer the necessity for a careful choice of words, this statement contains a modicum of truth. But only a modicum." G.H. Vallins, *The Best English* 28 (1960; repr. 1973).
- **Signaling an emphatic appositive:** "Disorder, redundancy, omission, ambiguity in general. These are the four by-ways into which we stray from the highroad of good English." Janet Rankin Aiken, *Commonsense Grammar* 32 (1936). / "Young editors and also so-called mature adults are sometimes unable to make publishing judgments because of certain emotional or mental blocks. The question of values arises. Integrity. Morality. Taste. Aesthetics. Standards. These virtues are sometimes obstacles to an editor's business judgment." William Targ, "What Is an Editor?" in *Editors on Editing* 4, 16–17 (Gerald Gross ed., rev. ed. 1985).
- **Negating:** "All a dying man could utter would be a prejudgement. Which is absurd." Christopher Ricks, *T.S. Eliot and Prejudice* 91 (1988).
- **Explanatory:** "For the compromise theory the question of justice is a question of balance, and the balance is both impersonal and intuitive. Impersonal because individuals become the instruments of achieving aggregate quantities—of equality as much as of utility. Intuitive because the correct balance must be a matter of inarticulate 'feel.'" Ronald Dworkin, *A Matter of Principle* 272 (1985).
- **Elaborating:** "Or he may confess and avoid: for instance, by admitting that the sheriff had a *capias* to arrest the servant but asserting that he had used excessive violence. And so on, until an affirmative is negatived." J.H. Baker, *An Introduction to English Legal History* 92 (3d ed. 1990).
- **Bolstering:** "One needs only to read Terence, Plautus, or Seneca to realize how little human nature has changed in two thousand years. (If it has changed at all, which I doubt.)" Frank Yerby, "How and Why I Write the Costume Novel," in *Writing in America* 125, 129 (John Fischer & Robert B. Silvers eds., 1960).
- **Recanting:** "The Age of Aquarius has finally dawned in Presidential politics. Sort of." Maureen Dowd, "2 Baby Boomers on 1 Ticket: A First, but Will It Work?" *N.Y. Times*, 13 July 1992, at A1.
- **Undercutting:** "In poetry, [Herbert Read] says, 'there is no time interval between the words and the thought.' A very rash assertion indeed." I.A. Richards, "Herbert Read's *English Prose Style*," in *Complementarities: Uncollected Essays* 178, 180 (John Paul Russo ed., 1976).
- **Imitating the mind's processing of information:** "What kind of boy was this? I had to know. I looked up. I looked directly at him. A skinny fellow with glasses. Small-boned and loose-limbed, and not so tall as I'd first thought. Wearing a loose-fitting jacket and baseball cap. Not, in my estimation, 'cute.'" Monty S. Leitch, "A New Edge to the Dangers of Youth," *Roanoke Times*, 13 Jan. 1997, at A5.
- **Urgent:** "Never mind the discounts and the espresso; patronize your independent bookseller. Soon. And often." Leonard Garment, "Mid-List Crisis," *Forbes*, 20 Oct. 1997, at 118.
- **Staccato:** "Men rather than women, black men if possible. Older people rather than younger. Discerning rather than deferential. Shepherds rather than sheep, football buffs rather than football widows, fans of 'L.A. Law' rather than 'NYPD Blue.' And though there are no longer any blank slates when it comes to O.J. Simpson . . . it's better that they get their news from 'MacNeil/Lehrer' or Newsweek than 'Geraldo!' or The Star. Among lawyers and jury consultants that is the consensus prescription for Mr. Simpson's ideal juror." David Margolick, "Ideal Juror for O.J. Simpson: Football Fan Who Can Listen," *N.Y. Times*, 23 Sept. 1994, at A1.
- **Summing up an emotional circumstance:** "Suppose that you and I are acquaintances and we're in my apartment having a conversation and that at some point I want to terminate the conversation and not have you be in my apartment anymore. Very delicate social moment." David Foster Wallace, "Tense Present," *Harper's Mag.*, Apr. 2001, at 39, 50.

Whatever the purpose, though, the incomplete or verbless sentence carries some degree of risk. You risk not being expert enough to carry it off adroitly. You risk your readers' being suspicious about whether you intended a rhetorical effect or simply failed to finish a complete sentence. You should therefore be wary: "Most writers . . . use the incomplete sentence sparingly, except in reports of conversation. It is a special device, to be used for special effects. In the hands of anyone but an expert, it is usually unsuccessful because the basic patterns have not been established, and missing ideas cannot be supplied." Robert M. Gorrell & Charlton Laird, *Modern English Handbook* 202 (2d ed. 1956).

Here, for example, is an ill-advised fragment: "While print people still have every right to be bemused by the rapid shift in conventional wisdom, they would be wise to avoid complacency. Because the industry stands at a very serious crossroads." Rem Reider, "At the Crossroads," *Am. Journalism Rev.*, Mar. 2001, at 6. The writer might have (1) put a dash before *because* (for emphasis), (2) used a comma (see **because (B)**), or (3) omitted the *because* and started a separate sentence. As the sentence stands, though, readers are likely to think they're reading a subordinate clause to be followed by a main clause. So the fragment results in a MISCUE. As a rule, any fragment starting with *because* is suspect for just these reasons.

Incomplete or verbless sentences of the acceptable type are not classified as "fragments," but technically they are precisely that. So it is possible, in good usage, to write fragments. Possible but difficult.

For examples of incomplete sentences beginning with *Which*, see **which (C).**

incongruous (= not having corresponding or appropriate characteristics; out of keeping) is often misspelled **incongrous*—e.g.:

- "Last night, she turned in an achingly soulful, sorrow-filled rendition of 'Hellhound,' followed by a wonderfully *incongrous* [read *incongruous*], bright and funky take on the violent '32-20 Blues.'" Michael Norman, "Paying Homage to a Master," *Plain Dealer* (Cleveland), 28 Sept. 1998, at D1.
- "Their tinkling calls, so *incongrous* [read *incongruous*] from such gigantic birds, carried across the water mingled

with the cries of gulls and whonks of geese." Mike Drew, "Portraits of Elegance," *Calgary Sun*, 3 Apr. 1999, at 33.

The word is preferably accented on the second rather than the third syllable: /in-**kong**-groo-əs/. For the distinction between *congruous* and *congruent*, see **congruent.**

LANGUAGE-CHANGE INDEX
incongruous misspelled *incongrous: Stage 1

in connection with is almost always a vague, loose connective, often used in reporting wrongdoing. Occasionally—very occasionally—it is the only connective that will do. Use it as a last resort—e.g.: "The F.B.I. was searching for Mr. Bailey *in connection with* the stabbing of his friend, Demming F. Rocker 3d." "Officer's Killer Was Told F.B.I. Sought Him, Detectives Say," *N.Y. Times*, 28 Nov. 1997, at B8. Here, Bailey may have been wanted for help in solving the crime rather than as a suspect.

But when criminal charges have officially been made, *in connection with* is almost always too fuzzy—e.g.:

- "Bonds, 26, whose last address was 4 Linden St., Winthrop, is wanted on multiple warrants *in connection with* [read *for*] an April armed robbery at a Dorchester pizza restaurant." Ann E. Donlan, "Cops Seeking Murder-Try Suspect," *Boston Herald*, 28 Nov. 1997, at 16.
- "Bowser, King and Meggerson were arrested shortly afterward and charged *in connection with* [read *with*] another robbery that occurred that day before Wood was wounded." Glenn E. Rice, "Trial Set for January for Three Men Accused in Shooting a Wyandotte County Deputy," *Kansas City Star*, 1 Sept. 2015, News §.

Cf. **in this connection.**

inconsistency; *__inconsistence.__* Writers on usage formerly tried to distinguish between the forms, reserving *inconsistency* for the sense "the general quality of being inconsistent" and making *__inconsistence__* mean "an inconsistent act; an instance of being inconsistent." Today, however, *inconsistency* has ousted *-ce* in all senses. Avoid *__inconsistence__* as a NEEDLESS VARIANT. Cf. **consistency.**

Current ratio: 143:1

in contrast with; in contrast to. These are equally good. See **contrast (A).**

__incontrollable.__ See **uncontrollable.**

__increasingly more__ is increasingly—or rather, more and more—common as a REDUNDANCY. E.g.: "As the business becomes *increasingly more* [read *increasingly* or *more*] competitive, do publishers care which books they publish or what shape the manuscripts are in when they hit the press?" Roger Cohen, "When a Best Seller Is at Stake, Publishers Can Lose Control," *N.Y. Times*, 12 May 1991, at E4.

The phrase *__increasingly less__* is a jarring OXYMORON that would be better rendered *less and less* or *decreasing*—e.g.: "[Alien pirates] were highly entertaining when we first saw them in the 'Star Wars' cantina 25 years ago; they've grown *increasingly less* [read *less and less*] so with every ripoff since." Joe Miller, "Don't Dig: 'Treasure' Isn't There," *News & Observer* (Raleigh), 27 Nov. 2002, at E1.

In fact, *increasingly* is a word that aspiring stylists might do well to jettison from their vocabulary—or at least use less and less.

LANGUAGE-CHANGE INDEX
1. *<i>increasingly more</i> for <i>more</i>: Stage 1
2. *<i>increasingly less</i> for <i>less and less</i>: Stage 1

incredible; incredulous. *Incredible* (= unbelievable) has become a VOGUE WORD to describe something that astounds, especially in a pleasing way—e.g.: "Moore combined this with meditations on the *incredible* [read *rare? priceless?*] paintings she found in a warehouse several months after Sargent's death in 1978." Susy Schultz, "Troubled Life Leads to Poetic Justice," *Chicago Sun-Times*, 2 June 1996, at 16.

Incredulous has long meant "disbelieving, doubting, skeptical" <she was incredulous when listening to the story>. E.g.:

- "It took Shoup about 10 minutes to convince George that he wasn't joking. Then he had to convince [George's] wife, who was equally *incredulous*." Susan A. Cantonwine, "Money Will Not Change Lotto Winner," *Dayton Daily News*, 23 July 1997, at Z41.
- "Secrets spin from his fertile imagination and into the *incredulous* ears of his passengers." Roger Ebert, "An Implausible 'Theory,'" *Chicago Sun-Times*, 8 Aug. 1997, at 33.

Although early writers, in the late 16th and early 17th centuries, used *incredulous* as a synonym for *incredible* (= unbelievable), the DIFFERENTIATION between the words has long been settled. Today it must be regarded as a mistake to use *incredulous* interchangeably with *incredible*—e.g.:

- "He said it is *incredulous* [read *incredible*] to accuse him of creating a deficit when he has cut spending by more than $70 million since he took office." Diane C. Walsh, "Essex Prosecutor Lashes Back at County Executive," *Star-Ledger* (Newark), 4 May 1999, at 41.
- "With every report from every scientific organization saying how much the Department of Energy has botched the science or, just as bad, not completed it before recommending the site to President Bush, . . . it seems *incredulous* [read *incredible*] that Bush would plow ahead." Brian Greenspun, "Yucca Fight Won't End," *Las Vegas Sun*, 12 Feb. 2002, at A13.

This distinction was firm even in the early to mid-20th century, when Wodehouse wrote the following: "'It contained an offer to swap the cow-creamer for Anatole, and Tom is seriously considering it!' [¶] "I stared at her. 'What? *Incredulous!*' [¶] "'*Incredible*, sir.' [¶] "'Thank you, Jeeves. *Incredible*! I don't believe it. Uncle Tom would never contemplate such a thing for

LANGUAGE-CHANGE INDEX (For the full key, see front matter pp. xxxi, l–li.)
Stage 1: Rejected. **Stage 2:** Widely shunned. **Stage 3:** Widespread but . . . **Stage 4:** Ubiquitous but . . . **Stage 5:** Fully accepted.
Invariably inferior forms marked by asterisk (*). • Ratios represent frequency of prevalent forms vs. variants in current books.

an instant.'" P.G. Wodehouse, *The Code of the Woosters* 91–92 (1938; repr. 1976). See **credible**.

LANGUAGE-CHANGE INDEX
incredulous misused for *incredible*: Stage 1
Current ratio (*it is incredible* vs.
**it is incredulous*): 133:1

incriminate; *criminate. The first is now more usual in both AmE and BrE. Although **criminate* was the more common word through the 19th century, today it is a NEEDLESS VARIANT.

Current ratio (*incriminated* vs. **criminated*): 20:1

incrustation; *encrustation. Although *encrust* (not **incrust*) is the verb, the spelling *incrustation* has predominated since the mid-18th century—apart from an anomalous period from 1975 to 2005 (inexplicably). The most prestigious dictionaries correctly put the main headword under *in-*. For more, see EN-.

incubus; succubus. An *incubus* is a male demon said to have sex with sleeping women. A *succubus* is a female demon said to have sex with sleeping men. (**Succuba* is a NEEDLESS VARIANT.) Each should be confined to its narrow sense, rather than being used broadly as a synonym for "demon"—e.g.: "Sainte-Croix promptly fled, whereupon Mme. de Brinvilliers leapt upon Briancourt's back like some crazed *incubus* [read *succubus* or, better, *demon*]." Anne Somerset, *The Affair of the Poisons* 27 (2003). In the mid-1990s, the Reebok shoe company made news by selling a women's running shoe called the *Incubus*. After being on sale for a year, the shoe was pulled off the market when ABC News reported the gaffe. Apparently the marketing wizards and the trademark lawyers all neglected to consult a dictionary.

The plural forms are *incubi* (or *incubuses*) and *succubi* (or *succubuses*). It might be better to adopt *succubuses*, though, than to lead writers into the inconsistent forms seen in the following sentence: "We discovered that we could fashion medieval *incubuses* and *succubi* [read *succubuses*] not only from blacks but from late 19th-century immigrant hordes." Florence King, "Current Need to Awaken Dormant Beelzebub," *Wash. Times*, 12 Nov. 1995, at B8. Some writers would write *incubi* and *succubi*, but see PLURALS (B). Others have wisely espoused *incubuses* and *succubuses* (well, the words, not the things denoted by them)—e.g.: "These days, there are no *incubuses* or *succubuses*, I suspect, but we still have nightmares." Michael G. Gartner, "Words, Words, Words," *Courier-J.* (Louisville), 8 Dec. 1991, at D3.

inculcatable. So spelled. See -ATABLE.

inculcate (into). A. And *indoctrinate*. *Inculcate* is sometimes misused for *indoctrinate*. Although these are both transitive verbs (i.e., they take direct objects), the nature of the objects is different. One *inculcates* values into people; and one *indoctrinates* people with certain values—e.g.: "Green schools can also *inculcate* green values in students at an impressionable

age." Bryan Walsh, "Little Green Schoolhouse," *Time*, 1 Oct. 2007, at 59. So one does not *inculcate* people, but rather values or beliefs or ideas. The mistake is common—e.g.:

- "A way must be found to *inculcate these youth with values* [read *inculcate values into these youths*]." Sharon Pratt Kelly, "Can We Win the Battle for America's Streets?" *USA Today* (Mag.), May 1994, at 22.
- "But [Chris] Burden said his obsession with such models sprang from some serious thinking over many years about the nature of toys. 'They're the tools we use to *inculcate* children into how to be adults, how to live in the world,' he said." Randy Kennedy, "An Artist's Vision," *N.Y. Times*, 8 June 2008, at A37. (A possible revision: *They're the tools we use to teach children how to be adults, how to live in the world*.)
- "Sexually loaded media is, unfortunately, a fact of life. The solution then is to *inculcate teens with the knowledge* [read *inculcate into teens the knowledge*] they need to protect themselves." O. Ricardo Pimentel, "Sex, Sex and More Sex. Got Your Attention?" *Milwaukee J. Sentinel*, 10 Aug. 2008, Crossroads §, at J4. (On *media is*, see **media**.)

H.W. Fowler noted this aberration and called it "a curious mistake" (*FMEU1* at 266). No longer is it curious, but it is still a mistake. See OBJECT-SHUFFLING. For more on *indoctrinate*, see **indoctrinate**.

LANGUAGE-CHANGE INDEX
inculcate misused for *indoctrinate*: Stage 3
Current ratio (*inculcated into him* vs.
**inculcated him with*): 4:1

B. And *instill. *Instill* usually follows the syntactic pattern of *inculcate* <a commander must instill confidence in the troops>. The terms overlap to a great degree, each one denoting compulsion by persistent repetition. But there are subtleties in their connotations. To *inculcate* a value or belief is to pound it in (a rare second sense of the word is "to trample"). To *instill* it is to build up the value or belief bit by bit (a rare second sense is to introduce a liquid drop by drop). So *instill* carries more positive connotations than *inculcate*, which is closer in nuance to *indoctrinate*. See **instill**.

***inculpable.** See **culpable** & **inculpatable**.

inculpatable, not *inculpable*, is the correct form of the word meaning "capable of being inculpated [i.e., incriminated]." (See -ATABLE.) *Inculpable* is, however, a negative form that generally means "not culpable; blameless; free from guilt." Use of *inculpable* may cause incriminating ambiguities. See **culpable**.

inculpatory; *inculpative. The standard form is *inculpatory* (= tending to incriminate)—e.g.: "When the room was finally checked, police found no *inculpatory* evidence." Kristen Delguzzi, "Jurors See Scene of Hotel Slaying," *Cincinnati Enquirer*, 15 Nov. 1996, at C1. **Inculpative* is a NEEDLESS VARIANT. Cf. **culpable** & **exculpatory**.

Current ratio: 108:1

***incumbrance.** See **encumbrance**.

incurrence; *incurment. Sometimes writers need a noun corresponding to the verb *incur*. *Incurrence* is the standard term; **incurment* is a NEEDLESS VARIANT. *Incurrence* is sometimes misspelled **incurrance*.

Current ratio (*incurrence* vs. **incurment*): 718:1

in danger. See danger (A).

indebtedness. A. Generally. *Indebtedness* = the state or fact of being indebted. E.g.:

- "Existing heavy bonded *indebtedness*, state-government budget woes and a lingering recession do not make for a healthy environment in which to issue new bonds." Ray Dussault, "Financing Dicier After Market Slips on Orange Peel," *Bus. J.—Sacramento*, 13 Feb. 1995, at 28.
- "O'Toole, for all his playfulness and his pub-crawling, is a serious student of the theater whose sense of its past—and his own *indebtedness* to that past—is powerful." Jonathan Yardley, "Loitering with Intent," *Int'l Herald Trib.*, 15 Feb. 1997, at 5.
- "The scale and quality of Western *indebtedness* versus Chinese investment was a contributory factor to the Great Financial Crisis of 2008." Nigel Wilson, "Our Rebirth as an Investing Economy Needs to Begin Now," *Sunday Telegraph*, 30 Aug. 2015, Bus. §, at 4.

The term is often used where the simpler word *debt* would be preferable—e.g.: "Holders of certain unsecured *indebtedness* [read *debts*] of the company have deferred payments until Feb. 28." "In Brief," *Ariz. Bus. Gaz.*, 16 Feb. 1995, at 26. In this sense, *indebtedness* is a NEEDLESS VARIANT of *debt*. But in some contexts one can hardly discern what is being referred to: the state of being indebted or the actual debt.

B. And **indebtment*. A NEEDLESS VARIANT of *indebtedness* or *debt*, **indebtment* was much more common up to the mid-20th century than it is today. Now it's confined to a few legal texts—where it would still be better replaced with *indebtedness* or *debt*.

INDEFINITE PRONOUNS. See PRONOUNS (D).

independence; *independency. Interestingly, **independency* was the standard term until shortly before the American colonies' Declaration of Independence (1776). Since then, *independence* has been the standard form in all varieties of World English.

Current ratio: 196:1

independent contractor; employee. Unlike an *employee*, an *independent contractor* is left free to do the assigned work and to choose the method for accomplishing it. And unlike an *employee*, an *independent contractor* does not, upon committing a wrong while carrying out the work, create liability for an employer that did not authorize the wrongful acts. For example, a taxi driver is an independent contractor, while a private chauffeur is an employee. A freelance writer is an independent contractor; a staff writer is an employee.

independent(ly). A. Preposition with. *Independent* should take the preposition *of*, not *from*—e.g.: "The International Criminal Court, which is *independent from* [read *independent of*] the United Nations, would have no mandate to try Mr. [Charles G.] Taylor." Lydia Polgreen & Marlise Simons, "Sierra Leone Asks to Move Liberian's Trial," *N.Y. Times*, 31 Mar. 2006, at A7.

B. Adverb or Adjective. The proper adverbial phrase is *independently of*. E.g.: "He said the men were flying *independently of* each other." Susan Gilmore et al., "The Lure of Ultralights," *Seattle Times*, 8 Aug. 1997, at A1. The phrase *independent of*, an adjective phrase, is sometimes wrongly asked to perform an adverbial function—e.g.: "In the summers in the South, people rise early to get work done before the heat comes up; Franklin does it *independent of* [read *independently of*] the weather." Paul Hendrickson, "Hope Is His Middle Name," *Wash. Post*, 6 Aug. 1997, at C1.

index. A. Plurals. For ordinary purposes, *indexes* is the preferable plural, not *indices*—e.g.:

- "The book is beautifully produced, [is] profusely illustrated, [and] contains scrupulous filmographies and two *indexes* (of boy actors and film titles)." Peter Parker, "Sweet Boys with Insufferable Parents," *Independent*, 12 Oct. 1996, Books §, at 6. (For the reasons behind the inserted words, see PARALLELISM.)
- "A list of contributors and several *indexes* are included." Anne C. Fullam, "Almanac Offers Insights to the Hudson," *N.Y. Times*, 12 Jan. 1997, Westchester §, at 17.

In modern print sources, the collocation *book indexes* greatly predominates over *book indices*. See PLURALS (B).

Indices (/**in**-də-seez/), though less pretentious than **fora* or **dogmata*, is pretentious nevertheless. Some writers prefer it to *indexes* in technical contexts, as in mathematics and the sciences. Though not the best plural for *index*, *indices* is permissible in the sense "indicators"—e.g.: "Various *indices*, from satellite photos of crops in the Third World, to emergency room reports of overdoses in America's inner cities, make possible rough estimates of the quantities of drugs being produced and reaching America's streets." George F. Will, "Put Blame Where Blame Belongs in War on Drugs," *Chattanooga Times*, 25 Sept. 1996, at A7. Cf. appendixes.

Writers who use the Latinate form, of course, should spell it correctly. Some misspell it with a medial *-e-* on the influence of *index*—e.g.: "Standard & Poor's Equity Services Group plans to add Newport News Shipbuilding to one of its equity *indeces* [read *indices*] after the shipyard is spun off." "S&P to Add Peninsula Yard to Equity Index," *Virginian-Pilot* (Norfolk), 6 Dec. 1996, at D1.

B. And **indice*. The erroneous BACK-FORMATION **indice* (/**in**-də-see/) has been around for a while.

LANGUAGE-CHANGE INDEX (For the full key, see front matter pp. xxxi, l–li.)
Stage 1: Rejected. Stage 2: Widely shunned. Stage 3: Widespread but . . . Stage 4: Ubiquitous but . . . Stage 5: Fully accepted.
Invariably inferior forms marked by asterisk (*). • Ratios represent frequency of prevalent forms vs. variants in current books.

Although the term is noted as the singular form of *indicia* (= indicators) in the *OED*, it is labeled both rare and obsolete; the surviving alternative, *indicium*, is also rare. What has happened is that the Latinate plural of *index*, namely *indices*, has confused people into using **indice* as a singular (instead of *index*). In September 1982, President Ronald Reagan mentioned economic *indices* and then used the singular, three-syllable **indice* where *index* might have been expected. See Alan R. Slotkin, "Media Watch," 58 *Am. Speech* 192 (1983).

Though heard fairly often from television announcers, **indice* is seldom seen in print. But it does appear—e.g.: "Kielholz firmly believes that a younger workforce will be more in tune with the knowledge-worker spirit. However, Kielholz's most important *indice* [read *index* or, perhaps, *criterion*] remains IQ." "Employer Meets Burden of Demonstrating Nondiscriminatory Reason for Termination," *N.Y.L.J.*, 17 May 2001, at 17.

LANGUAGE-CHANGE INDEX
*indice for *index*: Stage 1

Indianan; *Indianian. See **Hoosier.**

indicable. See -ABLE (D) & -ATABLE.

*indicant. See **indicative.**

indicate shouldn't appear where *say, state, show,* or *suggest* will suffice—e.g.:

- "Memos between White House staffers *indicated* [read *said* or *suggested*] that McAuliffe had checked to make sure the call had been made." Leah Garchik, "Happy Birthday, Mr. Fat Cat," *S.F. Chron.*, 6 Mar. 1997, at E10.
- "Homicide Bureau detectives could not be reached to comment Saturday, but law enforcement officials *indicated* [read *said*] that the probe is continuing." Dan Herbeck, "Woman Pressing Police to Step Up Probe of Death of Twin," *Buffalo News*, 23 Nov. 1997, at B5.

indicated, to be. This phrase is common medical JARGON, as in "Further medication is *indicated* [i.e., advisable]." Better for Dr. X to say, "You should continue taking your medicine." Cf. **contraindicate.**

indicative; *indicant; *indicatory; indicial. *Indicative* is the usual adjective corresponding to the noun *indication*. **Indicant* and **indicatory* are NEEDLESS VARIANTS except in archaic medical contexts. *Indicial* is the adjective corresponding to both *indicia* and *index*; it means (1) "of the nature of an indicia; indicative"; or (2) "of the nature or form of an index." See **indicia.**

indices. See **index (A).**

indicia; indicium. *Indicia* (/in-**dish**-ə/ or /in-**dish**-ee-ə/), the plural of *indicium* (= an indication, sign, token), is usually treated as a mass noun forming the plurals *indicia* and **indicias*, the former being preferred: "The 1980s takeover cases identified several *indicia* of due care in a board's deliberation." Harvey L. Pitt, "Ten Commandments for Takeover in the 1990s,"

Corporate Board, Jan. 1992, at 21. The singular *indicium* is, in this sense, obsolescent.

But *indicium* is a live singular in the sense "a graphical element on printed matter that indicates paid postage"—e.g.: "It uses a two-dimensional bar code; the *indicium*, or 'stamp,' includes both machine-readable and human-readable information." Cheryl Currid, "Creating Stamps on Printer Is Another Hassle Made Easy," *Houston Chron.*, 27 Aug. 1999, Tech. §, at 3. See **index (B)** & **indicative.**

indicial. See **indicative.**

indicium. See **indicia.**

indict; indite. Both words are pronounced /in-**dɪt**/. The former means "to charge formally with a crime"; the latter, "to write, compose, dictate." A literary term, *indite* is rarely used today. But it isn't unknown—e.g.:

- "Its principles hold for drafting a policy memorandum to the head of a business firm or for *inditing* a letter to a friend." Gorham Munson, *The Written Word* 9 (rev. ed. 1949).
- "I would take it to one of my dupes who would *indite* a blackmail demand to the young man's father." Donald Thomas, "The Case of the Talking Corpse," in *Sherlock Holmes and the Voice from the Crypt* 223, 318 (2002).
- "Max, who supposedly *indites* these confessions in the year 1930, . . . has survived a number of the young century's crises." John Updike, "Mind/Body Problem," *New Yorker*, 26 Jan. 2004, at 90.

Cf. **extradite.**

indictment usually takes *of*, but *against* has also been fairly common since the 19th century. The prosecutors may have a *case against* a suspect, but the *indictment* can be either *of* or *against* the suspect. In journalism, *against* is quite common—e.g.:

- "The order is the prelude to possible detention and multiple *indictments against* [or *indictments of*] Milosevic." Smita Nordwall, "After Years of Urging, China Ratifies Human Rights Treaty," *USA Today*, 1 Mar. 2001, at A6.
- "In a motion Thursday to dismiss the *indictment against* [or *indictment of*] John Cumbee, Jed Stone argued that his client's case should not be heard again in McHenry County." Dave Barnes, "Cop Seeks Change of Venue for His Retrial," *Chicago Trib.*, 2 Mar. 2001, at 1.
- "Wolf . . . is presiding over the 1995 racketeering *indictment against* [or *indictment of*] Bulger and Flemmi." Shelley Murphy, "Renewed Strain for Bulger Squad," *Boston Globe*, 3 Mar. 2001, at B1.

For more on *indictment*, see **arraignment.**

LANGUAGE-CHANGE INDEX
*indictment against for *indictment of*: Stage 5

indifference; *indifferency. The latter is an ARCHAISM and a NEEDLESS VARIANT.

Current ratio: 336:1

indifferent takes *to*, preferably not *as to*—e.g.:

- "If we're intelligent about how we design and deploy them, we'll be *indifferent as to* [read *indifferent to*] how consumers use them." Rebecca Cantwell, "Business Person of the Year Tele-Visionary," *Rocky Mountain News* (Denver), 20 Dec. 1998, at G1.

- "Brokers will be *indifferent as to* [read *indifferent to*] whether the funds their customers buy are load funds or no-load funds." Patrick McGeehan & David Franecki, "Monthly Mutual Funds Review," *Wall Street J.*, 2 Aug. 1999, at R1.

See **as to.**

indigence; indigency. Since 1700, *indigence* has been the predominant form in general English-language sources—by a significant margin. But in legal sources *indigency* predominates. Although there is no DIFFERENTIATION between the terms other than that contextual one, neither can be declared a NEEDLESS VARIANT.

Current ratio: 9:1

indigenous. In Canada and Australia, *indigenous* (= native to a place) is capitalized when it refers to the land's original inhabitants <the Indigenous tribes> but lowercase when it refers to other things <the indigenous flora>. This practice has not taken root in either the U.S. or the U.K.

indigenous American. See **Native American.**

indigent, n. See FUNCTIONAL SHIFT (C).

indigestion. For the pronunciation, see **digestion.**

INDIRECT QUESTIONS. See QUESTIONS, DIRECT AND INDIRECT.

indiscernible; *indiscernable. The former spelling is standard. See -ABLE (A) & **discernible.**

Current ratio: 71:1

indiscreet; indiscrete. *Indiscreet* = lacking discretion in the sense of prudence, circumspection, and cautious reserve; *indiscrete* = not divided into distinct parts. *Indiscreet* is a common term, *indiscrete* a rare one. And, perhaps not surprisingly, some writers choose the wrong form—e.g.:

- "Mr. Pavelic concluded . . . that Mr. Shapiro may have been set up to look *indiscrete* [read *indiscreet*]." David Margolick, "Uneasy Quiet After Turmoil on the Team for Simpson," *N.Y. Times*, 17 Jan. 1995, at A12.
- "The brouhaha that broke out over an NDP MLA's somewhat *indiscrete* [read *indiscreet*] Facebook photos following the stunning crush of the governing Progressive Conservative party points to a gross trend in politics in the social media age." Tyler Dawson, "Average Albertans Replacing Political Pros," *Edmonton J.*, 11 May 2015, at A15.

See **discrete.**

LANGUAGE-CHANGE INDEX
indiscrete misused for *indiscreet*: Stage 1

indisputable is pronounced either /in-di-**spyoo**-tə-bəl/ or (formerly, and sometimes still in BrE) /in-**dis**-pyoot-ə-bəl/.

indisputably (= unquestionably) is the usual word, not *indisputedly*, which is an odd hybrid between

indisputably and *undisputedly* (= without challenge). E.g.:

- "She is the mother of three sons, which *indisputedly* [read *indisputably*] makes her the only justice to have experienced pregnancy." "All Eyes on Justice O'Connor," *Newsweek*, 1 May 1989, at 34.
- "The third is 'Shadow of a Doubt' (1943), in which [Teresa] Wright starred—'his favorite film,' Dr. [Ruth] Prigozy said, and *indisputedly* [read *indisputably* or *undisputedly*] first-class." Alvin Klein, "Scholarly Regard for a Master of Suspense and the Cinema," *N.Y. Times*, 17 Oct. 1999, § 14, at 15.
- "As the composer of one *indisputedly* [read *indisputably*] great musical ('A Chorus Line') . . . Hamlisch is still reaching for the sustained depth found in the mentors he often cites: Cole Porter, Richard Rodgers, Jerome Kern and so on." Andrew Adler, "Hamlisch Still Seeking the Depth of His Mentors," *Courier-J.* (Louisville), 25 Nov. 2001, at D3.

LANGUAGE-CHANGE INDEX
indisputedly for *indisputably* or *undisputedly*: Stage 1
Current ratio (*indisputably* vs. *indisputedly*): 364:1

indistinguishable; *undistinguishable. The former has been standard since about 1870 in AmE and 1880 in BrE; the latter is a NEEDLESS VARIANT.

Current ratio: 23:1

indite. See **indict.**

individual was formerly thought to be a newfangled barbarism as a noun substituting for *man, woman,* or *person.* Certainly, those more specific terms are generally to be preferred over *individual,* but this word has made a place for itself in contexts in which the writer intends to distinguish the single person from the group or crowd.

Some writers grossly overuse the term for no apparent reason—e.g.:

> Several corollary points flow from this concept of style and its application to political biography. The first is that *an individual's* [read *a person's*] style may conflict with the requirements of his office; it is just such a condition that may lie at the base of political failure. The possibility of such "misfit" between style and role is greatest when *an individual* [read *someone*] comes to a new and demanding office . . . late in life . . . . It is thus crucial to examine the fit between *an individual's* [read *the person's*] style and the requirements of his political roles, and whether those requirements change *as the individual moves through his* [read *during the person's*] career.
>
> Moreover, the use of the concept of style makes it imperative to examine that point in a subject's early life at which his style was first formed and applied successfully . . . . It is at this point that we may find the key to *an individual's* [read *the person's*] later political behavior. This creation of a political style will often be part of an identity crisis in young adulthood; the *individual's* [read *person's*] psychological equilibrium may therefore depend upon the creation and successful application of a particular style. H.N. Hirsch, *The Enigma of Felix Frankfurter* 7 (1981).

LANGUAGE-CHANGE INDEX (For the full key, see front matter pp. xxxi, l–li.)
Stage 1: Rejected. **Stage 2:** Widely shunned. **Stage 3:** Widespread but . . . **Stage 4:** Ubiquitous but . . . **Stage 5:** Fully accepted.
Invariably inferior forms marked by asterisk (*). • Ratios represent frequency of prevalent forms vs. variants in current books.

In the page following that passage, 11 more *individuals* crowd the text. And after reading that page, one is tempted to banish the word altogether. But some writers use the word more responsibly, and they shouldn't have it taken away from them.

Much of the teeth-gnashing this word causes can be blamed on police-blotter JARGON—e.g.: " 'Two people were attacked by several *individuals* [read *other people*] at this *location* [read *place*],' Denver police spokesman Detective John White said in a prepared statement." Jim Kirksey, "Officer Wounds Alleged Attacker," *Denver Post*, 27 Jan. 2003, at B6. (Overprepared, most stylists would agree.)

individualize; individuate. These words, which have basically the same sense ("to make individual in character, to give individuality to"), have undergone DIFFERENTIATION. *Individualize* is the ordinary term—e.g.: "While the strategies for just how to prepay your mortgage can be *individualized* to fit your own cash flow, there are some other general rules to follow." Don Hunt, "Full Speed Ahead," *Chicago Trib.*, 8 Aug. 1997, at 1.

Individuate is often used in scientific contexts and in Jungian psychology in highly technical senses, and it should generally be confined to these uses. E.g.: "Not that the Bob Joneses and Jane Smiths of the world aren't *individuated*, as the Jungians say." Bill Tammeus, "Newt Should Have Known Enough to Be Wary of Guys with Goofy Names," *Milwaukee J. Sentinel*, 3 Aug. 1997, at 6.

indoctrinate is sometimes displaced by **indoctrine*, an obsolete variant that has rarely appeared in Modern English. E.g.:

- "If one generation of parents—that's all it takes, just one— could be *indoctrined* [read *indoctrinated*] with valid child-rearing concepts, those children *will* [read *would*] grow up to pass on those universal truisms to their children." Lendon H. Smith, "Where Have They Been?" *Health News & Rev.*, 22 Sept. 1993, at 7.
- "African American women often are *indoctrined* [read *indoctrinated*] with the belief that there's something wrong, unattractive, about their curvy bodies, broad noses, full lips and kinky hair, the women said." Norma Martin, "Austinites Experience 'Exhale,' " *Austin Am.-Statesman*, 24 Dec. 1995, at E1, E5.

LANGUAGE-CHANGE INDEX
*indoctrine for *indoctrinate*: Stage 1
Current ratio (*indoctrinated* vs.
*indoctrined): 1,405:1

indorse. See **endorse.**

*indow. See **endow.**

induce. See **deduce (B).**

inducement; induction; inductance. *Inducement* ordinarily means "that which induces or persuades." *Induction*, in the context of reasoning, means "the establishment of a general proposition from a number of particular instances." *Inductance* is a technical electrical term.

inducible. So spelled—not **induceable*. Cf. **deducible.**
Current ratio: 4,825:1

inductance. See **inducement.**

induction. See **deduce (B)** & **inducement.**

*indue. See **endue.**

indulge. When the target of the indulgence is a habit, custom, or form of gratification, this verb is usually intransitive: one *indulges in* a given habit. Here, the writer got the idiom wrong: "Employees in a New York City office building have to trek outside to *indulge their habit* [read *indulge in their habit*]." Christopher John Farley, "The Butt Stops Here," *Time*, 18 Apr. 1994, at 59.

But when the target of the indulgence is the person seeking that gratification, the verb is transitive and the person is the verb's direct object—e.g.:

- "*Indulge* your inner Sue Ellen with this Ciner Torsade necklace with freshwater pearls, crystal, onyx and jet beads, $495, at Saks." Jan Tyler & Susan Abrams, "Blast from the Past," *Newsday* (N.Y.), 5 Dec. 2002, Home & Gardens §, at B31.
- "While they *indulge themselves* in adult interaction, their little ones are in nearby rooms being tended to by professional preschool teachers." Kathy Barberich, "Helping Moms, Helping Kids," *Fresno Bee*, 26 Jan. 2003, at H1.

industrious; industrial. *Industrious* corresponds to *industry* in the general sense of a person's work ethic. *Industrial* corresponds to *industry* in the narrow sense of manufacturing goods. *Industrious* typically refers to people <an industrious worker>; *industrial* typically refers to manufacturing activities or productive enterprises <an industrial town>. *Industrial* is pronounced in four distinct syllables: /in-**dəs**-tree-əl/—not /in-**dəs**-trəl/.

-INE. See **-ILE.**

ineffectual; ineffective; inefficacious; inefficient. See **effective.**

INELEGANT VARIATION. H.W. Fowler devised the name "elegant variation" for the ludicrous practice of never using the same word twice in the same sentence or passage. When Fowler named this vice of language in the 1920s, *elegant* was almost a pejorative word, commonly associated with precious overrefinement. Today, however, the word has positive connotations. E.g.: "The book is exceedingly well edited, and several essays are *elegantly* written."

Lest the reader think that the subject of this article is a virtue rather than a vice in writing, it has been renamed unambiguously: *inelegant variation*. The rule of thumb with regard to undue repetition is that one should not repeat a nearby word if it can be felicitously avoided; this is hardly an absolute proscription, however.

Variety for variety's sake in word choice can confuse readers. If you call a car "the BMW" in one place and "the sporty import" in another, can your reader be certain that you're referring to the same car? If you write about a person's "candor" in one sentence and "honesty" in the next, is the reader to infer that you are distinguishing between two traits, or using different words to refer to the same one?

The more formal the writing, the worse fault this lack of clarity can be. It is a maxim in interpreting legal language that if different words are used, different meanings must have been intended. In less formal contexts, variety is more forgivable—but there are always limits.

Perhaps the most famous example is *elongated yellow fruit* as the second reference for *banana*. Hence Charles W. Morton named "the elongated-yellow-fruit school of writing," citing examples such as these:

billiard balls	=	the numbered spheroids
Bluebeard	=	the azure-whiskered wifeslayer
Easter-egg hunt	=	hen-fruit safari
milk	=	lacteal fluid
oysters	=	succulent bivalves
peanut	=	the succulent goober
songbird	=	avian songster
truck	=	rubber-tired mastodon of the highway

Morton, "The Elongated Yellow Fruit," in *A Slight Sense of Outrage* 99, 99–102 (1955). As Morton explains, this sin "lies somewhere between the cliché and the 'fine writing' so dreaded by teachers of English Composition. . . . It does bespeak an author who wishes to seem witty, knowledgeable, and versatile . . . . It can also bespeak an author who is merely pompous." *Ibid.* at 100. Other commentators have been less charitable—e.g.: "The attempt to ring the changes on a word is often positively vicious." Paul M. Fulcher, "These But the Trappings . . . ," in *Foundations of English Style* 189, 204 (Paul M. Fulcher ed., 1927).

There is even a book full of these things, in which a minister is "an old pulpit pounder," a prizefighter is "a braggart of the squared circle," and a vegetarian is "a confirmed spinach-addict." See J.I. Rodale, *The Sophisticated Synonym Book* (1938).

The basic type of variation found objectionable by Fowler is the simple change from the straightforward term to some slightly more fanciful or formal synonym, as here:

- "This is Allen's first *directing* bid since 1989's 'Crimes and Misdemeanors'—he won the *helming trophy* [read *directing trophy* or *best-director Oscar*] for 1977's 'Annie Hall'—and his 11th writing nomination." Kathleen O'Steen, "Hit Happens: 'Gump' Nods at 13," *Daily Variety*, 15 Feb. 1995, at 1.
- "Pakistan's top court has ruled that male doctors may no longer perform *autopsies* on female corpses, saying *postmortems* [read *autopsies*] by the opposite sex show disrespect for the dead." "Autopsies Segregated," *Fresno Bee*, 28 Mar. 1996, at A12.
- "[The price controls] imposed by this budget will cause more distortions, more animosity among patients, hospitals and *doctors* and more thoughts among *physicians*

[read *doctors*] of quitting and joining labor unions." "Medicare Balances the Budget," *Asian Wall Street J.*, 4 Aug. 1997, at 12.

Equally common in modern prose is the switch from one form of a word to another—e.g.:

- "But it's not just those with a *sanguinary* view. Those with a *sanguine*—make that *super-sanguine*—view are eyeing California, too." Don Bauder, "Don Bauder" [series], *San Diego Union-Trib.*, 30 Aug. 1989, at E1. See **sanguine.**
- "During the hoopla about Vice President Dan Quayle's remark about Murphy Brown, his critics reminded him that she is a *fictional* character. Well, Murphy might be *fictitious*, but so am I, according to the same critics." Lisa Hirsh, "Traditional Families Aren't Modern Fiction," *St. Louis Post-Dispatch*, 23 July 1992, at C3. On that use of *fictitious*, see **fictional.**
- "Now just 27, he's a thoughtful and gifted writer, but he's in something of a *collegiate* rut. Or maybe the patience of those of us not in a *collegial* rut has just worn thin." Jeremy Gerard, "Wonderful Time," *Variety*, 15–21 Jan. 1996, at 135. See **collegial.**
- "For delayed coking, this means having to cope with greater quantities of vacuum *residuum* with a higher carbon *residue*." A. Stefani, "Debottleneck Delayed Cokers for Greater Profitability," *Hydrocarbon Processing*, June 1996, at 99. See **residue.**

Certain pairs may lend themselves to this snare: *arbiter* and *arbitrator*, *adjudicative* and **adjudicatory*, *investigative* and *investigatory*, *exigency* and **exigence*. In fact, it sometimes seems that amateurish writers believe that NEEDLESS VARIANTS were made for this specific stylistic purpose.

Sometimes the variation leads to real confusion. For example, in the following headline, the reader must wonder at first whether *victim* and *loved one* refer to the same person: "Victim's Family Can Witness Death of Loved One's Killer," *Austin Am.-Statesman*, 17 Nov. 1995, at A11. The solution there would be to delete *Victim's*.

"The point to be observed," wrote H.W. Fowler, "is that, even if the words meant exactly the same, it would be better to keep the first selected on duty than to change guard" (*FMEU1* at 132).

inept. See **inapt.**

inertia (= resistance to movement, change, or effort) is occasionally confused with a nearly opposite sense, resulting in a MALAPROPISM—e.g.: "Other business incubators evolve from local entrepreneurs, [James] Segedy said, and provide business support to help the businesses gain *inertia* [read *momentum*] needed to survive their first year." Michael Wanbaugh, "Argos Residents Look to the Future," *South Bend Trib.*, 24 Jan. 2003, at A2. Perhaps the confusion is with *impetus* (= incentive; encouragement). See WORD-SWAPPING.

LANGUAGE-CHANGE INDEX
inertia misused for *momentum*: Stage 1

LANGUAGE-CHANGE INDEX (For the full key, see front matter pp. xxxi, l–li.)
Stage 1: Rejected. **Stage 2:** Widely shunned. **Stage 3:** Widespread but . . . **Stage 4:** Ubiquitous but . . . **Stage 5:** Fully accepted.
Invariably inferior forms marked by asterisk (*). • Ratios represent frequency of prevalent forms vs. variants in current books.

inessential. See **nonessential.**

inestimable. See **estimable.**

inevitability; *inevitableness. The latter is a NEEDLESS VARIANT.

Current ratio: 37:1

inevitable. See ADJECTIVES (B).

in excess of is verbose for *more than, exceeding,* or some other word—e.g.: "Within hours a storm with maximum wind velocities *in excess of* [read *exceeding*] a hundred miles an hour swept across southern England and Wales." Thomas Levenson, "At the Speed Limit," *Atlantic Monthly,* Mar. 1990, at 40.

*inexpense is a NONWORD that first appeared (wraith-like) in the late 19th century and has been spotted from time to time since. It's not listed in any major unabridged dictionary, and it doesn't really fill a need in the language—e.g.:

- "The *relative inexpense* [read *relatively low price*] of much of [Kurt] Strobach's work doesn't make him less worthy of recognition than artists and craftsmen who sell their work for much more money." Steve Stanek, "A Cut Above," *Chicago Trib.,* 3 Nov. 1991, Tempo Northwest §, at 1.
- "The *relative inexpense* [read *affordability*] with which a band can record and manufacture a disc has blown open the playing field to anyone with a credit card who has the yen to be a rock star; in turn, there's a plethora of product from bands that aren't, let's say, quite ready for mass consumption." Joan Anderman, "How Do Local CD's Stack Up?" *Boston Globe,* 25 Dec. 1998, at C17.
- "Because of the ease and relative *inexpense* [read *relatively low cost*] of obtaining spices today, we forget how rare, costly and sought-after they were in earlier ages." Andrew Jayasundera, "Spices of Influence," *Seattle Times,* 24 Sept. 2000, at 10.

See BACK-FORMATIONS & NEOLOGISMS.
LANGUAGE-CHANGE INDEX
*inexpense for *affordability*: Stage 1

inexpert, adj.; **nonexpert,** adj. An important distinction exists. *Inexpert* = unskilled <the novice's inexpert shooting caused a real danger to observers>. *Nonexpert* = not of or by an expert, but not necessarily unskilled <even nonexpert drivers can handle this course>. Whereas *inexpert* has been in common use since the 18th century, *nonexpert* did not appear with any frequency till about 1900.

inexplicable (= unexplainable) is accented on the second syllable (/in-**ek**-spli-kə-bəl/) or the third (/in-ek-**splik**-ə-bəl/). Cf. **explicable.**

inexpressible; *inexpressable. The former spelling is standard. See -ABLE (A).

Current ratio: 364:1

inexpressive; *unexpressive. The first is standard; the second is a NEEDLESS VARIANT.

Current ratio: 4:1

infanticide = (1) the killing of a baby; or (2) a parent who kills a baby, or someone who kills a baby esp. with a parent's consent. Sense 2 invariably takes an article <a merciless infanticide>, whereas sense 1 only sometimes takes an article <the infanticide committed by a deranged father> <infanticide committed by a mother with postpartum depression>.

In law, strictly speaking, not every killer of a baby has committed infanticide. The killing of another person's child is simple murder or manslaughter. Infanticide, by definition, must be by or on behalf of a parent. See Glanville Williams, *The Sanctity of Life and the Criminal Law* 13 (1957).

Despite the legal meaning of *infant* (= a person under the age of majority, usu. 18 years old), the word *infanticide* is restricted to baby-killing. A parent who kills a 17-year-old child would not be called an "infanticide" (sense 2). (In England, the Infanticide Act applies to the killing of a child up to one year old.) The slightly broader term *child-slaying,* however, might cover situations in which children who are old enough to walk—and up to the age of 18—are killed. By contrast, the most restrictive term is *neonaticide,* which refers to the killing of a newborn. Among the three terms—*infanticide, child-slaying,* and *neonaticide*—the first two are the most emotive terms because they are widely known, and the third is a clinical, abstract description that many would read or hear without understanding. See -CIDE.

in fault. See **at fault.**

infeasible; *unfeasible. Though once standard, the latter has become a NEEDLESS VARIANT.

Current ratio: 2:1

infect. See **infest (A).**

infectious is sometimes erroneously rendered **infectuous*—e.g.: "A note of caution: *West End Christmas* possesses a humor that's *infectuous* [read *infectious*]." Lynne Cline, "West End Christmas," *Santa Fe New Mexican,* 6 Dec. 1996, Pasatiempo §, at 6. See **contagious.**
LANGUAGE-CHANGE INDEX
infectious misspelled **infectuous*: Stage 1
Current ratio: 6,813:1

infer. A. Meaning. Properly used, *infer* means "to deduce from evidence; to reason from premises to a conclusion"—e.g.:

- "We get no sense of the man himself from this book except what we can *infer* from the biographical facts that Mr. Magida presents." John B. Judis, "Maximum Leader," *N.Y. Times,* 18 Aug. 1996, § 7, at 24.
- "FBI spokesmen have told us that we are not to *infer* that Richard is guilty of anything merely because he is a suspect, among others." Larry Maddry, "FBI Should Charge Jewell or Cut Him Some Slack," *Virginian-Pilot* (Norfolk), 26 Aug. 1996, at E1.
- "Research shows that a daily glass or two of wine is associated with greater longevity than drinking either more or less alcohol. So it's irresistible *to infer* that modest amounts of alcohol cause a person to live longer." "The Art of Being Smart," *Daily Telegraph,* 15 Aug. 2015, at 1.

B. And *imply*. Writers frequently misuse *infer* when *imply* (= to hint at; suggest) would be the correct word—e.g.:

- "So they obliged him, publishing his life story in its March 24th issue, without *inferring* [read *implying*] that he was going to die." Lennie Grimaldi, "Connecticut Q&A: Robert Pelton," *N.Y. Times*, 7 Apr. 1991, Conn. §, at 3.
- "One [response] was a bright and chatty letter that clearly *inferred* [read *implied*] that Grandma had put her message across." June Lejeune, "Thanks or No Thanks," *Sarasota Herald-Trib.*, 12 Feb. 1997, at B4.
- "Pulis said yesterday he would decide whether to select the 22-year-old once he had spoken to him in training. But he *inferred* [read *implied*] Berahino is still too distracted to perform to his best." "Midweek Knocks Hamper Brunt and McManaman," *Birmingham Mail* (U.K.), 29 Aug. 2015, at 34.

Remember: a speaker or writer *implies* something without putting it expressly. A listener or reader *infers* beyond what has been literally expressed. Or, as Theodore Bernstein put it, "The *implier* is the pitcher; the *inferrer* is the catcher." *The Careful Writer* 227 (1965).

Don't be swayed by apologetic notes in some dictionaries that sanction the use of *infer* as a substitute for *imply*. Stylists agree that the important distinction between these words deserves to be maintained.

LANGUAGE-CHANGE INDEX
infer misused for *imply*: Stage 3

inferable; *inferrable; *inferrible. The preferred form *inferable*, pronounced /in-**fər**-ə-bəl/, was standard by the mid-19th century. **Inferrable* is a variant spelling. Through the mid-1950s, some commentators considered **inferrible* the best spelling because of the rule that a consonant should be doubled after a stressed syllable. *Inferable*, which has now ousted the other forms, is anomalous in its spelling. Cf. **deferrable** & **transferable**.

Current ratio (in order of headwords): 20:3:1

inference. Traditionally, one *draws*, not *makes*, inferences. If one says "to make an inference" (like "to make a deduction"), many listeners will confuse *inference* with *implication*. The verb *draw* is therefore clearer. Concededly, however, since the early 1960s the collocation *make inferences* has appeared in print somewhat more frequently than *draw inferences*. Hence the widespread confusion about the precise meaning of *inference*—properly a conclusion arrived at through reasoning, not suggestion. See **infer**.

inferentially. This fancy word often displaces a more common substitute, such as *seemingly* or *we can infer that*. The *OED* states that *inferentially* means "in an inferential manner," but allows that it is used "sometimes qualifying the whole clause or statement [and meaning] as an inference, as may be inferred." This use is common especially in writing about technical

and legal subjects—e.g.: "In 1926, the Supreme Court *inferentially* [read, perhaps, *seemingly*] decided, in Myers v. U.S., that President Johnson was right in principle on this issue." Martin D. Tullai, "A Senator Saved the Presidency," *Plain Dealer* (Cleveland), 29 Mar. 1994, at B7. See SENTENCE ADVERBS. Cf. **hopefully** & **thankfully**.

In AmE, *inferentially* was once almost exclusively a lawyers' word, but it's passing into general use—e.g.: "Clinton, on CBS, *inferentially* conceded that Congress might not approve either element." "Oh Noooo!" *Time*, 14 Mar. 1994, at 35.

inferior takes *to*, not *than* (which requires a grammatical comparative, not a notional one)—e.g.: "Neither Drew nor Ryan offered the same offensive potential as Refsnyder, whose glove is considered to be far *inferior than* [read *inferior to*] his counterparts [read *those of his counterparts* or *his counterparts' gloves*]." Alex Schiffer, "Beltran Gets Right Back to Work with Bat," *Star-Ledger* (Newark), 21 July 2015, at 28.

Current ratio: 355:1

*inferrable; *inferrible. See **inferable**.

infest. A. And *infect*. *Infest* (= to inhabit either as a parasite or in menacingly large numbers) is sometimes confounded with *infect* (= [of a germ or virus] to introduce a disease into an organism). In general, living things are *infected*; places are *infested*. And while an infestation may result in disease, the cause of the disease will be infection. Some writers miss that distinction, typically with *infest* displacing *infect*—e.g.:

- "I'm thinking, is our opposition to the archbishop's point of view a classic case of Seattle overhang? That's the disease that rapidly *infests* [read *infects*] editorial offices and gives us in these towers the eyesight to see things only from under Seattle's roof." James Vesely, "Classic Seattle Overhang and the Cross We Carry," *Seattle Times*, 19 Mar. 2001, at B4.
- "Once the germs *infest* [read *infect*] wildlife populations, the wild animals can just as easily spread it to other domestic herds through the same mechanisms." Editorial, *Denver Post*, 1 May 2001, at B8.
- "Citrus canker is a bacterial disease that *infests* [read *infects*] the leaves of trees and causes lesions on the fruit." Bill Rufty, "Officials Iron Out Canker Plan," *Ledger* (Lakeland, Fla.), 12 Mar. 2002, at E1.

The opposite error, in which *infect* ousts the proper word *infest*, is rare but not entirely exterminated—e.g.: "There were no demons in his past, but night after night demons would *infect* [read *infest*] his dreams to the point that he was beginning to question his sanity." A.S. Mott, "In His Head," in *Fireside Ghost Stories* 9, 9 (2003).

LANGUAGE-CHANGE INDEX
1. *infest* misused for *infect*: Stage 1
2. *infect* misused for *infest*: Stage 1

LANGUAGE-CHANGE INDEX (For the full key, see front matter pp. xxxi, l–li.)
Stage 1: Rejected. **Stage 2:** Widely shunned. **Stage 3:** Widespread but . . . **Stage 4:** Ubiquitous but . . . **Stage 5:** Fully accepted.
Invariably inferior forms marked by asterisk (*). • Ratios represent frequency of prevalent forms vs. variants in current books.

B. And *invest*. *Infest* is sometimes, in a gross MALA-PROPISM, confused with *invest*—e.g.:

- "Cited: Harvest from about 1,470 Boise National Forest acres in Logging Creek and French Creek drainages will thin stands of *insect-invested* [read *insect-infested*] trees." "Idaho," *USA Today*, 17 Dec. 1991, at A10.
- "The resulting *crime-invested* [read *crime-infested*] tenement becomes uninviting to would-be renters." Willard Woods, "Landlords See Basketball Camp for Kids as Way to Cut Apartment Problems," *Star Trib.* (Minneapolis), 3 July 1993, at H22.
- "Channel 39 will dip its toe into the *shark-invested* [read *shark-infested*] waters known as late-night talk beginning in the fall of 1995." Mike McDaniel, " 'Juvenile Justice' Series Picked Up by 40 Stations," *Houston Chron.*, 17 Dec. 1994, Houston §, at 5.

LANGUAGE-CHANGE INDEX
invest misused for *infest*: Stage 1

infinite (= unimaginably large in degree or amount) doesn't work well with qualifiers in phrases such as **almost infinite* or **nearly infinite*, which are examples of ILLOGIC—e.g.:

- "There have been *an almost infinite number of* [read *countless*] studies." Earl W. Buxton, *Looking at Language* v (M.H. Scargill & P.G. Penner eds., 1969).
- "The world that asks for the maximum information in the minimum time creates a problem of *nearly infinite* [read *infinite* or *seemingly infinite*] possibilities." Sara S. Kennedy, "American Society's Fast Track to Oblivion," *Hartford Courant*, 26 Nov. 2000, at G3.
- "Picasso's also has quite an extensive pizza menu, featuring pies that can be topped in *almost infinite* [read *many*] combinations." Angela Shah, "Grill Makes a Palette of Italian Favorites," *Dallas Morning News*, 23 Jan. 2003, Garland §, at S9.

The word is also often a sign of hyperbole, as those examples show. See ADJECTIVES (B).

LANGUAGE-CHANGE INDEX
*almost infinite for *countless*: Stage 1

infinitely. A. And *eminently*. *Infinitely* (= endlessly, limitlessly) for *eminently* (= to a high degree) is either gross OVERSTATEMENT or a MALAPROPISM. It's a surprising error even in our hyperbole-ridden culture—e.g.:

- "The voice is quite pleasant, really. Low, well-modulated and *infinitely* [read *eminently*] reasonable, it is the voice of a good person." Karla Peterson, "Sandra Bernhard: Shocking Ms. B. Has Her Warm and Comfy Side," *San Diego Union-Trib.*, 23 June 1994, Entertainment §, at 11.
- "Riggins used to train bird dogs in his spare time. Some observers might suggest that experience makes him *infinitely* [read *eminently*] qualified to instruct the Cardinals' 1994 staff." Dan O'Neill, "Credentials of Riggins Rate Triple A All the Way," *St. Louis Post-Dispatch*, 26 Oct. 1994, at D5.
- "But for readers desiring a richly poetic treatment of [Robert] Frost in all his splendid contrariety—kindly/surly, selfish/magnanimous, caring/distant, childish/*infinitely* [read *eminently*] wise—this is a book to savor." Marjorie Kehe, "When Robert Frost Met Khrushchev,"

Christian Science Monitor, 8 Apr. 2008, Book §, at 13.

LANGUAGE-CHANGE INDEX
infinitely misused for *eminently*: Stage 1
Current ratio (*eminently successful* vs.
*infinitely successful): 488:1

B. And Comparatives. When *infinitely* modifies a comparative adjective or adverb, the result is almost always either illogical or at least hyperbole—e.g.:

- "Barron, a game-fowl breeder who has about 200 roosters, said the average gamecock lives a lot longer than the average broiler chicken and agrees with Rubio that their game birds are *infinitely* [read *far*] better cared for." Stella Davis, "Fighting Fowl," *Santa Fe New Mexican*, 30 Nov. 2002, at B1.
- "The source of that speed comes in a very different package, and gaining horsepower requires a lot less grease and *infinitely* [read *much*] more RAM." Michael Yount, "Imported Speed," *Salt Lake Trib.*, 1 Dec. 2002, at S1.
- "Self-acceptance is *infinitely* [read *far* or *so much*] sexier and more appealing than the relentless racing after eternal youth." Joy Rothke, "50 May Not Be So Fabulous, but at Least She's Still Here," *Chicago Trib.*, 4 Dec. 2002, Woman News §, at 6.

See ADJECTIVES (B).

Occasionally, though, the usage is justified when the thing designated could truly be infinite—e.g.: "[Ornette] Coleman opened the door to improvisation based on melodic and rhythmic lines. It was a door that opened *infinitely* more doors." Dean Kuipers, "Break the Music Mold," *L.A. Times*, 5 Dec. 2002, Calendar Weekend §, pt. 5, at 2. Here, the number of variations in an improvisational performance really is infinite.

LANGUAGE-CHANGE INDEX
infinitely used with a comparative: Stage 1

infinitive. See BE-VERBS & SPLIT INFINITIVES.

infinity; **infinitude*. The latter term, though dating from the 17th century, remains little more than what H.W. Fowler labeled it in 1926: a NEEDLESS VARIANT of *infinity*. It occurs where *infinity* would surely be the better word—e.g.: "Electron microscopes have revealed the nearly incomprehensible complexity and *infinitude* [read *infinity*] of the subvisible world." Charles Siebert, "Quantum Leaps," *N.Y. Times*, 29 Sept. 1996, § 6, at 137. The word appears often in theological contexts, perhaps seeming to lend some concreteness to the idea being discussed—e.g.: "In prayer we find that the trustworthy place wherein to feel at home is the *infinitude* of God, divine Love." "A Home of Your Own," *Christian Science Monitor*, 28 June 1996, at 17.

LANGUAGE-CHANGE INDEX
*infinitude for *infinity*: Stage 2
Current ratio (*infinity of* vs. **infinitude of*): 5:1

inflame; **enflame*. The first is standard; the second is a NEEDLESS VARIANT.

Current ratio: 18:1

inflammable. See **flammable** & **inflammatory**.

inflammatory; inflammable. Surprisingly, *inflammable* (= combustible) is occasionally misused for *inflammatory* (= provocative of an angry or violent reaction). While both words are synonymous with *incendiary*, *inflammable* is always literal <the arsonist used an inflammable liquid to spread the fire>, *inflammatory* always figurative <the inflammatory rhetoric almost caused a riot>. It's a well-known distinction, but writers occasionally take a wrong turn halfway through spelling *inflammatory*—e.g.:

- "Newman's a veteran; he knows better than to incite the opposition with such *inflammable* [read *inflammatory*] bulletin-board material." Mike Penner, "1987 Revisited? Braves Say No," *L.A. Times*, 25 Oct. 1991, at C1.
- "Why is it so hard to understand that the social fabric of our society can be tragically destroyed by the *inflammable* [read *inflammatory*] words of the dividers and haters among us?" Letter of Charles L. Deremer, *Morning Call* (Allentown, Pa.), 1 May 1995, at A8.
- "Her opponents this time were the *inflammable* [read *inflammatory*] words of her father, who accused a player and the tennis world of racism, and a persistent pack of reporters." Shaun Powell, "U.S. Open: All Eyes Focused on Venus," *Newsday* (N.Y.), 8 Sept. 1997, at A54.

This confusion provides yet one more reason why *flammable* is to be encouraged over *inflammable*, which should be ignited and consumed. See **flammable.**

LANGUAGE-CHANGE INDEX
inflammable misused for *inflammatory*: Stage 1

*inflatus. See **afflatus.**

inflict; afflict. *Inflict* takes *on*; *afflict* takes *with*. Nonliving objects, especially scourges or punishments, are *inflicted on* people; living things, especially humans, are *afflicted with* diseases.

But misusing *inflict* for *afflict* is increasingly common—e.g.:

- "While other urban superintendents were trying to hide the depths of the problems *inflicting* [read *afflicting*] their school systems, Alice Pinderhughes, who passed away last Thursday at age 74, was at least honest." "Alice Pinderhughes," *Baltimore Sun*, 20 Nov. 1995, at A10.
- "This lack of freedom of speech is what people in Russia and many other countries have dealt with in the past, and are *inflicted* [read *afflicted*] with now." Susan DeBow, "Society Stifles Freedom of Speech," *Cincinnati Post*, 3 July 2000, at A19.
- "The speakers . . . dismissed concerns . . . that some oak trees are *inflicted* [read *afflicted*] with Sudden Oak Death disease." Maria Brosnan Liebel, "Quick Action Ordered on Lafferty," *Press Democrat* (Santa Rosa), 14 Nov. 2000, at B1.

See OBJECT-SHUFFLING.

The reverse error is also surprisingly frequent—e.g.:

- "The whole reason for reaching this settlement was to make Big Tobacco financially accountable for the health costs its addictive product has *afflicted* [read *inflicted*] on

the nation." Editorial, "Tobacco Plan Worth the Wait," *Morning Call* (Allentown, Pa.), 22 June 2001, at A14.
- "Although the nation has . . . been spared from another Sept. 11, a repeat of the kind of horror *afflicted* [read *inflicted*] on New York City, the Pentagon and airliners on that day is not out of the question." Editorial, "Addressing Aftermath of an Attack," *Daily Herald* (Chicago), 16 Feb. 2002, News §, at 10.
- "Some of the myriad hassles *afflicted* [read *inflicted*] on air travelers come from federal security mandates, among them the much-hated random searches." Editorial, "Get Some Hassles Out of Air Travel," *Herald-Sun* (Durham, N.C.), 22 Oct. 2002, at A10.

LANGUAGE-CHANGE INDEX
1. *inflict* misused for *afflict*: Stage 1
Current ratio (*afflicted with* vs. *inflicted with): 15:1
2. *afflict* misused for *inflict*: Stage 1
Current ratio (*inflicted on* vs. *afflicted on): 177:1

influence. The first syllable receives the primary accent (/**in**-floo-ənts/), not the second (/in-**floo**-ənts/). That's so whether it's used as a noun or as a verb. See PRONUNCIATION (B).

influence-peddlers. This term should refer to the politicians who sell their influence, not to the people who try to buy it. Yet many politicians get it backwards—e.g.: "He [Patrick J. Buchanan] even updated his stump graphics with a giant mock check at his side made out for hundreds of millions of dollars to the major parties and signed *Influence Peddlers* [read, perhaps, *Special Interests*]." Francis X. Clines, "Buchanan Wraps Himself in McCain's Flag of Reform," *N.Y. Times*, 17 Mar. 2000, at A17.

The distinction is hardly a fine line, though. Officeholders and government officials often avail themselves of the "revolving door" option to make more money as private-sector lobbyists. But they still retain some influence through friendships and political connections and could be seen as peddling that advantage.

*inforce. See **enforce (A).**

informant; informer. Both terms are used in reference to those who confidentially supply police with information about crimes. *Informant* is now more than four times as common in AmE and BrE alike. The Evanses wrote that *informant* is neutral, whereas *informer*, which acquired strong connotations of detestation in the 17th and 18th centuries, remains a connotatively charged term (*DCAU* at 245). Although that statement doesn't hold true for legal writing, it does in most other contexts. See INELEGANT VARIATION.

informative; informatory. The latter is a NEEDLESS VARIANT, except in bridge (the card game).
Current ratio: 378:1

informer. See **informant.**

LANGUAGE-CHANGE INDEX (For the full key, see front matter pp. xxxi, l–li.)
Stage 1: Rejected. **Stage 2:** Widely shunned. **Stage 3:** Widespread but . . . **Stage 4:** Ubiquitous but . . . **Stage 5:** Fully accepted.
Invariably inferior forms marked by asterisk (*). • Ratios represent frequency of prevalent forms vs. variants in current books.

infrequent; *unfrequent. The latter, predominant till about 1880, is now a NEEDLESS VARIANT.

Current ratio: 25:1

infringe. See **impinge.**

infusable; infusible. These two words—found primarily in medical and other technical fields—are sometimes confused. *Infusable* = capable of being infused. *Infusible* = not capable of being fused. The latter appears much more frequently in print.

in future. This phrase is BrE, perhaps through direct translation of the Latin phrase *in futuro* or perhaps because of the BrE pattern of usage without the definite article <she's in hospital>. AmE uses the definite article: *in the future.* So does BrE occasionally. For the phrase *in the near future,* see **future.**

-ING. See DIMINUTIVES (H).

ingenious; ingenuous. These words are virtual antonyms, yet *ingenious* (= clever, skillful, inventive) is sometimes displaced by *ingenuous* (= artless, simple, innocent)—e.g.:

- "They're no different from Kenneth Lay or Jeffrey Skilling at Enron, who either claimed ignorance of the crimes that were going on around them or found *ingenuous* [read *ingenious*] ways to cover them up." Sheryl McCarthy, "Church Needs to Do Some Serious Spring Cleaning," *Newsday* (N.Y.), 15 Apr. 2002, at A26.
- "Clocking in at about three hours (the original play ran six), it is a handsome venture, equipped with an *ingenuous* [read *ingenious*] set of modular walls by Andrew Jackness, sensitive lighting by Jennifer Tipton and sinister gongs-and-crickets music by John Gromada." Misha Berson, "Despite Fine Efforts, O'Neill's 'Electra' Showing Its Age," *Seattle Times,* 29 Apr. 2002, at E2.

Ingenuous is also misused for its other opposite, *disingenuous* (= tricky; feigning ignorance in order to deceive)—e.g.:

- "With all due respect, isn't it a bit *ingenuous* [read *disingenuous*] to say that we haven't made the decision whether or not to go to war yet, because absent our going in there and kicking him out to get the regime change, we don't expect him to step aside." Charlie Gibson, interviewing Secretary of Defense Donald Rumsfeld on ABC's *Good Morning America,* 9 Sept. 2002.
- "Obfuscating and *ingenuous* [read *disingenuous*] comments are often made by guests of all political and social persuasions, including Islamic spokespersons appearing on his show. He is indeed a 'no-spin doctor' when he forthrightly cuts through the sand-in-your-eyes kind of bull appearing in Omar's opinion piece." Kenneth Yerington, "Hate Is Not as Rampant as Writer Claims It Is," *Iowa City Press-Citizen,* 3 Nov. 2002, at A9.

LANGUAGE-CHANGE INDEX
1. *ingenuous* misused for *ingenious:* Stage 1
2. *ingenuous* misused for *disingenuous:* Stage 1

ingenuity once corresponded to *ingenuous,* and *ingeniosity (last used with any validity in 1608) to *ingenious.* Through a curious historical reversal of the role of *ingenuity,* it came to mean "ingeniousness."

Ingenuousness was the only term left to do the work of the noun corresponding to the adjective *ingenuous.* So although *ingenuity* appears to be the correlative of *ingenuous,* it no longer is.

LANGUAGE-CHANGE INDEX
ingenuity as the noun corresponding to
ingenious: Stage 5

ingenuous. See **ingenious.**

ingraft. See **engraft.**

ingratiate (= to bring [oneself] into favor [with]) should always be reflexive in modern usage <they ingratiated themselves to the company>. Nonreflexive uses are unidiomatic—e.g.:

- "Rep. Phil English['s] . . . conservative voting record and responsiveness to the large, integrated steel mills has *ingratiated him with* [read *endeared him to*] steel lobbyists." Nancy E. Kelly, "Labor Has Its Day in Democratic Politics," *Am. Metal Market,* 30 Aug. 1996, at 1.
- "And even if you present a memo listing every inaccurate event she's related, she may be so *ingratiated with* [read *close to*] the boss that a report will have little effect." Lindsey Novak, "Bad Sign: Boss' Editing Changes Put Employee in a Bind," *Chicago Trib.,* 26 Jan. 1997, at C1.

LANGUAGE-CHANGE INDEX
ingratiate used nonreflexively: Stage 1

ingress; egress. The correct prepositions are illustrated by this sentence: "The company breached its duty to furnish Collins with a safe means of *ingress to* and *egress from* the vessel."

-ING WORDS. See GERUNDS, FUSED PARTICIPLES & DANGLERS (B), (D).

*inhabitability. See **habitability.**

inhere. **A. Preposition with.** *Inhere* takes the preposition *in*—not *within.* E.g.: "Of course that fusion *inheres within* [read *inheres in*] Judaism." Alisa Solomon, "What's God Got to Do with It?" *Village Voice,* 18 Apr. 1995, at 33.

Current ratio (*inhere in* vs. *inhere within): 29:1

B. For *inure*. Whereas *inhere* means "to exist as a basic quality in" <a conscience inheres in every well-adjusted child>, *inure* means either "to become accustomed" <inured to the honking horns> or, at law, "to take effect to (someone's) advantage" <inured to the heir's benefit>. Using *inhere* in place of *inure* is a stunning MALAPROPISM—e.g.: "Plaintiff alleges that such strategy *inhered* [read *inured*] to the financial benefit of defendant Carter when Carter subsequently sold the mortgage loans to other financial institutions." Steven P. Bann, "Case Digests: Banks—Mortgages," *N.J.L.J.,* 19 Dec. 1994, at 60. See **inure.**

LANGUAGE-CHANGE INDEX
inhere misused for *inure:* Stage 1

inherent (/in-**heer**-ənt/ or /in-**hair**-ənt/) takes the preposition *in*—e.g.: "They say the extreme risks now *inherent in* Mexican investments may not be fully reflected in the securities' prices." Tom Petruno, "To Vultures, Mexico a Different Animal," *L.A. Times*, 22 Feb. 1995, at D1. Some writers mistakenly use *to*.

inheritable. See **heritable.**

inhibitory; *inhibitive. The latter is a NEEDLESS VARIANT.

Current ratio: 68:1

inhospitable (= [1] (of a place) difficult to live or stay in because of adverse conditions, or [2] (of a person) not welcoming visitors in a friendly way) is traditionally pronounced /in-**hos**-pi-tə-bəl/—though today /in-hah-**spit**-ə-bəl/ is probably more frequent throughout the English-speaking world. Cf. **hospitable.**

inimical (/i-**nim**-i-kəl/) means "hostile, injurious, adverse." It often appears where *adverse* otherwise might <a position inimical to the best interests of the university>. **Inimicable* (a NONWORD) for *inimical* is a fairly common error. The *OED* records **inimicable* as a "rare" adjective, but it should be extinct—e.g.:

- "An international treaty that imposes new concepts of guaranteed rights and benefits is *inimicable* [read *inimical*] to a sovereign nation and a free society." Edwin Meese III & Andrew J. Cowin, "Domestic Policy Courtesy of the U.N.," *San Diego Union-Trib.*, 19 Nov. 1993, at B7.
- "Luke's Jedi powers, Leia's level-headed leadership and Han Solo's seat-of-the-pants swashbuckling are all put to the test by an alien society that is *inimicable* [read *inimical*] to humans and truly menacing." Andrew Smith, "Sci-Fi Novels Excel, Repel in Spinoff Mode," *Commercial Appeal* (Memphis), 18 May 1997, at G2.
- "These issues have taken on totemic significance in the mainstream in the broadside against both multiculturalism in general and non-European immigration in particular as though they were *inimicable with* [read *inimical to*] the principles of social equality." Gary Younge, "Comment: Gay Equality Can't Yet Be Claimed a Western Value, but It Is a Human Right," *Guardian*, 7 June 2010, at 27.

Cf. *unequivocable* (discussed under **unequivocal**).

LANGUAGE-CHANGE INDEX
**inimicable* for *inimical*: Stage 1
Current ratio (*inimical* vs. **inimicable*): 244:1

initial, vb., makes *initialed* and *initialing* in AmE, *initialled* and *initialling* in BrE. See SPELLING (B).

INITIALESE. See ABBREVIATIONS (C).

INITIALISMS. See ABBREVIATIONS.

initiate—a FORMAL WORD for *begin*, *open*, or *introduce*—is appropriate when referring to taking the first step in an important matter. Although you may *begin* an interview, *begin* a conversation, or *begin* a lecture, you *initiate* a series of high-level negotiations. But it is ludicrous to say that you *initiate* an ordinary telephone call. Cf. **inaugurate.**

injunction. See **enjoinder.**

injunctive; *injunctional; *injunctory. *Injunctive* is the standard term. The others are NEEDLESS VARIANTS.

Current ratio: 2,092:2:1

in lieu of. A. Generally. The phrase *in lieu of* (= in place of) is now English, and *instead of* will not always suffice in its stead—e.g.: "The two were arraigned before a town of Montezuma justice and sent to the Cayuga County Jail *in lieu of* $100,000 bond or $50,000 cash bail." Jeff Stage, "Troopers Find 43 Pounds of Marijuana in Car," *Syracuse Herald-J.*, 8 Aug. 1997, at B1. But *instead* is usually better whenever it naturally fits—e.g.: "The stations originated in Europe as rest stops for travelers walking long distances or for those making pilgrimages to local cathedrals *in lieu of* [read *instead of*] going to the Holy Land." "Walking in Jesus' Steps," *Patriot Ledger* (Quincy, Mass.), 22 Mar. 1997, at 44.

B. For *in view of* or *in light of*. The day after President Clinton announced his healthcare plan in the fall of 1993, a radio host, broadcasting from the White House lawn, said to his listeners: "This morning we're going to discuss what state health care means *in lieu of* the President's new federal plan." This mistake—which is spreading—results from a confusion of *in lieu of* with *in view of* or *in light of*, either of which would have sufficed in that sentence. As it is, *in lieu of* is a MALAPROPISM when used for either of the other phrases.

LANGUAGE-CHANGE INDEX
in lieu of in the sense "in view of": Stage 1

in like Flynn. This phrase, meaning "assured of success," first became widespread during World War II as an allusion to the actor Errol Flynn's legendary prowess in seducing women. (In 1942, Flynn was prosecuted for the statutory rape of two teenage girls—and was acquitted.) Today the phrase has generally lost any sexual connotation—e.g.:

- "By these standards, Gore should be *in like Flynn*." Kevin Phillips, "The Bush Restoration," *Memphis Commercial Appeal*, 13 Feb. 2000, at B3.
- "Based on the results of our Triangle Census, you'll be *in like Flynn*." Joe Miller, "Road Rage, Grits and Biscuits," *News & Observer* (Raleigh), 27 Mar. 2000, at E1.
- "Follow the formula, and you're *in like Flynn*." Kerry Capell, "Tiny Telecom, Terrific Results," *BusinessWeek*, 7 Aug. 2000, at 26.

The phrase has been the subject of wordplay and consequent confusion. In 1966 appeared *Our Man Flint*, a film starring James Coburn and spoofing the James Bond series; the following year, its sequel, *In Like Flint*, was released. The popularity of these films—especially the latter with its pun on *in like Flynn*—sparked lingering confusion about what the proper phrase should be. So, for example, during

LANGUAGE-CHANGE INDEX (For the full key, see front matter pp. xxxi, l–li.)
Stage 1: Rejected. **Stage 2:** Widely shunned. **Stage 3:** Widespread but . . . **Stage 4:** Ubiquitous but . . . **Stage 5:** Fully accepted.
Invariably inferior forms marked by asterisk (*). • Ratios represent frequency of prevalent forms vs. variants in current books.

coverage of the 2000 Republican Convention, Mark Shields, a PBS commentator, said that George W. Bush might be "in like Flynn, or in like Flint—whatever we say" (PBS Convention Coverage, 3 Aug. 2000). This confusion had already surfaced in print—e.g.:

- "Yep, with my peacoat, I was in like *Flint* [read *Flynn*], I thought, able to hubbub with the highbrows or hang with the homeboys." Liz McGehee, "Nice in the Offseason" (pt. 2), *News & Observer* (Raleigh), 11 Jan. 1998, at H1 (in this example, *hubbub* should probably be *hobnob*).
- "If you want to be 'in like *Flint* [read *Flynn*],' there has to be a measure of exclusivity." Larry Lipson, "Westside Supper Club Very Inviting, Once You Find It," *Daily News* (L.A.), 27 Aug. 1999, at L55.
- "Finder praises Gawande as a quick learner. If he failed to incorporate advice initially, says Finder, 'the second time he was in like *Flint* [read *Flynn*].'" Vanessa E. Jones, "Reporter from the OR," *Boston Globe*, 10 Nov. 1999, at F1.

Although **in like Flint* occasionally appears in tongue-in-cheek references to Flint, Michigan, and to flint as stone, it shouldn't appear in sentences such as those just quoted. Errol Flynn is reported to have resented the phrase, but it will always be linked etymologically to him. See James Ross Moore, "Errol Flynn," 8 *Am. Nat'l Biography* 155, 156 (1999).

LANGUAGE-CHANGE INDEX
*in like Flint for *in like Flynn*: Stage 2
Current ratio (*in like Flynn* vs. **in like Flint*): 9:1

in line, stand. See **stand in line.**

inmate. Strictly speaking, anyone who shares a dwelling with others, whether involuntarily or not, is an *inmate* of that dwelling. The usual reference is to a prisoner or to a patient in an asylum, other uses of the term having become archaic. Even when used in contexts not involving institutionalization, the word still usually carries unpleasant connotations—e.g.: "The houses are large, drafty places where fires are slow to draw, meals are protracted, and the *inmates* often feel physically uncomfortable." Lesley Chamberlain, "Torments of Pretense," *L.A. Times*, 10 June 2001, at 14.

in memoriam is sometimes misspelled **in memorium*—e.g.: "Alfred Lord Tennyson reputedly staged the first reading of 'In *Memorium* [read *Memoriam*]' to a group of Irish nuns in the Asgard room." George Kimball, "Golfers Are Discovering the 'Garden of Ireland,'" *Boston Herald*, 17 Mar. 1996, Travel §, at 7-1. Unfortunately, one unsure about the spelling may have difficulty looking it up in a dictionary. That's because *memoriam* exists in English only in this phrase, which is alphabetized under *I* rather than *M*.

LANGUAGE-CHANGE INDEX
in memoriam misspelled **in memorium*: Stage 1
Current ratio: 40:1

inmost. See **innermost.**

innately is sometimes misused for *inherently*. What is *innate* is inborn—the term should be confined

to living things. But *inherent* (= essential, intrinsic) applies best (but not exclusively) to nonliving things such as objects or ideas. The error of misusing *innate* for *inherent* is becoming widespread—e.g.:

- "Natural disasters are not *innately funny* [read *funny in themselves*], but they can produce humor." Mike Harden, "What Makes Good Comedy?" *Star Trib.* (Minneapolis), 28 July 1994, at E4.
- "Why the idea of Belgium should be so *innately* [read *inherently*] funny is a bit of a mystery." A.A. Gill, "Descending into Bad Habits," *Sunday Times* (London), 18 June 1995, Style §, at 29.
- "The hushed natural setting fits a genre that's *innately* [read *inherently*] human-scale—much more so than, say, full-blown orchestral music." Amy Biancolli, "Ticklish Situation," *Times Union* (Albany), 27 Aug. 2015, at V14.

LANGUAGE-CHANGE INDEX
innately misused for *inherently*: Stage 1

*innavigable. See **unnavigable.**

innermost; inmost. Both mean "farthest inward" or "most intimate." If any substantive difference exists, it's that *innermost* is more emphatic about being deep inside <innermost thoughts>. In any event, *innermost* is far more common than *inmost*, which has become a purely literary word.

innervate. See **enervate.**

innocence; *innocency. The latter is an obsolete variant.

Current ratio: 80:1

innocent. See **not guilty (A).**

innovate. So spelled. See SPELLING (A).

innovative; *innovational. The latter is a NEEDLESS VARIANT.

Current ratio: 635:1

innuendo. Pl. *innuendoes*—not **innuendos*. See PLURALS (D).

Current ratio: 1.2:1

innumerable. See **enumerable.**

*innundate. See **inundate.**

inoculation. So spelled. This word is often misspelled **innoculation* or **inocculation*. See SPELLING (A).
Current ratio (*inoculation* vs. **innoculation* vs. **inocculation*): 1,759:12:1

*inopposite. See **inapposite.**

in order to; in order for; in order that. The phrase *in order to* is often wordy for the simple infinitive—e.g.: "*In order to* [read *To*] control class sizes, the district will also place seven portable classrooms at the four schools." David Woolsey, "Meridian Board Caps 4 Schools' Enrollment," *Idaho Statesman*, 28 Feb. 1995, at B1. The primary exception occurs when another infinitive is nearby in the sentence—e.g.: "The controversy illustrates how the forces of political correctness pressure government *to grow* in size and arbitrariness *in order to pursue* a peculiar compassion mission." George F. Will, "Fresh Dispatches from the Frontlines of Indignation," *Baltimore Sun*, 9 Mar. 1995, at A19.

In order for, which is followed by a clause, is often wordy for *for*—e.g.: "*In order for* [read *For*] the RCE scheme to be reliable, both detectors must get exactly the same amount of illumination." Gail Robinson, *Electronic Eng'g Times*, 10 Mar. 1997, at 37.

Finally, *in order that*, which often needs no reduction, begins a subordinate clause expressing purpose. It is usually followed by *may* or *might*—e.g.:

- "They are glad that the big guy closed down the shop for three days this week *in order that* the lads *might* grab some holiday cheer." Steve Buckley, "Tuna Talk Drills in Fun," *Boston Herald*, 28 Dec. 1996, Sports §, at 43. (Here, *so* would be an improvement over *in order*.)
- "*In order that* the child reader *may* emulate the generous whale, the first three books in the series . . . all come with a peel-off sticker on the back cover." Valerie Cruice, "Heartening Lessons of Winslow Whale," *N.Y. Times*, 16 Feb. 1997, Conn. §, at 10.
- "Sacrificing jobs *in order that* some *might* enjoy higher pay may soon start to feel much less clever a policy." Allister Heath, "Fasten Your Seatbelts—There's a Little Economic Turbulence Ahead," *Daily Telegraph*, 13 Aug. 2015, at 16.

*inorganic food. See **organic.**

in other words. The following readerly sentiment is fairly commonplace: " 'In other words' is likely to prompt the question, 'Why not have used the right words the first time?' To be sure, a subtle or complicated thought may need to be clarified by a careful restatement. But too often, repetition is merely a habit—almost a reflex—inviting inattention or boredom from the reader or hearer." Ellsworth Barnard, *English for Everybody* 107 (1979). In other words, writers should take heed.

in part. See **in whole.**

*inplane. See AIRLINESE.

in point of fact. See **fact (D).**

in prison. This idiom does not ordinarily take an indefinite article: *he is in prison*, not **he is in a prison*. But if an adjective modifies *prison* and the term therefore becomes more concrete, the article should be inserted—e.g.: "Mr. Bararella, now *in* [read *in a*] high-security prison, wears [his wife's] wedding band [on a chain] around his neck, traditionally a sign of mourning." Celestine Bohlen, "As Omerta Crumbles, the Mafia Changes the Rules," *N.Y. Times*, 11 Oct. 1995, at A3.

input, n. & v.t. This jargonmonger's word—dating from the 18th century as a noun and from the mid-1940s as a verb—is one that careful writers tend to avoid.

Although the word can almost always be improved on, it can fairly be described as ubiquitous—e.g.:

- "They want to help devise the budget and have more *input* [read *say*] in whether deans and vice presidents receive tenure." Judy H. Longshaw, "Winthrop Faculty Wants More Involvement," *Herald* (Rock Hill, S.C.), 1 Mar. 1997, at B1.
- "After last week's loss to the Flyers, though, Campbell has wondered aloud if, even with the great effort and *input* [read *contributions*] of his stars, the Rangers have enough talent to enjoy more than spasmatic success." Stu Hackel, "Campbell's Soup: Can Anyone Coach the Rangers?" *Village Voice*, 11 Mar. 1997, at 125. (On the use of **spasmatic* in that sentence, see **spasmodic.**)
- "Parental *input* [read *influence*] is still more powerful than teacher–child interactions in school." Mary Newton Brudner, *The Grammar Lady* 22 (2000).

For the verb *input*, as with the IRREGULAR VERB *put*, the usual past-tense form is *input*—e.g.: "Some people had middle initials *inputted* [read *input*] and others didn't, and some names were misspelled." Peter Beinart, "Doing the Inaugural Hustle," *New Republic*, 3 Feb. 1997, at 22. See COMPUTERESE. But the verb use is less well accepted than the noun use.

LANGUAGE-CHANGE INDEX
1. *input* as a noun in nontechnical senses: Stage 5
2. *input* as a verb: Stage 4
3. **inputted* as a past tense: Stage 2
Current ratio (*been input* vs. **been inputted*): 7:1

inquire; *enquire. *Inquire* is a FORMAL WORD for *ask*. In AmE and BrE alike, *in-* is the preferred spelling. At least one sophisticated newspaper, however, uses the archaic *en-* spelling in its name (*The Cincinnati Enquirer*). See EN- & **inquiry.**

inquirer; inquisitor. *Inquirer* is the more general of the two terms, meaning "someone who asks questions or investigates." *Inquisitor*, not to be used where *inquirer* is called for, means "someone who examines others to obtain information," and carries with it historical connotations of the Spanish Inquisition.

inquiry. A. Pronunciation. *Inquiry* may be pronounced either /in-**kwir**-ee/ or /in-kwə-ree/. The former has long been the dominant AmE pronunciation. It is the only standard pronunciation in BrE.

B. And *enquiry*. In AmE, *inquiry* is the standard spelling in all senses. In BrE, *enquiry* is equivalent to *question*, whereas *inquiry* means "an official investigation." See EN-.

C. And *query*. While *query* refers to a single question, *inquiry* may refer also to a series of questions or a sustained investigation. Occasionally writers misuse *query* for *inquiry*—e.g.:

- " 'You've really got a couple of things that are problematic, notwithstanding the idea that a married woman could be counted as unmarried because she kept her maiden name,' said Richard Steffen, a Speier staffer who launched *a query*

[read *an inquiry*] into the state's record-keeping system."
Ramon G. McLeod, "Maiden Names Skew Birth Data,"
S.F. Chron., 2 May 1996, at A16.
- "Those months of *query* [read *inquiry*] also produced the figures—get ready for the math—to back up its findings." Cathy Gant-Hill, "Arts Scene Is Pretty as a Picture," *News & Record* (Greensboro), 2 Jan. 1997, at D1.

LANGUAGE-CHANGE INDEX
query misused for *inquiry*: Stage 1

inquisitive; inquisitorial; *inquisitional. *Inquisitive* = given to inquiry or questioning <a highly inquisitive mind>. *Inquisitorial* has quite different connotations: "of the character of an inquisitor; offensively or impertinently inquiring, prying" (*OED*). (To contrast *inquisitorial* with *accusatorial*, see **accusatory**.) **Inquisitional* is a NEEDLESS VARIANT of *inquisitorial*.
Current ratio (*inquisitorial* vs. **inquisitional*): 12:1

inquisitor. See **inquirer.**

inquisitorial. See **inquisitive.**

in re; re. Known to nonlawyers as a legalistic term, *in re* (= regarding, in the matter of) was once commonly used at the outset of legal documents and is now often used before case names (particularly in uncontested proceedings) <*In re Wolfson's Estate*>.

In business correspondence, *in re* is usually shortened to *re* as a signal or introductory title announcing the subject of the letter. But *re* is often criticized as unnecessary JARGON: "Even if the caption must be used, as it seldom has to be, the *Re:* is totally unnecessary, as the mere giving of prominence to the item tells the reader it is going to be the subject of the letter. Notice how some of the formality is lost by the omission of this little 'throwback' to early letter-writing days.

Re: Your letter of March 10	Your letter of March 10
Re: August Sales Contest	August Sales Contest
Re: Order No. 8873	Order Number 8873"

L.E. Frailey, *Handbook of Business Letters* 242–43 (rev. ed. 1965). Another business-writing text says that *re* "is giving way to *subject*." Charles T. Brusaw et al., *The Business Writer's Handbook* 540 (3d ed. 1987).

This trend has been hurt, though, and may have been doomed by the ubiquitous use of *Re:* in e-mails, for two reasons. First, the short form fits right in with the hurried style of the medium (tho YMMV :o). More important, e-mail software routinely changes the subject line on a reply message by adding *Re* followed by a colon.

*in receipt of. This phrase, to be avoided as OFFICIA-LESE and COMMERCIALESE, is invariably inferior to *have received* or *has received*. Instead of **We are in receipt of your letter*, say *We have received your letter*.

in regard to. See **regard (A).**

in respect of. See **respect.**

insanitary. See **unsanitary.**

inside (of). The word *inside* shouldn't typically be followed by *of* <the ball was inside the 40-yard line>. See **of (B).**
Current ratio (*inside the* vs. **inside of the*): 9:1

insidious; invidious. Although these words look and sound similar and convey negative ideas, their meanings are nothing alike. *Insidious* = (of people and things) lying in wait or seeking to entrap or ensnare; operating subtly or secretly so as not to excite suspicion—e.g.: "Many Indians still fear that economic liberalization will bring with it cultural imperialism of a particularly *insidious* kind—that 'Baywatch' and burgers will supplant Bharatanatyam dances and bhelpuri." Shashi Tharoor, "India Poised to Become an Economic Superpower," *Wash. Post*, 10 Aug. 1997, at C1.

Invidious = offensive; repulsive; arousing ill will or resentment. This term is often applied to discrimination, as it has been for more than two centuries—e.g.: "The example familiar to us is segregation. In 1896, the justices said there was nothing *invidious* about separating black people unless they chose to see it that way. That pretense . . . could hardly be maintained in 1954." Anthony Lewis, "Justice Spoke to Our Better Angels," *Times-Picayune* (New Orleans), 4 Aug. 1997, at B5.

The two words generally ought not to be used in the same sentence because sound might appear to triumph over sense—e.g.: "At a time when 'difference' and 'identity' are the potent and inevitable terms in a new comparatism grounded in 'culture,' it may be important to remind ourselves how *insidious* comparison can be, how *invidious* and odious." W.J.T. Mitchell, "Why Comparisons Are Odious," *World Literature Today*, 1 Mar. 1996, at 321.

insightful. See **inciteful.**

insignia; *insigne. Today *insignia* (technically plural) is regarded as the singular, *insignias* as its plural. E.g.: "Roses bearing this *insignia* have undergone two years of comparison with other new varieties." Diane Relf, "Rose Blooms, Rose Facts," *Roanoke Times*, 20 June 1996, at 9. Cf. **indicia.**

The Latin singular **insigne* is rarely used. When it does appear, it would be better as *insignia*—e.g.: "Mr. Robb . . . later learned that a red-white-and-blue tie he wore Sept. 5 when he was endorsed by Bobby Scott—the state's only black congressman—was adorned with the *insigne* [read *insignia*] of the Confederacy." Laurie Kellman, "Robb Urged to Fight Harder to Keep Seat," *Wash. Times*, 7 Oct. 1994, at A1.

LANGUAGE-CHANGE INDEX
*insigne for *insignia*: Stage 1
Current ratio (*an insignia* vs. **an insigne*): 48:1

insipient. See **incipient.**

insist takes the preposition *on*, not *in*—e.g.: "In a society that *persists and insists in* [read *persists in and insists on*, if the rhyming is really necessary] permitting its citizens to own and possess weapons, it becomes necessary to determine who may and who may not acquire them."

insistence; *insistment. The latter is a NEEDLESS VARIANT. *Insistence* is often misspelled **insistance.*

Current ratio (*insistence* vs. **insistment*): 42,536:1

insofar as (= in such degree as) is spelled thus in AmE and *in so far as* in BrE. (See **inasmuch as.**) But perhaps, as H.W. Fowler suggested, it shouldn't be spelled at all: "He must have a long spoon that sups with the devil; and the safest way of dealing with *in so far* is to keep clear of it. The dangers range from mere feebleness or wordiness, through pleonasm or confusion of forms, and inaccuracy of meaning, to false grammar" (*FMEU1* at 276). As the following examples illustrate, modern writers are often chargeable with each of the offenses just mentioned.

- **Wordy:** "[Bill Cosby] knows this is a hurt that will never go away, but *insofar as* [read *if*] humanly possible, he wants people to move back to the time where they saw him as someone who brings laughter into their lives." Lawrie Mifflin, "Cosby Asks to Grieve with Dignity," *Austin Am.-Statesman*, 31 Jan. 1997, at F1.
- **Pleonastic:** "This is particularly true *insofar as* [read *because*] Mr. Dellums' ascendancy comes at a very sensitive moment." Frank Gaffney Jr., "Furrowed Brows on the Defense Front," *Wash. Times*, 28 Dec. 1992, at E1.
- **Ungrammatical:** "His name has surfaced in connection with Commerce Department lobbying *insofar as* [read *because of*] his success in winning Cellular Communications Inc." Jeffrey Silva, "Nextwave Ownership Edict Begs Question," *Radio Comm. Rep.*, 13 Jan. 1997, at 1. (*Insofar as* isn't a preposition and therefore can't govern *success*; a preposition such as *because of* is needed.)

Sometimes *insofar as* leads to a false economy. The two words *in* and *so* could be simplified to *as*, so that you end up with *as far as* instead of *insofar as*. The choice is then between three words (and three syllables) and two words (but four syllables). To some, this seems a trivial worry, but to the writer cultivating a lean style it is serious business. And part of the problem with *insofar as* is that it "feels" wordy—e.g.: "Boyer . . . seems to be viewed as a bit more of a dark horse by Republicans interviewed last week—at least *insofar as* [read *as far as*] the top job goes." Michael Silence & Tom Humphrey, "Pope Campaign Trying to Cover All of 1st District," *Knoxville News-Sentinel*, 16 June 1996, at B1.

But sometimes a sentence containing *insofar as* isn't easily simplifiable. And where (not *insofar as*!) that is so, the phrase can hardly be faulted—e.g.: "His suggestion that government . . . has no business regulating private behavior amounts to a claim that representative democracy is illegitimate, at least *insofar as* it does not comport with his morality." J. Stewart Brams, "Outlawing Drug Use Does Not Violate Privacy," *Pitt. Post-Gaz.*, 5 Aug. 1996, at A10. To replace *insofar as* with *to the extent that* would

make the sentence wordier. To clip it down to *as* would be too elliptical.

On this term's spelling, see **inasmuch.**

insoluble; unsolvable; *insolvable. *Insoluble* is used in reference both to substances that will not dissolve in one or more liquids and to problems that cannot be solved. E.g.:

- "Her duties included making calamine lotion from water-*insoluble* powders." Brian Brennan, "Pharmacy Was Fascinating," *Calgary Herald*, 26 Sept. 1995, at B2.
- "The problem, you see, is delicate. I sometimes fear that it is *insoluble*." Daniel Horch, *The Angel with One Hundred Wings* 135 (2002).

Unsolvable is used only in reference to problems that cannot be solved. Most stylists prefer it to *insoluble*—e.g.: "In both Iraq and North Korea the drive to contain proliferation has made George Bush the point man in an *unsolvable* problem." Stefan Halper, "Negotiating the Korean Rift," *Wash. Times*, 20 Jan. 2003, at A17.

*Insolvable should be avoided as a NEEDLESS VARIANT.

in some circumstances. See **circumstances (c).**

insomuch—always one word—is usually best replaced by a less stilted phrasing, such as *in (that), so (as),* or *so (that).* As the following examples illustrate, both *insomuch as* and *insomuch that* are sometimes used, but they are both easily replaceable—e.g.:

- "*Insomuch as* [read *Since*] Towey was held to a standard few officials could live up to, yes, killing the confirmation was unfair. And *insomuch as* [read *since*] the Republicans, despite their surface politeness, handled it with all the grace of a demolition derby." Louis Lavelle, "Caesar's Ghost," *Tampa Trib.*, 21 May 1995, Commentary §, at 1.
- "The '93 season, Wilhelm's last, was memorable *insomuch that* [read *because* or *in that*] the Tigers needed to win two of three at FSU to finish 11–11 in the league." Frank Dascenzo, "Wilhelm Can't Stay Away from Game," *Herald-Sun* (Durham, N.C.), 16 May 1996, at B6.
- "*Insomuch as* [read *As far as*] the immediate postmatch stats can be trusted, he was credited with being Ireland's leading tackler (with 13)." Gerry Thornley, "Fearless Ireland Cut New Dash in Dramatic Race for Prize," *Irish Times*, 23 Mar. 2015, Sport §, at 3.

Cf. **inasmuch as.**

insouciant (= cheerfully unconcerned; unworried) may be pronounced either /in-**soo**-see-int/ or /in-**soo**-shənt/, the latter being a more anglicized version.

in spite of. See **despite.**

inst.; ult.; prox. F.T. Wood writes that *inst.* (short for *instant*) was "once a quite respectable legal term, now a piece of commercial jargon for 'the present month' (e.g., 'We beg to recognise the receipt of your letter of the 25th inst.'). Use the name of the month instead."

Wood, *Current English Usage* 123 (1962). The advice is well taken.

Likewise, *ult.* (L. *ultimo* "of last month") and *prox.* (L. *proximo* "of next month") should be replaced with the straightforward *last month* and *next month*—or with a precise reference naming the month. See COMMERCIALESE.

installment is the standard AmE spelling. *Instalment* is the BrE spelling.

instance; instancy. *Instance* "in the sense of urgent solicitation or insistence [always in the phrase *at the instance of*] is a useful word; in any other sense it is useless." Percy Marks, *The Craft of Writing* 53 (1932). Another legitimate meaning of the word is "an illustrative example," as in *for instance.*

But in the phrase *in a majority of instances* (= usually), the word is indeed useless—e.g.: "*In the vast majority of instances,* the company about to be acquired hires an outside firm to vet the proposed purchase price by reviewing details of the transaction and then comparing them with similar deals." Rick Brooks, "Some Investment Banks Assess Their Own Acquisitions," *Wall Street J.*, 9 Jan. 1998, at B2. (Read: *The company about to be acquired usually* [or *almost always*] *hires an outside firm . . . .*)

Instancy, a rare term, means "urgency; pressing nature; imminence" <the instancy of the danger was apparent to all>.

instantly; instantaneously. *Instantly* = at once, directly and immediately. *Instantaneously* = (1) (of two events that occur) so nearly simultaneously that any difference is imperceptible; or (2) done in an instant.

instigation (= the act of inciting or fomenting) is sometimes misused for *initiation* or *installation*—e.g.: "The cover celebrates the 650th anniversary of the *instigation* [read *initiation*] of the Order of the Garter, the UK's highest civil and military honour." David McManus, "The British Philatelic Bureau," *Precision Marketing*, 1 June 1998, at 25. (The writer also errs in describing his subject: the Order is a chivalric honor, neither civil nor military.)

LANGUAGE-CHANGE INDEX
instigation misused for *initiation*: Stage 1

instill; instil. The preferred spelling is *instill* in AmE, *instil* in BrE. This word takes the preposition *in(to),* not *with* <he instilled character as well as knowledge into his students>. *With* results from confusion of *inspire* with *instill* or *infuse*. See OBJECT-SHUFFLING & **inculcate (B).** Cf. **imbue.**

instillation; *instillment. The latter is a NEEDLESS VARIANT.

Current ratio: 265:1

instinctive; *instinctual. The latter is a NEEDLESS VARIANT. More than most such variants, it appears in respectable publications—e.g.: "Men notice women's vulnerabilities with a falcon's eye—it's surely *instinctual* [read *instinctive*]—yet not just for predatory purposes: also protectively." Edward Hoagland, "Sex and the River Styx," *Harper's Mag.*, Jan. 2003, at 49, 54.

Current ratio: 4:1

institute is a FORMAL WORD for *begin* or *start.* Cf. **commence.**

in-store (= being or occurring within a shop or store) is a PHRASAL ADJECTIVE so hyphenated—preferably not solidified into **instore.* The term became popular in AmE in the 1940s and in BrE in the 1960s <in-store promotions> <in-store displays>.

insubstantial; *unsubstantial. Although H.W. Fowler preferred **unsubstantial* and it predominated till about 1950, it is rarely seen now and should be classed a NEEDLESS VARIANT. *Insubstantial,* the standard term, is much more common than **unsubstantial* in modern print sources.

Current ratio: 3:1

*insue is an archaic spelling of *ensue.* See **ensue.**

insult, in medical and scientific JARGON, often means "something that disturbs normal functions; a trauma"—e.g.:

- "American experience . . . could be useful in reminding [Russians] that government still has a vital role in repairing the cruel injuries inflicted by chemical and nuclear *insults* to the environment." "Russia's Ravaged Environment," *Boston Globe,* 5 Aug. 1995, at 8.
- "What auxologists call 'environmental *insults*' can slow or stop this growth. Obvious '*insults*' are poor nutrition, illness, lack of hygiene, polluted surroundings and overcrowded housing." Rod Usher, "A Tall Story for Our Time," *Time,* 14 Oct. 1996, at 64.
- "The evidence of increased danger from teenage smoking is also important, the researchers said, because it's consistent with the idea 'that environmental *insults* are most deleterious during breast development.' " Robert Cooke, "Study Links Smoking, Breast Cancer," *Newsday* (N.Y.), 13 Nov. 1996, at A4.

See **trauma.**

insupportable. See **unsupportable.**

insurable. So spelled.

insurance. A. And *assurance.* *Insurance* answers to both *insure* and *ensure* (the spelling **ensurance* now being obsolete). (See **assure.**) Usually, *insurance* refers to indemnification against loss (from the verb *insure*). In this legal sense, insurance is of two kinds. One is insurance against accidents: buildings burning, ships sinking, cars colliding, bodies being injured, and the like. The other—in BrE frequently called *assurance*—is provision for designated people on the occurrence of death: *life insurance* (AmE) or *life assurance* (BrE).

In AmE, *assurance* (which answers to *assure*) chiefly means "pledge" or "guarantee"—e.g.: "But the *assurances* China provided to the Clinton Administration have not been made public." James Przystup & Robert

A. Manning, "Clinton's Inscrutable China Policy," *Nat'l Rev.*, 8 Dec. 1997, at 22. It sometimes also means "self-confidence"—e.g.: "Countertenor Robert Harre-Jones, tenors Charles Daniels and Angus Smith and baritone Donald Greig spun out the florid, long, trailing melodic lines of Dufay and Ockeghem motets with delicate *assurance.*" Cecelia Porter, "Orlando Consort at Dumbarton Church," *Wash. Post*, 10 Nov. 1997, at B7.

B. Pronunciation. This word is preferably pronounced with the primary accent on the second syllable: /in-**shuur**-ənts/—not /in-shər-ənts/ (a dialectal pronunciation). See PRONUNCIATION (B) & DIALECT.

> LANGUAGE-CHANGE INDEX
> *insurance* mispronounced /**in**-shər-ənts/: Stage 2

insure. See **assure.**

insured, n., like *deceased* and *accused*, forms an awkward plural <several insureds> and possessive <the insured's liability>. This infelicity can be avoided in one of two ways: (1) by using *insured* as an adjective <both insured representatives> or (2) by using an equivalent term <both insurants> <the policyholder's claim>. If you are using *insured* as a noun, though, use an *of*-phrase for the possessive <the liability of the insured>. See POSSESSIVES (J).

insurer; *insuror. The latter is a NEEDLESS VARIANT.

> Current ratio: 3,145:1

insurgence; insurgency. These words have undergone DIFFERENTIATION, but the distinction is a fine one. *Insurgence* = an act or the action of rising against authority; a revolt <the military quelled an insurgence in Bangkok this morning>. *Insurgency* = the state or condition of being in revolt <no deaths occurred during the three-week insurgency>.

*insuror. See **insurer.**

insurrectionary; *insurrectional. The latter is a NEEDLESS VARIANT.

> Current ratio: 6:1

in sync. See **sync.**

integer is pronounced /**in**-tə-jər/, with a soft -*g*-.

integrable. This is the standard adjective corresponding to *integrate*—not **integratable.* See -ATABLE.

> Current ratio: 29:1

integral; integrant. The second is a NEEDLESS VARIANT of the first as an adjective, but it exists legitimately as a fancy equivalent of *component*—e.g.: "Hauy defines the mineral species to be: 'a collection of matter whose *integrant* molecules are all alike, and composed of the same elements united in the same proportion.'" Robert Jameson, "A Brief History of Systematic Mineralogies," *Mineralogical Record*, 1 July 1995, at 49. It is pronounced /**in**-tə-grənt/.

Integral (/**in**-tə-grəl/) is often misspelled *intergral—e.g.: "Before long the slender, shy immigrant became an *intergral* [read *integral*] part of the New York art scene." Amy Sutherland, "When Yasuo Kuniyoshi Was Still Plain Folk," *Portland Press Herald*, 26 Jan. 1997, at E1. Avoid also the mispronunciation /in-**teg**-rəl/.

> LANGUAGE-CHANGE INDEX
> *integral* misspelled *intergral: Stage 1

*integratable. See **integrable.**

integration. See **desegregation.**

intelligent. A. And *intelligible.* *Intelligent* means "(of people) having mental power or grasp." *Intelligible* means "(of statements) understandable."

B. And *intellectual,* adj. Someone who is *intelligent* has an innate ability to learn quickly and to solve problems easily <an intelligent young child>. Someone who is *intellectual* enjoys using his or her intelligence for scholarly or philosophical pursuits <a quiet, intellectual woman who spends most of her time in bookstores>.

intelligentsia is the standard spelling. *Intelligentzia is a variant.

In the early 20th century, some purists pronounced the Russian loanword with a hard -*g*-, as in *get*. But the pronunciation quickly conformed to a soft -*g*- on the analogy of the cognates *intelligent* and *intelligence*. Only /in-tel-i-**jent**-see-ə/ is now considered the standard pronunciation.

> Current ratio: 341:1

intense; intensive. The conventional advice—to shun *intensive* wherever *intense* will fit the context—is sound. *Intensive* is really a philosophical and scientific term best left to philosophers and scientists. Other writers can work well enough with *intense*—e.g.: "Anti-tobacco lawyers complain that the *intensive* [read *intense*] scrutiny serves another purpose too—intimidating some clients into giving up their claims to keep embarrassing personal information from becoming public." Myron Levin, "Private Eyes' Probing Armed Big Tobacco for Court Battles," *Houston Chron.*, 3 Aug. 1997, at 12.

But *intensive* is now customary in jargonistic PHRASAL ADJECTIVES such as *capital-intensive, labor-intensive, time-intensive,* and the like.

Intensive is sometimes wrongly made **intensitive.* This is commented on, along with **preventative,* in an old book: Austin Phelps & Henry Allyn Frink, *Rhetoric: Its Theory and Practice* 24 (1895). Cf. **preventive.**

Back to the present: *intense* has also become a low CASUALISM for "very interesting" <"He showed up at the party half naked." "Really? That's intense!">.

> LANGUAGE-CHANGE INDEX
> *intensive* misused for *intense*: Stage 4

LANGUAGE-CHANGE INDEX (For the full key, see front matter pp. xxxi, l–li.)
Stage 1: Rejected. **Stage 2:** Widely shunned. **Stage 3:** Widespread but . . . **Stage 4:** Ubiquitous but . . . **Stage 5:** Fully accepted.
Invariably inferior forms marked by asterisk (*). • Ratios represent frequency of prevalent forms vs. variants in current books.

INTENSIVE PRONOUNS. See PRONOUNS (E).

*__intensive purposes, for all.__ For this error, see **for all intents and purposes.**

intently (= with rapt concentration or attention, eagerly) is sometimes misused for *intensely* (= to a very great degree, forcefully)—e.g.: "Ah, the Roseanne people love. Or love to hate. Or maybe just dislike *intently* [read *intensely*]." Dusty Saunders, "'Saturday Night Special' Loaded for Targets of Roseanne's Shtick," *Rocky Mountain News* (Denver), 10 Apr. 1996, at D12.
                                LANGUAGE-CHANGE INDEX
            intently misused for *intensely*: Stage 1

intents and purposes. See **for all intents and purposes.**

INTER-; INTRA-. These prefixes have quite different meanings. *Inter-* means "between, among." *Intra-* means "within, in." So *interstate* means "between states" and *intrastate* means "within a state." American bureaucrats and businesspeople have recently created any number of NEOLOGISMS with these prefixes, primarily with *inter-* (e.g., *interagency, interbranch, intercorporate, intermunicipal*) but also with *intra-* (e.g., *intranet, intrapreneur*).

interact with one another. This is a glaring REDUNDANCY that should almost always be trimmed to *interact*—e.g.: "It's the best thing to do in the long run, especially as patients *interact with one another* [read *interact*] and form bonds." Ronell Smith, "Families Find Adult Day Care a Comfort," *Augusta Chron.*, 27 Jan. 2003, at B5. The same is true of *interact with each other*. See **each other.**

__inter alia; inter alios.__ The best course, undoubtedly, is to use *among others*, a phrase that can refer to people or things. The Latin is not so simple. Whereas *inter alia* (= among other things) refers to anything that is not human, *inter alios* (= among other people) refers to human beings. (The Latin form *inter alias* means "among other female persons.")

interceptor; *intercepter. The two forms vied for predominance till about 1930, when *interceptor* became the standard term and **intercepter* a NEEDLESS VARIANT.

                                Current ratio: 111:1

interesting is pronounced /**in**-trə-sting/—not /**in**-ə-res-ting/. See PRONUNCIATION (B).

interestingly. See SENTENCE ADVERBS.

interface, v.i. Outside COMPUTERESE, this verb is jargonmongers' talk. E.g.:

• "Team members were delegated a project-related job that required minimal *interfacing* [read *interaction*] with others." Deborah S. Kezsbom & Katherine A. Edward, *New Dynamic Project Management* 252 (2001).
• "Making contact and *interfacing* [read *dealing*] with others from another culture can be stressful and lead to culture

shock." Wallace V. Schmidt, *Communicating Globally* 84 (2007).
                                LANGUAGE-CHANGE INDEX
    interface to denote interaction between people <the
        editor must interface with the writer>: Stage 2

interfusible. So spelled—not **interfusable*. See -ABLE (A).

INTERJECTIONS. See FUNCTIONAL SHIFT (H).

interline. See AIRLINESE.

interment; internment. *Interment* = burial <interment will take place just after the funeral service>. *Internment* = detention, especially of aliens in wartime <internment camps for hundreds of enemy aliens>.
    Interment is sometimes, especially in obituaries, confounded with *internment*—e.g.:

• "Graveside ceremony and *internment* [read *interment*] will be at Hillside Cemetery in Peekskill immediately following." "Stark, Rosalie White," *Times Union* (Albany), 22 Aug. 2000, at B7.
• "Memorial services have been planned for a later date *in* [read *on*] Cape Cod, with *internment* [read *interment*] in the Dennis Cemetery." "Obituaries," *Ariz. Republic*, 29 Oct. 2000, at B8.
• "*Internment* [read *Interment*] will follow at Middleton Cemetery." "Deaths," *Idaho Statesman*, 5 Dec. 2000, at 7.
                                LANGUAGE-CHANGE INDEX
        internment misused for *interment*: Stage 1

intermezzo is pronounced /in-tər-**met**-soh/ or /in-tər-**med**-zoh/, but not /-**mez**-oh/. Pl. *intermezzos* or (pretentiously) *intermezzi*. See PLURALS (B).
        Current ratio (*intermezzi* vs. *intermezzos*): 4:1

intermittent; intermitting. Both words mean "occurring at intervals." The distinction is that *intermittent* connotes random intervals, whereas *intermitting* connotes cyclic repetition. The first word is far more common; in fact, *intermitting* is almost never seen in general writing. But in technical writing, and especially medical writing, *intermitting* conveys a useful distinction—e.g.:

• "By the 17th century, *synochus* had been distinguished from *synocha*, a term Galen did not use. The former continued to be a continuous fever, whereas the latter could be *intermitting*, and was sometimes linked with the periodicities we associate with malaria." Bill Bynum, "Synochus," *Lancet*, 21 Sept. 2002, at 956.
• "The cure was as ugly as the disease: *intermitting* doses of chemotherapy, radiation and painful spinal taps." Carol Sowers, "Woman with Leukemia Urges Minorities to Donate," *Ariz. Republic*, 15 July 2005, at B6.
• "This method uses an *intermitting* technique, along with a free traveling plunger in the tubing string that acts as an interface between the liquid phase and the gas phase." "A Pump for All Reasons," *Oil & Gas J.*, 24 June 2006, at 4.

in terms of is often indefensibly verbose. Whenever you can replace it with a simple preposition, do so—e.g.:

- "Each of the paintings 'rates' a different area of Wisconsin, *in terms of* [read *for*] the quality of its towns." James Auer, "$2 Million Grant to Met Museum Has Ties to Milwaukee," *Milwaukee J. Sentinel*, 26 Nov. 1997, Cue §, at 2.
- "Many arts groups have indeed been too exclusive *in terms of* [read *in*] their offerings, he said, and they have been guilty of the sin of elitism." Elsa Brenner, "Arts Centers Open Doors for Hire to Survive," *N.Y. Times*, 30 Nov. 1997, Westchester §, at 1.
- "*In terms of* [read *In*] the overall expenditure on the Trident replacement, this is a tiny amount." "He's the Chancer of the Exchequer," *Daily Record* (Glasgow), 1 Sept. 2015, News §, at 8.

But in the sense "expressed by means of," the phrase is quite defensible—e.g.: "At the same time, he describes Sibelius's symphonies *in terms of* visual, personal drama, evoking not only smashings and submersions, but also dreamlike journeys through forests and snow." Leslie Kandell, "Tribute to a Long-Lived Voice from the North," *N.Y. Times*, 30 Nov. 1997, N.J. §, at 20.

internecine. As originally used in English, and as recorded by Samuel Johnson in 1755, *internecine* means "mutually deadly; destructive of both parties." In best usage it still bears the sense of devastation—e.g.: "As Zaman portrays himself, he is the civil warlord. He was the one to avoid the *internecine* bloodshed that continues to plague Afghanistan." Michael A. Lev, "In Power Shift, Afghan Warlord Now Out of Loop," *Chicago Trib.*, 7 May 2002, News §, at 6.

The word is now routinely used in extended senses, with the suggestion that internecine warfare has a winner. Often, in fact, it is used to mean nothing more than "internal"—e.g.:

- "But whoever emerges victorious from the *internecine* [delete *internecine*] Internet wars, the one sure winner is guaranteed to be the business and residential consumer." Paul Spillenger, "Internet Access Wars Heat Up," *Ark. Bus.*, 1 July 1996, at 1.
- "If handled right, *internecine* [read *internal*] struggle can pay off for winners and losers alike." Bill Walsh, "Managing the Monster," *Executive Excellence*, Nov. 1996, at 19.
- "It is in the nature of bureaucrats to fight for turf and for money. The goal of winning these fights becomes more important than the formal goals of an agency, because winning the *internecine* [read *interagency*] battles for money and turf is seen as a matter of survival." Andrew Greeley, "Merger Making Homeland Insecure," *Times-Union* (Albany), 30 Nov. 2002, at A11.

Today, these uses are so common that they can no longer be called solecisms. But careful writers will respect the word's traditional roots in belligerency and find other words to describe petty squabbles.

The word is pronounced in several ways, the best perhaps being /in-tər-**nee**-sin/. But other pronunciations are acceptable: /in-tər-**nee**-sɪn/, /in-**tər**-nə-sin/, /in-**tər**-nə-seen/, and /in-tər-**ne**-seen/.

LANGUAGE-CHANGE INDEX
internecine misused for *internal*: Stage 3

Internet. Capitalized thus—not **internet*. E.g.: "Mercifully, Lasch did not live to see the *internet* [read *Internet*] or the full digital revolution that the personal computer spawned." Stewart Weaver, Introduction to Christopher Lasch, *Plain Style* 39 (Stewart Weaver ed., 2002). The word is legitimately viewed as a proper noun. See **World Wide Web.**

internment. See **interment.**

interoffice. One word.

interpellate. See **interpolate.**

interpersonal. "What this [word] adds to 'personal' except five letters and a superficial impression of scientific exactness, I do not see—except, perhaps, in a particular context where 'intergroup' relations might also be involved." Ellsworth Barnard, *English for Everybody* 34 n.12 (1979). Point well taken.

interpolate; interpellate. The first /in-**tərp**-ə-layt/ means "to insert into a text or writing"; the second /in-tər-**pel**-ayt/), used in legislative reports, means "to question formally; to seek information."

interpret; *interpretate. The latter is an obsolete BACK-FORMATION and a NEEDLESS VARIANT of *interpret*—e.g.: "The essence of ice dancing is the inventiveness of the performance, how the music is *interpretated* [read *interpreted*] and how the dance steps are choreographed." Lee Shappell, "International Flair," *Ariz. Republic*, 20 Jan. 1993, at D1.

LANGUAGE-CHANGE INDEX
*interpretate for *interpret*: Stage 1
Current ratio (*interpreting* vs.
*interpretating): 1,494:1

interpretive; interpretative; *interpretational. Generally, one forms the adjective on the model of the noun form of a word. Hence *prevention* yields *preventive*, not **preventative*; *determination* yields *determinative*, not **determinive*; *administration* yields *administrative*, not **administerive*. And with *interpretation*, the traditionally correct adjective is *interpretative* (= having the character or function of interpreting; explanatory). E.g.:

- "You will misuse it . . . if you substitute the dictionary for the exercise of your own *interpretative* judgment in reading." Mortimer Adler, "How to Read a Dictionary" (1941), in *Words, Words, Words About Dictionaries* 53, 59 (Jack C. Gray ed., 1963).
- "Crews continue to work on restrooms, a parking lot and *interpretative* displays near the McMillin Bridge off Washington 162, he said." Rob Tucker, "Foothills Trail 2.3 Miles Closer to Completion," *News Trib.* (Tacoma), 6 Aug. 1997, at B9.

But *interpretive* has gained ground since the mid-20th century—so much so that it's about twice as

LANGUAGE-CHANGE INDEX (For the full key, see front matter pp. xxxi, l–li.)
Stage 1: Rejected. **Stage 2:** Widely shunned. **Stage 3:** Widespread but . . . **Stage 4:** Ubiquitous but . . . **Stage 5:** Fully accepted.
Invariably inferior forms marked by asterisk (*). • Ratios represent frequency of prevalent forms vs. variants in current books.

common in print as *interpretative*. The shorter form surpassed the longer in frequency of use in print sources in the early 1960s. Today it is standard—e.g.:

- "Morrison, also a founding member of Bolsa Chica Conservancy, said her first goal will be to train more volunteer hosts for the conservancy's *interpretive* center." Kimberly Brower, "Bolsa Chica Group Fills Education Post," *L.A. Times*, 30 July 1997, at B2.
- "Signs along the *interpretive* walkway urge visitors not to eat the fruit, but the temptation to savor an exotic fruit plucked fresh from a tree is almost irresistible." Pat Stein, "Quail's Subtropical Garden an 'Opportunity for Discovery,'" *San Diego Union-Trib.*, 10 Aug. 1997, at H21.
- "The Northern Ireland home of influential socialist and Easter Rising leader James Connolly is to be turned into a museum and *interpretive* centre." Maurice Fitzmaurice, "Museum Plan for Connolly's Home," *Mirror* (U.K.), 31 Aug. 2015, at 14.

Refight an old fight, if you like, and stick to *interpretative*. But *interpretive* has already taken hold.

Interpretational is a NEEDLESS VARIANT—e.g.: "Therein lies the *interpretational* [read *interpretive*] logjam, the slippery definitions of 'tradition' and 'honor' that wreak the most havoc on open dialogue." Lynell George, "When Mascots Unite," *L.A. Times*, 8 June 1997, at E3.

LANGUAGE-CHANGE INDEX
1. *interpretive* for the traditional *interpretative*: Stage 5
Current ratio (*interpretive* vs. *interpretative*): 2:1
2. *interpretational* for *interpretive*: Stage 1

interregnum. Pl. *interregnums* or *interregna*—AmE writers being inclined to the former and BrE to the latter. See PLURALS (B).
Current ratio (*interregnums* vs. *interregna*): 1.1:1

interrogate is a FORMAL WORD for *question*; it suggests formal or rigorous questioning.

interrogatee; *interrogee. *W3* lists **interrogee* (= someone interrogated), not *interrogatee*, but the *OED* lists *interrogatee*, not **interrogee*. Since the agent noun is *interrogator*, it makes more sense to prefer the corresponding passive form, *interrogatee*. This longer form is more than twice as common in modern print sources.
Current ratio: 2:1

interrogative; *interrogatory, adj.; *interrogational. *Interrogative* (= of, relating to, or resembling a question) is the standard term. E.g.: "Wimsey smiled at Harriet, an odd, *interrogative* smile." Dorothy L. Sayers, *Gaudy Night* 364 (1936; repr. 1995). The others are NEEDLESS VARIANTS. In legal contexts, *interrogatory* is a noun meaning "a written question (usu. in a set of questions) submitted to an opposing party in a lawsuit as part of discovery" (*Black's Law Dictionary* 947 [10th ed. 2014]).
Current ratio (*interrogative* vs. *interrogatory* vs. *interrogational*): 52:5:1

***interrogee.** See **interrogatee.**

interrupter; *interruptor. The first spelling has long predominated in print sources and is considered standard. See -ER (A).
Current ratio: 20:1

interstate; intrastate. These adjectives should not be used adverbially, as here: "Organized crime operates *interstate* [read *in interstate commerce* or *across state lines* or *throughout the states*]." See INTER-.

interstitial (= situated within gaps) is the standard spelling. It's pronounced /in-tər-**stish**-əl/. **Intersticial* is a variant spelling.
Current ratio: 1,162:1

intervener. Preferably so spelled—*intervenor* being an exclusively legal spelling.
Current ratio: 2:1

***intervenience.** See **intervention.**

***intervent,** a misbegotten BACK-FORMATION from *intervention*, is incorrect for *intervene*—e.g.:

- "Chilean banking officials will close at least four of the eight banks and finance companies in which the Government *intervened* [read *intervened*] last November." Mary Helen Spooner, "Chile to Close 'At Least 4 Financial Institutions,'" *Fin. Times*, 26 Mar. 1982, § I, at 4.
- "Key congressional leaders indicated they might be willing to wait until the end of the week before *interventing* [read *intervening*] in the labor dispute." Frank Swoboda, "Hill in No Hurry to Settle Railroad Shutdown," *Wash. Post*, 25 June 1992, at A1.
- "NATO *intervented* [read *intervened*] the following year and has inherited the issue now that Serb-led Yugoslav forces have left." John Ward Anderson, "A Battle Brews in the Buffer Zone," *Wash. Post*, 14 Mar. 2001, at A18.

LANGUAGE-CHANGE INDEX
intervent for *intervene*: Stage 1
Current ratio (*intervened* vs. *intervented*): 19,299:1

intervention; *intervenience. The latter is a NEEDLESS VARIANT.
Current ratio: 65,794:1

in the affirmative. See **affirmative.**

in the amount of. See **check (B).**

in the ascendant. See **ascendant.**

in the circumstances. See **circumstances (A).**

in the context of. See **context of.**

in the course of is often wordy for *during* or *while*—e.g.: "Billingsley got to know the widow Doss pretty well *in the course of* [read *during*] the investigation." Bill Thomas, "He Can Name Tune but Can't Find Lyrics," *Jupiter Courier* (Fla.), 26 Nov. 1997, at A9.

in the event. See **event.**

in the final analysis; in the last analysis. Both CLICHÉS are likely to detract from your prose. Try to state the proposition without this tepid lead-in.

in the light of; in light of. Both are CLICHÉS. *In the light of* is the more traditional phrasing dating back to the 16th century. Increasingly, in figurative contexts other than the SET PHRASE *in the light of day*, the shorter form has come to be the standard form <in light of how much our bags weigh, it's understandable that we'd have to pay extra>. See **in lieu of (B).**

in the midst of. See **amid (B).**

in the negative. See **affirmative.**

in the offing. See **offing.**

in the process of. See **process (B).**

in the throes of. See **throes of.**

in this connection. All in all, one can understand a mid-20th-century editor's denunciation of the phrase: "Of all the superfluous baggage carried by the journalistic or literary pilgrim, this seems to me the supreme specimen of uselessness. Study this combination of words through a hundred of its innumerable intrusions into printed text, and then say if it is not a monster of futility. It is not merely unnecessary verbiage, it is an actual clogging and cluttering of the channels of clear, concise utterance. To me, as an editor, it seems to suggest desire to consume rather than to conserve paper and typewriter ribbons." Edward N. Teall, *Putting Words to Work* 276 (1940). Cf. **in connection with.**

***inthrall; *inthral.** See **enthrall.**

***intice.** See **entice.**

intimately. For a misuse of *intricately* for this word, see **intricately.**

intimidatable. So formed—not **intimidable*. E.g.: "Sloan was perhaps the least *intimidatable* player in league history." Ray Ratto, "Nobody Sings the Blues Louder than the Jazz," *News & Observer* (Raleigh), 6 June 1997, at C1. See -ATABLE.

Current ratio: 2:1

into. See **in.**

in toto (= completely, entirely, wholly, in full) is a LATINISM expressing such a fundamental notion, and having so many ready English synonyms, that it is seldom if ever justified. E.g.:

- "I asked and received permission from editor Max Brantley to reproduce it here *in toto* [read *in full*]." Meredith Oakley, "Why Not a Recall Now?" *Ark. Democrat-Gaz.,* 15 Sept. 1997, at B7.
- "Scientists had thought that given the considerable commitment of male sea horses to child care, sex roles would be swapped *in toto* [read *in full*], and the males would sit back peacefully while the females thrashed it out with one

another over the right to mate with them." Natalie Angier, "When (and Why) Dad Has the Babies," *N.Y. Times,* 28 Oct. 1997, at F1.

INTRA-. See INTER-.

intramural = conducted within the limits of an organization or body, esp. of an educational institution. The term is misused when the sense extends beyond one college or university—that is, it is impossible to have a competition remain intramural if there are competitors from elsewhere: "They are also trying to determine if there has been any recent contact between Harvard and Dartmouth, like *intramural* sports." "Link Sought Between Sicknesses at Two Colleges," *N.Y. Times,* 6 Dec. 1994, at A12.

There is no counterpart *intermural* meaning "between colleges, etc." Instead, *intermural* is an exceedingly rare "dictionary word" (attested in the *OED* only in early lexicons) meaning "between walls."

intransigence (= stubborn refusal to accommodate or compromise) is standard. **Intransigeance* and **intransigency* are NEEDLESS VARIANTS.

intrastate. See **interstate.**

intravenous (= through or into a vein) is pronounced /in-trə-**vee**-nəs/—not /in-trə-**vee**-nee-əs/. See PRONUNCIATION (B).

intricately (= in a detailed or complicated way) is sometimes misused for *intimately* (= in a close, personal way)—e.g.:

- "Hill has also been *intricately* [read *intimately*] involved with CEPA's operations at Southern Energy and has a good working relationship." Matthew C. Quinn, "Southern Co. Replaces Old Asian Hand with Georgian," *Atlanta J.-Const.,* 14 June 1997, at E1.
- "Carolyn J. Schutz, 61, the secretary of Elmhurst's Epiphany Evangelical Lutheran Church who was *intricately* [read *intimately*] involved in relief work for the area's poor, died Sunday in Elmhurst Memorial Hospital." Deborah Kadin, "Carolyn J. Schutz," *Chicago Trib.,* 11 Sept. 1997, at 9.
- "'Paul was checking off the boxes,' said SMG executive Doug Thornton, who managed the Superdome for the state and was *intricately* [read *intimately*] involved in the process." Jeff Duncan, "How the Saints Were Saved in 2005," *Times-Picayune* (New Orleans), 30 Aug. 2015, at C1.

LANGUAGE-CHANGE INDEX
intricately misused for *intimately*: Stage 1

intrigue, v.i., has traditionally meant "to carry on a plot or secret love affair." But today the word most commonly functions as a mere equivalent of *interest* or *fascinate*. Many editors object to the word when used in this newer sense—e.g.: "Seeing the heads of all four networks gathered in the same room last week is extraordinary enough. Even more *intriguing*

LANGUAGE-CHANGE INDEX (For the full key, see front matter pp. xxxi, l–li.)
Stage 1: Rejected. **Stage 2:** Widely shunned. **Stage 3:** Widespread but . . . **Stage 4:** Ubiquitous but . . . **Stage 5:** Fully accepted.
Invariably inferior forms marked by asterisk (*). • Ratios represent frequency of prevalent forms vs. variants in current books.

[read *fascinating*], however, were the downcast eyes and somber expressions." "Networks Under the Gun," *Newsweek*, 12 July 1993, at 64. (The example also shifts tense from present in the first sentence to past in the second.) In the end, however, the traditional use of *intrigue* seems doomed. The word might justifiably be considered among the SKUNKED TERMS.

LANGUAGE-CHANGE INDEX
intrigue in the sense "to interest" <this idea intrigues policy-makers>: Stage 4

introductory should never be used in the phrase *be introductory of* (something); one should instead write *introduce*. E.g.: "This first section *is introductory of* [read *introduces*] some of the tenets that constitute part of that framework." See BE-VERBS (B).

As a noun, *introductory* sometimes serves as a chapter title, but it is inferior to *introduction*.

introvert (= one whose interests are inwardly directed for the most part, often tending toward solitude) is the standard spelling. *Intravert is a variant. See **extrovert**.

Current ratio: 971:1

intrusive; obtrusive. As with the verbs *bring* and *take*, *come* and *go*, and *immigrate* and *emigrate*, some writers have trouble with the ins and outs of these adjectives. *Intrusive* means "butting in" or "prone to impose upon others against their wishes"—e.g.: "It's naggy and *intrusive*. Windows Vista is always popping up warnings and messages, making you wish you could just be left alone." David Pogue, "Hate Vista? You May Like the Fix," *N.Y. Times*, 22 Jan. 2009, at B1. *Obtrusive* means "jutting out"—e.g.: "But I like many of today's thinner TV stands because they are less *obtrusive* and come in a variety of styles." Mary Carol Garrity, "Flat-Screen TVs Offer Decorating Options," *Detroit News*, 17 Jan. 2009, at H10. But just as *bring* and *take* depend on the point of view, so do *intrusive* and *obtrusive*, to the point that the words do overlap. If you're being *intrusive*, thrusting yourself upon me against my wishes, I may find your *obtrusive* behavior rude. So are you being *intrusive* or *obtrusive*? Both, really. Or consider this example: "Part of the appeal of using a viral technique lies in the less *obtrusive* nature in which a user is confronted by it . . . ." James L. Johnston et al., "Widgets in Online Marketing Campaigns—A Balancing Act," *Metropolitan Corporate Counsel*, Jan. 2009, at 16. Either adjective might work there, though a good argument could be made that the more familiar *intrusive* fits better in this type of figurative context.

***intrust.** See **entrust.**

intuit, a mid-19th-century BACK-FORMATION from the noun *intuition*, is often useful—e.g.:

- "Perhaps Scott McNealy—the avowed anti-intellectual who once told an interviewer that his favorite book of all time was *How to Putt Like the Pros*—simply *intuited* that the day would come when Sun and Microsoft would directly face off against one another." Randall E. Stross,

"Sun's Secret Weapon," *U.S. News & World Rep.*, 26 Feb. 2001, at 49.
- "Waking from a dream of a snake swallowing its own tail, he *intuited* the structure of the benzene ring, the central mystery of his scientific quest." Rob Brezsny, "Free Will Astrology," *Village Voice*, 10 Apr. 2001, at 22.
- "Abakanowicz makes visible what is usually only *intuited*." Mary Thomas, "Sculptor Treats Art as a Sacred Creation," *Pitt. Post-Gaz.*, 6 June 2001, at E1.

LANGUAGE-CHANGE INDEX
intuit: Stage 5

***inumerable.** See **enumerable.**

inundate. So spelled, though it is often misspelled *innundate—e.g.: "The wave of children produced by baby boomers is now *innundating* [read *inundating*] the schools." Ralph Jimenez, "Local-Tax Bills Spell R-e-l-i-e-f New Ways," *Boston Globe*, 26 Jan. 1997, N.H. Weekly §, at 1.

LANGUAGE-CHANGE INDEX
inundate misspelled *innundate: Stage 1
Current ratio (*inundated* vs. *innundated): 662:1

inure; *enure. The first is the standard spelling. *Inure* = (1) to take effect, come into use <the trust money inures to the symphony's benefit>; or (2) to make accustomed to something unpleasant; habituate <she became inured to the nuisance of her neighbors' shouting and, after a time, stopped complaining>. The noun is *inurement*.

For the misuse of *inhere* for *inure*, see **inhere (B).**

Current ratio (*inured* vs. *enured): 40:1

invaluable. See **valuable.**

invent. See **discover.**

inventable; *inventible. Despite the early-19th-century predominance of *inventible, the spelling *inventable* is now standard—as it has been since about 1850. See -ABLE (A).

Current ratio: 2:1

inverse, n. See **converse.**

INVERSION. Awkward are most, though not all, grammatical inversions (like the one that begins this sentence). They seem to be on the rise in journalism—e.g.: "*Said* the silver-haired Rotblat, a professor emeritus of physics at the University of London: 'I hope the recognition will help other scientists to recognize their social responsibility.'" William D. Montalbano, "Anti-Nuclear Scientists Win Nobel Peace Prize," *L.A. Times*, 15 Oct. 1995, at A1.

The inversions especially to be avoided are the ones that suggest amateurish literary striving. The problem with these is that, "like the atmospheric inversion that is blamed for smog, the inversion of sentences creates a kind of linguistic smog that puts the reader to work sorting out the disarranged elements, causes his eyes to smart, and perhaps makes him wish he were reading something else. . . . Straining for variety in sentence structure is usually the cause. Tired of starting with the subject and adding the predicate, some writers make a mighty effort and jump out of the frying pan into the smog." Roy H. Copperud, *American Usage and Style* 210 (1980).

Inversions are probably intended to signal emphasis, but in fact they often convey preciosity—e.g.:

- "Brief and powerless is man's life. On him and all his race the slow sure doom falls pitiless and dark." Bertrand Russell, "A Free Man's Worship," 1 *Independent Rev.* 415 (1903). (Russell later called this essay "florid and oratorical"—and the inversions doubtless contributed to this effect. See *The Autobiography of Bertrand Russell 1944–1969* 247 (1969).)
- "Very careful must the writer be." Paul M. Fulcher, "The Seven Lamps of Style," in *The Foundations of English Style* 3, 13 (Paul M. Fulcher ed., 1927).
- "Write for an audience and not purely for himself, every true writer does." Gorham Munson, *The Written Word* 49 (rev. ed. 1949).
- "This it is which leads us into false comparisons and gloomy thoughts." Jacques Barzun, "English as She's Not Taught" (1953), in *A Language Reader for Writers* 189, 191 (James R. Gaskin & Jack Suberman eds., 1966).
- "In such desperately sad circumstances one is tempted to let grammatical faults pass. But a fault it is nevertheless." Robert W. Burchfield, *Points of View* 112 (1992).
- "Unaffected would be the marriage benefit of the current law, which gives a married couple a lower effective tax rate than an unmarried couple if one spouse has much less income than the other." Kathy M. Kristoff, "Tax Cuts: How They Might Affect You," *L.A. Times*, 7 Apr. 1995, at 3. (A possible revision: *The marriage benefit of the current law would be unaffected. It gives a married couple . . . .*)
- "He never wavered from his crusade. Listen he always did. Respect he always had. Love from his generous soul he always offered." John Hurt, "Eulogy of Quentin Crisp," *Time*, 6 Dec. 1999, at 41.
- "Death I thought I understood." Harold Orlans, "Old Age and Frustration," *Am. Scholar*, Winter 2001, at 115, 116.

Some inverters mar their grammar as well as their style. They have problems with singulars and plurals, being unable to distinguish the inverted predicate from the subject—e.g.:

- "Our oldest son is now driving, and with privilege *comes* [read *come*] new challenges and more gray hair for me." George Olson, "Why Did We Have Four Children?" *Orlando Sentinel*, 21 Sept. 1996, at A17. (A *his* before *privilege* would help the reader through that sentence.)
- "With increased life expectancy *comes* [read *come*] increased expectations." Stephanie Shapiro, "Down Model Shows Exceptional Talents," *Las Vegas Rev.-J.*, 27 Feb. 1997, at E3.

For an archaic verb that appears only in inverted constructions, see **quoth.**

invest. For the blunder of using *infest* for *invest*, see **infest.**

investigable. So spelled—not **investigatable.* See -ABLE (D) & -ATABLE.

Current ratio: 4:1

investigative; investigatory. *W3* calls *investigatory* "chiefly British," but it occurs almost as commonly as *investigative* in American law-enforcement contexts. There is no need for the two variants to coexist. We might be well advised to throw out *investigatory* and stick with *investigative*, or to develop some DIFFERENTIATION.

Current ratio: 10:1

invidious. This term is sometimes mistakenly, through METATHESIS, written **indivious*—e.g.: "Indivious [read *Invidious*] discrimination is not pervasive anymore." Luis Wilmot, "Affirmative Action," *San Antonio Express-News*, 25 June 1995. For more on this word, see **insidious.**

LANGUAGE-CHANGE INDEX
invidious misspelled **indivious*: Stage 1
Current ratio: 4,073:1

in view of. See **in lieu of (B).**

in view of the fact that is a weak equivalent of *because*.

inviolate; inviolable. Although the words are often used interchangeably in practice, careful writers distinguish between them. *Inviolate* suggests that something has not been violated; *inviolable* suggests that it is incapable of being violated. The more common term has always been *inviolable*.

*in virtue of. See **virtue of.**

invite. Use it in the traditional way—as a verb. Avoid it as a noun displacing *invitation*—e.g.:

- "In the meantime, he isn't counting on many *invites* [read *invitations*] to cocktail parties." Jeffrey H. Birnbaum, "Don't Show Them the Money!" *Fortune*, 3 Mar. 1997, at 116.
- "Apple Inc. will hold an *invite-only* [read *invitation-only*] event Sept. 9 at the Bill Graham Civic Auditorium in San Francisco, where it is expected to reveal the iPhone 6s." Andrea Chang, "Apple Plans Product Event at Larger Venue," *L.A. Times*, 28 Aug. 2015, Bus. §, at 2.

In conversational writing, the casual use is more at home—e.g.: "An *invite* to the porch is not an *invite* to the house." Garrison Keillor, *Lake Wobegon Days* 131 (1985).

LANGUAGE-CHANGE INDEX
invite as a noun: Stage 4

inviter; *invitor. The first spelling is standard. See -ER (A).

Current ratio: 7:1

invocable (= [1] that can be appealed to, or [2] that can be put into effect or operation) has been the standard term since the early 19th century. **Invokable* is a variant spelling. Both are pronounced /in-**voh**-kə-bəl/.

Current ratio: 2:1

LANGUAGE-CHANGE INDEX (For the full key, see front matter pp. xxxi, l–li.)
Stage 1: Rejected. **Stage 2:** Widely shunned. **Stage 3:** Widespread but . . . **Stage 4:** Ubiquitous but . . . **Stage 5:** Fully accepted.
Invariably inferior forms marked by asterisk (*). • Ratios represent frequency of prevalent forms vs. variants in current books.

in vogue is sometimes mistakenly rendered **en vogue*, doubtless as an affectation—e.g.: "Only the most optimistic or oblivious would buy a personal computer for a 13-year-old this Christmas and assume that [the] same machine would still be *en vogue* [read *in vogue* or, better, *up to date*] come college." Shaun Schafer, "Hardware Hunting," *Tulsa World*, 7 Dec. 1996, at E6.

Language-Change Index
*en vogue for *in vogue*: Stage 1
Current ratio (*in vogue* vs. **en vogue*): 36:1

invoke. See **evoke.**

in whole; in part. Wilson Follett wrote that *in whole* is unidiomatic for *as a whole*, the former phrase having been created as a needed parallel of *in part* (*MAU* at 246). He was wrong, unless we want to count as idiomatic only pre-16th-century language and to ignore steady uses up till the present time. Both *in whole* and *as a whole* (or *on the whole*) are acceptable idioms; indeed, they are not even used in quite the same way. Both refer to a complete thing, but while *as a whole* is the general phrase <as a whole, the chorus performed wonderfully>, *in whole* is always a correlative of *in part* <letters may be reprinted in whole or in part>.

-ion. See zombie nouns.

Iowan; *Iowegian. The first is standard; the second is a rare variant. See denizen labels.

I personally, a phrase that grew enormously in popularity during the 20th century, is usually prolix for a simple *I*. Occasionally, though, it legitimately contrasts one's personal opinion with a contrary stance or action <I personally don't care if you smoke, but the city ordinance says you can't do it here, and I can get fined if I let you>. See first person. For *I myself*, see **myself** & pronouns (e).

ipse dixit (lit., "he himself said it") = something said but not proved; a dogmatic statement. E.g.:

- "Cogent legal reasoning was subordinated to *ipse dixit*." "Benchmarks of the Administration," *Wash. Times*, 11 Jan. 1994, at A14.
- "[Justice Brennan's] real doctrine always showed through. It was the doctrine of *ipse dixit*: He has said it, so it must be so." "Death with Dignity," *Richmond Times-Dispatch*, 30 Apr. 1996, at A8.
- "As with the whole article, this is just so much *ipse dixit*, without a shred of proof." Clive Stafford Smith, "All Talk and No Trousers," *Guardian*, 9 Aug. 2009, Comment §.

ipsissima verba. See **verbatim.**

ipso facto (= by the fact or act itself; by its very nature) is sometimes replaceable by a more direct wording, such as *necessarily* or *in itself*—e.g.:

- "Tales of oppression are *innately* [read *inherently*] dramatic. That doesn't *mean—ipso facto—*[read *necessarily mean*] they make good plays." Laurie Winer, " 'To Take Arms' Struggles to Find Real-Life Drama," *L.A. Times*, 14 Feb. 1997, at F8. (On the misuse of *innately* in that sentence, see **innately.**)

- "What interests me is Dixon's notion that talking about polygamy and same-sex unions in the same breath is, *ipso facto* [read *in itself*], offensive." David Reinhard, "Polygamy and Gay Marriage," *Oregonian* (Portland), 22 June 2008, Editorial §, at 5.

But the latinism is sometimes undeniably useful—e.g.: "H.L. Mencken, who began his career as a police reporter in Baltimore, wrote that he quickly encountered what he called the 'police mentality': Every person accused or suspected of a crime is *ipso facto* guilty of that offense." Jack Wardlaw, "Reacting to a Harmful TV Story," *Times-Picayune* (New Orleans), 12 Jan. 1997, at B7. The phrase need not be italicized.

Iran. In educated speech, the country's name is pronounced either /i-**rahn**/ (preferred) or /i-**ran**/ (more anglicized). Avoid the xenophobic yokel's pronunciation /ɪ-**ran**/ or /ɪ-ran/.

The corresponding adjective and denizen label is *Iranian*, pronounced /i-**rahn**-ee-ən/ (preferred) or /i-**ray**-nee-ən/. Avoid /i-**ran**-ee-ən/ and especially /ɪ-**ray**-nee-ən/ or /ɪ-ray-nee-ən/. See names (c).

Iraq. In educated speech, the country's name is pronounced either /i-**rahk**/ (preferred) or /i-**rak**/ (more anglicized). Avoid /ɪ-**rak**/ and /ɪ-rak/, which smack of ignorance and perhaps enmity.

The corresponding adjective and denizen label is *Iraqi*, pronounced /i-**rahk**-ee/ (preferred) or /i-**rak**-ee/. Avoid /ɪ-**rak**-ee/ and /ɪ-rak-ee/. See names (c).

iridescent. So spelled. **Irridescent* is a common misspelling—e.g.: "The Corrente was positively *irridescent* [read *iridescent*] in a French impressionist manner." Richard Dyer, "Schepkin Masterfully Projects Emotional Conflict," *Boston Globe*, 2 Nov. 1996, at C3. (On the use of *masterfully* in the title of that article, see **masterful.**)

Language-Change Index
iridescent misspelled **irridescent*: Stage 1
Current ratio: 77:1

ironic; ironical. *Ironic* is standard. **Ironical* is a needless variant that used to be the preferred form; it is still occasionally seen in BrE.

Ironic denotes (1) feigned ignorance used against an adversary to elicit information or to point up fallacy in the adversary's position; (2) a feigned attitude used to produce an effect opposite of what that attitude would seem to convey, such as faint praise used to express contempt, or apparent scorn used to express enthusiasm; or (3) a situation or event that has the opposite outcome of what might have been expected; a twist of fate. Senses 1 and 2 are classic, even classical. Sense 3 is modern, now predominant, and apt to raise the hackles of classicists.

Sense 1, often called *Socratic irony*, is typified by Plato's chronicling of his teacher's conversation, in which Socrates assumed a philosophical position similar to that of his Sophist counterpart, leading to situations where faulty reasoning behind those positions became obvious. This device is still used in American law schools and elsewhere (the *Socratic method*).

Sense 2, often called *literary irony* or *romantic irony*, also involves communication or a situation that is not what it appears to be, though typically the audience or another character understands the intent. Examples abound, among the most famous being Jonathan Swift's satirical *A Modest Proposal*, in which the solution to the Irish famine is suggested to be the eating of children.

Sense 3, often called *situational irony*, is more extended—some would say overextended. It takes in any situation or run of events "that seems deliberately contrary to what was or might be expected; an outcome cruelly, humorously, or strangely at odds with assumptions or expectations" (*OED*). How broad is that? One critic goes so far as to say that "all genuine fiction is, by nature, ironic. For fiction, whether comic or tragic, dramatizes the interplay of compelling opposites . . . ." R.W.B. Lewis, *The American Adam* 91 (2009).

For many, though, the singer Alanis Morissette crossed the line with "Ironic," a song on her 1995 album *Jagged Little Pill*. That tune itemizes such misfortunes as rain on your wedding day, a fly in your wine, and a traffic jam when you're running late. All amount to tough luck, but they are hardly ironic.

ironically. See SENTENCE ADVERBS.

Iroquois (the Indian tribe) is pronounced /**ir**-ə-kwoy/ or /**ir**-ə-koy/—not /**ir**-ə-kwoyz/ or /**ir**-ə-kwah/. The plural is *Iroquois*, pronounced identically.

irrebuttable; irrefutable. To see how these words should be differentiated, see the entry on *rebut* and *refute* under **rebut**. On the pronunciation of *irrefutable*, see **refutable**.

***irregardless**, a semiliterate PORTMANTEAU WORD from *irrespective* and *regardless*, should have been stamped out long ago. But it's common enough in speech that it has found its way into all manner of print sources—e.g.:

- "*Irregardless* [read *Regardless*] of the Big Ten outcome, Knight said he is gratified with IU's improvement over last season." Stan Sutton, "Hoosiers, with Help from Iowa, Could Share Big Ten Crown," *Courier-J.* (Louisville), 10 Mar. 1991, at C1.
- "A similar result for the case of finitely repeated games establishes that, *irregardless* [read *regardless*] of whether the number of repetitions is finite or infinite, the swing producer strategy is one possible strategy for achieving profits." James M. Griffin & William S. Neilson, "The 1985–86 Oil Price Collapse and Afterwards," *Economic Inquiry*, Oct. 1994, at 543.
- "Pensions were awarded by the states in which veterans lived after the war, *irregardless* [read *regardless*] of which state the veteran served in." Laura C. Edwards, *Three Centuries in America* 205 (1999).

Perhaps the most surprising instance of this barbarism occurs in a linguistics text, four times on a single page (what follows is a representative instance): "Compounds that were presented without a space received shorter gaze durations (*irregardless* [read *regardless*] of how they were supposed to be spaced)." Barbara J. Juhasz, Albrecht W. Inhoff & Keith Rayner, "The Role of Interword Spaces in the Processing of English Compound Words," in *Current Issues in Morphological Processing* 291, 305 (Pam Frost et al. eds., 2005).

Although this widely scorned NONWORD seems unlikely to spread much more than it already has, careful users of language must continually swat it when they encounter it.

LANGUAGE-CHANGE INDEX
*irregardless for *regardless* or *irrespective*: Stage 2
Current ratio (*regardless* vs. **irregardless*): 572:1

IRREGULAR VERBS. A. The Forms. There are two types of verbs—regular (or "weak") and irregular (or "strong"). Irregular verbs form the past tense or past participle in unpredictable ways, usually by changing the vowel of the present-tense form, without the addition of an ending (e.g., *begin, began; rise, rose; wring, wrung*). Regular verbs, by contrast, form the past tense by adding *-ed, -d,* or *-t* to the present tense.

Irregular verbs are sometimes called "strong" verbs because they seem to form the past tense from their own resources, without calling an ending to their assistance. The regular verbs are sometimes called "weak" verbs because they cannot form the past tense without the aid of the ending (most often *-ed*).

All told, English now has fewer than 270 live irregular verbs. The trend is against the irregular forms: "For many centuries there has been a steady loss in favor of the weak class." George O. Curme, *English Grammar* § 42.B.2, at 73 (1947). Here are the most common irregular forms:

Present Tense	Past Tense	Past Participle
abide	abode	abode
arise	arose	arisen
be	was	been
bear	bore	borne
beat	beat	beaten
become	became	become
beget	begot	begotten
begin	began	begun
behold	beheld	beheld
bend	bent	bent
beseech	besought	besought
beset	beset	beset
bet	bet	bet
bid (express)	bade	bidden
bid (offer)	bid	bid
bind	bound	bound
bite	bit	bitten
bleed	bled	bled
blow	blew	blown

LANGUAGE-CHANGE INDEX (For the full key, see front matter pp. xxxi, l–li.)
Stage 1: Rejected. **Stage 2:** Widely shunned. **Stage 3:** Widespread but . . . **Stage 4:** Ubiquitous but . . . **Stage 5:** Fully accepted.
Invariably inferior forms marked by asterisk (*). • Ratios represent frequency of prevalent forms vs. variants in current books.

break	broke	broken		make	made	made
breed	bred	bred		mean	meant	meant
bring	brought	brought		meet	met	met
broadcast	broadcast	broadcast		mistake	mistook	mistaken
build	built	built		overcome	overcame	overcome
burst	burst	burst		overtake	overtook	overtaken
buy	bought	bought		pay	paid	paid
cast	cast	cast		put	put	put
catch	caught	caught		quit	quit	quit
choose	chose	chosen		read	read	read
cleave (= to split)	cleft	cleft		rend	rent	rent
cling	clung	clung		rid	rid	rid
come	came	come		ride	rode	ridden
cost	cost	cost		ring	rang	rung
creep	crept	crept		rise	rose	risen
cut	cut	cut		rive	rove	riven
deal	dealt	dealt		run	ran	run
dig	dug	dug		say	said	said
dive	dove (AmE)	dived		see	saw	seen
do	did	done		seek	sought	sought
draw	drew	drawn		sell	sold	sold
drink	drank	drunk		send	sent	sent
drive	drove	driven		set	set	set
dwell	dwelt	dwelt		sew	sewed	sewn
eat	ate	eaten		shake	shook	shaken
fall	fell	fallen		shed	shed	shed
feed	fed	fed		shine	shone	shone
feel	felt	felt		shoot	shot	shot
fight	fought	fought		show	showed	shown
find	found	found		shrink	shrank	shrunk
fit	fit	fit		shut	shut	shut
flee	fled	fled		sing	sang	sung
fling	flung	flung		sink	sank	sunk
fly	flew	flown		sit	sat	sat
forbear	forbore	forborne		slay	slew	slain
forbid	forbade	forbidden		sleep	slept	slept
forecast	forecast	forecast		slide	slid	slid
forget	forgot	forgotten		sling	slung	slung
forgive	forgave	forgiven		slink	slunk	slunk
forsake	forsook	forsaken		slit	slit	slit
forswear	forswore	forsworn		smite	smote	smitten
freeze	froze	frozen		sow	sowed	sown
get	got	gotten (AmE), got (BrE)		speak	spoke	spoken
				speed	sped	sped
give	gave	given		spend	spent	spent
go	went	gone		spin	spun	spun
grind	ground	ground		spit	spat	spat
grow	grew	grown		split	split	split
hang (a picture)	hung	hung		spread	spread	spread
have	had	had		spring	sprang	sprung
hear	heard	heard		stand	stood	stood
hide	hid	hidden		steal	stole	stolen
hit	hit	hit		stick	stuck	stuck
hold	held	held		sting	stung	stung
hurt	hurt	hurt		stink	stank	stunk
keep	kept	kept		strew	strewed	strewn
kneel	knelt	knelt		stride	strode	strode
know	knew	known		strike	struck	struck
lay (= to place)	laid	laid		string	strung	strung
lead	led	led		strive	strove	striven
leap	leapt	leapt		swear	swore	sworn
leave	left	left		sweep	swept	swept
lend	lent	lent		swim	swam	swum
let	let	let		swing	swung	swung
lie (= to rest)	lay	lain		take	took	taken
light	lit	lit		teach	taught	taught
lose	lost	lost		tear	tore	torn

tell	told	told
think	thought	thought
throw	threw	thrown
thrust	thrust	thrust
tread	trod	trodden
undergo	underwent	undergone
understand	understood	understood
undertake	undertook	undertaken
undo	undid	undone
uphold	upheld	upheld
upset	upset	upset
wake	woke	woken (or waked)
wear	wore	worn
weave	wove	woven
weep	wept	wept
win	won	won
wind	wound	wound
withdraw	withdrew	withdrawn
withhold	withheld	withheld
withstand	withstood	withstood
wring	wrung	wrung
write	wrote	written

B. Past-Participial Adjectives No Longer Used as Verb Forms. Many past participles no longer exist as verbs in good usage, but continue as adjectives. For examples discussed in entries throughout this book, see **behold** (the adjective being *beholden*), **cleave** (*cloven*), **laden, melt** (*molten*), **mow** (*mown*), **proved** (*proven*), **saw** (*sawn*), **shape** (*misshapen, well-shapen*), **shave** (*shaven*), **stricken** & **swell** (*swollen*). Some adjectives of this type persist only as ARCHAISMS; see **engrave** (*engraven*) & **gnaw** (*gnawn*).

C. AmE vs. BrE. Sometimes the choice between two past-tense or (more commonly) past-participial forms depends on which major strain of English one is working in. AmE prefers *gotten*, BrE *got*. See **get (B).** A similar pair is *hewed* (AmE) and *hewn* (BrE).

D. Dialectal Forms. One characteristic of DIALECT is the use of past participles in place of past-tense verbs—e.g., *it begun a moment ago, *he swum, *the shirt shrunk, *the grass sprung up, *she sung loudly. For examples discussed in various entries, see **drink** (*I drunk it all*), **sink** (*he sunk*) & **swim** (*she swum*).

Another dialectal trait is the use of past-tense verbs for past participles—e.g., *she had began piano lessons, *he's been bit by a snake. See **begin (c)** (*had began*), **bite** (*had bit*), **drink** (*had drank*) & **shake** (*was shook*).

Still another characteristic of dialect is the use of regular past forms for irregular verbs—e.g., *the shirt shrinked, *the bee stinged me, *he sweared he'd never let it happen, *he swinged at the ball. For examples discussed in various entries, see **bet** (*betted*), **cast** (*casted*), **deal** (*dealed*), **drive** (*drived*), **shrink** (*shrinked*) & **strew** (*strewed*).

Finally, dialects have many irregular past forms differing from those of STANDARD ENGLISH. See **bring (A)** (*brung*), **buy (A)** (*boughten*), **chide** (*chid, *chidden*),

climb (A) (*clomb and *clumb*), **drag** (*drug*), **drown (A)** (*drownded*), **overflow** (*overflown*), **pleaded** (*pled*), **ride** (*rid*), **sling** (*slang*), *snuck & **swell** (*swoll, *swole*). Over time an irregular form might become standard; for example, see **fit.**

For the related issue of phrases such as *might should have, see DOUBLE MODALS.

E. Derived Nouns Used as Verbs. Often, when an irregular verb forms a noun (especially a compound noun) and that noun is then used as a verb, the inflection is regular rather than irregular. For example, in baseball a ball that is hit into the air is a *fly ball*, often shortened to a *fly*. When a batter hits one, we say that he *flied* (not *flew*) out to left field. (See **fly.**) When the ball makes a beeline to an outfielder without touching the ground, we say that the batter *line-drived* (not *line-drove*) it. (See **drive.**) When someone gets the cold-shoulder treatment from associates, we may even say, colloquially, that the person has been *deep-freezed, though in this particular instance most fastidious editors would prefer *deep-frozen*. (See **deep-freeze.**) Essentially the root verb is removed from its native grammatical form when it is made into a noun (*fly, line-drive, deep-freeze*), and when the noun is then used as a verb it demands regular inflections in order to maintain a close association with the derived noun. Otherwise, the reader is distracted by a MISCUE, such as seeing the batter actually flying or driving.

F. Choice Between -*ed* and -'*d*. See -ED.

irrelevance; irrelevancy. The DIFFERENTIATION is as follows: *irrelevance* states a quality <the irrelevance of the documents>, while *irrelevancy* cites an instance <one irrelevancy after another>. The only plural form, therefore, is *irrelevancies*. See **relevance.**

irrelevant is sometimes, through METATHESIS, made *irrevelant. And this spurious form appears in otherwise literate publications—e.g.:

- "The world trade talks are *irrevelant* [read *irrelevant*] to much of the U.S. trade debate." R.C. Longworth, "Global Trade Talks May End as Boon, or a Mouthful of Air," *Chicago Trib.*, 7 Dec. 1993, News §, at 1.
- "Democrats know that if Bush chalks up a string of big victories early on, they run the risk of becoming politically *irrevelant* [read *irrelevant*]." Sue Kirchhoff & Susan Milligan, "Ten-Year Tax Cut Plan Battered by Winds of Politics," *Boston Globe*, 19 Feb. 2001, at A13.

The two words are also confused in speech, by mispronunciation, much like *calvary* and *cavalry*. See **calvary.**

LANGUAGE-CHANGE INDEX
irrevelant for *irrelevant*: Stage 1
Current ratio (*irrelevant* vs. *irrevelant*): 2,140:1

irreligious; unreligious; nonreligious. All three words essentially mean "not religious." But the *ir*-prefix usually marks a dichotomy (e.g., *rational* vs.

LANGUAGE-CHANGE INDEX (For the full key, see front matter pp. xxxi, l–li.)
Stage 1: Rejected. **Stage 2:** Widely shunned. **Stage 3:** Widespread but . . . **Stage 4:** Ubiquitous but . . . **Stage 5:** Fully accepted.
Invariably inferior forms marked by asterisk (*). • Ratios represent frequency of prevalent forms vs. variants in current books.

irrational), so *irreligious* often suggests conscious indifference or even hostility toward religion. It is a judgmental term. *Unreligious* is less negative, but *non-religious* is the most common and the most reliably neutral. Cf. **sacrilegious.**

irreparable is pronounced /i-**rep**-ə-rə-bəl/—not /eer-ə-**pair**-ə-bəl/. Cf. **reparable.**

irrepressible. So spelled—not **irrepressable*. See -ABLE (A).

> Current ratio: 2,242:1

irresistible. So spelled—preferably not **irresistable*. See -ABLE (A).

> Current ratio: 158:1

irrespective of = regardless of. E.g.: "*Irrespective of* the bomb's part in the outcome of World War II, we all owe President Truman our gratitude for another reason." "Bomb's Lessons," *Phoenix Gaz.*, 13 Feb. 1995, at B12. Confusion of the words *irrespective* and *regardless* has given rise to the semiliterate **irregardless*. See **irregardless*.

*irresponsive. See **unresponsive.**

irrevocable; **unrevokable; *irrevokable.* The first—the preferred form—is pronounced /i-**rev**-ə-kə-bəl/, not /ir-ə-**voh**-kə-bəl/. (See PRONUNCIATION (B).) **Unrevokable* is a NEEDLESS VARIANT. **Irrevokable* is simply a misspelling.

On *irrevocable* as a noncomparable adjective, see ADJECTIVES (B).

> LANGUAGE-CHANGE INDEX
> *irrevocable* mispronounced /ir-ə-**voh**-kə-bəl/: Stage 4

irruption. See **eruption.**

-ISE. See -IZE.

is is. As early as the 1980s, a doubled *is* (called a reduplicative copula) became common in American speech <what I meant is is that . . .>. This is not the type of double that is sometimes grammatically required <what it is is a major ripoff>. (See **what it is is.**) Rather, the second *is* is grammatically superfluous <the thing that concerns me is is that I'm late>. Rarely is this form found in writing, even when speech containing it is transcribed. In any event, it isn't an expression for careful speakers.

For a detailed linguistic explanation of this sloppy phrasing—or, as the authors of the study chastely put it, its "teleological raison d'être"—see Michael Shapiro & Michael C. Haley, "The Reduplicative Copula *Is Is*," 77 *Am. Speech* 305–12 (2002). Although the authors trace this construction back only to the 1990s, it certainly existed in 1984: the minister who performed my wedding service in May of that year used it habitually (I thought anomalously).

> LANGUAGE-CHANGE INDEX
> *is is* for *is*: Stage 2

isolable, not **isolatable*, is the standard form—e.g.: "They are more genetically *isolatable* [read *isolable*]

right now than any ethnic group or gay people." David Berreby, "Up with People," *New Republic*, 29 Apr. 1996, at 14. See -ABLE (D) & -ATABLE.

> LANGUAGE-CHANGE INDEX
> **isolatable* for *isolable*: Stage 4
> Current ratio (*isolable* vs. **isolatable*): 2:1

isosceles. So spelled. See SPELLING (A).

Israel (the country) is pronounced /**iz**-ree-əl/ or /**iz**-ray-əl/—not /**iz**-rəl/. In some hymns and other ecclesiastical vocal works, the name is given special pronunciations, such as /**iz**-rı-el/ and /**is**-rı-el/. These have no place in ordinary speech. See NAMES (C).

issue. A. *At issue; in issue.* *At issue* = (1) (of people) in controversy; taking opposite sides of a case or contrary views of a matter; at variance <his views are at issue with mine>; or (2) (of matters or questions) in dispute; under discussion; in question <the allegations at issue> (*OED*). The *OED* notes that *in issue* shares sense 2 of *at issue*, but calls it rare. Having originated in mid-19th-century legal contexts, *in issue* is common in law but rare elsewhere. *At issue* is the ordinary idiomatic phrase.

B. *Issue as to whether; issue of whether.* These phrases are prolix for *issue whether*. Cf. **question whether.** See **as to (B)** & **whether (B).**

C. In the Sense of "offspring" or "descendants." In the drafting of wills and trusts, the word *issue* invites litigation. English courts—as well as courts in New York and New Jersey—have held that it means all descendants, however remote. Other courts have held that the word refers only to children and not to more remote descendants. And whether it covers adopted children is a question that courts will answer differently. In sum, the word is best avoided altogether.

But anyone who uses it should use it grammatically, and that is not difficult. The question sometimes arises whether the word should be treated as a singular or as a plural noun. The answer is either—e.g.: "Any *issue who is a minor* [or *issue who are minors*] will be assigned a guardian."

D. *Have issues with.* Although the colloquial use of *issue* to mean *problem* is becoming common, many people find it grating. It especially stands out in the trendy construction *have issues with*—e.g.:

- "Both kids *have issues with* [read *are troubled by*] their parents' sexuality." Roger Ebert, *Roger Ebert's Movie Yearbook 2007* 655 (2006).
- "This is the third time he's had his left knee repaired, and I'm hard-pressed to name another golfer—a top-flight one—who's had the knee *issues* [read *problems*] he's had." Dan Daly, "Woods' Forbidden Apple Pays Off," *Wash. Times*, 18 June 2008, at C1.

Outside the *have issues with* construction, *issue* and *problem* are often close to synonymous—e.g.: "Cleveland's version of Phalen Boulevard—a proposed 2¾-mile stretch of road from Interstate 490 to University Circle—has been bottled up by money *issues*." Jim Nichols, "Proposal for Corridor Faces Major Obstacles," *Plain Dealer* (Cleveland), 13 July 2008, at A10. In this example, *issues* denotes matters of public interest, but those issues probably involve money *problems*.

E. And *edition*. In the newspaper business, the two terms are distinguished. At *The New York Times*, "[a]n issue means all the copies printed on a given day. There may be several *editions* of one *issue*." *The New York Times Manual of Style and Usage* 117 (1999).

Istanbulite; Istanbullu. A citizen of Istanbul, Turkey, is known predominantly in English as an *Istanbulite*. The Turkish *Istanbullu* is a variant term sometimes encountered. See DENIZEN LABELS.

isthmus is pronounced /**is**-məs/ or /**isth**-məs/. The latter is almost unpronounceable, and there's no good reason to try. Pl. *isthmuses*. The word derives from the Greek *isthmos*, and it is an error to make the plural—as some do—**isthmi*. See HYPERCORRECTION (A).
     Current ratio (*isthmuses* vs. **isthmi*): 2:1

is to do with. See **has to do with.**

it. This EXPLETIVE and pronoun often appears too many times in one sentence. Careful writers restrict it (*it*, that is) to one meaning in a given sentence—no more. The problems with using more than one in a sentence are threefold. First, ambiguity may arise if each of two pronominal *its* refers to a different antecedent from the other. Second, the sentence may well contain a MISCUE if readers can't immediately distinguish the pronoun *it* from an expletive *it*. And third, having one *it* followed closely by another often impairs euphony.

The most common sloppiness is to use the expletive *it* and the personal pronoun *it* in the same passage—e.g.:

- "For anyone who really watches the program, *it* is obvious that *it* is not a 'political attack' on Catholicism." Andrew M. Greeley, "TV Series No Threat to Catholics," *Salt Lake Trib.*, 1 Nov. 1997, at B3. (A possible revision: *Anyone who watches the program will see that it is not a "political attack" on Catholicism.*)
- "Despite the sharp rise in inequality, *it* does not look as if inequality will be an issue in the year 2000 elections. Maybe America will just learn to live with much higher levels of inequality. India does—and *it* is, after all, a democracy. But then again, maybe *it* won't." Lester C. Thurow, "Inequalities in Wealth a Political, Not Economic Problem," *USA Today*, 23 Nov. 1999, at A19. (The problem there is that *it* refers, in the next-to-last sentence, to *India*. But in the final sentence, *it* refers to *America*, which occurs two sentences before. One solution would be to put the next-to-last sentence in parentheses. [It's a parenthetical thought, after all.] Another solution would be to write *But then again, maybe America won't learn to tolerate this type of inequality.*)
- "More people work in retail than any other business sector in Canada, but few *it* seems view *it* as a real career." Hollie Shaw, "Changing the Perception of Retail as Career," *Nat'l Post* (Can.), 1 Sept. 2015, at 4. (A possible revision: *Though the retail sector employs more Canadians than any other, it seems that few in the industry view their jobs as real careers.*)

Also, avoid the double expletive—two filler words in a single phrase. One filler *it* will do—e.g.:

- "*It* is evident that *it* will become necessary to hike taxes from year to year as federal and state dollars dwindle." "Unfair Tax Proposal," *Miami Times*, 8 May 1997, at A4. (A possible revision: *The city will surely have to hike taxes each year as federal and state dollars dwindle.*)
- "Now, coach Dave Wannstedt says, *it* is apparent that *it* will take more time for Hughes to acclimate himself to the backfield." Melissa Isaacson, "Nasty Weather Creates Nasty Situations," *Chicago Trib.*, 17 Aug. 1997, at 9. (A possible revision: *Now, coach Dave Wannstedt says, Hughes will need more time to acclimate himself to the backfield.*)

When used after a passive-voice verb, *it* often gives the misimpression that it's a pronoun with an antecedent. E.g.:

- "The burial was to take place at Highgate, and *it* was intended to take the body by train from Winooski to Cambridge Junction over the defendant's road and thence over the connecting road to Highgate." (The full passive is *it was intended (by someone) to take the body*; yet, on first reading, *it* appears to refer to *burial*.)
- "Despite her prediction that the economic recovery will be slow, *it* is expected that the company will flourish during the next few quarters." (*It* seems at first to refer to *economic recovery* when in fact it is merely an expletive.) See MISCUES.

In short, delete *it* when you can; and if you need it, keep it to one meaning within a sentence.

ITALICS. A. Generally. H.W. Fowler cautioned that many people, though competent in their own special subjects, don't have enough writing experience to realize that they shouldn't try to achieve emphasis by italicizing something in every tenth sentence (*FMEU1* at 304). With experience comes the competence to frame sentences so that emphatic words fall in emphatic places. (See SENTENCE ENDS.) Also, the writer learns the techniques of subtle repetition—the type that reinforces an idea without cloying.

Ralph Waldo Emerson overstated the case: "'Tis a good rule of rhetoric [that] Schlegel gives—'In good prose, every word is underscored,' which, I suppose, means, Never italicize." "Lectures and Biographical Sketches," in 10 *Complete Works of Emerson* 169 (1904). By the same reasoning, of course, one might say that we should abolish question marks, exclamation points, and even commas. The point is to italicize only when one must.

B. Foreign Phrases. If an imported term hasn't been fully naturalized, it should appear in italics—e.g.: *au mieux* (Fr. "on the best terms"); *cogito, ergo sum* (L. "I think, therefore I am"); *dolce far niente* (Ital. "sweet idleness"); *Weltschmerz* (Ger. "depression or pessimism caused by comparing the world's actual circumstances with ideal ones"). But because English is such a diverse language—having drawn from the resources of dozens of other languages—it

LANGUAGE-CHANGE INDEX (For the full key, see front matter pp. xxxi, l–li.)
Stage 1: Rejected. **Stage 2:** Widely shunned. **Stage 3:** Widespread but . . . **Stage 4:** Ubiquitous but . . . **Stage 5:** Fully accepted.
Invariably inferior forms marked by asterisk (*). • Ratios represent frequency of prevalent forms vs. variants in current books.

is quite hospitable to foreign-looking words. That is, they become naturalized easily. And when that happens, the terms are written in ordinary roman type. (See GARNER'S LAW.) The words in the following list are italicized here only because they're being referred to as words—e.g.: *caveat emptor* (L.), *décolletage* (Fr.), *gestalt* (Ger.), *glasnost* (Russ.). A good dictionary usually provides guidance on which words should be italicized.

For more on foreignisms, see GALLICISMS & LATINISMS.

Italy (the country) is pronounced /it-ə-lee/, the corresponding adjective being *Italian* /i-**tal**-yən/—never /ɪ-**tal**-yən/ (characteristic of uneducated speech). See NAMES (C).

itemization is often unnecessary for *list*.

iterate. Although *iterate* (= to repeat) is not an equivalent of *underscore* or *ensure*, some writers apparently think so—e.g.: "The always-busy [Quincy] Jones is currently completing an ambitious project that *iterates* [read *underscores*] his place in American music annals, an album of new songs and updated classics called *Q's Jook Joint*." John H. Ostdick, "The Joint Is Jumping," *Am. Way*, 15 Oct. 1995, at 16. See **reiterate.**

LANGUAGE-CHANGE INDEX
iterate misused for *underscore* or *ensure*: Stage 1

it goes without saying. See **goes without saying.**

it is I; it is me. Generally, of course, the nominative pronoun (here *I*) is the complement of a linking verb <this is she> <it was he>. But *it is me* and *it's me* are fully acceptable, especially in informal contexts: "both forms, 'It is I' and 'It is me,' are correct—one by virtue of grammatical rule, the other by virtue of common educated usage." Norman Lewis, *Better English* 186–87 (rev. ed. 1961).

The phrasing has elicited a great deal of comment over the years, mostly in its defense—e.g.:

- " 'It is me' is not frequent till the first half of the eighteenth century. Before that, 'It is I' was general." W. Murison, "Changes in the Language Since Shakespeare's Time," 14 *Cambridge History of English Literature* 434, 446 (1932).
- "Such a change [as] from *It is I* to *It's me* is probably a benefit to the English language. It involves no ambiguity, simplifies grammar, and is intrinsically as euphonious as the alternative form." Janet Rankin Aiken, *Commonsense Grammar* 26 (1936).
- "The facts surrounding the case of 'It is *me*' are: 1. This expression is in accepted use in informal situations. 2. It is preferable to 'It is *I*' whenever the speaker wishes to emphasize his own personal identity. It is so used and has been so used by dozens of reputable writers from Shakespeare to the present, including such men as Emerson, Meredith, and Stevenson. 3. So far as anyone knows, it has been in good colloquial use for three or four centuries, though for most of that time, the grammarians have been grumbling about it. 4. Many careful, sensitive speakers and writers employ both 'It is *me*' and 'It is *I*,' depending on the desired shade of meaning." Walter Barnes, "Stepchildren of the Mother Tongue," 95 *Review of Reviews*, Mar. 1937, at 59–60.

- "By the rules of grammar and the dictates of the pedant, it's heinous. But if everybody who says it were to be hanged, the trees would be full of strange fruit, and soon there would be nobody left to string the culprits up. The second pronoun is in apposition with the first, and should agree with it in number, gender and case. But 'It's I' is awfully straitlaced." Edward N. Teall, *Putting Words to Work* 298–99 (1940).

Of course, those with even a smattering of French know that *It's me* answers nicely to *C'est moi*. Good writers have long found the English equivalent serviceable—e.g.:

- "*It is* not *me* you are in love with." Richard Steele, *The Spectator*, No. 290, 1 Feb. 1712.
- "But Silver . . . called out to know if *that were me*." Robert Louis Stevenson, *Treasure Island* 72 (1883; repr. 1985).
- "Not more than four people know that *it is me*." Raymond Paton, *Autobiography of a Blackguard* 42 (1924).
- "*It's* only *me*." Ian Anderson, "Aqualung" (1971) (song lyric).
- "Begin *talking* out your thoughts on paper as if you were explaining a concept to a friend. Imagine that *it's me*." John R. Trimble, *Writing with Style* 22 (2d ed. 2000).

E.B. White told an amusing story about the fear that so many writers have of making a mistake: "One time a newspaper sent us to a morgue to get a story on a woman whose body was being held for identification. A man believed to be her husband was brought in. Somebody pulled the sheet back; the man took one agonizing look, and cried, 'My God, it's her!' When we reported this grim incident, the editor diligently changed it to 'My God, it's she!' " E.B. White, "English Usage," in *The Second Tree from the Corner* 150, 150–51 (1954).

Similar problems arise in the third person, as in *it is him*. When the contraction appears, *Newsweek* makes the phrase *it's him*—e.g.: "Rostenkowski simply signed an expense-account voucher for stamps that Smith converted into cash. The first time he says he witnessed the alleged scheme, in 1989, 'I was no doubt taken aback when I saw his [Rostenkowski's] name on the [$2,000] voucher. I couldn't believe it was him.' Most Democrats on Capitol Hill still can't believe *it's him*." Jonathan Alter, "Rostenkowski Reeling," *Newsweek*, 2 Aug. 1993, at 20. See PRONOUNS (B).

it is important to note that; it is interesting to note that. These sentence nonstarters merely gather lint. They should be abolished.

it is me. See **it is I.**

its; it's. The possessive form of *it* is *its*; the contraction for *it is* is *it's*. But the two words are often confounded—e.g.:

- "Potter County was ordered by the state to do something about overcrowding in *it's* [read *its*] system." Zachary Walker, "Randall Needs Jail Space," *Canyon News* (Tex.), 13 Jan. 1994, at 1.
- "For all *it's* [read *its*] faults, . . . this is a pretty interesting film." Craig Kopp, "Fox Film Mixes Wit, Horror," *Cincinnati Post*, 19 July 1996, at B1.
- "The best moment . . . brings out some energy and droll humor, but *its* [read *it's*] not enough to keep this unfocused

piece from meandering off to nowhere." Mike Steele, "Avant-Garde Roots, Performing Charisma Unite 'Three Women at the Fore,'" *Star Trib.* (Minneapolis), 16 Jan. 1998, at B5.

Confusion is just as much a problem in BrE as it is in AmE—e.g.:

- "With insurgent country providing some of the most clearly defined American rock since grunge, it was never going to be long before the movement found *it's* [read *its*] very own Nirvana." Tom Cox, "This Week's Pop CD Releases," *Guardian*, 16 Jan. 1998, at T16.
- "But fear not because fashion does award *it's* [read *its*] very own New Year's Honour's list of modern classics." James Sherwood, "Real Shopping, Police Style," *Independent*, 16 Jan. 2000, at 8.

See SPELLING (A).

Also, the possessive *its* should never be used—as it sometimes is—as a personal pronoun in place of *his*, *her*, or *his or her*.

> LANGUAGE-CHANGE INDEX
> 1. *it's* misused for *its*: Stage 2
> Current ratio (*its own* vs. **it's own*): 494:1
> 2. *its* misused for *it's*: Stage 2
> Current ratio (*it's not* vs. **its not*): 41:1

it's me. See **it is I.**

I wonder. See QUESTIONS, DIRECT AND INDIRECT.

-IZE; -ISE. Adding the suffix *-ize* (or *-ise* in BrE) to an adjective or noun is one of the most frequently used ways of forming new verbs. Many verbs so formed are unobjectionable—e.g.: *authorize, baptize, familiarize, recognize, sterilize,* and *symbolize.* The religious leader Norman Vincent Peale helped popularize (ahem) the suffix in the mid-20th century: "'*Picturize, prayerize,* and *actualize*' was Peale's key formula." Tim Stafford, "God's Salesman," *Christianity Today*, 21 June 1993, at 35.

But NEOLOGISMS ending in *-ize* are generally to be discouraged, for they are usually ungainly and often superfluous. Hence we have no use for *artificialize, audiblize, cubiclize, fenderize* (= to fix a dented fender), *funeralize, ghettoize, Mirandize, nakedize, obituarize,* and so on. Careful writers are wary of new words formed with this suffix. See, for example, **Mirandize,** ***operationalize** & **prioritize.**

J

jaguar (= a large South American wildcat) is pronounced /jag-wahr/ in AmE and /jag-yoo-ə/ in BrE—preferably not /jag-yoo-ahr/ or /jag-wir/.

jail; gaol. The first is the AmE spelling; the second, a BrE variant. Note, however, that since about 1935 the spelling *jail* has predominated in the print sources of BrE. Both words, of course, are pronounced /jayl/.
> Current ratio: 16:1

jam (= [1] a fruit jelly; or [2] a congested or otherwise difficult situation) is sometimes misused for *jamb* (= the vertical sidepost of a doorway, window frame, or other framed opening)—e.g.:

- "The wide woodwork around the *door jams* [read *doorjambs*] highlights the Victorian wallpaper." Marilyn K. Wempa, "From Eyesore to Eye Pleaser," *Pitt. Post-Gaz.*, 10 June 1997, at B3.
- "The deputy found a .380 semiautomatic pistol on the floorboard and a marijuana cigar on the driver's *door jam* [read *doorjamb*]." Paul Purpura, "Mental Exam Ordered After Carjack," *Times-Picayune* (New Orleans), 12 Feb. 2015, at A10.

> LANGUAGE-CHANGE INDEX
> **doorjam* for *doorjamb*: Stage 1

James's; James'. See POSSESSIVES (A).

janissary (= a loyal, subservient follower) has been the standard spelling since the 18th century. It is capitalized only when used to mean "a Turkish infantry soldier in the sultan's guard." **Janisary* and **janizary* are variant forms.
> Current ratio (*janissary* vs. **janisary* vs. **janizary*): 273:31:1

jarful. Pl. *jarfuls*, not **jarsful*. See PLURALS (G).
> Current ratio: 6:1

JARGON refers to the special, usually technical idiom of any social, occupational, or professional group. It arises from the need to streamline communication, to save time and space—and occasionally to conceal meaning from the uninitiated. The subject has a magnified importance today because we live "in an age when vague rhetoric and incomprehensible jargon predominate." Oliver Letwin, "Good Servant, Bad Master," *Times* (London), 25 May 1995, Books §, at 37.

Jargon covers a broad span of vocabulary. For the commonplace medical phrase *heart bypass surgery*, a range of jargon is available. There's the much more technical (and more verbose) *coronary artery bypass graft*. From that phrase comes the acronym *CABG*, pronounced the same as *cabbage* <we're going to have to give him a CABG>. Some heart surgeons, who would have nothing to do with such SLANG, prefer the pompously arcane *myocardial revascularization*. But whatever the name, it's all bypass surgery.

LANGUAGE-CHANGE INDEX (For the full key, see front matter pp. xxxi, l–li.)
Stage 1: Rejected. **Stage 2:** Widely shunned. **Stage 3:** Widespread but . . . **Stage 4:** Ubiquitous but . . . **Stage 5:** Fully accepted.
Invariably inferior forms marked by asterisk (*). • Ratios represent frequency of prevalent forms vs. variants in current books.

Other examples of medical jargon abound:

black eye = bilateral periorbital ecchymosis
  (/ek-i-**moh**-sis/)
boil = furuncule (/**fyuur**-əng-kəl/)
bruise = contusion, ecchymosis
chicken pox = varicella (/var-i-**sel**-ə/)
chilblain = pernio (/**pər**-nee-oh/)
clubfoot = talipes (/**tal**-i-peez/)
cut = laceration
drunk = suffering from a hyperingestion of ethanol
headache = cephalalgia (/sef-əl-**al**-jee-ə/)
heartburn = pyrosis (/pɪ-**roh**-sis/)
kidney stone = renal calculus
measles = morbilli (/mohr-**bil**-ɪ/)
mumps = infectious parotitis (/par-ə-**tɪ**-tis/)
removal of a lung = pneumonectomy
  (/noo-moh-**nek**-tə-mee/)
scrape = abrade, abrasion
set of symptoms = presentation
short of breath = SOB
sneeze = sternutation (/stər-nyoo-**tay**-shən/)
spot on the lung = probable bronchogenic carcinoma
syphilis = lues (/**loo**-eez/)
throat = pharynx (/**fair**-ingks/)
urinate = micturate (/**mik**-chə-rayt/)
vomiting = emesis (/**e**-mə-səs/)
wisdom tooth = dens serotinus (/denz see-**roh**-ti-nəs/)

Doctors will say things such as *Patients rarely present with* [i.e., have symptoms of] *pleurisy in quite this way*, or *This is an unusual presentation for pleurisy.* Maybe it's understandable that some physicians would use *emesis* as a EUPHEMISM for *vomiting* when speaking among themselves in front of a patient. But surely no one is comforted by being called *the SOB patient.* (Some within the medical profession have started changing *SOB* to *SOA* [= short of air] for this very reason.)

Doctors have several ways of saying that a patient is on a respirator (or ventilator). Some, of course, say that a patient is *on the respirator* or *on the ventilator.* Others, being fond of slang, say that the patient is *on the blower.* But then there are the stuffed-shirt doctors who say precisely the same thing in the most pretentious possible way: the patient is *being given positive-pressure ventilatory support.*

Few took note when James C. Leary wrote these wise words in 1957: "Some medical writers tend to overload their pieces with unnecessary technical terms—words like 'ipsilateral' for 'on the same side,' for instance. Few medical [readers] remember enough Latin or Greek to puzzle out the meanings of unnecessarily difficult words and, if they come too frequently, the writer has lost his reader's interest and usually his reader. A good rule for medical writers to follow would be to use simple English words unless there is none exact enough to express the idea sought." Leary, "Medical Writing as Seen by a Layman," in *A Group of Papers on Medical Writing* 16, 16–17 (1957).

Of course, jargon is hardly the exclusive province of such fields as medicine and law. (See LEGALESE.) It can be found in virtually any other specialized field, such as social work (*equality-proofing, food-insecure*);

healthcare (*retroactive disenrollment*); statistics (*disaggregated data*); engineering (*tunnel-jacking, soil-freezing*); investments (*portfolio optimization, derivative leveraging, allocated income streams*); business and management (*suboptimized multifunctionality, integrator global-value proposition, redundant 24/7 b2b solution*); and computing (*kernel panic, embedded protocol*).

And don't forget linguistics, here represented in a straight-faced passage: "Rules of construal associate antecedents and anaphors, let us say, by the device of coindexing." Noam Chomsky, "On Opacity," in *Studies in English Linguistics* 1, 1 (Sidney Greenbaum et al. eds., 1979). "On Opacity" indeed! In that sentence, which looks at first like a fragment, the verb is *associate.*

The linguist Dwight Bolinger disapprovingly quotes an example of jargon from an article on linguistics: "In traditional linguistics it has been assumed that the analysis of sentences can be performed upon examples isolated from the process of interaction within which they naturally emerge." He then deflates the jargon to this: "Traditional linguists thought that sentences could be analyzed out of context." See Dwight Bolinger, *Language: The Loaded Weapon* 129 (1980).

One of the more prominent types of jargon—one to which most travelers are exposed—is AIRLINESE. In the late 1990s, a captain announced, in midflight: "We're about to *traverse an area of instability*, so I've *illuminated* the fasten-seatbelts sign." When a flight attendant was asked how she would say the same thing, she said: "We're going to *encounter some light chop*, so I've *turned on* the fasten-seatbelts sign." Another said, "We're about to *go through some choppy air*, so please fasten your seatbelts." Those quotations progress from the most to the least jargonistic—or, to put it judgmentally from the passenger's perspective, from the least to the most admirable.

True, jargon is sometimes useful shorthand for presenting ideas that would ordinarily need explaining in other, more roundabout ways for those outside the specialty. Jargon thus has a strong in-group property, which is acceptable when one specialist talks with another.

But at other times, jargon is no time-saver at all. It can be obtuse and actually inhibit communications. In his book *On the Art of Writing* (2d ed. 1943), Sir Arthur Quiller-Couch set out the two primary vices of jargon: "The first is that it uses circumlocution rather than short straight speech. It says: '*In the case of* John Jenkins deceased, the coffin' when it means 'John Jenkins's coffin'; and its yea is not yea, neither is its nay nay; but its answer is *in the affirmative* or *in the negative*, as the foolish and superfluous *case* may be. The second vice is that it habitually chooses vague wooly abstract nouns rather than concrete ones" (*ibid.* at 105). "To write jargon is to be perpetually shuffling around in a fog and cotton-wool of abstract terms" (*ibid.* at 117). See ABSTRACTITIS, DOUBLESPEAK & ABBREVIATIONS (C).

Jargon is unacceptable when its purpose is to demonstrate how much more the speaker or writer knows as a specialist than ordinary listeners or readers do. The intended audience, then, is the primary consideration in deciding which words will be most immediately intelligible. See OBSCURITY & PLAIN LANGUAGE.

Among the better treatments of the subject are *Languages and Jargons: Contributions to a Social History of Language* (Peter Burke & Roy Porter eds., 1995); Walter Nash, *Jargon: Its Uses and Abuses* (1993); Tom Fahey, *The Joys of Jargon* (1990); Jonathon Green, *Newspeak: A Dictionary of Jargon* (1984); Don Ethan Miller, *The Book of Jargon* (1981); Joel Homer, *Jargon: How to Talk to Anyone About Anything* (1979); Kenneth Hudson, *The Jargon of the Professions* (1978). An older guide worth looking at is James Le Sure, *Guide to Pedaguese: A Handbook for Puzzled Parents* (1965).

jargonistic; *jargonish; *jargonic. The first has been standard in AmE since the early 1940s and in BrE since the early 1950s. The second and third, both much rarer than the first, are NEEDLESS VARIANTS.

Current ratio (in order of headwords): 15:1.2:1

*jarsful. See **jarful.**

jealousy; envy. The careful writer distinguishes between these terms. *Jealousy* is properly restricted to contexts involving emotional rivalry, especially regarding the sex instinct; *envy* is used more broadly of resentful contemplation of a more fortunate person.

But of course there's more to it than just that. For a fascinating study of the nuances (not for the prudish), see T. M. Ankles, *A Study of Jealousy as Differentiated from Envy* (1939).

LANGUAGE-CHANGE INDEX
jealousy for *envy* (of things, not
love interests): Stage 2

Jehoshaphat, the name of a king of Judah mentioned in the Old Testament, is often misspelled **Jehosophat*—e.g.: "The two children hurry to see Baba-Ali, the sword swallower, and watch the daring *Jehosophat* [read *Jehoshaphat*] walk on red-hot coals." Barnhardt Myl, "To Market, To Market," *News & Record* (Greensboro), 7 Apr. 1996, at F5.

The name is properly pronounced /ji-**hahsh**-ə-fat/. The mispronunciation /ji-**hoh**-sə-fat/, popularized in the habitual interjection (*Jumpin' Jehoshaphat!*) of Yosemite Sam in the Bugs Bunny cartoons, is based on an erroneous reading of the word (ignoring the -*sh*-), coupled perhaps with the influence of *Jehovah* (/ji-**hoh**-və/). (Yosemite Sam seems never to hit the books.) But the phrase became so ubiquitous that the interjection would call undue attention to itself if pronounced in any way other than Yosemite's. Not many people today use the phrase.

LANGUAGE-CHANGE INDEX
Jehoshaphat misspelled **Jehosophat*: Stage 1
Current ratio: 12:1

jejune /jə-**joon**/ = (1) shallow, insubstantial, dull, insipid; (2) (of nourishment or agricultural lands) scanty, meager, barren; or (3) puerile, childish. The late Jacques Barzun, among others, disapproved of sense 3: "The great usagist [Jacques Barzun] took issue with a political comment . . . about the President's *jejune jitters*. 'The meaning "youthful, childish" for *jejune*,' Barzun noted, 'has got into the dictionaries only as a concession to the misusers.' The original meaning of *jejune*—'empty of food, meager'—led to its modern sense of 'dull, insipid.' Probably because the word sounded like *juvenile*, it picked up a meaning of 'puerile, childish,' which is the way it is most commonly used today. . . . I say *jejune* means *puerile* now. And, besides, it goes with *jitters*." William Safire, "On Language," *N.Y. Times*, 16 Oct. 1994, § 6, at 18, 20.

Sense 1 now predominates in BrE—e.g.: "Major's toffy cabinet ministers in their pinched Saville Row suits, lisping languidly in accents Oxonian, remind many Brits just how rotten and irrelevant the old aristocracy has become. These *jejune* relics belong to the 19th century, not the 21st." Eric Margolis, "Major Deserves His Fate," *Toronto Sun*, 27 Mar. 1997, at 12. And it still sometimes appears in AmE—e.g.: "Michael Kinsley wrote that Jewish Americans envied Israelis for living out history in a way that made the comfort and security of life in New York seem *jejune*." Geoffrey Wheatcroft, "The Big Kibbutz," *N.Y. Times*, 2 Mar. 1997, § 7, at 6.

Despite disapproval, sense 3 predominates in AmE—e.g.:

- "Svich . . . launch[es] her poetry in speeches that are sometimes beautiful and sometimes embarrassingly *jejune* or stickily romantic." Bill Von Maurer, "There's Little Chemistry in 'Alchemy,'" *Sun-Sentinel* (Ft. Lauderdale), 10 Dec. 1996, at E3.
- "My wife had given me carte blanche and other credit cards for the evening and I felt positively *jejune* again . . . . I stood at the corner of Dow and Jones, wondering where to begin." Herb Caen, "7 Decades of Baghdad by the Bay," *S.F. Chron.*, 3 Feb. 1997, at H2.
- "The show . . . will delight those who find this sort of frolicsome caper ingenious rather than *jejune*." Charles McNulty, "'Murder for Two' a Frantic Bid for Musical Amusement," *L.A. Times*, 5 June 2015, at 11.

The unfortunate thing about this double meaning is that it's sometimes hard to tell what the writer means. *Jejune* is a put-down, but is the writer calling something "dull" or "adolescent"? In the following sentence, you can't really tell: "This poor translation of a hastily withdrawn French comedy . . . bumps along in a way that makes one yearn for the *jejune* raunchiness of 'Private Parts.'" Malcolm Johnson, "Machete Needed to Wade Through 'Jungle,'" *Hartford Courant*, 8 Mar. 1997, at E1. Maybe, in fact, the word has a tinge of both, as the meanings merge: "The self-indulgent

---

LANGUAGE-CHANGE INDEX (For the full key, see front matter pp. xxxi, l–lii.)
Stage 1: Rejected. **Stage 2:** Widely shunned. **Stage 3:** Widespread but . . . **Stage 4:** Ubiquitous but . . . **Stage 5:** Fully accepted.
Invariably inferior forms marked by asterisk (*). • Ratios represent frequency of prevalent forms vs. variants in current books.

'Girls Only' . . . is pointless and aimless, offering up tired or *jejune* observations best confined to a [schoolgirl's] diary." Joanne Kaufman, "'Girls Only': A Memoir Resting on a Shaky Foundation," *Chicago Trib.*, 2 Feb. 1997, at C3.

Maybe, then, the best definition today—in AmE, at least—is "insipidly adolescent" or "intellectually insubstantial as a result of juvenility."

LANGUAGE-CHANGE INDEX
jejune in the sense "puerile": Stage 3

Jekyll and Hyde. See LITERARY ALLUSION.

jemmy. See **jimmy.**

jeopardize; **jeopard;* **enjeopard.* H.W. Horwill wrote that in AmE "*jeopard* is preferred to *jeopardize*, the common term in England." *Modern American Usage* 178 (2d ed. 1944). This wasn't true in 1944, and it isn't true today—e.g.:

- "Mr. Connelly said no federal funds were *jeopardized* by the ordinance." Joyce Price, "Allentown Feels HUD's Wrath over 'English-Only' Law," *Wash. Times*, 5 Apr. 1995, at A1.
- "Overfishing had *jeopardized* the survival of some species." "News Summary," *N.Y. Times*, 3 Apr. 1997, at A2.
- "The Broncos don't want Sanders to suffer a setback that would *jeopardize* his availability for the season opener Sept. 13." Troy E. Renck, "Broncos Briefs," *Denver Post*, 26 Aug. 2015, at B3.

*Jeopard and **enjeopard* are NEEDLESS VARIANTS that, though extremely rare, still sometimes appear—e.g.: "He quit, *jeoparding* [read *jeopardizing*] more than 20 years of integrity in one day." Kelley Steve, "James Abandons His Sinking Ship," *Des Moines Register*, 24 Aug. 1993, Sports §, at 1.

jerry-build. See **jury-rig.**

*jerry-rig. See **jury-rig.**

jetsam (= goods abandoned at sea and submerged indefinitely) is so spelled—not **jetsom*. E.g.: "A box contains the flotsam and *jetsom* [read *jetsam*] she collects to make impressions in the sand." Larry Maddry, "Artist Finds a Home for Her Creative Spirit via the Sand of Virginia," *Virginian-Pilot* (Norfolk), 25 Oct. 1995, at E1. It is pronounced /jet-səm/.

LANGUAGE-CHANGE INDEX
jetsam misspelled **jetsom*: Stage 1
Current ratio: 73:1

jewelry; jewellery. The first is the AmE spelling; the second is BrE. In cultivated AmE and BrE speech, the word is pronounced /**joo**-wəl-ree/—not (through METATHESIS) /**jool**-ə-ree/. And *jewel* is /**joo**-wəl/, in two audible syllables—not /jool/ or /juul/.

jibe. See **gibe.**

jimmy; jemmy. A burglar's crowbar is spelled *jimmy* in AmE, *jemmy* in BrE. The same is true for the verbs as well.

jingoism. See **chauvinism (B)** & **jingoist.**

jingoist; jingo. The former has come to displace the latter as the agent noun corresponding to *jingoism*. A *jingoist* is a belligerent patriot and nationalist who favors an aggressive foreign policy. The word almost always carries pejorative connotations—e.g.:

- "The Duma's *jingoists* seem to care little that the obligations of START-2 are finely balanced." "Russia's Surly Answer to NATO," *Economist* (U.S. ed.), 1 Feb. 1997, at 47.
- "Many Serbs . . . escaped the war of the *jingoists* by fleeing or deserting." Peter Schneider, "The Writer Takes a Hike," *New Republic*, 3 Mar. 1997, at 34.
- "One customary explanation is that the people who ran covert operations at the C.I.A. from 1947 to 1967 were not right-wing *jingoists*." Louis Menand, "A Friend of the Devil," *New Yorker*, 23 Mar. 2015, at 84.

Jingo has pretty much been driven out, unless a pun is needed—e.g.: "*Jingo* bells, *jingo* bells, jingoism all the way on MTV this season." "The Best of Cable & Satellite," *Independent*, 21 Dec. 1996, at 57. Otherwise, it appears mostly in the phrase *by jingo*, a mild oath expressing affirmation or surprise <I'll do it, by jingo!>.

jinni. See **genie.**

*jiujutsu. See **jujitsu.**

jive. See **gibe.**

jobsite. One word. Cf. **worksite.**

jocular; jocose; jocund. *Jocular* (/**jok**-yə-lər/) has been the most common since the mid-19th century. But the other two aren't quite NEEDLESS VARIANTS. *Jocular* and *jocose* (/joh-**kohs**/) both mean "given to joking" or "intended jokingly; humorous." But *jocular* suggests a playful disposition <her jocular manner endeared her to others> or deliberate facetiousness <jocular remarks during the business meeting>, while *jocose* often connotes mischievous (sometimes feeble) attempts at humor <his jocose wisecracks wore thin>. *Jocund* (/**jok**-ənd/), a broader yet more bookish word, means "jolly, merry, lighthearted" <jocund New Year's Eve revelers>. The following quotations well illustrate typical usage:

- "*Jocular*, tanned and smooth-voiced, he gave the impression he'd rather be at a shrimp boil, getting things accomplished without seeming to strain too hard at it." Tom Baxter, "Cheerful Dixon Packs Up, Heads for TV Screen," *Atlanta J.-Const.*, 1 Apr. 1997, at B2.
- "Its violence is facetiously cartoonish, its sexuality just a hint in the air and its *jocose* sense of silliness right out of Nick at Nite." Michael McWilliams, "Sam Raimi Makes a Successful Play for the Funny Bone with 'Spy Game,'" *Detroit News*, 3 Mar. 1997, at B3.
- "It's as good a place as any to start trying to lay the foundation for the *jocund* artist's goofily cheeky world view." Murray Whyte, "On the Road Too Fully Travelled," *Toronto Star*, 20 Mar. 2014, at E3.

jodhpur /**jod**-pər/ is an eponym for the city of Jodhpur, India. The word (almost invariably used in the plural) refers to a type of flared-at-the-thigh pants used in English horse-riding. Through a kind of visual

METATHESIS, the word is often mispronounced /jod-fər/. And believe it or not, this error became pervasive in the horse-riding industry in the mid-20th century.

The mispronunciation sometimes results in the obvious misspelling—e.g.: "Wealthy suburbanites clad in fancy *jodphurs* [read *jodhpurs*] and riding boots will replace overall-clad cowboys like Mizer." Meghan Meyer, "Old Feed Store Fading into the Sunset," *Palm Beach Post*, 14 July 2002, at B1.

By inevitable extension, the misspelling also goes back to the source of the word—e.g.: "His name is Ali Akbar Khan, above, whose family traces its musical roots to the 16th century, when an ancestor was court musician to the Emperor Akbar, as Ali Akbar Khan was to the Maharaja of *Jodphur* [read *Jodhpur*] in his 20's." Lawrence Van Gelder, "Footlights," *N.Y. Times*, 7 Nov. 2002, at E1.

How did Jodhpur, a town in central India, come to be famously associated with riding pants? It seems that Rao Raja Hanut Singh, who represented Jodhpur at Queen Victoria's 60th jubilee in 1897, had designed some comfortable riding trousers that ballooned at the thigh and narrowed at the knee so that they could be tucked into boots. While in London, he had the pants copied by a London tailor, who then began making and selling them. By 1899, the pants were well on their way to international popularity.

LANGUAGE-CHANGE INDEX
jodhpur misspelled and
mispronounced **jodphur*: Stage 2
Current ratio (*jodhpurs* vs. **jodphurs*): 57:1

Johnny-come-lately. Pl. *Johnny-come-latelies*—not **Johnny-come-latelys* or **Johnnies-come-lately*. See PLURALS (E) & (G).
Current ratio (plural forms in order): 4:1.3:1

joint cooperation is a REDUNDANCY.

join together is a REDUNDANCY that should be allowed to survive only in the traditional marriage service, and there only because it is a bona fide remnant of Elizabethan English.

jollily. See ADVERBS (B).

Joneses. See PLURALS (E).

Jones's. See POSSESSIVES (A).

jostle (= to bump roughly) has been the standard spelling since the 18th century. **Justle* is a variant.
Current ratio (*jostled* vs. **justled*): 208:1

joust. The traditional view is that this word should be pronounced either /jəst/ or /joost/. See *NBC Handbook of Pronunciation* 189 (3d ed. 1964) (listing only /joost/); William H.P. Phyfe, *20,000 Words Often Mispronounced* 421 (1937) (listing only /jəst/ and /joost/). But almost all Americans say /jowst/; this pronunciation must be considered not just acceptable, but—because of its overwhelming prevalence, coupled with no good reason for opposing it—preferable. Let the orthoepic jousting cease.

Jr.; Sr. See NAMES (B).

jubilant (= rapturously happy because of a success) is pronounced /**joo**-bi-lənt/—never /**joob**-yə-lənt/. The corresponding noun is *jubilation* /joo-bi-**lay**-shen/—not /joob-yə-**lay**-shən/. The mispronunciations were a rather constant habit of former NBC News anchor Brian Williams.

Judaism (the Jewish religion based on the Hebrew Scriptures) is preferably pronounced in four syllables: /**joo**-dee-iz-əm/, /**joo**-day-iz-əm/, or /**joo**-də-iz-əm/—not /**joo**-diz-əm/. The cognate terms are pronounced as follows:

Judea (or *Judaea*): /joo-**dee**-ə/ or /joo-**day**-ə/
Judean (or *Judaean*): /joo-**dee**-ən/ or /joo-**day**-ən/
Judaic: /joo-**day**-ik/
Judaica: /joo-**day**-i-kə/
Judeo: /joo-**dee**-oh/ or /joo-**day**-oh/—not /**joo**-dee-oh/ or /**joo**-day-oh/

judge; justice. In AmE, as a general rule, judges sitting on the highest appellate level of a jurisdiction are known as *justices*. Trial judges and appellate judges on intermediate levels are generally called *judges*, not *justices*.

New York, California, and Texas depart from these rules of thumb. In New York, *justices* sit on the trial court of general jurisdiction (the Supreme Court, oddly), whereas *judges* sit on the state's highest court, the Court of Appeals. The anomaly of calling trial judges *justices* is a matter of tradition, the "Supreme Courts of Judicature" having been established in 1691. In California, *justices* sit on the intermediate appellate courts (the *Courts of Appeal*) as well as on the Supreme Court. In Texas, *justices* sit on the courts of appeals (between the trial court and the Supreme Court—the latter being the highest civil court, which is also composed of *justices*); *judges* sit on trial courts and on the Court of Criminal Appeals, the highest criminal court.

H.W. Horwill wrote that "*judge* carries with it in America by no means such dignified associations as it possesses in Eng. It may mean [in AmE] no more than a *magistrate* of a police court." *Modern American Usage* 180 (2d ed. 1944). *Justice* may also denote, in AmE and BrE alike, a low-ranking judge or inferior magistrate, as in the phrases *justice of the peace* and *police justice*. Cf. **Chief Justice of the United States.**

judgeable. So spelled.

judgement. See **judgment** (A).

judging. For *judging* as an acceptable dangling modifier, see DANGLERS (E).

LANGUAGE-CHANGE INDEX (For the full key, see front matter pp. xxxi, l–li.)
Stage 1: Rejected. **Stage 2:** Widely shunned. **Stage 3:** Widespread but . . . **Stage 4:** Ubiquitous but . . . **Stage 5:** Fully accepted.
Invariably inferior forms marked by asterisk (*). • Ratios represent frequency of prevalent forms vs. variants in current books.

judging from; judging by. Meaning "if we are to judge by," each of these phrases is an acceptable dangler or disguised conjunction <judging from your smile, the interview must have gone well>. (See DANGLERS (E).) The phrases became especially common in print sources beginning about 1800. Since that time, *judging from* has been the more common of the two in AmE; since the 1930s, *judging by* has been somewhat more common in BrE.

> Current ratio (*judging from* vs. *judging by* in World English): 1.1:1

***judgmatic.** See **judgmental.**

judgment. A. Spelling. *Judgment* is the preferred form in AmE and in British legal texts, even as far back as the 18th century. *Judgement* is prevalent in British nonlegal texts and was thought by H.W. Fowler to be the better form (*FMEU1* at 310). Cf. **abridgment** & **acknowledgment.** See MUTE E.

B. AmE and BrE Legal Senses. In AmE, a *judgment* is the final decisive act of a court in defining the rights of the parties <the judgment constituted the final decree>. In BrE, *judgment* is commonly used in the sense in which *judicial opinion* is used in AmE.

C. Court judgment. This phrase is a REDUNDANCY, though an understandable one when the likely readers are nonlawyers. For example, the following book's title might have misled general readers if the word *court* had been removed: Gini G. Scott et al., *Collect Your Court Judgment* (1991).

judgmental; *judgmatic. *Judgmental* = (1) judging when uncalled for; or (2) of, relating to, or involving judgment. Although the newer sense 1 is now more common <a judgmental critic>, sense 2 still appears—e.g.: "In October 1985, police Chief Sid Klein took away Welch's summons book and said he couldn't write any more tickets, citing Welch's 'lack of *judgmental* ability.'" "Officer Saw Discipline as Harassment," *St. Petersburg Times*, 2 Apr. 1996, at A4. **Judgmatic*, which H.W. Fowler called a "facetious formation" because of its irregular formation on the analogy of *dogmatic*, is a NEEDLESS VARIANT of *judicious*. See **judicial.**

***judicative.** See **adjudicative.**

judicial; judicious. *Judicial* = (1) of, relating to, by, or involving the court <judicial officers>; (2) in court <judicial admissions>; (3) legal <the Attorney General took no judicial action>; or (4) of, relating to, or involving a judgment <judicial interest at the rate of 4% annually>. Sense 4, which is confined to legal contexts, is suspect because it hasn't yet gained admission to most dictionaries.

Judicious is a much simpler word, meaning "well considered, discreet, wisely circumspect." E.g.:

- "The duo put on a lively show that was highlighted by the *judicious* use of video and an inflatable cow skull." Claudia Perry, "Brooks, Dunn Turn Dome into Honky-Tonk Heaven," *Houston Post*, 28 Feb. 1995, at A6.

- "He spoke [about] . . . the need to be *judicious* in helping emerging democracies develop institutions to thrive in this changed geopolitical landscape." Stuart Ingis, "Law Students with Laptops Link Bosnia to the Internet," *Christian Science Monitor*, 28 Feb. 1997, at 19.

- "There's not much to it: a smattering of the usual suspects (ginger, garlic, scallions), a *judicious* sprinkling of Sichuan peppercorn, some soy and a bit of black vinegar to balance it." T. Susan Chang, "From a London Blogger, Pages of In-Your-Face Flavor," *Wash. Post*, 2 Sept. 2015, at E1.

See **judgmental.**

judiciary is pronounced either /joo-**dish**-ee-er-ee/ or /joo-**dish**-ə-ree/. Cf. **beneficiary.**

judicious. See **judicial.**

jujitsu; *jujutsu; *jiujutsu. Although the Japanese term is *jū-jūtsu*, the phonetic spelling *jujitsu* became the established form in both AmE and BrE during the mid-20th century. The others are variant forms in English.

> Current ratio (in order of headwords): 23:8:1

juncture. The phrase *at this juncture* should be used in reference to a crisis or a critically important time—e.g.: "*At this* critical *juncture* in history, the people of China need and deserve our support and friendship." Samuel D. Ling, "China's Challenge," *Chicago Trib.*, 27 Feb. 1997, at 22. Such phrases as *critical juncture* (a CLICHÉ) and *pivotal juncture* are redundant, since *juncture* alone will typically suffice in place of those phrases.

But the phrase *at this juncture* isn't equivalent merely to "at this time" or "now." When used with these meanings—as by the first President George Bush and popularized by his impersonator, Dana Carvey—it's a pomposity. E.g.:

- "While the city has not initiated the program with much grace or deftness, that is no reason to make things even messier at this late *juncture* [read *date*]." "Stick to Your Sticker Guns," *Austin Am.-Statesman*, 26 Feb. 1997, at A10.

- "*At this juncture* [read *This time*] last season, with the same total of two points, the Toon Army had declared war on manager Alan Pardew and owner Mike Ashley." Craig Hope, "Grim Up North," *Daily Mail*, 1 Sept. 2015, at 79.

Sometimes *junction* gets mistakenly substituted, especially in speech—e.g.: "'It would be advisable for the Virginia legislature to reconsider this at this *junction* [read *juncture*] . . . ,' she said." "Va. Schools Forge Ahead with National Motto: In God We Trust," *Wash. Post*, 28 July 2002, at B1. The error occurs in writing as well, but much less often—e.g.: "The new contract pointed toward his release at this *junction* [read *juncture*] before a roster bonus came due." Don Hammack, "Saints Roster Taking Shape with Moves," *Sun Herald* (Biloxi, Miss.), 21 Mar. 2002, at B1.

> LANGUAGE-CHANGE INDEX
> 1. *at this juncture* meaning "now": Stage 3
> 2. *at this junction* for *at this juncture*: Stage 1

Junior. On whether to include a comma with the abbreviation *Jr.*, see NAMES (B).

junkie (= [1] a drug addict, or [2] an avid aficionado) is the standard spelling. **Junky* is a variant.

Current ratio: 5:1

junta; junto. Of Spanish origin, *junta* (= a political or military group in power, esp. after a coup d'état) is pronounced either /**hoon**-tə/ or /**jən**-tə/. It is much more common in AmE than its altered form, *junto* /**jən**-toh/, which has undergone slight DIFFERENTIA-TION to mean "a self-appointed committee having political aims." Ernest Gowers wrote that *junto* "is an erroneous form" (*FMEU2* at 319), but it appears frequently in BrE where an American would write *junta*—e.g.: "Even so, a compliant civilian government may not be easy for the deeply unpopular *junto* to achieve." "Myanmar: Deja Vu," *Economist* (Am. ed.), 16 Jan. 1993, at 34.

jurisprudent, n.; **jurisprude.** *Jurisprudent*, though appearing to be an adjective, is a noun meaning "a jurist" or "a learned lawyer." *Jurisprude*, not recorded in the *OED*, is listed in *W3* as a BACK-FORMATION from *jurisprudence* with the meaning "a person who makes ostentatious show of learning in jurisprudence and the philosophy of law or who regards legal doctrine with undue solemnity or veneration." The word deserves wider currency, preferably with recognition of its pejorative connotations (with the pun on *prude*). Yet today most scholars in the field of jurisprudence call themselves jurisprudes without any hint of self-deprecation.

LANGUAGE-CHANGE INDEX
jurisprude as a nonpejorative equivalent of
jurisprudent, n.: Stage 3
Current ratio (*jurisprudents* vs. *jurisprudes*): 6:1

jurist. A. Generally. In BrE, this word is reserved for someone who has made outstanding contributions to legal thought and legal literature. In AmE, it is loosely applied to every judge of whatever level, and sometimes even to nonscholarly practitioners who are well respected.

B. For *juror*. This is a surprising error. On the front page of the *Oakland Tribune*, a deck line states: "Group may recommend better pay for *jurists*." The meaning of that statement isn't clear until you read the body of the story: "The panel also is expected to recommend *jurors*—who are increasingly reluctant to serve on trials—be paid more money." "Jury Changes Would Drop Requirement for Unanimity," *Oakland Trib.*, 30 Apr. 1996, at A1. Nowhere does the story mention judges' pay. See **juror.**

juror ought to be distinguished from *potential juror* or *veniremember*—e.g.: "When the court was cleared of unchosen *jurors* [read *veniremembers*],

the spectators waiting in the corridor were allowed inside." John Bryson, *Evil Angels* 346 (1985). The difference is that a *potential juror* or *veniremember* hasn't yet been selected to sit on the jury, but is merely in the pool of people who might be selected; a *juror* is someone who has been empaneled on a jury. For a surprising misuse, see **jurist (B).**

Juror is preferably pronounced /**juur**-ər/, though it is frequently overpronounced in AmE /**juur**-ohr/ to distinguish the syllables—especially by lawyers and judges. In BrE, it is simply /**juur**-ə/.

jury. In AmE, this is a COLLECTIVE NOUN, and it therefore takes a singular verb <the jury has spoken>. To emphasize the individual members of the jury, we have the word *jurors* <the jurors have spoken>. In BrE, however, it is common to see a plural verb with *jury* <the jury have spoken>, just as with other collective nouns.

jury-rig; jerry-build; *jerry-rig; *gerry-rig. The first is an authentic nautical phrase, dating from the early 17th century. Derived from *jury-mast* (= a temporary replacement for a ship's broken mast), the *jury* part here has nothing to do with 12 peers deciding someone's fate. Instead, according to Barnhardt's *Dictionary of Etymology*, it probably derives from the Old French word *ajurie* (= help). The second is something of a PORTMANTEAU WORD combining *jury-rig* with a 19th-century BrE CASUALISM, *jerry-built* (= shoddy; poorly made to last a short time).

Jerry-build is sometimes used transitively to refer to something assembled from bits and pieces of other things. E.g.:

- "These passages faithfully capture the flavor of Jacobs's interminable book: corny, juvenile, smug, tired. Jacobs—a poor man's Dave Barry; no, a bag person's Dave Barry—has a modus operandi: to drift through the encyclopedia he supposedly read, yank out an entry, tear open his Industrial-Strength Comedy Handbook and *jerry-build* a lame wisecrack." Joe Queenan, "A Little Learning Is a Dangerous Thing," *N.Y. Times*, 3 Oct. 2004, § 7, at 13.
- "If history repeats itself, this budget, like the last six, will continue to limit what the universities can charge while the NDP *jerry-builds* something it hopes will keep the province's three degree-granting institutions from collapsing completely under financial strain." "Scrap Cap on Tuition," *Winnipeg Free Press*, 20 Feb. 2006, at A10.
- "Two-time Oscar winner Leo McCarey had to borrow [Robert] Walker footage from Alfred Hitchcock's Strangers on a Train, filmed a year earlier, to *jerry-build* his finale." Mike Clark, "Film Star's Death Can Be a Boost or a Hurdle," *USA Today*, 8 Feb. 2008, at E10.

*Gerry-rig is a fairly recent American NEEDLESS VARIANT of the mistaken **jerry-rig*—e.g.: "A 150-ton specialized tank landing craft was *gerry rigged* [read *jury-rigged*] to her deck. She weighed anchor and riding low in the water sailed for England." Sgt. Paul

LANGUAGE-CHANGE INDEX (For the full key, see front matter pp. xxxi, l–li.)
Stage 1: Rejected. **Stage 2:** Widely shunned. **Stage 3:** Widespread but . . . **Stage 4:** Ubiquitous but . . . **Stage 5:** Fully accepted.
Invariably inferior forms marked by asterisk (*). • Ratios represent frequency of prevalent forms vs. variants in current books.

Kane, "Ship That Saved Hundreds at Normandy, Still Proudly Sails," Dept. of Defense U.S. Marine Corps news release, 26 Oct. 2006. Unless you're writing a legal brief—where *jury-rigged* might create a felonious MISCUE—stick with that authentic original.

Current ratio (*jury-rigged* vs. **jerry-rigged* vs. **gerry-rigged*): 71:38:1

just, like *only,* must be carefully placed—e.g.: "Texas' Danny Peoples . . . had a two-run double and *just* hit foul a ball that could have been a two-run, game-tying homer." Kirk Bohls, "Dallas Baptist Assaults Texas Pitching 10–5," *Austin Am.-Statesman,* 26 Apr. 1994, at E1, E6. *Just* probably modifies *foul*—it might arguably modify *could*—but it certainly doesn't modify the word that it precedes, *hit,* which might indicate that he had hit the foul immediately before. Perhaps the writer was so eager to indicate how the ball was barely foul that he put the *just* in too early.

Another example: " 'America needs a decade of renewal and reform,' he [Richard D. Lamm, a presidential candidate] said. 'It *just doesn't* [read *doesn't just*] need a new President—it needs a whole decade of reform and renewal.' " Ernest Tollerson, "Lamm, Ex-Governor of Colorado, Seeks Reform Party's Nomination," *N.Y. Times,* 10 July 1996, at A1, A12. See **only.**

just as soon. This idiom is occasionally mangled into the unintelligible MALAPROPISM **just assume*—e.g.:

- "[O]ffice courtships have become as much a fixture in the workplace as fax machines and desktops. And it's one area most executives would *just assume* [read *just as soon*] not govern, a new survey shows." Teresa M. McAleavy, "Unwritten Rules Govern Office Wooing," *Record* (Bergen Co., N.J.), 17 Feb. 2002, Bus. §, at B6.
- "If Tampa Prep coach A.J. Hendrix has his way, he would *just assume* [read *just as soon*] not *to see* [omit *to*] Shorecrest's Anthony Katchuk again." Brandon Wright, "Shorecrest Downs Tampa Prep Again," *St. Petersburg Times,* 30 Mar. 2006, at C8.
- "I'm not a social butterfly and *just assume* [read *would just as soon*] spend my free time studying the teachings of Aradia." Nicholas Hanna, *Coven of Rats* 3 (2007).

LANGUAGE-CHANGE INDEX
*just assume for *just as soon*: Stage 1

just deserts (= the treatment one truly deserves) is occasionally misrendered **just desserts.* Sometimes, of course, it's a playful pun, as when a bakery is called *Just Desserts.* But sometimes it's sloppiness or pure ignorance—e.g.: "The deliciously wicked Francis Urquhart gets his *just desserts* [read *just deserts*] in this third installment of the story [the film *The Final Cut*]." "Best Bets," *Commercial Appeal* (Memphis), 21 Feb. 1997, at E2. In that example, the adverb *deliciously* creates a nonsensical echo in the wrong word *desserts.*

LANGUAGE-CHANGE INDEX
just deserts misspelled *just desserts*: Stage 3
Current ratio: 3:1

just exactly. Although this REDUNDANCY is common in speech, it shouldn't appear in careful writing (apart from dialogue)—e.g.: "*Just exactly* [read *Just*] how good are the big, fast and skillful Flyers?" Stephen Harris, "Hockey: B's Can't Cool Red-Hot Flyers," *Boston Herald,* 8 Jan. 1997, Sports §, at 8.

For a similar phrase involving *exact,* see **exact same.**

justice. See **judge.**

juvenile (= [1] of, relating to, or involving young people who aren't yet adults, or [2] typical of a silly child or adolescent) is correctly pronounced either /**joo**-və-nəl/ or (esp. in BrE) /**joo**-və-nɪl/.

juvenilely. See ADVERBS (B).

juvenocracy. See GOVERNMENTAL FORMS.

juxtaposition is a noun, not a verb. Although one may *position* a thing, one may not *juxtaposition* two things. *Juxtapose* is the correct verb form—e.g.: "The intended irony of Luther's skewed morality *juxtapositioned* [read *juxtaposed*] against the President's lack of morality is not particularly subtle or original." "It Takes a Sensitive Thief," *Pantagraph* (Bloomington, Ill.), 21 Feb. 1997, at D3. Likewise, the participial adjective is *juxtaposed,* not *juxtapositioned*—e.g.: "And Martha [Stewart], well, let's check her magazine's calendar, . . . with its *juxtapositioned* [read *juxtaposed*] reminders to 'prune roses' and 'climb Mt. Kilimanjaro.' " Jean Marbella, "Just So," *Baltimore Sun,* 8 Nov. 1996, at E1. See FUNCTIONAL SHIFT (D).

LANGUAGE-CHANGE INDEX
*juxtapositioned for *juxtaposed*: Stage 1
Current ratio (*juxtaposed* vs. **juxtapositioned*): 421:1

K

kabala; **kabbala; **kabbalah.* See **cabala.

*kabob. See **kebab.**

kaleidoscope. So spelled. See SPELLING (A).

karat. See **carat.**

karate (the Japanese martial art), a loanword adopted into English in the 1950s, has the settled English pronunciation /kə-**rah**-tee/. Avoid /kə-**rah**-tay/ and /kə-**rat**-ee/.

*kasher. See **kosher.**

Kazakhstan. So spelled—with the medial -h-. The inhabitants of this former Soviet republic are called *Kazakhs*. See DENIZEN LABELS.

kebab; *kabob; *kebob; *cabob. The first of these spellings—the one closest to the Turkish etymon— had become standard by the early 1940s. The others are variant forms.

Current ratio (in order of headwords): 254:41:7:1

*Kelt; *Keltic. See **Celt.**

kempt. See **unkempt.**

kennel, vb. (= to put or keep in a kennel—that is, a place where dogs are cared for), makes *kenneled* and *kenneling* in AmE, *kennelled* and *kennelling* in BrE. The divergences in spelling date back to about 1800.

kerb. See **curb.**

kerchief. Pl. *kerchiefs*—not **kerchieves*. See PLURALS (C).

Current ratio: 508:1

kerosene is the standard spelling. **Kerosine* is a variant.

Current ratio: 114:1

ketchup; catsup; catchup. The first spelling greatly predominates in modern usage and has done so since about 1850 in BrE and about 1985 in AmE. It has the advantages of phonetically approximating and of most closely resembling the word's probable source, either the Cantonese *k'ē chap* or the Malay *kēhap*, both referring to a kind of fish sauce. The pronunciation is either /**kech**-əp/ or /**kach**-əp/; /**kat**-səp/ is pretentious.

kettledrum. One word. See **timpani (A).**

khaki (= a brownish-yellow fabric of twilled cotton or wool) is frequently misspelled **kahki*—e.g.: "Tuesday is D-day. But don't look for Audie Murphy or a whole lot of *kahki* [read *khaki*]." Lawrence van Gelder, "The Glory and Glamour of Dietrich," *N.Y. Times*, 31 Mar. 1996, § 12, at 51.

LANGUAGE-CHANGE INDEX
khaki misspelled **kahki*: Stage 1

Khrushchev. So spelled, with three *h*'s, though often misspelled with two (**Khruschev*) or even one (**Kruschev*).

kibbutz /ki-**buutz**/ (= a farm in Israel where many people live and work together) forms the Hebrew plural *kibbutzim* in all varieties of World English— not **kibbutzes*. A member of a *kibbutz* is known as a *kibbutznik*.

Current ratio (*kibbutzim* vs. **kibbutzes*): 39:1

kibitz (= [1] to comment unhelpfully and annoyingly when someone is doing something, or [2] to speak tediously about obvious things) is a Yiddishism introduced into English in the 1920s. The word is accented on the first syllable: /**kib**-itz/. The agent noun is *kibitzer* /**kib**-it-zər/. The variant spellings **kibbitz* (vb.) and **kibbitzer* (n.) have not become predominant in any variety of World English.

Current ratio (*kibitz* vs. **kibbitz*): 4:1
Current ratio (*kibitzer* vs. **kibbitzer*): 10:1

kibosh (= the stopping of a plan or idea from developing or progressing; veto), a word of unknown origin dating in English from the early 19th century, refers to an action or decision that halts further progress on a plan, idea, or activity. It usually appears in the phrase *to put the kibosh on* (something). It was widely adopted in BrE in the 1830s and in AmE in the 1870s. The word is normally pronounced /**kɪ**-bosh/ in both AmE and BrE, but /ki-**bosh**/ is also an acceptable AmE pronunciation.

kidnapping. A. Spelling. Spell-check programs notwithstanding, the spelling with -pp- is preferred, by convention. But the inferior spelling **kidnaping* occasionally appears.

That spelling has its defenders—e.g.: "The form with a single 'p' is to be preferred because it is a general rule of spelling that the accent determines whether or not to double the letter when the suffix is to be added to a word ending in a *single consonant* preceded by a *single vowel* . . . . [T]he final consonant is *not* doubled if the word has more than one syllable and the accent is not on the last." Rollin M. Perkins, *Criminal Law* 134 n.1 (1957) (citing the examples of *develop*, *offer*, and *suffer*).

Perkins's final statement, explaining the general rule, is sound. But it overlooks the exceptional nature of *kidnapping*. First, the word is formed on the model of the shorter verb: *nap, napping*. Second, up to the 19th century, *kidnap* was generally accented on the second syllable. Third, *kidnapping* is much more common than **kidnaping* in modern print sources. See SPELLING (B).

Current ratio: 32:1

B. Sense. *Kidnapping* = the act or an instance of taking or carrying away a person without his or her consent, by force or fraud, and without lawful excuse. Does *kidnapping* refer only to the nabbing of kids? No. At common law, it was defined as the forcible abduction or stealing away of a man, woman, or child from his or her own country and taking him or her into another. Originally, the "kids" who were napped were not children at all, but laborers who were taken by force or by guile for service on early American plantations.

LANGUAGE-CHANGE INDEX (For the full key, see front matter pp. xxxi, l–li.)
Stage 1: Rejected. **Stage 2:** Widely shunned. **Stage 3:** Widespread but . . . **Stage 4:** Ubiquitous but . . . **Stage 5:** Fully accepted.
Invariably inferior forms marked by asterisk (*). • Ratios represent frequency of prevalent forms vs. variants in current books.

The law therefore distinguishes between *adult-kidnapping*, which includes the element of force or fraud, and *child-kidnapping*, which often does not, because, for example, there might be no force or fraud involved in making off with a baby-stroller.

kill . . . dead is a REDUNDANCY popularly promoted (alas) in television commercials touting insecticides that, it is said, will "kill bugs dead." It's certainly an emphatic, attention-getting phrase.

kiln is pronounced either /kil/ or /kiln/. According to one authority, "the pronunciation [kil] appears to be used only by those concerned with the working of kilns." Daniel Jones, *Everyman's English Pronouncing Dictionary* 283 (14th ed. 1967). Another says: "If you want to show that you know something more about this word than how to spell it, say KIL. If you think saying KIL will make you sound pedantic or weird, or both, pronounce the *n*." Charles Harrington Elster, *BBBM* at 279.

kilometer; kilometre. Denoting a distance of 10,000 meters, the word is spelled *kilometer* in AmE, *kilometre* in BrE. In AmE, the second syllable tends to be stressed: /ki-**lom**-i-tər/. In BrE, the first syllable tends to be stressed: /**kil**-ə-meet-ər/.

kiltie (= [1] someone who wears a kilt—esp. the thick tartan skirt-like garment traditionally worn by Scotsmen, or [2] a decorative tuft of leather or leatherlike material with serrated ends, traditionally worn atop golf shoes) is predominantly so spelled. In sense 1, *kilty* is a variant spelling that appears almost as frequently as *kiltie*.

Current ratio: 3:1

kimono (= a long, loose Japanese robe) is frequently misspelled **kimona*—e.g.: "Over her fireplace in Maryland hangs a portrait of her in a *kimona* [read *kimono*] from the year she lived in Japan." Patricia Meisol, "Migration Pattern," *Baltimore Sun*, 28 Oct. 1997, at E1. The proper pronunciation is /ki-**moh**-noh/; the common but inferior pronunciation /ki-**moh**-nə/ probably accounts for the misspelling.

LANGUAGE-CHANGE INDEX
kimono misspelled **kimona*: Stage 1
Current ratio: 64:1

-KIN. See DIMINUTIVES (I).

kind. See **class** & **type of.**

kindergarten. This German loanword for "children's garden" has been in use in English since at least the mid-18th century with its foreign spelling intact. It is sometimes misspelled as if it were anglicized—e.g.: "Lexington is the largest school in the state for the profoundly deaf and hard-of-hearing, and educates students from pre-*kindergarden* [read *kindergarten*] to age 21." Nicole Bode, "Deaf Get into the Act," *Daily*

News (N.Y.), 6 June 2002, Suburban §, at 1. The word may be pronounced /**kin**-dər-gahrt'n/ or /-gahrd'n/.

LANGUAGE-CHANGE INDEX
kindergarten misspelled **kindergarden*: Stage 1

kindergartner has been the standard spelling since the 19th century. **Kindergartener* is a variant.

Current ratio: 3:1

kindly, adv. This word is now frequently misplaced in sentences. Traditionally, it has meant something close to *please*, as in *Kindly take your seats* (= please take your seats). This usage has long been more common in BrE than in AmE. Perhaps that is why Americans have begun to misplace *kindly*, by having it refer not to the person who is requested to do something but to the person doing the requesting—e.g.: "We *kindly* ask you to take your seats." This linguistic misstep has become fairly common in AIRLINESE.

LANGUAGE-CHANGE INDEX
kindly in reference to the requester instead of the person requested: Stage 2

kind of. A. Meaning "somewhat." *Kind of* is a poor substitute for *somewhat*, *rather*, *somehow*, and other adverbs. It properly functions as a noun, however, signifying category or class in phrases such as *this kind of paper*. Cf. **sort of.** See **these kind of.**

B. *What kind of (a)*. With this phrasing, the *a* is not only unnecessary but also typical of uncultivated speech. Thus *It depends on what kind of vacation you want*, not **It depends on what kind of a vacation you want*. See CLASS DISTINCTIONS.

LANGUAGE-CHANGE INDEX
*what kind of a . . . for *what kind of . . .* : Stage 3
Current ratio (*what kind of person* vs.
*what kind of a person): 6:1

Kingdom of the Netherlands. See **Netherlands.**

kingly; queenly; royal; regal. The first two words should be reserved for specific references to the male or female monarch. *Royal* is the more general word, meaning "of, relating to, or involving a monarch" <the royal family>. It's sometimes metaphorical, as in *a royal touch*. The term *regal* can also be used broadly—in the sense "splendid, stately, magnificent"—but almost always in reference to a person <regal posture>; *royal* occasionally shares this sense <royal treatment>. Of course, *royal* can also mean "huge, significant" <royal pain> <royal screw-up>.

king-size, adj., is the standard spelling in AmE and BrE alike. **King-sized* is a variant.

Current ratio: 2:1

kismet (= fate; the foreordained events of one's life) is pronounced /**kiz**-mət/, /**kis**-mət/, or either of those first syllables with /-met/.

kitchenette is the standard spelling. **Kitchenet* is a variant.

kitty-cornered. See **catty-cornered.**

kiwifruit. One word in AmE, generally two in BrE.

kleptomania has been the standard spelling since the 19th century. **Cleptomania* is a variant.
Current ratio: 122:1

knackwurst. See **knockwurst.**

knapsack (= a lightweight frameless backpack) is frequently misspelled **napsack*—e.g.:

- "Safe to say, although Schmidt contends he is still merely exploring, he has all the right equipment in his *napsack* [read *knapsack*]." Kurt Erickson, "The Gauntlet Is Thrown," *Pantagraph* (Bloomington, Ill.), 16 Feb. 1997, at A4.
- "Of the 53 players a certain notorious owner jammed into his *napsack* [read *knapsack*] and hustled off to Baltimore, only 18 are still with the Ravens as they prepare to meet the Cincinnati Bengals today." Bob Hunter, "Ravens Haven't Taken Off in Baltimore Yet," *Columbus Dispatch*, 7 Sept. 1997, at E1.
- "Thousands of troops returned from Second World War battles with battered copies in their *napsacks* [read *knapsacks*]." Ian Hernon, "Author's Words Are Still Relevant Today," *Liverpool Echo*, 26 Jan. 2011, at 10.

LANGUAGE-CHANGE INDEX
knapsack misspelled **napsack*: Stage 1
Current ratio: 865:1

knave (= a rogue) is sometimes confused with *nave* (= the main body of a church)—e.g.:

- "As he spoke, the audience sat quietly near the red and turquoise *knave* [read *nave*] of the church, eating cookies and cheese curls." Nathaniel Sheppard Jr., "At Rally in Chicago, a Load of Facts, 16 Listeners and One Determined Cause," *N.Y. Times*, 12 Oct. 1980, § 1, at 34.
- "She told me to enter the *knave* [read *nave*] of the church, then step into a small room where there was a wooden partition in the wall." Jacqueline Higuera McMahan, "Sweet Tamales Are Holiday Tradition," *S.F. Chron.*, 15 Dec. 1993, Food §, at 10.
- "Many institutions chipped in with money and advice—including English Heritage, the diocese, and the Churches Conservation Trust, a charity funded by the state and the Church Commissioners that looks after churches put to other uses (one has a swimming pool in the *knave* [read *nave*])." "Saving Churches for Their History—Not Religion," *Guardian*, 3 July 2010, at 29.

LANGUAGE-CHANGE INDEX
knave misused for *nave*: Stage 1

kneel > knelt > knelt. In modern print sources, the past-tense and past-participial *knelt* is more than five times as common as its variant **kneeled*. See IRREGULAR VERBS.
Current ratio (*knelt down* vs. **kneeled down*): 6:1

knees. See **hands and knees.**

knickknack is so spelled, with a *-kk-* in the middle. Some writers mistakenly omit one of them—e.g.: "Eddy's daffy, disintegrating mother gets caught climbing in windows or pinching *knicknacks* [read *knickknacks*]." Arion Berger, "Absolutely Frightening," *Village Voice*, 13 June 1995, at 45. **Nicknack* is a variant spelling.

LANGUAGE-CHANGE INDEX
knickknack misspelled **knicknack*: Stage 1
Current ratio: 32:1

knife. Pl. *knives.* See PLURALS (C).

knight-errant. Pl. *knights-errant.* See PLURALS (G).

Knight Templar. The traditional plural is *Knights Templars* (pluralizing both the noun *knight* and the POSTPOSITIVE ADJECTIVE *templar*). This has been so since the 1600s.

The historic *Knights Templars* were members of a military and monastic Augustinian order founded in 12th-century Jerusalem during the First Crusade. Members were called the Knights of the Temple or *Knights Templars* because their quarters were in a palace next to the building called Solomon's Temple. The order was suppressed in the 14th century for religious and political reasons.

Although a modern international organization called the Knights Templar (no *-s*) exists, its connection to the monastic order is apocryphal. So although many writers err, the differing plural spellings for the ancient order and the modern organization should be carefully observed.

knit > knitted > knitted. The usual past tense is *knitted*, except in the phrase *close-knit family*. E.g.:

- "Or has Andy MacPhail, without Ed Lynch mucking things up, simply *knitted* together an amazing patchwork quilt?" Jay Mariotti, "Cubs Are for Real," *Chicago Sun-Times*, 7 May 2001, at 91.
- "Australia's fairy penguins are all set for winter and any oil spills after 1,000 tiny woolly sweaters were specially *knitted* and sent from as far away as Japan to the Australian island state of Tasmania." *Daily News* (N.Y.), 27 May 2001, at 44.

The usual phrase is *knitted brow*, not **knit brow*—e.g.:

- "Akeara, Freeman's 7-year-old daughter, is sprawled on the floor, her hair standing on end, her brow *knitted* as she draws a picture." Daniel A. Grech, " 'Home Doesn't Have to Be Perfect,' " *Wash. Post*, 19 Sept. 1999, Prince William Extra §, at 1.
- "He claimed that it reigned supreme in eating quality, but (and here his brows *knitted*) only in its area of origin, north of Sacramento." David Karp, "Gems Among the Stones," *L.A. Times*, 23 May 2001, at H1.
- " 'I just want to get back to playing basketball,' Swoopes says, gripping and shaking an imaginary ball, her brow

LANGUAGE-CHANGE INDEX (For the full key, see front matter pp. xxxi, l–li.)
Stage 1: Rejected. **Stage 2:** Widely shunned. **Stage 3:** Widespread but . . . **Stage 4:** Ubiquitous but . . . **Stage 5:** Fully accepted.
Invariably inferior forms marked by asterisk (*). • Ratios represent frequency of prevalent forms vs. variants in current books.

knitted into an angry sneer." W.H. Stickley, "Memorable Past, Uncertain Future," *Houston Chron.*, 26 May 2001, Sports §, at 1.

Cf. **fit.**

Current ratio: 3:1

knock out; knock up. See PHRASAL VERBS.

knockwurst (= a thick, spicy sausage common in German cuisine) is the standard spelling today. Although *knackwurst* is the traditional German spelling, the form *knockwurst*, an accurately phonetic respelling, has predominated in AmE since the 1950s and in BrE since the 1970s.

Current ratio: 4:1

Knopf. The well-known publishing house is pronounced /kə-**nahpf**/—with /k/ distinctly sounded.

knot. A *knot* is a unit of speed equal to one nautical mile per hour. The term originated over 200 years ago when a ship's speed was measured with a log line, a length of twine or rope marked at intervals by colored knots and attached to a circular log weighted with lead. This float stayed relatively stationary in the water and pulled the log line over the ship's side. After 28 seconds (if using markers set 47.33 feet apart) or 30 seconds (if using markers set 50.75 feet apart), the line was hauled back. The number of knots that had passed over the side was the measure of the ship's speed. In the 19th century, the nautical mile (and the *knot*) was standardized as 6,076 feet, compared with 5,280 feet to a mile on land. Today, both watercraft and aircraft measure speed in *knots*.

Since a *knot* is a measure of speed and not distance, a REDUNDANCY results if you append a time element such as *per hour*—e.g.:

- "An effective speed is 1.5 to 1.6 *knots per hour* [read *knots*], or just fast enough to keep the herring rolling slowly." Fenton Roskelley, "Hunting & Fishing," *Spokesman-Rev.* (Spokane), 19 Nov. 1999, at C4.
- "They usually work best at slow trolling speeds, no more than 2.5 *knots per hour* [read *knots*]." J. Michael Kelly, "Slammin' Salmon," *Post-Standard* (Syracuse), 24 Aug. 2000, at D9.
- "Ships must negotiate 12 sharp turns in waters that flow anywhere from 3 to 7 *knots per hour* [read *knots*]." Louis Meixler, "Oil Tankers Pose Risk on Bosporus," *L.A. Times*, 1 July 2001, at A8.

LANGUAGE-CHANGE INDEX
**knots per hour* for *knots*: Stage 2

know, through careless error, is sometimes written *now*—e.g.: "Gempler said he didn't *now* [read *know*] why the union produced the report." Hannelore Sudermann, "Teamsters Attack Apple Industry over Core Issues," *Spokesman-Rev.* (Spokane), 23 July 1997, at A10.

knowledgeable. So spelled—not **knowledgable*.

Current ratio: 139:1

known /nohn/ is often mispronounced /**noh**-ən/, as if it had two syllables.

known quantity. See **unknown quantity.**

Koran; Qur'an; Quran. These English translations of the Arabic name for Islam's holy book are phonetic. Although *Koran* long predominated in AmE and BrE, *Qur'an* and *Quran* are now predominant in World English print sources. The second syllable is stressed: /kə-**rahn**/ or /kə-**ran**/.

kosher is the standard spelling. **Kasher* is an archaic variant.

Current ratio: 117:1

kowtow (= to behave subserviently) has been the standard spelling in AmE since about 1930 and in BrE since about 1960. **Kotow* is a variant. See SPELLING (A).

Current ratio: 16:1

kudos (best pronounced /**kyoo**-dahs/ or /**kyoo**-dohs/, with no *-z* sound at the end) derives from the Greek word *kydos* "glory." A singular noun meaning "praise, glory," it is sometimes erroneously thought to be a plural—e.g.:

- "Dresser . . . has received *several kudos* [read *much kudos* or *several rave reviews*] for 'Better Days' since it premiered in 1986." Mark Chalon Smith, " 'Better Days' Makes Best of Hard Times," *L.A. Times*, 27 Nov. 1992, at F1.
- "The winning team gave *many kudos* [read *much kudos*] to its 'anchor,' chamber member Mark Sharon." Ken O'Brien, "Chamber Teams Raise Funds, Fun Through Olympics," *Chicago Trib.*, 19 May 1996, Tempo Southwest §, at 2.
- "Last week, he was nominated for best breakthrough performance by the Independent Spirit Awards, and more *kudos* [read *honors*] seem in the offing." Lou Lumenick, "The 'Fisher' King," *N.Y. Post*, 16 Dec. 2002, at 37.

As a result of that mistake, **kudoes* (a mistaken plural) and **kudo* (a false singular) have come to plague many texts—e.g.:

- "This is a great-looking show, too: *Kudoes* [read *Kudos*] to the costumer (Ambra Wakefield) and choreographer (Lee Martino)." Eric Marchese, "Curtain Call," *Orange County Register*, 20 July 1996, at F3.
- "Whether you nail me when you think I'm wrong or toss me *a kudo* [read *kudos*] when you agree, I rely on you for ideas and criticism." Dan Gillmor, "Looking Back on the Year's Miscues and Boo-Boos," *St. Louis Post-Dispatch*, 29 Dec. 1997, at 13.
- "[Army] Archerd is the first [journalist] to receive the humanitarian *kudo* [read *kudos*], which will be presented Jan. 28 at the BevWilshire." "Archerd to Receive Scopus," *Daily Variety*, 16 Sept. 2002, at 2.

The mistaken plural use, as well as the back-formed singular **kudo*, came into vogue in World War II. See Atcheson L. Hench, "Singular 'Kudos' and Plural 'Kudos,' " 38 *Am. Speech* 303–04 (1963). But the print evidence of the plural use dates back to the 1920s.

LANGUAGE-CHANGE INDEX
1. *kudos* as a false plural <many kudos>: Stage 4
Current ratio (*kudos is* vs. **kudos are*) (sadly): 1:1.1
2. **kudo* as a false singular: Stage 2
Current ratio (*a kudos* vs. **a kudo*): 10:1
3. **kudoes* as a false plural: Stage 1

Ku Klux Klan. So spelled. The more thoroughly alliterative misspelling *_Klu Klux Klan_ is fairly common—e.g.: "Two grandsons . . . said that they had never heard him refer to the bombing or to his membership in the _Klu Klux Klan_ [read _Ku Klux Klan_]." David Lamb, "Jury Begins Deliberating '63 Church Bombing Case," _L.A. Times_, 22 May 2002, at A14.

LANGUAGE-CHANGE INDEX
Ku Klux Klan misspelled *_Klu Klux Klan_: Stage 1
Current ratio: 53:1

***kummerbund.** See **cummerbund.**

kumquat (= a small citrus fruit resembling a tiny orange) has been the standard spelling since about 1900 (a little later in BrE). *_Cumquat_ is a variant.

Current ratio: 10:1

Kuwait is accented on the second syllable: /kuu-**wayt**/, /koo-**wayt**/, or /kə-**wayt**/. Avoid /kyuu/ and /-wɪt/.

L

label, vb., makes _labeled_ and _labeling_ in AmE, _labelled_ and _labelling_ in BrE. See SPELLING (B).

labor, v.t. See **belabor.**

laboratory (= a special building or room in which scientific tests are made or substances prepared) is preferably pronounced /**lab**-rə-tor-ee/ in AmE and /lə-**bor**-ə-tor-ee/ in BrE. The shortened form _lab_, once considered a CASUALISM, is thoroughly established as standard.

Labour Party; Labor Party. In Great Britain, the spelling is _Labour Party_; in Australia, the spelling is _Labor Party_. How should Americans spell the name of the British party? Most newspapers Americanize the spelling, making it _Labor_, but the better practice is to spell this proper name, like any other, the way the nameholder spells it—e.g.:

- "Opposition leader John Smith died from a heart attack Thursday, creating a crisis for the _Labor_ [read _Labour_] Party just as it was looking strong enough to regain control of government." "British Opposition Leader Dies," _Dallas Morning News_, 13 May 1994, at A10.
- "Mr. Blair, the 43-year-old leader of the _Labor_ [read _Labour_] Party, entered 10 Downing Street to the jubilant cheers of flag-waving supporters." Warren Hoge, "Blair Takes Charge, Vowing 'Practicable' Policies," _N.Y. Times_, 3 May 1997, at 1.
- "When warned by a colleague focused to some extent on winning elections that a particular policy would alienate the voters, a British _Labor_ [read _Labour_] Party leader high-mindedly declared that 'there must be no compromise with the electorate.'" Barney Frank, "They Won't 'Compromise' with Voters," _Portland Press Herald_, 16 Aug. 2015, at 4.

See -OR.

labyrinthine; ***labyrinthian.** The first, the usual form, is much more common than the second, a NEEDLESS VARIANT. The word is pronounced /lab-ə-**rin**-thin/.

Current ratio: 33:1

-laced. Although _straitlaced_ is formed from an adjective (_strait_), the modern combining form -_laced_ (meaning "filled with") should follow a noun: _arsenic-laced meal_, _metaphor-laced speech_, etc. It shouldn't be combined with an adjective—e.g.: "After the game, Isaiah Rider, who scored 16 points, questioned his teammates' will to win with a _profane-laced_ [read _profanity-laced_] diatribe." "Shaq's Monster Night Lifts L.A.," _Austin Am.-Statesman_, 30 Dec. 1999, at D4.

lachrymose; ***lacrimose.** This word, meaning "tearful," is generally spelled _lachrymose_, which is about 52 times as common as *_lacrimose_ in modern print sources. Both forms have ancient origins: the classical Latin term is _lacrima_ (= teardrop), but the -_chry_- spelling crept into medieval Latin (_lachrymalis_). That newer spelling has been standard since the 18th century. E.g.:

- "It seems like 'Dying Rose' is a bit too _lacrimose_ [read _lachrymose_], with an image too forced." Jay Miller, "Ontario's Mae Moore Keeps Positive View," _Patriot Ledger_ (Quincy, Mass.), 1 Sept. 1995, at 13.
- "Nestled cozily in chintz couches, surrounded by cuddly stuffed bunnies and kitties and puppies, the confessors sprinkle their _lachrymose_ monologues with the same catchphrases and catechismal confessions." Ruth Shalit, "Dysfunction Junction," _New Republic_, 14 Apr. 1997, at 24.

lackadaisical is often mistakenly written and misspoken *_lacksadaisical_, probably under the influence of _lax_—e.g.:

- "There's a sitcomlike airiness to her _lacksadaisical_ [read _lackadaisical_] attitude toward family life." Chloe Veltman, "Mom's the Word," _S.F. Weekly_, 2 May 2007 at N.
- "After a _lacksadaisical_ [read _lackadaisical_] freshman year, Gordon was academically ineligible for his sophomore campaign." Rob Shore, "Making the Most of a Second Chance," _Charlotte Sun_ (Port Charlotte, Fla.), 2 Oct. 2013, at 6.

In fact, the influence of _lax_ is made clear in the misspelling *_laxadaisical_ (a much less common error), the scourge of those who write letters to newspaper editors. Here a columnist lets loose on sports

LANGUAGE-CHANGE INDEX (For the full key, see front matter pp. xxxi, l–li.)
Stage 1: Rejected. **Stage 2:** Widely shunned. **Stage 3:** Widespread but . . . **Stage 4:** Ubiquitous but . . . **Stage 5:** Fully accepted.
Invariably inferior forms marked by asterisk (*). • Ratios represent frequency of prevalent forms vs. variants in current books.

commentators: "I have been able to get away with a slightly *lackadaisical* (or '*laxadaisical*' if you listen to the football pundits on BBC Radio 5 Live) approach to pop." David Whetstone, "Ever Get the Feeling Everyone Else Is Going in the Opposite Direction?" *The Journal* (Newcastle, England), 28 May 2014, at 45. In 2002, a Grand Rapids folk-rock band named the Four Lincolns released an album called *Laxadaisical*. Perhaps the band knew they were making a portmanteau pun (see PORTMANTEAU WORDS), but many of their fans surely didn't. Folk-rock laxity.

> LANGUAGE-CHANGE INDEX
> 1. *lacksadaisical* for *lackadaisical*: Stage 2
> Current ratio (*lackadaisical* vs. *lacksadaisical*):
> 1,204:1
> 2. *laxadaisical* for *lackadaisical*: Stage 1

lackey (= a bootlicker, toady) has been the standard spelling since the mid-19th century. *Lacquey* is a variant.

> Current ratio: 13:1

*lacrimose. See **lachrymose.**

lacuna is a FORMAL WORD for *gap*—e.g.:

- "'London Bridge' . . . isn't likely to answer the question, since it simply fills a literary *lacuna*." Book Rev., "Celine Away," *Village Voice*, 11 July 1995, at 12.
- "Female gymnasts inhabit a very strange and specific *lacuna* between girl and woman." Jonathan Van Meter, "Shannon! Jaycie! Dominique! And Again!" *N.Y. Times*, 20 Oct. 1996, § 6, at 58.
- "These sorts of responses are an entirely understandable response to a social media environment that broadcasts failures of or *lacunas* in our legal and moral systems and encourages us to feel a jolt of fury with each and every outrage." Alyssa Rosenberg, "Justice for Lions," *Nat'l Post* (Can.), 31 July 2015, at A11.

The word has two plurals, *lacunae* and *lacunas*. Although *lacunas* might be thought preferable as the native-English plural, *lacunae* appears to be well established as a foreign plural. See PLURALS (B).

> Current ratio: 16:1

lacy. So spelled—not *lacey.* For an example of this error, see **bassinet.**

> Current ratio: 19:1

lade (= to load) is an ARCHAISM in all senses, except in shipping contexts. See **laden.**

laden. A. As a Past Participle Equivalent to *loaded.*
Laden survives today as a participial adjective <a laden barge> and not as a past participle. (See IRREGULAR VERBS (B).) To use *laden* as a part of the verb phrase is to be guilty of ARCHAISM, although it is still used in shipping contexts <the ship was laden by union workers>. But sometimes, in literary contexts, *laden* is simply the right word <with rue my heart is laden>. See **lade.**

Although *ladened* is permissible in Scottish English—since *laden* is the Scottish equivalent of *lade*, v.t. & v.i.—it is a solecism elsewhere. E.g.:

- "She stares out from the magazine cover, line-free, mascara-*ladened* [read *laden*] and pouting, looking something like a teenage daughter who's petulant after being asked to do the dishes." Abigail Trafford, "Mythical Flauntin' of Youth," *Wash. Post*, 26 Nov. 1996, Health §, at Z6.
- "How would you like to be able to eat any fat-*ladened* [read *laden*] goody you want . . . without gaining weight?" Bill Hendrick, "Gene May Be Key to Raising Metabolism," *Atlanta J.-Const.*, 3 Mar. 1997, at C3.

> Current ratio (*laden* vs. *ladened*): 473:1

B. For *ridden*. *Ridden* is the more general term, meaning "infested with," "full of," or "dominated, harassed, or obsessed by." *Laden* has not shed its strong connotation of "loaded down." Hence a place might be *laden* with things if they had been stacked there; or, more plausibly, a truck or barge might be *laden* with goods. But figuratively, *laden* fails as an effective adjective if the original suggestion of loading is ignored. E.g.: "This winter she's going to teach herself how to use the GIS computerized mapping system so she can map out *mosquito-laden* [read *mosquito-ridden*] areas and make it easier on the workers." Pam Starr, "The Bug Lady: No One Knows Insects Like Dreda McCreary," *Virginian-Pilot* (Norfolk), 15 Oct. 1997, at E1.

> LANGUAGE-CHANGE INDEX
> -*laden* for -*ridden* (in the sense "infested with"): Stage 2

ladies' man; lady's man. The phrase is commonly written both ways, but *ladies' man* (the predominant form since the late 19th century) is more in keeping with the sense of *many* women. Some dictionaries seem to misdefine the phrase: "a man very fond of the company of women and very attentive to them" (*WNWCD*); "a man who shows a marked fondness for the company of women or is esp. attentive to women" (*W11*). The main element is missing there because such a man could still be so oafish as to seem repulsive to women. That is, a *ladies' man* must be not only fond of women but also popular with them. See **lady.**

> Current ratio: 4:1

lady. This word has become increasingly problematic. Though hardly anyone would object to it in the phrase *ladies and gentlemen* or on a restroom sign, most other uses of the term might invite disapproval—depending on the readers' or listeners' views about SEXISM. It isn't a SKUNKED TERM, but it's gradually becoming something like one. And this process has been occurring since at least the mid-20th century: "I don't know any word that has been so beaten down in modern usage as 'lady.'" Edward N. Teall, *Putting Words to Work* 286 (1940).

The linguist Cecily Raysor Hancock of Chicago observed in 1963 that Americans are divisible into three groups when it comes to using *lady*: (1) those who use *lady* in preference to *woman* when referring to female adults of any social class (a group that has steadily dwindled); (2) those who generally use *woman* in preference to *lady*, but who use *lady* in reference to social inferiors; and (3) those who use *woman* uniformly regardless of social class or familiarity, except in a few set formulas such as *ladies and gentlemen*. See "*Lady and Woman*," 38 *Am. Speech* 234–35 (1963). Hancock rightly notes that "the use of *lady* at present apparently gives more sociological information about its user than about the person described," adding: "*woman* is probably the safer choice of the two." *Ibid.* at 235.

lady's man. See **ladies' man.**

***laesae majestas;** *laesae majestatis.* See **lese majesty.**

Lafayette. The Marquis de Lafayette's name was pronounced /lah-fay-**et**/. The name of the Louisiana city is /laf-ee-**yet**/.

laid; lain. See **lay.**

laissez-faire; ***laisser-faire.** The former spelling has long been standard. Some British publications, however, continue to use the outmoded spelling (*laisser*)—e.g.:

- "Should Hongkong's *laisser-faire* [read *laissez-faire*] government do an about-face to build Hongkong Inc?" "Farewell to Adam Smith," *Economist*, 30 Sept.–6 Oct. 1989, at 71.
- "This is bonkers, though par for the course for a Bush administration that is all for *laisser faire* [read *laissez-faire*] except when US companies whine about foreign competition." Robert Peston, "The Stock Exchange Drops Its American Dream," *Sunday Telegraph*, 13 Oct. 2002, at 3.

The phrase is pronounced /les-ay **fair**/—not /lah-zay/ or /lay-zay/.

Current ratio: 69:1

lam, on the. See **on the lam.**

lama; llama. A *lama* is a Buddhist priest in Tibet or Mongolia—Tibetan Buddhism also being known as Lamaism. A *llama* is the South American long-necked animal with thick wool-like hair.

lambaste; lambast. Although both spellings are well attested, *lambaste* is truer to the putative ETYMOLOGY (*lam* "to beat" + *baste* "to thrash") and, in any event, has vastly predominated in AmE since the mid-20th century. *Lambast*, however, has been the usual form in BrE since the late 1960s. In World English today, *lambaste* predominates by a 3-to-1 ratio.

The word is pronounced /lam-**bayst**/, /**lam**-bast/, or /**lam**-bayst/. The second is the most frequent pronunciation; that explains, no doubt, why people have trouble with the spelling in AmE. The traditionally correct pronunciation—and the one with by far the most authority—is the first one listed.

LAMBDACISM. See PRONUNCIATION (C).

lament, v.t., should not be made intransitive by the addition of a preposition—e.g.:

- "They should be used to it by now, having *lamented over* [delete *over*] one-point defeats to both Kansas City and San Francisco." Greg Pogue, "Seattle Surprise," *Nashville Banner*, 4 Nov. 1996, at E1.
- "I *lamented over* [delete *over*] my lost opportunity to dissent." Jon T. Ferrier, "Sounds of Jazz Leave Our Days," *Grand Rapids Press*, 6 July 1997, at E1.
- "While Defenbaugh steadfastly defends the work of his task force, others, including conspiracy theorists in a number of books about the bombing, *lament over* [delete *over*] leads not followed." Max B. Baker, "America Remembers the OKC Bombing 20 Years Later," *Ft. Worth Star-Telegram*, 17 Apr. 2015, News §.

LANGUAGE-CHANGE INDEX
lament used intransitively <lamented over the loss> instead of transitively <lamented the loss>: Stage 1
Current ratio (*lamented the* vs. *lamented over the*): 58:1

lamentable is pronounced either /**lam**-ən-tə-bəl/ or /lə-**men**-tə-bəl/. Traditionally, the first of these pronunciations has been considered the better one.

landowner has been written as one word in both AmE and BrE since the early 19th century. The same is true of *landownership*.

landward(s). See DIRECTIONAL WORDS (A).

***laniard.** See **lanyard.**

lanolin (= a fatty substance in cosmetics and emollients) is the standard spelling in AmE and BrE alike. *Lanoline* is a variant.

Current ratio: 20:1

lanyard, a word referring to various types of cords or ropes, has been predominantly so spelled since the mid-19th century. *Laniard* is a variant spelling.

lapelled (= [of a coat or jacket] having a front that is joined to the collar and folded back on each side) is so spelled in AmE and BrE alike. Why is the final -l- doubled in AmE, though not in *leveled*? Because the final -l- in *lapelled* occurs in an accented syllable. See SPELLING (B).

lapsable. So spelled—preferably not *lapsible*. See -ABLE (A).

Current ratio: 8:1

***lapsus linguae;** *lapsus calami.* These LATINISMS are fancy ways of referring to slips of the tongue (*linguae*) or of the pen (*calami*). The phrase *lapsus linguae* /**lap**-səs **ling**-gwee/ is the more common one—e.g.: "In a *lapsus linguae*, Pam Weiger, a Fire Department spokeswoman, said, 'We ended up transporting sick of them, I mean six of them, to Mount Vernon

LANGUAGE-CHANGE INDEX (For the full key, see front matter pp. xxxi, l–li.)
Stage 1: Rejected. **Stage 2:** Widely shunned. **Stage 3:** Widespread but . . . **Stage 4:** Ubiquitous but . . . **Stage 5:** Fully accepted.
Invariably inferior forms marked by asterisk (∗). • Ratios represent frequency of prevalent forms vs. variants in current books.

Hospital.' " Frank Wolfe, "Students Take Ill at Mount Vernon," *Wash. Times*, 18 June 1991, at B4.

As for *lapsus calami* (/**lap**-səs **kal**-ə-mı/), which means "a slip of the pen," examples abound in this book, in entries such as **toe the line** (mistakenly written *tow the line*) and **row to hoe** (mistakenly written *road to hoe*).

On the Latinity of these phrases, see LATINISMS & SESQUIPEDALITY.

larceny. See **burglary.**

large, unlike *great*, is not a word that can be idiomatically coupled with other words denoting measure, such as *breadth, depth, distance, height, length, weight,* and *width*. But writers often misuse *large* when *great* would be the right word—e.g.:

- "About 46 percent of the state's bridges are not wide or high enough, have lanes that are too narrow or can't handle *large* [read *great*] weights or high speeds." Mei-Ling Hopgood, "Missouri's City Highways All Choked Up," *St. Louis Post-Dispatch*, 6 Feb. 1997, at A1.
- "Every so often, gravity from a planet acts like a 'slingshot,' Mumma said, hurtling a comet *large* [read *great*] distances from the sun." Diedtra Henderson, "Unlocking Comets' Secrets," *Seattle Times*, 18 Mar. 1997, at A12. (Because gravity is a property rather than an emanation, the phrase *the gravity of a planet* would be more logical in that sentence than *gravity from a planet*.)

LANGUAGE-CHANGE INDEX
large for *great* with words of measure <great distance>: Stage 1

large-sized; large-size, adj. This PHRASAL ADJECTIVE is usually redundant. The predominant form (twice as common) is *large-sized*. Although *large-sized apparel* is defensible, *large-sized business* is not.

largesse; largess. *Largesse* (= generous giving; munificence) has long been the standard spelling in English. The GALLICISM was first borrowed into Middle English and was fully anglicized as *largess* by the 16th century. AmE mostly stuck with that spelling through about 1950, while BrE had reverted to the Frenchified spelling *largesse* by 1900. Today *largesse* predominates in AmE as well as BrE. Although the preferred pronunciation is the anglicized /lahr-**jes**/, the word is often pronounced in the French way, that is, /lahr-**zhes**/.

larva (= a newly hatched insect) predominantly forms the plural *larvae* (/**lahr**-vee/) in AmE and BrE alike. Avoid pronouncing the plural form as /**lahr**-vɪ/ or /**lahr**-vay/.

Current ratio (*larvae* vs. *larvas*): 201:1

larynx /**lar**-ingks/ is sometimes, through METATHESIS, mispronounced /**lar**-ə-niks/ or /**lahr**-niks/. From the latter mispronunciation comes the inevitable misspelling—e.g.:

- "[Ken] Raabe [a puppeteer] uses an object called a swazzle, a kind of small artificial *larnyx* [read *larynx*] placed at the back of his throat, to make the traditional shrill, raspy

voice of Punch." Nancy Maes, "Clowns at Custer's Last Stand," *Chicago Trib.*, 15 June 2001, at 35.
- "[Bob] Schwartz rarely takes his eyes (or his *larnyx* [read *larynx*]) off New Mexico." Jeff Commings, "Rush, Meet Bob," *Albuquerque Trib.*, 26 Apr. 2002, at C3.

LANGUAGE-CHANGE INDEX
larynx misspelled and mispronounced *larnyx*: Stage 1
Current ratio: 679:1
Current ratio (*larynxes* vs. *larynges* as pl.): 1:1

lasagna, denoting a popular Italian dish, is the standard spelling in AmE. *Lasagne* (the Italian plural) predominates in BrE.

Current ratio (*lasagna* vs. *lasagne*): 4:1

lasso. Pl. *lassos*, not *lassoes*. See PLURALS (D).

last analysis, in the. See **in the final analysis.**

last but not least. First and foremost, it needs to be said that this tired expression is best avoided. Second, please realize that *least* is the most emphatic word in the phrase, thereby suggesting the opposite of what is being asserted. Try *finally* instead.

last name. See NAMES (D).

last rites (= a sacrament in which a priest blesses and prays for a person who has fallen critically ill or been grievously injured) is occasionally misrendered *last rights*—e.g.: "Less than a year later, he would give her son, Albie, his *last rights* [read *last rites*] as he lay dying in a hallway." Peter Gelzinis, "Charlestown's Rev. Coyne Is Worthy of Name 'Father,' " *Boston Herald*, 16 June 1996, at 16. Cf. **rite of passage.**

A former term for *last rites* is *extreme unction*, but the Roman Catholic Church changed the name in 1972 to shift the focus from dying to healing, spiritually and physically. Today the rite is called, variously, *sacrament of the sick, anointing of the sick,* and *sacrament of healing.*

LANGUAGE-CHANGE INDEX
last rights for *last rites*: Stage 1
Current ratio (*last rites* vs. *last rights*): 30:1

late. A. The late. This expression is elliptical for *lately* (i.e., recently) *deceased*. How long this can be used of a dead person depends on how recently that person died, but anything more than five years or so is going to strike most readers as odd (e.g., *the late John F. Kennedy*). Of course, there's no absolute statute of limitations; the question is whether a fair number of reasonable readers would know or need to be reminded that the person has died. But the expression serves as more than just a reminder. It also offers a note of respect—and perhaps even a touch of sorrow. So in the fall of 1997 people said *the late Princess Diana* not because anybody needed to be reminded that she had died in August of that year—everyone knew it—but because people mourned her death. By the same token, a widowed spouse might continue to use *my late husband* or *my late wife*.

The late is also helpful in historical contexts to indicate that someone has recently died <the Civil Rights Act of 1964 was seen at the time as a tribute to the late John F. Kennedy>.

B. Late residence. The usage *his (or her) late residence*, common in obituaries from the late 20th century, was first mentioned in usage commentary in 1984. See David L. Gold, "Media Watch: *His Late Residence*," 59 *Am. Speech* 96 (1984). But in fact the phrase dates back to the 18th century and was fairly common in the 19th. Because *late* means "recently deceased," this is an odd instance of HYPALLAGE. It makes little sense. The best editorial practice is to let the context make clear that a decedent's residence is being referred to—e.g.:

- "Born Jan. 21, 1938, in Chicago, she passed away Friday, March 28, 2008, at her *late residence* in Shorewood." "Lucille K. Eakins" (obit.), *Daily Herald* (Arlington Heights, Ill.), 31 Mar. 2008, Bus. §, at 6.
- "A celebration of Frances' life will be held at her *late residence*, 6545 Murano Way, Lakeworth, FL on Saturday, Apr. 26, 2008 from 1-5 PM." "Funeral Notices" (Frances (Sweeney) Foster), *Palm Beach Post*, 24 Apr. 2008, at B8.
- "Died May 26, 2008, peacefully, at Slieve Dhu Nursing Home. Funeral from her *late residence*, 11 Whiteforth Road, Aughlisnafin, Castlewellan, tomorrow (Wednesday) at 2.00 p.m. for service in Clough Non Subscribing Presbyterian Church, followed by interment in adjoining churchyard. Friends welcome to call at her *late residence*." "Wilson, Sarah Jane (Sadie)" (obit.), *Belfast Telegraph* (Ireland), 27 May 2008.

later. A. Without Temporal Context. *Later* should not be used unless a proper time frame has already been established. E.g.: "As Salman Rushdie, *later the target of an Islamic fatwa calling for his death* [read *who was to become the target of an Islamic fatwa calling for his death*], stated in 1985, ..."

B. Later on. The distinction between *later* and *later on* rests on two points: euphony and formality. Occasionally, *later on* simply sounds better in a sentence. It is always less formal—e.g.:

- "*Later on*, I realized it was a good thing I had paid Billy's reputation that trite little compliment." Larry McMurtry, *Anything for Billy* 14 (1988).
- "What you spend today sets the course for how much you'll 'need' *later on*." Lisa Reilly Cullen, "Are You Where You Want to Be?" *Money*, Dec. 1997, at B1.

Cf. **early on.**

late residence. See **late (B).**

lath; lathe. A *lath* /lath/ is a long narrow piece of wood used as an underlay for some other building material, such as plaster or tile. A *lathe* /laythe/ is a machine that shapes wood or metal by having it rotated against a sharp tool within the machine.

LATINISMS. In the English language, Latin words and phrases typically fall into one of six categories:

(1) those that are now so common that they're barely recognizable as Latin (*bonus, data, vice versa*); (2) those that are reduced to abbreviations in scholarly contexts (*e.g., i.e., ibid., id.*); (3) those used in JARGON of doctors, lawyers, and scientists (*metatarsus, habeas corpus, chlorella*); (4) the mottoes and maxims used especially in ceremonial contexts (*E pluribus unum, Sic transit gloria mundi*); (5) those that literate people know and occasionally find useful (*ipse dixit, non sequitur, rebus, mutatis mutandis*); and (6) the truly rare ones that characterize SESQUIPEDALITY (*ceteris paribus, hic et ubique, ignoratio elenchi*). Increasingly, the view among stylists is that unless you know that your audience is fairly erudite, categories 3 through 6 are dangerous territory.

For an interesting list of Latinate adjectives describing various animals, see ANIMAL ADJECTIVES. On whether to italicize words borrowed from Latin and other languages, see ITALICS (B). On pluralizing Latin terms, see PLURALS (B) & HYPERCORRECTION (A).

Latino; Latina. See **Hispanic.**

latter. See **former.**

latterly, an ARCHAISM characteristic of 19th-century prose, is essentially equivalent to *later* or *lately*. It occurs seldom in AmE but occasionally in BrE—e.g.:

- "*Latterly* he professed himself increasingly saddened by the manipulative nature of the business he had helped to create." "Edward L. Bernays" (obit.), *Daily Telegraph*, 13 Mar. 1995, at 23.
- "In the early years, its work was mainly inspections of long-stay hospitals; *latterly*, it moved into thematic reviews of services." David Brindle, "Demise of the Eyes," *Guardian*, 2 Apr. 1997, at 6.

When the word does appear in AmE, it is usually in a literary context—e.g.: "A novelist himself, once a New York editor, formerly director of the Iowa Writers' Workshop and *latterly* of the Napa Valley Writers' Conference, these days Leggett lives and writes here in the Bay Area." David Kipen, "Saroyan as Monstrous Narcissist," *S.F. Chron.*, 10 Nov. 2002, Sunday Rev. §, at 1.

laudatory; *laudative; laudable. The first two both mean "expressing praise." But *laudative* is a NEEDLESS VARIANT of *laudatory*, the much more common word. *Laudable*, in contrast, means "deserving praise." The distinction is the same as that between *praiseworthy* (= *laudable*) and *praiseful* (= *laudatory*).

The misuse of *laudatory* for *laudable* is lamentably common—e.g.:

- "Indeed, like Nixon before him, a jaundiced view of Clinton and his motives causes many to oppose or at least look askance at even his most *laudatory* [read *laudable*] goals." Jeff Rivers, "Cast Aside National Cynicism Left Over from Watergate," *Hartford Courant*, 4 Aug. 1994, at A2.

LANGUAGE-CHANGE INDEX (For the full key, see front matter pp. xxxi, l–li.)
Stage 1: Rejected. **Stage 2:** Widely shunned. **Stage 3:** Widespread but . . . **Stage 4:** Ubiquitous but . . . **Stage 5:** Fully accepted.
Invariably inferior forms marked by asterisk (*). • Ratios represent frequency of prevalent forms vs. variants in current books.

- "But for all its *laudatory* [read *laudable*] achievements, the council-manager model can be aloof, even distant, from the people who are paying for it." "Government Merger," *Herald-Sun* (Durham, N.C.), 8 Sept. 1994, at A12.
- "The New York legislation on self determination at the end of life is *laudatory* [read *laudable*] but insufficient." Alan Pfeffer, "Let Patient Decide When It's Time to Die," *Times Union* (Albany), 14 July 2015, at D2.

LANGUAGE-CHANGE INDEX
laudatory misused for *laudable*: Stage 2
Current ratio (*laudable goal* vs. **laudatory goal*): 39:1

launch has become a VOGUE WORD when used in the sense "to begin, initiate"—e.g.:

- "USAir Chairman Seth Schofield . . . is visiting Pittsburgh to *launch* a new service to Mexico City today." Steve Creedy, "Travel Agents Slap Airlines over Fee Caps," *Pitt. Post-Gaz.*, 15 Feb. 1995, at F1.
- "DuPage County is *launching* an innovative 'last chance' educational initiative for students expelled from school because of drug selling." Casey Banas, "Last Chance Offered to Kids Facing Expulsion," *Chicago Trib.*, 12 Feb. 1997, at D1.

The related noun <the first launch in California will be in San Diego> is much the same.

laundromat is sometimes misspelled **laundry mat*—e.g.:

- "Winkler got the idea for immortalizing T-shirts one day during the spin cycle at the *laundry mat* [read *laundromat*]." "Last-Minute Gifts Tip for Holiday Procrastinators," *Virginian-Pilot & Ledger Star*, 22 Dec. 1996, at 6.
- "He followed the scent to the vent fan on the nearby *laundry mat* [read *laundromat*], then to the dryers inside where bulging pillow cases were tumbling." R.K. Shull, "Waiting for the Smoke to Clear," *Indianapolis News*, 19 July 1999, at C1.
- "Someone stole a car from a *laundry mat* [read *laundromat*]." "Police Log," *Orlando Sentinel*, 2 Sept. 1999, at D10.
- "The Rizzo family returned to the *laundry mat* [read *laundromat*]." Alex Lizzi Jr., *Bonding the Rizzo's* [read *Rizzos'*] *Family Vacation* 100 (2007).

Although *laundromat* appears to be a PORTMANTEAU WORD, perhaps derived from *laundry* and *automat*, it is actually a servicemark for a brand of washing machines, and, briefly, a chain of do-it-yourself laundries.

LANGUAGE-CHANGE INDEX
*laundry mat for *laundromat*: Stage 1
Current ratio (*laundromat* vs. **laundry mat*): 18:1

*lava bread. See **laver bread.**

lavaliere; *lavalier; *lavalliere; *lavallière. *Lavaliere* is the standard spelling for the word meaning (1) "a microphone that is clipped to clothing and used typically in broadcast studios and theaters"; or (2) "a style of jewelry and clothing." (The microphone was so named because it was originally hung around the neck like jewelry.) Although the term derives from the name of a French courtesan, Louise de la Vallière (1644–1710), the anglicized *lavaliere* is pronounced

/lav-ə-**leer**/. The other three spellings are variant forms, the last two being overt GALLICISMS (pronounced /lah-vahl-**yair**/).

Current ratio (in order of headwords): 57:34:17:1

laver bread (= a Welsh dish consisting of seaweed that is boiled, dipped in oatmeal, and fried) is sometimes wrongly written **lava bread*, doubtless because one unfortunate but common pronunciation of *laver* is almost identical with that of *lava*. E.g.:

- "One specialty is *lava* [read *laver*] bread fried (really a form of seaweed)." "Amtrak's Auto Train: English Breakfasts," *Wash. Post*, 3 Sept. 1989, at E3.
- "We started with a trip to the Lleyn Peninsula in North Wales, dreaming of mountains and seascapes and *lava* [read *laver*] bread with dinner." Mary Dejevsky, "Happiness Is Rediscovering Nationhood," *Independent*, 9 Apr. 2010, Comment §, at 42.

The better pronunciation—the only one recognized in most current dictionaries—is /**lay**-vər/.

LANGUAGE-CHANGE INDEX
*lava bread for *laver bread*: Stage 2
Current ratio (*laver bread* vs. **lava bread*): 4:1

lavish, vb. As a transitive verb, *lavish* takes a direct object, but it is traditionally a thing, not a person. That is, you lavish gifts on a person, not a person with gifts. But since the late 1970s, writers have engaged in OBJECT-SHUFFLING with this verb—e.g.:

- "The NCAA will announce Notre Dame's first major rules infraction in the school's history today, ending a two-year investigation into the relationship between players and former boosters who *lavished them with gifts, money and trips* [read *lavished gifts, money, and trips on them*], an NCAA source said." Malcolm Moran, "No Luck: Notre Dame Faces Sanctions," *Austin Am.-Statesman*, 17 Dec. 1999, at C4.
- "Mayor Willie Brown welcomed Philippine President Joseph Estrada with open arms Tuesday, *lavishing him with compliments* [read *lavishing compliments on him*] and encouraging him to maintain ties with the Bay Area." Pia Sarkar, "Philippine 1st Couple to Get Royal Welcome," *S.F. Examiner*, 26 July 2000, at A4.
- "The Bulls, shut out by other top free agents, could *lavish him with money* [read *lavish money on him*]." Ethan J. Skolnick, "New Era for Heat," *Palm Beach Post*, 1 Aug. 2000, at C1.

Despite those desirable edits, this nontraditional usage does seem to give the language more versatility when the thing being lavished takes many words to express—e.g.: "She had *lavished him* with the adoration and protectiveness of a childless woman who has borrowed a precious gift, especially a gift from God." Sharon Rab, "The Red Dress," *Dayton Daily News*, 6 Aug. 2000, at C3. That sentence is particularly challenging to try to rewrite by using the traditional idiom. One solution would be to make it the idiomatic *lavished on him the adoration* . . . . Another would be to replace *lavished* with another verb, such as *showered*: *She had showered him with the adoration and protectiveness of a childless woman who* . . . . A third would be to allow this extension in the use of *lavish*. Linguistic conservatives will prefer the first two solutions; liberals will be perfectly happy with the third.

LANGUAGE-CHANGE INDEX
*lavishing someone with gifts for lavishing gifts on someone: Stage 4
Current ratio (lavished gifts on him vs. *lavished him with gifts): 1.2:1

lawful. See **legal.**

lawsuit. Journalists often misuse *lawsuit* (one word in both AmE and BrE) for *complaint* or *petition* (= the paper that is filed to start a lawsuit)—e.g.:

- "In its 18-page *lawsuit* [read *complaint*], Viacom-owned CBS alleged: ' "Celebrity" was consciously designed to mimic "Survivor" and unfairly trade on its success.' " Meg James, "CBS Sues to Block New ABC Program," *L.A. Times*, 7 Nov. 2002, Bus. §, pt. 3, at 3.
- "The allegations in his 144-page *lawsuit* [read *complaint*] read like a Robin Cook novel." Lynne Tuohy, "Pfizer Trials Called Cruel, Immoral," *Hartford Courant*, 6 Dec. 2002, at A1.
- " 'Defendants knew he couldn't control his gambling addiction,' according to the 29-page *lawsuit* [read *complaint*]." Becky Yerak, "Gamblers Sue over Addiction," *Detroit News*, 8 Dec. 2002, at D1.

The *lawsuit* is the whole process; the document (however many pages long) is only an instrumental part of it.

LANGUAGE-CHANGE INDEX
lawsuit misused for *complaint* or *petition*: Stage 1

lawyer; attorney; counsel; counselor. The two most common among these, *lawyer* and *attorney*, are not generally distinguished even by members of the legal profession—except perhaps that *lawyer* is often viewed as having negative connotations. So one frequently hears about *lawyer-bashing*, but only the tone-deaf write *attorney-bashing*—e.g.: "*Attorney-bashing* [read *Lawyer-bashing*] always will be a popular pastime." Christopher Smith, "Injury Lawyer May Be Utah's Best—Bar None," *Salt Lake Trib.*, 7 Feb. 1994, at A1.

Technically, *lawyer* is the more general term, referring to one who practices law. *Attorney* literally means "someone who is designated to transact business for another." An *attorney*—archaically apart from the phrases *power of attorney* and, less commonly, *attorney-in-fact*—may or may not be a lawyer. Hence Samuel Johnson's statement that *attorney* "was anciently used for those who did any business for another; now only in law." *A Dictionary of the English Language* (1755).

From the fact that an *attorney* is really an agent, Bernstein deduces that "a *lawyer* is an *attorney* only when he has a client. It may be that the desire of *lawyers* to appear to be making a go of their profession has accounted for their leaning toward the designation *attorney*." Theodore M. Bernstein, *The Careful Writer* 60 (1965). Yet this distinction between *lawyer* and *attorney* is rarely, if ever, observed in practice.

In AmE, *counsel* and *counselor* are both, in one sense, general terms meaning "one who gives (legal) advice," the latter being the more formal term. *Counsel* may refer to but one lawyer <opposing counsel says> or, as a plural, to more than one lawyer <opposing counsel say>. See **counsel (B).**

lay; lie. A. The Distinction. Very simply, *lie* (= to recline, be situated) is intransitive—it can't take a direct object <he lies on his bed>. But *lay* (= to put down, arrange) is always transitive—it needs a direct object <please lay the book on my desk>. The verbs are inflected as follows:

Verb	Present Tense	Past Tense	Past Participle	Present Participle
lay, v.t.	lay	laid	laid	laying
lie, v.i.	lie	lay	lain	lying

Because *lie* is intransitive, it has only an active voice <lie down for a while>. And because *lay* is transitive, it may be either active <he laid the blanket over her> or passive <the blanket was laid over her>. See PASSIVE VOICE.

To use *lay* without a direct object, in the sense of *lie*, is nonstandard <I want to lay down> <he was laying in the sun>. But this error is very common in speech—from the illiterate to the highly educated. In fact, some commentators believe that people make this mistake more often than any other in the English language. Others claim that it's no longer a mistake—or even that it never was. But make no mistake: using these verbs correctly is a mark of refinement.

The most unusual of these inflected forms, of course, is *lain*, but most writers have little difficulty getting it right—e.g.:

- "Katrina Kuratli said she and her husband, Dan, had just *lain* down in their bedroom when the bomb went off around 10:45 p.m." Mack Reed, "Pipe Bomb Rips Car, Jolts Simi Neighborhood," *L.A. Times*, 30 Apr. 1994, at B9.
- "Prosecutors later claimed the witness had *lain* down next to two of the murder victims, expecting to die." Tom Jackman, "Witness in Three Murder Cases Pleads Guilty to Conspiracy," *Kansas City Star*, 28 June 1994, at B1.
- "Massive seed banks that have *lain* dormant for decades are expected to re-emerge from freshly exposed muck." James F. McCarty, "Project Set to Restore Mentor Marsh," *Plain Dealer* (Cleveland), 31 Aug. 2015, at A6.

See **lie** & IRREGULAR VERBS.

B. *Lay* for *lie*. This is one of the most widely known of all usage errors—e.g.:

- "Mr. Armstrong [debating against Alan Dershowitz] was not to be outdone . . . . But Mr. Dershowitz did not *lay* [read *lie*] down." William Glaberson, "Face to Face, 2 Lawyers Feud Away, Slap for Slap," *N.Y. Times*, 19 Jan. 1991, at 15.
- "The girls were ordered to *lay* [read *lie*] face down on the floor and were told they would have their throats slit if they yelled." "Girls' Final Hours Detailed in Court," *Amarillo Sunday News-Globe*, 15 May 1994, at A17.

LANGUAGE-CHANGE INDEX (For the full key, see front matter pp. xxxi, l–li.)
Stage 1: Rejected. **Stage 2:** Widely shunned. **Stage 3:** Widespread but . . . **Stage 4:** Ubiquitous but . . . **Stage 5:** Fully accepted.
Invariably inferior forms marked by asterisk (*). • Ratios represent frequency of prevalent forms vs. variants in current books.

- "If you've got an extra $79,800 *laying* [read *lying*] around you could become the proud owner of two vacant buildings on the southeast corner of the Canyon square." Bill Rogers, "Buildings Priced at $79,800," *Canyon News* (Tex.), 30 Oct. 1994, at 1.
- "This Christmas give a gift that's been *laying* [read *lying*] around for twelve years." Advertisement for Glenlivet Scotch Whisky, *Atlantic Monthly*, Dec. 1994, at 13.
- "But Walters did not ask any questions, investigators said. He ordered the two to get out of the car and *lay* [read *lie*] on the ground, according to Strouse's girlfriend." Peter Fimrite, "Deadly End to Sunday Drive on Dusty, Rural Road," *S.F. Chron.*, 23 May 1995, at A13.

Similarly, although a sickness can *lay you low*, if you're in that position you're *lying low*—e.g.: "Back when James A. Baker 3d was *lying low* over at the White House, the first invisible chief of staff, cynics in the West Wing said he was trying to avoid being tied too closely to a Presidential campaign that seemed headed for the political dump." "Baker Takes New Role, Leading 'Winnable' Bid," *N.Y. Times*, 31 Oct. 1992, at 8. But American journalists get it wrong as often as they get it right—e.g.:

- "Another reason I *laid low* [read *lay low*] was to be in a position to help a friend back out of what he now must know to be a dead end." William Safire, "Buchanan's Campaign," *N.Y. Times*, 16 Dec. 1991, at A15.
- "A wan-sounding D'Amato said he has been *laying low* [read *lying low*], nursing a bad cold at home on Long Island, since Giuliani announced his endorsement of Cuomo." Bob Liff & Charles V. Zehren, "D'Amato Tries to Hide from Spotlight," *Newsday* (N.Y.), 27 Oct. 1994, at A25.
- "Lately allegedly told a killer to *lay low* [read *lie low*] after a homicide and tried to thwart a police investigation into the crime." George Hunter & Holly Fournier, "Bond Lowered for Detroit Cop Facing Charges in Murder Plot," *Detroit News*, 27 Aug. 2015, at A6.

Another common mistake is *laying in wait* for *lying in wait*—e.g.:

- "Police say several armed assailants may have been *laying* [read *lying*] in wait at East 39th Street and Park Avenue." Erica Franklin, "14 Unsolved Murders Are Possibly Tied to Drug Sales," *Indianapolis Star*, 11 Oct. 1994, at A1.
- "Dunlap has been accused of *laying* [read *lying*] in wait until closing time at the Chuck E Cheese restaurant, then systematically shooting the five employees still on duty." Ginny McKibben, "Ex-Friend Links Dunlap to Burger King Robbery," *Denver Post*, 1 Apr. 1995, at B4.

Some blame the confusion in part on the children's prayer that begins, "Now I *lay* me down to sleep." But there, *lay* is properly transitive (*me*, meaning "myself," being its object). It is grammatically equivalent to "Now I *lie* down to sleep," though metrically speaking the latter doesn't have a prayer.

LANGUAGE-CHANGE INDEX
1. *lay* misused for *lie*: Stage 4
2. *lay low for *lie low* (as a present-tense form): Stage 4
Current ratio (*to lie low* vs. *to lay low): 1.2:1
3. *laid low for *lay low* (as a past form): Stage 4
Current ratio (*they lay low* vs. *they laid low): 1.8:1

C. *Laid* for Past-Tense *lay*. The *lay*-for-*lie* error also occurs with the past-tense forms—e.g.: "He *laid* [read *lay*] down flat on the ground and looked around for an object or landmark he might have missed from a higher angle." "Pumpkin Place," *Amarillo Daily News*, 4 Mar. 1996, at C1.

LANGUAGE-CHANGE INDEX
laid misused for past-tense *lay*: Stage 4
Current ratio (*he lay down on* vs. *he laid down on): 9:1

D. *Laid* for *lain*. Not surprisingly, the same mistake occurs with the past participles as well—e.g.:

- "The players—performers—will take on a problem that has *laid* [read *lain*] dormant since Peter Ueberroth caved in to the umps." Peter Gammons, "KC May Start Enjoying Some Royalties," *Boston Globe*, 25 Nov. 1990, at 58.
- "Or the epilepsy might have *laid* [read *lain*] dormant, triggered by the ball's blow, she says." Susan H. Thompson, "Boy Loses Chunk of Brain, Regains His Life," *Tampa Trib.*, 16 Sept. 1996, Baylife §, at 1.
- "Foes have lashed out with claims that the plan was hastily worked out over the past few weeks after the deregulation idea had *laid* [read *lain*] dormant for two years." Dave Sheingold, "Landline Oversight Fading," *N.J. Record*, 20 May 2015, at A1.

LANGUAGE-CHANGE INDEX
laid misused for past-participial *lain*: Stage 4
Current ratio (*had lain idle* vs. *had laid idle): 29:1

E. *Lain* for the Past-Participial *laid*. This is a ghastly example of HYPERCORRECTION, that is, choosing the more far-fetched (and, as it happens, wrong) term in a contorted attempt to be correct—e.g.:

- "Earlier in the day, several people had '*lain hands*' [read '*laid hands*'] on Zachary and prayed for him. This is common at the crusades, as many people seem to think that God has anointed them." Mike Thomas, "The Power and the Glory," *Orlando Sentinel*, 24 Nov. 1991, at 9.
- "But to me it seemed like the kind of thoughtless destructiveness that has *lain* [read *laid*] waste to much of the city." Ed Zotti, "Supporters Fervent About Rogers Park's Future," *Chicago Enterprise*, May 1994, at 30.
- "The goal of the bill is to both avoid the pattern of attempted murder charges being pleaded down to misdemeanor offenses and to make sure the severity of the act is *lain* [read *laid*] out plainly." Abigail Goldman, "Metro Keeps Close Tabs on Fury in the Home," *Las Vegas Sun*, 18 Mar. 2009, Metro §, at 1.

LANGUAGE-CHANGE INDEX
lain for past-participial *laid*: Stage 1
Current ratio (*had laid the foundation* vs. **had lain the foundation*): 153:1

lay low. See **lie low.**

layman; layperson; lay person. *Layman*, the most common among these terms, is generally regarded as unexceptionable—in reference to members of both sexes, of course. E.g.:

- "James Wilkinson, the 55-year-old *layman* who carried the cross at the head of Princess Diana's funeral procession, said he had never experienced anything like Saturday's ceremony." Mary Williams Walsh, "1961–1997," *L.A. Times*, 7 Sept. 1997, at A22.

- "One of the hormones has been postulated to cause the post-prandial—in *layman's* terms, after-meal—mechanism that brings on drowsiness." Diane Lacey Allen, "Feeling Full," *Ledger* (Lakeland, Fla.), 27 Nov. 1997, at D1.

Still, modern writers increasingly avoid *layman* on grounds of SEXISM.

Lay person (two words) dates from the early 18th century, but the one-word compound *layperson* is an Americanism dating from the early 1970s. Though much less common than *layman*, it frequently appears, especially today in the one-word form—e.g.:

- "Since [1979], the school's principals have been *laypersons*, and most of the sisters have given up teaching duties." George Morris, "Still Serving: Group of Sisters at St. Aloysius Has Seen Lots of Things Change," *Advocate* (Baton Rouge), 2 Mar. 1997, at H1.
- "Some would require coverage for surgical procedures such as mastectomies or for emergency care in cases where a 'prudent *layperson*' would think it necessary." Mary Agnes Carey, "Patients' Rights Are Hot Item in Congress," *St. Louis Post-Dispatch*, 25 Nov. 1997, at A4.
- "To the *layperson*, those numbers suggest that refineries are using low oil prices to gouge the public." Whit Richardson, "Why Aren't Gas Prices Lower? It's Complicated," *Portland Press Herald*, 23 Aug. 2015, at 1.

For the reasons for avoiding *layperson*, like all other words ending with the suffix *-person*, see SEXISM (C).

LANGUAGE-CHANGE INDEX
layperson for *layman*: Stage 4
Current ratio (*layman* vs. *layperson*): 4:1

lay off. See **fire.**

lay of the land; lie of the land. The first is the usual AmE form, the second the BrE, for this phrase meaning (1) lit., "the arrangement of an area's terrain; topography"; or (2) fig., "the facts of a given situation; the current state of affairs." *Lay of the land* was predominant in AmE by 1840, *lie of the land* in BrE by 1880.

lay waste. The traditional idiom is an unusual one: either *they laid waste the city* or (a variant form) *they laid the city waste*. *Lay* is the verb; *city* is the object; and *waste* is an adjective serving as an objective complement. The structure of *they laid waste the city* is like that of the unobjectionable *they laid bare the problems*.

In 1965, an academician polled about 100 college students in New York, only a quarter of whom preferred the traditional phrasing; half preferred the phrasing *laid waste to the city*. In that version, *lay* is the verb; *waste* is a noun serving as a direct object; and a prepositional phrase follows. The phrasing doesn't make any literal sense.

A look at relative frequencies in 2003 suggested that in modern print sources, the version with the superfluous *to* outnumbered the one without it by a 3-to-1 ratio. Even *Newsweek* editors had adopted the preposition: "Old-time carpet-bombing laid waste to great swaths of territory." John Barry & Evan Thomas, "The Fog of Battle," *Newsweek*, 30 Sept. 2002, at 36. It looked as if the new idiom was laying waste the old one—that is, laying waste *to* the old one. But by 2008 a more extensive linguistic corpus showed that the traditional transitive version had retained the lead by a 2-to-1 ratio.

lead > led > led. So inflected. The past tense of the verb *lead* (/leed/)—meaning "to guide or direct"— is *led*. But as a noun, *lead* (pronounced /led/) refers either to a metallic element or to a thin stick of marking substance in or for a pencil (though the graphite in pencils has not contained the metal lead for many years). Writers often mistake the past-tense spellings, as if this verb were analogous to *read–read*—e.g.:

- "Dr. Stewart, a co-author of the study, established her reputation in the field of radiation and health with her findings, published in 1956, that prenatal X-rays had *lead* [read *led*] to an increase in cancer deaths among children in Britain." Matthew L. Wald, "Pioneer in Radiation Sees Risk Even in Small Doses," *N.Y. Times*, 8 Dec. 1992, at A2.
- "Representative David E. Bonior, left, the Democratic minority whip who *lead* [read *led*] the all-night delay, rubbed his eyes at the end of a leadership caucus on several issues before the House." "Irate Democrats Tie Up the House Till Daylight," *N.Y. Times*, 30 June 1995, at A10 (photo caption).
- "After an upset win over No. 2 Stanford on Friday, Texas made it clear there would be no letdown against the Mustangs as Aldrich posted 10 kills and Doran *lead* [read *led*] the defense with 11 digs en route to claiming the first set in 15 minutes." David Crabtree, "Horns Make Short Work of SMU," *Austin Am.-Statesman*, 8 Sept. 1999, at C3.

See IRREGULAR VERBS. Cf. **mislead.**

LANGUAGE-CHANGE INDEX
led, the past tense, misspelled *lead*: Stage 2
Current ratio (*had led to the* vs.
*had lead to the): 117:1

leaf. Pl. *leaves.* See PLURALS (C).

leafleting; *leafletting. The spelling *leafleting* has been predominant in AmE and BrE alike since about 1960. **Leafletting* is a variant. See SPELLING (B).
Current ratio: 5:1

lean > leaned > leaned. The form **leant* /lent/ as a past tense and past participle is largely obsolete, though still appearing occasionally in BrE.
Current ratio: 20:1

leapt; leaped. Both are acceptable past-tense and past-participial forms for the verb *leap*. Because *leapt* is pronounced /lept/, the mistaken form **lept* is frequently encountered—e.g.:

- "John J. Sirica *lept* [read *leapt*] to his feet, shouting, 'It ain't fair. It ain't fair!'" "Sirica, 88, Dies; Persistent Judge in Fall of Nixon," *N.Y. Times*, 15 Aug. 1992, at 1, 11.

LANGUAGE-CHANGE INDEX (For the full key, see front matter pp. xxxi, l–li.)
Stage 1: Rejected. **Stage 2:** Widely shunned. **Stage 3:** Widespread but . . . **Stage 4:** Ubiquitous but . . . **Stage 5:** Fully accepted.
Invariably inferior forms marked by asterisk (*). • Ratios represent frequency of prevalent forms vs. variants in current books.

- "The booming, friendly Texas drawl didn't just come across the telephone line, it *lept* [read *leapt*] across it and grabbed the person on the other end." David Hanners, "LBJ Phone Conversations Provide Shadings of Epochal Era," *Dallas Morning News*, 26 Sept. 1993, at A47.
- "Sharon Kelly . . . *lept* [read *leapt*] to her feet in joy when the award was announced." Julie Irwin, "Five City Schools Share $25,000 for Excellence," *Cincinnati Enquirer*, 30 Oct. 1997, at C2.

Leapt, which used to be the more common form in 20th-century BrE (but not in the 19th century), is steadily being displaced by *leaped*. In frequency of use, the two forms are neck-and-neck in modern BrE print sources, but *leaped* has been predominant in AmE since the 18th century.

LANGUAGE-CHANGE INDEX
leapt misspelled **lept*: Stage 1

learned; learnt. In AmE, the past tense is *learned*; in BrE, it's often *learnt*. To use *learnt* in AmE is an affectation.

As an adjective, *learned* has two syllables /**lǝr**-nǝd/, and as a past-tense verb, one /lǝrnd/. The adjective means "possessing or showing broad or systematic knowledge; erudite."

leasable. So spelled.

lease, vb.**; let.** *Let* (10th c.) is 300 years older than *lease* (13th c.) in the sense "to grant the temporary possession and use of (land, buildings, rooms, movable property) to another in return for rent or other consideration." But both are well established, and they are equally good. As used by (real) estate agents in BrE, the term "To Let" is more common than the phrase "For Rent," the usual term in AmE.

To say that one *leases* property nowadays does not tell the reader or listener whether one is lessor or lessee. From its first verbal use in the 13th century, *lease* meant "to grant the possession of," but in the mid-19th century the word took on the additional sense "to take a lease of; to hold by a lease." This ambiguity has made the preposition used important to clarity: the lessor *leases to* and the lessee *leases from*. See **rent,** vb.

*leasor; *leasee. These are aberrations in Modern English for *lessor* and *lessee*. E.g.:

- "The city would require the *leasee* [read *lessee*] to construct at least 55,000 square feet of maintenance hangar space." "Government Actions," *Wash. Post*, 12 Apr. 1990, at V5.
- "The City Council repealed the archaic law that gave land *leasors* [read *lessors*] exclusive rights to the first 100 feet of water." Scott Richardson, "McLean County Lakes Offer Hot Fishing Prospects," *Pantagraph* (Bloomington, Ill.), 6 Mar. 1997, at B7.

See **lessor.**

LANGUAGE-CHANGE INDEX
1. **leasor* for *lessor*: Stage 1
Current ratio (*lessor* vs. **leasor*): 1,283:1
2. **leasee* for *lessee*: Stage 1
Current ratio (*the lessee must* vs. **the leasee must*): 103:1

*least worst. This phrase, like its kissing cousin **least worse*, doesn't make literal sense: it should be *least bad*. If you have several undesirable options with varying levels of undesirability, only one can be the *worst*. All the others are *less bad*, and the least undesirable is the *least bad*. With a superlative adverb such as *least*, it's incorrect to use either a comparative or a superlative adjective: hence *bad* is correct.

In each of the following examples, the illogical phrase—most often it's a spoken error, but sometimes (especially in BrE sources) it's the writer's fault—should be replaced by *least bad*. E.g.:

- "Lamar Alexander, trying to convince voters he was more than the *'least worse'* [read *'least bad'*] choice, had to roll out a refreshened agenda." Nancy Gibbs & Michael Duffy, "The Secret Test of New Hampshire," *Time*, 26 Feb. 1996, at 20.
- "'There's no good solution,' agreed Jason Catlett, chief executive of Junkbusters Corp., an antispam concern based in Green Brook, N.J. 'It's a matter of which is the *least worst* [read *least bad*].'" Jared Sandberg, "Recipe for Halting Spread of 'Spam' Is Proving Elusive," *Wall Street J.*, 13 June 1997, at B1.
- "It is difficult to say which is the *least worst* [read *least bad*] pairing." Benedict Nightingale, "Where All Is for the Worst," *Times* (London), 20 Aug. 1997, at 31.
- "The England–France 'friendly' at Twickenham, heralding the Rugby World Cup, seemed a so-so game in which the *least worst* [read *least bad*] team triumphs, sort of." Peter McKay, "The England–France 'Friendly' at Twickenham," *Daily Mail*, 17 Aug. 2015, at 17.

Cf. **worse comes to worst.** See COMPARATIVES AND SUPERLATIVES & ILLOGIC.

LANGUAGE-CHANGE INDEX
*least worst or **least worse* for *least bad*: Stage 3
Current ratio (*least bad* vs. **least worst* vs. **least worse*): 22:9:1

leave alone; let alone. Traditionally, there has been a distinction: *leave me alone* means "leave me by myself (in solitude)"; *let me alone* means "stop bothering me." But only extreme purists will fault someone who uses *leave alone* in the nonliteral sense. Today that phrase is far more common than *let alone*. E.g.:

- "Good Samaritan VanVelkinburg told them to *leave him alone* and go away." Angela Cortez, "Kin, Friends Laud Samaritan," *Denver Post*, 21 Nov. 1997, at A1.
- "And who wants to be thrown into a car-insurance pool with 80-year-olds from Miami? Just *leave me alone!*" Linda Stasi, "Drop Dead," *Village Voice*, 2 Dec. 1997, at 20.

Before 1920, the collocation *let him alone* (or *let her alone*) appeared far more frequently in print. But that trend was reversed by about 1915 in BrE and 1930 in AmE.

Let alone is also used to mean "not to mention" or "much less" <he no longer drinks beer or wine, let alone bourbon or tequila>.

LANGUAGE-CHANGE INDEX
leave alone in nonliteral sense: Stage 5

lectureship; *lecturership. Even though **lecturership* is more logical (being analogous to *professorship* and *ambassadorship*, for example), it hasn't established itself as a standard term. The usual word is the age-old *lectureship*, which is now about 30 times as common in print sources—e.g.: "His extra-curricular activities include guest *lectureships* at Juilliard and charities like Paul Newman's Hole in the Wall Camp for seriously ill children." Joe Williams, "Busy Kevin Kline Makes Time for His Hometown," *St. Louis Post-Dispatch*, 22 Nov. 2002, Mag. §, at F1.

Those who write **lecturership*—and today it is mostly confined to BrE—are likely to be thought pretentious. The following sentence suggests, no doubt unwittingly, that Oxford is a more pretentious place than Liverpool: "After a *lecturership* [read *lectureship*] at Merton College, Oxford, and an assistant *lectureship* at Liverpool University, Roberts was elected, aged 26, Professor of History at the Rhodes University College." "Professor Michael Roberts" (obit.), *Daily Telegraph*, 25 Jan. 1997, at 13.

LANGUAGE-CHANGE INDEX
*lecturership for *lectureship*: Stage 1
Current ratio (*lectureship* vs. **lecturership*): 30:1

lede, n. This bit of newspaper JARGON usually refers to the first paragraph of an article, the *lead*. Typically, for example, an editor may tell a reporter to "punch up the *lede*," or a wire service may transmit a revised *lede* for a breaking story. It may also refer to the top story in an edition. Outside those contexts, though, the spelling is an aberration and *lead* is standard. When it is used in general writing, it should be labeled as newspaper jargon for the reader's benefit—e.g.: "There are few worse sins in journalism than 'burying the lede,' and here I'm going to have to plead no contest." Dwight Garner, "Cooking," *N.Y. Times*, 8 Dec. 2002, § 7, at 50.

leery (= suspicious, wary) is the standard spelling. **Leary* is a variant. Though criticized as SLANG (from *leer*) in the 18th century, the word has long been respectable. *Leery* was the predominant spelling in AmE by 1900 and in BrE by 1910.

Current ratio: 32:1

leftward(s). See DIRECTIONAL WORDS (A).

legal; lawful; licit. *Legal* is the broadest term, meaning either (1) "of, relating to, or involving law, falling within the province of law," or (2) "established, permitted, or not forbidden by law." These two senses are used with about equal frequency.

Lawful and *licit* share sense 2 of *legal*: "according or not contrary to law, permitted by law." *Lawful* is quite common <driving in a lawful manner>. The least frequent of these three terms is *licit* <licit acts> <the licit use of force>, which usually occurs in direct contrast to *illicit*.

Lawful should not be used in sense 1 of *legal*, as it sometimes is—e.g.: "The judgment must be affirmed if there is sufficient evidence to support it on any *lawful* [read *legal*] theory, and every fact issue sufficiently

raised by the evidence must be resolved in support of the judgment." See **illegal.**

LEGALESE. Despite popular prejudices, not all uses of legal language are bad. But unnecessarily complex legal JARGON—or "legalese"—is widely viewed by legal scholars as the source of many problems: (1) it alienates people from their legal system; (2) it besots its users—namely, lawyers—who think they're being more precise than they really are; and (3) it doesn't communicate efficiently, even to other lawyers, despite occasional claims to the contrary. (See OBSCURITY.) For solid treatments, see *Garner's Dictionary of Legal Usage* (3d ed. 2011); Bryan A. Garner, *Legal Writing in Plain English* (2013); Joseph Kimble, *Lifting the Fog of Legalese* (2006); David Mellinkoff, *The Language of the Law* (1963); and Richard C. Wydick, *Plain English for Lawyers* (5th ed. 2005). For a law dictionary that explains all the arcana, see *Black's Law Dictionary* (10th ed. 2014).

legal holiday; bank holiday. A *legal holiday* is a day designated by law as a holiday, accompanied by the closing of most public offices and paid leave for most public employees. Observance of a legal holiday by the private sector is voluntary. A legal holiday may be established by the national government (e.g., July 4 as Independence Day) or a state government (e.g., March 2 as Texas Independence Day).

A *bank holiday* is a day designated by law for the closing of banks and paid leave for bank employees. *Bank holidays* are standardized in many countries, but are not observed in the United States.

legally. See SENTENCE ADVERBS.

legal separation. See **divorce (c).**

legation. See **embassy.**

legislator. In proper governmental terms, a governor is the executive, not a legislator: "Utah Gov. Mike Leavitt and *other legislators* [read *several legislators*] discuss their support for a balanced-budget amendment with reporters on Thursday." "EPA Has Been Flexible on Missions, Official Says," *Austin Am.-Statesman*, 10 Feb. 1995, at A10 (photo caption). The caption-writer wasn't observing the separation of the branches of government.

legitimacy; legitimation; *legitimization; *legitimatization. *Legitimacy* = the fact of being legitimate. *Legitimation* is the best word for the sense (1) "the action or process of rendering or authoritatively declaring (a person) legitimate"; or (2) "the action of making lawful; authorization" (*OED*). E.g.: "Both halves of the grand bargain outlined then—security and *legitimation* for Israel, land and power for Palestinians—are now in doubt." Barton Gellman, "Israel–Palestinian Peace Process 'Hanging by a Thin

LANGUAGE-CHANGE INDEX (For the full key, see front matter pp. xxxi, l–li.)
Stage 1: Rejected. **Stage 2:** Widely shunned. **Stage 3:** Widespread but . . . **Stage 4:** Ubiquitous but . . . **Stage 5:** Fully accepted.
Invariably inferior forms marked by asterisk (∗). • Ratios represent frequency of prevalent forms vs. variants in current books.

Thread,'" *Pitt. Post-Gaz.*, 25 Mar. 1997, at A3. **Legiti-mization* and **legitimatization* have been NEEDLESS VARIANTS since they first appeared in the 19th century.

legitimate, vb. See **legitimize.**

*legitimatization. See **legitimacy.**

*legitimatize. See **legitimize.**

*legitimization. See **legitimacy.**

legitimize; legitimate, vb.**; *legitimatize.** *Legitimate* is the oldest of these verbs, dating from 1531, but it's not the most frequent. *Legitimize* outnumbers the traditionally preferred *legitimate* by a large margin in modern print sources. It refers to establishing the legitimacy of anything or anyone (except with regard to parentage)—e.g.:

- "Joel Aranson . . . need only flash his ticket stub from Game 6 of the 1996 World Series to *legitimize* his friend-ship with Torres." Tom Keegan, "Joe's Brother Keeps on Tickin,'" *N.Y. Post*, 25 Oct. 2000, at 12.
- "If Bush scores a decisive Florida win, an eventual high court ruling in his favor could *legitimize* his claim on the presidency and shatter Gore's White House dreams." Andrew Miga, "Suddenly, All Eyes," *Boston Herald*, 25 Nov. 2000, at 4.
- "What matters to the three is domestic power built upon a base of nationalism that they believe *legitimizes* their poli-cies." Tad Szulc, "Three Amigos Who Bear Close Watch-ing," *L.A. Times*, 24 Dec. 2000, at M2.

Legitimate, as a verb (/lə-**jit**-ə-mayt/), though given priority by most dictionaries and preferred by vari-ous authorities, is a NEEDLESS VARIANT in all but one sense: "to make an otherwise illegitimate child into a legitimate one." E.g.:

- "Gober asked why Brown had not *legitimated* his 3-year-old daughter, Morgan." Mark Bixler, "Judge Back in Spot-light," *Atlanta J.-Const.*, 25 Jan. 1998, at C2.
- "Fathers of children born out of wedlock cannot categori-cally be held accountable for not *legitimating* the child by marrying the expectant mother." Wolfgang P. Hirczy de Mino, "From Bastardy to Equality," *J. Comp. Family Stud-ies*, 1 Apr. 2000, at 231.
- "Juvenile Court Judge Kenneth Turner . . . said his court in the past 35 years has *legitimated* 122,884 children." Shir-ley Downing, "Push to Collect Support Comes to Shove," *Commercial Appeal* (Memphis), 19 Nov. 2000, at B3.

This DIFFERENTIATION between *legitimate* and *legiti-mize* has become fairly well marked in recent years. We should encourage it.

*Legitimatize was formerly considered preferable to *legitimize* on principles of word formation. For example, both H.L. Mencken and G.H. Vallins used this longer form. Today the penultimate syllable would be dropped—e.g.:

- "His neologism . . . enters into sound idiom and is presently wholly *legitimatized* [read *legitimized*]." H.L. Mencken, "The Nature of Slang" (1919), in *A Language Reader for Writers* 150, 156 (James R. Gaskin & Jack Suberman eds., 1966).
- "'Nearby' is, as yet, an unlawful union, but common usage is tending to *legitimatise* [read *legitimize*] it." G.H. Vallins, *Good English: How to Write It* 196 (1951).

- "There is one idiom in which attraction *legitimatizes* [read *legitimizes*], as it were, an otherwise false agreement." G.H. Vallins, *Better English* 16 (4th ed. 1957).

Today, however, **legitimatize* occurs quite rarely. It is a NEEDLESS VARIANT.

LANGUAGE-CHANGE INDEX
1. *legitimize*: Stage 5
2. *legitimate* (/lə-**jit**-ə-mayt/) in the specialized mean-ing "to make [a nonmarital child] legitimate": Stage 5
3. **legitimatize* for *legitimize*: Stage 1
Current ratio (*legitimized* vs. **legitimatized*): 54:1

leisure (= time spent in relaxation or at ease) is pro-nounced /**lee**-zhər/ in AmE or /**lezh**-ər/ in World English—but preferably not /**lay**-zhər/ anywhere.

leitmotif (= a recurrent musical or metaphorical theme associated throughout the work with a specific character or situation) is the standard spelling. **Leit-motiv*, though more faithful to the German loanword, is but a variant in English. That is, the word was angli-cized to make it align with an older import into the English language: *motif*. In fact, though, the mean-ing of *leitmotif* (which smacks of SESQUIPEDALITY) is so close to that of *motif* that one wonders why it is ever needed. The pronunciation is /**lɪt**-moh-teef/. See GERMANICISMS.

lend > lent > lent. So inflected. **Lended* is an error that has occasionally appeared since the early 19th century—e.g.:

- "The $27 black windbreakers emblazoned with 'Crown Casting Co.' *lended* [read *lent*] credibility in the final min-utes before 'Action!'" Ann E. Donlan, "54 Bad 'Actors' Answer Police 'Casting Call,'" *Boston Herald*, 9 June 1997, at 5.
- "Kukoc *lended* [read *lent*] an assist on the boards with eight and scored 19 points." Daryl Van Schouwen, "Ener-gized Worm Back as Chairman of Boards," *Chicago Sun-Times*, 27 Apr. 1998, at 7.
- "As cheesy as the acting was in *Resident Evil*, I thought it *lended* [read *lent*] a B-movie charm to the proceedings." Jeff Kapalka, "Future Dreams and Nightmares from the Past," *Syracuse Herald Am.*, 27 Sept. 1998, at 12.

See IRREGULAR VERBS & **loan.**

LANGUAGE-CHANGE INDEX
*lended for *lent*: Stage 1
Current ratio (*lent him* vs. **lended him*): 1,557:1

length (= an end-to-end measurement of size, distance, time, etc.) is pronounced /lengkth/ or /leengkth/—but not /lenth/ or /laynth/.

lengthwise; *lengthways. The former has been the established standard form since about 1800. The lat-ter is a NEEDLESS VARIANT.

Current ratio: 7:1

lengthy. Throughout the 19th century, many BrE speakers considered this word an ugly American-ism. But it is now standard throughout the English-speaking world. The only restriction is that it should refer to books, talks, or arguments, with the implica-tion of tedium. It shouldn't refer to physical distances, as here: "Women longshoremen sometimes have to drive *lengthy* [read *long*] distances to find one [a toilet] or to locate someone with a key." Joan C. Stanus, "Working on the Docks," *Virginian-Pilot & Ledger Star* (Norfolk), 10 Apr. 1997, at 6.

LANGUAGE-CHANGE INDEX
lengthy for *long* in senses not referring to distance: Stage 5

leniency; *lenience. The former has been standard since 1800. The latter is a NEEDLESS VARIANT. E.g.: "Shas Party leader Aryeh Deri . . . is alleged to have demanded Bar-On's appointment in expectation of *lenience* [read *leniency*] in his own trial on charges of fraud in his party's finances." Barton Gellman, "Netanyahu's Indictment Sought," *Wash. Post*, 17 Apr. 1997, at A1.

LANGUAGE-CHANGE INDEX
lenience for *leniency*: Stage 1
Current ratio (*leniency* vs. *lenience*): 16:1

lens. So spelled—not *lense*. But the misspelling occurs fairly often, as something like a BACK-FORMATION from the plural—e.g.:

- "Raunchy Lisa 'Left Eye' Lopez—who got her nickname after wearing a condom over one *lense* [read *lens*] of her glasses—makes no apologies for her behavior." John Dingwall, "Latest Flame," *Daily Record* (Baltimore), 8 Feb. 1996, at 23.
- "You will . . . pay a price for such surreal sensationalism—a single *lense* [read *lens*] is $150." Sylvi Capelaci, "For Your Eyes Only," *Toronto Sun*, 24 June 1997, at 42.
- "His [Alex Rocco's] most famous role came in 1972's 'The Godfather,' in which he played the humbled casino owner who meets his fate on a massage table, with a bullet through a thick eyeglass *lense* [read *lens*]." "Was Moe Greene in 'The Godfather'?" *Wash. Post*, 21 July 2015, at B4.

LANGUAGE-CHANGE INDEX
lens misspelled *lense*: Stage 1
Current ratio (*a lens* vs. **a lense*): 462:1

lent. See **lend.**

***lept.** See **leapt.**

lesbian. See **gay** (B).

lese majesty; *lèse majesté; *laesae majestatis; *leze majesty; *lèse majesty; *laesae majestas. The preferred form of this originally legal term—meaning "a crime against the state, esp. against the ruler" or "an attack on a custom or traditional belief"—is the anglicized *lese majesty*. The variant spellings should be avoided. In BrE, the phrase tends to be hyphenated; in AmE, it usually isn't. E.g.:

- "Ad posters for the film fail to take into account Thai sensibilities by picturing Foster above the king. This is considered a great insult by Thais and a possible *lese majesty*. Thai royals must be pictured above commoners." James East & Dana Harris, "Thailand Picks a Sword Fight with 'Anna' Pic," *Hollywood Reporter*, 22 Nov. 1999, at 4.

- "[Bill] Richardson's true *lese majesty*, however, was not his one-time no-show on a security question that within days was forgotten. It was his continuing opposition to congressional larding of pet projects into appropriations bills." Robert Novaks, "Energy Secretary Feels Senators' Wrath for Scorning Pork Legislation," *Augusta Chron.*, 13 Sept. 2000, at A4.

The anglicized pronunciation is /leez **maj**-ə-stee/.
Current ratio (first four headwords): 26:13:11:1

less. A. And *fewer*. Strictly, *less* applies to singular nouns <less tonic water, please> or units of measure <less than six ounces of epoxy>. *Fewer* applies to plural nouns <fewer guests arrived than expected> or numbers of things <we have three fewer members this year>. The empirical evidence in print sources bears out the distinction: the collocation *fewer people* is about seven times as common in books published today as **less people*.

If you have trouble distinguishing the two words, try substituting a phrase. If "not as much [as]" fits, make it *less*. If "not as many [as]" is better, use *fewer*. See COUNT NOUNS AND MASS NOUNS & **fewer.**

The exception in using *fewer* occurs when count nouns essentially function as mass nouns because the units are so very numerous or they aren't considered discrete items (the idea of individual units becomes meaningless). Hence *less* is used correctly with time and money: one isn't, ordinarily, talking about the number of years or the number of dollars but rather the amount of time or the amount of money. E.g.:

- "On that mantra, Larry Clark has built a $45 million-a-year company in *less* than five years." Max Jarman, "Homebuilder on Fast-Grow Track," *Ariz. Bus. Gaz.*, 30 Nov. 1995, at 17.
- "Okay, how about $50 a month for such an apartment—*less* than two dollars a day?" J.A. Lobbia, "Getting Skewed on Rent," *Village Voice*, 29 Apr. 1997, at 49.

Fewer, in fact, is incorrect when intended to refer to a period of time—e.g.: "You can run from sea level to the sky and back to earth in as fast as 45 minutes (so far), but even today, going round-trip in *fewer* [read *less*] than 60 minutes carries a special cachet." Lew Freedman, "Their Own Mountain," *Anchorage Daily News*, 29 June 1997, at D1. But if the units of time are thought of as wholes, and not by fractions, then *fewer* is called for <fewer days abroad> <fewer weeks spent apart>.

Hence we say *less documentation* but *fewer documents*; *less argumentation* but *fewer arguments*; *less whispering* but *fewer remarks*; *less ambiguity* but *fewer ambiguities*; *less of a burden* but *fewer burdens*; *less material* but *fewer items*; *less fattening* but *fewer calories*.

The degree to which *less* occurs where *fewer* would be the better word is a matter of some historical dispute. In 1969, a linguist reported that "the use of *less* in referring to discrete countables is very rare" in edited English. Louise Hanes, "*Less* and *Fewer*," 44 *Am. Speech* 234, 235 (1969). But earlier that decade, another writer

LANGUAGE-CHANGE INDEX (For the full key, see front matter pp. xxxi, l–li.)
Stage 1: Rejected. **Stage 2:** Widely shunned. **Stage 3:** Widespread but . . . **Stage 4:** Ubiquitous but . . . **Stage 5:** Fully accepted.
Invariably inferior forms marked by asterisk (∗). • Ratios represent frequency of prevalent forms vs. variants in current books.

had nearly called the usage standard American English: "Modern writers and contemporary educated speakers often ignore the distinction between *less* and *fewer*, and you will find *less* frequently used with plural nouns in current magazines, newspapers, and books, and will hear it even more frequently from the lips of educated people. Such being the case, *less* cannot realistically or effectively be restricted to singular nouns." Norman Lewis, *Better English* 252 (rev. ed. 1961).

Although the modern evidence seems to suggest that Lewis was more accurate than Hanes in describing what you'll find in edited English, fastidious writers and editors preserve the old distinction. But the loose usage crops up often—e.g.:

- "She says it, but fact is, she's a linguist—a student of words. We need more of them, not *less* [read *fewer*]; more words, more students." Lorene Cary, "As Plain as Black and White," *Newsweek*, 29 June 1992, at 53.
- "There were *less* [read *fewer*] than 300,000 marriages in 1993, the lowest level since the second world war, leaving clerics with little to do on Saturday mornings but twiddle their thumbs." Nick Gardner, "Secure Your Future by Tying the Knot," *Sunday Times* (London), 6 Aug. 1995, § 5, at 5. (Why, with a number like 300,000, isn't the idea of an individual increment meaningless? Because, although one might think of dollars in that light, one doesn't think of marriages in that way.)
- "You will have *less* [read *fewer*] people to call and haunt about paying for their outfits and buying their accessories." "Advice for the Bride," *Boston Herald* (Mag.), 19 Oct. 1997, at 6.

The linguistic hegemony by which *less* has encroached on *fewer*'s territory is probably now irreversible. What has clinched this development is something as mundane as the express checkout lines in supermarkets. They're typically bedecked with signs cautioning, "15 items or less." These signs are all but ubiquitous in the United States. But the occasional more literate supermarket owner uses a different sign: "15 or fewer items."

Finally, even with the strict usage, it's sometimes a close call whether a thing is a mass noun or a count noun, and hence whether *less* or *fewer* is proper. Take, for example, a percentage: should it be *less than 10% of the homeowners were there* or *fewer than 10% of the homeowners were there*? One could argue that a percentage is something counted (i.e., 10 out of 100) and therefore requires *fewer*. One could also argue that a percentage is a collective mass noun (akin, e.g., to *money*), and so requires *less*. The latter is the better argument because most percentages aren't whole numbers anyway. Even if it were a toss-up between the two theories, it's sound to choose *less*, which is less formal in tone than *fewer*.

LANGUAGE-CHANGE INDEX
less for *fewer* in reference to a plural count noun: Stage 3
Current ratio (*fewer people* vs. *less people): 7:1

B. One less or *one fewer? If, in strict usage, *less* applies to singular nouns and *fewer* to plural nouns, the choice is clear: *one less golfer* on the course, not *one fewer golfer. This is tricky only because *less* is

being applied to a singular count noun, whereas it usually applies to a mass noun. Burt Bacharach got it right in "One Less Bell to Answer" (1970). Since at least 1700, most published authors have gotten it right. And most contemporary writers get it right—e.g.:

- "I couldn't care less that NFL players will receive *one less* game check." "Capital-Journal," *Topeka Capital-J.*, 16 Sept. 2001, at X2.
- "Some Middle Georgia cancer patients may have *one less* thing to worry about this time next year." Charlie Lanter, "Pulaski Hospital to Build Cancer Treatment Center," *Macon Telegraph*, 15 Nov. 2001, at 3.
- "Some industry observers worry about a deal that will lead to *one less* independent news organization." Mark Kempner, "In a Merger, CNN, ABC May Shoot for the Stars," *Atlanta J.-Const.*, 3 Nov. 2002, Bus. §, at 1.

Nearly one-tenth of the time, however, writers use *one fewer, an awkward and unidiomatic phrase. One can't help thinking that this is a kind of HYPERCORRECTION induced by underanalysis of the *less*-vs.-*fewer* question—e.g.:

- "But Boras points out that Park had only *one fewer* [read *less*] quality start than Randy Johnson and Curt Schilling of the Arizona Diamondbacks." Jason Reid, "Silence Speaks Loudly to Park Baseball," *L.A. Times*, 19 Nov. 2001, at D1.
- "In studies, women given the gel during open pelvic surgery had only *one fewer* [read *less*] internal scar but almost twice the risk of infection." Lauran Neergaard, "FDA Reverses Decision on Gel," *State* (Columbia, S.C.), 20 Nov. 2001, at A8.
- "Energy Secretary Spencer Abraham . . . has *one fewer* [read *less*] hat than we said the other day." Al Kamen, "Cheney Losing His Voice," *Wash. Post*, 21 Nov. 2001, at A21.

Current ratio: 12:1

C. And *lesser*. *Lesser*, like *less*, refers to quantity, but is confined to use as an adjective before a singular noun and following an article <the lesser crime> or alone before a plural noun <lesser athletes>, thus performing a function no longer idiomatically possible with *less*. Dating from the 13th century, this formal usage allows *lesser* to act as an antonym of *greater*.

Occasionally, *lessor* (= landlord) is misused for *lesser*—e.g.:

- "The nuclear-arms race has produced 70,000 nuclear bombs by the United States and a *lessor* [read *lesser*] amount [read *number*] by the former U.S.S.R." Letter of Minerva Rees Massen, "In the Wake of Hiroshima and Nagasaki," *S.F. Chron.*, 5 Aug. 1995, at A20.
- "Washington residents pay 2.2 percent of the sticker price of a new car for the first two years, and then *lessor* [read *lesser*] amounts each year on a sliding scale." Tom Koenninger, "License-Plate Cheats Cause Neighbors to Pay More Tax," *Columbian* (Vancouver, Wash.), 6 Oct. 1996, at B9.

See **lessor.**

D. Adjective for Noun. As a noun, *less* means "a smaller amount" or "something not as important." Occasionally, writers make it an adjective when it should be a noun—e.g.: "He wants business to make money and everyone to pay *less taxes* [read *less in taxes*]." "The New, Improved Powell," *N.Y. Times*, 13 Sept. 1995, at 14.

lessor; lessee. *Landlord* and *tenant* are simpler equivalents that are more comprehensible to most people. For a mistake involving *lessor* and *lesser*, see **less (c).** See also **lease** & ***leasor.**

lest. A. Sense. Because *lest* means "for fear that," it should be followed by a negative idea. It isn't equivalent with *in case*—one can't rightly say, "She plans to take along a camera *lest* [read *in case*] she find a breathtaking view." Indeed, the negative idea is overwhelming in modern usage—e.g.: "Its members would do well to study up, *lest* they find themselves met by a wall of suspicion, or worse yet indifference." Betty Winston Baye, "Ralph Reed: The Black Messiah?" *Courier-J.* (Louisville), 20 Feb. 1997, at A11.

Some passages present close calls. Yearning for something that you've just discovered isn't generally considered a negative thing unless you've just planned the opposite. In the following example, in which just that problem emerges, the probable sense is *or, or else,* or *because*: "If you've just remodeled your kitchen into a high-tech wonderland, do not read Viana La Place's new book *lest* [read *or, or else,* or *because*] you might find yourself yearning for a serene, minimal kitchen like hers." S. Irene Virbila, "Our Annual Cookbook Special," *L.A. Times,* 12 Dec. 1996, at H11.

B. Mood Following. *Lest* is best followed by a verb in the SUBJUNCTIVE mood, not in the indicative, because *lest* points to something that is merely possible, not definite. E.g.:

- "*Lest* there *be* any doubt about the extent of the trouble, Archuletta points to the fact that most production companies now routinely include in their filming budgets some money to pay off harassers." Cynthia H. Craft, "Acts of Extortion Steal the Scene from Film Crews," *L.A. Times,* 15 Mar. 1995, at A1.
- "As with any spice, however, it shouldn't be overheated *lest* it *burn.*" Ann Steiner, "Color from Paprika Gives Food a Boost," *Houston Chron.,* 4 Dec. 1996, at 13.
- "The Bosnian Serb military leader is reportedly leery of leaving the self-proclaimed republic of Srpska, *lest* he *be* dragged off to The Hague where an international tribunal seeks to try him for crimes against humanity." James Ledbetter, "Waiting for Radovan," *Village Voice,* 11 Mar. 1997, at 34.

Occasionally, though, writers ill-advisedly use the indicative—e.g.: "Certain foreign policy experts urged . . . that the West shouldn't press Mikhail Gorbachev too hard to liberate his dissidents *lest* it *makes it harder* [read *become harder*] for him to do other good things." Suzanne Fields, "Trouble Ahead for Israel's Labor Party," *Wash. Times,* 16 Mar. 1995, at A19.

Idiomatically speaking, if a modal verb follows *lest,* it should be *might* (or perhaps *should*), not *will* or *would*—e.g.:

- "I feared for a fortnight to walk the streets of Seattle *lest* I *would* [delete *would*] be thwacked soundly about the head

and ears by a blackthorn cudgel." Jon Hahn, "Ack! These Columns Really Stepped in It," *Seattle Post-Intelligencer,* 29 Dec. 2001, at E2.

- "Other justices found it strange that judicial candidates could talk about old cases, but never current ones, *lest* it *would* [delete *would*] be regarded as prejudging a case." Tom Webb, "Judicial Elections Argued," *Pioneer Press* (St. Paul), 27 Mar. 2002, at A1.
- "Jonathan Clark nipped him at the wire, *lest* he *would* [read *should*] have three straight titles." Dave Hickman, "Westfall Wraps Up Fourth Title with Final-Round 68," *Charleston Gaz. & Daily Mail,* 29 June 2002, at B1.

-LEST. See DIMINUTIVES (J).

let, v.t. See **lease.**

let. For the use of this word in opposite senses, see CONTRONYMS.

let alone. See **leave alone.**

let go. See **fire.**

let's. A. *Let's you and I.* First, think of *let's: let us. Us* is in the objective case. Another form of the phrase (still in the objective case) would be *let you and me* (*you and me* agreeing with *us*). The construction *let you and I* is ungrammatical—and fairly rare.

But what about *let's you and I*? That is, *let us, you and I.* This, too, is ungrammatical—*us* and *you and I* being in apposition. (See APPOSITIVES.) It's an error of some literary standing. T.S. Eliot began "The Love Song of J. Alfred Prufrock" (1917) in this way: "Let us go then, you and I." In that sentence, *go* is an infinitive without an express *to* (sometimes called a "bare infinitive"), and an infinitive has as its subject a pronoun (*us*) in the objective case—not the nominative case. Yet the appositive for *us*—namely, *you and I*—is in the nominative case. This is an oddity, but today *let's you and I* [+ verb] is common in spoken and written English alike. H.W. Fowler might have called it a "sturdy indefensible"—e.g.:

- "This upcoming Father's Day weekend, *let's you and I* renew our commitments to our kids and be the dads we always intended to be." Doug Hall & Russ Quaglia, "Dad's Resolution," *Seattle Post-Intelligencer,* 14 June 1999, at E2.
- " '*Let's you and I* think about it for a second,' he said during lunchtime." Cheryl Blackerby, "West Palm's Sudden Fame Trumps Palm Beach," *Palm Beach Post,* 18 Nov. 2000, at B1.
- " '*Let's you and I* be fair with one another.' " Jacob M. Schlesinger & Michael M. Phillips, "Surprising Choices," *Wall Street J.,* 19 Mar. 2001, at A1 (quoting Senator Robert Byrd).

Nevertheless, in print sources that have appeared since 1900, the phrasing *let's you and me* has predominated slightly over *let's you and I*—so take heart if you prefer the more grammatically rigorous phrasing.

Current ratio: 1:1

B. *Let's us.* This phrase is nonstandard for *let's.*

LANGUAGE-CHANGE INDEX (For the full key, see front matter pp. xxxi, l–li.)
Stage 1: Rejected. **Stage 2:** Widely shunned. **Stage 3:** Widespread but . . . **Stage 4:** Ubiquitous but . . . **Stage 5:** Fully accepted.
Invariably inferior forms marked by asterisk (*). • Ratios represent frequency of prevalent forms vs. variants in current books.

C. **Let's don't.* This phrase is nonstandard for *let's not.*

leukemia (a type of blood cancer) is now the standard spelling in all varieties of World English. From about 1940 to 1970, **leukaemia* was standard BrE, but since 1970 *leukemia* has become predominant even there.

Current ratio: 5:1

levee. See **levy,** n.

level, vb., makes *leveled* and *leveling* in AmE, *levelled* and *levelling* in BrE. See SPELLING (B).

leverage, v.t. & v.i., is a mid-20th-century Americanism <a leveraged portfolio = one with a high amount of debt>. The term has definite meaning, but it may be characterized as a term used primarily by financial jargonmongers. See JARGON.

levy, n.; **levee.** *Levy* may act as a noun in two senses: (1) "the imposition of a fine or tax, or the fine or tax so imposed"; and (2) "the conscription of men for military service, or the troops so conscripted." The plural is *levies*—e.g.: "During the housing boom, voters passed hundreds of open-space tax *levies* to control growth and sprawl." Dennis Cauchon, "Officials Open Coffers for Open Space," *USA Today,* 28 May 2008, at A3.

Levee, meanwhile, is the noun meaning "a river embankment; dike; pier." In BrE, primarily, it also has the sense "a formal reception." Occasionally *levee* is used as a verb, meaning "to provide with a levee (dike)." The plural is *levees,* but misspellings are common—e.g.: "Insurers are estimated to have paid as much as $60 billion for damages caused by Hurricane Katrina, but about $25 billion of that was considered the result of flooding when the *levies* [read *levees*] broke in New Orleans." Randy Diamond, "Storm Model Raises Doubts," *Palm Beach Post,* 4 May 2007, at A1.

Levee is fairly often misspelled *levy*—e.g.: "The *levy* [read *levee*] broke about five blocks away, split like a cheap pair of pants and turned an industrial canal into a raging wall of water." Scott Ostler, "Football in New Orleans," *S.F. Chron.,* 3 Dec. 2006, at C1.

LANGUAGE-CHANGE INDEX
levy misused for *levee*: Stage 1

levy, v.t., = (1) "to impose (as a fine or a tax) by legal sanction" <the court levied a fine of $500>; (2) "to conscript for service in the military" <the troops were soon levied>; (3) "to wage (a war)" <the rebels then levied war against the government>; or (4) to take or seize (property) in execution of a judgment <the creditor may levy on the debtor's assets>.

In sense 1, this verb is sometimes mangled through OBJECT-SHUFFLING: "He quit hours after the football program was *levied* with sanctions that included a two-year ban on post-season play, a loss of 10 scholarships for each of the next two recruiting classes, and removal from the Pac-10's television revenue-sharing pool for 1993, costing the program an estimated $1.4

million." Jim Cour, "Coach Quits in Protest," *Austin Am.-Statesman,* 23 Aug. 1993, at C1. A program (or person) is not *levied with* a penalty; rather, the penalty is *levied against* the program (or person).

The word is pronounced /le-vee/; it's sometimes wrongly pronounced like the surname *Levy* (usually /lee-vee/).

lexicography; lexicology. *Lexicography* is the making of dictionaries; *lexicology* is the study of words and their origins, meanings, and uses.

*leze majesty. See **lese majesty.**

liability. See **disability** (A).

liable (= subject to or exposed to) should not be used merely for *likely.* *Liable* best refers to something the occurrence of which risks being permanent or recurrent. E.g.:

• "What you don't know is *liable* to hurt you—and your building." Maureen Patterson, "See You in Court!" *Buildings,* Feb. 1997, at 48.
• "Taking away any function for more than a few days is *liable* to result in loss of that capability." Richard J. Ham, "After the Diagnosis," *Post Graduate Medicine,* June 1997, at 57.

In law, *liable* also means "responsible" or "subject to a penalty" <the landowner may be liable if someone is injured while on the land>.

Liable has three syllables (/lɪ-ə-bəl/), not two, and so is pronounced differently from *libel.*

liaise, v.i., is a BACK-FORMATION from *liaison,* meaning "to establish liaison" or "to act as a liaison officer" <diplomats who liaise with Soviet officials>. First used in the 1920s, this word is still stigmatized in some quarters as being cant or JARGON. It is pronounced /lee-**ayz**/. The word is more common in BrE than in AmE—e.g.:

• "The FA's marketing and media team are here in force, *liaising* with sponsors such as Nationwide and Umbro." Richard Williams, "Team England Thriving on an Army of Helpers," *Guardian,* 14 June 2002, at 6.
• "The CCS had the ostensible aim of getting department heads together, *liaising* better with local authorities and business." "Task of Ensuring That Cover Is More than Just a Front," *Fin. Times,* 22 June 2002, at 4.
• "His possible dismissal attracted huge attention among West Bankers, many of whom regard him with distaste—partly because he has *liaised* with Israel and the CIA." Phil Reeves, "Security Chiefs Refuse to Accept Dismissal by Arafat," *Independent,* 4 July 2002, at 13.

The word occasionally crops up in AmE—e.g.: "For 10 to 20 hours during an average week, she's the neighborhood's chief advocate, cook and bottle-washer, *liaising* with the cops, pols, bureaucrats, and merchants who interact with her domain." David Nyhan, "A Rare Natural Resource Known as Annisa," *Boston Globe,* 21 Nov. 1999, at C4.

LANGUAGE-CHANGE INDEX
liaise as a word: Stage 5

liaison is pronounced either /lee-**ay**-zahn/ or /lee-ə-zahn/, the first being more common in both AmE and

BrE; /**lay**-ə-zahn/ is a mispronunciation. (See PRONUN-CIATION (B).) The nontechnical senses of the word are (1) n., "an illicit love affair"; (2) n., "communication established for the promotion of mutual understanding; someone who establishes such communication"; and (3) adj., "acting as an intermediary" <liaison officer>.

The word is commonly misspelled *laison and (especially) *liason.

libel /lɪ-bəl/. Pronounce it carefully. The word is often mispronounced, through epenthesis, the way *liable* /lɪ-ə-bəl/ is pronounced. See PRONUNCIATION. For the sense of the word, see **defamation.**

liberty. See **freedom** (A).

libido. Although dictionaries once recorded /li-**bɪ**-doh/ as the preferred pronunciation, /li-**bee**-doh/ is now the established preference in AmE. The plural is *libidos*—not *libidoes*.

Current ratio (*libidos* vs. *libidoes*): 208:1

library is pronounced /lɪ-brer-ee/—not /lɪ-ber-ee/. See PRONUNCIATION (B).

licit. See **legal.**

licorice (/lik-ə-rish/) has been the standard spelling in AmE since about 1900. *Liquorice* has been the standard spelling in BrE since the 18th century. This word shouldn't be confused with its uncommon homophones, *lickerish* (= lascivious, lecherous) and *liquorish* (= tasting like liquor).

lie > lay > lain. So inflected (except when *lie* means "to utter a falsity"—see below). A murderer may *lie in wait.* Yesterday he *lay in wait.* And for several days he has *lain in wait*—e.g.: "The Ramseys say an intruder may have *lay* [read *lain*] in wait for hours before killing the 6-year-old beauty queen." "Ramseys' Mission: Find the Killer," *Austin Am.-Statesman,* 18 Mar. 2000, at B8. See IRREGULAR VERBS & **lay.**

In the sense of telling an untruth, the verb is inflected *lie > lied > lied.*

LANGUAGE-CHANGE INDEX
lay for past-participial *lain*: Stage 1
Current ratio (*had lain* vs. *had lay*): 91:1

liege, a term recorded in English from the 14th century, is a kind of CONTRONYM: it can denote either a medieval vassal sworn to allegiance to a feudal lord or the feudal lord to whom the vassal swears allegiance. In fuller phrasing, the vassal is a *liegeman,* the lord a *liege lord.* The main point of this entry, however, is to note the pronunciation: /leej/—not /leezh/. Cf. **siege.**

lie low; lay low. The latter phrase is common but loose. The two phrasings both appear in print, but the correct *lying low* is three times as common as *laying low.* See **lay** (B).

lien, n. (= a legal right or interest that a creditor has in another's property, lasting usu. until a debt that it secures is satisfied), is pronounced most properly /**lee**-ən/, or commonly /leen/ or /lin/.

lie of the land. See **lay of the land.**

lieu /loo/. See SPELLING (A).

life-and-death; *life-or-death. Though the sense is "relating to a matter of life *or* death," idiom has long sanctioned *and* in this phrase, not *or. Life-and-death* has vastly predominated in print sources since the phrase became popular in the early 19th century. It still predominates—e.g.:

- "Easy's temperament lets him saunter his way into any number of *life-and-death* situations and barely break a sweat." Adina Hoffman, "Denzel: So Noir and Yet So Far," *Jerusalem Post,* 1 July 1996, Arts §, at 5.
- "It's a *life-and-death* issue, with the potential to affect any Canadian adults." "Make Euthanasia an Election Issue," *Alberni Valley Times* (Can.), 1 Sept. 2015, at A4.

LANGUAGE-CHANGE INDEX
life-or-death for *life-and-death*:
Stage 3
Current ratio (*life-and-death* vs. *life-or-death*): 2:1

lifelong; livelong. *Lifelong* = lasting for all or most of one's life <Seymour's lifelong dream was to conduct the New York Philharmonic>. *Livelong* = (of a time period, esp. a day or a night) whole, entire <"the eyes of Texas are upon you, all the livelong day">. *Livelong* was once more prevalent than *lifelong,* especially during the early 19th century, but then the fortunes of these two words reversed about 1860. Since then, instances of *lifelong* have steadily risen in modern print sources. Confusion of these words isn't as uncommon as it ought to be—e.g.:

- "Born in Providence, a son of the late Peter Gomes and the late Mary Fortes, he had been a *livelong* [read *lifelong*] resident of Providence, moving to Brockton eight years ago." "Late Obituary: Bernard D. 'Chicken' Fortes," *Providence J.-Bull.,* 18 Jan. 1995, at C6.
- "Berning pursued a *livelong* [read *lifelong*] interest in the golf swing." Larry Bohannan, "Making Ends Meet," *Desert Sun* (Palm Springs), 12 Feb. 2002, at C8.
- "A native and *livelong* [read *lifelong*] resident of the Tampa area, he attended Riverview High School." "McGowan, Mitchell Curtis" (obit.), *St. Petersburg Times,* 4 Sept. 2002, at B7.

LANGUAGE-CHANGE INDEX
livelong misused for *lifelong*: Stage 1

***life-or-death.** See **life-and-death.**

life-size, adj., has been the standard term from the beginning, in the first half of the 19th century. *Life-sized* is a NEEDLESS VARIANT.

Current ratio: 3:1

LANGUAGE-CHANGE INDEX (For the full key, see front matter pp. xxxi, l–li.)
Stage 1: Rejected. **Stage 2:** Widely shunned. **Stage 3:** Widespread but . . . **Stage 4:** Ubiquitous but . . . **Stage 5:** Fully accepted.
Invariably inferior forms marked by asterisk (*). • Ratios represent frequency of prevalent forms vs. variants in current books.

lifestyle. When this word was viewed as a NEOLO-GISM—in the 1960s through the 1980s—it was often disparaged as an unnecessary innovation and as a VOGUE WORD. But today it seems serviceable as denoting a concept widely regarded as important.

LANGUAGE-CHANGE INDEX
lifestyle: Stage 5

lighted; lit. Both are standard past-tense and past-participial forms. The most traditional forms are *lighted* as an adjective <a lighted torch> and as a past participle <have you lighted the fire yet?>. *Lit* is unimpeachable as a past tense—e.g.: "He *lit* another cigarette, inhaling deeply as the executives ran through several more subjects." Ken Auletta, "Beauty and the Beast," *New Yorker*, 16 Dec. 2002, at 65, 67. See IRREGULAR VERBS.

Although *he lighted the fire* was the predominant phrase in print sources from 1700 to 1900, during the 20th century *he lit the fire* became predominant beginning about 1915. Let your ear guide you.

Current ratio (*he lit the* vs. *he lighted the*): 4:1

lightning; lightening. The first is the flashing phenomenon that occurs in an electrical storm. The second is the process of getting lighter, either in color or in weight. Sometimes, however, writers misuse *lightening* for *lightning*—e.g.: "After all, given the inroads the group made last year and absent a presidential *lightening* [read *lightning*] rod in the form of Ms. Showalter . . . ." Courtney Leatherman, "From Insurgents to the Establishment," *Chron. of Higher Educ.*, 17 Dec. 1999, at A18. The opposite error rarely if ever occurs.

LANGUAGE-CHANGE INDEX
lightning misspelled *lightening*: Stage 1

light-year; parsec. Despite their appearance, these terms measure distance, not time. A *light-year* is the distance that light travels in one year in a vacuum (about 5.88 trillion miles). Although some figurative uses accurately reflect distances <the next town seemed light-years away>, the popular mind makes the term refer to time—e.g.:

- "And needless to say, the special effects are *light years* ahead [read *way ahead*] of what Disney had in the '60s." Dan Taylor, "'Anastasia' a Flub? 'Flubber' Fine Art?" *Press Democrat* (Santa Rosa), 7 Dec. 1997, at Q27.
- "Although it seems like *light years* [read *ages*] since Rick Pitino departed, and his name rarely comes up in interviews these days, O'Brien made reference to the former Celtics coach and president during Sunday's postgame media conference." Mark Cofman, "Anderson Having a Ball in Playoffs," *Boston Herald*, 23 Apr. 2002, at 78.
- "*Light years* [read *Long*] ago, while working late in a darkened computer lab at the University of Seattle, Joe Loughry became fascinated with the lights blinking on the face of his modem." "Those Blinking Lights Could Be a Security Risk," *Milwaukee J. Sentinel*, 21 May 2002, at E3.

Joan Baez misused the term in her 1975 ballad "Diamonds and Rust": "And here I sit / Hand on the telephone / Hearing a voice I'd known / A couple of light years ago / Heading straight for a fall." It's a lovely song but lousy science and loose usage.

A *parsec* has to do with *second*—not as a measure of time but as a measure of angle (circle = 360 degrees; 1 degree = 60 minutes; 1 minute = 60 seconds). A *parsec* is the distance that a star would be from the earth if its apparent position in the sky (its parallax, hence the *par* in *parsec*) shifted by one second of arc as the earth orbits the sun. It is equivalent to about 3.26 light-years. While *parsec* appears in print far less frequently than the better-known *light-year*, when used outside astronomy it is often used incorrectly. Even Han Solo (Harrison Ford) got it wrong in the original *Star Wars* movie when he bragged that his spaceship, the *Millennium Falcon*, "made the Kessel run in less than 12 parsecs." The purported meaning of the word varies widely—e.g.:

- "Just what is a 'Battle Droid with STAP,' anyway? Apparently, it's some kind of bad-guy robot on an upright, flying motorcycle. He was in your local Target and Toys 'R' Us stores for about a *parsec* [read *second*] before fans snatched them all up." Hank Stuever, "Space Junk Clears Path for 'Star Wars,'" *Dayton Daily News*, 22 Nov. 1998 (implying a very short time).
- "The Matrix: Hardware cinema blasted several *parsecs* [read *centuries*?] into the future with this endlessly ingenious sci-fi psych-out." Bob Strauss, "A Pioneering Masterpiece," *Daily News* (L.A.), 30 Dec. 1999 (implying a very long time).
- "'Star Trek: Nemesis' is better than the tepid 'Star Trek: Insurrection'; falls short of 'First Contact' because the villain (Tom Hardy) couldn't pick the lint off Borg Queen Alice Krige's cape; and finishes *half a parsec (a nose)* [read *a nose*] ahead of 'Generations.'" Arthur Salm, "Attack of the Clone," *San Diego Union-Trib.*, 12 Dec. 2002, Entertainment §, at 14 (implying a very short distance).

Once again, these examples illustrate bad science and poor usage.

likable (= [of a person] pleasant to be with and easy to like) has been predominantly so spelled in AmE since the 1890s. The standard BrE spelling, *likeable*, was established in the 18th century. Cf. **livable** & **lovable.**

like. A. As a Preposition. The object of a preposition should be in the objective case—you say *They are very much like us*, not **They are very much like we*. When the second-person pronoun is used, no problem arises: "I, like you, believe that Mozart was the greatest composer of all time." But apart from the second person (in which the form remains the same), writers often get confused on this point, as with first-person pronouns—e.g.:

- "She, like *I* [read *me*], instantly fell in love with his beautiful face, huge blue eyes, unusually soft fur, and gentle disposition." Patricia Livingston, "New Cat Forced Out but Finds Nice Home," *Times-Picayune* (New Orleans), 3 Feb. 2000, at B11. (A suggested improvement: *Like me, she instantly fell . . . .*)
- "He, like *I* [read *me*], just can't find any proof about the NHTAS's cries that unhelmeted motorcyclists truly are an undue burden on society." Letter of Donald Smith, "Helmet Law Will Not Solve Problem," *Charleston Gaz.*, 22

Feb. 2000, at A4. (A suggested improvement: *Like me, he just can't find . . . .*)

- "'He, like *I* [read *me*], sees with abhorrence executions of innocent people,' Mr. Smith said." Sean Scully, "Senators Seek Greater Safeguards in Capital Cases," *Wash. Times*, 8 June 2000, at A6 (quoting Senator Gordon H. Smith). (A suggested improvement: *Like me, he sees with abhorrence . . . .*)

The same problem afflicts the third-person pronouns—e.g.:

- "We, like *they* [read *them*], thought we were the coolest things on the floor." Rochelle Riley, "Reunion Means Remembering, Rejoicing," *Fla. Today*, 22 Dec. 1998, at A12. (A suggested improvement: *Like them, we thought . . . .*)
- "And we, like *they* [read *them*], do so at our peril." Mike Pence, "Explaining the Appeal of *Titanic*," *Saturday Evening Post*, 1 May 1999, at 40. (A suggested improvement: *And like them, we do so at our peril.*)
- "'Let them say of us that we believed that we care and we—like *they* [read *them*]—looked up to the next generation.'" Tony Yapias, "Millard County Honors Veterans with Memorial," *Salt Lake Trib.*, 5 Nov. 2000, at B10 (quoting Governor Mike Leavitt of Utah). (A suggested improvement: *Let them say of us that we cared and that, like them, we looked up to the next generation.*)

As all the parenthetical revisions suggest, the most natural solution is to open the clause with *like* and keep the subject and verb together (*Like me, he agrees*). The awkwardness in the original wordings results from the odd pairing of a nominative and an objective pronoun in what looks like a parallel construction (*He, like me, agrees*). See PRONOUNS (B).

LANGUAGE-CHANGE INDEX
Prepositional *like* introducing nominative pronoun: Stage 1

B. As a Conjunction. In traditional usage, *like* is a preposition that governs nouns and noun phrases, not a conjunction that governs verbs or clauses. Its function is adjectival, not adverbial. Hence one does not write, properly, **The story ended like it began*, but *The story ended as it began.* If we change the verbs to nouns, *like* is correct: "The story's ending was like its beginning." Frequently, then, *like* needs to be replaced by the proper conjunction *as* (or *as if*)—e.g.:

- "It looks *like* [read *as if*] the sales clerks are ahead of the hitters so far." Dan O'Neill, "Morning Briefing," *St. Louis Post-Dispatch*, 16 Mar. 1995, at D2.
- "*Like* [read *As*] I said: so far, so good." John Naughton, "Television When Less Is More Desirable," *Observer*, 16 July 1995, at 21.
- "Star-crossed lovers, they are—*like* [read *as*] in the play—sprung from two households, both alike in dignity." Alisa Valdes, "Romeo & Juliet," *Boston Globe*, 17 Oct. 1995, at 59.
- "And it looks *like* [read *as if*] local football teams will be just as good in 2015, maybe even better with a little luck." Kevin Lytle, "Local High School Football Programs Are on the Rise," *Ft. Collins Coloradoan*, 2 Sept. 2015, at D3.

This relatively simple precept is generally observed in writing, but has been increasingly flouted in American speech. Although examples of *like* used conjunctively can be found throughout the Middle English period, the usage was widely considered nonstandard from the 17th through the mid-20th centuries. Then defenders came along, raising it to the level of a standard CASUALISM—e.g.:

- "The use of *like* as a conjunction is a usage on the borderline of acceptability in American English." Robert C. Pooley, *Teaching English Usage* 153 (1946).
- "Anyone who complains that its use as a conjunction is a corruption introduced by Winston cigarettes ought, in all fairness, to explain how Shakespeare, Keats, and the translators of the Authorized Version of the Bible came to be in the employ of the R.J. Reynolds Tobacco Company." Bergen Evans, "Grammar for Today," *Atlantic Monthly*, Mar. 1960, at 80, 81.
- "A colloquialism *like* as a conjunction may be, but indefensible it certainly is not. It is first of all a widespread custom of speech, it has arisen naturally and in the same way that *as* has, and unless one starts from the *a priori* position that there is only one legitimate form of expression for every idea in speech, it makes as strong a bid for favor as the conjunction *as*." George Philip Krapp, *Modern English: Its Growth and Present Use* 271 (Albert H. Marckwardt ed., 2d ed. 1969).
- "It is a generally accepted fact that *like* is widely used as a subordinating conjunction in colloquial and popular speech and in writing that reflects colloquial usage." C. Dale Whitman, "*Like* as a Conjunction," 49 *Am. Speech* 156, 156–57 (1974).
- "In many kinds of written and spoken English *like* as a conjunction is struggling towards acceptable standard or neutral ground. It is not quite there yet. But the distributional patterns suggest that the long-standing resistance to this nippy little word is beginning to crumble as a new century approaches." Robert W. Burchfield, *Points of View* 135 (1992).

Although this use of *like* can no longer be considered an outright solecism, as it once was, it hasn't moved far from the borderline of acceptability. It is acceptable casual English; it isn't yet in the category of unimpeachable English.

LANGUAGE-CHANGE INDEX
1. *like* as a conjunction: Stage 4
Current ratio (*as they do* vs. *like they do*): 14:1
2. *like* for *as if* or *as though*: Stage 4
Current ratio (*acts as if he* vs. *acts like he*): 1.2:1

C. *As* for *like*. This is a form of HYPERCORRECTION—trying so hard to avoid error that you end up falling into an opposite error. Ernest Gowers saw the problem: "A fashion seems to be growing, even among some good writers, to prefer *as* to *l.* not only, rightly, as a conjunction, but also, ill-advisedly, as a prepositional adjective" (*FMEU2* at 336). E.g.: "*As* [read *Like*] most people, I have been fortunate to have many mentors in

LANGUAGE-CHANGE INDEX (For the full key, see front matter pp. xxxi, l–li.)
Stage 1: Rejected. **Stage 2:** Widely shunned. **Stage 3:** Widespread but . . . **Stage 4:** Ubiquitous but . . . **Stage 5:** Fully accepted.
Invariably inferior forms marked by asterisk (*). • Ratios represent frequency of prevalent forms vs. variants in current books.

life." John B. Simon, "Seymour F. Simon," *CBA Record*, Oct. 1993, at 14. Cf. **in common with.**

LANGUAGE-CHANGE INDEX
as misused for the preposition *like*
<as you, I agree with that>: Stage 2

D. Overused. Like any other word, *like* can entangle a sentence if used indiscriminately—e.g.: "I have been buying most of my books from Barnes & Noble, whose two new superstores have come down on my old neighborhood shop *like* the Assyrians who came down *like* the wolf on the fold." Victor Navasky, "Buying Books: Theory vs. Practice," *N.Y. Times*, 20 June 1996, at A13. The two *like* phrases are especially jarring because they come at the end of an already involved sentence.

E. As a Vogue Word and Verbal Tic. California is often falsely and invidiously charged with popularizing *like* as a space-filler: "California's biggest contribution to the American language is the use of the most versatile word ever—you guessed it, 'like.' Like, a word preceding every, like, noun and, like, verb, is almost the only description needed in a world where adjectives are, like, becoming a dying breed." Mark Egan, "Like, the Language Has Lots of Baggage," *Wash. Times*, 29 Sept. 1997, at A2.

In a 2008 study, a Midwestern teenager was asked why social networking was so important to her. She responded:

> It sounds stupid and everything but like once you like get into it it's really like addicting—just like everything. Like you have your song and like you write like all this stuff about yourself and like all my friends basically have it. So like we always like read each other's pages and like call each other and like kind of, and like you put like 300 pictures up so . . . people's pictures and stuff and comments.
> Don Campbell, "Plugging In, Tuning Out," *USA Today*, 10 Sept. 2008, at A11.

One is surprised only by the keenness of her first three words—that it sounds stupid.

Since the 1980s, *be like* has also been a low CASUAL-ISM equivalent to *said* in relating a conversation, especially among juveniles—e.g.: "And I'm like, 'Yes, I do.' But he's like, 'No, you don't.' And so I'm like, 'If you're just going to contradict me, then . . . .'" In teenagers, this usage is all but ubiquitous. In adults, it shows arrested development. Cf. BE-VERBS (C) & **go (B).**

LANGUAGE-CHANGE INDEX
like as a spoken space-filler <I was, like, ready an hour ago>: Stage 2

F. *The likes of.* Is *the likes of* (= people or things of the same type as) disparaging? The linguist Dwight Bolinger calls the phrase, which didn't become widespread till the 19th century, "dysphemistic" (*Language: The Loaded Weapon* 122 (1980)). Sometimes it's disparaging, but not always. In fact, it's more commonly positive than negative:

- Positive: "We may be able to ring in the new year with a fireworks show *the likes of* which nobody's seen for a century." David Kipen, "A Literary Hodgepodge," *S.F. Chron.*, 24 Dec. 2000, at 35.

- Positive: "The country vocalist evokes the spirits of powerhouses past (Kitty Wells and Patsy Cline) as well as the present-day *likes of* Patty Loveless and Mandy Barnett." "Best of Song," *People*, 25 Dec. 2000, at 35.
- Neutral or Ambiguous: "They'll do floor exercises, uneven bars, rings and other things to songs by *the likes of* Christina Aguilera and the Backstreet Boys." Scott Mervis, "Hot List," *Pitt. Post-Gaz.*, 17 Nov. 2000, at 2.
- Negative: "This is similar to putting *the likes of* David Duke and Pat Buchanan in charge of affirmative action or anti-discrimination." Letter of Chris Ahmed, "Israel Ties Strong," *Atlanta J.-Const.*, 25 Oct. 2000, at A15.
- Negative: "The GIC buys health coverage for all state employees, retirees and their families, while occasionally fending off politically charged attacks by *the likes of* Joe Kennedy and Mark Montigny." "Pols & Politics," *Boston Herald*, 24 Dec. 2000, at 19.

But variations of the phrase, *so-and-so and his* [or *her*] *like* and *something-or-something and the like*, often have a more discernible tinge of negativity—e.g.:

- "Supporters of private accounts . . . mistakenly count Moynihan *and his like* as true allies in this cause." Jack Kemp, "Move Ahead on Social Security Reform," *San Diego Union-Trib.*, 10 Jan. 2001, at B8.
- "Jonathan Sacks *and his like* stand for exclusivity." Graham Turner, "Jew Against Jew Is a Greater Threat," *Daily Telegraph*, 12 Apr. 2001, at 24.
- "Steve Drowne *and his like*, the middle-of-the-road jockeys who take work where they can get it, can afford no such protest." Alan Lee, "Jockeying for the Right to Have a Day Off," *Times* (London), 4 June 2001, Sports §, at 6.

See **ilk (B).**

G. Faulty Comparisons with *like*. See ILLOGIC (B).

likely. Traditionally, this word had to be preceded by a modifier such as *very* or *quite* <they will quite likely require additional supplies>. Today, however, it is common to use *likely* as an equivalent of *probably* and not to insist on the modifier <they will likely require additional supplies>. See **apt (B).**

LANGUAGE-CHANGE INDEX
likely as an equivalent of *probably* (as in *We'll likely be on time*): Stage 5

likes of. See **like (F).**

-LILY. See ADVERBS (B).

limbo. Pl. *limbos*. See PLURALS (D).

limit; limitation. A *limit* is whatever marks an end to something, as in *city limits* or *speed limit*. A *limitation* is the extent of one's capacity or a constraint that voids, as in *physical limitations* or *statute of limitations*.

linchpin (= [1] a locking pin, as in an axle, or [2] anything crucial to holding the parts of something together), a term dating back to Middle English, is preferably (and predominantly) so spelled. **Lynchpin*, which falsely suggests an association with *lynch*, is a chiefly BrE variant.

Current ratio (*linchpin* vs. **lynchpin*): 3:1

line. See **stand in line; wait in line.**

lineage; linage. The first is a common term meaning "ancestry." The second is (1) an uncommon term meaning "the number of lines of something (such as a newspaper article)"; or (2) a bowling term for the number of games played. Although most dictionaries give *lineage* as a variant of *linage*, *lineage* should certainly not be considered a NEEDLESS VARIANT given the DIFFERENTIATION just described.

Linage has two syllables: /**lɪ**-nij/. *Lineage* has three: /**lin**-ee-ij/.

line-drived. See **drive.**

-LING. See DIMINUTIVES (K).

lingerie. This French word emerged in the English language in the 1830s as a word denoting linen clothes. It soon became a EUPHEMISM for *women's underwear*. A true French pronunciation is difficult in English, since the first syllable is a French nasal with no precise equivalent in English. Although the French pronunciation is something like /la[n]-**zhree**/—and that is the approximate BrE pronunciation—the established AmE pronunciation is /lon-jə-**ray**/. No advertiser would consider affecting a French pronunciation for an American audience. See HYPERCORRECTION (K).

linguine; *linguini. This word, pronounced /ling-**gwee**-nee/, is predominantly spelled *linguine*—not *linguini*.
                                Current ratio: 2:1

linguist; linguistician. *Linguist* = (1) a student of linguistics, or (2) a person fluent in many languages. Sense 1 is the specialist's one; sense 2 is the popular one. The potential AMBIGUITY of the term has led to the coining of another term, *linguistician*—"a rather self-conscious title which linguistics scholars themselves never use, but which is sometimes useful to help avoid confusing the two senses of 'linguist.'" David Crystal, *Linguistics* 36 (1971). The *OED* dates *linguistician* from 1895. Though comparatively rare, it does appear from time to time—e.g.:

- "The primary interest of the *linguistician* . . . is the sound of a language." Lincoln Barnett, *The Treasure of Our Tongue* 272 (1964).
- "[M]ost literary critics are not certain if the *linguisticians* can tell them anything about what makes literary text valuable." Vasant Anant Shahane, *Focus on Forster's Passage to India* 78 (1975).

linguistics; philology. Both, broadly speaking, refer to the study of language. But there are differences. *Linguistics* = the scientific study of language, comprising etymology, semantics, phonetics, morphology, grammar, and syntax. *Philology* = (1) literary or classical scholarship; or (2) a specialized branch of linguistics dealing with changes in language over time. In sense 2, *philology* is sometimes known as *classical* or *historical linguistics*.

Etymologically, *philology* denotes the love of 'logos' (speech, word, or reason). Since the English Renaissance, it has denoted the love of learning and literature—in a broad sense. Since the 18th century, it has also meant the humanistic study of language or languages, especially in a historical or comparative way. But the word has been very much out of academic fashion since about the mid-20th century.

lip-sync, vb.; lip-synch. To *lip-sync*, of course, is to move one's lips silently in synchronization with recorded vocals, either one's own or someone else's. Although the dictionaries are split between the *sync* and *synch* forms, the slight leader in print is *lip-sync*. But this is true only for the uninflected form: *lip-synching*, *lip-synched*, and *lip-syncher* are far more prevalent than the anomalously formed *lip-syncing*, *lip-synced*, and *lip-syncer*. Oddly, however, the inflected forms of *sync* (when used alone) are more common than those of *synch*. In the interests of uniformity—to keep the language in some degree of harmony, if not sync—the *syncing–synced* forms should be preferred in all derivative phrases. See **sync.** So *lip-sync* seems destined to prevail.

Occasionally people misunderstand the phrase and write *lip-sing*—e.g.: "'This is where freshmen and seniors together do wacky performances and where teachers *lip sing* [read *lip-sync*] in front of the students,' Sullivan said." Grace Camacho, "A Golden Birthday," *Orange County Register*, 16 Nov. 2000, at 1.
                                LANGUAGE-CHANGE INDEX
                                lip-sing for *lip-sync*: Stage 2

liquefy. So spelled. *Liquify*, which predominated till about 1750, is now considered a misspelling. E.g.: "McClintock doesn't want any news of the existence of the virus—a fast-acting strain that *liquifies* [read *liquefies*] internal organs and has a 100 percent mortality rate—to leak out." James Verniere, "Germ of an Idea," *Boston Herald*, 10 Mar. 1995, at S3. Cf. **rarefy** & **stupefy.** See -FY. See also SPELLING (A).
                                LANGUAGE-CHANGE INDEX
                                liquefy misspelled *liquify*: Stage 2
                                Current ratio: 8:1

liqueur. See **liquor.**

liquid. See **fluid.**

***liquify.** See **liquefy.**

liquor; liqueur. Although *liquor* /**lik**-ər/ is any alcoholic drink in BrE (including beer and wine), it is generally only a strong alcoholic drink in AmE (gin, vodka, rum, etc.). In all varieties of English, *liqueur* /li-**kuur**/ is a strong sweet alcoholic drink usually taken in a small quantity after a meal. *Liquor* often wrongly displaces *liqueur*—e.g.:

LANGUAGE-CHANGE INDEX (For the full key, see front matter pp. xxxi, l–li.)
Stage 1: Rejected. **Stage 2:** Widely shunned. **Stage 3:** Widespread but . . . **Stage 4:** Ubiquitous but . . . **Stage 5:** Fully accepted.
Invariably inferior forms marked by asterisk (*). • Ratios represent frequency of prevalent forms vs. variants in current books.

- "The drinks group is to unveil a £25 million promotional campaign for Baileys—its biggest investment in the cream *liquor* [read *liqueur*] brand." "Need to Know," *Times* (London), 4 Nov. 2008, at 40.
- "So what exactly is a Bushwacker? It's a milkshake mix, coffee *liquor* [read *liqueur*], chocolate *liquor* [read *liqueur*], and white rum, according to Carmichael." Kevin Robinson, "Bushwacker Fest Cools Summer Heat," *Pensacola News J.*, 4 Aug. 2013, at C10.
- "The new expanded dessert menu will include Sexy Bananas Foster, which is bananas caramelized with dark brown sugar, flambéed with rum and banana *liquor* [read *liqueur*], and served with a scoop of vanilla ice cream." Laura McFarland, "The Cajun Experience Opens New Restaurant," *Winchester Star* (Va.), 21 May 2014, Life §, at 4.

liquorice. See **licorice.**

lissome; lissom. See **lithe.**

listen; hear. To *listen* is to try to hear, especially in order to understand, appreciate, or identify something. To *hear* is simply to perceive with the ear, whether with effort or not.

Listserv. See **e-mail list.**

lit. See **lighted.**

litany; liturgy. Etymologically speaking, a *litany* is a series of prayers; a *liturgy* is the canon of a religious service. In addition, *litany* has taken on the extended sense "a long and often repetitive recitation or listing" <a litany of complaints>.

litchi. See **lychee.**

liter (the basic measure of liquid in the metric system) is so spelled in AmE, *litre* in BrE. See -ER (B). The AmE spelling became firmly established about 1900.

literally = (1) with truth to the letter; or (2) exactly; according to the strict sense of the word or words. *Literally* in the sense "truly, completely" is a SLIPSHOD EXTENSION. E.g.: "Behavioralists and postbehavioralists alike, *literally* or figuratively, learn what they know of science from the natural sciences, from the outside." (Read: *Behavioralists and post-behavioralists alike learn what they know of science from the natural sciences, from the outside.*)

When *literally* is used figuratively—to mean "emphatically," "metaphorically," or the like—the word is stretched paper-thin (but not literally). E.g.:

- "When I got to practice, I was stunned by the overwhelming fear the press had of Lombardi . . . *literally* petrified. He held everyone at bay and did very few interviews." Nick Canepa, "First Game Was a Battle of TV Aerials," *San Diego Union-Trib.*, 28 Jan. 1988, Super Bowl §, at 22. (Because we know it is a metaphor, simply say: *When I got to practice, I was stunned that the press was overwhelmingly petrified by Lombardi. He held everyone at bay and did very few interviews.*)
- "His coaches said BYU threw a different look at the Aztecs than last November, when he *literally* [delete *literally*] bombed the Cougars for 52 points." Tom Krasovic,

"Aztecs Thinking Aerial Route Is the Way to Go," *San Diego Union-Trib.*, 22 Sept. 1992, at C1.
- "For Chip Sullivan, former club professional turned PGA Tour pro, life *literally* [delete *literally*] has been turned upside down." Randy King, "PGA Life Different *than* [read *from*] Being Home on the Range," *Roanoke Times*, 15 Jan. 1997, at B1. (On the use of *different* in that headline, see **different (A).**)

A *New Yorker* cartoon that appeared on 28 February 1977 (p. 54), by Lorenz, had this funny bit of dialogue: "Confound it, Hawkins, when I said I meant that literally, that was just a figure of speech."

Although *W3* (1961) acknowledged that *literally* could be used to mean "in effect, virtually," it didn't record the complete reversal in sense that led *literally* to mean "metaphorically" or "figuratively." This reversal appears to have been first recognized in the early 1970s. See "What Is *Literally* Literally?" 48 *Am. Speech* 210 (1973).

Language-Change Index

literally for *figuratively* <we're literally toast>: Stage 3

Literary Allusion. An allusion, if it isn't too arcane, can add substantially to the subtlety and effectiveness of writing. To work, the allusion should refer to a common body of literature with which every cultured person is familiar. Increasingly, though, there isn't any such body of literature. Even Shakespeare's *Hamlet* is hopelessly recondite to many modern readers. So it's hard to bring off a good allusion if it doesn't relate to current events or popular culture.

The effective writer is wary on the one hand of hackneyed allusions, and on the other hand of allusions so learned that they're inaccessible to the average educated reader. The following Shakespearean allusion, with the word *heir*, is likely to befuddle many readers: "He worries about graffiti. He knows the recession has hit the buildings' owner, so he worries about the paint job and *the thousand shocks a building is heir to* in a rough neighborhood where people have things besides architectural design on their minds." Lawrence Christon, "A Lasting Imprint," *L.A. Times*, 15 Oct. 1995, at E1. This passage alludes to Hamlet's famous to-be-or-not-to-be soliloquy: "and the thousand natural shocks that flesh is heir to" (*Hamlet* 3.1.61–62). The allusion works well even for the reader who doesn't recognize the Shakespearean echo. Ideally, the words in an allusion flatter those who recognize it while not bothering those who don't.

Of course, if an allusion is worthwhile, then it's worth getting right. Johnnie Cochran, the famous defense lawyer in the O.J. Simpson murder trial, referred to *Dr. Jekyll and Mr. Hyde*, but his memory of the plot failed him: "Eleanor Knowles Dugan is the first of several to point out that Johnnie Cochran got himself all upscrewed when he said, 'The prosecution is trying to portray Fuhrman as Mr. Hyde but he's really Dr. Jekyll.' Jekyll was the good guy, Johnnie." Herb Caen, "Is It Friday Yet?" *S.F. Chron.*, 15 Sept. 1995, at A20.

*literateur. See littérateur.

literati, the Italian plural of literato ("lettered person"), corresponding to the Latin litteratus, is established as a plural in English. The closest singular is the GALLICISM littérateur (= a literary person). Whoever misuses lite-rati as a singular is indisputably not a littérateur—e.g.:

- "Among the more remarkable things about the guide is that Bartholomew, scarcely a literati [read a littérateur], never dreamed of writing it at all." Charlie Meyers, "If Books Could Thrill," Denver Post, 28 Jan. 1998, at D16.
- "In the entries . . . are gems of her novels, but the writings are not the self-conscious renderings of a literati [read a littérateur] writing for posterity." Marcy Smith Rice, "Dawn Powell's Time to Be Reborn," News & Observer (Raleigh), 25 Oct. 1998, at G5.
- "He is a literati [read a littérateur], musician, bon vivant, surfer dude and fly fisherman." Phil Richards, "Colts' Debut: Indy's Good Catch," Indianapolis Star, 9 Sept. 2012, at A1.

See littérateur.

Some writers use literati as a mass noun and match it with a singular verb, as if it were equivalent to a word like bourgeoisie, as in *the literati holds these ideas dear.

LANGUAGE-CHANGE INDEX
1. literati misused to refer to a single person: Stage 1
2. literati as a mass noun with a singular verb: Stage 3

literatim. See verbatim.

literature is pronounced /**lit**-ər-ə-chuur/—not /**lit**-ər-ə-tyoor/ (or /**lit**-ər-chuur/). See PRONUNCIATION (B).

lithe; lissome; lissom; *lithesome. Lithe = supple; flexible; limber. Lissome (sometimes spelled lissom, especially in BrE) is synonymous with lithe, except that lissome additionally suggests graceful movement <perhaps the most lissome ballet dancer in the troupe>. Although *lithesome dates from the late 18th century and is illustrated in the OED with three examples from the 19th, it remains a NEEDLESS VARI-ANT of lithe.

litigator; litigant. When it originated in the late 19th century, litigator was a NEEDLESS VARIANT of litigant. But now those two terms have been differentiated. While a litigant is a party to a lawsuit, a litigator is a lawyer who conducts lawsuits. See DIFFERENTIATION.

litigious (= eager to resolve disagreements through lawsuits) is three syllables: /li-**tij**-əs/—not /li-**tee**-jəs/ or /li-**tij**-ee-əs/.

littérateur (= a literary person), a GALLICISM, is some-times misspelled *literateur—e.g.: "However, poets and literateurs [read littérateurs], unwilling or unable to risk all in writing a Homeric epic from scratch, sol-dier on with their translations of epic poetry." Marshall de Bruhl, "La Victoria de Santa Anna," L.A. Times, 9

Mar. 1997, Book Rev. §, at 6. Omitting the acute accent from the first -e- is acceptable. See literati.

LANGUAGE-CHANGE INDEX
littérateur misspelled *literateur: Stage 1
Current ratio: 16:1

littler; littlest. These forms—the comparative and superlative for little—are perfectly good, although some writers have gotten the odd idea that they're not.

liturgy. See litany.

livable (= [1] bearable, endurable, or [2] suitable to an agreeable arrangement in life), dating from the early 19th century, is predominantly so spelled in AmE and BrE alike. *Liveable is a chiefly BrE variant. Cf. likable & lovable.

Current ratio (livable vs. *liveable): 5:1

livelong. See lifelong.

liven (up). See enliven & PHRASAL VERBS.

living in sin. This phrase, which reached its zenith in the 19th century, is on the wane. Even the Church of England has proclaimed that living in sin is a "most unhelpful" way of describing unmarried couples who cohabit. The Church estimates that four out of five couples live together before marrying. A major Church report in 1995 therefore concluded that the phrase should be dropped. Ruth Gledhill, " 'Living in Sin' Is No Longer Sinful, Says Church Report," Times (London), 7 June 1995, at 1.

llama. See lama.

load, n.; lode. Although they have similar etymolo-gies, their meanings have fully diverged. Load (in its basic senses) means "a quantity that can be carried at one time" or, by extension, "a burden" <a load of work> <a load off my mind>. Lode carries the narrow meaning "a deposit of ore," as well as the figurative sense "a rich source or supply."

The correct phrase, then, is mother lode (= an abun-dant supply), not *mother load. Although dozens of headline writers have used mother load as a pun (usu-ally in reference to pregnant women), some have fallen into true error—e.g.:

- "She worked as a computer programmer, but kept plug-ging away at the music. And finally, she hit the mother load [read mother lode]." Tony Kiss, "Messina Never Gave Up Dream of Music Career," Asheville Citizen-Times (N.C.), 3 Nov. 1996, at F1.
- "This site is a mother load [read mother lode] of investing and financial planning information." Ted Sickinger, "Web Review," Kansas City Star, 6 Apr. 1997, at F23.

LANGUAGE-CHANGE INDEX
*mother load for mother lode: Stage 1
Current ratio (the mother lode vs.
*the mother load): 11:1

LANGUAGE-CHANGE INDEX (For the full key, see front matter pp. xxxi, l–li.)
Stage 1: Rejected. **Stage 2:** Widely shunned. **Stage 3:** Widespread but . . . **Stage 4:** Ubiquitous but . . . **Stage 5:** Fully accepted.
Invariably inferior forms marked by asterisk (*). • Ratios represent frequency of prevalent forms vs. variants in current books.

load factor. See AIRLINESE.

*****loadstar.** See **lodestar.**

loadstone. See **lodestone.**

loaf. Pl. *loaves.* See PLURALS (C).

loan; lend. In strict usage, *lend* is the verb and *loan* the noun. The verb *loan* has long been considered permissible, however, when used to denote the lending of money (as distinguished from the lending of things). But both types of *loaning* are common. In print sources from 1600 to the present day, the collocation *he lent* has predominated over *he loaned*—in AmE and BrE alike.

> LANGUAGE-CHANGE INDEX
> 1. *loan* (money) for *lend* (money): Stage 5
> Current ratio (*lend money* vs. *loan money*): 3:1
> 2. *loan* (a thing) for *lend* (a thing): Stage 4
> Current ratio (*lend me a car* vs. **loan me a car*): 1.5:1

loathe; loath; *****loth. *Loathe* (/lohth/) is the verb meaning "to abhor, detest." *Loath* (/lohth/), with its NEEDLESS VARIANT **loth,* is an adjective meaning "reluctant." The verb spelling is often wrongly used for the adjective—e.g.:

- "If you are at a dinner, sitting at the head table, you may be *loathe* [read *loath*] to stand up and walk away because you are on display up there." Charles Osgood, *Osgood on Speaking* 80–81 (1988).
- "Even young fans, usually *loathe* [read *loath*] to adopt the musical tastes of their parents, are bewildered." Edna Gundersen, "Pink Floyd's Retrogressive Progression," *USA Today,* 25 Apr. 1994, at D1.
- "They have done little but dither, insisting they are *loathe* [read *loath*] to interfere in the market." Barbara Yaffe, "Sales Will Slow, but Prices Won't Back Down," *Vancouver Sun,* 1 Sept. 2015, at C1.

> LANGUAGE-CHANGE INDEX
> *loathe* for the adjective *loath*: Stage 2
> Current ratio (*am loath to* vs. **am loathe to*): 7:1

loathsome. So spelled, even though the first syllable sounds like the verb rather than the adjective (see **loathe**). Perhaps as a result of the sound association, many writers err by writing **loathesome*—e.g.:

- "An array of *loathesome* [read *loathsome*] characters drifts through this anthropology of the urban undead." Chris Kidler, "Tama Janowitz's 'A Certain Age,'" *Baltimore Sun,* 8 Aug. 1999, at F10.
- "Severed Fingers and Toes (Gasworks) are extremely *loathesome* [read *loathsome*]-looking gummy chews, available at party stores." Charles Perry, "Extreme Treats," *L.A. Times,* 27 Oct. 1999, at H1.
- "The characters we first meet in 'Nurse Betty' are terminally dim, risible or *loathesome* [read *loathsome*]." James Verniere, "Zellweger Is a Reason to Love 'Nurse Betty,'" *Boston Herald,* 8 Sept. 2000, at S21.

> LANGUAGE-CHANGE INDEX
> *loathsome* misspelled **loathesome*: Stage 1

*****lobbier.** See **lobbyist.**

lobby. The legislative senses derive ultimately from the architectural sense of the word. In 19th-century AmE, *lobby* came to denote (through the linguistic process known as metonymy) the people who habitually haunt the lobby of a legislative chamber to carry on business with legislators and especially to influence their votes.

As a verb, *lobby* has come to mean: (1) to frequent legislative chambers for the purpose of influencing the members' official business <the group lobbied against the proposed reforms>; or (2) to promote or oppose (a measure) by soliciting legislative votes <the organization lobbied a measure through the House>.

The agent noun is *lobbyist,* meaning "someone who lobbies." The term originated during the American Civil War. See **lobbyist.**

lobbyist; *****lobbyer; *****lobbier. The second and third forms are NEEDLESS VARIANTS. See **lobby.**

> Current ratio (in order of headwords): 3,751:2:1

location; locale; locality. All three terms are frequently used. They are generally equivalent, but only *locale* has the sense "the setting or scene of action or of a story."

loc. cit. See *ibid.*

locution. See **elocution.**

lode. See **load.**

lodestar (= a guiding light or principle) is so spelled—not **loadstar.*

lodestone; loadstone. The term meaning "something that strongly attracts" is predominantly spelled *lodestone* in AmE and *loadstone* in BrE. The BrE spelling vastly predominated throughout the 18th and 19th centuries. In the mid-19th century, the word was respelled to make it correlate more strongly with its etymology (fr. the OE *lode,* meaning "way") and with its cognate *lodestar.* During the 20th century, this respelled version surpassed *loadstone* in AmE and still might in BrE.

Cf. **lodestar.**

lodgment; lodgement. This word (denoting [1] accommodations, shelter, lodgings; [2] the placing of something or someone into a fixed or stationary position; or [3] a place where something is positioned) is predominantly spelled *lodgment* in AmE, *lodgement* in BrE. But the medial *-e-* seems to be dropping in frequency in BrE. See MUTE E.

LOGIC. See ILLOGIC.

logical fallacy. See **grammatical error.**

logically. See SENTENCE ADVERBS.

lollipop is the standard spelling. **Lollypop* is a variant.

> Current ratio: 11:1

lone; alone. *Lone* comes before the noun, *alone* after. Misusing *alone* for *lone* is an odd error: "Anything we fully do is *an alone* [read *a lone*] journey." Natalie

Goldberg, *Writing Down the Bones* 169 (1986). See POSTPOSITIVE ADJECTIVES.

LANGUAGE-CHANGE INDEX
alone misused for *lone*: Stage 1

long-lived, adj. The traditional AmE preference, both in this phrase and in *short-lived*, has been to pronounce the second syllable /lɪvd/, not /lɪvd/. (The sense is "having a long life," and the past-participial form has been made from *life* [/lɪf/], not the ordinary verb *live* [/liv/].) But the predominant practice today—and the BrE preference—is /lɪvd/. The AmE tendency to make it a short *-i-* is perhaps explainable on the analogy of the ordinary word *lived*; the BrE tendency may be influenced additionally by the phrase *long live the Queen*.

long-standing, adj. So spelled (with the hyphen).

longtime, adj. So spelled (without the hyphen).

*look badly. See **badly (A).**

look over. See **overlook.**

loom large. See **bulk large.**

loose, v.t.; **loosen.** See **lose (A).**

Lord, a traditional term for the Christian God, has come under attack: "Some U.S. churches are beginning to question the title of Lord for Jesus Christ, reports the *Washington Post*, noting that the word is laden with negative meaning; some groups are replacing the title with gender-neutral terms such as Redeemer, Comforter or Friend. Rev. James Crawford of Boston's Old South Church said his United Church of Christ should be seeking 'metaphors for Ultimate Reality that do not assume a cosmos or creation where . . . some male-like figure or being is in charge.' " "Religion Watch," *Globe & Mail*, 24 Aug. 1993, at A16. Whether the term will continue to flourish or dwindle in use remains to be seen, but a long struggle seems assured. See SEXISM.

For more on the title in British nobility, see **Tennyson.**

Lord Tennyson. See **Tennyson.**

*Los Angelean. See **Angeleno.**

lose. A. And *loose*, v.t.; **loosen.** *Lose,* v.t., = to suffer the deprivation of; to part with. *Loose* is both an adjective meaning "unfastened" and a verb meaning "to release; unfasten." *Loosen* bears a similar meaning, but whereas *loose* generally refers to a complete release <loosing criminals on the community>, *loosen* generally refers to a partial release <loosening one's belt>. Additionally, *loosen* is figurative more often than *loose* is.

Loose is sometimes misused for *lose*—e.g.: "The Imperial Irrigation District also stands to *loose* [read *lose*] about seven percent of its allotment." Dean E.

Murphy, "California Water Users Miss Deadline on Pact for Sharing," *N.Y. Times*, 1 Jan. 2003, at A11.

LANGUAGE-CHANGE INDEX
lose misspelled *loose*: Stage 1

B. *Lose no time.* The phrase *no time should be lost* is famously ambiguous, suggesting either that something is urgently needed or that it's so futile that it's not worth the effort. "Urgently needed" is the usual sense, but not without a potential MISCUE—e.g.: "The General Assembly last Friday overwhelmingly passed a bill abolishing parole and reforming sentencing in Virginia, fulfilling in part Gov. George Allen's central campaign promise. The House and Senate, however, did not at the same time approve a funding mechanism to make the plan a reality. *No time should be lost on this.*" "Parole Abolition Passes," *Virginian-Pilot & Ledger-Star* (Norfolk), 5 Oct. 1994, at A14.

C. *Lose out.* See PHRASAL VERBS.

lot. See **a lot.**

*loth. See **loathe.**

lotus. Pl. *lotuses*. See PLURALS (A).

loudhailer (BrE for "a bullhorn") is so spelled—not **loudhaler*. See **hale.**

Louisianian; *Louisianan. The first is standard and traditional. The second is a variant that has grown in popularity since the 1940s. See DENIZEN LABELS.

lour. See **lower.**

lovable (= worthy of or attracting love), dating from the Middle English period, has been predominantly so spelled in both AmE and BrE since the mid-19th century. **Loveable* is a variant spelling. Cf. **likable** & **livable.**

Current ratio: 6:1

lovelily. See ADVERBS (B).

low; lowly. Each can function as both adjective and adverb: *a low profile; the supplies ran low; a lowly peasant; soar lowly through the clouds*. Because of the potential ambiguity, ensure that either word's meaning is clear from the context.

lower; lour, vb. *Lower*—as a virtual synonym of *glower* (= to scowl), and pronounced with the same vowel sounds /low-ər/—is so spelled in most AmE dictionaries. It also means (of the sky or a storm) to be dark and menacing. *Lour*, the standard BrE spelling, is listed as a variant form. That's unfortunate because the spelling *lower* is an instant and inevitable MISCUE. We'd be well advised to use *lour* instead, as the British do—e.g.:

• "The visceral shock of the Scarpia theme, hammered out tutta forza in the opening bar of the piece, was here

---

underlined by his *louring* presence—an ominous figure picked out of the darkness in an unforgiving shaft of light." Edward Seckerson, "Leap in the Dark," *Independent*, 16 Sept. 1994, at 23.
- "His first lead was in Terence Fisher's 'The Curse of the Werewolf' (1961), where his *louring* looks were seen to advantage." W. Stephen Gilbert, "They Live Again," *Observer*, 30 June 1996, at 6.
- "The chorus moves like zombies and wears meaningless Jeff Koons cartoon-character heads, as bully boys in uniforms threaten violence and avenging angels *lour* from the heavens." Rupert Christiansen, "Tchaikovsky's Magical Card Dealt with a Dead Hand," *Daily Telegraph*, 8 June 2015, at 23.

low-key, adj., is the standard form. **Low-keyed* is a variant.
Current ratio: 22:1

lowly. See **low.**

lubricious; *lubricous. This term—meaning (1) "lecherous, lewd" <a man known for becoming lubricious while drinking>; (2) "tricky, shifty" <a lubricious character who repeatedly eluded questioning>; or (3) "physically slippery" <a lubricious pole>—is preferably spelled *lubricious*. This form more accurately suggests the corresponding noun, *lubricity*. **Lubricous*, the standard form till about 1920, is now a NEEDLESS VARIANT.
Current ratio: 10:1

Lucullan (= lavish, luxurious) has been the standard term since the 18th century. **Lucullian* and **Lucullean* are variant forms.
Current ratio (*Lucullan* vs. **Lucullian* vs.
*Lucullean): 9:2:1

luggage. See **baggage.**

Luna. See **earth.**

lunatic does not have the respectable medical background of words such as *moron* and *idiot*, once-technical terms that were lost to popular usage and abandoned. Its past lurks more in superstitious folklore: derived from *Luna*, it originally denoted someone whose mad behavior was governed by the phases of the moon. Those connotations have faded, however, and today the term merely denotes an insane person. It is useful in that sense, and also as an adjective <lunatic fringe>. But since it's a term of opprobrium <are you some kind of lunatic?>, it should be used cautiously, if at all.

lunge, vb., traditionally makes the present participle *lunging* /lən-jing/, not **lungeing*. Cf. **tinge.**
Current ratio (*lunging at* vs. **lungeing at*): 132:1

lustful; lusty. *Lustful* is the narrower word, meaning "driven or excited by sexual lust" <long, lustful looks>. E.g.:
- " 'The only great sex I have had has been in a loving relationship. It's still pretty *lustful*.' " Lester Middlehurst, "Question of Sex," *Daily Mail*, 6 Apr. 1996, at 45 (quoting Paul Carrack, the singer).

- "People of any sexual orientation can be violent or *lustful*." "Breakthrough on TV as Nation Faces Gay, Lesbian Issues," *USA Today*, 27 Mar. 1997, at A12.

Lusty is broader and typically lacks the other word's sexual connotations; it means either "vigorous, robust, hearty" <a lusty appetite> or "spirited, enthusiastic" <a lusty performance of *The Tempest*>. E.g.:
- "He tries desperately to reclaim his character's *lusty* youthful bravura." Lucia Mauro, "Next Theatre Takes Bard on Stylish Romp," *Chicago Sun-Times*, 3 Apr. 1997, Features §, at 34.
- "The 57-year-old Lovett and his ace collaborators . . . spent more than two hours showcasing their prodigious skills, blending gospel fervor with country's endearing wit, the blues' *lusty* urgency and folk's spare, elegant beauty." Preston Jones, "Review: Lyle Lovett and His Large Band at Bass Hall," *Ft. Worth Star-Telegram*, 24 Aug. 2015, Entertainment §.

Sometimes writers misuse *lusty* for *lustful*—e.g.: "The affair included 400 e-mail communications, cyber sex and, finally, long and *lusty* [read *lustful*] phone calls." Kathleen Kernicky, "Caught in the Net," *Sun-Sentinel* (Ft. Lauderdale), 3 Nov. 1996, at E1.
LANGUAGE-CHANGE INDEX
lusty misused for *lustful*: Stage 2

lustrum (= half a decade; a five-year period) must be one of the most overlooked yet most potentially useful words in the English language. The standard plural is *lustra*, not **lustrums*.

lusty. See **lustful.**

lutenist; *lutanist. One might well simply choose to say *lute player*. But if one of the *-ist* forms is called for, make it *lutenist* (the predominant form since about 1850).
Current ratio: 5:1

luxurious; luxuriant. These two words long ago underwent DIFFERENTIATION. *Luxurious* = characteristic of luxury <luxurious hotel>. *Luxuriant* = growing abundantly; lush <luxuriant foliage>. Cf. **spartan.**

Each word is sometimes confused with the other. Most commonly, *luxurious* is wrongly used for *luxuriant*—e.g.:
- "But during December, holly's *luxurious* [read *luxuriant*] leaves and brightly colored berries become all but indispensable." Lindsay Bond Totten, "Christmastime Less Colorful Without Holly in the Garden," *Chicago Sun-Times*, 23 Dec. 2001, at C5.
- "Streets and yards are densely covered with the vines and flowers and *luxurious* [read *luxuriant*] vegetation of many semi-tropical varieties." Melinda Kanner, "Savannah After Midnight," *Harv. Gay & Lesbian Rev.*, 1 May 2002, at 22.
- "Frida Kahlo . . . was so proud of her *luxurious* [read *luxuriant*] facial hair that she painted it right on to her self-portraits." Stephanie Mencimer, "The Trouble with Frida Kahlo," *Wash. Monthly*, 1 June 2002, at 26.

But the opposite error, *luxuriant* for *luxurious*, also sometimes occurs—e.g.: "The Hostess House has the feeling of a large, *luxuriant* [read *luxurious*] home with plush velvet furnishings, an oak dance floor, a large fireplace and enclosed decks and patios." Lori Taff, "Services Abound to Assist Party Planners," *Columbian* (Vancouver, Wash.), 30 Apr. 1996, Special §, at 2. (On the use of *home* and *house*, see **house**.)

Language-Change Index

1. *luxurious* misused for *luxuriant*: Stage 2
2. *luxuriant* misused for *luxurious*: Stage 2

luxury (= a very great pleasure or comfort that isn't absolutely required) is pronounced either /**luk**-zhə-ree/ or /**lug**-zhə-ree/.

lychee (the small round fruit of a Chinese tree of the soapberry family) is now predominantly so spelled in AmE and BrE alike—though the variant spelling *litchi* (prevalent in AmE and BrE from 1930 to 1980) remains popular in many parts of the English-speaking world. **Lichi* is another variant spelling—one that has fallen out of favor since the early 20th century.

lyings-in. See PLURALS (G).

*lynchpin. See **linchpin**.

lyricist; lyrist. A *lyricist* /**lir**-ə-sist/ writes lyrics. Eric Partridge erroneously called it a "rare word" (*U&A* at 176), but in fact it's quite common.

A *lyrist* /**lir**-ist/ plays the lyre. Although *lyrist* has occasionally been used as a synonym for *lyricist*, in that sense it's a NEEDLESS VARIANT.

M

ma'am. This contraction of *madam* can be found pretty much throughout the English-speaking world. But it especially characterizes Southern, Midwestern, and Western AmE on the one hand, and British aristocratic speech (but only in reference to royalty) on the other. E.g.:

- "Greetings *Ma'am*: The Queen, in the only public appearance on her 70th birthday, is given flowers at the Church of St. Mary Magdalen at Sandringham yesterday." "70th Birthday Flowers for the Queen," *Independent*, 22 Apr. 1996, at 5 (photo caption).
- "Yes, *ma'am*, the museum's architect is Shreveport's own, Mike McSwain." "You'll Find Van Cliburn on the Left, Just Past Elvis," *Times* (Shreveport, La.), 27 Aug. 2015, at C10.

macabre is pronounced /mə-**kahb**-r[ə]/ or /mə-**kahb**/—preferably the former.

macaroni; *maccaroni. The first has been the preferred spelling since the 18th century.

Current ratio: 30:1

macerate (= [1] to cause to waste or wither away from lack of nourishment, or [2] to steep or soak [something] in fluid so as to soften and separate into component parts) is pronounced /**mas**-ə-rayt/—not /**may**-sə-rayt/.

machete is best pronounced /mə-**shet**-ee/ or /mə-**chet**-ee/.

Machiavellian; *Machiavelian. The first has been the preferred spelling since the 18th century.

Current ratio: 55:1

machination. The first syllable is more properly pronounced /mak/, not /mash/.

machismo /mah-**cheez**-moh/ (= the quality of being macho; exaggerated masculine pride) is sometimes mispronounced /mah-**keez**-moh/. It's acceptable to say the first syllable with a schwa sound (/mə-/). The anglicized /-chiz-/ for the second syllable is gaining acceptance.

macho (= aggressively manly), borrowed from Spanish in the early 20th century, is best reserved for adjectival uses <macho bluster> <macho posturing>. Although the word has come into use as a noun synonymous with *machismo*, the latter term is more appropriate for that sense. See **machismo**.

mackintosh; McIntosh; Macintosh. A *mackintosh* (often, in BrE, shortened to *mack*) is a waterproof raincoat. Although the inventor was Charles Macintosh, the 19th-century Scottish chemist, the garment's name has come to be spelled differently, with the internal -*k*-. Some writers spell the word according to the man's correct name—*macintosh*—but this remains a mere variant, and the chance of reverting to that spelling is probably long past. A *McIntosh* (also termed a *McIntosh red*) is a late-maturing apple known for its juiciness and tang. And of course, a *Macintosh* is a brand of personal computer. Orally, the three terms can be confusing: "I ate the only *McIntosh* I could find," "I took my *mackintosh* with me," etc. As one writer put it, "Even *Macintosh*, which once meant a type of raincoat [still does!] or a particular type of apple [ditto], now means something else to millions." James Coates, "Its Future Uncertain as Buyout Rumors Persist," *Chicago Trib.*, 25 Jan. 1996, at N1.

Macron. See DIACRITICAL MARKS.

mad. Although this word has various nuances, the two primary senses are (1) "demented, insane," and (2) "angry." Unfortunately, sense 2—though predating Shakespeare and actually used by him—became stigmatized during the early 20th century as somehow

LANGUAGE-CHANGE INDEX (For the full key, see front matter pp. xxxi, l–li.)
Stage 1: Rejected. **Stage 2:** Widely shunned. **Stage 3:** Widespread but . . . **Stage 4:** Ubiquitous but . . . **Stage 5:** Fully accepted.
Invariably inferior forms marked by asterisk (*). • Ratios represent frequency of prevalent forms vs. variants in current books.

substandard. The stigma should never have attached. The word is less formal than *angry*, *ireful*, *wrathful*, or **wroth*, but it's perfectly acceptable and has been for centuries.

*madamoiselle. See **mademoiselle.**

madding crowd; *maddening crowd. By historical convention, *madding crowd* is the idiom, dating from the late 16th century. Unlike *maddening*, which describes the effect on the observer, *madding* (= frenzied) describes the crowd itself. Thomas Gray's "Elegy in a Country Churchyard" (1749) and Thomas Hardy's novel *Far from the Madding Crowd* (1874) helped establish this idiom, especially Gray's "far from the *madding crowd*'s ignoble strife." In modern writing, *madding crowd* remains more than six times as common as its corrupted form.

But some writers get it wrong—e.g.:

- "Far from the *maddening* [read *madding*] crowd of shoppers and away from the tinsel and mistletoe, Grinches, apparently, are everywhere." Mike Pellegrini, "Bah! Humbug!" *Pitt. Post-Gaz.*, 22 Dec. 1996, at G9.
- "'Being typecast would bother me if my career weren't flourishing outside of the show,' the 47-year-old Williams says earnestly in a tiny office away from the *maddening crowd* [read *madding crowd*]." Joel Reese, "Here's the Story, of a Man Named Williams," *Chicago Daily Herald*, 13 Aug. 2002, Suburban Living §, at 1.

LANGUAGE-CHANGE INDEX
*maddening crowd for *madding crowd*: Stage 2
Current ratio (*madding crowd* vs.
*maddening crowd): 6:1

mademoiselle. So spelled. **Madamoiselle* is a frequent misspelling—e.g.:

- "Photo of Sherry Francis as Madame de Volanges, Mary Lilly as Madame La Marquise de Merteuil, Erica Welborn as *Madamoiselle* [read *Mademoiselle*] Cecile Volanges." "A Stitch in Time," *Sunday Advocate* (Baton Rouge) (Mag.), 24 Sept. 1995, at 14 (photo caption).
- "A few days later, *Madamoiselle* [read *Mademoiselle*] Agnes, a reporter for French television with a lot of *moxy* [read *moxie*], turned up at the Balenciaga show in a vintage embroidered shearling coat." Kate Betts, "The Trends That Just Blew In," *N.Y. Times*, 17 Feb. 2002, § 9, at 4.

The term is abbreviated *Mlle.* in the singular, *Mlles.* in the plural. In BrE, the period after the abbreviation is normally omitted.

maelstrom, originally a Dutch word referring to a grinding or turning stream, is frequently misspelled **maelstorm*—e.g.: "The *maelstorm* [read *maelstrom*] resulting from the refusal of Denver Nuggets basketball player Mahmoud Abdul-Rauf to stand for the national anthem has prompted some to wonder if the line between reverence and disrespect isn't . . . [hard] to delineate these days." Karen Crouse, "Degrees of Respect Vary in NHL Arenas," *Orange County Register*, 24 Mar. 1996, at C12.

LANGUAGE-CHANGE INDEX
maelstrom misspelled **maelstorm*: Stage 1
Current ratio: 1,375:1

Mafia; *Maffia. The latter—the Italian spelling—is merely a variant in English and ought to be avoided. The term is normally capitalized except when it refers figuratively to a non-Italian group <Chinese mafia>.

mafioso; mafiosi. A *mafioso* is a member of the Mafia, a secret criminal society. The Italian plural *mafiosi* is far more common than the anglicized **mafiosos*. The feminine form *mafiosa* is rarely seen.

Although *Mafia* is predominantly capitalized in modern print sources, *mafioso* traditionally isn't.

Magdalen(e). The (more famous) Oxford college is *Magdalen*; the Cambridge college is *Magdalene*. They're spelled differently but pronounced the same. Although the Magdalen Islands, in Quebec, have an intuitive English pronunciation (/**mag**-də-lən/), the colleges are both pronounced /**mawd**-lən/. In fact, that pronunciation gave rise to the English word *maudlin* (= excessively sentimental), from Mary Magdalene's traditional depiction as a sobbing penitent. Although her name is spelled with an *-e* on the end, the islands and the Oxford college omit it.

Magi (the three wise men who, according to the Bible, brought gifts to the baby Jesus) is pronounced /**may**-jı/ (rhymes with *pay by*)—not /**maj**-ı/. The singular *Magus* /**may**-gəs/ is much less commonly encountered.

magic, adj.; **magical.** Native speakers of English don't have nearly as much trouble using these words appropriately as lexicographers have classifying the uses adequately. Both may mean either (1) "of, relating to, or involving mystical powers that allow impossible things to be accomplished," or (2) "of, relating to, or involving the performance of tricks for entertainment, esp. by sleight of hand." *Magic* tends to be used attributively as a means of identification <magic word> <magic spell>, while *magical* tends to be more descriptive <with magical speed> <a magical evening together>. Hence *magical* often means "enjoyable, exciting, or romantic in an unusual way" <what a magical vacation>. Only *magical* functions as a predicate adjective <the effect was magical> <the rescuer must have been magical>. In the predicate position, *magic* tends to be perceived as a noun <It was magic!>.

magisterial; magistral; *magistratic; *magistratical. Although *magisterial* carries connotations of nobility, command, and even dictatorialness, it is also the preferred adjective corresponding to the noun *magistrate*. In this latter sense, **magistratic* and **magistratical* are NEEDLESS VARIANTS. *Magistral* = (1) of a master or masters <an absolutely magistral work>; or (2) formulated by a physician <a magistral ointment>.

magistracy; *magistrature; *magistrateship. The first of these is the standard term either for the office, district, or power of a magistrate, or for a body of magistrates. **Magistrature* and **magistrateship* are NEEDLESS VARIANTS.

Current ratio (in order of headwords): 1,022:62:1

magistral. See **magisterial.**

*magistrateship; *magistrature. See **magistracy.**

*magistratic; *magistratical. See **magisterial.**

*magistrature. See **magistracy.**

Magna Carta. A. And **Magna Charta****.** The usual—and the better—form is *Magna Carta. Time* magazine used the variant spelling and found itself on the defensive: "We were unfairly reproved for our spelling of the document Magna Charta [*Living*, Nov. 11]. Although many publications use the more familiar Magna Carta, most dictionaries prefer the word we used, *charta*, from the Latin word for paper." "Going by the Rules," *Time*, 16 Dec. 1991, at 9. Which dictionaries? Not *W3, RH2, AHD, W11*, or the *OED*—the last of which shows that the great document was known exclusively as *Magna Carta* from the 13th to the 17th centuries. And the leading British textbooks on the subject, by W.S. McKechnie and J.C. Holt, use *Carta*. For the full history of the vicissitudes of the two spellings, see Bryan A. Garner, "A Lexicographic Look at Magna Carta," in *Magna Carta: Muse and Mentor* 85 (Randy J. Holland ed., 2014).

And what about the *Time* editors' argument that *charta* is the Latin word for "paper"? That argument is empty: *charta* and *carta* are variant forms bearing the same meaning in Latin.

Current ratio: 2:1

B. Article with. Traditionally, *Magna Carta* did not take a definite article: one said *Magna Carta*, not *the Magna Carta*. This traditional usage is still followed closely in London and, less rigorously, elsewhere in England—e.g.:

- "The Declaration of Arbroath was a century after *Magna Carta*: and the baronial limitations on kingship in the earlier document were also to filter down, to give all a dim sense of being 'freemen.'" John Lloyd, "Brave Heart's Campaign Trail," *Fin. Times*, 4 Jan. 2003, Books §, at 5.
- "Although *Magna Carta* expressly forbids it, torture has often been a part of judicial procedures in England." "The Sight of the Rack," *Economist* (U.S. ed.), 11 Jan. 2003, Special Report §, at 1.
- "It was Wilberforce's hatred that abolished slavery. It was hatred of fascism that won the war. It was hatred that forged the Health Service, marched for civil rights, wrote *Magna Carta*." A.A. Gill, "The Red Lion," *Sunday Times* (London), 26 Jan. 2003, Features §, at 48.

But writers outside England—even elsewhere in the U.K., in Commonwealth countries, and in former colonies, including the U.S.—rarely follow suit. E.g.:

- "There have been many detested monarchs from bad King John, despite the fact that he signed *the Magna Carta*, onwards." Brian Meek, "Why They Still Long to Reign over Us," *Herald* (Glasgow), 26 Nov. 2002, at 14.

- "It takes a long time for a culture of democracy to emerge. . . . Arguably, the British experience began with *the Magna Carta* in 1215." Keith Suter, "Africa Sinks into Danger of No Return," *Canberra Times*, 14 Jan. 2003, at A11.
- "They believe that the White House is trying to usurp their legislative power of the purse—a power, their staffers point out, that dates to *the Magna Carta*." Michael Grunwald, "Washington's Loudest Voice for Frugality," *Wash. Post*, 20 Jan. 2003, at A1.

magnate; magnet. A *magnate* (/**mag**-nayt/) is a tycoon, a person who has grown rich in a field that is usually specified <oil magnate>. A *magnet* (/**mag**-net/) is a piece of metal that attracts iron and aligns with the earth's north and south poles (or with another magnetic field).

Magnate is occasionally misspelled *magnet*, an unattractive error—e.g.:

- "He even adds appearances by railroad *magnet* [read *magnate*] James J. Hill and novelist Sinclair Lewis." Jeremy C. Shea, "Browsing: Mysteries," *St. Louis Post-Dispatch*, 26 Sept. 1999, at F10.
- "A sign outside the apartment building where Storm and Harrison live chronicles the history of Phillipsburg from 1654 . . . to 1887, when the town famous for its 'beautiful architecture, excellent schools and churches' attracted bankers, artisans and railroad *magnets* [read *magnates*] and South Main Street 'was affectionately known as millionaire's row.'" Nancy Averett, "Fire Damages Structure in P'burg Historic District," *Morning Call* (Allentown, Pa.), 30 May 2000, at B1.
- "Railroad *magnet* [read *magnate*] Henry Flagler had hardly noticed the place when building the Florida East Coach Railroad southward in the 1890s to his new playground for the rich, Palm Beach." Elliott Jones, "Creation of a Garden," *Press J.* (Vero Beach, Fla.), 16 Nov. 2001, at C1.

Before the Gilded Age of the late 19th century, the terms *magnate* and *tycoon* both referred to prominent people in business and politics. In that era, however, the words were applied to super-rich industrialists such as Andrew Carnegie and John D. Rockefeller; the words suggest massive wealth and are still used more commonly with older industries. Hence it is more common today to read of a *railroad magnate* or an *oil tycoon* than a *software magnate* or a *telecom tycoon*.

LANGUAGE-CHANGE INDEX
*railroad magnet for *railroad magnate*: Stage 1

magnifico (= a high-ranking or extremely prominent person; grandee) forms the plural *magnificoes*—preferably not *magnificos. See PLURALS (D).

Current ratio: 1.5:1

magniloquent (= characterized by high-flown, bombastic speech) should be restricted to contexts involving language. Strictly speaking, it can't be about gesturing—e.g.: "To my nervous question about a tailcoat, he pointed *magniloquently* [read *grandiosely*] to the closet and said

LANGUAGE-CHANGE INDEX (For the full key, see front matter pp. xxxi, l–li.)
Stage 1: Rejected. **Stage 2:** Widely shunned. **Stage 3:** Widespread but . . . **Stage 4:** Ubiquitous but . . . **Stage 5:** Fully accepted.
Invariably inferior forms marked by asterisk (*). • Ratios represent frequency of prevalent forms vs. variants in current books.

encouragingly, 'Try it.'" Dietrich Fischer-Dieskau, *Reverberations* 131 (Ruth Hein trans., 1989).

LANGUAGE-CHANGE INDEX
magniloquent meaning "grandiose" but not in reference to language: Stage 1

maharaja; *maharajah. This historical term, meaning "an Indian prince who rules over a province," has been predominantly spelled *maharaja* since the mid-20th century—first in BrE and then in AmE. The spelling *maharajah is obsolescent.

Current ratio: 2:1

maharani; *maharanee. This term, meaning "the wife of a maharaja," is predominantly spelled *maharani*—*maharanee being an obsolescent variant.

Current ratio: 4:1

Mahican; *Mohican; Mohegan. Although James Fenimore Cooper's *Last of the Mohicans* (1826) popularized the *-o-* spelling, the preferred and predominant spelling of the name of the American Indian confederacy is *Mahican*. The *Mohegans* were one tribe within that Algonquian confederacy.

Mahomet. See **Muhammad.**

*maihem. See **mayhem (c).**

mail carrier. See SEXISM (c).

maim. See **mayhem (b).**

main, adj. See ADJECTIVES (b).

mainstream, v.t., is a jargonistic VOGUE WORD. It originated in the mid-1970s when Congress mandated that handicapped children be accommodated in regular classrooms. The following use is typical—e.g.: "Adrienne Lissner of St. Louis advocates *mainstreaming* autistic children in school." Joan Little, "Dealing with the Myths and Reality of Autism," *St. Louis Post-Dispatch*, 12 Jan. 1997, at C12. (A possible revision: *Adrienne Lissner of St. Louis advocates putting autistic children into regular classes*. Or: *Adrienne Lissner of St. Louis advocates keeping autistic children in regular schools*.)

In the 1980s the word came to be used more and more to denote the integration of any subculture into the main culture—e.g.:

- "'It means Hispanics are *mainstreaming themselves* [read *moving into the mainstream*],' said Robin Rorapaugh, Texas director for the Clinton campaign." Sam Attlesey, "Texas Politics," *Dallas Morning News*, 22 Mar. 1992, at A46.
- "Borne up by popular culture, including the wildly successful 'Friends' sitcom, single momhood has been *mainstreamed*, even romanticized." Tom Jackson, "Where, Oh Where, Is the New Virginity?" *Tampa Trib.*, 8 Dec. 2002, Pasco ed., at 1.
- "Other elements of black college subculture were *mainstreamed* by Spike Lee's 1988 movie 'School Daze' and the 1987–93 TV sitcom 'A Different World.'" Natalie Hopkinson, "Nick Cannon, Big Shot," *Wash. Post*, 9 Jan. 2003, at C1.

See FUNCTIONAL SHIFT (D).

majority. A. For *most*. When *most* will suffice, use it in place of *majority*—e.g.: "The majority [read *Most*] of the budget increase is due to the long-awaited expansion or replacement for city hall." Dave Nicholson, "Public Hearings Set on Budget," *Tampa Trib.*, 6 Sept. 1997, at 1. *Majority* is most helpful in discussing votes—e.g.: "And let's not forget that a *majority* of Michigan voters approved term limits." Joseph A. Morton, "Should Michigan Kill Term Limits?" *Detroit News*, 6 Sept. 1997, at C14.

B. Number. *Majority* is sometimes a COLLECTIVE NOUN that takes a singular verb, but sometimes (through SYNESIS) it's a plural demanding a plural verb—e.g.:

- "But the clear *majority reach*, or at least attempt to reach, that level where quality dwells." Jack Valenti, "Lights! Camera! Rhetoric!" *Wash. Post*, 4 Feb. 1996, at C4.
- "It is unwise, however, to become complacent, especially when the *majority seems* to have done just that." "Insider Trading," *Tulsa Trib. & Tulsa World*, 24 Aug. 1997, at E4.

Especially in the phrase *a majority of (people or things)*—with the *of*-phrase spelled out—the word *majority* is generally treated as a plural in both AmE and BrE. E.g.: "Since the *majority* of shops that will open tomorrow *were* also open last Sunday, most shoppers will be hard put to notice the difference that the law has made." Tim Jackson, "Open All Hours (Well, Almost)," *Independent*, 27 Aug. 1994, at 11. Still, the sentence could be advantageously recast: *Since most shops that will open tomorrow were . . . .*

C. And *plurality*. *Majority* and *plurality* are most often used in reference to elections and other types of surveys. A *majority* (sometimes termed an *absolute majority*, although there is no distinction) is either (1) a number of votes that is more than half the total <the referendum passed with a 53% majority>, or (2) the numerical spread by which the majority won <when Jeffords bolted, the Democrats took control of the Senate with a one-vote majority>. *Majority* is often used as an adjective to designate the bloc with the most votes or members <some committee members dissented from the majority report>.

In a contest with three or more candidates or questions, a *plurality* is either (1) the largest vote, or (2) the difference between the largest vote and the second-largest vote. It is often contrasted with a *majority* because a *plurality* may be smaller than 50% <Hirsch won a plurality in the first mayoral election, but third-party candidates drew off enough votes to deny her a majority and force a runoff>.

The terms *majority* and *plurality* are usually distinguished, so that the results of an election are announced as one or the other depending on whether one candidate or question won more than 50% of the vote. In this commonly observed distinction, a *plurality* is less than a *majority*. That can make a difference in the outcome (see the example in the paragraph above) or in the strength of the winner's mandate. For example, a *plurality* opinion by the Supreme Court (i.e., one that is signed by fewer than five justices) may carry less weight as precedent than a *majority* opinion. But if rules merely call for a *plurality* election, the distinction disappears: a *majority* is always a *plurality* as well.

majuscule. See **minuscule.**

make an attempt; make an effort; make efforts. These phrases are verbose for *try*—e.g.:

- "The association said that if a mass disaster occurs, it will *make efforts* [read *try*] to warn disaster victims that they may be approached by 'parachute lawyers.'" "Arundel Digest," *Capital* (Annapolis), 11 Jan. 1997, at C1.
- "Although Larson *makes an attempt* [read *tries*] to paint a psychological portrait of Holmes, his portrait of Burnham is as dry as fallen leaves in December." Cathy Frisinger, "A Long-Winded Chicago Sage," *Ft. Worth Star-Telegram*, 16 Feb. 2003, at D6.
- "Although Brown says her family generally avoids discussing the murders, they do *make an effort* [read *try*] to tell Sydney and Justin about Nicole." Thomas Fields-Meyer et al., "O.J.'s Kids Now," *People*, 17 Feb. 2003, at 69.

make-believe (the pretense that something unreal actually exists) is the standard term—*make-belief being a variant. *Make-believe* can also be an adjective meaning "pretended or imaginary" <make-believe friends>.
Current ratio: 66:1

make do (= to manage with what happens to be available, however inadequate it may be) is distressingly often written *make due, a blunder—e.g.:

- "The Bulls will have to *make due* [read *make do*] until Rodman returns to the lineup Saturday night." Terry Armour, "Bulls Heed Call for All Rebounders," *Chicago Trib.*, 12 Dec. 1996, Sports §, at 6.
- "The state is trying to *make due* [read *make do*] by asking the State Patrol to pay particular attention in the area to driving that can cause accidents." Kery Murakami, "When a Single Driver Can Use HOV Lane," *Seattle Post-Intelligencer*, 13 Jan. 2003, at B1.
- "As much as I treasure Roberto and the kids, living free of the hierarchy, we're *making due* [read *making do*] with a loose network of other runaways, outcasts, antisocials." Cynthia Leitich Smith, *Tantalize* 45 (2007).

For more on this type of verb, see PHRASAL VERBS.
LANGUAGE-CHANGE INDEX
*make due for *make do*: Stage 1
Current ratio (*make do with* vs.
*make due with): 40:1

make efforts. See **make an attempt.**

make up. See **comprise (c).**

malaise (= a vague feeling of being slightly sick or unwell, often suggesting the onset of an illness), a GALLICISM first used in English in the mid-18th century, is preferably pronounced /mə-**layz**/, /mə-**lez**/, or /mal-**ayz**/—always with the accent on the second syllable. Avoid stressing the first syllable.

MALAPROPISMS are words that, because they are used incorrectly, produce a humorous effect. The term derives from the character Mrs. Malaprop in Richard Brinsley Sheridan's play *The Rivals* (1775). Mrs. Malaprop loves big words, but she uses them ignorantly and creates hilarious solecisms and occasionally embarrassing double entendres. One of Mrs. Malaprop's famous similes is *as headstrong as an allegory on the banks of the Nile*. Elsewhere, she refers to the *geometry* of *contagious countries*.

What most sources do not point out is that Sheridan borrowed the device from Shakespeare, who used it quite often for comic effect, always in the mouths of lower-class characters who are unsuccessfully aping the usage of their social and intellectual betters and saying something quite different (sometimes scandalously different) from what they meant to say. For example, Elbow, the incompetent constable in *Measure for Measure*, says of a bawdy house that it is "a respected [read *suspected*] house" (2.1.162). Several equally hilarious misusages—in this scene and others—have the judge standing bemused as both the accused and the accuser get their meanings tangled up.

A well-known example of a Shakespearean malapropism that skirts sacrilege is Bottom the Weaver's garbled version of 1 Corinthians 2:9, delivered near the end of *A Midsummer Night's Dream*: "The eye of man hath not heard, the ear of man hath not seen, man's hand is not able to taste, his tongue to conceive, nor his heart to report, what my dream was" (4.1.211–14).

Modern examples aren't hard to come by. One lawyer apparently mistook *meretricious* (= superficially attractive but false, like a prostitute) for *meritorious*, with embarrassing consequences: he asked a judge to rule favorably on his client's "meretricious claim." See **meretricious.** Similarly, Senator Sam Ervin recalled a lawyer who, in arguing that his client had been provoked by name-calling (*epithets*), said: "I hope that in passing sentence on my client upon his conviction for assault and battery, your honor will bear in mind that he was provoked to do so by the *epitaphs* hurled at him by the witness." Paul R. Clancy, *Just a Country Lawyer* 121 (1974). See **epithet (b).**

Other examples are *infinitesimal* (= very small) for *infinite* (= boundless), e.g.: *across the infinitesimal universe*; *nefarious* (= evil) for *multifarious* (= greatly varied), e.g.: *ties, shirts, shoes, belts, socks, and all the other nefarious parts of one's wardrobe*; *voracity* (= greediness with food) for *veracity* (= truthfulness), e.g.: *How dare you attack my voracity!*; and *serial* for *surreal*, e.g.: *it was truly a serial experience*.

For yet other examples, see **advert; allusion (a); apposition; attain; attribute, v.t.; beggar description; behest; climactic; confess (b); deep-seated; disparaging; effrontery (a); equivalent (b); for all intents and purposes; gambit (b); guerrilla; heart-rending;**

LANGUAGE-CHANGE INDEX (For the full key, see front matter pp. xxxi, l–li.)
Stage 1: Rejected. **Stage 2:** Widely shunned. **Stage 3:** Widespread but . . . **Stage 4:** Ubiquitous but . . . **Stage 5:** Fully accepted.
Invariably inferior forms marked by asterisk (*). • Ratios represent frequency of prevalent forms vs. variants in current books.

Hobson's choice (C); illicit; impotence (B); inclement; infest (B); infinitely (A); inhere (B); in lieu of (B); moot (C); odious; penile; perpetuate; perspicuous; pillar; *uncategorically; & *unmercilessly. Cf. WORD-SWAPPING.

male, adj.; **masculine; manly; manlike; mannish.** All these terms mean "of, relating to, or involving men," but their uses can be finely distinguished. *Male* is the most neutral <male-pattern baldness>. *Masculine* shares this neutral sense <masculine traits>, but often suggests the positive qualities traditionally associated with men <his masculine confidence was no charade>. *Manly* carries the positive connotations of *masculine* <manly strength and vigor>. *Manlike* most often refers to nonhumans <a tribe of manlike apes>. *Mannish* typically has negative connotations, especially in reference to a woman <she had a mannish appearance>.

Although these terms bear interesting historical distinctions, in modern usage some of them—particularly *manly* and *mannish*—are considered politically incorrect: *manly* because it suggests that women don't possess the admirable qualities denoted, and *mannish* because it typically applies to women in a derogatory sense. Cf. **female.** See SEXISM (C).

malefaction. See **malfeasance.**

malefactor has four syllables: /**mal**-ə-fak-tər/.

***malefeasance.** See **malfeasance.**

malevolent; maleficent. Whereas the former means "desirous of evil to others," the latter means positively "hurtful or criminal to others." Hence *malevolent* has to do with malicious desires and *maleficent* with malicious actions. Cf. **beneficent.**

Maleficent is pronounced /mə-**lef**-i-sənt/—not /mə-**lif**-ə-sənt/. Cf. **beneficent.**

malfeasance; *malfeazance; *malefeasance; misfeasance; malefaction. Because the words *malfeasance* and *misfeasance* are imprecise in AmE, we begin with the clear-cut BrE distinctions. In BrE, *malfeasance* refers to an unlawful or intentionally wrongful act, whereas *misfeasance* refers to an otherwise lawful act performed in a wrongful manner. *Malfeazance* and *malefeasance* are obsolete spellings of *malfeasance*.

In AmE, *malfeasance* has traditionally been associated with misconduct by a public official. But more and more it is used to denote wrongdoing by anyone in a position of trust—e.g.: "Lawyers, accountants, corporate consultants, executive recruiters and retired chief executives are selling themselves as experts on the federal law passed last year to crack down on corporate *malfeasance*." Ameet Sachdev, "Corporate Governance Becomes Go-To Field," *Chicago Trib.*, 20 Jan. 2003, Bus. §, at 1. See **malfeasant.**

Misfeasance is a more general word meaning "transgression, trespass"—e.g.:

• "As stated above, most of those who do not receive a high-quality education are members of minority groups

or come from low-income families. No nation in the 21st century will be able to sustain this type of educational *misfeasance* and expect to remain a leader among nations." Mary H. Futrell et al., "Teaching the Children of a New America: The Challenge of Diversity," *Phi Delta Kappan*, 1 Jan. 2003, at 381.

• "Kyle, 65, resigned the job of legislative auditor, the head of the principal agency ferreting out *misfeasance* in state and local governments." Lanny Keller, "Running for Office Takes Different Kind of Skills," *Advocate* (Baton Rouge), 23 Jan. 2003, at B9.

Misusage of *misfeasance*, as by referring to something of great seriousness, is relatively common—e.g.: "The death of children while under the supposed protection of the state is not only tragic but evidence of *misfeasance*." Editorial, "Child Deaths Expose Systemic Failures," *Indianapolis News*, 20 Feb. 2003, at A14. A child's death goes beyond being a mere transgression or trespass, even if it is the result of a public official's or agency's neglect in performing duties. The writer probably meant *malfeasance*.

Malefaction (= crime, offense) has become an ARCHAISM.

malfeasant, adj., corresponds to the noun *malfeasance*. See **malfeasance.**

***malfeazance.** See **malfeasance.**

MALFORMATIONS. See MORPHOLOGICAL DEFORMITIES.

malignancy; malignity. *Malignancy* = a cancerous tumor. The word is well known. *Malignity* = wicked or deep-rooted ill will or hatred; malignant feelings or actions. E.g.: "[Tom] Paulin is also famous for having led the attack on T.S. Eliot for his anti-Semitism—he argued in a passionate review of a book on the subject that you can't separate the poetry from the poet's *malignity*." Judith Shulevitz, "Senescent Prejudices," *N.Y. Times*, 12 Jan. 2003, § 7, at 23.

malignant. See **benign.**

mall. See **maul.**

malodorous. See **odorous.**

malpractice (= the failure of a usu. licensed professional to render competent services) is preferably pronounced /mal-**prak**-tis/—not /**mal**-prak-tis/.

maltreat. See **mistreat.**

mammilla /ma-**mil**-ə/ (= a female mammal's nipple) has been the standard spelling in AmE since about 1830. It was long the standard spelling in BrE as well, but beginning in the mid-1960s the variant spelling *mamilla* took hold in BrE. One might predict that this anomaly, based on a Latin diminutive spelling, won't last—given all the etymologically related words that double the -*m*- (*mamma, mammiferous, mammilate, mammography*, etc.). But a resolution in favor of *mammilla* in BrE may well take decades. The plural is *mammillae* /ma-**mil**-ee/.

-MAN. See SEXISM (C).

man. See SEXISM (C).

man and wife. Since the 1960s, this phrase has been steadily decreasing in frequency. The reason, presumably, is that it does not accord the woman an equal status—i.e., she is referred to only by her marital status. A more balanced phrasing is *husband and wife*. See SEXISM (E). Interestingly, the collocation *husband and wife* has predominated over *man and wife* in print sources since the mid-18th century.

mandatory; mandatary. *Mandatory* is the usual word, meaning "obligatory, compulsory." *Mandatary* is much rarer; it's either a noun meaning "a person or entity holding a mandate; an agent" or an adjective meaning "of, relating to, or involving an agency relationship." For purposes of DIFFERENTIATION, *mandatory* should not be used as a noun where *mandatary* can work in its place.

mandolin. The stringed instrument is so spelled—not *mandoline*. A *mandoline* is a food-slicing device.

maneuver has been the predominant AmE spelling since the 1930s. *Manoeuvre* has always predominated in BrE.

mango. Pl. *mangoes*. See PLURALS (D).

mangy (= [1] suffering from the skin disease called mange; or [2] unhygienic, filthy) is so spelled—not *mangey. E.g.: "Six years ago, [Michael] Cecchi, an actor, had rescued a *mangey* [read *mangy*] Luca from a kennel in New Jersey." Alexandra Zissu, "After the Breakup, Here Comes the Joint-Custody Pet," *N.Y. Times*, 22 Aug. 1999, § 9, at 1.

manic depression (dating from 1911), known also as *manic-depressive illness* (dating from 1951), denotes a mental disorder characterized by alternating episodes of depression and mania. By the late 20th century, the terms were seen by mental-health professionals as DYSPHEMISMS, perhaps because they had entered the popular consciousness and had begun appearing in nonclinical senses. Hence a new term was created in the late 1970s: *bipolar disorder*, in reference to the alternating extremes in mood. Today *bipolar disorder* is by far the most common term for the illness—so much so that it has entered everyday speech <he's so bipolar!>. A new clinical term may one day be required if the term becomes widely abused.

manicure; pedicure. A. Sense. *Manicure* = (1) a cosmetic treatment or care for hands, esp. the fingernails; or (2) a person who provides such treatments or care. The second sense has been almost wholly replaced by *manicurist*.

B. As Verb. *Manicure* = (1) to give cosmetic treatments to another's hands, esp. trimming, polishing, and grooming the fingernails; or (2) to trim closely and neatly; to make neat and attractive. In its second, extended sense, golf-course fairways, hedges, and the like are manicured.

C. And *pedicure*. As a noun, *pedicure* = (1) a cosmetic treatment or care for the feet, esp. the toenails; (2) the care or cosmetic treatment of an animal's claws or hooves; (3) medical treatment of the feet for minor problems such as corns or bunions; or (4) a person who provides medical or cosmetic treatments for feet. It also has a verb sense (= to treat the feet cosmetically or surgically) and may be transitive or intransitive. Although it has been used since 1896, it has never been as common as *manicure*.

Because *mani-* denotes something related to the hand, and *pedi-* to the foot, these terms are restricted to those specific body parts. Some writers misunderstand this. Hence:

Noun:

- "Webster pampers her feet with weekly *manicures* [read *pedicures*], moisturizers, and a pumice rock." Luisa Yanez, "Fancy Footwork," *Sun-Sentinel* (Ft. Lauderdale), 27 Feb. 1998, at B3.
- "Another girl fussed while giving her toenails a quick *manicure* [read *pedicure*]." Billy Sloan, "The Other Day I Could Feel My Eggs Ticking," *Sunday Mail* (Scotland), 31 Oct. 1999, at 45.

Verb:

- "He's started having a girl massage him and *manicure* [read *pedicure*] his toes." Nigel Rosser, "Andrew's Fixer," *Evening Standard*, 22 Jan. 2001, at 10.
- "Female workers were subject to the sexual and other whims of the owner, who forced them to clip and *manicure* [read *pedicure*] his toenails, and watched them shower and lie in their cots." Malia Zimmerman, "U.S. Probes American Samoan Firm," *Wash. Times*, 30 Mar. 2001, at A14.

Past-participial adjective:

- "We wouldn't want those *manicured* [read *pedicured*] toes to get dirty now, would we?" Jennifer D. Braun, "Canine Couture from the House of Poochie," *Star-Ledger* (Newark), 16 July 2000, at 1.

LANGUAGE-CHANGE INDEX
manicure misused for *pedicure*: Stage 2

manifest, adj. See ADJECTIVES (B).

manifesto. Pl. *manifestos*—not *manifestoes. See PLURALS (D).

Current ratio: 3:1

manifold; manyfold. *Manifold* (/**man**-ə-fohld/) means "many and varied" <the reasons are manifold>, or (as a noun) a multichannel air chamber such as the one in an automotive engine <exhaust manifold>. *Manyfold* (/**men**-ee-fohld/) applies to something multiplied many times <a manyfold increase>.

LANGUAGE-CHANGE INDEX (For the full key, see front matter pp. xxxi, l–li.)
Stage 1: Rejected. **Stage 2:** Widely shunned. **Stage 3:** Widespread but . . . **Stage 4:** Ubiquitous but . . . **Stage 5:** Fully accepted.
Invariably inferior forms marked by asterisk (*). • Ratios represent frequency of prevalent forms vs. variants in current books.

Manifold is occasionally misspelled with a -*y-* —e.g.: "Concept cars, or dream cars, as they were once known, are wondrous and magical creations. The reason for their existence is *manyfold* [read *manifold*]." Arv Voss, "Chrysler's Concept Cars Depict Real Intent," *Wash. Times*, 19 Feb. 1999, at E4. (Given the automotive context, however, even the correct spelling would look odd there.)

> LANGUAGE-CHANGE INDEX
> *manyfold* misused for *manifold*: Stage 1

manikin; *mannikin; mannequin. The first and third forms, though etymologically the same, have undergone DIFFERENTIATION. *Manikin* = (1) a little man; a dwarf; or (2) a model showing the anatomical parts of the human body, used in medical training, art classes, and the like. (*Mannikin is a variant spelling of the word.) *Mannequin* = a human-like model for displaying clothes and the like. Although sense 2 of *manikin* seems close to the sense of *mannequin*, the *manikin* is typically more anatomically correct—while *mannequins* often have exaggerated (or, sometimes, missing) features.
> Current ratio (*manikin* vs. *mannikin): 3:1

mankind. See **humankind, womankind** & SEXISM (C).

manly; manlike; mannish. See **male.**

manned flights. See SEXISM (C).

mannequin. See **manikin.**

manner, in a ——. This phrase typifies a sluggish style. *In a professional manner* should be *professionally*; *in a rigid manner* should be *rigidly*; *in a childish manner* should be *childishly*. Good editors do not leave such phrases untouched.

Still, some phrases cannot be made into -*ly* adverbs: *in a Rambo-like manner*; *in a determined manner* (few editors would choose *determinedly*—see -EDLY); *in a hit-them-over-the-head manner*. In many such phrases, though, the word *way* would be an improvement over *manner*. See ADVERBS. Cf. **nature.**

manner born, to the. This Shakespearean phrase—meaning "accustomed from birth to a certain habit or custom"—first occurred in *Hamlet* (1603), when the melancholy protagonist bemoans the king's drunken revelry: "Though I am a native here / And to the manner born, it is a custom / More honored in the breach than the observance." 1.4.16–18. The phrase is sometimes misunderstood as **to the manor born*. This confused view of the text was persuasively refuted by the Evanses in 1957 (*DCAU* at 290).

But confusion in the popular mind was aggravated by a clever pun in the title of the BBC television series *To the Manor Born* (1979–1981), which ran frequently on American PBS stations. The actress Penelope Keith played an heiress who, having lived her entire life on an English manor that has been in the family for generations, is forced, through financial straits, to sell the manor to a supermarket magnate.

After she moves into a smaller house on the manor, the heiress and the businessman gradually fall in love and eventually marry.

Yet as one linguist has observed in reference to similar phrases, "what one generation says in game the next generation takes in earnest." John Algeo, "Editor's Note," 54 *Am. Speech* 240 (1979). What begins as a pun can spread into genuine linguistic confusion—e.g.:

- "A few players seem to the English *manor* [read *manner*] born, and the rest at least have the general idea." Richard Christiansen, "Wordplay a Little Wobbly in Challenging 'Superman,'" *Chicago Trib.*, 16 Jan. 2001, at 2.
- "Many of the more than 100 designers who showcased their collections at the Bryant Park tents shared an affinity for military-themed outfits or upper-crust clothes cut to exude the aura of one clearly to the *manor* [read *manner*] born." Cheryl Lu-Lien Tan, "Fashion Week Finishes in Style," *Baltimore Sun*, 17 Feb. 2001, at E1.
- "If you were not to the *manor* [read *manner*] born, consider staying at a hotel where a guest can feel like a country squire." Barrett J. Brunsman, "Virginia's Vintages," *Cincinnati Enquirer*, 18 Mar. 2001, at T3.

Sometimes it's not clear whether the phrase is a pun or simply a blunder—e.g.: "She is landed gentry, so to speak; *to the manor born*, some would say." Lynne Duke, "On the Inside Looking Out," *Wash. Post*, 23 Apr. 2001, at C1. And sometimes it's a lame pun at best—e.g.: "As befits a privy *to the manor born*, Berman's stucco outhouse has a louvered cupola and plaster walls." Marty Crisp, "Privy Preview," *Lancaster New Era*, 1 Apr. 2001, at B1. In the last example just quoted, the phrase *to the manner born* wouldn't really work, since the reference is obviously to real estate (in fact, a toilet)—not to human behavior or experience.

> LANGUAGE-CHANGE INDEX
> **to the manor born* for *to the manner born*: Stage 1

manner in which is often unnecessarily verbose for *how* or *way*—e.g.: "Those larger issues—the foreign money contributions, the conduit money, the virtual merging of Clinton campaign and Democratic Party coffers and the generally reckless *manner in which* [read *way*] the Democrats raised funds for the 1996 presidential campaign—continue to demand vigorous investigation and prosecution." "An Independent Counsel?" *Wash. Post*, 26 Nov. 1997, at A18.

*mannikin. See **manikin.**

manoeuvre. See **maneuver.**

*manor born, to the. See **manner born.**

manpower. See SEXISM (C).

mantle; mantel. *Mantle* means, among other things, "a loose robe." It is frequently used in figurative senses <mantle of leadership> <mantle of greatness>. E.g.: "The tributes flowing in suggest a *mantle* of modern sainthood falling upon her." Polly Toynbee, "Will Diana's Ghost Haunt the Monarchy?" *San Diego Union-Trib.*, 7 Sept. 1997, at G6. The word frequently appears in the phrase *take on the mantle of* or *take up* *the mantle of* (a predecessor, etc.). You can also just *take the mantle*, but the PHRASAL VERBS *take on* and *take up* appear more frequently.

Mantel is a very different word, meaning "a structure of wood or marble above or around a fireplace; a shelf." E.g.: "Display some of your prized possessions on a shelf or on top of a *mantel* or windowsill." Chris Casson Madden, "Wake Up a Drowsy Bedroom," *San Diego Union-Trib.*, 7 Sept. 1997, at H19.

Each word is sometimes confused with the other—e.g.:

- "With key veterans like Byron Scott and Kenny Gattison gone from the inaugural season team, the *mantel* [read *mantle*] of leadership fell to Anthony and Edwards." Gary Kingston, "Toothless Grizzlies Look for Leadership to Spark Next Season," *Vancouver Sun*, 19 Apr. 1997, at C1.
- "That's where he hopes to get that intercepted pass that will finally go on his *mantle* [read *mantel*]." Jonathan Jones, "Undrafted Rookie Dean Marlowe Trying to Latch on with Carolina Panthers," *Charlotte Observer* (N.C.), 30 Aug. 2015, Sports §.

LANGUAGE-CHANGE INDEX
1. *mantle* misused for *mantel*: Stage 1
2. *mantel* misused for *mantle*: Stage 1

manuscript. Although the ETYMOLOGY of this term refers to a handwritten document [L. *manu-* "hand" + *script* "written"], today the term most frequently refers to a word-processed (or typewritten) document. Eric Partridge urged a bright-line distinction between a *manuscript* and a *typescript* (*U&A* at 179), but scholars and antiquarian booksellers are the only people who observe it, and today *typescript* is probably obsolescent.

The abbreviation *ms.* shouldn't be written *Ms.*; nor should it be italicized. Pl. *mss.*

many; much. *Many* is used with count nouns (i.e., those that denote a number of discrete or separable entities). *Much* is used with mass nouns (i.e., those that refer to amounts as distinguished from numbers). Hence, *many people* but *much salt*. Here *much* is used incorrectly: "We do not have *much* [read *many*] facts here." (Cf. *less* for *fewer*, noting that *less* is the correlative of *much*, whereas *fewer* is the correlative of *many*.) See COUNT NOUNS AND MASS NOUNS. See also **less (A).**

Sometimes the writer must decide whether a word such as *data* is a count noun (as it traditionally has been) or a mass noun (as it has come to be). E.g.: "But *much* [read *many*?] of the data in present personnel files is highly subjective." William O. Douglas, *Points of Rebellion* 21 (1970). Of course, the choice of the singular verb *is* shows that Justice Douglas considered *data* a mass noun—so *much* was the appropriate word. See **data.**

LANGUAGE-CHANGE INDEX
much misused for *many*: Stage 3

many a. This idiom requires a singular verb <many a new father has fretted about whether he is helping enough in caring for the newborn>. Essentially, because the idiom is distributive rather than aggregate in sense, the verb is singular.

But as H.W. Fowler pointed out in 1926 (*FMEU1* at 343), writers sometimes incorrectly make the verb plural when using an inverted construction with *there*. The trouble is still with us—e.g.:

- "There *are* [read *is*] many a person I have met and worked with who simply deride themselves into taking some action." Michael Dirda, "An Unnerving Tale of Spirit Visitations, Uncertainty, Dread and Premonitions of Regret," *Wash. Post*, 31 Mar. 2002, Book World §, at 15. (A possible revision: *Many people I have met and worked with have simply derided themselves into taking some action.*)
- "I'm sure there *are* [read *is*] many a trader/producer who will feel relieved to see the meat futures close April 12." Sue Martin, "Emotional Week in the Meat Futures Market," *Grand Forks Herald*, 15 Apr. 2002, at A13.
- "There *have* [read *has*] been many a night on the Naples Naval Support Activity base that postal clerk chief John Mowry just can't sleep." Marc J. Spears, "Military Personnel Abroad Try to Keep Score," *Denver Post*, 21 May 2002, at D1.

LANGUAGE-CHANGE INDEX
*there are many a person for *there is many a person*: Stage 1

manyfold. See **manifold.**

maraschino is pronounced either /ma-rə-**skee**-noh/ or /ma-rə-**shee**-noh/. Although the first of those is more technically correct and is preferred by pronunciation authorities, the second predominates in AmE and must be accepted as standard.

mariage de convenance. See **marriage of convenience.**

marijuana; *marihuana. The former spelling now overwhelmingly predominates and should be preferred. Supreme Court Justice Lewis F. Powell, speaking in 1986 at a luncheon, stated: "The big problem we had in the Court this past Term was how to spell *marijuana*. We were about equally divided between a 'j' and an 'h' and since I was supposed to be the swing vote on the court, and just to show my impartiality, I added a footnote in a case . . . in which I spelled *marijuana* with a 'j' once and an 'h' in the same sentence." Quoted in *ABA J.*, 1 Oct. 1986, at 34.

Current ratio: 40:1

marinade, n. & vb.; **marinate,** vb. Although *marinade* has been recorded as a verb as well as a noun, it's predominantly a noun <he soaked the steak in a pineapple-sauce marinade>. When a verb is needed, *marinate* is better: it's older and much more common <he marinated the steak overnight>.

LANGUAGE-CHANGE INDEX (For the full key, see front matter pp. xxxi, l–li.)
Stage 1: Rejected. **Stage 2:** Widely shunned. **Stage 3:** Widespread but . . . **Stage 4:** Ubiquitous but . . . **Stage 5:** Fully accepted.
Invariably inferior forms marked by asterisk (✻). • Ratios represent frequency of prevalent forms vs. variants in current books.

marked is pronounced /markt/, as one syllable. The pronunciation /**mar**-kəd/, in two syllables, is a vestige of the correct adverbial pronunciation /**mar**-kəd-lee/.

LANGUAGE-CHANGE INDEX
marked mispronounced /**mar**-kəd/ instead of /markt/: Stage 2

marriage; wedding. Although dictionaries such as the *OED* and *W2* suggest that one sense of *marriage* is "entry into wedlock," in general usage today the word is gradually growing narrower in sense to refer exclusively to the ongoing relationship. The *wedding* is the ceremony that solemnizes the relationship. Hence using *marriage* in the older, broader sense can result in confusion. For example, the following sentence suggests that fewer than 300,000 married couples lived in Great Britain in 1993—an unlikely state of affairs for a country with more than 50 million people: "There were *less* [read *fewer*] than 300,000 *marriages* [read *weddings*] in 1993, the lowest level since the second world war, leaving clerics with little to do on Saturday mornings but twiddle their thumbs." Nick Gardner, "Secure Your Future by Tying the Knot," *Sunday Times* (London), 6 Aug. 1995, § 5, at 5. Although using *marriage* in this way is defensible, it is ill-advised. See **wed.**

marriage of convenience; *mariage de convenance. Since the 18th century, the anglicized version has always predominated over the GALLICISM. But it should be understood rightly: *marriage of convenience* is not "an ill-considered marriage that happens to be convenient to the parties involved," but instead "a marriage contracted for social or financial advantages rather than out of mutual love."

Current ratio: 23:1

married spouse. See **spouse.**

marshal, n. **A. And *martial*,** adj. *Marshal* = (1) a military officer; (2) a person performing duties, as a person in charge of ceremonies or an officer for a court; or (3) a law-enforcement officer. *Martial* = (1) of, relating to, or involving warfare; or (2) warlike.

These words are often confused in three contexts.

The first is *martial arts*, which is wrongly written **marshal arts*—e.g.:

- "Dr. Thompson's curious blend of the *marshal arts* [read *martial-arts*] philosophy and tactical communication reflects his own hybrid background." Kate Stone Lombardi, "Verbal Persuasion for Police," *N.Y. Times*, 19 Mar. 1995, Westchester §, at 1.
- "Mestre Cafuringa has been hired to teach children how to express themselves through capoiera, a *marshal art* [read *martial art*] from Brazil." Betty L. Martin, "Kids Learn Life Skills Through Art," *Houston Chron.*, 20 June 2002, This Week §, at 1.
- "Artist Phyllis Parun will conduct a workshop in Taoist ink painting and poetry from 10 a.m. to 2 p.m. on Sunday at the Shaolin Do *marshal arts* [read *martial-arts*] studio." *Times-Picayune* (New Orleans), 27 Sept. 2002, Lagniappe §, at 20.

The second is *court marshal* (= a judicial officer) for *court-martial* (= a military court)—e.g.: "We should be engaged in saving our at-risk young people, not rounding them up for *court-marshal* [read *court-martial*]." Arthur A. Jones & Robin Wiseman, "How Does the Chief Really Intend to Fight the Gang War?" *Daily News* (L.A.), 12 Jan. 2003, at V1. When the subject is a court officer rather than a military court, *court marshal* (with no hyphen) may be correct—e.g.: " 'They're very thin,' she confided to a *court marshal* as she filed out of the courtroom during the lunch break. 'You can see the filling in them.' " Kim Martineau, "New Venue for Tombstone Feud," *Hartford Courant*, 20 Nov. 2002, at B1. In other words, *marshal* as a noun is always a person. So in *court marshal*, *marshal* is the noun and *court* is adjectival. In *court-martial*, *court* is the noun and *martial* is a POSTPOSITIVE ADJECTIVE. See **court-martial (B).**

The third is *martial law* (= military rule imposed by a country's government under an asserted claim of necessity), which is incorrectly made **marshal law*, especially in loose uses of the term—e.g.: "Fourteen months later, the control board's imposed system of *marshal* [read *martial*] law hasn't made a marked difference." Adrienne T. Washington, "Finally, a Court Puts Limits on D.C. Board," *Wash. Times*, 9 Jan. 1998, at C2. This error was spread when a made-for-TV movie entitled *Marshal Law* was released in 1996: it was about a marshal who was ruthless with violent criminals. How many viewers caught the pun?

LANGUAGE-CHANGE INDEX
*marshal law for *martial law*: Stage 1
Current ratio (*martial law* vs.
*marshal law): 208:1

B. Spelling. *Marshal* is frequently misspelled **marshall*—e.g.: "Spokane Valley firefighters helped save 30 tons of the hay, but the loss still reached about $12,000, said Kevin Miller, deputy fire *marshall* [read *marshal*] for Valley Fire." "Haystack Fire Deemed Suspicious," *Spokesman-Rev.* (Spokane), 16 Jan. 2003, at V11. The error is undoubtedly encouraged by the frequency of the proper name *Marshall*.

LANGUAGE-CHANGE INDEX
marshal as noun misspelled **marshall*: Stage 1
Current ratio (*fire marshal* vs. **fire marshall*): 14:1

marshal, v.t. (= to arrange in order), makes the past-tense and participial forms *marshaled* and *marshaling* in AmE, *marshalled* and *marshalling* in BrE. (See SPELLING (B).) But misspellings with the doubled -*l*- frequently occur in AmE—e.g.: "The picture did feature an intelligently *marshalled* [read *marshaled*] series of '50s, '60s and '70s decor." Henry Sheehan, "The 'Other' Awards," *Orange County Register*, 26 Mar. 1995, at F14.

Although the inflected form is *marshalled* in BrE, the uninflected form is still *marshal*, as in AmE. But this, too, is subject to error—e.g.: "That means two large and one smaller country combining together can *marshall* [read *marshal*] the 23 votes needed to block new proposals." John Williams, "The Net Is Closing In," *Daily Mirror*, 29 Mar. 1994, at 6.

Like the noun, the verb *marshal* is often misspelled **marshall*—e.g.: "Many in the crowds seemed undeterred—even invigorated—by the steady and seemingly inexorable march toward a possible war, perhaps in a few weeks, as the United States and a few allies *marshall* [read *marshal*] troops, naval flotillas and air wings in a rapidly escalating mobilization in the Persian Gulf region." Lynette Clemetson, "Thousands Converge in Capital to Protest Plans for War," *N.Y. Times*, 19 Jan. 2003, § 1, at 12.

LANGUAGE-CHANGE INDEX
marshal as verb misspelled **marshall*: Stage 1

*marshal law. See **marshal, n. (A).**

marshmallow is so spelled—not **marshmellow* (under the influence of the adjective *mellow*). But the misspelling is fairly common—e.g.: "Everything hinged on the *marshmellow-throwing* [read *marshmallow-throwing*] left arm of Brian Anderson, the Diamondbacks' starter." Lisa Olson, "D-Backs' Shot Rests with Curt," *Daily News* (N.Y.), 31 Oct. 2001, at 70.

LANGUAGE-CHANGE INDEX
marshmallow misspelled **marshmellow*: Stage 1
Current ratio: 422:1

marten; martin. A *marten* is an arboreal weasel-like mammal found in North American and Eurasia; it is hunted for its fur in many northern countries. A *martin* is a songbird of the swallow family, but it has a less strongly forked tail than most swallows.

martial, adj. See **marshal, n.**

martial law. See **marshal, n. (A).**

martin. See **marten.**

marvel, vb., makes *marveled* and *marveling* in AmE, *marvelled* and *marvelling* in BrE. See SPELLING (B).

marvelous; marvellous. The first is the AmE spelling (standard since about 1915); the second is BrE (standard since the 17th century).

masculine. See **male.**

MASCULINE AND FEMININE PRONOUNS. See SEXISM (B).

massacre, v.t., makes *massacring* (not **massacreing*)—e.g.: "If I were *massacring* English, he would grimace at my linguistic butchery, wouldn't he?" "Interview with Czech Defector Ivo Moravec," *Ottawa Citizen*, 16 Apr. 1997, at A17.

MASS NOUNS. See COUNT NOUNS AND MASS NOUNS.

master. Traditionally, *master* was used in reference to a boy up to the age of 12—especially in addressing an envelope. Today the practice has largely fallen into disuse, except in formal circumstances. The custom thrives chiefly in the southern United States, as this sampling illustrates:

• "I have loved receiving mail since I was a boy sitting on the front porch waiting for mailman Mike Houser. . . . I wondered why they [my correspondents] addressed me as '*master*,' and it must have been when I was in college that I learned that this is a term used for a boy too young to be called 'mister.'" Harold Julian, "Hail to the Mail," *Knoxville News-Sentinel*, 21 May 2000, at E9.
• "Serving as honorary ring bearers were nephews of the bride, *Masters* Joseph Alexander and Jacob Thomas, twin sons of Destry and Dawn Hill Harding, and *Master* Jamie Nick Timmers of Druten, son of the groom." "Celebrations—Timmers–Smith Wedding," *Roanoke Times*, 11 Nov. 2001, Extra §, at 5.
• "*Master* Thomas Ray Kinard, infant, died November 29, 2001." "Death Notices," *Charlotte Observer*, 1 Dec. 2001, at B6.
• "Pages were *Master* Michael Owen Barry Jr., son of Mr. and Mrs. Barry; and *Master* John Villars Baus III, son of Mr. and Mrs. Baus Jr." "Proteus Takes Trip to the Bayou to Inventory 'Flora and Fauna,'" *Times-Picayune* (New Orleans), 12 Feb. 2002, Living §, at 2.

masterful; masterly. Traditionally, *masterful* has described a powerful, even bullying, superior; *masterly* has described the skill of a master of a profession or trade. A master craftsman is *masterly*; a boorish tyrant is *masterful*. Which is the correct term in the following sentence? "Though Britain's Derek Jacobi looks about as much like Adolph Hitler as Archie Bunker, he evokes the Fuhrer with *masterful* verve." Harry F. Waters, "Hitler, Göring, Speer and Co.," *Newsweek*, 10 May 1982, at 65. (The actor is *masterly*; Hitler was *masterful*.)

Perhaps one reason the two words are so frequently confounded is that when an adverb for *masterly* is needed, *masterfully* seems more natural than *masterlily*. (See ADVERBS (B).) "He writes *masterfully*" strikes one as much less stilted than "He writes *masterlily*." This problem with the adverbial form threatens to destroy a useful distinction between the two adjectival forms. So if an adverb is needed, try *in a masterly way*.

Oddly enough, though many today think of *masterly* as an unusual word, it was much more common than *masterful* until the mid-1980s, when it mysteriously fell into disfavor. The slide had begun in the 1970s. Masterly writers continue to like *masterly*.

LANGUAGE-CHANGE INDEX
masterful misused for *masterly*: Stage 4
1920 ratio (*masterly performance* vs.
masterful performance): 16:1
Current ratio (*masterly performance* vs.
masterful performance): 1:1.2

master's degree. So written.

MATCHING PARTS. See PARALLELISM.

materfamilias (= the mother of a family; a woman who heads a household) is pronounced /may-tər-fə-mil-ee-əs/. Pl. *matresfamilias*, the form **materfamili-ases* being virtually unknown. Both forms are rare. See PLURALS (A), (B). Cf. **paterfamilias.**

material, n.; **materiel.** *Material* is the general word meaning "constituent substance or element" <raw materials>. *Materiel* (sometimes written the French way, *matériel*) means "the equipment and supplies used by an organization, esp. the military"; the term is often distinguished from *personnel. Materiel* is preferably pronounced /mə-teer-ee-**el**/.

materialize = (1) to assume a physical form <the ghost suddenly materialized>; (2) to come into existence <a new style of architecture materialized in the 19th century>; or (3) to appear suddenly <the waiter materialized at our table>. All three senses are standard. Sense 2 is now most widespread.

materiel. See **material.**

math; maths. The first is the standard shortened form of *mathematics* in AmE. The second is standard in BrE.

matinee (= a daytime movie showing or theater performance) is so written today, without the acute accent over the first *-e-*. See DIACRITICAL MARKS.

matrix. Pl. *matrices* or (much less commonly) *matrixes.* See PLURALS (B).

Current ratio: 32:1

matzo; *matzoh; *matzah; *matza; *matsah. The first is the standard spelling <matzo-ball soup>. The others are variant spellings.
Current ratio (*matzo ball* vs. **matzoh ball* vs. **matzah ball*): 8:4:1

maudlin. See **Magdalen.**

maul, n. & vb.; **mall,** n. *Maul* = (n.) a heavy mallet or hammer <they nailed the railway ties by driving wedges with mauls>; or (vb.) (1) to injure by pounding <Ali mauled Foreman>; or (2) to injure by treating very roughly, often in a life-threatening way <the tiger had been mauling the trainer for 15 minutes before anyone noticed>. *Mall* = (1) the game of pall-mall (pronounced /pel-**mel**/), or the mallet used in that game; (2) a lane used for playing pall-mall; (3) any shaded walkway or promenade; or (4) a shopping center, usu. enclosed.

Although the first meanings listed for each term are related to each other, the two words have grown in radically different directions. Today the primary confusion—an outright mistake—is to use *mall* where the verb *maul* is intended. The error occurs especially in figurative uses—e.g.: "In girls Division 4, Ashley Harrison, Nichelle McRorie and Lacey Erickson scored as the Stingers *malled* [read *mauled*] the Tustin Cheetahs,

3–1." Jason Thornbury, "Hat Trick Not Enough for United Sweetness," *Orange County Register,* 19 Sept. 1996, Community §, at 14.

LANGUAGE-CHANGE INDEX
mall misused for *maul*: Stage 1

mausoleum (= a building containing a tomb or tombs) predominantly forms the plural *mausoleums* in all varieties of World English—though the variant **mausolea* appears from time to time in BrE.

Current ratio: 4:1

mauve (= a pale bluish purple color) is preferably pronounced /mohv/ (rhyming with *stove*)—not /mawv/.

maxilla (the jaw or jawbone) predominantly makes the Latinate plural *maxillae* (/mak-**sil**-ee/)—not **maxillas.*

Current ratio: 27:1

maximum, n. & adj.; **maximal,** adj. More and more frequently, *maximum* (like *minimum*) acts as its own adjective. E.g.:

• "When Janet sees bargains like that, she buys the *maximum* quantity the market allows and freezes it." Marilee Spanjian, "Free Lunch? No, but It's Close," *Tennessean,* 25 Aug. 1997, at W1.

• "The officials can levy the *maximum* amount under the cap and refund taxes if budget projections remain intact." Ted Gregory, "Township Gives Back Green for Holidays," *Chicago Trib.,* 26 Nov. 1997, at D1.

Maximal usually means "the greatest possible" rather than merely "of, relating to, or constituting a maximum." E.g.:

• "Hill says upgrades in both insulation and ventilation must be made for *maximal* effectiveness." C.J. Autry, "Protect Your Home from Winter," *Asheville Citizen-Times* (N.C.), 12 Jan. 1997, at G1.

• "Most women . . . may not know that, for *maximal* results, they need calcium and exercise in tandem." Diane Guernsey, "In Your 40s," *Town & Country,* Oct. 1997, at 208.

See **minimal.**

The plural of the noun *maximum* is either *maximums* or *maxima,* increasingly the former in AmE—e.g.:

• "These optional cash payments range from minimums of $10–$100 to annual *maximums* of $100,000 or more in many cases." Charles Carlson, "No-Fuss Investing," *Barron's,* 1 Dec. 1997, at 24.

• "The district has the region's largest class sizes and is pressing up against state *maximums* in many grades." "Many Changes in Store for New School Year," *Wash. Post,* 31 Aug. 2015, at B2.

Yet *maxima* vastly predominates in AmE and BrE alike. See **minimum** & PLURALS (B).

Current ratio (*maxima* vs. *maximums* in World English): 10:1

may; might. These words occupy different places on a continuum of possibility. *May* expresses likelihood <we may go to the party>, while *might* expresses a stronger sense of doubt <we might be able to go if our appointment is canceled> or a contrary-to-fact hypothetical <we might have been able to go if George hadn't gotten held up>.

Some sentences present close calls—e.g.: "If one of his coaches did something wrong, he says, he *may* [or *might*] be able to forgive." Debra E. Blum, "Coaches as Role Models," *Chron. of Higher Education*, 2 June 1995, at A35, A36. If that statement comes on the heels of alleged wrongdoing by a coach, then *may* is the better word. But if it's a purely hypothetical question, *might* is preferable.

Difficulties are especially common in negative forms, in which *may not* can be misread as meaning "do not have permission" <you may not come with me>. If the writer is using a negative in supposing or hypothesizing or talking about future possibilities, the phrase should probably be *might not*—e.g.: "This myth assumes that the softness of the breasts in the very early postpartum period will last for three days; it *may* [read *might*] not." Kathleen G. Auerbach, "Myths vs. Reality," *Mothering*, 22 Dec. 1997, at 68.

Misusing *might* for *may* runs contrary to the tendency to suppress SUBJUNCTIVES in modern English. But it does occur—e.g.:

- "An American Eagle flight that crashed Tuesday killing 15 people apparently had an engine 'flame-out' and *might* [read *may*] have stalled in the minutes before it approached the Raleigh-Durham airport, the National Transportation Safety Board said late Wednesday." Don Phillips, "Plane *Might* [read *May*] Have Stalled Before Crashing," *Austin Am.-Statesman*, 15 Dec. 1994, at A1. (*Might* erroneously suggests that the stall didn't happen; the probability is that it did.)
- "Power surges *might* [read *may*] have triggered outages for up to 2 million people." Richard Cole, "Western Cities in the Dark After 8-State Mystery Blackout," *Austin Am.-Statesman*, 15 Dec. 1994, at A6. (*Might* suggests that the outages didn't occur; they did.)

For the distinction between *may* and *can*, see **can (A).**

***may can.** See DOUBLE MODALS.

mayhem. A. Senses. *Mayhem* = (1) malicious injury to or maiming of a person, orig. so as to impair or destroy the victim's capacity for self-defense; (2) violent and damaging action, violent destruction; or (3) rowdy confusion, disruption, chaos. Sense 3 is inappropriately attenuated because the word, strictly speaking, should involve some type of serious injury or damage—e.g.: "Dash Rip Rock calls New Orleans home, but band members don't call their root-rock *mayhem* [read *clamor*? *rumpus*? *ruckus*? *tumult*?] anything other than rock 'n' roll." Kenn Rodriguez, "Hard-to-Describe Sound of Country, Punk," *Albuquerque J.*, 1 Dec. 1995, Venue §, at F22.

LANGUAGE-CHANGE INDEX
mayhem misused for *ruckus*: Stage 2

B. And *maim,* n. Though etymologically identical, *mayhem* and *maim* have undergone DIFFERENTIATION. In the best usage, *mayhem* refers to the crime (sense 1 above) and *maim* to the type of injury required for the crime.

C. And ***maihem. This spelling amounts to nothing more than a NEEDLESS VARIANT. It has been so since the 18th century.

mayonnaise (the thick white sauce) is so spelled. See SPELLING (A). The word is preferably pronounced in three distinct syllables: either /**may**-ə-nayz/ or /may-ə-**nayz**/—not /**may**-nayz/ or /**man**-ayz/.

mayoralty (= a mayor's office or term of office) is sometimes wrongly made ***mayorality**—e.g.: "He recalled that early in his *mayorality* [read *mayoralty*], he spoke of New York as the financial capital of the world." Beth Piskora, "Rudy Says, 'Ask the Pope,'" *N.Y. Post*, 1 July 2001, at 63.

When pronouncing the word, make it four syllables (not three), with stress on the first: /**may**-ər-əl-tee/. The corresponding adjective is *mayoral* /**may**-ər-əl/, not /may-**or**-əl/.

LANGUAGE-CHANGE INDEX
mayorality for *mayoralty*: Stage 1
Current ratio (*mayoralty* vs.
mayorality): 112:1

***may should.** See DOUBLE MODALS.

***may supposed to.** See DOUBLE MODALS.

***may used to.** See DOUBLE MODALS.

***may will.** See DOUBLE MODALS.

McIntosh. See **mackintosh.**

me; I. See FIRST PERSON & PRONOUNS (A), (B).

meager; meagre. The first has been the AmE spelling since about 1915; the second has been standard in BrE since the 17th century. See -ER (B).

mealy-mouthed, adj., is so written, with a hyphen. In less than one-third of the instances in modern print sources, the word is written solid: ***mealymouthed.** This solid spelling has been pretty steadily on the rise since about 1800.

mean, adj., = (1) small; (2) cruel; (3) ignoble; (4) stingy; or (5) average. Readers today often misunderstand sense 1, believing that a *mean-spirited* person is malevolent, evil, or malicious—e.g.: "His stunts ranged from sophomoric—punching holes in Styrofoam coffee cups—to *mean-spirited* [read *malicious*]—calling up the wives of fellow cops and in an uncannily realistic feminine voice pretending to be their husband's mistress." Todd Lighty, "Former Cop Crossed Line, Destroyed It," *Chicago Trib.*, 19 Jan. 2003, News §, at 18. Actually, a *mean-spirited* person merely has a small spirit, a petty mind—e.g.: "Yet, more and more, voyeuristic, fundamentally *mean-spirited* shows like

---

LANGUAGE-CHANGE INDEX (For the full key, see front matter pp. xxxi, l–li.)
Stage 1: Rejected. **Stage 2:** Widely shunned. **Stage 3:** Widespread but . . . **Stage 4:** Ubiquitous but . . . **Stage 5:** Fully accepted.
Invariably inferior forms marked by asterisk (*). • Ratios represent frequency of prevalent forms vs. variants in current books.

this appear to be the wave of the future in TV. Say it ain't so, Joe." Noel Houston, "This 'Joe' Ain't Shoeless, Just Soulless," *Newsday* (N.Y.), 20 Jan. 2003, at B2.

LANGUAGE-CHANGE INDEX
mean-spirited in the sense "malicious": Stage 3

mean, n.; **median.** Please distinguish between these two words. The *mean* (also called the *arithmetic* [/ar-ith-**met**-ik/] *mean*) is what is usually understood by the term *average*: the sum of a set of values divided by the number of elements in the set. The *median* is the point in a series of numbers above which is half the series and below which is the other half. Selectively using one or the other is a common way to make statistics lie. The *median* income among an unemployed person, a burger-flipper making minimum wage, and Bill Gates may be $17,000, but the *mean* salary would make some less-critical readers think they were all multimillionaires.

meaningful has followed the way of its semantic cousin, *significant*, and become a VOGUE WORD—e.g.:

- "To a significant extent, a *meaningful* childhood requires *meaningful* time with parents and other caring adults." "Childhood Cherished," *Christian Science Monitor*, 21 Dec. 2000, at 10. (Notice the *significant* that opens this sentence.)
- "We make little effort to conserve or save energy, and we still fail to produce *meaningful* amounts of solar, wind and geothermal energy." Jonathan Marshall, "Sun Power," *Ariz. Republic*, 30 Mar. 2001, at 2.
- "We'll have an opportunity to shift a *meaningful* degree of authority back to parents and communities." John Boemer, "Empower Parents and Kids," *Wash. Times*, 22 May 2001, at A19.
- "A typical parent and child engage in *meaningful* conversation for only 20 minutes a week." Rob Brezsny, "Free Will Astrology," *Village Voice*, 29 May 2001, at 22.

Because of this indiscriminate overuse, *meaningful* is fast becoming meaningless.

mean-spirited; meanspirited. The hyphenated form is standard. Some make it a solid word—e.g.: "Ms. Phillips is accustomed to being called *meanspirited*." Anita Gates, "Return to L.A.," *N.Y. Times*, 18 Feb. 1996, § 7, at 21. But the hyphenated form remains more than seven times as common in print as the solid form. See **mean,** adj.

meantime; meanwhile. People use *in the meantime* and *meanwhile* to perform essentially the same adverbial function. *In the meanwhile* is unidiomatic. Because *meanwhile* saves two words, professional editors often prefer it—e.g.:

- "Three other Palestinians were killed as they tried to cross the Gaza border with Israel. *Meanwhile*, the Israeli army said attacks have declined since Arafat's cease-fire call two weeks ago." "What's News," *Wall Street J.*, 31 Dec. 2001, at A1.
- "The full story of the Enron debacle . . . will take months to emerge. *In the meantime* [read *Meanwhile*], no one disagrees with Berardino's diagnosis that there's a crisis in accounting." Jeremy Kahn, "One Plus One Makes What?" *Fortune*, 7 Jan. 2002, at 88.

Both *meanwhile* and *meantime* can be used alone, though the former more naturally so <meanwhile, they saw Jan approaching the 18th green>.

Meanwhile, *meantime* at the head of a sentence is nontraditional and not fully idiomatic—e.g.: "The bonds are no longer traded and the stock is delisted. *Meantime* [read *Meanwhile*], Ross and Zell learned a tough lesson." Kerry A. Dolan & Luisa Kroll, "Sweet and Sour," *Forbes*, 7 Jan. 2002, at 1.

measles is sometimes misspelled **measels*—e.g.: "Proximity to children also exposes teachers to the gamut of childhood illnesses, including chicken pox and *measels* [read *measles*]. And then there is head lice." Gary White, "A Virus for the Teacher," *Ledger* (Lakeland, Fla.), 16 Oct. 2002, at D1.

LANGUAGE-CHANGE INDEX
measles misspelled **measels*: Stage 1
Current ratio: 980:1

measure, n. & vb., is pronounced to rhyme with *pleasure*—hence /**mezh**-ər/—not /**may**-zhər/.

*meat out. See **mete out.**

meatus /mee-**ay**-təs/ (= a passage or opening leading to the interior of the body) is a fourth-declension noun in Latin: hence the Latinate plural does not change its form—*meatus*. The anglicized plural *meatuses* is sometimes encountered—as is the mistaken form **meati*. Even in medical journals, one can imagine that it's less confusing to refer to *two meatuses* than to *two meatus*.

Current ratio (*two meatus* vs. **two meati* vs. *two meatuses*): 2:1.1:1

medal, vb. Although the *OED* records *medal* as a verb in a transitive sense—"to decorate or honour with a medal; to confer a medal upon"—the modern trend is to use the word intransitively, as by saying that an athlete *medaled* in an event. In this sense, it is roughly equivalent to *place*. A headline: "Golfer Gonzales *Medals* at Ivy Championships," *Harvard Univ. Gaz.*, 30 Apr. 1998, at 7.

Medal, vb., makes *medaled* and *medaling* in AmE, *medalled* and *medalling* in BrE. See SPELLING (B).

media; medium. Strictly speaking, the first is the plural of the second <the media were overreacting>. But *media*—as a shortened form of *communications media*—is increasingly used as a mass noun <the media was overreacting>—especially in a collocation such as *social media* <social media is an especially important aspect of medium marketing>. While that usage still makes some squeamish, it must be accepted as standard. In modern print sources, the phrasing *the media is* is somewhat more prevalent than *the media are*. See COUNT NOUNS AND MASS NOUNS & **social media.** Cf. **criterion** & **phenomenon.**

But it's still possible (and preferable) to draw the line at **medias*, a double plural that has recently raised its ugly head—e.g.:

- "He is one of just a few actors to appear in the same role in all three *medias* [read *media*]—stage, TV and screen." Crosby Day, "Stewart Delights in 'Harvey,'" *Orlando Sentinel*, 31 Mar. 1996, at 49.
- "LinkedIn is one of the best but least understood social *medias* in today's business marketplace." "Local Business Calendar," *Worcester Telegram & Gaz.*, 30 Aug. 2015, News §, at 2. (A possible revision: *LinkedIn is one of the most useful but least understood social-media platforms in today's business marketplace.*)

Mediums is the correct plural when the sense of *medium* is "a clairvoyant or spiritualist"—e.g.:

- "Contact is initiated by the deceased, and no psychics, *mediums* or devices are involved." Kim Gilmore, "Workshop Discusses Messages from the Dead," *St. Petersburg Times*, 14 Oct. 1996, Citrus Times §, at 1.
- "Now, with us as witnesses, Carol was about to perform what is known as 'channeling'—a technique commonly used by many psychics and *mediums*." Chris Morton & Ceri Louise Thomas, "Secret of the Crystal Skulls: Day Two," *Daily Mail*, 4 Nov. 1997, at 28.

It is also normal in a collocation such as *happy mediums*. E.g.: "This no doubt is the case with almost all happy *mediums*." Charles Macomb Flandrau, *Prejudices* 167 (1911).

Otherwise, the form should be avoided in favor of *media*—e.g.:

- "Reporters for printed *mediums* [read *media*] also focus criticism on television for using all-purpose experts to express an opinion on a wide variety of subjects." Charles Rothfeld, "On Legal Pundits and How They Got That Way," *N.Y. Times*, 4 May 1990, at B10.
- "The message of the Mona Lisa is transmitted through all three *mediums* [read *media*]." Sean Hall, *This Means This This Means That: A User's Guide to Semiotics* 40 (2d ed. 2012).

LANGUAGE-CHANGE INDEX
1. *media* as a mass noun: Stage 5
2. **medias* as a plural for *media*: Stage 1
3. *mediums* in reference to spiritualists: Stage 5
4. *mediums* misused for *media*: Stage 3

median; medium. These words occasionally get confounded in two ways. First, *medium* (= midrange) sometimes displaces *median* (= midpoint) in SET PHRASES such as *median income*—e.g.: "The gap between the *medium* [read *median*] incomes of white families versus black families is wide." Les Payne, "What Would King Say?" *Newsday* (N.Y.), 19 Jan. 2003, at A28. Second, *medium* is sometimes substituted for *median* in its physical manifestation as a roadway divider—e.g.: "Angela carries the greatest guilt, seeing this truck driver's face as he flew over the highway *medium* [read *median*], and the faces of the drivers in the oncoming cars. If he had not swerved to miss her, she would be the one in the obituary." Adair Lara, "Fellow Drivers Are Not Your Enemies,"

S.F. Chron., 19 Mar. 1996, at E8. For more on *median*, see **mean,** n.

LANGUAGE-CHANGE INDEX
medium misused for *median*: Stage 1
Current ratio (*median income* vs.
*medium income): 21:1

*medias. See **media.**

mediation. See **arbitration (B).**

medicable (= treatable, curable) is the correct form—not **medicatable*. See -ABLE (D) & -ATABLE.

medical; medicinal. The first applies to all aspects of a physician's practice, the second only to what is associated with medicines.

medical marijuana; *medicinal marijuana. The former is the more common phrase for the use of the *Cannabis sativa* plant to ease the symptoms of some medical conditions (such as AIDS) or treatment (such as chemotherapy). It is found more than eight times as often as **medicinal marijuana* in World English print sources, and three to four times as often in legal sources. Since *medical marijuana* is the plainer, simpler, and shorter phrase, **medicinal marijuana* should be considered a NEEDLESS VARIANT. See **marijuana.**

*medicatable. See **medicable.**

*medicinal marijuana. See **medical marijuana.**

medicine; medication; medicament. *Medication* has traditionally meant "the action of treating medically," but in the mid-20th century it came to have the sense "a medicinal substance, medicament" (a sense recorded in *W2* [1934] but not in the second edition of the *OED* [1989]). Because *medicine* and *drug* are both available, careful writers tend to avoid *medication* in this sense. But their refined style is lost on the great mass of speakers and writers who refer to *new medications* and being *on medication*.

Medicine and *medicament* are essentially synonymous in the sense today given to *medication*. *Medicament* is little used in AmE.

medieval; *mediaeval. *Medieval* (= of, relating to, or involving the Middle Ages) has been the predominant spelling in AmE since the 1920s and in BrE since the 1930s. **Mediaeval*, the standard until the shift occurred, is now a mere variant. *Medieval* is preferably pronounced /med-ee-vəl/ (three syllables), /med-i-ee-vəl/, or /meed-i-ee-vəl/. The last two (four-syllable) pronunciations are arguably pedantic. Avoid /mid-/ in the first syllable.

Current ratio: 9:1

medium. See **media** & **median.**

LANGUAGE-CHANGE INDEX (For the full key, see front matter pp. xxxi, l–li.)
Stage 1: Rejected. **Stage 2:** Widely shunned. **Stage 3:** Widespread but . . . **Stage 4:** Ubiquitous but . . . **Stage 5:** Fully accepted.
Invariably inferior forms marked by asterisk (*). • Ratios represent frequency of prevalent forms vs. variants in current books.

medley (= a mixture) is sometimes confused with—and, through METATHESIS, pronounced like—*melody* (= a tune). The error is especially common with a dish that became popular in the late 20th century: *fruit medley*. E.g.:

- "The menu includes a Caesar salad, Jamaican jerk chicken, Caribbean pasta with shrimp sauce, tropical fruit *melody* [read *medley*], steamed vegetables, island peach crepes, tea and coffee." Kathryn Straach, "Name Your Vehicle for Texas Victuals," *Dallas Morning News*, 8 June 1997, at G7.
- "Customers can choose from a variety of favorites including English toffee, fruit *melody* [read *medley*], red apple caramels, hand-dipped chocolate covered pretzels in milk chocolate or dark chocolate." Kim Mikus, "Sister Working Hard to Ensure Quality of Chocolate Gift Baskets," *Daily Herald* (Arlington Heights, Ill.), 25 Sept. 2001, at 1.

LANGUAGE-CHANGE INDEX
*fruit melody for *fruit medley*: Stage 1

*meet out. See **mete out.**

meet up with. See PHRASAL VERBS.

*meld together is a fairly common REDUNDANCY that originated in the 1920s and has steadily spread since the 1960s.

melée (= [1] group hand-to-hand fighting, or [2] mass confusion and struggle), a GALLICISM borrowed into English in the 17th century, has lost one DIACRITICAL MARK but retained another: originally *mêlée*, it is now usually written *melée* or just *melee*. In BrE it is pronounced /**mel**-ay/, but in AmE it is usually either /**may**-lay/ or /may-**lay**/.

*meliorate. See **ameliorate.**

melody. See **medley.**

melt > melted > melted. *Molten* is now only a past-participial adjective <molten lava>. It shouldn't be used as a verb, even within JARGON-ridden specialties—e.g.: "This segregation behavior and the phase separation seem to imply that the equiaxed zone was *molten* [read *melted*] during welding and then resolidified." Kamal K. Soni et al., "SIMS Imaging of Al-Li Alloy Welds," *Advanced Materials & Processes*, 1 Apr. 1996, at 35. See IRREGULAR VERBS (B).

LANGUAGE-CHANGE INDEX
molten for past-participial *melted*: Stage 1
Current ratio (*had melted* vs. **had molten*): 219:1

meme, n. A *meme* (/meem/) is a type of behavior or an idea that becomes widely mimicked or adopted by others within a culture or subculture; esp., a humorous video, phrase, illustration, or other symbol or depiction that is suddenly and widely spread by and mimicked or parodied on the Internet. The NEOLOGISM arose in the 1970s, as a shortening of Greek *miméme* ("same, alike").

memento. So spelled—not **momento.* The misspelling, which has lurked in the language since the 17th century, was never widely used until the late 20th century. The ETYMOLOGY has to do with the Latin

verb *meminisse* "to remember." It has nothing to do with *moment.* Yet in both AmE and BrE, *memento* outranges **momento* by only a 2-to-1 margin. Pl. *mementos.* See PLURALS (D). The word is pronounced /mə-**men**-toh/—not /moh-**men**-toh/.

memorandums; memoranda. *Memorandum* is always the singular noun. Either *memorandums* or *memoranda* is correct as a plural. Shakespeare used *memorandums* (*Henry IV, Part 1* 3.3.158). One nice thing about *memorandums* is that it will help curb the tendency to misuse *memoranda* as a singular, as in the erroneous phrasing **This memoranda is late.* But the plural *memoranda* has been far more common than *memorandums* in print sources since the early 19th century.

Current ratio (*memoranda* vs. *memorandums*): 8:1

memoriam, in. See **in memoriam.**

ménage; manège. Both are French loanwords, hence GALLICISMS. The first refers to the management of one's household. The second refers to the care and feeding of one's horses.

mendacity; mendicity; mendicancy. *Mendacity*, the most common of these terms, denotes deceptiveness or lying—e.g.: "The word classicism has connotations of formal logic and balance, and to apply it to the dog's breakfast of impressionist clichés in this concert was an act of intellectual *mendacity*, a cynical willingness to play on the layman's uninformed stereotypes." Kyle Gann, "Gentrification: Uptown Makes a House Call," *Village Voice*, 8 Apr. 1997, at 66. The corresponding adjective is *mendacious* (= lying, untruthful).

Mendicity is beggarliness—e.g.: "For Alexander it was just another day in the 1995 campaign, a marathon of *mendicity* that will do much to determine which G.O.P. hopefuls will survive to compete in the 1996 campaign. . . . [H]e needs to raise $20 million by the end of this year." Michael Duffy, "The Money Chase," *Time*, 13 Mar. 1995, at 93. Many cities in England have "mendicity societies," which look after the poor. The more concrete synonym, which is slightly more common, is *mendicancy*—which more closely corresponds to the adjective and noun *mendicant* (= [adj.] begging; [n.] beggar). *Mendicancy* suggests the begging of a friar or monk who has taken a vow of poverty; *mendicity*, by contrast, suggests a less virtuous type of begging.

menstruation (= the monthly discharge of blood from the uterus of a fertile but nonpregnant female primate) is pronounced /men-stroo-**ay**-shən/—not /men-**stray**-shən/ (a mispronunciation resulting from syncope) or /men-i-**stray**-shən/ (a mispronunciation caused by epenthesis plus syncope).

menstruum (= a solvent, esp. one used for extracting a drug from a plant) forms the plural *menstrua*—or sometimes *menstruums.* See PLURALS (B).

Current ratio (*menstrua* vs. *menstruums*): 5:1

mental attitude is a common REDUNDANCY that arose in the late 19th century. The phrase might have made good sense when it was common to think of a person's *physical attitude* (i.e., posture and carriage), but those days are no more. E.g.: "Positive *mental attitude* [read *attitude*] will be the topic addressed by former University of Tennessee basketball coach Ray Mears." "State Mental Health Consumers' Group Meets Here Saturday," *Knoxville News-Sentinel*, 17 Apr. 1997, at B4.

mentee (= protégé; a person who has a mentor) arose in the mid-1960s to correspond to *mentor* (which itself dates from the mid-1700s). The main oddity about the pair is that unlike most pairs ending in *-or* and *-ee*, these are not from a verb stem. That is, almost every other pair derives from a verb—*grantor–grantee, licensor–licensee, mortgagor–mortgagee*, and so on. But there is no verb *to ment*, and *mentor* derives from the eponym *Mentor*, the name of a guide or adviser in Homer's *Odyssey*. Yet the *mentor–mentee* correlatives have become established as VOGUE WORDS, especially in education and business—e.g.:

- "One major candidate from a major university had an extremely distinguished sponsor who was apparently intent on emphasizing his special closeness to the *mentee*." David Damrosch, "Mentors and Tormentors in Doctoral Education," *Chron. of Higher Educ.*, 17 Nov. 2000, at B24.
- "But Spane has managed to fashion a flip-flop in their *mentor–mentee* relationship." Linda Helser, "Client Turns Teacher for Mentor," *Ariz. Republic*, 13 Dec. 2000, at 1.
- "Mentors and *mentees* should talk on the phone at least once a week and get together at least once a month." "Mentors Needed for Teens in Phillipsburg," *Star-Ledger* (Newark), 11 Jan. 2001, at 3.

The alternative term, *protégé*, may sound affected, but *mentee* is hardly an improvement.

mentor (= an experienced person who tutors and helps a less experienced person) is preferably pronounced /**men**-tər/, but the overpronounced /**men**-tor/ is probably dominant today in AmE.

meow; *miaow; *miaou; *miaul; *meou. According to a solid majority of dictionaries, the standard word for a cat's sound is *meow*. Some cats, presumably ill trained, use variant pronunciations. See **mewl.**
Current ratio (in order of headwords): 295:33:3:2:1

Mephistophelean; Mephistophelian. The first, which is not quite as common (but nearly!), should be preferred for the same reasons that *Shakespearean* is preferred. It is pronounced /mə-**fis**-tə-**fee**-lee-ən/ or /mef-is-tə-**fee**-lee-ən/. See **Euclidean & Shakespearean.**

Current ratio (*Mephistophelian* vs.
Mephistophelean): 1.2:1

mercantile (= involving trade and commerce) is most traditionally pronounced /mər-kən-tıl/ in BrE and /mər-kən-til/ in AmE—but since the early 20th century /**mər**-kən-teel/ has become the standard AmE pronunciation.

Mercedes-Benz. The plural is *Mercedes-Benzes*, but some writers wrongly leave off the *-es*—e.g.: "And last week that élite group of electors arrived at the Hong Kong Convention Center in a procession of Rolls-Royces and *Mercedes-Benz* [read *Mercedes-Benzes*] to cast their ballots for a winner anointed long before." Sandra Burton, "Beijing's Capitalist," *Time*, 23 Dec. 1996, at 47.

But what if the name is shortened, as it so frequently is, to *Mercedes*? The plural is then *Mercedeses*—e.g.: "He is so wild about his car, Young says, that sometimes when he stops other *Mercedeses* along the highway, 'I check the interiors, the dash.'" Laura Blumenfeld, "Gentlemen, Start Your Imaginations," *Wash. Post*, 30 Dec. 1996, at D1. Although it is true that many people say *Mercedes* as a plural, this usage flouts the age-old rule for pluralizing names. See PLURALS (F).

merchandise; *merchandize. The first is standard. The second is a misbegotten verb and noun. **Merchandize* emerged as a variant of *merchandise* in both the noun and verb senses during the 17th century and flourished until the mid-19th century. Today, it's an anomaly as either part of speech—e.g.: "The goal should be to make it harder for criminals to pay or receive money for stolen *merchandize* [read *merchandise*], he said." Jaikumar Vijayan, "The Identity Underworld," *Christian Science Monitor*, 6 May 2015. See -IZE.

Current ratio: 41:1

mercifully. See SENTENCE ADVERBS.

mercilessly. See **unmercilessly.*

mercy killing. See euthanasia (A).

meretricious (= alluring by false show) has not lost its strong etymological connection with the Latin word for "prostitute" (*meretrix*). A *meretricious marriage* is one that involves either unlawful sexual connection or lack of capacity on the part of one party. Outside law, though, the word is typically figurative, meaning "tawdry and showy without substance or merit"—e.g.: "Of course, there's also another reason to spurn some of these costly new mansions. . . . They look like starter homes on steroids, like Disney cartoons, like health clubs and encyclopedias of kitsch. We're talking bad taste. Tacky, gross, ostentatious, *meretricious*, vulgar, fake, phony, dreadful." Colin Campbell, "Historic Real Estate Market Exists Far Afield," *Atlanta J.-Const.*, 27 Nov. 2001, at B3.

merge together, a REDUNDANCY dating from the early 19th century, is a blemish. See **together.**

LANGUAGE-CHANGE INDEX (For the full key, see front matter pp. xxxi, l–li.)
Stage 1: Rejected. **Stage 2:** Widely shunned. **Stage 3:** Widespread but . . . **Stage 4:** Ubiquitous but . . . **Stage 5:** Fully accepted.
Invariably inferior forms marked by asterisk (*). • Ratios represent frequency of prevalent forms vs. variants in current books.

meridiem; meridian. See **a.m.**

meringue. So spelled. See SPELLING (A).

Meritage. "Some people find the word 'Meritage' meritorious. Others find it meretricious. But most people
have no idea what it means." John Kessler, "Drinkers
Confused over 'Meritage' Label," *Denver Post*, 8 June
1994, at E1. Dictionaries provide little help: as of late
2015, few major dictionaries had an entry on the
term—which has an interesting history.

In 1987, California winemakers sponsored an
international contest to create an upscale term for
a table wine blended from two or more Bordeaux
varietals grown in the United States. A California
grocery-store wine buyer won the contest with *Meritage*, a PORTMANTEAU WORD formed by combining
merit with *heritage*. The word rhymes with *heritage*;
it's pronounced /**mer**-ə-tij/. Yet many wine enthusiasts mistakenly give it a Frenchified pronunciation
(/mer-i-**tahzh**/), which has become lamentably widespread. The term isn't a GALLICISM at all.

The wine producers trademarked the term, which is
now available only to members of the Meritage Association. To qualify as a Meritage under current guidelines, a wine must:

- Be a blend of two or more U.S.-grown Bordeaux grape
  varieties (meaning, for red wines, cabernet franc, cabernet
  sauvignon, carmenere, gros verdot, malbec, merlot, petit
  verdot, and St. Macaire; and for white wines, sauvignon
  blanc, sauvignon vert, and semillon). No variety can make
  up more than 90% of the final combination.
- Be bottled and produced by a U.S. winery from grapes that
  carry a U.S. appellation.
- Be the winery's best wine of its type.
- Be limited to 25,000 cases per vintage.

What's the reason for all this? Under U.S. law, a varietal
such as cabernet sauvignon must have at least 75% of
that one grape. Blended table wines, a fine tradition in
Bordeaux, have traditionally been snubbed by American wine-lovers, like mutts at dog shows. Hence the
idea to fabricate a fancy new name for good blends.
It was a clever stroke to choose a linguistic blend
(another term for a portmanteau word). The marketing ploy has worked: since 1988, Meritage wines have
grown more and more successful (and more and more
expensive). To help keep prices reasonable, insist on
the unpretentious pronunciation rhyming with *heritage*. With the faux-French affectation, things will
surely get out of hand. Cf. **claret.**

mesalliance; misalliance. *Mesalliance*, a GALLICISM,
means "a marriage with a social inferior; a morganatic
marriage." *Misalliance* is best kept distinct in the sense
(1) "an improper alliance," or (2) "a marriage in which
the partners are ill suited for each other." A *mesalliance*
(either /may-zə-**li**-ənts/ or /may-zahl-**yahns**/) may be
a happy marriage, but a *misalliance* (/mis-ə-**li**-ənts/)
never is.

Messrs. is the abbreviation for *messieurs*, the plural of
the French *monsieur*. In English it acts as the plural of
Mr. The female equivalent is *mesdames* (*Mmes.*).

metal for *mettle* (= natural temperament; courage) is
a blunder—e.g.: "We have yet to test the *metal* [read
mettle] of our response capabilities." "Coordinators
Rank Top Challenging Issues," *Emergency Mgmt.
Update* (Va. Dep't of Emergency Servs.), Jan. 1995,
at 1.

LANGUAGE-CHANGE INDEX
metal misused for *mettle*: Stage 1
Current ratio (*test their mettle* vs.
*test their metal): 22:1

METAPHORS. A. Generally. A *metaphor* is a figure
of speech in which one thing is called by the name
of something else, or is said to be that other thing.
Unlike *similes*, which use *like* or *as*, metaphorical
comparisons are implicit—not explicit. Skillful use of
metaphor is one of the highest attainments of writing;
graceless and even aesthetically offensive use of metaphors is one of the commonest scourges of writing.

Although a graphic phrase often lends both force
and compactness to writing, it must seem contextually
agreeable. That is, speaking technically, the *vehicle* of
the metaphor (i.e., the literal sense of the metaphorical
language) must accord with the *tenor* of the metaphor
(i.e., the ultimate, metaphorical sense), which is to say
that the means must fit the end. To illustrate the distinction between the vehicle and the tenor of a metaphor, in the statement *that essay is a patchwork quilt
without discernible design*, the makeup of the essay is
the tenor, and the quilt is the vehicle. It is the comparison of the tenor with the vehicle that makes or breaks
a metaphor.

A writer would be ill-advised, for example, to use
rustic metaphors in a discussion of the problems of air
pollution, which is essentially a problem of the bigger
cities and outlying areas. Doing that mismatches the
vehicle with the tenor.

B. Mixed Metaphors. The most embarrassing
problem with metaphors occurs when one metaphor
crowds another. It can happen with CLICHÉS—e.g.:

- "It's on a day like this that the cream really rises to the
  crop." (This mingles *the cream rises to the top* with *the
  cream of the crop*.)
- "He's really got his hands cut out for him." (This mingles *he's got his hands full* with *he's got his work cut out
  for him*.)
- "This will separate the men from the chaff." (This mingles
  separate the men from the boys with *separate the wheat
  from the chaff*.)
- "It will take someone willing to pick up the gauntlet and
  run with it." (This mingles *pick up the gauntlet* with *pick
  up the ball and run with it*.)
- "From now on, I am watching everything you do with
  a fine-toothed comb." (*Watching everything you do* isn't
  something that can occur with *a fine-toothed comb*.)

The purpose of an image is to fix the idea in the reader's or hearer's mind. If jarringly disparate images
appear together, the audience is left confused or sometimes laughing, at the writer's expense.

The following classic example comes from a speech
by Boyle Roche in the Irish Parliament, delivered in
about 1790: "Mr. Speaker, I smell a rat. I see him floating

in the air. But mark me, sir, I will nip him in the bud." Perhaps the supreme example of the comic misuse of metaphor occurred in the speech of a scientist who referred to "a virgin field pregnant with possibilities."

C. Dormant Metaphors. Dormant metaphors sometimes come alive in contexts in which the user had no intention of reviving them. In the following examples, *progeny*, *outpouring*, and *behind their backs* are dormant metaphors that, in most contexts, don't suggest their literal meanings. But when they're used with certain concrete terms, the results can be jarring—e.g.:

- "This Note examines the doctrine set forth in *Roe v. Wade* and its *progeny*." "Potential Fathers and Abortion," 55 *Brooklyn L. Rev.* 1359, 1363 (1990). (*Roe v. Wade*, of course, legalized abortion.)
- "The slayings also have generated an *outpouring of hand wringing* from Canada's commentators." Anne Swardson, "In Canada, It Takes Only Two Deaths," *Wash. Post* (Nat'l Weekly ed.), 18–24 Apr. 1994, at 17. (Hand-wringing can't be poured.)
- "But managers at Hyland Hills have found that, for whatever reasons, more and more young skiers are *smoking behind their backs*. And they are worried that others are setting a bad example." Barbara Lloyd, "Ski Area Cracks Down on Smoking," *N.Y. Times*, 25 Jan. 1996, at B13. (It's a fire hazard to smoke behind your back.)

Yet another pitfall for the unwary is the CLICHÉ-metaphor that the writer renders incorrectly, as by writing **taxed to the breaking point* instead of *stretched to the breaking point*. See SET PHRASES.

METATHESIS. This term refers to the transposition of letters or sounds in a word or phrase. Historical examples abound (e.g., the modern words *bird* and *third* from Old English *bridd* and *thridda*). But modern examples—such as *ax* for *ask* (typical of modern DIALECT, but with historical antecedents), **irrevelant* for *irrelevant*, **progidy* for *prodigy*, and the like—are to be avoided in STANDARD ENGLISH. For entries discussing various modern examples, see **anemone, calvary, chaise longue, diminution, irrelevant, jodhpur, medley, nuclear** & **relevant.** See also **quick (B).**

meteor. See **meteoroid.**

meteoric rise. This phrase is another example of how idiom trumps logic. Meteors always fall toward the earth. They never actually rise, and even their apparent path is as likely to be falling toward the horizon as rising away from it. Still, the idiom *meteoric rise* is about 30 times as common in print as *meteoric fall*. In fact, it's so much more common that *meteoric* standing alone is now understood to signify quick success—e.g.: "The last time the IRL produced a *meteoric star* of Hornish's caliber, the driver was Tony Stewart." Ed Hinton, "Driver Dust-ups Good Box Office," *Chicago Trib.*, 30 Mar. 2002, Sports §, at 11. A word-frequency graph for the phrase from 1900 to 2000 shows an almost straight-line upward trend—in other words, the very thing commonly denoted by the phrase.

meteoroid; meteor; meteorite. The headwords are listed in astronomical order. That is, a *meteoroid* (a piece of rock or metal traveling through space) becomes a *meteor* if it enters the earth's atmosphere and a *meteorite* when it hits the earth's surface.

The adjective *meteoric* means not only "of, relating to, or involving meteors" but also "resembling a meteor in speed or sudden brilliance" <a meteoric rise to stardom>.

meteorologist (= a professional student of weather), a nonsexist equivalent to the old-fashioned term *weatherman*, is pronounced /mee-tee-ə-**rol**-ə-jist/, in six syllables—not /mee-tə-**rol**-ə-jist/. Meteorologists often mispronounce the word themselves—as daily newscasts throughout the United States will bear out.

mete out, v.t. (*mete* from an Old English word for "measure"), is the correct phrase, not **meet out* or **meat out*—e.g.:

- "He said, 'It's not a matter of enforcement, but a problem of *meating out* [read *meting out*] justice' in dealing with juveniles." Mark J. Bell, "Mall Developers Coming to City," *Intelligencer* (Wheeling, W. Va.), 1 Apr. 1992, Bus. §, at 1.
- "Given this standard, no international court would *meet out* [read *mete out*] justice any Westerner would recognize as such." Donald Devine, "All for a World Court?" *Wash. Times*, 7 Dec. 1999, at A16.
- "If indeed it turns out that Enron's managers were engaged in shabby financial practices then shame on them and let the law *meet out* [read *mete out*] its punishments." Terrence L. Barnich, "Free Markets and the Fall of Enron," *Chicago Trib.*, 2 Dec. 2001, Commentary §, at 21.

This phrase is also sometimes incorrectly written **meter out*—e.g.: "The coach has *metered out* [read *meted out*] discipline with all the predictable consistency of spilled mercury, having no hard-and-fast punishment standards." Nick Horvath Jr., "Don't Turn That Page," *Patriot-News* (Harrisburg), 25 Oct. 2000, at C1.

LANGUAGE-CHANGE INDEX
1. **meat out* for *mete out*: Stage 1
2. **meet out* for *mete out*: Stage 1
3. **meter out* for *mete out*: Stage 1

methinks (= it seems to me) is an ever-popular ARCHAISM, thanks to Shakespeare: "The lady doth protest too much, methinks" (*Hamlet* 3.2.230). Note, however, that Shakespeare put *methinks* at the end of the line, not at the beginning. The following, then, is something of a misquotation—and there are countless others like it: "*Methinks* Scott Hicks protests too much about the 'Shine' backlash." Paul Willistein, "Oscars Declare Their 'Independents,'" *Morning Call* (Allentown, Pa.), 23 Mar. 1997, at F1.

Methinks also appears frequently without the accompanying "protest too much" language—e.g.:

- "The problem—*methinks* it obvious—was in Foxborough." Michael Madden, "Olson Couldn't Get Out of Spotlight,

So She'll Get Out of Country," *Boston Globe*, 26 May 1991, Sports §, at 44.

- "*Methinks* he'll have quite a lot of people keeping him company when that day comes." Sean Kilfeather, "Slipped DISC at the Mansion House," *Irish Times*, 5 June 1993, Weekend Sport §, at 17.
- "Tracking the source of this one could be a Nile-esque expedition, but *methinks* the answer lies in one body who wanted to hype King of the Hill." David Holthouse, "Surf the Jungle Telegraph Debris," *Anchorage Daily News*, 7 Apr. 1995, Weekend §, at 25.
- "*Methinks* that those making the fuss over our excellent dinner of calamari and lasagna would object if planning commission members were found to be members of the Rhododendron Society." Letter of Neil M. Ridgeley, "How Did We Become the 'Gang' of Seven?" *Baltimore Sun*, 23 Mar. 1997, at B4.

methodology, strictly speaking, means "the science or study of method." But it is now widely used as an equivalent of *method* or *methods*—e.g.:

- "Defenders of *scientific methodology* [read either *scientific methods* or *the scientific method*] were urged to counterattack against faith healing, astrology, religious fundamentalism and paranormal charlatanism." Malcolm W. Browne, "Scientists Deplore Flight from Reason," *N.Y. Times*, 6 June 1995, at C1.
- "Some Fulton commissioners, guided by the grumbling of employees who did not get raises, complained about the study's *methodology* [read *method* or *methods*] and results." Carlos Campos, "County Medical Examiner Plans to Retire," *Atlanta J.-Const.*, 5 June 1997, at E12.
- "This means that if this survey were repeated using the same questions and the same *methodology* [read *methods*], 19 times out of 20, the findings would not vary from the percentages shown here by more than plus or minus 4.9 percentage points." Jennifer Jacobs, "Many Endorse Roundup Plan," *Des Moines Register*, 2 Sept. 2015, at A1.

Prefer *method* or *methods* whenever you can.

LANGUAGE-CHANGE INDEX
methodology for *method*: Stage 5

metropolis. Pl. *metropolises*—preferably not **metropoles* /mi-**trop**-ə-leez/.
Current ratio: 3:1

metrosexual, n. & adj., is a PORTMANTEAU WORD made by combining *metropolitan* with *heterosexual*. The term refers to a probably heterosexual man who takes pains to present an upscale dapper appearance through fastidious clothing selections and impeccable grooming as evidenced, for example, by eyebrow-plucking, waxing of the trunk, and highlighting of the hair. A metrosexual is thought to have many of the habits and sensibilities of a sophisticated urban gay man. Coined in 1991, the term has risen steadily in use in AmE and BrE alike.

mettle. See **metal.**

mewl; mew; meow. *Mewl*, a verb only, means "to cry like a baby; whimper." *Mew* and *meow* each mean (1) n., "the sound a cat makes," or (2) vb., "to make this sound." But because *mew* also has other, unrelated meanings—and because *meow* is more popularly associated with cats—*meow* might be the better spelling for these senses. (For variants, see **meow.**)

Unless you want to emphasize the crying sound in a cat's voice, *mewl* should yield to *meow* in feline contexts. In these sentences, however, *mewl* seems right:

- "Suddenly we hear the whirring refrigerator in the kitchen, a cat *mewling* in the alley." Lisa Sack, "Don't Touch That Dial," *Village Voice*, 18 Oct. 1994, at 87.
- "Of course, it's hard not to notice a cat who starts *mewling* and ramming your bedroom door with her head at 6 every morning." Ray Recchi, "A Vacation Is Nice," *Sun-Sentinel* (Ft. Lauderdale), 1 July 1997, at E1.

Mexican-American. See **Hispanic.**

*miaow; *miaou; *miaul. See **meow** & **mewl.**

miasma. Pl. *miasmas*—preferably not **miasmata* (the Greek plural that predominated in English-language contexts till about 1900). See PLURALS (B).
Current ratio: 3:1

mic. See **mike.**

mice. See **mouse.**

mice type. This JARGON refers to the fine print in an advertisement, warranty, or other document, specifically copy that takes away what the big headline promises—e.g.:

- "Fine print cost Jeffrey Vigneault $500. Vigneault . . . shelled out $3,500 in December 2000 for a Power Mac computer, attracted by its prowess for video and promise of a $500 rebate from Apple. He sent in his paperwork three weeks later, and faster than you can say 'Steve Jobs,' it was rejected: He'd missed the deadline, a relative speck at the bottom of the form, buried amid 20 lines of what advertisers, regulators, and consumer advocates call '*mice type*.'" "Buyer Beware," *Consumer Reports*, Jan. 2002, at 15.
- "Whenever I get these solicitations, I immediately turn to the '*mice type*.' That's where you find the 'gotchas,' the information the companies don't want to tell you." Clark Howard, "Zero-Percent Cards Hide the 'Gotchas,'" *Atlanta J.-Const.*, 17 June 2006, at FE5.

Michigander; Michiganian; *Michiganite. By popular consensus, *Michigander* is the predominant form, appearing more than three times as often in print as *Michiganian* (the form once decreed by state statute). **Michiganite* is a rare variant used by the U.S. Government Printing Office. See DENIZEN LABELS.
Current ratio (in order of headwords): 20:6:1

microbrewery; craft brewery. *Microbrewery* is the predominant term for a small, usually local beer-maker, appearing in print about 60 times as often as the more upscale term *craft brewery*. Oddly, though, in 2015 the Associated Press preferred *craft brewery* in its influential *Stylebook*, explaining that it's more descriptive. Whether this stylistic endorsement will have much impact on actual usage remains to be seen.

mid; midst. See **amid.**

Middle West; Middle Western. See **Midwest.**

midnight. See **a.m.** (C).

Midwest; Midwestern; Middle West; Middle Western. The one-word forms, which have eclipsed the two-word forms in popularity, should now be considered standard. Of course, a difficulty with geographic terms such as these is where to draw their boundaries: in Wichita Falls, Texas, there's a school called "Midwestern University." This despite the ordinary understanding that the Midwest's most southwestern state is Kansas.

midwife, v.t.; *__midwive.__ The first is the standard form for the verb as well as the noun—e.g.:

- "The milling district of Minneapolis . . . *midwived* [read *midwifed*] some of its most prominent companies." Steve Brandt, "Reclaiming Mill City's River Roots," *Star Trib.* (Minneapolis), 18 Dec. 1996, at B1.
- "Welles *midwived* [read *midwifed*] the notion that you do not have to know much about the film process to make a good, even a great film." Neil Norma, "What If . . . ," *Evening Standard*, 14 Apr. 1997, at 23.

LANGUAGE-CHANGE INDEX
midwived for *midwifed*: Stage 1
Current ratio (*midwifed* vs. *midwived*): 5:1

midwifery (= the skill or work of a specially trained nurse who helps in childbirth) is predominantly pronounced /mid-**wif**-ə-ree/ or /mid-**wif**-ree/ in BrE, but /mid-**wif**-ə-ree/ or /mid-**wif**-ree/ in AmE. Yet as Elster notes, the most traditional 18th- and 19th-century pronunciations had an initial syllable stress: /**mid**-wif-ree/ or /**mid**-wif-ə-ree/. *BBBM* at 314.

mien (= demeanor, appearance, bearing) often carries connotations of formidableness <his imposing mien>. The word is pronounced /meen/.

might. See **may** & SUBJUNCTIVES.

*__might can.__ See DOUBLE MODALS.

*__might could.__ See DOUBLE MODALS.

*__might had better.__ See DOUBLE MODALS.

*__might ought.__ See DOUBLE MODALS.

*__might should have,__ a dialectal subjunctive, is much less common than the equally poor *__might could.__ But it occasionally appears in print—e.g.: "He *might should have* [read *might have* or *should have*] considered it, given the Tigers' meek at-bats during the first seven innings, despite finishing with 12 hits." Kirk Bohls, "Redman Strikes Down Auburn," *Austin Am.-Statesman*, 5 June 1994, at E8. See DOUBLE MODALS.

LANGUAGE-CHANGE INDEX
might should have for *might have* or *should have*:
Stage 1

*__might supposed to.__ See DOUBLE MODALS.

*__might've used to.__ See DOUBLE MODALS.

*__might would.__ See DOUBLE MODALS.

mighty. In AmE, this word can function as (1) an attributive noun <the meek and the mighty alike>; (2) an adjective <the mighty river overswelled its banks>; or (3) an adverbial intensifier <she felt mighty proud>. Sense 3 is largely confined to the South and Southwest.

mike; mic. As a shortened form of *microphone*, both *mike* and *mic* are used in AmE and BrE alike—but *mike* in this sense has traditionally predominated. The standard form in dictionaries such as *AHD*, *W11*, and *WNWCD* is *mike*. But whereas *mike* more immediately suggests the pronunciation, *mic* more immediately suggests the longer form. Still, *mic* looks as if it's pronounced "mick" and therefore probably leads to misreadings of its own. *Newsweek*, like many other publications, uses the standard form—e.g.:

- "White House officials see House Speaker-to-be Newt Gingrich as a formidable foe—not the least because of his discipline before an open *mike*." "On Message," *Newsweek*, 28 Nov. 1994, at 6.
- "And he needs to establish some distance between himself and the ever-present *mike*, as well as himself and the ever-present crowd." Meg Greenfield, "Dole's Problem," *Newsweek*, 3 June 1996, at 82.

The spelling *mic*, endorsed in 2010 by the Associated Press but not yet listed in most dictionaries, is also common—e.g.:

- "The sound of the *mic* [read *mike*] is warm, not the tinny, junky sound you'd expect from an inexpensive *mic* [read *mike*]." "Videotests," *Video Mag.*, Apr. 1994, at 22.
- "He's hosting the weekly open-*mic* [read -*mike*] shows, 8 p.m. Tuesday at the Grey Eagle Tavern and Music Hall." Tony Kiss, "Entertainment This Week," *Asheville Citizen-Times* (N.C.), 1 Jan. 1995, at L1.
- "Every night has a theme, from killer reggae on Sundays to open *mic* [read *mike*] on Thursdays." Kristine Eco & Melissa Bauer, "Java Talk," *Sun-Sentinel* (Ft. Lauderdale), 18 Sept. 1996, at 12.

This spelling (*mic*) seems to be a holdover from port labels on old stereos and tape players. Yet people had long since decided that the pronunciation spelling *mike*, which dates from the 1920s, was more sensible and convenient. After all, the verb uses *__miced__ and *__micing__ present serious problems; *miked* and *miking* have no such problems.

Current ratio (*open mike* vs. *open mic*): 1:1

mileage is the standard spelling in AmE and BrE alike. *__Milage__ is a variant.

Current ratio: 237:1

milieu (/meel-**yuu**/ or /mil-**yuu**/) is sometimes misspelled *__mileau__—e.g.: "Morton was a pianist, composer and band leader who emerged from the New Orleans jazz *mileau* [read *milieu*] to become one of the most famous musicians in America during the 1920s." Iris Fanger, "Actor's Right at Home in 'Jelly'

LANGUAGE-CHANGE INDEX (For the full key, see front matter pp. xxxi, l–li.)
Stage 1: Rejected. **Stage 2:** Widely shunned. **Stage 3:** Widespread but . . . **Stage 4:** Ubiquitous but . . . **Stage 5:** Fully accepted.
Invariably inferior forms marked by asterisk (*). • Ratios represent frequency of prevalent forms vs. variants in current books.

Role," *Boston Herald*, 23 Feb. 1996, at S12. The plural *milieus* is preferable to *milieux*. See PLURALS (B).

LANGUAGE-CHANGE INDEX
milieu misspelled **mileau*: Stage 1
Current ratio: 1,757:1

militate. See **mitigate.**

*milktoast. See **milquetoast.**

millenarian (= someone who believes in a thousand-year age of blessedness beginning with the second coming of Christ) is so spelled despite the *nn* in *millennium*. The difference in spelling relates to ETYMOLOGY: like the adjective *millenary*, the term *millenarian* derives from the Latin term *milleni* "a thousand each." An arcane synonym for *millenarian* is *chiliast* (/**kil**-ee-ast/), from the Greek term *chilioi* "a thousand." Hence a thousand-year period is known not only as a *millennium* (fr. L. *mille* "a thousand") but also as a *chiliad* (/**kil**-ee-ad/). These are words for only the heartiest vocabularians.

millennium [L. *mille* "thousand" + *annus* "year"] forms two plurals: *millennia* and *millenniums*. The predominant plural is *millennia* in AmE and BrE alike. See PLURALS (B). Although *millenniums* was the predominant plural in print sources from about 1850 to 1935, a major reversal of fortune occurred in the 1930s and 1940s: the Latinate plural *millennia* gained ascendancy in both AmE and BrE. Today it predominates in World English by a 19-to-1 ratio (17-to-1 in AmE).

A few major AmE publications continue to use *-iums*. E.g.:

- "For decades, La Selva, a lush, dripping jungle filled with towering trees and swinging vines, has served as the quintessential example of the pristine rain forest, untouched and unchanged for *millenniums*." Carol K. Yoon, "Rain Forests Seen as Shaped by Human Hand," *N.Y. Times*, 27 July 1993, at B5.
- "Abruptly, the two sexes—who had gone for *millenniums* without exchanging any more than the few grunts required for courtship—were expected to entertain each other with witty repartee over dinner." Barbara Ehrenreich, "Burt, Loni and Our Way of Life," *Time*, 20 Sept. 1993, at 92.
- "I reminded him that for *millenniums*, Europe has brimmed with white people who have hated and fought each other." Dawn M. Turner, "White Separatist Echoes Trump," *Chicago Trib.*, 1 Sept. 2015, at 3.

The spelling of the word shouldn't be any mystery: "*Millennium* has been spelled *millennium* for about a millennium. It links the Latin *mille* (thousand) and *annus* (year) . . . . When *annus* bonds with another word, the *a* becomes an *e*." Barry Newman, "Mil(l)en(n)ium," 13 *English Today* 17, 18 (1997). But the word is commonly misspelled in all sorts of ways, as Newman's article details.

The word is especially often deprived of one *-n-* and misspelled **millenium*—e.g.: "Does anybody really think a new TSU athletic director will be selected and in place before the next *millenium* [read *millennium*]?"

David Climer, "Molasses Moves Faster than TSU," *Tennessean*, 3 Sept. 1997, at C1. In fact, this misspelling has even found its way into proper names, such as the hotel that (until 11 Sept. 2001) was across the street from the World Trade Center in New York City, and also the car manufactured by Mazda (both spelled "Millenium"). Perhaps that should be called not a proper name but an improper name. See SPELLING (A).

LANGUAGE-CHANGE INDEX
millennium misspelled **millenium*: Stage 1
Current ratio: 39:1

milliard. See **billion.**

millionaire is so spelled—not, like *questionnaire*, with *-nn-*. But writers frequently get it wrong—e.g.: "Riordan, a 66-year-old *millionnaire* [read *millionaire*] who works for $1 a year, was elected the year after the 1992 riots, promising to 'turn the city around.'" Jonathan T. Lovitt, "Riordan Re-elected Mayor in L.A.," *USA Today*, 9 Apr. 1997, at A3. For another word susceptible to this problem—*doctrinaire*—see **doctrinal.** Cf. **questionnaire.**

LANGUAGE-CHANGE INDEX
millionaire misspelled **millionnaire*: Stage 1
Current ratio: 58:1

millipede has been the standard spelling since about 1875. **Millepede* is a variant.

Current ratio: 43:1

milquetoast (= a weak, timid person who is easily led) is the standard spelling. Even though the name derives from Harold T. Webster's early-20th-century comic strip *The Timid Soul*, in which the character is named Caspar Milquetoast, the word has been so fully assimilated that the *m-* shouldn't be capitalized. **Milktoast* is a variant spelling, not recommended.

Current ratio: 27:1

mimic, v.t., makes *mimicked* and *mimicking*. Cf. **panic** & **picnic.**

minable is the standard spelling in AmE, *mineable* in BrE. See MUTE E.

Current ratio (*mineable* vs. *minable*
in World English): 1.3:1

mineralogy (= the scientific study of minerals) is pronounced /min-ə-**ral**-ə-jee/—not /-**rahl**-ə-jee/. Cf. **genealogy.**

*minify. See **minimize (B).**

minima. See **minimum.**

minimal; minimum, adj. Both words are used adjectivally. *Minimal* is always an adjective, and *minimum* is used as an attributive adjective in phrases such as *minimum wage*. The words mostly overlap, but in one sense there is a distinction: *minimal* may or may not be absolute, but *minimum* always is. *Minimum* = the least possible, practical, legal, etc. <the minimum age to serve as President is 35>. *Minimal* = (1) the least; or

(2) few, little <win with minimal effort> <enact over minimal opposition>. Some authorities object to the use of *minimal* in a nonabsolute sense; presumably if they had their way a *minimalist* musical composition would consist of one note played one time on one instrument. Cf. **maximum.**

LANGUAGE-CHANGE INDEX
minimal in reference to a small amount (e.g., *a minimal amount of salt*): Stage 5

*minimalize. See **minimize (c).**

minimize. A. Meanings. In best usage, *minimize* means "to keep (something) to a minimum"—e.g.: "To *minimize* its exposure to the failings of any one technology, the agency has long relied on a 'layered' system of diverse detectors, from software for spotting anomalies in shipping manifests to X-ray scanners." David Stipp, "Detecting the Danger Within," *Fortune*, 17 Feb. 2003, at 104.

But the word is also used to mean "to misrepresent (something) as less significant than it really is; to belittle or degrade"—e.g.: "Mr. Kelly sought to *minimize* differences between Mr. Roh and the administration on North Korea and other issues, suggesting that those differences might have been unfairly magnified during the heat of the campaign." Howard W. French, "Seoul May Loosen Its Ties to U.S.," *N.Y. Times*, 20 Dec. 2002, at A1. Some authorities have criticized use of *minimize* in the latter sense. Among them is Theodore Bernstein, who was an assistant managing editor of *The New York Times*. But as this citation from the same newspaper suggests, the new sense is thoroughly ingrained in our usage today. It has become standard.

LANGUAGE-CHANGE INDEX
minimize in the sense "to play down" (as in *In the news conference, the officials minimized their role in the decision*): Stage 5

B. And *minify. Both H.W. Fowler and Eric Partridge considered **minify* a NEEDLESS VARIANT of *minimize* (*FMEU1* at 355–56; *U&A* at 186). But Theodore Bernstein liked the term as an alternative to *minimize* in the second sense discussed in (A): "The word is not used as much as it should be, but let us not *minify* it." Bernstein, *The Careful Writer* 278 (1965). Too late.

Current ratio: 1,945:1

C. And *minimalize. **Minimalize* is a NONWORD bearing an extra syllable—e.g.:

- "Paperwork has been *minimalized* [read *minimized*]." David Fettig, "Drive to Improve Cash Flow Yields Productivity Gains," *Fedgazette*, Apr. 1995, at 1.
- "TV director Brian Large *minimalizes* [read *minimizes*] the damage by relying on closeups." Jeff Bradley, "PBS's 'Cosi' Showcases Mezzo Cecilia Bartoli," *Denver Post*, 28 Dec. 1996, at E10.
- "Insufficient technology and bandwidth shuts down teacher/student computer access and *minimalizes* [read

minimizes] the education during excessive testing." Cindi Andrews, "Common Core Test Flaws Are Obvious," *Cincinnati Enquirer*, 8 Mar. 2015, at F4.

LANGUAGE-CHANGE INDEX
*minimalize for *minimize*: Stage 1
Current ratio (*minimized* vs. **minimalized*): 302:1

minimum, n. The predominant plural is *minima*, but few aside from scientists use it—e.g.: "The maxima of one fringe pattern will be superimposed on the *minima* of the other, and vice versa." Andreas Maurer, "Cardboard Double-Star Interferometer," *Sky & Telescope*, Mar. 1997, at 91. The form *minimums*, though not recorded in many dictionaries, has been on the rise since the 1940s and ought to be accepted as standard. It's now fairly common—e.g.:

- "New Jersey's requirements were already higher than the new *minimums*." Karen W. Arenson, "Standard for Equivalency Degree Is Raised," *N.Y. Times*, 9 Apr. 1997, at B10.
- "Often, governments set the *minimums* below subsistence levels to attract foreign investment, the critics said." William Branigan, "Clinton, Garment Makers Hail Accord on Sweatshops," *Wash. Post*, 15 Apr. 1997, at A10.
- "Although credit card companies might scream loudest for their money, they can wait—although paying the *minimums* on the cards is far preferable to not paying at all." Gregory Karp, "How to Survive Job Loss," *Chicago Trib.*, 31 Aug. 2015, Bus. §, at 1.

Cf. **maximum.** See PLURALS (B).

LANGUAGE-CHANGE INDEX
minimums as a plural: Stage 5
Current ratio (*minima* vs. *minimums*): 4:1

*miniscule. See **minuscule.**

minister, vb. See **administer.**

minor, adj. See ADJECTIVES (B).

*minor woman—an odd combination of EUPHEMISM, MISCUE, and OXYMORON—displaces a more natural wording such as *girl, female minor*, or, if the sex of the person is obvious, *minor*. E.g.: "His reference to a 'mature' woman means he does not favor the right of a *minor woman* [read *minor*] to choose to have an abortion without parental or judicial consent." Susan Yoachum, "Wilson Campaign Sticks to Familiar Topics," *S.F. Chron.*, 2 Nov. 1990, at A21.

minuscule. So spelled, not **miniscule*. The word derives from the word *minus*; it has nothing to do with the prefix *mini-*. But the misspelling has spread since about 1950—e.g.:

- "Mouth hanging open, Harry saw that the little square for June thirteenth seemed to have turned into a *miniscule* [read *minuscule*] television screen." J.K. Rowling, *Harry Potter and the Chamber of Secrets* 242 (Am. ed. 1999).
- "Even as some people questioned the practical effect of saving such a *miniscule* [read *minuscule*] portion of the

---

LANGUAGE-CHANGE INDEX (For the full key, see front matter pp. xxxi, l–li.)
Stage 1: Rejected. **Stage 2:** Widely shunned. **Stage 3:** Widespread but . . . **Stage 4:** Ubiquitous but . . . **Stage 5:** Fully accepted.
Invariably inferior forms marked by asterisk (*). • Ratios represent frequency of prevalent forms vs. variants in current books.

state budget, they were mostly willing to forgo cynicism." Kathleen Burge, "Forgoing of Salaries Gets Mixed Reviews," *Boston Globe*, 2 Jan. 2003, at B5.

- "Consider Iowa, with only a *miniscule* [read *minuscule*] African-American population." Abigail Thernstrom & Stephen Thernstrom, "Racial Gerrymandering Is Unnecessary," *Wall Street J.*, 11 Nov. 2008, at A20.

See SPELLING (A). Even so, the correct spelling has always vastly predominated in print sources.

The counterpart—a rarity—is *majuscule*. Today that term is used only in printing, to denote a capital letter.

In both AmE and BrE, *minuscule* is now pronounced /**min**-ə-skyool/—though before the 1960s the standard pronunciation stressed the second syllable: /mi-**nəs**-kyool/. Avoid /**min**-yə-skyool/.

LANGUAGE-CHANGE INDEX
minuscule misspelled **miniscule*: Stage 4
Current ratio: 2:1

minutia (= a trivial detail; a trifling matter) is the singular of the plural *minutiae*. Though much less common than the plural, *minutia* is hardly unknown. Unfortunately, it is almost always misused for the plural—e.g.:

- "But his first response when asked about vulnerabilities is to pull from his suit jacket pocket one of the approximately 4,000 small spiral notebooks he has filled with the *minutia* [read *minutiae*] of his days since 1974." George F. Will, "A Cassandra Candidacy?" *Wash. Post*, 12 Jan. 2003, at B7.
- "I won't bore you with the *minutia* [read *minutiae*], but I will say that as our 'to do' list has grown longer our tempers have grown shorter." Winda Bennett, "Leap of a Lifetime," *Seattle Post-Intelligencer*, 13 Jan. 2003, at C1.
- "In life, that translates into them being mired in personal *minutia* [read *minutiae*], focusing on their real or imagined minor physical faults." Bryan Rourke, "When You Can't See Face Value," *Providence J.-Bull.*, 21 Jan. 2003, at E1.

The phrases should be *lost in the minutiae, statistical minutiae*, and *day-to-day minutiae*—never *minutia*. But occasionally *minutia* is the right word—e.g.: "With audio commentary by Tsiaras . . . , no *minutia* is left unexamined (body donor Jernigan is a near perfect specimen, save one missing testicle)." Ty Burr & Kipp Cheng, "The Week," *Entertainment Weekly*, 21 Mar. 1997, at 78.

The plural is often mispronounced as if it were the singular word (/mi-**n[y]oo**-shee-ə/ or, less good, /mi-**n[y]oo**-shə/). But the traditional and most proper pronunciation of *minutiae* is /mi-**n[y]oo**-shee-ee/.

LANGUAGE-CHANGE INDEX
minutia for the plural *minutiae*: Stage 2
Current ratio (*lost in the minutiae* vs.
*lost in the minutia): 5:1

Mirandize, vb. Since the 1970s, *Mirandize* (= to read an arrestee his rights under *Miranda v. Arizona*, 384 U.S. 436 [1966]) has become common as police-officer SLANG in the United States. It's therefore becoming common generally—e.g.: "They are read their rights ('*mirandized*') and interrogated." Robin T. Lakoff, *Talking Power: The Politics of Language in Our Lives* 87

(1990). The word has even started taking on extended senses—e.g.: "So since I would be popping antibiotics from hours before the operation until a week or more after, everyone *Mirandized* me about the, oh by the way, if you happen to, be sure to, etc." Samantha Bennett, "Toothless Wisdom," *Pitt. Post-Gaz.*, 29 July 1997, at C2.

Some believe this NEOLOGISM to be a blemish in place of another phrasing, such as *to read* (an arrestee) *his Miranda rights*. Only 23% of the usage panelists for the *Harper Dictionary of Contemporary Usage* (2d ed. 1985) considered the word "a useful addition to the language." The other 77% disapproved. (See -IZE.) Given its precipitate rise in popularity since about 1985, the word seems destined to lose its objectionableness as long as *Miranda* remains good law.

mirror is pronounced /**mir**-ər/ or /**meer**-ər/—not /**mir**-ə/ or, worse, /**meer**/. See PRONUNCIATION (B), (C).

misalliance. See **mesalliance.**

misappropriate. See **appropriate** (A).

misbelief. See **disbelief.**

miscellaneous must be followed by a plural COUNT NOUN; it does not work with an abstract mass noun. Though one might refer to *miscellaneous languages* (and thereby include Chinese, English, French, Thai, and Vietnamese), it makes no sense to write *miscellaneous contract language*, as in Mark M. Grossman, *The Question of Arbitrability* 57 (1984) (section title). Exceptions are SET PHRASES such as *miscellaneous shower* and *miscellaneous income*.

mischievous /**mis**-chə-vəs/ is so spelled. **Mischievious* is an impishly common misspelling and mispronunciation /mis-**chee**-vee-əs/—e.g.:

- "I could not imagine them driving, getting mouthy, moody or *mischievious* [read *mischievous*], let alone going to drinking parties at the homes of friends whose parents were out of town." Eleanor Mallet, "The Tranquility of School Age," *Plain Dealer* (Cleveland), 25 Feb. 1995, at E1.
- "Mayan Indians considered this place hell's fun house, inhabited by *mischievious* [read *mischievous*] gods who had to be soothed with heaping food bowls and the occasional human sacrifice." Judith Wynn, "Lodge Guests Settle In Among Tropical Wildlife," *Boston Herald*, 26 Dec. 2002, at 38.

See PRONUNCIATION (B). Cf. **grievous.**

LANGUAGE-CHANGE INDEX
mischievous misspelled or mispronounced
*mischievious: Stage 2
Current ratio: 383:1

MISCUES. A miscue is an inadvertent misdirection that causes the reader to proceed momentarily with an incorrect assumption about how—in mechanics or in sense—a sentence or passage will end. The misdirection is not serious enough to cause a true ambiguity because, on reflection, the reader can figure out the meaning. Thus:

The court decided the question did not need to be addressed.

The mere omission of *that* after the verb *decided* induces the reader to believe that *the question* is the direct object—that is, to believe (if only for an immeasurably short moment) that the court decided the question. In fact, of course, the court decided not to decide the question. See (F).

Miscues are of innumerable varieties; the only consistent cure is for the editor or self-editor to develop a keen empathy for the reader. Part of what the editor or self-editor must do, then, is to approach the text as a stranger might. Further, though, a good edit must involve the kind of skeptical reading in which one imagines how one reader in ten might misread the sentence.

Following are discussions of six of the most common causes of miscues.

A. Unintended Word Association. Sometimes two words in a passage seem to go together—because they frequently *do* go together—but in the particular instance aren't intended to. This commonly occurs in two ways.

First, a word appearing late in a passage sometimes seems to echo an earlier word to which it really has no relation. For example, in the final clause of the following passage, *barred* suggests some relation to *disbarred* in the opening sentence: "In 1948 he was found guilty of unprofessional conduct and *disbarred* for three years by a federal judge. The decision was appealed and reversed three years later. In 1958 Fisher, a thin-faced, thinning-haired socialite, was censured by the Illinois Supreme Court for actions against clients— but the Chicago Bar Association had asked that he be *barred* from practice for five years." Murray T. Bloom, *The Trouble with Lawyers* 158 (1970).

Second, readers can be misled into WORD-SWAPPING. For example, the phrase *visual imagery* suggests picturesqueness (as opposed to picaresque) in the following sentence: "Given the rich *visual imagery* of Cervantes's *picaresque* romance, this is certainly a production that can appeal to both deaf and hearing audiences." Graham Hassell, "New Tilt at Old Tale with Signs of Enchantment," *Evening Standard*, 12 Oct. 1995, at 46. (To eliminate the miscue, replace *picaresque* with some other word such as *comic* or *panoramic*. See **picaresque**.) Similarly, the phrase *army regimen* suggests *regiment* (= a military unit): "She shows Rabin, full of grandfatherly pride at the family's third generation of warriors for Israel, his prime ministerial curiosity about how the *army regimen* had changed since his day." Judith Dunford, "Good-Bye, Grandpa," *Chicago Sun-Times*, 5 May 1996, at 14. Cf. **calvary.**

In the following examples, some interesting things occur on first reading. Clothes are laid down, flattery induces a woman to have sex, fans are kept from going, and somebody engages in murderous attacks:

- "The Tudor justices enforced laws against Roman Catholic recusants, regulations *laying down the clothes* people might wear and the price they should pay for them." Alan Harding, *A Social History of English Law* 72 (1966). (Did 16th-century judges mandate nudity for Roman Catholics?)
- "Flattery induced a woman to submit to intercourse by pretending to perform a surgical operation. He was convicted of rape." Glanville Williams, *Textbook of Criminal Law* 514 (1978). (A man named Flattery committed a crime, but his name suggests the wile he might have used in committing it. The miscue might be removed by referring to *Mr. Flattery* instead of *Flattery*.)
- "Texas and Dallas officials said they would be disappointed to lose the game and said they were taking steps in an attempt to *keep* fans *from* both schools *going* to Dallas." Arnold Hamilton, "Moving of Game Is Urged," *Dallas Morning News*, 12 Aug. 1993, at A1. (*Keep* means "retain" in that sentence, but the proximity of *from* makes it read as if it meant "prevent.")
- "Small-minded, episodic *murder attacks* the basis of our taken-for-granted values so fundamentally that it generates anxiety." David Canter, "Anxious, Appalled . . . but Still Drawn to Horror," *Sunday Times* (London), 13 Mar. 1994, at 4–6. (It looks on first reading as if the noun phrase *murder attacks* is the subject, but *murder* is the subject and *attacks* is the verb.)

B. Misplaced Modifiers. When modifying words are separated from the words they modify, readers have a hard time processing the information. Indeed, they are likely to attach the modifying language first to a nearby word or phrase—e.g.:

- "The 39-year-old San Francisco artist has beaten the odds against him by living—no, thriving—with the virus that causes AIDS for 14 years." Christine Gorman, "Are Some People Immune to AIDS?" *Time*, 22 Mar. 1993, at 49. (Does the virus cause AIDS for 14 years?)
- "Both died in an apartment Dr. Kevorkian was leasing after inhaling carbon monoxide." "Kevorkian Victory: 3d Judge Says Suicide Law Is Unconstitutional," *N.Y. Times*, 28 Jan. 1994, at A9. (This word order has Dr. Kevorkian inhaling carbon monoxide and then leasing an apartment.)
- "On November 6, 1908, most historians agree that either a company of Bolivian cavalry, or four local police officers from el pueblo de la San Vicente, . . . shot Butch [Cassidy] and the [Sundance] Kid to death when they were discovered to be in possession of a stolen mule." J. Lee Butts, *Texas Bad Girls* 112 (2001). (This seems to say that the historians reached an agreement on November 6, 1908, not that they agree about the events of that date. A possible rewrite: *Most historians agree that on November 6, 1908 . . . .*)

C. Clear Referents. When a word such as a pronoun points back to an antecedent or some other referent, the true referent should generally be the closest appropriate word—e.g.:

- "Until recently, the inns showed themselves particularly ill-equipped to handle the overseas students, including many Africans and such future statesmen as Mr. Nehru, who by 1960 made up two thirds of all those called to the

English bar." Alan Harding, *A Social History of English Law* 389 (1966). (This sentence involves a REMOTE RELATIVE that makes Mr. Nehru sound like a very big man indeed.)

- "There are various reasons that juries hang, some better than others." Robin T. Lakoff, *Talking Power: The Politics of Language in Our Lives* 126 (1990). (The writer means *some reasons*, not *some juries*, but some readers will not see this immediately.)
- "They [judicial appointments] are often given to those with political connections, which may handicap women." "A Woman's Place Is in the Law," *Globe & Mail* (Toronto), 24 Aug. 1993, at A14. (Political connections may handicap women? No: The fact that judicial appointments are often given to those with political connections may handicap women. The *which* has a vague referent in the quoted sentence.)

Proximity isn't the only signal of what referent a word is pointing to, though. Number and gender are often clear signals <my briefcase and my friends were right at the door when I left, but I still forgot to bring it with me>. Case may also matter, but it can't sort out a hopeless sentence: in "the boys were rude to the girls because they didn't like them," the fact that *boys* and *they* are nominative while *girls* and *them* are objective does not make the meaning of the sentence clear. The syntactic strength of the referent also bears on clarity. Subjects and objects of main verbs make the strongest referents, while objects of prepositions, even if closer to the referring word, are usually weaker.

The only way to avoid these ambiguities is to read copy carefully and repeatedly. Reading aloud is also helpful.

D. Failure to Hyphenate Phrasal Adjectives. Forgetting to put hyphens in PHRASAL ADJECTIVES frequently leads to miscues. For example, does the phrase *popular music critic* refer to a critic in popular music or to a sociable music critic? If it's a critic of popular music, the phrase should be *popular-music critic*. See PUNCTUATION (J).

E. Misleading Phraseology. *Emigrate from* and *immigrate to* are the idioms, and sometimes the blunder **emigrate into* or **immigrate from* appears. Here, there is no blunder, but the phrase beginning with *emigrate* might at first appear to be one: "International agreements signed by virtually every state have recognized the right to emigrate as a fundamental right on which limitations can be imposed only under exceptional circumstances. These agreements have woven the right to *emigrate into* the fabric of international law." Jeffrey Barist et al., "Who May Leave: A Review of Soviet Practice," 15 *Hofstra L. Rev.* 381, 394 (1987). See **immigrate.**

Some writers omit a needed object, leaving readers to deduce an incorrect one. For example, according to the following sentence, with whom did Nicole Simpson talk? "Nicole Simpson talked about her troubles with O.J. only 'when she was having a really bad day.'" Christine Spolar & Lloyd Grove, "Nicole and O.J.: Scenes from a Volatile Relationship," *Wash. Post*, 24 June 1994, at A1, A23. The writer means to

say, "Nicole Simpson talked *to friends* about her troubles with O.J.," but as written the sentence looks as if it might be, "Nicole Simpson talked *with O.J.* about her troubles." The original might have been improved merely by inserting *to friends* after *talked*.

Sometimes, as in the following example, the confusing syntax results from a preposition—e.g.:

- "Here there is no problem in using blanks for which of several payment plans the borrower wants to use." Barbara Child, *Drafting Legal Documents* 138 (2d ed. 1992). (*For* appears to have a single-word object [*which*], as opposed to a phrasal object [*which of several payment plans*].)
- "An FBI agent, Douglas Deedrick, said hairs resembling Simpson's were present at the crime scene—on the bloodied shirt of victim Ronald Goldman and on a knit cap found by Goldman's feet." Larry Reibstein, "The Simpson Strategy," *Newsweek*, 10 July 1995, at 47. (The phrase *found by* suggests we're about to learn who [*Goldman's feet?*] found the knit cap. To prevent the miscue, the writer should have said *near* or *beside* instead of *by*.)

Yet again, the first word in an adverbial phrase (*up the coast of New England*) sometimes seems to be part of a verb (*blew up*): "The storm also blew up the coast of New England." John J. Goldman, "Northeast Slammed by Storm; 7 Killed," *Austin Am.-Statesman*, 12 Dec. 1992, at A1.

F. Ill-Advisedly Deleted *that*. The widespread but largely unfounded prejudice against *that* leads many writers to omit it when it is necessary—e.g.:

- "Following comments from the public, the council decided the issue needed further study by a committee of citizens and private haulers." Ann Marie Halal, "San Diego Addresses Crusade," *Waste News*, 23 Dec. 1996, at 14. (Insert *that* after *decided*.)
- "Commissioner Karen Sonleitner pointed out any policy changes approved after Sept. 1 could be subject to the state's Property Rights Act." Tara Trower, "Travis Debates Regulations for Flood Plain," *Austin Am.-Statesman*, 30 July 1997, at B2. (Insert *that* after *pointed out*.)
- "Skinner said he believes many prisoners contract AIDS behind bars." Tim Novak, "Prisons Hit by Soaring AIDS Costs," *Chicago Sun-Times*, 3 Nov. 1997, at 1. (Insert *that* after *believes*.)

See **that (B).**

*misdoubt, vb., is an archaic variant—and now a NEEDLESS VARIANT—of the verb *doubt. *Misdoubt* can also mean "to fear, suspect," but this sense too should be avoided because it can lead to some awkward double negatives—e.g.: "I misdoubt the ladies won't like it" (*SOED*). See NEGATIVES (A). The word has steadily waned since 1900.

misfeasance. See **malfeasance.**

mishap should refer to a minor accident, not one in which people are killed. Yet this error is common—e.g.:

- "*U.S. News & World Report* magazine notes this week that 1,144 people died in train *mishaps* [read *accidents*] last year." Rod Watson, "Private Sector vs. Government in Valujet Crash," *Buffalo News*, 23 May 1996, at B3.
- "On a single Sunday afternoon last August, three people died as a result of Jet Ski *mishaps* [read *accidents*] in

Southampton, N.Y." Alexandra Alger, "Here They Come Again," *Forbes*, 3 June 1996, at 182.

- "Miscellaneous *mishaps* [read *incidents*]—such as motorcycle accidents, falls and drownings—account for a handful of deaths each year." Bob von Sternberg, "Every Other Day, an American Cop Dies in the Line of Duty," *Star Trib.* (Minneapolis), 4 Aug. 2002, at A1.

When government agencies use the word for tragic accidents, the reader suspects a deliberate attempt to soften the edges—e.g.:

- "Major accidents are known in the military as Class A *mishaps* if they cause death, permanent injury or at least $1 million in losses." Alan C. Miller & Kevin Sack, "Far from Battlefield, Marines Lose One-Third of Harrier Fleet," *L.A. Times*, 15 Dec. 2002, News §, at 1.
- "NASA also has its own *Mishap* Investigation Team." Carl Hulse, "Critics Seek a Broader Shuttle Panel," *N.Y. Times*, 5 Feb. 2003, at A23.

LANGUAGE-CHANGE INDEX
mishap misused in reference to a major accident:
Stage 1

misinformation. See **disinformation.**

mislead > misled > misled. As with the verb *lead*, the past forms of *mislead* are sometimes mistakenly rendered—e.g.:

- "Don't be *mislead* [read *misled*] by the inflated score." Jason Cohn, "Joseph Weathers Attack Until Toronto Storms to 7–4 Victory," *Toronto Star*, 14 Dec. 2000, Sports §, at 1.
- "It is important that the voting public not be *mislead* [read *misled*]." Rosalie Pedalino Porter, "Debate on Bilingual Education Should Correct Misconceptions," *Telegram & Gaz.* (Worcester, Mass.), 2 Sept. 2001, at C2.
- "Hay said many small business customers have complained that they were *mislead* [read *misled*] by telemarketers for NOS." "Hay Plans to Contest Company's Actions," *Las Vegas Rev.-J.*, 11 July 2002, at D2.

Cf. **lead.**

LANGUAGE-CHANGE INDEX
mislead misused for the past-tense *misled*: Stage 1
Current ratio (*were misled by* vs.
*were mislead by): 49:1

misnomer. Speakers and writers frequently misuse this word, meaning "an inappropriate name," to mean "a popular misconception"—e.g.: " 'The last I remember, only 7 percent of Division I programs operate in the black. The common *misnomer* [read *misunderstanding*] is that people see this as a multi-million-dollar business.' " "College Arena a Marketplace," *Times Union* (Albany), 24 Dec. 2000, at C1 (quoting Syracuse assistant athletic director Michael Veley). Oddly enough, this mistake is itself a kind of misnomer based on a misconception.

Although the error is less common in edited text, it does surface—e.g.:

- "The idea is to break down the stigmas, myths and *misnomers* [read *misunderstanding*] surrounding suicide by showing teens and others that death is never a solution to a problem." Eric Bradley, "Group Looks to Prevent Teen Suicide," *Oshkosh Northwestern*, 13 Sept. 2002, at A1.
- "The old theory that was heard at UW for years is that the school needs a big-name coach. That's really a *misnomer* [read *misconception*] because UW usually has succeeded in developing its own big-name coach." Larry Birleffi, "Choosing Coach Requires Work," *Wyo. Trib.-Eagle* (Cheyenne), 21 Nov. 2002, at B2.

Typically, when the term is used correctly it will accompany a misleading word or title, often in quotation marks—e.g.: "Old countries are sometimes world-weary and cynical, urging a 'realism' that is sometimes a *misnomer* for the moral corruption they know so very well." Richard Cohen, "Nobel Winners and Losers," *Wash. Post*, 15 Oct. 2002, at A19.

LANGUAGE-CHANGE INDEX
misnomer misused for *misconception* or
misunderstanding: Stage 1

MISPLACED MODIFIERS. See DANGLERS, ILLOGIC (C) & MISCUES (B).

misquote. See **quote.**

misremember means "to remember incorrectly," not "to forget." E.g.: "In the first group, children affirmed about 15 percent of the false allegations of wrongdoing—bad enough for those who think that children never lie, *misremember* or make things up." Carol Tavris, "Day-Care Witch Hunt Tests Massachusetts Justice," *Tulsa Trib. & Tulsa World*, 24 Apr. 1997, at A15. As the following quotation suggests, *misremember* is often a EUPHEMISM for *lie*—e.g.: "Despite the fact many of our respondents had a tendency to, let us say, *misremember*, other poll questions suggest some are more likely to have voted than others." John Ibbitson, "Election Polls Bring Out the 'Best' in Some People," *Ottawa Citizen*, 1 Oct. 1994, at B2.

missing, to go. See **go missing.**

*missis. See **missus.**

*Missouran. See **Missourian.**

Missouri. The pronunciation of this state name has provoked much strife. Although most Americans say /mi-**zuur**-ee/, many Missourians say /mi-**zuur**-ə/. In and around St. Louis, many say /ee/, but /ə/ has traditionally predominated in other parts of the state. Both pronunciations are standard. Yet it is a telling point that politicians running for statewide office are careful to say /ə/—to seem folksy and avoid sounding like an auslander. (Cf. **Nevada.**) But interestingly, the final-syllable /ə/ pronunciation seems to be for

LANGUAGE-CHANGE INDEX (For the full key, see front matter pp. xxxi, l–li.)
Stage 1: Rejected. **Stage 2:** Widely shunned. **Stage 3:** Widespread but . . . **Stage 4:** Ubiquitous but . . . **Stage 5:** Fully accepted.
Invariably inferior forms marked by asterisk (*). • Ratios represent frequency of prevalent forms vs. variants in current books.

insiders only—all non-Missourians being expected to say /ee/.

The information in the preceding paragraph is the result of my frequent travel during two decades through different parts of the state, in the course of which I have routinely quizzed locals and polled lawyer-audiences in seminars that I've taught—including all 180+ lawyers in the state attorney general's office and all the state appellate judges. The results, strongly favoring /mi-**zuur**-ə/ for native Missourians outside St. Louis, are essentially the same as those in Allen Walker Read's study, "The Pronunciation of the Word 'Missouri,'" 8 *Am. Speech* 22–36 (Winter 1933). For a very different view, insisting that /mi-**zuur**-ee/ is preferred throughout the state, see Charles Harrington Elster, *BBBM* at 319–22.

An early commentator, the noted linguist E.H. Sturtevant, attributed the final-syllable /-ə/ to HYPERCORRECTION. It's a surprising but quite plausible argument: "In the dialect of Missouri and the neighboring states, final *a* in such words as 'America,' 'Arizona,' 'Nevada,' becomes *y*—'Americy,' 'Arizony,' 'Nevady.' All educated people in that region carefully correct this vulgarism out of their speech; and many of them carry the correction too far and say 'Missoura,' 'praira,' etc." E.H. Sturtevant, *Linguistic Change* 79 (1917).

Missourian; *Missouran. The newspaper in Columbia, Missouri, is called *The Missourian*. And interestingly, even though most people in Columbia pronounce the name of their state /mi-**zuur**-ə/, they pronounce the name of their newspaper /mi-**zuur**-ee-ən/. In fact, Missourian informants say that the four-syllable pronunciation is universal within the state. See DENIZEN LABELS.

Current ratio: 3,062:1

misspelling, believe it or not, is often misspelled *mispelling. See SPELLING (A).

Current ratio: 159:1

missus (from *Mrs.*) has been the standard spelling since the 17th century. *Missis is a variant.

Current ratio: 4:1

mistake > mistook > mistaken. Mercifully, the correct forms are seldom mistaken, though indeed they sometimes are—e.g.: "Finally, Fly almost *mistaked* [read *mistook*] El Sid Fernandez for a bat when he showed up in Sarasota at 225, down 40 from fightin' weight." "Caught on the Fly," *Phoenix Gaz.*, 15 Apr. 1995, at D2. See IRREGULAR VERBS.

LANGUAGE-CHANGE INDEX
*mistaked for *mistook*: Stage 1
Current ratio (*mistook* vs. *mistaked): 3,496:1

mistreat; maltreat. Most usage critics have differentiated between these terms. "To *mistreat*," say the Evanses, "is to treat badly or wrongly. The word suggests a deviation from some accepted norm of treatment and a deviation always towards the bad. To *maltreat*, to abuse, to handle roughly or cruelly, is to

mistreat in a special way. The words are often used interchangeably (Horwill believes that Americans prefer *mistreat* and English *maltreat*), but *maltreat* is usually restricted to the rougher forms of mistreating" (*DCAU* at 302). From 1700 to about 1960, *maltreat* was the more common term in all varieties of English. But *mistreat* overtook it in frequency about 1960.

mistrustful. See **distrustful.**

misusage (= [1] maltreatment; or [2] the incorrect use of language) is increasingly misused for *misuse*, n. (= unauthorized use; misapplication)—e.g.: "It monitors and analyzes companies' telecommunications networks to measure call traffic and to find *misusage* [read *misuse*] of the systems." Maria Carlino, "AAC de Latinoamerica Inc.," *J. of Commerce*, 13 Oct. 1995, at A5. Cf. **usage.**

LANGUAGE-CHANGE INDEX
misusage misused for *misuse*: Stage 2

miter; mitre. The first is the AmE spelling; the second is BrE. See -ER (B).

mitigable. So formed—not *mitigatable. See -ATABLE.
Current ratio: 14:1

mitigate; militate. *Mitigate* = to make less severe or intense <the new drug mitigates the patient's discomfort>. *Militate* = to exert a strong influence <Harry's conflicting schedule militates against an October 17 meeting>.

*Mitigate against for *militate against* is an error that emerged about 1900 and spread precipitately from 1950. Edmund Wilson called it "William Faulkner's favorite error." *The Bit Between My Teeth* 570 (1965). Faulkner's failings aside, the error is surprisingly common—e.g.:

- "Together we will surely arrive at the means to end the many obstacles that appear to *mitigate* [read *militate*] against our success." Chelsea Quinn Yarbro, *Darker Jewels* 295 (1993).
- "In general, the speed of mass communication *mitigates* [read *militates*] against exploring an issue carefully as people's attention span decreases in correlation with shorter, rapid-fire presentation." Barry R. McCaffrey, "Perspective on Illegal Drugs," *L.A. Times*, 2 Jan. 1997, at B7.
- "It is the one thing that most *mitigates* [read *militates*] against the Patriots winning their last two games." Ron Borges, "Two-Game Series for Patriots," *Boston Globe*, 18 Dec. 2002, at E1.

Today, *mitigate* is almost invariably transitive, a synonym of *alleviate*. (The *OED* recognizes an intransitive sense, meaning "to grow milder or less severe," but labels it rare. Even that label is generous.) Using it with *against* is nonstandard—e.g.: "The show's excellent 57-page guide *mitigates against* [read *mitigates*] its density, as does the curators' healthy respect for the impact of real things." Roberta Smith, "Icy Genius with a Taste for Order," *N.Y. Times*, 29 Nov. 2002, at E37.

Militate against—as well as its antonym *militate in favor of* or *militate for*—is perfectly acceptable. E.g.:

- "The campaign he ran *militates against* the historic presidency he would like to lead." Jonathan Rauch, "Self-Inflicted Budget Woes," *U.S. News & World Rep.*, 18 Nov. 1996, at 94.
- "Two things *militate in favor of* a deal." "Turkish Tangle," *Fin. Times*, 27 Feb. 1996, at 15.

But **militate toward* is unidiomatic.

LANGUAGE-CHANGE INDEX
*mitigate against for *militate against*: Stage 3
Current ratio (*militate against* vs.
*mitigate against): 3:1

mitre. See **miter.**

mnemonic; pneumonic. *Mnemonic* (= [1] of, relating to, or involving memory; or [2] esp., designed to assist memorization) is the more common word, often in the phrase *mnemonic device* or an equivalent—e.g.: "Heck, use the book to create a lesson and ask kids to come up with rhymes or alliterative phrases for all their vocabulary words. Poetry and song are the best *mnemonic* tools." David Ross, "Some Odds and Ends, Mostly Ends," *Press-Telegram* (Long Beach), 25 Nov. 2000, Lifestyle §, at 4. The word derives from the Greek term *mnemon* (= memory). As more than one wit has pointed out, the word's spelling should be easier to memorize.

Pneumonic (= [1] of, relating to, or involving pneumonia; or [2] of, relating to, or involving the lungs)—e.g.:

- Sense 1: "Their excited breaths were agitated [by] their bronchitic and *pneumonic* coughs." Nelsy Rodriguez, "St. Nick Tours JFK Hospital," *Desert Sun* (Palm Springs), 20 Dec. 2006, at B1.
- Sense 2: "The plot unfolds like this: A terrorist releases an airborne or 'weaponized' form of *pneumonic* plague in the Metrodome during a game with 43,000 in attendance." Maura Lerner, "Drill Covers 'What-Ifs' of Health Disaster," *Star Trib.* (Minneapolis), 17 May 2007, at B3.

The word derives from the Greek term *pneumon* (= lung).

The two words are similarly pronounced, with only the vowel sound in the first syllable differing. *Mnemonic* is pronounced /ni-**mahn**-ik/ (not /mi-**nahn**-ik/); *pneumonic* is pronounced /noo-**mahn**-ik/.

Perhaps because the pronunciations are so close, *pneumonic* occasionally displaces *mnemonic*—e.g.:

- "'When I grew up in Minneapolis, the weather ball was quite a deal,' [Ethan P.] Seltzer says. 'There was this little jingle that went with it and that you could use like a *pneumonic* [read *mnemonic*] device to figure out what the weather ball was telling you.'" Spencer Heinz, "Planet Portland: A Simple Pleasure Blinks On in Tricolor," *Oregonian* (Portland), 14 Dec. 2006, Metro §, at 7.
- "Eric Jensen, a San Diego-based advocate whose work has been adopted across the country, thinks of it as 'ESP'—*pneumonic* [read *mnemonic*] devices are key in brain-based teaching—or 'engagement of strategies that are based on principles of brain research.'" Erika Hobbs,

"How Was School Engaging?" *Orlando Sentinel*, 7 Jan. 2007, at B1.
- "Use *pneumonics* [read *mnemonics*]: Tuesday is trash day; Wednesday is watering day." Amara Willey, "Fresh Start," *Courier News* (Bridgewater, N.J.), 1 Apr. 2007, Features §, at 2.

An even stranger error is confusing *pneumonic* and *pneumatic* (= of, relating to, or involving gas, esp. air pressure)—e.g.: "They purchased casters with eight large *pneumonic* [read *pneumatic*] tires. Meyer said the air-filled tires did the trick and made Santa's ride better." Karla Breister, "Club Lends Santa a Hand," *Reporter* (Fond du Lac, Wis.), 31 Dec. 2006, at C3.

LANGUAGE-CHANGE INDEX
1. *pneumonic* misused for *mnemonic*: Stage 1
Current ratio (*mnemonic device* vs.
*pneumonic device): 125:1
2. *pneumonic* misused for *pneumatic*: Stage 1

M.O. See **modus operandi.**

mobile, adj. & n.; **Mobile.** As an adjective, *mobile* means "movable" and is pronounced /**moh**-bəl/ in AmE—BrE and Canadian speakers preferring /**moh**-bɪl/. As a noun referring to a sculpture or decoration consisting of small objects tied to wires or strings and hung up so that the objects can be set into motion by air currents, *mobile* is pronounced /**moh**-beel/ in AmE but /**moh**-bɪl/ in BrE (as with the adjective). The proper noun denoting the city in Alabama (*Mobile*) is pronounced /moh-**beel**/ (as locals say it)—not /**moh**-beel/.

moccasin. So spelled. See SPELLING (A).

mode; module. There must be something in the root: these words, like *modality*, are inflated VOGUE WORDS.

In proper usage, *mode* means "manner," and *module* means "a unit of size." President George H.W. Bush often entered the "*mode* mode," as when he told a crowd in Los Angeles: "I am not here in the *mode* of politics, I am not here in the *mode* of partisanship, I am not here in the *mode* of blame. I am here to learn from the community." Quoted in Robert B. Gunnison & Susan Yoachum, "Bush Visits Riot Zone," *S.F. Chron.*, 8 May 1992, at A1. Such talk proved fruitful for Russell Baker's lively column in *The New York Times*:

> President Bush says he is about to enter "campaign mode." Does this mean America will then have president *á la mode*? Absolutely not. Do you think the President is a slice of pie?
>
> This is the same answer I had from Mr. Bush's mode handler .... The mode Mr. Bush will enter is not a dessert, but a new technological product of the space program. Space-news fans will have noticed that multitudes of modes pour out of NASA press releases.
>
> There is launch mode, re-entry mode, recapture-the-lost-satellite mode, two-hour-snooze mode, expense-account-dinner mode and dozens more, including

LANGUAGE-CHANGE INDEX (For the full key, see front matter pp. xxxi, l–li.)
Stage 1: Rejected. **Stage 2:** Widely shunned. **Stage 3:** Widespread but . . . **Stage 4:** Ubiquitous but . . . **Stage 5:** Fully accepted.
Invariably inferior forms marked by asterisk (*). • Ratios represent frequency of prevalent forms vs. variants in current books.

Washington-by-night mode. A typical Washington-by-night mode is entered when two variously sexed Government employees finish a two-bottle dinner and one says, "Let's not go back to the Pentagon, let's go to your place."

The mode has recently been joined by the module, which is hard to distinguish from the old-fashioned model except that the "e" is misplaced and a "u" is thrown in for reasons NASA would rather not talk about. It seems pretty obvious though that NASA had an embarrassing excess of "u's" stockpiled and wanted to get rid of some before the press began fuming about "u"-gate.

Why doesn't Mr. Bush enter one of the new-fangled modules? Too risky. Since modules are much newer than modes, the Secret Service refuses to let Mr. Bush enter one until the manufacturers use stronger materials for holding the things together.

> Russell Baker, "In the Mode Mood," *N.Y. Times,* 15 Aug. 1992, at 15.

model, vb., makes *modeled* and *modeling* in AmE, *modelled* and *modelling* in BrE. See SPELLING (B).

*mode of operandi. See **modus operandi.**

modern-day, a phrase that spread dramatically after 1950, is invariably inferior to *modern*—e.g.:

- "[In] Walt Disney's syndicated kid show 'Gargoyles,' . . . animated 1,000-year-old stone creatures are transplanted to *modern-day* [read *modern*] Manhattan to ward off evildoers." Cathy Hainer, "Good-Guy Gargoyles Ringing Up Big Sales," *USA Today,* 17 Mar. 1995, at D1.
- "These *modern-day* [read *modern*] pioneers are the home-school parents." Joe Rohner, "Free-Market Principles Should Apply to Education as Well," *Idaho Statesman,* 19 Apr. 1995, at A9.

modernity (= the quality of being modern) is preferably pronounced /mə-**dər**-ni-tee/ or /mah-**dər**-ni-tee/—but not /**dair**/ in the second syllable.

modernly (= in modern times), formerly common as a SENTENCE ADVERB, is accurately described by the *OED* as being "now rare." Today (not to say modernly), it can usually be replaced by *today* or *now*—e.g.: "Brick sidewalks line the legendary Great Stage Road, *modernly* [read *now*] known as Main Street." Joanne Anderson, "Jonesborough, Tenn., Is the Town," *Roanoke Times,* 25 Sept. 1994, at F8.

module. See **mode.**

modus operandi (= a method of operating; a manner of procedure) is often just a fancy substitute for *method.* Yet it is well established. But the plural form—*modi operandi*—is fairly rare. See PLURALS (B). The abbreviation *M.O.* is popular with police detectives. The phrase is sometimes misrendered **mode of operandi*—e.g.:

- "As companies evolve from control and command as their primary *modes of operandi* [read *modus operandi*], they become more open to new ways of working." Tom McWhinnie et al., "Companies Wise to Consider Day Care Options," *Seattle Post-Intelligencer,* 23 Oct. 1995, at B5.

- "Marshall (1–2) gets that chance and what is becoming a regular *mode of operandi* [read *modus operandi*], so will numerous other MAC teams." "Herd Eye Kansas St.," *Lancaster Eagle-Gaz.,* 17 Sept. 2003, at B1.

> LANGUAGE-CHANGE INDEX
> **mode of operandi* for *modus operandi*: Stage 1

Mohammed. See **Muhammad.**

Mohave; Mojave. The former is the traditional spelling for the American Indian people; the latter is the spelling for the desert in Southern California. Today, however, there is a decided tendency to use *Mojave* for both. Cf. **Navajo.**

*Mohican; Mohegan. See **Mahican.**

Mojave. See **Mohave.**

mold; mould. For all three meanings (hollow container, growth of fungal hyphae, soft loose earth), *mold* is standard in AmE, *mould* in BrE.

molest. While the traditional meaning of the word is "to interfere maliciously" and the connotations have almost always been negative, this word did not denote sexual assault until recently. Despite being a EUPHEMISM originally, it has become a fairly harsh word. Today it would confuse most readers if used in its original sense, with no sexual aggression implied.

molten. See **melt.**

momenta. See **momentum.**

momentarily. Strictly speaking, this word means "for a moment," not "in a moment." But the latter sense is now widespread, and the word has therefore become occasionally ambiguous—e.g.: "I'll be able to talk with you *momentarily.*" When the latter sense is meant, it is much clearer to say, "I'll be able to talk with you in a moment." Cf. **presently.**

> LANGUAGE-CHANGE INDEX
> *momentarily* in the sense "in a moment": Stage 4

*momento. See **memento.**

momentum. Pl. *momentums* or *momenta.* Though one might understandably consider the latter a pretension, in fact it has always predominated in print sources—e.g.: "Heisenberg proposes that these 'particles' are in reality a field of potential masses and *momenta.*" Karen G. Evans, "Chaos as Opportunity," *Pub. Admin. Rev.,* Sept.–Oct. 1996, at 491. See PLURALS (B).

> Current ratio (*momenta* vs. *momentums*): 21:1

Monacan; Monegasque. For a citizen of Monaco, the first has long been the standard term; the second is a colorful variant that arose in the 19th century; though common, it has never really predominated in usage. See DENIZEN LABELS.

monarchical; *monarchic; *monarchial; monarchal. *Monarchical* (= of, relating to, or characteristic of a monarchy) is the standard form. It predominates in modern usage by a 6-to-1 ratio over *monarchic, and by a 17-to-1 ratio over *monarchial. Both of those terms are NEEDLESS VARIANTS. But *monarchal* (= of, relating to, or characteristic of a monarch), the least frequent of these words, is different because it relates to the person and not to the institution.

MONDEGREENS. A mondegreen is a misheard lyric, saying, catchphrase, or slogan. The word was coined by the Scottish writer Sylvia Wright in a 1954 article in *Harper's Magazine*. There she wrote that, as a child, she had misinterpreted the lyrics of a Scottish ballad called "The Bonny Earl of Moray." One of the lines in the song is this: "They hae slain the Earl o' Moray and laid him on the green." She had thought it went, "They hae slain the Earl o' Moray and Lady Mondegreen."

Indeed, many mondegreens are essentially children's misinterpretations. Consider the examples just from the Christmas season. A child sings "Silent Night" in this way: "Holy imbecile, tender and mild." Of course, the actual words are "Holy infant, so tender and mild." In the same song, "Christ the sailor is born" is a mangled version of "Christ, the Savior, is born." And "round yon Virgin" can mistakenly become "round John Virgin." In "The Twelve Days of Christmas," some have interpreted the true love's gift of the first day as being "a part-red gingerbread tree" instead of "a partridge in a pear tree." In "Jingle Bells": "Bells on cocktails ring, making spareribs bright"—a metamorphosis of "Bells on bobtail ring, making spirits bright." And in "Rudolph, the Red-Nosed Reindeer," some have thought that there's a tenth reindeer: "Olive, the other reindeer" (for "All of the other reindeer").

Many mondegreens occur in transcribed speech. A secretary or court reporter doesn't quite hear the words and comes up with a plausible guess. "Attorney and notary public" becomes "attorney and not a republic." "County surveyor" becomes "Countess of Ayr." "Juxtaposition" becomes "jock strap position."

Perhaps the most interesting of all, though, are those that result from listening to songs. Often the lyrics aren't readily available to listeners, and often the lyrics are sung a little indistinctly. So listeners create their own plausible versions, some of which in sheer creativity rival the originals—e.g.:

- "A girl with kaleidoscope eyes." (Beatles)
  "A girl with colitis goes by."
- "A Merry Conceit." (Folk tune)
  "American Seat."
- "Don't it make my brown eyes blue." (Crystal Gayle)
  "Donuts make my brown eyes blue."
- "Gladly, the Cross I'd Bear." (Name of hymn)
  "Gladly, the Cross-Eyed Bear."
- "Lead On, O King Eternal." (Hymn title)
  "Lead On, O Kinky Turtle."
- "Livin' is easy with eyes closed." (Beatles)
  "Livin' is easy with nice clothes."

- "Revved up like a deuce, another runner in the night." (Manfred Mann adapting Bruce Springsteen)
  "Wrapped up like a douche in the middle of the night."
- "'Scuse me while I kiss the sky." (Jimi Hendrix)
  "'Scuse me while I kiss this guy."
- "Secret Agent Man." (Johnny Rivers)
  "Secret Asian Man."
- "She's got a ticket to ride." (Beatles)
  "She's got a tick in her eye."
- "Somewhere over the rainbow, way up high." ("Somewhere Over the Rainbow")
  "Somewhere over the rainbow, weigh a pie."
- "The answer, my friends, is blowin' in the wind." (Bob Dylan)
  "The ants are my friends, it's blowin' in the wind."
- "There's a bad moon on the rise." (Creedence Clearwater Revival)
  "There's a bathroom on the right."

Sometimes a misheard phrase does more than just confuse the listening public. In 1979, Bonnie Raitt recorded Jackson Browne's lovelorn song "Sleep's Dark and Silent Gate." As Browne composed the song, one line goes: "I found my love too late." But Raitt sang this line differently: "I found my love today." So Raitt's version is (unwittingly?) less forlorn than Browne's.

There are websites and books devoted to collecting interesting and humorous mondegreens (many of which, unfortunately, are implausible attempts at humor rather than actual misunderstandings). The leading books on the subject are by Gavin Edwards (including '*Scuse Me While I Kiss This Guy* [1995], *He's Got the Whole World in His Pants* [1996], *When a Man Loves a Walnut* [1997], and *Deck the Halls with Buddy Holly* [1998]), Martin Toseland (*The Ants Are My Friends: Misheard Lyrics, Malapropisms, Eggcorns, and Other Linguistic Gaffes* [2007]), and J. A. Wines (*Mondegreens: A Book of Mishearings* [2007]). There are also websites that list mondegreens and make musical lyrics widely available. It is easier than ever to verify a lyric that one might be unsure of.

Although mondegreens were much written about in the late 20th century, only two major dictionaries as of 2015 had recorded the word *mondegreen*. This is an indication not of the word's feebleness, but of lexicographic oversight. Many journalists had discussed mondegreens at length, often season after season: for example, Margie Boulé in the *Oregonian* (Portland); Jon Carroll in the *San Francisco Chronicle*; Philip Howard in *The Times* (London); Richard Lederer in the *Patriot Ledger* (Quincy, Mass.); William Safire and Jack Rosenthal in *The New York Times*; Elizabeth Weise in *USA Today*. By the turn of the 21st century, there were hundreds of published references to mondegreens. There's no doubting the utility and widespread currency of the word—or its legitimacy.

Some of the bungles collected in this book are essentially mondegreens: *beckon call* for *beck and

LANGUAGE-CHANGE INDEX (For the full key, see front matter pp. xxxi, l–li.)
Stage 1: Rejected. **Stage 2:** Widely shunned. **Stage 3:** Widespread but . . . **Stage 4:** Ubiquitous but . . . **Stage 5:** Fully accepted.
Invariably inferior forms marked by asterisk (✳). • Ratios represent frequency of prevalent forms vs. variants in current books.

call; *for all intensive purposes for *for all intents and purposes*; *hone in for *home in*; and *to the manor born for *to the manner born*.

Monegasque. See **Monacan.**

monetize; *monetarize. *Monetize* = (1) to put (coins or currency) into circulation as money; (2) to give fixed value as currency; or (3) to purchase (debt), thereby freeing up moneys that would otherwise be used to service the debt. *Monetarize* is a NEEDLESS VARIANT that occurs most commonly in senses 2 and 3—e.g.:

- Sense 2: "A new approach will enable us to take into account social values without forcing ourselves to *monetarize* [read *monetize*] values [that] intrinsically cannot be evaluated in dollar or peso terms." Larry R. Kohler, "Introduction to the Issues," *Ecumenical Rev.*, 1 July 1996, at 279.
- Sense 3: "No single jurist could . . . limit the rate at which Washington prints currency or *monetarizes* [read *monetizes*] its debt." "No Automatic Pay Raises," *Las Vegas Rev.-J.*, 16 Dec. 1994, at B16.

LANGUAGE-CHANGE INDEX
*monetarize for *monetize*: Stage 1
Current ratio (*monetize* vs. *monetarize*): 45:1

moneyed; *monied. The first is standard—e.g.:

- "There is a spot of trouble here in Cheever country [Greenwich, Conn.], the suburban promised land where *moneyed* executives ride the train to Manhattan." Blaine Harden, "Nonresident Sues Over Park Access Litigation," *L.A. Times*, 7 Sept. 1997, at A12.
- "Bailey came from a *moneyed* family." Jeffrey Toobin, "Candide," *New Yorker*, 16 Dec. 2002, at 42, 44.

Cf. **honeyed.**

Current ratio: 3:1

moneys; *monies. The first is the more logical and the editorially preferred form, but *monies* is a frequent variant. Their history is interesting. *Monies* (an archaic plural similar to *attornies*) was prevalent from 1750 to 1850. *Moneys* swelled into predominance from 1850 until 1975—at one point during that period achieving a 7-to-1 advantage in comparative word frequency. Although 20th-century usage authorities almost unanimously recommended *moneys* (and thought the question settled), in 1970 or so the two forms once again became close contenders—to the dismay of many traditionalists. See PLURALS (E).

But why do we need a plural at all? Why doesn't the COLLECTIVE NOUN *money* suffice? The answer lies in idiom. While *money* generally functions in collective senses <we made a lot of money on that deal>, *moneys* is frequently used, especially in financial and legal contexts, to denote "discrete sums of money" or "funds" <many federal and state moneys were budgeted for the disaster relief>.

Current ratio (*moneys* vs. *monies*): 1:1.5

mongolism; mongoloid. See **Down syndrome.**

mongoose forms the plural *mongooses*, not *mongeese*. But the mistaken form is hardly unknown—e.g.:

"They joined Pruno, Yorick and Tucky, along with a pair of *mongeese* [read *mongooses*], two guinea pigs, an assortment of snakes and a barfing crane named (what else?) Ichabod." Bill Ruehlmann, "Heartwarming Tale of Living Like Animals," *Virginian-Pilot & Ledger Star* (Norfolk), 9 Mar. 1997, at J3.

LANGUAGE-CHANGE INDEX
*mongeese for *mongooses*: Stage 1
Current ratio (*mongooses* vs. *mongeese*): 26:1

monied. See **moneyed.**

monies. See **moneys.**

moniker; *monicker. *Moniker* outnumbers the variant *monicker* by a huge margin. If either form can be called etymologically superior, it's *moniker*, since the word seems to derive from the Irish term *munnik*.

Current ratio: 56:1

monition. See **admonition (A).**

monitory; monitorial. See **admonitory.**

monologue (= a speech or skit delivered by a single performer) is the standard spelling. *Monolog* is a variant. The agent noun is *monologuist* /mon-ə-lawg-ist/, preferably not *monologist* /mə-**nol**-ə-jist/, the former being slightly more common—e.g.: "Then in 1986, a friend took him to see a performance by *monologuist* Spalding Gray, and it turned out to be a revelation." Jan Breslauer, "It All Adds Up Now," *L.A. Times*, 17 Aug. 1997, at 49.

monotonous; monotonic. Although these terms have an overlapping sense—"having little or no variation in tone"—they have undergone substantial DIFFERENTIATION. *Monotonous* is now predominantly figurative, meaning "tediously lacking in variety; uninteresting because unvarying." *Monotonic* should be reserved for the literal sense "of, relating to, or consisting of a single tone."

Monseigneur (= a French title given to someone of high birth or rank, or an important church office-holder) forms the plural *Messeigneurs*—preferably not *Monseigneurs*. The term is used before a title of office or rank <Monseigneur the Prince>, never before a personal name. It is pronounced /mahn-sen-**yuur**/.

Current ratio (*Messeigneurs* vs.
Monseigneurs): 13:1

monsieur /mə-**syuu**/ (the French equivalent of *Mr.* or *Sir*) forms the plural *messieurs* (/mes-[y]ərz or may-**syuu**/). The term is abbreviated *M.* (singular) or *MM.* (plural).

Monsignor /mon-**seen**-yər/ (= a title given to certain dignitaries within the Roman Catholic Church) forms the plural *Monsignori* or (less frequently) *Monsignors*.

Current ratio: 2:1

mooch (= [1] to beg, cadge; or [2] to steal, filch) is the standard spelling <he mooched off me for two years!>. *Mouch* is a variant form prone to MISCUES.

Current ratio: 25:1

moon. See **earth.**

moot. A. As an Adjective. The *OED* lists only the sense "that can be argued; debatable; not decided, doubtful." Hence a *moot point* was classically seen as one that is arguable. A *moot case* was a hypothetical case proposed for discussion in a "moot" of law students (i.e., the word was once a noun). In U.S. law schools, students practice arguing hypothetical cases before appellate courts in *moot court.*

From that sense of *moot* derived the extended sense "of no practical importance; hypothetical; academic." This shift in meaning occurred about 1900 <because the question has already become moot, we need not decide it>. Today, in AmE, that is the predominant sense of *moot.* Theodore M. Bernstein and other writers have called this sense of the word incorrect, but it is now a fait accompli, especially in the SET PHRASE *moot point.* To use *moot* in the sense "open to argument" in modern AmE is to create an ambiguity and to confuse readers. In BrE, the transformation in sense has been slower, and *moot* in its older sense retains vitality.
> LANGUAGE-CHANGE INDEX
> *moot* in the sense "of no significance": Stage 5

B. As a Verb. Historically, the verb *moot* meant "to raise or bring forward (a point, question, candidate, etc.) for discussion." That sense was formerly common in AmE but today is current mostly in BrE—e.g.:

- "Air New Zealand and Brierley Investments, a significant shareholder in Air NZ, have been *mooted* as potential buyers." Nikki Tait, "News Chief Plans Talks on Future of Ansett," *Fin. Times,* 5 Apr. 1995, at 33.
- "Swansong was created by Rambert's current artistic director Christopher Bruce back in the 1980s, long before he was *mooted* as saviour of the ailing company." Jenny Gilbert, "Bussell and Guillem Slug It Out," *Independent,* 30 Mar. 1997, at 13.

In American legal usage, a new sense of *moot* has taken hold: "to render (a question) moot or of no practical significance" (*Black's Law Dictionary* 1161 [10th ed. 2014]). E.g.: "A challenge to an abortion statute will be *mooted* after nine months by the birth of the child." William M. Landes & Richard A. Posner, "The Economics of Anticipatory Adjudication," *J. Legal Studies* 683, 717 (1994).

C. Confused with *mute*. Sometimes the phrase **mute point* is used as a not-so-clever pun—e.g.:

- "If money talks, then gender equity is becoming a *mute point* among Idaho high school basketball coaches." Stephen Dodge, "Boys, Girls Coaches Receive Equal Pay," *Idaho Statesman,* 9 Jan. 1995, at C2.
- "A *mute point*: Big question at practice Monday was whether Michael Jordan is happy. It's not known because he's still not talking." Sam Smith, "Ankle Better, Longley Hopes to Play in Game 5," *Chicago Trib.,* 16 May 1995, at N10.
- "Whether he was going to talk to the media has turned from a *mute point* to a moot one, at least in Vancouver." Gary Kingston, "No National Debt Owed by Caps," *Vancouver Sun,* 25 Aug. 2015, at F1.

But in many other instances, no pun is in sight. It's simply a MALAPROPISM that spread in the late 20th century—e.g.:

- "In a separate development that could make the dispute a *mute* [read *moot*] point, the Canon building and nearby properties have been sold to Federated Department Stores, which plans to erect Bloomingdale's West Coast flagship store on the Canon block." Don Shirley, "'Shakespeare' Vows to Remain at Canon," *L.A. Times,* 18 Feb. 1995, at F16.
- "Authority members agreed that the penalty for a corporation that purchases open market securities after entering into a Slugs subscription—a sixth-month ban on purchasing Slugs—is a *mute* [read *moot*] point since the corporation that issued the bonds is defunct as well." Angela Shah, "Texas Public Finance Agency Close to Defeasing Super Collider Debt," *Bond Buyer,* 18 May 1995, at 24.
- "Petrie said these scenarios are *mute* [read *moot*] points: 'The likelihood of KMart going bankrupt is minuscule.'" Paul Gargaro, "As KMart Woes Go . . . ," *Crain's Detroit Bus.,* 20 Nov. 1995, at 2.

Even the verb *moot* is susceptible to this confusion—e.g.: "But Gramley believes such a range would *mute* [read *moot*] the point of having a numerical target." "Congress May Redefine Fed's Job to New Focus on 'Price Stability,'" *Investor's Bus. Daily,* 22 Sept. 1995, at B1.

> LANGUAGE-CHANGE INDEX
> **mute point* for *moot point*: Stage 1

morale; moral, n. H.W. Fowler spent a page and a half discussing the difficulties with these words (*FMEU1* at 361–62), but today problems are rarely encountered. *Morale* = the mental or emotional condition of a person or group, esp. as exhibited by confidence, discipline, or zeal; spirit. *Moral* = (1) the lesson of a fable, story, etc.; or (2) (pl.) principles of right and wrong. For more on *morals,* see **ethics (B).**

moratorium. Both *moratoriums* and *moratoria* are fairly common plurals. On the reasons for preferring the native plural *moratoriums,* see PLURALS (B). But the fact is that *moratoria* has always appeared more frequently in post-1900 print sources. Before that, the words weren't used much.
> Current ratio (*moratoria* vs. *moratoriums*): 2:1

more; most. See COMPARATIVES AND SUPERLATIVES & **all (C).**

more difficult than necessary. For an odd error, see **possible (B).**

more honored in the breach. See **breach, more honored in the.**

more important(ly). As an introductory phrase, *more important* as a sentence-starter has historically been considered an elliptical form of "What is more important . . . ," and hence the *-ly* form is sometimes thought to be the less desirable. From 1850 to 1950, *more important* appeared frequently in print sources

LANGUAGE-CHANGE INDEX (For the full key, see front matter pp. xxxi, l–li.)
Stage 1: Rejected. **Stage 2:** Widely shunned. **Stage 3:** Widespread but . . . **Stage 4:** Ubiquitous but . . . **Stage 5:** Fully accepted.
Invariably inferior forms marked by asterisk (∗). • Ratios represent frequency of prevalent forms vs. variants in current books.

as a sentence-starter. Beginning in 1950, *more importantly* also began appearing frequently—and by 2000 it was rivaling the no-*ly* form. For now, the two coexist in literary language, but momentum seems to be on the side of the -*ly* form—which now predominates by a 2-to-1 ratio in BrE (it's 1-to-1 in AmE).

Three points militate against the position that the -*ly* form is undesirable. First, if we may begin a sentence "*Importantly*, the production appeared first off Broadway . . . ," we ought to be able to begin it, "*More importantly*, ..." See SENTENCE ADVERBS.

Second, the ellipsis does not work with analogous phrases, such as *more notable* and *more interesting*. Both of those phrases require an -*ly* adverb—e.g.:

- "*More notably*, the Dust Brothers are responsible for the production of Beck's Grammy-winning album, 'Odelay.'" Josh Newman, "Group's Career Is Sweet," *Grand Rapids Press*, 24 July 1997, at D13.
- "*More interestingly*, the robot's untimely end touched all sorts of people with no involvement in the project." "Strange Kindness and Familiar Robots," *Globe & Mail* (Toronto), 6 Aug. 2015, at A10.

And third, if the position is changed from the beginning of the sentence in any significant way, the usual ellipsis becomes unidiomatic and -*ly* is quite acceptable—e.g.: "Shrage believes that the strategy should not be to reverse the intermarriage rate, as some activists argue, but to make sure that intermarried couples embrace Judaism and, *more importantly*, commit to raising their children as Jews." Diego Ribadeneira, "Jewish Community Flourishing, New Report Says," *St. Louis Post-Dispatch*, 6 Sept. 1997, at 32.

The criticism of *more importantly* and *most importantly* has always been rather muted and obscure, and today it has dwindled to something less than muted and obscure. So writers needn't fear any criticism for using the -*ly* forms; if they encounter any, it's easily dismissed as picayunish pedantry. See **importantly**.

LANGUAGE-CHANGE INDEX
more importantly for *(what is) more important*: Stage 5

more perfect. This phrase appears in the preamble to the U.S. Constitution: "We the People of the United States, in Order to form a *more perfect* Union." Some critics object that *perfect*, as an absolute quality, should not take a comparative adjective. The answer to those critics is an old one: "It is pedantic to object to the colloquial use of such expressions as 'more universal' [and] '*more perfect*' . . . . Of course, superficially viewed, these expressions are incorrect, as there cannot be degrees of universality or of perfection . . . ; yet what is really meant by 'more perfect,' for example, is 'more nearly perfect.'" Harry T. Peck, "What Is Good English?" in *What Is Good English? and Other Essays* 3, 16–17 (1899). See ADJECTIVES (B).

Although we tend to think of the phrase as having been coined for the Constitution, in fact it was in general currency during the 17th century. Its idiomatic standing was never questioned until the 19th century.

***more possible.** See ADJECTIVES (B).

***more preferable.** See ADJECTIVES (B) & **preferable.**

***more . . . rather than.** See **rather** (C).

mores (= the customs, social behaviors, and moral values of a given society or subset of it) is preferably pronounced /**mor**-ayz/ or /**maw**-rayz/—not /**moh**-rays/ or /morz/.

more so. Two words, not one.

more than. See **over** (A) & SUBJECT–VERB AGREEMENT (I).

more . . . than. A. Parallel Constructions. To maintain parallel phrasing with this construction, it's often important to repeat the preposition. Here, for example, the second *by* is necessary to clarity: "What saddens Ms. Showalter is her conviction that the Allbucks and thousands like them would stand a better chance of obtaining cures if they could accept that their symptoms would be treated *more effectively by* psychotherapy *than by* endless inconclusive medical tests [that] encourage paranoia while obfuscating science." John Carlin, "It's All in the Mind, Bud," *Independent*, 27 Apr. 1997, at 18. See PARALLELISM.

B. **More . . . than all.* See **all** (D).

***more unique.** See ADJECTIVES (B).

moribund (= dying) does not mean "dead." Yet many writers misuse the word in this way—e.g.: "If Brian O'Neill's controversial proposal to end the fight over the Boundary Waters Canoe Wilderness isn't *totally moribund* [read *a dead letter* or *quite dead*], it's clearly in deep trouble." Dean Rebuffoni, "Embattled BWCA Plan Has Led to More Proposals," *Star Trib.* (Minneapolis), 4 Dec. 1996, at B1.

LANGUAGE-CHANGE INDEX
moribund used to mean "dead" instead of "dying": Stage 2

***morning dove.** See **mourning dove.**

MORPHOLOGICAL DEFORMITIES are words derived from other languages, usually Latin or Greek, whose morphemes are so put together as to clash with the lending or borrowing language's principles of word-formation. In some philologists' view, one does not combine the inseparable particle *dis-* with nouns to form English verbs (e.g., *dismember*) because it is impermissible by Latin morphology. In Latin, *dis-* was joined only with verbs to form privative verbs (e.g., *disentitle, disregard*).

But all this is irrelevant. What is permissible in another language has no bearing on what is permissible in ours (splitting infinitives, for example, or ending sentences with prepositions)—and there's no tenable reason why it should. It's preposterous to contend that Latin morphology should govern English morphology—as preposterous as suggesting that modern law should conform to Roman law.

Modern English contains any number of examples of putatively ill-formed words made up of classical morphemes:

asylee
breathalyzer
deflation
drunkometer
homophobe
prosumerism (a PORTMANTEAU WORD from
  pro-consumerism)
simulcast
speedometer
stagflation
teletype
urinalysis
workaholic

Our playfulness and inventiveness with morphemes like these are what makes English such a vital language. Gone are the days when H.W. Fowler's words had any hope of resonating: "Word-making, like other manufactures, should be done by those who know how to do it; others should neither attempt it for themselves, nor assist the deplorable activities of amateurs by giving currency to fresh coinages before there has been time to test them" (*FMEU1* at 241). No doubt the apathy that even most educated Americans feel about this issue results largely from the stubborn monolingualism rampant in the United States. Cf. HYBRIDS.

mortgagor; *mortgager. *Mortgagor* has always been the standard spelling. **Mortgager* is a variant. See -ER (A).

Current ratio: 69:1

mortise (= a hole or groove put into wood or stone for making a joint) is the standard spelling in AmE and BrE alike. **Mortice* is a variant.

Current ratio: 7:1

Moscow (the Russian city), an exonym for *Moskva* /məsk-və/, is legitimately pronounced either /**mos**-koh/ or /**mos**-kow/.

Moslem. See **Muslim.**

mosquito. Pl. *mosquitoes.* See PLURALS (D).

most—in the sense "quite, very"—is an established CASUALISM. Today it is STANDARD ENGLISH, though less formal than *quite*—e.g.:

- "Cerulli's findings are *most* inauspicious for the banking industry." "Can US Bank Funds Survive?" *Retail Banker Int'l*, 7 Mar. 1995, at 4.
- "The shredded lamb, encased in a flaky crust, was seasoned deliciously and was *most* enjoyable." Pat Bruno, "A Field Day," *Chicago Sun-Times*, 21 Nov. 1997, at 32.

See **very** (A). See also COMPARATIVES AND SUPERLATIVES & **all** (C).

*most especially is redundant for *especially*—e.g.: "Stendhal's imaginative relation to his protagonists, *most especially* [read *especially*] to Julien, . . . is inseparable from a consideration of the kind of narrator or dramatized persona he invents to serve as his intermediary." Robert Alter, *A Lion for Love* 191 (1979) (biography of Stendhal).

most important(ly). See **more important(ly).**

*most number of things. This phrasing is incorrect for *most things* or (more verbosely) *greatest number of things* or *highest number of things*—e.g.:

- "The team had the *most number of* [read *most*] wins in the history of the school with a 15–1 record." Harper Mar, "Grimsley Swimmer Places in Pan Am Games," *News & Record* (Greensboro), 26 Mar. 1995, at 6.
- "The party winning the *most number of* [read *most*] seats traditionally gets the first crack to form the government." Loh Hui Yin, "Markets, Business Root for Democrat Win in Thai Polls," *Bus. Times*, 16 Nov. 1996, at 4.
- "There's surely a place for them in the record books for *most number of* [read *most*] past members." John Meagher, "In the Court of King Richard, Folk Royal," *Irish Independent*, 29 Aug. 2015, at 16.

Grammatically, *most* does not properly modify a singular COUNT NOUN such as *number*. In fact, the incorrectness of the phrasing is highlighted when the comparative is substituted for the superlative: you can't say **more number of things*, etc.

LANGUAGE-CHANGE INDEX
*most number of for *greatest number of*: Stage 1
Current ratio (*greatest number of* vs.
*most number of): 19:1

mother lode. See **load.**

motion. See **resolution.**

motion seconded. This parliamentary idiom has recently become mangled, through sound association, into the phrase **notion seconded*. Perhaps the phrase needed is *notion confirmed*—e.g.:

- "Common Cause asked the House ethics committee to investigate Rostenkowski. A *New York Times* editorial *seconded that notion* [read *approved that idea*?] and urged House Democrats to 'call on Mr. Rostenkowski to step aside as chairman.'" Peter Carlson, "Dan Rostenkowski Goes Down in History," *Wash. Post* (Mag.), 17 Oct. 1993, at 35.
- "Hamister says he believes in fan-friendly ownership, that he'll be out and about, attentive and accountable. Berman, who has the majority financial stake, *seconded the notion* [read *agreed*]." Todd Berman, "Sabres Deal Brings Out Kid in Berman," *Buffalo News*, 22 Nov. 2002, at B1.
- "Teresinski said Scott's location and small user base have always made the town's participation in the authority problematic—a *notion seconded* [read *notion confirmed*] by others close to the project." Peter Rebhahn, "Scott May Leave Water Authority," *Green Bay Press-Gaz.*, 14 Jan. 2003, at B1.

No doubt part of the blame goes to Smokey Robinson and the Miracles for the 1967 hit "I Second That Emotion."

LANGUAGE-CHANGE INDEX
*notion seconded for *notion confirmed*: Stage 1
Current ratio (*notion confirmed* vs.
*notion seconded): 8:1

LANGUAGE-CHANGE INDEX (For the full key, see front matter pp. xxxi, l–li.)
Stage 1: Rejected. **Stage 2:** Widely shunned. **Stage 3:** Widespread but . . . **Stage 4:** Ubiquitous but . . . **Stage 5:** Fully accepted.
Invariably inferior forms marked by asterisk (*). • Ratios represent frequency of prevalent forms vs. variants in current books.

motto. Pl. *mottoes.* See PLURALS (D).

*mouch. See **mooch.**

mould. See **mold.**

mourning dove; mourning warbler. The *mourning dove*, a grayish-brown medium-sized bird common throughout North and Central America, is said to be so called because its plaintive sound suggests grieving. The *mourning warbler*, a small species of songbird found in eastern and central North American forests, is said to be so called because its dark breast suggests one in mourning (the *OED* quotes the *Atlantic Monthly* from 1866 to say that ornithologists were evoking the dark breast). In neither name does the etymology have anything to do with the AM (hence it's not *morning dove or *morning warbler)—e.g.:

- "The abundance of woods and dead trees, he said, *have* [read *has*] brought the sightings of more cardinals and *morning* [read *mourning*] doves." Maureen Costello, "Guardian of the Land," *Boston Globe*, 21 Jan. 2001, Globe West §, at 1.
- "*Morning* [read *Mourning*] doves coo and sea gulls circle." Darragh Johnson, "The Man Behind the Speedo," *Wash. Post*, 1 Mar. 2001, at T12.
- "He's constantly revising his routines, and is quite proud of his white *morning* [read *mourning*] doves (part of a classic appearing-disappearing trick that has become a staple in his show)." Miriam Di Nunzio, "Berwyn Teen Makes TV Magic," *Chicago Sun-Times*, 16 Mar. 2001, Weekend Plus §, at 10.

LANGUAGE-CHANGE INDEX
*morning dove for *mourning dove*: Stage 1
Current ratio (*mourning dove* vs.
*morning dove): 11:1

mouse. The plural of this word, in reference to small rodents, is (of course) *mice.* In reference to computer gadgets, usage has changed rapidly. Many usagists in the late 1990s recommended *mouses* over *mice* (on the analogy of *louse,* which forms *louses* in reference to cads but *lice* in reference to insects). As recently as 2007, the *Associated Press Stylebook,* which most newspapers follow, was silent on the issue, and *mouses* prevailed—e.g.: "[Mark] Bolger said Microsoft has found that surface computing is more intuitive than computer *mouses,* which require training." Howard Wolinsky, "At Your Fingertips; Finally, a Real Hands-on Computer," *Chicago Sun-Times,* 25 Oct. 2007, Fin. §, at 49. But in 2008, the *AP Stylebook* recommended the form *mice,* which had already become standard in commerce—e.g.: "In March, the EPA fined a Southern California company, IOGEAR, $208,000 for making unsubstantiated antimicrobial claims about its nanosilver-coated computer *mice* and keyboards." Margaret Woodbury, "The Allure of Nanosilver," *L.A. Times,* 4 Aug. 2008, Health §, at F3. See PLURALS (H). Any real debate seems now at an end: the collocation *computer mice* is eight times more common in print than **computer mouses.* Those who advocated *mouses* analogized valiantly, but they should concede their editorial loss and move on. See **snoot.**

*mousey. See **mousy.**

moustache. See **mustache.**

mousy (= [1] of, like, or involving a mouse or mice, or [2] timorous, meek, nervous, and drab) has been the predominant spelling in AmE and BrE alike since about 1900—*mousey being a variant.
Current ratio: 6:1

mouthful. Pl. *mouthfuls.* See PLURALS (G).

movable has been predominantly so spelled in AmE since about 1840 and in BrE since about 1870. *Moveable* is a variant spelling. See MUTE E.
Current ratio: 3:1

mow > mowed > mowed. The past-participial *mown* is best reserved for adjective uses—e.g.: "You can practically smell the *mown* outfield grass and taste the dirty-water hot dogs." Don Mayhew, "Opening Day Hits," *Fresno Bee,* 1 Apr. 1997, at E1. See IRREGULAR VERBS (B).
Current ratio (*has mowed* vs. *has mown): 2:1

Mr.; Mrs.; Ms. In AmE, the first two terms are considered abbreviations, so they have a period at the end. *Ms.* originated in the 1950s as a blend of *Mrs.* and *Miss.* American dictionaries do not define *Ms.* as an abbreviation or contraction, but it is written with a period anyway to conform to the style of *Mr.* and *Mrs.*

Because contracted abbreviations (with letters deleted from the middle of the word) don't take a period in BrE, British writers use these three forms without a period <Mr Whitaker> <Mrs Kerr> <Ms Denning>.

ms. See **manuscript.**

Ms. See SEXISM (E) & **Mr.**

much. See **many.**

much less. This phrase requires the writer to put the less rigorous word first, the more rigorous last. But here they're reversed: "Recent history amply illustrates the difficulties in *adapting, much less surviving* [read *surviving, much less adapting*]." Shelley von Strunckel, "What the Stars Say About Them," *Sunday Times* (London), 18 June 1995, Style §, at 36. Surviving is easier than surviving and adapting. Therefore, the phrasing in the original is illogical. Fowler recommends *let alone* as a less troublesome substitute. See ILLOGIC.

*muchly is nowadays considered a jocular NON-WORD—though several centuries ago it was not so stigmatized. *Much* is the preferred form in all adverbial contexts. But *muchly occasionally finds its way into print—e.g.:

- "More of this would have been *muchly* [read *much*] appreciated." Jennifer Barrs, "Roy Clark Still Strong on Strings," *Tampa Trib.,* 1 Mar. 1996, Florida/Metro §, at 4.
- "*Thanks muchly* [read *Thank you*] to Rafael Palmeiro, whom the Cubs traded because he showed little power potential." Bob Verdi, "Ah, a Ballpark with Warmth—and

People," *Chicago Trib.*, 11 Sept. 1996, Sports §, at 1. (For more on *thanks much*, see **thank you**.)

- "Merl is survived by his father and one brother, both named Sam. He's already *muchly* [read *deeply* or *sorely*] missed." Vic Fleming, "Man of His Words," *Ark. Democrat-Gaz.*, 28 Aug. 2015, at 17.

For other adverbs with a superfluous *-ly*, see ADVERBS (C).

LANGUAGE-CHANGE INDEX
muchly for *much*: Stage 1
Current ratio (*much appreciated* vs.
muchly appreciated): 2,534:1

much-needed is often used nonsensically. That is, it's common to read about **much-needed voids* and **much-needed gaps*, when the true reference is to voids or gaps that need to be filled—e.g.: "He said the four division chairmen will fill a *much-needed gap* that occurs when a committee chairman takes the floor to push a certain bill." Frank Phillips, "Finneran Plans Bigger Bonuses for Four Allies," *Boston Globe*, 27 Mar. 1997, at A1. If the gap is much needed, then the division chairs will spoil things by filling it. See ILLOGIC.

mucus, n.; **mucous,** adj. These two ought to be kept separate, *mucus* for the slimy substance and *mucous* for the adjective describing whatever contains or secretes mucus. So **mucus membrane* is a mistake—e.g.: "If a person already has herpes, chlamydia, gonorrhea, or syphilis and is exposed to HIV, he or she is more likely to contract the virus because of openings in the *mucus* [read *mucous*] membranes and skin." "Increased Research Leads to Dramatic Declines in Sexually Transmitted Diseases," *USA Today* (Mag.), Feb. 1995, at 11.

In medical literature, *mucous ball* and *mucus ball* are about equally common. This is a closer case than *mucous membrane*, however, because *mucus ball* is a ball of mucus, and the noun is justifiably used in an attributive sense—e.g.: "Over the ensuing six months, there has been no further problem with *mucus balls*, his level of dyspnea, or edema." Edward M. Harrow et al., "Respiratory Failure and Cor Pulmonale Associated with Tracheal Mucoid Accumulation [etc.]," *Chest*, Feb. 1992, at 580. But the best course, outside medical literature, might be to find a EUPHEMISM.

LANGUAGE-CHANGE INDEX
*mucus membrane for *mucous membrane*: Stage 1
Current ratio (*mucous membrane* vs.
*mucus membrane): 31:1

Muhammad; Mohammed; Mahomet; Muhammed. How do you spell the name of the founder of Islam (who lived from 570 to 632)? The spelling *Mahomet* predominated from 1600 till about 1880, when *Mohammed* became predominant throughout the English-speaking world. The retransliterated *Muhammad* overtook all rivals about 1945 and is now standard.

Current ratio (in order of headwords): 25:11:2:1

multiply is an adverb /məl-ti-plee/ as well as a verb /məl-ti-plı/. Because the word is ordinarily a verb, the adverbial use can give rise to MISCUES—e.g.: "The St. Christopher-Ottilie Residential Treatment Center [is] a home for *multiply* handicapped children." Joe Krupinski & Mike Candel, "High School Notebook," *Newsday* (N.Y.), 30 Nov. 1994, at A66. But writers can arrange the sentence parts to ensure that the word is read correctly—e.g.: "Buying toys for a severely or *multiply* handicapped child can be difficult." Andale Gross, "Learning to Fit the Toys to the Child," *Kansas City Star*, 10 Dec. 1994, Olathe §, at 3. Putting *multiply* on a parallel course with *severely* minimizes the possibility of a reader miscue.

murder. A. And *homicide; manslaughter; man-killing*. *Homicide* is the killing of another human being; it is the general legal term. (See **homicide**.) *Murder* is the unlawful killing of a human being with malice aforethought. It is the most heinous kind of criminal homicide. At common law, *murder* was not subdivided; but in most American jurisdictions statutes have created *first-degree murder, second-degree murder,* and *third-degree murder* (in descending order of reprehensibility). Indeed, *second-degree murder* is the same as common-law murder, as defined above. *First-degree murder*, a statutory crime, is the common-law crime of murder with an added element (such as arson, rape, robbery, burglary, larceny, or kidnapping) that aggravates the crime.

Manslaughter, which has a lower degree than *murder*, is homicide committed without malice aforethought.

Man-killing is a nonlegal synonym for *homicide*, used sometimes of nonhuman killers <man-killing isn't something tigers do unless they're physically provoked or very hungry>. But it's a sexist term: see SEXISM (C).

B. *Unintentional murder*. This phrase may strike some readers as an OXYMORON, but it has been fairly widespread since the late 18th century. E.g.:

- "On Tuesday, the [California Supreme Court], in a major break with a 4-year-old precedent, ruled that a killer can be executed for an *unintentional murder*." "Calif. Death Sentence Upheld," *L.A. Times*, 15 Oct. 1987, § 1, at 1.
- "One of McDonagh's gifts is knowing that the darker the subtext, the more outrageous the lines can be, because what would ordinarily seem offensive becomes significant in light of a true disaster: the *unintentional murder* of a child." John Anderson, "Bumbling Hit Men Score Bulls-Eye in Darkly Droll 'Bruges,'" *Wash. Post*, 8 Feb. 2008, at C6.

And it is entirely proper to speak of an *unintentional murder*, as when someone, for no good reason, shoots a gun into an occupied room and kills somebody inside. But traditionally, intent is the very distinction between murder and manslaughter, so unless this is a legal term of art you are stuck with, use *unintentional killing* instead.

LANGUAGE-CHANGE INDEX (For the full key, see front matter pp. xxxi, l–li.)
Stage 1: Rejected. **Stage 2:** Widely shunned. **Stage 3:** Widespread but . . . **Stage 4:** Ubiquitous but . . . **Stage 5:** Fully accepted.
Invariably inferior forms marked by asterisk (*). • Ratios represent frequency of prevalent forms vs. variants in current books.

murex (= a flesh-eating snail abounding in tropical seas) traditionally formed the plural *murices*. But since the late 1940s in AmE and the early 1970s in BrE, *murexes* has become predominant in English-language print sources.

murk, n.; **murky,** adj. These are preferably so spelled. **Mirk* and **mirky* are variant spellings.

Current ratio (*murk* vs. **mirk*): 7:1
Current ratio (*murky* vs. **mirky*): 577:1

Muslim; Moslem. Both terms mean "a follower of Islam" and appear in English-language works from the 15th century on. *Moslem* was the standard spelling until the 1940s, when *Muslim* became predominant in World English. Curiously, BrE and AmE lagged behind the shift. *Muslim* became predominant in BrE about ten years later. *Muslim* overtook *Moslem* in AmE in 1963, possibly influenced by the prominence of the *Black Muslims*, an alternative name for the Nation of Islam, during the civil-rights movement. Worldwide, *Muslim* is now 20 times as common as *Moslem*.

mustache; moustache; mustachio. A latent DIFFERENTIATION has begun to take hold. *Mustachio*, tinged with ARCHAISM, has come to suggest a large, bushy mustache. E.g.: "In Italian *baffi* means handlebar mustache; George's own substantial *mustachio* is insured by Lloyd's of London." Don Freeman, "If Only George Could Give Those Cigars Away," *San Diego Union-Trib.*, 20 Jan. 1995, at E2.

Sometimes, too, *mustachio* has come to mean "one side of a big mustache." Though the dictionaries have been slow to recognize this sense, it is fairly common—e.g.:

- "Back in Toronto in the 1880s, he cultivated a southwestern appearance, with free-falling *mustachios* and the sort of long linen duster favoured by drovers and outlaws." Douglas Fetherling, "Bob Bob Bobbin' Along," *Saturday Night*, Sept. 1996, at 87.
- "A villain named Hurwitz Murkowski (hiss) ties Smokey Bear to the tracks, twirls his waxed *mustachios* and then, with a snarl, yelps, 'Curses, foiled again!' (huzzah)." "White Hats to the Rescue," *S.F. Examiner*, 7 Oct. 1996, at A16.
- "I can picture Monsieur Henny, twirling his *mustachios* and flashing his cleaver as he gestures to his display of lapin, before helping Mme. Wells select the best one." Tucker Shaw, "The Fixer," *Denver Post*, 19 Jan. 2011, at D1.

The corresponding adjectives are *mustached* (generic) and *mustachioed* (for the big ones). Although *mustachioed* is most commonly mentioned as the adjective, *mustached* is common and entirely respectable—e.g.: "Handsome, *mustached*, expensively suited, he can't move without conjuring up images of Johnnie Cochran." Lloyd Rose, " 'Chicago': Going Gangbusters Again," *Wash. Post*, 18 Apr. 1997, at C1.

Moustache is the BrE spelling of *mustache*, predominant there since about 1830. *Mustache* has predominated in AmE since about 1940.

*must could have. See DOUBLE MODALS.

muster. See **pass muster.**

mutatis mutandis (= the necessary changes having been made; taking into consideration or allowing for the changes that must be made) might seem a useful LATINISM in some literary contexts, since the English equivalents are wordier. But in most actual uses of the phrase, it can be simplified. The phrase is hardly needed for a straightforward comparison in which readers are sure to know that two things aren't identical—e.g.:

- "The anti-smoking movement affords a recipe for success that, *mutatis mutandis*, [delete the phrase and the commas] can be useful to many other social movements." Peter L. Berger, "Furtive Smokers," *News & Record* (Greensboro), 7 Aug. 1994, at F1.
- "Hughes's Harlem has pimps and number-runners and illegitimate babies and alcohol and marijuana—but none of these things, *mutatis mutandis*, is unknown in 'polite society,' as both Hughes and his readers are well aware." Helen Vendler, "The Unweary Blues," *New Republic*, 6 Mar. 1995, at 37. (A possible revision: *but all these things have their equivalents in 'polite society'* . . . .)
- "If 'Pink Flamingos' offered a geeky, low-rent version of 'The Godfather,' the movie's narrative structure is, *mutatis mutandis*, the same as 'Star Wars.' " J. Hoberman, "The Naked & the Dead," *Village Voice*, 15 Apr. 1997, at 67. (A possible revision: *is similar to that of 'Star Wars.'*)

Sometimes the phrase is entirely superfluous. In the following sentence, its purpose seems to be to impress, and the writer (ironically) becomes less intelligible with its use: "So, if one can use 'yellow' and 'good' intelligently and intelligibly—if others can understand what one means by them—then, for practical purposes, both words, *mutatis mutandis*, are meaningful." John Hill, "Can We Talk About Ethics Anymore?" *J. Bus. Ethics*, Aug. 1995, at 585. Cf. **ceteris paribus.** See SESQUIPEDALITY.

mute. See **moot (c).**

MUTE E. In English, a verb's unsounded final *-e* is ordinarily dropped before the *-ing* and *-ed* inflections: *create, creating, created; rate, rating, rated; share, sharing, shared*. Exceptions to this rule are verbs ending in *-ee, -ye,* and *-oe*; these do not drop the *-e* before *-ing*, but they do drop it before *-ed*: *agree, agreeing, agreed; dye, dyeing, dyed; hoe, hoeing, hoed*.

The suffix *-able* often causes doubt when it is appended to a base ending in a mute *-e*. Usually, the *-e* is dropped when *-able* is added, but a number of exceptions exist in BrE (e.g., *hateable, hireable, mineable, nameable, rateable, ropeable, saleable, sizeable, unshakeable*). See -ABLE (E). Oddly, though, the spellings *livable* and *movable* predominate in BrE. For all these *-able* adjectives—apart from *hateable, nameable,* and *ropeable*—AmE drops the medial *-e-*.

Although the general rule in AmE is to drop the *-e* before a vowel, the almost universal exception to this rule is to keep the *-e* if needed to indicate the soft sound of a preceding *-g-* or *-c-*, as in *change, changeable; hinge, hingeing; trace, traceable*. Yet even this exception to the rule is not uniform: *lunge* yields *lunging*, and *impinge* yields *impinging*. A less common exception retains the mute *-e* to distinguish a word from another with a like spelling, as in *dye*, *dyeing*. Because the given form of a word when inflected is easily forgotten and often the subject of disagreement even among lexicographers, the best course is to keep an up-to-date and reliable dictionary at hand.

One other difference between AmE and BrE is noteworthy: in AmE, the mute *-e* is dropped after *-dg-* in words such as *acknowledgment, fledgling,* and *judgment,* whereas the *-e* is typically retained in BrE (*acknowledgement, fledgeling,* and *judgement*). Even so, British legal writers usually prefer the spelling *judgment.* See **judgment (A).**

*mute point. See **moot.**

mutual. A. And *common*. It's possible to refer to a couple's *mutual* devotion, but not their *mutual* devotion to their children. The reason is that whatever is *mutual* is reciprocal—it's directed by each toward the other. E.g.: "So consider the matter a quid pro quo, a *mutual* exchange of affection between Zereoue and Mountaineer fandom." Michael Dobie, "More-Famous Amos," *Newsday* (N.Y.), 14 Nov. 1997, at A103.

But when the sense is "shared by two or more," then the word is *common*—not *mutual*. *Friend in common* has traditionally been thought preferable to *mutual friend,* although the latter has stuck because of Dickens's novel (the title to which, it is sometimes observed, comes from a sentence mouthed by an illiterate character). Some careful writers continue to use *friend in common.* But *mutual friend* has in fact predominated since the 18th century—today by a 60-to-1 ratio.

Language-Change Index
mutual friend for *friend in common:* Stage 5

B. In Redundancies. *Mutual* creates any number of redundancies. E.g.: "The 25-page motion . . . claims that multimillion-dollar misstatements are strewn along a Symington paper trail that consists of a series of *mutually contradictory* [read *contradictory* or *inconsistent*] financial statements." Jerry Kammer & Pat Flannery, "Judge Asked to Rule Symington Lied on Financial Statement," *Ariz. Republic,* 22 Mar. 1997, at B5. Some of the more common prolixities with this word are *mutual agreement and **mutual cooperation.* Cf. **together.**

Redundancies are especially common when *mutual* appears with *both*—e.g.: "And Hongkong, he adds, will be there to serve China to the *mutual benefit of both parties involved* [read *mutual benefit of the parties* or *benefit of both parties*]." Rahita Elias, "A Tough Act to Follow for HK's New Port Development Board Chief," *Bus. Times,* 17 Oct. 1996, Shipping Times §, at 1.

The phrasing **mutual . . . each other* is a fairly common redundancy—e.g.:

- "They have a deep, *mutual respect for each other* [read *mutual respect*] even when they bump heads over draft picks." Mike Preston, "Savage Finds Diamonds in the Rough," *Baltimore Sun,* 18 Jan. 2001, at D1.
- "My father was a Roman Catholic and my mother a Protestant and . . . they *had a mutual respect for each other's religion* [read *respected each other's religion*]." Dale Turner, "The Simple Favor of an Introduction Can Change a Life," *Seattle Times,* 20 Jan. 2001, at A11.

See **reciprocity** & REDUNDANCY.

my and your house. See POSSESSIVES (E).

Myanmarese; Myanmaran. See **Burmese.**

my bad. This low colloquialism gained popularity in the mid-1980s, apparently growing out of American sports SLANG and meaning "Sorry, my mistake." It was well enough established by 1986 to be listed in a collection of campus slang published by the University of North Carolina, and it soon became a staple in pop culture. The phrase now seems to be on the wane.

myriad is more concise as an adjective <myriad drugs> than as a noun <a myriad of drugs>. Here the shorter use is illustrated:

- "June 1996: Telectronics resumes production after wrangling over *myriad* legal and manufacturing issues." Al Lewis, "Pacemaker Firm Pulls Plug," *Rocky Mountain News* (Denver), 14 Dec. 1996, at B1.
- "Back when we still thought America was a melting pot instead of a collection of hyphens, the crux of combining *myriad* nationalities into one was in that oath." Pat Truly, "The Choice All Immigrants Must Make," *Baltimore Sun,* 14 Jan. 1997, at A9.
- "That color change prompted some to erroneously fear the rocket exploded, when they were actually witnessing a second-stage ignition of additional boosters, according to *myriad* media reports." Adam Linhardt, "Early Risers Catch Glimpse of Rocket," *Key West Citizen,* 3 Sept. 2015, at A1.

But the mere fact that the adjective is handier than the noun doesn't mean the latter is substandard. The noun (ca. 1555) has been with us more than 200 years longer than the adjective (ca. 1791), and the choice is a question of style, not correctness. Yet in print sources since 1850, the shorter adjectival use has been much more frequent.

Current ratio (*myriad reasons* vs.
a myriad of reasons): 1.2:1

myself is best used either reflexively <I have decided to exclude myself from consideration> or intensively <I myself have seen that> <I've done that myself>. The word shouldn't appear as a substitute for *I* or *me* <my wife and myself were delighted to see you>. Using it that way, as an "untriggered reflexive," is

LANGUAGE-CHANGE INDEX (For the full key, see front matter pp. xxxi, l–li.)
Stage 1: Rejected. **Stage 2:** Widely shunned. **Stage 3:** Widespread but . . . **Stage 4:** Ubiquitous but . . . **Stage 5:** Fully accepted.
Invariably inferior forms marked by asterisk (*). • Ratios represent frequency of prevalent forms vs. variants in current books.

thought somehow to be modest, as if the reference were less direct. Yet it's no less direct, and the user may unconsciously cause the reader or listener to assume an intended jocularity, or that the user is somewhat doltish. E.g.:

- "Those ins and outs are largely a self-learning process, though knowing the experience of someone like *myself* [read *me*] might make the learning shorter, easier, and a lot less painful." Mark H. McCormack, *What They Don't Teach You at Harvard Business School* xii (1984).
- "The exclusion of women and women's concerns is self-defeating. For instance, *myself and other women in Hollywood* [read *many women in Hollywood, including me,*] would deliver millions of dollars of profit to the film industry if we could make films and television shows about the lives of real women." Rita Mae Brown, "In Flight from the Female," *L.A. Times*, 22 Oct. 1989, Book Rev. §, at 4.
- "A number of readers, like *myself* [read *me*], will doubtless feel that this exposure has given them a clear professional sense of Rogers." Michael Patrick Gillespie, "A Composition of Place," *Irish Lit. Supp.*, Fall 2015, at 27.

See PRONOUNS (E) & FIRST PERSON. Cf. **I personally.**

LANGUAGE-CHANGE INDEX
1. *myself* for *me* <He was an avid golfer like myself>: Stage 3
2. *myself* for *me* in a compound predicate <Give it to John or myself>: Stage 2

mystical; mystic, adj. These words, about equally common, have long been regarded as more or less interchangeable. Margaret Nicholson suggested that "*mystical*, not *mystic*, is now used in reference to theological mysticism" (*DAEU* at 356). But that doesn't appear to be true: in 1992, for example, David S. Ariel published a book entitled *The Mystic Quest: An Introduction to Jewish Mysticism*. Further, *mystical* appears predominantly in nontheological contexts.

Perhaps the best thing that might be said is that euphony should govern the choice of term—e.g.:

- "A maverick, however, he hewed to a poetic surrealism despite the polemics of abstraction that surrounded him, using figurative elements to evoke the mythic and the *mystical*." Grace Glueck, "Art in Review," *N.Y. Times*, 6 June 1997, at C22.
- "The chords of memory are not *mystic* anymore." Leon Wieseltier, "Immemorial," *New Republic*, 9 June 1997, at 50.
- "They are awestruck to finally enter this *mystic* fraternity." Bryan Hendricks, "Fowl Ball!" *Ark. Democrat-Gaz.*, 16 Aug. 2015, Sports §, at 32.
- "Her recent poetry is more political, but also more *mystical*, and less interested in women's issues." Sarah Berry, "Medbh McGuckian's Ex-Centric Obscurity," *Irish Lit. Supp.*, Fall 2015, at 19.

Since 1600 or so, *mystical* has prevailed over *mystic* in frequency of use in English-language print sources—with the exception of the period from 1870 to 1930 (a mystic period).

N

Nabokov, Vladimir (1899–1977). How do you pronounce the writer's name? It's /vla-**deem**-ər/ (rhyming with *redeemer*) /**nab**-ə-kawf/ (rhyming with *have a cough*). According to Justice Ruth Bader Ginsburg, who studied closely with Nabokov as her teacher at Cornell, that's how the man pronounced his own name. See Bryan A. Garner, Interview with Justice Ginsburg, 10 *Scribes J. Legal Writing* 133, 135 (2010).

naiad (/**nay**-ad/ or /**nɪ**-ad/) = a river nymph. This permissibly forms the Greek plural *naiades* /**nay**-ə-deez/—even in English-language contexts—but *naiads* (/**nay**-adz/ or /**nɪ**-adz/) has always predominated. For the principles governing foreign plurals, see PLURALS (B).

Current ratio (*naiads* vs. *naiades*): 21:1

naive; *naïve; naif; *naïf. The standard adjective is *naive* (without a diaeresis), the standard noun *naif* (again, no diaeresis). The others are variant forms. *Naive* (= amusingly ingenuous) is sometimes misused for the noun *naif* (= a naive person)—e.g.: "But you are not a political *naive* [read *naif*]." A.M. Rosenthal, "Arianna, Go Home!" *N.Y. Times*, 20 June 1995, at A15 (addressing Arianna Stassinopoulos Huffington). Maybe the author thought that, because he was addressing a woman, he should feminize the form. But in English, *naif* is not considered sex-specific.

The adjective is pronounced /nah-**eev**/, the noun /nah-**eef**/.

LANGUAGE-CHANGE INDEX
naive misused as a noun for *naif*: Stage 1

naiveté; *naivete; *naïveté; naivety; *naiveness. The first of these—a half-GALLICISM that keeps the accent but loses the diaeresis—is the standard form in AmE. Avoid the variants. The word is pronounced /nah-eev-**tay**/ or /nah-ee-və-**tay**/.

Naivety, which is chiefly BrE, is pronounced /nah-**eev**-tee/ or /nah-**ee**-və-tee/.

*Naiveness is an artless anglicization created by simple, unaffected people deficient in worldly wisdom and informed judgment.

nameable. So spelled in both AmE and BrE—not **namable*. See MUTE E.

Current ratio: 4:1

named for; named after; named from. *Named for* means "to be named in honor of (someone or something)" <the Nobel Prize was named for Swedish scientist Alfred Nobel>—e.g.: "Saturday's ceremony preceded the Albany Alligators–Fort Worth Cats game at the Paul Eames Sports Complex, *named for* Paul in honor of his decades of work on behalf of baseball and youth sports in Albany." Tim Tucker, "It's a Golden Play at the Plate," *Atlanta J.-Const.*, 24 July 2001, at E2.

Named after means that a person's or thing's name was given to another person or a place after the namesake was born or achieved fame. It does not necessarily connote an honor, but it may—e.g.: "Bradlee seemed to be betting Mrs. Graham's newspaper on the reporting of a couple of then obscure, young city-desk reporters, Bob Woodward and Carl Bernstein, who were in turn relying on anonymous sources, chiefly one *named after* a porn movie, 'Deep Throat.'" Evan Thomas, "An American Original; Katharine Graham 1917–2001," *Newsweek*, 30 July 2001, at 42.

Named from (the least prevalent phrasing) applies to things, not people, and means that a name was inspired by something else that isn't necessarily well known or worthy of honor. In some contexts, it signals an implicit memorialization of a predecessor that bore the same name—e.g.: "A new development called Lost Creek proposed by Don Simon Homes in Madison near the town of Blooming Grove has all of its streets *named from* Beatles' song titles." George Hesselberg, "Where the Streets Have Odd Names," *Wis. State J.*, 15 July 2001, at G1. See **eponymous.**

namely is generally preferable to *viz.* or *to wit*. But often all three expressions can be avoided—e.g.: "There's a big, juicy, column-ready event hanging out there, *namely* the Microsoft CEO summit." Kevin Maney, "Computer Spins Technology Tale," *USA Today*, 15 May 1997, at B5. (A possible revision: *There's a big, juicy, column-ready event hanging out there: the Microsoft CEO summit.*) See **viz.** & **to(-)wit.**

Namely is customarily followed by a comma, as are equivalent terms such as *to wit, for example,* and *that is*. But writers increasingly skip the comma after this single-word introduction—e.g.: "[Meyer] Schapiro's understanding of Romanesque art is based on an essential belief about humankind, *namely* [read *namely,*] that individuality—the sense of it, the yearning for it, the struggle for it—is quite simply the core of the human." Jed Perl, "The Varieties of Artistic Experience," *New Republic*, 30 Oct. 2006, at 23.

This type of phrase or clause specifies, clarifies, or gives one or more examples of what preceded. Because it's nonrestrictive, it should be set off from the sentence. Not doing so usually results in a sentence that's tough to get through—e.g.: "That's tricky when some *signals namely equity markets* [read *signals, namely, equity markets,*] hitting new highs are bullish." Jon Birger, "Can the Economy Survive the Housing Bust?" *Fortune*, 13 Nov. 2006, at 189 (*namely, equity markets* might also be set off by em-dashes or parentheses).

NAMES. A. Capitalization. Many complex rules govern the capitalization of names—too many to cover here. But a few especially important ones merit mention. First, names that are proper nouns—such as names of people, places, books, articles, and the like—are capitalized <President Ronald Reagan> <Atlanta, Georgia> <*Gone with the Wind*>. That's the rule that everybody knows. Second, when a name such as *Hockaday School* is reduced to a shortened form (the *School*) after the first reference, even the common noun *school* may be capitalized because it's a short-form proper noun. This practice is common for in-house publications such as annual reports. And in legal writing, a statute is commonly referred to as *the Act* after the first reference, and the court one is addressing is always *the Court*. Keep in mind, though, that in most prose the practice can get out of hand: "[D]o not capitalize a short form unless it clearly warrants the importance, distinction, or emphasis that capitalization conveys." *Gregg Reference Manual* Rule 310 (10th ed. 2004). And third, when a name for some idiosyncratic reason isn't usually capitalized <k.d. lang>, the first letter must be capitalized when it begins a sentence <K.d. lang sang a few of her hit songs>. (Some editors would write her name K.D. Lang regardless of her preference for lowercase. Cf. **Cummings.**) For a full coverage of the many complexities of capitalizing names, see *The Chicago Manual of Style*. See CAPITALIZATION (A).

B. Jr.; Sr.; III; etc. There are four traditional rules about the use of these labels—most of them forgotten in modern usage though scattered throughout etiquette books.

First, a father should not adopt the *Sr.* label, nor should others refer to him that way without good reason. That's what the etiquette mavens have long said—e.g.:

- "A gentleman who represents the head of the senior branch of his family is privileged to use a card engraved simply, 'Mr. Brown.'" 1 *Correct Social Usage* 212 (1907) (suggesting that 'Mr. Henry A. Brown Sr.' does not properly exist).
- "Senior cannot be used with a man's name. No matter how famous the son, he is junior to his father as long as his father is alive." Millicent Fenwick, *Vogue's Book of Etiquette* 557 (1948).
- "'Senior' is never used after a man's name." Nancy Loughridge, *Dictionary of Etiquette* 105 (1955).
- "A man never uses 'Sr.,' though on occasion it is correct for others to add 'senior' to the name of the older man when referring to him (though not when addressing a letter to him) if confusion with his son would otherwise result." Llewellyn Miller, *The Encyclopedia of Etiquette* 393 (1967).

Second, a son drops *Jr.* when his father dies (with exceptions noted below). Again, that's what the experts have consistently said—e.g.:

- "At the death of his father, he is no longer junior." Margery Wilson, *Pocket Book of Etiquette* 105 (1937).
- "A man is 'Mark Strand Jr.' only while his father is alive and, of course, he bears his father's exact name." Nancy Loughridge, *Dictionary of Etiquette* 105 (1955).

LANGUAGE-CHANGE INDEX (For the full key, see front matter pp. xxxi, l–li.)
Stage 1: Rejected. **Stage 2:** Widely shunned. **Stage 3:** Widespread but . . . **Stage 4:** Ubiquitous but . . . **Stage 5:** Fully accepted.
Invariably inferior forms marked by asterisk (✱). • Ratios represent frequency of prevalent forms vs. variants in current books.

• "Names are traditionally numbered only among the living." Judith Martin, *Miss Manners' Guide for the Turn-of-the-Millennium* 60 (1990).

Even modern newspapers agree: "Normally, when a father dies, the son drops the 'Jr.'" "Racing Family Tries to Shake Grief," *Rock Hill Herald*, 26 Feb. 2001, at A1.

This rule was once widely followed. There were, for example, father-and-son Oliver Wendell Holmeses. As soon as the father (the poet) died in 1894, the son (the jurist) dropped *Jr.* despite his father's great renown. (And, of course, during his lifetime the poet never used *Sr.* on his name.) As a more modern example, the actor Jason Robards dropped *Jr.* after his father, a stage actor, died in 1963.

There are two exceptions to the second rule: (1) If the deceased father was quite famous, the son may retain *Jr.*: "The rule that a man does not continue to use 'Jr.' after the death of his father is correctly disregarded if the older man was extremely prominent and continues to be mentioned frequently in the press and elsewhere after his death. In such case, the son properly continues to use 'Jr.' to avoid confusion." Llewellyn Miller, *The Encyclopedia of Etiquette* 393 (1967). There are good examples, such as Frank Sinatra Jr. and Hank Williams Jr. (they rightly kept their labels). (2) Some authorities have suggested that a son who earns a title should not use *Jr.*, presumably because the differentiating label that *Jr.* represents then becomes unnecessary: "A son who acquires a title ('Dr.,' 'Colonel,' 'Rabbi,' for example) drops 'Jr.' unless his father also has the same title as well as the same name." Llewellyn Miller, *The Encyclopedia of Etiquette* 393 (1967).

Today, these first two rules are frequently ignored. Many men seem to become *Jr.* for life (e.g., William F. Buckley Jr.). And some fathers do adopt *Sr.* Perhaps the niceties are lost as fewer and fewer sons are named after their fathers; the convention is certainly much rarer than it was in the early 20th century. In 2000, the advice columnist Abigail Van Buren repeated the customary guidance about dropping *Jr.* on the father's death but added that "if you desire, there is nothing illegal or improper about retaining the 'Jr.'" Abigail Van Buren, "Dear Abby," *Charleston Gaz.*, 22 June 2000, at D3. One etiquette book adds that a son's retaining the *Jr.* after his father dies "helps to differentiate between his wife and his mother if the latter is still living and does not wish to be known as 'Mrs. Jones, Sr.'" Elizabeth L. Post, *Emily Post's Etiquette* 26 (1992). This approach certainly makes good sense. Perhaps the new convention is to keep *Jr.* to honor the father.

Even if a "Jr." drops the label, there's some evidence that others won't—e.g.: "Edwin Llwyd Ecclestone was a 'Jr.' for most of his life, but he dropped the 'Jr.' from his name after his father's death in 1981 and can't understand why people and the press don't honor that." "The Power Hitter E. Llwyd Ecclestone Born March 8, 1936," *Palm Beach Post*, 19 Dec. 1999, Special §, at 98.

Third, *Jr.* and *Sr.* aren't used unless the names are identical—forename, middle name, and surname. So the second Bush president (George W. Bush) is not a junior, the father's name being George Herbert Walker Bush. But some journalists, especially in Great Britain, use *Jr.* and *Sr.* as a kind of loose shorthand—e.g.: "George Bush Sr [said it] in his campaign for the US presidency in 1988." Philip Howard, "Who Said That?" *Times* (London), 23 Mar. 2001, § 2, at 5. (Of course, the British, as in that example, omit any period after *Sr.* because it is a contracted abbreviation. See **Mr.**)

Many American writers use *Sr.* to distinguish an older man, especially a father, with the same name, even if the younger man does not use *Jr.*—e.g.: "*Stacy Keach Sr.*, a character actor, director and producer who was also the father of actor *Stacy Keach* and director James Keach, died Thursday at Providence-St. Joseph Medical Center in Burbank, Calif." "Stacy Keach Sr." (obit.), *Dallas Morning News*, 15 Feb. 2003, at A39.

Fourth, when a male shares a name with both his living father and his living grandfather, he is called "3rd" or "III." (The Arabic numeral appears less pretentious.) If the grandfather dies first among the three, the grandson becomes "Jr." If the father dies before the grandfather, the grandson stays "3rd." When both the father and grandfather have died, the grandson drops all distinguishing labels. So getting into "5th," "6th," and so on isn't yet possible—though medical breakthroughs may one day result in such longevity. Kings and queens, by the way, aren't subject to this rule.

Finally, there's the question of punctuation. *Jr.* and *Sr.*, which are increasingly used restrictively, may appear with no comma—e.g.: "Louis V. Gerstner Jr., the new chairman of I.B.M., began his campaign yesterday to revive the world's largest computer maker by announcing an $8.9 billion program to cut the company's costs sharply." Steve Lohr, "I.B.M. Chief Making Drastic New Cuts; 60,000 Jobs to Go," *N.Y. Times*, 28 July 1993, at A1. Journalistic stylebooks—such as the AP's and the UPI's—prefer this approach, probably because newspapers generally disfavor optional commas.

And the comma-less *Jr.* has logic on its side. That's why E.B. White was persuaded to change the text of *The Elements of Style*. The first and second editions had said: "The abbreviations *etc.* and *jr.* are parenthetic and are always to be so regarded. James Wright, Jr." *Elements of Style* at 3 (1959; 2d ed. 1972). The text changed in the third edition, however, after Thomas B. Lemann of New Orleans prompted White: "Although *Junior*, with its abbreviation *Jr.*, has commonly been regarded as parenthetic, logic suggests that it is, in fact, restrictive and therefore not in need of a comma. James Wright Jr." *Elements of Style* at 3 (3d ed. 1979).

But in the mid-1990s, the president of the American Law Institute, Charles Alan Wright, canvassed the views of 25 eminent lawyers and judges who bore the abbreviation at the ends of their names. They unanimously stated a preference for the comma. That's the traditional approach.

Both forms are correct. Besides logic, the comma-less form probably has the future on its side; for one thing, it makes possessives possible (*John Jones Jr.'s book*). The with-comma form has recent (not ancient) tradition on its side. Posterity will be eager to discover, no doubt, how this earth-shattering dilemma is resolved in the decades ahead. One consideration that militates in favor of the comma-less form is that, in a sentence, one comma begets another: "John Jones, Jr. was elected" seems to be telling Jones that Jr. was elected. With a comma before *Jr.*, another is needed after: "John Jones, Jr., was elected."

C. Pronunciation of Foreign Names. As the international lingua franca, English has achieved a greater degree of eclecticism than any other language in history. It has borrowed words from most other major languages, often copiously. It has almost universally anglicized its borrowings—using English phonemes (speech sounds) to approximate the sound of a word in the language of the word's origin. The English word *ketchup*, for example, derives from the Cantonese term *k'ē chap*, which is not authentically pronounceable with English phonemes. No sensible speaker of Cantonese, when visiting the United States, would object that Americans "mispronounce" *ketchup*, any more than a sensible American would object that Thais, when speaking Thai, say something like /kahm-pyoo-**tuu**-[ə]/ for *computer* or /a-**pən**/ for *apple* (both of which are Thai borrowings from English).

A borrowing language, in other words, makes loanwords more native—more pronounceable—by using the closest available phonemes. What results, when the usage becomes widespread, is a "correct" pronunciation in the borrowing language. A speaker striving to be correct shouldn't reach for an affected pronunciation using foreign phonemes unavailable to other speakers of the borrowing language.

Four major principles follow from this line of reasoning.

(1) *If a name is well known to the English-speaking world, use the pronunciation most common among speakers of English.* Trying to outdo one's neighbors with "correct" pronunciations of foreign names is a silly affectation. It may be good German to say *Bach* with a guttural end (/bahkh/), but it isn't good English. And when the German composer's name appears in an English sentence, it should be a simple /bahk/. Examples abound:

Barcelona (/bahr-sə-**loh**-nə/, not /bahr-thə-**loh**-nə/)
Budapest (/**boo**-də-pest/, not /**boo**-də-pesht/)
Caracas (/kə-**rahk**-əs/, not /kə-[d]ahk-əs/)
Cuba (/**kyoo**-bə/, not /**koo**-bə/)
Hawaii (/hə-**wɪ**-ee/, not /hə-**vɪ**-ee/)
Mexico (/**mek**-si-koh/, not /**me**-hee-koh/)

Moscow (/**mos**-koh/ or /**mos**-kow/, not /məsk-vəh/)
Paris (/**pair**-is/, not /pah-**ree**/)
Salzburg (/**sahltz**-bərg/, not /**zahlz**-boorg/)
Van Gogh (/van **goh**/, not /van **gok**/)

(2) *When pronouncing foreign names that aren't well known, use English phonemes that most nearly approximate those in the original language—and avoid un-English phonemes.* It is hard for most Americans to say the name of the Czech composer Leos Janacek in a way that's satisfactory to a native speaker of the Czech language. (It's hard enough to get the DIACRITICAL MARKS right: Leoš Janáček.) A simple /**lay**-ohs yah-**nah**-chek/ is as close as most English speakers will ever get. And besides, most speakers of English would put the main accent on the first syllable: /**yah**-nah-chek/. That's about as close as anyone needs to get in an English-language context. Likewise, Hispanic names such as *Herrera* and *Guatemala* needn't—and shouldn't—be given hispanicized pronunciations with rolled *r*'s and guttural *g*'s.

On the other hand, Americans are fully capable of saying /ee/ and /ɪ/, so we shouldn't have the trouble that we do with the German *ei* (/ɪ/) and *ie* (/ee/). Perhaps the problem comes from inconsistently pronounced names such as Einstein (/**ɪn**-stɪn/) and Goldstein (/**gohld**-steen/). Chess Grandmaster Jacques Mieses liked to tell a story about an American who addressed him saying, "Are you Mister Meises [/**mis**-tər **mɪ**-zəz/]?" "No," came the reply, "I am Meister Mieses [/**mɪz**-tər **mee**-zəz/]."

Sometimes, though, the choices aren't so stark. After the terrorist acts of 11 September 2001, the group al-Qaeda came to be well known. Some speakers of Arabic criticized American television commentators for saying /al-**kɪ**-də/ or /al-**kay**-də/, insisting that it should be /al-kah-**ee**-də/. But English isn't hospitable to this separation of the middle syllables: it collapses the two into a diphthong. Hence /al-**kɪ**-də/ (the preferable pronunciation) or /al-**kay**-də/.

(3) *Avoid chauvinistic distortions of foreign names that are fully pronounceable with English phonemes.* It's fairly common to call enemies by distorted names. But this isn't an endearing quality of Americans or any other speakers of English. A few examples of distorted pronunciations come readily to mind (last in each list):

Arab (/**ar**-əb/, not /**ay**-rab/)
Begin, Menachem (/mi-**nahk**-əm **bay**-gin/, not /**bee**-gin/)
Gandhi (/**gahn**-dee/, not /**gan**-dee/)
Hiroshima (/hi-roh-**shee**-mə/, not /hi-**roh**-shi-mə/)
Hussein, Saddam (/sə-**dahm** hoo-**sayn**/, not /**sad**-əm/)
Iran (/i-**rahn**/, not /ɪ-**ran**/)
Iraq (/i-**rahk**/, not /ɪ-**rak**/)
Italian (/i-**tal**-yən/, not /ɪ-**tal**-yən/)
Milosevic (/mi-**loh**-sə-vich/, not /mi-**loh**-sə-vik/)
Vietnam (/vee-ət-**nahm**/, not /vee-ət-**nam**/)

LANGUAGE-CHANGE INDEX (For the full key, see front matter pp. xxxi, l–li.)
Stage 1: Rejected. **Stage 2:** Widely shunned. **Stage 3:** Widespread but . . . **Stage 4:** Ubiquitous but . . . **Stage 5:** Fully accepted.
Invariably inferior forms marked by asterisk (✳). • Ratios represent frequency of prevalent forms vs. variants in current books.

(4) *Within the English-speaking world, follow local preferences for place names.* This is a slightly weaker principle than the others. For example, with *Hawaii* it yields to #1. (See **Hawaii (C).**) Many names are pronounced idiosyncratically in different locales:

- Berlin (Germany): /bər-**lin**/
  Berlin (New Hampshire): /**ber**-lən/
- Cairo (Egypt): /**kɪ**-roh/
  Cairo (Illinois): /**kay**-roh/
- DeKalb County (Illinois): /de-**kalb**/
  DeKalb County (Georgia): /de-**kab**/
- Edinburg (Texas): /**ed**-in-bərg/
  Edinburgh (Scotland): /**ed**-in-bər-ə/
- Humble (Texas): /əm-bəl/ (see **humble**)
- Lima (Peru): /**lee**-mə/
  Lima (Ohio): /**lɪ**-mə/
- Mexia (Texas): /mə-**hay**-ə/
- Milan (Italy): /mi-**lahn**/ *or* /mee-**lahn**/
  Milan (Michigan): /**mɪ**-lan/
- Palestine (historic): /**pal**-ə-stɪn/
  Palestine (Texas): /**pal**-ə-steen/
- Pedernales (Texas): /pər-di-**nal**-əs/ (see METHATHESIS)

D. Names with Particles. Many names contain particle prefixes such as *al, d', de, della, der, du, el, la, mac, ten, ter, van,* and *von.* If a prefix has been compounded with the remainder of the surname, the correct form takes little thought <Lafarge> <Debussy> <Vandergriff>. But things can become more complicated with proper names having separate particles. When used with a person's full name or with a title, the particle is retained as part of the surname <Count von Zeppelin> <Princess Marie de Bourbon> <Justice van Zandt> <Professor Ahmad al-Hariq> <Mrs. La Ruiz>. By contrast, when the surname is used alone, whether the particle remains depends on the name's origin, the particle's function (that is, whether it's a preposition, an article, or an expression of descent), and certain customary usages.

In Romance languages (such as French, Spanish, Italian, and Portuguese), particles that are also prepositions meaning "of," "from," or "at" are not capitalized. If the main part of the surname is a single syllable, the preposition is retained when the surname is used alone—hence *Charles de Gaulle* becomes *de Gaulle* and *Pierre de Weck* becomes *de Weck.* If a surname is longer than one syllable, the preposition is usually dropped—hence *Simon de Montfort* becomes *Montfort* and *Eduardo de Carvalho* becomes *Carvalho.* When *d'* is used, it is normally retained, regardless of the length of the surname—e.g., *Jean d'Arc* becomes *d'Arc* and *Tullio d'Attore* becomes *d'Attore.* All other particles are always capitalized and are retained in the surname—so *John Dos Passos* becomes *Dos Passos, Jacques La Motte* becomes *La Motte,* and *Georges Des Périers* becomes *Des Périers.* If a name contains a preposition plus another particle, the preposition remains lowercase and is dropped when the surname stands alone—e.g., *Françoise de La Tour* yields *La Tour* and *Tomas de La Ruiz* yields *La Ruiz.* The one exception to lowercasing prepositions occurs when a preposition has been compounded with the remainder of the name, as in *Claude Debussy* (*Debussy*) and *Henri Darnley* (*Darnley*).

Exceptions abound when names with Romance-language particles appear in anglicized forms. For example, *la, le,* and *les* are very rarely contracted to *l'* in French, but the contraction appears frequently in anglicized French names—e.g., *Philip L'Estrange* (instead of *le Estrange*) and *Charles L'Alique* (instead of *le Alique*). Most particles are lowercase, and they are usually retained when the surname is used alone <della Francesca> <de la Renta> <du Maurier>. This is so even if the main surname has more than one syllable <de Havilland> <de Tonnancour>. Sometimes the prepositions are capitalized <Luca Della Robbia> <Thomas D'Avenant>, sometimes not <Cecil B. de Mille> <Juan de Las Casas>. Anglicized names may not have a space between the particle and the main surname. And the particle may or may not be capitalized, while the main name is always capitalized <LeTourneau> <DeLaRosa> <deNiverville>. See **De Quincey.**

In German, a particle in a surname always contains a preposition, usually *von;* occasionally, the Flemish preposition *van* appears. Sometimes an article will appear with the preposition <von dem> <von der>. Particles are never capitalized and are always dropped when the surname stands alone—hence *Manfred von Richthofen* becomes *Richthofen, Gerhard von der Burg* becomes *Burg,* and *Ludwig van Beethoven* becomes *Beethoven.* When anglicized, the particles in German names are ordinarily (but not always) lowercase <Klaus von Bülow> <Wernher Von Braun> and are usually retained—so *Friedrich von Steuben* becomes *von Steuben* and *Erich von Stroheim* becomes *von Stroheim.* The person's own preference, which shouldn't be hard to determine, is the ultimate guide.

The most common particle in Dutch and Flemish surnames is the preposition *van,* sometimes coupled with an article <van der> <van de>; other common particles are *ten* and *ter.* A particle is never dropped when the surname stands alone, even if the particle means "of" or "from"—so *Vincent van Gogh* becomes *van Gogh, Jan ten Broeck* becomes *ten Broeck,* and *Roger van der Weyden* becomes *van der Weyden.* Capitalization of particles differs depending on whether the named person is Dutch or Flemish. In a Dutch name, the particle is usually capitalized only if it follows a title and there is no intervening personal name or initial <Prof. Van Leeuwenhoek> <Prof. H. J. van Leeuwenhoek>. But in Flemish names, the first particle is always capitalized unless the person is explicitly noble; then it is lowercase <Prof. Van de Waele> <Baron van de Waele>. When anglicized, the particle *van* is often capitalized; a conjoined article may or may not be <Martin Van Buren> <Erik Van den Broeck> <Peter Van Der Water>. It is also common to see surnames of Dutch and Flemish derivation compounded in myriad ways—e.g., *van der Bild* becomes *Vanderbild, van Brugh* becomes *Vanbrugh,* and *van de Kieft* becomes *Vande Kieft.* Again, hew to the person's preference.

Arabic surnames often have particles, such as articles or words that express a relationship; these include *Abu* (father of), *Abd* (servant of), *Abdel,*

Abdul (worshiper of), *ad, al, an, ar, bin* (son of), *bint* (daughter of), *el, ibn* (son of), and *umm* (mother of). Note that some Arabic prefixes are always capitalized; some require hyphens. All particles are capitalized when the surname stands alone—hence *Noor al Hussein* becomes *Al Hussein, Ahmad el-Ahmiad* becomes *El-Ahmiad,* and *Jasmine umm Kulthum* becomes *Umm Kulthum.* As a rule, particles are retained <bin Laden>, but there are exceptions, usually in the names of well-known people—e.g., *Anwar al-Sadat* becomes *Sadat, Hafez al-Assad* becomes *Assad,* and *Zine el-Abidine Ben-Ali* becomes *Ben-Ali.*

Celtic names are often preceded by *à, ab, ap, Fitz, M', Mac, Mc,* or *O,* all of which express descent. The particle is always retained with the surname. Except for the Welsh particles *ab* and *ap* <ab Llewellyn> <ap Rhys> and the Irish particle *à* <à Broin>, a particle should be capitalized when the surname stands alone <Fitz Simmons> <MacHeath>. In Irish usage, a space always follows the Irish particle *O* or *à* <O Reilly> <à Colm>, but anglicized versions of *O* are customarily followed by an apostrophe and no space <O'Brien>. The particles *Mac, Mc,* and *M'* are used in both Scottish and Irish surnames, traditionally with no space between the particle and the rest of the name <MacDonald> <McAlister> <M'Naughton>. There can be more than one version of a name depending on whether the particle has been absorbed <MacPherson> <Macpherson> <McPherson>. The same is true of *Fitz* <Fitz Patrick> <Fitzpatrick>. The Welsh particles *ab* and *ap* usually have a space separating them from the rest of the surname <ab Eynon> <ap Rhodri>, but there is a trend toward eliminating the space <apEvans> <apRoberts>.

Some surnames in English and Romance languages take the form of saints' names <Charles St. John> <Georges Saint Sebastien> <Phillipe San Pedro> <Camille Saint-Saëns> <Carlos Santo Domingo>; the correct spelling depends on the established usage or the name holder's preference. The *saint* particle is always retained and capitalized as part of the surname—e.g., *Yves St. Laurent* becomes *St. Laurent* and *Camille Sainte-Beuve* becomes *Sainte-Beuve.* But if the surname also contains a particle, that particle is dropped when the surname is used alone—e.g., *José de San Martín* becomes *San Martín* and *Francesco da San Germanno* becomes *San Germanno.*

Some names were anglicized long ago and won't be familiar if the anglicized form isn't used. On the other hand, a name that is written other than by the appropriate convention can tag the writer as careless or biased. Care is required.

A final note: despite the myriad conventions here discussed, every lowercase particle gets capitalized at the beginning of a sentence—e.g., *Bin Laden ranted about . . . , D'Arc presented a problem . . . , De la Renta's fashion show was . . . , De Mille's final epic demonstrated . . . .* See (A).

E. British Practices with American Place Names. British writers do a strange thing with American place names: they use the adjectival form ending in *-n* where Americans wouldn't change the name at all. Hence the British might refer to Bill Clinton's *Arkansan property,* as opposed to his *Arkansas property.* And notice what British writers do in the following examples—wrongly from the American's perspective:

- "He died Friday night at his *Californian* [read *California*] ranch in Big Sur." Clive Cookson, "Linus Pauling: Leader in Chemistry," *Fin. Times,* 22 Aug. 1994, at 4.
- Peter Tory, "Delicious *Texan* [read *Texas*] Recipe for Criminal 'Appetites,'" *Daily Express* (London), 26 Aug. 1994, at 9.

F. Proper Names as Adjectives. See ADJECTIVES (D).

G. Pluralizing Proper Names. See PLURALS (F).

H. Names for Place Residents and Natives. See DENIZEN LABELS.

I. Other Sources. For good general studies, see Justin Kaplan & Anne Bernays, *The Language of Names* (1997), and Elsdon C. Smith, *Treasury of Name Lore* (1967). For books on how proper names have become everyday words, see Eugene Ehrlich, *What's in a Name?* (1999); Andrew Sholl, *Wellingtons, Watts & Windsor* (1997); and Rosie Boycott, *Batty, Bloomers and Boycott* (1983). For a source on possessive phrases made from proper names (e.g., *Achilles' heel, Adam's rib, Halley's comet*), see Dorothy Rose Blumberg, *Whose What?* (1969).

nankeen (= a type of cotton cloth) is the standard spelling in AmE and BrE alike. **Nankin* is a variant.

Current ratio: 8:1

nanny (= a nursemaid) is the standard spelling. **Nannie* is a primarily BrE variant (yet uncommon even there).

Current ratio: 435:1

naphtha. A. Misspelled. *Naphtha* /**naf**-thə/ (= a liquid distilled from petroleum and used as a solvent or fuel) is sometimes misspelled (and mispronounced) **naptha*—e.g.:

- "The facility would produce about 20,000 barrels per day of distillates and *naptha* [read *naphtha*] and be scheduled for startup in 2002." "Phillips Eyes Qatar Plant," *Tulsa World,* 17 July 1997, at E1.
- "The facility, which will employ oil- and *naptha* [read *naphtha*]-burning generators and perhaps one that burns coal, is planned for a 17-acre parcel in Puhi." Joan Conrow, "New Kauai Power Plant Would Double Capacity," *Honolulu Star-Bull.,* 2 Aug. 1997, at A4.
- "The fire erupted on the barge carrying *naptha* [read *naphtha*]." "Barges Collide; Fire Is Extinguished," *San Antonio Express-News,* 21 July 2015, Metro §, at 7.

LANGUAGE-CHANGE INDEX
naphtha misspelled and
mispronounced **naptha*: Stage 1
Current ratio: 18:1

LANGUAGE-CHANGE INDEX (For the full key, see front matter pp. xxxi, l–li.)
Stage 1: Rejected. **Stage 2:** Widely shunned. **Stage 3:** Widespread but . . . **Stage 4:** Ubiquitous but . . . **Stage 5:** Fully accepted.
Invariably inferior forms marked by asterisk (*). • Ratios represent frequency of prevalent forms vs. variants in current books.

B. Long Form: *naphthalene;* **naphthaline;* **naph-thalin.* The first is the standard spelling in AmE and BrE alike. The others are variant forms.

*napsack. See **knapsack.**

narcissism (= excessive interest in oneself; self-love) is the standard term. **Narcism* is a NEEDLESS VARIANT that appeared sporadically from about 1920 to 1960.

Current ratio: 559:1

narcissus. Since about 1870, the predominant plural has been the Latin *narcissi,* not the native plural **narcissuses* (which is excessively sibilant)—e.g.:

- "All my laboriously naturalized daffodils and *narcissi* will gradually emerge in my absence." Maxine Kumin, "Florida Spring Has Her Missing Mud Season," *Star Trib.* (Minneapolis), 23 Mar. 1995, at A15.
- "And I wanted to see the dwarf *narcissi* dance around the koi pond." Irene Virag, "Living Color," *Newsday* (N.Y.), 6 Apr. 1997, at E9.

But from 1800 to 1860, the homegrown plural was the more common of the two. See PLURALS (B).

Current ratio (*narcissi* vs. **narcissuses*): 9:1

narrator; **narrater.* The first is the standard form, the second a variant to be avoided.

Current ratio: 41,805:1

nary a (= not a; not one; no) was long considered dialectal AmE dating from the 18th century. In fact, though, it appears today in highly literate writing—e.g.:

- "There's *nary a* decorated interior these days that isn't testimony to a flurry of veneer-stripping, sanding and hand-rubbing." Stephanie Gutmann, "Rusticated," *New Republic,* 3 Apr. 1995, at 14.
- "The settlement ended a sex discrimination suit filed in April 2002 by three female employees after a yearlong campaign by the employee union to get coverage had received *nary* a word from company officials." *Columbia Journalism Rev.,* Mar. 2003, at 9.
- "The Canadian Museum of Civilization, after a promising start under new management in 1998, has yet to move away from the bland exhibits of a previous era, when *nary* a dark shadow was to be seen." Victor Suthren, "A Museum of Tolerance," *Maclean's,* 17 Mar. 2003, at 42.

The expression grew in prevalence and stature beginning about 1850.

national; federal. In a nation with a federal system of government, these two terms might seem interchangeable. But the founders of the United States carefully distinguished them—particularly James Madison, who wrote:

> [T]he Constitution is to be founded on the assent and ratification of the people of America, given by deputies elected for the special purpose; but, on the other [hand], . . . this assent and ratification is to be given by the people, not as individuals composing one entire nation, but as composing the distinct and independent States to which they respectively belong. It is to be the assent and ratification of the several States, derived from the supreme

authority in each State—the authority of the people themselves. The act, therefore, establishing the Constitution will not be a *national* but a *federal* act.

The Federalist No. 39, at 243 (James Madison)

(Clinton Rossiter ed., 1961).

So as Madison explained, the foundation of the Constitution is *federal;* the operation of governmental powers under the Constitution is *national;* and the method of introducing amendments is *mixed. Ibid.* at 246.

Native American. The term *Native American* proliferated in the 1970s to denote groups served by the federal Bureau of Indian Affairs: American Indians as well as the Eskimos and Aleuts of Alaska. Later, the term was interpreted as including Native Hawaiians (see **Hawaiian**) and Pacific Islanders, and it fell into disfavor among some Indian and Alaskan groups, who came to prefer *American Indian* and *Alaska Native.* Yet views are unpredictable: some consider *Native American* more respectful than *American Indian.*

As an equivalent to *American Indian,* the phrase *Native American* was long thought to be a 20th-century innovation. See *Second Barnhart Dictionary of New English* 316 (1980); Sidney I. Landau, "Native American," 69 *Am. Speech* 202 (1994). In fact, the phrase *Native American*—though it proliferated in the early and mid-1970s—dates back to at least 1737 in this sense. See Fred Shapiro, "Computer-Assisted Evidence for the Antiquity of the Term *Native American,*" 76 *Am. Speech* 109 (2001). And it made literal sense (for the most part) in 1737, since at that time most people who had been born in the New World were indigenous—not of European descent.

By the 19th century, when the term *Native American* was fairly common, it had become ambiguous, since it often referred to any person born in the United States, whether of indigenous or of European descent. Here, in a mid-20th-century passage, it refers to place of birth: "Dr. Flesch . . . was born in Vienna, but writes more like a *native American* than do most native Americans; in fact, he teaches the natives how to write like natives; it is always amazing to recall that he came to America as lately as the 1930's." Gorham Munson, *The Written Word* 196 (rev. ed. 1949).

The phrase *indigenous American,* which is more logically and etymologically correct, does have some support—e.g.:

- "He alleged he and other American Indians were being illegally excluded from serving as jurors in San Juan County, where more than half the residents are descended from *indigenous Americans.*" Dawn House, "Jury Still Out on Navajos' Role in Utah Courts," *Salt Lake Trib.,* 7 Feb. 2001, at D2.
- "Hundreds of high schools and colleges have dropped their Indian symbols over the past 30 years as many *indigenous American* groups and their members have called for sports teams to drop the names." David McKay Wilson, "Rules Due on School Mascots," *J. News* (Westchester Co., N.Y.), 3 June 2002, at B1.
- "Bartolome de Las Casas . . . preached justice for *indigenous Americans* in the 16th century." Stephanie Nichols,

"Shrine Will Promote Understanding," *Commercial Appeal* (Memphis), 8 Aug. 2002, Neighbors §, at 2.

Not surprisingly, the synonymous phrase *autochthonous American* has never caught on.

*native-born citizen. This phrase, though it has been fairly common since the 19th century, reeks of REDUNDANCY—e.g.: "Some immigrants come to America as boat people, dirt poor and speaking no English, and within a decade are part of the professional class—suggesting that any poor *native-born* [read *native*] citizen has only his own sloth to blame." Robert Kuttner, "The Delusion of a Classless America," *San Diego Union-Trib.*, 29 July 1997, at B7.

The modern temptation to brace the adjective *native* may come from two sources. First, in American law, the noun *native* has come to mean either (1) "a person born in the country"; or (2) "a person born outside the country of parents who are (at the time of the birth) citizens of that country and who are not permanently residing elsewhere." Sense 2 represents a slide in meaning, but the writer quoted above could not possibly have wanted to protect against that extended meaning. Second, the phrase *Native American*, meaning *American Indian*, has recently popularized a secondary meaning of *native*, one having to do with heritage and not with birthplace: "one of the original or usual inhabitants of a country, as distinguished from strangers or foreigners; now *esp.* one belonging to a non-European race in a country in which Europeans hold political power" (*OED*).

LANGUAGE-CHANGE INDEX
native-born citizen for *native citizen*: Stage 4
Current ratio (*native citizen* vs. *native-born citizen*): 1.3:1

natural child is a EUPHEMISM for *bastard, illegitimate child*, or *nonmarital child*. But the phrase is nearly meaningless, all children being natural. See **illegitimate child.**

nature, of a ——. Good editors routinely revise this stilted phrase, which takes four words to do the work of one. If, for example, you can say that someone is *of a generous nature*, you can invariably say that the person is simply *generous*. Cf. **manner.**

naught; nought. These are different spellings of the same word, meaning "nothing." By convention, *nought*—especially in BrE—has come to signify the number zero (0). *Naught* is conventionally used in all nonmathematical contexts in which "nothing" is meant, usually accompanied by some form of *come* or *go*—e.g.:

- "Fujimori's dramatic bid to move the hostage impasse off dead center by seeking Cuba's assistance apparently came to *naught*, but he deserves credit for the effort." "Heading for Havana?" *Pitt. Post-Gaz.*, 5 Mar. 1997, at A10.

- "Rodriguez' efforts went for *naught*." Gary Brooks, "Sanders' Woes Continue," *News Trib.* (Tacoma), 19 Apr. 1997, at C1.

See **aught (B) & dreadnought.**

Sometimes *nought* ill-advisedly appears where the conventional word would be *naught*—e.g.:

- "Plans to sell a large portion of Meador Park to the owner of the Battlefield Mall came to *nought* [read *naught*] last week." Clarissa A. Franch, "Simon DeBartolo Declines to Purchase Meador Park," *Springfield Bus. J.* (Mo.), 21 Oct. 1996, at 3.
- "But all of Henry's machinations to get a male heir came to *nought* [read *naught*]." Peggy Brown, "Heirs to the Crown," *Newsday* (N.Y.), 9 Sept. 1997, at A30.

LANGUAGE-CHANGE INDEX
came to nought for *came to naught*:
Stage 1
Current ratio (*came to naught* vs.
came to nought): 5:1

nausea (= the feeling one has just before vomiting) is pronounced /**naw**-zee-ə/, /**naw**-zhə/, or /**naw**-shə/. The corresponding verb is *nauseate* /**naw**-zee-ayt/.

nauseous (= inducing nausea) for *nauseated* (= experiencing nausea) is becoming so common that to call it an error is to exaggerate. Even so, careful writers tend to be sickened by the slippage and to follow the traditional distinction in formal writing. That is, what is *nauseous* makes one feel *nauseated*—e.g.: "No one in Mrs. Thompson's crew would ever be so *nauseous* as to try to get everybody to pray aloud or form a prayer circle, but you can still tell what they're all doing." David Foster Wallace, "The View from Mrs. Thompson's," in *Consider the Lobster* 140 (2006). Through 2008, the U.S. Supreme Court, in its seven uses of either word, had maintained a perfect record—e.g.: "It is made up entirely of repetitive descriptions of physical, sexual conduct, 'clinically' explicit and offensive to the point of being *nauseous*; there is only the most tenuous plot." *Kaplan v. California*, 413 U.S. 115, 116–17 (1973).

But other writers have spread the peccadillo, especially since the late 20th century—e.g.:

- "At first, she didn't worry too much when she felt *nauseous* [read *nauseated*] and had a few more headaches than usual." Laura Bendix, "Factory Stores Workers Worry About Illnesses," *Santa Fe New Mexican*, 12 May 1995, at A1.
- "He takes $30,000 worth of AIDS-related drugs a year, which leave him horribly *nauseous* [read *nauseated*]." Dave Saltonstall, "Cops Clip 61 at Pot Rally," *Daily News* (N.Y.), 4 May 1997, at 6.

Nauseous is pronounced /**naw**-shəs/.

LANGUAGE-CHANGE INDEX
nauseous misused for *nauseated*: Stage 4
1940 ratio (*felt nauseated* vs. *felt nauseous*): 9:1
Current ratio: 1:1.5

LANGUAGE-CHANGE INDEX (For the full key, see front matter pp. xxxi, l–li.)
Stage 1: Rejected. **Stage 2:** Widely shunned. **Stage 3:** Widespread but . . . **Stage 4:** Ubiquitous but . . . **Stage 5:** Fully accepted.
Invariably inferior forms marked by asterisk (*). • Ratios represent frequency of prevalent forms vs. variants in current books.

nautilus (the mollusk with a spiral shell) has traditionally formed the plural *nautili* (/**nawt**-i-LI/), but since about 1970 *nautiluses* has been strongly predominant in AmE. In BrE and in World English, the two plurals have been locked in close competition since about 1920.

Navajo; *Navaho. Although *Navaho was the predominant spelling as recently as the mid-1960s, today *Navajo* is standard. That's probably because it more closely resembles the Spanish etymon, *navajó*. Cf. **Mohave.**

Navajo has three plurals: *Navajos* (best), *Navajo* (second best), and *Navajoes* (not best at all). See PLURALS (D).

> Current ratio (*Navajo* vs. *Navaho*): 13:1
> Current ratio (*Navajos* vs. *Navajoes*): 25:1

naval; navel. *Naval*, adj., = of, relating to, or involving ships or a navy. *Navel*, n., = belly button. The correct phrase is *navel orange*, which has a navel-like depression at the top. But the mistaken phrase *naval orange* is fairly common—e.g.:

- "Riverside, home of the *naval* [read *navel*] orange, celebrates its orange history with a 'gourmet grove' of orange delicacies." Mary Frances Smith, "Festivals, Feasts & Fairs," *L.A. Times*, 7 Apr. 1996, at 3.
- "Sun Pacific, the largest *naval orange* [read *navel-orange*] grower in California and largest kiwi grower in the United States, is exporting half the oranges it normally ships because of the port impasse." Peter Fimrite, "Hard-Hit Citrus Growers Crushed by Port Dispute," *S.F. Chron.*, 14 Feb. 2015, at A1.

> LANGUAGE-CHANGE INDEX
> *naval orange* for *navel orange*: Stage 1
> Current ratio (*navel orange* vs.
> *naval orange*): 22:1

nave. See **knave.**

Nazi (= [1] an adherent to the tenets of Adolf Hitler's National Socialist Party in Germany (1933–1945), or [2] someone who exercises authority with excessive strictness and cruelty) is pronounced /**naht**-see/ or (in old-fashioned films, etc.) /**nat**-see/—but never /**nah**-zee/ or /**naz**-ee/.

N.B. is the abbreviation for the Latin *nota bene* (= note well; take notice).

né. See **née.**

Neanderthal (= [1] a hominid that lived some 30,000 to 200,000 years ago, [2] a big, ugly, and stupid man, or [3] a person with backward ideas and resolute opposition to change) is a technical term in sense 1 and a disparaging label in senses 2 and 3. The word is predominantly pronounced /nee-**an**-dər-thawl/ in AmE and /nee-**an**-dər-tawl/ in BrE. The latter is a slightly anglicized version of the German place name for which the species was named. Many American scientists have adopted this pronunciation perhaps to dissociate themselves from the derogatory connotations of senses 2 and 3.

Neapolitan. As a noun, *Neapolitan* denotes an inhabitant of Naples, Italy. (See DENIZEN LABELS.) As an adjective, it identifies the noun it goes with as being from or connected with Naples. *Neapolitan* ice cream, with layers of different flavors (commonly chocolate, vanilla, and strawberry), originated in the 19th century, supposedly in Naples. The word is pronounced /nee-ə-**pahl**-i-tən/, not /nee-ah-/ or /nee-oh-/.

The term is misspelled *Neopolitan* surprisingly often—e.g.:

- "'Italian,' once a derogatory ethnic label, is now understood to have emerged as a social construct derived from many regional identities—*Neopolitan* [read *Neapolitan*], Calabrian, Sicilian—that once characterized early immigration from Italy to the United States." Alex P. Oberle & Daniel D. Arreola, "Resurgent Mexican Phoenix," *Geographical Rev.*, 1 Apr. 2008, at 171.
- "That classic *Neopolitan* [read *Neapolitan*] ice-cream trio is delicious on the eye, too." "Color My Wedding," *Brides*, Sept.–Oct. 2008, at 140.
- "It was not unlike floating through an enormous block of *Neopolitan* [read *Neapolitan*] ice cream." Helen Olsson, "Nebraska, with a Paddle," *N.Y. Times*, 3 Oct. 2008, at F1.

> LANGUAGE-CHANGE INDEX
> *Neapolitan* misspelled *Neopolitan*: Stage 1
> Current ratio: 68:1

near should not be used adverbially in place of *nearly*. That use of the word is dialectal—e.g.: "It's long all right, but not *near* [read *nearly*] as long as the money shadow Tiger figures to cast by the time he's ready for the rocking chair alongside the 19th hole." Peter Finney, "Year One: A Gauge into Woods' Future," *Times-Picayune* (New Orleans), 27 Aug. 1997, at D1. See DIALECT.

> LANGUAGE-CHANGE INDEX
> *near* misused for the adverb *nearly*: Stage 1
> Current ratio (*not nearly as* vs. *not near as*): 40:1

nebula /**neb**-yə-lə/ (= an interstellar cloud consisting of gas and dust sometimes visible in the night sky) has two plurals, *nebulae* and *nebulas*. Although many dictionaries record only the Latinate plural (-*ae*), the -*as* form isn't uncommon—e.g.: "Designer Tony Walton's fiber-optic light backdrops created *nebulas* and fountains of colored lights to show off the dancers." Maggie Hall, "Miami's 'Jewels' Is a Gem of a Show," *Tampa Trib.*, 19 Apr. 1995, Metro §, at 6. Still, *nebulae* (/**neb**-yə-lee/) has been strongly predominant since the word came into use in the 1700s. See PLURALS (B).

> Current ratio (*nebulae* vs. *nebulas*): 9:1

necessary; necessitous. *Necessary*, the more common word, means "essential." *Necessitous* = placed or living in a condition of necessity or poverty; hard up; needy. One of the most famous statements using the word was Franklin Delano Roosevelt's: "As President Roosevelt said in justifying his bill of rights, '*necessitous* men are not free men.'" "Constitutional Amendments," *L.A. Times*, 4 July 1995, at B8.

necessitarianism. See **fatalism.**

necessitate (= to make necessary) is often inferior to *require*—e.g.: "A bored tunnel also *necessitates* [read *requires*] deeper stations, which cost more to build and ventilate." Mei-Ling Hopgood, "When the Tracks Meet the Trees," *St. Louis Post-Dispatch*, 24 Aug. 1997, at B1. Yet *require* isn't always a satisfactory substitute—e.g.: "Early-season struggles could *necessitate* a change." Mark Didtler, "USF Starts, and So Does Barnhardt," *Orlando Sentinel*, 6 Sept. 1997, at B4. What explains the difference? *Necessitate* sounds less rigid and absolute than *require*.

necessitous. See **necessary.**

neck-and-neck. This metaphorical phrase, from horse racing, is sometimes wrongly written **neck-in-neck*—e.g.: "The top contenders in both the Republican Senate primary and the Democratic race for governor are *neck-in-neck* [read *neck-and-neck*] in the latest polls." Richard L. Berke, "With 3 Primaries Tuesday, Michigan Voters Go Fishing," *N.Y. Times*, 1 Aug. 1994, at A7. The mistaken form doubtless results from the common pronunciation, as if it were *neck-'n'-neck*.

LANGUAGE-CHANGE INDEX
*neck-in-neck for *neck-and-neck*: Stage 1
Current ratio (*neck-and-neck* vs. **neck-in-neck*): 23:1

neckwear (= clothing worn about the neck) is sometimes misspelled **neckware*, on the false analogy of *hardware* or *software*—e.g.:

- "Ms. Keys, 31, had been a *neckware* [read *neckwear*] designer, concentrating on women's scarves, when someone gave her husband a fancy-looking Italian tie." James Barron, "Oh, to Be Sneaky and Well Dressed," *N.Y. Times*, 1 Sept. 1996, § 1, at 47.
- "Dean Mullin, owner of Knotz Apparel Corp., a New Hope *neckware* [read *neckwear*] and graphic design company, said HPNet called him Tuesday." John Wilen, "ISP Abandons Clients to Move West, Fast," *Phil. Bus. J.*, 28 Mar. 1997, at 9.
- "After her stellar performance Sunday in the women's slopestyle competition, she has a new piece of *neckware* [read *neckwear*]: an Olympic gold medal." Rick Maese, "Anderson Rides 'Good Vibes' to Snowboarding Gold," *Wash. Post*, 10 Feb. 2014, at D7.

LANGUAGE-CHANGE INDEX
*neckware for *neckwear*: Stage 1
Current ratio (*neckwear* vs. **neckware*): 30:1

nectarous; *nectareous; *nectarean; *nectareal. Though all these adjectives are infrequent, the first is standard. The others are NEEDLESS VARIANTS.

Current ratio (in order of headwords): 99:94:50:1

née; né. This GALLICISM (meaning "born") denotes a person's original name. The feminine form, *née*, often precedes a married woman's maiden name <Mrs. David Smith (*née* Mary Jones)>. Either form (*né* is masculine) may also follow a changed name, such as a pen name

<Mark Twain (*né* Samuel Clemens)> or a screen name <Marilyn Monroe (*née* Norma Jean Baker)>.

In AmE, the accent mark is often omitted. But especially in the uncommon masculine form, the two characters are apt to be mistaken as a typographical error—so the accent is recommended. See DIACRITICAL MARKS.

The two forms are pronounced the same: /nay/.

The feminine form is often misapplied to men's names—e.g.:

- "The movement's founding troika—Ed 'Big Daddy' Roth, Von Dutch (*nee* [read *né*] Kenneth Howard) and Robert Williams—started out, back in the '50s, as hot-rod enthusiasts who worked on cars instead of canvas, proudly raising middle fingers to snobby high-art aficionados." Jessica Dawson, " 'Second Childhood': The Mechanics of 'Low Brow,' " *Wash. Post*, 19 July 2001, at C5.
- "Benjamin Graham (*nee* [read *né*] Grossbaum), father of modern security analysis, mentor of Warren Buffett." Jason Grunberg & Cybele Weisser, "Give Us Your (Moderately) Poor," *Money*, 1 Aug. 2001, at 24.

By SLIPSHOD EXTENSION, *nee* is used to mean "formerly" and applied to nonliving objects—e.g.:

- "Sporting News Radio, *nee* [read *formerly*] One on One, now mostly exists as a promotional tool for everything Sporting News, from the weekly magazine to its website." Phil Mushnick, "All Ads, All the Time," *N.Y. Post*, 22 July 2001, at 94.
- "If the Bayer (*nee* [read *formerly*] Alcoa) sign hadn't been on Mount Washington all these years, we would be just as well without it." Editorial, "Lighting Their Ire: Signs on Buildings Bring Out the Art Critic in Everyone," *Pitt. Post-Gaz.*, 22 July 2001, at E3.

LANGUAGE-CHANGE INDEX
1. *née* for *né* in reference to a man: Stage 3
2. *née* for *formerly* in reference to an inanimate object: Stage 1

needle in a haystack; needle in a bottle of hay. Although the latter expression looks odd to most people, it's the older one. The word *bottle* is used there in the sense "bundle"—a sense that is now obsolete (except in the expression). The phrase *needle in a haystack* predominates in modern usage.

Current ratio (*needle in a haystack* vs. *needle in a bottle of hay*): 43:1

NEEDLESS VARIANTS, two or more forms of the same word without nuance or DIFFERENTIATION—and seemingly without even hope for either—teem in the English language. They're especially common in the outer reaches of the language—in technical vocabulary. Unfortunately, the unnecessary coexistence of variant forms (e.g., adjectives ending in *-tive* and *-tory*) leads not to precision in technical writing but to uncertainties about authorial intention. The trusting reader silently thinks, "The writer used *investigative* on the previous page but now has pressed *investigatory* into service—is a distinction intended?"

"It is a source not of strength," wrote H.W. Fowler, "but of weakness, that there should be two names for the same thing [by-forms differing merely in suffix or in some such minor point], because the reasonable assumption is that two words mean two things, and confusion results when they do not" (*FMEU1* at 373). The confusion is perhaps greatest when the writer who is fond of INELEGANT VARIATION discovers the boundless mutations of form that exist in unabridged dictionaries: *submission* will appear in one sentence, *submittal in the next; *quantify* on one page, *quantitate on the next; and so on.

"On the other hand," Fowler advises us, "it may be much too hastily assumed that two words do mean the same thing; they may, for instance, denote the same object without meaning the same thing if they imply that the aspect from which it is regarded is different, or are appropriate in different mouths, or differ in rhythmic value or in some other matter that may escape a cursory examination" (*FMEU1* at 373). Hence the nonlawyer should not jump to assume that *necessaries* is uncalled for in place of *necessities*; that *acquittance* has no place alongside *acquittal*; that *recusancy* is yet another needless variant of *recusal*; that *burglarize* is as good for a British audience as it is for an American one; and so forth.

Any number of entries throughout this work attempt to ferret out and discriminate between cognate words with established or emerging distinctions and those that seem, at present, to have neither. To the extent possible, words and phrases rightly classifiable as needless variants ought to be dropped from the language.

negative, in the. See **affirmative, in the.**

NEGATIVES. A. Negative Prefixes. The primary negative (or "privative") prefixes in English are *in-* (assimilated in many words to *il-, im-, ir-*), *un-, non-, anti-,* and *a-*. For purposes of simple negation, *in-* is the most particularized of these prefixes, since it generally goes only with certain Latin derivatives (e.g., *inaccessible, inarticulate, intolerant*). *Un-* usually precedes most other adjectives, including Latin derivatives ending in *-ed* (e.g., *undiluted, unexhausted, unsaturated*). *Non-* is the broadest of the prefixes, since it may precede virtually any word. It often contrasts with *in-* or *un-* in expressing a nongradable contrast, rather than the opposite end of a scale—e.g.: *nonscientific* (= concerned with a field other than science) as opposed to *unscientific* (= not in accordance with scientific principles). *Anti-*, of course, has the special sense "against." *A-* (= not, without) appears mostly but not exclusively with Greek derivatives (e.g., *theist/ atheist, symmetrical/asymmetrical*) and scientific terminology (e.g., *mitosis/amitosis*). Because this prefix is easily confused with the defunct Old English prefix *a-* (which is not a negative), it is best kept to established pairings.

As a general rule, try to find the most suitable particularized prefix—and if no other is really suitable, try *non-*.

But consistency is often difficult to find with particular roots. For example, *unsaturated fats* has the corresponding noun *nonsaturation*, not *unsaturation. Likewise, we have *indubitable* but *undoubted*, *irresolute* but *unresolved*, *irrespective* but *unrespected*. From a typographical standpoint, negative prefixes cause trouble with PHRASAL ADJECTIVES, as in *uncross-examined witness*. Wordings that are less compressed are usually preferable; hence *a witness who wasn't cross-examined*.

With few exceptions, the prefix *non-* does not take a hyphen unless it is attached to a proper noun, as with *non-European*. See PUNCTUATION (J).

B. Not un-; not in-. Double negatives such as *not untimely* are often needlessly used in place of more straightforward wordings such as *timely*. When the negatives serve no such identifiable purpose, they ought to be avoided. To say, for example, that the point is *not uninteresting* or that somebody's writing is *not unintelligible* is probably to engage in a time-wasting rhetorical flourish.

This type of litotes (the negation of an opposite) often makes language convoluted. George Orwell ridiculed it with this example: "A not unblack dog was chasing a not unsmall rabbit across a not ungreen field." "Politics and the English Language" (1946), in 4 *Collected Essays, Journalism and Letters of George Orwell* 127, 138 n.1 (1968).

C. Periphrastic Negatives. Generally *we disagree* is preferable to *we do not agree*—except that the latter may be slightly more emphatic. Directness is better than indirectness; hence *violate* rather than *fail to comply with*; *violate* rather than *do not adhere to*, and the like. See PERIPHRASIS.

D. Not . . . all. On the problems caused by this phrasing, see **all (B).**

neglectful; *neglective. The latter has always been a NEEDLESS VARIANT that is rare or obsolete.

Current ratio: 486:1

negligee; *negligée; *negligé; *négligé. Some will say that it's good in any form. But in fact *negligee* is standard. The other three are variants—*négligé being a GALLICISM.

negligence; *negligency. The latter has always been a NEEDLESS VARIANT.

Current ratio: 6,196:1

negligible. So spelled—not *negligeable. See -ABLE (A).

negotiate (= to discuss [something] for the purpose of reaching a bargain or other agreement) is preferably pronounced /nə-**goh**-shee-ayt/, not /nə-**goh**-see-ayt/.

neither. A. Pronunciation. In AmE generally, /**nee**-thər/ is the traditionally preferred pronunciation; /**nı**-thər/ is a mildly pretentious variant in most parts of the country. But in BrE, /**nɪ**-<u>th</u>ər/ is usual. Cf. **either** (A).

B. Number. As a pronoun, *neither* is construed as a singular. That is, it should take a singular verb, and any word for which *neither* is an antecedent should also be singular. Hence *neither of the offers was a good one* is grammatically better than **neither of the offers were good ones*. E.g.:

- "The fact is that *neither* of these men *were* [read *was*] an expert on language." John McWhorter, *The Word on the Street* 63 (1998).
- "Two new research papers add to the debate. *Neither dispute* [read *Neither disputes*] the idea that evolution plays a role in shaping behavior, but *they* [read *both*] question the evidence that jealousy evolved differently in men and women." Erica Goode, "Jealous? Sexes Wired Differently, Psychologist Claims," *San Diego Union-Trib.*, 16 Oct. 2002, at F1.

But often it's not that simple. In the first example below, the plural *themselves* is necessary to avoid an awkward or sexist construction (though it would be better to recast the sentence). In the second and third examples, however, there is no danger of SEXISM because the company isn't mixed—and therefore the singular would be the better choice. E.g.:

- "Even though I was the first born (a common entrepreneurial trait), *neither* of my parents worked for *themselves*, and that was a strike against me." Teresa Burney, "Need Job Advice? Break Out the Chivas (Disc, That Is)," *St. Petersburg Times*, 9 June 1996, at G1. (A suggested revision: *neither of my parents was self-employed*.)
- "*Neither* of these two men placed *themselves* [read *himself*] into the police and fire retirement system." Letter of William Blake Brandywine, "Letters to the Editor—Portsmouth," *Virginian-Pilot* (Norfolk), 17 Nov. 1996, Portsmouth Currents §, at 6.
- "Defense attorneys said *neither* of the women had acknowledged *their* [read *her*] pregnancy to *themselves* [read *herself*] or anyone else and said both were distraught and irrational facing the moment of birth." Pat Wiedenkeller, "Pregnancy, Denial, Tragedy," *Newsday* (N.Y.), 21 Nov. 1996, at A27.

LANGUAGE-CHANGE INDEX
neither as a pronoun erroneously construed
with a plural verb: Stage 3
Current ratio (*Neither of them is* vs.
**Neither of them are*): 5:1

C. Beginning Sentences with. It is permissible to begin a sentence with *neither*—just as it is with *nor*—when embarking on yet another negative subject. E.g.:

- "*Neither* must we suppose that the size of the book makes any difference: big books are not necessarily scholarly, nor small ones superficial." Frank Wilson Cheney Hersey, *English Composition* 9 (1921).
- "*Neither* are they outraged at themselves for playing racial politics by insidiously implying, or outright accusing, every black Clinton Cabinet member of being either

a crook or incompetent, or both." Letter of Thomas E. Davis, "GOP Expresses Outrage, but Its Conduct Is Outrageous," *Nashville Banner*, 2 July 1996, at A4.

See **nor** (A).

neither . . . nor. A. Singular or Plural Verb. This construction takes a singular verb when the alternatives are singular or when the second alternative is singular—e.g.:

- "*Neither* the radiator *nor* the water pump *leak* [read *leaks*]." Ray Magliozzi & Tom Magliozzi, "Duplicate Cars Means Customer Pays More for Name," *Amarillo Daily News*, 21 Aug. 1993, at B5.
- "*Neither* the Health Department *nor* the governor's office *were* [read *was*] aware of the changes until the governor received the bills, along with hundreds of others, the following week." Russell Garland, "Plummer Bill Proves Perils of Last-Minute Legislation," *Providence J.-Bull.*, 21 July 1997, at A1.
- "*Neither* Haley *nor* Rowell *were* [read *was*] charged with setting the Macedonia fire." "Prosecutor Drops Kevorkian Case," *St. Louis Post-Dispatch*, 2 Aug. 1997, at 25.
- "But *neither* the airlines *nor* the FAA *were* [read *was*] willing to adopt bag-matching domestically." Holman W. Jenkins Jr., "Airport Security Is Better than You Think," *Wall Street J.*, 2 Jan. 2002, at A19.

Cf. **either** (D).

Moreover, the traditional position is that the verb should precisely match the form mandated by the second of the alternatives. E.g.: "*Neither* Barton *nor* I *am* saying that equities aren't a great long-term place to be." Robert Farrell, as quoted in "Can Stocks Still Rise?" *Fortune*, 18 Aug. 1997, at 68. But in fact, this "rule" has almost never been followed in actual practice when the second element is first person (thereby mandating *am*). As an empirical matter, **neither he nor I am* has never been as common in print as **neither he nor I are*. Both are editorially subpar. Yet apart from *am* constructions, there are several possible variations, among them these:

Neither you nor he *is* right.
Neither I nor she *is* right.
Neither he nor you *are* right.
Neither I nor you *are* right.

As we have already seen, errors frequently occur—e.g.: "Neither you nor I *is* likely to change the world." Jefferson D. Bates, *Writing with Precision* 82 (rev. ed. 1988). Because any choice there is likely to sound wrong, it's a good idea to write around the problem instead. Reversing the order of the elements would improve the sound of the sentence: *Neither I nor you are likely . . .*, or better yet *Neither one of us is likely . . . .* See PREVENTIVE GRAMMAR.

Of course, when both alternatives are plural, the verb is plural—e.g.: "*Neither* those goals *nor* the overall themes of the conference *fit* the extremist image conjured up by some critics of the gathering, like Senators

---

LANGUAGE-CHANGE INDEX (For the full key, see front matter pp. xxxi, l–li.)
Stage 1: Rejected. **Stage 2:** Widely shunned. **Stage 3:** Widespread but . . . **Stage 4:** Ubiquitous but . . . **Stage 5:** Fully accepted.
Invariably inferior forms marked by asterisk (*). • Ratios represent frequency of prevalent forms vs. variants in current books.

Bob Dole and Phil Gramm." "A China Agenda for Mrs. Clinton," *N.Y. Times*, 30 Aug. 1995, at A14.

LANGUAGE-CHANGE INDEX
neither . . . nor with singular alternatives erroneously paired with a plural verb: Stage 3

B. Number of Elements. These CORRELATIVE CONJUNCTIONS best frame only two elements, not more. Though it's possible to find modern and historical examples of *neither . . . nor* with more than two elements, these are unfastidious constructions. When three or more are involved, it's better not to say **They considered neither x, y, nor z.* Instead, say *They didn't consider x, y, or z.* Or it's permissible to use a second *nor* emphatically in framing three elements: *They considered neither x, nor y, nor z.* Cf. **either (B).**

LANGUAGE-CHANGE INDEX
neither . . . nor with more than two elements: Stage 3

C. Parallelism. Not only should there be just two elements, but also the elements should match each other syntactically. (See PARALLELISM.) E.g.:

- "At the same time, many of Aristide's followers express concern that some ex-members of the army and its paramilitary allies who carried out a campaign of terror here have *neither been disarmed nor brought* [read *been neither disarmed nor brought*] to justice." Douglas Farah, "Aristide: U.S. Occupation of Haiti a 'Great Success,'" *Wash. Post*, 31 Mar. 1995, at A1.
- "But Indonesia's ongoing record of improving the quality of life for all East Timorese should *neither be overlooked nor undone* [read *be neither overlooked nor undone*] by those who seek to exploit historical divisions among the East Timorese people for political gain." Letter of D. Budiman, "Indonesian Government Brooks No Room for Divisive Terrorists," *Wash. Times*, 17 Dec. 1997, at A20.
- "Secret Service spokesman Jim Makin said Merletti intended *neither to offend nor infringe* [read *neither to offend nor to infringe*] on agents' free-speech rights." "After JFK Tell-All, Agents Told to Zip It," *Chicago Sun-Times*, 19 Dec. 1997, at 37.

D. *Neither . . . or. This phrasing is either a serious grammatical lapse or a serious typographical error—e.g.:

- "Practically speaking, though, language is *neither* a mirror *or* [read *nor*] a prison." Dennis Baron, *Declining Grammar and Other Essays on the English Vocabulary* 4 (1989).
- "The arrangement has worked because *neither* Fennig *or* [read *nor*] Hmiel *seem* [read *seems*] bent on grabbing glory or control for *themselves* [read *himself*]." Bob Zeller, "Martin Stays Patient in Midst of Drought," *News & Record* (Greensboro), 4 May 1997, at C1.
- "*Neither* lineups of movies *or* [read *nor*] celebrity guests are announced until one day before the festival begins." Steve Persall, "Almost Heaven: Telluride Film Festival," *Tampa Bay Times*, 3 Sept. 2015, at W15.

LANGUAGE-CHANGE INDEX
*neither . . . or for *neither . . . nor*: Stage 2

NEOLOGISMS, or invented words, are to be used carefully and self-consciously. Usually they demand an explanation or justification, since the English language is already well stocked. New words must fill demonstrable voids to survive, and each year a few good ones get added to the language. Some become VOGUE WORDS; others are slow to achieve acceptance; still others, denoting scientific innovations, might never become widely known. Fortunately, lexicographers monitor new entrants into the language and periodically publish compilations such as these: John Ayto, *20th Century Words* (1999); Stuart Berg Flexner & Anne H. Soukhanov, *Speaking Freely* (1997); Sara Tulloch, *The Oxford Dictionary of New Words* (1991); John Algeo, *Fifty Years Among the New Words* (1991).

It is sobering to record what the greatest of late-20th-century lexicographers said about the slow acceptance of new words: "It usually takes slightly more than a century for a word to reach such a state of maturity that it is not recognizably or instinctively felt to be a newcomer." Robert W. Burchfield, *Points of View* 103 (1992).

Yet the explosion of electronic media in the second half of the 20th century has compressed time, and the standards for "maturity" are dropping. For whatever reason, we seem perfectly comfortable today with terms such as *workaholic* (1971), *talk radio* (1972), *couch potato* (1973), *PC* (a personal computer in the 1980s, political correctness in the 1990s), *sound bite* (1980), and terms from the 1950s and 1960s such as *do-it-yourself, glitch, mall, meritocracy, middle management, nitty-gritty,* and *prime time*. For an excellent discussion about speculating on the success of neologisms, see Allan Metcalf, *Predicting New Words* (2002).

Neologism is pronounced /nee-**ahl**-ə-jiz-əm/—not /nee-ə-**loh**-jiz-əm/ or /nee-uh-**lawg**-iz-əm/.

neologist; *neologizer. The first is standard, the second a NEEDLESS VARIANT. E.g.: "Sir Thomas Elyot, the great *neologizer* [read *neologist*], deliberately set out to improve and promote English by introducing new words into the language." Ronald Wardhaugh, *Proper English: Myths and Misunderstandings About Language* 76 (1999).

Current ratio: 11:1

neonaticide. See **infanticide.**

*Neopolitan. See **Neapolitan.**

nephew; niece. Legally speaking, are the children of a spouse's siblings one's *nephews* and *nieces*? No: it's only by courtesy that they're so called.

nepotism is best reserved for the sense "bestowal of official favors upon members of one's family," and not attenuated to refer to friends or political connections. The root sense of *nepot-* in Latin is "nephew, grandson."

nerve-racking (= exasperating) is so spelled—not **nerve-wracking.* See **rack.**

Current ratio: 1.4:1

Netherlands, the; Kingdom of the Netherlands; Holland; Dutch; The Hague. A. Generally. The European country is called *the Netherlands.* The Netherlands—together with Aruba, Curaçao, and St.

Maarten—makes up the *Kingdom of the Netherlands*. In 2010, Bonaire, St. Eustatius, and Saba became special municipalities of the Netherlands. Strictly speaking, *Holland* refers to two coastal provinces of the Netherlands (North Holland and South Holland), and not to the country's ten other provinces. Still, *Holland* is commonly used to refer to the Netherlands as a whole. The people, language, and culture are called *Dutch*. Although the country's capital is Amsterdam, its government is located in The Hague.

B. Capitalization, Number, and Possessive Form. The article *the* is not capitalized in *the Netherlands* (though it always is in *The Hague*). The country's name is plural in form but grammatically singular. This means that it takes a singular verb <the Netherlands is home to the International Court of Justice> but forms a plural possessive <the Netherlands' population is over 16 million>.

C. Denizens. The predominant noun for a citizen of the Netherlands has consistently been *Hollander* from 1680 to the present day. *Netherlander*, an alternative term, was common in the mid-1600s but fell into relative decline. **Netherlandian* is a NEEDLESS VARIANT. See DENIZEN LABELS.

> Current ratio (*Hollanders* vs. *Netherlanders*): 3:1
> Current ratio (*Netherlander* vs. **Netherlandian*): 231:1

neurofibroma. See **neuroma.**

neurological; *neurologic. Although some doctors use the shorter form, it's a NEEDLESS VARIANT that occurs in print much less frequently than the longer form—e.g.: "Treatment of RSDS begins with a prompt and serious attempt to find the nerve lesion, using available *neurologic* [read *neurological*] examinations." Allen Douma, "Pain Syndrome Can Be Difficult to Beat and to Understand," *Chicago Trib.*, 16 Dec. 2001, Health & Fam. §, at 8.

> Current ratio: 2:1

neuroma; neurofibroma. These synonyms denote a usually benign tumor formed on a nerve-cell sheath. The first has consistently been used more frequently in English-language print sources than the second. Although the standard plurals before 1940 were **neuromata* and **neurofibromata*, usage shifted in the mid-20th century toward the anglicized plurals *neuromas* and *neurofibromas*, first in AmE and then in BrE.

Nevada is pronounced /nə-**vad**-ə/ inside the state but /nə-**vah**-də/ throughout much of the rest of the country—perhaps on the analogy of *enchilada* and names such as *Estrada* and *Prada*. Given the sovereign right of citizens to choose how their place names are pronounced, the short *a* in /nə-**vad**-ə/ should be preferred.

One is tempted to say that /nə-**vah**-də/ is incorrect, since the native people's preference ought to be determinative—but things are not so simple. Many highly refined people throughout the U.S. believe that /**vah**/ is the better pronunciation. Given this circumstance, one can only conclude that both pronunciations are acceptable. But if you're in the state, you'd be wise to say /**vad**/. Cf. **Missouri.**

never expected. Eric Partridge criticized this phrase as "incorrect—or, at best, loose—for *expected never*" (*U&A* at 202). But in fact the two phrases don't mean precisely the same thing. Idiomatically, it's quite proper to say that you *never expected* something that simply didn't enter your mind. But to say that you *expected never* means that you thought about it seriously and were skeptical. Imagine how the following passage would change if *never expected* were changed to *expected never* (with the necessary adjustments in syntax made): "Laloo *never expected* the Rapid Action Force to surround the chief minister's residence on that fateful Friday afternoon. He *never expected* to be told to resign by 3 p.m. or face dismissal. He *never expected* to be confronted by his children in tears. And, most important, he *never expected* the administration to cut itself off from him." Swapan Dasgupta & Farzand Ahmed, "The Education of Rabri Devi," *India Today*, 11 Aug. 1997, at 18.

nevertheless. See ***but nevertheless.**

New Hampshirite; *New Hampshireite; *New Hampshireman. The first is standard; the second is a variant spelling (not nearly as common); the third, with its *-man* suffix, is a form that some find objectionable as being tinged with SEXISM. See DENIZEN LABELS.

*new innovation. Because an *innovation* is something new or different, the phrase **new innovation* is redundant—e.g.:

- "To work, a sequel must return you to the familiar but then lead you into new territory. There have to be new developments, in terms of the narrative and characterization, and it must include *new innovations* [read *innovations*] in terms of structure or setting." Jane Roscoe, "With Right Stuff, Sequels Top Originals," *Newsday* (N.Y.), 29 May 2001, at A27.
- "*Totally new innovations* [read *Innovations* or perhaps *Notable* or *Remarkable innovations*] also were apparent at NeoCon, especially in floor coverings." Lisa Skolnik, "For Office or Home, Mixing It Up Is the Way to Go," *Chicago Trib.*, 24 June 2001, H&G §, at 1.

See REDUNDANCY.

New Jerseyan; New Jerseyite. The first is standard; the second is a variant used by the U.S. Government Printing Office. Although the *-ite* form predominated until the 1980s, the *-an* form is now significantly more common. See DENIZEN LABELS.

> Current ratio: 2:1

LANGUAGE-CHANGE INDEX (For the full key, see front matter pp. xxxi, l–li.)
Stage 1: Rejected. **Stage 2:** Widely shunned. **Stage 3:** Widespread but . . . **Stage 4:** Ubiquitous but . . . **Stage 5:** Fully accepted.
Invariably inferior forms marked by asterisk (*). • Ratios represent frequency of prevalent forms vs. variants in current books.

New Orleanian; *New Orleansian. The first is standard; the second is a fairly rare variant that many New Orleanians consider erroneous. Even though /**leenz**/ isn't an accepted pronunciation of the final syllable of the city's name (see **New Orleans**), *New Orleanian* is pronounced /noo ohr-**lee**-nee-ən/. See DENIZEN LABELS.

Current ratio: 196:1

New Orleans is acceptably pronounced either /noo or-lee-ənz/ or /noo **or**-lənz/. Some natives say /noo orl-yənz/, /**nahr**-lənz/, or /**naw**-lənz/. Avoid /noo or-**leenz**/.

news. For most of its life, *news* was used as both a singular and a plural. It was only in the 19th century that the singular became the exclusively standard usage. The word continues to be regarded as singular—e.g.:

- "By now, such good *news has* become commonplace." Tom Saler, "Earnings Help Explain the Bull's Endurance," *Milwaukee J. Sentinel*, 4 Aug. 1997, at 13.
- "Since *news has* come out of the medical-device manufacturer's generosity, some 800 requests for assistance have flooded in." Steve Cranford, "James Question on NB's Tax Deal," *Bus. J.* (Charlotte), 8 Sept. 1997, at 1.

newsstand. So spelled—not *newstand.

nexus. The acceptable plural forms are *nexuses* (English) and *nexus* (Latin). Naturally, the English form is preferable—e.g.: "The *nexuses* of activity for both rooms are the counters where the marijuana is dispensed." Glen Martin, "The Tokin' Joint," *S.F. Chron.*, 24 Aug. 1997, at Z1. Some writers have betrayed their ignorance of Latin by writing *nexi, as if it were a second-declension noun. (Actually, because *nexus* is a fourth-declension noun, it doesn't change its form in the plural.) In Latin, *nexi refers to people who have been reduced to quasi-slavery for debt! Cf. **apparatus** & **prospectus.** See HYPERCORRECTION (A) & PLURALS (B).

nice = (1) subtle, precise <a nice question> <a nice distinction>; or (2) good, attractive, agreeable, pleasant <they're nice people> <it's a nice vacation package>. Although purists formerly objected to sense 2, it's now universally accepted among reputable critics. Still, the word is so vague in that sense—as a generalized expression of approval—that stylists work to find a more concrete term to express their meaning.

nicety = (1) scrupulousness, fastidiousness, accuracy; (2) subtlety, difficulty, the quality of requiring a high level of precision; or (3) something elegant or refined; a luxury. Sense 3 is attested from the 15th to the 20th centuries <clean linen and other niceties of apparel> and has continued into the 21st. Given the primacy of senses 1 and 2, though, one wonders whether *luxuries* might not be a better word than *niceties* in the following sentences:

- "Prior proposed certain *niceties* for the remodeled spa, including fancy ceiling tiles, nameplates labeling each

room after mesquites, creosotes and other 'healing powers of the desert' and a slight aroma of herbs and oils." Melissa Prentice, "Westward Look's New Spa Wants Its Clients to Relax," *Ariz. Daily Star*, 4 Dec. 1996, at E6.
- "For luminaries like . . . Barbra Streisand and others, there are certain *niceties* that the studios will automatically provide." Dan Cox, "They Asked for What?" *Newsday* (N.Y.), 8 July 1997, at B7.
- "Findings like those cast [early childhood family education] not as a *nicety* for the affluent or a leg up for the poor, but as an essential component of general public education." Editorial, "ECFE Cuts Are a Step Backward," *Star Trib.* (Minneapolis), 27 Mar. 2003, at A22.

niche is best pronounced /nich/. The pronunciation, predominant in AmE, has led to the phonetic misspellings *nitche and *nitch—e.g.:

- "Bob said they are planning on more servicing and looking for a *nitche* [read *niche*] that others can't [fill]." Joan Pritchard, "Zide Brothers Travel American Way with Sporting Goods," *Parkersburg News* (W. Va.), 27 Nov. 1994, at 1.
- "Others, like Ken Hammond and John Carter, have found their *nitch* [read *niche*] in the International and American Leagues after initial lucrative stints in the NHL." Buzz Gray, "Hockey Purgatory," *Times Union* (Albany), 15 Jan. 1995, at D1.
- "He found his *nitch* [read *niche*] as a field engineer, he says." Carol Humphreys, "New England Feast in South Laguna," *Orange County Register*, 18 Aug. 1997, at E1.

Although the pronunciation /neesh/ is heard among educated speakers, many consider it a pretentious deanglicization of a word that has been anglicized since the 1700s. See PRONUNCIATION (D).

LANGUAGE-CHANGE INDEX
niche misspelled *nitch or *nitche: Stage 1

***nicknack.** See **knickknack.**

nictitate (= to wink or blink rapidly) is the standard form. (*Nictate is a NEEDLESS VARIANT.) This word verges on SESQUIPEDALITY.

nidus /**nɪ**-dəs/ (= a nest or breeding place), a Latinate technical term, conventionally forms the plural *nidi* /**nɪ**-dɪ/—not *niduses*. The related term *nidology* denotes the study of birds' nests.

niece. See **nephew.**

Nietzsche. So spelled—though often misspelled *Nietsche. The name is pronounced /**neet**-chə/—not /neetsh/ or /**neet**-chee/.

Niger (the African country) has the anglicized pronunciation /**nɪ**-jər/, which is preferred in English-language contexts. Locals mostly use the Frenchified pronunciation /nee-**zhair**/.

niggardly (= grudging, stingy) derives from an Old Norse word (*hnøggr* "covetous, stingy"); it has nothing to do with the racial slur that it sounds similar to. E.g.: "A tall, heavy-set, good-looking Irishman, he was never *niggardly* about attorney fees." Murray T. Bloom, *The Trouble with Lawyers* 272 (1970). Even so, prudent speakers and writers have come to shun it just to avoid misunderstandings. The word has been in decline in English-language print sources since 1950.

Unfortunately, the word itself is sometimes misspelled because of such misunderstandings—e.g.: "Mr. Graham carries a reputation for being *niggeredly* [read *niggardly*] but he insists there is a difference between shrewd investment and frivolous spending." "Soccer: No Denying Graham's Right to Title," *Daily Telegraph*, 13 May 1991, at 35.

nightie (= a woman's or child's nightgown), a DIMINU-TIVE dating from the late 19th century, has been predominantly so spelled in AmE since about 1915 and in BrE since about 1955. *Nighty* is a variant spelling.
Current ratio: 4:1

nihilism is pronounced /nɪ-ə-li-zəm/ or /nee-ə-li-zəm/. The *-h-* is silent.

nimbus (= [1] a dark cloud that may bring rain, or [2] a halo) has two plurals, *nimbuses* and *nimbi*, which are about equally common. *Nimbuses* might be considered preferable as the anglicized plural—e.g.: "Happy faces and halos (she calls them *nimbuses*) are parts of her visual vocabulary." Donald Miller, "Welcome the Mystery," *Pitt. Post-Gaz.*, 31 Mar. 1995, Weekend Mag. §, at 2. See PLURALS (B).

nimrod. According to the standard dictionaries—such as *W11* and the *SOED*—this word means "a skillful hunter." The term comes from the name of a king of Shinar (Nimrod), described in Genesis as a mighty hunter. The word is often used in this traditional sense—e.g.: "Some sportsmen, of course, would say Mealey has a fatal flaw . . . . *Nimrods* and anglers believe he's too cozy with groups as varied as ranchers, miners, loggers and even environmentalists." D.F. Oliveria, "Unattended Youngsters at Great Risk in the Water," *Spokesman Rev.* (Spokane), 5 Aug. 1997, at B4.

In late-20th-century SLANG, though, the word came to mean "a simpleton; dunderhead; blockhead"—e.g.:

- "Hey all you mack daddies (cool guys) out there: if you don't want to sound like a *nimrod* (geek) on your next trip to kili cali (Southern California), don't get all petro (worried)." "New in Paperback," *Wash. Post*, 20 July 1997, at X12.
- "Thus we wind up with the tableau of several hundred more or less disgruntled *nimrods* trudging along like cattle through a process that is at best inefficient, at worst absurd." Charlie Meyers, "Waiting, Waiting in Line for Leftovers," *Denver Post*, 15 Aug. 1997, at D4.
- "Before they know it, they've become the sort of uptight *nimrod* who writes passive-aggressive tweets to their rail operator whenever they fail to get a seat in the mornings." Stuart Heritage, "I Can't Afford to Bring Up a Child in the Capital," *Guardian*, 1 Oct. 2014, at 5.

Though this sense isn't recorded in most standard dictionaries, it certainly exists and is well known among

the generations that grew up watching Bugs Bunny—who used the term snidely in reference to the hunter Elmer Fudd. For now, this usage remains slang. But it surely threatens to kill off the hunter sense. For the fascinating origins of this slang meaning, see p. xlix.

LANGUAGE-CHANGE INDEX
nimrod in the sense "simpleton": Stage 5

*nitch(e). See **niche.**

nitroglycerin; *nitroglycerine. The first is the standard spelling in AmE and BrE alike.
Current ratio: 3:1

no. Pl. *noes*, preferably not **nos*. See PLURALS (D). Cf. **yes.**

nobody. See **no one** & PRONOUNS (D).

no-brainer (= a solution or course of action so obviously right that it needn't be thought about much) is AmE SLANG dating from the 1950s. It surged into popularity in the mid-1980s and has since become something of a VOGUE WORD not only in AmE but in World English as well.

no doubt. See ***doubtlessly.**

Noel; Noël; Nowell. The song "The First Noel" has been traced back to a book of English carols dated 1833, with the spelling *Nowell*. Although the song is known to have originated in rural western England, the composer is unknown. The song title was spelled *nowell* through most of the 19th century, and this spelling made perfect sense. According to the *OED*, *nowell* is "a word shouted or sung as an expression of joy, originally to commemorate the birth of Christ"; it dates, somewhat surprisingly, from the 1300s. Chaucer used it in "The Franklin's Tale": "And *nowel* crieth every lusty [i.e., joyful] man." The word fell into disuse in the 16th century.

Sometime after the song's early-19th-century debut, probably in the late 19th or early 20th century, someone "corrected" the spelling of the song title (and verses) to *noel*, which is a French word meaning "a Christmas carol." To make it even more Frenchified, some writers gave it a diaeresis (*noël*). Although this word is recorded in the English language from 1811, the *OED* contains only three illustrative quotations.

Most American adults who came of age in the 20th century are familiar with the spelling "The First Noel" and with front-yard Christmas signs that spell out *Noel* (or *Noël*). Yet many hymnals, such as the Episcopal Hymnal, consistently used the original spelling. This one makes more historical sense for two reasons. First, the song is English, not French. Second, the traditional English meaning is more in line with what most people intend today: someone with a Christmas display that says "Noel" probably doesn't mean "a

LANGUAGE-CHANGE INDEX (For the full key, see front matter pp. xxxi, l–li.)
Stage 1: Rejected. **Stage 2:** Widely shunned. **Stage 3:** Widespread but . . . **Stage 4:** Ubiquitous but . . . **Stage 5:** Fully accepted.
Invariably inferior forms marked by asterisk (*). • Ratios represent frequency of prevalent forms vs. variants in current books.

Christmas carol," but instead something like "Christ is born!" Yet *noel* is the predominant form and will probably remain so, apart from a few stalwart hymnals and songbooks.

no expense has been spared (= somebody has spent a lot of money) is both hackneyed and crass. It's typically the sort of phrase one expects to hear from a social climber. Cf. **no object.**

no fewer. See **no less (A).**

no holds barred. The METAPHOR comes from wrestling: in some matches, no wrestling holds are illegal. When used as a PHRASAL ADJECTIVE, of course, it is hyphenated <a no-holds-barred matchup>.

Some writers, though, misunderstand the phrase and write **no-holes-barred*—e.g.:

- "Preaching what he calls a message of self-help and self-love to the black man, Farrakhan's in-your-face, *no-holes-barred* [read *no-holds-barred*] approach has been condemned by Vice President Al Gore and members of Congress." Robbie Morganfield, "Farrakhan Urges End to 'Tide of Violence,'" *Houston Chron.*, 12 Apr. 1994, at A1.
- "The party has long needed an open and *no-holes-barred* [read *no-holds-barred*] debate on the subject." "An Election with the Wrong Candidates," *Independent*, 1 July 1995, at 16.
- "If Phil Mickelson is ever going to win a major—or even the 'fifth major' they are playing at TPC Sawgrass this week—he will not do it backing down from his *no-holes-barred* [read *no-holds-barred*] style of play." Hank Gola, *Daily News* (N.Y.), 23 Mar. 2003, at 50.

LANGUAGE-CHANGE INDEX
*no holes barred for *no holds barred*: Stage 1
Current ratio (*no holds barred* vs.
*no holes barred): 74:1

noisome is often misconstrued as meaning "noisy; loud; clamorous." In fact, it means "noxious; malodorous." (Cf. **fulsome.**) The word is related etymologically to *annoy*.

LANGUAGE-CHANGE INDEX
noisome in the sense "noisy": Stage 3

no less. A. And *no fewer.* The phrase *no less*, like *less*, preferably refers to amounts or to mass nouns, not countable numbers. *No fewer* is the better phrase when discussing numbers of things. (See **less (A).**) But many good writers nod on this point—e.g.:

- "In this annual, there are *no less* [read *no fewer*] than five painters banking on wax for beauty." Regina Hackett, "A Chance to Shine in Bellevue," *Seattle Post-Intelligencer*, 19 July 1997, at C1.
- "Chinese officials . . . have issued *no less* [read *no fewer*] than three condemnations of the congressman's trip." "Back from Tibet," *Wash. Times*, 30 Aug. 1997, at A15.
- "During his career he had *no less* [read *no fewer*] than 43 fellow Corsicans as generals in his army." Christopher McCooey, "A Hike Through the Scented Corsican Hills," *Fin. Times*, 6 Sept. 1997, at 17.

When the sense is *nothing short of*, that phrase (or *nothing less than*) typically improves the sentence—e.g.: "Among the local newspapers, 'The Hartford

Daily Courant' proclaimed that *no less than* [read *nothing short of*] an 'orthographical mania' was afoot in Hartford because a competing spelling bee was scheduled on the same spring night." Joe Duffy, "Twain Floored by 'Spelling Epidemic,'" *Hartford Courant*, 31 Aug. 1997, at H1.

LANGUAGE-CHANGE INDEX
no less for *no fewer* in reference to
a count noun: Stage 4

B. And *not less.* *No less* connotes surprise <he weighs no less than 300 pounds>. The phrasing in the example expresses astonishment that he weighs so much. *Not less* is more clinical and dispassionate <he weighs not less than 300 pounds>. That example states matter-of-factly that he weighs at least that much and maybe more.

no longer requires oxygen. This bit of medical JARGON is a peculiar brand of ILLOGIC. The true sense, of course, is that the patient no longer requires *supplementary oxygen*—e.g.: "Since the operation, he says, he's put on more than 10 pounds of muscle, *no longer requires oxygen* [insert *supplementary* before *oxygen*], and feels liberated to do practically whatever he wants." Joe Rojas-Burke, "Health Plan OKs Tests for Teen," *Oregonian* (Portland), 15 June 2000, at A1. The phrase is, however, perfectly proper when used by morticians.

nom de plume; nom de guerre. See **pseudonym.**

nomenclature (= a formal system of naming things, esp. in science and allied disciplines) is pronounced /**noh**-mən-klay-chər/ in AmE and /noh-**men**-klə-chər/ in BrE.

nominal = in name only, but not in reality. The *nominal* head of a university department is one whose power is questionable; *nominal* is a put-down word. By extension, what is *nominal* may be real but not significant <the popular incumbent faced only nominal opposition>, so the word has taken on the sense of "very little."

In grammar, *nominal* has an additional meaning: "of, relating to, or functioning as a noun" <a nominal clause>—though *noun* is often its own adjective <a noun clause>. And in this context *nominal* can itself be a noun, denoting a word or group of words functioning as a noun.

NOMINALIZATIONS. See ZOMBIE NOUNS.

NOMINATIVE ABSOLUTES. See ABSOLUTE CONSTRUCTIONS.

NOMINATIVE AND OBJECTIVE CASES. See PRONOUNS (A), (B).

no more than; not more than. The first is the more natural idiom—and historically by far the more common one. Cf. **no less (B).**

Current ratio: 3:1

NON-. See NEGATIVES (A).

nonage (= the period of someone's minority or youth) is pronounced /**non**-ij/ in AmE and /**noh**-nij/ in BrE.

nonbelief. See **disbelief.**

nonbeliever. See **atheist.**

noncomparable. See **incomparable.**

Noncomparable Adjectives. See **adjectives (b).**

nonconstitutional; unconstitutional. These terms have distinct meanings. *Nonconstitutional* = of, relating to, or involving some legal basis or principle other than those of the U.S. Constitution <a nonconstitutional doctrine>. *Unconstitutional* (the more familiar word) = in violation of, or not in accordance with, principles found in the U.S. Constitution <an unconstitutional and therefore void statute>. See **constitutional.**

none = (1) not one; or (2) not any. Hence it may correctly take either a singular or a plural verb. To decide which to use, substitute the phrases to see which fits the meaning of the sentence: *not one is* or *not any are.* E.g.:

- "Sexton stressed—several times—that all the meats are farm-raised and USDA-approved and *none are* endangered." Bob Walter, "Buffalo Bob's Food Business Takes Walk on the Wild Side," *Sacramento Bee,* 1 Sept. 1997, at B4.
- "There are many lessons that society can learn from Mother Teresa's life . . . . But *none is* as powerful as the lessons that Mother Teresa said she learned from the poor." "A Powerful Voice," *Orlando Sentinel,* 6 Sept. 1997, at A18.

Generally speaking, *none is* is the more emphatic way of expressing an idea. But it's also the less common way, particularly in educated speech, and it therefore sounds somewhat stilted. The problem is exacerbated by the unfortunate fact that some stylists and publications insist that *none* is always singular, even in the most awkward constructions. Cf. **no one.**

LANGUAGE-CHANGE INDEX
none in the sense "not any," with a plural verb: Stage 5
Current ratio (*none is* vs. *none are*): 1.5:1
Current ratio (*none of them is* vs.
none of them are): 1:1

noneconomic. See **uneconomical.**

***nonenforceable.** See **unenforceable.**

nonessential; inessential; unessential. Although most American dictionaries list *unessential* as the usual term, it is the least common of these words (and has been since about 1940). *Inessential* is somewhat more common, but *nonessential* is by far the most common <nonessential computer storage>. *Nonessential* has predominated in print since about 1940.
Current ratio (in order of headwords): 3:1:1

nonesuch; nonsuch. The first spelling is etymologically superior, the word being a combination of *none* and *such. Nonsuch* is a chiefly BrE variant. Regardless of spelling, the first syllable is pronounced /nən/.

Nonesuch functions both as a noun (= a person or thing without equal) and as an adjective (= unparalleled, incomparable).
Current ratio: 2:1

nonetheless. One word in AmE, three (frequently) in BrE.
Current ratio (one word vs. three words): 6:1

nonexpert, adj. See **inexpert.**

nonincentive. See **disincentive.**

nonmarital child. See **illegitimate child.**

nonmaterial. See **immaterial.**

nonorganic food. See **organic.**

nonplus, the verb meaning "to baffle or confound unexpectedly," preferably makes *nonplussed* and *nonplussing* in AmE and BrE alike, because the second syllable is stressed. (See SPELLING (b).) But the variant **nonplused* appears in some American writing—e.g.:

- "Betancourt looks *nonplused* [read *nonplussed*]." Barbara Peters Smith, "Legislating, Up Close," *Ledger* (Lakeland, Fla.), 19 Apr. 1995, at A7.
- "Almost daily, we were *nonplused* [read *nonplussed*] by the breaking revelations during the testimony." "The Wonder of Welfare Fraud," *L.A. Times,* 13 Apr. 1997, at B7.
- "Everything about her was otherworldly and astonishing: Her eyes were big and brown, her nose was tiny and upturned, and her mouth was set in a *nonplused* [read *nonplussed*] purse." Curtis Sittenfeld, "Bad Latch," *Wash. Post,* 9 Aug. 2015, at A15.

Since the 1990s there has arisen a mystifying notion that *nonplussed* is essentially synonymous with its near-antonym *unfazed.* That is a nonplussing misperception.

LANGUAGE-CHANGE INDEX
1. *nonplussed* misspelled **nonplused*: Stage 1
Current ratio (*nonplussed* vs. **nonplused*): 9:1
2. *nonplussed* as meaning "unfazed": Stage 2

nonprofit; not-for-profit. The first is more common, but the second is increasingly used in AmE for greater accuracy. The phrase *nonprofit corporation* misleadingly suggests that the corporation makes no profits, but such a corporation actually does earn profits and then applies them to charitable purposes. *Not-for-profit* is thought to reveal more accurately that the purpose is not for private gain, though indeed the organization may profit. The hyphenated form of the word, **non-profit*, which sometimes appears in corporate literature and in unedited copy, is always ill-advised. See NEGATIVES (A).

LANGUAGE-CHANGE INDEX (For the full key, see front matter pp. xxxi, l–li.)
Stage 1: Rejected. **Stage 2:** Widely shunned. **Stage 3:** Widespread but . . . **Stage 4:** Ubiquitous but . . . **Stage 5:** Fully accepted.
Invariably inferior forms marked by asterisk (∗). • Ratios represent frequency of prevalent forms vs. variants in current books.

nonresponsive. See **unresponsive.**

NONRESTRICTIVE RELATIVE PRONOUNS. See **that (A).**

non sequitur (= [1] a conclusion that does not follow from the premises; or [2] a statement or response that is unrelated to the one before it) means, in Latin, "it does not follow." The phrase should be spelled as two words, not hyphenated or spelled as one word; and because it has been fully naturalized, it should not be italicized. The phrase is frequently misspelled *-tor*, *-tar*, or *-ter* in the last syllable—e.g.: "The second half was almost a complete *non-sequitor* [read *non sequitur*], musically: The Marcia Ball Band from New Orleans." Barbara Zuck, "Booming Cannons and Brass Kick Off Lancaster Festival," *Columbus Dispatch*, 20 July 1995, at G7.

In the following sentence, the phrase is not only misspelled but also misused because the idea of something following (or not following) something else is missing: "To compare the suffering of Americans of Japanese ancestry to the suffering of the European Jews is a *non sequitor* [read *non sequitur*]." "The Manzanar Lesson," *Press-Enterprise* (Riverside, Cal.), 30 Sept. 1996, at A9. A non sequitur, strictly speaking, must be a conclusion that does not follow from the premises. A mere inaccurate or exaggerated comparison—as in the example just quoted—isn't a non sequitur.

LANGUAGE-CHANGE INDEX
non sequitur misspelled **non sequitor*: Stage 1
Current ratio: 89:1

nonsuch. See **nonesuch.**

NON-U. See CLASS DISTINCTIONS.

NONWORDS. H.W. Fowler's formidable American precursor, Richard Grant White, wrote incisively about words that aren't legitimate words:

> [A]s there are books that are not books, so there are words that are not words. Most of them are usurpers, interlopers, or vulgar pretenders; some are deformed creatures, with only half a life in them; but some of them are legitimate enough in their pretensions, although oppressive, intolerable, useless. Words that are not words sometimes die spontaneously; but many linger, living a precarious life on the outskirts of society, uncertain of their position, and cause great discomfort to all right-thinking, straightforward people.
>
> *Words and Their Uses* 184 (rev. ed. 1899).

His polemical tone and hyperbole were characteristic and purposeful.

Among the words that he labeled nonwords are three that might still be considered so: **enthused, *experimentalize, *preventative.* But with most of the others he mentioned, he proved anything but prophetic—they're now standard: *accountable, answerable, controversialist, conversationalist, donate, exponential, jeopardize, practitioner, presidential, reliable, tangential.* The lesson is that in any age, stigmatizing words is a tough business—no matter how good the arguments against them might be.

This book contains entries on dozens of terms that might be considered nonwords by White's standards. Among the more prominent ones are these (each of which is treated separately in this book):

> *affrontery (see **effrontery (B)**)
> *analyzation (see **analysis**)
> *annoyment (see **annoyance**)
> *discomforture (see **discomfit (D)**)
> *dispersement (see **disburse**)
> *doubtlessly
> *fastly
> *forebearance (see **forbearance**)
> *furtherest
> *illy (see **ill**)
> *improprietous
> *inclimate (see **inclement**)
> *inexpense
> *inimicable
> *intervent
> *irregardless
> *muchly
> *optimalize
> *paralyzation
> *preplan
> *proprietous
> *quelch
> *seldomly (see **seldom**)
> *thusly (see **thus (B)**)
> *uncategorically
> *unmercilessly
> *unrelentlessly

The term *nonword* might appear to be a nonword itself because until recently it did not appear in most dictionaries. Today that has changed, though: *W11,* for example, defines it as "a word that has no meaning, is not known to exist, or is disapproved," and dates it from 1961. It also appears in *RH2* and the *OED.*

no object. This phrase, literally speaking, should mean "not a goal; not something considered worth achieving." In fact, though, writers use it to mean "no obstacle" or "no objection"—e.g.:

- "Culpin sees teleworking as capable of making a great contribution to economic growth in a global marketplace where distance *is no object* [read *is irrelevant* or *is no obstacle*]." Claire Gooding, "The Ups and Downs of Teleworking," *Fin. Times,* 5 Apr. 1995, at xviii.
- "If you would love a fast, handsome car, and if money is *no object* [read *no obstacle*], take a close look at the 911." Richard Truett, "Staying True to Form," *Fresno Bee,* 4 May 1996, at D1.
- "But if size is *no object* [read *not an objection* or *of no concern*], take heart that in the heat of competition, one can purchase superior 2-megapixel cameras from the major brands for less than $200." Stephen Williams, "Marketplace Reflections On a Grab Bag of Trends," *Newsday* (N.Y.), 24 Dec. 2002, at A42.

The nonsense of the phrase is apparent especially in the following example, in which *object* bears a double sense, through ZEUGMA: "So now it's on to Florida and the Marlins, where money is *no object* but winning is." Patrick Zier, "Leyland Must Produce," *Ledger* (Lakeland, Fla.), 30 Mar. 1997, at C1. In that sentence, seemingly, money is no object (= no obstacle) but winning is an object (= a goal); hence *object* means different things with the different subjects. And strictly speaking, the final word (*is*) should be followed by *one* to counteract the fact that the entire phrase (*no object*) seems to carry over as UNDERSTOOD WORDS—not just the noun *object*. Cf. **no expense has been spared.**

noon. See **a.m.** (C).

no one; nobody. *No one* is more common than *nobody*. In AmE, both terms are treated as singular nouns and therefore as singular antecedents <no one in his right mind would care>. But today, as indefinite pronouns, they're often treated as plural to avoid SEXISM—e.g.:

- "Yes, Germany was ringed by enemies, but this was just the right time for a bold move, the fuhrer figured. *No one* in *their* right mind would expect it." James Kindall, "The Battle of the Bulge," *Newsday* (N.Y.), 15 Dec. 1994, at B3.
- "The narrator promises us early that *no one* gets killed, but *they* get really nasty boo-boos." Louis B. Parks, "AAA-a-aa-a-a-ah!: 'George' is Fun for Everybody," *Houston Chron.*, 16 July 1997, at 1.
- "It seems they're charging roughly the same amount, and no one wants to lower *their* fees." Jim Dillon, "ATM Fees Increasingly Attacked," *Dayton Daily News*, 3 Aug. 1997, at B7.

Fewer readers than ever seem to be bothered by this type of construction. My informal surveys suggest that 10–20% of a wide readership would think that such a construction lessens the writer's credibility. That's enough to give any serious writer pause. Although the usage seems inevitable in the long run, careful writers of AmE will probably wait until the opposition dwindles even further. In 2008, *no one . . . his* constructions still greatly outnumbered *no one . . . their* constructions in print sources. See CONCORD, PRONOUNS (D) & SEXISM (B). Cf. **none.**

In BrE it is especially common for *no one* and *nobody* to act as antecedents of indeterminate number—e.g.: "How the Elizabethans reacted is, alas, unknown, since *nobody* thought Shakespeare's plays important enough to bother recording *their* impressions." John Carey, "Stages of Hatred," *Sunday Times* (London), 4 Oct. 1992, § 6, at 8.

LANGUAGE-CHANGE INDEX
no one or *nobody . . . their*: Stage 4

no one, not even [+ pl. n.]. When this phrasing precedes the verb, it leads to constructions that are either clumsy or ungrammatical. The merely clumsy constructions get the grammar right, with a singular verb—e.g.:

- "*No one*, not even the prosecutors, *was* sure Boria would give the same version of events she had given to two grand juries." Juan Gonzalez, "Her Bravery Shatters Blue Wall," *Daily News* (N.Y.), 27 Sept. 1996, at 21.

- "She is a nobody, the girl or guy that *no one*, not even the teachers, *likes.*" Kristi Wright, "In the Dollhouse," *Omaha World-Herald*, 1 Oct. 1996, at 35.

The ungrammatical constructions botch the SUBJECT–VERB AGREEMENT, which in modern English is a more serious type of CONCORD than noun–pronoun agreement (see **no one**). E.g.:

- "*No one*, not even the Orioles, *were* [read *was*] supposed to match Boston's awesome run-scoring machine." Bob Klapisch, "Sox Arrive . . . with Holes," *Record* (N.J.), 1 July 1996, Sports §, at 1.
- "But *no one*, not even the wireless providers, *know* [read *knows*] what the future will look like." Debra Sparks, "Hold That Call," *Fin. World*, 12 Aug. 1996, at 33.

Which number to use becomes obvious if you mentally move the phrase to the end of the sentence <no one *knows* what the future will look like, not even the wireless providers>.

*no other . . . except. See **other** (B).

no other . . . than. See **other** (B).

*noplace. This dialectal word, answering to the standard *anyplace*, was fairly common in the 18th century, but it became stigmatized by the mid-19th century. Although it was moderately on the rise in print sources during the 1980s and 1990s, it remains nonstandard for *nowhere* or *no place*—e.g.: "As the Joads' plight continues to worsen there's no work, no food, *noplace* [read *nowhere* or *no place*] decent to live." Doug Mason, "Power of Steinbeck's Book Evident on Stage," *Knoxville News-Sentinel*, 4 Feb. 1995, at B6. Cf. ***anyplace** & **someplace.**

LANGUAGE-CHANGE INDEX
*noplace for *nowhere*: Stage 2
Current ratio (*nowhere* vs. **noplace*): 706:1

no problem. See **thank you** (B).

no pun intended. See WORD PATRONAGE.

nor. A. Beginning a Sentence. *Nor*, like *neither*, may begin a sentence. It must follow either an express NEGATIVE or an idea that is negative in sense <This is not economical. Nor is it entirely satisfactory . . . >. E.g.:

- "The uttering of a word is not a consequence of the uttering of a noise, whether physical or otherwise. *Nor* is the uttering of words with a certain meaning a consequence of uttering the words." J.L. Austin, *How to Do Things with Words* 114 (1965).
- "Walter did not begrudge his son such precautions. *Nor*, for his part, had Peter protested his father's trading the townhouse on Blake Street for a corrode." Candace Robb, *The Riddle of St. Leonard's* 19 (large-print ed. 1997).
- "None of that mattered to Judge James P. Kleinberg in Santa Clara. *Nor* did extensive government-sponsored studies showing that the best thing to do with lead paint is to leave it right where it is." Daniel Fisher, "Public Nuisances," *Forbes*, 7 Sept. 2015, at 50.

LANGUAGE-CHANGE INDEX (For the full key, see front matter pp. xxxi, l–li.)
Stage 1: Rejected. **Stage 2:** Widely shunned. **Stage 3:** Widespread but . . . **Stage 4:** Ubiquitous but . . . **Stage 5:** Fully accepted.
Invariably inferior forms marked by asterisk (*). • Ratios represent frequency of prevalent forms vs. variants in current books.

In this construction, of course, the word *nor* needn't follow a *neither*. See **neither** (c). See also **also not**.

B. For *or*. When the negative of a clause or phrase has appeared at the outset of an enumeration, and a disjunctive conjunction is needed, *or* is generally better than *nor*. The initial negative carries through to all the enumerated elements—e.g.:

- "There have been *no* bombings *nor* [read *or*] armed attacks by one side against the other." William D. Montalbano, "Links to IRA Seen in Rash of Violence in Northern Ireland," *L.A. Times*, 12 Jan. 1996, at 1.
- "This is *no* longer practical *nor* [read *or*] desirable." Helene Crane, "Overcoming Fear of Fear," *Calgary Herald*, 1 June 1996, at A9.
- "The road has *no* sidewalks, shoulders, *nor* [read *or*] crossing guard. There is no other route to school." Charles T. Bowen, "A Chance to Impact New Schools," *Tampa Trib.*, 3 Aug. 1997, at 1. (On the use of *impact* in that title, see **impact**.)

Sometimes the best solution is to replace *nor* with *and no*—e.g.:

- "Although he has almost *no* name recognition *nor* [read *and no*] political cash, Unruhe appears undaunted." Carlos V. Lozano, "23rd Congressional District," *L.A. Times*, 30 Oct. 1996, at B1.
- "Florida, with its large elderly population, has *no income nor* [read *no income tax and no*] estate tax." Sonya Zalubowski, "With Taxes on Homes Going Through the Roof, We Need Solution," *Oregonian* (Portland), 31 Oct. 1996, at 2.

See **not** (B).

nor'easter. This CASUALISM denotes a storm that brings high winds and rain or snow to the upper Atlantic Coast. The storm is so named because although the cyclonic storm itself moves northeasterly up the coast, the inland winds on its west side blow from out of the northeast.

While the folksy pronunciation might evoke images of a Yankee seafarer in some, the contracted term is neither authentic nor accurate. New Englanders tend to drop their *r* sounds and are more likely to pronounce *northeaster* as /naw-**thees**-tə/. As *Boston Globe* wordsmith Jan Freeman noted, "The facts, however, have not slowed the advance of *nor'easter*. Even in print, where it's probably less common than in speech, it has practically routed *northeaster* in the past quarter-century or so. . . . [I]t would take a mighty wind, at this point, to blow *nor'easter* back into oblivion."

The style guides at *The New York Times* and the *Boston Globe* ban the contracted form. But it is now established.

normality; *normalcy*. The first has long been considered superior to the second—and it is more than twice as common in modern print sources. Born in the mid-19th century and later popularized by President Warren G. Harding, *normalcy* has never been accepted as standard by the best writing authorities. It still occurs less frequently than *normality*, and it ought to be treated as a NEEDLESS VARIANT. Careful editors continue to prefer *normality*—e.g.: "Set to emerge officially from the University of Chicago next week,

the landmark study, called the 'National Health and Social Life Survey,' shatters many preconceptions in its attempts to define *normality*." Peter Gorner, "Sex Study Shatters Kinky Assumptions," *Chicago Trib.*, 6 Oct. 1994, § 1, at 1.

LANGUAGE-CHANGE INDEX
normalcy for *normality*: Stage 4
Current ratio (*normality* vs. *normalcy*): 2:1

north; northward(s); northerly. See DIRECTIONAL WORDS.

*nosey. See **nosy**.

no sooner . . . than; *no sooner . . . when. The first phrasing is better because *sooner* is a comparative that should take the word *than*, not *when*. Although the correct phrasing is vastly predominant, the loose phrasing is lamentably common—e.g.:

- "*No sooner* did he hear a description of the suspects' car *when* [read *than*] he saw the car himself." Paul Sullivan, "Tommy Tajima, at 47, Newspaper Photographer," *Boston Herald*, 22 Dec. 1999, at 39.
- "He had *no sooner* gotten into the 1996 Mercury Sable *when* [read *than*] he saw a police car chasing them down Old Highway 441." Frank Stanfield, "Man Convicted in Bank Heist," *Orlando Sentinel*, 10 Nov. 2000, at 2.
- "So *no sooner* had he arrived in Mykonos *when* [read *than*] he headed back to Santorini." Nancy Cooren Guerin, "Love Means Going the Extra Mile," *Times Union* (Albany), 6 Dec. 2000, at F3.

LANGUAGE-CHANGE INDEX
no sooner . . . when for *no sooner . . . than*: Stage 3

nostalgia /nah-**stal**-jə/—not /nah-**stahl**-jə/ or /nah-**stal**-jee-ə/.

nostrum (/**nos**-trəm/ or /**nohs**-trəm/), meaning either "a quack medicine" or "a panacea," forms the plural *nostrums*, not *nostra*—e.g.: "If it wants to move into the global economy, [India] must give up many of the *nostrums*, such as the need to preserve small businesses, [that] are deeply enshrined in its social policy." Peter Montagnon, "Old Protectionism Restricts Progress," *Fin. Times*, 19 Nov. 1996, at 4. See PLURALS (B). Cf. **rostrum**.

nosy (= unduly inquisitive; prying) has been the standard spelling since about 1950 in AmE and BrE alike. **Nosey*, once the predominant form, is now a variant.
Current ratio: 3:1

not. A. Placement of. When used in a construction with *all* or *every*, *not* is usually best placed just before that word. E.g.:

- "But *every* team *does not* expect more. Kansas does." Jonathan Feigen, "College Basketball Preview," *Houston Chron.*, 10 Nov. 1996, at 21. (A possible revision: *But not every team expects more. Kansas does.*)
- "While *every* letter *cannot* be answered, your stories may be used in future columns." Eileen Ogintz, "Children Connect on a Caribbean Cruise," *News & Observer* (Raleigh), 31 Aug. 1997, at H7. (A possible revision: *While not every letter can be answered . . . .*) See **all** (B).

B. *Not . . . nor.* This construction should usually (when short phrases or clauses are involved) be *not . . . or.* E.g.:

- "As parents, we need to encourage our children to focus on our inner character, *not* on our superficial traits, *nor* on marketing-driven peer expectations." Ellen J. Dewey, "Dispelling a Myth," *Lancaster New Era*, 17 Aug. 1997, at P3. (A possible revision: *As parents, we need to encourage our children to focus on our inner character, not on our superficial traits or on marketing-driven peer expectations.*)
- "The Ramona trial . . . did *not* reunite the Ramonas, *nor* did it convince Steph Ramona that she may have been wrong." Ann Rule, "Recalling an Elusive Past," *Wash. Post*, 7 Sept. 1997, Book World §, at 6. (A possible revision: *The Ramona trial did not reunite the Ramonas or even convince Steph Ramona that she might have been wrong.*) See **nor** (B).
- "The shooter was *not* a convicted felon *nor* does it appear his mental health history would have triggered sufficient alarm." "The Parkers' 'Sound Cause,'" *Baltimore Sun*, 3 Sept. 2015, at A16. (A possible revision: *The shooter did not have a prior felony conviction or a mental-health history that would have triggered sufficient alarm.*)

C. In Typos. *Not* is a ready source of trouble. Sometimes it becomes *now*, and sometimes it drops completely from the sentence. This tendency helps explain why some newspapers use CONTRACTIONS such as *shouldn't* and *wouldn't*: the negative is unlikely to get dropped. See **not guilty** (A).

D. *Not* [this] but [that]. This construction sometimes leads to MISCUES if the negative isn't well placed—e.g.: "The dungeon is the center of a debate over *not* the effectiveness of pedagogic hard labor *but* the race of the punished and the race of the punishers." Jon D. Hull, "Do Teachers Punish According to Race?" *Time*, 4 Apr. 1994, at 30. (A possible revision: *The dungeon is the center of a debate not over the effectiveness of pedagogic hard labor but over the race of the punished and the race of the punishers.*)

E. *Not only . . . but also.* See **not only . . . but also.**

notable. See **noticeable.**

not all. See **all** (B).

not all that. See **all that.**

notarize, originally an Americanism dating from the 1920s, is now commonplace in AmE and BrE alike—e.g.: "Patrick Henry Talbert, a minister who *notarizes* some Greater Ministries documents, has been sued twice in the past three years by people claiming he bilked them of their investments." Michael Fechter, "IRS Probes Ministry's Gift Program," *Tampa Trib.*, 25 Aug. 1997, at 1.

notary public. Pl. *notaries public*—not **notary publics.* E.g.: "County Clerk Mary Jo Brogoto said *notary publics* [read *notaries public*] should call the office at 881-1626 before picking up their commissions in Independence." "Metro Digest: Independence," *Kansas City Star*, 28 July 1997, at B2. See PLURALS (G) & POSTPOSITIVE ADJECTIVES.

LANGUAGE-CHANGE INDEX
*notary publics for *notaries public*: Stage 1
Current ratio (*notaries public* vs. **notary publics*): 3:1

*not as good of a . . . . See **as . . . as** (D).

notate. See **note,** vb.

not . . . because. See **because** (C).

note, vb.; **notate.** The latter, a BACK-FORMATION from *notation* dating from 1871, is a NEEDLESS VARIANT except in reference to musical notation.

not . . . either. See **either** (E).

not even. See **no one.**

not every. See **not** (A).

noteworthy. See **noticeable.**

not-for-profit. See **nonprofit.**

not guilty. A. And *innocent.* It used to be that only journalists made the mistake of writing *plead innocent* rather than *plead not guilty*, but now this phrase has made it even into judges' writing. Lawyers should avoid the phrase, since there is no such thing as a plea of *innocent.* Journalists, on the other hand, avoid *not guilty* merely because *not* might get accidentally dropped or changed to *now*:

> Many newspapers—and it tends to drive lawyers a little crazy—but many newspapers insist on saying that a defendant "pleaded innocent"; they will not report that he or she "pleaded not guilty." I've gone to clients for many years and said, "That's wrong. People don't plead innocent; they are not found innocent. They plead and are found 'not guilty.'" Now I realize that newspaper writers live in perpetual fear of the word *not* either being dropped by a printer or being changed from *not* to *now*. Therefore, whenever possible, they shy away from the word *not*, even at the expense of strict accuracy. . . .
>
> The lesson is simply this: Before you dismiss others' workmanship, do understand why they have said what they have said; there may be a good reason for it.
>
> Robert Sack, "Hearing Myself Think:
Some Thoughts on Legal Prose,"
4 Scribes J. Legal Writing 93, 98–99 (1993).

Fair enough. But writers who do have enough time for careful proofreading shouldn't sacrifice accuracy in this way.

Strictly speaking, *not guilty* and *innocent* aren't quite synonymous. To be *innocent* is to be blameless. To be *not guilty* is to have been exonerated by a jury of a crime charged—regardless of actual blame. So in a sentence such as the following one, many can't help thinking that the writer is blurring a distinction—e.g.: "A San Francisco jury found him *innocent* [read *not* guilty] of the charge in 1988." Robert Hilburn, "Way Beyond Center Field," *L.A. Times*, 4 May 1997, at 5.

LANGUAGE-CHANGE INDEX
plead innocent for *plead not guilty*: Stage 4

B. *Not guilty beyond a reasonable doubt. This phrasing is ambiguous. The standard by which a jury decides criminal charges is this: a defendant is guilty only if the evidence shows, beyond a reasonable doubt, that he or she committed the crime. Otherwise, the defendant is not guilty. So we say that a defendant was not found *guilty beyond a reasonable doubt*.

But it doesn't follow that we should also say that a defendant was found **not guilty beyond a reasonable doubt*. Is that *not guilty (beyond a reasonable doubt)* or *not guilty-beyond-a-reasonable-doubt*? The latter idea makes more sense—e.g.: "The question is whether a judge can reach a contrary conclusion on the second charge—deciding that though a defendant was *not guilty beyond a reasonable doubt*, he nonetheless probably committed the crime." "High Court's Highhanded Decision," *Chicago Trib.*, 26 Jan. 1997, at 20.

Yet many readers will misconstrue the phrase. Regardless of the writer's intention, some will think of **not guilty beyond a reasonable doubt* as a strong vindication—rather than as the slight vindication it is (we, the jury, had the slightest bit of reasonable doubt, so we had to find the defendant not guilty). The writer might have gotten it right in the following sentence, but nonlawyers are likely to be misled: "When you know all the facts [of the O.J. Simpson case], you'll see that the prosecutors failed to meet their burden of proof, and how, contrary to the court of public opinion, the jury arrived at their verdict of 'not guilty beyond a reasonable doubt.'" Patricia A. Jones, "Uncensored: Authors Answer Questions Left with Simpson Verdict," *Tulsa World*, 1 Dec. 1996, at G5.

If somebody is found not guilty, say *not guilty*. Omit the standard (*beyond a reasonable doubt*) to prevent a MISCUE.

*not hardly. This robust barbarism is fine if your purpose is to show DIALECT, but it doesn't otherwise belong in the serious writer's toolbox—e.g.:

- "Is there a more logical place for Moorpark than the Marmonte League? *Not hardly*. [Read *Hardly*.] But logic often has nothing to do with it." Paige A. Leech, "Time to Get Real on Realignment," *L.A. Times*, 16 Feb. 1997, at C10.
- "End of the problem? *Not hardly*. [Read *Hardly*.] In February, the state filed criminal charges." Jerry Spangler, "Fight Brews over Out-of-State Spirits," *Deseret News* (Salt Lake City), 29 July 1997, at B4.
- "Liberal alarmist hype? *Not hardly*. [Read *Hardly*.]" Cy Wood, "Indescribably Inane," *Valley Times-News* (Lanett, Ala.), 6 Aug. 2015, News §, at 4.

LANGUAGE-CHANGE INDEX
*not hardly for *hardly*: Stage 1
Current ratio (*can hardly* vs. **can't hardly*): 98:1

noticeable; notable; noteworthy; noted. These words overlap to a degree. *Noticeable* = easily seen or noticed (as, e.g., scars)—the word is generally confined to physical senses. *Notable* = (1) prominent; excellent <notable books of the season>; or (2) easily seen or noticed (applied to qualities as well as to material things) <her notable industriousness>. *Noteworthy* = worthy of notice or observation; remarkable <a noteworthy commencement address>. *Noted* = famous; celebrated; well known <a noted biographer>.

It is worth noting that a noted or notable person may not be noticeable; that a noticeable person may not be at all notable or noted; but that noteworthy achievements may lead one to become noted or notable—and perhaps, after some media attention, even noticeable.

On *noticeable* as a frequently misspelled word, see SPELLING (A).

no time should be lost. See **lose (B)**.

not in-. See NEGATIVES (B).

not in a position to. This phrase is often wordy for *cannot, can't, could not*, or the like—e.g.: "Granted, we're talking about hockey players, who, unlike their basketball and football counterparts, usually *are not in a position to* [read *can't*] reap immediate financial rewards if they leave early." Michael Hunt, "Bound by a Common Goal," *Milwaukee J. Sentinel*, 27 Mar. 1997, Sports §, at 1.

*notion seconded. See **motion seconded.**

not less. See **no less (B)**.

not more than. See **no more than.**

not only . . . but also. These CORRELATIVE CONJUNCTIONS must frame syntactically identical sentence parts—e.g.:

- "Many board games, electronic toys and computer programs *are not only enjoyable but also provide* [read *not only are enjoyable but also provide*] educational benefits." Jeffrey L. Derevensky & Rina Gupta, "Christmas Without Elmo," *Montreal Gaz.*, 19 Dec. 1996, at B3. (In that revision, the conjunctions frame two verb phrases. Another possible revision: *Many board games, electronic toys, and computer games are not only enjoyable but also educational.* The conjunctions frame two adjectives.)
- "It *not only* will save construction costs *but also* the cost of land acquisition and demolition." Donna Leslie, "Stadium Belongs on the Riverfront," *Cincinnati Enquirer*, 23 Nov. 1997, at D3. (A possible revision: *It will save not only construction costs but also the cost of land acquisition and demolition.* The conjunctions correctly frame two noun phrases.)
- "These foundation-like funds are useful *not only* for small donors *but also* for big donors who don't want to hassle with the red tape." Susan Lee, "Loosen Up a Bit, Folks," *Forbes*, 15 Dec. 1997, at 64. (The conjunctions frame two *for*-phrases.)

See PARALLELISM.

One common issue in *not only* constructions is whether it's permissible to omit the *also* after *but*. The answer is yes, the result being a CASUALISM—e.g.:

- "Commissioner Pete Rozelle assured Harris County officials that if they made some $67 million in improvements, the Astrodome would be *not only* adequate *but* worthy of a Super Bowl." "NFL Inadequacies," *Houston Chron.*, 6 Sept. 1995, at A20.

- "[Perret] seeks to secure Grant's reputation *not only* as a successful general *but* as a military genius." Eric Foner, "The Very Good Soldier," *N.Y. Times*, 7 Sept. 1997, § 7, at 13.

So how do you decide whether to include *also* (which will always result in a correct construction)? It's merely a matter of euphony and formality: let your ear and your sense of natural idiom help you decide in a given sentence.

Another way to complete the construction is *not only . . . but . . . as well*. But a writer who uses this phrasing should not add *also*, which is redundant with *as well*—e.g.: "Feminist methods and insights [must] be adopted *not only* by female scholars, *but also* by males *as well*." J.M. Balkin, "Turandot's Victory," 2 *Yale J. Law & Humanities* 299, 302 (1990). In that sentence, *also* should have been omitted.

No comma is usually needed between the *not only* and *but also* elements, and—as the last citation above shows—to put one in merely introduces an awkward break.

notorious may mean either "infamous" (the usual sense) <a notorious killer> or "famous" (an archaic sense). The word's negative connotations are firmly established in modern usage. Yet the corresponding noun, *notoriety*, is more neutral <achieved notoriety by saving several lives>. Gradually, though, the noun is becoming tinged with the unpleasant connotations of its adjectival form <achieved notoriety for drug-peddling charges>.

not proven. See **proved.**

Notre Dame, University of. The predominant pronunciation among stuffed shirts is /noh-trə **dahm**/ (which, however, is the correct pronunciation for the Paris cathedral). The predominant pronunciation among university officials and alumni is /noh-trə **daym**/. The predominant pronunciation among all other Americans is /noh-tər **daym**/.

not un-. See NEGATIVES (B).

notwithstanding is a FORMAL WORD used in the sense "despite," "in spite of," or "although." In general English-language contexts, it has experienced a steady decline in use since about 1760. E.g.: "*Notwithstanding* an outpouring of editorial opinion on either side of this issue, there are no easy answers." Richard Baum, "Perspective on China," *L.A. Times*, 30 Nov. 1997, at M5.

The question that literalists ask is, What doesn't withstand what else? Is the outpouring of opinion "not withstanding" (i.e., subordinated to) the lack of easy answers, or is the lack of easy answers "not withstanding" (subordinated to) the outpouring of editorial opinion? Because the former is the correct reading, some believe that *notwithstanding* should be sent to the end of the phrase in which it appears: *The family's objection to the marriage notwithstanding*, as opposed to *Notwithstanding the family's objection to the marriage*.

But the literalist argument is very much in vain, as the *OED* attests with a 14th-century example of *notwithstanding* as a sentence-starter. This usage has been constant from the 1300s to the present day. In fact, the construction with *notwithstanding* following the noun first appeared more than a century later, and has never been as frequent. The *Century Dictionary* explains: "As the noun usually follows [the word *notwithstanding*], the [word] came to be regarded as a prep. (as also with *during*, ppr.), and is now usually so construed." 3 *Century Dictionary and Cyclopedia* 4029 (1914). The word is not a DANGLER because it does not function as a participle.

nought. See **naught.**

NOUN PLAGUE is Wilson Follett's term for the piling up of nouns to modify other nouns (*MAU* at 229). When a sentence has more than two nouns in a row, it generally becomes much less readable. The following sentence is badly constructed because of the noun-upon-noun syndrome, which (sadly) is more common now than in Follett's day: "Consumers complained to their congressmen about *the National Highway Traffic Safety Administration's automobile seat belt 'interlock' rule*." One can hardly make it to the SENTENCE END to discover that we're talking about a rule. (Even worse, many writers today would leave off the possessive after *Administration*.) In the interest of plague control, the following rewrite is advisable: *the 'interlock' rule applied to automotive seat belts by the National Highway Traffic Safety Administration*. A few prepositional phrases and an adjective (*automotive*) do the job.

Readability typically plummets when three words that are ordinarily nouns follow in succession, although exceptions such as *fidelity life insurance* certainly exist. But the plague is unendurable when four nouns appear consecutively, as when writers refer to a **participation program principal category* or the **retiree benefit explanation procedure*. Occasionally one encounters even longer strings: in 1997, a major national bank circulated a form entitled *Government Securities Dealership Customer Account Information Form*—which might be something of a record.

It is true, of course, that noun-stacking really involves making all but the last noun into adjectives. But the problem is that many readers will think that they've hit upon the noun when they're still reading adjectives. Hence a MISCUE occurs. For more on the use of nouns as adjectives, see FUNCTIONAL VARIATION (B).

Finally, it is worth cautioning against loading a single statement with too many abstract nouns ending in *-tion*. The effect isn't pleasing:

- "Police must [study] . . . how to defuse volatile *situations* and how to instruct victims on *prosecution* and *protection options* the law provides." Jim Nichols, "Domestic Violence Cases Soar in Medina," *Plain Dealer* (Cleveland), 30 Dec. 1993, at B1.
- "This work led to a *consideration* of additional important attributes of *information* and *communication* media within *organizations*." Ralph H. Sprague, "Electronic Document Management," *MIS Q.*, Mar. 1995, at 29.
- "All of the 'classic' *assumptions* that are at the basis of the terms 'culture' and 'intercultural differences' find *expression* in this *intervention*. That is why the *situation* at the Center is not a *question* of organizational change." Micha Popper, "The Glorious Failure," 33 *J. Applied Behavioral Science* 27 (1997).

For more on words ending in *-tion*, see ZOMBIE NOUNS. See also SOUND OF PROSE.

NOUNS AS ADJECTIVES. See FUNCTIONAL SHIFT (B).

NOUNS AS VERBS. See FUNCTIONAL SHIFT (D).

no use. Eric Partridge labeled this "incorrect—or, at best, colloquial—for *of no use*" (*U&A* at 203). Yet *it's no use* has greatly outranked *it's of no use* in print sources since about 1830. Although some readers and listeners would consider *no use* colloquial, the following examples certainly aren't incorrect:

- "There's *no use* crying about it." Dana Parsons, "Apocalypse When?" *L.A. Times*, 27 Aug. 1995, at B1.
- "It is *no use* comparing this city to others, because there is no other city in the world like it." Dennis Duggan, "The Battle in Defense of Hearth and Home," *Newsday* (N.Y.), 8 May 1997, at A8.
- "But it's *no use*." George Howe Colt, "The Strange Allure of Disasters," *Life*, June 1997, at 58.
- "She knows it's *no use* forcing the feisty elders of Ferry County." Erica Curless, "'The Fire Ain't Going to Get Us,'" *Spokesman-Rev.* (Spokane), 3 Sept. 2015, at A1.

The longer phrase, *of no use*, would be of no use in any of these citations unless the sentences were rearranged—and made slightly longer.

nouveau riche. A. Generally. *Nouveau riche* (= [1] a newly rich person; or [2] newly rich people collectively) is sometimes misspelled *nouveau rich—e.g.: "It will be for Deng's heirs to deal with problems such as the widening gap between China's *nouveau rich* [read *nouveau riche*] and rural poor." James Cox, "Deng Xiaoping: 1904–1997," *USA Today*, 20 Feb. 1997, at A1.

The phrase keeps the French plural *nouveaux riches*, as it has since it was first used in the 1790s. But some mistakenly write *nouveau riches or even (as a plural) *nouveau rich—e.g.:

- "But the customers here are China's *nouveau riches* [read *nouveaux riches*] from one of the wealthiest of the Middle Kingdom's southern cities." Keith B. Richburg, "China Attracts Western Retailers Willing to Learn Its Ways," *L.A. Times*, 16 Feb. 1997, at D15.
- "Even for those *nouveau rich* [read *nouveaux riches*] with the spare change and audacity to have their own personal

guard posted at the entrance, it still takes a moment." "Back Porch," *S.F. Examiner*, 22 Dec. 1996, at E3.

See PLURALS (B).

Some writers seem to believe that the phrase refers not to people but to newfound wealth—e.g.:

- "Unlike Donald Trump and his ilk, [Ralph] Lauren spends his *nouveaux riches* [read *newfound wealth*] with old-money restraint." Claudia Glenn Dowling, "He Has Fame, Fortune, Family, and His Health," *Life*, May 1989, at 136.
- "The Victorians couldn't blow their bucks on big-screen TVs. Instead, their *nouveau riches* [read *newfound wealth*, or merely *wealth*] went toward embellishing their houses." M.J. McAteer, "A Touch of Class," *Wash. Post*, 16 Apr. 1997, at D9.

The singular and plural forms are pronounced /noo-voh **reesh**/.

LANGUAGE-CHANGE INDEX
1. *nouveau rich for *nouveau riche*: Stage 1
Current ratio (*nouveau riche* vs. *nouveau rich): 50:1
2. *nouveau riches as a plural for
nouveaux riches: Stage 1
Current ratio (*nouveaux riches* vs.
*nouveau riches): 17:1
3. *nouveau riche* in reference to
newfound wealth: Stage 1

B. And Its Near-Synonyms: *parvenu*; *arriviste*. The GALLICISMS *parvenu* (/**pahr**-və-noo/) and *arriviste* (/ah-ree-**veest**/) are synonymous, meaning "a person who is newly rich; an upstart." *Arriviste* can also refer to someone who has recently acquired power or success that isn't necessarily monetary.

Although *nouveau riche* is by far the most widespread of these terms, the others are hardly uncommon—e.g.:

- "Movie stars and chief executives sipped champagne and knocked mallets with the likes of Prince Charles and Princess Michael of Kent at snobby residential polo clubs. The *parvenus* and wannabes followed at slightly less exclusive clubs." June Fletcher, "Equestrian Communities Hitting Stride Again in the '90s," *Salt Lake Trib.*, 21 July 1996, at G4.
- "Even the models, draped in wide stripes and emergency colors, are posed to look like vogue-ish, fad-worn *arrivistes*, sporting smiles of complete incomprehension." Jeff Danziger, "A Catalog of Horrors," *Wall Street J.*, 8 Nov. 1996, at A18.
- "Like any subculture, WAGS have their own hierarchy, with wives ruling the roost and mere girlfriends seen as gold-digging *parvenus*." Kevin McDonough, "Lives of Jocks Fascinate Fans of 2 Reality Shows," *Commercial Appeal* (Memphis), 18 Aug. 2015, at 5.
- "The people at the *arriviste* tech companies sometimes consult with him to see what the neighbourhood wants." Alec Scott, "Medium Rare," *Globe & Mail* (Toronto), 1 Sept. 2015, at L1.

But *parvenu* and *arriviste* are uncommon enough that they smack of SESQUIPEDALITY.

novella forms the plural *novellas* or (less good) *novelle. See PLURALS (B).

Current ratio: 5:1

novelty does not mean "an extreme rarity." Rather, it denotes something new (and possibly rare). In the sentence "Mother–son incest is so rare as to be regarded as a *novelty*," the writer could have better written, "Mother–son incest is an extreme *rarity*." *Oedipus Rex* belies any claim that incest might have to novelty. And the connotations of *novelty* are positive, so linking it to something as negative as incest makes this use even stranger (but not more novel).

novitiate; *noviciate. This word—meaning (1) "the period during which a person is a novice"; (2) "a building where novices are housed"; or (3) "a novice"—is preferably spelled *novitiate*. *Noviciate is a variant spelling that was common from only about 1750 to 1850. The word is sometimes misspelled *novitate—e.g.: "Last year the case was transferred to the Diocese of Allentown, since that is where Ciszek was born and where he is buried at the Jesuit *novitate* [read *novitiate*]." Anne Rodgers-Melnick, "Journey Toward Sainthood Long, Complex," *Pitt. Post-Gaz.*, 14 Sept. 1997, at A11.

Current ratio (*novitiate* vs. *noviciate): 17:1

now. People go to great lengths to use genteelisms instead of this simple, straightforward word—especially *at the present time* and *at this time*. For a fairly common misspelling involving *now*, see **know.** See **at the present time** & **at this time.**

Nowell. See **Noel.**

nowhere; *nowheres. The first is standard. The second is a dialectal word. See DIALECT. Cf. **anywhere.**
LANGUAGE-CHANGE INDEX
*nowheres for *nowhere*: Stage 1
Current ratio (*nowhere* vs. *nowheres): 412:1

nowhere near as is a CASUALISM for *not nearly as*. During the 20th century, it became fairly common in both AmE and BrE—e.g.:

- "Admittedly, Tony Blair is *nowhere near as* [or *not nearly as*] terrifying as Mrs. T." Nicholas Lloyd, "Spin Doctors in Overdose," *Times* (London), 6 Aug. 1997, at 21.
- "The technology, which is *nowhere near as* [or *not nearly as*] sophisticated as a flux generator bomb, could easily move from law enforcement to the criminal and terrorist population." "Cyber Terrorism," *Am. Banker*, 8 Sept. 1997, at 43.

no worries. This Australianism, meaning "no problem" or "don't worry," appeared first in the mid-1960s. The OED records a singular use from Sydney in 1965: "*No worry* . . . it's amazing what a few schooners of jolly does for a bloke." The *Australian National Dictionary* records the plural *no worries* in a 1967 book by J. Hibberd entitled *White with Wire Wheels*: " 'Well. How was she?' . . . 'Who, Sue? No worries.' " Other uses are attested from the late 1960s to the mid-1980s.

The actor and writer Paul Hogan popularized the phrase outside Australia in his Crocodile Dundee movies (the memorable one of 1986, the less memorable sequel of 1988, and the wholly forgettable second sequel of 2001). Hogan's catchphrase was *No worries, mate.* The wide appeal of those movies made the phrase something of a vogue expression, sometimes with and sometimes without *mate* tacked on the end. In many examples, American and British writers make clear that the phrase is an Australianism—e.g.:

- "Not since John McEnroe was thrown out five years ago had the laid-back, *no-worries-mate* Australian Open rocked the way it did Monday." "Australian Fans Rock, but Agassi Still Rolls," *Wash. Post*, 24 Jan. 1995, at C7.
- "[I]t would be scarcely worth turning up to play against a team that includes Wallaby full-back Mat Rogers, living personification of that ubiquitous Aussie catchphrase, '*no worries, mate.*' " Huw Richards, "Rogers Learns to Handle the Pressure," *Fin. Times*, 20 Nov. 2003, at 16.
- " '*No worries,*' said Lonie, an Australian who was the only non-Californian signed by Tedford." Jay Heater, "Cal Didn't Venture Far in Finding Strong Recruiting Class," *San Jose Mercury News*, 5 Feb. 2004, Sports §, at 3.

But beginning about the year 2000, the expression had spread into mainstream AmE without any hint of its foreignness. The phrase now commonly appears without any reference to Australia at all, as in the title of Chris Tomasson's March 2004 article: "No Ball? No Basket? *No Worries,*" *Rocky Mountain News* (Denver), 19 Mar. 2004, at C7. Sometimes the phrase is part of the syntax <they had no worries about the weather that afternoon>, but often it's a catchphrase used as an INCOMPLETE SENTENCE (and this is the quintessential Australianism)—e.g.:

- "Rachel McQuillan joined the million-dollar club more than four years ago, an elite group mostly occupied by players known by their first names. And she owns an Olympic bronze medal in doubles from Barcelona in 1992. *No worries,* right?" Lisa Dillman, "First Round Is All Good for Lucky Loser Tennis," *L.A. Times*, 9 Mar. 2001, at D9.
- "Jimmy, my man. You had Wisconsin Parrotheads worried there for a while. Up until this week, Jimmy Buffett had not penciled in any dates for a concert. . . . [H]e promised he'd be coming back. And indeed he is. . . . See? *No worries.*" Rob Thomas, "Gotta-Have-It List," *Wis. State J.*, 18 Mar. 2004, Rhythm §, at 2.
- "Once at the arena, UW players shot around for an hour, with maybe 150 people watching and cheering on their various shooting and dunking contests. Still, the UAB press lingers. *No worries.*" Dan Raley, "Tempo to Tell Tale in Huskies' NCAA Opener," *Seattle Post-Intelligencer*, 19 Mar. 2004, at C1.

nuance. Although in French this word is spoken with stress on the second syllable, in English the best (and commonest) pronunciation is /**n**[**y**]**oo**-ahnts/.

nuclear. In standard AmE, this word is pronounced /**n**[**y**]**oo**-klee-ər/—not /**n**[**y**]**oo**-kyə-lər/, a "spectacular

___
LANGUAGE-CHANGE INDEX (For the full key, see front matter pp. xxxi, l–li.)
Stage 1: Rejected. **Stage 2:** Widely shunned. **Stage 3:** Widespread but . . . **Stage 4:** Ubiquitous but . . . **Stage 5:** Fully accepted.
Invariably inferior forms marked by asterisk (*). • Ratios represent frequency of prevalent forms vs. variants in current books.

blunder" (in Burchfield's words) induced by false analogy with words such as *muscular, spectacular,* and *vernacular.* Though politicians and other educated people have had difficulty saying the word correctly, if you can do it you should. See PRONUNCIATION (B). Cf. METATHESIS & DIALECT.

William Safire has suggested that because Presidents Eisenhower, Carter, Clinton, and Bush (George W.) have used the mistaken pronunciation, speechwriters begin printing *new-clear* in place of this word in the versions of speeches that presidents read. "On Language," 20 May 2001, § 7, at 24, 26. Not a bad idea.

In 2012, in a public forum, I asked Andrew Card— President George W. Bush's chief of staff—whether the pronunciation of *nuclear* had ever been discussed in his presence in the Oval Office. His entirely serious answer: "Endlessly."

LANGUAGE-CHANGE INDEX
nuclear mispronounced /**noo**-kyə-lər/: Stage 2

nucleus. In traditional senses, the plural is *nuclei*—not *nucleuses.* E.g.:

- "He said the genetic therapy company scientists hope to target the mutation by injecting a small molecule made of DNA, the basic material of all cell *nucleuses* [read *nuclei*]." Mark Guidera, "Oncor to Develop Gene Therapy for Obesity," *Baltimore Sun,* 26 Mar. 1996, at C2.
- "[For DNA testing to work,] there have to be cell *nuclei* present, and hair that has been pulled away from its roots doesn't contain any *nuclei*." Laurie P. Cohen, "Inside the Cell," *Wall Street J.,* 19 Dec. 1997, at A1.
- "He said there are no queen bees or larvae in either of the *nucleuses* [read *nuclei*], rendering them useless." W.T. Eckert, "Beekeeper Allegedly Stings Clients," *Journal* (Ogdensburgh, N.Y.), 2 Sept. 2014, News §, at 3.

But in sports talk—in which *nucleus* means "a core of strong players on a team"—*nucleuses* is standard. E.g.:

- "The Islanders, with two potential lottery picks in the 1997 draft, plus one of the better young *nucleuses* in the National Hockey League, could afford to surrender the five No. 1 draft picks required to sign either Sakic or Forsberg." Eric Duhatschek, "Cash Crunch," *Calgary Herald,* 15 Feb. 1997, at D4.
- "Christie Burden, Megan Frank and Latoya Robinson all started a year ago and along with Selwyn make for one of the best—if not tallest—*nucleuses* around." Michael S. Snyder, "Strongest in Decades," *Sun-Sentinel* (Ft. Lauderdale), 19 Nov. 1997, at 22.
- "Clearly, *nucleuses* win games, not just one player." Benjamin Hochman, "LeBron's Legacy Could Be on Line," *Denver Post,* 30 May 2013, at B1.

See PLURALS (B).

Current ratio (*nuclei* vs. *nucleuses*): 1,223:1

nuke, v.t., is a slangy word that means not only "to attack with nuclear weapons" but also "to destroy, demolish" or "to microwave (food)." The following examples illustrate the three senses:

- "I don't think I've watched my video of the movie 'Fail Safe,' in which New York City gets *nuked,* more than 30 or 40 times." Mike Royko, "Read On, Gluttons for Punishment," *Chicago Trib.,* 12 Mar. 1987, at C3.

- "Jordan *nuked* the Knicks . . . and settled the double-teaming controversy, too." "Eastern Lowlights Make for Strange Playoff Race," *Commercial Appeal* (Memphis), 2 Apr. 1995, at D8.
- "Remember this the next time you rip open a freshly *nuked* bag of microwave popcorn: You're really getting a whiff of rotten eggs." "Popping-Good Smell Is Old Eggs," *Daily News* (L.A.), 31 Mar. 1997, at L2.

See SLANG.

*****numbedness.** See **numbness.**

number. See **amount.**

number of. A. *A number of.* Some pedants think that correctness dictates *a number of people is.* One critic, for example, refers to "the growing habit of using plural verbs with singular nouns," adding: "'A number of voters were unhappy' illustrates the offense." F. Thomas Trotter, "Out on the Campaign Trail, English Grammar Trampled," *Nashville Banner,* 12 Sept. 1996, at A13.

But *a number of* is quite correctly paired with a plural noun and a plural verb, as in *there are a number of reasons*—e.g.:

- "But when asked, a surprising *number* of Cubans *seem* not to know exactly what it is they should be celebrating on December 25." Pascal Fletcher, "Mixed Blessings for Castro's Christmas Decree," *Fin. Times,* 20 Dec. 1997, at 3.
- "Although most Jefferson scholars have considered the rumor unlikely, a gradually increasing *number*—including late historians Page Smith and Fawn Brodie—*have* given credence to the Hemings story." Barbra Murray, "Clearing the Heirs," *U.S. News & World Rep.,* 22 Dec. 1997, at 54.
- "A *number* of clubs, particularly on the continent, *operate* with a head coach and a technical director who plays a major role in talent spotting." "Tim: Buck Stops with Me Over Signings," *Birmingham Mail* (U.K.), 3 Sept. 2015, Sports §, at 64.

This construction is correct because of the linguistic principle known as SYNESIS, which allows some constructions to control properties such as number according to their meaning rather than strict syntactical rules. Since the meaning of *a number of things* is *many things* (or *several things*), and since *some things* is plural, the verb must be plural.

The question becomes a close one, however, when an adjective precedes *number* <a significant number of them [is] [are]>. Because the adjective emphasizes *number* as a noun, some writers make the verb singular—e.g.:

- "What matters more than this . . . is that there *is* abroad in the world these days a *substantial number of* groups and individuals whose varied labors make inevitable a deepening sense of self." Wendell Johnson, *Verbal Man: The Enchantment of Words* 123 (1956; repr. 1965).
- "There *is a substantial number* (perhaps on the order of fifty) of standard verbs ending in -en that have been formed from adjectives." Robert W. Burchfield, *Points of View* 91 (1992).

But these writers are strongly outnumbered by those who, even with the qualifying adjective, see the idiom as being *a number of,* necessitating a plural verb.

Linguistic authorities have a long tradition of preferring the plural here—e.g.:

- "As the Greeks understood, there *are an infinite number* of degrees of simplicity, ranging from the simple colloquial to the simple grand." A.R. Orage, *Readers and Writers (1917–1921)* 76 (1922; repr. 1969).
- "As everybody knows, there *are a vast number* of words in the language . . . which were deliberately coined to imitate a sound." Guy N. Pocock, "Sound and Sense," in *Foundations of English Style* 180, 182 (Paul M. Fulcher ed., 1927).
- "As men are now constituted, there *are a great number* who ever come to feel this surrender to be a sacrifice." Otto Jespersen, *Mankind, Nation, and Individual from a Linguistic Point of View* 117 (1946).
- "We know, for example, that there *are a significant number* of differences." Albert Marckwardt, "Regional and Social Variations" (1958), in *A Language Reader for Writers* 65, 70 (James R. Gaskin & Jack Suberman eds., 1966).
- "There *are* still *a large number* of unanswered questions about this grammar-building activity." Graham Wilson, Foreword, *A Linguistics Reader* xxii (Graham Wilson ed., 1967).
- "*A large number* of our teachers of English *have* had such a meager scientific training that they cannot give their students what they need." George Curme (as quoted in James Sledd, "Grammar or Gramarye?" in *A Linguistics Reader* 125, 135 (Graham Wilson ed., 1967)).
- "There *have* been *an almost infinite number* of studies." Earl W. Buxton, *Looking at Language* v (M.H. Scargill & P.G. Penner eds., 1969).
- "There *are a remarkable number* of words in standard English that are very easy to confuse." David Crystal, *Who Cares About English Usage?* 11 (1984).
- "There *are a surprising number* of words that seem to us perfectly innocent and acceptable . . . which at one time or another were anathema in usage circles." Dennis Baron, *Declining Grammar* 92 (1989).

Few usage critics have ever discussed this particular point. One who did, G.H. Vallins, labeled those who insisted on the singular "purists" (a derogatory term in his mind). (See Vallins, *Good English: How to Write It* 17 [1951].) Better to stick with the plural.

LANGUAGE-CHANGE INDEX
a number of with plural noun and plural verb: Stage 5
Current ratio (*a number of them were* vs. **a number of them was*): 82:1

B. The number of. When the phrase is used with the definite article *the*, everything changes. Now, instead of talking about the multiple things, we're talking about the number itself, which is singular <the number of students planning to attend college is steadily rising>.

C. With *most*. See **most number of things*.

NUMBERS. See NUMERALS.

numbness; *numbedness. The latter is a NEEDLESS VARIANT.

Current ratio: 9,252:1

numbskull. See **numskull.**

NUMERALS. A. General Guidance in Using. The best practice is to spell out all numbers ten and below and to use numerals for numbers 11 and above. This "rule" has five exceptions:

1. If numbers recur throughout the text or are being used for calculations—that is, if the context is technical or quasi-mathematical—then numerals are usual.
2. Approximations are usually spelled out (*about two hundred years ago*).
3. In units of measure, words substitute for rows of zeros where possible (*$10 million, $3 billion*), and numerals are used (*3 inches, age 24, 3:15 PM*).
4. Percentages may be spelled out (*eight percent*) or written as numerals (*8 percent* or *8%*).
5. Numbers that begin sentences must always be spelled out. (See (B).)

B. Not Beginning Sentences with. It is generally considered stylistically poor to begin a sentence—or a paragraph—with a numeral <2002 was a good year for new mystery novels>. Some periodicals, such as *The New Yorker*, would make that sentence begin *Two thousand two was . . . .* But most writers and editors would probably begin the sentence some other way, as by writing, *In 2002, no fewer than 3,700 mystery novels were published.* Sometimes the revision requires significant reworking of the sentence—e.g.: "*1942* saw the publication of the first major dictionary of its kind." Robert Allen, "The Big Four," 12 *English Today* 41, 41 (1996). (A suggested revision: *In 1942, the first major dictionary of its kind was published.* [On the change of the zombie noun *publication* to the passive-voice *was published*, see the final paragraph of ZOMBIE NOUNS.]) More often, especially with years, the problem can be fixed simply by beginning the sentence with *The year.* So that quotation could also be fixed by starting the sentence with *The year 1942 saw.*

Numbers other than years present more problems. Generally, it is acceptable to simply spell out the number rather than using a numeral. That's no problem with small numbers—most styles call for spelling out small numbers anyway. The trouble comes with larger numbers, and the larger the number, the more troubling it can be. But the rule of reason applies here. When the number can be expressed briefly, or when precision is not an issue, simply write out the number <A hundred years ago we didn't have these problems>. But rather than writing *Thirty-four thousand eight hundred seventy-one people voted for the bond issue*, it's better to reword the sentence: *Nearly 35,000 people . . . .*

C. Round Numbers. Except when writing checks or other negotiable instruments, omit double zeros after a decimal: *$400* is better form than *$400.00*.

D. Decades. As late as the 1970s, editors regularly changed *1970s* to *1970's*. More recently, the tendency is to omit the apostrophe. That cleaner style should be encouraged, though *The New York Times* and some

LANGUAGE-CHANGE INDEX (For the full key, see front matter pp. xxxi, l–li.)
Stage 1: Rejected. **Stage 2:** Widely shunned. **Stage 3:** Widespread but . . . **Stage 4:** Ubiquitous but . . . **Stage 5:** Fully accepted.
Invariably inferior forms marked by asterisk (*). • Ratios represent frequency of prevalent forms vs. variants in current books.

other newspapers still use the apostrophe. See DATES (D) & PUNCTUATION (A).

E. Votes and Scores. The preferred method for reporting votes and scores is to use numerals separated by an en-dash <a 5–4 decision> <the Cowboys won 38–3>. This method, which gives the reader more speed than spelling out the numbers, is standard today.

F. Cardinal and Ordinal. A *cardinal number* expresses amount (e.g., *one, two, three*). An *ordinal number* expresses place in a series (e.g., *first, second, third*). Occasionally, cardinal numbers are mistakenly used for ordinal numbers—e.g.: " 'It wasn't really a ballet class. It was more of a modern dance class, sort of an introduction to ballet,' Roy explained with the weariness of someone reciting a response for the *umpteenth million* [read *umpteen-millionth*] time." Randy Riggs, "Roy: Building a Better Linebacker Through Ballet," *Austin Am.-Statesman*, 24 Aug. 1995, at D8.

G. Repetition. The repetition of numbers by spelling them out and then using numerals typifies LEGALESE and should never be used outside legal drafting <the sum of forty-one dollars and thirty-seven cents ($41.37)>. Even in modern legal documents it is largely uncalled for—the convention harks back to the days of legal scribes, who doubled words and numerals to prevent fraudulent alterations (words controlled over numerals). See Bryan A. Garner, *Legal Writing in Plain English* 115–16 (2001). Occasionally, the redundant convention can be seen in informal situations where it is unintentionally funny <they have two (2) children, a son age thirteen (13) and a daughter age seven (7)>.

H. In Names. See NAMES (B).

numerical; numeric. These words overlap when they mean "of, relating to, or involving numerals" <numerical display> <numeric keypad>. But *numerical* is the broader (and more common) term, with the additional meaning of "mathematical" <numerical analysis> <numerical advantage>. When the sense of "numeral" involved is a measurement rather than a symbol, *numerical* is the better choice—e.g.: "These reputed traditional families registered an increase of 5.7 percent during the 1990s, in contrast to *numeric* [read *numerical*] decreases during the previous two decades." William H. Frey, "Married with Children," *American Demographics*, Mar. 2003, at 2.

NUMERICAL PREFIXES. English is a major debtor to the world's other languages, especially to Latin and Greek. The extent of borrowing from the classical languages is mind-boggling. One of the early editors of the *OED*, the great Henry Bradley, put it this way: "The Latin element in modern English is so great that there would be no difficulty in writing hundreds of consecutive pages in which the proportion of words of native English and French etymology, excluding particles, pronouns, and auxiliary and substantive verbs, would not exceed five per cent of the whole." Henry Bradley, *The Making of English* 94 (1904; repr. 1951).

Among the combining forms that we have inherited are those relating to numbers. Especially in technical contexts, the English language can express numerical relationships through words formed from classical elements. Anyone who takes the time to learn these elements will understand many otherwise unfamiliar words on sight. What follows is a list of the classically derived prefixes that make up English words, with some representative examples. Among these words are several HYBRIDS and MORPHOLOGICAL DEFORMITIES (e.g., *kilowatt, milliwatt, monokini*), but most have been devised with some attention to word-formation principles.

one
uni- (Latin)
  unicellular
  unicorn
  unicycle
  unilateral
  unique
  unit
mono- (Greek)
  monodactylous
  monogamy
  monoglot
  monogram
  monokini
  monologue
  mononucleosis
  monophthong
  monopoly
  monorail
  monotonous

two
du(o)- (Latin)
  duet
  duodecillion
  duodrama
  duologue
  duomachy
  duopoly
  duplicate
deuter(o)- (Greek)
  deuteragonist
  deuteride
  deuterium
  deuterogamy
  deuterograph
  deuterostome

twice
bi- (Latin)
  bicycle
  biennial
  bifocals
  bigamy
  bilateral
  binary
  biped
  bisect
  bisexual
di- (Greek)
  dichromatic
  *digamy
  dilemma

  dioxide
  diphthong

three
tri- (Latin & Greek)
  triangle
  triathlon
  triceratops
  tricycle
  triennial
  trimester
  tripartite
  triplicate
  tripod
  triumvirate
  trivium

four
quadr- (Latin)
  quadrant
  quadrennial
  quadriceps
  quadrilateral
  quadrille
  quadripartite
  quadriplegic
  quadrivium
  quadrumanous
  quadruped
tetra- (Greek)
  tetracycline
  tetrad
  tetragon
  tetrahedron
  tetralogy
  tetrapod
  tetrastich

five
quin(que)- (Latin)
  quinary
  quincentennial
  quinquelateral
  quinquennial
  quinquepartite
  quinternion
  quintessential
  quintet
  quintuple
penta- (Greek)
  pentagon
  pentagram
  pentarch
  pentastich

pentathlon

six
sex- (Latin)
  sexagenarian
  sexangular
  sexcentennial
  sexennial
  sexpartite
  sextet
  sextuplets
  sextuplicate
hexa- (Greek)
  hexachlorophane
  hexagon
  hexagram
  hexameter
  hexapod
  hexarchy

seven
sept- (Latin)
  September
  septemvirate
  septenarius
  septennial
  septet
  septipartite
  septuagenarian
  septuplets
hept- (Greek)
  hebdomadal [Late
    Greek]
  heptad
  heptagon
  heptameter
  heptarchy
  heptathlon
  heptose

eight
oct(o)- (Latin & Greek
  [*okto*])
  octagenarian
  octagon
  octarchy
  octennial
  October
  octopartite
  octopus

nine
nona- (Latin)
  nonagenarian
  nonagon
  nonamer
  nonary
nove(m)- (Latin)
  novemarticulate
  November
  novemdecillion
  novena
  novendial
  novennial
ennea- (Greek)
  ennead

enneagon
enneahedron
enneastyle

ten
dec(em)- (Latin)
  December
  decempedal
  decemvir
  decennial
deca- (Greek)
  decadal
  decade
  decagon
  decahedron
  decameron
  decangular
  decasyllabic
  decathlon

hundred
cent- (Latin)
  centenarian
  centennial
  centesimal
  centigrade
  centiliter
  centimeter
  centipede
  centurion
  century
hect(o)- (Greek)
  hectare
  hectogram
  hectoliter
  hectometer

thousand
mill(e)- (Latin)
  millecuple
  millennial
  milliampere
  milliliter
  million
  millipede
  millirem
  milliwatt
kilo- (Greek)
  kilogram
  kiloliter
  kilometer
  kiloton
  kilowatt
chili- (Greek)
  chiliad

**ten thousand (or
"countless")**
myri- (Latin)
  myriad
  myriametric
  myriapod
  myriogram
  myriotheism

numerous is often just an inflated equivalent of *many*—e.g.: "Exhibits in the two-story Virginia Room provide an overview of the *numerous* [read *many*] Civil War battles fought in Virginia." Randy Mink, "Shenandoah Valley Abounds in Hospitality," *Denver Post*, 18 May 1997, at T1. Avoid it.

numismatist (= a coin collector) is pronounced /n[y]oo-**mis**-mə-tist/ or /n[y]oo-**miz**-mə-tist/—not /n[y]oo-miz-**mat**-ist/. The most common cognates are the adjective *numismatic* /n[y]oo-miz-**mat**-ik/ and the noun *numismatics* /n[y]oo-miz-**mat**-iks/ (avoid the erroneous /n[y]oo-**miz**-mə-tiks/). *Numismatics* is plural in form but singular in construction <numismatics is a terrific hobby for those with a historical bent>.

numskull (= a dolt or dunce) was long the standard spelling (from about 1770 till 2000). *Numbskull*, though an etymologically accurate spelling, was long considered a variant. But it has become more frequent in print sources since 2000.
    Current ratio (*numbskull* vs. *numskull*): 1.1:1

nuptial; nuptials. Although *nuptial* is in good use as an adjective, the noun *nuptials* (= wedding) is generally a pomposity to be avoided. It should be left to its ineradicable place in newspaper reports of weddings, where grubstreet hacks engage in (not to say become engaged to) INELEGANT VARIATION.
    Nuptial is pronounced /**nəp**-shəl/—not /**nəp**-shə-wəl/ or (worse) /-chə-/. See **prenuptial.**

*nurseling. See **nursling.**

nursing one's wounds. Occasionally, by MALAPROPISM, the phrase is mangled into **nurturing one's wounds*, as if wounds were to be cultivated and developed further—e.g.: "The other young women *nurtured* [read *nursed*] his wounds and cooled his skin with sponges soaked in a special herbal solution." Lawrence Patrick, *Inner Journey* 26 (2003).

LANGUAGE-CHANGE INDEX
*nurturing wounds for *nursing wounds*: Stage 1

nursling (= [1] a baby still being nursed; or [2] anything that is being cared for tenderly) has been the standard spelling since the 18th century. **Nurseling* is a variant.

Current ratio: 10:1

nurturance looks like a NEEDLESS VARIANT of *nurture*, but the words have diverged in their connotations. Whereas *nurture* means either "upbringing" or "food," *nurturance*—a 20th-century NEOLOGISM dating from 1938—means "attentive care; emotional and physical nourishment." If this DIFFERENTIATION persists, then *nurturance* will earn a permanent position in the language. For now, it remains relatively uncommon—e.g.:

- "Moral *nurturance* comes next, linking self-discipline to self-reliance." Paul Rosenberg, "Examining Morals in

LANGUAGE-CHANGE INDEX (For the full key, see front matter pp. xxxi, l–li.)
Stage 1: Rejected. **Stage 2:** Widely shunned. **Stage 3:** Widespread but . . . **Stage 4:** Ubiquitous but . . . **Stage 5:** Fully accepted.
Invariably inferior forms marked by asterisk (*). • Ratios represent frequency of prevalent forms vs. variants in current books.

Politics and the Media," *Christian Science Monitor*, 10 June 1996, Features §, at 14.

- "Bailey sets four criteria he says are essential to proper human development: safety, wellness, *nurturance* and stimulation." "Is Smart Start Getting the Critical Look It Deserves?" *News & Observer* (Raleigh), 24 Mar. 1997, at A8.
- "He makes it clear that like the environment, the protection, maintenance and *nurturance* of our libraries is a cause so worthy it is beyond debate." Charlotte Duggan,

"Save Our Stacks," *Winnipeg Free Press*, 30 May 2015, at A1.

*nurturing one's wounds. See **nursing one's wounds.**

Nutmegger; Connecticuter. The first is the standard name for someone who hails from or lives in Connecticut. The second is a less common equivalent. See DENIZEN LABELS.

Current ratio: 5:1

O

O; Oh. Although the distinction isn't always observed, there is one: *O* denotes either a wish or a classically stylized address <Praise the Lord, O Jerusalem—Psalm 147>, while *Oh* expresses a range of emotions from sorrow to pain to shock to longing to momentary hesitation <Oh! You frightened me!> <Oh? You want me to get that?>. *O* is always capitalized, comes just before a noun, and is usually not followed by any punctuation—e.g.: "*O* Dionysus, it would be so humiliating to have a seizure now!" Gillian Bradshaw, *Cleopatra's Heir* 379 (2002).

Oh may be lowercase if it occurs in midsentence and is always set off by commas inside a sentence <I was just thinking that, oh, I miss my home>.

oaf. Pl. *oafs.* See PLURALS (C).

oasis forms the plural *oases*—not **oasises.*

oats, sowing wild. See **sow (B).**

obbligato (= a musical accompaniment traditionally viewed as obligatory in performing a piece) has been predominantly so spelled since 1880—when **obligato* became just a variant spelling. Pl. *obbligatos.* See PLURALS (B) & SPELLING (A).

obeisance (= a strong respect for and deference to another) is preferably pronounced /oh-**bay**-sən[t]s/—though /oh-**bee**-sən[t]s/ is also acceptable.

obelisk (= a stone pillar erected usu. as a memorial) is preferably pronounced /**ob**-ə-lisk/—not /**oh**-bə-lisk/.

obfuscate (= to render [a subject] impenetrable to understanding, esp. by means of incomprehensible language) is preferably pronounced /**ob**-fəs-kayt/—not /**ob**-fyoo-skayt/. Before the 20th century, the traditional pronunciation was /ob-**fəs**-kayt/.

object, no. See **no object.**

objectify; objectivize. *Objectify*, dating from the mid-19th century, means either (1) "to make into an object," or (2) "to render objective." *Objectivize*, dating from the late 19th century, means "to render objective." It would be convenient for the words to undergo DIFFERENTIATION, so that *objectify* would be confined to its sense 1, while *objectivize* would preempt *objectify* in the latter's sense 2. See **reify.**

objectionable; objectional. *Objectionable* (= open to objection; unacceptable; offensive) is the ordinary word. *Objectional* (= of, relating to, or like an objection), a rare word, is frequently misused for *objectionable*—e.g.:

- "Two Vista High School students . . . were suspended for publishing an underground newspaper that school officials said was *objectional* [read *objectionable*] and contained sexually explicit material." "Student Paper Suit," *San Diego Union-Trib.*, 20 Feb. 1985, at B2.
- "The plan is *objectional* [read *objectionable*] to some because it envisions free-standing retail businesses along Crabapple Road, which residents want to keep residential." Diane R. Stepp, "City Council Action," *Atlanta J.-Const.*, 15 Sept. 1994, at H4.
- "Stull has drawn attention to many *objectional* [read *objectionable*] aspects of the meat and poultry industries." Barb Shelly, "'Pink Slime' Product of Cheap-Beef Economy," *Tulsa World*, 13 Apr. 2012, at A19.

LANGUAGE-CHANGE INDEX
objectional misused for *objectionable*:
Stage 1

objectivize. See **objectify.**

OBJECT-SHUFFLING. This term describes what unwary writers often do with verbs that require an indirect as well as a direct object. E.g.: "He continued the medicine a few days longer, and then *substituted the penicillin with tetracycline* [read *substituted tetracycline for the penicillin* or *replaced the penicillin with tetracycline*]." This use of *substitute* for *replace*, resulting from a confusion over the type of object that each verb may take, is labeled "incorrect" in the *OED*.

Unfortunately, there is no simple rule for determining which verbs are reversible and which are not. (See ERGATIVE VERBS.) One must rely on a sensitivity to idiom and a knowledge of what type of subject acts upon what type of object with certain verbs. It is perfectly legitimate, for example, either to *inspire* a person *with* courage or to *inspire* courage *in* a person; but the switch does not work with similar words such as *instill* and *inculcate*. Good teachers *instill* or *inculcate values into* students, but cannot properly be said to **instill students with values* or to **inculcate students with values*. See **inculcate.** For additional examples, see **arrogate, cite, diagnose, impart, inflict & levy.**

obligatory; obligative. The general term is *obligatory* (= required, mandatory). *Obligative* is a grammatical term for the mood of verbs expressing obligation or necessity.

oblivious has traditionally taken the preposition *of* in its strictest (an increasingly rare) sense of "forgetful" <an oblivious dotage> <oblivious of her pending appointment>. The more popular meaning of *oblivious* today is "unmindful; unaware; unobservant"; this construction typically (but not always) uses the preposition *to* <oblivious to signs of a financial disaster>. *Oblivious of* was the predominant phrasing in English language print sources till about 1968, when it was overtaken by *oblivious to*.

Although *to* is now the more common mate of *oblivious*, some fastidious speakers and writers continue to use *of*, regardless of whether the meaning is "forgetful" or "unaware"—e.g.: "He confesses that he was *oblivious to* [or *oblivious of*] his son, and the evidence he supplies is persuasive." Malcolm Jones Jr., "The Man Who Sired a Monster," *Newsweek*, 7 Mar. 1994, at 67. Both prepositions are standard.

LANGUAGE-CHANGE INDEX
oblivious to for *oblivious of*: Stage 5
1934 ratio (*oblivious of* vs. *oblivious to*): 2:1
Current ratio (*oblivious to* vs. *oblivious of*): 4:1

OBSCURITY, generally speaking, is a serious literary offense. Simple ideas are often made needlessly difficult, and difficult ideas are often made much more difficult than they need to be.

Obscurity has myriad causes, most of them rooted in imprecise thought or lack of consideration for the reader. The following examples are winners of a "Bad Writing Contest" held in New Zealand in 1997. All three are by English professors—the first two American and the third British:

- "The visual is *essentially* pornographic, which is to say that it has its end in rapt mindless fascination; thinking about its attributes becomes an adjunct to that, if it is unwilling to betray its object; while the most austere films necessarily draw their energy from the attempt to repress their own excess (rather than from the more thankless effort to discipline the viewer)." Fredric Jameson, *Signatures of the Visible* 1 (1992).
- "If such a sublime cyborg would insinuate the future as post-Fordist subject, his palpably masochistic locations as ecstatic agent of the sublime superstate need to be decoded as the 'now all-but-unreadable DNA' of the fast deindustrializing Detroit, just as his RoboCop-like strategy of carceral negotiation and street control remains the tirelessly American one of inflicting regeneration through violence upon the racially heteroglassic wilds and others of the inner city." Rob Wilson's essay in an anthology entitled *The Administration of Aesthetics* (1994) (as quoted in Ray Lilley, "No Contest: English Professors Are Worst Writers on Campus," *Sacramento Bee*, 18 May 1997, at A13).

- "The lure of imaginary totality is momentarily frozen before the dialectic of desire hastens on within symbolic chains." Frederick Botting, *Making Monstrous: Frankenstein, Criticism, Theory* (1991) (as quoted in Lilley).

One might try to defend this obtuseness on grounds that the subjects are metaphysical, but the defense will be to little avail.

Things have gotten so bad in some fields that even the experts sometimes can't distinguish brilliance from gibberish. For example, in 2002 *The New York Times* reported that two French physicists (twin brothers named Bogdanov) had attracted a great deal of attention to their theory about what preceded the Big Bang. Here's a sample of their prose: "Then we suggest that the (pre-)spacetime is in thermodynamic equilibrium at the Planck-scale and is therefore subject to the KMS condition." According to one editor of a professional journal—a journal in which their work was published before the editors had "raised their standards"—the paper was "essentially impossible to read, like 'Finnegans Wake.'" While a professor in France and another in Boston called the Bogdanovs' work potentially valuable, a professor in New York called it "nonsense" and another in Santa Barbara called it "nutty." The New York professor, a physicist at Columbia University, said: "Scientifically, it's clearly more or less complete nonsense, but these days that doesn't much distinguish it from a lot of the rest of the literature." The Bogdanovs defended themselves by saying, "Nonsense in the morning may make sense in the evening or the following day." For a full account of the affair, see Dennis Overbye, "Are They a) Geniuses or b) Jokers?" *N.Y. Times*, 9 Nov. 2002, at A19. This tale illustrates the beauty of obscurity: it's all but impossible to judge its content.

The root of the problem is largely psychological: "Most obscurity, I suspect, comes not so much from incompetence as from ambition—the ambition to be admired for depth of sense, or pomp of sound, or wealth of ornament." F.L. Lucas, *Style* 74 (1962). More bluntly still: "The truth is that many writers today of mediocre talent, or no talent at all, cultivate a studied obscurity that only too often deceives the critics, who tend to be afraid that behind the smoke-screen of words they are missing the effectual fire, and so for safety's sake give honour where no honour is due." G.H. Vallins, *The Best English* 106 (1960).

Excessive treatment of details often leads either to this substantive emptiness or to a self-defeating accuracy, in which it's difficult for the reader to discern the major points because of the cascading minutiae. In writing of this kind, sentences are often so heavily qualified that they become unreadable. Edgar Allan Poe put the point well: "In one case out of a hundred a point is excessively discussed because it is obscure; in the ninety-nine remaining it is obscure

---
LANGUAGE-CHANGE INDEX (For the full key, see front matter pp. xxxi, l–li.)
Stage 1: Rejected. **Stage 2:** Widely shunned. **Stage 3:** Widespread but . . . **Stage 4:** Ubiquitous but . . . **Stage 5:** Fully accepted.
Invariably inferior forms marked by asterisk (*). • Ratios represent frequency of prevalent forms vs. variants in current books.

because excessively discussed" (as quoted in Ashbel G. Gulliver, *Cases on Future Interests* 13 [1959]).

A final point. If you're going to be obscure, don't promise simplicity. Calling your message easy and direct when it isn't will engender resentment in your readers. Consider this opening sentence from an article on healthcare law: "The message of this article is simple and straightforward: If you represent non-integrated provider-controlled contracting networks purporting to operate as messenger arrangements but which in actuality are fixing prices, the time has come to fix them so they comply with section 1 of the Sherman Act." Jeff Miles, "Ticking Antitrust Time Bombs: A Message to Messed-Up Messenger Models," *Health Lawyers News*, Nov. 2002, at 5. Now try rereading it slowly to see if you can make out any glimmer of a point. Guess what. The healthcare lawyers who sent it to me as an example of poor prose didn't understand it either.

For more on different types and causes of obscurity, see ABBREVIATIONS (c), ABSTRACTITIS, AIRLINESE, BUREAUCRATESE, COMMERCIALESE, COMPUTERESE, JARGON, LEGALESE, OFFICIALESE & WOOLLINESS. For the antidote, see PLAIN LANGUAGE.

obsequies; obsequious. These words are unrelated in meaning. *Obsequies* (/**ob**-si-kweez/), the plural noun (the singular *obsequy* is rare), is a FORMAL WORD for *funeral. Obsequious*, the adjective, means "overeager to please or agree with powerful people." It is pronounced /əb-**see**-kwee-əs/ or /ob-**see**-kwee-əs/.

observance; observation. The DIFFERENTIATION between these two words is complete. *Observance* = the act of heeding or obeying; an instance of following a custom or rule; a ritual. *Observation* = scrutiny; study; a judgment or inference from what one has seen.

obsess. This verb can be either intransitive <Philip obsessed about his lost love> or transitive—although the latter appears usually in the passive voice <Sylvia was obsessed with the idea>. Only rarely does *obsess* appear as an active transitive verb—e.g.: "Striving to decipher Picasso's ambiguous blend of fierce misogyny and gaga woman-worship, Mailer ventures that women *obsessed* him because they were 'the last available manifestation of that Creator whose secrets he had hoped to capture.' " Francine du Plessix Gray, "Stud Wars," *L.A. Times Book Rev.*, 15 Oct. 1995, at 1, 15.

obsessive; obsessional. Except in the psychological term *obsessional neurosis, obsessional* is a NEEDLESS VARIANT.

obsolete; obsolescent. See **archaic.**

obstetric; *obstetrical. The more common, and the preferred, form is *obstetric*. The longer form held sway from about 1910 to 1958 but was then superseded.
Current ratio: 3:1

obstinacy, not *obstinance, is the noun corresponding to *obstinate* (= stubborn)—e.g.: "Gundolf informed George that he had chided Rausch for his *obstinance* [read *obstinacy*]." Robert E. Norton, *Secret Germany* 419 (2002).

LANGUAGE-CHANGE INDEX
obstinance for *obstinacy*: Stage 1
Current ratio (*obstinacy* vs. *obstinance*): 155:1

obstructive; *obstructional; *obstructionary. The second and third are NEEDLESS VARIANTS.

obtain. See **attain.**

obtainment; *obtention; *obtainance; *obtainal. What noun corresponds to the verb *obtain*? Though none of these four is common, *obtainment* is the most natural and the most frequent. The others are NEEDLESS VARIANTS. Of course, the gerund *obtaining* is always available for use, and it's more frequent than *obtainment*.

Current ratio (in order of headwords): 382:275:2:1

obtrusive. See **intrusive.**

obverse, n. See **converse,** n.

obviate. Some modern dictionaries define *obviate* as meaning "to make unnecessary." And some writers actually use the word this way—e.g.: "Volunteering does not, I repeat does not, *obviate* government's role in providing social services." Betty Winston Baye, "Volunteers Won't Be Enough," *Courier-J.* (Louisville), 1 May 1997, at A13.

But that definition is unduly restrictive. In fact, the *OED* doesn't even list this sense. *Obviate* more usually means "to meet and dispose of or do away with (a thing); to prevent by anticipatory measures" (*OED*). E.g.:

- "Human influence is a natural part of planetary evolution that might need to be tempered but certainly not *obviated*." "Environment: Facing Facts," *Richmond Times-Dispatch*, 6 Dec. 1995, at A10.
- "Mr. Kasparov said he had missed the draw because the computer had played so brilliantly that he thought it would have *obviated* the possibility of the draw known as perpetual check." Bruce Weber, "Kasparov Sings the Deep Blues," *Int'l Herald Trib.*, 13 May 1997, at 1.
- "I am also aware that if I capitulate, ceding my claim without contesting the other claim, I will raise the very suspicions I am seeking to *obviate*." Chelsea Quinn Yarbro, *Communion Blood* 23 (1999).

See **circumvent.** Cf. **vitiate.**

In the sense "to make unnecessary," *obviate* often appears correctly in the phrase *obviate the necessity of* or *need for*. These phrases are not redundancies, for the true sense of *obviate the necessity* is "to prevent the necessity (from arising)," hence to make unnecessary—e.g.: "Not insignificantly, it may also *obviate the need for* some government tuition aid." John Kolbe, "Small Steps Creating Tax Revolution," *Ariz. Republic*, 4 May 1997, at H5.

Obviate is sometimes misunderstood as meaning "to make obvious"—e.g.: "This is just another study *obviating* the obvious." Gregory Stanford, "Surprise! Safety Net Does Work," *Milwaukee J. Sentinel*, 8 Dec. 1996, Crossroads §, at 3. (A possible revision: *This is just another study making obvious things obvious.* Or: *This is just another study making obvious things more obvious.*)

obviously, like other dogmatic words (*clearly, undeniably, undoubtedly*), is one that writers tend to rely on when they're dealing with difficult, doubtful propositions. Be wary of it. See **very** & WEASEL WORDS. Cf. **clearly.**

Occam's razor; Ockham's razor. In the 14th century, William of Ockham (1285–1349), an Englishman, wrote a book entitled *Commentary on the Sentences.* In it, he devised what is now known as *Occam's razor* (the preferred spelling): *Entia non sunt multiplicanda praeter necessitatem* (lit., "entities are not to be multiplied beyond necessity"). In plain English, this means that the simplest of competing theories is preferable to the more complex ones, or that the parts of an argument should never be multiplied any more than necessary. Although many philosophers still use *Ockham*, the spelling *Occam* appears more than twice as often in modern print sources. Another term for *Occam's razor* is the *law of parsimony.*
Current ratio (*Occam's razor* vs. *Ockham's razor*): 2:1

occupant; occupier. Although both refer to a person who occupies a particular place, AmE greatly prefers *occupant* for most purposes, while BrE distinguishes between the words based on time. In BrE, *occupant* connotes a short-term stay, whether in a taxi, a theater seat, or a hotel room <that room's occupant will check out on Friday>; *occupier* connotes a long-term resident or tenant <my uncle has been the sole occupier since the house was built> or an occupying military force <the occupier of France during World War II>. E.g.: "While at first these unions were formed with the blessing of the *occupier*, they could be transformed into spaces of resistance against that *occupier* . . . ." *Japan as the Occupier and the Occupied* 79 (Christine de Matos & Mark E. Caprio eds., 2015).

occurred. So spelled. But **occured* is a common misspelling—one of the most common, in fact, in the language. See SPELLING (B).
Current ratio: 272:1

occurrence. So spelled. Various misspellings (such as **occurence* and **occurance*) are fairly common. (See SPELLING (A).) The word's first syllable is best pronounced /ə-/, not /oh-/.

oceanic (= of, relating to, or involving one or more oceans) is pronounced /oh-shee-**an**-ik/—not /oh-**see**-an-ik/.

ochlocracy. See GOVERNMENTAL FORMS.

ochre; *ocher. Meaning "a clay from which a dark-yellow pigment is produced," **ocher* is usually so spelled in AmE dictionaries. *Ochre* is the spelling found in BrE dictionaries. But American writers have long used both spellings, and since the late 18th century they have always preferred *ochre*. It's now twice as common as **ocher*. See -ER (B).
Current ratio (AmE): 2:1
Current ratio (World English): 4:1

-OCK. See DIMINUTIVES (L).

Ockham's razor. See **Occam's razor.**

octet (= [1] a group of eight, esp. of musicians; or [2] a musical composition for eight musicians) is the standard spelling in AmE and BrE alike. **Octette* is a variant.
Current ratio: 268:1

octopus. Because this word is actually of Greek origin—not Latin—the classical plural is *octopodes* /ok-**top**-ə-deez/, not **octopi*. But the standard plural in AmE and BrE alike is *octopuses*—which has vastly predominated in print sources since the early 20th century. Still, some writers mistakenly use the supposed Latin plural—e.g.:

- "Winnik did a column on the sex life of *octopi* [read *octopuses*], but it's not the kind of thing that should be in a family newspaper." Bob Krauss, "Our Honolulu," *Honolulu Advertiser*, 5 Feb. 2003, at 1.
- "Had he won the thing after having won last week at the Bob Hope, the fans would have tossed hats or *octopi* [read *octopuses*] onto the 18th green." Scott Ostler, "Bank Shot Is Given Hole New Meaning," *S.F. Chron.*, 10 Feb. 2003, at C1.
- "Mr. Cranston concentrates on one class of marine mollusk: cephalopods. That means *octopi* [read *octopuses*], nautili, cuttlefish, and squid." Anita Gates, "Cuttlefish and *Octopi* [read *Octopuses*, even though it spoils the rhyme] and Squid, Oh My!" *N.Y. Times*, 17 Dec. 2005, at A30.

See PLURALS (B) & HYPERCORRECTION (A). Since 1900, *octopuses* has greatly predominated in English-language print sources.

Occasionally the pedantic *octopodes* appears, but it is relatively rare—e.g.: "The baby octopus salad, made with finger-sized *octopodes*, whole and purplish, were marinated in a tasty, sesame oil dressing and lightly sprinkled with sesame seeds." Rose Kim, "Food Day," *Newsday* (N.Y.), 19 Oct. 2001, at B23.
LANGUAGE-CHANGE INDEX
*octopi for *octopuses*: Stage 3
Current ratio (*octopuses* vs. **octopi*): 3:1

ocular is turgid for *visual* or *with one's eyes* <ocular inspection>. The word is sometimes misspelled **occular.*

LANGUAGE-CHANGE INDEX (For the full key, see front matter pp. xxxi, l–li.)
Stage 1: Rejected. **Stage 2:** Widely shunned. **Stage 3:** Widespread but . . . **Stage 4:** Ubiquitous but . . . **Stage 5:** Fully accepted.
Invariably inferior forms marked by asterisk (*). • Ratios represent frequency of prevalent forms vs. variants in current books.

oculist; ocularist. See **ophthalmologist.**

odalisque (= [1] a female slave or concubine in a harem; or [2] an exotic, sexy woman, esp. a reclining nude as a theme in a painting) is the standard spelling. **Odalisk* is a variant. The word is pronounced /**oh**-də-lisk/. See SPELLING (A).

Current ratio: 13:1

oddly. See SENTENCE ADVERBS.

odds. *Odds are* is a familiar locution. But when *odds* is separated from the verb, a mistake in SUBJECT–VERB AGREEMENT often appears—e.g.:

- "The *odds* that a woman might have more than one *is* [read *are*] extremely low." Sandra Coney, "Full Cancer Evaluation—Now," *Sunday Star-Times*, 16 May 1999, at C4.
- "The *odds* of hitting all six numbers *is* [read *are*] one in 18 million." Harrison Sheppard, "Lotto Number: $56 Million," *Daily News* (L.A.), 17 Aug. 1999, at N4.
- "The *odds* of an instrument being contaminated *is* [read *are*] slight to begin with." Sandi Doughton, "Clinic Warns of Infection Risk," *Seattle Times*, 27 Aug. 2015, at A1. (On the failure to use a possessive before the gerund *being* in that example, see FUSED PARTICIPLES.)

LANGUAGE-CHANGE INDEX
*odds . . . is: Stage 1

*odiferous. See **odorous.**

odious (= hateful, repulsive) derives from *odium* (= hatred; the reproach that attaches to an act that people despise). E.g.: "The other problem with this legislative effort is that it came about in reaction to citizen disgust with an earlier, more *odious* plan advanced by Rep. Kay O'Connor of Olathe—who has espoused using state tax money to support private education vouchers." Laura Scott, "Cramped View of 'The Basics,'" *Kansas City Star*, 4 Mar. 1997, at C6.

Odious has nothing to do with *odor*—the extended sense of "repulsive" means repulsion based on hatred, not on stench. But some writers, mistakenly believing that it does, commit a MALAPROPISM—e.g.:

- "They were impassable in spring and unbearable in summer (largely due to *odious* [read *odorous* or *malodorous*] horse effluence)." John Clayton, "Roll the Snow, Stick the Gum, and ??? the Cats," *Union Leader* (Manchester, N.H.), 15 Jan. 1996, at A1.
- "The oil business has pretty much dried up in Luling, where empty stores dot the main street. What remains is the pall of *an odious* [read *a malodorous*] smell from the natural gas flared off when pressure builds inside the wells." Philip Hersh, "'In This Day . . . Why Are We Dying?'" *Chicago Trib.*, 2 Sept. 2001, News §, at 1.
- "As I walk closer to the baths I notice that they are filled with excrement. The stench is *odious* [read *nauseating*?]." Patti Thorn, "Incest and Empathy: A Counselor's Tale," *Rocky Mountain News* (Denver), 16 Nov. 2002, at D7.

See **odorous.**

LANGUAGE-CHANGE INDEX
odious in olfactory sense: Stage 1

odor (= a smell) is so spelled in AmE, *odour* in BrE. The AmE spelling took hold in the early 1840s. The corresponding adjective is *odorous* in all varieties of World English. See -OR; -OUR.

odorous; odoriferous; malodorous. In practice, *odorous* (= having a pronounced odor) is neutral in connotation <an odorous bouquet> <an odorous locker room>. Although in 1957 the Evanses insisted that *odorous* be "strictly confined to pleasant fragrances" (*DCAU* at 333), today it is used with a negative sense about twice as often as a positive one. *Malodorous* carries even stronger negative connotations <a malodorous bathroom>. *Odoriferous*, a frequently misused term, has historically had positive connotations in the sense "fragrant" <odoriferous rose gardens>. It shouldn't be used in reference to foul odors—e.g.: "The only thing that gave him trouble was finding a toad; the rest of the stuff, though mostly nasty and *odoriferous* [read *odorous* or *malodorous*], was obtained with little difficulty." Theodore R. Cogswell, "The Wall Around the World" (1953), in *The Mammoth Book of Fantasy* 1, 12 (Mike Ashley ed., 2001).

*Odiferous is an erroneous shortening of *odoriferous* that sprang up about 1920. It's often misused for *odorous* or *malodorous*—e.g.: "I was in the Texas Panhandle, typically maligned for its harsh weather, *odiferous* [read *malodorous*] feedlots, and dull, windwhipped landscape—flat as a tortilla and practically treeless." Joe Nick Patowski, "Grand Canyons," *Texas Monthly*, Aug. 1997, at 130. Only someone familiar with garlic plants knows whether the odor in the following example is nice or foul (probably the latter): "They are underplanted with useful plants ranging from fragrant peppermint to *odiferous* [read *malodorous*, *odorous*, or *odoriferous*] garlic chives." Rosemary Herbert, "New England Gardening," *Boston Herald*, 3 Aug. 1997, at 53.

Just as *odious* (= offensive) is sometimes misused to describe a foul smell, so *odoriferous* is sometimes misused to mean "corrupt" or at least "suspicious"—e.g.: "There does seem to be something *odoriferous* underfoot." Kathleen Parker, "American Fatwa Coming to a Bookstore Near You," *Orlando Sentinel*, 29 Dec. 2002, at G3. Unfortunately, the use is common enough that at least one dictionary (*W11*) lists "morally offensive" as an alternative definition of *odoriferous*. In one sense that's understandable, because corruption and bad smells have always been associated (the usage passes the sniff test). But in a larger sense it's unfortunate, since we can't clearly distinguish all the *odor* words we already have—and it just continues the degeneration of the word's connotations. It would be far better to think of this loose extension as an ineffectual METAPHOR rather than as a definition. See **odious.**

LANGUAGE-CHANGE INDEX
1. **odiferous*: Stage 2
2. *odoriferous* in the sense "foul-smelling": Stage 2
Current ratio (*odoriferous* vs. **odiferous*): 5:1

oenology. See **enology.**

-OES. See PLURALS (D).

of. A. Signaling Verbosity. However innocuous it may appear, the word *of* is, in anything other than small doses, among the surest indications of flabby writing. Some fear that *of* and its resulting flabbiness are spreading: "Clearly, *of* is now something more than a mere preposition. It's a virus." "All About Of," *N.Y. Times*, 8 Mar. 1992, at 14. The only suitable vaccination is to cultivate a hardy skepticism about its utility in any given context. If it proves itself, fine. Often, though, it will merely breed verbosity—e.g.:

- "In spite *of* the fact that a great percentage *of* the media coverage *of* Muslims mainly targets the negative actions *of* some splinter groups and several individuals, there are still a shrinking number *of* people who are still under the false impression that Al-Islam is a 'bloody and dangerous religion,' as the Bishop puts it." Frederick Qasim Khan, "Muslims Do Not Denounce Christians," *Call & Post* (Cleveland), 4 Jan. 1996, at A5. (A possible revision: *Because the media frequently put Muslims in a negative light, some continue to believe that Al-Islam is a "bloody and dangerous religion," as the Bishop puts it.* [Five *of*s to none; 56 words to 28; and heightened logic in the revision.])
- "By the mid-1980s, many *of* these politicians were seen as a big part *of* the problem not only in terms *of* poor economic performance but also in terms *of* political authoritarianism." Julius E. Nyang Oro, "Critical Notes on Political Liberalization in Africa," *J. Asian & Afr. Studies*, 1 June 1996, at 112. (A possible revision: *By the mid-1980s, many of these politicians were seen as having contributed to the problem both through poor economic performance and through political authoritarianism.* [Four *of*s to one; 32 words to 25.])
- "In light *of* the high number *of* requests from retail investors, the Treasury can expect to top the million mark in terms *of* numbers *of* small shareholders participating in the privatization." Deborah Ball, "Telecom IPO in Italy Has Strong Start," *Wall Street J. Europe*, 21 Oct. 1997, at 13. (A possible revision: *Given the high demand from retail investors, the Treasury can expect that more than a million small shareholders will participate in the privatization.* [Four *of*s to none; 31 words to 23.])

As the examples illustrate, reducing the *of*s can, even at the sentence level, make the prose much more brisk and readable. See PREPOSITIONS (A).

B. Intrusive *of*. The word *of* often intrudes where it doesn't idiomatically belong, as in **not that big of a deal* (read *not that big a deal*), **not too smart of a student* (read *not too smart a student*), **somewhat of an abstract idea* (read *a somewhat abstract idea*), etc. E.g.: "Spurs guard Mario Elie doesn't seem to think the Spurs will have *that difficult of a time* [read *a difficult time*] handling the Knicks in these Finals." "Elie Attacks," *Fla. Today*, 17 June 1999, at C2. Cf. **all** (A), **as . . . as** (D) & **too** (C).

For the opposite tendency—omitting a necessary *of*—see **couple** (C).

C. Superfluous in Dates. *December of 1987* should be *December 1987*. See DATES (B).

D. For *have*. Because the spoken *have* (especially in a contraction) is often identical in sound with *of* <I should've done it>, semiliterate writers have taken to writing **should of*, **could of*, and **would of* (aka **shoulda*, **coulda*, and **woulda*). But the word is *have*, or a contraction ending in *'ve*, and it should be written so. This error has typified uneducated usage since about the time of World War I. Instances of it are legion—e.g.:

- "'He may *of* [read *have*] been otherwise occupied by his other legal troubles,' Lanza said. 'Other than that, I don't know.'" Jack Sherzer, "Spotz Suit Against Officers Dismissed," *Harrisburg Patriot*, 1 Aug. 1996, at B4 (quoting David J. Lanza, who can't be faulted for the mistranscription).
- "Humans are great with second-guessing and hindsight, but the truth is that we only know this reality and not the one that might *of* [read *have*] been." Richard Kohn, "Politics Is Harmful to Heroes' Health," *News & Record* (Greensboro), 23 Aug. 1998, at F3.
- "When it turned out Watson was up north, he changed his story, admitted he might *of* [read *have*] done the job himself, called it self-defense." Peter Matthiessen, "The Killing of the Warden," *Audubon*, 1 Nov. 1998, at 36.
- "Not bad, but I could *of* [read *have*] eaten three of them." Steve Hopkins, "Kiwi Blokes Like 'Em Extra Large," *New Truth & TV Extra*, 24 Nov. 2000, at 9.
- "Beethoven never would *of* [read *have*] made the cut either." Letter of Elizabeth A. Pickett, *Hartford Courant*, 2 Dec. 2000, at A14.

See **had have.*

LANGUAGE-CHANGE INDEX
of misused for *have*: Stage 1

E. *Of a . . . nature*. See **nature.**

F. *Of*-genitive vs. Possessive. See **of** (A) & POSSESSIVES (H).

*of a. The collocation [adj.] + of *a* + [noun] is unrefined usage. See **of** (B).

off. See **off of.*

off-color (= [1] varying from a given color; or [2] in poor taste; risqué) is the standard term. **Off-colored* is a variant form with nothing to recommend it.
Current ratio: 21:1

offence. See **offense.**

offendable; **offendible*. The former is standard, the latter a variant spelling. See -ABLE (A).

offense; offence. The first has been the AmE spelling since about 1910; the second has always been standard BrE. In AmE and BrE alike, the word is preferably accented on the second syllable: /ə-**fen**[t]s/. Unfortunately, because athletes and sports announcers put the accent on the first syllable (/**of**-en[t]s/), many American speakers have adopted this pronunciation

LANGUAGE-CHANGE INDEX (For the full key, see front matter pp. xxxi, l–li.)
Stage 1: Rejected. **Stage 2:** Widely shunned. **Stage 3:** Widespread but . . . **Stage 4:** Ubiquitous but . . . **Stage 5:** Fully accepted.
Invariably inferior forms marked by asterisk (*). • Ratios represent frequency of prevalent forms vs. variants in current books.

even in the word's legal sense. The sound of it puts the literate person's teeth on edge. Cf. **defense.**

In BrE, and to a lesser extent in AmE, lawyers commonly distinguish *crimes* (at common law) from *offenses* (created by statute). It is common in both speech communities to use *offense* for less serious infractions and *crime* for more serious ones. Lawyers would not speak of the "offense" of murder. Nor would they refer to the "crime" of parking a car in the wrong place.

LANGUAGE-CHANGE INDEX
1. *offense* pronounced with accent on first syllable in sports usage: Stage 5
2. *offense* (= infraction, crime) pronounced with accent on first syllable: Stage 2

offeror; *offerer. The first is standard in AmE and BrE alike—and has been so since the mid-20th century. But see **profferer.**

Current ratio: 5:1

offhand, adj.; ***offhanded.** Although *offhand* (not **offhanded*) is the standard adjective, *offhandedly* is the standard adverb—in AmE and BrE alike.

Current ratio (*offhand* vs. **offhanded*): 12:1

office, vb., has become a commonplace expression in the American business world, but not among fastidious users of language. Although *office* is recorded as a verb from the 16th century, the new vogue began in the Southwest during the 1980s within the oil-and-gas industry. Gradually it has spread to other fields and has started to overrun the country. No one seems to *have an office* anymore; instead, everyone *offices.* E.g.:

- "*Officing* in Irvine, Calif., Carlisle will be responsible for business development in the eleven western states." *Oil & Gas J.*, 25 July 1983, at 172.
- "The Uptown area is most attractive to prospective tenants wanting the lure of downtown without the high costs associated with *officing* there." Anne Belli, "Uptown Looking Up," *Dallas Bus. J.*, 2 May 1988, at A18.
- "A few months ago, Tali Blumrosen and Chris Pierini formed a new PR firm, B&P, *officing* out of their homes." Maxine Mesinger, "Life's a Party for Birthday Trio," *Houston Chron.*, 25 Sept. 1996, Houston §, at 1.
- "*Officed* at the corporate location today, she began her career across the street in bookkeeping using a crank adding machine." Rosemary Horvath, "Business Milestone," *Sentinel-Standard* (Ionia, Mich.), 29 Nov. 2014, Mich. News §, at 1.

This is a classic example of the issue discussed under FUNCTIONAL SHIFT (A), (D).

LANGUAGE-CHANGE INDEX
office as a verb: Stage 3

OFFICIALESE = the language of officialdom, characterized by bureaucratic turgidity and insubstantial fustian; inflated language that could be readily translated into simpler terms. E.g.: "To promote the successful completion of our customary mid-diurnal paradigm regarding the procurement of necessary nutritional supplementation and the advancement of the contemporaneous, spontaneous, and coterminous interdialoguing of affiliated human-services assets, the present contingent should initiate both direct and lateral movements as appropriate to minimize and at the end of the day eliminate the physical separation between the target population and the aliment-preparation and -dispensation facilities." As translated: "Let's talk over lunch."

Officialese is governed by four essential rules. First, use as many words as possible. Second, if a longer word (e.g., *utilize*) and a shorter word (e.g., *use*) are both available, choose the longer. Third, use circumlocutions whenever possible. Fourth, use cumbersome connectives when possible (*as to, with regard to, in connection with, in the event of,* etc.).

Among the linguistically unsophisticated, puffed-up language seems more impressive. Hence police officers never *get out of their cars*; instead, they *exit their vehicles.* They never *smell* anything; rather, they *detect it by inhalation.* They *proceed* to a *residence* and *observe* the suspect *partaking of food.* They never *arrest a person*; rather, they *apprehend an individual.* Rather than *sending* papers to each other, officials *transmit* them (by hand-delivery, not by fax). And among lawyers, rather than *suing*, one *institutes legal proceedings against* or *brings an action against.* For sound guidance on how to avoid officialese, see Ernest Gowers, *The Complete Plain Words* (2d ed. 1973); J.R. Masterson & W.B. Phillips, *Federal Prose: How to Write in and/or for Washington* (1948). See OBSCURITY. Cf. BUREAUCRATESE.

officiate. The verb, meaning "to perform the duties of an official," has traditionally been intransitive—that is, it doesn't take a direct object; instead, it has a preposition after it. A priest *officiates at* a wedding, and a referee *officiates at* a sports event. Only up to the early 1700s was the word ever transitive, and then only rarely. But this usage is now undergoing something of a resurgence. One sees it most often in the PASSIVE VOICE—e.g.:

- "A memorial Mass *was officiated* [read *was led*] by Rev. Nathanael Foshage on Wednesday, Sept. 26 at St. Michael's Catholic Church in Delta." "Allinson" (obit.), *Chicago Trib.*, 27 Sept. 2001, at 7. [Or read: *The Rev. Nathanael Foshage officiated at the memorial mass on Wednesday . . . .*] (On the use of *Rev.* in the original sentence, see **Reverend.**)
- "The ceremony *was officiated* by Rabbi Sherwin Wine." Nancy Chipman Powers, "Three New Rabbis Share Secular Humanist Heritage," *Detroit Free Press*, 5 Dec. 2001, at B2. [Read *Rabbi Sherwin Wine officiated at the ceremony.*]
- "The game *was officiated* very tightly." David Steinle, "Belaire, Capitol in Final," *Advocate* (Baton Rouge), 15 Dec. 2001, at D9. [Read *The referees officiated over the game very tightly.*]

Some writers attempt to preserve intransitivity by writing *was officiated at*—e.g.: "Limbaugh—a conservative of such clout that his 1994 marriage to third wife Marta Fitzgerald *was officiated at* by Justice Clarence Thomas—is determined to stay on the air." Lori Rozsa, "Rush Limbaugh Reveals He Is Going Deaf,"

People, 22 Oct. 2001, at 60. But the passive form necessarily means that the verb is being used transitively: to say that *Justice Thomas officiated at the wedding* can't properly be rendered as *the wedding was officiated at by Justice Thomas*. See ERGATIVE VERBS.

officious. In Samuel Johnson's day, *officious* had positive connotations ("eager to please"). Today, however, it means "meddlesome; interfering with what is not one's concern." E.g.: "Over the years, the most *officious* and obnoxious customs officials I encountered were those in India." Thomas Sowell, "On Busybodies, Young 'Adults' and Self-Respect," *Atlanta J.-Const.*, 6 Sept. 1995, at A10.

In the context of diplomacy, the word has a strangely different sense: "having an extraneous relation to official matters or duties; having the character of a friendly communication, or informal action, on the part of a government or its official representatives" (*OED*) <an officious communication>.

The word has been subjected to SLIPSHOD EXTENSION. Some mistakenly think it means "official-looking"—e.g.: "He still lived in the same old dormitory, but in a bigger and more *officious* room." Still others take it to mean "official-sounding" or merely "official"—e.g.:

- "A dead person is the 'decedent' in the *officious lingo* [read *jargon*] of the medical examiner, for example, and ballistics experts often refer to 'the signature of the weapon.'" Phil Reisman, "Firsthand Look at the Ease of Getting an Indictment," *J. News* (Westchester Co., N.Y.), 9 Jan. 2003, at B1.
- "In an *officious-sounding* [read *official-sounding*] voice, he warns victims they've ignored multiple summonses for jury duty." Dan Casey, "'Jury Duty' Scam Targets Unwary Residents," *Roanoke Times*, 8 Jan. 2015, at B1.

LANGUAGE-CHANGE INDEX
officious in the sense "official-looking": Stage 3

offing, in the. This is the correct, idiomatic phrase meaning "likely to occur soon"—not *on the offing*.

***off of** is idiomatically inferior to *off* without the preposition—e.g.:

- "It wasn't as though Porch was looking for a tall bridge to jump *off of* [read *off*] after last week's loss." Brian J. French, "Porch Makes Amends for Fumble, Carries the Tribe Past Boston U," *Virginian-Pilot & Ledger Star* (Norfolk), 28 Sept. 1997, at C5.
- "As I raked, I knew all the leaves and the people that had planted the trees they fell *off of* [read *off*]." Adyne Wakefield, "Raking Up the Past as Winter Nears," *Oregonian* (Portland), 21 Nov. 1997, at D19.
- "When Witty arrived at UC in 2010, the Bearcats were coming *off of* [read *off*] their glorious Sugar Bowl season (12–1) under Brian Kelly." Tom Groeschen, "UC Yearns to Be Back in Top 25," *Cincinnati Enquirer*, 3 Sept. 2015, at C8.

In print sources since 1500, the collocation *off the* has been in constant use, while *off of the* occurs only seldom. Cf. **outside.**

LANGUAGE-CHANGE INDEX
off of for *off*: Stage 3
Current ratio (*off the* vs. *off of the*): 42:1

offspring (= one or more children or descendants) is either singular or—more commonly—plural <many parents aren't teaching their offspring these days>. There is no plural form *offsprings*, but this escapes some writers. E.g.: "And with three horses—his mare and two *offsprings* [read *offspring*]—at nearby Crestwood Farm, he is well on his way." Mark Woods, "Hard-Hitting Cat Has Soft Spot for Horses," *Courier-J.* (Louisville), 11 Sept. 1997, at C1.

LANGUAGE-CHANGE INDEX
offsprings for plural *offspring*: Stage 1
Current ratio (*several offspring* vs.
several offsprings): 72:1

***oft.** See **often (B).**

often. A. Pronunciation. The educated pronunciation is /**of**-ən/, but the less adept say /**of**-tən/. To put it another way, the silent-*t* pronunciation is U; the spoken-*t* pronunciation is distinctly non-U. (See CLASS DISTINCTIONS & PRONUNCIATION (B).) Similar words with a silent -*t*- are *chasten, fasten, hasten, listen, soften,* and *whistle.*

LANGUAGE-CHANGE INDEX
often pronounced /**of**-tən/: Stage 4

B. And *oftentimes*; *oft*; *ofttimes*. *Oftentimes* is a common synonym of *often*; it often seems to add weight and perhaps quaintness to a pronouncement. The second and third are literary ARCHAISMS and NEEDLESS VARIANTS. Substituting *often* is almost always (not merely often) better—e.g.:

- "Bessette and Gleason know that *oftentimes* [read *often*] it's the little things they do that make the most difference." Ashley Clemente-Tolins, "The Night Shift," *Oregonian* (Portland), 21 Dec. 1995, at 1.
- "Although she *oft* [read *often*] made it to the lane, Sadler (7 points on 2-for-13 shooting) was usually greeted by Hillwood's Latonia Clay, a 5-11 center with a penchant for altering shots." Jeff Pearlman, "Szamier Smooths Out Hillwood's 49–36 Romp," *Tennessean*, 10 Jan. 1996, at C4.
- "Smoke and smells from nearby concession stands *ofttimes* [read *often*] wafted over the courts." Frederick C. Klein, "Plenty of Lunch Seating, but U.S. Open Stadium Isn't All for the Masses," *Wall Street J.*, 29 Aug. 1997, at B4.

About the only time *oft* is justified is when it's part of a PHRASAL ADJECTIVE <an oft-quoted passage>. Cf. **once** & **then (A).**

***ofttimes.** See **often (B).**

LANGUAGE-CHANGE INDEX (For the full key, see front matter pp. xxxi, l–li.)
Stage 1: Rejected. **Stage 2:** Widely shunned. **Stage 3:** Widespread but . . . **Stage 4:** Ubiquitous but . . . **Stage 5:** Fully accepted.
Invariably inferior forms marked by asterisk (*). • Ratios represent frequency of prevalent forms vs. variants in current books.

ogle (= to stare in a flirtatious or sexually suggestive way) is preferably pronounced /**oh**-gəl/—not /**ah**-gəl/ or /**aw**-gəl/.

ogreish (= rather like an ogre) is the standard spelling in AmE and BrE alike. *Ogrish* is a variant.

Oh. See **O.**

***oinology.** See **enology.**

okay; OK; O.K. Each of these is okay. Although *OK* predominates in highly informal contexts, *okay* has an advantage in edited English: it more easily lends itself to cognate forms such as *okays, okayer, okaying,* and *okayed.* The term is a CASUALISM in any event, but *okay* is slightly more dressed up than *OK.* Some purists prefer *OK* simply because it's the original form. It is, after all, the most successful Americanism ever—perhaps the best-known word on the planet.

A few publications, such as *The New Yorker,* prefer the periods—e.g.: "It's *O.K.* Take your time." Arthur Miller, "The Bare Manuscript," *New Yorker,* 16 Dec. 2002, at 82, 91. For more on the presence or absence of periods, see ABBREVIATIONS (A).

okina. For a brief discussion of this DIACRITICAL MARK in Hawaiian English, see **Hawaii (B).**

Oklahoma Citian; *Oklahoma Cityan. The first is the standard spelling; the second is a variant. See DENIZEN LABELS. Cf. **Kansas Citian; Twin Citian.**

Oklahoman; *Oklahomian; Okie. The first is standard; the second is a NEEDLESS VARIANT that rarely appears in print; the third is a common CASUALISM considered derogatory by many Oklahomans. See DENIZEN LABELS.

ol'. See **olde.**

old adage. See **adage.**

olde; ole; ol'. These affected variants of *old* come in two distinct flavors. *Olde* is a 20th-century invention intended to mimic Old English <Ye Olde Pub>. The spurious coinage has become tediously popular in an age of mass-produced quaintness. The spuriousness is compounded in the example above when *ye* is pronounced as it is spelled. The first letter of the authentic Middle English term was a *thorn,* identical in form to the letter *y* but pronounced with a voiced *th,* as in *this.*

By contrast, *ole* and *ol'* are 19th-century inventions used mostly in dialogue to signify DIALECT <Grand Ole Opry> <Bubba's a good ol' boy>.

The spelling *olde* is distinctly out of place when used in a rural rather than Old World context—e.g.: "Texas *Olde* [read *Ol'* or *Ole*] Time Fiddlers Jam." "Best Bets," *Austin Am.-Statesman,* 19 July 2002, at E2.

olden. Apart from the SET PHRASES *olden times* and the *olden days,* this adjective doesn't generally appear in good writing (except in that of Shakespeare and his contemporaries). Today, the word describes itself: it's a creaky ARCHAISM.

older; oldest. See **elder.**

ole. See **olde.**

oligarchy. See GOVERNMENTAL FORMS.

oligopoly; oligopsony. The former denotes control or domination of a market by a few large sellers; the latter, control or domination of a market by a few large customers.

ombudsman; ombuds; *ombudsperson. *Ombudsman* = (1) an official appointed to receive, investigate, and report on private citizens' complaints about the government; or (2) a similar appointee in a nongovernmental organization. Originally a Swedish word denoting a commissioner, *ombudsman* spread throughout the world during the mid-20th century as governments and other institutions saw the wisdom of having such an official. Though the word entered the English language only as recently as the mid-1950s, it has caught on remarkably well.

But despite its prevalence throughout the English-speaking world, this word might prove to have a short life span. Because of the *-man* suffix, many writers consider it sexist. (See SEXISM (C).) Some have taken to lopping off the suffix, and though the word *ombuds* looks distinctly un-English and remains unrecorded in most English dictionaries, it is surprisingly common—e.g.: "To resolve disputes with managers, lab employees can go to the *ombuds* office, where a neutral mediator tries to facilitate resolutions informally and confidentially." Adam Rankin, "Lab Vows to Win Worker Trust," *Albuquerque Trib.,* 28 Jan. 2003, at D3.

Several writers have tried *ombudsperson,* but that coinage should be allowed to wither. Others have experimented with *ombuds officer,* which at least satisfies one's desire to have a word that looks as if it denotes a person—e.g.: "Columbia University last week named its first 'ombuds officer' as a reference point on campus for people who have grievances within the university and are looking for options to deal with them." "Campus Life: Columbia," *N.Y. Times,* 14 July 1991, § 1, pt. 2, at 31.

In 2008, *ombudsman* remained more than ten times as common in print sources as its rivals.

Current ratio (*ombudsman* vs. *ombuds* vs. *ombudsperson*): 12:1.5:1

omelet; omelette. American dictionary publishers are in step with current usage, which prefers *omelet* to *omelette* by a 2-to-1 ratio. But in BrE, *omelette* is about 3 times more common.

omissible. So spelled—not *omissable.* (See -ABLE (A).) *Omittable* is a NEEDLESS VARIANT.

Current ratio (*omissible* vs. *omittable* vs. *omissable*): 39:3:1

on; upon. These synonyms are used in virtually the same ways. The distinctions are primarily in tone and connotation. *On*, the more usual word since the mid-18th century, is generally preferable: it's better to write *put the groceries on the counter* than *put the groceries upon the counter*. But *upon* is the better word for introducing a condition or event—e.g.: *Upon receiving the survey, you should fill it out completely.* See **upon.**

on behalf of. See **behalf.**

onboard; on board. As an adjective, *onboard* is a closed compound <an onboard navigation system>. As an adverbial phrase, *on board* remains a preposition with its object <loading cargo on board>. Writers occasionally flounder—e.g.: "The man had brought nothing *onboard* [read *on board*], the movie screen wasn't working, and apparently all he could do for entertainment was tap on the window and sing to himself." Joshua Kurlantzick, "The Agony and Ecstasy of 18 Hours in the Air," *N.Y. Times*, 2 July 2006, § 5, at 3. Cf. **online.** See also **aboard.**

once. By convention, *once* isn't hyphenated either adverbially <a once powerful monarch> or adjectivally <the once and future king>. Cf. **often (b)** & **then (a).**

once in a while. So written. The phrase is occasionally disfigured into a MONDEGREEN—e.g.:

* "The recipes are usually interesting, and I may even try one *once and while* [read *once in a while*]." Dan Macdonald, "Ingenuity in Kitchen Can Stop the Tears," *Fla. Times-Union*, 22 July 1999, at F1.
* "The father said he could not ask for anything more out of his son. Except maybe for letting the old man make a better-tasting omelet every *once and while* [read *once in a while*]." Tom Reed, "Fraternal Instinct," *Akron Beacon J.*, 17 Aug. 2001, at E7.
* "*Once in while* [read *Once in a while*], I'll part with some [buttery caramel corn] for special friends." Kathie Jenkins, "Better than Store-Bought," *Pioneer Press* (St. Paul), 7 Dec. 2001, at F3.

For the mistake of writing **ever once in a while* for *every once in a while*, see **ever (b).**

LANGUAGE-CHANGE INDEX
1. **once and while* for *once in a while*: Stage 1
Current ratio (*once in a while* vs. **once and while*): 1,482:1
2. **once in while* for *once in a while*: Stage 1
Current ratio (*once in a while* vs. **once in while*): 199:1

one. A. The Overdone *one*. In AmE, *one* (= any person indefinitely) is extremely formal. To most American speakers, it seems bookish and pedantic. It's rare to find anyone who goes this far, especially in speech: "So if *one* does *one's* best, *one* recognizes that sometimes *one's* best is not going to bring all of the changes that *one* would hope for, but it doesn't mean there hasn't been progress." Bob Krueger (interviewed by Diane Jennings, *Dallas Morning News*, 31 Dec. 1995,

at J1). For ordinary purposes, *you* is a better, more relaxed choice. The passage above, for example, might have read: *So if you do your best, you recognize that sometimes your best isn't going to bring all the changes that you would hope for, but it doesn't mean there hasn't been progress.* See **you.**

One can only sympathize with the student whose essay was revised by a teacher to read this way: "Does *one* ever feel bereft when *one* picks up *one's* chips to light *one's* fire for *one's* evening meal? Or when *one* washes *one's* milk pail before milking *one's* cow? *One* would fancy not." In discussing this editorial travesty, a linguist asks: "Is it possible that the impeccable '*one*' can be overdone? *One* fancies, from this illustration and others that *one* knows, that it can." Dora Jean Ashe, "One Can Use an Indefinite 'You' Occasionally, Can't You?" in *A Linguistics Reader* 63, 64 (Graham Wilson ed., 1967).

Or as another linguist wryly put it: "One has only to listen to one's pseudo-educated and superprecise friends to get one's ear full." Lodwick Hartley, "Provocative Pronouns for Precise People" (1959), in *A Language Reader for Writers* 107, 108 (James R. Gaskin & Jack Suberman eds., 1966).

B. *One . . . he*. This expression, though historically condemned as inferior to *one . . . one*, actually predominates in AmE usage. But its future probably isn't bright: *one . . . he* bothers strict grammarians as being less than fully grammatical, and it bothers other readers as being sexist. See SEXISM (B). So it should probably be improved—e.g.:

* "When *one* is writing exposition, surely *he* should not indulge himself in poetic prose." Leo Kirschbaum, "Style" (1961), in *Perspectives on Style* 56, 61 (Frederick Candelaria ed., 1968). (A possible revision: *Surely a person writing exposition should not indulge in poetic prose.*)
* "*One* does not sacrifice *his* individuality by using such means of communication." Ellsworth Barnard, *English for Everybody* 35 (1979). (A possible revision: *You don't sacrifice your individuality by using such means of communication.*)
* "I hate it when the rock stars of *my* youth die. Not only does it draw *one* uncomfortably close to *his* own mortality, but a little piece of *yourself* goes toes up with them." Buddy Blue, "A Spoonful-Sized Tribute to a Supersized Talent," *San Diego Union-Trib.*, 26 Dec. 2002, Mag. §, at 14. (Why not just stick with the FIRST PERSON throughout? Touching all three bases—first [*my*], second [*yourself*], and third [*his*]—is impressive, but it's no home run.)

See **you.**

LANGUAGE-CHANGE INDEX
one . . . he: Stage 4

C. *One* [+ name]. Using *one* as an adjective before a proper name, as in "*one* Howard James," is a pretentious legalism with a valid pedigree in English, but generally without justification in modern prose. It might even hint at biblical echoing, for the *OED* quotes from the Bible: "and of *one* Jesus, which was

---
LANGUAGE-CHANGE INDEX (For the full key, see front matter pp. xxxi, l–li.)
Stage 1: Rejected. **Stage 2:** Widely shunned. **Stage 3:** Widespread but . . . **Stage 4:** Ubiquitous but . . . **Stage 5:** Fully accepted.
Invariably inferior forms marked by asterisk (*). • Ratios represent frequency of prevalent forms vs. variants in current books.

dead, whom Paul affirmed to be alive" (Acts 25:19). Today, however, the word *one* usually looks askance at any name following it. But occasionally it can be neutral in connotation, when the writer wants to hint that the person named is not someone the reader is probably familiar with <at the table were Madonna, Elton John, and one Harold Pfister of Des Plaines>.

one and one (is) (are). See SUBJECT–VERB AGREE-MENT (G).

one and the same, a phrase dating from the 16th century, is occasionally misrendered *one in the same.*
                                    Current ratio: 39:1

one another. See **each other.**

one-armed bandit (= a slot machine) is the preferred spelling. *One-arm bandit* is a variant.
                                    Current ratio: 8:1

***one fewer.** See **fewer.**

one . . . he. See **one (B).**

180-degree turnaround; *360-degree turnaround. In nontechnical contexts, when you use measurements of geometric degrees, you'll probably want either *90 degrees* (a right angle, as for a left- or right-hand turn) or *180 degrees* (a complete turnaround). The phrase *360 degrees* refers to a full-circle turn <a 360-degree skid> or a panorama—e.g.: "On the fourth floor, windows provide a *360-degree* view of the treetops." Ruth Ryon, "Living Above It All in Converted Water Tower," *L.A. Times,* 6 Apr. 2003, at K14. To turn 360 degrees is to be facing the same direction you started with.

By contrast, *180 degrees* from one direction is the opposite direction. In the common idiom, to make a *180-degree turnaround* is to change circumstances completely—e.g.: "NBC's *180-degree* turn between Sunday, when it defended [Peter] Arnett's decision to grant the Iraqi TV interview, and yesterday, when he was fired, was an eyebrow-raiser." Melanie McFarland, *Seattle Post-Intelligencer,* 1 Apr. 2003, at E1.

Sometimes writers turn the idiom too far, referring absurdly to a *360-degree turnaround,* which would logically denote "full circle" or (to change the geometrical metaphor) "back to square one"—e.g.:

- "[Christina] Aguilera, when she wasn't dressed as a wannabe New Orleans hooker for the 'Lady Marmalade' performance, did a *360-degree* [read *180-degree*] turn from last year's Grammy fashion fiasco." Monica L. Haynes, "O J-Lo, Where Art Thou?" *Pitt. Post-Gaz.,* 28 Feb. 2002, at D1.
- "For rock fans, the 'alternative rock' music scene out there today is quite disappointing—the music sounds too manufactured and fake and isn't very original. The Used is a *360-degree* [read *180-degree*] turn from all of this." Melissa Ortiz, "A Utah Alternative," *Buffalo News,* 13 Nov. 2002, at N4.
- "[Joe] McCarthy, arguably the top boys basketball player in the 1A North Star League, has done a *360-degree* [read *180-degree*] turnaround since arriving in Clark Fork in November 2000." Greg Lee, "New Spin on Life," *Spokesman Rev.* (Spokane), 16 Jan. 2003, at C1.

See ILLOGIC.

LANGUAGE-CHANGE INDEX
360-degree turnaround for *180-degree turnaround*:
Stage 1
Current ratio (*180-degree turnaround* vs.
360-degree turnaround): 13:1

one in [number] is; *one in [number] are. In this construction, a singular verb is required because *one* is the subject. But writers frequently get it wrong—e.g.:

- "Only one in five *believe* [read *believes*] that their parents had more fun as teenagers than they are experiencing now." Bob Dart, "A New National Study of Teen Attitudes Reveals a Remarkably Gloomy View," *Chicago Trib.,* 3 Aug. 1988, Style §, at 12. (In this sentence the words *their* and *they* also create a number problem. See CONCORD (B) & PRONOUNS (D).)
- "Research has found that only one in six *think* [read *thinks*] that political agreement is important for a successful marriage." Cherrill Hicks, "'How on Earth Can You Live with a Tory?'" *Independent,* 22 Mar. 1992, at 24.
- "One in six *think* [read *thinks*] motor insurance companies are not doing enough to combat crime, while 53% similarly accuse car manufacturers." "Car Stolen Every Two Minutes, Says RAC," *Herald* (Glasgow), 11 Jan. 1994, at 5.
- "A CBS-*New York Times* poll of 867 adults found only one in five *believe* [read *believes*] the Clintons did anything wrong in Whitewater." "The Polls," *Dayton Daily News,* 13 Mar. 1994, at A3.
- "Nearly one in two Brazilian women of childbearing age *have* [read *has*] been sterilized, according to a 2001 government survey." John Jeter, "Infertile Ground Is Sown in Brazil," *Wash. Post,* 11 June 2004, at A14.

The same holds true when the construction is *one of five,* etc. See SUBJECT–VERB AGREEMENT (K).
LANGUAGE-CHANGE INDEX
one in three believe for *one in three believes*: Stage 2

***one in the same.** See **one and the same.**

one less. See **fewer.**

one of [number]. See **one in [number] is.**

one of the [+ pl. n.] who (*or* **that**). This construction requires a plural verb in the relative clause, not a singular one. After the *who* or *that,* the verb should be plural because *who* or *that* is the subject, and it takes its number from the plural noun to which *who* or *that* refers—e.g.:

- "*One of the most insidious perils that waylay* the modern literary life is an exaggerated success at the outset of a career." Edmund Gosse, "Making a Name in Literature" (1889), in *A Reader for Writers* 86, 97 (William Targ ed., 1951).
- "When we look at living creatures from an outward point of view, *one of the first things that strike us* is that they are a bundle of habits." William James, *Habit* 3 (1890; repr. 1914).
- "This is *one of those spurious truisms that are* not intelligently believed by anyone." Henry Bradley, "Spoken and Written English" (1913), in *The Collected Papers of Henry Bradley* 168, 168 (1928; repr. 1970).
- "It is *one of the colloquial terms that worry* me." Anthony Burgess, *A Mouthful of Air* 23 (1992).

The reason for this construction becomes apparent when we reword any of those sentences: "Of the insidious perils that waylay the modern literary life, this is one." / "Of the first things that strike us, one is that . . . ." / "Of those spurious truisms that are not intelligently believed by anyone, this is one." / "Of the colloquial terms that worry me, this is one."

Yet many writers erroneously believe that *one* is the (singular) subject—e.g.:

- "*One of the things that is* very interesting to know is how you are feeling inside." Gertrude Stein, "Poetry and Grammar" (1935), in *Perspectives on Style* 44, 45 (Frederick Candelaria ed., 1968). (A possible revision: *One thing that is very interesting to know is how you are feeling inside.*)
- "'Very' is *one of the words that contributes* [read *contribute*] to flabby writing." Lester S. King, *Why Not Say It Clearly* 55 (1978).
- "Social class is *one of the extralinguistic factors that* often *shows* [read *show*] a correlation with language variation." Ronald K.S. Macaulay, *Locating Dialect in Discourse* 13 (1991).
- "'Chemistry' is *one of those words that* always *makes* [read *make*] me a little suspicious." Ron Hoff, *I Can See You Naked* 95 (1992).
- "[David] Frum is *one of those who has* [read *have*] undergone a conversion (or two)." Patricia Cohen, "Conservative Thinkers Think Again," *N.Y. Times*, 20 July 2008, at WK3.

As the following quotations illustrate, British writers have just as much trouble with this phrasing as Americans—e.g.:

- "*One of the words that dangles* [read *dangle*] to worst purpose is *because* after a negative statement." Basil Cottle, *The Plight of English* 87 (1975).
- "Here we have *one of those* packagings that *decays* [read *decay*] with time rather faster than the contents." Christopher Hitchens, *For the Sake of Argument* 280 (1993).
- "Bulkiness is *one of the things that makes* [read *make*] them costly." "The Different Engine," *Economist*, 5 Feb. 1994, at 85.
- "At moments like these I am *one of those people who finds* [read *find*] refuge in that lame line: 'I don't know much about art, but I know what I like.'" Nicholas Woodsworth, "A Week in the Louvre," *Fin. Times* (Weekend ed.), 6–7 Aug. 1994, § II, at 1.
- "It is clearly *one of those words which has* [read *that have*] become a marker for intellectual unreliability." Minette Marrin, "Bish Talks Bosh," *Sunday Telegraph*, 11 June 1995, at 31. (In that sentence, *a marker* should be *markers*.)
- "I've just completed *one of those loathsome but entirely necessary tasks which serves* [read *that serve*] as a reminder of just how unnecessary a lot of our exchanges with our fellow human beings are." Jonathan Ross, "The Past Is All in the Cards," *Sunday Times* (London), 18 June 1995, Style §, at 2. (For the reason for changing *which* to *that* in the last two sentences, see **that (A)**.)

So how adamant should we be about observing this distinction? The great linguist Otto Jespersen was unbudgeable: "It is not proof of logical or grammatical narrowmindedness to set oneself against expressions such as 'he is one of the kindest men that has ever lived,' instead of 'that have ever lived.' One can be the enemy of pedantry without surrendering one's liking for clear logic." *Mankind, Nation, and Individual from a Linguistic Point of View* 106–07 (1946). The grammarian Wilson Follett was even more resolute: "Let three thousand say *one of those who believes* while only three say *those who believe*; and as long as the three thousand do not also say *we believes, you believes, they believes*, the three thousand will be wrong from the only point of view that is relevant here, the point of view of form" (*MAU* at 24). But Follett's position won't hold up if the tide of usage is so strongly against this linguistic nicety as he hypothetically posits. The tide isn't nearly so strong. And yet this is one of the grammatical points that trip (not *trips*!) up even the "experts" (see the quotations in the second paragraph above).

The linguist Dwight Bolinger gave up on the traditional usage back in 1980: "I believe that the question is no longer an issue in American English—that, for better or worse, it is close to being decided in favor of the singular." "Progress Report on *One of Those Who Is* . . . ," 55 *Am. Speech* 288, 288 (1980). To some, that announcement was probably welcome news; to others, it amounted to a rash surrender.

For the traditionalist, perhaps the most sensible course is to prefer the traditional usage in your own writing, to adhere to it when editing or correcting others' work, but not to despair unduly as the age-old preference continues eroding.

LANGUAGE-CHANGE INDEX
**one of the few that is* for *one of the few that are*:
Stage 4
Current ratio (*one of those who are* vs.
**one of those who is*): 9:1

onerous (= burdensome) for *heinous* (= shockingly evil; abominable) is an occasional error—e.g.:

- "We can all take pride in the fact that this *onerous* [read *heinous*] crime was ferreted out and nipped before it could destroy the neighborhood." Letter of Albert P. Johnson, "Community Activist Remembered," *St. Petersburg Times*, 23 Jan. 1988, at 2.
- "There can't be any of this revolving-door justice where penalties for *onerous* [read *heinous*] crimes are reduced to tut-tutting, decorated cells and a few years." "Murder, They Wrote," *Toronto Sun*, 2 Sept. 1995, Editorial §, at 1.
- "Because Saudi Arabia has the most *onerous* [read *heinous*] violations among the 15 countries cited, the report said, the U.S. government needs to get serious about pressuring the desert kingdom to reform." Julia Duin, "Saudis Top Violators of Religious Rights," *Wash. Times*, 14 May 2003, at A1.

The word is pronounced either /**on**-ər-əs/ (like *honor us*) or /**oh**-nər-əs/ (like *owner us*).

LANGUAGE-CHANGE INDEX
onerous misused for *heinous*: Stage 1

LANGUAGE-CHANGE INDEX (For the full key, see front matter pp. xxxi, l–li.)
Stage 1: Rejected. **Stage 2:** Widely shunned. **Stage 3:** Widespread but . . . **Stage 4:** Ubiquitous but . . . **Stage 5:** Fully accepted.
Invariably inferior forms marked by asterisk (*). • Ratios represent frequency of prevalent forms vs. variants in current books.

*onery. See **ornery.**

oneself; *one's self. *Oneself* became the predominant spelling of the reflexive pronoun about 1900. **One's self* is an archaic variant that was already becoming old-fashioned when this passage was written: "The first and probably the most important one is production discipline, making *one's self* [read *oneself*] write whether one feels like it or not. The second is revision discipline; the third, rejection-slip discipline." Anne Hamilton, *How to Revise Your Own Stories* vii (1946). By the late 20th century, the two-word version had become distinctly nonstandard and pedantic-looking. Yet it still appears occasionally—e.g.:

- "Going to work for *one's self* [read *oneself*] often proved the only solution to bridging gaps in a work record." Mary Agria, "Flexibility Is Key for Working at Home," *Telegraph Herald* (Dubuque), 22 Sept. 1996, at D3.
- "Talk about hard to look at *one's self* [read *oneself*]." Bob Petrie, "Teen Scenes Allow Art to Imitate Life," *Ariz. Republic*, 10 Apr. 1997, Gilbert §, at EV1.
- "One Web site even suggests mailing a valentine to *one's self* [read *oneself*] as a kind of affirmation." Mark Woolsey, "Valentine's Isn't Hearts, Flowers for Everyone," *Atlanta J.-Const.*, 13 Feb. 2003, N. Fulton §, at 4.

The two-word construction is correct, however, when referring to one's *self* in a psychological or spiritual sense—e.g.: "The desire to pass on something of *one's self*, whether genetically in offspring, materially in prized possessions or inheritance, or spiritually in writing, art or music, is a near universal human inclination." Philip Chard, "Time Does Its Best to Erase Our Legacies," *Milwaukee J. Sentinel*, 11 Feb. 2003, at F1.

Current ratio: 7:1

one-time, an ambiguous term that can mean either "former" <a one-time professional wrestler> or "occurring only once" <a one-time opportunity>, is generally so hyphenated. AmE has moved toward solidifying the word—as given in *W11*—but the process is slow.

*one . . . you. This shift from third person to second is even worse than *one . . . he.* (See **one (B).**) Typically the best solution is to prefer *you* over *one*—e.g.:

- "*One* hears—and if *you* are like me, *you* acquiesce in— many complaints about the decline of civility in Western society." Clifford Orwin, "Civility," 60 *Am. Scholar* 553, 553 (1991). (A possible revision: *You hear—and if you are like me, you acquiesce in—many complaints . . . .*)
- "But actually, no other act is stronger than saying *you* are wrong about something to God, to another human being, [and] to *one's self* [read *yourself*]." Carol McGraw, "Yom Kippur Brings 'Another Chance,'" *Orange County Register*, 22 Sept. 1996, at B6. (For more on the spelling **one's self*, see **oneself.**)

online; on-line. Although *on-line* (with the hyphen) remains common for references to being connected to the Internet, the hyphen is probably doomed to disappear. The closed form is already predominant, whether the word is used as an adjective or an adverb—e.g.:

- Adjective: "Besides, all these hip Web savants were smugly pronouncing that *online* journalism was the future." Rem Reider, "At the Crossroads," *Am. Journalism Rev.*, Mar. 2001, at 6.
- Adverb: "Go *online*. Hundreds of restaurants are listed at www.opentable.com." Erica Marcus, "Advice for Making This a Valentine's Day Dinner to Remember," *Newsday* (N.Y.), 12 Feb. 2003, at B16.

In JARGON, the phrase *on line* (unhyphenated) has been extended to mean "into service" <the new power plant will be coming on line in June>, and the corresponding adjective is solid <an online power plant>.

Current ratio: 12:1

on line, stand. See **stand in line.**

only. A. Placement. *Only* is perhaps the most frequently misplaced of all English words. Its best placement is precisely before the words intended to be limited. The more words separating *only* from its correct position, the more awkward the sentence; and such a separation can lead to ambiguities. (Cf. **just** & **solely.**) Yet the strong tendency in AmE is to stick *only* right before the verb or verb phrase regardless of the ILLOGIC—e.g.:

- "The prosecution was hindered from seeking a conviction on attempted manslaughter charges because Seles elected not to testify at the hearing and *only provided her medical records shortly before* [read *provided her medical records only shortly before*] the trial was to begin." Cindy Shmerler, "WTA Still Working for Harsher Sentence," *USA Today*, 28 Apr. 1994, at C11.
- "So far, the county proposes that PDA [planned-development agriculture] *only be allowed for about* [read *be allowed for only about*] 15 areas in the eastern county." Dale White, "Instead of Homes on Huge Lots, Houses Could Be Clustered Around Open Land," *Sarasota Herald-Trib.*, 19 Nov. 1997, at B1.
- "In the U.S., boys *only seem to go for girl heroes when* [read *seem to go for girl heroes only when*] they are teamed up with male partners, as in the Power Rangers." Philip Murphy, "Kidvid Producers Cautiously Optimistic," *Variety*, 1 Dec. 1997, at 70.
- "You'd *only* need an apostrophe if you used a noun after the possessive." Mary Newton Bruder, *The Grammar Lady* 106 (2000). [A suggested revision: *You'd need an apostrophe only if you used a noun after the possessive.*]

The great H.W. Fowler was surprisingly permissive on this point back in 1926: "There is an orthodox position for the adverb, easily determined in case of need; to choose another position that may spoil or obscure the meaning is bad; but a change of position that has no such effect except technically is both justified by historical & colloquial usage & often demanded by rhetorical needs" (*FMEU1* at 405–06). The problem with Fowler's view is that what is merely "technically" obscure for one person may for another person be a full-fledged ambiguity.

Fowler's American contemporary, John F. Genung, was more sensible in his approach (writing somewhat earlier): "Capable of being either an adjective or an adverb, [*only*] can modify almost any part of speech; so if not placed immediately before the word (or phrase) to which it belongs its force is liable to be stolen by what comes between." *Outlines of Rhetoric* 71 (1893).

More than a century before Genung and Fowler wrote those passages, the rhetorician Hugh Blair summed up the rationale for being careful about placing *only* and similar words. It holds true even today: "The fact is, with respect to such adverbs as *only, wholly, at least,* and the rest of that tribe, that in common discourse, the tone and emphasis we use in pronouncing them generally serves to show their reference, and to make the meaning clear; and hence, we acquire a habit of throwing them in loosely in the course of a period [i.e., a sentence]. But in writing, where a man speaks to the eye, and not to the ear, he ought to be more accurate; and so to connect those adverbs with the words which they qualify, as to put his meaning out of doubt upon the first inspection." Hugh Blair, *Lectures on Rhetoric and Belles Lettres* vol. 1, at 245 (1783; 11th ed. 1809).

LANGUAGE-CHANGE INDEX
only separated from the word it limits: Stage 3

B. In Doublespeak. A paltering *only* sometimes reflects DOUBLESPEAK. Consider the signs that, beginning in the mid-1990s, appeared at American Airlines gates throughout the United States: *Beverages only in main cabin.* The airline is saying that while first-class passengers will get both meals and drinks, coach-class passengers will get only drinks. If the sign read *Meals only in first class,* the syntax would work pretty well, but the majority of passengers (in coach) would be miffed. If it said *No meals in coach class,* the sense of upset would only intensify. If it said *Only beverages in coach class,* the sense would be right—but once again the coach passengers might feel as if they were being shorted. So the sign-writers changed *coach class* to *main cabin* (a kind of EUPHEMISM) and then worded the sign as if it were an honor being bestowed: *Prizes only for the winners. Jackpots only for the lucky few. Beverages only in main cabin.* It sounds as if everyone else on board must do without: no drinks for those in the cockpit or in first class. But of course that isn't so. First-class passengers don't complain about the sign because they know they'll be fed and get all the drinks they reasonably want. Coach passengers don't complain because they don't think through what the sign really means. See AIRLINESE.

C. As Noncomparable Adjective. See ADJECTIVES (B).

D. And *sole.* See sole.

only if. See if (B).

onomatopoeic; *onomatopoetic. The first is now standard for the adjective corresponding to *onomatopoeia* (= the formation or use of a word that sounds like the action or object it denotes); the second is a

NEEDLESS VARIANT that confusingly suggests an inherent linkage with poetry. Since about 1950, the *-poeic* form has outnumbered the *-poetic* form by a wide margin—e.g.:

- "A vast number of words in the language—*onomatopoeic* words they are called—. . . were deliberately coined to imitate a sound." Guy N. Pocock, "Sound and Sense," in *Foundations of English Style* 180, 182 (Paul M. Fulcher ed., 1927).
- "The Italian playwright and performer Dario Fo has a similar routine, called Grummelot, an *onomatopoeic* babble that communicates the sense of a speech through rhythm and tone rather than words." Ryan McKittrick, "'Archimedes' an Inventive Play on Words," *Boston Globe,* 7 Dec. 2001, at D3.
- "Ever since Eric Clapton and Jimi Hendrix popularized the wah-wah pedal—a foot-operated device that derives its *onomatopoeic* name from the reverb sound it creates—guitarists have used their toes to do more than tap along to the beat." "Horizons' Wah-Wah Rings," *Christian Science Monitor,* 8 May 2008, Innovation §, at 14.

One historian of the English language has suggested *echoic* as a simpler substitute: "One theory is that words imitated natural sounds, such as the cries of animals or the noises made by rapidly moving or colliding objects. Words that had this origin are sometimes said to be *onomatopoetic,* but the term *echoic* is to be preferred as being shorter, easier to spell, and more obviously descriptive of what is intended." G.L. Brook, *A History of the English Language* 17 (1958).

Onomatopoeic is pronounced /on-ə-mat-ə-**pee**-ik/. Take care not to use the sloppy pronunciation /on-ə-mon-ə-**pee**-ik/.

Current ratio: 3:1

on the contrary. See contrary (B).

on the grounds that. See because (D).

on the lam (= on the run from law-enforcement authorities) began as American SLANG. Although the expression has been traced back to the late 19th century, its precise origin remains obscure. The phrase didn't become common till about 1930. It is fairly widespread today—e.g.:

- "A former Bank of the Desert loan officer, who has been *on the lam* since May, was arrested in Las Vegas this week on federal bank fraud and money-laundering charges." Don McAuliffe, "Former Desert Bank Executive Arrested," *Press-Enterprise* (Riverside, Cal.), 28 Aug. 1999, at D3.
- "Grauman was *on the lam* after escaping from both the South Dakota prison and a jail in Wyoming." "Escapee Charged with Murder," *Rocky Mountain News* (Denver), 15 June 2000, at A33.
- "He fled after the conviction, living *on the lam* for six months before being arrested in Las Vegas and sentenced to 30 years in prison." James C. McKinley Jr., "Jamiel A. Chagra, 63, Drug King, Dies," *N.Y. Times,* 29 July 2008, at B6.

Occasionally the phrase is mistakenly made **on the lamb*—e.g.: "The owner of a local clothing company

LANGUAGE-CHANGE INDEX (For the full key, see front matter pp. xxxi, l–li.)
Stage 1: Rejected. **Stage 2:** Widely shunned. **Stage 3:** Widespread but . . . **Stage 4:** Ubiquitous but . . . **Stage 5:** Fully accepted.
Invariably inferior forms marked by asterisk (*). • Ratios represent frequency of prevalent forms vs. variants in current books.

was arrested Tuesday and an employee of the company is *on the lamb* [read *on the lam*], in the wake of a raid by the state Department of Industrial Relations." Yomi S. Wronge, "Agents Stage Raid on an Unlicensed Garment Producer," *Orange County Register*, 16 Oct. 1997, at 2.

LANGUAGE-CHANGE INDEX
on the lamb for *on the lam*: Stage 2
Current ratio (*on the lam* vs. *on the lamb*): 6:1

on the other hand. It is pure pedantry to insist that this contrastive phrase must always be paired with *on the one hand*. In fact, to do so in most cases would be verbose. *On the other hand* has been in common use without a preceding *on the one hand* since the 17th century. For a similar problem, see **former.**

on the part of. This phrase is usually verbose—e.g.:

- "Watterson is somewhat self-effacing about how he comes up with such metaphysical thoughts *on the part of* [read *for*] the kid, such cogent comments by the cat." "After a Highly Successful Decade, Cartoonist Is Pulling the Plug on 'Calvin & Hobbes,'" *Asbury Park Press* (Neptune, N.J.), 3 Dec. 1995, at C3.
- "Although the election rerun is the result of illegal financial actions *on the part of* [read *by*] the Carey campaign, Cherkasky's first job will be to investigate possible financial irregularities in the Hoffa campaign." Frank Swoboda, "Overseer Named for Rerun of Teamsters' Vote," *Wash. Post*, 3 Dec. 1997, at A19.
- "It's more of a pause and reassessment *on the part of* [read *by*] the developer, rather than pulling the plug." Paul Grondahl & Eric Anderson, "Retail Project Near TU Stalls," *Times Union* (Albany), 2 Sept. 2015, at C10.

on the whole has been a SET PHRASE since the 17th century. Some writers mistakenly make it *on a whole*—e.g.: "Economic matters are by far the biggest concern among those polled, and *on a whole* [read *on the whole*], people seem to feel they are not doing badly." Michael Winerip, "Backers of Bush in '92 Are Turning to Clinton," *N.Y. Times*, 27 May 1996, at 10. *On a whole* appears to be a dialectal phrase found in rural Minnesota and other nearby states. See DIALECT.

LANGUAGE-CHANGE INDEX
on a whole for *on the whole*: Stage 1

op. cit. See **ibid.**

open-ended(ness) should be hyphenated so that it won't look too monstrous. See PUNCTUATION (J).

opera. See **opus.**

operable; operative; operational. *Operable* is now commonly used in two senses: (1) "practicable; capable of being operated"; and (2) "(of a tumor or other bodily condition) capable of being ameliorated through surgery." In sense 1, the word is occasionally, and wrongly, written *operatable*—e.g.: "In Focus Systems will move into new emerging market segments by . . . producing smart and wireless projectors or making [its projectors] *operatable* [read *operable*] on batteries." "Lightest Multimedia Projector Makes Debut," *Bus. Times*, 7 Mar. 1997, at 7. See -ABLE (D) & -ATABLE.

Operative = (1) having effect; in operation; efficacious <the regulations are now operative>; or (2) having principal relevance <*may* is the operative word of the statute>. As a noun, *operative* most commonly means "a secret agent" or "a detective"—e.g.: "The most elaborate [scheme] involved an attractive young female *operative* on a bike. . . . When the winsome *operative* staged an accident, two Warriors came to her aid. She talked her way into their house, looking for evidence." Peter Elkind, "Blood Feud," *Fortune*, 14 Apr. 1997, at 90.

Operational = engaged in operation; able to function; used in operation. E.g.: "The $69 million adult medium-security prison, which would be built on a 120-acre site, would employ more than 200 construction workers and have about 450 full-time employees once it becomes *operational*." Courtney Challos, "Town Sees Prisons as Freedom from Economic Woes," *Chicago Trib.*, 31 Mar. 1997, at N1. Sometimes, though, the word appears in phrases where it probably shouldn't. For example, the idea denoted by *operational costs* is more usually expressed as *operating costs*—e.g.: "But commissioners discussed two possible options that would bring in money for *operational* [read *operating*] costs." Angela Cortez, "Facilities' Upkeep a Concern," *Denver Post*, 1 Apr. 1997, at B2.

LANGUAGE-CHANGE INDEX
operatable for *operable*: Stage 1

operationalize, dating from the 1950s, smacks of pure JARGON. Some businesspeople talk about *operationalizing objectives* when all they mean is *working toward goals* or *translating objectives into operating procedures*. Others use it in equally fuzzy ways, often as a fancy substitute for *use*—e.g.:

- "Indeed, the merit of this contribution is arguably in illustrating how the previous approach can be more fully *operationalized* [read *used*] and empirical results readily interpreted." Ben Fine & John Simister, "Consumption Durables: Exploring the Order of Acquisition," 27 *Applied Economics* 1049 (1995).
- "Though not often *operationalized* [read *used*?] in this way, FLC is basically a process theory." Louis G. Pol & Sukgoo Pak, "Consumer Unit Types and Expenditures on Food Away from Home," *J. Consumer Affairs*, 22 Dec. 1995, at 403.
- "Clinton commended Gore for educating the public about global warming, which earned Gore a Nobel Peace Prize. 'The sale's been made,' he said of Gore's work. 'But now what we have to do is figure out how to *operationalize* [read *implement*] this.'" Anna-Louise Jackson, "Clinton Promotes Going Green," *Chicago Defender*, 9 Nov. 2007, at 6.

See -IZE.

LANGUAGE-CHANGE INDEX
operationalize: Stage 1

operative. See **operable.**

ophthalmologist; oculist; optometrist; optician; ocularist. The first two designate a doctor trained in a school of medicine (an M.D.) whose specialty is the eye, although *ophthalmologist* is now much more usual than *oculist*. An *ophthalmologist* may perform intraocular surgery as well as other procedures and may prescribe drugs and glasses or contact lenses. An *optometrist* is a doctor trained in a school of optometry (an O.D.) and is licensed to examine the eyes, diagnose problems, and prescribe drugs, glasses, and contact lenses—and may even perform minor surgical procedures. An *optician* makes or sells lenses and, like a pharmacist, fills prescriptions (for glasses). Finally, an *ocularist* makes, colors, and fits artificial eyes.

Ophthalmologist is pronounced /of-thə[l]-**mol**-ə-jist/—not /op-thə[l]-**mol**-ə-jist/. See PRONUNCIATION (D).

LANGUAGE-CHANGE INDEX
ophthalmologist mispronounced /op-thə[l]/
instead of /of-thə[l]/: Stage 4

ophthalmology is sometimes misspelled **ophthamology*, **opthalmology*, or **opthamology*. Pronouncing the /l/ in the second syllable is more cultivated than not pronouncing it. To omit it is to invite the first and third of the misspellings just noted.

opine. A. Generally. *Opine* today often connotes the forming of a judgment on insufficient grounds. It can suggest the giving of an idle or facetious opinion—e.g.: "At Boardinghouse, a South Shore shop catering exclusively to snowboarders, the young staffers on duty *opined* that skiers are as doomed as the dinosaurs." Glen Martin, "Ski Season Coasts In," *S.F. Chron.*, 1 Dec. 1997, at A1.

The word can carry many nuances. Sometimes *opine* seems intended to cheapen the opinion given—e.g.:

- "The couple . . . were often berated on Boston radio shows as greedy careerists who had entrusted their sons to an inexperienced sitter in order to save a few dollars. ('Apparently the parents didn't want a kid,' *opined* one talk show caller. 'Now they don't have a kid.')" Bill Hewitt et al., "Murder or Not?" *People*, 17 Nov. 1997, at 54.
- "According to Benson, education is not a state responsibility but is 'the responsibility of the local people.' He *opines* that is 'what it says in the (New Hampshire) constitution.'" Alf E. Jacobson, "Benson Is Wrong," *Union Leader* (Manchester, N.H.), 3 Feb. 2003, at A8.

Often the word suggests mild ridicule (as in the first example below), folksiness (as in the second), or jocularity (as in the third)—e.g.:

- "'I think there's a real nobility to public service,' *opines* Ben [Affleck] ever-so-Kennedyesquely in the March [*Vanity Fair*]." Gayle Fee & Laura Raposa, "Affleck on a Roll to Congress?" *Boston Herald*, 4 Feb. 2003, News §, at 16.
- "Of the [con men], Huck *opines* that 'they've got more schemes than a possum has ticks.'" Ivan M. Lincoln, "Buoyant, Moving 'Big River' Docks at Hale Centre," *Deseret News* (Salt Lake City), 4 Feb. 2003, at C6.
- "'Matrimony' proudly tromps through a musical wilderness of pain and suffering. But not without a high level of

humor. Musselwhite *opines*, 'life will be better when you're not in it.'" Richard L. Eldredge, *Atlanta J.-Const.*, 11 Feb. 2003, at E9.

The word is also used in the sense "to express or pronounce a formal or authoritative opinion" (*OED*). Although the *OED* calls this sense rare, it's anything but rare in AmE. In law, it routinely denotes the testimony of an expert witness. It is also fairly common elsewhere—e.g.: "When Intel Chief Executive Craig Barrett visited the ancient Chinese city of Xi'an last spring, thousands of students at Xi'an University packed a hall to hear him *opine* about the future of technology." Ted Sickinger, "State Must Risk to Keep Tech Edge," *Oregonian* (Portland), 4 Feb. 2003, at A1.

Since the word sometimes implies authoritativeness, sometimes disingenuousness, and sometimes ridicule, it's perfect for denoting political spin control—e.g.: "Almost as the applause still echoed, the audience practically sprinted out to parse, *opine* and analyze beneath the bright television lights set up in a marble chamber near the House floor." Bob Dart, "State of the Union," *Atlanta J.-Const.*, 29 Jan. 2003, at A6.

B. And *opinion, vb. When used as a verb, *opinion* is at best a NEEDLESS VARIANT of *opine*, at worst a NONWORD. E.g.:

- "The court *opinioned* [read *opined*] that people 'might resist' joining the guerrillas." Stephen F. Gold, "A Travesty of Justice," *Christian Science Monitor*, 3 Mar. 1992, at 18.
- "In the same edition, E.J. Montini *opinioned* [read *opined*] that there are far worse things than flag burning to worry about." "Worse Things to Worry About," *Ariz. Republic*, 15 Mar. 1995, at B8.
- "One poster helpfully linked to the Dec. 9 Dallas Morning News, in which columnist Rod Dreher *opinioned* [read *opined* or *wrote*] that 'Alberto Gonzales, the bumblefutz U.S. attorney general who defenestrated himself from the Department of Justice . . . , is surely the Texan of the Year.'" Linda P. Campbell, "Objection! Objection! Law," *Ft. Worth Star-Telegram*, 27 Dec. 2007, at B13.

LANGUAGE-CHANGE INDEX
*opinioned for *opined*: Stage 1

opossum; possum. *Opossum* (/ə-**pos**-əm/), long said to be standard, has never been as common in AmE or BrE as *possum*. The colloquially shortened form of this Algonquian term, *possum*, is more than twice as common in journalistic sources, and it is even more common in speech (because of the unaccented first syllable of *opossum*). *Possum* quite rightly appears in the CASUALISM *play possum* (= to play dead or pretend to be asleep). It also appears in DIALECT and in literary rendering of dialect. While *possum* is generally thought to be Southern dialect, in fact it is seen throughout the English-speaking world—e.g.:

- "Today, the eighth-grader at the Williams School in New London owns about 200 dummies. These include Freddy, a *possum* who tries to cross the road." Joanna Mechlinski,

LANGUAGE-CHANGE INDEX (For the full key, see front matter pp. xxxi, l-li.)
Stage 1: Rejected. **Stage 2:** Widely shunned. **Stage 3:** Widespread but . . . **Stage 4:** Ubiquitous but . . . **Stage 5:** Fully accepted.
Invariably inferior forms marked by asterisk (*). • Ratios represent frequency of prevalent forms vs. variants in current books.

"Look Who's Not Talking," *Hartford Courant*, 3 Feb. 2003, at D3.

- "Ryan knew they were animal tracks—raccoons, *possum*, squirrels, birds." Denis Hamill, "No Furr-giving Ryan's Cat Lady," *Daily News* (N.Y.), 4 Feb. 2003, Suburban §, at 3.
- "But, he said, the feed and chickens can attract coyotes, *possums* and rats." Deana Poole, "Fans of Pet Chickens Plead for Zoning Change," *Olympian* (Olympia, Wash.), 4 Feb. 2003, at B1.
- "We raised chickens and ducks; the yard was host to quail, mourning doves, snakes, *possums* and a variety of other creatures." Jon Love, "Kindness Cuts Across Borders," *Fresno Bee* (South Valley ed.), 7 Feb. 2003, at 13.
- "Months later, amid an otherwise subdued dawning, a *possum* brought us both out of bed as he stalked across our deck." Neil Morgan, "It Was High Noon at Night in Cuyamacas," *San Diego Union-Trib.*, 9 Feb. 2003, at B2.

The misspellings **opposum* and **oppossum* have arisen doubtless from the influence of *opposite*—e.g.:

- "The ratlike *opposum* [read *opossum*] is prevalent in the area." Tom Long, "Time to Stock Up, Bed Down for Winter," *Boston Globe*, 2 Nov. 1994, at 77.
- "There seem to be enough people who are interested in studying the 48 discrete movements between an *oppossum's* [read *opossum's*] slow-walk and its bound." Barbara Stewart, "Work on the Wild Side," *N.Y. Times*, 7 Apr. 1996, N.J. §, at 4.

LANGUAGE-CHANGE INDEX
1. *possum* for *opossum*: Stage 5
Current ratio (*possums* vs. *opossums*): 1.2:1
2. *opossum* misspelled **opposum* or **oppossum*: Stage 1
Current ratio (*opossum* vs. **oppossum* vs. **opposum*): 129:1:1

opportunistic; opportune. *Opportunistic* describes someone who is motivated by expediency and self-interest—e.g.: "Everybody—greedy players, lying owners, feeble commissioner, slimy lawyers, *opportunistic* Congressmen—pretends to tell us the precise nature of baseball's labor problems." Bob Hunter, "Steinbrenner Spends to Win, but Won't Hide His Intentions," *Columbus Dispatch*, 19 July 2002, at C3.

Opportune describes something that is convenient, fit, suitable, appropriate, or well-timed—e.g.: "This would be an *opportune* time for a Latino candidate to run for the City Council." Sam McManis, "Latinos Lack Political Pull in Concord," *S.F. Chron.*, 9 Aug. 2002, Contra Costa §, at 1.

But *opportunistic* is now sometimes misused to mean *opportune*—e.g.:

- "At a crucial and *opportunistic* [read *opportune*] moment, he [Emperor Hirohito of Japan] risked his throne to bring his people's suffering to an end." E. Barry Keehn, "The Emperor's Mask After the War," *San Diego Union-Trib.*, 24 Sept. 2000, Books §, at 1.
- "Now is the most *opportunistic* [read *opportune*] time for this type of product." Cecile B. Corral, "Suppliers Hope Retailers Get the 'Basic' Idea," *Home Textiles Today*, 26 Nov. 2001, at 13.
- "Some of Stuckey's more exciting plays couldn't have come at more *opportunistic* [read *opportune*] times." Chris

Hughes, "Stuckey Will Leave Large Legacy at Northside," *Macon Telegraph*, 14 June 2002, at C1.

LANGUAGE-CHANGE INDEX
opportunistic misused for *opportune*: Stage 1

opposition. For an odd misusage, see **apposition.**

oppress; repress. *Oppress* = to subject (a person or a people) to inhumane or other unfair treatment; to persecute. *Repress* = (1) to keep under control; (2) to reduce (people) to subjection; (3) to inhibit or restrain; or (4) to suppress. The negative connotations of *oppress* are greater than those of *repress*.

oppressible. So spelled—preferably not *oppressable* (which has become common since about 2000). See -ABLE (A).

oppugn. See **impugn (A).**

opt (= to choose or decide) is usually followed by *for* or *to*—e.g.:

- "Few women have *opted for* careers in mathematics, engineering and the natural sciences." Mike Bowler, "In Math, Women a Plus," *Baltimore Sun*, 4 Oct. 1995, at B2.
- "After being left off the postseason roster in a decision manager Mike Hargrove called 'very difficult,' Winfield *opted to* sit in the dugout and travel on the road." John Giannone, "'Peeved' Winnie Along for Ride," *Daily News* (N.Y.), 4 Oct. 1995, at 56.

Readers may find *opt for* (a CASUALISM) a bit too jaunty for some contexts.

The phrase *opt between* is unusual and unnecessary—e.g.: "For one thing, a patient choosing medical care doesn't have the leisure, knowledge or power enjoyed by a consumer *opting* [read *choosing*] between a Big Mac and a Whopper." "Why Wait for Hillary?" *Newsweek*, 28 June 1993, at 38, 40. That example illustrates INELEGANT VARIATION, from an ill-founded fear of repeating the verb *choose*.

Opt out (of), meaning "to choose not to participate [in]," is a bit of LEGALESE that has entrenched itself in the public consciousness through class-action lawsuits, contracts, and governmental regulations—e.g.:

- "Roughly $5.2 million will be distributed by formula among the settlement class members, unless they *opt out*." Ken Harney, "Some Reverse Mortgages Are Perilous for the Unwary," *Baltimore Sun*, 9 Feb. 2003, at L1.
- "Under a new set of rules drafted by the Environmental Protection Agency, the businesses could *opt out of* the current requirement to reduce toxic fumes from their plants to the maximum extent possible." Gary Polakovic, "EPA Plans to Relax Toxic Emission Standards," *L.A. Times*, 11 Feb. 2003, News §, at 18.
- "McGrady and Hill can *opt out of* their deals after the 2004–05 season. Rivers is signed through the 2005–06 season." Jerry Brewer, "Magic Miscalculations," *Orlando Sentinel*, 11 Feb. 2003, at D1.

*opthalmology. See **ophthalmology.**

optician. See **ophthalmologist.**

optimize (= to make the best use of) is the word, not *optimalize*—e.g.: "Insulin dosage was *optimalized* [read *optimized*] by the study physician." Julio Wainstein et al., "The Use of Continuous Insulin Delivery Systems in Severely Insulin-Resistant Patients," 24 *Diabetes Care* 1297 (1 July 2001). See NONWORDS.

LANGUAGE-CHANGE INDEX
optimalize for *optimize*: Stage 1
Current ratio (*optimized* vs. *optimalized*): 7,885:1

optimum. *Optimum* is the noun, but *optimal* is—optimally speaking—the better adjective. Hence the phrase should be *optimal advantage*, not *optimum advantage*. The reason is that there's no need for *optimal* if we use *optimum* both as a noun and as an adjective. It serves the principle of DIFFERENTIATION to distinguish between the two forms. But the adjectival *optimum* seems to be edging out *optimal* in practice, and the latter may one day be just a NEEDLESS VARIANT.

optometrist. See **ophthalmologist.**

opt out. See **opt.**

opus. Pl. *opuses*—preferably not *opera* (except in references to operatic works). See PLURALS (B).

opusculum; opuscule; *opuscle. Although the Latinate *opusculum* (= a minor literary or musical work) was long ago anglicized to *opuscule*, the latter has never occurred as frequently in English-language print sources as the former. And although one might expect *opuscules* to be more convenient to readers of English than the plural *opuscula*, in fact the more bookish term has predominated in all varieties of English. *Opuscle* is a variant form. For nonscholars, of course, all these terms are hopelessly pedantic.

-OR; -ER. See -ER (A).

-OR; -OUR. Although all agent nouns except *saviour* (BrE) take *-or* in both AmE and BrE (e.g., *actor, investor*), the general distinction is that of the other nouns that end in either of these forms, AmE nouns tend to be spelled *-or*, and BrE nouns *-our*. That distinction occurs primarily in abstract nouns. Hence the British write *behaviour, colour, flavour,* and *humour*, whereas Americans write *behavior, color, flavor,* and *humor*. The following words, however, end in *-or* on both sides of the Atlantic: *error, horror, languor, liquor, pallor, squalor, stupor, terror, torpor,* and *tremor*. *Glamour* is the primary exception to the *-or* rule in AmE.

In BrE, nouns ending in *-our* change to *-or* before the suffixes *-ation, -iferous, -ific, -ize,* and *-ous* (e.g., *coloration, honorific*). But *-our* keeps the *-u-* before *-able, -er, -ful, -ism, -ist, -ite,* and *-less* (e.g., *honourable, labourer, colourful*). At least one British writer has suggested that BrE would be better off hastening

toward the AmE spellings. G.H. Vallins refers to the "slow process in English (we have *terror, horror, governor*, all of which were once spelt with a *u*)," adding that this process "merely needs quickening up by a few journalists and novelists with confidence and vigour enough to defy convention." G.H. Vallins, *Better English* 116 (4th ed. 1957). (Make that *vigor*, G.H.!) See **Labour Party.**

or. See **and/or.**

oral. See **aural** & **verbal.**

orangey (= suggestive of an orange—the fruit or the color) has been the standard spelling since the early 1970s. *Orangy* is a variant.

orangutan; *orangutang; *orang-utan; *orangoutan; *orangoutang. The spelling of this word—deriving from the Malay term *oran utan* ("forest man")—has been settled since about 1950: *orangutan*. The others are variant spellings. The standard AmE pronunciation is /ə-**rang**-[g]ə-tan/. But the other pronunciation (/ə-**rang**-[g]ə-tang/) remains quite common, possibly because the reduplicative rhyme makes the word easier to say.

orate, a BACK-FORMATION from *oration*, was once widely considered objectionable or merely humorous. But it has almost completely lost this stigma. It sometimes suggests that the speaker is pompous, but the word itself no longer strikes most readers or listeners as being facetious—e.g.:

- "Whether he was *orating* from the House dais or taking an operatic pie in the face at the Bushnell, Weicker thrived on center stage." Michele Jacklin, "Weicker Leaves Office as He Governed: On His Own Terms," *Hartford Courant*, 1 Jan. 1995, at A1.
- "Helping inestimably to evoke the era are Charles Corcoran's effective set and Jill Nagel's sound design, which subtly adds echo to Roosevelt's voice as he *orates* from a small balcony." Andy Webster, "The Amazing Adventures of a Gregarious Dissident," *N.Y. Times*, 16 May 2008, at E3.

For the misuse of *perorate* for *orate*, see **perorate.**

orchestrate, in nonmusical contexts, is a CLICHÉ and a VOGUE WORD. But it is arguably useful in indicating that an (apparently spontaneous) event was clandestinely arranged beforehand. Cf. **choreograph.**

order of protection. See **protective order.**

ordinal numbers. See **cardinal numbers** & NUMERALS (F).

ordinance; ordnance; ordonnance. *Ordinance* (= a municipal [i.e., city] law) is common in AmE but rare in BrE, where *byelaw* serves this purpose. *Ordnance* =

LANGUAGE-CHANGE INDEX (For the full key, see front matter pp. xxxi, l–li.)
Stage 1: Rejected. **Stage 2:** Widely shunned. **Stage 3:** Widespread but . . . **Stage 4:** Ubiquitous but . . . **Stage 5:** Fully accepted.
Invariably inferior forms marked by asterisk (*). • Ratios represent frequency of prevalent forms vs. variants in current books.

military supplies; cannon; artillery. *Ordonnance* = the ordering of parts in a whole; arrangement.

Occasionally *ordnance* is misused for *ordinance*—e.g.:

- "His municipal government adopted its own standards in May 1994 as a city *ordnance* [read *ordinance*]." Kevin Petrie, "TCI Promises Cities Better Service Record," *Denver Bus. J.*, 19 Apr. 1996, at A9.
- "He said noise and parking are addressed specifically by city *ordnances* [read *ordinances*]." Martin Luttrell, "Bands Might Not Play On," *Worcester Telegram & Gaz.*, 16 Jan. 2006, at B1.

The opposite error, *ordinance* for *ordnance*, also occurs—e.g.:

- "It coordinates civilian organizations clearing mines and unexploded *ordinance* [read *ordnance*] across Kosovo." Carlotta Gall, "U.N. Aide in Kosovo Faults NATO on Unexploded Bombs," *N.Y. Times*, 23 May 2000, at A3.
- "There are a number of unexploded small *ordinance* [read *ordnance*] scattered about the entire island." Andrew Doughty & Harriett Friedman, *Maui Revealed* 141 (2001).
- "They are reluctant veterans of detonating unexploded *ordinance* [read *ordnance*]." Amy Waldman, "A Nation Challenged," *N.Y. Times*, 23 Nov. 2001, at B4.

LANGUAGE-CHANGE INDEX
1. *ordnance* misused for *ordinance*: Stage 1
2. *ordinance* misused for *ordnance*: Stage 1

Oregon. Some natives of the state insist on a long medial *-e-*: /**or**-ee-gən/. Others, though, are perfectly happy putting a short vowel or schwa in the middle syllable: /**or**-i-gən/ or /**or**-ə-gən/. No full-blooded Oregonian (/or-i-**goh**-nee-ən/), though, countenances rhyming the last syllable with *gone*. It's *gun*, not *gone*.

organdy (= a sheer cotton or silk fabric) has been the standard spelling since the late 1930s. *Organdie* is a variant.

organic. This adjective traditionally means (to a chemist) "carbon-based" or (to a physician) "of, relating to, or involving a body organ." Purists may object to its odd extensions in reference to plant foods that are grown without chemicals, pesticides, or genetic manipulation, but the phrase is here to stay—it's even codified in federal law. The phrase *inorganic food* is, strictly speaking, an OXYMORON, since all foods contain carbon. Use *nonorganic food* instead.

orient; *orientate*. The latter is a NEEDLESS VARIANT of *orient*, which means "to get one's bearings or sense of direction"—e.g.: "It's doubly daunting for foreign players trying to *orientate* [read *orient*] themselves to the USA." Chris Colston, "For Some, a World of Change," *USA Today*, 22 Jan. 2008, at C5.

The longer variant (a BACK-FORMATION from *orientation*) is more common in BrE than in AmE—e.g.:

- "Not everyone, even in *market-orientated* [read *market-oriented*] America, is wholly happy with what is happening." *Sunday Times* (London), 11 Dec. 1988, at H1.

- " 'Vampires aren't very *family orientated* [read *family-oriented*].' " Terry Pratchett, *Carpe Jugulum* 151 (1998).
- "As excited as she had been to be reunited with Connor, she had felt *disorientated* [read *disoriented*] by leaving the Vampirate ship—and her friends there—so precipitately." Justin Somper, *Vampirates: Tide of Terror* 79–80 (2007).

Cf. **disorient.**

LANGUAGE-CHANGE INDEX
orientate for *orient*: Stage 2
Current ratio (*oriented* vs. *orientated*): 22:1

ornery (= recalcitrant; mean-spirited) is the standard spelling of this word, which is pronounced /**or**-nə-ree/. *Onery* is a variant spelling influenced by the dialectal pronunciation /**on**-[ə]-ree/. Interestingly, *ornery* was originally an alteration of the word *ordinary*, but today (of course) it no longer bears that sense. See DIALECT.

Current ratio: 37:1

orphan. See **widow.**

orphanhood; *orphancy*; *orphandom*. The first is the usual word, the other two being NEEDLESS VARIANTS.

orthopedics (= the branch of medicine dealing with correcting problems with bones and muscles) is so spelled in AmE, *orthopaedics* in BrE. The divergence in spelling occurred in the first decade of the 20th century.

orthoscopic. See **arthroscopic.**

-os. See PLURALS (D).

ostensible; ostensive. *Ostensible* (the usual term) = seeming; apparent <her ostensible opinion isn't supported by her actions>. *Ostensive* = clearly displaying; directly demonstrative <his behavior was ostensive of his debased character>. Though some dictionaries sanction the usage, it's an error to use *ostensive* synonymously with *ostensible*—e.g.:

- "His main effort, and the *ostensive* [read *ostensible*] purpose of this book, is a description of a tour of Vietnam he took in 1993." "Jill Ker Conway Recalls 'Future of a Woman Alone in the 1950s,'" *Roanoke Times*, 26 Feb. 1995, Book §, at 6.
- "The convention's charge is to select three candidates, *ostensively* [read *ostensibly*] to help the governor make a final selection for the board." "The School Convention Worked," *Baltimore Sun*, 27 June 1995, at A10.
- "The fun—and there is quite a bit to be had—derives in part from the over-the-top performance by Sizemore and the sometimes painfully ordinary 'insights' of the *ostensive* [read *ostensible*] geniuses, but the film is surprisingly free of cant." Philip Martin, "Review: The Genius Club," *Ark. Dem.-Gaz.*, 1 Feb. 2008, Moviestyle §, at 1.

LANGUAGE-CHANGE INDEX
ostensive misused for *ostensible*: Stage 1

osteopathy. *Osteopathy* is the drug-free alternative-medicine discipline that focuses on treating muscular and skeletal problems primarily by using noninvasive manual therapies. In the United States, *osteopathic* *medicine* is distinct. Its practitioners are *osteopathic physicians*, who must be fully trained as medical doctors and receive specialized training in the musculoskeletal system to earn the degree Doctor of Osteopathic Medicine, or D.O. In much of the rest of the world, an *osteopath* is not a physician but a person specially trained only in treating musculoskeletal conditions through manual techniques, such as applying pressure to or moving muscles and bones.

Osteopathy is pronounced /os-tee-**op**-ə-thee/—not /**os**-tee-ə-path-ee/.

ostler. See **hostler.**

other. A. **Other . . . other than.** Repeating *other* in this way is a fairly common REDUNDANCY—e.g.: "The fractional approach typically does not integrate with any *other* type of social insurance program *other than* Social Security." Carolyn M. Burton et al., "Disability Insurance with Social Integration," *J. Am. Soc'y of CLU & ChFC*, Sept. 1995, at 56. Either one of the *others* should be dropped.

LANGUAGE-CHANGE INDEX
*other . . . other than: Stage 1

B. *No other . . . than.* This phrase often gets mangled into **no other . . . except*, which is a piece of ILLOGIC. The correction is typically *no . . . other than*—e.g.:

- "The Bruce Willis supernatural thriller has grossed $20 million for the fifth consecutive weekend, accomplishing what *no other film has done except 'Titanic'* [read *what no film other than 'Titanic' has done* or *no film has done except 'Titanic'*]." Robert W. Welkos, "Weekend Box Office," *L.A. Times*, 8 Sept. 1999, at F3.
- "Some people may believe we will have *no other choice except* [read *no other choice than*] light rail." Jay Tibshraeny, "Chandler to Study Transit Woes, Options," *Ariz. Republic*, 21 Feb. 2001, at 4.
- "He desires *no other woman except* [read *no woman other than* or *no other woman than*] his absent fiancée." Loren King, "Rohmer Films, in Focus at Brattle, More than Just Talk," *Boston Globe*, 23 Feb. 2001, at D5.

Very occasionally, the *no other . . . except* phrasing is actually correct—e.g.: "Vojtas has testified repeatedly that he earned less than $50,000 a year as a police officer and that he had *no other* source of income *except for* gifts from his mother." Bruce Keidan, "Brentwood Drops Vojtas Appeal," *Pitt. Post-Gaz.*, 10 Feb. 2001, at A1. Here the word *other* refers to something already mentioned (the $50,000 salary), as opposed to referring to something in a yet-to-be-completed *than*-clause.

LANGUAGE-CHANGE INDEX
*no other . . . except for *no other . . . than*: Stage 1
Current ratio (*no other person than* vs. **no other person except*): 10:1

C. And *otherwise.* See **otherwise (A).**

otherwise. A. And *other.* Pedants insist that *other* is the adjective, *otherwise* the adverb—and that it's wrong to use *otherwise* as an alternative to an adjective <no real impact, substantial or otherwise>. Wilson Follett believed that "to pronounce this *otherwise* inadmissible would be to fly in the face of a strongly established usage. But usage, which can allow it on sufferance, cannot prevent it from being rejected by more exact writers" (*MAU* at 242–43). In fact, though, this usage is so strongly established that—to most educated speakers—*other* would sound incorrect. E.g.: "Cowboys simply aren't cowboys—urban or *otherwise*—without a pair of boots between them and the ground." Dan R. Barber, "Boot Bonanza," *Dallas Morning News*, 11 Sept. 1997, at A33.

Of course, *otherwise* often functions adverbially as well—e.g.: "Paul Sanchez . . . said his business has been booming, financially and *otherwise*." David Snyder, "Vendors Confident Fair Will Be Successful," *Albuquerque Trib.*, 5 Sept. 1997, at A8.

B. As a Conjunction Meaning "or else." This slipshod usage, which leads to RUN-ON SENTENCES, occurs primarily in BrE. *Otherwise* shouldn't connect two clauses in a compound sentence—e.g.:

- "It's got to be attractive, *otherwise* people won't go there." George Martin, "Why My Montserrat Is More than Just a Home for Retired Rockers," *Evening Standard*, 11 Sept. 1997, at 23. (Put a period or semicolon after *attractive* and a comma after *otherwise*. Or else change *otherwise* to *or else*.)
- "The alliance needs to receive clearance from London, Washington and Brussels by November *otherwise* BA and American may not be able to launch joint services in time for next summer's timetable." Michael Harrison, "Brussels Urged to Relax Stance on BA Alliance," *Independent*, 12 Sept. 1997, at 21. (Put a period or semicolon after *November* and a comma after *otherwise*. Or else change *otherwise* to *or else*.)
- "But they cannot afford to do this, since they must believe that their view is correct, *otherwise* why would they be bothering to put it forward." Richard J. Evans, "Bound by the Web of Facts," *Fin. Times*, 13 Sept. 1997, at 4. (Put a period or semicolon after *correct* and a comma after *otherwise*.)

In each of those sentences, a period or semicolon should precede *otherwise*; after *otherwise*, the comma is optional but preferred.

otiose (= unneeded; not useful) is a word used more by literary critics than by other writers. You might say that the word itself is otiose—e.g.: "*Otiose* happens to be a word whose meaning the formidable William F. Buckley Jr. once confessed kept escaping him. Does the rather plain context of [Niall] Ferguson's passage warrant ransacking the language for a term so arcane that it baffles a Buckley?" Frederic Morton, "Dynasty:

LANGUAGE-CHANGE INDEX (For the full key, see front matter pp. xxxi, l–li.)
Stage 1: Rejected. Stage 2: Widely shunned. Stage 3: Widespread but . . . Stage 4: Ubiquitous but . . . Stage 5: Fully accepted.
Invariably inferior forms marked by asterisk (*). • Ratios represent frequency of prevalent forms vs. variants in current books.

The House of Rothschild," *L.A. Times*, 21 Nov. 1999, Book §, at 4. It appears much more commonly in BrE than in AmE—e.g.:

- "The question is *otiose*; they won't touch those things because they are politically dangerous." Richard Hoggart, "A Charge Too Far," *Observer*, 8 Dec. 1996, at 25.
- "Commentary on this novel seems *otiose*, after the recent brouhaha." "Journey with the Goods," *Guardian*, 20 Mar. 1997, Features §, at T15.
- "This set turns out to be a plea against pandering to stereotypes, against one generation preaching to another, against modern-day mediocrity in all its *otiose* reality-TV, electronic-tablet, Coke Light forms." Mark Monahan, "Comedy," *Daily Telegraph*, 22 Aug. 2015, at 19.

An alternative definition ("idle, at leisure") is labeled archaic in *NOAD*. It's certainly rare.

The preferred pronunciation in AmE is /**oh**-shee-ohs/. The BrE pronunciation /**oh**-tee-ohs/ sounds affected here.

otolaryngology; otorhinolaryngology. These are essentially synonymous words denoting the medical field dealing with the ears, nose, and throat. The *-rhino-* version manages to work in explicit reference to the nose, but the resulting word is downright proctological. So the shorter form, which is more widespread in medicine, is preferable. But most people don't say *otolaryngologist*; they say *ear, nose, and throat specialist*.

The words are pronounced as follows: *otolaryngology* /**oh**-toh-ler-in-**gol**-ə-jee/; *otorhinolaryngology* /**oh**-toh-**rī**-noh-ler-in-**gol**-ə-jee/.

Current ratio (in order of headwords): 5:1

ought. A. Infinitive Following. *Ought* (an old past tense and past participle of *owe*, now a modal auxiliary verb) should always be followed by a full infinitive, whether the phrase is *ought to* or *ought not to*—e.g.:

- "Clinton to this day insists his day-and-night shakedown of contributors constituted, at one and the same time, action that *ought to be* illegal, but an innocent exercise in democracy and the free play of ideas." John Hall, "Few Mourn End of Thompson's Hearings, and That Is a Shame," *Richmond Times-Dispatch*, 6 Nov. 1997, at A9.
- "Editors *ought not to have been* so thin-skinned when asked to participate in the recent forums." William McGaughey Jr., "Star Tribune Should've Taken Part in Media and Public Forums," *Star Trib.* (Minneapolis), 22 Nov. 1997, at A23.
- "Cats *ought not to be* let out at night in a coyote's range." "Cape Elizabeth Coyotes," *Portland Press Herald*, 1 Dec. 1997, at A4.

As if striving to earn some type of scholastic badge, some writers omit the particle *to*, especially when the expression is in the negative or interrogative. But there is no warrant for the bare infinitive—e.g.:

- "A postmodern view of organizational culture argues that we *ought not think* [read *ought not to think* or *should not think*] of socialization as a series of social acquisitions that occur in unchanging contexts." William G. Tierney, "Organizational Socialization in Higher Education," *J. Higher Educ.*, 1 Jan. 1997, at 1.

- "But what happened in southwest Iowa *ought not be* [read *ought not to be* or *shouldn't be*] repeated." "Human Factor Needed in Redistricting," *Omaha World-Herald*, 28 Nov. 1997, at 28.
- "The service area's outgoing board *ought not do* [read *ought not to do* or *shouldn't do*] anything in its final month to earn even greater opprobrium." "Distrust in Kearns," *Salt Lake Trib.*, 1 Dec. 1997, at A10.

LANGUAGE-CHANGE INDEX
*ought not be for *ought not to be*: Stage 2
Current ratio (*ought not to be* vs. **ought not be*): 13:1

B. And *should*. *Ought* should be reserved for expressions of necessity, duty, or obligation; *should*, the slightly weaker but more usual word, especially in speech, expresses appropriateness, suitability, or fittingness.

C. **Had ought*. This phrasing is nonstandard in place of *ought*—e.g.:

- "You *had ought* [read *ought*] to see some of the aeroplanes travel here and see some of the battles in the clouds." Norm Maves Jr., "Rats the Size of Half-Grown Mules Visit Trenches," *Oregonian* (Portland), 8 Nov. 1994, at B1.
- "I shall now inform readers of The Press-Enterprise of a high-class, real keen, really cool culture and entertainment institution that they *had ought* [read *ought*] to know about and go to some time." T.E. Foreman, "Bowled Over by Hollywood Amphitheater," *Press-Enterprise* (Riverside, Cal.), 17 Sept. 1995, at E2.
- "If anything, the players *had ought* [read *ought*] to go on strike." Zac Gershberg, "The Sordid Business of Football," *Idaho State J.*, 7 Sept. 2014, at 15.

See DOUBLE MODALS.

LANGUAGE-CHANGE INDEX
*had ought for *ought*: Stage 1

D. *Oughtn't*. This quaint CONTRACTION sometimes appears. The same principles govern its use as those governing *ought*. That is, it should be followed by the full infinitive, not a bare infinitive—e.g.:

- "Kennedy and his top aides scratched their heads at the revelation, wondering if something *oughtn't* to be done." Paul Berman, "The Patriot," *L.A. Times*, 2 July 2000, Book §, at 9.
- "It *oughtn't* [read *oughtn't to*] be allowed to sit in a vault, or even in a glass case in a museum." Joseph Epstein, "The Master's Ring," *Commentary*, 1 Oct. 2000, at 49, 56.
- "Well, they *oughtn't* to try it with 'Crime in Suburbia.'" Marc Mohan, "Crime and Punishment in Suburbia," *Oregonian* (Portland), 5 Jan. 2001, at 33.

Most writers would use the far more natural word *shouldn't*.

E. **Ought to could*. See DOUBLE MODALS.

F. Confused with *aught*. See **aught** (c).

-OUR. See -OR.

ours, an absolute possessive, is sometimes wrongly written **our's*—e.g.:

- "'We don't have nearly the physical challenge here that we had there,' Barnett conceded. '*Our's* [read *Ours*] is more mental.'" B.G. Brooks, "Back in Focus," *Rocky Mountain News* (Denver), 29 Aug. 1999, at N10.

- "Our selectmen are bypassing the intent of federal law for cases such as *our's* [read *ours*] because they think that in being more accommodating to Massport, they will somehow win special relief." Lori Eggert, "Bedford Town Meaning to Air Participation in FAA Suit," *Boston Globe*, 14 Jan. 2001, Northwest Weekly §, at 5.
- "'*Our's* [read *Ours*] is a good market,' Embry said of the Tri-County Area." Steve Tarter, "Home Sales Hit New High," *Peoria J. Star*, 13 Feb. 2001, at C1.

See POSSESSIVES (C).

LANGUAGE-CHANGE INDEX
our's for *ours*: Stage 1
Current ratio (*ours* vs. *our's*): 555:1

ourself; ourselves; *theirself. *Ourself* is technically ill formed, since *our* is plural and *self* is singular. In the preferred form, *ourselves*, both parts are plural. *Ourself* is established, though, in the editorial or royal style—e.g.: "You'd be surprised how hard it is to write a column from the shower. *We've* been stuck in here, hosing *ourself* down, since watching Michael Jackson creep the hell out of the entire country." Tim Goodman, "Jackson Show Is Over, but He's Still Creeping Us Out," *S.F. Chron.*, 12 Feb. 2003, at D1. But *theirself for *themselves*, increasingly common since 1900, is indefensible (see SEXISM (B)).

out. A. As an Unnecessary Particle in Phrasal Verbs. *Out* is usually superfluous in phrases such as *calculate out, *cancel out, *distribute out, *segregate out, and *separate out. (Colloquially, it occurs in *figure out*, *lose out*, *make out*, *test out*, *try out*, and *work out*.) See PHRASAL VERBS.

But sometimes *out* is quite necessary—e.g.: "At the time of the crash, the FAA said potentially explosive sparks had been '*designed out*' of all big-jet fuel tanks." Robert Davis, "FAA Agrees to Fuel-Tank Changes," *USA Today*, 4 Dec. 1997, at A4. The phrase *design out* (= to rid of [an undesirable characteristic]) is common in patent contexts.

B. As a Noun. This usage <she was looking for an out> is a CASUALISM.

outbid > outbid > outbid. So inflected. *Outbidden is an error confined mostly to BrE and Australian English—e.g.: "They admit to feeling plenty of pressure to find their dream home in the current market, having been *outbidden* [read *outbid*] on numerous occasions." Andrew Carswell, "House Price Frenzy," *Daily Telegraph*, 2 Oct. 2013, at 15.

outdoor(s); out-of-door(s). *Outdoor* is the better, more economical choice for the adjective <outdoor activities>. *Out-of-door* is a formal and awkward equivalent <an out-of-door affair>, and *out-of-doors* is even creakier.

Outdoors and *out-of-doors* are both adverbs. Once again, *outdoors* is the better choice.

And, of course, *outdoors* is also a noun <the great outdoors>.

out loud. See **aloud.**

out-of-door(s). See **outdoor(s).**

out of sync. See **sync.**

outside does not need *of*—hence *outside the house*, not **outside of the house*. E.g.: "Italian goods have done well *outside of* [read *outside*] the Continent because the lira has fallen 15% vs. the U.S. dollar in the past year." James C. Cooper & Kathleen Madigan, "Sprinting Toward Entry in the EMU," *Business Week*, 15 Sept. 1997, at 31. In modern print sources, the collocation *outside the* occurs about five times as often as *outside of the. See **of (B).** Cf. ***off of.**

When *outside of appears in the sense *apart from* or *aside from*, either of those phrases would be more serviceable—e.g.: "*Outside of* [read *Apart from* or *Aside from*] economies of scale in purchasing and merged back-room operations, Pillowtex reaps Fieldcrest's well-known brands in sheets, comforters, [and] towels." Jennifer Steinhauer, "Pillowtex to Acquire Fieldcrest for $400 Million," *N.Y. Times*, 12 Sept. 1997, at D6.

LANGUAGE-CHANGE INDEX
outside of for *outside*: Stage 4
Current ratio (*outside the* vs. *outside of the): 5:1

outsized; outsize, adj. The first is standard AmE. The second is standard BrE.

Current ratio (*outsized head* vs. *outsize head* in AmE): 3:1
Current ratio (*outsize head* vs. *outsized head* in BrE): 1.3:1

outward(s). See DIRECTIONAL WORDS (A).

ova. See **ovum.**

over. A. For *more than*. In one of its uses, the prepositional *over* is interchangeable with *more than* <over 600 people were there>—and this has been so for more than 600 years. The charge that *over* is inferior to *more than* is a baseless crotchet. E.g.:

- "Reagan won the election by *over* a million votes." Gerard De Groot, "Reagan's Rise," *History Today*, Sept. 1995, at 31.
- "He breaks off . . . from reporting the injustices inflicted on Beethoven's Fifth Symphony (well *over* a hundred pages) to voice vigorous approval of Carlos Kleiber." Paul Griffiths, "What's the Score?" *N.Y. Times*, 24 Aug. 1997, § 7, at 11. Cf. **above (A).**

In 2014 even the Associated Press came around, finally sanctioning *over* "in all uses to indicate greater numerical value." One curmudgeonly copyeditor snapped back: "More than my dead body!"

LANGUAGE-CHANGE INDEX
over in the sense "more than": Stage 5

LANGUAGE-CHANGE INDEX (For the full key, see front matter pp. xxxi, l–li.)
Stage 1: Rejected. **Stage 2:** Widely shunned. **Stage 3:** Widespread but . . . **Stage 4:** Ubiquitous but . . . **Stage 5:** Fully accepted. Invariably inferior forms marked by asterisk (*). • Ratios represent frequency of prevalent forms vs. variants in current books.

B. *Over-* as a Combining Form. See **overly.*

overall is a VOGUE WORD, often a lame SENTENCE ADVERB. Many sentences would read better without it—e.g.:

- "*Overall, Wada* [read *Wada*] says Toyota has doubled its engineering output over the past four years." Alex Taylor III, "How Toyota Defies Gravity," *Fortune,* 8 Dec. 1997, at 100.
- "*Overall, Berea's statistics* [read *Berea's statistics*] speak worlds about the demand for affordable higher education; this year, the college accepted only 22 percent of its applicants." Tamar Lewin, "With No Frills or Tuition, a College Draws Attention," *N.Y. Times,* 21 July 2008, at A12.

overarching /oh-vər-**ahr**-ching/. The *-ch-* is sometimes mispronounced with a /k/ sound.

overdo; overdue. The first is the verb (= to do too much), the second the adjective (= past due, late). But the two are sometimes confounded—e.g.:

- " 'If you have blue eyes, bring them out. But when you do, don't *overdue* [read *overdo*] it with too much makeup or jewelry.' " "By Design," *L.A. Times,* 16 June 1994, at E3 (quoting Homer Prefontaine).
- "The Izod Center—eaten alive by the Xanadu mess at the Meadowlands—needs millions in long-*overdo* [read *over-due*] improvements for it to continue as a viable home." Steve Politi, "It's Time to Bring Nets to Newark," *Star-Ledger* (Newark), 2 May 2008, at 31.

LANGUAGE-CHANGE INDEX
1. *overdo* misused for *overdue*: Stage 1
2. *overdue* misused for *overdo*: Stage 1
Current ratio (*overdo them* vs.
*overdue them): 59:1

overestimate. See **underestimate.**

overflow > overflowed > overflowed. Some writers mistakenly use *overflown* as the past participle of *overflow*—e.g.:

- "But water has *overflown* [read *overflowed*] the levee at least four times since it was built." Missy Baxter, "Levee Project Halted After Flood Proves New Wall Would Have Failed," *Courier-J.* (Louisville), 14 Apr. 1997, at B2.
- "Though waste was found in a lagoon at the farm, some waste had *overflown* [read *overflowed*] at a lift station designed to pump it from four hog houses to the lagoon." Hannah Mitchell, "Hog Waste Feared Leaking into River," *Morning Star* (Wilmington, N.C.), 10 July 1997, at B1.

See IRREGULAR VERBS (D). For a short, interesting study of this term, see Ann Eljenholm Nichols, "The Past Participle of 'Overflow': 'Overflowed' or 'Over-flown,' " 41 *Am. Speech* 52 (Feb. 1966).

LANGUAGE-CHANGE INDEX
overflown misused for *overflowed* as past participle
of *overflow*: Stage 1
Current ratio (*overflowed its banks* vs.
*overflown its banks): 44:1

overfly > overflew > overflown. Oddly, this verb dates from the 14th century. Though never common, it's become more so in the age of flight—e.g.: "It'll be the first time the shuttle crew has *overflown* the heartland since the 2003 Columbia tragedy." Mark Carreau, "Shuttle Begins Journey Home," *Houston Chron.,* 6 Nov. 2007, at A4.

overlay; overlie. To *overlay* is to spread (something) on top of; to overspread <she intended to overlay the culture plates with bacteria>. To *overlie* is either to lie above <the preserve overlies vast oil deposits> or to smother by lying on <ash from an eruption would overlie valuable winery fields>.

As with *lay* and *lie,* the most common error is to use *overlay* when the proper word is *overlie.* One signal of the misuse is putting the present participle *overlaying* at the beginning of the sentence—e.g.:

- "*Overlaying* [read *Overlying*] all this was a perfectionism so intense that it was difficult to get products out of the lab, let alone to market." Betsy Morris, "Big Blue," *Fortune,* 14 Apr. 1997, at 68, 71.
- "*Overlaying* [read *Overlying*] these hypernaturalistic scenes are evocations of the slain woman's spirit intoning nonsense rhymes in a high girlish voice." Stephen Holden, "Deadliness of Military Life," *N.Y. Times,* 2 May 1997, at C33.
- "*Overlaying* [read *Overlying*] all of [delete *of*] this is the recent Supreme Court ruling upholding Obamacare exchanges." "Upheaval in Health Care Hitting Region," *Beaumont Enterprise* (Tex.), 2 July 2015, at 6.

See **lay.**

LANGUAGE-CHANGE INDEX
overlay misused for *overlie*: Stage 3

overlook; oversee; look over. To *overlook* is to neglect or disregard. To *oversee* is to supervise or superintend. To *look over* is to examine.

Although historically *overlook* bore the meanings of *oversee* and *look over* (see *OED*), the word has narrowed its sense in STANDARD ENGLISH. Today it's sloppy to use it interchangeably with *oversee*—e.g.: " 'It will improve the quality of the water,' said Mark Norton, who *overlooks* [read *oversees*] projects for a joint powers agency." Vanessa Colon, "Underwater Propellers to Save Fish," *Press-Enterprise* (Riverside, Cal.), 31 Jan. 2003, at B1. See **oversight.**

LANGUAGE-CHANGE INDEX
overlook misused for *oversee*: Stage 2

*overly. Although it's old, dating from about the 12th century, **overly* was never much used until about 1950. It is almost always unnecessary because *over-* may be prefixed at will: *overbroad, overrefined, overoptimistic, overripe,* etc. When *overly* is not unnecessary, it's merely ugly. Some authorities consider **overly* semiliterate, although the editors of the Merriam-Webster dictionaries have used it in a number of definitions. Certainly this adverb should be avoided whenever possible, though admittedly *over-* as a prefix sometimes just doesn't sound right (*overburdensome*). Yet it usually serves well—e.g.: "To supporters, Duke's initiative was a worthy, if *overly ambitious* [read *overambitious*], effort." Peter Applebome, "Duke Learns of Pitfalls in Promise of Hiring More Black Professors," *N.Y. Times,* 19 Sept. 1993, at

1. When *over-* is awkward or ugly-sounding, another word is invariably at the ready—e.g.:

- "Hence the UN inspectors were not *overly* [read *especially*] skeptical when they started their work of scrutinizing Iraq's arsenal of weapons of mass destruction." "Saddam's UN Nemesis," *Boston Globe*, 8 June 1997, at D6.
- "There are certain things that are correct in one context but *overly* [read *unduly*] formal or stuffy in another." Mary Newton Brudner, *The Grammar Lady* 6 (2000).
- "The harsher attacks create some risk for McCain, analysts say, because he may come off as *overly* [read *too*] negative." Jill Zuckman, "McCain Ad Fights Rival's Celebrity Head-On," *Chicago Trib.*, 31 July 2008, News §, at 1.

LANGUAGE-CHANGE INDEX
overly instead of *unduly* or the prefix *over-*: Stage 4
Current ratio (*overeager* vs.
overly eager): 3:1

oversea(s), adj. The standard form is *overseas* <we didn't send brochures to overseas clients>. *Oversea* is a variant form.

Current ratio: 106:1

oversee. See **overlook.**

oversight. A. As a Noun. *Oversight* = (1) an unintentional error; or (2) intentional and watchful supervision. For sense 2, *oversight* is an unfortunate choice of word: *supervision* is preferable, or perhaps even *monitoring*. Indeed, *administrative oversight* sounds less like a responsibility than a bureaucratic botch. See CONTRONYMS.

B. As a Jargonistic Verb. In some fields, people have begun using *oversight* as a verb in place of *oversee*—or, more often, *oversighting* in place of *overseeing* or the simple *oversight* itself. The usage is common in Australia, but elsewhere it occurs primarily in speech—e.g.:

- "'The whole company is reviewing and *oversighting* [read *overseeing*] what is going on at the Zion station,' Reed said at a meeting." Robert Enstad, "Edison Says It's Fixing Zion Plan," *Chicago Trib.*, 1 Feb. 1991, at C4 (quoting a utility company's senior vice president).
- "Of that 66 percent, there're likely to be a whole lot who voted to put [Tom] Udall into Congress, and they might be very annoyed over Congress wasting its time in such *oversighting* [read *oversight*]!" Letter of William R. Dales, "Phone Taps OK," *Santa Fe New Mexican*, 16 May 2006, at A5.
- "The investigative mechanism of Congress will be brought to bear fully on Iraq. Because that's the mechanism by which Democrats tell their activists they're dealing with Iraq: 'Hey, we're investigating. We're *oversighting* [read *overseeing*] them.'" Bill Steigerwald, "Now Come the Dems" (interview with reporter Major Garrett), *Pitt. Trib.-Rev.*, 6 Jan. 2007.

See JARGON & **overlook.**

LANGUAGE-CHANGE INDEX
oversighting for *overseeing*: Stage 1

oversized; *oversize, adj. The first is standard <an oversized box>. The second is a NEEDLESS VARIANT.

Current ratio (*oversized engine* vs.
oversize engine): 3:1

OVERSTATEMENT. In persuasive or even polemical prose, such words as *clearly, patently, obviously,* and *indisputably* generally weaken rather than strengthen the statements they preface. They have been debased by overuse. Critics have noted that a writer who begins a sentence with one of these words is likely to be stating something questionable. See **clearly** & SENTENCE ADVERBS.

Unconscious overstatement is also a problem. It is never good to overstate one's case, even in minor, unconscious ways, since doing so will make the writing less credible. Unless the purpose is to be humorous or satirical, good writers avoid exaggeration.

overthrow, n.; ***overthrowal.** The latter, a NEEDLESS VARIANT that cropped up in the 1830s and has persisted, isn't recorded in most dictionaries. But it does, unfortunately, occur—e.g.:

- "The military says more than 2,000 people had been killed in insurgency-related incidents since the February *overthrowal* [read *overthrow*] of President Ferdinand Marcos." "Philippine Rebel Leader in Favor of Peace Talks," *Chicago Trib.*, 13 Nov. 1986, at C4.
- "It was just completed at the time of his *overthrowal* [read *overthrow*] and death in 1989, and the present Parliament uses it now." Elizabeth Shannon, "Flair, Mystery Fill Romania," *Boston Globe*, 7 Mar. 1999, at M5.

LANGUAGE-CHANGE INDEX
overthrowal for the noun *overthrow*: Stage 1
Current ratio (*the overthrow of* vs.
the overthrowal of): 1,028:1

overweening (= presumptuous, arrogant, or immoderate) is so spelled—but the misspelling *overweaning* is common. The word derives from the Old English verb *wenan*, meaning "to hope or believe." It has nothing to do with the verb *to wean* (see **wean**). E.g.:

- "Bush has a certain self-confidence, as one Democrat put it, so that he doesn't exude an *overweaning* [read *overweening*] need to fill up every corner of every room with his magnificent presence, or be right all the time." Carolyn Lochhead, "The Name of the Game," *S.F. Chron.*, 12 Feb. 2001, at A25.
- "The law of averages trumped Rivera's *overweaning* [read *overweening*] pride." Stephen Cannella, "Inside Baseball," *Sports Illustrated*, 23 Apr. 2001, at 78.

The word is sometimes misused for *overwhelming*. Jacques Barzun cites the example of a suggestion "greeted with *overweening* [read *overwhelming*] disapproval." *Simple and Direct* 30 (1975).

LANGUAGE-CHANGE INDEX
1. *overweening* misspelled *overweaning*: Stage 1
2. *overweening* misused to mean "overwhelming":
Stage 1

LANGUAGE-CHANGE INDEX (For the full key, see front matter pp. xxxi, l–li.)
Stage 1: Rejected. **Stage 2:** Widely shunned. **Stage 3:** Widespread but . . . **Stage 4:** Ubiquitous but . . . **Stage 5:** Fully accepted.
Invariably inferior forms marked by asterisk (*). • Ratios represent frequency of prevalent forms vs. variants in current books.

ovum (= the female reproductive cell; egg cell) forms the plural *ova*—not **ovums*. See PLURALS (B).

Current ratio: 644:1

owing, adj.; **owed.** Although *owing* in the sense of *owed* is an old and established usage <$45 was owing on the bill>, the more logical course is simply to write *owed* where one means *owed*. That's precisely what most writers and editors do today: beginning about 1970, the collocation *amount owed to* overtook *amount owing to* in frequency of use in print sources. The active participle may sometimes cause MISCUES—e.g.:

- "I examine company reports for details of money *owing from* [read *owed by*] customers." Kevin Goldstein-Jackson, "Can You Trust the Accounts?" *Fin. Times,* 22 Feb. 1997, at 2.
- "Taxpayers who owe taxes for 1996 still have to pay the balance *owing* [read *owed*] by April 30." Michael Kane, "Fewer than Half Have Yet to File," *Vancouver Sun,* 26 Apr. 1997, at H1.

See PASSIVE VOICE.

Current ratio (*amount owed to* vs. **amount owing to*): 3:1

owing to (= because of) is an acceptable dangling modifier now primarily confined to BrE—e.g.: "Prolonged rain in the West Country has caused today's meeting at Newton Abbot to be abandoned *owing to* waterlogging." "Racing: Newton Abbot Off Due to Waterlogging," *Independent,* 2 Dec. 1997, at 29.

Yet it does occur in AmE—e.g.:

- "There's a great deal of humor in the story, *owing to* the ironic distance that this method of telling lends to the tale." Marion Garmel, "Scrooge's Timeless Tale at IRT Showcases Strong Ensemble Work," *Indianapolis Star,* 2 Dec. 1997, at E3.
- "*Owing to* years of screaming at each other across the newsroom of the Washington Post, hosts Tony Kornheiser and Mike Wilbon have the same comic timing as Bob Hope and Bing Crosby." David Barron, "A Look at Best of Sports TV as 2002 Ends," *Houston Chron.,* 30 Dec. 2002, Sports §, at 7.
- "The stalking, which continues sporadically today, is at once bizarre, terrifying and, *owing to* Paul's deep pockets, maddeningly relentless and difficult to trace, according to the book." Andy Newman, "Stalked: A Decade on the Run," *N.Y. Times,* 31 July 2008, at G1.

Cf. **due to.** See DANGLERS (E).

OXFORD COMMA. See PUNCTUATION (D).

oxidize, oddly, forms the noun *oxidation,* not **oxidization.* But some writers mistakenly use the longer form—e.g.:

- "While the shelving wasn't in danger of collapsing, it was expanding as it rusted—a natural result of *oxidization* [read *oxidation*]." J. Linn Allen, "Prudential Face Lift Draws Some Frowns," *Chicago Trib.,* 21 Dec. 1996, at 1.
- "Beans or tomatoes . . . are quite acidic and may turn black when *oxidization* [read *oxidation*] occurs from an improperly seasoned pan." Sylvia Carter, "Cast Iron, the Metal of a Good Cook," *Newsday* (N.Y.), 19 Feb. 1997, at B19.

- "Grapes were left on the vine for too long and then once picked weren't chilled long enough, resulting in *oxidization* [read *oxidation*]." "Scottish Wine Still Needs Refining," *Winnipeg Free Press,* 25 July 2015, at D14.

Meanwhile, **oxidate* is a NEEDLESS VARIANT of *oxidize.*

LANGUAGE-CHANGE INDEX
1. **oxidization* for *oxidation*: Stage 1
Current ratio (*oxidation* vs. **oxidization*): 178:1
2. **oxidate* for *oxidize*: Stage 1
Current ratio (*oxidize* vs. **oxidate*): 129:1

OXYMORONS. A. Generally. This term, originally a Greek word meaning "keenly foolish" or "sharply dull," denotes an immediate contradiction in terminology. Thus:

amateur expert	intense apathy
baby grand	mandatory choice
build down	nonworking mother
conspicuous absence	organized mess
exact estimate	pretty ugly
executive secretary	standard deviation
found missing	sure bet

Among language aficionados, collecting and inventing cynical oxymorons is a parlor game; they enjoy phrases that seem to imply contradictions, such as *military intelligence, legal brief,* and *greater Cleveland* (this last being quite unfair to a great city).

Writers sometimes use oxymorons to good effect—e.g.: "And there was, moreover, an irresponsibly giddy antigovernment fervor among the more *sophomoric House freshmen.*" Joe Klein, "The Unabomber and the Left," *Newsweek,* 22 Apr. 1996, at 39. The main thing to avoid is seemingly unconscious incongruity such as **increasingly less* or **advancing backwards.*

B. Plural. Although most dictionaries list only the Greek plural *oxymora,* Margaret Nicholson listed *oxymorons* first in 1957 (*DAEU* at 403). In fact, *oxymorons* is now about six times as common as *oxymora* in print sources, and it ought to be accepted as standard—e.g.: "*Oxymorons,* like beauty, seem to be in the eye of the beholder." Mary Newton Bruder, *The Grammar Lady* 166 (2000). See PLURALS (B).

Today, *oxymora* looks pedantic—e.g.:

- "If time is money, then Florida's 'toll-free' consumer hot lines are *oxymora* [read *oxymorons*]." "State Tries to Make Its Hot Lines More Efficient, Less Expensive," *Orlando Sentinel,* 23 Oct. 1995, at C1.
- "During a fall month of a Major League Baseball season, former catcher/manager Yogi Berra, the king of *oxymora* [read *oxymorons*], once noted that it was getting 'later earlier.'" "July Was 2nd Driest on Record," *Indianapolis Star,* 6 Aug. 1997, at B4.
- "Add this to your list of government *oxymora* [read *oxymorons*]: Priority Mail." Rick Brooks, "Priority Mail Fails Test of Time," *Times Union* (Albany), 30 May 2002, at A1.

LANGUAGE-CHANGE INDEX
oxymorons as the plural for *oxymoron*: Stage 5
Current ratio (*oxymorons* vs. *oxymora*): 6:1

P

pabulum; pablum. *Pabulum* /**pab**-yə-ləm/ = (1) food, nourishment; (2) nourishment for the mind; or (3) a soft, bland cereal for babies. *Pablum*, with a capital *P*, is a trademark for a brand of the cereal *pabulum* (sense 3). The lowercase *pablum* (formed through syncope) has taken on the figurative sense "bland, trite, or simplistic writing or ideas"—e.g.: "Still, the raw charm of her pipes is strong enough to turn *pablum* such as 'Just Missed the Train' and Ms. Warren's 'Some Kind of Miracle' into pure ear candy." Thor Christensen, "A Voice Carries Only So Far," *Dallas Morning News*, 20 Apr. 2003, at G12. *Pabulum* sometimes carries this meaning also, but in modern print sources *pablum* outnumbers it by more than two to one in this sense— e.g.: "With 'Butterfly,' Carey moves further away from the gorgeously sung pop *pablum* . . . and into her role as the Barbra Streisand of her generation." Michael Corcoran, "Mariah Carey Takes Flight on 'Butterfly,'" *Austin Am.-Statesman*, 16 Sept. 1997, at E1. Other than that one use, however, the longer word has always appeared much more frequently in print.

pace, prep. (/**pay**-see/ or /**pah**-chay/), is a LATINISM meaning originally "with peace to," and today "with all due respect to." It is used most often when the writer expresses a contrary position—e.g.:

- "*Pace* Mr. Spalding, the church's traditional condemnation of abortion is constant and unchanging." Letter of Brian J. Shanley, "Constant on Abortion," *Wash. Post*, 14 Feb. 1995, at A14.
- "[Visual artistry] shouldn't even try [to do what a novel does], Henry James says in the preface to 'The Golden Bowl' (incidentally, a novel that—*pace* Ms. Ozick—I'm about to make into a film, my third joyful encounter with Henry James)." Letter of James Ivory, "Novels on Film," *N.Y. Times*, 19 Jan. 1997, § 2, at 6.
- "A democracy, *pace* Mr Salmond, is a permanent discussion, an endless negotiation." Chris Deerin, "Salmond Called it a 'Dark Star' but London Is a Beacon That Befits Us All," *Scottish Daily Mail*, 26 May 2014, at 14.

The word was at its literary height in 1900; it has since become much less frequent in print.

pacifist; *pacificist; passivist. *Pacifist* (= one opposed to war or other physical conflict) is the established form. Etymologists formerly argued that **pacificist* is the better-formed word, but it's no picnic to pronounce—which is probably why today it's no more than a NEEDLESS VARIANT. Although R.W. Burchfield says that "the shorter form is now the only one in use" (*FMEU3* at 566), the longer form is lamentably common in AmE—e.g.: "And then there are the *pacificists* [read *pacifists*], groups like the historic American Friends Service Committee founded by Quakers in 1917, which plans to host an exhibit called 'The Costs of War,' detailing how the $720 million spent each day on the war could be spent on education and housing." Colleen O'Connor, "Activists to Color Democratic Convention," *Houston Chron.*, 22 June 2008, at A19.

The term *passivist* (= one with a passive attitude or way of life) is usually set against *activist*—e.g.:

- "Sitting-in seems more *passivist* than activist, but activism can apparently take many shapes, including simple relentlessness." Russell Baker, "Activism Epidemic!" *N.Y. Times*, 28 June 1994, at A17.
- "McCain also seems stunningly unaware that the justices he simplistically lauds as 'judicial *passivists*' are nothing of the sort." Geoffrey R. Stone, "McCain's Justice: Conservative Activism Gone Wild," *Chicago Trib.*, 7 May 2008, at C23.

LANGUAGE-CHANGE INDEX
pacificist for *pacifist*: Stage 1
Current ratio (*pacifist* vs. **pacificist*): 104:1

paean. A. And *pean; paeon; peon. A *paean* (/**pee**-in/) is a joyous tribute. (**Pean* is a variant spelling.) A *paeon* (/**pee**-in/ or /**pee**-ahn/) is a four-syllable metrical foot in classical or English prosody. The two words have a common origin (the Greek word *paiōn*) and came into English at about the same time—1589 and 1603, respectively—but have been differentiated almost all that time. (See DIFFERENTIATION.) A *peon* (/**pee**-ahn/) is a low-level worker or drudge, especially one held in compulsory servitude. There are two plurals: *peons* (preferred) and **peones* (/pay-**oh**-neez/—a Portuguese plural). See PLURALS (A).

B. *Paean of praise. Because a *paean* is specifically a song of praise or thanksgiving, the phrase **paean of praise* is a REDUNDANCY intended perhaps to provide contextual clues to those with an etiolated vocabulary— e.g.: "She recited a moving *paean of praise* [read *paean*] when the order 'Pour le Mérite' was conferred on me." Dietrich Fischer-Dieskau, *Reverberations* 313 (Ruth Hein trans., 1989).

***paederast.** See **pederast.**

paella (the Spanish dish made with rice, meats, and vegetables) is pronounced /pah-**ay**-yə/ or /pɪ-**el**-ə/.

pail. For the mistaken phrase **beyond the pail*, see **pale.**

pailful. Pl. *pailfuls*. See PLURALS (G).

pair. A. Plural Form. The preferred plural of *pair* is *pairs*—a choice that became predominant by 1850, when the matter should have been settled. In nonstandard usage, *pair* often appears as a plural—e.g.:

LANGUAGE-CHANGE INDEX (For the full key, see front matter pp. xxxi, l–li.)
Stage 1: Rejected. **Stage 2:** Widely shunned. **Stage 3:** Widespread but . . . **Stage 4:** Ubiquitous but . . . **Stage 5:** Fully accepted.
Invariably inferior forms marked by asterisk (*). • Ratios represent frequency of prevalent forms vs. variants in current books.

"The ASU outburst matched a 9-year-old record set ironically enough by Miami when Greg Ellena and Rusty DeBold hit two apiece in a five-homer game against Stanford in 1985. In addition to Cruz's and Williamson's *pair* [read *pairs*], Todd Cady hit a solo shot—his 11th—for the team's first run." Kirk Bohls, "Devils Oust Miami," *Austin Am.-Statesman*, 8 June 1994, at E1.

Language-Change Index
pair as a plural for *pairs*: Stage 3
Current ratio (*two pairs* vs. *two pair*): 6:1

B. *Pair of twins.* Is it right to speak of a *pair of twins*—that is, does this phrase denote two people or four? Because twins are always two per birth, a *pair of twins* is two people. (Shoes also come in pairs, and a *pair of shoes* is two—not four—shoes.) Four twins are two pairs of twins. But the redundant phrase *pair of twins* can be found in print sources fairly steadily from 1800 to the present day.

pajamas; pyjamas. The former is the AmE spelling, the latter BrE. The word is best pronounced /pə-**jah**-məz/, not /pə-**jam**-əz/.

pale, beyond the. This phrase, which means "bizarre, outside the bounds of civilized behavior," derives from the legal sense of *pale* from English history ("a district or territory within specific bounds, or subject to a particular jurisdiction"). In medieval Ireland, the district around Dublin, settled by the English and considered a law-abiding area, was known as the *Pale* or *within the Pale.* The land beyond that area was characterized as wild "bandit country." Today, whatever is *beyond the pale* is a forbidden area or subject.

Modern writers occasionally mangle the phrase by writing *beyond the pail instead of *pale*, a blunder that spread especially after 1950. E.g.:

- "To have a panel of citizens and the Commonwealth's Attorney . . . call for the board members' resignations with such harsh and demeaning language, however, is beyond the *pail* [read *pale*]." "School Board Members' Resignation Letters," *Virginian-Pilot & Ledger Star* (Norfolk), 10 Mar. 1996, at 7.
- "Justice [William] Brennan, who authored the opinion in *Roth* that placed obscenity *beyond the pail* [read *beyond the pale*] of First Amendment protection, now dissented." John E. Semouche, *Censoring Sex* 45 (2007). (Here, though, *beyond the pale* would also be inappropriate, unless you consider the First Amendment "outside the bounds of civilized behavior.")

Language-Change Index
*beyond the pail for *beyond the pale*: Stage 1
Current ratio (*beyond the pale* vs.
*beyond the pail): 398:1

palette; palate; pallet. *Palette* (= [1] a board used by artists for mixing colors; or [2] a set or range of colors) is sometimes misused for its homophone *palate* (= [1] the roof of the mouth; or [2] the sense of taste). It's an exquisite solecism, if there is such a thing:

- "When Ginny Lang moves from Georgetown to Los Angeles, one of the places she will miss most is Sugar's, a Georgetown convenience store that for 50 years has served a range of tastes, from sophisticated *palettes* [read *palates*] to the junk food preferences of college students." Tara Stevens, "A Stool at Sugar's Is a Special Spot in Georgetown," *Wash. Post*, 27 Sept. 1984, at D1.
- "Dr. Bill Magee, a plastic surgeon and founder of Operation Smile, was there and fixed the cleft *palette* [read *palate*] of the girl, Meng Fang." Mya Frazier, "Doctor Learns of Love Through Chinese Man's Travails," *Columbus Dispatch*, 24 June 1995, at C5.

Language-Change Index
palette misused for *palate*: Stage 1

pall; pallor. *Pall* = (1) a piece of cloth draped over a coffin or tomb, or (2) a shortened form of *pallium*, a robe worn by a bishop or by a monarch at a coronation. It is sense 1 that appears figuratively in the set phrase *to cast a pall over* (a situation), meaning to have a sense of gloom and defeat settle in. *Pallor* = paleness of face, esp. a deathly lack of color.

Both words suggest that things aren't right. But there the difference ends: a *pallor* is a paleness in the face, while a *pall* is something that causes gloom. Only a *pall*, not a *pallor*, is cast or hung. One grows pallid at the thought of these misuses:

- "In fact, a *pallor* [read *pall*] hung over the Coming Out Week activities at the University of Minnesota, said Kjersten Reich, 20, of the Queer Student Cultural Center." Rosalind Bentley, "Many Say Shepard Symbolizes Struggle of Gays and Lesbians," *Star Trib.* (Minneapolis), 14 Oct. 1998, at A1.
- "The strong-arm tactics cast a *pallor* [read *pall*] over the once-lustrous Espy name." Charles Whitaker, "Mike Espy: Bruised but Unbowed," *Ebony*, 1 Apr. 1999, at 98.
- "Commerce students said the noontime fights cast a *pallor* [read *pall*] on the rest of the day." Mary Ellen O'Shea, "5 Arrested at Commerce After Fights," *Springfield Union-News*, 19 Oct. 2002, at B1.

Language-Change Index
pallor misused for *pall*: Stage 1

palmetto. Pl. *palmettos*—not *palmettoes. See plurals (d).

Current ratio: 9:1

palomino. So spelled. See spelling (a).

palpable (lit., "touchable") = tangible; apparent. There is nothing wrong with using this word in figurative senses <palpable weaknesses in the argument>, as it has been used since at least the 15th century.

What is nonsensical, however, is to say that the *level* of frustration, tension, etc. is palpable—e.g.:

- "While Tyagachev and his colleagues conveyed a degree of ambiguity about what could force the delegation to leave before the closing ceremony or to boycott the Athens Games, *their level of frustration and anger was palpable* [read *their frustration and anger was palpable*]." Michael Janofsky, "Russians Threaten to Pull Out of Games," *N.Y. Times*, 22 Feb. 2002, at D1.
- "When they share a scene, *the energy level is palpable* [read *the energy is palpable*]." David Bianculli, "Net Goes 0 for 2," *Daily News* (N.Y.), 24 Sept. 2002, at 79.
- "Even in America's heartland, far from the sniper and terrorist attacks, the *anxiety level* [omit *level*] is palpable."

Kay Lazar, "Anxiety Gripping the U.S. Despite Drop in Violence," *Boston Herald*, 27 Oct. 2002, News §, at 8.

The word is occasionally confused with *palatable* (= [of food or drink] tasty; or [of a situation] acceptable)—e.g.: "As a foreigner, especially having come from the relative political docility of Australia, this tension was *palatable* [read *palpable*], almost like he could smell it coming from the fear of the populace." Gregory Paul Broadbent, *On the Obsidian Sea* 263 (2014).

pamphlet. This word is pronounced with the *-ph-* as if it were an *-f-*: /**pam**-flət/. Many people incorrectly say /**pam**-plət/. See PRONUNCIATION (B), (F).

panache (= admirable flair, verve, and style) is preferably pronounced /pə-**nash**/—not /pə-**nahsh**/.

pandemic = (of a disease) prevalent over the whole of a country or continent, or over the whole world. The word is usually an adjective but may be used as a noun—e.g.: "The 1918 flu *pandemic* killed 20 million." Shannon Brownlee, "The Disease Busters," *U.S. News & World Rep.*, 27 Mar. 1995, at 48. Cf. **epidemic.**

pander. The oldest use of this word—dating from about 1530—is as a noun meaning "a go-between in a sexual rendezvous; procurer." The sense was long ago extended to "someone who caters to others' base desires."

By the 1600s, the word had come to be a verb meaning (1) "to act as a go-between in a sexual rendezvous," or (2) "to exploit the weaknesses of others." Sense 2 is now more common—e.g.:

- "While the mayor will *pander* to almost any group when the time and place are right, he has made surprisingly few efforts to ingratiate himself in the city's black communities." Joseph Dolman, "Police Scandal Is About Power, Rather than Race," *Newsday* (N.Y.), 21 Aug. 1997, at A54.
- "Talk shows like Sally, Ricki Lake, Jerry Springer and Jenny Jones generally *pander* to the worst in our natures, parading a sideshow of freaks and social misfits before the cameras." Michael Storey, "Rosie Swaps Places with Sally," *Ark. Democrat-Gaz.*, 9 Sept. 1997, at E3.

The word still sometimes appears as a noun, but now the verb has become so widespread that few consider the word a noun. Meanwhile, in the mid-19th century, the noun *panderer* sprang up. It has now gone far toward displacing the noun *pander*—e.g.:

- "Even the O.J. saga, which already has set the standard for future tabloid *panderers*, is beginning to wane on the gawk-o-meter." Steve Otto, "Bizarre World Helps Create Sick Humor," *Tampa Trib.*, 29 Nov. 1994, Metro §, at 1.
- "During his three-decade career, Bowie has been both a bold explorer and a sad *panderer*." Richard Cromelin, "Bowie Gives a Focused Show in Intimate Small-Club Setting," *L.A. Times*, 12 Sept. 1997, at F20.
- "Don't expect the weak-kneed *panderers* to actually solve tough problems or work to make life better for

Alabamians." "Alabama Legislators Fail to Reflect Will of the People," *Birmingham News* (Ala.), 7 Aug. 2015, at A8.

panegyric (= a rapturous encomium) is pronounced /pan-i-**jir**-ik/—not /pan-i-**jɪ**-rik/.

panel, vb., makes *paneled* and *paneling* in AmE, *panelled* and *panelling* in BrE. See SPELLING (B).

panic, v.i., makes *panicked* and *panicking*. Usually intransitive, *panic* can also be a transitive verb meaning "to affect with panic"—e.g.: "British director Bernard Rose will try to *panic* audiences with a new fiend known as 'Candyman.'" "Sweet Terror," *Wash. Times*, 11 Oct. 1992, at D1. Cf. **mimic** & **picnic.**

pants; pant. Clothing retailers lack standardization when referring to trousers. Neiman Marcus uses *pant*—"9H. Women's Pant 305.00." Bloomingdale's uses *pants*—"E. Clam Digger Pants." And Silhouettes alternates (without any apparent reason) between *pant* and *pants*.

This inconsistency has been around for a long time. The *OED* quotes A.L. Hench from 1936 as follows: "For six or seven years now, I have been hearing clothes dealers speak of a pair of pants as 'a fine pant.' The reasoning seems to be that if a pile of pairs of pants is *pants*, then one pair is a *pant*."

Pant may appear to be a false singular of *pants* or even a BACK-FORMATION. But both words are actually abbreviations of *pantaloons*, and have been so used since the late 19th century when H.A. Shands noted that in Mississippi, "They say: 'I have a pant that I can sell you,' etc. Of course, *pants* is a well-known abbreviation, but I think *pant* is rather a new word."

papal (= of, relating to, or involving the Pope) is pronounced /**pay**-pəl/—not /**pap**-əl/.

paparazzi (= photographers who follow celebrities, often aggressively, in hopes of snapping candid photos) is a plural; *paparazzo* is the singular. Originally Italian—invented for Federico Fellini's film *La Dolce Vita* (1960)—the term first surfaced in English in the mid-1960s. Unfortunately, because the singular form is so rare, some writers have begun using the misbegotten double plural *paparazzis—e.g.:

- "The *paparazzis* [read *paparazzi*] even left the Clintons to find her [Princess Diana] on the Vineyard." J.M. Lawrence, "From Tonya to O.J.," *Boston Herald*, 25 Dec. 1994, at 25.
- "*Paparazzis* [read *Paparazzi*]. Seven-foot Oscar statues. And local actor Ben Tyler announced guests' names as they walked down the red carpet." Kathy Shocket, "Stars Shine on Hollywood Night," *Ariz. Republic*, 12 May 1997, at C1.
- "We would feel fully entitled to turn around and reject a new framework, on the grounds that we did not hack phones, or pay *paparazzis* [read *paparazzi*], or bribe public servants." "A Royal Charter Alone Will Not Restore Trust," *Independent*, 18 Mar. 2013, at 14.

On 31 August 1997, the day Princess Diana died after a car crash while being chased by paparazzi, many television commentators used the incorrect form—no doubt spreading the mistake among millions of viewers. See SPELLING (A).

LANGUAGE-CHANGE INDEX
*paparazzis for the plural paparazzi: Stage 1

paperwork. One word.

papier-mâché. So spelled—not *paper-mâché or *paper-mache. E.g.: "This morning, when the gates open at 8 a.m., the lifesized paper-mache [read papier-mâché] band will start to play with the flick of a switch in the Circus Museum." Kate Gurnett, "Altamont Fair Awaits August Crowds," Times Union (Albany), 14 Aug. 1995, at B1. Although American dictionaries spell the phrase with the DIACRITICAL MARKS, it's often spelled without the circumflex over the -a-.

Even so, the phrase is best pronounced /pay-pər-mə-**shay**/—not /pah-pyay-/ or /pap-yay-/.

LANGUAGE-CHANGE INDEX
papier-mâché misspelled *paper-mâché or
*paper-mache: Stage 1

papilla (= a nipple-like projection such as a tastebud) is pronounced /pə-**pil**-ə/—the plural being papillae /pə-**pil**-ee/.

paprika (the piquant red powdered spice) is pronounced /pa-**pree**-kə/ or /pə-**pree**-kə/ in AmE or /**pap**-ri-kə/ sometimes in BrE.

papyrus /pa-**pɪ**-rəs/ (= [1] a tall sedge native to northern Africa, [2] the pith of this plant made into paperlike writing material, or [3] a manuscript written on this material) overwhelmingly makes the plural papyri /pa-**pɪ**-rɪ/—not papyruses.

par. See subpar.

***parachronism.** See anachronism.

paradigm. A. Sense. Paradigm = (1) an example, pattern; (2) a pattern of grammatical changes within a language; (3) a theoretical framework; or (4) a prevailing attitude, esp. within education or scholarship.

B. Plural. The preferred plural is paradigms, as opposed to *paradigmata. See PLURALS (B).

C. For paragon. The term paragon (= a model of perfection) is sometimes displaced by paradigm, especially in the phrase paragon of virtue—e.g.:

- "A person might be called a paradigm [read paragon] of virtue if their [read his or her] behaviour is to be emulated." Alexander Bird, Philosophy of Science 276 (1998).
- "Mr. McCain, once regarded as a paradigm [read paragon] of virtue and accessibility by many in the media who follow him, also is facing criticism." Ralph Z. Hallow, "McCain's Shining Star Dims Republicans," Wash. Times, 11 Jan. 2000, at A1.
- "Swans were long held out as the paradigm [read paragon] of virtue, but it turns out they aren't all that faithful either." Stephanie Brenowitz, "A Biological Explanation for Infidelity," Columbus Dispatch, 12 Aug. 2001, at F7.

D. Pronunciation. Paradigm is pronounced /**pa**-rə-dɪm/—though it was /**pa**-rə-dim/ in both AmE and BrE through the early 20th century.

LANGUAGE-CHANGE INDEX
paradigm misused for paragon: Stage 1

paradox. A paradox is a seeming contradiction or a statement that appears on its face to be contrary to reason, but whose incongruity sometimes resolves itself on closer analysis—e.g.: "What explains this poor-in-wealth, rich-in-health mystery? That's exactly what Hayes-Bautista hopes to discover and what health experts have dubbed the 'Latino epidemiological paradox.'" Yvette Cabrera, "Latina Mothers Poor in Wealth, Rich in Health," Milwaukee J. Sentinel, 11 Aug. 2002, Lifestyle §, at L3.

In strict usage, a paradox is not an unresolvable problem—e.g.: "Two months shy of kicking off its 2002 campaign, United Way of South Hampton Roads officials are faced with the paradox [read problem] of a bad economy. Community needs rise. And too often, donations go down." Janie Bryant, "Economy, Scandal May Affect Fund-raising in the Region," Virginian-Pilot (Norfolk), 19 July 2002, at B4.

Nor is it an incongruous situation—e.g.: "The Texas prison system doesn't provide inmates with condoms, but it still wants its 143,000 prisoners to be as educated as possible about AIDS. If there is a paradox [read an inconsistency] there, no one mentioned it at the Darrington Prison Unit, where 128 convicts from 16 state prison units gathered to get the latest information about AIDS and other infectious diseases." Steve Olafson, "Inmates Learn About AIDS at First Conference of Its Kind," Houston Chron., 18 July 2002, at A27.

And since a paradox is an apparent contradiction, the phrase *apparent paradox is a REDUNDANCY—e.g.: "And how does one solve the Democratic Party's apparent paradox [read paradox] that a Republican flying the Stars and Bars is explicitly wrong while a Democrat doing the same is implicitly okay?" Editorial, "Paradox," Richmond Times-Dispatch, 20 July 2002, at A8.

paradoxically. See SENTENCE ADVERBS.

paragon. See paradigm (c).

paralipsis; *paralepsis; *paraleipsis. Although the more classical spelling *paraleipsis predominated until about 1960, paralipsis has become standard among rhetoricians since that time. *Paralepsis is the second most common spelling. Let's not fully discuss the degree to which *paraleipsis has fallen into disfavor. For the meaning of this rare term, see p. 1019.

Current ratio (in order of headwords): 3:2:1

parallel, vb., makes paralleled and paralleling in AmE and BrE alike—not *parallelled and *parallelling. See SPELLING (B).

PARALLELISM. A. Generally. Parallelism—the matching of sentence parts for logical balance—helps satisfy every reader's innate craving for order and rhythm. In a list, for example, you might have noun + noun + noun, or verb + verb + verb, or adjective + adjective + adjective. By phrasing parallel ideas in parallel grammatical constructions, you show the reader how one idea relates to another. You supply correspondences. Stylists have long emphasized the importance of matching phrase to like phrase:

- "One of the first requisites for the writing of good clean sentences is to have acquired the art of enumeration, that is, of stringing together three or four words or phrases of identical grammatical value without going wrong." H.W. Fowler, *FMEU1* at 142.
- "Everyone who tries to write—at least, everyone not afflicted with what is sometimes called a tin ear—has a degree of natural instinct for putting like thoughts into like constructions. Some have the instinct *in excelsis*. . . . [But] most of us possess the instinct for matching parts in no more than a variable and inferior degree and must strengthen it by self-discipline and taking thought." Wilson Follett, *MAU* at 211.
- "How do you make ideas parallel? In a series, all the items should be alike, whether all nouns, all gerunds, all infinitives, all phrases or all clauses. If a series of verbs is used, they should all be in the same tense, voice and mood. Subjects of parallel clauses should be in the same person and number. When two phrasal prepositions or conjunctions are used together, both need to be present in their entirety." Brian S. Brooks & James L. Pinson, *Working with Words* 73 (2d ed. 1993).
- "No long complex sentence will hold up without parallel construction. Paralleling can be very simple. Any word will seek its own kind, noun to noun, adjective to adjective, infinitive to infinitive." Sheridan Baker, *The Practical Stylist* 101 (8th ed. 1998).

B. Parts of Speech. With CORRELATIVE CONJUNCTIONS and with lists (even short ones), noun should be matched with noun, adjective with adjective, adverb with adverb, etc. Avoid mixtures—e.g.:

- "The poem is derivative, ceremonial, and *an elegy* [read *elegiacal*]." D.S. Brewer, *Chaucer* 44 (2d ed. 1960). (Another possible revision: *The poem is a derivative and ceremonial elegy.* The original list consisted of adjective + adjective + noun.)
- "John Baker is conservative and *a traditionalist*." Murray Teigh Bloom, *The Trouble with Lawyers* 223 (1970). (A possible revision: *John Baker is conservative and traditional.* Or: *John Baker is a conservative and a traditionalist.* The original list consisted of adjective + noun.)
- "Webb, who batted .104 last season, had two doubles, three walks *and scored three times* [read *and three runs*]." Rick Cantu, "Freshman Sits in Driver's Seat as Longhorns Cruise," *Austin Am.-Statesman*, 5 Feb. 1995, at E1, E8. (The original list consisted of noun + noun + verb phrase.)
- "Her French-Canadian husband, Jean Marc, 50, was *gentle, generous and a millionaire* [read *a gentle, generous millionaire*]." Adam Fresco & Ian Cobain, "Weetabix Wife Lived a Life of Novel Charm," *Times* (London), 23 Mar. 2001, at 5. (The original list consisted of adjective + adjective + noun.)

A clear thinker presents lists logically so that grammatical and commonsense relationships are clear.

C. Phrases and Clauses. One of the most common mistakes in falling into a nonparallel construction involves mixing phrases and clauses by introducing a verb late in the game. "Orthopedic surgeons study for four years in a college or university, four years in an orthopedic residency program and may have one optional year of specialized education." "Podiatry vs. Orthopedics," *USA Today*, 14 Apr. 2003, at D7. The writer follows two *four years* phrases with the clause *may have one optional year of specialized education.* Worse, the first two elements are objects of the shared preposition *for*, a job that the *may have* clause can't serve. A suggested revision: *Orthopedic surgeons study for four years in a college or university and four years in an orthopedic residency program; they may have one optional year of specialized education.*

D. Content. To the true stylist, mere grammatical parallelism isn't enough: the grammar should match the ideas. That is, you should strive for notional parallelism. It seems obvious that you shouldn't say that someone is *hungry, tall, and Italian*. But subtler problems arise: "The poetic opening stiffens, dreamily relaxes, then mightily reclenches: an instability of mood and texture both *symptomatic* of the mature Schubert and *disorienting* to generations of frustrated admirers, beginning with Robert Schumann." Joseph Horowitz, "A Symphony Is Where You Find It," *N.Y. Times*, 24 May 1992, § 2, at 1. Although both *symptomatic* and *disorienting* begin adjective phrases, the ideas expressed aren't coordinate. A possible revision: *The poetic opening stiffens, dreamily relaxes, and then mightily reclenches. The instability of mood and texture—symptomatic of the mature Schubert—has been disorienting to generations of frustrated admirers, beginning with Robert Schumann.* The revision subordinates one phrase (*symptomatic*) to the other (*disorienting*), so that frustrated readers themselves aren't disoriented by writing that is symptomatically unparallel.

paralyse. See **paralyze.**

paralysis; *paralyzation. The first is standard. The second is a NONWORD that arose in the 19th century and today appears with some frequency—e.g.:

- "Part 1 includes a special-effects shot depicting the *paralyzation* [read *paralysis*] of New York City." Tom Shales, "Doomsday: The Miniseries," *Wash. Post*, 7 May 1994, at G1.
- "Already, *paralyzation* [read *paralysis*] of arterial expressways running through the Kobe area from Tokyo and Nagoya to Hiroshima and Fukuoka was beginning to take a toll." Sam Jameson, "Criticism of Quake Response Rises in Japan," *L.A. Times*, 19 Jan. 1995, at A1.
- "A federal appeals court tossed out his conviction, calling the *paralyzation* [read *paralysis*] 'shocking to the

conscience." Jamie Satterfield, "Judge Allows Lawsuit to Proceed," *Knoxville News-Sentinel*, 14 Apr. 2015, at A1.

For the similar NONWORD **analyzation*, see **analysis**.

> LANGUAGE-CHANGE INDEX
> **paralyzation* for *paralysis*: Stage 1
> Current ratio (*paralysis* vs.
> **paralyzation*): 959:1

paralyze; paralyse. The first is the AmE spelling; the second is the predominant BrE spelling.

parameters. A. Generally. Technical contexts aside, this jargonistic VOGUE WORD is not used by those with a heightened sensitivity to language. To begin with, only a specialist in mathematics or computing knows precisely what it means: elsewhere it is a mush word. Second, when it does have a discernible meaning, it is usurping the place of a far simpler and more straightforward term, such as *boundaries*, *limits*, or *guidelines*. Although this 20th-century VOGUE WORD abounds in AmE, it doesn't occur in the best writing—e.g.:

- "Similarly, his [Frank Zappa's] music broke down barriers even as it expanded *parameters*." Harry Sumrall, "Mother of Invention," *Austin Am.-Statesman*, 18 May 1995, Entertainment §, at 13. (How could it not expand "parameters" if it is breaking down barriers? A possible revision: delete *even as it expanded parameters*.)
- "In March, school board members set *parameters* [read *guidelines*] for the search, saying they would consider only those with superintendent experience and a doctorate." Forrest White, "Schools Superintendent Job Draws 38 Applications," *Post & Courier* (Charleston, S.C.), 30 Apr. 1997, at B4.
- "At 14 months, babies already know a lot about the *parameters* [read *limits*] of their safe little world." Elisabeth Kallick Dyssegaard, "The Danes Call It Fresh Air," *N.Y. Times*, 17 May 1997, § 1, at 19.

Rarely is the word used in the singular, but it does occur: "How many corporations inhabit a world so neat that one *parameter* can summarize it?" "The Limitations of WACC," *Harv. Bus. Rev.*, May–June 1997, at 136.

B. And *perimeter*. Sometimes *perimeter*, the meaning of which has influenced the senses of *parameter*, is used ostensibly so that the writer can sidestep any criticisms for the use of *parameter*. Although this usage makes literal sense, a clearer expression is available—e.g.: "Some of the nation's foremost experts in medicine, law and politics will discuss the 25th Amendment to the U.S. Constitution, which *sets perimeters for* [read *establishes procedures in the event of*] presidential disability and [determines] when the president must transfer power to the vice president." "Wake Forest Forum Features Address by President Ford," *News & Record* (Greensboro), 10 Nov. 1995, at B2. And in any event, *perimeter* is best left to physical senses <the fort's perimeter>.

> LANGUAGE-CHANGE INDEX
> 1. *parameters* for the idea of limits, guidelines, or characteristics: Stage 4
> 2. *perimeters* for the same idea: Stage 1

paramount means "superior to all others" or "most important"—not merely "important." E.g.: "It is *extremely paramount* [read *extremely important* or *paramount*] that effective deployment of sworn deputies must begin with the distribution of these workers on a proportionate-need basis." Letter of Michael J. Robinson, "Sheriff's Defeatist Attitude Is a Cop-Out," *St. Petersburg Times*, 13 Sept. 1989, at 2. See **tantamount** & ADJECTIVES (B). Cf. **penultimate**.

> LANGUAGE-CHANGE INDEX
> *paramount* in the sense "important" (rather than "most important"): Stage 2

paramountcy is the noun corresponding to the adjective *paramount*. It's not often seen but quite proper—e.g.: "Deng Xiaoping the economic pragmatist was always shadowed by Deng Xiaoping the political ideologue, who asserted, at every critical juncture, the *paramountcy* of the Chinese Communist Party in his nation's affairs." Frank Viviano, "China's Supreme Leader Dies," *S.F. Chron.*, 20 Feb. 1997, at A1. **Paramouncy* is a variant spelling to be avoided.

A more familiar word, such as *supremacy* or *preeminence*, will almost always be a better choice.

Current ratio (*paramountcy* vs. **paramouncy*): 70:1

*paramutual; *paramutuel. See **parimutuel**.

paraphrase, n. & vb., is sometimes misspelled **paraphraze*.

paraplegic (= someone who is immobile from the waist down) has four syllables: /par-ə-**plee**-jik/—not /par-ə-pə-**lee**-jik/ (with an epenthetic schwa).

parasitic (= [1] living on other organisms, as a parasite does, or [2] fawning for favors; sycophantic) is the predominant form of the word in all varieties of World English. **Parasitical* is a NEEDLESS VARIANT.

parasol. So spelled. See SPELLING (A).

parcel, vb., makes *parceled* and *parceling* in AmE, *parcelled* and *parcelling* in BrE. See SPELLING (B).

pardon, v.t. See **commute (B)**.

pardon me. See **excuse me**.

paren. This CASUALISM for *parenthesis*, based on the term's long-standing abbreviation, is gaining in popularity—e.g.:

- "As far as I know, I'm the first one who did colon, minus, *paren*." Katie Hafner, "Emoticon at Age 20 Continues to Stir :-)," *Chicago Trib.*, 23 Sept. 2002, Bus. §, at 4 (quoting Scott E. Fahlman of Carnegie Mellon University).
- "Besides singing, my favorite thing to do is to connect people for business, romance, or just because,' Manisha Shahane wrote to me. Perhaps it was her final earnest set of *parens* that grabbed my attention: '(Ask anyone who knows me!).'" Kristen Paulson, "The Single File," *Boston Globe*, 12 Dec. 2002, Cal. §, at 8.

Part of the reason for this trend may be that the singular (*paren*) and the plural (*parens*) are formed according to the regular manner—whereas *parenthesis* gives some speakers and writers trouble in its various uses. See **parenthesis.**

parental (= of, relating to, or involving being a parent and esp. being responsible for a child's safety and development) is pronounced /pə-**ren**-təl/—not /**par**-ən-təl/.

PARENTHESES. See **parenthesis** & PUNCTUATION (K).

parenthesis /pə-**ren**-thə-sis/, the singular noun, forms the plural *parentheses* /pə-**ren**-thə-seez/. But because the plural is more common than the singular, some speakers use the mistaken BACK-FORMATION *parenthese (wrongly pronounced /pə-**ren**-thə-see/). The error occurs occasionally in writing as well as in speech.

LANGUAGE-CHANGE INDEX
*parenthese as false singular in place
of *parenthesis*: Stage 1
Current ratio (*parenthesis* vs. *parenthese): 155:1

parenting; grandparenting. *Parenting*, a VOGUE WORD meaning "the raising of a child by its parents," is a fairly recent coinage: *W11* dates it from 1958. It began as JARGON used by psychologists, sociologists, and self-help practitioners, but spread into the general language during the 1980s. Its relative *grandparenting* is much rarer—e.g.: "*Grandparenting* Styles Differ," *Charleston Daily Mail*, 10 Oct. 1995, at A8.

Of course, the gerund *parenting* implies a verb, but that form appears less often than the noun. It's more jarring, and there's usually a handy and simple substitute—e.g.:

- "The group says other clients are trying to have babies that will genetically match children they have already *parented* [read *given birth to*] and lost." "Cloning Facts," *Denver Post*, 29 Dec. 2002, at A6.
- "He admits that marriage isn't the silver bullet for social ills but observes that *well-parented* [read *well-reared*] kids often cause less crime or other problems, thus costing society and the government less money." Abraham McLaughlin, *Christian Science Monitor*, 13 Jan. 2003, USA §, at 1.
- "This legislation is a slap in the face to them and to hundreds like them across Iowa who are *parenting* [read *raising children*] and *foster-parenting* [read *providing foster homes*], with all of the challenges and little of the recognition that 'traditional' couples receive." Letter of Heather L. Adams, "No Evidence for Adoption Ban," *Des Moines Register*, 17 Feb. 2003, at A10.

LANGUAGE-CHANGE INDEX
parenting in the sense "child-rearing": Stage 4

parimutuel, n., = a form of gambling in which those who have bet on winning numbers share in the total stakes, after deduction of a management fee. The word is borrowed from French, in which *pari mutuel* means "mutual stake." The word is sometimes misspelled *paramutual, *paramutuel, or *parimutual—e.g.:

- "Between 1984 and 1994 the annual amount bet on legalized gaming—including casinos, lotteries, *parimutual*

[read *parimutuel*] betting and sports books—jumped by 137%." "Taking a Hard Look at Gambling," *L.A. Times*, 5 Mar. 1996, at B6.
- "These bets—like those at the *paramutual* [read *parimutuel*] windows—are based on bloodlines, sires, dams and history of siblings." Bruce A. Scruton, "How Much for That Horse?" *Times Union* (Albany), 7 Aug. 1996, at C1.
- "Alamo Downs: Originally a well-known horse-racing track that turned to motor sports when Texas outlawed *paramutuel* [read *parimutuel*] wagering." Bruce Mabrito, "S.A.-Area Motor Sports," *San Antonio Express-News*, 7 July 2015, Metro §, at 4.

LANGUAGE-CHANGE INDEX
parimutuel misspelled in various ways: Stage 1

Parisian (= a citizen or resident of Paris) is pronounced /pə-**rizh**-ən/ or /pə-**ree**-zhən/ in AmE but /pə-**riz**-ee-ən/ in BrE.

parley; parlay. A. As Nouns. A *parley* (/**pahr**-lee/) is a discussion of disputed matters, especially a negotiation between warring parties to end hostilities. A *parlay* (/**pahr**-lay/) is a series of all-or-nothing wagers made in hopes of eventually accumulating large winnings.

Each word is sometimes misused for the other—e.g.:

- "Tickets can also be earned when you cash an Action Cash voucher, make a $10 *parley* [read *parlay*] bet in the sports book, or play live bingo or in the pit." Dave Zweifel, "Jerry's Nugget Celebrating 40th Anniversary with Giveaways," *Las Vegas Rev.-J.*, 8 Oct. 2004, at J8.
- "What was that the sources were saying Friday about an 'enormous breakthrough' in the Yahoo-Microsoft negotiations? Obviously what they meant to say was 'enormous breakdown.' Steve 'Not A Dime More' Ballmer and Jerry 'Not A Dime Less' Yang held one last *parlay* [read *parley*] on Saturday, and as dawn broke Sunday, the Yahoo generals looked out from their battlements on a dusty, empty field, tents and equipment abandoned—no giant wooden horse, no nothing." John Murrell, "Good Morning Silicon Valley," *San Jose Mercury News*, 30 Mar. 2007, at C3.

B. As Verbs. *Parley* = (1) to discuss differences of opinions, or (2) to negotiate an agreement or settlement, esp. an end to a war. *Parlay* = (1) to repeatedly wager the original stake plus the accumulated winnings, or (2) in an extended sense, to use something on which to build momentum or to use as a foundation.

Although misuses are rare, they do occur—e.g.:

- "Edwards, whose popularity had been sinking badly in the polls since his 1991 victory over David Duke, now stands ready to *parley* [read *parlay*] his casino winnings into a credible bid for re-election in 1995." Jack Wardlaw & Peter Nicholas, "Breaking Casino Impasse May Help Edwards in '95," *Times-Picayune* (New Orleans), 29 Aug. 1993, at A1.
- "How can we possibly be so deluded as to think such negotiations this time will not produce results akin to those of previous efforts to *parlay* [read *parley*] with

LANGUAGE-CHANGE INDEX (For the full key, see front matter pp. xxxi, l–li.)
Stage 1: Rejected. **Stage 2:** Widely shunned. **Stage 3:** Widespread but . . . **Stage 4:** Ubiquitous but . . . **Stage 5:** Fully accepted.
Invariably inferior forms marked by asterisk (*). • Ratios represent frequency of prevalent forms vs. variants in current books.

other totalitarians: confirming their contempt for Western interlocutors, reinforcing the despots' sense of inevitable victory and encouraging more aggressive behavior by the latter to achieve that outcome on an accelerated basis?" Frank J. Gaffney Jr., "What Were They Thinking?" *Wash. Times*, 10 July 2007, at A14.

LANGUAGE-CHANGE INDEX
1. *parley* misused for *parlay*: Stage 1
2. *parlay* misused for *parley*: Stage 1

Parliament. The definite article (*the*) is unnecessary before this word when it is used as a proper noun (i.e., in reference to a particular parliament) <Parliament voted to make such conduct illegal>. Cf. **Congress.**

parliamentary need not be capitalized unless one is referring to the doings of a particular parliament. Unlike *congressional*, which should not be capitalized, *parliamentary* as a lowercase adjective has other senses, most commonly in denoting procedural rules for governing meetings. So there may be more justification for the uppercase *Parliamentary* than an uppercase *Congressional.* See **congressional.**

parochial = (1) of or related to a church parish; or (2) confined in range or outlook. The *OED* dates sense 1 to Chaucer in the early 15th century, and it is still current—e.g.: "It took less than a year for Algene Patrick to learn all she needed to know about William H. Brazier Elementary School . . . . The grandmother decided enough was enough, and she put Lawrenesha in *parochial* school." Elizabeth Weiss Green, "Grade School Goes Corporate," *U.S. News & World Rep.*, 7 May 2007, at 50.

But the figurative sense 2, in use since the 1850s, is unobjectionable—e.g.:

- "Financially the United States heretofore has been *parochial.* Unlike England, Scotland, Germany, France, Canada, and South Africa, we have not had tremendously powerful banking organizations." Susan Adams, "90 Years Ago in Forbes," *Forbes*, 7 May 2007, at 38.
- "[B]efore the Giuliani campaign got off the ground, many Republican operatives believed that a major liability for the candidate would be his dependence on this closed circle of *parochial* advisers, none of whom is experienced in national elections." Thomas B. Edsall, "Party Boy," *New Republic*, 21 May 2007, at 26.
- "[David Buss] was accused of being *parochial*: Though the surveys had been distributed in 37 countries, his critics argued that the populations surveyed were still mostly Western or Westernized." Karen Olsson, "Human Mate Selection Is a Many-Splendored Thing," *Texas Monthly*, June 2007, at 138.

paroxysm (= a sudden spasm or attack of pain, coughing, shaking, etc.) is preferably pronounced /**par**-ək-siz-əm/, not /pə-**rok**-siz-əm/.

parricide; patricide. *Parricide,* the more usual word, means (1) "the murder of one's own father"; or (2) "someone who murders his or her own father." Sense 1: "According to Mones, there are about 300 *parricide* cases a year in the United States. . . . About 70 percent

of all *parricides* involve adolescent boys killing a father." Regina Brett, "Defense of Abused Teen in His Father's Slaying Made Ohio Court History," *Buffalo News*, 21 Apr. 1997, at C1. Sense 2: "The contention that quadriplegia is 'punishment enough'—like the *parricide*'s claim that he deserves mercy as an orphan—is one addressed to the sentencing court's discretion alone." *United States ex rel. Villa v. Fairman*, 810 F.2d 715, 717–18 (7th Cir. 1987).

It is also used in extended senses, such as "the murder of the ruler of a country" and "the murder of a close relative." These are not examples of SLIPSHOD EXTENSION, however, for even the Latin etymon (*parricida*) was used in these senses. See -CIDE.

Patricide is a NEEDLESS VARIANT.

parsec. See **light-year.**

parsimony, law of. See **Occam's razor.**

part. See **portion.**

partake is construed with either *in* or *of* in the sense "to take part or share in some action or condition; to participate." *In* is the more common preposition in this sense—e.g.: "From 5 to 5:30 p.m., members will meet and *partake in* a wine and cheese reception." Joan Szeglowski, "Town 'N' Country," *Tampa Trib.*, 10 Sept. 1997, at 4.

Of is the correct preposition when the sense is "to receive, get, or have a share or portion *of* "—e.g.: "So should one *partake of* Chinese cuisine, British history and Clint Eastwood?" T. Collins, "Carryout, Videos Make Dating Like Staying Home," *Courier-J.* (Louisville), 12 Sept. 1997, at W27. All in all, the collocation *partake of* has always been more prevalent than *partake in.*

partially. A. And *partly.* Whenever either word can suffice in a given context, *partly* is the better choice. *Partially* occasionally causes ambiguity because of its other sense "in a manner exhibiting favoritism." E.g.: "The case was *partially* heard on May 31, 1995." Lydia Barbara Bashwiner, "Aubrey Family-Member Rule Is Applied Prospectively Only," *N.J. Lawyer*, 24 Feb. 1997, at 36. But aren't cases supposed to be heard impartially?

The first edition of *AHD* (1969) notes that *partly,* which has wider application, "is the choice when stress is laid on the part (in contrast to the whole), when the reference is to physical things, and when the sense is equivalent to *in part, to some extent*" <partly to blame> <a partly finished building>. "*Partially* is especially applicable to conditions or states in the sense of *to a certain degree*; as the equivalent of *incomplete*, it indirectly stresses the whole" (*AHD*) <partially dependent> <partially contributory>. The third edition (1992) dropped this helpful distinction.

Another way of thinking about the distinction is that *partly* deals with a part, while *partially* deals with the whole, but only to a partial extent or degree.

B. As an antonym of *impartially.* Often this usage causes no real ambiguity—e.g.:

- "The EU, by considering the unilateral application of Greek South Cyprus for membership, has acted *partially*." Letter of Hakki Muftuzade, "EU Has Only Stirred the Cyprus Pot," *Wall Street J. Europe*, 15 Feb. 2000, at 11.
- "Ruddock has handled a difficult portfolio with a deal of success. But his copious interventions have allowed media criticism that he might have acted *partially*." Tony Harris, "Public Interest, or Private?" *Australian Fin. Rev.*, 6 Feb. 2001, at 42.

But sometimes it can cause real confusion—e.g.:

- "The other 37 decisions were decided *partially* [read *partly*? *tendentiously*?] in favor of the patients." "Protecting Patients," *Dallas Morning News*, 22 July 1999, at A26.
- "Blayney concedes that some planners' anti-annuity bias may be *partially* [read *partly*? *unfairly*?] based on self-interest." Mary Beth Franklin, "Steady Flow of Income," *Kiplinger's Personal Finance*, 1 Oct. 2001, at 102.
- "A world *very partially* [read *only partly*? *cliquishly*?] unified by technology still has no collective consciousness or collective solidarity." Stanley Hoffmann, "Clash of Globalizations," *Foreign Affairs*, 1 July 2002, at 104.

participatory; *participative. The latter is a NEEDLESS VARIANT.

Current ratio: 6:1

PARTICLES IN NAMES. See NAMES (D).

parti-colored (= many-colored, multihued) is the correct form. But **party-colored* is a fairly common misspelling, perhaps from the festiveness suggested by the word's meaning—e.g.: "The lawn grows lush and is bordered by . . . scattered groupings of annuals such as *party-colored* [read *parti-colored*] seed dahlias." Kym Pokorny, "Presidential Bouquet," *Oregonian* (Portland), 18 Aug. 1996, at L11. See ETYMOLOGY (D). **Parti-color*, adj., is a NEEDLESS VARIANT.

LANGUAGE-CHANGE INDEX
parti-colored misspelled **party-colored*: Stage 3
Current ratio: 3:1

particular (= of, relating to, or involving a single person or thing) is pronounced /pər-**tik**-yə-lər/—not /pə-**tik**-lər/. The adverb *particularly* has five distinct syllables: /pər-**tik**-yə-lər-lee/—though in DIALECT it can be shortened to three (/pə-**tik**-lee/). For more on the adverb, see the next entry.

particularly. The phrase *and particularly* is usually unnecessary for *particularly*—e.g.: "But the law, *and particularly* [read *particularly*] its quota system, has been sharply criticized by the Council of Europe and other Western organizations that Latvia hopes to join someday." Alessandra Stanley, "Divided Latvians Awaiting Clinton," *N.Y. Times*, 6 July 1994, at A1, A5. Once the *and* is deleted, the reader is comfortable with the phrase *particularly its quota system* as a mere APPOSITIVE—and is comfortable with the singular verb.

partisan; partizan. The first is the preferred spelling in both AmE and BrE. Although the term denotes "someone who takes part or sides with another," it has connotations of "a blind, prejudiced, unreasoning, or fanatical adherent" (*OED*).

Current ratio: 76:1

partition is often mispronounced as if it were *petition*.

partly. See **partially.**

party is a legalism that is unjustified when it merely replaces *person*. If used as an elliptical form of *party to the contract* or *party to the lawsuit*, *party* is quite acceptable as a term of art. E.g.: "Either *party* may enforce the terms of this contract, and in the event that either *party* must use attorneys to effect such enforcements, then such expenses and other fees may be charged against the other *party*." Fred Rodell's quip is worth remembering: "Only The Law insists on making a 'party' out of a single person." Rodell, *Woe Unto You, Lawyers!* 28 (1939; repr. 1980).

The word has become something of a popularized technicality on restaurant waiting lists <the Butterworth party>—a usage so convenient and so commonplace now that any objection is bootless.

*party-colored. See **parti-colored.**

parvenu. See **nouveau riche (B).**

passable; possible. *Passable* = (1) capable of being passed, open; or (2) acceptable. *Possible* (a rare term) = feeling; susceptible to pain or suffering. The primary error is to misuse *possible* for *passable*, especially in sense 2—e.g.: "They get *possible* [read *passable*] fake identification like driver's licenses in the border states and then look for work." Jack Sherzer, "Company Is Fined \$150,000," *Patriot & Evening News* (Harrisburg), 29 Mar. 1996, at B4. See -ABLE (A). Cf. **impassible.**

LANGUAGE-CHANGE INDEX
possible misused for *passable*: Stage 1

passage. See **voyage.**

pass away. This phrase—sometimes shortened to *pass* <she passed last week>—is the most common EUPHEMISM for *die*. Characteristic of non-U speech, it was most common during the Victorian era. See CLASS DISTINCTIONS.

passcode. See **password.**

passed is sometimes misused for *past*—e.g.: "He said that in addition to the organizers' decision to exclude the openly homosexual group from the parade, 'there have been other efforts as well to eliminate some of the other excesses associated with the parade, the drinking and rowdy behavior present in years *passed* [read *past*].'" Pam Belluck, "Irish March Stars Cardinal O'Connor," *N.Y. Times*, 18 Mar. 1995, at 16.

The opposite error also occurs—e.g.: "Before you know it, thirty minutes has *past* [read *passed*], and you are done." Carter G. Phillips, *Advocacy Before the United States Supreme Court*, 15 T.M. Cooley L. Rev. 177, 190 (1988). See **past.**

LANGUAGE-CHANGE INDEX
1. *passed* misused for *past*: Stage 1
2. *past* misused for *passed*: Stage 1

passerby. Pl. *passersby*—not **passerbys*. See PLU-RALS (G).

Current ratio: 199:1

passible. See **passable.**

passim (lit., "throughout") is used in citing an author-ity in a general way and indicates that the point at hand is treated throughout the work. It's a fairly erudite citation signal—e.g.: "There is a curious reluctance on the author's part to let go of linear frameworks—from 'differentiation to integration' (p. 13), 'dependence to interdependence' (p. 19), 'childhood to maturity' (p. 25), and on to ever-higher 'states of consciousness' (*passim*)." Michael Edwards, "Popular Development: Rethinking the Theory and Practice of Development," *J. Dev. Studies*, Apr. 1997, at 581.

PASSIVE VOICE. A. Generally. Many writers talk about passive voice without knowing exactly what it is. In fact, many think that any BE-VERB signals passive voice, as in:

> The quotation is applicable to this point.

But that sentence is actually in active voice—even though it's badly in need of editing. Most professional editors would change *is applicable* to *applies*, but they wouldn't call it "passive" because it's not. It's just a flabby *be*-verb.

The point about passive voice is that the subject of the clause doesn't perform the action of the verb. Instead, you back into the sentence:

> Passive: The deadline was missed by the applicant.
> Active: The applicant missed the deadline.

And, of course, in the passive form, it's possible to omit the actor altogether—a prime source of unclar-ity. Sometimes it amounts to responsibility-dodging:

> Passive: The deadline was missed.

As anyone who follows political discourse knows, the passive voice is a staple of politicians <mistakes were made>.

The unfailing test for passive voice is this: you must have a *be*-verb (or *get*) plus a past participle (usually a verb ending in *-ed*). Hence constructions such as these are passive:

is	discussed
are	believed
was	sent
were	delivered
been	served
being	flattered
be	handled
am	given
get	stolen

Sometimes, though, the *be*-verb or *get* won't appear. It's simply an implied word in the context. For example:

> Recently I heard it suggested by a friend that too many books appear with endnotes.

Grammatically speaking, that sentence contains the implied verb *being* after the word *it*, so it's in the pas-sive voice. To make it active, you'd write:

> Recently I heard a friend suggest that too many books appear with endnotes.

What's the real problem with using passive voice? There are three. First, passive voice usually adds a cou-ple of unnecessary words. Second, when it doesn't add those extra words, it fails to say squarely who has done what. That is, the sentence won't mention the actor with a *by*-phrase (*The book was written* vs. *The book was written by Asimov*). Third, the passive subverts the normal word order for an English sentence, mak-ing it harder for readers to process the information. To put it a little more dramatically, "The impersonal passive voice [is] an opiate that cancels responsibil-ity, hides identity, and numbs the reader." Sheridan Baker, "Scholarly Style, or the Lack Thereof" (1956), in *Perspectives on Style* 64, 66 (Frederick Candelaria ed., 1968).

The active voice has palpable advantages in most contexts: it saves words, says directly who has done what, and meets the reader's expectation of a normal actor–verb–object sentence order.

The hedging in the previous sentence—"in most contexts"—is purposeful. That is, sometimes you'll be justified in using the passive voice. There's no absolute prohibition against it—and anyone who tries carrying out such a prohibition would spoil a piece of writing. Among the times when you'll want the passive in a given sentence are these:

- When the actor is unimportant.
- When the actor is unknown.
- When you want to hide the actor's identity.
- When you need to put the punch word at the end of the sentence.
- When the focus of the passage is on the thing being acted on.
- When the passive simply sounds better.

Still, professional editors find that these six situations account for only about 15% to 20% of the contexts in which the passive appears.

That means you ought to have a presumption against the passive, unless it falls into one of the cat-egories just listed.

B. The Double Passive. The problem here is using one passive immediately after another. E.g.:

- "This document refers to the portion of the votes *entitled to be cast* by virtue of membership in the union." (Votes are not *entitled to be cast*; rather, union members are *enti-tled to cast* votes.)
- "Had the new vaccine *been intended to have been injected* into the patient, he would have been warned to avoid drinking alcohol." (A possible revision: *If the new vaccine had been intended for injection into the patient . . . .*)

The problem is common with the verb *seek* (and sometimes *attempt*), especially in legal contexts—e.g.:

- "But the inference *sought to be drawn* in such a case would have to be that the parties had, at the time of the acquisition of the property, communicated to one another a common intention to acquire the property in equal shares." Shiranikha Herbert, "Home Truths About Sharing the Mortgage," *Guardian*, 29 Apr. 1992, at 23. (A possible revision: *But the inference in such a case would have to be that when the parties acquired the property, they communicated to one another a common intention to acquire it in equal shares.*)
- "There is no evidence that any improper influence *was sought to be exercised* by me or anybody else over any official decision." President Bill Clinton, as quoted in "The Whitewater Inquiry," *N.Y. Times*, 8 Mar. 1994, at D20. (A possible revision: *There is no evidence that I or anybody else tried to influence any official decision.*)
- "The investigation began after fake $20 bills *were attempted to be passed* at Key Bank on Main Street." Ben Beagle, "Funny Money Still a Mystery," *Livingston County News* (Geneseo, N.Y.), 11 June 2015, at A4. (A possible revision: *The investigation began after fake $20 bills were recognized at Key Bank on Main Street.*)

H.W. Fowler wrote that "monstrosities of this kind . . . are as repulsive to the grammarian as to the stylist" (*FMEU1* at 121).

A few double passives are defensible—e.g.: "Offerings made in compliance with Regulation D *are not required to be registered* with the SEC under the Securities Act." As Ernest Gowers noted, "In legal or quasi-legal language this construction may sometimes be useful and unexceptionable: *Diplomatic privilege applies only to such things as are done or omitted to be done in the course of a person's official duties. / Motion made: that the words proposed to be left out stand part of the Question*" (*FMEU2* at 139). But these are of a different kind from *are sought to be included* and *are attempted to be refuted*, which can be easily remedied by recasting. The principle is that if the first passive-voice construction can be made active—leaving the passive infinitive intact—the sentence is correctly formed. Here, in Fowler's famous example, a recasting of the first passive verb form into the active voice clarifies the sense:

Passive/Passive:	The prisoners were ordered to be shot.
Active/Passive:	He ordered the prisoners to be shot.
Active/Passive:	He ordered the prisoners shot.

But in the following example, a recasting of the first passive verb into the active voice does not make sense:

Passive/Passive:	The contention has been attempted to be made.
Active/Passive:	He attempted the contention to be made.

The last-quoted sentence is un-English. Sense can be restored to it by casting both parts in the active voice:

Active/Active:	He attempted to make the contention.

A final caution against the passive: "The difference between an active-verb style and a passive-verb style—in clarity and vigor—is the difference between life and death for a writer." William Zinsser, *On Writing Well* 111 (5th ed. 1994).

passivist. See **pacifist.**

pass muster. This phrase began as a military term meaning "to undergo review without censure." In widespread use since the 18th century, by the 19th it had spread into the language generally, in the sense "to prove worthy"—e.g.:

- "[The prize] goes only to firms that meet a stringent set of criteria and *pass muster* in detailed on-site inspections." Will Astor, "From a Two-Bay Garage to the Baldridge," *Rochester Bus. J.*, 15 Nov. 1996, at 10.
- "When the deal was announced in April, Gingrich's aides were confident it would *pass muster* in the ethics panel." Marc Lacey & Janet Hook, "Panel Stiffens Terms for Gingrich to Pay Penalty," *Ariz. Republic*, 16 May 1997, at A1.

The phrase is mangled in various ways, as by writing **past muster*—e.g.:

- "None of these shows, with their puppets and stuntmen in rubber suits, would *past* [read *pass*] muster with today's video-savvy youngsters." Stephen Kopfinger, "Old Shows Still Beat Modern TV," *Lancaster New Era*, 7 Jan. 1996, at B2.
- "Despite such strong backing, the design must *past* [read *pass*] muster with the Secretary of the Interior . . . ." Steve Litt, "The Mall, Unhallowed," *Plain Dealer* (Cleveland), 11 May 1997, at I8.

Quite apart from that error, the phrase invites condiment-inspired puns—e.g.: "The seventh and newest Wienermobile to crisscross America is a bite-sized vehicle compared to Oscar Mayer's beloved hot-dog fleet. But the 'mini' has proved this summer to, um, *pass mustard*." Tom Alesia, "Oscar Mayer Takes Bite Out of Wienermobile," *Wis. State J.*, 6 Aug. 2008, at A1. Sadly, it's no joke sometimes—e.g.:

- "Asked about albums he digs from the past decade, [Joel] O'Keeffe cites Iron Maiden and Judas Priest's latest. For O'Keeffe, not even a heavy Jack White riff *passes mustard* [read *passes muster*]." Jed Gottlieb, "Motorhead Gets Airbourne's Rock Engines 'Runnin','" *Boston Herald*, 27 Mar. 2008, at 36.
- "Cleanup hitters are judged much more by their run production than their on-base percentage, but Jeff Crawford could *pass mustard* [read *pass muster*] on either count." Chris Kennedy, "Crawford Igniting Bombers," *Republican* (Springfield, Mass.), 10 June 2008, at C2.

LANGUAGE-CHANGE INDEX
1. **past muster* for *pass muster*: Stage 1
Current ratio (*pass muster* vs. **past muster*): 277:1
2. **pass mustard* for *pass muster*: Stage 1
Current ratio (*pass muster* vs. **pass mustard*): 1,389:1

LANGUAGE-CHANGE INDEX (For the full key, see front matter pp. xxxi, l–li.)
Stage 1: Rejected. **Stage 2:** Widely shunned. **Stage 3:** Widespread but . . . **Stage 4:** Ubiquitous but . . . **Stage 5:** Fully accepted.
Invariably inferior forms marked by asterisk (*). • Ratios represent frequency of prevalent forms vs. variants in current books.

password; passcode. The latter is a NEOLOGISM created in an effort to keep up with modern technology. In the computer age, a *password* is often not a word at all; instead, it's merely a combination of characters (letters and numbers). Hence the term *passcode*, born in the early 1990s.

Like many other neologisms, this one may be short-lived: *password* isn't likely to be bumped from the language. Indeed, those who object to a *password* that consists of the digits in one's birthdate, for example, are probably being too literal.

past. This word occurs in many redundant phrases, such as **past history*, **past track record*, and **past experience*, in which the noun denotes something that by its very nature is rooted in the past. See REDUNDANCY. For a misuse, see **passed.**

> LANGUAGE-CHANGE INDEX
> *past* in redundancies such as **past history*,
> **past experience*: Stage 3

pastille (= [1] a solid air-freshener; or [2] a soothing throat lozenge) is the standard spelling. **Pastil* is a variant.

> Current ratio: 9:1

pastime is sometimes misspelled **pasttime*. The misspelling derives from a misunderstanding of the word's origin: *pastime* derives from *pass* (v.t.) + *time*, not *past* + *time*.

> LANGUAGE-CHANGE INDEX
> *pastime* misspelled **pasttime*: Stage 1
> Current ratio: 231:1

past master (= a true expert) is now so spelled, though originally (in the 18th century) the phrase was **passed master*. Today, though, **passed master* is considered erroneous.

*past muster. See **pass muster.**

pastoral (= [1] typical of country life; involving a peacefully bucolic existence, or [2] of, relating to, or involving the duties of a priest or minister toward his or her congregation) is pronounced /**pas**-tə-rəl/ (AmE) or /**pahs**-tə-rəl/ (BrE)—not /pa-**stor**-əl/.

pastorale /pas-tə–**ral**/ (= a piece of music evoking rustic or bucolic life), an Italian loanword, predominantly forms the plural *pastorales*. The Italianate plural *pastorali* is a chiefly BrE variant.

> Current ratio: 2:1

PAST-PARTICIPIAL ADJECTIVES. See IRREGULAR VERBS (B) & ADJECTIVES (F).

*pasttime. See **pastime.**

patella (= kneecap) has predominantly formed the Latinate plural *patellae* (/pə-**tel**-ee/) since the 18th century. *Patellas* is a homegrown variant that is seldom used.

> Current ratio (*patellae* vs. *patellas*): 12:1

patent, n., v.t. & adj. In the adjectival sense of "obvious, apparent," the preferred pronunciation is /**payt**-ənt/. In all other senses and uses, the pronunciation is /**pat**-ənt/.

paterfamilias (= [1] the male head of a household, [2] a patriarch, or [3] a male leader of a movement, campaign, discipline, etc.) is pronounced /pat-ər-fə-**mil**-ee-əs/. Pl. *patresfamilias*—the anglicized variant **paterfamiliases* being extremely uncommon. See PLURALS (A), (B). Cf. **materfamilias.**

> Current ratio: 8:1

pathos. See **bathos.**

patina (/**pat**-ə-nə/ or [less good] /pə-**tee**-nə/)—meaning "a film or crust on an object formed from age or use"—has been the standard form since the 18th century. **Patine* is a NEEDLESS VARIANT.

> Current ratio: 62:1

patricide. See **parricide.**

paucity (= dearth, scarcity) indicates a small quantity, not a complete lack of something, as this sentence erroneously suggests: "It would have had the inevitable result of demonstrating the *total paucity or lack* [read *lack* or *absence*] of evidence from which any jury could conclude that a reasonable man would have acted as the appellant did." "Provocation Issue for Jury," *Times* (London), 18 July 1994, Features §. The mistaken phrases **complete paucity* and **total paucity* emerged in the 1940s and 1950s. Cf. **plethora.**

> LANGUAGE-CHANGE INDEX
> *paucity* misused to mean "a complete absence": Stage 1

pause, vb., is now sometimes used transitively. The major dictionaries differ in their treatment of the transitive sense <President Bush paused his vacation for a press conference>. The first edition of the *OED* (1928) listed *pause* as an intransitive verb only. In the *OED Supp.* (1982), R.W. Burchfield defined *pause* transitively in the sense "to cause to stop temporarily," with but two examples, from 1542 and 1908. *W2* (1934) notes that the transitive—more specifically, the reflexive—sense is "obsolete." American dictionaries didn't start recording the transitive sense as a live form until the early 1990s.

Although the transitive sense was historically marginal at best, something happened in the 1970s and 1980s to change all that: people started *pausing* their cassette tapes and later their VCRs instead of *putting them on pause*. So a simple technological change probably led to the revival of a long-dormant idiom.

pavilion. See SPELLING (A).

pay. A. Inflected Forms: *pay > paid > paid*. **Payed* is a startlingly frequent error for *paid*—e.g.:

- "He got charged with harassment after a supermarket fistfight, a violation, and *payed* [read *paid*] a $250 fine." Al Baker, "Bounty Hunter Tom Evangelista Comes Armed with a Big Gun, Lots of Patience, and a Plan to Get His Man," *Newsday* (N.Y.), 9 Nov. 1997, at G8.
- "He *payed* [read *paid*] $387,500 in 1995, according to the records." David Montgomery, "Embassy Neighbors Try to Dig Up Dirt on Tunnel," *Wash. Post*, 11 Mar. 2001, at C1.

B. And *pay up*. The PHRASAL VERB *pay up* means "to discharge (a debt) completely." *Pay* may refer to partial or total payments. Because of this slight DIF-FERENTIATION, *up* is not a needless particle. See PHRASAL VERBS.

C. *Put paid*. See **put paid to**.

pay dirt. Two words in AmE and BrE alike.

payer; payor. Although *payor* (corresponding to *payee*) predominates in legal writing, *payer* is better and much more common in other contexts. See -ER (A).

Current ratio: 3:1

pay (one's) respects (= to show polite respect for someone by appearing personally) is the SET PHRASE, but some writers have begun to write the singular *respect* instead of *respects*: "McGovern and his wife tried to tour the building and view the displays, but it wasn't easy with well-wishers seeking to pay their *respect* [read *respects*]." John Knaggs, "McGovern Easy to Admire," *Austin Am.-Statesman*, 12 Oct. 1995, at A15. That wording may be more logical than the accepted usage *to pay their respects*; the well-wishers each showed the same *respect* for McGovern. But logic must yield to the universally accepted idiom.

To *pay one's last respects* is to show respect for a dead person by attending a funeral or visiting a grave.

payor. See **payer**.

payroll is occasionally misspelled **payrole*, a blunder dating from the early 1900s—e.g.:

- "The courts may put you on the *payrole* [read *payroll*] yet." Mike Causey, "Want U.S. Job? Three Ways to Still Get One," *Wash. Post*, 17 Feb. 1981, at C2.
- "One of the most appealing ideas they floated is lowering the *payrole* [read *payroll*] tax." "A Budgetary Train Wreck," *Rocky Mountain News* (Denver), 23 Dec. 1994, at A47.
- "It reports that Barca are keen to remove the Dutch striker from their *payrole* [read *payroll*]." Niall Couper, "Football: Press Watch," *Independent*, 24 May 2004, Sport §, at 54.

For the confusion between *role* and *roll*, see **role**.

LANGUAGE-CHANGE INDEX
payroll misspelled **payrole*: Stage 1
Current ratio: 24,905:1

pay up. See **pay (B)**.

peaceful; peaceable. Generally, *peaceful* refers to a state of affairs <reach a peaceful resolution> <a peaceful morning spent fly-fishing>; *peaceable* refers to the disposition of a person or a nation <as calming and peaceable a show as *Mister Rogers' Neighborhood*> <peaceable kingdom>. The two words overlap some, but the DIFFERENTIATION is worth encouraging.

Although we now think of *peaceful* as the more usual word, from 1650 to 1800 *peaceable* occurred with far greater frequency. Such are the vicissitudes of words.

peace of mind; piece of (one's) mind. Whereas *peace of mind* is calm assurance, a *piece of one's mind* is something a person says in a fit of pique. But the two are surprisingly often confounded—e.g.:

- "After experimenting with this, the thought of regaining control of your destiny and *piece* [read *peace*] of mind will be comforting." Greg Brozovich, "Ditch Work for Great Front Range Snow," *Denver Post*, 14 Dec. 1995, at D10.
- "Although it is a little more expensive, it is a small price to pay for *piece* [read *peace*] of mind, Marusak said." Michael Farrell, "Comfortex Corp. Gets Ready to Roll Out New Line of Shades," *Capital District Bus. Rev.*, 14 July 1997, at 3.
- "But once people take the step of dealing with them, there's a relief and *piece* [read *peace*] of mind." Dell Warner, "Seniors: Lawyers at Legal Center Give Seniors Advice on How to Protect Their Assets," *Detroit News*, 29 Aug. 1997, at D8.

LANGUAGE-CHANGE INDEX
*piece of mind for *peace of mind*: Stage 1

peaked, adj., = sickly, pale, anemic-looking. The word is pronounced /**pee**-kəd/, not /**pik**-əd/ or (worse yet) /peekt/.

*peak (one's) interest. See **pique**.

*pean. See **paean**.

pearl. In the context of knitting, see **purl**.

pecan (= [1] a long thin sweet nut with a dark red shell, or [2] the tree that produces this nut) is predominantly pronounced /pi-**kahn**/ in AmE—but also, in certain regions, /pi-**kan**/. The latter is a BrE pronunciation, along with /**pee**-kan/.

peccadillo. Pl. *peccadilloes*—not **peccadillos*. See PLU-RALS (D). Cf. **armadillo**.

Current ratio: 6:1

pecs. This is the standard CASUALISM, a shortened form of the word *pectorals* (= chest muscles). The word is used figuratively as well as literally—e.g.: "Democrats got a chance to flex their political *pecs*." Reynolds Holding, "California Candidate for the Supreme Court," *S.F. Chron.*, 15 Sept. 2002, at D3. Cf. **biceps, quadriceps** & **triceps**.

Two variant forms are **pects* and **pecks*, but they are comparatively infrequent and should be discouraged—e.g.: "Clad only in bathing trunks, they posed, flexed and strutted. West leered, inspected lats, delts and *pects* [read *pecs*] and fluttered her eyelashes in excitement." K.J. Evans, "Bill Miller (1904–): Mr. Entertainment," *Las Vegas Rev.-J.*, 2 May 1999, at A56.

Pectoral is pronounced /**pek**-tə-rəl/, not /pek-**tor**-əl/.

peculate. See **defalcate (A)**.

pecuniary; pecunious. The suffixes distinguish these words. *Pecuniary* = relating to or consisting of money. *Pecunious* = moneyed; wealthy. Its opposite is *impecunious* (= destitute). See **impecunious**.

LANGUAGE-CHANGE INDEX (For the full key, see front matter pp. xxxi, l–li.)
Stage 1: Rejected. **Stage 2:** Widely shunned. **Stage 3:** Widespread but . . . **Stage 4:** Ubiquitous but . . . **Stage 5:** Fully accepted.
Invariably inferior forms marked by asterisk (✳). • Ratios represent frequency of prevalent forms vs. variants in current books.

The adverb corresponding to *pecuniary* is *pecuniarily*—e.g.: "As even the *pecuniarily* impaired can tell you, the greenback is graced by George Washington." Jack Cox, "Baron of Boodle," *Denver Post*, 10 July 1997, at E1.

pedagogue (= a teacher, often a pedantic one) is the standard spelling. *Pedagog is a variant. (Cf. **analog, catalog(ue)** & **dialogue**.) For a comment on the potential decline of the *-ue* form, see -AGOG(UE).

pedagogy (= the study or practice of effective teaching) is predominantly pronounced /ped-ə-goh-jee/ in AmE, but sometimes also /ped-ə-gah-jee/. The latter is the BrE pronunciation.

The standard corresponding adjective is *pedagogical* (/ped-ə-**goh**-ji-kəl/ *or* /ped-ə-**gah**-ji-kəl/)—*pedagogic being a NEEDLESS VARIANT.

pedal, vb., makes *pedaled* and *pedaling* in AmE, *pedalled* and *pedalling* in BrE. See SPELLING (B).

peddler (= an itinerant seller) has been the standard AmE spelling since about 1860. *Pedlar* is standard BrE, *pedler being a chiefly BrE variant.

pederast (= a male homosexual pedophile) is so spelled in AmE and BrE alike. *Paederast is a chiefly BrE variant.

Current ratio: 20:1

pedestal (= a base or foundation) is sometimes, in a wild error, misused for *pestle* (= a tool for pounding or grinding substances in a mortar)—e.g.: "Not at all pretty is the way Oklahoma State plays, all stumble and grunt, a mortar-and-*pedestal* [read *pestle*] kind of basketball." Bernie Lincicome, "These Cowboys Don't Look Capable of Roping a Mule," *Austin Am.-Statesman*, 28 Mar. 1995, at E5.

LANGUAGE-CHANGE INDEX
pedestal misused for *pestle*: Stage 1

pediatric; podiatric. These words both emerged about 1900. *Pediatric* (/pee-dee-**a**-trik/) = of, relating to, or involving the branch of medicine dealing with children. *Podiatric* (/poh-dee-**a**-trik/) = of, relating to, or involving the branch of medicine dealing with the human foot.

pediatrician; *pediatrist. The first is the common, preferred term for a doctor who deals with children and their illnesses. (In BrE, it's spelled *paediatrician*.) The second, a NEEDLESS VARIANT, has the liability of being confused with *podiatrist* (= a foot doctor); it is not used in modern medical practice.

pedicure. See **manicure.**

pedlar; *pedler. See **peddler.**

pedophile (= someone who is sexually attracted to children) is pronounced /ped-ə-fil/; in BrE it's *paedophile* /pee-də-fil/. The term was not in common use until the 1970s.

peel; peal. See **eyes peeled.**

peer over (= to look above and past) for *peer at* (= to look at) is an error that might have resulted from confusion with *look (something) over*—e.g.: "Inside the Israeli police compound in Shati, security guards *peered over* [read *peered at*] the end of a suicide attack. The remains of 19-year-old Bahaa al-Din al-Najr were still in the parking lot where he died hours earlier in a burst of gunfire that set off explosives strapped to his waist." John Kifner, "Dedicated Extremists Present Twin Threat to Peace in Mideast," *N.Y. Times*, 15 Sept. 1993, at A1, A8 (photo caption). You *peer over* an object, not an event. The guards were peering *at* the suicide bomber.

pejorative (= [of a word or phrase] having negative connotations and tending to insult or disparage) is so spelled, though often mistakenly spelled *perjorative from the mid-20th century to the present day—e.g.:

• "By 'radical' I mean not the commonly used political *perjorative* [read *pejorative*] but the original definition." Susan Jacoby, "Hers," *N.Y. Times*, 14 Apr. 1983, at C2.
• "He coined the *perjorative* [read *pejorative*] term 'inside the Beltway.'" David Warsh, "Who Is Bob Bartley?" *Boston Globe*, 17 Mar. 1996, at 77.
• "Words like 'union,' 'public' and 'government' are, sadly, *perjoratives* [read *pejoratives*]." James Warren, "Labor's Fleeting Moment on Stage," *Daily News* (N.Y.), 1 Sept. 2013, Editorial §, at 28.

Though once pronounced /pee-jər-ay-tiv/ (or, in BrE, /pee-jər-ə-tiv/), the predominant (and fully acceptable) pronunciation today is /pə-**jor**-ə-tiv/.

LANGUAGE-CHANGE INDEX
pejorative misspelled *perjorative*: Stage 1
Current ratio: 130:1

Peking. See **Beijing.**

pelvis (= the wide, curved bones on which the spine sits and to which the legs are joined) has two plurals: the ordinary *pelvises* and the Latinate *pelves*. In AmE, *pelvises* bumped out *pelves* as the predominant form in 2003. In BrE, *pelvises* is on the upswing but still remains second to *pelves* in frequency of occurrence—doubtless especially in medical writing.

penal; punitive; penological. These words have distinct senses. *Penal* = of, relating to, or involving punishment or retribution. *Punitive* = serving to punish; intended to inflict punishment. *Penological* = of, relating to, or involving the study of the philosophy and methods of punishment and treatment of people found guilty of crime.

For a MALAPROPISM, see **penile.**

penalize (= [1] to subject to punishment, or [2] to treat unfairly) is most traditionally pronounced /pee-nə-liz/ in AmE and BrE alike. Today, however, /pen-ə-liz/ is widespread and acceptable in AmE.

penchant. Although the Gallic pronunciation /paw[n]-shaw[n]/ is standard in BrE, it's almost unknown in AmE—in which the anglicized /**pen**-chənt/ is standard. See GALLICISMS.

pencil, vb., makes *penciled* and *penciling* in AmE, *pencilled* and *pencilling* in BrE. See SPELLING (B).

pendent; pendant. *Pendent,* adj., = hanging, suspended. *Pendant,* n., = something suspended, as an object on a chain around one's neck.

pending; impending. Both terms apply to things that are about to occur, but in the best usage they denote very different things. What is *pending* is awaiting an outcome—e.g.: "Another precedent has resulted from a *pending* suit by the parents of an American-born teenager killed in a terrorist attack in Israel." Bob Egelko, "11 Families Sue Saudis, Sudan for $3 Trillion," *S.F. Chron.,* 16 Aug. 2002, at A1. What is *impending* is imminent (in the literal sense of the word, "hanging over one's head") and harmful—e.g.: "The phrase 'Back to School' strikes a chord of *impending* doom for most students." Patrick Dunn, "Enrollment Rises in St. Thomas Aquinas's 3rd Year," *Albuquerque J.,* 15 Aug. 2002, West Side J. §, at 4.

Yet it is not uncommon for writers to use *impending* for *pending,* perhaps because they think the extra syllable adds gravitas. Whatever the reason, the SLIP-SHOD EXTENSION threatens to deprive us of a useful word, as *impending* loses its connotations of danger or evil—e.g.:

- "The California Department of Water Resources is planning to issue $11.95 billion of power bonds. XLCA is now poised to insure part of the *impending* [read *pending*] issue." Aaron T. Smith, "MBIA Pushes for Tax Law Change That Could Affect Competitors," *Bond Buyer,* 16 Aug. 2002, at 3.
- "Oxford University scholar and literary biographer Hermione Lee assesses the *impending* [read *pending*] republication of 'On Being Ill,' one of Virginia Woolf's 'most daring, strange and original essays.'" Tim Rutten, "Regarding Media," *L.A. Times,* 16 Aug. 2002, So. Cal. Living §, pt. 5, at 1.
- "He has had some good reasons for playing poorly in the majors this year—an inner-ear infection before the Masters, the *impending* [read *pending*] birth of his daughter at the U.S. Open, and being a new father at the British Open." "Funk, Furyk Lead by One," *Pitt. Post-Gaz.,* 16 Aug. 2002, at B8.

Occasionally, *pending* is used where the context calls for the more ominous connotations that *impending* provides—e.g.: "A blend of myth, history and contemporary comment, much affected by premonitions of the *pending* [read *impending*] World War II, it aptly conveys Orozco's dour, apocalyptic vision of human fate." Grace Glueck, "A Fire Born of Revolution," *N.Y. Times,* 16 Aug. 2002, at E29.

LANGUAGE-CHANGE INDEX
1. *impending* misused for *pending*: Stage 1
2. *pending* misused for *impending*: Stage 1

pendulum (= a swinging weight suspended from a pivot) forms the plural *pendulums* in all varieties of English—not **pendula.*

Current ratio: 2:1

penetrable. So formed—not **penetratable.* See -ABLE (D) & -ATABLE.

Current ratio: 376:1

penile (= of, relating to, or involving the penis) is sometimes mistakenly written *penal* (= of, relating to, or involving punishment)—e.g.:

- "For men whose impotence can't be solved simply by switching medications, he said there are a growing number of treatment options, including hormonal treatment, medication injected directly into the penis, external vacuum pumps that can be used to produce an erection or *penal* [read *penile*] implants." Mary Powers, "Impact on Sex Drive Often Left Unspoken," *Commercial Appeal* (Memphis), 8 Dec. 1991, at C3. (This example cries out for a serial comma.)
- "[T]alk shows [would later feature] lesbian mothers who had won custody of their children, mistresses who discussed the pain of dating married men, William Masters and Virginia Johnson discussing Americans' sexual practices and problems, a film of an actual abortion, parents of gays, and *penal* [read *penile*] implants." Eva S. Moskowitz, *In Therapy We Trust* 262 (2001).

See MALAPROPISMS.

Whereas *penal* is pronounced /**pee**-nəl/, *penile* is pronounced /**pee**-nɪl/.

LANGUAGE-CHANGE INDEX
*penal implants for *penile implants*: Stage 1

penitentiary (= a state or federal prison) is an Americanism in its modern sense—the word once having denoted a place in a monastery for the confinement of those doing penance. Pennsylvania Quakers used the term in the late 18th century to name their prisons, where they instituted solitary confinement. Traditional BrE equivalents are *house of correction* and (in London) *bridewell,* both of which had become old-fashioned by the end of the 19th century.

Penitentiary is preferably pronounced /pen-i-**ten**-shə-ree/, in five syllables. Avoid the six-syllable /pen-i-**ten**-shee-er-ee/.

pen name. See **pseudonym.**

penological. See **penal.**

pentathlon. See -ATHLON.

*penuchle; *penuckle. See **pinochle.**

penultimate (= next-to-last) is sometimes misused for *ultimate* or *quintessential*—e.g.:

- "The classic surfer movie, 'The Endless Summer,' caught a new wave this week in Superior Court here. . . . In the complaint, *Hynson v. Brown,* 694180, Hynson claims that August was set up with a new car, a tavern and, eventually, a surfboard business by Brown, with proceeds from the *penultimate* [read *ultimate* or *quintessential*] surfer movie." Marty Graham, "'Endless Summer' Surfer Says He Never Was Paid," *L.A. Daily J.,* 13 Nov. 1995, at 32. (Could any movie be dubbed the next-to-last surfing movie of all time?)

LANGUAGE-CHANGE INDEX (For the full key, see front matter pp. xxxi, l–li.)
Stage 1: Rejected. **Stage 2:** Widely shunned. **Stage 3:** Widespread but . . . **Stage 4:** Ubiquitous but . . . **Stage 5:** Fully accepted.
Invariably inferior forms marked by asterisk (*). • Ratios represent frequency of prevalent forms vs. variants in current books.

- "As our cover story points out, data warehouses have been sold by many vendors as the *penultimate* [read *quintessential*?] business solution." Alan Alper, "Warehouse Wonders?" *ComputerWorld*, 1 Apr. 1996, at 7.
- "If you took Lachemann at his word, he was either the *penultimate* [read *quintessential*] 'players' manager'—covering up for each and every transgression—or flatly unqualified for the position." Mike Penner, "Taking One for the Team," *L.A. Times*, 7 Aug. 1996, at C1.

Sometimes, too, the word is misspelled **pentultimate* (perhaps through sound association with *pent-up*)—e.g.: "When Poole secured a 4–2 in the *pentultimate* [read *penultimate*] race the scores were level at 42–42." Nigel Pearson, "Champion Rickardsson Is Great Leveller," *Birmingham Evening Mail*, 8 Apr. 2003, at 51. Cf. **paramount, tantamount** & **ultimately.**

LANGUAGE-CHANGE INDEX
1. *penultimate* misused for *ultimate*: Stage 2
2. *penultimate* misspelled **pentultimate*: Stage 1
Current ratio: 10,608:1

penumbra. Though most dictionaries list only the plural *penumbrae*, one could hardly be faulted for anglicizing to *penumbras*. (See PLURALS (B).) E.g.: "They embroider controversial opinions with qualifiers, exemptions, tripartite analyses, *penumbras* and other devices that enable them to wriggle out of positions that infuriate Washington hostesses or the editors of the New York Times." Tony Snow, "Clarence Thomas, No Excuses," *Cincinnati Enquirer*, 7 July 1995, at A14.
Current ratio (*penumbras* vs. *penumbrae*): 3:1

penumbral; *penumbrous. The latter is a NEEDLESS VARIANT.
Current ratio: 107:1

peon. See **paean.**

people. A. And *persons*. The traditional distinction—now a pedantic one—is that *people* is general, *persons* specific. So one refers to *300 people who had assembled* but to *the twelve persons on the jury. Persons* has been considered better for small, specific numbers. But *twelve persons on the jury* seems stuffy to many readers, and most native speakers of English (since about the mid-1970s) would say *twelve people on the jury*. In contexts like that, *people* has long been used and has come to be viewed as the more natural phrasing. Consider these examples:

- "Some *persons* take delight in the felicities of language." Lester S. King, *Why Not Say It Clearly* 81 (1978).
- "Of course, some *persons* do not consider the National Lawyers Guild respectable." Ellsworth Barnard, *English for Everybody* 21 (1979).

To the modern reader or speaker, these sentences seem a little unnatural or strained. By 1865 in BrE and 1880 in AmE, the collocation *some people* was more common in print sources than *some persons*. It's understandable why the Associated Press and *The New York Times* recommend using *people* over *persons* except in

quotations and in SET PHRASES (e.g., *Missing Persons Bureau, third persons*).

LANGUAGE-CHANGE INDEX
people for *persons* in reference to small, specific groups: Stage 5
Current ratio (*three people* vs. **three persons*): 2:1

B. And *state*. A *people* (collectively) is a great many persons united by a common language and by similar customs—usually the result of common ancestry, religion, and historical circumstances. A *state* is a great many persons, generally occupying a given territory, among whom the will of the majority—or of an ascertainable class of persons—prevails against anyone who opposes that will. A *state* may coincide exactly with one *people*, as in Japan, or may embrace several, as in the United States.

Pepys. The last name of Samuel Pepys (1633–1703), the English diarist, is pronounced counterintuitively: /peeps/. The adjective *Pepysian* is correspondingly pronounced /**peep**-see-ən/.

PER- as a prefix typically means "through," as in *perspire* (= to emit sweat through the pores) and *pervade* (= to spread throughout). But in certain ARCHAISMS—such as *perchance, perfervid*, and *perforce*—it's an intensive. It's a hidden intensive in *peruse*.

per. See **a (B)** & ***as per.**

per annum is unnecessary for *a year, per year*, or *each year*. Cf. **per diem.**
Occasionally, the phrase is misspelled *per anum*—an embarrassment because the latter means "through the anus" (a medical EUPHEMISM actually appearing in some discussions of sex crimes). E.g.:

- "The interest rates are aggressively pitched—currently 5 per cent gross *per anum* [read *per annum*] on credit balances." Neasa Macerlean, "Bank on New Tesco Card," *Observer*, 9 June 1996, at 10.
- "[I]ndustrial growth in the same period averaged between 9 and 10 percent *per anum* [read *per annum*]—an impressive performance by any standard." Atul Kohli, *State-Directed Development* 187 (2004).

Whatever the interest rate a debtor must be charged, it's revolting to think of money being paid that way. Surely it's better to pay in the traditional way: through the nose.

LANGUAGE-CHANGE INDEX
per anum misused for *per annum*: Stage 1
Current ratio (*percent per annum* vs.
*percent per anum): 414:1

per capita; per caput. The first is the frequently used plural ("by heads"), the second the rare singular ("a head; by the head").

percent; per cent; per cent.; per centum. This sequence illustrates in reverse the evolution of this word, originally a phrase. The solid word became predominant in AmE about 1968; in BrE the two-word form predominates.

The plural of *percent* is *percent*; adding an *-s*, though not uncommon, is substandard.

In most writing, *75%* is easier to read than *75 percent* or (worse yet) *seventy-five percent*. Prefer the percentage sign when you can. Many styles, however, insist on spelling out *percent*.

AmE writers refer to something's being *at* such-and-such a percent; BrE writers refer to its being *on* the percent—e.g.: "According to a MORI poll in today's Times, Labour finds itself *on 56 per cent* and the Conservatives on 23." Stephen Bates & Martin Linton, "Tory Poll Rating Hits Record Low," *Guardian*, 26 Aug. 1994, at 1. Note also the BrE two-word spelling of *per cent*.

percentage. A. Number. Even though this word is technically a singular, it's usually construed with a plural verb when followed by *of* plus a plural noun (or when the *of*-phrase is implied)—e.g.:

- "Women often have little say about finances at home or at work, while a greater *percentage* than ever before *are* the sole breadwinners." Amy Kaslow, "Helping Women Seen as Boosting World Prosperity," *Christian Science Monitor*, 24 Aug. 1995, Economy §, at 1.
- "A lower *percentage* of over-50s . . . *leave* benefits for work." Richard Adams, "The 'Grey Army' Makes New Push Back to Work," *Fin. Times*, 30 Aug. 1997, at 1.

But when the sentence is inverted, and the verb precedes the noun, a singular verb is required. That is, even though you say *a higher percentage of them are*, you also say *there is a higher percentage of them*. E.g.: "No statistics exist to prove or disprove the widespread perception that there *are* [read *is*] a higher percentage of lesbians than of gay men in the military." "A (Quiet) Uprising in the Ranks," *Newsweek*, 21 June 1993, at 60.

B. And *percentage point*. Writers must be careful with *percentages* and *percentage points*. For example, if the unemployment rate rises from 4% to 6%, both of these statements are true: *Unemployment is up two percentage points*, and *Unemployment is up 50%*. If you're a politician, which sentence you decide to use probably depends on whether your party is in or out of office.

per centum. See **percent.**

perceptible. So spelled—not **perceptable*. See -ABLE (A). For a misuse, see **perceptive.**

Current ratio: 1,309:1

perceptive (= keenly intuitive) for *perceptible* (= appreciable, recognizable) is an infrequent error—e.g.:

- "The Chiefs won yesterday because they made no *perceptive* [read *perceptible*] mistakes offensively." Bob Slocum, "Chiefs Embarrass Jumpy Raiders," *San Diego Union-Trib.*, 26 Nov. 1990, at D7.

- "These are but some of the protests against Ottawa's waste—something the auditor general documents every year with no *perceptive* [read *perceptible*] effect on Ottawa's spending." Peter Worthington, "MP Details Ottawa Waste," *Toronto Sun*, 13 Feb. 1996, at 11.

LANGUAGE-CHANGE INDEX
perceptive misused for *perceptible*: Stage 1

perchance is archaic for *perhaps*. It's often used in mockery or self-mockery—e.g.:

- "Because his offensive skills run to zero, Dennis Rodman baits whomever he can into rutting with him, *perchance* to draw the technical [foul], *perchance* better to forward his image that night on SportsCenter." Thomas Stinson, "Murder and Mayhem? No, It's the NBA," *Atlanta J.-Const.*, 13 May 1995, at F7.
- "The composition of the crowd began to change as exultant figures of the left and centre came to partake of the excellent champagne, and *perchance* to gloat." Rian Malan, "Election '97: One Last Spin Precedes a New Messiah," *Independent*, 4 May 1997, at 18.

See ARCHAISMS.

percolate (= [1] [of a liquid, light, or air] to pass slowly through a permeable material, or [2] [of ideas] to spread as if by effervescence) is pronounced /pər-kə-layt/—not /pər-kyə-layt/.

per diem, a LATINISM, means "for or by the day" <per diem fee>. Sometimes it makes more sense to write *a day* <$50 a day> or *daily* <daily fee>. (See **a (B).**) Although it has been defended when it is positioned before the noun it modifies <per diem allowance>, *daily* is usually an improvement. When used as an adjective, *per diem* is rarely the best available phrase.

As a noun (an Americanism), *per diem* has designated a daily stipend, especially for travel and living expenses, since the early 1800s. It is firmly established and well accepted. Cf. **per annum.**

peremptory. See **preemptive.**

perfect. See ADJECTIVES (B) & **more perfect.**

perfectible. So spelled—preferably not **perfectable*. See -ABLE (A).

Current ratio: 23:1

perfervid. See **fervent.**

perimeter. See **parameters (B).**

period-dots. See PUNCTUATION (F).

periodic; periodical. These two have undergone DIFFERENTIATION. *Periodic*, the more general word, means "occurring at regular intervals" <periodic reviews of employee performance>. (The word also has specialized meanings in mathematical and scientific contexts.) *Periodical* is now usually restricted

LANGUAGE-CHANGE INDEX (For the full key, see front matter pp. xxxi, l–li.)
Stage 1: Rejected. **Stage 2:** Widely shunned. **Stage 3:** Widespread but . . . **Stage 4:** Ubiquitous but . . . **Stage 5:** Fully accepted.
Invariably inferior forms marked by asterisk (*). • Ratios represent frequency of prevalent forms vs. variants in current books.

to mean "published at regular intervals" <periodical newsletters>. And, of course, *periodical* is used as a noun meaning "a publication issued at regular intervals" <the doctor's office subscribed to a dozen or more periodicals>.

period of, for a. This phrase is usually verbose—e.g.: "If your grandchildren or great-grandchildren lived with you *for a period of a year or more* [read *for a year or more*], section (d) of this bill would ensure that they would always be able to visit with the grandparent that kept them." "Grandparents Visitation Bill Far Better than Existing Law," *Ark. Democrat-Gaz.*, 10 Feb. 1991.

period of time is usually unnecessary in place of either *period* or *time*. Cf. **time period.*

PERIODS. See PUNCTUATION (L).

PERIPHRASIS (/pə-**rif**-rə-sis/) = a roundabout way of writing or speaking. Many a technical writer uses "jargon to shirk prose, palming off periphrasis upon us when with a little trouble he could have gone straight to the point." Arthur Quiller-Couch, *On the Art of Writing* 108 (2d ed. 1943). See DOUBLESPEAK, EUPHEMISMS, JARGON & REDUNDANCY.

perjure (= to swear falsely) is now used only as a reflexive verb—e.g.:

- "So which is it that bothers you—that wives no longer obey their husbands, or that they no longer *perjure* themselves by promising to do so?" Judith Martin, "Dive into Problem," *Houston Chron.*, 27 July 1997, at 2.
- "This is a society, Griffin said, where . . . 'a bigot can disguise himself as a police officer' and *perjure* himself during O.J. Simpson's high-profile murder trial." Lola Sherman, "Diversity in Workplace Called Essential by Barrios Panelists," *San Diego Union-Trib.*, 13 Aug. 1997, at B3.
- "He also said the feds encouraged witnesses to *perjure* themselves by giving false testimony and gave 'sweetheart deals' to witnesses who should face criminal charges." Michael O'Keeffe, "Oxi Morons," *N.Y. Daily News*, 3 July 2015, at 62.

perjured, adj.; **perjurious; *perjurous; *perjurial; *perjuried.** *Perjured* is now the usual adjective (a past-participial adjective) corresponding to *perjury*—e.g.: "One defendant was acquitted, and the case against another was dismissed before trial after the *perjured* testimony was exposed." Robert D. McFadden, "Three More in Precinct Are Accused," *N.Y. Times*, 7 Apr. 1995, at B1.

Perjurious is somewhat broader because it means "involving perjury" as opposed to the more specific sense of *perjured* (= characterized by perjury). So it's possible to speak of a person's *perjurious* tendencies but not of *perjured* tendencies. **Perjurous* and **perjurial* are NEEDLESS VARIANTS.

*Perjuried is an infrequent blunder for *perjured*—e.g.: "They committed fraud on the court by misrepresenting and concealing evidence, sponsoring *perjuried* [read *perjured*] testimony, and presenting false evidence." David Cohn, "Court Rejects Asbestos Liability Case," *J. of Commerce*, 28 Nov. 1989, at A13. See **subornation of perjury.**

LANGUAGE-CHANGE INDEX
*perjuried for *perjured*: Stage 1

perjurer. So spelled in AmE and BrE alike—not **perjuror.*

Current ratio: 69:1

*perjurial; *perjuried; perjurious; *perjurous. See **perjured.**

*perjuror. See **perjurer.**

permanence; permanency. These two, both of which appear frequently, share the sense "the quality or state of being permanent." But while *permanence* emphasizes durability <the permanence of the snow>, *permanency* emphasizes duration <the permanency of death>. Since the 1830s, *permanence* has occurred more frequently in English-language print sources than *permanency*.

permissible. So spelled—not **permissable.* See -ABLE (A).

Current ratio: 288:1

permission; acquiescence. *Permission* connotes an authorization to do something, whereas *acquiescence* connotes the passive failure to object to someone's doing something.

permissive; *permissory. The latter is a NEEDLESS VARIANT.

Current ratio: 1,473:1

permit. As a noun meaning "an official document granting the right to do something," *permit* is stressed on the first syllable: /**pər**-mit/. As a verb meaning either "to consent to expressly or formally" or "to enable," *permit* is stressed on the second syllable: /pər-**mit**/. It is a FORMAL WORD. See **allow.**

permute; *permutate. *Permute* is both older and more common than **permutate*, a BACK-FORMATION and NEEDLESS VARIANT.

Current ratio: 10:1

pernickety. See **persnickety.**

perorate (/**pər**-ə-rayt/) = to conclude a formal address. E.g.: "But he makes clear that he believes in an escape from suffocating rules and a return to initiative. Civil servants should be given guidelines, but to get things done they must seize the day. As he *perorates*: 'One basic change in approach will get us going: [etc.—to end of speech].' In short, what Mr. Howard is trying to do with this thoughtful little book is drive us all sane." Christopher Lehmann-Haupt, "A Call to Deregulate Rules and Regulations," *N.Y. Times*, 19 Jan. 1995, at C22.

But the word is sometimes misused for *orate*—e.g.:

- "As directed by Kirk Jackson, the best moments fashion Wadsworth's body into a conflation of father and son: While *perorating* [read *orating*] on homosexuality's evils, Daddy is annoyed by the wig he finds on his head." Steven Drukman, "Cameos," *Village Voice*, 13 Sept. 1994, at 104.
- "Means is fond of *perorating* [read *orating*] endlessly about the Oneness of Nature and Family-ness of All Creatures even as he disparages and excoriates those who would dare question his weltanschauung." Bruce Olds, "Where White Men Fear to Tread," *L.A. Times*, 21 Jan. 1996, Book Rev. §, at 2.
- "McCaughey doesn't merely talk. He expounds. He *perorates* [read *orates*]. He declaims. Ask him what time it is, and he'll tell you how to build a watch." Sinclair Stewart, "The Outsider," *Globe & Mail* (Toronto), 29 Sept. 2006, at 32.
- "For the first time they joined forces with financially hard-pressed hipsters and performance artists who tossed up protest Web sites and trooped to City Hall to *perorate* [read *orate* or *rail*] against the plan." Michael Powell, "A Condo Tower Grows in Brooklyn," *Wash. Post*, 21 Feb. 2007, at C1.

The noun is *peroration* (/pər-ə-**ray**-shən/)—e.g.: "Even before the *peroration*—'Fellow Americans, fellow Democrats, I offer you for the Presidency of the United States, that son of the Texas hills, that tested and effective servant of the people: Lyndon B. Johnson'—the big Texas delegation had begun to roar." Robert A. Caro, *The Years of Lyndon Johnson: Master of the Senate* 821 (2002).

LANGUAGE-CHANGE INDEX
perorate misused for *orate*: Stage 1

perpetrate. See **perpetuate.**

perpetuable. So formed—not **perpetuatable*. See -ABLE (D) & -ATABLE.

perpetual (= continuing forever; everlasting) is sometimes misused for *continuous*—e.g.: "Mr. Rushdie, 46, has lived in almost *perpetual* [read *continuous*] hiding since Feb. 14, 1989, when his novel 'The Satanic Verses' was condemned as blasphemous by Ayatollah Ruhollah Khomeini of Iran, who called for his death." Douglas Jehl, "In a Rebuke to Teheran, Clinton and His Top Aides Meet Rushdie," *N.Y. Times*, 25 Nov. 1993, at A1. At the writing of that sentence, Rushdie had not yet lived forever; it couldn't have been *perpetual* hiding. See ADJECTIVES (B).

LANGUAGE-CHANGE INDEX
perpetual misused for *continuous*: Stage 2

*perpetuatable. See **perpetuable.**

perpetuate (= to make last indefinitely; prolong) and *perpetrate* (= to commit or carry out) are surprisingly often confounded. Although *MWDEU* says that "actual examples of mistaken use are in extremely short supply," the following list could easily be multiplied:

- "But Maxwell could not single-handedly have *perpetuated* [read *perpetrated*] his frauds." Tom Bower, "Cost of Cap'n Bob's Shilling," *Guardian*, 4 May 1992, Features §, at 21.
- "In 1988, Federal District Judge James L. Kinf dismissed the suit as baseless, accused Mr. Shean of knowingly *perpetuating* [read *perpetrating*] a fraud and fined the Christie Institute." Michael Kelly, "Perot Shows Penchant for Seeing Conspiracy," *N.Y. Times*, 26 Oct. 1992, at A10.
- "They assemble to pray for an end to the violence *perpetuated* [read *perpetrated*] on an innocent member of the human race." Letter of Nell Keim, "Abortion Clinic Protests," *Sacramento Bee*, 22 Jan. 1995, at F6.
- "Of course, a good detective may have a clear idea of who has *perpetuated* [read *perpetrated*] the crime." Terence A. Hockenhull, "Getting the Edge in Professional Selling: Doing It Like a Private Eye," *BusinessWorld*, 11 Mar. 1997, at 6.

See MALAPROPISMS.

LANGUAGE-CHANGE INDEX
perpetuate misused for *perpetrate*: Stage 3
Current ratio (*perpetrating crimes* vs.
*perpetuating crimes): 20:1

perquisite; prerequisite. *Perquisite* (often shortened to *perk*) = a privilege or benefit given in addition to one's salary or regular wages <executive perquisites such as club memberships>. *Prerequisite* = a previous condition or requirement <applicants must satisfy all five prerequisites before being interviewed>. Although *MWDEU* says there is "almost no evidence of the words' being interchanged," the confusion certainly does occur—e.g.:

- "Have executive salaries, bonuses and other corporate *prerequisites* [read *perquisites*] been cut, or will the proposed rate increase maintain them?" "Sorry, Wrong Numbers," *Wash. Post*, 11 July 1993, at C8.
- "Then, it needs to start selling permanent seat licenses, luxury boxes and club seats, all the wonderful *prerequisites* [read *perquisites* or *perks*] an NFL owner requires." Ken Rosenthal, "Forget Legal Avenues, Take Baltimore's Route to NFL," *Baltimore Sun*, 30 Nov. 1995, at D1.
- "The five-year contract has an effective date of March 1. In addition to salary, it also provides for negotiated *prerequisites* [read *perquisites* or *perks*] and compensation features." Doug Hensley, "Tech, Dickey Agree to $1 Million Deal," *Amarillo Daily News*, 7 May 1996, at D1.
- "Job descriptions are detailed and present information on duties, salaries, *prerequisites* [read *perquisites*], employment and advancement opportunities, relevant organizations, and special advice for getting into the desired field." Kent Anderson, Book Rev., *School Arts*, 1 Dec. 1996, at 46.

See **prerequisite.**

LANGUAGE-CHANGE INDEX
prerequisite misused for *perquisite*: Stage 1

per se (lit., "through [or *in*, *by*, *of*] itself") = (1) standing alone; in itself; or (2) as a matter of law. The phrase is both adverb and adjective. Formerly used

---

LANGUAGE-CHANGE INDEX (For the full key, see front matter pp. xxxi, l–li.)
Stage 1: Rejected. **Stage 2:** Widely shunned. **Stage 3:** Widespread but . . . **Stage 4:** Ubiquitous but . . . **Stage 5:** Fully accepted.
Invariably inferior forms marked by asterisk (*). • Ratios represent frequency of prevalent forms vs. variants in current books.

almost always after the adjective or noun it modifies, today it is often used before, especially in legal contexts—e.g.:

- "Derivatives are not *per se* unsuitable or risky." Interview with Richard Cortese, *Compliance Rptr.*, 15 May 1995, at 9.
- "Another reason is that in *Town of Newton*, the Supreme Court decided 5–4 that release-dismissal agreements are not *per se* invalid." Monroe Freedman, "Treading On, or Trading Off, Rights?" *Recorder* (S.F.), 17 May 1995, at 6.

When used in this way, *per se* typically means "always," "absolute," or "absolutely."

When in its usual position as a POSTPOSITIVE ADJECTIVE, the phrase takes no punctuation, even though its English equivalents (*in itself, of itself, as such*) are ordinarily framed by commas. E.g.:

- "Design standards, *per se*, [delete commas] were not part of the 1937 Housing Act." Diana Scott, "A Time-Eroded Vision of Public Housing," *S.F. Examiner*, 17 May 1995, Habitat §, at 2.
- "And no one wants to know why 'jobs' *per se* don't 'pay' for many of those who hold them." Loretta Mock, "Public Money Fattens Private Profits," *Newsday* (N.Y.), 18 May 1995, at A36.

The former AmE pronunciation (/pər **see**/) has lost out to /pər **say**/, which is now almost universal.

That pronunciation may explain the phonetic misspelling that occurs surprisingly often (**per say*)—e.g.:

- "But [Tony] Kushner, being Kushner, is not content to lay it all out in such a pat manner. He's less interested in history, *per say* [read *per se*], than the soul of history—and the soul of now." Nina Metz, " 'Bright Room' Has Unshakable Impact," *Chicago Trib.*, 22 Oct. 2005, Weekend §, at 30.
- " 'I don't think this is going to solve the poverty problem in New York *per say* [read *per se*], but it's real money and it's a serious beginning towards a larger strategy,' he said." Jill Gardiner, "Mayor Budgets Anti-Poverty Outlays," *N.Y. Sun*, 19 Dec. 2006, N.Y. §, at 1 (quoting Michael Bloomberg).
- " 'The limitations aren't going to be the dollars *per say* [read *per se*] as to what we can pay a coach.' " Jeff Shelman, "Questions and Answers," *Star Trib.* (Minneapolis), 8 Mar. 2007, at C7 (quoting Joel Maturi, University of Minnesota athletic director).

LANGUAGE-CHANGE INDEX
*per say for *per se*: Stage 1
Current ratio (*per se* vs. **per say*): 445:1

persecute. See **prosecute.**

persevere is pronounced /pər-sə-**veer**/. Because the word is frequently a victim of the intrusive *-r-* (/pər-sər-**veer**/), it is often misspelled **perservere*. The corresponding noun, *perseverance* (/pər-sə-**veer**-ən[t]s/), has been similarly victimized. See PRONUNCIATION (B), (C) & SPELLING (A).

persistence (= tenacity of purpose; doggedness) has been the predominant form of the word in all varieties of English since the 18th century. **Persistency* is a NEEDLESS VARIANT.

Current ratio: 24:1

persnickety; pernickety. The older form, *pernickety*, has been standard BrE since the word was first used in the early 19th century. It was also standard AmE till about 1980, when *persnickety* became predominant. Today *persnickety* is about five times as common in print as *pernickety* in AmE—e.g.:

- "We adore *persnickety* bachelor Jerry Seinfeld." Marge Colburn, "TV Decor: What We See Is What We Get," *Chicago Sun-Times*, 23 Dec. 1994, at 5.
- "When a *persnickety* neighbor comes over to complain about your paint peeling off your fence, you thank him ever so much for caring and hand him a paintbrush." Steve Wilson, "In Freemen Standoff, Patience Is Virtue for Only So Long," *Ariz. Republic*, 24 May 1996, at A2.
- "Normally we're pretty *persnickety* about cheese steak sandwiches, but Skinny J's version . . . was, while not authentic, pretty darn good." Eric H. Harrison, "Skinny J's Choices Are Wide," *Ark. Democrat-Gaz.*, 3 Sept. 2015, Style §, at 51.

-PERSON. See SEXISM (C).

persona is singular, not plural—*personas* (which is preferable) or *personae* being the plural. But writers sometimes also misuse *personae* as a singular—e.g.: "But instead of writing another original screenplay, Tarantino has staked his reputation on a different approach: he has acquired rights to a best-selling crime novel from the hot author of *Get Shorty* and adapted it around the retro-hip *personae* [read *persona*] of the ultimate 1970s blaxploitation babe, Pam Grier." Jeffrey Ressner, "Back in the Action," *Time*, 18 Aug. 1997, at 70.

LANGUAGE-CHANGE INDEX
personae misused as a singular: Stage 1

persona non grata (/pər-**soh**-nə non **gray**-tə/ or /**grah**-tə/) [L. "an unwanted person"] is so spelled. In law the phrase refers most commonly to a diplomat who is not acceptable to a host country, but generally the phrase refers to anyone who is unwelcome. E.g.: "Whitney was believed to be damaged goods and was marked as *persona non grata* at the end of his three-plus years with the Florida Panthers." Michael Arace, "All-Star Billing," *Columbus Dispatch*, 17 Jan. 2003, at D1.

Some writers get misled by the much more common LATINISM *gratis* (/**grat**-is/), meaning "free, without charge," and proceed to mangle the phrase—e.g.:

- "Couples who should know better are quickly becoming *persona non gratis* [read *persona non grata*] in several circles." Judy Wells, "The Wells Watch," *Fla. Times-Union*, 13 Feb. 2000, at D2. (Because of the plural sense, another wording would be preferable. See below.)
- "Through mid-August they . . . were *persona non gratis* [read *persona non grata*] to their fans." Jay Greenberg, "Yes, It Really Is Happening," *N.Y. Post*, 23 Sept. 2001, at 106. (Ditto.)
- "When he questioned the wisdom of being listed as her newest book club selection, he traded in her seal of approval for a *persona non gratis* [read *persona non grata*] label instead." Lisa Tramontana, "Corrections: Bestseller Achieves Success Without Oprah's Boost," *Advocate* (Baton Rouge), 27 Jan. 2002, Mag. §, at 13.

The Latin plural is *personae non gratae* (/pər-**soh**-nee non **gray**-tee/, not /pər-**soh**-nɪ/ or /-**nay**/), which can't be readily anglicized: **personas non grata* doesn't work, and neither does **persona non gratas* (or, worse yet, **personas non gratas*). In the first two quotations above, a plural is called for: the writers would have been well advised to use *unwelcome, unacceptable, ostracized*, or some other word. But what seems to be happening today is that *persona non grata* is becoming freely singular or plural, as the sense requires.

The antonym of *persona non grata* is the less common *persona grata* (= a person who is welcome). While the negative form occurs in both AmE and BrE, the positive form (infrequent as it is) appears far more often in BrE than in AmE.

LANGUAGE-CHANGE INDEX
*persona non gratis for *persona non grata*: Stage 1
Current ratio (*persona non grata* vs.
*persona non gratis): 142:1

*personation. See **impersonation.**

persons. See **people** (A).

person . . . they; person . . . them. See CONCORD (B).

perspective. See **prospective.**

perspicuous; perspicacious. *Perspicuous* is to *perspicacious* as *intelligible* is to *intelligent*. *Perspicuous* (/pər-**spik**-yoo-əs/) may be defined etymologically as "see-through-it-ive-ness." It means "clear, lucid," and it is applied to thought and expression—e.g.: "Jackson's new lyrics are *perspicuous*, leaving no doubt as to their meaning." Bill Eichenberger, "Jackson Wraps Sophisticated Sounds Around Naive Messages," *Columbus Dispatch*, 21 July 1995, at E10. *Perspicacious* (/pər-spi-**kay**-shəs/) = penetrating in thought; acutely discerning; keen; shrewd <a writer as perspicacious as Susan Sontag>.

The noun corresponding to *perspicuous* is *perspicuity* (/pər-spi-**kyoo**-ə-tee/)—e.g.: "The making of distinctions is the task of all philosophy, of course, but no one does it with the *perspicuity* and finesse of Isaiah Berlin." Robert Craft, "Sir Isaiah's Philosophical Bestiary," *Wash. Post*, 16 Aug. 1992, Book World §, at 11.

The noun corresponding to *perspicacious* is *perspicacity* (/pər-spi-**kas**-ə-tee/), meaning "keenness, insight, great intelligence." Sometimes *perspicuity* incorrectly displaces it—e.g.:

- "Dangerous even then, but what's not to trust in a guy who orders orange juice with his dinner and showed the *perspicuity* [read *perspicacity*?] not to be excited about being bound for the Bills in Buffalo?" Cheryl Johnson, "Trial Brings Flashback to '69: Married O.J. Put a Move on Her," *Star Trib.* (Minneapolis), 5 Oct. 1995, at B3.
- "Indeed, His Gray Eminence believes that, if only those at City Hall had his visionary *perspicuity* [read *perspicacity*], Long Beach would now have a major football stadium, an NFL team, clean ocean water, great waves, a

surplus of downtown parking, a surplus of tax revenue, no red ink-draining fish tank, and enough tourist trade to guarantee almost every businessperson in the city a profit." Doug Krikorian, "Taking a Wait, See Approach to Torre," *Long Beach Press-Telegram*, 2 Nov. 2007, at C1.
- "Before Japanese bosses celebrate, they may want to consider that this golden opportunity is hardly the result of business *perspicuity* [read *perspicacity*]. Japanese companies had such a surfeit of unused capital because of poor corporate governance and fiscal management." "Mergers and Acquisitions: The Japanese Are Coming (Again)," *Economist*, 4 Oct. 2008, at 92.

Worse yet, through WORD-SWAPPING people have begun to confuse *perspicacity* with *pertinacity* (= unyielding persistence, obstinacy)—e.g.: "It is still possible to beat the bogey of passenger airlines undercutting cargo rates; all it takes is good old persistence and *perspicacity* [read *pertinacity*] in finding the right product mix." Brian Johnson-Tomas, "Look to Charters for Competitive Edge," *Air Cargo World*, 1 Mar. 1994, at 17. On 31 August 1997, the day Princess Diana died after a car crash in Paris while being pursued by paparazzi, one television commentator referred to the "dogged perspicacity" of the photographers who hound celebrities. That's a MALAPROPISM: he certainly didn't mean to praise those photographers for being intelligent.

LANGUAGE-CHANGE INDEX
1. *perspicuity* for *perspicacity*: Stage 1
2. *perspicacity* for *pertinacity*: Stage 1

persuadable; *persuadible; *persuasible. The preferred form is *persuadable*. The others are NEEDLESS VARIANTS. See -ABLE (A).

What follows may seem like a one-off error, but usage mistakes are like cockroaches and ants: where you find one, you're bound to find others. **Persuasibility* (a variant of *persuadability*) has been misused for *persuasiveness* (= the quality of engendering belief or commitment) here: "Where status equality exists, then other factors such as the inherent *persuasibility* [read *persuasiveness*] of the arguments may be salient." Elizabeth Chell, *The Psychology of Behaviour in Organizations* 103 (1987). Arguments can be persuasive but never persuadable. The fanciness of **persuasibility* may have misled the writer.

persuade; convince. In the best traditional usage, one *persuades* another *to do* something but *convinces* another *of* something. The idea was to avoid *convince to*—the phrasing **she convinced him to resign* is traditionally viewed as less good than *she persuaded him to resign.*

Either *convince* or *persuade* may be used with a *that*-clause. Although *persuade that* occurs mostly in legal contexts, it does appear elsewhere—e.g.:

- "But at the same time he's *persuaded that* he has to take advantage of the message of tolerance that is part of

LANGUAGE-CHANGE INDEX (For the full key, see front matter pp. xxxi, l–li.)
Stage 1: Rejected. **Stage 2:** Widely shunned. **Stage 3:** Widespread but . . . **Stage 4:** Ubiquitous but . . . **Stage 5:** Fully accepted.
Invariably inferior forms marked by asterisk (*). • Ratios represent frequency of prevalent forms vs. variants in current books.

Muhammad's legacy." Carl Bernstein & Marco Politi, "Power and the Pope," *San Diego Union-Trib.*, 18 Oct. 1996, at E1.

- "The merger has received preliminary approval from the UC Board of Regents, which was *persuaded that* the agreement would avert financial problems at UCSF." Lisa M. Krieger, "Bills May Threaten UC–Stanford Merger," *S.F. Examiner*, 22 May 1997, at A6.

LANGUAGE-CHANGE INDEX
convince as an equivalent of *persuade*: Stage 5

*persuadible; *persuasible. See **persuadable.**

pertain. See **appertain.**

pertinence; *pertinency. Although both forms were fairly common till 1850, about that time *pertinence* became predominant. It is now about 12 times as common as **pertinency*, which is merely a NEEDLESS VARIANT. See -CE.

peruse (= to read with great care) is pompous and stilted in business correspondence. That is, the word shouldn't be used merely as a fancy substitute for *read*. It is pronounced /pə-**rooz**/; the corresponding noun is *perusal* /pə-**rooz**-əl/.

Some writers misuse the word as if it meant "to read quickly" or "scan" (in the colloquial sense of that word)—e.g.:

- "Combs takes off his round sunglasses, quickly *peruses* [read *skims*] the stack of documents, asks a few questions and then signs several, but requests changes in others." Chuck Philips, "Bad Boy II Man," *L.A. Times*, 25 May 1997, Calendar §, at 8.
- "While both teams anxiously milled about in front of their dugouts and restless fans voiced their opinions, Thornton hurriedly *perused* [read *read* or *scanned*] the rule book." "One Giant Step for Merchants," *Lewiston Morning Trib.* (Idaho), 5 Aug. 1997, at B1.
- "It is now a bit awkward so I do as I'm told and very briefly *peruse* [read *look over*] the authors, seeing Dickens, Kipling, Steinbeck, Günter Grass, Don DeLillo, Virginia Woolf." Helena de Bertondano, "I Hear Obama Did Read the Book," *Sunday Telegraph*, 26 Sept. 2010, Features §.

That SLIPSHOD EXTENSION has become common enough to be listed in some dictionaries. But since it's the opposite of the word's traditional meaning, that usage is best shunned.

LANGUAGE-CHANGE INDEX
peruse for *skim* or *glance over*: Stage 2

*pervade throughout. This phrase is redundant, since *pervade* means "to be throughout; spread throughout"—e.g.: "The bold use of color *pervades throughout* [read *pervades*] the first floor rooms." Frances Jaques, "Decor Delight," *Capital* (Annapolis), 10 May 1997, at D1. See REDUNDANCY.

LANGUAGE-CHANGE INDEX
*pervade throughout for *pervade*: Stage 1

petard; petar. See **hoist(ed) with one's own petar(d).**

petitio principii. See **beg the question.**

petit jury; petty jury. The first spelling is standard in AmE, the second in BrE. The terms are pronounced identically: /**pet**-ee **juur**-ee/.

pettifog, n., is a NONWORD in place of *pettifogger* (= [1] a petty or disreputable lawyer; or [2] someone who quibbles over trivial matters). It's a fairly unusual error—e.g.: "Yet though [H.W. Fowler] was a stickler, he was no pedant. Apart from newspaper writers, whose mangling of the language kept him supplied with horrible examples, nothing aroused his derision like the *pettifog* [read *pettifogger*]." William P. Cheshire, "The Man Who Kept the Light Burning in the Twilight," *Ariz. Republic*, 14 July 1991, at C4. But *pettifog* does appear correctly as a verb <he wastes most of his time pettifogging over trivialities>, a BACK-FORMATION from the noun.

LANGUAGE-CHANGE INDEX
pettifog misused for *pettifogger* as a noun: Stage 1

petty jury. See **petit jury.**

-PH-. See PRONUNCIATION (D).

phalanx (/**fay**-langks/) = (1) a body of troops in close array; (2) a massed or organized group of individuals; or (3) a finger bone or toe bone. In senses 1 and 2, the plural is *phalanxes*; in sense 3, it's *phalanges*. See PLURALS (B).

phallus. Pl. *phalluses* or (less good) **phalli*. In modern print sources, *phalluses* is much more common—and has been so since about 1980. See PLURALS (B).

Current ratio: 2:1

phantasm (= a specter or ghost) is the standard spelling in AmE and BrE alike. **Fantasm* is a variant.

Current ratio: 42:1

phantasmagoria (= a constantly shifting scene that is colorful or bizarre) is singular, not plural—e.g.: "An intimate, inward piece, it was a *phantasmagoria* of sound effects." Ellen Pfeifer, "'Sneakers' Gives Tiny Audience a Big Treat," *Boston Herald*, 31 July 1997, at 36.

The plural is *phantasmagorias*, but *phantasmagoria* is sometimes misused as a plural—e.g.: "The real-life Marshall Applewhite and his followers had already done that far more effectively than any of the *phantasmagoria* [read *phantasmagorias*] conjured up by Chris Carter and his award-winning team." Damian Thompson, "The Brainwashing of America," *Daily Telegraph*, 9 Aug. 1997, Features §, at 15.

LANGUAGE-CHANGE INDEX
phantasmagoria misused as a plural: Stage 1

*phantasy. See **fantasy.**

Pharisaic; *Pharisaical; *pharisaic; pharisaical. The first is the predominant word meaning "of, relating to, or involving the Pharisees," members of an ancient Jewish sect who strictly observed the written laws and traditions of religion but who were criticized in the

New Testament as being hypocritically self-righteous. By extension, the lowercase word *pharisaical* (note the *-al*) has come to mean "observing the letter but not the spirit of religious doctrine; sanctimonious." *Pharisaic* is pronounced /fa-rə-**say**-ik/, *pharisaical* /fa-rə-**say**-i-kel/.

Pharisaical and *pharisaic* are NEEDLESS VARIANTS.

pharmaceutical; *pharmaceutic. The latter is a NEEDLESS VARIANT.

Current ratio: 519:1

phase. See **faze.**

phase out. See PHRASAL VERBS.

Ph.D. (L. *Philosophiae Doctor* "Doctor of Philosophy") requires the lowercase *-h-* and (traditionally) both periods—although increasingly the periods are omitted.

phenom. See **phenomenon (c).**

phenomena. See **phenomenon (A).**

phenomenalism (= in philosophy, the theory that knowledge is limited to phenomena, i.e., things that can be perceived or observed) is the standard spelling. **Phenomenism* is a variant.

Current ratio: 18:1

phenomenon. A. And *phenomena*. *Phenomenon* is the singular form, *phenomena* the plural. Writers have misused the plural form as if it were singular since the mid-19th century. The error persists—e.g.:

- "Not only was this *phenomena* precipitated by the final growth in the price of gas, but by such other disclosures as prospective shallow water zones." Dev George, "Emphasis on Economy Continues as Industry Adjusts to Lower Prices," *Offshore*, May 1994, at 29. (Read: *This phenomenon was precipitated not only by the final growth in the price of gas but also by* . . . . [See PARALLELISM.])
- "No social *phenomena* [read *phenomenon*] highlights the change better than the explosive growth of religious cults." Merrill Goozner, "Dispirited Young Japanese Swelling the Ranks of Cults," *Chicago Trib.*, 24 Mar. 1995, at 1.
- "'One to One' marketing has become the mantra of Internet commerce. . . . Customers who experience the One to One *phenomena* [read *phenomenon*] feel special." William Cunningham, "How to Win Truly Loyal Customer," *Cincinnati Post*, 21 Aug. 2000, at B7.
- "If the sky is clear during the moon's early crescent phases, it's also possible to see the entire dark disc of the moon faintly illuminated as well. This *phenomena* [read *phenomenon*] is possible because of earthshine, the reflection of sunlight off Earth and over to the moon." Dan Malerbo, "Vernal Equinox, New Moon," *Pitt. Post-Gaz.*, 16 Mar. 2015, at D7.

See PLURALS (B).

Surprisingly, the word is often misspelled **phenomenum*, especially in BrE—e.g.:

- "In Argentina, ego deflation on a national scale was first encountered as a local *phenomenum* [read *phenomenon*]."

Glenn Gibbons, "Euro 96: Scotland So Far but No Further," *Observer*, 2 June 1996, Sports §, at 5.
- "But to those trying to get a grip on the Hingis *phenomenum* [read *phenomenon*], it didn't matter." Charles Bricker, "1 More Step: 16-Year-Old Martina Hingis Is About to Cap Her Meteoric Rise by Succeeding," *Sun-Sentinel* (Ft. Lauderdale), 18 Mar. 1997, at C1.
- "A press release from the publication arrives in the inbox saying that the social networking *phenomenum* [read *phenomenon*] has become 'a left-wing attack tool.'" "Business Diary," *Independent*, 18 Nov. 2009, at 42.

LANGUAGE-CHANGE INDEX
1. *phenomena* as a singular: Stage 2
Current ratio (*a rare phenomenon* vs.
*a rare phenomena): 60:1
2. *phenomenon* misspelled **phenomenum*: Stage 1
Current ratio: 20,877:1

B. As a Plural. Conversely, the singular *phenomenon* is sometimes mistakenly used as a plural—e.g.: "These irregularities could explain several *phenomenon* [read *phenomena*] in the earth including the well-known jerkiness in the planet's rotational rate." George Alexander, "Cat Scans Used to Explore the Earth," *N.Y. Times*, 16 Dec. 1986, at C3. Cf. **criterion** & **media.**

LANGUAGE-CHANGE INDEX
phenomenon as false plural for *phenomena*: Stage 1

C. And *phenomenons, phenom(s)*. Even though *phenomena* is the accepted plural, some people erroneously write *phenomenons*—e.g.:

- "The seven-day week, alone among the components of the calendar, has always been thought to be a product of divine instruction or social convention, not set by natural *phenomenons* [read *phenomena*] as the day, month and year are." Jon Nordheimer, "Sunday Afternoon Blues," *Kansas City Star*, 13 Oct. 1991, at G1.
- "One of the strangest *phenomenons* [read *phenomena*] in nature is the way a moose can disappear." Craig Medred, "Are You Looking to Bag Moose?" *Anchorage Daily News*, 17 Aug. 1997, at F1.
- "These *phenomenons* [read *phenomena*] change sign for time-reversed magnetic domains." Hans Schmid, "Magnetoelectric Effects in Insulating Magnetic Materials," in *Introduction to Complex Mediums for Optics and Electromagnetics* 167, 182 (Werner S. Weiglhofer & Akhlesh Lakhtakia eds., 2003).

But in the popular sense "a talented person who is achieving remarkable success and popularity," *phenomenon* makes the plural *phenomenons* <Garth Brooks and Clint Black, two great phenomenons of country music, were present>. E.g.: "*Phenomenons* need not be phenomenal every week, especially when they fulfill so many agendas—youth and commercial, color and culture." Bud Shaw, "All Types of Fans Just Talkin' Tiger," *Plain Dealer* (Cleveland), 23 Aug. 1997, at D1.

In this last sense, the word is often replaced by the CASUALISM *phenom* (the result of apocope)—e.g.:

- "He will join Loyola's Colin Falls and Ohio high school *phenom* LeBron James in the game." Marlen Garcia,

LANGUAGE-CHANGE INDEX (For the full key, see front matter pp. xxxi, l–li.)
Stage 1: Rejected. **Stage 2:** Widely shunned. **Stage 3:** Widespread but . . . **Stage 4:** Ubiquitous but . . . **Stage 5:** Fully accepted.
Invariably inferior forms marked by asterisk (*). • Ratios represent frequency of prevalent forms vs. variants in current books.

"Ex-Proviso East Coach Faces Trouble in Peoria," *Chicago Trib.*, 21 Feb. 2003, Sports §, at 11.

- "'Come Away' is now a certifiable *phenom*, an album that caught on with grown-ups, starting with NPR instead of MTV and then moving to younger audiences as the months went by." David Segal, "Yes, Norah!" *Wash. Post*, 24 Feb. 2003, at C1.

LANGUAGE-CHANGE INDEX
1. *phenomenons* as false plural for *phenomena*: Stage 3
2. *phenomenons* in reference to notable people <the popularity of Peyton Manning and Jordan Spieth makes them true sports phenomenons>: Stage 4

philanderer (= a man who engages in brief love affairs) is the standard form. *Philander*, n., is a NEEDLESS VARIANT. Of course, *philander* is the invariable verb <after a life of philandering, he had little to show for it but nine illegitimate children whom he hardly knew>.

philatelist (= a stamp collector) is pronounced /fi-**lat**-əl-ist/ in AmE and BrE alike—not /fi-**layt**-əl-ist/ or /fi-**laht**-əl-ist/. The most common cognates are *philately* /fi-**lat**-əl-ee/ and *philatelic* /fil-ə-**tel**-ik/. Cf. **numismatist.**

Philippine Islands, often shortened to *Philippines*, is so spelled. The native islanders are known as *Filipinos*, a word deriving from the country's name when it was a Spanish possession: *Islas Filipinas.*

philology. See **linguistics.**

philosophical (= of, relating to, or involving philosophers or philosophy) has been the standard form since the late 17th century. *Philosophic* is a variant. See -IC.
                                                            Current ratio: 10:1

phlegmatic (= having a slow, calm temperament) is pronounced /fleg-**mat**-ik/, with a hard -*g*-. This despite the silent -*g*- in the corresponding noun *phlegm* (= [1] mucus produced in the nose and throat, or [2] calm, steady equanimity in all situations).

phony (= false, sham) is the standard spelling. *Phoney* is a variant.
                                                            Current ratio: 7:1

PHRASAL ADJECTIVES. A. General Rule. When a phrase functions as an adjective preceding the noun it modifies—an increasingly frequent phenomenon in 20th- and 21st-century English—the phrase should ordinarily be hyphenated. Hence *the soup is burning hot* becomes *the burning-hot soup*; *the child is six years old* becomes *the six-year-old child*. Most professional writers know this; most nonprofessionals don't.

The primary reason for the hyphens is that they prevent MISCUES and make reading easier and faster. Following are examples drawn from four University of Chicago Press books published from 1987 to 2002:

absurd-sounding orders
across-the-board discounts
acute-care treatment

agreed-upon answer
AIDS-related complexes
Anglo-American court
average-cost compilation
basing-point pricing
best-known one
bid-rotation schemes
big-ticket item
black-haired eagle-faced professor
brain-bisected monkey
broad-stroked depictions
business-tort law
certificate-of-need laws
choice-of-evil situation
class-action lawyers
classical-formalist legal thinking
common-carrier industries
common-law character
computer-software firms
cost-minimizing output
cost-reducing advantages
court-imposed deadline
court-ordered separation
criminal-law sense
dealer-service theory
death-producing acts
delivered-price systems
demand-creating activity
downward-sloping line
early-nineteenth-century settlers
easy-credit charge account
electrical-equipment conspirators
English-speaking people
evil-minded aggressor
exclusive-dealing contracts
face-to-face meetings
far-ranging and free-thinking eclecticism
first-run motion pictures
five-judge tribunal
flesh-and-blood individuals
foreign-sounding name
for-profit firms
French-lace smuggler
full-blown cartel
garden-variety exclusive-dealing case
government-owned business
hard-and-fast, cut-and-dried, open-and-shut issue
hard-core sexual conduct
hard-eyed view
hard-to-read writing
head-on collision
head-to-head competition
high-echelon FBI officials
higher-price outlet
high-volume manufacturer
hit-and-run statute
HIV-negative person
identical-looking ships
identity-determining memories
illusion-ridden jurists
industry-wide price-fixing committees
information-technology personnel
ink-dispensing writing utensil
intellectual-property markets
interest-group pressures
Internet-related firms

Jaguar-driving playboy
joint-stock company
joint-venture route
judge-made rules
kidney-dialysis machine
large-scale production
law-school-sponsored training
long-run costs
long-standing problems
long-term care
loose-knit arrangement
low-cost sellers
lower-paying job
make-believe world
marginal-revenue curve
market-clearing level
market-definition cases
market-share trends
merger-to-monopoly movement
most-favored-nation clause
narrow-minded and out-of-date productions
never-published introductory essay
new-economy industries
nineteenth-century judge
no-distribution constraint
no-fault divorce
not-for-profit firms
now-classic treatise
odd-numbered license plates
office-supply stores
one-way window
original-equipment market
output-reducing effects
patent-misuse cases
pension-fund investments
point-by-point defense
policy-analysis spectrum
potential-competition doctrine
price-discriminating monopolist
price-fixing conspiracies
private-brand equivalent
profit-seeking efforts
quality-adjusted price
quality-enhancing advantages
raw-material costs
razor-sharp minds
restricted-distribution cases
right-hand side
right-wing group
run-of-the-mill cases
safe-driving billboard
sealed-bid basis
second-run showing
self-enforcing agreements
seventeen-year-old boy
shoe-machinery firms
short-run effects
single-firm monopoly
single-spaced pages
single-store grocery
sleeping-car business
small-business standpoint

still-mourned wartime president
subsequent-run motion pictures
supplier-customer relation
tacit-collusion case
third-party physician
third-year medical student
three-part harmony
thumbs-up sign
time-honored method
trademark-sharing cases
trade-secret law
treble-damage suits
Ulysses-and-the-Sirens strategy
university-educated, middle-class males
war-weary jury
well-authenticated cases
well-designed system
well-publicized suicide
well-recognized exception
writ-copying apprenticeship
yes-or-no question
zero-sum game

Reputable newspaper publishers are as conscientious about this point as reputable book publishers. What follows is a sampling of phrasal adjectives found in *The Wall Street Journal* during one week:

11-mile split
20-year lows
24-hour-a-day guards
30-year fixed loan
50-odd brands
$55-a-barrel oil
across-the-board cuts
anthrax-tainted letters
banking-supervision committee
believe-it-or-not category
big-is-better philosophy
blue-blood, country-club Republicans
bond-trading activities
cash-starved telecom outfits
cellular-phone networks
central-bank officials
client-confidentiality rules
crop-dusting manuals
decade-old U.N. sanctions
Democrat-led Senate
distressed-debt investors
DVD-viewing programs
energy-trading colossus
farm-subsidies issue
fast-track authority
full-body patdown
health-care coverage
higher-income earners
highest-ranking officers
high-school students
high-stakes bid
homeland-security director
inhaled-anthrax infection
law-enforcement official

---

little-known presidential candidate
low-end commitment
low-income workers
market-share figure
me-too competition
mom-and-pop retail outlet
movie-theater industry
national-security briefing
natural-gas pipeline
no-documentation loans
note-receivable assets
one-way flight
optical-scan ballots
precinct-count device
precinct-counted optical-scan ballots
private-sector employees
public-health pandemics
punch-card ballots
real-estate prices
right-wing militia
round-the-clock bargaining
search-and-rescue operation
second-largest army
securities-trading unit
shell-shocked mothers
state-sponsored terrorism
stepped-up air campaign
stock-crippled Yahoo
third-largest oil producer
third-quarter loss
three-day visit
top-executive team
tough-girl raiment
treaty-member countries
U.S.-led campaign
venture-backed tech start-ups
Washington, D.C.-based airline-industry trade group
well-armed guerrilla fighters
wire-transfer services
working-class jury
zero-interest new-car loans

In any single issue of that newspaper, you will find many more hyphenated phrasal adjectives than these.

Upon encountering a phrasal adjective, the reader isn't misled into thinking momentarily that the modifying phrase is really a noun itself. In other words, the hyphens greatly clarify the meaning. It matters a great deal, for example, where you put hyphens in *last known criminal activity report*.

Some guides might suggest that you should make a case-by-case decision, based on whether a misreading is likely. You're better off with a flat rule (with a few exceptions noted below) because almost all sentences with unhyphenated phrasal adjectives will be misread by *someone*. (See PUNCTUATION (J).) The following examples demonstrate the hesitation or lack of clarity caused by a missing hyphen:

- "One last pop on this whole question of incivility of discourse, the *much argued over* [read *much-argued-over*] issue of whose speech has been more inflammatory and socially destructive than whose." Meg Greenfield, "It's Time for Some Civility," *Newsweek*, 5 June 1995, at 78. (After *much argued*, the reader expects a noun; then *over* appears, unsettling the reader for a moment; then, in two

milliseconds, the reader adjusts to see that *much-argued-over* is a phrasal adjective modifying *issue*.)
- "O'Neill is serving a 20- to 40-year state prison sentence in Dallas, Luzerne County, for a Northampton County conviction in 1994 on *statutory rape, involuntary deviate sexual intercourse and corruption of minors charges.*" Bob Laylo, "Children Testify on Sex Ring Abuse," *Morning Call* (Allentown, Pa.), 20 Sept. 1996, at B1. (Read either *statutory-rape, involuntary-deviant-sexual-intercourse, and corruption-of-minors charges* or [better] *charges of statutory rape, involuntary deviant sexual intercourse, and corruption of minors.* [On the change from *deviate* to *deviant*, see **deviant (A)**.)
- "*Business telephone call protocol* is crucial." Mary Newton Bruder, *The Grammar Lady* 84 (2000). (A possible revision: *Business telephone-call protocol is crucial.*)
- "This *English as a second language text* presents the different speaking styles for international students." *Ibid.* at 243. (A possible revision: *This English-as-a-second-language text presents the different speaking styles for international students.*)

Readability is especially enhanced when the hyphens are properly used in two phrasal adjectives that modify a single noun—e.g.:

13-year-old court-ordered busing plan
24-hour-a-day doctor-supervised care
county-approved billboard-siting restriction
long-latency occupational-disease cases

Some writers—those who haven't cultivated an empathy for their readers—would omit all those hyphens.

Following are examples in which enlightened writers or editors supplied the necessary hyphens:

- "As a reader you are alerted by that direct, *straight-to-the-heart-of-the-matter statement.*" Lucile V. Payne, *The Lively Art of Writing* 65 (1965).
- "The petition . . . argues that the ruling 'took a major step away from settled law' in the First Amendment's *free-exercise-of-religion clause.*" Wade Lambert & Wayne E. Green, "Subway-Begging Ban Is Backed on Appeal," *Wall Street J.*, 11 May 1990, at B8, B11.
- "The survey was conducted by telephone Jan. 12–16, before the radio ads promoting the *official-English bill* were broadcast on Atlanta radio stations." Elizabeth Kurylo & Rhonda Cook, "*English-Only Bill* Splits Georgians," *Atlanta J.-Const.*, 20 Feb. 1994, at A1.
- "The *English-language bill*'s sponsor, Sen. Mike Crotts (R-Conyers), said he is confident the legislation will pass the Senate." *Ibid.* at A14.
- "They lived in a *first-floor apartment* in a *six-story rent-controlled, union-subsidized housing development* in Flushing, Queens." Ken Auletta, "Beauty and the Beast," *New Yorker*, 16 Dec. 2002, at 65, 70.
- "'Out of the way, out of the way!' sang Mrs. Weasley, coming through the gate with what appeared to be a giant, *beach-ball-sized Snitch* floating in front of her." J.K. Rowling, *Harry Potter and the Deathly Hallows* 119 (1st Am. ed. 2007).

For more on these hyphens, see PUNCTUATION (J).

B. Exception for *-ly* Adverbs. When a phrasal adjective begins with an adverb ending in *-ly*, the convention is to drop the hyphen—e.g.: "With the *hotly-contested* [read *hotly contested*] Second Congressional District primary six days away, supporters of Sen. Bob

Smith gathered last night just as curious about a race two years away and a candidate who hasn't said yet whether he's running." M.L. Elrick, "Kemp Coy on Plans for 1996," *Concord Monitor*, 8 Sept. 1994, at B1. But if the *-ly* adverb is part of a longer phrase, then the hyphen is mandatory (*the not-so-hotly-contested race*).

Meanwhile, be sure not to confuse adjectives ending in *-ly* with adverbs. A hyphen is proper—e.g.: "She was a *curly-haired* gamine, ghosting through the hawthorn hedge that bordered the main path." Charles de Lint, "Merlin Dreams in the Mondream Wood" (1990), in *The Merlin Chronicles* 434, 442 (Mike Ashley ed., 1995).

C. Suspensive Hyphens. When two phrasal adjectives have a common element at the end, and this ending portion (usually the last word) appears only with the second phrase, insert a suspensive hyphen after the unattached words to show their relationship with the common element. The hyphens become especially important when phrases are compounded in this way—e.g.:

- "Detroit is . . . positioning the new class of compacts as the centerpiece of an old-fashioned, *'50s- and '60s-style* all-out autumn advertising blitz." Janice Castro, "Small Cars, High Hopes," *Time*, 12 Sept. 1994, at 58.
- "Disney money also permitted Bob Weinstein to launch Dimension Films, a division devoted to the revenue-producing *horror-* and *teen-movie* market." Ken Auletta, "Beauty and the Beast," *New Yorker*, 16 Dec. 2002, at 65, 75.
- "It was a *four-* or *five-times-a-year* indulgence, if that." Arthur Miller, "The Bare Manuscript," *New Yorker*, 16 Dec. 2002, at 82, 85.

Occasionally writers omit the hyphens, resulting almost invariably in readers' puzzlement—e.g.: "They lived in the small city of Apopka, Florida, located *in the fern and foliage growing region* [read instead *in the fern- and foliage-growing region*] north of Orlando."

D. Duration or Amount. When phrasal adjectives denote durations or amounts, plurals should be dropped—e.g.: "The report doesn't disclose whether Annie Bell was born after a normal *nine months pregnancy* [read *nine-month pregnancy*]." Likewise, one should write *14-hour-a-day schedule*, *three-week hiatus*, *32-year-old Kansan*, *2,000-bottle wine cellar*, and *25,000-volume library*. The exception is with fractions, in which the plural is retained <a two-thirds vote>.

E. The Compound Conundrum. When the first or last element in a phrasal adjective is part of a compound noun, it too needs to be hyphenated: *post-cold-war norms*, not **post-cold war norms*. Otherwise, as in that example, *cold* appears more closely related to *post* than to *war*. Writers frequently blunder by omitting one of the necessary hyphens—e.g.:

- "Agnes Manyara's *smooth kidney bean-colored complexion* [read *smooth kidney-bean-colored complexion*] is interrupted by a row of tiny, barely visible tribal markings

etched beneath each eye." Toni Y. Joseph, "Scarring Ritual," *Dallas Morning News*, 18 Apr. 1993, at A1.
- "If Dian Parkinson has paid a price for leaving 'The Price Is Right' after 18 years, you'd never know it. The bubbly former model, 41, just did a week of *game show-spoofing* [read *game-show-spoofing*] cameos on David Letterman's show, and she's launching an acting career." "Life After 'Price' Is Right," *USA Today*, 19 Nov. 1993, at D2.
- "I see vegetables in abundance, fresh green salads drenched in healthy *olive oil-based* [read *olive-oil-based*] dressing overflowing their bowls." Robert C. Atkins, *Dr. Atkins' New Diet Revolution* 5 (2002).

Sometimes attaching a modifier to a one-word compound noun may require separating its elements. The problem arises when the adjective specifically modifies the first element of the compound, creating a new phrase that in turn modifies the second element. For example, *pillbox* is always written as a single word, but a box containing sleeping pills would have to be a *sleeping-pill box* (not a *sleeping pillbox* or a *sleeping-pillbox*). Similarly, in baseball we always make the term *baseline* a one-word compound when it stands alone, but when we use it to identify the line from home plate to first or third base, we have to split the elements to make *first-base line* or *third-base line*. Two more examples: although a *bookstore* is where we buy books, for secondhand books we go to a *used-book store* (not a *used bookstore* or a *used-bookstore*); and although a *schoolteacher* teaches school, a *Sunday-school teacher* teaches Sunday school. Cf. **watermark.**

F. Proper Nouns. When a name is used attributively as a phrasal adjective, it ordinarily remains unhyphenated. E.g.: "The *Terry Maher strategy* put immediate pressure on rival bookshop chains." Raymond Snoddy, "Book Price War Looms in Britain," *Fin. Times*, 28–29 Sept. 1991, at 1. This becomes quite awkward, though, when the two words in a proper noun are part of a longer phrasal adjective <the King County-owned stadium> <a New York-doctor-owned building>. The only reasonable thing to do is rewrite <the stadium owned by King County> <a building owned by a New York doctor>.

G. Phrasal Adjectives Following the Noun. When they occur in the predicate, phrasal adjectives usually aren't hyphenated: "This rule is *well worn*"—but "This is a *well-worn* rule." Some exceptions are always hyphenated. Among them are these:

cost-effective	old-fashioned
crystal-clear	risk-averse
dyed-in-the-wool	short-lived
high-spirited	time-sensitive
ill-advised	wild-eyed

H. Foreign Phrases. When used as adjectives, phrases taken from foreign languages generally hold together without the need for hyphens to prevent MIS-CUES <hors d'oeuvre tray> <habeas corpus petition> <ad hoc committee> <ex parte communications>.

LANGUAGE-CHANGE INDEX (For the full key, see front matter pp. xxxi, l–li.)
Stage 1: Rejected. **Stage 2:** Widely shunned. **Stage 3:** Widespread but . . . **Stage 4:** Ubiquitous but . . . **Stage 5:** Fully accepted.
Invariably inferior forms marked by asterisk (*). • Ratios represent frequency of prevalent forms vs. variants in current books.

PHRASAL VERBS are verbs that comprise more than one word, often a verb and a preposition (acting as an adverbial particle). Hence politicians *put up with* the press, and vice versa; striking workers *hold out* for more benefits; arguing family members *work out* their problems; campers must *make do* with the supplies they have; legacies are *handed down* from one generation to the next; gardeners work to *get rid of* weeds; overworked employees, like candles left too long, *burn out*; boxers are *knocked out*—and pregnant women (in the vulgar DYSPHEMISM) *knocked up*. For a collection of these verbs, see G.W. Davidson, *Chambers Pocket Guide to Phrasal Verbs* (1982).

Rhetoricians have taken two positions on these verbs. On the one hand, some recommend using them whenever they're natural-sounding because they lend a relaxed, confident tone—hence *get rid of* instead of the Latin-derived *eliminate*, *phase out* instead of *gradually discontinue*. On the other hand, because phrasal verbs often add to the number of words (though not syllables) in a phrase, some rhetoricians prefer avoiding them—hence *handle* instead of *deal with*, *resolve* instead of *work out*. In the end, this tension can't be worked out as a matter of general principle: one's judgment will depend on the context.

Four caveats are in order with phrasal verbs.

First, when using one, include the entire phrase and not just the primary verb. Don't say that two things *cancel each other* if what they're really doing is *canceling each other out* (or *canceling out each other*). And don't say that you're *drawing the resources* if you're *drawing on the resources*.

Second, don't use a phrasal verb if the adverbial particle is simply baggage that doesn't add to meaning. So don't say *meet up with* if *meet* suffices. Don't say *connect up* or *divide up* if *connect* or *divide* suffices. The same is true of other phrasal verbs, such as *calculate out* (*calculate*); *continue on* (*continue*); and *separate out* (*separate*). E.g.: "Competition in high schools . . . has not *slackened off* [read *slackened*]." Roger Buckley, *Japan Today* 93 (2d ed. 1990). It is true that DIFFERENTIATION has occurred with several phrases, such as *die off* (*die*), *face up to* (*face*), and *lose out* (*lose*). With these phrases, the particles add a nuance to the verb.

Third, although the corresponding nouns are often solid (*breakdown, holdup, lockout, meltdown, phaseout, pushover, shutout, spinoff, workout*), the verb forms should remain two words. Some writers, especially in BrE, tend to use hyphens that don't belong in the verbs—e.g.: "But Mr. Bush's speech suggests that the administration has overcome its initial doubts and is determined to *lock-in* [read *lock in*] still further nuclear weapons reductions." "Bush Ready for Further Nuclear Arms Cuts," *Fin. Times*, 28–29 Sept. 1991, at 1.

Fourth, because phrasal verbs are idioms that give the main verb a unique spin, don't compound the phrase's particle or preposition with another preposition—e.g.: "A2Z is incorporated in Idaho, a state where unclaimed-property laws do not specifically

address gift cards, allowing Amazon.com to *hang onto* [read *hang on to*] unused value." Peter Lewis, "New Law Will Ban Gift-Card Expiration," *Seattle Times*, 27 June 2004, at B1. Here, *hang on* is the phrasal verb and *to* is the preposition that attaches to *unused value*. A similar problem crops up with phrases such as *give in* [to] and *brush up* [on]. See **give in to temptation.**

phraseology (= the way in which words and phrases are used in a particular utterance, subject, or language) is unusually formed, suggesting by the *-ology* suffix that it might denote a discipline or study of some type. Originally, in the 16th century, the term referred to a collection or handbook of idiomatic phrases—the coiner, according to the *OED*, having chosen an "erroneous form" for his title. In any event, by the 18th century *phraseology* took on its modern sense: the choice and arrangement of words to express ideas. The word is pronounced /fray-zee-**ol**-ə-jee/, in five syllables—not /fray-**zol**-ə-jee/.

*****phrenetic.** See **frenetic.**

*****phrensy; *phrenzy.** See **frenetic.**

phylum (= [1] in taxonomy, one of the primary divisions of the animal kingdom; or [2] in linguistics, a group of related languages) forms the plural *phyla*—not *phylums*. See PLURALS (B).

Current ratio (*phyla* vs. *phylums*): 209:1

physician-assisted suicide. See **euthanasia (B).**

pianist is pronounced either /pee-**an**-ist/ or /**pee**-ə-nist/. The first is the traditional and unpretentious AmE pronunciation; the second is the traditional BrE one. If you use the latter, be sure to pronounce the final *-t*!

piazza (= an open square in an Italian town) has predominantly made the anglicized plural *piazzas* since the 18th century. The Italianate plural *piazze* is little used in English.

Current ratio (*piazzas* vs. *piazze*): 9:1

picaresque; picturesque. These words are quite different. *Picaresque* = roguish. *Picturesque* = fit to be the subject of a picture; strikingly graphic.

Picaresque, adj. & n., can give rise to a MISCUE when used in conjunction with a reference to visual imagery. For a good example of this confusion, see MISCUES (A).

picayune. So spelled. See SPELLING (A).

pickaxe. So spelled—preferably not *pickax*. See **ax.**

picnic, v.i., makes *picnicking* and *picnicked*. Cf. **mimic & panic.**

picture (referring to a painting, drawing, photograph, or depiction), in STANDARD ENGLISH, is pronounced /**pik**-chər/—neither /**pich**-ər/ (sloppy) nor /**pik**-tyoor/ (pedantic and pretentious).

picturesque. See **picaresque.**

pidgin (fr. the Chinese pronunciation of the English word *business*) = a simplified form of language used for communication between nonnative speakers of a language <pidgin English>. Although some mid-19th-century writers used the form **pigeon English*, that form is now regarded as mistaken—e.g.:

- "Spottiswood said he couldn't stand the thought of having the actors speak the kind of *pigeon* [read *pidgin*] English often used in films about the Japanese." David Zurawik, "Docudrama Eloquently Adds Fiction to Fact, but the Total May Not Add Up to History," *Baltimore Sun*, 5 Aug. 1995, at D1.
- "Her now 13-year-old son . . . has been raised 'native' and speaks *pigeon* [read *pidgin*] English like a two-year-old." Bruce Kirkland, "Humor, Style Lost in the Jungle," *Toronto Sun*, 7 Mar. 1997, Entertainment §, at 6.
- "The next few pages offered . . . sentences written in brief, almost *pigeon-English* [read *pidgin-English*] format that showed no flare or conscience for being creative, [but] rather just the primitive and somewhat failed first attempts at writing." W.D. Jordan, *The Boatman* 199 (2010). (On the misuse of *flare* for *flair* in that sentence, see **flare**.)

It's pronounced like *pigeon*—namely, /**pij**-ən/.

LANGUAGE-CHANGE INDEX
*pigeon English for *pidgin English*: Stage 2
Current ratio (*pidgin English* vs. **pigeon English*): 6:1

piebald; skewbald. These terms refer to spots or blotches of color on animals' coats. Although there is some overlap between the two, the basic distinction is this: *piebald* = spotted white and black; *skewbald* = spotted white and a color other than black (usu. brown).

Both words can function as either adjective or noun, and both most often refer to horses.

piece of (one's) mind. See **peace of mind.**

Pierre, the capital of South Dakota, is pronounced /peer/, not /pee-**air**/.

*pigeon English. See **pidgin.**

*pigmy. See **pygmy.**

pilaf; pilau; *pilaw. What do we call the dish consisting of rice, vegetables, and sometimes meat? In AmE, it's *pilaf* (/**pee**-lahf/—not /pi-**lahf**/). In BrE, it's traditionally *pilau* (/**pee**-low/)—though since the 1960s *pilaf* has come into currency in BrE and since the mid-1990s seems to have been steadily ousting *pilau*. **Pilaw* is a variant spelling.

pillar for *pillory* is a MALAPROPISM, as Mr. Rush points out: "Norman Rush, author of the acclaimed novel *Mating*, reviewed a litany of malapropisms from television ('I heard a Democratic congressman complain that in the House bank scandal, members of his party were being "pillared"—which sounds kind of

honorific to me') to explain the problems of 'language not anchored in a text.'" Peter Whoriskey, "Paradise Lost? Books' Future Debated," *Miami Herald*, 20 Nov. 1994, at A1. When the error occurs, it is mostly in speech—e.g.: "'None of this is any fun. The school board has been frugal and is being *pillared* [read *pilloried*] for it,' he said." Karl J. Karlson, "School Cuts Trouble Rice Lake," *Pioneer Press* (St. Paul), 24 Apr. 1994, at B1.

LANGUAGE-CHANGE INDEX
pillar misused for *pillory*: Stage 1

pilsner (= a lager beer) has established itself as the standard spelling. **Pilsener* is a variant that predominated in AmE till 1953 and in BrE till 1977. Some capitalize the first letter—after the Czech place name *Pilsen* (also *Plzen*)—but the word has been fully naturalized into English and needs no capital.

Current ratio (*pilsner* vs. **pilsener*): 9:1

pimento; pimiento. Both words come from the Spanish *pimienta* (= pepper), and both denote the European sweet pepper best known in the U.S. for its use in stuffed green olives. *Pimento*—which also denotes allspice and the allspice tree—is the more common spelling today. It's the standard form in combinations such as *pimento cheese* and *pimento grass* (= St. Augustine grass). In reference to the pepper, though, *pimento* is more than twice as common as *pimiento* in general-interest publications, while *pimiento* is the accepted style in food magazines such as *Bon Appetit* and *Gourmet*. So neither form is realistically cancelable as a NEEDLESS VARIANT.

Current ratio (*pimento cheese* vs. *pimiento cheese*): 2:1

Current ratio (*pimiento pepper* vs. *pimento pepper*): 1:1

pinky; pinkie. In both AmE and BrE, *pinky* is an adjective meaning "rather pink." But a distinction exists for the noun referring to the smallest finger: AmE prefers *pinky*, and BrE *pinkie*. Hence Americans write *pinky ring*, while Britons write *pinkie ring*.

PIN number. For this redundant acronym, see ABBREVIATIONS (B).

pinochle; *pinocle; *penuchle; *penuckle. The first has been the standard spelling for the name of the card game since it began in the mid-19th century. The others are variant forms.

Current ratio (for first three headwords): 162:5:1

pint-sized, adj., is the standard spelling in AmE and BrE alike. **Pint-size* is a variant.

Current ratio: 2:1

piquant (= [1] pleasingly tart or spicy, or [2] agreeably provocative) is pronounced /**pee**-kənt/—preferably not

LANGUAGE-CHANGE INDEX (For the full key, see front matter pp. xxxi, l–li.)
Stage 1: Rejected. **Stage 2:** Widely shunned. **Stage 3:** Widespread but . . . **Stage 4:** Ubiquitous but . . . **Stage 5:** Fully accepted.
Invariably inferior forms marked by asterisk (*). • Ratios represent frequency of prevalent forms vs. variants in current books.

/**pee**-kahnt/ and certainly not /pee-**kahnt**/, /**pee**-kant/, /**pee**-kwant/, or /**pik**-wənt/.

pique (/peek/), vb., = (1) to irritate; or (2) to excite or arouse. The most common phrase in sense 2 is *pique one's interest*—e.g.: "He views the Internet primarily as a way to *pique* the interest of potential customers and to familiarize them with his gallery." Holly Selby, "Galleries Reach Past Their Walls on Web Sites," *Houston Chron.*, 23 July 1997, Houston §, at 4. But some writers erroneously make the phrase **peak one's interest*—e.g.:

- "What really *peaked* [read *piqued*] Jones's interest was McVeigh's attempted phone call to Strassmeir." James Ridgeway, "The Fall Guy?" *Village Voice*, 9 Apr. 1996, at 28.
- "If the Oscar-winning film 'Braveheart' *peaked* [read *piqued*] your interest about Scottish culture, stop by the 13th annual Tam O'Shanter Scottish Highland Games and Festival today." Joan T. Collins, "Weekending," *Boston Herald*, 3 Aug. 1996, at 16.
- "Travels to southern Italy *peaked* [read *piqued*] his interest in earthquakes and volcanoes, and in 1638 he climbed the rumbling Mt. Vesuvius to observe the crater first-hand, and this began a life-long interest in subterranean phenomena." Nick Kanas, *Star Maps* 195 (2012).

See ERGATIVE VERBS.

LANGUAGE-CHANGE INDEX
*peak one's interest for *pique one's interest*: Stage 1
Current ratio (*piqued my interest* vs.
*peaked my interest): 10:1

pitiable; pitiful; piteous; pitiless. *Pitiable* = calling for or arousing pity. E.g.: "Most interesting is the resourcefulness of the little girl, who manages to engage her captor—who is equal parts monster and *pitiable* child—skillfully enough to keep herself alive." Chris Petrakos, "A Peach of a Puzzle on Plum Island," *Chicago Trib.*, 18 May 1997, at C6.

Etymologically, *pitiful* means "feeling pity," but in modern speech and writing it is almost always used in the sense "contemptible"—e.g.: "How offensive. How disgusting. And what a *pitiful* way for a serious process to start." Editorial, "Recall Petition Is No Call for City Hall Celebration," *Idaho Statesman*, 13 Feb. 2003, at 8.

The word *piteous* (originally "pious" or "compassionate") "had become misused for *pitiable* as early as Shakespeare's time: for him hearts could be *piteous* in the active sense and corpses in the passive." Ivor Brown, *I Give You My Word & Say the Word* 235 (1964). Today *piteous* is an archaic and poetic synonym of *pitiable*—not a word for ordinary uses.

Pitiless = showing no pity. E.g.: "The corporate Caesar pound[s] his chest about his *pitiless* determination to increase profits." Russell Baker, "Lean, Mean, Love Ya," *N.Y. Times*, 13 May 1997, at A21.

Pittsburgher; *Pittsburger. The first is the standard spelling; the second is a variant form.

Current ratio: 9:1

pixelate; *pixellate; *pixilate; *pixillate. The first is the standard verb meaning "to divide (an image) into pixels [minute areas of illumination on a display screen], esp. for display or storage in a digital format." The other spellings are variant forms. The single *-l- pixelated* predominates in AmE and BrE alike.

Current ratio (in order of headwords): 23:4:4:1

pixie (= a fairy or elf) has been the standard spelling since the 1920s. **Pixy* is a variant.

*pixilate. See **pixelate.**

pizzeria. The word for a restaurant specializing in pizza is often (if understandably) misspelled **pizzaria*—e.g.:

- "Gennaro Lombardi and Anthony Totonno pose outside Lombardi's, the first licensed *pizzaria* [read *pizzeria*] in the United States." "Crispy, Droopy or Chunky: The True American (Pizza) Pie," *N.Y. Times*, 29 June 2006, at E5 (photo caption).
- "Old Chicago, a *pizzaria* [read *pizzeria*], moved into that building just four months later." Terry Anderson, "You'll Never Go Hungry in Ashwaubenon," *Green Bay Press-Gaz.*, 27 Aug. 2006, at E1.

LANGUAGE-CHANGE INDEX
pizzeria misspelled **pizzaria*: Stage 1
Current ratio: 270:1

pizzicato (= a musical direction that a stringed instrument is to be plucked instead of bowed), an Italian loanword from the mid-19th century, has two plurals: *pizzicatos* and *pizzicati*. In both AmE and BrE, *pizzicati* has slightly predominated in recent years; *pizzicatos* has been closing the gap.

Current ratio (*pizzicati* vs. *pizzicatos*): 2:1

PLACE NAMES. A. As Adjectives. See ADJECTIVES (D).

B. British Practices with American Place Names. See NAMES (E).

C. Pronunciation of Foreign Names. See NAMES (C).

D. Names for Residents and Natives. See DENIZEN LABELS.

place of abode. See **abode.**

place where. This phrase is perfectly idiomatic. There is no good reason to insist on *place that.* Cf. **reason why.**

plagiarize is often misspelled **plagarize* or **plagerize*. E.g.:

- "The article accused the author of leaning heavily—far too heavily—on editorial assistance, even *plagarizing* [read *plagiarizing*] the idea for his acclaimed novel, 'Being There.'" Leslie Holdcroft, "'Jerzy Kosinski: A Biography,'" *Seattle Times*, 18 Aug. 1996, at M2.
- "Auggie and Iz are on a mission to find a famous jazz artist [and] rescue their *plagerized* [read *plagiarized*] music from Cosmo LaRue." Lonnie Brown, "Program Takes Kids on a Mission," *Ledger* (Lakeland, Fla.), 8 Feb. 1997, at D1.
- "Corelli's style was easier to *plagarize* [read *plagiarize*] than Haydn's; Haydn's contemporaries and successors

were more taken with being original than being imitators." John H. Baron, *Chamber Music* 1507 (2010).

LANGUAGE-CHANGE INDEX
plagiarize misspelled **plagarize* or **plagerize*:
Stage 1
Current ratio (*plagiarize* vs. **plagarize*): 2,058:1

plaguy (= annoying, disagreeable) is the standard spelling in AmE and BrE alike. **Plaguey* is a variant.
Current ratio: 2:1

*plain geometry. See plane geometry.

PLAIN LANGUAGE. A. Generally. Albert Einstein once said that his goal in stating an idea was to make it as simple as possible but no simpler. He also said: "Most of the fundamental ideas of science are essentially simple, and may, as a rule, be expressed in a language comprehensible to everyone." *The Evolution of Physics* 29 (1938). If that's true of science, surely it's true of most other subjects.

But there is little reason for hope when so many writers seem to believe that to appear competent or smart, they must state their ideas in the most complex manner possible. Of course, this problem plagues many fields of intellectual endeavor, as the philosopher Bertrand Russell noted:

> I am allowed to use plain English because everybody knows that I could use mathematical logic if I chose. Take the statement: "Some people marry their deceased wives' sisters." I can express this in language [that] only becomes intelligible after years of study, and this gives me freedom. I suggest to young professors that their first work should be written in a jargon only to be understood by the erudite few. With that behind them, they can ever after say what they have to say in a language "understanded of the people." In these days, when our very lives are at the mercy of the professors, I cannot but think that they would deserve our gratitude if they adopted my advice.
> Bertrand Russell, "How I Write" (1954), in *The Basic Writings of Bertrand Russell* 63, 65 (Robert E. Egner & Lester E. Denonn eds., 1961).

But the professors have not heeded Russell's advice. Since he wrote that essay in the mid-1950s, things have gotten much worse in fields such as biology, economics, education, law, linguistics, literary criticism, political science, psychology, and sociology.

Consider the following passage from a tax statute, a 260-word tangle that is as difficult to fathom as any mathematical theorem:

> 57AF(11) Where, but for this sub-section, this section would, by virtue of the preceding provisions of this section, have in relation to a relevant year of income as if, for the reference in sub-section (3) to $18,000, there were substituted a reference to another amount, being an amount that consists of a number of whole dollars and a number of cents (in this sub-section referred to as the "relevant number of cents")—

> (a) in the case where the relevant number of cents is less than 50—the other amount shall be reduced by the relevant number of cents;

> (b) in any other case—the other amount shall be increased by the amount by which the relevant number of cents is less than $1.

> (12) Where, but for sub-section (5), this section would, by virtue of the preceding provisions of this section, have effect in relation to a relevant year of income as if, for the reference in sub-section (3) to $18,000, there were substituted a reference to another amount, being an amount that consists of a number of whole dollars and a number of cents (in this sub-section referred to as the "relevant number of cents") then, for the purposes of the application of paragraph 4(b)—

> (a) in a case where the relevant number of cents is less than 50—the other amount shall be reduced by the relevant number of cents; or

> (b) in any other case—the other amount shall be increased by the amount by which the relevant number of cents is less than $1.

> Income Tax Assessment Act [Australia] § 57AF(11), (12)
> (as quoted in David St. L. Kelly, "Plain English in Legislation," in *Essays on Legislative Drafting* 57, 58 [David St. L. Kelly ed., 1988]).

That is the type of prose that prompts an oft-repeated criticism: "So unintelligible is the phraseology of some statutes that suggestions have been made that draftsmen, like the Delphic Oracle, sometimes aim deliberately at obscurity." Carleton K. Allen, *Law in the Making* 486 (7th ed. 1964). See OBSCURITY.

With some hard work, the all-but-inscrutable passage above can be transformed into a straightforward version of only 65 words:

> If either of the following amounts is not in round dollars, the amount must be rounded off to the nearest dollar (or rounded up to the next whole dollar if the amount is 50 cents or more):

> (a) the amount of the motor-vehicle-depreciation limit; or

> (b) the amount that would have been the motor-vehicle-depreciation limit if the amount had equaled or exceeded $18,000.

> Revision based on that of Gavin Peck
> (quoted in Kelly at 59).

Few would doubt that the original statute is unplain and that the revision is comparatively plain. True, to comprehend the revision, the reader must understand what a "motor-vehicle-depreciation limit" is, but some things can be stated only so simply.

But shouldn't learned professionals be allowed complex verbiage? That is, shouldn't they express themselves in more sophisticated ways than nonprofessionals do?

These questions need serious answers because they present the most serious impediment to the

---

LANGUAGE-CHANGE INDEX (For the full key, see front matter pp. xxxi, l–li.)
Stage 1: Rejected. **Stage 2**: Widely shunned. **Stage 3**: Widespread but . . . **Stage 4**: Ubiquitous but . . . **Stage 5**: Fully accepted.
Invariably inferior forms marked by asterisk (*). • Ratios represent frequency of prevalent forms vs. variants in current books.

plain-language movement. There are essentially four answers.

First, those who write in a difficult, laborious style risk being unclear not only to other readers but also to themselves. Because writing reflects thinking, if your thinking is obscure and convoluted your prose will be, too. And you'll be less likely to appreciate the problems that are buried under such convoluted prose.

Second, obscure writing wastes readers' time—a great deal of it, when the amount is totaled. An Australian study conducted in the 1980s found that lawyers and judges take twice as long deciphering legalistically worded statutes as they do plain-language revisions. See Law Reform Commission of Victoria, *Plain English & the Law* 61–62 (1987). The same is surely true in other fields as well.

Third, simplifying is a higher intellectual attainment than complexifying. Writing simply and directly is hard work, and professionals ought to set this challenge for themselves. In fact, the hallmark of all the greatest stylists is precisely that they have taken difficult ideas and expressed them as simply as possible. No nonprofessional could do it, and most specialists can't do it. Only extraordinary minds are capable of the task. Still, every writer—brilliant or not—can aim at the mark.

Fourth, the very idea of professionalism demands that writers not conspire against nonspecialists by adopting a style that makes their writing seem like a suffocating fog. We should continually ask ourselves how the culture stacks up when we consider the durable truth expressed by Richard Grant White: "As a general rule, the higher the culture, the simpler the style and the plainer the speech." *Words and Their Uses* 31 (1870; repr. 1899).

B. A Plain-Language Library. Those wishing to consult further sources in the field may find the following books helpful:

- Rudolf Flesch, *The Art of Readable Writing* (1949).
- Rudolf Flesch, *The Art of Plain Talk* (1951; repr. 1978).
- Robert Gunning, *The Technique of Clear Writing* (rev. ed. 1968).
- Rudolf Flesch, *How to Write Plain English: A Book for Lawyers and Consumers* (1979).
- *How Plain English Works for Business: Twelve Case Studies* (U.S. Dep't of Commerce, Office of Consumer Affairs, 1984).
- Ernest Gowers, *The Complete Plain Words* (Sidney Greenbaum & Janet Whitcut eds., 3d ed. 1986).
- Robert D. Eagleson, *Writing in Plain English* (1990).
- *Plain Language: Principles and Practice* (Erwin R. Steinberg ed., 1991).
- Richard Lauchman, *Plain Style: Techniques for Simple, Concise, Emphatic Business Writing* (1993).
- Martin Cutts, *The Plain English Guide* (1995).
- Joseph Kimble, *Lifting the Fog of Legalese* (2006).
- Joseph Kimble, *Writing for Dollars, Writing to Please* (2012).
- Bryan A. Garner, *Legal Writing in Plain English* (2d ed. 2013).

plainly. See **clearly.**

plan. See *preplan.

plane geometry—so written—is sometimes mistakenly made **plain geometry.* E.g.: "Unlike most suckers, I never had to take *plain* [read *plane*] geometry or trig." Gary Dunford, "Blame It on X-Factor, Eh," *Toronto Sun*, 15 May 1997, at 6.

LANGUAGE-CHANGE INDEX
*plain geometry for *plane geometry*: Stage 1
Current ratio (*plane geometry* vs.
*plain geometry): 42:1

planetarium (= [1] a model of the solar system, or [2] a building or room for projecting images of the solar system), a word dating from the early 18th century, has predominantly made the plural *planetariums* since about 1800. But the Latinate plural *planetaria* has always been a rival, especially in BrE. In AmE, the decided preference today is for *planetariums*.

plantain (= [1] a popular garden plant with broad leaves spread close to the ground; or [2] a type of banana or banana plant) is pronounced /**plan**-tin/, not /**plan**-tayn/ or /plan-**tayn**/.

plantar fasciitis (= inflammation and soreness of the bottom of the foot) is so spelled. *Plantar* derives from the Latin word *planta*, meaning "the sole of the foot." The *fascia* [L. "a band or sash"] is the thin layer of tissue that encases or connects muscles, organs, and bones. There are *fasciae* (that's the predominant plural, although *fascias* also exists) throughout the body. Literally, *fasciitis* is the inflammation (-*itis*) of the *fascia*.

The phrase is pronounced /**plan**-tər fash-ee-ɪ-tis/ or (less well) /fay-shee-ɪ-tis/. Some people blur the middle syllables of *fasciitis*, making it /fash-ɪ-tis/, but this indistinct pronunciation probably accounts for misspellings—and so is to be avoided.

Not surprisingly, the phrase is often misspelled. Sometimes *plantar* becomes *planter*—e.g.: "Camby suffers from *planter* [read *plantar*] *fasciitis.*" Frank Isola, "Skidding Knicks Look Lost," *Daily News* (N.Y.), 12 Nov. 2001, at 67. At other times, *fasciitis* loses one of its medial vowels because of the common mispronunciation—e.g.: "Francis . . . has been suffering from *plantar fascitis* [read *fasciitis*] in his left foot." Elliott Teaford, "Clipper Report," *L.A. Times*, 26 Nov. 2001, at D13. And sometimes the whole phrase is mangled, with a superfluous possessive to boot (and boot hard)—e.g.: "She also developed *planter's fascitis* [read *plantar fasciitis*], a painful strain on the bottom of the foot." "The Goal Is to Tri," *Herald Am.* (Syracuse), 30 July 2000, at AA1.

LANGUAGE-CHANGE INDEX
plantar fasciitis misspelled in various ways: Stage 2

plantar wart (= a wart on the sole of the foot) is often wrongly transformed into **planter's wart*, probably on the false analogy of *planter's punch* and *Planter's Peanuts*—e.g.:

- "Hayes said June had complained of *planter's* [read *plantar*] warts on her feet." Winifred Yu, "Troy Housing Group

Axes 1st Minority Administrator," *Times Union* (Albany), 8 July 1995, at B6.
- "Now he will be off his feet for a while after surgery for *planter's* [read *plantar*] warts." Reid Hanley, "Season Too Short for Fremd's Ridge," *Chicago Trib.*, 29 July 1998, at 5.
- "Clean your feet to avoid getting *planter's* [read *plantar*] warts." Chris Heidenrich, "Five Minutes with . . . ," *Daily Herald* (Chicago), 23 Dec. 1998, at 1.

It doesn't help that *plantar* and *planter* are homophones: both are pronounced /**plan**-tər/.

This example of folk etymology was first noted by Robert L. Chapman in 41 *Am. Speech* 238 (1966). For the etymology of *plantar*, see **plantar fasciitis.** For more on folk etymology, see ETYMOLOGY (D).

LANGUAGE-CHANGE INDEX
plantar wart mistakenly written
**planter's wart*: Stage 1
Current ratio: 17:1

plastically is the adverb corresponding to *plastic*, adj. But some writers misspell it *plasticly, maybe on the analogy of *publicly*—e.g.: "Then the boys escape and begin to track down Wolf's long-lost brother, who lives out West in a strange colony of die-hard TV fans who have been *plasticly* [read *plastically*] altered to resemble Captain Kirk, the Honeymooners, Perry Mason and so on." Carolyn See, "Improvising a Brave New Nuked World," *L.A. Times*, 1 June 1987, § 5, at 4. See -IC.

LANGUAGE-CHANGE INDEX
plastically misspelled *plasticly: Stage 1
Current ratio: 391:1

plateful. Pl. *platefuls*, not *platesful. See PLURALS (G).
Current ratio: 63:1

platitude; plaudit. A *platitude* is a cliché statement—especially one that is expressed as if it were fresh and insightful <his speech was full of platitudes such as "Keep your chin up!">. A *plaudit* is an expression of praise or congratulation <as mayor, she won the plaudits of environmentalists and developers alike>.

David Broder, the Washington journalist, pointed out that Greg Gumbel of CBS blended the two in a comment about the Denver Broncos' quarterback, John Elway: "Elway is receiving all the *platitudes* [read *plaudits*] he deserves." See David S. Broder, "The Politics of So-So," *Wash. Post*, 20 Jan. 1999, at A27. This mistake sometimes crops up in print—e.g.: "I can't think of very many area coaches who deserve the *platitudes* [read *plaudits*] Druckenmiller's former athletes give him." Ron Kohl, "Coach 'Druckie' Is Fondly Remembered as One of a Kind," *Morning Call* (Allentown, Pa.), 10 Sept. 1999, at C9 (an appreciative obituary).

LANGUAGE-CHANGE INDEX
platitude misused for *plaudit*: Stage 1
Current ratio (*received plaudits* vs.
**received platitudes*): 47:1

platypus. Pl. *platypuses*. As one writer warns: "Don't expect platypus spotting to be a close-up, cuddly affair. Platypuses (never platypi) are shy and elusive." Sue Neales, "In Pursuit of the Platypus," *The Age*, 2 Nov. 1996, at 3. Although H.W. Fowler and other respected usage commentators have always promoted the native-grown plural, writers sometimes go astray—e.g.:
- "How do you even start to invent a fractured, empty soul for your generation while there are kangaroos and duck-billed *platypi* [read *platypuses*] boinging past your window?" Bruno Maddox, "Australia: Not That Boring," *N.Y. Times*, 23 Feb. 1997, § 7, at 11.
- "The *platypi* [read *platypuses*] of Tidbinbilla Nature Reserve will earn their free worms this autumn." "Millennial Moments," *Canberra Times*, 10 Mar. 1998, at 7.
- "*Platypi* [read *Platypuses*] were dissected in an attempt to show that they were fakes. We now know that *platypi* [read *platypuses*] are indeed real animals and can explain their odd characteristics in the light of what we now know about the unique evolution of the animal life of the Australian land mass." Ian Marsh, *Theory and Practice in Sociology* 16 (2014).

Even if the first example was intended to be jocular, the humor would not have been diminished by the doubly alliterative *-puses* form.

LANGUAGE-CHANGE INDEX
*platypi for *platypuses*: Stage 1
Current ratio (*platypuses* vs. *platypi): 23:1

plaudit. See **platitude.**

plausible. So spelled—not *plausable. See -ABLE (A).

playwriting; *playwrighting. The second, a corrupt form of the first, is lamentably common—e.g.:
- "[A] professor in the English department at the University of Cincinnati counts *playwrighting* [read *playwriting*] among the courses she teaches." Jackie Demaline, "Playhouse Booking Good for Local Playwrights," *Cincinnati Enquirer*, 16 Mar. 2003, at E2.
- "Kist said *playwrighting* [read *playwriting*] is a way for her to communicate her ideas." Melissa Hollander, "Festival Brings Playwright's Words to Life," *Daily Herald* (Chicago), 18 Apr. 2003, Neighbor §, at 1.
- "She is a recent recipient of the prestigious National Endowment for the Arts/Theatre Communication Group *playwrighting* [read *playwriting*] residency." Holly Johnson, "The Sky's the Limit," *Oregonian* (Portland), 25 Apr. 2003, Arts & Living §, at 5–6.

See SPELLING (A). For a similar error, see **copyright.**

LANGUAGE-CHANGE INDEX
*playwrighting for *playwriting*: Stage 1

pleaded; *pled; plead (as a past tense). *Pleaded* has always been the predominant past-tense and past-participial form. From the early 1600s, *pleaded* has appeared much more frequently in print sources than its rivals. Commentators on usage have long preferred it, pouring drops of vitriol onto *has pled and *has plead:

LANGUAGE-CHANGE INDEX (For the full key, see front matter pp. xxxi, l–li.)
Stage 1: Rejected. **Stage 2:** Widely shunned. **Stage 3:** Widespread but . . . **Stage 4:** Ubiquitous but . . . **Stage 5:** Fully accepted.
Invariably inferior forms marked by asterisk (*). • Ratios represent frequency of prevalent forms vs. variants in current books.

- "*Plĕad*, sometimes wrongly used as the pret. of *plead*. The correct form is *pleaded*." John F. Genung, *Outlines of Rhetoric* 324 (1893).
- "Say, 'He *pleaded* guilty' (not '*pled*' or '*plead*')." Sherwin Cody, *Dictionary of Errors* 118 (1905).
- "Careful speakers use *pleaded*." Frank H. Vizetelly, *A Desk-Book of Errors in English* 167 (1906).
- "The past tense is *pleaded*. The use of *pled* or *plead* is colloquial." C.O. Sylvester Mawson, *Style-Book for Writers and Editors* 178 (1926).
- "These past tense forms [*plead* and *pled*] are by some authorities condemned as entirely incorrect, and by others classified as colloquial. The correct past tense of *plead* is *pleaded*, as 'He pleaded illness as an excuse.'" Maurice H. Weseen, *Crowell's Dictionary of English Grammar and Handbook of American Usage* 470 (1928).
- "The surely correct forms of the verb *to plead* in the past tense and past participle are *pleaded*, *has pleaded*. Colloquially, *plead* and *pled* are used as the past tense." Clarence Stratton, *Handbook of English* 245 (1940).
- "*Pleaded* is the approved past tense of *plead*. THUS: He *pleaded* (not '*pled*' or '*plead*') *not guilty*." Alexander M. Witherspoon, *Common Errors in English and How to Avoid Them* 135 (1943).
- "The past and p.p. are *pleaded*. *Pled* is now colloq. or dial. (or Sc.)." Margaret Nicholson, *DAEU* at 427.

The problem with these strong pronouncements, of course, is that the past forms *pled and *plead* have gained some standing in AmE, as the Evanses noted in the 1950s (although they mentioned only *pled): "In the United States *pleaded* and *pled* are both acceptable for the past tense and for the past participle. In Great Britain only the form *pleaded* is used and *pled* is considered an Americanism" (*DCAU* at 372).

Indeed, *pled, dating from the 16th century, is nearly obsolete in BrE, except as a dialectal word. Nor is it considered quite standard in AmE, although it is a common variant in legal usage—e.g.: "For his part, Igusa has *pled* [read *pleaded*] not guilty and could not be reached for comment." "A Nest of Software Spies?" *BusinessWeek*, 19 May 1997, at 100. It is less common outside legal writing, but it still shows up—e.g.: "'I didn't mean anything—hey, are you okay? Don't cry, Bella,' he *pled* [read *pleaded*]." Stephanie Meyer, *Eclipse* 479 (2007).

Still, *pleaded*, the vastly predominant form in both AmE and BrE, is always the best choice—e.g.:

- "Only Nadia knew of his plans, and she *pleaded* with him not to leave her." David Tarrant, "Bela Karolyi," *Dallas Morning News*, 25 Feb. 1996, at E1.
- "On Friday, Rice, now 70, of Glenview, *pleaded* guilty to the bank robbery." Matt O'Connor, "Man, 70, Admits Robbing Bank," *Chicago Trib.*, 17 May 1997, at 5.
- "Many an interviewer has asked, begged and unsuccessfully *pleaded* with him to come clean and reveal his name." Aldore Collier, "Sinbad Talks About His Divorce, Single Parenthood and His Real Name," *Ebony*, June 1997, at 84.
- "Abelardo Rojas, who ran Bustamante's stash houses in New York, got caught, was extradited, and *pleaded* guilty." Jeffrey Robinson, *The Takedown* 231 (2011).

The spelling *plead as a past tense (for *pled) appeared in the 18th century, apparently on the analogy of *read* > *read*. (Cf. **lead.**) If one needed a dialectal past tense, though, *pled is surely the better choice because it can't be mistaken as a present-tense verb—but better yet (of course) is *pleaded*. E.g.:

- "Shaffer never complied with requests and in March he *plead* [read *pleaded*] no contest to 41 building and fire code violations at three complexes." Jody Kleinberg, "Sr. Landlord Fined $8,750 over Repairs," *Press Democrat* (Santa Rosa), 15 Oct. 1997, at B1.
- "Kaczynski, who was not present at Friday's hearing, has *plead* [read *pleaded*] not guilty to a 10-count indictment alleging that he was responsible for four bombings, including two fatal blasts in Sacramento." "Mental Defense Faces Challenge," *Times Union* (Albany), 1 Nov. 1997, at A2.
- "Finally, there is the case law allowing a defendant who has *plead* [read *pleaded*] guilty to a drink driving charge to argue special reasons, including 'laced drinks' in mitigation of sentence." Niamh Nic Daeid, *Fifty Years of Forensic Science* 112 (2010).

See IRREGULAR VERBS (D).

LANGUAGE-CHANGE INDEX
1. *pled as a past tense for *pleaded*: Stage 3
Current ratio (*he pleaded guilty* vs.
*he pled guilty): 3:1
2. *plead* as a past tense for *pleaded*: Stage 3
Current ratio (*he pleaded guilty* vs.
*he plead guilty): 13:1

plead guilty to is the correct phrasing, not *plead guilty of (an unidiomatic phrasing that arose in the 19th century)—e.g.:

- "Mr. Krikava's wife, Carol, and son, Kevin, pleaded guilty *of* [read *to*] perjury and received only probation, since the guidelines allow leniency for defendants who plead guilty." Dirk Johnson, "A Farmer, 70, Saw No Choice; Nor Did the Sentencing Judge," *N.Y. Times*, 20 July 1994, at A1, A9.
- "In a report released yesterday, the Commodity Futures Trading Commission ruled that Merrill Lynch & Co.'s investigation into an employee who later pleaded guilty *of* [read *to*] wire fraud was 'inadequate.'" Aaron Lucchetti, "Merrill Lynch & Co. Rebuked by CFTC in Probe of Broker," *Wall Street J.*, 20 Mar. 1997, at B2.
- "Tony Yengeni, former chief whip for South Africa's ruling African National Congress, pleaded guilty *of* [read *to*] fraud and was convicted by a Pretoria magistrate yesterday." Nicol Degli Innocenti, "ANC Politician Guilty of Fraud," *Fin. Times*, 14 Feb. 2003, at 6.

This phrasing results from confusing related idioms: one pleads *to* a charge, but one is guilty *of* a crime. Cf. **not guilty.**

LANGUAGE-CHANGE INDEX
*plead guilty of for plead guilty to: Stage 1
Current ratio (*plead guilty to* vs.
*plead guilty of): 31:1

plead innocent. See **not guilty** (A).

*please find enclosed. See ***enclosed please find.**

*please RSVP. See **RSVP.**

plectrum (= a musical pick for plucking a stringed instrument) has predominantly formed the plural *plectra* since the 18th century—though the home-grown plural *plectrums* began striking a chord in the 1990s.

Current ratio: 3:1

*pled. See **pleaded.**

pledgeable. So spelled.

pledgor; pledger; *pledgeor. The most logical spelling is *pledger*, not *pledgor* or **pledgeor*—and *pledger* is 20 times as common as *pledgor* in AmE journalistic writing. But in legal contexts, *pledgor* is 50 times as common as *pledger*, largely because it is the regular correlative of *pledgee*. That spelling also predominates in books printed throughout the world. See MUTE E.

Current ratio (*pledgor* vs. *pledger* vs. **pledgeor* in World English): 156:44:1

plenary (/**plee**-nə-ree/ or /**plen**-ə-ree/) is a FORMAL WORD for *full, complete,* or *entire.* E.g.:

- "It is an axiom of the criminal law, in Massachusetts as in Michigan, that judges have *plenary* power to see that justice is done in their courtrooms." "Nanny Trial: Too Lenient," *Detroit News,* 12 Nov. 1997, at A12.
- "One of the *plenary* sessions at a recent meeting of the National Council of Catholic Women addressed environmental concerns." Jeffrey Weiss, "Christians Work to Save Environment," *Fresno Bee,* 15 Nov. 1997, at B6.

plenitude. So spelled. The word is derived from the Latin *plenus* "full"—the etymon also for *plenary.* Unfortunately, through confusion with the word *plenty,* the misspelling **plentitude* (which first appeared in the 18th century) has become common—e.g.:

- "In its scant 181 pages (including a well-organized index), the reader will find a *plentitude* [read *plenitude*] of good shopping theory." Georgia Brown, "Gonzo Shopper," *Wash. Times,* 2 Jan. 1997, at C11.
- "On one hand, the new image of feminine pleasure played into fantasies of sexual *plentitude* [read *plenitude*] that have long characterized pornography." Kristen Hatch, "The Sweeter the Kitten the Sharper the Claws," in *Bad: Infamy, Darkness, Evil, and Slime on Screen* 143, 150 (Murray Pomerance ed., 2004).
- "Tissot . . . interviewed rabbis and Bedouins in order to understand Christ in the *plentitude* [read *plenitude*] of his reality." James Gardner, "So What Was the Fuss All About?" *Wall St. J.,* 17 Dec. 2009, at D6.

Of course, the phrase *a plenitude of* can very often be shortened to a simple *much* or *many.*

LANGUAGE-CHANGE INDEX
plenitude misspelled **plentitude*: Stage 1
Current ratio: 11:1

plentiful; plenteous. No distinction in meaning being possible, writers should prefer the prevalent modern form, *plentiful. Plenteous* is archaic and poetic.

*plentitude. See **plenitude.**

plethora. According to the *OED* and most other dictionaries, this word refers (and has always referred) to an overabundance, an overfullness, or an excess. The phrase *a plethora of* is essentially an ornate equivalent of *too many*—e.g.: "Our electoral politics now is beset with *a plethora of* [read *too many*] players and a confusing clutter of messages." Steven E. Schier, "From Melting Pot to Centrifuge," *Brookings Rev.,* 1 Jan. 2002, at 16. But sometimes, when not preceded by the indefinite article, the word is genuinely useful—e.g.:

- "Critics say the *plethora* of scrip circulating in Argentina risks running out of control." Matt Moffett & Michelle Wallin, "Investors Question Argentine Currency Proposal," *Wall Street J.,* 26 Dec. 2001, at A6.
- "For readers who can't peruse hundreds of periodicals or read the *plethora* of short-fiction collections published each year, it offers the opportunity to dive into the current trends and fresh voices that define the modern American short story." Jean Blish Siers, " 'Short Story' Series Strikes Gold Again," *Chicago Trib.,* 10 Jan. 2002, Tempo §, at 2. (One hopes that the writer intended to suggest that there are too many such collections published each year.)
- "Mr. Daniels has said he plans to streamline cabinet agencies, citing for example their *plethora* of public-relations shops." Jeanne Cummings & John D. McKinnon, "Bush Budget Focuses on Homeland Defense and Economy," *Wall Street J.,* 10 Jan. 2002, at A14.

Unfortunately, through misunderstanding of the word's traditional sense, many writers use it as if it were equivalent to *plenty* or *many.* Although *W11* seems to countenance this meaning, it is unrecorded in the *OED* and in most other dictionaries. And it represents an unfortunate degeneration of sense—e.g.:

- "Buffalo may seem like a boring city, but we've managed to produce *a plethora* [read *plenty*] of famous people, the Goo Goo Dolls, Ani Difranco, David Boreanaz and now, Chad Murray." Amanda Pendolino, "Chad Murray: Tales from the 'Creek,' " *Buffalo News,* 8 Jan. 2002, at N2.
- "The cookbook does offer *a plethora* [read *plenty*] of possibilities and a wide range of recipes bound to find a place in every home cook's culinary hall of fame." Diane Peterson, "Modern Classics," *Press Democrat* (Santa Rosa), 9 Jan. 2002, at D1.
- "The old policies did not anticipate a *plethora* [read *series* or *group* or *lot*] of suicide bombers." Letter of Scott Sutherland, "Body Scan," *Orlando Sentinel,* 10 Jan. 2002. (One suicide bomber is too many—so *plethora* doesn't work.)

Phrases such as **a whole plethora of* are likewise ill-considered—e.g.: "Then, once you get to the airport ticket counter, there's *a whole plethora* [read *a whole range* or *a wide variety*] of biometric identifiers you could use to tie the background checks you've done to the individuals who present themselves at the ticket counter." Michael O. Hulley, "Secure in High-Tech Future," *Boston Globe,* 6 Jan. 2002, at F2. Cf. **paucity.**

LANGUAGE-CHANGE INDEX (For the full key, see front matter pp. xxxi, l–li.)
Stage 1: Rejected. **Stage 2:** Widely shunned. **Stage 3:** Widespread but . . . **Stage 4:** Ubiquitous but . . . **Stage 5:** Fully accepted.
Invariably inferior forms marked by asterisk (*). • Ratios represent frequency of prevalent forms vs. variants in current books.

The word is pronounced /**pleth**-ə-rə/, not /plə-**thor**-ə/.

LANGUAGE-CHANGE INDEX
a plethora of misused to mean "plenty of": Stage 1

pleurisy; *pleuritis. The first is the ordinary word for inflammation of the lining of the chest cavity. The second is a NEEDLESS VARIANT used by some in the medical profession.

Current ratio: 4:1

plexus (= a complex network) forms various plurals. *Plexuses* is the English plural (preferred). *Plexus* is the Latin plural. And **plexi* is an outright error. See PLURALS (B) & HYPERCORRECTION (A).

plow, n. & vb., is the standard spelling in AmE. *Plough* has been the predominant BrE form since the 18th century.

plum; plumb. As well as being the name of a fruit and of the reddish-purple color of that fruit, *plum* is used figuratively as an adjective meaning "desirable," especially to describe a job <a plum ambassadorship>. *Plumb* as an adjective describes something that is truly vertical <plumb line>. Writers sometimes commit a MALAPROPISM by misusing *plumb* for *plum*—e.g.:

- "Mark Golin, the one-time editor of *Maxim* and *Details*, is said to be a top contender to land the *plumb* [read *plum*] job of editing *Rolling Stone.*" Keith J. Kelly, "Golin Is Strong Candidate to Run New Rolling Stone," *N.Y. Post*, 30 Apr. 2002, at 29.
- "How did Tisdale land such a *plumb* [read *plum*] assignment?" Tannette Johnson-Elie, "For Brewers, She Calls Sales Pitches," *Milwaukee J. Sentinel*, 2 July 2002, at D1.

The opposite error also occurs, though less frequently—e.g.: "Accompanying the boats are scores of suspended plaster *plum bobs* [read *plumb bobs*] that look like huge rain drops frozen in flight . . . . *Plum bobs* [read *Plumb bobs*] symbolize security because they stay level, even as a boat tosses in the waves." Doug McCash, "3 Shows Venture Out of the Gallery Mainstream," *Times-Picayune* (New Orleans), 1 June 2001, Lagniappe §, at 36.

The adjective *plumb*, "perfectly straight, vertical," by dialectal extension of the "perfectly straight" sense, has come to mean "entirely, wholly" <I'm plumb tired>. But some writers confuse the spelling by associating it somehow with fruit—e.g.: "Shelley, a 13-week-old springer spaniel, looks *plum-tired* [read *plumb tired*] during an obedience class at Temple Terrace Recreation Center on Tuesday night." "Inside," *St. Petersburg Times*, 16 Jan. 1993, Community Times §, at 1 (photo caption). See DIALECT.

Plumb is also a verb meaning "to measure depth, esp. of water." The confusion with *plum* occasionally persists with this sense as well—e.g.: "Her poetry is insightful in a way you might expect from someone who *plums the depths* [read *plumbs the depths*] of emotions and the mind." Paula Wachowiak, "For Masters

of Verse, It's All Work and Word Play," *Buffalo News*, 6 Sept. 2000, at D1.

LANGUAGE-CHANGE INDEX
1. **plumb assignment* for *plum assignment*: Stage 1
Current ratio (*plum assignment* vs.
*plumb assignment): 80:1
2. **plum tired* for *plumb tired*: Stage 3
Current ratio (*plumb tired* vs. **plum tired*): 3:1
3. **plum the depths* for *plumb the depths*: Stage 1

plurality. See **majority (C).**

PLURAL POSSESSIVES. See POSSESSIVES (B).

PLURALS. A. Generally. Most nouns form their plurals simply by adding *-s*—thus *books, songs, xylophones*. But if a word ends with the sound of /s/, /sh/, /ch/, or /z/, the plural is formed by adding *-es*—thus *buses, thrushes, churches*, and *buzzes*. Occasionally, a single final consonant is doubled—thus *fez* makes *fezzes*.

Several exceptions exist in words derived from Old English, such as *child–children, foot–feet, goose–geese, louse–lice, man–men, mouse–mice, ox–oxen, tooth–teeth, woman–women*.

B. Borrowed Words. References to this subentry appear throughout this book. That's not to say that each such term is discussed here but only that the principles governing the words are explained here.

Words imported into the English language from other languages—especially Greek, Latin, French, and Italian—present some of the most troublesome aspects of English plurals. Many imported words become thoroughly naturalized; if so, they take an English plural. But if a word of Latin or Greek origin is relatively rare in English—or if the foreign plural became established in English long ago—then it typically retains its foreign plural. See GARNER'S LAW.

One reliable guide is this: if in doubt, use the native-English plural ending in *-s*. That way, you'll avoid the mistakes involved in HYPERCORRECTION, which is rampant with false foreign plurals (as when people say or write **ignorami* instead of *ignoramuses*, thereby betraying something quite ironic). H.W. Fowler called the benighted stab at correctness "out of the frying-pan into the fire" (*FMEU1* at 416). Many writers who try to be sophisticated in their use of language make mistakes such as **ignorami* and **octopi*—unaware that neither is a Latin noun that, when inflected as a plural, becomes *-i*. The proper plural of the Greek word *octopus* is *octopodes*; the proper English plural is *octopuses*.

Those who affect this sort of sophistication may face embarrassing stumbles—e.g.: "A 'big city' paper with an editor as eminently qualified as I'm sure you are should know that the plural of *campus* is **campi* (not *campuses*). Just like the plural of *virus* is **viri* (not *viruses*), and the plural of *stadium* is **stadia* (not *stadiums*)." Letter to the Editor, *Dallas Morning News*, 22 Sept. 2002, at J3 (name withheld for obvious reasons). Although **stadia* has some basis as a plural in English (see **stadium**), **campi* and **viri* are ludicrous, and this attempted comeuppance reeks of ignorance.

Again, if it's a close call, use the native plural. In music, it's better to say *allegros* than *allegri*; *concertos* than *concerti*; *contraltos* than **contralti*; *solos* than **soli*; *sopranos* than **soprani*; and *virtuosos* than **virtuosi*. In publishing, it's better to say *appendixes* than *appendices*; *compendiums* than *compendia*; and *Festschrifts* than *Festschriften* (from German). It's pedantic and prissy to say that politicians attend **fora*, enter **auditoria*, ascend **rostra*, and speak in favor of *referenda*.

But exceptions certainly exist. Literate people say *crises*, not **crisises*; *criteria*, not **criterions*; *hypotheses*, not **hypothesises*; *phenomena*, not *phenomenons*; and *timpani*, not **timpanos*. Medical and biological researchers say *bacilli*, not **bacilluses*; *fungi*, not **funguses*; *ova*, not **ovums*; *stimuli*, not **stimuluses*; and *thalami*, not **thalamuses*. Few other people ever use those words, although *fungi* and *stimuli* aren't uncommon.

Some are extremely close calls, or vary according to context. *Cactuses* predominates in common usage, but *cacti* is the more frequent form in print. *Formulas* is generally better than *formulae* (and *spectrums* than *spectra*), but not in scientific contexts. There is significant movement toward *honorariums*, but *honoraria* still predominates; the same is true of *penumbras* and *penumbrae*. *Millenniums* and *millennia* were long neck-and-neck, though *millennia* has pulled ahead. See **millennium**.

A few variant forms have started undergoing DIFFERENTIATION. *Phalanxes* is the plural referring to groups of people; *phalanges* is the term for bones in the fingers and toes. *Protozoans* is the term for a few microorganisms that go by that name, but *protozoa* is typically used for large numbers. *Staff* generally makes *staffs*, but the musical staff is pluralized *staves*. *Stigmas* is better than *stigmata* except in religious contexts <the stigmata of Christ>.

French words also present problems. *Bête noire* makes *bêtes noires*; *chargé d'affaires* makes *chargés d'affaires*; *fait accompli* makes *faits accomplis*; *force majeure* makes *forces majeures*; *nouveau riche* makes *nouveaux riches*. But the trend is to anglicize fully French plurals. Hence the common phrase *bon mots* is now often printed in roman type without the French double plural: **bons mots*. Likewise, the phrases in the left column outnumber those in the right:

bon vivants	**bons vivants
chaise longues	**chaises longues
cul-de-sacs	**culs-de-sac
filet mignons	**filets mignons

If you're really stumped by a question of this kind, try looking at the Google Ngram Viewer, which will tell you which one of two or more possible plurals predominates in English-language books.

C. Nouns Ending in *-f*. Some words change in the plural from a final *-f* to *-ves*, but others simply become *-fs*. Following are the main ones that change:

beef, beeves	scarf, scarves
(fattened cattle)	self, selves
calf, calves	sheaf, sheaves
elf, elves	shelf, shelves
half, halves	staff, staves (in music)
hoof, hooves	thief, thieves
knife, knives	wharf, wharves
leaf, leaves	wife, wives
life, lives	wolf, wolves
loaf, loaves	

And these are the ones that preferably don't change:

beef, beefs (types of meat or complaints)
dwarf, dwarfs
handkerchief, handkerchiefs
kerchief, kerchiefs
oaf, oafs
proof, proofs
roof, roofs
staff, staffs (except in music)

Note, however, that the plural of *still life* is *still lifes*.

D. Nouns Ending in *-o*. No consistent rules are possible for plurals of words ending in *-o*. But some weak guidelines can be ventured. First, nouns used quite often in the plural tend to end in *-oes* (*embargoes*, *heroes*, *noes*, *potatoes*, *vetoes*). The following plurals ending in *-oes* are predominant in English:

archipelago	archipelagoes
buffalo	buffaloes
calico	calicoes
cargo	cargoes
desperado	desperadoes
domino	dominoes
echo	echoes
embargo	embargoes
fresco	frescoes
go (*a go at it*)	goes
grotto	grottoes
hero	heroes
hobo	hoboes
innuendo	innuendoes
magnifico	magnificoes
mango	mangoes
mosquito	mosquitoes
motto	mottoes
no	noes
peccadillo	peccadilloes
portico	porticoes
potato	potatoes
stucco	stuccoes
tomato	tomatoes
tornado	tornadoes

LANGUAGE-CHANGE INDEX (For the full key, see front matter pp. xxxi, l–li.)
Stage 1: Rejected. **Stage 2:** Widely shunned. **Stage 3:** Widespread but . . . **Stage 4:** Ubiquitous but . . . **Stage 5:** Fully accepted.
Invariably inferior forms marked by asterisk (*). • Ratios represent frequency of prevalent forms vs. variants in current books.

torpedo	torpedoes
veto	vetoes
volcano	volcanoes

Some are close calls. For example, American dictionaries tend to list *peccadilloes* before *peccadillos*, but that term is surely no more naturalized than *banjo* (which forms *banjos*).

Second, alien-looking words (e.g., *imbroglio*), proper names (e.g., *the Florios*—that is, the Florio family), words that are seldom used as plurals (e.g., *bravados*), words in which *-o* is preceded by a vowel (e.g., *portfolios*), and shortened words (e.g., *photo*) typically don't take the *-e-*. Among the many plurals that don't have an *-e-* before the pluralizing *-s* are these:

albinos	embryos
arpeggios	folios
avocados	gazebos
cameos	mementos
crescendos	piccolos
curios	tuxedos
dynamos	

Good dictionaries contain the preferred spellings. If it's possible to cite a trend, the plurals with *-e-* seem very slightly on the decline. But it's a slow, weak trend.

E. Nouns Ending in -y. If a word ends in a *-y* preceded by a vowel, the plural is formed by adding an *-s*—e.g.:

alloy, alloys	money, moneys
chimney, chimneys	monkey, monkeys
donkey, donkeys	moray, morays
journey, journeys	osprey, ospreys

But if a word ends in a *-y* that isn't preceded by a vowel, the plural is formed by omitting the *-y* and substituting *-ies*—e.g.:

bankruptcy, bankruptcies	pony, ponies
gully, gullies	story, stories
mercy, mercies	sty, sties
opportunity, opportunities	supply, supplies

There are two exceptions in the second category. First are proper names: *Busby* becomes *Busbys*, *Kingsly* becomes *Kingslys*, and so on. (See (F).) Second are words ending in *-quy*: *colloquy* becomes *colloquies*, and *soliloquy* becomes *soliloquies*.

Writers err especially by treating words in the first category as if they belonged in the second—e.g.:

- "[It seems] a small enough price to pay, though, for the joy of watching *donkies* [read *donkeys*] year-round." Rebecca Jones, "Kicking Up Their Heels," *Rocky Mountain News* (Denver), 20 Jan. 1996, at D2.
- "Spurred on by this warning, they all continue with their mortal *journies* [read *journeys*] by connecting in ways that will, in the case of death, make their last moments worthwhile." Mary Houlihan-Skilton, "'Fat Tuesday' Needs More Louisiana Magic," *Chicago Sun-Times*, 3 Apr. 1996, at 44.
- "Stephen M. Halajko, 2 Chris Dr., [was awarded a building permit] for two one-flue *chimnies* [read *chimneys*] and a fireplace valued at $4,000." "Building Permits," *Providence J.-Bull.*, 9 Jan. 1997, at C4.

F. Proper Names. Although few books on grammar mention the point, proper names often cause problems as plurals. The rule is simple: most take a simple *-s*, while those ending in *-s*, *-x*, or *-z*, or in a sibilant *-ch* or *-sh*, take *-es*. Thus:

Singular Form	Plural Form
Adam	Adams
Adams	Adamses
Bush	Bushes
Church	Churches
Cox	Coxes
Flowers	Flowerses
Jones	Joneses
Levy	Levys
Lipschutz	Lipschutzes
Mary	Marys
Rabiej	Rabiejs (the *-j-* is silent)
Shapiro	Shapiros
Sinz	Sinzes
Thomas	Thomases

Plurals such as these are often erroneously formed by calling, say, Mr. and Mrs. Sinz **the Sinz*, **the Sinz'*, or **the Sinz's*. The last two forms, with apostrophes, merely result from confusion with possessives—and not even good possessives: the correct possessive is *Sinz's* in the singular and *Sinzes'* in the plural. See PUNCTUATION (A) & POSSESSIVES (B).

Otherwise well-schooled people have a hard time with names that end in *-s*. The Flowers couple really should be known as the *Flowerses*—that's the only known plural that any traditional English grammar would countenance. When in February 2003 *The New York Times* ran a big article on the Jukes clan, the *Times* correctly (and repeatedly) referred to the family as the *Jukeses*—e.g.: "Now new information about the *Jukeses* has been found in archives at the State University of New York at Albany." Scott Christianson, "Bad Seed or Bad Science?" *N.Y. Times*, 8 Feb. 2003, at A19. But the article also cited an 1877 book erroneously titled *The Jukes: A Study in Crime, Pauperism, Disease, and Heredity*. To the list of evils in that title, the 19th-century author might have added "poor editing."

G. Compound Nouns. Certain compound nouns and hyphenated terms make their plurals by adding *-s* to the main word—e.g.:

aides-de-camp	knights-errant
battles royal	maids of honor
brothers-in-law	men-of-war
commanders-in-chief	mothers-in-law
consuls general	notaries public
courts-martial	poets laureate
editors in chief	postmasters general
fathers-in-law	rights-of-way
hangers-on	sergeants-at-arms
heirs presumptive	sisters-in-law
holes in one	

The American and British practices differ on the method of pluralizing *attorney general*. See **attorney general.** See also POSTPOSITIVE ADJECTIVES.

A term in which the noun is more or less disguised adds *-s* at the end, as with all compounds ending in *-ful*:

armfuls	handfuls	roomfuls
bagfuls	jarfuls	scoopfuls
barrelfuls	lapfuls	shovelfuls
basketfuls	lungfuls	spoonfuls
bottlefuls	mouthfuls	tablefuls
bucketfuls	pailfuls	tablespoonfuls
cupfuls	platefuls	teaspoonfuls
forkfuls	pocketfuls	tubfuls
glassfuls	potfuls	

A few phrases fall into this category, such as *cul-de-sacs* (see (B)) and *Johnny-come-latelies.*

But when the addition is merely a preposition, the -s- is added internally, as in *hangers-on, listeners-in, lookers-on* (more typically *onlookers*), *lyings-in,* and *passersby.*

H. Differentiated Forms. Despite the exceptional forms mentioned in (A)—the ones deriving from Old English (e.g., *foot–feet*)—in one instance there is an exception to the exception. When *louse* refers to a scoundrel or cad, the plural is always *louses.* See **mouse.**

I. Acronyms and Abbreviations. In general, form the plural of an acronym or initialism merely by adding -s with no apostrophe: CEO, CEOs; FAQ, FAQs; IPO, IPOs; PC, PCs; PIN, PINs; POW, POWs; and so on. (But see (L).) This style, consistent with the overall modern trend toward simplicity, also applies where the short form ends in a sibilant sound <IMAXs> <MASHs> <SOSs>. Cf. DATES (D).

There are two practical reasons for this preference. First, the acronym or initialism may also be used as a possessive—a form that does require an apostrophe—so the apostrophe should distinguish the two forms <the CEO's schedule> <NASA's budget>. Second, using an apostrophe to form a plural is one of the most common and persistent spelling errors, especially with names (as when someone erroneously refers to *the Bingham's* instead of [correctly] to *the Binghams*). Using apostrophes to form plurals of these short forms encourages that error.

Still, apostrophes are sometimes necessary. They are traditionally used with abbreviations containing capital letters and periods <M.B.A.'s>. They are needed to avoid confusion where the form uses lowercase letters <gif's>. See (L).

Abbreviations—as distinguished from acronyms—usually form the plural by adding -s before the period <paras. = paragraphs> <assocs. = associates>. Some abbreviations, especially in citations, are formed by doubling one of the prominent letters in the word <exx. = examples> <MSS. = manuscripts> <pp. = pages>. Abbreviations of measurement generally do not change form <2 in.> <40 mi.>.

As with *POW* and *WMD,* even if the first word is the main noun in the spelled-out form (*prisoner of war, weapon of mass destruction*), and the spelled-out version would pluralize that noun (*prisoners of war, weapons of mass destruction*), the abbreviated plural

is nevertheless formed with -s at the end of the abbreviation (*POWs, WMDs*). A few writers mistakenly use the singular form as if the plural were internally understood—e.g.: "With it comes the end, I hope, of the hoopla and parades of the three *POW* [read *POWs*] that wandered aimlessly into enemy territory and were taken as prisoners for a few days." Letter of Violet Fredericks, *Press-Enterprise* (Riverside, Cal.), 20 June 1999, at A16.

Using *RBI* as a plural form (meaning "runs batted in") isn't usual, but it does sometimes ill-advisedly appear—e.g.:

- "Jeter . . . is hitting .233 (10-for-42) in the postseason with no homers and only three *RBI* [read *RBIs*]." Jeff Horrigan, "Jeter's Short at Plate," *Boston Herald,* 30 Oct. 2001, at 90.
- "Dave McGrath got the win, three hits, three *RBI* [read *RBIs*], scored three runs and went deep." Kevin Callanan, "Sun and Fun Senior Softball League," *Orlando Sentinel,* 5 Dec. 2001, at 8. (That sentence also illustrates both a lack of PARALLELISM and an odd anticlimax.)
- "His bat came alive in the postseason, when he was 8-for-19 with three doubles, a triple and three *RBI* [read *RBIs*]." Tony Jackson, "Reds Acquire Pirates Pitcher," *Cincinnati Post,* 21 Dec. 2001, at B3.

J. Mass (Noncount) Nouns. A recent trend in the language is to make plurals for mass nouns—i.e., general and abstract nouns that cannot be broken down into discrete units and that therefore should not have plural forms. One example of this phenomenon is the psychologists' and sociologists' term *behaviors* (= actions), suggesting that the ways in which people behave are readily categorizable and therefore countable. Granted, one can have good or bad behavior, but not, traditionally speaking, *a* good behavior or *a* bad behavior. This is JARGON.

Increasingly, though, speakers of English think of *technologies* and *methodologies* as being discrete things. And to weather forecasters, it makes perfect sense to speak of *humidities* and *accumulations.* In part, this trend seems to show two things: first, an affection for abstract terms; and second, a resulting tendency to reify those abstract terms. See COUNT NOUNS AND MASS NOUNS.

K. Numbers and Decades. The modern trend is to form the plural of numbers and decades by adding -s with no apostrophe <par 4s> <the 2010s>. Some publication styles, notably that of *The New York Times,* still use the -'s form with decades <the 1990's>. But the reason for that newspaper's unusual style does not apply to most writers: "Many publications omit such apostrophes, but they are needed to make . . . all-cap headlines intelligible and are therefore used throughout the paper for consistency." *New York Times Manual of Style and Usage* 261–62 (1999).

L. Words and Letters. The best way to form the plural of a word used as a word is to italicize it and append -s in roman type <trim the number of *of*s to

LANGUAGE-CHANGE INDEX (For the full key, see front matter pp. xxxi, l–li.)
Stage 1: Rejected. **Stage 2:** Widely shunned. **Stage 3:** Widespread but . . . **Stage 4:** Ubiquitous but . . . **Stage 5:** Fully accepted.
Invariably inferior forms marked by asterisk (*). • Ratios represent frequency of prevalent forms vs. variants in current books.

tighten prose>. With letters, too, that approach usually works best <roll call was up to the *Hs*> <mind your *ps* and *qs*>. If italic type is unavailable, the apostrophe may be unavoidable <straight *A's*> <no *if's*, and's, or but's>. And to some writers, when the letter to be pluralized is *s*, the apostrophe may be irresistible <a straightaway followed by a series of *S's*>. But two points bear emphasis. First, avoid the apostrophe if possible because its use as an incorrect plural form is so widespread that any use at all encourages error. Second, if despite that advice you do use the apostrophe to form the plural of one word or letter, use it the same way with plural words and letters elsewhere in the document to keep your style consistent.

    M. Plural Possessives. See POSSESSIVES (B).

plus, n., forms the plural *pluses* in AmE and BrE alike—preferably not **plusses*.

ply (= fold) forms the plural *plies*. **Plys* is incorrect. See PLURALS (E).

p.m. See **a.m.**

pneumonic. See **mnemonic.**

pocketful. Pl. *pocketfuls*—not **pocketsful*. See PLURALS (G).

podcast > podcast > podcast. Avoid **podcasted*.

podia. See **podium.**

podiatric. See **pediatric.**

podiatry. See **chiropody*.

podium = (1) a low wall serving as an architectural foundation; (2) a raised platform that a speaker or orchestra conductor stands on; dais; or (3) a stand for holding a speaker's notes; lectern. Sense 3, once widely condemned as a misuse, has become commonplace. But careful writers should avoid it—e.g.:

- "Verne Lundquist and Pat Haden work the game, which is fine, as long as they don't pull a stunt like last week's 'debate,' in which they stood behind *podiums* [read *lecterns*] and discussed the merits of the Houston–Cincinnati game minutes before the presidential debate." Bill Goodykoontz, "With Irvin Back, Cowboys Serve Up Tough Test for Cards," *Ariz. Republic*, 13 Oct. 1996, at F3.
- " 'My day started optimistically enough at 6:30 this morning,' says the tall, ethereally pale novelist [Joyce Carol Oates] as she arranges her notes at the *podium* [read *lectern*]." Robin Vaughn, "A Quick Read on the Art of Style," *Boston Herald*, 27 June 1997, at S24.
- "Moving out from behind the *podium* [read *lectern*] allows . . . more of a connection between the speaker and the audience." Raymond Greenlaw, *Technical Writing, Presentational Skills, and Online Communication* 130 (2012).

    The plural is *podiums* or *podia*. Although the latter long predominated in print sources, the two are close rivals now. See PLURALS (B).

LANGUAGE-CHANGE INDEX
podium misused for *lectern*: Stage 4
Current ratio (*podia* vs. *podiums*): 1.4:1

poem (= a writing in verse) has two syllables: /**poh**-əm/—not /poym/ or /pohm/. The cognate *poetry* is /**poh**-ə-tree/—not /**poy**-tree/ or /**pwet**-tree/.

poetize; poeticize. The two have undergone DIFFERENTIATION. Although both originally meant "to compose poetry," only *poetize* (dating from the late 16th century) properly bears that sense today. *Poeticize* (dating from the early 19th century) means "to imbue with poetic qualities; to impart an aesthetic or emotional impact suggestive of poetry." Historically, *poetize* has been the more common word—since the 18th century—and it remains so. Only in the last 25 years of the 20th century did *poeticize* rival it in frequency.

poet laureate. Pl. *poets laureate*—preferably not **poet laureates*. Consider Walter Hamilton, *The Poets Laureate of England* (1879). See PLURALS (G).

Current ratio: 1.1:1

pogrom (= a planned, purposefully executed mass murder, esp. amounting to genocide), a Russian loanword dating from about 1900, is pronounced /pə-**grom**/ or /**poh**-grəm/ in AmE and /**pog**-rəm/ in BrE.

poinsettia. The preferred pronunciation has four syllables: /poin-**set**-ee-ə/. Although /poin-**set**-ə/ spread far and wide during the 20th century—and is even listed as the first pronunciation in *WNWCD*—it is not yet standard. Another mispronunciation that adds an erroneous -*t*- to the first syllable (/point-**set**-ə/) is common in uncultivated speech.

pointillism (= a style of painting that uses small spots of color all over the canvas as opposed to brushstrokes) is pronounced mostly in an anglicized way in AmE: /**poyn**-ti-liz-əm/—although /**pwan**-ti-liz-əm/ is also current and predominates in BrE. The fully Frenchified /**pwan**-tee-yiz-əm/ is an affectation in English-speaking contexts.

POINTING WORDS. A. Generally. Pointing words (technically known as "deictic terms")—words like *this, that, these, those,* and *it*—point directly at an antecedent. A pointing word should always have an identifiable referent. But this doesn't mean that *this* or *these* must always have a noun immediately following it. Most grammarians take a more relaxed position: "The antecedent of *this* and *that* may be any single noun . . . . *This* and *that* may also refer to a phrase, clause, or sentence, or even to an implied thought. Reference of this kind must, however, be immediately clear and apparent; otherwise the thought will be obscure." James C. Fernald, *English Grammar Simplified* 40 (Cedric Gale ed., rev. ed. 1979). Fernald is not alone: "*This*, like *that*, is regularly used to refer to the idea of a preceding clause or sentence: 'He had always had his own way at home, and this made him a poor roommate.'/'The company trains their salesmen in their own school. This [more formally: This practice] assures them a group of men with the same sales methods.' " Porter G. Perrin, *Writer's Guide and Index to English* 794 (rev. ed.

1950) (bracketed language in original). Perrin's notation in his second example accurately describes the difference between *this* and *this practice*: it is a question of formality, not of correctness.

Actually, the grammarians' rule against vague reference is just that—a rule that forbids ambiguities of the kind illustrated here: "The most important activity is the editing of a college newspaper. *This* has grown with the college." (Ex. drawn fr. Richard Summers & David L. Patrick, *College Composition* 129 (1946).) What has grown with the college? Editing? The newspaper? The importance of editing the college newspaper? You simply cannot tell what the writer intended—if indeed the writer knew.

What the writer needs is a sensitivity to antecedents, whether explicit or implicit. Good writers routinely use pointing words to refer to something that, although clear, is less specific than a particular noun. Often the *this* or *that* functions as a summarizing word and means, essentially, "what I've just said"—e.g.:

- "As a language [English] is highly unified; more so than many tongues spoken by a far smaller number of people. *This* raises the question of the probable future of English." Albert H. Marckwardt, *American English* 170 (1958).
- "Kanemaru and Takeshita have come so close to differing publicly in recent months that some analysts believe an open split may be only a question of time. *This*, however, overlooks the historical relationship between the two men." C. Smith, "Splitting Headache," *Far Eastern Econ. Rev.*, 31 May 1990, at 15.
- "Over the past several weeks government bonds have recovered about half the ground they lost as interest rates rose earlier this year. *That* has evidently prompted money managers at investing institutions to pump some of their large cash reserves into stocks." "Prices Retreat for 3rd Session," *Mainichi Daily News*, 9 June 1990, at 5.
- "The Puritan hatred of Laud was well nigh insane. A leading MP speaks of the 'wicked tenets' of his Arminianism. *This* because the poor Archbishop believed in free will." A.L. Rowse, "Civil War Revisited," *Fin. Times* (Weekend), 27–28 Apr. 1991, at xviii.
- "By this fall, the Hollywood gossip was that Miramax might suffer huge losses on 'Gangs,' but Weinstein denies *this*." Ken Auletta, "Beauty and the Beast," *New Yorker*, 16 Dec. 2002, at 65, 69.

The test for knowing when the word *this* is acceptable in such a context is this: ask yourself, This what? If an answer comes immediately to mind, the word *this* is probably fine. If none comes immediately to mind, you probably need to add a noun. But a word of warning: inserting an abstract noun or noun phrase such as *fact*, *idea*, *practice*, or *state of affairs* often mars the style.

For a related problem with the relative pronoun *which*, also a pointing word, see REMOTE RELATIVES.

B. *This* vs. *that*. It isn't easy to explain precisely when to use the pointing word *this* and when to use *that*, or when to use the plural *these* and when to use *those*. Essentially *this* connotes proximity and immediacy in relation to the speaker or writer <this hat on my head>, while *that* connotes some distance and remove <that hat over there>. The difference can be quite subtle, and often either word works as well as the other.

point in time. This phrase, well known as mere verbiage, occurs most commonly in reported speech. But sometimes it sneaks into print—e.g.:

- "Corzine says the proposals would add only an extra $60 billion to federal spending when fully implemented, a *point in time* [read *time*] even he concedes may never come." Charles Stile & Jeff Pillets, "McCain, Giuliani and Franks Attack Corzine," *Record* (N.J.), 2 Nov. 2000, at A16.
- "At some *point in time* [read *point*], the family moved to Oklahoma City." "Jane Elizabeth Good Eckroat" (obit.), *Daily Oklahoman*, 6 June 2001, at D8.
- "Although still just sticks at this *point in time* [read *point*], roses will soon reward with new foliage and flowers." Judy Sharpe, "Time to Come Up Roses," *Newcastle Herald*, 9 June 2001, at 17.

The clumsy phrase is occasionally made worse by being preceded by *particular*. Stick with a simple substitute such as *time, point, now, moment*, and the like.

point of fact. See fact (D).

point of view. See viewpoint.

point out; point to; point up. *Point out* = to call attention to <she pointed out the four withering geraniums> <he pointed out the health benefits of eating lots of vegetables>. *Point to* = to direct attention to (as an answer or solution) <they could point to no good reason for closing the facility>. *Point up* = to illustrate <this case points up a key pitfall of the prosecutors' seeking capital punishment>.

poky; pokey. *Poky*, adj., = (1) inactive, sluggish, slow <the poky golfers in front of us>; (2) cramped and uncomfortable <a poky lecture hall>; or (3) badly dressed, shabby <the poky teenage styles of the 1990s>. *Pokey*, n., is a CASUALISM meaning "jail."

pole. See poll.

poleaxe. So spelled—preferably not *poleax. See ax.
                                                    Current ratio: 2:1

polemic, n.; **polemical,** adj. Although *polemic* can be an adjective as well as a noun, it is better confined to noun uses <a long-winded polemic>. Reserve *polemical* for the adjectival uses <polemical writings>.

police, though a COLLECTIVE NOUN, is generally construed as a plural both in AmE and in BrE <the police aren't here yet>. The word is pronounced /pə-**lees**/— not /**poh**-lees/. See PRONUNCIATION (B).

police officer. See SEXISM (C).

LANGUAGE-CHANGE INDEX (For the full key, see front matter pp. xxxi, l–li.)
Stage 1: Rejected. **Stage 2:** Widely shunned. **Stage 3:** Widespread but . . . **Stage 4:** Ubiquitous but . . . **Stage 5:** Fully accepted.
Invariably inferior forms marked by asterisk (*). • Ratios represent frequency of prevalent forms vs. variants in current books.

policy; polity. *Policy*, by far the more common word, means "a concerted course of action followed to achieve certain ends; a plan." It is more restricted in sense than *polity*, which means (1) "the principle upon which a government is based"; or (2) "the total governmental organization as based on its goals and policies." Sense 2 is more usual—e.g.: "[Here is] what Therese perceives to be the problem: excessive tolerance and liberal hand-wringing by a *polity* too faint to punish and hold accountable those who daily erode a sense of safety and well-being for the majority of citizens in our small metropolis." Jere W. Chapman, "View from the Streets," *Star Trib.* (Minneapolis), 31 Aug. 1997, at A23.

policyholder; *policyowner. *Policyholder* is preferably spelled as one word. **Policyowner* is a NEEDLESS VARIANT.

policy-making should be hyphenated. See **decision-making.**

*policyowner. See **policyholder.**

POLITICAL CORRECTNESS today primarily refers to the phenomenon of stifling views and attitudes contrary to those of the enlightened intelligentsia of the left, especially as regards social and political issues. It is a kind of planned intolerance for the expression of ideas that run counter to liberal orthodoxies. One sees it in language, when a vocal minority insists on the avoidance of certain terminology considered discriminatory or offensive, and especially insists on the use of EUPHEMISMS and DOUBLESPEAK; in debate, when contrarian views are excoriated for their very utterance; and in everyday life, when the timid refuse to express an idea in any but the most anodyne way. A host of new sensitivities have been launched: ableism, ageism, lookism, sizeism, weightism, and the like.

Of course, the phrase *politically correct* in its modern applications was originally intended as a kind of self-mocking OXYMORON, since political views by their nature cannot be "correct" or "incorrect." Surprisingly, the phrase dates back to the 1930s, but it wasn't until the late 1980s that the idea spread and came into vogue. The abbreviation *PC* or *P.C.* spread with equal rapidity.

In all social arguments in which not just public intellectuals but also propagandists become embroiled, words and phrases get distorted as accusations and counteraccusations are hurled by one side against the other. Meaningful debate can become impossible. Even the phrase *political correctness* sometimes seems to lose all meaning.

For two entries in which the question of political correctness is at the fore, see **anchor baby** and **illegal immigrant.**

*politicalize. See **politicize.**

politically; politicly. *Politically* (/pə-**lit**-i-klee/) = in a political way; in a way that involves politics. *Politicly* (/**pol**-i-tik-lee/) = in a politic (i.e., judicious or prudent)

way. The latter, of course, is much less common—e.g.: " 'Is that a duck or a cormorant?' Bruce Babbitt asked, resting his paddle on his chino-covered leg, looking at a distant water bird. 'We have both,' raft guide Katy Strand told him *politicly*." Peter Bacque, "Babbitt Links Cleaner James to Federal Law," *Richmond Times-Dispatch*, 19 Oct. 1995, at B1. Cf. **impolitic.**

politicize; *politicalize. The first is standard. It means (1) "to talk about or engage in politics"; or (2) "to make (something) political or to make (a person, group, or the like) politically aware or active." **Politicalize*, a NEEDLESS VARIANT, is less than 1% as frequent. But it does occur—e.g.: "This incident demonstrates the ability of special interest groups to *politicalize* [read *politicize*] the research funding process." Tammy L. Lewis & Lisa A. Vincler, "Storming the Ivory Tower," 20 *J. College & Univ. Law* 417, 460 n.149 (1994). See **politick.**

LANGUAGE-CHANGE INDEX
*politicalize for *politicize*: Stage 1
Current ratio (*politicize* vs. **politicalize*): 301:1

politick, v.i.; **politicize.** *Politick*, a BACK-FORMATION from *politics*, was formerly disparaged as a NONWORD. But today it is fully accepted as meaning "to engage in partisan political activities." *Politicize* has the similar sense "to act the politician," but also the broader sense "to render political" <politicizing judicial elections>.

politicly. See **politically.**

politics may be either singular or plural. Today it is more commonly singular than plural <politics is a dirty business>, although formerly the opposite was true. As with similar *-ics* words denoting disciplines of academics and human endeavor, *politics* is treated as singular when it refers to the field itself <all politics is local> and as plural when it refers to a collective set of political stands <her politics were too mainstream for the party's activists>. Cf. **semantics.**

polity. See **policy.**

poll (= [1] the place where one votes in an election, [2] the number of votes recorded in an election, or [3] a survey conducted to gauge candidates' support in a campaign) is sometimes confounded with its homophone *pole* (= [1] a long stick or post, [2] the northernmost or southernmost point on a planet, [3] one of two opposite ideas or beliefs, or [4] one of two points at the ends of a magnet or battery). E.g.:

- "Turner said yesterday that he will never again pay workers to haul voters to the *poles* [read *polls*]." John Stamper, "Senator Gets Home Detention," *Lexington Herald-Leader* (Ky.), 24 Apr. 2007, at C1.
- "Together, they help illustrate two passionate, opposite *polls* [read *poles*] in our national debate about improving schools." Joe Nathan, "Parents Question Journalists, Teacher Unions," *Stillwater Gaz.* (Minn.), 16 Mar. 2012, Columns §.

polyandry. See **polygamy.**

polyarchy (= a democratic political structure with no entrenched majority but equally contesting minorities) is sometimes confused as meaning "a group of states" or something less clear—e.g.: "Looking to the future, Brown sees a world in which superpower bipolarity, the cohesion of alliances and the sovereignty of states have all eroded, moving the world toward a system of '*polyarchy*' with new problems and challenges." John C. Campbell, "New Forces, Old Forces and the Future of World Politics," *Foreign Affairs*, Summer 1988, at 1114. See GOVERNMENTAL FORMS.

polygamy; polyandry; polygyny. The first is the broadest term, referring to a person's being simultaneously married to more than one spouse. *Polyandry* is the practice of having more than one husband; *polygyny* is the practice of having more than one wife. See **bigamy.**

　Polygamy is pronounced /pə-**lig**-ə-mee/. *Polyandry* is pronounced /**pol**-ee-an-dree/ or /pol-ee-**an**-dree/. *Polygyny* is pronounced /pə-**lij**-ə-nee/.

polygraph. Although *polygraph* is pronounced /**pol**-ee-graf/, the related forms are pronounced quite differently: *polygraphy* /pə-**lig**-rə-fee/, *polygrapher* /pə-**lig**-rə-fər/, *polygraphic* /pol-ee-**graf**-ik/. The pronunciations are analogous to those involving *photograph* and its cognates.

polygyny. See **polygamy.**

pomace (= [1] the residue left after squeezing the juice out of a fruit, vegetable, fish, etc., or [2] something smashed into a pulpy mass) is pronounced /**pəm**-is/—not /**pom**-is/.

pommel; pummel. *Pommel* should be reserved for the noun meaning "a knob on the hilt of a sword or at the front of a saddle." It commonly appears in the gymnastics phrase *pommel horse*. *Pummel* is the preferred spelling of the verb meaning "to hit with, or as with, the fists." The verb derives from the noun: a person sometimes *pommeled* another with the hilt of a sword, back when that sort of thing was fashionable. Gradually, however, the -*u*- spelling began to appear—probably because of the word's traditional pronunciation: /**pəm**-əl/ (/**pom**-əl/ is a variant pronunciation for the noun). Today, *pummel* is about 15 times as common as the verb *pommel* in print. The gerund *pummeling* means "a beating."

　Although *pommel* occasionally appears as a verb, the DIFFERENTIATION outlined above should be favored—e.g.: "A sophomore at Sylvan Hills High School, Don Baker *pommeled* [read *pummeled*] himself." Charles Allbright, "Career Choices," *Ark. Democrat-Gaz.*, 3 Feb. 1997, at E1.

LANGUAGE-CHANGE INDEX

*take a pommeling for *take a pummeling*: Stage 1
Current ratio (*pummel him* vs. **pommel him*): 15:1

pompom; pompon. The decorative tuft of strands used by cheerleaders was originally called by its French name, *pompon*, which in English dates from the late 19th century. This spelling is still quite common, even preferred in some current dictionaries. E.g.: "In case Red Bone wasn't enough, the Chinese organizers brought in a red-clad cheerleading squad which danced to Latin beat music waving little fans instead of *pompons* during breaks." Peter Fimrite, "Jumpin' Cyclists Are Smash in China," *S.F. Chron.*, 22 Aug. 2008, at D8.

　But usage has shifted toward *pompom* in recent years because so many people misheard the word, and because of the linguistic tendency toward reduplicative sounds—e.g.:

- "Home of the state champion *pompom* squad and a General Motors Buick plant, it turned out to be a potential lodging industry jewel." Fred R. Bleakley, "On the Prowl," *Chicago Trib.*, 13 Aug. 1995, at C5.
- "The viewing party clustered around a television and met [Sarah] Palin's speech at the Republican convention in Minnesota with raucous cheers, applause and waving of McCain posters and red *pompoms*." Noelene Clark, "It's About Time," *Seattle Times*, 4 Sept. 2008, at A8.

Today, the newer form, *pompom*, is sanctioned both by the *AP Stylebook* (2008) and by *The New York Times Manual of Style and Usage* (1999). And *pompom* outranks *pompon* by a 4-to-1 ratio in modern journalism and by a 2-to-1 ratio in books. It has been the predominant form only since the 1990s.

　Pompom (with the variant spelling *pompon*) is also a generic name for flowers with small blossoms that resemble the decorative tufts, such as dahlias and chrysanthemums. About as far from that pleasant mental picture as you can get is another definition for the hyphenated *pom-pom*: an automatic gun or cannon mounted as part of a set (especially pairs), as on a battleship.

LANGUAGE-CHANGE INDEX

pompom for *pompon*: Stage 5
Current ratio (*pompoms* vs. *pompons*): 2:1

ponderous = (1) (of a thing) heavy, slow, awkward, or (2) (of writing or ideas) long and tedious, even impenetrable. The *ponder* part may hint at meditation, but while heavy thought may be *ponderous*, ordinary self-reflection is not—e.g.: "I was away at college during his illness, however, and barely got to know that gentler man. It would take many years, and many *ponderous* [read *contemplative*] walks, to understand his absence in my life." Sandra Miller, "The Man in the Park," *Hartford Courant*, 9 June 2002, Northeast §, at 3.

　The word is sometimes misspelled without the medial -*e*-, perhaps on the analogy of *wondrous*—e.g.: "Such a *pondrous* [read *ponderous*] thing is only fit to be buried at the bottom of the sea." Paul Edward Parker,

---

LANGUAGE-CHANGE INDEX (For the full key, see front matter pp. xxxi, l–li.)
Stage 1: Rejected. **Stage 2:** Widely shunned. **Stage 3:** Widespread but . . . **Stage 4:** Ubiquitous but . . . **Stage 5:** Fully accepted.
Invariably inferior forms marked by asterisk (∗). • Ratios represent frequency of prevalent forms vs. variants in current books.

"Harpooner's Diary: Two More Whales, Boys, and We'll Go Home," *Providence J.-Bull.*, 25 Sept. 1996, at C2.

LANGUAGE-CHANGE INDEX
1. *ponderous* misused for *contemplative*: Stage 1
2. *ponderous* misspelled *pondrous: Stage 1
Current ratio: 795:1

pontifex (= [1] a high priest, or [2] the Pope) makes the Latinate plural *pontifices*. In most contexts, *pontiff* and *pontiffs* suffice.

Pontius Pilate is so spelled, but increasingly it is incorrectly written *Pontius Pilot—e.g.:

• "A song addressed to *Pontius Pilot* [read *Pontius Pilate*] was done in the style of Billie Holliday's 'God Bless the Child.'" Rick Mattingly, "Arms Are Too Short to Box with God," *Courier-J.* (Louisville), 26 Apr. 1996, at C8.
• "[A referendum] would allow the commission to play *Pontius Pilot* [read *Pontius Pilate*] and wash their hands of responsibility." Tony Boylan, "Williams Wise Not to Force Special Election," *Fla. Today*, 31 May 1997, at B1.
• "He is no Joan of Arc or Joseph of Arimathea; no Mary Magdalene or *Pontius Pilot* [read *Pontius Pilate*]." Kathleen J. Martin, *Indigenous Symbols and Practices in the Catholic Church* xv (2013).

Current ratio: 144:1

populace. A. And *population*. Both refer to the human inhabitants of a geographic region. The difference is in connotation: *population* is a neutral term, while *populace* suggests the rabble or common folk—with a rather superior tone.

B. And *populous*. The adjective *populous* (= heavily populated) is surprisingly often confused with the noun *populace*—e.g.:

• "The four most *populace* [read *populous*] states—California, New York, Texas and Florida—are concerned about it." Patrick K. Lackey, "Keep the Immigrants Coming," *Virginian-Pilot* (Norfolk), 15 Apr. 1995, at A6.
• "Short on the mountains and oceans of more *populace* [read *populous*] states, we work doubly hard to stake our claim in long-term prosperity and economic growth." Renzi Stone, "3 Solutions for a Creative Class," *Daily Oklahoman*, 19 Oct. 2003, at A9.
• "And this is how—in part—the body politic will select the governor of the nation's fourth most *populace* [read *populous*] state." Daniel Ruth, "Say Hello to the Lieutenant of Obscurity," *Tampa Trib.*, 16 Sept. 2006, Metro §, at 1.

LANGUAGE-CHANGE INDEX
populace misused for *populous*: Stage 1
Current ratio (*more populous* vs.
*more populace): 996:1

populous; populist. *Populous* (= thickly populated) for *populist* (= of, relating to, or involving a movement claiming to represent the whole of the people) is a startling error—e.g.:

• "The advent of the Jacksonian era and its emphasis on democratic *populous* [read *populist*] ideals . . . promoted . . . the notion that . . . judges should be popularly elected." Norman Krivosha, "Acquiring Judges by the Merit Selection Method," 40 *Sw. L.J.* 15 (1986).
• "'It seems to me that we take this grand *populous* [read *populist*] approach when we want to avoid responsibility

for that decision,' said South Central Los Angeles member Rita Walters. 'The board needs to be the one making the decision. We are the elected officials.'" Beth Shuster, "L.A. Board to Vote on Year-Round Plans," *Daily News* (L.A.), 30 Jan. 1990, at N1.
• "Our national gambling revolution did not result from a *populace* [read *populist*] movement. It emerged almost exclusively through the combined efforts of the gambling industry, its wealthy lobbyists, and our desperately receptive legislators/politicians." V. Thomas Mawhinney, "Gambling Creates Governmental, Personal Problems," *South Bend Trib.*, 22 July 2001, at B7.

Populist is also sometimes misused for *popular*—e.g.: "In the 1992 election, the lines blurred even further, as candidates sought to expand the ways in which they used *populist* [read *popular*] media forums, becoming regulars on talk shows, like Larry King's, usually reserved for authors publicizing books or actors promoting pictures." Maureen Dowd, "Selling Chips? Or Is It Quayle? It's All a Blur," *N.Y. Times*, 29 Jan. 1994, at 6.

For a similar mistake—*populace* for *populous*—see **populace (B)**.

LANGUAGE-CHANGE INDEX
1. *populace* misused for *populist*: Stage 1
2. *populous* misused for *populist*: Stage 1
3. *populist* misused for *popular*: Stage 1

porcupine (the animal with quills) is pronounced /**por**-kyə-pin/—not /**por**-kee-pin/ (a childish pronunciation).

pore (= to read intently) is sometimes misspelled *pour* (= to make [a liquid] flow downward). This blunder occurs in writing not pored over carefully enough by a good proofreader—e.g.:

• "Ms. Besso . . . now spends her evenings *pouring* [read *poring*] over brochures from Boston, Boulder, Colo., and Nashville." Sara Rimer, "Fleeing Los Angeles: Quake Is the Last Straw," *N.Y. Times*, 18 Feb. 1994, at A1, A10.
• "*Pouring* [read *Poring*] through the book, one is struck *both by* [read *by both*] the warmth and depth of the musicians." Jeff Bradley, "James Comes into Its Own," *Denver Post*, 24 Nov. 1996, at G15. On the lack of PARALLELISM there, see **both (A)**.
• "Banking was arguably already the most regulated industry in America. Even at Carver—a small player on a field of financial giants—four government regulators *pour* [read *pore*] over our books annually and impose financial controls." Deborah C. Wright, "A Hit on Harlem," *N.Y. Post*, 9 Oct. 2006, at 21.

This mistake probably appears primarily because the verb *pore* appears less often in print than in speech.

LANGUAGE-CHANGE INDEX
*pour over books for *pore over books*: Stage 2
Current ratio (*pore over books* vs.
*pour over books): 14:1

porpoise. The standard pronunciation is /**porp**-əs/, not /**por**-poyz/ (a spelling pronunciation). Cf. **tortoise**.

Porsche (the car) is acceptably pronounced /porsh/ or /**por**-shə/.

porte cochere (/port koh-**shair**/) = (1) a large gateway and passage that allows vehicles to pass into an inner courtyard; or (2) an overhanging structure, usu. projecting from a building's entrance, that protects vehicles and their occupants from the elements. Although Margaret Nicholson termed sense 2 "erroneous" (*DAEU* at 433), it has long been standard AmE. In fact, it's the primary sense today.

Although the French phrase is written *porte cochère*, the grave accent is now omitted in AmE. See DIACRITICAL MARKS.

portend (= to foretell or foreshadow), like *forebode*, has negative connotations—e.g.:

- "A Washington Post report from a fishing village near the mouth of the Mississippi River *portends* more of the same kind of trouble—only this time on an unexpectedly massive scale." William Snider, "Fish Kills Are Spreading Nationwide," *News & Record* (Greensboro), 28 Sept. 1997, at F3.
- "At the end of October the crash of Hong Kong's stockmarket seemed briefly to *portend* a global crash." "The IMF and Asia," *Economist*, 22 Nov. 1997, at 20.
- "Disgustingly graphic yet not specifically threatening expressions may sometimes *portend* disruption." Jill Joline Myers et al., *Responding to Cyber Bullying* 67 (2011).

It's unwise to try to use the word in neutral or positive senses. Some other verb, such as *augur* or *presage*, might suffice, or maybe even a simpler word such as *bring*—e.g.: "Most medical advances *portend* [read *bring*] hope for the sick and the disabled." Barbara Yost, "No. 7 Proved to Be Lucky in Pregnancy—This Time," *Ariz. Republic*, 23 Nov. 1997, at EV2.

portentous (= [1] ominous, prophetic; [2] wondrous; [3] solemn; or [4] self-important, self-consciously somber) is so spelled. But the word is sometimes incorrectly written **portentious* or (less often) **portentuous*. E.g.:

- "Told in a discontinuous, cinematic style, 'Amnesia' is often *portentuous* [read *portentous*]." Chauncey Mabe, "Everything's Coming Apart in Amnesia," *Sun-Sentinel* (Ft. Lauderdale), 12 June 1994, at D1.
- "Most *portentious* [read *portentous*] is an article in May's *Esquire* magazine by the radio personality and Sinatra expert Jonathan Schwartz, which states the widespread rumor (and half hopes) that the elder Mr. Sinatra, who turns 80 in December, has finally decided to stop performing." John Marchese, "Owning the Name but Not the Fame," *N.Y. Times*, 30 Apr. 1995, § 1, at 45.
- "Given all the *portentious* [read *portentous*] state-of-the-world rhetoric that has surrounded the project, the big surprise at the Refugio hearing was how comfortingly normal the objections seemed." Peter Canellos, "Texans Ponder Where Superhighway Might Take Them," *Boston Globe*, 4 Mar. 2008, at A2.

Dwight Bolinger explains the origin of the error: "*Portentous* sounds like *pretentious*, there is a vague association of meaning, and the suffix *-tious* is more substantial and possibly more frequent than simple *-ous*, so we begin to get *portentious*." *Language: The Loaded Weapon* 42 (1980).

LANGUAGE-CHANGE INDEX
1. *portentous* misspelled **portentious*: Stage 1
Current ratio: 104:1
2. *portentous* misspelled **portentuous*: Stage 1
Current ratio: 1,630:1

portion; part. There are connotative differences. *Portion* = share (as of an estate or of food). It is an entity cut (or as if cut) away from the whole <his portion of the profits> <her portion of the grain>. *Part*, in contrast, merely connotes a constituent piece of the whole <part of a house, a country, etc.>.

portmanteau. Pl. *portmanteaus* or (less good) **portmanteaux*. The homegrown plural *portmanteaus* has predominated since the word first came into common use in the 18th century. See PLURALS (B).

Current ratio: 3:1

PORTMANTEAU WORDS. Lewis Carroll improvised this term to denote words formed by combining the sounds and meanings of two different words. (Linguists use the term *blend*.) Carroll gave us *chortle* (chuckle + snort) and *galumph* (gallop + triumph). Thus *aerobicise* derives from *aerobic exercise*; *insinuendo* combines *insinuation* with *innuendo*; and *quasar* is from *quasi* and *stellar*. Other recent innovations are *avigation*, from *aviation* and *navigation*; *pictionary* for *picture-filled dictionary*; and *videbut* for *video debut*.

Most portmanteau words are nonce-words that do not gain currency; others, like *brunch* (breakfast + lunch), become standard. Among portmanteau coinages are these:

advertorial (*advertisement + editorial*)
Amerasian (*American + Asian*)
asylee (*asylum + refugee*)
breathalyzer (*breath + analyzer*)
brotel (*brothel + hotel*)
cockapoo (*cocker spaniel + poodle*)
defamacast (*defamatory + broadcast*)
docudrama (*documentary + drama*)
emoticon (*emotion + icon*)
executary (*executive + secretary*)
Franglais (*Francais + Anglais*)
frenemy (*friend + enemy*)
futilitarian (*futile + utilitarian*)
galimony (*gal + alimony*)
glumpy (*gloomy + grumpy*)
guesstimate (*guess + estimate*)
infomercial (*information + commercial*)
jazzercise (*jazz + exercise*)
jocoserious (*jocose + serious*)
labradoodle (*Labrador retriever + poodle*)
liger (*lion + tiger*)
metrosexual (*metropolitan + heterosexual*)
mockumentary (*mock + documentary*)

LANGUAGE-CHANGE INDEX (For the full key, see front matter pp. xxxi, l–li.)
Stage 1: Rejected. **Stage 2:** Widely shunned. **Stage 3:** Widespread but . . . **Stage 4:** Ubiquitous but . . . **Stage 5:** Fully accepted.
Invariably inferior forms marked by asterisk (*). • Ratios represent frequency of prevalent forms vs. variants in current books.

motel (*motor* + *hotel*)
netiquette (*Internet* + *etiquette*)
Oxbridge (*Oxford* + *Cambridge*)
palimony (*pal* + *alimony*)
perma-press (*permanent* + *press*)
quelch (*quell* + *squelch*) (see **quelch*)
radiocast (*radio* + *broadcast*)
simulcast (*simultaneous* + *broadcast*)
slumlord (*slum* + *landlord*)
slurk (*slink* + *lurk*)
smog (*smoke* + *fog*)
Spanglish (*Spanish* + *English*)
sportscast (*sports* + *broadcast*)
stagflation (*stagnation* + *inflation*)
sweedle (*swindle* + *wheedle*)
televangelist (*television* + *evangelist*)
threepeat (*three* + *repeat*)
uprighteous (*upright* + *righteous*)
weathercast (*weather* + *forecast*)

Some portmanteau words lend an air of jocularity—e.g.: "The skinny [on Federal Express]? When you *absotively posilutely* have to get it there." Stephen Lynch, "Surfing with a Purpose," *Buffalo News*, 19 Dec. 1995, at B7.

For a good collection, see Dick Thurner, *Portmanteau Dictionary: Blend Words in the English Language, Including Trademarks and Brand Names* (1993).

possess. The phrase *is possessed of* is an old-fashioned phrase meaning "possesses, owns" <they are possessed of three houses>. The phrase *is possessed by* or *is possessed with* means "is obsessed by" or "has no control over" (usu. something undesirable, even demonic) <he is possessed by the need to control others> <she is possessed with her desire for food>. Sometimes *possessed of* gets dispossessed of its rightful place—e.g.:

- "Even though Scott *is possessed with* [read *is possessed of*] such a talent, he labored in obscurity until only recently." Steve Bryant, "Singer's Voice Among a Pantheon of Great Artists," *Phil. Trib.*, 14 Nov. 1997, at E3.
- "And, Caruso added, his old friend *is possessed with* [read *is possessed of* or, better, *has*] an uncanny ability to change people's minds." Tony Freemantle, "Livingston's Background Speaks Well," *Houston Chron.*, 16 Nov. 1998, at 1.
- "He also *is possessed with* [read *is possessed of*] an on/off switch and a tremendous grasp of diplomacy." Steve Buckley, "Love–Hate with Subban," *Boston Herald*, 8 May 2014, at 60.

LANGUAGE-CHANGE INDEX
is possessed with misused for *is possessed of*: Stage 1
Current ratio (*is possessed of* vs. *is possessed with*): 11:1

possessive; possessory. The terms *possessive* and *possessory* have undergone DIFFERENTIATION. *Possessive* = (1) exhibiting possession or the desire to possess <she dealt with him in a possessive, domineering way>; (2) [in grammar] denoting possession <a possessive pronoun>. *Possessory* = (1) of, relating to, or involving a possessor <her possessory rights over the farm>; (2) arising from possession <possessory interest>; or (3) that is a possessor <possessory caretaker>.

POSSESSIVES. A. Singular Possessives. To form a singular possessive, add *-'s* to most singular nouns—even those ending in -*s*, -*ss*, and -*x* (hence *Jones's*, *Nichols's*, *witness's*, *Vitex's*). E.g.: "Noting *Congress's* move to regulate maternity hospitalization, managed-care advocates predict that politicians would legislate health care." Kent Jenkins et al., "Health Care Politics," *U.S. News & World Rep.*, 1 Dec. 1997, at 24. The traditional approach of the *AP Stylebook* (see, e.g., the 1996 6th ed.) was to use nothing more than an apostrophe if the word already ends in -*s*. In the 2002 edition, the AP editors came up with a hairsplitting rule to use only the apostrophe (no additional -*s*) for (1) a word that ends in -*s* if it is followed by a word that begins with *s*-, and (2) a singular name that ends in -*s* (pp. 200–01). But most authorities who aren't newspaper journalists demand the final -*s* for virtually all singular possessives (e.g., *Bill Forbis's farm*, not *Bill Forbis' farm*). See the very first rule of William Strunk Jr. & E.B. White, *The Elements of Style* 1 (3d ed. 1979).

There are four exceptions to this rule. (1) The possessives of personal pronouns do not take apostrophes (*ours*, *yours*, *its*, *theirs*). In particular, the word *its* is possessive; *it's* is the contraction of *it is* (see **its**). (2) Biblical and Classical names that end with a /zəs/ or /eez/ sound take only the apostrophe:

Aristophanes' plays
Jesus' suffering
Moses' discovery
Xerxes' writings

No extra syllable is added in sounding the possessive form. (3) If a corporate or similar name is formed from a plural word, it takes only the apostrophe. Hence *General Motors* makes *General Motors'*, not **General Motors's*—e.g.: "A merger by General Motors will excite great interest in an enforcement agency simply because of *General Motors's* [read *General Motors'*] size." E.W. Kintner, *An Antitrust Primer* 95 (2d ed. 1973). And *United States* has always made *United States'*, not **United States's*. (4) According to the traditional rule, a sibilant possessive before *sake* takes merely an apostrophe, without an additional -*s*—hence *for appearance' sake*, *for goodness' sake*, and *for conscience' sake*. See (N).

B. Plural Possessives. For most plural possessives, use the ordinary plural form and add an apostrophe to the final -*s*: *Smiths'*, *Joneses'*, *bosses'*, *octopuses'*. The one exception is for plurals not ending in -*s*, for which -*'s* is added as in the singular possessive: *brethren's*, *children's*, *men's*, *women's*.

Writers sometimes confound the singular and plural possessives, most commonly by misusing the singular for the plural—e.g.:

- "Asses were 'generally the property of the poor,' who used to keep them as beasts of burden and for their milk, which is more nutritious and closer to human milk than *cow's* [read *cows'*] milk is; in the 1750s, some London shops sold *ass's* [read *asses'*] milk, usually under the sign 'Ass and Foal.'" Tony Fairman, "How the Ass Became a Donkey," 10 *English Today* 29, 34 (1994).
- "I don't much admire the *Wales's* [read *Waleses'*] taste in expensive schools." Peter Preston, "Good Schooling Is Just

a Passing Fancy," *Guardian*, 16 June 1995, at 9. (The reference was to the Prince and Princess of Wales.)

- "Arielle found me in the *girl's bathroom* [read *girls' bathroom* (because it's a school bathroom)] on the floor, during my math class." Paige Love-Rose, *Beauty* 106 (2011).

C. Absolute Possessives. The words *hers, ours, theirs,* and *yours* are sometimes termed "absolute" or "independent" possessives because they occur when no noun follows. No apostrophe appears in these words, which are often in the predicate <the house was ours> <the fault was theirs>. Sometimes, though, they can occur as subjects <hers was a gift that anyone would envy>. See UNDERSTOOD WORDS.

Occasionally, an absolute possessive occurs when it shouldn't—usually in combination with ordinary possessives. E.g.: "If a new relationship breaks up, your teen may feel very protective of you and feel stress about both *yours* [read *your*] and his or her vulnerability." Jeff Lindenbaum, "Dating After Divorce?" *Seattle Times*, 2 Nov. 1994, at E2.

D. Double Possessives. Some people erroneously stigmatize *a friend of mine* or *an acquaintance of John's*, in which both an *of* and a possessive form appear: "The double possessive is redundant, and it should be avoided in careful speech and formal writing. In short, don't be too 'possessive,' i.e., redundant, when indicating possession or ownership in your writing or speech. Form the possessive case by adding an *'s* or by using the preposition *of.* Just don't get carried away and do both at the same time." Michael G. Walsh, "Grammatical Lawyer," *Practical Lawyer*, Jan. 1996, at 12.

But this age-old idiom has appeared consistently since the days of Middle English. And it is widely approved:

- "The double genitive [i.e., double possessive] is required whenever a word indicating ownership is placed after *of.* For example, *he found a bone of the dog's* and *he found a bone of the dog* mean different things; and *he found a toy of the child* is meaningless." DCAU at 142–43.
- "By an old and well-established English idiom, sometimes called the double genitive, possession may be shown by two methods at the same time, by an *of*-phrase and by a possessive form of the substantive. 'You are no friend of mine.' [Possession is shown by the prepositional *of*-phrase and by the possessive form *mine.*]" R.W. Pence & D.W. Emery, *A Grammar of Present-Day English* 345 (2d ed. 1963).
- "Using both the *s*- and *of*-genitives together is an English idiom of long and respectable standing. It is especially common in locutions beginning with *that* or *this* and usually has an informal flavor: 'that boy of Henry's'; 'friends of my father's'; 'hobbies of Jack's.' It is useful in avoiding [an] ambiguity . . . : 'Jane's picture' is resolved either as 'the picture of Jane' or 'the picture of Jane's.'" Porter G. Perrin, *Writer's Guide and Index to English* 625 (Karl W. Dykema & Wilma R. Ebbitt eds., 4th ed. 1965).

The double possessive appears in good writing and typically causes no trouble. Occasionally, however, it can be improved on—e.g.: "Many *colleagues of Dr. Siegel's* [read *of Dr. Siegel's colleagues*] have said they were shocked by the allegations about a man whom they have long considered to be a reserved, somewhat academic person." Elisabeth Rosenthal, "Hospital Chief Denies Harassing Aide," *N.Y. Times*, 1 Sept. 1995, at A13.

Of course, the double possessive is impossible to avoid in constructions with personal pronouns <a friend of mine> <that attitude of his>.

LANGUAGE-CHANGE INDEX
a friend of John's: Stage 5

E. Joint Possessives: *John and Mary's house.* For joint possession, an apostrophe goes with the last element in a series of names. If you put an apostrophe with each element in the series, you signal individual possession. E.g.:

John and Mary's house. (Joint)
John's and Mary's houses. (Individual)
America and England's interests. (Joint)
America's and England's interests. (Individual)

In the last two examples, *interests* is plural (regardless of the possessives) merely as a matter of idiom: we typically refer to *America's interests*, not *America's interest*. With pronouns, each element is always possessive <your and his time-share>.

On consecutive pages of a book, Frank Rich gets the rule reversed: "The remainder of the time . . . is devoted to *Lawrence Kasha's and David Landay's book* [read *Lawrence Kasha and David Landay's book*]." Frank Rich, *Hot Seat* 168 (they coauthored it). / "They've also performed radical surgery on *Molière and Coward's famous heroes* [read *Molière's and Coward's famous heroes*]." *Ibid.* at 169 (Molière and Noel Coward never cowrote anything!).

Again: "At times *Mr. Levinson's and Mr. Link's script* [read *Mr. Levinson and Mr. Link's script*] threatens to rekindle durable narrative devices from *Damn Yankees* and *Camelot*." Frank Rich, *Hot Seat* 207 (1998) (they coauthored the script). And again: "Ms. Howe takes a specific character's concern—the battle-scarred Ariel's hatred of men, Faith's ecstatic anticipation of motherhood, *Holly's and Leo's* [read *Holly and Leo's*] growing sexual attraction—and distills it into a concentrate of intoxicating feeling." *Ibid.* at 499 (the attraction is mutual). Yet again: "To see *Hecht's and MacArthur's* [read *Hecht and MacArthur's*] 1928 valentine to the press now, in Jerry Zaks's attractively cast and appropriately slam-bang revival at the Vivian Beaumont, is also to appreciate it as a play." *Ibid.* at 501 (Hecht and MacArthur were coauthors).

Other reputable writers have likewise been thrown off—e.g.: "Plays of this kind had become very popular on the London stage, with dramas such as *Beaumont's and Fletcher's* [read *Beaumont and Fletcher's*] recent *Philaster* and the revival of the favourite *Mucedorus*." Peter Ackroyd, *Shakespeare* 481 (2005) (they were coauthors).

LANGUAGE-CHANGE INDEX (For the full key, see front matter pp. xxxi, l–li.)
Stage 1: Rejected. **Stage 2:** Widely shunned. **Stage 3:** Widespread but . . . **Stage 4:** Ubiquitous but . . . **Stage 5:** Fully accepted.
Invariably inferior forms marked by asterisk (✳). • Ratios represent frequency of prevalent forms vs. variants in current books.

F. Names as Adjectives. When a proper name is used as an adjective, it isn't a possessive and therefore doesn't take an apostrophe. Hence "the Cubs [not *Cubs'*] game is at 1:00 today." The following example incorrectly uses an apostrophe because the name *Fields* (referring to a single person) is being used adjectivally: "One source who attended the fundraiser said it generated at least $50,000 for the *Fields'* [read *Fields*] campaign." "Scuttlebutt," *Gambit* (New Orleans), 14 Nov. 1995, at 8. With a title instead of a name, the apostrophe would be needed <the mayor's campaign>.

G. Possessives of Names Made with Possessives. It is common for businesses to be named with a proper single name in possessive form, such as *McDonald's*. Although possessive in form, these are functionally nouns, as in *McDonald's brings you a new kind of meal.* How, then, does one make a possessive of the noun *McDonald's*? Literally, it would be *McDonald's's*, as in *Try McDonald's's dinner combos!* But good phrasing requires *the dinner combos at McDonald's.* It is also quite defensible to write *McDonald's dinner combos* (the name functioning as a kind of possessive) or *the McDonald's dinner combos* (the name functioning attributively).

H. Inanimate Things. Possessives of nouns denoting inanimate objects are generally unobjectionable. They have risen steadily in frequency of occurrence since the late 19th century, perhaps chiefly because they allow writers to avoid awkward uses of *of*—e.g.: *at day's end, at the water's edge, the book's title, the article's main point, the system's hub, the envelope's contents, the car's sticker price.* See **of (A)**.

The old line was that "it's better to use an "*of* phrase rather than the *'s* to indicate possession when the possessor is an inanimate object. Write *foot of the bed*, not *the bed's foot*." Robert C. Whitford & James R. Foster, *Concise Dictionary of American Grammar and Usage* 96 (1955). *Foot of the bed*, of course, is a SET PHRASE, so the example is not a fair one. As a general principle, though, whenever it's not a violation of idiom, the possessive in *'s* is preferable <the hotel's front entrance> <the earth's surface>.

But such possessives can be overdone. For example, avoid using the possessive form of a year—e.g.: "Mr. Rogers, 41, took the show by storm in 1993, winning 28 blue ribbons and the Show Sweepstakes with a total of 1,120 points (which really upped the ante: *1992's winner* [read *the 1992 winner*] scored only 387 points)." Anne Raver, "A Big Flower Show One Loves to Hate," *N.Y. Times*, 2 Mar. 1995, at B5.

I. Phrasal Possessives. Avoid phrasal possessives when possible, so that you don't end up with sentences like this: "That strange man who lives down the block's daughter was arrested last week." (Read: *The daughter of that strange man who lives down the block was arrested last week.*) The form with *of*, though slightly longer, is correct. Sometimes, too, the sentence can be fixed in some way other than by inserting an *of*—e.g.: "These statements do let women in on *the man in question's view* of our half of humanity." (Read: *These statements do let women in on how the man in question views our half of humanity.*)

As always, there are exceptions—two of them. With a phrase such as *mother-in-law*, the possessive is acceptable and widely used <my mother-in-law's sister>. The other established phrasal possessives are variations on *anybody else's*: "Once alerted, the janitor could find *no one else's* umbrella." See **else's**.

J. Attributive Nouns Ending in -*ed*. Words ending in -*ed* become awkward as possessives. This happens primarily in law. With such phrases as *the insured's death* and *the deceased's residence*, it's better to use an *of*-phrase—hence *the death of the insured* and *the residence of the deceased*. (Or you might try *the decedent's residence*.) See **insured**.

K. Possessives Followed by Relative Pronouns. The relative pronoun *who* stands for a noun; it shouldn't follow a possessive because the possessive (being an adjective, not a noun) can't properly be its antecedent. In the sentence that follows, *Esterhazy's* is a possessive adjective modifying the UNDERSTOOD WORD *voice*, but the writer meant *who* to refer to *Esterhazy*: "Or there may have been inimical voices raised among the committee, such as Palffy's or Nikolaus Esterhazy's, *who* just then had had an unpleasant brush with the composer." George R. Marek, *Beethoven* 382 (1969). (Read: *Or inimical voices may have been raised within the committee, such as those of Palffy or Nikolaus Esterhazy. The latter had just had an unpleasant brush with the composer.*) The poor grammar in the original sentence raises another question: to whom does the *who* refer—Esterhazy alone, or both Esterhazy and Palffy? The revision assumes that the reference is to Esterhazy alone. Otherwise, the wording would be *both of whom*.

L. Units of Time or Value. The idiomatic possessive should be used with periods of time and statements of worth—hence *30 days' notice* (i.e., notice of 30 days), *three days' time, 20 dollars' worth*, and *several years' experience*. E.g.:

- "Under Japanese law, 10 judges of the 15-member Supreme Court, the nation's top court, must be legal experts with at least *10 years experience* [read *10 years' experience*]." "Japanese Supreme Court May Soon Seat 1st Woman," *Ariz. Daily Star*, 15 Jan. 1994, at A2. In that sentence, of course, it would also be possible to write *with at least 10 years of experience*.

- "The three fashion-industry veterans with more than *80 years experience* [read *80 years' experience*] among them were clearly ready for a vacation." William Kissel, "Fashioning a Home," *Celebrated Living*, Fall 2002, at 54.

This usage was dealt a real setback in 2002 with the release of the hit movie *Two Weeks Notice* [read *Two Weeks' Notice*], starring Hugh Grant and Sandra Bullock. It might have been an even bigger hit if the good-usage crowd hadn't boycotted the movie on principle. Cf. *six months pregnant* under **pregnant**.

M. Titles of Books, Films, and the Like. Do you say *Turabian's "A Manual for Writers"* or *Turabian's*

"Manual for Writers"? That is, if you're introducing a title with a possessive, do you include an article (*A* or *The*) that begins the title? Including the article gets the full title of the book, but omitting it seems less stilted. Eric Partridge liked the former phrasing (*U&A* at 333); others prefer the latter (e.g., *Words into Type* 136 [3d ed. 1974]). In fact, though, either style is likely to bother some readers.

Kingsley Amis has found a sensible approach: "Speakers of English understandably feel that a noun, or modifier-plus-noun, will take a maximum of one article or possessive or other handle and shy away from saying anything like 'Graham Greene's *The Confidential Agent*' or 'Anthony Burgess's *A Clockwork Orange*' or 'A.N. Other's *He Fell Among Thieves*.' . . . To behave properly you have to write, for instance, 'Graham Greene's thriller, *The Confidential Agent*' and 'Anthony Burgess's fantasy of the future, *A Clockwork Orange*' and 'Kafka's novel [or whatever it is] *The Castle*.'" *The King's English* 121 (1997).

N. *Goodness' sake* and *conscience' sake.* The traditional view is that in the phrases *for goodness' sake* and *for conscience' sake*, no final *-s* is added to the possessive. In practice, writers follow this exception with *goodness* but not with *conscience* (the prevalent form in AmE being the almost unpronounceable *conscience's sake*). The reason is probably that *for goodness' sake* is so common. In fact, 50% of the time in modern prose, writers omit the possessive altogether, making it **for goodness sake.*

The best course is probably to stick with the traditional forms so that they're parallel: *goodness' sake* and *conscience' sake*. See **conscience' sake.**

O. **Fused Participles.** On the need for the possessive case before an *-ing* participle, see FUSED PARTICIPLES.

POSSESSIVE WITH GERUND. See FUSED PARTICIPLES.

possessory. See **possessive.**

possible. A. And *practicable*. *Practicable* (= feasible; possible in practice) is only a little narrower than *possible* (= capable of happening or being done). The more problematic words are *practical* and *practicable*. See **practical.**

For a mistake related to these words, see **impracticability.**

B. **For *necessary*.** This error occasionally appears in the odd, unidiomatic phrase **more difficult than possible*—e.g.: "The movie goes overboard trying to make the parents' day more difficult than *possible* [read *necessary*]." Frank Gabrenya, "All in a Day's Work," *Columbus Dispatch*, 20 Dec. 1996, at E14.

C. **As a Noncomparable Adjective.** See ADJECTIVES (B).

possum. See **opossum.**

post facto. See **ex post facto.**

posthaste is obsolete in all but its adverbial sense (= quickly). And even that is archaic-sounding and fairly rare—e.g.:

- "The animal should be carefully field dressed at once or, at the least, taken *posthaste* to the nearest butcher or abattoir." Jim Casada, "Learning to Appreciate the Culinary Delights of Venison," *Herald* (Rock Hill, S.C.), 1 Nov. 1996, at C4.
- "Drink it *posthaste*; fruit shakes separate if they sit around." Cathy Thomas, "Go Absolutely Bananas," *Buffalo News*, 30 Apr. 1997, at C2.
- "After listening to their stories, I asked Agent Findley to initiate a case report with Officer Stoinski's report attached and get it to me *posthaste*." Terry Grosz, *The Thin Green Line* 295 (2004).

post hoc (= [of, relating to, or involving] the fallacy of assuming causality from temporal sequence) for *ex post facto* or *after-the-fact* is a common error. E.g.: "They argue that . . . the Court's written opinions are therefore just '*post-hoc* [read *after-the-fact*] rationalizations' of their earlier decision on the merits." Forrest Maltzman & Paul J. Wahlbeck, "Strategic Policy Considerations and Voting Fluidity on the Burger Court," *Am. Pol. Sci. Rev.*, 1 Sept. 1996, at 581.

LANGUAGE-CHANGE INDEX
post hoc misused for *ex post facto* or
after-the-fact: Stage 1

post hoc, ergo propter hoc (L. "after this, therefore because of this") denotes the fallacy of confusing sequence with consequence. E.g.: "The Feb. 5 Dispatch editorial linking the major decrease in the number of licensed gun dealers with a minor decrease in homicides illustrates the first fallacy taught in any logic course: *post hoc, ergo propter hoc* (after this, therefore because of this). The rooster's crow does not cause the sun to rise." Letter of Kevin Cantos, "Licensing Unrelated to Drop in Slayings," *Columbus Dispatch*, 22 Feb. 1997, at A11.

Two common usages, *since* for *because* (acceptable) and *consequent* for *subsequent* (unacceptable), exemplify the fallacy: they originated when speakers and writers confused causality with temporality. See **post hoc.**

posthumous, introduced into English in the early 17th century, acquired a nonetymological *-h-* from its very beginnings as an English word. The Latin etymon *postumus* means "last" or "late-born." But the *-h-* was added in a 1619 book about Ben Jonson: "He [Jonson] . . . was *posthumous*, being born a month after his father's death." (Quoted in *OED*.) The *OED* notes that the *-h-* was added "through erroneous attribution to *humus* the earth, or (as explained by Servius) *humāre* to bury." So *exhume* is not in fact cognate with *posthumous* at all. In any event, the well-established

LANGUAGE-CHANGE INDEX (For the full key, see front matter pp. xxxi, l–li.)
Stage 1: Rejected. **Stage 2:** Widely shunned. **Stage 3:** Widespread but . . . **Stage 4:** Ubiquitous but . . . **Stage 5:** Fully accepted.
Invariably inferior forms marked by asterisk (*). • Ratios represent frequency of prevalent forms vs. variants in current books.

but erroneous -*h*- should have no bearing on the pronunciation, which is properly /**pos**-chuu-məs/—not /pohst-**hyoo**-məs/ or /pahst-**hyoo**-məs/.

postilion (= a person who rides the leading left-side horse of a team of horses drawing a carriage) has been the standard spelling since the 1840s. *Postillion* is a primarily BrE variant.

postmortem. See **autopsy.**

POSTPOSITIVE ADJECTIVES follow the nouns they modify, generally because they follow Romance rather than Germanic (or English) syntax. They exist in English largely as a remnant of the Norman French influence during the Middle Ages, and especially in the century following the Norman Conquest. The French influence was most pronounced in the language of law, politics, religion, and heraldry.

In fields in which French phrases were adopted wholesale—syntax and all—they often passed into the English language unchanged, even though in English, adjectives otherwise almost invariably precede the nouns they modify. Following is a list of frequently used phrases with postpositive adjectives:

accounts payable	court-martial
accounts receivable	heir apparent
ambassador-designate	knight-errant
annuity certain	minister extraordinary
attorney general	notary public
battle royal	postmaster general
body politic	president-elect
condition precedent	secretary general
condition subsequent	steak tartare

On the troublesome issue of pluralizing the nouns in phrases such as these, see PLURALS (G).

At least two common English nouns, *matters* and *things*, often take postpositive adjectives that are ordinarily prepositive. Hence we say that someone is interested in *matters philological* or *things philosophical*.

Sometimes a writer will attempt to create a prepositive adjectival phrase where properly the phrase would normally and most idiomatically be postpositive. The result is ungainly indeed: "*The complained-of injuries* [read *The injuries complained of*] occurred on the practice field late Thursday."

There is, however, a tendency in modern writing to make prepositive PHRASAL ADJECTIVES out of what would formerly have been postpositive. So instead of having *payments past due*, we just as often see *past-due payments*.

postscript. See **P.S.**

potable drinking water. This phrasing is redundant, since what is potable is drinkable—e.g.: "By hygiene I mean not only the use of toilets and the preservation of *potable drinking water* [read *potable water*] but a rational acceptance of birth control and an attitude neither phobic nor reckless toward sex." William A. Henry III, *In Defense of Elitism* 29–30 (1994). See REDUNDANCY. Its having appeared as early as 1900 is

no recommendation of it. The phrase spread rapidly from 1960 to 2000.

potency; ***potence.*** Oddly, *potency* is more common in the positive, and *impotence* in the negative. See **impotence.**

Current ratio (*potency* vs. *potence*): 126:1

potentiality, dating from the 17th century, is jargonistic when used (as it usually is) merely for the noun *potential.* E.g.: "They must seek to find meaning for their life, and to give something unique from their *potentiality* [read *potential*] for experience." Catherine Proctor, "Recovering Addicts Are Encouraged to Realign Their Ideals," *Asheville Citizen-Times,* 10 May 1997, at A9.

The one justifiable sense of *potentiality* is "the state or quality of possessing latent power or capacity capable of coming into being or action" (*SOED*)—e.g.: "In every child who is born, under no matter what circumstances, . . . the *potentiality* of the human race is born again." James Agee (as quoted in John Kolbe, "Grandpa's Words of Wisdom," *Ariz. Republic,* 6 July 1997, at H5).

LANGUAGE-CHANGE INDEX
potentiality for *potential*: Stage 1
Current ratio (*their potential* vs. *their potentiality*): 169:1

potful. Pl. *potfuls*—not *potsful*. See PLURALS (G).

pour. For the misuse of this verb for *pore,* see **pore.**

P.P.S. See **P.S.**

practical; practicable. Though similar, these words should be distinguished. *Practical* = manifested in practice; capable of being put to good use. Its opposite is *theoretical.*

Practicable (/**prak**-ti-kə-bəl/) = capable of being accomplished; feasible; possible. E.g.:

- "Officers were instructed to hold the apprehended person for delivery to an officer of the other jurisdiction as soon as *practicable.*" Mark A. Hutchison, "Legality of Police Pacts Questioned," *Sunday Oklahoman,* 6 Apr. 1997, at 1.
- "On the basis of emerging ITU standards, videoconferencing should become *practicable* over standard telephone lines." George Black, "Videoconferencing," *Fin. Times,* 10 Sept. 1997, at 12.

For a mistake related to this word, see **impracticability.** For comments on the negative forms, see **impractical.**

Occasionally *practicable* is misused for *practical*—e.g.: "The articles in The Syracuse Newspapers and comments by the Syracuse SkyChiefs Board of Directors were very interesting and extremely *practicable* [read *practical*]." Letter of John Anthony, "There's Already Doubt About '98 SkyChiefs," *Post-Standard* (Syracuse), 11 Sept. 1997, at D2. See **possible** (A).

In both words, the first syllable is stressed: /**prak**-ti-kəl/ and /**prak**-ti-kə-bəl/.

LANGUAGE-CHANGE INDEX
practicable misused for *practical*: Stage 1

practice; practise. In AmE, *practice* is both the noun and the verb. (Until about 1915, *practise* was the standard verb in AmE. For some reason AmE adopted *practice* as the verb about the time of World War I.) In BrE, *practice* is the noun and *practise* the verb.

praying mantis is the correct spelling, not **preying mantis*. Even though this insect preys on others, its name comes from the way it holds its front legs raised, as if in prayer. But some writers misunderstand the ETYMOLOGY—e.g.: "On Sunday, the 6-10 *preying mantis* [read *praying mantis*] look-alike pitched seven innings, whiffed 14 and retired after throwing 130 pitches." Frank Luksa, "Series Reaches Striking Climax," *Dallas Morning News*, 14 July 1997, at B1.
LANGUAGE-CHANGE INDEX
praying mantis misspelled **preying mantis*: Stage 1
Current ratio: 17:1

preachify, a derogatory word dating from the 18th century, means "to preach in a factitious or a tedious way" (*OED*). E.g.: "The Rev. John Crum was *preachifying* when a loud voice bellowed 'Salvation,' which was followed by a snort that folks said sounded like a frightened horse." John Switzer, "Leatherwood God Left Villagers Divided," *Columbus Dispatch*, 31 July 1994, at C8. See **speechify.**

precede; proceed. These words are sometimes confused even by otherwise literate people. Both may mean "to go ahead," but in different senses. *Precede* = to go ahead of; to come before <the husband preceded his wife by ten steps>. *Proceed* = to go ahead; to continue <they proceeded into the hall>.
*Preceed, a misspelling, confuses the two words. It occurs in print surprisingly often—e.g.: "He asked the audience to vote for politicians who solve problems, instead of focusing on the storms that *preceed* [read *precede*] the solutions." Anne Michaud, "Solving Problems Stressed for County," *Cincinnati Enquirer*, 18 Apr. 1997, at C1.
The same is true of the misuse of *proceed* for *precede*—e.g.: "Representative Charles B. Rangel of New York, the senior Democrat on the Ways and Means Committee, and one of the leading liberals in Congress, *proceeded* [read *preceded*] Mr. Archer to the microphone." Jerry Gray, "Bills to Balance the Budget and Cut Taxes Pass the Senate," *N.Y. Times*, 1 Aug. 1997, at A12.
LANGUAGE-CHANGE INDEX
1. *precede* misspelled **preceed*: Stage 1
2. *proceed* misused for *precede*: Stage 1

precedence. A. And **precedency*. Today *precedence* is the standard term. **Precedency*, a NEEDLESS VARIANT, was common through the first half of the 19th century.
Current ratio: 72:1

B. Pronunciation. Although the traditional pronunciation of *precedence* was /pri-**seed**-ənts/, today the standard pronunciation in all the major varieties of World English is /**pres**-i-dənts/. Hence the word is now typically a homophone of *precedents*.

C. And *precedent*. *Precedence* (= priority) and *precedent* (= [1] an established convention, or [2] a model) are sometimes misused for each other. For example, *precedent* sometimes displaces *precedence* in the phrase *take precedence*—e.g.: "Criminal cases, because of speedy-trial requirements, take *precedent* [read *precedence*] over civil cases." Stuart Eskenazi, "Texas Files $4 Billion Tobacco Lawsuit," *Austin Am.-Statesman*, 29 Mar. 1996, at A1, A10. Misusages of this type are extremely common among journalists not accustomed to writing about the law.
Likewise, *precedence* sometimes ousts *precedent* in the phrase *set a precedent*—e.g.:

- "The state Supreme Court earlier set the *precedence* [read *precedent*] for Brantley's ruling." Michelle Hillier, "Go to Vote on Park Tax, Backers Say," *Ark. Democrat-Gaz.*, 4 Nov. 1994, at A13.
- "Judice isn't setting *precedence* [read *a precedent*] with his career move." Jeff Davis, "Judice Makes Pitch to Save Baseball Career," *Fresno Bee*, 2 July 1995, at D5.
- "Jones set a *precedence* [read *precedent*] by seeking approval from the Continental Congress before accepting the foreign decoration." David T. Zabecki, "Medals and Decorations," in 2 *A Companion to American Military History* 899, 913 (James C. Bradford ed., 2009).

LANGUAGE-CHANGE INDEX
1. **taking precedent* for *taking precedence*: Stage 1
Current ratio (*taking precedence* vs.
*taking precedent): 44:1
2. **setting a precedence* for *setting a precedent*: Stage 1
Current ratio (*setting a precedent* vs.
*setting a precedence): 101:1

precedent, adj., is inferior to *previous* or *prior*, except when used as a POSTPOSITIVE ADJECTIVE in a phrase such as *condition precedent*. E.g.: "This rule in no respect impinges on the doctrine that one who makes only a loan on such paper, or takes it as collateral security for a *precedent* [read *prior*] debt, may be limited in his recovery to the amount advanced or secured." This adjective is best pronounced /pri-**seed**-ənt/, although /**pre**-si-dənt/ is acceptable. For the noun form of *precedent*, see **precedence (B), (C).**

*preceed. See **precede.**

preceptorial (= teacherly) is the standard form. **Preceptoral* is a NEEDLESS VARIANT.
Current ratio: 14:1

precipitancy; *precipitance. See **precipitation.**

LANGUAGE-CHANGE INDEX (For the full key, see front matter pp. xxxi, l–li.)
Stage 1: Rejected. **Stage 2:** Widely shunned. **Stage 3:** Widespread but . . . **Stage 4:** Ubiquitous but . . . **Stage 5:** Fully accepted.
Invariably inferior forms marked by asterisk (*). • Ratios represent frequency of prevalent forms vs. variants in current books.

precipitate, adj.; **precipitous**; *__precipitant.__ These words are quite different, though often confused. *Precipitate* /pri-**sip**-i-tət/ = sudden; hasty; rash; showing violent or uncontrollable speed. This word is applied to actions, movements, or demands. *Precipitous* = like a precipice; steep. It is applied to physical things—rarely to actions, unless the METAPHOR of steepness is apt.

Precipitous is frequently misused for *precipitate*—e.g.:

- "We are not asking for a *precipitous* [read *precipitate*] decision on the directorship." John R. Day, "Get Moving on Mental Health Director," *Chicago Trib.*, 16 Jan. 1995, at 12.
- "Even more troubling is the *precipitous* [read *precipitate*] decline—42 percent—in cash contributions in the first quarter of 1995." "Let Them Eat Cake Mix?" *Baltimore Sun*, 1 May 1995, at A8.
- "This type of hypertonic dysfunction often results in *precipitous* [read *precipitate*] labor—labor that lasts less than 3 hours from the start of uterine contractions to birth." 1 N. Jayne Klossner, *Introductory Maternity Nursing* 432 (2006).

Perhaps the second example is excusable if we picture a graph with a sharp drop, or if we visualize a decline; but if "sudden" is meant, *precipitate* is the word.

*__Precipitant,__ adj., is a NEEDLESS VARIANT for *precipitate*—e.g.: "Easley's lawyer . . . [contended] that the forged document caused Easley's *precipitant* [read *precipitate*] decline in academic and community standing." Ted Gup, "University 'Prank' Ruined Life, Student's Suit Charges," *Wash. Post*, 21 Sept. 1978, at A1. But *precipitant* is a useful noun meaning "a cause or stimulus"—e.g.: "Sleep deprivation is another *precipitant* of somnambulism." Pat Guiteras, "Parent Worries Sleepwalker Will Go Too Far," *Chapel Hill Herald*, 5 Apr. 1995, at 6.

LANGUAGE-CHANGE INDEX
precipitous misused for *precipitate*: Stage 4

precipitation; precipitancy; *__precipitance.__ *Precipitation* = (1) something that condenses from a vapor and falls (as rain or snow) <a forecast of freezing precipitation overnight>; or (2) the bringing about of something suddenly or unexpectedly <precipitation of a riot>. *Precipitancy* = sudden or rash haste <we shouldn't act with precipitancy>. Although *precipitation* has sometimes overlapped with *precipitancy*, this overlap is undesirable. Finally, *__precipitance__ is a NEEDLESS VARIANT of *precipitancy*.

precipitous. See **precipitate.**

precision; precisian; precisionist. *Precision* = accuracy. *Precisian* = a person who adheres to rigidly high standards (often with regard to moral conduct). (The first two are homophones: /pri-**sizh**-ən/.) *Precisionist* = a person who prizes absolute correctness of expression and performance, esp. in language and ritual.

preclusive; *__preclusory.__ The latter is a NEEDLESS VARIANT.

*__precondition,__ a 19th-century NEOLOGISM, is usually unnecessary in place of *condition*—e.g.: "For months the Government tried in vain to persuade him that he and the ANC should abandon some of the cornerstones of their strategy as a *pre-condition* [read *condition*] for future negotiations." Fred Bridgland, "Freedom Brings Mandela His Greatest Challenge," *Sunday Telegraph*, 11 Feb. 1990, at 3.

predacious; *__predaceous.__ See **predatory.**

predate = (1) /pree-**dayt**/ to have existed before (something else); or (2) /pri-**dayt**/ to devour as prey; prey upon. Sense 2, not recorded in most dictionaries, is a newfangled BACK-FORMATION from *predation*. And it doesn't fill a void: *prey* is an age-old verb that does the job. E.g.:

- "The colorful fish are easily seen and *predated* [read *preyed*] upon, and once a dominant male disappears, a remarkable event occurs." Natalie Angier, "If You've Got It, Flaunt It," *Courier-J.* (Louisville), 13 Jan. 1992, at A5.
- "If the wolf population becomes too large, these meat animals are *predated* [read *preyed*] upon, thus diminishing the supply of food for the hunters and their families." "Wolf Overpopulation Cuts into Food Supply," *Anchorage Daily News*, 18 Feb. 1996, at D2.
- "Some additional differences exist between predatory and herbivorous sea snails in details of the shell, but some of these stem from the fact that predatory sea snails themselves are *predated* [read *preyed*] upon." Joseph Heller, *Sea Snails* 152 (2015).

For sense 1, see **antedate.**

LANGUAGE-CHANGE INDEX
predate misused for *prey*, vb.: Stage 1

predatory; *__predative; *predatorial; predacious; *predaceous.__ For the sense "preying on other animals," *predatory* is the most usual term. *__Predative__ and *__predatorial__ are rare NEEDLESS VARIANTS.

Predacious and *__predaceous__ might also be classed as NEEDLESS VARIANTS. But because *predatory* has extended senses <a company's predatory actions against its competitors> <predatory young men who target naive girls>, some biologists prefer *predacious*. Even if we allow that term—though the possibility of true DIFFERENTIATION seems remote—the by-form *__predaceous__ should still be avoided.

predestine, vb.; *__predestinate,__ vb. Although Merriam-Webster dictionaries might lead you to believe otherwise, *predestine* has been the standard form since the mid-19th century. *__Predestinate,__ as a verb, is a NEEDLESS VARIANT. But the adjective by the same spelling is a synonym of *predestined*: it is pronounced /pri-**des**-ti-nət/. It might be considered a NEEDLESS VARIANT as well. But none of these pronouncements were foreordained.

Current ratio (*predestined* vs. *__predestinated__): 10:1

predicable; *__predicatable.__ *__Predicatable__ is an error for either *predicable* (= capable of being asserted) or (more predictably) *predictable*—e.g.: "The conclusion is *predicatable* [read *predictable*], but what comes before it is good, old-fashioned fun." Diane Holloway, "Annie's Wig Needs Work," *Austin Am.-Statesman*, 17 Nov. 1995, at F1. See -ABLE (A) & -ATABLE.

predominant; predominate, adj. The latter is a NEEDLESS VARIANT for *predominant*. In good usage, *predominate* is the verb, *predominant* the adjective. Readers may be confused by *predominate* as an adjective because it is the same form as the verb, so *predominant* should be reserved for this job—e.g.:

- "Jazz must still undergo [de-ghettoizing] to dispel the *predominate* [read *predominant*] images of it as banal happy-time entertainment and primitive, spontaneous emotionalism." Peter Watrous, "Finally, a Lincoln Center for American Music," *N.Y. Times*, 20 Jan. 1991, § 2, at 28.
- "In Pittsburgh, our *predominate* [read *predominant*] groups are black and white." Jane Miller, "YWCA's Center for Race Relations Stresses Awareness," *Pitt. Post-Gaz.*, 2 Feb. 1997, Metro §, at 2.
- "As he looked images would suggest themselves and he would select and paint the one that he wished to impose as the *predominate* [read *predominant*] image." Peter Banks & Jonathan Evens, *The Secret Chord* 44 (2012).

Cf. **preponderant.**

LANGUAGE-CHANGE INDEX
predominate misused as an adjective
for *predominant*: Stage 1
Current ratio (*predominant role* vs.
*predominate role): 96:1

predominate, vb.; **dominate.** *Predominate* is an intransitive verb: either it stands alone, or it needs a preposition after it, such as *in, on,* or *over*. But some writers have begun making it transitive, with a direct object. The trend should be resisted—e.g.:

- "The younger Harley, 33, a skinny, ruddy-faced fellow, looks like a kid amid the grandmotherly members who *predominate the group* [read *predominate in the group*]." Beth Jackendoff, "A Fugue of Personalities, Teaneck Chorus Turns 50," *Record* (N.J.), 4 Jan. 1988, at B2.
- "Those who frequent coffee shops are generally mild-mannered, said Sen. Cohen, adding that liquor won't *predominate the menu* [read *predominate on the menu*]." Michael Finn, "Coffee House Liquor Gets Reprieve," *Chattanooga Free Press*, 21 May 1997, at B8.
- "Today, trucks, boots, cowboy leather jackets and Mexican rock *predominate the scene* [read *predominate*] on a Saturday night at the *zocalo* (main plaza), 'machismo' vibrates in the air, stories of flashy money mingle with drug trafficking." Kirsten Appendini, "'From Where Have All the Flowers Come?'" in *Women Working the NAFTA Food Chain* 128, 135 (Deborah Barndt ed., 2004).

Dominate, by contrast, can be either transitive <the challenger dominated the champ from the opening bell> or intransitive <athletes dominate over scholars in the school's social hierarchy>.

LANGUAGE-CHANGE INDEX
predominate used as a transitive verb: Stage 1

preeminent. What is *preeminent* is unique: it stands above all others of its kind. So an indefinite article (*a* or *an*) is usually illogical with the word—e.g.: "The second [day] will be devoted to the archive of Charles Negre, *a pre-eminent* [read *an eminent* or *the preeminent*] practitioner of French primitive photographs." Carol Vogel, "Inside Art," *N.Y. Times*, 1 Feb. 2002, at E34.

To call more than one person or thing *preeminent* in the same field is to break the word's sense—e.g.: "Kissell said that Williams and Stan Musial, two of the *preeminent* [read *best*] hitters of their generation, got their hits in different ways." Tom Timmermann, "Martinez Is Unhappy with First Half but Feels More Relaxed at Plate," *St. Louis Post-Dispatch*, 6 July 2002, Sports §, at 4.

preemptive; peremptory; preemptory. The adjectives most commonly used and distinguished are *preemptive* and *peremptory*. *Preemptive* = (1) of, relating to, or involving preemption <the agency's preemptive powers>; or (2) preventive, deterrent <a preemptive strike>. *Peremptory* = (1) incontrovertible; or (2) imperious, domineering. Sense 1: "Fortunately, Deaver gave Henry the hook before he could issue the usual *peremptory* command." Alexander Cockburn, "The End: Convention Seals Post-History Case," *Phoenix Gaz.*, 17 Aug. 1996, at B9. Sense 2: "In these books, the author's twisty, improbable plots feel implausible and contrived; her poised authorial manner, *peremptory* and pinched." Michiko Kakutani, "Her Serene Tyranny, a Mistress of Mayhem," *N.Y. Times*, 16 May 1997, at C29.

Preemptory (= of, relating to, or involving a preemptor) properly appears only in rare legal uses. Yet it is sometimes confused with *preemptive*—e.g.:

- "In a statement, Continental said it was disappointed the city had filed the *preemptory* [read *preemptive*] suit and noted it has been negotiating for several months to get modifications to the lease." Beverly Narum, "Denver Sues Continental over Lease," *Houston Post*, 23 Feb. 1995, at C1.
- "Financial marketeers [hope] to make Federal Reserve policy makers nervous enough to snug up interest rates as a *preemptory* [read *preemptive*] move against inflation." Jerry Heaster, "Economy Has Survived Half of 1996," *Kansas City Star*, 30 June 1996, at F1.
- "When stress is certain to occur, *preemptory* [read *preemptive*] emotional reactions tend to mimic (predict) those that will subsequently occur in response to the expected stressor." Christian Waugh et al., *Biobehavioral Resilience to Stress* 117, 125 (Brian J. Lukey & Victoria Tepe eds., 2008).

And it's also occasionally misused for *peremptory*, no doubt from a false association with *preempt*—e.g.:

- "On Friday, Judge John Ouderkirk of State Superior Court dismissed a black woman after a challenge for cause and a black man after a *preemptory* [read *peremptory*] challenge by the prosecutor. In making *preemptory* [read *peremptory*]

LANGUAGE-CHANGE INDEX (For the full key, see front matter pp. xxxi, l–li.)
Stage 1: Rejected. **Stage 2:** Widely shunned. **Stage 3:** Widespread but . . . **Stage 4:** Ubiquitous but . . . **Stage 5:** Fully accepted.
Invariably inferior forms marked by asterisk (✳). • Ratios represent frequency of prevalent forms vs. variants in current books.

challenges, lawyers do not have to give a reason for wanting a prospective juror dismissed." "Jury Queries Resume in Beating Case," *N.Y. Times*, 8 Aug. 1993, at 17.

- "Like Barkley's Suns then, Barkley's Rockets toyed with the Timberwolves in a *preemptory* [read *peremptory*], rub-your-nose-in-it fashion." Dan Barreiro, "Barkley Toys with the Wolves Again," *Star Trib.* (Minneapolis), 25 Apr. 1997, at C1.
- "Seven African Americans were discharged from the jury because of *preemptory* [read *peremptory*] challenges from the defendant's attorneys." John A. Kirk, "The Long Shadow of Carnell Russ' Death," *Ark. Times*, 4 Sept. 2014, at 15.

LANGUAGE-CHANGE INDEX
1. *preemptory* misused for *preemptive*: Stage 1
Current ratio (*preemptive strike* vs.
preemptory strike): 209:1
2. *preemptory* misused for *peremptory*: Stage 1
Current ratio (*peremptory challenges* vs.
preemptory challenges): 57:1

preestablished. So spelled.

preexisting. So spelled.

preface; foreword. Technically, a *preface* is a book's front matter that is written by the author. A *foreword* is contributed by someone other than the author. See **foreword.**

prefatory; *prefatorial; *prefacial; *prefatial. The last three terms are NEEDLESS VARIANTS of the first.
Current ratio (in order of headwords): 8,818:84:10:1

prefect (= [1] a chief administrative officer or magistrate; or [2] [esp. in BrE] a senior student in private school vested with disciplinary authority) has the corresponding adjective *prefectorial* <prefectorial authority>. The term *prefectoral* is a NEEDLESS VARIANT.

The similarly spelled *prefectural* is in good use as the adjective corresponding to *prefecture* (= [1] an administrative district; or [2] the office of a prefect). Sometimes *prefectural* is wrongly displaced by one of the other terms—e.g.: "The Duke of Kent this morning met Mr. Toshitami Kaihara, Governor of Hyogo *Prefectoral* [read *Prefectural*] Government, Kobe." "Court Circular," *Times* (London), 25 Nov. 1996, at 26. *Prefectual* is a misspelling that appears from time to time—e.g.: "Donations from the seminar will be used toward the construction of the Okinawan *Prefectual* [read *Prefectural*] Martial Arts Pavilion, to open in 1997 in Okinawa." James Black, "Karate: Demonstration at Nassau CC," *Newsday* (N.Y.), 23 Feb. 1995, at A59.

LANGUAGE-CHANGE INDEX
1. *prefectoral* misused for *prefectural*: Stage 1
Current ratio (*prefectural* vs. *prefectoral*): 17:1
2. *prefectural* misspelled *prefectual*: Stage 1
Current ratio: 178:1

prefer. It is quite idiomatic to prefer one thing *to* another, or one thing *over* another. But the two things being compared must be grammatically and logically parallel: "Everyone, after all, would *prefer* working in a

pleasant working environment *to* an unpleasant one." Robert Levering, *A Great Place to Work* ix (1988). (A possible revision: *Everyone, after all, would prefer a pleasant working environment to an unpleasant one.*) See PARALLELISM.

It is not idiomatic, however, to couple *prefer* with *than*, as sometimes occurs with the infinitive—e.g.: "I *prefer* to write things out in longhand *than* to type them up." Perhaps this instead: *I prefer to write things out in longhand rather than to type them up.* Or: *I prefer to write things out in longhand, not to type them up.*

preferable, inherently a comparative adjective, shouldn't be preceded by *more*—e.g.:

- "All hands involved have decided that inconveniencing Suns fans is *eminently more preferable than* [read *much preferable to*] risking the chance that just one person in the known universe misses a chance to see Michael Jordan." Milton Kent, "Baseball Catches Up in Ratings," *Baltimore Sun*, 26 Apr. 1995, at C2.
- "The fact that they won after bowling so badly in Glamorgan's first innings was a reminder of how four-day cricket is infinitely *more preferable* [read *preferable*]." "Cricket: Cronje Calls Up Heavy Artillery," *Daily Telegraph*, 2 Sept. 1995, at 21. (On the use of *infinitely* in this example, see **infinitely (B).**)
- "If, instead of considering size as an attribute or criterion, we focus on our objectives, we can say that, with respect to safety, the large car is *more preferable* [read *preferable*]." Ernest H. Forman & Mary Ann Selly, *Decision by Objectives* 21 (2001).

See COMPARATIVES AND SUPERLATIVES & ADJECTIVES (B).

Also, the word takes *to*, not *than*—e.g.:

- "The timing of eating candy is also crucial, he said, adding that once a day after dinner is *preferable than* [read *preferable to*] all day long when bacteria can build up and cause tooth decay." Barri Bronston, "Trick or . . . Toothpaste?!" *Times-Picayune* (New Orleans), 27 Oct. 1997, at C1.
- "The complexity of intensional contexts aside, Levinson's argument that there could not be a state of affairs that necessitated another state of affairs *more preferable than* [read *preferable to*] it is simply not convincing." Jay David Atlas, *Logic, Meaning, and Conversation* 178 (2005).
- "For definiteness suppose that all criteria are positively oriented, i.e. their larger values are *more preferable than* [read *preferable to*] the smaller ones." Vadim P. Berman et al., "Interval Value Tradeoffs Methodology and Techniques of Multicriteria Decision Analysis," in *User-Oriented Methodology and Techniques of Decision Analysis and Support* 144, 145 (Jaap Wessels & Andrzej P. Wierzbicki eds., 2013).

Preferable is accented on the first syllable, not the second: /**pref**-ər-ə-bəl/, not /pri-**fər**-ə-bəl/. See PRONUNCIATION (B) & CLASS DISTINCTIONS.

LANGUAGE-CHANGE INDEX
1. *more preferable* for *preferable* or
much preferable: Stage 3
Current ratio (*much preferable to* vs.
more preferable than): 2:1
2. *preferable than* for *preferable to*: Stage 1
Current ratio (*preferable to* vs.
preferable than): 121:1
3. *preferable* mispronounced /pri-**fər**-ə-bəl/: Stage 2

PREFIXES, NEGATIVE. See NEGATIVES (A).

pregnant. The phrase *six months pregnant* takes neither a hyphen before nor an apostrophe after *months*. The construction is not analogous to the idiomatic possessive with units of time or value that it superficially resembles (e.g., *six months' time*). In those phrases, the main word (e.g., *time*) is a noun, whereas *pregnant* is an adjective. Further, the sense of the construction is different: "six months *of* time" (idiomatic possessive) vs. "pregnant *for* six months" (no possessive at all). E.g.: "Mrs. Bennett, *three months pregnant*, works at a mental-retardation facility in neighboring Temple." Nathan Levy, "Strain on a Small Town," *Wash. Times*, 27 Mar. 2003, at C11. For more on the idiomatic possessive with units of time or value, see POSSESSIVES (L).

preheat. The prefix generally adds nothing to the verb. In recipes and other food contexts, make it "heat the oven to 325°."

prejudge; forejudge. The latter, in one of its senses, is a NEEDLESS VARIANT of *prejudge*, the usual term. See **forejudge.**

prejudgment (= the act of prejudging) has been predominantly so spelled throughout the English-speaking world since the 18th century. **Prejudgement* is a variant spelling. Cf. **judgment.**

Apart from the noun sense, the word is used adjectivally in law to describe something that takes place before a judgment has been rendered <prejudgment garnishment of wages> <prejudgment interest>.

prejudice, n. & v.t. In addition to the well-known sense of *bias* (n.) or *to make biased* (vb.), *prejudice* is also a legalism for *harm* (n.) or *to harm* (v.t.). In ordinary discourse, it is a lawyer's pomposity—e.g.: "After the 1994 courtroom defeat, Ms. Sullivan sued her attorneys, arguing that they had pressured her to sell stock in 1989 to ensure that their legal fees would be paid, despite her fears that this would *prejudice* [read *hurt*] her case." Ellen Joan Pollock, "The Long Goodbye," *Wall Street J.*, 19 May 1997, at A1.

Sometimes the past participle *prejudiced* in this legal sense can cause a MISCUE because some readers might take it to mean "having a strong bias against (something)"—e.g.: "The Louisiana revocatory action is available to a creditor who is *prejudiced* at the time by a fraudulent transfer made by his debtor." Albert Tate Jr., "The Revocatory Action in Louisiana Law," in *Essays on the Civil Law of Obligations* 133 (Joseph Dainow ed., 1969).

prejudicial. A. And *prejudiced*. *Prejudicial* (= tending to injure; harmful) applies to things and events; *prejudiced* (= harboring prejudices) applies to people. The

meaning of a sentence can frequently be made clearer by using *harmful* in place of *prejudicial*.

Occasionally, writers misuse *prejudicial* for *prejudiced*, especially in the negative form—e.g.: "AIDS is *unprejudicial* [read *unprejudiced*], knows no gender bias and should be everyone's nightmare." Letter of Sandy Sagen, "AIDS Stereotype," *Sacramento Bee*, 18 Oct. 1996, at B9. Actually, of course, it would be an understatement to say that AIDS is highly prejudicial: the writer said the opposite of what she meant.

B. And *pre-judicial*. The hyphen makes an important difference. *Pre-judicial* = of, relating to, or involving the time before a person became a judge <pre-judicial career>. Cf. RE- PAIRS.

prelate (= a bishop, cardinal, or other important priest in a Christian church) is pronounced /**prel**-it/—not /**pree**-layt/.

preliminary to for *before* is a silly pomposity—e.g.: "She brings in to him the 'last water,' *preliminary to* [read *before*] saying grace." Sylvia Barack Fishman, *Follow My Footprints* 121 (1992). Cf. **prior.**

prelude is pronounced either /**prel**-yood/ or (less good) /**pray**-lood/.

*premia. See premium.

premier, adj.; **premiere,** n. Aside from the part-of-speech distinction, three observations are in order. First, *premier*, the adjective meaning "first in importance or rank," is often pretentious in place of *first* or *foremost*. Second, *premiere*, the noun meaning "a first performance," has come into standard use as a verb <the new sitcom premieres in October>. (See FUNCTIONAL SHIFT (D).) Third, the accent is no longer used in the noun—hence *premiere*, not **première*. See DIACRITICAL MARKS.

In AmE, the two words are homophones: both are preferably pronounced /pri-**meer**/. In BrE, *premier* is pronounced /**prem**-yə/, and *premiere* is pronounced /**prem**-ee-ə/.

premise; *premiss. In the sense "a previous statement or proposition from which another is inferred as a conclusion," *premise* has always predominated in AmE and has predominated in BrE since about 1950. **Premiss* is a chiefly BrE variant.

premises (= a house or building) has a curious history. Originally, it denoted in law the part of a deed that sets forth the names of the grantor and grantee, as well as the things granted and the consideration. Then, through HYPALLAGE, it was extended to refer to the subject of a conveyance or bequest, specified in the premises of the deed. Finally, it was extended to refer to a house or building along with its grounds. In short, someone who says, "No alcohol is allowed on

LANGUAGE-CHANGE INDEX (For the full key, see front matter pp. xxxi, l–li.)
Stage 1: Rejected. **Stage 2:** Widely shunned. **Stage 3:** Widespread but . . . **Stage 4:** Ubiquitous but . . . **Stage 5:** Fully accepted.
Invariably inferior forms marked by asterisk (*). • Ratios represent frequency of prevalent forms vs. variants in current books.

these premises" is unconsciously using a popularized technicality.

The term is always used in the plural—e.g.:

- "The paint was peeling from its exterior, its rooms were empty and the *premises were* condemned by selectmen." Fred Hanson, "Old School Becomes a Jewel," *Patriot-Ledger* (Quincy, Mass.), 3 Oct. 1994, at F8.
- "These *premises were* originally let in 1957 by the appellant's predecessor in title." Paul Magrath, "Variation of Lease Did Not Create New Tenancy," *Independent*, 14 Sept. 1995, at 12.
- "The movements of pigs, feedstuffs, vehicles, and people onto and off the *premises* were traced to identify possible sources of the virus and limit the spread of infection." Anna Rovid Spickler et al., "Descriptions of Recent Incursions of Exotic Animal Diseases," in *Emerging and Exotic Diseases of Animals* 52, 58 (Anna Rovid Spickler et al. eds., 4th ed. 2010).

It is pronounced /**prem**-i-siz/, not /-seez/.

Unfortunately, some people (misunderstanding the term and its history) have begun referring to **this premise* when they mean "this piece of property." In 2003, a famous San Francisco steakhouse sported an unidiomatic, ill-premised sign inside the front door: "No alcohol may be taken off this premise." The sign is still there in 2016.

*premiss. See **premise.**

premium. The standard plural has been *premiums* since the 18th century. The form **premia* is hopelessly pedantic—e.g.:

- "Suppose that an insurance scheme is established and administered in such a way that insurance *premia* [read *premiums*] are not affected by riskiness of the portfolio." Philip Perry, "Regulation Q and Federal Deposit Insurance," *Am. Banker*, 2 Mar. 1983, at 4.
- "Substantial increases in insurance *premia* [read *premiums*] will further tip the balance." Letter of Kieran Murphy, "Doctors Foot the Bill," *Fin. Times*, 18 Nov. 1988, at I25.
- "This means that assets associated with nondiversifiable risks will carry risk *premia* [read *premiums*]. But, how can we measure such risk *premia* [read *premiums*] objectively when buying assets is essentially a matter of subjective preferences?" Salih N. Neftci, *Principles of Financial Engineering* 315 (2d ed. 2008).

See PLURALS (B).

LANGUAGE-CHANGE INDEX
*premia for *premiums*: Stage 1
Current ratio (*premiums* vs. **premia*): 22:1

premonition (= an odd feeling that something bad is imminent) was traditionally pronounced /**pree**-mə-nish-ən/, but in the mid-20th century /**prem**-ə-nish-ən/ became standard in both AmE and BrE alike.

prenuptial; antenuptial. From 1800 to about 1960, *antenuptial* was the predominant term in all varieties of English. About 1955, *prenuptial* became predominant in BrE, and by the 1970s AmE had followed suit. Oddly, *antenuptial* is omitted from many English-language dictionaries, although it appears routinely in legal writing in AmE; it's a NEEDLESS VARIANT.

Prenuptial is pronounced /pree-**nəp**-shəl/ or /pree-**nəp**-chəl/. But some speakers wrongly add an extra syllable: /pree-**nəp**-chə-wəl/. This mispronunciation sometimes occurs with *nuptial* as well. See **nuptial.**

A *prenuptial agreement* is commonly if informally called a *prenup*. See CASUALISMS (C).

preowned. In the 1970s, *preowned* became a common EUPHEMISM for *used*. Used-car dealers are especially fond of this DOUBLESPEAK—e.g.: "Why settle for an Accord or Taurus when you can have a *preowned* Cadillac for about the same price?"

preparatory; *preparative, adj. *Preparatory* is the standard term. **Preparative*, adj., is a NEEDLESS VARIANT. But as a noun, *preparative* legitimately means "something that prepares the way for something else."

Preparatory, adj., is pronounced /**prep**-ə-rə-tor-ee/ or /prə-**par**-ə-tor-ee/.

When used in the sense "to prepare for," *preparatory to* is pure JARGON. E.g.: "Personnel of the 582nd Medical Ambulance Co. are trying to create a mailing list *preparatory to holding* [read *to prepare for*] their first reunion." "Military Reunions," *News & Record* (Greensboro), 10 Sept. 1997, at R2. The phrase is likewise pretentious in place of *before*—e.g.: "That was the same campaign in which [Clinton] attacked the Bush administration for doing too little to stop the slaughter in Bosnia, *preparatory to* [read *before*] getting elected president and letting it continue for another four years." Paul Greenberg, "Communist China: Our Most-Favored Tyranny," *Tulsa Trib. & Tulsa World*, 22 Feb. 1997, at A12. Cf. **preliminary to** & **prior.**

*preplan, a NONWORD that took root in the 1930s and 1940s, is illogical for *plan* because planning must necessarily occur beforehand. E.g.:

- "Ninety percent of wasting time and standing in line can be eliminated with a little *preplanning* [read *planning*] and some common sense." Mark H. McCormack, *What They Don't Teach You at Harvard Business School* 212 (1984).
- "In return you get an interactive touch screen display that will beep a warning if you take a wrong turn and stray from its *preplanned* [read *planned*] route." Michael Koster, "No Need to Ask Directions," *Santa Fe New Mexican*, 26 Apr. 1997, at C1.
- "The success of a rescue operation is predicated upon the *preplanning* [read *planning*] that an organization employs in advance of the mission. A written *preplan* [read *plan*] identifies the hazards within the local jurisdiction, the need for specific types of rescue capabilities, and the operational procedures for conducting rescue tasks." Tom Vines & Steve Hudson, *High-Angle Rope Rescue Techniques: Levels I & II* 208 (4th ed. 2014).

See ILLOGIC (A).

LANGUAGE-CHANGE INDEX
*preplan for *plan*: Stage 2
Current ratio (*planned* vs. **preplanned*): 192:1

preponderant; *preponderate, adj. The latter is a NEEDLESS VARIANT that often occurs predominantly in the adverb *preponderately*—e.g.: "The statistical patter . . . has thus far indicated that AIDS and its transmission are *preponderately* [read *preponderantly*] linked to homosexual practices." "AIDS: At Risk from Being Too Squeamish," *Daily Mail*, 29 June 1992, at 6.

Use *preponderate* only as a verb—e.g.: "Its market share has declined each year as cars equipped for unleaded gasoline have *preponderated*, and lead gas is projected essentially to disappear by about 1990." Daniel Rosenheim, "Getting the Lead Out Won't Be a Gas," *Chicago Trib.*, 17 Feb. 1985, at C1. Cf. **predominant.**

LANGUAGE-CHANGE INDEX
preponderately for *preponderantly*: Stage 1
Current ratio (*preponderantly* vs.
preponderately): 47:1

PREPOSITIONS. A. The Preposition Quotient. In lean writing, it's a good idea to minimize prepositional phrases. In flabby prose, a ratio of one preposition for every four words is common; in better, leaner writing, the quotient is more like one preposition for every ten or fifteen words.

Five editorial methods can tighten sentences marred with too many prepositions. First, the prepositional phrase can be deleted as surplusage; for example, it's often possible in a given context to change a phrase such as *senior vice president of the corporation* to *senior vice president*—if the corporate context is already clear. Second, uncovering ZOMBIE NOUNS often eliminates as many as two prepositions each time; hence *is in violation of* becomes *violates*. Third, it's sometimes possible to replace a prepositional phrase with an adverb; so *she criticized the manuscript with intelligence* becomes *she criticized the manuscript intelligently*. Fourth, many prepositional phrases resolve themselves into POSSESSIVES; hence *for the convenience of the reader* becomes *for the reader's convenience*. And finally, a change from PASSIVE VOICE to active often entails removing a preposition; so *the ball was hit by Jane* becomes *Jane hit the ball*. See **of (A).**

B. Ending Sentences with Prepositions. The spurious rule about not ending sentences with prepositions is a remnant of Latin grammar, in which a preposition was the one word that a writer could not end a sentence with. But Latin grammar should never straitjacket English grammar. If the SUPERSTITION is a "rule" at all, it is a rule of rhetoric and not of grammar, the idea being to end sentences with strong words that drive a point home. (See SENTENCE ENDS.) That principle is sound, of course, but not to the extent of meriting lockstep adherence or flouting established idiom.

The idea that a preposition is ungrammatical at the end of a sentence is often attributed to 18th-century grammarians. But that idea is greatly overstated. Bishop Robert Lowth, the most prominent

18th-century grammarian, wrote that the final preposition "is an idiom, which our language is strongly inclined to: it prevails in common conversation, and suits very well with the familiar style in writing." *A Short Introduction to English Grammar* 137 (rev. ed. 1782). The furthest Lowth went was to urge that "the placing of the preposition before the relative is more graceful, as well as more perspicuous; and agrees much better with the solemn and elevated style." *Ibid.* That in itself is an archaic view that makes modern writing stuffy; indeed, Lowth elsewhere made the same plea for *hath*: "*Hath* properly belongs to the serious and solemn style; *has* to the familiar." *Ibid.* at 56. But in any event, Lowth's statement about prepositions was hardly intended as a "rule."

Winston Churchill's witticism about the absurdity of this bugaboo should have laid it to rest. When someone once upbraided him for ending a sentence with a preposition, he rejoined, "That is the type of arrant pedantry up with which I shall not put." Avoiding a preposition at the end of the sentence sometimes leads to just such a preposterous monstrosity.

Perfectly natural-sounding sentences end with prepositions, particularly when a verb with a preposition-particle appears at the end (as in *follow up* or *ask for*). E.g.: "The act had no causal connection with the injury complained *of*." When one decides against such formal (sometimes downright stilted) constructions as *of which*, *on which*, and *for which*—and instead chooses the relative *that*—the preposition is necessarily sent to the end of the sentence: "This is a point on which I must insist" becomes far more natural as "This is a point that I must insist on." And consider the following examples:

Correct and Natural	Correct and Stuffy
people worth talking to	people to whom it is worth talking
What are you thinking about?	About what are you thinking?
the man you were listening to	the man to whom you were listening
a person I have great respect for	a person for whom I have great respect
a habit I want to stick to	a habit to which I want to stick

In 1947, a scholar summed up the point: "Those who insist that final prepositions are inelegant are taking from the English language one of its greatest assets—its flexibility—an advantage realized and practiced by all our greatest writers except a few who, like Dryden and Gibbon, tried to fashion the English language after the Latin." Margaret M. Bryant, "The End Preposition," 8 *College English* 204 (Jan. 1947). Is more authority needed? Here it is:

- "If the sense is clear and the effect is smooth, there is no reason for avoiding the final preposition. It would be absurd to object to *What are you looking for?* and require

LANGUAGE-CHANGE INDEX (For the full key, see front matter pp. xxxi, l–li.)
Stage 1: Rejected. **Stage 2:** Widely shunned. **Stage 3:** Widespread but . . . **Stage 4:** Ubiquitous but . . . **Stage 5:** Fully accepted.
Invariably inferior forms marked by asterisk (*). • Ratios represent frequency of prevalent forms vs. variants in current books.

the very awkward *For what are you looking?*" Janet Rankin Aiken, *Commonsense Grammar* 149 (1936).

- "Nor did the obsession that English sentences should ape classical models unduly influence [Joseph] Addison, an eighteenth-century writer remarkable for his fluent, easy, and polished diction. Indeed, so frequently did he end his sentences with a preposition that such a conclusion has been referred to as 'the Addisonian termination.' And, whatever pedants may say to the contrary, English people will continue to say, easily and unselfconsciously: 'He is the man I spoke to.' 'This is what I was thinking of.' 'What are you talking about?' 'Who did you go with?' 'Speak when you are spoken to.'" W.P. Jowett, *Chatting About English* 176 (1945).

- "Though by its very name a preposition is 'placed before' a noun, modern English idiom allows, and has always allowed, it to be placed after, and often as the last word in the sentence." G.H. Vallins, *Good English: How to Write It* 154 (1951).

- "In some expressions the preposition is by the custom of the language forced to the end." G.H. Vallins, *Better English* 61 (4th ed. 1957).

- "In regard to the placing of the preposition, we should do well to divest ourselves of the notion that it is 'an inelegant word to end a sentence with' and that, just because it is called a *pre-position*, it must therefore 'be placed before.'" Simeon Potter, *Our Language* 101 (rev. ed. 1966).

- "Though I doubt that many persons still take it seriously . . . , perhaps there are still those who need to be gently told that no self-respecting writer or speaker has ever bothered to conform to this most errant of all imagined rules of 'grammar.'" Ellsworth Barnard, *English for Everybody* 101 (1979). / "Nobody would ask, 'To what is the world coming?' rather than 'What is the world coming to?'" *Ibid.* at 111.

Good writers don't hesitate to end their sentences with prepositions if doing so results in phrasing that seems natural:

- "'[E]ntire unanimity' refers to unanimity among those who constitute the greatest number thought *of.*" Harry Thurston Peck, "What Is Good English?" in *What Is Good English? and Other Essays* 3, 16–17 (1899).

- "Whatever truth may be, it is worth staying *for.*" Paul M. Fulcher, "The Seven Lamps of Style," in *The Foundations of English Style* 3, 6 (Paul M. Fulcher ed., 1927).

- "When we grow older and have something to write about we often don't write letters because we are afraid of being dull. And that is a very good thing to be afraid *of.*" S.P.B. Mais, *The Writing of English* 22 (1935).

- "Ganesa, who is every reader, found his attention continually held and did not ask to be let *off.*" Gorham Munson, *The Written Word* 31 (rev. ed. 1949). / "Falling into the wrong word-environment for your new word is a hazard to watch out *for.*" *Ibid.* at 91.

- "The great majority of reviews give an inadequate or misleading account of the book that is dealt *with.*" George Orwell, "I Write as I Please," in *Shooting an Elephant and Other Essays* 164, 167 (1950).

- "The peculiarities of legal English are often used as a stick to beat the official *with.*" Ernest Gowers, *Plain Words: Their ABC* 13 (1954).

- "In the structure of the 'coherent sentence,' such particles are necessary, and, strip the sentence as bare as you will, they cannot be entirely dispensed *with.*" G.H. Vallins, *The Best English* 30 (1960).

- "Poetry, as Dr. Johnson said, is untranslatable and hence, if it is good, preserves the language it is written *in.*" Anthony Burgess, *A Mouthful of Air* 156 (1992).

- "It was the boys in the back room, after all, whom Marlene Dietrich felt comfortable drinking *with.*" Russell Baker, "Sexwise It's the Pits," *N.Y. Times*, 17 Apr. 1993, at 15.

See **which, that** & FUNCTIONAL SHIFT (F).

C. Redundant Prepositions. Writers often repeat prepositions unnecessarily when there are intervening phrases or clauses. E.g.: "Sue is survived by her beloved husband, Roy C. Walker, *with whom* she shared her life *with* for 63 years." "Sue A. 'West' Walker" (obit.), *Austin Am.-Statesman*, 14 July 1995, at B4. (Delete the second *with*.) Paul McCartney, in his hit song "Live and Let Die," made a similar error: "But if this ever-changing world *in which* we live *in* makes you give in and cry, just live and let die." McCartney might have improved the lyrics by writing *in which we're livin'.*

D. The Wrong Preposition. A marginally useful guide in determining what preposition goes with a given verb is to look to the verb's prefix. Thus *inhere in, comport with* (L. *com-* "with"), *attribute to* (L. *ad-* "to"), and so on. But the exceptions are many. For example, *impute* takes *to, prepare* takes *for,* and *recoil* takes *from.*

In any event, more and more writers seem to have difficulty using the right preposition in various idioms—e.g.:

- *Down* used superfluously: "'Free the Juice,' a street picketer's sign proclaimed in one of the opening scenes last year as the grand circus trial *pitched down* [read *pitched*] its tent." Francis X. Clines, "And Now, the Audience Rests," *N.Y. Times*, 8 Oct. 1995, at 4. (One *puts up* a tent or *pitches* it, but does not erect it by *pitching it down*.)

- *In* for *to:* "We may even live in a style *in* [read *to*] which we never *dreamed* we could become accustomed." Sheridan Baker, "Scholarly Style, or the Lack Thereof" (1956), in *Perspectives on Style* 64, 72 (Frederick Candelaria ed., 1968).

- *Of* for *about:* "National League umpire Bruce Froemming, angered by Montreal pitcher Jeff Fassero's critical *comments of* [read *comments about*] a fellow umpire, rebutted the Expos starter's complaints Tuesday." "Ump Cries Foul at Remarks Made by Montreal's Fassero," *Austin Am.-Statesman*, 29 May 1996, at C5. (One makes *comments on* a thing or *about* a person. One makes *criticism of* a person or a thing. But here the writer confounded the two phrases.)

- *On* for *into:* "After a slow start, Henderson began putting up All-America numbers, but the Longhorns went *on* [read *into*] a tailspin in which they lost six of eight games." Randy Riggs, "Six of One . . . ," *Austin Am.-Statesman*, 4 Mar. 1995, at C4.

- *To* for *in:* "To show he is serious, Mr. Kwasniewski resigned his membership on Saturday *to* [read *in*] the political party that he founded." Jane Perlez, "Polish Leader Vexed by Final Hurdle: His Past," *N.Y. Times*, 29 Nov. 1995, at A3. (BrE would make it *membership of,* but in AmE it's *membership in.*)

- *To* for *of:* "The military . . . can only hope that these same children will remain ignorant *to* [read *of*] the military's history of sacrificing the long-term health of its troops for short-term political and military goals." Letter of Dan Fahey, "Joining the Army Is Hazardous to Health," *N.Y. Times*, 19 Nov. 1995, at 14.

Many other prepositions are treated throughout this book in entries for verbs they accompany. Readers with an interest in a more detailed, comprehensive treatment of this subject may benefit from consulting the following works: Morton Benson et al., *The BBI Combinatory Dictionary of English: A Guide to Word Combinations* (1986); Frederick T. Wood, *English Prepositional Idioms* (1967); and A.P. Cowie & R. Mackin, *The Oxford Dictionary of Current Idiomatic English* (1975).

E. Prepositions as Particles or Adverbs. See FUNCTIONAL VARIATION (F).

prerequisite. A. And *requisite*. Rarely is *prerequisite* used with the degree of punctilio that Eric Partridge prescribed: "Properly, a *prerequisite* has to be obtained or fulfilled before a *requisite* can be attended to. In short, *prerequisite* is rarely permissible." "Vigilans" [Eric Partridge], *Chamber of Horrors* 114 (1952). Probably it is more accurate to say that *prerequisite* includes a built-in time element, whereas *requisite* does not.

B. And *perquisite*. See **perquisite**.

prerogative (= a right that someone has by reason of position or prominence) is pronounced /pri-**rog**-ə-tiv/—not /pə-**rog**-ə-tiv/.

presage, n. & vb. A *presage* (/**pres**-ij/) is either an omen—something that portends a future occurrence—or an intuition that something is going to happen, especially something bad. To *presage* (/**pres**-ij/ or /pri-**sayj**/) is to foreshadow, foretell, or predict. Elster recommends distinguishing the pronunciation of the verb from that of the noun (*BBBM* at 389).

prescience (= foreknowledge or foresight) is preferably pronounced /**presh**-ənts/ in AmE and /**pres**-ee-ənts/ in BrE. The old-fashioned AmE pronunciations were /**pree**-shints/ and /**pree**-shee-ints/.

   The corresponding adjective *prescient* is similarly /**presh**-ənt/ (AmE) or /**pres**-ee-ənt/ (BrE)—or, in old-fashioned AmE, /**pree**-shint/ or /**pree**-shee-int/.

prescribe. See **proscribe**.

presentation (= a talk, an award ceremony, a way of showing something, etc.) is pronounced /prez-ən-**tay**-shən/ or (less good) /pree-zən-**tay**-shən/.

presentiment; presentment. A *presentiment* is an odd feeling that something bad will soon happen; a premonition. The word is pronounced /pri-**zen**-ti-mənt/—not /pri-**sen**-ti-mənt/ or /pree-**zen**-ti-mənt/. A *presentment* is (1) a formal statement of an issue to

be decided by a court of law, (2) a grand jury's formal written accusation made on its own initiative, or (3) the formal production of a negotiable instrument for acceptance or payment. The word is pronounced /pri-**zent**-mənt/.

presently contains an ambiguity. In the days of Shakespeare, it meant "immediately." Soon its meaning evolved into "after a short time" (perhaps because people exaggerated about their promptitude). This sense is still current. Then, chiefly in AmE, it took on the additional sense "at present; currently." This use is poor, however, because it both causes the ambiguity and displaces a simpler word (*now* or, if more syllables are necessary, *at present* or *currently*)—e.g.:

- "Carol *presently* [read *now*] has a one-elephant show (I am not making this up) going at the Clarion Hotel in downtown San Diego." Mike Harden, "Writer, Elephant Paint a Pretty Picture Amid GOP Circus," *Columbus Dispatch*, 14 Aug. 1996, at A6.
- "But the waiting list for such a kidney is *presently* [read *now*] 35,000 patients long." Richard Jerome, "A Father's Gift," *People*, 26 May 1997, at 52.
- "A truly innovative program, such as the original Windows operating system, might well receive a degree of protection akin to that *presently* [read *now*] available." Mathias Klang & Andrew Murray, *Human Rights in the Digital Age* 133 (2005).

Cf. **momentarily.** See also **at the present time.**

LANGUAGE-CHANGE INDEX
presently for *now* or *currently*: Stage 4

present time, at the. This phrase is wordy for *now*.

present writer. Unless self-mockery is intended, this phrase is today generally considered inferior to *I* or *me*. Common throughout the late 19th and 20th centuries, it is now in decline. See FIRST PERSON.

preservation; *preserval. The latter is a NEEDLESS VARIANT.

Current ratio: 118,003:1

presidency. A. And *presidence*. *Presidency* = the office or function of a president. *Presidence* = the action or fact of presiding.

   B. And *president*. In AmE, you can either *run for the presidency* or *run for president*. Technically, the former is better, but the latter is extremely common among educated speakers.

Presidents' Day; *President's Day; *Presidents Day. The spelling as a plural possessive is best and most common. It's also the original spelling. Until 1971, Lincoln's Birthday (12 February) and Washington's Birthday (22 February) were both observed as federal holidays. In 1971, President Richard Nixon proclaimed that the two holidays would be combined

LANGUAGE-CHANGE INDEX (For the full key, see front matter pp. xxxi, l–li.)
Stage 1: Rejected. **Stage 2:** Widely shunned. **Stage 3:** Widespread but . . . **Stage 4:** Ubiquitous but . . . **Stage 5:** Fully accepted.
Invariably inferior forms marked by asterisk (*). • Ratios represent frequency of prevalent forms vs. variants in current books.

into one, "the Presidents' Day," honoring all past presidents of the United States. He also proclaimed that the holiday would be observed on the third Monday in February. But *Presidents' Day* is not a federal legal holiday; *Washington's Birthday* is the name officially adopted by the federal government. Even so, several states call it *Presidents' Day*—perhaps so that Lincoln's birthday, no longer a legal holiday, can be celebrated jointly. Cf. **Veterans Day.**

The singular possessive—*President's Day*—is clearly wrong but still occasionally appears.

Current ratio (in order of headwords): 5:3:1

presiding juror. See **foreman (B).**

prestigious (= admired as one of the best and most important within a category) is preferably pronounced /pre-**stij**-əs/ in AmE and BrE alike—not /pri-**stee**-jəs/.

presume. See **assume.**

presumption. See **assumption.**

presumptive; presumptuous. *Presumptive* = (1) giving reasonable grounds for presumption or belief; warranting inferences; or (2) based on presumption or inference. Sense 1: "In investigating deaths, '50 is used as a *presumptive* age for natural death,' says David Campbell." Kathleen Doheny, "'Natural' Death Is No Stranger to the Young," *L.A. Times*, 23 May 1995, at E3. Sense 2: "He's also running on a slate with Larry Forgy, the party's *presumptive* nominee for governor." Joseph Gerth, "Scott Seems Confident in Attorney General Race," *Courier-J.* (Louisville), 21 May 1995, at B8.

Presumptuous = arrogant, presuming, bold, forward, impudent. The word is so spelled, though **presumptious* is a common error (especially in BrE)—e.g.:

- "'Of course, it's *presumptious* [read *presumptuous*] of him,' said Tim Graham, editor of the conservative MediaWatch newsletter. 'But Gingrich makes the bold and *presumptious* [read *presumptuous*] move, and he rattles people's cages.'" Ed Bark, "Gingrich Shoots for Prime Time," *Dallas Morning News*, 7 Apr. 1995, at A37.
- "It is a disgraceful and *presumptious* [read *presumptuous*] neglect of what is a compelling battle." Alan Lee, "Teamwork Makes Warwickshire the Title Favourites," *Times* (London), 21 Aug. 1995, Sport §.
- "We may have been a little *presumptious* [read *presumptuous*] in reacting as we did but we were not *presumptious* [read *presumptuous*] in a degree that the agent could seriously condemn." Philip Pettit, "The Capacity to Have Done Otherwise," in *Relating to Responsibility: Essays for Tony Honoré on his Eightieth Birthday* 21, 33 (Peter Cane & John Gardner eds., 2001).

See **SPELLING (A).** Pronounced properly, the word has four syllables: /pri-**zump**-choo-əs/, not /pri-**zump**-shəs/.

Presumptive is often misused for *presumptuous.* In June 1999, presidential candidate George W. Bush said that it would be "*presumptive* [read *presumptuous*] for someone who doesn't even have the nomination yet to be laying out the list of potential vice presidents."

George W. Bush (as quoted in Ken Herman, "Bush Ticket Could Be Split on Abortion," *Austin Am.-Statesman*, 24 June 1999, at A1). He wasn't alone:

- "I'm the lamest of lame ducks, and I am not advocating any radical changes to the new governor or the Legislature. That would be highly *presumptive* [read *presumptuous*]." Philip E. Batt, "Keep Idaho's Balanced Tax System Intact," *Idaho Statesman*, 11 Dec. 1998, at B9.
- "But she thinks it would be *presumptive* [read *presumptuous*] of them to think they could attract endangered animals to their little habitat, which now includes about 45 acres." Sue Lowe, "Onetime Cornfield Now Prairie, Wetlands," *South Bend Trib.*, 1 Feb. 1999, at B1.
- "Former Secretary of State Warren Christopher, a Gore representative, complained yesterday that Bush was being *presumptive* [read *presumptuous*] by assuming he's president-elect before the courts have ruled on the issue of hand recounts in Florida." Zachary Coile, "Bush Using Electoral Timeout to Practice Being Presidential," *S.F. Chron.*, 4 Dec. 2000, at A5.

LANGUAGE-CHANGE INDEX
1. *presumptuous* misspelled **presumptious*: Stage 1
Current ratio: 140:1
2. *presumptive* misused for *presumptuous*: Stage 1

pretence. See **pretense.**

pretend as though for *pretend that* (by analogy to *act as though*) is unidiomatic.

pretense; pretence. The first is the AmE spelling; the second is BrE.

preterit(e), n. & adj. This grammatical term refers to past tenses, but it fell into disuse during the 20th century because of the ambiguity contained within it. That is, some writers have used it to mean "the simple past tense," but others want it to include past participles. And in any event it smacks of SESQUIPEDALITY, since *past* expresses the same idea. But if you must know how to spell it, *preterite* is standard in AmE and BrE alike. *Preterit* is a chiefly AmE variant.

pretermit (/pree-tər-**mit**/) = to overlook or ignore purposely—e.g.: "I *pretermit*, because it is unworthy of serious notice, the argument from social welfare priorities." William A. Stanmeyer, "Toward a Moral Nuclear Strategy," *Policy Rev.*, Summer 1982, at 59 n.13.

The word doesn't properly mean "to prevent, preclude, or obviate," but some writers use it that way—e.g.:

- "ACUS based its rule on a supposed lack of 'clear indication' that Congress meant to *pretermit* [read *preclude*] agency review." David O. Stewart, "The Equal Access to Justice Act," *Nat'l L.J.*, 21 May 1984, at 20.
- "To *pretermit* [read *prevent* or *obviate*] a reprise of the Bork confirmation ordeal, Mr. Bush blacklisted . . . 10 glittering candidates associated with ideas subversive of fashionable legal orthodoxy." Bruce Fein, "Better to Avoid the Cobwebs?" *Wash. Times*, 28 Aug. 1990, at G3.

LANGUAGE-CHANGE INDEX
pretermit misused for *prevent*, *preclude*, or *obviate*: Stage 1

preternatural (/pree-tər-**nach**-ər-əl/) has several meanings, all with the core idea of "unnatural." It may mean "unexplainable," similar to *supernatural* <preternatural phenomenon>. It used to mean "contrary to nature," often to describe a symptom of disease <preternatural swelling>, but that usage has faded. A new meaning has emerged, though: "extraordinary," especially to describe a talent <a preternatural gift for music>. Sometimes the word's senses collide when the writer means "extraordinary" but not at all "unnatural"—e.g.: "Scherfig is as warm and welcoming as her movie. A *preternatural* [read *natural*? *stunning*?] blonde, like many Scandinavians, she has a robust laugh that echoes through a hotel room." Ruthe Stein, "The Language of Love," *S.F. Chron.*, 2 Feb. 2002, Sunday Datebook §, at 51.

pretextual (= based on a pretext), coined in the 1950s, is sometimes wrongly written *pretextural: "If the employer satisfies this burden, then the employee is provided with a 'full and fair opportunity' to demonstrate that the employer's rationale is *pretextural* [read *pretextual*], i.e., that it was not the actual motivating pretext, then the issue of discrimination must be submitted to a jury for a determination." Hyman Lovitz & Sidney L. Gold, "Standard of Proof Set in Title VII Cases," *Legal Intelligencer*, 26 Oct. 1993, at 8. Cf. **contextual** & **contractual**.

LANGUAGE-CHANGE INDEX
pretextual misspelled *pretextural: Stage 1

pretty, adv., is still considered informal or colloquial <a pretty good drawing>. It sometimes conveys a shade of doubt—*pretty clear* being less certain in some readers' minds than *clear*. E.B. White called *pretty*, *rather*, *very*, and *little* "leeches that infest the pond of prose, sucking the blood of words." *The Elements of Style* 73 (4th ed. 1999). See WEASEL WORDS.

prevalent is accented on the first, not the second, syllable: /**prev**-ə-lənt/.

prevaricate = to avoid telling the truth, esp. by equivocating; to lie—e.g.: "[I]mpressed by Maggie's brashness and her amazing ability to lie on a dime and *prevaricate* at will, Kaz installs her in their guest house." Michael Wilmington, "Ugly Duckling Tale Doesn't Lay an Egg, but Never Takes Flight," *Chicago Trib.*, 8 June 2007, Movies §, at 5.

Oddly, the word is sometimes confounded with *procrastinate*, especially in BrE—e.g.: " 'I never make art in the studio,' says [Cornelia] Parker. 'I make it in the space. That way, you have to make very good, quick decisions. You can't *prevaricate* [read *procrastinate*]. You just have to get on with it.' " Geoff Edgers, *Boston Globe*, 6 Dec. 2006, at K14. See WORD-SWAPPING.

Occasionally, it's hard to decipher what the writer intended—e.g.: "There is certainly no other evidence from any source that Einstein was ever romantically interested in this young woman, whose mother he eventually married and who thus became his beloved stepdaughter. But the author *prevaricates* [read *waffles*? *doesn't elaborate*?], leaving the reader with the hint that perhaps there was more to this letter." Amir D. Aczel, "Eternal Einstein," *Boston Globe*, 15 Apr. 2007, at D5. Whatever the meaning, surely there is no suggestion here that the author evaded the truth.

LANGUAGE-CHANGE INDEX
prevaricate misused for *procrastinate*: Stage 1

prevent. In AmE, this verb takes *from*, but in BrE the preposition is frequently omitted—e.g.:

- "Fortunately for us, the earth's atmosphere absorbs gamma rays and *prevents them doing* any damage to life or property here." Clive Cookson, "Headed This Way from a Galaxy Near You," *Fin. Times*, 17 May 1997, at 2. (AmE would insert *from* after *them*.)
- "That did not *prevent him keeping* Australia at bay at Lord's." Rob Steen, "James Lets His Runs Do the Talking," *Sunday Times* (London), 31 Aug. 1997, Sports §, at 9. (AmE would insert *from* after *him*.)

Prevent there causes verbose, awkward constructions—e.g.:

- "This is likely to require some tightening in the stance of macroeconomic policy to *prevent there being* [read *prevent*] any inflationary impact." Garry Young, "The UK Economy," *Nat'l Inst. Econ. Rev.*, 1 Oct. 1996, at 7.
- "Last year they went to court claiming amnesty would *prevent there* from ever being a criminal trial in his death." "In South Africa, the Truth and Nothing But," *Wash. Times*, 4 Feb. 1997, at A18. (A possible revision: *Last year they went to court claiming that amnesty would prevent a criminal trial for his death.*)
- "But Russell's paradox does not *prevent there being* [read *prevent* or *preclude*] something else—a *class* of all sets—which is an extensional entity behaving in some respects as sets do." Michael Potter, *Set Theory and Its Philosophy* 312 (2004).

preventable. So spelled in AmE and BrE alike—no longer *preventible (the predominant spelling through about 1880). See -ABLE (A).

Current ratio: 53:1

preventive; ***preventative.** The strictly correct form is *preventive* (as both noun and adjective), though the corrupt form with the extra internal syllable is unfortunately common—e.g.:

- "Many owners don't do *preventative* [read *preventive*] maintenance, said HouseMaster president Ken Austin." Joe Catalano, "Buying into Costly Repairs," *Newsday* (N.Y.), 2 Feb. 1996, at D6.
- "The scientific discoveries . . . have led biotech researchers to develop two classes of vaccines: *preventative* [read *preventive*], such as traditional inoculations against polio, influenza, or rubella; and therapeutic, where the immune system is primed to fend off the recurrence of certain diseases such as skin cancer." Ronald Rosenberg,

---

LANGUAGE-CHANGE INDEX (For the full key, see front matter pp. xxxi, l–li.)
Stage 1: Rejected. **Stage 2:** Widely shunned. **Stage 3:** Widespread but . . . **Stage 4:** Ubiquitous but . . . **Stage 5:** Fully accepted.
Invariably inferior forms marked by asterisk (*). • Ratios represent frequency of prevalent forms vs. variants in current books.

"Not Your Kid's Vaccine," *Boston Globe*, 10 Sept. 1997, at D1.

- "As shadow health minister she has championed *preventative* [read *preventive*] health care; promoting dieting, exercise and stop-smoking programmes, for example." "Liz Kendall's High-Stakes Workout," *Economist*, 30 May 2015, at 56.

In modern print sources, *preventive* is about five times as common as **preventative*, a NEEDLESS VARIANT.

LANGUAGE-CHANGE INDEX
*preventative for *preventive*: Stage 3
Current ratio (*preventive* vs. **preventative*): 5:1

PREVENTIVE GRAMMAR. Occasionally a grammarian or editor will be asked a question such as, "Should it be *It's both of their second marriage* or *It's both of their second marriages?*" The expert to whom the question has been posed will demur and recommend a rewrite: *It's a second marriage for each of them*, or even *It's a second marriage for them both*. Or perhaps *the* for *a*. The questioner will persist: "But which of the original wordings is correct? Assume a rewrite is impossible."

But of course a rewrite is never impossible. Although questions of this kind might fascinate philologasters, they're a nuisance to both the true philologist and the true stylist. The best recourse is a rewording. Why perpetrate a sentence that's awkward but arguably defensible? A sentence that's only defensible will raise doubts in the reasonable reader's mind.

Often you'll be presented with a sentence that is correct, according to strict grammatical tradition, but that sounds either stuffy or downright wrong. During the 20th century, for example, some grammarians insisted that *Neither you nor I am a plumber* is correct phrasing. Using *are* or *is* in place of *am* would be quite incorrect. These grammarians relied on the "rule of proximity": in *neither–nor* constructions, the second element controls the verb for both number and person. Hence *neither you nor I am*. See, e.g., Roy Ivan Johnson et al., *English Patterns* 426 (1941) ("When two subjects are connected by the correlative conjunctions *either . . . or* or *neither . . . nor*, the verb agrees with the subject which stands nearer to it: . . . One thing is certain: either you or I *am* responsible."). See **neither . . . nor (A).**

But this "correct" wording sounds awful. It sounds wrong. And now the empirical evidence shows that published authors have never used it much. In every period of Modern English, **neither you nor I are* (grammatically poor) has occurred more frequently than **neither you nor I am*. The grammarians who insisted on *am* were simply out of touch with the practice of authors who actually used the phrase—and they were insisting on a kind of linguistic unreality. Their position was unsound.

The point of this entry is that you're better off avoiding awkward solutions entirely. If you're a smart writer, you won't create unnecessary frictions between you and your reader. It would be better to write or say, *You're not a plumber, and neither am I*. That would

be seriously inconvenient only if you were trying to use *am a plumber* as a rhyme in a poem. In ordinary prose, it's typically to your advantage to write around a problem, thus eliminating doubts completely rather than creating merely defensible solutions to them. You want to convey a message, not defend the way you expressed it.

Many of the words discussed under SKUNKED TERMS fall under this principle: if some number of readers, either those in the know or the linguistic know-nothings, are going to think you've gotten something wrong, your best course may be to reword. Even so, you must draw the line somewhere. If you mention "preventive grammar," and your interlocutor says it should surely be "preventative grammar," it would be understandable for you simply to write off your interlocutor altogether.

preview, n. & vb., is the standard spelling. **Prevue* is a variant.

Current ratio: 729:1

*previous to for *before* is highfalutin—e.g.:

- "*Previous to* [read *Before*] this award, the Police Department had received at least $11 million under the 1994 crime bill alone." Emily Bazar & Janine DeFao, "City Cops Receive Big Grant," *Sacramento Bee*, 16 July 1997, at A1.
- "During the nine years *previous to* [read *before*] their reign, 1980–88, the Chiefs appeared on ABC's prime-time game one time." Greg Hall, "Chiefs' Performance Worthy of Prime Time," *Kansas City Star*, 9 Sept. 1997, at 3.

Cf. **prior** & ***subsequent to.**

*preying mantis. See **praying mantis.**

pricey. This CASUALISM, meaning "expensive," is preferably so spelled in AmE and BrE alike—not **pricy* (a variant spelling).

Current ratio: 24:1

prideful. See **proud.**

prier (= someone who pries) is the standard spelling. **Pryer* is a variant.

Current ratio: 27:1

primal; primordial; primeval; *primaeval. All these words essentially mean "first in time; original." But in the JARGON of scientists, each is usually confined to a distinct scientific context: *primal* to psychology <primal therapy>, *primordial* to biology <primordial soup>, and *primeval* to geology or paleontology <primeval forests>. **Primaeval* is a chiefly BrE variant of *primeval*.

primer (= an elementary or introductory textbook) is pronounced /**prim**-ər/ in AmE but /**prī**-mər/ in BrE. Interestingly, the AmE pronunciation probably represents the older form, and BrE usage seems to have shifted during the 20th century: the original *OED* in 1909 gave precedence to the pronunciation with a short *i*.

primeval. See **primal.**

primogeniture; primogenitor. *Primogeniture =* (1) the fact or condition of being the firstborn child of the same parents; or (2) (at common law) the right of succession or inheritance belonging to the firstborn, often involving the exclusion of all other children.

Primogenitor = the first parent; earliest ancestor. Loosely, it's used for *progenitor* (= forefather, ancestor).

primordial. See **primal.**

primrose path. See **garden path.**

principal; principle. A. The Senses. These two words, though often confused and used incorrectly and interchangeably, share no common definitions. Generally, it's enough to remember that *principal* (= chief, primary, most important) is usually an adjective and that *principle* (= a truth, rule, doctrine, or course of action) is virtually always a noun. Although *principle* is not a verb, we have *principled* as an adjective.

But *principal* is sometimes a noun—an elliptical form of *principal official* <Morgan is principal of the elementary school> or *principal investment* <principal and interest>.

B. Principal misused for principle. This is a fairly common blunder—e.g.:

- "The Ways and Means bill approved today, after more than a month of deliberation and voting, preserves two of the central *principals* [read *principles*] put forth by the President: universal coverage and the requirement that employers assume 80 percent of its cost for their workers." Robin Toner, "Clinton Wins One, Then Loses as 2 Panels Vote on Health Bill," *N.Y. Times,* 1 July 1994, at A1.
- "The three repeatedly pointed to their own steadfast adherence to *principals* [read *principles*], trying to draw contrast between themselves and Mr. Dole." "Ignoring G.O.P. Rivals, Dole Says He Can 'Smell Victory,'" *N.Y. Times,* 10 Mar. 1996, at 11.

LANGUAGE-CHANGE INDEX
principal misused for *principle*: Stage 1
Current ratio (*fundamental principles* vs. **fundamental principals*): 305:1

C. Principle misused for principal. This mistake is perhaps even more common—e.g.:

- "Employed with CISD for 29 years and served as CISD *Principle* [read *Principal*] for 26 years." Advertisement for Dave Corley, running for city commission, *Canyon News,* 28 Apr. 1994, at 2. (This misuse—in which *principal,* if correctly used, would be a noun—appears less commonly than the adjectival misuse.)
- "Audio CDs are a *principle* [read *principal*] source of material for making music with samples." Geary Yelton, "From Disk to Disk," *Electronic Musician,* June 1994, at 48.
- "Bowers was a *principle* [read *principal*] figure in one of college basketball's nastiest scandals in recent years after she made allegations of NCAA violations by the Baylor men's

team in memos to university officials." Randy Riggs, "Calm on the Court," *Austin Am.-Statesman,* 21 Jan. 1995, at C1.

LANGUAGE-CHANGE INDEX
principle misused for *principal*: Stage 2
Current ratio (*principal reasons* vs. **principle reasons*): 17:1

D. Principal as a Noncomparable Adjective. See ADJECTIVES (B).

prior; previous. The adjectives *prior* and *previous* for *earlier* are each within the stylist's license; **prior to* and **previous to* in place of *before* are not.

In fact, **prior to*—one of the most easily detectable symptoms of BUREAUCRATESE, COMMERCIALESE, and LEGALESE—is terribly overworked. As Theodore Bernstein once pointed out, one should feel free to use **prior to* instead of *before* only if one is accustomed to using **posterior to* for *after.* See *The Careful Writer* 347 (1979). Cf. **previous to* & **subsequent to.*

prioritize; *priorize. Writers with sound stylistic priorities avoid these words. *Prioritize,* dating from the mid-1960s, typifies bureaucratic bafflegab—e.g.: "The rate at which an objective is achieved should reflect the degree to which that component of the plan has been *prioritized.*" (Read: *Do the most important things first.*) Instead of *prioritize,* conservative writers tend to use *set priorities* or *establish priorities.* In time, of course, *prioritize* might lose its bureaucratic odor. But that time has not yet arrived.

Much less common than *prioritize* is the illogically formed **priorize,* a fairly obscure Canadianism—e.g.:

- "Of course, the finance minister will, for the benefit of his colleagues, '*priorize*' [read *establish priorities for*] the promises made by the new regime." Dalton Camp, "Grits Can Be Ruthless," *Toronto Star,* 7 Nov. 1993, at H3.
- "Two months later, not only must a prospective comrade share all of our 'isms'; s/he must also *priorize them* [read *view their relative importance*] exactly as we do." "The Left's First Deadly Sin: Ideological Elitism," *Canadian Dimension,* 19 Sept. 1997, at 3. (On the use of *s/he* in that sentence, see SEXISM (B).)
- "In consequence, the triple criteria used in this work can help to *priorize* [read *arrange*] several clusterings and to find the more reliable patterns from a set of data." Dante Conti & Karina Gibert, "The Use of the Traffic Lights Panel as a Goodness-of-Clustering Indicator," in *Artificial Intelligence Research and Development* 19, 27 (David Riaño et al. eds., 2012).

See -IZE & BUREAUCRATESE.

LANGUAGE-CHANGE INDEX
1. *prioritize*: Stage 4
2. **priorize*: Stage 1
Current ratio (*prioritize* vs. *establish priorities* vs. **priorize*): 1,728:69:1

*prior to. See **prior.**

LANGUAGE-CHANGE INDEX (For the full key, see front matter pp. xxxi, l–li.)
Stage 1: Rejected. **Stage 2:** Widely shunned. **Stage 3:** Widespread but . . . **Stage 4:** Ubiquitous but . . . **Stage 5:** Fully accepted.
Invariably inferior forms marked by asterisk (*). • Ratios represent frequency of prevalent forms vs. variants in current books.

prise. See **prize**.

prison. See **in prison**.

pristine (= [1] unspoiled and undamaged, as if new, or [2] extremely fresh or clean) is pronounced /pri-**steen**/ in AmE and /**pris**-teen/ in BrE. Two old-fashioned pronunciations, both archaic, are /**pris**-tin/ and /**pris**-tɪn/.

privation. See **deprivation**.

privilege is often misspelled *priviledge* (a common spelling till about 1700, but now justly regarded as a mistake)—e.g.: "A season badge, which includes grounds and clubhouse *priviledges* [read *privileges*] throughout the tournament, is $80." "Motorola Western Open Facts," *Chicago Sun-Times*, 30 June 1996, at 25. (On the poor title of that article, see NOUN PLAGUE.) See SPELLING (A).

The word is permissibly pronounced with either three syllables (/**priv**-ə-lij/) or two (/**priv**-lij/).

LANGUAGE-CHANGE INDEX
privilege misspelled *priviledge*: Stage 1
Current ratio: 642:1

prize; prise. Although *prise* is the better spelling in the sense "to pry or force open," *prize* often appears in this sense. But the DIFFERENTIATION is worth promoting. *Prize* is the spelling for all other senses.

proactive = (of a person, policy, etc.) creating or controlling a situation by taking the initiative or anticipating events; ready to take initiative, tending to make things happen (*SOED*). Though, as a VOGUE WORD, *proactive* is widely viewed with suspicion, it's occasionally useful as an antonym of *reactive*. It seems to fill a gap in the language—one not adequately filled by *assertive* or any other common word. Cf. **reactionary**, n.

LANGUAGE-CHANGE INDEX
proactive as an antonym for *reactive*: Stage 5

pro and con; pro et con. The latter phrase is the Latin for "for and against." The English rendering—*pro and con*—is standard. The phrase may function as a noun <the pros and cons>, as an adverb <people argued pro and con>, or as an adjective <arguments pro and con>.

Pro and con has also been used as a verb phrase <to pro-and-con the issue>, and although today this use sounds somewhat odd, it has the sanction of long standing: the *OED* dates it from 1694. The *OED* also records the phrase as a preposition <arguments pro and con the proposal>, but *for and against* would be better.

Current ratio: 320:1

probably /**pro**-bə-blee/ is frequently mispronounced /**prob**-lee/ and even /**prol**-ee/. See PRONUNCIATION (B).

probity (= honesty; integrity) is sometimes misused for *propriety*—e.g.:

• "We should also openly discuss the major difference between the ethical *probity* [read *propriety*] of euthanasia,

with which many concur, and its legality." Faith Fitzgerald, "Physician Aid in Dying—Finding a Middle Ground," 157 *Western J. Medicine* 193 (1992).
• "The Clintons and their political allies have built careers on criticizing the 'get-rich-quick' attitudes of the 'greedy 80s,' when all sorts of unscrupulous scoundrels were making money on deals of dubious ethical *probity* [read *propriety*]." "Whitewater Rafting," *Orange County Register*, 2 Feb. 1994, at B8. (People have or lack probity; deals don't.)

LANGUAGE-CHANGE INDEX
probity misused for *propriety*: Stage 1

problematic; problematical. Both forms appear in modern writing. Though *problematic* is now much more usual, euphony may occasionally recommend *problematical*.

How *problematic* came to denote "troublesome" isn't puzzling. The word *problem* derives from the Latin and Greek term for "something put forward, esp. for discussion and perhaps resolution." This sense lives on, for example, in the math *problems* that a teacher assigns for homework. In English, this original sense of *problem* goes back at least to the 1300s.

It wasn't until two centuries later that *problem* came to be used in the sense of "difficulty." Even so, *problematic* continued to be married to the original sense of "poser" or "riddle," until quite recently. Today, though, it is commonly used to describe something that creates trouble—e.g.: "But the jet can't travel nonstop to Pelosi's home district in San Francisco . . . . For security reasons, refueling stops are considered *problematic*." Edward Epstein, "Pelosi Finds Unlikely Ally in Flight Fuss," *S.F. Chron.*, 9 Feb. 2007, at A1. Indeed, that sense has drowned out the former sense of *problematic* as "uncertain" or "doubtful."

So is that trend troublesome? Not really. The word neatly fills a void in the language, and the meaning is intuitively recognizable. It ought to be considered standard.

LANGUAGE-CHANGE INDEX
problematic meaning "troublesome": Stage 5

problematize (= to question the premises on which an argument is based), a term actually coined by the playwright Ben Jonson in the 1630s, took root and became fashionable in the 1970s. It has unfortunately become common in academic JARGON, especially in cultural studies, social science, and literary theory—e.g.:

• "War and work, bedrocks of masculinity, were now *problematized* by changes in dominant cultural narratives." Kenneth Rufo, "Stiffed: The Betrayal of the American Man," 66 *So. Communication J.*, 1 Oct. 2000, at 97.
• "As discussed below, studies in the 1990s both continued and *problematized* this conceptualization of housework." Scott Cotrane, "Research on Household Labor," 62 *J. Marriage & the Family*, 1 Nov. 2000, at 568.
• "Pelagius's treatment of Demetrias's *nobilitas* in his construction of her asceticism, however, becomes still more complex. The language of 'honor and riches' is distinctly *problematized* at the end of the letter by the invocation of the recent disaster that has brought Demetrias and her family to African shores." Andrew S. Jacobs, "Writing Demetrias," 69 *Church History*, 1 Dec. 2000, at 719.

Question is often cleaner. *Complicate* is occasionally a good, uncomplicated substitute.

proboscis /proh-**bos**-is/ (= [1] the trunk of an elephant or snout of an animal, or [2] any similar tubular organ on an insect or other life-form), a Greek loanword dating from the 17th century, traditionally formed the classical plural *proboscides* in English-language contexts. But the anglicized plural *proboscises* became predominant in AmE in the late 1970s, and it has competed closely with the Greek plural in BrE since the mid-1980s. See PLURALS (B).

Current ratio (*proboscises* vs. *proboscides* in World English): 1.2:1

proceed. See **precede.**

proceed forward, dating from the 17th century, is an age-old REDUNDANCY—e.g.:

- "And now, in the first days of this Maple Leafs training camp, it is difficult to *proceed forward* [read *move forward*] without first looking back." Steve Simmons, "It's Make or Break Time for Leafs' Yushkevich," *Toronto Sun,* 12 Sept. 1997, at 16.
- "*Proceed forward* [read *Proceed*] from the intersection where the road takes on a new identity as Glacier Drive." Tom Vanden Brook, "Seasonal Colors to Fall For," *Milwaukee J. Sentinel,* 10 Oct. 1997, Ozaukee Wash. §, at 1.
- "When you work repeatedly with people who are familiar, then repetition will always remain the basis from which to *proceed forward* [read *proceed*]." Graham Firth & Mark Barber, *Using Intensive Interaction with a Person with Social or Communicative Impairment* 71 (2011).

proceeds, n. (= the value of land, goods, or investments when converted into money), takes a plural verb. But some writers want to write *proceeds is* instead of the correct form, *proceeds are.* This noun is pronounced /**proh**-seeds/, with the accent on the first syllable.

process, n. & vb. **A. Pronunciation.** A *process* is a series of purposeful actions to which something is subjected or a series of things that occur naturally and result in a gradual change <fermentation is both a biological and a chemical process>. The word is pronounced /**prah**-ses/ in AmE and /**proh**-ses/ in BrE. To *process* something is either to deal with or handle it in some way, especially through established procedures, or to subject it to some special treatment <we haven't yet processed the applications>. This verb is pronounced just as the noun is: /**prah**-ses/ in AmE and /**proh**-ses/ in BrE.

But *process* can also be another verb entirely—meaning "to move in a procession"—as a BACK-FORMATION from *procession.* In this chiefly BrE sense, the word is pronounced /prə-**ses**/.

For the plural of the noun, the preferred pronunciation is /**prah**-ses-iz/ in AmE and /**proh**-ses-iz/ in BrE—not /-seez/ in the final syllable.

B. *In the process of.* This phrase never adds anything to the sentence in which it appears. You can safely omit it and thereby tighten your sentence—e.g.:

- "I have on my desk a little manuscript from the fourteenth century written by an unknown author, which I am *in the process of* [delete *in the process of*] editing." Donald J. Lloyd, "Our National Mania for Correctness," in *A Linguistics Reader* 57, 58 (Graham Wilson ed., 1967).
- "Appropriately for a community that was *in the process of* [delete *in the process of*] acquiring the sophistication of golf and drugs, this was not a case of a mean little robbery gone wrong but a thoroughly contemporary killing." Owen Harris, "A Long Time Between Murders," *Am. Scholar,* Winter 2001, at 71, 79.

processable; *processible. Although many American dictionaries continue to give priority to the archaic-looking **processible,* the spelling *processable* is now more than five times as common in modern print sources. It looks more natural, and it ought to be accepted as standard. See -ABLE (A).

Current ratio: 5:1

prochronism. See **anachronism.**

proconsulship; * proconsulate. The latter is a NEEDLESS VARIANT.

Current ratio: 2:1

procreative; *procreational. The former is standard, **procreational* being a NEEDLESS VARIANT.

Current ratio: 15:1

procuration; *procurance; procuracy. See **procurement.**

procure is a FORMAL WORD for *get* (the ordinary word) or *obtain* (a semiformal word).

procurement; procuration; *procurance; procuracy. *Procurement* (= the act of obtaining) is the generic noun corresponding to *procure*—e.g.:

- "Judicial Watch represents five of the 900 former White House staffers in a suit seeking $90 million in damages for what they allege was the Clinton administration's improper *procurement* of the files." Jerry Seeper, "Ruling Expected in Secret Files Suit," *Wash. Times,* 24 May 1997, at A4.
- "It is unfortunate that the *procurement* of infants for needy adults has created a market in babies." Letter of Cecily Catherine Marangos, "More to Say on Adoption Law," *N.Y. Times,* 25 May 1997, § 13, at 17.

Procurement has another, more restricted sense in legal contexts: "the act of persuading or inviting another, esp. a woman or child, to have illicit sexual intercourse" (*Black's Law Dictionary* 1401 [10th ed. 2014]). E.g.: "Police alleged that they were required to perform duties of a very personal nature for the governor on official time . . . , [including] the *procurement* of women for sex and concealment of the governor's adulterous relationships." "Political Discrimination," *Ark. Democrat-Gaz.*, 19 Feb. 1994, at B9. **Procurance* is a NEEDLESS VARIANT.

Procuration = (1) the act of giving someone a power of attorney; or (2) the authority given to someone with a power of attorney. Hence *procuration fees* are agent fees. E.g.: "There are over 40 lenders who offer advisers a *'procuration fee.'* This is a cash payment made to advisers by lenders for bringing them the business." James Hipwell, "Place a Mortgage and Win a Motor," *Independent*, 24 Sept. 1995, at 13.

Procuracy = (1) a letter of agency; the document giving someone a power of attorney; (2) the office of a procurator, i.e., an official charged with managing the financial or legal affairs of a geographic region; or (3) the region within a procurator's jurisdiction. Though rare, the term is still used, primarily in senses 2 and 3—e.g.:

- "After some initial progress in getting the Municipal *Procuracy* to investigate and acknowledge that the allegations were 'basically correct,' the efforts of these staff members were obstructed by high officials." Orville Schell, "China's 'Model' State Orphanages Serve as Warehouses for Death," *L.A. Times*, 7 Jan. 1996, at M2.
- "While in Russia, he presented his idea to members of the former Soviet *Procuracy*, the Russian version of the Justice Department." Christian D. Berg, "A Chat with Atty. Paul Walsh of Bristol County," *Providence J.-Bull.*, 5 Aug. 1996, at C1.

prodigal. To be *prodigal* is to be prone to wasteful spending, especially to frittering away one's savings on hedonistic indulgence. In the biblical parable, the *prodigal* son leaves home, squanders his inheritance, almost starves to death, and is still greeted with open arms when he returns to his father.

Most people today associate *prodigal* with the part of the parable about wandering afar and coming home repentant, with no connotation left of squandering money—e.g.:

- "Tucker is another of the Royals' *prodigal* sons. . . . [T]he Royals traded him to Atlanta for Dye. Tucker then swung the bat for the Cincinnati Reds and the Chicago Cubs before the Royals made a trade to bring him back this year." Kendrick Blackwood, "You Gotta Love These Guys!" *Pitch Weekly* (Kansas City), 25 Apr. 2002, at 1.
- "Our hero is a *prodigal* son (David Arquette) returned home to revive the family gold mine and rekindle an old flame with the foxy lady sheriff (Kari Wuhrer)." Brian Miller, "Scream," *Seattle Weekly*, 18 July 2002, at 78.

The word is unrelated to *prodigy* and *prodigious*, both of which today generally carry positive connotations.

LANGUAGE-CHANGE INDEX
prodigal in the sense "returning": Stage 3

prodigality; profligacy. The former means "lavishness, extravagance." The latter means primarily "given to overindulgence in vice, licentiousness," but it also shares the sense of the former.

prodigious (= [1] amazing, marvelous; [2] enormous; or [3] abnormal) for *prestigious* (= having prestige) is a

MALAPROPISM—e.g.: "The rich and famous of decades gone by came here to float in serenity. In 1984, the *prodigious* [read *prestigious*] hotel was accorded National Historic Landmark status." John Hawkins, "Spruced-Up Homestead Bids for Greater Draw," *Wash. Times*, 5 Apr. 1994, at B6.

LANGUAGE-CHANGE INDEX
prodigious misused for *prestigious*: Stage 1

producible. So spelled in AmE and BrE alike—not **produceable*. But the misspelling is common—e.g.: "To reiterate, clothes only work when there is something of quality inside, and in too many cases that something is not easily *produceable* [read *producible*] or findable—or certainly not on the fashion pages." Barnett Singer, "What's Happened to the Gentleman?" *Buffalo News*, 21 July 1995, at C3. See -ABLE (A).

Current ratio: 35:1

pro et con. See **pro and con.**

profane; profanatory. What is *profane* is irreverent or blasphemous <a profane insult>; what is *profanatory* tends to make something profane <drink had a profanatory influence on him>.

PROFANITY. To put it politely, profanity is generally beyond the scope of this book. For the definitive works, see Ashley Montagu, *The Anatomy of Swearing* (1967) and Geoffrey Hughes, *Swearing: A Social History of Foul Language, Oaths and Profanity in English* (1991). On the loss of taboo for sexual and excretory terms, see Robert S. Wachal, "Taboo or Not Taboo: That Is the Question," 77 *Am. Speech* 195–206 (2002). For practical guidance on reducing your swearing, see James V. O'Connor, *Cuss Control: The Complete Book on How to Curb Your Cussing* (2000). For practical guidance on increasing the variety and imaginativeness of your swearing, see Reinhold Aman, *Opus Maledictorum: A Book of Bad Words* (1996).

profession. This word has been much debased in recent years, primarily at the hands of egalitarians who call any occupation a profession. In many American cities today, a person seeking a job as a barber, manicurist, or convenience-store manager turns in the classified ads to the section titled "Professions." A physician looking for a change in jobs turns to "Advanced Degree Required," a section of its own rather than a subsection of "Professions."

Traditionally there have been but three professions: theology, law, and medicine. These were known either as *the three professions* or as *the learned professions*. The term was ultimately extended to mean "one's principal vocation," which embraces prostitution as well as medicine. (*The oldest profession* originally had an irony much stronger than it has today.)

The restricted sense of *profession* no doubt strikes many people as snobbish and anachronistic. What about university professors, atomic physicists, and engineers? Perhaps three professions are not enough, but we ought to use at least *some* discrimination, with emphasis on "prolonged specialized training in a body of abstract knowledge." William J. Goode, "Encroachment, Charlatanism, and the Emerging Profession," 25 *Am. Soc. Rev.* 902, 903 (1960). Professional training "must lead to some order of mastery of a generalized cultural tradition, and do so in a manner giving prominence to an *intellectual* component." Talcott Parsons, "Professions," 12 *Int'l Encycl. Soc. Sci.* 536, 536 (1968).

professoriate (= collectively, the professors of an academic institution) has been the standard term since the mid-19th century. Before that, **professorate* was standard; it is now a NEEDLESS VARIANT of either *professoriate* or *professorship*. Avoid the variant spelling **professoriat*.
Current ratio (*professoriate* vs. **professorate* vs. **professoriat*): 7:2:1

profferer. So spelled—not **profferor*. For a curiosity, though, see **offeror**. See also -ER (A).

profligacy. See **prodigality.**

progenitor. See **primogeniture.**

progeny (= offspring) is usually plural in sense—e.g.: "The day before is the annual Alumnae Baby Party, when mothers and grandmothers (perhaps even a great-grandmother or two) will be showing off their *progeny* who've become students at the school." Betty Guillard, "VIPs Rounded Up for Cowboy Month," *Times-Picayune* (New Orleans), 7 May 1997, at E3. So it takes a plural verb. It's not a COLLECTIVE NOUN that takes a singular verb—e.g.: "Their *progeny was* [read *progeny were*] many, and all of them came back from World War II and worked in the business." "All in the Family," *Footwear News*, 16 Oct. 1995, at S26.
The word is sometimes used as a singular in place of *son, daughter,* or *child,* but only when the writer wants to be facetious—e.g.:

- "It took this nervous first-time father a minute or two to realize that my poor tiny *progeny* was born without the old gluteal fold, i.e., a butt." Robert Glenn, "Dad Has Two Arguments Against Abortion Option," *Seattle Post-Intelligencer,* 28 Sept. 1996, at A7.
- "Ashley Hamilton, who not only is the *progeny* of George Hamilton but was once married to the infamous Shannen Doherty of Beverly Hills 90210 for about 20 minutes, is going to get himself spliced . . . to Angie Everhart." Roger Anderson, "Glitterati," *Commercial Appeal* (Memphis), 4 Oct. 1996, at E7.

For the insensitive use of *progeny* as a metaphor, see METAPHORS.

prognosis; prognostication; prognostic, n. *Prognosis* is ordinarily used in medicine to mean "a forecast of the probable course and termination of an illness." (See **diagnosis.**) *Prognostication* is more general,

denoting "a prediction or prophecy" or "a conjecture of some future event formed upon some supposed sign." E.g.: "But not quite everyone is convinced that Mr. Greenspan's latest *prognostication*—or, for that matter, the unbroken economic expansion since 1991—proves that he has all the answers." Peter Russell, "Erring on the Side of Fighting Inflation at the Expense of Jobs," *N.Y. Times,* 10 Apr. 1997, at D2. *Prognostic* = an indication or omen.

program; programme. The first is the AmE spelling; the second is BrE. *Program* is used in BrE, however, in reference to computer programs.
The word is best pronounced /**proh**-gram/ in AmE and BrE alike—but /**proh**-grəm/, with an anomalous schwa sound, is widespread and acceptable today.

program(m)er; program(m)ing. The best spellings use -*mm*-, whether in AmE or BrE. The -*mm*- in AmE appears to derive from *programme,* the BrE spelling. Although some American dictionaries have given priority to **programer* and **programing,* these forms are rare and undesirable: they suggest a long -*a*- in the penultimate syllable. See SPELLING (B).
Current ratio (*programmer* vs. **programer*): 843:1
Current ratio (*programming* vs. **programing*): 357:1

progress, n. & vb. The noun *progress* (= [1] slow or steady movement in a determinate direction, [2] advancement toward an objective, or [3] gradual betterment) is pronounced /**prah**-gres/ in AmE and /**proh**-gres/ in BrE. The verb *progress* (= [1] to move forward, [2] to move to a better or more advanced phase, or [3] to continue) is pronounced /prə-**gres**/ in AmE and BrE alike.

prohibit takes the preposition *from* <the bylaws prohibit us from doing that>. Formerly, this verb could be construed with *to* <the bylaws prohibit us to do that>, but now this construction is an ARCHAISM. Cf. **forbid.**

prohibitive; prohibitory. These terms have undergone a latent DIFFERENTIATION that deserves encouragement. *Prohibitive* may mean generally "having the quality of prohibiting," but more and more in modern prose it has the sense "tending to preclude consumption or purchase because of expense" <the costs are prohibitive>. *Prohibitory* has carved out a niche in the law in the sense "expressing a prohibition or restraint" <prohibitory injunction>.

project, n. & vb. The noun *project* (= [1] a carefully planned piece of work, [2] an ambitious undertaking, or [3] a part of a school or college course involving a formulated task, esp. one requiring research) is /**prah**-jekt/ in AmE and BrE alike. Avoid /**prah**-jek/. The verb *project* (= [1] to plan, configure, estimate,

LANGUAGE-CHANGE INDEX (For the full key, see front matter pp. xxxi, l–li.)
Stage 1: Rejected. **Stage 2:** Widely shunned. **Stage 3:** Widespread but . . . **Stage 4:** Ubiquitous but . . . **Stage 5:** Fully accepted.
Invariably inferior forms marked by asterisk (*). • Ratios represent frequency of prevalent forms vs. variants in current books.

or extrapolate, [2] to present for consideration, [3] to stick out beyond an edge or surface, [4] to display outwardly, [5] to send out with great force, or [6] to ascribe to another [one's own attitudes or feelings, etc.]) is pronounced /prə-**jekt**/.

prolificacy; *****prolificness.** The standard noun corresponding to *prolific* is *prolificacy*, not *****prolificness*—e.g.:

- "Alas, Ms. Oates—whose work I deeply admire—has paid a price for her prolificacy." Jay Parini, "On Being Prolific," in *Writers on Writing* 199, 204 (Robert Pack & Jay Perini eds., 1991).
- "Allen's *prolificness* [read *prolificacy*] is legendary." John Beifuss, "So-So 'Love You' Says: Woody Allen Needs a Hiatus," *Commercial Appeal* (Memphis), 17 Jan. 1997, at C1.
- "The first problem that has to be confronted in relation to Ruiz's oeuvre is its sheer *prolificness* [read *prolificacy*]." Michael Goddard, *Impossible Cartographies* 1 (2013).

Cf. **genericness.**

LANGUAGE-CHANGE INDEX
*****prolificness* for *prolificacy*: Stage 1
Current ratio (*prolificacy* vs. *****prolificness*): 3:1

prolifically is the adverb corresponding to *prolific*, adj. But some writers misspell it *****prolificly*, maybe on the analogy of *publicly*—e.g.: "No wonder I wrote so easily, and *prolificly* [read *prolifically*]." Jeanne Crownover, "She'd Be a Writer . . . Except She Has Too Much Tranquility," *Sacramento Bee*, 1 Jan. 1995, Scene §, at 6. See -IC.

LANGUAGE-CHANGE INDEX
prolifically misspelled *****prolificly*: Stage 1
Current ratio: 2,100:1

*****prolificness.** See **prolificacy.**

prologue. So spelled—not *****prolog.**

promisor; promiser. Usage commentators have long said that the former is the legal spelling (as it is), the latter the everyday spelling. In fact, though, lawyers have much more call to use the term, so *promiser* is comparatively infrequent in print sources.

Current ratio: 15:1

promissory. So spelled.

promoter. So spelled in AmE and BrE alike—not *****promotor.** E.g.: "Meanwhile, the city's attorneys have been meeting with concert *promotors* [read *promoters*]." Ruth S. Intress, "City's Legal Stance Still Unsure on Concert Ban," *Richmond Times-Dispatch*, 21 Apr. 1997, at B1.

LANGUAGE-CHANGE INDEX
promoter misspelled *****promotor*: Stage 1
Current ratio: 79:1

promotive (= tending to promote) tends to be used in wordy constructions—e.g.: "Thought that is faithful to God *is promotive of* [read *promotes*] health, while thinking that tends away from God undermines health." "On the Subject of Thinking," *Christian Science Monitor*, 21 Feb. 1997, at 17. See BE-VERBS (B).

*****promotor.** See **promoter.**

promulgate (= [1] to put into effect [a new law, regulation, etc.], or [2] to proclaim or make known to as many people as possible) is pronounced /**prahm**-əl-gayt/ in STANDARD ENGLISH today—though it was traditionally pronounced /prə-**məl**-gayt/ before the mid-20th century.

prone; prostrate; supine. To lie *prone* or *prostrate* is to lie facedown. To lie *supine* is to lie face up. But in 1997, when a mass suicide occurred in San Diego, a local officer spread an incorrect usage to millions of listeners: " 'They were lying *prone* on their backs,' the San Diego sheriff's spokesman told the TV camera." Richard K. Shull, "Fatal Dose of Copspeak," *Indianapolis News*, 1 Apr. 1997, at A11. Within seconds of that televised statement, "an earnest broadcast reporter, eager to set the record straight, declared, 'They were *prostrate* on their backs.' " *Ibid.* The word that each speaker wanted, of course, was *supine*.

For more on *prostrate*, see **prostate (B).** See also **supine.**

PRONOUNS. A. The Basics. The personal pronouns in English are as follows:

Singular Pronouns

	Nominative	*Objective*	*Possessive*
First Person	I	me	my, mine
Second Person	you	you	your, yours
Third Person	he, she, it	him, her, it	his, her, hers, its

Plural Pronouns

	Nominative	*Objective*	*Possessive*
First Person	we	us	our, ours
Second Person	you	you	your, yours
Third Person	they	them	their, theirs

There are four essential rules concerning personal pronouns. First, if the pronoun is the subject of a clause, it must always be in the nominative case <she is friendly>. Second, if the pronoun is the object of a verb, it must be in the objective case <He thanked her>. Third, if a pronoun is the object of a preposition, it must always be in the objective case <it was the fault of them, not their children>. If a prepositional phrase contains two or more objects, all the objects are in the objective case <please tell only me and him>. *Like*, a preposition, is followed by the objective case <you're starting to sound like me> <they looked like us>. Fourth, if the pronoun is the subject of an infinitive, it must be in the objective case <she wanted him to sing another song>.

B. Confusion of Nominative and Objective Cases. One might think that a work of this kind, catering as it does to serious writers, could pass over the differences between subjects and objects in pronouns. But debilitated grammar seems ubiquitous—e.g.:

- "My mother was busy raising my brother and *I* [read *me*]." / "Give Al Gore and *I* [read *me*] a chance to bring America back." Bill Clinton, accepting the Democratic nomination for President of the United States, 16 July 1992.
- "Thompson said the final step in the university grievance process will be for *he* [read *him*] and Chandler to meet."

Zachary Walker & Brad Tooley, "Marshall Gets Temporary Restraint on University," *Canyon News*, 26 June 1994, at 1, 13.

- "She must have watched John and *I* [read *me*] when we all met at a party one evening." Susan Elliott, "The Day Denholm Said He Wanted an Open Marriage," *Daily Mail*, 22 Aug. 1994, at 28, 29.
- "That tax of course is passed on to you and *I* [read *me*] through a franchise fee on our electric bills. Boiling it down, our city charges you and *I* [read *me*] for the electric company to use our city easements." "WT Should Be Appreciated," *Canyon News*, 20 Aug. 1995, at 4. (Consistency isn't always a virtue.)
- "Choice is available to *I* [read *me*], a member of Congress." Senator Judd Gregg of New Hampshire, U.S. News Debate Series, PBS, 20 Oct. 1995.
- "As for *we* [read *us*] poor slobs who were out of the loop—any loop—we did what Dallasites had always done: We took it on faith that the city was virtually recession-proof." Jim Atkinson, "The Great Dallas Bust," *D Mag.*, Dec. 1995, at 91, 92.
- "What the public knows about Mr. Kelly's life at home since his surrender in Switzerland is more or less what he, his parents and Mr. Puccio have chosen to disclose: scenes of Mr. Kelly passing the time with vigorous exercise and of *he* [read *him*] and his parents declaring his innocence, as seen on a recent broadcast of ABC's 'Turning Point.'" George Judson, "Ex-Fugitive from Rape Charge Seeks to Shape Image and Trial," *N.Y. Times*, 2 May 1996, at A12.
- "Tokens predicting the future were buried in each dish . . . a coin for one who would become wealthy and a ring for *he or she* [read *him or her*] who would marry." Edythe Preet, "Good Cheer," *Irish America*, 31 Oct. 1996, at 66.
- "But they are not like *you and I* [read *you and me*], Po." Peter David, *Sir Apropos of Nothing* 110 (2001).
- "'If he had not forgiven *we* [read *us*] who lost faith at that time, he would have very few followers left.'" J.K. Rowling, *Harry Potter and the Half-Blood Prince* 27 (1st Am. ed. 2005).

For **between you and I*, see **between (B)** & HYPERCORRECTION (B). For *it's me*, see **it is I**. For pronouns after *than*, see **than (C)**.

Occasionally, writers avoid the strictly correct form merely to avoid seeming pedantic. One trying for a natural tone might understandably shrink from *I* in this example: "There are now so many casinos in the Upper Midwest that somebody has actually written a guidebook for gamblers who want to know what the places are like. [¶] And that somebody is *me*." David Hawley, "New Guidebook Has the Scoop," *Pioneer Press* (St. Paul), 22 Oct. 1994, at D1. The word *I*, technically, should serve as the predicate nominative after the linking verb *is*. That is, the pronoun in the predicate denotes the same person as the subject (*somebody*), so the predicate takes the nominative form because of that interchangeability. But *me* is much more common today in a sentence like that one.

Ernest Gowers gave sound advice here: "The prepositional use of *than* is now so common colloquially

(*He is older than me; they travelled much faster than us*) that the bare subjective pronoun in such a position strikes the readers as pedantic, and it is better either to give it a more natural appearance by supplying it with a verb or to dodge the difficulty by not using an inflective pronoun at all" (*FMEU2* at 620). Following are several good examples involving comparatives in which, strictly speaking, a pronoun in the nominative case should follow the word *than*:

- "What makes the story even juicier is that Pamela, 74, has allegedly been feuding for years with her two former stepdaughters, both of them slightly older than *her*—and one of whom may face financial difficulties." Mark Hosenball, "Clifford Pleads Ignorance," *Newsweek*, 3 Oct. 1994, at 46. (*Than she is* would also work well.)
- "He's much dumber than *me*." *Newsweek*, 24 Oct. 1994, at 4 (characterizing the message of Governor Mario Cuomo's advertisements aimed at defeating his successor, George Pataki). (*Than I am* would also work.)
- "'It's clear that actually a lot of people they protect are in more danger than *me*—if you're a member of the royal family or, more recently, if you were the secretary of state for Northern Ireland.'" Sarah Crichton, "Caught Between East and West, Rushdie Keeps On," *Newsweek*, 6 Feb. 1995, at 59 (quoting Salman Rushdie, who could also have said *than I am*).
- "I remember Paul Sann, a fabled old-time, cynical, swashbuckling New York tabloid editor, whose girlfriend, a leggy, undernourished model maybe thirty years younger than *him*, was my wife's friend." Edward Hoagland, "Sex and the River Styx," *Harper's Mag.*, Jan. 2003, at 49, 59. (*Than he was* would also work.)
- "Bobby, a Regular Army Veteran, was about ten years older than *me*." Gardner Botsford, *A Life of Privilege, Mostly* 41 (2003). (*Than I was* would also work.)

For *than whom*, see **than (D)**.

C. Underused in Specialized Writing. Some specialized writers—especially legal writers—have overlearned the lesson that pronouns sometimes have unclear referents. So they (the writers, not the referents) swear off ever using them (the pronouns, not the writers). The resulting style is quite stiff and unnatural—e.g.:

- "Frankfurter was unprepared for what was to come. *Frankfurter* [read *He*] did hold opinions about the Court's role in handling civil liberties, but these opinions were sometimes contradictory, extremely fuzzy, inarticulate, and unrefined." H.N. Hirsch, *The Enigma of Felix Frankfurter* 133 (1981).
- "Frankfurter was also convinced that he could easily handle his judicial colleagues. Throughout his life *Frankfurter* [read *he*] had excelled at 'personalia.'" *Ibid.* at 138.
- "Throughout the spring of 1941, as Black, Douglas, and Murphy continued to agree with Frankfurter only in minor cases, Frankfurter stepped up his efforts at instruction. By the end of the term, *Frankfurter* [read *he*] was clearly exasperated with his colleagues." *Ibid.* at 155.

D. Indefinite Pronouns: Number. Traditionally, indefinite pronouns (*anybody, anyone, everybody, everyone, nobody, no one, somebody,* and *someone*)

LANGUAGE-CHANGE INDEX (For the full key, see front matter pp. xxxi, l–li.)
Stage 1: Rejected. **Stage 2:** Widely shunned. **Stage 3:** Widespread but . . . **Stage 4:** Ubiquitous but . . . **Stage 5:** Fully accepted.
Invariably inferior forms marked by asterisk (*). • Ratios represent frequency of prevalent forms vs. variants in current books.

have been considered invariably singular. Indeed, as the subject of a verb, each of those terms must be singular—e.g.:

- "There's just one problem: Hardly *anybody* is riding." William LaRue, "Bootlegger's Secret," *Post-Standard* (Syracuse), 16 Dec. 1997, at A8.
- "He releases bad news when *nobody* is looking." "Public Pulse," *Omaha World-Herald*, 19 Dec. 1997, at 28.
- "*Everyone* was gleeful, full of the spirit of Hanukkah." Beverly Levitt, "If It's Hanukkah, It's Latke Time," *Denver Post*, 21 Dec. 1997, at D1.

For an example of *anyone . . . are*, see **anyone (D)**.

But often, as in the following sentences, the sense undoubtedly carries the idea of plurality from an antecedent pronoun to a referent one: "Since *everyone* there was Japanese, and none of *them* had ever traveled abroad, *they* needed a translator." / "*Everybody* was crouched behind furniture to surprise me, and *they* tried to. But I already knew *they* were there." Try changing *them* to *him* and *they* to *he*, and you end up with deranged writing. SYNESIS dictates that the logical sense trumps the strict rules of grammar with these words in transition.

Other sentences present closer calls, but the trend is unmistakable—e.g.:

- "We are therefore appealing to *anyone* working on a literary, social, or other historical text who has found a discrepancy between the material with which *they* are working and an entry in the *OED*, no matter how trivial, to send *their* comments to us." Letter of John Simpson & Edmund Weiner [coeditors of the *OED*], "Revision of the Oxford English Dictionary," *TLS*, 5 Nov. 1993, at 15.
- "Being so down-to-earth she accepts *everybody* for who *they* are, and so is unlikely to treat *them* any differently from the way she deals with anybody else." Shelley von Strunckel, "What the Stars Say About Them," *Sunday Times* (London), 18 June 1995, Style §, at 36.

Although *everybody* and *everyone* carry the strongest suggestions of plurality, the other indefinite pronouns are almost as natural as antecedents with *they* and *them*. That's because *they* has increasingly moved toward singular senses. (See SEXISM (B).) Disturbing though these developments may be to purists, they're irreversible. And nothing that a grammarian says will change them.

E. Reflexive Pronouns. The reflexive pronouns—*herself, himself, itself, myself, oneself, ourselves, themselves, yourself, yourselves*—have two uses. First, they may serve as the object of a reflexive verb (one that has the subject acting on itself), as either a direct object <they flatter themselves> or an indirect object <she gave herself a break>. Second, they may give their antecedent special emphasis. The antecedent may be the subject <Gayle herself would never admit it> <Gayle would never admit it herself> or an object <give it to Gayle herself>.

The key to the use of reflexive pronouns is that each one should reflect an antecedent. They are misused when they just stand in for personal pronouns—e.g.: "It is only right and just, Ms. Flamel, that the assets

of the partnership should now be divided equally *between yourself and me* [read *between you and me*]." Fred Saberhagen, *A Coldness in the Blood* 152 (2002). See **myself**.

Nonstandard reflexive pronouns, such as **hisself* and **theirselves*, typify DIALECT.

F. Overeager Pronouns. See ANTICIPATORY REFERENCE.

G. Restrictive and Nonrestrictive Relative Pronouns. See **that (A)**.

H. *One* as a Pronoun. See **one**.

I. Noun–Pronoun Disagreement. See CONCORD (B).

J. Relative Pronoun–Antecedent Disagreement. See CONCORD (D).

pronunciation is sometimes mistakenly said (and written) **pronounciation*—e.g.:

- "Gloria Estefan stopped by to discuss her new movie with Meryl Streep—Couric checked the *pronounciation* [read *pronunciation*] of her name seconds before air time." Eric Deggans, "Dawn's Early Fight," *St. Petersburg Times*, 1 Nov. 1999, at D1.
- "Discussions will range from players who appeared on baseball cards without ever making it into a game to the *pronounciation* [read *pronunciation*] of names." Joe Capozzi, "It's Geek to Us," *Palm Beach Post*, 21 June 2000, at C1.
- "Collora, who reads stories to a third- and fourth-grader on alternate weeks, also helps them with their *pronounciation* [read *pronunciation*] and comprehension." Betty Ommerman, "School Mentors Who Are Doing Their Homework," *Newsday* (N.Y.), 29 Oct. 2000, at G24.

LANGUAGE-CHANGE INDEX
*pronounciation for *pronunciation*: Stage 1
Current ratio (*pronunciation* vs.
*pronounciation): 165:1

PRONUNCIATION. A. General Principles. The best course is to follow the pronunciation current among educated speakers in one's region. A few words have universally accepted pronunciations and rejected mispronunciations; where prescriptions on pronunciation appear in this book, the preferred pronunciation is generally preferred across geographic boundaries.

H.W. Fowler still speaks to us with clarion wisdom: "The ambition to do better than our neighbours is in many departments of life a virtue; in pronunciation it is a vice; there the only right ambition is to do as our neighbours" (*FMEU1* at 466).

But when it comes to words that are seldom pronounced by English-speaking people—as with any learned word—the advice to conform with our neighbors' pronunciation becomes problematic. For here we find diversity, not uniformity—the result of the infrequent occasions when the words are pronounced. And when opinions diverge among reasonable and educated people, there must be considerable leeway.

For a misspelling of *pronunciation*, see **pronunciation**.

B. Commonly Mispronounced Words. Many troublesome words are listed throughout this book, with the correct pronunciation noted. Here are some of the most frequently mispronounced words in AmE:

	Correct	*Incorrect*
affluent	**af**-loo-ənt	ə-**floo**-ənt
album	**al**-bəm	**al**-bləm
almond	**ah**-mənd	**al**-mənd
applicable	**ap**-li-kə-bəl	ə-**plik**-ə-bəl
arctic	**ahrk**-tik	**ahr**-tik
asked	askt	ast, aksd
asterisk	**as**-tə-risk	**as**-tə-rik
athlete	**ath**-leet	**ath**-ə-leet
cement	sə-**ment**	**see**-mint
comparable	**kom**-pə-rə-bəl	kəm-**pair**-ə-bəl
comptroller	kən-**troh**-lər	**komp**-troh-lər
concierge	kon-see-**airzh**	kon-see-**air**
coupon	**koo**-pon	**kyoo**-pon
descent	di-**sent**	**dee**-sent
Detroit	di-**troyt**	**dee**-troyt
ebullient	i-**buul**-yənt	**eb**-yə-lənt
ecstatic	ek-**stad**-ik	e-**stad**-ik
escape	es-**kayp**	ek-**skayp**
espresso	es-**pres**-oh	ek-**spres**-oh
et cetera	et **set**-ə-rə	ek set-ə-rə
extraordinary	ek-**stror**-di-ner-ee	ek-strə-**or**-di-ner-ee
fifth	fifth	fith
flaccid	**flak**-sid	**flas**-əd
grocery	**grohs**-[ə]-ree	**groh**-shree
height	hɪt	hɪtth
heinous	**hay**-nəs	**hee**-nəs, **hee**-nee-is
hindrance	**hin**-drin[t]s	**hin**-də-rin[t]s
hundred	**hən**-drəd	**hən**-ərd, **hən**-drit
hypnotize	**hip**-nə-tɪz	**hip**-mə-tɪz
Illinois	il-ə-**noy**	il-ə-**noyz**
influence	**in**-floo-ənts	in-**floo**-ənts
insurance	in-**shuur**-ənts	in-**shər**-ənts
interesting	**in**-trə-sting	in-ə-**res**-ting
intravenous	in-trə-**vee**-nəs	in-trə-**vee**-nee-əs
irrevocable	i-**rev**-ə-kə-bəl	ir-ə-**voh**-kə-bəl
liaison	**lee**-ə-zahn, lee-**ay**-zahn	**lay**-ə-zahn
library	**lɪ**-brer-ee	**lɪ**-ber-ee
literature	**lit**-ər-ə-chuur	**lit**-ər-ə-tyoor, **lit**-ər-chər
mirror	**mir**-ər	**mir**-ə, meer, mər
mischievous	**mis**-chə-vəs	mis-**chee**-vee-əs
nuclear	**noo**-klee-ər	**noo**-kyə-lər
often	**of**-ən	**of**-tən
pamphlet	**pam**-flət	**pam**-plət
persevere	pər-sə-**veer**	pər-sər-**veer**
police	pə-**lees**	**poh**-lees
preferable	**pref**-ər-ə-bəl	pri-**fər**-ə-bəl
probably	**pro**-bə-blee	**prob**-lee, **pro**-lee
pronunciation	proh-nən-see-**ay**-shən	pron-**nown**-see-ay-shən
realtor	**reel**-tər	**reel**-ə-tər
schism	**siz**-əm	**skiz**-əm, **shiz**-əm
secretary	**sek**-rə-ter-ee	**sek**-ə-ter-ee
sherbet	**shər**-bət	**shər**-bərt
specifically	spi-**sif**-i-klee	pə-**sif**-i-klee

substantive	**sə**-stən-tiv	sə-**stə**-nə-tiv, sə-**stan**-tiv
wash	wahsh	wahrsh
zoology	zoh-**ol**-ə-jee	zoo-**ol**-ə-jee

Some CONTRACTIONS are also commonly mispronounced. For example, *couldn't, didn't,* and *wouldn't* are sometimes mouthed as if the *-d-* were part of the unemphasized second syllable: /**kuu**-dənt/, rather than the correct /**kuud**-ənt/, etc. Sometimes, too, careless speakers syncopate contractions into such sounds as /kuunt/ and /wuunt/.

On pronunciations as class indicators, see CLASS DISTINCTIONS.

C. Recessive and Progressive Stresses. In English pronunciation, two forces seem to be constantly at work: pushing back the accent in certain words (recessive stress) and pushing it forward in others (progressive stress). Hence pronunciations shift very gradually. Recessive stress—usually by which the accent gets moved from the first to the second syllable—sometimes yields what have come to be seen as accepted pronunciations, but many of the recessive stresses here listed typify unrefined speech (stages 1 to 3 of the Language-Change Index). Most of the terms listed here are more fully discussed in entries at their alphabetical places in this book.

Traditional Stress	**Recessive Stress**
admirable	ad**mir**able (LCI Stage 1)
affluent	aff**lu**ent (LCI Stage 2)
amicable	am**ic**able (LCI Stage 1)
applicable	app**lic**able (LCI Stage 2)
armistice	arm**is**tice (LCI Stage 1)
clitoris	clit**or**is (LCI Stage 2)
comparable	com**par**able (LCI Stage 2)
congruent	con**gru**ent (LCI Stage 4)
despicable	des**pic**able (LCI Stage 5)
disparate	dis**par**ate (LCI Stage 1)
explicable	ex**plic**able (LCI Stage 5)
exquisite	ex**quis**ite (LCI Stage 5)
formidable	form**id**able (LCI Stage 3)
gondola	gon**do**la (LCI Stage 1)
hospitable	hos**pit**able (LCI Stage 4)
influence	in**flu**ence (LCI Stage 2)
integral	in**teg**ral (LCI Stage 1)
lamentable	lam**ent**able (LCI Stage 4)
mayoral	may**or**al (LCI Stage 3)
pastoral	pas**tor**al (LCI Stage 2)
preferable	pref**er**able (LCI Stage 2)
revocable	rev**oc**able (LCI Stage 3)
vehement	ve**he**ment (LCI Stage 1)

With other terms, though, the force of change is in the opposite direction, from second syllable to first. Again the shift from the traditional pronunciation to the new stress sometimes typifies unrefined speech. But note that many more of the progressively stressed words have reached Stage 5 of the Language-Change Index—meaning full acceptability in STANDARD ENGLISH.

LANGUAGE-CHANGE INDEX (For the full key, see front matter pp. xxxi, l–li.)
Stage 1: Rejected. **Stage 2:** Widely shunned. **Stage 3:** Widespread but . . . **Stage 4:** Ubiquitous but . . . **Stage 5:** Fully accepted.
Invariably inferior forms marked by asterisk (*). • Ratios represent frequency of prevalent forms vs. variants in current books.

Traditional Stress	Progressive Stress
ac**cli**mate	**ac**climate (LCI Stage 5)
a**cu**men	**ac**umen (LCI Stage 3)
ce**ment**	**ce**ment (LCI Stage 3)
con**fis**cate	**con**fiscate (LCI Stage 5)
con**tra**ry	**con**trary (LCI Stage 5)
de**ba**cle	**deb**acle (LCI Stage 2)
de**scent**	**de**scent (LCI Stage 2)
De**troit**	**De**troit (LCI Stage 1)
il**lus**trative	**il**lustrative (LCI Stage 2)
in**cul**cate	**in**culcate (LCI Stage 5)
in**sur**ance	**in**surance (LCI Stage 2)
mi**nus**cule	**min**uscule (LCI Stage 5)
ob**fus**cate	**ob**fuscate (LCI Stage 5)
po**lice**	**po**lice (LCI Stage 1)
precedence	pre**ce**dence (LCI Stage 5)
sonorous	so**nor**ous (LCI Stage 4)
va**ga**ries	**va**garies (LCI Stage 5)

Much depends on what one linguist calls the "dynamics of utterance." Dwight L. Bolinger, "Stress and Information," 33 *Am. Speech* 5–20 (1958). Stress shifts in certain words are an indication of DIALECT and of regional preferences. They may also be affected by the presence or absence of stress in neighboring words. See Arthur J. Bronstein, *The Pronunciation of American English* 256 (1960).

D. De-anglicized Pronunciations. English speakers who learn another language often busy themselves with using the "correct" pronunciation of loanwords long since anglicized: *ambiance* /ahm-bee-**ahns**/ for /**am**-bee-ən[t]s/ (*ambience*); *guillotine* /**gee**-yə-teen/ for /**gil**-ə-teen/; *homage* /oh-**mahzh**/ for /**hom**-ij/; *San Jacinto* /san hah-**seen**-toh/ for /san jə-**sin**-toh/; and even place names such as *Torino* for *Turin*. These speakers display not so much their learning of another tongue as their ignorance of English pronunciation. Cf. HOBSON-JOBSONISM.

E. Lambdacism and Rhotacism. These are two of the most common defects in pronunciation: *lambdacism* denotes the imperfect or superfluous sounding of -*l*- (as by making it sound like an -*r*- or -*y*-), and *rhotacism* denotes the imperfect or superfluous sounding of -*r*- (as by making it a -*w*- or -*l*-). In some children, these mispronunciations occur at an early stage of development and are soon outgrown; for them, *Mary had a little lamb* can sound like *Mawy had a yitto yam*. Sometimes, though, these defects are never outgrown; they become minor speech impediments. Sometimes, too, pronunciations exhibiting rhotacism characterize regional speech, as in President John F. Kennedy's pronunciation of *idea* /ı-**deer**/ and *Cuba* /**kyoo**-bər/. In the words listed in (B), one sees the intrusive -*r*- (*persevere*) and the omitted -*r*- (*mirror*), both of which are types of rhotacism; and the intrusive -*l*- (*album*), which is a type of lambdacism.

F. The Mispronounced -*ph*-. In several words—notably, *diphtheria, diphthong, naphtha, ophthalmology,* and *pamphlet*—people tend to change the /f/ sound of the -*ph*- to a /p/ sound. Avoid these mispronunciations.

For an example of a -*ph*- that has simply dropped out of a word, see **apothegm**. Cf. **jodhpur**.

G. Names. See NAMES (C).

H. *Pronunciation* and *enunciation*. *Enunciation* = (1) clear articulation of words, sentences, and thoughts; or (2) a formal announcement, proclamation, or statement. In sense 1, *enunciation* includes correct *pronunciation* of words, but it is a much broader term. When *enunciation* is used without a modifier of quality, the understood connotation is positive <the speaker is known for her enunciation>; *pronunciation*, on the other hand, is connotatively neutral <the president is known for his pronunciation>.

I. Bibliography. For the best guidance on pronouncing the most troublesome words, see Charles Harrington Elster, *The Big Book of Beastly Mispronunciations* (2d ed. 2005). For an excellent guide to proper nouns, see John K. Bollard, *Pronouncing Dictionary of Proper Names* (2d ed. 1998). For still other references, see the Select Bibliography at the end of this book.

proof. Pl. *proofs.* See PLURALS (C).

propaganda, typically a singular mass noun, makes the (rare) count-noun plural *propagandas* (which has been around since the 18th century)—e.g.: "Colin Jacobson has amassed a startling collection of banned or suppressed photographs that clashed with prevailing *propagandas* of a particular era or were seen as ideologically dangerous." Mona Reeder, "Images to Savor for Months to Come," *Dallas Morning News*, 20 Dec. 2002, at C4. The word *propaganda* is sometimes mistaken to be a plural in the class of *data* and *strata*— e.g.: "Ideological and political *propaganda were* [read *propaganda was*] being used to bolster their objective, too." "Developing Nations Moving Towards Debt Trap," *Statesman*, 17 Feb. 1997.

LANGUAGE-CHANGE INDEX
propaganda misused as a plural: Stage 1

propagate (= to reproduce or extend) is occasionally confused with *promulgate* (= to proclaim; put [a policy, law, etc.] into action)—e.g.: "The EC tends to impose its will by regulatory edict rather than by statutes enacted by elected representatives. It *propagates* [read *promulgates*] regulations daily, at an annual rate of several thousands." "Taking Sides: Stranglehold of the Eurocrats," *Sunday Telegraph*, 29 July 1990, at 21.

LANGUAGE-CHANGE INDEX
propagate misused for *promulgate*: Stage 1

propellant, n.; **propellent,** adj. As the headwords show, the noun and the adjective aren't spelled the same.

*propelment. See **propulsion**.

properly. How you place this word in relation to a linking verb can affect meaning: *be properly* means something different from *properly be*. The latter phrase means that the thing in question (the subject) is proper, or that it is proper for the thing to be done <parents may properly be notified in these circumstances>, while the former means that the thing should be done in a proper way <parents must be properly notified—not orally, but in writing>. See BE-VERBS.

Proper Names. See names.

proper noun; common noun. These phrases are antonyms. A *proper noun* is the name of a specific person <Noah Webster>, place <Vancouver, British Columbia>, or thing <Gateway Arch>. A *common noun* is the name of a general class of people <teacher>, places <mountain>, or things <iron ore>. Some writers mistakenly believe that the antonym of *proper noun* is *improper noun*—e.g.: "Capitalization of *improper* [read *common*] nouns and the lack thereof for proper nouns, sentence fragments and run-on sentences are unacceptable abuses of the English language." Lloyd Bockstruck, "Even Basics Are Wrong in These Basic Books," *Dallas Morning News*, 19 May 2001, at C8.

prophesy; prophecy. *Prophesy* (/**pro**-fə-sı/) is the verb meaning "to predict or foretell"; *prophecy* (/**pro**-fə-see/) is the noun meaning "a prediction or foretelling." The two words are sometimes confounded—e.g.:

- "When he was finished he acknowledged the applause in good form before the chorus surged onto the stage to tell him of the Vestal's *prophesy* [read *prophecy*]." Chelsea Quinn Yarbro, *Communion Blood* 369 (1999).
- "Meanwhile, the gods finagle a meeting between Helen and young Paris (Matthew Marsden), a shepherd born to royalty, who was cast off as a baby because his birth was *prophecied* [read *prophesied*] to signal the destruction of Troy." Allan Johnson, " 'Helen' a Soap Opera in Greek Clothing," *Chicago Trib.*, 18 Apr. 2003, Tempo §, at 5.
- "Denied the constitutional option of a tie, it's a sure thing that in the day (or days? weeks? months?) ahead, millions of sore losers will be screaming bloody murder, *prophecying* [read *prophesying*] doom and acute gloom." Logan Jenkins, "A Monday in the Doldrums as Moby Dick Circles," *San Diego Union-Trib.*, 1 Nov. 2004, at B2.

To complicate matters further, the verb *prophesy* has sometimes been incorrectly made *prophesize*, especially since the 1950s—e.g.:

- "As Jesus rode through Jerusalem, many of the Jews waved palm branches and hailed him as the king of Israel because of clues . . . that had been *prophesized* [read *prophesied*] in Scripture." Betty Beard, "Holy Celebrations Have Similar Roots," *Ariz. Republic*, 26 Mar. 1994, at E9.
- "The Fox double triumph was perhaps *prophesized* [read *prophesied*] earlier this season." Jerry Krupnick, " 'The Simpsons' and 'X-Files' Win Peabodys," *Star-Ledger* (Newark), 4 Apr. 1997, at 39.
- "Mariammal's brother, too, reportedly continues to *prophesize* [read *prophesy*] and perform healings in his own small temple in the village." Tracy Pintchman, "From Local Goddess to Locale Goddess," in *Inventing and Reinventing the Goddess* 89, 94 (Sree Padma ed., 2014).

Language-Change Index
1. *prophecy* (n.) misspelled *prophesy*: Stage 3
2. *prophesize* for *prophesy*: Stage 2
Current ratio (*prophesied* vs. *prophesized*): 29:1

proponent. See **protagonist (B).**

proportion, v.t.; **proportionate,** v.t.; **proportionalize.** The second and third are needless variants.
Current ratio (*proportioned* vs. *proportionated* vs. *proportionalized*): 1,845:1:1

proportional; proportionate; proportionable. The distinction to be observed is between *proportional* and *proportionate*. Admittedly, at times the distinction is foiled by the frequent interchangeability of the terms. Nevertheless, it is possible to formulate a nuance. *Proportional* = (1) of, relating to, or involving proportion; or (2) in due proportion. *Proportionate* = proportioned; adjusted in proportion. As a Latinate perfect passive participle, *proportionate* suggests the conscious proportioning of an agent. See **proportion.**

This nice distinction aside, *proportional* is more than five times as common in print as *proportionate*—e.g.:

- "In all, 120 legislators will be elected to the Knesset (parliament) on the basis of *proportional* representation." John Battersby, "Israeli Election Plunges into Unknown," *Christian Science Monitor*, 1 Apr. 1996, at 7.
- "Some schools have shown that *proportional* numbers of male and female athletes can be achieved without eliminating men's teams." Letter of Lawrence H. Berger, "Level Playing Field," *Times* (London), 26 May 1997, at 12.

The exception, however, is in the negative form of the word: *disproportionate* is nearly 30 times as common as *disproportional*. E.g.:

- "Miller spends a *disproportionate* share of his waking hours crushing soda cans and organizing neighborhood seminars on sibling rivalry in Sino-Tibetan society." Allen Rose, "Mulletropolis Cogitation Is Out in the Ozone," *Orlando Sentinel*, 17 May 1996, at D1.
- "This is a real community, warts and all, with a *disproportionate* share of dysfunctional elements." Luis H. Fracia, "Speech Lessons," *Village Voice*, 27 May 1997, at 63.

Proportionable is an archaism that still sometimes occurs—e.g.: "If this is exceeded, then area payments will be *proportionably* [read *proportionately*] reduced in the offending countries." "£20m Rise in Cost of Support for Arable Farming Sector," *Extel Examiner*, 7 Jan. 1995, at 22. It has no place today. See **pro rata.** Cf. **commensurate.**
Current ratio (in order of headwords): 117:26:1

propose; proposition, vb. *Propose* (= to offer or suggest [some course of action]) has no particular connotations except when used in the sense of asking someone to marry. The word dates from the 14th century. *Proposition*, on the other hand, is an Americanism dating only from the early 20th century; it almost always carries a negative connotation. In its original uses, it usually implied that some unsavory or illegal action was suggested. It soon began to denote specifically an invitation to another person to engage in illicit sex.

propound. See **expound.**

LANGUAGE-CHANGE INDEX (For the full key, see front matter pp. xxxi, l–li.)
Stage 1: Rejected. **Stage 2:** Widely shunned. **Stage 3:** Widespread but . . . **Stage 4:** Ubiquitous but . . . **Stage 5:** Fully accepted.
Invariably inferior forms marked by asterisk (*). • Ratios represent frequency of prevalent forms vs. variants in current books.

proprietary; proprietorial; *proprietory. The last is an erroneous form. The adjective form corresponding to the noun *proprietor* is either *proprietary* or *propri-etorial*. *Proprietary* also means "of, relating to, or holding as property."

In the following sentence, *proprietorial* is almost certainly misused for *proprietary*: "The contracts were negotiated not with the band's company, The Beatles, Ltd., which held the rights, but with NEMS, which did not possess any *proprietorial* [read *proprietary*] rights whatsoever, being simply a management organization." Albert Goldman, *The Lives of John Lennon* 335 (1988).

> LANGUAGE-CHANGE INDEX
> *proprietorial* misused for *proprietary*: Stage 1

*proprietous is a NONWORD that occasionally displaces *proper*—e.g.: "Besides regular guests, a *propri-etous* [read *proper*] attitude infects bellmen, waiters, bartenders and the managing director of 32 years, Andrew Anspach." Diana Nelson Jones, "Revising the Round Table," *Pitt. Post-Gaz.*, 2 Apr. 1997, at B1. A BACK-FORMATION from *propriety*, the word is highly improper. Cf. *improprietous.

> LANGUAGE-CHANGE INDEX
> **proprietous* for *proper*: Stage 1
> Current ratio (*proper* vs. **proprietous*): 146,385:1

propriety. This word may mean either "fitness, rightness" or "correctness in behavior or morals." But some writers have come to use it in the sense of *property*, perhaps as a kind of misguided BACK-FORMATION from the adjective *proprietary*—e.g.: "Between 1869 and his death in 1931, at age 84, Thomas Alva Edison was granted more than a thousand patents for inventions familiar and eccentric: from the typewriter, electric pen, electric light, phonograph, motion picture camera and alkaline storage battery—to the talking doll and a concrete house that could be built in one day from a cast-iron mold. [¶] From the start, Edison endeavored to 'keep a full record' of his progress— and the *propriety* of his ideas." Neil Baldwin, "Eureka: Thomas Alva Edison's Notebooks, Brought to Light," *N.Y. Times*, 14 May 1995, § 6, at 30.

For an odd misusage involving *propriety*, see **probity**.

propulsion; *propelment. The latter is a NEEDLESS VARIANT.

> Current ratio: 5,799:1

propulsive; *propulsory. The latter is a NEEDLESS VARIANT.

> Current ratio: 440:1

pro rata, adv. & adj., should be spelled as two words <their shares will be reduced pro rata> <the companies will each exchange their 5.6 percent pro rata equity interest>. The phrase *on a pro rata basis* is wordy for *pro rata*—e.g.: "TPI shareholders will have the right to receive contingent shares that will permit them to receive—*on a pro rata basis* [read

pro rata]—any cash proceeds resulting from TPI's ongoing lawsuit." Mary Hance, "Shoney's Acquiring Franchise," *Nashville Banner*, 5 Sept. 1995, at D1. The tendency to use the wordier expression signals the decline of the adverbial *pro rata* and the rise of the adjective. See **basis (A).**

Proportionate(ly) can often serve in place of *pro rata*—e.g.: "His 22-page financial disclosure to the Office of Government Ethics showed he received $1,141,578 from Kirkland & Ellis and $25,000 from NYU. He also received a *pro rata* [read *proportionate*] share of the counsel's salary." Frank J. Murray, "Starr Busy in Private Practice," *Wash. Times*, 13 Sept. 1995, at A4. See **proportionate.**

proscenium (= the front part of a stage, esp. in front of the curtain) has predominantly formed the plural *prosceniums* in all varieties of World English since about 1920. Before that, the Latinate plural *proscenia* (for this ultimately Greek term) was standard.

> Current ratio (*prosceniums* vs. *proscenia*): 2:1

proscribe; prescribe. *Proscribe* = to prohibit. *Prescribe* = to impose authoritatively. But some writers apparently think that *proscribe* is simply a fancier form of *prescribe*—e.g.:

- "Built-in safeguards prevent shifts that could cause damage when rpm's are beyond *proscribed* [read *prescribed*] limits for the particular year." Bob Hill, "Advertorial Drivetime," *Oregonian* (Portland), 15 Mar. 1997, at DT1.
- "An amendment . . . merely authorizes the enactment of a litany of laws dictating the punishment of citizens interpreted to have committed an act of physical desecration upon a banner *proscribed* [read *prescribed* or *defined*] to be a flag." Keith A. Kreul, "But There Are Better Solutions," *Wis. State J.*, 14 June 1997, at A7.
- "Whenever a manager does follow instinct, rather than the investment style *proscribed* [read *prescribed*] to him, one mistake causes investors to flee." Charles A. Jaffe, "A Return to Our Roots," *Boston Globe*, 21 Mar. 1999, at C6.

Sometimes, but much less often, the opposite error occurs—e.g.: "Most of these rules of grammar have no real justification and there is therefore no serious reason for condemning the 'errors' they *prescribe* [read *proscribe*]." Frank Palmer, *Grammar* 14 (1971). Given the ability and reputation of Mr. Palmer, that instance is almost certainly a printer's error.

> LANGUAGE-CHANGE INDEX
> 1. *proscribe* misused for *prescribe*: Stage 1
> 2. *prescribe* misused for *proscribe*: Stage 1

PROSE, SOUND OF. See SOUND OF PROSE.

prosecute; persecute. *Prosecute* = to begin a case at law for punishment of a crime or of a legal violation. *Persecute* = to oppress, coerce, treat unfairly, often out of religious hatred. Occasionally the two are confounded—e.g.: "Asked why they figure Philips has not actively *persecuted* [read *prosecuted*] violators, sources cite 'pure negligence' and a 'lack of organization' on the part of the company." Paul Verna, "Replicators

Cite Growing Burden of CD Patent Fees," *Billboard*, 16 Aug. 1997.

LANGUAGE-CHANGE INDEX
persecute misused for *prosecute*: Stage 1

prosecutorial; prosecutory; *prosecutive; *prosecutional. Among these, the most common term in criminal-law texts is *prosecutorial*; but many dictionaries omit the term. Instead, most dictionaries define *prosecutory* and its NEEDLESS VARIANT **prosecutive*—less common words—as "of, relating to, or involving prosecution." E.g.: "Law enforcement, shelter and support agencies, medical personnel, legal and *prosecutory* agencies, child-abuse treatment and intervention personnel all needed special interdisciplinary training and better." Dee Aker, "The World Is Watching," *Chicago Trib.*, 11 Aug. 1996, Womanews §, at 1.

But *prosecutorial* serves as the adjective corresponding to *prosecutor*—e.g.:

- "Not only did he lack the maturity and courage to face me, but he was irresponsible to have leaked my *prosecutorial* demise to the press the day before it occurred." Paul Richwalsky, "Richwalsky Replies to Hawpe," *Courier-J.* (Louisville), 19 Sept. 1997, at A15.
- "Now she has shaken up her *prosecutorial* staff." "Reluctance of Reno Looks Worse Now," *Dayton Daily News*, 19 Sept. 1997, at A14.
- "Until 2010, the notion of positive complementarity was primarily one of *prosecutorial* strategy." Olympia Bekou, "Building National Capacity for the ICC," in *The International Criminal Court in Search of Its Purpose and Identity* 133, 139 (Triestino Mariniello ed., 2015).

This word is hundreds of times as common in print as *prosecutory*—and has been since the 1970s.

*Prosecutional is but a NEEDLESS VARIANT—e.g.: "Marcia Clark, leader of that magnificent *prosecutional* [read *prosecutory* or *prosecutorial*, depending on the meaning] botch, has received a \$2 million advance for her literature." Blackie Sherrod, "Simpson Trial Has Attracted the Jackals," *Dallas Morning News*, 5 Dec. 1996, at A37.

LANGUAGE-CHANGE INDEX
*prosecutional for *prosecutory* or *prosecutorial*: Stage 1

prosecutrix. See SEXISM (D).

proselytize; proselyte, v.t. The former is preferred for three reasons: (1) despite the -IZE suffix, it's more euphonious and easier to say; (2) *proselyte* is primarily a noun, and using it as a verb causes MISCUES; and (3) *proselytize* is nine times as common in print. Because it is transitive, not intransitive, *proselytize* typically takes a direct object (without *to* or any other preposition)—e.g.: "According to the suit, Osborn had *proselytized to* [read *proselytized*] one of his players and had tried to persuade the player to attend his church." Jack McCallum & Richard O'Brien, "Of

Passes and Prayers," *Sports Illustrated*, 22 Apr. 1996, at 20.

Current ratio (*to proselytize* vs. **to proselyte*): 9:1

prospective; perspective. *Prospective* (adj.) = (1) likely to become <prospective member>; or (2) expected <prospective profits>. *Perspective* (n.) = (1) the angle from which something is viewed <we gained a better perspective on the hill>; or (2) the relative proportions and positions of people and things within a scene <everything in the drawing seemed to be in perspective>. The noun *perspective* is sometimes used attributively—that is, it functions as an adjective, especially in art contexts <perspective painting>.

Misusing *perspective* for *prospective* amounts to a MALAPROPISM—e.g.:

- "Manis is expected to call 1,500 *perspective* [read *prospective*] jurors, or more than three times the usual number for a case, to look for 12 unbiased jurors." Lee Mungin, "Al-Amin Case," *Atlanta J.-Const.*, 6 Jan. 2003, at D1.
- "A jury questionnaire will help prosecutors and defense lawyers determine if the *perspective* [read *prospective*] jurors have predisposed biases in the case." Andy Nelesen, "Hill Trial in Toddler's Death Set for Monday," *Green Bay Press-Gaz.*, 16 Feb. 2003, at B7. (On the use of *if* in that sentence, see **if (A).**)

LANGUAGE-CHANGE INDEX
perspective misused for *prospective*: Stage 1

prospectus. The correct English plural is *prospectuses*—and it is the only form listed in English dictionaries. The Latin plural is *prospectus* (a fourth-declension noun), not **prospecti* (the product of ignorant HYPERCORRECTION originally in the 18th century)—e.g.:

- "No charts, printouts, graphics, maps, blueprints, or *prospecti* [read *prospectuses*]." Robert Stone, "Maximum Bob," *Village Voice*, 6 June 1995, at 75.
- "The proposed change would follow the commission's current initiative to streamline mutual fund *prospecti* [read *prospectuses*]." "SEC May Change Disclosure Rules for Fund Portfolios," *Dallas Morning News*, 18 Mar. 1997, at D4.

See **conspectus** & PLURALS (B). Cf. **apparatus** & **nexus.**

LANGUAGE-CHANGE INDEX
*prospecti for the plural *prospectuses*: Stage 1
Current ratio (*prospectuses* vs.
*prospecti): 111:1

prostate. A. And *prostatic*. Whereas most people, when referring to the disease, use *prostate cancer*, specialists often use *prostatic cancer*. That form can be found even in popular sources—e.g.:

- "This study, reported in the Journal of the National Cancer Institute, showed that 10 servings of tomatoes a week reduced the incidence of *prostatic cancer* by an amazing 45 percent." Dr. Kenneth Walker, "Researchers Link Bad

LANGUAGE-CHANGE INDEX (For the full key, see front matter pp. xxxi, l–li.)
Stage 1: Rejected. **Stage 2:** Widely shunned. **Stage 3:** Widespread but . . . **Stage 4:** Ubiquitous but . . . **Stage 5:** Fully accepted.
Invariably inferior forms marked by asterisk (*). • Ratios represent frequency of prevalent forms vs. variants in current books.

Gums with Cardiovascular Disease," *Chicago Sun-Times,* 1 Sept. 1996, at 45.

- "And how does sex affect the PSA test to detect *prostatic cancer?*" Dr. Gifford-Jones, "Fear of Being Buried Alive Well-Founded," *Toronto Sun,* 19 Sept. 1996, at 59.

In fact, though, the phrase *prostate cancer* is about 100 times as common in print now as the more technical-sounding version. For example, in his 1996 book, Michael Korda used the title *Man to Man: Surviving Prostate Cancer.* That's the form that reflects common usage. The other is something of an affectation best left confined to the medical dictionaries.

B. And *prostrate*. These are very different words, but they are sometimes confused. In the verb sense, to *prostrate* oneself is to kneel down in humility or adoration. As an adjective, *prostrate* means either "lying facedown" or "emotionally overcome." (See **prone**.) The noun *prostate,* by contrast, refers to the gland found in male mammals, surrounding the urethra at the base of the bladder.

The most common mistake is to write **prostrate gland* instead of *prostate gland*—e.g.:

- "For operations on major blood vessels and the *prostrate* [read *prostate*] gland, the death rate was 200." "How Practice Makes Perfect," *Newsweek,* 7 Jan. 1980, at 39.
- "Brans are popular, as are palmetto products, which are said to help prevent the *prostrate* [read *prostate*] gland from becoming enlarged." Ronda Robinson, "Be Healthy," *Knoxville News-Sentinel,* 3 Dec. 1995, at E12.
- "During emission, the capsule of the *prostrate* [read *prostate*] gland contracts simultaneously with the contractions of the vas deferens so that the thin, milky fluid of the *prostrate* [read *prostate*] glands adds further to the bulk of the semen." Ritu Jain, *Secrets of Homoeopathy* 167 (2007).

LANGUAGE-CHANGE INDEX
*prostrate gland for *prostate gland*: Stage 1
Current ratio (*prostate gland* vs.
*prostrate gland): 97:1

prostrate. See **prone** & **prostate (B)**.

protagonist. A. Generally. Literally, *protagonist* = the chief character in a drama. By extension, it means "a champion of a cause." It should not be used loosely in reference to any character in a drama or any supporter of a cause—only to the chief one. But the SLIPSHOD EXTENSION is commonplace—e.g.:

- "Its half-dozen intertwined *protagonists* [read *characters*], all played by fine, serious actors, are sensitive, right-thinking human beings who worry about the world." Kenneth Turan, " 'Canyon': Trying to Bridge Life's Chasms," *L.A. Times,* 25 Dec. 1991, at F1.
- "In a national daily yesterday, half a dozen leading Festival *protagonists* [read *supporters*] were asked for a bet on the meeting." Chris Mcgrath, "Banking on Mulligan," *Sporting Life,* 11 Mar. 1997, at 2.

LANGUAGE-CHANGE INDEX
protagonist in the sense "any character": Stage 2

B. And *proponent*. Perhaps the most objectionable watering-down of the meaning of *protagonist* occurs when it is used as an equivalent of *proponent*—e.g.:

"Rep. Henry Gonzalez, the Texas Democrat who chairs the housing subcommittee, is the *protagonist* [read *proponent*] of this legislation that also would increase the number of adjustable rate mortgages the FHA may insure." "Senate Panel Action Gives Housing a User-Tax Victory," *San Diego Union-Trib.,* 27 Apr. 1986, at F23.

LANGUAGE-CHANGE INDEX
protagonist in the sense "proponent": Stage 2

C. And *antagonist*. Some writers mistakenly use *protagonist* when the word they were looking for was *antagonist* (= opponent)—e.g.:

- "Once again, longtime *protagonists* [read *antagonists*] Frank Thomas and Jerry Manuel are the focal points of a very public spat." Paul Sullivan, "Simple Resolution to Feud," *Chicago Trib.,* 9 July 2002, Sports §, at 1.
- "Uniting these longtime political *protagonists* [read *antagonists*] in a common cause underscores the inaugural's theme of 'bringing Californians together,' [Gabriel] Sanchez said." Gregg Jones, "Low-Key Inauguration Planned for Davis' Second Term," *L.A. Times,* 29 Dec. 2002, Cal. Metro §, pt. 2, at 1.
- "The two longtime *protagonists* [read *antagonists*], in a plot development that seems too good to be true given their relationship of late, will play together today in the final group in the final round of the Buick Invitational." Steve Elling, "Woods, Mickelson Ready to Rumble," *Orlando Sentinel,* 16 Feb. 2003, at C1.

LANGUAGE-CHANGE INDEX
protagonist misused for *antagonist*: Stage 2

D. Plural Use. If the *protagonist* is the main character in a play <Oedipus>, may we address more than one main character as *protagonists* <Romeo and Juliet>? H.W. Fowler decried the extensions of *protagonist* discussed in (B) and (C), but he also called the plural use "absurd." The *OED* disagrees, contending that "limitation to the singular is strictly relevant only in the context of ancient Greek drama." Today the plural is widely used and just as widely accepted—e.g.: "Everyone did a very good job, starting with the *protagonists,* Mitchell Bennett Schor as Little Joe and Eve Levin as Annette." Anne Midgette, "Sweet Take for a Child, but a Dark Side, Too," *N.Y. Times,* 18 Feb. 2003, at E3.

protectable; *protectible. The former now predominates: it's about three times as common as its variant. See -ABLE (A).

Current ratio: 3:1

*protected order. See **protective order.**

protective; *protectory. As an adjective, the latter is a NEEDLESS VARIANT.

Current ratio: 9,951:1

protective order (= a restraining order or an order preventing some type of conduct) is sometimes incorrectly rendered **protected order*—e.g.: "Russell William McKay, 38, was arrested Sept. 18, for violation of *protected* [read *protective*] order." Police Blotter, *Tennessean,* 3 Nov. 2002, at W14. In some states, the variant *order of protection* is standard, especially in relation to domestic violence.

LANGUAGE-CHANGE INDEX
protected order for *protective order*: Stage 1
Current ratio (*protective order* vs.
*protected order): 610:1

protégé (= someone whose career has been cultivated and promoted by a prominent mentor) has two acute accents. (See DIACRITICAL MARKS.) Although the term is not usually considered sex-specific, English has borrowed the feminine form as well from French: *protégée*. Both forms were first used in the 18th century.

protein used to be pronounced as three syllables. Today it's almost always /**proh**-teen/ instead of /**proh**-tee-ən/.

pro tem is a now-anglicized term derived from the abbreviation for *pro tempore* (= for the time being). No longer should this fairly common LATINISM be italicized. It is used as a POSTPOSITIVE ADJECTIVE in phrases such as *mayor pro tem*. Although it formerly required a period (i.e., *tem.*), today it is commonly and correctly used without one—e.g.:

- "Led by co-chairs Lt. Governor Jack Riggs, Idaho, and Indiana Deputy Speaker *Pro Tem* Susan Crosby, committee members approved four resolutions." "Health Capacity Task Force Committee Meets," *State Government News*, 1 June 2002, at 32.
- "Last Wednesday, police suspect a Superior Court *pro tem* judge got sauced, got into his Mercedes and proceeded to hit and kill an 18-year-old high school senior." Laurie Roberts, "Latest Road Outrage Doubly Outrageous," *Ariz. Republic*, 9 Apr. 2003, at B3.

protest, n.; **protestation.** The difference is that *protest* (/**proh**-test/), the ordinary word, usually refers to a formal statement or action of dissent or disapproval, whereas *protestation*, a learned word, generally denotes a solemn affirmation <protestations of love>.

protest, vb., is transitive or intransitive in AmE, but solely intransitive in most BrE writing. In BrE one writes, "They *protested against* discrimination," but not "They *protested* discrimination." Although he was writing on British usage only, Eric Partridge considered the latter, AmE usage incorrect and quoted an American writer as an offender against idiom (*U&A* at 248). The phrase *protest against* is common also in AmE <they protested against the government's decision>. In AmE, however, *against* is routinely omitted <they protested the government's decision>. The verb is preferably pronounced /prə-**test**/ in AmE and BrE alike.

protestation. See **protest,** n.

protester is the standard spelling. *Protestor* is a mere variant in all but one sense, in which the word is

capitalized: "a Scottish Presbyterian who protested against the union with the Royalists in 1650." Not common.

***prototypal.** See **prototypical.**

prototype. See **archetype.**

prototypical; ***prototypic;** ***prototypal.** The first is the usual and preferred form. The others are NEEDLESS VARIANTS. See **archetype.**

Current ratio (in order of headwords): 48:4:1

protozoan (= any of various single-celled organisms) is the standard spelling. *Protozoon is a variant. *Protozoan* makes the plural *protozoans* or, especially in collective reference, *protozoa*. See PLURALS (B).

protuberate is sometimes misspelled and mispronounced as if it were *protruberate, perhaps out of confusion with *protrude*. The noun and adjective, likewise, are *protuberance* and *protuberant*, without the invasive -*r*-:

- "Sylt-Ost—or 'eastern' Sylt, the *protruberance* [read *protuberance*] that seems to form the handle of the ax—is a rich expanse of green meadow, not unlike the flat North German plain." J.S. Marcus, "Germany's Fragile North Sea Playground," *N.Y. Times*, 5 June 1994, § 5, at 8.
- "Yayoi Kusama . . . became notorious in the 1960's for covering surfaces with phalluses. In the catalogue is a photograph of a room filled with furniture bristling with such *protruberances* [read *protuberances*], which, seemingly, are cast in plaster." Vivien Raynor, "An Exhibition Emphasizing the Feminist Role in Politics," *N.Y. Times*, 7 May 1995, § 13, at 24.

LANGUAGE-CHANGE INDEX
protuberate misspelled and mispronounced
*protruberate: Stage 1

proud; prideful. The connotative distinction to bear in mind is that *prideful* suggests excessive pride, haughtiness, and disdain. *Prideful* is also moralistic in tone.

proved; proven. Since the 17th century, *proved* has been the preferred past participle of *prove*. It has always been the preponderant form. But *proven* often ill-advisedly appears—e.g.:

- "Yet it was another 'Game of the Century,' matching teams that had *proven* [read *proved*] thus far to be unbeatable." Mark Blaudschun, "There's Always Time for a Turnaround," *Boston Globe*, 19 Sept. 1997, at D13.
- "He hasn't been *proven* [read *proved*] wrong yet." Thom Loverro, "Should Cal Take a Seat?" *Wash. Times*, 19 Sept. 1997, at B1.

In AmE, *proven*, like *stricken*, properly exists only as an adjective—e.g.:

- "All in all, the theory of group selection needs some beefing up before it steps onto the mat with the *proven* champion, individual selection, say both supporters and

---

LANGUAGE-CHANGE INDEX (For the full key, see front matter pp. xxxi, l–li.)
Stage 1: Rejected. **Stage 2:** Widely shunned. **Stage 3:** Widespread but . . . **Stage 4:** Ubiquitous but . . . **Stage 5:** Fully accepted.
Invariably inferior forms marked by asterisk (*). • Ratios represent frequency of prevalent forms vs. variants in current books.

critics." Virginia Morell, "Genes vs. Teams," *Science*, 9 Aug. 1996, at 739.

- "But that strategy of occupation and settlement is a *proven* failure—if the object is peace." "Stop Mideast Violence by Starting Peace Talks," *Palm Beach Post*, 31 July 1997, at A12.

Proven has survived as a past participle in legal usage in two phrases: first, in the phrase *innocent until proven guilty*; second, in the verdict *Not proven*, a jury answer no longer widely used except in Scots law. As for *Not proven*, one writer has defined this verdict as meaning, "Not guilty, but don't do it again." William Roughead, *The Art of Murder* 131 (1943). See IRREGULAR VERBS (B).

LANGUAGE-CHANGE INDEX
proven as a past participle: Stage 4
Current ratio (*experience has proved* vs.
experience has proven): 4:1

provenance. A. And *provenience*. Both are FORMAL WORDS for *origin* or *source*. *Provenance* (/**prah**-və-nints/ or /-nənts/) is the more usual word throughout the English-speaking world, usually in reference to art, antiques, artifacts, and other fields in which proof of authenticity is an issue. *Provenience* (/prə-**vee**-nyən[t]s/) is a chiefly AmE variant.

Current ratio: 19:1

B. Misused for *province*. *Provenance* is sometimes misused for *province* (= domain), a MALAPROPISM—e.g.:

- "Where 'The Full Monty' makes something akin to a political gesture is in drawing attention to the nude male body, a subject more typically the *provenance* [read *province*] of avant-garde artists and photographers than of big Broadway musicals." Reed Johnson, "Bare Truths of Character," *L.A. Times*, 21 Apr. 2002, § 6, at 8.
- "Large, complex documents, once the *provenance* [read *province*] of professional printers, were brought in-house to word processing departments years ago." Greta Ostrovitz, "Cadwalader Finds a Better Way to Train Staff," *N.Y.L.J.*, 28 May 2002, at 5.
- "If it thinks about it at all, popular opinion may hold that just intonation—the use of purely consonant tunings based on the overtone series—is the *provenance* [read *province*] of math geeks with synthesizers." Kyle Gann, "Overtones of Eternity," *Village Voice*, 4 June 2002, at 117.

LANGUAGE-CHANGE INDEX
provenance misused for *province*: Stage 1

provided that; providing that. The phrase *provided that* (= on condition that; if; as long as) is a shortened form of the ABSOLUTE CONSTRUCTION *it being provided that*. E.g.:

- "New Orleans restaurateur Ralph Brennan . . . may serve on the board of directors of a bank that does business with those two agencies, *provided that* he does not vote on matters involving the bank." Matt Scallan, "Ethics Officials Can't Fill in for Judges, Colleagues Say," *Times-Picayune* (New Orleans), 19 Sept. 1997, at B8.
- "If one parent is more affluent than the other, adequate child support from the better-off parent can permit the child to remain with the less wealthy parent, *provided that*

the custodial parent will manage the support money to benefit the child." Sara P. Schechter, "Tell Them to Stop Fighting," *Mothering*, 22 Sept. 1997, at 70.

*Providing that is a variant form that some grammarians consider inferior because it's not readily classifiable according to traditional grammar. (For an example of mid-20th-century disapproval of *providing* in this use, see Sophie C. Hadida, *Your Telltale English* 45 [rev. ed. 1942].) In fact, **providing that* frequently causes MISCUES <he predicted that the church would prosper and gave some $100,000, providing that support could be found also from other donors>. As a practical matter, **providing that* is especially apt to cause a miscue when *that* is elided—e.g.: "St. Luke's requested the tax exemption based on parts of state law that allow tax exemptions for property, *providing the company* [read *provided that the company*] doesn't profit by it." Ken Miller, "St. Luke's Tax Status Hinges on Definitions," *Idaho Statesman*, 20 July 1997, at A1. See **given (that)** & **that (B)**.

In fact, though, nine times out of ten the word *if* is a better choice than either *provided that* or **providing that*.

province. See **provenance (B)**.

provocative; *provocatory. The latter is a NEEDLESS VARIANT.

prox. See **inst.**

proximate; proximal. Both mean "lying very near or close." Yet *proximal* is primarily a technical, scientific term, whereas *proximate* is the ordinary term with the additional senses (1) "soon forthcoming; imminent"; (2) "next preceding"; and (3) "nearly accurate; approximate." See **approximate.**

prudent; prudential. "To call an act *prudent*," wrote H.W. Fowler, "is normally to commend it; to call it *-ial* is more often than not to disparage it" (*FMEU1* at 473). *Prudent* = exhibiting prudence <the detective's prudent withholding of judgment on the killing proved brilliant in the end>. *Prudential* = relating to, considered from the point of view of, or dictated by prudence <the senator opposed the policy on both moral and prudential grounds>. Writers sometimes use *prudential* where the shorter and simpler *prudent* would be a better fit—e.g.: "The Carnegie Endowment for International Peace recently released a thoughtful report arguing that the *prudential* [read *prudent*] course of action at present is to allow the inspections to continue." Joe Roidt, "Preventive War," *Charleston Gaz.*, 11 Feb. 2003, at A5.

LANGUAGE-CHANGE INDEX
prudential misused for *prudent*: Stage 1

prurience; *pruriency. The latter, standard through the 1930s, has become a NEEDLESS VARIANT.

Current ratio: 4:1

*pryer. See **prier.**

P.S.; postscript. The former (usually in capitals and with periods) is, of course, an abbreviation for the latter. In ordinary writing, you're better off spelling out the word—that is, "The postscript added nothing substantial to the letter" is clearer and smoother than "The P.S. added nothing substantial to the letter."

In letter-writing, a second postscript is abbreviated *P.P.S.* (for *post-postscript*).

pseudonym; alias; pen name; nom de plume; nom de guerre. A *pseudonym* is a fictitious name, especially (but not necessarily) one used by a writer. It is synonymous with *alias*, but is free of the criminal connotations that *alias* often carries. (See **alias.**) A *pen name* is a writer's pseudonym. *Nom de plume* is French for "pen name"—although most etymologists agree that the phrase was coined in English during the early 19th century from the French words. *Nom de guerre* is genuine French borrowed in the 17th century (lit., "war name"), denoting "an assumed name under which a person fights or engages in some other action or enterprise" (*SOED*)—e.g.: "On his first day there, he said, he met Mr. bin al-Shibh, known by his *nom de guerre*, Obeida." Desmond Butler & Don Van Natta Jr., "A Qaeda Informer Helps Investigators Trace Group's Trail," *N.Y. Times*, 17 Feb. 2003, at A1.

Unless a stylistic flourish is the desired effect, the two GALLICISMS are to be avoided.

For a truly outré error involving *pseudonym*, see **synonym.**

psych, vb.; **psyche,** n. & vb. *Psych* /sɪk/ = (1) to analyze psychologically <don't try to psych my behavior>; (2) to figure out and anticipate correctly <I psyched out my professors and made all A's>; (3) to use intimidating ploys against <but all his gamesmanship didn't psych her out>; or (4) to get mentally prepared for an event <she psyched herself up before the competition>. It is SLANG in all these senses. As a verb, *psyche* is a variant spelling. The predominant spelling of the PHRASAL VERB is *psych out*, not **psyche out*.

Psyche /sɪ-kee/ is best confined to its noun sense: "the human mind or soul."

Current ratio (*to psych out* vs. **to psyche out*): 2:1

*psychal. See **psychic.**

psychedelic. So spelled—not **psychodelic*.

psychiatry (= the branch of medicine dealing with mental illness and behavioral disorders) is preferably and predominantly pronounced /sɪ-kɪ-ə-tree/ in AmE and BrE alike—with a long *-i-* sound in the first syllable. The pronunciation that makes the first syllable *sick* is unfortunate, to say the least. The same goes for all three cognates (*psychiatrist, psychiatric, psychiatrically*). For the difference between *psychiatry* and *psychology*, see **psychology.**

psychic; psychical; *psychal; psychological. *Psychic* = (1) of, relating to, or involving the psyche; (2) spiritual; or (3) paranormal. *Psychical* (= of, relating to, or involving the mind) is contrasted with *physical*. **Psychal* is a NEEDLESS VARIANT. *Psychological* = (1) of, relating to, or of the nature of psychology; dealing with psychology; or (2) of, relating to, or involving the objects of psychological study; of, relating to, or involving the mind; mental (*OED*). The *OED* states that sense 2 of *psychological* is a loose usage, but it is now firmly established.

psycho. See **psychopath.**

*psychodelic. See **psychedelic.**

psychological. See **psychic.**

psychological moment entered the English language as the result of a misinterpretation. The phrase *das psychologische Moment* has been traced back to the 1870 German siege of Paris. A German magazine urged that the bombardment of the city be delayed until it would have the greatest psychological momentum (*das psychologische Moment*) to build on famine, disorder, and other effects of the siege and act as the final blow to crush French morale. A French translator misinterpreted *das Moment* ("momentum") as *der Moment* ("the moment"). The phrase was fashionably ridiculed in France, where it was rendered *moment psychologique* (= the moment in which the mind anticipates something that will happen).

The phrase was quickly picked up by English newspapers in a still more mistaken sense of "the psychologically appropriate moment." By 1926 it was overused to the point of becoming "hackneyed," according to H.W. Fowler's *Dictionary of Modern English Usage*. Today it is often used in reference to a psychological effect—e.g.: "Resources were measured, conserved and released at just the right *psychological moments*. Beethoven knew, and Delfs knows, that convincing emotional outburst paradoxically requires patience. Thus the extraordinary amount of 'waiting music' in this symphony, long moments where the composer marks time between themes or between spike events in the score. The patient calm enlarged the fury of the storm." Tom Strini, "Concerto's Elements a Perfect Fit," *Milwaukee J. Sentinel*, 16 June 2001, at B6.

But the phrase is often used loosely to mean "the critical moment" or even "the nick of time," with reference to neither psychology nor the mind—e.g.: "Gately loves the complexity of the opera. 'It's an opera director's delight. You can really direct it like a play. . . . The action never stops, or when it does, it's a deep *psychological moment* [read *critical moment*] that doesn't feel like the action has stopped.'" Catherine Reese

---

LANGUAGE-CHANGE INDEX (For the full key, see front matter pp. xxxi, l–li.)
Stage 1: Rejected. **Stage 2:** Widely shunned. **Stage 3:** Widespread but . . . **Stage 4:** Ubiquitous but . . . **Stage 5:** Fully accepted.
Invariably inferior forms marked by asterisk (*). • Ratios represent frequency of prevalent forms vs. variants in current books.

Newton, "A Knight at the Opera: At Utah Opera, Verdi's Final Masterpiece, 'Falstaff,'" *Salt Lake Trib.*, 27 Feb. 2000, at D1.

psychology; psychiatry. *Psychology* is the science of the mind and behavior; *psychiatry* is the branch of medicine dealing with mental or behavioral disorders. A *psychiatrist* holds an M.D., whereas a *psychologist* does not.

psychopath; sociopath; antisocial personality; antisocial, n. The term *psychopath* is no longer common in clinical use among psychiatrists and psychologists because of the word's pejorative associations. The disparaging clipped form *psycho* undoubtedly contributed to the need for a shifting of vocabulary.

Instead, *sociopath* or *antisocial personality*—and the corresponding terms *sociopathy* /so-see-**ahp**-ə-thee/ and *antisocial personality disorder*—are now the generally accepted nomenclature among specialists. Not all sociopaths commit heinous crimes; indeed, many enter the professions and make a steady living (though not a good life). A sociopath is essentially someone who (1) is a pathological liar and misleader; (2) has a minimal investment in moral values; (3) has no conscience—i.e., feels no remorse for harm caused to others; (4) has little or no regard for others' rights, safety, and property; (5) is often angry or hostile; (6) exhibits callousness toward others' feelings; (7) tends to defend shortcomings or failures by going on the offensive against others; (8) tries to manipulate others' emotions; and (9) tends to act impulsively, without regard for the consequences. See *Psychodynamic Diagnostic Manual* 601 (2006). One study, Martha Stout's *The Sociopath Next Door* (2005), reports that 4% of the population is afflicted with antisocial personality disorder—more men than women.

Often *antisocial personality* is shortened to *antisocial*—e.g.: "[With] the covetous *antisocial* . . . , aggrandizement, the desire to possess and dominate, is seen in a distilled form: These individuals feel that life has not given them 'their due'; they have been deprived of their rightful amount of love, support, or material reward; and others have received more than their share." Theodore Millon et al., *Personality Disorders in Modern Life* 158 (2d ed. 2004).

Although *psychopath* and *sociopath* are generally thought to be interchangeable with *antisocial*, some writers suggest a distinction: "[O]ne often used distinction between *psychopath* and *sociopath* is the user's belief in the origins of the disorder. Psychopaths are believed to possess some constitutional disposition to the syndrome. In contrast, sociopaths are biologically normal, but develop antisocial characteristics through incompetent or hostile socialization, mainly defective parenting." *Ibid.* at 153.

pubes (= [1] a person's external genitals; or [2] pubic hair) has two syllables /**pyoo**-beez/. It's often mispronounced /pyoobz/.

Language-Change Index
pubes /**pyoo**-beez/ mispronounced /pyoobz/: Stage 4

public, a collective noun, usually takes a singular verb in AmE <public is> and a plural verb in BrE <public are>.

publicly, not **publically*, is the adverb—e.g.:

- "Marlin Fitzwater, the President's spokesman, said Mr. Bush felt assured that Dr. Sullivan, whatever his private views might be, would *publically* [read *publicly*] support the President's policy of opposing abortion in almost all cases." Steven V. Roberts, "Bush Will Stand by Nominee to Health Post, Officials Say," *N.Y. Times*, 25 Jan. 1989, at 1.
- "But McCurdy was *publically* [read *publicly*] critical of Clinton after losing a Senate race in Oklahoma this year." Chris Black, "CIA Candidate List Has 2 from Region," *Boston Globe*, 30 Dec. 1994, Nat'l §, at 2.

See -IC.

Language-Change Index
publicly misspelled **publically*: Stage 1
Current ratio: 194:1

pudendum forms the plural *pudenda* (= the external genitals, esp. those of the female). The plural form, pronounced /pyoo-**den**-də/, is much more common—even when the reference is to one person. (See plurals (b).) In the following sentence, it's not clear which one of two noted writers might have misused the plural as a singular (perhaps it was both): "Erica Jong raised her hand to say, 'I think we should talk about how men hate women writers. Paul Theroux once called me *a* giant *pudenda*.'" Leah Garchik, "War Between the Literary Sexes," *S.F. Chron.*, 2 Apr. 1997, at E8. The usage point—that it should have been *a giant pudendum*—gets lost in the far-fetched metaphor.

puerile (= childishly silly; ridiculously juvenile) is pronounced /**pyoor**-əl/ in AmE and /**pyoor**-il/ in BrE. *Puerility*, however, is the same in both: /pyuu-**ril**-i-tee/.

puissant (= strong, powerful), a gallicism borrowed into English in the 15th century and frequently used by Shakespeare, is preferably pronounced /**pwis**-ənt/ or /**pwee**-sənt/ in AmE and BrE alike. Avoid such doubly anglicized and decoupled diphthongs as /**pyoo**-i-sint/ and /pyoo-**is**-ənt/.

Pulitzer. The name is preferably pronounced /**puul**-it-sər/, not /**pyoo**-lit-sər/.

pummel. See **pommel.**

pumpkin is often misspelled **pumkin*—e.g.: "It will begin with ravioli stuffed with pureed *pumkin* [read *pumpkin*] in a nutmeg cream." Chris Sherman, "Gala Night to Have Grand Menu Series," *St. Petersburg Times*, 5 Nov. 1996, at B2. The word is pronounced /**pəmp**-kin/, not /**pəng**-kin/—unless, as Elster says, "you're joking or using it as a term of endearment for a child" (*BBBM* at 399).

Punctuation is the cuing system by which writers signal their readers to slow down, pause, speed up, supply tonal inflections, and otherwise move more smoothly through sentences. Punctuation is an aspect of rhetoric: a way of giving emphasis and rhythm and achieving clarity. Meanwhile, punctuation problems are often a prime indicator of poor writing: "Most errors of punctuation arise from ill-designed, badly shaped sentences, and from the attempt to make them work by means of violent tricks with commas and colons." Hugh Sykes Davies, *Grammar Without Tears* 167 (1951).

The basic marks—and their uses—are well known. Yet each one sometimes presents difficulties. Even the best writers should pay close attention to these matters because the more sophisticated the writing is, the subtler and more varied the punctuation becomes. And punctuating well is essential to writing solid sentences.

A. Apostrophe [']. This punctuation mark does three things. First, it often indicates the possessive case <Charles Alan Wright's treatise> <Jane Ortiz's appointment>. See POSSESSIVES. Second, it frequently marks the omission of one or more elements and the contracting of the remaining elements into a word (or figure)—e.g.: *never* into *ne'er*; *will not* into *won't*; *1997* into *'97*. See CONTRACTIONS. Third, it is sometimes used to mark the plural of an acronym, initialism, number, or letter—e.g.: *CPA's* (now more usually *CPAs*), *1990's* (now more usually *1990s*), and *p's and q's* (still with apostrophes because of the single letters). See DATES (D) & NUMERALS (D).

Two contradictory trends—both bad—are at work with apostrophes.

First, careless writers want to form plurals with wayward apostrophes—e.g.: "The *bishop's* [read *bishops*] of the United Methodist Church have issued an urgent appeal for funds to assist the victims of flooding in the Midwest." Monte Marshall, "Special Offering for Flood Relief," *United Methodist Rep.*, 3 Sept. 1993. The same problem occurs in third-person-singular verbs: In the early 1990s, a sign at an Austin service station read, "Joe *say's*: It's time to winterize your car." And a distressing number of signs on mailboxes and entryways are printed, e.g., *The Smith's* [read *The Smiths*].

The second unfortunate trend is to drop necessary apostrophes: there is a tendency to write *the hotels many shops* or *Martins Pub*. The only possible cure is increased literacy.

Finally, U.S. place names drop possessive and associative apostrophes by government policy, so what was once Harper's Ferry, West Virginia, became Harpers Ferry. President Theodore Roosevelt charged the U.S. Board on Geographic Names in 1906 with standardizing place names. One resulting policy is that each name become a "fixed label" so that, under this questionable rationale, "[t]he need to imply possession or association no longer exists." ("Principles, Policies, and Procedures," geonames.usgs.gov/docs/pro_pol_pro.pdf, at 42.) Contracting apostrophes <Lake O' the Pines> and surname apostrophes <O'Bannon Mill> remain.

B. Bullet [•]. This mark draws the eye immediately to one of several enumerated items. When you don't mean to imply that one thing in a list is any more important than another—that is, when you're not signaling a rank order—and when there is little likelihood that the list will need to be cited, you might use bullet dots. They enhance readability by emphasizing salient points. Examples appear throughout this book (see, for example, the bullets under (C)).

There is a notable difference, however, between how the bullets appear in this book and how they ought to appear in most documents. Although here the bullets fall at the left margin, they should generally be indented at least as far as a paragraph indent or perhaps a little more. They are not indented here because the double-column format would make indentation look strange.

Here are seven more tips on using bullets well: (1) end your introduction with a colon, which serves as an anchor; (2) keep the items grammatically parallel (see PARALLELISM); (3) if you begin each item with a lowercase letter, put a semicolon at the end of each item, use *and* after the next-to-last item, and put a period after the last item; (4) if you begin each item with a capital—by convention, "fragments" are acceptable units here—end each with a period; (5) use hanging indents, which are extremely important in giving each bullet its full weight (see DOCUMENT DESIGN (H)); (6) ensure that the bullets are well proportioned both in their size and in their distance from the text they introduce, preferably with no more than one blank character-space between the bullet and the first word; and (7) resist the temptation to play with hollow characters, smiley faces, check marks, and the like—unless you're trying for an offbeat appearance, use real bullet dots.

C. Colon [:]. This mark, which promises the completion of something just begun, has five uses.

First, it may link two separate clauses or phrases by indicating a step forward from the first to the second: the step may be from an introduction to a main theme, from a cause to an effect, from a general statement to a particular instance, or from a premise to a conclusion. E.g.:

- "Boeing left some chips on the table: It agreed to give up the exclusive-supplier agreements it had negotiated with American Airlines, Delta Air Lines, and Continental Airlines." "Boeing–McDonnell Gets a Thumbs-Up," *Business-Week*, 4 Aug. 1997, at 42.
- "Economists point to day care's problems as a classic case of 'market failure': Large numbers of parents need the service so they can work, but they are not willing to pay the fees that would be necessary for the well-trained, highly motivated workers they would like their children to have." Victoria Pope, "Day-Care Dangers," *U.S. News & World Rep.*, 4 Aug. 1997, at 31, 34.
- "My assignment: Identify and contact the CIOs for 100 companies that were selected on the basis of their

LANGUAGE-CHANGE INDEX (For the full key, see front matter pp. xxxi, l–li.)
Stage 1: Rejected. **Stage 2:** Widely shunned. **Stage 3:** Widespread but . . . **Stage 4:** Ubiquitous but . . . **Stage 5:** Fully accepted.
Invariably inferior forms marked by asterisk (*). • Ratios represent frequency of prevalent forms vs. variants in current books.

productive and innovative use of information technology." Megan Santosus, "Putting Along," *CIO*, Aug. 1997, at 118.

- "Nor did the evidence submitted resolve the real question: whether Jackson is in fact Cosby's daughter." Matt Bai & Allison Samuels, "No Laughing Matter," *Newsweek*, 4 Aug. 1997, at 33.

As in the examples just quoted, what follows the colon may be either a full clause or just a phrase.

Authorities agree that when a phrase follows a colon, the first word should not be capitalized (unless, of course, it's a proper noun). But when a complete clause follows the colon, authorities are divided on whether the first word should be capitalized. The first three bulleted examples in the preceding paragraph follow the prevalent journalistic practice: the first word is capitalized. But the other view—urging for a lowercase word following the colon—is probably sounder: the lowercase (as in this very sentence) more closely ties the two clauses together. That's the style used throughout this book. It's also the house style for *The New Yorker*—e.g.:

- "Though active, El Misti isn't doing anything at the moment, but Arequipa is: it has spread up the volcano's flanks along the gullies where lava and ash will someday begin to flow." Tad Friend, "Disaster!" *New Yorker*, 16 Dec. 2002, at 36, 38.
- "Party lines are not to be confused with chat lines, party planners, or escort services: they are a prehistoric phone technology of copper-loop circuits." Susan Orlean, "Party Line," *New Yorker*, 16 Dec. 2002, at 52.

Although the uppercase convention is a signpost to the reader that a complete sentence is ahead, that signpost generally isn't needed.

Those who follow the lowercase convention typically recognize an exception and capitalize what follows the colon when the colon introduces a series of sentences: "He made three points: He wanted some water. He needed to sleep. And he wanted to go home."

Second, the colon can introduce a list of items, often after expressions such as *the following* and *as follows*—e.g.: "The meetings are as follows: Central, Dec. 11 at the Municipal Auditorium, 5:30 p.m.–7:30 p.m.; South, Dec. 15 at the Mexican Cultural Institute, 5:30 p.m.–7:30 p.m." Megan Kamerick, "Main Plaza Considered as Site of Museum on Mexico's History," *San Antonio Bus. J.*, 12 Dec. 1997, at 6.

Third, the colon formally introduces a wholly self-contained quotation, whether short or long. If the quotation is in block form, the colon is mandatory, but if it's run in with the text, a comma is also permissible. E.g.: "By 1776 it seemed clear to numerous inhabitants of the western areas of the Connecticut River valley that the fight against tyranny had assumed a two-fold character: 'We are contending against the same enemy within, that is also without.'" Gordon S. Wood, *Creation of the American Republic* 186 (1972).

Fourth, the colon often appears after the salutation in formal correspondence <Dear Ms. Johnsonius:>.

Finally, the colon separates elements such as a book's title and subtitle <*Will Rogers: A Biography*>,

chapter and verse in a biblical citation <John 3:16>, hour and minute in time <9:05 PM>, and similar uses.

Avoid four common misuses of the colon. (1) Don't put one between a verb and its object or complement <she enjoys watching plays, films, and TV shows> (no colon after *watching*). (2) Don't put a colon between a preposition and its object <they are enamored of rare books, bone china, and etched glass> (no colon after *of*). (3) Don't put a colon after the conjunction *that* <he declared that all the plants on board must be quarantined>. (4) Don't put a colon after an introductory word or phrase such as *for example, including, such as*, or *that is* <several dignitaries were present, including Vice President Joseph Biden, Senator John Cornyn, and Justice Antonin Scalia> (no colon after *including*). Even so, as noted above, a colon is often appropriate after a phrase that more formally announces a list (e.g., *as follows, the following, including these*).

D. Comma [,]. This punctuation mark, the least emphatic of them all, is the one used in the greatest variety of circumstances. Two styles result in different treatments. The "close" style of punctuation results in fairly heavy uses of commas; the "open" style results in fairly light uses of commas. In the 20th century, the movement was very much toward the open style. The byword was, "When in doubt, leave it out." Indeed, some writers and editors went too far in omitting commas that would aid clarity. What follows is an explanation tending slightly toward the open style, but with a steady view toward enhancing clarity.

Essentially, the comma has nine uses.

First, the comma separates items (including the last from the next-to-last) in a list of more than two—e.g.: "The Joneses, the Smiths, and the Nelsons." In this position, it's called, variously, the serial comma, the Oxford comma, or the Harvard comma. Whether to include the serial comma has sparked many arguments. But it's easily answered in favor of inclusion because omitting the final comma may cause ambiguities, whereas including it never will—e.g.: "A and B, C and D, E and F[,] and G and H." When the members are compound, calling for *and* within themselves, clarity demands the final comma. (See ENUMERATIONS (B).) Although newspaper journalists typically omit the serial comma as a "space-saving" device, virtually all writing authorities outside that field recommend keeping it—e.g.:

> When you write a series of nouns with *and* or *or* before the last one, insert a comma before the *and* or *or*. "The location study covered labor, tax, freight, and communications costs, all in terms of 1972 prices." While this rule is not observed by all publishers, it is valid and helpful. Professional magazines follow it frequently, and such authorities as David Lambuth support it. The reason is that the comma before the *and* helps the reader to see instantly that the last two adjectives are not joined. In the example cited, suppose the last comma in the series is omitted; *freight and communications costs* could then be read as one category, though it is not meant to be.
>
> David W. Ewing, *Writing for Results in Business, Government, and the Professions* 358 (1974).

Examples abound. In the following sentence, for example, is Toby the terrier a gift, or is Toby the terrier getting a little plastic surgery? "Federal officials said that the Delle Donnas received $26,700 in cash and gifts from Ms. Medrano, including gift cards for Macy's, plastic surgery for Mrs. Delle Donna and a Yorkshire terrier named Toby valued at $2,300." Jonathan Miller, "Mayor Is Convicted in Extortion Case," *N.Y. Times*, 30 Apr. 2008, at B3. The serial comma would prevent the MISCUE.

Second, the comma separates coordinated main clauses—e.g.: "Cars will turn here[,] and coaches will go straight." There are two exceptions: (1) when the main clauses are closely linked <Do as I tell you [no comma] and you won't regret it>; and (2) when the subject of the second independent clause, being the same as in the first, is not repeated <Policies that help prevent crime are often better for the public [no comma] and are closer to the ideal of effective public administration>. (Another way of referring to the construction in that sentence is that it contains a "compound predicate.") Omitting the comma before the *and* in a compound sentence often causes an ambiguity or MISCUE:

- "I would love to see her and the baby and I will be here all day." (Insert a comma after *baby*; otherwise, it might appear that the baby and the writer will be there all day.)
- "No one claimed responsibility for the attack nor for once were Chechen guerrillas seen as the prime suspects." Sander Thoenes, "Russia Rivals Trade Insults over Moscow Bombing," *Fin. Times*, 13 June 1996, at 2. (Insert a comma after *attack*; otherwise, it looks as if *for once* is parallel to *for the attack*.)

Third, the comma separates most introductory matter from the main clause, often to prevent misunderstanding. The introductory matter may be a word <Moreover,>, a phrase <In the meantime,>, or a subordinate clause <If everything goes as planned,>. Matter that is very short may not need this comma <On Friday we leave for Florida>, but phrases of three or more words usually do—and even the shortest of subordinate clauses always do <That said,>. On the other hand, a comma may prove helpful for clarity even with shorter phrases <For now, we must assume the worst>. It may even be imperative <Outside, the world goes on>.

Fourth, the comma marks the beginning and end of a parenthetical word or phrase, an appositive, or a nonrestrictive clause—e.g.: "I am sure[,] however[,] that it will not happen."/ "Fred[,] who is bald[,] complained of the cold." Some writers mistakenly omit the second comma—e.g.: "After graduating from Rosemary Hall, an exclusive Greenwich girls' school in 1965, Ms. Close began touring with Up With People, the squeaky-clean pop group." Betsy Sharkey, "Glenn Close: So Visible a Star, So Distant," *N.Y. Times*, 27 Mar. 1994, at 2-1, 2-30. (Insert a comma after *school*

or, better, put *in 1965* after *graduating*.) Still others omit both commas, often creating a MISCUE: "Our customers must be at a minimum priority concerns of everyone." (Insert a comma after *be* and after *minimum*; otherwise, one might read *at a minimum priority* as a single phrase.)

Fifth, the comma separates adjectives that each qualify a noun in the same way <a cautious[,] reserved person>. If you could use *and* between the adjectives, you'll need a comma—e.g.: "Is there to be one standard for the *old, repulsive* laws that preferred whites over blacks, and a *different, more forgiving* standard for new laws that give blacks special benefits in the name of historical redress?" Linda Greenhouse, "Signal on Job Rights," *N.Y. Times*, 25 Jan. 1989, at 1. But when adjectives qualify the noun in different ways, or when one adjective qualifies a noun phrase containing another adjective, no comma is used. In these situations, it would sound wrong to use *and*—e.g.: "a distinguished [no comma] foreign journalist"; "a bright [no comma] red tie." Writers often include the comma when it isn't necessary—e.g.: "The centerpiece of the Senate GOP package, which could be presented to the Senate Finance Committee for a vote as early as next week, is a *permanent, $500-per-child* [read *permanent $500-per-child*] tax credit for families. . . . Effective in 1996, families would be granted a *new, $500* [read *new $500*] tax credit for each child." Jonathan Peterson, "Key GOP Senators OK $245 Billion in Tax Cuts," *L.A. Times*, 15 Oct. 1995, at A1. See ADJECTIVES (C).

Sixth, the comma separates a direct quotation from its attribution <"Honey, I'm home," Desi said>, but it is not used to separate quoted speech that is woven into the syntax of the sentence <TV loves catchphrases such as "Honey, I'm home">.

Seventh, the comma separates a participial phrase, a verbless phrase, or a vocative—e.g.: "Having had breakfast[,] I went for a walk."/ "The sermon *over* [or *being over*], the congregation filed out."/ "Fellow priests[,] the clergy must unite in reforming the system of electing bishops." Note, however, that no comma is needed within an absolute construction—e.g.: "The sermon [no comma] being over, we all left." (See ABSOLUTE CONSTRUCTIONS.) Nor is a comma needed with restrictive expressions such as "my friend Professor Wright" or "my son John" (assuming that the writer has at least one other son—see APPOSITIVES).

Eighth, in informal letters the comma marks the end of the salutation <Dear Mr. Crosthwaite[,]> <Dear Rebecca[,]> and the complimentary close <Very truly yours[,]> <Yours sincerely[,]>. In formal letters, the salutation is separated from the body by a colon <Dear Sir[:]> <Dear Madam[:]>.

Finally, the comma separates parts of an address <#8 Country Club Dr., Amherst, Massachusetts> or a date <March 2, 1998>. Note that in these examples,

LANGUAGE-CHANGE INDEX (For the full key, see front matter pp. xxxi, l–li.)
Stage 1: Rejected. **Stage 2:** Widely shunned. **Stage 3:** Widespread but . . . **Stage 4:** Ubiquitous but . . . **Stage 5:** Fully accepted.
Invariably inferior forms marked by asterisk (∗). • Ratios represent frequency of prevalent forms vs. variants in current books.

the state in the address and the year in the date are parenthetical, so each would ordinarily take a comma or some other punctuation after it (unless the place name or date were used as an adjective—see ADJECTIVES (D) & DATES (C)). Note also that no comma is needed between the month and year in dates written "December 1984" or "18 December 1984"; a comma is required only when the date is written "December 18, 1984." See DATES (B).

Writers cause needless confusion or distraction for their readers when they insert commas erroneously. This typically occurs in one of four ways.

(1) Some writers insert a comma before the verb—something that was once standard. But the practice has been out of fashion since the early 20th century, and today it's considered incorrect—e.g.: "Whether or not the shoes were bought at our store, [omit the comma] is not something we have yet been able to ascertain."/ "Only if this were true, [omit the comma] could it be said that John F. Kennedy was a great president." Even those who understand this principle are sometimes tempted to place a comma after a compound element that doesn't require one. Avoid the temptation—e.g.: "Teachers who do not have a Ph.D., a D.M.A., or an M.A., [omit the comma] do not qualify for the pay raise."

(2) Commas frequently set off an adverb that doesn't need setting off. The result is a misplaced emphasis—e.g.: "We, *therefore*, [read *therefore* without the embracing commas] conclude that the mummy could not be authentic." Note that if the emphasis in that sentence is intended for some reason to fall on *We*—as clearly separated from some other group and its thinking—the commas should stand; but if the emphasis is to fall on *therefore* as a simple consequence of reasoning from the evidence, then the commas should be omitted. See **therefore (A).**

(3) In compound sentences, an unnecessary comma is sometimes inserted before a second independent clause when the subject is the same as in the first clause. (As some grammarians put it, a comma shouldn't appear before the second part of a "compound predicate.") As explained above in the second rationale for using this mark, no comma appears before the conjunction when the second clause has an understood subject—e.g.: "They did their spring cleaning, and then had a picnic." (Delete the comma.) Sometimes, though, a comma is needed for clarity—e.g.: "We like to have wine and ham it up on weekends." (Insert a comma after *wine*.)

(4) Some writers (even some otherwise excellent ones) mistakenly use a comma as if it were a stronger mark—a semicolon or a period. The result is a comma splice—e.g.: "He said he didn't want to look, he wanted to remember her as she was in life." (Replace the comma with a semicolon; see RUN-ON SENTENCES.) This also occurs in series of phrases or clauses that themselves contain commas. Semicolons rather than commas are often needed to separate the elements in complex series—e.g.: "We celebrate the

Fourth by flying the red, white, and blue; honoring baseball, Mom, and apple pie; and shouting hip, hip, hooray as the fireworks burst."

E. Dash. There are two kinds of dashes, which printers are able to distinguish by their length: the em-dash and the en-dash. See (G), (H).

F. Ellipsis Dots [. . .]. Ellipsis points—also called "period-dots"—come in threes. Each one is typographically identical to the period, but together they perform a special function: they signal that the writer has omitted something, usually from quoted matter. Consider the following sentence: "Shakespeare's speech—as exhibited in his works, at least—seems to have represented rather well the cultivated usage of Elizabethan England, particularly in the area around London; and what is more, it was sensitive to social levels." Carroll E. Reed, *Dialects of American English* 10 (1967). If you quoted that sentence but omitted some words from the middle and at the end, it would look like this: "Shakespeare's speech . . . seems to have represented rather well the cultivated usage of Elizabethan England, particularly in the area around London . . . ." The final period-dot in that quotation, which is spaced evenly with the other three, is simply the period for the sentence; it's not technically part of the ellipsis.

For a more detailed explanation of ellipses, see QUOTATIONS (E).

G. Em-Dash [—]. The *em-dash*, which is as wide as the capital *M*, is used to mark an interruption in the structure of a sentence. In typewriting, it is commonly represented by two hyphens, often with a space at each end of the pair (--). Word-processing programs can place a true em-dash, but the procedure varies among programs. A pair of em-dashes can be used to enclose a parenthetical remark or to mark the ending and the resumption of a statement by an interlocutor. E.g.: "The last time I saw him I asked him if he still believed—as he once had written—'that we are at this moment participating in one of the very greatest leaps of the human spirit to a knowledge not only of outside human nature but also of our own deep inward mystery.'" Bill Moyers, Introduction to Joseph Campbell, *The Power of Myth* xix (Betty Sue Flowers ed., 1988).

The em-dash can also be used to replace the colon—e.g.:

- "On July 22, the company was awarded the largest privatization contract ever for a prison—a 2,048-bed minimum-security facility in Taft, Calif." "Wackenhut Wins Its Prison Bid," *BusinessWeek*, 4 Aug. 1997, at 42.
- "She returned to singing in 1996—after a stroke and complications from diabetes forced her to have both legs amputated." Suzanne Braun Levine, "My Secret Predawn Rite," *Newsweek*, 4 Aug. 1997, at 12.

The em-dash is perhaps the most underused punctuation mark in American writing. Whatever the type of writing, dashes can often clarify a sentence that is clogged up with commas—or even one that's otherwise lusterless. Imagine the following sentences if commas replaced the well-chosen em-dashes:

- "It is noteworthy that the most successful revolutions—that of England in 1688 and that of America in 1776—were carried out by men who were deeply imbued with a respect for law." Bertrand Russell, "Individual and Social Ethics" (1949), in *The Basic Writings of Bertrand Russell* 357, 358 (1961).
- "Unfortunately, moral beauty in art—like physical beauty in a person—is extremely perishable." Susan Sontag, *Against Interpretation* 55 (1966).
- "When David Nemer sat down with his 12-year-old daughter one night recently to watch a television sitcom—a treat for finishing her homework early—he was shocked by the behavior he saw in his living room." Daniel Howard Cerone, "Adult Programming Invades Family Hour," *L.A. Times*, 15 Oct. 1995, at A1.
- "I heard this anecdote from Mikhail Gorbachev—who had heard it from Gromyko himself—when I paid him a visit, earlier this year, to talk about the vodka anniversary." Victor Erofeyev, "The Russian God," *New Yorker*, 16 Dec. 2002, at 56.
- "She tried not to think that all his verses about her—the sonnets, the villanelles, the haiku—were merely ploys to prepare her for this ridiculous rubber balloon." Arthur Miller, "The Bare Manuscript," *New Yorker*, 16 Dec. 2002, at 82, 86.

Sometimes, perhaps as a result of an ill-founded prejudice against dashes, writers try to make commas function in their place. Often this doesn't work. In fact, the commas can result in a comma splice (one of two types of RUN-ON SENTENCE)—e.g.: "Don't worry about making it pretty, they will do that, just make sure the mathematics is right." "Get Out Your Pencils," *Newsweek*, 4 Apr. 1994, at 8. (A possible revision: *Don't worry about making it pretty; they will do that. Just make sure the mathematics is right.*)

When using dashes, be sure to place them logically so that the PARALLELISM of the sentence remains intact. Sometimes writers put them in odd places—e.g.:

- "Criminologist Marvin Wolfgang compiled arrest records for every male born—and raised in Philadelphia—in 1945 and 1958." James Wootton, "Lessons of Pop Jordan's Death," *Newsweek*, 13 Sept. 1993, at 12. (A possible revision: *Marvin Wolfgang, a criminologist, compiled arrest records for every male who was both born in Philadelphia in either of two years—1945 and 1958—and raised there.* On the reason for changing the position of *criminologist* in that sentence, see TITULAR TOMFOOLERY.)
- "There were other cellars beyond an arch, containing nothing more than rats and rubbish *but—and that was—important*, they couldn't be seen from the cages." Terry Pratchett, *Night Watch* 167 (2002). (Perhaps the writer meant to put *important* before the second dash. Even if that were true, though, the sentence would have a problem with ANTICIPATORY REFERENCE—since the word *that* refers to something that hasn't yet been mentioned.)

Generally, two em-dashes are all a sentence can handle. With three, the reader loses track of what material is part of the main sentence and what is parenthetical. A long sentence might contain distinct pairs of em-dashes far apart without creating problems, but it's better to observe the two-em-dash limit.

Consider putting a letter space before and after an em-dash. Although most book publishers omit the spaces, outside fine typography the spaces help prevent awkward line breaks.

H. En-Dash [–]. The *en-dash*, which is half as wide as the *em-dash*, is distinct (in print) from the *hyphen*. It joins pairs or groups of words to show a range, and also indicates movement or tension (rather than cooperation or unity). It is often equivalent to *to* or *versus* <the 1914–1918 war> <the nature–nurture debate> <the Dallas–Toronto–Quebec route> <the Fischer–Spassky match> <the Marxist–Trotskyite split>. The en-dash is also used, however, for joint authors <the Prosser–Keeton text>. But it's not used for one person with a double-barreled name—e.g.: "Lord Baden-Powell's organization" (that's a hyphen, not an en-dash).

Some editors use the en-dash for a PHRASAL ADJECTIVE in which the individual elements contain spaces or internal hyphens <a Pulitzer Prize–winning author> <a Christopher Ricks–type literary critic><the secretary-treasurer–elect> <pre–Civil War society>.

In typewriting and in newspaper journalism, the en-dash is commonly represented by a single hyphen. Word-processing programs can insert a true en-dash, but the procedure varies among programs.

In circumstances involving a disjunction, the en-dash is usually preferable to the virgule—e.g.: "If we manage to get that far, the absurdity of attempting to preserve the 19th-century possessive–genitive dichotomy [not *possessive/genitive dichotomy*] will have become apparent." See (Q).

I. Exclamation Point [!]. This mark is used after an exclamatory word, phrase, or sentence. It usually counts as the concluding full stop—e.g.: "I can almost hear the producer saying, 'Cut! Too much talk!'" Phillip Lopate, "The Last Taboo," in *Dumbing Down: Essays on the Strip Mining of American Culture* 164, 173 (1996). If used within square brackets in or after a quotation, it expresses the quoter's amusement, dissent, or surprise.

J. Hyphen [-]. This mark has been called "the pest of the punctuation family" (Sophie C. Hadida, *Your Telltale English* 133 [rev. ed. 1942]). Generally, AmE is much less hospitable to hyphens than BrE. Words with prefixes are generally made solid: *displeasure* (not *dis-pleasure*), *preshrunk* (not *pre-shrunk*), *postdebate* (not *post-debate*), *preordain* (not *pre-ordain*). This no-hyphen style seems aesthetically superior, but reasonable people will differ on such a question. They can agree, however, that the hyphen must appear when an ambiguity or MISCUE is possible without it—e.g., *pre-judicial* (career), *re-sign* (the letter). See CO- & RE- PAIRS.

LANGUAGE-CHANGE INDEX (For the full key, see front matter pp. xxxi, l–li.)
Stage 1: Rejected. **Stage 2:** Widely shunned. **Stage 3:** Widespread but . . . **Stage 4:** Ubiquitous but . . . **Stage 5:** Fully accepted.
Invariably inferior forms marked by asterisk (*). • Ratios represent frequency of prevalent forms vs. variants in current books.

But in one context, AmE is quite hospitable to the hyphen. That's in the realm of PHRASAL ADJECTIVES. Here's the rule: if two or more consecutive words make sense only when understood together as an adjective modifying a noun that follows, those words (excluding the noun) should be hyphenated. So you hyphenate *special-interest money*, but only because *money* is part of the phrase; if you were referring to this or that *special interest*, a hyphen would be wrong. Thus:

credit card	*but*	credit-card application
electoral college		electoral-college procedures
forest products		forest-products stocks
high frequency		high-frequency sounds
natural gas		natural-gas pipeline
small business		small-business perspectives
used record		used-record store

Wilson Follett had it right when he said, in reference to this phrasal-adjective hyphen: "Nothing gives away the incompetent amateur more quickly than the typescript that neglects this mark of punctuation or that employs it where it is not wanted" (*MAU* at 428).

K. Parentheses [( )]. These marks enclose words, phrases, and even whole sentences (but usually no more than a whole paragraph). If what is enclosed is a full sentence, the closing parenthesis follows the end punctuation; if not, the end punctuation is placed outside, as in the previous sentence here. More specifically, parentheses are used in four ways. First, they indicate interpolations and remarks by the writer of the text <Mrs. X (as I shall call her) now spoke>. Second, they specify, in one's own running text, an authority, definition, explanation, reference, or translation <according to Fowler (*FMEU1* at 64), it is correct to . . . >. Third, in reporting a speech, they sometimes indicate interruptions by the audience <"Finally—(laughter)—no, I'm really coming to an end now—(laughter)—let me say . . .">. Fourth, parentheses separate reference letters or figures that do not need a full stop, e.g., (1)(a).

The first of those uses comes into play most frequently. The main test for whether a parenthetical construction works is whether the rest of the sentence makes sense without it. That's because words contained within parentheses do not affect the syntax of the rest of the sentence. E.g.: "We must determine whether each (or both) children are entitled to tickets." The writer of that sentence could have avoided this error (*each children are*) by reading the sentence without the parenthetical phrase.

Virtually any punctuation mark is subject to an annoying overuse, but this is especially true of parentheses, which to be effective must be used sparingly. When they appear at all frequently, they tire the reader's eye, add to the burden of decoding, and deaden the reader's interest. Sentences can sag with all the qualifying parentheticals.

On the use of parentheses with appositives, see APPOSITIVES.

L. Period [.]. This mark is used for two purposes. First, it ends all sentences that are not questions or exclamations. The next word normally begins with a capital letter. Second, it has traditionally indicated abbreviations, but this use is on the decline. See ABBREVIATIONS (A).

If a point marking an abbreviation comes at the end of a sentence, it also serves as the closing full stop. E.g.: "She also kept dogs, cats, birds, etc." But where a closing parenthesis or bracket intervenes, a period is required: "She also kept pets (dogs, cats, birds, etc.)." When a sentence concludes with a quotation that ends with a period, question mark, or exclamation mark, no further period is needed. E.g.: "He cried, 'Be off!' [no period] But the child would not move."

M. Question Mark [?]. A question mark follows every question for which an answer is expected. Typically, the next word begins with a capital letter. "He asked me, 'Why are you here?' A foolish question." But it's also possible to have a midsentence question mark—e.g.: "Why should what is supposed to be a sacrament be performed with everyone looking on?—with that most desolating of all assemblages, a family reunion." Edmund Wilson, "Things I Consider Overrated" (1920), in *From the Uncollected Edmund Wilson* 127 (1995). Most authorities recommend not placing a comma after the question mark in such a sentence; yet, though it seems a little old-fashioned, Wilson's em-dash after the question mark is quite acceptable.

A question mark is not used after indirect questions <He asked me why I was there>. See QUESTIONS, DIRECT AND INDIRECT.

A question mark may be placed in brackets after a word, phrase, or date whose accuracy is doubted <Cardinal Wolsey (1475?–1530)>.

N. Quotation Marks [" "]. Reserve quotation marks for five situations: (1) when you're quoting someone; (2) when you're referring to a word as a word <the word "that">, unless you're using italics for that purpose; (3) when you mean so-called-but-not-really <if he's a "champion," he certainly doesn't act like one>; (4) when you're creating a new word for something—and then only on its first appearance <I'd call him a "mirb," by which I mean . . . >; and (5) when you're marking titles of TV and radio programs, magazine articles, book chapters, poems, short stories, and songs <having been put on the spot, she sang "Auld Lang Syne" as best she could>.

In marking quotations, writers and editors of AmE and BrE have developed different conventions for quotation marks (or "inverted commas," as the British call them). In AmE, double quotation marks are used for a first quotation; single marks for a quotation within a quotation; double again for a further quotation inside that; etc. In BrE, the practice is exactly the reverse at each step.

With a closing quotation mark, practices vary. In AmE, it is usual to place a period or comma within the closing quotation mark, whether or not the punctuation so placed is actually a part of the quoted matter. In BrE, by contrast, the closing quotation mark comes before any punctuation marks, unless these marks form a part of the quotation itself (or what is quoted is *less* than a full sentence in its own right). Thus:

AmE: (1) "Joan pointedly said, 'We won't sing "God Save the Queen."'"
     (2) "She looked back on her school years as being 'unmitigated misery.'"

BrE: (1) 'Joan pointedly said, "We won't sing 'God Save the Queen.'"'
     (1) 'She looked back on her school years as being "unmitigated misery".'

In both sets of examples, the outermost quotation marks indicate that a printed source is being quoted directly.

With respect to question marks and exclamation marks, AmE and BrE practice is the same. They're either inside or outside the ending quotation mark depending on whether they're part of what's being quoted—e.g.: (AmE) "Did Nelson really say 'Kiss me, Hardy'?"/ (BrE) 'Did Nelson really say "Kiss me, Hardy"?' And: (AmE) "Banging her fist on the table, she exclaimed, 'And that's *that!*'"/ (BrE) 'Banging her fist on the table, she exclaimed, "And that's *that!*"' (Note that when the end of an interrogatory or an exclamatory sentence coincides with the end of another sentence that embraces it, the stronger mark of punctuation is sufficient to end *both* sentences. A period need not also be included.)

Colons and semicolons are placed outside quotation marks—e.g.: "John didn't shout 'Fire!'; he did, however, say that he smelled smoke."

As to quotations that are interrupted to indicate a speaker, AmE and BrE again show different preferences. In AmE, the first comma is placed within the quotation mark <"Sally," he said, "is looking radiant today">; in BrE, the first comma (usually) remains outside the inverted comma, just as though the attribution could be lifted neatly out of the speaker's actual words <'Sally', he said, 'is looking radiant today'>. See QUOTATIONS (D).

Finally, be cautious about using gratuitous quotation marks. The emphatic use is a sign of amateurish writing (and advertising). Don't use them for PHRASAL ADJECTIVES, don't use them to be cute, and don't use them to suggest that the marked word or phrase is somehow informal or slangy—it usually isn't. If you mean what you say, say it without hesitation. If you don't, then use other words. The following examples could be improved by removing the quotation marks and tweaking the sentences:

- "Features are the characteristics of a product or service that are 'built-in' when you buy it—in other words, 'the things it already comes with.'" Erica Levy Klein, *Write Great Ads* 33 (1990).
- "The individual, however, who truly 'made it happen' is our senior vice president, Jim Savage. . . . Since he and I are virtually always on the 'same page' in our philosophy and thoughts, I had a double advantage of having a

dedicated, experienced, bright collaborator who made a magnificent contribution." Zig Ziglar, *Ziglar on Selling* 16 (1991).

O. Semicolon [;]. This mark—a kind of "super-comma"—separates sentence parts that need a more distinct break than a comma can signal, but that are too closely connected to be made into separate sentences. Typically these will be clauses of similar importance and grammatical construction.

Four uses are common.

First, the semicolon is sometimes used to unite closely connected sentences; typically, as in this very sentence, there is no conjunction between clauses. E.g.: "But Shakespeare's language appears entirely familiar to us, although it is almost 400 years old; the spelling, the vocabulary, the shapes of the words and phrases seem to have changed but little in that time." W.F. Bolton, *A Short History of Literary English* 15 (1972). Often, such a semicolon signals an antithesis—e.g.:

- "He did not lead; he followed." John Wain, "Byron: The Search for Identity," in *Essays on Literature and Ideas* 85, 91 (1963).
- "The evil lover is not prudent; he is simply wicked." W. Ross Winterowd, *Rhetoric: A Synthesis* 13 (1968).
- "Malamud promises an oeuvre; Bellow, at fifty-one, has already achieved one." Anthony Burgess, "The Jew as American," in *Urgent Copy* 131, 132 (1968).

Some editors would argue that in the first two examples, the clauses are so short and interconnected that a comma could have been used instead of a semicolon, especially since there is no other internal punctuation. But the better practice is to use a semicolon rather than a comma. See the final paragraph of (D).

Second, the semicolon sometimes separates coordinate clauses in long, complex sentences. This use was much more common in the 19th century than it is today—e.g.:

- "But Elizabeth was not formed for ill-humour; and though every prospect of her own was destroyed for the evening, it could not dwell long on her spirits; and having told all her griefs to Charlotte Lucas, whom she had not seen for a week, she was soon able to make a voluntary transition to the oddities of her cousin, and to point him out to her in particular notice." Jane Austen, *Pride and Prejudice* 80 (1813; repr. 1990).
- "The system which had addressed him in exactly the same manner as it had addressed hundreds of other boys, all varying in character and capacity, had enabled him to dash through his tasks, always with fair credit, and often with distinction; but in a fitful, dazzling way that had confirmed his reliance on those very qualities in himself, which it had been most desirable to direct and train." Charles Dickens, *Bleak House* 211 (1853; repr. 1985).
- "If the memory which we have uncovered does not answer our expectations, it may be that we ought to pursue the same path a little further; perhaps behind the first traumatic scene there may be concealed the memory of a

LANGUAGE-CHANGE INDEX (For the full key, see front matter pp. xxxi, l–li.)
Stage 1: Rejected. **Stage 2:** Widely shunned. **Stage 3:** Widespread but . . . **Stage 4:** Ubiquitous but . . . **Stage 5:** Fully accepted.
Invariably inferior forms marked by asterisk (✳). • Ratios represent frequency of prevalent forms vs. variants in current books.

second, which satisfies our requirements better and whose reproduction has a greater therapeutic effect." Sigmund Freud, "The Aetiology of Hysteria" (1896), in *The Freud Reader* 100 (Peter Gay ed., 1989).

Third, the semicolon separates items in a series when any element in the series contains an internal comma—e.g.:

- "Greek developments include *pimplemi* and *pletho*, 'to fill'; *pleres*, *pleos*, 'full'; *poly*-, 'much,' with comparative *pleios* and superlative *pleistos*; *polemos*, 'war'; and *polis*, 'city.'" Mario Pei, *The Families of Words* 229 (1962).
- "I wish to acknowledge the valuable help of a number of superior editors in the composition of this book: Neal Kozodoy of *Commentary*; Erich Eichmann, and Hilton Kramer of *The New Criterion*; John Gross, formerly of the *Times Literary Supplement*; and Carol Houck Smith, of W.W. Norton." Joseph Epstein, *Plausible Prejudices: Essays on American Writing* 9 (1985).
- "Between 1815 and 1850 Americans constructed elaborate networks of roads, canals, and early railroad lines; opened up wide areas of newly acquired land for settlement and trade; and began to industrialize manufacturing." Sean Wilentz, "Society, Politics, and the Market Revolution," in *The New American History* 62 (Eric Foner ed., 1997).

Fourth, the semicolon sometimes appears simply to give a weightier pause than a comma would. This use is discretionary. A comma would do, but the writer wants a stronger stop—e.g.: "There is never anything sexy about Lautrec's art; but there also is never anything deliberately, sarcastically anti-feminist in it." Aldous Huxley, "Doodles in the Dictionary" (1956), in *Aldous Huxley: Selected Essays* 198, 206 (1961).

The most common misuse of the semicolon is to place it where a colon belongs. So it's not uncommon to see, in a business letter, a semicolon after the salutation: "Dear Sarah; . . . ." But the semicolon stops the forward movement of a statement, whereas a colon marks a forward movement. In any given published example, the error might simply be a typographical error. But it happens too commonly to be routinely a typo—e.g.: "In addition to those whose names appear as contributors, I am especially grateful to the following for their valuable assistance in the preparation of the Second Edition; Luciano Berio, Juilliard School of Music; David Burrows, New York University; . . . ." Willi Apel, *Harvard Dictionary of Music* v–vi (2d ed. 1972). In that sentence, the first semicolon should be a colon; the others are correct.

P. Square Brackets ([ ]). These enclose comments, corrections, explanations, interpolations, notes, or translations that were not in the original text but have been added by subsequent authors, editors, or others. E.g.: "My right honorable friend [John Smith] is mistaken."/ "They [Whig members of Congress] couldn't thwart President Jackson's legislative agenda." Unfortunately, many journalists use parentheses for this purpose—a slipshod practice.

Also, brackets often show parentheses within parentheses <Smith and her commander (Robert Parnell, also a [helicopter] pilot) both survived the crash>. But in some fields, such as law, it's not only acceptable but customary to use parentheses within parentheses <(citing Leonard Baker, *John Marshall: A Life in Law* 14 (1974))>. The "nesting" parentheses at the end of that citation appear throughout this book in parenthetical cross-references to subparts; for example, toward the end of PLURALS (G), a cross-reference reads, "(see (B))."

In scholarly writing, brackets are sometimes used for adjustments in quoted matter, such as making lowercase a letter that was uppercase in the source of the quotation <"It is not surprising, in Alison Lurie's view, that '[i]nnovations in language are always interesting metaphorically'"> or signifying the omission of a word's inflection <"Good writers . . . sometimes prove[ ] to be among the toughest of editors themselves">. (Here, the *-d* has been omitted from the past-tense *proved*.) Some writers and editors, though, tacitly change the capitalization to keep their text free of brackets. Too many bracketed edits can certainly clutter a quotation. In fact, the practice is so distracting that it should be used only where the quotation must be rigorously accurate.

Q. Virgule [/]. Known popularly as the "slash," arcanely as the "solidus," and somewhere in between as the "diagonal," the virgule is a mark that doesn't appear much in first-rate writing. Some writers use it to mean "per" <50 words/minute>. Others use it to mean "or" <and/or> or "and" <every employee/independent contractor must complete form XJ42A>. Still others use it to indicate a vague disjunction, in which it's not quite an *or* <the novel/novella distinction>. In this last use, the en-dash is usually a better choice. (See (H).) In all these uses, there's almost always a better choice than the virgule. Use it as a last resort.

But the virgule has legitimate uses as well: (1) to separate run-in lines of poetry <To be, or not to be: that is the question: / Whether 'tis nobler in the mind to suffer / The slings and arrows of outrageous fortune>; (2) to show pronunciations (as they're shown throughout this book) <*ribald* is pronounced /**rib**-əld/>; (3) to separate the numerator and the denominator in a fraction <19/20>; (4) in Internet addresses <http://www.oed.com>; and (5) in informal jottings, to separate the elements in a date <11/17/98>.

R. Bibliography. For books on punctuation, see the Select Bibliography at the end of this book (p. 1049).

pundit (= [1] a wise, learned teacher, or [2] an acknowledged expert who is paid to opine about matters of public interest, esp. through the mass media) is pronounced /**pən**-dit/. Of Hindi and ultimately Sanskrit origin, the word was introduced into English in the late 1600s and first became widely popular about 1800. The derivative *punditry* (= the quality or state of being a pundit) arose in the 1920s, and *punditocracy* (= government by pundits) in the 1980s. By the latter date, *pundit* had come to be tinged with negative connotations—the sense often being that the person is not so much an acknowledged expert as a putative one.

Today there is a widespread mispronunciation of the word involving an epenthetic *-n-* in the second syllable: /pən-dint/. It arose in the late 20th century and has been spreading ever since. You can avoid it by dint of good memory and care in enunciation.

punitive; *punitory. The latter is a NEEDLESS VARI-ANT. See **penal.**

Current ratio: 751:1

PUNS. After centuries of disrepute, puns (= humorous verbal ambiguities) now appear in straight-faced writing more than ever. It's easy to see why they're sometimes considered lame—e.g.: "Hip hotelier Ian Schrager has brought a *Starck* change to San Francisco's historic Clift Hotel. He and celebrated designer Philippe Starck have teamed up to reopen the stately hotel." "Nifty New Clift," *Am. Way,* 15 Nov. 2001, at 18. On the other hand, it's easy to admire a seafood restaurateur who's willing to put money at risk with the name "Just for the Halibut."

Puns are generally beyond the scope of this book, but a good treatment can be found in Walter Redfern, *Puns* (1984). For some amusing books on punning, see especially Richard Lederer's many books, including *Get Thee to a Punnery* (1988), *The Play of Words* (1991), *Puns and Games* (1996), *Word Circus* (1999), and *Have a Punny Christmas* (2000). For a special kind of pun treated here, see WELLERISMS.

pupilage (= the state or period of being a pupil) is the standard AmE spelling. *Pupillage* is the predominant BrE spelling—but that has been so only since the 1970s.

purchase. See **buy (B).**

purl is a knitting term denoting a type of stitch. *Pearl* is a variant form to be avoided—e.g.:

- "Key trends . . . include: cotton cable knee socks and cotton *pearl* [read *purl*] stitch knee socks, $12." Sylvi Capelaci, "Legs Long on Style," *Toronto Sun,* 23 Aug. 1994, Imagination §, at 38.
- "With four hours of free time, a basic knowledge of the knit-and-*pearl* [read -*purl*] stitch and a creative mind, critter mittens were formed." Faith Mayer, "Critter Mittens Win Magazine Prize," *Telegram & Gaz.* (Worcester), 28 Feb. 1997, at B4.
- "Knotted *pearl* [read *purl*] stitch produces a wide, rather open band with a knotted surface." Eaglemoss Publications, *The Complete Illustrated Stitch Encyclopedia* 83 (2001).

LANGUAGE-CHANGE INDEX
pearl misused for *purl*: Stage 1
Current ratio (*purl stitch* vs. *pearl stitch): 13:1

purport, vb., = to be intended to seem <the bill purported to be a $100 bill>. Because the sense is already passive, this verb shouldn't be put into the PASSIVE VOICE—e.g.:

- "Three people were arrested Sunday at the Smithsonian Institution's Air and Space Museum after pouring what *was purported* [read *purported*] to be human blood and

ashes on the Enola Gay, which dropped the first atomic bomb on Japan." "Blood, Ashes Thrown at Enola Gay Exhibit," *Chicago Trib.,* 3 July 1995, at 10.

- "The paperback also included a cassette tape containing what *was purported* [read *purported*] to be a phone call from the supposedly dead Elvis." Joel Selvin, "Flipping Through the Pages of a Unique Life," *S.F. Chron.,* 3 Aug. 1997, at 33.
- "Even the Canadian trial, which was *purported* [read *purported*] to be designed to evaluate women between the ages of 40 and 49 separately, was actually too small to evaluate women in this age group." Daniel B. Kopans, *Breast Imaging* 163 (2007).

purposeful. See **purposive.**

purposely; purposefully. *Purposely* = on purpose; intentionally. *Purposefully* = with a specific purpose in mind; with the idea of accomplishing a certain result. Some writers fall into INELEGANT VARIATION with these words—e.g.: "For someone to be guilty of witness tampering, they must have acted *purposely*. Accidentally interfering with a witness, for example, does not qualify. Because the indictments did not specify Montgomery acted *purposefully* [read *purposely*], Mohl 'quashed,' or voided, the indictments." "Man, 22, Gets 5–12 Years for Rape," *Union Leader* (Manchester, N.H.), 23 Nov. 1996, at A7. Cf. **right,** adj.

LANGUAGE-CHANGE INDEX
purposefully misused for *purposely*: Stage 1

purposive; purposeful. H.W. Fowler and the *OED* editors objected to *purposive* as an ill-formed hybrid. Today, however, it is usefully distinguished in one sense from *purposeful* (= [1] having a purpose; or [2] full of determination). *W11* records under *purposive* the sense "serving or effecting a useful function though not as a result of planning or design."

But in other senses it is a NEEDLESS VARIANT of *purposeful*—e.g.: "The raw materials for John Wayne the persona were Wayne's imposing physique and an economical, *purposive* [read *purposeful*] body language, which combined with the famous Wayne voice . . . to convey an air of inevitability and control." Michiko Kakutani, "The Making of a Myth Who Rode into the Sunset," *N.Y. Times,* 25 Feb. 1997, at C14.

LANGUAGE-CHANGE INDEX
purposive misused for *purposeful*: Stage 1

pursuant to (= in accordance with; under; in carrying out) is rarely—if ever—useful. Lawyers are the main users of the phrase, and they often use it imprecisely. Following are some well-taken edits that show how multihued the phrase has become:

- "The virus-infected trees constitute 'a public nuisance *pursuant to* [read *as defined by*] the Civil Code and Food and Agricultural Code,' Wallace wrote in his ruling." Steven Mayer, "Kern County Judge Orders Removal of Infected Trees," *Fresno Bee,* 21 Nov. 1997, S. Valley §, at 11.

LANGUAGE-CHANGE INDEX (For the full key, see front matter pp. xxxi, l–li.)
Stage 1: Rejected. **Stage 2:** Widely shunned. **Stage 3:** Widespread but . . . **Stage 4:** Ubiquitous but . . . **Stage 5:** Fully accepted.
Invariably inferior forms marked by asterisk (*). • Ratios represent frequency of prevalent forms vs. variants in current books.

- "Actually, the college has some male students, but *pursuant to its incorporation* [read *in accordance with its articles of incorporation*], men are not accepted into the college's liberal arts school." Donna Greene, "New Chief Helps Define Women's College," *N.Y. Times*, 7 Dec. 1997, Westchester §, at 3. (*Pursuant to its incorporation* is briefer, to be sure, but it doesn't make much sense.)
- "CenterSpan owes Sony Music Entertainment a $500,000 content fee and $750,000 in quarterly payments *pursuant to* [read *under*] a deal it struck to put the major's content on its peer-to-peer network." Matthew Benz, "CenterSpan May Cease Operations," *Billboard*, 12 Apr. 2003, at 34.

Eric Partridge was wrong to call this phrase "officialese for *after*" (*U&A* at 257). It may be OFFICIALESE, but it does not, ordinarily, mean "after."

pushback. See AIRLINESE.

put paid to = (1) to put a stop to (something) as an object of interest; or (2) to deal effectively with (a person). The phrase seems to derive from the practice of stamping invoices as "paid," at which time they stop being of any interest to the creditor. Sense 1 is far more common—e.g.:

- "But if Perlman's audience thought it was going to be able to bask in gorgeous, mellow romanticism, the concert's all-Bartok second half *put paid to* that idea." Judy Gruber, "Itzhak Perlman," *Wash. Post*, 14 Nov. 1994, at D6.
- "In passing, they *put paid to* some favorite urban legends." Marina Warner, "Tom, Dick and Xtmeng," *N.Y. Times*, 16 Feb. 1997, § 7, at 7.
- "This, however, was not to be: the attack on the USSR meant that the war changed its focus and *put paid to* any hopes of Spain playing a role." Joan Maria Thomàs,

Roosevelt and Franco During the Second World War 161 (2008).

See PHRASAL VERBS.

putrefy (= to make or become putrid; decay; rot) is so spelled—and has been since about 1800. It is often misspelled **putrify* (an archaic form that has persisted in the linguistic shadows)—e.g.: "To adult tastebuds, Mega Warheads' initial assault on the senses is akin to licking the corroded terminals of a storage battery while inhaling *putrified* [read *putrefied*] air from an ancient innertube." J. Taylor Buckley, "Warheads Candy Sets Taste, Sales Explosion," *USA Today*, 11 June 1997, at B3. See -FY. Cf. **liquefy, rarefy** & **stupefy**.

LANGUAGE-CHANGE INDEX
putrefy misspelled **putrify*: Stage 1
Current ratio: 7:1

put up with. See PHRASAL VERBS.

pygmy, n., has been the standard spelling since about 1935. **Pigmy* is a variant form. The adjective form is the same: *pygmy*. So **pygmaean* and **pygmean* are NEEDLESS VARIANTS.

Current ratio (*pygmy* vs. **pigmy*): 2:1

pyjamas. See **pajamas.**

pyorrhea (= periodontitis) is so spelled in AmE, *pyorrhoea* in BrE. But the word is periodontologically old-fashioned: since the early 1950s in AmE and the late 1950s in BrE, *periodontitis* has become the usual term.

Q

Qatar (the Middle Eastern country) is preferably pronounced /kət-ər/ throughout the English-speaking world—not /kah-tahr/, /kə-**tahr**/, /kay-**tahr**/, /**kay**-tahr/, /**gah**-tər/, or /gət-ər/. Although older dictionaries list those variants, as the nation has risen in prominence internationally more and more speakers of English have realized that it's easy to pronounce a homophone of *cutter*.

qua, conj. & adv. (= in the capacity of; as; in the role of), is often misused and is little needed in English. "The real occasion for the use of *qua*," wrote H.W. Fowler, "occurs when a person or thing spoken of can be regarded from more than one point of view or as the holder of various coexistent functions, and a statement about him (or it) is to be limited to him in one of these aspects" (*FMEU1* at 477). Here is Fowler's example of a justifiable use: "*Qua* lover he must be condemned for doing what *qua* citizen he would be condemned for not doing." But *as* would surely work better in that sentence; and in any event, this use of *qua* is especially rare in AmE.

One is hard-pressed to divine any purpose but rhetorical ostentation or idiosyncrasy in the following examples:

- "Such developments . . . do not explain why students *qua* students have played such an important role in stimulating protest." Seymour Martin Lipset, "Why Youth Revolt," *N.Y. Times*, 24 May 1989, at A31.
- "The proposal that a physician *qua* physician (or a medical ethic as such) is the necessary or best authority for the existential decision of rational suicide misrepresents medical knowledge and skills." Steven H. Miles, "Physician-Assisted Suicide and the Profession's Gyrocompass," *Hastings Ctr. Rep.*, May 1995, at 17.
- "The second [aspect of Plato's account] concerns his views about the content of the knowledge of the choric poet, i.e. what kind of knowledge the choric poet possesses *qua* choric poet." Antony Hatzistavrou, "'Correctness' and Poetic Knowledge: Choric Poetry in the *Laws*," in *Plato and the Poets* 361, 361 (Pierre Destrée & Fritz-Gregor Herrmann eds., 2011).

Similarly, *as* is better in unemphatic uses, in which Fowler rightly objected to *qua*—e.g.:

- "As a colleague explained to a small group of students: 'We don't do that *qua* [read *as*] physicians, . . . but *qua* [read *as*] friends, as an act of charity.'" Charles Lefevre, "In France, Terminal Stage Medicine Is Not Hopelessly Ill," *Hastings Ctr. Rep.*, Aug. 1988, at S19.
- "Psychiatrists *qua* [read *as*] physicians should never deprive individuals of their lives, liberties, and properties, even if the security of society requires that they engage in such acts." Thomas Szasz, "Mental Illness Is Still a Myth," *Society*, May 1994, at 34.
- "A state (here South Korea) has the right to protect itself—*qua* government—even if its population were not threatened by nuclear death and would, perhaps, in the face of a conventional attack, rather be Red than dead." Jeremy J. Stone, "Less than Meets the Eye," *Bull. of Atomic Scientists*, Sept. 1996, at 43. (Here the writer seems to mean *through* government; he would have been better off deleting the dashes and the phrase within them.)

The term is pronounced /kwah/—preferably not /kway/, even though the latter is the first pronunciation listed in many dictionaries.

QUADRA-. See **QUADRI-.**

quadrennial; *quadriennial. *Quadrennial* (= occurring every four years; lasting four years) is now standard: the etymologically proper *-i-* was dropped from the word in the 18th century. Today **quadriennial* is merely a variant spelling to be avoided. See QUADRI-.
> Current ratio: 42:1

QUADRI-; QUADRU-; QUADRA-. In Latinate words denoting four of something, *quadri-* is the usual form, as in *quadripartite* (= having four parts), *quadrillion* (= 10^{15} [consisting of four groups of three zeros after 1,000]), and *quadrivium* (= the four subjects of study in the higher division of the medieval curriculum, consisting of arithmetic, geometry, astronomy, and music).

Quadru- is the usual form for words in which the second element begins with a *-p-*, as in *quadruped* (= a four-legged animal), *quadruple* (= to multiply by four), and *quadruplet* (= one of four children born at one birth). The two words in which *quadru-* precedes a word without a *-p-* are rare: *quadrumanous* (= four-handed) and *quadrumvirate* (= a group of four men united in some way).

Although Eric Partridge said that *quadra-* is "always wrong" (*U&A* at 257), it appears unexceptionably in many terms deriving from Late Latin, such as *quadragesimal* (= of, relating to, or involving Lent) and *quadrangle* (= a four-sided figure). And 20th-century word coiners have devised words such as *quadraphonic* (= of, relating to, or involving a sound system with four loudspeakers) and *quadrathlon* (= an athletic contest involving four events).

But in one word especially—*quadriplegia*—the medial *-i-* is sometimes wrongly made *-a-*. About

10% of the time in print, the misspelling **quadraplegia* appears—e.g.: "The sudden bending of the neck . . . can lead to spinal cord injury and permanent paralysis of both arms and legs (known as *quadraplegia* [read *quadriplegia*])." G. Timothy Johnson, "So Long, Readers—The Doctor Is Out," *Chicago Trib.*, 22 Aug. 1986, at C2.

LANGUAGE-CHANGE INDEX
quadriplegia misspelled **quadraplegia*: Stage 1

quadriceps. While the correct term for these thigh muscles is *quadriceps* in both singular and plural forms, it is common when writing of a single muscle to drop the *-s*—e.g.: "Brown had no update on the condition of kick returner Josh Davis, who suffered a *quadricep* [read *quadriceps*] injury against Missouri." Eric Olson, "NU's Ball-Control Keyed Win," *Omaha World-Herald*, 14 Oct. 2002, at C1. It's better to stick with the singular form *quadriceps*, by far the more commonly used form. But given the acceptance of *bicep* as a singular, *quadricep* probably can't be far behind. Cf. **bicep, pecs** & **triceps.**
> Current ratio (*left quadriceps* vs.
> **left quadricep*): 7:1

*quadriennial. See **quadrennial.**

quadriplegia. So spelled. See QUADRI-.

QUADRU-. See **QUADRI-.**

quagmire (= [1] a bog, or [2] an especially difficult or complicated situation) is pronounced /**kwag**-mɪr/ in AmE and either that way or /**kwahg**-mɪr/ in BrE.

*quai. See **quay.**

qualifiedly (= with qualifications or reservations) is an adverb usually signaling that the sentence ought to be rewritten—e.g.:

- "The sage of Israel defense analysts, Zeev Schiff, believes that a compromise with Syria *is*, as he wrote in Haaretz on Dec. 8, *qualifiedly optimistic* [read, perhaps, *has . . . a qualified optimism* or *is . . . fairly optimistic*]." Amos Perlmutter, "Syria's Mideast Peace Gambit," *Wash. Times*, 26 Dec. 1995, at A14.
- "Burundi's prime minister, Antoine Nduwayo, a Tutsi, *has also qualifiedly backed a security force* [read, perhaps, *has also backed a security force, though with qualifications* or *has also backed a security force, but not without qualifications*]." "Burundi at the Edge," *N.Y. Times*, 25 July 1996, at A22.

Since the 19th century, the word has appeared more frequently in AmE than in BrE. See -EDLY.

qualitative; *qualitive. The first is standard in AmE and BrE alike. The second is a NEEDLESS VARIANT—e.g.: "That result, though, suggests a *qualitive* [read *qualitative*] difference between the approach of period

LANGUAGE-CHANGE INDEX (For the full key, see front matter pp. xxxi, l–li.)
Stage 1: Rejected. **Stage 2:** Widely shunned. **Stage 3:** Widespread but . . . **Stage 4:** Ubiquitous but . . . **Stage 5:** Fully accepted.
Invariably inferior forms marked by asterisk (*). • Ratios represent frequency of prevalent forms vs. variants in current books.

wind instrumentalists to their craft and that of their keyboard or string counterparts." Andrew Clements, "Tan and Hoeprich," *Fin. Times*, 27 Sept. 1988, at I27. *Qualitative* corresponds to *quality* in the sense of character or nature, not in the sense of merit or excellence. Cf. **quantitative.**

> LANGUAGE-CHANGE INDEX
> **qualitive* for *qualitative*: Stage 1
> Current ratio (*qualitative* vs. **qualitive*): 6,531:1

quality. When used as an adjective meaning "of high quality," this is a VOGUE WORD and a CASUALISM <a quality bottling company> <quality time>. Use *good* or *fine* or some other adjective of better standing.

For a misuse of *quality*, n., for *quantity*, see **unknown quantity.**

> LANGUAGE-CHANGE INDEX
> *quality* as an adjective
> meaning "of high quality": Stage 4

quandary (/**kwahn**-də-ree/ or /**kwahn**-dree/) = a state of befuddlement or pervasive doubt <now that he's been told the truth, he's in a quandary about his next step>. The word best describes a state of mind and should not be detached from mental processes. That is, it shouldn't be used as a synonym of *problem, challenge, issue, dilemma,* or *quagmire*—e.g.:

- "One of the most difficult *quandaries about* [read *issues with*] assisted suicide stems from the uncertainty of medicine." "The Courts and Assisted Suicide," *Tampa Trib.*, 5 Feb. 1997, at 10.
- "If Lugar follows through on his threats, Senate Majority Leader Trent Lott, R-Miss., faces a difficult *quandary* [read *challenge* or *problem*]: how to keep the dueling chairmen in line and prevent gridlock in the two key committees." Terry M. Neal & Ceci Connolly, "Senate Giants Wait to See Who Blinks," *Record* (N.J.), 9 Aug. 1997, at A8.

Because the *-ary* is unstressed, the misspelling **quandry* sometimes appears—e.g.:

- "Now, he's in a *quandry* [read *quandary*]." Bob Snyder, "Hole-in-One Truth," *Post-Standard* (Syracuse), 25 June 1997, at D6.
- "The arrival of the REITs is putting the titans in a *quandry* [read *quandary*]." Peter G. Gosselin, "Investors Muscling In on Realty Titans' Domain," *Boston Globe*, 10 Aug. 1997, at A1.

> LANGUAGE-CHANGE INDEX
> 1. *quandary* misused in the sense "dilemma," "problem," "issue," or the like: Stage 1
> 2. *quandary* misspelled **quandry*: Stage 1
> Current ratio: 107:1

quanta. See **quantum.**

*quantificational. See **quantitative.**

quantify; *quantitate. The latter is a NEEDLESS VARIANT newly popular with social scientists, whose word choice should never be treated as a strong recommendation.

> LANGUAGE-CHANGE INDEX
> **quantitate* for *quantify*: Stage 1
> Current ratio (*quantify* vs. **quantitate*): 27:1

quantitative; *quantificational; *quantitive. The preferred form is *quantitative*, not **quantitive*. Avoid variants such as **quantificational* as well. Cf. **qualitative.**

> Current ratio (in order of headwords): 869:8:1

quantum (= amount; measure) forms the plural *quanta*, an exception to the maxim to avoid foreign plurals. (See PLURALS (B).) Actually, though, for the most part the word itself is easily simplified and should be avoided—e.g.: "If necessary, he will enter into arrangements with financial institutions and stockbrokers to place out an appropriate *quantum* [read *number*] of PWE shares to ensure its continued listing." Jennifer Jacobs, "Ting Makes Offer for 6.56m PWE Shares at RM7.75 Each," *Bus. Times*, 14 May 1996, at 6.

quantum leap; quantum jump. These terms, once technical but now part of the popular idiom, date from the early 20th century. They denote "a sudden, extensive change (usu. an improvement) in the rate of progress." Although purists insist that, in physics, the change is merely abrupt but not necessarily large or dramatic, anyone using the term in that sense is sure to be misunderstood in most contexts—even technical ones. The popular sense, involving a massive change, seems genuinely useful. Its only disadvantage is that it's now a VOGUE WORD and a CLICHÉ.

The phrase *quantum leap* is 20 times as common in print today as *quantum jump*. But this disparity represents a reversal: from 1920 to 1980 *jump* was more frequent in print sources. The alternative term leapt ahead in 1980.

quarrel, v.i., makes *quarreled* and *quarreling* in AmE, *quarrelled* and *quarrelling* in BrE. See SPELLING (B).

quarter is best pronounced /**kwor**-tər/—not /**kor**-tər/.

*quarternary. See **quaternary.**

quartet; *quartette. The former is standard in AmE and BrE alike. The latter is an infrequent variant. Cf. **quintet.**

> Current ratio: 13:1

quarto (= a type of page size or book) forms the plural *quartos*. See PLURALS (D).

quash. See **squash.**

quasi—pronounced /**kway**-zɪ/ or /**kwah**-zee/—means "as if; seeming or seemingly; in the nature of; nearly." In legal writing, *quasi* may stand alone as a word, but as a prefix it's generally hyphenated. The term has been prefixed to any number of adjectives and nouns, e.g., *quasi-compulsory, quasi-domicile, quasi-judicial,* and *quasi-monopoly.*

quaternary, adj. & n., is often misspelled **quarternary, *quarternary,* or **quatenary.* The adjective means "consisting of four parts," the noun "a set of four things." The word is pronounced either /**kwah**-tər-ner-ee/ or /kwə-**tər**-nər-ee/.

quay is the standard spelling. **Quai* is a variant. The word is pronounced /kee/ or /kay/—preferably not /kway/.

queasy is the standard spelling in AmE and BrE alike. **Queazy* is a variant.

Current ratio: 358:1

Quebec (the French Canadian province) was long ago anglicized in pronunciation: /kwə-**bek**/. To say /kay-**bek**/ in an English-speaking context is to engage in affectation.

queenly. See **kingly.**

*quelch is an unconsciously made PORTMANTEAU WORD formed from *quell* (= [1] to overwhelm, or [2] to pacify) or *quash* (= to suppress) and *squelch* (= to crush or silence), perhaps through a false association with *quench*. Although few dictionaries record this NONWORD, it's hardly uncommon. Either *squelch* or *quell*, both standard words that dictionaries have long recognized, will serve better. Sometimes *squelch* seems like the right choice—e.g.:

- "He aggravated scholars even further by *quelching* [read *squelching*] hopes that he might release reams of hitherto unread Joyceana sealed in a suitcase in the Irish national library." John Engstrom, "Actor Goes Galactic," *Boston Globe*, 9 July 1990, at 33. (On the use of *aggravate* for *irritate* in that sentence, see **aggravate**.)
- "But she was equally scornful of the school for trying to *quelch* [read *squelch*] individuality." Sam McManis, "High School Backs Dress Code," *S.F. Chron.*, 25 Aug. 2001, at A13.
- "Already this year, Haug had to *quelch* [read *squelch*] rumors that it was appropriate for teachers to use 'hand signals' to cue students during testing." Nancy Mitchell, "Jeffco School Under Review over CSAP," *Rocky Mountain News* (Denver), 21 Mar. 2002, at A32.

At other times, *quell* seems to fill in better—e.g.:

- "But a baserunning blunder by the slow-footed Kmak, who tried to stretch a single into a double, *quelched* [read *quelled*] one potential rally." Joseph A. Reaves, "As Streak Ends, Cubs See Errors of Ways," *Chicago Trib.*, 3 Aug. 1995, at N1.
- "Security used pepper spray to try to *quelch* [read *quell*] the mob." Editorial, "It's Just a Game," *Ariz. Daily Star*, 27 Nov. 2002, at B6.

What's the principle for deciding between *squelch* and *quell*? *Squelch* is better for the idea of stifling talk, emotions, thoughts, and the like. *Quell* is better for the idea of stifling a violent uprising or competitive bid.

LANGUAGE-CHANGE INDEX
*quelch for *squelch*: Stage 1
Current ratio (*squelch* vs. **quelch*): 275:1

querist. See **questioner.**

querulous (= habitually fretful, whiny, and complaining) is pronounced /**kwer**-yə-ləs/ or /**kwer**-ə-ləs/—not /**kweer**-/.

query (= a question designed to elicit particular information or to check the accuracy of something) is pronounced /**kweer**-ee/—not /**kwair**-ee/. For the difference between *query* and *inquiry*, see **inquiry (C).**

*questionary. See **questionnaire.**

*question as to whether. See **question whether.**

question-begging. See **beg the question.**

questioner; querist. The first is now the ordinary, more natural term. But from 1700 to about 1840, *querist* (now old-fashioned) was predominant. Today it would doubtless be misunderstood in speech.

Current ratio: 39:1

QUESTION MARKS. See PUNCTUATION (M).

questionnaire; *questionary. *Questionnaire*, the standard term, is occasionally misspelled **questionaire*—e.g.: "The *questionaires* [read *questionnaires*] ask several kinds of questions." Steven Amick, "Community's Views on Policing Needs Solicited," *Oregonian* (Portland), 16 Sept. 1997, at B2. Cf. **doctrinal** & **millionaire.**
*Questionary is a NEEDLESS VARIANT.

LANGUAGE-CHANGE INDEX
questionnaire misspelled **questionaire*: Stage 1

*question of whether. See **question whether.**

QUESTIONS, DIRECT AND INDIRECT. A direct question—one explicitly posed—ends with a question mark. E.g.:

- "How can demand be controlled and stimulated?" Helen E. Haines, *Living with Books* 39 (2d ed. 1950).
- "There are [other cultures that] seem to have largely succeeded in taming or repressing [envy]. What causes such differences? Is it perhaps the varying frequency of certain types of personality and character?" Helmut Schoeck, *Envy: A Theory of Social Behavior* 10 (1970).
- "Does he or she have pockets deep enough to finance future rounds?" Roberta Reynes, "Venturing Out for Rapid Growth," *Nation's Bus.*, 1 Nov. 1997, at 54.

But an indirect question—one posed at a distance from the actual asking—ends with a period. E.g.:

- "In Clarksdale, Miss., a motel desk clerk diplomatically inquired what we were doing in that city, having noted we were from Florida." Red Marston, "Every Place Has a Story to Tell," *St. Petersburg Times*, 25 Nov. 1997, at G16.
- "Reamer himself, when asked what value he added, once replied, 'absolutely none.'" Bethany McLean, "Sure Bets?" *Fortune*, 8 Dec. 1997, at 256.
- "I wondered what he was thinking." Dori Butler & Sheila Kitzinger, "They Saw It All," *Mothering*, 22 Dec. 1997, at 58.

LANGUAGE-CHANGE INDEX (For the full key, see front matter pp. xxxi, l–li.)
Stage 1: Rejected. **Stage 2:** Widely shunned. **Stage 3:** Widespread but . . . **Stage 4:** Ubiquitous but . . . **Stage 5:** Fully accepted.
Invariably inferior forms marked by asterisk (*). • Ratios represent frequency of prevalent forms vs. variants in current books.

Writers sometimes err by putting a question mark after an indirect question, especially one beginning with *I wonder*—e.g.:

- "Come to think of it, *I wonder* if the weapon in question is one he confiscated from the OU football dorm?" Jim Donaldson, "A Tale of a Gunslinger and a Smoking Gun," *Providence J.-Bull.*, 6 Aug. 1997, at D1.
- "*I wonder* whether the NAACP would have considered it proper if the Ku Klux Klan had similarly paid off the plaintiffs in Brown v. Board of Education?" "Lost Opportunity," *Fresno Bee*, 27 Nov. 1997, at B14.

In both those examples, the question mark should be a period.

question whether; *question of whether; *question as to whether. The first has a long literary lineage: it properly uses the noun clause beginning with *whether* in apposition to *question*. The other two are minor prolixities—e.g.: "There is also the *question of whether* [read *question whether*] talk of values—in the context of adultery and the like—will resonate in 2004 as it once did." Jeffrey Toobin, "Candide," *New Yorker*, 16 Dec. 2002, at 42, 48. See **whether (B).**

Current ratio (in order of headwords): 6:6:1

*quethen. See **quoth.**

quetzal (/ket-**sahl**/) = [1] a colorful, long-tailed bird common to Mexico and Central America; or [2] the basic monetary unit of Guatemala. **Quezal* is a variant spelling.

Current ratio: 300:1

queue (/kyoo/), vb., makes *queued* and *queuing* (not *queueing*). For the sense of the noun as well as the verb, see **cue.**

*quezal. See **quetzal.**

quick. A. And *quickly.* Although *quick*, as an adverb, dates back to Middle English, *quickly* has long been considered preferable in serious writing. To say *she learns quick* is so casual as to be slangy. But some exceptions occur in SET PHRASES such as *Come quick!* (sometimes also *Come quickly!*) and *get-rich-quick schemes*. Some instances are close calls—e.g.: "Police said they believe that the explosives were stolen and dumped in the A.B. Jewell water reservoir by someone who wanted to get rid of them *quick*." "Police Remove Explosives from Oklahoma Reservoir," *Dallas Morning News*, 30 July 1997, at D12. Cf. **slow.**

B. Meaning "alive." *Quick* originally meant "alive" and continued to do so up to the 19th century, as in the Apostles' Creed: "From thence he shall come to judge the *quick* and the dead." Except in allusion to that well-known sentence, this usage is now archaic. See ARCHAISMS.

The illogical phrase *quick with child*—referring to a pregnant woman—began in the 15th century as a METATHESIS of the strictly logical *with quick child*. The *OED* labels the phrase "rare or obsolete," but writers continue to use it: "Under the common law, abortion was allowed with the consent of the woman and before she was '*quick with child*' (i.e., the time when the first movements of the child were felt by the woman, around the end of the first trimester)." Maggie Jones Patterson et al., "Abortion in America," *J. Consumer Research*, 1 Mar. 1995, at 677.

*quick claim. See **quitclaim.**

quid pro quo (= this for that; tit for tat) is a useful LATINISM since the only English equivalent is *tit for tat*, which seems too colloquial in many contexts. E.g.: "Here, then, is a lobbying group pointedly offering something of value to a public official as a *quid pro quo* for a political favor." Jim Brunelle, "Paper's Series Shows How Irredeemably Corrupt System Is," *Portland Press Herald*, 19 Sept. 1997, at A11. And the word *exchange* often doesn't quite capture the right sense—e.g.: "Congress will evade its intent with subversive language or will collude with the executive, engaging in *quid pro quo* at the pork barrel." Letter of Bill Weiss, "Line-Item Veto Law Can Prod Press to Find, Feds to Cut Pork," *Columbus Dispatch*, 6 Sept. 1997, at A9.

The best plural is *quid pro quos*. *Quids pro quos* is a pedantic alternative. **Quids pro quo* is simply incorrect; it's a good example of HYPERCORRECTION. See PLURALS (B).

quiescence; *quiescency. *Quiescence* (/kwee-**es**-ənts/ or /kwɪ-/) is standard, **quiescency* being a NEEDLESS VARIANT. **Quiesence* is a fairly common misspelling—e.g.: "The apparent *quiesence* [read *quiescence*] and resignation of the Iowa electorate is a source of deep frustration for Iowa Democrats." James R. Dickenson, "Hip-Deep in Farm Crisis, Iowa Favors Republican," *Wash. Post*, 10 Oct. 1986, at A16.

LANGUAGE-CHANGE INDEX
1. *quiescence* misspelled **quiesence*: Stage 1
Current ratio: 469:1
2. **quiescency* for *quiescence*: Stage 1
Current ratio (*quiescence* vs. **quiescency*): 1,204:1

quiescent (= [1] characterized by inactivity or tranquility, or [2] causing no trouble or symptoms for the time being) is pronounced either /kwee-**es**-ənt/ or (less commonly) /kwɪ-**es**-ənt/. See SPELLING (A).

quiet, n.; quietness; quietude. *Quiet* = silence; stillness; peace <the quiet of Wolfson College when the students had departed>. *Quietness* = the condition of being silent or still <they had mistakenly attributed her quietness to shyness>. *Quietude* = a state or period of repose; tranquility <after a three-month quietude, he resumed work>.

quiet, v.t.; quieten. The preferred verb form is *quiet*. Chiefly a Briticism, *quieten* was considered a superfluous word by H.W. Fowler (*FMEU1* at 479). Avoid it.

Current ratio (*quieted* vs. *quietened*): 11:1

quietness; quietude. See **quiet,** n.

quietus (= [1] the end of something, or [2] someone's death) is pronounced /kwɪ-**ee**-təs/—preferably not

/kwɪ-**ay**-təs/ or /**kwɪ**-ə-təs/. The plural is *quietuses*. See PLURALS (B). Avoid bare bodkins.

Quincey, Thomas De. See **De Quincey, Thomas.**

quintet; *quintette. The first is standard in AmE and BrE alike. The latter is a NEEDLESS VARIANT; though uncommon, it still occasionally appears. Cf. **quartet.**

Current ratio: 30:1

quit = (1) to stop; or (2) to leave. For sense 1, the past tense is *quit* <he finally quit snoring>. (See IRREGULAR VERBS.) For sense 2, which is more common in BrE than in AmE, the past tense is *quitted*—e.g.:

- "By page 290 Robin has long *quitted* the suburbs, met a nice girl at Oxford, done his war service, [etc.]." David Hughes, "You Can't Do Both," *Mail on Sunday*, 11 Sept. 1994, at 36.
- "As he *quitted* the palace, the whole Court crowded about him to pay their compliments." "The Jacobite File," *Scotsman*, 30 Sept. 1996, at 12.
- "It was heard from Indian River in a few days more that Blueskin had *quitted* the inlet and had sailed away to the southeast; and it was reported, by those who seemed to know, that he had finally *quitted* those parts." Howard Pyle, "Blueskin the Pirate," in *Ghost Pirates* 97, 119 (Tom McCarthy ed., 2007).

quitclaim (= the formal release of a potential right, esp. of any claim to ownership) often appears in the legal phrase *quitclaim deed*. The word is occasionally mangled into **quick claim*—e.g.:

- "Adult children also abuse their elderly parents by gaining control over their money. The parents sign over their home via a *quick-claim* [read *quitclaim*] deed, the children put them in a nursing home and then leave the area with the proceeds from the sale of the home." Steve Heisler, "Women Reach Out to Those Left Alone," *Sarasota Herald-Trib.*, 10 Oct. 2007, at BM4.
- "The board approved Caron to execute the land swap through a *quick claim* [read *quitclaim*] deed." "School Approves Land Swap," *Hartford Courant*, 5 Jan. 2008, at B2.
- "Cascade County commissioners approved a resolution Tuesday allowing mortgages, *quick claim* [read *quitclaim*] deeds, power of attorney, land transfers, condominium bylaws, subdivision covenants and other documents to be posted on the county's Web site." Karl Puckett, "County Will Begin Posting Documents on Web Site," *Great Falls Trib.*, 10 Sept. 2008, at M1.

See MONDEGREENS.

LANGUAGE-CHANGE INDEX
*quick claim for *quitclaim*: Stage 1

quite = (1) entirely, completely; (2) very; or (3) fairly, moderately. Sense 3 occurs in BrE only, in which the word has undergone pejoration. To say that something is *quite good* is a compliment in AmE but nearly the opposite in BrE: "Some years ago I was hired by an American bank. I received a letter from the head of human resources that started: 'Dear John, I am quite pleased that you have decided to join us.' That 'quite' cast a cloud. Then I discovered that in American English 'quite' does not mean 'fairly' but 'very.'" John Mole, "Body Language of World Business," *Sunday Times* (London), 8 July 1990, § 6, at 1.

AmE differs somewhat from BrE in the placement of the indefinite article with *quite*. Although Americans and Britons alike say *quite a long time*, Britons also sometimes say *a quite long time*. Eric Partridge preferred the latter (*U&A* at 258). E.g.: "They're in the food chain, in the water supply, and according to the New Yorker of some years ago, they've been creating vile, barren mutant fish in our oceans for *a quite long time* now." Deborah Orr, "The Childless Future Facing Men," *Independent*, 29 June 2001, at 5. But that usage strikes the modern ear as pedantic and unidiomatic, while *quite a long time* is perfectly natural—e.g.:

- "On Saturday in Columbus, Ohio, there was a loss that figured to tempt your average fan to wallow for *quite a long time*." Dan Barreiro, "Admit It Clem, 'U' Played Badly," *Star Trib.* (Minneapolis), 27 Feb. 1995, at C1.
- "It may take *quite a long time* before your loved one takes any action of any kind." Meg Nugent, "Straight from the Heart," *Star-Ledger* (Newark), 11 Feb. 2003, at 35.

For the advantage of *quite* over *very* with a past-participial adjective, see **very (B).**

quite the contrary. See **contrary (B).**

quitter; quittor. For "someone who quits," *quitter* is preferred. *Quittor* = an inflammation of the feet, usu. in horses.

quixotic (= impractically based on wholly unrealistic dreams of improving the world) is pronounced /kwik-**sot**-ik/—not /kee-**hoh**-tik/. True, the adjective derives from the name of Cervantes's character Don Quixote, but the adjective acquired the anglicized pronunciation as early as the 18th century. And even though Cervantes's *Don Quixote* is /dahn kee-**oh**-tee/, Lord Byron's *Don Quixote* is anglicized as /dahn **kwik**-sət/ by long-established convention.

quoin (= [1] the distinctive corner or cornerstone of a building, or [2] the keystone of an arch) is pronounced /koyn/—preferably not /kwoyn/.

quondam (= former) is an ARCHAISM more common in BrE than in AmE—e.g.: "Most of the descendants of the original immigrants have melted into the gentrified suburbs and only a few remain, but those few—like Joe the baker and Sadie the barber and *quondam* beauty-queen—leapt at the chance." Sue Gaisford, "Radio: Lest the Promised Land Be Forgotten," *Independent*, 4 May 1997, at 13.

LANGUAGE-CHANGE INDEX (For the full key, see front matter pp. xxxi, l–li.)
Stage 1: Rejected. **Stage 2:** Widely shunned. **Stage 3:** Widespread but . . . **Stage 4:** Ubiquitous but . . . **Stage 5:** Fully accepted.
Invariably inferior forms marked by asterisk (*). • Ratios represent frequency of prevalent forms vs. variants in current books.

The word is sometimes misspelled *quandam, and misused also—e.g.: "This would have been the perfect time to meet . . . what used to be called The Wife, the *quandam* [read *quondam*?] little woman who, theory has it, might be able to influence what is written." Richard Cohen, "Press Party Symbolizes Carter Administration," *Wash. Post*, 26 Jan. 1978, at B1. Is the writer suggesting that she is no longer little? At best the sentence involves a MISCUE.

The word has several synonyms: *erstwhile, sometime,* and *whilom.* See **erstwhile.**

quorum. Pl. *quorums*—not **quora.* See PLURALS (B).
Current ratio: 34:1

QUOTATION MARKS. See PUNCTUATION (N).

QUOTATIONS. A. Use of Quoted Material. The deft and incidental use of quotations is a rare art. Poor writers are apt to overuse block quotations (see (B)). Those who do this abrogate their duty, namely, to *write.* Readers tend to skip over single-spaced mountains of prose, knowing how unlikely it is that so much of a previous writer's material pertains directly to the matter at hand.

Especially to be avoided is quoting another writer at the end of a paragraph or section, a habit infused with laziness. Skillful quoters subordinate the quoted material to their own prose and use only the most clearly relevant parts of the previous writing. And even then, they weave it into their own narrative or analysis, not allowing the quoted to overpower the quoter.

B. Handling Block Quotations. The best way to handle them, of course, is not to handle them at all: quote smaller chunks. Assuming, though, that this goal is unattainable—as many writers seem to think it is—then the biggest challenge is handling a quotation so that it will actually get read. The secret is in the lead-in.

Before discussing how a good lead-in reads, let us look at the way many of them read. They're dead:

- According to one authority: . . . .
- The author went on to state: . . . .
- The article concludes as follows: . . . .
- As stated by one critic: . . . .

Anyone who wants to become a stylist must vow to try *never* to introduce a quotation in this way. Readers are sure to skip the quotation.

With a long quotation, the better practice is to evoke the gist of the quotation in the lead-in. Hence the lead-in becomes an assertion, and the quotation becomes the support. Feeling as if the writer has asserted something concrete, the reader will often, out of curiosity, want to verify that assertion.

Consider, for example, how nicely three literary critics introduce quotations. First is Randall Jarrell, in his *Third Book of Criticism* (1965):

- "His poetic rhetoric is embarrassingly threadbare and commonplace, as when he writes about his own lost belief: . . . ."

- "What he says about his childhood is true of his maturity: . . . ."
- "His obsessions, at their worst, are a moral and intellectual disaster and make us ashamed for him: . . . ."

Second is William Empson, in *Argufying: Essays on Literature and Culture* (1987):

- "The first reply of Lamb (3 October) begins with the words, 'Your letter was an inestimable treasure to me,' but the next one grieves that Coleridge is not settling down to a serious course of life, and the third (24 October) questions the doctrines that Coleridge has preached: . . . ."
- "Mr. Piper sometimes admits that a use of words by a Romantic is bad, but even so he considers it bad in a different way from what we think: . . . ."
- "He quotes from 'A General Introduction for My Work' (1937) about the undirected hatred that sprouts in the modern world: . . . ."

Third is Hermione Lee, in her essay entitled "*Power*: Women and the Word," in *The State of the Language* (Christopher Ricks & Leonard Michaels eds., 1990):

- "Adrienne Rich, in an essay called 'Power and Danger,' gives a feminist history of the word as used against women: . . . ."
- "Any rewriting of women's history, as in this neutrally uninformative passage, has to center on the word: . . . ."
- "Toril Moi (arguing with Irigaray over the word *power*) writes these heartening words: . . . ."

How does such a lead-in work in the fuller context? Here's an example from the masterly Christopher Ricks:

> William Blake knew, whether or not torment may hereafter prove eternal, that eternity may itself be a torment to contemplate:
>
>> Time is the mercy of Eternity; without Time's swiftness Which is the swiftest of all things: all were eternal torment.
>
> Christopher Ricks, *Beckett's Dying Words* 24 (1993).

When the writer gives the upshot in the introductory words, readers aren't left hunting for the quotation's central idea.

This method has the benefit not only of ensuring that the quotation is read, but also of enhancing the writer's credibility. For if the lead-in is pointed as well as accurate, the reader will agree that the quotation supports the writer's assertion.

C. Punctuating the Lead-In. Writers usually have four choices: a colon, a comma, a period (i.e., no lead-in, really—only an independent sentence before the quotation), or no punctuation. A long quotation ordinarily requires a colon—e.g.:

> My concern today is with what might be called the Higher Bibliography (*bibliology* would be a better word), and in particular with the superior historical certainty increasingly claimed for such investigations. Here, as a sample, is a characteristic pronouncement:
>
>> When bibliography and textual criticism join [*sc.* in the editing of a definitive text], it is impossible to imagine one without the other. Bibliography may be said to attack textual problems from the mechanical point of view, using evidence which must deliberately avoid being colored by literary considerations.

Nonbibliographical textual criticism works with meanings and literary values. If these last are divorced from all connection with the evidence of the mechanical process that imprinted meaningful symbols on a sheet of paper, no check-rein of fact or probability can restrain the farthest reaches of idle speculation. [Fredson Bowers, *On Editing Shakespeare and the Elizabethan Dramatists* 34–35 (1955).]

On the contrary, I shall argue, the only check-rein on idle critical speculation is critical speculation that is *not* idle.

> F.W. Bateson, "The New Bibliography
> and the 'New Criticism,'" in
> *Essays in Critical Dissent* 1–2 (1972).

Some writers, though, let the lead-in and the quotation stand as separate sentences; that is, Bateson might have used a period instead of the colon when leading in to the Bowers quotation. But the colon helps tie the quotation to the text and is therefore generally superior, especially when the quotation is introduced by a sentence using *here* or *consider* or a similar word. A period would leave the quotation in a sort of syntactic limbo.

A comma typically introduces a short quotation that isn't set off from the rest of the text—e.g.:

> True, I can't quite match [Barzun's] example of the novelist who submitted a manuscript in which one of his characters spoke about seeing a play starring the Lunts; it came back to him from his publisher with the marginal suggestion, "Wouldn't the Hunts be better?"
>
> John Gross, "Editing and Its Discontents," in
> *The State of the Language* 282, 285
> (Christopher Ricks & Leonard Michaels eds., 1990).

A colon would be permissible in place of that comma, but it would introduce the quotation more formally and give a stronger pause. With the comma, the reader glides more easily into the silly suggestion that Gross quotes.

When is it best to use no punctuation at all? Only when the introductory language moves seamlessly into the quoted material. E.g.:

> Thus, Wilson is able to say of the Dickens family penury and of Charles's childhood humiliations that they are
> biographical data worth knowing and bearing in mind, because they help us to understand what Dickens was trying to say. He was less given to false moral attitudes or to fear of respectable opinion than most of the great Victorians; but . . . the meaning of Dickens's work has been obscured by that element of the conventional which Dickens himself never quite outgrew.
>
> Janet Groth, *Edmund Wilson:*
> *A Critic for Our Time* 25 (1989).

The mere fact that what is being introduced is a block quotation does not mean that some additional punctuation is necessary.

D. American and British Systems. In AmE, quotations that are short enough to be run in to the text (usually fewer than 50 words) are set off by pairs of *double* quotation marks ("..."). In BrE, quoted text that is not long enough to be a block quotation is set off by *single* quotation marks ('...'). See PUNCTUATION (N).

E. Ellipses. A good way to trim down a bloated quotation—and to increase the odds of having it read—is to cut irrelevant parts. When you omit one or more words, you show the omission by using ellipsis points (a series of three period-dots) with one space before, after, and between them:

> In several scenes . . . the players bear down and the camera bores in with an intensity that suggests the sense of liberty, even in matters irrelevant to censorship, that freedom from the Hays code can bring.

Use a fourth period-dot when the omission falls between sentences in the quoted material or when your ellipsis ends a sentence.

The spacing between the last quoted word and the first ellipsis point depends on whether the word before the ellipsis ends a sentence. In the following example, *charming* is the last word of the first sentence, and it therefore ends with a period followed by three ellipsis points:

> Both he and the children are very charming. . . . But I would like still better to see any sufficiently intelligent attack on the new kinds of soul-destroyer—those heirs of the healers of the recent past who have learned the words ever so earnestly but, lacking the remotest ear for the tune, do their work by the book.

But if *charming* were not the last word of the first sentence, then the three ellipsis points would come first, and the (typographically identical) period after. The only difference would be the space between *charming* and the first dot:

> Both he and the children are very charming . . . . But I would like still better to see any sufficiently intelligent attack on the new kinds of soul-destroyer—those heirs of the healers of the recent past who have learned the words ever so earnestly but, lacking the remotest ear for the tune, do their work by the book.

This distinction—a hairsplitting distinction, in the minds of some—is one that careful writers should adhere to. Otherwise, careful readers will justifiably wonder whether the end of the sentence has been lopped off.

Finally, when you omit one or more paragraphs in a block quotation, use a whole line for the three ellipsis points (centered), which should have five to seven spaces between them—e.g.:

> It seems to me that the title *Something to Declare* encapsulates the tragedy of foreign films in America. Though many foreign films don't make it over here, those that do are not necessarily the best. Popular success, sensationalism, or the mere fact of coming from some major film industry—French, German, Italian—may be more important than quality. But if a good foreign film does make it to America—if distributors and exhibitors do not deem it uncommercial—all kinds of duties are levied on it because it has "something to declare."
>
> .   .   .

LANGUAGE-CHANGE INDEX (For the full key, see front matter pp. xxxi, l–li.)
Stage 1: Rejected. **Stage 2:** Widely shunned. **Stage 3:** Widespread but . . . **Stage 4:** Ubiquitous but . . . **Stage 5:** Fully accepted.
Invariably inferior forms marked by asterisk (*). • Ratios represent frequency of prevalent forms vs. variants in current books.

The problem with the better foreign films is that—unlike the majority of American movies, even the superior ones—they have . . . something to say. They are not just devices for killing a couple of hours, not just movie-movies. They do not merely entertain but also, by provoking thought, sustain. And for this, they incur the heavy duty of disregard. A public afraid to confront a little reality, to feel more strenuously committed—to think—simply stays away. Such films have something to declare, but virtually no one to declare it to.

> John Simon, *Something to Declare* xv (1983).

For more on ellipses, see PUNCTUATION (F).

quote (properly a verb) for *quotation* is a CASUAL-ISM that has been very much on the rise since the 1950s. E.g.:

- "While browsing through the *Oxford Dictionary of Quotations,* I came across several *quotes* attributed to Benjamin Disraeli." Letter of Terry Clapp, "Disraeli's Views," *Press Democrat* (Santa Rosa), 6 Aug. 1997, at B4.
- "Most of his really good *quotes,* which have an off-the-cuff originality when heard at a campaign rally, are rehashes from the book." William Murphy, "Pols & Politics," *Newsday* (N.Y.), 19 Sept. 1997, at A30.
- "A *quote* has an even more powerful effect if we presume not just a particular author behind it, but God, nature, the unconscious, labor, or difference." Boris Groys, *Under Suspicion: A Phenomenology of the Media* 90 (Carsten Strathausen trans., 2012).

The problem with *quotation* is that, to the writer who hopes to deliver goods quickly, the three syllables sound and read as if they are slowing the sentence down. The single syllable of *quote,* meanwhile, sounds apt to such a writer. And it sounds more and more natural all the time, as it seems to predominate in spoken English. So although it remains informal for now, it's gaining ground in formal prose.

The negative form, too, is a casualism—e.g.: "I need to correct several *misquotes* printed in the article by Kristi O'Brien, 'Crosses Set in Protest of Abortions.'" Letter of Vicki Rice, "Claims Misquoting in Article About Abortions," *State J.-Register* (Springfield, Ill.), 23 May 1997, at 8. See **cite,** v.t.

> LANGUAGE-CHANGE INDEX
> *quote* for *quotation*: Stage 4

quoth, an ARCHAISM, appears chiefly in historical contexts or jaunty prose. The word is always part of an inverted phrase. That is, *quoth* precedes its subject—e.g.: "*Quoth* the Ravens, 'Charge ever more.' The average ticket price for the new [Baltimore] Ravens is $40.05, compared to $32.61 last year when the team was the Cleveland Browns." Jerry Stack, "Morning Briefing: Eye Openers," *St. Louis Post-Dispatch,* 12 Aug. 1996, at C2. (That sentence is, of course, a play on Edgar Allan Poe's famous line, "Quoth the Raven, 'Nevermore.'") See INVERSION.

The word should be used only in the past tense (for "said"). The present-tense verb **quethen* is obsolete.

Quran. See **Koran.**

R

rabbet; rebate. In carpentry, a *rabbet* is a kind of groove cut into the edge of a board. *Rebate* (in this sense) is a variant form.

rabbi; *rabbin. *Rabbi,* the standard term, forms the plural *rabbis*—not **rabbies. *Rabbin,* an archaic form, is a NEEDLESS VARIANT—except that it gives us the adjective *rabbinic.* We also have the cognate noun *rabbinate* (= [1] the position, tenure, or office of a rabbi; or [2] collectively, a body of rabbis).

rabbit. See **Welsh rabbit.**

rabid (= [1] [of an animal] afflicted with rabies, or [2] having extreme and unreasonable opinions) is pronounced /**rab**-id/—not /**ray**-bid/.

raccoon; *racoon. The animal is North American, and the AmE spelling is *raccoon.* The traditional BrE spelling—a variant form in AmE—is **racoon.* But since 1950 the AmE spelling has become predominant also in BrE. *Raccoon* should be considered standard in all varieties of English.

> Current ratio (World English): 13:1

racial discrimination; race discrimination. The first phrase predominates in print sources and is slightly better because, other things being equal, an adjective is preferable if it has the form as well as the function of an adjective (hence *racial*). But predictably, idiomatic English is not consistent: we speak of *racial equality* but *race relations,* and of *racial tension* but *race riots.* Cf. **sex,** adj.

> Current ratio (in order of headwords): 9:1

racism; *racialism. Both terms date from the early 20th century—**racialism* (1907) is more than two decades older than *racism* (1933)—yet both terms remained relatively obscure until the late 1950s. **Racialism* stayed obscure, but *racism* shot to ever greater levels of prominence beginning in the 1960s—first in AmE and later in BrE. *Racism* = (1) unfair treatment of people on grounds of their ethnicity or race, or (2) the belief that some races of people are inherently superior to others.

rack; wrack. The word *rack* is a complicated one with many senses. The important thing to know about the two spellings is that *wrack* is predominant in only one specialized sense: "seaweed" or "kelp." In all other senses and idioms, *rack* is the word. In the sense "to torture," *rack* has been vastly predominant since the

18th century <racking his brains> <racked with guilt> <nerve-racking>. In the sense "destruction," *rack and ruin* has always been the standard phrase from the mid-18th century—not **wrack and ruin*. Yet **wrack and ruin* predominated over *rack and ruin* in print sources from the early 19th century to about 1920.

The spelling *rack* actually accounts for nine different nouns and seven different verbs. If you're willing to cudgel your brains for an hour, perhaps while chewing dried wrack, study the entries in a couple of unabridged dictionaries. (With acknowledgments to my late friend Bob Burchfield.)

racket; racquet. For the implement used in net games, *racket* is standard in AmE and BrE alike. The variant form *racquet* appears in some proper names (e.g., the Palm Springs Racquet Club) seemingly because the "fancy" spelling looks more high-toned. Perhaps that also explains why, in the sport of squash, *racquet* has somehow become the predominant spelling. The same is true of *racquetball*, the related sport using short-handled rackets.

racketeer, n. & v.i. The noun *racketeering* refers to the business of racketeers—a system of organized crime traditionally involving the extortion of money from business firms by intimidation, violence, or other illegal methods. Oddly, this noun (as well as the verb *racketeer*) is characterized by the *OED* as an Americanism, whereas the adjective *racketeering* is exemplified in that dictionary only by British quotations. If the verb and its derivative forms began as Americanisms, they will inevitably spread to BrE, given the inroads already made.

In 1970, Congress passed the Racketeer Influenced and Corrupt Organizations Act (RICO), which led to a resurgence of the word in AmE. Today *racketeering* often has the broad sense "the practice of engaging in a fraudulent scheme or enterprise."

*racoon. See **raccoon.**

racquet. See **racket.**

radiance (= [1] a soft, gentle light, or [2] a beaming happiness that emanates from someone) has always been the standard term in all varieties of English. **Radiancy* is a NEEDLESS VARIANT.

Current ratio: 103:1

radical, adj., = (1) of, relating to, or involving a root or foundation <the radical selfishness of human nature>; or (2) far-reaching, extreme, sweeping <a radical proposal>. It's sometimes misspelled *radicle*—e.g.: "This *radicle* [read *radical*] approach to bifurcation would make any class certification a foregone conclusion." "Ninth Circuit Denies Red Cross

Mandamus Request in AZ Blood Class Action," *Pharmaceutical Litig. Rptr.*, July 1996, at 11,449.

Actually, *radicle* is a noun meaning "a small root"—e.g.:

- "If everything's in sync, the acorn germinates. Its hard brown shell is cracked by the emerging root, or *radicle*, which burrows downward." Irene Virag, "Li Life," *Newsday* (N.Y.), 3 Nov. 1996, at E9.
- "Often the *radicle* (root) has already begun to emerge." Paul Rogers, "Don't Lose Growing Days," *Telegram & Gaz.* (Worcester), 29 May 1997, at C11.

radiocast > radiocast > radiocast. So inflected. The solecism **radiocasted* almost never appears despite the problems that arise with analogous verbs such as *broadcast*. See -CAST & IRREGULAR VERBS.

radius. The Latin plural *radii*, traditionally the preferred form, greatly outnumbers *radiuses* in modern print sources from all varieties of English. E.g.: "During a turn, the two skis cut different *radii*—the outside ski carving a wider turn than the inside ski." Greg Johnston, "All Aboard!" *Seattle Post-Intelligencer*, 23 Oct. 1997, at 8.

LANGUAGE-CHANGE INDEX
radiuses for *radii*: Stage 2
Current ratio (*radii* vs. *radiuses*): 76:1

radix (= [1] a plant root, or [2] the base of a system of numbers or algorithms) has always predominantly formed the plural *radices*—not **radixes*.

Current ratio: 14:1

railroad; railway. As nouns these words are virtually equivalent. *W2* makes the following distinction: "*Railroad* . . . is usually limited to roads [with lines or rails fixed to ties] for heavy steam transportation and also to steam roads partially or wholly electrified or roads for heavy traffic designed originally for electric traction. The lighter electric street-car lines and the like are usually termed *railways*." But that distinction has largely faded, as *railway* appears comparatively seldom in AmE. In BrE, the term *railway* is more common. Streetcar lines in England are commonly called *tramlines* and the vehicles *tramcars* or *trammy cars*.

Railroad is used universally as a verb <passenger railroading>, figuratively as well as literally—e.g.: "But we're Brooklynites, so watch out; we will not be *railroaded*." Dick D. Zigun, "Can Coney Come Back?" *N.Y. Times*, 9 Aug. 1997, § 1, at 23. This sense is now used in BrE as well as AmE.

raise. A. And *rear.* The old rule, still sometimes observed, is that crops and livestock are *raised* and children are *reared.* But today the phrase *born and raised* is about nine times as common in print as *born and reared.* And *raise* is now standard as a synonym for *rear*—e.g.:

LANGUAGE-CHANGE INDEX (For the full key, see front matter pp. xxxi, l–li.)
Stage 1: Rejected. **Stage 2:** Widely shunned. **Stage 3:** Widespread but . . . **Stage 4:** Ubiquitous but . . . **Stage 5:** Fully accepted.
Invariably inferior forms marked by asterisk (*). • Ratios represent frequency of prevalent forms vs. variants in current books.

- "We parents so often blow the business of *raising* kids, but not because we violate any philosophy of child *raising*." Bill Cosby, *Fatherhood* 20 (1986).
- "He earlier had worked in the candy-making business in Pittsburgh, where he was born and *raised*." "John J. Martin Dies at 74," *Wash. Post*, 8 Aug. 1997, at B4.
- "My mother *raised* me to be polite." Mary Newton Brudner, *The Grammar Lady* 57 (2000).
- "However, of the thirty-one young people born in Britain, five of them were sent back to Hong Kong and partly *raised* there, before returning to Britain. Individuals *born and raised* predominantly in Hong Kong and those *born and raised* in Britain (or brought to Britain by primary school age) tended to have different expectations about family and work." Miri Song, *Helping Out* 106 (2010).

Indeed, *born and reared* is now likely to sound affected in AmE—even though it was predominant over *born and raised* till about 1950.

As a matter of word frequency, *raising children* (as opposed to *rearing children*) became the predominant usage in AmE in 1968 and in BrE by 1974.

Language-Change Index
raise meaning "to bring up (children)": Stage 5
Current ratio (*raise children* vs. *rear children*): 9:1

B. And *rise*. The straightforward distinction is that *raise* (raise > raised > raised) is transitive, while *rise* (rise > rose > risen) is intransitive. Here the rule is followed: "For 40 years the farmer has *risen* at 4:00 in the morning to tend to his crops and *raise* his chickens." But the following example incorrectly uses *raise* as an intransitive verb: "Then it [an alligator] *raised up* [read *rose*] on all four legs and charged." Jeff Klinkenberg, "Boardwalk on the Wild Side," *St. Petersburg Times*, 26 Dec. 1995, at D1.

Language-Change Index
raise misused for the intransitive *rise*: Stage 2

Raising. See **can't seem** & **don't think.**

rallentando. See **ritardando.**

rambunctious is sometimes misspelled **rambunctuous*—e.g.:

- " 'I try to keep a semblance of order here,' she says, in between a couple of well-placed reminders to the occasional student getting too *rambunctuous* [read *rambunctious*]." Tom Snyder, "Grinding Out the Meals," *Orange County Register*, 8 Aug. 1996, at 1.
- "From the grungy tub-thumping, through the soul and reggae covers and the rave-up Winning Ugly, *Dirty Work's* all over the shop, loud and *rambunctuous* [read *rambunctious*] and in your face." Christopher Sandford, *Keith Richards: Satisfaction* 280 (2004).

Cf. **bumptious** & **rumbustious.**

Language-Change Index
rambunctious misspelled **rambunctuous*: Stage 1
Current ratio: 633:1

rampant means "widespread, unrestrained," usually in a pejorative sense <a rampant epidemic>. Hence bad things become *rampant in* places; places don't become **rampant with* bad things. Yet some writers get this backwards—e.g.: "Officials and residents in the area want to revive and showcase the glory that was Bronzeville before it becomes *rampant* [read *rife*] with large *tracks* [read *tracts*] of vacant land and dilapidated buildings." "Revival of 'Black Metropolis' Blossoms," *Telegraph Herald* (Dubuque), 24 Sept. 1996, at A7. (For the second error in that sentence, see **track.**)

Language-Change Index
*rampant with for *rife with*: Stage 1

*ramsack. See **ransack.**

rancor (= a feeling of anger and hatred toward someone) is so spelled in AmE—and has been since about 1850. *Rancour* has always been the BrE spelling. See -**or**; -**our.**

rankle (= to irritate or embitter) is traditionally a transitive verb, not an intransitive one. Something rankles someone—it doesn't **rankle with* someone. Most writers get this right in the overwhelming majority of instances. Yet in both AmE and BrE, the superfluous *with* has begun insinuating itself alongside *rankle*—e.g.:

- "The decision still *rankles with* [read *rankles*] Parnevik, who said: 'It didn't surprise me—the guy in charge never surprises me.' " Dale Rankin, "Golf: Jesper Risks Ryder Chop," *Scottish Daily Record*, 25 Jan. 2000, at 37.
- "It must *rankle with* [read *rankle*] Rawley indeed that this bastard brother was seated at the same table. And *rankle with* [read *rankle*] his father as well." Diane Gaston, "A Reputable Rake," in *Rapturous Rakes Bundle* 7, 230 (2007).
- "I am slightly nervous that the memory of the photographs of our wild dance at Atlantic on the cover of the *Star* and the *Enquirer* might still *rankle with* [read *rankle*] her estranged husband, Bruce Willis, who will be attending the premiere that night." Christopher Ciccone, *Life with My Sister Madonna* 257 (2009).

Language-Change Index
*rankle with for *rankle*: Stage 3
Current ratio (*rankled him* vs.
*rankled with him): 4:1

ransack (= to search thoroughly, esp. for loot; pillage) is occasionally misspelled **ramsack*—e.g.: "After Kentland was *ramsacked* [read *ransacked*] by Union troops during the Civil War, Kent rebuilt Kentland." Robert Freis, "Grand Land with a History as Rich as Its Soil," *Roanoke Times*, 10 Oct. 1995, at 8.

Language-Change Index
ransacked misspelled **ramsacked*: Stage 1
Current ratio: 1,529:1

rap (= a negative allegation or reputation) typically appears in the phrase *bad rap* or *bum rap*. It's occasionally confused with the word *wrap* (= a material for covering something)—e.g.:

- "Aldermen Terry Cavanagh and Allan Bolstad feel their failing grades are a bum *wrap* [read *rap*]." Jim Farrell, "Phair Tops Council in Arts Body Rating," *Edmonton J.*, 17 Aug. 1995, at B3.
- "Even though Edgar Allan Poe gets a bum *wrap* [read *rap*] for 'just dying here,' his genealogy is deeply rooted in this

city's history." Letter of Christine Merrill, "Ravens Name Is Perfect for City," *Baltimore Sun*, 15 Apr. 1996, at A6.

LANGUAGE-CHANGE INDEX
*bum wrap for *bum rap*: Stage 1
Current ratio (*bum rap* vs. **bum wrap*): 49:1

rappel (= to engage in the mountain-climber's maneuver of descending a precipice with a double rope) is sometimes confounded with the similar-sounding *repel*—e.g.:

- "She performs back flips while strapped in a *repelling* [read *rappelling*] harness attached to bungee cords." Bill Buchalter, "Olympic Fire Burns in Brandy," *Orlando Sentinel*, 3 Mar. 1992, at D1.
- "Without hesitation I wrapped the rope around me preparing for the *repel* [read *rappel*] down to the floor below." David Patton & Debbie Patton, *A Promise* 131 (2008).
- "The reason for *repelling* [read *rappelling*] is a given; all Marines must know how to *repel* [read *rappel*] in case we come to a cliff and need to get down, or if we're required to make a window entry and have to *repel* [read *rappel*] down a building." Bob Cannady, *Through the Scope* 37 (2013).

Because the verb is accented on the second syllable (/ra-**pel**/ or /rə-**pel**/), its inflected forms have a double *-l*: *rappelled, rappelling*. See SPELLING (B).

LANGUAGE-CHANGE INDEX
repel misused for *rappel*: Stage 1

rapprochement (= the formal establishment of good relations between two countries that have gone through a period of strained relations), though it entered English as a loanword as early as 1809, has more or less kept its French pronunciation: /rap-rohsh-**mahn**/, with the accent on the final syllable. Avoid /ra-**prohsh**-mahn/.

rapt (= captivated, enthralled, spellbound) is sometimes erroneously made **wrapt*, an obsolete past-tense and past-participial form of *wrap*. This error seems to occur mostly in BrE—e.g.:

- "In a bid for equilibrium, I picked up my new biography of Evelyn Waugh and was soon *wrapt* [read *rapt*] in absorption by the flickering fire." Mary Killen, "Danger at Every Turn," *Sunday Telegraph*, 29 Jan. 1995, at 13.
- "She enters with a large suitcase out of which she creates some puppet magic [that] held the young audience *wrapt* [read *rapt*]." Laurie Atkinson, "Puppet Magic Simply Charming," *Evening Post*, 24 Jan. 1996, at 15.
- "Instruct the group that the point of the exercise is to see the effects of attention and inattention. For this end, they are to pay *wrapt* [read *rapt*] attention to Advisor A and little or no attention to Advisor B." E.H. McGrath, *Basic Managerial Skills for All* 197 (2011).

This error is traceable to 17th-century prose but has appeared infrequently over time in comparison with the standard usage.

LANGUAGE-CHANGE INDEX
*wrapt attention for *rapt attention*: Stage 1
Current ratio (*rapt attention* vs.
*wrapt attention): 71:1

rapture is susceptible to a blunder analogous to the one that occurs with *rapt*. That is, some writers make it **wrapture*. Sometimes, of course, it's simply a facetious formation—e.g.: "Whatever you do, don't forget the glue gun, the real key to true *wrapture*." Kathy Legg, "Inspirations for Wrapping It All Up," *Wash. Post*, 7 Dec. 1995, at T12. But uses of that kind—and the fact that some women's apparel stores call themselves *Wrapture*—are likely to cause some popular confusion in years ahead.

rara avis (/**rair**-ə ay-vis/, lit., "rare bird") is, as H.W. Fowler once noted, "seldom an improvement on *rarity*" (*FMEU1* at 483). The plural is *rara avises* or (more commonly, believe it or not) *rarae aves*. See PLURALS (B).

rare; scarce. In the best usage, *rare* refers to a consistent infrequency, usually of things of superior quality <diamonds having more than three carats remain quite rare>. *Scarce* refers to anything that is not plentiful, even ordinary things that are temporarily hard to find <job opportunities are scarce this year>. Writers sometimes misuse *rare* for *scarce*—e.g.: "Flowers are frequent, usually in the warmer months, but fruit is *rare* [read *scarce*] in the Tampa Bay area." Bette Smith, "Plant Profile," *St. Petersburg Times*, 17 May 1997, at D3.

rarebit. See **Welsh rabbit.**

rarefaction /rair-ə-**fak**-shən/ = (1) the act or process of making less dense; the state of being less dense; or (2) the act or process of purifying; the state of being purified. The forms **rarefication*, **rarification*, and **rarifaction* are erroneous—e.g.:

- "Occasionally, signs of fibrinous pericarditis and a *rarefication* [read *rarefaction*] of intramyocardial vessels suspicious for chronic vasculitis can be found. Angiographically, this type of *rarefication* [read *rarefaction*] of intramyocardial vessels is seen as a 'burned tree' angiogram." *Textbook of Angiology* 290 (John B. Chang ed., 2012).
- "The Presocratics are believed to have suggested a sundry of underlying 'stuff' such as air or water; proposed processes of alteration involving, for example, *rarification* [read *rarefaction*] and condensation; and, of course, they offered opinions about opposites." Edward Schiappa, *Protagoras and Logos* 95 (2d ed. 2013).
- "The solution consists of the high pressure gas expanding into the low pressure gas, sending a shock wave ahead and a *rarifaction* [read *rarefaction*] wave in the other direction." Pijush K. Kundu et al., *Fluid Mechanics* 278 (6th ed. 2015).

LANGUAGE-CHANGE INDEX
rarefaction misspelled **rarefication*, **rarification*, or **rarifaction*: Stage 1
Current ratio (in order of LCI): 256:4:4:1

rarefy (/**rair**-ə-fɪ/) = (1) to make or become less dense or solid; or (2) to purify. Although the standard spelling has been fixed since about 1740, the variant

LANGUAGE-CHANGE INDEX (For the full key, see front matter pp. xxxi, l–li.)
Stage 1: Rejected. **Stage 2:** Widely shunned. **Stage 3:** Widespread but . . . **Stage 4:** Ubiquitous but . . . **Stage 5:** Fully accepted.
Invariably inferior forms marked by asterisk (*). • Ratios represent frequency of prevalent forms vs. variants in current books.

spelling *rarify has persisted since that time. Today the latter is generally regarded as a misspelling—e.g.:

- "Penny-pinching skiers can even spend a week or two in the *rarified* [read *rarefied*] air of the Colorado Rockies." David Gonzales, "Hostels Are Hostile to High Prices," *Times-Picayune* (New Orleans), 29 Jan. 1995, at E1.
- "Too often, when we wonder why government and its institutions cost so much, we gaze down for solutions, look to the bottom of the pond where real life goes on instead of peering into that murky but *rarified* [read *rarefied*] algae bloom." Royal Ford, "It's Time to Challenge the Chancellor," *Boston Globe*, 23 Feb. 1997, at 2.
- "Sam Ranzulla [is] a 23-year-old veteran of these *rarified* [read *rarefied*] quarters." John Husar, "A Look at the Bulls' Drive," *Chicago Trib.*, 23 May 1997, Sports §, at 7.

See -FY. See also SPELLING (A). Cf. **liquefy** & **stupefy**.

LANGUAGE-CHANGE INDEX
rarefy misspelled **rarify*: Stage 4
Current ratio: 5:1

*rarely ever. A. Self-Contradictory Idiom. Though old, the phrase *rarely ever* is literally nonsensical—as many idioms are, of course. But this one is easily corrected to *rarely, rarely if ever,* or *rarely or never*—e.g.: "Norv Turner is a conservative, low-key, play-them-one-game-at-a-time coach who *rarely ever* [read *rarely*] gushes." Bill Free, "National Spotlight Pumps Up Redskins," *Baltimore Sun*, 13 Oct. 1997, at C7. Since 1800, *rarely if ever* has steadily occurred much more frequently in print. Cf. ***seldom ever.**

LANGUAGE-CHANGE INDEX
rarely ever for *rarely* or *rarely if ever*: Stage 1
Current ratio (*rarely if ever* vs. **rarely ever*): 2:1

B. And *rarely or ever*. The phrasing *rarely or ever* has no justification at all. It's erroneous in place of *rarely or never* or *rarely if ever*—e.g.:

- "Among those who have *rarely or ever* [read *rarely or never*] camped out is 9-year-old Kurt Davidson of Tujunga." Tom Schultz, "Sunland-Tujunga Program Teaches Kids Wonders of Outdoors," *L.A. Times*, 24 July 1998, at B3.
- "Because thousands of fully certified teachers *rarely or ever* [read *rarely if ever* or *rarely or never*] come near a classroom, it's likely that one out of five . . . of those who actually stand in front of kids each morning are uncertified." Carl Campanile & Stefan Friedman, "They Flunk and Stay in School," *N.Y. Post*, 4 Mar. 2002, at 26.
- "Scientists *rarely or ever* [read *rarely if ever*] explain their methods sufficiently to allow replication, and anyway few scientists ever bother to replicate work done elsewhere." William Gaver, "Science and Design," in *Ways of Knowing in HCI* 143, 149 (Judith S. Olson & Wendy A. Kellogg eds., 2014).

LANGUAGE-CHANGE INDEX
rarely or ever for *rarely or never*: Stage 1
Current ratio (*rarely or never* vs. **rarely or ever*): 34:1

*rarify. See rarefy.

*rase. See raze.

ratable; rateable. The spelling *ratable* is standard in AmE, *rateable* in BrE. See MUTE E.

ratatouille (= a spiced vegetable stew made of tomatoes, eggplant, zucchini, squash, onions, peppers, etc.) is pronounced /rat-ə-**too**-ee/. If there was any serious contention by the variant pronunciation /rah-tə-**too**-ee/, it was ended in 2007 by the popular animated film *Ratatouille*, in which Remy the rat (/rat/) cooked up a critically acclaimed dish of *ratatouille*. In the popular mind, there is no rival pronunciation.

ratchet, n. & vb. So spelled—not **rachet*. E.g.: "Kallstrom said security was being 'racheted [read ratcheted] up,' not only in New York but in other cities." "2 Held in N.Y. Bomb Plot Allegedly Tied to Hamas," *Houston Chron.*, 2 Aug. 1997, at 1.

The verb is inflected as *ratcheted* and *ratcheting*—not **ratchetted* and **ratchetting* (formerly preferred in BrE).

rateable. See ratable.

rate of speed is a REDUNDANCY that became especially common after 1850. *Speed* alone normally suffices.

rather. A. *Rather than*. This phrase can function either as a conjunction or as a preposition. As a conjunction (the more common use), *rather than* demands that the constructions on each side of it be parallel: "If we can, we will solve this problem diplomatically *rather than* forcibly." But as a preposition, *rather than* can connect nonparallel constructions: "*Rather than* staying home on a Saturday night, we went out to six different bars."

When *rather than* separates two verbs, it's often less awkward to convert the verbs into gerunds: "I've always liked *going* out rather than *staying* in." But sometimes *rather than* appears between simple verbs—e.g.: "With due respect to Shakespeare and others, we want our girls to *communicate* freely with the live world around them *rather than plunge* into musty old books." Vladimir Nabokov, *Lolita* 179 (1955; repr. 1982). Many modern writers would make that *rather than plunging*.

B. **Rather . . . instead of*. This phrasing, an example of SWAPPING HORSES, sometimes displaces what should be a straightforward *rather . . . than*—e.g.: "The tragedy of Ms. Charen's column is that it reveals a writer who would *rather* be glib and sarcastic *instead of* [read *than*] measured and sincere." William Roberts, "Column on Princess Was Callous," *Syracuse Herald-J.*, 12 Sept. 1997, at A8.

C. **More . . . rather than*. It's poor syntax to write *more . . . rather than*—e.g.: "His ideological convictions . . . were defined *more* by present-day concerns *rather* [delete *rather*] *than* by thirteenth-century conditions." Robert E. Norton, *Secret Germany* 667 (2002).

rather unique. See ADJECTIVES (B).

rathskeller (= a basement, pub, or tavern), a GERMANICISM dating from the mid-18th century, is pronounced either /**raht**-skel-ər/ or /**rath**-skel-ər/.

ratiocination; rationalization. *Ratiocination* /rash-ee-os-ə-**nay**-shən/ = the process or an act of reasoning. *Rationalization* = (1) an act or instance of explaining (away) by bringing into conformity with reason; or (2) (colloq.) the finding of "reasons" for irrational or unworthy behavior. Sense 2 is responsible for the negative connotations of the word.

rational. See **reasonable.**

rationale (= a reasoned exposition of principles; an explanation or statement of reasons) is not to be confused with *rationalization.* (See **ratiocination.**) *Rationale* routinely has three syllables (/rash-ə-**nal**/), despite H.W. Fowler's belief that it should be four syllables based on its Latin ETYMOLOGY (-*ale* being two syllables). Today, his pronunciation (/rash-ə-**nay**-lee/) would sound terribly pedantic in most company. The final syllable is now pronounced like that in *morale* or *chorale.*

Occasionally the noun *rationale* is confused with the adjective *rational*: " 'The *rational* [read *rationale*] that they used in that *defies* [read *escapes*] me.' " Bill Martin, "All Dressed Up . . . ," *Austin Am.-Statesman,* 24 May 1994, at C8 (quoting Wayne Graham, the Rice baseball coach). Although the second error in that sentence is surely the speaker's, the *rational–rationale* mistake is probably the journalist's.

LANGUAGE-CHANGE INDEX
rational misused for *rationale*: Stage 1

rationalization. See **ratiocination.**

ravage; ravish. *Ravage* (= destruction or devastation, usu. through repeated acts over a sustained period) is sometimes confused with *ravish* (= [1] to abduct and rape, or [2] to enrapture)—e.g.:

- "Still, to see the *ravishes* [read *ravages*] of too much salinity in the river continues to upset residents as well as environmentalists." Janis D. Froelich, "Hillsborough River Too Salty, Friends Say," *Tampa Trib.,* 14 Dec. 2000, at 1.
- "People fleeing the *ravishes* [read *ravages*] of Eastern Europe, Africa and elsewhere are confined for months at a time while their paperwork is 'processed.' " Eric Harrison, " 'Last Resort' Builds on a Dream," *Houston Chron.,* 30 Mar. 2001, at 5.
- "Marcus was about to ask how the mechanism had withstood the *ravishes* [read *ravages*] of time, but David merely said he had no idea." Johan Minto, *The Heliopolis Scrolls* 216 (2009).

As in those examples, the word *ravage* typically occurs in a plural construction <the ravages of time>. *Ravage* is also occasionally used as a verb meaning "to ruin, destroy" <tornadoes ravaged the area>.

The opposite error (*ravage* for *ravish*) is rare, but it does occur—e.g.: "If necessary, I would claim that I went to visit my friend Mariana and that he attempted to *ravage* [read *ravish*] me, but I doubted it would come to that." Peter Robinson, "The Duke's Wife," in *Much Ado About Murder* 284, 292 (2002).

The word *ravish*, now literary or archaic, should be avoided in nonfigurative contexts. The primary problem with *ravish* is that it has romantic connotations: it means not only "to rape" but also "to fill with ecstasy or delight." The latter sense renders the word unfit for acting as a technical or legal equivalent of *rape.* The term describing the act should evoke outrage; it should not be a romantic abstraction, as *ravish* is.

Still, the word *ravishing* (= captivating, enchanting) is generally considered a perfectly good and complimentary adjective.

LANGUAGE-CHANGE INDEX
ravish misused for *ravage*: Stage 1
Current ratio (*the ravages of* vs.
*the ravishes of): 438:1

ravel. For the use of this verb in opposite senses, see CONTRONYMS.

raven; ravin. For the verb meaning "to plunder, devour greedily," *raven* is the standard spelling <they ravened their meal>. *Ravin* is a variant spelling.

But for the related noun meaning either (1) "a violent plundering" <the utter ravin of the town>, or (2) "something preyed upon" <the town was their ravin>, *ravin* is standard and *raven* the variant. Perfectly logical and intuitive, no?

ravish. See **ravage.**

raze (= to tear down) is the standard spelling. **Rase,* a variant, is chiefly BrE.
For the misuse of *raze* for *raise,* see **hair-raising.**

RBI (= run batted in) makes the plural *RBIs,* not *RBI.* See PLURALS (I).
Current ratio (*three RBIs* vs. *three RBI): 2:1

re. See **in re.**

RE- PAIRS. Many English words beginning with the prefix *re-* take on different meanings depending on whether the word is hyphenated or closed. Some of these words, whose two different senses with and without the hyphen should be self-explanatory, are:

re(-)bound	re(-)mark
re(-)call	re(-)move
re(-)claim	re(-)place
re(-)collect	re(-)present
re(-)count	re(-)prove
re(-)cover	re(-)search
re(-)create	re(-)sent
re(-)dress	re(-)serve
re(-)form	re(-)sign
re(-)fund	re(-)sound
re(-)join	re(-)store
re(-)lay	re(-)treat
re(-)lease	

-RE; -ER. See -ER (B).

LANGUAGE-CHANGE INDEX (For the full key, see front matter pp. xxxi, l–li.)
Stage 1: Rejected. **Stage 2:** Widely shunned. **Stage 3:** Widespread but . . . **Stage 4:** Ubiquitous but . . . **Stage 5:** Fully accepted.
Invariably inferior forms marked by asterisk (*). • Ratios represent frequency of prevalent forms vs. variants in current books.

reactionary, n.; *****reactionist;** *****reactionarist; reactive.** *Reactionary* (= ultraconservative) is the standard form. **Reactionist* and **reactionarist* are NEEDLESS VARIANTS.

Reactive = (1) of, relating to, or characterized by reactions <Jones's reflexes made him an extraordinarily reactive athlete>; or (2) occurring in response to a stimulus <reactive depression>. Occasionally *reactionary* is misused for *reactive*—e.g.:

- "A strong chairman should give Mr. Barley the push he needs to make the MPO a pro-active—rather than *reactionary* [read *reactive*]—player on transportation matters." "Get Moving in 1997," *Orlando Sentinel*, 5 Jan. 1997, at G2.
- "Dan Footman, an outstanding athlete who tends to underachieve and is not a great *reactionary* [read *reactive*] player, will take [an injured player's] place." Vic Carucci, "Bills Better Be Wary of Cornered Colts," *Buffalo News*, 19 Oct. 1997, at B9.

Cf. **proactive.**

LANGUAGE-CHANGE INDEX
reactionary misused for *reactive*: Stage 1

reader-friendly. See -FRIENDLY.

ready, willing, and able. In law, this SET PHRASE traditionally refers to a prospective buyer of property who can legally and financially consummate the deal. A less common variant is *ready, able, and willing.*

real, *adj.* Since the early 18th century, *real* has been considered dialectal when used for *very*—e.g.:

- "Competition in recent years hasn't been *real* [read *very*] friendly." L. Gordon Crovitz, "Even Gentlemanly Yachtsmen Go to Court, but Why Let Them?" *Wall Street J.*, 16 May 1990, at A17.
- "But he said it *real nice* [read *very nicely*]." Gordon Edes, "Little Is Preparing a Forceful Response," *Boston Globe*, 11 Feb. 2003, at F1.
- "This was a *real* [read *very*] big deal and even I got into the countdown business." J.V. Trott, *The Cleavers Didn't Live on Our Street* 95 (2009).

The phrasing **real good* likewise is dialectal, *really good* or *quite good* (adverb + adjective) being standard—e.g.:

- "'I think the two BU teams were really talented and were *real* [read *really* or *quite*] good on special teams.'" John Connolly, "Champions Return to BU," *Boston Herald*, 4 Dec. 2000, at 86 (quoting Peter Yetten).
- "'I don't think anybody is feeling *real* [read *really*] good about him [Al Gore] right now.'" "Missing Man," *Newsweek*, 11 Dec. 2000, at 43 (quoting Miami mayor Alex Penelas).
- "A *real* [read *really*] good mortgage lender can tell within five minutes if he can give you a loan from looking at your report." Carl Agard, *Getting the Real Out of Real Estate* 65–66 (2007).

See DIALECT.

LANGUAGE-CHANGE INDEX
real for *really* <*he's feeling real bad>: Stage 3
Current ratio: 3:1
Current ratio (*feeling really bad* vs.
**feeling real bad*): 5:1

real-estate agent. See **realtor.**

real facts. See **fact** (C), (E).

realtor; real-estate agent; estate agent. *Realtor* (= a real-estate agent or broker) has two syllables, not three: /**reel**-tər/, not /**reel**-ə-tər/. (See PRONUNCIATION (B).) This Americanism is a MORPHOLOGICAL DEFORMITY, since the *-or* suffix in Latin is appended only to verb elements, and *realt-* is not a verb element. But the term is too well established in AmE to quibble with its makeup. Its shortness commends it.

Some authorities suggest that it should be capitalized and used only in its proprietary trademark sense, that is, "a member of the National Association of Realtors"; that organization invented and registered the trademark in 1916. Few people seem to know about the trademark, and consequently in AmE the term is used indiscriminately of real-estate agents generally. In BrE, *real-estate agents* are known as *estate agents*, *realtor* is virtually unknown, and the phrase *real estate* is only a little better known.

LANGUAGE-CHANGE INDEX
realtor mispronounced with three syllables: Stage 1

realty (= a property in the form of land and buildings or other fixtures attached to the land) is pronounced in two syllables: /**reel**-tee/—not /**reel**-ə-tee/.

rear. See **raise** (A).

rearward(s). See DIRECTIONAL WORDS (A).

reasonable; rational. Generally, *reasonable* means "according to reason; sensible." *Rational* means "having reason." Yet *reasonable* is often used in reference to people in the sense "having the faculty of reason" <reasonable person>. When applied to things, the two words are perhaps more clearly differentiated: "In application to things *reasonable* and *rational* both signify according to *reason*; but the former is used in reference to the business of life, as a *reasonable* proposal, wish, etc.; *rational* to abstract matters, as *rational* motives, grounds, questions, etc." George Crabb, *Crabb's English Synonymes* 589 (John H. Finley ed., 2d ed. 1917).

*****reasonable-minded** is a REDUNDANCY that sprang up in the late 19th century, first in BrE in the late 1860s and then in AmE in the late 1870s. It persists—e.g.:

- "It's the kind of hard work that any *reasonable-minded* [read *reasonable*] person would go to extreme lengths to avoid." Arthur Hoppe, "The Secret Key to Fitness," *S.F. Chron.*, 3 July 1994, at 1.
- "Operation Rescue turns off *reasonable-minded* [read *reasonable*] people when it harasses women at abortion clinics." Joseph Perkins, "Animal Rights Extremists Are Hurting Own Cause," *Rocky Mountain News* (Denver), 22 May 1997, at A68.

reasonableness; *reasonability. The former has been standard since the 17th century. The latter has been a NEEDLESS VARIANT ever since.

*****reason is because.** This construction is loose because *reason* implies *because* and vice versa. Robert

W. Burchfield, the distinguished *OED* lexicographer, put it well: "Though often defended by modern grammarians, the type 'the reason . . . is because' (instead of 'the reason . . . is that') aches with redundancy, and is still as inadmissible in Standard English as it was when H.W. Fowler objected to it in 1926." *Points of View* 116 (1992).

After *reason is*, you'll need a noun phrase, a predicate adjective, or a clause introduced by *that*. The best cure for **reason is because* is to replace *because* with *that*—e.g.:

- "Marcello (Jean Reno) has one frantic mission in life: to keep anyone from dying in the small Italian village where he lives. The *reason is because* [read *reason is that*] there are only three plots left in the local cemetery and his terminally ill wife, Roseanna (Mercedes Ruehl), wishes only that she be buried next to their daughter." "Ticket," *Star-Ledger* (Newark), 27 June 1997, at 14.
- "The second *reason is because of* [read *reason relates to*] the different research perspectives taken in regard to the causes of dyslexia." Denis Lawrence, *Understanding Dyslexia* 29 (2009).
- "There are varying opinions about how a financial model should look. One *reason is because* [read *reason is that*] modeling is a relatively recent practice." Jack Avon, *The Handbook of Financial Modeling* xiii (2013).

As an empirical matter, STANDARD ENGLISH has embraced *reason is that* over **reason is because* since the late 18th century. The predominance of the former has been most stark since 1900.

Variations such as **reason is due to* are no better—e.g.: "It's a challenge for any athlete to come back after four years of inactivity. The challenge is even greater when *the reason is due to injury* [read *the layoff is due to injury* or *injury is the cause*]." Barry Lewis, "Long Wait Is Over: Kojima's on Mound," *Tulsa Trib. & Tulsa World*, 4 May 1997, at B1. Cf. **reason why.**

LANGUAGE-CHANGE INDEX
1. **reason . . . is because*: Stage 4
Current ratio (*reason is that* vs. **reason is because*): 22:1
2. **reason . . . is due to*: Stage 4

*reasons account for. This odd, illogical construction appears to result from writers' seeking to avoid both the noun *things* (and therefore resort to *reasons*) and the construction *there are* (see **there is**). But either of those choices is preferable to the idea that a reason can account for something. There can be several reasons for a phenomenon; or several things can account for it. But idiomatically speaking, the reasons don't account—e.g.:

- "Several *reasons account* for the trend, specialists say, but most point to one reason: experience." Raphael Lewis, "Teen Drivers Said to Pose Increased Risk," *Boston Globe*, 16 Mar. 2000, at B4. [A suggested revision: *Several things account for the trend, specialists say, but most point to one: experience.* Or: *There are several reasons for the trend.*]

- "Michael Wilson, professor of geosciences at Fredonia State College, said *a number of reasons account* [read *that there are a number of reasons*] for the lake's good condition." Terry Frank, "Report Calls for Improving Lake Condition," *Buffalo News*, 12 Dec. 2000, at C2.
- "The first is that an agent necessarily knows what his or her reasons are (*reasons account for* intentional behavior, while causes might account for accidents or unintentional behaviors)." Kelly Shaver, *The Attribution of Blame* 127 (2012). (A possible revision: . . . *what his or her motivations are (motivations account for intentional behavior . . .).*)

reason why; reason that. Both forms are correct. It's an unfortunate SUPERSTITION that *reason why* is an objectionable REDUNDANCY. True, it is mildly redundant (as are *time when* and *place where*), but it has long been idiomatic. The *OED*, under *why* (5a), has examples from 1225 to 1908. The collocation *reason why* has consistently occurred more frequently than *reason that* in print sources since the early 17th century—with a steady variance since about 1680. Good writers routinely use *reason why*—e.g.:

- "The *reason why* I object to Dr. Johnson's style is that there is not discrimination, no variety in it." William Hazlitt, "On Familiar Style" (1822), in *Perspectives on Style* 112, 113 (Frederick Candelaria ed., 1968).
- "The *reason why* these things are as they are is that the people who use the language have agreed that they should be so, and not otherwise." Brainerd Kellogg, *A Text-Book on Rhetoric* 16 (1881).
- "Indeed, one of the *reasons why* we have syntactical doubts and questions is that idiom influences and sometimes defies pure 'grammar.' " G.H. Vallins, *Good English: How to Write It* 9 (1951).
- "The sentence also tells us the *reasons why* this is so." Lester S. King, *Why Not Say It Clearly* 39 (1978).
- "No, immortality was not the *reason why* my wife and I produced these beloved sources of dirty laundry and ceaseless noise." Bill Cosby, *Fatherhood* 15–16 (1986).
- "The *reason why* this unimportant wedding had been chosen was precisely that it was redundant." Frank Kermode, *Not Entitled* 244 (1995).
- "Yet, as one former regulator points out, there are sound *reasons why* the prudential ratios applied to banks are stricter than those applied to non-banks, such as insurance companies." Peter Martin, "Birth of Brown's Brainchild," *Fin. Times*, 23 May 1997, at 21.
- "Prime-time programming may drain your brain, but there's no *reason why* your TV set should." Anita Hamilton, "Cool Stuff," *Time*, 1 June 1997, at 16.

It is true, however, that *why* might have been omitted in all but the King and Martin examples.

The phrasing *reason that* is often a poor substitute for *reason why*—as in any of the examples just quoted—just as *time that* and *place that* are poor substitutes when adverbials of time and place are called for. Cf. the indefensible redundancy ***reason is because.**

LANGUAGE-CHANGE INDEX
reason why: Stage 5
Current ratio (*reason why* vs. *reason that*): 1.5:1

LANGUAGE-CHANGE INDEX (For the full key, see front matter pp. xxxi, l–li.)
Stage 1: Rejected. **Stage 2:** Widely shunned. **Stage 3:** Widespread but . . . **Stage 4:** Ubiquitous but . . . **Stage 5:** Fully accepted.
Invariably inferior forms marked by asterisk (*). • Ratios represent frequency of prevalent forms vs. variants in current books.

rebate. See **rabbet.**

rebound; re-bound. See RE- PAIRS. For an error involving *rebound*, see **redound.**

rebus (= [1] a representation of a word or phrase by pictures or symbols, such as a drawing of an eye for *I*; or [2] a riddle using these pictures or symbols) forms the plural *rebuses*, not **rebi*. E.g.: "His iconoclastic experimentation with clay included asymmetry, *rebuses*, animals, flowers and explicit sexual images expressed in fantastic forms." J.J. McCoy, "Watch This Space," *Wash. Post*, 29 May 1997, at T4.

rebut; refute. *Rebut* means "to attempt to refute." *Refute* means "to defeat (an opponent's arguments)." Hence someone who *rebuts* certainly hopes to *refute*; it is immodest to assume, however, that one has *refuted* another's arguments. *Rebut* is sometimes misspelled **rebutt*. See **refute.**

recall; re-call. See RE- PAIRS.

recant; recount. *Recant* = to publicly repudiate a previous statement, belief, or accusation. *Recount* = to narrate a past event, esp. from personal experience. *Recant* sometimes erroneously displaces the similar-sounding *recount*—e.g.:

- "Keep a 'holiday memories' book and ask each guest to write a small passage describing a special moment of the evening or past year. This will provide a great opportunity for guests to *recant* [read *recount*] past holiday stories and memories year after year." "A Time for Traditions," *Topeka Capital-J.*, 8 Dec. 2001, at A2.
- "Dressed in a top hat and tails, [Mel] Garrett chats with his riders and *recants* [read *recounts*] tales of Weston's glory days." Patti Brown, "Relish Vintage Feel of Missouri River Town," *Des Moines Register*, 19 May 2002, at F5.
- "[Jason] Heath *recants* [read *recounts*] his brief history in the sport of bouldering." Scott Keepfer, "A Little Time and a Little Effort," *Greenville News* (S.C.), 22 Oct. 2002, at D2.

The *OED* does give "recount" as one sense of *recant* but labels it obsolete and rare. The most recent example is from 1611.

Recant is best reserved for use with personal statements and public positions (think *cant* = "sing"). Other words are better suited when the thing taken back is something other than words—e.g.:

- "The state's consumer counsel has asked state regulators to *recant* [read *reverse*] a recent decision under which she said Yankee Gas ratepayers would bear all of the costs of the company's proposed multimillion-dollar system expansion." "Gas Rate Decision 'Fatally Flawed,' " *Hartford Courant*, 14 Feb. 2002, at E6.
- "Why do I feel like I'm listening to a deathbed confession by someone who's been a bastard all his life and suddenly, at the 11th hour, is terrified and wants to *recant* [read *make up for* or *renounce*?] his evil ways?" Fred Pfisterer, "Helms' Apologies Somewhat Unmoving," *Daily News Leader* (Staunton, Va.), 5 Mar. 2002, at A9.
- "Worcester was a special hotbed of revolt. On August 27, 1774, an estimated 3,000 people gathered on the Common to watch Timothy Paine *recant* [read *resign*] his

appointment to the Governor's Council." Albert B. Southwick, " 'First' American Revolution Began in Worcester, Towns," *Sunday Telegram* (Worcester), 7 Apr. 2002, at C3.

Recant may be transitive (as in the first use in the following example) or intransitive (as in the second): "Police have a follow-up interview scheduled with Olowokandi's former girlfriend, Suzanne Ketcham, who says she plans to *recant* her original statements to them and a representative of the district attorney's special victims unit. [¶] 'It's not unusual for victims of domestic abuse to *recant*,' Nilsson said." Elliott Teaford, "Olowokandi Case Will Go to D.A.," *L.A. Times*, 7 Dec. 2001, Sports §, at 5.

LANGUAGE-CHANGE INDEX
1. *recant* misused for *recount*: Stage 1
2. *recant* misused for *reverse, renounce,* or *resign*: Stage 1

receipt, v.t., began as an Americanism in the 18th century and soon spread to BrE, reaching the pinnacle of its popularity about 1920. It is COMMERCIALESE, but there is no grammatical problem in writing *the bill must be receipted* or *the sale was receipted*. The verb appears most often in the PASSIVE VOICE—e.g.:

- "Items are supposed to be *receipted*, stored and disposed of properly." Kevin Murphy, "Liquor Control Supervisor Fired," *Kansas City Star*, 9 May 1997, at C3.
- "Hence on noticing a *receipted* invoice, the auditor should verify that neither the original nor the duplicate thereof has already been entered in the Purchase Day Book." Arun Kumar & Rachana Sharma, *Auditing* 207 (2001).
- "Many auditors now practicing will recall that invoices were mailed with checks—to be *receipted* and returned to the payers." Harvey Cardwell, *Principles of Audit Surveillance* 276 (2005).

receipt of, in. See **in receipt of.**

receivables (= debts owed to a business and regarded as assets) began in the mid-19th century as an Americanism but is now current in BrE as well. It is the antonym of *payables*. See ADJECTIVES (C) & FUNCTIONAL SHIFT (C).

receive. See SPELLING (A).

recense. See **revise.**

recension (= the revision of a text) is not to be confused with *rescission*. See **rescission.**

recess, n. & vb. The noun *recess* is preferably pronounced /ri-**ses**/ in reference either to an alcove or niche in the wall of a room or to a secluded place where things are hidden. It is preferably pronounced /**ree**-ses/ for a brief period of rest, play, or inactivity between sessions, lessons, etc. The verb *recess* (= [1] to place within an indentation, [2] to make an indentation in, or [3] to take a break) is pronounced /ri-**ses**/ in STANDARD ENGLISH.

recidivist, n. & adj.; **recidivistic; *recidivous.* *Recidivist* can be both a noun (meaning "a habitual criminal") and an adjective (meaning "habitually criminal") <recidivist behavior> <recidivist offenders>. The adjectives *recidivistic and *recidivous are NOW NEEDLESS VARIANTS.

Current ratio (*recidivist offenders* vs. *recidivistic offenders*): 6:1

reciprocity; reciprocation. *Reciprocity* = (1) the state of being reciprocal <over the years they achieved a satisfactory reciprocity>; or (2) the mutual concession of advantages or privileges for purposes of commercial or diplomatic relations <their reciprocity in according favors worked to each one's advantage>. *Reciprocation* = the action of doing something in return <a concession made without hope of reciprocation>.

Coupling either word with *mutual* creates a REDUNDANCY—e.g.: "We also witness a touching emotional resolution of the situation and learn of the long-standing *mutual reciprocation* [read *reciprocity*] between the two." Joan Hinkemeyer, "Ferroll Sams Authors 3 Hopeful Looks at the Human Condition," *Rocky Mountain News* (Denver), 28 May 1995, at A80. See **mutual.**

*recision; *recission. See **rescission (A).**

recital; recitation. These words overlap, but are distinguishable. Aside from a (usually) solo musical or dance performance, *recital* may mean "a rehearsal, account, or description of some thing, fact, or incident" <a recital of all the incidents would be tedious>. *Recitation* usually connotes an oral delivery before an audience, whether in the classroom or on stage. Yet it is more often the general noun meaning "the act of reciting"—e.g.: "This continuing tension is realized in a series of formal tropes: angry monologues, *recitations* of dreams, discussions of cartographic representation of Greenland and what they call their 'truth game.'" Ben Brantley, "Whimsy as a Tool to Deal with AIDS," *N.Y. Times*, 29 June 1995, at C11.

recitative, n. & adj., is preferably pronounced /res-ə-tə-**teev**/ as a noun (meaning "a type of vocal music delivered in a declamatory style") and /ri-**sit**-ə-tiv/ or /ri-**si**-tə-tiv/ as an adjective (meaning "narrative or repetitive"). See Victor Fell Yellin, "The Pronunciation of 'Recitative,'" 43 *Am. Speech* 291–96 (1968).

reckless. So spelled. In a fairly gross error, the word is frequently misspelled **wreckless*, which appears to denote precisely the opposite of what it's supposed to mean. As literacy in the higher sense has become ever shakier, this error has become disturbingly common—e.g.:

• "It begins with the cast making mindless revelry; the quality of movement is disturbingly loose and *wreckless* [read *reckless*]." Nancy Goldner, "'Speaking in Tongues' World Premiere at the Annenberg," *Phil. Inquirer*, 11 Nov. 1988, at 15.

• "Racette was charged with *wreckless* [read *reckless*] operation of a motor vehicle, speeding and failure to keep right, police said." "10 Injured in Fiery Dracut Accident," *Boston Globe*, 4 Feb. 1990, at 66.

• "Ohio Wesleyan played aggressively—often *wrecklessly* [read *recklessly*]—in the first quarter in building its lead." Gene Wang, "Hobart Wins 13th NCAA Title," *Wash. Post*, 31 May 1993, at C9.

• "But while Clinton is in Portland this week, the hope here is that he'll reconsider his administration's *wreckless* [read *reckless*] course." "To: The President, II," *Oregonian* (Portland), 26 June 1995, at B6.

• "Raabe faces several charges, including third-degree assault and *wreckless* [read *reckless*] driving." "2 Denver Traffic Cops Hit, Injured by a Car," *Denver Post*, 7 Dec. 2001, at B3.

The second and fifth examples are particularly ironic misspellings, given the contexts. For the sense of the word *reckless*, see **wanton.**

LANGUAGE-CHANGE INDEX
reckless misspelled **wreckless*: Stage 1
Current ratio: 1,072:1

reclaim; re-claim. See RE- PAIRS.

recognizance; reconnaissance; *reconnoissance. *Recognizance* = a bond or obligation, made in court, by which a person (called the *recognizor*) promises to perform some act or observe some condition (as to appear when called on, to pay a debt, or to keep the peace). E.g.: "The suspect was released on his own *recognizance.*"

In BrE, the *-g-* in *recognisance* (as it is spelled in BrE) is silent. But in AmE, the *-g-* is regularly sounded.

Reconnaissance = a preliminary survey; a military or intelligence-gathering examination of a region. **Reconnoissance* is an archaic French spelling of *reconnaissance*; it is also a NEEDLESS VARIANT of *recognizance* and of *recognition*. The verb corresponding to *reconnaissance* is *reconnoiter*. See **reconnoiter.**

recognize /**rek**-əg-nɪz/ is often mispronounced /**rek**-ə-nɪz/, without the *-g-* sounded.

recollect. A. And *remember*. The distinction is a subtle one worth observing. To *remember* is to retrieve what is ready at hand in one's memory. To *recollect* is to find something stored further back in the mind. As the *OED* puts it, "*Recollect*, when distinguished from *remember*, implies a conscious or express effort of memory to recall something [that] does not spontaneously rise in the mind."

B. And *re-collect*. As with other RE- PAIRS, the hyphen is crucial: *recollect* means "to remember, recall"; *re-collect* means (1) "to collect (something) again," or (2) "to gather or compose (oneself)."

recompense—both a noun ("payment in return for something") and a transitive verb ("to repay, compensate")—is a FORMAL WORD equivalent to but more

LANGUAGE-CHANGE INDEX (For the full key, see front matter pp. xxxi, l–li.)
Stage 1: Rejected. **Stage 2:** Widely shunned. **Stage 3:** Widespread but . . . **Stage 4:** Ubiquitous but . . . **Stage 5:** Fully accepted.
Invariably inferior forms marked by asterisk (*). • Ratios represent frequency of prevalent forms vs. variants in current books.

learned than *compensation* or *compensate*. In BrE, the noun is sometimes spelled *recompence*. *Recompense* is more frequently a noun than a verb—e.g.:

- "Serving both interests would be fitting *recompense* for the government's role in grossly polluting Chattanooga Creek." Letter of Harry Austin, "The Right Cleanup Decision," *Chattanooga Times*, 26 June 1995, at A6.
- "In *recompense* for his acceptance of NATO expansion, Yeltsin got the privileges appropriate to a leader of one of the world's eight most advanced economies." "A Summit of Symbols," *Boston Globe*, 24 June 1997, at A14.
- "The blogger then published her own version of events, saying she deserved suitable *recompense* for writing a post she claimed would take eight hours." Emma Lunn, "When Bloggers Are Expecting a Meal Ticket, Why Should We Trust Their Reviews?" *Independent*, 22 Aug. 2015, at 52.

See **compensate (B)**.

recondite (= difficult to understand) is traditionally pronounced /ri-**kon**-dɪt/, but /**rek**-ən-dɪt/ is now usual.

reconnaissance; *reconnoissance. See **recognizance**.

reconnoiter; reconnoitre. The verb form corresponding to the noun *reconnaissance* is predominantly spelled *-er* in AmE, *-re* in BrE. See -ER (B) & **recognizance**. It is pronounced /ree-kə-**noy**-tər/ or /rek-ə-**noy**-tər/.

recount. On the difference between *recount* and *re-count*, see RE- PAIRS. For the misuse of *recant* for *recount*, see **recant.**

recountal (= a narration or recital) is the noun corresponding to the verb *recount* (as opposed to the verb *re-count* [= to count again]). It dates from the early 19th century. **Recountment* is an obsolete variant used by Shakespeare.

Current ratio: 21:1

recoup; recuperate. *Recoup*, dating from the 15th century as an English word, is a transitive verb with two senses: (1) "to get back (lost money, etc.)"; and (2) "to pay back (money owed, etc.)." Although sense 2 is older, sense 1 is now predominant. *Recuperate*, dating from the mid-16th century, is now almost always intransitive with the sense "to get well; to regain one's strength after a medical procedure or an illness."

The *OED* illustrates the misuse of *recoup* for *recuperate* with two quotations (from 1939 and 1955). The mistake is still in our midst—e.g.:

- "Still *recouping* [read *recuperating*] from foot surgery and planning to strike a long-term performance deal in Las Vegas for early next year, Cassidy kicked back and watched hours of rare footage of the Rats in action." Michael Paskevich, "Desert Rats," *Las Vegas Rev.-J.*, 23 July 1999, at J3.
- "*Recouping* [read *recuperating*] from recent triple-bypass surgery, 32-year-old John Jackson Jr. has told Fox Sports he'll try to pull a Letterman comeback." Tom Hoffarth, "What Smokes," *Daily News* (L.A.), 31 Mar. 2000, at S6.
- "Parnes, who wishes there were a break this time of year so children could *recoup* [read *recuperate*] from illnesses, warned that she foresees a long winter ahead." Linda

Perlstein, "Illness Brings Rise in School Absenteeism," *Wash. Post*, 1 Feb. 2001, at T3.

A related mistake is the misspelling **recouperate*—e.g.: "Lance Diamond, the godfather of Buffalo soul, is in Mercy Hospital *recouperating* [read *recuperating*] from a flu-like illness." Anthony Violante, "Diamond in the Rough," *Buffalo News*, 30 Nov. 2000, at C2.

The *OED* records two examples of "recuperating" losses—from 1891 and 1924—noting that they are rare. They are actually misuses of *recuperate* for *recoup*, an occasional error even today—e.g.:

- "The funeral provider would have to file a civil lawsuit to *recuperate* [read *recoup*] its money, Yabuno said." Sharyn Obsatz, "Ex-Mortuary Firm Executive Pleads Guilty," *Press-Enterprise* (Riverside, Cal.), 19 July 2000, at B1.
- "Pemex invested about $4.7 million. . . . It expects to *recuperate* [read *recoup*] the money in about 18 months, Ramirez said." "Pemex to Go Online with Natural Gas," *Houston Chron.*, 29 July 2000, Bus. §, at 2.
- "The mayors of Montreal and Laval have pledged to do everything in their power to *recuperate* [read *recoup*] money stolen from taxpayers over the past two decades." Monique Muise, "Montreal Won't Take Action Against Former Employees," *Montreal Gaz.*, 6 Aug. 2014, at A6.

LANGUAGE-CHANGE INDEX
1. *recoup* misused for *recuperate*: Stage 3
2. *recuperate* misused for *recoup*: Stage 2
Current ratio (*recoup the loss* vs.
*recuperate the loss): 7:1

recourse; resource. These words are unrelated. To have *recourse* to something is to turn to it for aid or protection <recourse to the law>; to be without *recourse* is to have no remedy <she thought about suing but found she had no recourse>. A *resource* is something that is available for use, such as wealth or books or other assets.

Sometimes one word gets swapped for the other—e.g.: "William Blake and Walt Whitman, whose main source for their renovation of poetry into free verse was the Bible, saw, without *resource* [read *recourse*] to the more extensive verse typography found in the revised versions, that the Bible was an endless fountain of poetry." Willis Barnstone, "Three Invisible Poets," *Southwest Rev.*, 22 Mar. 2001, at 412. See WORD-SWAPPING.

LANGUAGE-CHANGE INDEX
resource misused for *recourse*: Stage 1
Current ratio (*without recourse* vs.
*without resource): 19:1

recover; re-cover. See RE- PAIRS.

recreate; re-create. A distinction is fading. *Recreate* = (1) to amuse oneself by indulging in recreation; or (2) (of a pastime) to agreeably occupy. *Re-create* = to create anew. Classically, the hyphen makes a great difference—e.g.:

- "Her days are divided between frolicking in the sand and *recreating* in a resort hotel." A. Scott Walton, "Peach Buzz," *Atlanta J.-Const.*, 19 Mar. 1995, at E2.

- "The dining rooms feature big, open rooms and vintage signs designed to *re-create* the airy, energetic atmosphere of 1940s Gulf seafood houses." Barbara Chavez, "City Reeling in Landry's Seafood Chain," *Albuquerque J.*, 21 Sept. 1995, at D6.

But *recreate* is so much more common than *re-create*—and the tendency to delete the hyphen after a prefix is so strong in AmE—that *recreate* is losing the senses listed above and is taking over the meaning of *re-create*. The process is now almost complete. Still, some careful editors continue to make the distinction. See RE- PAIRS.

recreational; recreative. *Recreational* is the standard adjective corresponding to the noun *recreation*; it's about a thousand times as common as its synonym *recreative*, a NEEDLESS VARIANT. But *recreative* is genuinely useful in the sense "tending to re-create"—e.g.: "The paradoxically destructive and *recreative* force of the mythical flood seemed as real to Friday's performers as it must have to the composer." Timothy Pfaff, "Innocence of Children Survives 'Noah's Flood,'" *S.F. Examiner*, 24 June 1995, at C1.

recriminatory; *recriminative. The former has been standard since the late 18th century. The latter has always been a NEEDLESS VARIANT.

Current ratio: 9:1

recruitment; *recruital. Since about 1950, *recruitment* has been the predominant noun in AmE and BrE alike. Though standard from the 1840s to about 1950, **recruital* has now become a NEEDLESS VARIANT.

Current ratio: 30,378:1

recuperate. See **recoup.**

recur; reoccur. The first means "to happen repeatedly, often at more or less regular intervals." The second (less common) means merely "to happen again." See **relapse.**

recurrence; *recurrency; reoccurrence. *Recurrence* refers to a repeated occurrence, especially at fairly regular intervals. **Recurrency* is a NEEDLESS VARIANT. *Reoccurrence* refers to another occurrence of something, with no suggestion that the thing happens repeatedly or at more or less regular intervals.

recusal; *recusation; *recusement; recusancy; *recusance. The preferred noun corresponding to the verb *recuse* (= to remove [oneself] as a judge considering a case) is *recusal*, though its earliest known use is only as recent as 1950: "On the 13th of April, Judge Longshore filed an order of *recusal* accompanied by an order vacating his former order." *Methvin v. Haynes*, 46 So. 2d 815, 817 (Ala. 1950). **Recusation* reigned supreme as STANDARD ENGLISH from the 18th century to the early 1970s, but mysteriously it is now

almost unknown; it has become a NEEDLESS VARIANT. **Recusement* (not listed in the *OED*), though once common, is also now a NEEDLESS VARIANT.

Recusancy is a different word, meaning "obstinate refusal to comply." **Recusance* is a NEEDLESS VARIANT of *recusancy*.

Current ratio (*recusal* vs. **recusation*): 19:1

redact. See **revise.**

redeemable; *redemptible. The first is standard. Avoid the second, which is pedantic, unnecessary, and irredeemable—in short, a NEEDLESS VARIANT.

redemptive; *redemptory; redemptional. *Redemptive* = tending to redeem, redeeming. **Redemptory* is a NEEDLESS VARIANT. *Redemptional* = of, relating to, or involving redemption.

redolent (= [1] strongly aromatic, scented, or [2] evocative or suggestive) is pronounced /**red**-ə-lənt/—not /ri-**dohl**-ənt/. When a preposition follows the word, idiom requires *of* <a potpourri redolent of lilacs> <an experience redolent of my boyhood>.

redoubtable (= [1] venerable; or [2] fearsome) is a 14th-century loanword from the Old French *redoutable* (= dreaded). Both senses are common:

- Sense 1: "Chipperfield and a number of 'britischer Architekten,' as Architectural Review notes in its April 2006 issue, have been leaving a *redoubtable* imprimatur on Germany's landscape." Suzanne Stephens, "David Chipperfield Architects Combines Modernism and Classicism with a Reductive Clarity in the New Modern Literature Museum in Marbach, Germany," *Architectural Record*, 1 Feb. 2007, at 102.
- Sense 2: "The Irish were *redoubtable* duellists, but so lacking in decorum when potting each other that, in 1777, delegates from five counties assembled to hammer out the Irish Code Duello." Arthur Krystal, "En Garde! The History of Duelling," *New Yorker*, 12 Mar. 2007, at 80. (On the spelling of *dueling* vs. *duelling*—and likewise *duelist* vs. *duellist*—see **duel.**)

The writer's meaning isn't always clear, though—e.g.: "As the new year approached, the man set to become the new Senate majority leader was the *redoubtable* Harry Reid, possibly the most interesting boring guy in Washington." Todd S. Purdum, "The Majordomo: Senator Harry Reid," *Vanity Fair*, Feb. 2007, at 130. (Is the "boring" senator being labeled fearsome? eminent? merely powerful?)

redound, now used most commonly in the verbose expressions *to redound to the benefit of* (= to benefit) and *to redound to one's credit*, may also be used in negative senses <to redound against or to the shame of>. E.g.: "If I leave before the new villa is complete, I will have more questions to answer than I would care to deal with, and I would leave behind speculation that

LANGUAGE-CHANGE INDEX (For the full key, see front matter pp. xxxi, l–li.)
Stage 1: Rejected. **Stage 2:** Widely shunned. **Stage 3:** Widespread but . . . **Stage 4:** Ubiquitous but . . . **Stage 5:** Fully accepted.
Invariably inferior forms marked by asterisk (*). • Ratios represent frequency of prevalent forms vs. variants in current books.

could *redound* to you." Chelsea Quinn Yarbro, *Communion Blood* 304 (1999).

Unfortunately, some writers confuse this word with *rebound*—e.g.:

- "If these remarks may be understood only as opinion, the words of Eros further emphasize Shakespeare's intention, *Eros* [read *Eros'*] statement being especially important because it deviates from the source where the indicated events *rebound* [read *redound*] largely to Anthony's discredit." J. Leeds Barroll, "Shakespeare and the Art of Character: A Study of Anthony," 5 *Shakespeare Studies* 159, 171 (1969).
- "Weavers are favored by karmic forces, and such endeavors as the saving of a weaver's life can *rebound* [read *redound*] to one's benefit at the most unexpected times." Peter David, *Sir Apropos of Nothing* 110 (2001).

The ETYMOLOGY of *redound* lies in the Latin *und* "wave," and the word implies an advancing and receding move.

LANGUAGE-CHANGE INDEX
rebound misused for *redound*: Stage 1
Current ratio (*redound to the benefit* vs.
*rebound to the benefit): 14:1

redress, n. & vb. The noun *redress* (= [1] the means of correcting a wrong, or [2] the act of correcting something wrong or unfair) is pronounced /**ree**-dres/ in AmE but /ri-**dres**/ in BrE. The verb *redress* (= [1] to set right, rectify, or remedy, or [2] to compensate or make up for) is uniformly pronounced /ri-**dres**/ in STANDARD ENGLISH. On *redress* vs. *re-dress*, see RE- PAIRS.

redressable. So spelled in AmE and BrE alike—preferably not **redressible*. But this represents a change in spelling from the 18th-century standard (*-ible*), which persisted into the 20th century. *Redressable* became the predominant form in AmE in the 1940s and in BrE as recently as the 1980s. See -ABLE (A).

red tape. Lawyers and government officials formerly used red ribbons (called "tapes") to tie their papers together. Gradually during the 19th century, these red ribbons came to symbolize rigid adherence to time-consuming rules and regulations. Writers such as Scott, Longfellow, and Dickens used the term *red tape*, and now it has become universal. But its origins are widely forgotten.

reducible. So spelled—not **reduceable*. See -ABLE (A).
Current ratio: 364:1

REDUNDANCY. Washington Irving wrote that "redundancy of language is never found with deep reflection. Verbiage may indicate observation, but not thinking. He who thinks much says but little in proportion to his thoughts." Those words are worth reflecting on.

This linguistic pitfall is best exemplified rather than discoursed on:

- "Ms. Kwok believed *the cause of the heavy rainfall was due to two major factors* [read *that two things caused the heavy rainfall*]." Andrew Laxton & Edward Laxton, "Sun to Take a Rain-Check as Expert Forecasts Gloom," *South China Morning Post*, 21 Aug. 1994, at 4. See **cause . . . is due to.**

- "Unaware of the spider's *poisonous venom* [read *venom* or *poisonous bite*], Martinez grabbed a *piece of tissue paper* [read *tissue*] to get rid of it the way she normally gets rid of critters." Hank Rosenblum, "Spider Bite Tip Helps Save Tot, 3," *Denver Post*, 29 Sept. 1994, at B1.
- "A woman with a permanent disability who claims she received a low *test* score for the law school entrance *exam test* because the test-givers wouldn't accommodate her has sued them for emotional distress." Lauren Blau, "LSAT Target of Woman's Suit," *L.A. Daily J.*, 15 Nov. 1995, at 3. (*Test* appears twice, once in the phrase *exam test*, tripling the redundancy.)
- "Bush also went high profile, *choosing* as one of his *picks* baseball legend Nolan Ryan for a six-year term." "Bush's Appointees Settle In Quickly," *Austin Am.-Statesman*, 24 Dec. 1995, at D11. (*Choosing as one of his picks* is tautological. If it read, less colloquially, *choosing as one of his choices* it would have been more obvious both to the writer and to the editors that the phrasing was redundant.)
- "Curtis and Company was a prosperous chemist's shop on Crawford Street, the nearest such to Baker Street; Holmes and I both *frequented* the establishment *on a regular basis*." Barbara Paul, "The Sleuth of Christmas Past," in *Holmes for the Holidays* 18, 19 (Martin H. Greenberg et al. eds., 1996). ("To frequent" means to "to visit (a place) often or habitually.")
- "That each creature from microbe to man is unique in all the world is amazing when you consider that every life form is assembled from *the same identical* [read *the same* or *identical*] building blocks." George Johnson, "Soul Searching," *N.Y. Times*, 2 Mar. 1997, § 4, at 1. See **identical.**
- "Building on those beginnings and armed with *new innovations* [read *innovations*], the industry today is staking its future on new territory." "Offshore Oil's Half-Century Mark," *Times-Picayune* (New Orleans), 16 Nov. 1997, at B6.
- "As local Chinese opera was performed on a stage on the balcony, a distinguished audience watched from the courtyard that was gardened with tall trees and elegant *dwarf bonsais*." Mark Kurlansky, *Salt: A World History* 375 (2002). (The author tried to create a distinction by using *tall* and *dwarf*, but bonsais are dwarfs by definition.)
- "*Religious hymns* [read *Hymns*] were playing in the background." Jennifer Emily, "Documents: Mom Thanked God After Attack," *Dallas Morning News*, 16 Dec. 2004, at B4.

Samuel Johnson once advised writers to "avoid ponderous ponderosity." His repetition of word roots, of course, was purposeful. But many writers engage in such repetitions with no sense of irony, as in the phrases *build a building, refer to a reference, point out points, an individualistic individual*. In the sentences that follow, the repetitions are thoughtless errors:

- "Other issues include preserving a minimum set of *state-required requirements* [read *state-imposed requirements* or *state requirements*] like class size and teacher benefits in home-rule districts." Kendall Anderson, "PISD Monitoring State Education Reform," *Dallas Morning News*, 23 Mar. 1995, at G1.
- "When Madison drafted the Constitution, he was concerned that *specifying certain specific rights* [read *specifying certain rights*] in the Bill of Rights might later be thought to exclude any rights not specifically listed." Mel Lipman, "Plenty of 'New Rights,'" *Las Vegas Rev.-J.*, 11 Aug. 1997, at B6.

Though many of those mistakes look like unique ones—the result of semiconscious writing—some redundancies are so commonplace that they've been all but enshrined in the language. Adept editors must be alert to such phrases as these:

> absolute necessity
> actual fact (see **fact**)
> advance planning
> basic fundamentals
> brief respite
> closely scrutinize
> collaborate together (see **together**)
> combine together
> completely full
> connect together
> consensus of opinion (see **consensus**)
> entirely eliminate
> fellow colleagues
> few in number (see ***few in number**)
> free gift (see ***free gift**)
> future forecast
> future plans
> general consensus of opinion (see **consensus**)
> interact with each other (see **each other**)
> many . . . abound
> merge together
> mingle together
> mix together
> mutual advantage of both (see **mutual**)
> new innovation
> new recruit
> pair of twins
> pause for a moment
> plead a plea
> pooled together
> reason is because (see ***reason is because**)
> reelected for another term
> refer back
> regress back
> serious crisis
> still continues to
> surrounded on all sides
> temporary reprieve
> throughout the entire
> unfilled vacancy
> visible to the eye

For examples of redundant acronyms, see ABBREVIA-TIONS (B).

Is a one-word redundancy possible? Certainly, with the help of suffixes and prefixes—e.g.:

- "Bipartisan bromides about the Bush administration are like Muzak—inescapable, unending and stultifying. . . . And, as Dubya would say, they '*misunderestimate*' him." Robert L. Borosage, "Operation Divide and Discredit," *Wash. Post*, 10 Jan. 2001, at A19.
- "When the first blasts echoed at 11:15 P.M., a young woman, *elfinlike* [read *elfin* or *elflike*] and angst-ridden, dashed from her home just off Regent's Park, looking for sanctuary." Colin Edwards, *The Father of Forensics* 74 (2006).

redundancy. See **tautology.**

reek; wreak. These homophones are occasionally confused. *Reek*, vb., = to give off an odor or vapor

<the house reeked of gas>. *Reek*, n., = an odorous vapor <the reek of garlic spoiled our conversation>. *Wreak* = to inflict, bring about <to wreak havoc>.

The misspelling **reek havoc* has been a frequent blunder since the 1980s, but only in AmE—e.g.:

- "Past hurricanes have *reeked* [read *wreaked*] havoc on this small fishing community of east Apalachicola." "The News in Brief," *Christian Science Monitor*, 6 June 1995, at 2.
- "Pesticides and mite infestations already have *reeked* [read *wreaked*] havoc on the population." "Across the USA: News from Every State," *USA Today*, 7 May 1996, at A8.

Also, *wreak* for *reek* is a surprisingly common slip-up—e.g.:

- "Watching Jagger, a grandfather, singing the songs of his youth is embarrassing—like watching an old tart plastered in powder, *wreaking* [read *reeking*] of cheap perfume, stumbling along the Champs-Elysees, leering at passersby." Natasha Garnett, "Focus: The Rolling Stones," *Daily Telegraph*, 7 Aug. 1994, at 14.
- "Though such a statement *wreaks* [read *reeks*] of hyperbole, Alexakis truly seemed more comfortable with the intimate give-and-take at this sold-out Middle East date on his solo tour." Tristram Lozaw, "Music: Alexakis Finds Comfort Zone," *Boston Herald*, 10 Apr. 1997, at 53.
- "Nate Newton has leaked a little information in response to reports that the Cowboys' dorm rooms at St. Edward's University *wreaked* [read *reeked*] of urine and were otherwise in a mess upon the team's checkout from training camp last week." Tim Price, "Newton Says Dorm Free of Any Pee," *San Antonio Express-News*, 21 Aug. 1997, at C1.

See **wreak (C).**

*Reak is a common misspelling of *reek*—e.g.:

- "The oil company subsequently hired a firm to clean the oil, but after six weeks of work and a declaration the house was inhabitable, the house still '*reaked* [read *reeked*] of oil,'" Hansen said." MaryAnn Spoto, "Suit Seeks Damages for Oil Spill Nightmare," *Star-Ledger* (Newark), 26 Sept. 1997, at 51.
- "Those who have briefly been able to visit the residential buildings have reported finding them filled with ash and *reaking* [read *reeking*] of rotting food." David Usborne, "America's Own Refugees: People Who Can't Go Home," *Independent*, 19 Sept. 2001, at 11.

And a DOUBLE BOBBLE results when the misspelling **reak havoc* displaces the correct form, *wreak havoc*— e.g.: "January arrived on the UW-Platteville campus and *reaked* [read *wreaked*] havoc with the men's basketball record." Nick Zizzo, "Pioneers Get Back on Track," *Wis. State J.*, 1 Feb. 2001, at E3.

LANGUAGE-CHANGE INDEX
1. **reek havoc* for *wreak havoc*: Stage 1
Current ratio (*wreak havoc* vs. **reek havoc*): 151:1
2. *wreak* misused for *reek*: Stage 1
Current ratio (*reek of* vs. **wreak of*): 174:1
3. **reak* as a misspelling of *wreak* or *reek*: Stage 1

reemerge, like many other words in which the vowel ending the prefix is also the first letter of the word proper, was once hyphenated—but no longer.

LANGUAGE-CHANGE INDEX (For the full key, see front matter pp. xxxi, l–li.)
Stage 1: Rejected. **Stage 2:** Widely shunned. **Stage 3:** Widespread but . . . **Stage 4:** Ubiquitous but . . . **Stage 5:** Fully accepted.
Invariably inferior forms marked by asterisk (*). • Ratios represent frequency of prevalent forms vs. variants in current books.

reenactment. No hyphen.

reenforce. See **reinforce.**

reenter; reentry. These terms are now solid.

reestablish, formerly hyphenated, no longer is.

refer. See **allude** (A).

referable; *referrible; *referrable. The vastly predominant form is *referable* (= capable of being referred to)—which, like *preferable*, is accented on the first syllable; otherwise, the final *-r-* would be doubled. (See SPELLING (B); cf. **conferrable.**) This spelling has held sway since the 16th century. **Referrable* and **referrible* are variant spellings that have never been serious rivals.

Current ratio (in order of headwords): 59:2:1

refer back is a common REDUNDANCY, *refer* alone nearly always being sufficient—e.g.: "Irons said he believes the judge's latest ruling *refers back* [read *refers*] to an original order in 1991 that did order the removal of the cross." Valerie Alvord & Gerry Braun, "San Diego Files Notice to Appeal Soledad Cross Ruling," *San Diego Union-Trib.*, 8 Oct. 1997, at B3.

Dating from the 18th century, the phrase *refer back* is justified when it means (as it occasionally does) "to send back to someone who or that which has previously been involved"—e.g.: "The full council wouldn't pass the plan and *referred* it *back* to the committee." Cindy Eberting, "Gaming Ads Could Stay at KCI," *Kansas City Star*, 5 June 1997, at C4. See **revert.** Cf. **relate back.**

reference, n. See **referral.**

reference, as a verb meaning "to provide with references," is defensible. E.g.: "The cross-*referenced* chapter contains two subsections." The evidence of this verb dates back to the 17th century, after which it lay quiescent till about 1950. Then it surged to an unprecedented popularity (as compared to its former self).

Since the latter half of the 20th century, the term has become a VOGUE WORD, however, as a synonym for *refer to*—e.g.:

- "You can add notes (10K) to your items, import, or simply *reference* [read *refer to* or *cite*] external files." Bill Howard, "Agenda: Lotus' Answer to Information Management," *PC Mag.*, July 1988, at 34.
- " 'And I would simply *reference* [read *refer to*] those of you who are out there working.' " "A Nominee's Withdrawal," *N.Y. Times*, 19 Jan. 1994, at A14 (quoting Bobby Ray Inman).
- "At one point, Kristof specifically *referenced* [read *referred to*] the impact that stricter gun laws can have on gun suicides." Louis Jacobson, "Columnist Correct on Calculation of Deaths," *Atlanta J.-Const.*, 4 Sept. 2015, at B1.

See FUNCTIONAL SHIFT (D) & COMPUTERESE.

LANGUAGE-CHANGE INDEX
reference in the sense "to refer to": Stage 4
Current ratio (*refer to the fact* vs.
*reference the fact): 55:1

referendum. Pl. *referendums* or *referenda.* In modern AmE journalistic sources, *referendums* is four times as common, but in AmE books, *referenda* predominates. In BrE books and journalism, the homegrown *referendums* has been dominant since about 2000. See PLURALS (B).

*referrable. See **referable.**

referral; reference. Both mean "the act of referring." *Reference* is the broader term. *Referral,* which began as an Americanism in the early 20th century but now is commonly used in BrE as well, means specifically "the referring to a third party of personal information concerning another" or "the referring of a person to an expert or specialist for advice."

*referrible. See **referable.**

referring to your letter of. See **replying to your letter of.**

reflection; *reflexion. The first spelling has been predominant in all varieties of English since the early 17th century. **Reflexion* is an archaic variant that enjoyed a brief floruit in mid-18th-century AmE. **Reflexion* was formerly common in British writing.

Current ratio: 101:1

REFLEXIVE PRONOUNS. See PRONOUNS (E).

reform; re-form. See RE- PAIRS.

refractive; refractory. These terms have undergone DIFFERENTIATION. *Refractive* = that refracts light <refractive lenses>. *Refractory* = stubborn, unmanageable, rebellious <refractory teenagers>.

refrain. See **restrain.**

refugee; evacuee. *Refugee* (= someone who flees home to seek safety) originally denoted French Huguenots who fled to England in the late 1680s to escape religious persecution. The word has another (rare) sense, denoting a fugitive on the run. *Refugee* had lost most of its connotations of foreignness or truancy when Hurricane Katrina forced thousands of New Orleans residents out of the city in August 2005. But many of those who fled objected to being referred to as *refugees* in news accounts and political discourse. Almost overnight the word was displaced by *evacuee* (= someone who withdraws from a place, esp. under an order from some authority). See -EE.

The words are pronounced /ref-yoo-**jee**/ or /**ref**-yoo-jee/ and /ee-vak-yoo-**ee**/.

refund, n. & vb. The noun *refund* (= an amount of money given back) is pronounced /**ree**-fənd/. The verb *refund* (= to return [money] by way of repayment or restitution) is pronounced /ri-**fənd**/. On the question of *refund* vs. *re-fund*, see RE- PAIRS.

refutable (= conclusively disprovable) is correctly pronounced either /ri-**fyoot**-ə-bəl/ or /**ref**-yə-tə-bəl/. Its antonym, *irrefutable,* is likewise either /ir-i-**fyoo**-tə-bəl/ or /i-**ref**-yə-tə-bəl/.

refutation; *refutal. The first is standard. The second is an unnecessary and ill-formed variant—e.g.: "In a point-by-point *refutal* [read *refutation*] of the 42-page civil action, Columbia/HCA . . . say in court documents that they were exercising 'independent business judgment.'" Roz Hutchinson, "Wesley Responds to Wichita Clinic Lawsuit," *Wichita Bus. J.* (Kan.), 22 Nov. 1996, at 5. Sometimes the word is misused for *denial*—e.g.: "Michael Shermer . . . has written a valuable primer debunking many of the crackpot obsessions of our time—alien abductions, creationist science, Holocaust *refutal* [read *denial*], the statistics-bespangled racism of the bell curve and pseudoscientific theology among them." Todd Gitlin, "Millennial Mumbo Jumbo," *L.A. Times*, 27 Apr. 1997, Book Rev. §, at 8.

> LANGUAGE-CHANGE INDEX
> *refutal for refutation or denial: Stage 1
> Current ratio (*refutation* vs. *refutal): 645:1

refutative; *refutatory. *Refutative* has predominated in BrE since the 1820s and in AmE since the 1930s. *Refutatory is a NEEDLESS VARIANT.

> Current ratio: 2:1

refute is not synonymous with *rebut* or *deny*. That is, it doesn't mean merely "to counter an argument" but "to disprove beyond doubt; to prove a statement false." Yet the word is commonly misused for *rebut*—e.g.: "Ontario Hydro strongly *refuted* [read *denied* or *rebutted*] the charges, saying none of its actions violate the Power Corporations Act." Tom Blackwell, "Local Utilities Sue Ontario Hydro over Pricing," *Ottawa Citizen*, 25 Apr. 1997, at D16. See **rebut.**

Sometimes the word is misused for *reject*—e.g.: "Two-thirds of people *refuted* [read *rejected*] [Nicholas Ridley's] belief that European Monetary Union is a 'German racket to take over the whole of Europe.'" Toby Helm, "Majority Back Euro Ideals," *Sunday Telegraph*, 15 July 1990, at 1.

Confute is essentially synonymous with *refute* in the sense "to prove to be false or wrong." It's probably the stronger term, but it's much rarer.

> LANGUAGE-CHANGE INDEX
> 1. *refute* misused for *rebut* or *deny*: Stage 1
> 2. *refute* misused for *reject*: Stage 1

regal. See **kingly.**

regard. A. As a Noun in *with regard to* and *in regard to*. In these phrases, the singular noun is standard. The plural form (as in *with regards to or *in regards to) is, to put it charitably, poor usage—e.g.:

- "In the case of Angel, it is [set] to a simple piano accompaniment, *and with regards to* [read *but with regard to* or, better, *but with*] Mimi and Roger, there is a musical gap when the line is spoken." Robert Sprayberry, "'Prescription' Results from an Under-Dose of 'Rent,'" *L.A. Times*, 20 Oct. 1997, at F3.

- "Single men and women are overwhelmed and confused by a barrage of information and advice on what to do and what not to do *in regards to* [read *in regard to*] finding Mr. Right and Ms. Girl-of-My-Dreams." Lynn Norment, "The Dos and Don'ts of the New Dating Rules," *Ebony*, Dec. 1997, at 46.

- "I've come to learn some complexities of our system, especially *in regards to* [read *with regard to*] its unique freedom of movement." David Staples, "School Success Depends on Parents," *Edmonton J.*, 4 Sept. 2015, at A4.

The acceptable forms are best used as introductory phrases. But even these may be advantageously replaced by a single word such as *concerning, regarding,* or *considering,* or even *in, about,* or *for.*

The plural *regards* is acceptable in this sense only in the phrase *as regards.* But some writers mistakenly use *with regards to—e.g.: "He became furious at the mere mention of George F. Will, the columnist who accused him recently of 'judicial exhibitionism' *with regards to* [read *with regard to*] his trade-agreement ruling." Ruth M. Bond, "At the Center of Trade-Accord Storm, Judge Bristles but Watches Image," *N.Y. Times*, 17 Sept. 1993, at B11. See **as regards.** Cf. **respect.**

> LANGUAGE-CHANGE INDEX
> 1. *in regards to for *in regard to*: Stage 3
> Current ratio (*in regard to* vs. *in regards to): 13:1
> 2. *with regards to for *with regard to*: Stage 2
> Current ratio (*with regard to* vs. *with regards to): 23:1

B. As a Verb in *highly regarded* and *widely regarded*. The verb *regard* commonly appears in these two combinations. The one phrase, *highly regarded*, is a vague expression of praise; the other, *widely regarded as*, usually leads to words of praise—though it would certainly be possible to say that someone is *widely regarded as beneath contempt*. It's a mistake, however, to truncate the latter phrase—to say *widely regarded* in place of *highly regarded*: "Crotty has published four novels since leaving the newspaper, and he's *widely regarded* [read *highly regarded*] by both fiction writers and journalists." Worse still is the error based on a mishearing of the already-erroneous phrase as *wildly regarded.

> LANGUAGE-CHANGE INDEX
> widely regarded for highly regarded: Stage 1

regarding is sometimes ambiguous. It can function as a preposition, meaning "with respect to; concerning; about" <I have no comment regarding the jury's verdict>. Or it can function as a gerund, meaning "consideration; taking into account" <regarding modern life in a contemplative way is understandably depressing>.

For *regarding* as an acceptable dangling modifier, see DANGLERS (E).

LANGUAGE-CHANGE INDEX (For the full key, see front matter pp. xxxi, l–li.)
Stage 1: Rejected. **Stage 2:** Widely shunned. **Stage 3:** Widespread but . . . **Stage 4:** Ubiquitous but . . . **Stage 5:** Fully accepted.
Invariably inferior forms marked by asterisk (*). • Ratios represent frequency of prevalent forms vs. variants in current books.

regardless (= without regard to) should not be used for *despite* (= in spite of). E.g.:

- "Take heart. *Regardless* [read *Despite*] what happened Saturday, the Broncos will be performing in the Super Bowl Sunday." Mark Wolf, "Get Over the Broncos: Others Need Support," *Rocky Mountain News* (Denver), 7 Jan. 1997, at C2.
- "He looked more like a public relations man than a football coach—*regardless* [read *despite*] what was printed on the large, white board." Randy Kindred, "New Illini Coach Turner 'Building Relationships,'" *Pantagraph* (Bloomington, Ill.), 6 June 1997, at B1.

Though longer, *regardless of* would also be acceptable in those sentences. See *irregardless.

LANGUAGE-CHANGE INDEX
regardless (without *of*) misused for *despite*: Stage 2

regardless of whether. This is the idiomatic phrasing, not *regardless whether*—e.g.:

- "When he wanted to send troops to help end the civil war a year ago, President Clinton told a skeptical public and Congress that they would be withdrawn in December 1996 *regardless whether* [read *regardless of whether*] peace had been achieved." "Bosnia Mission Is Not Justified," *Fla. Times-Union*, 21 Nov. 1996, at A10.
- "One proposal . . . would require the companies to pay $6 billion a year, indefinitely, to compensate tobacco farmers—*regardless whether or not* [read *regardless of whether*] their crop is needed." "The Farmers' Cut," *Courier-J.* (Louisville), 22 June 1997, at D2.

See **whether (C).**

LANGUAGE-CHANGE INDEX
regardless whether for *regardless of whether*: Stage 2
Current ratio (*regardless of whether* vs.
regardless whether): 44:1

regards. See **regard (A)** & **as regards.**

regime (= [1] a particular government, esp. one whose legitimacy is questioned, [2] a specific system for doing something under a given plan or management, or [3] a special plan of exercise and diet intended to improve one's health; a regimen) is pronounced /ri-**zheem**/ in AmE or /ray-**zheem**/ in either AmE or BrE. Avoid /ri-**jeem**/ and /ray-**jeem**/.

In exercise and other health-related contexts, *regimen* (= a systematic routine designed to improve a person's health and fitness) predominates in AmE, *regime* in sense 3 in BrE—e.g.:

- "Many people, fat or fit, can't keep up a strenuous 30-minute *exercise regimen*, day in and day out." Aaron E. Carroll, "Diet, Not Exercise, Is Crucial to Weight Loss," *N.Y. Times*, 18 June 2015, at A3.
- "She does not bore on about her *dietary or health regime*, or engage in competitively self-deprecating 'fat talk.'" Hannah Betts, "Flirtatious, but Never Rapacious," *Daily Telegraph*, 24 Apr. 2014, Features §, at 27.

regiment (= a military unit made up of several battalions) is coming to be misused for *regimen* (= a systematic plan designed to improve health, skills, etc.)—e.g.:

- "Wealthy people plagued with weak nerves and 'autointoxication' flocked to the San, as it was known, from all over the world to undergo a strict *regiment* [read *regimen*] of sinusoidal baths, Vibrotherapy, laughing exercises and five enemas a day." Laurie Muchnick, "In Battle Creek, Not All Flakes Were Made of Corn," *Miami Herald*, 6 June 1993, at I3.
- "No one wants to return to a strict *regiment* [read *regimen*] of dreary alphabet drills." Mike Berry, "Whole-Language Dives into Words," *Orlando Sentinel*, 9 Apr. 1995, at K1.
- "As he heads toward his 58th birthday on May 13, Dill is playing some of the best golf of his career, thanks to better equipment, a strict training *regiment* [read *regimen*] and a successful diet." Raul Dominguez Jr., "Thanks to a Fresh Start, This Dill's Not in a Pickle," *San Antonio Express-News*, 26 Mar. 1997, at D3.

Cf. **calvary.**

LANGUAGE-CHANGE INDEX
regiment misused for *regimen*: Stage 1
Current ratio (*strict regimen* vs.
strict regiment): 35:1

register; registrar. Both designate a governmental officer who keeps official records. The *OED* notes that *register* was commonly used in this sense from 1580 to 1800 and that *registrar* is now the usual word. But in AmE *register* retains vitality: various levels of government have *registers of copyrights, registers of deeds, registers of patents, registers of wills*, and the like. As a matter of AmE usage, a *registrar* is usually a school official, whereas a *register* is usually someone who records documents for state or local government.

Apart from the agent-noun sense, the usual meaning of *register* is "a book or other record in which entries are made during the course of business."

registrable (/**rej**-is-trə-bəl/) is so spelled in AmE and BrE alike—e.g.: "The stakes are open to all AKC *registrable* pointing breeds." Doug Smith, "Walleyes Are Hot on Mille Lacs," *Star Trib.* (Minneapolis), 26 May 2002, at C19. This form was thoroughly established in 19th-century BrE and in early-20th-century AmE. *Registerable* can now be regarded as a misspelling—e.g.:

- "[In] *KanPopper*, the inevitable deformation of the name . . . makes it *registerable* [read *registrable*] as a trademark." Dennis Baron, *Declining Grammar and Other Essays on the English Vocabulary* 195 (1989).
- "Those under 21 with a *registerable* [read *registrable*] blood alcohol level of 0.02 or higher are in violation of the law." Andrew J. Skerritt, "Highway Patrol Investigates Teen's Death," *Herald* (Rock Hill, S.C.), 10 Sept. 2002, at B1.

LANGUAGE-CHANGE INDEX
registrable misspelled *registerable*: Stage 1
Current ratio: 10:1

registrant /**rej**-i-strənt/ does not rhyme, in the final syllable, with *restaurant*. Yet somehow, within the influential Securities and Exchange Commission in Washington, D.C., the pervasive pronunciation is /**rej**-i-stront/, with a moderately strong final syllable.

registrar. See **register.**

registrate, though dating from the 18th century, is an ill-conceived BACK-FORMATION from *registration*, the verb *register* being standard—e.g.:

- "Listeners can qualify by *registrating* [read *registering*] at various local sites." "Tuned In," *York Daily Record*, 10 May 1994, at 1.
- "Those interested must apply and be interviewed before *registrating* [read *registering*] for the class." "Hospice Training Scheduled," *Richmond Times-Dispatch*, 28 Feb. 1996, at M8.

It is true, however, that *registrate* is correctly used when denoting the setting of pipe-organ stops. But this usage is rare outside the American Guild of Organists.

Language-Change Index
registrate misused for *register*: Stage 1
Current ratio (*registered* vs. *registrated*): 7,650:1

regret. See **resent (B).**

regretful; regrettable. Errors made are *regrettable*; the people who have made them should be *regretful*. The most common error is to misuse *regretful* for *regrettable*, especially in the adverbial forms—e.g.:

- "Yet *regretfully* [read *regrettably*], there may be less than full understanding that MARTA's rail-service areas are really a function of trip volume densities and urban economics." Ray Magliozzi & Tom Magliozzi, "Is MARTA Just a Downtown Train?" *Atlanta J.-Const.*, 4 Mar. 1992, at A14.
- "*Regretfully* [read *Regrettably*], the articles reflect a failure of contemporary liberalism and progressive politics." Mark H. Hornung, "Don't Argue with GOP, U. of C. Success," *Chicago Sun-Times*, 10 Nov. 1993, at 49.
- "But realistically and *regretfully* [read *regrettably*], we can't pick and choose." "The Postal Code," *Globe & Mail* (Toronto), 11 Aug. 2015, at A10.

See SENTENCE ADVERBS.

Language-Change Index
regretfully misused for *regrettably*: Stage 4
Current ratio (*regrettably not* vs. **regretfully not*): 10:1

regulable (/**reg**-yə-lə-bəl/), meaning "able to be regulated; susceptible to regulation," has long been standard in AmE. It was in BrE, too, until the 1970s, when the longer *regulatable* became predominant in BrE by a significant margin. Even so, in AmE the longer word is a blemish—e.g.: "Where the highway leads is cloudy, but the traffic keeps growing and does not seem to be readily *regulatable* [read *regulable*]." Walter Goodman, "At Age 9, Light-Years Ahead," *N.Y. Times*, 13 Apr. 1995, at C16. (The sentence would sound better if *readily* were changed to *easily*. See SOUND OF PROSE.) See -ABLE (D) & -ATABLE.

regularly; routinely. These are nearly synonymous, but *regularly* implies a more orderly sequence at predictable intervals <Karl regularly eats cereal for breakfast> <Gillian routinely checks her car's oil and tires before taking a trip out of town>.

regulatory; regulative. Although both adjectives were once common, *regulatory* achieved vast predominance

in AmE beginning in 1920 and in BrE beginning in 1960. It's accented in AmE on the first syllable (/**reg**-yə-lə-tor-ee/), in BrE often on the third (/reg-yə-**lay**-tə-ree/). *Regulative* might generally be regarded as a NEEDLESS VARIANT, but in theology *regulative principle* is a SET PHRASE.

Current ratio: 30:1

reify (= to make material, or to convert mentally into a thing) is a transitive verb—e.g.:

- "In his first two years, Clinton's single biggest mistake was seeking to *reify*, in one great leap, his panoramic revelation of the perfect healthcare system." Ronald Brownstein, "Expect Newt Gingrich to Renew Debate About Government's Role," *Dayton Daily News*, 22 Nov. 1994, at A11.
- "Taste, touch, sight, smell, sound—all these senses are at work here, in order to *reify* those abstractions that hover at the backs of our minds." Peter Thorpe, "Our Senses Frolic in Poet's 'Multi-Media' Approach," *Rocky Mountain News* (Denver), 28 May 1995, at A80.

It shouldn't be used intransitively—e.g.: "I'm reminded of younger abstract painters like Robert Harms, in whose work objects threaten to emerge, whereas in Park's they threaten to *reify* into paint or glance." Eileen Myles, "Darragh Park at Tibor de Nagy," *Art in America*, July 1994, at 94. The meaning of that sentence is unclear even given the greater context, which (like much other art commentary) is infected with ABSTRACTITIS.

rein; reign. Like many other homophones, these words are frequently mistaken for each other in print—but perhaps no other pair is confused in so many different ways. Besides the blunders below, see **free rein.**

Rein in, not **reign in*, is the correct phrase for "to check, restrain." The metaphorical image is of the rider pulling on the reins of the horse to slow down (i.e., "hold your horses")—e.g.:

- "Though the White House has tried to *reign him in* [read *rein him in*], Roger Clinton (Secret Service code name: 'Headache') has ambitions to become more than the President's dysfunctional younger brother." Walter Scott, "Personality Parade," *Parade*, 1 Aug. 1993, at 1.
- "With every disclosure it becomes clearer that Yeltsin is unwilling or unable to *reign in* [read *rein in*] his protégé." Richard Beeston, "The Power Behind the Force," *Times Mag.* (London), 11 Mar. 1995, at 11.
- "The university also has turned down thermostats, turned out its lights and *reigned in* [read *reined in*] its use of express mail." Brad Heath & Janet Vandenabeele, "U-M Braces for $42 Million in Cuts," *Detroit News*, 21 Feb. 2003, at A1.

The error also occurs with the noun forms: one holds the *reins*, not the *reigns*. E.g.:

- "Ron Low has a hold of the Oilers' *reigns* [read *reins*] for now, but should he not work out, look for former Canucks and Flyers coach Bob McCammon to take

LANGUAGE-CHANGE INDEX (For the full key, see front matter pp. xxxi, l–li.)
Stage 1: Rejected. **Stage 2:** Widely shunned. **Stage 3:** Widespread but . . . **Stage 4:** Ubiquitous but . . . **Stage 5:** Fully accepted.
Invariably inferior forms marked by asterisk (*). • Ratios represent frequency of prevalent forms vs. variants in current books.

over as coach next season." Roy Cummings, "Old Pros Attempt to Regain Past Glory," *Tampa Trib.*, 16 Apr. 1995, Sports §, at 4.

- "Now, Tony DiCicco, the goalie coach in 1991, is holding the *reigns* [read *reins*] and has worked to build the U.S. from the back." Shari Rampenthal, "Williams Targets High Jump," *Wis. State J.*, 10 May 1995, at D2.

- "In other cases, the computer recommended keeping tighter *reign* [read *rein*] on inventory, pressing the vendor for more discounts, or raising prices." Saul Hansell, "Listen Up! It's Time for a Profit," *N.Y. Times*, 20 May 2001, § 3, at 1, 14.

As further evidence of Murphy's Law at work, the opposite error (*rein* for *reign*) occurs as well—e.g.:

- "His *rein* [read *reign*] as Fort Meade's tobacco-chewing, play-calling leader ended abruptly in September 1993." Tom Ford, "Fort Meade's Jamison Brings Stability, Nostalgia," *Tampa Trib.*, 1 Sept. 1995, at 2.

- "Rarely do Oscar voters make the right choice for Best Foreign Language Film, and their reliably incorrect instincts *reined* [read *reigned*] supreme again earlier this year with the anointing of the peculiar Dutch import, 'Character.'" David Baron, "'Character' Has Some Serious Flaws," *Times-Picayune* (New Orleans), 29 May 1998, Lagniappe §, at 28.

- "Confusion *reined* [read *reigned*] when everyone within a five-mile radius was asked to evacuate." Cheryl Jane Kountze, "May 1976's Deadly Fog," *Houston Chron.*, 4 Jan. 2003, at 35.

LANGUAGE-CHANGE INDEX
1. **reign in* for *rein in*: Stage 2
2. **hold the reigns* for *hold the reins*: Stage 1
Current ratio (*hold the reins* vs. **hold the reigns*): 23:1
3. **rein supreme* misused for *reign supreme*: Stage 1
Current ratio (*reign supreme* vs. **rein supreme*): 195:1

reinforce (= to strengthen) has been the universal form since the early 17th century. That's an anomaly, since the base verb is *enforce*, not **inforce*. (Likewise with *reinstate*.) Rather than making the word solid (*reenforce*) or retaining the *-e-* with a hyphen or diaeresis (*re-enforce, reënforce*), the *-e-* in such words was changed to *-i-* whenever the prefix was added. *Reenforce* is sometimes seen in AmE, but always in a special sense: "to enforce again."

reiterate, -tion; iterate, -tion. It is perhaps not too literalistic to use *iterate* in the sense "to repeat," and *reiterate* in the sense "to repeat a second time [i.e., to state a third time]." But the distinction is observed by only the most punctilious writers, *reiterate* being the usual term in either sense. See **iterate**.

Since an *iteration* repeats a former event, the term can't logically apply to the *first* anything—e.g.:

- "Allison's first *iteration* [read *appearance*] in 1989 drenched Houston. It returned last year as a system that caused historic destruction in the nation's fourth-largest city, earning retirement as an Atlantic storm name." "Voter Turnout, Elections Top NAACP Agenda," *Sun-Sentinel* (Ft. Lauderdale), 7 July 2002, at A3.

- "Its first *iteration* [read *version*], in 1947, was such a disaster that it had to be redrawn two years later—and was still being amended 37 years after that." Fred Hiatt, "Operation Tough: Revamping Government," *Newsday* (N.Y.), 16 July 2002, at A25.

- "Many of the most daring are being commissioned by an emerging online force—such corporate giants as Nestle USA, Pepsi, Coca-Cola and General Motors that sat out the first *iteration* [read *generation*] of Web advertising while the rest of the nation went dot-com crazy." Doug Bedell, "On the Web, in Your Face," *Dallas Morning News*, 25 July 2002, at A1.

LANGUAGE-CHANGE INDEX
*first iteration for *first version*, etc.: Stage 1

*reknowned. See **renowned.**

relapse; recur. The patient relapses; the illness recurs. Let us hope this wording blunder doesn't recur: "Prostate cancer is less likely to *relapse* [read *recur*] in men who are treated by more experienced surgeons, according to a new study." "Experience Matters in Prostate Surgery," *N.Y. Times*, 26 July 2007, at A15.

LANGUAGE-CHANGE INDEX
relapse misused for *recur*: Stage 1

relate back. Except in law, this phrase is generally a REDUNDANCY. Since the 18th century, lawyers have used it to mean that something done at one point is considered to have been done at an earlier time. For more, see *Garner's Dictionary of Legal Usage* 764 (3d ed. 2011). See **revert.** Cf. **refer back.**

relatedly. See -EDLY.

relate to (= to empathize with) is a voguish expression characteristic of popular American cant from the 1970s on <Southern writers can relate to what it's like growing up in Atlanta>. It is unlikely to lose that stigma anytime soon. Cf. **identify.**

LANGUAGE-CHANGE INDEX
relate to in the sense "empathize with": Stage 4

relation. A. And *relative*. These terms are interchangeable in the sense "a person with familial connections to another," although currently *relative* is much more usual.

B. And *relationship*. *Relation* is the broader term in this pair, since *relationship* refers either to kinship or to the fact of being related by some specific bond, especially a social or emotional bond. The phrase *in relationship with* is almost always incorrect for *in relation to*. To be correct, the phrase would almost have to be *in his* (or *her*) *relationship with*, etc.

relative to (= in relation to; in comparison with) is, in Eric Partridge's words, "gobbledygook" (*U&A* at 263). Though that pronouncement is a bit strong, the phrase can be easily replaced to good advantage—e.g.:

- "If you made a list of the worst banking crises *relative to* [read *in relation to*] a nation's GDP over the past 15 to 20 years, America's S&L crisis doesn't even make the top 50." Rob Norton, "The Big Costs of Policy Mistakes," *Fortune*, 29 Sept. 1997, at 44.

- "The estimates obtained here for fathers and sons are low *relative to* [read *compared with*] those found in Solon (1992), Zimmerman (1992), and Altonji and

Dunn (1991)." Kenneth A. Couch & Thomas A. Dunn, "Intergenerational Correlations in Labor Market Status," *J. Human Resources*, 22 Dec. 1997, at 210.

Although *relative to* is shorter than most phrases that can replace it, its meaning tends to be less clear, as illustrated in the examples above.

Relatively to is a comparatively rare—and unidiomatic—equivalent. E.g.: "It points to the benefits [that] such countries as the UK, Italy and Sweden have enjoyed by allowing their currencies to weaken *relatively to* [read *in relation to*] those of France and Germany." Robert Chote, "IMF Report Upsets Paris and Bonn," *Fin. Times*, 30 Mar. 1996, at 3.

relay; re-lay. See RE- PAIRS.

release; re-lease. See RE- PAIRS.

relegate; delegate. To *relegate* is to consign to an inferior position <because first class was full, he was relegated to coach>. To *delegate* is to commit (powers or duties) to an agent or representative <Shirley delegated the task to her associate>, or to appoint (a person) as one's agent <I'll delegate you as my stand-in for tomorrow's meeting>.

relevance; *relevancy. The former has been the predominant form in both AmE and BrE since about 1930. See **irrelevance.**

Current ratio: 29:1

relevant. The misspelling *revelant is a classic example of METATHESIS, or the transposition of sounds in a word. The error is more frequent in speech than in writing, but it does appear surprisingly often in print—e.g.:

- "Right or wrong, the quote becomes *revelant* [read *relevant*] now because Brasseur and Eisler will defend their 1993 world championships in Japan next Tuesday and Wednesday and neither Russian couple is expected to take part." Jim Proudfoot, "Open Ice Ahead for Canadian Figure Skaters," *Toronto Star*, 18 Mar. 1994, at E4.
- "With drastic service cuts just around the corner for many New Yorkers, Schnieder's film and the subsequent discussion are as *revelant* [read *relevant*] as they were when Abe Beame was mayor." "Outings," *Newsday* (N.Y.), 23 Apr. 1995, at A67.
- "Today's commemorations of the 52 people who died when Khan and his co-conspirators attacked London's transport network on 7 July 2005 will make the continuing questions over racial and cultural divisions in this corner of Yorkshire seem especially *revelant* [read *relevant*]." Richard Garner, "'Segregated' Areas Link Up for Cricket in Home Town of 7/7 Ringleader," *Independent*, at 18.

President Harry S. Truman is said to have blundered often in this way.

LANGUAGE-CHANGE INDEX
relevant misspelled *revelant: Stage 1

reliable, despite some earlier objections, is perfectly sound English. The word dates back to the 16th century but wasn't widely used until the 19th century, during the middle of which a furor arose over it. Critics thought it badly formed because the *-able* suffix, they said, works only with transitive verbs; that is, *eatable* means "able to be eaten," but *reliable* doesn't mean "able to be relied." It was also incorrectly denounced as an Americanism—this though it was born more than 200 years before Americanisms were ever talked about. Some writers therefore suggested that it should be *rely-on-able* or *rely-upon-able* (analogous to *come-at-able*). The critics' voices have long since been silenced, and nobody today pauses over the word. See -ABLE (C).

reluctant. For the misuse of *reticent* for *reluctant*, see **reticent.**

remain. In correspondence, it was once common to include the phrase *I remain* or *we remain* in a complimentary close such as *Yours sincerely* or *Very truly yours*. Today, the phrase *I remain* is not only stilted but also lame.

remark; re-mark. See RE- PAIRS.

remedial; remediable. *Remedial* = (1) providing a remedy; corrective <remedial measures>; or (2) designed to improve one's deficiencies in a given field <a remedial-reading class>. *Remediable* = capable of being remedied; curable <remediable problems>.

remediate, a BACK-FORMATION from *remediation*, is generally either a NEEDLESS VARIANT of *remedy* or a piece of gobbledygook. There's only one exception: in environmental law, *remediate* is a term of art. It's common for environmental lawyers to speak of polluted property or of pollutants on property to be remediated—e.g.: "The evidence suggested that there was little groundwater pollution and that any such contamination *was remediated* [read *had been remedied*]." E.E. Mazier, "Removal of Underground Tanks to Preempt Oil-Leak Liability Did Not Constitute 'Damages,'" *N.J. Lawyer*, 12 Aug. 1996, at 28.

Otherwise, though, the word itself is a pollutant—e.g.: "Students who don't pass will be allowed to take the test again in a couple of weeks, will be *remediated* [read *tutored? coached?*] until they feel ready to take the test again or will be allowed to retake the course." Tara Tuckwiller, "Putnam Doesn't Act on Pay Raises," *Charleston Gaz.*, 24 June 1997, at C3.

LANGUAGE-CHANGE INDEX
remediate for *remedy* (outside environmental law): Stage 1

remember. See **recollect** (A).

remembrance (= [1] an instance of remembering or being remembered, [2] the power of someone's memory, [3] a particular memory or recollection, [4] the duration of time over which someone can remember, [5] a keepsake or memento, or [6] a commemoration

LANGUAGE-CHANGE INDEX (For the full key, see front matter pp. xxxi, l–li.)
Stage 1: Rejected. **Stage 2:** Widely shunned. **Stage 3:** Widespread but . . . **Stage 4:** Ubiquitous but . . . **Stage 5:** Fully accepted.
Invariably inferior forms marked by asterisk (*). • Ratios represent frequency of prevalent forms vs. variants in current books.

or memorial) is pronounced in three syllables: /ri-**mem**-brənts/. An epenthetic schwa sound shouldn't occur after the -*b*-.

reminisce (= to think or talk about events in one's past, esp. pleasant ones) is a stubbornly intransitive verb. In other words, you *reminisce* about things. You don't **reminisce* things*—e.g.:

- "Don loved *reminiscing his* [read *reminiscing about his*] Navy years with his veteran buddies." "Wilhelm, Donald Calvin" (obit.), *Tampa Bay Times*, 8 Jan. 2013, at B6.
- "Each Trojet had a wonderful time *reminiscing their* [read *reminiscing about the*] 2013–2014 season." Kennedy Valinevicius, "Trojets Hold Banquet," *JG–TC* (Mattoon–Charleston, Ill.), 12 Apr. 2014, at C6. (On the *each . . . their* issue in that sentence, see **each** (A).)

Current ratio (*reminisce about the past* vs. **reminisce the past*): 26:1

remissible. So spelled—not **remissable*. See -ABLE (A).

Current ratio: 42:1

remission; *remittal; remittance; *remitment. *Remission* = (1) forgiveness; or (2) diminution of force, effect, degree, or violence. Sense 2 is especially common in reference to virulent diseases—e.g.: "Hall opens [the book] with a case: a cancer patient in 1993 receiving a new treatment called T.N.F. (tumor necrosis factor), which initially looks like a brilliant achievement but turns out to be all too fleeting—after some *remission* the patient dies before Hall manages to interview this testament to modern medicine." Roy Porter, "Offering Resistance," *N.Y. Times*, 29 June 1997, § 7, at 9. **Remittal* is a NEEDLESS VARIANT.

Remittance means "money sent to a person, or the sending of money to a person"—e.g.: "The hospital bill sent last week to Mark Davis was straightforward: $605 for services provided May 29. *Remittance* due in 10 days." Mark Patinkin, "Hospital Bill Exacts Toll on Bereaved Family," *Providence J.-Bull.*, 19 June 1997, at F1. **Remitment* has been a NEEDLESS VARIANT since the 18th century.

remonstrate. AmE preferably stresses the second syllable: /ri-**mon**-strayt/. BrE stresses the first: /**rem**-ən-strayt/; this pronunciation is also acceptable in AmE.

remorselessly. A. And *unremorsefully. These two terms are essentially equivalent. *Remorselessly* is far more common and somewhat more pejorative.
   B. Mistakenly Made *remorsely. Although **remorsely* isn't recorded in the *OED* or other dictionaries, some writers have taken to using it—apparently as a contracted form of *remorselessly*. E.g.:

- "Ever since then, the belt stars have been slowly but *remorsely* [read *remorselessly*] rising in the sky." Graham Hancock, "Riddle of Sphinx Lies in the Stars," *Daily Mail*, 5 Apr. 1995, at 42.
- "The Ivanhoe Theatre is dominated by a large, faceless clock, suspended in the rear of the stage above the actors

and ticking away *remorsely* [read *remorselessly*] as Dr. Faustus, after spending 24 years in the pursuit of power and pleasure, nears the hour of his damnation." Richard Christiansen, "Stage Tricks Can't Spare Ivanhoe's Doomed 'Faustus,'" *Chicago Trib.*, 20 July 1995, at 26.
- "Does Pellegrini feel any sympathy for the Liverpool captain, who will be *remorsely* [read *remorselessly*] reminded of what happened tomorrow evening at the Etihad Stadium by the City supporters?" "Pellegrini Wants Credit for City's Class, Not Cash," *Sunday Telegraph*, 24 Aug. 2014, Sport §, at 6.

The error is more common in BrE than in AmE.
                LANGUAGE-CHANGE INDEX
**remorsely* for *remorselessly*: Stage 1
Current ratio (*remorselessly* vs. **remorsely*): 124:1

REMOTE RELATIVES. A. Generally. "Every relative word which is used shall instantly present its antecedent to the mind of the reader, without the least obscurity." Hugh Blair, *Lectures on Rhetoric* 65 (Grenville Kleiser ed., 1911). Surprisingly few modern grammarians discuss what has become an increasingly common problem: the separation of the relative pronoun (*that, which, who*) from its antecedent. For example, in the sentence "The files sitting in the office that I was talking about yesterday are in disarray," the word *that*—technically—modifies *office*, not *files*. But many writers today would intend to have it modify *files*. They would loosely employ a "remote relative."

The best practice is simply to ensure that the relative pronoun immediately follows the noun it modifies. As the following examples illustrate, lapses involving *which* are extremely common:

- "There is a story told in the *Shabbat* about the famous Jewish scholar Rabbi Hillel *which* has some pertinence to the text before you." Neil Postman & Charles Weingartner, *Linguistics: A Revolution in Teaching* ix (1966). (*Which* modifies *story*—12 words and 4 nouns before. A possible revision: *A story told in the* Shabbat *about the famous Jewish scholar Rabbi Hillel has some pertinence to the text before you.* Or: *There is a story told in the* Shabbat *about the famous Jewish scholar Rabbi Hillel—a story that has some pertinence to the text before you.*)
- "Legislators are constantly making decisions about law reform *which* depend on moral values." Simon Lee, *Law and Morals* 3 (1986). (*Which* modifies *decisions*—4 words and 2 nouns before. A possible revision: *Legislators are constantly making decisions about law reform, and many of these decisions depend on moral values.*)
- "This will take the game back to its roots in the 1920s, when we had the Decatur Staleys, owned by Staley's starch company, *which* later became the Chicago Bears." John Rothchild, "Rooting for the Federal Expresses," *Time*, 30 May 1994, at 53. (*Which* modifies *Decatur Staleys*—6 words and 2 nouns before. The Chicago Bears started out as Staley's starch company? Fascinating. Actually, the problem is the parenthetical phrase *owned by Staley's starch company*. A possible revision: *This will take the game back to its roots in the 1920s, when we had the Decatur Staleys, owned by Staley's starch company. That team later became the Chicago Bears.*)
- "I looked at the dead body of my mother, *which* Astel was just in the process of covering with a sheet." Peter David, *Sir Apropos of Nothing* 127 (2001). (*Which* modifies *body*,

4 words and 2 nouns before. A possessive phrase—*my mother's dead body*—would have prevented the problem.)

But the relative pronoun *that* is almost as troublesome, and when used remotely is even more likely to cause confusion—e.g.:

- "There is a word unrecognizable even to some crossword puzzle addicts *that* is useful in describing my strategy of survival between May and October. I estivate." Leslie Hanscom, "Some Don't," *Newsday* (N.Y.), 21 May 1989, Mag. §, at 9. (*That* modifies *word*—8 words and 2 nouns before. A possible revision: *A word unrecognizable even to some crossword-puzzle addicts describes my strategy of survival between May and October. I estivate.*)
- "Justice Blackmun's tone was urgent, as if in the twilight of his career he wanted to reopen a dialogue on the death penalty *that* had all but disappeared from the Court with the retirement of Justices William J. Brennan Jr. and Thurgood Marshall, who both believed that the death penalty was inherently unconstitutional." Linda Greenhouse, "Death Penalty Is Renounced by Blackmun," *N.Y. Times*, 23 Feb. 1994, at A1, A10. (*That* modifies *dialogue*—5 words and 2 nouns before. A possible revision: *Justice Blackmun's tone was urgent, as if in the twilight of his career he wanted to reopen a dialogue on the death penalty. That dialogue had all but disappeared from the Court with the retirement of Justices William J. Brennan Jr. and Thurgood Marshall, who both believed that the death penalty was inherently unconstitutional.*)
- "The Census Bureau has a remedy for the next scheduled head count, in 2000. It is called sampling, a method similar to that used in public opinion polls *that* extrapolates the characteristics of a large group by talking to a representative part of it." Steven A. Holmes, "2 Communities, Poles Apart, Illustrate Debate on Census," *N.Y. Times*, 30 Aug. 1997, at 1. (*That* modifies *method*—9 words and 2 nouns before. A possible revision: *The Census Bureau has a remedy for the next scheduled head count, in 2000. It is called sampling, a method similar to that used in public-opinion polls. It extrapolates the characteristics of a large group from a representative sample.*)
- "C-130 aircraft packed with radio transmitters flew lazy circles over the Persian Gulf broadcasting messages in Arabic to the Iraqi people *that* were monitored by reporters near the border." Patrick E. Tyler, "War Imminent as Hussein Rejects Ultimatum," *N.Y. Times*, 19 Mar. 2003, at A1. (*That* modifies *messages*—7 words and 3 nouns before. Probably the best edit would be to make a second sentence: *The messages were monitored by reporters near the border.*)

Even *who* and *whose* are used remotely, and just as confusingly (especially if more than one person has been mentioned nearby)—e.g.:

- "Patricia Buthmann and Tim Tyroler on Tuesday lost their effort to block being evicted from the Casa Carranza apartments . . . because they allowed a woman to stay with them *who* possessed two syringes suspected to be drug paraphernalia." Kris Mayes, "Renters Run Afoul of Eviction Law," *Phoenix Gaz.*, 29 Sept. 1994, at B1. (At first, the relative pronoun *who* may seem to modify *them* as part of an archaic construction; in fact, it modifies *woman*—5 words and 2 nouns before. A possible revision: *Patricia Buthmann and Tim Tyroler on Tuesday lost*

their effort to block being evicted from the Casa Carranza apartments . . . because a woman who had stayed with them was found to possess two syringes that appeared to be drug paraphernalia.*)

- "She is the mother of four children *who* at age 15 aborted what would have been her first child, and evidently she seeks to redress that wrong." William F. Buckley, "Both Sides Gearing Up on Abortion," *Fresno Bee*, 26 Jan. 1995, at B9. (Who aborted whom? It reads as if the woman's 15-year-old quadruplets aborted what would have been her first child—a time-warp problem. *Who* is intended to modify *mother*—4 words and 2 nouns before. A possible revision: *The mother of four children, she at age 15 aborted what would have been her first child, and evidently she seeks to redress that wrong.*)
- "Just last year, they succeeded in removing a Victorian house near the Capitol Building, *whose* owner had refused every entreaty to leave for half a century." Peter S. Canellos, "The Second Battle of Concord," *Boston Globe* (Mag.), 29 Sept. 1996, at 14. (*Whose* refers to *house*—5 words before—but seems at first to refer to *Capitol Building*. A possible revision: *Just last year, they succeeded in removing a Victorian house near the Capitol Building; its owner had refused every entreaty to leave for half a century.*)
- "Clearly 'Cruyff' mustn't be confused with that autocrat Dutchman with a similar name *who* used to manage Ajax and Barcelona." "Let's Have a Bit of a Blow for Battling," *Daily Telegraph*, 2 Apr. 1997, at 44. (*Who* refers to *Dutchman*—5 words and 2 nouns before. A possible revision: *Clearly, "Cruyff" mustn't be confused with the similarly named autocratic Dutchman who used to manage Ajax and Barcelona.*)

At times, the remote relative may even appear in a phrase such as *in which*—e.g.: "The unexpected announcement renewed speculation about the 74-year-old Pope's broader state of health, particularly because he planned an important speech at the United Nations on the family *in which* he was expected to discuss the Vatican's views of the recent population conference in Cairo." Alan Crowell, "Pope, Citing His Health, Cancels His Planned Trip to New York," *N.Y. Times*, 23 Sept. 1994, at A1. (*In which* modifies *speech*—8 words and 3 nouns before. A possible revision: *The unexpected announcement renewed speculation about the 74-year-old Pope's broader state of health, particularly because he planned an important speech at the United Nations on the family. In that speech, he was expected to discuss the Vatican's views of the recent population conference in Cairo.*)

As in many of the examples quoted above, remote relatives often seem to result from the writer's ill-advised combining of two sentences into one. Among the advantages of avoiding remote relatives—preventing MISCUES and even AMBIGUITY—is an improved average SENTENCE LENGTH.

For more on relative pronouns, see that (A). For a similar problem with prepositional phrases, see ILLOGIC (E).

B. The Exceptional *which*. Some exceptionally well-edited publications, including *The New Yorker*

LANGUAGE-CHANGE INDEX (For the full key, see front matter pp. xxxi, l–li.)
Stage 1: Rejected. **Stage 2:** Widely shunned. **Stage 3:** Widespread but . . . **Stage 4:** Ubiquitous but . . . **Stage 5:** Fully accepted.
Invariably inferior forms marked by asterisk (*). • Ratios represent frequency of prevalent forms vs. variants in current books.

and *The Atlantic Monthly*, adhere to the *that–which* rule but nonetheless use *which* instead of *that* to signal that the relative clause is separated from its antecedent. E.g.: "Before joining the Bush Administration, he [Richard Haass] had held the job at the Brookings Institution *which* James Steinberg now holds." Nicholas Lemann, "How It Came to War," *New Yorker*, 31 Mar. 2003, at 36, 39. (A possible revision: *Before joining the Bush Administration, he had held a job at the Brookings Institution—the job now held by James Steinberg.* Or: *Before joining the Bush Administration, he had held the job that James Steinberg now holds at the Brookings Institution.*)

The estimable Barbara Wallraff, formerly senior editor at *The Atlantic Monthly*, defends the exceptional *which*: "When another noun intervenes between the noun being modified by the restrictive clause and the clause itself, and that second noun might be misread as the antecedent, we use *which* without a comma to signal the connection to the first noun." *Word Court* 116 (2000). For example, to mitigate the remote relative *a book about movies that I enjoyed* (where it is the book and not the movies that were enjoyed), the exceptional *which* would make it *a book about movies which I enjoyed*. While the device might be more effective if it were widely understood and used, it can't clear up the ambiguity in this example. And it is further hampered by the still-widespread use of *which* in restrictive clauses. As long as that practice continues, *which* can never be a reliable signal because the reader can't be sure whether the clause is restrictive or nonrestrictive. The far better approach will always be to keep the antecedent and relative clause side by side.

remove; re-move. See RE- PAIRS.

remuneration. So spelled. **Renumeration* is an all-too-common misspelling and mispronunciation—e.g.:

- "Joseph Cammarata . . . said he . . . would recommend rejecting any settlement that did not include financial *renumeration* [read *remuneration*] for Jones." Robert Kilborn & Lance Carden, "News in Brief," *Christian Science Monitor*, 2 June 1997, at 2.
- "I'm at school at 6:30 a.m., work through my lunch hour and prep period (tutoring, revising essays with students, giving makeup tests, and/or grading papers—all without 'extra' *renumeration* [read *remuneration*], by the way), and I leave school anywhere between 3:30 and 5:30 p.m., depending on after-school meetings and student appointments." Cindy Haworth, "Nurse's Notion Is Fallacy," *Ariz. Republic*, 15 July 1997, at E7.

See METATHESIS.

LANGUAGE-CHANGE INDEX
remuneration misspelled **renumeration*: Stage 1
Current ratio: 320:1

renaissance (= [1] a rebirth, or [2] [capitalized] the European period from the 15th to the 17th centuries, when art, literature, and scientific ideas blossomed) is pronounced /**ren**-i-sahns/ in AmE and /ri-**nay**-səns/ in BrE. The pronunciation /ren-ə-**sahns**/ is a pedantic affectation.

rencontre; rencounter. The dictionaries provide little certainty about these words. *W11* lists the main entry under *rencontre*; the *COD* lists the main entry under *rencounter*, as does *W2*. Under *rencontre*, the *COD* labels both spellings archaic, although the Merriam-Webster dictionaries list *rencontre* as current in the senses (1) "a hostile meeting or contest between forces or individuals; combat"; and (2) "a casual meeting." The *OED* adds the sense "an organized but informal meeting of scientists," dating from 1975 in BrE.

The empirical evidence shows that although *rencounter* predominated in AmE and BrE alike, since 1820 or so *rencontre* has been the predominant spelling in both varieties and for all senses.

rend > rent > rent. But **rended* has long been a variant past-tense and past-participial form, perhaps for fear that *rent* might cause a MISCUE. A misreading seems more likely in the first sentence that follows than in most others, but it's probably better to use the traditional form—e.g.:

- "Unlike 'Uncle Tom's Cabin,' Ms. Seaquist's work, thus far, assumes that we all not only understand the issues that have *rended* [read *rent*] Bosnia and led to the horror, but that the issues allow only one legitimate position." Joel Henning, "Bosnia: A Phone Call to Action," *Wall Street J.*, 18 Dec. 1996, at A18. (On the ungrammatical lack of PARALLELISM in that sentence, see **not only . . . but also.**)
- "Veronica's dream of singing in Johannesburg floods Abraham with memories and he refuses to have his heart *rended* [read *rent*] again." Michael Eck, "Fugard's 'Valley Song' a Mesmerizing Drama," *Times Union* (Albany), 19 July 1997, at B11.
- "If you're not winning, then you're out in public, garments *rended* [read *rent*], whipping yourself so everyone can see." Cathal Kelly, "Panic Time in Washington," *Toronto Star*, 19 Sept. 2013, at S4.

See IRREGULAR VERBS. Whenever the past-participial *rent* might be confusing, try *torn apart* or *broken* instead.

For the MALAPROPISM of misusing *render* for *rend*, see **heart-rending.**

LANGUAGE-CHANGE INDEX
*rended for past-tense *rent*: Stage 1
Current ratio (*have rent* vs. **have rended*): 58:1

rendezvous, n. Pl. *rendezvous*, not **rendezvouses*. The singular is pronounced /**ron**-day-voo/, the plural /**ron**-day-vooz/.

rendezvous, vb. Dating from the 17th century, this verb makes *rendezvouses* /**ron**-day-vooz/ in the third-person present tense and *rendezvoused* /**ron**-day-vood/ in the past tense. The present participle is *rendezvousing* /**ron**-day-voo-ing/.

renege; *renegue; *renig. The first is the standard form in AmE and BrE alike. The second is a chiefly BrE variant. The third is a chiefly AmE variant.

renounce. See **denounce.**

renounceable; *renunciable. The former is standard in AmE and BrE alike. The latter is a NEEDLESS VARIANT.

Current ratio: 28:1

*renouncement. See renunciation.

renowned (= famous) is so spelled. *Reknowned is wrong but fairly common for renowned. E.g.: "Byatt is reknowned [read renowned] for her intelligence." Mira Stout, "What Possessed A.S. Byatt," N.Y. Times, 26 May 1991, § 6, at 13, 14.

The noun form is renown; there is no verb (despite the past-participial adjective renowned). The adjective is sometimes wrongly written *reknown or renown—e.g.:

- "Michaels became reknown [read renowned] for 'The War Song.'" "The Week in Music," San Diego Union-Trib., 15 Mar. 1984, Panorama §, at 6.
- "There will be a DVD viewing of a lecture by the renown [read renowned] author Doug Tallamy." "What's Happening," Orlando Sentinel, 21 May 2015, at G1.

The adjective is pronounced /ri-nownd/.

LANGUAGE-CHANGE INDEX
1. renowned misspelled *reknowned: Stage 1
Current ratio: 687:1
2. *reknown for renowned: Stage 1
Current ratio (renowned vs. *reknown): 807:1

rent, n.; rental, n. Generally, prefer rent instead of the noun rental whenever it will suffice. Reserve rental for a record of rent payments received <the Grosvenor Estate rentals were incomplete> or the property itself <he owns only one small rental>.

rent, vb.; lease, vb. In AmE, these terms are used both for what the tenant does and for what the landlord does. In BrE, the lessor leases (or lets) and the lessee rents. So in AmE, rent is ambiguous since it may refer to the action taken by either party. The word has had this double sense from at least the 16th century. Both the lessee and the lessor are renters, so to speak, though this term is usually reserved for tenants. See lease.

rental, n. See rent, n.

*renumeration. See remuneration.

*renunciable. See renounceable.

renunciation; *renouncement. The former has long been standard in AmE and BrE alike. The latter is a NEEDLESS VARIANT.

Current ratio: 42:1

reoccur. See recur & relapse.

reoccurrence. See recurrence.

rep (= corded cloth) is the standard spelling <a rep tie>. *Repp is a variant spelling.

reparable; repairable. Although the latter has traditionally been something of a NEEDLESS VARIANT, some DIFFERENTIATION seems to be taking place. Reparable is now often relegated to metaphorical, abstract senses <are the two countries' diplomatic problems reparable?>, while repairable increasingly appears in literal, concrete senses <is the bicycle chain repairable?>. The antonyms are irreparable and unrepairable.

In frequency of occurrence in print sources, repairable overcame reparable in BrE in the 1870s, and in AmE nearly a century later, in the 1960s. But both remain in fairly common use.

Reparable is pronounced /rep-ə-rə-bəl/. (Cf. irreparable.) Repairable is pronounced /ri-pair-ə-bəl/.

reparative; *reparatory. Since the early 19th century, the former has been standard in AmE and BrE alike. The latter is a NEEDLESS VARIANT.

Current ratio: 20:1

repartee (= rapid conversation that is replete with intelligent and amusing remarks and replies) is pronounced /rep-ər-tee/ or /rep-ahr-tee/—preferably not /-tay/.

*repay back. Although this REDUNDANCY dates back to the 18th century, it is considered poor style. Use repay or pay back—e.g.: "Students who obtain Stafford loans borrow at a reduced interest rate and wait until after graduation to repay them back [read repay them or pay them back]." Mike Bucsko, "Grove City to Stop Federal College Aid," Pitt. Post-Gaz., 11 Oct. 1996, at A1.

LANGUAGE-CHANGE INDEX
*repay back for repay or pay back: Stage 1
Current ratio (pay back vs. *repay back): 471:1

repeal, a transitive verb meaning "to remove from the statute books by legislative action," doesn't take from (which is implied from its definition). When the preposition from is needed, another verb is called for—e.g.: "Unlimited sick leave would be repealed [read removed] from state law." Randy McClain, "Panel Sends Teacher Sick-Leave, Sabbatical Bills to Senate," Advocate (Baton Rouge), 16 Apr. 1999, at A7.

repeat, whether as adjective, noun, or verb, is best pronounced /ri-peet/—not /ree-peet/.

*repeat again; *repeat back. Both are needless redundancies. See REDUNDANCY.

*repeat the same. This phrase is redundant—e.g.: "Gov. Parris N. Glendening repeated the same [read repeated those] sentiments in a letter May 8 to foundation members and cited a $2.8 million expansion plan

LANGUAGE-CHANGE INDEX (For the full key, see front matter pp. xxxi, l–li.)
Stage 1: Rejected. Stage 2: Widely shunned. Stage 3: Widespread but . . . Stage 4: Ubiquitous but . . . Stage 5: Fully accepted.
Invariably inferior forms marked by asterisk (*). • Ratios represent frequency of prevalent forms vs. variants in current books.

for the museum." Dan Thanh Dang, "Black Caucus Is Asked to Probe Firing at Annapolis Museum," *Baltimore Sun*, 15 May 1997, at B8. See REDUNDANCY.

repel. A. And *repulse*. Although both verbs mean "to drive back," the traditional distinction is that *repulse* is primarily physical <after repeated warnings, he was repulsed from the premises>; *repel* is primarily figurative <the body odors on the subway repelled her>. Hence *repel* is the verb corresponding more closely in meaning to the adjective *repulsive*. You can find this distinction in any number of older usage books— e.g.: "The person who feels repulsion is *repelled*, not *repulsed*; *repulsed* means 'rejected.'" H.A. Treble & G.H. Vallins, *An A.B.C. of English Usage* 155 (1936). See **repellent**.

Some writers observe that distinction, using *repulse* for what beats back and *repel* for what disgusts—e.g.:

- "After initial setbacks, Israeli troops *repulsed* the attack." "A History of Conflict," *Milwaukee J. Sentinel*, 14 July 2002, at J1.
- "The army *repulsed* the attack after exchanging fire." "The World in Brief: Uganda," *L.A. Times*, 18 Sept. 2002, at A4.
- "Capsaicin oil on seeds and grains [will] make them edible for birds but repulsive to squirrels. The seeds and grains *repel* squirrels but don't harm them in any way." Janice Mawhinney, "Birdseed Claims to Keep Squirrels at Bay," *Toronto Star*, 25 Feb. 2001, Life §, at 3.
- "While the marigold's pungent smell apparently *repelled* these pests, the odor was also repulsive to many humans." Diana Blowers, "Kettering's Mari-Golden Anniversary," *Dayton Daily News*, 23 May 2002, at C1.

Today, however, the verbs are as likely to be used interchangeably, perhaps because *repulse* seems to answer to *repulsive* (= disgusting, obnoxious) and *repel* to *repellent* (= that pushes away or beats back)—e.g.:

- "Whatever *repulses* you in others will *repulse* others if you have it. Cultivate habits that attract people when you're young." Tom Gardner & David Gardner, "S&P 500 Makes Up Lion's Share of Market," *Atlanta J.-Const.*, 23 June 2002, at C5 (paraphrasing Warren Buffett).
- "The middle passages contain grotesque parts about ways that the body both attracts and *repulses*." Patrick Z. McGavin, "'Cremaster 3' Offers a Stunning Concept," *Chicago Trib.*, 13 Sept. 2002, Movies §, at 9.
- "The last time residents recall their sleepy county being the center of international news was 139 years ago, when the Confederate Army successfully *repelled* advancing Union troops in the Battle of Chickamauga, north of Noble." Brian Basinger, "Quiet Area's Last Horror Was a Civil War Battle," *Augusta Chron.*, 25 Feb. 2002, at B6.
- "Renegade soldiers tried to take over three garrisons in the capital but were *repelled* by loyalist troops." "Last of Mutineers Yield to Troops," *Chicago Trib.*, 11 Aug. 2002, at 5.

Because this tendency seems irreversible, you might take any of three tacks. First, you might keep (for now) to the traditional distinction, which is fading. Just don't be the last to cling to it. Second, you might embrace the reversal in meaning; everyone will know what you mean, and the risk to credibility is slight because so few people ever learned the old distinction. Third, you might treat these verbs as SKUNKED

TERMS and avoid them altogether for the next couple of centuries while the new meanings solidify.

B. And *rappel*. See **rappel**.

repellent; repulsive. Both mean, literally, "causing to turn away." *Repulsive* is stronger; it applies to whatever physically pushes back <repulsive forces> or disgusts or offends in the extreme <Fred's constant posing before mirrors and self-adulatory talk are only two examples of his repulsive narcissism>. *Repellent* is often more dispassionately descriptive and (typically) nonmetaphorical <a sunblock that is repellent to insects>. Avoid **repellant*, a variant spelling of *repellent*. See **repel (A)**.

repercussion (= an effect resulting from an act or event, esp. a bad one that will last for some time), a word most commonly used in the plural, is pronounced /ree-pər-**kəsh**-ən/—not /rep-/.

repertoire; repertory. Although these terms are etymological doublets, they have undergone a good deal of DIFFERENTIATION. *Repertoire* = (1) all the pieces of music, dances, or plays that a performer or group knows and can perform <they have no classical music in their repertoire>; or (2) the total number of things that someone or something can do <the behavioral repertoire of toddlers>. *Repertory* = a type of theater in which the troupe alternates plays on different nights as opposed to performing the same play night after night <repertory company> <repertory theater>.

repetitive; repetitious; *repetitional; *repetitionary. The first two terms are undergoing DIFFERENTIATION. *Repetitive* generally means "repeating; containing repetition" <repetitive cadences>. It is a largely colorless term. *Repetitious*, which has taken on pejorative connotations, means "full of tedious repetitions" <a highly repetitious essay in need of pruning>. Neither word was in frequent use until the early 20th century; since 1915 or so, *repetitive* has occurred with much greater frequency than *repetitious*.

*Repetitional and **repetitionary* are NEEDLESS VARIANTS of *repetitive*.

Current ratio (in order of headwords): 8,811:780:5:1

replace. See **substitute**, vb.

replace; re-place. See RE- PAIRS.

replete means not "complete," but "abundantly supplied with; full to overflowing." **Repleat* is an infrequent misspelling—e.g.: "A representative for People for the Ethical Treatment of Animals, asked for the organization's position on trapping, faxed *The Sun* a two-page fact sheet *repleat* [read *replete*] with lurid descriptions of 'gruesome deaths.'" Debbie Price, "New Generation of Trappers in the Hunt," *Baltimore Sun*, 2 Mar. 1997, at B1. Admittedly, **repleat* was a variant spelling in the early 18th century, but it was laid to rest by 1750 and is revived today only by error.

LANGUAGE-CHANGE INDEX
replete misspelled **repleat*: Stage 1
Current ratio: 855:1

replicable, not **replicatable,* has always been the standard form since the word emerged in the 1940s—e.g.: "Theoretically still required to shed all programming *replicatable* [read *replicable*] by a commercial channel, Alan Yentob's BBC1 thumbed its nose at Birtist teachings, notably via the Lottery." John Dugdale, "The Woof and the Smooth," *Guardian,* 2 Jan. 1995, at T14. See -ABLE (D) & -ATABLE.

LANGUAGE-CHANGE INDEX
*replicatable for *replicable:* Stage 1
Current ratio (*replicable* vs. **replicatable*): 201:1

replying to your letter of; referring to your letter of. Commonly found in business correspondence, these participial openers are widely condemned as weak and stilted. Also, they typically result in DANGLERS. E.g.: "*Replying to your letter of March 7,* the report you inquired about is soon to be acted on by the standing committee." (A possible revision: *The standing committee will soon act on the report that you asked about in your letter of March 7.*)

reportage (= the reporting or depiction of events, esp. through journalism) is preferably pronounced /rep-ər-**tahzh**/ in AmE and BrE alike. Although some American dictionaries record /ri-**por**-tij/, an anglicized pronunciation, it is rarely if ever heard in AmE today.

reportedly. See -EDLY.

repository; **repositary.* The first has been the standard spelling since the 17th century. The second is a NEEDLESS VARIANT. Cf. **depositary.**

Current ratio: 2,720:1

reprehensible. So spelled—not **reprehensable.* See -ABLE (A).

represent; re-present. See RE- PAIRS.

repress. See **oppress.**

repressible. So spelled—not **repressable.* See -ABLE (A).

Current ratio: 102:1

reprise; reprisal. *Reprise* = (1) /ri-**prIz**/ an annual deduction, duty, or payment out of a manor or estate, as an annuity or the like; or (2) /ri-**preez**/ (in music) a repetition of a theme or (in the performing arts) a repetition of a performance or role. In sense 2 the word is often metaphorical. *Reprisal* /ri-**prI**-zəl/ = an act of retaliation, usu. of one nation against another but short of war. *Reprisal* for *reprise* is a MALAPROPISM— e.g.: "Unless one party backs down, the battle could escalate into a *reprisal* [read *reprise*] of the partisan strife that paralyzed the Senate for several weeks over the summer." Jeremy W. Peters, "Between Democrats and a Push for Filibuster Change, One Nominee," *N.Y. Times,* 30 Oct. 2013, at A12. A clearer choice here would be *repeat.*

Another odd MALAPROPISM is the substitution of *reprise* for *reprieve* — e.g.: "It remains true that because of the acceptance of the trade dollar, and its subsequent circulation in the United States, the inflationary interests were granted a *reprise* [read *reprieve*] on the issue between 1873 and 1876, when the trade dollar's coinage was discontinued." Richard Hofstadter, *The Paranoid Style in American Politics, and Other Essays* 279–80 (2012).

reprove; re-prove. See RE- PAIRS.

repudiatory; **repudiative.* Although both forms were common from the mid-19th century to the mid-20th, since the 1970s *repudiatory* has become the standard term. **Repudiative* is now a NEEDLESS VARIANT.

Current ratio: 14:1

repugn. See **impugn** (A).

repulse. See **repel** (A).

repulsive. See **repellent.**

reputation. See **character.**

requiescat in pace. See R.I.P.

require. See **necessitate.** For a misusage of *adjure* to mean *require,* see **abjure** (C).

requisite. See **prerequisite** (A).

*requisite requirement is a patent REDUNDANCY.

requital; **requitement.* The former has been predominant since the early 16th century. The latter is a NEEDLESS VARIANT.

Current ratio: 154:1

rescindable; **rescissible.* The first is older (18th c.), more prevalent, and more recognizable in relation to the verb. It is the only form listed in the *OED*; W3 contains both. The second is a NEEDLESS VARIANT.

Current ratio: 1.2:1

rescission. A. And **recision; *recission; *rescision.* For "an act of rescinding, annulling, vacating, or canceling," *rescission* is the standard and the etymologically preferable spelling. It has been vastly predominant since about 1800.

But some writers have been misled by their smattering of Latin: perhaps they have realized that **recision* is from the Latin noun *recisio,* meaning "a cutting back, or lopping off." And through the process known as folk etymology, these writers may have wrongly thought **recision* to be the correct form, *rescission* a corruption. (See ETYMOLOGY (D).) Yet *rescission* is the true Latin form (fr. the accusative *rescissionem*) and English form. *Rescission* is preferable also because of its consistency with the verb *rescind.*

LANGUAGE-CHANGE INDEX (For the full key, see front matter pp. xxxi, l–li.)
Stage 1: Rejected. **Stage 2:** Widely shunned. **Stage 3:** Widespread but . . . **Stage 4:** Ubiquitous but . . . **Stage 5:** Fully accepted.
Invariably inferior forms marked by asterisk (*). • Ratios represent frequency of prevalent forms vs. variants in current books.

*Recission and *rescision are common misspellings resulting from combinations of the other forms.

Current ratio (in order of headwords): 243:5:4:1

B. Pronunciation. The sound of the -ss- in rescission is like that in *precision*, not that in *permission*. This is one of very few English words in which the -ss- has the sound /zh/ instead of /sh/. Two others are *abscission* and *fission* (commonly in AmE—but also pronounced /sh/). See **fission.**

C. And *rescindment. This is yet another NEEDLESS VARIANT of *rescission*. It flourished for a brief period in the late 18th century. See (A).

research, whether as adjective, noun, or verb, is best pronounced /ri-**sərch**/—although /**ree**-sərch/ is also common in AmE.

research; re-search. See RE- PAIRS.

resent. A. For *begrudge. Unlike *begrudge*, *resent* shouldn't be used with a direct and an indirect object—e.g.: "It is easy for women to *resent men their easy access* to sexual arousal since our own is often wrapped in thick layers of guilt and insecurity." Celia Barbour, "Looking at Pictures," *N.Y. Times*, 23 Apr. 1994, at 15. The idiom should be *to begrudge men their easy access* because the verb *resent* always takes a simple direct object.

B. For *regret. If it's within your control and you've done it, you *regret* it; if it's foisted on you, you *resent* it. E.g.: "'I think that every person I know who likes me, who talked with Gail Sheehy, frankly *resents* [read *regrets*] having done so, because she so systematically manipulated and was so totally dishonest in the article.'" Greg Pierce, "Gingrich v. Sheehy," *Wash. Times*, 11 Sept. 1995, at A5 (quoting Speaker of the House Newt Gingrich).

LANGUAGE-CHANGE INDEX
resent misused for *regret*: Stage 2

C. And *re-sent. See RE- PAIRS.

reserve; re-serve. See RE- PAIRS.

residence; residency. See **citizenship.**

resident. See **citizen (A).**

residual; residuary, adj.; ***residuous.** In most contexts, *residual* is the general adjective meaning "relating to or constituting a residue; leftover" <residual effects>. But in the specialized context of estates and trusts, *residuary* is the preferred adjective meaning "of, relating to, or involving all the property and money that remains after someone's death and after any bills have been paid." E.g.: "A person who is entitled to the *residuary* estate (what is remaining after all legacies and other outgoings have been paid) is entitled to receive such an account, which should show that everything has been dealt with correctly." "Briefcase," *Fin. Times*, 27 Sept. 1997, at 7. ***Residuous** is a NEEDLESS VARIANT of the other two words.

residue; residuum; residual, n.; **residuary,** n. Both *residue* and *residuum* mean "that which remains."

Residue is the usual and preferred term for most contexts. *Residuum* is a technical term used correctly in chemical contexts. *Residual*, n., = a remainder; an amount still remaining after the main part is subtracted or accounted for (*OED*). *Residuary*, n., is a NEEDLESS VARIANT except in legal contexts. See **residual.**

***residuous.** See **residual.**

residuum. See **residue.**

resign; re-sign. See RE- PAIRS.

resilience (= [1] the ability of a substance such as a resin to return to its original shape after it has been beaten or pressed, or [2] the ability to become strong, successful, or happy again after a difficult or trying circumstance) has been the standard noun since the 18th century. ***Resiliency** is a NEEDLESS VARIANT.

Current ratio: 5:1

resister; resistor. *Resister* (= someone who resists) is the agent noun dating from the 14th century. *Resistor* (= a piece of wire or other substance increasing electrical resistance) is the electrical term dating from the early 20th century.

resistible. So spelled—preferably not ***resistable.** See -ABLE (A).

Current ratio: 24:1

resistor. See **resister.**

resolution; motion. These terms carry distinct meanings in parliamentary procedure. When a deliberative assembly passes a *resolution*, the assembly is formally expressing its opinion about something—but no official action is taken. But when an assembly member raises a *motion*, the assembly is considering a formal proposal for action—and if the motion carries, the action will be taken.

resolvable; *resolvible; resoluble. *Resolvable* has always been the predominant term, since the 17th century, in meaning "able to be resolved." *Resoluble* has the liability of meaning also "capable of being dissolved again." Avoid the variant spelling ***resolvible.** Cf. **soluble.**

resound; re-sound. See RE- PAIRS.

resource. See **recourse.**

respect. The phrases *with respect to* and *in respect of* are usually best replaced by single prepositions. E.g.:

- "Clinton . . . has continued to enjoy stronger support from women than men even *with respect to* [read *in*] the Paula Jones case." Susan Estrich, "Will Clinton Stoop to Conquer?" *Denver Post*, 5 June 1997, at B11.
- "Notices stating the action taken *in respect of* [read *against* or *on*] each licensee have been placed on the Consumer Credit Public Register." "Mortgage Lenders Warned by OFT," *Fin. Times*, 29 June 1995, at 8.
- "Dublin's Philip McMahon and Mayo's Cillian O'Connor will not face any further action *in respect of* [read *for*] other

incidents." Sean Moran, "Proposed Ban Likely to Rule Connolly Out," *Irish Times*, 1 Sept. 2015, Sport §, at 14.

Cf. **regard (A)**.

respecting. For *respecting* as an acceptable dangling modifier, see DANGLERS (E).

respective; respectively. These terms, the adjective and adverb, respectively, meaning "each according to its own situation," ought to be used only when the distinction matters—e.g.: "Only 7% of married women and 8% of single women describe their financial personality as 'confident'; 15% and 24%, *respectively*, call themselves 'confused.'" Walter Updegrave, "Pitching Policy," *Money Mag.*, 1 Feb. 2003, at 27. There, the writer wants to make it clear that the 15% figure goes with married women and 24% with single women.

But as often used, these are heavily pedantic terms. As H.W. Fowler wrote, "Delight in these words is a widespread but depraved taste; like soldiers and policemen, they have work to do, but, when the work is not there, the less we see of them the better; of ten sentences in which they occur, nine would be improved by their removal" (*FMEU1* at 500).

Here, for example, it makes no difference which vessel weighs 100 tons and which weighs 120 tons, so *respectively* is superfluous: "As the two craft, weighing *respectively* 100 and 120 tons, dock the problems will be both technical and linguistic." "Bread-and-Salt Welcome as Atlantis Crew Greet 'Aliens from Space,'" *Daily Telegraph*, 29 June 1995, at 11. It would be more natural to write, "As the two craft—one 100 tons, the other 120—dock, the problems will be both technical and linguistic."

Often, then, both *respective* and *respectively* aren't needed at all—e.g.:

- "Even those as young as 2 offered opinions on the Indian princess Pocahontas and the English explorer John Smith, voiced by Irene Bedard and Mel Gibson *respectively* [delete *respectively*]." Melissa Myers, "You Are the Critic," *Des Moines Register*, 29 June 1995, at 7.
- "Both men also realized a long time ago that, despite the caliber of their *respective games* [read *games* or *play*], careers as touring professionals were not in their future." Leonard Shapiro, "Two Golfers Hope to Play Home Holes," *Wash. Post*, 11 May 1997, at D6.

For an example in which *respectively* seems useful, see **paean (A)** (fourth sentence).

respiratory is preferably pronounced /**res**-pər-ə-tor-ee/, not /ri-**spi**-rə-tor-ee/.

respite (= a short period of relief or rest) is preferably pronounced /**res**-pit/—not /**res**-pit/ or /ri-**spit**/.

resplendence (= the quality or state of being beautiful, bright, and impressive; splendor) has been the standard noun in all varieties of English since 1800. **Resplendency* is a NEEDLESS VARIANT.

Current ratio: 6:1

respond back. Because the prefix *re-* means "back," this phrase is usually a REDUNDANCY—e.g.:

- "Perrin also recommended no additional action be taken until the county *responds back* [read *responds*] to the municipality with respect to its willingness to front-end the associated costs." Ian McCallum, "Sewer Plan Shelved," *Times Journal* (St. Thomas, Ont.), 15 Aug. 2005, News §, at 1. (The verbing of *front-end* in that sentence may also irritate some readers.)
- "Any member needing a baby sitter e-mails the monthly coordinator a week prior to [read *before*] the date needed. Members who are available to baby-sit at that time *respond back* [read *respond*] to the coordinator and the requesting member chooses a sitter." Molly Kozik, "Baby Sitting Co-op Gives Parents a Source of Relief," *Daily Herald* (Chicago), 16 July 2006, North Aurora §, at 1.

Sometimes, though, the *back* is justified—e.g.: "I respond by pointing to my kayak at the water's edge and he *responds back* with a huff." Robert Hughes, "They Make War, Not Love with Nature," *Fla. Today*, 4 Sept. 2006, Sports §, at D-2.

-RESS. See SEXISM (D).

restaurateur. So spelled, as a French loanword from the late 18th century. **Restauranteur*, with an intrusive *-n-*, is a common error that began appearing in the mid-19th century and spread especially after 1960. It occurs in writing as well as in pronunciation—e.g.:

- "Corporate spending is way down, *restauranteurs* [read *restaurateurs*] and caterers say." Ellen Debenport, "Second-Term Inaugurals Often a Little Lackluster," *St. Petersburg Times*, 19 Jan. 1997, at A1.
- "Tom and Mickey Kopp, seated, were recently named Central New York's outstanding *restauranteurs* [read *restaurateurs*]." Larry Richardson, "Chittenango Restaurant Savors Regional Award," *Post-Standard* (Syracuse), 19 June 1997, at 15 (photo caption).

The mispronunciation—resulting, of course, from the spelling of *restaurant*—may also be influenced by *raconteur*. See SPELLING (A).

LANGUAGE-CHANGE INDEX
restaurateur misspelled **restauranteur*: Stage 2
Current ratio: 19:1

restful. See **restive**.

rest in peace. See **R.I.P.**

restitutionary; *restitutive; *restitutional; *restitutory. Unabridged dictionaries generally record only **restitutive* and **restitutory*, the two words that predominated in print sources from 1870 to 1930. But in law—where the subject of restitution is most common—the standard term has been *restitutionary* since about 1985. It is now vastly predominant. All other forms can now be regarded as NEEDLESS VARIANTS.

Current ratio (in order of headwords): 36:13:3:1

LANGUAGE-CHANGE INDEX (For the full key, see front matter pp. xxxi, l–li.)
Stage 1: Rejected. **Stage 2:** Widely shunned. **Stage 3:** Widespread but . . . **Stage 4:** Ubiquitous but . . . **Stage 5:** Fully accepted.
Invariably inferior forms marked by asterisk (*). • Ratios represent frequency of prevalent forms vs. variants in current books.

restive = (1) intractable, stubborn, unmanageable; or (2) restless, nervous, impatient. Although sense 1 is older, sense 2 has become more common. Some critics lament this development, but it seems irreversible—e.g.:

- "Many of the movers and shakers who control so much of New York's economic and financial life are already quite *restive* about the possible huge tax burden on those who live or work in New York." "Time for New York to Simplify Its Income Tax," *N.Y. Times*, 14 Apr. 1985, § 4, at 22.
- "Each time I brought up the subject of how much he was paid, he became *restive*." Marie Brenner, "The Unquiet American," *Wash. Post*, 21 Sept. 1997, Mag. §, at 6.
- "Fiorina's support in the polls is driven in part by *restive* voters who are frustrated by the status quo and are seriously considering outsiders such as her, businessman Donald Trump and Dr. Ben Carson." Seema Mehta, "Attacks Are a Good Sign for Fiorina," *L.A. Times*, 3 Sept. 2015, at 6.

The more serious problem is that *restive* is sometimes misused for *restful*—e.g.: "*Restive* [read *Restful*] moment. Lori takes a time out from sports to relax in her living room." "Armed with Attitude," *Fresno Bee*, 4 Sept. 1997, at E6 (photo caption).

LANGUAGE-CHANGE INDEX
1. *restive* in the sense "nervous": Stage 5
2. *restive* in the sense "restful": Stage 2

rest on one's laurels. The *laurel* in this phrase refers literally to the leaf of the bay laurel tree. It is typically used figuratively to denote honors or victories (as, in antiquity, a laurel wreath awarded in athletic events or military campaigns). To *rest on one's laurels* is to stop competing and bask in the glow of past successes. The phrase doesn't work as well with the verb *sit* (that's no way to show off the symbol of one's triumphs). Yet **sit on one's laurels* has become fairly common in AmE—e.g.:

- "But American colleges cannot *sit* [read *rest*] on their laurels if they are to remain what they tend to consider themselves: the very best." Niall Ferguson, "Still the Head of the Class?" *L.A. Times*, 22 Aug. 2005, at B11.
- "Our State Fair is the best state fair, but why *sit* [read *rest*] on our laurels?" Ken Fuson, "Big Bellies and Beer Men: Let's Spice Up Iowa State Fair," *Des Moines Register*, 18 Aug. 2006, News §, at A13.
- "Not one to *sit on her laurels and rest* [read *rest on her laurels*], Shayna is also active with the local Society for the Prevention of Cruelty to Animals, and is a singer and songwriter." Cindy Elavsky, "Stephanie Speeds Her Way into Salem," *Tulsa World*, 27 Aug. 2006, Television §, at 47.

Of course, people resting on their laurels might also be sitting on their hands.

LANGUAGE-CHANGE INDEX
**sitting on laurels* for *resting on laurels*: Stage 1
Current ratio (*resting on their laurels* vs.
**sitting on their laurels*): 11:1

restoration; *restoral. The former has been standard since it was first used in the 14th century. The latter is a NEEDLESS VARIANT.

Current ratio: 2,836:1

restore; re-store. See RE- PAIRS.

restrain; refrain. These words were once almost interchangeable, but have long since been distinguishable. *Restrain* (= [1] to hold [a person or thing] back from an action; or [2] to deprive of liberty) is now almost exclusively a transitive verb. Although the *OED* records occasional intransitive uses—in which *restrain* is construed with *to* or *from*—these are historical. And although from the late 16th century to the mid-19th century *restrain* was occasionally used as a synonym for the intransitive *refrain* (= to hold [oneself] back), that use is now rare and ill-advised. *Refrain* always concerns oneself in the sense "to abstain" <he refrained from exchanging scurrilities with his accuser>, whereas *restrain* concerns either someone else <the police illegally restrained the complainant from going into the stadium> or oneself (reflexively) <I couldn't restrain myself>.

In the following sentences, *refrain* would have been the better choice—e.g.:

- "Mr. Clinton will make the case that the United States will lack the moral authority to press India and Pakistan to *restrain* [read *refrain*] from testing nuclear weapons until the Senate approves the test ban treaty." John M. Broder, "Clinton to Urge More Control on Aid to Schools: to Stick to Policy, Not His Trial, in State of the Union Address," *N.Y. Times*, 18 Jan. 1999, at A1, A10.
- "Under the terms of the agreement, Alpine and the Carroll brothers have agreed . . . that they will *restrain* [read *refrain*] from selling or offering for sale 'any securities of any kind.'" David Robb, "Film Solicitor Reined In Again," *Hollywood Rptr.*, 25 Aug. 1999, at 3.
- "Pseudo-omniscient, mouthy sports journalists who try to belittle readers with supercilious text will *restrain* [read *refrain*] from speaking their all-too-correct opinions and just report." Mac Engel, "With Start of School Come Some 'Realistic' Predictions," *Ft. Worth Star-Telegram*, 18 Aug. 2000, at 15.
- "The demotion was harder for Chiaverini to take, but he *restrained* [read *refrained*] from saying anything inflammatory after Palmer's original comments." Tony Grossi, "Chiaverini Down but Not Out," *Plain Dealer* (Cleveland), 15 Sept. 2000, at D1.

Refrain is sometimes misused for *restrain*, as a reflexive verb—e.g.: "I had to *refrain myself* [read *restrain myself* or *refrain*] from snapping that I wasn't quite ready to date." Miriam Sagan, "How to Talk to a Widow," *Albuquerque J.*, 2 Mar. 1997, at 14.

LANGUAGE-CHANGE INDEX
1. *restrain* misused for *refrain*: Stage 2
2. *refrain oneself for *restrain oneself*: Stage 1
Current ratio (*restrain oneself* vs.
*refrain oneself): 58:1

RESTRICTIVE AND NONRESTRICTIVE RELATIVE PRONOUNS. See **that (A).**

résumé. So spelled, preferably, with both accents. The first acute accent is often dropped for three reasons. First, the word is typically pronounced /**rez**-[y] ə-may/, not /**ray**-zyoo-may/. Second, the accent over the final syllable (*resumé*) sufficiently distinguishes this noun from the verb *resume*. Third, AmE is inhospitable to unnecessary DIACRITICAL MARKS, and many desktop dictionaries (*W11* being a notable exception) have ditched the two-accent version. See **vita.** Cf. **protégé** & **soufflé.**

LANGUAGE-CHANGE INDEX
resumé for *résumé*: Stage 2
Current ratio (*résumé* vs. *resumé*): 12:1

resurface, like *surface*, may be intransitive or transitive, though the meanings differ. *Resurface* = (1) to come to the top again <he resurfaced in the middle of the pond>; or (2) to put a new top on <the state resurfaced the road>.

resuscitate. So spelled. See SPELLING (A).

retaliatory; retaliative. The two forms have undergone DIFFERENTIATION. The first means "of, relating to, or constituting retaliation" <retaliatory eviction>, whereas the second means "vindictive, tending to retaliation" <a retaliative landlord>. But there is a tendency for *retaliatory* to assume both senses.

retch, v.i. This verb, meaning "to vomit or try to vomit," is amazingly often misspelled *wretch*—e.g.:

• "A few weeks ago I found myself stretching out on the couch and *wretching* [read *retching*] into a bowl, nursing a headache the size of Montana." Deborah Halter, "Never Underestimate the Power of the Mighty Television," *Ark. Democrat-Gaz.*, 6 July 1997, at J3.
• "Chris Webber returned to the training-camp [after spending] the previous 3 1/2 days *wretching* [read *retching*] his insides out." "Pro Basketball," *Columbus Dispatch*, 9 Oct. 1997, at D2.

Wretch, of course, is a noun meaning either "a miserable person" or "a contemptible lowlife." A person who is *retching* often feels like a *wretch* but is probably in no condition to think of the usage issue.

LANGUAGE-CHANGE INDEX
wretch misused for the verb *retch*: Stage 1
Current ratio (*retching* vs. *wretching*): 89:1

reticent = reserved; unwilling to speak freely; taciturn. E.g.:

• "He's silent in the locker room, *reticent* in team meetings and uncomfortable among reporters." Randy Covitz, "Chiefs' Defense Needs Young Starters to Step Up," *Kansas City Star*, 30 Aug. 1997, at D1.
• "Making the album was a difficult process, but unlike their *reticent* singer, the band seem to enjoy discussing Portishead's agonizing creation." Rob Brunner, "Class Trip-Hop Portishead Follows 'Dummy' with a Smart New Disc," *Entertainment Weekly*, 17 Oct. 1997, at 76.

But the word is frequently misunderstood as being synonymous with *reluctant*—e.g.:

• "Malinowski said Pi-Pa-Tag officials have been wary about the earth-capping proposal from its inception, but now they're even more *reticent* [read *reluctant*] to approve

such a plan." David Pedreira, "Asbestos Concerns Stauffer Neighbors," *Tampa Trib.*, 29 July 1997, at 1.
• "Although the Marlins also have been *reticent* [read *reluctant*] to run (two steals in as many attempts), leadoff batter Devon White was hit by a pitch Sunday, promptly stole second and scored the first Florida run on Bobby Bonilla's single." Joe Gergen, "Marlins vs. Braves," *Newsday* (N.Y.), 14 Oct. 1997, at A73.
• "Now that the Wizards' playoff hopes are gone, Jordan can take time to soak in the farewells he was previously *reticent* [read *reluctant*] to embrace." Joseph White, "Wizards Set for Jordan's Final Home Game," *Commercial Appeal* (Memphis), 14 Apr. 2003, at D4.

The corresponding noun is *reticence*, not **reticency* (a NEEDLESS VARIANT). In the noun as well as the adjective, the difference between taciturnity and reluctance is extremely subtle—e.g.: "Many cases go unreported because of a *reticence* on the part of the victims to publicly accuse close relatives, much like the silence that often cloaks child abuse." Jon Nordheimer, "A New Abuse of Elderly: Theft by Kin and Friends," *N.Y. Times*, 16 Dec. 1991, at A1.

LANGUAGE-CHANGE INDEX
reticent in the sense "reluctant": Stage 4
Current ratio (*reluctant to* vs. **reticent to*): 62:1

retina (= the back-of-the-eye membrane that receives light and sends an image of what has been seen to the brain) has predominantly made the plural *retinas* since the 1950s in AmE and since the 1980s in BrE. Before that, the Latinate plural *retinae* (/ret-ən-ee/) was prevalent in all varieties of English. See PLURALS (B).

Current ratio: 4:1

retirement; *retiral; *retiracy. *Retirement*, of course, is the usual word. **Retiral* (= the act of retiring) and **retiracy* (= the state of being retired) are now NEEDLESS VARIANTS.

Current ratio (in order of headwords): 7,778:2:1

retractable; *retractible. The word wasn't used much till the 1920s, and since then there has been no serious competition between the spellings: *retractable* is vastly predominant in AmE and BrE alike—hence standard. See -ABLE (A).

Current ratio: 256:1

retraction; *retractation. In the figurative sense "the act of recanting" or "a statement in recantation," *retraction* has been the usual term in AmE since 1800 and in BrE since 1860. After the mid-19th century, **retractation* became a chiefly BrE variant. In both varieties of English, *retraction* is the noun corresponding to *retract* in literal senses as well ("to draw back," etc.).

Current ratio: 33:1

retreat; re-treat. See RE- PAIRS.

LANGUAGE-CHANGE INDEX (For the full key, see front matter pp. xxxi, l–li.)
Stage 1: Rejected. **Stage 2:** Widely shunned. **Stage 3:** Widespread but . . . **Stage 4:** Ubiquitous but . . . **Stage 5:** Fully accepted. Invariably inferior forms marked by asterisk (*). • Ratios represent frequency of prevalent forms vs. variants in current books.

*retreat back is a common REDUNDANCY dating back to the 17th century—e.g.: "There is no way out of that blind alley but to *retreat back* [read *retreat*] into the very language that brought one in." Joseph Brodsky, *Less than One* 287 (1986). Cf. ***return back** & **revert**.

retributive; retributory; *retributional; *retributionary. *Retributive* = of or characterized by retribution. E.g.: "But justice will be served if the settlement is preventive, not just *retributive*." "The Cigarette Pact," *Boston Globe*, 25 June 1997, at A20. *Retributory* has the added sense "causing or producing retribution." E.g.: "Many of the investment banks . . . were hit by *retributory* legislation." Robert Sobel, "Kicking and Screaming," *Barron's*, 20 May 1996, at A43. Although euphony can govern the choice, it's worth knowing that *retributive* has been vastly predominant in print sources since about 1770.

*Retributional and **retributionary* are NEEDLESS VARIANTS sometimes used but omitted from the major dictionaries.

Current ratio (in order of headwords): 2,850:47:16:1

retrofit, n. & v.t. The noun *retrofit*—dating from the early 1950s—is a HYBRID meaning "a modification of equipment or a building to include developments not available at the time of original manufacture or construction." The term has been extended to verb uses. The past tense is *retrofitted*, not *retrofit*—e.g.: "The Tickells, 21, were driving the Veggie Van, a 3-ton Winnebago splashed with yellow daisies and *retrofitted* to run on used cooking oil." Connie Koenenn, "Sunday Brunch," *L.A. Times*, 21 Sept. 1997, at E3.

RETRONYMS. In the beginning there was the *telephone*. Each one had the same essential features, including a dial. (For convenience, the word was shortened to the CASUALISM *phone*.) Then came another type: the *push-button telephone* (often referred to by the trademark *Touch-Tone telephone*). So a NEOLOGISM had to be developed to refer to the original type with a dial: the *rotary telephone*. That term is an example of a retronym—a word or phrase invented to denote what was originally a genus term but has now become just one more species in a larger genus. Retronyms are usually occasioned by cultural, historical, and technological developments.

Retronyms aren't a recent phenomenon. When *roller skates* were invented in the 19th century, it became necessary to refer to the kind used on ice—originally just *skates*—as *ice skates*. When cars began appearing on turn-of-the-century roads, old-style carriages came to be called *horse-drawn carriages* to distinguish them from the new *horseless carriages*. In the 1910s, when sound first came to be synchronized with motion pictures (in *talking movies* or *talkies*), the original type of movie came to be known as the *silent movie*. That is, nobody ever referred to *silent movies* until sound was added to the newer type. In the mid-20th century, what had been known as the *Great War* became known as *World War I* (it certainly wasn't called that in its day). A little later, when people started traveling in *jet airplanes*, the original type was distinguished by the phrase *propeller airplanes*. In the 1970s, when *unleaded gasoline* was developed, the original gasoline became known as *leaded gasoline*. And in the 1980s, cola drinkers rejected *New Coke* in favor of what then had to be renamed *Coke Classic*. The list of retronyms is constantly growing.

Original	New Species	Retronym
book	paperback book	hardback *or* hardcover book
business	e-business	brick-and-mortar business
coffee	decaffeinated coffee	regular coffee *or* caffeinated coffee
college	two-year college	four-year college
computer	desktop computer	mainframe computer
	laptop computer	
	notebook computer	
conference	teleconference	face-to-face conference
	videoconference	
contacts	color contacts	clear contacts
diaper	disposable diaper	cloth diaper
door	hollow-core door	solid-core door
fabric	synthetic fabric	natural fabric
guitar	electric guitar	acoustic guitar
Internet connection	broadband Internet connection	dial-up Internet connection
mail	e-mail	snail mail
milk	skim milk	whole milk
parent	adoptive parent	biological parent *or* natural parent
partner	life partner	business partner
pen	ballpoint pen	fountain pen
performance	recorded performance	live performance
photo(graph)	color photo	black-and-white photo
play	radio play	stage play
	teleplay	
razor	safety razor	straight razor
	electric razor	
soda	diet soda	regular soda
steering	power steering	nonpower steering
store	online store	brick-and-mortar store
tape	videotape	audiotape
television	color television	black-and-white television
transmission	automatic transmission	manual transmission
turf	artificial turf	natural turf, organic turf
typewriter	electric typewriter	manual typewriter
watch	digital watch	analog watch

William Safire, who first wrote about retronyms in his "On Language" column in *The New York Times* (27 July 1980), credits Frank Mankiewicz, then president of National Public Radio, with coining the term and collecting the first examples. As of September 2008, most printed dictionaries did not list the term, but it seems destined to full recognition in dictionaries of the future.

*return back is a fairly common REDUNDANCY. Its heyday was the 18th century through the mid-19th, after which period it was largely stifled in print sources. But it still occasionally crops up—e.g.: "An initial examination by orthopedic specialist Frank Jobe had shown that Jaha might be able to *return back* [read *return*] shortly after the all-star break." Andrew Cohen, "Powerless: Jaha Out for Season," *Wis. State J.*, 18 June 1997, at B1. Cf. *retreat back & revert.
> Current ratio (*soon returned to* vs. *soon returned back to*): 344:1

reurge; re-urge. In AmE, the word is solid: *reurge*.

reuse; re-use. In AmE, the word is solid: *reuse*.

revenge. See avenge.

revere; *reverence, v.t. The former has been the standard, predominant verb only since about 1950. It means "to admire greatly." The latter is a more formal equivalent that was prevalent from the mid-17th century to about 1950; it threatens to become a NEEDLESS VARIANT.
> Current ratio (*revered* vs. *reverenced*): 10:1

reverend. In denoting a member of the clergy, this term has traditionally been restricted to adjectival uses, as one newspaper acknowledged after being upbraided by a careful reader: "We referred correctly to the *Rev.* Wiley Drake, . . . but an inside subhead read, 'The *reverend* says.' Some dictionaries recognize *reverend* as a colloquial noun form referring to a member of the clergy, but our stylebook doesn't; the word is an adjective." Pat Riley, "The Rev. Robert Ross Offers Some Righteous Observations," *Orange County Register*, 3 Aug. 1997, at B4. The noun uses without the article—as in *Reverend Harold Myers* as opposed to *the Reverend Harold Myers*—have long been stigmatized as poor usage. And if the stigma is wearing off, it's doing so very gradually.

reverie (= a daydream) has been the standard spelling in AmE and BrE alike since the 17th century. *Revery is a chiefly AmE variant; don't use it.
> Current ratio: 13:1

*reversable. See reversible.

reversal; reversion. The first corresponds to the verb *reverse* <a reversal of fortune>, the second to the verb *revert* <a dangerous reversion to prewar policies>. Roughly speaking, a *reversion* is a throwback.

reverse, n. See converse.

reversible. So spelled in AmE and BrE alike—not *reversable. See -ABLE (A).
> Current ratio: 1,733:1

reversion. See reversal.

revert = (1) to return to a former state, condition, or posture; (2) to go back in thought, speech, or action; or (3) (of property) to return to the former owner or to that owner's heirs. Sense 1 is most common—e.g.: "Christina Martin, Gingrich's spokeswoman, later dismissed a suggestion that he was *reverting* to the tougher rhetoric that characterized his first term as speaker." Judy Holland, "Gingrich Rips Clinton's Violations, Backs End to Limits on Donations," *News & Observer* (Raleigh), 26 Sept. 1997, at A8.
> *Revert back is a REDUNDANCY common in AmE— e.g.: "Medieval town centers, once built for people on foot and a few carts and carriages, have partly *reverted back* [read *reverted*] to strollers." Marlise Simons, "Amsterdam Plans Wide Limit on Cars," *N.Y. Times*, 28 Jan. 1993, at A5. Cf. refer back, relate back & *retreat back.
> Current ratio (*reverted to* vs. *reverted back to*): 12:1

revertible. So spelled in AmE and BrE alike. *Revertable is a chiefly AmE variant. See -ABLE (A).
> Current ratio: 9:1

*revery. See reverie.

review, n.; *reviewal. The latter is a NEEDLESS VARIANT. For a misuse of *review*, see revue.
> Current ratio (*a review* vs. *a reviewal*): 13,597:1

revile (= to assail with vituperative language) is occasionally misused for *repulse* (= to arouse feelings of disgust) or *repel* (= [1] to drive back, esp. by physical force; or [2] to reject [a statement, etc.]). The headline from an article appearing on the first page of the *Amarillo Globe-Times* reads: "Thought of Parent Testimony Reviles [read *Repulses*] Many," 17 Feb. 1998.
> LANGUAGE-CHANGE INDEX
> *revile* misused for *repel* or *repulse*: Stage 1

revisable. So spelled in AmE and BrE alike—not *revisible. See -ABLE (A).
> Current ratio: 166:1

*revisal. See revision.

revise; redact; recense. The first is the ordinary word. The second and third refer specifically to revising texts with close scrutiny. *Redact* = (1) to make a draft of; or (2) to edit. In American law, it is often used in the sense "to edit out or mask the privileged, impertinent, or objectionable matter in a document." *Recense* is more of a literary term; it relates to scholarly editing of ancient texts and the like.

reviser; *revisor. The first has been the predominant spelling in AmE and BrE alike since the word first came into use in the 18th century. See -ER (A).
> Current ratio: 8:1

revision; *revisal. The latter is a NEEDLESS VARIANT.

LANGUAGE-CHANGE INDEX (For the full key, see front matter pp. xxxi, l–li.)
Stage 1: Rejected. Stage 2: Widely shunned. Stage 3: Widespread but . . . Stage 4: Ubiquitous but . . . Stage 5: Fully accepted.
Invariably inferior forms marked by asterisk (*). • Ratios represent frequency of prevalent forms vs. variants in current books.

revisionary; *revisional; revisory; revisionist.
Revisionary = of, relating to, or made up of revision
<revisionary methods>. *Revisional* is a NEEDLESS
VARIANT. *Revisory* = having power to revise; engaged
in revision <a revisory board>. *Revisionist* = having
the purpose of changing the conventional beliefs
about something, esp. in a political way.

revisionism (= the practice of rethinking traditionally accepted notions about events or ideas in light of
later developments and revelations), a 20th-century
word, is sometimes neutral in connotation—e.g.: "The
author of this book covers familiar ground in unfamiliar ways. Eva Sheppard Wolf's *revisionism* begins
with her reduced estimate of slaves freed in the 1780s."
James Oakes, "Race and Liberty in the New Nation:
Emancipation in Virginia from the Revolution to Nat
Turner's Rebellion," *The Historian*, 22 Dec. 2008, at
808. But in practice, *revisionism* (like the agent noun
revisionist) carries pejorative connotations—e.g.:

- "Days later, Cheney took pains to single out [Rep. John]
  Murtha as 'a good man, a Marine, a patriot,' before going
  on to declare those who charge that the nation was
  deceived into war guilty of '*revisionism* of the most corrupt and shameless variety.'" Julie Schfeld Davis, "Point
  Man Cheney Viewed as Liability," *Baltimore Sun*, 25 Nov.
  2005, at A1.
- "Rodney Stark comes out swinging right from the bell in
  'The Victory of Reason,' his fiercely polemical account of
  the rise of capitalism.... 'The success of the West, including the rise of science, rested entirely on religious foundations, and the people who brought it about were devout
  Christians,' he argues in this provocative, exasperating,
  and occasionally baffling exercise in *revisionism*." William
  Grimes, "Capitalism, Brought to You by Religion," *N.Y.
  Times*, 30 Dec. 2005, at E42.

***revisor.** See **reviser.**

revisory. See **revisionary.**

revitalize has become a VOGUE WORD among politicians and businesspeople <to revitalize the inner
city>. Avoid it.

revocability is pronounced /rev-ə-kə-**bil**-i-tee/.

revocable; *revokable. The first has been vastly predominant since the 16th century; it is pronounced
/**rev**-ə-kə-bəl/. *Revokable* (as well as *revokeable*) is a
NEEDLESS VARIANT. See **irrevocable.**

Current ratio: 121:1

***revocate.** See **revoke.**

revoke (= to declare officially that a law, decision,
or agreement is no longer effective) is the standard
verb. *Revocate*, a misbegotten BACK-FORMATION, has
occasionally appeared since the mid-20th century. It
remains an error.

Current ratio: 1,818:1

revolutionary, n.; ***revolutionist,** n. Although *revolutionist* is the older term in English (1710), it is now
merely a NEEDLESS VARIANT of *revolutionary*, which

overthrew its rival during the first half of the 20th
century.

Current ratio (*a revolutionary is* vs.
a revolutionist is): 6:1

revue (= a musical show) is so spelled. Avoid the erroneous variant *review* in this sense—e.g.: "Grapevine's
Runway Theatre is performing 'Leader of the Pack,' a
musical *review* [read *revue*] of popular songs of the
1960s written by songwriter Ellie Greenwich." "Arts
Roundup: For a Limited Time," *Dallas Morning News*,
24 July 1997, at G5.

LANGUAGE-CHANGE INDEX
review misused for *revue*: Stage 1

rewind > rewound > rewound. So inflected. *Rewinded* is an infrequent error—e.g.: "Scenes can be freeze-
framed and advanced, *rewinded* [read *rewound*] and
fast-forwarded with the push-button precision of CD
audio or laser disc players." Steve Persall, "To DVD or
Not to DVD?" *St. Petersburg Times*, 19 Feb. 1999, at 20.
See IRREGULAR VERBS.

LANGUAGE-CHANGE INDEX
rewinded for past-tense *rewound*: Stage 1
Current ratio (*rewound* vs. *rewinded*): 227:1

rewrite is both noun and verb, although *write* itself
cannot be a noun. E.g.:

- "The play, meanwhile, could stand a good *rewrite*." Scott
  Collins, "'Pants on Fire': A Smothered Attempt," *L.A.
  Times*, 21 Oct. 1994, at 26.
- "A good *rewrite* of the Endangered Species Act would bal-
  ance the costs and benefits of preserving each and every
  species and subspecies." "Endangered Species," *San Diego
  Union-Trib.*, 18 Mar. 1995, at B6.
- "It was Mr. Kenney who took over the *rewrite* of the rules."
  John Ibbitson & Campbell Clark, "Immigration Minister
  'Flat-Footed' on Crisis," *Globe & Mail* (Toronto), 4 Sept.
  2015, at A3.

rhapsodic (= [1] of, relating to, or involving the recitation of an epic poem, or [2] written or spoken rapturously, with excited extravagance or overenthusiasm)
has vastly predominated in print sources over its rival
rhapsodical in AmE since 1920 and in BrE since the
late 1930s. The longer form is now a NEEDLESS VARI-
ANT. See -IC.

Current ratio: 5:1

rhetoric = (1) the art of using language persuasively;
the rules that help one achieve eloquence; (2) the persuasive use of language; (3) a treatise on persuasive
language; and (4) prose composition as a school subject. These are the main senses outlined in the *OED*,
which also records "ironical or jocular" uses from the
late 16th century to the mid-19th century (such as this
from 1742: "The rhetoric of John the hostler, with a
new straw hat, and a pint of wine, made a second conquest over her"). There should probably be added a
new sense, related to but distinct from the first sense:
(5) "the bombastic or disingenuous use of language to
manipulate people."

Older books defined *rhetoric* in line with sense 1:

- "Rhetoric is the Art of speaking suitably upon any Subject." John Kirkby, *A New English Grammar* 141 (1746).
- "Rhetoric is the art of aggrandizing and bringing out into strong relief, by means of various and striking thoughts, some aspect of truth which of itself is supported by no spontaneous feelings, and therefore rests upon artificial aids." Thomas De Quincey, "Rhetoric" (ca. 1835), in 10 *De Quincey's Works* 21, 29–30 (1862).
- "Rhetoric is the art of adapting discourse, in harmony with its subject and occasion, to the requirements of a reader or hearer." John F. Genung, *The Working Principles of Rhetoric* 1 (1902).

But the slippage toward the pejorative sense 5 began early. William Penn suggested its iniquitous uses in the 17th century: "There is a Truth and Beauty in Rhetorick; but it oftener serves ill Turns than good ones." William Penn, "Some Fruits of Solitude" (1693), in 1 *Harvard Classics* 329, 352 (Charles W. Eliot ed., 1909). By the 20th century, some writers with a classical bent were trying hard to reclaim the word—e.g.: "No one who reads [ancient authors] can hold the puerile notions of rhetoric that prevail in our generation. The ancients would have made short work of the cult of the anti-social that lies behind the cult of mystification and the modern hatred of rhetoric. All the great literary ages have exalted the study of rhetoric." Van Wyck Brooks, *Opinions of Oliver Allston* 291 (1941). But T.S. Eliot probably had it right when he acknowledged that the word is essentially ambiguous today—generally pejorative but with flashes of a favorable sense: "The word [*rhetoric*] simply cannot be used as synonymous with bad writing. The meanings which it has been obliged to shoulder have been mostly opprobrious; but if a precise meaning can be found for it this meaning may occasionally represent a virtue." Eliot, " 'Rhetoric' and Poetic Drama," in *The Sacred Wood* 78, 79 (7th ed. 1950).

For a good, well-rounded reference work on rhetoric, see *The Encyclopedia of Rhetoric* (Thomas O. Sloane ed., 2001).

*rhodomontade. See **rodomontade.**

rhombus. Pl. *rhombuses* or (less good) **rhombi.* See PLURALS (B).

    Current ratio (*rhombuses* vs. **rhombi*): 1.3:1

RHOTACISM. See PRONUNCIATION (C).

*rhumba. See **rumba.**

rhyme; rime. *Rhyme* means generally (1) "the correspondence of sound in words or lines of verse"; or (2) "a poem or poetry." *Rime* means "the icy crystals on a freezing surface; frost." Because of this long-standing DIFFERENTIATION, *rime* as a variant of *rhyme* ought to be discouraged.

Historically, though, *rime* is correct for "poetry." But a linguist once incorrectly traced the native Middle

English word *rime* to a Greek antecedent, and as a result generations of schoolchildren have learned to use the more difficult—and technically wrong—spelling *rhyme.* It's now standard.

Rime still appears for *rhyme* on rare occasions. But unless it's in a historical or jocular context (or there's an ancient mariner involved), use the modern spelling—e.g.: "This informative section also includes suggestions for helping children read and write by using letter-onset/*rime* [read *rhyme*] analogies, and for encouraging bilingual children's writing." Cathy J. Morton, "Writing in the Elementary Classroom: A Reconsideration," *Childhood Educ.*, 1 Oct. 2002, at 54.

rhyme royal; rime royale; *rhyme royale. *Rhyme royal* (= a seven-line stanza in iambic pentameter, with the rhyme scheme *ababbcc*) is standard in both AmE and BrE. *Rime royale* (sometimes anglicized as *rime royal*) is the standard French phrase. **Rhyme royale* is a mistaken mixture of the two.

    Current ratio (in order of headwords): 70:1.5:1

rhythmic; *rhythmical. H.W. Fowler said, "Both forms are too common to justify any expectation of either's disappearance" (*FMEU1* at 506). But he did think that **rhythmical* is the more ordinary term. In fact, though, *rhythmic* (the less rhythmic word) has outnumbered **rhythmical* in print sources since 1890 by a wide margin. Cf. **eurythmics.**

    Current ratio: 7:1

ribald (= of, relating to, or involving coarse, sexually suggestive or even sexually explicit humor or remarks) is pronounced /**rib**-əld/—not /**rɪ**-bahld/ or /ri-**bahld**/. The corresponding noun *ribaldry* (= the quality, state, or fact of being ribald—or an instance of it) is /**rib**-əl-dree/.

riboflavin. So spelled in AmE and BrE alike—not **riboflavine.*

    Current ratio: 89:1

rickety. So spelled. See SPELLING (A).

ricochet, vb., makes *ricocheted* /rik-ə-shayd/ and *ricocheting* /rik-ə-shay-ing/ in AmE. Those are the preferred forms as well in BrE, which also has the variants **ricochetted* /rik-ə-shet-əd/ and **ricochetting* /rik-ə-shet-ing/. The *-tt-* form was superseded in AmE by 1930 and in BrE by 1950.

    Current ratio (*ricocheted* vs. **ricochetted*): 27:1

rid > rid > rid. **Ridded* is a variant form to be avoided—e.g.:

- "The fish-eating public had a heyday the last time Williams and Badger were *ridded* [read *rid*] of non-game fish." Rich Landers, "State Won't Take Chance with Rotenone," *Spokesman-Rev.* (Spokane), 21 Sept. 1995, at C1.
- "When the night was over, Shaw had made $20 and had *ridded* [read *rid*] the world of one more TV set." Paul

LANGUAGE-CHANGE INDEX (For the full key, see front matter pp. xxxi, l–li.)
Stage 1: Rejected. **Stage 2:** Widely shunned. **Stage 3:** Widespread but . . . **Stage 4:** Ubiquitous but . . . **Stage 5:** Fully accepted.
Invariably inferior forms marked by asterisk (*). • Ratios represent frequency of prevalent forms vs. variants in current books.

Glader, "Bright Ones Bust the Boob Tube," *Indianapolis Star*, 17 Apr. 1997, at A14.

- "In one bold swoop Friday, the Yankees all but *ridded* [read *rid*] themselves of two players owner George Steinbrenner wanted no part of anymore." "Vaughn to Yankees Done Deal," *Chicago Trib.*, 5 July 1997, Sports §, at 4.

See IRREGULAR VERBS.

LANGUAGE-CHANGE INDEX
ridded for *rid* as past tense and
past participle: Stage 1
Current ratio (*had rid* vs. *had ridded*): 41:1

ridden. See **laden (B).**

ride > rode > ridden. In DIALECT, *rid* is sometimes used as a past participle. See IRREGULAR VERBS.

Current ratio (*had ridden in* vs. *had rid in*): 765:1

ridiculous has moved a long way from its etymological suggestion of "causing laughter," so that people nowadays often call *ridiculous* what causes them anger, frustration, distress, or even sadness. In other words, by SLIPSHOD EXTENSION it is frequently used when people are far from laughing. Today it is unrealistic to insist on etymological rigor with this word. For the sense "causing laughter," *risible* is now the better term. See **risible.**

rife; ripe. While a tree may be *rife* (= abundant) with fruit, and that fruit may be *ripe* (= fully mature), the terms are unrelated. To confuse them is a surprisingly common MALAPROPISM—e.g.:

- "Iowa State . . . made an impression in Florida, *ripe* [read *rife*] with high school players coach Dan McCarney's staff would love to lure to Ames." Miller Bryce, "Worth Every Penny," *Des Moines Register*, 26 Aug. 2002, at C6.
- "The movie is *ripe* [read *rife*] with fond allusions to earlier 007 flicks." David Germain, "Top Picks for Fall Films," *Cincinnati Post*, 26 Sept. 2002, at 14.
- "Exotic yet wholly approachable and *ripe* [read *rife*] with top-notch musicianship and infectious energy, this 'Revolution de Amor' is hard to resist." Scott D. Lewis, "CD of the Week," *Oregonian* (Portland), 30 Sept. 2002, at E1.

LANGUAGE-CHANGE INDEX
ripe misused for *rife*: Stage 2
Current ratio (*rife with* vs. *ripe with*): 5:1

riff; rift. These two are sometimes confused. *Riff* is now largely confined to jazz and pop-music contexts. It refers to a melodic phrase, usually repeated and often played in unison by several instruments; sometimes it's a variation on a tune, and it may be either an accompaniment to a solo or the only melodic element. E.g.: "With guitar *riffs* so rudimentary they seem to have been made up on the spot, . . . the U.K. sextet played with rude ebullience." Gret Kot, "No Stretching for Elastica," *Chicago Trib.*, 29 Sept. 2000, at 2.

In these senses, the term dates only from the mid-20th century—and has little discernible relation to the older, mostly obsolete senses of *riff* (= [1] a string of onions, [2] the diaphragm, and [3] the mange; an itchy rash). That's probably because this particular *riff* seems to have originated as a truncated form of the musical term *refrain*.

By extension, the word came to apply to a comic's take on a particular subject, especially an extemporaneous tirade—e.g.: "The comedian Richard Lewis says he was knocked out when he first heard a [Jonathan] Winters album at the age of thirteen: . . . 'I asked to sit next to him at a Stanley Kramer dinner, and just leaning over for a string bean he'd go into a whole *riff* about where that string bean came from and that I was insane for eating it. Nothing can go by him.'" Gerald Nachman, *Seriously Funny* 621 (2004).

Rift arose in Middle English in the sense "a fissure or divide; a split or crack"—the meaning it still carries. E.g.: "Word out of Washington is that Bondra wants to change teams because of a *rift* with coach Ron Wilson." Nancy Marrapese-Burrell, "End-of-the-Year Sale," *Boston Globe*, 1 Oct. 2000, at D2. Occasionally the term also refers to the rapids formed by rocks protruding from the bed of a stream. It formerly also meant "a burp"—a sense long obsolete.

Although the *OED* records two early-17th-century uses of *riff* in the obsolete sense "rift, chink," the modern use of the word in that sense appears to be nothing more than rank WORD-SWAPPING resulting from sound association—e.g.:

- "[Roone Arledge] was angered, sources say, that ABC Daytime had effectively gone behind his back to snare Walters. Walters told him that it was a fait accompli. Thus, 'The View' has now caused a minor *riff* [read *rift*] between the two." Verne Gay, "The Daytime View," *Newsday* (N.Y.), 11 Aug. 1997, at B3.
- "The mayor of South Jordan says the city has not abandoned a plan to construct a 111-acre wildlife preserve along the Jordan River, despite a major *riff* [read *rift*] with the U.S. Fish and Wildlife Service." Brent Israelsen, "S. Jordan to Revive Preserve," *Salt Lake Trib.*, 4 Dec. 1999, at D3.
- "The way he sees it, things aren't bad at all. No *riffs* [read *rifts*] between him and crew chief Todd Parrott." Skip Wood, "Yates Works to Vault Jarrett Back to the Top," *USA Today*, 26 May 2000, at F9.
- "When the *riff* [read *rift*] between the forest monk and the nation's financial wizards became public, it caused many Thais to wonder how an elderly Buddhist monk could have forced powerful government leaders to explain the machinations of their fiscal policy." Sarah Rooney, "Monk vs. the Machine," *S.F. Chron.*, 26 Sept. 2000, at A11.

Careful users of language preserve the age-old fissure between the words.

LANGUAGE-CHANGE INDEX
riff misused for *rift*: Stage 1

*rigamarole. See **rigmarole.**

right, adj.; **righteous; rightful.** These terms are sometimes confused. *Right* = correct, proper, just. *Righteous* = morally upright, virtuous, or law-abiding. This term has strong religious connotations, often of unctuousness. *Rightful* = (1) (of an action) equitable, fair <a rightful solution>; (2) (of a person) legitimately entitled to a position <the rightful heir>; or (3) (of an office or piece of property) that one is entitled to <his rightful inheritance>. Cf. **purposely.**

right, n. For some common errors, see **last rites** & **rite of passage.**

right, vb.; ***righten.** The latter is a NEEDLESS VARIANT—e.g.: "Walter Orange plays the comic constable, Dogberry, who *rightens* [read *rights*] the situation between Claudio and Hero." T.E. Foreman, "'Much Ado,' Much Updated," *Press-Enterprise* (Riverside, Cal.), 2 Aug. 1996, at A19.

Current ratio (*righted* vs. **rightened*): 490:1

righteous; rightful. See **right,** adj.

right-of-way is hyphenated whether used as a PHRASAL ADJECTIVE <a right-of-way easement> or as a noun <yield the right-of-way>. The plural has always been *rights-of-way,* not **right-of-ways.* See PLURALS (G).

Current ratio (pl. form): 8:1

right to die. As a noun phrase, *right to die* is three words <advocates of the right to die>. But as a PHRASAL ADJECTIVE, it should be hyphenated: "Both sides of a *right-to-die* case received a skeptical hearing today at the Supreme Court." Linda Greenhouse, "*Right-to-Die* Case Gets First Hearing in Supreme Court," *N.Y. Times,* 7 Dec. 1989, at 1.

right-to-lifer (= an opponent of abortion rights) is journalists' JARGON—and is often used as a pejorative. E.g.: "The cast of characters includes . . . Attorney General Dick Thornburgh, a strident *right-to-lifer* who took the questionable step of asking the court to reconsider *Roe.*" "The Battle over Abortion," *Newsweek,* 1 May 1989, at 28.

right to privacy is three words as a noun phrase, but hyphenated as a PHRASAL ADJECTIVE <right-to-privacy case>.

rigmarole (= a senselessly cumbersome, hassle-filled procedure) is the standard spelling. **Rigamarole* is a variant spelling that is less than half as common in print. Despite its spelling, *rigmarole* is often pronounced /**rig**-ə-mə-rohl/, though the dictionaries record /**rig**-mə-rohl/.

Current ratio: 14:1

rigor (= [1] exacting thoroughness, or [2] severe austerity) has been predominantly so spelled in AmE print sources since the late 1840s. In BrE, the spelling *rigour* has always been standard. See -OR; -OUR.

rill; *rille. *Rill* = (1) a brook or stream; or (2) a long, narrow trench or valley on the moon's surface. **Rille* is a variant spelling for sense 2, but there is little reason to promote it.

rime. See **rhyme.**

rime royale. See **rhyme royal.**

ring > rang > rung; ringed. Senses that relate to encircling take the regular *-ed* inflections in the past tense and past participle <the enemy ringed the encampment>. Senses that relate to sound—the more usual senses—take the irregular inflections *ring > rang > rung* <the telephone rang>.

The past-participial *rung* is often misused as a simple-past verb—e.g.:

- "Another time, he *rung* [read *rang*] a shot off the goalpost." Gretchen Flemming, "Cyclones Power Past Griffins, 5–3," *Grand Rapids Press,* 28 Feb. 1998, at C1.
- "She *rung* [read *rang*] up the purchase, put it in a bag, and handed me the change." Neil Steinberg, "Steering Shy of Facts of Life," *Chicago Sun-Times,* 30 June 1998, at 36.
- "Rich Pilon is not known for his soft hands but his hard fists; he *rung* [read *rang*] up 291 penalty minutes last season." Keith Gave, "Eastern Conference Preview," *Dallas Morning News,* 4 Oct. 1998, at Q14.

See IRREGULAR VERBS.

The opposite error—*rang* as a past-participial form in place of *rung*—is much more common in BrE than in AmE:

- "His father, Mr Charles Smith, told Birmingham Coroner's Court he had *rang* [read *rung*] his son's mobile telephone the previous evening." "Suicide Son's Final Message by Mobile Phone," *Birmingham Post,* 19 Mar. 1998, at 4.
- "He said the phone had *rang* [read *rung*] all day with messages from well-wishers—'even complete strangers.'" Michael Howie, "Home at Last to Hug from Mum and Dad," *Aberdeen Press & J.,* 22 July 2000, at 1.
- "She got a message that Alice had *rang* [read *rung*]." Peter Allen, "I Fled the Flames Crying I'm Alive," *Daily Mail,* 27 July 2000, at 10.

But it does appear in American sources—e.g.: "Abdin (25–2–3) got up at [the count of] eight, after the bell had *rang* [read *rung*]." "It's a Giant Party in Volunteer Land," *Buffalo News,* 31 Jan. 1999, at D14. See also **wring.**

LANGUAGE-CHANGE INDEX
1. *rung* misused for simple-past *rang:* Stage 1
Current ratio (*he rang* vs. **he rung*): 26:1
2. *rang* misused for past-participial *rung:* Stage 1
Current ratio (*had rung* vs. **had rang*): 47:1

rinsable. So spelled in AmE and BrE alike—not **rinsible.* See -ABLE (A).

R.I.P. These initials stand for the Latin phrase *requiescat in pace* (= may he [or she] rest in peace), not the English *rest in peace.*

ripe. See **rife.**

riposte; *ripost. *Riposte* /ri-**pohst**/ (= a sharp comeback or swift retort) is the standard spelling in AmE and BrE alike. **Ripost* is a variant.

Current ratio: 318:1

***risable.** See **risible.**

rise. See **arise** & **raise** (B).

risible (= laughable, ludicrous) is so spelled—not **risable.* (See -ABLE (A).) It rhymes with *visible.* See **ridiculous.**

LANGUAGE-CHANGE INDEX (For the full key, see front matter pp. xxxi, l–li.)
Stage 1: Rejected. **Stage 2:** Widely shunned. **Stage 3:** Widespread but . . . **Stage 4:** Ubiquitous but . . . **Stage 5:** Fully accepted.
Invariably inferior forms marked by asterisk (*). • Ratios represent frequency of prevalent forms vs. variants in current books.

risqué (= verging on indecency) is occasionally—in the speech of the marginally literate—misused for *risky*. The feminine *risquée* doesn't properly exist in English.

ritardando (= a musical direction to slacken the tempo gradually) predominantly makes the plural *ritardandos* in AmE, but the Italianate *ritardandi* in BrE. Oddly enough, the synonymous *rallentando* predominantly makes *rallentandos* in AmE and BrE alike—not **rallentandi*. See PLURALS (B).

rite of passage; *rite de passage.* Because the English expression is synonymous with (and more recognizable than) the French one, the latter should be considered an unnecessary GALLICISM.

Occasionally, *rite* is misspelled *right* in this phrase—e.g.:

- "Many consider drinking a normal *right-of-passage* [read *rite of passage*] for college students and complain about police barging into bars, forcing them to present proof of age." James Thorne, "Chapel Hill Fights Heavy Drinking Image," *News & Record* (Greensboro), 24 Aug. 1995, at B1.
- "The circumcision was identified as a *right* [read *rite*] of passage from girlhood to womanhood, representing cleanliness, chastity and purity." Letter of Barbara Johnson, "Circumcision," *Indianapolis Star*, 14 Oct. 1995, at A11.
- "He plans to do an email blast to fraternal and masonic organizations, *rights-of-passage* [read *rites-of-passage*] groups and anyone connected to mentorship." Barry Carter, "Men, It Is Time to Step Up Again," *Star-Ledger* (Newark), 4 Sept. 2015, N.J. §, at 15.

Cf. **last rites.**

LANGUAGE-CHANGE INDEX
right misused for *rite*: Stage 2
Current ratio (*rite of passage* vs. **right of passage*): 9:1

rivaled; rivalled. See **unrivaled.**

*road to hoe. See **row to hoe.**

robbery. See **burglary.**

rock 'n' roll; rock-'n'-roll; rock'n'roll; rock and roll; rock-and-roll; rock & roll. Each of these is listed in at least one major American dictionary. *Rock 'n' roll* is probably the most common; appropriately, it has a relaxed and colloquial look. *Rock and roll* and *rock-and-roll* are somewhat more formal than the others and therefore not very fitting with the music itself. The others are variant spellings—except that *rock-'n'-roll*, with the hyphens, is certainly preferable when the term is used as a PHRASAL ADJECTIVE <the rock-'n'-roll culture of the 1960s>.

Fortunately, the editorial puzzle presented by these variations has largely been solved: almost everyone today refers to *rock music* or simply *rock*. Increasingly, *rock 'n' roll* carries overtones of early rock—the 1950s-style music such as "Rock Around the Clock," by Bill Haley and the Comets.

rococo /rə-**koh**-koh/ is so spelled. See SPELLING (A).

rodomontade; *rhodomontade. This word, meaning "boastful talk" and pronounced /rod-ə-mən-**tayd**/, has been predominantly spelled *rodomontade* since about 1915. The *rh-* spelling was characteristic of the period from 1790 to 1915.

Current ratio: 1.2:1

roister; *royster. *Roister* (= [1] to brag and swagger; or [2] to engage in bumptious merrymaking) has been the standard spelling since the 1930s. **Royster* is a variant.

role; roll. These are sometimes confused. *Roll* has many senses, including breadstuff, but the only sense that causes problems is "a list or register; roster" <the teacher took roll>. *Role*, by contrast, means "a function or part, as in a drama." E.g.:

- "She has no children with names such as Johnny, John, Peter, Paul, Mary or Martha. Instead, a sampling of names on one of her *roles* [read *rolls*] includes Tiana, Victoria, Carmen, Melissa, Christopher, Phillip, Tyler and Allegra." Marlene Feduris, "What's in a Name?" *Amarillo Globe-News*, 24 May 1992, at D1.
- " 'What *roll* [read *role*] will the faculty have in deciding on the curriculum?' Durbin asked." "New Division," *Daily Texan*, 7 Oct. 1992, at 8, 9.
- " 'Everyone played their *roll* [read *role*].' " Mark Rosner, "UConn Nails Horns 96–86," *Austin Am.-Statesman*, 16 Dec. 1993, at E1, E5 (quoting B.J. Tyler, a college basketball player, who should not be charged with this error).

LANGUAGE-CHANGE INDEX
1. *role* misused for *roll* (= list): Stage 1
2. *roll* misused for *role*: Stage 1

Roma. See **gypsy.**

Romania; *Rumania; *Roumania; *România. *Romania* (/roh-**may**-nee-ə/) became the predominant spelling about 1975. **Rumania* was once the standard spelling; it was touted in linguistic literature as the preferred form, since it reflects the correct pronunciation (see Merritt Ruhlen, " 'When in Rome, Do as the Romanians Do,' " *Am. Speech* 154, 155 [1970]). But it is now a mere variant. The other variant, **Roumania*, is a GALLICISM. The circumflex over the medial *-a-* is unnecessary in English-language contexts.

The choice in spelling has on occasion been an emotionally fraught issue: "A university press once made a book of papers by seven professors, each dealing with his own specialty in world affairs. One author insisted his paper would be unavailable unless the spelling 'Rumania' appeared in it, and another announced that his article would be withdrawn if he could not spell it 'Roumania,' retaining the *o* as a heritage from 'Rome.' " Edward N. Teall, *Putting Words to Work* 123 (1940). Presumably neither one of those authors would be happy with today's preference for *Romania*.

Current ratio (in order of headwords): 92:7:5:1

Romany (= [1] a Gypsy; or [2] the language of Gypsies) is the standard spelling—preferably not **Rommany.* See **gypsy.**

Current ratio: 12:1

roof, n. Pl. *roofs*, not **rooves*, for as long as the word has been recorded. But the mistaken plural occurs with some frequency—e.g.:

- "But the view from the classroom (which his son uses to run a cramming school) is of *rooves* [read *roofs*] and television aerials, so the farmers' cause seems already lost." "The Last of the Left," *Economist*, 4 Feb. 1995, at 32.
- "The birds scoured yards for food, roosted in eaves and pooped liberally on tile *rooves* [read *roofs*]." Susan M. Loux, "Dairy Pigeons Spot New Targets," *Press-Enterprise* (Riverside, Cal.), 20 July 1996, at B1.
- "Now Violeta shows off snapshots of Puerto Rico that evoke dusty palm trees and hot clay *rooves* [read *roofs*] and heavy blue skies." Diana Michele Yap, "'Met Violeta, Liked Her a Lot,'" *Providence J.-Bull.*, 10 Oct. 1996, at H8.

Cf. **hoof**. See PLURALS (C).

LANGUAGE-CHANGE INDEX
*rooves for *roofs*: Stage 1
Current ratio (*roofs* vs. **rooves*): 535:1

roofed, not **rooved*, has been the standard form since the 17th century—e.g.:

- "These new state farms and cooperatives—clusters of *tin-rooved* [read *tin-roofed*] huts nestling in valleys—have been attacked repeatedly by the rebels." Peter Ford, "What War Means for Nicaragua's Peasants," *Christian Science Monitor*, 10 July 1987, Int'l §, at 1.
- "Salt is in a deep valley, with *flat-rooved* [read *flat-roofed*] houses built into the hillsides, where protesters took up position, leaving the police at a severe disadvantage." Alan Cowell, "Unrest in Jordan Gains Islamic Tone," *N.Y. Times*, 22 Apr. 1989, § 1, at 1.
- "Alberobello, Italy is home to whitewashed, *conical-rooved* [read *conical-roofed*] houses known as trulli." Maggie Galehouse, "Top 10 Weird, Wonderful Places to See Before You Die," *Houston Chron.*, 15 Jan. 2012, Good Life §, at 1.

Cf. **hoofed**.

LANGUAGE-CHANGE INDEX
*rooved for *roofed*: Stage 1
Current ratio (*roofed* vs. **rooved*): 2,335:1

roomful. Pl. *roomfuls*—not **roomsful*. See PLURALS (G).

root around (= to poke about) is preferably so spelled—not **rout around* or **route around*. But the illogical slips are fairly common—e.g.:

- "Maybe he should *rout* [read *root*] around in the attic for that pirate flag." "The Fall of an American Icon," *Business-Week*, 5 Feb. 1996, at 34.
- "Some of these [hotels] are available via Planet Hawaii, though users might have to *route* [read *root*] around for them." Donna Marino, "Surfing the 'Net," *Tour & Travel News*, 8 May 1995, at 44.

To *route around* is to establish a route that bypasses something—e.g.: "Meanwhile, doctors began perfecting bypass surgery, in which a blood vessel is grafted into position to *route around* a clogged artery." Eric B.

Schoch, "Helping Heal Heartache," *Indianapolis Star*, 2 Feb. 1997, at C1.

LANGUAGE-CHANGE INDEX
root around misspelled **rout around* or
*route around: Stage 1
Current ratio (*root around* vs. **rout around*): 40:1

*rooves. See **roof**.

ropeable. So spelled in both AmE and BrE—not the easily misread **ropable*. See MUTE E.

Current ratio: 2:1

rosary; rosery. The first is a string of prayer beads or a set of prayers. The second is a garden or section of a garden devoted to roses. The terms are sometimes confounded—e.g.:

- "Like Albert, the two women stayed some time in front of the casket. Mrs. Minelli said a decade of the *rosery* [read *rosary*]." Elaine Bergstrom, *The Door Through Washington Square* 204 (1998).
- "Katrina remembered the *Echo* in the suitcase and before you could say *rosery beads* [read *rosary beads*], she had it in front of her face saying 'take my picture.'" Jessica Flynn, "Neil's Dead-Good Way to Read His Newspaper," *South Wales Echo*, 29 June 2012, News §, at 27.
- "Now roses are lovely, of course, but the problem with formal *rosaries* [read *roseries*] is that they tend to look horrible outside the summer—whatever the rose growers tell us in their propaganda." Tim Richardson, "Japanese Gardens: Mysterious or Kitsch?" *Daily Telegraph*, 3 Feb. 2014, Lifestyle §.

rostrum. Pl. *rostra* or *rostrums*, the former having been long predominant in World English. See PLURALS (B). Cf. **nostrum**.

Current ratio: 5:1

rotary; rotatory. *Rotary* is the everyday adjective describing something that spins on an axis, especially a mechanical object <rotary razor>. In technical and scientific writing, *rotatory* describes something subject to or causing a spinning force <optical rotatory dispersion>.

rouble. See **ruble**.

rouche. See **ruche**.

rough-hewn. See **hew** (B).

*Roumania. See **Romania**.

round. See **around**.

rouse. See **arouse**.

route is pronounced either /root/ or /rowt/. For quite some time, pronunciation specialists have heavily favored /root/. But even those who say that they're planning a cross-country route (/rowt/) would surely also say Route (/root/) 66. Cf. **en route**. For a misusage of *route*, see **root around**.

LANGUAGE-CHANGE INDEX (For the full key, see front matter pp. xxxi, l–li.)
Stage 1: Rejected. **Stage 2:** Widely shunned. **Stage 3:** Widespread but . . . **Stage 4:** Ubiquitous but . . . **Stage 5:** Fully accepted.
Invariably inferior forms marked by asterisk (*). • Ratios represent frequency of prevalent forms vs. variants in current books.

routinely. See **regularly.**

routinize (= to develop into a regular schedule) is pronounced either /**roo**-tə-nɪz/ or /roo-**tee**-nɪz/. Although this word (dating from the early 1920s) sometimes smacks of gobbledygook, it's also difficult to replace—e.g.:

- "The raunchiness that some, at least, admired in the earlier book has been replaced by *routinized* descriptions of the hydraulics of moderately unroutine sex." K. Anthony Appiah, "Identity Crisis," *N.Y. Times*, 17 Sept. 1995, § 7, at 42.
- "Moreover, teachers can be trained to teach a particular subject, texts can be targeted, and many lessons can be standardized and techniques *routinized*." Albert Shanker, "Education Reform: What's Not Being Said," *Daedalus*, 22 Sept. 1995, at 47.
- "At present there are concerted moves on the part of the government and industry to develop a set of regulations that will *routinize* the use of drones in Canada." Shayna Gersher, "Drone Surveillance in Canada Needs Regulations," *Ottawa Citizen*, 11 Apr. 2014, at A10.

See -IZE.

row to hoe is an agricultural or gardening METAPHOR meaning "a challenging and perhaps arduous project" <it's going to be a tough row to hoe>. Sometimes it's ludicrously written as the MONDEGREEN **road to hoe*, especially in sportswriting—e.g.:

- "Though victories over Newcastle and Aston Villa showed Leicester how they can preserve their status, it will be a hard *road* [read *row*] to hoe this winter." Michael Henderson, "Leicester Dig in for Long, Hard Winter," *Times* (London), 25 Nov. 1996, at 33.
- "Even if David Robinson comes back, it will be a hard *road* [read *row*] to hoe to make it into the playoffs." "NFL Has Finally Gone Too Far with Super Bowl Hype," *San Antonio Express-News*, 2 Feb. 1997, at C5.
- "Red-hot North Carolina has a tough *road* [read *row*] to hoe." "UNC Faces Tough Road," *Star-Ledger* (Newark), 19 Feb. 1997, at 54. (The error is elliptically repeated in the title.)

See **lapsus linguae.**

LANGUAGE-CHANGE INDEX
*road to hoe for *row to hoe*: Stage 1
Current ratio (*row to hoe* vs. **road to hoe*): 16:1

royal. See **kingly.**

*royster. See **roister.**

RSVP; rsvp; R.S.V.P.; r.s.v.p. The first is the usual abbreviation of the French phrase *répondez s'il vous plaît* (= respond if you please)—the phrase for requesting responses to invitations. Because the phrase contains the polite idea of "please," it's a REDUNDANCY to say **please RSVP*.

Increasingly, AmE is making the acronym a verb meaning either "to respond" <have you RSVP'd yet?> or "to make reservations" <admission is free, but be sure to RSVP at least two days beforehand>. That's probably why **please RSVP* is becoming so common—e.g.:

- "If you have received an invitation, *please RSVP* [read *please respond*] . . . so the newspaper will be prepared to

honor your organization." "Political Town Hall Meeting to Be Held at Afro-Awakenings," *Ft. Worth Star-Telegram*, 19 Sept. 1996, at 2.
- "*Please RSVP* [read *Please respond*] to the concierge at (317) 636-2121, ext. 1690." "What's in Store," *Indianapolis Star*, 11 Sept. 1997, at 9.

See ABBREVIATIONS (B).

LANGUAGE-CHANGE INDEX
*please RSVP for *RSVP*: Stage 3

ruble /**roo**-bəl/ (the Russian monetary unit) has been predominantly so spelled in AmE since the 1930s. Although that spelling has also made inroads into BrE, *rouble* is standard there.

ruche /roosh/ (= pleated or fluted cloth, esp. for garment trimmings) has been the standard spelling since the 18th century. **Rouche* is a variant.

Current ratio: 17:1

ruin, n.; **ruination.** *Ruin* is the ordinary term. *Ruination*, which is quite common, has traditionally been humorous and colloquial, but today often seems to convey a special earnestness or acknowledged hyperbole—e.g.:

- "The increasing involvement of player agents is leading to the *ruination* of professional sports, claims columnist Tom Powers of the St. Paul Pioneer Press." Shav Glick, "Morning Briefing," *L.A. Times*, 14 Oct. 1995, at C2.
- "They're liable to slip in a bit about their faith, and you can't have that nonsense because, Lord knows, it could be the *ruination* of the country." John Downing, "Maybe the End Is at Hand," *Toronto Sun*, 29 June 1997, at C3.
- "For the opposition parties, bad economic news on Prime Minister Stephen Harper's watch is manna from heaven. They have, in truth, been starved for *ruination* until now, notwithstanding their own best efforts." "About That 'Recession,'" *Nat'l Post* (Can.), 2 Sept. 2015, at A8.

*Rumania. See **Romania.**

rumba (the Cuban dance) has been the standard spelling since the word was first used in the early 20th century. **Rhumba* is a variant.

Current ratio: 7:1

rumbustious (= boisterous, rambunctious)—a term that sprang to life as an 18th-century Briticism—is sometimes misspelled **rumbustuous*. E.g.: "Harle makes a marvellous case for the lyrically reflective, eventually *rumbustuous* [read *rumbustious*] and jazzy three-movement saxophone concerto, launched at the 1984 Proms." Paul Driver, "Classical," *Sunday Times* (London), 15 June 1997, Culture §, at 26. Cf. **rambunctious.**

LANGUAGE-CHANGE INDEX
rumbustious misspelled **rumbustuous*: Stage 1
Current ratio: 30:1

RUN-ON SENTENCES do not stop where they should. The problem usually occurs when the writer is uncertain how to handle PUNCTUATION or how to handle such adverbs as *however* and *otherwise*, which are often mistakenly treated as conjunctions.

Some grammarians distinguish between a "run-on sentence" (or "fused sentence") and a "comma splice" (or "run-together sentence"). In a run-on sentence, two independent clauses—not joined by a conjunction such as *and*, *but*, *for*, *or*, or *nor*—are incorrectly written with no punctuation between them. Hence a run-on sentence might read: "I need to go to the store the baby needs some diapers." Correctly, it might read: "I need to go to the store; the baby needs some diapers."

With a comma splice, two independent clauses have merely a comma between them, again without a conjunction—e.g.: "I need to go to the store, the baby needs some diapers."

The presence or absence of a comma—and therefore the distinction between a run-on sentence and a comma splice—isn't usually noteworthy. So most writers class the two problems together as run-on sentences.

But the distinction can be helpful in differentiating between the wholly unacceptable (true run-on sentences) and the usually-but-not-always unacceptable (comma splices). That is, most usage authorities accept comma splices when (1) the clauses are short and closely related, (2) there is no danger of a MIS-CUE, and (3) the context is informal. Thus: "Jane likes him, I don't." But even when all three criteria are met, some readers are likely to object. And in any event, a dash or a semicolon seems preferable to a comma in a sentence like that one.

Unjustified comma splices are uncommon in non-fiction writing, but they do sometimes occur—e.g.: "The remnants of Hurricane Opal will move north through the Tennessee Valley as a tropical storm this morning. Winds near the center of the storm will diminish rapidly, *however*, wind gusts over 60 miles an hour will persist around the storm center." "Weather Report," *N.Y. Times*, 5 Oct. 1995, at B8. In that sentence, the mispunctuation makes for an ambiguous modifier because *however* could go with either the clause before or the clause after. The context suggests that the reading should be with a semicolon after *rapidly*. The best edit would be to replace *however* with *but*—and to delete the comma after it. See HOWEVER (D).

*run the danger. See **danger** (B).

run the gantlet. See **gantlet.**

rustically (= in a rural, countrified manner) is the adverb corresponding to *rustic*, adj. But some misspell it **rusticly*, maybe on the analogy of *publicly*—e.g.: "If you haven't already guessed, Newport is not for the '*rusticly* [read *rustically*] challenged.' " Adam Mertz, "State of Seclusion," *Milwaukee J. Sentinel*, 14 Oct. 1994, at B5. See -IC.

LANGUAGE-CHANGE INDEX
rustically misspelled **rusticly*: Stage 1

S

's. See POSSESSIVES.

saccharin, n.; **saccharine,** adj. In AmE and BrE alike, *saccharin* is the noun <saccharin is a well-known sweetener>, *saccharine* the adjective <saccharine television shows>.

sacerdotal (= priestly) is best pronounced /sas-ər-**doh**-təl/; /sak-/ is a variant pronunciation.

sacrilegious (= violative of something sacred; profane) is so spelled. **Sacreligious*, under the influence of *religious*, has been a fairly common misspelling since about 1800—e.g.:

- "A second demand was that the film 'Mohammad, Messenger of God' be removed from this country on grounds that the Hanafis regarded it as *sacreligious* [read *sacrilegious*], the jury was told." J.Y. Smith, "Hanafi Lawyer Argument Highly Praised by Judge," *Wash. Post*, 20 July 1977, at C1.
- "There's something almost *sacreligious* [read *sacrilegious*] about Nick Cave and the Bad Seeds playing outdoors in the midday sun." Ed Masley, "Nick Cave Steps Out of the Dark," *Pitt. Post-Gaz.*, 29 July 1994, Arts & Entertainment §, at 19.

- "There will surely be some who will find the pleasantly profane deity's observations seriously *sacreligious* [read *sacrilegious*]." Michael D. Reid, "Second Coming Will Have You Rolling in the Aisles," *Victoria Times Colonist* (Can.), 30 Aug. 2015, at C9.

Still another persistent misspelling is **sacriligious*—e.g.: " 'O Holy Night,' with ukulele accompaniment, borders on the *sacriligious* [read *sacrilegious*]." Jay Orr, "Merry Christmas BABY!" *Nashville Banner*, 5 Dec. 1996, at C16.

The correct spelling can be remembered easily with either of two mnemonic devices: (1) recall the noun *sacrilege* (similar to *privilege*); (2) reverse the first two vowels of *religious*.

The preferred pronunciation today is /sak-ri-**lij**-əs/, which has displaced /sak-ri-**lee**-jəs/. See SPELL-ING (A).

LANGUAGE-CHANGE INDEX
sacrilegious misspelled **sacreligious*: Stage 1
Current ratio: 119:1

sacrosanct, literally "most sacred," is now often ironic. Sometimes the irony appears unintentional—e.g.:

LANGUAGE-CHANGE INDEX (For the full key, see front matter pp. xxxi, l–li.)
Stage 1: Rejected. **Stage 2:** Widely shunned. **Stage 3:** Widespread but . . . **Stage 4:** Ubiquitous but . . . **Stage 5:** Fully accepted.
Invariably inferior forms marked by asterisk (*). • Ratios represent frequency of prevalent forms vs. variants in current books.

"Ray Kroc, who founded the McDonald's empire, wrote that the french fry was '*sacrosanct*,' its preparation 'a ritual to be followed religiously.'" Danny Penman, "Judgment Day for McDonald's," *Independent*, 19 June 1997, at 20.

sadly. See SENTENCE ADVERBS.

safe-deposit box. This is the original and predominant term, not **safety-deposit box*—e.g.: "He'll just go quietly, back to his day job at Home Depot, doing business with customers who don't know about that silver medal in his *safety-deposit box* [read *safe-deposit box*]." Mike Downey, "Bobsled Pioneer Prepares for a Slower Lifestyle," *Chicago Trib.*, 13 Feb. 2003, Sports §, at 1. The extra syllable in *safety* probably originated as an auditory error: people heard the phrase and associated the *de-* prefix on *deposit* with the *-ty* suffix on *safety*, and then duplicated the sound. In modern print sources, *safe-deposit box* is six times as common as **safety-deposit box*.

The PHRASAL ADJECTIVE *safe-deposit* always requires a hyphen in this term.

LANGUAGE-CHANGE INDEX
*safety-deposit box for *safe-deposit box*: Stage 2
Current ratio (*safe-deposit box* vs.
*safety-deposit box): 6:1

said, adj. Legal writers formerly used this word as a supposedly more precise equivalent of *the*, *this*, *that*, *these*, or *those*. But as lawyers have generally learned that it isn't any more precise—and, indeed, that it can lead to various technical problems—the term has become much less frequent. Still, some writers use it for a mock-legal flavor—e.g.:

- "If you call an invention, an idea, or a suggestion 'practicable,' you are voicing the opinion that *said* [read *the*] invention, idea, or suggestion can be translated from theory into actuality." Norman Lewis, *Better English* 127 (rev. ed. 1961).
- "The complement of a copulative infinitive is in the objective case, agreeing with the subject of *said* [read *the*] infinitive, if the infinitive has a subject." *Ibid.* at 347.
- "A telephone Christmas is a much less stressful Christmas, especially if *said* [read *the*] phone is left off the hook." Robert Kirby, "Christmas by Telephone Has a Nice Ring," *Salt Lake Trib.*, 2 Dec. 1997, at B1.

As the edits suggest, you're generally well advised to cut the LEGALESE unless you're being very much tongue-in-cheek—e.g.: "Any regular Joe who isn't the boy toy of a fabulously rich ($800 million) pickle heiress could have gotten exactly the same consideration from City Hall if *said* Joe Sixpack had asked to have a fire hydrant outside his $2 million Beacon Hill mansion moved." "Pols & Politics," *Boston Herald*, 18 May 1997, at 31. Cf. **same (A)** & **such (A)**.

sailor; sailer. A *sailor* is someone who sails—always in reference to a person. A *sailer* is a vessel or vehicle that sails or that moves by the use of a sail—e.g.: "The second part of the project is to launch an operational solar *sailer* with eight sails to be tested in an 850-km. (528-mi.) circular orbit, also using a Volna rocket." Michael

A. Dornheim, "Solar Sail Test to Launch This Week," *Aviation Week & Space Tech.*, 16 July 2001, at 42.

It isn't unusual to see *sailer* misused for *sailor*—e.g.: "The current exercises involve about 15,000 *sailers* [read *sailors*] and Marines, and include cruisers and destroyers, with nonexplosive bombs dropped from the air, according to the Associated Press." Mark Skertic & Lynn Sweet, "Ordeal Awaited Gutierrez After Vieques Arrest," *Chicago Sun-Times*, 30 Apr. 2001, at 3.

LANGUAGE-CHANGE INDEX
sailor misspelled *sailer*: Stage 1

Saint Nicholas. See **Santa Claus**.

sake. See POSSESSIVES (N).

salaam. So spelled. See SPELLING (A).

salable; saleable; *sellable. The standard spellings are *salable* in AmE and *saleable* in BrE. (See MUTE E.) *Sellable*, arguably a more logical form, was formerly used by some writers but never gained widespread currency. Cf. **unsalable**.

sale. Something *for sale* is simply being offered for a specified price. Something *on sale* is being offered at a discounted price. See **hard sell**.

saleable. See **salable**.

salesperson; salesman. To avoid SEXISM, many prefer the former. *Salesperson* seems to be one of the few words in which *-person* isn't particularly grating. Even so, as a matter of word frequency, *salesman* today holds a slight edge in AmE and a bigger one in BrE.

salesroom; saleroom. The former is standard in AmE, the latter in BrE. That split has remained fixed since the mid-19th century.

salience; *saliency. The former is standard in AmE and BrE alike. The latter is a NEEDLESS VARIANT.
Current ratio: 6:1

saline. Although the better pronunciation was once thought to be /**say**-lin/, both that pronunciation and /**say**-leen/ are now standard.

salinization. See **desalination**.

salmon is pronounced /**sam**-ən/, not /**sal**-mən/. But *salmonella* is pronounced with the *-l-*: /sal-mə-**nel**-ə/.

salutary; *salutiferous; salubrious. *Salutary* = beneficial; wholesome. **Salutory* is a common misspelling, especially in BrE—e.g.:

- "Fans of the gone-but-not-forgotten Butterflies should rush to see Wendy Craig in this *salutory* [read *salutary*] tale about how not to treat your relatives." "Pick of the Day: Sleeping Beauty," *Independent*, 19 Dec. 1995, at 10.
- "The *Mirror's* coverage of the subsequent inquiry provides a *salutory* [read *salutary*] reminder of how much has changed in popular journalism." Niall Dickson, "Child Protection: Press and the Pendulum," *Guardian*, 23 Oct. 1996, at 2.

- "Sanctions are as old as time. So are the *salutory* [read *salutary*] lessons." Ambrose Evans-Pritchard, "US Final Showdown with Russia Is More Dangerous Than It Looks," *Daily Telegraph*, 17 Apr. 2014, Bus. §, at 2.

*Salutiferous is a NEEDLESS VARIANT of *salutary*.

Salubrious, a near-synonym of *salutary*, means "healthful; promoting health or well-being." E.g.:

- "While we wish Hunt a long and healthy life, even the *salubrious* atmosphere of Holly Pond isn't going to keep him around that long." "Hunt's Denial: Fourth Appeal Unsuccessful," *Montgomery Advertiser*, 3 Sept. 1996, at A6.
- "And stepping into the spa is still a *salubrious* experience, with its soft new age music and ylang-ylang and citrus-scented air." Elizabeth Evans, "A Better Fit for Fit Eaters," *Orange County Register*, 29 Nov. 1996, at F33.

LANGUAGE-CHANGE INDEX
*salutory for *salutary*: Stage 1
Current ratio (*salutary* vs. *salutory): 109:1

salvable. See **savable.**

Salvadoran; *Salvadorean; *Salvadorian. For a citizen of El Salvador, the first is standard in AmE and BrE alike; the other two are variant forms. See DENIZEN LABELS.

salvage, n.; **selvage.** *Salvage* = (1) the rescue of property (as at sea or from fire); or (2) the discovery and extraction of something valuable or useful from rubbish. *Selvage* = the edging of cloth. See **selvage.**

salvageable. See **savable.**

salvo. Pl. *salvos*—preferably not *salvoes. See PLURALS (D).

Current ratio: 3:1

same. A. As a Pronoun. This usage, commonly exemplified in the phrase *acknowledging same*, is a primary symptom of LEGALESE and COMMERCIALESE. In 1926, when the usage was at its height, H.W. Fowler wrote trenchantly that it "is avoided by all who have any skill in writing" and that those who use it seem bent on giving the worst possible impression of themselves (*FMEU1* at 511). The words *it*, *them*, and the noun itself (e.g., *the envelope*) are words that come naturally to us all. *Same* or *the same* is an unnatural expression:

- "Even though such a witness discloses a new lead, it is better to make note of *same* [read *that fact*], but not to depart from the original objective until its possibilities have been exhausted." Asher L. Cornelius, *The Cross-Examination of Witnesses* 18–19 (1929).
- "Equity enabled them to hold any kind of property in trust for their own benefit, and to dispose of *the same* [read *it*] at pleasure." Stephen Pfeil, "Law," 17 *Encyclopedia Americana* 86, 90 (1953).

As these examples illustrate, the phrase is rendered sometimes with the definite article, sometimes without. Cf. **said** & **such** (B).

Unfortunately, the pretentious construction has spread to general writing—e.g.:

- "It appears that Hagler and Spinks—who are in the midst of multimillion dollar fights or arranging *same* [read *them*]—don't seem too put out about the forced abdications." Jack Fiske, "Governing Bodies Conduct Strip Search," *S.F. Chron.*, 28 Feb. 1987, at 45.
- "Two more yards and it would have been Young's first NFL touchdown. Noting *same* [read *that fact?*], he spat out a wad of smokeless tobacco before leaving the dressing room." John Crumpacker & Gwen Knapp, "Sacks Coming in Bunches for the Line with No Name," *S.F. Examiner*, 3 Dec. 1996, at B5.

In fact, when used as a pronoun, *same* is even less precise than *it* (transparently singular) or *they* (transparently plural). *Same* can be either and is therefore often unclear.

Interestingly, an ambiguous *same* once gave rise to a major constitutional question: whether John Tyler was in fact the tenth President of the United States. When President William Henry Harrison died on April 4, 1841, Article II of the Constitution read as follows:

> In case of the removal of the President from office, or of his death, resignation, or inability to discharge the powers and duties of the said office, the *same* shall devolve on the Vice-President. [U.S. Constitution, Art. II, § 1.]

There was some uncertainty whether *same* referred to *the powers and duties of the said office* or to *the said office* itself. (Note that an *it* or a *they* would have prevented the ambiguity.)

For some time, senators debated whether Tyler—after being inaugurated on April 9—had assumed the presidency or only the President's powers (and continued as Vice President). Although Congress passed a resolution referring to Tyler as "the President of the United States" (Cong. Globe, 27th Cong., 1st Sess. 4, 5), one scholar more than a century later asserted that "constitutional historians are in unanimous agreement that the framers intended the Vice-President to act as President but not to be President" (Clinton Rossiter, *The American Presidency* 209 [2d ed. 1960]). But the conundrum was quite complex: in a thoughtful essay on the point, David P. Currie concludes that "it is inconceivable either that Tyler became President or that he did not; I see no satisfactory way out of the box" ("His Accidency," 5 *Green Bag* [2d series] 151, 154 [2002]). Ultimately, it all hinged on the ambiguity of *same*.

In 1967, the 25th Amendment remedied the ambiguity by providing that if the President dies, resigns, or is removed, "the Vice President shall become President" (U.S. Constitution, Amend. 25, § 1). If the President is disabled, the Vice President assumes the office's powers and duties as "Acting President" as long as the disability continues (*ibid.* §§ 3, 4).

B. *Same . . . as are. *Are* often appears superfluously when writers state that two or more things are identical—e.g.:

LANGUAGE-CHANGE INDEX (For the full key, see front matter pp. xxxi, l–li.)
Stage 1: Rejected. **Stage 2:** Widely shunned. **Stage 3:** Widespread but . . . **Stage 4:** Ubiquitous but . . . **Stage 5:** Fully accepted.
Invariably inferior forms marked by asterisk (*). • Ratios represent frequency of prevalent forms vs. variants in current books.

- "Savage punishments are accepted with the *same* resigned acceptance *as are* [read *as*] the tragic accidents that occur with regularity in this fundamentally hostile land." Lisa Jardine, "Milton Agonistes," *L.A. Times*, 27 Apr. 1997, Book Rev. §, at 9.
- "Tucson officials say they are not in the *same* financial straits *as are* [read *as*] officials in Boston, where bankruptcy remains a possibility." Stephanie Innes, "Damage Done: Church Plagued by Loss of Trust," *Ariz. Daily Star*, 28 Dec. 2002, at A1.

See **as . . . as** (C).

If the verb seems desirable after the *as*—because the reader wouldn't automatically supply it—then it's best to avoid INVERSION. That is, instead of writing that **horses are required to undergo the same veterinary examination as are Hereford cattle*, write that *horses are required to undergo the same veterinary examination as Hereford cattle are*. E.g.: "They're targeted at the *same* high-risk groups *as are flu shots* [read *as flu shots are*]—those over 65 and anyone with a chronic health problem." "Pneumonia, Other Vaccinations Available," *Tampa Trib.*, 24 Oct. 1995, at 1.

C. **Same difference*. This phrase is an illogical AmE CASUALISM that is to be avoided not only in writing but in speech as well. "It's all the *same*," "It's the *same* thing," etc. are better. (See ILLOGIC.) But: *Six minus three yields the same difference as seven minus four.*

LANGUAGE-CHANGE INDEX
*same difference: Stage 2

D. **Same identical*. See **identical**.
E. **Repeat the same*. See **repeat the same*.
F. *Exact same*. See **exact same**.

Sammarinese. Citizens of the ancient country near Italy, San Marino, are so called. **San Marinese* is a NEEDLESS VARIANT. See DENIZEN LABELS.

Current ratio: 3:1

*sanatarium. See **sanatorium**.

sanative; *sanatory. See **sanitary**.

sanatorium; *sanitarium; *sanitorium; *sanatarium. The standard spelling is *sanatorium* (= an institution for the treatment of chronic diseases or care of long-term convalescents; a health resort). The others are NEEDLESS VARIANTS—e.g.:

- "Early Tuesday, Carter—the first former or current American president to visit Castro's Cuba—was to visit Cuba's AIDS *sanatarium* [read *sanatorium*] and a farm cooperative, both on the outskirts of Havana." "Carter Debates Castro on Rights, Democracy," *Deseret News* (Salt Lake City), 14 May 2002, at A4.
- "More than 47,000 people were hospitalized in the state tuberculosis *sanitarium* [read *sanatorium*]." Karen Bair, "Looking Back," *Herald* (Rock Hill, S.C.), 24 Feb. 2003, at D1.

Although the traditional plural is *sanatoria*, the anglicized *sanatoriums* has also been widespread since the late 19th century and today predominates in AmE. (See PLURALS (B).)

Although some writers have tried to distinguish **sanitorium* as a facility for physical healthcare from

sanatorium as one for mental healthcare, the distinction has never taken hold.

Current ratio (in order of headwords): 119:78:5:1

sanction = (1) to approve; or (2) to penalize. The word is generally understood as bearing sense 1. Hence lawyers, who use it primarily in sense 2, are likely to be misunderstood. See CONTRONYMS.

As a noun, *sanction* is burdened by the same ambiguity, meaning either (1) "approval" <governmental sanction to sell the goods>, or (2) "penalty" <the statute provides sanctions for violations of the act>. In phrases such as *give sanction to*, the word means "approval"—while *issue sanctions against* shows disapproval.

sanctionable, like *sanction*, carries a double sense of approval and disapproval. Most often, *sanctionable* means "deserving punishment"—e.g.: "'It had never been suggested that a physician's discussion of marijuana as a medical option was illegal or otherwise *sanctionable*,' the suit states." Mike McKee, "Doctors Fight Back on Prop 215," *Recorder* (S.F.), 15 Jan. 1997, at 1.

But the word sometimes means "approvable." Avoid it in this sense—e.g.: "In Massachusetts, Gov. William Weld has weighed in with a proposal that medical use [of marijuana] be *sanctionable* [read *approvable*] by a panel of physicians." D.A. Mittell Jr., "Legalizing Pot Is Not Just a Question of Medicine," *Patriot Ledger* (Quincy, Mass.), 8 Feb. 1997, at 19.

sanguine; sanguinary; sanguineous; sanguinolent. All these words share the Latin root *sang-* "blood" (also found in the French loanword *sangfroid* "cold-bloodedness"). *Sanguine* (= happy and confident about the future; optimistic) is the most common of the four <sanguine disposition>. The relation to blood has to do with the ancient idea of bodily humors—blood being predominant in a sanguine temperament. *Sanguinary* (= [1] involving bloodshed and killing <sanguinary plays like *Titus Andronicus*>, or [2] bloodthirsty, murderous <sanguinary killers>) invokes the idea of blood in an entirely different way. *Sanguineous* (= [1] blood red <sanguineous paint>, or [2] of, relating to, or involving blood <sanguineous relations>) is the most connotatively neutral—neither positive nor negative—except when functioning as a NEEDLESS VARIANT of *sanguinary* in sense 1. *Sanguinolent* (= tinged with blood) is the most bookish of them all <sanguinolent sputum>. Cf. **consanguineous.**

In the sense "optimistic, confident," *sanguine* is sometimes confounded with *sanguinary* (= [1] involving bloodshed; or [2] bloodthirsty)—e.g.: "Unfortunately, not all the members of the administration's environmental team appear to share the *sanguinary* [read *sanguine*] views of Hunt and Howes on the future of clean water." "Water Quality Advancing to the Rear," *Herald-Sun* (Durham, N.C.), 3 Jan. 1996, at A10.

LANGUAGE-CHANGE INDEX
sanguinary misused for *sanguine*: Stage 1

sanitary; sanative; *sanatory. *Sanitary* = of, relating to, or involving health or, more usu., cleanliness <sanitary surgical tools>. *Sanative* = health-producing; healthful <sanative treatments>. **Sanatory* is a NEEDLESS VARIANT.

*sanitorium; *sanitarium. See **sanatorium.**

sank. See **sink.**

San Marinan; *San Marinoite. For a citizen of San Marino, California, the first is standard; the second is a NEEDLESS VARIANT. For a citizen of the world's fifth-smallest country—San Marino—see **Sammarinese.** See also DENIZEN LABELS.

sans is an archaic literary GALLICISM to be avoided, unless a tongue-in-cheek or archaic effect is intended. *Without* is virtually always preferable to *sans* (as long as one is using the English language)—e.g.:

- "The same curatorial team, *sans* [read *without* or *minus*] Moore, organized a small show at Gracie Mansion's semi-private gallery." Bill Arning, "Days with Art," *Village Voice*, 10 Dec. 1996, at 95.
- "Sears said I should eat just one [bowl of Thai salad], *sans* [read *without*] noodles." Molly Martin, "Lunching in the Zone with Author Barry Sears," *Seattle Times*, 16 Mar. 1997, at 6.
- "It was here, originally *sans* [read *without*] dancers and dance moves, that the singer actually became the star." Mike Bell, "Janet Jackson Delivers Hits and Misses," *Calgary Herald*, 3 Sept. 2015, at C2.

As an English word, it's pronounced /sanz/, not /sahnz/. In fact, though, its most frequent use in English is as part of a larger French phrase <sans doute> <sans culottes>, in which it would normally take more of a French pronunciation.

sans serif; *sans-serif; *sanserif. The first is the standard spelling; the others are variant forms. It's pronounced /san **ser**-if/, not /sə-**reef**/. See DOCUMENT DESIGN (A).

Current ratio (in order of headwords): 14:8:1

Santa Claus; *Santa Klaus; Father Christmas; St. Nicholas; Saint Nick. The ubiquitous name *Santa Claus* dates from the late 18th century as a loanword from the Dutch *Sinterklaas*, or its dialectal variant *Sint Klaas* "Saint Nicholas." Originally an Americanism that has been traced to a New York publication of 1773, it did not come into widespread AmE use until the mid-19th century, especially after 1840. The variant spelling **Santa Klaus* made infrequent appearances in print from about 1850 to 1950.

In BrE, the traditional name is *Father Christmas*, which dates from the mid-17th century but didn't come into common use until about 1820. Interestingly, the Americanism *Santa Claus* has overtaken *Father Christmas* in BrE print sources since 1960, now predominating by a nearly 2-to-1 ratio.

By far the oldest term in English is *St. Nicholas* (*St.* usually abbreviated thus), referring to the 4th-century bishop of Myra in Asia Minor, who is known as the patron saint of Russia and Greece, as well as of sailors and children. After the Reformation in the 16th century, his popularity died out in Protestant Europe—except in Holland. Dutch colonists brought *Sinterklaas* to New York, then known as "New Amsterdam." In English-language print sources, *St. Nicholas* appeared more commonly than *Santa Claus* until the mid-20th century. The ratio today for *Santa Claus/St. Nicholas/Father Christmas* in World English print sources is 6:3:1. The shortened forms *St. Nick* and *Saint Nick* typically occur in jocular contexts.

sarcoma (= a malignant tumor within the body's connective tissues) predominantly makes the plural *sarcomas* (standard since the late 19th century). The etymologically correct Greek plural **sarcomata* was in sharp decline by 1910 and had been thoroughly eclipsed in frequency of use by 1940.

Current ratio: 87:1

sarcophagus. A. Plural. The standard plural is *sarcophagi* (/sahr-**kof**-ə-jɪ/). The anglicized form *sarcophaguses* rarely appears. See PLURALS (B).

Current ratio: 58:1

B. And *sarcophagous*. *Sarcophagus* is a noun meaning "stone coffin"; *sarcophagous* is an adjective meaning "meat-eating, carnivorous." Interestingly, the two words share their ETYMOLOGY: the Greek *sarkophagos* (= flesh-eating) referred to a kind of limestone thought to decompose the flesh of corpses placed in it.

Today, the DIFFERENTIATION is complete: *sarcophagus* is the noun and *sarcophagous* (or its variant, *sarcophagic*) the adjective. But like other homophonic pairs, some writers keep them straight while others don't—e.g.:

- "He can never please his parents, particularly his frosty mother, who has the glazed look of a gold Egyptian *sarcophagus*." Stephen Hunter, "Early Fassbinder Film Gives Hint of Director's Greatness," *Baltimore Sun*, 3 Nov. 1994, at D7.
- "The walls were painted to resemble old stone, with bits of dried moss creeping out from between them. The *sarcophagous* [read *sarcophagus*], left, is about 4 inches tall and is on the dining room table." Renee Garrison, "Pyramid Power," *Tampa Trib.*, 27 July 1996, Home & Garden §, at 1.

LANGUAGE-CHANGE INDEX
sarcophagous misused for the noun *sarcophagus*: Stage 1

sari; *saree. Meaning "a long piece of cloth wrapped around one's body like a dress (esp. common in India)," the word is most commonly spelled *sari* throughout World English, though **saree* is also sometimes found.

Current ratio: 8:1

LANGUAGE-CHANGE INDEX (For the full key, see front matter pp. xxxi, l–li.)
Stage 1: Rejected. **Stage 2:** Widely shunned. **Stage 3:** Widespread but . . . **Stage 4:** Ubiquitous but . . . **Stage 5:** Fully accepted.
Invariably inferior forms marked by asterisk (*). • Ratios represent frequency of prevalent forms vs. variants in current books.

SASE. See **self-addressed stamped envelope.**

SAT. This term originated in 1926 as an initialism for the *Scholastic Aptitude Test*, developed by Princeton psychology professor (and eugenicist) Carl C. Brigham from an IQ test he had created for the U.S. Army during World War I. It was first administered to high-school students that same year, and was later adopted by Harvard. In 1948, the Educational Testing Service (ETS) in Princeton, New Jersey, first administered the test for the College Board. From the beginning, the test was known primarily in its shortened form: SAT (with each letter individually sounded).

In 1993, faced with controversy that the test was culturally biased and did not accurately measure *aptitude*, ETS changed the name of the test to the *Scholastic Assessment Test*. Some wondered what a *test* could be other than an *assessment*, and four years later ETS took the position (which it has maintained since) that SAT is not an initialism (or, loosely, an acronym—see ABBREVIATIONS (A), (B)) at all: the name of the test is the SAT, they declared, and the letters don't stand for anything. (The College Board now calls it the SAT Reasoning Test on its website.) But in popular usage, the original full name and the redundant interregnal name are still used routinely—e.g.:

- "Though Massachusetts has a reputation as a high-performing state, its combined scores of the *Scholastic Assessment Tests* have generally mirrored national averages and have pulled ahead only in the last six years." Anand Vaishnav, "Massachusetts Students Post Modest Gains in SAT Scores," *Boston Globe*, 28 Aug. 2002, at B1.
- "New Yorkers scored a 494 on the verbal portion of the *Scholastic Aptitude Test*, or one point lower than last year." Carl Campanile, "New York's SAT Disgrace," *N.Y. Post*, 28 Aug. 2002, at 2.

The declaration that the letters of a well-known initialism no longer stand for what most people assume they do was not entirely unprecedented. In 1963, Texas Agricultural & Mechanical University (better known as Texas A&M) did the same thing. But the PR people did not try to change the school's strong traditions: the students remain *Aggies*. Likewise, in the mid-1990s, Microsoft declared that OLE no longer stood for "object linking and embedding"—that OLE simply stood for OLE.

satirical; *satiric; satyric. The first two are adjectives that emerged in the early 16th century. They correspond to *satire*. *Satirical* is the usual word, **satiric* being a NEEDLESS VARIANT.

Satyric means "of, relating to, or involving *satyrs* (= half-human, half-goat figures in Greek mythology)." Hence *satyric drama* is a form of ancient Greek play having a chorus of satyrs.

satyric. See **satirical.**

Saudi; *Saudi Arabian. For a citizen of Saudi Arabia, the first is the standard term; the second is a NEEDLESS VARIANT. By contrast, *Arab* denotes not citizenship but race.

Current ratio: 32:1

savable; salvable; salvageable. *Savable* (so spelled—not **saveable*) means "capable of being saved." Originally this word was used in theological senses, and it still carries religious connotations. *Salvable*, too, has a theological sense ("admitting of salvation"), as well as the sense (used of ships) "that can be saved or salvaged." *Salvageable*, dating from the 1910s in AmE, has become common in the sense "that can be salvaged"—e.g.: "The NTSB will study the engine and other *salvageable* parts to try to determine if there was a mechanical failure." Tom Wells, "Skydive Survivor May Quit the Sport," *Chattanooga Times*, 27 May 1997, at A6.

Current ratio (*savable* vs. **saveable*): 3:1

savanna (= a grazing plain in the subtropics) is the standard spelling in AmE and BrE alike, *savannah* being a variant. But the city and the river in Georgia are spelled *Savannah*.

save, in the sense "except," is an ARCHAISM best avoided. But as the following examples illustrate, it still occasionally appears—e.g.:

- "Everyone, *save* [read *except*] for a handful of brief, part-time employees, came back." Lauri Githens, "The Club That Wouldn't Die," *Buffalo News*, 1 Apr. 1994, Gusto §, at 16.
- "He was named the Final Four's most outstanding player, an award that seemed absolutely deserving to everyone *save* [read *except*] Dean E. Smith." Mark Bradley, "1995 Men's Basketball Championship," *Atlanta J.-Const.*, 19 Mar. 1995, at F8.
- "He did, however, have six runner-up finishes in that time period—one in each year, *save* [read *except*] for 1986 when he had two." "Rose Thinking Green These Days," *Chattanooga Free Press*, 28 Mar. 1997, at H2.

*saveable. See **savable.**

*save and except is a fairly common but unjustifiable REDUNDANCY that arose in the 18th century and has persisted—e.g.: "LifeCo is 'basically prepared to go forward with obtaining a final judgment of foreclosure *save and except for the fact* [read *except*]' that it does not yet have a complete list of tenants renting space in the garage." Alex Finkelstein, "LifeCo, Insurer Continue to Dog Juarez," *Orlando Bus. J.*, 8 July 1994, § 1, at 7. (Granted, the journalist was merely quoting the company.) Worse yet is the collapsed phrase **save except*, a solecism—e.g.: "There are leagues for bowlers of all ages, *save except* [read *except*] infants and toddlers." Rachel Gordon, "When the Hour Is Late and You're Still on a Roll," *S.F. Examiner*, 26 Mar. 1994, at A5.

saving(s). In refined prose, write *a saving of $100*, not **a savings of $100*. Technically, *savings* is a plural, not a singular. Yet as an adjective in the phrases *savings bank, savings account*, and the like, the plural form is unimpeachable. Cf. **daylight saving(s) time.**

Current ratio (*a saving of* vs. **a savings of*): 1.1:1

savior; saviour. The first is AmE, the second BrE. The AmE spelling did not become predominant until the early 1930s. See -OR; -OUR.

savor; savour. The first is AmE (predominant since about 1840), the second BrE (always predominant). The corresponding adjective is *savory* (AmE) or *savoury* (BrE). See -OR; -OUR.

saw > sawed > sawed. The past participle *sawn* is mostly archaic except as an adjective <sawn lumber> and as a past form in BrE <it was sawn through>. *Sawed-off* is the overwhelming favorite in AmE, *sawn-off* the overwhelming favorite in BrE. But in the past few decades, *sawn-off* (whether in reference to shotguns, antlers, or branches) has made small inroads against *sawed-off* in American writing. Canadians stick closer to BrE on this score—e.g.: "A *sawn-off* sweatshirt worn by the beach blonde [Pamela Anderson] is on the auction block for an estimated $1,500 to $2,000." Rita Zekas, "And This Is Just In . . . ," *Toronto Star*, 7 May 1997, at SW4. In American print sources, *sawed-off shotgun* outnumbers *sawn-off shotgun* by an 17-to-1 ratio. See IRREGULAR VERBS (B).

As a verb form, *sawed* has long been thought to be the preferable past participle, though it still vies closely with *sawn*—e.g.: "The complex could use many of the logs previously chipped for pulp or *sawn* [read *sawed*] into log-grade lumber, company officials said." "The Bottom Line," *Oregonian* (Portland), 23 May 1997, at B1.
LANGUAGE-CHANGE INDEX
sawn for *sawed* as a past participle: Stage 3
Current ratio (*be sawed into* vs. *be sawn into*): 1:1.1

say; state, vb. Whenever possible, use *say* rather than *state*. The latter typically sounds stilted. But there is a substantive as well as a tonal difference: *say* means "to tell; to relate," while *state* means "to set out (formally); to make a specific declaration." See **tell.**

Theodore Bernstein, the assistant managing editor of *The New York Times*, ridiculed his colleagues' overreliance on synonyms of *said*: "In the days of our forefathers Tom Swift almost never said anything; he usually *averred*, *asseverated*, *smiled*, *chuckled*, *grinned* (plainly or mischievously), *groaned*, *expostulated*, *ejaculated*, *declared*, or *asserted*. . . . The simple verb *said* never seems to be good for more than one inning; then writers or editors feel they must rush in all kinds of bush-league relief pitchers." *The Careful Writer* 283–84 (1965).

sc., the abbreviation for *scilicet* (= that is to say; namely), is a pedantic abbreviation. Because the equivalent terms *namely* and *i.e.* are more widely known, they generally serve better. Even *viz.* is better known than *sc.* See **viz.**

scalawag; scallywag; *scallawag. For this Americanism meaning "a scruffy, disreputable person" dating from the mid-19th century, the first is the standard spelling. Though the word predates the American Civil War, it was popularized during Reconstruction to denote a white Southerner who cooperated with freedmen and carpetbaggers to control state and local governments. It still retains this limited sense in historical writing. In BrE, the variant spelling *scallywag* has predominated since about 1900. *Scallawag* is still another variant.

scallop; *scollop. The standard form has been *scallop* since about 1800. *Scollop* is a variant.

scaly. So spelled—not *scaley.

scampi (= large prawns), though itself plural, is considered a mass noun when it refers to a dish that includes large prawns <I ordered the scampi *or* I ordered scampi>. Though common, the REDUNDANCY *shrimp scampi* is best avoided.
Current ratio (*the scampi* vs. **the shrimp scampi*): 3:1

scan is ambiguous: it may mean either (1) "to examine carefully, scrutinize," or (2) "to skim through, look at hurriedly." In AmE, as it happens, sense 2 now vastly predominates. That usage may be bolstered by the ubiquitous electronic scanner, which contributes to the idea of haste. See CONTRONYMS.

scapula (= a shoulder blade) makes the plural *scapulae* (/**skap**-yə-lee/)—the homegrown *scapulas* being a secondary variant.
Current ratio: 15:1

scarce. See **rare.**

scarcely any is sometimes displaced by the dialectal double negative *scarcely no* (even, as the example shows, in BrE)—e.g.: "It is a pity that it got *scarcely no* [read *scarcely any*] publicity because Liffe's performance was little short of stunning." Anthony Hilton, "Facts of Liffe Set the Scene for the Future," *Evening Standard*, 8 Jan. 1997, at 33. *Scarcely* has enough negative force that negatives should be avoided with it.
LANGUAGE-CHANGE INDEX
scarcely no for *scarcely any*: Stage 1
Current ratio (*scarcely any* vs. **scarcely no*): 364:1

scarf, n. & vb. Although the plural noun *scarfs* is listed in most dictionaries as standard, *scarves* is more than eight times as common in modern print sources. Having been vastly predominant since the 1940s, *scarves* should be accepted as the preferred form. See PLURALS (C).

As a form of the verb *scarf* (= [1] to wrap with a scarf, or [2] to eat ravenously), *scarfs* is correct <the designer scarfs the models with Indian silks> <John usually scarfs down lunch>.

scarify; scorify. *Scarify* (from *scar*) means (1) "to make superficial marks or incisions in; cut off skin from"; (2) "to break up the surface of (the ground) with a spiked machine [a scarifier] for loosening soil

LANGUAGE-CHANGE INDEX (For the full key, see front matter pp. xxxi, l–li.)
Stage 1: Rejected. **Stage 2:** Widely shunned. **Stage 3:** Widespread but . . . **Stage 4:** Ubiquitous but . . . **Stage 5:** Fully accepted.
Invariably inferior forms marked by asterisk (*). • Ratios represent frequency of prevalent forms vs. variants in current books.

or building roads"; or (3) "to pain by severe criticism." Sense 1 is most common—e.g.:

- "Rub the seed across some sandpaper to weaken the hard seed coat or *scarify* it with a knife for better germination." Robert Stiffler, "Scotts' Soil-Test Kit Promises Quicker Results," *Virginian-Pilot* (Norfolk), 20 Apr. 1997, at G2.
- "Native Americans did no surgery. Some injuries were *scarified*." Jim Carty, "Plant Products Filled Pantries, Pharmacies of Native Americans," *Columbian* (Vancouver, Wash.), 15 May 1997, Neighborhood §, at 6.
- "Buy *scarified* Bahia grass seed to increase germination." "What to Do This Month," *Tampa Tribune*, 12 Apr. 2003, Baylife §, at 10.

Sense 1 applies also to body adornment by cutting and scraping—e.g.: "Worse, once piercing becomes commonplace among people like, well, Leslie, the trendsetters up the ante with other forms of body alteration: cutting (*scarification* as adornment), branding (searing flesh with high heat in artistic patterns) and—please don't eat during this next sentence—tongue splitting, in which the tongue is cleaved nearly in half so as to cause it to fork like a lizard's." Buzz McClain, "Is There a Ring in Your Future?" *Wash. Post*, 11 Feb. 2003, at F1. So goes the march of civilization.

Sense 3 is also fairly common—e.g.: "With a combination of dazzling philosophical acumen and *scarifying* wit, Stove does for irrationalism in Karl Popper's philosophy . . . what the Romans did for Carthage in the Third Punic War." Roger Kimball, "Who Was David Stove?" *New Criterion*, Mar. 1997, at 21.

A separate *scarify*, based on the root word *scare*, dates from the late 18th century but remains mostly dialectal. It often carries a lighthearted connotation—e.g.:

- "The cost-of-living index had taken a *scarifying* new jump of 1.2 percent in February, to an annual rate of 15 percent." Peter Goldman, "Carter's New Energy Plan," *Newsweek*, 2 Apr. 1979, at 27.
- "Saturday the attraction is the high-jump, a *scarifying* attempt to better the world horse-jumping record of 7 feet 7 1/2 inches over a wall for a bonus prize of $5,000." Angus Phillips, "For Horse Show Set, It's Cash and Carry," *Wash. Post*, 27 Oct. 1988, at D1.
- "Soon everyone begins to look like a suspect in the death of Sir Charles Baskerville: the convict, perhaps the heir, maybe even the butler with a secret. And, of course, the hound itself—brought to *scarifying* life with the aid of computer-generated special effects." Deniece Washington, "The Fun Is Elementary," *Boston Globe*, 19 Jan. 2003, TV §, at 4.

It would be helpful if the two words were pronounced differently, but dictionaries record no such distinction. Both are pronounced with the first syllable sounding like *scare*: /**skair**-i-fı/.

Scorify = to reduce to dross or slag. The term surfaces most commonly in cognate forms, such as *scorifier*—e.g.: "Hanging adjacent to the furnace are the specialized tongs for handling crucibles, cupels and the dishlike ceramic containers called *scorifiers*." "Silver City's Fargo Stage Comes to Silver City, Idaho," *Bulletin* (Bend, Or.), 2 Apr. 1997, at T14.

scavenge, vb.; **scavenger**, vb. The verb *scavenge* is a BACK-FORMATION from the noun *scavenger*. *Scavenge* having taken hold as the predominant verb in the late 19th century—first in BrE and then in AmE—the verb *scavenger* should be considered a NEEDLESS VARIANT.

Current ratio (*scavenged* vs. *scavengered): 364:1

sceptic. See **skeptic.**

sceptre; *scepter. The spelling *sceptre* has been standard in AmE and BrE alike since the 18th century—though many American dictionaries spell the word *scepter. See -ER (B).

Current ratio: 2:1

schema (= a plan, diagram, outline, or preliminary draft) is pronounced /**skee**-mə/. In frequency of use, the anglicized plural *schemas* overtook the Greek plural *schemata* during the 1990s in both AmE and BrE.

Current ratio: 3:1

scherzo; scherzando. Although the musical term *scherzo* (= a playful, sprightly composition) has predominantly formed the plural *scherzos* since the late 19th century, the story is different for *scherzando* (= a musical direction to perform playfully). Only the Italianate plural *scherzandi* exists for this term.

schism (= division, separation) is now almost always used figuratively—e.g.:

- "The issue has also created a *schism* within the Orange County agency, which bears the greatest responsibility for child protection." Matt Lait, "Policy Lets O.C. Agency Ignore Some Sex Crimes," *L.A. Times*, 6 Sept. 1996, at A1.
- "Confronting the *schism* between Blacks and Koreans, two women are discovering a recipe for friendship and healing in a two-bedroom West Hollywood apartment where the aromas of kimchee and corn bread mingle in the air." Helie Lee & Stephanie Covington, "Kimchee and Corn Bread," *Essence*, Apr. 1997, at 94.
- "There is also a generational *schism*, with retired people and those aged over 55 still very much in favour of remaining part of the UK." Ben Borland, "Sturgeon Knows She Wouldn't Win New Referendum," *Express* (U.K.), 4 Sept. 2015, at 12.

Pronunciation experts have long agreed that the word is pronounced /**siz**-əm/, not /**skiz**-əm/ or /**shiz**-əm/. Yet the traditional pronunciation grows rarer year by year. See PRONUNCIATION (B).

schismatic; *schismatical. The shorter term has been predominant throughout the English-speaking world since about 1850.

Current ratio: 5:1

schizophrenic; schizoid. Each of these words can function as both adjective (= characterized by schizophrenia) and noun (= a person with schizophrenia). But both words are most often adjectives, and *schizophrenic* is the more common term. If any difference exists, it's that a *schizoid* (or *schizoid personality*) is someone who is seclusive, shut in, and unsociable, whereas a *schizophrenic* (or *schizophrenic* *personality*) has a serious psychological disorder involving greater dissociation between the intellect and the emotions.

The words are pronounced /skit-sə-**fren**-ik/ and /**skit**-soyd/.

scholium (= a marginal note or comment, esp. of an erudite kind) has always predominantly made the naturalized classical plural *scholia*. The variant *scholiums* has rarely been used.

Current ratio: 211:1

***schtick; *schtik.** See **shtick.**

scilicet. See **sc.**

scintilla (= a minute particle; a trace) forms the plural *scintillas* or (less good) *scintillae*. (See PLURALS (B).) The word is pronounced /sin-**til**-ə/, not /skin-/.

Current ratio: 2:1

***scirocco.** See **sirocco.**

scissors. As a term for the cutting instrument, *scissors* has been treated as a plural since the 14th century, and that is the preferred modern construction <where are the scissors?>. But the phrase *a pair of scissors*, which first appeared in the 15th century, is singular because the noun *pair* controls the verb, not the prepositional phrase *of scissors* <a pair of scissors is in the drawer>.

Since the mid-19th century, *scissors* has occasionally been construed with a singular verb. Although this usage has never been the usual form in AmE or BrE, it does occur—e.g.: "An efficient tool for this purpose, a nose (safety) *scissors is* small, has rounded blunt-tipped ends, and costs about $24." Lois Fenton, "Philbin's Monochromatic Look Catches On," *Commercial Appeal* (Memphis), 16 Apr. 2000, at G4.

As a term used in sports (e.g., wrestling, gymnastics), *scissors* always takes a singular verb <the scissors is a classic wrestling move> <in the pommel-horse competition, the scissors is a demanding display requiring great gymnastic skill>.

sclerosis (= a disease that causes an organ or soft tissue to harden) forms the (rarely needed) plural *scleroses*.

***scollop.** See **scallop.**

scone (= a small round cake usu. eaten with butter) predominantly rhymes with *gone* in BrE and with *tone* in AmE.

score, as in *fourscore and seven*, means "20," though various other numbers are often mistakenly attached to the word. So *fourscore and seven* = 87.

scoria (= [1] the slag produced by smelting ore, or [2] loose lava resembling this slag) is, despite its appearance, a singular noun—the plural being *scoriae*

(/**skor**-i-ee/). Avoid construing the singular noun with a plural verb, as well as the false singular **scorium*.

scorify. See **scarify.**

Scotch, adj. & n.; **Scottish,** adj.; **Scots,** adj. & n. As adjectives, *Scots* generally applies to people <Scotsman> and *Scottish* to things <Scottish golf>. But the distinction is far from rigid. Some things, usually those associated with people, have names that use *Scots* instead of *Scottish*, e.g., *Scots law, Scots Guards, Scots goose, Scots pine*. And there are many things with fixed names, such as *Scottish Rite* and *Scottish Rifles*. The noun *Scots* usually refers to the form of English spoken in Scotland <speaks a lilting Scots> or to the people <the Scots of the Highlands>.

Scotch, an adjective of English origin, is a contracted form of *Scottish*. Although it was used for a long time in Scotland, and appears in the writings of eminent figures such as James Boswell, Robert Burns, and Sir Walter Scott, it is now often considered offensive. Limit its use to SET PHRASES such as *Scotch broth* and *Scotch egg*. But even some of those names are undergoing change. For instance, **Scotch terriers* are now called *Scottish terriers* or even *Scots terriers*. And a *Scotch bonnet* pepper is more often called a *habanero* pepper.

As a noun, *Scotch* refers only to whisky distilled in Scotland. See **whisky.**

Scotticism (= a word, phrase, or expression typical of Scottish English) is so written—not **Scottishism*. Cf. **Briticism.**

scrimmage; *scrummage. Since about 1825, *scrimmage* has greatly preponderated over **scrummage* in frequency of use.

Current ratio: 25:1

scriptorium (= a room in which scribes, esp. in medieval monasteries, do their copying) predominantly makes the Latinate plural *scriptoria*—which makes sense for people who historically were writing primarily in Latin. We don't have many scriptoria these days, but if we did we might well call them *scriptoriums*.

scrumptious (= delicious, extremely pleasant) is so spelled, not **scrumptuous*—e.g.:

- "Naturally lower-fat cheeses star in some *scrumptuous* [read *scrumptious*] sandwiches." Marlene Parrish, "Cheese ABCs," *Pitt. Post-Gaz.*, 8 Mar. 1995, at D1.
- "I try a *scrumptuous* [read *scrumptious*] raspberry-chocolate bash." Marcia Schnedler, "Where Life Is a Big Chocolate Chip," *Kansas City Star*, 24 Sept. 1995, at H1.

Cf. **bumptious.**

LANGUAGE-CHANGE INDEX
scrumptious misspelled **scrumptuous*: Stage 1
Current ratio: 206:1

LANGUAGE-CHANGE INDEX (For the full key, see front matter pp. xxxi, l–li.)
Stage 1: Rejected. **Stage 2:** Widely shunned. **Stage 3:** Widespread but . . . **Stage 4:** Ubiquitous but . . . **Stage 5:** Fully accepted.
Invariably inferior forms marked by asterisk (*). • Ratios represent frequency of prevalent forms vs. variants in current books.

*sculduggery; *scullduggery. See skulduggery.

scull. See skull.

sculpt; sculpture, v.t.; *sculp. Although the preferred verb was long thought to be *sculpture* <to sculpture a bust>, *sculpt* (a BACK-FORMATION from *sculptor*) is now the predominant form and should be accepted as standard. *Sculp* is a NEEDLESS VARIANT.

The predominance of *to sculpt* over *to sculpture* is a more recent phenomenon than you might suspect: the linguistic coup occurred in AmE in the late 1980s and in BrE in the early 1990s.

For the agent noun, *sculptor* is preferred over *sculpturer.

LANGUAGE-CHANGE INDEX
sculpt as a verb: Stage 5
Current ratio (in order of headwords): 86:60:1

scurvy, adj. & n.; scurfy, adj. *Scurvy* (= contemptible) is a metaphorical term expressing scorn. Typical of Elizabethan English, and now an ARCHAISM, it appears mostly in jocular contexts—e.g.: "If Dwayne Rudd does anything wrong, anything, which leads to the Brownies losing again, he will be fed to the Bengals. No, not those *scurvy* Cincinnati Bengals—the ones at the Cleveland zoo." Jerry Greene, "Rudd's Fine Excuse for Inexcusable Act," *Orlando Sentinel*, 15 Sept. 2002, at D11.

As a noun, *scurvy* denotes the disease, common among sailors up to the 19th century, brought on by a deficiency in vitamin C. The chief symptoms are spongy, bloody gums and loose teeth, as well as bloody mucous membranes. For another delightful entry (suggested by that description), see mucus.

Scurfy means "(of an organism) full of dandruff or similar white flakes occurring as a result of disease or parasites." E.g.: "Right about now is the time to treat euonymus scale (the *scurfy* white stuff) on euonymus and pachysandra and other scale insects on mugo pines, lilacs, peach, plum and cherry trees." Carol Bradford, "Sequence of Garden Events Remains the Same Year In, Year Out," *Post-Standard* (Syracuse), 7 Apr. 2002, Garden §, at 26.

scutum (= a bony or horned plate or scale found on some reptiles and insects) makes the plural *scuta*. But the anglicized shortened form *scute*, made by apocope, has the straightforward plural *scutes*. Since about 1875, *scutes* has occurred with greater frequency than *scuta* in English-language print sources worldwide.

Current ratio (*scutes* vs. *scuta*): 7:1

Scylla and Charybdis, between. As described by Homer, *Scylla* /sil-ə/ was a sea monster who had six heads (each with a triple row of teeth) and twelve feet. Though primarily a fish-eater, she was capable of snatching and devouring (in one swoop) six sailors if their ship ventured too near her cave in the Strait of Messina. (In the accounts of later writers, she is rationalized into a rocky promontory.) Toward the opposite shore, not far from Scylla's lair, was *Charybdis*

/kə-**rib**-dis/, a whirlpool strong enough thrice daily to suck into its vortex whole ships if they came too close.

Hence to say *between Scylla and Charybdis* is a close literary equivalent of *between a rock and a hard place* or *between the devil and the deep blue sea*. The main difference between the phrases is that there is no comfort between a rock and a hard place; there is a safe, though precarious, way to proceed between Scylla and Charybdis. All three phrases are CLICHÉS. See LITERARY ALLUSION.

sear. See sere.

seasonable; seasonal. *Seasonable* = (1) appropriate to the season; opportune <for us, an August trip to Aspen is quite seasonable: we don't ski>; (2) timely <your letter was not seasonable>; or (3) (of weather) suitable to the time of year <seasonable April showers>. *Seasonal* = (1) of, relating to, or characterizing the seasons of the year, or any one of them <El Niño has caused seasonal changes in weather>; or (2) dependent on the seasons, as certain trades <seasonal shipping patterns>.

Interestingly, *seasonable* was the much more common word till about 1900, when a reversal in word frequency occurred with this pair.

Seattleite; *Seattlite. The first is the standard spelling; the second is a variant form. See DENIZEN LABELS.
Current ratio: 12:1

seaward(s). See DIRECTIONAL WORDS (A).

seaworthy. One word—not hyphenated. See -WORTHY.

secede. See cede.

second-guess, v.t. So hyphenated.

second language. See foreign language.

secretariat (= the position or quarters of a secretary) is the standard spelling. *Secretariate is a variant.

*secretariship. See secretaryship.

secretary is pronounced /sek-rə-tar-ee/—not /sek-ə-tar-ee/. See PRONUNCIATION (B).

secretaryship; *secretariship. The first spelling has always been standard. The second is a variant form.
Current ratio: 5,549:1

secrete = (1) to hide; or (2) to exude or ooze through pores or glands; to produce by secretion. Although *secrete away* is technically redundant, it avoids the possible MISCUE from the conflicting senses <then, in a frenzy, he secreted away all the contraband drugs>. Sense 1 is increasingly confined to literary and legal contexts.

secretive; secretory. The first is the adjective ("inclined to secrecy, uncommunicative") corresponding to sense 1 of *secrete* (just above). The second is the adjective ("having the function of secreting") corresponding to sense 2 of *secrete*. *Secretive* is best pronounced /**see**-krə-tiv/ for sense 1 and /si-**kree**-tiv/ for sense 2. *Secretory* is pronounced /si-**kree**-tə-ree/.

seducible. So spelled—not *seduceable. See -ABLE (A).
Current ratio: 12:1

see, n. See **bishopric.**

see > saw > seen. So inflected. Using the past tense for the past participle, and vice versa, is typical of DIALECT. Usually these errors occur only in reported speech—e.g.:

- "'If I *was* [read *had been*] here on time, I would have *saw* [read *seen*] what happened and the guy or gal who did this would be caught.'" Giovanna Fabiano, "Vehicle Hits, Kills Woman in Raritan," *Courier-News* (Bridgewater, N.J.), 7 Sept. 2002, at A2 (quoting Louie Dellatorca).
- "He said, 'I *seen* [read *saw*] when you got that [interception], but you almost got it slapped away.'" Steve Ellis, "A Son Never Forgets," *Tallahassee Democrat*, 21 Sept. 2002, at 1 (quoting Alonzo Jackson).

LANGUAGE-CHANGE INDEX
seen as a simple past for *saw*: Stage 1
Current ratio (*I saw* vs. *I seen): 37:1

seem. On the sequence of tenses in phrases such as *seemed to enjoy* (as opposed to *seemed to have enjoyed*), see TENSES (A).

segment, v.t.; ***segmentalize**; ***segmentize.** The first has been standard since the mid-19th century. The second and third forms are NEEDLESS VARIANTS. See -IZE.
Current ratio (*segmenting* vs. *segmentalizing vs. *segmentizing): 3,457:1.3:1

segue is a noun (meaning "a seamless transition") and an intransitive verb (meaning "to transition smoothly"). (It's also a transitive verb, but only in music.) The misspelling *segway (except in the trademarked company name) is particularly embarrassing—e.g.:

- "[Barack Obama] applauded the work of junior Joe Pearson, of Barrington, who works under lead biodiesel research Professor Ihab Farag. It was a good *segway* [read *segue*] to Obama's own proposal that would reduce the amount of carbon in the fuel Americans pump into their tanks." "Obama, in Nashua, Pledges to Get U.S. Out of War," *Union Leader* (Manchester, N.H.), 21 Apr. 2007, at A2.
- "For almost 30 years, Larry Monroe has been spinning records and CDs on KUT-FM radio.... Monroe's signature is the '*segway*' [read *segue*]. He takes pride in piecing together creative set lists in which the songs are united by theme, a condition of heart or climate, or an artist's affinity for a single word in a refrain." Brad Buchholz, "Sharing the Language of Dylan," *Austin Am.-Statesman*, 13 Sept. 2007, at E1.

LANGUAGE-CHANGE INDEX
*segway for *segue*: Stage 1
Current ratio (*segue* vs. *segway): 68:1

seigneur; ***seignior.** *Seigneur* /say-**nyuur**/, a 16th-century borrowing from Middle French, refers to a man of rank or authority, especially a feudal lord—or else (today) to a Canadian member of the landed gentry. *Seignior is a variant spelling.
Current ratio: 7:1

seise; seize. These homophones are related, but they have undergone DIFFERENTIATION. *Seize* is principally a nontechnical lay word meaning: (1) "to take hold of (a thing or person) forcibly or suddenly or eagerly"; (2) "to take possession of (a thing) by legal right" <to seize contraband>; or (3) "to have a sudden overwhelming effect on" <to be seized by fear> (*OAD*). *Seize* should be confined to these senses. In the legal sense "to put in possession, invest with the fee simple of," the spelling *seise* is standard in both AmE and BrE; it corresponds better with the noun *seisin*.

seldom. Because this word is an adverb as well as an adjective, the NONWORD *seldomly is never (not merely seldom) needed—e.g.:

- "Hogan was a man so focused that he *seldomly* [read *seldom*] noticed what was going on around him." Jeff Babineau, "Hogan's Legacy," *Orlando Sentinel*, 3 Aug. 1997, at C4.
- "There, one obviously bored soldier checks identifications, and *seldomly* [read *seldom*] exercises his prerogative of looking inside bags and purses." "Deadly Biowarfare Collection Amid Disrepair in Russian Lab," *San Antonio Express-News*, 10 Aug. 1997, at A4.

It isn't even listed in most dictionaries. For other adverbs ending in a superfluous -*ly*, see ADVERBS (C).

LANGUAGE-CHANGE INDEX
*seldomly for *seldom*: Stage 1
Current ratio (*seldom* vs. *seldomly): 1,002:1

***seldom ever.** In this phrase—which seems to be a collapsed form of *seldom if ever*—the word *ever* is superfluous. True, the usage dates back to the 17th century, but it can hardly be recommended despite that history. E.g.: "And as everyone knows, Fleck, who *seldom ever* [read *seldom*] missed a meeting, will attend those sessions as long as he is able." Madeleine Mathias, "'Lafayette Treasure' Gets New Title at 98," *Morning Call* (Allentown, Pa.), 27 May 1997, at B1. Since the late 18th century, *seldom if ever* has steadily occurred more frequently in print. Cf. ***rarely ever.**

LANGUAGE-CHANGE INDEX
*seldom ever for *seldom*: Stage 2
Current ratio (*seldom* vs. *seldom ever): 617:1

self. Pl. *selves.* See PLURALS (C).

self-addressed stamped envelope. Though sometimes condemned, this phrase is now firmly entrenched in AmE (especially in the abbreviated form SASE). *Self-addressed* isn't merely "addressed by oneself," but commonly means "addressed for return to the sender." The prefix *self-* prevents vagueness: an envelope that's merely *addressed* could be addressed to anybody.

LANGUAGE-CHANGE INDEX (For the full key, see front matter pp. xxxi, l–li.)
Stage 1: Rejected. **Stage 2:** Widely shunned. **Stage 3:** Widespread but . . . **Stage 4:** Ubiquitous but . . . **Stage 5:** Fully accepted.
Invariably inferior forms marked by asterisk (*). • Ratios represent frequency of prevalent forms vs. variants in current books.

How should one pronounce SASE? And which indefinite article should it take, *a* or *an*? Dictionaries say that each letter should be enunciated /ess-ay-ess-ee/. But in informal speech, many people prefer to sound it out /**say**-zee/. It would seem logical in formal writing to treat SASE as if each letter were sounded out <an SASE>. Yet *an* has a slight lead over *a* as its introductory article in all varieties of World English.

Current ratio (*an SASE* vs. *a SASE*): 1.2:1

*self-admitted, like **self-confessed,* is a REDUN-DANCY—e.g.:

- "Hawkes is *a self-admitted* [read *an admitted*] toy buff." Amy Wu, "Toycrafter Sales Spinning Up," *Rochester Democrat & Chron.*, 21 Dec. 2002, at D9.
- "He's commercially successful—selling just about everything he paints—and a *self-admitted* [read *self-described* or delete *self-admitted*] happy man." Scarlet Cheng, "A Life Rich in Possibilities," *L.A. Times*, 18 Jan. 2003, at E1.

Cf. ***self-confessed.**

LANGUAGE-CHANGE INDEX
*self-admitted for *admitted*: Stage 3
Current ratio (*an admitted* vs.
*a self-admitted): 20:1

*self-complacent is redundant, *complacent* being sufficient—e.g.:

- "You will remind the *self-complacent* [read *complacent*] to stop and think of their fellow men." Joe Fitzgerald, "Unsung Heroes Suffer While Pols Play Budget Games," *Boston Herald*, 11 Jan. 1996, at 18.
- "In the end, . . . his approach strikes one as limited in its conservatism and a trifle *self-complacent* [read *complacent*]." Michael K. Holleran, "Total Parish Ministry," *Nat'l Catholic Rep.*, 9 Aug. 1996, at 15.
- "Being arrogantly *self-complacent* [read *complacent*] or self-satisfied, to use the dictionary definition of the word, does not go down well with voters." Peter MacMahon, "A Big Mistake to Underestimate the Lib Dems' Electoral Appeal," *Scotsman* (Edinburgh), 7 Apr. 2007, at 33.

LANGUAGE-CHANGE INDEX
*self-complacent for *complacent*: Stage 1
Current ratio (*a complacent* vs.
**a self-complacent*): 26:1

*self-confessed is a REDUNDANCY that has come to be widespread. Yet it is not above editorial reproach—e.g.: "A court that frees a *self-confessed* [read *confessed*] murderer on a technicality would seem to bear responsibility for any harm that criminal may do in the future." Mario Pei, *Words in Sheep's Clothing* 86 (1969). Cf. ***self-admitted.**

LANGUAGE-CHANGE INDEX
*self-confessed for *confessed*: Stage 4
Current ratio (*confessed spy* vs.
**self-confessed spy*): 3:1

self-deprecating; self-depreciating. See **deprecate.**

selfie (= a photo taken of oneself by oneself, typically with a cellphone camera) is so spelled—not **selfy.*

self-killing; self-murder; self-slaughter. See **suicide (A).**

sell, n. See **hard sell.**

*sellable. See **salable.**

selvage; selvedge. *Selvage* (= a specially made edge of fabric or paper) is the spelling in AmE, *selvedge* in BrE.

semantics (the study of the meaning of words and phrases) is construed as a singular <semantics is a subset of linguistics>. Cf. **politics.**

semestral is the preferred adjective corresponding to *semester* in AmE and BrE alike—not **semestrial.* Cf. **trimestral.**

SEMI-. See BI-.

semiannual (AmE); **half-yearly** (BrE). See **biannual.** On the hybrid form *semi-yearly,* see HYBRIDS.

SEMICOLONS. See PUNCTUATION (O).

semimonthly. See BI-.

semiweekly. See BI-.

send; transmit. For general purposes, *send* is much preferable to *transmit,* which has been justly criticized as a word overworked in official documents. The Evanses note that *transmit* "is labored elegance unless it carries the definite idea of passing something through or over an intermediary" (*DCAU* at 187).

senhor; senhora; senhorita. See **señor.**

señor, señora, señorita; senhor, senhora, senhorita; signor, signora, signorina. The first three are courtesy titles in Spanish: *señor* /say-**nyor** or sen-**yor**/ (for a man—equivalent to *Mr.*); *señora* /say-**nyor**-ə or sen-**yor**-ə/ (for a married woman—equivalent to *Mrs.*); *señorita* /say-nyə-**ree**-tə or sen-yə-**ree**-tə/ (for an unmarried woman—equivalent to *Miss*).

The Portugese or Brazilian counterparts are *senhor* /sen-**yor**/, *senhora* /sen-**yaw**-rə/, and *senhorita* /sen-yə-**ree**-tə/.

The Italian counterparts are *signor* /seen-**yor**/ (formerly often *signior), *signora* /seen-**yor**-ə/ (formerly sometimes *signiora), and *signorina* /seen-yə-**reen**-ə/ (no recorded instances of the alternative *signiorina).

For the Spanish forms, the tilde over the *n* is traditionally optional, but the relative ease of producing it today on computer screens and handheld devices militates in its favor. See DIACRITICAL MARKS.

sensational; sensationalistic. *Sensational* answers to *sensation* (excitement) and may mean either "awesome" <a sensational performance by the orchestra> or "commanding attention" (in the sense, actually, of "awful") <the sensational O.J. Simpson trial>. *Sensationalistic* (= overblown; distorted to shock the emotions), answering to *sensationalism,* always carries strongly negative connotations—e.g.: "Print media are being just as *sensationalistic* as TV. The Oct. 21 cover of Newsweek featured the figure of a skeleton carrying a scythe and the screaming headline 'The Tarot Card Killer' (ah, they have given him a name—part of the tradition)." Tom Shales, "Sniper Shootings Have Everyone Running Off to Join Media Circus," *San Diego Union-Trib.*, 18 Oct. 2002, at E7. Because *sensationalistic* cannot be ambiguous, it is the better choice for signaling disapproval—e.g.: "CBS and NBC did far less sweeps stunting than Fox and ABC, which blew out almost its entire schedule for *sensational* [read *sensationalistic*] Michael Jackson exposés and The Bachelorette's infatuation of the moment." Tom Jicha, "Ratings Reality," *Sun-Sentinel* (Ft. Lauderdale), 28 Feb. 2003, at D1.

LANGUAGE-CHANGE INDEX
sensational misused for *sensationalistic*: Stage 1

*****sensatory.** See **sensory.**

sense. Generally, when *sense* means "logic" or "sensibleness," it's followed by *in* <what's the sense in delaying any further?>. An exception: when *sense* denotes "meaning," it's followed by *of* <what is the sense of that word?>.

sensitize; *sensitivize. Although in 1926 H.W. Fowler championed the latter, the former is now standard in AmE and BrE alike. **Sensitivize*, a rare word, is now rightly seen as eccentric. See -IZE.

LANGUAGE-CHANGE INDEX
sensitize: Stage 5
Current ratio: 1,802:1

sensor. See **censor.**

sensorium (= the body's sensory apparatus) predominantly makes the plural *sensoria*—not **sensoriums*.

Current ratio: 4:1

sensory; *sensorial;*sensatory. *Sensory* = of, relating to, or involving sensation or the senses. **Sensatory* and **sensorial* are NEEDLESS VARIANTS.

Current ratio (in order of headwords): 10,226:202:1

sensuous; sensual. Although these words derive from the same root (*sens-*, meaning "appeal to the senses"), they have undergone DIFFERENTIATION. *Sensuous* = of, relating to, or involving the five senses; arousing any of the five senses. The word properly has no risqué connotations, though it is gravely distorted by hack novelists. Here it is correctly used: "Words thus strung together fall on the ear like music. The appeal is *sensuous* rather than intellectual." W. Somerset Maugham, "Lucidity, Simplicity, Euphony," in *The Summing Up* 321, 322 (1938).

Sensual = relating to gratification of the senses, esp. sexual; salacious; voluptuous <sensual desires>. This is the word intended by the hack novelists who erroneously believe that *sensuous* carries sexy overtones. *Sensual* is correctly used here: "Lartigue shows a land where a benevolent sun shines on women and water, cars, painted fingernails, tennis champs, swimmers—a

sensual topography of blonde and brunette." Rosemary Ranck, "Where Sorrow Never Came," *N.Y. Times*, 14 Dec. 1997, § 7, at 23. And it's badly misused here: "There is something special about naked babies, a purely *sensual* [read *aesthetic*?] sight devoid of sexuality." Gail Stewart Hand, "Oh, Baby, You Look Great in the Buff," *San Diego Union-Trib.*, 6 Jan. 1997, at E3.

LANGUAGE-CHANGE INDEX
1. *sensuous* misused for *sensual* (carrying sexual overtones): Stage 4
2. *sensual* misused for *sensuous* (relating to the senses): Stage 2

SENTENCE ADVERBS qualify an entire statement rather than a single word in the sentence. A sentence adverb does not resolve itself into the form *in a — manner*, as most adverbs do. So in *Happily, the bill did not go beyond the committee*, the introductory adverb *happily* conveys the writer's opinion on the message being imparted. The following words are among the most frequent sentence adverbs ending in *-ly*:

accordingly	fortunately	oddly
admittedly	importantly	paradoxically
apparently	interestingly	regrettably
arguably	ironically	sadly
certainly	legally	strangely
concededly	logically	theoretically
consequently	mercifully	
curiously	naturally	

Improvising sentence adverbs from traditional adverbs like *hopefully* (= in a hopeful manner) and *thankfully* (= in a thankful manner) is objectionable to many stylists but seems to be on the rise. Avoid newfangled sentence adverbs of this kind. And in formal prose, even those like *hopefully* and *thankfully* shouldn't appear. Though increasingly common, they have a tarnished history. See **hopefully** & **thankfully.**

Because sentence adverbs reveal the writer's own thoughts and biases, writers often overuse them in argumentation—but danger lurks in words such as *clearly, obviously, undoubtedly,* and *indisputably.* See **clearly** & OVERSTATEMENT.

SENTENCE ENDS. Rhetoricians have long emphasized that the punch word in a sentence should come at the end:

- "The most emphatic place in a clause or sentence is the end. This is the climax; and, during the momentary pause that follows, that last word continues, as it were, to reverberate in the reader's mind. It has, in fact, the last word. One should therefore think twice about what one puts at a sentence-end." F.L. Lucas, *Style* 39–40 (1955).
- "A word or phrase gains importance by being placed at the beginning or the end of a sentence. The end is the more important position of the two, for the sentence that trails off in a string of modifiers runs downhill in interest. By saving an important part of the predicate till the end, you emphasize the main idea." Alan H. Vrooman, *Good Writing: An Informal Manual of Style* 131 (1967).

LANGUAGE-CHANGE INDEX (For the full key, see front matter pp. xxxi, l–li.)
Stage 1: Rejected. **Stage 2:** Widely shunned. **Stage 3:** Widespread but . . . **Stage 4:** Ubiquitous but . . . **Stage 5:** Fully accepted.
Invariably inferior forms marked by asterisk (*). • Ratios represent frequency of prevalent forms vs. variants in current books.

- "Because the end of a sentence is the last thing a reader sees, it is a position of emphasis. Don't use it to express minor thoughts or casual information. Don't write 'Both candidates will appear here in July, if we can believe the reports.' (This is correct only if you want to stress the doubt-fulness of the reports.) Don't write 'Pray for the repose of the soul of John Bowler, who died last week in Cleveland.' (Your reader will start wondering what he was doing in Cleveland.)" Daniel McDonald, *The Language of Argument* 219 (5th ed. 1986).

Yet the point eludes writers who end sentences with a flat phrase such as *in many cases*, with a date that isn't critical, or with the very noun phrase that appeared at the beginning.

One way to test how effective your sentences are is to read them aloud, exaggerating the last word in each sentence. If the reading sounds awkward or foolish, or if it seems to trail off and end on a trivial note, the sentence should probably be recast.

SENTENCE FRAGMENTS. See INCOMPLETE SENTENCES.

SENTENCE LENGTH. What is the correlation between sentence length and readability? No one knows pre-cisely. Rhetoricians and readability specialists have long suggested aiming for sentences of varying lengths, but with an average of about 20 to 25 words. And empirical evidence seems to bear out this rough guideline. In 1985, three authors calculated figures for several publications, using extensive samples:

Publication	Average Sentence Length
Pittsburgh Press	20
Reader's Digest	20.4
Popular Mechanics	21.8
Science Digest	22
Field & Stream	22.8
Newsweek	24
Time	24.4
Scientific American	24.9
New York Times	26.6
Wall Street Journal	27

Source: Gary A. Olson, James DeGeorge & Richard Ray, *Style and Readability in Business Writing* 102 (1985).

They arrived at a provocative conclusion: "Varying your sentence length is much more important than varying your sentence pattern if you want to produce clear, interesting, readable prose." *Ibid.*

If you're aiming for an average sentence length of 20 to 25 words, some sentences probably ought to be 30 or 40 words, and others ought to be 3 or 4. Variety is important, but you must concern yourself with the overall average.

Standards have changed, of course, with time. In the 18th and 19th centuries, the long sentence was much more common than it is today. For many mod-ern readers, long sentences are less and less readable. They are plodding. They waste time. Long sentences slow the reading and create a solemn, portentous impression; short sentences speed the reading and the thought. For the modern writer, it's "a counsel of perfection never to write a sentence without asking,

'Might it not be better shorter?'" F.L. Lucas, *Style* 103 (1962). (For more on this phrasing, see **counsel of perfection.**)

For a good technique to shorten sentences, see REMOTE RELATIVES.

separate. So spelled—not **seperate*. See SPELLING (A).
Current ratio: 1,468 :1

*separate between. This phrase often appears ill-advisedly in place of *distinguish between* or *separate from*—e.g.:

- "Second, [be sure to] *separate between* [read *distinguish between*] direct and indirect salespersons' costs." Melissa Campanelli, "Can Managers Coach?" *Sales & Mktg. Mgmt.*, 1 July 1994, at 58.
- "You marvel at the distance that *separates between that ancient time and* [read *separates that ancient time from*] this one." Joshua Siskin, "You Didn't Plant It, Don't Know About It, but There It Is," *Daily News* (L.A.), 11 Nov. 1995, at L16.
- "Just as Shen Wei does not separate cultural influences in his art, he increasingly does not *separate between the mediums* [read *distinguish between the media*] he uses to express himself." Jordan Levin, "Chinese Choreographer Shen Wei to Debut Painting & Dance Show During Art Basel Miami Beach," *Miami Herald*, 26 Nov. 2014, Enter-tainment §. (On the change from *mediums* to *media*, see **media.**)

LANGUAGE-CHANGE INDEX
*separate between for *separate from* or *distinguish between*: Stage 1
Current ratio (*distinguish between* vs. **separate between*): 256:1

*separate out. See PHRASAL VERBS.

*seperate. See **separate.**

septet (= a group of seven) is the standard spelling in AmE and BrE alike. **Septette* is a variant.
Current ratio: 28:1

sepulchre; *sepulcher; sepulture. Oddly enough, *sepulchre* is the standard spelling in AmE as well as BrE—not **sepulcher*. The word means "burial place, tomb," and is pronounced /sep-əl-kər/. *Sepulture*, sometimes a NEEDLESS VARIANT of **sepulcher*, jus-tifies its separate form in the sense "burial." These words are formal, even literary.

sequential; sequacious. *Sequential* = forming a sequence or consequence <a sequential narrative>. *Sequacious* = slavishly servile <she is surrounded by sequacious protégés>.

sequential order is a REDUNDANCY that has spread since about 1950—e.g.: "These [Ernest Hemingway–Maxwell Perkins] letters contain long—emphasize long—discussions of money, of advances on work, royalties, serializations, advertising and the *sequential order* [read *sequence* or *order*] in which stories should be published in collections." John Balzar, "Fragments of Friendship," *L.A. Times*, 19 Jan. 1997, Book Rev. §, at 9.

sequester, v.t.; **sequestrate.* Generally, **sequestrate* means nothing that *sequester,* the more common term, does not also mean. Both terms are old: *sequester* dates from the 14th century, **sequestrate* from the early 16th century. *Sequester* = (1) to set aside; separate <the judge sequestered the jury>; or (2) to temporarily remove (something) from the owner's possession; esp., to seize (a debtor's property) until creditors' claims are paid <the judge sequestered the bankrupt estate's remaining assets>.

Apart from arcane legal uses, **sequestrate* is a NEEDLESS VARIANT.

Current ratio: 14:1

seraph /**ser**-əf/, referring to a six-winged angel, has two plurals: a Hebrew one (*seraphim*) and a native English one (*seraphs*). *Seraphim* is about three times as common in print as *seraphs,* and it sometimes even appears alongside the anglicized plural for *cherub*— e.g.: "Her 'Angels' is a similar exposition, where the angelic hierarchy (angels, *seraphim,* and cherubs) is displayed in the bright upper part of the painting." Sylvia Krissoff, "Show Covers Opposite Ends of Spectrum," *Grand Rapids Press,* 14 Dec. 1997, at B5. Cf. **cherub.** See PLURALS (B).

The double plural **seraphims* is erroneous—e.g.: "Dolly Epstein, who says she has collected more than 100 angels since 1991, began collecting *seraphims* [read *seraphim* or *seraphs*] two years ago." Carmen Duarte, "Customers at Angelic Gift Shop Get Spiritual Lift with Purchases," *Ariz. Daily Star,* 9 Sept. 1998, at E6.

LANGUAGE-CHANGE INDEX
*seraphims for *seraphim* or *seraphs*: Stage 2
Current ratio (*seraphim* vs. *seraphs* vs. **seraphims*): 17:6:1

sere; sear. Although both spellings have been used for the adjective meaning "dried and withered," *sere* is standard. In that sense, *sear* is a variant to be avoided. But *sear* has legitimate senses, first as a verb: (1) "to burn quickly with powerful heat"; (2) "to have an extremely strong sudden and unpleasant impact on, as by scorching"; or (3) "to briefly cook the surface of (food) at high temperature." *Sear* is also two nouns: first, referring to a scar or mark by the quick burns of searing; and second, the catch that holds the hammer of a gun's lock.

serendipity (= luck in making happy accidental discoveries) forms the adjective *serendipitous,* a useful term of recent vintage (ca. 1943).

sergeant; serjeant. In medieval times, this word (ultimately deriving fr. L. *servient* "serving") came to mean someone performing a specific function in the household or jurisdiction of a king, lord, or deliberative assembly and reporting directly to the top authority under which that person served. Of the more than 50

variant spellings of the term over the centuries, the preferred spelling in AmE today is *sergeant.* In BrE, there is some DIFFERENTIATION between spellings: *sergeant* is largely military <sergeant-major> and *serjeant* largely legal <serjeant-at-arms>. **Sargeant* is a common misspelling stemming from the pronunciation of *sergeant* /**sar**-jənt/ and perhaps also from the CASUALISM *sarge.*

SERIAL COMMA. See PUNCTUATION (D).

series. Though serving as a plural when the need arises, *series* is ordinarily a singular <the series is quite popular>. But it is also a noun of multitude, so that phrases such as *a series of things* take a plural verb—e.g.:
- "There *have* been a *series of* such *incidents* as refugees from both sides have begun reconstructing houses." "Muslim Homes Explode in Serb Area," *Ariz. Republic & Phoenix Gaz.,* 11 Nov. 1996, at A17.
- "A *series of* motivational *meetings were* held in the early evening." Joanna Schmitcke, "Lifetime of Wrestling Pays Off," *Sacramento Bee,* 2 Feb. 1997, at N6.
- "In the 1960s and 1970s *a series of articles were* published, sketching out the main characteristics of European class structure and its changes during the postwar decades." Max Haller, *Class Structure in Europe* xi (2003).
- "A *series of studies have* since identified a number of factors, including heat transferred into deep oceans and small volcanic eruptions, that affected the temperature at the surface of the Earth." Karl Mathiesen, "Global Warming Has Not Slowed, Data Shows," *Irish Times,* 6 June 2015, at 10.

See SYNESIS. Even so, the collocation *there has been a series* has predominated over *there have been a series* in print sources since the phrasing became common about 1800. The same is true for *there is a series,* which has consistently predominated over *there are a series.* Cf. **species.**

Series keeps the same form in the plural. The form **serieses* is an archaic plural that still occasionally appears—e.g.:
- "The Braves have posted an unfathomable 6–0 mark at Busch this year, winning three-game *serieses* [read *series*] in April and July." Dave Reynolds, "Stopping Braves a Breeze at Busch?" *Peoria J. Star,* 12 Oct. 1996, at D1.
- "She's led the Cowgirls to nine conference titles and five Women's College World *Serieses* [read *Series*]." Berry Tramel, "Softball Needs New Identity," *Daily Oklahoman,* 9 May 1997, at 27.

LANGUAGE-CHANGE INDEX
*serieses as plural of *series*: Stage 1

serjeant. See **sergeant.**

serum (= [1] a liquid injected into a person's blood to fight infection or poison, [2] the thin part of blood, or [3] the liquid from a plant) forms the plural *sera* or *serums.* The former has always preponderated in English-language print sources.

LANGUAGE-CHANGE INDEX (For the full key, see front matter pp. xxxi, l–lii.)
Stage 1: Rejected. **Stage 2:** Widely shunned. **Stage 3:** Widespread but . . . **Stage 4:** Ubiquitous but . . . **Stage 5:** Fully accepted.
Invariably inferior forms marked by asterisk (*). • Ratios represent frequency of prevalent forms vs. variants in current books.

service, n. & vb. Originally a noun in the 13th century, *service* came into use as a transitive verb as early as the 16th century—but infrequently until the mid-20th century. As a verb, *service* may mean "to provide service for" <the mechanic serviced the copying machine>, "to pay interest on" <to service a debt>, or generally "to perform services for." Ordinarily, the verb *to serve* ought to be used in broad senses. *Service,* v.t., should be used only if the writer believes that *serve* would not be suitable in idiom or sense, especially since *service* can also denote the male animal's function in breeding.

servicemark (= a name, phrase, or other device intended to identify the services of a certain business) is now preferably one word, not two and not hyphenated. See **trademark.**

serviette (= a napkin), which first sprang into widespread use in the 1770s in BrE, has always occurred more frequently in that variety. It was at its height of popularity in BrE from about 1910 to 1950. Nancy Mitford made much of its non-U status. See CLASS DISTINCTIONS.

SESQUIPEDALITY is the use of big words, literally those that are "a foot and a half" long. Although the English language has an unmatched wealth of words available for its users, most of its resources go untapped. The *OED* contains more than 600,000 words, yet even educated people have only about 10% of that number in their working vocabulary. See David Crystal, *The Cambridge Encyclopedia of the English Language* 123 (1995); Tom McArthur, *The Oxford Companion to the English Language* 1091–92 (1992).

This discrepancy gives rise to a tension between two ideals. On the one hand, vocabulary-builders have long maintained that a rich personal word-stock is your key to success:

- "A rich vocabulary is the most common and invaluable possession of the leaders in every profession, in every commercial enterprise, and in every department of active living. . . . Vocabulary is so intimately tied up with success that from now on we might as well talk of the two as though they were one and the same thing." Wilfred Funk, *The Way to Vocabulary Power and Culture* 1 (1946).
- "You are likelier to succeed (both in school and after) if you have the words you need at your command. You can, by using this book diligently, attain not only a *larger* vocabulary but, even more, an *improved* vocabulary." Arthur Waldhorn & Arthur Zeiger, *Word Mastery Made Simple* 8 (1957).
- "It has been stated on the basis of a study of student academic mortality at one large university that the lack of an adequate vocabulary is the most important single factor contributing to failure in college." Donald M. Ayers, *English Words from Latin and Greek Elements* xiv (rev. Thomas D. Worthen, 2d ed. 1986) (citing G. Rexford Davis, *Vocabulary Building* 1 [1951]).

On the other hand, writing guides are full of advice to shun big words:

- "There is a tendency, almost an instinct in the American, to use and prefer high-sounding words. The American,

as such, likes to be unsimple and grandiloquent when it comes to his manner of expression." Richard Burton, *Why Do You Talk Like That?* 124 (1929).
- "It is a habit, amounting almost to mania, among inexperienced and ignorant writers to shun simple words. They rack their brains and wear out their dictionaries searching for high-sounding words and phrases to express ideas that can be conveyed in simple terms." Edward Frank Allen, *How to Write and Speak Effective English* 57 (1938).
- "Those who run to long words are mainly the unskillful and tasteless; they confuse pomposity with dignity, flaccidity with ease, and bulk with force." H.W. Fowler, *FMEU2* at 342.
- "The more you surrender to the temptation to use big words . . . the further you are apt to stray from your true feelings and the more you will tend to write in a style designed to impress rather than to serve the reader." John R. Trimble, *Writing with Style* 80 (1975).

Which of these two views is correct? It's entirely possible to resolve the seeming paradox and to hold that they're both essentially right. Build your vocabulary to make yourself a better reader; choose simple words whenever possible to make yourself a better writer.

The last part of that antithesis is hard for some wordsmiths to accept. And it needs tempering, because hard words have a legitimate literary tradition. English has inherited two strains of literary expression, both deriving ultimately from ancient Greek rhetoric. On the one hand is the plain style now in vogue, characterized by unadorned vocabulary, directness, unelaborate syntax, and earthiness. (This style is known to scholars as Atticism.) On the other hand we have the grand style, which exemplifies floridity, allusiveness, formal and sometimes abstruse diction, and rhetorical ornament. Proponents of this verbally richer style (called Asiaticism) proudly claim that the nuances available in the "oriental profusion" of English synonyms make the language an ideal putty for the skilled writer to mold and shape precisely. The Asiaticist sees the opulence of our language as providing apt terms for virtually every conceivable context.

Still, using the abundant resources of English is widely, if not wisely, discouraged. This attitude is as old as Modern English. During the 16th century, when our language had just begun to take its modern form, learned Englishmen who enriched their lexically impoverished tongue with Latin and Greek loanwords were vilified as "smelling of inkhorn" or as "inkhornists." One of the more notable borrowing neologists of the Renaissance, Sir Thomas Elyot, author of *The Governour*, wrote in 1531: "Divers men, rather scornying my benefite ['beneficence,' i.e., adding to the English word-stock] than receyving it thankfully, doo shew them selves offended (as they say) with my straunge termes." The "straunge termes" this redoubtable inkhornist gave us include *accommodate, education, frugality, irritate, metamorphosis, persist,* and *ruminate*. He sought not to parade his formidable erudition, but rather "to augment our Englyshe tongue, wherby men shulde as well expresse more abundantly the thynge that they conceyved in theirs hartis (wherefore language was ordeyned) havinge wordes apte for the purpose." In retrospect, of course, the efforts of Elyot and others like him were not in vain because they enriched the language.

The problem, though, remains: to what extent is it advisable to use big words? The Fowler brothers generally thought it inadvisable: "Prefer the familiar word to the far-fetched." H.W. Fowler & F.G. Fowler, *The King's English* 14 (3d ed. 1931). But "prefer" raises an important question: how strong is this preference to be? Sheridan Baker elaborates the idea more fully, and quite sensibly:

> "What we need is a mixed diction," said Aristotle, and his point remains true 24 centuries and several languages later. The aim of style, he says, is to be clear but distinguished. For clarity, we need common, current words; but, used alone, these are commonplace, and as ephemeral as everyday talk. For distinction, we need words not heard every minute, unusual words, large words, foreign words, metaphors; but, used alone, these become bogs, vapors, or at worst, gibberish. What we need is a diction that weds the popular with the dignified, the clear current with the sedgy margins of language and thought.
> Sheridan Baker, *The Practical Stylist* 133 (8th ed. 1998).

Intermingling Saxon words with Latin ones gives language variety, texture, euphony, and vitality. The best writers match substance with form. They use language precisely, evocatively, even daringly. So we shouldn't assume that Hemingwayan spartanism is the only desirable mode, unless we're ready to indict T.S. Eliot, H.L. Mencken, Vladimir Nabokov, John Updike, Edmund Wilson, and many another masterly writer.

Having established a reputable pedigree for the judicious employment of unfamiliar words, we can approach a standard for discriminating between useful and relatively useless abstrusities. Consider words as analogues to mathematical fractions, both being symbols for material or conceptual referents: would a self-respecting mathematician say *12/48* instead of *1/4* just to sound more erudite? Certainly not. Likewise, a writer or speaker generally should not say *obtund* when the verbs *dull* and *blunt* come more readily to mind. Nor would one say *saponaceous* for *soapy*, *dyslogistic* for *uncomplimentary*, *macrobian* (or *longevous*) for *long-lived*, *arenaceous* or *sabulous* for *sandy*, *immund* for *dirty*, *nates* for *buttocks*, or *venenate* for the verb *poison*.

Of course, it's impossible to set down absolute rules about which words are and are not useful. Still, it's almost always degenerate to avoid the obvious by clothing it in befogged terminology. In the words of Samuel Taylor Coleridge, "Whatever is translatable in other and simpler words of the same language, without loss of sense or dignity, is bad."

But what about the mathematician who arrives at 15/16? Is it really best to round off the fraction to 1?

Maybe in some contexts, but not in all—certainly not in the professional context. Likewise with the writer who, when describing an asthenic person, should not balk at using *asthenic* rather than the vaguer *weak*, because the former evokes the distinct image of muscular atrophy, which the latter lacks. And why engage in circumlocutions when a single word neatly suffices?

One could make similar arguments for thousands of other English words. *Coterie* and *galere* have almost identical meanings—something like "a group of people united for a common interest or purpose"—but no everyday word exists for this notion. The same is true of *cathexis*, *eirenicon*, *gravamen*, *obelize*, *oriflamme*, *protreptic*, and any of numberless other examples. Samuel Johnson came closest to rationalizing his sesquipedalian penchant when he wrote: "It is natural to depart from familiarity of language upon occasions not familiar. Whatever elevates the sentiments will consequently raise the expression; whatever fills us with hope or terror, will produce some perturbation of images and some figurative distortions of phrase."

Certainly you might have occasion to use abstruse vocabulary for reasons other than stylistic dignity or the lack of a simpler term. Three stand out. First, it's often desirable to avoid the apt but voguish word. To select one of several examples, in the days when *aggravate* was first coming to be widely used for "irritate, annoy," the fastidious speaker or writer could either combat the word's debasement and use it correctly or seek refuge in *exacerbate*. As a result, *exacerbate* is no longer an unusual word. (And of course, *make worse* is always an available standby.)

Second, big words can often have a humorous effect, though the fun is limited to those who can understand them. Such jocular phrases as *campanologist's tintinnabulation* (= bell-ringer's knell), *alliaceous halitosis* (= garlic breath), *pernoctative nepotation* (= riotous carousing through the night), and *bromidrotic fug* (= sweaty stench) can be delightfully amusing.

A third reason for waxing lexiphanic is to soften one's scurrility—to abstract it so that one's audience does not immediately visualize an unpleasant image. For example, R. Emmett Tyrell, the political analyst, once used *fecalbuccal* to describe certain politicians. He couldn't—and wouldn't—have said that if he'd been forced to simplify. For a similar example of my own use of *stercoraceous*, see the last paragraph under **copse**.

In the end, there seem to be three legitimate stances for the writer. The first is that if you truly want to communicate with a wide readership, you have to build your core of small, familiar words. The second is that if one of your purposes is to edify, use challenging words while allowing the context to reveal their meanings, as in the following examples:

- *umbrelliferous*: "His arms were like pipes, and had a way of branching from his shoulders at sharp angles so that the

LANGUAGE-CHANGE INDEX (For the full key, see front matter pp. xxxi, l–li.)
Stage 1: Rejected. **Stage 2:** Widely shunned. **Stage 3:** Widespread but . . . **Stage 4:** Ubiquitous but . . . **Stage 5:** Fully accepted.
Invariably inferior forms marked by asterisk (*). • Ratios represent frequency of prevalent forms vs. variants in current books.

umbrella-bearing, or *umbrelliferous*, limb, for example, shot up on a steeply ascending vertical before articulating crisply at the elbow into a true vertical." Patrick McGrath, *Blood and Water and Other Tales* 68 (1988).

- **enucleate** [A psychiatrist is talking to a woman in love with a madman]: "Appearances to the contrary, Edgar Stark is a deeply disturbed individual." "I know this, Jack." "I wonder if you do. Do you know what he did to that woman after he killed her?" She said nothing. "He decapitated her. Then he *enucleated* her. He cut her head off, and then he took her eyes out." *Ibid.* at 72.
- **synaesthesia**: "The *synaesthesia* (mixing of senses) of 'visible sob' might seem too rich to apply to a golf ball, if it didn't occupy the climactic position in the description." David Lodge, *The Art of Fiction* 148 (1992).

The third stance is that if you know you're writing for a specific audience with a prodigious, specialized vocabulary—whether one particular reader or the intelligentsia generally—then use hard words that are truly unsimplifiable. But question your motives: are you doing it to express yourself well, or are you just showing off?

For those who wish to do the second or third of those three things, there is no shortage of books on the subject. These are among the best:

- Robert H. Hill, *A Dictionary of Difficult Words* (1st Am. ed. 1971).
- Russell Rocke, *The Grandiloquent Dictionary* (1972).
- I. Moyer Hunsberger, *The Quintessential Dictionary* (1978).
- J.N. Hook, *The Grand Panjandrum: And 1,999 Other Rare, Useful, and Delightful Words and Expressions* (1980).
- George S. Saussy, *The Oxter English Dictionary: Uncommon Words Used by Uncommonly Good Writers* (1984).
- Paul Hellweg, *The Insomniac's Dictionary: The Last Word on the Odd Word* (1986).
- *Dictionary of Uncommon Words* (Laurence Urdang ed., 1991).
- Norman W. Schur, *2000 Most Challenging and Obscure Words* (1994).
- David Grambs, *The Endangered English Dictionary: Bodacious Words Your Dictionary Forgot* (1994).
- Josefa Heifetz Byrne, *Mrs. Byrne's Dictionary of Unusual, Obscure, and Preposterous Words* (2d ed. 1994).
- Charles Harrington Elster, *There's a Word for It: A Grandiloquent Guide to Life* (1996).
- Eugene Ehrlich, *The Highly Selective Dictionary for the Extraordinarily Literate* (1997).
- Erin McKean, *Weird and Wonderful Words* (2002).

session; cession. *Session* = (1) a meeting of a body of people; an assembly; (2) the term or period of such a meeting; or (3) a period of time devoted to a particular activity. *Cession* = (1) the act of ceding or giving up (as by treaty); or (2) a thing ceded.

sessional; *sessionary. The first is the standard adjective corresponding to the noun *session*. The second is a NEEDLESS VARIANT.

Current ratio: 951:1

set one's sights. See **site**.

SET PHRASES. Bits of language sometimes become fossilized, and when they do it's foolish to try to vary them. Hence *carved in stone* should never become

carved in shale, or whatever other variation one might lamely invent. Nor, to cite another example, should one change *comparing apples and oranges* to *comparing apples and pomegranates*. Wilson Follett called set phrases "inviolable" (if not quite inviolate): "The attempt to liven up old clichés by inserting modifiers into the set phrase is a mistake: the distended phrase is neither original, nor unobtrusive, nor brief, and sometimes it has ceased to be immediately clear, as in *They have been reticent to a tactical fault*" (*MAU* at 303).

In addition to the fault of inserting modifiers into set phrases, three other faults commonly occur.

First, it is wrong to force a set phrase into ungrammatical contexts—e.g.: "This was reported to *we the people*." Although the well-known phrase *we the people* derives from the Preamble to the Constitution, it was necessarily in the nominative case there as the subject of the sentence.

Second, it's poor style to aim at novelty by reversing the usual order of a phrase, as by writing **well-being and health* instead of *health and well-being*, or *hearty and hale instead of *hale and hearty*. Cf. INELEGANT VARIATION & CLICHÉS.

Third, if the set phrase isn't used in its common sense, it can cause a MISCUE—e.g.: "Mehrunnissa washed her hands, fed Ladli her dinner, ate something herself, and *put* her daughter *to sleep* [read *put . . . to bed*]." Indu Sundaresan, *The Twentieth Wife* 307 (2002) (The set phrase *put to sleep* is a EUPHEMISM for *euthanize*. But Mehrunnissa did not kill Ladli.)

seven seas. This figurative term has been used since antiquity, but its meaning has varied among cultures. To the ancient Romans, the *seven seas* were a group of saltwater lagoons near what is now Venice. At about the same time, the Persians called the streams that flowed into the Oxus River the *seven seas*. Much later in Europe, the *seven seas* were the North, the White, the Baltic, the Aegean, the Mediterranean, the Adriatic, and the Black Seas.

In modern usage, the term denotes all the planet's seas and oceans, not any seven in particular—e.g.: " 'If they want to sail the *seven seas*, the Air Force can't give them that.' " Lindsay Tozer, "First Coast Military Recruiters Say Navy Not the Only Option," *Fla. Times-Union*, 21 July 2001, at B1 (quoting M.Sgt. Alister Alford, a recruiter).

sew. For a blunder involving *sowing wild oats*, see **sow (B)**.

sewage; sewerage. *Sewage* is the waste matter conveyed through sewers; *sewerage* means either the removal of sewage or the system of removal.

sewn up (= [of an outcome] made certain) is sometimes mistakenly written *sown up, as if the METAPHOR had to do with *sowing* (as opposed to *sewing*)—e.g.:

- "It seems that the powerful had the game *sown* [read *sewn*] up from the start." James Gill, "Justice for Those

Who Can Pay," *Times-Picayune* (New Orleans), 26 Feb. 1999, at B7.

- "Gallegos aide and LaPuente Mayor Edward Chavez . . . has *sown* [read *sewn*] up endorsements from his boss and others in the Legislature's Latino caucus." Jean Merl, "Finish Line Close in Some Districts," *L.A. Times*, 2 Mar. 2000, at B1.

Interestingly, the mistake occurs much more frequently in BrE than in AmE—e.g.:

- "No formal deal has yet been tabled but there is speculation that the deal could be *sown* [read *sewn*] up in the next couple of days." Chris Morley, "Refuge from the Tax Man," *Evening Mail*, 29 Sept. 2000, at 37.
- "Psychological therapy is such a fundamentally difficult activity that all of us sometimes think that if only we had one more theory or technique up our sleeves we would finally have it all *sown* [read *sewn*] up." Frank Wills & Diana Sanders, *Cognitive Behaviour Therapy* vi (3d ed. 2012).

LANGUAGE-CHANGE INDEX
sown misused for *sewn*: Stage 1
Current ratio (*sewn up* vs. **sown up*): 21:1

sex, adj.; **sexual**. Both *sex discrimination* and *sexual discrimination* are widely used. The former predominates, perhaps because *sexual* has come to refer more to sexual intercourse and things pertaining to it. Hence *sexual* is becoming rare in contexts not involving intercourse or the drive to engage in it. Today, *sexual education* seems to suggest something rather different from *sex education*—e.g.: "Family planning officials at MexFam said they hope that this legislation will improve the quality of *sexual education* [read *sex education*] and promote the use of condoms." Abigail Davis, "Value of Safe Sex Stressed in Mexico," *Dallas Morning News*, 30 July 1993, at A22. See **gender**. Cf. **racial discrimination**.

sex, n. See **gender**.

Sexism. A. Generally. If you start with the pragmatic premise that you want to avoid misleading or distracting a significant percentage of your readers, then you'll almost certainly conclude that it's best to avoid sexist language. Regardless of your political persuasion, that conclusion seems inevitable—if you're a pragmatist.

But does avoiding sexism mean resorting to awkward devices such as **he/she*? Surely not, because that too would distract many readers. What you should strive for instead—if you want readers to focus on your ideas and not on the political subtext—is a style that doesn't even hint at the issue. So unless you're involved in a debate about sexism, you'll probably want a style that, on the one hand, no reasonable person could call sexist and, on the other hand, never suggests that you're contorting your language to be nonsexist.

B. The Pronoun Problem. English has a number of common-sex general words, such as *person, anyone, everyone*, and *no one*, but it has no common-sex singular personal pronouns. Instead, we have *he, she*, and *it*. The traditional approach has been to use the masculine pronouns *he* and *him* to cover all people, male and female alike. That this practice has come under increasing attack has caused the most difficult problem in the realm of sexist language. Other snarls are far more readily solvable.

The inadequacy of the English language in this respect becomes apparent in many sentences in which the generic masculine pronoun sits uneasily. Lawyers seem to force it into the oddest contexts—e.g.: "If a testator fails to provide by will for *his* surviving spouse [a *she*?] who married the testator after the execution of the will, the omitted spouse shall receive the same share of the estate *he* [i.e., the spouse] would have received if the decedent left no will." Unif. Probate Code § 2-301(a) (1989).

As H.W. Fowler noted (with contributions from Ernest Gowers):

> There are three makeshifts: first, *as anybody can see for himself or herself*; second, *as anybody can see for themselves*; and third, *as anybody can see for himself*. No one who can help it chooses the first; it is correct, and is sometimes necessary, but it is so clumsy as to be ridiculous except when explicitness is urgent, and it usually sounds like a bit of pedantic humour. The second is the popular solution; it sets the literary man's [!] teeth on edge, and he exerts himself to give the same meaning in some entirely different way if he is not prepared to risk the third, which is here recommended. It involves the convention (statutory in the interpretation of documents) that where the matter of sex is not conspicuous or important the masculine form shall be allowed to represent a person instead of a man, or say a man (*homo*) instead of a man (*vir*).
>
> *FMEU2* at 404.

Although some writers make that *him-* or *herself*, which is perhaps even more obtrusive, at least two other makeshifts are now available.

The first is commonly used by American academics: *as anybody can see for herself*. Such phrases are often alternated with those containing masculine pronouns, or, in some writing, appear uniformly. Whether this phraseology will someday stop sounding strange to most readers only time will tell. This is one way, however, of: (1) maintaining a grammatical construction; and (2) avoiding the awkwardness of alternatives such as *himself or herself*.

But the method carries two risks. First, unintended connotations may invade the writing. In the 1980s, a novel was published in two versions, one using generic masculine pronouns and the other using generic feminine pronouns; the effects on readers of the two versions were reported to have been startlingly different in ways far too complex for discussion here. Second, this makeshift is likely to do a disservice to women in the long run, for it would probably be adopted by only

LANGUAGE-CHANGE INDEX (For the full key, see front matter pp. xxxi, l–li.)
Stage 1: Rejected. **Stage 2:** Widely shunned. **Stage 3:** Widespread but . . . **Stage 4:** Ubiquitous but . . . **Stage 5:** Fully accepted.
Invariably inferior forms marked by asterisk (*). • Ratios represent frequency of prevalent forms vs. variants in current books.

a small minority of writers: the rest would continue with the generic masculine pronoun.

A second new makeshift has entered Canadian legislation: *as anybody can see for themself*; *if a judge decides to recuse themself*. (Donald L. Revell et al., "'Themself' and Nonsexist Style in Canadian Legislative Drafting," 10 *English Today* 10 [1994].) The word *themself* (attested from the early 19th century—but nonstandard) may fill the need for a gender-neutral reflexive pronoun, but many readers and writers—especially Americans—bristle at the sight or the sound of it. So for the legal writer, this makeshift carries a considerable risk of distracting readers.

Typographical gimmickry may once have served a political purpose, but it should be avoided as an answer to the problem. Tricks such as *s/he*, *he/she*, and *she/he*—and even the gloriously misbegotten double entendre, *s/he/it*—are trendy, ugly, distracting, and often unpronounceable. If we must have alternatives, *he or she* is the furthest we should go. See **he or she**.

For the persuasive writer—for whom credibility is all—the writer's point of view matters less than the reader's. So if you're writing for an unknown or a broad readership, the only course that does not risk damaging your credibility is to write around the problem. For this purpose, every writer ought to have available a repertoire of methods to avoid the generic masculine pronoun. No single method is sufficient. In a given context, you might consider doing any of the following:

- Delete the pronoun reference altogether. E.g.: "Every manager should read memoranda as soon as they are delivered *to him* [delete *to him*] by a mail clerk."
- Change the pronoun to an article, such as *a* or *the*. E.g.: "An author may adopt any of the following dictionaries in preparing *his* [read *a*] manuscript."
- Pluralize, so that *he* becomes *they*. E.g.: "A student should avoid engaging in any activities that might bring discredit to *his* school." (Read: *Students should avoid engaging in any activities that might bring discredit to their school.*)
- Use the relative pronoun *who*, especially when the generic *he* follows an *if*. E.g.: "If a student cannot use Standard English, *he* cannot be expected to master the nuances of the literature assigned in this course." (Read: *A student who cannot use Standard English cannot be expected to master the nuances of the literature assigned in this course.*)
- Repeat the noun instead of using a pronoun, especially when the two are separated by several words. E.g.: "When considering a manuscript for publication, the editor should evaluate the suitability of both the subject matter and the writing style. In particular, *he* [read *the editor*] . . . ."

For a sensible discussion of the generic masculine pronoun, see Beverly Ray Burlingame, "Reaction and Distraction: The Pronoun Problem in Legal Persuasion," 1 *Scribes J. Legal Writing* 87 (1990).

Though the masculine singular personal pronoun may survive awhile longer as a generic term, it will probably be ultimately displaced by *they*, which is coming to be used alternatively as singular or plural. (See CONCORD (B).) This usage is becoming common—e.g.:

- "It is assumed that, if *someone* is put under enough pressure, *they* will tell the truth, or the truth will emerge despite the teller." Robin T. Lakoff, *Talking Power: The Politics of Language in Our Lives* 90 (1990).
- "*Anyone* planning a dissertation on Hollywood's fling with yuppie demonology will want to include 'The Temp' in *their* calculations." Janet Maslin, "A Perfect Secretary, Temporarily," *N.Y. Times*, 13 Feb. 1993, at 8.
- "*Everybody* from President Vicente Fox to governors and mayors regularly *visit their* country-folk here, to participate in community festivities and crown Mexican-American beauty queens." Eduardo Porter, "Mexico Woos Its Citizens Living in U.S.," *Wall Street J.*, 24 Oct. 2002, at B1.

Speakers of AmE resist this development more than speakers of BrE, in which the indeterminate *they* is already more or less standard. That it sets many literate Americans' teeth on edge is an unfortunate obstacle to what promises to be the ultimate solution to the problem.

For a good historical treatment of this issue, see Robert Eagleson, "The Singular *They*," 5 *Scribes J. Legal Writing* 87 (1994–1995).

For a similar etymological progression, see **none**.

C. Words with man- and -man. "For the lawyer more than for most men, it is true that he who knows but cannot express what he knows might as well be ignorant." That sentence opens Chapter 1 of Henry Weihofen's *Legal Writing Style* (2d ed. 1980)—a sentence that, ironically, is flanked by warnings against sexist language (pp. vii, 19–20). If Weihofen were writing today, no doubt he would express himself in neutral language.

Throughout the English-speaking world, writers' awareness of sexism rose most markedly during the 1980s. In September 1984, the Commonwealth Attorney-General's Department in Canberra, Australia, issued a press release entitled "Moves to Modify Language Sex Bias in Legislation." The release states that "the Government accepts that drafting in 'masculine' language may contribute to some extent to the perpetuation of a society in which men and women see women as lesser beings." The press release recommends, "where possible and appropriate, avoidance of the use of words ending in *man*, such as *chairman, serviceman, seaman,* and so on." See "The De-Masculinisation of Language in Federal Legislation," 58 *Aus. L.J.* 685, 685–86 (1984).

In a similar vein, American businesspeople and journalists have begun to write in more neutral language, sometimes obtrusively neutral—e.g.:

- "The ice cream mixture is placed in the frozen canister and turned automatically, thus eliminating the use of salt, ice and *personpower* [read *labor* or *toil*]." Vivian Taylor, "A Passion for Ice Cream," *Fresno Bee*, 14 Aug. 1996, at E1.
- "The University of Iowa *Office of the Ombudsperson* [read *Ombuds Office*?] saw 386 new clients during fiscal 1996–97, up 7 percent from a year ago." "More Clients Visit U of I *Ombudsperson* [read *Ombuds*]," *Des Moines Register*, 16 Aug. 1997, Metro §, at 5.
- "When the blow-dried *anchorperson* [read *anchor*] on the 11 o'clock news tells you the market rose or fell 100 points, you have learned absolutely nothing." Martin Sosnoff, "Where Are the Analysts' Yachts?" *Forbes*, 6 Oct. 1997, at 144.

- "The *chairperson* [read *chair*] must consider the point of order immediately and make a decision as to whether it is valid or not." Beverley Weynton, *Manage Meetings* 48 (2002).

As a nonsexist suffix, *-person* leaves much to be desired. For every *chairperson, *anchorperson, *draftsperson, *ombudsperson, and *tribesperson, there is a superior substitute: *chair*, *anchor*, *drafter*, *ombuds*, and *tribe member*. Words ending in *-person* are at once wooden and pompous. Many words that ended in *-man* have been successfully transformed without using *-person*, among them *police officer*, *firefighter*, and *mail carrier*.

Some of the extremes to which the trend has been taken seem absurd, such as *herstory (to avoid *his*), *womyn (to avoid *men*), and the like. For the more ardent reformers, the line-drawing often doesn't seem to be tempered with good sense. For example, in 1992, *Time* magazine reported:

> NASA will no longer refer to "manned" flights but will describe the missions as "habitated" and "uninhabitated," or "crewed" and "uncrewed." Says a NASA spokesman: "We have been ordered to delete any reference by sex, on the grounds that 'manned' flight is crude and 'crewed' is p.c." Even so, some sociologists are still not satisfied. They prefer "space flight by human beings." Female astronauts find these linguistic aerobics foolish. Says one: "Common sense is the victim of all this rhetoric."
>
> "Lost in Space: Common Sense," *Time*, 6 July 1992, at 13.

For other entries dealing with this and related issues, see **chairman, foreman, humankind, male & ombudsman.**

D. Differentiated Feminine Forms. Several word endings mark feminine forms (as in *authoress*, *comedienne*, *confidante*, *heroine*, *majorette*, and *tutrix*). As a whole, these are very much on the wane.

For example, words ending in *-ess*, such as *poetess* and *authoress*, are mostly archaic in AmE. (BrE is more hospitable to them; it's not unusual to see references to *manageresses* in British newspapers.) At some point they acquired a derogatory tinge, and they've never been the same. The quite understandable tendency has been to avoid sex-specific terms if the person's sex is beside the point. And it usually is beside the point when identifying a *poet*, an *author*, or a *waiter*. Not everyone agrees that this is true of *actors*: although some women insist that they are *actors*, the Academy of Motion Picture Arts and Sciences retains the "Best Actor," "Best Actress," "Best Supporting Actor," and "Best Supporting Actress" categories. Still, the support for *actress* seems to be eroding.

One word that has persisted (especially in workaday journalism) is *songstress*, which unlike *singer* suggests "female singer-songwriter." The feminine form has long been more common than its male counterpart (*songster*). It is jarring to hear phrases such as *lady lawyer, *woman doctor, **female booksalesman*, or the Air Force's *female airman. It sounds condescending, even if that wasn't intended. But it isn't at all jarring—except to insufferable pedants—to read or hear about a woman's being an *author* or *waiter*.

As for words ending in *-trix*, the law seems to be one of two last bastions for such terms—e.g.: *executrix*, *prosecutrix*, *testatrix*. But even in law these terms are moribund. Increasingly, lawyers refer to women as *executors*, *prosecutors*, and *testators*. The other bastion? Sadomasochism—with *dominatrix*.

For other words with differentiated suffixes, see the entries at **bacchant, blond, brunet(te), comedian, coquette, distrait, doyen, fiancé, heiress & waiter.**

E. Equivalences. Among the subtler problems of nonsexist usage is to refer to men and women in equivalent terms: not *man and wife*, but *husband and wife*; not *chairmen* and *chairs* (the latter being female), but *chairs* (for all); not *men* and *girls* (a word that diminishes the status of adult females), but *men* and *women*.

Even *Mr.*, on the one hand, as contrasted with *Miss* or *Mrs.*, on the other, causes problems on this score. Differentiating between one woman and another on the basis of her marital status is invidious, really, if we do not make the same distinction for men. The idea that it matters as an item of personal information whether a woman is married—but that it doesn't matter whether a man is married—is surely an outmoded one. Though many people once considered *Ms.* an abomination, today it is accepted as the standard way of addressing a married or unmarried woman. Unless the writer knows that a woman prefers to use *Mrs.* or *Miss*, the surest course today is to use *Ms.* (/miz/).

F. Statute of Limitations. Those committed to nonsexist usage ought to adopt a statute of limitations that goes something like this: in quoted matter dating from before 1980, passages containing bland sexism—such as the use of the generic *he* or of *chairman*—can be quoted in good conscience because in those days the notions of gender-inclusiveness were entirely different from today's notions. Although it is quite fair to discuss cultural changes over time, it is unfair to criticize our predecessors for not conforming to present-day standards. How could they have done so? Therefore, using "[*sic*]" at every turn to point out old sexist phrases is at best an otiose exercise, at worst a historically irresponsible example of mean-spiritedness. For a choice discussion of a textbook that uses hundreds of *sics* in this way, see James R. Nafziger, "A Sicness unto Death," 1 *Scribes J. Legal Writing* 149 (1990).

G. Bibliography. For those wishing to inquire further into this interesting subject, the following books are worth consulting:

- Merriellyn Kett & Virginia Underwood, *How to Avoid Sexism: A Guide for Writers, Editors and Publishers* (1978).

LANGUAGE-CHANGE INDEX (For the full key, see front matter pp. xxxi, l–li.)
Stage 1: Rejected. **Stage 2:** Widely shunned. **Stage 3:** Widespread but . . . **Stage 4:** Ubiquitous but . . . **Stage 5:** Fully accepted.
Invariably inferior forms marked by asterisk (*). • Ratios represent frequency of prevalent forms vs. variants in current books.

- Mary Vetterling-Braggin ed., *Sexist Language: A Modern Philosophical Analysis* (1981).
- Barrie Thorne et al. eds., *Language, Gender and Society* (1983).
- Michelene Wandor ed., *On Gender and Writing* (1983).
- Bobbye D. Sorrels, *The Nonsexist Communicator* (1983).
- Dennis Baron, *Grammar and Gender* (1986).
- Casey Miller & Kate Swift, *The Handbook of Nonsexist Writing* (2d ed. 1988).
- Francine Wattman Frank & Paula A. Treichler, *Language, Gender, and Professional Writing* (1989).
- Val Dumond, *The Elements of Nonsexist Usage* (1990).
- Dale Spender, *Man Made Language* (2d ed. 1990).
- Rosalie Maggio, *The Bias-Free Word Finder* (1991).
- Jane Mills, *Womanwords* (1993).
- Casey Miller & Kate Swift, *Words and Women* (3d ed. 2001).

sext (= to send a sexually explicit text message, esp. a pornographic selfie) is inflected *sext > sexted > sexted.* The definiendum is to be avoided. Cf. **text,** vb.

sextant; sexton. A *sextant* is an old-fashioned instrument used in navigation. A *sexton* is an officer who handles day-to-day affairs at a church or synagogue, with varying responsibilities depending on the religious institution. The two words are occasionally confounded, especially in obituaries—e.g.:

- "He was a parishioner of Holy Ghost Church, where he served as a *sextant* [read *sexton*]." "Obituaries," *Providence J.-Bull.*, 17 Oct. 2000, at C3.
- "He was a member of St. John the Baptist Catholic Church and served for more than 50 years as *sextant* [read *sexton*] and treasurer of the St. John's Cemetery." "Deaths and Funerals," *Dayton Daily News*, 18 Nov. 2000, at B2.
- "Mr. Whitehurst was a member of New Saint Mark Baptist Church . . . , where he was a past chairman; member of Deacon Board; past president of the Floral Club; Pastor's Aide; Trustee Board; past treasurer of the church; and *Sextant* [read *Sexton*]." "David R. Whitehurst Sr." (obit.), *Virginian-Pilot & Ledger Star* (Norfolk), 29 Nov. 2001, at B8.

LANGUAGE-CHANGE INDEX
sextant misused for *sexton*: Stage 1

sextet (= a group of six) is the standard spelling in AmE and BrE alike. *Sextette* is a variant.

sexton. See **sextant.**

sexual. See **sex,** adj.

shakable; shakeable. The first spelling is standard in AmE, the second in BrE. See MUTE E.

shake > shook > shaken. So inflected. Occasionally *shook* appears erroneously as the past-participial form—e.g.:

- "Exercise rider Kelly Rycroft was *shook* [read *shaken*] up Wednesday morning when a horse he was pulling up was struck from behind by a bolting horse." Dennis Feser & Jan Alta, "Astro Force Renew Rivalry in Richmond Stakes," *Vancouver Sun*, 26 Apr. 1996, at D3.
- "Melissa Cromley was next door watching a movie when she heard a muffled sound, saw a bright flash and then was *shook* [read *shaken*] by an explosion." John Beauge,

"Sewer Explosion Caused by Flushed Gasoline," *Harrisburg Patriot*, 2 June 1997, at B6.
- "The culture was *shook* [read *shaken*] at 200 rpm overnight at 37°C and was very turbid the next morning." Joshua Hampton Hunter, *Biochemical Analysis of the Mycobacterium Tuberculosis Thymidylate Synthases* 127 (2008).

Shaked is sometimes misused as a past tense (rarely as a past participle)—e.g.:

- "Still going nowhere on third-and-10 from the Carolina 40, Petty *shaked* [read *shook*] loose from blitzing State safety Pig Prather and threw a hanging 35-yard pass." Ron Higgins, "Bulldogs Fall to Carolina's Miracle Workers," *Commercial Appeal* (Memphis), 24 Sept. 2000, at D1.
- "After Goode came down with the catch, he *shaked* [read *shook*] off a defender and streaked half the field for the game-tying score." Josh Gajewski, "Willowridge Too Goode in Overtime," *Houston Chron.*, 21 Oct. 2000, at 11.
- "Keep believing that the way those votes *shaked* [read *shook*] out are a fluke, not a warning." Tonya Weathersbee, "Election Results Are Proving This Is the Time to Discuss Race," *Fla. Times-Union*, 20 Nov. 2000, at B7.

The weak form (*shaked*) is perhaps justifiable in the facetious reduplicative phrase *shaked and baked*—e.g.:

- "He had *shaked* and baked, turning the St. Ignatius gym into his personal oven." E.L. Rogers, "Medina 62, St. Ignatius 61," *Plain Dealer* (Cleveland), 12 Dec. 1999, at C15.
- "Missouri quarterback Darius Outlaw scrambled. He passed. He *shaked* and baked." Gary Estwick, "Inconsistency Catches Up with QB Outlaw," *Austin Am.-Statesman*, 22 Oct. 2000, at D4.

But *shaked* is probably pointless when it appears alongside other weak verbs, the verb here falling victim to false analogy—e.g.: "He jumped. He skipped. He pointed. He shimmied. He *shaked* [read *shook*]." "Around the NFL," *Cincinnati Enquirer*, 9 Sept. 1996, at D5. See IRREGULAR VERBS.

LANGUAGE-CHANGE INDEX
1. *shook* misused for *shaken* (past participle of *shake*): Stage 1
Current ratio (*had shaken* vs. *had shook*): 43:1
2. *shaked* for *shook*: Stage 1
Current ratio (*he shook off* vs. *he shaked off*): 1,462:1

shakeable. See **shakable.**

Shakespeare; *Shakspere; *Shakespere; *Shakspeare; *Shakespear. Although each of these variations has appeared at one time or another in scholarly writing, *Shakespeare* has been the standard spelling since the mid-19th century.

Shakespearean; *Shakespearian. The first spelling is now standard in AmE and BrE alike. On the merits, *Shakespearean* is preferable because it preserves the final vowel in the great bard's name. *Shakespearian* is a variant. Cf. **Euclidean** & **Mephistophelean.**
Current ratio: 5:1

shall; will. Grammarians formerly relied on the following paradigm, which now has little utility:

Simple Futurity		
First person	I shall	we shall
Second person	you will	you will
Third person	he will	they will

Determination, Promise, or Command		
First person	I will	we will
Second person	you shall	you shall
Third person	she shall	they shall

But with only minor exceptions, *will* has become the universal word to express futurity, regardless of whether the subject is in the first, second, or third person. *Shall* is now mostly restricted to two situations: (1) interrogative sentences requesting permission or agreement <shall we all go outside?> <shall I open the present now?>; and (2) legal documents, in which *shall* purportedly imposes a duty <the tenant shall obtain the landlord's permission before making any changes to the premises>. In both of those situations, *shall* seems likely to persist, but in law it is declining because of increased recognition of its hopeless ambiguity as actually misused by lawyers. See *Garner's Dictionary of Legal Usage* 952–55 (3d ed. 2011).

Professor Gustave Arlt of the University of California summed it up well, writing in the late 1940s: "The artificial distinction between *shall* and *will* to designate futurity is a superstition that has neither a basis in historical grammar nor the sound sanction of universal usage. It is a nineteenth-century affectation [that] certain grammarians have tried hard to establish and perpetuate. . . . [T]hey have not succeeded." Quoted in Norman Lewis, *Better English* 270 (rev. ed. 1961).

And if the distinction isn't real, there's simply no reason to hold on to *shall*. The word is peripheral in AmE.

LANGUAGE-CHANGE INDEX
will for old-school *shall* with first-person nouns: Stage 5

shamefacedly. Although *shamefaced* is two syllables, *shamefacedly* is four: /shaym-**fay**-səd-lee/. Cf. **allegedly.**

***shammy; *shamois; *shamoy.** See **chamois.**

shanghai, v.t., = (1) to drug or otherwise make insensible and then abduct for service on a ship needing crew members; or (2) to influence by fraud or compulsion. The inflected forms are *shanghaied* and *shanghaiing.*

The verb has its origin in the SLANG of 19th-century San Francisco. When gold was discovered in California, many sailors deserted their ships in the San Francisco Bay to seek their fortunes in the goldfields. So ship captains constantly needed new crewmen, willing or not. More than a few men in San Francisco passed out from drugs or alcohol and woke up to find themselves on extended voyages, especially to Shanghai, a major Chinese seaport and trading center. Hence, to be *shanghaied* soon meant to be kidnapped and impressed.

Sense 2 became common by the end of World War I.

shapable; shapeable. The first spelling is standard in AmE, the second in BrE. See MUTE E.

shape > shaped > shaped. The archaic past participle *shapen* exists only in the forms *misshapen, ill-shapen,* and *well-shapen.* The latter two, though much less common than *misshapen,* still occur—e.g.:

- "At the back of the restaurant, the Pinup Lounge pays homage to Vargas Girls, those idealized images of *well-shapen* women painted by Alberto Vargas during and after World War II and for years afterwards." Matt Kelley, "Runza Pioneer Sitting Back in the Saddle," *Omaha World-Herald,* 28 May 1995, Bus. §, at 1.
- "He gave to every worthy cause and outstretched palm that found its way to his corner office in *ill-shapen,* yellow-bricked Cleveland Municipal Stadium." Jon Morgan, "Life of a Salesman," *Baltimore Sun,* 19 Apr. 1997, at D1.

See IRREGULAR VERBS (B).

***sharable.** See **shareable** & MUTE E.

share. This word appears in various redundant phrases, such as **share in common, *share together,** and **both share**—e.g.:

- "Elway and Dan Marino have been playing contract leapfrog with Elway always getting the last leap. They *both share* [read *have*] the same agent, Marvin Demoff of Los Angeles, and that's the way he's always done it, ever since they were rookies." Joseph Sanchez, "Tom Dempsey's Record 63-Yarder Turns 25," *Denver Post,* 5 Nov. 1995, Sports §, at C3.
- "This is one book families may want to own so it can be pulled out often to *share together* [read *look at together* or *share*]." Sue Struthers, "Poetry Allows Every Child to Taste Words," *Press-Enterprise* (Riverside, Cal.), 1 Dec. 1996, at D5.
- "Madison and St. Clair counties *share common* [read *share* or *have common*] roots emerging from basically working-class people." "Did Racism Cause Defeat of Garcia?" *St. Louis Post-Dispatch,* 7 Dec. 1996, at 34.
- "Coincidentally, although they *shared* [read *had*] little else *in common* and perhaps never even met, they both owed it to Heidelberg that they were admitted into George's world." Robert E. Norton, *Secret Germany* 624 (2002).

See REDUNDANCY.

shareable; *sharable. The spelling *shareable* has long been standard in AmE and BrE alike. That's anomalous for AmE (see MUTE E), but the reason undoubtedly has to do with how easily *sharable* can be misread.

Current ratio: 1.3:1

LANGUAGE-CHANGE INDEX (For the full key, see front matter pp. xxxi, l–li.)
Stage 1: Rejected. **Stage 2:** Widely shunned. **Stage 3:** Widespread but . . . **Stage 4:** Ubiquitous but . . . **Stage 5:** Fully accepted.
Invariably inferior forms marked by asterisk (*). • Ratios represent frequency of prevalent forms vs. variants in current books.

shareholder; stockholder; *shareowner. All three terms refer to someone who owns stock in a corporation. The first is the most common in both AmE and BrE, the second a fairly common equivalent, and the third so much less frequent that it has become a NEEDLESS VARIANT.

Current ratio (in order of headwords): 440:62:1

shares. See **stock.**

shat. See **shit.**

shave > shaved > shaved. *Shaven* exists only as a past-participial adjective <clean-shaven face> <his shaven chin>. See IRREGULAR VERBS (B). Cf. **proved.**

LANGUAGE-CHANGE INDEX
shaven for *shaved* as a past-tense verb: Stage 1
Current ratio (*had shaved* vs. **had shaven*): 22:1

*s/he. See SEXISM (B).

sheaf. Pl. *sheaves.* See **sheaves** & PLURALS (C).

sheath, n.; **sheathe,** vb. It's an error to use *sheathe* (/sheeth/) as a noun or *sheath* (/sheeth/) as a verb—e.g.:

- "The device features a mechanism that secures the needle, point and all, inside a plastic *sheathe* [read *sheath*] at the same time that the user withdraws it from the skin." Jeff Hawkes, "Safer Needles Are Now Available," *Lancaster New Era,* 20 Feb. 1996, at A1.
- "Madame de Sevigne's friend, the Sun King, tamed his subjects by urging them to *sheath* [read *sheathe*] their swords and help with his nightshirt or hold his candle as he got undressed." Jackie Wullschlager, "Maman Dearest," *Fin. Times,* 4 Nov. 1996, at 21.

Just remember the difference between the analogous terms *breath* (n.) and *breathe* (vb.). See **breath.**

Sheath forms the plural *sheaths,* not *sheathes*—e.g.: "Don Davis makes each of the hand-tooled leather *sheathes* [read *sheaths*] that come with his knives." "The Cutting Edge," *Denver Post,* 6 Aug. 1997, at F1 (photo caption).

LANGUAGE-CHANGE INDEX
1. *sheathe* misused as noun for *sheath*: Stage 1
Current ratio (*a sheath* vs. **a sheathe*): 325:1
2. *sheath* misused as a verb for *sheathe*: Stage 4
Current ratio (*to sheathe* vs. **to sheath*): 1.1:1

sheaves, n., is the plural both of *sheaf* (= a bundle) and of *sheave* (= a pulley). Avoid **sheafs,* which has never been standard.

Current ratio: 40:1

shed > shed > shed. Avoid the erroneous **shedded*—e.g.: "Prosecutors plainly want to suggest that the missing bags contained both the knife they believe Mr. Simpson used to murder Nicole Brown Simpson and Ronald L. Goldman, and blood-soaked clothes he quickly *shedded* [read *shed*] before boarding his flight to Chicago." David Margolick, "Five Bags or Three Bags? Simpson Prosecutor Asks," *N.Y. Times,* 30 May 1995, at A14. See IRREGULAR VERBS.

LANGUAGE-CHANGE INDEX
*shedded for *shed* as past tense of *shed*: Stage 1
Current ratio (*shed leaves* vs. **shedded leaves*): 277:1

she'd better; *she better. See **better** (A).

sheikh (= [1] an Arab chieftain; or [2] a Muslim official) has been the standard spelling in AmE and BrE alike. **Sheik* is a primarily AmE variant. The word is pronounced /sheek/ or /shayk/.

Current ratio: 2:1

shelf. Pl. *shelves,* not **shelfs.* See PLURALS (C).

shellac, n. & vb., is the standard spelling. But the proper inflections for the verb are *shellacked* and *shellacking.* See -C-.

sherbet /**shәr**-bәt/ is commonly mispronounced with an intrusive *-r-:* /**shәr**-bәrt/. Because of this mispronunciation, the word is sometimes wrongly spelled **sherbert.* See PRONUNCIATION (B).

LANGUAGE-CHANGE INDEX
1. *sherbet* mispronounced /**shәr**-bәrt/: Stage 2
2. *sherbet* misspelled **sherbert*: Stage 2
Current ratio: 32:1

*sheroot. See **cheroot.**

*shily. See **shy.**

shine. As a transitive verb, it's inflected *shine > shined > shined* <he shined his shoes>. As an intransitive verb, it's inflected *shine > shone > shone* <the sun shone brightly>. Hence the standard collocations are *shone on* and *shone forth,* not **shined on* or **shined forth.*

Writers occasionally use *shined* where *shone* is the word they want—e.g.: "And neither *shined* [read *shone*] like the oft-dormant Texas running game that has produced only two 1,000-yard rushers since Earl Campbell and none since Eric Metcalf in 1987." Kirk Bohls, "Texas Starts from the Ground Up," *Austin Am.-Statesman,* 19 Aug. 1993, at E1.

Still others confuse *shone* with *shown*—e.g.:

- "As March turns into April, there are houses here where it has been weeks since the sun has *shown* [read *shone*] through the windows, so high are the snowbanks." Lorna Colquhoun, "Winter Just Won't Quit," *Union Leader* (Manchester, N.H.), 31 Mar. 1997, at A1.
- "The lights *shown* [read *shone*] bright and sparkly blue in the picture window." John Przybys, "Christmas Memories," *Las Vegas Rev.-J.,* 24 Dec. 2000, at J1.
- "I feel such a deep gratitude for the light *shown* [read *shone*] forth in you, this church." Stephen Goyer, "Tragedy, Prayer and the Power of God," *Charlotte Observer,* 13 Aug. 2001, at A11.

Rarely, a writer will slip the other way and spell *shown* as *shone*—e.g.: "Former No. 1 Pick *Shone* [read *Shown*] to Sonic Door." Headline, *Seattle Post-Intelligencer,* 1 Nov. 1996, at E6. See IRREGULAR VERBS.

LANGUAGE-CHANGE INDEX
1. *shined* misused for *shone*: Stage 2
Current ratio (*sun shone brightly* vs. **sun shined brightly*): 26:1
2. *shown* misused for *shone*: Stage 1
Current ratio (*light shone down* vs. **light shown down*): 21:1

shipowner. One word.

shirk. In the modern idiom, this word is almost exclusively a transitive verb, as in the expression that someone has *shirked* his or her duties. But the misformed phrase *shirk from* has recently emerged, probably out of confusion with *shrink from*—e.g.:

- "[Children] must have teachers who never *shirk* [read *shrink*] from challenging them to do their best." "Motivated Children Learn," *Baltimore Sun*, 18 June 1997, at A10.
- "Kennedy . . . did not *shirk* [read *shrink*] from the hard work of getting America ready for the modern age and infusing that effort with the idealism and commitment that bore fruit in Project Apollo and the Peace Corps." David M. Shribman, "When Mud Is Splattered on the History Books," *Boston Globe*, 30 Nov. 1997, at D3.
- "The film doesn't *shirk* [read *shrink*] from conveying the keen sense that in the face of so much agony, an act of compassion had as random an impact in saving a life as did the mortar shells in ending so many." James L. Graff, "The Way It Was," *Time*, 11 Dec. 1997, at 82.

LANGUAGE-CHANGE INDEX
shirk misused for *shrink*: Stage 1
Current ratio (*shrink from* vs. *shirk from*): 40:1

shish kebab. See kebab.

shit > shat > shat. So inflected. *Shitted* is nonstandard. To many people, all forms of the word are considered objectionable.

Current ratio: 5:1

*shivaree. See charivari.

*shoe-in. See shoo-in.

shone. See shine.

shoo-in (= a candidate or competitor who is sure to win), a CASUALISM deriving from the idea of "shooing" something (as a pet), is so spelled. Yet *shoe-in* is a frequent error that has spread since the mid-20th century—e.g.:

- "Besides being a *shoe-in* [read *shoo-in*] for the Hall of Fame, Woodson has been a model player and member of the community." Butch Otey, "Woodson Belongs Here," *Pitt. Post-Gaz.*, 24 May 1997, at B3.
- "Gray . . . is considered a *shoe-in* [read *shoo-in*] for re-election." Craig Timberg, "Robey Ponders Run for Executive," *Baltimore Sun*, 28 Sept. 1997, at B1.
- "This move leaves James Hoffa, son of the late You-Know-Who, as a *shoe-in* [read *shoo-in*] for the upcoming vote." "The Week That Was," *Post-Standard* (Syracuse), 22 Nov. 1997, at A6.

LANGUAGE-CHANGE INDEX
shoe-in for *shoo-in*: Stage 3
Current ratio (*shoo-in* vs. *shoe-in*): 3:1

shoot, n.; chute. The latter means (1) "an inclined channel or passage"; (2) "a waterfall or water slide"; or (3) "a parachute." *Shoot* is the standard spelling for all other senses.

Chute is sometimes misspelled *shute*—e.g.:

- "The river sucked me right down the *shute* [read *chute*] of a Class Two rapid." Heather Summerhayes Cariou, "Taking the Plunge," *Sun-Sentinel* (Ft. Lauderdale), 4 Sept. 1994, at 6.
- "I . . . could only laugh with relief that I was no longer hurtling out of control down an ice *shute* [read *chute*]." James Bedding, "Sixty Seconds of Sublime, Stupefying Terror," *Daily Telegraph*, 4 Jan. 1997, at 21.

LANGUAGE-CHANGE INDEX
shute for *chute*: Stage 1

shortcut > shortcut > shortcut. So inflected. The erroneous past-tense and past-participial *shortcutted*, which first emerged in the 1920s, sometimes appears—e.g.: "Calyx and Corolla *short-cutted* [read *shortcut*] the route by contracting a network of growers." "Flower Catalog Cuts Middleman," *Milwaukee J. Sentinel*, 14 Jan. 1996, at 12. See IRREGULAR VERBS.

LANGUAGE-CHANGE INDEX
shortcutted for the past tense *shortcut*: Stage 1

short-lived. See long-lived.

should; would. *Should* appears with the first, second, or third person to express a sense of duty <I really should go with you>; a condition <if Bess should call, tell her I'll be back at 4 o'clock>; or an expectation <they should be here in five minutes>. *Would* appears with any of the three persons to express habitual practice <every day the golfers would start lining up at 6:30 AM>; a hypothetical <she would do it if she could>; or a preference <I would choose the maroon shirt>. *Should* can take the place of *would*, however, in some idiomatic exclamations <I should think so!> <I should hope not!>. See would.

*shouldn't ought. See DOUBLE MODALS.

shouldn't wonder. This phrase should be followed by an affirmative, not a negative, construction. That is, *I shouldn't wonder if he were elected* is correct; *I shouldn't wonder if he weren't elected* is confusing.

*should of. See of (D).

*should ought. See DOUBLE MODALS.

shovel, vb., makes *shoveled* and *shoveling* in AmE, *shovelled* and *shovelling* in BrE. See SPELLING (B).

*shovelboard. See shuffleboard.

shovelful. Pl. *shovelfuls*. See PLURALS (G).

shovel pass; *shuffle pass. The words *shuffle* and *shovel* cause confusion in a term from American football: *shovel pass*, in which the ball is scooped or flipped forward underhand as one might shovel dirt or snow. Some sportswriters have wrongly written *shuffle pass*—e.g.: "'But as I'm watching, they're doing something about our game with the Bills and they show Buffalo running a play on film—(Jim) Kelly throwing

LANGUAGE-CHANGE INDEX (For the full key, see front matter pp. xxxi, l–li.)
Stage 1: Rejected. **Stage 2:** Widely shunned. **Stage 3:** Widespread but . . . **Stage 4:** Ubiquitous but . . . **Stage 5:** Fully accepted.
Invariably inferior forms marked by asterisk (*). • Ratios represent frequency of prevalent forms vs. variants in current books.

a *shuffle pass* [read *shovel pass*] to Thurman Thomas.'"
"So They Say . . . ," *Austin Am.-Statesman*, 13 Mar.
1994, at E2 (quoting Jimmy Johnson, then coach of
the Dallas Cowboys).

LANGUAGE-CHANGE INDEX
*shuffle pass for *shovel pass*: Stage 1

show > showed > shown. The standard past participle
has been *shown*, not *showed*, since the 17th century.
Hence *has shown*, not **has showed*. In the PASSIVE
VOICE, *shown* is mandatory <he was shown to have
lied>. See IRREGULAR VERBS.

shred > shredded > shredded. So inflected. Some people erroneously believe that this is an IRREGULAR VERB
that continues as *shred* in the past forms—e.g.: "Earlier
this year, Mr. Lumbers attracted national attention after
he *shred* [read *shredded*] 17,000 open edition prints
holding a retail value of about $600,000." Kim Hanson,
"Artists Urged to Change Approach to Business," *Nat'l
Post*, 29 June 1999, at C8.

LANGUAGE-CHANGE INDEX
shred misused for past-tense *shredded*: Stage 1
Current ratio (*had shredded* vs. **had shred*): 60:1

shrink > shrank > shrunk. So inflected in STANDARD
ENGLISH since the mid-19th century. In informal
usage, the past participle often displaces the simple
past, as in the movie title *Honey, I Shrunk the Kids*
(1989). But examples are hardly scarce in formal
writing—e.g.:

- "Flunkies grumbled when he forced them to recite anti-
corruption hymns, and again when he *shrunk* [read
shrank] official dinners from lavish feasts to nothing more
than one soup and four dishes." John Colmey et al., "Zhu's
Leap Forward," *Time* (Int'l ed.), 16 Mar. 1998, at 16.
- "He *shrunk* [read *shrank*] Donna Mills' big hair of the '80s
to scrunchy curls and later to a more refined shag." Barbara Thomas, "Beauty Remember: A New 'Do Can Mean
a New You," *L.A. Times*, 25 Dec. 1998, at E3.
- "Paris, with 2,115,757 [people] within the city limit
and nearly 11 million in the metropolitan area, *shrunk*
[read *shrank*] by 1.7 percent." Craig R. Whitney, "Paris Is
Shrinking," *N.Y. Times*, 7 July 1999, at A4.
- "From 1990 to 1999, aircraft quantities *shrunk* [read
shrank] by 69 percent, but their unit costs rose by 32 percent. Similarly, the quantity of ships *shrunk* [read *shrank*]
by 84 percent, but their unit costs rose by 50 percent."
Jacques S. Gansler, *Democracy's Arsenal* 31 (2011).

Some writers mistakenly use **shrinked* as a past
tense and past participle—e.g.:

- "Taxol has *shrinked* [read *shrunk*] the tumors in 25 percent to 30 percent of ovarian cancer patients and eliminated them in others." Ruth SoRelle, "Ovarian Cancer
Drug Approved," *Houston Chron.*, 30 Dec. 1992, at A1.
- "Texas country-folk chanteuse Katy Moffatt's latest album
needs to be *shrinked* [read *shrunk*] before it's played."
"Discs: Social D Sees the 'White' in Dark," *Boston Herald*,
20 Oct. 1996, Entertainment §, at 44.
- "As regards the role of communication facility, the world
has *shrinked* [read *shrunk*] and has become smaller." A.K.
Shukla, *Women Chief Ministers in Contemporary India*
204 (2007). (Note the REDUNDANCY in that sentence.)

See IRREGULAR VERBS. Cf. **proved** & **stricken (A)**.

Shrunken is exclusively a past-participial adjective <a shriveled and shrunken appearance>. Avoid
it as a verb—e.g.: "Upon return, the child found that
the room and its contents had been *shrunken* [read
shrunk]." David H. Uttal, "On the Relation Between
Play and Symbolic Thought," in *Contemporary Perspectives on Play in Early Childhood Education* 97, 106
(Olivia N. Saracho & Bernard Spodek eds., 2003).

For *shirk* misused for *shrink*, see **shirk**.

LANGUAGE-CHANGE INDEX
1. *shrunk* for simple past: Stage 3
Current ratio (*she shrank* vs. **she shrunk*): 8:1
2. **shrinked*: Stage 1
Current ratio (*he shrank* vs. **he shrunk* vs.
*he shrinked): 654:108:1
3. *shrunken* as past-participial verb
(not participial adjective): Stage 1
Current ratio (*has shrunk* vs.
*has shrunken): 31:1

shrivel, vb., makes *shriveled* and *shriveling* in AmE,
shrivelled and *shrivelling* in BrE. See SPELLING (B).

shtick (= a routine that one frequently performs) is
the standard spelling. **Schtick*, **schtik*, and **shtik*
are variants.

Current ratio (in order): 286:68:9:1

shuffleboard; **shovelboard*. The original term was
either **shove board* or **shovel board*, but the standard
term since about 1890 has been *shuffleboard*.

Current ratio: 44:1

*shuffle pass. See **shovel pass**.

*shute. See **shoot**.

shy, *adj.* Since about 1800, the comparative of this
word has been predominantly spelled *shyer*, the superlative *shyest*—in AmE and BrE alike. (*W11* gives priority to the wrong forms: **shier* and **shiest*.) *Shyly* is so
spelled—not **shily*. Cf. **sly** & **spry**.

Siamese twins. For the phrase *conjoined twins* as a
nonethnic substitute, see **conjoin**.

sibylline (= prophetic; of, relating to, or involving
fortune-telling) is often misspelled **sybilline*—and
has been so since the early 19th century, doubtless
through the influence of the etymologically distinct
word *sybarite*. E.g.: "There were Joan's often *sybilline*
[read *sibylline*] remarks—'Of course, we always do
Tibet from the north.'" Nicholas Haslam, "Joan Lady
Camrose: Family Fortunes," *Guardian*, 29 May 1997,
at 17. The word is pronounced /**sib**-ə-lin *or* -leen/.

sic. A. Generally. *Sic* (= thus, so), invariably bracketed and preferably set in italics, indicates that a
preceding word or phrase in a quoted passage is
reproduced as it appeared in the original document.
Sic at its best is intended to aid readers, who might
be confused about whether the quoter or the quoted

writer is responsible for the spelling or grammatical anomaly. This interpolation has been much on the rise: in published writings, its use has skyrocketed since the mid-20th century.

B. Benighted Uses. Some writers use *sic* meanly—with a false sense of superiority. Its use may frequently reveal more about the quoter than about the writer being quoted. For example, a recent book review of an English book contained a *sic* in its first sentence after the verb *analyse*, which was so spelled on the book's dust jacket. In AmE, of course, the preferred spelling is *analyze*; in BrE, however, the spelling *analyse* is not uncommon and certainly does not deserve a *sic*. In fact, all the quoter (or overzealous editor) demonstrated was an ignorance of British usage.

Finally, *sic* is easily overused when quoting from a source that uses many archaic forms.

sic, vb.; **sick,** vb. *Sic* means to direct a person or an animal to chase or attack someone or something. *Sick*, once the dominant form, is a variant spelling today—e.g.: "We have tried *sicking* [read *siccing*] the dog on him but it just winds up being overcome by the somnolent vapors that fill the room and falls asleep by his side." David Grimes, "Waking Up Is So Hard to Do," *Sarasota Herald-Trib.*, 7 Nov. 2002, at E1.

sick, adj.; **sickly,** adj. & adv.; ***sicklily,*** adv. While *sick* means "ill," *sickly* (adj.) means "habitually ill" <a sickly young man> or "associated with sickness" <a sickly complexion>. Because *sickly* is an adverb as well as an adjective, the term **sicklily* can justifiably be regarded as a NEEDLESS VARIANT. See ADVERBS (B).

sideswipe; ****sidewipe.*** *Sideswipe* (= to strike a glancing blow), dating from the early automotive age (1926), is the term to use. **Sidewipe*, an artificial form that appeared occasionally in the early 20th century, has no valid standing.

Current ratio: 304:1

siege (= [1] a military blockade of a fortress, city, etc., or [2] a relentless attack or persistent threat) is preferably pronounced /seej/—not /seezh/.

sight. See **site.**

sight unseen. From a strictly logical point of view, the phrase makes little sense. In practice, however, it has an accepted and useful meaning: "(of an item) bought without an inspection before the purchase." In this sense, it dates from late-19th-century AmE, but now it is used throughout the English-speaking world. See ILLOGIC (A). The phrase has been common since the early 20th century. Having arisen in late-19th-century AmE, it is now used throughout the English-speaking world.

Sometimes the phrase is erroneously written **site unseen*—e.g.: "Experts say the Web could be even more dangerous than the telephone because the medium will soon showcase virtual walk-throughs of property and homes for sale, in which purchases could be hustled *site unseen* [read *sight unseen*]." Bradley Inman, "Real Estate on the Web," *San Diego Union-Trib.*, 20 July 1997, at H3. See **site.**

LANGUAGE-CHANGE INDEX
sight unseen misspelled **site unseen*: Stage 1
Current ratio: 80:1

signal, vb., makes *signaled* and *signaling* in AmE, *signalled* and *signalling* in BrE. See SPELLING (B).

signatory, n.; ****signatary;*** ****signator.*** H.W. Fowler and George P. Krapp both recommended in the 1920s that **signatary* be adopted as the preferred noun (*FMEU1* at 534; *A Comprehensive Guide to Good English* 540 [1927]). Today, however, **signatary* is virtually never used. Most dictionaries record only *signatory*, and that form vastly predominates in modern print sources—e.g.: "And since U.N. documents are designed to be inoffensive to their *signatories*, they contain language that offers an escape hatch." Marilyn Greene, "Forums' Value: Waste of Money or Time to Bond?" *USA Today*, 30 Aug. 1995, at A11.

Signatory may be an adjective as well as a noun (Krapp considered it the only adjectival form)—e.g.: "They would also be allowed to visit commercial chemical companies in *signatory* nations." Peter Grier, "No Quick Farewell to Chemical Arms," *Christian Science Monitor*, 29 Aug. 1995, at 1.

*Signator, modeled on Latinate agent nouns, is a NEEDLESS VARIANT of *signatory*.

For those who like plain English, of course, *signer* is always available. It has been fairly common since the 17th century.

signee = a high-profile recruit, often an athlete, who is signed up by a school, employer, etc. Although the *signee* is the one who signs (active voice), the passive -EE makes sense in most contexts because the *signee* "is signed" by an organization. E.g.:

- "Prairie has Husky *signee* Dan Dickau and is expected to challenge for the Greater St. Helens League title with Evergreen of Vancouver." "Times Stars of the Week," *Seattle Times*, 10 Dec. 1996, at C5.
- "The Wildcats had five football players sign national letters of intent to attend major colleges, the most *signees* in recent memory." Celeste E. Whittaker, "Westminster Sends Five to Major-College Programs," *Atlanta J.-Const.*, 13 Feb. 1997, at D9.
- "Such is the case with South West Philly's General, the freshest *signee* to Blackground Records." Damon C. Williams, "General Leading the Charge," *Phil. Daily News*, 24 Jan. 2003, at 61.

LANGUAGE-CHANGE INDEX (For the full key, see front matter pp. xxxi, l–li.)
Stage 1: Rejected. **Stage 2:** Widely shunned. **Stage 3:** Widespread but . . . **Stage 4:** Ubiquitous but . . . **Stage 5:** Fully accepted.
Invariably inferior forms marked by asterisk (∗). • Ratios represent frequency of prevalent forms vs. variants in current books.

But in other situations—where the person who signs can in no way be said to have "been signed" by anyone—the passive construction is silly. Substitute the active agent noun or reword—e.g.:

- "After a local newspaper printed the names of the people who signed the integration petition, dozens of the *signees* [read *signers*] asked to have their names removed." Hannah Mitchell, "Threats and Triumphs: 35 Years at the NAACP," *Charlotte Observer*, 6 Dec. 2002, at V1.
- "Each morning, according to Walker, the Phone Assurance Line volunteers telephone the *signees on the list* [read *those who signed the list*]." Bryan Dye, "Service Tells of Programs for Seniors," *Press-Enterprise* (Riverside, Cal.), 29 Jan. 2003, at B2.

LANGUAGE-CHANGE INDEX
signee misused for *signer*: Stage 1

significance; signification. These should be distinguished. *Significance* = (1) a subtly or indirectly conveyed meaning; suggestiveness; the quality of implying; or (2) the quality of being important or significant. *Signification* = (1) the act of signifying, as by symbols; or (2) the purport or sense intended to be conveyed by a word or other symbol.

signor. See **seigneur.**

silex (= [1] silica-containing material, or [2] heat-resistant glass) has predominantly formed the plural *silices* since the 18th century. *Silexes* is a rarely used 20th-century variant.

Current ratio: 10:1

siliceous (= of, like, or containing silica) has been the standard spelling since the 18th century. **Silicious* is a variant.

Current ratio: 5:1

*sillabub. See **syllabub.**

sillily. See ADVERBS (B).

*silvan. See **sylvan.**

simpatico. Like *sympathy*, this word derives from the Greek word *sympátheia* (= sympathy). But *simpatico* (= mutually fond or understanding) came to English in the 19th century as a loanword from either Italian (*simpatico*) or Spanish (*simpático*)—probably the former. In good English the word has always had the *sim-* spelling. Stumbling on the pattern of *sympathy*, writers often misspell the word—e.g.:

- "In the meantime, [Sleepy] Brown lost a lot of momentum. While he may have now found a *sympatico* [read *simpatico*] partner in Big Boi's label, there's been tension with that imprint's distributor, Virgin Records." Jim Farber, "The Legend of Sleepy Ain't Hollow," *Daily News* (N.Y.), 24 Sept. 2006, Sunday Now §, at 20.
- "The Bulls, thought to be a contender with several new arrivals, notably Ben Wallace, lost six in a row and now are dealing with Wallace's blatant insurrection by insisting on wearing a headband, which the team does not allow. He and coach Scott Skiles are, for the moment, not *sympatico* [read *simpatico*]." Peter May, "East Teams Have Gone South," *Boston Globe*, 28 Nov. 2006, at E3.

- "[Iris] meets humorous, energetic Miles (Jack Black), another composer attached to a sexy actress (Shannyn Sossamon) but much more *sympatico* [read *simpatico*] with Iris, who doesn't know that she's a knockout until her new friends in L.A. tell her." Michael Sragow, " 'Holiday' Sweet," *Baltimore Sun*, 8 Dec. 2006, at C1.

Although *simpatico* is an adjective, some err by wielding it as a noun—e.g.: "Iowans this Sunday will want to see if there is some '*simpatico* [read, perhaps, *affinity*], is there a gut feeling about this person. . . . They want to feel his cloth, they want to see just how real this guy is,' [Sen. Tom] Harkin said." Lynn Sweet, "Dems 'Confused,' Obama Writes," *Chicago Sun Times*, 15 Sept. 2006, News §, at 22 (quoting Senator Tom Harkin on the subject of presidential nominee Barack Obama). That type of misusage repels sympathy.

LANGUAGE-CHANGE INDEX
1. *simpatico* misspelled **sympatico*: Stage 1
Current ratio: 14:1
2. *simpatico* used as a noun
(not as an adjective): Stage 2

simplex (= [1] a simple word, [2] archaically, a single-needle telegraph, or [3] some other rudimentary construct, esp. in mathematics) has three possible plurals. *Simplices* is the oldest and still the predominant form. *Simplexes* is a 20th-century anglicization that frequently appears. **Simplicia* is an old variant that rarely appears except in sense 1.

simplistic, a pejorative adjective meaning "oversimple, facile," became a VOGUE WORD during the 1980s and 1990s: "With adults, a word catches on and it becomes a hobbyhorse that we ride to death. Remember when early critics of President Reagan's economic plans called them 'simplistic'? It was a word seldom used until then, but once let loose in the '80s, it was on every tongue. When someone didn't like something but couldn't articulate why, he'd call it 'simplistic.' " Michael Skube, "Let's Bring Closure to Adult Slang, Which Just Isn't Cool," *Atlanta J.-Const.*, 17 June 1997, at B3.

Some misuse the word as a synonym for *simple*— that is, not as a pejorative at all. E.g.:

- "Replay is not the answer. That sounds like a nice, *simplistic* [read *simple*] fix but what the NFL really needs is to improve its officiating and have better coordination among the officials." Ira Miller, "Replay Not Answer to Many Blown Calls," *S.F. Chron.*, 6 Oct. 1995, at E3.
- " 'We try to be *simplistic* [read *simple*] in our pricing and we try to keep it *simplistic* [read *simple*] for our new releases,' he says." Diane Garrett, "What Is a New Release?" *Video Store*, 15 June 1997, at 14 (quoting Craig Wilson, a Seattle video-store owner).

*Too simplistic is a venial REDUNDANCY—e.g.: "Tom Dimmit, principal of Golden High School in the Jefferson County school district, says even that [proposal] is *too simplistic* [read *simplistic*]." Janet Simons, "The Great Homework Debate," *Rocky Mountain News* (Denver), 17 Aug. 1997, at F5.

LANGUAGE-CHANGE INDEX
simplistic in the nonpejorative sense "simple": Stage 3

simulacrum (= something made to look like something else) predominantly forms the plural *simulacra*—the homegrown plural **simulacrums* being an uncommon variant.

Current ratio: 79:1

simulcast > simulcast > simulcast. So inflected. **Simulcasted* is a frequent error—e.g.:

- "TNT . . . actually produced the game broadcast that Channel 56 *simulcasted* [read *simulcast*]." Howard Manly, "Ratings Points, Few for Style," *Boston Globe*, 16 Sept. 1997, at C7.
- "'Kickoff' will be *simulcasted* [read *simulcast*] on Channel 13 and Home Team Sports." Milton Kent, "With New Kids on NFL Block, Fox Pregame in for Showdown," *Baltimore Sun*, 4 Sept. 1998, at D2.
- "MSNBC, which *simulcasted* [read *simulcast*] much of NBC News' impeachment coverage, averaged a 1.0 rating for the day (455,000 households)." "It's Good News for Networks," *Hollywood Rptr.*, 23 Dec. 1998, at 5-1.

See -CAST, IRREGULAR VERBS & PORTMANTEAU WORDS.

LANGUAGE-CHANGE INDEX
*simulcasted for past-tense *simulcast*: Stage 1

since. This subordinating conjunction may bear a sense either of time or of logical connection. Despite the canard that the word properly relates only to time, the causal meaning has existed continuously in the English language for more than a thousand years. In modern print sources, the causal sense is almost as common as the temporal sense. Typically, *since* expresses a milder sense of causation than *because* does—e.g.:

- "In the next sentence, *since* the 'while' is not a mere connective but implies antithesis, its use is justifiable." G.H. Vallins, *Better English* 29 (4th ed. 1957).
- "*Since* the normal teaching load at L.S.U. was then 12 hours, this arrangement meant that we taught three courses in addition to our editorial work." Cleanth Brooks, "The Life and Death of an Academic Journal," in *The Art of Literary Publishing* 97 (Bill Henderson ed., 1995).
- "*Since* it's hard for the IRS to find all the taxpayers using these shelters, it wants promoters to rat them out." Janet Novack, "Client Beware," *Forbes*, 12 Aug. 2002, at 48.
- "[This] is, of course, nonsense—especially *since* some companies spend billions of dollars a year buying back shares to keep options dilution from affecting earnings per share." Justin Fox, "The Only Option," *Fortune*, 12 Aug. 2002, at 110.
- "And thousands may be unknowingly infected, *since* the virus produces symptoms in only 1 percent of victims." Geoffrey Gagnon, "Back with a Vengeance," *Newsweek*, 12 Aug. 2002, at 30.

See SUPERSTITIONS & as (A).

Be careful, though, of starting a sentence with *since* and then using a past-tense construction, which can lead to ambiguity—e.g.: "*Since* Memphis exposed Louisville's main weaknesses . . . in a humbling loss for

the Cardinals at Freedom Hall, the Cards have struggled." Mike Strange, "Selection Sunday Conference-by-Conference Breakdowns," *Sporting News*, 17 Mar. 2003, at 21. The reader wonders, at least momentarily, whether the Cards have struggled *because of* or just *after* the upset. See MISCUES (A).

*since . . . then mangles the syntax of a causal construction—e.g.: "*Since* he was mad Saturday, *then* he should get even today." Greg Johnson, "It's Expect the Unexpected at Buick Open," *Grand Rapids Press*, 10 Aug. 1997, at E1. The problem is remedied by omitting *then*. Or the writer could have deleted *Since* and changed *then* to *so*.

sine die (= without a day being fixed) is used to indicate that no date has been set for resumption. The phrase is OFFICIALESE for "indefinitely." E.g.: "The court adjourned *sine die.*" *Appointment of Iredell*, 2 U.S. (2 Dall.) 400, 400 (1790) (term notation). *Sine die* is used exclusively in reference to adjournment taken with no date set for resumption of the proceedings or meeting. A linguist complains that the phrase is "horribly mispronounced to the point where the first part sounds like the trigonometric function and the second like a synonym for 'perish.'" Mario Pei, *Words in Sheep's Clothing* 83 (1969). But /**sı**-ni **dı**-ee/ has long been established as the usual English-language pronunciation. Even so, /**see**-nay **dee**-ay/ is common in BrE.

sine qua non /**sı**-nee kwah **non** *or* sin-ay kwah **nohn**/ (L. "without which not") = an indispensable condition or thing. This LATINISM is common in both lay and legal writing and should remain unmolested by plain-English reform—e.g.:

- "Ambiguity of constitutional language and uncertainty about constitution-makers' intent is the very *sine qua non* of judicial review as it has operated in the United States." Robert G. McCloskey, *The American Supreme Court* 117–18 (1960).
- "While knowledge of the right to refuse consent is one factor to be taken into account, the government need not establish such knowledge as the *sine qua non* of an effective consent." *Schneckloth v. Bustamonte*, 412 U.S. 218, 227 (1973) (per Stewart J.).
- "The *sine qua non* of copyright is originality." *Feist Publications, Inc. v. Rural Tel. Serv. Co.*, 499 U.S. 340, 345 (1991) (per O'Connor J.).
- "Attracting crowds is not merely an unforeseen byproduct of street performing, it is its *sine qua non*: A street performer who never gathers an audience would give up the pursuit very quickly." *Berger v. City of Seattle*, 569 F.3d 1029, 1073 (9th Cir. 2009).

Cf. **but for.**

sing > sang > sung. So inflected. Although the past-participial *sung* was often used as a simple-past verb

---

LANGUAGE-CHANGE INDEX (For the full key, see front matter pp. xxxi, l–li.)
Stage 1: Rejected. **Stage 2:** Widely shunned. **Stage 3:** Widespread but . . . **Stage 4:** Ubiquitous but . . . **Stage 5:** Fully accepted.
Invariably inferior forms marked by asterisk (*). • Ratios represent frequency of prevalent forms vs. variants in current books.

through the mid-19th century, today the usage should be regarded as an error—e.g.:

- "She *sung* [read *sang*] the title track." Timothy Finn, "Williams Rocks, Sways Through Raw, Earnest Concert," *Kansas City Star*, 13 Dec. 1998, at B8.
- "But the poet's more than 1,500 songs, including many soulful lyrics that he *sung* [read *sang*] for films, also stirred the hearts of his poorer country members." "Pradeep, Hindi Poet, Songwriter," *L.A. Times*, 14 Dec. 1998, at A27.
- "Her co-star as she *sung* [read *sang*] her latest hit was a huge white python slung over her bare shoulders." Kirk Montgomery & Mark Harden, "Aiming for Triple Crown," *Denver Post*, 9 Nov. 2001, Weekend §, at 1 (referring to Britney Spears).

See IRREGULAR VERBS.

LANGUAGE-CHANGE INDEX
sung misused for simple-past *sang*: Stage 1
Current ratio (*she sang* vs. *she sung*): 22:1

single; singular. A. As Adjectives. *Single* = (1) only one in number; sole; individual <a single strand of hair at the crime scene>; or (2) unmarried <single white male seeks single female for conversation and possible romance>. *Singular* = (1) exceptional, remarkable, one-of-a-kind <a singular achievement>; or (2) odd, eccentric <singular behavior>. In the following example, the writer uses *singular* once correctly (in the sense "one-of-a-kind") and once incorrectly (for *single*) in a forced attempt at a parallel: "It was not supposed to end this way. His final story was to have an Omaha dateline, where he was carried triumphantly off the field at majestic Rosenblatt stadium, his players propping up their *singular* coach whose career was driven by a *singular* [read *single*] goal. One more win." Kirk Bohls, "The Memories Will Be Treasured Even if the Unthinkable Is True," *Austin Am.-Statesman*, 18 July 1996, at A1.

B. As Nouns: *single* for *singular*. "*Criteria* and *phenomena*, heard everywhere as *singles* [read *singulars* or *singular nouns*], are encountering stern opposition from people who take care to speak of *a graffito*, but never say *a confetto*." Robertson Cochrane, "Verbum Sap," 21 *Verbatim* 11, 11 (1994).

singlehanded, adv.; **singlehandedly.** When the word follows the verb, the preferred adverb is *singlehanded* <she did it singlehanded>. When the adverb precedes the verb, *singlehandedly* is called for <she singlehandedly brought the corporation back from the brink of bankruptcy>.

single most. This venial REDUNDANCY (*single* adds nothing to the superlative it precedes) appears most often in quoted speech, but it's also common in edited text. Rare before 1950, it has spread like a contagion since then. It arguably adds emphasis—e.g.:

- "To see or not to see? Stratford is a must for every big-bus tour in England, and probably the *single most* [read *most*] popular side-trip from London." Rick Steves, *Rick Steves' Great Britain 2008* 269 (2008).
- "Yves Saint Laurent, widely considered the *single most* [read *most*] influential fashion designer of the second half

of the 20th century, died Sunday at age 71 at his Paris home after a long illness." Wendy Donahue, "Yves Saint Laurent: 1936–2008," *Chicago Trib.*, 2 June 2008, News §, at 1.
- "[Anna] Wintour is an intimidating but somewhat elusive presence in the movie, but when she lets her bobbed hair down she reveals surprising insecurity for someone widely considered to be the *single most influential person* [read *most influential person*] in the $300 billion worldwide fashion industry." Lou Lumenick, "It's a Cold Wintour," *N.Y. Post*, 18 Jan. 2009, at 11.

single out (= to select or distinguish from others) is a PHRASAL VERB that has been common since the 17th century. Although it's simplistically literal to insist that this idiom cannot refer to more than one thing, to couple it with a word such as *many* or *several* can be jarring. E.g.: "In both reviews, she *singled out* [read *focused on*? *spotlighted*?] several dancers for praise, including Yuan Yuan Tan in 'Chi Lin' and Lorena Feijoo in Yuri Possokhov's 'Damned.'" David Wiegand, "Making It Big in New York," *S.F. Chron.*, 16 Oct. 2002, at D3. (A possible rewrite: *In each review she praised individual dancers, including Yuan Yuan Tan in "Chi Lin" and Lorena Feijoo in Yuri Possokhov's "Damned."*)

singular. See **single.**

sink > sank > sunk. The standard inflections have been fixed only since about 1880—and still there is some flux in print sources. The past participle often ousts the simple-past form from its rightful place—e.g.:

- "When the Montreal Expos announced that they had selected outfielder Errick L. Williams in the annual Rule 5 draft, it caused barely a ripple of interest. Until it *sunk* [read *sank*] in exactly who Errick L. Williams was." Larry Stone, "Montreal Picks, Plans to Trade Heisman-Toting Ricky Williams," *Seattle Times*, 15 Dec. 1998, at E4. (On the second sentence in that example, see INCOMPLETE SENTENCES.)
- "Elsewhere in Times Square, investors stand to lose the $30 million they *sunk* [read *sank*] into the magic-themed restaurant of David Copperfield, which may never open." Paul Tharp, "'Baywatch' Bistros Bet on Bucking Trend," *N.Y. Post*, 30 Dec. 1998, at 23.
- "He *sunk* [read *sank*] 15 of 23 shots (65 percent)." Marvin Pave, "Barzey Doing Bang-Up Job Off the Bentley Bench," *Boston Globe*, 10 Jan. 1999, at 12.
- "A 28-year-old man attending last year's Oktoberfest, Munich's celebration of beer-drinking and frivolity, was dancing on a table top when a woman he had never met came up behind him and *sunk* [read *sank*] her teeth into his leg." Sheryl Gay Stolberg, "Ein Bier, Bitte, but Watch Out for Biters," *N.Y. Times*, 17 Aug. 1999, at F9.

See IRREGULAR VERBS.

The past-participial form *sunken* is used exclusively now as an adjective <sunken vessel> <sunken cheeks>.

LANGUAGE-CHANGE INDEX
sunk misused for simple-past *sank*: Stage 2
Current ratio (*the boat sank* vs. *the boat sunk*): 9:1

sinus. Although the plural in Latin is *sinus* (it's a fourth-declension noun), in English *sinuses* has been the standard plural since the 18th century. To write *several sinus* is to engage in befuddling pedantry.

siphon (= a bent tube for transferring liquid) is now the standard spelling in AmE and BrE alike. **Syphon* is a variant.

Current ratio: 6:1

sirloin. So spelled—not **sirlion*. But even the correct spelling is a historical corruption of *surloin* (fr. Fr. *sur* "above" + *loin*). Folk etymologists claim that a Tudor or Stuart king "knighted" the cut of beef ("Sir Loin"), but the tale has no historical basis.

sirocco; *scirocco. Meaning "an extremely hot and blighting wind," *sirocco* has been predominantly so spelled since it was first used in the 17th century. **Scirocco* is a variant spelling that in recent years has been outnumbered in print sources by a 6-to-1 ratio.

Current ratio: 6:1

sistren. See **brethren.**

sit > sat > sat. So inflected. Except as part of the compound verb *babysit*, the mistaken form **sitted* rarely appears as a past tense (and even with *babysit* it's wrong—see **babysit**). When it does appear, **sitted* is usually a mistake for *seated*—e.g.: "Tony Janetta, a local plumber who takes a keen interest in city government, raised Mayor Betty Jo Rhea's ire a week ago when he began punctuating his remarks by pointing a pencil at council members *sitted* [read *seated*] a few feet away." "Second Reading," *Herald* (Rock Hill, S.C.), 11 Jan. 1993, at A4.

LANGUAGE-CHANGE INDEX
*sitted for *seated*: Stage 1
Current ratio (*seated* vs. **sitted*): 5,834:1

site; sight. This is yet another example of homophonic confusion. A *site* is a place or location; a *sight* is (among other things) something seen or worth seeing.

This example is an unusually close call: "The intern liked to ask the 42-year-old lawyer, who was working for the firm as an independent contractor, for advice ranging from how to maintain integrity as a lawyer to what *sights* [read *sites*?] he should visit in California." "Victims of Chance in Deadly Rampage," *N.Y. Times*, 7 July 1993, at A7. Why a close call? Because a *site* is a place, but one talks about *seeing the sights*.

This one isn't: "The *site* [read *sight*], therefore, of Fudge stepping out of the fire once more, looking disheveled and fretful and sternly surprised that the Prime Minister did not know exactly why he was there, was about the worst thing that had happened in the course of this extremely gloomy week." J.K. Rowling, *Harry Potter and the Half-Blood Prince* 10 (1st Am. ed. 2005).

The phrase *set one's sights* is a SET PHRASE with its origins in gunmanship. It means "to aim at" or "to have as one's ambition." Writers sometimes mangle the phrase, most commonly by writing *sites* for *sights*—e.g.:

- "He set his *sites* [read *sights*] on a law career early." Scott Fornek, "Inner-City Success Story Turns Tragic," *Chicago Sun-Times*, 20 Sept. 1994, at 3.
- "Miller and Laura lost their re-election bids in November and will be replaced by Republican commissioners who had set their *sites* [read *sights*] on eliminating Harrison's job." Hector Gutierrez, "Golden Manager to Get Extra Severance Pay," *Rocky Mountain News* (Denver), 25 Dec. 1996, at A36.
- "The defeat of British troops by the Mahdists in the Sudan in the 1880s encouraged Belgian king Leopold II and French expansionists to set their *sites* [read *sights*] on the Nile Valley." Richard A. Bradshaw, "Central African Republic: Nineteenth Century: Gbaya, Banda, and Zande," in 1 *Encyclopedia of African History* 398, 399 (Kevin Shillington ed., 2013).

Cf. **sight unseen.** For other errors with *site*, see **cite, n.** (B).

LANGUAGE-CHANGE INDEX
1. *sight* misused for *site*: Stage 2
2. *site* misused for *sight*: Stage 2

*sit on one's laurels. See **rest on one's laurels.**

*sitted. See **sit.**

situation has, in one of its senses, become a VOGUE WORD and is often used superfluously—e.g.: "When most Americans are reminded of *the starvation situation* [read *starvation*] in Africa, they probably recall the vivid pictures displayed on their television screens of thousands of sick and dying Somalis." "Starving Continent," *Houston Chron.*, 17 July 1993, at C12. In fact, *situation* typifies one kind of ABSTRACTITIS, as the linguist Dwight Bolinger explains: "The general favorite [abstract noun] for a number of years has been *situation*—empty enough to cover any situation. . . . The operator explains, *Yes, we know, everyone's having the same trouble—we're in a slow-talk situation*. A radio report says that *the weather does not permit a helicopter to maintain a landing situation*. Two people in a fight are in a *conflict situation*. The result of no rain is a *drought situation*. The nice thing about *situation* is that you can add it to any self-sufficient action noun: *crime situation, inflation situation, strike situation, attack situation, retreat situation*." Dwight Bolinger, *Language: The Loaded Weapon* 131 (1980). Used in this way—and even standing alone as in the television-crime-show CLICHÉ *we've got a situation here*—the word is a EUPHEMISM for *problem*.

sizable; sizeable. The preferred spellings are *sizable* in AmE, *sizeable* in BrE. See MUTE E.

skeptic is the standard spelling in AmE, *sceptic* in BrE. The BrE variant occasionally surfaces in AmE—e.g.: "How far toward *scepticism* [read *skepticism*] may students be led by their possible bewilderment?" James Sledd, "Hans Kurath on English Pronunciation," 40

LANGUAGE-CHANGE INDEX (For the full key, see front matter pp. xxxi, l–li.)
Stage 1: Rejected. **Stage 2:** Widely shunned. **Stage 3:** Widespread but . . . **Stage 4:** Ubiquitous but . . . **Stage 5:** Fully accepted.
Invariably inferior forms marked by asterisk (*). • Ratios represent frequency of prevalent forms vs. variants in current books.

Am. Speech 201, 205 (1965). Yet the AmE preference for *skeptic* has been fixed since about 1940.

skew; skewer. To *skew* is to change direction; to *skew* statistics is to make them misleading, especially by including some factor that is irrelevant to the inquiry. To *skewer* is (1) to impale, or (2) figuratively, to satirize or criticize. As a noun, a *skewer* is (1) a stick or rod that food is impaled on for cooking; or (2) something that skews something, esp. statistics or perception. *Skewer* is occasionally misused for the verb *skew*—e.g.:

- "The boycotts of Los Angeles (1984) and Moscow (1980) *skewer* [read *skew*] the results and make them irrelevant." Skip Myslenski, "Mind Your Medals," *Chicago Trib.*, 19 July 1996, Sports §, at 1.
- "Not only do they compete with their truly wild counterparts for food and habitat, their numbers *skewer* [read *skew*] population counts of migratory Canadas." Bill Burton, "Undesirables Create Fowl Condition," *Capital* (Annapolis), 13 July 1997, at C12.
- "Critics of the system say the danger of open primaries is that crossover voters will intentionally *skewer* [read *skew*] the results of the opposition party's races in hopes of nominating a candidate who can be defeated by their own party." Will Anderson, "Officials See Significant Cross-Ticket Voting in Primary," *Atlanta J.-Const.*, 15 July 2000, at G3.

As a noun in sense 2, *skewer* is used correctly here: "'What was he doing in that bathroom with that girl at five in the morning, drunk?' Bucher asked. 'Alcohol is the number one *skewer* of reality.'" Sandy Nelesen, "Tight End Emotional as Verdict Delivered," *Green Bay Press-Gaz.*, 4 Feb. 2001, at A1 (quoting Waukesha County District Attorney Paul Bucher).

LANGUAGE-CHANGE INDEX
skewer misused for *skew*: Stage 1

skewbald. See **piebald.**

skid > skidded > skidded. *Skid* is an incorrect past tense that occurs only in AmE—e.g.:

- "Deputies said Brooks' southbound car *skid* [read *skidded*] out of control on a curve." "Two Men Are Killed, Two Injured in Overnight Crashes," *Indianapolis News*, 19 Mar. 1996, at D7.
- "He then overcorrected and the car *skid* [read *skidded*] across the double yellow line into the path of a 1990 Nissan 300ZX driven by Jessica Graves." "Traffic Collision Injures 2 People," *Press-Enterprise* (Riverside, Cal.), 7 Nov. 1996, at B7.

LANGUAGE-CHANGE INDEX
skid misused for past tense *skidded*: Stage 2
Current ratio (*car skidded* vs. **car skid*): 11:1

skied is the past tense of both the verb *ski* <she skied (/skeed/) down the advanced slopes> and the verb *sky* <he skied (/skid/) his tee shot, and it went only 100 yards>. For the second of these, **skyed* is a variant spelling that might have served well for purposes of DIFFERENTIATION, but usage in golf, baseball, and basketball has now settled on *skied*. In the present participle, *ski* becomes *skiing* and *sky* becomes *skying*.

skillful. A. And *skilful*. The AmE spelling is *skillful*, the BrE *skilful*. Cf. **willful.**

B. And *skilled*. Since the 16th century, the adjective *skilled* has commonly appeared in such collocations as *skilled artisan*, *skilled engineer*, and *skilled seaman*. *Skilled* has always predominated in word frequency over *skillful*—which can refer to professionals but often appears in collocations such as *skillful diligence* and *skillful management.*

skill-less—so hyphenated—is sometimes misspelled **skilless*. E.g.: "'Regardless of what people think, it's not a *skilless* [read *skill-less*] job,' said a clerk at a west end Safeway." Mike Sadava, "No Stores to Shut if Strike Hits Safeway," *Edmonton J.*, 21 Mar. 1997, at B3. See PUNCTUATION (J).

skim milk; skimmed milk. Though the latter was the original form in the 18th century, *skim milk* is now standard AmE, outstripping the other in frequency of use by a 5-to-1 ratio. Yet in BrE, *skimmed milk* remains (just barely) the predominant form. See ADJECTIVES (F). Cf. **fine-toothed comb, iced tea** & **stained glass.**
Current ratio (World English): 3:1

skulduggery; skullduggery; *sculduggery; *scullduggery. *Skulduggery* (= trickery; unscrupulous behavior) has traditionally been the standard spelling in AmE and BrE alike. It remains so in BrE. But in the mid-1990s, about the time of the Clinton–Lewinsky scandal, AmE sources began predominantly using *skullduggery*—and this predominance has continued. It's in keeping with similar AmE spellings such as *skillful* and *willful*, for both of which BrE drops the first -*l*-. The other two are variant forms.

skull; scull. *Skull* = the head of a skeleton. *Scull* = (1) a small light racing boat for use by one, two, or four persons; (2) one of a pair of oars used with such a boat; or (3) a single oar used at the stern of a boat to propel it forward by working the oar from side to side.

SKUNKED TERMS. When a word undergoes a marked change from one use to another—a phase that might take ten years or a hundred—it's likely to be the subject of dispute. Some people (Group 1) insist on the traditional use; others (Group 2) embrace the new use, even if it originated purely as the result of WORD-SWAPPING or SLIPSHOD EXTENSION. Group 1 comprises various members of the literati, ranging from language aficionados to hard-core purists; Group 2 comprises linguistic liberals and those who don't concern themselves much with language. As time goes by, Group 1 dwindles; meanwhile, Group 2 swells (even without an increase among the linguistic liberals).

A word is most hotly disputed in the middle part of this process: any use of it is likely to distract some readers. The new use seems illiterate to Group 1; the old use seems odd to Group 2. The word has become "skunked."

Hopefully is a good case in point. Until the early 1960s, the word appeared only infrequently—almost always with the meaning "in a hopeful manner" <she watched hopefully as her son, having teed off, walked

down the first fairway>. Then a new use came into vogue, in the sense "one hopes; I hope; it is to be hoped" <hopefully, they'll get it done on time>. The Group 1 objectors were vocal (for reasons explained under **hopefully**), and for a time the word acquired a bad odor. But with time the odor has faded, so that only a few diehards continue to condemn the word and its users.

To the writer or speaker for whom credibility is important, it's a good idea to avoid distracting *any* readers or listeners—whether they're in Group 1 or Group 2. On this view, *hopefully* is now unusable: some members of Group 1 continue to stigmatize the newer meaning, and any member of Group 2 would find the old meaning peculiar.

Among the skunked terms discussed at their own entries are **data, decimate, effete, enormity, fulsome, impassionate, intrigue** & **transpire**. (Among the other candidates for inclusion are *celibate, chauvinism,* and *jejune.*) For an early discussion of skunked terms (not using this label), see Edward A. Stephenson, "Stenochoric Patterns and Avoidance Choices," 43 *Am. Speech* 309–11 (1968).

sky, vb. See **skied.**

skyjack; hijack. Today airline hijackings are still sometimes termed *skyjackings.* But *hijacking* remains the more common word. See **hijack** & PORTMANTEAU WORDS.

slacken (off). See PHRASAL VERBS.

slain. See **slay.**

slander. See **defamation.**

*****slanderize** is a NEEDLESS VARIANT of *slander,* vb. It seems to occur mostly in speech—e.g.:

- " 'If you're a politician, you should give an awful lot of thought to what you're saying, particularly when you're going to *slanderize* [read *slander*] your opponent.' " Sam Howe Verhovek, "Sticking with One of Their Men," *N.Y. Times,* 24 Oct. 1992, § 1, at 25 (quoting Alan Riley, a sports-card dealer).
- " 'In principle, we're also opposed to any form of popular culture that *slanderizes* [read *slanders*] African American women.' " Elmer Smith, "Shakur's 'Image' Problem," *Sacramento Bee,* 22 Jan. 1994, at B7 (quoting Don Rojas, an NAACP representative).

LANGUAGE-CHANGE INDEX
slanderize for the verb *slander:* Stage 1
Current ratio (*slander,* vb. vs. *slanderize*): 2,009:1

SLANG, a notoriously difficult term to define, has potentially four characteristics: (1) it is markedly lower in dignity than STANDARD ENGLISH; (2) it typically surfaces first in the language of people with low status or with a low level of responsibility; (3) it is more or less taboo in the discourse of those with high

status or a high degree of responsibility; and (4) it displaces a conventional term to protect the user either from discomfort caused by the conventional term or from the annoyance of fully elaborated expression. See Bethany K. Dumas & Jonathan Lighter, "Is Slang a Word for Linguists?" 53 *Am. Speech* 5, 14–15 (1978). A term meeting any two of those four criteria probably qualifies as slang. *Ibid.* Most slang is linguistically rebellious—purposely infra dig. It is a mistake to think of slang as being the same as DIALECT, although the two may overlap.

It can hardly be surprising that reactions to slang vary widely. The famously nonconformist Walt Whitman called slang "an attempt of common humanity to escape from bald literalism, and express itself illimitably, which in the highest walks produces poets and poems." "Slang in America" (1885), in 2 *The Collected Writings of Walt Whitman* 572, 573 (Floyd Stovall ed., 1964). Others have extolled it in hardly less exalted terms:

- "Pedants, prigs, purists, precisians, and all dry-witted and thin-witted persons naturally hate slang, because it is alive. But men of rich natures love slang. It is the wild game of language." *Educational Review* (1892) (as quoted in C.H. Ward, *What Is English?* 391–92 [1925]).
- "[A]n accustomed word sometimes seems to lose its force through familiarity, and the substitution of a picturesque or ludicrous metaphor enlivens the dullness of ordinary straightforward speech. This impulse accounts for the growth of what we call slang." Henry Bradley, *The Making of English* 174–75 (1904; repr. 1951).
- "Slang originates in the effort of ingenious individuals to make the language more pungent and picturesque—to increase the store of terse and striking words, to widen the boundaries of metaphor, and to provide a vocabulary for new shades of difference in meaning." H.L. Mencken, "The Nature of Slang" (1919), in *A Language Reader for Writers* 150, 155 (James R. Gaskin & Jack Suberman eds., 1966).

Although prescriptive linguists are often depicted as stern opponents of slang, the most prescriptive of them all saw its place: "A little racy slang may well be used in the course of one's daily talk; it sometimes expresses that which otherwise would be difficult, if not impossible, of expression." Richard Grant White, *Words and Their Uses, Past and Present* 42 (1870). A decade later, in another book, White wrote a little more expansively: "Slang has, in many cases, a pith and pungency which make it not only pardonable, but tolerable. It often expresses a feeling, if not a thought, of the passing day, which could not be so forcibly expressed—for the day—in any other phraseology." *Every-Day English* 484 (1880).

Other commentators, though, have described slang much less flatteringly:

- "Slang is to a people's language what an epidemic disease is to their bodily constitution; just as catching and just as inevitable in its run. . . . Like a disease, too, it is severest where the sanitary conditions are most neglected, where there is least culture and thought to counteract it." John F. Genung, *Outlines of Rhetoric* 32 (1893).

- "Slang words belong to a generally unauthorized vocabulary, which every speaker of English should be able to do without." H.N. MacCracken & Helen E. Sandison, *Manual of Good English* 3 (1917).
- "The man and the woman who interlard their speech with colloquialisms and slang are like the individual who picks up weeds when he might gather flowers." Frank H. Vizetelly, *How to Use English* 21 (1933).
- "[Slang is] the sluggard's way of avoiding the search for the exact, meaningful word." John C. Hodges, *Harcourt College Handbook* 197 (1967).

So where does the truth lie? Perhaps somewhere in between the two views. If the focus is on speech, then slang undoubtedly has its place in every normal person's mouth. Some will use it more than others. It grows out of a desire for novelty (freshness), experience shared with others (specialization), a sense of humor and a delight in metaphor (playfulness), an economy of words (pithiness), and sometimes a desire to be part of an in-group (secrecy).

One commentator has unscientifically suggested an archetypal pattern for the spread of much slang: from the underworld to the lower classes, then to hip middle-class youths, then to Madison Avenue and TV comedians, and then to the general population. See Frances D. Ross, "The Spread of Slang," 52 *Am. Speech* 97 (1977). She notes that "steps are sometimes skipped or reversed" with a given slang term and that "there is generally a three- to fifteen-year lag between its first appearance and its wide use or understanding." This may accurately describe how some slang develops and spreads, but certainly not all—since slang is produced by linguistic mavericks of all descriptions.

Most slang is ephemeral; it never makes its way into the general language. One linguist estimates that the "half-life of a slang expression is of the order of magnitude of one year, which implies that about one specimen in a thousand will survive for ten years." Martin Joos, *The Five Clocks* 26–27 (1961). So a slang term can make writing look noticeably dated. But some of it does survive and become standard (e.g., *fad, joke, redeye flight, rubbernecking, skyscraper, slump*).

Slang is one of the main sources by which the language is renewed. We shouldn't think of it as something new and threatening; it is old and for the most part wholesome. It has always been with us, and with our forebears from time immemorial—or should this be *for gee whiz, who knows how long*?

For more on slang, see the following books:

- *Random House Historical Dictionary of American Slang* (J.E. Lighter ed., 1994, 1997) (only two of the projected four volumes have appeared).
- Ronald M. Harmon, *Talkin' American: A Dictionary of Informal Words and Expressions* (1995).
- John Ayto, *The Oxford Dictionary of Slang* (1998).
- Richard A. Spears, *NTC's Dictionary of American Slang and Colloquial Expressions* (3d ed. 2000).
- *A Dictionary of Slang and Unconventional English* (Eric Partridge & Paul Beal eds., 8th ed. 2002).

- Robert L. Chapman et al., *Dictionary of American Slang* (4th ed. 2007).

SLASH. See PUNCTUATION (Q).

slay > slew > slain. A. Generally. *Slay* = (1) to kill; or (2) to overwhelm, often with delight. In sense 1, the verb has gradually been disappearing from common use except in poetry, headlines, and references to crime victims—e.g., *her son was slain by a stranger in 2002.* Even that usage is unusual; the more usual word would be *killed* or *murdered.*

But as a past-participial adjective, *slain* has few if any suitable alternatives—e.g.: "He was the host at a Rose Garden ceremony in which he signed into law bills to fight legal drugs, keep track of sex offenders and provide college funds for the children of *slain police officers.*" Adam Nagourney, "Clinton in North, Dole in South, Study for Debate," *N.Y. Times,* 4 Oct. 1996, at A1. Many would use a wordier phrase such as *police officers killed in the line of duty.*

B. *Slayed for slew. Although *slew* is the preferred past-tense form in both senses, the variant *slayed sometimes appears—e.g.:

- "As the candidate who politically *slayed* [read *slew*] the powerful Phillips in a strongly Democratic district, she has been a magnet for media attention." Richard D. Walton, "Indiana's Freshmen Hope to Offer Fresh Perspective," *Indianapolis Star,* 5 Jan. 1995, at A1.
- "They named and *slayed* [read *slew*] the various dragons of political correctness." James Ledbetter, "Press Clips," *Village Voice,* 21 May 1996, at 25.
- "Simon *slayed* [read *slew*] the Wildcats at the free-throw line, where he was 14 of 17." Timothy W. Smith, "Simon and Bibby: Ice Under Pressure," *N.Y. Times,* 1 Apr. 1997, at B17.

This nonstandard variant also commonly appears in sense 2—e.g.:

- "Andy Kindler's comedic style caught his audiences off-guard, and *slayed* [read *slew*] them, in 1996." Jim Slotek, "They Got a Licence for Laughs," *Toronto Sun,* 23 Dec. 1996, Entertainment §, at 44.
- "Fifty times, Albert Brooks *slayed* [read *slew*] the audience with his comedy routines on Johnny Carson's 'Tonight Show.'" Virginia Rohan, "Mother Trouble," *Record* (N.J.), 26 Dec. 1996, Your Time §, at Y1.
- "The Weeknd, who *slayed* [read *slew*] the stage with a flame-throwing rendition of Can't Feel My Face, will perform at Tampa's Amalie Arena on Dec. 17." Jay Cridlin, "Your VMAs Hangover Cure," *Tampa Bay Times,* 2 Sept. 2015, at 21.

See IRREGULAR VERBS.

LANGUAGE-CHANGE INDEX
*slayed for *slew*: Stage 1
Current ratio (*slew* vs. *slayed): 78:1

sleight of hand. This term—meaning "a hand-trick or other display of dexterity"—is the native English equivalent of *legerdemain.* *Sleight* (/slɪt/) derives from the Middle English word *sleahthe* (= wisdom, cleverness). Although in the early 14th century it was recorded as *slight,* the word we now know by that spelling is a quite different Anglo-Saxon word. Because the two words are homophones, writing *slight of hand* instead of *sleight of hand* has long been a fairly common error—e.g.:

- "There is no Joycean word-play to puzzle over; no ingenuous narrative *slight* [read *sleight*] of hand." Merle Rubin, "New Yorker Writer's Miniature Novels," *Christian Science Monitor*, 15 Jan. 1997, at 15. (If sleight of hand was involved, the intended word must have been *ingenious*—not *ingenuous*. See **ingenious**.)
- "Some choose not to practice the magick of witchcraft—spelled differently to distinguish it from the *slight* [read *sleight*] of hand tricks magicians use." Susan Seibel, "Witches Brew Some Magic: Psychic-Pagan Fair Raises Money for Children's Hospital," *Pitt. Post-Gaz.*, 2 May 2001, at W1.
- "Budgets were only 'balanced' with the use of one-time revenues from land sales, diversions of sewer and water funds (almost $100 million) and other budget *slights* [read *sleights*] of hand." Mary Ball & Scott Barnett, "Solving San Diego's Fiscal Problems," *San Diego Union-Trib.*, 6 May 2001, at G3.

LANGUAGE-CHANGE INDEX
slight of hand for *sleight of hand*: Stage 2
Current ratio (*sleight of hand* vs. *slight of hand*): 13:1

slew, n. (= a large number), which most commonly appears in the phrase *whole slew*, is sometimes miswritten *slough* (= a stagnant bog—pronounced /sloo/)—e.g.:

- "Watch for a whole *slough* [read *slew*] of indictments to be issued today stemming from a major cargo theft ring involving baggage handlers at O'Hare Airport." Michael Sneed, "Tipsville," *Chicago Sun-Times*, 22 May 1992, at 2.
- "Naturally, this has stimulated the introduction of a whole *slough* [read *slew*] of books." Claude F. Whitmyer, "Internet: An Expensive, Popular Way to Communicate," *The Office*, Oct. 1993, at 22.
- "There are winter onions, Egyptian onions and a whole *slough* [read *slew*] of other types grown only by onion aficionados." David Robson, "The Onion Has Its Day in the Sun," *State J.-Register* (Springfield, Ill.), 28 Jan. 1995, at 13.

Sometimes, too, it's wrongly made *slue* (= an act of rotating or veering)—e.g.:

- "'GoldenEye' . . . has one insane villain, two beautiful women (one good, one bad) and a *slue* [read *slew*] of high-tech gadgets." Jonathan Tucker, "Brosnan's Bond Makes 'GoldenEye' a Hit," *San Antonio Express-News*, 9 Dec. 1995.
- "Leo's Grill features a Spanish-style wooden facade surrounded by a *slue* [read *slew*] of tall trees." Barbara Rivera, "Family Grill Near Port Offers Home Cookin'," *Tulsa Trib. & Tulsa World*, 22 Oct. 1997, at 4.
- "Many companies and organizations have decided having a *slue* [read *slew*] of managers or directors wasn't good enough and have handed out vice president titles like they were Ad Sheets on a downtown street corner." "Government Needs Change," *Iowa City Press-Citizen*, 7 July 2005, at A7.

For still further confusions between these words, see **slough** & **slue**.

LANGUAGE-CHANGE INDEX
1. *slough* misused for *slew*: Stage 1
Current ratio (*whole slew* vs. *whole slough*): 89:1
2. *slue* misused for *slew*: Stage 1
Current ratio (*a slew of* vs. *a slue of*): 256:1

slew, vb. See **slay.**

slicked-back hair. That's the phrase, not *slicked-backed hair*—e.g.: "Wearing *slicked-backed* [read *slicked-back*] hair, a series of sleek evening outfits, and a raffish smile, he's more than a dancer." Frank Rich, *Hot Seat* 59 (1998).

LANGUAGE-CHANGE INDEX
slicked-backed for *slicked-back*: Stage 1

slide > slid > slid. So inflected. A few older grammar books listed *slidden* as an alternative or even a preferred past-participial form. See, e.g., O.M. Hanna & Joseph S. Taylor, *1600 Drill Exercises in Corrective English* 71 (rev. ed. 1936) (listing *slidden* before *slid*). Today most dictionaries don't even list *slidden*, which occurred mostly in the 18th and 19th centuries, but never as commonly as the past-participial *slid*. It still occasionally appears, especially as a past-participial adjective (and most frequently in the adjective *backslidden*)—e.g.: "He's been a devout Pentecostal Christian and a *back-slidden* agnostic and suffered his share of chronic depression and nervous breakdowns." John La Briola, "Devil in the Details," *Denver Westword*, 26 July 2001. As a past-participial verb, the nonstandard *slidden* is somewhat more common in BrE—e.g.: "I don't think there was physical space for the gun even to have *slidden* beneath the car." John Macleod, "The Death of Willie McRae," *Herald* (Glasgow), 28 Mar. 1995, at 10. It's not recommended in AmE.

The past-tense form *slided* is standard only in the compound *slip-slided*—e.g.: "For most of the day, [Ruston] Boucher had *slip-slided* through other subdivisions and sauntered up to a retirement home." Tim Bryant & Stephen Deere, "No Street Slick Enough to Keep Florists from Getting Valentine's Flowers to You," *St. Louis Post-Dispatch*, 14 Feb. 2007, at A1. In other constructions, it's erroneous—e.g.:

- "The puck *slided* [read *slid*] down the ice." Steven Bruss, "Pro Hockey," *Atlanta J.-Const.*, 17 Feb. 1996, at G6.
- "Over the years, the [National Baptist Convention] has changed and matured, [Jesse Jackson] added, claiming the laws of the nation have *slided* [read *slid*] during that time." Harold McNeil, "Baptist Gathering Hears Jackson Call for Return to Activism," *Buffalo News*, 7 Aug. 1997, at C5.
- "They helped Bezanson put on a life jacket after he crawled onto the truck's hood, then got him into a basket that was *slided* [read *slid*] across the ladder to land." "N.H. Divers Rescue Driver from Icy River," *Seattle Times*, 19 Apr. 2001, at A2.

LANGUAGE-CHANGE INDEX (For the full key, see front matter pp. xxxi, l–li.)
Stage 1: Rejected. **Stage 2:** Widely shunned. **Stage 3:** Widespread but . . . **Stage 4:** Ubiquitous but . . . **Stage 5:** Fully accepted.
Invariably inferior forms marked by asterisk (*). • Ratios represent frequency of prevalent forms vs. variants in current books.

See IRREGULAR VERBS.

LANGUAGE-CHANGE INDEX
*slided for slid: Stage 1
Current ratio (had slid vs. *had slided): 225:1

*slier; *sliest; *slily. See **sly.**

*slight of hand. See **sleight of hand.**

sling > slung > slung. So inflected in AmE and BrE alike. As a past-tense form, *slang* is dialectal (see DIALECT). As a past participle meaning "placed in a sling," *slinged* can be convenient, but it can also be startlingly ambiguous—e.g.: "Pediatric experts such as Dr. William Sears claim *slinged* babies are more alert." Sue Gleiter, "Baby on Board: Sling Allows Moms to Enjoy Hands-Off Freedom," *Post-Standard* (Syracuse), 9 Sept. 2007, at I4. Outside that limited sense, the NONWORD *slinged* is an infrequent error—e.g.:

- "Now before you make the Irish-restaurant-is-an-oxymoron joke, Wilcox says his partner, Robert Lionette—who formerly *slinged* [read *slung*] haute hash at the tony Oyster Bar in Oak Bluffs—is going to update some of the old recipes from Old Sod." Gayle Fee & Laura Raposa, "Inside Track," *Boston Herald*, 29 Apr. 1996, at 8.
- "But [Ramon] Ortiz *slinged* [read *slung*] his way through eight innings and 92 pitches, holding the Yankees to that one run on seven hits." LaVelle E. Neal III, "Putting an End to the Party," *Star Trib.* (Minneapolis), 12 Apr. 2007, at C1.
- "Starting quarterback Anthony Morelli threw the game's only interception and was sacked twice, but he said it was no big deal. 'I just went out and *slinged* [read *slung*] it around a little bit,' he said." Bernard Fernandez, "Size Could Pay Off for Lions," *Phil. Daily News*, 23 Apr. 2007, Sports §, at 107.

See IRREGULAR VERBS.

LANGUAGE-CHANGE INDEX
1. slang for slung as past tense of sling: Stage 1
Current ratio (had slung vs. *had slang): 120:1
2. *slinged for slung as past tense of sling: Stage 1
Current ratio (slung vs. *slinged): 1,786:1

slingshoot > slingshot > slingshot. Although the word is most often a noun, the corresponding verb is so inflected. The erroneous past-tense and past-participial form *slingshooted* sometimes appears—e.g.: "It also *sling-shooted* [read *slingshot*] Schreyer into this week's U.S. Open." Jim Benson, "Hot Putter Fuels Big Comeback," *Pantagraph* (Bloomington, Ill.), 9 June 1997, at B1. See IRREGULAR VERBS.

LANGUAGE-CHANGE INDEX
*slingshooted for past-tense slingshot: Stage 1

slink > slunk > slunk. So inflected. **Slank* and **slinked* are nonstandard variants in the past tense and past participle—e.g.:

- "The advent of the riders bruited by scurvid curs that howled woundedly and *slank* [read *slunk*] among the crumbling walls." Cormac McCarthy, *Blood Meridian, Or, The Evening Redness in the West* 97 (1992). (On the fragmentary nature of that sentence, see INCOMPLETE SENTENCES.)

- "As the minutes ticked away and it dawned on him that he wouldn't be getting any money, he *slinked* [read *slunk*] toward the door and—well—stole away." Robert Kilborn & Lance Carden, "Money in the Bank," *Christian Science Monitor*, 18 Nov. 1998, at 20.
- "The boys slid off the table and *slinked* [read *slunk*] away." Pat Shellenbarger, "Flair," *Grand Rapids Press*, 13 Dec. 1998, at J1.
- "He rolled the flag into a ball and *slinked* [read *slunk*] off the track. His bronze medal was gone. [Wallace] Spearmon had been DQd for weaving out of his lane too many times." Mike Downey, "Runaway Reign," *Chicago Trib.*, 21 Aug. 2008, Sports §, at 1.

Meanwhile, the erroneous form **slunked* sometimes appears as a past-tense verb or participle—e.g.:

- "They grew impatient when he *slunked* [read *slunk*] along like the rest of the team and finally dumped him and his $800,000 yearly salary." Dan Raley, "Smitten with Whiten," *Seattle Post-Intelligencer*, 6 Sept. 1996, at E1.
- "Party leaders would have roared their disapproval and Bysiewicz and Lecce would have *slunked* [read *slunk*] off, licking their wounds." Michele Jacklin, "Primary Candidates Are Willing to Roll the Dice," *Hartford Courant*, 26 Aug. 1998, at A13.
- "[Bonnie] Murchison, standing with two of her friends, said she had a boyfriend, which wasn't exactly the truth. The boy *slunked* [read *slunk*] away." Francis X. Donnelly, "Teens Decry Fairlane's New Curfew," *Detroit News*, 3 May 2004, at B1.

See IRREGULAR VERBS.

LANGUAGE-CHANGE INDEX
1. *slank for slunk as past tense of slink: Stage 1
Current ratio (slunk away vs. *slank away): 198:1
2. *slinked for slunk as past tense of slink: Stage 2
Current ratio (slunk off vs. *slinked off): 9:1
3. *slunked for slunk as past tense of slink: Stage 1
Current ratio (slunk out vs. *slunked out): 245:1

SLIPSHOD EXTENSION. Several entries in this dictionary refer to this type of misusage. "Slipshod extension" denotes the mistaken stretching of a word beyond its accepted meanings, the mistake lying in a misunderstanding of the true sense. It occurs most often, explained H.W. Fowler, "when some accident gives currency among the uneducated to words of learned origin, and the more if they are isolated or have few relatives in the vernacular" (*FMEU1* at 540). Today, one might rightly accuse not only the uneducated but also the educated of the linguistic distortion of *literally* and *protagonist*, to name but two of many possible examples. See **literally** & **protagonist.** For other examples, see **ad hoc, alibi, compound, dilemma, egoism, factor, hopefully, medicine, veracity, verbal, viable** & **vitiate.**

slither, vb.; **sliver.** *Slither* = to slide over a surface with twisting or side-to-side motions, as a snake does <we slithered down the muddy slope>. *Sliver* = a thin piece or shard of something that has been cut or broken off <a sliver of cheese> <not a sliver of evidence>. The most common error with these words is to misuse *slither* for *sliver*—e.g.: "There's not a *slither* [read *sliver*] of difference between Rudd and

Gillard on policy." Terry McCrann, "Labor in Crisis," *Advertiser* (Aus.), 23 Feb. 2012, at 6. The opposite error also occurs—e.g.: "For the connoisseur like Joe there's Boa, his constrictor, *slivering* [read *slithering*] down the banisters, her tongue darting expectantly for the kiss he always gives her." Sue Arnold, "Why You Should Never Give a Dog a Clone," *Independent*, 6 Aug. 2005, at 38.

sliver. See **slither.**

slough. A. Pronunciation. Depending on the meaning, this word can rhyme with *through, bough,* or *rough.*

As a noun, *slough* /sloo/ = (1) a muddy bog; or (2) a place ridden with immorality. (*Slew* and *slue,* which are frequent misspellings of this word, are actually different words. See **slew** & **slue.**)

As a verb, *slough* is pronounced /sləf/ (see (B)).

The pronunciation /slow/ is a chiefly BrE variant in the noun senses.

B. Misspelled *sluff* as a Verb. *Slough off* (= [1] to shed an outer skin; or [2] to cast off, discard) is sometimes incorrectly written **sluff off* (a phonetic spelling)—e.g.: "As he delves deeper into a lousy world in which people steal children for money, he expands, *sluffs* [read *sloughs*] off his lethargy and assumes the role of avenger." Chris Meehan, "Child's Kidnapping for Baby Broker Triggers Tale of Love and Vengeance," *Grand Rapids Press*, 12 Jan. 1997, at J7.

As a SLANG term, *sluff* means "to be lazy; shirk responsibilities" <Johnny, have you been sluffing again?>. In this sense the phonetic spelling is passable. See Robert L. Chapman, *American Slang* 406 (1987). Although Chapman cites *sluff* without *off,* more often the PHRASAL VERB **sluff off* is used <Jaynie, have you been sluffing off again?>.

LANGUAGE-CHANGE INDEX
slough off (the phrasal verb) misspelled
*sluff off: Stage 1
Current ratio: 68:1

slow has long been treated as an immediate adverb, i.e., one not requiring the *-ly* suffix. It is ill-informed pedantry to insist that *slow* can be only an adjective. Though *slowly* is the slightly more common adverb— and has been since the 17th century—*slow* is often just as good in the adverbial sense. In deciding whether to use *slow* or *slowly* as the adverb, let rhythm and euphony be your guides. For example, Coleridge wrote, in "The Complaint of a Forsaken Indian Woman": "I'll follow you across the snow, / You travel heavily and *slow.*" The usage is common today—e.g.:

- "While his proposal doubtless goes too *slow* for some legislative leaders, he is wise to steer a moderate tax-cutting course." "State of the Presidency," *Post & Courier* (Charleston, S.C.), 26 Jan. 1995, at A10.

- "Lincoln's remote location made development move *slow.*" Mike McCarthy, "Lincoln Project Would Offer Shelters to High-Tech Crowd," *Bus. J.—Sacramento,* 15 May 1995, § 1, at 2.
- "I have Windows 95, but now I'm running out of memory, plus it runs too *slow* at times." "Upgrading Makes Sense," *Tampa Trib.,* 5 May 1997, at 4.

You'll undoubtedly prefer *slowly* in most situations, but occasionally *slow* will sound better. As the mystery writer Rex Stout once quipped, "Not only do I use and approve of the idiom 'Go slow,' but if I find myself with people who do not, I leave quick" (as quoted in Norman Lewis, *Better English* 69 [rev. ed. 1961]). Cf. **quick (A).**

LANGUAGE-CHANGE INDEX
go slow (with *slow* in adverbial sense): Stage 5
Current ratio (*go slow* vs. *go slowly*): 1.1:1

sludge; slush; slurry. These messy-sounding words, perhaps onomatopoeic, have pretty well-defined contours. But all could be sloshed around in. *Sludge* = (1) thick sediment or mud at the bottom of a liquid; (2) the solid matter that is left after industrial waste or sewage has been cleaned; or (3) thick dirty oil within an engine or similar machinery. *Slush* = (1) partly melted snow; (2) soft mud; a marshy mire; (3) greasy refuse left after frying; (4) trashy, pollyannish writing; or (5) unsolicited submissions for publication in a magazine. *Slurry* = a watery mixture of mud, coal, animal waste, plaster of Paris, or similar insoluble materials.

slue, vb. (= to swing or slide centrifugally), is the standard spelling. E.g.: "At one point we *slued* so sharply toward the edge that I inadvertently clutched at the Nepali interloper sitting next to me." Karen Swenson, "On the Road to Tibet," *Wall Street J.,* 16 Sept. 1994, at A8. *Slew,* however, is a variant form particularly common in BrE. But especially because that term has other meanings, the language would be well served if everyone followed the majority of American dictionaries and stuck to *slue* for this sense. Cf. **slew** & **slough.**

*sluff off. See **slough (B).**

slumberous; *slumbrous. Although **slumbrous* is older, *slumberous* has become the standard form in both AmE and BrE. The shift occurred in the early 19th century. **Slumbrous* occurs mostly in BrE.

Current ratio: 2:1

slurry. See **sludge.**

slush. See **sludge.**

sly (= wily, cunning, sneaky) preferably makes *slyer, slyest,* and *slyly*—whether in AmE or BrE. Some writers misguidedly use the variant spellings **slier, *sliest,* and **slily*—e.g.:

LANGUAGE-CHANGE INDEX (For the full key, see front matter pp. xxxi, l–li.)
Stage 1: Rejected. **Stage 2:** Widely shunned. **Stage 3:** Widespread but . . . **Stage 4:** Ubiquitous but . . . **Stage 5:** Fully accepted.
Invariably inferior forms marked by asterisk (*). • Ratios represent frequency of prevalent forms vs. variants in current books.

- "The land has been creeping *slily* [read *slyly*] out to sea for the last twenty centuries or so." Steven Moore, "The Beast in the Vatican," *Wash. Post*, 15 Sept. 1996, Book World §, at 4.
- "This is not a Michael Jordan-light-up-a-planet smile but something *slier* [read *slyer*], more subtle, the expression of a man who has a private joke." Michael Farber, "Cat Quick," *Sports Illustrated*, 2 June 1997, at 68.
- "Two years after his song 'Accidental Racist' sparked a firestorm he said was the result of being misunderstood, Paisley—one of Nashville's *sliest* [read *slyest*], smartest songwriters—is taking extra care to present his positions clearly." Mikael Wood, "Paisley Follows Simpler Pattern," *L.A. Times*, 8 June 2015, Calendar §, at 1.

Cf. **shy** & **spry**.

> Current ratio (*slyest* vs. *sliest): 8:1
> Current ratio (*slyly* vs. *slily): 12:1

smell > smelled > smelled. So inflected today in AmE and BrE alike. *Smelt* is now an exclusively BrE variant.

smite > smote > smitten. So inflected in AmE and BrE alike. This verb almost always appears in biblical allusions—almost never in purely secular contexts. So when it does appear in a secular setting, it can seem almost facetious—e.g.: "American and British readiness to *smite* Iraq has forced Mr. Hussein to listen, and he is now beginning to negotiate some of the terms for opening up suspected weapons sites to United Nations inspection, senior American, French and British officials say." "Putting Steel in Democracy to Scare the Iraqis," *N.Y. Times*, 11 Feb. 1998, at A1, A6. See IRREGULAR VERBS.

Smithsonian Institution. This is the name—not **Smithsonian Institute*.

smoky, adj., is so spelled—not *smokey. But the lovable mascot's name is *Smokey Bear* (or *Smokey the Bear*).

smolder; smoulder. *Smolder* (= to burn slowly without flame) is the standard spelling in AmE, *smoulder* in BrE. The shift in American spelling (from *smoulder* to *smolder*) occurred in the late 1930s.

smooth, vb.; *smoothen. The latter is a NEEDLESS VARIANT—e.g.: "But eventually, Dr. Toaff insists, the knobs and bulges will *smoothen* [read *smooth*] out." Natalie Angier, "One Woman's Decision Against a Hysterectomy," *N.Y. Times*, 18 Feb. 1997, at C1.

The verb is often misspelled *smoothe, doubtless on the analogy of *soothe* and *teethe*—e.g.: "They are also using a polishing process that *smoothes* [read *smooths*] the metal that sits above the circuitry." Benjamin Fulford, "Another Dimension," *Forbes*, 22 July 2002, at 173. This misspelling may also be influenced by the past-tense form: *smoothed*.

LANGUAGE-CHANGE INDEX
1. *smoothe for the verb *smooth*: Stage 1
Current ratio (*to smooth* vs. *to smoothe): 151:1
2. *smoothen for the verb *smooth*: Stage 1
Current ratio (*smoothed* vs. *smoothened): 81:1

smoulder. See **smolder**.

snaky (= [1] teeming with snakes, or [2] resembling a snake) is the standard spelling in World English—*snakey being an uncommon variant.

Current ratio: 20:1

sneak > sneaked > sneaked. So inflected. See **snuck**.

snivel, vb., makes *sniveled* and *sniveling* in AmE, *snivelled* and *snivelling* in BrE. See SPELLING (B).

snoot. In the April 2001 issue of *Harper's*, the late David Foster Wallace introduced his family's acronym for *syntax nudnik of our time* or, alternatively, *Sprachgefühl necessitates our ongoing tendance*. (A fuller version of Wallace's influential essay, purportedly a review essay of the first edition of this book, appears in Wallace's *Consider the Lobster* [2006], at pp. 66–127, under the title "Authority and American Usage.") The word denotes a well-informed language-lover and word connoisseur. It aptly captures the linguistic snootiness of those who weigh their words, value verbal nuances, resist the societal tendency to blur useful distinctions, reject newfangled usages without strong redeeming qualities, and concern themselves with linguistic tradition and continuity.

Here's what Wallace himself had to say about the subject:

> There are lots of epithets for people like this—Grammar Nazis, Usage Nerds, Syntax Snobs, the Language Police. The term I was raised with is SNOOT. The word might be slightly self-mocking, but those other terms are outright dysphemisms. A SNOOT can be defined as somebody who knows what *dysphemism* means and doesn't mind letting you know it. . . . A fellow SNOOT I know likes to say that listening to most people's English feels like watching somebody use a Stradivarius to pound nails.
>
> Wallace, "Tense Present," *Harper's*, Apr. 2001, at 39, 41.

As he suggested, the language needs a neutral-to-positive word for this idea, and Wallace's deserves a permanent place in the language.

A well-executed usage book systematically records the linguistic predilections of snoots at a given time, as well as the reasons underlying those predilections. The great snoots of the 18th century were Samuel Johnson and Robert Lowth; of the 19th, Lindley Murray and Richard Grant White; of the 20th, H.W. Fowler and Theodore M. Bernstein. Snoots have gotten better with time because, with the constant progress of scholarship and technology, they have become better-informed about the actual state of the language. Less guesswork is involved.

As in the quotation above, Wallace capitalized *snoot*. Actually, he used small caps. But his own capitalization practices throughout the essay were idiosyncratic, and the better approach—if the word is going to win its way—is surely to treat it more like *radar* or *scuba* and make it lowercase. Time and snoots will tell.

The corresponding abstract noun is *snootitude*.

snuck is a nonstandard past tense and past participle of *sneak* common in American speech and writing. The standard past form *sneaked* has predominated in AmE and BrE alike for hundreds of years. The form *snuck* sneaked into the language about 1915 and began spreading wildly about 1970. Surprisingly, **snuck* appears almost as often as *sneaked* in modern print sources—e.g.:

- "They include all that weird wording *snuck* [read *sneaked*] into bills to assure that the gravy train stops at your station." Steve Tidrick, "The Budget Inferno," *New Republic*, 29 May 1995, at 17. (On the misuse of *assure* for *ensure* in that example, see **assure.**)
- "He says he *snuck* [read *sneaked*] to female friends' homes to play with their dolls, since his mother, a Southern Baptist, answered with a big N-O to his request for a 'Solo in the Spotlight' Barbie, and his father 'flipped out.'" Taylor Ward, "Ken—and His Barbies," *St. Petersburg Times*, 6 Dec. 1996, Time Out §, at 4.
- "The next day, Gowdy and I *snuck* [read *sneaked*] off camera to a mesquite thicket where birds were flying thick and fast." Bob Whitaker, "Fishy Stories of Wildlife Conquests, Comedy," *Ariz. Republic*, 29 May 1997, Out There §, at 1.
- "I *snuck* [read *sneaked*] behind the scenes at yesterday's party preparations and lived a day in the life of the A-list." Julie Hannah, "Getting Ready for a Night on the Styles," *Daily Record* (Glasgow), 4 Sept. 2015, at 22.

See DIALECT. See also IRREGULAR VERBS (D).

For a similar word that in STANDARD ENGLISH is a regular verb (*drag > dragged > dragged*) but has a nonstandard past form (**drug*), see **drag.**

One odd point about this dialectal past-tense form is that it couldn't have been influenced by analogy from some other verb ending in *-eak* or *-eek*, most of which are weak verbs (e.g., *creak, freak, leak, peek, reek, streak*). Even the IRREGULAR VERBS don't end in *-uck* (e.g., *seek–sought, break–broke–broken*).

LANGUAGE-CHANGE INDEX
*snuck for *sneaked*: Stage 4
Current ratio (*sneaked* vs. **snuck*): 1.3:1

so. A. Beginning Sentences with. Like *And* and *But, So* is a good word for beginning a sentence (no comma following). Each of these three is the informal equivalent of a heavier and longer conjunctive adverb (*Additionally, However,* and *Consequently* or *Therefore*). Rhetoric, not grammar, is what counts here. The shorter word affords a brisker pace—e.g.:

- "After more than tripling the magazine's newsstand sales, she was hired by Hearst Magazines to start the U.S. version of *Marie Claire . . . .* The 1994 start-up became the most successful in the company's history. *So* she was picked to succeed Brown." Janny Scott, "New Cosmo Editor's Life Is a Page Right Out of the Magazine," *San Diego Union-Trib.*, 1 June 1997, at D5.
- "The world they've been living in has been broken, says he. *So* they cling to football: an old ritual to get them through New Year's Day." William Green, "The Sky Was Falling," *Forbes*, 2 June 1997, at 208.

See **and** (A) & **but** (A).

Of course, in STANDARD ENGLISH the sentence-starting *so* should follow from what has been said

before. It should introduce a conclusion. If it's a message-starting *so*—for example, the first word of an e-mail or text message—it's nothing but a speech tic reduced to writing. And it's a tic that will annoy readers who are traditionalists, especially those born before 1980 or so. The message-starting *so* is a bit of trendy, youthful SLANG.

B. For *very*. In traditional usage, *so* is a comparative adverb <so cold I could die> <so cumbersome that I don't want it> <he's not so tall as she is>. Gradually, speakers and writers began dropping the final part of the comparison <he's so tall!> <she's so smart> <it's so cold>. Essentially, *so* became an intensifier without any necessary sense of comparison—much as *that* is now doing. (See **that** (E).) This use of *so* for *very* remains a CASUALISM.

C. **So therefore*. Coupling *so* with *therefore* typically results in a REDUNDANCY—e.g.:

- "*So therefore* [read *Therefore,*] wise British businesses should carry on with the notion of sterling as a generally strong currency in the medium term." Hamish McRae, "What Will Happen to the Pound Outside the Eurozone?" *Independent*, 23 Jan. 2003, at 22.
- "*So, therefore,* [read *So*] with all the opportunity for armchair psychoanalyzing, getting to know the real Mr. Archer should be a slam dunk, right?" Carol Herman, "Peer Disgraced but Managing to Thrill, Still," *Wash. Times*, 2 Feb. 2003, at B6.

D. The Construction *so . . . as*. See **as . . . as** (A).

sobriquet; **soubriquet*. *Sobriquet* (/**soh**-bri-kay/) is the standard spelling of this term for an assumed name, a nickname, or an epithet. **Soubriquet* is a variant form that has never predominated and has been relatively uncommon since about 1900.

Current ratio: 6:1

social. A. And *societal*; **societary*. Although the two main words overlap to some degree, they are distinguishable. *Social* = (1) living in companies or organized communities <man is a social animal>; (2) concerned with the mutual relations of (classes of) human beings <the social compact>; or (3) of or in or toward society <social intercourse> (*COD*).

Societal has replaced **societary* (now merely a NEEDLESS VARIANT) in the sense "of, relating to, or dealing with society." E.g.:

- "Teenagers are more likely to have unprotected sex when they have been drinking. And that can lead to other *societal* concerns." Ralph Hingson, "Tough Laws, Enforcement Slow Teenage Drinking," *Boston Globe*, 5 Oct. 1997, at E1.
- "Experts point to parental and *societal* influences that portray violence as a way to solve problems." Deborah Sharp, "Student Gun Violence Creeps into Small-Community Schools," *USA Today*, 3 Dec. 1997, at A2.

B. And *sociable*. *Sociable* = ready for companionship; quick to unite with others; gregarious. *Social* = relating to people in society.

LANGUAGE-CHANGE INDEX (For the full key, see front matter pp. xxxi, l–li.)
Stage 1: Rejected. **Stage 2:** Widely shunned. **Stage 3:** Widespread but . . . **Stage 4:** Ubiquitous but . . . **Stage 5:** Fully accepted. Invariably inferior forms marked by asterisk (*). • Ratios represent frequency of prevalent forms vs. variants in current books.

social media. Among the many changes ushered in by the use of *social media* is the tendency to treat *media* as a mass noun that takes a singular verb. In print sources worldwide, *social media* has much more commonly been treated as singular since the term really caught on in about 2003. See **media**.

sociopath. See **psychopath**.

sodomite; *sodomist. The first outnumbers the second by a 20-to-1 ratio in modern print sources, so that **sodomist* might be fairly classified as a NEED- LESS VARIANT. Of course, either term is objectionable as an excessively hidebound and moralistic pejorative for "someone who engages in sodomy"—e.g.: "Loeb immediately took up the cause and has continued a campaign against the GSO [Gay Students Association] for two years, preferring to call the GSO 'sodomites' for headline purposes in the [Manchester, N.H.] *Union Leader*." Kevin Cash, *Who the Hell Is William Loeb?* 383 (1975). For "an inhabitant of Sodom," the word is capitalized: *Sodomite*.

sodomy. This ambiguous term can include almost any kind of "unnatural" sex, though it is most often confined to anal intercourse and bestiality. *Sodomy* was not a traditional common-law offense, though an early statute criminalizing it became a part of the common law of many American jurisdictions. These statutes have been nullified by Supreme Court decisions.

***software program.** Avoid this REDUNDANCY. Either word will do, though *software* will usually be the better choice because it's the narrower term.

soi-disant = self-proclaimed. This French affectation is inferior both to the translation just given and to *self-styled*. E.g.:

- "What it may need instead is an establishment with the nerve to tell the *soi-disant* [read *self-proclaimed*] victims: Stop kvetching." Michael S. Greve, "Remote Control Tuning for Speech," *Wash. Times*, 9 Nov. 1996, at D3.
- "Our group was my wife, Olivia; my son, Nicholas, the *soi-disant* [read *self-styled*] surfer; [et al.]." Warren Hoge, "Where Wildlife Meets Wild Surf," *N.Y. Times*, 16 Feb. 1997, § 5, at 11.

Sometimes the GALLICISM is misused for *so-called*— e.g.: "When Paul Robeson sang the song in the London production of Show Boat in 1928, the biggest problem he had was wrapping his beautiful, impeccable vowels around the *soi-disant* [read *so-called*] dialect lyric." Mark Steyn, "Paint It Black," *Am. Spectator*, Mar. 1997, at 44, 46.

Sol. See **earth**.

solace /sahl-əs/ (= comfort in sorrow or trouble; relief from distress) should not be used merely as a synonym of *comfort*, without the circumstance of grief or distress being implied. The misuse occurs here: "Companies with the greatest market share often have a tendency to 'sit on a lead.' They will take *solace* [read *undue pride*?] in their numbers, become complacent, and lose their competitive edge." Mark H. McCormack, *What They Don't Teach You at Harvard Business School* 205–06 (1984).

sola topi (= a pith helmet, originating in India, made from the sola plant) is sometimes misspelled **solar topi* (and has been since the 19th century)—e.g.:

- "But she kept the English cricketing cap and the *solar topi* [read *sola topi*]." Joan Bridgman, "Mad Dogs, English-women and Nureyev," *Contemp. Rev.*, 1 Apr. 1995, at 213.
- "The other common headgear, popular particularly among officers and commissars, was the *casque colonial or solar topi* [read *sola topi*], made of cork or pressed fibre covered with cloth." Martin Windrow, *The Last Valley* 157 (2004).
- "Most importantly for the health of Anglo-Indians was the *solar topi* [read *sola topi*], a sort of fetish that demonstrated British ability to overcome debilitating heat." Steven Patterson, *The Cult of Honor in British India* 112 (2009).

Once in a while the error is compounded into a MALAPROPISM—e.g.: "Imperialism is back in vogue. With global stability threatened by failed states (or near states) like Afghanistan and Palestine, the literature on international affairs is suddenly rife with articles whose authors seem to be channeling Rudyard Kipling. . . . All the President needs is a *solar toupee* [read *sola topi*] and a cut-glass English accent." Michael Elliott, "George W. Kipling," *Time*, 8 July 2002, at 35. See DOUBLE BOBBLES.

It is pronounced /**soh**-lə **toh**-pee/. **Sola topee* is an alternative spelling.

> LANGUAGE-CHANGE INDEX
> *sola topi* misspelled **solar topi*: Stage 3
> Current ratio: 2:1

sole (= the one and only; single) should not be used with a plural noun, as it sometimes is. *Only* is the better choice—e.g.:

- "Pakistan's soldiers seem to be the *sole* [read *only*] people in the country with a sense of duty and national responsibility." Eric Margolis, "Pakistan's Rid of Bhutto, but Other Woes Remain," *Toronto Sun*, 9 Feb. 1997, at C5.
- "The first [flawed premise] is that grade point average (GPA) and SAT scores are the *sole* [read *only*] criteria for ranking students." Letter of Mark L. Liquorman, "Quotas Still Needed," *St. Petersburg Times*, 30 Nov. 1997, at D2.

> LANGUAGE-CHANGE INDEX
> *sole* followed by a plural noun: Stage 2

solecism. Generally, *solecism* (/**sahl**-ə-siz-əm/) refers to a grammatical or syntactic error, often a gross mistake. E.g.:

- "Robert Faggan edited with a touching, if somewhat irritating, respect for the exact orthography of the original letters, even keeping misspellings and blatant *solecisms*." Christopher Bernard, "A Touching Tracking of Our God-Hunger," *Ft. Worth Star-Telegram*, 23 Mar. 1997, at 9.
- "I once spoke French well enough to teach in a Marseille lycee—but that was 25 years ago and today I could hardly string two sentences together without committing some gross *solecism*." Michael Dirda, "The Lingo Kid," *Wash. Post*, 18 May 1997, Book World §, at 15.

A solecism can also be a social impropriety, especially in BrE—e.g.: "'This [feeding fruitcake to the royal corgis] is always regarded as an unforgivable *solecism* at the Palace, where only the Queen is permitted to augment her dogs' diets in this way,' says my man at the palace." Tim Walker, "News–Mandrake–Black Looks," *Sunday Telegraph*, 10 Nov. 2002, at P38.

Yet the word has been extended to figurative senses in AmE as well—e.g.:

- "Yet in the end Siddiqui's artistry overrides even the *solecisms* of the [musical] score." Jenny Gilbert, "Delicate Hands, Feet of Artistry," *Independent*, 23 Mar. 1997, at 15.
- "It is full of junk history, such as the rustic ideal of the country cottage, which he appears not to realize is an entirely modern idea; or the tiresome *solecism*, that everyone likes 'Georgian' architecture, but that 'speculative development' is necessarily bad." Boaz Ben Manasseh, "Spirit and Place," *Architectural Rev.*, 1 Nov. 2002, at 96.

solely. Like *only*, this word is sometimes misplaced syntactically—e.g.: "Orick said that although the educational programs are sponsored by Purdue University, they are not *solely related* [read *related solely*] to preservation of agricultural farmlands." Welton W. Harris II, "Land-Use Plan Sessions Scheduled," *Indianapolis News*, 2 Dec. 1997, Metro N. §, at 1. See **only.**

Also, the word is fairly frequently misspelled **soley*—e.g.: "Since playing basketball as a freshman, Prentiss has concentrated *soley* [read *solely*] on softball." John Hines, "Buffaloes Figure to Roam Farther," *San Antonio Express-News*, 9 Feb. 1997, at C8. Cf. **agilely** & **futilely.** See ADVERBS (B).

solemnness is sometimes misspelled **solemness* and has been since the early 19th century. E.g.: "Contrast *solemness* [read *solemnness*] and spooky guitar noise with bright melodies and a flair for rocking." Kieran Grant, "Love and Rockets Still Setting Off Fireworks," *Toronto Sun*, 8 Apr. 1996, Entertainment §, at 36. Surprisingly, the *OED* lists the misspelling as a variant; it surely doesn't warrant that standing, since it violates every sound principle of word formation. In any event, a far better choice is to use the familiar *solemnity.*

Current ratio (*solemnity* vs. *solemnness* vs. **solemness*): 680:1.1:1

solicit. A. For *elicit*. To *solicit* a response is to request it. To *elicit* a response is to get it. But some writers confuse the two, usually by misusing *solicit* for *elicit*—e.g.: " 'The way the question was worded didn't *solicit* [read *elicit*] the type of response I think we were looking for,' Ekberg said." Geordie Wilson, "Three Levies on One Ballot a Possibility for Voters," *Seattle Times*, 15 Aug. 1991, at C3. The following example contains an ambiguity—is the core group to ask 4,000 people or to get 4,000 to cooperate? "Sentient representatives expect the core group to *solicit* [read *elicit*?] responses from about 4,000 people." Carolene Langie, "Buena Park to Ask About Goals, Issues," *Orange County Register*, 28 June 1990, at 1.

LANGUAGE-CHANGE INDEX
solicit misused for *elicit*: Stage 1

B. And **solicitate*. **Solicitate*, a NEEDLESS VARIANT of *solicit*, is an erroneous BACK-FORMATION from *solicitation*. Though it is old—having originated in the 18th century—it serves no purpose—e.g.:

- "Among those Watson has *solicitated* [read *solicited*] advice from was Roy Williams." Steve Hershey, "Ryder Cup Caps Career for Watson," *USA Today*, 24 Sept. 1993, at B1.
- "Packwood *solicitated* [read *solicited*] jobs for his estranged wife." Glenn Kessler, "Diaries Paint a Bleak Image of Washington," *Charleston Daily Mail*, 9 Sept. 1995, at A1.

LANGUAGE-CHANGE INDEX
*solicitate for *solicit*: Stage 1
Current ratio (*solicited* vs. **solicitated*): 9,248:1

solicitude = (1) protectiveness; or (2) anxiety. Because of these two quite different senses, the word is often ambiguous. But sense 1 is now more common—e.g.: "Afterward, in a show of *solicitude* rarely displayed during his five months at St. Stanislaus, he comforted parishioners distraught by the death of their beloved Father Willie." Mark Gillispie, "An Unlikely Murder Suspect," *Plain Dealer* (Cleveland), 12 Jan. 2003, at A1.

SOLIDUS. See PUNCTUATION (Q).

solo. Pl. *solos*—preferably not **soli*. See PLURALS (B).

solon, journalese for *legislator*, is derived from the name of Solon, an Athenian statesman, merchant, and poet (ca. 640–560 B.C.). In the early 6th century B.C., Solon achieved important political, commercial, and judicial reforms that greatly improved life in the city-state of Athens. He reversed the trend of converting impoverished Athenians into serfs at home or of selling them abroad as slaves. He also standardized Athenian coinage and its system of weights and measures, granted citizenship to immigrant craftsmen, and enhanced the prosperity and independence of Athenian farmers.

In modern times, his name has been used to denote either "a sage" or, used sarcastically or ironically, "a wise guy." Today, the term "may be inescapable, and thus grudgingly admissible, in headlines, where *legislator, senator*, or *representative* will not fit, but in text it is to be avoided." Roy Copperud, *Webster's Dictionary of Usage and Style* 368–69 (1964).

soluble; solvable. *Soluble* is usually applied to dissolvable substances, whereas *solvable* is usually applied to problems. But *soluble* is also sometimes used in reference to problems; this usage is acceptable, though less and less common by the year. The phrase *solvable problems* overtook *soluble problems* in frequency of occurrence in print sources in the early 1970s, and the disparity is ever-increasing. Cf. **resolvable.**

somber; sombre. The first is AmE, the second BrE. See -ER (B). Interestingly, *somber* became the predominant AmE form only as recently as 1940.

LANGUAGE-CHANGE INDEX (For the full key, see front matter pp. xxxi, l–li.)
Stage 1: Rejected. **Stage 2:** Widely shunned. **Stage 3:** Widespread but . . . **Stage 4:** Ubiquitous but . . . **Stage 5:** Fully accepted.
Invariably inferior forms marked by asterisk (*). • Ratios represent frequency of prevalent forms vs. variants in current books.

somebody; someone. The words are equally good; euphony should govern the choice. *Someone* is often better by that standard. Although both of these indefinite pronouns date from the 14th century in English, *somebody* predominated through the 18th and 19th centuries; only in the 1920s did *someone* surpass *somebody* in frequency of occurrence in print sources. That trend has continued ever since. Each is traditionally a singular noun that, for purposes of CONCORD, is the antecedent of a singular pronoun. *Some body and *some one as two words are obsolete spellings.

On treating these terms as singular or plural, see PRONOUNS (D). Cf. **anyone (B).**

someday; some day. For the adverbial sense "at some unidentifiable time in the future, esp. the distant future" the one-word *someday* is standard <You'll be a star someday.> <Someday you'll be thankful we did this!>. When *day* retains its noun sense in reference to a discrete 24-hour period, the two-word *some day* is standard <Let's agree on some day next week for the meeting.> <We'll pick some day when we're all in town.>.

someone. See **somebody.**

someplace for *somewhere* is out of place in formal prose. But it's acceptable as a CASUALISM in speech. This word first surged into popular use in the 1930s—and it has steadily increased ever since. Having originated in the late 19th century, it began seriously spreading in the mid-20th. Cf. ***anyplace** & ***noplace.**

Current ratio (*somewhere* vs. *someplace*): 19:1

somersault; *somerset; *summersault. *Somersault* is the standard spelling in AmE and BrE alike—preferred not only over the two listed, but also over *somersaut, *somersalt, *summerset, and other odd variations.

Current ratio (in order of headwords): 22:1.3:1

-something. From the late 1980s, this term has combined with multiples of 10 (beginning with 20) to designate a cohort of people within an age group, especially so as to emphasize perceived similarities in lifestyle or mind-set. Normally hyphenated, the compounds provide a rough estimate of someone's age, or else they allow people (especially older ones) to make generalizations about those of a certain age—e.g.: *twenty-somethings, thirty-somethings, forty-somethings, fifty-somethings,* and *sixty-somethings.* What's the most common of these compounds in print sources? By far the favorite is *twenty-somethings,* followed by *thirty-somethings.* Octogenarians are rarely if ever referred to as *eighty-somethings.* A popular American television drama titled *thirtysomething* (one word, lowercase) premiered in September 1987 and ran for four seasons. It depicted the lives of a group of baby boomers in their thirties. The group's bond stemmed from the similarities in their youthful lives—growing up in the culture of the 1960s—as contrasted with what they became: parents in middle-class America.

sometime. A. And *some time.* *Sometime* = at an indefinite or unspecified time; esp., at a time in the future <we'll see each other sometime>. *Some time* = quite a while <they spent some time together>. The difference may be illustrated by contrasting the senses of these two sentences: (1) "It was not until *sometime* later that George quit." (The precise time is unknown to the writer.) (2) "It was not until *some time* later that George quit." (George waited quite a while before quitting.)

Each is sometimes misused for the other, and has been for quite some time—e.g.:

- "I spent *sometime* [read *some time*] searching for new or pre-construction apartments that would work out to under 33 percent of what the average household makes in Miami." Ricardo Mor, "Can an Average Joe Find a Place Around Here?" *Miami Herald,* 19 Aug. 2015, Opinion §.
- "They heard about a plan to have the district's gifted program studied and evaluated by a nationally recognized educator *some time* [read *sometime*] this school year." Susan Snyder, "ASD Schools to Try Out Uniforms," *Morning Call* (Allentown, Pa.), 4 Oct. 1996, at A1.

LANGUAGE-CHANGE INDEX
1. *sometime* misused for *some time*
(= quite a while): Stage 1
Current ratio (*some time ago* vs.
*sometime ago): 18:1
2. *some time* misused for *sometime* (= at an
indefinite future time): Stage 2
Current ratio (*call me sometime* vs.
**call me some time*): 7:1

B. As an Adjective Meaning "former." This is a slightly archaic sense of *sometime* <my sometime companion>. The word does not properly signify "on-again-off-again" or "occasional"—as it appears to in the following quotation (as suggested by the incorrect use of *sometimes*): "Jack Kemp, the former Congressman and Housing Secretary and a *sometimes-supporter* [read *sometime supporter*] of Mr. Dole, said in a television interview on Saturday that several Republican leaders, including Speaker Newt Gingrich, were planning such a meeting in two weeks." Katharine Q. Seelye, "A G.O.P. Policy Meeting May Put Pressure on Dole," *N.Y. Times,* 15 July 1996, at A8. See **erstwhile.**

LANGUAGE-CHANGE INDEX
sometimes misused for *sometime* (= former): Stage 1

somewhat. The phrasing *somewhat of a has traditionally been considered poor because it treats *somewhat*—principally an adverb—as a pronoun. Instead of **somewhat of a lackluster performance,* write either *a somewhat lackluster performance* or *something of a lackluster performance.* E.g.:

- "So when the district needed help with its accounting work, it found itself in *somewhat* [read *something*] of a quandary." Lynn Shea, "Tiny District Tries to Get Help with Its Accounting," *Pitt. Post-Gaz.,* 24 Sept. 1997, at W7.
- "Neuheisel . . . is *somewhat* [read *something*] of a natural when he's chatting up one of his guys, even with towels flying." Jack McCallum, "Always a Dull Moment," *Sports Illustrated,* 24 Nov. 1997, at 72.

- "After all, the Jayhawks had six seniors on last season's team, . . . making this *somewhat* [read *something*] of a rebuilding season for Kansas." Josh Barr, "Kansas Shows Its Staying Power," *Wash. Post*, 5 Dec. 1997, at B4.

The collocation *something of a* has a greatly predominated over **somewhat of a* since the 17th century in print sources. The disparity became most pronounced during the 20th century. See of (B) & WEASEL WORDS.

LANGUAGE-CHANGE INDEX
*somewhat of an expert for
something of an expert: Stage 3
Current ratio (*something of an expert* vs.
*somewhat of an expert): 5:1

somewhere. See **someplace.**

songstress. See SEXISM (D).

sonorous is pronounced /**sahn**-ə-rəs/, /**sohn**-ər-əs/, or /sə-**nor**-əs/. Although the last was traditionally considered best in AmE, the first now predominates among speakers at all levels.

*sooner rather than later. Not only is this idiom redundant; it isn't entirely logical because the comparison is never completed. Sooner and not later than what? *Soon* is usually an improvement—e.g.:

- "If so, that could dampen fears that the Federal Reserve will act *sooner, rather than later,* [read *soon*] to boost interest rates again." William Goodwin, "Jobs Report Fails to Shake Up Markets," *Am. Banker*, 10 Oct. 1994, at 48.
- "They argue that subjects such as Jerusalem are so central to the debate that they should be dealt with *sooner rather than later* [read *soon*]." Rebecca Trounson, "Ready to Tackle the Tough Issues, Netanyahu Says," *L.A. Times*, 8 Oct. 1996, at A1.

The phrase **sooner rather than later* originated in the late 19th century but wasn't widely used until the late 20th.

LANGUAGE-CHANGE INDEX
*sooner rather than later: Stage 4

sophic; sophical. See **sophistic(al).**

sophist; sophister. *Sophister* is, except in historical contexts denoting a certain rank of student, a NEEDLESS VARIANT of *sophist* (/**sof**-ist/ or /**sah**-fist/), which today has primarily negative connotations in the sense "a person who uses fallacious arguments; a specious reasoner." Formerly, *sophist* was a respectable word meaning "a person distinguished for erudition; a scholar."

sophistic(al); sophic(al). These words have opposite connotations. The former (usually *sophistical*—though *sophistic* is gaining ground) means "quibbling, specious, or captious in reasoning." The latter (usually *sophical*) means "learned; intellectual."

Sophistical, the disparaging term, is the more common—e.g.:

- "His *sophistical* alibi that he has a duty and responsibility to bless the rest of the nation with his political genius has more the smell of naked ambition than selfless magnanimity." "Wilson Can't Hide for Long," *S.F. Chron.*, 27 Mar. 1995, at A18. (On the use of *alibi* in that sentence, see **alibi (A).**)
- "It doesn't require state attorneys general filing *sophistical* lawsuits to 'recover' smokers' medical costs." Jeff Jacoby, "So the Tobacco Industry Lied," *Austin Am.-Statesman*, 8 Apr. 1997, at A11.

soprano. Pl. *sopranos*—preferably not **soprani*. See PLURALS (B).

Current ratio: 29:1

*sorb. See **absorb.**

sort. For **these sort of,* see ***these kind of.**

sortie (= [1] a raid, esp. an unexpected attack from a besieged position; [2] by extension, an excursion) is occasionally misspelled **sortee*—e.g.:

- "NATO says it has flown 1,700 *sortees* [read *sorties*] as of Wednesday, a quarter of which were bombing runs." Lance Gay, "The Daily Cost: Approximately $40 Million," *Pitt. Post-Gaz.*, 1 Apr. 1999, at A4.
- "Perhaps it was the conversation I had the other day with one of the reporters who works with me covering news in Bar Harbor that provided the inspiration for a *sortee* [read *sortie*] last weekend to that tourist mecca." Jeff Stout, "Cold Walk Brings Hot Tea to Boil," *Bangor Daily News*, 10 Feb. 2007, at D6.

LANGUAGE-CHANGE INDEX
sortie misspelled **sortee*: Stage 1
Current ratio: 1,921:1

sort of, adv., a CASUALISM that hedges what would otherwise be a direct statement, should be avoided in polished writing. Both the following sentences would be improved by dropping it:

- "It used to be easy to think of McElwee as a *sort of* [delete *sort of*] literary novelist, but one with no chance of getting a movie option." Abby McGanney Nolan, "Ross McElwee: Man with a Movie Camera," *Village Voice*, 27 Jan. 1998, at 72.
- "Watch who talks, who changes the course of the discussion, who *sort of* [delete *sort of*] drops in and out of the conversation." Sarah McGinty, "How You Speak Shows Where You Rank," *Fortune*, 2 Feb. 1998, at 156.

See ***these kind of** & **type of.** Cf. **kind of (A).**

SOS. The signal for emergency help, especially at sea, is not an abbreviation (as folk etymology would have it) for "save our souls" or "save our ship." (See ETYMOLOGY (D).) It was adopted by the International Radio Telegraph Convention in 1908 as a universal code because it is easy to remember, easy to send, and easy to recognize by light or sound: three short pulses, three long pulses, three short pulses. Because it was

---

LANGUAGE-CHANGE INDEX (For the full key, see front matter pp. xxxi, l–li.)
Stage 1: Rejected. **Stage 2:** Widely shunned. **Stage 3:** Widespread but . . . **Stage 4:** Ubiquitous but . . . **Stage 5:** Fully accepted.
Invariably inferior forms marked by asterisk (*). ● Ratios represent frequency of prevalent forms vs. variants in current books.

never an abbreviation, there has never been a need to use periods. The plural form is SOSs.

*so therefore. See **so** (c).

sotto voce (Ital., lit. "under the voice"), having been fully anglicized, is no longer italicized in English. It is pronounced /**sot**-oh **voh**-chee/.

*soubriquet. See **sobriquet**.

soufflé /soo-**flay** or **soo**-flay/ takes the acute accent over the final -*e*. (See DIACRITICAL MARKS.) Yet because the word has been fully anglicized, it should not be italicized. (Cf. **résumé**.) Although in almost no conceivable context could the word be confounded with *souffle*—an archaic medical term (without the accent mark) denoting a heart murmur or some similar sound heard through a stethoscope—the very existence of that homograph counsels in favor of retaining the accent for the French dish.

sound bite (= a pithy, catchy comment or catchphrase), a term that sprang into popular use in the 1980s, is predominantly written as two words. Although the solid form *soundbite* seems intuitively right and even inevitable, it remains less common today by a 4-to-1 ratio.

The spelling **sound byte* is an error—e.g.: "Although this was a fairly logical prediction to make, knowing the teams, their styles, and their media sound *bytes* [read *bites*] throughout the week, Kawakami hit the nail on the head." "For His Next Trick: Tonight's Winning Lottery Numbers," *L.A. Times*, 22 Mar. 1997, at C3. The METAPHOR is of a bite-sized quotation, especially on video. *Byte*, on the other hand, denotes a string of eight binary digits (*bits*) processed as a unit by a computer.

LANGUAGE-CHANGE INDEX
sound bite misspelled **sound byte*: Stage 1
Current ratio: 18:1

SOUND OF PROSE. Every writer is occasionally guilty of having a tin ear. But the effective writer is self-trained not to write in a way that distracts with undue alliteration, unconscious puns, accidental rhyming, or unseemly images. These clunkers are sure to irritate some readers. And although clunkers are never entirely escapable, writers can learn to minimize them—most helpfully by acquiring the habit of reading their prose aloud.

A. Undue Alliteration or Rhyme. I.A. Richards, in a classic book, wrote: "But in most *prose*, and more than we ordinarily *suppose*, the opening words have to wait for *those* that follow to settle what they shall mean." *The Philosophy of Rhetoric* 50 (1936). This type of wordplay—assuming that it is wordplay—should be undertaken cautiously because it declares that the writer is being wry or coy.

Intentional but ineffective alliteration is one thing. Thoughtless alliteration is quite another—e.g.:

- "The Jaguars also signed wide receiver Jimmy Smith to a new contract, and came *to terms to two* other draft picks."

"Brackens, Jags Agree to Terms of Contract," *Austin Am.-Statesman*, 29 May 1996, at C3. (There are too many *tos* and *twos* here, particularly because one comes to terms *with* someone, not *to* someone.)

- "That makes some *sense, since* [read *sense, because*] a child who has mouth-runs is going to have a hard time winning friends." Saundra Smokes, "Breaking the Silence on the Tattletales Among Us," *Times Union* (Albany), 5 Jan. 1997, at E5.

Other phrases susceptible to this problem include *instead of a steady, tempted to attempt, net debt schedule*, and *need not know*. See ALLITERATION.

B. Awkward Repetition. Too much repeating of sounds can enfeeble your style, especially if two different forms of the same root appear close together—e.g.:

- "The major role of *legislative* liaisons is to answer *legislators'* [read *lawmakers'*] questions about the impact of proposed *legislation* [read *bills*] on various agencies." Editor's Note to a letter to the editor, *Chicago Sun-Times*, 22 June 1992, at 18.
- "The next stop is the House–Senate *conference*, where *conferees* [read *legislators*] will try to reconcile differences." Susie T. Parker, "Energy Bill Faces Possible Sinking, DOE Aide Warns," *Oil Daily*, 16 July 1992, at 1.
- "If you're getting the *impression* [read *idea*] we weren't *impressed* with our $20,000 test truck, you're right." Tom Incantalupo, "Pickup Was Hard Ride," *Newsday* (N.Y.), 24 Feb. 1995, at C6.
- "It set aside $3.25 million . . . to cover expected losses from *liquidating* [read *selling*] liquid crystal display screens and other assets left over from the Epson deal." Robert Trigaux, "Jabil Circuit Takes Loss on Contract," *St. Petersburg Times*, 17 Mar. 1995, at E2.
- "Critics of this new approach say it squelches distinctive programming by pushing stations to adopt more successful, *uniform formats* [read *consistent formats*]." Andrea Adelson, "A Wider Public for Noncommercial Radio," *N.Y. Times*, 10 Feb. 1997, at D8.

soundtrack is so written (or sometimes *sound track*)—not **sound tract*. The *track* in the phrase denotes the segment in a motion picture or videotape where sound, as opposed to visual camera work, is reproduced. But some writers err by writing *tract*—e.g.:

- "Some of the *sound tracts* [read *soundtracks*] may have to be 'bleeped.' " Bob Brister, "Sporting Clays All in Family Now," *Houston Chron.*, 16 June 1992, Sports §, at 7.
- "A superb example of this type of media cross-pollination appeared last week, when the official *sound tract* [read *soundtrack*] CD to the Fox series 'Party of Five' was released by Reprise Records." David Bianculli, "Tune In to Series CDs," *Austin Am.-Statesman*, 17 Nov. 1996, Show World §, at 5.

For other misuses, see **track**.

LANGUAGE-CHANGE INDEX
*sound tract for *soundtrack*: Stage 1
Current ratio (*soundtrack* vs. **sound tract*): 4,606:1

sour grapes is one of the most commonly misused idiomatic METAPHORS. It is not a mere synonym of *envy* or *jealousy*. Rather, as in Aesop's fable about the fox who wanted the grapes he could not reach, *sour grapes* denotes the human tendency to disparage as undesirable what one really wants but can't get (or hasn't gotten). For example, a high-school boy who asks a girl for a date and is turned down might then insult her in all sorts of puerile ways. That's a case of sour grapes.

But the traditional and correct use of the phrase seems to be on the wane. Some uses are downright incoherent—e.g.: "Great Britain's reaction [in the Falklands War] was more a case of *sour grapes* and wounded pride than any genuine desire to right a terrible wrong." Letter of Philip Naff, "Falklands Furor," *Time*, 10 May 1982, at 5. (The British reaction couldn't have been "sour grapes" because [1] Great Britain did not disparage the Falklands as undesirable—it wanted to keep them as a territory; and [2] Britain was successful in the effort.) The more typical misuse looks like this: "Is someone trying to jinx *Good Will Hunting*'s chances for a screenwriting Oscar? Perhaps a competitor's *sour grapes* [read *envy*] over the film's success?" Nick Madigan, "Bad Vibes Haunt 'Good Will' Nom," *Daily Variety*, 16 Mar. 1998, at 36.

LANGUAGE-CHANGE INDEX
sour grapes in the sense "envy": Stage 3

south; southward(s); southerly. See DIRECTIONAL WORDS.

sovereignty; *sovranty. The first is the standard spelling. The second is an experimental shortening that some British writers tried in the 19th and 20th centuries—but it didn't catch on.

Current ratio: 3,926:1

sow, vb. A. Inflection: *sow* > *sowed* > *sown*. In the past participle, *sowed* is a variant form. In modern print sources, *sown* predominates by a 4-to-1 ratio. See IRREGULAR VERBS.

B. *Sowing wild oats*. To *sow* is to scatter seed. By extension, to *sow one's wild oats* is to engage in youthful promiscuity or other excess. Some writers, though, mistake *sow* (/soh/) with its homophone *sew* (= to stitch with needle and thread)—e.g.:

- "Primarily, Ios attracts a young Scandinavian crowd that spends the summer *sewing* [read *sowing*] its oats on the nude beaches and in the wild discos." "Not for the Sedate," *L.A. Times*, 6 Aug. 1989, § 7, at 25.
- "Kevin Kilner's handsome gentleman caller . . . is a study in masculine poise, exuding the relaxed confidence of a one-time high school heartthrob who has *sewn* [read *sown*] his last wild oat." Jan Stuart, "A 'Glass' You Can See Things In," *Newsday* (N.Y.), 16 Nov. 1994, § II, at B7.
- "Timber Rattlers manager Matt Erickson has been part leader, part instructor and part counselor, guiding an age group that otherwise might be *sewing* [read *sowing*] wild oats in college somewhere." Tom Haudricourt, "Growing, Pitch by Pitch," *Milwaukee J. Sentinel*, 6 June 2015, at B1.

Sometimes the METAPHOR appears to be misunderstood. A father, for example, cannot sow the son's oats: "Snelling's *oats were sewn* [*sic*] early in big-time college basketball by his father, Ray Snelling, who played at Southwest Missouri State University in the late 1960s." Kevin E. Boone, "Snelling Will Be Temp in Flat River,"

St. Louis Post-Dispatch, 10 Aug. 1989, at 7. It's hard to suggest a solution for that sentence, which reflects woolly thinking. But perhaps a better phrasing would be *roots were planted*.

Also, this is traditionally a male-only metaphor, since only males have the seed to sow. Only if you take the phrase as a dead metaphor does it work in reference to females. But many readers will find the following sentences hopelessly incongruous:

- "Are they women who are *sowing their wild oats* before they get married—or are they really married women who are afraid to tell the truth?" Abigail Van Buren, "Survey: Wives Are More Faithful," *Chicago Trib.*, 10 Sept. 1987, at C17.
- "But how does a '90s girl *sow her wild oats*?" Polly Shulman, "A Restless Flock," *Newsday* (N.Y.), 14 Aug. 1994, at 40. How indeed?
- "Jamie, a salon owner, met him before she was out of her teens, but at 25, she wonders aloud whether she needs to *sow her wild oats*." Joanne Weintraub, "Turning Another Page in Reality TV," *Milwaukee J. Sentinel*, 13 June 2006, at E1.

LANGUAGE-CHANGE INDEX
**sew wild oats* for *sow wild oats*: Stage 1

***spacial.** See **spatial.**

spade. See **spay.**

spaghetti and meatballs. On the question whether this phrase takes a singular or plural verb, see SUBJECT–VERB AGREEMENT (D).

spartan; sparse. *Spartan* is the antonym of *luxurious*, and *sparse* the antonym of *luxuriant*. (See **luxurious.**) But there the similarities end.

In ancient Greece, the people of Sparta were known as being stoical, frugal, simple, laconic, brave, disciplined, and indifferent to comfort or luxury. From them we get the adjective *spartan*, which describes someone with the qualities just listed <the spartan pioneers of the American West>. By extension, a person's surroundings, diet, or lifestyle can be spartan when comforts or luxuries are few <a spartan life on the prairie>. E.g.: "He doesn't like the idea of Elke entering his home and seeing how bare he keeps it, how *spartan* his life is." Donna Jo Napoli & Richard Tchen, *Spinners* 85 (1999).

The word *sparse* means "not densely packed; scattered" <sparse trees on the plain> <a sparsely populated area>.

Undoubtedly through mistaken sound-association, people have begun misusing *sparse* for *spartan*—e.g.:

- "It is to be her retirement home, so she takes only a few of her worldly possessions and intends to live a *sparse* [read *spartan*] life." Kay Rohrer, "'Winter Solstice' Exhibits Heartfelt Depth," *Sunday Patriot-News* (Harrisburg), 8 Oct. 2000, at E3.
- "The cramped front hall remains pretty much as it was more than 100 years ago. Visitors instantly get a sense of

LANGUAGE-CHANGE INDEX (For the full key, see front matter pp. xxxi, l–li.)
Stage 1: Rejected. **Stage 2:** Widely shunned. **Stage 3:** Widespread but . . . **Stage 4:** Ubiquitous but . . . **Stage 5:** Fully accepted.
Invariably inferior forms marked by asterisk (*). • Ratios represent frequency of prevalent forms vs. variants in current books.

the hunkered-down, *sparse* [read *spartan*] existence of the [tenement] building's residents." Patrick Connolly, "Walking Tour Peeks at the Past," *Tennessean*, 7 Apr. 2002, at G1.

- "Spec. Kevin Conforti's temporary home is a tent where about 17 soldiers sleep in sleeping bags on cots. A small stove at the end provides heat. Despite the rather *sparse* [read *spartan*] accommodations, Conforti, of Okmulgee, says the training is very good." Barbara Hoberock, "Oklahoma Guard Troops Prepare to Deploy Overseas," *Tulsa World*, 17 Dec. 2002, at A11.

See WORD-SWAPPING.

LANGUAGE-CHANGE INDEX
sparse misused for *spartan*: Stage 1

spasmodic; *spasmodical; *spasmatic; spastic. *Spasmodic* = (1) of, relating to, or characterized by a spasm; or (2) intermittent, sporadic, unsustained. *Spasmodical and *spasmatic are NEEDLESS VARIANTS. *Spasmatic is labeled "rare or obsolete" by the *SOED*, but of those two labels only "rare" is accurate—e.g.:

- "Likewise, human history is a *spasmatic* [read *spasmodic*], seemingly random rise from a lake, through evolution, to the high points of history." Ernest Tucker, "Laughs Fail to Work in AIDS Farce," *Chicago Sun-Times*, 17 Nov. 1994, at 48.
- "After last week's loss to the Flyers, though, Campbell has wondered aloud if, even with the great effort and input of his stars, the Rangers have enough talent to enjoy more than *spasmatic* [read *spasmodic*] success." Stu Hackel, "Campbell's Soup: Can Anyone Coach the Rangers?" *Village Voice*, 11 Mar. 1997, at 125.

Spastic has literal, figurative, and slangy senses in AmE: (1) (lit.) "of, relating to, or characterized by a spasm" <spastic paralysis>; (2) (fig.) "highly excitable, agitated" <a spastic child>; and (3) (rude slang) "bumbling, klutzy, incompetent" <the comedian's signature sketch was acting like a spastic high-schooler on a date with the homecoming queen>.

LANGUAGE-CHANGE INDEX
*spasmatic for *spasmodic*: Stage 1

spatial. So spelled in all varieties of English—not *spacial.

Current ratio: 355:1

spay (= to neuter by removing the ovaries from [a female animal]) is used so often in the past-tense and past-participial form (*spayed*) that it's sometimes confused with *spade*—e.g.:

- "Task force will probe way to curb county's animal population. Suggestions: mandatory *spade and neuter* [read *spaying-and-neutering*] laws." "Arizona," *USA Today*, 22 Aug. 1991, at A8.
- "The Society for the Prevention of Cruelty to Animals found that the animals are fed well and are *spade* [read *spayed*] and neutered." Krista Paul, "In Sea Cliff, 1 House, 70 Pets and a 911 Call," *Newsday* (N.Y.), 8 July 1993, at 22.
- "Event sponsors hope to raise $50,000 for the Humane Society's *spade and neuter* [read *spay-and-neuter*] clinic." "Yogarama 2000 to Raise Funds for Animal Support," *Atlanta J.-Const.*, 22 Apr. 2000, at E6.

LANGUAGE-CHANGE INDEX
spade misused for *spayed* as past form of *spay*: Stage 2

speaking. This word is among the few "acceptable danglers" or "disguised conjunctions" when used as a sentence adverb—e.g.:

- "Speaking realistically, Ritchey still only hopes to 'capture' a small margin of the commuting population." Thomas Hackett, "Riders Take Public Transportation for Diverse Reasons," *News & Observer* (Raleigh), 2 Apr. 1996, at B1. (This might be a paraphrase of Ritchey, but the sentence barely has him speaking, if at all; the comment is the writer's.)
- "Economically *speaking*, the ACC basketball tournament and the Greater Greensboro Chrysler Classic are the only other sporting events that pump more money into the local economy." Craig T. Greenlee, "Soccer Tourney," *News & Record* (Greensboro), 25 May 1997, at C7. (Any competent reader knows that the sporting events aren't speaking; the writer is.)
- "Practically *speaking*, the proponents of government-funded health insurance for kids ignore the likeliest result of their plan." "Siren Song for Kids," *Gaz. Telegraph* (Colo. Springs), 26 May 1997, at 4. (Again, the reader knows that the proponents aren't doing the speaking; the writer is.)

See DANGLERS (E) & SENTENCE ADVERBS.

spec = (1) specification <in accordance with your specs>; (2) speculation (in the sense of a business venture) <built on spec> <spec home>; or (3) *pl.*, spectacles <Put on your specs!>.

special. See **especial**.

specialty; speciality. *Specialty* has been the predominant form in AmE since the 18th century. In BrE, *speciality* predominated from the 1870s to the 1970s—but now *specialty* is once again on the rise. It appears that *specialty* is the standard term worldwide.

Current ratio: 8:1

species is both singular and plural. As a singular noun, it means "a group of similar plants or animals that can breed among themselves but not outside the group." From that sense the word's meaning has naturally been extended to "class" or "type" <a problem of this species is best left to the family to work out>. As a plural, *species* means "all the groups of similar plants or animals that can breed [etc.]." In the title of Charles Darwin's great work, *The Origin of Species* (1859)—among the most important books ever published—*species* is plural. Unfortunately, many publications insert a spurious *the* before *Species*, as if Darwin had considered only the human species. Cf. **series**.

Some writers erroneously make *specie* a singular of *species*—e.g.: "The shrub, also known as southern spicebush, was listed in 1986 as an endangered *specie* [read *species*] by the U.S. Fish and Wildlife Service." Ron Maxey, "Church to House Synergy Residents," *Commercial Appeal* (Memphis), 23 Feb. 1996, at B3. (*Specie*, in its correct form, means "coined money." As a mass noun, it has no plural, unless one means to refer to different types of coined money.)

And sometimes people mistake *species* for *sex*—e.g.:

- "And she was on the whole glad she didn't have to play the scene in which her co-star, Patsy Kensit, is attacked by moths, which required her to have 'rubber rings impregnated with female sex pheromones' sewn into her dress to attract the sex-starved *male species* [read *males*]." Sheila Johnston, "Terrifying, Brittle, Arrogant, Icy," *Independent*, 7 Dec. 1995, Features §, at 10.

- "In an annual ritual, pollen released by the males drifts through the air until it reaches the *female species of tree* [read *female of this species* or *female trees*]." Linda Weiford, "High Tree-Pollen Counts Hammer the Allergic," *Anchorage Daily News*, 8 June 1997, at A1.
- "Beach volleyball has become one of the most popular Olympic sports, especially for the male-dominated TV audience. Some would crudely suggest that it's the uniforms. I have a higher opinion of *the male species* [read *men*] than that." Mark McCarter, "Sights, Sounds, Sand," *Huntsville Times* (Ala.), 14 Aug. 2008, at D1.

The pronunciation is /**spee**-sheez/ or /**spee**-seez/. Cf. **genus.**

LANGUAGE-CHANGE INDEX
1. *specie* as a false singular of *species*: Stage 2
Current ratio (*endangered species* vs.
endangered specie): 833:1
2. *species* for *sex* in, e.g., "male species": Stage 2

specious; spurious. The two words are related in sense but not at all in etymology (L. *speciosus* "beautiful, plausible"; L. *spurius* "bastard"). What is *specious* is seemingly true but actually false <specious arguments>. What is *spurious* is illegitimately produced <spurious offspring>; sham, counterfeit, or forged <spurious bank drafts>; or else insincere <spurious praise>. While *specious* more often refers to reasoning and arguments, *spurious* more often refers to fake things or conditions. Although *specious* appeared more frequently than *spurious* in print throughout the 17th century to the early 19th, *spurious* has appeared somewhat more frequently than *specious* since about 1850.

specs. See **spec.**

spectator. So spelled—not **spectater.*

specter; spectre. This word is preferably spelled *-er* in AmE, *-re* in BrE. Curiously, however, many Americans cling to the British spelling—perhaps because *specter* didn't become standard in AmE till about 1940. (See -ER (B).) The word is sometimes misspelled *spector—e.g.: "He also raises the *spector* [read *specter*] of a duplicate stone." Irene Gardner Castleton, "Stone of Scone Belongs in Scotland, Not Ireland," *Times Union* (Albany), 12 Jan. 1997, at E4.

spectrum. The plural *spectra* vastly predominates over *spectrums* in print sources and has consistently done so since the 18th century. See PLURALS (B).
Current ratio: 84:1

speculative; *speculatory. The first is standard; the second is a NEEDLESS VARIANT.
Current ratio: 2,780:1

speculator. So spelled—not **speculater.*

speculum (= [1] a medical instrument inserted into the body for inspection, or [2] an astrological drawing or table) has predominantly formed the Latinate plural *specula* since the 17th century—not *speculums*.
Current ratio: 5:1

speechify = to deliver a speech. The word is used in a mocking or derogatory way. See **preachify.**

speed > sped > sped. The best past-tense and past-participial form is *sped*, not *speeded. It has been so since the 17th century. But there's one exception: the PHRASAL VERB *speed up* (= to accelerate) <she speeded up to 80 m.p.h.>. See IRREGULAR VERBS. See **rate of speed.**

LANGUAGE-CHANGE INDEX
*speeded for *sped* as past tense
and past participle of *speed*: Stage 2
Current ratio (*sped* vs. *speeded): 6:1

spell > spelled > spelled. So inflected in AmE (since 1850) and mostly in post-1980 BrE, though *spelt* is the more traditional past form in BrE.
Current ratio (World English): 4:1

SPELLING. A. Common Misspellings. Computerized spell-checkers have begun to eliminate many misspellings. But they don't catch all misspellings if the word is actually a different word, as when *not* is mistyped *now*. And to the extent that the word lists in the spell-checkers aren't sound, certain misspellings may become more widespread. For example, one spell-checker stops at *restaurateur*, recommending that it be replaced with the incorrect form *restauranteur. All in all, though, spell-checkers are quite helpful.

Here are some of the most commonly misspelled words in the English language. Naturally, they're spelled correctly here:

aberration	conniption	idiosyncrasy
accommodate	consensus	impostor
acknowledg-	corroborate	impresario
ment	croupier	inadvertent
acoustic	definitely	independent
ad nauseam	dependent	innovate
aficionado	desiccate	inoculate
aggressive	disappoint	interrupt
allotted	ecstasy	irresistible
anoint	embarrass	isosceles
asinine	emperor	judgment
assassination	espresso	kaleidoscope
barbiturate	expedite	knowledge
bizarre	friend	kowtow
cacophony	gauge	lackadaisical
camaraderie	glamorous	liaison
canister	graffiti	lieu
category	grammar	liquefy
cemetery	harass	loathsome
committee	hors d'oeuvre	lollipop

mayonnaise	pavilion	sacrifice
meringue	persevere	sacrilegious
millennium	persistent	separate
minuscule	personnel	siege
misspelling	pharaoh	sophomore
moccasin	picayune	souvenir
mortgage	playwright	stratagem
newsstand	poinsettia	successful
nickel	possession	supersede
niece	presumptuous	surprise
notable	privilege	tattoo
noticeable	publicly	threshold
obbligato	quiescent	titillate
occasion	rapport	tongue
occurrence	rarefy	tourniquet
ophthalmology	receive	truncheon
palomino	rendezvous	ukulele
paparazzi	restaurateur	unforeseen
paralleled	resuscitate	unwieldy
parasol	rhythm	vermilion
parishioner	rickety	weird
pastime	rococo	you're

Three CONTRACTIONS are also constantly being misspelled: *it's*, *they're*, and *you're*. (See **its, their** & **your.**) Among the less usual words that are difficult to spell are *iridescent*, *kimono*, *naphtha*, and *syzygy*.

Of course, English orthography is riddled with anomalies of various types—and for various reasons. Sometimes a word seems to be analogous to another in its formation but for etymological reasons isn't (e.g., one word ends in *-tuous*, another *-tious*). Or related words may have been borrowed from a source language at different times (e.g., 13th-century *feme sole* but 20th-century *femme fatale*). Then again, it could be that two loanwords that seem to have similar properties aren't at all analogous (e.g., the sing.–pl. Latin pairs *fungus–fungi* and *apparatus–apparatus*, the latter being a fourth-declension noun—and *apparatuses* being the preferred English plural). And perhaps most commonly, etymologically unrelated words sometimes have a coincidence of sound that misleadingly makes speakers think of them as analogues (*democracy*, *idiosyncrasy*). What follows are some of the marked irregularities in English spelling. Some of the words in this list appeared in the list above, but they're included here to show the misleading analogy to another word.

acquiesce but *aqueduct*
affinity but *aficionado*
airplane but *aeronautics*
anal but *anilingus*
ascendable but *descendible*
Belgium but *Belgian*
bombast but *lambaste*
bookstore but *used-book store*
Britain but *Brittany*
bumptious but *presumptuous*
clamor but *glamour* (yet *glamorous*)
comrade but *camaraderie*
coup de grace but *foie gras*
criticize but *advertise*
cumbrous but *slumberous*
de jure but *du jour*
democracy but *idiosyncrasy*

despoil but *despoliation*
dexterous but *ambidextrous*
elves but *dwarfs*
embarrass but *harass*
enforce but *reinforce*
enjoin but *injunction*
enumerate but *remunerate*
example but *exemplary*
express but *espresso*
face but *artifice*
fantasy but *phantasm*
femme fatale but *feme sole*
fire but *fiery*
fractious but *anfractuous*
fungi but *apparatuses* (or L. *apparatus*)
fusillade but *fuselage*
garden but *kindergarten*
gardener but *kindergartner*
Glasgow but *Glaswegian*
hammer but *grammar*
Herbert but *sherbet*
hooves but *roofs*
idea but *ideology*
important but *inadvertent*
impressive but *impresario*
infectious but *tempestuous*
innocuous but *inoculate*
irreversible but *iridescent*
jam but *doorjamb*
juror but *perjurer*
literati but *littérateur*
load but *mother lode*
madam but *mademoiselle*
mellow but *marshmallow*
millennium but *millenarian*
millionaire but *questionnaire*
miniskirt but *minuscule*
moment but *memento*
muffle but *duffel*
munition but *diminution*
noblesse but *largess*
obelisk but *odalisque*
obligation but *obbligato*
paper but *papier-mâché*
pass but *impasse*
patriot but *expatriate*
personal but *personnel*
Philippines but *Filipino*
pizza but *pizzeria*
playwright but *playwriting*
plenty but *plenitude*
politically but *impoliticly*
ponderous but *wondrous*
precede but *supersede*
pretentious but *portentous*
primacy but *apostasy*
proceed but *precede*
pruritis but *tinnitus*
publicly but *plastically*
religious but *sacrilegious*
repair but *reparable*
restaurant but *restaurateur*
salami but *salaam*
scarify but *rarefy*
Shaw but *Shavian*
spoil but *spoliation*
storm but *maelstrom*

strategy but stratagem
sufferance but suffrage
summery but wintry
temple but templar
tendency but tendance
tendon but tendinitis
until but till (not 'til)
venom but antivenin
vinegar but vinaigrette
violin but violoncello
wean but overweening
weasels but measles
wondrous but splendorous

B. Doubling of Final Consonants in Inflected Verbs. Apart from words ending in *-l* and exceptions noted below, all English-speaking countries follow the same rules on doubling. When a suffix beginning with a vowel is added, the final consonant of the word is repeated only if (1) the vowel sound preceding the consonant is represented by a single letter (hence *bed, bedding* but *head, heading*); or (2) the final syllable bears the main stress (hence *oc-'cur, oc-'curred* but *'of-fer, 'of-fered*). Among the more commonly misspelled words are these: *biased, focused, benefited, transferred.*

There are exceptions. Unaccented syllables in inflected words are often spelled differently in AmE and in BrE. Americans generally do not double a final *-l* before the inflectional suffix, whereas the British generally do. Thus:

AmE	BrE
canceled, canceling	cancelled, cancelling
counseled, counseling	counselled, counselling
dialed, dialing	dialled, dialling
dueled, dueling	duelled, duelling
funneled, funneling	funnelled, funnelling
imperiled, imperiling	imperilled, imperilling
initialed, initialing	initialled, initialling
labeled, labeling	labelled, labelling
leveled, leveling	levelled, levelling
marshaled, marshaling	marshalled, marshalling
marveled, marveling	marvelled, marvelling
modeled, modeling	modelled, modelling
parceled, parceling	parcelled, parcelling
penciled, penciling	pencilled, pencilling
signaled, signaling	signalled, signalling
sniveled, sniveling	snivelled, snivelling
squirreled, squirreling	squirrelled, squirrelling
stenciled, stenciling	stencilled, stencilling
swiveled, swiveling	swivelled, swivelling
totaled, totaling	totalled, totalling
toweled, toweling	towelled, towelling
trammeled, trammeling	trammelled, trammelling
traveled, traveling	travelled, travelling
unraveled, unraveling	unravelled, unravelling

The British–American split is seen also in words such as *jewel(l)er, pupil(l)age, tranquil(l)er,* and *travel(l)er,* the British preferring *-ll-* over the *-l-* used by Americans. But there are exceptions: British writers use the forms *paralleled, paralleling*—just as Americans

do—presumably to avoid the ungainly appearance of four *-l*-s in quick succession.

BrE doubles the final consonant after a fully pronounced vowel in words such as *kidnapped, -ing* and *worshipped, -ing.* (One exception is *galloped, galloping.*) In AmE, *kidnapping* and *worshipping* are preferred over *kidnaping (see **kidnapping (A)**) as exceptional forms (as with *formatted, formatting*). The same is true of *worshipped, worshipping.* (See **worship.**) *Programmed* and *programming* are the preferred spellings on both sides of the Atlantic, the single *-m-* spellings being secondary variants in AmE; for the probable reason underlying this American inconsistency, see **program(m)er.**

There are a few other exceptions in AmE. *Chagrined, combated,* and *coroneted* are all exceptional because the final consonant isn't doubled even though the final syllable of their uninflected forms is accented. But these forms are few. With the verb *combat,* the possibility of a MISCUE seems great enough that *combatted* and *combatting* ought to be preferred—despite what the dictionaries say.

Writers and editors should make themselves aware of these minor transatlantic differences in spelling and avoid inserting a bracketed *sic* when quoting a foreign text. See **sic.**

C. Words with *-ie-* or *-ei-*. The old rule—*i* before *e,* except after *c,* or when sounded as *a,* as in *neighbor* and *weigh*—generally holds. But there are many exceptions, such as *counterfeit, either, feisty, forfeit, height, leisure, seize, their,* and *weird.* Several words of foreign (especially German) derivation also violate the rule, such as *Fahrenheit, meister,* and *zeitgeist*—as well as words in which the *-i-* and *-e-* are both pronounced, such as *deity, society,* and *spontaneity.* The except-after-*c* proviso also has its exceptions, such as *concierge* and *financier.*

D. Compounds. The normal process in Modern English is for separate words used habitually to become hyphenated, and then fused into a single word (e.g., *to day* became *to-day* in the 19th century and then *today* in the 20th). Because the process is constantly at work, it's difficult to be definite about the status of some terms. For example, *database* went rapidly from *data base* through *data-base* to *database*; and many writers simply skipped the intermediate step. The same tendency is now seen as people begin to write *wordprocessing* as a solid word. See **word processing.**

spew (= to gush or vomit) is sometimes misspelled *spue—e.g.: "The enemy must be loathed where it is not feared, and let the consequent emotions *spue* [read *spew*] where they may." Hugo Young, "The Phobia That Lies Behind the Sneers," *Guardian,* 11 Mar. 1997, at 15.

LANGUAGE-CHANGE INDEX
spew misspelled *spue: Stage 1

LANGUAGE-CHANGE INDEX (For the full key, see front matter pp. xxxi, l–li.)
Stage 1: Rejected. **Stage 2:** Widely shunned. **Stage 3:** Widespread but . . . **Stage 4:** Ubiquitous but . . . **Stage 5:** Fully accepted.
Invariably inferior forms marked by asterisk (*). • Ratios represent frequency of prevalent forms vs. variants in current books.

sphinx. Pl. *sphinxes.* The alternative plural **sphinges* is obsolete in English.

spicy. So spelled in AmE and BrE alike—not **spicey.*

spiel is best pronounced /speel/, not in the mock-Yiddish fashion that has become so common (/shpeel/), which is jocular.

spill > spilled > spilled. So inflected in both AmE (from 1900) and BrE (from 1956). The archaic past form *spilt* still sometimes appears in metaphorical references to *spilt milk* ("Don't cry over spilt milk"), particularly in BrE. But *spilled milk* is more common in AmE.

spin > spun > spun. This IRREGULAR VERB is so inflected in AmE and BrE alike. *Span* is obsolete as an inflected form of *spin,* though some writers so use it (more commonly in BrE than in AmE)—e.g.:

- "The hot road *span* [read *spun*] away behind her." Dorothy L. Sayers, *Gaudy Night* 4 (1936; repr. 1995).
- "Christy *span* [read *spun*] a yarn about discovering hidden treasure on a coral reef and meeting dolphins, crabs and stingrays." "Marine Life Inspires Two Young Writers," *Bristol Evening Post,* 7 Dec. 1999, at 12.
- "The flutey Ballet des Sylphes brought a smile to the face, while the Cleveland strings *span* [read *spun*] silky threads of sound in the Menuet des Follets. Simply ravishing!" Hugh Canning, "Arias on a Shoestring," *Sunday Times* (London), 20 Aug. 2000, at 18.
- "Gingerly, I lined up the shot with the camera laid on the ice, trotted into position, *span* [read *spun*] round and went flying backwards off an ice ridge." Andrew James, "A Winter's Tale," *Independent,* 23 Dec. 2000, at 5.

LANGUAGE-CHANGE INDEX
span as a past tense for *spun*: Stage 1

spiral, vb., makes *spiraled* and *spiraling* in AmE, *spiralled* and *spiralling* in BrE. See SPELLING (B).V

spirea (= a rosy shrub) has been predominantly so spelled in AmE since 1930. The spelling *spiraea* has predominated in BrE since the early 19th century.

spiritual; spiritualistic; spirituous; *spiritous; spirituel; spirituelle; spirited. *Spiritual* is the broadest of these terms, meaning "of the spirit as opposed to matter; of the soul esp. as acted on by God; concerned with sacred or religious things" (*COD*). *Spiritualistic* = of, relating to, or involving spiritualism, i.e., the belief that departed spirits communicate with and show themselves to the living, esp. through mediums. *Spirituous* = alcoholic. E.g.: "The purveyors of *spirituous* liquors have lately taken to advertising on TV after years of voluntarily absenting themselves." Tom Teepen, "Purge the Vices, Ignore a Crisis," *Austin Am.-Statesman,* 7 Apr. 1997, at A11. **Spiritous* is an ARCHAISM in the sense of "highly refined or dematerialized," and is also a NEEDLESS VARIANT of *spirituous.* *Spirituel* (masculine) or *spirituelle* (feminine) means "witty" or "of a highly refined character or nature, esp. in conjunction with liveliness or quickness of mind" (*OED*). Finally, *spirited* means "full of spirit; lively; energetic" <a spirited debate>.

spiritualism; *spiritism. The first has always been the predominant form since coming into frequent use in the early 19th century.

*spirt. See **spurt.**

spit (= to force out the contents of one's mouth) is inflected in three possible ways:

> spit > spat > spat
> spit > spat > spit
> spit > spit > spit

Good authority can be found for the first two; the third finds less enthusiastic support. The recommendation here is to follow the first—e.g.:

- "On Tuesday night, he shook hands with John Hirschbeck, the umpire in whose face he *had spat* seven months earlier." Gordon Edes, "Exploits Finally Bring Cheer," *Boston Globe,* 27 Apr. 1997, at F9.
- "The Conservatives said the strictly Orthodox Jews, known more commonly as the haredim, *had spat* on them and pelted them with garbage and feces." "Mixed-Gender Prayer Assailed in Jerusalem," *Austin Am.-Statesman,* 13 June 1997, at A6.
- "Then the man *spat.* Tobias was shocked and thought the man *had spat* at him, but he did not feel anything." Bernard Dionne, *I Can See* 104 (2012).

Admittedly, however, the collocation *had spit* has historically predominated over *had spat* for most of the era since 1800 (the two forms having closely vied in print sources from 1915 to 1980). Yet *has spat* has predominated over *has spit* for most of the same period. Writers have wavered on how best to expectorate. See IRREGULAR VERBS.

Avoid *spit* as the past-tense form. It has never been the predominant form in AmE or BrE, and it sounds dialectal—e.g.:

- "She had *spit* [read *spat*] the words at him venomously, in utter contempt, before she left, refusing to ever see him face-to-face again." Rick Hutchins, *The RH Factor* 87 (2005).
- "They were just lucky as hell that no one *spit* [read *spat*] in my face; it only landed on my clothes. I didn't care how small I was or how much anyone preached non-violence. If someone had *spit* [read *spat*] in my face, I was going to beat the living hell out of them or die trying." Freya Anderson Rivers, *Swallowed Tears* 214 (2012).
- "Once when a group of East End Jews had come to protest at one of his rallies, her father had *spit* [read *spat*] on one of the demonstrators." Laura L. Sullivan, *Love by the Morning Star* 150 (2014).

Spit (= to use a spit or skewer) makes *spitted* as the past tense and past participle—e.g.:

- "We saw *spitted* small birds being barbecued at the Oktoberfest." John Gould, "Lobsters Debut and Disappear in Germany," *Christian Science Monitor,* 22 Nov. 1996, Home Forum §, at 17.
- "Gilbert and Sullivan must be revolving like *spitted* chickens in their graves." Richard Farr, "Cat-Like Tread: It's Inventive, Theatrical and Shocking," *Seattle Times,* 7 Apr. 1997, at F5.

LANGUAGE-CHANGE INDEX
spit as past tense or past participle of *spit*: Stage 4

spite of, in. See **despite.**

spitting image. A. Etymology. *Spitting image* (= the exact likeness; an identical duplicate) is actually a corruption of *spit and image*, from the notion of God's using spit and dust to form the clay to make Adam in his image. As far back as the early 1800s, the phrase *the very spit of* was used in this sense <the child is the very spit of his grandfather>. By the mid- to late 1800s, *spit* was coupled with *image* (or *fetch* or *picture*) to form *spit and image*. But around the turn of the 20th century, *spitting image* (or *spittin' image*) appeared. It became the more common form in AmE and BrE at about the same time in the late 1950s. Though originally an error, it's so common today— some 23 times as common in print as *spit and image*— that most dictionaries fully countenance it without recording *spit and image*. E.g.:

- "He remains the father of two children—a son who is growing into his *spitting image* and a daughter who has no memory of him." Mike McAndrew, "Slain Officer's Legacy Lingers," *Post-Standard* (Syracuse), 30 Oct. 1995, at A5.
- "Robby Unser, the 29-year-old *spittin' image* of three-time Indy 500 king Bobby Unser, delivered his best effort by qualifying fourth fastest." Robin Miller, "Cart Notebook," *Indianapolis Star*, 1 June 1997, at C10.
- "Reggie Jr. says he is the *spitting image* of his father." Andy Baggot, "On the Fast Track," *Wis. State J.*, 1 June 1997, at D1.

A contrarian view comes from *WNWCD*, which records only *spit and image*. It's a much rarer form—e.g.:

- "And the blondish-brown-haired infant is the *spit and image* of his daddy." Nancy Luna, "A Lot Like Daddy," *Orange County Register*, 25 Sept. 1996, at A1.
- "But in the real world we have to eyeball one face to pronounce it the *spit and image* of another." Mike McGough, "Cloning Around with Uncanny Resemblances," *Pitt. Post-Gaz.*, 3 May 1997, at A7.
- "Bobby Mauch, who played the pauper (or was it the prince?) in the rambunctious 1937 film of Mark Twain's *Prince and the Pauper* opposite his *spit-and-image* twin brother, Billy, who portrayed the prince (or was it the other way around?), died Oct. 15 near his home in Santa Rosa, Calif." "Bobby Mauch" (obit.), *Dallas Morning News*, 29 Oct. 2007, at B5.

LANGUAGE-CHANGE INDEX
spitting image: Stage 5
Current ratio (*spitting image* vs. *spit and image*): 23:1

B. And *splitting image. This odd variant, another chip off the old *spit and image* block, usually appears as a pun. But occasionally (and sadly), a sober-sided writer will err with it—e.g.:

- "He's the *splitting image* [read *spitting image*] of his brother, Tampa Bay Buccaneers cornerback Ronde Barber. And why not? Ronde and Tiki Barber, the Giants' leading rusher, are identical twins." Chris Harry, "Giants," *Orlando Sentinel*, 23 Jan. 2001, at D4.
- "But these pumped-up fans . . . were already bubbly, chatty and, in many cases, the *splitting images* [read *spitting image*]

of the star singers." Lisa Jones Townsel, "Star-Inspired Duds," *St. Louis Post-Dispatch*, 12 July 2003, Lifestyle §, at 26.
- "The 2004 Titan full-size pickup has brought along its older brother for the ride: A revamped 2005 Nissan Frontier is the *splitting image* [read *spitting image*] of the company's Mississippi-made truck." Josee Valcourt, "Redesigns Lead the Way," *Clarion-Ledger* (Jackson, Miss.), 6 Jan. 2004, at C1.

LANGUAGE-CHANGE INDEX
*splitting image for *spitting image*: Stage 1
Current ratio (*spitting image* vs.
*splitting image): 30:1

splendid; splendiferous; splendorous; *splendrous. *Splendid* is the ordinary choice of these words meaning "distinguished, illustrious, out-of-the-ordinary" <a splendid achievement>. *Splendiferous* is usually a comic or colloquial equivalent <the show featured dazzling dancers and splendiferous special effects>. *Splendorous*, meaning "brilliant, magnificent, glorious," is a seriously enthusiastic word <the Republicans celebrated by throwing a splendorous inaugural ball>. *Splendrous is a variant of *splendorous*.

split > split > split. So inflected. But some wayward writers have split from the age-old idiom—e.g.: "Fabri-Centers of America (Hudson, OH), a fabric and craft retailer, has *splitted* [read *split*] its stock to increase shares' liquidity." "Fabri-Centers Splits Stock to Pursue Strategy," *Akron Beacon J.*, 3 Aug. 1995, at B2. See IRREGULAR VERBS.

LANGUAGE-CHANGE INDEX
*splitted for past-tense *split*: Stage 1
Current ratio (*has split* vs. *has splitted): 834:1

SPLIT INFINITIVES. A. Generally. H.W. Fowler divided the English-speaking world into five classes: (1) those who neither know nor care what a split infinitive is; (2) those who do not know, but care very much; (3) those who know and condemn; (4) those who know and approve; and (5) those who know and distinguish (*FMEU1* at 558). It is this last class to which, if we have a good ear, we should aspire.

An infinitive is the tenseless form of a verb preceded by *to*, such as *to dismiss* or *to modify*. Splitting the infinitive is placing one or more words between *to* and the verb, such as *to summarily dismiss* or *to unwisely modify*. For the infinitive to be truly split, the intervening word or words must follow *to* directly <to satisfactorily have finished>. E.g.: "Supporters of defense projects and opponents of how the president used his new line-item veto power joined forces yesterday *to decisively reject* President Clinton's line-item veto of military construction programs." "Congress Votes to Undo Clinton Veto," *San Diego Union-Trib.*, 9 Nov. 1997, at A7. If the adverb follows any other part of the infinitive, there's no split <to have satisfactorily finished>.

LANGUAGE-CHANGE INDEX (For the full key, see front matter pp. xxxi, l–li.)
Stage 1: Rejected. **Stage 2:** Widely shunned. **Stage 3:** Widespread but . . . **Stage 4:** Ubiquitous but . . . **Stage 5:** Fully accepted.
Invariably inferior forms marked by asterisk (*). • Ratios represent frequency of prevalent forms vs. variants in current books.

Although few armchair grammarians seem to know it, some split infinitives are regarded as perfectly proper:

- "The evidence in favor of the judiciously split infinitive is sufficiently clear to make it obvious that teachers who condemn it arbitrarily are wasting their time and that of their pupils." Sterling A. Leonard, *Current English Usage* 124 (1932).
- "Sometimes it is necessary to split an infinitive or to cast the sentence in another mould. In the sentence beginning, 'I want to inform you clearly . . .' there is no justification for splitting, but what about this one: 'It compelled the principal to at least review the case under discussion'? If you change that for either 'It compelled the principal at least to review the case under discussion' or 'It compelled the principal to review at least the case under discussion,' you have changed the meaning." W.P. Jowett, *Chatting About English* 185 (1945).
- "The split infinitive is in full accord with the spirit of modern English and is now widely used by our best writers." George O. Curme, *English Grammar* § 70.B, at 148 (1947).
- "[The English language gives us] the inestimable advantage of being able to put adverbs where they will be most effective, coloring the verbs to which they apply and becoming practically part of them. . . . If you think a verb cannot be split in two, just call the adverb a part of the verb and the difficulty will be solved." Joseph Lee, "A Defense of the Split Infinitive," 37 *Mass. L.Q.* 65, 66 (1952).
- "To deliberately split an infinitive, puristic teaching to the contrary notwithstanding, is correct and acceptable English." Norman Lewis, *Better English* 287 (rev. ed. 1961).
- "Splitting an infinitive is preferable both to jamming an adverb between two verbs, where everyone must puzzle out which verb it modifies ('They *refused* boldly *to go* so far away'), and to 'correcting' a split in a way that gives an artificial result ('They wanted *to shorten greatly* the length of the trip'). Sometimes those are the only choices we have, except for rewriting the sentence, and my point is that we needn't rewrite." Barbara Wallraff, *Word Court* 99 (2000).

See SUPERSTITIONS (B).

LANGUAGE-CHANGE INDEX
split infinitives where they feel natural: Stage 5

B. Splits to Be Avoided. If a split is easily fixed by putting the adverb at the end of the phrase and the meaning remains the same, then avoiding the split is the best course:

| Split: | "It is not necessary *to here enlarge* upon those points." |
| Unsplit: | "It is not necessary *to enlarge* upon those points *here*." |

Such capriciously split infinitives only jar the reader. Similar examples turn up frequently—e.g.:

- "Maybe the intense distrust many voters feel toward their government institutions have led them *to almost automatically vote* [read *to vote almost automatically*] against anything the Legislature supports." Marty Latz, "Democrats Take Ideas Straight to Voters for 'Wins,'" *Ariz. Republic/Phoenix Gaz.*, 30 May 1995, at B7. (Notice also the subject–verb disagreement: *distrust* is the subject, and the verb should be *has*.)
- "Last year three-time Doral champion Raymond Floyd revamped the course, adding, among other things, 18 bunkers *to, he says, 'put* [read *in order, he says, to 'put*]

the teeth back in the monster.'" "Doral-Ryder Open," *Sports Illustrated*, 10 Mar. 1997, at 6.

Wide splits are generally to be avoided, especially with piled-on adverbs—e.g.: "We encourage both spouses to utilize the best efforts *to understandingly, sympathetically, and professionally try* to work out a compromise." (A possible revision: *We encourage both spouses to try to work out a compromise understandingly, sympathetically, and professionally.*) But sometimes—for effect—they may be justified: "If there is no other way to make our point, we ought to boldly go ahead and split. We should also be willing to sometimes so completely, in order to gain a particular effect, split the infinitive as to practically but quite consciously run the risk of leaving the *to* as far behind as the last runner in the London Marathon. Grammar is made for man, not man for grammar." "To Split or Not to Split," *Times* (London), 1 Aug. 1995, at 15.

With CORRELATIVE CONJUNCTIONS, a split infinitive simply displays carelessness—e.g.: "There are already enough problems with trying to get all parents *to either make sure* their children are in car seats *or* in seat belts." Sharon K. Woulfe, "Most Should Keep Air Bags On," *Pantagraph* (Bloomington, Ill.), 19 Nov. 1997, at A12. (A possible revision: *There are already enough problems with trying to get all parents to make sure their children are protected by either car seats or seat belts.*) See PARALLELISM.

C. Justified Splits. A number of infinitives are best split. Perhaps the most famous is from the 1960s television series *Star Trek*, in which the opening voice-over included this phrase: *to boldly go where no man* (or, in the revival of the 1980s and 1990s, *where no one*) *has gone before*. The phrase sounds inevitable partly because it is so familiar, but also because the adverb most naturally bears the emphasis, not the verb *go*.

And that example is not a rarity. Consider: *She expects to more than double her profits next year.* We cannot merely move the adverbial phrase in that sentence—to "fix" the split, we would have to eliminate the infinitive, as by writing *She expects that her profits will more than double next year*, thereby giving the sentence a different nuance. (The woman seems less responsible for the increase.)

Again, though, knowing when to split an infinitive requires a good ear and a keen eye. Otherwise, the ability to distinguish—the ability Fowler mentioned—is not attainable. *To flatly state*, for example, suggests something different from *to state flatly*. In the sentences that follow, unsplitting the infinitive would either create an awkwardness or change the sense:

- "White House officials said they hope Wellstone and Moseley-Braun can be persuaded *to quietly drop* their objections and allow the bill to pass when the Senate returns from its vacation." Pam Louwagie, "Wellstone Continues to Put Pressure on Administration over Budget Cuts," *Star Trib.* (Minneapolis), 7 July 1995, at A15.
- "With no ready templates available—the only other 'nearby' track, in Vancouver, was judged too dark, static and simplistic—the two had *to pretty well make up* Speed

Zone Go Kart Raceway from scratch." Alan Kellogg, "Entrepreneurs Get Checkered Flag for Go-Cart Venture," *Edmonton J.*, 11 Apr. 1997, at B1.

- "Issues that most feminists support, such as abortion rights and equal treatment for gays and lesbians, seem *to directly contradict* Christian teachings." Cristina Smith, "Women of the Cloth," *News & Observer* (Raleigh), 3 Oct. 1997, at E1.
- "Some in the audience said they were unhappy that the council could not honor a previous council's agreement allowing homeowners *to voluntarily connect* to the public sewer for $750 each." Kelly Ryan, "Keller Considers Sewer Hookups," *Dallas Morning News*, 5 Oct. 1997, at S1.

Distinguishing these examples from those under (B) may not be easy for all readers. Those who find it difficult might advantageously avoid all splits.

D. Awkwardness Caused by Avoiding Splits. Occasionally, sticking to the old "rule" about split infinitives leads to gross phrasing. The following sentences illustrate clumsy attempts to avoid splitting the infinitive. In the first example, the adverb may be placed more naturally than it is without splitting the infinitive; in the second and third examples, a split is called for:

- "Linda Dishman . . . said Monday that Mahony was *attempting unfairly to deflect* attention away from what she said was illegal demolition of a city-protected landmark." Larry Gordon, "Battle over Cathedral's Fate Intensifies," *L.A. Times*, 4 June 1996, at A1. (What was unfair: the attempting or the deflecting? Read either *was unfairly attempting to deflect* or *was attempting to unfairly deflect*.)
- "Democrats fought for an increase in the minimum wage and *hope quickly to pass* [read *hope to quickly pass*] an expansion of the family leave act." Judy Packer-Tursman, "Comp-Time Proposal Polarizes 2 Parties," *Pitt. Post-Gaz.*, 5 Feb. 1997, at C7.
- "The ordinance is not *expected immediately to solve* [read *expected to immediately solve*] problems with the throbbing, low-frequency bass notes from a local club in the Cromwell Square Shopping Center." Stacy Wong, "In Cromwell, Votes on Noise, Large-Pet Laws," *Hartford Courant*, 15 May 1997, at B1.

E. Ambiguities. When the first of several infinitives is split and the initial *to* is the only one, an ambiguity results—e.g.: "The legislation would make it a federal crime *to physically block* access to clinics, damage their property or injure or intimidate patients and staff." "Congress OKs Protections for Abortion Clinics," *Dallas Morning News*, 13 May 1994, at A1. There's a problem in interpretation: does *physically* modify the verbs *damage*, *injure*, and *intimidate*, as well as *block*? One hopes that the problem is merely with the journalist's paraphrase and not with the legislation itself.

***splitting image.** See spitting image (B).

splutter; sputter. These words are largely synonymous. But *splutter* is the newer word: it probably formed as a blend of *splash* and *sputter*. (See

PORTMANTEAU WORDS.) Though the words were about equally common from 1800 to 1950, since then *sputter* has greatly predominated.

spoil > spoiled > spoiled. So inflected in AmE and BrE alike. *Spoilt*, a common variant of the past-tense spelling especially in BrE, has never predominated even in that variety of English.

Current ratio (*spoiled* vs. *spoilt*): 4:1

spoil, n.; spoils. The plural form is standard in SET PHRASES <the spoils of war> <to the victor belong the spoils> and in similar uses when multiple objects are referred to <the looters carried off their spoils>—e.g.:

- "The *spoils* of unmanned space exploration are clear—conveniences of modern life such as mobile phones and satellite television would not function without the vast fleets of satellites that orbit the Earth." Anjana Ahuja, "Why Man Will Always Reach for the Stars," *Times* (London), 3 Feb. 2003, at 4.
- "Now, China is crossing the sea in the other direction, bringing home *spoils* from Japan." Peter S. Goodman & Akiko Kashiwagi, "Imperial Irony Building in Japan," *Wash. Post*, 6 Feb. 2003, at E1.

The singular form is very rare, but occasionally seen: "We, the sales professionals steeped in knowledge and cunning, [are] ever testing each other, encouraging each other, ever eager for chase, and no more ashamed to be called by our proper name, and to take our fair share of the *spoil*." Mark Borkowski, "Electronics Sales People and Hunters," *Canadian Electronics*, 1 Nov. 2002, at 4.

spoliation; despoliation; *despoilment. A learned word, *spoliation* /spoh-lee-**ay**-shən/ means the act of ruining, destroying, or spoiling something. In the hands and mouths of the less-than-learned, it's often misspelled and mispronounced **spoilation* (an example of METATHESIS). The difference between the form of the verb and of the noun arises from different paths by which the words came into English: in the 14th century, *spoil* was borrowed from Old French (*espoille*), whereas in the 15th century *spoliation* was borrowed from Latin (*spoliātio*).

Despoliation (= pillaging, plundering) is often misspelled **despoilation*—a blunder that can spoil otherwise highly literate writing—e.g.:

- "The horrors of gulag and the environmental *despoilations* [read *despoliations*] of the Soviet era both get their due here." Martin Sieff, "Russia's Epic Effort to Conquer Siberia," *Wash. Times*, 27 Feb. 1994, at B7.
- "The severed head of an elephant fashioned from foam and paint . . . seems to be a straightforward reminder of the *despoilation* [read *despoliation*] of natural habitats." Mary Abbe, "Art Review: Dead Heads," *Star Trib.* (Minneapolis), 4 Sept. 2009, at E18.
- "'Environment' has become a narrow, bitterly focused word turning exclusively on hurts or *despoilations* [read *despoliations*] of nature." Rex Murphy, "A Triumph for the

---

LANGUAGE-CHANGE INDEX (For the full key, see front matter pp. xxxi, l–li.)
Stage 1: Rejected. **Stage 2:** Widely shunned. **Stage 3:** Widespread but . . . **Stage 4:** Ubiquitous but . . . **Stage 5:** Fully accepted.
Invariably inferior forms marked by asterisk (*). • Ratios represent frequency of prevalent forms vs. variants in current books.

Human 'Environment,'" *Nat'l Post* (Can.), 17 Mar. 2012, at A22.

Oddly, though, the corresponding verb is *despoil*. Why the discrepancy in spelling? The answer again lies in the vagaries of linguistic history. English borrowed the verb in the 13th century from Old French (*despoillier*) but the noun in the 17th century from Latin (*despoliatio*). And those two forms—for centuries, at any rate—stuck. The Frenchified noun coined in the early 19th century, *despoilment, never rose above being a NEEDLESS VARIANT.

LANGUAGE-CHANGE INDEX
1. *spoliation* misspelled *spoilation: Stage 1
Current ratio: 66:1
2. *despoliation* misspelled *despoilation: Stage 1
Current ratio: 26:1

sponge, vb., makes *spongeable* (not *spongable) but *sponging* (not *spongeing). *Sponge,* n., makes the corresponding adjective *spongy* (not *spongey). Please absorb all that.

spoonfuls; *spoonsful. The former is standard. See PLURALS (G).

Current ratio: 16:1

sports car—not *sport car—is the standard term. But *sport coat* and *sport shirt* are standard phrases that predominate over *sports coat and *sports shirt.

sport utility vehicle; *sports utility vehicle. The first is standard in AmE and BrE alike. The second is a NEEDLESS VARIANT.

Current ratio: 2:1

spouse. Whenever you know that you're referring to a *husband* or *wife,* use one of those terms. *Spouse,* which carries a legalistic flavor, should appear only when the context is not sex-specific. *Married spouse* is an infrequent REDUNDANCY.

sprain > sprained > sprained. So inflected. An erroneous *sprang* sometimes springs up—e.g.:

- "A Web site has been created on the Internet for people to send quick get-well wishes to Kerri Strug, who *sprang* [read *sprained*] her ankle Tuesday night." *Times-Picayune* (New Orleans), 25 July 1996, at A1 (photo caption).
- "'I *sprang* [read *sprained*] my ankle twice dancing to karaoke,' McCormick says." Thomas Ropp, "Couple Share Curse of the Karaoke," *Ariz. Republic,* 16 Dec. 1996, at C1.

Of course, *sprang* is the correct past-tense form of the verb *spring.* See **spring.**

LANGUAGE-CHANGE INDEX
*sprang ankle for *sprained ankle*: Stage 1

spread > spread > spread. So inflected. The weak form of the verb (*spreaded) is erroneous—e.g.:

- "According to Ms. Lucas, Deborah Isabelle's character and 'motivation' *spreaded* [read *spread*] to other students." Antonio R. Harvey, "Bright Futures," *Sacramento Observer,* 21 June 1995, at A9.
- "He *spreaded* [read *spread*] the wealth around, throwing to eight different receivers." Ken Brazzle, "ASU Kealy Gets

Support He Needs for USC Win," *Tucson Citizen,* 13 Oct. 1997, at C3.
- "Bobby's clean-shaven face *spreaded* [read *spread*] in a wide smile." John W. Fountain, "For Teammates, Challenges Continue Off the Field," *Wash. Post,* 5 July 1998, at A1.

See IRREGULAR VERBS.

LANGUAGE-CHANGE INDEX
*spreaded for past-tense *spread*: Stage 1
Current ratio (*is spread* vs.
*is spreaded): 1,525:1

sprightly (= [1] lively, airy; or [2] zesty, esp. spicy, in flavor) is subject to the mischievous misspelling *spritely—e.g.:

- "Will she end up a bitter, washed-up star a la Baby Jane, psychologically torturing her *spritely* [read *sprightly*] sis Jamie-Lynn? Let's recap Britney's recent bizarre behavior." Tamara Ikenberg, "Not So 'Lucky,'" *Courier-J.* (Louisville), 10 Mar. 2007, at S4.
- "Jesse Aarons (Josh Hutcherson, 'Kicking and Screaming') is in middle-school hell. He's bullied in class and ignored at home. Enter Leslie Burke (AnnaSophia Robb, 'Charlie and the Chocolate Factory'), a *spritely* [read *sprightly*] new student with an enchanting perspective on life despite being treated as an outsider herself." "This 'Bridge' Is Best Uncovered," *Boston Herald,* 17 June 2007, Edge §, at 32.
- "This is when you want to reach for one of the stalwarts of the California wine trade. . . . Also consider the *spritely* [read *sprightly*] Firehose 2006 California Off-Dry Riesling ($9), a new release from Trinchero Family Estate in Napa Valley; the floral and delicately sweet Cameron Hughes 2006 Lot 50 Mosel-Saar-Ruwer Riesling ($9); and the big, peachy and spicy Peltier Station 2006 Viognier ($14)." Mike Dunne, "Good Deals to Pair with Your Backyard Meals," *Sacramento Bee,* 21 May 2008, at F1.

LANGUAGE-CHANGE INDEX
sprightly misspelled *spritely: Stage 1
Current ratio: 33:1

spring > sprang > sprung. So inflected. But *springed* is correct when the sense is "equipped with springs" <a springed mattress> <springed hinges> or "to spend the season of spring" <they springed in Europe>. (The latter usage will strike many readers as more than a little odd.)

The real challenge with these words is to get the past-tense and past-participial forms in their proper places. Some writers spring an erroneous *sprung* on their readers—e.g.:

- "Teachers can obtain study guides that describe the history of the dances and the cultures from which they *sprung* [read *sprang*]." "School Notes," *S.F. Chron.,* 19 Dec. 1997, at 2.
- "They *sprung* [read *sprang*] out of the gate with a string of initiatives that culminated with the president's 1993 budget victory." Clarence Page, "Clinton's Legacies Continue to Be a Work in Progress," *Chicago Trib.,* 18 Jan. 1998, at 19.
- "Then they *sprung* [read *sprang*] a backdoor play on Grimsley." Jeff Carlton, "Dudley Turns Corner, Makes Little Four Final," *News & Record* (Greensboro), 30 Dec. 1998, at C1.

The opposite misuse—*sprang* for *sprung*—is less common:

- "Some of these trade-terms may *have originally sprang* [read *have originally sprung*] up as slang." Otto Jespersen, *Mankind, Nation, and Individual from a Linguistic Point of View* 147 (1946).
- "Bob Horne . . . said that there are more than 300 truckers' ministries that *have sprang* [read *have sprung*] from the original, the Ministry of Transport, founded by Canadian chaplain Jim Keys in 1951." Sue Anne Pressley, "Truck-Stop Ministry Offers Comfort in the Odd Hours," *Wash. Post*, 3 Nov. 1996, at A3.
- "A number of competitors *have sprang* [read *have sprung*] up." Larry Kanter, "Furniture Trade," *L.A. Bus. J.*, 23 June 1997, at 40.

See IRREGULAR VERBS.

For a misuse of *sprang* for *sprained*, see **sprain.**

LANGUAGE-CHANGE INDEX
1. *sprung* misused for simple-past *sprang*: Stage 4
Current ratio (*vessel sprang a leak* vs.
vessel sprung a leak): 1.3:1
2. *sprang* misused for past-participial *sprung*: Stage 1
Current ratio (*have sprung* vs. **have sprang*): 105:1

*spritely. See **sprightly.**

spry (= active and nimble despite advancing age) makes *spryer* and *spryest*—preferably not **sprier* and **spriest*. Cf. **shy** & **sly.**

*spue. See **spew.**

spumoni; spumone. The Italian term for this ice-cream dessert is *spumone* (/spyoo-**moh**-nee/). Although that used to be the preferred spelling in English as well, dictionaries are now almost equally divided. In English print sources, *spumoni* appears about 16 times as often as *spumone*. *Spumoni* has predominated in English since the 1920s.

spurious. See **specious.**

spurt; *spirt. Most AmE dictionaries list **spirt* merely as a variant of *spurt*. In 1926 H.W. Fowler suggested a DIFFERENTIATION: use **spirt* in the sense "gush, jet, flow" <a spirt of blood> <oil spirts up from the ground>, and reserve *spurt* for "sprint, burst, hustle" <work done in spurts> <Bailey spurted past>. But this distinction never took hold.

Current ratio (*spurted* vs. **spirted*): 25:1

sputter. See **splutter.**

squalor /skwah-lər/ is so spelled in BrE and AmE alike—not **squalour*. See -OR; -OUR. Cf. **glamour.**

Current ratio: 136:1

SQUARE BRACKETS. See PUNCTUATION (P).

squash; quash, vb. *Squash* (= to flatten or soften [something] by forceful crushing or squeezing) is not a substitute for *quash* (= to overturn or make legally invalid; to suppress, as a rebellion). Many writers err on this point—e.g.:

- "The Alabama story ends for the moment with criminal indictments, and with Windom not only installed as lieutenant governor but also successfully seeing through the tort-reform legislation his opponents had tried to *squash* [read *quash*]." Arianna Huffington, "Happy Ending No Savior in Political Horror Story," *Chicago Sun-Times*, 1 Sept. 1999, at 45.
- "The Hartford Courant's motion to *squash* [read *quash*] a subpoena duces tecum issued by the Journal Publishing Co. is granted." "Connecticut Opinions—Connecticut Superior Court Reports," *Conn. Law Trib.*, 26 Feb. 2001, at 212.
- "They fear that the West Freeport rebellion could hamper the town's future planning efforts and *squash* [read *quash*] other, more moderate proposals to revamp the town's zoning laws." Tom Bell, "Zoning Controversy Defines Council Race," *Portland Press Herald*, 1 Nov. 2001, at B1.

LANGUAGE-CHANGE INDEX
squash misused for *quash*: Stage 3
Current ratio (*quash the rebellion* vs.
*squash the rebellion): 3:1

squeeze > squeezed > squeezed. So inflected. **Squoze* is a dialectal past-tense form dating from the early 19th century. E.g.: "As we lifted it to our lips, the onions, bell peppers, yellow squash and smoked gouda cheese, all melted and gooey, *squoze* [read *squeezed*] out from their roasted bread blankets onto the paper wrapping we used as a plate." "Truckin' at Green Cuisine," *Arkansas Times*, 8 Dec. 2010.

Current ratio (*squeezed* vs. **squoze*): 2,276:1

squelch. See ***quelch.**

squirearchy (= the class of landed gentry or country proprietors) is predominantly so spelled in all varieties of English—not **squirarchy*.

Current ratio: 17:1

squirrel, vb., makes *squirreling* and *squirreled* in AmE, *squirrelling* and *squirrelled* in BrE. See SPELLING (B).

Sr. See NAMES (B).

Sri Lankan; *Ceylonese. A citizen of Sri Lanka (known as Ceylon until 1972) is today known as a *Sri Lankan*, not a **Ceylonese*. See DENIZEN LABELS.

Current ratio: 9:1

stabilize; *stabilify; *stabilitate. The first has been standard since it was coined in the mid-19th century. The second and third are NEEDLESS VARIANTS.

stadium. Although dictionaries traditionally gave priority to **stadia* as the plural, *stadiums* is the more natural and now the more usual form. *Stadiums* has been the predominant form in English print sources since the mid-1980s—e.g.:

- "Dozens of *stadiums* have sprouted up all over the country in recent years." Lisa Respers, "Funds Sought for Stadium in Aberdeen," *Baltimore Sun*, 28 Apr. 1997, at B1.

LANGUAGE-CHANGE INDEX (For the full key, see front matter pp. xxxi, l–li.)
Stage 1: Rejected. **Stage 2:** Widely shunned. **Stage 3:** Widespread but . . . **Stage 4:** Ubiquitous but . . . **Stage 5:** Fully accepted.
Invariably inferior forms marked by asterisk (*). • Ratios represent frequency of prevalent forms vs. variants in current books.

- "The other 25 percent of the money would go for 'regional attractions' like baseball and football *stadiums* in Pittsburgh." Tom Barnes, "New Tax Bill Gives Counties More Backers," *Pitt. Post-Gaz.*, 30 May 1997, at A1.

See PLURALS (B).

LANGUAGE-CHANGE INDEX
stadiums: Stage 5

staff. In most senses, the plural is *staffs*. But in music (as well as some archaic senses), the preferred plural is *staves*—though *staffs* occasionally appears even in musical contexts. See PLURALS (C).

stained glass, not *stain *glass*, is the standard form—e.g.: "One of the most prominent features will be a round *stain glass* [read *stained-glass*] window above the altar." Elizabeth Crooker, "It Took Seven Years, but They Finally Have Church," *Union Leader* (Manchester, N.H.), 21 Mar. 1997, at A5. (On the reason for the hyphen in that correction, see PHRASAL ADJECTIVES.) Cf. **fine-toothed comb, iced tea** & **skim milk.**

LANGUAGE-CHANGE INDEX
*stain *glass* for *stained glass*: Stage 1
Current ratio (*stained glass* vs.
*stain *glass*): 119:1

stalactite; stalagmite. They're both deposits of calcium carbonate found in caves and caverns. The difference is that a *stalactite* hangs from the ceiling, while a *stalagmite* rises from the floor. Writers sometimes fall into error by using *stalagmite* for *stalactite*—e.g.:

- "The Dripstone Trail Tour is a leisurely hour-plus trek known for delicate sodastraw formations and totem pole *stalagmites* [read *stalactites*] hanging from cave ceilings." Bob Puhala, "Weekend Grand Tour," *Chicago Sun-Times*, 2 Jan. 1994, Travel §, at 1.
- "Walking into a slip house [i.e., part of a ceramics plant] and seeing *stalagmites* [read *stalactites*] of clay hanging from the ceiling caused by an earlier line break indicates a lack of interest in cleanliness." Paul Kiesow, "Cleanliness: A Component of Quality Often Overlooked," *Ceramic Indus.*, 1 Feb. 1996, at 32.

But *stalactite* for *stalagmite* is hardly unknown—e.g.:

- "Guided tours offer glimpses of spectacular *stalactites* [read *stalagmites*] rising from the cave floor to underground waterfalls." Bob Puhala, "Weekend Grand Tour," *Chicago Sun-Times*, 2 Jan. 1994, Travel §, at 1.
- "If a *stalagmite* [read *stalactite*] on the ceiling joined a *stalactite* [read *stalagmite*] on the floor, they made a column." Winifred Yu, "Framed by the Ages," *Times Union* (Albany), 18 Feb. 1996, at G11.

A mnemonic device popular among schoolchildren holds that the -*c*- in *stalactite* stands for *ceiling*, while the -*g*- in *stalagmite* stands for *ground*. Another useful one is "hang tight."

In AmE, the accent for both words falls on the second syllable. In BrE, the first syllable is stressed in both words.

LANGUAGE-CHANGE INDEX
1. *stalagmite* misused for *stalactite*: Stage 1
2. *stalactite* misused for *stalagmite*: Stage 1

stamen (= the pollen-producing male part of a flower) forms the plural *stamens*. The classical plural *stamina* has an entirely different sense in English—a strong sense that shows no signs of flagging.

stamping ground. See **stomping ground.**

stanch. See **staunch.**

STANDARD ENGLISH. This is a troublesome term: we all think we know what it is, but a definition proves elusive. Broadly speaking, it is the English used by educated people. Some Britons contend that it is the English used by educated Britons, and that whatever is used by educated people in the United States is Standard American English. Some Americans refer to Standard British English, to differentiate it from American English. Among commentators, some believe that there is a Standard English that subsumes both AmE and BrE. Still others suggest that each English-speaking nation has its own standard: whatever happens to be the most prestigious dialect within that nation.

Although no comprehensive universal definition exists for the whole of Standard English, there is a range of normally accepted linguistic behavior within a given country. As long as deviations from that range are few and insignificant, the standard is maintained.

One major purpose of this book is to detail what is and is not Standard English. In some instances that means Standard Written English (some commentators dislike the capitals because they make the phenomenon seem too monolithic and institutionalized, but capitals are widely used among linguistic commentators). In other instances that means Standard Colloquial English. Since this book is principally about English in its written form, it is easy enough to exclude accent (as many linguists prefer to do) in discussing the linguistic standard. Mostly, the differences between Standard English and dialect have to do with grammar, vocabulary, spelling, and punctuation (though undeniably also the pronunciation of certain words, such as *can't*, for which /kant/ is standard and /kaynt/ is nonstandard).

Throughout the 20th century, commentators noted (sometimes in strong terms) the social disapproval that attaches to nonstandard English. Mostly this is put in negative terms. If you don't speak Standard English, you're at a social and professional disadvantage—e.g.:

- "The intelligent people of America use reasonably pure English. If the speaker falls below this level he simply disgusts." John P. Altgeld, *Oratory: Its Requirements and Its Rewards* 9 (1901).
- "Anyone who cannot use the language habits in which the major affairs of the country are conducted, the language habits of the socially acceptable of most of our communities, would have a serious handicap." Charles Carpenter Fries, *American English Grammar* 14 (1940).
- "Talking the Standard Language . . . is to [people's] advantage, not merely materially, because they can more easily obtain positions in society which now—whether one approves of it or not in the abstract—are given by

preference to people whose speech is free from dialect, but also because they thus escape being looked down on on account of their speech and are therefore saved from many unpleasant humiliations. Apart from all this, merely by reason of their way of speaking they have a better chance of coming in contact with others and getting a fuller interchange of ideas." Otto Jespersen, *Mankind, Nation, and Individual from a Linguistic Point of View* 70–71 (1946).

- "A standard has the advantages of uniformity, general utility, and presentability. Whoever writes it knows two things: he *will* be understood; he will *not* be regarded with condescension, amusement, or contempt." A.P. Rossiter, *Our Living Language* 75 (1953).
- "Native deviators from standard English—ours—are suspected of being vulgar, uneducated, or simply rustic." Graham Wilson, *A Linguistics Reader* 86 (Graham Wilson ed., 1967).
- "People, whether male or female, who use a substandard or less prestigious form of speech often pay a social penalty for doing so." Peter Farb, *Word Play* 57 (1974).
- "Deviations from standard English, or what people take to be deviations, are more likely to arouse fury, pity, or scorn than admiration for the deviator's individuality." Barbara Wallraff, *Word Court* 9 (2000).

So there's the neatly compiled answer to why Standard English is worth trying to attain: without it, you won't be taken seriously. Many people, especially educated people, will regard you with condescension, amusement, and contempt; they'll consider you vulgar, uneducated, rustic, and possibly even disgusting; you might well arouse fury, pity, or scorn.

Although some linguists are fond of saying that a standard language is preferred not for any *linguistic* reason but merely for *social* reasons, the social factors that affect language users can't readily be—and shouldn't be—divorced from linguistics. That is one of the tenets underlying the field known as sociolinguistics. Social pressures are inextricably intertwined with language.

And so what began as one of many 14th-century dialects has risen, by a series of historical events, to become the literary language of the English-speaking world. This dialect wasn't inherently superior to the other dialects; it was the language used by the people with social and political influence. It became the medium of exchange in politics, diplomacy, law, medicine, technology, and other fields involving intellectual discipline. This rise coincided with literary cultivation and enhanced stability.

Despite the tone that commentators have occasionally taken, encouraging people to use Standard English is not a matter of snobbery. It is a matter of (1) cultural cohesion, (2) continuity with a great literary tradition, and (3) equal opportunity. Learning it does not mean rejecting one's origins; rather, it is (to some speakers) the equivalent of learning another language—becoming essentially bidialectal. "Its virtue," as the writer and

linguist Anthony Burgess put it, "lies in its neutrality, its lack of purely local associations, its transparency, its clarity, its suitability for intellectual discourses or dispassionate government pronouncements." *A Mouthful of Air* 22 (1992).

For related discussions, see CLASS DISTINCTIONS & DIALECT.

standby. Pl. *standbys*—not **standbies.*

*standee. See -EE.

stand in line; stand on line. While both phrases must be accepted as standard, *stand in line* predominates throughout the English-speaking world. The regionalism *stand on line* prevails in the New York City area and elsewhere in the Northeast, and it is heard (and read) elsewhere too often to be dismissed as a NEEDLESS VARIANT. Yet it does smack of DIALECT. Cf. **wait in line.**

standpoint. See **viewpoint.**

Star-Spangled Banner. Keep the hyphen. See PHRASAL ADJECTIVES.

start. See **begin (B)** & **commence.**

statable. So spelled in AmE and BrE alike—not **stateable.* See MUTE E.

> Current ratio: 4:1

state, n. See **people (B).**

state, vb. See **say.**

*stateable. See **statable.**

stated otherwise, when used at the very beginning of a sentence, is a pompous version of *in other words.* The phrase emerged in the late 19th century and became widespread during the 20th. It shows no signs of waning—e.g.:

- "*Stated otherwise* [read *In other words*], while conservatives contend UDI by Quebec after a victorious Yes vote would be revolutionary and seditious, pragmatists claim Ottawa's refusal to heed the clearly expressed wishes of a majority in the province would be dictatorial." Louis-Philippe Rochon, "Two Federalist Solitudes," *Montreal Gaz.,* 16 Oct. 1996, at B3.
- "*Stated otherwise* [read *In other words*], if the largest S&L in the United States cannot attract new investment capital with which to lend and grow, the industry cannot survive." Elliot B. Smith, "S&Ls Want Bank Market," *Orange County Register,* 19 Feb. 1997, at C1.

But toward the end of a sentence, the phrase is often quite natural (in the sense "disagreed")—e.g.:

- "The FAA, airport management and controllers say the airport is safe, and that the flying public has little to worry about, though union representatives *stated otherwise* less than two weeks ago." Cheryl Meyer, "Trouble in the Tower," *Lancaster New Era,* 3 Mar. 1997, at A1.

LANGUAGE-CHANGE INDEX (For the full key, see front matter pp. xxxi, l–li.)
Stage 1: Rejected. **Stage 2:** Widely shunned. **Stage 3:** Widespread but . . . **Stage 4:** Ubiquitous but . . . **Stage 5:** Fully accepted.
Invariably inferior forms marked by asterisk (*). • Ratios represent frequency of prevalent forms vs. variants in current books.

- "Press accounts *stated otherwise*." Jo Mannies, "'Finally'— Haas Revels in His Victory," *St. Louis Post-Dispatch*, 7 Apr. 1997, at C2.

Cf. **in other words.**

statelily. See ADVERBS (B).

state of the art, n.; **state-of-the-art,** adj. These VOGUE WORDS illustrate the interests of a fast-changing society with rapidly effected technological innovations <state-of-the-art products>. For the moment, they are tainted by association with salesmen's JARGON.

***stati.** See **status.**

stationary; stationery. The first is the adjective (= remaining in one place, immobile), the second the noun (= writing materials, esp. paper with envelopes). For a mnemonic device, think of the *-er* in *paper*.

On *stationary* as a noncomparable adjective, see ADJECTIVES (B).

statistic (= a single term or datum in a statistical compilation) is a BACK-FORMATION from *statistics* dating from the late 19th century. Today its correctness is beyond challenge. E.g.:

- "This *statistic* is a dramatic turnaround from surveys done as recently as five years ago." Vince Vawter, "Snapshot Shows City Growing in Multiple Ways," *Evansville Courier*, 5 Oct. 1997, at A20.
- "He did not cite the source of that *statistic*." "Lawyer Asks High Court to Target Police Chase," *News & Observer* (Raleigh), 10 Dec. 1997, at A10.

LANGUAGE-CHANGE INDEX
one statistic: Stage 5

statistics = (1) the mathematics of collecting and analyzing numerical data; or (2) numerical data. Sense 1 is singular <statistics is an exacting discipline>. Sense 2 is plural <the statistics aren't yet in>.

status (/**stat**-əs/ or /**stay**-təs/) forms the plural *statuses* (or, in Latin, *status*), not **stati*. See HYPERCORRECTION (A) & PLURALS (B).

status quo; *status quo ante;* ***status in quo.** Status quo* means "the state of affairs at present"; hence **current status quo* is a REDUNDANCY. *Status quo ante* (= the state of affairs at a previous time) is generally confined to legal contexts. (So are the adverbial LATINISMS *in statu quo* and *in statu quo ante*, both meaning "in the same state of affairs as existed earlier.") **Status in quo* is an archaic variant of *status quo*.

statutory; ***statutorial.** Statutory* = (1) of, relating to, or involving legislation <statutory construction>; or (2) legislatively created <the law of patents is purely statutory>.

**Statutorial* is a NEEDLESS VARIANT not recognized in the dictionaries. But it sometimes appears in print—e.g.:

- "The dedication would be *statutorial* [read *statutory*]." "Gas Tax Hike," *Star Trib.* (Minneapolis), 3 May 1994, at A12.

- "Now if you think this *statutorial* [read *statutory*] change is something that would cause heavy breathing only among communications lawyers, consider the fact that it will open competition." Robert Haught, "Potomac Junction," *Daily Oklahoman*, 8 Aug. 1996, at 4.
- "Gov. Bobby Jindal also soon weighed in, saying the levee board didn't have the *statutorial* [read *statutory*] authority to retain outside counsel on a contingency fee basis." Lauren McGaughy, "Tort Reform Receiving a Renewed Push," *Times-Picayune* (New Orleans), 19 Dec. 2013, at A1.

The adverb *statutorily* is sometimes wrongly written **statutorially* or **statutorally*—e.g.:

- "At an interest rate *statutorally* [read *statutorily*] set at 10 percent, Detroit Diesel would have two to five years to repay the loan, said Nelson." Lara Jones, "Engine Remanufacturer Could Create 450 New Utah Jobs," *Enterprise* (Salt Lake City), 8 July 1996, at 1.
- "Nothing compels him, *statutorally* [read *statutorily*] or ethically, to give up on the job." "Tobacco: Unregulated Remarks," *Virginian-Pilot* (Norfolk), 6 Mar. 1997, at B10.

LANGUAGE-CHANGE INDEX
1. **statutorial* for *statutory*: Stage 1
Current ratio (*statutory* vs. **statutorial*): 22,299:1
2. **statutorally* for *statutorily*: Stage 1
Current ratio (*statutorily* vs. **statutorally*): 1,905:1
3. **statutorially* for *statutorily*: Stage 1
Current ratio (*statutorily* vs. **statutorially*): 3,241:1

***statutory legislation** is a REDUNDANCY—e.g.: "Only after the Civil War did *statutory legislation* [read *statutes* or *legislation*] become widespread, replacing common law." Janet Pearson, "Roe vs. Wade," *Tulsa World*, 26 Jan. 1997, at G1.

statutory rape (= sexual intercourse with a female below the age of consent, regardless of whether it occurs against her will) is an Americanism that originated in the 19th century. Originally, statutory-rape laws applied only to female victims, but today the great majority of American states have sex-neutral legislation dealing with this offense. *Statutory rape* is a popular term, not (ironically) a statutory one.

staunch; stanch. *Staunch* is predominant both as the adjective ("trustworthy, loyal") and as the verb ("to restrain the flow of [usu. blood]"). As verbs, both headwords were common from about 1830—about equally so. But since about 1960, *staunching the flow* has for the most part overtaken *stanching the flow* in AmE and BrE alike—e.g.:

- "Until now, his most notable move was *staunching* the flow of red ink by closing New York Newsday in 1995." Mark Jurkowitz, "Shakeups May Signal Sea Change for Press," *Boston Globe*, 10 Oct. 1997, at C1.
- "Selman stumbled off to try and *staunch* the flow from a severed artery while Outlaw staggered into Utah Street and collapsed." J. Lee Butts, *Texas Bad Girls* 32 (2001). (For more on *try and* in this quotation, see **try and.**)
- "He did not know what he felt as he saw Snape's white face, and the fingers trying to *staunch* the bloody wound at his neck." J.K. Rowling, *Harry Potter and the Deathly Hallows* 657 (1st Am. ed., 2007).

Although there is no sound objection to that wording, *stanching* the flow has predominated in AmE since about 1990.

LANGUAGE-CHANGE INDEX
Current ratio (*staunching the flow* vs. *stanching the flow* in World English): 1:1

stave > stave > staved. So inflected. Avoid the variant past form *stove*.

steadfast, adj., has been the standard spelling since the early 19th century. **Stedfast* is a variant that predominated during the 17th and 18th centuries.

steal. See **embezzle.**

steamroll; *steamroller, v.t. Although **steamroller* was once considered the standard verb, *steamroll* surpassed it in the early 1990s: it's now twice as common in print. E.g.: "From there, Levens *steamrolled* on three runs and a reception, scoring from the 3." Don Pierson, "Packers 27, Vikings 11," *Chicago Trib.*, 2 Dec. 1997, Sports §, at 1.
Current ratio (*steamrolled* vs. **steamrollered*): 2:1

stemma (= [1] a family tree, or [2] a diagram showing the relationships among literary works) predominantly forms the plural *stemmata*—not *stemmas*.
Current ratio: 2:1

stencil, vb., makes *stenciled* and *stenciling* in AmE, *stencilled* and *stencilling* in BrE. See SPELLING (B).

stereotypical; stereotypic. The longer form is standard in figurative senses—e.g.: "Despite the wide variety of women who adhere to feminism, the *stereotypical* thinking that feminists are radicals lives on." Martha Ezzard, "South Can Use Fonda's Brand of Activism," *News & Record* (Greensboro), 30 Nov. 1997, at F2. *Stereotypic* is standard for the narrow sense "of or produced by stereotypy (the process of printing from stereotype plates)."

sterility. See **impotence (A).**

sternum. Surely if this word were in common use, English speakers would say and write the plural form as *sternums*. But because it invariably appears in medical and technical writing, the Latinate plural *sterna* has consistently predominated since the 17th century.

stewardess. In standard usage, this term was overtaken by *flight attendant* in AmE in the mid-1990s. The feminine suffix made it politically incorrect (see SEXISM (B))—and more and more men now have this occupation. So a hypernym was needed, and *flight attendant* was coined in the 1940s to fill the void. It did not surge into widespread use in AmE till the 1970s. In BrE, however, *flight attendant* still doesn't seriously rival *stewardess* in frequency of use in print sources. See POLITICAL CORRECTNESS.

stick > stuck > stuck. So inflected. The exception occurs in hockey and other sports, in which *sticked* (= [1] hit with a stick, or [2] having used a stick) is ubiquitous—e.g.:

- "No one has *pogo-sticked* farther." John Walters, "The Question Is Why?" *Sports Illustrated*, 2 Nov. 1998, at 16.
- "Lightning forward Darcy Tucker had been sent to the box for six minutes for challenging Pittsburgh goalie Tom Barrasso, who had *sticked* him to the mouth." Roy Cummings, "Lightning Take Small Steps in Loss," *Tampa Trib.*, 22 Nov. 1998, at 1. See IRREGULAR VERBS.

stick to; stick with. Both phrases are acceptable in figurative senses <stick with it!> <stick to it!>. *Stick to* predominates in both AmE and BrE. *Stick with* is a chiefly AmE variant.
Current ratio: 2:1

stigma. A. Plural. *Stigma* (/stig-mə/) can be pluralized in two ways: *stigmas* and *stigmata* (/stig-**mah**-tə/). The English plural (-*mas*) is preferable in most contexts. But *stigmata* carries the specialized sense "bodily marks resembling the crucifixion wounds of Jesus Christ." In this sense the word is sometimes pronounced /**stig**-mə-tə/, after the Greek and Latin. See PLURALS (B).
Current ratio (*stigmata* vs. *stigmas*): 1.4:1

B. And *stigmatism*. *Stigmatism* (= [1] the absence of astigmatism, or [2] the condition of being afflicted with unhealthy spots on the skin, esp. spots that bleed) is frequently confounded with *stigma* (= a mark of disgrace)—e.g.:

- "'South Park's' edgy creators are fighting the *stigmatism* [read *stigma*] that they're all about gross-out and shock-value." Anthony D'Alessandro, "'Bush' League Project," *Daily Variety*, 30 Mar. 2001, at A8.
- "Millions of men and women who opened the closet door, 'came out,' risked social *stigmatism* [read *stigma*], as well as the loss of their jobs and careers." "We've Come a Long Way," *S.F. Chron.*, 16 Oct. 2001, at A16.
- "A possible reason for this may be to avoid the *stigmatism* [read *stigma*] that accompanies such a label ['aggression'] being applied to a State." Dan Sarooshi, "The Peace and Justice Paradox," in *The Permanent International Criminal Court* 95, 113 (Dominic McGoldrick et al. eds., 2004).

For further misuse of **stigmatism,** see **astigmatism.**
LANGUAGE-CHANGE INDEX
stigmatism misused for *stigma*: Stage 1

stiletto. Pl. *stilettos*. See PLURALS (D).

still life. Although the usual plural of *life* is *lives*, the art phrase *still life* makes the plural *still lifes*. See PLURALS (C).
Current ratio (*painted still lifes* vs. **painted still lives*): 28:1

LANGUAGE-CHANGE INDEX (For the full key, see front matter pp. xxxi, l–li.)
Stage 1: Rejected. **Stage 2:** Widely shunned. **Stage 3:** Widespread but . . . **Stage 4:** Ubiquitous but . . . **Stage 5:** Fully accepted.
Invariably inferior forms marked by asterisk (*). • Ratios represent frequency of prevalent forms vs. variants in current books.

stimulus. Pl. *stimuli.* This word has not traditionally made a native-English plural, but a few writers have nevertheless experimented with *stimuluses—e.g.:

- "The octopus is meant not to symbolize industry or productivity, but as an example of the kind of visual *stimuluses* [read *stimuli*] that America is producing." Robert W. Duffy, "Ceos' Tentacles Embrace Arts," *St. Louis Post-Dispatch*, 28 July 1996, at C4.
- " 'You can get [gross domestic product] up, you can get it to appear to be growing strongly. But if you have structural impediments in the system, those *stimuluses* [read *stimuli*] are transitory.' " Greg Ip, "Greenspan Says Japan, Europe Face 'Rigidities,' " *Wall Street J. Europe*, 20 Nov. 2002, at UKA 3 (quoting Alan Greenspan).

See PLURALS (B).

LANGUAGE-CHANGE INDEX
*stimuluses for *stimuli*: Stage 1
Current ratio (*stimuli* vs. *stimuluses): 36,863:1

sting > stung > stung. So inflected. See IRREGULAR VERBS.

stink > stank > stunk. So inflected. *Stinked is a dialectal past tense and past participle (see DIALECT). *Stunk* often appears erroneously as a simple-past form, especially in figurative uses—e.g.:

- "When I coached, the calls *stunk* [read *stank*] then and the calls stink now." Howard Manly, "Patriots, Ch. 4 Winners," *Boston Globe*, 8 Dec. 1998, at E5.
- "The Patriots *stunk* [read *stank*]." Steve Buckley, "Blow a Gasket, Pete," *Boston Herald*, 28 Dec. 1998, at 100.
- "Your timing *stunk* [read *stank*]." David Landis, "Beat the Street," *Kiplinger's Personal Finance*, 1 Feb. 2003, at 56.

See IRREGULAR VERBS.

LANGUAGE-CHANGE INDEX
1. *stinked as past tense of *stink*: Stage 1
Current ratio (*stank* vs. *stunk* vs. *stinked): 603:198:1
2. *stunk* for simple-past *stank*: Stage 4
Current ratio (*they stank* vs. *they stunk): 3:1

*stirafoam; *stirofoam. See **Styrofoam.**

stochastic. See **aleatory.**

stock; shares. *Stock* = (1) the capital or principal fund raised by a corporation through subscribers' contributions or the sale of shares; (2) the proportional part of this capital credited to an individual shareholder and represented by the number of units owned; or (3) the goods that a merchant has on hand.

Whereas *stock* is a mass noun, *shares* is a count noun closely related to sense 2 of *stock*. *Shares* = the units of capital that represent an ownership interest in a corporation or in its equity. See COUNT NOUNS AND MASS NOUNS.

stockholder. See **shareholder.**

stogie (= a long, thin cigar) has been the standard spelling in BrE since the 1920s and in AmE since the 1940s. *Stogy (predominant in AmE till about 1940) and *stogey are variants.
Current ratio (*stogie* vs. *stogy vs. *stogey): 59:11:1

stoic, adj.; ***stoical.** H.W. Fowler argued in 1926 that *stoical* appears more often as a predicate adjective <his behavior was stoical>, while *stoic* is better used attributively <stoic indifference> (*FMEU1* at 565). No such distinction is maintained today, and the historical evidence is against Fowler. What can safely be said today is that *stoic* predominates over *stoical in all uses in AmE and BrE alike. The longer form appears to be moribund. Unless specifically referring to the ancient Greek school of philosophy, *stoic* should not be capitalized. See -IC.

Current ratio: 3:1

stomping ground; stamping ground. The traditional phrase is *stamping ground*, first used in the late 18th century and still predominant in BrE. *Stomping ground*, a 19th-century Americanism, spread in AmE throughout the 20th century and achieved predominance in the early 1990s. Today it outnumbers its more traditional rival by a 2-to-1 ratio in AmE print sources. When the first edition of this book appeared in 1998, only one major American dictionary listed *stomping ground*. Now almost all dictionaries have it, and about half give it priority over *stamping ground*.

It's perfectly idiomatic to say either *stomping ground* or *stomping grounds*—e.g.:

- "Sanchez and Charlton are from Tampa, while Bender hails from Clemson, S.C., head coach Jackie Hadel's old *stomping grounds*." Scott Kauffman, "Freshmen Serve Up Volleyball Success," *Orlando Sentinel*, 21 Sept. 1997, at K9.
- "Smith, 51, just completed four consecutive nights at CBGB, her old *stomping ground* and the birthplace of New York punk." Jim Sullivan, "Patti Smith Finds 'Peace' Outside Rock," *Boston Globe*, 2 Dec. 1997, at E1.

LANGUAGE-CHANGE INDEX
1. *stomping ground* for *stamping ground*: Stage 5
2. *stomping grounds* for *stomping ground*: Stage 5

stony. So spelled in AmE and BrE alike—not **stoney.* See MUTE E.

Current ratio: 90:1

storey. See **story.**

story; storey. For the floor or level of a building, *story* is AmE and *storey* BrE. Surprisingly, the BrE preference for *storey* did not take hold until the late 1940s. The plural forms are *stories* and *storeys.* See PLURALS (E).

straight. As an antonym of *gay*, *straight* dates from the early 1940s as AmE slang. It moved from SLANG into Standard Written English in the 1990s. (See **gay.**) The more formal antonyms, of course, are *heterosexual* and *homosexual.*

straight and narrow; *strait and narrow. The King James Version of the Bible contains this sentence: "Because strait is the gate, and narrow is the way which leadeth unto life, and few there be that finde it." Matthew 7:14. Although the phrase **strait and narrow* predominated in English-language print sources throughout the 18th century, by 1850—doubtless through folk etymology (see ETYMOLOGY

(D))—*straight and narrow* became the vastly preponderant form. It is now unquestionably the standard phrase.

Current ratio: 13:1

straightaway. See **straightway.**

straighten; straiten. These two verbs have different meanings. *Straighten* = to make or become straight. *Straiten* = (1) to make narrow, confine; or (2) to put into distress, esp. financial hardship. Because *straiten* is the rarer word, it is sometimes wrongly displaced by *straighten*—e.g.:

- "Brookes may pride itself on a different sort of education—mature and part-time students, flexible courses—but in these financially *straightened* [read *straitened*] times, does it not look with envy towards its neighbour, well on the way to meeting its £340 million target for its fund-raising appeal?" James Meikle, "New Universities: Oxford Leaves Its Blues Behind," *Guardian*, 23 Mar. 1993, at E4.
- "While most farmers were in *straightened* [read *straitened*] circumstances and too old-fashioned to want machinery, he believed Gridley Gerhardt to be forward-looking and prosperous." John Gould, "Phil Sugg's Struggle with a Mighty Machine," *Christian Science Monitor*, 13 Sept. 1996, at 17.
- "So it has fallen to Villas-Boas to manage the transition in comparatively *straightened* [read *straitened*] circumstances while handling egos that rub against each other like tectonic plates." Oliver Holt, "Lamps Has Put AVB in a Whole New Light," *Mirror* (U.K.), 13 Dec. 2011, Sport §, at 56.

LANGUAGE-CHANGE INDEX
straighten misused for *straiten*: Stage 2
Current ratio (*straitened circumstances* vs. *straightened circumstances*): 9:1

straight-faced. So spelled—not *strait-faced*. Perhaps by false analogy to *straitlaced*, some writers get it wrong—e.g.: "The splendour of the frocks and hats would shock this *strait-faced* [read *straight-faced*] economist." "Paying the High Price for Conspicuous Consumption," *Canberra Times*, 6 Nov. 2007, at 17.

straightway; straightaway. *Straightway* was first used in the 15th century as an adverb meaning either "directly" <the ball rolled straightway into the cup> or "immediately" <he went straightway to the King>. The word has stayed mostly adverbial, though it occasionally functions as an adjective <a straightway valve>.

In the 17th century—perhaps through epenthesis combined with the influence of *away*—the variant form *straightaway* emerged, first as an adverb <she straightaway ran to the church>, then in the 19th century as an adjective <a straightaway track> and as a noun (esp. as part of a racecourse) <caught up with the competition in the straightaway>. *Straightaway*, in short, has proved to be a versatile word.

In both AmE and BrE, *straightway* has consistently occurred with greater frequency in print sources—apart from a brief period from about 1980 to about 2005, when *straightaway* overtook it first in BrE and then in AmE. Since 2005, though, *straightway*, the more formal word, has once again been predominant. The word *straightaway* has the feel of a CASUALISM. The rivalry between the words is not yet at an end—or even in the final stretch.

Current ratio (in order of headwords): 2:1

***strait and narrow.** See **straight and narrow.**

straiten. See **straighten.**

straitjacket. The *strait* in this word means "close-fitting." *Straightjacket* is a common but mistaken variant that has lingered (and even swelled a little) since the mid-19th century. E.g.: "Teachers of the subject assigned editorials by rhetorical types until it was realized that such *straightjacketing* [read *straitjacketing*] of students was destructive of talent, not a developer of it." Curtis D. MacDougall, *Principles of Editorial Writing* 81–82 (1973).

As with many other compound nouns, this term has been spelled as two words, as a hyphenated compound, and as a single word. Today the single word is by far the most common form and should be accepted as standard—e.g.:

- "A white-coated psychiatrist flips his notebook, as The Woman, in a *straight-jacket* [read *straitjacket*], hallucinates her way through a therapy session." Janelle Gelfand, "Enthralling Performances, Design Double Operas' Intensity," *Cincinnati Enquirer*, 1 July 2001, at E2.
- "Skip the wrap shirt, an invention that feels more like a *straight jacket* [read *straitjacket*] than a garment of leisure." Jill Radsken, "Dive In to End-of-Season Sales Racks," *Boston Herald*, 12 July 2001, at 50.

LANGUAGE-CHANGE INDEX
straightjacket for *straitjacket*: Stage 3
Current ratio (*straitjacket* vs. *straightjacket*): 3:1

straitlaced (= rigidly narrow in moral matters; prudish) referred originally, in the 16th century, to a tightly laced corset—*strait* meaning "narrow" or "closely fitting." Over time, writers have forgotten the ETYMOLOGY (or they never learned it in the first place) and have confused *strait* with *straight*. Hence the erroneous form *straightlaced*—e.g.:

- "He is also *straightlaced* [read *straitlaced*], though a much more interesting person than Sgt. Friday." Mike Klis, "Girardi Turning Wednesdays into Big Bat Nights," *Gaz. Telegraph* (Colo. Springs), 11 May 1995, at C1.
- "Perhaps this city is just too *straightlaced* [read *straitlaced*] to learn how bikes and cars can coexist." Philip Lerman, "Get It in Gear, Washington!" *Wash. Post*, 3 Aug. 1997, at C1.

LANGUAGE-CHANGE INDEX (For the full key, see front matter pp. xxxi, l–li.)
Stage 1: Rejected. **Stage 2:** Widely shunned. **Stage 3:** Widespread but . . . **Stage 4:** Ubiquitous but . . . **Stage 5:** Fully accepted.
Invariably inferior forms marked by asterisk (✻). • Ratios represent frequency of prevalent forms vs. variants in current books.

Once hyphenated in AmE, the term has been solid since the late 1970s. In BrE, the term is still predominantly hyphenated <strait-laced>.

LANGUAGE-CHANGE INDEX
*straightlaced for straitlaced: Stage 3
Current ratio (straitlaced vs. *straightlaced): 4:1

strangely. See SENTENCE ADVERBS.

strata. See **stratum.**

stratagem. So spelled—though the mistaken form *strategem, on the analogy of strategy, appears about 20% as often as the correct spelling. Though the words stratagem and strategy are etymologically related, they came into English by different routes, and their spellings diverged merely as a matter of long-standing convention. What happened is that the Latin strategema became stratagema in Romance languages such as French. (The Century Dictionary calls the Romance spelling "erroneous.") Stratagem came into English in the 15th century, through French. But it wasn't until the early 19th century that English and American writers borrowed strategy (originally a Greek term) from Latin. Hence our incongruous spellings today. See SPELLING (A).

Current ratio (stratagem vs. *strategem): 31:1

strategic (= [1] done as part of a plan, esp. in a particular situation, [2] useful or right for a specific purpose, or [3] of, relating to, or involving warfare) is the standard term. *Strategical is a NEEDLESS VARIANT.

Current ratio: 185:1

stratum. Pl. *strata.* (See PLURALS (B).) Although strata is not a singular, it is sometimes misused that way— e.g.: "By contrast with the atmosphere of, say, Sinclair Lewis's 'Main Street,' in which an afternoon call or the purchase of a shirtwaist might occasion endless talk among every strata [read stratum] of a community, minding our own business has become a cardinal virtue." Anna Quindlen, "The Price of Privacy," N.Y. Times, 28 Sept. 1994, at A23.

LANGUAGE-CHANGE INDEX
strata for stratum as a singular: Stage 2
Current ratio (a stratum vs. *a strata): 10:1

stratus (= a type of cloud) forms the plural *strati,* not *stratuses.* See PLURALS (B).

street clothes. See **civilian clothes.**

strew. A. As a Verb: *strew > strewed > strewn.* So inflected. The past-participial strewn was not fixed as the standard form until about 1860—simultaneously, oddly enough, in both AmE and BrE. The archaic strewed as a past participle persists, but only as a sporadic variant—e.g.:

- "The plane's tail broke off and debris was strewed [read strewn] across the canyon." "Searchers Find 'Black Box' in Peru Crash," Toronto Star, 2 Mar. 1996, at A28.
- "It's been 13 years since her [Georgia O'Keeffe's] ashes were strewed [read strewn] over the glorious New Mexico landscape by her assistant and principal heir." Jo Ann Lewis, "The Ghosts of Abiquiu," Wash. Post, 10 Jan. 1999, at G1.

- "There were shelves and there were storage areas. Both were strewed [read strewn] with a jungle of junk through which Shier would attempt to navigate on his way to fill the requisitions." Skip Vogel, Constant Bearing—Decreasing Range 2006: A Makeover for Sailor Sam 41 (2006).

See IRREGULAR VERBS & **strow.**

LANGUAGE-CHANGE INDEX
strewed for past-participial strewn: Stage 3

B. As a Noun. *Strew* is uncommon as a noun <a strew of papers on the desk>. W3 defines it as "a number of things scattered about; a disorderly mess." Because it is so rare, a good replacement might be the better-known, similar-sounding *slew*—e.g.: "Ordinary people could be heard earnestly offering a strew [read slew] of views that, at their most human turning, veered toward the confessional." Francis X. Clines, "At $50 a Pop, Specialists Listen to the Vox Pop," N.Y. Times, 2 Mar. 1996, at 8.

stricken. A. Generally. Though *stricken* often appears as a past participle, grammatical authorities have long considered it inferior to *struck*, which in any event has always been the predominant past participle. It's an ARCHAISM except when used as an adjective <a stricken community>. The past-participial use is ill-advised—e.g.: "A noncompete agreement that bans a person from ever setting up a competing company in the same geographical location will be stricken [read struck] down by the courts as too restrictive." Joseph T. Leone, "Family Businesses Need to Play It Safe," Wis. State J., 16 Feb. 1997, at E4. Cf. **proved** & **shrink.**

LANGUAGE-CHANGE INDEX
stricken for past-participial struck: Stage 4
Current ratio (will be struck vs. *will be stricken): 9:1

B. *Strickened.* The participial usage has given rise to the mistaken use of *stricken* for *strike*, and therefore to the DOUBLE BOBBLE *strickened (attested from the early 19th century on)—e.g.:

- "He was strickened [read stricken] Friday night while doing what he loved—watching the Attleboro High football team play." "City & Town Report," Providence J.-Bull., 26 Oct. 1994, at D2.
- "Cintron competed at the state meet while strickened [read stricken] with a bad cold." Michael Russo, "Matching Dominance," Sun-Sentinel (Ft. Lauderdale), 14 Mar. 1996, at C16.
- "Malone's enthusiasm after Game 6 was tempered because of his concern for a cancer-strickened [read stricken] 13-year-old boy, whom he has befriended." Tom Knott, "Malone's Class Could Teach the NBA a Lesson," Wash. Times, 4 June 1996, at B1.

See **strike** & IRREGULAR VERBS.

LANGUAGE-CHANGE INDEX
*strickened for stricken: Stage 1
Current ratio (stricken vs. *strickened): 1,999:1

stride > strode > strode. So inflected. The variant past participle *stridden (attested in the OED from 1576 to 1970) rarely appears today. Another past-participial form, *strid, was current before 1800 but is now obsolete.

The form *strode* serves as both the simple past and the past participle. Hence there is no full correspondence with the seemingly analogous *ride > rode > ridden*. E.g.:

- "It was 12:15, a mere 15 minutes after McQueen had *strode* into the chamber." Jim Adams, "The Death Penalty in Kentucky," *Courier-J.* (Louisville), 2 July 1997, at A1.
- "My father had *strode* in and told me to stop." Elisa Seagrave, "Mother, I Hardly Knew You," *Independent*, 28 July 1998, at 9.
- "Let's call Kevin Downtown Brown, because that's where Michael Tucker took him with two men on in the eighth, mere minutes after Brown, Atlanta's uber-nemesis of late, had *strode* heroically in from the bullpen." Dale Robertson, "Padres Still Trying to Keep the Faith," *Houston Chron.*, 13 Oct. 1998, at 1.

Some writers erroneously treat *stride* as a weak verb and use the misbegotten form **strided*—e.g.:

- "Imitating Lowe's in-court identification of Aleman last week, McNally *strided* [read *strode*] across the courtroom and pointed to a spectator." Lorraine Forte, "Aleman Trial Headed to Jury," *Chicago Sun-Times*, 30 Sept. 1997, at 3.
- "Stewart knew he hadn't run out of bounds but was momentarily confused when, after he *strided* [read *strode*] into the end zone, no one immediately signaled a touchdown." Kevin Paul Dupont, "Stewart Proves the Playmaker in This Game," *Boston Globe*, 4 Jan. 1998, at F13.
- "A man in a tie *strided* [read *strode*] into the G.I. Joe's Lottery Agent on Smith Hill in Providence yesterday afternoon and placed $1,500 in cash on the counter." Ariel Sabar, "World's Biggest Jackpot, Up for Grabs," *Providence J.-Bull.*, 21 May 1998, at A19.

See IRREGULAR VERBS.

> LANGUAGE-CHANGE INDEX
> 1. *strode* as a past participle: Stage 5
> Current ratio (*had strode* vs. **had stridden*): 3:1
> 2. **strided* for *strode*: Stage 1
> Current ratio (*strode* vs. **strided*): 262:1

strike > struck > struck. So inflected. The form **striked* is erroneous—e.g.:

- "The No. 8 Hillbillies *striked* [read *struck*] next when Jack McDaniels returned an interception 97 yards to knot the score at 7." "N. Marion Breezes over Huntington," *Charleston Gaz.*, 22 Nov. 1997, at B4.
- "As recently as the late Sixties, British post-war race relations hit a low when white workers at the Bristol Omnibus Company *striked* [read *struck*] in protest against the employment of non-whites." Lindsay Baker, "The Slow Burn," *Guardian*, 28 Mar. 1998, at T17.
- "'Okie from Muskogee' was for his father, he said, as the band *striked* [read *struck*] it up." Chris Varias, "Merrier Merle's Mere Hour Better than '97 Show," *Cincinnati Enquirer*, 2 Oct. 1998, at E2.

See IRREGULAR VERBS & **stricken.**

> LANGUAGE-CHANGE INDEX
> **striked* for *struck*: Stage 1
> Current ratio (*struck* vs. **striked*): 7,115:1

string > strung > strung. The verb is so inflected. (See IRREGULAR VERBS.) But the past-participial adjective for fiddles, violas, cellos, etc. is *stringed* <stringed instruments>.

strive > strove > striven. So inflected. The form **strived* is erroneous both as the simple past and as the past participle—e.g.: "Negotiators *strived* [read *strove*] to get South African power-sharing talks back on track." *Wall Street J.*, 20 May 1991, at A1. See IRREGULAR VERBS.

Although **had strove* was fairly common in the 18th century, since 1820 or so *had striven* has greatly predominated in print sources. **Had strived* is another variant form that has barely been used in print.

> LANGUAGE-CHANGE INDEX
> **strived* for *strove* or *striven*: Stage 3
> Current ratio (*we strove* vs. **we strived*): 5:1
> Current ratio (*have striven* vs. **have strived*): 6:1

stroma (= [1] a cushion-like mass of fungus, or [2] the connective tissue forming the framework of a bodily organ), a technical biological term, has predominantly formed the plural *stromata* since about 1800—not **stromas*.

> Current ratio: 8:1

*strow, a by-form of *strew*, occurred with some frequency during the 18th century—but not nearly as often as *strew*. Today it is a barely used NEEDLESS VARIANT.

struma (= a swelling of the thyroid or other gland; esp., goiter), a technical medical term, has predominantly formed the plural *strumas* since the mid-19th century—not the Latinate *strumae* or **strumata*.

> Current ratio: 7:3:1

strychnine (= a poisonous alkaloid used in small doses for medicinal purposes) is the standard spelling in AmE and BrE alike—not **strychnin*.

> Current ratio: 33:1

stucco. Since 1900 or so, the plural *stuccoes* has been predominant in AmE and BrE alike—not **stuccos*. See PLURALS (D).

> Current ratio: 1.3:1

stultify formerly meant "to attempt to prove mental incapacity." By modest extension, it came to mean either "to make or cause to appear foolish" or "to put in a stupor." E.g.:

- "Rote liturgy can *stultify* as well as edify." Daniel B. Clendenin, "Why I'm Not Orthodox," *Christianity Today*, 6 Jan. 1997, at 32.
- "[This] gratuitous act of philistinism . . . threatens to *stultify* the nation still further." Auberon Waugh, "Way of the World," *Daily Telegraph*, 22 Jan. 1997, at 25.

Then, by SLIPSHOD EXTENSION, it took on the sense "to make useless or futile; to undermine; to negate or retard." Avoid this loose usage—e.g.:

- "Nostalgia . . . can *stultify* [read *sap*] a restaurant's vitality." William Rice, "Nostalgia Is a Sweet Menu Item," *Chicago Trib.*, 28 July 1995, at 4.
- "Finally, many fear the political chaos will *stultify* [read *undermine*] peace talks with the Palestinians." "Israeli

---

LANGUAGE-CHANGE INDEX (For the full key, see front matter pp. xxxi, l–li.)
Stage 1: Rejected. **Stage 2:** Widely shunned. **Stage 3:** Widespread but . . . **Stage 4:** Ubiquitous but . . . **Stage 5:** Fully accepted. Invariably inferior forms marked by asterisk (*). • Ratios represent frequency of prevalent forms vs. variants in current books.

Political Scandal Not Over Yet," *State J.-Register* (Springfield, Ill.), 27 Apr. 1997, at 12.

The word is sometimes misunderstood in two ways. First, it's sometimes (by still further extension) misused for *squelch* or *stifle*—e.g.: "These labels in all areas of our political life *stultify* [read *squelch* or *stifle*] discussion . . . as well as fostering intolerance throughout the political spectrum." Guy Charlton, "Cultures Must Be Respected," *Wis. State J.*, 8 May 1993, at A7. Second, it's sometimes misused for *disgrace* or *dishonor* (or perhaps *stupefy*)—e.g.: " 'Nonconformity' is Algren's last great cry against injustice, a howl against all that would *stultify* [read *stifle*] the human spirit." Tom Grimes, " 'Nonconformity' a Last Cry for Society's Injustices," *Austin Am.-Statesman*, 1 Dec. 1996, at E6.

LANGUAGE-CHANGE INDEX
stultify misused to mean *stifle* or *undermine*: Stage 1

stupefy. So spelled today, as it has been since the mid-19th century. The archaic spelling **stupify* is now regarded as a misspelling—e.g.:

- "Insurance agents will *stupify* [read *stupefy*] their clients with [obscure] notations." James W. Johnson, *Logic and Rhetoric* 197 (1962).
- "Drugs like heroin and cocaine typically *stupify* [read *stupefy*] and immobilize the user." Richard Morin, "New Facts and Hot Stats from the Social Sciences," *Wash. Post*, 27 Mar. 1994, at C5.
- "It is, he said, that which *stupifies* [read *stupefies*]." "The Advocate and Introduction of Jagermeister," *Baton Rouge Advocate*, 18 Apr. 2010, at F4.

See -FY. Cf. **liquefy** & **rarefy.**

LANGUAGE-CHANGE INDEX
stupefy misspelled **stupify*: Stage 2
Current ratio: 6:1

stupid. See **ignorant.**

St. Valentine's Day. See **Valentine's Day.**

sty (= an inflammation on the eyelid) is the standard spelling. (**Stye* is a variant form.) The plural is *sties*. See PLURALS (E).

Another word spelled *sty* (= a pen for pigs) also has the plural *sties*.

stylish; stylistic. *Stylish* = in style, in vogue <a stylish hat>. *Stylistic* = (1) having to do with style (of general application) <stylistic criticisms that were off the mark>; or (2) in the appropriate style (of music) <his stylistic flourishes were typical of the baroque period>.

stymie; **stymy*. This term, a Scotticism from golf, is best spelled *stymie*. It can function as a noun <a serious stymie>, but more commonly it's a verb—e.g.:

- "Danielle Odom brings quiet pathos to the damaged little girl—though the tongue-twisting lines she's handed once she arrives in heaven would *stymie* virtually any child actor." Everett Evans, " 'Slavs!' Has Some Peaks but Falls Short of 'Angels,' " *Houston Chron.*, 15 Sept. 1995, Houston §, at 1.

- "These puzzlements *stymie* many investors." Reed Abelson, "To Find New-Issue Players, Use a Scorecard," *N.Y. Times*, 17 Sept. 1995, § 3, at 1.

The verb is inflected *stymie > stymied > stymieing.*
Current ratio (*stymie* vs. **stymy*): 165:1

Styrofoam, a trademark, is sometimes misspelled **stirafoam* or **stirofoam*. If you're not referring to the trademarked product (which should have a capital *S*), *plastic foam* is a better choice.

subconscious. See **unconscious.**

subject, n. See **citizen (B).**

SUBJECT–COMPLEMENT DISAGREEMENT. See CONCORD (C).

subject matter is two words as a noun phrase and is hyphenated as a PHRASAL ADJECTIVE. Formerly, even the noun uses were hyphenated, but the phrase lost its hyphen in AmE during the 1920s and in BrE during the 1960s.

SUBJECT–VERB AGREEMENT. A. General Rule. The simple rule is to use a plural verb with a plural subject, a singular verb with a singular subject. But there are complications. If a sentence has two or more singular subjects connected by *and*, use a plural verb. Yet if the subjects really amount to a single person or thing, use a singular verb <the apple of his eye and the source of his inspiration is Heather>. And if the sentence has two singular subjects connected by *or*, *either . . . or*, or *neither . . . nor*, use a singular verb <let me know if you or your client has any questions>. See CONCORD (A). See also **either (D)** & **neither . . . nor (B).**

B. False Attraction to Noun Intervening Between Subject and Verb. This subheading denotes a mistake in number usually resulting when a plural noun intervenes between a singular subject and the verb. The writer's eye is thrown off course by the plural noun that appears nearest the verb—e.g.:

- "The stalled barges and the towboats that push them along are costing the industry as much as $500,000 a day, but the ripple effect of these disruptions *are* [read *is*] incalculable." Michael deCourcy Hinds, "River Shippers Squirm as Profits Wash Away," *N.Y. Times*, 7 July 1993, at A7.
- "Evaluation of rookies and free agents *are* [read *is*] the fundamental reason for playing these games." Tim Cowlishaw, "Switzer Exhibits Restraint," *Dallas Morning News*, 31 July 1994, at B1.
- "Its history of domination by neighboring countries *sharpen* [read *sharpens*] a stubborn independence." John Darnton, "Left at Altar by Norway, Europe Tries Stiff Upper Lip," *N.Y. Times*, 30 Nov. 1994, at A3.

This error sometimes occurs when two nouns, seeming to create a plural, intervene between the subject and the verb—e.g.: "Barefaced *defiance* of morals and law *were* [read *was*, because the subject is *defiance*] illegal." Lawrence M. Friedman, *Crime and Punishment in American History* 131 (1993). See SYNESIS.

The reverse error, plural to singular, also occurs—e.g.: "While the types of illness covered *varies* [read *vary*] from one insurer to another, most pay out for heart disease, certain types of cancer and strokes." Digby Larner, "For Parents, Just One Word: Insurance," *Int'l Herald Trib.*, 1–2 July 1995, at 17.

C. False Attraction to Predicate Noun. Occasionally a writer incorrectly looks to the predicate rather than to the subject for the noun that will govern the verb. The "correct" way of phrasing the sentence is often awkward, so the writer is well advised to find another way of stating the idea—e.g.:

- "You can use live or artificial bait to catch these fish. My favorite *are* top-water plugs, plastic jigs and live green backs or shrimp." Mike Manning, "Captain's Corner," *St. Petersburg Times*, 30 July 1997, at C2. (Read: *My favorites are* or *My favorite bait is . . . .*)
- "It has been placed in the grave on top of *old bones which* presumably *is* the skeleton of Declan." Peter Tremayne, "Corpse on a Holy Day," in *And the Dying Is Easy* 291, 295 (2001). (Because *which* takes its number from its antecedent *bones*, the verb should be *are*. Also, a comma should precede the *which*. [See **that (A).**] Hence, *old bones, which are presumably the skeleton of Declan*.)

D. Compound Subjects Joined Conjunctively. If two or more subjects joined by *and* are different and separable, they take a plural verb—e.g.:

- "At the same time, the democratic process and the personal participation of the citizen in his government *is* [read *are*] not all we want." Charles P. Curtis Jr., *Lions Under the Throne* 49 (1947). (*The democratic process* and *personal participation* are different things.)
- "Few golfers appreciate the time, money and technical know-how that *goes* [read *go*] into making a golf product." John Steinbreder, "Perfection Takes Time for Clubs, Balls," *Golfweek*, 25 Jan. 2003, at 36. (*Time, money*, and *know-how* are different things.)

But sometimes the two subjects joined by *and* express a single idea, and hence should take a singular verb <their confusion and uncertainty is understandable>. This is the case with *spaghetti and meatballs*, which denotes a single dish and therefore takes a singular verb. The third writer below recognized this, but the other two didn't:

- "Spaghetti and meatballs *are* [read *is*] on the menu." David Polochanin, "Prime Time Today," *Providence J.-Bull.*, 23 Jan. 1997, at C1.
- "For instance, spaghetti and meatballs *are* [read *is*] regional." Michael Ardizzone, "Emilia-Romagna: Heart of Italian Cuisine," *Travel Weekly*, 8 May 1997, at E3.
- "The spaghetti and meatballs *is* great comfort food." Michael Bauer, "A Full Plate," *S.F. Chron.*, 24 Aug. 1997, at 42.

See **bread and butter.**

E. Misleading Connectives. The phrases *accompanied by, added to, along with, as well as, coupled with,* and *together with* do not affect the grammatical number of the nouns preceding or following them. When such a phrase joins two singular nouns, the singular verb is called for—e.g.:

- "For example, he says, America's declining ability to compete in the global sale of automobiles and other manufactured products, *as well as* its status as the world's leading debtor nation, *are* [read *is*] partly the result of the declining cognitive abilities of workers and administrators." Malcolm W. Browne, "What Is Intelligence, and Who Has It?" *N.Y. Times*, 16 Oct. 1994, § 7, at 3, 41.
- "The absence of crude petroleum and iron ore, *coupled with* limited indigenous supplies of coal and natural gas, *ensures* that Japanese industry must import to survive." Roger Buckley, *Japan Today* 67 (2d ed. 1990).

Similarly, a phrase introduced by the preposition *like*, after a singular subject, does not make the number plural. The following example of misusage in a major airline's publication may well qualify as one of the worst 11-word sentences ever written: "The room, *like* he and I [*sic*], *are* [read *is*] a work in progress." Jim Shahin, "Wired for Weirdness," *Am. Way*, 1 Feb. 2003, at 46, 47. A possible revision: *The room is a work in progress, like him and me.* For the reason why the object of the preposition *like* should be objective and not nominative, see **like (A).**

F. Plural Units Denoting Amounts. In AmE, a plural noun denoting a small unit by which a larger amount is measured generally takes a singular verb—e.g.:

- "Five hours *are* [read *is*] enough time."
- "Fifteen minutes *pass* [read *passes*] more quickly than you might think."

See COLLECTIVE NOUNS & SYNESIS.

G. *One and one (is) (are).* Both forms are correct. It's possible to treat *one and one* as a single mathematical idea, so that the appropriate verb is *is*. Or it's possible to treat the two *ones* separately—hence *are*. Since the 18th century, the plural has predominated.

The same is true of multiplication: both *four times four is sixteen* and *four times four are sixteen* are correct. But here the singular is much more common and more natural in modern usage.

H. *Thing after thing (is) (are).* This construction takes a singular verb—e.g.:

- "Assault after assault on the M'Naghten Rules *were* [read *was*] beaten off until 1957." H.L.A. Hart, "Changing Conceptions of Responsibility," in *Punishment and Responsibility* 186, 191 (1968).
- "Study after study *has* shown that in heterosexual couples, perpetrators are overwhelmingly men and victims are overwhelmingly women." Kathleen Waits, "Domestic Violence," in *The Oxford Companion to American Law* 222 (2002).

I. *More than one is; *more than one are.* The phrase *more than one* generally takes a singular verb, not a plural one <more than one was there>—even though the sense is undeniably plural. If the noun is supplied before the verb, the construction is necessarily

LANGUAGE-CHANGE INDEX (For the full key, see front matter pp. xxxi, l–li.)
Stage 1: Rejected. **Stage 2:** Widely shunned. **Stage 3:** Widespread but . . . **Stage 4:** Ubiquitous but . . . **Stage 5:** Fully accepted.
Invariably inferior forms marked by asterisk (∗). • Ratios represent frequency of prevalent forms vs. variants in current books.

singular <more than one woman was there>. But without the noun, the construction becomes a little trickier. H.W. Fowler insisted on the singular (*FMEU1* at 363), and most professional writers use it—e.g.:

- "Each ticket costs 50 cents and more than one *is* usually necessary." Tom Bayles, "Seafood Fest Rolls Four Events into One," *Sarasota Herald-Trib.*, 11 Apr. 1999, at B1.
- "The variable for parental age represents the age of the oldest parent, if more than one *is* alive." Kenneth A. Couch, "Time? Money? Both? The Allocation of Resources to Older Parents," *Demography*, 1 May 1999, at 219.

The only exception is a narrow one: it occurs in a more or less pedagogical context when the phrase denotes the plural form of a word, as opposed to the singular—e.g.:

- "Sondra Katzen of the Brookfield Zoo said platypuses (more than one *are* also called *platypi*) are not found at zoos in the U.S. because the animal cannot breed in captivity." J. Hope Babowice, "Kids Warm Up to Mammals, Learn What Sets Them Apart," *Daily Herald* (Chicago), 21 May 1998, at 1.
- "One gladiolus is a gladiolus . . . . More than one *are* gladioluses or gladioli." Cass Petersen, "Spike Your Garden with Striking Glads," *San Diego Union-Trib.*, 14 Feb. 1999, at H25. (On whether *gladiola* is an acceptable singular, see **gladiolus**.)
- "Remember that one animal is an animal, but more than one *are* animaux, ending in *aux*." Vince Passaro, "Unlikely Stories," *Harper's Mag.*, 1 Aug. 1999, at 80.

Apart from that one situation—or when the number given is greater than one <more than four golfers were in the group>—a plural verb should not follow. To say **more than one are present* is unidiomatic at best—e.g.:

- "This column looks at the job description of the personal representative or representatives if more than one *are* [read *is*] named." Julie Tripp, "How to Administer an Estate," *Oregonian* (Portland), 27 Jan. 1997, at B12.
- "The charge is $40 for the first policy illustration and $30 after that, if more than one *are* [read *is*] analyzed at the same time." William Giese, "Insurance You Can Do Without," *Kiplinger's Personal Fin. Mag.*, 1 Feb. 1997, at 71.
- "Some of the emotional elements affecting a decision may be: What sort of mood is the person in at the time; the relationship between the individuals when more than one *are* [read *is*] involved in the decision." David Crook, "Why Do People Buy?" *Glass Age*, 1 May 1997, at 16.

J. Plural Subject Intended to Denote Area or Statistic. Some writers fall into the habit of implicitly prefacing plural nouns with UNDERSTOOD WORDS such as *the idea of*, *the field of*, or even *the fact of*. To be sure, some of these wordings are perfectly idiomatic <mathematics is where my talent lies>.

But the habit should not extend beyond the reach of idiomatic comfort. Consider the following title, over an article by Ray and Tom Magliozzi: "Duplicate Cars Means Customer Pays More for Name," *Amarillo Daily News*, 21 Aug. 1993, at B5. In that title, there is an implied subject—something like *the fact of having . . . means*. But the phrasing looks sloppy.

As in the example just cited, this mistaken idiom seems to occur most frequently with the verb *mean*—e.g.: "There, all-scarlet clothes *means* [read *mean*] disease in the house." Tamora Pierce, *Circle of Magic: Sandry's Book* 141 (1997). If the writer really wants a singular *means*, then the subject should be a gerund (as in *someone's wearing scarlet clothes means . . .*).

Sometimes a plural noun is intended as a singular statistic, but the grammar is mangled—e.g.: "Amid controversy over numbers, 37 million Hispanic people *is* just shy of 37.7 million black citizens in new Census Bureau estimates." "Hispanics Close to Outnumbering Blacks," *USA Today*, 22 Jan. 2003, at A3. This isn't a problem involving a singular *people* as opposed to plural *peoples*. It's a problem of comparing one singular numerical amount with another. A possible revision: *Amid controversy over numbers, the Hispanic population (37 million) is just shy of the black population (37.7 million) in new Census Bureau estimates.*

K. One in five; one of every five. When the first number is *one*, this construction takes a singular: *one in three is not admitted, one of every five achieves a perfect score*, etc. See **one in [number] is.**

L. Decades. Decades customarily take plural verbs: *the 1930s were a tough time in America.* The following is unidiomatic: "The 1950s *is* [read *are*] remembered more for *its* [read *their*] sociology than for *its* [read *their*] politics." R.Z. Sheppard, "Golden Oldies," *Time*, 19 July 1993, at 61.

M. An Unusual Plural. By convention—and through the principle of SYNESIS—a singular abstract noun may take a plural verb if it's modified by two or more adjectives referring to different varieties of things denoted by that noun. E.g.:

- "*Eastern* and *Western* art *differ* in many fundamental ways."
- "*Classical* and *modern* philosophy *are* not radically different fields of study."

One way of analyzing those sentences is to say that the first adjective has an implied noun after it. See UNDERSTOOD WORDS.

N. Nouns of Multitude. See SYNESIS.

O. *A number of people (is) (are).* See **number of** & SYNESIS.

P. *One of those who (is) (are).* See **one of the [+ pl. n.] who (or that).**

Q. *Each* as Subject. See **each (A).**

R. *What* as Subject. See **what.**

S. Inversion. See INVERSION & **there is.**

T. Alternatives. See **either (D)** & **neither . . . nor (A).**

SUBJECT–VERB SEPARATION. The core words in a sentence are the subject and the verb. They are related both in sense and in grammar. And related words should go together. If you separate them too much, the sentence goes asunder—e.g.:

- "Jurors' *need* to hear that testimony again just minutes before reaching a verdict *puzzled* experts." Haya El Nasser & Sally Ann Stewart, "Verdict Revealed Today," *USA*

Today, 3 Oct. 1995, at A1. (A possible revision: *When jurors said they needed to hear that testimony again, and just minutes later reached a verdict, the experts were puzzled. Or: The experts were puzzled when jurors said they needed to hear that testimony again, and just minutes later reached a verdict.*)

- "*Plans* unveiled Wednesday for a pair of looping reliever roads connecting vast tracts of land south of Forest Drive *have* been roundly panned by many residents." Jeff Nelson, "Many Skeptical of Forest Drive Plans," *Capital* (Annapolis), 28 July 1996, at D1. (A possible revision: *Many residents have criticized plans unveiled Wednesday for a pair of looping reliever roads connecting vast tracts of land south of Forest Drive.*)

SUBJUNCTIVES. In modern English, the subjunctive mood of the verb appears primarily in six contexts: (1) conditions contrary to fact <if I were king> (where the indicative would be *am*); (2) suppositions <if I were to go, I wouldn't be able to finish this project> (where the indicative would be *was*); (3) wishes <I wish that I were able to play piano> (where the indicative would be *was*); (4) demands and commands <I insisted that he go> (where the indicative would be *goes*); (5) suggestions and proposals <I suggest that she think about it a little longer> (where the indicative would be *thinks*); and (6) statements of necessity <it's necessary that they be there> (where the indicative would be *are*).

Although subjunctives are less common in English than they once were, they survive in those six contexts. While suppositions and wishes are the most common examples in conversation, the others are most common in writing. And they're worth keeping. Following is some evidence of slippage (along with four correct uses).

Counterfactual conditions:

- "But the truth is, if it *wasn't* [read *hadn't been*] for a last-minute infusion of cash by an out-of-state lobbying group, the initiative would not have even garnered enough signatures to qualify for the ballot." Jack Fischer, "Populist Rhetoric Masks Measure Aimed at Congress," *San Jose Mercury News*, 21 Oct. 1992, at A1.
- "I felt as though I *was* [read *were*] using an alias, a well-used and permanent one as the years went by, but an alias nevertheless." Mary Willis, "How I Gave Up My Alias," *N.Y. Times*, 16 Oct. 1994, § 6, at 32. (The writer is talking about giving up her married name—thus it's contrary to fact.)
- "Even if he *was to* [read *were to* or *does*] endorse another candidate, he actually has little in the way of a political operation to pass on." Bill Turque, "A Pilgrimage to Perot," *Newsweek*, 7 Aug. 1995, at 32.

Demands and commands:

- "Britain's farmers are worried that consumers and more supermarkets are going to start demanding that all British beef *comes* [read *come*] from herds free from confirmed cases of BSE." R. Palmer & I. Birrell, "Vets Question the Safety of UK Sausages," *Sunday Times* (London), 10 June 1990, § 1, at 3.

- "Ike directed that every effort *be* made to do so." Frank Whitsitt, "They Also Served Who Bark and Sniff," *Wall Street J.*, 20 May 1996, at A18.

Suggestions and proposals:

- "His plans reduced to regrets, he suggests that his informant *checks* [read *check*] with Israeli intelligence." Leslie Thomas, "Mega-Nerds Meet the Mega-Villains," *Sunday Times* (London), 15 Apr. 1990, at H7.
- "And France proposes that the EC *commits* [read *commit*] itself to a single currency by 1999." Rory Watson & Nicholas Comfort, "Maastricht Deal Will Shape Our Destiny," *European*, 6–12 Dec. 1991, at 1.
- "Circuit Judge John E. McCormick is expected to propose Tuesday that Milwaukee County judges *be* elected by county-supervisor districts." Chester Sheard, "Judge to Urge District Judicial Elections," *Milwaukee J. Sentinel*, 18 Oct. 1994, at A5.

Statements of necessity:

- "His entrance into the military made it necessary that he *use* the birth-certificate version [of his name]." Mike Elfland, "Outspoken Burke Says City Hall Needs Harder Sell to Lure Businesses," *Telegram & Gaz.* (Worcester), 19 Sept. 1997, at B1.
- "It will be necessary that he or she *have* a solid understanding of school finances." Alyssa Roggie, "Candidates Target Budget, Openness," *Intelligencer J.* (Lancaster, Pa.), 30 Oct. 1997, at B1.
- "When the position potentially involves exercising the power of life or death over citizens, it is essential that screening procedures *are* [read *be*] in place to keep from hiring people who are temperamentally unsuited for the work." "Is Screening Sufficient?" *Herald* (Rock Hill, S.C.), 15 Dec. 1997, at A9.

Formerly, writers used subjunctives with every type of condition, whether contrary to fact or not. Today most of these sound like not-so-quaint ARCHAISMS—e.g.:

- "Its very existence is, therefore, a bulwark against oppression and tyranny, no matter who *be* the potential oppressor or tyrant." Leslie Scarman, *English Law—The New Dimension* 6 (1974).
- "The word processor is a marvelous machine, and no sensible writer, *if such there be*, should scorn it." Stephen White, *The Written Word* 74 (1984).

Subjunctives also persist in a few idiomatic phrases, such as *Long live the Queen, as it were, be that as it may, far be it from me*, and the literary *would (that) it were*. Another example is *be they*—e.g.: "In social situations, a conversation with Justice Brennan is likely as not to focus on the interests of those with whom he is speaking, *be they* judges, politicians and journalists, or waitresses, secretaries and gardeners." Martin Tolchin, "Brennan Described as Self-Effacing, Sociable Irish Pol," *Dallas Morning News*, 22 July 1990, at A12. They also endure in statements of fear or anxiety with the word *lest*. See **lest (B).** See also TENSES (A).

sublimate; sublime, vb. These verbs overlap, but only in their secondary senses; they're best kept separate. The primary sense of *sublimate*, the more common word, is "to transmute (an instinct) from one form to another, esp. to a more socially acceptable form"—e.g.: "The current popular outrage about corporate governance is mostly *sublimated* concern about declining stock prices." Michael Kinsley, "Bulls, Bears and Chickens," *Wash. Post*, 26 July 2002, at A33. Most often, the instinct that gets changed relates to sex—e.g.:

- "Many clergy do keep their vow of celibacy. But a blocked instinct has to go somewhere, and not everyone succeeds at *sublimating*." Letter of Sylvia Sturgis, "Fathers' Fall from Grace," *Boston Globe*, 24 Feb. 2002, at E8. (In this example, the object of sublimating—namely, *it*—seems to be implied.)
- "Nathan (Tim Robbins) was a boy raised by parents so strict that his entire sexual drive was *sublimated* into the desire to train others as mercilessly as he was trained." Roger Ebert, "'Human Nature' Takes Comic Look at Sexuality," *Chicago Sun-Times*, 12 Apr. 2002, Weekend §, at 27.
- "Some patrons may, indeed, be offended, concerned that nudity, even when *sublimated* in art, may generate some kind of libidinous charge." Owen McNally, "Stark, Naked," *Hartford Courant*, 5 May 2002, at 61.

Sometimes the word suggests that what is *sublimated* is suppressed—e.g.: "There's an erotic spark between them, but it remains *sublimated*." Todd Lothery, "A Good 'Read,'" *News & Observer* (Raleigh), 23 Aug. 2002, What's Up §, at 23. If the sense is merely to suppress without transforming, then *suppress* is the better choice.

Sublime = (1) to change or be changed from a solid to a vapor (and possibly back to solid again); (2) to purify; (3) to make sublime; to raise in dignity; or (4) to enhance the worth of. Most of these senses are rather rare, *sublime* being far more common as an adjective meaning "uplifted; exalted; lofty; supreme." Sense 1 is most usual in technical contexts—e.g.:

- "Once *sublimed* into the vapor state, the titanium is allowed to condense on the internal array or on a portion of the inner surface of the chamber." Phil Danielson, "How to Use Getters and Getter Pumps," *R&D*, 1 Feb. 2001, at 53.
- "Children also inhaled a whiff of carbon dioxide as it *sublimed* from dry ice to vapors." Kathryn Grondin, "Show Yields Discoveries for Kids," *Daily Herald* (Chicago), 25 Mar. 2001, News §, at 3.

Although *sublimate* can be used in this sense, *sublime* is preferable (to encourage DIFFERENTIATION)—e.g.: "The ice '*sublimated*' [read '*sublimed*']—turned to gas and escaped into space—prematurely." Frank D. Roylance, "Hubble Camera Finding Baby Stars," *Baltimore Sun*, 6 June 2002, at A4. Many dictionary definitions suggest that the vapor gets changed back to a solid again (see *OED*, *W11*, etc.).

Sometimes the sense of *sublime* as a verb isn't easy to decipher. In the purple prose that follows, it seems to bear sense 4 ("to enhance the worth of"), but one can

hardly be sure what the sentence means at all: "This is a manifesto . . . for language brutishly simple and hideously complex, as mandarin as oranges *sublimed* in cans and clean as a paper cut, for effusive language that soaks itself in the spume of its words." Vanessa Place, "The Radical Romantic," *L.A. Weekly*, 31 Aug. 2001, at 41. Indeed, that passage seems soaked in that very way.

submersible; *submergible; *submergeable. Though the second might seem simpler (cf. *persuadable* and **persuasible*), the first has always been more common in both AmE and BrE. **Submergeable* is a NEEDLESS VARIANT. See -ABLE (A).

Current ratio (in order of headwords): 1,491:19:1

submissible; *submissable; *submittable. Though labeled "rare" in the *OED*, *submissible* occurs with some frequency in AmE and BrE alike. **Submissable* and **submittable* are NEEDLESS VARIANTS.

Current ratio (*submissible* vs. **submittable* in World English): 5:1

submission; *submittal. *Submission* (= [1] the act of submitting; or [2] something submitted) is the standard word. **Submittal* is a NEEDLESS VARIANT of *submission*—e.g.: "Town code requires members to act on applications within 180 days of *submittal* [read *submission* or *their being submitted*]." Jonathan McNeilly, "New Rite Aid Plans Rejected in Henniker," *Union Leader* (Manchester, N.H.), 1 May 1997, at A5.

Current ratio: 118:1

*submittable. See **submissible.**

SUBORDINATION AND COORDINATION. People like being coordinated; they dislike being subordinated. So the terminology in this entry is a little counterintuitive because in writing subordination is good, and coordination often less so.

An elementary point of composition—one that really could be called "advanced," given how many writers overlook it—is the importance of using subordinate sentence structures as opposed to coordinate ones. Coordination involves creating compound sentences: two independent clauses of equal importance joined by a conjunction such as *and*. E.g.:

> We needed to send our letter first, and we sent it last week. (Poor)

Subordination involves making one of the clauses dependent. That is, it couldn't stand on its own as a complete sentence. It's less important. A subordinate clause normally begins with a subordinating conjunction such as *although* or *because*. (See **although** & **because.**) E.g.:

> Because we needed to send our letter first, we sent it last week. (Better)

Competent editors frequently insert subordinating conjunctions at crucial points in a piece of writing. For nonfiction writers, perhaps the handiest subordinate conjunctions are *although* (for addressing counterpoints) and *because* (for stating your own reasons). The word *although*, which is especially useful at the outset of a sentence, ensures that your undercutting of a contrary point will appear in the main clause. In a sentence of under 30 words, that structure is normally more effective than *but* positioned between independent clauses. Consider:

> The deadline passed last Thursday, but Johnson was never told about it. (Mediocre)

vs.

> Although the deadline passed last Thursday, Johnson was never told about it. (Better)

vs.

> Although Johnson was never told about it, the deadline passed last Thursday. (Better)

With subordination, the phrasing immediately shows that one clause is more important than the other. You're amplifying the one and diminishing the other. The prose starts flowing better almost immediately.

When the more important idea is put into a subordinate clause, the result is what composition teachers call "upside-down subordination":

> The deadline passed last Thursday, although Johnson was never told about it. (Poor)

That sentence is poorly phrased. In fact, most sentences with *although* tacked on the end (as opposed to the beginning) have been poorly constructed. The writer's point is weakened, and the reader may be misdirected.

Some otherwise advanced writers have problems with overcoordinating their clauses. Take for example a British professor who teaches college courses in rhetoric and critical thinking. The opening paragraph of his book *The Logic of Real Arguments* consists of eight sentences, five of which are compound (all without the requisite comma before the conjunction in the compound sentence). Here's the opening line of his book:

> We learn most of what we know from teachers and experts of one kind and another and this is not surprising in a highly specialised modern society. [Alec Fisher, *The Logic of Real Arguments* 1 (2d ed. 2004).]

This sentence has several faults. First, it contains three *and*s. Second, it has no internal punctuation—which makes it more difficult to tell which one of the three *and*s connects clauses as opposed to noun elements. Third, without subordination, it's hard to say precisely what the main point of the sentence is, especially given how it ends.

Let's try using subordination with the sentence, casting it three different ways:

- Given the highly specialized society in which we live, it's hardly surprising that we learn most of what we know from teachers and experts.
- We learn most of what we know from teachers and experts—hardly surprising given how highly specialized modern society has become.

- It can hardly come as a surprise that we learn most of what we know from teachers and experts. After all, we live in a highly specialized society.

Each of those versions has a slightly different emphasis based on the words at the beginnings and ends of the sentences. The end, of course, is of paramount importance. (See SENTENCE ENDS.) The third revision creates two sentence ends and therefore two points of emphasis. Doing that also improves the average sentence length. (See SENTENCE LENGTH.)

In the second sentence of our author's book, the flaw of overcoordinating surfaces again:

> However, it is possible to rely too heavily on experts and this approach to learning and knowledge tends to encourage passivity and receptiveness rather than inventiveness and imagination. [Alec Fisher, *The Logic of Real Arguments* 1 (2d ed. 2004).]

This sentence, containing four *and*s, begins with the clunky *However*. (See **but (A)**.) Once again, someone wanting to use subordination instead of coordination could devise three more appealing versions:

- Yet if we rely too heavily on experts for our learning and knowledge, we tend to become passive and receptive rather than inventive and imaginative.
- But this heavy reliance on others to learn may encourage passivity and receptiveness rather than inventiveness and imagination.
- Yet when it comes to learning and knowledge, an overreliance on experts can encourage passivity and receptiveness rather than inventiveness and imagination.

Note once again that the revisions are shorter. Subordination typically promotes economy with words. It also makes the syntax more interesting because there's more variety. The prose is more than a series of compound sentences with undifferentiated main clauses linked by conjunctions.

Now let's look at the final two sentences of our author's first paragraph, once again mispunctuated:

> Confidence in one's own judgement is another key to understanding and a secondary objective of this book is to give the reader such confidence. It's like learning to ride a bicycle—you will have some falls on the way but once you can do it you'll realise you can do a great deal on your own. [Alec Fisher, *The Logic of Real Arguments* 1 (2d ed. 2004).]

With five of the eight sentences in the paragraph constructed this way—coordinating conjunctions linking independent clauses—the reader, subconsciously if not consciously, begins to sense monotony ahead. Figuring out what's a main thought and what's an ancillary one will take up the reader's time and energy. Once again, the passage can be revised for enhanced readability and clarity:

> Another purpose of this book is to give you confidence in your own judgment—always a key to understanding. It's like learning to ride a bicycle: although you'll have

some falls on the way, once you can do it you'll feel more self-sufficient.

Something similar might be said of subordination. It's always a key to good writing. It's like learning to ride a bike: although you'll occasionally produce less-than-pellucid sentences, once you've learned the technique of subordination, you'll write better more and more automatically.

subornation of perjury. This legal phrase refers to the crime of trying to persuade another person to commit perjury. In the press (and, embarrassingly enough, even in judicial opinions), it is occasionally rendered *subordination of perjury*, a persistent MALAPROPISM that can be traced back to the 18th century. E.g.:

- "The Parliament noted that when nothing was in writing, contract terms were 'commonly endeavored to be upheld by perjury and *subordination of perjury* [read *subornation of perjury*].'" John Roska, "Oral Contract to Buy House Requires Proof of Basic Issues," *St. Louis Post-Dispatch*, 1 Apr. 2004, St. Clair–Monroe §, at 2.
- "Hirschfeld faces one count of conspiracy to obstruct justice, one count of obstruction of justice, one count of *subordination of perjury* [read *subornation of perjury*] and one count of perjury." Carlos Santos, "Flamboyant Lawyer Back in the News," *Richmond Times-Dispatch*, 17 Oct. 2004, at B1.
- "Based on the State's delay in notifying defense counsel of its *subordination of perjury* [read *subornation of perjury*] allegations, Mora claims the prosecution 'deliberately interfered with [his] constitutional right to the effective assistance of counsel.'" *Mora v. Williams*, 111 Fed. App'x. 537, 548 (10th Cir. 2004) (O'Brien, J.).

LANGUAGE-CHANGE INDEX
subordination of perjury for *subornation of perjury*: Stage 1
Current ratio (*subornation of perjury* vs. *subordination of perjury*): 25:1

subpar. This VOGUE WORD has a curious double meaning. In ordinary contexts, of course, it means "below average, not measuring up to normal standards" <a child's subpar report card>. But in golf, the term means "below par for a hole, round, or match"—par being the standard number of strokes for a hole or course <three subpar rounds in his last four tournaments>. Oddly enough, then, it's desirable to be subpar in golf but not in other aspects of life.

subpoena. A. Sense. W3 lists *subpoena* as an adverb meaning "under penalty" (or "under pain"). This, of course, is its etymological sense. Yet it virtually never appears in modern writing with this meaning, and it should be considered obsolete in that sense.

The modern use is as a noun. Even in medieval English practice, *subpoena* served as a noun denoting the writ that commenced civil proceedings by ordering the defendant to attend under pain of a monetary penalty. Today, its meaning is "a court order commanding the presence of a witness or production of things, such as documents, under a penalty for noncompliance."

B. Spelling. *Subpena* appears in any number of federal statutes because that was, until 1986, the spelling recommended by the *Government Printing Office Style Manual*. Yet *subpoena* is by far the more common spelling and for that reason alone is to be preferred. The form with the digraph *æ* (*subpœna*) is pedantic at best in modern writing.

C. Plural. Although *subpoena* is a singular English noun dating from the late 15th century, it was never a Latin noun. Rather, the English word *subpoena* derived from the Latin phrase *sub poena*, meaning "under penalty" or "under pain." The plural *subpoenas* appeared in English law as early as 1509 in the title of a statute "for Subpoenas and Privy Seals." That was the only plural until the early 19th century, when *subpoenae* first appeared—in a misquotation from Coke's *Institutes* (Coke actually wrote *sub poena*). So the false Latin plural *subpoenae* is a HYPERCORRECTION and, in fact, not a Latin word at all. But because the *-ae* does show up in the correct past-tense verb form *subpoenaed*, the confusion may have been compounded.

LANGUAGE-CHANGE INDEX
subpoenae for *subpoenas*: Stage 1
Current ratio (*subpoenas* vs. *subpoenae*): 447:1

D. Subpoena, v.t. The inflected forms of this verb, which dates from the early 17th century, are *subpoenaed* and *subpoenaing*. The miscast forms *subpoened* and *subpoening* have appeared sporadically since the 19th century. The mistaken form *subpoenaeing* is a 20th-century American error. *Subpoena'd* is an old BrE past-tense variant that was never as common as the standard form *subpoenaed*.

E. Pronunciation. The word is pronounced /sə-**pee**-nə/ as both noun and verb.

subscribe. For the misuse of *ascribe* for *subscribe*, see **ascribe.**

subsequently. A. For *later*. Using the four-syllable word in place of the two-syllable word is rarely, if ever, a good stylistic choice.

B. And *consequently*. Though both words contain the sense "following" or "occurring later," *consequently* has primarily a causal nuance: "occurring because of." Frequently *subsequently* (which has no connotation of causation) is misused for *consequently*—e.g.: "My taste tends to be masculine to begin with. Chintz is not on my radar screen. *Subsequently* [read *Consequently*] I don't attract frou frou clients." Peter Marino, in "Peter Marino, Architect," *Celebrated Living*, Fall 2008, at 88, 89 (interview). See **consequent.**

LANGUAGE-CHANGE INDEX
subsequently misused for *consequently*: Stage 1

subsequent to is a pomposity for *after* or *later*, just as *prior to* is for *before*. E.g.:

- "Such an atmosphere was created *subsequent to* [read *after*] the June 1989 Tiananmen Square massacre." "Most Favored Nation Doing the Right Thing," *Ariz. Republic*, 29 Apr. 1997, at B4.
- "Therefore, private investment can only be attracted *subsequent to* public sector land preparation." Craig Johnson, "Brownfield Funding Issue Is About More than Clean Soil," *Star Trib.* (Minneapolis), 22 May 1997, at A23.

(A possible revision: *Therefore, private investors will be attracted only after the public sector has helped clean up the land.*)

Cf. **prior** & ***previous to.**

subsidence (= the act or process of settling or sinking) is pronounced /səb-**sıd**-əns/ or /**səb**-si-dens/. The word is sometimes misspelled *subsidance*—e.g.: "Saltwater intrusion is a by-product, of sorts, of conversion and *subsidance* [read *subsidence*] in combination with tidal surges." Doug Pike, "Saving the Wetlands," *Houston Chron.*, 8 May 1997, at 13.

subsistence is occasionally misspelled *subsistance*—e.g.: "Fuller rightly observes that the causes of Third World deforestation are complex, varied and largely attributable to the *subsistance* [read *subsistence*] needs of local people." Ted Ferrioli, "Maybe if We Called Loggers 'Rural Natives' It Would Help," *Oregonian* (Portland), 28 June 1996, at C7.

Current ratio: 196:1

substantiate. So spelled—not *substantuate.*

substantive. A. Pronunciation. *Substantive*—a commonly mispronounced word—has three, not four, syllables: /**səb**-stən-tiv/. The common error in AmE is to insert what is technically known as an epenthetic *-e-* after the second syllable: /**səb**-stə-nə-tiv/. Still another blunder is to accent the second syllable: /səb-**stan**-tiv/. See PRONUNCIATION (B).

LANGUAGE-CHANGE INDEX
substantive mispronounced with four syllables:
Stage 2

B. For *substantial.* *Substantial* is the more general word, meaning "of considerable size, quantity, or importance; real; ample." *Substantive* is more specialized, appearing most often in old-fashioned grammars (in which *substantive* means "noun") and in law (in which it serves as the adjective corresponding to *substance* and as the antonym of *procedural* <substantive rights>). Some writers misuse *substantive* for *substantial*—e.g.: "Facing a $290 million deficit this year, L.A. is hard pressed to meet the cops' demands for a *substantive* [read *substantial*] raise." "Mayhem as a Negotiating Tactic," *Newsweek*, 28 Mar. 1994, at 7.

LANGUAGE-CHANGE INDEX
substantive misused for *substantial*: Stage 1

substitute, vb.; replace. These verbs are hardly interchangeable. You substitute something *for* something else <the recipe allows you to substitute tofu for chicken>, but you *replace* something *with* something else <the recipe allows you to replace chicken with tofu>.

subterfuge is pronounced /**səb**-tər-fyooj/, not /-fyoozh/.

subtle; *subtile.* The former is standard in AmE and BrE alike. The latter is an ARCHAISM and NEEDLESS VARIANT that has steadily waned since about 1780.

Current ratio: 68:1

subtly. So spelled, not *subtlely*—e.g.: "The disparity can give retail brokers an incentive to *subtlely* [read *subtly*] dissuade a customer from selling IPO shares right after an offering." Kathleen Day, "NASD to Toughen Penalties," *Wash. Post*, 29 July 2002, at A8.

succinct. The first *-c-* has a /k/ sound: /sək-**sinkt**/. Cf. **accessory** (B) & **flaccid.**

succubus. See **incubus.**

such. A. As a Demonstrative Adjective. *Such* is properly used as an adjective when reference has previously been made to a category of people or things: hence *such* means "of that kind" <such a person> <such people>. It isn't properly equivalent to *this, that, these,* or *those.*

With this word two points should be kept in mind. First, when used as a demonstrative adjective to modify a singular noun, *such* typifies LEGALESE. And contrary to what some think, *such* isn't any more precise than *the, that,* or *those.* Second, *such* is a POINTING WORD that must refer to a clear antecedent. In the following sentence, *such* is used once vaguely (without an antecedent), once clearly: "The Association agreed to compile data on all conventions that will occur in cities where there are interested Gray Line members and to forward *such* report to *such* members." The first *such* (along with *forward*) would best have been omitted; no reports have been referred to—only the compilation of data, which is not necessarily the same as a report. The second *such*, less objectionable because it refers to the *members* previously mentioned, would read better as *those.* Cf. **said.**

B. As a Pronoun. Although the pronoun use of *such* has ancient history on its side—it dates from the 9th century—today it is best regarded as an ARCHAISM except in a few phrases on the model of *such is life.* E.g.: "Mr. Richler's main business as a novelist has been puncturing pretension; and *such is* the rich pretentiousness of contemporary culture . . . that he need never worry about being out of work." Joseph Epstein, "The Pleasures of Nastiness," *Wall Street J.*, 19 Dec. 1997, at A16. Except in that type of idiom, *such* as a pronoun is barbarous-sounding <we never received such>. Indeed, Krapp called it a "crude low colloquialism." George P. Krapp, *A Comprehensive Guide to Good English* 568 (1927). Cf. **same** (A).

***suchlike.** Born in the 15th century and common by the 16th, this pronoun waned in the 18th century and declined even more in the 19th. Today it is found mostly in DIALECT, not in STANDARD ENGLISH.

LANGUAGE-CHANGE INDEX (For the full key, see front matter pp. xxxi, l–li.)
Stage 1: Rejected. **Stage 2:** Widely shunned. **Stage 3:** Widespread but . . . **Stage 4:** Ubiquitous but . . . **Stage 5:** Fully accepted.
Invariably inferior forms marked by asterisk (*). • Ratios represent frequency of prevalent forms vs. variants in current books.

Sudan, Sudanese; *Soudan, *Soudanese. The spellings *Sudan* and *Sudanese* are standard. The longer forms predominated until about 1905, but they are now all but obsolete. See DENIZEN LABELS.

sudden, all of a. See **all of a sudden.**

suffer. To *suffer from* is to have (an affliction). To *suffer with* is to feel pain as a result of (an affliction).

sufferance. So spelled. **Suffrance* is an infrequent misspelling.

Current ratio: 71:1

suffice it to say is the SUBJUNCTIVE form of *it suffices to say*. It has been in common use since the mid-18th century, usually at the beginning of a sentence but not always—e.g.:

- "*Suffice it to say* that the plotters, once their plan has been set into motion, aren't content to leave well enough alone." Janet Maslin, "'Deathtrap' with Michael Caine," *N.Y. Times*, 19 Mar. 1982, at C8.
- "When her students were asked how they liked working with her, *suffice it to say* that they gushed." Natalie Angier, "Scientist at Work," *N.Y. Times*, 30 May 1995, at C1.
- "*Suffice it to say* that the film concerns a British-born inspirational speaker named Michael Stone." Steven Zeitchik, "Leaders of the Pack," *L.A. Times*, 4 Sept. 2015, Calendar §, at 1.

See SUBJUNCTIVES.

The phrase is sometimes wrongly metamorphosed into **suffice to say*, without the *it*—e.g.: "In a following chapter we shall have much to say about reasoning and inference, but for now *suffice to say* [read *suffice it to say*] that it is easier to argue a case after it has been adequately elaborated and illustrated." V.A. Howard & J.H. Barton, *Thinking on Paper* 59 (1986). Maybe the writers were concerned with the number of *its* already in the sentence—a valid concern. But they could have fixed the problem in some other way. (A possible revision: *Later, we'll have something to say about reasoning and inference. But for now, suffice it to say that you can more easily argue a case after adequately elaborating and illustrating your points.*)

LANGUAGE-CHANGE INDEX
*suffice to say for *suffice it to say*: Stage 4
Current ratio (*suffice it to say* vs. **suffice to say*): 2:1

sufficiency; *sufficience. The former has always been standard in AmE and BrE alike. The latter is a NEEDLESS VARIANT.

Current ratio: 1,726:1

sufficient. See **adequate** (A) & **enough.**

sufficiently . . . as to can usually be simplified to *enough to*—e.g.:

- "He sees little evidence of Asian economies being *sufficiently supple as to* [read *supple enough to*] be able to change direction quickly." Peter Aspden, "Life in the Old Tortoise Yet," *Fin. Times*, 30 Sept. 1997, Survey §, at 1.
- "His recommendations, while satisfactory, are not *sufficiently notable as to* [read *notable enough to* or *so notable*

as to] make a lasting impression." Vaughn A. Carney, "Where Does the Nation Go from Here?" *Chicago Trib.*, 30 Nov. 1997, at 19.

*sufficient number of, a. Although this phrase is certainly old, dating back to the 17th century, it is also certainly verbose for *enough*—e.g.:

- "As might be expected, he found *a sufficient number of* [read *enough*] legislators receptive to the state's crying need to legalize betting." O.K. Carter, "Races' Old Patron Would Be Proud," *Ft. Worth Star-Telegram*, 17 Apr. 1997, at 1.
- "But the 1996 farm law requires the department to transfer sales to the private sector if *a sufficient number of* [read *enough*] agents were available in each state." "Farm Law Passed in 1996 Required Change," *Chicago Trib.*, 25 May 1997, at 2. (Note also the poor tense-shifting: *were* [five words from the end] should be *are*.)

suffrage (= [1] the right to vote, or [2] a short prayer) is occasionally misspelled **sufferage*—e.g.:

- "[C]lass formation in the cultural and political sense—as well as in the sense of economic identification—entails, among other things, the determined struggle of nascent working-class factions for *sufferage* [read *suffrage*]." Stanley Aronowitz, *The Politics of Identity* 132 (1992).
- "Issue of Voting Rights for Blacks Roiled Early *Sufferage* [read *Suffrage*] Movement." Headline, *Telegram & Gaz.* (Worcester), 28 Feb. 2008, at A11.
- "To better oppose the increasingly oppressive apartheid laws, [Helen] Suzman and 10 others broke away to form the Progressive Party—though she initially did not support universal, one-man-one-vote *sufferage* [read *suffrage*]." Denis Goldberg, "Appraisal: Suzman's Courage Failed Her," *The Forward*, 16 Jan. 2009, at 4.

Current ratio: 995:1

suffragist; suffragette. The broad term for a person who believes that a disenfranchised class of people should have the right to vote is *suffragist*. That term dates back to the early 19th century. In AmE, it extends especially to women's suffrage. *Suffragette* (referring specifically to any woman who participated in the movement to give women the right to vote) is not recorded before the first years of the 20th century. The diminutive suffix *-ette* was adopted by two groups that made strange bedfellows: the movement's most scornful opponents and its most radical proponents.

Today, many people object to the term *suffragette* as sexist—e.g.: "'My mother was a *suffragette*,' she said in the opening line of Ken Burns' documentary on the *suffragists* . . . . Her choice of words was surprising, said her daughter, Penelope Carter, of Rochester. 'The word *suffragette* reminded her of the Rockettes,' Ms. Carter said. 'She was a *suffragist*.'" Douglas Martin, "Ruth Dyk, Champion of Women's Suffrage, Dies at 99," *N.Y. Times*, 26 Nov. 2000, § 1, at 57.

Nevertheless, *suffragette* remains about twice as common as *suffragist*. The terms are often used interchangeably (sometimes, as in the first example below, for INELEGANT VARIATION)—e.g.:

- "Anti-*suffragists* feared voting rights would escort in the destruction of the American family, and many

Southerners were suspicious of the Northerners who arrived to sway legislators. American *suffragettes* tended to be well-educated, well-heeled women of social stature, although the underprivileged and working classes actually gained the most by ratification." Lisa A. DuBois, "The Perfect 36," *Variety*, 13 May 1996, at 79.

- "Sojourner Truth . . . was at a meeting with her sister *suffragettes* when a man wandered in and began taunting the women about their desire to vote." Judy Wells, "EVE Awards Presented to 3 Winners," *Fla. Times Union*, 9 June 2001, at B1.
- "Youngsters will . . . have an opportunity to learn about *suffragists* such as Sojourner Truth, Susan B. Anthony and Anna Howard Shaw." "Camp Features Lessons on Prominent Women," *Lansing State J.*, 9 July 2002, at 4.

Despite popular usage, however, *suffragist* has overtaken *suffragette* in English-language print sources published since the early 1970s. The votes seem to be in—at least for scholarly writing.

*****suffrance.** See **sufferance.**

suggest. See **allude** (C).

suggestible. So spelled in AmE and BrE alike—not **suggestable.* See -ABLE (A).

Current ratio: 288:1

suicide. A. And *self-killing; self-murder; self-slaughter; felo-de-se.* The five terms are generally synonymous, though *self-murder* and *self-slaughter* are charged with extremely negative connotations. *Suicide* and *self-killing* are broad terms that include every instance in which a person intentionally causes his or her own death. *Suicide* used to be included within the definition of *homicide* (= the killing of a human being by a human being), but the modern trend has been to distinguish the one from the other by defining *homicide* as "the killing of a human being by *another* human being." The Latin phrase *felo-de-se* is a EUPHEMISM either for a person who commits suicide or for the act of suicide. See -CIDE.

B. As an Agent Noun. In the early 18th century, *suicide* took on the secondary sense of "someone who dies by his or her own hand," and the word has been steadily used in this meaning ever since—e.g.: "Both the elder of Anne's sisters, Jane, and an aunt, Frances, were *suicides*." John Simon, "Connoisseur of Madness, Addict of Suicide," *New Criterion*, Dec. 1991, at 58, 59. Earlier synonyms, now less frequently employed, include *self-destroyer, self-killer, self-murderer, self-slayer*, and *felo-de-se.*

C. As a Verb. The verb has been used intransitively <he suicided>, reflexively and redundantly <he suicided himself>, and transitively and ridiculously <he suicided her (i.e., drove her to suicide)>. In the intransitive and reflexive uses, the senses are self-evident. The most common use is the intransitive one—e.g.:

- "He called his homeland the new Nazareth, and *suicided* at the age of 30 in 1925." Paul Greenberg, "As Boris Yeltsin Ascends, So Do the Hopes of His Nation," *Chicago Trib.*, 21 June 1991, at C23.
- "At age 42, he slowly *suicided*." Dwight Cunningham, "Cigarettes at Work," *Crain's Small Bus.* (Detroit), 3 Oct. 1994, at 8.
- "Not long afterwards, my good friend Grand Chief Stan Beardy asked me to accompany him to the Wunnumin Lake First Nation to do what we could to comfort the families of three young people who had *suicided*." James K. Bartleman, "Creating Hope," *Nat'l Post* (Can.), 29 Mar. 2010, at A14.

But all these verb uses sound trendy and semiliterate.

*****suicide victim,** a seeming OXYMORON, is a phrase that suggests a dogmatic stand on the issue whether suicide is ever justifiable. The phrase became popular in the mid-20th century. The less doctrinaire equivalent, *suicide* (n.), is probably more suitable in most contexts. E.g.:

- "The series responded with a moving episode in which Crosetti's body was found, an obvious *suicide victim* [read *suicide*]." Steve Hall, "Worthwhile Watching," *Indianapolis Star*, 28 May 1995, TV Week §, at 1.
- "Senator Bob Kerrey's tribute to disabled Vietnam veteran and *suicide victim* Lewis B. Puller Jr. [was] never delivered." Diane Daniel, "Words of Eulogy Live On After Death," *Boston Globe*, 26 May 1997, at C6. (A possible revision: *Senator Bob Kerrey's tribute to Lewis B. Puller Jr., a disabled Vietnam veteran who committed suicide, was never delivered.*)

sui generis; sui juris. *Sui generis* /soo-ee jen-ə-rəs/ (= of its own kind; individual; like only to itself) is an acceptable LATINISM because of its familiarity. An arty equivalent of *unique*, it first came into frequent use in the late 18th century. The phrase is singular only, and it should not be used with plural nouns. E.g.:

- "The Third Reich was a *sui generis* horror: a state resting on systematic mass murder as a central goal." "Dangerous Dreams," *Village Voice*, 16 Apr. 1996, at 24.
- "Even considered as one of the troika of Schubert's last quartets, . . . 'Death and the Maiden' is truly *sui generis*." John Henken, "Schubert Soars with Alban Berg Quartet," *L.A. Times*, 19 May 1997, at F4.
- "Opened this summer, the museum adeptly tells the *sui generis* neighbourhood's story through multimedia exhibits about its past and walking tours through its present." Alec Scott, "Medium Rare," *Globe & Mail* (Toronto), 1 Sept. 2015, at L1.

Sui juris /soo-ee juur-əs/ = (1) of full age and capacity; or (2) having full social and civil rights. The term is pretty much confined to legal contexts. But even there, the LATINISM is often better translated into ordinary English.

suite. In the phrase *bedroom suite*, the standard pronunciation of *suite* is /sweet/; in DIALECT, the word becomes /soot/ (like *suit*). Occasionally, the dialectal

LANGUAGE-CHANGE INDEX (For the full key, see front matter pp. xxxi, l–li.)
Stage 1: Rejected. **Stage 2:** Widely shunned. **Stage 3:** Widespread but . . . **Stage 4:** Ubiquitous but . . . **Stage 5:** Fully accepted.
Invariably inferior forms marked by asterisk (*). • Ratios represent frequency of prevalent forms vs. variants in current books.

pronunciation affects the printed word (*bedroom suit*)—e.g.: "When I was in Denver, Colorado, in the '60s, I bought quite a bit of furniture, a bedroom *suit* [read *suite*] and a dining room *suit* [read *suite*]." Anon., "Meet the Woodworkers," *Chambersburg Public Opinion* (Pa.), 16 Dec. 2007, Local §, at 1.

LANGUAGE-CHANGE INDEX
bedroom suit for *bedroom suite*: Stage 1

sulfur; sulphur. The first has been standard AmE since about 1940. Although the second has been standard BrE since the 18th century, the *-f-* spelling is making strong headway there. In World English, *sulfur* has predominated since about 1950. Professional chemists worldwide use only the *-f-* form, as in *sulfide, sulfate,* and *sulfurous.* Both terms are sometimes misspelled **sulfer* or **sulpher,* even in technical sources—e.g.:

- "The *sulpher* [read *sulphur*] dioxide gas released was completely absorbed in an excess of dilute aqueous sodium hydroxide (Step 2)." E.N. Ramsden, *Calculations for A-Level Chemistry* 98 (1995).
- "Potassium bicarbonate or wettable *sulfer* [read *sulfur*] may cause damage to some plants. Spray foliage of plants once every one to two weeks after first signs of disease are discovered." Nancy Robitaille & Eugenie Robitaille, *Insects, Pests, and Diseases of the African Violet Family* 175 (2005).

Current ratio (*sulfur* vs. *sulphur*): 1.4:1

sumac (= a plant of the cashew family) is predominantly so spelled—in AmE from 1910 and in BrE from 1950. **Sumach* is a variant form. The word is pronounced /**shoo**-mak/ or /**soo**-mak/.

*summersault. See **somersault.**

summons. Pl. *summonses* (in AmE and BrE alike). E.g.: "Littering is illegal, yet smokers seem strangely immune to the threat of *summonses* or public rebuke for their thoughtless actions." Letter of Alexander B. Grannis, "Smokers Litter Our Streets Without a Thought," *N.Y. Times,* 31 May 1995, at A20.

sumptuous; sumptuary. These words have almost opposite senses. *Sumptuous* = excessively luxurious; made or produced at great cost <a sumptuous feast>. *Sumptuary* = relating to or designed to regulate expenditures <sumptuary regulations>.

Sumptuous is sometimes misspelled **sumptious,* perhaps under the influence of *scrumptious*—e.g.:

- "If you have a leftover fish, you can convert it into a *sumptious* [read *sumptuous* or, depending on meaning, *scrumptious*] soup in a matter of minutes." Adrian Cornell, "Cook Goes Fishing, Turns Up Good News," *St. Louis Post-Dispatch,* 15 Feb. 1997, at 26.
- "Last Wednesday the chief executive of Heron International hosted a *sumptious* [read *sumptuous* or, depending on meaning, *scrumptious*] lunch at the Savoy." Doug Morrison, "Ronson Reunited," *Daily Telegraph,* 2 Mar. 1997, at 7.

LANGUAGE-CHANGE INDEX
sumptuous misspelled **sumptious*: Stage 1

sum total of. This phrase is technically a REDUNDANCY—*sum* meaning "total"—but it's a venial one not likely to disappear from the modern lexicon. The phrase can be especially useful for emphatic purposes in such lines as *the sum total of our knowledge*—although a few sticklers would probably prefer *totality* there.

sun. See **earth.**

sundry (= various) is, in AmE, a quaint term with literary associations. The redundant expression *various and sundry,* dating from the 19th century, ought to be avoided even in the most casual contexts. *Sundries* (= miscellaneous small items) has been in common use since the 18th century.

sunk. See **sink.**

*supercede. See **supersede (A).**

supererogatory has two almost opposite sets of connotations, some positive and others negative. The core sense is "going beyond what is required." On the one hand, the word may connote "superfluous," and it is often used in this way—e.g.: "The best opera directors accept this primacy of music in creating theatrical illusion; the worst ones swamp it with overblown stage effects [that] make the music, as it were, *supererogatory.*" Terry Teachout, "Words, Music, Opera," *Commentary,* Dec. 1995, at 57. On the other hand, it may mean "performing more than duty or circumstances require; doing more than is minimally needed"—e.g.: "She believed that . . . Christian morality . . . requires *supererogatory* acts toward one's neighbor, even the neighbor who is an enemy." Vigen Guroian, "The New Nationalism & the Gospel Witness," *Commonweal,* 14 July 1995, at 11.

superior, adj., takes *to*—not *than.*

SUPERLATIVES. See COMPARATIVES AND SUPERLATIVES.

supernumerary is a fancy adjective meaning (1) "extra"; (2) (of an employee) "engaged only in case of special need"; or (3) "superfluous." The word is sometimes wrongly written **supernumery*—e.g.: "He was . . . a former *supernumery* [read *supernumerary*] police officer in East Windsor and had also served with the U.S. Navy." "John F. Corbett" (obit.), *Hartford Courant,* 7 May 1997, at B10.

The same error occurs in the noun use, in which *supernumerary* means "an extra person or thing"—e.g.:

- "The chorus hung around like *supernumeries* [read *supernumeraries*]." Andrew Clark, "Where Opera Goes from Strength to Strength," *Fin. Times,* 28 July 1994, at 15.
- "The good burghers of Cannes . . . don't like to be treated as *supernumeries* [read *supernumeraries*]." Derek Malcolm, "Cannes 96," *Guardian,* 8 May 1996, at T6.

LANGUAGE-CHANGE INDEX
supernumerary misspelled **supernumery*: Stage 1
Current ratio: 176:1

supersede. A. Spelling. This word—from the Latin root -*sed*- "to sit," not -*ced*- "to move"—is properly spelled with an internal -*s*-, not a -*c*-. But so many other English words end in -*cede* or -*ceed* that many writers unconsciously distort the spelling of *supersede*. The misspelling has persistently occurred since the 17th century, though quite infrequently in comparison with the correct spelling. The error appears in some surprising places—e.g.:

- "The decision sends a strong message to lumber companies that claim their property rights *supercede* [read *supersede*] environmental concerns." Daniel Sneider, "Species Act Survives Challenge," *Christian Science Monitor*, 21 Feb. 1997, at 3.
- "For now, their legal battle in California mostly centers on jurisdiction, whether the state's gun laws *supercede* [read *supersede*] those enacted locally." Lynda Gorov, "Calif. Gun Battle," *Boston Globe*, 18 Apr. 1997, at A1.
- "For example, a federal statute may *supercede* [read *supersede*] or 'preempt' a similar state statute, and a state statute may *supercede* [read *supersede*] or 'preempt' a similar county or city ordinance." William A. Kaplin & Barbara A. Lee, *The Law of Higher Education* 673 (2011).

See SPELLING (A).

LANGUAGE-CHANGE INDEX
supersede misspelled *supercede: Stage 2
Current ratio: 12:1

B. Corresponding Noun. *Supersession* is the standard noun form, meaning either "the act of superseding" or "the state of being superseded." E.g.: "School Board 12 is the sixth community school board that has had part of its operations superseded by Mr. Fernandez and his aides. *Supersession* is a more lenient step than suspension." Joseph Berger, "School District Stripped of Fiscal Power," *N.Y. Times*, 7 Dec. 1991, at 27. As with the verb, the internal -*s*- is sometimes incorrectly made -*c*-.

Supersedure, a NEEDLESS VARIANT in all contexts but beekeeping, occasionally appears where it doesn't belong—e.g.: "Sharpton said Pataki's dramatic *supersedure* [read *supersession*] of Johnson violated a provision of the Voting Rights Act." Dan Morrison, "Sharpton: Pataki Stole Case," *Newsday* (N.Y.), 24 Mar. 1996, at A4. As for the bees, *supersedure* means "the replacement of an old, weakened queen bee by a younger, more vigorous one"—e.g.: "A deficit of queen pheromones might be the cause of queen rearing by worker honey bees during swarming and queen *supersedure*." David J.C. Fletcher & Murray S. Blum, "Regulation of Queen Number by Workers in Colonies of Social Insects," *Science*, 21 Jan. 1983, at 312.

Current ratio (*supersession* vs. *supersedure*): 16:1

C. Misused for *surpass* or *beat*. Sportswriters have begun using this word as a synonym of *beat*: hence one team is said to "supersede" another when it wins a game. E.g.: Tim Cowlishaw, "Cowboys *Superseded* [read *Beaten*] by Redskins: Dallas Defense

Overpowered in 35–16 Loss," *Dallas Morning News*, 7 Sept. 1993, at B1. And other writers have misused the word for *surpass*—e.g.: "Arguably, Russia *supersedes* [read *surpasses*] even England in the publication of Shakespeare's works and the staging of his plays." Melor Sturua, "O.J. Through Russian Eyes," *Wall Street J.*, 21 Sept. 1994, at A14.

SUPERSTITIONS. In 1926, H.W. Fowler used the term *superstitions* to describe, in the field of writing, "unintelligent applications of an unintelligent dogma" (*FMEU1* at 586). Experts in usage have long railed against them as arrant nonsense, yet they retain a firm grip—if not a stranglehold—on the average person's mind when it comes to putting words on paper. Indeed, these superstitions are bred in the classrooms in which children and adolescents learn to write.

Most of these superstitions are treated elsewhere in this book, in the entry to which the reader is referred at the end of each subentry. For additional perspectives on these points, see the brief statements by respected authorities on style, grammar, and usage that are collected below.

A. The False Notion That You Should Never End a Sentence with a Preposition.

- "The origin of the misguided rule is not hard to ascertain. To begin with, there is the meaning of the word 'preposition' itself: stand before. The meaning derives from Latin, and in the Latin language prepositions do usually stand before the words they govern. But Latin is not English. In English prepositions have been used as terminal words in a sentence since the days of Chaucer, and in that position they are completely idiomatic." Theodore M. Bernstein, *Miss Thistlebottom's Hobgoblins: The Careful Writer's Guide to the Taboos, Bugbears, and Outmoded Rules of English Usage* 177 (1971).
- "Ending a sentence with a preposition can be as dangerous as stepping on a crack in a sidewalk." Allan Metcalf, "Double or Nothing: An End to Final Prepositions," 62 *Am. Speech* 182, 182 (1987).

See PREPOSITIONS (B).

B. The False Notion That You Should Never Split an Infinitive.

- "There is a busybody on your staff who devotes a lot of his time to chasing split infinitives. Every good literary craftsman splits his infinitives when the sense demands it. I call for the immediate dismissal of this pedant. It is of no consequence whether he decides to go quickly or quickly to go or to quickly go. The important thing is that he should go at once." George Bernard Shaw, Letter to *The Times* (19th c.) (as quoted in *Best Advice on How to Write* 259–60 (Gorham Munson ed., 1952)).
- "Anybody who doesn't wish to see too wide a division between the spoken and the written speech will not be too severe against the split infinitive. A man may write 'to tell really' or 'really to tell', but he will probably say 'to really tell'. It seems to us that there are phrases in which the split infinitive is the more direct and instinctive form." "The Split Infinitive" (1898), in *Casual Essays of the Sun* 238, 240 (1905).

LANGUAGE-CHANGE INDEX (For the full key, see front matter pp. xxxi, l–li.)
Stage 1: Rejected. **Stage 2:** Widely shunned. **Stage 3:** Widespread but . . . **Stage 4:** Ubiquitous but . . . **Stage 5:** Fully accepted.
Invariably inferior forms marked by asterisk (✳). • Ratios represent frequency of prevalent forms vs. variants in current books.

- "The practice of inserting an adverb between the infinitive sign [*to*] and the infinitive has steadily increased during the last hundred years, and goes on increasing still. Even a slight examination of the best and the worst contemporary production, in both England and America, will make clear that the universal adoption of this usage is as certain as anything in the future well can be." Thomas R. Lounsbury, *The Standard of Usage in English* 259 (1908).
- "The notion that it is a grammatical mistake to place a word between *to* and the simple form of a verb, as in *to quietly walk away*, is responsible for a great deal of bad writing by people who are trying to write well. Actually the rule against 'splitting an infinitive' contradicts the principles of English grammar and the practice of our best writers." *DCAU* at 469.
- "There is no point in rearranging a sentence just to avoid splitting an infinitive unless it is an awkward one." Porter G. Perrin, *Writer's Guide and Index to English* 828 (4th ed. 1965).

See SPLIT INFINITIVES (A).

C. The False Notion That You Should Never Split a Verb Phrase.

- "In a compound verb (*have seen*) with an adverb, that adverb comes between the auxiliary and the participle ('I have *never* seen her'); or, if there are two or more auxiliaries, immediately after the first auxiliary ('I have *always* been intending to go to Paris'); that order is changed only to obtain emphasis, as in 'I never have seen her' (with stress on 'have') . . . . There is, however, a tendency to move an adverb from its rightful and natural position for inadequate reasons, as in 'Oxford must *heartily* be congratulated.'" Eric Partridge, *U&A* at 224.
- "Because of their misconception as to what a split infinitive really is, some have reached the erroneous conclusion that an adverbial modifier must never be placed between parts of a compound verb phrase, with the result that they write in such an eccentric style as 'I greatly have been disappointed' instead of writing naturally 'I have been greatly disappointed.'" R.W. Pence & D.W. Emery, *A Grammar of Present-Day English* 320 n.69 (1963).
- "With a compound verb—that is, one made with an auxiliary and a main verb—the adverb comes between auxiliary and main verb (*He will probably telephone before starting / I have often had that thought myself / The clock is consistently losing five minutes a day*)." Wilson Follett, *MAU* at 53.

See ADVERBS (A).

D. The False Notion That You Should Never Begin a Sentence with *And* or *But*.

- "Next to the groundless notion that it is incorrect to end an English sentence with a preposition, perhaps the most wide-spread of many false beliefs about the use of our language is the equally groundless notion that it is incorrect to begin one with 'but' or 'and.' As in the case of the superstition about the prepositional ending, no textbook supports it, but apparently about half of our teachers of English go out of their way to handicap their pupils by inculcating it. One cannot help wondering whether those who teach such a monstrous doctrine ever read any English themselves." Charles Allen Lloyd, *We Who Speak English* 19 (1938).
- "There is no reason why sentences should not begin with *and*." Roy H. Copperud, *American Usage: The Consensus* 15 (1970).

- "There is a persistent belief that it is improper to begin a sentence with *And*, but this prohibition has been cheerfully ignored by standard authors from Anglo-Saxon times onwards." R.W. Burchfield, *Points of View* 109 (1992).
- "Many of us were taught that no sentence should begin with 'but.' If that's what you learned, unlearn it—there's no stronger word at the start." William Zinsser, *On Writing Well* 74 (6th ed. 1998).

See **and** (A) & **but** (A).

E. The False Notion That You Should Never Write a One-Sentence Paragraph.

- "A paragraph may contain but one sentence . . . [or] two sentences; but usually it contains more than two." Adams S. Hill, *The Foundations of Rhetoric* 23–24 (1896).
- "To interpose a one-sentence paragraph at intervals—at longish intervals—is prudent. Such a device helps the eye and enables the reader (especially if 'the going is heavy') to regain his breath between one impressive or weighty or abstruse paragraph and the next." Eric Partridge, *U&A* at 224–25.
- "Three situations in essay writing can occasion a one-sentence paragraph: (a) when you want to emphasize a crucial point that might otherwise be buried; (b) when you want to dramatize a transition from one stage in your argument to the next; and (c) when instinct tells you that your reader is tiring and would appreciate a mental rest." John R. Trimble, *Writing with Style* 92–93 (2d ed. 2000).

F. The False Notion That You Should Never Begin a Sentence with *Because*.
So novel and absurd is this superstition that few authorities on writing have countered it in print. But here's one: "This proscription ['Never begin a sentence with *because*'] appears in no handbook of usage I know of, but the belief seems to have a popular currency among many students." Joseph M. Williams, *Style: Ten Lessons in Clarity and Grace* 168 (1981). It appears to result from concern about fragments—e.g.: "Then the group broke for lunch. Because we were hungry." Of course, the second "sentence" is merely a fragment, not a complete sentence. (See INCOMPLETE SENTENCES (A).) But problems of that kind simply cannot give rise to a general prohibition against starting a sentence with *because*. Good writers do so frequently—e.g.:

- "*Because* of the war the situation in hospitals is, of course, serious." E.B. White, "A Weekend with the Angels," in *The Second Tree from the Corner* 3, 6 (1954).
- "*Because* the relationship between remarks is often vague in this passage, we could not rewrite it with certainty without knowing the facts." Donald Hall, *Writing Well* 104 (1973).

See **because** (E).

G. The False Notion That You Should Never Use *since* to Mean *because*.

- "There is a groundless notion current both in the lower schools and in the world of affairs that *since* has an exclusive reference to time and therefore cannot be used as a causal conjunction. . . . No warrant exists for avoiding this usage, which goes back, beyond Chaucer, to Anglo-Saxon." Wilson Follett, *MAU* at 305.
- "It is a delusion that *since* may be used only as an adverb in a temporal sense ('We have been here since ten o'clock').

It is also a causal conjunction meaning *for* or *because*: 'Since it is raining, we had better take an umbrella.'" Roy H. Copperud, *American Usage and Style: The Consensus* 349 (1980).

See **as (A)**.

H. The False Notion That You Should Never Use *between* **with More than Two Objects.** "When Miss Thistlebottom taught you in grammar school that *between* applies only to two things and *among* to more than two, she was for the most part correct. *Between* essentially does apply to only two, but sometimes the 'two' relationship is present when more than two elements are involved. For example, it would be proper to say that 'The President was trying to start negotiations between Israel, Egypt, Syria and Jordan' if what was contemplated was not a round-table conference but separate talks involving Israel and each of the other three nations." Theodore M. Bernstein, *Dos, Don'ts & Maybes of English Usage* 29 (1977). See **between (A)**.

I. The False Notion That You Should Never Use the First-Person Pronouns *I* **and** *me.* "If you want to write like a professional just about the first thing you have to do is get used to the first person singular. Just plunge in and write 'I' whenever 'I' seems to be the word that is called for. Never mind the superstitious notion that it's immodest to do so. It just isn't so." Rudolf Flesch, *A New Way to Better English* 49 (1958). See **FIRST PERSON**.

J. The False Notion That You Should Never Use Contractions. "Your style will obviously be warmer and truer to your personality if you use contractions like 'I'll' and 'won't' when they fit comfortably into what you're writing. 'I'll be glad to see them if they don't get mad' is less stiff than 'I will be glad to see them if they do not get mad.' There's no rule against such informality—trust your ear and your instincts." William Zinsser, *On Writing Well* 117 (3d ed. 1985). See **CONTRACTIONS (A)**.

K. The False Notion That You Should Never Use *you* **in Referring to Your Reader.**

• "Keep a running conversation with your reader. Use the second-person pronoun whenever you can. Translate everything into *you* language. *This applies to citizens over 65* = if you're over 65, this applies to you. *It must be remembered that* = you must remember. *Many people don't realize* = perhaps you don't realize. Always write directly to *you*, the person you're trying to reach with your written message. Don't write in mental isolation; reach out to your reader." Rudolf Flesch, *How to Be Brief: An Index to Simple Writing* 114 (1962).

• "Not only does the use of *you* eliminate the passive and make sentences more readable, it directs the writing where it should be directed: to the reader. The 'you attitude' is reader-oriented rather than writer-oriented." Gary A. Olson, James DeGeorge & Richard Ray, *Style and Readability in Business Writing* 96 (1985).

See **you.**

supervise is occasionally misspelled **supervize*—e.g.: "And when any out-of-state parolee is under New Hampshire's jurisdiction, it is the Granite State's parole board [that] *supervizes* [read *supervises*] parole." Pat Grossmith, "Humphrey's Criminal Record Wasn't Shared Between Region's States," *Union Leader* (Manchester, N.H.), 19 Oct. 1994, at 4.

Current ratio: 1,294:1

supervisory; supervisorial. *Supervisory* = of, relating to, or involving supervision. *Supervisorial* = of, relating to, or involving a supervisor.

supine. Because the word means "lying on one's back," the phrase **supine on (one's) back* is a REDUNDANCY. It cropped up in the 19th century and still occasionally appears—e.g.: "Evans was to be laid *supine on his back* [read *supine*] as all four limbs were strapped with leather binds to a bed." Joe Domanick, "How California Failed Kevin Evans," *L.A. Times*, 26 Aug. 2001, Mag. §, at 10. See **prone.**

supplely, adv. (= in a supple manner), is better than *supply*, which causes a MISCUE by suggesting the noun or verb spelled that way. E.g.: "Her three-octave voice, *supplely* roaming from a lower register to breathy soprano, blasted through a pounding eight-man combo." Jan Stuart, "Basia's Siren Songs," *Newsday* (N.Y.), 16 Nov. 1994, at B9. The word has been infrequently used since the 19th century. Cf. **subtly.**

supplement, n.; **complement,** n. A *supplement* is simply something added <a dietary supplement>. A *complement* is a wholly adequate supplement; it's something added to complete or perfect a whole <that scarf is a perfect complement to your outfit>.

For misuses of *compliment* for *complement*, see **compliment.**

supplementary; supplemental; suppletory; *suppletive. *Supplementary* has been the standard term since about 1800. The other forms have the same meaning, namely, "of the nature of, forming, or serving as a remedy for the deficiencies of something." Outside the law—which uses special phrases such as *supplemental pleading* and *suppletory oath*—the terms *supplemental*, *suppletory*, and **suppletive* are NEEDLESS VARIANTS.

supplicant; suppliant. *Supplicant* is the standard noun meaning "someone who earnestly beseeches; a humble petitioner"—e.g.:

• "Upstairs in a darkened room of the Edina home in which he was staying, Sakya Trizin, supreme head of one of Tibetan Buddhism's four branches, received a constant stream of *supplicants*." Kay Miller, "Buddhism from Tibet Pursues Energy of West," *Star Trib.* (Minneapolis), 8 July 1995, at A1.

• "Yeltsin has been cut out of some crucial discussions and sometimes treated as a needy *supplicant*." Cragg Hines,

LANGUAGE-CHANGE INDEX (For the full key, see front matter pp. xxxi, l–li.)
Stage 1: Rejected. **Stage 2:** Widely shunned. **Stage 3:** Widespread but . . . **Stage 4:** Ubiquitous but . . . **Stage 5:** Fully accepted.
Invariably inferior forms marked by asterisk (*). • Ratios represent frequency of prevalent forms vs. variants in current books.

"Yeltsin Signs NATO Accord, Agrees to Redirect Missiles," *Houston Chron.*, 28 May 1997, at 1.

- "It's true that Priebus came to Trump Tower for a pledge-signing ceremony, as if the party were a *supplicant* and Trump the grantor of favors." Eugene Robinson, "He Pledged. Now What?" *Wash. Post*, 4 Sept. 2015, at A21.

As a noun, *suppliant* is a NEEDLESS VARIANT because it occurs much less frequently and because it less closely matches the corresponding verb, *supplicate*. But as an adjective meaning "humbly beseeching" or "earnestly entreating," *suppliant* is standard. In sum, use *suppli-cant* as a noun and *suppliant* as an adjective.

supposable; suppositious; supposititious; suppositional; *suppositive. *Supposable* = capable of being supposed; presumable. E.g.: "He learns more about himself and the *supposable* dimension of man's future." Dick Richmond, "A Sequel to 'The Celestine Prophecy,'" *St. Louis Post-Dispatch*, 16 May 1996, at G7.

Suppositious and *supposititious* sometimes cause confusion. Although some modern dictionaries list these as variants, some DIFFERENTIATION is both possible and desirable. *Suppositious* should be used to mean "hypothetical; theoretical; assumed." E.g.:

- "House Speaker Thomas Foley . . . said: 'I never answer questions like that. They are what are called *suppositious* questions.'" Michael Karnish, "Clinton Receives a High Court List," *Boston Globe*, 16 Apr. 1994, at 1.
- "It is exactly here that I think the roots of Charles's tragicomedy lie, and not in the wholly *suppositious* notion of 'parricide' advanced by the Robert Redford movie 'Quiz Show.'" Jeffrey Hart, "'Van Doren' and 'Redford,'" *Nat'l Rev.*, 7 Nov. 1994, at 78.

Supposititious (the most frequently occurring of all the headwords in this entry) should be confined to its usual sense: "illegitimate; spurious; counterfeit." E.g.: "This *supposititious* mortal mind, not God, is the parent of all oppression and abuse, individual and collective." "The Circle of Love," *Christian Science Monitor*, 11 Sept. 1996, at 17. Interestingly, one user of the word has complained that not everyone grasps its precise meaning: "People who write about musical manuscripts find it difficult if not impossible to get the word *supposititious* into print ('fraudulently substituted in the place of another thing; not genuine, spurious') without someone suggesting it should be *suppositious* ('based on supposition')." Fritz Spiegl, "Usage and Abusage," *Daily Telegraph*, 8 July 1995, at 32.

Sometimes *suppositious* appears to be misused for its longer sibling—e.g.: "Lo finally has her baby by the side of a stream, with Elaine assisting. (The tidily achieved birth is the script's one *suppositious* [read *supposititious*] touch.)" Stanley Kauffman, "Manny and Lo," *New Republic*, 12 Aug. 1996, at 26.

Suppositional = conjectural, hypothetical. It has much the same sense as *suppositious*, and is perhaps generally the clearer word. And it's a little more common—e.g.: "Most of the play takes place in a tent, where Hale and Montresor argue their opposing world views, hopes and passions—a highly *suppositional* but dramatically irresistible approach, Ford

admitted." Paul Hodgins, "Short Memory an Asset for 'Nathan Hale,'" *Orange County Register*, 3 Nov. 1995, at 29.

Suppositive is a NEEDLESS VARIANT of *supposititious* and *suppositional*.

***supposably.** See **supposedly.**

supposal; *suppose, n. See **supposition.**

supposedly (= as is assumed to be true; presumably) is the proper adverb corresponding to *supposed*—not *supposably* (which, properly, means something like *arguably*). The form *supposably* is becoming quite common in speech, but fortunately it's still rare in print. See -EDLY.

Current ratio: 1,130:1

supposed to (= expected to) wrongly made *suppose to* has been a fairly common error since the 1940s—e.g.:

- "We're *suppose* [read *supposed*] to feel her greatest humiliation in this scene." Avis L. Weathersbee, "Judging TV's Black Images," *Chicago Sun-Times*, 8 Apr. 2001, Showcase §, at 1.
- "'The Price of Milk' is *suppose* [read *supposed*] to be a surreal romantic comedy about two young lovers who encounter a series of strange encounters and situations." Paul Stevens, "So Sour," *Buffalo News*, 18 May 2001, at G6.
- "He was *suppose* [read *supposed*] to be a lawyer, in fact was in his second year of law school at Florida State University, when he had an epiphany." "Artistic Tribute to 4-Legged Victims," *Atlanta J.-Const.*, 26 May 2001, Features §, at C2.

Cf. **used to.**

In constructions in which *suppose* means "to assume," an infinitive may follow the verb <I suppose this to be your answer>.

LANGUAGE-CHANGE INDEX
is suppose to for *is supposed to*: Stage 1
Current ratio (*is supposed to* vs. *is suppose to*): 181:1

supposition; supposal; *suppose, n. *Supposition* is the ordinary word; the others are NEEDLESS VARIANTS. But *supposal* is sometimes used by logicians.

suppositious; supposititious; suppositional; *suppositive. See **supposable.**

suppressible. So spelled in AmE and BrE alike—not *suppressable.* See -ABLE (A).

Current ratio: 42:1

suppressor. So spelled—not *suppresser.*

surcease. See **death.**

Surinamese; *Surinamer. For a citizen of Suriname, the first is standard; the second is a NEEDLESS VARIANT. See DENIZEN LABELS.

Current ratio: 172:1

surlily. See ADVERBS (B).

surmise. A. Spelling. As noun and verb, the word is so spelled—not *surmize.* E.g.: "Other officials even extended their optimism to *surmize* [read *surmise*] that 'a new climate has begun.'" Ana Martinez-Soler, "Madrid Cheers as France Quashes ETA Terrorists," *Christian Science Monitor*, 17 Jan. 1984, at 7.

B. And *surmisal. The word **surmisal* has long been a NEEDLESS VARIANT of the noun *surmise*—e.g.:

- "On Long Island, the vacuum of knowledge is filled with assumptions and *surmisals* [read *surmises*], the latest being that Iran may have been involved in the bomb explosion aboard TWA 800—that is, if it was a bomb explosion." Daniel Schorr, "Tripping over Terrorism," *Christian Science Monitor*, 9 Aug. 1996, at 19.
- "Just 32 months away from 12 years in office, Democratic Colorado Gov. Roy Romer recently offered a rather ironic *surmisal* [read *surmise? appraisal?*] of his cumulative effect on our state's Republican Legislature." "Put It to a Vote," *Gaz. Telegraph* (Colo. Springs), 13 May 1997, at 6.

LANGUAGE-CHANGE INDEX
*surmisal for *surmise*: Stage 1
Current ratio (*the surmise* vs. **the surmisal*): 300:1

surname; Christian name; forename; given name. The *surname* (or *family name*) denotes (wholly or partly) one's kinship. In many cases it was derived from physical characteristics, occupations, or locations and later transmitted to descendants (e.g., Smith); in other cases it indicated paternity (e.g., Davidson). Such names came to be called *surnames*. The modern custom is that a woman who marries may, but need not, add her husband's surname to her own (e.g., Hillary Rodham Clinton). In medieval England the *Christian name* was the baptismal name and was the only name that many people bore. Surnames were given later to differentiate (e.g., Robert the Younger).

The personal name of a non-Christian (and perhaps of anyone) is better called a *forename* (if it comes first) or *given name*—or simply *personal name*. E.g.: "'Suraphol' is the *personal name* [or *forename* or *given name*] and 'Apaiwongse' the *family name* [or *surname*] of my friend in Bangkok." The phrases *first name* and *last name* can be misleading because of the naming practices of different cultures. See NAMES (D).

surprise, n. & vb., is surprisingly often misspelled **surprize*. True, that was a variant spelling through the mid-19th century, but today it can justifiably be regarded as an error—e.g.: "There are other benefits that come from engaging an investment counselor who is paid for service: . . . fewer *surprizes* [read *surprises*] from volatile returns." Jonathan Chevreau, "Define Your Goals Before Investing," *Fin. Post*, 25 Nov. 1995, at 73. The misspelling **suprise* is also common—e.g.: "A pair of high school sweethearts winds up with a *suprise* [read *surprise*] pregnancy in a small town in South Dakota." Morain Michael, "Hollywood Hits Iowa's Red Carpet," *Des Moines Register*, 30 Dec. 2008, at E1.

Current ratio: 243:1

*surrounding circumstances. See circumstances (B).

surveil; *surveille. *Surveil* is a relatively new, and decidedly useful, verb corresponding to the noun *surveillance*. It is, in fact, a BACK-FORMATION from the noun. The present-participial and past-tense forms are *surveilling* and *surveilled*. E.g.: "Instead, Young has spent a fair amount of time since 1979 *surveilling* Clifford Antone for the Organized Crime Control Task Force." Robert Draper, "Clifford's Blues," *Texas Monthly*, Oct. 1997, at 140. *W11* gives 1914 as the year of its first recorded use. It was in fairly widespread use in AmE by the 1970s and in BrE by the 1990s. The spelling **surveille* is a variant form.

Current ratio: 6:1

surveyor. So spelled—not **surveyer*.

Current ratio: 1,113:1

survivor. So spelled—not **surviver*.

Current ratio: 2,455:1

susceptible—properly sounded /sə-**sep**-tə-bəl/—is sometimes mispronounced, even by educated speakers, /sək-**sep**-tə-bəl/.

suspect, n. A *suspect* is someone suspected of committing a crime. The person who commits the crime is a criminal (or a robber, thief, murderer, or the like). But in police reports it is common for writers (and, more commonly, broadcast reporters) to describe how "the *suspect*" committed the crime. Not only is this often absurd (if there *is* no suspect at that time), it is also potentially false and libelous (if there is a suspect but the suspect is not guilty). Unfortunately, the slack usage seems to be an infection that some writers catch from hanging around police JARGON too long—e.g.:

- "When confronted, the other man punched him in the eye. The *suspect* [read *assailant*] fled on foot, leaving the lawnmower." Jeremy Jarrell, "Woman Reports She Saw Man," *Herald-Dispatch* (Huntington, W. Va.), 31 May 2002, at C3.
- "On Friday officers watched as two *suspects* [read *men*] stole hand tools from the bait vehicle and another vehicle, DuBusk said. The *suspects* [read *suspected thieves*] fled when marked police units got in behind them, DuBusk said." Jim Balloch, "1 Arrested, Another Sought in Construction Site Theft," *Knoxville News-Sentinel*, 1 June 2002, at B5. (Perhaps the writer should have used a different verb, such as *took*, instead of *stole*. The suspects took tools, but did they steal them? Only a judge or a jury can decide. Neutral, balanced writing in crime reports is very difficult.)
- "After being given an undisclosed amount of cash, the *suspect* [read *robber*] fled north on foot." "For the Record," *Salt Lake Trib.*, 1 June 2002, at B2.

suspect, adj.; **suspicious.** These adjectives have always overlapped a good deal. *Suspect* = (1) not likely to be completely true <some highly suspect evidence>; (2) not likely to be completely forthright or honest <a suspect character>; (3) likely to have or to cause

LANGUAGE-CHANGE INDEX (For the full key, see front matter pp. xxxi, l–li.)
Stage 1: Rejected. **Stage 2:** Widely shunned. **Stage 3:** Widespread but . . . **Stage 4:** Ubiquitous but . . . **Stage 5:** Fully accepted.
Invariably inferior forms marked by asterisk (*). • Ratios represent frequency of prevalent forms vs. variants in current books.

problems <as we investigated the leak, we concluded that the second-floor door threshold is quite suspect>; or (4) likely to be involved in criminal activity <a suspect SUV>.

Suspicious = (1) having serious doubts about whether someone is behaving properly or honestly <we became suspicious of his conduct>; (2) feeling distrust of someone or something <suspicious of people generally> <suspicious of big government>; or (3) arousing thoughts that something bad or illegal is occurring <suspicious circumstances> <alert the authorities if you see anything suspicious>.

The convergence in meaning occurs especially with sense 4 of *suspect* and sense 3 of *suspicious*. So, for example, the collocation *suspect van* occurs just as frequently in print sources as *suspicious van*. But *suspicious circumstances* and *suspicious activities* dwarf *suspect circumstances* and *suspect activities* in word frequency and have done so since the mid-18th century. Many of the collocations are phrase- or idiom-specific.

suspendable; *suspendible; *suspensible. The first is standard in AmE and BrE alike; the second and third are NEEDLESS VARIANTS. Though *suspendible is the only form listed in *W3* and the *OED*, suspendable is five times as common. See -ABLE (A).
Current ratio (in order of headwords): 11:2:1

suspense; suspension. *Suspense* is the feeling of anxiety or excitement you experience when you don't know what will happen next. *Suspension* can be (1) the official stopping of something for a period <suspension of hostilities>; (2) the disallowing of someone to carry on for a time, esp. as a form of punishment <the player's suspension for four games was amply justified>; (3) the part of a vehicle attached to the wheels to make the ride more comfortable on bumpy roads <a car with superb suspension>; or (4) a liquid mixture in which minute bits of solid material are contained without dissolving <flecks of gold floating in the suspension>.

suspicion, as a verb, is dialectal for *suspect*. This usage emerged in the early 19th century and has persisted in the linguistic shadows, occasionally appearing in print—e.g.:

- "My guest hunter, who had never seen a gobbler called up, was trembling with turkey fever, and I *suspicioned* [read *suspected*] he was about to shoot." Bob Brisyer, "The Small Stuff: Shooting Techniques," *Field & Stream*, Feb. 1995, at 76.
- "Tests may include . . . bone density when osteoporosis is *suspicioned* [read *suspected*] or a woman is at risk for osteoporosis." Ron Surowitz, "Hormone Treatment May Be an Option for Menopause," *Jupiter Courier* (Fla.), 12 Mar. 1997, at A10.

See DIALECT.

LANGUAGE-CHANGE INDEX
suspicioned for *suspected*: Stage 1
Current ratio (*he suspected* vs. *he suspicioned*): 564:1

suspicious. See **suspect,** adj.

sustained injuries is OFFICIALESE for *was injured*. Dating from the late 18th century, it became frequent over the course of the 20th century—e.g.: "Also since the series, parents have filed lawsuits alleging two area children *sustained injuries* [read *were injured*] at unsafe play areas." Rosa Salter, "L.V. Dad Envisions Playground Safety Network," *Morning Call* (Allentown, Pa.), 25 Nov. 1996, A.M. Mag. §, at D1. Why prefer an edit that introduces the PASSIVE VOICE? This edit illustrates the principle that passive voice is usually preferable to a ZOMBIE NOUN (*injuries*).

To *sustain injuries to (a body part)* is usually verbose for *injure*—e.g.:

- "The woman *sustained injuries to her head and neck* [read *injured her head and neck*] in the accident at 11:40 a.m. Jan. 11." "Police Report," *Milwaukee J. Sentinel*, 18 Jan. 1996, at 14.
- "Kennard, in her mid-30s, *sustained injuries to her jaw, neck and shoulder* [read *injured her jaw, neck, and shoulder*], and has severe headaches, Collins said." Ted Cilwick, "Jury Awards Woman Who Slipped in Mall Half-Million Dollars," *Salt Lake Trib.*, 26 Nov. 1996, at B4.

To argue that those edits make the victim sound responsible for his or her injuries is to ignore an age-old English idiom. A football player might hurt his arm in a game—might even break his arm—and no one would be led to think that it was a self-inflicted wound.

swab (= [1] a mop; or [2] a cotton wad or cloth used for cleaning) is the standard spelling in AmE and BrE alike. *Swob is a variant.
Current ratio: 719:1

swale (= a depression in the land) is sometimes misspelled *swail—e.g.: "Mickelson . . . played it safe at 13 and banked his tee shot off the right fringe. 'It caught the right *swail* [read *swale*] and caught the bottom of the cup,' Mickelson said." Melanie Hauser, "TPC Leaves Players Amazed at High Scores," *Houston Post*, 25 Mar. 1995, at B5.

LANGUAGE-CHANGE INDEX
swale misspelled *swail: Stage 1
Current ratio: 175:1

*swang. See **swing.**

swap (= to exchange) is the standard spelling in AmE and BrE alike. *Swop is a chiefly BrE variant.
Current ratio (*swapping* vs. **swopping*): 122:1

SWAPPING HORSES while crossing the stream is H.W. Fowler's term for vacillating between two constructions (*FMEU1* at 589). Thus someone writes that *the rate of divorce is almost as high in Continental Europe, other things being equal, than it is in the United States.* The first *as* needs a second one in answer, but instead is ill greeted by *than*. See **as . . . as (E).**

Examples don't exactly abound in modern prose, but they're not rare either—e.g.:

- "He has given the Tilden, Simonsen, Hugo Muller and Pedler *lectureships* [read *lectures*] of the Royal Society of

Chemistry." "Isotechnica Inc." (announcement), *Fin. Post*, 12 Apr. 1997, at 33. (He has been given—or awarded— lectureships and has given lectures, but he hasn't given lectureships. See **lectureship**.)

- "Beardstown coach Don Dillon would *rather* have Maltby handing off *instead of* [read *than*] catching passes." Jim Benson, "Moroa Faces Beardstown in 'Third Round,'" *Pantagraph* (Bloomington, Ill.), 31 Oct. 1997, at B3. (*Rather* is completed by *than*, not *instead of*; but *instead of* would suffice if *rather* were omitted.)

SWAPPING WORDS. See WORD-SWAPPING.

swat (= to swing at [something] with a slapping movement) is the standard spelling in AmE and BrE alike. **Swot* is a variant.

Current ratio (*swatted* vs. **swotted*): 74:1

swathe, n. & vb.; **swath,** n. Let's first consider the nouns. In AmE, *swathe* generally denotes a wrapping, bandage, or other material in which something is enveloped. *Swath*, meanwhile, denotes a space cut by a scythe or mower; the grass or other low plants left within such a space; or a strip, belt, or lengthwise extent of something (especially land). To *cut a wide swath* is to make an ostentatious display or to attract attention.

In BrE, things are different: as a noun, *swathe* is taking over all senses—or has taken over. *Swath* is very much in decline even as a noun.

But in both AmE and BrE, the verb *swathe* means (1) to wrap up closely or fully, (2) to bandage or otherwise bind, or (3) in a figurative sense, to enwrap or enfold; to envelop as with a wrapping.

Swathe is pronounced /sway<u>th</u>/ as both noun and verb. *Swath* is pronounced /swoth/ or /swah<u>th</u>/.

swear > swore > sworn. So inflected. Swear off using the weak form **sweared*—e.g.:

- "Goodwin, whom [read *who*] Reds manager Jack McKeon suggested needed a bit of an attitude adjustment Thursday, stormed out of McKeon's office, *sweared* [read *swore*] a bit, told teammates he was quitting, changed into street clothes and left the clubhouse." Dan Hoyt, "The Rundown," *Kansas City Star*, 8 Aug. 1997, at D4.
- "To many of Jarvis' former Tribune colleagues, who also once *sweared* [read *swore*] by the place but thought it defunct, the ephemeral nature of Danny's was confounding." Charles Leroux, "An Italian Brigadoon," *Chicago Trib.*, 12 Jan. 2003, Mag. §, at 17.

See IRREGULAR VERBS.

LANGUAGE-CHANGE INDEX
1. **sweared* for *swore* or *sworn*: Stage 1
Current ratio (*swore* or *sworn* vs. **sweared*): 3,795:1
2. *Swore* as a past participle in place of *sworn*: Stage 1
Current ratio (*had sworn* vs. **had swore*): 302:1

SWEARING. See PROFANITY.

sweat > sweated > sweated. Although *sweat* is a variant past tense and past participle, *sweated* has been the

standard form since the early 20th century in AmE and BrE alike—e.g.:

- "He was dressed in white cowboy hat and boots, and a pearl-gray western jacket that he *sweat* [read *sweated*] through." Daniel Gewertz, "Legendary Dylan Rocks 'n' Rolls," *Boston Herald*, 14 Apr. 1997, at 31.
- "Neil Hord didn't mind the heat as he *sweat* [read *sweated*] under his hard hat at a construction site on Greene Street." Rich McKay, "Hot Streak Expected to Continue," *News & Record* (Greensboro), 4 July 1997, at B1.
- "His hands *sweated* if he found himself on the way to a new place on his own, a place that was to mean something to him, a place where he had to prove himself. They had *sweated* last autumn in the train to Gommern, they were sweating again today." Julia Franck, *Back to Back* 217 (2013).

Before 1910, *sweat* was an irregular verb (*sweat > sweat > sweat*); since that time, it has become regular in AmE and BrE alike.

In quasi-figurative phrases <we really sweated over that one!> <they sweated it out>, the only possible past forms are *sweated*—e.g.:

- "Remington Park fans have *sweated* their way through another summer quarter horse meeting." Bob Forrest, "See Spot Run During Final Remington Week," *Tulsa Trib. & Tulsa World*, 6 July 1996, at B3.
- "Inside, you'll find . . . a celebration of the valedictorians, who have *sweated out* straight A's and are finishing high school at the top of their respective classes." "'97 Graduation," *Spokesman-Rev.* (Spokane), 5 June 1997, at V1.
- "The result of this was she wanted to meet my parents. I really *sweated* that one out. I *sweated* out what my parents would say." Clyde A. Weber, *Church in the Wildwood* 68 (2013).

LANGUAGE-CHANGE INDEX
sweat as past form in place of *sweated*
<**he sweat heavily*>: Stage 3
Current ratio (*he sweated* vs. **he sweat*): 4:1

sweep > swept > swept. So inflected. Yet the weak form **sweeped* has erroneously swept into print—e.g.:

- "Ben Maidment *sweeped* [read *swept*] in on the left wing and converted a feed from Dana Mulvihill five seconds after a power play expired." Joe Concannon, "Bernard Rules in Eagles' Barn," *Boston Globe*, 30 Nov. 1997, at C17.
- "Jason Arnott *sweeped* [read *swept*] in a rebound from Patrik Elias' missed shot on Nikolai Khabibulin." Bob McManaman, "Coyotes Have No Answers for Devils," *Ariz. Republic*, 29 Mar. 1998, at C5.
- "A few homes were totally *sweeped* [read *swept*] away, leaving nothing to go home to." David Hefner, "Shelters Are Home Away from Home," *Tennessean*, 18 Apr. 1998, at A6.

See IRREGULAR VERBS.

LANGUAGE-CHANGE INDEX
*sweeped for *swept*: Stage 1
Current ratio (*swept* vs. **sweeped*): 5,683:1

LANGUAGE-CHANGE INDEX (For the full key, see front matter pp. xxxi, l–li.)
Stage 1: Rejected. **Stage 2:** Widely shunned. **Stage 3:** Widespread but . . . **Stage 4:** Ubiquitous but . . . **Stage 5:** Fully accepted.
Invariably inferior forms marked by asterisk (*). • Ratios represent frequency of prevalent forms vs. variants in current books.

sweetbrier; sweetbriar. The rosy-pink European rose is *sweetbrier* in AmE (predominantly since 1850) and *sweetbriar* in BrE (consistently since the late 18th century).

swell. A. Inflection: *swell > swelled > swelled.* So inflected in AmE. The form *swollen*—quite correct as an adjective <swollen ankles>—is a variant past participle in AmE. But in BrE *swollen* is the normal past participle <her ankles had swollen to twice their ordinary size>.

In 1936, two British usage critics (preferring *swollen*) said that "'*swelled* head' is the only phrase which has the weak form of the participle." H.A. Treble & G.H. Vallins, *An A.B.C. of English Usage* 173 (1936). E.g.: "After two Oscar wins, several nominations and many blockbuster hits, beloved actor Tom Hanks has developed a *swelled* head." Jennie Punter, "Apollo 13," *Globe & Mail* (Toronto), 21 Sept. 2002, at R19 (referring comically to computer enlargement). In fact, we've developed the SLANG noun *swellhead* to denote an egotist. *Swollen head* (a fine distinction in AmE) tends to refer to a diseased or injured one.

Despite Treble and Vallins's singular exception, modern writers tend to use the past-participial *swelled* whenever the sense is "grown in number"—e.g.:

- "The region's Arab-American population had *swelled* to an estimated 70,000 people." Robert L. Smith, "When Terror Hits Home," *Plain Dealer* (Cleveland), 11 Sept. 2002, at S5.
- "The number of patients in his Framingham practice had *swelled* to 4,000." Rhonda Stewart, "Doctors Take a Large Dose of Change," *Boston Globe*, 15 Sept. 2002, Globe West §, at 1.

This usage is about five times as common in print as the metaphorical use of *swollen* in similar contexts. And judge for yourself, but *swollen* feels unnatural here: "By the time the group reached Times Square, the number of marchers had *swollen* [read *swelled*] into the hundreds." Crocker Stephenson, "Observers Step in Line as Bands Head to Ground Zero," *Milwaukee J. Sentinel*, 12 Sept. 2002, at A15.

And in AmE, the more usual past participle is *swelled* in other senses as well—e.g.: "Tests showed his brain had *swelled* [or *swollen*], a condition that can be fatal." Ed White, "West Nile Sidelines Kids' Radio Bible Voice," *Grand Rapids Press*, 15 Sept. 2002, at A21. See IRREGULAR VERBS (B).

B. Dialectal Variants. The term **swoll* is a dialectal form sometimes encountered, usually in recorded speech—e.g.:

- "Tackle Steve Wallace explained: 'New Orleans *swoll* up on the goal line. And they stopped us. And we *swoll* up after. It was a theme all week. They would swell up and we had to swell up bigger.'" Don Pierson, "49ers Aren't Well but They're Looking Swell," *Chicago Trib.*, 3 Dec. 1991, at C8.
- "Up to the time I started to get all *swoll'* up like a pizened pup, it had been a fairly remarkable weekend." Herb Caen, "The Rambling Wreck," *S.F. Chron.*, 24 Nov. 1992, at B1.

*Swole is a variant spelling of this word, both in AmE DIALECT and in BrE—e.g.:

- "We heard an unprecedented number of Dan Ratherisms, including every single colorful Texas simile except, '*Swole* up like an old mule's prostate.'" Bob Garfield, "MCI Fails to Connect with Melodramatic Ad," *Advertising Age*, 16 Nov. 1992, at 46.
- "Her legs *swole up* [read *swelled*] like sausages on a barbecue, I did feel sorry forrah." Russell Davies, "The Liver Birds Are Now Single Liver Mums," *Daily Mail*, 1 Dec. 1995, at 9.

See IRREGULAR VERBS (D).

LANGUAGE-CHANGE INDEX
1. **swoll* as a past form of *swell*: Stage 1
Current ratio (*swelled up* vs. **swoll up*): 102:1
2. **swole* as a past form of *swell*: Stage 1
Current ratio (*swelled up* vs. **swole up*): 42:1

swim > swam > swum. So inflected since the late 19th century in AmE and BrE alike. Yet *swam* often appears erroneously as a past participle—e.g.:

- "The Red Devils have *swam* [read *swum*] at the current site since 1952." Mary Jo Monnin, "Noteworthy," *Buffalo News*, 4 Feb. 1997, at D4.
- "Because Lindberg *already had swam* [read *had already swum*], a Senior National qualifying time in the 100 back, she could not enter the 100 backstroke final." Andy Mendlowitz, "After a Back Injury, Stroke of Good Luck Returns to Lindberg," *Wash. Post*, 1 Apr. 1998, at V10.
- "Within three hours of arriving at his new home, Keiko was reported to be vocalizing with a dolphin that had *swam* [read *swum*] between the pen and the shore." "'Free Willy' Star Returns to Atlantic," *Chicago Trib.*, 11 Sept. 1998, at 4.

And *swum* is sometimes misused for *swam*—e.g.: "They *swum* [read *swam*] on." Carol Benefell, "Dramatic Rescue Near Goat Rock," *Press Democrat* (Santa Rosa), 8 Apr. 1996, at B1. See IRREGULAR VERBS.

LANGUAGE-CHANGE INDEX
1. *swam* for past-participial *swum*: Stage 2
Current ratio (*have/had swum* vs. **have/had swam*): 6:1
2. *swum* for simple-past *swam*: Stage 2
Current ratio (*they swam down* vs. **they swum down*): 5:1

swine. When used in the literal sense of a pig, *swine* does not change its form in the plural <we raise swine at the farm>. In the derogatory sense of a crude boor, the plural may be either *swine* or *swines* <they're such swine> <they're both swines>.

swing > swung > swung. So inflected. The dialectal **swang* has occurred sporadically in print since the 18th century. It persists—e.g.:

- "One of [the boys] *swang* [read *swung*] erratically, topping his ball, which rattled a few yards along the grass and disappeared into a drainage ditch." Don Gillmor, "Scot on the Rocks," *Sun-Sentinel* (Ft. Lauderdale), 27 Feb. 1994, at J1.
- "As the youngster performed the [baseball] drill, he *swang* [read *swung*] away." Rich Kaipust, "Mavs Lose Pair to Injuries," *Omaha World-Herald*, 7 Apr. 1998, Sports §, at 30.
- "Donald bowled at excitingly high pace and while his partner Shaun Pollock was not as rapid he *swang* [read *swung*] the ball excessively." Stephen Brenkley, "Cricket: Hapless Return of Old England," *Independent*, 21 June 1998, Sport §, at 18.

See DIALECT.

The weak form *swinged is also an infrequent error—e.g.: "The game swinged [read swung] on an outstanding rebounding charge led by Pete Corzine and Cody Fallace." Suzanne Mapes, "Lakers Use Defense to Propel Offense in Win," *Orange County Register*, 19 Dec. 1996, at 16. Actually, swinged /swinjd/ is the correct past-tense form of swinge (= to beat or chastise). See IRREGULAR VERBS.

LANGUAGE-CHANGE INDEX
1. *swang for swung: Stage 1
Current ratio (swung vs. *swang): 790:1
2. *swinged for swung: Stage 1
Current ratio (swung vs. *swinged): 2,212:1

swivel, vb., makes *swiveled* and *swiveling* in AmE, *swivelled* and *swivelling* in BrE. See SPELLING (B).

*swob. See **swab.**

*swoll; *swole. See **swell (B).**

swollen. See **swell (A).**

swoon, vb., means either (1) "to faint" or (2) "to be overjoyed or enraptured"—e.g.:

- "Like a latter-day St. Theresa *swooning* in ecstasy, her visage is simultaneously lost in a spiritual trance and abandoned in carnal reverie." Christopher Knight, "Branching Out: Victor Estrada's Work at Santa Monica Museum Is Both Inventive, Grim," *L.A. Times*, 28 Oct. 1995, at F1.
- "I am of an age to have *swooned* over Elvis when he caused such havoc among teenagers." Lois Reagan Thomas, "Writing on 'The King,'" *Knoxville News-Sentinel*, 12 Oct. 1997, at F6.

But *swoon* does not mean "to slump or fade," as some writers think, and the word should not ordinarily be used to describe the actions of inanimate things—e.g.:

- "Whether the legal profession is suffering from a lack of respect or just a lack of good jobs, applications to law schools have *swooned* [read *slumped* or *declined*] in the nation in recent years, down to 78,000 this year, from a peak of 94,000 in 1991." "Law School Is Losing Its Luster," *S.F. Chron.*, 22 Sept. 1995, at A18.
- "Nevertheless, Baltimore-area townhouse sales *swooned* [read *declined*]." "New-Home Sales in Howard Counter Decline for Area," *Baltimore Sun*, 12 Oct. 1997, at L1.

LANGUAGE-CHANGE INDEX
swoon misused for *decline*: Stage 1

*swop. See **swap.**

*sworn affidavit has been a fairly common REDUNDANCY since the late 19th century. See **affidavit.**

*swot. See **swat.**

swum. See **swim.**

*sybilline. See **sibylline.**

syllabification; *syllabication. Although these are synonyms (= the act or process of forming syllables, or

of dividing words into syllables), prefer *syllabification*, since it corresponds to the more common verb *syllabify* (as opposed to *syllabicate*). Although the two nouns were once almost equally common, since 1985 or so *syllabification* has predominated—e.g.:

- "Teachers spend at least four weeks of valuable instructional time teaching children to bubble-in the scantron sheet and to memorize such trivia as *syllabication* [read *syllabification*] rules." Letter of Deidra W. Frazier, "Let Them Write to Pass Exam," *Advocate* (Baton Rouge), 8 Aug. 1996, at B8.
- "Swensen, whose razor sharp *syllabication* [read *syllabification*] made for some superb diction, delivered her lines expressively." David Abrams, "Mechetti Wins Gamble with Mahler 3rd," *Post-Standard* (Syracuse), 17 May 1997, at C1.
- "Obama is the first five-letter, three-syllable president in history. The last names of John Adams, John Quincy Adams, John Tyler, Ulysses Grant, Rutherford Hayes and Richard Nixon matched his in letter count but not *syllabication* [read *syllabification*]." Joe Blundo, "'O-ba-ma' Inspires Syllabic Brainteasers," *Columbus Dispatch*, 23 Dec. 2008, at D1.

Current ratio: 4:1

syllabub (= a sweet dessert or drink made from cream, sugar, and either wine or fruit juice) has been predominantly so spelled since the mid-18th century—not *sillabub*.

Current ratio: 13:1

syllabus. Pl. *syllabuses* or *syllabi*. American teachers are fond, perhaps overfond, of the Latin plural. Ernest Gowers wrote that "the plural *-buses* is now more used than *-bi*" (FMEU2 at 610). He was right about BrE, where *syllabuses* edges out *-bi* by a 1.4-to-1 ratio. But in AmE the ratio is 6-to-1 the other way. And in legal writing, the ratio is 10-to-1 *syllabi* over *-buses*. See PLURALS (B).

LANGUAGE-CHANGE INDEX
syllabuses as plural of *syllabus*: Stage 5
Current ratio (syllabi vs. syllabuses
in World English): 2:1

SYLLEPSIS. See ZEUGMA.

sylvan (= of, relating to, or living in the woods) has always been the predominant spelling, from the 17th century on. Fowler's 1926 objection to it on etymological grounds looks quirky today, given that the Latin word for *wood* could be spelled either *silva* or *sylva*. *Silvan* is a variant spelling that has never had much currency in English print sources.

Current ratio: 24:1

symbolic; *symbolical. The first has been standard—and vastly predominant—since the late 19th century. The second is a NEEDLESS VARIANT.

symbology (the study of symbols) has been so written since the mid-19th century—not *symbolology*.

Current ratio: 751:1

sympathy. See **empathy** & **simpatico.**

*sympatico. See **simpatico.**

symposium. Pl. *symposia* (standard from the 18th century)—not *symposiums.* The latter is defensible—though it appears less often in English-language print sources by a 5-to-1 ratio. See PLURALS (B).

synagogue, n., is the standard spelling in AmE and BrE alike. *Synagog* is a variant. See -AGOG(UE).

Current ratio: 852:1

sync; *synch. This word, a truncated form of *synchronization* (or, as a verb, *synchronize*), is spelled *sync* in print nearly six times as often as it's spelled *synch.* It occurs most frequently in the phrases *in sync* (= correctly timed, compatible, in agreement), *out of sync* (meaning the opposite), and *lip-sync.* The inflected forms are *synced* /sinkt/ and *syncing* /**sink**-ing/, both of which unfortunately suggest a sibilant -*c*-. But the alternatives, *synched* and *synching*, are hardly better, since they might suggest a -*ch*- sound instead of the proper -*k*- sound. Most dictionaries are in (ahem) tune with the prevalent usage.

Interestingly, lexicographers have traced the verb (1929) back further than the noun (1937). It might be that the verb preceded the noun in actual usage, but this would be mildly surprising. More likely, earlier occurrences of the noun will be found to predate 1929. See **lip-sync.**

synchronous; synchronic; *synchronal. *Synchronous* = occurring at the same time or operating at the same speed. *Synchronic* = (of an analysis, study, etc.) dealing with events at one time without considering historical antecedents. (Cf. **diachronic.**) *Synchronal* is a NEEDLESS VARIANT of *synchronous.*

SYNESIS. In some contexts, meaning—as opposed to the strict requirements of grammar or syntax—governs SUBJECT–VERB AGREEMENT. Henry Sweet, the 19th-century English grammarian, used the term "antigrammatical constructions" for these triumphs of logic over grammar. (Expressions in which grammar triumphs over logic are termed "antilogical.") Modern grammarians call the principle underlying these antigrammatical constructions "synesis" (/**sin**-ə-sis/).

The classic example of an antigrammatical construction is the phrase *a number of* (= several, many). It is routinely followed by a plural verb, even though technically the singular noun *number* is the subject <a number of people were there>. (See **number of.**) Another example occurs when a unit of measure has a collective sense. It can be plural in form but singular in sense—e.g.: "*Three-fourths is* a smaller quantity than we had expected."/ "*Two pounds* of shrimp *is* all I need."

If these constructions are grammatically safe, similar constructions involving COLLECTIVE NOUNS are somewhat more precarious. The rule consistently announced in 20th-century grammars is as follows: "Collective nouns take sometimes a singular and sometimes a plural verb. When the persons or things denoted are thought of as individuals, the plural should be used. When the collection is regarded as a unit, the singular should be used." George L. Kittredge & Frank E. Farley, *An Advanced English Grammar* 101 (1913). Generally, then, with nouns of multitude, one can justifiably use a plural verb.

Among the common nouns of multitude are *bulk, bunch, flood, handful, host, majority, mass, minority, multitude, percentage, proportion,* and *variety.* Each of these is frequently followed by *of* [+ plural noun] [+ plural verb]—e.g.:

- "A great *variety* of clays *were* available to Mississippian potters in the Southeast." Vincas P. Steponaitis et al., "Large-Scale Patterns in the Chemical Composition of Mississippian Pottery," *Am. Antiquity,* 1 July 1996, at 555.
- "Republicans in California see Boxer as a vulnerable target, and a *host* of them *are* actively considering the race." Cathleen Decker, "New Welfare Law Should Be Amended, Boxer Says," *L.A. Times,* 16 Jan. 1997, at A3.
- "Of these 3,000, however, just a small *proportion are* enrolled in courses such as Foundations of Health or Human Sexuality." Richard A. Kaye & Theodore Markus, "AIDS Teaching Should Not Be Limited to the Young," *USA Today* (Mag.), 1 Sept. 1997, at 50.
- "A *handful* of them *are* world-class operations." Linda DuVal, "World-Class Spas Let Visitors Indulge Themselves and Relax," *Gaz. Telegraph* (Colo. Springs), 26 Oct. 1997, at T&B4.
- "The *majority* of them *were* brought over by the autocratic tyrant, led astray, divided, slandered and finally violently suppressed." "'The Democratic Banner Cannot Be Obscured,'" *Wall Street J.,* 18 Nov. 1997, at A22.
- "Only a small *percentage are* chosen as All-America Selections." Ted Fisher, "Four Award-Winning Plants Offer Beauty, Reliability," *Austin Am.-Statesman,* 6 Dec. 1997, at C7.

These nouns of multitude are preferably treated as plural when they're followed by *of* and a plural noun. Perhaps the best-known example is *a lot,* which no one today thinks of as having a singular force <a lot of people were there>. See **a lot.**

Occasionally an ambiguity arises—e.g.: "There is now *a variety of* antidepressant drugs that can help lift these people out of their black moods." If the sense of *a variety of* is "several," then *are* is the appropriate verb; if the sense of the phrase is "a type of," then *is* is the appropriate verb. Either way, though, a writer would be wise to reword a sentence like that one.

But the nouns *amount, class,* and *group* all typically call for singular verbs—e.g.:

- "This *class* of organizations *was* far more prevalent in the developing countries." Lester M. Salamon & Helmut K. Anheier, "The Civil Society Sector," *Society,* 11 Jan. 1997, at 60.
- "A small *group* of conservative congressmen *are* [read *is*] thinking about drafting a bill requiring U.S. companies to translate the names of their businesses locating here into Spanish." Paul de la Garza, "Hooters in Mexico May Prove Challenge," *San Antonio Express-News,* 25 Nov. 1997, at C1.
- "The total dollar *amount* of savings *was* not immediately available." Karen Herzog, "UW System Cuts 36 Positions," *Milwaukee J. Sentinel,* 13 Sept. 2015, at A4.

There may be little or no logical consistency in the two sets of examples just given—justifiable plurals and table 887

less justifiable ones—but the problem lies just outside the realm of logic, in the genius of the language. It is no use trying to explain why we say, on the one hand, *that pair of shoes is getting old*, but on the other hand, *the pair were perfectly happy after their honeymoon.*

For more on grammatical agreement generally, see CONCORD & COLLECTIVE NOUNS.

synonym for *pseudonym* (= a pen name) is a bizarre error—e.g.: "All of the contributors used *synonyms* [read *pseudonyms*]: Etienne George signed himself as Edmund Delorme, a name he would use again in a subsequent publication; Georg Böttcher wrote verses in French under the name G. Tonnelier; Arthur Stahl, in honor of a promenade in his hometown of Friedberg known as the 'Rumania,' assumed the pen name Rumanophile." Robert E. Norton, *Secret Germany* 29–30 (2002). See **pseudonym.**

LANGUAGE-CHANGE INDEX
synonym misused for *pseudonym*: Stage 1

synonymous (= equivalent in meaning) is sometimes confused with *antonymous* (= opposite in meaning)—e.g.: "The phrase 'subsequent to' is a preposition, with the same meaning as 'after' or 'since.' It is *synonymous* [read *antonymous*] with 'prior to,' which is also a preposition." Gertrude Block, "The Punctuated Lawyer," *Fed. Lawyer*, Jan. 1996, at 21. *Subsequent to* is obviously antonymous—not synonymous—with *prior to*. In tone, it is analogous to *prior to*. There would have been no confusion if the author had written, "It is the opposite of *prior to.*"

Synonymous is often misspelled *synonomous*—e.g.: "Woodrow Wilson 'Woody' Hite, the man whose name was *synonomous* [read *synonymous*] with big band music in Portland for decades, died Tuesday, Nov. 4, 1997, in Camarillo, Calif." John Foyston, "Big Band Leader Woody Hite Dies at 82," *Oregonian* (Portland), 7 Nov. 1997, at D12.

synonymy; *synonymity. Since the 18th century, *synonymy* has been the preferred form in AmE and BrE alike.

Current ratio: 6:1

synopsis (= a short summary of the main events or ideas in a book, film, play, etc.) makes the plural *synopses* /si-**nop**-seez/.

syntactic (= of, relating to, or involving the way words are arranged into sentences) is the standard adjective—**syntactical* being a variant form. See -IC.

Current ratio: 9:1

synthesis (= [1] something made by combining different things, or [2] the process of combining things) makes the plural *syntheses* /**sin**-thə-seez/.

synthesize; *synthetize. Although H.W. Fowler called the latter spelling "the right formation" (*FMEU1* at 593), *synthesize* has now fully taken hold, and **synthetize* should be considered a NEEDLESS VARIANT. It has never been more than a linguistic cipher in either AmE or BrE.

Current ratio: 461:1

*syphon. See **siphon.**

systematic; systemic. *Systematic* = (1) carried out according to an organized plan; or (2) habitual, deliberate. *Systemic* = affecting an entire system; systemwide. Typically, *systemic* should be replaced by *systematic* unless the reference is to systems of the body <autoimmune and other systemic disorders> or METAPHORS based on bodily systems <our political order has been debilitated by a series of systemic problems>.

systematize; *systemize. The former is standard in AmE and BrE alike. The latter is a NEEDLESS VARIANT.

Current ratio: 15:1

systemic. See **systematic.**

systole (= a rhythmically occurring contraction, esp. by the heart when blood is forced through the circulatory system) is pronounced /**sis**-tə-lee/.

syzygy (= a straight-line configuration of three celestial bodies within the same celestial system, as happens, for example, during a solar or lunar eclipse) is pronounced /**siz**-ə-jee/.

T

table, v.t., has nearly opposite senses in AmE and BrE. By *tabling* an item, Americans mean postponing discussion for a later time, while Britons mean putting forward for immediate discussion. Hence Americans might misunderstand the following sentences:

- "MPs from both sides of the Commons will tomorrow *table* parliamentary questions demanding to know what

official action has been taken to uncover the facts." John Furbisher & Richard Caseby, "'God's Policeman' Keeps Head Down as Bricks Fly," *Sunday Times* (London), 10 June 1990, § 1, at 4.
- "Ian Gibson, the Labour MP for Norwich North, warned that colleagues would *table* Commons motions condemning the pay increase at a time when Gordon Brown, the Chancellor, was demanding pay restraint from the public

LANGUAGE-CHANGE INDEX (For the full key, see front matter pp. xxxi, l–li.)
Stage 1: Rejected. **Stage 2:** Widely shunned. **Stage 3:** Widespread but . . . **Stage 4:** Ubiquitous but . . . **Stage 5:** Fully accepted.
Invariably inferior forms marked by asterisk (*). • Ratios represent frequency of prevalent forms vs. variants in current books.

sector workers." Colin Brown, "Lord Irvine Gives Up His Extra £22,000 a Year," *Sunday Telegraph*, 9 Feb. 2003, at 1.

tableau. Pl. *tableaux* or (less frequently) *tableaus.* See PLURALS (B).

Current ratio: 13:1

taboo; *tabu. Although the two forms were close rivals throughout the 18th and 19th centuries, beginning in the 1890s *taboo* established itself as the standard spelling.

For the verb *taboo* (= to forbid or prohibit because of tradition or custom), the past tense is *tabooed* rather than **taboo'd.* E.g.: "In golf's rubric, the serious mention of those two words [Grand Slam] had long held the same *tabooed* rank as a discourse on the shanks." Barker Davis, "Old Blue Gives a Wake-Up Call," *Wash. Times*, 17 June 1997, at B1.

Current ratio (*taboo* vs. *tabu): 7:1

tack; tact. In sailing, a *tack* is a change in course made by turning the vessel or the sail so that the wind strikes the other side of the sail. To change *tack*, then, is to change course. Sometimes writers using this idiom pick the more familiar *tact* (= discretion, diplomacy), possibly because the idiom suggests an unrelated but similar word (changing *tactics*)—e.g.:

- "Rumsfeld, Ashcroft Take Different *Tact* [read *Tack*] on Enemy." Headline, *Richmond Times-Dispatch*, 9 Dec. 2001, at B2.
- "Or if the administration wants to take a radically different *tact* [read *tack*] on financial matters, it could hire Jill Q. Baer, the creative services director of the Maryland State Lottery Agency." Rob Blackwell et al., "Washington People," *Am. Banker*, 29 Apr. 2002, at 4.
- "He tries to explain, telling her it's the U.S. Open venue. She mistakenly thinks he's playing in the Open. After a deep breath, he tries a different *tact* [read *tack*]." Rich Cimini, "Getting Tee Time on Bethpage's Black Doesn't Happen Overnight," *Daily News* (N.Y.), 19 May 2002, at 98.

LANGUAGE-CHANGE INDEX
tact misused for *tack*: Stage 1
Current ratio (*different tack* vs. *different tact): 21:1

tactile; *tactual. *Tactile* is the standard word meaning either "of, relating to, or involving touch" or "touchable, tangible." *Tactual is a NEEDLESS VARIANT.

Current ratio: 17:1

takable. So spelled in AmE and BrE alike. *Takeable is a chiefly BrE variant. See MUTE E.

Current ratio: 1.5:1

take. A. Inflection: *take* > *took* > *taken.* So inflected. The form *tooken is low DIALECT that occasionally shows up in quoted speech—e.g.:

- "And how he absolutely hated 'to get *tooken* [read *taken*] out of a ball game.'" Garret Mathews, "Ol' Diz Would Have Struck Out in Broadcasting Today," *Evansville Courier & Press*, 22 Jan. 1999, at B1 (quoting Dizzy Dean).
- "Testimony showed Sokolowski told another man he 'had *tooken* [read *taken*] care of' Ellwood." "Sentence Upheld in Grisly Murder," *News & Record* (Greensboro), 4 Dec. 1999, at B6C.

- "'We just had a tornado up there in Clinton. I got my house *tooken* [read *taken*] away,' said 22-year-old Johnnie Arnold." Jon Gambrell, "Risky Business," *St. Louis Post-Dispatch*, 20 Apr. 2008, at D4.

Though unusual, the form *tooken isn't new: it first appeared in print in the 18th century and has persisted as nonstandard.

LANGUAGE-CHANGE INDEX
*tooken: Stage 1
Current ratio (*taken* vs. *tooken): 23,970:1

B. And *bring.* See **bring** (B).

*takeable. See **takable.**

take a decision. See AMERICANISMS AND BRITICISMS (C).

take for granted is sometimes written *take for granite, occasionally as a play on words—e.g.: "Just because she etches art in stone doesn't mean Leda Miller's work is *taken for granite*." David Templeton, "Art on a Headstone," *Pitt. Post-Gaz.*, 7 May 1995, at W1. But sometimes it's just a MALAPROPISM—e.g.: "There's a huge demographic out there who appreciates good film and shouldn't be taken for *granite* [read *granted*]." Stephen Lynch, "Reality Fails to Bite When It Comes to Generation X," *Orange County Register*, 23 Aug. 1994, at F2. In the literature on usage, this mistake was first recorded in the 1952 edition of a well-known college text: Norman Foerster & J.M. Steadman Jr., *Writing and Thinking* 340 (James B. McMillan ed., 5th ed. 1952).

LANGUAGE-CHANGE INDEX
*take for granite for *take for granted*: Stage 1
Current ratio (*take for granted* vs.
*take for granite): 2,829:1

taken aback. This phrase (meaning "shocked or stunned, usu. by something someone has done") is sometimes wrongly written—or wrongly said—**taken back.* E.g.:

- "Never one to be *taken back* [read *taken aback*] by a new situation, even at the age of eight, Paula had learned a technique for disarming people." Walter B. Barbe, "My Friend Paula" (1958), in *Readings in the Language Arts* 468, 469 (Verna Dieckman Anderson et al. eds., 1964).
- "I was quite *taken back* [read *taken aback*] by her [Molly Ivins's] referring to the reappointment of Alan Greenspan as chairman of the Federal Reserve Board as 'disgusting.'" Letter of Richard H. Hinz, "Column, Not Greenspan, 'Malodorous,'" *Palm Beach Post*, 6 Apr. 1996, at A9.
- "'Nothing to do with me?' She was completely *taken back* [read *taken aback*]. 'I can't just stand by and see Sarah being cheated on.'" Isobel Stewart, "What Jenny Saw," *Good Housekeeping*, Aug. 1996, at 137.

LANGUAGE-CHANGE INDEX
*taken back misused for *taken aback*: Stage 2
Current ratio (*somewhat taken aback* vs.
**somewhat taken back*): 19:1

takeover, n. One word.

taking account of; taking into account. For the use of these phrases as acceptable dangling modifiers, see DANGLERS (E).

talc, vb. (= to apply talcum powder to), anomalously makes *talced* and *talcing,* not **talcked* and **talcking.* See -c-.

talisman. Pl. *talismans.* Sometimes the erroneous **talismen* appears for the singular or plural, especially the latter—e.g.:

- "The boy soldiers wear old shredded Zairian army uniforms or jeans and T-shirts, often with *talismen* [read *talismans*] or plastic rosary beads around their necks." Chris Tomlinson, "Child Warriors Believe Magic Makes Them Unbeatable," *Plain Dealer* (Cleveland), 14 Dec. 1996, at A10.
- "The round, clay pieces follow the African tradition of *talismen* [read *talismans*], worn around the neck and blessed for good luck." Richard Taliaferro Jr., "Cultures Tied for Down-Home Fun," *Richmond Times-Dispatch,* 17 Aug. 1997, at B1.

Language-Change Index
*talismen as a false plural for *talismans*: Stage 1
Current ratio (*talismans* vs. **talismen*): 98:1

talk to; talk with. The first suggests a superior's advising or reprimanding or even condescending <I want to talk to you about the work you're doing> <a movie star wants to talk to me?>. The second suggests a conversation between equals, with equal participation <I want to talk with you about our project> <I can always talk with my husband after class>. The distinction is chiefly relevant when the parties have different levels of power, authority, or prestige.

Tallahasseean. So spelled. See DENIZEN LABELS. Cf. **Tennessean.**

tamable; tameable. The first is AmE, the second BrE. See MUTE E.

tangential (= peripheral, incidental) is the standard form in AmE and BrE alike. **Tangental* is a NEEDLESS VARIANT. Occasionally the word is misspelled **tangenital,* which is something of a MALAPROPISM resulting from METATHESIS—e.g.: "In an effort to ensure at least a *tangenital* [read *tangential*] spot in boxing, Hearns in January will don a new suit of clothes." W.H. Stickney Jr., "'Hit Man' Gets into Promoting," *Houston Chron.,* 1 Oct. 1995, at 30.

tantalize = to torment by sight or promise of a desired thing kept just out of reach. The verb *tantalize* is derived from the Greek myth about Tantalus, the son of Zeus and the nymph Pluto. After becoming the king of Lydia, he offended the gods by divulging their secrets to mortals. Because the father of Tantalus was divine, Tantalus (though not a god) was himself immortal and so could not be executed for his crime. Instead, as an eternal punishment, he was plunged into a lake of Hades, up to his chin, while overhead boughs of edible fruit hung temptingly near. Whenever he dipped to drink, the water receded; whenever he stretched to eat, a wind blew the laden boughs out of reach.

Through SLIPSHOD EXTENSION, *tantalize* is now gradually being stretched to mean "to stimulate desire or the senses"—e.g.:

- "They're currently scrambling to raise big money for TV ads, because they rightfully fear that Romney will have the money to saturate the airwaves with upbeat imagery and *tantalizing* sound bites." Dick Polman, "GOP Outsider Charms Mass.," *Phil. Inquirer,* 30 May 2002, at A4.
- "After I tracked down the *tantalizing* fragrance, I was quite surprised to find out it was coming from a petunia!" "These Plants Will Provide Pleasing Aromas All over Your Yard," *Macon Telegraph,* 3 Oct. 2002, at 3.
- "Smoke frequently drifted over the glass divider between the bar and the dining area, interfering with the *tantalizing* odors emanating from the plates of those seated nearby." Dale Rice, "A Mediterranean Getaway in Downtown Austin," *Austin Am.-Statesman,* 28 Nov. 2002, at 8.

For the time being, careful writers will probably resist this extension—but it may inevitably become a legitimate sense.

Although it's sometimes hard to be sure from the context, *tantalize* often seems to be misused for *titillate* (= to excite sensually)—e.g.:

- "Kama Sutra tells the truth about eros: that no matter how *tantalizing* [read *titillating*?] sex can be, without love, it is unruly, destructive and lonesome-making." Rod Dreher, "Lush 'Kama Sutra' Sensual, Not Sexy," *Sun-Sentinel* (Ft. Lauderdale), 7 Mar. 1997, Showtime §, at 6.
- "More sweet than sexy, more tender than *tantalizing* [read *titillating*?], the film is one that even a prime time audience could love." Lauren Kern, "Warm! Fuzzy! Gay!" *Houston Press,* 22 May 1997.

Language-Change Index
tantalize misused for *titillate*: Stage 1

tantamount (= equivalent) is sometimes misused for *paramount* (= supreme, preeminent)—e.g.:

- "With quality a *tantamount* [read *paramount*] concern, the Cecils always are looking for the right factories to produce items made exactly to their specifications." Sheila Gadsden, "Tin Isn't Coppersource's Cup of Tea," *S.F. Bus. Times,* 24 July 1989, § 1, at 1.
- "Clearly written contracts, carefully outlining duties and functions, are of *tantamount* [read *paramount*] importance." Martha Stewart, "Good Planning Enhances the Chance of Success of Any Party," *Patriot & Evening News* (Harrisburg), 21 Mar. 1996, at C3.
- "But his requirement that Phil Jackson stay on for another season is of *tantamount* [read *paramount*] importance." "Celtics' $22 Million Offer Lures Knight from Lakers," *Rocky Mountain News* (Denver), 6 July 1997, at C5.

See **paramount.** Cf. **penultimate.**

Language-Change Index
tantamount misused for *paramount*: Stage 1
Current ratio (*paramount importance* vs.
*tantamount importance): 338:1

tape-record, v.t. This verb is always hyphenated.

taqueria (= an informal Mexican restaurant specializing in tacos) is pronounced /tahk-ə-**ree**-ə/—not

LANGUAGE-CHANGE INDEX (For the full key, see front matter pp. xxxi, l–li.)
Stage 1: Rejected. **Stage 2:** Widely shunned. **Stage 3:** Widespread but . . . **Stage 4:** Ubiquitous but . . . **Stage 5:** Fully accepted.
Invariably inferior forms marked by asterisk (*). • Ratios represent frequency of prevalent forms vs. variants in current books.

/tə-**kwer**-ee-ə/ (on the mistaken analogy of *cafeteria*). Although it did not occur in English until the late 1970s, today it is common especially in AmE.

tarlatan /**tahr**-lə-tən/ (= a fine, stiff cotton fabric) is the standard spelling in AmE and BrE alike. **Tarletan* is a variant.

Current ratio: 4:1

tarsus (= [1] the ankle, together with the small bones that make it up, or [2] a small plate within the eyelid) forms the plural *tarsi* /**tahr**-sɪ/—not **tarsuses*.

tartar; tartare. *Tartar* has several meanings: (1) "a solid acid present in grape juice and deposited as a reddish sediment in wine casks"; (2) "this same substance partly purified to make a cream used in cooking"; (3) "a hard, yellowish crusty substance that forms on teeth as a result of how saliva interacts with food particles; calculus."

In AmE, *tartar* is the standard form in *tartar sauce* (derived from sense 2 above); in BrE, however, the normal spelling is *tartare sauce* (occasionally rendered as the GALLICISM *sauce tartare*, with a POSTPOSITIVE ADJECTIVE).

The one instance in which *tartare* is standard in AmE is in the phrase *steak tartare*, a dish (and name) borrowed from the French in the 1920s.

As a postpositive adjective, *tartare* is pronounced /tahr-**tahr**/. The *SOED* suggests that all pronunciations of that spelling in BrE follow that form, but Briticized as /tah-**tah**/. The pronunciation of *tartar* in AmE is /**tahr**-tər/, in BrE /**tah**-tə/.

Tartar; Tatar. These are historically the same word, the first borrowed into Middle English from Medieval Latin, the second reintroduced into English from Persian or Turkish in the mid-19th century. The term refers to (1) a member of the Mongolian and Turkic peoples who, led by Genghis Khan (1202–1227), invaded central and western Asia, as well as eastern Europe, in the Middle Ages; (2) a descendant of those people, esp. someone whose family comes from European Russia, Crimea, or parts of Asia; or (3) any of the Turkic languages of these people. Although *Tartar* /**tahr**-tər/ has predominated in print sources since Middle English, *Tatar* /**taht**-ər/ has become almost equally frequent since the mid-20th century, and it is considered the preferable term for ethnological references.

One reason for the decline of *Tartar* in technical references is that the word took on a derogatory sense beginning in the 17th century (often capitalized also in this sense): "a savage; a violent, tempestuous, uncontrollable person." Another reason is the etymological spuriousness of *Tartar*: in the 1300s, the Persian word *Tatar* was corrupted through false association with the Latin word *Tartarus*, meaning "hell." Hence the scholarly trend in recent decades has been to prefer *Tatar*.

Taser is the trademarked name of an electrical stun gun and the company that invented it. For that reason,

it is properly capitalized, and usually appears so even when used as a verb or an adjective—e.g.: "Find out what happened before the patient was Tasered .... All Tasered patients are considered to have experienced a fall until proven [read *proved*] otherwise." Fire Chiefs Association of Broward County, *Florida Regional Common EMS Protocols* 162 (2010). But the margin isn't wide—it's lowercase nearly as often, especially when used as a verb.

The company capitalizes its entire name (TASER) as an acronym of "Thomas A. Swift Electric Rifle," based on a Tom Swift book that was a childhood favorite of its inventor, Jack Cover.

task, v.t. Although modern word aficionados tend to think of the verb *to task* as a newfangled innovation, this usage dates from the 1500s. It means "to put to work on" or "to compel (someone) to undertake an assignment." The verb was widely popular in the mid-19th century and then experienced a precipitate lull from about 1910 to the mid-1970s. So when the word inexplicably regained widespread currency in the 1980s and beyond—when English speakers were accustomed to the word only as a noun—many decried it as an annoying example of FUNCTIONAL SHIFT. Nothing I say here is likely to dissipate the visceral annoyance that purists may feel. But it's worth the reminder to examine the history of words before excoriating them. On the other hand, *task* is legitimately subject to some gentle scorn on grounds of being a VOGUE WORD.

tassel (= a hanging ornament made of threads or strips) is sometimes misspelled **tassle*—e.g.: "Shauvin spends at least an hour on weekends polishing and fixing her motorcycle with the shiny, gold skulls and long leather *tassles* [read *tassels*]." Virginia de Leon, "Va-Va-Va-Vroooom," *Spokesman Rev.* (Spokane), 10 Aug. 1997, at E1.

As a verb, *tassel* makes *tasseled* and *tasseling* in AmE, *tasselled* and *tasselling* in BrE. See SPELLING (B).

tasty; tasteful. Although *tasteless* serves as the antonym of both—and although *tasteful* once meant "appetizing"—the DIFFERENTIATION between the words has been complete since the late 19th century. *Tasty* (= pleasing to the palate; delicious; appetizing) is literal. *Tasteful* (= having and displaying refinement in manners, the arts, and other matters of aesthetic judgment) is figurative.

Tatar. See **Tartar.**

tattoo, vb. Inflected *tattooed* and *tattooing*.

taught. See **taut (A).**

taunt, n. & v.t. See **taut (B).**

taut. A. And *taught*. *Taut* (= [1] tightly stretched; [2] tense; or [3] well-disciplined) is surprisingly often written *taught* (the past tense of *teach*)—e.g.:

- "*Taught* [read *Taut*] ropes sprawling this way and that anchored them to the ground." Charlene Baumbich,

"Memorable Days and Nights at Camp," *Chicago Trib.*, 22 July 1990, at 1.

- "Muscles *taught* [read *taut*], bodies bent, the dancers' breath became an integral part of the piece, their gasps, groans, shrieks and explosive exhalations providing a rhythmic counterpoint to the movement. The piece is laced with tension, and the dance is built around *taught* [read *taut*] muscles, twitching fingers and bent bodies." Kip Richardson, "Rousseve's Work a Touching Tribute," *Oregonian* (Portland), 24 Jan. 1993, Lively Arts §, at 3.
- "Also in deference to American tastes, [BMW] added touches of wood and began installing seats with wrinkled, rather than *taught* [read *taut*], leather." James Bennet, "Luxury Car Fight Turns Uncivilized," *N.Y. Times*, 30 Aug. 1994, at D1.

In that last example, *wrinkled leather*, as opposed to **taught leather*, must come from old cows as opposed to educated ones.

B. And *taunt*, n. & vb. *Taunt* is both a verb ("to provoke with sarcasm or insults") and a noun ("a sarcastic, provocative gibe"). Unfortunately, writers are increasingly confusing that word with the adjective *taut* (= tightly stretched [literally or figuratively])—e.g.:

- "He and Tucker, who goes by the name Chongo, tinkered with the rope, tuning it *taunt* [read *taut*] like a violin string." Nora Zamichow, "A Spiritual Quest on a Rope," *L.A. Times*, 28 Nov. 1998, at A1.
- "The shoulders are still broad and round with muscles, the biceps *taunt* [read *taut*]." Elton Alexander, "Phills Takes Charge as Hornets' Leader," *Plain Dealer* (Cleveland), 18 Apr. 1999, at C17.
- "Kai's eyes gleamed as he waited by his partner's feet, muscles *taunt* [read *taut*] under his golden fur as he anticipated the coming command." LaDonna Nicholson, "Four-Legged Enforcement," *Orange County Register*, 30 Mar. 2000, at 1.

LANGUAGE-CHANGE INDEX
taunt misused for *taut*: Stage 1
Current ratio (*stretched taut* vs.
*stretched taunt): 73:1

tautological, dating from the early 17th century, has been the standard form since the 18th century. It's six times as common as **tautologous*, a NEEDLESS VARIANT.
Current ratio: 6:1

tautology; redundancy. *Tautology*, a term found mostly in discussions of logic and rhetoric, refers to a restatement of something already said within the immediate context—in words that are different but do not add anything new. E.g.: "Some people in Europe seem to think international bureaucracies and global treaties automatically generate good policy. Indeed, they define good policy as anything that is produced by this process—a rather convenient *tautology*." Daniel J. Mitchell, "European Cult of Multinationalism," *Wash. Times*, 7 Nov. 2002, at A25. *Redundancy*, which is a more general term, refers to a word or phrase that adds nothing to the overall meaning because its sense has already been expressed <advance planning>. See REDUNDANCY.

taxi, n. Pl. *taxis*, not **taxies*. Likewise, *taxis* is the present-tense third-person singular of *taxi*, vb.

taxiing. So spelled in AmE and BrE alike—not **taxying*.
Current ratio: 19:1

taxpayer. One word.

taxwise = (1) adv., viewed with taxes in mind <today, real estate is a better investment taxwise than it was a few years ago>; or (2) adj., (of an investment) undertaken in a way that minimizes taxes <the fund encourages taxwise investing>; (of an investor) prudent in taking measures to avoid taxes <when you set up a retirement account, be taxwise>. For more on sense 1, see -WISE.

teach > taught > taught. So inflected. **Teached* is a form that isn't taught anywhere and is no part of STANDARD ENGLISH. But it sometimes appears in print—e.g.:

- "Bert John Berghorst worked with the Hope Summer Repertory Theatre and formerly *teached* [read *taught*] at the West Ottawa schools." "Teacher, Theater Figure Discovered Dead in Home," *Grand Rapids Press*, 26 Sept. 1995, at A10 (story deck).
- "Royston said he *teached* [read *taught*] youngsters and adults to either cover a grease fire before it spreads or put it out with baking soda." Caryl R. Lucas, "Belleville Kids Honored for Saving Their Moms in Separate House Fires," *Star-Ledger* (Newark), 11 Nov. 1998, at 43.
- "In addition to traditional subjects, the school *teached* [read *taught*] functional skills and has a vocational job program." "Specialty Schools," *Enquirer-J.* (Monroe, N.C.), 25 June 2015, at A31.

See IRREGULAR VERBS.

LANGUAGE-CHANGE INDEX
*teached for *taught*: Stage 1
Current ratio (*taught me* vs. **teached me*): 1,900:1

tear gas, n.; **teargas,** v.t. This term is spelled as two words for the noun, one for the verb. The inflected forms are *teargassed* and *teargassing* in AmE and BrE alike.

techie, n.; **techy,** adj. A technology whiz or a computer repairer is a *techie*—e.g.: "So when it's your home computer that's on the fritz (a very pre-digital expression), you hire a computer technician, or 'techie,' to save you from your ignorance." Philip Schmidt, *Don't Sweat It, Hire It* 70 (2007). The corresponding adjective is usually spelled *techy*—e.g.: "For photographers who are new to digital, the histogram's *techy*-looking graph can initially be confusing or even intimidating." Matt Paden, *Great Photos with Your Digital SLR* 28 (2009).

*technic. See technique.

technical; technological. The distinction is sometimes a fine one. *Technical* = (1) of, relating to, or involving

LANGUAGE-CHANGE INDEX (For the full key, see front matter pp. xxxi, l–li.)
Stage 1: Rejected. **Stage 2:** Widely shunned. **Stage 3:** Widespread but . . . **Stage 4:** Ubiquitous but . . . **Stage 5:** Fully accepted.
Invariably inferior forms marked by asterisk (*). • Ratios represent frequency of prevalent forms vs. variants in current books.

a particular science, art, or handicraft; or (2) of, relating to, or involving vocational training. *Technological* = (1) of, relating to, or involving the science of practical or industrial arts; or (2) of, relating to, or involving innovative gadgetry and computers. *Technological* connotes recent experimental methods and development, whereas *technical* has no such connotation.

technique; *technic. *Technique* has always been standard in AmE and BrE alike. **Technic* is a variant spelling to be avoided—e.g.: "I have heard this remedy [eye-muscle exercises] praised by those whom it has helped (the novelist Aldous Huxley has written a glowing and laudatory book about this *technic* [read *technique*])." Norman Lewis, *Better English* 238 (rev. ed. 1961).

Current ratio: 312:1

technological. See **technical.**

techy. See **techie.**

teeming with (= to abound; be in plentiful supply) should be followed by a count noun <the pond is teeming with fish> <our suggestion box is teeming with slips>. But sometimes it's misused for *rich in*, when applied to abstract noncount nouns—e.g.:

- "Lancaster County is *teeming with* [read *rich in*] history." Donald Wagner, "Touring Historic Manheim," *Lancaster New Era*, 31 May 1997, at A6.
- "The University of Arizona is *teeming with* [read *rich in*] tradition—and will soon have a place to put it on display." "'New' McKale Puts UA on Level with Great Sports Schools," *Tucson Citizen*, 14 Aug. 1997, Sports §, at 1.

Teeming is also sometimes misspelled *teaming*—e.g.:

- "Helen King of Riverside wasn't surprised when I recently reported that Mystic Lake is *teaming* [read *teeming*] with fish." Bob Pratte, "Pogs Go the Way of All the Fads," *Press-Enterprise* (Riverside, Cal.), 1 May 1995, at B3.
- "Gerber, with the help of other scouts, cut a swath through brush and a swampy area *teaming* [read *teeming*] with mosquitoes." Judy Hartling, "Troop at Church Adds Three Eagle Scouts," *Hartford Courant*, 8 Aug. 1996, Manchester Extra §, at 5.

LANGUAGE-CHANGE INDEX
teaming with misused for *teeming with*: Stage 1
Current ratio (*teeming with life* vs. **teaming with life*): 19:1

teenage, adj.; ***teenaged; *teen-age; *teen-aged.** The first has been the standard spelling since the early 1960s. The others are variant forms. In its 2002 revision, the *AP Stylebook* finally dropped the hyphenated forms.

Current ratio (in order of headwords): 147:12:2:1

teenager (so written, without a hyphen) is best understood literally as an adolescent aged 13 to 19—at least in any context in which precision is expected <20% discount today for all teenagers>. *Adolescent* (= a young person who is developing into an adult) is a somewhat broader term.

*teepee. See **tepee.**

tee shirt. See **T-shirt.**

teetotaler; teetotaller. The first is AmE; the second is BrE. This geographic distinction was fixed by the early 20th century. But in all varieties of English, *teetotalism* is the standard spelling. Cf. SPELLING (B).

telecast > telecast > telecast. So inflected. Avoid **telecasted*—e.g.:

- "NBC, which *telecasted* [read *telecast*] the event, could not have been pleased by the card." Doug Chapman, "Women's Final a Lackluster Battle Between Geezers," *Providence J.-Bull.*, 5 July 1998, at E13.
- "Last season, 100 Mets games were *telecasted* [read *telecast*] by FSNY." "Mets' Huskey, McMichael Have Knee Procedures," *N.Y. Post*, 13 Oct. 1998, at 69.
- "A year later, a new sports network called ESPN *telecasted* [read *telecast*] its second game ever." Ed Hardin, "After 13 Years, Blue Moon Shines on Cullowhee," *News & Record* (Greensboro), 22 Nov. 1998, at C1.

See -CAST & IRREGULAR VERBS.

LANGUAGE-CHANGE INDEX
*telecasted for *telecast* as a past tense: Stage 1
Current ratio (*was telecast* vs. **was telecasted*): 51:1

teleconferencing. See **conferencing.**

telegraph, vb.; **telegram,** n. To *telegraph* is to send a *telegram*. Although *telegram* has also been recorded as a verb since the mid-19th century, it has only sporadically so appeared and has never become standard—e.g.:

- "He *telegrammed* [read *telegraphed*] the governor." H.N. Hirsch, *The Enigma of Felix Frankfurter* 100 (1981).
- "When [Oscar Levant] was suspended for insulting a local sponsor, Frank Lloyd Wright, not noted for his TV viewing, *telegrammed* [read *telegraphed*] support for Oscar." Ian Whitcomb, "Such Happy Songs," *L.A. Times*, 12 June 1994, Book Rev. §, at 1.
- "Rockne *telegrammed* [read *telegraphed*] Iris Trippeer: 'George some improved. Still critical. Wishes to see you today.'" John U. Bacon, "This Is the Real Story of . . . : The Gipper, Part 1," *Detroit News*, 5 Jan. 1997, at D1.

LANGUAGE-CHANGE INDEX
telegram misused for *telegraph*: Stage 1
Current ratio (*telegraphed* vs. **telegrammed*): 39:1

telephonee. See -EE.

telephonic. Although *telephone* ordinarily serves as its own adjective <telephone call> <telephone directory>, *telephonic* proves useful to avoid MISCUES in some contexts—e.g.: "Just when you thought you were learning to live with voice mail, a new *telephonic* plague is about to sweep the business world—'on-hold marketing.'" Richard Tomkins, "Sold to the Person on Hold," *Fin. Times*, 22 Sept. 1997, at 16. (*Telephone plague* might suggest a surfeit of telephones—as opposed to telephone calls.) *Telephonic* was coined as early as 1840 and came into widespread use as early as 1880.

televise, vb., is so spelled—not **televize.* The word (dating from the 1920s) is a BACK-FORMATION from *television.*

Current ratio (televised vs. *televized): 308:1

tell; say. These verbs have distinct uses that most native speakers of English instinctively understand. Idiomatically speaking, you *say* that something is so, or you *tell* someone that something is so. *Tell,* in other words, needs a personal indirect object. You don't *tell* that something is so, but instead *tell someone* that something is so—e.g.:

- "After reviewing emergency procedures, he *told* [read *said*] that he would let me fly it." Gibson Armstrong, "He Hitches Ride in Wild Blue Yonder," *Lancaster New Era,* 5 Jan. 1997, at B8.
- "He *told* [read *said*] that he trained until he was nauseous and pulled his muscles." Patricia de Martelaere & Kendall Dunkelberg, "Scars," *Literary Rev.,* 22 Mar. 1997, at 527. (On the use of *nauseous* in that sentence, see **nauseous.**)
- "Mention the LSU fan he dumped into a garbage can and Knight will *tell* [read *say*] that *if he had have* [read *if he had*] been out of control, he'd have decked the guy." Mike Littwin, "Self-Tarnished Knight Needs Same Tough Love," *Rocky Mountain News* (Denver), 15 May 2000, at C2.

Still, it's permissible to say *tell that to your father* and the like—e.g.: "OK, RWD is better for towing, but *tell that to the owner* of a 4-cylinder engine." Jim Mateja, "Sienna Makes Up for Rare Toyota Miscue," *Chicago Trib.,* 21 Sept. 1997, at 1. In this usage, *tell that to* is a SET PHRASE.

LANGUAGE-CHANGE INDEX
tell misused for say: Stage 1

temblor; trembler. A *temblor* /**tem**-blər/ is an earthquake. A *trembler* is (1) a person who shakes with fear or whose religious practices include shaking, or (2) a species of songbird. The first use of *temblor* recorded in the *OED* is dated 1876. That was followed in 1913 by the first recorded use of **tremblor,* labeled plausibly enough as a variant of *temblor* influenced by *trembler*—a historical DOUBLE BOBBLE. Today, *temblor* is by far the dominant form, appearing in print 47 times as often as **tremblor.* Even *trembler* appears about as often as *tremblor—e.g.:

- "Aftershocks continued Sunday after a magnitude 5.4 *tremblor* [read *temblor*] hit three miles north of Big Bear City early Saturday morning." "Aftershocks Still Rattle Inland Cities," *Press-Enterprise* (Riverside, Cal.), 24 Feb. 2003, at B6.
- "More than 135 years ago, on April 24, 1867, the Humboldt Fault triggered a 5.1-magnitude *trembler* [read *temblor*] in Wamego, 15 miles from the dam site, that toppled chimneys and cracked plaster walls." Matt Moline, "Project to Reinforce Dam Extends Controversy of Past 50 Years," *Topeka Capital-J.,* 10 Nov. 2002, at B2.

Although *temblor* originated as a Spanish term naturalized in English in the late 19th century, the plural was fully anglicized by 1910: *temblors.* The Spanish plural *temblores is listed in some dictionaries as a variant plural. See PLURALS (B).

LANGUAGE-CHANGE INDEX
trembler or *tremblor for temblor: Stage 1

temerarious. See **timorous.**

temerity (= rash boldness) is sometimes confused with *timidity.* In the following example, the writer's meaning isn't at all clear—e.g.: "There's a wonderful moment when Hal actually has the *temerity* to place his hand on his father's shoulder, a *timid* gesture of affection that he immediately is made to regret." Lloyd Rose, " 'Henry IV': Shortened and Sweet," *Wash. Post,* 27 Sept. 1994, at D1.

temperature. A. Pronunciation. *Temperature* is pronounced /**tem**-pə-rə-chər/ or /**tem**-prə-chər/, not /**tem**-pə-rə-tyuur/, which is extremely pedantic, or /**tem**-pə-chər/, which is slovenly. A combination of the precious and the slovenly, /**tem**-pə-tyuur/ is ridiculously affected.

B. For *fever.* In colloquial English, *temperature* has been used in the sense "fever" since the late 19th century. But this usage is illogical because everything has a temperature, in the general sense of the word. The better choice is *fever*—e.g.:

- "Mustang Joe, a finalist in the Wimbledon Derby, came down badly with the sickness and was running a *temperature* [read *fever*]." Roger Jackson, "Jo's the Best," *Sporting Life,* 20 Nov. 1995, News §, at 1.
- "One day recently, Christopher was running a *temperature* [read *fever*]." Patricia A. Russell, " 'Chris Is a Child Like Any Other Child,' " *Providence J.-Bull.,* 24 Apr. 1997, at C1.

Of course, it's acceptable to say that someone is *running a temperature of 104*—because the word *temperature* makes perfect sense when it's coupled with a specific number.

LANGUAGE-CHANGE INDEX
temperature misused for fever: Stage 3
Current ratio (running a fever vs.
running a temperature): 3:1

tempestuous; tempestive. *Tempestuous* (a common word) = stormy <Jane has a tempestuous relationship with her mother>. *Tempestive* (an extremely arcane word) = timely, seasonable <a tempestive delivery>. The latter is sometimes misused for the former—e.g.: "In the past year, competition has become *tempestive* [read *tempestuous*], said Dominique Decoudray, M & S chief buyer for fresh products in Europe." Suzanne Lowry, "Paris Life," *Daily Telegraph,* 2 June 1994, at 15.

LANGUAGE-CHANGE INDEX
tempestive misused for tempestuous: Stage 1

temporize. A. And *temporalize.* *Temporize* (fairly common since the 17th century) = (1) to gain time by evasion or indirection <the tough financial

solutions have long been apparent, but policymakers have temporized>; or (2) to behave as the circumstances require, esp. by complying or yielding <after Jill threatened to leave, Jack temporized and wore a dark suit to the wedding>.

Temporalize (never a common word) = (1) to become a part of earthly life; secularize; or (2) to place in time. Sense 1: "Still, having '*temporalized*' Himself in the act of creation, and having allowed Himself to be affected by human suffering, His all-powerfulness *already underwent* [read *had already undergone*] a diminution." Richard Wolin, "Mortality and Morality," *New Republic*, 20 Jan. 1997, at 30. Sense 2: "What might it suggest, 1890s writers asked, for 'Woman' to be understood as 'New'—for the apparently 'natural' category of the feminine to be *temporalized*?" Jennifer L. Fleissner, "The Work of Womanhood in American Naturalism," *Differences*, 1 Mar. 1996, at 57.

B. And *extemporize*. *Extemporize* = to speak or perform extemporaneously; improvise. E.g.:

- "Many Americans recall how Clinton, speaking on health care to Congress last September, had to *extemporize* after finding the wrong speech scrolling on his Teleprompter screen." John Aloysius Farrell, "Life on the Edge Marks Presidency," *Boston Globe*, 13 June 1994, at 1.
- "Marvin Jones had to *extemporize* Wednesday in front of Orlando's Downtown Athletic Club, the organization that awarded him the 1992 Butkus Award as the nation's top linebacker." Carter Gaddis, "Improvising Will Be Key as Jets' Jones Hits Camp," *Tampa Trib.*, 13 July 1997, at 6.

tenant. See **tenet.**

tend = (1) to be predisposed to [something]; or (2) to look after or care for [someone or something]. Sense 2 is a Middle English shortening of *attend*, and the two words are generally interchangeable in AmE <tend to business>. In BrE, the two words are interchangeable in limited contexts such as fires <tending to a fire> <attending to a fire> or first aid <tend (to) a patient> <attend to a patient>. In golf talk in AmE as well as BrE, it is common to ask a fellow player or a caddie to *tend the pin* (i.e., to hold the pin while a player on or near the green plays a shot and to pull the pin as soon as the shot has been made).

Tend is sometimes wrongly made *tender*, more commonly in BrE than in AmE—e.g.:

- "She witnessed Neilson fall repeatedly into her carefully *tendered* [read *tended*] flower beds." "Savage Deeds in the Garden," *Evening Post*, 22 June 1998, TV §, at 15.
- "Their plants, lovingly and carefully *tendered* [read *tended*], are their pride and joy." Danielle Gusmaroli, "'Gardeners' Dig In for Flower Pot Fight," *Evening Standard*, 12 Feb. 2001, at 9.
- "Kevin, a black teenager in South Africa, proudly shows off his well *tendered* [read -*tended*] garden and a small hut which he calls home." Hardev Kaur, "Blacks Continue to Live in Poverty," *New Straits Times*, 23 May 2001, at 10.

See **exhibit a tendency.**

LANGUAGE-CHANGE INDEX
*well-tendered garden for well-tended garden: Stage 1

tendentious. A. Generally. *Tendentious* = (of a writing, etc.) tending to promote a given viewpoint; biased. The word appears much more commonly in BrE than in AmE—e.g.:

- "The Whitehall information code says no press release should contain *tendentious* or politically biased material." David Hencke, "Whitehall Press Officers Sound Off," *Guardian*, 17 Oct. 1997, at 4.
- "The usual reason for producing expressions like 'says a survey,' 'according to a new report,' 'latest research indicates,' 'scientists have discovered' or 'say doctors' is to add authority to some partisan or *tendentious* argument." Auberon Waugh, "A Plague on All 'Health Surveys,'" *Sunday Telegraph*, 26 Oct. 1997, at 37.
- "Politicians love to use history as a tool to justify policy.... The tendency drives historians mad, however. They argue that such a shallow use of the past is selective, *tendentious*, and sometimes just factually incorrect." Mark Rice-Oxley, "In Arguing for War, Blair Enlists History as His Ally," *Christian Science Monitor*, 7 Mar. 2003, World §, at 7.

Avoid the variant spelling *tendencious.
    Current ratio (*tendentious* vs. *tendencious): 97:1

B. With People. The word doesn't properly apply to people, in the sense *prejudiced* or *biased*—e.g.: "Bretecher's world is peopled by *tendentious* [read *prejudiced* or *biased*] hippies who turn into pretentious yuppies." Mary Schmich, "Accent on Agony," *Chicago Trib.*, 3 Aug. 1997, at 18.

LANGUAGE-CHANGE INDEX
tendentious misused in reference to a person,
as opposed to an argument, statement,
presentation, etc.: Stage 1

C. For *contentious*. *Tendentious* is occasionally confused with *contentious* (= combative)—e.g.:

- "The structure represents Selig's vision for his sport—the opportunity to soar beyond the *tendentious* [read *contentious*] labor struggles that have bedeviled baseball for decades and into an era of not only prosperity, but peace." Teri Thompson, "Selig: A New View for Baseball," *Daily News* (N.Y.), 21 Oct. 2001, at 76.
- "The reordered priorities promise a *tendentious* [read *contentious*] fight that will test the president's newfound political capital—and will set the tone for the 2002 midterm elections." Francine Kiefer & Abraham McLaughlin, *Christian Science Monitor*, 5 Feb. 2002, USA §, at 1.
- "'Why Orwell Matters' suggests that neither camp is likely to win a lasting victory in the *tendentious* [read *contentious*] tug of war for the allegiance of a polemicist as gifted, and refractory, as Hitchens." Jim Barloon, "Why Orwell Matters," *Houston Chron.*, 5 Jan. 2003, Zest §, at 18.

LANGUAGE-CHANGE INDEX
tendentious misused for *contentious*: Stage 1

D. For *tendinitis*. A surprising error is the substitution of *tendentious* for *tendinitis* (= inflammation of tendons in a joint). It probably results from trigger-happy users of spell-checkers—e.g.:

- "'However, I don't think my body can go another year at this intensity. I have had some lower back problems and patellar *tendentious* [read *tendinitis*] (jumper knees) so I want to leave the game healthy.'" "Long and Fruitful

Career," *Spokesman-Rev.* (Spokane) (Idaho ed.), 17 Nov. 2001, at H14 (quoting Lindsay Herbert).

- "The fashion-merchandising major did not compete as a sophomore because of knee surgery. She had struggled with patellar *tendentious* [read *tendinitis*] throughout her freshman year." Chuck Cavalaris, "Simpson Sprints to Lead at Marshall," *Knoxville News-Sentinel*, 16 May 2002, at D2.
- "About 45 minutes before Sunday's game, Nets coach Byron Scott said starting point guard Jason Kidd was going to sit out because of *tendentious* [read *tendinitis*] in his left foot." John Reid, "Nets' Kittles Returns Home as a Pro," *Times-Picayune* (New Orleans), 10 Mar. 2003, Sports §, at 6.

LANGUAGE-CHANGE INDEX
tendentious misused for *tendinitis*: Stage 1

tender, v.t., is a FORMAL WORD for *offer* or *give*. For a growing misuse of the word, see **tenure**.

tenderfoot (= a newcomer or beginner) forms the plural *tenderfeet* in AmE and BrE alike—not **tenderfoots.*
Current ratio: 4:1

tendinitis; *tendonitis.* *Tendinitis* (= inflammation of a tendon), dating from about 1900, takes its spelling directly from the Late Latin word. **Tendonitis*, incorrectly arrived at by association with the spelling of the English noun *tendon*, has become fairly common since the 1950s. See SPELLING (A).
Current ratio: 1.4:1

tenet (= a doctrine or basic belief, dogma) is sometimes confounded with the similar-sounding *tenant* (= [1] someone who has a leasehold, a lessee; or [2] an inhabitant, dweller). The result is linguistically untenable—e.g.:

- "The Clinton legislation, which embraces many of the *tenants* [read *tenets*] supported in education legislation passed in the Bush Administration, calls for the reconfiguration of American public schools." William Celis III, "Annenberg to Give Education $500 Million over Five Years," *N.Y. Times*, 17 Dec. 1993, at A1, A15.
- "This new view is called 'community-based conservation.' One of its fundamental *tenants* [read *tenets*] is that trust is central to devising long-term solutions to environmental problems." Pete Geddes, "Building Trust and Respect in the West," *Seattle Times*, 3 July 1996, at B5.
- "[Robert Blake] said the church's fundamental *tenant* [read *tenet*] is 'creation of man, fall of man, redemption through Jesus Christ.'" Brian Morelli, "New Nondenominational Christian Church at UI," *Iowa City Press-Citizen*, 24 Aug. 2007, at A3.

LANGUAGE-CHANGE INDEX
tenant misused for *tenet*: Stage 2
Current ratio (*fundamental tenet* vs. **fundamental tenant*): 70:1

Tennessean; *Tennesseean.* The first has been standard since the 1930s, before which time the second (now but a variant) was somewhat more common. Although the final *-e* is dropped in this word, it's

retained in the similar term *Tallahasseean*. See DENIZEN LABELS.
Current ratio: 7:1

Tennyson. The formal name of the 19th-century poet laureate is Alfred, Lord Tennyson. But writers often mistakenly write **Lord Alfred Tennyson* (and have done so since the late 19th century)—e.g.:

- "Harrogate had become the culture capital of Northern England, attracting such celebrities as Charles Dickens, *Lord Alfred Tennyson* [read *Alfred, Lord Tennyson*], George Bernard Shaw and Sir Edward Elgar, as well as most of Europe's royalty." David Yeadon, "Hear, Hear, Harrogate!" *Wash. Post*, 16 July 1995, at E1.
- "Poets John Keats, Wordsworth, *Lord Alfred Tennyson* [read *Alfred, Lord Tennyson,* or simply *Tennyson*] and Scott eloquently wrote of their impressions." Lisa Marlowe, "Lingering on Mull," *L.A. Times*, 5 May 1996, at L1.
- "There's a poem by *Lord Alfred Tennyson* [read *Alfred, Lord Tennyson,*] and a reference to the Woody Allen movie 'Annie Hall.'" Emily Parker, "Forget Big Brother—Fear Many Little Brothers," *Wash. Post*, 22 Mar. 2015, at B7.

The reason it's an error is that, with an English baron, *Lord* is almost always coupled with a last name instead of a first. The decision lies with the recipient. But usage can get complicated: *W2* notes that "Lord Henry Derby" and "Lord Philip Derby" would be possible "for the younger sons of dukes and marquises." Remember that.

TENSES. A. Generally. The following table shows the basic tenses in English with the verb *be* conjugated. The labels *1st, 2nd,* and *3rd* stand for first person, second person, and third person.

Indicative Mood

Present Tense

	Singular	Plural
1st	I am	We are
2nd	You are	You are
3rd	He is	They are

Past Tense

	Singular	Plural
1st	I was	We were
2nd	You were	You were
3rd	She was	They were

Future Tense

	Singular	Plural
1st	I will be	We will be
2nd	You will be	You will be
3rd	He will be	They will be

Present-Perfect Tense

	Singular	Plural
1st	I have been	We have been
2nd	You have been	You have been
3rd	She has been	They have been

Past-Perfect Tense

	Singular	Plural
1st	I had been	We had been
2nd	You had been	You had been
3rd	He had been	They had been

LANGUAGE-CHANGE INDEX (For the full key, see front matter pp. xxxi, l–li.)
Stage 1: Rejected. **Stage 2:** Widely shunned. **Stage 3:** Widespread but . . . **Stage 4:** Ubiquitous but . . . **Stage 5:** Fully accepted.
Invariably inferior forms marked by asterisk (*). • Ratios represent frequency of prevalent forms vs. variants in current books.

Future-Perfect Tense

	Singular	Plural
1st	I will have been	We will have been
2nd	You will have been	You will have been
3rd	She will have been	They will have been

Subjunctive Mood

Present Tense (Suggestions, Requirements)

	Singular	Plural
1st	(that) I be	(that) we be
2nd	(that) you be	(that) you be
3rd	(that) he be	(that) they be

Past Tense (Present/Future Reference)

	Singular	Plural
1st	(If) I were	(If) we were
2nd	(If) you were	(If) you were
3rd	(If) he were	(If) they were

Past-Perfect Tense (Past Reference)

	Singular	Plural
1st	(If) I had been	(If) we had been
2nd	(If) you had been	(If) you had been
3rd	(If) she had been	(If) they had been

Cf. SUBJUNCTIVES.

B. Sequence of. The term *sequence of tenses* refers to the relationship of tenses in subordinate clauses to those in principal clauses. Generally, the former follow from the latter.

In careful writing, the tenses agree both logically and grammatically. The basic rules of tense sequence are easily stated, although the many examples that follow belie their ostensible simplicity.

(1) When the principal clause has a verb in the present (*he says*), present perfect (*he has said*), or future (*he will say*), the subordinate clause has a present-tense verb. Grammarians call this the primary sequence.

(2) When the principal clause is in past tense (*he said, he was saying*) or past perfect (*he had said*), the subordinate clause has a past-tense verb. Grammarians call this the secondary sequence.

(3) When a subordinate clause states an ongoing or general truth, it should be in the present tense regardless of the tense in the principal clause—thus *He said yesterday that he is Jewish*, not **He said yesterday that he was Jewish*. This might be called the "ongoing-truth exception."

Examples may be readily found in which the primary sequence is mangled—e.g.: "Mrs. Yager faces a possible sentence of up to 60 years in prison, although neither side expects that the maximum sentence *would* [read *will*] be imposed if she *was* [read *is*] convicted." Peter Applebome, "Child Abuse 'Rescuer' Is Now the Accused," *N.Y. Times*, 27 Apr. 1992, at A1.

But the secondary sequence also causes problems when the writer begins with a past-tense verb in the principal clause and then switches to the present or future tense in the subordinate clause—e.g.:

- "Mr. Noriega limited his own movements even further, avoiding windows and even the shaded palm court out of fear that snipers *will* [read *would*] gun him down." Kempe, "So Noriega Is Ours," *Wall Street J.*, 4 Jan. 1990, at A1, A14.

- "The term 'request' *implied* that you *have* [read *had*] a choice in the matter." Eoin Colfer, *Artemis Fowl: The Arctic Incident* 112 (Am. ed. 2002).

An exceedingly common problem occurs with (tenseless) infinitives, which, when put after past-tense verbs, are often wrongly made perfect infinitives—e.g.:

- "Remembering how busy General Maxwell Taylor must have been as Chairman of the Joint Chiefs of Staff in 1963, how would you have liked *to have been* [read *to be*] in his shoes when he received the following cablegram, dated October 31, 1963, from General Paul Harkins, United States commander in Vietnam?" David W. Ewing, *Writing for Results in Business, Government, and the Professions* 111 (1974).

- "Guest . . . had had plenty of time *to have challenged* [read *to challenge*] on either side." Geoff Lester, "Guest's Up and Downer!" *Sporting Life*, 15 Nov. 1996, at 19.

- "It would have been unfair to the co-authors, he said, *to have listed* [read *to list*] Dr. Lu among them." Nicholas Wade, "Scientists Find a Key Weapon Used by H.I.V.," *N.Y. Times*, 19 Apr. 1997, at 1, 9.

This problem occurs frequently with the verbs *seemed* and *appeared*—e.g.:

- "Ripken *appeared to have enjoyed* [read *appeared to enjoy*] passing Kinugasa more than he enjoyed passing Gehrig." Mark Maske, "Officially, Ripken Is on Top of the World," *Wash. Post*, 15 June 1996, at H1.

- "Other residents, however, *seemed to have enjoyed* [read *seemed to enjoy*] the storm as they ventured into the hail-covered streets." Ibon Villelabeitia, "Let It Snow, Let It Snow, Let It . . . Er, Hail," *Orange County Register*, 16 Jan. 1997, Community §, at 1.

Cf. **would have liked.**

Finally, some writers mistakenly ignore the ongoing-truth exception—e.g.: "It hadn't escaped my notice that many modern texts, like many older ones, *were* [read *are*] self-referential, or concerned with the pleasures of 'recognition.'" Letter of Claude Rawson, *London Rev. of Books*, 18 May 1989, at 5.

On a related subject, see DOUBLE MODALS.

C. Threatened Obsolescence of Perfect Tenses. Perhaps the heading here is overdrawn, but a distressingly large number of educated speakers of English seem at least mildly hostile to perfect tenses. There are three: the present perfect, the past perfect (or pluperfect), and the future perfect. And they're worth some attention.

First, the present-perfect tense is formed with *have* [+ past participle], as in *I have done that*. Either of two qualities must be present for this tense to be appropriate: indefiniteness of past time or a continuation to the present. This tense sometimes represents an action as having been completed at some indefinite time in the past—e.g.:

> I *have played* more than 1,000 rounds of golf.

> They *have seen* Ely Cathedral before.

But sometimes, too, the present perfect indicates that an action continues to the present—e.g.:

> I *have played* cards nonstop since 3:00 yesterday.

> They *have toiled* at the project for three years now.

If neither of those qualities (imprecision about time or, if the time is precise, continuation to the present) pertains to the context, then the present perfect isn't the right tense.

Apart from the urge to convert this tense to simple past when the present perfect is needed, the most common error is to use the present-perfect form when the time is definite but the action doesn't touch the present—e.g.: "I *have played* [read *played*] cards nonstop from 3:00 to 5:00 PM yesterday."/ "They *have toiled* [read *toiled*] at the project for three years until last month." If, as in those examples, the action is wholly in the past—and the time is relatively definite—the simple past is called for.

Second, the past-perfect tense is formed with *had* [+ past participle], as in *I had done that.* This tense represents an action as completed at some definite time in the past—that is, before some other past time referred to. E.g.:

I *had* already *taken* care of the problem when you called yesterday.

By June 26 the money *had disappeared.*

Third, the future-perfect tense is formed with *will* (or *shall*) [+ *have* + past participle], as in *I will have done that.* This tense represents an action that will be completed at some definite time in the future—e.g.:

She *will have published* her second book by the time she's 30.

They *will have gone* to sleep by midnight.

Of these three types, the present perfect causes the most confusion. Some writers mistakenly equate it with PASSIVE VOICE—to which it has no relation. Others simply want to cut *have*, thereby converting the continuing action to a completed action. They may call this economizing, but it's almost always a false economy. And if the *have*-cutters ever become numerous enough, they will have done (that's future perfect) the language serious harm.

tentative (/**ten**-tə-tiv/) is often mispronounced, and therefore mistakenly written, as if the word were **tenative*—e.g.:

- "At the all-star break, he was making 42 percent (126 of 300) of his field goals, looking *tenative* [read *tentative*] with the ball." David Aldridge, "Harvey Grant Has Found That He Could Get to Like Starting After All," *Wash. Post*, 16 Apr. 1990, at C6.
- "The department and USEC have reached a *tenative* [read *tentative*] agreement on allowing the Department of Energy to take over USEC's plant in Paducah, Kentucky if the company ceases production there." Carter Dougherty, "Energy Department, USEC Near Pact on Nuclear Power," *Wash. Times*, 11 Feb. 2002, at A6.
- "Those first, *tenative* [read *tentative*] forays at Cathedral and White Horse ledges led to a winter ascent of Mount Washington, then to 14,000-foot peaks in Colorado."

Michael O'Connor, "Up to Challenge," *Boston Herald*, 4 May 2002, at 38.

Current ratio: 4,159:1

tenterhooks. A *tenter* is a frame for stretching cloth to dry, and *tenterhooks* are the hooks or nails placed in the tenter to hold the cloth. The SET PHRASE *on tenterhooks*, then, refers to being stretched, therefore strained and nervous. Because the unfamiliar word *tenterhook* is rarely seen outside that phrase, it is prone to being misspelled **tenderhook*, perhaps under the influence of *tenderfoot* or *tinderbox*—e.g.:

- "They did see the smoke from the huge Sioux and Cheyenne encampment, and were on *tenderhooks* [read *tenterhooks*] until Custer's scout, Curley, arrived on the morning of the 27th bearing confirmation of their fears." Frederic Smith, "Civilian Grant Marsh Played Major Role in Bighorn Story," *Bismarck Trib.*, 25 June 2001, at A1.
- "Nittoli said she was put on *tenderhooks* [read *tenterhooks*] in July, when she decided to leave Morristown Memorial Hospital and got a letter from Kalleberg suggesting she not quit the hospital because her job as SART and SANE coordinator was in jeopardy." Peggy Wright, "Prosecutor's Office Scrambles After Resignations," *Daily Record* (Morristown, N.J.), 13 Jan. 2004, at A1.
- "There was That Guy, and he's in every line, the guy who declares to the people in front of and behind him that in Europe, they're on *tenderhooks* [read *tenterhooks*] to see if we mess this one up, too." Rachel Sauer, "New Voting Reality: A Long Wait in Line," *Palm Beach Post*, 3 Nov. 2004, at D1.

The error first occurred in AmE in the early 19th century and had spread into BrE by 1900. Cf. **tinderbox.**

LANGUAGE-CHANGE INDEX
tenterhook misspelled **tenderhook*: Stage 1
Current ratio (*tenterhooks* vs. **tenderhooks*): 85:1

tenure; tender. *Tenure* (= [1] a holding by right, as of an elected office; [2] the time spent in such an office; or [3] an entitlement to a professional position, esp. at a university, with protection against dismissal) is sometimes used where the intent was *tender*, vb. (= to offer something, esp. in settlement of a debt or a dispute). When the thing being tendered is a resignation, this MALAPROPISM is particularly absurd—e.g.:

- "The acting Governor refused to get involved, and so McClure *tenured* [read *tendered*] his resignation." David G. Tosifon, "Mass. Boxing Chief Spars with Fellow Commissioner, Resigns," *Bay State Banner*, 20 Aug. 1998, at 2.
- "In an executive session Monday, Farkas *tenured* [read *tendered*] her resignation, offering 60 days' notice." Meghan Hershey, "Mount Joy Manager Resigns After 5 Months," *Lancaster New Era/Intelligencer Journal*, 3 Oct. 2001, at B6.
- "Talley, who *tenured* [read *tendered*] his resignation letter Friday, said he was stepping down . . . because he is too busy." Tony J. Taylor, "Talley Resigns from Converse Board," *Spartanburg Herald-J.* (S.C.), 14 Nov. 2001, at C1.

LANGUAGE-CHANGE INDEX
tenure misused for *tender*: Stage 1

LANGUAGE-CHANGE INDEX (For the full key, see front matter pp. xxxi, l–li.)
Stage 1: Rejected. **Stage 2:** Widely shunned. **Stage 3:** Widespread but . . . **Stage 4:** Ubiquitous but . . . **Stage 5:** Fully accepted.
Invariably inferior forms marked by asterisk (*). • Ratios represent frequency of prevalent forms vs. variants in current books.

tepee (= a conical tent made by American Indians of the Plains and Great Lakes regions) is the standard spelling of this quintessentially American word, whether in AmE or BrE. **Teepee* and **tipi* have been variants since the 18th century.

 Current ratio (*tepee* vs. **tipi* vs. **teepee*): 2:1.5:1

tercentenary; *tricentennial; *tercentennial; *tricentenary. Since the mid-19th century, the first has been the usual spelling for both the noun meaning "a period of 300 years" and the adjective meaning "of, relating to, or involving a 300-year period." The other three are variant forms. See **centennial.**

 Tercentenary is pronounced /tər-sən-**ten**-ə-ree/ or /tər-**sen**-tə-ner-ee/.

 Current ratio (in order of headwords): 23:3:2:1

termagant (= a quarrelsome, overbearing woman) is pronounced /**tər**-mə-gənt/, not /-jənt/. The mispronunciation occurs twice in the movie *Stepsister from Planet Weird* (2001).

terminable, adj. So written—not **terminatable.* See -ATABLE.

terminal. See **terminus.**

terminate. See **fire.**

terminus; terminal, n. *Terminus* = the place at the end of a travel route, esp. a railroad or bus line. Pl. *termini* or (much less commonly) *terminuses.* (See PLURALS (B).) *Terminal* = (1) a station on a transportation route; (2) a computer workstation; or (3) a point for connecting wires in an electrical circuit.

terra cotta. The noun is so written <a bust in terra cotta>, but the adjective is *terra-cotta* <a terra-cotta bust>.

terrain; terrane. *Terrain* (dating from the mid-18th century) = the topography of a given region or piece of land. *Terrane* (dating from the mid-19th century) = (1) a specific geological formation in a given region; or (2) the rocks associated with such a formation. Although it originated as an altered spelling of *terrain, terrane* is now a standard geologist's term.

terrine. See **tureen.**

territory; dependency; commonwealth. The distinctions in AmE are as follows. *Territory* = a part of the United States not included within any state but organized with a separate legislature (*W11*). Guam and the U.S. Virgin Islands are *territories* of the United States; Alaska and Hawaii were formerly *territories. Dependency* = a land or territory governed, but not formally annexed, by a geographically distinct country. The Philippines was once a *dependency* of the United States. *Commonwealth* = a political unit having local autonomy but voluntarily joined with the United States. A few states are called *commonwealths,* but mostly one thinks of Puerto Rico and the Northern Mariana Islands as *commonwealths.* Puerto Rico is sometimes referred to as a *dependency,* but its proper designation is *commonwealth.*

 In BrE, *commonwealth* = a loose association of countries that recognize one sovereign <the British Commonwealth>. See **commonweal.**

tessera (/**tes**-ər-ə/) = (1) a small square tablet used in ancient Rome as a token; or (2) a small square block used in mosaic. The plural is *tesserae* (/**tes**-ər-ee/) or *tesseras.* See PLURALS (B).

 Current ratio (*tesserae* vs. *tesseras*): 180:1

testatrix (= a female maker of a will, or female testator) is increasingly viewed as archaic. *Testator* is generally viewed as a non-sex-specific term. See SEXISM (D).

testimony. See **evidence (A).**

tetchy; techy. See **touchy.**

tête-à-tête. Although the DIACRITICAL MARKS are mandatory, the term is ordinarily printed in roman type, not italics. The plural *tête-à-têtes* (italicized here only because it's referred to as a phrase) is pronounced identically: /tet-ə-**tet**/.

text, vb.; **texting.** As a verb, *text* (= to send a text message) sprang into favor in the late 1990s with the popularity of instant-messaging systems—e.g.: "If you're shopping for a new plan, analyze your calling, *texting* and data-download patterns." Liz F. Kay, "Finding New Ways to Trim Your Cell Phone Expenses," *Baltimore Sun,* 22 Jan. 2009, at A8. The term was almost instantly familiar and filled a new need in the language, so it's bootless to grouse about its success. See FUNCTIONAL SHIFT (D).

 Of course, the verb is inflected *text > texted > texted.* Cf. **sext.**

text message is increasingly shortened to *text* (= a written message that is sent electronically, usu. from one handheld device to another).

textual; textuary. As an adjective, the latter is a NEEDLESS VARIANT. As a noun, however, *textuary* denotes a biblical scholar.

thalamus (= [1] a part of the brain that relays sensory impulses; or [2] the receptacle of a flower) forms the plural *thalami.* Though not unknown in AmE, *thalamuses* is rare. See PLURALS (B).

 Current ratio: 431:1

than. A. Verb Not Repeated After (*than is, than has*). Often it's unnecessary (though not ungrammatical) to repeat *be*-verbs and *have*-verbs after *than,* especially when a noun follows—e.g.:

- "Derby (pronounced Darby) is far more typical of English life *than is* [read *than*] London—in the same way that Dubuque is more typical of American life than New York City." Ann Miller Jordan, "Derby Filled with History, Charm—and Ghosts," *Ft. Worth Star-Telegram,* 26 Oct. 1997, at 1.
- "Both major female hormones, estrogen and progesterone, can be given at any age to strengthen bones, and the combination can be far more effective *than is* [read *than*] estrogen alone." Gabe Mirkin, "Looking to Control Body Fat?" *Wash. Times,* 27 Oct. 1997, at B12.

- "Akron is more respected this season *than is* [read *than*] Central Michigan." Berry Tramel, "Oklahoma Gets Baptism in Mid-American Conference Football," *Oklahoman*, 18 Aug. 2015, at 13.

See COMPARATIVES and SUPERLATIVES (C).

B. For *then*. This error is so elementary that one might fairly wonder whether it is merely a lapse in proofreading. But it occurs with some frequency—e.g.: "Mr. Bennett did wake up several times, hoping to hear good news, if not about himself, *than* [read *then*] at least about the two stars of the film, Nigel Hawthorne, nominated for best actor, or Helen Mirren, nominated for best actress." Sarah Lyall, "For Alan Bennett, Home Is Where He's Heartened," *N.Y. Times*, 19 Oct. 1995, at B3. This error is extremely common, perhaps because the two words are almost homophones in some dialects of AmE. In any given instance, though, the error might be typographical. For the opposite error, see **then** (B).

LANGUAGE-CHANGE INDEX
than misused for *then*: Stage 1

C. Case of Pronoun After: *than me* or *than I*? Traditional grammarians have considered *than* a conjunction, not a preposition—hence *He is taller than I (am)*. On this theory, the pronoun after *than* gets its case from its function in the completed second clause of the sentence—though, typically, the completing words of the second clause are merely implied. See UNDERSTOOD WORDS.

That view has had its detractors, including Eric Partridge, who preferred the objective case: *You are a much greater loser than me* (*U&A* at 330). Even William Safire plumps for the objective case: "The hard-line Conjunctionites have been fighting this battle a long time. Give them credit: they had to go up against the poet Milton's treatment of *than* as a preposition—*than whom* in 'Paradise Lost'—and against Shakespeare's 'a man no mightier than thyself or me' in 'Julius Caesar.'" Safire, "Than Me?" *N.Y. Times*, 16 Apr. 1995, § 7, at 16. See (D).

For formal contexts, the traditional usage is generally best; only if you are deliberately aiming for a relaxed, colloquial tone is the prepositional *than* acceptable. Often it seems ill-advised—e.g.:

- "So many of our students seem to struggle . . . . Are we really that much smarter than *them* [read *they*]?" John B. Mitchell, "Current Theories on Expert and Novice Thinking," 39 *J. Legal Educ.* 275 (1989).
- "What makes the story even juicier is that Pamela, 74, has allegedly been feuding for years with her two former stepdaughters, both of them slightly older than *her* [read *she*]—and one of whom may face financial difficulties." Mark Hosenball, "Clifford Pleads Ignorance," *Newsweek*, 3 Oct. 1994, at 46.
- "Scrambling to improve his chances, Donald Skelton, a safe-deposit manager at Chase, plans to go to night school this summer at age 46. He had a rude awakening after 25 years at the bank when he learned that his daughter, fresh

out of college, earned more than *him* [read *he*]." "At the New Workplace, an Unnerving Game of Musical Chairs," *N.Y. Times*, 4 Mar. 1996, at A10 (photo caption).
- "The sun on the runway illuminated their hair, which was bobbed to shoulder length and styled to the same tint—all in their thirties (he was fifty-eight at the time), twenty years younger than *him* [read *he*?], and of the same height." Edward Hoagland, "Sex and the River Styx," *Harper's Mag.*, Jan. 2003, at 49, 59.

See PRONOUNS (B).

What about "My mother likes the dog more than me?" vs. "My mother likes the dog more than I?" These sentences say different things, even though *than* acts as a conjunction, seemingly, in the first as well as the second. The first means *more than (she likes) me*, the second *more than I (like the dog)*. The Beatles presented this dilemma in their song "If I Fell" (1964), in which John Lennon sang: "I must be sure, from the very start, that you would love me more than her." Either this is bad English, or Lennon was envisioning a bisexual lover contemplating same-sex and different-sex lovers. But the latter has never seemed plausible—and the objective case is probably the speaker's maladroit attempt to suggest that two women are vying for his affections. (Consider: it was the Beatles in the 1960s.) But even if *than* is taken as a conjunction in *than her*—as short for *than (you love) her*, it represents unexemplary English.

LANGUAGE-CHANGE INDEX
than with an objective pronoun
<he's taller than me>: Stage 4
Current ratio (*taller than he* vs. **taller than him*): 3:1

D. *Than whom*. In the awkward and (fortunately) now-rare inverted construction (e.g., *T.S. Eliot, than whom few critics could be considered better*), one might expect the nominative *who* to be the preferred pronoun. *Than* is treated as a conjunction in formal usage, not a preposition (see (C)), so the preferable relative pronoun in formal writing would seem to be the nominative *who* rather than the objective *whom*. But the anomalous phrasing has been traditional since the latter part of the 16th century. The *OED* states that *than whom* "is universally recognized instead of *than who.*"

A late-19th-century American rhetorician objected to the phrase: "*Than whom*, as in the sentence, 'Wilfred, than whom no truer friend to me exists, counsels this course,' is an anomalous expression (*than* being treated as if it were a preposition with an object, whereas it is a conjunction) which it is better to avoid. The high example of Milton has given currency to the phrase." John F. Genung, *Outlines of Rhetoric* 57 (1893). But most 20th-century authorities accepted it. One of them, G.H. Vallins, explained that "usage has triumphed over 'grammar' and the ordinary speaker or writer over the pedant." G.H. Vallins, *Good English: How to Write It* 85 (1951).

LANGUAGE-CHANGE INDEX (For the full key, see front matter pp. xxxi, l–li.)
Stage 1: Rejected. **Stage 2:** Widely shunned. **Stage 3:** Widespread but . . . **Stage 4:** Ubiquitous but . . . **Stage 5:** Fully accepted.
Invariably inferior forms marked by asterisk (*). • Ratios represent frequency of prevalent forms vs. variants in current books.

Still, very few "ordinary" speakers or writers ever use the phrase, which is essentially a literary idiom. It's hardly surprising to find it in the writings of Hazlitt—e.g.: "I once knew a very ingenious man, *than whom*, to take him in the way of common chit-chat or fireside gossip, no one could be more entertaining or rational." William Hazlitt, "On the Conversation of Authors" (1820), in *A Reader for Writers* 275, 291 (William Targ ed., 1951). But it would be surprising to find it in an informal essay written in the 21st century.

E. *Prefer . . . than.* See **prefer.**

F. *Different than.* See DIFFERENT (A).

thankfully = in a manner expressing thanks; gratefully <after being saved so unexpectedly, they thankfully said goodbye>. E.g.: "Obligations are *thankfully* acknowledged to a long line of etymologists, lexicographers, and philologists, whom it would be mere pedantry to call by name." James Bradstreet Greenough & George Lyman Kittredge, *Words and Their Ways in English Speech* v (1901).

In the mid-1960s, the word came into frequent use in the sense "thank goodness; I am (or we are) thankful that"—that is, as a SENTENCE ADVERB analogous to *hopefully*. (See **hopefully.**) It occurred first in BrE and then spread to AmE. Although this use of *thankfully* is now fairly common, it has become a SKUNKED TERM in the minds of snoots. (See **snoot.**) *Gratefully* will often communicate the idea "in a thankful manner" more clearly. Or for sentence-adverb revisions, try *thank goodness* or *fortunately*—e.g.:

- "Rest assured, there will be no singing, no dancing and, *thankfully* [read *thank goodness*], no hokey Disney presentation." Milton Kent, "Big Weekend for Channel Surfing," *Baltimore Sun*, 31 Mar. 1995, at C2.
- "Ms. Sanday, in other words, wants to rewrite the rules of sex, as though sex—and courtship—were responsible for an egregious crime. *Thankfully,* [read *Thank goodness*] this is not the case." Karen Lehrman, "When 'No' Means 'No,'" *N.Y. Times*, 9 June 1996, § 7, at 24.
- "*Thankfully* [read *Luckily*], Spin publicist Jason Roth is still allowed to make more or less direct statements." James Ledbetter, "Press Clips," *Village Voice*, 1 Apr. 1997, at 32.
- "At two, she spoke in phrases incomprehensible to anyone but me. . . . *Thankfully* [read *Fortunately*], by two and a half, she had graduated to complex sentences." Mary Newton Bruder, *The Grammar Lady* 97 (2000).

LANGUAGE-CHANGE INDEX
thankfully as a SENTENCE ADVERB meaning "thank goodness": Stage 4

thanking you in advance. This bit of COMMERCIALESE arose in the late 19th century and had become widespread by the early 20th. It has been somewhat on the decline since about 1960. See **thank you.**

Thanksgiving Day; Thanksgiving. Either term is acceptable for the November holiday. But *Thanksgiving Day* more clearly denotes the day itself <the family's traditional touch-football game on Thanksgiving Day>, while *Thanksgiving* may suggest the entire holiday period <are you going home for Thanksgiving this year?>.

thank you. A. Generally. This phrase remains the best, most serviceable phrase, despite various attempts to embellish it or truncate it: *thanking you in advance* (presumptuous and possibly insulting), *thank you very much* (with a trailer of surplusage), *thanks* (useful on informal occasions), *many thanks* (informal but emphatic), **much thanks* (archaic and increasingly unidiomatic), **thanks much* (confusing the noun with the verb), and **thanx* (unacceptably cutesy).

Thank-you, n., is so hyphenated <a thousand thank-yous>.

B. Response. The traditional response to *Thank you* is *You're welcome*. Somehow, though, in the 1980s, *You're welcome* came to feel a little stiff and formal, perhaps even condescending (as if the speaker were saying, "Yes, I really did do you a favor, didn't I?"). As a result, three other responses started displacing *You're welcome*: (1) "No problem" (as if the speaker were saying, "Don't worry, you didn't inconvenience me too much"); (2) the slightly longer *Not a problem* (same implication); and (3) "No, thank *you*" (as if the person doing the favor really considered the other person to have done the favor). The currency of *You're welcome* seems to diminish little by little, but steadily. Old-fashioned speakers continue to use it, but its future doesn't look bright. Other traditional responses are *Don't mention it* and *Not at all*. Other nontraditional responses include *You bet* and *No worries*. See **no worries.**

than whom. See **than** (D).

that. A. And *which*. You'll encounter two schools of thought on this point. First are those who don't care about any distinction between these words as relative pronouns, who think that *which* is more formal than *that*, and who point to many historical examples of copious *whiches*. They say that modern usage is a muddle. Second are those who insist that both words have useful functions that ought to be separated, and who observe the distinction rigorously in their own writing. They view departures from this distinction as "mistakes."

Before reading any further, you ought to know something more about these two groups: those in the first probably don't write very well; those in the second just might.

So assuming you want to learn the stylistic distinction, what's the rule? The simplest statement of it is this: if you see a *which* without a comma (or preposition) before it, nine times out of ten it needs to be a *that*. The one other time, it needs a comma. Your choice, then, is between comma-*which* and *that*. Use *that* whenever you can.

Consider the following sentence: "All the cars that were purchased before 2008 need to have their airbags replaced." It illustrates a *restrictive* clause. Such a clause gives essential information about the preceding noun (here, *cars*) so as to distinguish it from similar items with which it might be confused (here, cars that were purchased from 2008 on). In effect, the clause restricts the field of reference to just this one particular case or class of cases—hence the term *restrictive*. Restrictive clauses take no commas (since commas would present the added information as an aside).

Now let's punctuate our sample sentence differently and change the relative pronoun from *that* to *which*: "All the cars, *which* were purchased before 2008, need to have their airbags replaced." This version illustrates a *nonrestrictive* clause. Such a clause typically gives supplemental, nonessential information. Presumably, we already know from the context which cars we're talking about. The sentence informs us that the cars need their airbags replaced—oh, and by the way, they were all bought before 2008. The incidental detail is introduced by *which* and set off by commas to signal its relative unimportance.

A restrictive clause is essential to the grammatical and logical completeness of a sentence. A nonrestrictive clause, by contrast, is so loosely connected with the essential meaning of the sentence that it could be omitted without changing the meaning.

Hence, three guidelines. First, if you cannot omit the clause without changing the basic meaning, the clause is restrictive; use *that* without a comma. Second, if you can omit the clause without changing the basic meaning, the clause is nonrestrictive; use a comma plus *which*. Third, if you ever find yourself using a *which* that doesn't follow a comma (or a preposition), it probably needs to be a *that*.

The most common problem is that people use *which* when the sentence really needs *that*—e.g.: "Despite all the uncertainty *which* [read *that*] surrounded the 1994 season—and the doubts *which* [read *that*] still linger like a hangover that just won't quit—Paul O'Neill was sure of one thing." Don Burke, "Yanks Ink O'Neill: 4 Years, $19M," *Star-Ledger* (Newark), 29 Oct. 1994, at 29. And this bad habit leads to even worse ones, such as overlong sentences and REMOTE RELATIVES.

Although the usual mistake is *which* for *that* as a restrictive pronoun, *that* is occasionally misused as a nonrestrictive pronoun—e.g.: "To me it's pretty certain no Republican national leader would call to the attention of the public these controversial subjects *that* have no definite solution." Letter of Brooks Norfleet Jr., "Clinton Facing Real Problems," *Dallas Morning News*, 30 Nov. 1993, at A16. (Delete *that* and insert a comma-*which*.)

British writers mostly ignore the distinction between restrictive and nonrestrictive relative pronouns. Most commonly *which* encroaches on *that*'s territory, but sometimes too a nonrestrictive *which* remains unpunctuated—e.g.:

- "Esa-Pekka Salonen, the boyish (36 going on 18) music director of the Los Angeles Philharmonic *which* plays the Proms at London's Albert Hall next week, says ...." Antony Thorncroft, "A Conductor Who Fits the Bill," *Fin. Times*, 26 Aug. 1994, at 11. (Insert a comma before *which*.)

- "The decision is the second defeat in five months for the French government *which* has been attempting to delay liberalising its domestic air transport market while it seeks to restructure its loss-making flag carrier." Paul Betts et al., "France Ordered to Open Two Internal Air Routes," *Fin. Times*, 27 Oct. 1994, at 1. (Insert a comma before *which*.)

- "Force Ouvrière, one of the French Unions *which* [read *that*] were most aggressive in calling for the industrial action that disrupted the country last year, yesterday lost control of the Caisse Nationale d'Assurance Maladie, the national health care agency, for the first time since 1967." "Hardline French Union Loses Role," *Fin. Times*, 13 June 1996, at 2.

One last thing. The Fowler brothers are often credited with "inventing" this distinction in *The King's English* (1906)—and the credit often seems to take the form of blame: "The ban on the restrictive *which* was made up suddenly by H.W. and F.G. Fowler in *The King's English* .... This spurious rule, which dismayed other grammarians, had no background in usage and cannot always be followed, notably in 'that which' clauses." Don Bush, "Grammatical Arthritis," *Technical Communication*, Feb. 1994, at 125. Although the Fowlers' exposition on this point is nothing short of brilliant, many earlier writers had already suggested the distinction. Note, however, that the first and third authors engage in the very misusage they talk about (both noted by a bracketed *n.b.*):

> Some critics have lately objected to the use of *that*, as a *relative*, conceiving *which* to be in all cases "the preferable word" [Hugh Blair, *Lectures on Rhetoric*]. But this is certainly a hasty and erroneous opinion. We have in English three relatives, *that*, *who*, and *which*; and, in their respective and appropriate use, we possess an advantage ... peculiar to our language, and which [*n.b.*] I hope we shall not be tempted to relinquish. [In the examples that Odell then gives, the *thats* are used restrictively, the *whiches* nonrestrictively.]
>
> James Odell, *An Essay on the Elements, Accents, and Prosody of the English Language* 49 (1806).

> "Which" is used in speaking of a *class generally*, and "that" when we mean to designate any particular *individual* of that class.
>
> Richard Dublin, *A Selection of English Synonyms* 21 (rev. ed. 1860).

> "That" the demonstrative is used as a relative, and is applied to both persons and things. It is often more appropriate than "who," or "which."
>
> It may be used for example, when the gender of the noun is doubtful; and where the antecedents refer to both persons and things: ....
>
> It is used before a restrictive clause after a superlative adjective, after "the same," and "who," and after an antecedent which [*n.b.*] is without the usual limiting demonstrative: as—
>
> "He was the best man *that* could be found for the place."
> "Even the same *that* I said unto you at the beginning."

LANGUAGE-CHANGE INDEX (For the full key, see front matter pp. xxxi, l–li.)
Stage 1: Rejected. **Stage 2**: Widely shunned. **Stage 3**: Widespread but . . . **Stage 4**: Ubiquitous but . . . **Stage 5**: Fully accepted.
Invariably inferior forms marked by asterisk (*). • Ratios represent frequency of prevalent forms vs. variants in current books.

"Who *that* is a sincere friend to it, can look with indifference on the attempts to shake the foundation of the fabric."—WASHINGTON.

"Thoughts *that* breathe, and words *that* burn."

> Joseph Angus, *Hand-Book of the
> English Tongue* 284 (1868).

Adjective clauses may be classified as restrictive and unrestrictive. Restrictive clauses limit the scope, or application, of the word they modify; as Water *that is stagnant* is unhealthful. Unrestrictive clauses do not so limit, or restrict, the application of the word they modify; as Water, *which is oxygen and hydrogen united*, is essential to life.

> Brainerd Kellogg, *A Text-Book on
> Rhetoric* 28 (1881).

Some teachers insist that the relative *that* should be used, instead of *who* or *which*, when the relative clause serves to restrict the meaning of the antecedent, and that *who* or *which* should be used, instead of *that*, when the relative clause adds something to the meaning of the antecedent, or explains it.

> Adams Sherman Hill,
> *Our English* 33 (1888).

The relative *who* or *which* may, and theoretically does, introduce a new fact about its antecedent; its office is, therefore, to head a coordinate clause, as may be shown by using its equivalent *and he, and it, and they*. The relative *that* is used only to introduce subordinate clauses necessary to define or restrict or complete our thought of the antecedent . . . . There are many cases where, for the sake of euphony or clearness, *who* or *which* has to be used though the meaning is restrictive. Such cases ought to be studied; and wherever *that* will go smoothly, use it. Do not be so careless in this respect as some writers are.

> John F. Genung, *Outlines of Rhetoric* 94–95 (1894)
> (elsewhere referring to "the restrictive *that*"
> and "the coordinate *which*").

The only retrospective blame that might lie with the Fowler brothers is that they pressed their point too diffidently. The distinction between *that* and *which* makes good sense. It enhances clarity. And the best American editors follow it.

Although linguists have generally been unsympathetic to maintaining the distinction, the distinguished Dwight Bolinger has urged its utility: "*Which* is used in nonrestrictive clauses not because of any rule about nonrestrictive clauses, but because such clauses are outside the flow of the sentence and call for a relative that will put the hearer on notice." Dwight Bolinger, *Language: The Loaded Weapon* 172 (1980).

LANGUAGE-CHANGE INDEX
which used with restrictive clauses: Stage 4

B. Wrongly Suppressed *that*. As a relative pronoun or conjunction, *that* can be suppressed in any number of constructions (e.g., *The dog you gave me* rather than *The dog that you gave me*). But in formal writing, *that* is often ill-advisedly omitted. In particular, the conjunction *that* should usually be retained to introduce clauses following verbs such as *acknowledge, ask, believe, claim, doubt,* and *said,* because without the conjunction what follows might be taken to be a noun complement. Dropping *that* after the verb can create a MISCUE, even if only momentarily—e.g.:

- "Son acknowledges being a member of a discriminated minority—his grandfather emigrated from the Korean Peninsula to work in the coal mines—may have helped him turn his eyes abroad early." Yuri Kageyama, "Softbank President Credited with Making Company an Industry Leader," *L.A. Times*, 21 June 1996, at D7. (Insert *that* after *acknowledges*.) For more on this use of *discriminated*, see **discriminate.**

- "They believed prisoners should be placed in isolation and educated." Mary Frain, "Criminal Justice—and Injustice," *Telegram & Gaz.* (Worcester), 27 Sept. 1996, at C1. (Insert *that* after *believed*.)

The writers who ill-advisedly omit *that* seem deaf to their ambiguities and miscues. When one instance occurs in a piece of writing, more are sure to follow. The following examples come from one article—which contains six more errors of the same variety:

- "But the state *charged the lease deal* [read *charged that the lease deal*], signed in 1991, sprang from a web of fraud and deceit." P.L. Wyckoff, "State Pays While Bankruptcy Delays Lease Suit," *Sunday Star-Ledger* (Newark), 11 Aug. 1996, § 1, at 25, 32.

- "During more than a year of negotiations and bureaucratic processing, the Karcher group *claimed the property* [read *claimed that the property*] was worth $2 million when it really was only worth $850,000, the state said." *Ibid.*

See MISCUES (F).

C. Used Excessively. Those who rabidly delete *that* (see (B)) seem to be overreacting to those who use it excessively—e.g.: "In a 1990 book of his successes and misadventures, *News of My Death . . . Was Greatly Exaggerated* (a tiresomely self-centered, but nonetheless bright and lucid analysis of the '80s boom-to-bust cycle), Hall points out, among other things, *that* while the problem as of '86 and '87 was *that* no one had any money, the bigger problem *that* had fomented *that* circumstance was *that* everyone had had too much money." Jim Atkinson, "The Great Dallas Bust," *D Mag.*, Dec. 1995, at 91, 92. (A possible revision: *In 1990 Hall wrote a book about his successes and misadventures:* News of My Death . . . Was Greatly Exaggerated. *It's tiresomely self-centered, but it's still a bright and lucid analysis of the '80s boom-to-bust cycle. In his view, although the problem in '86 and '87 was that no one had any money, this had resulted from an even bigger problem: in the early '80s, everyone had too much money.* [Five *thats* to one.])

D. Unnecessarily Repeated as Conjunction. One must be careful not to repeat the conjunction *that* after an intervening phrase. Either suspend it till just before the verb or use it early in the sentence and omit it before the verb—e.g.: "Mr. Siefker has gone through half a dozen lawyers, each thinking *that* with a little bit of work *that* he, too, could claim a piece of that magical work." David Margolick, "At the Bar," *N.Y. Times*, 8 Dec. 1989, at 27. (Delete the second *that*.)

E. For *very* or *so*. In certain negative constructions, *that* commonly functions adverbially—as a loose equivalent of *very* <I don't like pasta that much> <I was never that good at biology>. Some writers have objected when the degree of comparison is vague (how much don't you like pasta, and how bad were you at biology?). Although no reasonable person objects to the adverbial *that* when the point of comparison is explicit <I got three scoops—even though I didn't want that much!>, usage becomes unmoored when no comparison is intended <I did it, but I didn't even try that hard!>. Yet this is now an established CASUALISM, more characteristic of speech than of writing. For a good discussion that dates the trend toward using *that* for *very* from the mid-20th century, see Richard K. Redfern, "Not That Bad: Comments on the Adverbial 'That,'" 40 *Am. Speech* 74–76 (1965). Cf. **so (B)**.

LANGUAGE-CHANGE INDEX
all that for *so very* <it's not all that interesting>: Stage 4

F. And *who*. Is it permissible to say *people that*, or must one say *people who*? The answer is that *people that* has always been good English, and it's a silly fetish to insist that *who* is the only relative pronoun that can refer to humans. See **who (D), (E)**.

G. As a Pointing Word. See POINTING WORDS.

that is. Conventional wisdom once held that if this phrase begins a sentence, the result is a sentence fragment. (See INCOMPLETE SENTENCES (A).) But good writers unimpeachably use the phrase in this way, in place of *in other words*—e.g.:

- "While adopting certain teaching techniques, we are more interested in communication than in composition. *That is*, with due respect to Shakespeare and others, we want our girls to *communicate* freely with the live world around them rather than plunge into musty old books." Vladimir Nabokov, *Lolita* 179 (1955; repr. 1982).
- "But the base and, I believe, the country want someone in the White House who doesn't sound like another George Bush. *That is*, they want someone who doesn't suffer from an infallibility complex, who can admit mistakes and learn from them." Paul Krugman, "Wrong Is Right," *N.Y. Times*, 19 Feb. 2007, at A15.

Because of the close relationship between what follows *that is* and what comes before, a semicolon or an em-dash often substitutes for a period before *that is*—e.g.:

- "Definitions, contrary to popular opinion, tell us nothing about things. They only describe people's linguistic habits; *that is*, they tell us what noises people make under what conditions." S.I. Hayakawa, *Language in Thought and Action* 171 (1949).
- "In other words, the propositions of philosophy are not factual but linguistic in character—*that is*, they do not describe the behavior of physical, or even mental, objects; they express definitions, or the formal consequences of definitions." A.J. Ayer, *Language, Truth, and Logic* 57 (2d ed. 1952).
- "Wages and salaries serve the same economic purposes as other prices—*that is*, they guide the utilization of scarce resources which have alternative uses." Thomas Sowell, *Basic Economics* 144 (rev. ed. 2004).

The longer phrase, *that is to say*, is usually wordy in place of *that is*—e.g.: "The real solution is to make college football and men's college basketball programs uniform across NCAA divisions. *That is to say* [read *That is*], make Division 1-A schools compete within the same rules as Division III schools." Letter of Jerome Peirick, "College Athletes," *St. Louis Post-Dispatch*, 18 Sept. 1997, at B6. Cf. **namely** & **viz.**

that said. See **having said that.**

that which. When this stiff-sounding noun phrase can be replaced with *what*, it generally should be—e.g.: "Why continue to weep for *that which* [read *what*] is lost?" "NFL Poll: Luv 'Em and Leave 'Em," *Houston Chron.*, 28 Aug. 1997, at 2. Sometimes the word that's needed is *whatever*—e.g.: "*That which* [read *Whatever*] was subversive was perceived as liberating." Rachel Campbell-Johnston, "The Way We Look Now," *Nat'l Rev.*, 13 Oct. 1997, at 41. (Another possible revision: *Anything subversive was perceived as liberating*.)

But when *that* has an antecedent, *that which* is needed—e.g.: "The best financial advice is *that which* makes you the most money, not *that which* calls market tops or bottoms." Laszlo Birinyi Jr., "The Relative-Performance Trap," *Forbes*, 13 Oct. 1997, at 426.

When *that* becomes, in plural, *those*, the second word in this construction may be either *which* or *that*. But *that* is better because the relative pronoun is restrictive—e.g.:

- "The Florida task force could [investigate] a variety of creatures, including *those that* cause poisonous red tides in salt water." Steve Patterson, "Task Force to Examine Toxic Algae," *Fla. Times-Union*, 9 Oct. 1997, at B1.
- "Why are the 'cool' annuals *those which* [read *those that*] are expensive, hard to get and harder to grow?" Ann Lovejoy, "When It Comes to Annual Plants, Sometimes What's Less Gives More," *Seattle Post-Intelligencer*, 9 Oct. 1997, at E3.
- "Deep-sea species tend to grow more slowly than *those which* live [read *those that live* or *those living*] near the surface." "Fisheries: Drawing the Line," *Economist*, 5 Sept. 2015, at 63.

We use *that which* in the singular because *that that* is intolerably awkward, but in the plural *those that* isn't awkward at all.

the. A. Pronunciation. The pronunciation rule for the definite article parallels the usage rule for the indefinite articles *a* and *an*. Before a word that starts with a vowel sound, say /thee/ </thee/ ant> </thee/ elephant>. Before a word that starts with a consonant sound, say /thə/ </thə/ bee> </thə/ condor>. There is a twist, however: when saying the word for emphasis, say /thee/ no matter what word follows <that was /thee/ worst movie I've ever sat through>.

Most of us, when speaking naturally, get THUH distinction between THEE and THUH right without even thinking about it. It's when we start dwelling on it and imposing a misguided standard of correctness on ourselves that we begin to make a fetish out of saying THEE [before consonant sounds]. Then our speech becomes stilted and stagy,

LANGUAGE-CHANGE INDEX (For the full key, see front matter pp. xxxi, l–li.)
Stage 1: Rejected. **Stage 2:** Widely shunned. **Stage 3:** Widespread but . . . **Stage 4:** Ubiquitous but . . . **Stage 5:** Fully accepted.
Invariably inferior forms marked by asterisk (*). • Ratios represent frequency of prevalent forms vs. variants in current books.

because we are always trying to say things <u>THEE</u> "right" way instead of <u>THUH</u> natural way.

Charles Harrington Elster, BBBM at 465.

B. Capitalization in Names. On the question whether to capitalize the definite article when it begins a name, see CAPITALIZATION (C).

theater; theatre. The first is the usual spelling in AmE, the second in BrE. Somewhat surprisingly, the AmE spelling was not fixed until the 1940s. See -ER (B). The word is pronounced /**thee**-ə-tər/, not /**thee**-ay-tər/ or /thee-**ay**-tər/.

the case of. This FLOTSAM PHRASE is almost always best omitted. See **case (A).**

the fact that. See **fact (B).**

theft. See **burglary.**

The Hague. See **Netherlands.**

their. A. And *they're.* A book like this one need not explain such elementary distinctions. So it will not. But: "Liberals are again trying to explain why they lost their fifth presidential election in 20 years. They've been talking about what *they're* [read *their*] party should be for." "What's a Liberal For?" *Wall Street J.,* 13 Jan. 1989, at A6. For still another common mistake, see **there.** See also SPELLING (A).

B. Singular Antecedent with *their.* See CONCORD (B).

LANGUAGE-CHANGE INDEX
they're misused for their: Stage 1

theirs, an absolute possessive that takes no apostrophe, is sometimes wrongly written **their's*—e.g.:

- "The Badgers read Bennett's intensity. He read *their's* [read *theirs*]." Vic Feuerherd, "Bennett's Gift," *Wis. State J.,* 14 Nov. 2000, at D1.
- "Apparently, it can happen even in a marriage such as *their's* [read *theirs*], which lasted 33 years." Anna L. Bisol, "Montachusett People," *Telegram & Gaz.* (Worcester), 25 Mar. 2001, at 2.
- "The soon-to-be expanded dump's operators offer assurance that the stink isn't *their's* [read *theirs*]." "What's That Smell?" *Daily News* (L.A.), 25 Apr. 2001, at N14.

See POSSESSIVES (C).

LANGUAGE-CHANGE INDEX
*their's for theirs: Stage 1
Current ratio (<i>theirs</i> vs. <i>*their's</i>): 214 :1

*theirself. See **ourself.**

*theirselves, though common in the speech of the uneducated, is poor English. With origins in the late 18th century, it seldom appears in print—e.g.: "He encouraged those in attendance to be leaders, but to go beyond devoting *theirselves* [read *themselves*] to their careers to devote time to their family and personal lives." "Brentwood Honors 5 Leaders," *Tennessean,* 7 Oct. 1996, at F6. See PRONOUNS (E).

LANGUAGE-CHANGE INDEX
*theirselves for themselves: Stage 1
Current ratio (<i>themselves</i> vs. <i>*theirselves</i>): 3,182:1

theism; deism. These denote different ways of believing in God. *Theism* = the belief in one God who created and guides the universe. *Deism* = the belief in one God who created but does not intervene in the universe. For a discussion of those who reject both of these beliefs, see **atheist.**

the late. See **late.**

the likes of. See **like (F).**

*themself. See SEXISM (B).

then. A. As an Adjective. *Then* should not be hyphenated when alone as an adjective meaning "that existed or was so at that time" <the then mayor of San Diego>. When the word is part of a PHRASAL ADJECTIVE, the phrase should be hyphenated <then-mayor Rudolph Giuliani>, but not when it occurs after the noun <Rudolph Giuliani, then mayor of New York, said . . .>. Cf. **once & often (B).**

B. For *than.* This is a distressingly common error, especially in newsprint—e.g.: "He enjoyed much more autonomy with 'Face/Off' *then* [read *than*] he did with his other movies." Douglas J. Rowe, "Director Woo Puts a New Face on American Family Values," *Salt Lake Trib.,* 4 July 1997, at C8. For the reverse error, see **than (B).**

LANGUAGE-CHANGE INDEX
then misused for than: Stage 1

thence; whence; hence. *Thence* = from that place or source; for that reason. *Whence* = from there. *Hence* = (1) for this reason; therefore; (2) from this source; (3) from this time; from now; or (4) from this place; away. They're literary ARCHAISMS—except for *hence* in sense 1. See **hence & whence.**

thenceforth; *thenceforward. Both are antique-sounding, having enjoyed their heyday before 1800. The first remains standard. The second is a NEEDLESS VARIANT. For the misuse of *henceforth* for *thenceforth,* see **henceforth (D).**

the Netherlands. See **Netherlands.**

the number of. See **number (B).**

theorem. So spelled—not **theorum* (a misspelling traceable to the mid-19th century).

Current ratio: 4,085:1

theoretical; *theoretic. The standard form is *theoretical* in AmE and BrE alike—not **theoretic.* See -IC.

Current ratio: 25:1

theoretically. See SENTENCE ADVERBS.

therapist; *therapeutist. The standard term has always been *therapist.* **Therapeutist,* sometimes used in the late-19th and early-20th centuries, is now obsolete in AmE and BrE alike.

Current ratio: 1,782:1

there for *they're* or *their* is an embarrassing confusion of homophones. It's the type of solecism one expects from a grade-school student, not from a professional writer or editor. But it is a common inadvertence in journalism—e.g.:

- "And that's where these radio stations are really missing the boat, because *there* [read *they're*] missing the folks who hold the purse strings to all the disposable income." Brad Tooley, "Canyon Views," *Canyon News*, 13 Jan. 1994, at 1, 2.
- "Many market observers expect to see lesser quantities of fuel oil purchased with each transaction as buyers keep *there* [read *their*] inventories low." Alan Herbst, "Tight Supplies Support U.S. Atlantic Residual Markets," *Platt's Oilgram Price Rep.*, 22 Apr. 1996, at 1.
- "With money saved by not paying property tax, people could keep *there* [read *their*] homes in better condition, afford vacations and buy more." Glenda F. Cunard, "Higher Sales Tax," *Indianapolis Star*, 19 July 1996, at A9.

See **their.**

LANGUAGE-CHANGE INDEX
1. *there* misused for *they're*: Stage 1
2. *there* misused for *their*: Stage 1

thereabouts; *thereabout. Although any writer might be well advised to avoid either term, the former is preferred and overwhelmingly more common <it all happened in 2006 or thereabouts>. Cf. **whereabout(s).**
Current ratio: 5:1

there are. See **there is** & EXPLETIVES.

thereby. See **therefore** (D).

therefore. A. Punctuation Around. One must take care in the punctuation of *therefore*. When a comma appears before *therefore*, the preceding word gets emphasized <it was John, therefore, who deserved the accolades> (suggesting that somebody else got the accolades but didn't deserve them). (Cf. **however** (B).) Or you can reverse the order of the words to put *therefore* just before the word needing emphasis, but without surrounding commas <it was therefore John who deserved the accolades>. But the word is often mispunctuated. To see the false emphasis in each of the following examples, read the word preceding *therefore* as if it were strongly stressed:

- "'I have continuously [read *continually*] heard from residents about their firm opposition to the influx [read *establishment*] of such a clinic, which would inevitably increase crime in our community,' said Harris, adding that she, *therefore*, had approached Kearse to reach a resolution." Sid Cassese, "Hempstead Wins Drug Clinic Battle," *Newsday* (N.Y.), 30 July 1997, at A23. (Read: . . . *adding that she had therefore approached Kearse to reach a resolution.* Part of the trouble in this example stems from faulty placement of the adverb. See ADVERBS (A).) For the misuse of *continuously* in that sentence, see **continual.**
- "He was a Roman Catholic and felt all citizens of the country should share his religious beliefs. He, *therefore*, began to arrest all Orthodox Catholics." "Catholics, Nazis

in World War II," *Providence J.-Bull.*, 22 Aug. 1997, at B7. (Read: *He therefore began to arrest all Orthodox Catholics.*)
- "The results would allow parents in Alabama to know how their children fared against children in Minnesota and they, *therefore*, could agitate for better instruction when their children fell behind." Jim Wooten, "Setting School Agenda," *Atlanta J.-Const.*, 10 Sept. 1997, at A12. (Read: *The results would allow parents in Alabama to know how their children fared against children in Minnesota, and they could therefore agitate for better instruction when their children fell behind.*)

B. Run-on Sentences with. One should take care not to create RUN-ON SENTENCES by joining two independent clauses with *therefore*—e.g.: "Byfield had hired him for a ridiculous reason: 'He grew up in New York, *therefore* I liked him.'" Kenneth Whyte, "Let Byfields Be Byfields," *Saturday Night*, 1 Feb. 1996, at 15 (mispunctuating an oral comment). (A possible revision: *He grew up in New York—therefore, I liked him.* Or: *He grew up in New York; therefore, I liked him.* Or: *He grew up in New York. Therefore, I liked him.*)

C. And *therefor*. *Therefore* (stress on first syllable), an adverbial conjunction, means "for that reason, consequently." It's the usual word. *Therefor* (stress on last syllable), adv., & adj., means "for that" or "for it" <he showed charity and was finally rewarded therefor> <the recognition therefor>. Some writers mistake the two terms, especially in law (where *therefor* appears most frequently). As Eric Partridge noted, "many quite good writers do not even know of the existence of *therefor*" (*U&A* at 332). Maybe that's because it's legal JARGON. If the good writers that Partridge mentions start overusing it, they'll risk no longer being called "good."

D. For *thereby*. *Therefore* shouldn't be confused, as it sometimes is, with *thereby* (= by that means; in that way)—e.g.: "The bank recently completed negotiations to offer a student lending package in conjunction with Columbia University in New York, *therefore* [read *thereby*] providing student loans to college students at an expensive school." Marian King, "Banks Given More Incentives to Offer Loans for Students," *Sun-Sentinel* (Ft. Lauderdale), 1 Jan. 1997, at 14.

LANGUAGE-CHANGE INDEX
therefore misused for *thereby*: Stage 1

E. *So therefore. See **so** (D).

there is; there are. A. As Signals of Clutter. These phrases, though sometimes useful, can also be the enemies of a lean writing style, as several commentators have observed—e.g.:

- "The habit of beginning statements with the impersonal and usually vague *there is* or *there are* shoves the really significant verb into subordinate place instead of letting it stand vigorously on its own feet." David Lambuth et al., *The Golden Book on Writing* 19 (1964).
- "The trouble with 'there' has nothing to do with grammar or with 'correctness' of any kind. It's a perfectly proper word, and it moves in the best circles; you will find it in

abundance in the work of the most distinguished writers. But the fact remains that it is one of the most insidious enemies a beginning writer faces in his search for style. It is the enemy of style because it seldom adds anything but clutter to a sentence. And nothing saps the vitality of language as quickly as meaningless clutter." Lucile Vaughan Payne, *The Lively Art of Writing* 64–65 (1965).

- "The *there* construction is not to be condemned out of hand; it is both idiomatic and common in the best literature; it is clumsy and to be avoided with a passive verb; and in view of the prejudice against it [for promoting wordiness], the writer who uses it discriminatingly should take heart and be prepared to defend himself, for defense is indeed possible." Roy H. Copperud, *American Usage and Style: The Consensus* 380–81 (1980).

When is the phrase *there is* defensible? When the writer is addressing the existence of something. That is, if the only real recourse is to use the verb *exist*, then *there is* is perfectly fine—e.g.:

- "*There is* unlimited competition for our entertainment dollars." Jason Whitlock, "Royals' Big Shots Must Go," *Kansas City Star*, 21 Sept. 1997, at C1.
- "*There is* no positive relationship between aid levels and economic growth." Doug Bandow, "Death to Foreign Aid Opinion," *Fortune*, 29 Sept. 1997, at 52.

Otherwise, though, the phrase should typically be cut—e.g.: "*There is* wide support among congressional Republicans for a flat tax." "IRS Faces New Round of Scrutiny," *Dallas Morning News*, 20 Sept. 1997, at F1. (A possible revision: *Congressional Republicans tend to support a flat tax.* Or: *Many congressional Republicans support a flat tax.*) The phrase *there is wide support* has become a CLICHÉ among political commentators. And it does exactly what Lambuth and Payne warn against: it robs the sentence of a good strong verb.

B. Number with. The number of the verb is controlled by whether the inverted subject that follows *is* or *are* is singular or plural. Mistakes are common—e.g.:

- "He said there *is* [read *are*] several truckloads of nuclear waste." Frank Munger, "State Bans DOE Nuke Waste," *Knoxville News-Sentinel*, 18 Apr. 1996, at A1.
- "With an onslaught of fresh new talented female R&B groups, there *is* [read *are*] several ways you, the consumer, can decipher whether or not you should purchase their products." Craig D. Frazier, "'Tha Truth,' a Group of Talented Young Female Rappers with Style," *N.Y. Amsterdam News*, 15 Mar. 1997, at 30.

Constructions with *seem to be* and *appear to be* follow the same model: the number of the inverted subject dictates the number of the verb. Again, mistakes are common—e.g.:

- "There *appears* [read *appear*] to be several possibilities for transporting the Algerian gas under a new contract." Robert D. Hershey Jr., "Christopher Will Lead Gas Talks with Algeria," *N.Y. Times*, 15 Apr. 1981, at D1.
- "There *seems* [read *seem*] to be two key reasons for Capriati's renaissance." Sandra Harwitt, "Capriati's Life Back in Focus," *USA Today*, 26 Jan. 2000, at C3.

Especially when followed by a negative, *there* has in many minds come to represent a single situation. It therefore often appears, though wrongly, with a

singular verb—e.g.: " 'There *wasn't* [read *weren't*] any other witnesses.' " Rebecca Thatcher, "Girl's Report of Abduction, Sexual Assault Investigated," *Austin Am.-Statesman*, 9 Dec. 1994, at B1 (quoting the Austin, Texas, police chief). The person who says "there wasn't . . . [plural]" here would never say "they was." See EXPLETIVES & INVERSION.

LANGUAGE-CHANGE INDEX
1. *there is* (or *there's*) with a plural subject
<there's three things>: Stage 2
Current ratio (*there are three things* vs.
**there's three things*): 43:1
2. *there is* (or *there's*) with a compound subject whose first member is singular <there's an outhouse and a sump pump out back>: Stage 4

thesaurus (= a book or online resource that supplies synonyms) has long formed the standard plural *thesauri*. But since about 1960, *thesauruses* has climbed in frequency, especially in AmE. (See PLURALS (B).) E.g.:

- "In addition, there are the computerized *thesauruses* included in most word-processing programs." Leslie T. Sharpe & Irene Gunther, *Editing Fact and Fiction* 204 (1994).
- "*Thesauruses* also increased in popularity, rising from 22nd in terms of numbers of adult purchasers in 1994, to 10th last year." Debbie Davies, "Mapping Out the Best of the Books," *Independent*, 31 May 1997, at 19.
- "Teaching students how to use dictionaries and *thesauruses* is essential since many English words have multiple meanings and students have to choose the appropriate meaning for the context." Betty Roe et al., *Secondary School Literacy Instruction* 136 (2010).

LANGUAGE-CHANGE INDEX
thesauruses: Stage 5
Current ratio (*thesauri* vs. *thesauruses*): 3:1

these. See POINTING WORDS.

***these kind of;** ***these type of;** ***these sort of.** These illogical forms were not uncommon in the 17th and early 18th centuries, but by the mid-18th they had been stigmatized. Today they brand the speaker or writer as slovenly. They appear most commonly in reported speech, but sometimes not—e.g.:

- "What's disheartening about this, from the Lebanon point of view, is what happens next for a Lebanon team that felt it was built for *these kind of challenges* [read *this kind of challenge*]." Mike Gross, "Berks Power Chops Down Cedars," *Patriot & Evening News* (Harrisburg), 6 Sept. 1997, at C1.
- "It's just that *these sort of things* [read *this sort of thing*] always seem[s] to happen to the Angels." J.A. Adande, "Shedding His Wings," *L.A. Times*, 17 Sept. 1997, at C1.
- "But by making *these type of incidents* [read *this type of incident*] racial, he not only is [read *not only is he*] doing his player a disservice, he is failing her as a father." Bill Stamps, "Who Is the Racist?" *L.A. Times*, 20 Sept. 1997, at B7. For more on the nonparallel construction in that sentence, see PARALLELISM.

Of course, it's perfectly acceptable to write *these kinds* or *these types* or *these sorts*, as many writers conscientiously do—e.g.:

- "It's *these kinds* of stories that are scary." David Horowitz, "Fight Back: What to Do When It's Time for New Doctor," *Daily News* (L.A.), 26 Apr. 1997, at L16.
- "I told my sister that setting up her own Website would allow her to propagate *these kinds* of activities." Stewart Alsop, "Alsop to Publishers: Wake Up!" *Fortune*, 29 Sept. 1997, at 257.

LANGUAGE-CHANGE INDEX
these followed by *kind, type,* or *sort* in the singular: Stage 2
Current ratio (*these kinds of* vs. *these kind of): 13:1

thesis (= [1] a long research paper prepared as part of a degree requirement, [2] an idea or opinion posited on a subject, or [3] the statement of an essay's primary point) makes the plural *theses* /**thee**-seez/.

they. A. Number. On the use of this word as a singular term, see CONCORD (B), PRONOUNS (D) & SEXISM (B). See also **no one.**

B. Corporate *they*. Just as the first-person *we* often carries a corporate sense (see FIRST PERSON (B)), the third-person *they* can express a corporate policy or plan. This usage is a CASUALISM—e.g.: "A magazine editor writes to say *they* are doing an article on the healing power of laughter." Andy Rooney, *Common Nonsense* 178 (2002).

they'd better; they better. See **better (A).**

they're. See **their.**

thief. Pl. *thieves*—not *thiefs. The mistaken plural occasionally appears in print—e.g.: "After decades of being in bed with some of the biggest *thiefs* [read *thieves*] in the world, the World Bank has announced that an internal investigation has revealed 'alarming information' about World Bank corruption." "Deep Shoveling in the World Bank Cleanup," *Wash. Times*, 23 July 1998, at A22. See PLURALS (C).

LANGUAGE-CHANGE INDEX
*thiefs for *thieves*: Stage 1
Current ratio (*thieves* vs. *thiefs): 499:1

thimbleful. Pl. *thimblefuls*, not *thimblesful. See PLURALS (G).

Current ratio: 13:1

thing after thing (is) (are). See SUBJECT–VERB AGREEMENT (H).

thingy; thingamajig; thingamabob. During the 18th and 19th centuries, the first two emerged as CASUALISMS to denote something one can't remember the name of or doesn't know the name of. Among the variant spellings are *thingumajig and *thingumabob. The word *thingy*—which also first appeared in the 18th century but isn't recorded in most dictionaries—was used with a frequency about equal to that of the

longer words until 1990 or so, when it suddenly surged in popularity.

Current ratio (in order of headwords): 15:3:1

think. See **don't think.**

think coming, another. See **another think coming.**

third person should be pluralized *third persons*, never *third people.

Current ratio: 84:1

Third World. Originally, this term denoted the group of underdeveloped nations (especially in Africa and Asia) not aligned with either Western democracies (i.e., the *First World*—or *Free World*) or Communist countries (i.e., the *Second World*) during the Cold War.

But as the world turns, so does the language. In his *New Political Dictionary* (1993), William Safire notes that "with the end of the bipolar geopolitical world in 1990, a multipolar world was spawned; the third world became the South in a North–South relationship." Safire quotes Henry Grunwald from *Foreign Affairs*: "The 'Third World' urgently needs to be renamed, and not only because the 'Second World' has collapsed. The inadequacy of a label covering everything from dysfunctional non-countries in Africa to emerging industrial powers in South America indicates a lack of press understanding and attention." *NPD* at 795.

As Safire's example above illustrates, capitalization styles differ on this phrase: *The New York Times* uses lowercase, while the *AP Stylebook* uses caps. The latter choice is more logical, since the original sense paralleled the always-capitalized *Free World*, which in turn had historical foundation in the always-capitalized *New World*.

this. See POINTING WORDS.

thither. See **hither.**

thitherto. See **hitherto.**

***tho.** See **although.**

thoroughgoing (a solid word) means "thorough," but it connotes zeal or ardor. It is not, therefore, merely a NEEDLESS VARIANT of *thorough*—e.g.:

- "There is no question the charter needs a *thoroughgoing* review and rewrite." "L.A. City Elections," *L.A. Times*, 16 Mar. 1997, at M4.
- "[The governor] hasn't risked one iota of political capital to put such *thoroughgoing* reform on the state's agenda." "Give Back the Money," *Sacramento Bee*, 12 May 1997, at B6.

those. See POINTING WORDS.

***those kind of;** ***those type of;** ***those sort of.** See ***these kind of.**

those which; those that. See **that which.**

LANGUAGE-CHANGE INDEX (For the full key, see front matter pp. xxxi, l–li.)
Stage 1: Rejected. **Stage 2:** Widely shunned. **Stage 3:** Widespread but . . . **Stage 4:** Ubiquitous but . . . **Stage 5:** Fully accepted.
Invariably inferior forms marked by asterisk (*). • Ratios represent frequency of prevalent forms vs. variants in current books.

though. See **although.**

thought leader (= a person or company with a reputation for innovation and success in a field) is a VOGUE WORD that has been around since the 1970s—e.g.: "To get the message across, Monsanto will aim its television advertising at people who write letters to editors and speak out on public issues. It will direct its magazine ads to '*thought leaders*' through campaigns in the three national general newsweeklies and National Geographic." Donald P. Burke, "Monsanto Speaks Out on Benefit/Risk," *Chemical Week*, 26 Oct. 1977, at 5.

Like many vogue words before and since, this one has suffered from its share of ridicule—e.g.: "Each day certain economists and others warn us that the American economy is in serious trouble. . . . This caterwauling would be amusing except that so many of our politicos and supposed *thought-leaders* take this stuff seriously." Malcolm S. Forbes Jr., "Major Problem with the American Economy: Hypochondria," *Forbes*, 9 Mar. 1987, at 33.

A true "thought leader" would never think of using such a term any more than such CLICHÉS as *cutting edge* or *thinking outside the box*.

though . . . yet. See **although . . . yet** & CORRELATIVE CONJUNCTIONS.

thrash; thresh. *Thrash* = (1) to beat soundly, flog; (2) to defeat decisively; or (3) to move or toss about violently. *Thresh*, which sometimes carries those meanings, should be restricted to the sense "to separate grain from chaff by beating."

threefold. See **twofold.**

***360-degree turnaround.** See **180-degree turnaround.**

threepeat, a PORTMANTEAU WORD dating from the late 1980s, denotes a third consecutive championship won by a competitor or team. It is wordplay that combines *three* and *repeat*. In sports talk, the term has become something of a VOGUE WORD. It is also used as a verb <Do you think the team might threepeat?>. It should be solid, as shown, not hyphenated.

threnody /thren-ə-dee/ (= a funeral song; elegy) is the standard spelling in AmE and BrE alike. **Threnode* is a variant.

Current ratio: 373:1

thresh. See **thrash.**

threshold. So spelled. **Threshhold*, a common misspelling that emerged in the 19th century, occasionally appears in print—e.g.: "We dared to cross the *threshhold* [read *threshold*] from sophisticated, drawing-room, strangulated drollery to the wilderness where we not only faced the lion's roar but smelled the breath of their bad habits." Letter of Richard Harris (the actor), "A Sharp Kick from a Man Called Horse," *Sunday Times* (London), 6 Aug. 1995, § 3, at 8. The word is not a compound of the verb *hold*, but rather a modern form of the Old English *thaerscwold* ("doorsill").

thrice (= three times) is a literary ARCHAISM that is sometimes useful. Common in the 17th and 18th centuries, it has steadily declined in use since about 1800. But it appears not to be going extinct—e.g.: "He's *thrice*-divorced and no longer the superstar of Brisbane radio." Steven Rosen, "'Serenade' Offbeat Comedy with Certain Dark Elements," *Denver Post*, 8 Aug. 1997, at F3. When *thrice* follows the verb—and is not, as in the previous example, part of a PHRASAL ADJECTIVE—it sounds pretentious. E.g.: "'He may like a hot dog,' says Steve Tobash, golf pro at the Army–Navy Country Club, where Clinton has played *thrice* [read *three times*] since rehabilitation. 'But if he eats a hot dog, he works it off.'" Kevin Walker, "Quips, Quotes, Quibbles & Bits," *Tampa Trib.*, 10 Aug. 1997, at 8.

thrive > thrived > thrived. *Thrived*, not **throve*, is now considered the better past tense—e.g.: "He released them and—with no natural predators—they *throve* [read *thrived*] in the abundant wetlands." William J. Kole, "Muskrats' Tunneling Imperils Dutch Dikes," *Plain Dealer* (Cleveland), 28 Aug. 1997, at A4. Likewise, *thrived*, not **thriven*, is the better past participle. The irregular forms persisted longer in BrE than in AmE, but in all varieties they were obsolescent by 1950. See IRREGULAR VERBS.

LANGUAGE-CHANGE INDEX
thrived as a past form: Stage 5
Current ratio (*thrived* vs. **throve*): 14:1

throes of, in the. In this phrase, meaning "struggling in the process of (something very painful or difficult)" <in the throes of childbirth>, *throes* is sometimes mistakenly spelled *throws* (an error that spread during the 1990s)—e.g.:

• "'I turned on the light and observed my much-loved pet in the *throws* [read *throes*] of a grand mal seizure.'" Liz Quinlan, "A Painful Decision Made Even Harder," *Syracuse Herald-J.*, 11 July 1997, at B8 (quoting an anonymous reader).
• "Winner Turner is still in the *throws* [read *throes*] of a battle with the British authorities over a positive drugs test." "Johnson 'Running for the Money,'" *Irish Times*, 18 Aug. 1997, at 63.

The word is misused when the situation does not involve serious pain or difficulty—e.g.:

• "The legal action took HBO executives by surprise, since they were in the *throes* [read *process*] of sweetening Gandolfini's deal for the upcoming season." Cara DiPasquale & Kris Kamopp, "Gandolfini Says HBO Violated His Contract," *Chicago Trib.*, 11 Mar. 2003, at 28.
• "The usual closing-time shenanigans . . . take an obtuse turn when it is revealed that Nate might actually be *in the throes of* [read *having*] serious feelings for bar regular Andrea." Julio Martinez, "King of Clubs," *Daily Variety*, 18 Mar. 2003, at 38.

LANGUAGE-CHANGE INDEX
1. **in the throws* for *in the throes*: Stage 1
Current ratio (*in the throes of* vs.
*in the throws of): 36:1
2. *throes* used without a sense of struggle: Stage 2

throw > threw > thrown. So inflected. **Throwed* is dialectal, appearing mostly in reported speech of nonstandard speakers—e.g.: "'He just changed direction on me real fast and *throwed* me,' he [a cowboy] said." Dan R. Barber, "Hell on Hooves," *Dallas Morning News*, 17 May 2001, at S1. See DIALECT & IRREGULAR VERBS.

***thru,** a variant spelling of *through*, can be traced to the 17th century, but it had little currency until the early 20th. It's a CASUALISM to be shunned in serious writing. Oddly, it appears in parts of the Internal Revenue Code applicable to "pass-thru" entities and "look-thru" rules.

Current ratio (*through* vs. ***thru*): 613:1

thrust > thrust > thrust. So inflected. **Thrusted* is a common error—e.g.:

- "They *thrusted* [read *thrust*] pens, paper, footballs and jerseys over the fence top for Young to sign." Gary Swan, "Young Already Trying to Run 49ers' Camp," *S.F. Chron.*, 20 July 1998, at C1.
- "Kournikova *thrusted* [read *thrust*] her fists and racket in the air." Don Norcross, "Anna Gets Her Guns Going," *San Diego Union-Trib.*, 5 Aug. 2000, at D1.
- "He lunged, he *thrusted* [read *thrust*], he parried and chopped." Marie Villari, "Ironing Out the Wrinkles in This Story," *Post-Standard* (Syracuse), 8 Mar. 2001, Madison §, at 5.

See IRREGULAR VERBS.

LANGUAGE-CHANGE INDEX
**thrusted* for past-tense *thrust*: Stage 1
Current ratio (*were thrust* vs. ***were thrusted*): 537:1

thunderous. So spelled in AmE and BrE alike—not **thundrous*.

Current ratio: 303:1

thus. A. General Senses. A formal adverb that dates from Old English, *thus* has four meanings: (1) in this or that manner <one does it thus>; (2) so <thus far>; (3) hence, consequently; and (4) as an example. In senses 3 and 4, *thus*, when it begins a clause, should usually have a comma after it.

B. *Thusly.* *Thus* itself being an adverb, it needs no *-ly*. Although the NONWORD **thusly* has appeared in otherwise respectable writing since it emerged in the late 19th century, it remains a lapse—e.g.:

- "Jackson, a counterpuncher by nature, responded *thusly* [read *thus*] yesterday to such thoughts: 'His people may think this is a circus, but . . . .'" Ron Borges, "Jackson Has a Rallying Cry vs. Lewis: 'No Surrender,'" *Boston Globe*, 5 May 1994, at 79.
- "A Seattle critic once reviewed Bosworth's big movie debut *thusly* [read *thus*]: 'To call "Stone Cold" garbage is to give garbage a bad name.'" Andy Edelstein, "The TV-Jock Hall of Fame," *Newsday* (N.Y.), 6 Apr. 1997, at C16.
- "He does not plan on becoming the next No. 1 singles champion in college as is his brother Ty and *thusly* [read *thus*] does not seek to put in that much work." Herky Cush, "Multi-Sport Existence Proves Just Bliss-Ful," *Orlando Sentinel*, 25 May 1997, at 11.

For other adverbs ending in a superfluous *-ly*, see ADVERBS (C).

LANGUAGE-CHANGE INDEX
**thusly* for the adverb *thus*: Stage 1
Current ratio (*thus* vs. ***thusly*): 1,016:1

tibia (= a bone in the front of the leg below the knee), perhaps because it appears mostly in technical contexts, forms the plural *tibiae* (/**tib**-i-ee/) much more often than *tibias*. Cf. **fibula.**

Current ratio: 3:1

tidbit; titbit. These by-forms denote (1) "a fine morsel of food," or (2) "a choice piece of information, esp. of a gossipy kind." Both date from the 17th century. In World English and AmE alike, the spelling *titbit* generally held sway until the late 19th century. Beginning in the 1880s, *tidbit* overtook it in frequency of occurrence in AmE. The same thing happened in World English in the late 1930s. Since 1980 the predominance of *tidbit* has been dramatic. Yet in BrE, the reduplicative *titbit* has always predominated. One might speculate that a puritanical resistance to prurient-sounding words accounts for the American changeover.

tie makes, in the present participle, *tying*. **Tieing*, though common, is incorrect—e.g.:

- "Cam Neely scored the *tieing* [read *tying*] and winning goals as Boston improved to 8–0–2 in its last 10 games against the Islanders." Doug Chapman, "Islanders Marooned by Bruins, Who Can't Be Beaten," *Providence J.-Bull.*, 19 Mar. 1995, at C9.
- "As Dillehay said, *tieing* [read *tying*] overhand knots is 'the kind of thing nature cannot do.'" David L. Chandler, "The First Humans Arrived Earlier than We Thought—But How Much Earlier?" *Boston Globe*, 17 Mar. 1997, at C1.

LANGUAGE-CHANGE INDEX
**tieing* for *tying*: Stage 1
Current ratio (*tying* vs. ***tieing*): 229:1

***tike.** See **tyke.**

***'til.** See **till.**

TILDE. See DIACRITICAL MARKS.

till; until. *Till* is, like *until*, a bona fide preposition and conjunction. Though perhaps a little less formal than *until*, *till* is neither colloquial nor substandard. As Anthony Burgess put it, "In nonpoetic English we use 'till' and 'until' indifferently." *A Mouthful of Air* 158 (1992). It's especially common in BrE—e.g.:

- "After the First World War, Hatay, named by Attaturk after the Hittites, fell into the hands of the French, who did not return it *till* 1939." Daniel Farson, "Rich Rewards in the Land of the Hittites," *Independent*, 1 Apr. 1995, at 37.
- "It was not *till* 1994 that the New Yorker unmasked Reage as journalist Dominique Aury—Paulhan's long-standing lover." Jonathan Romney, "Story of O and S&M," *Guardian*, 21 Mar. 1997, at T9.

LANGUAGE-CHANGE INDEX (For the full key, see front matter pp. xxxi, l–li.)
Stage 1: Rejected. **Stage 2:** Widely shunned. **Stage 3:** Widespread but . . . **Stage 4:** Ubiquitous but . . . **Stage 5:** Fully accepted.
Invariably inferior forms marked by asterisk (*). • Ratios represent frequency of prevalent forms vs. variants in current books.

- "He works from dawn *till* dusk, six days a week." Adrian Brewer, "The House of God That Justo Built," *Daily Telegraph*, 31 Mar. 1997, at 17.

And it still occurs in AmE—e.g.: "In medium skillet, sauté the garlic *till* golden. Add onion, wait *till* brown." Jan Norris, "Latin, Asian Fests Add Spice to Weekend," *Palm Beach Post*, 23 Mar. 1995, at FN1.

But the myth of the word's low standing persists. Some writers and editors mistakenly think that *till* deserves a bracketed *sic*—e.g.: " 'Trading in cotton futures was not practiced *till* [*sic*] after the close of the Civil War, spot cotton being quoted like other stocks in cents, halves, quarters, etc.' " J. Steve Oliver & B. Kim Nichols, "Early Days," *School Science & Mathematics*, 1 Apr. 1997, at 216 (in which the *sic* appeared in the original source being quoted).

If a form deserves a *sic*, it's the incorrect ***'til: the word has no literary history as a contraction. Not until the 1980s was it widely perceived to be one. Worse yet is ***'till, which is abominable—e.g.: "A month or two remain *'till* [read *till*] you grab your dancing shoes, plus a crew of pals or that special date." Francine Parnes, "Primping for the Prom," *Denver Post*, 21 Mar. 1997, at E1.

Language-Change Index
1. ***'til for *till*: Stage 2
Current ratio (*till* vs. ***'til): 73:1
2. ***'till for *till*: Stage 1
Current ratio (*till* vs. ***'till): 150:1

timbal. See **timpani** (A).

timbre; timber. These are different words in both BrE and AmE. *Timbre* (/**tim**-bər/ or /**tam**-bər/) is primarily a musical term meaning "tone quality." E.g.: "Nor was his voice, when he spoke, of a *timbre* calculated to lull any apprehensions which his aspect might have inspired." P.G. Wodehouse, *The Return of Jeeves* 116 (1954). *Timber* (/**tim**-bər/) is the correct form in all wood-related senses. Cf. -ER (B).

timeout, in sportswriting and parenting, is increasingly spelled as one word. The plural is *timeouts*, not **timesout*. See PLURALS (G).

*time period is a common REDUNDANCY that became widespread in the late 20th century. The word *period* is almost always sufficient—e.g.:

- "And the average low drops from 70 to 62 for the same *time period* [read *period*]." Bill Bair, "September a Wet Month, but It Wasn't a Soggy One," *Ledger* (Lakeland, Fla.), 1 Oct. 1996, at B3.
- "That is why Barlow said his company requires that the right of easement be good for a certain *time period* [read *period*], such as 10 years." Judy Harriman, "Clearing the Path for Condo Sale," *St. Petersburg Times*, 1 Nov. 1996, at D2.

Cf. **period of time.**

*times less than. See ILLOGIC (G).

*times more than. See ILLOGIC (H).

time when. See **reason why.**

timorous; temerarious. These similar-sounding words are antonyms. *Timorous* (/**tim**-ə-rəs/) = fearfully reluctant to act. (It's related to *timid*.) *Temerarious* (/tem-ə-**rair**-ee-əs/) = foolhardily daring; rash and reckless. (It's related to *temerity*. See **temerity.**) The latter, a literary word, has never been in widespread use.

timpani. A. A Tale of Two Words. First, there's the Latinate word *tympanum*, which denotes (1) the eardrum, (2) the middle ear, (3) the diaphragm in an old-fashioned telephone, (4) in architecture, the vertical recessed face of a pediment, as over a door, (5) a hand drum of ancient Greece or Rome, (6) a modern kettledrum, or (7) a drumhead—that is, the stretched membrane of a drum. The plural is *tympana* in senses 1–4 and *tympani* in the drum senses (5–7).

Second, there's the Italianate *timpano*, denoting a kettledrum. The plural is *timpani*.

In music, the words are almost always used in the plural. *Tympani* has a long tradition in English-language print sources, tracing back to the 18th century. Its rival, *timpani*, didn't take root in the language until the 1920s, first in BrE and then in AmE. From 1950 to the present day, the two spellings have been jostling for predominance in BrE print sources; the competition did not become close in AmE print sources until the 1980s. But over the sweep of the period known as Modern English, *tympani* has long held sway.

What happened is that in the early 20th century, musicians and musicologists recognized *timpani* as an Italian word—the most frequent singular being *timpano*. A leading mid-20th-century musical encyclopedia has this entry (in full): "**timpani.** The Italian word for kettledrums. Printers and copyists often substitute *y* for *i* in this word; a mistake, since the letter *y* does not exist in the Italian language." 8 *Grove's Dictionary of Music and Musicians* 480 (Eric Blom ed., 1954).

In AmE journalism, *timpani* now preponderates by a significant margin. This might have come about because *timpani* is perceived as the direct Italian etymon, whereas *tympani* goes back to a Latin spelling. The singular being *timpano*, musicians and musicologists might have thought the *-y-* simply wrong—mixing an Italian spelling with a Latinate one, the Latin singular being *tympanum*. Yet *tympani* is the traditional plural for the Latin word in drum senses.

Language-Change Index
timpani spelled *tympani*: Stage 5
Current ratio (*tympani* vs. *timpani*
in World English): 2:1

B. Singular or Plural. The word *timpani*—though borrowed into English as the plural form of the Italian singular *timpano*—has become interchangeable singular or plural. Most commonly, of course, the word is plural—e.g.: "The Jefferson Symphony Orchestra has been awarded a $14,110 grant by the Bonfils-Stanton Foundation for a set of four new *timpani*." "Good for You," *Rocky Mountain News* (Denver), 3 Oct. 1996, at

D14. But it's often singular as well. Even professional musicians commonly refer to *a timpani*, not *a timpano. E.g.:

- "[It is an opera] house where Mozart's double-bass or *timpani* is heard as clearly as the soprano." Anthony Lewis, "To Love and Be Wise," *N.Y. Times*, 11 July 1994, at A15.
- "I hear a *timpani*." "Hot Ticket Items," *Sacramento Bee*, 17 May 1996, at TK3.
- "The incessant beat of an Aztec drum, which looks like a bongo but booms like a *timpani*, permeates the entire building." Hsiao-Ching Chou, "Fiddle Fervor Woman Passes on Legacy of Unique Instrument," *Denver Post*, 28 Aug. 1996, at G1.

See PLURALS (B).

LANGUAGE-CHANGE INDEX
timpani as a singular: Stage 5

C. **Timpani drum.* This phrase is a REDUNDANCY that had little currency till the late 20th century. It should be halved—e.g.:

- "The pit . . . is made up of 14 people on xylophones, marimbas, chimes, gongs, *tympani drums* [read *timpani* or *kettledrums*], glockenspiels, bells, triangles, tambourines and more." Michael Colton, "Esprit de Corps," *Boston Globe*, 17 Aug. 1994, at 73.
- "A *timpani drum* [read *timpani* or *kettledrum*], its head torn, . . . was serving as a trash can." Sandy Strickland, "Paxon Band on the Run in Search of Donations," *Fla. Times-Union*, 28 Aug. 1996, at 1.
- "Percussive instruments can also be played in an expressive sustaining fashion, such as a roll on a snare or *timpani drum* [read *timpani* or *kettledrum*], where the drum is struck repeatedly." Ethan Winer, *The Audio Expert* 626 (2012).

LANGUAGE-CHANGE INDEX
*timpani drum for *timpani* or *kettledrum*: Stage 1
Current ratio (*timpani* vs. *kettledrum* vs.
*timpani drum): 123:32:1

tinderbox (= [1] a box for holding kindling, or [2] a source of incitement, esp. to violence) is sometimes misspelled *tenderbox—e.g.:

- "But the detention center is an emotional *tenderbox* [read *tinderbox*], with tensions running high, said Dr. Don R. Heacock, a psychiatrist, who explained that residents are 'very often frightened and anxious about being incarcerated.'" Elsa Brenner, "Trying to Avoid Giving Up on Young Offenders," *N.Y. Times*, 3 Aug. 1997, § 13WC, at 1.
- "The number of people whose immune systems are suppressed to support transplanted organs or to fight cancer added to the *tenderbox* [read *tinderbox*]. In the 1980s, in areas of Africa devastated by political upheaval and AIDS, the white plague flickered, caught fire and exploded." Jon Franklin, "One Patient at a Time," *News & Observer* (Raleigh), 27 Feb. 2000, at A1.

LANGUAGE-CHANGE INDEX
tinderbox misspelled *tenderbox: Stage 1

tine (= a prong on a fork, pitchfork, or antlers) is the standard spelling. *Tyne is a variant.

Current ratio: 37:1

tinge, vb., traditionally makes the present participle *tinging* in AmE and BrE alike—not *tingeing.

tinker's damn (= something valueless) is the standard spelling. The phrase's mid-19th-century origin is unknown, but it probably alludes to the tinkers' reputation for profanity. **Tinker's dam* is a variant spelling, said to have originated from the tinker's little dam of bread to keep solder from running through a hole in a pot being mended. See ETYMOLOGY (D).

Current ratio: 3:1

tinnitus (= a ringing or other sound in the ears not caused by external stimulus) is so spelled, not *tinnitis. (The suffix *-itis* means "inflammation," and this word has nothing to do with it.) But the erroneous spelling is hardly uncommon—e.g.: "A free presentation on brain stem pressure, which can cause *tinnitis* [read *tinnitus*] and dizziness, will be held at 5:30 p.m. today." "Health Watch," *Pantagraph* (Bloomington, Ill.), 29 Jan. 2001, at D2. The word is best pronounced /ti-**NI**-təs/, not /**tin**-i-təs/.

LANGUAGE-CHANGE INDEX
tinnitus misspelled *tinnitis: Stage 1
Current ratio: 378:1

tinsel, vb., makes *tinseled* and *tinseling* in AmE, *tinselled* and *tinselling* in BrE. See SPELLING (B).

tintinnabulum (= a small tinkling bell) forms the plural *tintinnabula*—not *tintinnabulums. (See PLURALS (B).) The corresponding adjective, *tintinnabulary*, is more common than the noun; it means "of, relating to, or involving bells or their sounds." E.g.: "Tunes like 'The Ukrainian Bell Carol' and 'Jingle Bells' clearly established the *tintinnabulary* idea but the densely textured arrangement rarely showcased the vocal capabilities of those accomplished singers." Rick Rogers, "Canterbury Singers Celebrate Tuneful Christmas," *Daily Oklahoman*, 11 Dec. 1996, at 17.

-TION. See ZOMBIE NOUNS.

***tipi.** See tepee.

tipper. See tipster.

tipstaff (= a court officer who acts as crier and otherwise helps the judge) predominantly forms the plural *tipstaves* in AmE and BrE alike. Although the homegrown plural *tipstaffs* has long vied closely, it remains a secondary variant.

tipster; tipper. Both mean "someone who gives a critical piece of information (i.e., a *tip*)." *Tipster* often refers to someone who gives tips to police in criminal investigations or sells tips relating to speculative or gambling subjects <an anonymous tipster called the police and implicated Mr. Kryder>.

LANGUAGE-CHANGE INDEX (For the full key, see front matter pp. xxxi, l–li.)
Stage 1: Rejected. **Stage 2:** Widely shunned. **Stage 3:** Widespread but . . . **Stage 4:** Ubiquitous but . . . **Stage 5:** Fully accepted.
Invariably inferior forms marked by asterisk (*). • Ratios represent frequency of prevalent forms vs. variants in current books.

Tipper shares with *tipster* the meaning of an informer who tips off police on illegal activities. But more commonly it signifies (1) "someone who gives a gratuity" <at restaurants, he's a lousy tipper>, or (2) in business parlance, "someone who gives or sells tips to securities and other investors" <we invested in the stock after talking to our tipper>.

tire; tyre. Although traditionally the spelling *tire* was AmE and *tyre* BrE, since about 1950 *tire* has seriously rivaled *tyre* in BrE print sources. The traditional BrE spelling appears to be losing air.

Current ratio (BrE): 2:1
Current ratio (World English): 9:1

tiro. See **tyro.**

titbit. See **tidbit.**

tithe (= a donation of 10% of one's income to support charitable or religious activities) derives from Middle and Old English words for *tenth*. That percentage is commonly understood—e.g.: "After her conversion, it took her three years to start giving the 10 percent, or *tithe*. Now she would never consider not giving it." Sara Miller Llana, "Wealth Gospel Propels Poor Guatemalans," *Christian Science Monitor*, 17 Dec. 2007, World §, at 1.

Given that familiarity, **ten-percent tithe* is surely a REDUNDANCY—e.g.: "Two weeks ago, Fellowship Bible Church had its Commitment Sunday. Members were asked to pledge chunks of money beyond the *10-percent tithe* [read *tithe*] every pastor hopes, in vain, that every congregant gives." Bill Sanders, "Fellowship in Black and White," *Atlanta J.-Const.*, 28 Oct. 2007, at M1. In fact, though, in loose usage *tithe* now commonly denotes a donation of whatever size—e.g.: "Both figures are well shy of the biblical *10 percent tithe*." Chrissie Thompson, "Church Tithing Continues to Ebb; Only 2.56 Percent Given in 2004," *Wash. Times*, 13 Oct. 2006, at A9. Cf. **decimate.**

LANGUAGE-CHANGE INDEX
tithe to mean a donation of other than 10% of income: Stage 3

titillate; titivate. *Titillate* = to cause arousal or excitement, esp. of a sexual nature <titillating photographs>. *Titivate* = to smarten or spruce up <speed-dating aficionados who relentlessly titivate themselves>. A variant spelling of the latter is **tittivate*. For the difference between *titillate* and *tantalize*, see **tantalize.**

titmouse (= a small songbird) is also known as a *tit*, but only serious birdwatchers use the shortened form (because of the vulgar homonym). The vastly predominant plural (and the one recognized by dictionaries) is *titmice*, not **titmouses*—e.g.: "In recent days chickadees, *titmice*, robins, cardinals, and white-breasted nuthatches seemed to celebrate the return of blue skies and sunshine." Scott Shalaway, "Birds First Sign of Spring," *Pitt. Post-Gaz.*, 16 Mar. 2003, at D16. The form **titmouses*, though

perhaps logical (since it's not a mouse at all), occurs so infrequently as to be ill-advised—e.g.: "Other visitors to the Gibbs' yard Monday were cardinals, white-throated sparrows, . . . *titmouses* [read *titmice*], chickadees, juncos, Carolina wrens, bluebirds and goldfinches." Sylvia Cooper, "Watch Out for the Birds," *Augusta Chron.*, 24 Jan. 2003, at D10.

LANGUAGE-CHANGE INDEX
*titmouses for *titmice*: Stage 1
Current ratio (*titmice* vs. **titmouses*): 134:1

TITULAR TOMFOOLERY. Nowadays almost any APPOSITIVE is likely to be treated as if it were a title. This trend is primarily the fault of newspapers and magazines, which create descriptive titles for people on the fly. So instead of *Timothy McVeigh, the convicted bomber*, journalists want to say *convicted bomber Timothy McVeigh*. Worse yet, some writers would even capitalize the descriptor, further elevating the common noun to title status—e.g.: *Convicted Bomber Timothy McVeigh*.

Acceptance of these false titles (though never the capitalized form) is partly attributable to their sanction by the Associated Press: "Other titles serve primarily as occupational descriptions: *astronaut John Glenn, movie star John Wayne, peanut farmer Jimmy Carter*." *Associated Press Stylebook* 251 (Norm Goldstein ed., 2002). But *The New York Times* gives better advice: "Only official titles—not mere descriptions—should be affixed to names. Do not, for example, write *pianist Lynn C. Arniotis* or *political scientist Tracy F. Baranek*. But in a reference to someone well known, a descriptive phrase preceded by *the* is acceptable: *the sociologist Merrill H. Cordero*." *The New York Times Manual of Style and Usage* 334 (Allan M. Siegal & William G. Connolly eds., 1999).

This trend resulted from an understandable desire for economy in both words and punctuation, since most appositives require an article (*a* or *the*) and commas. Yet the result is often a breeziness that hardly seems worth the effort of repositioning the words from their traditional placement—e.g.:

- "They played *eventual champion Arkansas* in the opening round last year." "Familiar Role for A&T," *Asheville Citizen-Times* (N.C.), 15 Mar. 1995, at D3. (Insert *the* before *eventual champion*, and put commas before and after *Arkansas*.)
- "*Frequent contributor Michael Kaplan* [read *Michael Kaplan, a frequent contributor,*] taps in to this energy in the interview gracing our cover, 'On the Record' . . . . *Frequent contributor Ken McAlpine* [read *Ken McAlpine, another frequent contributor,*] does some hip-hop and flip-flop of his own as he checks out the guys who wear the striped shirts and whistles for the National Football League." John H. Ostdick, "The Joint Is Jumping," *Am. Way*, 15 Oct. 1995, at 16.

A true title of authority, such as *general* or *mayor*, is properly capitalized before a person's name <General Tommy Franks> <Mayor Willie Brown>. Job descriptions are not <flutist Ian Anderson>. Just where to draw the line can be an exercise in frustration. But even titles of authority are not capitalized when used as appositives following the name <Andrew Cuomo, governor of New York>.

TMESIS, the practice of separating parts of a compound word by inserting another word between those parts, seldom occurs today. Typically, it occurs either in humorous passages or in low colloquial language—e.g.: "The crowds and the loud music and the X Games are miles and miles and miles away, *a whole 'nother country away.*" Chris Jenkins, "Hell of a Race," *San Diego Union-Trib.*, 24 June 1997, at D1. (See SET PHRASES.) But tmesis occurs in other phrases as well—e.g.: "'[H]e might be in Florida *some-damn-where,*' says Fred Haselrig, Carlton's father." Michael Silver, "Invisible Man," *Sports Illustrated*, 18 Dec. 1995, at 66. In a similar vein, Joseph Pulitzer (1847–1911) of the *New York World* had a pet word: *indegoddampendent.* This type of interpolated profanity use is common in BrE with *bloody*—e.g.: "It is also, as her fans Down Under rightly proclaim, *abso-bloody-lutely* wonderful." Paul Cole, "Special Kasey," *Sunday Mercury* (U.K.), 21 Apr. 2002, at P38. In AmE, far stronger language is commonly inserted, as moviegoers know only too well.

The traditional form of tmesis, however, occurs with formal words ending in *-soever.* It has an archaic ring to it, and most readers probably encounter it primarily in the King James Version of the Bible—e.g.:

- "*What things soever* ye desire, when ye pray, believe that ye receive them and ye shall have them." Mark 11:24.
- "Then answered Jesus and said unto them, 'Verily, verily, I say unto you, The Son can do nothing of himself, but what he seeth the Father do: for *what things soever* he doeth, these also doeth the Son likewise.'" John 5:19.

The modern tendency, of course, is to write *whatever things.*

Tmesis is pronounced /tə-**mee**-sis/ or /**mee**-sis/. Contemporary linguists often call *tmesis* "infixing." For an impressive study, see James B. McMillan, "Infixing and Interposing in English," 55 *Am. Speech* 163–83 (1980).

to all intents and purposes. See **for all intents and purposes.**

to begin. See **begin** (A).

to cast aspersions. See **aspersions.**

Tocqueville, de. See NAMES (D).

toe the line; toe the mark. These phrases—meaning "to conform to the rules; to do one's duty"—derive from track-and-field events in which the contestants were once told to put one foot on the starting line. (Now the shouted instruction is *On your marks!*) The phrases appear to be Americanisms that originated in the early 19th century. See Charles Earle Funk, *Heavens to Betsy! and Other Curious Sayings* 136–37 (1955; repr. 1986).

Especially in the phrase *toe the line*, the METAPHOR is sometimes badly distorted from *toe* to *tow*—e.g.:

- "Wood's bill prohibits gag clauses, but the House version eliminates provisions that would have required health insurers to disclose the financial incentives (or penalties) that can persuade physicians to *tow* [read *toe*] the line in much the same way." Tom Paulson, "Doctors Still Hope for State Help on Insurance Issue," *Seattle Post-Intelligencer*, 1 Mar. 1996, at C1.
- "Meanwhile the Bosnian Serb Republic's ruling Serb Democratic Party, covertly led by Mr. Karadzic, has threatened to oust the territory's president, Biljana Plavsic, unless she *tows* [read *toes*] the line." "Voting Ban on Karadzic," *Guardian*, 2 July 1997, at 17.
- "Pressure from such microscopic scrutiny suggests that China will have to *tow* [read *toe*] the line, or world powers will retaliate with trade sanctions." M. Ray Perryman, "Hong Kong Shows How the Child Can Also Be the Parent," *San Antonio Bus. J.*, 25 July 1997, at 55.
- "*Tow* [read *Toe*] **the line:** carry one's load; follow set rules or orders strictly. Every employee needs to *tow* [read *toe*] the line around here." Joseph Melillo & Edward M. Melillo, *American Slang* 210 (2005).

See **lapsus linguae.**

Although *toe the line* is about five times as common as *toe the mark* in print sources today, the latter idiom has not entirely disappeared—e.g.: "In his latest tape, Osama bin Laden denounced Muslim countries that don't *toe his mark* as 'tyrannical and apostate regimes, which are enslaved by America.'" Ron Grossman, "Also-Rans Snipe at U.S.," *Chicago Trib.*, 2 Mar. 2003, Perspective §, at 1.

LANGUAGE-CHANGE INDEX
tow the line for *toe the line*: Stage 2
Current ratio (*toe the line* vs. *tow the line*): 8:1

together appears in many a REDUNDANCY, such as **blend together, *connect together, *consolidate together, *couple together,* and **merge together.* These phrases should be avoided, except when part of a SET PHRASE (e.g., *join together* in a marriage ceremony). Cf. **mutual** (A).

For the distinction between *altogether* and *all together,* see **altogether.**

together with. See SUBJECT–VERB AGREEMENT (E).

to include. See **include.**

tolerance; toleration. The former is the quality, the latter the act or practice. As a matter of word frequency, *toleration* occurred much more often in print sources than *tolerance* during the 17th to 19th centuries, but the position was reversed about the time of World War I: since 1914, *tolerance* has consistently appeared in print more frequently than *toleration.*

tome refers not to any book, but only to one that is imposingly or forbiddingly large (the one you're holding comes to mind).

LANGUAGE-CHANGE INDEX (For the full key, see front matter pp. xxxi, l–li.)
Stage 1: Rejected. **Stage 2:** Widely shunned. **Stage 3:** Widespread but . . . **Stage 4:** Ubiquitous but . . . **Stage 5:** Fully accepted.
Invariably inferior forms marked by asterisk (*). • Ratios represent frequency of prevalent forms vs. variants in current books.

tony (= fashionable and expensive) is so spelled in all varieties of World English. The word is occasionally misspelled *toney*.

too. A. Beginning Sentences with. It is poor style to begin a sentence with *too* (= also), although there is a tendency in facile journalism to use the word this way. Instead of *Too, we shouldn't forget*, write *Also, we shouldn't forget* or, better, *And we shouldn't forget*. Words such as *moreover*, *further*, and *furthermore* are also serviceable in this position—though they are heavy.

B. For *very*. This informal use of *too* almost always occurs in negative constructions <it's not too common>. But there are exceptions <you're too kind>.

C. *Too* [+ adj.] *a* [+ n.]. This idiom being perfectly acceptable, there is no reason to insist on the artificiality of *a too* [+ adj. + n.]; that is, *too good a job* is better than **a too good job*. E.g.: "But Monica is *too nice a person* for that kind of behavior." Dale Robertson, "For Seles, What Could Have Been Radiates in Hingis," *Houston Chron.*, 6 June 1997, at 1. For the bad form **too good of a*, see **of (B)**.

*tooken. See **take (A)**.

topography. See **typography**.

Torino. See **Turin**.

tornadic (= of, relating to, or involving a tornado or tornadoes) was coined in the late 19th century as an adjective corresponding to the 16th-century word *tornado*. The newer word can be seen as a pomposity because *tornado* generally serves as its own adjective <tornado activity>. But some writers seem to like the mock-technicality of *tornadic*—e.g.: "The peak of the storm hit Brockton and Mary D in Schuylkill Township, where *tornadic* [read *tornado*] damage was a quarter-mile wide." Kristen Klick, "Schuylkill Was Ripped by Twister," *Morning Call* (Allentown, Pa.), 15 May 1996, at B1.

Tornadic is pronounced either /tor-**nay**-dik/ or /tor-**nad**-ik/.

tornado. Pl. *tornadoes*—not **tornados*. See PLURALS (D).

Current ratio: 7:1

torpid. See **turbid**.

torsibility. For the use of this noun in opposite senses, see CONTRONYMS.

tortellini; tortelloni. *Tortellini*, the more usual word, normally denotes small squares of pasta that are formed into rings or hat shapes after stuffing. While *tortellini* is both singular and plural in English, the Italian singular is *tortellino* (= a small cake or fritter). Depending on the cookbook you consult, *tortelloni* either refers to a larger version of *tortellini* or is another name for *ravioli*.

tortfeasor (= someone who commits a civil wrong) was once spelled as two words (*tort feasor*), then was hyphenated, and now has been fused into a single word.

tortious. See **tortuous**.

tortoise. The standard pronunciation is /**tort**-əs/, not /**tor**-toyz/ (a spelling pronunciation). Cf. **porpoise**.

tortuous; torturous; tortious. *Tortuous* (/**tor**-choo-əs/) = full of twists and turns <a tortuous path through the woods>. *Torturous* (/**tor**-chər-əs/) = of, characterized by, or involving torture <torturous abuse>. *Tortious* (/**tor**-shəs/) = (1) of, relating to, or involving a civil wrong (i.e., a tort) for which a person can sue <tortious liability>; or (2) constituting a tort <a tortious act>. Two mistakes are fairly common—both involving *tortuous*.

First, that word is occasionally misused for *torturous*—e.g.: "Dozens of deaf Mexican immigrants huddled around Spanish-speaking interpreters in Queens and, using Mexican and American sign language, vividly described their long and *tortuous* [read *torturous*] ordeal at the hands of the smuggling ring, which forced them to sell $1 trinkets on the subway from morning until night." "Deaf Immigrants Exploited Over 10-Year Period in City," *N.Y. Times*, 22 July 1997, at A2.

Second, *tortuous* is sometimes misused for *tortious* (the least common of the three words)—e.g.:

- "The Masiarczyks accuse Anania of '*tortuous* [read *tortious*] conduct,' which they said has resulted in 'humiliation, embarrassment and other damages.'" Sarah Webster, "Badlands Battle Brews over Club," *Gaz. & Daily Mail* (Charleston, W. Va.), 29 Aug. 1996, at A8.
- "In return, Bocwinski agreed to drop the three other allegations, which were described in the settlement agreement as '*tortuous* [read *tortious*] acts.'" Pat Clawson, "Village Approves Lawsuit Settlement," *Chicago Trib.*, 7 Oct. 1996, at 3.
- "Bridas, meanwhile, are suing Unocal for '*tortuous* [read *tortious*] interference' in their business." J.J. Fergusson, "Western Oil Firms Face Central Asia's Political Minefield," *Independent*, 15 May 1997, at 12.

In those examples, it's hard to know who made the error: the quoter or the original writer. But somebody did.

LANGUAGE-CHANGE INDEX
1. *tortuous* misused for *torturous*: Stage 2
Current ratio (*torturous interrogation* vs. **tortuous interrogation*): 6:1
2. *tortuous* misused for *tortious*: Stage 1
Current ratio (*tortious act* vs. **tortuous act*): 14:1

total, vb., makes *totaled* and *totaling* in AmE, *totalled* and *totalling* in BrE. See SPELLING (B).

*totally obsolescent. For this phrase, see **archaic**.

to the contrary. See **contrary (B)**.

to the effect that is often verbose for *that*.

to the manner born. See **manner born**.

totting up (= adding up, calculating) is sometimes incorrectly made *toting up* (which means "carrying up")—e.g.: "*Toting* [read *Totting*] up a lifetime of 35 campaigns, in primaries and general elections, looking back on the proud history of a district once represented by the Speaker of the House, William B. Bankhead (Tallulah's father), Mr. Bevill maintained that the weight of history was on the Democrats' side." Robin Toner, "Retirements a Hurdle for Dixie's Democrats," *N.Y. Times*, 7 July 1996, at 1, 8.

touchy; tetchy; techy. *Touchy* = (1) oversensitive; irritable <he was a bit touchy during the interview>; or (2) requiring caution or tact in handling <a touchy subject>. Even though it predates *touchy*, *tetchy* (as well as its alternative spelling *techy*) is now a variant form (in sense 1). *Tetchy* occurs more often in BrE than in AmE.

For *techy* as an adjective meaning "involving one or more techies" (technology whizzes), see **techie.**

toupee is so written in English—not **toupée*, though the form **toupéé* might be suggestively mimetic.

tourniquet is so spelled. See SPELLING (A). It is pronounced /tər-ni-kət/ in AmE and /tə-ni-kay/ in BrE.

toward. A. And *towards*. Since about 1900, *toward* has been the predominant and editorially preferred form in AmE; *towards* has always been predominant in BrE. See DIRECTIONAL WORDS (A).

B. Pronunciation. The word is preferably pronounced /tord/ (to rhyme with *board*), not /tword/ or /tə-**word**/. See CLASS DISTINCTIONS.

C. Misused for *to* or *against*. *Toward* implies movement. It shouldn't be used when the sentence would be served by *to* or *against*—e.g.:

- "The parks and recreation department has no objections *toward* [read *to*] selling the West Suffield School." Rubaina Azhar, "Suffield Holds Off on Sales," *Hartford Courant*, 14 Mar. 1997, at B1.
- "Perhaps he should consider his own attitude, which appears to be one of prejudice *toward* [read *against*] people from certain parts of the country." Cameron T. Shalamunec, "No One Has Come Here to Make Others Unhappy," *Rocky Mountain News* (Denver), 24 Sept. 1997, at A48.
- "The author, Jan Murphy, suggests that our library officials acted with prejudice *toward* [read *against*] Laura Bast, who desired to volunteer with the library." "Story Overdramatized," *Patriot & Evening News* (Harrisburg), 6 Oct. 1997.

towel, vb., makes *toweled* and *toweling* in AmE, *towelled* and *towelling* in BrE. See SPELLING (B).

to(-)wit. The ordinary progression in such common phrases is from two words, to a hyphenated form, to a single word. Though some writers have experimented with the single-word version, and the hyphenated form was once common, today it seems that *to wit* is destined to remain two words—if indeed its destiny is not oblivion. *To wit* is a legal ARCHAISM in the place

of which *namely* is almost always an improvement. Cf. **namely** & **viz.**

toxic, n.; toxin. It's true that *toxic*, which is mostly an adjective <toxic substances>, has been a noun meaning "a poisonous substance, chemical or otherwise" since the late 19th century <releasing toxics into the air>. It's also true that *toxin* is narrower in scope: technically speaking, it means "a poisonous substance produced by a living organism, esp. a disease-causing substance." Despite those inconvenient facts, though, *toxic* is almost invariably used as an adjective today; to use it as a noun in general writing invites confusion and probably suspicion that the writer has blundered.

toxicology; toxology. *Toxicology* = the science of poisons. *Toxology* = the branch of knowledge dealing with archery.

toxin. See **toxic.**

toxology. See **toxicology.**

trachea (= the tube that takes air from the throat to the lungs; windpipe) has traditionally formed the classical plural *tracheae* (/**tray**-ki-ee/)—but then again the plural form is rarely needed outside medical and biological writing. Since about 1980 the homegrown *tracheas* has begun to rival its Greek sibling in all varieties of English.

tracheotomy; tracheostomy. The two are distinct. *Tracheotomy* (dating from the early 18th century) refers to any surgical cutting through the skin into the trachea. *Tracheostomy* (dating from the early 20th century) refers to the surgical formation of a hole through the neck and into the trachea to allow the passage of air. Since the early 1960s, *tracheostomy* has appeared more frequently in print.

track; tract. *Track* (= a course or beaten path) is sometimes misused for *tract* (= a parcel of land) in the phrase *tract of land*. Less common than it once was, the error still occurs—e.g.:

- "The banks had become owners of vast *tracks* [read *tracts*] of land through foreclosures." Gary Marsh, "David Bohannon Dies," *Bus. J.*, 27 Mar. 1995, at 8.
- "It's easy to be saddened by change, especially when that change means development gobbling up what longtime Floridians remember as vast *tracks* [read *tracts*] of vacant land, fields of flowers and quiet beaches." Karen Haymon Long, "Changes Come to All Lovely Places," *Tampa Trib.*, 9 June 1996, Travel §, at 1.
- "In the early 1990s, a very large underground circular tunnel about 85 feet underground was being dug on a huge *track* [read *tract*] of land south of Dallas, Texas, to house equipment for a very high-energy circular particle accelerator." Robert E. Krebs, *The History and Use of Our Earth's Chemical Elements* 365 (2d ed. 2006).

LANGUAGE-CHANGE INDEX (For the full key, see front matter pp. xxxi, l–li.)
Stage 1: Rejected. **Stage 2:** Widely shunned. **Stage 3:** Widespread but . . . **Stage 4:** Ubiquitous but . . . **Stage 5:** Fully accepted.
Invariably inferior forms marked by asterisk (*). • Ratios represent frequency of prevalent forms vs. variants in current books.

The opposite error has also sometimes occurred since the late 19th century. E.g.:

- "The prompt will always display the path of the current directory to help you keep *tract* [read *track*] of where you are in the filing system." T. Sheldon, "Building an Orderly Hard Disk," *PC Mag.*, 15 May 1984, at 269.
- "CBS Sports executive Len DeLuca (on phone) helps fellow vice president Rick Gentile (in cap) keep *tract* [read *track*] of action during the first day of the NCAA Tournament." "In the Eye of the Storm," *Dallas Morning News*, 22 Mar. 1995, at B1 (photo caption).

The same error occurs, though less often, when the subject is the *digestive tract*—e.g.: "Doctors diagnosed Crohn's, an autoimmune disease that confuses the immune system and causes inflammation in the digestive *track* [read *tract*]." Greg Bishop, "A Couple Grapple for Love, and Love of Achievement," *N.Y. Times*, 12 June 2008, at D6. Cf. **soundtrack.**

LANGUAGE-CHANGE INDEX
1. *track* misused for *tract*: Stage 1
Current ratio (*tract of land* vs. **track of land*): 90:1
2. *tract* misused for *track*: Stage 1
Current ratio (*kept track of* vs. **kept tract of*): 950:1

tradable. So spelled in AmE and BrE alike—not **tradeable*. See MUTE E.

trademark; tradename. Today in AmE, *tradenames* identify businesses; *trademarks* identify goods produced by or services provided by businesses. Since the mid-20th century, each term has been solidified (no hyphen) in AmE and BrE alike. See **servicemark.**

traditionalist; *traditionist. The first is the standard term; the second has been a NEEDLESS VARIANT since the late 19th century.

Current ratio: 46:1

traffic, v.i., forms the participles *trafficking* and *trafficked*, and the agent noun is *trafficker*. But the adjective is *trafficable*. See -C-.

tragic; *tragical. *Tragic* is standard. Although **tragical* predominated before 1750 and competed closely till 1800, it has been a NEEDLESS VARIANT in decline since then.

Current ratio: 35:1

trammel (= to bind, shackle, or otherwise restrain) makes *trammeled* and *trammeling* in AmE, *trammelled* and *trammelling* in BrE. See SPELLING (B).

tranquillity; *tranquility. Since about 1980, the two spellings have been about equally common. But since the 17th century, *tranquillity* has been considered the standard spelling, and **tranquility* a variant form. This despite the spelling **tranquility* in the preamble to the U.S. Constitution.

Current ratio: 2:1

transatlantic; *trans-Atlantic. The former has been the standard spelling since the 18th century—on both sides of the Atlantic. *Transpacific* follows the same standard—except that *trans-Pacific* is curiously prevalent in BrE.

transcendent; transcendental. *Transcendent* = surpassing or excelling others of its kind; preeminent. It is loosely used by some writers in the sense "excellent." *Transcendental* = supernatural; mystical; metaphysical; superhuman. The adverbial forms are *transcendently* and *transcendentally.*

transcript; transcription. The former is the written copy, the latter the process of producing it.

transfer, n.; **transferral; *transferal; transference.** The first is the standard term. The second and third are NEEDLESS VARIANTS—though if you must use one, **transferral* is the better spelling. *Transference* justifies its separate existence primarily in psychological contexts, in the sense "the redirection of feelings or desires" <one twin felt guilt by transference even though he was nowhere near when his brother committed the crime>.

transfer, v.t., is traditionally accented on the second syllable, hence the past-tense spelling *transferred*, not **transfered*. See SPELLING (B).

transferable. Since the 18th century, the word has been so spelled in AmE and BrE alike—not **transferrable* or **transferrible*. This despite the accent on the second syllable: /tranz-fər-ə-bəl/. In this way, the word is anomalous. Cf. **deferrable** & **inferable.**

Current ratio (*transferable* vs. **transferrable* vs. **transferrible*): 6,696:75:1

*transferal; *transferral; transference. See **transfer,** n.

TRANSFERRED EPITHET. See HYPALLAGE.

transfixion; transfiction. These homophones are distinct. The first denotes the state or condition of being transfixed. The second is a NEOLOGISM referring to a type of fiction involving or appealing to transgender people.

transformational; transformative. *Transformational* is the broader term, meaning "of or characterized by a change of form or substance." *Transformative* means "causing or (less commonly) susceptible to such a change."

transfusable. Despite the worldwide predominance of *fusible*, not **fusable*, the spelling *transfusable* has become standard in AmE and BrE alike. That spelling overtook the traditional **transfusible* in the 1960s and 1970s and is now unquestionably preponderant. See -ABLE (A).

Current ratio: 2:1

transgender; transgendered. The precise meaning of this new term (dating only to the mid-1970s) is hard to pin down, but it's most commonly used as a broad adjective describing people whose self-identity does not match the sex they were labeled with at birth—e.g.: "[Dr. Norman] Spack subjects his patients to a lengthy evaluation process before recommending hormone therapy. Kids undergo a battery of interview-based psychological tests to see if they meet the medically established criteria for gender-identity disorder. . . . There are many mysteries about the *transgendered*. This could clear up one of them." Laura Fitzpatrick, "The Gender Conundrum," *Time*, 19 Nov. 2007, at 59. The term is not necessarily an identification of sexual orientation.

Transgender is the broader and more common term. The participle *transgendered* might suggest some form of physical alteration—e.g.: "Rhiannon O'Donnabhain is suing the IRS in a case advocates for the *transgendered* are hoping will force the tax agency to treat sex-change operations the same as appendectomies, heart bypasses and other deductible medical procedures." "Around the Nation," *Record* (N.J.), 17 July 2007, at A6.

transgression for *transition* is a MALAPROPISM—e.g.: "Ms. Ash said the laser center 'is a natural *transgression* [read *transition*] into a new technology.'" Raquel Santiago, "Firms Turn Eyes to Laser Surgery," *Crain's Cleveland Bus.*, 29 Jan. 1996, at 3.

LANGUAGE-CHANGE INDEX

transgression misused for *transition*: Stage 1

*tranship. See **transship.**

transience; *transiency. The latter is a NEEDLESS VARIANT.

Current ratio: 9:1

transient, adj.; **transitory; transitive.** *Transient* = coming and going; impermanent; temporary <transient workers>. *Transitory* (= fleeting) has virtually the same meaning but is more commonly applied to things or events than to people <transitory renown>. *Transitive* is a grammatical term denoting a verb that takes a direct object <transitive verbs>.

Transient is best pronounced /**tran**-shənt/ in AmE. In BrE it is pronounced with three syllables: /**tran**-zee-ənt/ or /-see-/.

translucent. See **transparent.**

transmissible. So spelled in AmE and BrE alike. *Transmissable is a variant. See -ABLE (A).

Current ratio: 89:1

transmit. See **send.**

transmittal; transmission; transmittance. *Transmittal* is more physical than *transmission*, just as *admittance* is more physical than *admission*. *Transmittal*, though labeled rare in the *OED*, is common in AmE, especially in the phrase *transmittal letter* (= a cover letter accompanying documents or other things being conveyed to another). E.g.: "Middleton noted in his *transmittal letter* that Trie was a friend of Clinton's and 'a major supporter.'" Sharon LaFraniere & Susan Schmidt, "White House Ignored Red Flags About Fundraisers," *Oregonian* (Portland), 15 Feb. 1997, at A1.

Transmittance is a scientific term dealing with the transfer of radiant energy, etc. <spectral transmittance> <thermal transmittance> <amplitude transmittance>.

The COMMERCIALESE appears on many cover sheets where the simple *fax* would do nicely. See **fax.**

transnational. So spelled.

transpacific. See **transatlantic.**

transparency. During the accounting scandals of 2001, when elaborate financial arrangements of major corporations were exposed as frauds on their stockholders, *transparency* became a VOGUE WORD for no-nonsense openness with information—e.g.: "'*Transparency* in financial reporting, both to investors and internally, would make a big difference,' [Michael] Synk added." Mark Watson, "Seminar Will Look at Ethics in Business," *Commercial Appeal* (Memphis), 15 Mar. 2003, at F2. The term proved so popular that it crowded out a former vogue phrase, *full disclosure*, in nonfinancial contexts as well—e.g.:

- "'I believe in *transparency*, and when I write a letter to Ashcroft, I expect an answer and I expect complete information,' [Sen. Charles] Grassley said." Eric Lichtblau & Adam Liptak, "On Terror, Spying and Guns, Ashcroft Expands Reach," *N.Y. Times*, 15 Mar. 2003, at A1.
- "If the arts board wants to improve its image, start by following its own rules, operating with *transparency* and abiding by the spirit of the open meeting laws." Randy Krebs, "Our View" (Editorial), *St. Cloud Times* (Minn.), 15 Mar. 2003, at B7.
- "The American Conference of Bishops has promised '*transparency*' in disclosing information on child sexual abuse, she said, and '*transparency* means letting the public know the truth.'" Gina Macris, "Abuse Victims Call for Full Disclosure," *Providence J.-Bull.*, 17 Mar. 2003, at B1 (quoting Ann Hagan Webb).

transparent; translucent. A *transparent* substance allows light to pass through it freely, so that objects beyond it may be seen clearly. On the other hand, a *translucent* substance allows light to pass through it but diffuses it, so that objects beyond it are not clearly visible. Hence ordinary glass is *transparent*, while frosted glass is *translucent*.

transpire. The traditionally correct meaning of this word is "to pass through a surface; come to light; become known by degrees." But that sense is now beyond redemption, though writers should be aware of it. Today, of course, the popular use of *transpire* is as a FORMAL WORD equivalent to *happen, occur,* or *take*

LANGUAGE-CHANGE INDEX (For the full key, see front matter pp. xxxi, l–li.)
Stage 1: Rejected. **Stage 2:** Widely shunned. **Stage 3:** Widespread but . . . **Stage 4:** Ubiquitous but . . . **Stage 5:** Fully accepted.
Invariably inferior forms marked by asterisk (*). • Ratios represent frequency of prevalent forms vs. variants in current books.

place. But when used in that way, *transpire* is a mere pomposity displacing an everyday word—e.g.:

- "The group all had an interest in what was *transpiring* [read *happening*] in the Catholic Church as the Second Vatican Council got under way in 1962, Martinelli said." Gerald Renner, "Witness Tells of Abuse by Priest," *Hartford Courant*, 22 Aug. 1997, at A1.
- "Satisfied that something unusual was indeed *transpiring* [read *happening*], the team then arranged for a visit to the house." David Lazarus, "Ghostbuster Snares Clients on Net," *S.F. Chron.*, 13 Oct. 2002, at G1.

Another loose usage occurs (not *transpires*) when *transpire* is used for *pass* or *elapse*—e.g.: "Three days *transpired* [read *passed*] between the call and discovery of the dead child." Steven K. Paulson, "911 Call Was Made from Mansion Before Body Found," *Times Union* (Albany), 10 Jan. 1997, at A3.

All in all, *transpire* fits the definition of a SKUNKED TERM: careful writers should avoid it altogether simply to avoid distracting readers, whether traditionalists (who dislike the modern usage) or others (who may not understand the traditional usage).

LANGUAGE-CHANGE INDEX
transpire for *happen* or *occur*: Stage 4

transportation; transportal; *transportment. The first is the usual word for the system, method, business, or process of taking goods or people from one place to another. The second is often used as a technical term for the conveyance of pollen, seeds, etc. from one place to another. The third is a NEEDLESS VARIANT.

transposition; *transposal. The latter is a NEEDLESS VARIANT.

Current ratio: 518:1

transsexual. So spelled—not *transexual.

Current ratio: 38:1

transship (= to transfer from one ship or vehicle to another) is so spelled—without a hyphen. The word is often misspelled *tranship—e.g.: "Japanese intelligence sources speculated that the shipment may have originated in China and been *transhipped* [read *transshipped*] through the North Korean port of Chongjin by a middleman." Richard Lloyd Parry, "North Korea: A Nation Exporting Food While Its Children Starve," *Independent*, 18 July 1997, at 16.

Current ratio: 1.3:1

trapezoid; trapezium. These words are traps for the geometrically unwary. In AmE, a *trapezoid* is a shape with four sides, two of which are parallel; in BrE, it is a four-sided shape with no parallel sides. In AmE, *trapezium* is the word for the latter sense (a four-sided shape with no parallel sides), while in BrE it bears the former sense (a four-sided shape with two parallel sides). The predominant plural of *trapezium* is *trapeziums* in both AmE and BrE (a recent development in both)—though in World English *trapezia* has predominated since about 1970. The two plurals have been locked in rivalry since the 18th century.

trauma, in pathology, means "a serious wound or shock to the body," but in popular contexts it has been largely confined to figurative (emotional) senses. Cf. **insult.** Pl. *traumas*—preferably not the pretentious *traumata (in steep decline since about 1960).

Current ratio (*traumas* vs. *traumata): 32:1

travel, vb., makes *traveled* and *traveling* in AmE, *travelled* and *travelling* in BrE. See SPELLING (B).

travelogue (= a lecture or film documentary about travel to a particular place) is the standard spelling in AmE and BrE alike. *Travelog is a variant. (See **catalog(ue), dialogue** & **pedagogue.**) For a comment on the potential decline of the -*ue* form, see -AGOG(UE).

trawl, vb.; **troll,** vb. *Trawl* = (1) to fish with a large cone-shaped net (called a *trawl*) that is dragged on the bottom of a sea or lake; or (2) to search through (documents, computer files, etc.) to gather information. *Troll* = v.t., (1) to roll (something) around and around; (2) to sing robustly; (3) to pull through water; (4) to try to obtain something from by searching or interrogating; v.i., (5) to catch fish by dragging a lure or a baited hook, esp. from a moving boat; (6) to talk quickly; or (7) to roam; wander. Each word seems sometimes to be displaced by the other—e.g.:

- "The cities are strung along the road like hooks on a *trawling* [read *trolling*] line." Richard Nilsen, "Northern Trek," *Orange County Register*, 26 July 1998, at D4.
- "It was the second day experts from Colorado Alligators, a farm near Alamosa, *trolled* [read *trawled*] the pond with a huge net." Carla Crowder, "Hundreds Hope, After a While, to Spy Elusive Critter," *Rocky Mountain News* (Denver), 19 Aug. 1998, at A4.

Then again, sense 2 of *trawl* is virtually indistinguishable from sense 4 of *troll*. The usual phrase today is *trolling the internet*, not *trawling*.

LANGUAGE-CHANGE INDEX
1. *trawl* misused for *troll*: Stage 2
2. *troll* misused for *trawl*: Stage 2

tread > trod > trodden. So inflected. *Trod* is a variant past participle. Although many American dictionaries (surprisingly) list *untrod as the standard adjective in preference to *untrodden*, the latter form is seven times as common.

Since the mid-20th century, many writers have tried to make *trod* into a present-tense verb. They're treading heavily on the language—e.g.:

- "The war's scars are still fresh and Albert's quick feet seem to be *trodding* [read *treading*] upon the corpses of the heroes of the Resistance." Jim Keogh, " 'Self-Made Hero' Makes Deception Look Easy," *Telegram & Gaz.* (Worcester), 18 Feb. 1998, at C5.
- "A truce was declared yesterday in the latest battle of Manassas, as state and federal officials announced a plan to widen a perilous intersection without *trodding* [read *treading*] on a sacred Civil War battleground." Dan Eggen, "Past Gives Ground to Safety," *Wash. Post*, 29 Oct. 1998, at B5.

The mistaken form *trodded appears as both a past tense and a past participle—e.g.:

- "For four hours the group of about 60 *trodded* [read *trod*] through patches of thick pine and oak." Elisa Crouch, "Residents Tell Officials About Concern for Land," *Providence J.-Bull.*, 9 Feb. 1998, at C1.
- "He *trodded* [read *trod*] on Cardinals' foreheads for 124 yards in the opener." Tim Tyers, "Key Match-Ups," *Ariz. Republic*, 15 Nov. 1998, at F4.
- "Kanika has *trodded* [read *trodden*] loyally down the road less traveled with Tarrik in the last four years of marriage." Mike Kiley, "Wife Helps Brock Keep Faith in Cubs," *Chicago Sun-Times*, 20 Mar. 2000, at 90.

See IRREGULAR VERBS.

Treaded is the accepted past tense and past participle only in the sense of treading water, both literally and figuratively—e.g.:

- "He reached the western wall and *treaded* water as he groped for a handhold along the frosted stone." Michael Allen Dymmoch, *The Cymry Ring* 8 (2006).
- "Connecticut *treaded* water for the first half of the year before beginning its jobs descent, losing 10,500 jobs in September–November." Kenneth R. Gosselin et al., "Battered and Bruised: The Year in Business," *Hartford Courant*, 1 Jan. 2009, at A12.

LANGUAGE-CHANGE INDEX
1. *trod* misused for present-tense *tread*: Stage 1
Current ratio (*treading on* vs. **trodding on*): 251:1
2. **trodded* for *trod*: Stage 1
Current ratio (*trod on* vs. **trodded on*): 526:1
3. **trodded* for *trodden*: Stage 1
4. *treaded* in reference to treading water: Stage 5

treasonable; treasonous. Ernest Gowers wrote in 1965 that of these synonymous words, "*treasonous* is now comparatively rare, and more likely to be met in verse" (*FMEU2* at 647). Modern desk dictionaries still seem to agree, listing *treasonous* only as a variant of the older word, *treasonable*. And in AmE legal writing, that remains true: *treasonable* is five times as common as *treasonous* in court decisions (although federal criminal statutes use them interchangeably). But in modern American journalism, *treasonous* has scored a coup: it's the more common variant today. In World English, however, *treasonable* predominates by a 2-to-1 ratio.

*treat with dignity. See **dignity.**

treble; triple. These words are distinguishable though sometimes interchangeable. Outside baseball contexts <he tripled to deep right field>, *trebled* is a common term—e.g.:

- "The last time Congress 'reformed' campaign finance, it *trebled* the amount of money that is taken out of the Treasury (your money) and given to presidential candidates." Theo Lippman Jr., "What Political Campaigns Need Is Lots More Money," *Baltimore Sun*, 26 Nov. 1996, at A13.
- "The Company's . . . American depositary receipts have *trebled* in value." Jonathan Friedland, "Latin American Retailer Fights Giants," *Wall Street J.*, 19 Sept. 1997, at A10.

- "By 1992 it [South Africa's HIV rate] had *trebled* to 2.2 per cent. By the time South Africans voted in their first free elections in 1994 it had *trebled* again to 7.6 per cent. When Nelson Mandela stepped down and Thabo Mbeki took over in 1999 it had *trebled* once more to 22.4 per cent." Peter Gill, *Body Count* 64 (2006).

But in general, the baseball habits have permeated the language as a whole, and people are likely to talk about the *tripling* of costs, revenues, etc., as opposed to *trebling*.

As an adjective, *treble* usually means "three times as much or as many" <treble damages>, whereas *triple* means "having three parts" <a triple bookshelf> <triple bypass surgery>.

trek, n., derives from the Dutch *trekken* "to march or travel." It's occasionally misspelled **treck*—e.g.:

- "Jordan Pond is a good spot to begin your mountain-bike *treck* [read *trek*] northward past Eagle Lake to Bar Harbor." Judith Wynn, "Work of Art," *Boston Herald*, 7 Aug. 1997, at 52.
- "Hawaii's many trails are great, and none is finer than the volcanic *trecks* [read *treks*] around Kilauea on the Big Island." Zeke Wigglesworth, "The Best of Hawaii, for First-Timers," *Austin Am.-Statesman*, 24 Aug. 1997, at E1.

As a verb, *trek* makes *trekked* and *trekking*. But the misspelling occurs with the verb as well—e.g.:

- "*Trecking* [read *Trekking*] through rice paddies to check out reports of beatings one day, . . . the Americans aren't even sure how far their new jurisdiction extends." Andrew Selsky, "With Haitian Police Gone, U.S. Troops Become Cops," *Orange County Register*, 2 Oct. 1994, at A13.
- "On Thursday, while some of his colleagues were *trecking* [read *trekking*] north to Hamilton Park, the Carsons were making their first trip to Slimbridge." Tony Stafford, "Success Breeds Success for a Real Winner," *Sunday Telegraph*, 14 Apr. 1996, at 5.

LANGUAGE-CHANGE INDEX
*trecking for *trekking*: Stage 1
Current ratio (*trekking* vs. **trecking*): 482:1

trembler; *tremblor. See **temblor.**

trespassers will be prosecuted. This phrase, which most readers would construe as referring to criminal proceedings, usually expresses an untruth. In most states (Louisiana is a notable exception), trespass to land is ordinarily a tort—not a crime. Although the landowner can sue, the district attorney won't prosecute. But a trespasser who causes damage, as by trampling crops or breaking windows, can be criminally prosecuted.

-TRESS. See SEXISM (D).

triage (= a utilitarian and humanitarian method of deciding who receives medical treatment first according to how serious the need is) is sometimes misused for *trio*—e.g.:

LANGUAGE-CHANGE INDEX (For the full key, see front matter pp. xxxi, l–li.)
Stage 1: Rejected. **Stage 2:** Widely shunned. **Stage 3:** Widespread but . . . **Stage 4:** Ubiquitous but . . . **Stage 5:** Fully accepted.
Invariably inferior forms marked by asterisk (*). • Ratios represent frequency of prevalent forms vs. variants in current books.

- "At points during the monstrous task of consumption, the flavors changed from just bacon and egg to the full *triage* [read *trio*] of bacon, eggs and beef, and then just beef and egg." BryAnn Becker, "Whisk & Chop Aims for Diner Feel, Misses Mark," *Argus Leader* (Sioux Falls), 9 May 2010, at D1.
- "Durham said that the *triage* [read *trio*] of drama, dance, and vocals was part of the what made the musical a success." "Leon High School Drama Students Performing in Musical '13,'" *Tallahasee Democrat*, 13 Mar. 2011, Breaking News §.

triathlon. See -ATHLON.

*tribesperson. See SEXISM (C).

*tricentenary; *tricentennial. See **tercentenary.**

triceps. While the technically correct term for these three-anchored muscles (especially the back muscle of the upper arm, called the *triceps brachii* by anatomists) is *triceps* in both singular and plural forms, it has become common since 1950 when writing of a single muscle to drop the -*s*. Hence *tricep* has become a variant form—e.g.: "Then a therapist thumps the *tricep* and bicep of the bad right arm." Katti Gray, "Healing Is a Matter of Time—and Love," *Newsday* (N.Y.), 29 Oct. 2002, pt. II, at B2. This variant appears mostly in listings of sports injuries. It is better to stick to the standard singular *triceps*, by far the more commonly used form. But given the acceptance of *bicep* as a singular, *tricep* probably can't be far behind. See **bicep.** Cf. **pecs** & **quadriceps.**

Current ratio (*left triceps* vs. *left tricep*): 4:1

trifecta (/trɪ-**fek**-tə/) is a wager to pick, in correct order, the first-, second-, and third-place winners of a race, especially a horse race. The term was coined in the 1970s on the model of *perfecta* (= a wager to pick the first two winners of a race), which itself dates from 1961.

trillion. In the United States and France, *trillion* means "a million millions"; but in Great Britain, it traditionally means "a million million millions." The difference is more than substantial. But British writers today generally follow the American usage. Cf. **billion.**

trim. For the use of this verb in opposite senses, see CONTRONYMS.

trimestral—not *trimestrial*—is the traditional, standard adjective corresponding to *trimester.* Cf. **semestral.**

Current ratio: 1:1

trimonthly (= [1] occurring once every three months; or [2] lasting for three months) is typically inferior to the more common *quarterly*—e.g.: "The money that they collect this month will allow them to continue to provide such services as publishing a *trimonthly* [read *quarterly*] newsletter." Darren Becker, "Montreal Centre Wages Campaign for Peace," *Montreal Gaz.*, 15 Dec. 1996, at D3.

It's wrong to use *trimonthly* in the sense "three times a month," as some writers do. Cf. BI-.

trio. For a curious error, see **triage.**

triple. See **treble.**

triumphant; triumphal. People are *triumphant* (= celebrating a triumph), but events and actions are *triumphal* (= of, relating to, or constituting a triumph). *Triumphant* has always been the more frequent term in Modern English.

triumvir (= one of three officers forming an administrative or rulemaking group, which is called a *triumvirate*) forms the plural *triumvirs* or (less good) **triumviri*. (See PLURALS (B).) The word is pronounced /tri-əm-vər/.

Current ratio (*triumvirs* vs. **triumviri*): 9:1

-TRIX. See SEXISM (D).

trod; trodden. See **tread.**

troll. See **trawl.**

trolley (= a wheeled carriage) is the standard spelling in AmE and BrE alike. **Trolly* is a variant.

Current ratio: 124:1

trompe l'oeil; *trompe d'oeil; *tromp d'oeil; *trump l'oeil. The first spelling of this GALLICISM, meaning "deceives the eye," is by far the most common. It's predominant in AmE and BrE print sources, and it's the spelling recorded in most dictionaries. The second spelling is less common. The last two are NEEDLESS VARIANTS, the last one rare. The phrase can apply to any illusion as well as to a highly realistic style of painting—e.g.:

- "In architecture, fashion, and art, the Baroque period is distinguished by elaborate accessories and embellishments, from Corinthian capitals on pillars to ribbons and laces on clothing to the grand display of *tromp d'oeil* [read *trompe l'oeil*] murals to the grand statues of Bernini." Chelsea Quinn Yarbro, *Communion Blood* 16 (1999).
- "The latest for high-flying male executives, says Forbes magazine, is a custom-crafted porcelain veneer for one's teeth. This *tromp d'oeil* [read *trompe l'oeil*] is pearly white, dazzling and very costly." Ros Davidson, "A Drug Invented for Chemical Warfare Has Taken Off Across America as a Beauty Treatment That Paralyses . . . ," *Sunday Herald*, 28 May 2002, at P8.

The phrase is pronounced (in English) /trawmp lə-ee/.

Current ratio (first three headwords in order): 342:7:1

troop; troupe. Both words have their origins in the medieval French term *troupeau*, meaning "crowd" or "herd." *Troop* = an assembled unit of soldiers <a troop of parachutists>. The plural form *troops* signifies soldiers <the troops were deployed along the crest of the ridge> and is usually modified by an adjective to indicate some special training or assignment <ski troops> <airborne troops> <desert troops>. An adjective may also designate the soldiers' command level or department <divisional troops> <corps troops> <army troops> <Allied troops>. In this sense, *troops* refers to individual soldiers <three troops were injured in the raid>, but only when the reference is plural. That is, a single soldier, sailor, or pilot would never be termed *a troop*.

While some object to the use of *troops* (always plural) to refer to individuals, the usage is hardly new—e.g.: "A Vera Cruz letter-writer says that in the course of the insurrection in that city, three of the Government *troops* were killed and five wounded." "Mexican News—Further Details," *N.Y. Times*, 17 June 1853, at 1. Today it's standard, despite the inherent ambiguity presented by the collective sense of *troop*.

Troupe = a company of actors, acrobats, or other performers <a troupe of actors> <a troupe of circus performers>. Some writers misuse *troop* for *troupe*—e.g.:

- "The 15-member *troop* [read *troupe*] that puts on the circus hasn't missed a show since the incident on Wednesday." Robert Farley, "The Show Must Go On," *Patriot & Evening News* (Harrisburg), 12 May 1997, at A1.
- "A writer, director and military scholar, Milius assembled a worthy *troop* [read *troupe*] of tough-guy actors for his brawny 'Rough Riders' miniseries." Lon Grahnke, "Charging Forth into History," *Chicago Sun-Times*, 18 July 1997, at 37.

LANGUAGE-CHANGE INDEX
troop misused for *troupe*: Stage 1
Current ratio (*theater/-re troupe* vs.
theater/-re troop): 41:1

trooper; trouper. *Trooper* = (1) a cavalry soldier or horse; (2) a police officer mounted on horseback; or (3) a state police officer. *Trouper* = (1) a member of an acting troupe; (2) someone who handles adversity well; or (3) a loyal, dependable person. The proper expression, traditionally, is *real trouper* (sense 2), not *real trooper*. Yet while the correct form remains more common in BrE, the incorrect form has been gaining ground since 1970, especially in AmE—e.g.:

- "Quite the *trooper* [read *trouper*], Rees; he never once complained about the heat or the jellyfish or anything." Doug Pike, "By Jove, English Chap Is a Real *Trooper* [read *Trouper*]," *Houston Chron.*, 17 Oct. 1993, Sports §, at 27.
- "A real *trooper* [read *trouper*], Hanson was back at work the next day—sporting crutches, of course." "On the Mend," *Ft. Worth Star-Telegram*, 3 Mar. 1996, at 1.
- "Recently, our beloved 16-year-old cat, Casey, was stricken with cancer. Nevertheless, she was a real *trooper* [read *trouper*] until the end." Percy Ross, "Mom Needs Refrigerator," *St. Louis Post-Dispatch*, 20 Aug. 1997, at E6.

LANGUAGE-CHANGE INDEX
real trooper for *real trouper*: Stage 3
Current ratio (*real trouper* vs. *real trooper* in BrE): 5:1
Current ratio (same in AmE): 1:2

trope (/trohp/) means (1) a figure of speech, esp. a word or phrase used metaphorically, or (2) a motif.

Sense 1 is the traditional one—e.g.: "And yet he has held on to the *trope* of product-launch-as-birth; as recently as the days following the launch of the iPhone, he surprised someone who's known him for more than a decade by speaking of the laborlike 'emotional trauma' of bringing the iPhone to market." Tom Junod, "Steve Jobs and the Portal to the Invisible," *Esquire*, 1 Oct. 2008, at 185.

But the second sense is far more common in AmE print sources today: e.g.— " 'Nick & Norah' is clearly more mainstream and formulaic than 'Victor Vargas.' . . . But [Peter] Sollett is able to take familiar teen *tropes* and transform them into low-key magic." David Ansen, "Love Me, Love My Mix Tape," *Newsweek*, 6 Oct. 2008, at 58. And even that sense has itself become more of a *trope* in the traditional meaning: the sense is often closer to "cliché" than "motif."

troubled; troublesome; troublous. *Troubled* = (1) anxious or worried <he had a troubled look>; or (2) having lots of problems <a troubled relationship>. *Troublesome* = causing many pesky problems <troublesome dietary restrictions>. *Troublous* = (1) stormy and difficult <these troublous times>; or (2) causing serious trouble; troublesome <a troublous position to take in the litigation>. *Troublous* is a literary, old-fashioned word.

troubleshoot > troubleshot > troubleshot. So inflected. The erroneous past-tense and past-participial form *troubleshooted* sometimes appears, especially in AmE—e.g.:

- "Throughout the evening she *troubleshooted* [read *troubleshot*], greeted guests, mourned the winning low bid on a set of top-notch golf clubs placed by mistake on the silent-auction table, and worried about how the crowd was responding to the new location." Nancy Bartley, "Far East Gala II," *Seattle Times*, 16 Sept. 1991, at C2.
- "She's budgeted, run elections outside the city, helped prepare tax bills, maintained vital records, taken County Board minutes, *troubleshooted* [read *troubleshot*] disputes, etc." "Peoria County Clerk: JoAnn Thomas," *Peoria J. Star*, 24 Oct. 1998, at A4.
- "The approach to troubleshooting will vary slightly depending on whether it is a new system being commissioned or an old system being *troubleshooted* [read *troubleshot*]." Deon Reynders et al., *Practical Industrial Data Communications* 405 (2005).

See IRREGULAR VERBS.

LANGUAGE-CHANGE INDEX
troubleshooted for *troubleshot*: Stage 1
Current ratio (*troubleshot* vs. *troubleshooted*): 10:1

trough (= [1] a long narrow container for animals' water or food, [2] a channel for moving water, [3] a short period of low activity, depressed prices, etc., [4] the hollow area between two waves, or [5] in meteorology, an area of low pressure) is pronounced /trof/ and mispronounced /troth/ or /troh/.

LANGUAGE-CHANGE INDEX (For the full key, see front matter pp. xxxi, l-li.)
Stage 1: Rejected. **Stage 2:** Widely shunned. **Stage 3:** Widespread but . . . **Stage 4:** Ubiquitous but . . . **Stage 5:** Fully accepted.
Invariably inferior forms marked by asterisk (*). • Ratios represent frequency of prevalent forms vs. variants in current books.

troupe. See **troop.**

trouper. See **trooper.**

trousseau /troo-**soh** or **troo**-soh/ (= the personal possessions that a woman brings with her into marriage) is an archaic word, to say the least. It has traditionally formed the French plural *trousseaux* in AmE and BrE alike. But since about 1970, *trousseaus* has made headway in AmE, while *trousseaux* has been somewhat in decline.

Current ratio (*trousseaux* vs. *trousseaus*): 2:1

truculence; *truculency. The first has been standard since about 1830. The second, though older in the language, is a NEEDLESS VARIANT that rarely appears.

Current ratio: 33:1

truculent = (1) cruel, savage; or (2) aggressively defiant; challengingly sulky; disagreeably feisty. Although sense 2 was once condemned as a SLIPSHOD EXTENSION, today it is the ordinary use—e.g.:

- "The Oilers acquired Edmonton native Brantt Myhres, a *truculent* left winger, from the Tampa Bay Lightning yesterday in exchange for a conditional draft pick." Tim Wharnsby, "Errey Will Sign with Stars," *Fin. Post,* 17 July 1997, at 56.
- "A *truculent* Nickles told Lenzner: 'You know I don't mind you messing with me, but I do mind you messing with my family.'" Susan Schmidt, "Witness Who Proposed Probe of Nickles Grilled by Senators," *Wash. Post,* 1 Aug. 1997, at A16.
- "This autumn, the film of the book is being released, starring Julia Ormond as the *truculent* and charming Smilla." Alexandra Shulman, "What a Grey Day," *Daily Telegraph,* 11 Aug. 1997, at 16.

Some usage books also condemn using *truculent* to mean "mercenary" or "base," but actual instances in which the word has those meanings are extremely rare.

*true facts. See **fact** (E).

*trump l'oeil. See **trompe l'oeil.**

truncheon. So spelled. See SPELLING (A).

trustee, n. **A. And** *trusty.* Trustee (/trəs-**tee**/) = a person who, having a nominal title to property, holds it in trust for the benefit of one or more others (the beneficiaries). *Trusty* (/**trəs**-tee/), n., is an Americanism meaning "a (trusted) convict or prisoner." E.g.: "Because five jail *trusties,* supervised by the St. John Sheriff's Office, provided the labor, the addition cost taxpayers less than \$12,000." "Room to Grow," *Times-Picayune* (New Orleans), 19 Sept. 1997, at B1.

B. And *executor.* In the context of wills and estates, people are frequently confused about the difference between an *executor* and a *trustee.* The *executor* collects the decedent's property, pays the debts, and hands over the remaining property to the people who are entitled to it under the will. A *trustee* becomes necessary only when the property must be held for a time because it cannot, for some reason, be handed over at once to the people entitled to it.

try and is, in AmE, a CASUALISM for *try to*—e.g.: "Mr. Kemp, who seemed intent on slowing his normally rapid speaking pace, accused the Administration of 'demagoguery' in using 'fear' to *try and* [read *try to*] panic older voters with charges that Republicans endanger the health of the Medicare program." Francis X. Clines, "Candidates Stick to the Issues, Not Ducking the Touchy Ones," *N.Y. Times,* 10 Oct. 1996, at A15. In BrE, however, *try and* is a standard idiom.

Current ratio (*try to* vs. *try and*): 9:1

tsar. See **czar.**

T-shirt; t-shirt; tee shirt; *tee-shirt; *T shirt. Although most writers prefer *T-shirt* (the predominant form since 1950), *tee shirt* is common and *t-shirt* acceptable (though it's not recorded in most dictionaries). But the hyphenated **tee-shirt* is so rare that it is properly labeled a NEEDLESS VARIANT. *Forbes* seems to be the only prominent publication that consistently uses the unhyphenated form **T shirt*—e.g.: "A charter airline called Hooters Air, owned by the restaurant chain known for its curvy waitresses in tight *T shirts* [read *T-shirts*] and hot pants, will take off by midyear—featuring flight attendants garbed in clingy warm-up suits." Aliya Sternstein, "Unfasten Your Seat Belts," *Forbes,* 17 Feb. 2003, at 52.

Current ratio (in order of headwords): 156:20:10:3:1

tubercular; tuberculous; tuberculoid; tuberculated. *Tubercular* = (1) of, relating to, or involving tuberculosis <tubercular disease>; (2) caused by the tubercle bacillus <tubercular meningitis>; (3) having lesions that are or seem like tubercles <tubercular matter>; or (4) of, relating to, involving, or resembling a tubercle <tubercular deposit>. *Tuberculous* = (1) involving or having tuberculosis <tuberculous patients>; or (2) caused by the tubercle bacillus <tuberculous meningitis>. *Tuberculoid* = resembling or mimicking tuberculosis <tuberculoid leprosy>. *Tuberculated* = having or covered by tubercles <tuberculated skin>.

In short, *tubercular* is the broadest, most multifaceted term, and it was the most popular of the terms in the 19th century. In its two senses, *tuberculous* has been more commonly used in medical literature since 1900—hence *tuberculous meningitis* was nearly 25 times as common as *tubercular meningitis* in 1960 and about 5 times as common in 2008. The most specific and least common terms are *tuberculoid* and *tuberculated.*

As long as this bacterial disease (formerly known as *consumption*) inhabits the globe, we are going to need all four adjectives.

tubful. Pl. *tubfuls*—not **tubsful.* See PLURALS (G).

Current ratio: 4:1

Tucsonan; *Tucsonian; *Tucsonite. The first is standard; the others are NEEDLESS VARIANTS. See DENIZEN LABELS.

Current ratio (*Tucsonan* vs. **Tucsonian*): 5:1

tumbril; *tumbrel. *Tumbril* (= a cart designed esp. for farm use) is the standard spelling—and has been since 1820 or so in both AmE and BrE. The variant spelling *tumbrel*, though accorded the primary status in many English-language dictionaries, has not clearly predominated in any variety of English since 1813.

Current ratio: 2:1

tunable. So spelled in AmE and BrE alike—not *tune-able*. See MUTE E.

Current ratio: 13:1

tuna fish. Strictly speaking, *tuna fish* is redundant because *tuna* is invariably a *fish*. Many have complained about this issue, which first arose about 1914—e.g.:

- "If he had his way, he would rid the world of 'tuna fish.' 'What else can a tuna be?' asks Anderson." Robert L. Miller, "Letter from the Publisher," *Sports Illustrated*, 9 July 1984, at 4.
- "Although grammatically correct, *tuna fish* is redundant. You wouldn't say trout fish, salmon fish or perch fish." Marlene Parrish, "Kick the Can," *Pitt. Post-Gaz.*, 16 Apr. 1995, at J9.
- "*Tuna fish* is redundant. It's tuna." Clint O'Connor, "Retired Printer Promotes Proper Use of Words," *Plain Dealer* (Cleveland), 3 Dec. 1996, at E9.

In fact, though, the phrase (dating from the early 20th century) denotes a useful nuance: *tuna fish* is the type of processed, canned fish that is commonly served in sandwiches, whereas *tuna* typically refers to fresher types such as those found in seafood restaurants and sushi bars. Cf. **apple cider.**

tunnel, vb., makes *tunneled* and *tunneling* in AmE, *tunnelled* and *tunnelling* in BrE. See SPELLING (B).

tu quoque /too **kwoh**-kwee/ (lit., "you also") = a retort in kind; accusing an accuser of a similar offense. Traditionally, the phrase serves as a noun—e.g.:

- "Another element of Ehrenreich's argument . . . can be summed up as *tu quoque*—or, you're another." Midge Decter, "Who Is Addicted to What?" *Commentary*, 1 Apr. 1994, at 53.
- "Such gatekeepers of the right as Irving Kristol and Robert Bartley blithely promote their flat-earth ideas with breathtaking intellectual dishonesty, and no amount of *tu quoque* can smear it away." Todd Gitlin, "Up from Conservatism," *Wash. Monthly*, 1 Sept. 1996, at 46.

The term is also frequently used as an adjective—e.g.:

- "But Mr. Wheatcroft's book is more than an extended *tu quoque* philippic against moralistic hypocrites in the West." Herb Greer, "The Ottomans," *Nat'l Rev.*, 15 Aug. 1994, at 68.
- "They managed to outflank the court's ban on *tu quoque* evidence (meaning, 'If I am guilty, you are, too'), a stricture aimed at keeping Allied excesses, notably the mass bombing of German cities, out of the trial." Robert Shnayerson, "Judgment at Nuremburg," *Smithsonian*, 1 Oct. 1996, at 124.

And it's awkwardly coming into use as a verb—e.g.:

- "Retiring Sen. Dennis DeConcini at first declined to answer her question, finally *tu quoque-ing* her with the question, 'What about your own pension, Miss Stahl?'" William F. Buckley Jr., "Pension Exposé Perfectly Timed," *Daily Oklahoman*, 5 Nov. 1994, at 8.
- "Even the new scandal over Clinton's shady ties to an Indonesian financial group, which date back to his early days in Arkansas politics, isn't helping Dole, who has also taken enough money from foreign donors that the Clinton campaign, unable to deny the charges, can '*tu quoque*' the issue." Joseph Sobran, "Not Different Enough," *News & Record* (Greensboro), 27 Oct. 1996, at F4.

See LATINISMS.

turbid; turgid; turpid; torpid. *Turbid* = (of water) muddy, thick; (fig.) disordered. *Turgid* = swollen, distended, bloated, as with fluid—and by extension, it means "pompous." *Turpid* is a rare word meaning "filthy, worthless"; it's related to the word *turpitude* (= baseness, depravity). *Torpid* = dormant, sluggish, apathetic.

Turbid is sometimes erroneously displaced by *turgid*—e.g.:

- "Is there some way for us in the media to escape the *turgid* [read *turbid*] river flowing from our cynical exploitation of Diana's death and hypocritical lynch-mob reporting of Bill Clinton's indiscretion?" Brandt Ayers, "Gossip Gone Mad Threatening to Hang the Media's Credibility," *Charleston Gaz.*, 9 Sept. 1998, at A7.
- "Onto these *turgid* [read *turbid*] waters Logan hopes to pour the oil of dispassionate science." James Ricci, "Life and Death Study," *L.A. Times*, 28 Apr. 2002, Mag. §, at 5.
- "Frazier serendipitously discovers (as I did as a boy, 60 years before) a stream in Montclair, N.J., called the Third River, which winds its tired way through suburban strip malls, mill towns, industrial wastelands, Environmental Protection Agency Superfund sites and *turgid* [read *turbid*] swamps to the Passaic River, Newark Bay and eventually the Atlantic Ocean." E. William Smethurst Jr., "Ian Frazier's Perfect Book on Fishing Is Quite a Catch," *Chicago Trib.*, 19 May 2002, Books §, at 4.

Turbid has two corresponding nouns: *turbidity* and *turbidness*. Although the *OED* gives preference to *turbidness*, the form *turbidity* appears hundreds of times as often in print sources, perhaps because of its resemblance to *morbidity*—e.g.:

- "The fish were stressed in recent weeks by increases in water temperature and *turbidity*, he said." "State Kills 3,500 Trout After Disease Spreads," *Baltimore Sun*, 18 Aug. 1995, at C12.
- "Reducing *turbidity*, or water disturbance, makes more oxygen available for fish and other water life." Chris Kelley, "Local Firm, National Leader Team Up on Dredging Plan," *Dallas Morning News*, 11 July 1997, at A1.

LANGUAGE-CHANGE INDEX
turgid misused for *turbid*: Stage 1

---

tureen; terrine. *Tureen* (/t[y]oo-**reen**/) = a large lidded dish used for serving vegetables or soup. This has been the standard spelling since the early 18th century. Etymologically, it was a corruption of the French word *terrine*—influenced perhaps by the spelling of the Italian city Turin. Beginning in the 1980s and 1990s, *terrine* began to appear on French-influenced ethnic menus throughout the English-speaking world in the sense of either a food made of cooked meat, fish, or fruit and served in a usually loaf-shaped dish; or else the loaf-shaped dish itself. The words are now doublets: they have more or less distinct meanings and forms even though they are etymologically identical <I own a soup *tureen* given to my parents at their wedding in 1951> <She frequently orders lamb-curry *terrine* at her favorite Moroccan restaurant>.

turf. Pl. *turfs* in AmE, *turves* in BrE. See PLURALS (C).

turgid; turpid. See **turbid.**

Turin; Torino. Since the 18th century, the anglicized name (or exonym) for the Italian city has been *Turin*—not *Torino*. We likewise say *Rome*, not *Roma*; *Florence*, not *Firenze*; *Venice*, not *Venezia*. Yet when NBC broadcast the Winter Olympics from *Turin* in 2006, all the broadcasters hewed to calling the city *Torino*. Perhaps it seemed more "authentic." Perhaps the exonym *Turin* was not considered well-enough known to English speakers with its anglicized name, or perhaps broadcasters were concerned that all the "Torino 2006" signs might confuse viewers. One wonders, though, what would happen if the site had been Venice or Florence.

Current ratio: 3:1

Turkmen. For a citizen of Turkmenistan, this is the standard term. The plural is *Turkmens*. See DENIZEN LABELS.

Two archaic variants are *Turcoman* (prevalent from the 18th century to about 1875) and *Turkoman* (prevalent from about 1875 to 1950). They formed their plurals in -*mans*, not -*men*. *Turkmen* has been vastly predominant since about 1950.

Current ratio (*Turkmen* vs. *Turkoman* vs. *Turcoman*): 7:2:1

turnaround, 180-degree. See **180-degree turnaround.**

tussah; tussore; tussar. A 16th-century Hindi loanword denoting a type of silk that first became widely popular in the late 19th century, *tussah* is the standard spelling in AmE; *tussore* in BrE; and *tussar* in Indian English. In World English, *tussah* has predominated since about 1990.

twilight; twilit. Though normally a noun, *twilight* can function as an adjective <her twilight years>. And in most contexts it's better than *twilit*, which suggests (wrongly) that there's a verb *to twilight*. But the form *twilit* is current and acceptable in the sense "lighted by twilight" <a twilit stadium>. Those who find that

phrase strange-looking can always resort to a roundabout wording <a stadium illuminated by twilight>. *Twilighted* is nonstandard. Cf. **light.**

Current ratio (*twilit* vs. *twilighted*): 24:1

Twitter. One *tweets* or *sends a tweet* on Twitter, the social-media website. At least I do from time to time: @BryanAGarner.

two and two (is) (are). See SUBJECT–VERB AGREEMENT (G).

twofold, threefold, fourfold, and the like should each be spelled as one word.

two halves. See **half** (D).

two worst. See **worst** (B).

tying. So spelled—not *tieing*. See **tie.**

Current ratio: 229:1

tyke (= [1] a mongrel dog, or [2] a child, esp. a small boy) is the standard spelling. *Tike* is a variant.

Current ratio (*tykes* vs. *tikes*): 4:1

tympani. See **timpani.**

tympanum (the eardrum) forms the standard plural *tympana*—*tympanums* being a variant.

Current ratio (*tympana* vs. *tympanums*): 4:1

tyne. See **tine.**

type. See **class.**

type of—like *kind of*, *sort of*, and *variety of*—is often used unnecessarily and inelegantly. But when the word *type* does appear, it must have its *of*—which is unfortunately dropped in the following examples. They are typical of the modern American colloquial trend:

- "The Cloister is exquisitely beautiful and fine for a different *type person* [read *type of person*]." Rheta G. Johnson, "Campfires, Swamps Hold Ancient Truths," *Atlanta J.-Const.*, 24 Mar. 1997, at D1.
- "Councilman Mike Tassin also opposed the project, saying this *type person* [read *type of person*] does not match others already in the area." Adrian Angelette, "Rodeo Bar Development Reined In," *Advocate* (Baton Rouge), 25 Mar. 1997, at B1.

Cf. **couple** (C).

For the phrase *these type of*, see *these kind of*.

LANGUAGE-CHANGE INDEX

type person for *type of person*: Stage 3
Current ratio (*type of person* vs. *type person*): 18:1

typescript. See **manuscript.**

typhoon. See **hurricane.**

typing; typewriting. *Typing* is the standard term for operating an alphanumeric keyboard whether done on a typewriter, a computer, a PDA, or any other device. *Typewriting* refers to typing on a typewriter; on other devices it's become an obsolescent variant. But *typewriting* continues to be a useful term for (1) the act of operating a typewriter, or (2) the words physically printed on paper by a typewriter.

typo (= a typographical error) forms the plural *typos*.

typographical; typographic. Generally speaking, the first is preferred in both AmE and BrE—but each appears on both sides of the Atlantic. (See -IC.) In AmE, *typographical* is the usual choice when the following word begins with a vowel. It's most often used in the SET PHRASE *typographical error*.

typography; topography. *Typography* = the study and techniques of using type in printing, esp. as a designer or a typesetter. *Topography* = the three-dimensional shape of terrain. On occasion the first word gets misused for the second—e.g.: "The highest and best use of the property is the mining of limestone, says the appeal, 'given the *typography* [read *topography*], the high grade of plattin limestone deposits, the character of the surrounding property and the historic use of the subject property and the surrounding property.'" Ralph Dummit, "Pressure Prompts Hearing on Quarry," *St. Louis Post-Dispatch*, 12 Aug. 1998, St. Charles Post §, at 1.

LANGUAGE-CHANGE INDEX
typography misused for *topography*: Stage 1

tyrannical; tyrannous. Though the senses often seem to merge, *tyrannical* means "of, relating to, or involving a tyrant," while *tyrannous* means "of, relating to, or involving a tyranny." *Tyrannical* is the more usual word in AmE and BrE alike. In the following example, it can be readily seen that a tyrant is being suggested: "Is Parks and Recreation Commissioner Harry Stern a *tyrannical* despot who deprives hobbyists of their natural right to troll for metallic treasure?" Rachel Malamud, "A Stern Confrontation," *Village Voice*, 29 July 1997, at 26.

Yet here the two forms provoke suspicions of INELEGANT VARIATION: "As for white fears of *tyrannical* black governments (there is no shortage of examples from black-ruled Africa), need I remind him that the victims of these *tyrannous* regimes are predominantly black people?" Milton Allimadi, "Democracy in S. Africa," *Newsday* (N.Y.), 6 Oct. 1990, at 14.

tyrannize, a verb introduced into the language in the 15th century, was originally an intransitive verb meaning "to exercise oppressive power" <he tyrannized over his people for two decades>. Since the late 19th century, the verb has more commonly been transitive in the sense "to oppress or rule over severely" <he tyrannized his people for two decades>.

tyre. See **tire.**

tyro (= a beginner, novice) is the standard spelling in AmE. *Tiro* predominates in BrE. Pl. *tyros* (or, in BrE, *tiros*). See PLURALS (D).

U

U AND NON-U. See CLASS DISTINCTIONS.

ugly is sometimes used in the sense "ill-tempered, mean" <Mike is being ugly again>. The *OED* dates *ugly* in the sense "cross, angry" from the 17th century, with examples up to the 19th century. *Ugly customer* (= a person who is difficult to deal with or likely to cause trouble) appears in Charles Dickens's *Martin Chuzzlewit* (1844) and several other 19th-century sources.

ukase (/yoo-**kays**/ or /**yoo**-kays/), originally a Russian term, meant literally "a decree or edict, having the force of law, issued by the Russian emperor or government" (*OED*). By extension it has come to mean "any proclamation or decree, esp. of a final or arbitrary nature." E.g.: "Robert Landauer, former editorial page editor of The Oregonian, says citizens see the planning as growing out of a participatory process and not from *ukases* issued by professional planners." E.J. Dionne, "Portland Has Cut Through Obstacles to Make Urban Planning Work," *News & Record* (Greensboro), 1 June 1997, at F4.

ukulele. Preferably so spelled in AmE and BrE alike—not **ukelele* (a variant spelling perhaps influenced by the clipped form *uke* (/yook/). See SPELLING (A).

Current ratio: 8:1

ulna (= the inner bone of the lower arm), perhaps because it appears mostly in technical contexts, forms the plural *ulnae* (/**əl**-nee/) much more often than *ulnas*.

Current ratio: 4:1

ult. See **inst.**

ultimate destination. See **destination.**

ultimately = (1) in the end <she ultimately changed her mind>; (2) basically; fundamentally <the two words are ultimately related>. Cf. **penultimate.**

ultimatum. Pl. *ultimatums.* The native plural *-ums* has long been considered preferable to the Latinate **ultimata*, which has been comparatively uncommon in print sources since about 1900. E.g.: "The 49ers president delivered an ultimatum to a town that doesn't

LANGUAGE-CHANGE INDEX (For the full key, see front matter pp. xxxi, l–li.)
Stage 1: Rejected. **Stage 2:** Widely shunned. **Stage 3:** Widespread but . . . **Stage 4:** Ubiquitous but . . . **Stage 5:** Fully accepted.
Invariably inferior forms marked by asterisk (*). • Ratios represent frequency of prevalent forms vs. variants in current books.

respond to *ultimata* [read *ultimatums*]." Ray Ratto, "This Ultimatum Goes Against Team Policy," *S.F. Examiner*, 12 Feb. 1997, at D1. See PLURALS (B).

Current ratio: 7:1

umbo (= a rounded protuberance in the middle of a shield) forms the plural *umbones* (/əm-**boh**-neez/)—not *umbos.

Current ratio: 2:1

umlaut; diaeresis. These words denote the same mark consisting of two raised dots (¨) placed over a vowel, but they serve different phonetic functions. An *umlaut* (pronounced /**oom**-lowt/) indicates that the vowel has a modified sound—especially in German, as in *Männer* (pronounced /**men**-ner/). Generally, when an umlaut is omitted from a German word or name, an *e* is inserted after the vowel that had the umlaut—so, for example, *Göthe* becomes *Goethe* and *Münster* becomes *Muenster*. A *diaeresis* (pronounced /dɪ-**er**-ə-sis/ and sometimes spelled *dieresis*) indicates that the second of two adjacent vowels is pronounced separately, as in *naïve*.

But the distinction is largely academic: even with modern word-processing capabilities, these marks are often omitted. See DIACRITICAL MARKS.

umpteenth is sometimes misspelled *umteenth—e.g.: "A House subcommittee is at work on Virginia's *umteenth* [read *umpteenth*] study of campaign-finance reform." "Campaign-Finance Reform: Mandate Disclosure," *Virginian-Pilot & Ledger Star* (Norfolk), 8 Aug. 1996, at A18.

Current ratio: 287:1

UN-. See NEGATIVES (A).

unable. See **incapable**.

*unadvisable. See **inadvisable**.

unalienable. See **inalienable**.

unalterable; *inalterable. The first is standard. The second is a NEEDLESS VARIANT.

Current ratio: 16:1

unanimous appears in various redundant phrases, such as **unanimously of one opinion*, **entirely unanimous*, and **completely unanimous*. See ADJECTIVES (B) & REDUNDANCY.

unapt. See **inapt**.

unartistic. See **inartistic**.

unavoidable. See ADJECTIVES (B).

unaware; unawares. Properly, *unaware* is the adjective <I am unaware of that book> and *unawares* the adverb <the rainstorm caught us unawares>. Hence *taken unaware and *caught unaware are mistakes for the SET PHRASES *taken unawares* and *caught unawares*, both of which have a continuous literary tradition in AmE and BrE from the 18th century. E.g.:

- "And Denver was taken *unaware* [read *unawares*] when huge telephone boxes began appearing curbside in residential neighborhoods." Joanne Ditmer, "Churches Define Sense of Place," *Denver Post*, 13 July 1997, at E2.
- "Reportedly, he has had the ailments for months but the Flyers were caught *unaware* [read *unawares*]." Nancy L. Marrapese, "Burning Ambition," *Boston Globe*, 28 Sept. 1997, at E13.

LANGUAGE-CHANGE INDEX
1. *taken unaware for *taken unawares*: Stage 2
Current ratio (*taken unawares* vs.
*taken unaware): 9:1
2. *caught unaware for *caught unawares*: Stage 4
Current ratio (*caught unawares* vs.
*caught unaware): 2:1

unbeknown; unbeknownst. George P. Krapp suggested that both forms are humorous, colloquial, and dialectal. *A Comprehensive Guide to Good English* 602 (1927). The *COD* likewise suggests that both are colloquial. Eric Partridge and John Simon have written, in conformity with the *OED*, that *unbeknown* is preferred over the dialectal *unbeknownst*.

These inconsistent pronouncements serve as confusing guides. We can perhaps accept as British orthodoxy the *COD*'s suggestion that in BrE the forms are colloquial (for *unknown*). In AmE, neither can really be called dialectal or colloquial, since the words are essentially literary. In current AmE usage, *unbeknownst* far outranges *unbeknown* in frequency, and it must therefore be considered at least acceptable. But *unbeknownst*, like other *-st* forms (e.g., *whilst*, *amidst*), seems to come less naturally to AmE. So there's something to be said for preferring *unbeknown*—e.g.:

- "*Unbeknown* to her, though, Christmas was the day a curse transformed him from a handsome but vain young prince into the ugly, angry Beast." Susan King, "The Untold Chapter," *L.A. Times*, 13 Nov. 1997, at F41.
- "*Unbeknown* to the landlord, the group installed chemistry equipment, sinks, and a fume hood." Aaron Zitner, "What Ever Happened to the Saga of RU-486?" *Boston Globe*, 23 Nov. 1997, at 18.
- "*Unbeknown* to the participants—either before or after—for some of the people, slipped into twenty of their thirty sets was a word linked to the negative aspects of ageing—words like *old, lonely, grey, forgetful, retired*, etc. The other participants, again quite *unbeknown* to them, saw only neutral words not linked to ageing." Ian Robertson, *The Winner Effect: How Power Affects Your Brain* 90 (2012).

See DIALECT.

From 1800 to about 1968, *unbeknown* was the predominant form in AmE print sources, and it was predominant in BrE till about 2000. Since then, *unbeknownst* has grown in frequency of occurrence and surpassed its rival. Though it shows no signs of retreating, it has not yet reached Stage 5 because some worthy opinion-makers still wrinkle their noses.

LANGUAGE-CHANGE INDEX
unbeknownst for *unbeknown*: Stage 4
Current ratio (*unbeknownst* vs.
unbeknown): 3:1

unbelief. See **disbelief.**

unbeliever. See **atheist.**

unbroken. See ADJECTIVES (B).

*uncategorically is a silly but distressingly common MALAPROPISM for *categorically* (= unconditionally, without qualification). Having first appeared about 1900 and spread during the latter half of the 20th century, it came to national prominence in 1991. Testifying before the Senate Judiciary Committee, Judge Clarence Thomas "uncategorically" denied that he had discussed pornographic materials with Ms. Anita Hill: "Senator, I would like to start by saying unequivocally, *uncategorically*, that I deny each and every single allegation against me today." "The Thomas Nomination," *N.Y. Times*, 13 Oct. 1991, § 1, at 12.

Even by then, the illogically formed NONWORD had already made its way into print—e.g.: " 'I adore Rourke,' Jean-Pierre Wagneur says *uncategorically* [read *categorically*]." Alessandra Stanley, "Can 50 Million Frenchmen Be Wrong?" *N.Y. Times*, 21 Oct. 1990, § 6, at 41. Cf. ***unmercilessly** & ***unrelentlessly.**
> LANGUAGE-CHANGE INDEX
> **uncategorically*: Stage 1
> Current ratio (*categorically* vs.
> **uncategorically*): 618:1

unceremonious. See **ceremonial.**

uncharted (= unmapped), as in *uncharted territory*, is often wrongly written *unchartered*. Although the erroneous form is not nearly as common as the correct one, it has been gradually spreading since the mid-1970s—e.g.:

- "He believes this latest frontier in communications is an *unchartered* [read *uncharted*] territory bound to attract Wild West–type outlaws." Stephen Rodrick, "Cyberstoned," *Star Trib.* (Minneapolis), 22 May 1995, at A10.
- "This was not the Africa of Tarzan lore, my friend. Rather, it was *unchartered* [read *uncharted*] territory, a presentation of a dignified Africa." Rhonda Chriss Lokeman, "From Africa, with Love," *Kansas City Star*, 20 June 1995, at B7.
- "The benefits of moving into *unchartered* [read *uncharted*] territory are often weighed up against the perceived dangers of allowing such open-ended opportunities to emerge." *Beginning Teachers: Reviewing Disastrous Lessons* 23 (Michael Crowhurst ed., 2015).

An airplane might be *unchartered* if it had no scheduled flights. But unknown territory is *uncharted*, not *unchartered*. Cf. **chartered plane.**
> LANGUAGE-CHANGE INDEX
> *unchartered* misused for *uncharted*: Stage 1
> Current ratio (*uncharted waters* vs.
> **unchartered waters*): 13:1

uncommunicative; *incommunicative. The former has been standard since about 1800. The latter is a NEEDLESS VARIANT.
> Current ratio: 13:1

*uncomparable. See **incomparable.**

unconscionably (= unreasonably, unscrupulously, outrageously) is sometimes misused for *unconsciously* or *unselfconsciously*—e.g.: "Educated speakers who *unconscionably* [read *unconsciously* or *unselfconsciously*] say 'It is *me*' generally shy away from 'It is *him*,' 'It is *her*,' 'It is *us*,' and the like." Norman Lewis, *Better English* 186 (rev. ed. 1961) (in which the author argues that "It is me" is "established, acceptable English"). See **conscionable.**
> LANGUAGE-CHANGE INDEX
> *unconscionably* misused for *unconsciously*: Stage 1

unconscious; subconscious. These words are most commonly adjectives. *Unconscious* = (1) lacking consciousness; senseless <the blow knocked him unconscious>; (2) unaware <she was unconscious of the danger>; (3) not perceived by oneself <an unconscious slip of the tongue>; or (4) not done on purpose; unintentional <an unconscious slight>. *Subconscious* = not fully or wholly conscious <a subconscious motive>.

But the words are also synonymous nouns meaning "the part of the human psyche that is inaccessible to consciousness and that is largely dominated by repressed desires and experiences that can't be recalled." Professional psychologists "tend to use the term 'unconscious' in preference to 'subconscious' nowadays. . . . [But] the preferred lay term seems to be 'subconscious.' " Donald Watson, *A Dictionary of Mind and Spirit* 326 (1991).

unconstitutional. See **nonconstitutional.**

uncontrollable; *incontrollable. The former has been standard since the 17th century. The latter is a NEEDLESS VARIANT.
> Current ratio: 207:1

UNCOUNTABLES. See COUNT NOUNS AND MASS NOUNS.

uncovered is often ambiguous. It may mean (1) "not covered" <because they forgot to put up the tarp, the plants were completely uncovered throughout the storm>; or (2) "having had the cover removed" <the winds blew the tarp and uncovered the plants>. Hence, to say *the plants were uncovered during the storm* creates an ambiguity.

unctuous (/əngk-choo-əs/) is so spelled. **Unctious* (/əng-shəs/) is a not-uncommon mispronunciation

---

LANGUAGE-CHANGE INDEX (For the full key, see front matter pp. xxxi, l–li.)
Stage 1: Rejected. **Stage 2:** Widely shunned. **Stage 3:** Widespread but . . . **Stage 4:** Ubiquitous but . . . **Stage 5:** Fully accepted.
Invariably inferior forms marked by asterisk (*). • Ratios represent frequency of prevalent forms vs. variants in current books.

and misspelling based on *unction*—e.g.: "Most unbelievably *unctious* [read *unctuous*]: Ginger Spice of the Spice Girls, after winning Best Dance Video: 'Lady Diana had real girl-power.'" Jim Sullivan, "MTV Awards: The Show, the Sex, the Stupidity," *Boston Globe*, 5 Sept. 1997, at C16.

LANGUAGE-CHANGE INDEX
unctuous misspelled *unctious: Stage 1
Current ratio: 68:1

undeniably. See **clearly.**

underestimate is often misused for *overestimate* when writers intend the phrase *impossible to overestimate*. The misuse renders the phrase illogical, even ludicrous—e.g.:

- "Claiming 'it's impossible to *underestimate* [read *overestimate*] the timidity of professors,' Mansfield [Harvey C. Mansfield Jr.] worries that too many scholars are studiously avoiding teaching the hot topics of the day." Anthony Flint, "Mansfield's Leaving Would Be Harvard's Loss," *Boston Globe*, 6 June 1993, at 41.
- "He also says it's impossible to *underestimate* [read *overestimate*] the value of positive role models for African American children." Michael Abramowitz, "Split Could Bar Election of Black Election in P.G.," *Wash. Post*, 15 Aug. 1994, at D1.
- "'It is impossible to *underestimate* [read *overestimate*] the amount of damage the health care bill did in shaping the image of President Clinton as a big-government proponent,' Mr. From said at a news conference." Richard L. Berke, "Centrist Democrats' Poll Warns Clinton of Unrest," *N.Y. Times*, 18 Nov. 1994, at A10.
- "If we venture beyond the belief that war is determined by structural factors outside human control, it is impossible to *underestimate* [read *overestimate*] the importance of political norms for handling conflict." Susan G. Sample, "Military Buildups: Arming and War," in *What Do We Know About War?* 165, 191 (John A. Vasquez ed., 2000).

This error is akin to using *could care less for *couldn't care less*. See **couldn't care less** & ILLOGIC.

Sometimes, though, the writer really means *underestimate*—e.g.: "A little subtlety would have greatly enhanced 'Hamburger Hill's' potential for tragic irony, but the film makers are rigorously dedicated to the proposition that it's impossible to *underestimate* the intelligence of moviegoers." Kevin Thomas, "'Hamburger Hill': On the Lean Side," *L.A. Times*, 28 Aug. 1987, § 6, at 1.

LANGUAGE-CHANGE INDEX
**impossible to underestimate* for *impossible to overestimate*: Stage 2
Current ratio (*impossible to overestimate* vs. **impossible to underestimate*): 7:1

underhanded; underhand, adj. The shorter form is much older <underhand dealings>—having become established in the early 18th century—but *underhanded* spread in the 19th century and is now about twice as common. It must be accepted as standard—e.g.: "Partisans accused each other of unnecessary delay and *underhanded* negotiating tactics." Jeff Mayers

& Mike Flaherty, "Senate GOP Could OK Budget Deal," *Wis. State J.*, 20 Sept. 1997, at B1. Increasingly, *underhand* is confined to literal senses <because he hurt his shoulder, the tennis champion is temporarily having to use an underhand serve>.

LANGUAGE-CHANGE INDEX
underhanded for *underhand*: Stage 5
Current ratio (*underhanded tactics* vs. *underhand tactics*): 2:1

underlay, n.; **underlayment.** Denoting material placed under a structure, as for support, or under a floor covering or rooftop, *underlay* is the traditional noun, dating from the 14th century. It is the noun in BrE. *Underlayment*, dating from 1949, is an Americanism that since 1970 has surpassed the old form in frequency of occurrence in AmE. But there the close linguistic rivalry continues—and lexicographers are said to be placing long-term wagers on one form or the other. My guess is that *underlayment* will be uncontested in AmE one day before long and that BrE will follow suit about 30 years later. But linguistic predictions are notoriously unreliable.

underlie; underlay, vb. *Underlie* is so spelled. *Underly is an infrequent blunder—e.g.:

- "They [want to restore] principles that some, maybe even most, people believe to *underly* [read *underlie*] the cornerstone of our cultures: human relationships, love, marriage." Susan E. Foley, "Fearmongering," *Santa Fe New Mexican*, 15 May 1997, at A9.
- "It is this belief, as well as other beliefs that devalue women and support male privilege and entitlement, that *underly* [read *underlies*] the violent behavior." Paul Lee, "Domestic Violence," *Oregonian* (Portland), 9 Aug. 1997, at C7. (On the reason for using the singular verb, see SUBJECT–VERB AGREEMENT (E).)
- "Monocultures of the mind, like agricultural monocultures, are vulnerable to parasitisation or sudden collapses to a degree that biodiverse systems are not; and as Robert Ulanowicz argues, apparently 'irrational' associations and even 'mistakes' seem to *underly* [read *underlie*] much human creativity." David W. Kidner, *Nature and Experience in the Culture of Delusion* 263 (2012) (footnotes omitted).

Writers fall into the error because they more commonly see the adjectival participle *underlying* than the uninflected verb.

Underlay is properly the past tense of *underlie*—e.g.: "Atkins gets the doggedness, the country-boy simplicity that *underlay* Dunne's unquestioning devotion to duty, as well as the fey quality of his madness." Marianne Evett, "Irishman's Story a Poignant Tragedy," *Plain Dealer* (Cleveland), 11 May 1997, Arts §, at 21. But the word is sometimes used wrongly for *underlie*—e.g.: "As the ground thaws in the spring, the moisture is kept from draining downward by the *underlaying* [read *underlying*] ice." "Beleaguered Vermont Endures Rite of Spring," *Providence J.-Bull.*, 6 Apr. 1997, at B2. As with the root verbs *lie* and *lay*, errors with the past tense and past participle are myriad—e.g.: "Under such circumstances, it was almost a natural solution, and the possibility had *underlied* [read *underlay*] everyone's thoughts for some time." Kojo Suzuki, *Paradise* 122 (Tyran Grillo trans., 1st Am. ed. 2006). See **lie (A), (D).**

> LANGUAGE-CHANGE INDEX
> 1. *underlie* misspelled **underly*: Stage 1
> Current ratio (*underlie the* vs. **underly the*): 72:1
> 2. *underlay* misused for *underlie*: Stage 1
> Current ratio (*the underlying rock* vs.
> **the underlaying rock*): 1,351:1

undermine. See **circumvent.**

undersigned, n. Eric Partridge said that this attributive noun <the undersigned agrees to the following terms and conditions> is "permissible in law; affected or tediously jocular elsewhere" (*U&A* at 340). But even in law it's a silly way of avoiding the FIRST PERSON.

UNDERSTOOD WORDS are common in English, and they usually aren't very troublesome if we can mentally supply them. Often they occur at the outset of sentences. *More important* is short for *what is more important*; *as pointed out earlier* is short for *as was pointed out earlier.*

In a compound sentence, parts of a verb phrase can carry over from the first verb phrase to the second, in which they are understood: "Gorbachev has demanded that Lithuania suspend the declaration of independence before the blockade can be lifted and *talks begun.*" (That sentence is considerably more elegant than it would have been if the second verb phrase had appeared in full: *talks can be begun.*)

On verbs supposedly "understood" whose absence detracts from clarity, see BE-VERBS (A).

under the circumstances. See **circumstances (A).**

underway; under way. Some dictionaries record the term as two words when used adverbially, one word when used as an adjective preceding the noun <underway refueling>. In the phrases *get underway* (= to get into motion) and *be underway* (= to be in progress), the term is increasingly made one word, and it would be convenient to make that transformation, which has been underway since the 1960s, complete in all uses of the word.

**Under weigh* for *underway* is a visual MALAPROPISM undoubtedly based on a mistaken association with the nautical phrase *to weigh anchor*—e.g.:

- "The plot doesn't get *under weigh* [read *underway*] again until the explorers return topside." Thomas M. Disch, "Journey to the Center," *Wash. Post*, 30 Sept. 1990, Book World §, at 11.
- "After driving off planes, both ships got *under weigh* [read *underway*] by cutting our mooring lines." Harry Levins, "The Chief Yelled, 'This Is No War Game!'" *St. Louis Post-Dispatch*, 6 Dec. 1991, at 6.

- "After all, the life dynamic at play aboard a sailing ship *under weigh* [read *underway*] is trust." Mark McGarrity, "Joining the Sail Century," *Star-Ledger* (Newark), 30 June 2000, at 1.

This error is nothing new: it has occurred with some frequency since the mid-18th century. Cf. **aweigh.**

Although most other compound words starting with *under-* are closed, until recently the major newspaper style manuals still made *underway* two words. That changed in 2013 when the *AP Stylebook*—used by most U.S. newspapers—accepted it as one word in all uses.

> LANGUAGE-CHANGE INDEX
> **under weigh* for *underway*: Stage 2
> Current ratio (*get underway* vs.
> **get under weigh*): 7:1

undistinguishable. See **indistinguishable.**

undocumented alien. See **illegal immigrant.**

undocumented immigrant. See **illegal immigrant.**

undoubtably* is an archaic NONWORD equivalent to the standard *undoubtedly* or *indubitably*. E.g.: "As quarterback Damian Poalucci begins his final campaign against New Haven Saturday, he's also starting a season where he will *undoubtably* [read *undoubtedly*] be the Warriors' most-watched player—by opponents and fans alike." Jeff Schuler, "Poalucci Has Gaudy Numbers to Live Up To," *Morning Call* (Allentown, Pa.), 12 Sept. 1997, at S9. See **doubtlessly. Cf. **supposedly.**

> LANGUAGE-CHANGE INDEX
> **undoubtably* for *undoubtedly*: Stage 1
> Current ratio (*undoubtedly* vs. **undoubtably*): 871:1

undoubtedly. See **doubtlessly* & **clearly.**

undue alarm is not always an illogical phrase—e.g.: "Committee Chairman Richard Lugar (R-Ind.), sponsor of the legislation, said the CFTC was reacting with 'perhaps *undue alarm.*'" Mike Dorning, "Futures Overseer Fights Plan to Ease Regulation," *Chicago Trib.*, 12 Feb. 1997, Bus. §, at 1 (implying that some amount of alarm might be justified). But it usually does signal ILLOGIC—e.g.:

- "[The inspectors] do not carry guns and do not wish to *cause farmers undue alarm* [read *alarm farmers*] when they come for inspections." Paul Oldham, "Farmers Briefed on Hiring," *Tennessean*, 22 Oct. 1996, at B1.
- "To prevent *undue alarm*, Wednesday's test [tornado-warning system] will occur only if weather conditions are fair." "Metro Report," *Dallas Morning News*, 10 Dec. 1996, at A24. (And if fair weather comes, only the right amount of alarm will occur?)
- "The topic need *cause the reader no undue alarm* [read *not alarm the reader*]." W. Bolton & R.A. Higgins, *Materials for Engineers and Technicians* 111 (6th ed. 2015).

LANGUAGE-CHANGE INDEX (For the full key, see front matter pp. xxxi, l–li.)
Stage 1: Rejected. **Stage 2:** Widely shunned. **Stage 3:** Widespread but . . . **Stage 4:** Ubiquitous but . . . **Stage 5:** Fully accepted.
Invariably inferior forms marked by asterisk (*). • Ratios represent frequency of prevalent forms vs. variants in current books.

unearned income, to one unskilled in accounting, may seem like an OXYMORON. The term refers to income derived from investments as opposed to wages.

uneconomical; uneconomic; noneconomic. Strictly speaking, *uneconomical* should be the antonym of *economical* (= using resources carefully and without waste) and *noneconomic* the antonym of *economic* (= of, relating to, or involving trade, industry, and monetary policy and performance). That is the position in AmE—the two polarities just described. *Uneconomic* is a NEEDLESS VARIANT of both words.

But in BrE, curiously, *uneconomic* has been the predominant antonym of *economical* since the early 20th century <large cars are uneconomic to run>. E.g.: "Manifestly *uneconomic* [read *uneconomical*] projects have been pursued . . . . Lavish spending on the new federal capital, Abuja, is at odds with economic [correct] realities." "Aid and Reform in Nigeria," *Fin. Times,* 6 Jan. 1992, at 10. But given that *uneconomical* has grown close to *uneconomic* in their BrE rivalry, one can justifiably hope that the anomalously missing *-al* from the negative form in that variety of the language will soon be restored. See **economic (A).**

LANGUAGE-CHANGE INDEX
1. *uneconomic* for *uneconomical* (AmE): Stage 1
2. *uneconomic* for *uneconomical* (BrE): Stage 4

unenforceable; *nonenforceable. The first is standard in AmE and BrE alike. The second is a NEEDLESS VARIANT.

Current ratio: 100:1

unequivocal; *unequivocable. The adjective *equivocal* (= deliberately unclear in conveying information or opinion) was first used as an English word in the mid-16th century. By the mid-18th century, the antonym *unequivocal* (= completely clear and without possibility of doubt) had come into use. By 1800, the two terms occurred in print sources with almost equal frequency. Since the 1940s in AmE and the 1960s in BrE, the negative term *unequivocal* has occurred with greater frequency than *equivocal.*

In the mid-19th century, the mistaken form **unequivocable* first appeared. It became more and more widespread during the 20th century, reaching its zenith of popularity in the early 1980s. It has tapered off significantly since then, perhaps with the rise of spell-checkers, but it still occurs—e.g.:

- "Coach Joan Stolarik can say *unequivocably* [read *unequivocally*] that her team will win when Wilson Hunt swims against Wilson Fike." Tim Stevens, "Two Rival Wilson Teams, One Coach," *News & Observer* (Raleigh), 27 Nov. 1996, at C10.
- "And yet it is in this same voice that Martha Ingram states *unequivocably* [read *unequivocally*] her answer to the question: What do you like most about business?" Anne Faircloth, "Minding Martha's Business," *Fortune,* 29 Sept. 1997, at 173.
- "The Fort Worth Seminary and several other agencies gave *unequivocable* [read *unequivocal*] affirmation." Stewart G. Cole, *The History of Fundamentalism* 289 (2008).

Interestingly, the supposed antonym of this NONWORD, namely **equivocable,* has never gained any currency.

Since the early 19th century, the false adverb **unequivocably* has occurred with even greater frequency than **unequivocable.* This adverbial form, in fact, is the only one included in *W11*—labeled "nonstandard." Like the other mistaken forms, it declined precipitately after about 1984 (perhaps with rise of spell-checkers). Fortunately, it has never seriously rivaled the correct adverb *unequivocally.*

Unequivocal is pronounced /ən-i-**kwiv**-i-kəl/. Cf. **inimicable* (discussed at **inimical**).

LANGUAGE-CHANGE INDEX
*unequivocable for *unequivocal*: Stage 1
Current ratio (*unequivocal* vs. **unequivocable*): 674:1

unessential. See **nonessential.**

unexceptionable; unexceptional. *Unexceptionable* (= not objectionable) is historically the far more usual term. E.g.: "The imperial Chinese went so far as to dub their country 'the Middle Kingdom' so as to reflect what to them seemed an *unexceptionable* truth." Paul Campos, "Self-Absorption American-Style," *Rocky Mountain News* (Denver), 11 Dec. 2001, at A33.

Unexceptional (= not unusual) didn't come into common use until the mid-19th century. It now occurs with almost equal frequency. E.g.: "Outfielder Matt Lawdon is fine but *unexceptional*." Rod Beaton, "Yankees Land Their Men Again," *USA Today,* 14 Dec. 2001, at C7. See **exceptional (A).**

*unexpressive. See **inexpressive.**

*unfeasible. See **infeasible.**

*unfrequent. See **infrequent.**

unhappily. See **happily.**

uniform. See ADJECTIVES (B).

unintentional murder. See **murder (B).**

uninterest. See **disinterest.**

uninterested. See **disinterested.**

unique. Strictly speaking, *unique* means "being one of a kind," not "unusual." Hence the phrases **very unique, *quite unique, *how unique,* and the like are slovenly. The *OED* notes that this tendency to hyperbole—to use *unique* when all that is meant is "uncommon, unusual, remarkable"—began in the 19th century. However old it is, the tendency is worth resisting.

Unless the thing is the only one of its kind, rarity does not make it unique. For instance, if a thing is one in a million, logically there would be two things in two million. Rare indeed but not unique.

So because uniqueness, unlike rarity, is an absolute quality, something cannot logically be more or less unique than something else—any more than it could be especially complete. But some modifiers can justifiably be paired with *unique*—e.g.:

- "I save a *truly unique* experience for my final day—skiing a glacier in summer in a T-shirt." Margo Pfieff, "British Columbia Whistler's Summers Keep Blood Pumping," *Houston Chron.*, 9 Aug. 2015, Escapes §, at 3.
- "It's a social trend that makes Britain *almost unique* among developed economies, which see mostly rural to urban migration." George Osborne & Elizabeth Truss, "With Our Plan, the Countryside Can Become Britain's Engine of Growth," *Daily Telegraph*, 20 Aug. 2015, at 18.

Who can demand responsible use of the language from an ad writer who is reckless enough to say, in a national advertisement, that a certain luxury sedan is "so unique, it's capable of thought"? And what are we to make of the following examples?

- "This year the consensus among the development executives seems to be that there are some fantastically funny, very exciting, *very, very unique* talents here." Larry Doyle, "Searching for Jerry Seinfeld," *Time*, 16 Aug. 1993, at 18.
- "Residents of college basketball's *most unique* unincorporated village were in place yesterday afternoon, the day before their Blue Devils will face North Carolina." Malcolm Moran, "On the Duke Campus, Fans Form Bivouac," *N.Y. Times*, 2 Feb. 1995, at B7.
- "Turns out the University of Wisconsin football team is in the process of doing something *quite unique*." "1-Point Wins Set UW Apart," *Wis. State J.*, 27 Oct. 1997, at D1.
- "It is *extremely unique* with its combination of Japanese and English dialogue as well as its combination of its own script and that of the uber popular classic 'Fargo.'" Patrick Dougas, "'Kumiko, The Treasure Hunter,' Unique," *Great Falls Trib.* (Mont.), 26 June 2015, at H11.

Arguably, our modern culture lacks and does not *want* absolutes, in intellectual life or in language. But stick with the noncomparable *unique*, and you may stand out as almost unique. See ADJECTIVES (B).

LANGUAGE-CHANGE INDEX
unique as a word of degree, as in **very unique*: Stage 3

unisex (= not distinguishing or discriminating between sexes; suitable for both sexes) was first recorded by the *OED* in a 1968 article in *Life* magazine that sounds quaint today: "With-it young couples . . . are finding that looking alike is good fashion as well as good fun. The *unisex* trend was launched by . . . the teen-agers." The NEOLOGISM proved so necessary to late-20th-century culture that it quickly appreciated as a CASUALISM and is well accepted today. It applies to all manner of fashion, and even on occasion to public facilities that are traditionally segregated <unisex boutique> <unisex restrooms>. It's a far better word than the cold JARGON that is its only reasonable alternative in most contexts: *gender-neutral*.

United Kingdom. See **Great Britain.**

United States. A. Number. By the late 19th century in AmE, this proper noun had "ceased to have any suggestion of plurality about it." Harry T. Peck, *What Is Good English?* 3, 16 (1899). That represented a change from the early days of the republic when states'-rights particularism was rampant. It was once usual to say *the United States have*, as Alexander Hamilton did in *The Federalist* No. 15, at 108 (Clinton Rossiter ed., 1961).

The plural use was predominant in AmE till 1880 and in BrE till about 1895. Ever since, the proper noun *United States* has predominantly taken a singular verb.

Today, it's unidiomatic to suggest plurality in referring to the United States. But some BrE writers still use the phrase in this way—e.g.: "It has been shown that under the law of *some of the United States* [read *some states in the United States* or *some American states*] there is a legal advantage." Glanville Williams, *The Sanctity of Life and the Criminal Law* 183–84 (1957; repr. 1972).

LANGUAGE-CHANGE INDEX
United States used as a plural: Stage 1

B. Possessive. Like other words that are singular in meaning but formed from a plural, *United States* forms the possessive by adding an apostrophe alone <United States' interests>. See POSSESSIVES (A).

universal. See ADJECTIVES (B).

unkempt. A. Sense and Use. *Unkempt* is often said to be a word with a "lost positive," one of those interesting negatives without a corresponding positive word (cf. *discombobulate, disgruntled, nondescript*). That is, the word *kempt* is thought to be obsolete while *unkempt* thrives. (Perhaps this says something about the state of the world.) *Unkempt* means "uncombed, disheveled" (another word with a lost positive), although some of the earliest uses from the 14th century were figurative: *unkempt rhymes* and *unkempt words*. By the 18th century, most uses were literal: *unkempt hair, unkempt locks, unkempt fellows, unkempt cotton*. By the 19th century, the word took on broader senses of untidiness and applied to other things, such as clothes and farms.

The degree to which *kempt* is a lost positive is greatly overstated. Although *W11* traces the word back only to 1929, in fact it has appeared in print sporadically from the late 18th century, usually in the phrases *well-kempt, ill-kempt, more kempt*, and *less kempt*. These uses have steadily appeared up to the present day.

B. And *unkept*. Beginning in the mid-20th century, some writers and speakers began using *unkept* for *unkempt*. This example of a change resulting from folk etymology was first noted in Atcheson L. Hench, "Folk Substitution: 'Unkempt' Yields to 'Unkept,'" 41 *Am. Speech* 76 (1966). One linguist noted the error in a 1967 letter from Governor Ronald Reagan of California and predicted that "*unkempt* will disappear from the language eventually." Edward A. Stephenson, "'Unkept' Demonstrators," 42 *Am. Speech* 309, 310 (1967). See ETYMOLOGY (D).

LANGUAGE-CHANGE INDEX (For the full key, see front matter pp. xxxi, l–li.)
Stage 1: Rejected. **Stage 2:** Widely shunned. **Stage 3:** Widespread but . . . **Stage 4:** Ubiquitous but . . . **Stage 5:** Fully accepted.
Invariably inferior forms marked by asterisk (*). • Ratios represent frequency of prevalent forms vs. variants in current books.

Most commonly, *unkept* appears (quite appropriately) in phrases such as *unkept promises, unkept commitments,* and *unkept vows*—e.g.: "The *unkept* vow involves the company's stated intent to make its wildly popular AOL Instant Messenger (AIM) software work with other instant-messaging programs." Steven Levy, "Time for an Instant Fix," *Newsweek,* 30 Sept. 2002, at 38.

But the erroneous usage has become fairly common—e.g.:

- "Calvin sported an *unkept* [read *unkempt*] shock of red hair and wore thick eyeglasses." Stephen Gurr, "Answers Elusive in 3 Slayings," *Fla. Times-Union,* 30 May 2000, at B1.
- "The Utah fan was depicted with a scraggly beard, *unkept* [read *unkempt*] and 'a bit scruffy-looking.'" Shinika Sykes, "Utah–BYU Humor Hits Nerve in Sensitive Time," *Salt Lake Trib.,* 25 Nov. 2001, at A2.
- "'These raids have made people angry,' said deputy provincial intelligence chief Hassan, whose long, *unkept* [read *unkempt*] red beard is reminiscent of those the Taliban required of all Afghan males." Kathy Gannon, "Residents of Afghan Province Oppose U.S. Military Presence," *San Diego Union-Trib.,* 9 Sept. 2002, at A2.

These sentences, however, don't reflect prevailing usage. In identical contexts—those involving beards, hair, appearance, and hygiene generally—*unkempt* remains about 100 times as common as *unkept.* The gap has increased. In an October 2002 search of the ALLNEWS database in WESTLAW, *unkept* occurred in the context of beards, hair, appearance, or hygiene only 70 times in a whole decade (1992–2002), while *unkempt* occurred 3,456 times. E.g.: "Reid tried to board an American Airlines flight, but his *unkempt* appearance and lack of baggage prompted airline security to question him closely, and he missed his flight." "Bomb Suspect Offers Guilty Plea," *Wash. Post,* 3 Oct. 2002, at A1.

Apart from the sonic similarity, it's perfectly possible to retrace how the confusion arose. You *keep house;* you *keep up your yard.* If you don't do these things, your house looks *unkept* (that's where the extension started)—e.g.: "Officer Jerry Fogt . . . said that the inside of the house was dirty and 'unkept.'" Lisa Perry, "Murder Victim's Relative Asks Why," *Dayton Daily News,* 19 Dec. 2000, at A1. Notice that the journalist used quotation marks around what she probably took to be poor usage.

If one's property isn't "kept up," and can therefore be said to be *unkept,* it's a short leap then to say not that a person's surroundings are *unkept,* but that the person is *unkept.* But this remains a minority usage and doesn't yet seriously threaten the traditional usage of *unkempt.* Careful writers and editors should continue resisting *unkept* in these senses; it looks unkempt.

LANGUAGE-CHANGE INDEX
unkept misused for *unkempt*: Stage 1
Current ratio (*unkempt hair* vs. **unkept hair*): 101:1

unknown quantity (= a person or thing whose characteristics haven't been assessed) was originally a mathematical phrase. It became popular in the mid-20th century. Since then, some people have misunderstood the phrase as *unknown quality*—e.g.: "'She is an unknown *quality* [read *quantity*] as a legislator, but you don't come in here and blow the lid off in your first term.'" Michele Kay, "Senate Race: A Survivor vs. an Upstart," *Austin Am.-Statesman,* 5 Sept. 1994, at A1, A7 (quoting John White, a Democratic consultant and former Texas agriculture commissioner).

LANGUAGE-CHANGE INDEX
known quality misused for *known quantity*: Stage 1

unlawful. See **illegal.**

unleash. The word is premised on the analogy of letting a threatening or vicious animal off a leash. But a surprising number of writers have misunderstood that and written the meaningless **unlease*—e.g.:

- "But Mr. Williams *unleases* [read *unleashes*] a fiery temper at managers who fail to make budget." Eric N. Berg, "Suntrust's Florida Ambitions," *N.Y. Times,* 24 Nov. 1986, at D1.
- "When the South Vietnamese balked, the American response was to *unlease* [read *unleash*] the B-52s for the Christmas bombing raids on Hanoi." "Henry Kissinger: A Man for Some Seasons," *Economist,* 3 Oct. 1992, at 96.
- "Carl Wolter couldn't have picked a better time to *unlease* [read *unleash*] a monstrous throw." Robert Flexer, "Outstanding in His Field," *Morning Call* (Allentown, Pa.), 13 June 1996, at N20.
- "The mind can be an incredible tool with the power to *unlease* [read *unleash*] much-needed lessons on those who persecute others." Roger Hurlburt, "'Matilda' a Witty Tale of Mischief," *Sun-Sentinel* (Ft. Lauderdale), 2 Aug. 1996, Showtime §, at 5.

LANGUAGE-CHANGE INDEX
*unlease for *unleash*: Stage 1
Current ratio (*unleashes* vs. **unleases*): 2,433:1

unlike in. Though some critics have called the phrase a "gaucherie" and worse, *unlike in*—in which *unlike* takes on an adverbial sense—is now common in AmE and BrE alike. Of all the instances in which *unlike* appears, it is followed by *in* about 2% of the time—meaning, statistically, that it's quite frequent. E.g.:

- "But *unlike in* the primary, Cropp won't be running with the support of John Ray's well-financed mayoral campaign." Rene Sanchez, "D.C. Council in the Throes of an Upheaval," *Wash. Post,* 13 Sept. 1990, at C7.
- "Britain's Department of Trade and Industry is set today to propose new rules for the country's auditing industry, but *unlike in* the U.S. it won't go so far as to ban a company's auditors from providing some nonaudit services." Silvia Ascarelli & Marc Champion, "Deals & Deal Makers: U.K. to Propose New Set of Rules for Audit Industry," *Wall Street J.,* 29 Jan. 2003, at C5.
- "*Unlike in* the days after the election, there was no grappling for meaning last night." Brigid Schulte, "Love Flows for Morella at Tribute to 24 Years," *Wash. Post,* 30 Jan. 2003, at B1.

In those examples, there's almost an elliptical *what happened* after *unlike,* so that the full phrase is *unlike what happened in the primary, in the U.S.,* or *in the days after the election.* This rationale may ultimately justify the phrasing. But careful writers will avoid it because some percentage of informed readers consider it poor usage.

As a matter of frequency in print sources, the phrase first appeared in the late 18th century, spread throughout the 19th century (especially in AmE), declined in the mid-20th century, and has undergone a resurgence since about 1970. It may yet lose any stigma attaching to it.

Language-Change Index
unlike in: Stage 4

*****unmercilessly** is a MALAPROPISM and NONWORD on the order of *uncategorically. It emerged and began spreading in the late 19th century. *Mercilessly*, of course, is the word, or *unmercifully*—e.g.:

- "He worked with top-flight professionals and drilled them *unmercilessly* [read *mercilessly*]." David Richards, "That Fosse Flair," *Wash. Post*, 27 Sept. 1987, at F12.
- "They were joined in their crime by the 'slashers' who cut away at the film gem *unmercilessly* [read *mercilessly*], undoubtedly to make room for all the commercials in its two-hour time slot." *L.A. Times*, 24 Dec. 1989, TV Times §, at 2.
- "Helmut Deutsch was admirable in the pianistic scene-painting, but thumped his way *unmercilessly* [read *mercilessly*] through 'Die Erlkonig' at the end of the evening." John Allison, "Individual Vocal Talent—Recitals," *Fin. Times*, 30 Nov. 1995, at 29.
- "For every Ian Keatley kick they *unmercilessly* [read *mercilessly*] booed." Alan Quinlan, "So, the Heineken Cup Odyssey Ended in Marseille," *Irish Times*, 30 Apr. 2014, Sport §, at 2.

Cf. *uncategorically & *unrelentlessly.
Though it is a syllable longer than *mercilessly*, *unmercifully* also suffices—e.g.: "And still, Stevie Wonder seemed intent on taking his sweet, soulful time, teasing us *unmercifully*, making us sweat for his presence." Patricia Smith, "He's Still a Wonder to Behold," *Boston Globe*, 4 Jan. 1995, at 53.

Language-Change Index
*unmercilessly for *mercilessly*: Stage 1
Current ratio (*mercilessly* vs. *unmercilessly*): 1,560:1

unmoral. See **immoral.**

unnavigable; *innavigable. The first has been standard in AmE and BrE alike since the 18th century. The second is a NEEDLESS VARIANT.

Current ratio: 8:1

unorganized. See **disorganized.**

unpractical. See **impractical (B).**

unprejudicial. See **prejudicial (A).**

unqualified. See **disqualified.**

unravel, vb., makes *unraveled* and *unraveling* in AmE, *unravelled* and *unravelling* in BrE. See SPELLING (B).

unreadable. See **illegible.**

unreason; unreasonableness; *unreasonability. *Unreason* = lack of reason; irrationality. *Unreasonableness* = (1) the quality of going beyond what is reasonable or equitable; or (2) an act not in accordance with reason or good sense. *Unreasonability* is a NEEDLESS VARIANT of *unreasonableness*.

*****unrelentlessly** is a 19th-century solecism for either *unrelentingly* or *relentlessly*. Ironically, this NONWORD literally suggests just the opposite of the intended meaning—e.g.:

- "He has *unrelentlessly* [read *relentlessly* or, better, *faithfully*] served as a committee person involved in parks and recreation, fire prevention, police and emergency services, highway management, budget control and youth and school advisory committees." Letter of Larry E. Rice, "Change Dewitt Leader," *Post-Standard* (Syracuse), 19 Oct. 1995, at 15.
- "This prime minister [Benjamin Netanyahu] is still under the shadow of public opinion, and the opposition will *unrelentlessly* [read *unrelentingly* or *relentlessly*] continue to fight against him through legal, moral and political means." Amos Perlmutter, "Dodging a Misguided Political Fusillade," *Wash. Times*, 22 Apr. 1997, at A14.

Cf. *uncategorically & *unmercilessly.
Language-Change Index
*unrelentlessly for *relentlessly*: Stage 1
Current ratio (*relentlessly* vs. *unrelentlessly*): 1,737:1

unreligious. See **irreligious.**

unremorsefully. See **remorselessly (A).**

unresponsive; nonresponsive; *irresponsive. The general, most prevalent term has been widely used since the late 19th century: *unresponsive* = not reacting to or affected by something. *Nonresponsive*, most frequently a legal term, means "(of an answer to a question, esp. while under oath) not directly answering the question asked." *Irresponsive* is a NEEDLESS VARIANT of the other two.

*****unrevokable.** See **irrevocable.**

unrivaled; unrivalled. The first has been standard AmE since about 1930. The second has been standard BrE since about 1710. See SPELLING (B).

unsalable; unsaleable; *unsellable. The standard spellings are *unsalable* in AmE and *unsaleable* in BrE. (See MUTE E.) *Unsellable has never been a standard spelling. Cf. **salable.**

unsanitary; insanitary. The first is now the usual form in AmE. *Insanitary* is a variant with slightly more negative connotations. That is, if a place is *unsanitary* it is merely dirty, but if it's *insanitary* it's so dirty that it is likely to endanger health.

LANGUAGE-CHANGE INDEX (For the full key, see front matter pp. xxxi, l–li.)
Stage 1: Rejected. **Stage 2:** Widely shunned. **Stage 3:** Widespread but . . . **Stage 4:** Ubiquitous but . . . **Stage 5:** Fully accepted.
Invariably inferior forms marked by asterisk (*). • Ratios represent frequency of prevalent forms vs. variants in current books.

unsatisfied. See **dissatisfied.**

unsolvable. See **insoluble.**

*****unsubstantial.** See **insubstantial.**

unsupportable; insupportable. Both forms are standard and have been since they were first recorded in English in the 16th century. *Unsupportable* is about twice as common as *insupportable* in American journalistic sources—e.g.: "[A]dding $212 a month for health insurance to food, transportation, and housing costs in this high-cost state might well prove an *unsupportable* burden." Editorial, "What's with This Health Law?" *Boston Globe*, 29 Dec. 2006, at A14.

But *insupportable* is about six times as common as *unsupportable* in World English. It appears regularly in edited text—e.g.: "[O]ne can only admire Hood for the effort she makes in this book to describe an *insupportable* grief." Julie Wittes Schlack, "Learning to Live After Losing a Child," *Boston Globe*, 18 Jan. 2007, at E6. For now, *insupportable* has the distinct edge in word frequency.

untenable; untenantable. *Untenable* means "indefensible" (figuratively) as well as "unable to be occupied." *Untenantable* means "not capable of being occupied or lived in" <untenantable apartment units>. In speech, many people say *untenantable* when they mean *untenable*.

until. In the phrase **up until*, the *up* is superfluous, though it's common in speech. Use either *until* or *up to*—e.g.: "*Up until* [read *Until*] about 30 years ago, Sisters of Mercy were the teachers; today, lay teachers dominate." Kym Soper, "St. James School Celebrating 75th Anniversary," *Hartford Courant*, 7 Aug. 1997, at 1. See **till.**

*****until the time when** is verbose for *until*: "He renounced the whole of womankind *until the time when* [read *until*] he met the sweet little daughter of the innkeeper." Jaroslav Hasek, *The Red Commissar* 252 (Cecil Parrott trans., 1981). This prolixity has occurred especially in BrE since the late 18th century.

untrammeled (= unfettered; free) has been predominantly so spelled in AmE from 1900. In BrE, the final consonant is doubled: *untrammelled*. A trammel is a restraint in the form of a net or shackle. E.g.: "When Bush leaves office . . . , the radical theory of *untrammeled* executive power propounded by his administration will leave, too." Richard Just, "House Hold," *New Republic*, 12 Mar. 2008, at 2.

The traditional sense can be stretched too far—e.g.: "A wilderness, in contrast with those areas where man and his own works dominate the landscape, is hereby recognized as an area where the earth and its community of life are *untrammeled* by man, where man himself is a visitor who does not remain." Wilderness Act of 1964, 16 U.S.C. § 1131(c). Perhaps the drafters were thinking of *untrampled*. A better word choice might have been *unchanged*, or some such word.

Unfortunately, and perhaps because of its sanction in that statute, this new "green" sense of *untrammeled* is trampling on the word's traditional sense—e.g.:

- "[Sara] Thomas understands the love of *untrammeled* [read *wilderness*] spaces." Sharon Gittleman, "Livingston County: Observers to Peek at Wilderness Habitat," *Detroit Free Press*, 13 May 2007, News §, at 4.
- "The Hudson River School artists typically painted landscapes *untrammeled* [read *untouched*] by man." Roy Proctor, "New River Views," *Richmond Times-Dispatch*, 17 June 2007, at G12.
- "The two senior Vauxes live on an idyllic spread at Lloyd's Neck, surrounded by *untrammeled* [read *untrampled*? *unspoiled*?] countryside." Ariella Budick, "Their Home Is Where the Art Is," *Newsday* (N.Y.), 20 June 2007, at B6.

LANGUAGE-CHANGE INDEX
untrammeled misused for *untrampled* or
unspoiled: Stage 1

untrod(den). See **tread.**

*****untypical.** See **atypical.**

unwed. See **wed.**

unwieldy, an adjective meaning "difficult to handle" <unwieldy packages>, often seems to be mistaken for an adverb ending in *-ly*—e.g.:

- "And it doesn't require an *unwieldly* [read *unwieldy*], lengthy tournament to improve the situation." Mark Kiszla, "Nittany Lions Left with Whine, Roses," *Denver Post*, 3 Jan. 1995, at C1.
- "The Riedel Sommelier Vintage Champagne, a 10-inch-tall tulip glass ($49.95), was *unwieldly* [read *unwieldy*]." Suzanne Hamlin, "A Tall Glass Makes the Best of Bubbles," *N.Y. Times*, 25 Dec. 1996, at C5.

See SPELLING (A).
Current ratio (*unwieldy* vs. **unwieldly*): 51:1

upmost. See **utmost.**

upon is a FORMAL WORD appropriate for formal occasions—e.g.: "Beneath his likeness sits a table *upon* [read *on*] which participants place the fabric after prostrating themselves three times." Norine Dresser, "Southern California Voices," *L.A. Times*, 8 Feb. 1997, at B7. But in most contexts *upon* is unnecessary in place of *on*—e.g.: "We can insist *upon* [read *on*] seat belts and obeying all road rules." Letter of Donna R. Duppstadt, "Other Issues Omitted," *Patriot & Evening News* (Harrisburg), 21 Sept. 1997, at B14.

Although some will argue that the two are interchangeable and the choice is just a question of euphony, rarely will *upon* prove more euphonious or natural. *On* is the shorter, simpler, and more direct preposition. See **on.**

Yet *upon* is quite justifiable when the sense is "on the occasion of," or "when (something) occurs"—e.g.:

- "*Upon* disembarking from their chartered plane and boarding the team bus on the tarmac, they proceeded to have a fender bender—with a 727." "Major League Log," *Pitt. Post-Gaz.*, 17 July 1997, at D3.
- "*Upon* her return, she perused the leaderboard closely, finding she was still on top." Michael Madden, "Harvey,

Neumann on Top of Games," *Boston Globe*, 19 Sept. 1997, at D1.

uprighteous is a PORTMANTEAU WORD, a combination of *upright* and *righteous*—e.g.: "You may recall the uproar over Atlanta pitcher John Rocker and his lowly opinions of New York City and its inhabitants. It was hardly an original view, but he said it to a magazine reporter, and the *uprighteous* sky fell on him." Blackie Sherrod, "Athletes Can Swallow Their Feet," *Dallas Morning News*, 3 May 2001, at A19. Few dictionaries recognize it, but *W2* records it as an adjective and *W3* as an adverb (*uprighteously*). It's fairly rare today.

upstairs, adj., as in *upstairs bedroom*, is sometimes wrongly made either *upstair or *upstair's. The false possessive is the more grievous error—e.g.: "Within hours of her move there, the third fire broke out in an *upstair's* [read *upstairs*] bedroom, authorities said." Colin Poitras, "Prosecution Rests in Arson Case," *Hartford Courant*, 19 July 1996, at B3. Cf. **downstairs.**

LANGUAGE-CHANGE INDEX
*upstair's bedroom for upstairs bedroom: Stage 1

up-to-date should be hyphenated as an adjective, unhyphenated as an adverb. Hence, "Once the log is brought *up to date*, we will have an *up-to-date* log."

up to now is a comfortably idiomatic equivalent of *heretofore* and *hitherto*—e.g.:

- "So why did Gaffney, *up to now* a staunch supporter of the deal and a close ally of the governor, create what is likely to be three months of political pandemonium?" Rick Brand, "Gaffney's Move Creates Fallout for Pataki," *Newsday* (N.Y.), 21 Aug. 1997, at A38.
- "*Up to now*, Alps printers have been somewhat pricey." Dan Littman, "Alps' Challenger to the Ink Jet," *PC World*, 1 Oct. 1997, at 108.
- "*Up to now*, looking for a rich uncle's will was an arduous endeavor, yet many tried, some by proxy." Ron Grossman, "A Wealth of Wills Now Available Online," *Chicago Trib.*, 2 Sept. 2015, News §, at 4.

*up to —— off and more. This bit of ILLOGIC crops up fairly often in print ads and store signs. At a sale touted as offering *up to 50% off and more*, for example, all we know is that the sale price is (1) less than 50% off, (2) 50% off, or (3) more than 50% off. The number itself, then, is meaningless and serves only as bait in big, bold type. The small type, as usual, taketh away.

Versions of the phrase appear in places other than signs announcing sales—e.g.:

- "Some lakes and forests devastated by acid rain will likely take *up to* 70 years *or more* to recover." Mark Weiner, "Region's Acid Rain Recovery Goes Slow," *Post-Standard* (Syracuse), 26 Mar. 2001, at A1. (A possible revision: *Some lakes and forests devastated by acid rain could take 70 years or more to recover.*)

- "Use live bait or cut bait for yellow perch *up to* 1 1/2 pounds *or more*." Deane Winegar, "Fishing Report: Freshwater," *Richmond Times-Dispatch*, 30 Mar. 2001, at D4. (A possible revision: *Use live bait or cut bait for yellow perch up to 1 1/2 pounds (possibly a little more).*)

upward(s). Although *upward* has been the predominant adverb and adjective in AmE since 1870, the form ending in *-s* has become established in the SET PHRASE *upwards of* (= more than), a phrase that became prevalent in the early 18th century. Even so, *more than* is usually better than *upwards of*—e.g.:

- "The company said that *upwards of* [read *more than*] 15 percent of the shares are now held by U.S. investors." Peter John & Martin Brice, "USfunds Buy Reckitt," *Fin. Times*, 1 July 1997, at 48.
- "If she's right, the stock could rise *upwards of* [read *more than*] 61% to $35 by the end of next year." Junius Ellis, "Investing Advice from a Professional," *Money*, 1 Oct. 1997, at 231.

See DIRECTIONAL WORDS (A).

In BrE, *upwards* is normally the adverb <he painted upwards> and *upward* the adjective <an upward trend in prices>.

Uranus. The traditional pronunciation of the planet and the mythical god is /**yoor**-ə-nəs/. The dominant pronunciation in AmE is /uu-**ray**-nəs/, even though that variant is a relative newcomer. As Charles Harrington Elster noted, "Until the middle of [the 20th] century nearly two hundred years after the planet's discovery in 1781, the only recognized pronunciation placed the accent on the first syllable. Thus there is no precedent (other than a popular misconception, perhaps based on a false notion of how the Latin was pronounced) for stressing the second syllable." *BBBM* at 480. Well, that and the occasional desire to launch sophomoric jokes.

urban; urbane. *Urban* = (1) of, relating to, or located in a city; or (2) characteristic of city life. *Urbane* = suave; sophisticated; debonair. Occasionally *urbane* is misused for *urban*—e.g.: "Looking at a computer as a miracle machine is akin to spouting the glories of dense *urbane* [read *urban*] living or fossil fuels." James Hague, "Maybe You Just Need a File Box and a Typewriter," *Countryside & Small Stock J.*, July 1995, at 37.

LANGUAGE-CHANGE INDEX
urbane misused for *urban*: Stage 1

U.S.; U.S.A. As the shortened forms for *United States of America*, these terms retain their periods, despite the modern trend to drop the periods in most initialisms (see ABBREVIATIONS (A)). *U.S.* is best reserved for use as an adjective <U.S. foreign policy>, although its use as a noun in headlines is common. In abbreviations incorporating *U.S.*, the periods are typically dropped <USPS> <USAF> <USNA>.

LANGUAGE-CHANGE INDEX (For the full key, see front matter pp. xxxi, l–li.)
Stage 1: Rejected. **Stage 2:** Widely shunned. **Stage 3:** Widespread but . . . **Stage 4:** Ubiquitous but . . . **Stage 5:** Fully accepted.
Invariably inferior forms marked by asterisk (*). • Ratios represent frequency of prevalent forms vs. variants in current books.

usable. So spelled in AmE and BrE alike—not **useable*. See MUTE E.

Current ratio: 8:1

usage generally refers to an idiom or form of speech, an occurrence of one, or forms of speech in general. E.g.:

- "The first three *usages* [of 'received pronunciation'] attested in *OED* indeed derive from his work, beginning in 1869." L.C. Mugglestone, "John Walker and Alexander Ellis," *Notes & Queries*, 1 Mar. 1997, at 103.
- "The word 'angler' in this *usage* has nothing whatever to do with playing the angles." Michael Pakenham, "After 344 Years, 'The Compleat Angler' Still Works Magic with the Human Heart," *Baltimore Sun*, 14 Sept. 1997, at F4.

Here, the use (not *usage*) of the word is poor: "My criticism is just a small one and concerns *language usage* [read *language* or *usage* or *the use of language*], rather than the argument of the editorial." Letter of Jean Kimble, *Tucson Citizen*, 29 Aug. 1997, at 19.

Whenever *use* is possible, *usage* shouldn't appear. But *usage* for *use* is not an uncommon error—e.g.: "Although reproductive-health clinics and college health services have been prescribing the 'emergency' Pill for more than a decade, the Food and Drug Administration sanctioned *this usage* [read *it*] only last summer." Hallie Levine, "The 10 Myths That Stand Between You and the Pill," *Cosmopolitan*, 1 Mar. 1997, at 150. Cf. **misusage.**

The opposite error—*use* for *usage*—is quite uncommon but does occur: "This *Concise Dictionary* is primarily a manual for people who aspire to write a clear and forceful American [English] in accord with current good *use* [read *usage*]." Robert C. Whitford & James R. Foster, *Concise Dictionary of American Grammar and Usage* v (1955). Given the title of the book, that sentence also illustrates INELEGANT VARIATION.

LANGUAGE-CHANGE INDEX
1. *usage* misused for *use*, n.: Stage 3
2. *use* misused for *usage*: Stage 1

use; utilize; utilization. *Use* is the all-purpose noun and verb, ordinarily to be preferred over *utilize* and *utilization*. If Wilson Follett overstated the case against what he called "the bad habit" of using *utilize*, it wasn't by much: "Exact synonyms are rare and there is always a feature in the apparent synonym, whether shade of meaning, connotation, length, or rhythm, by which it can make itself useful. Yet some words at some times and others at all times can be shown to be unnecessary. *Utilize* is one of the second class. . . . If *utilize* and *utilization* were to disappear tomorrow, no writer of the language would be the poorer." *MAU* at 221–22. *Utilize* is both more abstract and more favorable connotatively than *use*.

used. See **preowned.**

used-book store. Preferably so written, not *used book-store*. E.g.: "We all have this vision of the perfect *used bookstore* [read *used-book store*]: it seems to come out of a Dickens story, or maybe the film version of *The Old Curiosity Shop*." Ian C. Ellis, *Book Finds: How to*

Find, Buy, and Sell Used and Rare Books 84 (2006). Concededly, however, since about 1985 instances of *used bookstore* are more frequent in print sources than the more logical *used-book store*—by a ratio of 5 to 1.

An apologist of the illogical phrasing might argue that it involves HYPALLAGE: it's a bookstore specializing in used stock. Then again, think about the ambiguity in its antonym: *new bookstore*.

LANGUAGE-CHANGE INDEX
used bookstore for *used-book store*: Stage 2

used not to. See **used to** (C).

used to. A. Generally. *Used to*, not **use to*, is the phrase meaning "formerly"—e.g.:

- "For those who don't know, Dagmar was a very big blond, what we *use to* [read *used to*] call in those days 'well-endowed.'" Nick Clooney, "Hanging Out with Rosie on Early TV," *Cincinnati Post*, 8 Jan. 2003, at B10. (Note that *in those days* produces a REDUNDANCY; changing *used to call* to *called* would eliminate it.)
- "Pilot was what we *use to* [read *used to*] call copperhead snakes." Billy Westbrook, "Think, and You Can Link Corn to Just About Anything," *Herald* (Rock Hill, S.C.), 19 Jan. 2003, Special §, at 3.

Cf. **supposed to.**

B. *Didn't used to; didn't use to.* The negative form—whichever you choose—doesn't occur nearly as often as the positive. *Did not use to* has been in constant use throughout the English-speaking world since about 1675. *Did not used to* didn't come into common use till the early 20th century—and didn't surpass the traditional form in AmE till the mid-1970s. In BrE, *did not use to* remains predominant, but the two forms have vied closely since the mid-1970s.

The phrasing denotes the idea that something never happened in the past but that it now happens often or regularly. It is the informal equivalent of *never used to* and the rarely encountered phrase *used not to*. In AmE, the contracted form *didn't used to* is a frequent CASUALISM—e.g.:

- "'Green' *didn't used to* be a popular word in the white world of skiing and snowboarding." Gary Olson, "Environment Gets a Lift from Skiers," *Ariz. Republic*, 30 Oct. 1994, at T1.
- "Ronnie Brown, Highland Park's parks and recreation director, said Christmas lights *didn't used to* be such a big deal in town." Dan R. Barber, "Lights Fantastic," *Dallas Morning News*, 11 Dec. 1996, at J1.
- "Choosing the car of the year is getting to be a messy business. It *didn't used to* be that way." Matt Nauman, "Here's How One Auto Writer Picks 'Of the Year' Nominees," *Times Union* (Albany), 19 Dec. 1996, at T10.

The question whether the phrase should be written *didn't use to* has stirred up some controversy among usage pundits. The argument goes that *didn't* supplies the past tense, and the main verb that follows should be in the present tense, as it is in a sentence such as *You didn't have* [not *had*] *to do that*. But *used to* can be seen as an idiomatic phrase based on an archaic meaning of *use* (= to be in the habit of).

On this view, the form of the verb is fixed in the positive *used to* and is unchanged in the far less common (and far less accepted) negative form, *didn't used to*.

How might we know this? After all, when the phrase is spoken, the *-d* of *used* is drowned out by the *t-* of *to*. The proponents of *didn't use to* make much of this, arguing that since we can't resolve the usage question by listening to speakers, we have to decide on the basis of traditional grammar. But in fact, we can draw an inference from pronunciation of the *-s-* in *use* (/**yooz**/) and *used* (/**yoost**/), and it supports the idiomatic phrase *didn't used to*.

In modern journalistic sources, *didn't used to* is almost twice as common as *didn't use to*. When *didn't use to* does appear, it commonly occurs in transcribed speech—e.g.: "'She was engulfed by a lake that *didn't use to* be there,' said Michael Foster, a case manager." Frank Stanfield & Lesley Clark, "Year's Heavy Rains Still Aren't Enough," *Orlando Sentinel*, 2 Dec. 1994, at 1.

But remember the standard form that can save you headaches: *never used to*. It avoids the grammatical problem of *did* + [past tense]. It keeps *used*. And it doesn't reek of DIALECT.

> LANGUAGE-CHANGE INDEX
> *didn't used to*: Stage 5
> Current ratio (*didn't used to be* vs.
> *didn't use to be*): 2:1

C. Contracted Form of *used not to*. In Irish speech, the formal phrase *used not to* is sometimes contracted (rather awkwardly) to *usen't to* or *usedn't to*—e.g.:

- "Ivy Reading, who worked there for 40 years, said: 'Saturdays we *usen't to be able to* [read *couldn't*] stop even for a cup of tea.'" Sarah Lonsdale, "Town Traders Crushed by Market Forces," *Sunday Telegraph*, 19 Sept. 1993, at 9.
- "'*Usen't we* [read *Didn't we used*] to beat these people?' complains Daly the bill collector." Jim Murray, "'Twas a Result Not Fit for Wearin' o' the Green," *L.A. Times*, 27 Nov. 1994, at C1.
- "'I *usedn't* [read *never used to*] agree with having to go back to Wexford for every training session.'" Sean Moran, "Dillon on Inter County Stage," *Irish Times*, 10 May 1996, at 16 (quoting Mick Dillon, a soccer player).

Both forms date from the early 19th century. *Usen't to* has consistently predominated over *usedn't to* since the late 1920s.

*used to could is dialectal for *used to be able to* or *could formerly*. It appears mostly in reported speech—e.g.:

- "'I was a lot stronger back then,' Webb said. 'I *used to could* [read *once could* or *used to be able to*] take a 100-pound bag and lift it over my head.'" Melissa Devaughn, "It Was a Grind, but Floyd County Miller Loved His Work," *Roanoke Times*, 23 Oct. 1994, at 19.
- "'You *used to could* [read *used to be able to*] read all the liner notes and see who wrote the songs and who played on whose album,' he said." Lori Buttars, "Silver Tongues Joe Flint," *Salt Lake Trib.*, 23 June 1996, at J1.

- "'I *used to could* [read *used to be able to*] rattle it off, knew the answers like the back of my hand,' he said." Ed Grisamore, "Longtime High School Football Coach 'Coming to Grips' with Dementia," *Macon Telegraph*, 3 Aug. 2014, at 965.

Dating from the early 19th century in AmE, the phrase had spread to BrE by the late 1830s. It has never been STANDARD ENGLISH. See DIALECT & DOUBLE MODALS.

> LANGUAGE-CHANGE INDEX
> **used to could*: Stage 2

user-friendly. See COMPUTERESE & -FRIENDLY.

*use to. See **used to.**

U.S. government. See **American government.**

*usually always. See ***generally always.**

usurpation; *usurpature. The former is standard in AmE and BrE alike. The latter is a NEEDLESS VARIANT.

Because *usurpation* begins with a /y/ sound, it takes the indefinite article *a*, not *an*—e.g.: "But, he insisted, it's not *an* [read *a*] usurpation." Mike Dunham, "Conference Heads into Home Stretch with Elliott Yet to Speak," *Anchorage Daily News*, 16 Aug. 1997, at E1. See a (A).

> Current ratio: 3,395:1

usury (/**yoo**-zhə-ree/) is a word whose content has changed considerably over time. Originally, *usury* meant "compensation for the use of money; the lending of money for interest." By the 18th century, however, its meaning had been narrowed to what it is today: "the lending of money at an excessive interest rate." The corresponding adjective is *usurious* (/yoo-**zhuur**-ee-əs/).

Because *usury* and *usurious* begin with a consonant sound, they should be preceded by *a* and not *an* when an indefinite article is called for. See a (A).

Utahn; Utahan. These two forms vie for predominance. The first has been standard since the late 19th century; the second is a variant spelling that wasn't very common except (oddly) in the 1930s, when it prevailed in print sources for a short time, and then again in a post-2000 resurgence. We await the outcome. See DENIZEN LABELS.

> Current ratio (*Utahan* vs. *Utahn*): 1.1:1

utilize; utilization. See **use.**

utmost, adj.; **upmost,** adj. The usual word is *utmost* (= most extreme; of the greatest urgency or intensity) <an issue of the utmost importance>. *Upmost* (= highest; farthest up) is a fairly uncommon variant of *uppermost*. Yet writers have begun misusing *upmost* in contexts where *utmost* is called for—e.g.:

- "In a competitive industry where repeat visitors are of *upmost* [read *utmost*] importance, how long can Legoland focus primarily on 3- to 12-year-olds?" Mike Freeman,

LANGUAGE-CHANGE INDEX (For the full key, see front matter pp. xxxi, l–li.)
Stage 1: Rejected. **Stage 2:** Widely shunned. **Stage 3:** Widespread but . . . **Stage 4:** Ubiquitous but . . . **Stage 5:** Fully accepted.
Invariably inferior forms marked by asterisk (*). • Ratios represent frequency of prevalent forms vs. variants in current books.

"Legoland Is Zoned for Kids," *San Diego Union-Trib.*, 19 Mar. 2000, at I1.

- "Hayes' death was of the *upmost* [read *utmost*] importance." Anwar Richardson, "We All Share Blame for Senseless Deaths," *Tampa Trib.*, 27 July 2000, at 10.
- "'The Cockettes,' a full-length documentary . . . , treats its subject with *upmost* [read *utmost*] respect." Ruthe Stein, "Cockettes Resurrected in Documentary," *S.F. Chron.*, 4 Aug. 2000, at C4.

The error occurs also in BrE—e.g.: "Britain is doing its *upmost* [read *utmost*], however, to ensure that the group's mandate and role are as limited as possible." Andrew Osborn, "UK Fights Plans for Regulator," *Guardian*, 17 July 2000.

> LANGUAGE-CHANGE INDEX
> *upmost* misused for *utmost*: Stage 1
> Current ratio (*utmost importance* vs.
> **upmost importance*): 477:1

uxorial; uxorious. The first is neutral, the second pejorative. *Uxorial* (= of, relating to, or involving a wife) is the less usual word, dating from 1800. E.g.: "Greer Garson became typecast in *uxorial*, middle-class roles." "Greer Garson" (obit.), *Daily Telegraph*, 8 Apr. 1996, at 19. *Uxorious* (= submissive to or exceedingly fond of one's wife) is both more common and older, dating from the 16th century. E.g.: "The new England manager is, at the time of his appointment, a notably level-headed individual, a devout Christian and *uxorious* husband. Should we read in four years' time that he is checking in to a sex-addiction clinic—having been found chanting 'God is dead!' in a hotel room while six prostitutes tug at the elastic of his football shorts—then we will know that fame destroys." Mark Lawson, "Ain't Misbehavin', Just Naturally Batty," *Guardian*, 6 May 1996, at 11.

V

v.; vs. Both are acceptable abbreviations of *versus*, but they differ in application: *vs.* is more common except in names of law cases, in which *v.* is the accepted abbreviation.

vacuum (= [1] a space devoid of matter, or [2] a cleaning tool that uses suctioning) predominantly forms the plural *vacuums* in both senses. In sense 1 (and its various allied subsenses in technical contexts), the Latinate plural *vacua* is also common.

vagina; vulva. The term *vagina* is now frequently used to denote not just the internal organ (the strict meaning), but also the external female genitals (the *vulva*, strictly speaking). The result is that *vulva* is falling into disuse, except in medical contexts.

Valentine's Day; *Valentines Day; *Valentine Day. Although the formal name is *St. Valentine's Day* (common in print till the 1970s), this is quite infrequent today. The standard term today is *Valentine's Day*. Avoid the two variant forms.

> Current ratio (in order of headwords): 100:5:1

vale of tears. In this age-old idiom, *vale* means "world"—and the full phrase means "this world of struggles and difficulties." But since the early 19th century, writers have sometimes mistakenly spelled it **veil of tears*—e.g.:

- "Edwin C. Daly left this *veil* [read *vale*] of tears on Monday (April 15, 1996) at his home in Tamarac, FL." "Edwin C. Daly" (obit.), *Hartford Courant*, 30 Apr. 1996, at B8.
- "'For my part, and I know some here will disagree, I'd like to have the right to terminate my stay in this *veil* [read *vale*] of tears and bow to no man with respect to maintaining a high measure of privacy as to my personal life,' Wright said." James Bradshaw, "Ex-Justice Says Courts Go Too Far to Call Assisted Suicide a Right," *Columbus*

Dispatch, 25 July 1996, at C5 (no doubt mistranscribing the quotation from Craig Wright, a former justice of the Ohio Supreme Court).

Because *vale* has so commonly been confounded with *veil*, some writers have begun using the latter noun as if it referred to a stream of tears covering the face (a watery veil)—e.g.:

- "This time, prosecutors were so eager to puncture the dissembling *veil* of tears that Lyle Menendez never took the stand to repeat his Oscar-caliber performance." "Justice for Two Killers," *Seattle Times*, 22 Mar. 1996, at B4.
- "Three weeks ago in a *veil* of tears, Abdur-Rahim announced he was leaving school to make himself available for the June 26 NBA draft." John Crumpacker, "Shareef Returning to Bears," *S.F. Examiner*, 30 May 1996, at D1.
- "In the feature film *Humoresque* of 1946, we see Joan Crawford gazing at us through a *veil* of tears as she sits at home, busily drinking herself into oblivion." Eva Rieger, *Richard Wagner's Women* 1 (Chris Walton trans., 2011).

Perhaps a pun was intended in each case, but the phrasing arouses the suspicion that the writer simply doesn't know any better.

> LANGUAGE-CHANGE INDEX
> **veil of tears* for *vale of tears*: Stage 2
> Current ratio (*vale of tears* vs. **veil of tears*): 6:1

valet is traditionally pronounced /**val**-it/ or /**val**-ay/ as a noun, or /va-**lay**/ as an adjective. The first was historically considered best, primarily in the sense "a gentleman's personal attendant who looks after his clothes etc." (*COD*). It's primarily to this archaic sense that *W2*'s comment applies: "*Valet* has been anglicized since the 17th century. Dr. Johnson (1755) gives val´ĕt, Buchanan (1766) văl´ĕt, Sheridan (1797) văl´ĕt, Smart (1836) văl´ĕt, and the best usage still prefers it." Yet that "preferred" usage is almost never heard, and even /**val**-ay/ is rare for the noun. The standard AmE pronunciation today for the noun is /va-**lay**/. But the most common AmE usage of the word is as an adjective, usually in reference to a parking attendant at a hotel or restaurant, where the accent is on the first syllable. In short, the word has been de-anglicized in AmE over the 20th century, while BrE continues with /**val**-it/.

valet, vb., makes *valeted* and *valeting* in both AmE and BrE.

valuable, adj.; **invaluable.** *Valuable* describes something that has measurable worth <a valuable necklace worth an estimated $20,000> or that possesses desirable qualities or characteristics <a valuable employee> <valuable information>. Despite its appearance, *invaluable* does not mean that something is worthless but rather that something (often intangible) is very highly valued or priceless <a dedicated employee can make invaluable contributions>.

valuation. For a fairly common REDUNDANCY, see **appraisal valuation.**

vane (= a device for showing wind direction) is sometimes mistakenly made *vain* or *vein*—e.g.:

- "The SPM buoy's top deck is designed to swivel, allowing a tanker to act like a weather *vain* [read *vane*] and remain head-on in the wind." L.R. Aalund, "Hawaii Offers Challenge and Opportunity to Refiner," *Oil & Gas J.*, 30 May 1994, at 43.
- "It seems a bit incongruous to find a store carrying Royall Bayrhum all purpose lotion, wind chimes, chess sets, patio grills, bocci balls, cupolas, weather *veins* [read *vanes*], and bird houses under the same roof with delicate crystal." Rod King, "Not Your Ordinary Giftshop," *Bus. People Mag.*, Nov. 1994, at 28.

LANGUAGE-CHANGE INDEX

vain or *vein* misused for *vane*: Stage 1
Current ratio (*weather vane* vs. **weather vein*): 330:1

vapid (= flat, dull, and intellectually barren) makes *vapidity*, preferably not **vapidness* (which is only one-tenth as common in print). E.g.: "Whatever was once unique and involving about its music has been usurped by synth-pop *vapidness* [read *vapidity*]." Greg Kot, "Faithful Followers," *Chicago Trib.*, 23 Apr. 1995, at C7. The adjective is pronounced /**vap**-id/, the noun /va-**pid**-i-tee/—preferably not with a long /ay/ in the first syllable.

variable, adj.; **variant,** adj.; **variational;** **variative. Variable* = subject to variation; characterized by variations. *Variant* = differing in form or in details from the one named or considered, differing thus among themselves (*COD*). *Variational* = of, pertaining to, or marked or characterized by variation. **Variative* shares the senses of *variational*; because it's the rarer word, it might be considered a NEEDLESS VARIANT.

Variable is pronounced /**va**-ree-ə-bəl/ (in four syllables)—not, as weather forecasters frequently mouth it, /**ver**-ə-bəl/.

variation; variance; variant, n. *Variation* = (1) a departure from a former or normal condition, action, or amount; a departure from a standard or type; or (2) the extent of this departure. E.g.: "For those who are willing to experiment, there are as many wonderful *variations* of kugel as imagination will allow." Marge Perry, "A Sweet New Year," *Record* (N.J.), 24 Sept. 1997, at F1.

Variance is used in two widely divergent senses: (1) "a difference or discrepancy between two statements or documents that ought to agree"; and (2) "a waiver of or exemption from a zoning law." *At variance* = (of people) in a state of discord; (of things) conflicting; in a state of disagreement or difference. E.g.: "So Gov. Wilson, championing Prop. 209 as leading to a 'color-blind society' in California, now wants the Legislature to repeal 35 laws he deems to be *at variance* with 209." "Prop 209's Legislative Headaches," *S.F. Examiner*, 12 Sept. 1997, at A21.

Variant = a form or modification differing in some way from other types of the same thing. E.g.: "Most of the goggles purchased for military aviation are produced by ITT . . . . They are *variants* of the F4949 model, . . . which has a 40-degree field-of-view, both horizontally and vertically." "Night Vision Goggles," *Tucson Citizen*, 18 Sept. 1997, at A6.

variational; **variative.* See **variable.**

variety. When the phrase *a variety of* means "many," it takes a plural verb—e.g.:

- "Words, songs and rituals are a few of the many things that color our experience, and *a variety of* them *are* found in religious services." William C. Graham, "Saving Signs, Wondrous Words," *Nat'l Catholic Rptr.*, 9 May 1997, at 15.
- "There *are a variety of* ' '90s-type' bills padding the typical household budget." "No Fed Action Expected," *Tampa Trib.*, 25 Sept. 1997, at 7.

In fact, it's erroneous in that context to use a singular verb—e.g.: "There *is* [read *are*] *a variety of* dwelling types, including houses, row houses and apartments, so that younger and older people, singles and families, poor and the wealthy, may live there." Steve Liewer, "Developers' Nostalgia Reaches Homebuyers," *Sun-Sentinel* (Ft. Lauderdale), 7 Sept. 1997, at B1. See SYNESIS.

When followed by a singular or COLLECTIVE NOUN, *a variety of* takes a singular verb—e.g.: "For the tests, *a variety* of equipment *is* attached to the helicopter's hard points and dropped in flight, including 2.75-inch rocket packs, auxiliary fuel tanks and dummy Hellfire and Sidewinder missiles." Jefferson Morris, "Upgraded Super Cobra Undergoing Stores Jettison Testing at Pax River," *Aerospace Daily*, 29 Jan. 2003, at 6.

LANGUAGE-CHANGE INDEX (For the full key, see front matter pp. xxxi, l–li.)
Stage 1: Rejected. **Stage 2:** Widely shunned. **Stage 3:** Widespread but . . . **Stage 4:** Ubiquitous but . . . **Stage 5:** Fully accepted.
Invariably inferior forms marked by asterisk (*). • Ratios represent frequency of prevalent forms vs. variants in current books.

various and sundry. See **sundry.**

*****various different** has been a fairly common REDUN-DANCY since the 18th century. E.g.: "Also available is a map that lets you take a self-guided native-trail walk through *various different* [read *various* or *different*] parts of the gardens." Karen C. Wilson, "Native-Plant Demonstration Gardens," *San Diego Union-Trib.*, 28 Sept. 1997, at H13. If **various different occasions* means "a number of different occasions," then the better wording is *several different.*

LANGUAGE-CHANGE INDEX
**various different* for *several different*: Stage 1
Current ratio (*several different* vs.
**various different*): 15:1

*****various of (the).** Although this phrasing dates from the late 18th century, it has traditionally been disapproved because *various* shifts from being used as an adjective to a pronoun. Although the phrasing is roughly analogous to *several of* or *many of*, it is not refined usage. Some improvement, including *various* alone, is always available—e.g.:

- "Even the most casual of swing band followers 50 years ago knew *various of the* [read *the various*] soloists in their favorite band." Philip Elwood, "A Standout Among Pianists in Swing Era," *S.F. Examiner*, 13 Jan. 1995, at D7. (In that quotation, *band* should be *bands*. See CONCORD (B).)
- "Both liberals and conservatives will take issue with *various of* [read *some of*] Morris's opinions." Jim Naughton, "'American Catholic' a Rare Work," *Rocky Mountain News* (Denver), 3 Aug. 1997, at E3.
- "Consider premarital sex, extramarital sex, birth control, abortion, homosexuality, and the ordination of women as clergy. *Various of* [read *Some or all of*] these will cause the leaders of most any church to make pronouncements appropriate for another century." Geneva Overholser, "Morals and Sexuality," *Chicago Trib*, 26 July 2000, at 17.
- "During the sequence, Gibson threatens to go the 'Tootsie' route, applying and trying on *various of the* [read *various*] female products, from mascara to panty hose." Dan Craft, "What Audiences Want from Mel," *Pantagraph* (Bloomington, Ill.), 21 Dec. 2000, at G2.

LANGUAGE-CHANGE INDEX
various used as a pronoun <various of my
colleagues agree>: Stage 2

vegan (= someone who strictly avoids foods of animal origin), a mid-20th-century NEOLOGISM, is pronounced /**vee**-gən/ or (less good) /**vej**-ən/.

vegetative; *****vegetive.** The first is the standard term. The second is a NEEDLESS VARIANT.
Current ratio: 2,065:1

veggie; *****vegie.** *Veggie* (= a vegetable) is the standard spelling of the colloquialism for *vegetable*. It is a mid-20th-century clipped form that adds the diminutive suffix *-ie* (see DIMINUTIVES (G)). **Vegie* is an alternative spelling found primarily in Australia and New Zealand. The *SOED* notes that *veggie* or **vegie* can also denote a vegetarian. See CASUALISMS (C).
Current ratio: 42:1

vehement is pronounced /**vee**-ə-mənt/, not /və-**hee**-mənt/.

vehicle. The *-h-* is not pronounced. Hence: /**vee**-i-kəl/. The word itself is often a prime example of OFFICIALESE, as when a police officer refers to *exiting the vehicle and engaging in foot pursuit* (= getting out of the car and running after a suspect). Some auto manufacturers have made their warranties easier to decipher by taking the simple step of substituting *car*, *truck*, *minivan*, or the like for the abstract *vehicle*. See ABSTRACTITIS & PLAIN LANGUAGE.

vehicular. A. *Vehicular homicide.* *Vehicular* /vee-**hik**-yə-lər/, an adjective dating from the 17th century, is not objectionable per se. Several states have *vehicular-homicide statutes*, in which there is no ready substitute for *vehicular*.

B. *Vehicular accident.* The phrase is pompous police JARGON for *traffic accident*, *car accident*, or (in BrE) *motoring accident*.

C. ****Vehicular unit.* The phrase is especially absurd for *car*: "The declaration sheet seeks to provide separate coverages for uninsured motorists on three *vehicular units*." If *cars* or *automobiles* were too specific, then *vehicles* would suffice.

D. Pronunciation. The *-h-* is pronounced in this word: /vee-**hik**-yə-lər/. Cf. **vehicle.**

*****veil of tears.** See **vale of tears.**

veld /velt/ (= an open, nearly treeless grassland) has been the standard spelling since about 1920. **Veldt* is a variant (chiefly in South African English).
Current ratio (World English): 1.5:1

venal; venial. *Venal* (= purchasable; highly mercenary; amenable to bribes; corruptible) has been the slightly more usual term since the mid-18th century. E.g.: "As the world rushes to congratulate Kabila for overthrowing Mobutu, the continent's most spectacularly *venal* dictator, terrible things are happening in the deep bush of this ruined country." "Genocide Stalks Tribal Rivalry," *Pitt. Post-Gaz.*, 2 June 1997, at A1.

Venial (= slight [used of sins]; pardonable; excusable; trivial) is most easily remembered by associating the *-ial* with that in *trivial*. It most frequently appears in the phrase *venial sin*. E.g.: "The 1992 election granted a kind of absolution, at least for *venial* sins, even though Clinton lied about them during the campaign." David Warsh, "Whitewater, Whitewater, and Munich," *Boston Globe*, 11 May 1997, at C1.

Writers sometimes misuse *venal* for *venial*, a recurrent error from the mid-19th century—e.g.:

- "Those are *venal* [read *venial*] sins compared to Rather walking off the set in 1987 when it looked as if a tennis match would run into the newscast." Phil Kloer, "'Equal Anchors' Idea at CBS Didn't Work," *Atlanta J.-Const.*, 22 May 1995, at C7.
- "The scandals of the Clinton Administration so far appear to be *venal* [read *venial*] sins, not cardinal ones." Robert J. Bresler, "Petty Scandals and Small Ideas," *USA Today* (Mag.), 1 May 1997, at 15.

- "At the left middle ground of the print Dürer shows the nude saint crawling on all fours as penance for his *venal* [read *venial*] sin while the woman's nudity might be understood as showing why the ascetic saint weakened before her beauty." Lisa Rosenthal, *Gender, Politics, and Allegory in the Art of Rubens* 51 (2005).

LANGUAGE-CHANGE INDEX
venal misused for *venial*: Stage 1
Current ratio (*venial sin* vs. **venal sin*): 39:1

vendible has been so spelled since the 17th century—not **vendable*. See -ABLE (A).

Current ratio: 15:1

vendor (= someone who sells) has been the standard spelling since the late 18th century. **Vender* is a variant. (See -ER (A).) *Vendor* is pronounced /**ven**-dər/, not /**ven**-dor/.

Current ratio (*vendor* vs. **vender*): 54:1

venerable = (of people) worthy of being venerated, revered, or highly respected and esteemed, on account of character or position; commanding respect by reason of age combined with high personal character and dignity of appearance; (of things) worthy of veneration or deep respect. The word is overblown when used merely for *old*. E.g.: "*More venerable* [read *Older* or, perhaps, *Senior*] citizens may recall the days when the electric chair was trucked around the state so that executions could be carried out at parish halls." James Gill, "Taking Executions on the Road," *Times-Picayune* (New Orleans), 20 June 1997, at B7.

LANGUAGE-CHANGE INDEX
venerable as a EUPHEMISM for *old*: Stage 4

venial. See **venal.**

venireman; venireperson; veniremember. All three denote "one of a panel of prospective jurors." *Venireman*, which dates from the late 18th century, has attracted criticism, especially in AmE, that it is sexist. See SEXISM (C). Yet it remains by far the most frequent of the three forms in AmE and BrE alike. American legal writers have experimented with *venireperson* since the mid-1970s and *veniremember* since the 1990s, but these innovations already appear moribund. What seems to be happening instead is that the longer synonym *prospective juror* has supplanted them all as the predominant term—doubtless a victory for PLAIN ENGLISH. This phrase became predominant in AmE about 1920 and in BrE about 1965.

Venire (= a panel of prospective jurors) is pronounced /və-**nɪ**-ree/ or (less good) /və-**nɪr**/ or /və-**neer**/.

venue = (1) the proper or a possible place for the trial of a lawsuit; or (2) the place where an event is held <the venue will be Madison Square Garden>. In sense 2, it's a VOGUE WORD—e.g.:

- "While large-market teams covet fancy *venues* [read *locations*] to boost revenues, small-market team executives say these buildings are sometimes vital for their mere survival in the league." Tony Bizjak & Clint Swett, "Kings Not Alone in Subsidy Patch," *Sacramento Bee*, 19 Jan. 1997, at A1. (Notice the awkward *venues . . . revenues*. See SOUND OF PROSE.)
- "After more than 300 years, the Covent Garden piazza is still London's most popular *venue* [read *place*] for street performers." William A. Davis, "British Polish Up Their Reputation with Colorful, Creative Retail Shops," *Plain Dealer* (Cleveland), 28 Sept. 1997, at K1.

Venus flytrap; *Venus's flytrap; *Venus' flytrap. All three were in frequent use from the mid-19th century. Not until the 1960s, in AmE and BrE alike, did the form without an apostrophe establish itself as standard. The others are variants to be avoided. See POSSESSIVES (A).

Current ratio (in order of headwords): 20:1.2:1

veracity = (1) truthfulness; observance of the truth; or (2) truth; accuracy. Sense 1, denoting a quality that people have, is the traditionally correct usage. Sense 2 began as a SLIPSHOD EXTENSION in the 18th century, and still might be so considered. But it's now common in law <the veracity of the affidavit>.

Veracity is not to be confused with *voracity* (= greediness in eating). See MALAPROPISMS.

veranda (= a roofed porch or portico) has been the standard spelling in AmE since 1850. **Verandah* is a chiefly BrE variant that predominated in that variety of English until about 1950.

Current ratio (World English): 1.5:1

*verbage. See **verbiage.**

verbal; oral. *Verbal* = (1) of, relating to, or expressed in words, whether written or oral; or (2) of, relating to, or expressed through the spoken word. *Oral* = (1) of, relating to, or involving the mouth; or (2) of, relating to, or expressed through the spoken word.

Many regard sense 2 as the exclusive province of *oral*, preferring that *verbal* not be used in this way. It's a matter, they might say, of SLIPSHOD EXTENSION. In fact, given the primary sense of *verbal*, the movie producer Samuel Goldwyn wasn't really very ironic when he remarked, "A *verbal* contract isn't worth the paper it's written on." After all, a written contract *is* verbal. The phrase requires *oral*.

The slippage is especially acute when *verbal* is opposed to *written*—e.g.: "Take care with words, *verbal* [read *oral*] and written." Sydney Omarr, "Horoscope," *Wash. Post*, 22 June 1997, at F2. Take care indeed!

In recent years, some people have said that they feel awkward using *oral* because of prurient connotations; that is, the word seems most often to appear in reference to oral sex. Why this should be so is hard to

LANGUAGE-CHANGE INDEX (For the full key, see front matter pp. xxxi, l–li.)
Stage 1: Rejected. **Stage 2:** Widely shunned. **Stage 3:** Widespread but . . . **Stage 4:** Ubiquitous but . . . **Stage 5:** Fully accepted.
Invariably inferior forms marked by asterisk (*). • Ratios represent frequency of prevalent forms vs. variants in current books.

fathom, since we have *oral surgery* and *oral reports*, not to speak of *oral commitments* and *oral communication*. If you think of *oral* in a narrow sexual sense, you should wash your mouth out with soap. Otherwise, we may be in danger of losing a perfectly good word.

LANGUAGE-CHANGE INDEX
verbal as a synonym for *oral*: Stage 4

VERBAL AWARENESS. To keep from making unconscious gaffes or MISCUES—as by referring to a *virgin field pregnant with possibilities*—writers must be aware of all the meanings of a word because its potential meanings can sabotage the intention. Careful users of language don't let a sign such as *Ears Pierced While You Wait* go unnoticed. Nor do they overlook the humor in the church bulletin that reads, *All women wishing to become Young Mothers should visit the pastor in his office.* Likewise, writers ought not to refer to *Roe v. Wade and its progeny*—though several prominent writers have done just that. Or consider how the writer must feel after seeing this in print: "[A] DNA study confirmed to the satisfaction of many that a male member of Jefferson's family had fathered at least one child with a mulatto slave named Sally Hemings." Anita Hamilton, "A Family Divided," *Time*, 5 July 2004, at 64. (The term *male member* is salaciously misleading there. *Male* could have been omitted: most readers would have known the father's sex.) A heightening of verbal awareness would save writers from such oddities—and potential embarrassments.

verbatim; literatim; *ipsissima verba.* These apparent synonyms carry slight nuances. *Verbatim* = word for word. *Literatim* = letter for letter. Sometimes the phrase *verbatim et literatim* is seen. *Ipsissima verba* (lit., "the selfsame words") = the exact language used by someone quoted (*W11*).

verbiage. This term has long had negative connotations, referring to language that is prolix or redundant. E.g.: "Fanatics sloughing through Stone's pseudo-Joycean jungle of *verbiage* might note . . . his overuse of sentence fragments and quick, cheap imagery." James Hannaham, "Hollywood Babble," *Village Voice*, 21 Oct. 1997, at 65. Still, the *SOED* records a "rare" neutral sense: "diction, wording, verbal expression." Unfortunately, this unneeded sense has been revived in recent years, so that it's sometimes hard to say whether pejorative connotations should attach. E.g.: "In the past, Spencer's public commentary has fallen short of the righteous, high-minded *verbiage* displayed in Diana's eulogy." Mary Voboril, "The Althorp Stories," *Newsday* (N.Y.), 18 Sept. 1997, at A6.

Strictly speaking, the phrase **excess verbiage* is a REDUNDANCY, given the predominant meaning of *verbiage*—e.g.: "None of the *excess verbiage* [read *verbiage*] would matter, of course, if 'Chasing Amy' had no aspirations beyond the windbag coarseness of a young director." Amy Biancolli, "'Chasing' Worthwhile, Yet Gritty," *Times Union* (Albany), 18 Apr. 1997, at D1. This phrase grew in prominence over the

20th century doubtless because the word *verbiage* was gradually losing its pejorative sense.

The syncopated form **verbage* for *verbiage* is a common error dating from the 19th century. Perhaps it was spawned by the analogy of *herbage*. E.g.: "But too often, investors need a magnifying glass and a law degree to get through the document's turgid, lengthy *verbage* [read *verbiage*]." David Lieberman, "Disney Overcomes Shareholder Protest," *USA Today*, 26 Feb. 1997, at B3. This error might result partly from the common mispronunciation: /vər-bij/, rather than the correct /vər-bee-ij/. Also, endings in *-iage* are less common in English than those in *-age*.

LANGUAGE-CHANGE INDEX
1. *verbiage* misused for *verbal expression* (with neutral connotation): Stage 4
2. **excess verbiage* for *verbiage*: Stage 3
3. *verbiage* misspelled **verbage*: Stage 1
Current ratio (*verbiage* vs. **verbage*): 122:1

VERBLESS SENTENCES. See INCOMPLETE SENTENCES.

VERBS. See TENSES.

verdict refers to a jury's pronouncement. It shouldn't be used in reference to a court's decision—e.g.: "Associate Justice Sandra Day O'Connor jerked forward in her black leather chair, visibly astonished. . . . The *verdict* [read *decision*] is expected next year." Keith C. Epstein, "Ohio Free Speech Case Shocks Supreme Court," *Plain Dealer* (Cleveland), 13 Oct. 1994, at A3.

LANGUAGE-CHANGE INDEX
verdict in reference to a judge's decision: Stage 2

Vergil. See **Virgil.**

vermilion. So spelled. See SPELLING (A).

verses; versus. *Verses* (/vər-siz/) are lines of a poem or song, sections of a song separated by the chorus, or subsections of chapters in books of the Bible. *Versus* (/vər-səs/) is a preposition from the Latin, meaning "facing," especially in law and sports. Writers sometimes misspell it *verses*—e.g.:

- "'Many rooms are semi-private and this idea sets up an obvious problem with the right to privacy *verses* [read *versus*] the need to know.'" Michael Lasalandra, "'Granny Cams' Bill Is Making Headway," *Boston Herald*, 17 Mar. 2002, News §, at 14 (quoting Ernie Corrigan).
- "'But it's the university. It's the people. A lot of kids have chosen to play for me *verses* [read *versus*] another school because they want to play for me.'" Hilary Krasu, "Murrell Finds Cougs Check Out OK," *Spokesman-Rev.* (Spokane), 26 Mar. 2002, at C1 (quoting Sherri Murrell).
- "The use of 10W/30 *verses* [read *versus*] 5W/30 is a recommendation from the manufacturer to get the gas mileage to a higher level to comply with CAFE requirements." "Auto Doc," *Newsday* (N.Y.), 3 May 2002, at D19.

For more on *versus*, see **v.**

LANGUAGE-CHANGE INDEX
verses misused for *versus*: Stage 1

vertebra (= a single bone that, together with similar bones, forms the spinal column) has two plurals: the standard *vertebrae* (/vər-tə-bree/ or /vər-tə-bray/) and the homegrown variant *vertebras* (/vər-tə-brəz/). (See PLURALS (B).) The Latinate plural (*vertebrae*) is so common that some writers mistake it for a singular—e.g.: "There were fears that he could be crippled after the fall, but an operation successfully treated a fractured *vertebrae* [read *vertebra*]." Charles Laurence, "Death Fall: British Skydiver Flies Home," *Daily Telegraph*, 5 July 1997, at 3.

LANGUAGE-CHANGE INDEX
vertebrae misused as a singular for *vertebra*: Stage 1

vertex; vortex. A *vertex* is either (1) the apex or highest point of something, or (2) the point at which two sides of a figure meet to form an angle. (Pl. *vertices*.) A *vortex* is swirling matter, such as a whirlpool or a tornado. (Pl. *vortices*.) The standard phrasing is *at the vertex* but *in the vortex*. The two terms are confounded fairly often—e.g.:

- "Members of the purported Seattle cell have . . . made pilgrimages to the North London Central Mosque in Finsbury Park, thought to be at the *vortex* [read *vertex*] of militant Islamic recruiting in Europe." Mike Carter et al., "Seattle Militants Investigated for Possible Ties to al-Qaida," *Seattle Times*, 12 July 2002, at A1. (Admittedly, this sentence might also take *in the vortex*.)
- "No longer does Tom Osborne command a squad of 150 young men on national television or stand at the *vortex* [read *vertex*] of Nebraska's football obsession." Matt Kelley, "Osborne Is at Home in the House," *Omaha World-Herald*, 21 July 2002, at A1. (Again, this sentence might also take *in the vortex*.)

See **vortex.**

vertical, adj., is sometimes misspelled **verticle*—e.g.: "To achieve that goal, the companies said they will test *verticle-takeoff* [read *vertical-takeoff*] and landing technology." "McDonnell–Boeing Aim: Cheaper Space Travel," *Orange County Register*, 16 June 1995, at C2.
Current ratio: 3,950:1

very. A. As a WEASEL WORD. This intensifier, which functions as both an adjective and an adverb, surfaces repeatedly in flabby writing. In almost every context in which it appears, its omission would result in at most a negligible loss. And in many contexts the idea would be more powerfully expressed without it—e.g.: "The *very* [delete *very*] outrageous statement by Earl Woods that his son would 'do more than anyone to change humanity' gives Woods a chance not only to survive his Miracle at the Masters, but to improve upon it." Blaine Newnham, "Tiger 'Knows What He's Doing,'" *Tulsa Trib. & Tulsa World*, 19 Apr. 1997, at B2. In that sentence—as in so many others—*very* actually weakens the adjective that follows. See **most.** Cf. **clearly** & **obviously.**

B. *Very disappointed*, etc. The strict, arch-conservative view is that *very* modifies adjectives (*sorry, sick*, etc.)

and not, properly, past participles (*disappointed, engrossed*, etc.). In 1966, Wilson Follett wrote that "finer ears are offended by past participles modified by *very* without the intervention of the quantitative *much*, which respects the verbal sense of an action undergone. Such writers require *very much disappointed, very much pleased, very much engrossed, very well satisfied*, etc." (*MAU* at 343). Four years later, Charlton Laird nodded at this stricture but suggested that it had become passé: "Half a century ago purists insisted that the past participle should never be preceded by *very* unless it was protected with an insulating *much*, and some of us were so imbued with this supposedly eternal truth that we still wince if we hear that anyone is *very pleased*." *Language in America* 493 (1970).

Of course, many past-participial adjectives have now lost their verbal force. Almost no one today would hesitate over *very depressed, very drunk, very interested, very tired*, or *very worried*. Although Follett and Laird would probably be very much displeased to learn this, *very pleased* also belongs in this list. The principle is that when a past participle has become thoroughly established as an adjective, it can indisputably take *very* rather than *very much*.

If there's any doubt about the phrasing, a good solution is to substitute *quite* or (a little more formally) *much*—or, again, possibly *very much*—for *very*. E.g.:

- "Now in their early 30s and *very changed* [read *very much changed*], they have a reunion." Louis B. Parks, "Mike Leigh Movies Wring the Best from Cast, Crew," *Houston Chron.*, 16 Aug. 1997, at 1.
- " 'Paul wrote in a time when women were *very subjugated* [read *quite subjugated*], so it was natural for him to take that point of view.' " Dana Sterling, "Retired Pastor Focused on People, Not Phrases," *Tulsa World*, 28 Nov. 1997, at A24 (quoting Roy Griggs).

C. Displaced by Other Words. See **so (B)** & **too (B).**

*very unique. See ADJECTIVES (B) & **unique.**

vestigial. So spelled. **Vestigal* is an infrequent misspelling that has recurred since the late 19th century.
Current ratio: 100:1

veteran. Once a veteran, always a veteran. Hence **former veteran*, a REDUNDANCY that spread during the mid-20th century, is erroneous—e.g.:

- "Many *former veterans* [read *veterans*] now work in the private sector and would have good reason to fear any disclosure of their possible exposure to Agent Orange." Shira A. Scheindlin, "Discovering the Discoverable: A Bird's Eye View of Discovery in a Complex Multi-District Class Action Litigation," 52 *Brook. L. Rev.* 397, 421 n.94 (1986).
- "Sometime after World War II, the Postal Service began to develop an inbred, bloated paramilitary culture. The 'generals'—many of them *former veterans* [read *veterans*]—who ran the place administered rigid rules from the Domestic Mail Manual, a tome the size of the New

LANGUAGE-CHANGE INDEX (For the full key, see front matter pp. xxxi, l–li.)
Stage 1: Rejected. **Stage 2:** Widely shunned. **Stage 3:** Widespread but . . . **Stage 4:** Ubiquitous but . . . **Stage 5:** Fully accepted.
Invariably inferior forms marked by asterisk (*). • Ratios represent frequency of prevalent forms vs. variants in current books.

York City telephone book." Bill McAllister, "Can Marvin Runyon Deliver?" *Wash. Post* (Mag.), 10 July 1994, at 16.

- "The *former veteran* [read *veteran*] sentinel wondered what was in the air this night." David M. Leyva, *Sunsprites and Other Miracles* 217 (2006).

LANGUAGE-CHANGE INDEX
former veteran for *veteran*: Stage 2

Veterans Affairs. So written—without an apostrophe. The phrase is short for the Department of Veterans Affairs, created by federal statute in 1988. Its predecessor was the Veterans Administration, a federal agency established in 1930.

Although the older name was predominantly written *Veterans' Administration* (with a plural possessive) from 1927 to 1942, from 1943 the plural was predominantly attributive in print sources—with no apostrophe.

Yet the standard form for the common-noun phrase is *veterans' benefits*, not **veterans benefits*.

Veterans Day; Veterans' Day. The spelling without the apostrophe has been predominant in AmE since the early 1960s and in BrE since the mid-1990s. In the U.S., the 1954 federal statute creating the federal holiday omitted the apostrophe and used the plural *Veterans* attributively. The former official name for the Nov. 11 holiday was *Armistice Day*. Cf. **Presidents' Day.**

Current ratio (*Veterans Day* vs. *Veterans' Day*): 4:1

via = (1) by way of (a place); passing through <they flew to Amarillo via Dallas>; or (2) by means of, through the agency of <we sent the letter via fax>. Sense 2, a CASUALISM, is questionable whenever a simple preposition would suffice. Ernest Gowers called it a vulgarism in *FMEU2*, and Wilson Follett (*MAU*) and Theodore Bernstein (*The Careful Writer*) concur. But like it or not—and there's no longer any reason not to like it—*via* is now standard in sense 2. It has come to supplant *through* whenever the latter word doesn't feel quite right—e.g.:

- "Tickets for the Knicks' two preseason games at Madison Square Garden go on sale at noon Thursday at the Garden box office and *via* Ticketmaster (507-8900 in New Jersey)." Dave D'Alessandro, "Camp Nellie Offers Softer Touch," *Asbury Park Press* (Neptune, N.J.), 27 Sept. 1995, at C4.
- "The archives prove that tens of thousands of Nazis and their collaborators arrived *via* the 'Rat Line,' an organization that helped wanted war criminals out of Europe and into South America." Jack Epstein, "Searching for South America's Nazi Gold," *Houston Chron.*, 20 Apr. 1997, at A23.
- "From its one store in Carytown, his company has sold furniture to customers throughout the country *via* its World Wide Web site." Betty Joyce Nash, "Doing Battle," *Richmond Times-Dispatch*, 1 Oct. 1997, at 3.

viable originally meant "capable of living; fit to live," a sense that still applies in many phrases, such as *a viable fetus*. By acceptable extension it has come to refer figuratively to any idea or thing that might flourish. But in this use it's a VOGUE WORD that can often be improved on—e.g.:

- "One of the strengths of the U.S. banking system is that *viable* [read *thriving*] banking companies exist outside the major metropolitan areas." Karen Kahler Holliday, "Sones Takes Leading Role Among Nation's 5,500 Independent Bankers," *Miss. Bus. J.*, 30 June 1997, at 18.
- "Mr. Montague will . . . have the responsibility of signing off commercially *viable* [read *promising*] projects before they are put out to tender." Michael Harrison, "Montague Named PFI Head," *Independent*, 15 July 1997, at 18.
- "They now have a *viable* [read *plausible*] successor to the Speaker in New York Congressman Bill Paxon." Sandy Hume, "Deja Coup II," *New Republic*, 29 Sept. 1997, at 10.

The word has lately been the victim of SLIPSHOD EXTENSION, when used in the sense "feasible, practicable" <a viable plan>. One writer has noted that "dictionaries now give [as definitions for *viable*] *real, workable, vivid, practicable, important,* newer definitions that seem only to confirm the critics' complaints that the word has had the edge hopelessly ground off it." Roy Copperud, *American Usage and Style* 405 (1980).

Hence it is sometimes hard even to know what a writer means with *viable*—e.g.:

- "Columbia Gulf estimated that it would cost $3.5 million to construct new facilities to connect South Pass to the closest *viable* [delete, or read *available* or *feasible*] interconnection with its East Lateral at Venice, Louisiana." "FERC Authorizes Reciprocal Leasing Arrangement by Tennessee and Columbia Gulf," *Foster Natural Gas Rep.*, 6 Mar. 1997, at 21.
- "The white cotton shirt is still *viable* [read *acceptable* or, possibly, *a possibility*], but it could also be traded for a softer, sheer-mesh top." Valli Herman, "Sharpsuiters," *Dallas Morning News*, 17 Sept. 1997, at E1.

Cf. **feasible.**

vice; vise. In AmE, a *vice* is an immoral habit or practice, and a *vise* is a tool with closable jaws for clamping things. But in BrE, the tool is spelled like the sin: *vice*.

vicegerent; viceregent. Both the spellings and the meanings of these two words are confusingly similar. A *vicegerent* (/vɪs-**jer**-ənt/ or /vɪs-**jeer**-ənt/) is a person appointed to administer the office of another (usually a sovereign or ruler). The word often refers to the Pope as God's representative on Earth.

A *viceregent* /vɪs-**ree**-jənt/ (the rarer word) is the deputy of a regent.

vice versa (= the other way around; just the opposite) should be the fulcrum for reciprocal referents. That is, *Mike likes Ellen and vice versa* says that Ellen also likes Mike. The subject and the object could be switched around, leaving the verb intact—e.g.:

- "I am sure I could have taught Jeffrey a couple of tricks, and *vice versa*." Vitali Vitaliev, "Outside Eye: Keep My Bar Stool Warm, Jeffrey," *Guardian*, 22 Sept. 1997, at T17. (The writer means that Jeffrey could have taught him a couple of tricks.)
- "You can adjust the slide to allocate more storage at the expense of programs or *vice versa*—up to a point." John D. Ruley, "Jog WinCE's Memory," *Windows Mag.*, 1 Oct.

1997, at 279. (The writer means that you can have more programs at the expense of storage.)

But some writers misuse the term in trying to imply something different from (or sometimes even analogous to) what they've just said—e.g.:

- "They have eased restrictions to an odd–even rationing system under which residents at odd addresses can water on odd days of the month, and *vice versa*." Lauren Dodge, "Battle Ground Now Awash in Water Issues," *Oregonian* (Portland), 18 Aug. 1997, at B2. (A possible revision: *... residents at odd addresses can water on odd days of the month, and those at even addresses on even days.*)
- "He'd rather have them beat up each other than someone else—and *vice versa*." "NFL Notebook," *Times Reporter* (New Philadelphia, Ohio), 20 Aug. 2015, at B3. (It's difficult to tell here exactly what the writer intended by *vice versa*: no rearrangement of the nouns in this sentence makes sense.)
- "Among the day's highlights, players said, were the inside run portions of the workout conducted on both fields (one field featured the Colts offense versus the Bears defense and *vice versa*)." Stephen Holder, "Colts, Bears Avoid Nastiness," *Indianapolis Star*, 20 Aug. 2015, at C1. (A possible revision: *... each field featured one team's offense versus the other's defense*).)

See ILLOGIC (B).

The phrase is pronounced either /vɪs **vər**-sə/ or (a little pedantically) /**vɪ**-sə **vər**-sə/.

vichyssoise (= a thick soup made with potatoes and leeks and usu. served cold) is often misspelled by transposing the double-*s* and the single-*s* (as if it were *vichysoisse), a fairly common error since the late 1930s. E.g.: "Entries like *vichysoisse* [read *vichyssoise*] and Lady Curzon consomme, which have all but vanished from the nouvelle world, appear, alongside specialties of the land." Catharine Reynolds, "Sedate Splendor on the Costa Brava," *N.Y. Times*, 17 July 1994, § 5, at 9. The word is pronounced /vish-ee-**swoz**/ or /vee-shee-swoz/. Remembering the -*z*-sound in the final syllable should help you think of the -*se* at the end of the word.

vicious; viscous. *Vicious* (= brutal) is sometimes confounded with *viscous* (= gummy)—e.g.:

- "Crouching just behind the service line, Agassi ran around his backhand to take a *viscous* [read *vicious*] rip at a return off Ferrero's timid serve." Selena Roberts, "Agassi Out as Ferrero Capitalizes on a Break," *N.Y. Times*, 7 June 2002, at D2.
- "Stealing a page from some old boxer's book, Douglas let Tyson punch himself out through the early rounds and then unleashed a *viscous* [read *vicious*] combination of sharp jabs and sharper shots on the champ." "Iron Bites," *Pitt. Post-Gaz.*, 7 June 2002, at B2.

LANGUAGE-CHANGE INDEX
viscous misused for *vicious*: Stage 1

vicious circle; vicious cycle. Both mean "a situation in which the solution to one problem gives rise to a second problem, but the solution to the second problem brings back the first problem." *Vicious circle*, the traditional phrase dating from the 18th century, remains more common than *vicious cycle* in modern print sources.

Although *vicious cycle* isn't recorded in the *OED*, it grew especially common in AmE during the 20th century and became slightly predominant in AmE print sources about 2000.

Current ratio (*vicious circle* vs. *vicious cycle* in World English): 1.3:1

victory. The phrase *win a victory is a common but venial REDUNDANCY—e.g.:

- "The United Auto Workers has *won a victory in Northeast Ohio in its bid to unionize seat plants owned by Johnson Controls Inc.* [read *won in its bid to unionize seat plants in Northeast Ohio owned by Johnson Controls Inc.*]" Brian Frasier, "UAW Wins Over Oberlin Plant," *Crain's Cleveland Bus.*, 24 June 1996, at 9.
- "Female athletes *won a victory* [read *won* or *were victorious* or *saw victory*] Monday in the Supreme Court." Woody Anderson, "Top Court Upholds Sex-Parity Rule for College Sports," *Hartford Courant*, 22 Apr. 1997, at A1.
- "Christianity had once *won a victory* [read *been victorious*] over the Romans." Harvey C. Mansfield, *Machiavelli's New Modes and Orders* 258–59 (2001).

A simple solution is to use *score* or *gain* instead of *win*.

victuals, pronounced /**vit**-əlz/, is spelled phonetically (*vittles*) only in colloquial usage. Related forms are *victualer* (= someone who provides food and drink for payment), *victualed*, and *victualing* in AmE; these three forms double the -*l*- in BrE. Cf. **chitterlings**. See SPELLING (B).

videlicet. See **viz.**

videoconferencing. See **conferencing.**

videodisc. The Associated Press and *New York Times* stylebooks both make this and most other *video*-compounds one word <videotape> <videoconference>. But when preceded by *digital*, the two-word form is far more common in print—no doubt because of the ubiquity of DVDs, popularly known as *digital video discs* (but see **DVD**). When the phrase appears without *digital*, the compound is usually made one word: *videodisc*.

viewpoint; point of view; standpoint. The first, which originated in the mid-19th century and became widespread in the early 20th, has been stigmatized by a few writers and grammarians who consider it inferior to *point of view*. Eric Partridge wrote that the term "has been deprecated by purists; not being a purist, I occasionally use it, although I perceive that it is

LANGUAGE-CHANGE INDEX (For the full key, see front matter pp. xxxi, l–li.)
Stage 1: Rejected. **Stage 2:** Widely shunned. **Stage 3:** Widespread but . . . **Stage 4:** Ubiquitous but . . . **Stage 5:** Fully accepted.
Invariably inferior forms marked by asterisk (∗). ● Ratios represent frequency of prevalent forms vs. variants in current books.

unnecessary" (*U&A* at 307). And John Simon says that "centuries of sound tradition have hallowed *point of view* as preferable to the Teutonism *viewpoint.*" *Paradigms Lost* 90 (1980).

Yet *viewpoint*, apart from being extremely common, conveniently says in one word what *point of view* says in three. The same holds true for *standpoint*. Today, no stigma should attach to either word.

LANGUAGE-CHANGE INDEX
viewpoint for *point of view*: Stage 5

vignette (= a brief depiction) is pronounced /vin-**yet**/, not /vin-**yay**/.

vilify is often misspelled **villify*—e.g.: "Democrats say they may wage [an ad campaign] to *villify* [read *vilify*] Republicans who voted against the proposal." Patrice Hill, "Dickering Almost Kills Deal on Budget," *Wash. Times*, 22 May 1997, at A1. No doubt the misspelling is influenced by *villain*, rather than the word's actual cognate, *vile*.

Current ratio: 39:1

vinaigrette (= an oil-and-vinegar salad dressing), a French loanword dating from the early 19th century, is so spelled. In French, the word simply means "vinegar sauce." But since the mid-19th century it has infrequently been misspelled on the model of the anglicized *vinegar*—e.g.: "Whisk together the red wine vinegar, olive oil, salt and pepper, and remaining mixture of fennel, rosemary, and orange zest to make a *vinegarette* [read *vinaigrette*]." John Edward Young, "Up to Your Gills in Canned Tuna? Try Fresh," *Christian Science Monitor*, 26 Jan. 2000, at 17.

Similarly, the word is often mispronounced. It should be /vin-ə-**gret**/, not /vin-ə-gə-**ret**/. See PRONUNCIATION.

LANGUAGE-CHANGE INDEX
1. *vinaigrette* misspelled **vinegarette*: Stage 1
Current ratio: 771:1
2. *vinaigrette* mispronounced in four syllables: Stage 3

vindicable. So formed in AmE and BrE alike—not **vindicatable*. See -ABLE (D) & -ATABLE.

vindictive; vindicatory; *vindicative. *Vindictive* = given to or characterized by revenge or retribution. *Vindicatory* = (1) providing vindication <a vindicatory eyewitness account>; or (2) punitive, retributive <vindicatory actions against the company>. Because sense 2 verges closely on the domain of *vindictive*, *vindicatory* should be reserved for sense 1. **Vindicative* is a NEEDLESS VARIANT that ill-advisedly displaces *vindictive*—e.g.: "Indeed, Chancellor suggests, those hostile feelings coupled with Patricia's compulsive need for things and recognition fuel her almost *vindicative* [read *vindictive*] toyings with Stanley." Simi Horwitz, "Deborah Findlay & Anna Chancellor Create the Muses in 'Stanley,' " *Back Stage*, 21 Feb. 1997, at 19.

violable. So formed in AmE and BrE alike—not **violatable*. See -ABLE (D) & -ATABLE.

Current ratio: 194:1

violate. See **contravene** (A).

violative. The phrase *to be violative of* is verbose for *to violate*. E.g.: "This proposal *is too flagrantly violative of the First Amendment* [read *violates the First Amendment too flagrantly*] to merit anything but condemnation." Walter G. Markum, "Campaign Finance Reform? Don't Bet on It," *Virginian-Pilot* (Norfolk), 13 Oct. 1997, at B10. See BE-VERBS (B).

The *OED* records *violative* from 1856 at the earliest, but the word appeared more than half a century before in a famous Supreme Court case, *Marbury v. Madison* (1803): "To withhold the commission, therefore, is an act deemed by the court not warranted by law, but *violative* of a vested legal right."

violoncello, not **violincello*, is the correct spelling for the bass member of the violin family. Not surprisingly, the word has often been misspelled through association with *violin*—e.g.:

- "He used a *violincello* [read *violoncello*] for the body of the female figure." Robert L. Pincus, "Surrealist Max Ernst Just Having Fun with Sculpture," *San Diego Union-Trib.*, 19 July 1992, at E2.
- "Edward Brewer is the keyboard artist, appearing with his wife, oboist Virginia Brewer, and Loretta O'Sullivan, playing Baroque *violincello* [read *violoncello*]." Robert Sherman, "Pulvermann Foundation in Fifth Concert Year," *N.Y. Times*, 19 May 1996, § 13, at 19.
- "Selections will include Beethoven's Ninth Symphony, Mozart's 'Marriage of Figaro' and Haydn's 'Concerto in C Major for *Violincello* [read *Violoncello*] and Orchestra.' " "Music Briefs," *Knoxville News-Sentinel*, 12 May 2002, at G4.

Of course, the safest approach is to use the simpler and much more recognizable *cello* instead.

LANGUAGE-CHANGE INDEX
violoncello misspelled **violincello*: Stage 1
Current ratio: 26:1

virago (= a harsh, shrewish woman) forms the plural *viragos* or (as a variant) *viragoes*. See PLURALS (D).

Current ratio (*viragos* vs. *viragoes*): 2:1

Virgil. Since the 17th century, *Virgil*, not *Vergil*, has been the standard spelling for the Roman poet who wrote the *Aeneid*—this despite his full Latin name, Publius Vergilius Maro.

Current ratio (*poet Virgil* vs. *poet Vergil*): 10:1

VIRGULES. See PUNCTUATION (Q).

virtual derives from the Latin root *virtus* (= virtue, effectiveness, strength, excellence). In its most traditional sense, the adjective means "in essence or effect, but not formally or titularly" <in Nicholas's absence, Rasputin became a virtual tsar>. By extension, it has come to denote "almost" <traffic came to a virtual standstill> or, quite loosely, "figurative" <we're buried in a virtual avalanche of paperwork>. Cf. **literally.**

In the 1980s, computer users and science-fiction writers adopted the term to describe data, software, interfaces, and the like that exist in electronic form only <virtual reality>. That's a handy term, filling a new need in the language. But it sets up the potential for some awkward mixed uses <the world is a virtual playground>.

virtue of, by; *in virtue of. *By virtue of*, not **in virtue of*, has been the standard phrase since the 17th century. The latter is an ARCHAISM.

Current ratio: 4:1

virtuoso. The plural is preferably *virtuosos*—not *virtuosi* (a pedantic form that is significantly less common in journalistic print sources). *Virtuosi* is more common in BrE than it is in AmE. In World English today, the two forms vie closely for supremacy in printed books. See PLURALS (B).

Current ratio (*virtuosi* vs. *virtuosos*): 1.5:1

virus. Pl. *viruses*.

vis-à-vis (lit., "face to face") is a multihued preposition and adverb in place of which a more precise term is often better. The traditional sense is adverbial, "in a position facing each other." But the word is most often figurative. And as a preposition, *vis-à-vis* has been extended to the senses "opposite to; in relation to; as compared with." Although more straightforward phrases are often available, they're sometimes longer—e.g.:

- "This shift appears to be based partly on the assumption that private equity returns provide some diversification (*vis-à-vis* traditional stock market investments)." "Plenty of Potential in Private Equity," *Fin. Times*, 21 July 1997, at 10. (Possibly *as compared with*?)
- "That would have done far more to bolster California's economic competitiveness *vis-à-vis* other Western states where income levies are considerably larger." "Progress at Last," *San Diego Union-Trib.*, 16 Sept. 1997, at B6. (Possibly *in comparison with*?)
- "Small, remote towns suffer from a number of deprivations—along with corresponding advantages—*vis-à-vis* big cities." Jonathan Chait, "Illiberal Arts," *New Republic*, 29 Sept. 1997, at 14. (Possibly *compared with*?)

But shorter substitutes are often available—e.g.:

- "A German mark sharply lower *vis-à-vis* [read *against*] the dollar and sterling has also helped boost exports." "Germany: Carmakers Show the Way," *BusinessWeek*, 15 Sept. 1997, at 88.
- "But I've often had this question *vis-à-vis* [read *about*] business lunches: Just how unusual and personalized can I be with them and not lose every client I've ever had?" Pamela Margoshes, "Power Lunches, in My Apartment," *N.Y. Times*, 28 Sept. 1997, § 3, at 14.
- "The present chapter delves into agencies' accountability *vis-à-vis* [read *to*] the European Parliament and the Council of the European." Madalina Busuioc, *European Agencies: Law and Practices of Accountability* 114 (2013).

viscera (= internal organs) is the plural of *viscus*. See PLURALS (B).

viscous. See **vicious.**

vise. See **vice.**

visible; visual. *Visible* means "capable of being seen; perceptible to the eye." *Visual* means "of, relating to, or involving vision or sight."

Hence the phrase for a blind or nearly blind person is *visually impaired*, not **visibly impaired*, which is something of a MALAPROPISM—e.g.:

- "Lyons also hopes to exhibit a sensory garden in Greeley Park that is accessible to the *visibly* [read *visually*] impaired and the physically challenged." Tammy Annis, "Barrier Awareness Day," *Union Leader* (Manchester, N.H.), 22 Aug. 1993, at B1.
- "Stovall is founder and president of the Narrative Television Network, which makes television accessible for blind and *visibly* [read *visually*] impaired people." "Baptist Official to Speak at Southern Hills," *Tulsa World*, 7 Sept. 1996, at D5.

Visibly impaired, however, is a phrase that police appropriately use in describing a person noticeably affected by alcohol.

LANGUAGE-CHANGE INDEX
visibly impaired misused for *visually impaired*: Stage 1

visit, n.; visitation. Dictionaries have long labeled these words synonyms, and for the most part their senses overlap. *Visitation*, for example, may denote simply the act or an instance of visiting—e.g.: "*Visitation* is seasonal; few guests come in winter." Jay Clarke, "Up Close with Six Florida Islands," *Chicago Trib.*, 21 Jan. 2007, Travel §, at 10.

But often, the words' connotations suggest a distinction. A *visit* is, in general, a casual or recreational meeting <a social visit>. *Visitation* connotes (1) the number of visits collectively; (2) a visit with a formal purpose or authorization, or (3) a supernatural or divine appearance. E.g.:

- Sense 1: "Daily temperatures can exceed the century mark in the summer months, when *visitation* is lowest." Tom Uhlenbrock, "Desert Park an Eco-tourist Playground," *Star-Ledger* (Newark), 29 Apr. 2007, Travel §, at 9.
- Sense 2: "There is one particularly amazing moment—a tribute to the subtlety of this film's writing, directing and acting—during his first allowed *visitation* at the nursing home." Barry Paris, "Love and Loss Among the Ruins of Alzheimer's," *Pitt. Post-Gaz.*, 18 May 2007, at E1.
- Sense 3: "Dancers regularly trot onstage to freeze as if overtaken by a sudden *visitation* of imagination or vibe." Apollinaire Scherr, "Morris Dances for the Sublime," *Newsday* (N.Y.), 21 Jan. 2007, Weekend §, at B7.

Without some suggestion of collectivity, formality, or transcendence, *visitation* often just sounds like a magniloquent substitute for the simpler word—e.g.: "[David] Bell is a gifted director and his fluid, lovely work here is extraordinary. This is a production that deserves *visitations* [read *visits*] from Broadway

LANGUAGE-CHANGE INDEX (For the full key, see front matter pp. xxxi, l–li.)
Stage 1: Rejected. **Stage 2:** Widely shunned. **Stage 3:** Widespread but . . . **Stage 4:** Ubiquitous but . . . **Stage 5:** Fully accepted.
Invariably inferior forms marked by asterisk (✳). • Ratios represent frequency of prevalent forms vs. variants in current books.

producers." Chris Jones, "Chris Jones Recommends," *Chicago Trib.*, 11 May 2007, On the Town §, at 9.

LANGUAGE-CHANGE INDEX
visitation misused for *visit*: Stage 1

visit, vb.; **visit with, to.** To *visit* someone is to call on that person, especially as an act of friendship or courtesy. To *visit* a place is to go there to see (as a sightseer might) or to oversee (as an official might). To *visit with* someone, in AmE, is merely to talk with that person for more than a moment, usually in a personal way (at a watercooler, in the front yard, on a city street, in a living room, etc.).

visor (= a projecting shade) has been the standard spelling since about 1825. *Vizor* is a variant.

Current ratio: 17:1

visual. See **ocular** & **visible.**

visualize does not mean "to see," but "to see in the mind's eye." So it's silly to say, as some do, that they can't *visualize* very well because of the fog.

vita [L. "life"] is nearly synonymous with *résumé.* The difference is that *vita* usually refers to an academic's accomplishments and is often longer than the typical one-page résumé. Despite the widespread notion to the contrary, the word *vita* /vee-tə/ is not a slangy, informal shortening of *curriculum vitae* [L. "course of one's life"], in which *vitae* is in the genitive case. Rather, *vita* is a perfectly good term in itself.

vitiate /vish-ee-ayt/ = (1) to impair the quality or reduce the value of (something); (2) to invalidate in whole or in part; or (3) to corrupt morally; debase. Sense 1 is the most widely used—e.g.: "Their whole approach is *vitiated* by the lack of historical (as opposed to literary) insight into the true social and cultural evolution of classical translation down the centuries." Peter Green, "The Slampam Blues," *New Republic,* 19 Feb. 1996, at 37. Sense 2 is the legal sense <a contract can be vitiated by illegal provisions>. Sense 3 is rare.

Vitiate is sometimes misused for its opposite, *ameliorate,* or for *obviate.* Although you might ameliorate or obviate a problem, you can *vitiate* something only if it's either neutral or good. Some writers even seem to think that *vitiate* means "to lessen"—e.g.: "As important as that development might be, one potential problem looms that could well *vitiate* [read *lessen*] the number of people who actually leave welfare rolls." "The Welfare Wagon," *Orange County Register,* 7 Aug. 1997, at B8. Still others think it means "to aggravate, exacerbate"—e.g.: "In India, religious conflict further *vitiates* [read *aggravates*] the problem." Joydeep Bhattacharya, "Just Changing the Guard Can't Save India from Asphyxiation," *L.A. Times,* 12 Feb. 1991, at B7. See **obviate** & SLIPSHOD EXTENSION.

LANGUAGE-CHANGE INDEX
1. *vitiate* misused for *lessen*: Stage 1
2. *vitiate* misused for *aggravate*: Stage 1

vittles. See **victuals.**

vituperative; **vituperous.* The former has always been the predominant adjective corresponding to *vituperation. *Vituperous* is a NEEDLESS VARIANT.

Current ratio: 96:1

viz. is an abbreviation of the Latin word *videlicet* (fr. *videbere* "to see" + *licet* "it is permissible"). The English-language equivalents are *namely* and *that is,* either of which is preferable. (See **namely** & **that is.**) Like its English counterparts, the Latin term signifies that what follows particularizes and explains a general statement. E.g.:

- "For too long Virginia's elitist Democrats (*viz.,* Don Beyer, L.F. Payne, Mark Warner, Chuck Robb et al. are—to a man—millionaires) have taken Virginia's African-Americans, including Wilder, for granted." "Election Clean-Up," *Richmond Times-Dispatch,* 8 Nov. 1997, at A8.
- "This tasted equally of its constituent parts: *viz.,* cabbage and chorizo sausage." A.A. Gill, "Country Roade," *Sunday Times* (London), 23 Nov. 1997, Style §, at 26.
- "John saw not only dimensions and building materials, he saw also the quality of life (a new Jerusalem), *viz.,* God would move into the city, there among the people." Abram Sangrey, "This Is God's House and Our Sacred Place," *Lancaster New Era,* 1 Dec. 1997, at A5.

The abbreviation raises three questions. First, how does one derive *viz.* from *videlicet?* The final -*z* in the abbreviation represents the medieval Latin symbol of contraction for *et* or -*et* (OED). Second, how does one pronounce *viz.?* Preferably by saying "namely." But if you want to say the Latin term, it's /vi-**del**-ə-sit/. Third, how do you punctuate it? As with *e.g.* and *i.e.,* the abbreviation is customarily set off from the rest of the sentence by a pair of commas (or, when it begins a sentence or a parenthetical expression, by one comma). See **e.g.** & **i.e.**

Current ratio (*namely* vs. *viz.*): 5:1

vocation. See **avocation.**

vociferous. A. And *voracious.* A *vociferous* person is loud, noisy, and clamorous; a *vociferous* crowd is characterized by unrestrained yelling. A *voracious* person or animal, meanwhile, devours food ravenously; a *voracious* reader has an insatiable desire for books, magazines, and other reading materials. In short, although the two words appear similar, they apply to very different types of behavior.

Through WORD-SWAPPING, they get confounded. *Vociferous* is sometimes misused for *voracious*—e.g.:

- "Monsignor Field [is] a nurturing mentor, with a depth that allowed him to be at once an aficionado of the opera, a *vociferous* [read *voracious*] reader and a fan of basketball." Susan Todd, "Rev. William Field, 84, a Priest's Priest," *Star-Ledger* (Newark), 4 Dec. 2000, at 67.
- "Atlanta's *vociferous* [read *voracious*] appetite for water isn't likely to wane anytime soon." "Protecting Our Water," *Greenville News* (S.C.), 19 Feb. 2002, at A6.

- "A *vociferous* [read *voracious*] reader who tears through several books a week and loves crime thrillers, Jackson applied for her first library card when she was 6 years old." Christina Headrick, "Nostalgia Marks Mazy Library's Final Day," *St. Petersburg Times*, 23 Mar. 2002, Clearwater §, at 1.

The opposite error is somewhat less common—e.g.:

- "Did everyone miss the target when the men's 4x100-meter relay team was so *voraciously* [read *vociferously*] condemned for its post-race antics?" David Steele, "At Least Olympics Seek Fix for Drugs," *S.F. Chron.*, 19 Oct. 2000, at E2.
- "Ironically, despite Olson's *voracious* [read *vociferous*] opposition to federal special prosecutors, one of his oldest, best friends is Kenneth Starr, the Clinton special prosecutor." Chuck Goudie, "Bush Attorney Held Keys to Operation Greylord," *Daily Herald* (Chicago), 15 Dec. 2000, at 10.

LANGUAGE-CHANGE INDEX
1. *vociferous* misused for *voracious*: Stage 1
Current ratio (*voracious reader* vs.
**vociferous reader*): 185:1
2. *voracious* misused for *vociferous*: Stage 1

B. And **vociferant.* *Vociferous* (in the sense given in (A)) has always (since the 18th century) been the standard term; *vociferant is a NEEDLESS VARIANT.

VOGUE WORDS. In the mid-1990s, colorful hair dye became all the rage. Teenagers used it. Thirty-somethings used it—and applied it to their young children's hair. Women of all ages used it. Even many middle-aged men used it. By 2001, the craze had long since spread over the globe. For example, in the summer of that year, it was difficult to spot, among hordes of young people at various places in Japan, a single undyed pate: seemingly everyone had light-brown or blond hair (if not some bolder color).

That's the way fads are. People latch on to them to make a statement about themselves. But the statement truly has little to do with individuality: it's all about groupism. You adopt a fad to show that you're with it, hip, or young at heart. You don't want to be left out or left behind. That's the essence of it.

Linguistic fads are much the same, but they often work at a less conscious level. Words and phrases sprinkled into conversation—as well as certain syntactic habits—have an effect that's somewhat analogous to that of ostentatiously dyed hair. Usage critics have traditionally grouped these phrases under the rubric of "Vogue Words."

Not surprisingly, various types of vogue words are used as badges to show that you belong to a certain group. If, in 2001, you wanted (subliminally or consciously) to show that you were sensitive to psychology, you'd have said that someone cannot bring *closure* to *issues* about *codependency* or *dysfunctional*

mentoring or *parenting* or *partnering*; that a *12-step program* will *empower recovering* addicts (or abusers, etc.) through *validation* and *transparency*. If you wanted to show that you were astute in business, you'd make a mantra of *growing* the business through *solutions* and *workable solutions*, especially *e-solutions* of various kinds. If you wanted to show that you were a cool person under the age of 25, you'd turn old laudatory adjectives into exclamatory nouns ending in *-ness* (*Coolness! Awesomeness! Greatness!*). If you didn't want to discuss something—or really did but wanted to add to the salaciousness of the discussion—you'd say, *Don't even go there!* or *I'm not even going to go there!* If you wanted to dismiss something that someone else had said to you or about you, you'd exclaim *Whatever!* (with the accent on the second syllable). (See **whatever (B).**) But if you were grateful for some small thing that someone had done for you, you'd exclaim hyperbolically, *You're my hero!* All these words and phrases, in short, say as much about the speaker's persona and attitude as about the speaker's supposed meaning.

During the late 1990s and early 2000s, a certain rhetorical question became voguish:

How good is *that*?
How fine is *that*?

Each one has a strong stress on the final word. Nobody would have been caught using plain old exclamations:

How good it is!
How fine it is!

The first group (the questions) sounded *au courant*; the second group (the exclamations) sounded as if they'd come out of mothballs.

Vogue expressions may have their origin in syntax, they may be NEOLOGISMS, or they may be old words used in novel uses or senses. (The name *vogue expressions* might be the more accurate name—but *vogue words* is pretty well established.) Often they quickly become either standard or hackneyed, and sometimes they pass into obscurity after a period of feverish popularity. The following list is a representative collection of fairly durable examples:

across-the-board
at the end of the day
basically
been there, done that
bottom line
cautiously optimistic
constructive
cool
cost-effective
cutting edge
definitely
dialogue, vb.
disconnect, n.
downside

LANGUAGE-CHANGE INDEX (For the full key, see front matter pp. xxxi, l–li.)
Stage 1: Rejected. **Stage 2:** Widely shunned. **Stage 3:** Widespread but . . . **Stage 4:** Ubiquitous but . . . **Stage 5:** Fully accepted.
Invariably inferior forms marked by asterisk (*). • Ratios represent frequency of prevalent forms vs. variants in current books.

downsize
empower; empowerment
environment
escalate (= to intensify)
eventuate
exposure (= liability)
facilitator
framework
gravitas
grow your business
identify with <I can identify with you>
impact, vb.
*incent, vb.
interface
in the final analysis
issues
-IZE words (e.g., *incentivize)
lifestyle
matrix
meaningful
methodology
need-to-know basis, on a
network, vb.
no-brainer
no-lose situation
no-win situation
office, vb.
on the cusp
on the same page
-oriented (e.g., cat-oriented)
overly
parameters
politically correct (or P.C.)
proactive
quantum leap
relate, v.i. <I can relate to that>
resonate <does that resonate with you?>
scenario
situation
state-of-the-art
synergy
transparency
upside
user-friendly (see COMPUTERESE)
venue (= the place for an event)
viable
wake-up call
win–win situation
world-class, adj.
worst-case scenario

When you put it all together, of course, it's ludicrous: "Language-wise, I am, like, majorly bummed by the way people abuse the mother tongue. This one's a no-brainer. Yo, I've got issues here, and this is my bottom line." Thomas B. Harrison, "Slang, Jargon Are Linguistic High Crimes," *Montgomery Advertiser*, 12 Jan. 1997, at C1.

voicemail. One word. The *OED* dates it back to 1980.

void, adj. See ADJECTIVES (B).

volitional; *volitive. *Volitional* (= of or belonging to volition [i.e., an act of willing or resolving]; pertaining to the action of willing) has been the standard term since the late 18th century. E.g.: "Mary Ann Sandoval . . .

testified that she believed Stuart's memory loss and behavioral problems were self-serving and *volitional*." Ginny McKibben, "Suspect Cleared for Slay Trial," *Denver Post*, 29 Oct. 1994, at B3. *Volitive* has long been a NEEDLESS VARIANT.

Current ratio: 43:1

voluptuous (= sexy; sensually gratifying) has occasionally been misspelled *voluptious since the late 18th century. E.g.: "It is a big wine, yet soft, *voluptious* [read *voluptuous*], and very fruity with fat, berrylike fruity flavors." Robert M. Parker Jr., "The Harvest of 1983," *Wash. Post*, 2 Nov. 1983, at E1.

Current ratio: 2,478:1

voracious. See **vociferous.**

voracity. See MALAPROPISMS & **veracity.**

vortex. Pl. *vortices* or *vortexes*. Although there is much to be said for the second of these as a homegrown plural, *vortices* is significantly more common in print. See PLURALS (B) & **vertex.**

Current ratio (*vortices* vs. *vortexes*): 12:1

votable. So spelled in AmE and BrE alike—not *vote-able*. See MUTE E.

votary; *votarist. The former has been standard since the 16th century. The latter is a NEEDLESS VARIANT.

Current ratio: 51:1

vouch; *avouch. The first is the word in current use. *Avouch* is obsolete, having been replaced by *vouch for* in the sense "to provide proof, to give a guarantee" <I'll vouch for her honesty>. *Vouch* itself is now almost always intransitive in this way (followed by *for*). As a transitive verb meaning "to call upon, rely on, or cite as authority," *vouch* is archaic.

vouchsafe ordinarily denotes "to grant something in a condescending way," or, more neutrally, "to grant something as a special favor." The word is often mildly sarcastic—e.g.: "Gen. Powell's opinions, as he has been *vouchsafing* them, were unformed or, where formed, oddly out of date." "America's Son," *Nat'l Rev.*, 27 Nov. 1995, at 12.

The term is sometimes misused in two ways. First, it's sometimes used as if it were equivalent to *grant*, *bestow on*, or *provide*—e.g.: "Last week, MTV *vouchsafed* [read *bestowed on*] him its Video Vanguard award, shortly after his sitcom, 'In the House,' went into its third season." Thomas Goetz, "Sell Sell," *Village Voice*, 16 Sept. 1997. Second, it's sometimes misused for *vouch for* (= to provide assurance of)—e.g.: "What do your other dealer friends and collectors think about it? Has a reliable restorer *vouchsafed* [read *vouched for*] its condition?" Edward Lewine, "How Not to Look Like a Dope in an Art Gallery," *N.Y. Times*, 14 Sept. 1997, § 13, at 1.

LANGUAGE-CHANGE INDEX
1. *vouchsafe* misused for *bestow on*: Stage 1
2. *vouchsafe* misused for *vouch for*: Stage 1

VOWEL CLUSTERS are not indigenous to the English language, although one finds them in our imported vocabulary, in words such as *giaour* (= one outside the Muslim faith), *maieutic* (= Socratic), *moueing* (= making a pouting face), *onomatopoeia* (= the use of imitative or echoic words, such as *click*, *fizz*, *plop*, and *splash*), and *queuing* (AmE) or *queueing* (BrE). In forming NEOLOGISMS, especially by agglutination, one should be wary of clumping vowels together in a way that would strike readers as un-English. Even three consecutive vowels may have this effect, as in **antiaircraft*, which is better hyphenated: *anti-aircraft*.

voyage; passage. A slight DIFFERENTIATION is possible. *Voyage* denotes a journey, especially by sea.

Passage is almost synonymous with *voyage* in that sense, but it does not have as much connotation of returning. That is, *passage* usually denotes some sort of one-way change, such as (1) a progression from one place or state to another <life passages>; (2) a route from one place to another <Northwest Passage>; (3) a ticket or other right to transportation <passage to Hawaii>; (4) part of a written work, esp. one read or cited <a passage from *Hamlet*>; or (5) the act of voting to enact a law <passage of the 1964 Civil Rights Law>.

vs. See **v.**

vulva. See **vagina.**

W

W. For the pronunciation, see **Dubya.**

waft (= [vb.] to float or be carried lightly) is pronounced /wahft/ or /waft/ (rhyming with *raft*).

wage; wages. The word can be indifferently singular <he earns a good wage> or plural <she earns good wages>, but the latter form has always predominated in all varieties of English. The plural, of course, is construed with a plural verb <your wages are now subject to a garnishment order>. The biblical phrasing *The wages of sin is death* (Romans 6:23) is regarded as a linguistic anomaly—and a SET PHRASE.

wagon; *waggon. The first has been standard AmE since about 1830 and standard BrE since about 1920. The second is a chiefly BrE variant.

wainscoting (= wood paneling lining an interior wall) has been the standard spelling in AmE and BrE alike since the 1820s. **Wainscotting* is a variant.

Current ratio: 10:1

waist; waste. Substituting *waste* for *waist* is most often a pun—e.g.: "County Is *Waste-Deep* in Reduction/Recycling Assistance" (headline), *Tampa Trib.*, 9 Nov. 2008, Local News §, at 3. But not always—e.g.:

- "Johnny Campbell, 22, tied a tow chain around his *waste* [read *waist*] and waded through *waste-deep* [read *waist-deep*] water to Guerrero's car, but as he touched her hand, a rush of water pushed the car out of his reach." Alex Branch & Scott Streater, "Flood Kills Mother, Child," *Ft. Worth Star-Telegram*, 2 May 2004, at A1, A23.
- "A prime spot for picture-taking is the fifth-floor rooftop of the City View Cafe on Dinh Tien Hoang Street, a few doors from the Thang Long Puppet Theatre where puppeteers stand *waste-deep* [read *waist-deep*] in water while manipulating fire-breathing dragons with bamboo sticks." Carol Pucci, "Hello, Hanoi," *Seattle Times*, 24 Feb. 2008, at L11.

- "While crossing a swollen, *waste-deep* [read *waist-deep*] creek linked arm-in-arm 45 minutes earlier, one member of the Sammamish teen's party had slipped and pulled two others underwater." Craig Hill, "Personal Locators Can Be a Lifesaver," *Mobile Register*, 14 Aug. 2008, Z §, at 9.

waistband is sometimes, in a gross error, written **wasteband* (sporadic through the 20th century)—e.g.:

- "The women sucked in their breath and tried to push their belly-buttons into fleshy balloons over their *wastebands* [read *waistbands*]." Rebecca Walsh, "Dancers at Fest Bare Their Bellies, Escape Daily Grind," *Salt Lake Trib.*, 28 Aug. 1994, at B1.
- "He allegedly pulled a gun from his *wasteband* [read *waistband*] and pointed it at Fuller's head." "Kamiah Man Faces Two Assault Counts," *Lewiston Morning Trib.* (Idaho), 4 Feb. 2003, at A11.

For more on this curiosity, see *Garner on Language and Writing* 259–60, 283 (2009).

Current ratio: 6,891:1

waistcoat (= [in BrE] a vest) is traditionally and best pronounced not as it's spelled, but instead /wes-kət/.

wait. See **await.**

waiter. If women can be actors and sculptors, then surely they can be *waiters*. Yet in looking for nonsexist alternatives to *waitress*, various groups have championed the silly terms **waitperson* and **waitron*. Let *waiter* (or, if need be, *server*) do for either sex. See SEXISM (D).

LANGUAGE-CHANGE INDEX
waiter as a gender-neutral term: Stage 5

wait in line; wait on line. The former is the standard AmE expression. The latter is a regionalism in the Northeast, especially in New York. Although some might think that it's the product of the computer age

LANGUAGE-CHANGE INDEX (For the full key, see front matter pp. xxxi, l–li.)
Stage 1: Rejected. **Stage 2:** Widely shunned. **Stage 3:** Widespread but . . . **Stage 4:** Ubiquitous but . . . **Stage 5:** Fully accepted.
Invariably inferior forms marked by asterisk (*). • Ratios represent frequency of prevalent forms vs. variants in current books.

(i.e., being *online*), in fact it dates back to the 19th century and became a common regionalism during the late 1960s. Cf. **stand in line.**

Current ratio (*wait in line* vs. *wait on line*): 29:1

*waitperson; *waitron. See **waiter.**

waive. A. Narrowing of Sense. This word has undergone what linguists call "specialization," its primary sense having gotten narrower with time. Originally, *waive* was just as broad as *abandon* <the fleeing thief waived the stolen goods>. But today, *waive* means "to relinquish voluntarily (something that one has the right to expect)" <the popular entertainer waived her usual fee>.

B. Confused with *wave*. *Waive* sometimes occurs where *wave* (= to move to and fro, esp. with the hand) belongs—e.g.:

- "The wife sat down and the presiding priest, *waiving* [read *waving*] aside the husband's lawyer as he had the wife's, asked to hear the husband's side of the case." John R. Allison, "Five Ways to Keep Disputes Out of Court," *Harv. Bus. Rev.*, Jan.–Feb. 1990, at 166.
- "But a new bidder—the Blockbuster Bowl, sponsored by the video store chain—threw the deal into doubt by *waiving* [read *waving*] a few extra dollars before the noses of our institutions of higher learning." Frederick C. Klein, "Who Cares Who's No. 1?" *Wall Street J.*, 3 Jan. 1992, at A5.
- "[Bobby] Cox thought it was better than borderline, and he let home plate umpire Chris Guccione know it with a waist-high *waive* [read *wave*] of his hand as he went to the mound to pull [Ron] Mahay for Tyler Yates." Vic Feuerherd, "Late Revival Meeting," *Wis. State J.*, 22 Sept. 2007, at C3.

LANGUAGE-CHANGE INDEX
waive misused for *wave*: Stage 1
Current ratio (*wave aside* vs. **waive aside*): 5:1

waiver. *Waiver* (= voluntary relinquishment of a right or advantage) is primarily a noun; *waver* (= to vacillate) is primarily a verb. It is a fairly common solecism to misuse *waiver* for *waver*—e.g.:

- "Mayor Koch . . . *waivered* [read *wavered*] between silence and support for months." "Bess Myerson Accused of Stealing $44 in Goods," *N.Y. Times*, 28 May 1988, at 9.
- "But when the defense lawyer found out the judge was *waivering* [read *wavering*], Mr. Polanski left the country." Caryn James, "A Life in Exile from America, from Memory," *N.Y. Times*, 17 Nov. 1993, at B1, B2.
- "'We continue our gentle adventure together. Our vows to disappear and our promises never to write another book have held for years . . . but sometimes they *waiver* [read *waver*].'" Walter Scott, "Personality Parade," *Parade*, 3 July 1994, at 2 (quoting Richard Bach, the author of *Jonathan Livingston Seagull*, on being married to the actress Leslie Parrish-Bach).
- "They get sensitive and uncomfortable, and *waiver* [read *waver*]." Julie Steelman, *The Effortless Yes* 29 (2011).

When *waivered* is not misused for *wavered*, it often displaces the more straightforward verb *waived*—e.g.: "While none have been approved by EPA, the three 'tertiary' ethers are chemically similar to MTBE

and would probably be *waivered* [read *waived*] by the EPA." George H. Unzelman, "U.S. Clean Air Act Expands Role for Oxygenates," *Oil & Gas J.*, 15 Apr. 1991, at 44.

Finally, *waver* occasionally ousts *waiver* from its rightful position—e.g.: "Out of the school's 575 students, 38 have signed *wavers* [read *waivers*] to allow them not to wear the uniform." Brian Hall, "Reaching Out," *Orange County Register*, 1 Feb. 1996, at 3.

LANGUAGE-CHANGE INDEX
1. *waiver* misused for *waver*: Stage 1
Current ratio (*waver between* vs.
*waiver between): 21:1
2. *waver* misused for *waiver*: Stage 1
Current ratio (*sign a waiver* vs. **sign a waver*): 109:1

wake; awake; awaken. The past-tense and past-participial forms of *wake* and its various siblings are perhaps the most vexing in the language. Following are the preferred declensions:

wake > woke > waked (or woken)
awake > awoke > awaked (or awoken)
awaken > awakened > awakened
wake up > woke up > waked up

See IRREGULAR VERBS. For the past participle, AmE prefers *waked*; BrE prefers *woken*.

wallet; billfold. The traditional distinction is that a *wallet* holds paper money unfolded and contains compartments for coins and the like, whereas a *billfold* (as the name suggests) holds it folded and does not contain extra compartments. But *wallets* now fold, so most people use the words interchangeably. And *billfold* is largely seen as sex-specific for males.

wallop (= to hit someone or something very hard, esp. either with one's hand or with something in one's hand) is inflected *walloped* and *walloping*. See SPELLING (B).

walrus. Pl. *walruses.*

wane; wax. *Wane* = to decrease in strength or importance. *Wax* (= [1] to increase in strength or importance; or [2] to become) is used primarily (in sense 1) as a correlative of *wane* <her influence waxed and waned>. In sense 2, it appears in such hackneyed expressions as *to wax poetic, eloquent*, etc.

wangle. See **wrangle.**

want, n. The usual sense, of course, is "something desired" or "a desire." But *want* has a long history as a FORMAL WORD meaning "lack," especially in the phrase *for want of*. Though this sense formerly had a literary cast, today it is fairly common even in informal writing—e.g.:

- "The Republican incumbent, William C. Cleveland, 48, a U.S. Capitol Police officer, said his motions often die for *want* of a second." Mike Allen, "GOP Struggles to Be Heard in Staunch Democratic Port," *Wash. Post*, 5 May 1997, at B3.
- "The kids are killing their parents at home for *want* of something to do, a place to go where they can be kids

and act like kids the way we adults did." Letter of Ben E. Thomas Sr., "Racial Bias Does Exist Here," *Anchorage Daily News*, 23 Sept. 1997, at B8.

The corresponding participle *wanting* (= lacking) is somewhat more common—e.g.:

- "It was not the intellectual gifts or probity of the three that the ABA found particularly *wanting*." Harvey Berkman, "ABA's 'Unqualified' Judges Doing Well," *Nat'l L.J.*, 13 Jan. 1996, at A1.
- "Broccoli sprouts may prove to be *wanting* in any number of these qualities." Natalie Angier, "Broccoli Sprouts Rated 'New' Wonder Food," *Denver Post*, 16 Sept. 1997, at A1.

wanton; reckless. In law, the word *wanton* usually denotes a greater degree of culpability than *reckless* does. A *reckless* person is generally fully aware of the risks and may even be trying and hoping to avoid harm. A *wanton* person may be risking no more harm than the *reckless* person, but he or she is not trying to avoid the harm and is indifferent about whether it results. In criminal law, *wanton* usually connotes malice, but *reckless* does not.

In nonlegal contexts, a *reckless* person is careless and irresponsible but may not have considered the possible consequences <a reckless skateboard rider>. And a *wanton* person is someone who is sexually unrestrained <a wanton lover>, or acts capriciously, cruelly, or maliciously <a wanton bully>. See **reckless.**

-WARD(s). See DIRECTIONAL WORDS (A) & **toward (A).**

warrant, v.t. Today, *warrant* most commonly means "to justify." And in modern idiom, one naturally says that acts or beliefs are *warranted*, but not so naturally that people are *warranted*. Thus *Such a conclusion warrants federal regulators in substituting their views for those of local officials* reads better this way: *Such a conclusion warrants federal regulators' substituting their views for those of local officials.* (On the possessive in that revision, see FUSED PARTICIPLES.)

Nevertheless, the *OED* contains examples of *warrant* used with personal objects from the 17th century. This usage remains current mostly in law, though sometimes it appears in other contexts—e.g.: "I wanted to hear what the reasons were, what could possibly *warrant* a woman to decide to do this." Renee Lynn Glembin, "Mothers and Motherhood," *Milwaukee J. Sentinel*, 11 May 1997, at 1.

Current ratio (*warranted his* vs. *warranted him*): 2:1

wary; weary. To be *wary* of something is to be on one's guard against it: cautious, watchful, and perhaps worried. E.g.: "Consumers remain *wary* of anthrax sent through the mail." Stephanie Miles, "Apparel E-tailers to Spruce Up for Holidays," *Wall Street J.*, 6 Nov. 2001, at B6.

To be *weary* is to be physically fatigued or, by extension, "sick and tired" of something and ready for it to end. E.g.: "Maryland players are apparently growing *weary* about being asked questions about Duke guard Jason Williams." Michael Murphy, "Final Four Summary," *Houston Chron.*, 31 Mar. 2001, at 8.

Doubtless by false association with *wary* and perhaps with *leery* (= suspicious and careful), writers sometimes misuse *weary*—e.g.:

- "As a general principle, Congress should be *weary* [read *wary*] of trading tax cuts for expensive new entitlements." "A Deal Republicans Must Refuse," *Wash. Times*, 29 June 2000, at A22.
- "Head coach Mike Novak, Steve's father, likes his team's chances but is *weary* [read *wary*] about being considered the favorite." Guy B. Stuller, "Brown Deer Stands Tall," *Milwaukee J. Sentinel*, 21 Nov. 2000, at S10.
- "A stamp might be the next tool that helps unite Americans at a time when some residents are *weary* [read *wary*] about opening the mail for fear of becoming a victim of a bioterrorist attack." Sean Adkins, "New Stamp Printed on Local Paper," *York Daily Record*, 25 Oct. 2001, at B5.

LANGUAGE-CHANGE INDEX
weary misused for *wary*: Stage 1

wash /wahsh/ is frequently mispronounced with an intrusive *-r-*: /wahrsh/. See PRONUNCIATION (B), (C).
LANGUAGE-CHANGE INDEX
wash mispronounced /wahrsh/: Stage 2

Washington's Birthday. See **Presidents' Day.**

waste, to lay. See **lay waste.**

*wasteband. See **waistband.**

wastebasket; wastepaper basket. Both terms came into use in the 1850s. For about a century, the shorter form *wastebasket* was regarded as an Americanism by speakers of BrE. But English speakers universally like economy of expression—anything to minimize syllables—and beginning about 1960 *wastebasket* rose rapidly in BrE, overtaking the longer form in frequency of use by 1990. Both terms are still in frequent BrE use, probably by different generations of speakers. In AmE, *trash can* appears more frequently even than *wastebasket*—but *trash can* may refer to a small receptacle within a house or office, to the larger receptacle within those places, or to the even larger receptacle put outside for collection (also, in this latter use, called a *garbage can* in AmE or *dustbin* or *litter bin* in BrE).

wastewater. One word.

watermark; water-mark; water mark. *Watermark* = (1) a line made by a body of water at its surface (as in a flood) and used to gauge the water's depth; or (2) a faint identifying mark pressed into fine paper during manufacture, or an analogous identifier embedded in a computer file by software. The word in sense 2 is

---

LANGUAGE-CHANGE INDEX (For the full key, see front matter pp. xxxi, l–li.)
Stage 1: Rejected. **Stage 2:** Widely shunned. **Stage 3:** Widespread but . . . **Stage 4:** Ubiquitous but . . . **Stage 5:** Fully accepted.
Invariably inferior forms marked by asterisk (*). • Ratios represent frequency of prevalent forms vs. variants in current books.

always written as a single compound, while in sense 1 it may also be hyphenated or made two words. When sense 1 is modified by adjectives such as *high* and *low*, the compound noun must be split since the adjective specifically modifies *water*, forming a PHRASAL ADJECTIVE that in turn modifies *mark* <the high-water mark of her career>. To write of a *high watermark is to invite MISCUES because the reader may think of a paper-company logo too near the top of a page—e.g.:

- "In between, though, the Dukes managed to overcome droughts (nothing in a half-dozen possessions en route to that *low-watermark* [read *low-water mark*] 17-point deficit) and poor shooting (32 percent the first half)." Chuck Finder, "Hard by the Hocking River," *Pitt. Post-Gaz.*, 30 Nov. 2001, at B1.
- "The oyster reached its *high watermark* [read *high-water mark*] here in the last decade of the 19th Century. At least half a dozen restaurants known as 'oyster houses' vied for the carriage trade with a variety of preparations." William Rice, "Raw Deal," *Chicago Trib.*, 23 June 2002, Mag. §, at 25.
- "In today's Information Age, work is accomplished—or should be—through a series of linked processes where client service, flexibility and cost containment have replaced volume as the *high watermark for* [read *high-water mark of*] success." John A. Uzzi, "What It Takes for Agencies to Thrive in the Information Age," *Nat'l Underwriter—Life & Health*, 30 Sept. 2002, at 29. (Unfortunately, correcting *high watermark hardly improves this COMMERCIALESE.)

water under the bridge; water over the dam. Both phrases allude to time gone by and events passed. Both date from the 19th century. Since about 1970, *water under the bridge* has been much more common. What *water over the dam* adds is the connotation of missed opportunities—e.g.:

- "Whether other prosecutions should have taken place under the Intelligence Identities Protection Act is another question, and it appears at this point to be *water over the dam* unless Mr. Fitzgerald and the Department of Justice have further plans in mind." Editorial, "Libby's Fate," *Pitt. Post-Gaz.*, 7 June 2007, at B6.
- "After a one-year hiatus—and a whole lot of *water under the bridge* since then—the World Bank is bringing back the office Christmas party." Amy Argetsinger & Roxanne Roberts, "Banking on Holiday Cheer," *Wash. Post*, 3 Dec. 2007, at C3.

The two expressions occasionally get mangled—e.g.: "As I've said before, Newark never should have dumped $210 million into the arena . . . . That, however, is *water over the bridge* [read *water under the bridge* or *water over the dam*] and into the sewer." Joan Whitlow, "Around Arena, Rubble, Rubble, Toil and Trouble," *Star-Ledger* (Newark), 5 Oct. 2007, Editorial §, at 19.

wave. See **waive** (B).

waver. See **waiver**.

wax. See **wane**.

waylay > waylaid > waylaid. Occasionally the past tense or past participle is misspelled *waylayed—e.g.:

- "Keggi's career was *waylayed* [read *waylaid*] in 1993 when she drank some bad water and was stricken with lingering symptoms from E-Coli bacteria." Paul Harber, "They're Going the Distance," *Boston Globe*, 24 Apr. 1997, at C10.
- "[T]he Trojans melted at 12:25 of the second half Friday, when [Taj] Gibson (team-high 16 points and 12 rebounds) was *waylayed* [read *waylaid*] with the fourth foul." Brian Hamilton, "Heels Rush In," *Chicago Trib.*, 25 Mar, 2007, Sports §, at 1.
- "Within the first three hours of the 26.2-mile event, hundreds of runners had been *waylayed* [read *waylaid*] by the heat and medical tents were filled with participants requiring treatment for dehydration and heat exhaustion." Michael Tsai, "Honolulu Marathon Feels Chicago's Heat," *Honolulu Advertiser*, 10 Oct. 2007, at D1.

Current ratio (*waylaid* vs. *waylayed): 400:1

way(s). In the sense "the length of a course or distance," *way* has long been considered the standard term <a long way>. In a singular sense, *ways* occurs frequently in AmE <quite a ways to go> but rarely in BrE. One might be tempted to call it dialectal, but the singular use in *a ways to go* actually occurs in AmE print sources about half as often as *a way to go*. E.g.: "This is premature, of course; Fox still has *a ways to go* [read *some way to go*?] before it's a full-fledged network." Larry Reibstein & Nancy Hass, "Rupert's Power Play," *Newsweek*, 6 June 1994, at 46. See DIALECT.

LANGUAGE-CHANGE INDEX
a ways to go: Stage 3

way which is typically erroneous for *way in which*. E.g.: "This column has as its main goal the empowerment of you, the reader, about *ways which* [read *ways in which*] you can become more informed and thereby take more responsibility for your own health." Glenn Ellis, "Using Herbs as a Method of Preventive Medicine," *Phil. Trib.*, 14 Jan. 1997, at B8.

But it's often quite natural and idiomatic to use *that* in place of *in which*, or even to omit the relative pronoun altogether. These phrasings are much more relaxed—e.g.:

- "*Ways that* they can help include volunteering to tutor." Letter of Janie Moore, "Parents' Help at Schools Is Good for Children," *Columbus Dispatch*, 7 Nov. 1997, at A10.
- "Well, that's the *way* they would do it in Mayberry." Letter of Kathy Heath, *Tampa Trib.*, 12 Sept. 1997, at 6.

LANGUAGE-CHANGE INDEX
*way which for *way in which*: Stage 1
Current ratio (*way in which* vs. *way which): 11:1

we. See FIRST PERSON & PRONOUNS.

weald. See **wield**.

wean means either "to cause (a child or young animal) to become accustomed to food other than the mother's milk" or, by extension, "to withdraw (a person) gradually from a source of dependence." Hence a person is typically *weaned off* something—e.g.:

- "Skeptics have claimed this decline in caseload would slow and then halt once the most employable welfare recipients were *weaned off* the rolls." Robert Rector, "Don't Listen to

Naysayers: Welfare Reform Is Working," *Las Vegas Rev.-J.*, 27 Apr. 1997, at D8.

- "The FDA recommends patients stop taking the drugs immediately. But some doctors say patients can experience depression unless they are *weaned off* them." "Q&A," *St. Petersburg Times*, 16 Sept. 1997, at A3.

But *weaned on*—used illogically in the sense "raised on, brought up with"—is a spreading contagion. E.g.:

- "For a culture *weaned on* [read *brought up on*] Hollywood's interpretation of romance, the very notion that any healthy, intelligent, attractive male might desire a woman over 35 is a radical concept." Shari Graydon, "There's Powerful Appeal in the Wrinkles of Age," *Vancouver Sun*, 25 May 1996, at D6.
- "We women were *weaned on* [read *nurtured on* or *brought up on*] tales of princes and princesses, fairy godmothers, ugly villains and comely heroes of noble character winning against the odds at every turn." Bea Perry, "The Dream Is Over," *Denver Post*, 12 Oct. 1997, at D5.
- "Brought up on a familial feed of Emersonian and Unitarian principles and then, Frank tells us, *weaned on* [read *nurtured by*] Sullivan's critical comments, the theory became Wright's touchstone." Donald Leslie Johnson, *On Frank Lloyd Wright's Concrete Adobe* 31 (2013).

See ILLOGIC. See also **overweening**.

LANGUAGE-CHANGE INDEX
weaned on for *raised on*: Stage 2

weaponize. For a long time—probably beginning in the 1950s—this *-ize* NEOLOGISM was in the exclusive domain of military and international-relations jargon. Uses were infrequent, but the word occurred in popular sources as early as 1984—e.g.:

- " 'Absolutely no work is being done to develop, manufacture, store or *weaponize* biological warfare agents,' the [Pentagon] statement says." R. Jeffrey Smith, "New Army Biowarfare Lab Raises Concerns," *Science*, 7 Dec. 1984, at 1176.
- "Iran also is very unlikely to '*weaponize*' a missile with chemical or nuclear material, a U.S. official said." Robin Wright, "U.S. Won't Halt Drive for Iran Ties," *L.A. Times*, 24 July 1998, at A12.

After September 11, 2001, when terrorists brought down the World Trade Center in New York and attacked the Pentagon, the general public became more aware of biological warfare and bioterrorism. Shortly after that event, cases of anthrax started appearing in cities scattered throughout the U.S., and the word sprang into general use—e.g.:

- "The United States suspected, but lacked the intelligence to ascertain (have they learned nothing?) that Iraq had, in militaryspeak, '*weaponized* anthrax and botulinum' for use in the Gulf War." Martin Levin, "The Bio-Warriors," *Globe & Mail* (Toronto), 22 Sept. 2001, at D16.
- "Not only did the incident lift the curtain on the Soviet Union's decades-long program to *weaponize* disease—hundreds of tons of anthrax, and a few dozen tons of plague and smallpox, were stored around the country for potential deployment in bombs and missiles—but it

brought home how vulnerable crowded urban areas are to biological warfare." Ken Alibek & Stephen Handelman, "Bioterror: A Very Real Threat," *Wall Street J.*, 11 Oct. 2001, at A22.

- "Because of the difficulty in '*weaponizing*' biological agents, she [Claudine McCarthy] concludes that even if the Florida incident does turn out to be some sort of attack, Americans have no reason to panic." Ronald Bailey, "Bioterrorism," *S.F. Chron.*, 14 Oct. 2001, at D3.

Although many neologisms ending in *-ize* are considered ugly and undesirable, the very thing that *weaponize* (as well as *weaponization*) denotes is horrific. And there's no other word for it. So this is a word whose coinage almost no one objects to: all the right-minded objections focus on the thing that the word denotes. See -IZE.

wear > wore > worn. So inflected—since the mid-18th century. The simple-past *wore* is sometimes mistakenly used as a past participle—e.g.:

- "And Imler turned out to be a pleasant surprise, using his quickness to create shots and gaining confidence at the point as the season has *wore* [read *worn*] on." John C. Cotey, "The 2 Faces of Pirates Series," *St. Petersburg Times*, 11 Dec. 1998, at 4.
- "By the latter stages of the first half, La Salle had *wore* [read *worn*] down the Clippers with its speed." Bob Leddy, "Boys' Basketball," *Providence J.-Bull.*, 6 Jan. 1999, at D5.
- "Bulls teammate Steve Kerr had said recently he thought the pressure of stardom and the grind of celebrity has *wore* [read *worn*] Michael down until he had nothing left." Brian Schmitz, "Bad News, NBA: No More Mike," *Orlando Sentinel*, 12 Jan. 1999, at C1.

See IRREGULAR VERBS.

LANGUAGE-CHANGE INDEX
wore as a past participle for *worn*: Stage 1
Current ratio (*had worn* vs. **had wore*): 308:1

we aren't. See **we're not**.

weary. See **wary**.

WEASEL WORDS. Theodore Roosevelt said, in a speech in St. Louis on May 31, 1916: "One of our defects as a nation is a tendency to use what have been called weasel words. When a weasel sucks eggs it sucks the meat out of the egg and leaves it an empty shell. If you use a weasel word after another there is nothing left of the other." Some writers have incorrectly assumed that the METAPHOR suggested itself because of the wriggling, evasive character of the weasel. In any event, sensitive writers are aware of how supposed intensives (e.g., *very*) actually have the effect of weakening a statement. Many other words merely have the effect of rendering uncertain or hollow the statements in which they appear. Among these are *candidly, clearly, compelling, duly, frankly, if practicable, manifestly, meaningful, obviously, perfectly, quite, rather, reasonable, seriously, significantly, somewhat,*

LANGUAGE-CHANGE INDEX (For the full key, see front matter pp. xxxi, l–li.)
Stage 1: Rejected. **Stage 2:** Widely shunned. **Stage 3:** Widespread but . . . **Stage 4:** Ubiquitous but . . . **Stage 5:** Fully accepted.
Invariably inferior forms marked by asterisk (✳). • Ratios represent frequency of prevalent forms vs. variants in current books.

substantially, *undue*, and *virtually*. See **clearly, obviously, somewhat** & **very**.

weatherman. See **meteorologist** & sexism (c).

weave > wove > woven. *Weaved* is correct only in the sense "moved in a winding or zigzag way"—e.g.: "Like scores of Saturday shoppers, Potter found himself in the middle of a 40-minute foot chase that began near the Capitol, *weaved* in and out of State Street buildings, and ended with the arrest of Shantell Washington, 19." Gwen Carleton, "Foot Chase on State St.," *Wis. State J.*, 30 Dec. 1996, at A3. Otherwise, the past tense is *wove*, and the past participle *woven*—e.g.:

- "That's art. So is the yarn he *weaved* [read *wove*] on a cardboard loom." Rochelle Carter, "Brushing Off False Ideas About Art," *Atlanta J.-Const.*, 14 July 1997, Gwinnett Extra §, at 1.
- "Boeing has *weaved* [read *woven*] together a company operating in every part of the space business." Jerry Hirsch, "Space, Boeing's Frontier," *Orange County Register*, 5 Aug. 1997, at C1.
- "The slogan *weaved* [read *wove*] its way into the fabric of American pop culture." Frank Sennett, "Trade in the Shades," *Writer's Digest*, 1 Sept. 1997, at 51.

See irregular verbs.

Language-Change Index
1. *weaved* misused for *wove*: Stage 2
Current ratio (*wove together* vs. **weaved together*): 6:1
2. *weaved* misused for *woven*: Stage 1
Current ratio (*had woven* vs. **had weaved* in most senses): 26:1

Web. See **World Wide Web.**

webpage. Preferably one word—e.g.: "When you click your mouse on a marked link on a *webpage*, here's what happens." H. Eric Branscomb, *Casting Your Net* 66 (2000). Yet *web page* is exceedingly common. Cf. **World Wide Web.**

Current ratio (*web page* vs. *webpage*): 6:1

website. One word, lowercase. Although *The Chicago Manual of Style* and the *AP Stylebook* both make it one word, lowercase, some stylesheets and dictionaries still specify **Web site* (a clunker). Cf. **World Wide Web.**

Current ratio (*website* vs. **Web site*): 1.1:1

we'd = (1) we would; or (2) we had. Sense 2 has not held as much favor as sense 1, but it is common and typically doesn't cause any confusion because the past participle follows closely—e.g.: "*We'd* just arrived in Colorado . . . . *We'd* gone to sleep gliding through the farmlands of Missouri." Sue Wunder, "Perfect, Thanks to Mulligan," *Christian Science Monitor*, 21 Aug. 1997, at 16.

wed. This verb is traditionally inflected *wed > wedded > wedded*. As a past-tense form, *wed* is a variant that *W2* labels "dialectal." It has become especially widespread since the mid-1970s. Stick to *wedded*—e.g.:

- "Last year, the singer [Dan Fogelberg] *wed* [read *wedded*] his longtime fiancée, Anastasia Savage, who shares his love of oil painting." Walter Scott, "Personality Parade," *Parade*, 3 Jan. 1993, at 4.
- "In one corner is lawyer Sanford Asher, who last month *wed* [read *wedded*] the ex-stripper convicted of plotting to kill his former wife and frame him for the crime." Larry Celona, "Doctor Sues Swiss Miss Hubby," *N.Y. Post*, 4 Feb. 2003, at 22.

In the negative, the proper adjective is *unwed* <unwed mothers>. That has been so since about 1920. Before that time, **unwedded* was the standard term.

Language-Change Index
wed as past tense for *wedded*: Stage 4
Current ratio (*has wedded* vs. **has wed*): 2:1

we'd better; *we better. See **better (A).**

wedding. See **marriage.**

Wedgwood. So spelled (for the fine pottery)—not **Wedgewood.*

Wednesday is pronounced /**wenz**-dee/ or /**wenz**-day/. But some precisians want to—and do—say /**wed**-nəz-day/, which is simply incorrect. The first *-d-* has long been silent.

weep > wept > wept. So inflected. The archaic form **weeped*, more common in the 18th century than today, should be regarded as erroneous—e.g.:

- "Players from both teams *weeped* [read *wept*] and prayed." Jarrett Bell, "Terrifying Injury Ends Player's NFL Career," *USA Today*, 23 Dec. 1997, at A1.
- " 'I can't stand up. I can't stand up,' [Carolyn] Sims *weeped* [read *wept*] as family moved her to the bench of a nearby bus stop near Capitol Drive and Oakland Ave." Linda Spice, "Mother Collapses After Speaking," *Milwaukee J. Sentinel*, 15 Mar. 2008, at B1.
- "We should have known it was a blunder that day, when [Cedric] Benson *weeped* [read *wept*] openly and then ripped other NFL teams who had questioned his character." Jay Mariotti, "The Joke's on Us, Chicago," *Chicago Sun-Times*, 8 June 2008, Sports §, at A78.

See irregular verbs.

Language-Change Index
*weeped for *wept*: Stage 1
Current ratio (*I wept* vs. **I weeped*): 926:1

weigh. For the mistaken use of **under weigh* for *underway*, see **underway.**

weight, vb.; **weigh.** "For purposes of calculating the scores, the questions are *weighted* for their difficulty." Should the word be *weight* or *weigh*? The answer is that *weight* (= to give value or assign importance to) is correct. To *weigh* something is to ascertain its weight (literally or metaphorically), not to establish it arbitrarily.

weird. So spelled. See spelling (A).

welcher. See **welsher.**

welder. So spelled in AmE and BrE alike—not **weldor.*

well, when forming an adjective with a past-participial verb, is hyphenated if placed before the noun (e.g., *a well-known person, a well-written book*), but it's typically not hyphenated if the phrase follows what it modifies (e.g., *a person who is well known, a book that is well written*). See PHRASAL ADJECTIVES (G).

well-being is hyphenated, not spelled as one word.

WELLERISMS. A *wellerism* (after Sam Weller or his father, two noted characters in Charles Dickens's *Pickwick Papers* [1836–1837]), is a statement, especially a proverbial or allusive one, in which the speaker puts the words in a new light or a surprising setting, often by means of punning. E.g.:

- " 'That's food for reflection,' as the goat said when it swallowed a mirror."
- " 'Spit is such a horrid word,' said the pig, as he was about to be barbecued."

For the definitive work, see Wolfgang Mieder & Stewart A. Kingsbury, *A Dictionary of Wellerisms* (1994).

welsher; welcher. The former is traditional in the sense "someone who shirks his or her responsibility." It most commonly refers to someone who does not pay gambling debts. E.g.: "But I don't suppose he had a fermenting punter after him shouting 'Welsher!' at the top of his voice." P.G. Wodehouse, *The Return of Jeeves* 22 (1954). (A punter is a wagerer; the speaker here is a bookmaker unable to pay off a winning bet.)

Many natives of Wales consider the word insulting, though there is no etymological evidence supporting a connection with *Welsh* (= of, relating to, or hailing from Wales). Even so, the popular mind makes this connection, and the careful writer must be heedful.

Current ratio (*welshed on a bet* vs. *welched on a bet*): 30:1

Welsh rabbit; Welsh rarebit. For the term denoting a dish of melted cheese on toast or crackers, *Welsh rabbit* has long been considered standard. It seems, however, that some 18th-century literalist, noting the absence of bunny meat in the dish, corrupted the term through false etymology to *rarebit*. *Welsh rarebit* didn't gain any real currency until about 1860 and didn't contend seriously with *Welsh rabbit* until about 1910. Today, both terms are still found, but unfortunately *Welsh rarebit* has been more common in print since the 1960s in BrE and the 1970s in AmE—perhaps to avoid offending the *Welsh*. But few have complained about this dish's name either way. See ETYMOLOGY (D).

Current ratio (*Welsh rarebit* vs. *Welsh rabbit*): 2:1

wench. See **winch.**

went missing. See **go missing.**

were. For the use of *were* in such expressions as *if it were* and *I wish I were*, see SUBJUNCTIVES.

we're not; we aren't. Although both forms are extremely common, *we're not* is about ten times as common in print as *we aren't.* And because the negative isn't contracted in *we're not*, the phrasing is more emphatic. E.g.: "*We're not* talking about a futuristic, Jetson-like electronic house where robots cook and clean. *We're not* even talking about so-called smart houses." Lew Sichelman, "Upgraded Wiring a Must in Homes," *San Diego Union-Trib.*, 31 Aug. 1997, at H1.

werewolf. So spelled—not **werwolf.* Pl. *werewolves.*

west; westward(ly); westerly. See DIRECTIONAL WORDS.

wet > wet(ted) > wet(ted). Since the 18th century, this verb has had both a regular and an irregular past and past participle form. In most contexts, *wet* is the predominant form—e.g.:

- "She *wet* her whistle with a sip of water." Warren Gerds, "Peters Pours on the Charm at Weidner Concert," *Green Bay Press-Gaz.*, 29 Sept. 2002, at A5.
- "And there are those other side effects: waking up to find your toddler *has wet* the bed, or waking up to the sound of puke hitting the bedspread." Deanna Weniger, "Bed-Sharing Charm Is Wearing Off," *Times Herald*, 28 Jan. 2003, at B4.
- "When applied to a hard surface and *wetted* down, this dry, relatively inexpensive white powder becomes ice slick." "When Killing Just Won't Do," *Harper's Mag.*, 1 Feb. 2003, at 17.

Wetted is used mostly in passive constructions <was wetted>, perhaps to eliminate the possible ambiguity that *wet*, in a phrase such as *was wet*, might be functioning as a predicate adjective and not as part of the verb phrase. The regular past form prevents any ambiguity—e.g.: "Cyanobacteria just beneath the surface appeared on the surface within minutes after the soil *was wetted*, and disappeared as the soil dried out." "Following the Water," *Tulsa World*, 7 Oct. 2001, at 7. See IRREGULAR VERBS.

For the misuse of *wet* for *whet*, see **whet.**

we the people. Many seem to consider these words a SET PHRASE—even if the phrasing is *hiding information from we* [read *us*] *the people*. In the best English, *we the people* is always a subject or a predicate nominative, but never the object of a verb or preposition. If the syntax calls for *us the people*, don't be afraid to use it.

From the 19th century on, such phrases as *for us the people* and *with us the people* have been standard. Only since 2000 has there been a serious upsurge in the ungrammatical phrases **for we the people* and **with we the people.*

wharf. The standard plural has been *wharves*—not **wharfs* —in AmE since the 18th century and in BrE since about 1860. The archaic form **wharfs*

LANGUAGE-CHANGE INDEX (For the full key, see front matter pp. xxxi, l–li.)
Stage 1: Rejected. **Stage 2:** Widely shunned. **Stage 3:** Widespread but . . . **Stage 4:** Ubiquitous but . . . **Stage 5:** Fully accepted.
Invariably inferior forms marked by asterisk (*). • Ratios represent frequency of prevalent forms vs. variants in current books.

predominated in BrE print sources from about 1700 to 1855 or so. See PLURALS (c). Cf. **dwarf.**

what. Eric Partridge opined that *what*, as the subject of a clause, generally takes a singular (third-person) verb regardless of what follows (not *what follow*) (*U&A* at 362). Thus:

- "What she wants *is* a new house."
- "What we need in this company *is* more type-A personalities."
- "What *is* at issue *is* assertions, not facts."
- "He put on what *is* called his trousers."
- "The two sides fear a deterioration in what *has* been amicable negotiations."

Those sentences reflect the most conservative usage. The last three sound pedantic, though, and good usage allows more variety than Partridge's straitjacketing advice. In fact, when used as a pronoun, *what* may be either singular or plural. The possibilities are several.

A. Singular *what* in the Noun Clause Followed by a Singular Predicate Noun. This construction is the easiest: *what* means "the thing that" and takes a singular verb. E.g.: "Unfortunately, *what is* needed *is* a return to terms and manners now maybe almost lost to our society." Elliott Brack, "Phone Manners Show We're Losing War for Civility," *Atlanta J.-Const.*, 27 Jan. 1997, at J2.

B. Singular *what* in the Noun Clause Followed by a Plural Predicate Noun. In this construction, as in (A), *what* means "the thing that." But the main verb is governed by the plural noun that follows it. That is, the construction exemplifies INVERSION—e.g.:

- "But *what worries* restaurateurs more *are* customers like Eric Wyka." Molly O'Neill, "Recession and Guilt Pare Dining Trade and Menus," *N.Y. Times*, 31 Mar. 1991, at 1. (This could also be rendered without the inversion: *Customers like Eric Wyka are what worries restaurateurs more.*)
- "But *what is* puzzling *are* the complaints of some—most notably ABC's Ted Koppel—that the conventions are so stage-managed as to be worthless from a news standpoint." Peter Callaghan, "A 'Managed' Convention Still Beats the Old Insider Game," *Morning News Trib.* (Tacoma), 25 Aug. 1996, at G1. (This could also be rendered without the inversion: *The complaints of some . . . are what is puzzling.*)
- "Unfortunately, *what's* needed *are* more working senators who will support it." "Only Congress Can Plug Campaign Cash Loopholes," *San Antonio Express-News*, 22 Mar. 1997, at B6. (This could also be rendered without the inversion: *More working senators who will support it are what is needed.*)

H.W. Fowler would have recommended rewriting the first of those sentences in this way: *What worries restaurateurs more is customers like Eric Wyka.* (*FMEU1* at 705–06.) That, in Fowler's view, would have been better because *customers* is a predicate noun that, despite being plural, shouldn't affect the verb preceding it. But neither version can be called wrong today, and O'Neill's original sentence typifies modern usage more than the Fowlerian revision does.

C. Plural *what* in the Noun Clause Followed by a Plural Predicate. In this construction, *what* means "the things that"—e.g.:

- "*What* the judge principally wants to hear *are* the relevant cases." Glanville Williams, *Learning the Law* 163 (11th ed. 1982).
- "Ebullience and eccentricity are to be found on every page but *what are* harder to discover *are* the depths of the Hailsham character." John Mortimer, "High Court Jester," *Sunday Times* (London), 8 July 1990, § 8, at 1.

Although some would say that the following sentence is just as acceptable as the two preceding ones, it probably violates idiom in changing the SET PHRASE *what matters most*: "*What matter* [read *What matters*] most in the exercise of focusing a collection *are* a lively imagination and an open mind." Nicholas A. Basbanes, "Preserving the Creative Past," *Biblio*, May 1997, at 8.

D. Undetermined *what* Followed by a Plural Predicate. In many contexts, *what* is the object in a noun clause; when that is so, the plural is three times as frequent as the singular. The *what* is hard to resolve into phrases such as "things that." E.g.:

- "Many places in Ohio, including Guernsey County, have *what are* considered naturally elevated levels of radon." Mike Lafferty, "Cleanup of Radioactive Slag Is Nearly Complete," *Columbus Dispatch*, 25 Aug. 1997, at C1.
- "Student evaluations instead should focus on *what are* called 'portfolio assessments' within the classroom." John Mooney, "N.J. Standard Testing Faulted," *Record* (N.J.), 24 Sept. 1997, at A2.

E. Plural *what* from Inverted *that*-Clause. Sometimes *what* signals an inverted relative clause, and when the inverted phrase has a plural subject, the construction *what have* (or *what are*, etc.) is called for—e.g.: "Japan and South Korea yesterday opened the way for an improvement in *what have been frosty relations* by announcing they will hold a summit next week." William Dawkins & John Burton, "S. Korea, Japan Aim to Defrost Relations Summit," *Fin. Times*, 13 June 1996, at 12. The *what*-clause is resolvable into *relations that have been frosty*, but with the INVERSION the *that* is changed to *what*.

whatever; whatsoever. A. Intensive Use. As an intensive (meaning "at all"), *whatsoever* is standard in AmE <he had no reason whatsoever>, though in all uses it is less frequent than *whatever*. Many American stylists prefer the shorter word, *whatever*—e.g.: "OPIC provides no grants or free benefits of any kind to any company or individual. None *whatever*." Stuart E. Eizenstat, "'Corporate Welfare' or Savvy Policy?" *Wash. Times*, 23 July 1997, at A15. In fact, in AmE and BrE print sources alike, *none whatever* occurred with much greater frequency than *none whatsoever* until the last two decades of the 20th century.

On phrases such as *what nature soever*, see TMESIS.

B. *Whatever* as an Interjection. *Whatever* has become a "Valley Girl" epithet for *Whatever you say* or *I couldn't care less.* See VOGUE WORDS.

what it is is. Sentences with this ungainly construction have been much on the rise since the beginning of the 20th century. E.g.: "*What* the O'Rourke study really *is is* simply a glorified set of examinations in grammar." Janet Rankin Aiken, *Commonsense Grammar* 244 (1936). Dating from the mid-19th century, the phrasing had become common by the 1960s—e.g.: "*What it is is* a judicious mixing of standard English with a large number of 'Scotchifications.' " Stanley Rundle, "Language and Dialect," in *A Linguistics Reader* 86, 88 (Graham Wilson ed., 1967).

Notice that neither of those writers put a comma before the second *is*. That's the way to punctuate it—with nothing at all. Only the last of these three more recent examples got the punctuation right:

- "Clearly, this is no high-level policy debate. *What it is, is* [delete the comma] payback time for middle-class voters." "Shaking the Washington Goody Tree," *Chicago Trib.*, 18 June 1997, at 20. (A possible revision: *Clearly, this is no high-level policy debate. Instead, it's payback time for middle-class voters.*)
- "It isn't poetic. *What it is, is* [delete the comma] unnerving." Mark Kreidler, "A Divisional Race That Will Not Die," *Sacramento Bee*, 11 Sept. 1997, at D1. (A possible revision: *It isn't poetic. It's unnerving.*)
- "The movie is not about stripping, and it's not likely to be among the top 10 or even 20 sexy movies you've ever seen. *What it is is* very funny, and what it's about, strangely enough, is self-respect and believing in yourself." Bob Fischbach, "Nudity Not Main Point of Funny 'Monty,' " *Omaha World-Herald*, 15 Sept. 1997, at 35. (A possible revision: . . . *you've ever seen. It's very funny, and strangely enough, it's about self-respect . . . .*)

What happens is that the noun clause (*what it is*) needs a verb (the second *is*). But a better method in many contexts is to avoid the *what*-construction altogether and make the sentence more direct. The suggested revisions show only a few of the myriad ways to do that. Cf. **is is.**

what kind of. See **kind of (B).**

whatsoever. See **whatever.**

what with. This phrase—meaning "in view of," "in consequence of," or "considering (one or more specified things)"—dates back to Old English. It begins an adverbial phrase—e.g.:

- "This is a city in perpetual health crisis, *what with* drugs, AIDS, and teenage pregnancy, not to mention the occasional appearance of the West Nile virus or sewage spill into the Jones Falls." Michael Ollove, "Dr. Baltimore," *Baltimore Sun*, 1 Oct. 2000, at E9.
- "You wouldn't want to give the vice president the morning drive shift, *what with* the danger of him causing freeway commuters to fall asleep at the wheel." Steve Harvey, "Has Rush Limbaugh Heard?" *L.A. Times*, 9 Dec. 2000, at B4. (On the question whether *him* should be *his* in the final part of that sentence, see FUSED PARTICIPLES.)

- "Once, Mussina was told, the Yankees were a difficult sell, *what with* a wild card of an owner and instability on the roster and in the managerial and coaching ranks." Tom Verducci, "Winning Pitch Sure," *Sports Illustrated*, 11 Dec. 2000, at 60.

when and if. See **if and when (B).**

whence (= from where; from which; from what source) is an especially FORMAL WORD that some readers consider stilted. Rudolf Flesch prematurely called it "obsolete," perhaps to reinforce his absolute recommendation to use *from where* instead. (See *The ABC of Style* 294 [1964].) But *from where* would hardly work in every context, and *whence* retains some vigor—e.g.: "If his method is to work at all, it must at least work in the sorts of economic cases *whence* it sprang." True, the writer might have said *cases from which it sprang*, but surely not *cases from where it sprang*.

From whence is technically redundant—because *whence* implies *from*—but the locution has appeared continually in the great writing from the 16th century: Shakespeare, Dryden, and Dickens all used the phrase. Still, it has seen a sharp decline in use since the early 18th century, just as *whence* has. *From whence* is less stilted than *whence* alone, which requires a greater literary knowledge for it to be immediately understandable. E.g.: "They cast the body into the water *from whence* it could not be reclaimed." Some people object to this usage, however well established; no one would object to *from which*. See **from hence, hence & thence.**

whenever; when ever. The usual expression is the solid *whenever* (= [1] at any time, or [2] every time that a specified thing happens). The two-word version is used as an emphatic extension of *when* in a question <When ever did you say such a thing?>.

where. A. *Where it's at.* The phrase **where it's at* and its variants have long set up parents' and teachers' classic grammatical correction: "Where's my lunchbox at?" "Between the *a* and the *t*." Besides the faux "sin" of ending a sentence with a preposition (see PREPOSITIONS (B)), the *at* is redundant, adding nothing to "where it is" or "where is it?" The usage is notoriously illiterate.

But the rebellious 1960s saw the phrase **where it's at* reborn in several new senses: "the truth" <the guru really knows where it's at>, "the current fad" <the Nehru jacket's dead; tie-dye is where it's at now>, or "the most important or current thing" <in racecar design, aerodynamics is where it's at>. These senses have stuck and remain common as CASUALISMS.

The idiom has become such a catchphrase that today it's once again used in the literal sense that parents and teachers have scolded children about, especially as a heading. An Internet search for the phrase returned thousands of hits, largely for sites giving directions to a place or listing an area's restaurants, clubs, and the like.

LANGUAGE-CHANGE INDEX (For the full key, see front matter pp. xxxi, l–li.)
Stage 1: Rejected. **Stage 2:** Widely shunned. **Stage 3:** Widespread but . . . **Stage 4:** Ubiquitous but . . . **Stage 5:** Fully accepted.
Invariably inferior forms marked by asterisk (*). • Ratios represent frequency of prevalent forms vs. variants in current books.

But it's no more grammatical today than it ever was, and when not used with a wink and a nudge, it's still a badge of non-U speech. See CLASS DISTINCTIONS.

In AmE and BrE print sources, instances of the query *Where is it at?* are extremely rare in comparison with *Where is it?*—and have always been so. The *at* was added in dialectal AmE in the 1860s and gradually spread. But it has always been stigmatized as nonstandard.

Current ratio (*Where is it?* vs. *Where is it at?*): 414:1

B. For *in which*. In formal prose, *where* should not be used as a relative pronoun instead of as a locative—hence not *case where* but *case in which*. But if you want a relaxed tone, *where* may be more suitable. In the following example, the contraction *I've* might not comfortably fit in the same sentence as *in which*—hence *where* is justifiable: "I've deliberately chosen an example *where* this unspeakable cluster did *not* stand out." Richard A. Lanham, *Revising Prose* 29 (1979).

C. For *when*. Sometimes the locative *where* is misused for the temporal *when*—e.g.: "If ever there was a year *where* [read *when*] athletes burned and raged at close of day, it was this one." David Steele, "Aging with Grace, Success," *S.F. Chron.*, 24 Dec. 2001, at C1.

whereabout(s). In all uses, *whereabouts* is the predominant form in AmE and BrE alike—as a noun <I don't know her whereabouts>, as an adverb <Whereabouts is the house?>, and as a conjunctive adverb <I don't know whereabouts he lives>. The use as a noun is most common—e.g.: "The silver BMW was discovered after authorities, checking a tip on the suspect's *whereabouts*, fanned out in the neighborhood." Robert Rudolph, "Suspect Surfaces in Search," *Star-Ledger* (Newark), 23 Sept. 1997, at 1.

The noun may take either a singular or a plural verb—e.g.:

- "Vicky (last name unknown) is Tom's girlfriend; her *whereabouts is* unknown." J.R. Hunter, *Over the Edge* 202 (2013).
- "The advantage of such a program is that the offender's *whereabouts are* known in a more real-time manner." Robert D. Hanser, *Introduction to Corrections* 147 (2012).

From 1850 to 1950 or so, the singular and plural uses vied closely for predominance, but beginning in the mid-20th century the plural uses took a decided advantage in both BrE (before 1950) and AmE (beginning in the 1960s). The plural use is now five times as common in print as the singular in modern sources. Cf. **thereabout.

Current ratio (*his whereabouts are* vs. *his whereabouts is*): 5:1

whereas has a cluster of literary senses, namely, "although; while on the one hand; on the contrary; but by contrast." These literary uses are a part of the general writer's idiom—e.g.: "*Whereas* both his parents have black hair, he has blond."

One usage critic has stated: "*Whereas* sounds stuffy. In spite of the objections of some grammarians, the common word is now *while*." Rudolf Flesch, *The ABC*

of Style 294 (1964). Yet *whereas* is better than *while* if the latter ambiguously suggests a time element, especially a clashing time element—e.g.: "*While* [read *Whereas* or *Although*] I brought her to the office, George took her home." See **while.**

whereby (= by means of which), though sometimes overworked, is more concise than alternatives such as *through which*. So it can be a useful word—e.g.: "Republican Congressman Ralph Regula of Ohio, chairman of the Appropriations subcommittee in charge of federal parks, is brokering a deal *whereby* Congress will appropriate $5 million and give it to California, which will in turn give it to the Reagans for the 100-year-old adobe house and grounds they paid $480,000 for in 1974." Margaret Carlson, "Lake Lucky, Here We Come!" *Time*, 29 Sept. 1997, at 19.

whet (= to sharpen or stimulate) commonly appears in the expression *whet the appetite*. Unfortunately, though, *whet* is often confused with *wet* (= to moisten, dampen, or drench)—e.g.:

- "More importantly, he *wet* [read *whetted*] the appetite of Atlanta and presumably much of the country for an Olympics that, at least in distances under a mile, could carry a red, white and blue tint." Jeff Metcalfe, "Johnson Breaks Record," *Ariz. Republic*, 24 June 1996, at D1.
- "Even Anheuser-Busch, the game's biggest advertiser, is hoping to *wet* [read *whet*] appetites and help it win the 'Ad Meter' popularity poll yet again." Holly M. Sanders, "YouTube Cracks Super Ads Code," *N.Y. Post*, 2 Feb. 2007, at 33.
- "That success has only *wet* [read *whetted*] the appetite of the Green Devils for the upcoming season." Mark Massoglia, "Wrestling Preview," *Marshfield News* (Wis.), 29 Nov. 2007, at B2.

The error might occur in part because people tend to salivate when their appetites are stimulated; that is, the mouth becomes *wet*. But it's still the wrong word.

The opposite error (*whet* for *wet*) also sometimes occurs—e.g.: "To *whet* [read *wet*] the whistle, Glazer's of New Orleans provided local libations, including a martini bar, spiced Cajun tea, and ambulance chasers." Tara McLellan, "Hospital Puts On Nighttime Fundraiser," *Times-Picayune* (New Orleans), 8 June 2008, Slidell §, at 13.

LANGUAGE-CHANGE INDEX
1. *wet* misused for *whet*: Stage 1
Current ratio (*whet your appetite* vs.
*wet your appetite): 28:1
2. *whet* misused for *wet*: Stage 1
Current ratio (*wet my whistle* vs.
*whet my whistle): 15:1

whether. A. *Whether or not.* Despite the SUPERSTITION to the contrary, the words *or not* are usually superfluous, since *whether* implies *or not*—e.g.:

- "In another essay, 'The Rules of the Game,' he discusses moral codes and *whether or not* [read *whether*] they work." Diane Hartman, "At Life's End, Carl Sagan Awed by Life's Unknowns," *Denver Post*, 22 June 1997, at D6.

- "Yet he seemed troubled by having to decide *whether or not* [read *whether*] to show the film at Venice." Ken Auletta, "Beauty and the Beast," *New Yorker*, 16 Dec. 2002, at 65, 68.
- "[It depends] on *whether or not* [read *whether*] the winds favor us, and *whether or not* [read *whether*] there's any trouble." Gary Blackwood, *Year of the Hangman* 27 (2002).

For a hilarious discussion of *whether or not*—and its variations, including *whether or not . . . or not*—see James Joseph Duane, "Avoiding the Curse of *Whetherornot*," 6 *Scribes J. Legal Writing* 41 (1996–1997).

But the *or not* is necessary when *whether or not* means "regardless of whether" <the meeting will go on whether or not it rains>. E.g.: "You can tap many of these resources *whether or not* you have an account with that fund company." Keith Kirkpatrick, "Picking Funds? Web Sites Can Help You Hit the Mark," *Home PC*, 1 Oct. 1997, at 181. If you add the word *regardless*, however, either it or *or not* is superfluous—e.g.: "[Who can use IRAs:] Couples with AGIs up to $150,000, singles to $95,000, *regardless of whether or not* [read *regardless of whether* or *whether or not*] they have retirement plans." Lisa Reilly Cullen, "How the New Breed of IRA Eases Retirement Saving," *Money*, 1 Oct. 1997, at 26.

B. As to whether. In *The King's English* 344 (3d ed. 1931), the Fowler brothers describe this phrasing as "seldom necessary." That judgment still stands—e.g.:

- "Surprisingly, most folks have never taken the time to learn this skill . . . , [which] may *mean the difference as to whether* [read *determine whether*] someone with no pulse or respiration will live or die." David Jennings, "We're All Obligated to Learn Basic Life-Saving Techniques," *Cincinnati Post*, 10 July 1997, at A20.
- "Mellot admits he 'doesn't have any facts' *as to* [read *about*] whether the curfew actually has cut crime." John Luciew, "Curfew's Legality Still Not Precise," *Patriot & Evening News* (Harrisburg), 24 Sept. 1997, at A1.

See **as to (B)** & **question whether.**

LANGUAGE-CHANGE INDEX
as to whether for whether: Stage 2

C. Of whether. *Whether* usually directly follows the noun whose dilemma it denotes: *decision whether, issue whether, question whether.* (See **question whether.**) But *regardless*, an adverb, makes *regardless of whether.* See *****regardless whether.**

Although *issue whether* is typically better than *issue of whether*, the latter phrase has certain justifiable uses in which *of* is obligatory, usually when *issue* is modified by an adjective. E.g.:

- "Thompson [referred to] . . . the narrow legal *issue of whether* fund-raising calls made by either Clinton or Gore violated a federal law barring solicitation on federal property." "Fund-Raising Law Not Broken, Clinton Says," *Chicago Trib.*, 23 Sept. 1997, at 11.
- "It also allowed trustees to avert the broader *issue of whether* the industrial park should become a residential

area in the future." Donna Kiesling, "Condos Rejected for Industrial Park Area," *Chicago Trib.*, 28 Sept. 1997, at I3.

LANGUAGE-CHANGE INDEX
*****question of whether</i> for <i>question whether</i>: Stage 4
Current ratio: 1:1

D. And if. See **if (A).**

which. A. Generally. This word, used immoderately, is possibly responsible for more bad sentences than any other in the language. Small wonder that James Thurber wrote: "What most people don't realize is that one 'which' leads to another. . . . Your inveterate whicher . . . is not welcome in the best company." "Ladies' and Gentlemen's Guide to Modern English Usage," in *The Ways of Language: A Reader* 142, 143 (Raymond J. Pflug ed., 1967). E.B. White was likeminded: "Careful writers, watchful for small conveniences, go *which*-hunting, remove the defining *whiches*, and by so doing improve their work." William Strunk Jr. & E.B. White, *The Elements of Style* 59 (4th ed. 2000).

For a full explanation of *which* vs. *that*, see **that (A).** Suffice it to say here that if you see a *which* with neither a preposition nor a comma, dash, or parenthesis before it, it should probably be a *that*.

B. Wrongly Applied to People. Unlike *that*—which can apply to either things or people—*which* applies only to things. If people are referred to, the nonrestrictive relative pronoun is *who*—e.g.: "Rights advocates and officials in Zaire protested the treatment of the illegal immigrants, some of *which* [read *whom*] were reportedly bound with tape." Youssef M. Ibrahim, "A Wary France Cracks Down on Its Muslims," *N.Y. Times*, 7 Sept. 1995, at A3. See **that (F).** Cf. **who (D).**

There is, of course, an exception for traditional wordings. For example, in Early Modern English, it was possible to cast the original version of the Lord's Prayer with a personal *which* <Our Father, which art in Heaven>.

LANGUAGE-CHANGE INDEX
which wrongly applied to people: Stage 1
Current ratio (<i>people who</i> vs. <i>people that</i> vs.
*****people which</i>): 119:15:1

C. Beginning Sentences with. Increasingly in modern prose, *Which* is being used to begin an INCOMPLETE SENTENCE. Is this permissible? Yes, the answer must be—primarily in three instances.

First, the introductory *Which* can be not only appropriate but also effective when the preceding sentence is long and the conclusion is so important that it shouldn't be a mere appendage—e.g.: "An audience thus captivated will surely come to marvel at Shakespeare's genius, but the hook that has skewered them is the dynamic of the narrative and the irresistible magnetism of his protagonists. *Which* is why 'Hamlet' generally fills theatres and Pericles empties them."

LANGUAGE-CHANGE INDEX (For the full key, see front matter pp. xxxi, l–li.)
Stage 1: Rejected. **Stage 2:** Widely shunned. **Stage 3:** Widespread but . . . **Stage 4:** Ubiquitous but . . . **Stage 5:** Fully accepted.
Invariably inferior forms marked by asterisk (✳). • Ratios represent frequency of prevalent forms vs. variants in current books.

Keith Baxter, "The Power of Priestley," *Daily Telegraph*, 29 Oct. 1994, Arts §, at 2.

Second, even after a short sentence, it can lend a dramatic effect to the *Which*-clause—e.g.:

- "All a dying man could utter would be a prejudgment. *Which* is absurd." Christopher Ricks, *T.S. Eliot and Prejudice* 91 (1988).
- "It means a comeback for the three-martini lunch. *Which* is a win-win situation." Tony Kornheiser, "There's a New Prescription for Better Exercise, Bending Elbows," *Detroit News*, 12 Oct. 1994, at C1.
- "Giuliani says the city still will take care of more people than any other city. *Which* is exactly his problem." Jimmy Breslin, "A Lousy Plan for the City," *Newsday* (N.Y.), 27 Oct. 1994, at A2.

Third, it's helpful when a thought is expressed in several sentences, and what follows—an inference, a summation, or the result of an alternative description—refers to all of it. E.g.:

- "Incidentally, the punctuation that has just been used, deliberately, is an illogical form that's enforced by publishers and their copyeditors. They cite the accursed *Chicago Manual of Style*. Logically, of course, the period should appear after the quotation marks. The quoted word is itself part of the sentence, and sentences end with periods (except old-time telegrams). The irrational custom is now too firmly established to be upset. Anytime soon, anyway. *Which* is another example of making a whole sentence of something that might follow a comma in a preceding sentence. *Which* is okay with me." Letter of Charles Rembar to Bryan A. Garner, 29 July 1993.
- "'We have our job cut out for us,' she said. 'There's an untapped hunger here for Memphis to learn about this incredible heritage, and we must do what we can to protect this legacy and ensure its continuation.' *Which* is where her Memphis Charitable Foundation comes in." Larry Nager, "Fittingly, New Local Award Goes to Phillips First," *Commercial Appeal* (Memphis), 30 Sept. 1995, at C3.

Often the paragraph ends, or a new paragraph begins, with a sentence starting with *Which*—e.g.: "In the process, the 31-year-old Mr. Rose has become a one-man cheering squad for the virtues of pet food. People may turn up their noses, but pet food is made under such stringent controls that it actually is fit for human consumption. 'It's pasteurized, sterilized and every other "ized,"' Mr. Rose says. [¶] *Which* doesn't mean most people want to spread a table cloth and share a few cans with Tabby, or with the guests." Judith Valente, "Edwin Rose's Palate Is Working Overtime on His Pet Theories," *Wall Street J.*, 29 June 1994, at A1.

D. *And which; but which*. To use either expression properly, a nonrestrictive *which*-clause parallel to the *and which* or *but which* must come first. E.g.: "Sutherland could have vetoed the $526 million budget, *which* he drafted this fall *and which* the council rewrote last month." Lisa Kremer, "Pierce Budget Won't Get Sutherland's Signature," *News Trib.* (Tacoma), 9 Dec. 1997, at B1. Without the preceding *which*, the *and which* puts the reader at sea—e.g.:

- "Eisner still has a huge chunk of stock options—about 8.7 million shares' worth—that he can't exercise yet *and which* will presumably increase in value over the next decade."

"Stock Options Give Eisner Record $565 Million Payday," *Newsday* (N.Y.), 5 Dec. 1997, at A79. (Change *and which* to *and that* so that the two relative clauses are parallel.)

- "He gladly revealed that Philadelphia—the city where he attended art school *and which* he has long criticized as bleak, cruel and gruesome—is his greatest influence." Samara Kalk, "Direct, but Not to the Point," *Wis. State J.*, 18 Dec. 1997, at A1. (A possible revision: *He gladly revealed that Philadelphia (where he attended art school)—a city he has long criticized as bleak, cruel, and gruesome—is his greatest influence.*)
- "The piece is a Brown original, a blues song that the MJQ has included as a primary entry in its repertoire for decades (*and which* served as the title track for a classic 1960 album)." Don Heckman, "Jazz Spotlight," *L.A. Times*, 28 Dec. 1997, at 65. (Change *and which* to either *and that* or *it*.)
- "How else to account for the explosive story Kirkham told the Voice from his cell at the Metropolitan Detention Center in Brooklyn—*and which* he repeated in a 'Dear Judge' letter he says he sent to Johnson." Frank Owen, "Club Buster," *Village Voice*, 30 Dec. 1997, at 49. (Insert *that* after *story* and change *and which* to *and that*.)

See **that (A)** & PARALLELISM.

E. For *who* or *whom*. See **who (E)**.

F. The Remote *which*. See REMOTE RELATIVES.

while for *although* or *whereas* is permissible and often all but necessary, despite what purists sometimes say about the word's inherent element of time. (See **although** & **whereas**.) *While* is a more relaxed and conversational term than *although* or *whereas*, and it works nicely when introducing a contrast—e.g.:

- "But *while* vertical malls like Manhattan Mall and nearby Herald Center have struggled, multi-story shops are becoming de rigueur for many big-name retailers from Barnes & Noble to Banana Republic." Amy Feldman, "Manhattan Mall on Sale Now," *Crain's N.Y. Bus.*, 17 Feb. 1997, at 1.
- "*While* police have no suspects, the owner said she heard two males laughing just before the mailbox exploded." Sara Olkon, "Homemade Bombs Set Off in a Roadside Mailbox," *Providence J.-Bull.*, 23 May 1997, at C1.
- "Five of the nine Dallas school board members are white, *while* only 11 percent of Dallas' schoolchildren are white." Chris Newton, "Turmoil Continues in Dallas Schools," *Pitt. Post-Gaz.*, 18 Sept. 1997, at A9.

The *OED* traces this use back to Shakespeare in 1588 (*Love's Labour's Lost*).

Though the use is quite proper, writers must be on guard for the occasional ambiguity. For instance, does it denote time or contrast in the following sentence? "[The] former spokeswoman . . . claim[s] she was fired in April because she is white, *while* the hospital's management was seeking to build bridges to Tampa's black community." "Cigar Maker From Spain to Purchase Havatampa," *Tampa Bay Bus. J.*, 19 Sept. 1997, at 4. The sense is surely a contrasting one, but the sentence undesirably causes the reader to hesitate.

Further, *while* shouldn't be used merely for *and*—e.g.: "Her father, J. Frank McKenna III, is a lawyer, *while* [read *and*] her mother, Colleen O'Shaughnessy McKenna, is the author of 17 children's books, many of which are set in Catholic schools." Mary Lee Gannon, "Catholic Has Service on Mind," *Pitt. Post-Gaz.*, 12 June 1996, at N9.

LANGUAGE-CHANGE INDEX
while used in nontemporal sense: Stage 5

*while at the same time is a common REDUNDANCY. Having first appeared in the late 1600s, it remained infrequent until the 19th century. Its rise has been fairly steady ever since. Yet editors typically remove the last four words as verbiage—e.g.:

- "Motivate them to keep selling the company *while at the same time* [read *while*] taking credit for their particular accomplishment." Mark H. McCormack, *What They Don't Teach You at Harvard Business School* 194 (1984).
- "He would not be the first national leader to talk peace *while at the same time* [read *while*] encouraging those who persist in terrorism." Alan Dershowitz, "Arafat Speaks of Peace as He Uses Terrorism," *Buffalo News*, 31 Oct. 1994, at B3.
- "The collapse of the Berlin Wall and the Soviet Union offer unparalleled opportunities for democracy worldwide, *while, at the same time,* [read *at a time when*] the level of ethnic and regional conflicts has never been greater." Ann Dale, *At the Edge* ix (2007).

while away; *wile away. The phrase *while away* (= to spend [time] idly) dates from the early 17th century and remains current—e.g.: "Guitarist Martin Barre doesn't *while away* his time listening to old Jethro Tull albums." Gene Stout, "Guitarist Barre Goes Beyond Jethro Tull," *Chicago Trib.*, 22 Nov. 1996, at 37.

*Wile away, a synonymous phrase dating from about 1800, began as a corrupt form but is included in modern dictionaries such as *W11* and *AHD* without any cautionary note. Most commonly, of course, *wile* is a noun meaning "a stratagem intended to deceive" or "trickery"; it may also function as a verb in the corresponding sense "to lure or entice." However old the mistaken form *wile away is—and never mind that Charles Dickens used it—it is still inferior to *while away* and has always been significantly less frequent in print sources. E.g.: "Before Kim Peek saw *Rain Man*, the 1988 award-winning movie loosely based on his life, he stayed home and *wiled* [read *whiled*] away the time working and reading books." Rhonda Smith, "Into the World," *Austin Am.-Statesman*, 28 Apr. 1994, at D1.

LANGUAGE-CHANGE INDEX
*wile away for *while away*: Stage 1
Current ratio (*while away* vs. *wile away): 14:1

whilom. See **erstwhile.**

whilst. Long characteristic of formal BrE, this conjunction fell into disuse in AmE over the course of the 19th and 20th centuries and became virtually obsolete, reaching its low point about 1990. Sentences like this one struck many American readers as reeking with pretension unless the source was British: "*Whilst* [read *While*] I was on vacation last week, it seems the Bethlehem Police Force got off the hook for killing a young man, John Hirko, in April." Paul Carpenter, "Just Makes You Feel Warm All Over," *Morning Call* (Allentown, Pa.), 21 Sept. 1997, at B1. But the word predominates in BrE—e.g.: "*Whilst* president of the Royal Statistical Society, he told statisticians that government is about asking questions." Ray Thomas, "Working Out the Figures," *Guardian*, 22 Sept. 1997, at 16.

But since the mid-1990s, the word has enjoyed a resurgence in AmE. See AMERICANISMS AND BRITICISMS (C). Still, it has not yet lost its odor of affectation.

Like its sibling *while*, it may be used for *although* or *whereas*. But again, this isn't entirely good usage in AmE. For *amongst*, see **among (A).**

LANGUAGE-CHANGE INDEX
whilst for *while* in AmE: Stage 2

whimsy (= fanciful or capricious humor) has been the standard spelling in AmE and BrE alike since about 1900. *Whimsey is a variant.

Current ratio: 24:1

whinge (= to keep complaining in a bothersome way), a Briticism, predominantly forms the present participle *whingeing*—not *whinging.

Current ratio: 2:1

whiny, adj. So spelled in AmE and BrE alike—not *whiney. Though dating from the 19th century, the term didn't emerge into widespread use until around the time of World War I.

Current ratio: 5:1

whir, n. & vb., has long been considered the standard spelling. *Whirr is a variant for both parts of speech. But the inflected forms, naturally, are *whirred* and *whirring*.

whisky; whiskey. If the liquor originated in Scotland, it's *whisky*. If it originated in the United States, it's *whiskey* <Kentucky whiskey>. To write *Scotch whiskey is a serious gaffe in the eyes of a Scot. In both AmE and BrE, however, the spelling *Irish whiskey* has predominated over *Irish whisky* since about 1950.

whither. See **hither.**

whitish; whity; *whitey. Both *whitish* (so spelled) and *whity*, as adjectives, mean "somewhat white." But *whitish* predominates in all varieties of English—perhaps because of the secondary contender's derogatory homophone, *Whitey* (= a white person or white society—thought of in an offensive way).

Whitsunday; *Whit Sunday; *Whitsun Day; Whitsuntide. The first three denote the seventh Sunday after Easter, on which the Christian festival of Pentecost is celebrated, commemorating the Holy Spirit's descent upon the apostles. *Whitsunday* is the standard spelling in AmE and BrE alike. **Whit Sunday* and **Whitsun Day* are chiefly BrE variants. *Whitsuntide* is either the full week beginning with Whitsunday or the first three days of that week.

whity. See **whitish.**

whiz, vb.; **whizz,** vb. In the sense "to move quickly," *whiz* is standard AmE (since about 1950), *whizz* standard BrE (since about 1920). But both are inflected *whizzes, whizzed,* and *whizzing.*

whiz-bang; whizz-bang. Dating from the early 20th century and meaning "something resembling fireworks for its conspicuous flash, noise, and startling effect," this term has varied in its spelling over time. The predominant forms are *whiz-bang* in AmE and *whizz-bang* in BrE—so hyphenated. Although *W11* lists only the solid forms **whizbang* and **whizzbang,* they occur in print sources much less often.

whiz kid (= a highly skillful or successful young person), dating from the mid-20th century, is so spelled in AmE and BrE alike. The variant spelling **whizz kid* was common in BrE from about 1960 to 1990, but it has steadily fallen in frequency of use since then. Today in BrE *whiz kid* predominates by a 3-to-1 ratio. The one-word variants (**whizkid* and **whizzkid*) are to be avoided.

> Current ratio (*whiz kid* vs. **whizkid* vs. **whizzkid* in World English): 37:1.4:1

who; whom. A. Generally. Edward Sapir, the philosopher of language, prophesied that "within a couple of hundred years from to-day not even the most learned jurist will be saying 'Whom did you see?' By that time the *whom* will be as delightfully archaic as the Elizabethan *his* for *its.* No logical or historical argument will avail to save this hapless *whom.*" *Language* 156–57 (1921; repr. 1949). A safer bet might be that no one will be spelling *to-day* with a hyphen. In any event, writers in the 21st century ought to understand how the words *who* and *whom* are correctly used.

Who, the nominative pronoun, is used (1) as the subject of a verb <it was Kate who rescued the dog>; and (2) as the complement of a linking verb, i.e., as a predicate nominative <they know who you are>. *Whom,* the objective pronoun, is used (1) as the object of a verb <whom did you see?>; and (2) as the object of a preposition <the person to whom we're indebted>.

It's true that in certain contexts, *whom* is stilted. That has long been so: "Every sensible English speaker on both sides of the Atlantic says *Who were you talking to?* [—not *Whom*—] and the sooner we begin to write it the better." J.Y.T. Greig, *Breaking Priscian's Head* 23 ([n.d.—ca. 1930]). But there are other constructions in which *whom* remains strong—and more so in AmE than in BrE. Although writers have announced the demise of *whom,* it persists in AmE—e.g.:

- "Even if things do come down to *whom* you know in this world, luck definitely figures in *whom* you meet." Jaclyn Fierman, "What's Luck Got to Do with It?" *Fortune,* 16 Oct. 1995, at 149, 150. (This is a little shaky: the modern bromide, a CASUALISM, is *It's not what you know, it's who you know.*)
- "Susan McDonough's classroom is filled with primary-school children of different ages, all of *whom* are lagging behind in reading skills." Ann O'Hanlon, "A New Take on an Old Problem," *Wash. Post,* 28 Sept. 1997, at V1.
- "He was implicated in the murder of a man *whom* his workers caught tampering with some stone blocks." Manuela Hoelterhoff, "Inconspicuous Consumer," *SmartMoney,* 1 Oct. 1997, at 183. (*That* might work more naturally in this sentence.)

The correct uses of *who* are sometimes tricky. But if the pronoun acts as the subject of a clause, it must be *who,* never *whom*—e.g.: "Alan Alda, *who* you quickly realize *is* sorely missed on TV, stars as Dan Cutler, a type-A personality advertising executive." Tom Jicha, "'White Mile' Shows How Men Will Be Boys," *Sun-Sentinel* (Ft. Lauderdale), 20 May 1994, at E6. (*Who* is the subject of *is.*)

While the subject of a finite verb is nominative (*I know she is good*), the subject of an infinitive is in the objective case (*I know her to be good*). The same is true of *who* and *whom.* But that brings us to the next section.

B. The Objective *who.* *Whom* is always the object of a verb, the object of a preposition, or the subject of an infinitive. E.g.: "Do all you can to develop your intuition—this will help you to know when to act and when to wait, *whom* to be cautious about and *whom* to trust." Susannah Rohland, "Today's Birthday," *Wash. Times,* 9 July 1997, at C16. If a horoscope writer like Rohland can get it right, then you'd think that other journalists would as well. But often they don't, perhaps because they consider the word stuffy—e.g.:

- "And he [nominee Stephen G. Breyer] promised, following the admonition of the late Justice Arthur Goldberg, *who* [read *whom*] he served as a law clerk 30 years ago, to do his best to avoid footnotes." Ruth Marcus, "Judge Breyer Gets Day in Rose Garden," *Wash. Post,* 17 May 1994, at A8.
- Kirk Bohls, "Life Was Easier When We Knew *Who* [read *Whom*] to Hate," *Austin Am.-Statesman,* 20 July 1994, at C1.
- "A polite, helpful 11-year-old *who* [read *whom*] everybody called Jake was fatally shot in his bedroom in this small rural town on Thursday, and a 13-year-old friend was charged hours later with killing him." Robert Hanley, "New Jersey Boy, 13, Is Charged with Killing 11-Year-Old Friend," *N.Y. Times,* 3 Sept. 1994, at 1. (*That* would also work naturally here.)
- "'Voters have a vital interest in learning the views of those who seek to govern them, for only through learning these views can the voter intelligently decide *who* [read *whom*] to vote for,' [one of the justices] wrote for the court." Phillip Carrizosa, "Political Flier Sponsors Must Identify Themselves," *S.F. Daily J.,* 29 Nov. 1994, at 1 (quoting the California Supreme Court's decision in *Griset v. Fair Political Practices Commission*). (The article accurately quotes the California Supreme Court's misuse of *who* for *whom* in a sentence so central to the holding that it was predictably quoted widely.)

- "Those friends include Myra Guarino, 62, of Valdosta, *who* [read *whom*] Mrs. Helms represents in a suit against the manufacturer of silicone breast implants." Ronald Smothers, "Small-Town Practice Proves Attractive for Rising Number of Lawyers," *N.Y. Times*, 7 July 1995, at A17.

In the examples just listed, *who* is defensible as a CASUALISM. But the objective *who* is not idiomatically normal after a preposition. For example, *one of whom* is something of a SET PHRASE—e.g.:

- "That sits well with local leaders, *one of who* [read *one of whom*] drew upon his own analogy to describe the party." Nancy Cook Lauer, "Maddox Named State Democratic Party Chief," *Tallahassee Democrat*, 5 Jan. 2003, at A1.
- "Parents proudly whooped it up for the players, not *one of who* [read *one of whom*] wore shoulder pads." Skip Wood, "San Diego Is Lukewarm to Hype of NFL Title Game," *USA Today*, 27 Jan. 2003, at C7.

LANGUAGE-CHANGE INDEX
1. *who* as an object not following a preposition: Stage 4
2. *who* as an object following a preposition: Stage 2

C. The Mistaken Nominative *whom*. Among the toughest contexts in which to get the pronouns right are those involving linking verbs. We say, for example, *who it is* for the same reason we say *This is he*, but some very good writers have nodded. In any event, *whom* shouldn't be used as the subject of any finite verb—e.g.:

- "The distinguished political and social philosopher Russell Kirk used the word 'energumen' to describe . . . *whom* [read *who*] it is I agitate against." William F. Buckley, *The Jeweler's Eye* 284 (1969). (*Who* is needed as the inverted subject of *is*: *it is who*, as in *it is he*.)
- " 'The side I saw was a kind, caring, loving man,' said Woodrich, *who* admitted that many people criticized him for fraternizing with a man *whom* [read *who*] they thought was the enemy." Lynn Bronikowski, "Lorenzo the Taskmaster Ultimately 'Burned Out,' " *Rocky Mountain News*, 10 Aug. 1990, at 74. (*Who* is needed as the subject of *was*.)
- "Police went to several addresses looking for a 17-year-old *whom* [read *who*] they thought was staying with his aunt." Phillip Matier et al., "S.F.'s 'Dirty Dozen' Teenagers Elude Police Trackers," *S.F. Chron.*, 20 Apr. 1994, at A15. (*Who* is needed as the subject of *was*.)
- "In the other corner are the anti-Stratfordians, the heretics and conspiracy theorists of literature, most of them devoted amateurs whose dogged sleuthing and amassing of evidence (albeit mostly circumstantial) continues to enlarge the body of contention that Shakespeare wasn't himself. But if not *he*, then *whom* [read *who*]?" Don Oldenburg, "Shakespeare's Raging Identity Crisis," *Wash. Post*, 17 May 1994, at C5. (*Who* is needed in a parallel phrasing with *he*.)
- "A free-lancer I knew once wrote what almost amounted to an obituary for a crusty old female journalist *whom* [read *who*] everyone thought was dying." Al Martinez, "A Street Named Merideth," *L.A. Times*, 13 Sept. 1994, at B3. (*Who* is needed as the subject of *was*.)
- "There are a number of people who might have wanted to kill Robert Nachtsheim in his Minneapolis flower shop early one morning in 1973, but the intervening two decades have failed to reveal *whom* [read *who*]." Kevin Diaz, "$4 Million Award's a Start Toward a Clean Slate," *Star Trib.* (Minneapolis), 22 Oct. 1994, at A1. (Although *whom* might seem to be the object of *reveal*, in fact the relative pronoun is the subject of an implied verb—*failed to reveal who* [*might have wanted to kill Robert Nachtsheim*]. Therefore, *who* is correct.)
- "A tense encounter with sheriff's deputies ended with the arrests of seven armed freemen *whom* [read *who*] authorities believed were bent on kidnapping a neighboring county prosecutor, and death threats from around the country directed at Bohlman and other county officials." Tom Kenworthy, "Standoff in Montana Tests Resolve to Avoid Bloodshed," *Wash. Post*, 19 Sept. 1995, at A1. (*Who* is needed as the subject of *were*.)
- "But [Chip] Beck ought to serve as an inspiration for a host of other superb golfers *whom* [read *who*] naysayers claim 'can't win the big ones.' " Michael Konik, "Birdies & Gentlemen: Some Memorable Moments in Ryder Cup Play," *Sky*, Sept. 1995, at 52, 57. (*Who* is needed as the subject of *can't win*.)
- "Sam divorced in 1969, and is survived by his son, Sam III, his wife, Angela, and their daughter, Samantha, of Clarksville, Tennessee; his daughter, Marguerite; the mother of Matthew and Grace, *whom* [read *who*] all lived with Sam in Austin." "Sam R. Baker Jr." (obit.), *Austin Am.-Statesman*, 10 Feb. 1996, at B4. (*Who* is needed as the subject of *lived*.)
- "The phrase 'natural-born citizen' should be given a meaning consistent with our transcendent right to select those *whom* [read *who*] we believe are most fit to govern." Michael I. Meyerson, "Citizen McCain," *N.Y. Times*, 17 July 2008, at A23. (*Who* is needed as the subject of *are*.)

See HYPERCORRECTION (F).

William Safire takes an interesting approach for those who fear seeming pedantic (by using *whom*) or being incorrect (by using *who* for *whom*): "When *whom* is correct, recast the sentence." "On Language," *N.Y. Times*, 4 Oct. 1992, § 6, at 12. So *Whom do you trust?* becomes, in a political campaign, *Which candidate do you trust?* The relative pronoun *that* can also substitute in many situations. For those who hesitate over these questions of case, this approach might seem quite sensible. See PRONOUNS (B).

But one commentator, Steven Pinker, calls Safire's suggestion an "unacceptable pseudo-compromise." *The Language Instinct* 389 (1994). And Pinker has a point: "Telling people to avoid a problematic construction sounds like common sense, but in the case of object questions with *who*, it demands an intolerable sacrifice. People ask questions about the objects of verbs and prepositions *a lot*." *Ibid.* Moreover, a phrase such as *which person* is wordier and slightly narrower than *who* or *whom*. So realistically, we're stuck with the continuing struggle between *who* and *whom*.

Perhaps the most sensible approach was the one taken by Robert C. Pooley in 1974: "Considering the importance some people place on mastery of [the textbook rules for *whom*], the schoolbooks may be justified in distinguishing the case forms for the relative pronouns for literary usage. But to insist that these literary

LANGUAGE-CHANGE INDEX (For the full key, see front matter pp. xxxi, l–li.)
Stage 1: Rejected. **Stage 2:** Widely shunned. **Stage 3:** Widespread but . . . **Stage 4:** Ubiquitous but . . . **Stage 5:** Fully accepted.
Invariably inferior forms marked by asterisk (*). • Ratios represent frequency of prevalent forms vs. variants in current books.

and formal distinctions be made in informal writing and speech as necessary to achieve 'correctness' is to do violence to the readily observed facts of current usage." *The Teaching of English Usage* 72 (2d ed. 1974).

LANGUAGE-CHANGE INDEX
whom misused as a subject: Stage 1

D. *Who* in Reference to Nonhumans (i.e., for *that* or *which*). *Who* is the relative pronoun for human beings (though *that* is also acceptable); *that* and *which* are the relative pronouns for anything other than humans, including entities created by humans. But writers too often forget this elementary point—e.g.:

- "Many companies, I believe, *who* [read *that*] are busy buying new businesses and bringing in new management teams haven't even tested the outside edge of their profitability." Mark H. MacCormack, *What They Don't Teach You at Harvard Business School* 203 (1984).
- "The best borrowers are grabbed by the banks and financial institutions *who* [read *that*] are in a position now to offer finer rates." "NBFCs Enter Cul-de-Sac," *Bus. Standard*, 25 Oct. 1997, at 13.

LANGUAGE-CHANGE INDEX
who in reference to nonhumans: Stage 2
Current ratio (*companies that* vs. **companies who*): 8:1

E. *Which* for *who* or *whom*. Some inattentive writers use *which* in referring to human beings—e.g.:

- "The bakery employs 11 people, two of *which* [read *whom*] are English (non-Amish) women, and one who is a salesman." Faith Whitcomb, "Bakery Relies on Generations of Amish Recipes," *Plain Dealer* (Cleveland), 13 June 1995, at 4.
- "Most of the students, *which* [read *who*] are evenly split between corporate clients and consumers, have taken the free course." Laura Castaneda, "Netting an Education," *S.F. Chron.*, 24 July 1997, at D1.
- "The driver of the first car, *which* [read *who*] was the only occupant, also died at the scene." "2 Killed in 3-Vehicle Crash on Highway 360," *Dallas Morning News*, 7 July 2003, at B2. (Because the writer used *which* instead of *who*, it seems at first as if the car was its own passenger and died in the accident.)

See **which (B).**

That, of course, is permissible when referring to humans: *the people that were present* or *the people who were present*. Editors tend, however, to prefer the latter phrasing.

F. Placement of the Relative Pronoun. See REMOTE RELATIVES.

whodunit (= a book, film, game, etc. about a murder case in which the culprit isn't revealed until the end) is an altered form of the dialectal question *Who done it?* Dating from the 1920s, this Americanism has always been predominantly spelled *whodunit* in AmE. When the term caught on in BrE, it was originally spelled the AmE way, but in the 1970s and 1980s the variant spelling **whodunnit* vied for predominance in BrE. Today in World English generally, including BrE, the settled spelling is *whodunit*.

Current ratio: 4:1

who else's. See **else's** & POSSESSIVES (I).

whoever; whomever. Here's the traditional rule about the nominative *whoever* and the objective *whomever*. If the word that completes the syntax after *-ever* is a verb, the correct choice is *whoever* <they praise whoever performs well>—even if there are a few intervening words <whoever, under these conditions, can deliver the goods on time will win the contract>. If the word that syntactically follows the *-ever* isn't a verb, the correct choice is *whomever* <he criticizes whomever he dislikes>—once again, even if there are a few intervening words <we'll help whomever, among the class members, the teachers recommend>. If you're unsure of the correct word, choose *whoever*; even when the objective *whomever* would be strictly correct, the *whoever* is at worst a CASUALISM (in other words, not bad except in formal contexts).

Like *who* and *whom*, this pair is subject to more than occasional HYPERCORRECTION—e.g.:

- "Both teams want to run, so *whomever* [read *whoever*] controls the boards and doesn't throw the ball away too much will win." David Dupree, "Western Conference Semifinals Analysis," *USA Today*, 6 May 1992, at C8.
- "But bringing religion into the schools, *whomever* [read *whoever*] originates it, opens a floodgate of problems." "Debate Heats Up on School Prayer," *Amarillo Daily News*, 9 Aug. 1995, at C1.
- "*Whomever* [read *Whoever*] the opposing pitcher was, the Sox never were at a disadvantage with Billy Pierce on the mound." Mike Imrem, "Sox' Pierce Was a Special Person and Player," *Daily Herald* (Arlington Heights, Ill.), 6 Aug. 2015, at 1.

See PRONOUNS (B) & **who (C).**

You can always be sure that the form **whomever's* is wrong. If it's intended as a possessive form, it's wrong for *whoever*; if it's intended as a contraction of *whomever is*, then the objective form *whomever* is wrongly acting as the subject of *is*. Yet this poor form often appears. Notice that in each of the following sentences, *whomever* looks like an object of a preposition or verb, but in fact it's simply part of a noun clause that should function as an object—e.g.:

- "It's up to the agent to get a copy of the contract to *whomever's* [read *whoever's*] going to close the sale." Julie Elman, "Ready, Set, Buy," *Virginian-Pilot & Ledger Star* (Norfolk), 1 June 2002, Real Estate §, at 1.
- "You can trust *whomever's* [read *whoever's*] behind the turntables." Eric Brace, "Deepflyte, House with 'Nooks and Crannies,'" *Wash. Post*, 9 Aug. 2002, at T6.
- "He tells *whomever's* [read *whoever's*] in charge that he wants to bring his wife by to look at the house—but never returns." Tom Spalding, "Ex-Con Sought in Theft Scam," *Indianapolis News/Star*, 27 Sept. 2002, at B1.

The slightly less common error is to make **whomever's* a possessive, where *whosever* (traditionally) should appear. (See **who(so)ever (C).**) If you're going to be formal enough to use a form of *whom*, though, it's probably better to stick to *whosever*—e.g.:

- "*Whomever's* [read *Whosever*] team wins in football has to play bailiff in open court for a day." Julie Kay,

"Hot-Tempered Broward Circuit Judge May Have a Lot of Enemies," *Miami Daily Bus. Rev.*, 27 Mar. 2002, at 1.

- "If the public is not satisfied, they have every right to ask for an inquiry into any City Judge, elected official, or *whomever's* [read *whoever*] record is in question." Letter of Diann Sams, "Sams Says Luster, Journal Are Real Demagogues," *Ithaca J.* (N.Y.), 22 July 2002, at A9.
- "Under whatever circumstances, by *whomever's* [read *whoever*] hand, Dominic's death is on the conscience of the system." Editorial, "Our View," *News-Leader* (Springfield, Mo.), 25 Aug. 2002, at A14.

whole, adj. See ADJECTIVES (B).

***whole entire.** This has been a fairly common REDUNDANCY since the 17th century—e.g.:

- "This has them ranked sixth in the *whole entire* [delete *whole entire*] nation, greatly reducing their margin of error for reaching their four-loss quota." Bob Wojnowski, "They're No Longer Many, So Here Are a Few Heartfelt Suggestions to Help Restore Irish Spring," *Detroit News*, 26 Sept. 1997, at D1.
- "Her sister, Doris G. Roupe, . . . was by her sister's side the *whole entire time of* [read *throughout*] her illness." "Cletis Opal Gibson Johnson" (obit.), *Roanoke Times*, 13 Nov. 1997, at B2.
- "Like snowflakes, there is only one you in *this whole entire* [read *the whole*] universe." Joel Goldman, *Yoga on the Moon and Beyond* 50 (2009).

***wholistic.** See **holistic.**

whom. See **who.**

whomever. See **whoever.**

whoop-de-do originated in the 1920s as a noun to denote either a lively social affair or a heated public debate. Today it is primarily an interjection used (without an exclamation mark) to show sarcastically that something isn't as impressive as someone else has suggested it would be <Well, we're here. Whoop-de-do.>. Although the original spelling was *whoop-de-do*, the variant spellings **whoop-de-doo* and **hoop-de-doo* became predominant for a time in the 1930s. Since the late 1930s, however, the standard spelling has been *do* in the final syllable. Whoop-de-do.

who's; whose. See **whose (B).**

whose. A. Meaning "of which." *Whose* may usefully refer to things <an idea whose time has come>. This use of *whose*, formerly decried by some 19th-century grammarians and their predecessors, is often an inescapable way of avoiding clumsiness—e.g.:

- "A book *whose* humor could have seemed tediously affected turns out to be entertaining and utterly useful." "Ready to Surf Web? Go Buy the Book," *Atlanta J.-Const.*, 24 Dec. 1995, at H4.
- "About $4.1 million is from buildings *whose* owners filed for bankruptcy, she said in an interview." D'Vera Cohn, "Water-Sewer Authority Weighs Delinquent Bills, Rate Increase," *Wash. Post*, 27 Sept. 1996, at B1.

- "Planetary scientists have wondered how the four smaller moons, *whose* orbits are closely packed together, manage to avoid colliding." Anne McGovern, "Solar System: Pluto's Perplexing Moons," *Sky & Telescope*, Sept. 2015, at 10.

The other possessive for *which*—namely, *of which*—is typically cumbersome. E.g.: "Western reluctance to intervene militarily in every foreign conflict is understandable. But it is disputable in the case of Bosnia, where fighting long ago turned from ethnic strife into a war of foreign aggression, *the continuation of which* [read *whose continuation*] would jeopardize European stability." Gideon Rafael, "NATO Plus Russia: A Humanitarian Relief Force," *Int'l Herald Trib.*, 19 July 1995, at 8.

LANGUAGE-CHANGE INDEX
whose referring to things: Stage 5

B. Mistakenly Written *who's*. Whereas *whose* is the possessive form, *who's* is a contraction for *who is*. But writers often confuse the two—e.g.:

- "Lee—*who's* [read *whose*] first hit recording was 1959's 'Ain't It So'—was only 16 in 1956." Richard Jinman, "Rock and Roll Down Under Hits the Big 40," *Weekend Australian*, 20–21 Jan. 1996, at 1.
- "Veteran comedian Richard Pryor was one of many *who's* [read *whose*] humor was considered rapid, rude, crude, and political." Charles Reeves, "The Changing Face of Comedy," *Phil. Trib.* (Mag.), 30 Apr. 1996, at 12.
- "*Who's* [read *Whose*] fault is this? That depends on whom you ask." Ellen Neuborne, "RSI Workers in Pain," *USA Today*, 9 Jan. 1997, at B1.
- "To learn nothing from the second half of the first Cleveland game—and that is certainly evident after being outscored, 55–13, in the past six quarters—points to a failure in preparation. Either that, or the players aren't very good, and *who's* [read *whose*] fault is that?" Gerry Dulac, "Report Card," *Pitt. Post-Gaz.*, 14 Oct. 2014, at E3.

LANGUAGE-CHANGE INDEX
who's misused for *whose*: Stage 1

whose else. See **else's** & POSSESSIVES (I).

who(so)ever, whom(so)ever; *whoso(ever), *whomso(ever). A. Choice of Term. The forms *whoever* and *whomever* are preferred in modern writing. But the ARCHAISMS **whosoever* and **whomsoever*, as well as **who(m)so*, appear sometimes in LEGALESE. Often these terms are superfluous, as here: "This is a right that avails against all persons *whomsoever* [delete *whomsoever*] in the world." Better: *This is a right against everyone else in the world.*

B. Case. The problem of proper case arises, just as it does with *who* and *whom*. E.g.: "*Whomever is* [read *Whoever is*] responsible for implementing the program is responsible for its faults." *OGEU* contains this rather poor advice: "Use *whoever* for the objective case as well as the subjective, rather than *whomever*, which is rather stilted" (p. 135). Stilted, perhaps, but correct—and really not very stilted in formal prose. See PRONOUNS (B).

C. Possessives. *Whosever* is the traditionally correct form, but it's very much on the wane. *Whoever's* is now the preferred colloquial form—e.g.:

- "'*Whoever's* bullpen does better is the team that's going to win that West.'" Chuck Ashmun, "Sideline Chatter," *Seattle Times*, 29 May 1997, at C2 (quoting Bip Roberts of the Kansas City Royals).
- "'*Whoever's* team loses has to follow the other guy around (in the post-season),' [Dwight] Gooden said." Marc Topkin, "Gooden Doesn't Know Where He'll Be in '98 Series," *St. Petersburg Times*, 7 Oct. 1997, at C4.
- "This is the kind of place, a coffin corner to kick off his patent-leather pumps after a good night's labors at *whoever's* jugular, feed the bats, floss his fangs and sigh, 'Be it ever so humble, there's no disgrace like home.'" Bud Collins, "Spooky Cellar Hides Burgundies to Die For," *Houston Chron.*, 19 Oct. 1997, at 2.
- "And as for calling it Flockstars, well, let's just say *whoever's* job it is to dream up pun-based names based on other shows' titles must be working overtime right now." Mike Ward, "Critic's Choice," *Express* (UK), 25 July 2015, at 47.

For examples of *whomever* used for *whosever*, see **whoever.**

Most strictly, *whoever's* is a contraction of *whoever is* (or, less commonly, *whoever has*)—e.g.: "One or two members work on equipment, *whoever's* left keeps the weapon close and an eye out for any 1,500-pound ursid wearing a white coat." Peter N. Spotts, "Arctic Scientists Tread Softly Around Natives," *Christian Science Monitor*, 23 Oct. 1997, at 3.

who's who is a shortened form of *who is who* (the second *who* being correct as a predicate nominative). But some writers—despite the popularity of various widely touted books called *Who's Who*—mangle the phrase into **who's whom*. E.g.:

- "The charade of *who's whom* [read *who's who*] and what's what gets stretched to absurd lengths." Jan Herman, "French Farce: All Dressed Up for a Tasty Snack," *L.A. Times*, 14 Jan. 1997, at F4.
- "Since so many of Tampa's servants of the people have been face down in the public trough for so long, pretty soon the only identifying feature one has to work with in figuring out when one glad-hander's term ended and another's commenced is [to try ascertaining] *who's whom* [read *who's who*] from the line-up of ever-expanding posteriors." Daniel Ruth, "Mr. Joey Corrects the Record," *Tampa Trib.*, 18 Mar. 1997, at 1.
- "All appearances to the contrary, they [the L.A. Lakers] weren't dethroned Sunday when the Boston Celtics walked all over them in a 109–96 object lesson in *who's whom* [read *who's who*] in the pecking order." Mark Heisler, "This Season, It Really Could Be Time to Worry," *L.A. Times*, 31 Jan. 2011, at 1.

The error sprang up in the early 20th century and spread especially after 1960. It apparently resulted from the mistaken sense that the final word is the verb's "object" (as opposed to a subjective complement, which it is). Writers who make this error have perhaps temporarily forgotten what's what.

LANGUAGE-CHANGE INDEX
**who's whom* for *who's who*: Stage 1

widely regarded. See **regard** (B).

widespread was, until the early 20th century, spelled as two words, but now it should always be one. For *widespreadly, see ADVERBS (B).

widow, n.; **widower.** A *widow* is a woman whose spouse has died; a *widower* is a man similarly bereft. Do the terms still apply when the surviving spouse remarries? No.

widow, vb., can make a past-participial adjective *widowed*, which may apply to either sex. Although *widowed man* may seem unnatural, it is common and unobjectionable—e.g.: "Schmidt himself is no less persnickety; once *widowed*, he asks his daughter . . . to tend him, telling her precisely how to make his lunch as if instructing troops in the loading of a gun." Anthony Lane, "Looking Back," *New Yorker*, 16 Dec. 2002, at 106.

widow; orphan. These words have special meaning in the terminology of typesetting and word processing. A *widow* is a paragraph's last line that is separated from the paragraph by a page break and carried over to the top of the following page. An *orphan* is a paragraph's first line that is similarly separated and left behind at the bottom of the preceding page. Most word-processing software packages have a feature called "widow/orphan protect" or something similar; you should use this feature so you won't carelessly leave any widows or orphans in an unsightly lurch. See DOCUMENT DESIGN.

widower. See **widow,** n.

wield; weald. The former is the verb meaning "to control; handle; hold and use" <he wields his power with good judgment>. The latter is the noun meaning "a forest" or "an uncultivated upland region."

wife. Pl. *wives.* See PLURALS (C).

Wi-Fi, a PORTMANTEAU WORD from *wireless fidelity*, came to prominence in the late 1990s. It is predominantly so spelled in all varieties of English, variants being *WiFi, *wi-fi, *wifi, and *Wifi. The hyphen and perhaps the second capital seem destined to disappear.

***wildly regarded.** See **regard** (B).

wild oats, sowing. See **sow** (B).

***wile away.** See **while away.**

will. See **shall.**

willful; wilful. *Willful* is the standard spelling in AmE, *wilful* in BrE. Curiously, the American spelling was not fully established in AmE until the 1940s. *Willfull, a misspelling, occasionally appears. Cf. **skillful.**

willy-nilly, adv. & adj., = (1) by compulsion <he forced his brother to accompany him willy-nilly>; or (2) in a haphazard, unplanned way <so far, all our meetings have occurred willy-nilly>. The phrase is sometimes, as the *OED* remarks, erroneously used for "undecided, shilly-shally" <a willy-nilly disposition>.

Wimbledon /wim-bəl-dən/ is often mispronounced / wim-bəl-tən/—and not just by simpletons.

*win a victory. See **victory**.

winch (= a cranking device that helps pull or haul) is sometimes confused with *wench* (= a young woman, esp. one with lewd propensities). The results are truly bizarre—e.g.:

- "By using a 1/4″ steel cable on the *wench* [read *winch*] and over the pulley, I was able to hoist up the logs and beams and maneuver them into place." Dick Sellers, "I Built a Log Cabin from Scratch for Under $11,000," *Mother Earth News*, Apr. 1993, at 34.
- "He slips the rope into a hydraulic *wench* [read *winch*], which hoists the 60-pound, wood-slatted box to the surface." Jerry Shriver, "Catching the Maine Attraction," *USA Today*, 14 July 1995, at D5.
- "Most drivers made it through the mud pit but some got stuck and had to be helped out with a *wench* [read *winch*]." Ryan Severance, "Some 75 Cars and Trucks Bring Rolling Thunder to Race," *Pueblo Chieftain* (Colo.), 2 Aug. 2015, Sport §.

LANGUAGE-CHANGE INDEX
wench misused for *winch*: Stage 1

wind, vb.; wound, vb.; winded. In most senses that are pronounced /wɪnd/, the preferred past-tense and past-participial forms of *wind* are *wound* (/wownd/) <the road wound through the countryside> <she hadn't wound the clock> <the luggage wound up in Boston>. In most senses pronounced /wind/ and related to breathing, airflow, and the sense of smell, the verb takes regular *-ed* endings <she became winded early in the race>. One uncommon sense defies this generalization, though: the preferred pronunciation of *wind* meaning "to blow a horn" is /wɪnd/, and the preferred inflections are both *wound*. See IRREGULAR VERBS.

wintry; *wintery. The former is the older and the standard spelling for the adjective meaning "of or like winter." It is much more common than the latter in modern print sources—e.g.: "The crowd of about 50 . . . mill about, sipping coffee and commenting on the *wintry* weather." Gay Jervey, "Workaholics Anonymous," *Fortune*, 3 Mar. 2003, at 150.
Current ratio: 31:1

wiry (= [1] of or like wire; [2] tall and thin; or [3] sounding like a vibrating wire) is so spelled. ***Wirey** is a common misspelling—e.g.: "The *wirey* [read *wiry*] Cuban will start the season as a reserve middle infielder." Ryan Corazza, "Wild Thing," *Chicago Trib.*, 31 Mar. 2008, at 14.
Current ratio: 327:1

-WISE. Generally, avoid *-wise* words or compounds when the suffix means "regarding" or some other frame of reference. They typically displace a more direct wording, and they're invariably graceless and inelegant—e.g.:

- "McCaskey (0–8) is the biggest school *population-wise*, but the smallest when it comes to youth soccer turnout." Eric Stark, "L-L Girls' Soccer '97," *Lancaster New Era*, 14 Apr. 1997, at C1. (A possible revision: *Although McCaskey (0–8) has the most students, it has the smallest turnout for youth soccer.*)
- "*Content-wise*, the slacker story reveals what other less mass-minded magazines revealed long ago: Slackers are not really job-averse at all." Bill Steigerwald, "Internet Can Satisfy a News Junkie Who Isn't Fussy About Convenience," *Commercial Appeal* (Memphis), 13 June 1997, at C4. (The best approach to revising that sentence is to delete *content-wise*.)
- "After a dull summer *book-wise* [read *in books* or *in the book trade*] . . . , the season of fairs, sales, readings and other book-related events gets off to a satisfying start this month." David Streitfeld, "Book Report," *Wash. Post*, 14 Sept. 1997, Book World §, at 15.
- "During the 1992 campaign, Democrats fared a little better, *grammarwise* [read *grammatically* or *grammatically speaking*]." Mary Newton Brudner, *The Grammar Lady* 37 (2000).

But some recent NEOLOGISMS seem to be earning their way. For example, *taxwise* is often better than *from the point of view of taxes* or some similar phrase—e.g.: "You can't fund an education IRA in any year you contribute to a prepaid tuition plan, now offered by 14 states. *Taxwise*, IRAs are better." Jane Bryan Quinn, "Dollars in, Dollars Out," *Newsweek*, 18 Aug. 1997, at 51. See **taxwise**.

Finally, some writers use the suffix playfully—e.g.: "In fact, *sex-wise* we are practically the weirdest creatures in the animal kingdom." Michael Thompson-Noel, "A Species of Sexual Weirdos," *Fin. Times*, 30 Aug. 1997, at 5.

wisteria; wistaria. Americans are often surprised to learn that the word for the flowery vine was once spelled *wistaria* (after Caspar Wistar, an anatomist), not *wisteria*. A prominent etymologist calls the change in spelling "apparently a misprint" in 1819. Robert K. Barnhart, *Dictionary of Etymology* 885 (1995). The original does still show up in American print sources, but usually in proper nouns—e.g.: "Last month they celebrated the annual *Wistaria* Festival in honor of a sprawling 114-year-old vine that is recognized as one of the world's largest blossoming plants." Joe Mozingo, "Fire Looms over Sierra Madre," *L.A. Times*, 29 Apr. 2008, at B3. Even when California papers are reporting on the *Wistaria* Festival, though, they spell the plant name *wisteria*.

Although the *OED* favors *wistaria*, American dictionaries list it as a variant spelling. It is so uncommon in AmE that some writers feel compelled to comment on it—e.g.: "[W.D.] Rose promised that the drink

LANGUAGE-CHANGE INDEX (For the full key, see front matter pp. xxxi, l–li.)
Stage 1: Rejected. **Stage 2:** Widely shunned. **Stage 3:** Widespread but . . . **Stage 4:** Ubiquitous but . . . **Stage 5:** Fully accepted.
Invariably inferior forms marked by asterisk (*). • Ratios represent frequency of prevalent forms vs. variants in current books.

would 'conjure up visions . . . of *wistaria* [sic] blooming in old patios, of sights and smells associated only
with the Vieux Carre.'" Amanda Hesser, "1935: Ramos
Gin Fizz," *N.Y. Times*, 15 June 2008, at MM67 (ellipsis
and "[sic]" notation are in the original).

The newer spelling with the medial -*e*- took awhile to
catch on: it became predominant in AmE print sources
in the 1940s and in BrE print sources in the 1970s.

> LANGUAGE-CHANGE INDEX
> *wisteria* so spelled: Stage 5
> Current ratio (*wisteria* vs. *wistaria*): 6:1

wit, to. See **to(-)wit.**

witenagemot, the historical term referring to the
Anglo-Saxon council of nobles and officials who
advised the king on administrative and judicial matters, has been predominantly so spelled since about
1800. The variant spelling *witenagemote* flourished
for a time in the 18th century but hasn't been widely
used in print sources since then. Whatever the spelling, the word is pronounced /**wit**-ən-ə-gə-moht/ or
/**wit**-ən-ə-yə-moht/.

To complicate spelling matters, a member of this
council was called a *witan*, from the Old English verb
of the same spelling (*witan* = to know). Note that the
fourth character is an *a*, not an *e* as in the longer compound. Hence the council term was also sometimes
spelled *witanagemot*, but this form of the word never
became standard.

with. A. As a Quasi-Conjunction. *With* is increasingly being used as a quasi-conjunction to introduce
a tag-on idea at the end of a sentence. The sense is
close to *and* <John went to Houston and Sarah went to
Minneapolis, with me going to Chicago>. Avoid this
sloppy construction—e.g.:

- "Labor also has an edge on unemployment and welfare
  and social issues, *with* the Coalition considered better able
  to handle the environment, interest rates and taxation."
  Michael Gordon, "Voters Swing Back to ALP on Issues,"
  Weekend Australian, 20–21 Jan. 1996, at 1. (A possible
  revision: *Labor also has an edge on unemployment and welfare and social issues; the Coalition is considered better able
  to handle the environment, interest rates, and taxation.*)
- "We separated, *with me carrying* [read *and I carried*] a
  couple thoughts [read *a couple of thoughts*] back to the
  office." Dana Parsons, "Life on the Outside of the American Dream," *L.A. Times*, 14 Nov. 1997, at B1.

> LANGUAGE-CHANGE INDEX
> *with* as a quasi-conjunction: Stage 3

B. In Absolute Constructions. See ABSOLUTE
CONSTRUCTIONS.

withal is an ARCHAISM for *besides, nevertheless, still,
with,* or *therewith*. Having gradually fallen into disuse
over the 19th and 20th centuries, it only occasionally
appears today, always with an antique sound—e.g.:

- "There is, *withal* [read *nevertheless*], much to admire in
  these memoirs and in the diplomacy they recount." David
  C. Hendrickson, "White House Years," *Foreign Affairs*, 19
  Sept. 1997, at 223.

- "*Withal* [read *Nevertheless* or *Still*], the Series will conclude in Miami tomorrow night or Sunday night." Frederick C. Klein, "A Not-So-Fall, Not-So-Classic October
  Interlude," *Wall Street J.*, 24 Oct. 1997, at B17.

withe (= a slender, flexible shoot, branch, or twig), a
Middle English term traceable to the 12th century, has
long predominated in print sources over its variant
withy (/**with**-ee/). The plurals are *withes* (/**with**z/) and
withies (/**with**-eez/). *Withy* has an additional sense as
a synonym of *willow* or *osier*.

wither is misused for *whither* in the following title:
John Darnton, "In Tory Vote, It's Not Just 'Wither
Major?' but 'Wither Britain?'" *N.Y. Times*, 2 July
1995, at 6. Because Britain was, at the time the article
appeared, withering under an unusual heat wave—the
worst since 1976—this might have seemed to be a joke.
But the misusage was in 24-point type. See **hither.**

within sometimes leads to ILLOGIC in announcing
scores—e.g.: "The play set up Michael Reeder's fourth
field goal to bring TCU to *within* 20–19." Suzanne Hal-
liburton, "Welcome Back," *Austin Am.-Statesman*, 19
Nov. 1995, at C8. TCU was not *within* 20–19, but right *at*
it. *Within* (not *to within*) would work in that sentence if
the preposition had a different object, e.g., *within a field
goal*, or (to avoid the repetition) *within a single point*.

without hardly. See **hardly.**

without impunity. See **impunity (A).**

without scarcely. This phrasing is an optical illusion: something of a REDUNDANCY while something of an OXYMORON. Whatever it is, though, it's
illogical—e.g.:

- "He shook hands *without scarcely* [read *without* or
  scarcely] noticing those who were there to encourage
  him." Godfrey Sperling, "The Power of a Candidate's
  Prose," *Christian Science Monitor*, 8 Mar. 1988, at 11.
- "How can a band keep plugging away—*without scarcely*
  [read *without* or *scarcely*] batting an eye—in the face of
  such departures?" Beach Patrick, "The Sound and the
  Spectacle," *Des Moines Register*, 12 June 1994, Entertainment §, at 1.

The same can be said of *without hardly*. Both phrases
have been dialectal since the 18th century.

> LANGUAGE-CHANGE INDEX
> *without scarcely* for *without* or *scarcely*: Stage 1

with regard to. See **regard (A).**

with respect to. See **respect.**

with the exception of, a popular phrasing in the 19th
century, is verbose for *except, except for, aside from*, or
apart from—e.g.:

- "The best-actress field is generally hale, *with the exception of* [read *aside from*] the cancer victim played by
  Diane Keaton in 'Marvin's Room.'" "A Sweep at Oscars
  May Be Hard to Get," *Tulsa Trib. & Tulsa World*, 24 Mar.
  1997, at A10.
- "European Union Members, *with the exception of* [read
  except for] Greece, recalled their envoys to Iran for

consultations over the court verdict." "Tehran Protesters Target German Embassy as Feud Deepens," *L.A. Times*, 12 Apr. 1997, at A4.

with the object of [+ vb. + -ing] is verbose for a simple infinitive—e.g., *with the object of preventing* in place of *to prevent.*

witness predominantly forms the possessive *witness's* in AmE, *witness'* in BrE. The BrE preference is anomalous, however, because BrE print sources show a decided preference for the singular possessive *Jones's* over *Jones'.* See POSSESSIVES (A).

woke; woken. See **wake.**

wolf. Pl. *wolves.* See PLURALS (C).

wolfish; *wolvish. The first has been standard since the 18th century; the second is a NEEDLESS VARIANT.
Current ratio: 50:1

wolverine; *wolverene. The latter is a NEEDLESS VARIANT. See ANIMAL ADJECTIVES.
Current ratio: 22:1

***wolvish.** See **wolfish.**

-WOMAN. See SEXISM (C).

woman. See **lady.**

womankind; *womenkind. The latter is erroneous, since *-kind* includes all the members of the sex. E.g.:

- "Now she feels she's pressured about what her roles will say to all of *womenkind* [read *womankind*]." Matthew Gilbert, "Fiorentino Sees 'Jade' Role as Reward, Not Selling Out," *Seattle Post-Intelligencer*, 16 Oct. 1995, at D1.
- "In the Neil Labute film, . . . two angry white men decide to avenge every wrong they think *womenkind* [read *womankind*] has inflicted on them by dating the same woman with the intent of emotionally traumatizing her." Duane Dudek, "Movie Stars Also Fight for Equality," *Milwaukee J. Sentinel*, 14 May 1997, at 8.

The analogous error would be **menkind* for *mankind.* See **humankind** & SEXISM (C).
LANGUAGE-CHANGE INDEX
**womenkind* for *womankind*: Stage 1
Current ratio (*womankind* vs. **womenkind*): 10:1

womanly; womanlike; womanish. See **female.**

***womenkind.** See **womankind.**

***womyn.** See SEXISM (C).

wont. Although Samuel Johnson reported in 1755 that this word had slipped from use, it hangs on today as a slightly whimsical way of expressing customary behavior. It is used almost exclusively as a predicate adjective <as he is wont to> or as a noun <as is her wont>, although other forms do exist. The dominant pronunciations are /wahnt/ and /wawnt/, although

/wohnt/ and /wənt/ are also accepted. Probably because it is usually a homophone for *want*, and because its meaning intertwines with that simpler term (someone who is *wont* to do something generally *wants* to do it), it is occasionally misspelled *want*—e.g.:

- "Montgomerie had been the target of catcalls from American fans all week. As is his *want* [read *wont*], he exacerbated the situation by letting the fans know how much they irritated him." Paul Kenyon, "Death Deals Golf a Cruel Blow," *Providence J.-Bull.*, 26 Oct. 1999, at D1.
- "Jackson, in his first season with the Lakers, waxed eloquent—as he is *want* [read *wont*] to do—on Perkins' star turn before Wednesday's Game 1." Karen Crouse, "Mt. Shaq Tough Hill for Perkins," *Daily News* (L.A.), 9 June 2000, at S1.
- "He was skinny all his life. But, as a body is *want* [read *wont*] to do, it's acquired an extra pound, or two or three, in its sunset years." Lisa Gutierrez, "Shawnee 'Santa' Hands Out Toys, Hands Down Art," *Kansas City Star*, 13 Dec. 2000, at F1.

The adjective *wonted* (= habitual), which invariably appears before the noun that it modifies <his wonted practice>, is archaic and literary. But it sometimes appears in popular writing—e.g.:

- "A few glancing high notes aside, she brought zest to 'Endless Pleasure' and lent 'O sleep, why dost thou leave me?' its *wonted* aura of lazy sensuality." Allan Ulrich, "Scintillating 'Semele,'" *S.F. Chron.*, 2 Nov. 2000, at B1.
- "Paul Plishka, however, demonstrated the meaning of the term veteran in the most respectful and complimentary sense as a droll Bartolo, despite his *wonted* vocal wobble." Anne Midgette, "Two Debuts, Planned and Unplanned," *N.Y. Times*, 12 Jan. 2002, at B13.
- "He has also claimed to have farmed out complaints to inattentive helpers—an act at variance with his *wonted* heavy hands-on approach to his pastoral duties." Editorial, "Why Is Cardinal Law Still in Office?" *Wash. Post*, 23 June 2002, at B7.

LANGUAGE-CHANGE INDEX
want misused for *wont*: Stage 1

woolen, adj.; **woollen,** adj. Whereas BrE has always had *woollen* as the standard spelling, AmE adopted *woolen* as its standard spelling shortly after 1900. Clothes made from *wool* are *woollens* in BrE but *woolens* in AmE. Yet *woolly* is the standard spelling of the related adjective in AmE and BrE alike—**wooly* being a nonstandard variant in AmE.

WOOLLINESS is the quality of being confused, hazy, indefinite, and indistinct in expression. Excessive cross-references, as in the Internal Revenue Code, are perhaps the apotheosis of woolliness—e.g.: "For purposes of paragraph (3), an organization described in paragraph (2) shall be deemed to include an organization described in section 501(c)(4), (5), or (6) which would be described in paragraph (2) if it were an organization described in section 501(c)(3)." I.R.C. § 509(a) (1984). See OBSCURITY.

LANGUAGE-CHANGE INDEX (For the full key, see front matter pp. xxxi, l–li.)
Stage 1: Rejected. **Stage 2:** Widely shunned. **Stage 3:** Widespread but . . . **Stage 4:** Ubiquitous but . . . **Stage 5:** Fully accepted.
Invariably inferior forms marked by asterisk (*). • Ratios represent frequency of prevalent forms vs. variants in current books.

WORDINESS. See REDUNDANCY.

WORD ORDER. See INVERSION.

WORD PATRONAGE is "the tendency to take out one's words and look at them, to apologize for expressions that either need no apology or should be quietly refrained from" (*FMEU1* at 733). A flourishing example today is *no pun intended.* But others are ready at hand as well—e.g.: "Hopefully—to use an ugly word— the dilemma will be solved by the proposed legislation." In his preface to *FMEU2*, Ernest Gowers indulged mildly in word patronage when he wrote: "This was indeed an epoch-making book in the strict sense of that overworked phrase" (p. iii). The tendency is not at all uncommon:

- "The Bloomsberries were also relentlessly elitist, *in the true sense of that much-misused word.*" "Time to Decry Woolf and All Her Bloomsbury Snobs," *Daily Telegraph,* 14 Sept. 1995, at 14.
- "How does a manager inspire those he supervises[?] . . . One answer is to 'empower' (*that horrid word!*) them." Ron Ashkenas et al., "The Boundaryless Organization," *Electronic News,* 22 Jan. 1996, at 40.
- "Ruth is meant to go through changes that give her some hint of—*pardon this ghastly word*—empowerment." Liz Braun, "Ruth Walks Line Between Laughter and Tragedy," *Toronto Sun,* 7 Feb. 1997, at 57.
- "In future, I'll explore alternative officing (*don't you hate all the new words?*) with an open mind." Lynette Evans, "Alternative Officing or How to Live Without People," *S.F. Examiner,* 3 Sept. 1997, Habitat §, at 1.
- "It is, *to use a term now in vogue in feminist art discourse,* a deeply gendered object, but it isn't feminist at all." Paul Richard, "Homer's Debut on Display in D.C.," *Portland Press Herald,* 7 Sept. 1997, at G1.

See **coin a phrase** & **if you will.**

word processing, n. Two words. But as a PHRASAL ADJECTIVE, the term is hyphenated <word-processing equipment>. The phrase once looked as if it might become solid, but the one-word form has fallen off in recent years. See SPELLING (D).

WORD-SWAPPING. It's something like a Murphy's Law of language: two words that can be confused will be confused. Sometimes the more popular word will encroach on the less popular (as when *demean* took over the sense *bemean* [= to make base or low; degrade]). At other times, the less well-known word encroaches on the better-known one. The following pairs are illustrative:

affect	*gets used for*	effect
alternate		alternative
averse		adverse
bizarre		bazaar
comprise		compose
contemptuous		contemptible
continuous		continual
corollary		correlation
effete		effeminate, elite
expedient		expeditious
foreboding		forbidding
formidable		formative

fortuitous	fortunate
incredulous	incredible
inflammable	inflammatory
inhere	inure
laudatory	laudable
luxurious	luxuriant
masterful	masterly
observance	observation
precipitous	precipitate
proscription	prescription
recant	recount
recoup	recuperate
recuperate	recoup
resource	recourse
reticent	reluctant
sparse	spartan
viscous	vicious
voracious	vociferous
vortex	vertex

This book records hundreds of other examples.

How does this happen? Because people enjoy experimenting with words—not going so far as to engage in true SESQUIPEDALITY, but merely using slightly offbeat words that everyone has heard before—they'll replace an "expected" word with one that strikes them as more genteel. And they'll do this without ever bothering to look the word up in a dictionary.

In the old days, this psychological impulse probably didn't have a great effect on the language. But in an age of mass communications—when millions of people can be simultaneously exposed to a barbarous error in speech—the effect can be almost immediate. One speaker's carelessness with the language spreads as never before.

And because writing follows speech—as it must— these confusions, over time, get embedded in the language. The dictionaries record that *infer* sometimes means *imply*; that *precipitous* sometimes means *precipitate* (adj.); and that *regretfully* sometimes means *regrettably*. It's the lexicographer's duty to record what's happening in the language; if various words are in flux, then the dictionaries will reflect it.

That's where a good dictionary of usage comes in: it helps people understand which words are worth continuing the struggle to preserve in their traditional senses; which words are all but lost in the short term (SKUNKED TERMS); and which words, though once confused, have undergone semantic changes that can't be objected to any longer. In any given age, various sets of words belong at different places on that continuum.

Rarely do the preservationists—the ones who want to keep traditional distinctions—prevail. Sometimes they do; more often they don't. But that doesn't mean the struggle is in vain. To the contrary: it means that these speakers and writers will be better equipped, among their contemporaries, to avoid stumbling and thrashing about in the language. Among astute listeners and readers, they'll have a higher degree of credibility. There's much to be said for that.

wordy does not mean "sesquipedalian," as many seem to suppose; it means, rather, "verbose, prolix."

workaholic. See -AHOLIC & MORPHOLOGICAL DEFORMITIES.

workaround, n., = a roundabout technique to accomplish something that can't easily be done more directly. First popular in the late 1980s, the word appears most often in computer contexts to denote a way of doing something that software doesn't specifically provide for. While the hyphenated form still occasionally appears (*work-around*), especially outside computer contexts, the word is most often a closed compound— e.g.: "Symantec, which makes the programs, has posted four *workarounds* to the problem, one more complicated than the next." "Subscription Glitch," *San Diego Union-Trib.*, 10 Mar. 2003, at E4.

As a PHRASAL VERB, *work around* is always two words—e.g.: "Before deciding on a notice system, board members discussed a variety of other ideas, though legally questionable, to *work around* the sunshine law." Kelly Yamanouchi, "Tourism Board Sets Up War Meeting Plan," *Honolulu Advertiser*, 14 Mar. 2003, at C1.

worker; *workman; *workingman. Because of the growing awareness of SEXISM, *worker* is the best choice. It has vastly predominated over the others in print sources from 1910 to the present day.

Current ratio (in order of headwords): 91:7:1

workers' compensation; workmen's compensation. These words contain a plural possessive, hence *workers'* and *workmen's*—not *worker's* and *workman's*. (See POSSESSIVES (A).) *Workers' compensation* now vastly predominates, doubtless because of a sensitivity to the SEXISM of the other. Another erroneously punctuated form is **workers compensation*.

workforce; workload. Each is one word.

working. Radio announcers throughout the Southwest commonly say that an accident is "working" at (say) Walnut Hill and Preston Road and that another is "working" on LBJ Freeway east of Midway. What they apparently mean is that a police officer or an emergency crew is at the scene and working to clear the way. The usage seems to have originated in police JARGON.

working class denotes "the class of people who work for wages to earn a living." The term usually refers to manual laborers and is often used pejoratively. But even doctors, lawyers, and the like work for a living.

So where does the phrase come from? Originally, *working class* was used in contrast to *leisure class*— people who, because of their independent means, can while away their time. But the leisure class is now virtually nonexistent. And although *working class* doesn't make much literal sense anymore, it's probably here to stay as a close synonym for *proletariat*.

workload. See **workforce**.

workman; workingman. See **worker**.

workmen's compensation. See **workers' compensation**.

workout, n.; **work out,** v.i. & v.t. Although the noun is one word <a good workout>, the verb should be two—e.g.: "The Longhorns will *workout* [read *work out*] once today, at 4:35 p.m." "Extra Points," *Austin Am.-Statesman*, 22 Aug. 1995, at C3. See PHRASAL VERBS. For more on *work out* in its intransitive use, see **calculate out**.

workplace. One word.

worksite. One word. Cf. **jobsite**.

workstation. One word.

World Wide Web is a proper noun, capitalized when written out in full and when shortened to *the Web*. When combined into compound form, though, it is usually lowercase <website>. Cf. **webpage** & **website**.

Because *the Web* is just one protocol (way of exchanging information) on the Internet—separate from mail and news protocols, for example—the terms *Web* and *Internet* are not interchangeable—e.g.:

- "Internet users have characterized *spam* as one of the biggest annoyances of using the *Web* [read *Internet*]." "AOL Eyes Spam Legislation," *San Diego Union-Trib.*, 24 Feb. 2003, at E3.
- "At least two of every five messages sent over the *Web* [read *Internet*] are spam, anti-spam software maker Brightmail says." "Microsoft Puts Limit on Hotmail," *Investor's Bus. Daily*, 26 Mar. 2003, at A2.
- "'It's a cat-and-mouse game,' said Ralph Sandridge, Lockheed Martin director of operational excellence, whose job is fighting spam and other *Web* [read *Internet*] menaces." Chris Cobbs, "Spammed!" *Orlando Sentinel Trib.*, 10 Apr. 2003, at C1.

worrisome; worrying, adj. In AmE, something that provokes worry is *worrisome*, but in BrE it's *worrying*—e.g.: "Most *worrying* for the Conservatives, the MORI poll shows Labour making more rapid gains among middle class and southern voters—key groups who have been solid Conservative supporters since 1979 and whom the party needs to win back to retain power." Stephen Bates & Martin Linton, "Tory Poll Rating Hits Record Low," *Guardian*, 26 Aug. 1994, at 1. This BrE usage, an example of HYPALLAGE, has begun to creep into AmE.

worse; worst; *worser. Writers seldom have trouble with the adjectives *bad* > *worse* > *worst*. But sometimes they yield to temptation with a little harmless wordplay—e.g.:

- "He beat his supposed betters, and *worsers*, clearly if not handily, taking the lead at the top of the homestretch and holding off by a length a rush by the 14-to-1 shot Victory Gallop at the end." Frederick C. Klein, "Long Course Favors Long Shot," *Wall Street J.*, 4 May 1998, at A20.

LANGUAGE-CHANGE INDEX (For the full key, see front matter pp. xxxi, l–li.)
Stage 1: Rejected. **Stage 2:** Widely shunned. **Stage 3:** Widespread but . . . **Stage 4:** Ubiquitous but . . . **Stage 5:** Fully accepted.
Invariably inferior forms marked by asterisk (*). • Ratios represent frequency of prevalent forms vs. variants in current books.

- "The Giants got a little worse. The Dodgers got worse than that. The Rockies got even *worser*." Ray Ratto, "Don't Expect a Comeback, Not Even, 'Oh Yeah?'" *S.F. Examiner*, 16 Sept. 1998, at D1.
- "I was so terrified at this prospect that I went straight home, washed down the better (or *worser*) part of a quart of gin, and cried myself to sleep." Jonathan Yardley, "High Anxiety in the Space Age," *Wash. Post*, 2 Nov. 1998, at E2.

worse comes to worst; worst comes to worst. The traditional idiom, evidenced in the *OED* consistently from the 16th century, is *worst comes to (the) worst* (= [if] things turn out as badly as possible). But the more modern and more logical idiom, *worse comes to worst*—with its progression from comparative to superlative—became predominant in the 1970s and has remained so. Except in BrE where both forms are frequent, *worse comes to worst* now outnumbers the traditional phrase in print sources—e.g.:

- "Why not just move . . . all the way? Another place where, if *worse comes to worst*, you can just blow up the bridge." Howie Carr, "Gang of Pirates Tries to Hack Through Cape," *Boston Herald*, 12 Aug. 1994, at 4.
- "But if *worse comes to worst*, there's nothing wrong with a little goof here or there in school pictures." "Planning Can Make School Photographs Just Picture-Perfect," *San Antonio Express-News*, 22 Sept. 1997, at D2.
- "Bring in an accountant. Bring in an economics graduate. *Worse comes to worst*, bring in a 12-year-old who runs a lemonade stand." Tim Hobson, "Get Some Real Pros," *Waterloo Region Record*, 21 July 2015, at A6.

Cf. *least worst.

Current ratio (*worse comes to worst* vs. *worst comes to worst* in World English): 1.1:1

worsen, vb., traceable to the 13th century, was once only a transitive verb <he worsened his situation>. But beginning in the late 18th century it took on intransitive uses as well <his situation worsened>. Today, in other words, *worsen* is an ERGATIVE VERB. Interestingly, the word wasn't used much in print until the 1930s—and it has climbed steadily ever since.

***worser.** See worse.

worship, vb. Although some American dictionaries give preference to the inflected forms *worshiped and *worshiping, these have never achieved predominance in AmE print sources. That is, *worshipped* and *worshipping* have steadily outranked the single-*p* forms in frequency of use despite the general rule about not doubling the final consonant in an inflected syllable that is unaccented. See SPELLING (B). The reason may have to do with the form of the second syllable (*nap* forms *napping*, and *ship* forms *shipping*) and the analogical associations that automatically arise in readers' minds. Even so, the single-*p* forms continue to vie with the double-*p* forms in AmE—doubtless because of the dictionaries' influence. In BrE, there has never been any real competition. On the evidence, though, one may deduce that *worshipped* and *worshipping* are standard AmE as well as BrE. Cf. **kidnapping (A).**

Current ratio (*worshipped* vs. *worshiped*): 3:1

worst. A. For *most.* *Worst* is a CASUALISM when used as an equivalent of *most* <what they need worst is food>. It is related to *badly in need*. It occurs chiefly in reported speech—e.g.:

- "'The library is the place that needs me the *worst*,' she said." Joy Murphy, "Library Volunteer, 71, Enjoys Books," *Ledger* (Lakeland, Fla.), 27 Sept. 1995, at F6 (quoting Dot Hart).
- "These reforms would help schools that need them *worst*—failing urban ones—where children have no alternatives." Tony Lang, "Entertainment 'Neighborhoods,'" *Cincinnati Enquirer*, 25 July 1997, at A18.

B. *Two worst*; **worst two.* The first, which is more logical than the second, has always predominated in print. **Worst two* is loose phrasing—e.g.: "Their *worst two* [read *two worst*] positions for offensive production have been catcher and third base." Phil Rogers, "Help Needed: Where Do Sox Turn?" *Chicago Trib.*, 26 June 1997, Sports §, at 10.

LANGUAGE-CHANGE INDEX
*worst two for *two worst*: Stage 3
Current ratio (*two worst* vs. **worst two*): 4:1

C. **Least worst.* See **least worst.

worst comes to worst. See **worse comes to worst.**

worth. When this word is used with an amount, the preceding term denoting the amount should be possessive. E.g.: "He bought a few dollars' *worth* of golf tees." See POSSESSIVES (L).
Current ratio (*dollars' worth* vs. **dollars worth*): 1.3:1

worthwhile. One word.

-WORTHY. This combining form means (1) "fit or safe for" <a seaworthy vessel> <a crashworthy minivan>; or (2) "deserving of" <a praiseworthy effort> <a creditworthy loan applicant>. As in the preceding examples, the form is almost always closed up with its root, not hyphenated. Only a few newfangled *-worthy* terms <an article-worthy celebrity> have hyphens.

***wot** (= to know) is an ARCHAISM that H.W. Fowler called a "Wardour Street" term, i.e., an "oddment" calculated to establish (in the eyes of some readers) the writer's claim to be someone of taste and the source of beautiful English. Today, it's an affectation unless ironic (and probably even then)—e.g.: "News is now at hand that for reasons I *wot* [read *know*] not, the White House kitchens will serve free-range chickens only." John Gould, "Pent-Up Pullets and White House Fowl," *Christian Science Monitor*, 20 May 1994, at 17. Even as an archaism, the word has experienced such a serious decline that many readers will not wot what you mean.

would. Writers often use *would* to condition statements that really ought to be straightforward—e.g.:

- "Mr. Kohl *would seem* [read *seems*] to have made another concession." Alan Riding, "European Leaders Give Their Backing to Monetary Plan," *N.Y. Times*, 9 Dec. 1989, at 1.
- "I *would submit to you* [read *submit to you*] that very few presentations end with the audience saying, 'Well, that

presenter really beat our brains out. He thrashed us good and proper.'" Ron Hoff, *"I Can See You Naked"* 58 (1992). (A better revision: *Very few presentations end with the audience . . . .*)

See **should** & SUBJUNCTIVES.

would have for *had*, in a conditional statement, is an example of a confused sequence of tenses. STANDARD ENGLISH calls for *if he had* or *if I had*, not **if he would have* [+ p.pl.] or **if I would have* [+ p.pl.]—e.g.:

- "If the trial judge *would have* [read *had*] allowed impeachment with a limiting instruction . . . , Robinson would be before this court arguing that this alternative solution was error." *United States v. Robinson*, 783 F.2d 64, 68 (7th Cir. 1986).
- "'It would have been more eventful today if we *would have* [read *had*] won.'" Mike Cochran, "Four's a Crowd: TCU Tops Tech, Shares in SWC Crown," *Austin Am.-Statesman*, 26 Nov. 1994, at C2 (quoting Spike Dikes, Texas Tech's coach).

Would have [+ p.pl.] for *had* [+ p.pl.] is especially common in the Southwest, probably from contamination by *could have* [+ p.pl.]. See TENSES (B).

LANGUAGE-CHANGE INDEX
*if I would have for *if I had*: Stage 2
Current ratio (*if I had gone* vs.
*if I would have gone): 26:1

would have liked. This phrase should invariably be followed by a present-tense infinitive—hence *would have liked to go, would have liked to read,* not **would have liked to have gone, *would have liked to have read.* The erroneous phrasings are becoming common—e.g.:

- "One *would have liked to have been* [read *would have liked to be*] present at the meeting in which the introduction of this equipment was ratified." Giles Smith, "'Replay' Ends Dispute over Hurst's Goal," *Daily Telegraph*, 16 Aug. 1997, at 21.
- "Clapp said he *would have liked to have seen* [read *would have liked to see*] more teams involved in postseason play." Richard Obert, "Expanded Playoffs Rejected," *Ariz. Republic*, 29 Aug. 1997, at C12.

Nor is it correct to say **would like to have done,* because the sequence of events is then off. See TENSES (B).

LANGUAGE-CHANGE INDEX
would have liked followed by perfect infinitive: Stage 4

wouldn't be surprised. Generally, a negative shouldn't appear after this phrase. That is, *I wouldn't be surprised if Ratliff has retired* means that I think Ratliff has retired; *I wouldn't be surprised if Ratliff hasn't retired* means, literally, that I suspect Ratliff is still working. But many people use the double-negative form, which is especially common in reported speech—e.g.:

- "Ethan Johnson, plan recorder for the Holden Arboretum in Kirtland, noted that one of the rhododendrons was

blooming, and 'I *wouldn't be surprised* if others *didn't have* [read *had*] flowers on them.'" Suzanne Hively, "Topsy-Turvy Winter Weather Unsettling to Sleeping Plants," *Plain Dealer* (Cleveland), 15 Jan. 2000, Your Home §, at 3.
- "'I *wouldn't be surprised* if they *didn't end* [read *ended*] up calling us back,' Prewitt said." Anita Mabante Leach, "'Charlotte' in 2 Languages," *Ariz. Republic*, 10 Mar. 2000, Sun Cities §, at 1.
- "'I *wouldn't be surprised* if she *didn't just stay* [read *just stayed*] right there,' Mr. Mathis said." Susan Vela, "Smith Youngest in State," *Cincinnati Enquirer*, 20 Dec. 2000, at B1.

LANGUAGE-CHANGE INDEX
wouldn't be surprised followed by a negative: Stage 2

*would of. See **of** (D).

would rather. See **had rather.**

wound. See **wind.**

wounds, nursing. See **nursing one's wounds.**

wove(n). See **weave.**

wrack; rack, vb. See **rack.**

*wrang. See **wring.**

wrangle; wangle. The two are occasionally confounded. *Wrangle* = to argue noisily or angrily. *Wangle* = (1) v.t., to accomplish or obtain in a clever way; (2) v.t., to manage (a thing) despite difficulties; or (3) v.i., to use indirect methods to accomplish some end. E.g.:

- "He has aptly demonstrated his advertising acumen by *wrangling* [read *wangling*] almost half a million dollars in free print media from *New York* Magazine." Letter of David Curry, *New York*, 23 Jan. 1989, at 9.
- "So, in 1990, he called the Detroit Lions and *wrangled* [read *wangled*] an invitation to camp." David Wharton, "Climbing Charts Again," *L.A. Times*, 9 Aug. 1997, at C10.

This confusion was all but unknown before the mid-1950s, but it has become common since 2000.

LANGUAGE-CHANGE INDEX
wrangle misused for *wangle*: Stage 4
Current ratio (*wangle an invitation* vs.
*wrangle an invitation): 2:1

*wrapt. See **rapt.**

*wrapture. See **rapture.**

wrathful; wroth. Both these literary adjectives mean "extremely angry," but *wroth* can be used predicatively only <waxed wroth> <he was wroth>. It would be wrong to speak of a **wroth man,* though *wrathful man* is perfectly acceptable. The words are pronounced /rath-fəl/ and /roth/. *Wrathful* is somewhat the more common of the two terms in print sources.

Both adjectives are FORMAL WORDS, and *wroth* in particular smacks of ARCHAISM—e.g.:

—————————

LANGUAGE-CHANGE INDEX (For the full key, see front matter pp. xxxi, l–li.)
Stage 1: Rejected. **Stage 2:** Widely shunned. **Stage 3:** Widespread but . . . **Stage 4:** Ubiquitous but . . . **Stage 5:** Fully accepted.
Invariably inferior forms marked by asterisk (*). • Ratios represent frequency of prevalent forms vs. variants in current books.

- "Ms. Eckert seemed to be quite *wroth* [read *angry*] with me, though if her theory . . . is accurate, she should be delighted with my work." Jack Kenny, "'Mean-Spirited Columnist' Hopes to Take Own Advice of Lightening Up," *Union Leader* (Manchester, N.H.), 25 July 2001, at A4.
- "Hosts at the on-air salon that is WSCR-AM are so *wroth* [read *angry*] they have urged fans to vandalize the screens and shoot down with BB guns any other sight-line obstructions the Cubs might float." Eric Zorn, "It's OK to Not See Eye to Eye About Screens," *Chicago Trib.*, 9 Apr. 2002, at 1.

The word is most often seen in the SET PHRASE *wax wroth* (= to become angry), which can be easily simplified—e.g.: "Pfeiffer has a ropy vein at her left temple that, when she *waxes wroth* [read *gets angry*], throbs noticeably." Leah Rozen, "Picks & Pans: Screen," *People*, 21 Oct. 2002, at 43.

Current ratio (*wrathful* vs. *wroth*): 1.2:1

wreak. A. Inflection: *wreak* > *wreaked* > *wreaked*. The past tense is not *wrought*, which is the archaic past tense and past participle of *work*.

B. Pronunciation. *Wreak* is pronounced /reek/—not /rek/.

C. *Wreak havoc*. The phrase *wreak havoc* (= to bring about difficulty, confusion, or chaos) is the established idiom in AmE and BrE alike. (In BrE, another traditional idiom is *play havoc*.) But *wreak havoc* has two variants to be avoided: *wreck havoc and *work havoc. E.g.:

- "An inner struggle was *working* [read *wreaking*] havoc on Tracey's normally cheerful demeanor." Jay McInerney, "Smoke," *Atlantic Monthly*, Mar. 1987, at 68.
- "The floods of 1997 have *wrecked* [read *wreaked*] havoc at some Northern and Central California dairies." Martha Groves, "Farming and Flood," *L.A. Times*, 9 Jan. 1997, at D2.
- "During [the character's] 15 years in the underworld, 113 of the most evil types escape back to earth, *wrecking* [read *wreaking*] havoc at will." M.S. Mason, "TV Goes Bump in the Night," *Christian Science Monitor*, 13 Nov. 1998, at B1.
- "Food intolerances to wheat or grains, as well as sugar, can promote inflammation, which can *wreck havoc* [read *wreak havoc*] on the body's joints." Angela McManus, "Any Tips to Deal with Arthritis?" *Evening Times* (Glasgow), 13 Aug. 2015, at 32.

The phrase *wreak havoc*, by the way, came into vogue only as recently as the 1970s. Before that time, such phrases as *wreak vengeance* and *wreak revenge* (both still used) were just as common as *wreak havoc*.

LANGUAGE-CHANGE INDEX
1. *wreck havoc for *wreak havoc*: Stage 1
Current ratio (*wreak havoc* vs.
*wreck havoc): 23:1
2. *work havoc for *wreak havoc*: Stage 1
Current ratio (*wreak havoc* vs. *work havoc): 33:1

D. And *reek*. For the confusion of *wreak* with *reek*, see **reek**.

wreath; wreathe. *Wreath* is the noun <a Christmas wreath>, *wreathe* the verb <they plan to wreathe the door in garlands>.

wreck and ruin. See **rack**.

***wreckless.** See **reckless**.

wretch. For an interesting mistake involving this word, see **retch**.

wrier; wriest. See **wry**.

wring. A. Inflection: *wring* > *wrung* > *wrung*. The past-tense and past-participial forms of *wring* (= to squeeze or twist) are sometimes erroneously written *rung*—e.g.:

- "On market days, it is possible to see a small boy grab a live chicken by the head and whip its body round and round in an arc until its neck is *rung* [read *wrung*]." Linda Greider, "Learning to Talk Turkey in French," *Wash. Post*, 16 Nov. 1978, at E1.
- "Wipe the upholstery with a cloth *rung* [read *wrung*] out very dry in a solution of one part denatured alcohol to one cup water." Helen Turk, "Are You Ready for Winter?" *Atlanta J.-Const.*, 30 Oct. 1992, Home & Garden §, at P3.
- "Cathy Turner had to guard the gold medal around her neck closely last night. If she wasn't careful, someone might have *rung* [read *wrung*] her neck with it." Mary Kay Cabot, "Turner's Gold Draws Heat," *Plain Dealer* (Cleveland), 25 Feb. 1994, at D1.

The erroneous past form *wringed sometimes appears—e.g.:

- "For the federal budget to be *wringed* [read *wrung*] clean of red ink near the start of the next millennium, the economy will have to continue a stretch of low inflation." Mike Meyers, "Seven Years? Ha! Try Seven Months!" *Star Trib.* (Minneapolis), 25 Jan. 1996, at A18.
- "[Willie] Nelson slowed it down and *wringed* [read *wrung*] it out when the world expected its outlaws to be wired to the gills." Michael Corcoran, "The 25 Best Austin Albums of All Time," *Austin Am.-Statesman*, 1 May 1997, at 32.
- "She *wringed* [read *wrung*] her hands as she prepared for the piercing." Lisa Jones Townsel, "Third Time's the Charm," *St. Louis Post-Dispatch*, 12 Sept. 1998, at 40.

Still another erroneous form, always as the past tense and not as a past participle, is *wrang—e.g.:

- "After she *wrang* [read *wrung*] out the clothes, Grandma hung them on the line to dry." Margaret Wente, "They'll Never Go Home Again," *Globe & Mail* (Toronto), 20 July 1996, at D7.
- "He *wrang* [read *wrung*] every ounce of bluesy longing out of 'I Want a Little Girl.'" Joe DeChick, "Better than Ever: CNY Jazz Orchestra," *Syracuse Herald-J.*, 16 Apr. 1997, at B4.
- "The moment he *wrang* [read *wrung*] from the shirt that was drenched with sweat and tears and celebration was not the single in the eighth inning that eased last night's conclusion." Steve Jacobson, "Brosius Hits the Heights," *Newsday* (N.Y.), 22 Oct. 1998, at A105.

See IRREGULAR VERBS.

LANGUAGE-CHANGE INDEX
1. *rung* misused for *wrung*: Stage 1
Current ratio (*wrung its neck* vs. *rung its neck): 29:1
2. *wringed for *wrung*: Stage 1
3. *wrang for *wrung*: Stage 1
Current ratio (*wrung his hands* vs.
*wrang his hands): 209:1

B. *Hand-wringing.* This phrase, in common use since the 1960s, is sometimes mangled into **hand-ringing*—e.g.:

- "Mary Tyler Moore now gets by without the haunting, *hand-ringing* [read *hand-wringing*] insecurity that once dogged her everywhere she went." Bob Thompson, "Rediscovering Mary," *Toronto Sun*, 10 Mar. 1996, at S3.
- "Don Wade . . . attended the United States–Greece basketball exhibition in Indianapolis and noted the *hand-ringing* [read *hand-wringing*] on the bench." "Cold War Heated Up Olympics," *Ark. Democrat-Gaz.*, 16 July 1996, at C2.

LANGUAGE-CHANGE INDEX
*hand-ringing for *hand-wringing*: Stage 1
Current ratio (*hand-wringing* vs.
*hand-ringing): 207:1

writable. So spelled in both AmE and BrE—not **writeable.* See MUTE E.

writ large. In this archaic CLICHÉ and in Omar Khayyam's "The Moving Finger Writes"—but virtually nowhere else—*writ* (for *written*) survives. E.g.: "Religion . . . is cheapened even more when it is mixed with pre-game military exercises—the baseball cap's 'God, Guns, and Guts' message *writ large.*" L.T. Anderson, "Public Prayer Needs Limits," *Charleston Daily Mail* (W. Va.), 24 Sept. 1997, at C1.

wrong; wrongful. The distinction is important. *Wrong* = (1) incorrect; unsuitable <the quoted figures were simply wrong> <it was wrong of us to expect them so soon>; or (2) contrary to law or morality; wicked <cloning just to get human organs is wrong>. *Wrongful* = (1) characterized by unfairness or injustice; contrary to law <Iraq's wrongful aggression against Kuwait>; or (2) (of a person) not entitled to the position occupied <the wrongful officeholder>.

wrongly; wrong, adv. Both are proper adverbs; *wrongly,* which is less common, appears before the verb modified <the suspects were wrongly detained>; *wrong* follows the noun <he answered the question wrong>.

wroth, adj. See **wrathful.**

wrought. See **wreak (A).**

wrought with ——. See **fraught (B).**

wrung. See **wring (A).**

wry (= drily humorous, sardonic) presents all lexicographers with a conundrum. Throughout the English-speaking world, *wrier* is more common as the comparative adjective than *wryer*—and has been since the early 19th century in all varieties of English print sources. Yet *wryest* predominates over *wriest* and has done so over the same period (except during the years 1940 to 1960). Very strange.

What's a dictionary to do? Recommend *wrier* but *wryest*? None seem to have made that choice. But they all list exclusively the adverb *wryly.* Doubtless for the sake of consistency, American dictionaries tend to recommend *wrier–wriest* (*W11* being an exception). British dictionaries tend to recommend *wryer–wryest.* My recommendation: use the -*y*- forms for consistency, and do so wryly.

Current ratio (*wrier* vs. *wryer*): 3:1
Current ratio (*wryest* vs. *wriest*): 2:1

X

xebec (= a type of three-masted ship once common in the Mediterranean) is the standard spelling in AmE and BrE alike. **Zebec* and **zebeck* are variants.

Current ratio (*xebec* vs. **zebec* vs. **zebeck*): 121:3:1

x-ed; **x'd; *x'ed; *xed. As the past tense for the verb meaning "to mark with an x, delete," the first is standard. The others are variant forms.

The present participle is preferably *x-ing,* not **x'ing.*

xerox is a registered trademark that is nevertheless used as a common noun <he made a xerox of the document>, an adjective <a xerox copy>, and a verb <to xerox an article>. Sometimes the word is capitalized, but usually not—e.g.: "Several readers *xeroxed* my Sept. 14 column." Alex Beam, "Looking Backward,"

Boston Globe, 21 Dec. 1992, at 19. Careful writers and speakers tend to use *photocopy* or some other similar word. **Zerox* is a common misspelling.

Xmas. This 16th-century abbreviation for *Christmas* spread into popular usage in the late 19th century. Today it is popular in advertising. The prejudice against it is unfounded and unfortunate. The X is not a Roman X but a Greek chi—the first letter in *Christ* (Gk. *Christos*). *Xmas* has no connection with Generation X, X-ray, or X as an algebraic variable.

According to the late poet and philologist John Ciardi, "Though commonly frowned upon by grammarians as slovenly and by the pious as profane, *X* has ancient antecedents as the symbol of Christ and the cross, so much so that illiterate Jews at Ellis Island

LANGUAGE-CHANGE INDEX (For the full key, see front matter pp. xxxi, l–li.)
Stage 1: Rejected. **Stage 2:** Widely shunned. **Stage 3:** Widespread but . . . **Stage 4:** Ubiquitous but . . . **Stage 5:** Fully accepted.
Invariably inferior forms marked by asterisk (*). • Ratios represent frequency of prevalent forms vs. variants in current books.

refused to sign with an *X*, insisting on making an *O*, called in Yiddish *kikl*, little circle." John Ciardi, *A Browser's Dictionary* 421 (1980).

Should you write *a Xmas gift* or *an Xmas gift*? The answer depends on how readers hear the word in the mind's ear. If readers hear "Christmas," then *a* is the correct indefinite article. If readers hear "Eksmas," then *an* would be correct. An informal survey suggests that most people say *Xmas* as "Christmas"; so *a* is probably the safer bet.

X-ray; x-ray. Either form is correct, although the first has predominated in both AmE and BrE in print sources since the late 19th century—the margin between the two being much less in AmE. Although *W11* suggests that the term is hyphenated as an adjective and verb (*X-ray*) but not as a noun (*X ray*), most other dictionaries hyphenate the term in all parts of speech. That makes good sense, and it's an easy rule to follow.

Current ratio (*X-ray* vs. *x-ray*): 2:1

Y

-**y.** See DIMINUTIVES (G).

y'all. A. Spelling. Dating back to the early 19th century, this sturdy Southernism is most logically *y'all*, not **ya'll*, and the better form is vastly predominant in print sources. Only the *you* of *you all* is contracted. And in modern print sources, *y'all* is five times as common. So **ya'll* (which misleadingly resembles *he'll*, *she'll*, and *we'll*) deserves an edit—e.g.:

- "If *ya'll* [read *y'all*] want to stink up your breath and your clothes and start forest fires and make other people sick and get heart disease and cancer . . . well, you just go right ahead." Jim Jenkins, "Thank Goodness Smoking Was Not Addictive," *News & Observer* (Raleigh), 26 May 1994, at A18.
- "'Ya'll [read Y'all] have got to help me a lot,' Bentley, a registered nurse at Chalmette Medical Center, told the students about class planning." Cassandra Lane, "Nunez Nurse Students Back in Classroom," *Times-Picayune* (New Orleans), 25 Feb. 1997, at A1.
- "'Geeeeeeez,' Puck yelled from above. 'Ya'll [read Y'all] look like ants from up here.'" Jim Souhan, "Forever," *Star Trib.* (Minneapolis), 23 May 1997, at C12.

In the late 20th century, some writers began spelling the term without an apostrophe: **yall*. See Jan Tillery & Guy Bailey, "Yall in Oklahoma," 73 *Am. Speech* 257 (1998). This spelling is not yet widespread (and not recommended).

Why has the spelling been so much trouble? *Y'all* is the only contraction in English in which a stressed form is contracted to an unstressed one. See Michael B. Montgomery, "A Note on Ya'll," 64 *Am. Speech* 273, 274 (1989). See also 5 *DARE* at 1132–34.

LANGUAGE-CHANGE INDEX
*ya'll for *y'all*: Stage 2
Current ratio (*y'all* vs. **ya'll*): 5:1

B. Number. Although the traditional use of *y'all* is plural, and although many Southerners have stoutly rejected the idea that it's ever used as a singular, there does seem to be strong evidence that it can refer to a single person—for example, *See y'all later* spoken to someone without a companion. One possibility is that the speaker means "you and anyone else who may be with you" or "you and anyone else who comes along."

Another possibility is that *y'all* may in fact refer to one person. Getting at the truth depends on understanding the speaker's state of mind. For good summaries of the debates over this point—they have sometimes been heated—see Nancy J. Spencer, "Singular *Y'all*," 50 *Am. Speech* 315 (1975); and Marvin K.L. Ching, "Plural *You/Y'All* by a Court Judge," 76 *Am. Speech* 115 (2001). For an argument that *y'all* can be singular, see Jan Tillery & Guy Bailey, "Yall in Oklahoma," 73 *Am. Speech* 257 (1998); for an opposing (and more persuasive) point of view, see Ronald R. Butters, "Data Concerning Putative Singular *Y'All*," 76 *Am. Speech* 335 (2001).

C. You all. Many speakers in the South and Southwest, even highly educated ones, use the uncontracted *you all* as the plural form of *you*. This is a convenient usage, since *you* alone can be either singular or plural—and therefore is sometimes ambiguous. (See PRONOUNS (A).) True, *you all* is unlikely to spread beyond regional usage. But speakers who (like the author of this book) grew up with the phrase won't be easily dispossessed of it. It's handy, and it's less susceptible to raised eyebrows than *y'all*.

There is, however, a noticeable tendency in urban areas to replace this phrase with *you guys*, even if those addressed include females. One Texas writer calls *you guys* a "horrid Yankee construction." Steve Blow, "What's Up with Y'all?" *Dallas Morning News*, 27 Sept. 2002, at A25. This may have resulted from the great influx of a geographically diverse population in major cities such as Dallas throughout the 1980s and 1990s, coupled with a growing sense among natives that *you all* and *y'all* signal provincialism.

yaws. See **frambesia.**

yay. See **yea.**

yclept (= called, by the name of) is an ARCHAISM still sometimes encountered—e.g.: "A World War II British codebreaker (many at Bletchley Park were female) would have been appropriately *yclept* Sadie O. Rylance [a spoonerism of *radio silence*]." Don Hauptman, "More Original Spoonerisms and Transposition Puns," 48 *Word Ways* 192 (1 Aug. 2015). It's the past participle of the long-obsolete verb *clepe* (= to call by the name of). As a revival of an Old English term attested from the 10th century, according to the *OED*, yclept was "much affected as a literary archaism by Elizabethan and subsequent poets," and "in less dignified writing [it was] often used for the sake of quaintness or with serio-comic intention." In recent centuries, it reached the height of its popularity in the 19th. The word has steadily declined in print sources since 1900.

ye. A. As Article Meaning "the." In phrases such as *Ye Olde Cheshire Cheese* (Samuel Johnson's favorite pub in London) and *Ye Olde Curiosity Shoppe*, the word *ye* is simply a variant spelling of *the*. The Middle English thorn (þ) represented the sound now represented in English by *th*. By 1500 or so, its form was identical to that of *y*. Hence the "proper" pronunciation of *ye* as a definite article is /thee/—not /yee/.

B. As Archaic Second-Person Pronoun. The personal pronoun *ye* (= you) was originally used, in the 10th century, only as a nominative plural <ye [you two] have my blessing> or in apposition with a vocative noun <ye gods>. By the 13th century it had come to be used as a singular equivalent to *thou*, at first as a way of showing respect to a superior <ye have my loyalty> and as an objective pronoun <I love ye> <Strange news to tell ye!>. Quaint by the 17th century, it now survives mostly in DIALECT, *you* having taken over all second-person responsibilities in STANDARD ENGLISH.

yea; yay; yeah. The first is an expression of assent, esp. in a vote. The second is an exuberant exclamation. The third is a CASUALISM for "yes."

year. For the possessive form in *five years' imprisonment*, etc., see POSSESSIVES (L).

yeoman service; *yeoman's service. The form *yeoman service* (= stalwart help and support in some endeavor) has been predominant in English-language print sources throughout the world since about 1900. Before that, **yeoman's service* was the standard term.
Current ratio: 3:1

yes. This word has two possible plurals: *yeses* and *yesses*. The better plural for the noun is *yeses* because, like *buses*, it follows the usual rule for nouns ending in -s. See PLURALS (A). Cf. **no**.

But the verb *yes* is inflected *yessed, yessing*. Therefore, the third-person singular verb is *yesses* <he's so uxorious that he yesses her constantly>.

yet. A. Beginning Sentences with. Like other coordinating conjunctions, *yet* is perfectly acceptable as a sentence-starter. It's a rank SUPERSTITION to believe otherwise. E.g.:

- "Yet if a student can—and this is most difficult and unusual—draw back, get a critical distance on what he clings to, come to doubt the ultimate value of what he loves, he has taken the first and most difficult step toward the philosophic conversion." Allan Bloom, *The Closing of the American Mind* 71 (1987).
- "*Yet* God must by now be hardened to blasphemous bulls." Christopher Ricks, *Beckett's Dying Words* 170 (1993).
- "Campaign professionals . . . are becoming the new breed of influence peddlers. *Yet* they don't need to register as lobbyists in Washington." Jeffrey H. Birnbaum, "Washington's Power 25," *Fortune*, 8 Dec. 1997, at 144.
- "*Yet* critics say the zone has instead become a mecca of gambling, prostitution and illicit trade." Jonathan Kaiman, "Zoning Gamble by Laos," *L.A. Times*, 8 Sept. 2015, News §, at 1.

Cf. **but** (A).

B. Idioms Involving *yet*. There are two common negative phrases revolving around this word: *no person has yet done something* and *the person has yet to do something*. Some writers have ill-advisedly conflated the two idioms to come up with their own brand of ILLOGIC—e.g.: "No artist has yet to capture the essence of the Thai sea." Advertisement of the Tourism Authority of Thailand, *Island* (Mag.), Fall 1995, at 7. The writer has inadvertently suggested that every artist has already captured the essence of the Thai sea.

C. Other Phrases. See **although . . . yet, as yet** & ***but yet**.

yodel, vb., makes *yodeled* and *yodeling* in AmE, but *yodelled* and *yodelling* in BrE.

yogurt; yoghurt. The Turkish loanword *yogurt* (= a thick cultured dairy product) is so spelled. *Yoghurt*, a variant spelling common (but not dominant) in BrE, is rare in AmE. In fact, *yogurt* is more than 23 times as common as *yoghurt* in American print sources. **Yoghourt* (predominant in BrE only during the 1950s) and **yogourt* are likewise variant spellings best avoided. Current ratio (*yogurt* vs. *yoghurt* in World English): 5:1

yoke; yolk. *Yoke* = (1) a twice-curved, usu. wooden beam with U-shaped brackets beneath to enclose the necks of two oxen or other draft animals <after a struggle, the oxen were fitted into the yoke>; or (2) a pair of animals suitable for yoking <a yoke of oxen>. *Yolk* = the yellow center of an egg <he liked omelettes made with egg whites—he didn't miss the yolks>. *Yoke* is sometimes a verb; *yolk* never is.

With this pair, WORD-SWAPPING is fairly common. Sometimes *yolk* is misused for *yoke*—e.g.:

- "A couple of Jacqueline Ott's sculptures are quite cunning: [for example,] two flat plywood umbrellas *yolked* [read *yoked*] together like Siamese twins." William Zimmer, "Spirited Shows in New Haven," *N.Y. Times*, 27 July 1986, § 11, at 26.

LANGUAGE-CHANGE INDEX (For the full key, see front matter pp. xxxi, l–li.)
Stage 1: Rejected. **Stage 2:** Widely shunned. **Stage 3:** Widespread but . . . **Stage 4:** Ubiquitous but . . . **Stage 5:** Fully accepted.
Invariably inferior forms marked by asterisk (*). • Ratios represent frequency of prevalent forms vs. variants in current books.

- "But now that information is king, members of the media monde have thrown off the *yolk* [read *yoke*] of oppression and now mostly cover each other, cutting out silly distractions." David Brooks, "Media Monde," *Wall Street J.*, 28 Apr. 2000, at W17.
- "She glances across the Cow Camp, studying the salted ham hanging from the shingles, the oxen *yolk* [read *yoke*] draped over the back fence, the spurs and the skillets and the bull skull nailed to the roof." Lane DeGregory, "The Cracker Life," *St. Petersburg Times*, 15 Feb. 2002, at D1.

The reverse error, though uncommon, does occur— e.g.: "I was stunned by the mix of aquamarine, luscious tans, dusty reds, yellow of egg *yoke* [read *yolk*], the turquoise as mute as a lizard." Sean Connolly, "One Nation, Cool and Damp," *Pitt. Post-Gaz.*, 30 Aug. 1997, at A9.

LANGUAGE-CHANGE INDEX
1. *yolk* misused for *yoke*: Stage 1
Current ratio (*yoked together* vs. **yolked together*): 283:1
2. *yoke* misused for *yolk*: Stage 1
Current ratio (*egg yolks* vs. **egg yokes*): 236:1

you. A. Used in an Exclusive Way. The point here is to be aware of your audience. If you're writing for the *New England Journal of Medicine*, it's probably safe to use *you* to mean "doctors." But consider how this opening paragraph of a news story would read to a person who isn't African-American: "The ever-changing black experience in America is being assessed with a new intensity. Skin color, how you talk, more specifically what you say and how you live your life, are examples of the tests used to determine what it means to be black in the 1990s." Lena Williams, "In a 90's Quest for Black Identity, Intense Doubts and Disagreement," *N.Y. Times*, 30 Nov. 1991, at 1. See SUPERSTITIONS (K).

B. In Legal Documents. The second-person pronoun is invaluable in drafting consumer contracts that are meant to be generally intelligible. Consider the difference between the following versions of a lease provision:

Resident shall promptly reimburse owner for loss, damage, or cost of repairs or service caused in the apartment or community by improper use or negligence of resident or resident's guests or occupants.

vs.

You must promptly reimburse us for loss, damage, or cost of repairs or service caused anywhere in the apartment community by your or any guest's or occupant's improper use.

Of course, the drafter must carefully define *you* and *us*, but doing so is usually a straightforward matter.

C. As an Informal Alternative to *one*, n. See **one** (A) & SUPERSTITIONS (K).

you all. See **y'all** (C).

you and I. For the mistaken phrase **between you and I*, see **between** (B).

you can't eat your cake and have it too; you can't have your cake and eat it too. The second phrasing, now the more common one, is sometimes stigmatized: "The first form makes sense: once you've eaten the damned thing, you can no longer have it. Not so the later, corrupt form: you can have your cake—enjoy looking at it, or keep it in the freezer, or have it set aside for you at the bakery—and then, at the proper moment, eat it, too. But some dolt somewhere along the line reversed the order, and it stuck." John Simon, Book Rev., *The New Criterion*, Mar. 1997, at 66, 69. In fact, though, it's not clear that the second form is illogical—much less impossible. Assume that the phrase were *you can't spend your money and save it too*; why couldn't you just as easily say *you can't save your money and spend it too*? Essentially, that idea is perfectly analogous to the one involving cake. Note too that one sense of *have* is "to partake of" <I'll have the scallops>.

But Simon is right that the *eat–have* sequence is the traditional one. That's the phrasing given both in *Brewer's Dictionary of Phrase and Fable* (14th ed. 1989) and in *Bartlett's Familiar Quotations* (16th ed. 1992). The latter book traces a form of the phrase back to John Heywood's collection of colloquial Elizabethan sayings: "Would ye both eat your cake and have your cake?" Heywood, *Proverbs* pt. I, ch. 9 (1546). The *OED* gives examples from 1562, 1711, 1815—all in the order that Simon prefers.

Yet the *have–eat* sequence has been the dominant one since about 1940—e.g.:

- "I want to *have my cake and eat it too*." Paul Gallico, "Mainly Autobiographical" (1946), in *A Reader for Writers* 30, 53 (William Targ ed., 1951).
- "Still wanting to *have your cake and eat it, too*, Gregory?" Patricia Wrede, *Mairelon the Magician* 244 (1991).
- "A theory that promises liberty as part of equality seems to allow us to *have our cake and eat it too*." K. Anthony Appiah, "Equality of What?" *N.Y. Rev. of Books*, 26 Apr. 2001, at 63.
- "Due to a recent change in law, you can keep working after reaching retirement age and not lose a penny of your Social Security retirement benefits. It's almost like *having your cake and eating it, too*." Jerry Freeman, "You Can Work and Get Benefits," *Fla. Today*, 9 Sept. 2002, People §, at 3.

Meanwhile, the *eat–have* sequence has steadily declined since the 1940s, so much so that many speakers of English have never encountered it.

LANGUAGE-CHANGE INDEX
you can't have your cake and eat it too: Stage 5
Current ratio (*have your cake and eat* vs. *eat your cake and have*): 6:1

you'd better; *you better. See **better** (A).

you guys. See **y'all** (C) & **guy**.

you know. For an early alarm against the spread of this linguistic virus, see James Thurber, "The Spreading *You Know*," in *Lanterns & Lances* 31–34 (1961).

you know what I'm saying? This has become a non-U catchphrase. See CLASS DISTINCTIONS.

your, the possessive form of the second person, is sometimes misused for *you're,* the contraction of *you are.* Often, as in the second and third examples below, the error is that of the journalist who reports speech:

- "Just saying *your* [read *you're*] going to get fit this year doesn't mean you will unless you define what you mean by the term 'fit' and establish some step-by-step goals to help you accomplish your fitness resolution." Lareta M. Tabor, "Have You Already Given Up Your New Year's Resolutions?" *Kansas City Star,* 15 Jan. 1994, at 19.
- "Gallagher said: 'They can accept it if *your* [read *you're*] older and time goes by.'" Malcolm Moran, "Some Final Goodbyes for a Fallen Fordham Player," *N.Y. Times,* 18 Oct. 1996, at B24.
- "'Jogging won't do much good if *your* [read *you're*] going to be hiking with a 50-pound pack,' says Hixson." Howard Meyerson, "The Elements: Are You Up to the Challenge?" *Grand Rapids Press,* 17 May 1997, at D1.

The opposite error also occurs, somewhat less commonly, but again most often in recorded speech—e.g.:

- "'Sometimes the kids taunt them and say, "*You're* [read *Your*] father has the ninja,"' he said. 'That hurts.' Ninja is slang for AIDS." Richard M. Nangle, "AIDS Rate High Behind Bars," *Sunday Telegram,* 4 Sept. 1994, at A1 (quoting Keith Williamson).
- "'In boxing you don't have that kind of luxury or time. If you mess up in a fight or two, *you're* [read *your*] career could be over.'" Maureen Landis, "Arroyo Wins Gold Gloves Title," *Lancaster New Era,* 29 May 1996, at 9 (quoting Ernie Arroyo).

See SPELLING (A).

LANGUAGE-CHANGE INDEX
1. *your* misused for *you're*: Stage 1
Current ratio (*you're better than* vs.
**your better than*): 92:1
2. *you're* misused for *your*: Stage 1
Current ratio (*your own* vs. **you're own*): 20,949:1

yours, an absolute possessive, is sometimes wrongly written **your's* (an 18th-century throwback that was effectively eradicated from STANDARD ENGLISH during the first half of the 19th century)—e.g.:

- "Outside the ring, Ontario's justice critic (*your's* [read *yours*] truly) tore up the bill and snarled for a large media scrum." Michael Bryant, "Why Ontario's Squeegee Cleanup Won't Wash," *Globe & Mail* (Toronto), 7 Feb. 2000, at A13.
- "'So, when's this big party of *your's* [read *yours*] happening?' asks the salesman." Peter Goddard, "Imperial Esso Man Still Slick as Ever," *Toronto Star,* 5 Aug. 2000, Entertainment §, at 9.
- "I believe all men have consciences that guide them; let *your's* [read *yours*] guide you this election." Letter of Dorothy Jean Paxton-Butler, "GOP Has Right Stance on

Morals, Decency, Life," *Pantagraph* (Bloomington, Ill.), 14 Aug. 2000, at A11.

Sometimes, too, it displaces the simple possessive *your*—e.g.:

- "With the many attractions now calling for *your's* [read *your*] and your family's attention, chances are you may have very little time left to visit the park." Cathy Summerlin, "The Mountains' Wild Side," *Tennessean,* 27 Aug. 2000, at G1.
- "Thanks, Dad . . . . It was through *your's* [read *your*] and Mom's hard work and guidance that I have come this far." Ginny Rudy, "Traveling in Memory of Dad," *Pitt. Post-Gaz.,* 26 Dec. 2000, at E3.

See POSSESSIVES (C), (E).

LANGUAGE-CHANGE INDEX
1. **your's* for *yours*: Stage 1
Current ratio (*letter of yours* vs.
**letter of your's*): 142:1
2. **your's* for *your*: Stage 1

*yous; *youse. These dialectal or low-prestige versions of the plural pronoun *you* have been attested in most parts of the English-speaking world. The spelling **yous* has been common for representing DIALECT since about 1700, and **youse* since the mid-19th century. The spelling **youse* gained predominance in AmE during the first half of the 20th century, but since then the two spellings have been about equally common. The low Americanism **youse guys* is universally so spelled. Cf. **y'all.**

Current ratio (*y'all* vs. **yous* vs. **youse*): 6:1.2:1

youth. Although this word can refer to a young person of either sex <several youths in the community>, it has traditionally had strong connotations of maleness. *W2* adds to its definition "esp., a young man," and Burchfield says of BrE that "its primary sense is a young male person" (*FMEU3* at 862). That has never been its primary sense in AmE, though any correct understanding of the word is heavily context-specific. The plural is preferably pronounced /yooths/—not /yoothz/.

Youth can also be a collective term for the young men and women of a country <all the youth in the land>. In this sense, of course, there is no plural. It would be hard to say *youths of the world* in the way that we might say *peoples of the world,* because in the plural form *youth* simply takes on the abstract sense of young people generally.

yuck; yuk. The standard words for expressing distaste are *yuck* and *yucky,* not the yuckier forms *yuk* and **yukky.* But *yuk* is a CASUALISM meaning (as a noun) a laugh <did it for the yuks> or (as a verb) "to jest or laugh" <yukking it up>.

LANGUAGE-CHANGE INDEX (For the full key, see front matter pp. xxxi, l–li.)
Stage 1: Rejected. **Stage 2:** Widely shunned. **Stage 3:** Widespread but . . . **Stage 4:** Ubiquitous but . . . **Stage 5:** Fully accepted.
Invariably inferior forms marked by asterisk (*). • Ratios represent frequency of prevalent forms vs. variants in current books.

Z

*zebec; *zebeck. See **xebec**.

zeitgeist. Though often capitalized as a German noun, this word may be treated as fully naturalized and therefore lowercased and printed in roman type. BrE sources tend to capitalize and italicize the term more than AmE sources.

zero. When used as an adjective (as it rarely is), *zero* should modify a plural noun, not a singular one. The only number that takes a singular noun is *one*. E.g.: "In 1985, New York City had 71 days that were out of compliance with the EPA standard for carbon monoxide; that number declined to two days in 1991 and *zero day* [read *zero days* or *no days*] last year." Gregg Easterbrook, "Winning the War on Smog," *Newsweek*, 23 Aug. 1993, at 29.

The plural is *zeros*, not *zeroes*—although *zeroes* is the correct verb form. See PLURALS (D).

zetetic; *zetetick. The adjective meaning "proceeding by inquiry or investigation" is preferably spelled *zetetic* in AmE and BrE alike. The Center for Scientific Anomalies at Eastern Michigan University publishes a journal called *The Zetetic Scholar*, devoted to the skeptical analysis of paranormal claims.

ZEUGMA. This figure of speech, literally a "yoking together," involves a word's being a part of two constructions. Sometimes it results in a grammatical error, but sometimes it's simply a felicitous way of phrasing an idea. For example, sometimes a verb or preposition is applied to two other words in different senses, often figuratively in one sense and literally in the other, as in *she took her oath and her seat*. Often, the phrasing is both purposeful and humorous—e.g.:

- "Time flies like an arrow; fruit flies like a banana." Groucho Marx, as quoted in Jim Shea, "Groucho Speaks," *Hartford Courant*, 18 Aug. 1997, at E1. (*Flies* is used in two senses; so is *like*.)
- "I just *blew my nose, a fuse, and three circuit breakers*." (A character on "The Jim Henson Hour," 16 July 1989.)
- "We would venture out into the Gulf of Mexico off Port Aransas, where we *found king mackerel* and *serenity*." Cactus Pryor, "He Called Me Puddin,'" *Tex. Monthly*, Feb. 1992, at 101, 134.
- Notice the title: "Cruel Flood: It Tore at Graves, and at Hearts," Isabel Wilkerson, *N.Y. Times*, 26 Aug. 1993, at A1.
- "You held your breath and the door for me." Alanis Morissette, "Head over Feet" [song] (1995).
- "He turned my life and this old car around." Sara Evans, "Three Chords and the Truth" [song] (1997).

For another good example, see **no object**.

But sometimes zeugma is a kind of grammatical error, as when a single word refers to two or more words in the sentence when it properly applies to only one of them. One type, the nontransferable auxiliary, plagues writers who habitually try to express their ideas in the alternative—e.g.:

- "At the same time, the number of people magnets Disney *has or will put* on its property has multiplied." Tom Brinkmoeller, "Warren Key in a Whole New Competitive World," *Orlando Bus. J.*, 9 Feb. 1996, at 24. (*Put* is made both a past-tense and a present-tense verb; insert another *put* after *has*.)
- "Although outside professionals *have and will be called* in to work on the station, firefighters will do most of the work." "Congrats Achievements," *Cincinnati Enquirer*, 18 July 1996, at B3. (Insert *been* after *have*; otherwise, *called* is nonsensically made both active and passive.)
- "U.S. policy toward Latin America *has and will continue to be held* hostage to the whims of the Senate Foreign Relations Committee and its chairman." Denise Dresser, "Helms' Opposition Makes Weld Look Fine to Mexico," *Houston Chron.*, 6 Aug. 1997, at 29. (*Has* doesn't match up with *be held*; insert *been* after *has*.)

Although commentators have historically tried to distinguish between *zeugma* and *syllepsis*, the distinctions have been confusing and contradictory: "even today agreement on definitions in the rhetorical handbooks is virtually nil." *The New Princeton Encyclopedia of Poetry and Poetics* 1383 (Alex Preminger & T.V.F. Brogan eds., 1993). We're better off using *zeugma* in its broadest sense and not confusing matters by introducing *syllepsis*, a little-known term whose meaning not even the experts agree on.

zibeline (= of, relating to, or involving sables) has predominated since the early 19th century in both AmE and BrE. *Zibelline* is a variant. The word is pronounced /**zib**-ə-lɪn/ or /-leen/. See ANIMAL ADJECTIVES.

Current ratio: 18:1

zinc, vb. (= to coat with zinc), vacillates in its inflected forms. The predominant spellings in AmE and BrE alike are the anomalous *zinced* and *zincing* (pronounced with a -*k*- sound), variants being *zincked* and *zincking*, as well as the willful misspellings *zinked* and *zinking*. See -C-.

Current ratio (*zinced* vs. *zincked*): 2:1

zither (= a type of stringed instrument) has always been the standard spelling since the word was first imported from German in the 18th century. *Zithern* is a variant.

Current ratio: 118:1

zombie; *zombi. The first spelling so predominates today—500-to-1 in a 2008 NEXIS search of AmE—that the original term is almost a lifeless corpse. *Zombi* derives from *nzambi*, the Bantu name of a West African python deity thought to raise the dead. A generally disparaging term in common use (in the sense "a dullard"), *zombie* was, for example, what Canadian army regulars called draftees in World War II. The notion of a *zombie* as a brain-eating monster evolved from horror movies, starting with *White Zombie* (1932), starring Bela Lugosi.

Current ratio (World English): 54:1

ZOMBIE NOUNS. Jargonmongers call them "nominalizations," i.e., verbs that have been changed into nouns. Without the JARGON, one might say that a verb has been buried in a longer noun—usually a noun ending in one of the following suffixes: *-tion*, *-sion*, *-ment*, *-ence*, *-ance*, *-ity*. Today such nouns are commonly called "zombie nouns." It is hardly an exaggeration (make that *one hardly exaggerates*) to say that when the verb will work in context, the better choice is almost always to use it instead of a zombie noun. Thus:

The Zombie Noun	The Verb Uncovered
arbitration	arbitrate
compulsion	compel
computerization	computerize
conformity, -ance	conform
contravention	contravene
dependence	depend
enablement	enable
enforcement	enforce
hospitalization	hospitalize
incorporation	incorporate
knowledge	know
maximization	maximize
mediation	mediate
minimization	minimize
obligation	obligate, oblige
opposition	oppose
penalization	penalize
perpetration	perpetrate
perpetuation	perpetuate
reduction	reduce
utilization	utilize, use
violation	violate

Naturally, you will sometimes need to refer to competition or litigation or regulation as a procedure, and when that is so you must say *competition* or *litigation* or *regulation*. But if a first draft says *the insurance industry's attempts at regulation of doctors*, you would be well advised to change that to *the insurance industry's attempts to regulate doctors*.

Why eliminate zombie nouns? Three reasons are detectable to the naked eye: first, you generally eliminate prepositions in the process (*perform an analysis of* becomes *analyze*); second, you often eliminate BE-VERBS by replacing them with so-called action verbs (*is in violation of* becomes *violates*); and third, you humanize the text by saying who does what—something often obscured by zombie nouns (*upon inspection of the letters* might become *when I inspected the letters*).

A fourth reason is not detectable to the naked eye, though. It is the sum of the three reasons already mentioned. For example, I might write this: "After the transformation of nominalizations, the text has fewer abstractions, so readers' visualization of the discussion finds enhancement." Or I could make the readers' job far more pleasant by writing this: "Uncovering zombie nouns makes writing more concrete, so readers can more easily see what you're talking about." See ABSTRACTITIS.

Though long neglected in books about writing, zombie nouns ought to be a sworn enemy of every serious writer. In technical writing, they often constitute an even more serious problem than PASSIVE VOICE.

zonal; zonary. In AmE and BrE alike, the adjective corresponding to *zone* is *zonal* in all but medical (obstetric) senses.

zonate (= arranged in zones) is the standard spelling in both AmE and BrE. **Zonated* is a variant.

Current ratio: 3:1

zoology is preferably pronounced /zoh-**ol**-ə-jee/—not /zoo-**ol**-ə-jee/. See PRONUNCIATION (B).

Zoroastrianism; *Zoroastrism. For the pre-Islamic religion in Persia, *Zoroastrianism* is the standard term in AmE and BrE alike. **Zoroastrism* is a NEEDLESS VARIANT.

Current ratio: 195:1

zwieback (= a sweetened bread that is baked and then sliced and toasted) is sometimes misspelled **zweiback*, and has been since the late 19th century in both AmE and BrE. E.g.: "At his school, *zwieback* [read *zwieback*], a type of German bread, was the preferred snack." Jane Tinsley Swope, "Calvert and Hillyer," *Baltimore Sun*, 26 Oct. 1994, at A15. The word is pronounced /**swee**-bak/ or /**swi**-bak/.

Current ratio: 16:1

LANGUAGE-CHANGE INDEX (For the full key, see front matter pp. xxxi, l–li.)
Stage 1: Rejected. **Stage 2:** Widely shunned. **Stage 3:** Widespread but . . . **Stage 4:** Ubiquitous but . . . **Stage 5:** Fully accepted.
Invariably inferior forms marked by asterisk (*). • Ratios represent frequency of prevalent forms vs. variants in current books.

GLOSSARY OF GRAMMATICAL, RHETORICAL, AND OTHER LANGUAGE-RELATED TERMS

abbreviation. 1. A shortened form of a word or phrase, created by omitting certain letters or words <New York = N.Y.> <received = rec'd>, or by substituting a symbol for a word <and = &>. • Common types of abbreviations include contractions <you'd = you would>, clipped words (e.g., *lab* from *laboratory*), acronyms, and initialisms. See ACRONYM; INITIALISM; CLIPPING. **2.** The process of shortening a word or phrase by omitting or substituting letters. See pp. 2–4.

ablative case. See CASE.

ablaut /**ab**-lowt/. The variation in the vowels of related words, usu. indicating a change in meaning or use. • This is typical of irregular verbs when they are conjugated <sing–sang–sung>. (See *irregular verb* under VERB.) Ablaut may be a change in a vowel's sound, or its omission, shortening, or lengthening. — Also termed *gradation*; *vowel gradation*.

absolute, n. A word that ordinarily functions as a sentence in itself, or as the nucleus of a sentence, but not as a component within a clause <ouch> <hello> <yes>.

absolute adjective. See *noncomparable adjective* under ADJECTIVE.

absolute comparative. See *dangling comparative* under COMPARATIVE.

absolute construction. A phrase grammatically independent of the rest of the sentence. • Such a construction functions as a sentence adverb or sentence modifier and may consist of (1) a nominative subject <*They having gone out of their way to see the monument,* the hosts knew that the tour shouldn't be rushed>; (2) an infinitive phrase <*To be honest,* I didn't like the cake much>; (3) a participial phrase with an express subject <*The play having been produced,* all that remained was to hope for positive reviews>; or (4) a prepositional phrase <*In isolation,* their actions might seem justified>. See pp. 9–10.

absolute degree. See DEGREE.

absolute form. A form of a possessive pronoun that stands alone without a noun <Mine is the one on the right> (*mine* being an absolute form) <This book is hers> (*hers* being an absolute form). — Also termed *independent form*.

abstractitis. Undesirable lack of concreteness in writing; vapid airiness in style. • Sir Ernest Gowers, who seems to have invented the word in

his second edition of H.W. Fowler's *Dictionary of Modern English Usage* (1965), characterized and described overused abstract language as a disease (hence the suffix -*itis*). He noted that afflicted writers habitually use polysyllabic, abstract words, convoluted syntax, and circumlocutions because of cloudy thinking that gets worse with time, until neither readers nor the writer can tell what a sentence means. But abstractitis can be effectively used in contexts such as parody. George Orwell mocked the trend toward abstractitis by "translating" a passage from Ecclesiastes into "modern" English. The original, in Elizabethan English, read: "I returned, and saw under the sun, that the race is not to the swift, nor the battle to the strong, neither yet bread to the wise, nor yet riches to men of understanding, nor yet favor to men of skill; but time and chance happeneth to them all." Orwell parodied it this way: "Objective consideration of contemporary phenomena compels the conclusion that success or failure in competitive activities exhibits no tendency to be commensurate with innate capacity, but that a considerable element of the unpredictable must invariably be taken into account."

abstract noun. See NOUN.

abstruse, adj. (Of a writing or subject matter) difficult to understand, esp. by reason of remoteness from everyday life or the usual course of thought; recondite.

academese /ə-kad-ə-**meez**/. The style typical of scholarly writing; esp., a mode of discourse that typifies the least appealing qualities of academic writing, namely, obscurity, pedantry, and pomposity. • Academese is characteristic of academicians who are writing for a highly specialized but limited audience, or who have a limited grasp of how to make their arguments clearly and succinctly.

accent. 1. A distinctive set of pronunciation features that characterize a region or social group; a distinctive manner of utterance <a Boston accent>. Cf. DIALECT. **2.** A special emphasis or stress placed on a particular syllable of a word <accent on the first syllable>. • The accent may shift when a word changes form. In *photographer,* the second syllable takes the accent. But in *photographic,* the accent shifts to the third syllable.

3. A diacritical mark (commonly ´) used in writing to show how a syllable should be stressed in pronunciation.

acute accent. In pronunciation, a diacritical mark (´) indicating that the letter or syllable is stressed or given a rising inflection. • In a loanword, especially those from French, the mark also indicates that the final letter or syllable is not silent <*flambé*>. Both stress and a nonsilent final vowel are shown by the acute accents in *résumé*. See DIACRITICAL MARK.

grave accent. A diacritical mark (`) indicating a falling pitch on a vowel (as in the French *père*) or that a final syllable is pronounced separately (as in Shakespeare's *perturbèd spirit*). • This mark most often appears in a word ending with -*ed*. It's uncommon in prose, although it's occasionally useful to distinguish an adjective (as in *learnèd friend,* meaning a well-educated lawyer) from a verb (*the friend learned,* meaning that a person acquired knowledge). See DIACRITICAL MARK.

accidence. 1. The field of grammar dealing with how word forms vary to express and distinguish number, case, person, mood, tense, and so on. • Affixes are one form of accidence. — Also termed *inflectional morphology.* See *inflectional affix* under AFFIX. Cf. MORPHOLOGY; SYNTAX. **2.** The system of inflection in a language; specif., the set of inflections, esp. suffixes and prefixes, that distinguish grammatical categories and relationships. • For instance, the suffix -*ed* often shows that a verb is in the past tense (as in *jog–jogged*), and the prefix *uni-* indicates that there is only one of something (as in *unicycle*). See INFLECTION.

accident. *Grammar.* A property attached to a word but not essential to it, as case, gender, or number.

accismus /ak-**siz**-məs/, n. *Rhetoric.* A feigned refusal of something ardently desired. • When people receive gifts or honors, they may use accismus by modestly declaring something like, "Oh, I couldn't possibly accept this!" or "I'm flattered, but I'm really not worthy of the honor." Political candidates and appointees sometimes engage in something like this tactic by declaring that they would really rather be doing something else than being involved in public life.

accusative case. See *objective case* under CASE.

acquisition. See LANGUAGE ACQUISITION.

acrolect /**ak**-roh-lekt/. The most prestigious variety of a particular language; a standard dialect. Cf. BASILECT.

acronym. 1. A word formed using the initials of a full name or phrase and spoken as a whole word. • For example, CALL is an acronym for Computer Assisted Language Learning. But not all acronyms are written with capital letters: *laser* is an acronym of *light amplification by stimulated emission of radiation*. An acronym is a type of ABBREVIATION. Cf. INITIALISM. **2.** Loosely, a word formed from the first few letters of a series of words (as in *Benelux*, from *Belgium*, the *Netherlands*, and *Luxembourg*). **3.** Loosely, INITIALISM. See pp. 2–3.

acrostic, n. A poem in which the first or last letter of each line, when taken in order, spell out a word, phrase, or sentence. Cf. TELESTICH.

action verb. See VERB.

active voice. See VOICE.

actor. The doer of an action. • Usually the actor is the subject and precedes the action. But in passive voice, the actor comes after it, usually in a prepositional phrase beginning with *by*. — Also termed *agent*. See *active voice* and *passive voice* under VOICE.

acute accent. See ACCENT.

additive coordinating conjunction. See *copulative conjunction* under CONJUNCTION.

adjectival /a-jik-tɪ-vəl/, adj. Of, relating to, or having the import of an adjective.

adjectival clause. See CLAUSE.

adjectival phrase. See PHRASE.

adjective. A word or phrase that describes or qualifies a noun or pronoun. • An adjective is usually placed before the noun it modifies <a blue lamp>, though sometimes it comes after the noun <court-martial>, or predicatively after a verb, such as a *be*-verb <It is hot> or a verb expressing a sense <The water looks choppy>. An adjective can also complement a noun <The options make the car expensive>. Many adjectives have a distinctive suffix such as *-able* <commendable>, *-al* <frontal>, *-ary* <legendary>, *-en* <golden>, *-ful* <helpful>, *-ible* <possible>, *-ic* <prolific>, *-ish* <squeamish>, *-ive* <preventive>, *-less* <pointless>, *-like* <rocklike>, *-ous* <tremendous>, *-some* <wholesome>, and *-y* <windy>. Most adjectives have three forms: POSITIVE <skillful>, COMPARATIVE <more skillful>, and SUPERLATIVE <most skillful>. See pp. 19–21.

absolute adjective. See *noncomparable adjective*.

attributive adjective. A usu. descriptive adjective that precedes the noun it qualifies or modifies; an adjective within a noun phrase <a golden thread> <the tattered envelope>.

compound adjective. 1. An adjective formed from two or more conjoined words <bedridden> <hardscrabble> <roughhewn>. **2.** See *phrasal adjective*.

coordinate adjective. An adjective that appears in a sequence with one or more related adjectives to modify the same noun. • The adjectives are separated by a comma or joined by *and* <calm, understanding manner> <a highly skilled and longtime employee>.

definitive adjective. An adjective that limits a noun by specifying "which one" or "how many"; an adjective that quantifies an exact or definite number <four people> <the first three editions> <He gave a fourth example>. • Definitive adjectives include ordinal and cardinal numbers <first class> <five toes>, definite and indefinite articles <the photograph> <a photograph>, and words such as *many*, *much*, and *some* <some keys won't work>. Other types of adjectives, including demonstrative adjectives such as *this* and *those* <those wands in the cabinet> and possessive adjectives <my cast-iron skillet>, may function as definitive adjectives. See *demonstrative adjective*; *possessive adjective*. Cf. DETERMINER.

demonstrative adjective. An adjective that modifies a noun merely by pointing to it, as opposed to describing it <this jewel>; an adjective that points to an antecedent. • The demonstrative adjectives are *this*, *that* (singular); *these*, *those* (plural); and *such* (preferably meaning "of that kind" and not "the very one just mentioned") <Such pages should be put into that pile over there>. See *definitive adjective*.

descriptive adjective. An adjective that defines the quality, type, or condition of something <positive outlook> <dry, hard soil> <nervous witness>.

distributive adjective. A type of adjective that qualifies a noun as one of a group <each person> <neither player>.

indefinite adjective. An indefinite pronoun used attributively for an indefinite number or quality of persons or things; an adjective that is the same as an indefinite pronoun in form but that modifies a noun <any college> <other people> <many years> <another day>. • Among

the indefinite adjectives are *another*, *any*, *both*, *each*, *either*, *neither*, *one*, *other*, and *some* <Both arguments are debated> <She interviewed other candidates>.

interrogative adjective. The interrogative pronoun *what*, *which*, or *whose* when used as a determiner to pose a question or to identify a particular noun or noun phrase. • An interrogative adjective is identical in form to its corresponding interrogative pronoun, but the pronoun stands alone, whereas the adjective is coupled with a noun or phrase. For example, *what* is an interrogative pronoun in *What do you want?* and an interrogative adjective in *What color are the tomatoes?*

irregular adjective. An adjective that has comparative and superlative forms that are not made by the normal rules <good–better–best> <bad–worse–worst>.

noncomparable adjective. An adjective that defines a state or condition that cannot be intensified or diminished because it is absolute; an adjective that denotes a quality that cannot be graded <unique> <unanimous>. — Also termed *absolute adjective*; *nongradable adjective*.

nongradable adjective. See *noncomparable adjective*.

phrasal adjective. A phrase that functions as a unit to modify a noun <the no-service-can-be-declined policy> <high-school cheerleader>. • With rare exceptions, phrasal adjectives are hyphenated. — Also termed *compound modifier*; *unit modifier*.

possessive adjective. An adjective that denotes ownership or possession and modifies a noun or noun phrase. • In form, a possessive adjective appears similar to a possessive pronoun, but possessive adjectives cannot stand alone. For instance, in response to the question, *Whose car is parked in the driveway?*, you could use the possessive pronoun *mine* <It's mine> or the possessive adjective *my* plus the noun <It's my car>. The possessive adjectives are *my*, *your*, *his*, *her*, *its*, *our*, *your*, and *their*. See *definitive adjective*.

predicate adjective. An adjective that modifies the subject, but comes after a linking verb and is not followed by a noun <Vanessa seems happy>. — Also termed *predicative adjective*.

predicative adjective. See *predicate adjective*.

pronominal adjective /proh-**nom**-ə-nəl/. A pronoun—other than a personal pronoun, *who*, or *none*—that modifies a noun <my> <your>

<his> <her>. • A pronominal adjective specifies a person, place, or thing. For example, in *his choice*, the pronoun *his* functions as an adjective and identifies who has the choice. — Also termed *adjective pronoun*.

proper adjective. An adjective that is derived from a proper noun and begins with a capital letter <American history> <the London Underground>.

qualitative adjective. A gradable adjective identifying a quality of a noun; specif., an adjective that tells what type, kind, class, or feature applies to a noun it modifies <tall cabinet> <green grass>.

quantitative adjective. An adjective that defines the quantity or order of a noun <First Amendment> <few leaders>.

relative adjective. An adjective that has the form of a relative pronoun but that qualifies a noun and introduces a relative clause; specif., an adjective introducing an adjectival clause or a noun clause <without checking who was at the door> <in late winter, by which time the snow will be deep>. • The relative adjectives are *which, that, who, whom, whose,* and *where* <He knew which way to go> <the writer whose book I read>.

adjective clause. See CLAUSE.

adjective complement. See COMPLEMENT.

adjective phrase. See PHRASE.

adjective pronoun. See PRONOUN.

adjectivism. The tendency to overuse adjectives. Cf. ADVERBISM.

adjunct. 1. In some grammatical systems, an adverb that adds detail to the action denoted by the verb, specifying such ideas as time <yesterday> <tomorrow> <nowadays>, place <abroad> <here> <upstairs>, manner <well> <swiftly> <sluggishly>, and extent <partly> <wholly> <mostly>. Cf. CONJUNCT; DISJUNCT; SUBJUNCT. **2.** A word or group of words having secondary importance in a phrase or sentence. — Also termed (in sense 2) *circumstance.*

adnomination /ad-nom-i-**nay**-shən/, n. Punning; paronomasia.

adoxography /ad-ahk-**sahg**-rə-fee/, n. Brilliant, elevated writing about a base, stultifying subject.

adverb. A word that modifies a verb <She wrote *quickly*>, an adjective <a *very* kind gesture>, or another adverb <uttered *quite* thoughtfully>, by expressing time, place, manner, degree, cause, or the like. • It is often distinguished by the suffix *-ly* and typically refers to the circumstances

or way in which an action occurs. Like adjectives, adverbs have three forms: POSITIVE <skillfully>, COMPARATIVE <more skillfully>, and SUPERLATIVE <most skillfully>. Adverbs traditionally fall into five categories: (1) adverbs of place or motion, such as *here, there, up, down*; (2) adverbs of time, such as *now, then, sometimes, never, always, often, ever*; (3) adverbs of manner or quality, such as *so, well, entirely, fully, sincerely*; (4) adverbs of measure or degree, such as *less, much, more, enough, sufficiently*; and (5) adverbs of modality, such as *certainly, not, maybe, perhaps, therefore*.

bare adverb. See *flat adverb.*

conjunctive adverb. An adverb (such as *therefore* and *whenever*) indicating a logical relationship between two clauses; specif., a connective word that combines the functions of a conjunction and an adverb by connecting two clauses while also qualifying a verb. • For example, in the sentence *I don't know when the concert is supposed to begin, when* qualifies the verb phrase *is supposed to begin*. A conjunctive adverb can have relative or interrogative force. — Also termed *connective adverb; adverbial conjunction; illative conjunction; introductory adverb; relative adverb*.

connective adverb. See *conjunctive adverb.*

consequential adverb. An adverb denoting inference, conclusion, or result.

flat adverb. An adverb that has the same form as its corresponding adjective <hard> <fast>. • Compare the examples *Go slow* and *Go slowly*, either of which is permissible (one with a flat adverb and one a normal *-ly* adverb. — Also termed *bare adverb*.

introductory adverb. See *conjunctive adverb.*

locative adverb. An adverb that indicates place or direction <The car moved forward>.

numeric adverb. An adverb indicating order or position <He played first>.

relative adverb. See *conjunctive adverb.*

sentence adverb. An adverb that modifies an entire independent clause, often connecting a sentence with the preceding one <fortunately> <moreover>. See p. 815.

simple adverb. A single-word adverb that qualifies a single part of speech <hardly visible> <entering now>.

adverb complement. See COMPLEMENT.

adverbial, adj. Of, relating to, or functioning as an adverb.

adverbial clause. See CLAUSE.

adverbial conjunction. See CONJUNCTION.

adverbialize, vb. To convert (a word or phrase that does not normally function as an adverb) into an adverb.

adverbial objective. A noun in an adverbial position after a verbal <He works *nights*>.

adverbial phrase. See PHRASE.

adverbism. The tendency to overuse adverbs. Cf. ADJECTIVISM.

adversative /ad-vər-sə-tiv/, adj. **1.** Expressing contrast, antithesis, or opposition <Although we were late for the wedding, we had to stop for gas> (the adversative *although* shows that the dependent clause it introduces was a hindrance to the action in the independent clause). • In professional writing, the most common adversative word is the sentence-starting *But*. **2.** DISJUNCTIVE. — **adversative,** n.

adversative conjunction. See CONJUNCTION.

affirmative. (Of a clause or phrase) positive, without any markers for negation.

affix, n. One or more letters or syllables attached to the beginning or end of a word, or inserted within a word, to modify the word's meaning; a bound morpheme attached to a root. See INFIX; PREFIX; SUFFIX; SYNTHETIC LANGUAGE.

derivational affix. An affix that, when added to a root, changes its part of speech.

inflectional affix. An affix that conveys grammatical information and does not change the root's part of speech.

agency comparative. See *dangling comparative* under COMPARATIVE.

agent. See ACTOR.

agent noun. See NOUN.

agglutination /ə-gloo-tə-**nay**-shən/. **1.** The process of compounding or combining several words into a single word, with minor or no changes to the forms or meanings of the constituent words. **2.** The addition of a suffix to a root to denote the word's grammatical function. **3.** The addition of affixes to a word's root. • The affixes produce new words with various functions. In some languages, especially some Native American languages, a word that has undergone agglutination may serve as a sentence.

agreement. The matching of words or word classes in terms of number (singular or plural), gender (masculine, feminine, or neuter), and person (first, second, or third). — Also termed *concord; congruence*. See CONCORD.

formal agreement. The conventional matching of nouns, demonstratives, personal pronouns, and verbs to mark them as singular or plural, as animate or inanimate, and as first-, second-, or third-person references <That sailor has made his bed> <Those sailors have made their beds>.

notional agreement. The matching of nouns and verbs according to sense as opposed to conventional grammar <A number of people were [not was] there>. See SYNESIS.

proximity agreement. The mismatching of a verb with a noun that intervenes between the grammatical subject and the verb and that differs in number from that subject <The state of the Olympic Games were [read was] uncertain>. Cf. FALSE ATTRACTION.

alexia /ay-lek-see-ə/. The inability to read correctly as a result of brain disease that affects someone who once could read. — Also termed *word-blindness*. — **alexic**, adj.

alingual, adj. (Of a person) not fluent in any language.

alliteration. *Rhetoric.* The repetition of a sound or letter at the beginning of consecutive or nearby words <a maker and model of melodious verse> <Her robe was ringed with rich, red ribbons>. • Alliteration can help make something memorable, but it can also look artificial or careless in prose. It is typically used in elevated oratory and in poetry. See EUPHONY. Cf. ASSONANCE; CONSONANCE. — **alliterative,** adj. See p. 37.

allonym /al-ə-nim/. 1. A (usu. historical) person's name that an author assumes as a pen name. 2. A work published under the name of someone other than the author. — **allony-mous** /ə-lon-ə-məs/, adj.

allomorph. A variation on a morpheme. • Only the sound of the morpheme changes, not the meaning. For example, the morpheme -*ed* indicates that a verb is in past tense. But it is not pronounced the same each time it appears. For example, it is /əd/ in *scolded*, but /d/ in *farmed*, and /t/ in *finished*. See MORPHEME.

allophone /al-ə-fohn/. A variation of a phoneme that is spelled the same but pronounced differently. • For instance, the *k* in *kit* is aspirated, but the *k* in *skit* is not; in these words, the *k* is an allophone of the phoneme *k*. See PHONEME.

allusion /a-loo-zhən/. A brief, usu. indirect reference to something or someone. • An allusion is effective only when the reader is familiar with the reference. Stating that someone is

"as tightfisted as Scrooge" presumes that the reader knows the Charles Dickens story *A Christmas Carol.*

alphabetism. See INITIALISM.

altiloquent /al-til-ə-kwent/, adj. Pompous; highfalutin; high-sounding. — **altiloquence,** n.

ambages /am-bə-jiz/, n. Indirections of speech; language characterized by quibbles, ambiguities, and circumlocutions <The weird sisters of Shakespeare's *Macbeth* are constantly mouthing ambages>. • Although the singular *ambage* exists, the plural form is customary.

ambiguity. 1. Uncertainty of meaning; the state of being equivocal or otherwise obscure. 2. Language that can be reasonably interpreted in two or more ways; a linguistic structure that is susceptible of more than one meaning. • A single word may be ambiguous if it has several meanings and the context does not make it clear what meaning applies. The statement *pain-relieving medicines are sold by frightening people* is ambiguous because *frightening* might mean "scary" or "putting fear into." — **ambiguous,** adj.

grammatical ambiguity. An ambiguity that results when a noun or noun phrase can be interpreted as having more than one grammatical role <The lamb is ready to eat> (meaning either that the meat is well cooked or that the animal is ready for feeding).

grouping ambiguity. An ambiguity that results when adjacent words can be grouped in different ways to impart different meanings <We decided on the airplane> (meaning either *we decided while on the airplane* or *we chose the airplane*).

lexical ambiguity. An ambiguity that results when a word has more than one plausible meaning in a sentence <That house is cold> (meaning either that the temperature is too low or that the feeling is artificial and unwelcoming).

linguistic ambiguity. Ambiguity in which an entire sentence may have more than one interpretation <Visiting relatives can be fun> (meaning either *it is fun to visit relatives* or *it is fun to have relatives visit*).

modification ambiguity. Ambiguity that results when a modifier can be interpreted as describing more than one part of the sentence <We looked at the huge president's portrait> (What was huge? The president? The portrait?).

structural ambiguity. Ambiguity that results from different possible analyses of grammatical structure <She

can't bear children> (meaning either that she dislikes children or that she cannot give birth to a child).

amelioration. See MELIORATION.

amphibology /am-fi-bahl-ə-jee/, adj. 1. The use of an ambiguous statement. 2. The ambiguous statement itself. — Also termed *amphiboly*.

amphiboly. See AMPHIBOLOGY.

amphigory /am-fi-gor-ee/, n. Nonsensical writing; a meaningless composition that has the semblance of sense. — **amphigoric,** adj.

ampollosity /am-pə-lahs-i-tee/, n. A bombastic, inflated prose style.

anacoluthon /a-nə-kə-loo-thon *or* -thən/. *Rhetoric.* A construction in which grammatical cohesion is lacking within a sentence, characterized by a change from one grammatical form to another, disharmonious form. • An anacoluthon usually occurs when the speaker suddenly changes the thought or point of view <He was warned that he had to shape up or what could he expect to happen?>. Sometimes it occurs as an instance of aposiopesis to heighten the rhetorical effect <If I don't find my keys in the next ten minutes—well, you don't want to know what will happen!>. See APOSIOPESIS.

anadiplosis /an-ə-di-ploh-sis/. *Rhetoric.* The repetition of a key word in consecutive clauses or sentences, appearing esp. at the end of one and the beginning of the next <It all comes down to money—money we don't have>. • Francis Bacon (1561–1626) used this device when he wrote, "Men in great places are thrice servants: servants of the sovereign or state; servants of fame; and servants of business." — Also termed *epanastrophe*.

anagoge /an-ə-goh-jee/. Mystical interpretation of a text. — **anagogic** /an-ə-goh-jik/, adj.

analogy /ə-nal-ə-jee/. 1. *Rhetoric.* The comparison of two different things by pointing out correspondences, usu. several of them, esp. to augment conceptual clarity. 2. *Philology.* The influence of the general pattern of a language (e.g., a plural ending in -*s*) to make an individual item (such as *woman*) conform to the pattern (making the plural form *womans*). • Analogy is often at work in children's speech (e.g., *That stinked!*) until the children master irregular forms. Sometimes analogy arises well past the stage of children's speech. Although *dive* and *drive* are similar in appearance, Standard English inflects them differently (*dive–dived–dived* vs. *drive–drove–driven*). Through analogy, *dove* is often used as the past tense of *dive*. (Yet nobody says, "I've diven in that pool before!")

analytic language. *Grammar.* **1.** A language in which every word has only one form and syntactical relationships such as tense, case, and number are shown by function words and word-order. • Context and pragmatic considerations are essential for understanding the meanings of words and sentences in analytic languages. A word or syllable may express a certain concept when it stands alone but express something else when combined with another. Chinese and Vietnamese are analytic languages. To some degree, English is also an analytic language. — Also termed *isolating language*. Cf. SYNTHETIC LANGUAGE. **2.** More loosely, a language that depends more on word-order than on inflections to indicate grammatical relationships, as English differentiates between "Man eats fish" and "Fish eats man."

ananym /**an**-ə-nim/, *n.* A name written backward (as with *Renrag* for *Garner*, or *Retsle* for *Elster*).

anaphora /ə-**na**-for-ə/. **1.** *Rhetoric.* The emphatic repetition of a sound, word, or phrase at the beginning of successive clauses, verses, or sentences. • Martin Luther King's repetition of *I have a dream* in his most famous speech is a kind of large-scale anaphora. — Also termed *epanaphora*; *epibole*. See SYMPLOCE. Cf. CATAPHORA; EPISTROPHE.

- Where is the wise? Where is the scribe? Where is the disputer of the world? (1 Corinthians 1:20)
- The heart of an Irishman is by nature bold, and he confides; it is tender, and he loves; it is generous, and he gives; it is social, and he is hospitable. (John Philpot Curran [1750–1817])
- We shall go on to the end, we shall fight in France, we shall fight on the seas and oceans, we shall fight with growing confidence and growing strength in the air, we shall defend our island, whatever the cost may be, we shall fight on the beaches, we shall fight on the landing grounds, we shall fight in the fields and in the streets, we shall fight in the hills; we shall never surrender. (Winston Churchill [1874–1965])

2. *Grammar.* The use of a word that refers to or substitutes for a word or group of words <Here are some books; read *one*>.

anaphoric /an-ə-**for**-ik/, *adj.* **1.** Of, relating to, or involving anaphora. See ANAPHORA. **2.** Of, relating to, or denoting reference to a preceding word or group of words. Cf. CATAPHORIC.

anaptotic, *adj.* (Of a language) characterized by deterioration and loss of inflected terms, as in English.

anaptyxis /an-ap-**tik**-sis/, *n.* Vowel epenthesis; the insertion of a superfluous vowel into the middle of a word or phrase <ellum> <thataway>. See EPENTHESIS.

anastrophe /ə-**nas**-trə-fee/. **1.** *Rhetoric.* An inversion of the usual order of words in a sentence <Uneasy lies the head that wears a crown> <echoed the hills>. • This device is most common in poetry. For example, T.S. Eliot used it in "The Journey of the Magi" (1927): *the ways deep and the weather sharp*. Anastrophe is sometimes seen in literary prose, too. See INVERSION. **2.** METATHESIS.

Anglo-Saxon. See OLD ENGLISH.

animate, *adj.* (Of an entity) conscious and able to act of its own will, or at least perceived as being able to do so. • In Indo-European languages (the family from which English descends), nouns were classified as animate (usually referring to living creatures but also to some nonliving things) and inanimate (usually referring to immobile things, especially ones that were never alive). In many languages, animate nouns were later subdivided into masculine and feminine genders, and inanimate nouns were assigned neuter gender. See *feminine gender, masculine gender,* and *neuter gender* under GENDER. Cf. INANIMATE.

animate noun. See NOUN.

antanaclasis /ant-ə-**nak**-lə-sis/. *Rhetoric.* **1.** A rhetorical tactic whereby a word or phrase appears twice in the same statement but in different senses <The lot I chose for my house is a lot bigger than I'd realized>. • Vince Lombardi (1913–1970) used this device when he said, "If you aren't *fired* with enthusiasm, you will be *fired* with enthusiasm." Cf. ZEUGMA. **2.** The repetition of a word or phrase after a parenthesis <I was saying—before I was so gently interrupted—I was saying how glad I am to be here>.

antanagoge /ant-ə-**nag**-ə-jee/, *n.* See TU QUOQUE.

antecedent. A noun or noun phrase to which a personal pronoun, a relative pronoun, or a pointing word refers. • The antecedent must agree in number with the referring word. In *although Alan left on time, he arrived late,* the singular masculine *Alan* is the antecedent with which the pronoun *he* agrees. And in *there were a dozen pictures to choose from, and those three are the best,* the plural *pictures* is the antecedent of *those.* See *pointing word*

under WORD; *relative clause* under CLAUSE. Cf. PRONOUN.

antepenult /an-ti-pen-**əlt**/ or /an-ti-**pee**-nəlt/. The third from the last syllable in a word, as with /mə/ in *accommodation.*

anthimeria. See FUNCTIONAL SHIFT.

anthorism /an-thə-**riz**-əm/, *n. Rhetoric.* A counterdefinition; a rhetorical technique of redefining something differently from how one's adversary has defined it.

anthypophora /an-thi-**pahf**-ə-rə/, *n. Rhetoric.* A rhetorical tactic of refuting an objection with a contrary inference or allegation <My opponent says that grammar is difficult to learn. That is so. But its uses are infinite.>.

anticlimax. *Rhetoric.* A sudden transition from a substantive or significant idea to one that is nonsensical or trivial, esp. after building up the importance of something.

antimetabole /an-tee-mə-**tab**-ə-lee/. *Rhetoric.* An inversion of the same words or ideas, usu. with a clever, ironic, or profound twist <a wit with dunces, and a dunce with wits (Alexander Pope [1688–1744]> <Never kiss a fool, and never let a fool kiss you>. See ANTISTROPHE.

antiphrasis /an-**tif**-rə-sis/. *Rhetoric.* The use of a word in a sense opposite to its established one. • For example, in teenage slang and some dialectal varieties of English, *He's bad! Real bad!* can mean "He's good." — **antiphrastic,** *adj.*

antistrophe /an-**tis**-trə-fee/. *Rhetoric.* The repetition of words in a transposed order; a reversal of the order of repeated words or phrases <the student of the professor and the professor of the student> <Ask not what your country can do for you, but what you can do for your country (President John F. Kennedy [1917–1963])>. — Also termed *antimetabole.* — **antistrophic,** *adj.*

antithesis. *Rhetoric.* The placement of contrasting or opposing ideas in a parallel construction <The prodigal robs his heir, as the miser robs himself>. • Examples:

- Not that I loved Caesar less, but that I loved Rome more. (Shakespeare, *Julius Caesar*)
- To err is human, to forgive divine. (Alexander Pope [1688–1744])
- Taste consists in the power of judging, genius in the power of execution. Taste appreciates; genius creates. (George Campbell [1719–1796])

antonomasia /an-ton-ə-**may**-zhə/. *Rhetoric.* **1.** The use of a proper noun in place of a common noun, as when a traitor is called an *Arnold,* a speaker a

Demosthenes, a lawmaker a *Solon,* or a patriot a *Washington.* **2.** The use of an epithet or official title instead of a person's proper name (as in *Mr. Chief Justice* for *Chief Justice John Roberts*).

antonym. A term with a meaning directly opposed to another, with which it can be paired by way of contrast; an opposite. • Many antonyms (such as *white–black; slow–fast*) are very different in appearance. But many words become antonyms of themselves by the addition of a negative prefix such as *in-, non-,* or *un-* <capable–incapable> <entity–nonentity> <happy–unhappy>. Cf. SYNONYM.

aorist /**ay**-ə-rist/, n. In Greek grammar, the simple past tense without limitations of aspect (e.g., completion or continuation) belonging to other past-tense forms. • The aorist corresponds to the simple past tense of English, as in *He sang.*

apagoge /**ap**-ə-goh-jee/, n. *Logic & Rhetoric.* Indirect proof; an argument based on establishing the contrary of a thesis to be impossible or absurd. — **apagogic,** adj.

aphaeresis /ə-**fer**-ə-sis/. The dropping of a word's unaccented initial letter or syllable, as in *coon* for *raccoon, mid* for *amid, possum* for *opossum,* and *squire* for *esquire.* • This commonly occurs in speech (as when *because* becomes *'cause,* and especially *becomes 'specially*) and in some types of writing, such as poetry (as when *it was* becomes *'twas*). Some names undergo aphaeresis (e.g., *Gene, Rita, Trina, Zandra*). — Also spelled *apheresis.* — Also termed *front-cut.* — **aphaeretic,** adj.

aphasia /ə-**fay**-zhə/, n. The loss or impairment of the ability to use or understand language. — **aphasic** /ə-**fay**-zik/, adj.

apheresis. See APHAERESIS.

aphesis /**af**-ə-sis/. The gradual loss of a short, unaccented vowel that begins a word. • Aphesis is a common type of aphaeresis—it might be termed *historical aphaeresis.* For example, the word *esquire* evolved into *squire.* — **aphetic** /ə-**fet**-ik/, adj. — **aphetize,** vb.

aphetism /**af**-ə-tiz-əm/, n. An aphetized word; a form resulting from the loss of a weak initial vowel (e.g., *possum* from *opossum*).

aphonia /ay-**foh**-nee-ə/, n. Loss of voice; inability to produce vocal sound, esp. because of damage to or disturbance of the vocal organs. — Also termed *aphony.* Cf. OBMUTESCENCE (1). — **aphonic,** adj.

aphthong /**af**-thong/, n. One or more letters that are customarily silent in the pronunciation of a word <in good speech, the *t* in *often* is an aphthong>.
• Examples: the first *d* in *Wednesday* /**wenz**-day *or* wenz-dee/, the *p* in *psychology* /sɪ-**kahl**-ə-jee/, the *p* in *pterodactyl* /ter-ə-**dak**-til/, the *th* in *isthmus* /**is**-məs/, and the *ue* in *tongue* /tung/.

apocope /ə-**pah**-kə-pee/. The loss of one or more sounds, syllables, or letters at the end of a word. • Quite a few English words have resulted from apocope, among them *cinema* (from *cinematograph*) and *photo* (from *photograph*). Names often undergo apocope (e.g., *Barb, Ben, Deb, Steph, Theo, Vince*). — Also termed *end-cut.* — **apocopate,** adj. — **apocopate,** vb. See HYPHAERESIS. Cf. CLIPPING.

apodosis /ə-**pahd**-ə-səs/. In a conditional sentence, the clause containing the consequence or result. • The apodosis is not always the last clause as in *if you want to have a picnic, we'll have to go to the market;* it may be the first. In *you can return the jacket if it isn't the right color,* the apodosis is *you can return the jacket* because that clause states the consequence of the mismatch. — Also termed *consequence clause; consequent; conclusion.* See PROTASIS.

apophasis /ə-**pahf**-ə-sis/. *Rhetoric.* The denial of an intention to mention something even while mentioning it <I won't even mention the fact that local and state officials failed to do their jobs>. • Several set phrases in our language signal apophasis, such as *not to mention, to say nothing of,* and *it goes without saying.* Cf. PARALEIPSIS.

aporia /ə-**pohr**-ee-ə/, n. *Rhetoric.* **1.** The suggestion or profession of uncertainty about how to begin, what to say, or what course to take <This may not be the best choice of words, but . . . >. **2.** An equivalency of reasons for and against a proposition.

aposiopesis /ap-ə-sɪ-ə-**pee**-sis/. The leaving of a sentence unfinished as a result of some powerfully intruding emotion or perception; esp., the breaking off of a thought as if from an inability or unwillingness to complete the sentence. • Examples:

• Ye winds, whom I—but it is better to calm the billows. (Virgil [70 B.C.–19 B.C.])
• I admit you are right. I myself . . . You see, a person I knew used to divide people into three categories: those who prefer nothing to hide rather than being obliged to lie, those who prefer lying to having nothing to hide, and finally those who like both lying and the hidden. (Albert Camus [1913–1960])

apostrophe /ə-**pahs**-trə-fee/. **1.** *Rhetoric.* The act or an instance of addressing an absent or dead person, or an abstract idea or imaginary object <Death, be not proud>. **2.** The mark ['], which indicates (1) the omission of one or more letters <can't>, (2) the possessive case <Caroline's book>, or (3) the plural of a letter or abbreviation <mind your p's and q's>. — **apostrophize,** vb.

greengrocer's apostrophe. *British English.* An apostrophe mistakenly placed before a plural *s* (as in *orange's* or *tomato's*). • Occasionally, the term refers to other blunders, such as the supposed plural *asparagu's.* — Also written (appropriately enough, there is no agreement on the point) *greengrocers' apostrophe.*

appellative /ə-**pel**-ə-tiv/, n. A name, esp. a common noun for a class of things.

apposition, n. **1.** The use of an adjunct word or phrase beside a principal word or phrase for reasons of identification, explanation, or commentary; esp., the setting of a noun or noun phrase beside another noun or noun phrase in a synonymous or identifying way, usu. with the force of a condensed clause <Margaret, his mother, . . . >. **2.** The relation of such an adjunct word or phrase to the principal word or phrase.

appositive, n. A word, phrase, or clause that follows another and gives more information about its predecessor; one used in apposition to another <Edward, King of England> <the river Thames>. • For example, in *My friend Leslie will visit in April,* the name *Leslie* is an appositive to *My friend;* it isn't set off by commas because it is restrictive (the speaker has more than one friend). In *Mel Brooks, the writer and comedian, took a cabana just beside ours,* the phrase *the writer and comedian* is an appositive to *Mel Brooks;* it's set off by commas because it's nonrestrictive. See p. 62.

appositive relative clause. See *nonrestrictive relative clause* under CLAUSE.

aptote /**ap**-toht/, n. In Greek grammar, an undeclinable noun; a noun that does not change its form depending on its case. Cf. MONOPTOTE; DIPTOTE; TRIPTOTE.

archaism /**ahr**-kay-iz-əm/. **1.** An old-fashioned or quaint word, phrase, or style. **2.** The revival of obsolete or obsolescent words to achieve some special literary effect.

argot /**ar**-gət *or* ar-goh/. A secret language or dialect that is unique to a certain group within a society. • The term often has a pejorative taint, since *argot* is especially associated with people in lower social strata or regard, such as thieves or hobos. Originally, the term denoted language used for purposes of disguise or concealment. — Also termed *cant*. See DIALECT. Cf. JARGON.

argument. **1.** A statement or series of statements calculated to persuade or convince. **2.** A disagreement or dispute, esp. a heated one. **3.** *Linguistics.* The complement of a verb (as, e.g., subject, direct object, or indirect object). • A verb must have at least one argument, because the argument distinguishes the verb grammatically. An intransitive verb requires only one argument, the subject <Paul writes and Dianne paints> <He laughed heartily>. A transitive verb needs at least two, the subject and a direct object, perhaps also an indirect object <The catcher dropped the ball> <You should send him a gift>.

arrestive, adj. (Of a conjunction such as *but*) tending to arrest.

article. A word such as *a*, *an*, or *the*, used before a word to limit it or to make it more or less definite; a limiting adjective that precedes a noun or noun phrase and determines the noun or phrase's use to indicate something definite (*the*) or indefinite (*a* or *an*). • An article might stand alone or be used with other adjectives (as in *a road* vs. *a brick road* vs. *the yellow-brick road*). Articles are also called *determiners* because they restrict or specify a noun in some way.

definite article. The word *the*. • It refers to a particular person or thing that (1) is understood without additional description (e.g., *the flowers are here* is a shortened form of *the flowers you ordered from Ecuador are here*); (2) is a thing that is about to be described <the hotel on Congress Street>; or (3) is important <the big one>. • The definite article can be used to refer to a group <the basketball team> or, in some circumstances, a plural <The ideas just kept flowing>.

indefinite article. The word *a* or *an*. • Each of these points to a nonspecific object, thing, or person that is not distinguished from the other members of a class. These things may be singular <a city in Texas>, or uncountable <a horde>, or generalized <a notion of truth>. *A* and *an* can't be used with plural nouns. Euphony governs which one should be used in speech and writing. If a word's first letter sounds like a consonant, use *a* <a unicycle> <a hammer>. If it's a vowel sound, use *an* <an unusual place> <an hour>. See EUPHONY.

zero article. An article that is implicitly present, usu. before a mass

or plural noun <The salespeople refolded shirts that shoppers had tried on> (*the* is implicit before *shirts*).

articulation. *Phonetics.* **1.** The use of movements of the organs of speech to produce sound. **2.** The resulting sound or utterance; esp., a consonant that affects syllabic division.

ascensive. See INTENSIVE.

aspect. A feature of a verb marked by an auxiliary form, changes in an internal vowel, or the addition or subtraction of an affix to express the duration and type of activity that a verb denotes. See MOOD; TENSE; VOICE; FORM. — **aspectual,** adj.

aorist aspect. A verb aspect that expresses past action as having occurred at some indefinite time, without implication of continuance or repetition. • This term is primarily used in reference to Greek and Sanskrit grammar. — Also termed *punctual aspect*; *momentaneous aspect.*

continuous aspect. See *progressive aspect.*

durative aspect. See *progressive aspect.*

frequentative aspect /free-**kwen**-tə-tiv/. A verb aspect expressing frequent recurrence or intensity of an action, state, or situation. • Unlike other languages, Standard English has no inflected forms for this purpose. But *-le* is a frequentative particle (e.g., in *chuckle*, *fizzle*, and *sparkle*). — Also termed *iterative aspect.*

imperfective aspect. A verb aspect that expresses action as (1) incomplete (or having no reference to completion), (2) continuing, or (3) repetitive <Thelma was singing>.

iterative aspect. A verb aspect that expresses action as being repeated several times.

momentaneous aspect. A verb aspect that expresses action as having been begun and terminated in an instant. — Also termed *aorist aspect*; *punctual aspect.*

perfective aspect. A verb aspect that expresses action as complete—or implies that it is so <Juan has collected seven witness statements>.

progressive aspect. A verb aspect (formed with a *be*-verb plus the main verb's present participle) showing that an action or state—past, present, or future—was, is, or will be unfinished at the time referred to. • For example, *I'm cooking dinner* is a current unfinished action. And in *I was reading a book when the package came,* *reading* was an unfinished

action at the time the event took place. — Also termed *continuous aspect*; *durative aspect.* See *main verb* under VERB; PARTICIPLE.

punctual aspect. See *aorist aspect*; *momentaneous aspect.*

aspirate /**as**-pə-rət/, n. **1.** A consonant that is articulated (*h* in *half*) or followed (*p* in *poo*) by a puff of air. **2.** The sound of the letter *h*. • Uneducated speakers of English in Great Britain often drop their aitches and are sometimes said to be weak in their aspirates. — **aspirate** /**as**-pə-rayt/, vb.

aspiration. An articulated sound that consists of a puff of breath, such as the *h*-sound in *how* or the slight puff following the *p*-sound in *pot*. Cf. ALLOPHONE.

assimilation. *Phonetics.* The influence of one sound on another that results in the two becoming more similar or even identical. • The word *assimilate* itself derives from Latin *ad-similo,* *commission* derives from L. *con-mis-sio,* *correlative* derives from L. *con-relativus,* *irrelevant* derives from L. *in-relevant,* etc. In *grandma,* the *-nd-* is assimilated to the following *-m-,* hence the pronunciation /**gram**-mə *or* **gram**-maw/.

assonance. The close resemblance or correspondence between vowel sounds in different syllables or words (e.g., *dimwit's inhibition*); the repetition of a sound, esp. a vowel sound, in adjoining or nearby words. • In *My Fair Lady,* Henry Higgins used assonance (a long *a* sound) as part of Eliza Doolittle's speech lessons: "The rain in Spain stays mainly in the plain." Often assonance consists of imperfect or partial rhymes—that is, a repetition of vowel sounds with different consonant sounds, as in *lady* and *baby,* *golden* and *molten,* *squealing* and *bleating,* and *penitent* and *reticent.* Cf. ALLITERATION; CONSONANCE.

asteism /**as**-tee-iz-əm/, n. *Rhetoric.* Politely clever mockery. • The garrulous brother of the taciturn Holy Roman Emperor Charles V once tried to cajole Charles into dinner conversation. Charles used asteism when he replied, "What need that brother, since you have words enough for us both?"

asyndeton /ə-**sin**-də-ton/. *Rhetoric.* The omission of conjunctions that normally join coordinate words, phrases, or clauses in a list. • Many great speakers have used asyndeton to produce memorable statements (e.g., Abraham Lincoln's declaration in the Gettysburg Address, "But, in a larger sense, we cannot dedicate, we cannot consecrate, we cannot hallow this ground"). Cf. POLYSYNDETON.

atonic /ay-**ton**-ik *or* ə-**ton**-ik/, adj. (Of a syllable or word) unaccented <an atonic vowel>.

attraction. See FALSE ATTRACTION.

attribute /**at**-tri-byoot/, n. A word or phrase that functions adjectivally; an adjective.

attributive /ə-**trib**-yə-tiv/, adj. Functioning as an adjective; specif., of, relating to, expressing, or having the nature of an attribute <an attributive noun>. • An attributive adjective directly precedes the noun it modifies (for instance, the word *lovely* in *lovely day*). See *attributive noun* under NOUN.

attributive adjective. See ADJECTIVE.

attributive noun. See NOUN.

augmentative. See INTENSIVE.

aureate diction. 1. The use of unusual words, usu. those borrowed from Latin or Greek, as a conscious stylistic flourish. **2.** The words used for that purpose. • During the Renaissance, influential writers introduced many words, often based on Latin or Greek, into English. Aureate diction was considered a mark of erudition. Among the now-familiar words that first appeared in the Renaissance are *alienate* (from Latin), *catastrophe* (from Greek), *encyclopedia* (from Latin & Greek), *jocular* (from French), *vacuum* (from Latin), and *virus* (from Latin). — Also termed *aureate language*. Cf. INKHORNISM.

autological, adj. (Of a modifying word) having the property denoted. • An autological word describes itself. Examples are *polysyllabic* (it has multiple syllables), *lexiphanic* (it's an ostentatious word), *sesquipedalian* (it's a long word), and *small* (it has only one syllable and five letters). Cf. HETEROLOGICAL.

auxesis /awk-**see**-səs/. *Rhetoric.* The use of a high-sounding word instead of a plain word to exaggerate the importance of something <Multitudinous rationales are extant for incorporating a prolegomenon (= There are many reasons for including a preface)>. • This is a type of hyperbole. — **auxetic** /awk-**set**-ik/, adj. See HYPERBOLE.

auxiliary verb. See VERB.

back-formation. A word formed from another word erroneously thought to be a derivative; the creation of a wrongly supposed original form by subtracting a supposed affix from what appears to be a derivative (as with *administrate* from *administration*, *liaise* from *liaison*, or *typewrite* from *typewriter*). • Some back-formations become standard

because no convenient word expresses the same meaning. For instance, the noun *sculptor* appeared in English in the early 17th century. The verb *sculpt* was derived from it almost two centuries later (possibly using the pattern of *act/actor*). But most back-formations are awkward and unnecessarily displace shorter established words. For example, the verb *orient* predates its derivative noun *orientation* by almost a century and is still in common use; the verb *orientate* was derived from *orientation* almost 50 years later. See p. 90.

badinage /**bad**-[ə]-nahzh/. Playful banter. Cf. PERSIFLAGE.

bahuvrihi /ba-hyoo-**vree**-hee/, adj. [Sanskrit "having much rice"] **1.** (Of a compound word) composed of an adjective plus a noun <redhead> <lazybones> <high-potency>. Cf. KARMADHARAYA. **2.** Forming a compound that is a part of speech different than its head <childless> <lice-ridden>. — **bahuvrihi,** n.

barbarism /**bahr**-bə-riz-əm/. *Rhetoric.* A stylistic flaw involving a misusage or dialectal form in what is intended to be a standard literary piece of writing.

barbarize /**bahr**-bə-riz/, vb. **1.** To speak or write like a barbarian. **2.** To violate grammatical rules.

bare adverb. See *flat adverb* under ADVERB.

bare infinitive. See INFINITIVE.

base, n. See ROOT.

base form. The simplest uninflected variant of a morpheme. See MORPHEME.

Basic English. A simplified version of the English language consisting of only 850 words and intended as a medium of international communication. • C.K. Ogden of Cambridge invented the system in the 1920s and wrote about it in such books as *Basic English* (1930). In this name, the word *Basic* was intended as an acronym for *British American Scientific International Commercial (English)*. — Often shortened to *Basic*.

basilect /**baz**-i-lekt *or* **bas**-i-lekt/, n. The least prestigious variety of a language; the lowest form of a language, typically spoken by the least well-educated members of society. Cf. ACROLECT. — **basilectal,** adj.

bathos /**bay**-thahs/, n. *Rhetoric.* A humorous descent from the sublime to the commonplace. — **bathetic** /bə-**thet**-ik/, adj.

battology /ba-**tahl**-ə-jee/, n. **1.** Idle talk; babbling. **2.** Needless repetition of words or ideas; tiresome repetitiousness. — **battological,** adj. — **battologist,** n.

bavardage /ba-vahr-**dazh**/. Foolish or idle chatter; prattle; twaddle.

belles-lettres /bel **let**-rə/. **1.** Literature regarded as an art form; literature valued for its aesthetic function rather than for its informative substance; esp., light but sophisticated literature. **2.** Literary criticism, esp. of the kind typical of the 19th century; the study of literature.—Also spelled *belles lettres*.

be-verb. See VERB.

bidialectal /bɪ-dɪ-ə-**lek**-təl/, adj. **1.** (Of a person) conversant in two dialects of a language, usu. the standard form and one other. **2.** (Of a speech community or teaching environment) using two linguistic varieties at different times, usu. the standard form and one other.

bilingual /bɪ-**lin**-gwəl/, adj. **1.** (Of a person) fluent or competent in two languages. **2.** (Of inscriptions, government instructions, ballots, etc.) written in two parallel versions with different languages. **3.** (Of an educational regime) involving instruction in two different languages. **4.** (Of a region) having a population among which two languages are commonly spoken.

bilingualism /bɪ-**lin**-gwə-liz-əm/, n. **1.** The ability to use two languages; the habitual use of two languages. **2.** The doctrine that promotes bilingual education. **3.** The coexistence of two official languages within a given polity, as both French and English are used in Canada.

billingsgate /**bil**-ingz-gayt/. Coarse and abusive language. • Originally, the term referred to the type of language one heard at the fish market formerly located in the Billingsgate area of London.

blandishment. Flattering language used as a subtle inducement for someone to do something.

blatherskite /**blath**-er-skɪt/. **1.** A person who talks at length yet says little or nothing of importance; someone whose speech has an exceedingly high ratio of words to ideas. **2.** Nonsense; foolish talk.

blend. A word derived by combining portions of two other words and retaining some of each word's essence. • Blends are relatively common in English. For example, we have *scurry* from *scatter* and *hurry*, and *smog* from *smoke* and *fog*. — Also termed *portmanteau word*. See pp. 711–12.

bloviate /**bloh**-vee-ayt/, vb. To speak garrulously, usu. with inflated rhetoric. — **bloviation,** n.

bound morpheme. See MORPHEME.

brachylogy /bra-**kil**-ə-jee/. **1.** Brevity; conciseness; condensed expression. **2.** An expression in which one or more words essential to the grammar has been omitted.

break Priscian's head. To violate the rules of grammar. • In the 6th century, Priscian [A.D. 500] wrote an 18-volume Latin grammar that was copied by almost every library in Europe and influenced writers for several centuries. He is reputed to have been so devoted to the study of grammar that making an error in his presence hurt him as much as a blow to the head. See PRISCIAN.

breve /breev *or* brev/. In pronunciation, a diacritical mark (˘) indicating that a vowel is short or unstressed. • For example, the mark shows that the vowel sound in *bet* is the short *eh* (/bĕt/). And in the pronunciation for *cooperate*, it indicates that the identical adjacent letters are not pronounced alike (/kŏŏpərāt/). The straight mark is a macron. See DIACRITICAL MARK. Cf. MACRON.

brogue /brohg/, n. **1.** An Irish accent in spoken English. **2.** Any strong regional accent or dialectal pronunciation. — **broguish,** adj.

bromide /broh-mɪd/. *Slang.* A banal or trite platitude or remark, meant to be soothing but suggesting insincerity or vapidity. — **bromidic** /broh-**mid**-ik/, adj.

bunkum. The practice of making insincere political speeches solely to please one's political constituents. — Also spelled *buncombe.* See p. 131.

buried verb. See *zombie noun* under NOUN.

by-form. A word that has an alternative form that is similar but less common <spelled–spelt> <apothegm–apophthegm>. • By-forms may have the same or nearly the same meanings unless they've undergone differentiation. See DIFFERENTIATION; NEEDLESS VARIANT.

cacoepy /kak-ə-wə-pee *or* kə-**koh**-ə-pee/. Bad or incorrect pronunciation. Cf. ORTHOEPY.

cacoethes loquendi /kak-ə-**wee**-theez loh-**kwen**-dɪ/. A mania for talking; esp., a morbid desire for gossip or speechmaking.

cacoethes scribendi /kak-ə-**wee**-theez skrɪ-**ben**-dɪ/. A mania for writing; specif., a morbid desire for authorship. • The term derives from the satires of the Roman poet Juvenal (ca. A.D. 55–127).

cacography /kə-**kahg**-rə-fee/, n. Bad writing; esp., poor spelling. — **cacographic** /kak-ə-**graf**-ik/, adj.

cacology /kə-**kahl**-ə-jee/, n. **1.** A bad use of words. **2.** Vicious mispronunciation.

caconym /**kak**-ə-nim/. An objectionable name or inappropriate term; esp., a term that violates the rules of a system for naming and should therefore not be used as a technical designation (for a start-up company, a newly discovered star, a newly developed drug, etc.). Cf. EUONYM.

cacophony /kə-**kahf**-ə-nee/. *Rhetoric.* An unpleasant or dissonant coupling of words; esp., harsh-sounding words; a harsh combination of sounds. Cf. EUPHONY.

cacozeal /kak-ə-zeel/. Inferior imitation in literary composition; an absurd affectation of writing.

calque /kalk/. See LOAN TRANSLATION.

cant. See ARGOT.

cardinal number. A number denoting quantity rather than place in a sequence (e.g., *three French hens*). Cf. ORDINAL NUMBER.

caritative. See HYPOCORISTIC.

carriwitchet /ka-ri-wich-et/. **1.** An absurd question that is intended to be facetious, such as "What's the distance from San Francisco to next Friday?" **2.** A play on words; PARONOMASIA.

case. 1. A grammatical category for the inflection of nouns and pronouns to indicate their function in a sentence; a noun or pronoun's change in form as a result of its change in function. • Nouns have two cases: common and possessive. Pronouns have three: nominative, objective, and possessive. (See DECLENSION.) Some older grammars, modeled on Latin grammars, recognized five cases: nominative (or subjective), genitive (or possessive), dative, accusative (or objective), and vocative. But modern grammarians have long held that clarity of analysis is gained by recognizing no more cases than the language's inflectional system demands. **2.** In an analytic language, as opposed to a synthetic one, the relation that a noun, adjective, or pronoun bears to some other word in the sentence—as opposed to its change in form.

ablative case. A grammatical case that exists in Latin and certain other Indo-European languages, but not in English, to mark a noun as carrying the sense "by, with, or from" with it. • Among the ablative phrases that English has borrowed from Latin are *ipso facto* (= by the very nature of the case) and *mutatis mutandis* (= with the necessary changes having been made).

accusative case. See *objective case.*

common case. The case of a noun that retains the same form whether it functions as a subject, direct object, or indirect object; esp., the uninflected form of a noun or pronoun, as distinct from its genitive or possessive form. • In English, all nouns have the common case. Some grammarians say that they have no case at all.

dative case. In some Indo-European languages, a case denoting the indirect object of a verb—that is, *to whom* or *for whom* we do a thing <Give the book *to James*>, or *to which* or *for which* we do a thing <Build a house *for Jill*>. The preposition is often omitted <Give *me* one good reason>.

genitive case. The case used to show a thing's source (as in *the car's exhaust*), a trait or characteristic (as in *women's intuition*), or possession or ownership (as in *our new house*). • In English, the genitive case is identical to the possessive case. With animate nouns, the genitive is generally indicated through inflection—the addition of *-'s* for a singular (e.g., *boy's*) or *-s'* for a plural (e.g., *boys'*). With inanimate nouns, the *of*-genitive is more common (e.g., *the purpose of the remark*).

nominative case. The case for the subject of a clause. • English nouns do not use inflections to show the nominative case, but languages such as Latin and Russian do. — Also termed *subjective case.*

objective case. The noun and pronoun case denoting either (1) the person or thing acted on by a verb in the active voice <The computer contains the file> (*file* is objective); or (2) the person or thing related to another element by a connective, such as a preposition <Slip the disk under the door> (*under* is a preposition, *door* is objective) <By whom was this done?> (*by* is a preposition, *whom* is objective). — Also termed *accusative case.*

oblique case. Any case of a noun or pronoun other than the common case or the nominative case.

possessive case. The noun and pronoun case denoting possession or ownership. • The possessive case is reflected in nouns by inflection (*'s* or *s'*) or by the periphrastic form [noun + *of the* + noun]. For example, in *Rachel's desk,* the apostrophe-plus-*s* shows that *Rachel's* is possessive; in *the money is theirs,* the form *theirs* is possessive.

subjective case. See *nominative case.*

casualism. A highly informal expression characteristic of conversation more than of edited prose. See pp. 148–49.

catachresis /kat-ə-**kree**-sis/. *Rhetoric.* **1.** The mistaken use of a word or phrase for another that is similar but does not have the same meaning. • Using *luxurious* (= elegant) for *luxuriant* (= profuse) is an example of catachresis. See MALAPROPISM. **2.** The strained use of a word or phrase without concern for its accepted sense, as occurs in a mixed metaphor. • It is sometimes used for rhetorical effect. In his farewell address, General Douglas MacArthur undoubtedly puzzled many listeners when he said, "I listen vainly, but with thirsty ear." **3.** Any forced use of a word. **4.** The use of a word falsely formed through folk etymology. See ETYMOLOGY (D). — **catachrestic,** adj.

cataphora /kə-**taf**-ə-rə/. *Rhetoric.* The use of a substitute to refer to or stand for a later word or phrase <Although it might be a good investment, the stock is too expensive> (the pronoun *it* having no antecedent but instead referring to *stock,* which occurs later in the sentence). Cf. ANAPHORA.

cataphoric /kat-ə-**for**-ik/, adj. Of, relating to, or denoting reference to a word or group of words occurring later in the sentence. Cf. ANAPHORIC.

catastasis /kə-**tas**-tə-sis/, n. The part of a speech, toward the beginning, in which the speaker sets forth the subject of discussion.

catenative verb. See VERB.

causerie /kohz-**ree** *or* koh-zə-ree/. An informal article, essay, or talk, usu. one of a series on a literary subject.

cedilla /sə-**dil**-ə/. In some Romance languages (e.g., French and Portuguese), a diacritical mark that appears under the letter *c* to indicate that the letter is pronounced softly as an *s* rather than hard as a *k.* • Most loanwords used in English that had cedillas are now usually spelled without <soupçon–soupcon> <garçon–garcon> <façade–facade>. See DIACRITICAL MARK.

cheville /shə-**veel**/. A repeated or meaningless word or phrase used to fill out the end of a sentence when euphony or balance with other sentences is desired. • The device is often used in poetry, as in Lewis Carroll's *Jabberwocky:* "O frabjous day! Callooh! Callay!" (in *Through the Looking Glass* 24 [1871; repr. 1993]).

chiasmus /kɪ-**az**-məs/. *Rhetoric.* The arrangement of adjoining parallel clauses or phrases with inverted word-order <I do not live that I may eat, but I eat that I may live>. • Normally, parallel clauses have an "a-b-a-b" arrangement. In a chiasmus, the order becomes "a-b-b-a." — **chiastic,** adj.

- The children ought not to lay up for the parents, but the parents for the children. (2 Corinthians 12:14)
- To Adam paradise was a home; to the good among his descendants, home is a paradise. (Julius Hare [1795–1855])
- Those gallant men will remain often in my thoughts and in my prayers always. (General Douglas MacArthur [1951])

choplogic. 1. Contentious, complicated, and often illogical or false argument based on trivial points. • Shakespeare used the word effectively in both senses in *Romeo and Juliet* (Act 3, scene 5). When Juliet's father announces he has chosen a husband for Juliet and she argues with him, her father dismisses her and her arguments as "choplogic." **2.** Someone who makes such an argument.

chrestomathy /kres-**tom**-ə-thee/, n. **1.** A collection of choice passages or short works from an author or authors. **2.** A collection of passages intended for use in learning a foreign language. — **chrestomathic** /kres-tə-**math**-ik/, adj.

chunk. *Linguistics.* **1.** A phrase or group of words, usu. learned as a unit when acquiring a language. **2.** A grouping of words customarily used together in a fixed expression, such as *It's a shame that, It's up to you,* or *To make a long story short.*

circumambage /sər-kəm-**am**-bəj/, n. **1.** *Usu. pl.* The use of roundabout or indirect speech or writing, often to avoid a particular subject; an instance of such indirectness. **2.** CIRCUMLOCUTION. See AMBAGES. — **circumambagious** /sər-kəm-am-**bay**-jəs/, adj.

circumflect, vb. To mark with the diacritical mark known as a circumflex. See CIRCUMFLEX.

circumflex. 1. A diacritical mark (ˆ) used over a vowel in a French word to show that a following *s* was elided <hospital–hôpital>. • Although French loanwords with circumflexes (such as *hôtel*) were used in the 19th century, the mark is uncommon today because so many loanwords have become naturalized. An exception is *fête.* It retains the circumflex in British English, but in American English it is a variant spelling of *fete.* See DIACRITICAL MARK. **2.** An accent or tone of voice in which a higher or acute tone is followed by a lower or grave tone within a single syllable.

circumlocution /sər-kəm-loh-**kyoo**-shən/. Roundabout speech or language, or the use of many words where one or two would suffice. — **circumlocutory** /sər-kəm-**lok**-yə-tohr-ee/, adj.

circumstance. See ADJUNCT.

clausal /**klaw**-zəl/, adj. Of, relating to, or consisting of a clause. • The word dates from the early 20th century. Cf. PHRASAL.

clause. A sentence part that contains a subject and verb. • While a clause has two essential elements (subject and predicate), a phrase consists of a group of two or more words not containing both of those elements. See PHRASE; WORD.

adjectival clause. A dependent clause that is used to expand a noun or noun phrase <She was delighted with the letter *that informed her of her admission to college*> <The evening *when we arrived* was eerily foggy> <I went to see the spot *where we met*>. — Also termed *adjective clause.* Cf. *relative clause.*

adverbial clause. A clause that indicates time, place, manner, degree, cause, or the like. • An adverbial clause can modify an adjective, an adverb, or a verb in the independent clause <You're better *than I ever was*> <I came *as soon as I knew you'd arrived*> <*Because you were still sleeping,* I waited *before I started practicing my flute*>. In the category of adverbial clauses some grammarians include (1) tag questions <He didn't go to the movie, *did he?*>, (2) interjected clauses <The dog, *he has declared,* must be fed promptly at 3:00 PM>, and (3) dependent clauses introduced by such words as *whoever* and *whichever* <*Whenever the play begins,* the children will settle down>.

appositive relative clause. See *nonrestrictive relative clause.*

comparative clause. A clause containing (and usu. introduced by) a comparative conjunction. See *comparative conjunction* under CONJUNCTION.

conditional clause. See PROTASIS.

consequence clause. See APODOSIS.

coordinate clauses. The individual clauses of a compound sentence, or the independent clauses of a compound–complex sentence; specif., clauses of the same rank.

defining relative clause. See *restrictive relative clause.*

dependent clause. A clause that, because it does not express a complete idea, must be joined with an independent clause to make sense, typically by a subordinating conjunction such as *before, though,* or *when.* • For example, in the sentence *I left after the mail arrived,* the clause following *after* is dependent. And in *I learned to drive when I was 16,* the clause beginning with *when* is subordinate. Dependent clauses may function as nouns <*That I am interested* should be obvious>, adjectives <Caroline, *who had never before been deep-sea fishing,* caught a shark>, or adverbs <*Because Alexandra scored two points,* the family celebrated>. — Also termed *subordinate clause; subclause.* See *subordinating* *conjunction* under CONJUNCTION. Cf. *independent clause*.

elliptical clause. A clause in which some of the words have been omitted as being understood <When [you are] hitting a golf ball, focus on just one "swing thought">.

embedded clause. A sentence that changes into a relative clause when combined with another sentence. • For example, the sentences *The boy is defending the goal well. The boy is my son.* can be combined into *The boy who is defending the goal so well is my son.* The relative clause *who is defending the goal so well* was derived from the first sentence.

independent clause. A clause that can stand alone as a complete sentence. • For example, in the sentence *I was present when the teacher walked in*, the clause *I was present* could stand alone. — Also termed *main clause*; *principal clause*; *matrix clause*; *superordinate clause*. Cf. *dependent clause*.

main clause. See *independent clause*.

matrix clause. See *independent clause*.

nominal clause. A dependent clause that functions as a noun or noun phrase. • Nominal clauses may begin with an interrogative (such as *who, when, how*) or a conjunction (such as *that, if, which*). For example, in the sentence *I couldn't imagine who would send an invitation*, the nominal clause *who would send an invitation* functions as the direct object. And in *The fact that he confessed is in his favor*, the nominal clause *that he confessed* is an appositive of *the fact*. Nominal clauses aren't as syntactically malleable as nouns because they have no plural form and can't take all the determiners and complements that a noun can. — Also termed *noun clause*.

nondefining relative clause. See *nonrestrictive relative clause*.

nonrestrictive relative clause. A clause beginning with *which, who,* or *whose* and adding nonessential information about the noun it modifies; a relative clause that narrows and identifies the head phrase. • The clause is always set off by commas <My aunt, who published a book recently, will be lecturing tonight>, and could be omitted without affecting the sentence's meaning (in the preceding example, *My aunt* is the subject of the complete sentence and the *who*-clause adds nonessential information). — Also termed *nondefining relative clause*; *appositive relative clause*.

noun clause. See *nominal clause*.

principal clause. See *independent clause*.

reduced relative clause. A relative clause that has lost either a relative pronoun plus a *be*-verb or an object relative pronoun.

relative clause. A dependent clause that modifies an antecedent and is most often expressly introduced by a relative pronoun such as *which, who, whose,* or *that*. See ANTECEDENT.

restrictive relative clause. A clause beginning with *that, who,* or *whose* that contains essential information about the noun or noun phrase it modifies; a relative clause that gives additional information about a noun element that has already been identified. • It is never set off with commas. If the clause were deleted, the meaning of the sentence would be affected. Compare *The room that I slept in was tastefully decorated* with *The room was tastefully decorated*. The restrictive relative clause *that I slept in* identifies a particular room. A restrictive clause never begins with *which*. — Also termed *defining relative clause*.

subordinate clause. See *dependent clause*.

superordinate clause. See *independent clause*.

cledonism /**klee**-də-niz-əm/, n. The practice of using euphemisms; the avoidance of seemingly ominous words.

cleft construction. See *cleft sentence* under SENTENCE.

cleft sentence. See SENTENCE.

cliché. A trite or hackneyed phrase that has been repeated so often as to have become meaningless. • Clichés can also be irritating. Consider this passage: *We chased a red herring and got the wool pulled over our eyes.* Few writers can turn one to effective use, although it can be done <let him who has never used a cliché cast the first stone> <football is a game of inches>. Avoid them. See FIGURE OF SPEECH; SET PHRASE. Cf. IDIOM. See p. 172.

climax. *Rhetoric.* The presentation of ideas or propositions so that each successive one is more forceful than the one preceding it—as in Caesar's *I came; I saw; I conquered*.

clipping. The process by which a word is shortened to produce a new word with the same meaning. • Clippings are abundant in English. For instance, *auto* comes from *automobile, fax* from *facsimile transmission,* and *fridge* from *refrigerator*. Cf. APOCOPE.

clitic /**klit**-ik/. An unstressed word that is pronounced and sometimes written as part of a neighboring word, often in contracted form (e.g., *sanserif* when so spelled, instead of *sans serif*). •

Although it is an independent word, it forms a phonological unit with the words that follow or precede it. There are two types of clitics: enclitics and proclitics. See ENCLITIC; PROCLITIC.

closed syllable. See SYLLABLE.

cognate /**kahg**-nayt/, adj. **1.** (Of two or more languages) descended from the same original language; belonging to the same linguistic family. **2.** (Of two or more words) deriving from the same root; representing the same original word, though having differences because of separate phonetic development <*provenance* is cognate with *provenience*>.

cognate, n. **1.** A word related to another by common origin, such as *provenance* (from French) and *provenience* (from Latin). **2.** A related word in a different language, as French *père* and Spanish *padre*. • The English word *mother*, the German *Mutter*, and the Latin *mater* all have the same meaning, similar forms, and a common origin. It is possible to trace commonality of origin back much further than Classical Latin or Classical Greek and to say that *brotherly* and *fatherly* are cognates because they derive from the same Indo-European root. **3.** *Phonetics.* A sound that is formed in the same place of articulation as another, such as *p, b,* and *m* (each formed with the lips).

cognate object. See OBJECT.

collective noun. See NOUN.

collocation /kol-oh-**kay**-shən/, n. **1.** A customary phrasing; the habitual pairing of one word with others. **2.** A group of words habitually grouped together in a particular order.

colloquial, adj. (Of language) informal; conversational. • Although traditionally the word applied to everyday words not thought to be admissible in formal settings, today— in what in some ways is a more relaxed age—*colloquial* language is considered one of the hallmarks of an effective style. The word *colloquial* is often misunderstood to be equivalent to *vulgar, low,* or *incorrect*. In fact, it describes words and phrases that rightly and frequently occur in ordinary conversation.

colloquy /**kol**-ə-kwee/. **1.** A conversation, a dialogue. **2.** A conference. — **colloquize** /**kol**-ə-kwɪz/, vb. — **colloquist,** n.

comma splice. See RUN-ON SENTENCE.

commatic, adj. (Of a composition) made up of short clauses or sentences; tersely phrased; concise.

comment clause. A clause, such as *I think* or *you know*, expressing an opinion or attitude and typically functioning as a politeness marker in speech. See Laurel J. Brinton, *The Comment Clause in English* (2012).

common, adj. **1.** Of, relating to, or involving the individuals that make up a class or the species that make up a genus. **2.** (Of a word) applicable to individuals of either sex <spouse> <humans>. See EPICENE.

common case. See CASE.

common gender. See GENDER.

common noun. See NOUN.

comparative, adj. Of, relating to, or involving a derived form of an adjective or adverb used, in the comparison of one thing to another, to show a higher degree of a quality or characteristic. See DEGREE.

comparative, n. **1.** The middle of three degrees of comparison for gradable adjectives and adverbs, showing that something has more of a quality than something else to which it is compared; the form of an adjective or adverb used to compare two things. • A comparative adjective or adverb is usually signaled by an *-er* suffix or by *more* or *less*. For example, *better* is the comparative of *good; more refreshingly* is the comparative of *refreshingly*. A comparative adjective compares a specified quality possessed by two things (e.g., in *Weekday newspapers are lighter than the Sunday edition,* the adjective *lighter* is comparative). A comparative adverb compares a specified action or condition common to two things (e.g., in *Lady Katherine speaks more eloquently than Ron does,* the adverbial phrase *more eloquently* is a comparative). — Also termed *comparative degree.* See ADJECTIVE; ADVERB; DEGREE. Cf. POSITIVE; SUPERLATIVE. **2.** A wording that implies comparison; esp., a statement that denotes a higher degree of a quality, relation, etc., from belonging to one object or set of objects as compared with another.

dangling comparative. An unfinished comparative that does not state the criterion or referent of the comparison <We work harder!> (than whom?). — Also termed *agency comparative; absolute comparative; hanging comparative; unfinished comparative.*

double comparative. A nonstandard construction such as *more better* or *more higher.* Cf. *double superlative* under SUPERLATIVE. See p. 187.

periphrastic comparative. A comparative adjective or adverb that changes degree by taking *more* or *less,* esp. when a one-word form ending in *-er* is available.

comparative clause. See CLAUSE.

comparative conjunction. See CONJUNCTION.

comparative degree. See COMPARATIVE.

comparative linguistics. See LINGUISTICS.

complement. 1. A word or group of words completing a grammatical construction in the predicate and describing or being identified with the subject or object (e.g., *long* in *The paragraph is long*). **2.** Any word or group of words that completes a grammatical construction, esp. in the predicate. • In sense 2, a complement may be an adverbial (e.g., *in the car* in *He left it in the car*), an infinitive (e.g., *to go* in *They wanted to go*), or an object (e.g., *the ball* in *She hit the ball*).

adjective complement. **1.** An adjective that completes a clause after a linking verb such as *appear, become, grow, prove,* or *seem* <Bob looks healthy>; a complement consisting of an adjective or adjective phrase. • As with a subject complement, the adjective complement modifies the subject <We are alone> <The water level is much higher>. **2.** An element following an adjective in an adjective phrase and completing the meaning of the adjective <Are you ready to go?> (in which *to go* completes the predicate adjective *ready*). — Also termed *adjectival complement.*

adverb complement. An element following an adverb in an adverbial phrase and completing the meaning of the adverb <Meet me in the lobby after the show> (in which *in the lobby* and *after the show* are adverb complements). — Also termed *adverbial complement.*

object complement. A complement that follows a linking verb and modifies or completes the sentence's object. • Generally, a verb expressing a perception, judgment, or change can allow its direct object to take an object complement: *I saw the driver sleeping.* The object and its complement can be rewritten as a sentence with a subject complement: *The driver was sleeping.*

prepositional complement. A complement that is linked to the verb by a preposition <I wandered around the shops and along the streets> (in which *the shops* completes *around* and *the streets* completes *along*).

subject complement. A complement that follows a linking verb and modifies or completes the sentence's predicate; specif., a noun or an adjective that modifies the subject of a sentence, comes after a linking verb, and completes the sentence. • For

example, in the statement *the grass becomes greener in spring,* the complement refers to the subject *grass,* not the linking verb *becomes,* and completes the grass's description.

compellation. 1. The act of addressing someone directly. **2.** The name, title, or other designation by which one is addressed; appellation.

complementary infinitive. See INFINITIVE.

complete predicate. See PREDICATE.

complete subject. See SUBJECT.

complex–compound sentence. See *compound–complex sentence* under SENTENCE.

complex preposition. See *phrasal preposition* under PREPOSITION.

complex sentence. See SENTENCE.

complex tense. See TENSE.

composition. 1. The art of arranging words into sentences, of sentences into paragraphs, and of paragraphs into various types of discourse. **2.** The production of written work. **3.** The combination of two or more words into a compound word.

compound. A grammatical unit composed of several independent elements. See *compound word* under WORD.

compound adjective. See *phrasal adjective* under ADJECTIVE.

compound–complex sentence. See SENTENCE.

compound conjunction. See CONJUNCTION.

compound indefinite pronoun. See PRONOUN.

compound modifier. See *phrasal adjective* under ADJECTIVE.

compound negation. See NEGATION (1).

compound noun. See NOUN.

compound personal pronoun. See PRONOUN.

compound predicate. See PREDICATE.

compound preposition. See PREPOSITION.

compound relative pronoun. See PRONOUN.

compound sentence. See SENTENCE.

compound subject. See SUBJECT.

compound word. See WORD.

conceit. 1. An elaborate or strained metaphor; a fanciful idea. **2.** An organizing theme or concept for a written work.

concessive, adj. (Of a preposition or conjunction) denoting a word, phrase, or clause that signals a reversal of an idea, opinion, viewpoint, or the like (e.g., introduced by *although, even though, in spite of*).

conciseness. The quality of expressing much in brief form; compact comprehensiveness.

conclusion. See APODOSIS.

concord. A grammatical relationship in which related parts of speech correspond in features such as number, gender, and person <I was> <you were> <they were>. • A subject and its verb must agree in person and number. A pronoun and its antecedent must agree in number, person, gender, and (sometimes, with linking verbs) case. — Also termed *agreement*. See also GENDER; SINGULAR; PERSON.

concrete noun. See NOUN.

conditional clause. See CLAUSE.

conditional conjunction. See CONJUNCTION.

conditional sentence. See SENTENCE.

conduplication /kon-d[y]oo-pli-kay-shən/. *Rhetoric.* The emphatic repetition of a word, with other words intervening between repetitions.—Also termed *conduplicatio.* Cf. EPIZEUXIS.

congruence. See AGREEMENT.

conjugate /kon-jə-gayt/. To inflect (a verb) according to voice, mood, tense, number, and person. — **conjugate** /kon-jə-gət/, adj.

conjugation. 1. The changing of a verb's forms to show voice, mood, tense, number, and person. **2.** A list of a verb's inflectional forms. • In some traditional grammars, the term *conjugation* applied not just to inflection but also to various sets of verb phrases—hence not just *rings* and *rang* but also *will ring, has rung, had rung,* and *will have rung.* This broader interpretation of conjugation was a holdover of Latin grammars. **3.** A class of verbs similarly conjugated <Latin verbs of the second conjugation>.

conjunct. In some grammatical systems, an adverb that connects one sentence or clause with another by expressing addition (e.g., *and* as a sentence-starter), contrast (e.g., *but* as a sentence-starter), or the like. • Although traditional grammarians use the term *conjunction* to cover both midsentence *and*s and sentence-starting *and*s, some modern grammarians call the former *conjunctions* and the latter *conjuncts.* Cf. ADJUNCT; DISJUNCT; SUBJUNCT.

conjunction. A particle (such as *and, or,* or *since*) that joins words, phrases, clauses, or sentences, and that indicates their relationship to one another.

additive coordinating conjunction. See *copulative conjunction.*

adverbial conjunction. See *conjunctive adverb* under ADVERB.

adversative conjunction /ad-vər-sə-tiv/. A conjunction that introduces a contrast or comparison to the first phrase or clause, e.g., *but, still,* and

yet <The roof and the walls are finished, yet there is a lot of inside work to do>. — Also termed *contrasting coordinating conjunction.*

comparative conjunction. A conjunction that expresses equality or difference of degree <as . . . as> <as if> <just as . . . , so . . .> <than>. See *comparative clause* under CLAUSE.

compound conjunction. A conjunction formed from the combination of two or more words, such as *nevertheless* and *notwithstanding.*

conditional conjunction. A conjunction that expresses contingency or some other condition <if> <unless>.

contrasting coordinating conjunction. See *adversative conjunction.*

coordinate conjunction. See *coordinating conjunction.*

coordinating conjunction. A conjunction that joins two elements of identical construction and of equal grammatical rank, such as *and* <Tom and I are going> or *or* <She is deciding whether to fly or drive>. — Also termed *coordinate conjunction; coordinator.*

copulative conjunction /kahp-yə-lə-tiv or kahp-yə-lay-tiv/. A conjunction that joins two coordinate phrases or clauses <and> <also>; esp., one that states an additional fact related to the first clause, e.g., *and, also,* and *moreover* <She is an excellent swimmer; moreover, she knows CPR>. — Also termed *additive coordinating conjunction.*

correlative conjunctions /kə-rel-ə-tiv/. Conjunctions that function as separable compound forms, occur in pairs, and have corresponding meanings <both . . . and> <either . . . or> <neither . . . nor>. See p. 224.

disguised conjunction. A conjunction that has the form of a participle but is used to introduce clauses (e.g., *considering, regarding,* and *supposing*).

disjunctive conjunction /dis-jənk-tiv/. A conjunction that expresses opposed or contrasting ideas; esp., one that denotes separation from or an alternative to the first phrase or clause. • Examples are *but, either, or,* and *nor.* — Also termed *separative coordinating conjunction.*

expletive conjunction /eks-plə-tiv/. A conjunction connecting two thoughts that are not expressed in the same sentence. • The conjunction refers back to a preceding thought or sentence (e.g., *So* in *So they say* and *thus* in *May it always be thus*).

final conjunction. A coordinating conjunction that denotes an inference or consequence. • It introduces

a clause that gives a reason or shows what has been or ought to be done in view of the first clause (e.g., *consequently, hence, so,* and *therefore* <I misread the map, hence my wrong turn>). — Also termed *illative conjunction.*

illative conjunction /il-ə-tiv or i-lay-tiv/. **1.** See *final conjunction.* **2.** See *conjunctive adverb* under ADVERB.

separative coordinating conjunction. See *disjunctive conjunction.*

simple conjunction. A single-word conjunction such as *and, but, if, or,* or *through.*

subordinating conjunction. A conjunction that introduces a dependent clause. — Also termed *subordinator.* See *dependent clause* under CLAUSE.

conjunctive /kən-jənk-tiv/, adj. Serving to connect words, phrases, clauses, and sentences. Cf. DISJUNCTIVE.

conjunctive adverb. See ADVERB.

connecting verb. See *linking verb* under VERB.

connective, n. A word that connects one sentence part to another; specif., a conjunction, preposition, or conjunctive adverb.

connective adverb. See *conjunctive adverb* under ADVERB.

connotation. Secondary meaning implied by a word or phrase, though not part of its literal meaning; semantic suggestiveness. • For example, the word *fire* has emotional associations with both "warmth" and "danger," depending on the context. Cf. DENOTATION.

consequence clause. See APODOSIS.

consequent. See APODOSIS.

consequential adverb. See ADVERB.

consonance. The repetition of a consonant sound in stressed syllables of two or more words <Catch and fetch, my dear pooch!>. • Consonance denotes especially the harmony of final consonant sounds, with unlike vowel sounds, as in *pull* and *call, black* and *fleck,* or *come* and *home.* Cf. ALLITERATION; ASSONANCE.

consonant. 1. One of a class of speech sounds (such as *g, l, n,* and *s*) that are enunciated by constricting or closing one or more points of the breath channel; a letter that represents such a sound (such as *g, l, n,* and *s*). See PHONEME. See **aorist. 2.** An alphabetic element other than a vowel. Cf. SEMIVOWEL; VOWEL.

constative /kon-stə-tiv/, adj. **1.** Of, relating to, or involving the aorist tense. See AORIST. **2.** (Of a statement) capable of being true or false.

constituent. A sequence of words grouped together and functioning as a grammatical unit.

constructio ad sensum /kən-**strək**-shee-oh ad **sen**-səm/. See SYNESIS.

construction. 1. The syntactic arrangement of words in a sentence. **2.** The connection between verbs and their objects or complements, between adjectives and their extensions, between prepositions and their objects. **3.** The explanation or interpretation of a statement or text; sense.

construe /kən-**stroo**/, vb. **1.** To combine a verb, adjective, preposition, or other part of speech with other words to which it is syntactically related <*oblivious* may be construed with *of* or *to*>. **2.** To analyze or explain the grammatical construction of a sentence. **3.** (Of a series of words) to be subject to grammatical analysis or interpretation. **4.** To explain the meaning of (a sentence, text, etc.); to interpret.

content word. A word that has intrinsic meaning in a lexicon. Cf. EMPTY WORD.

continuant. See FRICATIVE.

continuous aspect. See *progressive aspect* under ASPECT.

contraction. 1. The combining of two words into one by shortening either or both of the words or by replacing letters with a symbol. • In Standard English, many contractions consist of a verb + *not*, such as when *do not* becomes *don't* and *will not* becomes *won't*. Auxiliaries often appear in contractions after personal pronouns <I've> <you'd> <mustn't>. **2.** Any word resulting from such a combination.

contrasting coordinating conjunction. See *adversative conjunction* under CONJUNCTION.

contronym /**kon**-trə-nim/. A word that bears contradictory senses, such as *oversight* ("supervision" or "neglect"). See p. 218.

conversion. See FUNCTIONAL SHIFT.

coordinate, adj. Having the same order or rank *with* something else; equal in degree or importance <coordinate clauses>. Cf. SUBORDINATE.

coordinate adjective. See ADJECTIVE.

coordinate clauses. See CLAUSE.

coordinate conjunction. See *coordinating conjunction* under CONJUNCTION.

coordinating conjunction. See CONJUNCTION.

coordination. The process or result of linking two parts of speech of equal status by using coordinating conjunctions. • Only words in the same class (e.g., nouns or verbs) can be properly coordinated <cup and glass> <run and jump>—not words in different classes <beautiful and oversee>. See *coordinating conjunction* under CONJUNCTION.

coprolalia /kahp-roh-**layl**-yə/, n. The use of extremely coarse or disgusting language, esp. as a result of a mental disorder.

copula. The part of a proposition that connects the subject and the verb; esp., a *be*-verb employed as a sign of predication. See *linking verb* under VERB. — **copulative,** adj.

copular verb. See *linking verb* under VERB.

copulative conjunction. See CONJUNCTION.

copulative verb. See *linking verb* under VERB.

copyediting. See LINE-EDITING.

correlative /kə-**rel**-ə-tiv/, adj. (Of a pair of words or phrases) having reciprocal or corresponding functions and typically being used together (but not side by side) in a sentence. See *correlative conjunctions* under CONJUNCTION.

correlative conjunctions. See CONJUNCTION.

correption /kə-**rep**-shən/. A shortening of a word's or syllable's pronunciation.

counter word. A word that has recently come into widespread use in a sense or use other than its traditional one.

count noun. See NOUN.

crasis /**kray**-sis/. The blending of two vowels belonging to two different words that come into contact with each other (as in *th'oar* for *the oar*). — Also termed *syncresis*. See SYNALOEPHA.

creole /**kree**-ohl/. A language that began as a pidgin but has become the first language for some speakers; specif., a language that has developed from a standard language, first being used as the second language of a group and then becoming the group's usual language, with changes in sounds, grammar, and vocabulary. Cf. PIDGIN.

cryptolect /**krip**-tə-lekt/, n. A secret language used by a particular group or a segment of society.

dangler. A participle or participial phrase that is not syntactically connected to the noun it is meant to modify; a nonfinite predicate that cannot be properly linked to a noun or noun phrase in the rest of the sentence. • For example, in *Waving in moderate winds, the golfer took dead aim at the flag,* the action of the introductory phrase wants to attach to the closest noun (*golfer* rather than *flag*). — Also termed *dangling modifier.* See *dangling participle* under PARTICIPLE.

dangling, adj. (Of a participle or other modifier) not part of a proper grammatical construction.

dangling participle. See PARTICIPLE.

dative case. See CASE.

decasyllable /**de**-kə-sil-ə-bəl/, n. A line or word of ten syllables. — **decasyllabic** /de-kə-si-**lab**-ik/, adj.

declamation, n. **1.** The act of reciting a passage or selected oration, esp. as an exercise in intonation, elocution, or delivery. **2.** A speech or passage to be recited from memory in public. **3.** Bombastic, turgid oratory; an impassioned rhetorical condemnation or tirade; a harangue. **4.** A speech or writing with more sound than sense. — **declamatory,** adj.

declarative /di-**klair**-ə-tiv/, adj. Characterizing a sentence in which the speaker makes a statement (e.g., *Our nieces are visiting from Bangkok*). Most sentences are declarative. See *declarative sentence* under SENTENCE.

declarative mood. See MOOD.

declarative sentence. See SENTENCE.

declension. 1. The inflection of nouns or pronouns, depending on how they are used; esp., the deviation of a noun or pronoun's form from that of its nominative case. • In English, declension does not play a major role because there are no case endings on nouns (as there are in Latin and Romance languages). English has only seven pronouns that are declined as follows (for each, the nominative, objective, possessive, and absolute forms are shown [possessives and absolutes are different only in the first set and the last two sets]): *I–me–my–mine*; *you–your–yours*; *he–him–his*; *she–her–hers*; *it–it–its*; *we–us–ours*; and *they–them–their–theirs.* — Also termed *paradigm.* **2.** A listing of the inflected forms of a noun or pronoun; the rehearsing of a noun or pronoun's inflections. — **decline,** vb.

declinable, adj. Having inflections. Cf. UNDECLINABLE.

decussation /dek-ə-**say**-shən/. See CHIASMUS.

deep structure. In transformational grammar, the set of underlying semantic and syntactic relationships in a sentence. Cf. SURFACE STRUCTURE.

defective, adj. (Of a noun, verb, etc.) lacking some of the usual forms of declension or conjugation.

defective verb. See VERB.

deferred preposition. See *terminal preposition* under PREPOSITION.

definiendum /di-fi-nee-**en**-dəm/. A word, phrase, or symbol that is defined.

definiens /di-**fin**-ee-enz/. A definition; the words or symbols used in defining something.

defining relative clause. See *restrictive relative clause* under CLAUSE.

definite article. See ARTICLE.

definitive adjective. See ADJECTIVE.

degree. An indicator of the extent to which gradable adverbs or adjectives compare in intensity. • In their changing forms, gradable adverbs and adjectives display greater or lesser intensity in each of three degrees called positive or absolute (the base degree), comparative (the second degree), and superlative (the third degree) <lively–livelier–liveliest> <bad–worse–worst>. — Also termed *grade*. See POSITIVE; COMPARATIVE; SUPERLATIVE.

degree modifier. See INTENSIFIER.

deictic /dɪk-tik or dayk-/, adj. (Of a word) showing or directly pointing to something, esp. something's identity or a time or place. • The referent is determined by the context of the surrounding words. For example, in *today, I need you here*, the words *today, I, you*, and *here* are deictic. Identifying the referent for each word depends on who speaks or writes the sentence, who is being spoken to, and when and where it is said. For example, the word *I* points to the person who produces the sentence, and *you* to the person receiving it. See *pointing word* under WORD.

deictic pronoun. See *demonstrative pronoun* under PRONOUN.

deictic term. See *pointing word* under WORD.

deletion. The suppression of one or more sounds in the pronunciation of a word (hence *probably* becomes /**prob**-lee/ or even /**prol**-ee/).

demonstrative /də-**mon**-strə-tiv/, adj. (Of an adjective or pronoun) distinguishing a referent based on its location relative to the speaker, esp. *this, that, these*, and *those*. • A demonstrative word can be used as a determiner (a type of adjective) <Please take those papers> or as a pronoun <Give him that>.

demonstrative adjective. See ADJECTIVE.

demonstrative pronoun. See PRONOUN.

denotation. The literal meaning of a word or phrase, unaffected by emotion, attitude, or color. • For example, the denotation of *red rose* is a bright-colored flower that grows on a prickly shrub. But it also has symbolic meanings that are not suggested by its definition, such as an expression of love. Cf. CONNOTATION.

deontic, adj. See *deontic modality* under MODALITY.

dependent clause. See CLAUSE.

derivation. The process of forming new words from other words or the roots of words by adding an affix; affixation. • For example, an affix can be added to change a noun into an adjective <inspiration–inspirational> or a verb into a noun <deliver–deliverance>. And different words are formed when different affixes are added to a root such as *graph*: *phonograph* (n.) and *graphic* (adj.).

derivational affix. See AFFIX.

derivative, n. A word in some way formed from another word, as by adding an affix.

descriptive adjective. See ADJECTIVE.

descriptive grammar. 1. The study of linguistic structures focusing on a language's actual use by speakers. • Descriptive grammar assumes that the acid test of acceptability in language is whether native speakers of the language actually use a particular wording. It is not concerned with standardizing rules or applying rules to all speakers—only with determining what rules are actually used by native speakers. See GRAMMAR. Cf. PRESCRIPTIVE GRAMMAR. **2.** A book that systematically records the findings of such a study.

descriptive linguistics. See LINGUISTICS.

descriptivism /di-**skrip**-ti-vi-zəm/. An approach to language study that analyzes how people use language without making value judgments in deciding what is correct or incorrect, effective or ineffective. Cf. PRESCRIPTIVISM.

determiner. A type of adjective that limits how a noun phrase applies, including articles (*a, an*, and *the*), demonstrative adjectives (*this, that, these*, and *those*), and indefinite adjectives (e.g., *all, any, each, every, some, few*). Cf. *definitive adjective* under ADJECTIVE.

deverbal, adj. (Of a word, esp. an agent noun) derived from a verb. See DEVERBATIVE.

deverbative, n. A word derived from a verb; a deverbal word <runner> <skier>. Cf. NOMINALIZATION.

diachronic /dɪ-ə-**kron**-ik/, adj. Of, relating to, or involving the historical development of a language over time. • The historical approach to linguistics is often called diachronic because it looks at linguistic phenomena through previous ages to see how the current language, or a particular element in it, has evolved. Cf. SYNCHRONIC.

diachronic linguistics. See *historical linguistics* under LINGUISTICS.

diacope /dɪ-**ak**-ə-pee/. See TMESIS.

diacritic. See DIACRITICAL MARK.

diacritical mark. An orthographical character indicating that a letter or syllable has a special phonetic quality; specif., a dot, line, or other mark added to or nearby a letter usu. for one of four reasons: (1) to distinguish it from a similar letter; (2) to give it a different phonetic value; (3) to show some particular accent, emphasis, or tone; or (4) to indicate exact pronunciation, as in a dictionary. • Diacritical marks are usually seen in pronunciation guides or loanwords. For example, a breve (˘) indicates that a vowel is short or unstressed. When first adopted into English, some loanwords had diacritical marks <hôtel> <façade> <coördinate> <résumé>, but over time the marks tend to fall into disuse. — Also termed *diacritic*. See *acute accent* and *grave accent* under ACCENT; BREVE; CEDILLA; CIRCUMFLEX; DIAERESIS; MACRON; OKINA; TILDE; UMLAUT. See p. 271.

diaeresis /dɪ-**er**-ə-sis *or* dɪ-**eer**-ə-sis/. **1.** A diacritical mark consisting of two dots (¨) placed over a vowel that adjoins another vowel to indicate that the marked vowel should be sounded separately from the adjacent vowel <naïve> <Chloë> rather than merged into a diphthong or left silent. • In modern American English, the diaeresis is often dropped, even in proper names, although the pronunciation does not change <coöperate–cooperate> <Brontë–Bronte>. Any vowel can take a diaeresis, but *e, o*, and *i* are the most common in English. — Also spelled *dieresis*. See DIACRITICAL MARK. Cf. UMLAUT. **2.** The evolution of one syllable into two, esp. through separating the vowel elements of a digraph or diphthong. • For example, *medieval* is usually pronounced /med-**ee**-vəl/, but sometimes /med-i-**ee**-vəl/. Cf. SYNAERESIS.

diagramming. The use of lines and words to break a sentence down into its component parts and show their relationships for analytical or pedagogical purposes. — Also spelled *diagraming*.

dialect. A linguistic variety peculiar to a particular geographical area or used by members of a specific social class or group; specif., the linguistic features of a particular locality or class, esp. as distinguished from the speech of educated people. • It may differ from the standard form in characteristics such as accent, pronunciation, vocabulary, and grammatical structures. See ACCENT; ARGOT; IDIOLECT; JARGON; NONSTANDARD ENGLISH; PATOIS; PROVINCIALISM; SLANG. Cf. STANDARD ENGLISH. See pp. 272–74.

dialectology /dɪ-ə-lek-**tahl**-ə-jee/, n. The study of dialects; esp., the branch of linguistics concerned with understanding and describing dialects. — **dialectologist,** n.

diallage /dı-**al**-ə-jee/, n. *Rhetoric.* An advocate's presentation of arguments from various points of view, concluding with the argument that one particular point of view is soundest and should govern the outcome.

dialogism /dı-**al**-ə-jiz-əm/, n. **1.** *Rhetoric.* The use of dialogue to explain a subject, with characters to whom the author imputes various ideas and feelings. • Plato's *Dialogues* are a prime example. **2.** A conversational phrase; a colloquialism. **3.** A conversational style.

diasynthesis. See SYNTAX (2).

diasyrm /dı-ə-sərm/, n. *Rhetoric.* Rhetorical disparagement or ridicule.

diction. 1. The manner of using words in literature, oratory, or song; the way in which something is expressed in words, including articulation, pronunciation, intonation, and punctuation. **2.** The part of rhetoric dealing with word choice and word arrangement.

dieresis. See DIAERESIS.

differentiation. A process by which similar words, esp. by-forms (e.g., *derisive* and *derisory*), diverge in meaning, so that each word becomes distinctly useful. • For example, the verb *estimate* was once used to mean (1) "to assess" or (2) "to regard highly." Meanwhile, *esteem* was used to mean (1) "to regard highly" or (2) "to assess." Today the differentiation between the words is complete, and sense 2 of each is obsolete. If by-forms don't undergo differentiation, prescriptivists are likely to label the less widely used form a "needless variant." See BY-FORM; NEEDLESS VARIANT. See pp. 277–78.

diffuseness. The state or quality of being unfocused, disorganized, and verbose in speech or writing. — **diffuse,** adj.

diglossia /dı-**glahs**-ee-ə/, n. The coexistence of two languages within a speech community, usu. standard form and a regional dialect. Cf. MONOGLOSSIA; TRIGLOSSIA.

diglot /**dı**-glot/, adj. **1.** Bilingual. **2.** Composed or translated into two languages.

digraph /**dı**-graf/. **1.** A combination of two letters to represent one sound, such as the initial and final consonant sounds in *thrush* or the two vowels in *boat*. **2.** A ligature of two vowels that are not diphthongs but are written together as a single character, such as æ (ae) and œ (oe). Cf. DIPHTHONG.

digression. A divergence or departure from the primary point or line of thought. — **digress,** vb. — **digressive,** adj.

diminutive, n. A word that expresses youth, endearment, or a diminished size or status, usu. through a suffix. • The principal diminutive suffixes in English are *-et*, *-ette*, *-ling*, *-ock*, *-in*, *-y*, *-ie*, *-kin*. — Also termed *hypocoristic*.

dimorphism /dı-**morf**-iz-əm/, n. The existence of a word in two or more forms called doublets <dent–dint> <fat–vat> <church–kirk>. • To be a true dimorphism, the source of the two words must be identical. See DOUBLET.

diphthong /**dif**-thong/. A pair of vowels blended into one syllable to produce a single sound; specif., a succession of two vowels joined in a single syllable by a continuous glide of the tongue and lips from one vowel position to another <loud> <noise>. • In a *proper diphthong*, both vowels are pronounced, but they are blended so as to form one syllable. In an *improper diphthong* (not really a diphthong at all), two or more vowels appear in one syllable to make a simple sound <each> <people>. Formerly, writers such as Samuel Johnson (1709–1784) used the term *diphthong* for what modern writers call a *digraph* (e.g., the *ae* in *aesthetic* or the *oe* in *oenology*). The word is sometimes mispronounced /**dip**-thong/.

diptote /**dip**-toht/, n. In certain Indo-European languages, a noun having only two cases. Cf. APTOTE; MONOPTOTE; TRIPTOTE.

direct object. See OBJECT.

discourse. 1. A sequence of statements that together constitute a unified communication. • Examples are conversations, lectures, letters, newspaper articles, short stories, and novels.

direct discourse. Direct quotation involving the repeating of someone else's precise words. • In print, direct discourse is marked by quotation marks or by an extended quotation that is set off by indenting it <He asked, "Do you feel bad?">. — Also termed *oratio recta*.

indirect discourse. The reporting of an earlier utterance without the use of direct quotation <He asked whether I felt bad>. — Also termed *oratio obliqua*.

2. Traditionally, a formal discussion of a subject; a dissertation or treatise.

discourse analysis. *Linguistics.* **1.** The close study of texts or utterances longer than one sentence for the purpose of understanding linguistic content or sociolinguistic context. **2.** The result of such study.

disguised conjunction. See CONJUNCTION.

disjunct. In some grammatical systems, an adverb that affects the interpretation of the whole clause or sentence by expressing either attitude toward the thought of the sentence <unfortunately> <regrettably> or the likelihood of something's occurrence <perhaps> <possibly>. Cf. ADJUNCT; CONJUNCT; SUBJUNCT.

disjunction. 1. A coordinating conjunction that signals a choice between conjoined elements. **2.** The grammatical structure created by such a coordinating conjunction.

disjunctive, adj. **1.** Signaling a relationship of alternatives, contrast, or opposition <rough but good> <neither wholly right nor wholly wrong>. **2.** ADVERSATIVE. Cf. CONJUNCTIVE.

disjunctive conjunction. See CONJUNCTION.

dissimilation. *Phonetics.* **1.** A process by which two nearby consonant sounds that are identical or similar gradually become less alike. • In English, *l* and *r* are the letters whose sounds are most often affected by dissimilation. Two nearby *r* sounds can be difficult to articulate, so dissimilation may change the second *r* to *l*. This process produced the English word *marble* from the French *marbre*. And in *colonel*, although the word is spelled with two *l*'s, the first *l* is pronounced as though it were an *r* (/**kər**-nəl/). Many words are still written with certain consonants that are often dropped altogether in speech <listen>. **2.** The dropping of a consonant sound when a similar or identical sound is repeated within a word. • For example, the first *r* in *governor* is usually dropped and the word pronounced /**gəv**-ə-nər/ instead of /**gəv**-ər-nər/. In *government*, the *n* is often dropped (/**gəv**-ər-mənt/). Those pronunciations are widely accepted, but others with dropped sounds are not. For example, failing to articulate the first *r* in *library* (e.g., saying /**lı**-bair-ee/) is considered dialectal. — **dissimilate,** vb.

dissyllable /di-**sil**-ə-bəl/, n. A word of two syllables. — Also spelled *disyllable*. — **dissyllabic** /dis-i-**lab**-ik/, adj.

distributive /di-**strib**-yə-tiv/, adj. Referring to things individually, not collectively, so as to express separation or emphasize individuality. • Adjectives such as *each*, *either*, and *every* are distributive. — **distributive,** n.

distributive adjective. See ADJECTIVE.

distributive pronoun. See PRONOUN.

disyllable. See dissyllable.

ditransitive, adj. (Of a verb) taking both a direct and an indirect object.

ditransitive prepositional verb. See VERB.

ditransitive verb. See VERB.

dittograph. One or more letters or words mistakenly repeated when printing or copying a writing. — **dittographic,** adj. — **dittography,** n.

dittography. The unintentional repetition of a written letter, syllable, word, or series of letters, syllables, or words, esp. when copying. • A person may copy mechanically, without thinking about what he or she has just copied, and so write "wizzard" for *wizard* and "competitition" for *competition.*

dodecasyllable /doh-**dek**-ə-sil-ə-bəl/, n. A line or word of 12 syllables. — **dodecasyllabic** /doh-de-kə-si-**lab**-ik/, adj.

doggerel /**dog**-ə-rəl/ or /**daw**-gə-/, adj. **1.** (Of poetry or verses) rhythmically irregular, usu. to heighten burlesque or comic content. **2.** (Of writing or verses) badly expressed or composed; trivial.

doggerel, n. **1.** Humorous poetry or verses that are loosely styled and have an irregular rhythm. **2.** Poetry or writing that is trivial or badly composed.

double comparative. See COMPARATIVE.

double-dash construction. A grammatical construction in which a pair of long dashes sets off part of a sentence to emphasize or distinguish its content. • This construction is stronger than using parentheses or a pair of commas. Compare *we saw—and understood— the message left on Roanoke* with *we saw (and understood) the message* or *we saw, (and understood, the message.*

double entendre /dəb-əl ahn-**tahn**-drə *or* doob-lə ahn-**tahn**-drə/. **1.** A word or phrase having two meanings, one of the two usu. being ribald or off-color. **2.** Ambiguity arising from the double sense of a word or phrase. • The phrase *double entendre* isn't native to French, the closest expression being *mot à double entente* "a word (or phrase) with a double meaning." The English phrase, dating from the late 17th century, appears to have originated as bungled French.

double negative. 1. A construction in which two negative words are used, usu. in dialect <I don't never get asked to do chores>. • Among the most common double negatives are combinations of *n't* with *hardly* <couldn't hardly think> and *n't* with *no* <I can't get no satisfaction>. Double negatives are one characteristic of nonstandard language. **2.** A type of understatement (litotes) in which two negatives express a kind of positive or neutral thought. • *Your argument is*

not unjustifiable contains *not* and the negative prefix *-un,* yet the sense is close to (but not quite as strong as) *Your argument is justifiable.*

doublespeak. Language intentionally used to deceive, esp. by concealing or misrepresenting facts. • Contrary to popular belief, this word wasn't used by George Orwell (1903–1950) in *1984;* it first appeared in the 1950s. But Orwell was the first to use -*speak* as a suffix, as in *newspeak* and *oldspeak,* and used the word *doublethink.* Doublespeak is most often used by bureaucracies, businesses, and the military. Doublespeak is present, for example, in euphemisms such as *enhanced coercive interrogation techniques* (meaning "torture") and *ethnic cleansing* (meaning "genocide"). See pp. 300–01.

double superlative. See SUPERLATIVE.

doublet. *Philology.* One of a pair of words that have similar meanings, forms, or origins. • Doublets are quite common in English today. They typically share the same root but may have entered the language by different paths. Some are nearly synonymous, but not all are interchangeable because the words are distinguished by subtle differences in application. For example, *royal* ("descended from monarchs; of or related to the monarchy") and *regal* ("of, relating to, or suited for a monarch") ultimately share the Latin root word *regalis,* but *the royal family* may not be at all the same thing as *a regal family.* As a historical matter, doublets usually consist of an older form (e.g., *benison* [14th c.], *malison* [13th c.], and *provenance* [18th c.]) and a more recent form (e.g., *benediction* [15th c.], *malediction* [14th c.], and *provenience* [19th c.]). Sometimes doublets are accidental variations of one original, with or without a differentiation in meaning (e.g., *alarm, alarum; unbeknown, unbeknownst*). And sometimes doublets consist of a standard literary form <lord> and a dialectal one <laird>.

do-**verb.** See VERB.

dual /d[y]oo-əl/, adj. Of, relating to, or involving an inflection expressing two or a pair.

dual, n. The grammatical form, midway between singular and plural, indicating that a word applies to precisely two people or two objects. • It is used in addition to the singular and plural forms in some languages, such as Old English, Arabic, and many Polynesian languages—but it is not a part of Modern English.

dummy subject. An expletive (such as *there* and *here* in *There is . . .* and *Here*

are . . .) that is in subject position at the beginning of a sentence but is not the subject itself.

dummy word. See EXPLETIVE.

durative aspect. See *progressive aspect* under ASPECT.

dvandva compound /**dvan**-dvə/. [Sanskrit] A compound word consisting of elements that are related to each other as if joined by *and* <prince-consort> <teacher-writer> <Dallas–Fort Worth>.

dysphasia /dis-**fay**-zhə/. Any difficulty of speech resulting from a brain disorder; derangement of a person's speech due to confusion or loss of ideas arising from a brain disease.

dysphemism /**dis**-fə-miz-əm/. **1.** An offensive word or phrase used in place of a neutral one (e.g., *gerund-grinder* for *grammarian*). **2.** The act of making such a substitution. See p. 312.

Early Modern English. The English language used from about 1500 to about 1700.

ecbatic /ek-**bat**-ik/, adj. (Of a conjunction or clause) denoting a result or consequence, as opposed to a purpose or an intention. • This term is used primarily in reference to Greek grammar.

echolalia /ek-oh-**layl**-yə/, n. **1.** Meaningless repetition of words and sounds spoken by another person. • In young children, echolalia is a natural part of language acquisition. In older children and adults, it is often involuntary and pathological, occurring sometimes as a symptom of a psychiatric disorder. **2.** Any meaningless repeated noises, esp. vocalized ones. Cf. PALILALIA — **echolalic** /ek-oh-**lay**-lik/, adj.

echo question. An interrogative that retains the structure of a declarative statement that precedes it.

ecthlipsis /ek-**thlip**-sis/. The suppression of one or more sounds in a word (as in the [correct] two-syllable pronunciation of *Wednesday*).

editorial *we.* The use of the first-person plural pronoun by an individual who is speaking on behalf of a group, such as an editorial board of a newspaper or other publication.

eisegesis /ɪ-sə-**jee**-sis/. A textual interpretation into which the reader has injected his or her own ideas.

elenchic. See ELENCTIC.

elenchus /i-**leng**-kəs/. *Rhetoric.* **1.** That which must be proved to refute an opponent's argument. **2.** A refuting argument; a refutation.

Socratic elenchus. The Socratic method of disproving a falsity by posing a series of questions that lead to the truth.

3. Loosely, a sophistical or fallacious refutation. Cf. IGNORATIO ELENCHI. — Also termed *elench*. Pl. **elenchi.**

elenctic, adj. (In logic) serving to refute; refuting. — Also termed *elenchic.*

elision, n. **1.** The omission of a vowel or syllable from a spoken word, usu. in poetry for metrical reasons <th'embattled warriors> or in rapid, casual speech <wuzzup?>. • All contractions involve elision. Weak vowels are sometimes elided, so *history* is often pronounced /**his**-tree/, and *suppose* becomes /spohz/. In some words, consonants are elided. For example, *Christmas* becomes /**kris**-məs/. In some words a syllable is dropped, so *library* comes out /**lɪ**-bree/. *Elision* is the general term for all the types of phonological reduction, such as apocope, haplology, hyphaeresis, paresis, synaeresis, and syncope. — Also termed *paresis*. Cf. HYPHAERESIS. **2.** In writing, the striking out of a word or phrase. — **elide,** vb.

ellipsis. 1. The omission of one or more words that are understood and necessary to make a construction grammatically complete <Who steals my purse steals trash> (the phrase *he who* being collapsed into *who* by ellipsis). • The reader or listener is expected to supply the full form. This figure of speech often enhances the vividness and energy of prose. Examples:

- I must to England. (William Shakespeare [1564–1616])
- And so to bed. (Samuel Pepys [1633–1703])
- This party objects, and that. (Thomas Carlyle [1795–1881])
- Liana walked out on Cambridge and in on me. (Anthony Burgess [1917–1993])

2. The three dots < . . . > showing that some portion of written text has been omitted, usu. in a quotation. • The dots, which are typographically identical to periods, each have a space before and after. An ellipsis always consists of only three dots. When the omitted material is inside a sentence, only the ellipsis appears <Micah received many . . . awards for his art>. When the omitted material appears between two sentences, the ellipsis is preceded or followed by a period, depending on whether part of the first sentence or part or all of the following sentence (or sentences) has been omitted. If the first sentence is complete and its last word is before the dots, then the period is in its usual place and followed by the three ellipsis dots <Those were good days. . . . We had time to enjoy life.>. If it is not, then the first three dots are ellipsis dots and the last is the sentence's period <Some people are committed to achieving their personal goals . . . . But are they too focused on the future?>. — Also termed *ellipsis dots*; *period dots*. — **elliptical,** adj.

ellipsis dots. See ELLIPSIS (2).

elliptical clause. See CLAUSE.

elocution. The art of training to improve public speaking, as by teaching a person to use a socially acceptable accent and to speak clearly and effectively. — **elocutionist,** n. — **elocutionary,** adj.

embedded clause. See CLAUSE.

embolophasia /em-boh-loh-**fay**-zhə/, n. *Rhetoric.* The use of sonorous but meaningless words.

empty word. A word that has little or no intrinsic meaning but primarily serves some grammatical function, such as a particle. — Also termed *form word; function word; grammatical word.* Cf. CONTENT WORD.

enallage /i-**nal**-ə-jee/. See FUNCTIONAL SHIFT.

enantiosis /i-nan-tee-**oh**-sis/, n. See IRONY.

enclisis /**eng**-kli-sis/, n. The pronunciation of a phrase in such a way that a word is compounded with an immediately adjacent (usu. preceding) word (as in *follow-up*, n.). • In speech, the enclitic part of the compound often, but not always, loses its emphasis. Cf. PROCLISIS.

enclitic /en-**klit**-ik/, adj. (Of a word) leaning or dependent on what precedes; esp., of, relating to, or involving an unstressed word that follows a stressed word (as in *stop him!* [*him* is unstressed] or *piece of cake* [*piece* is stressed; *of* is not]). • Sometimes an enclitic word becomes joined with the preceding word (as with *thee* in *prithee* [*pray* + *thee*] or *not* in *cannot*). See CLITIC. Cf. PROCLITIC. — **enclitic,** n.

end-cut. See APOCOPE.

enneasyllable /**en**-ee-ə-sil-ə-bəl/, n. A line or word of nine syllables. — **enneasyllabic** /en-ee-ə-si-**lab**-ik/, adj.

enthymeme /**en**-thə-meem/. *Logic.* A syllogism in which one of the premises is unexpressed, as in *Because it is autumn, the leaves are falling from the trees* (implying that leaves fall from trees in the autumn). Cf. SYLLOGISM. — **enthymematic,** adj.

enthymeme of the first order. An enthymeme with an unexpressed major premise <Because Socrates is a man, he is mortal> (implying that all men are mortal).

enthymeme of the second order. An enthymeme with an unexpressed minor premise <Because all men are mortal, Socrates is mortal> (implying that Socrates is a man).

epagoge /**ep**-ə-goh-jee/, n. *Logic & Rhetoric.* **1.** Inductive reasoning; the drawing of a general conclusion from particular instances. **2.** An argument that relies on inductive reasoning. — **epagogic,** adj. Cf. APAGOGE.

epanadiplosis /ep-ə-nə-di-**ploh**-sis/. *Rhetoric.* Emphasis produced by repeating a word or phrase at the beginning and end of a sentence or clause <severe to his servants, to his servants severe> <an eye for an eye, a tooth for a tooth>. • This is a subspecies of epanalepsis. Examples:

- *Believe* not all you can hear; tell not all you *believe*. (American Indian proverb)
- In *times like these*, it is helpful to remember that there have always been *times like these*. (Paul Harvey [1918–2009])
- *A minimum wage* that is not a livable wage can never be *a minimum wage*. (Ralph Nader [1934–])
- *Justice*—that's all I ask—*justice*. (delivered by Denzel Washington in the movie *The Hurricane* [1999])

epanados /e-**pan**-ə-dohs/. *Rhetoric.* **1.** A recapitulation of topics, item by item, often in reverse order. **2.** Inverted repetition. **3.** A return to the subject of discussion after a digression.

epanalepsis /ep-ə-nə-**lep**-sis/. *Rhetoric.* The repetition of a word, phrase, or clause after intervening words <It was both a curse and a blessing—a curse in that . . .>. • Examples:

- *Weep no more*, woeful shepherds *weep no more*, for Lycidas, your sorrow, is not dead, sunk though he be beneath the watery floor. (John Milton [1608–1674])
- *Control*, control—you must learn *control!* (Frank Oz as Yoda in the movie *The Empire Strikes Back* [1980])
- Inflation was reduced the old-fashioned way—a recession; two years of massive unemployment; *more hungry*, in this world of enormous affluence, the United States of America, *more hungry*. (Mario Cuomo [1932–2015])

Cf. EPANADIPLOSIS. — **epanaleptic,** adj.

epanaphora. See ANAPHORA.

epanastrophe. See ANADIPLOSIS.

epanorthosis /ep-ə-**north**-ə-sis/, n. A figure of speech in which a writer or speaker uses a word and then takes it back to substitute a more accurate term <There was a clear reference to Marilyn Monroe—well, I suppose allusion would be more accurate because she was not actually named>.

epenthesis /i-**pen**-thə-sis/. In speech, the insertion of a sound or an unetymological letter into the body of a word. • Epenthesis commonly occurs in the mispronunciation of the words *athlete* and *realtor*, both of which are often mispronounced with an additional vowel sound in the middle (/**ath**-ə-leet/ instead of the correct /**ath**-leet/, and /**reel**-ə-tər/ instead of /**reel**-tər/). Children and others sometimes say *fambly* for *family*. One-syllable words are also subject to epenthesis, especially in dialect, so that words such as *elm*, *film*, and *chimney* are spoken /**el**-əm/, /**fil**-əm/, and /**chim**-ə-nee/. Historically, of course, epenthesis has been commonplace in the English language, and no sensible person objects to forms established long ago. All of the following resulted originally from epenthesis: the internal *n* in *messenger*, *nightingale*, and *passenger*; the *g* in *impregnable*; the internal *d* in *jaundice*, *kindred*, and *thunder*; and the second *r* in *bridegroom*. For subspecies of epenthesis, see ANAPTYXIS and PLEOPHONY. — **epenthetic**, adj.

epeolatry /ep-ee-**ahl**-ə-tree/, n. Word-worship. Cf. GRAMMATOLATRY. — **epeolatrous**, adj.

eperotesis. See EROTESIS.

epexegesis /e-pek-sə-**jees**-əs/. **1.** The addition of a word or words to clarify meaning. **2.** The word or words so added. — **epexegetical**, adj.

epibole /ee-**pib**-ə-lee/, n. **1.** ANAPHORA. **2.** The use in successive clauses of initial words that have a similar or (occasionally) the same meaning.

epicene /**ep**-ə-seen/, adj. (Of a word) having only a gender-neutral form. • For example, a *blonde* is a woman (*blonde* is a female-specific form), but a *redhead* could be a man or a woman, so *redhead* is an epicene word. Similarly, a *stallion* is understood to be a male horse, but *horse* alone is epicene. In languages in which nouns typically have gender, *epicene* means that a word has the same form for the masculine and feminine genders. — Also termed *common*.

epigram. 1. A concise, pointed, and usu. clever saying <If you haven't anything nice to say about someone, come sit by me—attributed to Alice Roosevelt Longworth> <A cynic is a man who knows the price of everything but the value of nothing—Oscar Wilde>. **2.** A short, witty poem. — **epigrammatic**, adj.

epigraph /**ep**-i-graf/. **1.** A thematic quotation at the beginning of a book, chapter, etc. **2.** An inscription, esp. on a building or statue.

epimone /ee-**pim**-ə-nee/. *Rhetoric*. The repetition of a phrase for emphatic effect. Cf. EPIZEUXIS.

epiphonema /ep-i-foh-**neem**-ə/, n. A strikingly expressed thought in the conclusion of a discourse to sum up what has preceded.

epiphora. See EPISTROPHE.

epiplexis /ep-i-**plek**-sis/, n. *Rhetoric*. The use of rebuke or reproach to convince someone of an argument. — Also termed *epitimesis*.

epiploce /i-**pip**-lə-see/, n. Climax; specif., the adding of one striking circumstance after another to culminate in a resounding argumentative finale.

epistolary /i-**pis**-tə-ler-ee/, adj. Of, relating to, or involving missives or other correspondence.

epistrophe /i-**pis**-trə-fee/. *Rhetoric*. The emphatic repetition of a sound, word, or phrase at the end of successive clauses, verses, or sentences <Charity beareth all things, believeth all things, hopeth all things, endureth all things>. • One of the best-known examples of epistrophe in American rhetoric is in the concluding sentence of Lincoln's Gettysburg Address: "and that government of *the people, by the people*, for *the people* shall not perish from the earth." It's also used in the statement, "Many people spend their lives pursuing *power*, consolidating *power*, and enjoying *power*." — Also termed *epiphora*. See SYMPLOCE. Cf. ANAPHORA. — **epistrophic**, adj.

episyllogism /ep-i-**sil**-ə-jiz-əm/. A syllogism one of whose premises is the conclusion of a previous syllogism. See SYLLOGISM. Cf. PROSYLLOGISM.

epithesis /ee-**pith**-ə-sis/, n. See PARAGOGE.

epithet /**ep**-i-thət/. **1.** A particularly apt description or label, whether the quality denoted is favorable or unfavorable. **2.** A verbal obscenity; a profane word or phrase.

epitimesis. See EPIPLEXIS.

epitrope /i-**pit**-rə-pee/, n. *Rhetoric*. **1.** A rhetorical tactic whereby one concedes the force of an opponent's claim in an attempt to gain an advantage, usu. by suggesting that the claim, though sound, is irrelevant to the debate at hand. **2.** A declaration of willingness to let disinterested others (e.g., a judge and jury) decide the merits of one's case, usu. made with the intention of showing that a favorable judgment is inevitable.

epizeuxis /ep-ə-**z[y]ook**-sis/. *Rhetoric*. The immediate, emphatic repetition of a word <All you care about is *me, me, me!*>. Cf. PLOCE; PALILOGY; CONDUPLICATION; EPIMONE. • Examples:

• Why are we going to fight? *Why, why?* (Esther Forbes [1891–1967])

• A monument . . . was erected to the memory of one of the best husbands by his "wretched widow," who records upon the marble that there never was such a man on the face of the earth before, and

never will be again, and that there never was anybody so miserable as she—no, never, never, never! (Oliver Wendell Holmes Sr. [1809–1897])

• Writing is at its best—always, always, always—when it is a kind of inspired play for the writer. (Stephen King [1947–])

eponym /**ep**-ə-nim/. **1.** A person, real or fictional, from whose name a person, thing, or place derives (or is believed to derive) its name. • Surnames are the most common source of eponyms. Examples are *boycott* (from Irish landlord Captain Charles Boycott), *sousaphone* (from American bandmaster and composer John Philip Sousa), and *malapropism* (from Mrs. Malaprop, a character in Richard Brinsley Sheridan's play *The Rivals*). But some are drawn from personal or other names, such as the month *August* (from Augustus Caesar), *cereal* (from Ceres, the Roman goddess of grain), and *America* (from Amerigo Vespucci). — Also termed *eponymous person*. **2.** A name that is so derived.

eponymous person. See EPONYM (1).

equational /i-**kway**-zhə-nəl/, adj. Of, relating to, or involving a construction showing that two elements have the same referent. • Equational elements in a sentence are interchangeable without affecting meaning (e.g., in *Mike's son is my daughter's teacher*, the nouns *son* and *teacher* refer to the same person, so the subject and the complement could be switched: *My daughter's teacher is Mike's son*).

equational verb. See *linking verb* under VERB.

equative /**ek**-wə-tiv/, adj. Of, relating to, or involving a construction showing that two separate things are equivalent in some way. • An *as . . . as* construction is equative (e.g., *the air smells as sweet as perfume*).

ergative verb. See VERB.

erotema /er-oh-**tee**-mə/. See EROTESIS.

erotesis /er-oh-**tee**-sis/. *Rhetoric*. **1.** A figure of speech used by the speaker in the form of interrogation to assert the opposite of the question asked or to imply an answer without plainly giving it or leading one to expect an answer; RHETORICAL QUESTION. **2.** An unbroken series of rhetorical questions. — Also termed *eperotesis*; *erotema*. See RHETORICAL QUESTION.

Esperanto /es-pə-**rahn**-toh/, n. An artificial language invented for universal use, with stems common to European languages and regularized endings. • Dr. Ludovik Lazarus Zamenhof (1859–1917), a Polish linguist whose pseudonym was Dr. Esperanto (= Dr. Hoping-One), invented the language in his 1887 book *Langue Internationale*. Cf. INTERLINGUA; PASIGRAPHY; PASILALY.

etymology /et-ə-**mahl**-ə-jee/. **1.** The study of the origin or derivation of words and how their meanings develop and change over time. • In dictionaries, the etymology of a term is shown after the pronunciation, part of speech, and variant spellings, or at the end of an entry. **2.** The history of a particular term, usu. including an account of its various forms and meanings. See pp. 350–52.

etymon /et-ə-**mahn**/. **1.** An earlier form of a word, in the same language or an ancestral language. **2.** A word in a foreign language that is the original form or source of a loanword. **3.** ROOT.

euonym /**yoo**-ə-nim/, n. A good name or appropriate term; esp., a term that conforms to the rules of a system for naming and is therefore available as a technical designation (for a start-up company, a newly discovered star, a newly developed drug, etc.). Cf. CACONYM.

euphemism. *Rhetoric.* **1.** The use of a more or less neutral word or phrase in place of an expression that is considered disagreeable in some way. **2.** An expression so substituted. • Euphemisms are often intended to prevent or soften negative responses. But they should be used only after careful consideration. To call a used car "pre-owned" is a semantic sleight of hand. But it is understandable for a hospital to have a "special-care clinic" where patients with sexually transmitted diseases are treated. — **euphemistic,** adj. — **euphemize,** vb.

euphony. The quality of having a pleasing sound or harmonious combination of sounds. • Euphony guides word choices, but it is not an objective concept. One listener may find the phrase *notorious notations* amusing, while another finds it irritating. — **euphonious,** adj. See ALLITERATION. See also *indefinite article* under ARTICLE. Cf. CACOPHONY.

euphuism /**yoo**-fyoo-iz-əm/. **1.** A pretentious, highly artificial literary style characterized by alliteration, high-flown words, antitheses, and strange expressions. **2.** Concocted elegance of language. Cf. GONGORISM; PERIERGIA. — **euphuistic,** adj.

exclamation. 1. An utterance expressing anger, pain, anguish, or surprise; a sentence used to express a feeling with added emphasis. — Also termed *exclamative*. **2.** INTERJECTION.

exclamative, n. See EXCLAMATION; *exclamatory sentence* under SENTENCE.

exclamatory sentence. See SENTENCE.

excrescent /ek-**skres**-ənt/, adj. (Of a sound in a word) not etymologically part of a word but instead appearing for reasons of euphony or ease of pronunciation. • Excrescent sounds occur in many common English words. For example, the *b* sound in *thimble* is not found in its Old English root word *thymel*, nor is the *d* sound of *thunder* part of its etymological precursors, *thoner* (Middle English) and *thunor* (Old English).

exegesis /ek-sə-**jee**-sis/. **1.** An expository discourse; specif., a critical analysis or interpretation of a passage or text. **2.** An explanatory note. — **exegete,** n. — **exegetical,** adj.

exempla /ek-**zem**-plə/. *Rhetoric.* Illustrations, esp. by way of anecdote, used to sustain an argument or to point to a moral. • Although the singular *exemplum* sometimes appears, the plural *exempla* is far more common in discussions of rhetoric.

exonym /**ek**-soh-nim/. A place name that one group of people uses to denote a foreign place when the denizens don't use that name as a matter of self-reference. • Examples are *Turin* (Torino), *Moscow (Moskva)*; *Vienna* (Wien), *Florence* (Firenze), *Morocco* (Maroc), *Angleterre* (England), and *Germany* (Deutschland).

expletive. 1. A word that serves as a noun in idiomatic expression but bears none of the lexical meaning that nouns usually bear; specif., a "dummy" constituent of a sentence with no inherent semantic content, such as *it* or *there* <It was raining> <There were celebrities present>. — Also termed *dummy word*; *prop word.* **2.** An exclamatory word or phrase, often profane. • Sense 2 is an extension of sense 1, profanities having once been considered as irrelevant words used to fill up space.

expletive conjunction. See CONJUNCTION.

expression. 1. The manifestation of an idea in words. **2.** A phrase or saying.

extrinsic modality. See *epistemic modality* under MODALITY.

factitive /**fak**-tə-tiv/, adj. (Of a transitive verb or a clause) expressing an action that leads to a result, esp. a change in a thing's state of being. • Verbs such as *appoint, build, destroy, elect,* and *make* are factitive (e.g., in *Munchie built a playhouse out of scrap lumber*, the action verb *built* is factitive because the lumber was transformed into a playhouse). The object of a factitive verb is sometimes called the *factitive object.* Some grammarians use the term *result* or *resultative*

as a synonym for *factitive*. The word is sometimes spelled (through syncope) *factive.*

factitive object. See FACTITIVE.

factitive verb. See VERB.

factive. See FACTITIVE.

false attraction. The influence exerted by a word on another word that causes it to take the incorrect form; esp., a mismatch between the number of a subject and its verb occurring when a phrase intervenes between the subject and the verb and misleads the writer into believing that the noun in the intervening phrase is the subject. • For example, when a subject is followed by a prepositional phrase with an object of a different number, the verb is often influenced by the closer noun. In *the correction of papers are a tough assignment*, the singular subject *correction* requires the singular verb *is*, but the plural *papers* influences the choice of the plural form *are*; it is incorrect because *papers* is a prepositional object, not the sentence's subject. — Also termed *attraction*.

feminine, adj. (Of a noun, pronoun, or suffix) indicating that the person or animal named is female. • In English, only the personal pronoun *she*, certain nouns such as *girl* and *doe*, and a few adjectives are feminine. — **feminine,** n. See GENDER.

figurative, adj. *Rhetoric.* **1.** Involving a rhetorical figure of any kind. **2.** Expressing an idea in words that normally denote another thing, as by analogy, simile, or metaphor. Cf. LITERAL.

figure of speech. *Rhetoric.* A special use of words; esp., the use of an expression in which a word or words are used for stylistic effect rather than for their literal meaning. • The expression "I'm starving!" means "I'm very hungry," usually not "I'm dying of hunger." "Starving" heightens the effect of the statement; it does not literally describe the person's condition. Figures of speech include metaphors and similes. The names of most figures of speech derive from ancient Greek and Latin. See CLICHÉ; HYPERBOLE; METAPHOR; SIMILE. Cf. TROPE (2).

final conjunction. See CONJUNCTION.

finite /**fɪ**-nɪt/, adj. (Of a verb) not in the infinitive mood—that is, limited by person and number.

finite verb. See VERB.

first person. See PERSON.

flat, adj. Not having a distinctive ending characteristic of a particular part of speech (e.g., an adverb that has the same form as an adjective or noun, or a noun used adjectivally without a change in form).

flat adverb. See ADVERB.

flection. See INFLECTION (1).

folk etymology. 1. A widespread but false notion about the origin of a word or phrase. **2.** The tendency of popular and mistaken beliefs about a word's origins to affect its use or form. • The adjective *posh* is a good example. It appeared relatively recently, in 1903, but its origins are unclear; it might have been derived from the slang noun *posh*, meaning *money* or a *dandy*. But according to folk etymology, wealthy people who traveled by ship between England and India paid more for cabins on the cooler side of the ship, port on the journey to India, and starboard returning. Hence *posh* was said to be an acronym for "port outward, starboard home." The story is entertaining, but researchers have not found any evidence that prices for cabins differed by which side of the ship they were on. **3.** A change in an unusual-looking word's form to a more usual form—based on a misunderstanding of the word's origin. See CATACHRESIS (4); ETYMOLOGY (D).

foot. The primary measure of poetic rhythm, corresponding to a bar of music.

footle /**fuut**-əl/, vb. To talk foolishly or nonsensically.

form. The way a word is spelled and pronounced according to how it is used in different tenses, cases, number, etc.; one of the inflected variations of a word. See ASPECT.

form word. See EMPTY WORD.

fossil. An old word or expression that persists only in certain set phrases or idioms (e.g., *hue* in the phrase *hue and cry*).

fragment. A sentence that lacks some essential component (esp. a predicate) to make it complete. • To determine whether a sentence is a fragment, rephrase it as a yes/no question. If you can't, it's not a complete sentence. A sentence fragment may result because the main clause doesn't have a main verb <peppers of all colors rolling down the slope>. Adding the verb *are* or *were* before *rolling* finishes the sentence. Incorrect punctuation may also create a fragment, especially when a dependent clause is separated from the main clause by a period instead of a comma: *The new doorknob came off in my hand. Which shouldn't have happened.* — Also termed *nonsentence*. See p. 501.

free morpheme. See MORPHEME.

frequentative aspect. See ASPECT.

Freudian slip. The inadvertent substitution of a wrong word for the intended word and presumably therefore revealing a subconscious thought or feeling. • The famous psychoanalyst Sigmund Freud (1856–1939) first described the phenomenon, which he called "faulty action," in 1901. Classically, Freudian slips suggest that the speaker's true thoughts have been exposed. For example, a speaker may intend to say "I'd like to thank all of you" but instead says "I'd like to spank all of you," before launching into a tirade. — Also termed *parapraxia*. See HETEROPHEMY.

fricative. A consonant sound made with a partial obstruction of the breath stream. — Also termed *continuant*.

front-cut. See APHAERESIS.

frothy, adj. (Of speech or writing) empty, insubstantial, and trivial.

full passive. See PASSIVE VOICE.

fulminate /**fəl**-mə-nayt/, vb. 1. To issue or utter (a threat, menace, denunciation, or criticism). 2. To thunder forth invective or censure.—**fulmination,** n.—**fulminatory,** adj.

functional shift. The use of a word or phrase that normally functions as one part of speech in a different way so that it functions as another. • Using *fun* (traditionally a noun) as an adjective (as in *This is a fun trip!*) is an example of functional shift. The most common types are noun-to-adjective shifts (*a hotel car*), verb-to-noun shifts (*an assist*), and noun-to-verb shifts (*to office on a particular floor of a building*). A noun, for example, may function as a verb <A truck jackknifed>. It may also function as an adjective <law report> <book report>. An adjective may also function as a verb <crimson'd with flowers> or as a noun <the poor>. — Also termed *functional change*; *conversion*; *enallage*; *anthimeria*. See p. 416.

function word. See EMPTY WORD; WORD.

fused participle. See PARTICIPLE.

fustian /**fəs**-chən/. Pretentious, bombastic verbiage; esp., an absurdly elevated style of speech or writing about a pedestrian subject. See TWADDLE.

future-perfect tense. See TENSE.

future tense. See TENSE.

galimatias /gal-ə-**may**-sh[ee-]əs/ or /-**mat**-ee-əs/. A confused and often pretentious jumble of words; a medley of meaningless talk; GOBBLEDYGOOK.

garrulity /gə-**rool**-i-tee/, n. Severe overtalkativeness; LOGORRHEA. — **garrulous,** adj.

gemination /jem-i-**nay**-shən/, n. **1.** The doubling of a consonant sound in a word. **2.** The doubling of a letter in the spelling of a word. • Many English words, such as *baggage* and *saddle*, have doubled letters, but only one is pronounced distinctly and the second only marginally, if at all. Often when gemination occurs in speaking a word such as *bottle* or *button*, and the second -*t*- is pronounced distinctly, the speaker is using a nonstandard pronunciation.

gender. A grammatical category by which a noun or pronoun is classified as masculine, feminine, or, in some languages, neuter, and articles and adjectives must take the masculine, feminine, or neuter form that agrees. • Although in some languages nouns have gender, in English most nouns have no set gender. Exceptions include animal names <buck–doe> <bull–cow> <cock–hen>, and the traditional use of feminine pronouns when referring to ships or boats. Only nouns and personal pronouns that expressly refer to a male or female person or animal are masculine or feminine. Personal pronouns (*he*, *she*) are most commonly affected by a noun's gender, but a very few adjectives are as well. For example, *blond* and *blonde* refer to yellow-haired males and females, respectively. Some nouns that once referred exclusively to a man (e.g., *actor*, *waiter*) now apply to both men and women. The noun still requires a masculine or feminine pronoun, but which one depends on the sex of the person referred to <George Clooney is my favorite actor>. Meanwhile, the sex-specific *actress* still lingers in some contexts <the Best Actress category>. See also CONCORD.

common gender. The gender of an inanimate noun or of a neutral classification of animate nouns. • Most English words are of common gender (e.g., a *doctor* may be a man or a woman), though there are many exceptions (e.g., a *father* is a man; a *mother* is a woman). Cf. *neuter gender.*

feminine gender. The gender of a noun or pronoun denoting a female person or animal (e.g., *daughter*, *doe*, *filly*). • Traditionally, many words were masculine in gender and changed to feminine by adding a suffix such as -*ess* (e.g., *steward–stewardess*). Many of those words are disappearing in favor of gender-neutral substitutes. (See SEXISM.) In other languages, nouns assigned the feminine gender have some semantic correlation with animation and the female sex. See ANIMATE; INANIMATE. Cf. *masculine gender.*

grammatical gender. Gender that depends on the form of a word and not primarily on its meaning, as in highly inflected Indo-European languages. Cf. *natural gender.*

masculine gender. The gender of a noun or pronoun denoting a male person or animal (e.g., *buck, ram, son*). • In other languages, nouns assigned the masculine gender have some semantic correlation with animation and the male sex. See ANIMATE; INANIMATE. Cf. *feminine gender.*

natural gender. Gender that depends not on the form of a word but on the sex of the thing denoted by the word, as in English. • According to this type of gender, only animate parts of speech have the notion of sex attached to them. So inanimate words are said to have no gender at all. See *common gender.* Cf. *grammatical gender.*

neuter gender. The gender of a noun or pronoun denoting an inanimate thing (e.g., *highway, shrub, weather*). In some languages other than English, the neuter gender is assigned to a noun or pronoun that has no semantic correlation to something animate (such as a human or higher animal). See ANIMATE; INANIMATE. Cf. *common gender.*

generalization. 1. The process by which a word with a fairly narrow meaning takes on a broader meaning. • For example, *barn* derives from Old English roots meaning "barley house," but has generalized to refer to a farm building for all kinds of storage. Cf. SPECIALIZATION. **2.** The extension of a linguistic feature from one item to a whole class. • *Overgeneralization* occurs when the feature is extended indiscriminately to all items in the class when the feature does not in fact apply to everything. Irregular verbs, for example, form the past tense by changing a vowel rather than taking an ending <sing–sang>.

general semantics. A field of study developed during the 20th century as a way to improve how people use language and other symbols, as well as their environment more generally. • It was developed by Alfred Korzybski (1879–1950) and popularized by S.I. Hayakawa (1906–1992) and Stuart Chase (1888–1985). Its basic tenets are that (1) a word is not the thing it represents ("the map is not the territory"); (2) words cannot say everything about anything ("a map does not represent the entire territory"); and (3) words are self-reflexive in the sense that explaining them requires other words, and others, and others ("a map would have to include a map

of the map, which in turn would have to include a map of the map of the map, etc."). Cf. SEMANTICS.

genitive case. See CASE.

gerund. A present-participial form that functions as a noun; a verbal noun. • A gerund is distinguishable from a participial verb, which is used only after a *be-*verb and functions as a main verb. A gerund can be the main verb's subject or object <Dancing is good exercise> <I like dancing>, and also the object of a preposition <I exercise every morning by walking two miles>.

gerundive, n. In Latin grammar, a future passive participle (e.g., *amandus* = to be loved) functioning as a verbal adjective to express necessity of performance. See PARTICIPLE.

gerundive phrase. See *gerund phrase* under PHRASE.

gerund phrase. See PHRASE.

gibberish. Unintelligible speech; incoherent talk.

gloss /glahs/, n. **1.** A word inserted into a text, esp. a historical one, by way of explanation or simplification. • Often a gloss makes explicit something that the original text left implicit. **2.** An explanatory statement in a reference book, such as a dictionary or glossary. **3.** More broadly, a comment, explanation, or interpretation. **4.** In a negative sense, a disingenuous "spin" on something; a tendentious interpretation.

glossary. 1. A partial dictionary that lists the definitions of technical terms in a field. — Also termed (rarely) *glossology.* **2.** A collection of glosses. See GLOSS.

glossolalia /glos-oh-**layl**-yə/. An ecstatic, unintelligible utterance usu. accompanying religious euphoria. • Glossolalia is also known as "speaking in tongues." — **glossolalic,** adj.

glossology /glah-**sahl**-ə-jee/, n. **1.** The scientific study of language. • This is an old-fashioned word for *linguistics.* — Also termed *glottology.* **2.** The marshaling and defining of the terminology used in any field of study. **3.** GLOSSARY (1).

glottal, adj. *Phonetics.* Of a sound, produced in the glottis, the upper part of the larynx between the two vocal cords.

glottal stop. *Phonetics.* A sound produced with complete closure of the glottis followed by an explosive release of breath. • You can hear a glottal stop in the middle of the interjection *uh-oh.* See OKINA.

glottochronology. A method of calculating the rate at which dialects and languages diverge by analyzing the rate at which vocabulary changes.

glottology. See GLOSSOLOGY (1).

gnome /nohm/. A concise statement of a principle, truth, or sentiment; a maxim, proverb, aphorism, or apothegm. — **gnomic,** adj.

gobbledygook. Complicated, pompous, and obscure verbiage, particularly that used by governments, businesses, or professions. • *Gobbledygook* was coined in 1944 by Maury Maverick, a former member of Congress who was serving in FDR's wartime government. He claimed that his inspiration was the turkey: "always gobbledy gobbling and strutting with ludicrous pomposity. At the end of his gobble, there was a sort of gook." It's not hard to find examples of gobbledygook, although they can be hard to comprehend <Forward-looking companies invest in quality asset projections> <We can revitalize the economy with regenerated policy innovations>. — Also spelled *gobbledegook.* Cf. LEGALDEGOOK.

gongorism /**gon[g]**-gə-riz-əm/, n. A pretentious, ornate writing style reminiscent of the 16th-century Spanish poet Góngora y Argote (1561–1627). — **gongoristic,** adj.

govern, vb. **1.** (Of a word, esp. a verb or preposition) to require (a noun or pronoun) to be in a certain case or (a verb) to be in a certain mood <Both verbs and prepositions govern pronouns that follow them as objects>. **2.** (Of a mood or case) to be required by a certain type of word <The genitive is governed by certain adjectives>. **3.** (Of a word) to be necessarily followed by (a specified case or mood) <The verb governs the objective case>.

government. The effect of one word on another according to usage, esp. in determining the case of a pronoun or the mood of a verb.

gradable, adj. Capable of being compared. See DEGREE.

gradation /grə-**day**-shən/. Inflection produced by changing a vowel in the root word (e.g., *drink–drank–drunk*). — Also termed *ablaut.* See *strong verb* under VERB.

grade. See DEGREE.

grammar. 1. The structural pattern of a language learned unconsciously by a child while acquiring his or her native tongue. **2.** A systematic, comprehensive description of this structural pattern. **3.** A pedagogical book in which a language is partially described, focusing primarily on the needs of native speakers. **4.** A book that seeks to describe a language comprehensively, as if to an alien, without reference to the pedagogical needs of native speakers. See DESCRIPTIVE GRAMMAR;

PRESCRIPTIVE GRAMMAR; TRANSFOR-
MATIONAL GRAMMAR; LINGUISTICS.

grammarian. 1. The author of a book on grammar. 2. A teacher of grammar. 3. One versed in grammar; a philologist.

grammatical, adj. 1. Of, relating to, or involving grammar. 2. According to the rules of grammar.

grammatical ambiguity. See AMBIGUITY.

grammatical function. The syntactic role that a word or phrase serves in a sentence (e.g., a noun or noun phrase may serve as subject or object) and the part of speech in which the word or phrase operates. — Also termed *grammatical relation.*

grammaticality, n. Correctness according to the rules of grammar. • Grammaticality is not a strict concept. Some forms of construction may be acceptable to all speakers of a particular dialect, while others may never be acceptable. But some forms may have more or less acceptance by at least some speakers.

grammatical relation. See GRAMMATICAL FUNCTION.

grammatical word. See EMPTY WORD.

grammaticaster /grə-**mat**-i-kas-tər/. An unknowledgeable grammarian; an amateur who comments incompetently on points of grammar. Cf. POETASTER; LOGICASTER.

grammaticism /grə-**mat**-i-siz-əm/. A grammatical rule, principle, or peculiarity.

grammaticize /grə-**mat**-i-sɪz/, vb. 1. To make (a sentence or construction) grammatically correct. 2. To display grammatical knowledge. 3. To expatiate on a point of grammar.

grammatolatry /gram-ə-**tahl**-ə-tree/. 1. The worship of grammar. 2. An unduly high regard for words as opposed to what they represent. Cf. EPEOLATRY. — **grammatolatrous,** adj.

grapheme /**graf**-eem/. The smallest distinguishable unit in a writing system. • Letters <A, c>, punctuation marks <?, !>, symbols <+, %>, and numbers <4, 7> are all types of graphemes.

grapholect /**graf**-ə-lekt/. A standard written language.

graphology /gra-**fol**-ə-jee/, n. 1. The study of handwriting. 2. The analysis of handwriting as an index to personality, intelligence, and other characteristics. 3. The study of the written symbols or printing systems in various languages. — **graphologist,** n. — **graphological,** adj.

grave accent. See ACCENT.

Great Vowel Shift. In the development of the English language, the period (ca. 1400–1700) when the pronunciation of stressed vowel sounds changed. • During this period, the pronunciation of stressed vowel sounds became systematically "raised," that is, pronounced higher in the mouth. So the word *each* in Chaucer's time was spelled *ech* and pronounced /ech/.

grouping ambiguity. See AMBIGUITY.

guideword. The word (or words) at the head of each page in an alphabetically arranged reference work such as a dictionary or encyclopedia, indicating typically the first or last word on the page.

guttural /**gət**-ər-əl/, adj. (Of a spoken sound) produced far back in the mouth (e.g., *g, k*). • *Guttural* is often misunderstood as meaning "produced in the throat," but guttural sounds are actually produced in the mouth, with the root of the tongue and the soft palate.

hanging comparative. See *dangling comparative* under COMPARATIVE.

hapax legomenon /**hap**-aks lə-**gah**-mə-nən/, n. 1. A word or phrase found only once in the written record of a language. 2. A word or phrase found only once in the work of a particular author. Pl. **hapax legomena.**

haplography. The unintentional omission of a written, repeated letter, syllable, word, or series of letters, syllables, or words, usu. while copying or reading. • In English, the word *idolatry* was derived from the Greek *idololatreia*; the repeated *-ol-* was lost through either haplography or syncope. (See SYNCOPE.) Haplography seems the more likely source of that shortening because the word probably appeared mostly in written contexts when the change occurred. Many instances of haplography result from the reader's eye jumping forward over similar symbols and seeing "endontics" instead of *endodontics*, and "tillate" instead of *titillate*. Cf. DITTOGRAPHY.

haplology /hap-**lahl**-ə-jee/. The contraction of a word by omitting syllables when the word is spoken. • For example, *probably* is often pronounced /**prob**-lee/ in rapid speech; in dialect, the haplology is taken even further: /**prol**-ee/. Cf. SYNCOPE.

head. 1. The most important word in a group of syntactically related words because it governs how the group performs in the sentence; the core word in a phrase. • In a relative clause, the head is the noun phrase to which the relative pronoun refers. • For example, in *the tall man in the front row*, the word *man* is the head of the noun phrase. — Also termed *headword.* 2. In typography, a headline, esp. one that summarizes a writing's topic.

headword. 1. The word that begins an entry in a reference work such as a dictionary or encyclopedia. 2. HEAD (1).

helping verb. See *auxiliary verb* under VERB.

hendecasyllable /hen-**de**-kə-sil-ə-bəl/, n. A line or word of 11 syllables. — **hendecasyllabic** /hen-de-kə-si-**lab**-ik/, adj.

hendiadys /hen-**dɪ**-ə-dəs/. *Rhetoric.* The use of two words connected by *and* to express the same idea as might be expressed with a single word and a qualifier; the separation of what is really one thing into two things <They drank from goblets and from gold> (they drank from golden goblets).

heptasyllable /hep-tə-sil-ə-bəl/, n. A word of seven syllables. — **heptasyllabic** /hep-tə-si-**lab**-ik/, adj.

hermeneutics, n. The art or science of interpreting texts. • The term is commonly used to refer to techniques of interpreting scripture, but it applies to any kind of text. — **hermeneutic,** adj.

heteric /hi-**ter**-ik/, adj. (Of a spelling) nonphonetic.

heteroclite. A word of irregular inflection; esp., a Latin noun irregular in declension. — **heteroclite,** adj.

heteroepy /het-ə-**roh**-ə-pee/. A variance from standard pronunciation. — **heteroepic** /het-ə-roh-**ep**-ik/, adj.

heterography /het-ə-**rahg**-rə-fee/, n. 1. A misspelling. 2. Irregular or inconsistent spelling (as in the orthography of English). Cf. HOMOGRAPHY.

heterological, adj. (Of a modifying word) not having the characteristic denoted. • A word that is heterological never describes itself. Examples are *long* (it has only four letters and one syllable) and *monosyllabic* (it has five syllables). Cf. AUTOLOGICAL.

heteronym. 1. A word that is spelled like another word but has a different meaning and is pronounced differently. • For instance, *lead* can mean "to guide" (/leed/) or "a metallic element" (/led/). Similarly, *alternate* can mean "the next choice" (/**awl**-tər-nit/) or "to switch back and forth" (/**awl**-tər-nayt/). 2. A phrase referring to a thing that is called by an entirely different name in a different geographical area. For example, an apple coated with hardened red-sugar syrup is called a *candy apple* in New York and a *taffy apple* in Pennsylvania. 3. A synonym; specif., a word that has the same meaning as another but is not written similarly and has a different origin. *Bucket* and *pail*, for instance, refer to the same object, but *bucket* derives from Anglo-Norman, while the origin of *pail* is unknown.

heterophemy. The inadvertent use of a word or phrase when another is meant. • Heterophemy usually results from a momentary lapse in concentration (as when a server writes an order for white wine instead of white rum). In speech, it is also called a slip of the tongue (*lapsus linguae*) and in writing a slip of the pen (*lapsus calami*). Freudian slips are a type of heterophemy. See FREUDIAN SLIP.

hexasyllable /**hek**-sə-sil-ə-bəl/, n. A word of six syllables. — **hexasyllabic** /hek-sə-si-**lab**-ik/, adj.

hiatus /hī-**ay**-təs/. A break in pronunciation between two adjacent vowels or vowel sounds that are not in the same syllable (e.g., *coowner*; *residuum*) or in different words (e.g., *to irritate*; *draw out*).

historical linguistics. See LINGUISTICS.

historical present tense. See TENSE.

Hobson-Jobsonism. The modification of a foreign word or phrase to fit the sound system of the borrowing language. • *Hobson-Jobson* is an anglicized corruption of the Shi'ite Muslim cry *Ya Hasan! Ya Hosain!*—used during the Festival of Muharram. The term became the popular name for the *Glossary of Anglo-Indian Colloquial Words and Phrases*, published in 1886. At the time, many of the hybrid terms in the *Glossary* were unique to British India. But some have become Standard English (e.g., *shawl*, *veranda*, *pajamas*, and *shampoo*). See p. 465.

holograph /**hahl**-ə-graf/, n. An entirely handwritten document—and all in one hand. — **holographic**, adj.

holophrasis /hoh-**lahf**-rə-sis/, n. The combination of many ideas in a single word, esp. a verb. — **holophrastic**, adj.

homeophony /hoh-mee-**ahf**-ə-nee/. Similarity in sound. — **homeophonic**, adj.

homily /**hom**-i-lee/. 1. A lecture, usu. on morality and often tedious. 2. A sermon. 3. A serious admonition or exhortation. 4. A platitude. — **homiletic** /hom-i-**let**-ik/, adj.

homograph. A word that has the same spelling as at least one other but has a different meaning. • It may be pronounced differently. Depending on the context, *fair* can mean an amusement <noun: the county fair>, attractive <adjective: a fair lady>, or just <adjective: a fair decision>. In all senses, the pronunciation is the same. Similarly, *lead* can be "to go first while others follow" <verb: I'll lead you home> or a metal <noun: a lead sinker>; if the word is spoken, it is differentiated by its pronunciation. If homographs have identical

pronunciations, they are also classified as homonyms. See HOMONYM. — **homographic**, adj.

homographic /hahm-ə-**graf**-ik/, adj. 1. Of, relating to, or involving a homograph. 2. Of, relating to, or involving homography.

homography /hə-**mahg**-rə-fee/, n. The representation of a language's sounds so that each sound is expressed by a single character, and no character represents more than that one sound. • The International Phonetic Alphabet is perhaps the best-known system of homography. Cf. HETEROGRAPHY (2).

homonym. 1. A word that is spelled identically with another but has a different pronunciation or meaning, and usu. a different origin; HOMOGRAPH. • The word *mood*, for example, in the sense of an emotion or state of mind derives from German (*Mut*) and Dutch (*moed*). But *mood* in the grammatical sense of verbs derives from Latin (*modus*). 2. HOMOPHONE. — **homonymous**, adj.

homophone. A word that is pronounced the same as another but has a different meaning and usu. spelling <rain–rein–reign> <rite–write–right–wright>. • Many nouns are homophones, such as *pair–pear*. Other parts of speech can also be homonyms. The verb *lie* means either (1) to say something that is not true, or (2) to be at rest, usu. (esp. of a living thing) in a horizontal position. The distinction becomes obvious when *lie* is conjugated in each sense: *lie–lied–lied* and *lie–lay–lain*. Homophones that have identical spellings are also homographs. — Also termed *paronym*. — **homophonous**, adj. — **homophony**, n.

hybrid. *Philology.* A word formed by combining elements of different languages. • For example, *amoral* is formed from the Greek negative prefix *a-* and the Latin root *moral*. *Hyperdrive* has the Greek prefix *hyper-* and the English *drive*. See p. 474.

hypallage /hi-**pal**-ə-jee *or* hī-/. *Rhetoric.* The reversal of the usual syntactic or semantic relationship of words; esp., the transference of an adjective from the person who has the quality denoted to some object (person or thing) with reference to which the person manifests that quality <flattering offer>. • A memorable example occurs in Byron's lines: "The night-winds sigh, the breakers roar, / And shrieks the wild seamew." (In the final clause, the subject–verb sequence is inverted to create a strikingly unparallel phrasing.) In Shakespeare's *Julius*

Caesar appears this example: "His coward lips did from their color fly." Shakespeare might have written, more ordinarily (and less memorably), "The color did fly from his coward lips." On a more down-to-earth level, hypallage frequently occurs in phrases such as *caring home* (it's not the home that's caring, but the people in it), *glad tidings*, *hopeless efforts*, *friendly glance*, *jealous look*, *joyful news*, *wise counsel*, and *treacherous plots*. — Also termed *transferred epithet*. See pp. 474–75.

hyperbaton. See INVERSION.

hyperbole /hī-**pər**-bə-lee/. *Rhetoric.* Overstatement; specif., exaggeration to distort facts by making them appear much more significant than they really are. • Hyperbole may be used to entertain or for serious purposes. Either way, it should be used with care. For example, calling a referee's poor decision "the crime of the century" is excessive. See AUXESIS; FIGURE OF SPEECH. Cf. IRONY; LITOTES; SARCASM. — **hyperbolic**, adj.

hyperbolism /hī-**pər**-bə-liz-əm/, n. 1. Addiction to hyperbole. 2. An instance of hyperbole.

hypercorrect, adj. 1. (Of an expression used by an imperfectly educated person) incorrectly formed from an erroneous attempt to use a prestigious form of language. 2. (Of an ill-educated speaker or writer) using erroneous expressions in a mistaken attempt to mimic educated usage. Cf. HYPERURBANISM. — **hypercorrection**, n. See pp. 475–77.

hypernym /**hī**-pər-nim/, n. A genus-word; a broad term that denotes something for which the language contains many more particular terms (as *red* is the hypernym for *crimson*, *oxblood*, *rubicund*, *ruddy*, *scarlet*, etc.). Cf. HYPONYM. — **hypernymy**, n.

hyperurbanism /hī-pər-**ər**-bə-niz-əm/, n. 1. An affected manner of speech or writing intended to avoid sounding rural or uneducated. 2. A hypercorrect phrasing used by someone who wants to sound sophisticated but instead achieves the opposite result. Cf. HYPERCORRECT. — **hyperurban**, adj.

hyphaeresis /hī-**fer**-ə-sis *or* hī-**feer**-ə-sis/. *Philology.* The omission of a letter, syllable, or sound from the body of a word. • For example, *whene'er* drops the *v* of *whenever* and thereby loses a syllable. Essentially, this word is synonymous with *syncope*. Cf. ELISION; HAPLOLOGY.

hypobole. See HYPOPHORA.

hypocorism /hī-**pahk**-ə-riz-əm/, n. A pet name or familiar name (e.g., *Billy* for *William*, *Lexi* for *Alexandra*).

hypocoristic /hɪ-pahk-ə-**ris**-tik/, adj. **1.** Of, relating to, or involving pet names or familiar names. **2.** DIMINUTIVE. — Also termed *caritative*.

hyponym /**hɪ**-poh-nim/, n. A species-word; a narrow term whose meaning is embraced within a broad category of meanings carried by a more general term (as *daisy, gladiolus, marigold, rose, stargazer, tulip,* and *violet* are hyponyms of the word *flower*). Cf. HYPERNYM. — **hyponymy,** n.

hypophora /hɪ-**pahf**-ə-rə/. *Rhetoric.* The posing and answering of questions, often at length; esp., the practice or an instance of raising and answering one or more questions that an opponent might raise about one's argument. Cf. PROLEPSIS (2). — Also termed *hypobole* /hɪ-**pob**-ə-lee/.

hypotaxis /hɪ-pə-**tak**-səs/. The subordination of one clause to another to show the logical relationship between ideas <We'll have to do the marketing tomorrow because I forgot to make a grocery list> (the conjunction *because* subordinates the dependent clause *I forgot to make a grocery list*). Cf. PARATAXIS. — **hypotactic,** adj.

hypozeuxis /hɪ-poh-**z[y]ook**-sis/. The use in one sentence of three or more parallel clauses in succession, each one with a subject and a verb.

hysteron proteron /**his**-tər-on **proh**-tər-on or **prot**-ə-ron/. *Rhetoric.* A construction in which the natural order of the elements is inverted to stress the more important event, even though it must occur later in time. • The command *put on your shoes and socks,* though literally absurd, is meant to put the emphasis on *shoes* over *socks.* — Also termed *hysterosis*.

hysterosis. See HYSTERON PROTERON.

idioglossia /id-ee-oh-**glos**-ee-ə/. The inability to pronounce guttural or palatal sounds in someone whose origins of speech are otherwise normal.

ideogram /**id**-ee-ə-gram/. A symbol that represents an idea rather than a particular word (e.g., the numeral *8* in contrast with the word *eight*). Cf. LOGOGRAM; PICTOGRAM.

idiolect /**id**-ee-ə-lekt/. An individual's distinctive language; a personal dialect. • Every person's language reflects word choices and other features that characterize that individual's speech and writing. See DIALECT; SLANG.

idiom /**id**-ee-əm/. **1.** A phrase that has a meaning greater than its constituent parts might suggest and that must therefore be learned independently of the traditional definitions of its constituent parts (e.g., *break wind, put up with, raining cats and dogs, top-shelf*). • For example, *kick the bucket* means

"die," and *red herring* means "something brought up to divert attention from the real issue." **2.** An expression that is widely used and accepted despite being illogical or formally ungrammatical (e.g., *a life-and-death situation* is illogical and *it's me!* is technically ungrammatical). Cf. SET PHRASE; CLICHÉ. — **idiomatic,** adj.

ignoratio elenchi /ig-nor-**ay**-she-oh i-**leng**-kee/, n. *Rhetoric.* The fallacy of arguing the wrong point. • Literally, this Latin phrase means "ignoring the refutation"—meaning that the advocate wastes time by trying to establish something not at issue. See ELENCHUS (3).

ignotum per ignotius /ig-**noh**-təm pər ig-**noh**-shəs/. [Latin "the unknown by the more unknown"] An attempt to explain something obscure in terms even more obscure <What does *habitation* mean? Why, it means "commorancy"!> <For those of you who don't understand the term *extirpate,* it's equivalent to *deruncinate*>. • The term is often applied when a word is defined opaquely or to an argument in which something that is not well understood is explained in terms even more arcane.

illative conjunction. 1. See *final conjunction* under CONJUNCTION. **2.** See *conjunctive adverb* under ADVERB.

illeism /**il**-ee-iz-əm/. Reference to oneself in the third person, either by the third-person pronoun (*he, she*) or by name or label. Two examples. In Shakespeare's *Julius Caesar* (1598), the eponymous character consistently uses illeism, saying at one point: "Caesar should be a beast without a heart / If he should stay at home today for fear" (2.2.42–43). In the 1996 presidential election, the Republican candidate, Bob Dole, was widely lampooned for his illeism ("Let me tell you what Bob Dole thinks.").

illocution /il-loh-**kyoo**-shən/, n. Speech or writing that itself constitutes an action, as by ordering, warning, or promising. Cf. PERLOCUTION.

imperative /im-**per**-ə-tiv/, adj. (Of verbs) expressing a command (*come here*), prohibition (*don't touch that*), request (*help me a minute*), warning (*stay out or else!*), or the like. A synonym is *jussive,* but *jussive* has a second sense that is narrower than *imperative.* Cf. JUSSIVE (2). See *imperative sentence* under SENTENCE.

imperative mood. See MOOD.

imperative sentence. See SENTENCE.

imperfective aspect. See ASPECT.

improper diphthong. See DIPHTHONG.

inanimate, adj. Of, relating to, or being a thing that lacks consciousness or is

inherently immobile, although it may be a living thing such as a plant. See *feminine gender, masculine gender,* and *neuter gender* under GENDER.

inanimate noun. See NOUN.

inceptive /in-**sep**-tiv/. See INCHOATIVE.

inchoative /in-**koh**-ə-tiv/. (Of a verb) showing that an action, state of being, or the like has begun. The term is also used as a noun to denote such a verb. — Also termed *inceptive; ingressive*.

incipit /**in**(t)-sə-pit/ or /**in**-kə-pit/, n. The first part or opening words of a writing, esp. when a work is untitled; specif., the beginning of a medieval manuscript.

indefinite adjective. See ADJECTIVE.

indefinite article. See ARTICLE.

indefinite pronoun. See PRONOUN.

independent clause. See CLAUSE.

independent form. See ABSOLUTE FORM.

indicative /in-**dik**-ə-tiv/, adj. (Of a verb) expressing a plain statement.

indicative mood. See MOOD.

indirect object. See OBJECT.

indirect-object inversion. The placement of an indirect object before the direct object (as in *John gave her the book* as opposed to *John gave the book to her*).

indirect question. See QUESTION.

indirect speech. See REPORTED SPEECH.

infinitive. A verb in its unconjugated form that can function as a noun but retains certain verb features, such as taking an object and being modified by adverbs. • The infinitive is usually preceded by "to" <to dance> or by an auxiliary or modal verb <You can take the camera>. The subject of an infinitive is always in the objective case <For him to prepare any less diligently would have been shocking>.

bare infinitive. An infinitive in which *to* is omitted. It almost always follows an auxiliary verb such as *should.* — Also termed *plain infinitive; pure infinitive; unmarked infinitive*.

complementary infinitive. An infinitive that functions as the principal verb <I am going to revise the manuscript next week> (in which *am going* has a modal quality).

marked infinitive. A verb form preceded by the word *to*.

plain infinitive. See *bare infinitive*.

pure infinitive. See *bare infinitive*.

split infinitive. An infinitive verb composed of *to* followed by one or more modifiers before the verb <to fully explain> <to deliberately split an infinitive>. See pp. 853–55.

unmarked infinitive. See *bare infinitive*.

infinitive phrase. See PHRASE.

infinitive verb. See INFINITIVE.

infix /in-fiks/, n. **1.** A sound element, such as a letter or syllable, inserted within a word. • In a string of suffixes, as in *cleanliness* where *-ly* and *-ness* are both suffixes, some grammarians treat all but the last-added syllable as infixes. Otherwise, infixes are comparatively rare in English. **2.** A word inserted between the parts of a compound word, often typical of slang (e.g., *some-damn-where, absobloodylutely*). See AFFIX. Cf. PREFIX; SUFFIX.

inflecting language. See SYNTHETIC LANGUAGE.

inflection. 1. The change of form that a word undergoes to distinguish its case, gender, mood, number, voice, or other characteristics. • Nouns, pronouns, and verbs are inflected either by affixation or by internal vowel change. Nouns are inflected to show that they are plural <goose–geese> <clock–clocks>. Verbs are inflected when conjugated <I have–it has> <jog–jogged>. — Also spelled *inflexion.* — Also termed *flection.* **2.** The study of how the endings of words may be used to show their relationship to one another; ACCIDENCE.

inflectional affix. See AFFIX.

inflectional morphology. See ACCIDENCE.

inflexion. See INFLECTION.

ingressive /in-**gres**-iv/, adj. See INCHOATIVE.

initialism. An abbreviation made from the initial letters (or most important initial letters) of a name, each letter being pronounced separately, such as *CPU, FBI,* and *r.p.m.* • The American Broadcasting Company is typically reduced to its initials: ABC. An initialism is a type of abbreviation. — Also termed *alphabetism.* See ABBREVIATION. Cf. ACRONYM.

inkhornism. *Rhetoric.* An arcane term; a bookish word. • An inkhorn was variously a portable case for holding writing materials or a portable ink bottle (originally made of horn). In the Renaissance, a pedantic, ostentatious writer would be said to "smell [or savor] a little of the inkhorn." Hence *inkhornism* came to be used in reference to a word that typifies a style with that particular odor. Before moving to define *intensifier,* I must pause to acknowledge the irony that so many of the rhetorical terms in this glossary are essentially inkhornisms. In self-defense, I merely note that I didn't make them up. I'm just reporting the linguistic facts. But in a glossary like this one, a little sesquipedality—for the right reader—can

be some fun. Who'd have known that terms like *epanadiplosis* and *hypophora* even existed? — Also termed *inkhorn term.*

intensifier /in-**ten**[t]-sə-fɪ-ər/. An adverb that emphasizes and heightens an adjective or some other adverb. • Intensive adverbs and adjectives include *extremely, fairly, quite, rather, so, too, very,* and (as negative intensifiers) *hardly* and *scarcely.* — Also termed *intensive* or *degree modifier.*

intensive, adj. Expressing intensity; emphatic. • The prefix *in-* can be either intensive (as in *intense* and *incense*) or negative (as in *incredible* and *indefensible*). — Also termed *ascensive; augmentative.* — **intensive,** n.

intensive, n. See INTENSIFIER; REFLEXIVE.

intensive pronoun. See PRONOUN.

interjection. A word or short phrase uttered as an exclamation with no literal meaning and having no grammatical connection with anything; an expression used as an exclamation, usu. one expressing a strong feeling (e.g., *Really? Oh, no! It can't be!*). • Interjections show emotion, particularly strong ones such as surprise and shock. They usually appear at the beginning of a sentence and are punctuated with a comma or an exclamation mark. Because an interjection has no grammatical function in a sentence, a meaningless utterance used as an introductory word can also be an interjection (e.g., *Well, I'll have to ask first*). Cf. EXCLAMATION; PASILALY.

Interlingua /in-tər-**ling**-gwə/, n. An artificial language invented for universal use, esp. the one promoted since the 1920s by New York's International Auxiliary Association. Cf. ESPERANTO; PASIGRAPHY; PASILALY.

interrogative /in-tə-**rah**-gə-tiv/, adj. Expressing a question (as in *Who is making that awful noise?* or *Why didn't the mail come today?*). • The word is also used as a noun to denote a question. See *interrogative sentence* under SENTENCE.

interrogative adjective. See ADJECTIVE.

interrogative mood. See MOOD.

interrogative pronoun. See PRONOUN.

interrogative sentence. See SENTENCE.

intervocalic, adj. *Phonetics.* (Of a sound) immediately preceded and followed by vowel sounds, as with /p/ in *occupy* and /d/ in *idea.*

intonation /in-tə-**nay**-shən *or* -toh-/. **1.** The rise and fall in the pitch of a person's speaking voice. • A question is generally marked by a rising intonation at the end of the sentence. And certain words, such as *only,* may vary

in sense according to the speaker's intonation. Except for questions, exclamations, and the like, American English tends to sound more monotone, with less intonational variation than British English. **2.** The system of pitch and tone patterns of a spoken language. See PITCH.

intransitive verb. See VERB.

intrinsic modality. See *deontic modality* under MODALITY.

introductory adverb. See *conjunctive adverb* under ADVERB.

invective, n. Abusive or insulting language. — **invective,** adj.

inversion. 1. A change in the normal order or relationship of words or other elements; esp., the placement of a verb or some part of the verb phrase before its subject <"I'm coming," calmly said he>. — Also termed *hyperbaton; metaplasm.* See ANASTROPHE. **2.** The transposition of the subject and the auxiliary verb for the purpose of posing a question (e.g., *He is a golfer* becomes *Is he a golfer?*).

iotacism /ɪ-**oht**-ə-si-zəm/. The conversion of other vowel sounds to that of iota (in English, a long *e*).

ipse dixit. *Rhetoric.* An unsupported assertion; something stated but not proved. • An ipse dixit rests only on the speaker's authority.

ipsissima verba /ip-**sis**-i-mə vər-bə/. The very same words used by someone who is being quoted; a verbatim rendition.

Irish bull. A statement that is incongruous, ludicrous, or logically absurd, often unintentionally. • Irish bulls are usually found in speech, but they occasionally make their way into print. Examples:

• It seems, from what I gather, to be one of those simple cases which are so extremely difficult. (Sir Arthur Conan Doyle [1859–1930])
• I don't like spinach, and I'm glad I don't, because if I liked it I'd eat it, and I just hate it. (Clarence Darrow [1857–1938])
• Always go to other people's funerals; otherwise they won't come to yours. (Yogi Berra [1925–2015])

irony /**ɪ**-rə-nee/. *Rhetoric.* A mode of speech in which the literal or implied meaning of the words is opposite that of the intended meaning; esp., a suggested meaning that differs from the apparent meaning. • A classic example of irony is Mark Antony's speech in Shakespeare's *Julius Caesar.* Although Antony declares, "I come to bury Caesar, not to praise him," and declares that the assassins are "honorable men," he means just the opposite. Irony can be used for many purposes, such as humor or to be rude without being directly confrontational <Of course the bride won't mind if you wear ripped jeans to her formal wedding>. — Also termed *enantiosis*. Cf. HYPERBOLE; LITOTES; SARCASM.

irregular adjective. See ADJECTIVE.

irregular verb. See VERB.

isocolon /ɪ-soh-**koh**-lən/. *Rhetoric.* **1.** The use of successive phrases, clauses, or sentences of similar length and parallel grammatical structure. **2.** A sentence composed of clauses of equal length. Pl. **isocola.** — **isocolic,** adj.

isolating language. See ANALYTIC LANGUAGE.

italic. 1. (adj.) Of, relating to, or involving a sloping style of typeface. **2.** (n.) (usu. pl.) In printing, the sloping typeface used for emphasis or distinction. See pp. 533–34.

iterative /**it**-ə-rə-tiv *or* -ray-/, adj. See *frequentative aspect* under ASPECT.

iterative aspect. See ASPECT.

jargon /**jahr**-gən/. The special, usu. technical idiom of a social, occupational, or professional group, often intended to streamline communication and save time and space, but sometimes also to conceal meaning from the uninitiated. Cf. ARGOT; DIALECT. — **jargonistic,** adj. See p. 535.

jawbreaker. A word that is particularly difficult to pronounce.

Johnsonese. An inflated, stilted, or pompous literary style that displaces plain English with long words and Latinate diction. • This pejorative term derives from the name and style of Dr. Samuel Johnson (1709–1784), the renowned lexicographer and writer. James Boswell recorded this example of how Johnson altered plain English:

> He seemed to take a pleasure in speaking in his own style; for when he had carelessly missed it, he would repeat the thought translated into it. Talking of the Comedy of The Rehearsal, he said, "It has not wit enough to keep it sweet." This was easy; he therefore caught himself, and pronounced a more round sentence: "It has not vitality enough to preserve it from putrefaction." (James Boswell [1740–1795])

Thomas B. Macaulay likewise noted how Johnson's style changed when writing a private letter and recounting the same incident for the public:

> His letters from the Hebrides to Mrs. Thrale are the original of that work of which the *Journey to the Hebrides* is the translation; and it is amusing to compare the two versions. "When we were taken upstairs," says he in one of his letters, "a dirty fellow bounced out of the bed on which one of us was to lie." This incident is recorded in the journey as follows: "Out of one of the beds on which we were to

repose started up, at our entrance, a man black as a Cyclops from the forge." (Thomas B. Macaulay [1800–1859])

Yet another classic example occurs in Johnson's definition of *network* in Johnson's *Dictionary of the English Language* (1755): "any thing reticulated or decussated, at equal distances, with interstices between the intersections."

jot. The least letter or character of any writing; hence, a minuscule part of anything. See TITTLE.

jus et norma loquendi /jəs et nor-mə loh-**kwen**-dɪ/. Collectively, the standards or rules of grammar, pronunciation, and other linguistic elements as established by the customs of the native users of the language.

jussive /jəs-iv/, adj. **1.** IMPERATIVE. **2.** Expressing a command directed to a third person (e.g., *let them eat cake; have them submit suggestions*). Cf. IMPERATIVE.

justification. In printing, the alignment of text so that one or both margins form a straight edge.

karmadharaya /kahr-mə-**dahr**-ə-yə/, n. [Sanskrit] A compound consisting of an adjective plus a noun <blackbird> <supernova> or an attributive noun plus a noun <fireworks> <lamppost>. Cf. BAHUVRIHI.

kernel sentence. In transformational grammar, a simple sentence that results from the application of a few required transformations, and that with further transformations can be expanded into more complicated sentences. • A kernel sentence is the stripped-down nucleus of a sentence of any complexity <Young people are often exceptionally polite even though the general coarsening of society has resulted in the lack of emphasis on good manners> (the kernel sentence being *People are polite*). — Also termed *simplex*.

kerning, n. In printing, the adjustment of spacing between characters or letters.

kinesics /ki-**nee**-siks/, n. The study of how body movements and gestures convey nonvocal meaning; the examination of body language as a part of communication.

King's English. The supposed apotheosis of BrE grammar, syntax, usage, punctuation, and pronunciation.— Also termed *Queen's English*.

koine. 1. A literary dialect. **2.** LINGUA FRANCA. **3.** A regional dialect or language that becomes the standard language for a wide area and loses its most pronounced local characteristics. • The term comes from the name of an ancient Greek dialect

that eventually became the common language of the eastern Mediterranean countries under the Greek and Roman empires.

laconism /**lak**-ə-niz-əm/. **1.** Brevity or succinctness of style or expression. **2.** A short, pithy sentence. — **laconic** /lə-**kon**-ik/, adj.

lallation /la-**lay**-shən/. **1.** Baby talk. **2.** LAMBDACISM (3).

lambdacism /**lam**-də-siz-əm/. **1.** The overuse or overfondness of the letter *l* in speaking or writing. **2.** The mispronunciation of *l*. **3.** The erroneous substitution of *l* for *r* in pronunciation. • In sense 3, *lambdacism* is synonymous with *rhotacism*. See RHOTACISM; LALLATION (2). See p. 738.

language. 1. The expression of human thought or emotion in words, whether written or spoken. **2.** The set of habits by which the members of a nation are accustomed to communicating with one another; the sum of a population's means of communicating information, including words and syntax as well as gestures and customs of behavior (as in *the English language*). **3.** The manner or style of writing or speech (as in *pompous language*). **4.** The vocabulary and phraseology of a group of people in a profession, industry, or the like (as in *medical language*).

language acquisition. The process or result of learning language, either as a whole or in part. — Sometimes shortened to *acquisition*.

langue. *Linguistics.* Language as an abstract system, the principles of which make speech possible. • The elements of langue include subsystems such as spelling, syntax, and grammar. These elements create meaning according to the principles by which they are arranged and how they relate to one another. Cf. PAROLE.

lapsus calami /**lap**-səs **kal**-ə-mɪ/. [Latin] A slip of the pen. See HETEROPHEMY.

lapsus linguae /**lap**-səs **lin**-gwee/. [Latin] A slip of the tongue. See HETEROPHEMY.

leading /**led**-ing/, n. In printing, the amount of blank space between every two lines of text.

left-branching sentence. A complicated sentence that has most of its complexity—the conditions, exceptions, etc.—before the principal verb; one that has a majority of its constituents on the left side of the tree diagram. Cf. RIGHT-BRANCHING SENTENCE.

legaldegook. A combination of legalese and gobbledygook; unclear or overtechnical legal language. See GOBBLEDYGOOK; LEGALESE.

legalese. 1. The jargon used by members of the legal profession. **2.** Language marked by the overuse of legal terms. See LEGALDEGOOK.

lemma /lem-ə/. 1. An ancillary proposition used as part of an argument. **2.** The heading or theme of a written argument. **3.** A word or phrase defined or discussed in a dictionary, glossary, encyclopedia, etc.; esp., a dictionary headword. Pl. **lemmas** (preferably not *lemmata*). — **lemmatical** /li-**mat**-i-kəl/, adj.

lemmatize /lem-ə-tIz/, vb. 1. To group together the inflected forms of a word and list them under a headword. **2.** To choose the headwords (or main entries) for a dictionary, glossary, encyclopedia, etc. — **lemmatization,** n.

letter. 1. A symbol in an alphabet, such as *Z.* **2.** A character representing a speech sound or sounds.

lexeme /lek-seem/. *Linguistics.* A word or phrase taken as a lexical unit in the abstract, without considering the forms it takes in specific constructions. — Also termed *lexical unit.*

lexical, adj. **1.** Of, relating to, or involving a word or words. **2.** Of, relating to, or involving the vocabulary of a language. **3.** Of, relating to, or involving a dictionary or lexicography.

lexical ambiguity. See AMBIGUITY.

lexical category. See PART OF SPEECH.

lexical meaning. The essential meaning of nouns, verbs, adjectives, and adverbs—i.e., of the words that carry the bulk of the semantic burden in any utterance.

lexical unit. See LEXEME.

lexicographer /lek-si-kog-rə-fər/. The writer or compiler of a dictionary. • In his great English dictionary of 1755, Samuel Johnson's famous definition read as follows: "a writer of dictionaries; a harmless drudge."

lexicography /lek-si-kog-rə-fee/. The art or process of compiling a dictionary or lexicon. — **lexicographic** /lek-si-kə-**graf**-ik/, adj.

lexicology /lek-si-kol-ə-jee/. The study of words and their derivation and signification.

lexicon. 1. The vocabulary of a language, group, or individual. **2.** A dictionary; wordbook.

lexigraphy /lek-sig-rə-fee/. 1. The representation of words by distinct characters, as in the Chinese alphabet. **2.** Loosely, LEXICOGRAPHY. — **lexigraphic,** adj.

lexiphanes /lek-sif-ə-neez/. Someone who indulges in sesquipedality or lexiphanicism to an extreme degree.

lexiphanic /lek-si-fan-ik/, adj. Of, realting to, or involving the use of many hard, pretentious words. — **lexiphanicism,** n.

lexis. *Linguistics.* The total vocabulary of a language, as distinct from the grammar.

ligature /lig-ə-chuur *or* **-chər** *or* **-tuur** *or* **-tyuur/.** A written character made up of two or more joined letters, such as *æ* and *ffi.*

light verb. See VERB.

line-editing. The spotting and fixing of problems in a manuscript—whether one's own or someone else's. • Several things can go wrong when you're editing: (1) you might miss a problem and fail to eliminate it; (2) you might spot a problem and propose a flawed solution, perhaps even a "solution" that worsens the text; or (3) you might misidentify something as a problem when in fact it's perfectly correct, so that your "solution" mars what was an unblemished text (rarely in such a situation is the editorial hand benign). So a good editor is surefooted, but the surefootedness depends on accurate knowledge of editorial problems and their solutions. — Also termed *copyediting.*

lingo. A variety of language rendered somewhat unintelligible to a generalist as a result of peculiarities of vocabulary or pronunciation.

lingua franca /ling-gwə frang-kə/. A language that is spoken commonly, esp. for business purposes, by people in many different lands. • In ancient times, Latin was spoken throughout the Roman empire and continued to be used in former Roman possessions as a trade language after the empire crumbled. By the Renaissance, French had become the lingua franca in Europe. Today, English is the global lingua franca.

linguist. 1. An expert in linguistics; a student of the history or science of language. **2.** Someone who is fluent in several languages.

linguistic ambiguity. See AMBIGUITY.

linguistics. The scientific study of language. See GRAMMAR; MORPHOLOGY; MORPHOPHONEMICS; PHONETICS; PHONOLOGY; PRAGMATICS; SEMANTICS; STYLISTICS; SYNTAX.

comparative linguistics. The branch of linguistics that focuses on the mutual relationships of languages believed to have a common origin or the historical development of a language between periods.

descriptive linguistics. A field of study that investigates how people actually use language, both in particular groups and broadly. Cf. *prescriptive linguistics.*

diachronic linguistics. See *historical linguistics.*

historical linguistics. The study of how one or more languages develop over time. — Also termed *diachronic linguistics.*

prescriptive linguistics. The study of language to derive or develop common rules and guide users in the use of standardized rules that aid communication. Cf. *descriptive linguistics.*

psycholinguistics /sI-koh-ling-**gwis**-tiks/. The study of how people learn, understand, and produce language.

sociolinguistics /soh-see-oh-ling-**gwis**-tiks *or* soh-shee-oh-ling-**gwis**-tiks/. The study of language in relation to society. • Social factors that affect language include class, region, and occupation.

structural linguistics. The analytical study of language as a system and the functions of linguistic units such as sounds, words, and sentences within the system.

linking verb. See VERB.

literal, adj. **1.** (Of a word or phrase) having the usual or most basic sense. Cf. FIGURATIVE. **2.** Unembellished.

literarism. 1. The use of unusual words by the literary or erudite. **2.** An addiction to literary language; an expression of literary language. **3.** A literary idiom or expression.

literatim /lit-ə-**ray**-tim/, adv. [Latin] Letter for letter.

literation. The representation of sounds or words by letters.

litotes /lI-tə-teez *or* **lit-ə-teez/.** *Rhetoric.* **1.** Understatement achieved by denying the opposite of an idea; affirmation of a thing by denying the truth of its opposite <a citizen of no mean city>. • Litotes is used to increase effect or to reduce censure. It's a very old tool in English rhetoric; examples are found in Anglo-Saxon literature right up to modern times. For example, *he's not the friendliest person* means *he's unfriendly.* And *it's not inconceivable that there will be a pop quiz* means *you'd better study: there will probably be a pop quiz.* Cf. HYPERBOLE; IRONY; SARCASM. **2.** An instance of such understatement.

loan translation. A word or phrase borrowed from another language by literally translating the components. • English has borrowed many terms from many languages, including Spanish (blue-blood = *sangre azul*), French (merciless = *sans pitié*), German (superman = *Übermensch*), and Latin (wisdom tooth = *dens sapientiae*). — Also termed *calque.*

loanword. *Philology.* A word borrowed or adopted from another language and partly or wholly naturalized. • Few or no changes are made to some adopted words such as *hotel* (from Fr. *hôtel*) and *kindergarten* (Ger.). For others, naturalization is evident. For instance, *extravert* was adapted from the German form *extravertiert*, which itself was compounded of the Latin *extra-* and *vertere*. The word evolved into *extrovert* when patterned on the established word *introvert*, derived from the Latin *introvertere*.

locative /**lahk**-ə-tiv/, adj. Expressing location; answering the question *where* or *in* (*at*) *what place*. • Some examples of locative words are directional words (e.g., *north*; *southwest*) and adverbs (e.g., *above*; *everywhere*; *here*; *inside*).

locative adverb. See ADVERB.

locution. 1. A mode of speaking. **2.** A word, phrase, or idiom; phraseology.

logicaster /**loj**-i-kas-tər/. An inferior logician; an illogical dabbler in logic. Cf. GRAMMATICASTER; POETASTER.

logocracy /lə-**gahk**-rə-see/, n. Government by the power of words. — **logocratic,** adj.

logodaedaly /log-ə-**ded**-ə-lee/, n. **1.** Skill in wordplay; verbal legerdemain. **2.** Wordplay.

logogram /**log**-ə-gram/. A written character such as a letter (e.g., *c.* for *century*) or a symbol (e.g., *$* or *%*) that represents a whole word, as in shorthand writing. — Also termed *logograph.* Cf. IDEOGRAM; PICTOGRAM.

logograph /**log**-ə-graf/. **1.** A written word. **2.** LOGOGRAM.

logogriph /**loh**-goh-grif/. A word riddle in which the solution requires the discovery of some word by a recombination of the letters or elements of specified words or by guessing and combining other words that, when correctly arranged, form the word to be guessed.

logolatry /loh-**gol**-ə-tree/. Excessive regard for verbal or literal accuracy. — **logolatrous,** adj.

logolept /**loh**-goh-lept/. A writer with a passion for sensational uses or combinations of words; a word maniac.

logology /lə-**gahl**-ə-jee/. The study of words with an emphasis on features such as length and letter patterns rather than meaning.

logomachy /lə-**gahm**-ə-kee *or* lah-**gahm**-ə-kee/, n. **1.** A dispute about words. **2.** A war of words; wordy strife without accompanying deeds. — **logomachist,** n.

logomancy /loh-goh-man[t]-see/. Divination through the use of supposedly magical words or phrases; verbal augury.

logomania /log-oh-**may**-nee-ə/. A type of insanity characterized by uncontrollable garrulity; mad loquacity. — **logomaniac,** n. — **logomaniacal,** adj.

logoneurosis /loh-goh-nuu-**roh**-sis/. A mental disorder resulting in defective use or forgetfulness of language. — **logoneurotic,** adj.

logopathy /loh-**gop**-ə-thee/. Disorder of speech caused by disease of the brain. — **logopathic,** adj.

logophobia /log-ə-**foh**-bee-ə/, n. A persistent fear, distrust, or dislike of words. — **logophobic,** adj.

logoplegia /loh-goh-**plee**-jee-ə/. A paralytic condition resulting in the inability to pronounce particular words.

logorrhea /log-ə-**ree**-ə/, n. Diarrhea of the mouth; excessive, often incoherent talkativeness. Cf. GARRULITY; LOQUACITY.

longueur /long-**guur**/. A long or boring passage, esp. in a writing. • This term originally applied to writings alone but is now extended to performing arts, including plays, music, and speeches. It almost always carries a hint of insult or disdain.

loose, adj. Of, relating to, or involving a syntactical element that is inessential to the meaning or grammatical construction <loose clause> <loose apposition>.

loquacity /loh-**kwas**-i-tee/, n. Talkativeness; fluency to a fault. Cf. GARRULITY; LOGORRHEA. — **loquacious,** adj.

lurry, n. **1.** Something recited by rote or delivered in a monotone; boilerplate speech. • John Milton (1608–1674), who disapproved of the Church of England's *Book of Common Prayer,* wrote that one effect of its use was "to turn prayer into a kind of lurry." **2.** A babble of voices; a hubbub.

macaronic /mak-ə-**ron**-ik/, adj. Using real or coined words mixed and mangled from various languages; linguistically jumbled.

macrolinguistics. 1. The study of all types of human communication, verbal or symbolic. • Defined most broadly, it includes both microlinguistics and prelinguistics. Cf. MICROLINGUISTICS; PRELINGUISTICS. **2.** The statistical analysis of large-scale linguistic phenomena, esp. involving more than one language.

macron /**may**-kron *or* mak-ron/. In pronunciation, a diacritical mark (ˉ) indicating that a vowel sound is long. • For example, the mark shows that the vowel sound in *beet* is a long *ee*

(/bēt/). And in *cooperate,* it indicates that the identical adjacent letters are not pronounced alike (/kōŏpərāt/). The curved mark is a breve. See DIACRITICAL MARK. Cf. BREVE.

main clause. See *independent clause* under CLAUSE.

main verb. See VERB.

malapropism /**mal**-ə-prop-iz-əm/. A grotesque misuse of a word, often one with some similarity in sound or stress pattern to another; the word so misused. • This sort of misuse is named for Mrs. Malaprop, a character in Richard Brinsley Sheridan's play *The Rivals* (1775), who frequently used words that sounded like the ones she meant to say, as in, "His physiognomy [phraseology] is so grammatical!" See CATACHRESIS. See p. 577.

malediction /mal-i-**dik**-shən/. A curse or imprecation; an invocation of evil.

mannerism. Constant or excessive recourse to a particular style or expression, syntactic feature, or literary treatment.

marked infinitive. See INFINITIVE.

masculine, adj. (Of a pronoun or noun) indicating that the person or animal named is male. • In English, only the personal pronoun *he,* certain nouns (such as *rooster*), and a few adjectives are masculine. Unlike in the feminine gender, masculine nouns and adjectives are not distinguished by suffixes. See GENDER. — **masculine,** n.

mass noun. See NOUN.

mataeology. Pointless or unproductive conversation or questioning; fruitless discourse. — **mataeologian,** n.

matrix clause. See *independent clause* under CLAUSE.

maxim. A pithy proposition or principle drawn from experience.

mechanics. Devices that lend clarity to writing, such as spelling, punctuation, and capitalization.

meiosis /mɪ-**oh**-sis/, n. *Rhetoric.* A figure of speech in which something's importance is intentionally understated or implied to be less significant or substantial than it really is. • The understatement actually heightens the force of the statement. For example:

- One nuclear bomb can ruin your whole day.
- Today, my wife left me, my dog bit me, and I lost my job, so I'm feeling a little down.
- I was somewhat worried when the psychopath ran toward me with a chainsaw.

— **meiotic,** adj.

melioration. *Linguistics.* The process by which over time a word elevates in meaning or gains a more positive connotation, so that a negative or derogatory word takes on a positive or favorable meaning. • For example, Old English *hláford* "keeper of the bread" was simplified and underwent melioration to Modern English *lord*. In Middle English, *luxury* and *lasciviousness* were synonyms. Today *luxury* means "something highly desirable but not a necessity," and *lasciviousness* refers to unrestrained sexual desire. Cf. PEJORATION. — Also termed *amelioration*.

melifluous /mi-**lif**-loo-əs/, adj. (Of an utterance, series of words or sentences, or voice) smoothly flowing; honey-like.

melliloquence. Pleasant-sounding speech; charming eloquence. — **melliloquent**, adj.

merism /**mer**-iz-əm/, n. *Rhetoric*. A type of synecdoche in which a totality is expressed by two contrasting parts <head-to-toe search> <come old and young alike>. — Also termed *merismus*.

metabasis /mə-**tab**-ə-sis/. *Rhetoric*. A transitional summary that links different sections of a writing; esp., a brief summing up of what has already been covered, followed by a précis of what will follow. — **metabatic**, adj.

metalanguage. *Linguistics*. Technical language used to describe or analyze an object of study, such as mathematics, philosophy, and esp. other languages. • When language is studied, it is called an *object language*. A metalanguage may be a natural language or a formal one that uses specific terms or formal models to discuss the elements or use of an object language. For example, the English sentence "Andrew shouts" might be rendered in a formal metalanguage as "S(a)," where *S* = *shouts* and *a* = *Andrew*. When addressing a natural language that is the same as the object language (e.g., English), writers conventionally use typographical means to distinguish between the metalanguage and the object language, usually by italicizing statements in the object language or surrounding them with quotation marks. See OBJECT LANGUAGE.

metalepsis /met-ə-**lep**-sis/, n. *Rhetoric*. **1.** The uniting of two or more figures of speech in one word or phrase. **2.** A word or phrase in which two or more figures of speech are united. — **metaleptic**, adj.

metalinguistics. 1. The study of language and its relationship to other elements within a culture or society. **2.** The study of linguists' methods of investigation and analysis.

metanalysis /met-ə-**nal**-i-sis/, n. The analysis of words or groups of words into new elements (e.g., historically *an ewt* became *a newt*, and *a napron* became *an apron*). Cf. PROTHESIS. — **metanalytical**, adj.

metanoia /met-ə-**noy**-ə/. *Rhetoric*. The tactic of correcting oneself or revising a previous statement for rhetorical effect. • Metanoia can serve a variety of rhetorical ends. Stopping to correct oneself disrupts the flow of discourse, drawing attention to and emphasizing the revision. Or, in a move similar to paralipsis, retracting a statement allows the speaker to introduce an idea or claim and then avoid responsibility for having done so. Sometimes strengthening an initially mild or uncontroversial statement (or qualifying an initially strong one) can persuade an audience by making the speaker seem more reasonable.

metanomen /met-ə-**noh**-mən/. A metaphorical name, esp. one used in poetic diction.

metaphor. *Rhetoric*. An implied comparison between two things by figuratively using a word or phrase in a sense analogous to its literal denotation <The fog creeps in on cat's feet> <a volley of words>. See FIGURE OF SPEECH; TROPE. Cf. SIMILE. Examples:

- Language is the amber in which a thousand precious thoughts have been safely embedded and preserved. (Richard Chenevix Trench [1807–1886])
- Style is the gossamer on which the seeds of truth float through the world. (George Bancroft [ca. 1800–1891])

metaphrase, n. A translation; esp., a literal, word-for-word translation.— **metaphrase,** vb. — **metaphrastic,** adj.

metaplasm /**met**-ə-plaz-əm/. **1.** *Grammar*. A change in a word's syllables or letters. **2.** *Rhetoric*. See INVERSION.

metastasis /mə-**tas**-tə-sis/. **1.** *Grammar*. The change of tenses, such as the use of the historical present tense. **2.** *Rhetoric*. A sudden change of subject; an abrupt transition.

metathesis /mə-**tath**-ə-sis/. Transposition of the usual sequences of letters, syllables, or sounds of a word (e.g., *aksed* for *asked*, or *irrevelant* for *irrelevant*). • Over time, metathesis may produce a permanent change in the language. See p. 591.

meter. 1. Poetic rhythm; esp., the technique by which such rhythm is achieved. **2.** The pattern of stressed and unstressed syllables in lines of poetry.

metonymy /mə-**tahn**-ə-mee/. *Rhetoric*. The use of a word or phrase to represent not just what it denotes but something it is closely associated with; specif., a metaphor by which something related to another thing becomes the word for that other thing. • For example, the *Beltway* refers to political Washington; *Broadway* refers to the New York theater; the *Crown* refers to a monarchy; *gray hairs* refers to old age; *Wall Street* refers to investments or American stock markets. — **metonymic,** adj. — **metonym,** n. See TROPE.

microlinguistics. 1. The direct study of a particular aspect of language, such as phonology, semantics, or grammar. Cf. MACROLINGUISTICS; PRELINGUISTICS. **2.** The study of one particular linguistic system and its peculiarities. Cf. MACROLINGUISTICS.

Middle English. The English language used from about A.D. 1100 to 1500.

missive /**mis**-iv/. A message in writing; esp., a letter.

misword, n. An ill-advised word used harshly or angrily.

misword, vb. To express erroneously; to word badly.

mixed construction. A phrasing that fuses two or more idiomatic constructions <as much or more than>.

modal, adj. Of, relating to, or imparting grammatical mood—that is, the distinct form of the verb that expresses factuality, command, question, counterfactual assertion, etc. See MOOD.

modal auxiliary. See *modal verb* under VERB.

modality. 1. The condition, fact, or quality of expressing mood or of otherwise being modal. **2.** A special linguistic attribute or emphasis that marks a statement in some way.

deontic modality. Modality that expresses permission or obligation <You may go> <You must go>. — Also termed *intrinsic modality.*

epistemic modality. Modality concerned with the truth of a proposition <You might be right> <You may be right>. — Also termed *extrinsic modality.*

modal verb. See VERB.

mode. See MOOD.

Modern English. The English language in use since about 1500.

modification ambiguity. See AMBIGUITY.

modifier. 1. *Grammar*. A qualifying word, such as an adjective or adverb. — Also termed *qualifier*. **2.** *Phonetics*. A diacritical sign used with a symbol to indicate that the marked word's sound is modified only by the symbol.

compound modifier. See *phrasal adjective* under ADJECTIVE.

momentaneous aspect. See ASPECT.

mondegreen /**mahn**-di-green/. A misheard lyric, saying, catchphrase, or slogan that is then repeated erroneously. • Sylvia Wright coined this word in a 1954 *Harper's Magazine* article entitled "The Death of Lady Mondegreen." She explained how, as a child, she had listened to a Scottish ballad called "The Bonny Earl of Moray," in which one line is "They hae slain the Earl o' Moray and laid him on the green." She heard it as "They hae slain the Earl o' Moray and Lady Mondegreen." Mondegreens often arise in popular songs, such as "Rudolph the Red-Nosed Reindeer" and the misinterpreted reference to "Olive, the other reindeer" (for "all of the other reindeer"). Some mondegreens become widespread, though not accepted, in speech (e.g., **for all intensive purposes* in place of *for all intents and purposes*). See pp. 603–04.

monogenesis /mon-oh-**jen**-ə-sis/, n. The theory that all languages have a single ancestral origin. Cf. POLYGENESIS.

monoglossia /mon-oh-**glahs**-ee-ə/, n. The existence of only one language within a speech community. Cf. DIGLOSSIA; TRIGLOSSIA.

monoglot. A person who speaks and understands only one language.

monophthong /**mahn**-əf-thong/. A single, simple vowel sound, formed with the organs of articulation in a fixed position; a pure vowel. • An example is the /e/ sound in the word *set.*

monoptote /**mon**-əp-toht/. A word that has only one case; esp., in Greek or Latin, a word that occurs only in a single oblique case. • Essentially, this term is synonymous with *aptote.* See APTOTE; DIPTOTE; TRIPTOTE.

monosemy /mə-**nah**-sə-mee/, n. A word's quality of having a single meaning. • Something characterized by monosemy is unambiguous. Cf. POLYSEMY.

monosyllable /**mon**-oh-sil-ə-bəl/, n. A word or utterance of one syllable. — **monosyllabic** /mon-oh-si-**lab**-ik/, adj.

monotransitive, adj. (Of a verb) taking only a direct object, not an indirect one as well. Cf. DITRANSITIVE.

monotransitive verb. See VERB.

mood. The characteristic of a verb's form that shows the speaker's attitude, and expresses whether the action or state it denotes is a fact, command, possibility, or wish. — Also termed *mode.* See MODAL. Cf. ASPECT; TENSE; VOICE.

declarative mood. The normal mood of a verb, in contrast to the imperative, interrogative, and subjunctive moods.

imperative mood. The mood used to express a command, or to instruct, incite, or encourage. • Imperatives are typically uninflected verbs used to state something firmly <Start now>, but they are tempered when trying to be polite or show respect <Bring that file here, please>.

indicative mood. The mood used to express an idea as objective fact.

interrogative mood. The mood used to show that something is a question. • Some grammarians consider this not to be a separate mood in English; they classify it as indicative.

optative mood. A mood that expresses a desire or hope. • Languages such as classical Greek have optative verb forms, but in English the subjunctive is used in expressions such as *Heaven help him!*

subjunctive mood. The mood that expresses an action or state not as a reality, but as a mental conception. • The subjunctive mood is not often used in modern English apart from a few expressions such as *if I were you.* See p. 869.

morpheme /**mor**-feem/. The smallest meaningful unit of a language; a word or part of a word that cannot be divided into smaller parts. • For instance, *outgoing* can be broken down into the preposition *out,* the verb *go,* and the suffix *-ing,* but none of those components can be further broken down, so they are morphemes. The word *girls* consists of two morphemes: *girl* and the plural suffix *-s.* But *mahogany* cannot be divided into smaller meaningful units. — **morphemic,** adj. See BASE FORM. Cf. PHONEME.

bound morpheme. A morpheme that cannot stand alone but must be attached to another morpheme. • Most prefixes and suffixes are bound morphemes. All inflectional morphemes are bound morphemes.

free morpheme. A morpheme that can occur as a stand-alone word. • Nouns such as *rule* and *place* are free morphemes.

inflectional morpheme. A morpheme that is added to a noun, verb, adjective, or adverb to change its grammatical role in some way. • Nouns have two inflectional suffixes (plural *-s* and possessive *-'s*); verbs have four of them (*-s, -ing, -ed,* and *-en*); and some adjectives and adverbs have two (*-er* and *-est*).

morphology /mor-**fahl**-ə-jee/. **1.** *Linguistics.* The study of how sounds are grouped into words, and how the constituents are arranged to signal meaning; esp., the study of how words are made from morphemes. **2.** The form

and structure of words; word formation. — **morphological,** adj. Cf. ACCIDENCE; SYNTAX.

morphophonemics /mor-foh-fə-**nee**-miks/. *Linguistics.* The analysis of grammatical and phonological facts that determine the forms of phonemes. — Also termed *morphophonology.* See PHONEME.

morphophonology. See MORPHOPHONEMICS.

motto. A word, phrase, or concise sentence that expresses a guiding rule of life, principle, or faith, and that has been adopted by a person or group of people.

mouillé /moo-**yay**/, adj. (Of a consonant) sounded with the tongue touching the palate (as with *l* and *n*).

mumpsimus. 1. A persistent adherent to an erroneous tenet or linguistic form, despite irrefutable correction. • The story runs that in the Middle Ages, an old priest was saying a prayer in Latin. The word *sumpsimus* (= we have received) he mispronounced as *mumpsimus.* When corrected, he insisted that he'd been saying *mumpsimus* for 30 years and would not change his "old mumpsimus" for the "new sumpsimus." In our own day, former President George W. Bush persisted in /**noo**-kyə-lər/ for /**noo**-klee-ər/ despite a deluge of corrections in the press. His pronunciational pertinacity might have earned him the title of mumpsimus. **2.** An erroneous tenet or linguistic form that someone tenaciously adheres to.

mutation. 1. The gradual, systematic change of a sound in a given language. **2.** The substitution or disappearance of a letter to form a new word. **3.** A change of vowel sounds, esp. as influenced by other sounds in the word or neighboring words. • The chief types are *consonant mutation* and *vowel mutation* (e.g., umlaut). Mutation accounts for shifting vowel pronunciations over time, and for irregular inflections as shown in spelling (e.g., *foot–feet; man–men*) and heard in pronunciation (e.g., the *-i-* in *child–children;* the *-o-* in *woman–women*). See GREAT VOWEL SHIFT.

mute, adj. (Of a letter) not pronounced.

mycterism. *Rhetoric.* Subtle mocking; a scornful gibe; an instance of sarcasm or irony. See SARCASM; IRONY.

narrowing. See SPECIALIZATION.

nasal /**nay**-zəl/, adj. (Of a spoken sound) produced by resonating air in the nose and mouth; of, relating to, or involving a speech sound made with air exiting the nose.

needless variant. An unnecessary deviation from the standard form of a word. • A writer or speaker who uses a needless variant may mislead the reader into believing that there is a distinction in the words. See BY-FORM; DIFFERENTIATION.

negation /ni-**gay**-shən/. **1.** The act or an instance of making what would otherwise be an affirmative statement into a negative one.

compound negation. The negation of a compound construction using *neither . . . nor.*

2. A negative statement.

negative, adj. Of, relating to, or involving a clause or phrase that contains a marker for negation.

neologism /nee-**ahl**-ə-jiz-əm/. A newly coined word or expression. — Also termed *neology.* — **neologist,** n. — **neologistic,** adj. See p. 624.

neoterism /nee-**ot**-ə-riz-əm/. The use of one or more newly invented words or phrases; the employment of a neologism. **2.** A neologism itself. — **neoteric,** adj.

neurolinguistics. The branch of linguistics that studies the relationship between language and the structure and functioning of the human brain.

neuter gender. See GENDER.

newspeak. Propagandistic language consisting of counter words, newfangled euphemisms, periphrasis, and doublespeak. • The term was coined by George Orwell in his novel *1984.*

nimiety (ni-**mi**-ə-tee). The state or quality of redundancy.

nomenclature. 1. A system of names applied to some field of study. **2.** A systematic listing of technical names or terms.

nominal, n. A word, phrase, or clause that is functionally equivalent to a noun. • The category embraces nouns, pronouns, noun phrases, and noun clauses. Cf. NOUN PHRASE.

nominal clause. See CLAUSE.

nominalization. The conversion of a part of speech into a nominal, as by making *false* into *falsity,* or *authorize* into *authorization.* See *zombie noun* under NOUN.

nominal phrase. See NOUN PHRASE.

nominative /**nah**-mə-nə-tiv/, n. The case of a sentence's subject or of a noun complement that follows a linking verb. • Only personal pronouns have a distinct nominative form (e.g., the first-person pronouns in *I lost my keys again* and *that's what we wanted*). — Also termed *subjective.*

nominative absolute. A phrase containing a subject and a participle that adverbially modifies the main clause of a sentence and has no other grammatical relation to that clause. • A nominative absolute is not part

of the sentence it qualifies by time, condition, cause, or circumstance. In essence, the nominative absolute (or *absolute phrase*) is a parenthetical comment (e.g., *Dinner having fizzled, we sat and watched television.* Or: *He being a friend of mine, I shouldn't comment publicly on his actions.*). See ABSOLUTE CONSTRUCTION.

nominative case, n. See CASE.

nonce-word. A word invented "for the nonce," that is, for one occasion only. • The first editor of the *Oxford English Dictionary,* James A.H. Murray (1837–1915), invented this expression for use in the *Dictionary*'s entries. There are related terms such as *nonce-borrowing* (= a word borrowed from a foreign language only for one occasion), *nonce-compound, nonce-expression,* and *nonce-meaning.*

noncomparable adjective. See **adjective.**

noncount noun. See *mass noun* under NOUN.

nondefining relative clause. See *nonrestrictive relative clause* under CLAUSE.

nonfinite verb. See INFINITIVE.

nongradable adjective. See *noncomparable adjective* under ADJECTIVE.

nonrestrictive, adj. (Of the modifier of a noun or phrase) adding information that is parenthetical but does not help identify the referent. • For example, in *The tents, which are on aisle 3, are on sale,* the clause *which are on aisle 3* is nonrestrictive because it does not identify which tents are on sale—presumably they all are. Similarly, in *Orrin Hatch, the Utah senator, spoke next,* the phrase *the Utah senator* is not needed to identify the person named, so it is a nonrestrictive appositive. Nonrestrictive matter is always set off from the rest of the sentence by commas. Cf. RESTRICTIVE.

nonrestrictive relative clause. See CLAUSE.

nonsentence. See SENTENCE.

non sequitur. 1. An absurd statement that produces a comic effect; esp., a statement or thought that does not logically follow what was just said. • In social situations, a non sequitur may indicate a misunderstanding or lack of attention, or it may be an effort to get away from an uncomfortable subject. **2.** A sudden, illogical turn in the dialogue or plot. • Would-be world-famous author Snoopy, the creation of Charles Schulz (1922–2000), committed non sequiturs repeatedly in his attempts at writing: "It was a dark and stormy night. Suddenly, a shot rang out! A door slammed. The maid screamed. Suddenly, a pirate ship appeared on

the horizon! While millions of people were starving, the king lived in luxury. Meanwhile, on a small farm in Kansas, a boy was growing up." **3.** A fallacious argument in which the conclusion does not follow from the premise or premises. • A classic example is the argument, "If A, then B. B is true. So A is true." But the conclusion is not necessarily related to the premises. For instance, "Dogs don't drink beer. I don't drink beer. Therefore, I am a dog." This doesn't exclude the possibility that the speaker is a human. Similarly, an *if–then* statement may be a non sequitur: "If I see four dachshunds today, then I'll have good luck tomorrow." Cf. ANACOLUTHON.

nonstandard, adj. (Of usage) not found in educated speech or writing.

nonstandard English. Informal English not used for educated speech or writing; colloquial English or dialects. See DIALECT. Cf. STANDARD ENGLISH.

non-U, adj. Of, relating to, or involving language or behavior characteristic of people who are neither in the upper social echelon nor among the better-educated in society. Cf. U.

nonverbal, adj. Without the use of words.

nonword. 1. A word that is not recorded in most major dictionaries <conversate>. **2.** A word that, even though it may be recorded in some dictionaries, is regarded by many as illegitimate because of its spurious origins <irregardless>. • Nonwords arise from many sources. They may be back-formations <orientate>, malapropisms <unmercilessly>, common misspellings <forebearance>, or neologisms <jumblicious>. Some move out of their shadowy existence if they prove to be useful or at least popular (e.g., *donate, stick-to-it-iveness*). But there is no sure way to tell whether a nonword will fade away or become standard. The term *nonword* itself was first coined in the 1890s and became standard only in the 1960s. See p. 630.

normative, adj. Concerned with the accepted standards or norms of usage.

normative grammar. See PRESCRIPTIVE GRAMMAR.

nosism. 1. An individual's use of the word *we* when speaking of or for himself or herself. **2.** The self-centered attitude of a group of people. • This is the collective form of *egotism.*

noun. A word that names something, whether abstract (intangible) or concrete (tangible).

abstract noun. A noun referring to something that has no physical existence, such as a feeling, quality, concept, or state of being. • Examples of abstract nouns are *education, fortune, love, quandary,* and *shamelessness.* Although an abstract noun is intangible, it may be countable <noises> <meetings> or uncountable <music> <happiness>. Sometimes the meaning of an abstract noun changes from singular to plural <kindness–kindnesses>. Cf. *concrete noun.*

agent noun. A noun that denotes a person who performs some action. • Agent nouns often have the suffix *-er* <traveler> or *-or* <collector>.

animate noun. A noun that refers to an animal or human.

attributive noun. A noun functioning as a modifier, usu. as an adjective. • An attributive noun may be a word or a noun phrase. When it is a phrase, it is hyphenated to prevent it from being mistaken for the subject or predicate object. • For example, *satellite dish* and *healthcare costs* begin with attributive nouns. — Also termed *noun adjunct.*

collective noun. A noun that names a group of people, animals, objects, or concepts; a noun that is grammatically singular but has a plural sense. • Some collective nouns may be singular or plural. You can usually tell which by looking at how the members of the group behave. If they act in unison with one another, then the collective noun is singular <The jury retires to deliberate>. But if the members behave as individuals, then the noun is plural <The jury disagree on a verdict and have told the judge they are deadlocked>. In American English, some collective nouns have distinct singular and plural forms (e.g., *team* and *teams*) and the accompanying verbs match them in number (e.g., *the team is* and *the teams are*). In British English, you'll often hear collective nouns, such as *team,* treated as plural <The team are playing very well today>. See pp. 179–80.

common noun. A general name for a person, place, or thing, capitalized only under certain circumstances, as when it begins a sentence or appears in a title. • Common nouns include *girl, police officer, teenager* (people); *office building, restaurant* (places); and *microwave, tractor* (things). A noun may function as a common noun when used in a general sense <times> <manor> and a proper noun when used for something specific <The Times> <Manor House Realty>. Common nouns ordinarily have singular and plural forms and are used with articles. Cf. *proper noun.*

compound noun. Two or more words that are joined (or, sometimes, hyphenated) to make a single noun <boyfriend> <landowner> <airplane>.

concrete noun. A noun referring to a person or thing that is perceptible through at least one of the five physical senses. Cf. *abstract noun.*

count noun. A noun that denotes an item that can be counted. • Count nouns have both singular and plural forms, usually made by adding *-s* or *-es.* In the plural, they frequently appear in constructions such as *two* ——, *several* ——, and *a large number of* ——. Cf. *mass noun.*

inanimate noun. A noun that refers to neither an animal nor a human.

mass noun. A noun that denotes an item that cannot be individually counted. • Examples: *meat, sugar, water.* Some mass nouns can also be count nouns on occasion <choose only the best meats>. But mass nouns do not usually have a plural form. — Also termed *noncount noun; uncountable noun.* Cf. *count noun.*

noncount noun. See *mass noun.*

proper noun. The name of a specific person, place, or thing, always written with a capital letter. • Proper nouns include *Jean Valjean* (character); *Jamaica, Abacus Restaurant* (places); and the *Eiffel Tower, Monday, the Fourth of July* (things). The names of holidays, days of the week and months, historical documents, organizations, religions, and the like are all proper nouns. — Also termed *proper name.* Cf. *common noun.*

recipient noun. A noun that denotes a person who receives some thing or action, or for whom something is done. • Recipient nouns often have the suffix *-ee* <honoree>.

zombie noun. A noun formed from a verb by addition of a suffix such as *-ance, -ity,* or *-tion* <performance–perform> <realization–realize>. • Such nouns often require prepositional phrases to elicit their meaning, and can result in wordiness. Recasting the sentence to use the simple verb is a good solution. — Also termed *nominalization; buried verb.*

noun adjunct. See *attributive noun* under NOUN.

noun-banging. See NOUNINESS.

noun clause. A clause that functions as a noun or noun phrase <When the car was dented is irrelevant>. Cf. NOMINAL.

object noun clause. A noun clause that plays the role of direct object in a sentence.

subject noun clause. A noun clause that plays the role of subject in a sentence.

noun-equivalent. See SUBSTANTIVE.

nouniness. The excessive use of nouns, noun phrases, and noun clauses, esp. in close succession. — Also termed *noun plague; noun-banging.* See p. 635.

noun phrase. A phrase with a noun as its head; a noun cluster that may include a determiner <the goat> and one or more adjectives <an old barn>. — Also termed *nominal phrase.* Cf. NOMINAL.

noun plague. See NOUNINESS.

number. A quality of a word that shows whether one object or more than one object is referred to; the grammatical marking of quantity. • In English, the two numbers are singular and plural.

numeric adverb. See ADVERB.

nuncupative /nən-**kyoop**-ə-tiv/, adj. (Of a will) spoken as opposed to written; oral.

obelize /**ahb**-ə-līz/, vb. **1.** To mark (part of a text) with an obelus (†) or other mark to indicate that it is spurious or doubtful. **2.** More broadly, to stigmatize (a word or expression) as being ungrammatical or unidiomatic.

object. A word denoting either (1) the person or thing acted on by a transitive verb in the active voice <The balloon carried a pilot and a passenger> (*pilot* and *passenger* are objective) or (2) the person or thing related to another element by a connective, such as a preposition <Place the slide under the microscope> (*under* is a preposition, *microscope* is objective). • Objects may be *direct* or *indirect.*

cognate object. An object that is derivationally related to the verb <Sing a song> <Die an untimely death>.

direct object. The noun or noun phrase that receives the action of a transitive verb or shows the result of that action <Brian enjoys golf>. • It answers the question *What?* or *Whom?* after an action verb.

indirect object. The noun or noun phrase representing the person or thing with reference to which the action of a ditransitive verb is performed; the noun or noun phrase that follows the verb and receives the action. • It answers the question *To whom?* or *For whom?* In English, an indirect object usually comes between the verb and the direct object. You can paraphrase it as the object of a preposition, often *to* or *for* (e.g., *He sent me a book* can be paraphrased as *He sent a book to me*). Although there can be a direct object without an indirect object, there must always be a direct object if there is an indirect object. Indirect objects are usually found with verbs such as *brought, give, offer, show,* and *take.*

object of a preposition. The noun or noun phrase that follows a preposition in a prepositional phrase.

retained object. An object that continues to function as an object when a passive sentence is rewritten in active voice. • For example, in the passive-voice sentence *He was given money by many trusting people* and the active-voice rewrite *Many trusting people gave him money, money* is the direct object. The passive-voice sentence *a gold watch was given to my father* will have two objects when rewritten in active voice, *The company gave my father a gold watch,* but only one, *my father,* is a retained object. In the passive sentence, it was the object of a preposition. In the active sentence, it is an indirect object.

object complement. See COMPLEMENT.

objective /ahb-**jek**-tiv/, n. The case in which the object of a transitive verb or preposition is expressed. • In present-day English, only the first- and third-person pronouns and *who* have an objective form that is different from the nominative form (i.e., *I–me, he–him, she–her, we–us, they–them,* and *who–whom*). Apart from those words, syntax determines the relationship that a word has to other words (e.g., in *the apple fell from the tree,* the word *tree* is the object of the preposition *from,* so [in the view of some traditional grammarians] it is in the objective case). Some grammarians call this the *accusative* case.

objective case. See CASE.

object language. *Linguistics.* A language that is being described, analyzed, or discussed. See METALANGUAGE.

object noun clause. See NOUN CLAUSE.

object of a preposition. See OBJECT.

obligative /ə-**blig**-ə-tiv/, adj. (Of a modal auxiliary) expressing a necessity or requirement (as with *must*). Cf. PERMISSIVE.

oblique case. See CASE.

obmutescence /ob-myoo-**tes**-en[t]s/. **1.** The loss of the ability to speak. Cf. APHONIA. **2.** Taciturnity; muteness.

obnubilation /ahb-n[y]oo-bi-**lay**-shən/. The beclouding of ideas; the act of making something obscure or indistinct. — **obnubilate,** vb.

obsolescent, adj. (Of a word or expression) gradually disappearing; becoming obsolete.

obsolete, adj. (Of a word or expression) no longer used; out of date.

occupatio /ahk-yə-**pay**-shee-oh/, n. See PARALIPSIS.

octosyllable /**ok**-tə-sil-ə-bəl/, n. A line or word of eight syllables. — **octosyllabic** /ok-tə-si-**lab**-ik/, adj.

officialese. The inflated, pompous, obscure language considered typical of bureaucrats' work, esp. in official documents and letters. • With effort, officialese can usually be translated into plain English. For instance, "The aforementioned office will, in its economic treatment, cease and terminate the distribution of moneys commencing as from May 1, 2007" becomes "Our office will stop making payments on May 1, 2007." See PLAIN ENGLISH. See p. 648.

okina /oh-**kee**-nə/. A diacritical mark resembling a right-facing apostrophe ('), used in the Hawaiian language to indicate a glottal stop or a consonant. • In Hawaiian, the name of the island group (and the biggest island) is sometimes written *Hawaiʻi.* See DIACRITICAL MARK; GLOTTAL STOP.

Old English. The Anglo-Saxon language, used in England from around A.D. 450 to 1100. • Unlike Middle English, Old English had a fully inflected grammar and had relatively few words borrowed from Latin and French. — Also termed *Anglo-Saxon.*

oligosyllable /**ol**-i-goh-sil-ə-bəl/, n. A line or word of few syllables. — **oligosyllabic** /o-li-goh-si-**lab**-ik/, adj.

onomasticon /on-ə-**mas**-ti-kon/. A dictionary of proper names; esp., the collection of Greek names compiled by Julius Pollux in the second century A.D.

onomastics /on-ə-**mas**-tiks/. **1.** The study of the origins and forms of proper names. **2.** The system that underlies the formation and use of proper names or of names used in a particular field. — **onomastic,** adj.

onomatology /on-ə-mə-**tol**-ə-jee/. **1.** The study and classification of names. **2.** The special vocabulary of any field of scientific study. **3.** A treatise on names.

onomatope /ə-**nahm**-ə-tohp/. An onomatopoeic word.

onomatopoeia /on-ə-mat-ə-**pee**-ə/. **1.** The formation of a word by imitating the sound it represents. • For example, *buzz* approximates the sound made by a flying insect, and *quack* is similar to a duck's voice. Other examples are *belch, crack, fizz, flutter, meow, plop, screech, smash, splash, squish, wham,* and *zoom.* **2.** The use of a word whose sound suggests its sense. Cf. SYNAESTHESIA. — **onomatopoeic,** adj.

open syllable. See SYLLABLE.

operator. 1. A grammatical element, such as a negative or determiner, that affects another element in a sentence. **2.** The first auxiliary verb in a verb phrase when the verb can be placed in front of the subject in order to change the mood of the sentence from declarative to interrogative (e.g., *Dan has been calling* becomes *Has Dan been calling?*).

optative /**ahp**-tə-tiv/, adj. (Of a verbal mood) expressing a hope or wish, esp. one that is realizable <may the best team win>.

optative mood. See MOOD.

oracy /**or**-ə-see/, n. **1.** Proficiency in speech; the ability to express oneself fluently and appropriately in speech. • Linguists have used this term since the mid-1960s. **2.** The oral transmission of information, esp. of cultural traditions and the like.

oral, adj. **1.** Of, relating to, or involving the mouth. **2.** Of, relating to, or involving the spoken word. **3.** Of, relating to, or involving a speech sound made with no air exiting through the nose.

oratio obliqua /or-**ray**-shee-oh oh-**blee**-kwə/. See *indirect discourse* under DISCOURSE.

oratio recta /or-**ray**-shee-oh **rek**-tə/. See *direct discourse* under DISCOURSE.

ordinal number. A number that denotes a position in a series rather than a quantity of things (e.g., *first; second; third*). • Ordinal numbers may function as adjectives (e.g., *first place*) or nouns (e.g., *Eustace is second*). Cf. CARDINAL NUMBER.

orismology /or-is-**mol**-ə-jee/. **1.** Technical terminology. **2.** The science of defining, esp. technical terms; lexicography for one or more technical fields. — **orismologic,** adj.

orthoepy /or-**thoh**-ə-pee *or* or-thə-wə-pee/. **1.** Correct or accepted pronunciation; the art of pronouncing words correctly. Cf. CACOEPY. **2.** The field of grammar concerned with pronunciation; specif., the study of how a writing or spelling system relates to the pronunciation of a language.

orthography /or-**thahg**-rə-fee/. **1.** The field of grammar that focuses on letters and spelling; the study of spelling and how letters are combined to represent sounds. **2.** The collective methods by which a language is conventionally reduced to its written form. **3.** The set of conventions that account for correct spelling.

orthophony /or-**thahf**-ə-nee/. Correct pronunciation and articulation.

otosis /oh-**toh**-sis/, n. **1.** The alteration or misuse of a word resulting from an erroneous impression of its sound. • Otosis was originally at work in the misrendering of *home in* (what homing pigeons do) as the increasingly widespread but erroneous *hone in*. **2.** The mishearing of spoken sounds.

overgeneralization. See GENERALIZATION.

oxymoron /ok-si-**mor**-on/. **1.** A pairing of contradictory or incongruous words; a paradoxical phrasing, usu. in two words <living death> <clingingly aloof>. **2.** *Rhetoric.* A paradox produced by juxtaposing words that seem contradictory <You must be cruel to be kind>. See p. 666.

palatal /**pal**-ə-təl/, adj. (Of spoken sounds) made by flattening the front of the tongue against or near the hard palate, as for the *y* in *yield*.

palaver /pə-**lav**-ər/. **1.** Empty flattering speech. **2.** A public conference or discussion; a powwow.

paleography /pay-lee-**og**-rə-fee/. **1.** Any ancient mode of writing. **2.** Collectively, ancient writings. **3.** The study of ancient writings and how to decipher them accurately.

palilalia /pal-ə-**layl**-yə/. A speech defect characterized by an abnormal repetition of syllables, words, or phrases. See VERBIGERATE. CF. ECHOLALIA; PALILOGY; PLOCE; EPIZEUXIS. — **palilalic** /pal-ə-**lay**-lik/, adj.

palilogy /pə-**lil**-ə-jee/, n. *Rhetoric.* The immediate repetition of a word or phrase, usu. for emphasis. Cf. EPIZEUXIS; PLOCE; PALILALIA.

palindrome. A word, phrase, or sentence that reads the same backward and forward (e.g., *Hannah*; *name no one man*). • Perhaps the most famous example is the one attributed to Napoleon when asked whether he could have invaded England: "Able was I ere I saw Elba."

palter /**pahl**-tər/, vb. To equivocate by speaking or writing unclearly; to speak in a tricky manner.

panegyric /pan-ə-**jeer**-ik/ or /-jI-rik/, n. A eulogistic oration or writing; elaborate or formal praise. — **panegyric,** adj.

paradiastole /pa-rə-dī-**as**-tə-lee/, n. The use of a euphemism to advance an argument by replacing an unfavorable term with a more favorable one— often one that fallaciously disregards part of the truth. • For example, in the debate over illegal immigration into the United States, those opposed to border control often replace *illegal alien* with *undocumented worker* (or even *worker*) and replace *illegal immigration* with *immigration* to obscure the illegality of the border crossings under debate.

paradigm /pa-rə-dɪm/. **1.** A pattern, exemplar, or prototype. **2.** *Grammar.* A model for the inflection of a class of words, as of verb conjugations or noun declensions <woman–woman's–women–women's> <ring–rings–rang–rung–ringing>. See DECLENSION (2). **3.** *Rhetoric.* An example or illustration of a point.

paradox. 1. A seemingly self-contradictory statement or belief; a seemingly absurd expression <never less alone than when alone>. **2.** *Rhetoric.* A figure of speech used to teach a lesson or evoke an impression by an unexpected or surprising turn of expression. **3.** A puzzling fact, observation, or person.

paragoge /pa-rə-**goh**-jee/. The addition of a sound or syllable at the end of a word <idea → idear> <unbeknown → unbeknownst>. • This term embraces not just vulgarisms such as *oncet*, but also more legitimate variations such as *amongst* for *among.* — Also termed *epithesis.* — **paragogic,** adj.

paragraph. A group of sentences in which a single topic is developed; a sequence of structurally related sentences. • A paragraph is traditionally begun on a new line, with a space separating the first word from the margin. Ideally, a paragraph is a unified statement of a particular point in the analysis or narrative.

paralanguage. In communication, the nonverbal elements used to modify meaning and convey emotion, such as intonation, volume, expressions, and gestures. • In written communications, particularly informal types such as e-mail and chatrooms, paralanguage appears in emoticons, capitalization, choice of fonts, and the like. — Also termed *paralinguistic features.*

paraleipsis. See PARALIPSIS.

paralinguistic, adj. Of, relating to, or involving paralanguage; relating to or designating nonverbal speech elements. See PARALANGUAGE.

paralinguistic features. See PARALANGUAGE.

paralinguistics. A branch of linguistics concerned with the nonphonemic aspects of speech, such as silence, tone of voice, facial expressions, gesticulation, body postures, and tempo. Cf. KINESICS.

paralipsis /pa-rə-**lɪp**-sis/. *Rhetoric.* A brief reference to something done in such a way as to emphasize the suggestiveness of the thing omitted <I'll mention only a few of the outrages committed by the Spanish Inquisition>. — Also spelled *paraleipsis; paralepsis* /pair-ə-**lep**-sis/. — Also

termed *preterition; pretermission; occupatio.* Cf. APOPHASIS.

parallelism. 1. The structural similarity of adjacent phrases, clauses, or sentences; esp., the presentation of ideas bearing equivalent weight by putting them into identical grammatical structures. **2.** A passage that illustrates such structural similarities. See pp. 670–71.

paramoion /pa-rə-**moy**-ən/, n. Alliteration of the initial sounds of two or more words in a sentence.

paraph /pə-**raf**/. A penned flourish at the end of or under a signature, often used to protect against forgery.

paraphrase, n. **1.** The restatement of a thought, passage, or text in words different from the original statement, and often with greater clarity and either more or less detail; an alternative wording that is faithful to the sense of another, earlier expression. **2.** Another wording of a grammatical structure to reveal its ambiguity. — **paraphrastic,** adj.

paraphrase, vb. To use one's own words to express the substance of what another writer or speaker has said (e.g., *To paraphrase Shakespeare, no matter what you call a rose, it still smells nice*).

parapraxia. See FREUDIAN SLIP & PARAPRAXIS.

parapraxis /pa-rə-**prak**-sis/. A moment of faulty memory, esp. as evidenced by a slip of the tongue. — Also termed *parapraxia.* Pl. **parapraxes.**

paraprosdokian /pa-rə-pros-**dohk**-ee-ən/. An unexpected linguistic shift at the end of a sentence, phrase, or passage, esp. one that suddenly changes the reader's interpretation of the first part. • The device is frequently used for comedic or dramatic effect. Examples:

- "I don't belong to an organized political party. I'm a Democrat." (Will Rogers)
- "Time flies like an arrow; fruit flies like a banana." (Groucho Marx)
- "War doesn't determine who is right— only who is left." (Anon.)

parasitic vowel. See SVARABHAKTI VOWEL.

parasynesis /pa-rə-**sin**-ə-sis/, n. The misconception of a word that results in a faulty form (as when *home in* [originally based on what homing pigeons do] becomes, through error, *hone in*).

parasyntheton /pa-rə-**sin**-thə-tahn/. A derivative word that consists of a root compounded with a particle <bylaws> <downtrodden> <uplifting>.

parataxis /pa-rə-**tak**-səs/. *Rhetoric.* The coordination of successive, equal clauses without expressly showing their syntactic relationship, so that the reader must infer how they are related <I'm ready; let's go>. Cf. HYPOTAXIS. — **paratactic,** adj.

parathesis /pə-**rath**-ə-sis/. Apposition; the placement of a word or phrase beside another with which it is syntactically parallel <my brother the flutist>. — **parathetic** /pair-ə-**thet**-ik/, adj. See APPOSITION.

paregmenon /pə-**reg**-mə-nahn/, n. *Rhetoric.* The use of a word in the same construction as another to which the first is cognate <die a death> <the victor's victory>.

parembole /pa-**rem**-bə-lee/. *Rhetoric.* An inserted phrase that modifies or explains the thought of a sentence. • A parembole differs from a parenthesis by having a more integral connection with the context. — Also termed *paremptosis.*

parenthesis. 1. A word, phrase, clause, or sentence inserted as an explanation or afterthought; an aside inserted into a sentence or paragraph. • In writing, it is usually set off by commas, em-dashes, or the curved brackets known as "parentheses" (see sense 2). **2.** A punctuation mark that sets off such a word, phrase, clause, or sentence— [(] as the opening mark and [)] as the closing one.

paresis /pə-**ree**-səs *or* pa-rə-/. See ELISION.

parisology /pa-ri-**sahl**-ə-jee/, n. Ambiguous or equivocal language. — **parisologist,** n.

parison /**pa**-ri-sən/, n. **1.** An even balance of clauses, words, syllables, or other elements in a sentence. **2.** A clause that balances another, as in an antithesis.

parlance. A manner of speaking or of using words, esp. within a particular social or professional group. • *Parlance* is usually combined with an adjective such as *common, film, legal, medical, military,* or *vulgar.*

parole. *Linguistics.* The actual use of language by speakers; written or spoken utterance. • Parole depends on the existence of a language and its systematic principles, but is not a system itself. Cf. LANGUE.

paromology /pa-rə-**mahl**-ə-jee/, n. *Rhetoric.* The concession of minor points in a debate as a way of enhancing one's credibility and strengthening one's position. — Also termed *paromologia.*

paronomasia /pa-rə-noh-**may**-zhə/. *Rhetoric.* The deliberate and humorous use of the double meanings of words and phrases; esp., a play on words in which the similarity of sound is a prominent characteristic;

a pun <The best of all acids is assiduity>. — Also termed *paronymy.* — **paronomastic,** adj.

paronym /**pa**-rə-nim/. **1.** A derived word having but a slight change in form from one in another language; esp., a word formed by adapting a foreign word (e.g., *civil* from Latin *civilis,* or *egality* from French *égalité*). **2.** A word derived from another in the same language (e.g., *analytical* from *analysis,* or *parasitic* from *parasite*). **3.** HOMOPHONE. — **paronymous,** adj.

paronymy /pa-**ron**-ə-mee/, n. **1.** The introduction of a word into a language by borrowing from another language and slightly changing it. **2.** The relationship between cognate words with related meanings. **3.** PARONOMASIA.

parrhesia /pə-**ree**-zhə/, n. **1.** Candor and frankness; bold outspokenness. **2.** The practice or an instance of seeking permission to be boldly outspoken.

parrotry /**pa**-rə-tree/, n. The mindless repetition of others' words or sayings; PSITTACISM.

parse, vb. **1.** v.t. To determine the parts of speech and the relationship between (the individual parts of a sentence). **2.** v.t. To describe (a word or phrase) by classifying its part of speech, its composition, its inflection, and its relation to other words in the sentence. **3.** v.i. (Of a sentence) to meet the standards of good grammar.

parsing. 1. The act or process of separating out the elements of a sentence so that the relationships between them can be analyzed. **2.** The grammatical analysis and description of a word, showing what part of speech it is and its relation to other words.

pars pro toto. See SYNECDOCHE.

participial phrase. See PHRASE.

participial preposition. See PREPOSITION.

participle. A verb form inflected for perfective aspect (for past participles such as *written, sold,* or *shrunk*) or progressive aspect (for present participles such as *carrying, flying,* or *lecturing*); esp., a word derived from a verb but having characteristics of both a verb and an adjective. • English participles are the verb forms used with a *be*-verb <am writing> or a form of *have* <had written>. A participle functions as an adjective when it modifies a noun or pronoun <walking stick>. — Also termed *gerundive.* See also *progressive aspect* under ASPECT.

dangling participle. A participle that is not properly connected to the sentence's subject. *Seeing* is a dangling participle in *seeing that there was a*

traffic jam ahead, the taxi turned left because *seeing* logically cannot refer to *taxi;* the taxi's driver did the seeing. — Also termed *dangler; misrelated participle.*

fused participle. A gerund used after a noun or noun phrase that would more properly be a possessive adjective. • In *The author having full rights to the work* means you must ask the *author for permission,* the participle *having* is fused with the preceding noun to form the subject *the author having.* Traditional grammarians prefer *The author's having full rights to the work means . . . .* See p. 419.

misrelated participle. See DANGLING PARTICIPLE.

past participle. A nonfinite verb form ending usu. in *-ed, -en,* or *-t* and used in verb phrases <has believed> <have taken> <has wept> to signal a perfective aspect. • Although past participles are often part of a verb phrase, they may also function adjectivally <proven fact> <used books>.

present participle. A nonfinite verb form ending in *-ing* and used in verb phrases to signal the progressive aspect <be + -ing> <was browsing> <am shopping>. • Although present participles are often part of a verb phrase, they may also function adjectivally <prevailing notions> <unremitting violence>.

particle. A word or wordlike element that cannot be inflected, has little meaning, and serves other functions, usu. as an affix or part of a phrasal verb. In English, particles include prepositions used in phrasal verbs (as in *take in, take off, take over,* and *take up*); a few spatial adverbs (such as *aback, ahead, aside, away, back, in front*); prefixes such as *un-* (as in *unremorseful*); and suffixes such as *-ness* (as in *fineness*).

partitive /**pahr**-tə-tiv/, adj. Setting off or referring to a particular part of a whole (e.g., *some money*) or only some portion of a collection (e.g., *most voters*). • The so-called *partitive genitive* indicates the whole of which the head of the construction is a part <a slice of bread> <a piece of pie>.

part of speech. One of a class of words (nouns, verbs, adjectives, and so on) that is distinguished by its normal function in a sentence. • Grammarians have traditionally recognized eight parts of speech: nouns, pronouns, verbs, adverbs, adjectives, prepositions, conjunctions, and interjections. The traditional definitions of these classes are based sometimes on meaning, sometimes on function or use. Modern linguists have therefore tended to abandon these eight labels in favor of other labels more theoretically "pure." — Also termed *word class*; *lexical category*.

pasigraphy /pə-**sig**-rə-fee/, n. An international system of writing; a universal written language. — **pasigraphic,** adj. Cf. ESPERANTO; INTERLINGUA.

pasilaly /**pas**-i-lal-ee/, n. An international system of speaking; a universal spoken language.

passive voice. The voice that makes the recipient of the verb's action the subject of the verb. • Compare *the tree was knocked down by the truck* (passive voice: the tree didn't knock but was the recipient of action) with *the truck knocked down the tree* (active voice: the truck was doing the knocking). See pp. 676–77.

full passive. A passive-voice construction that includes the doer of the action.

truncated passive. A passive-voice construction that omits the doer of the action.

past participle. See PARTICIPLE.

past-perfect tense. See TENSE.

past tense. See TENSE.

pathopoeia /path-ə-**pee**-ə/, n. **1.** A speaker's or writer's arousal of an audience's or reader's emotions. **2.** A passage designed to arouse listeners' or readers' emotions. — Also spelled *pathopeia*.

patient. Whatever is denoted by the word that is directly affected by the action of a verb (e.g., the object of a transitive verb).

patois /**pat**-wah *or* **pah**-twah/, n. **1.** A regional dialect that differs markedly from the standard language. See DIALECT. Cf. STANDARD ENGLISH. **2.** The jargon of a particular age group, profession, or other discrete and insular group.

patrial /**pay**-tree-əl/, n. A noun derived from a country's name and denoting an inhabitant of that country <American> <Iraqi>. — **patrial,** adj.

patter. 1. Glib, rapid talk. **2.** Illiterate chatter or gossip.

pedant /**ped**-ənt/. Someone who makes an ostentatious display of learning, esp. of superficial erudition. — **pedantic,** adj.

pedantry /**ped**-ən-tree/. **1.** An excessive display of or reverence for learning, usu. characterized by close attention to details, however trivial. **2.** An instance of pedantic behavior or a pedantic form of expression. — Also termed *pedanticism*.

pejoration /pee-jə-**ray**-shən/. A change in the meaning of a word from one that is positive or neutral to one that is negative or borders on the negative. • For example, *notorious* once meant "widely known" and implied nothing about reputation, but now it means "infamous." Cf. MELIORATION.

pejorative, n. A linguistic form, such as a word or morpheme, that expresses disparagement. — **pejorative,** adj.

pentasyllable /**pen**-tə-sil-ə-bəl/, n. A word of five syllables. — **pentasyllabic** /pen-tə-si-**lab**-ik/, adj.

penult /**pen**-əlt/. A word's next-to-last syllable.

perfective aspect. See ASPECT.

perfect tense. See *present-perfect tense* under TENSE.

pericope /pə-**rik**-ə-pee/. An extract or selection from a book, esp. a passage from the Bible. — **pericopal** /per-i-**koh**-pəl/, adj.

periergia /per-i-**ər**-jee-ə/, n. The use of ornate, embellished language to discuss a commonplace thing; pompous, bombastic language. Cf. EUPHUISM; GONGORISM.

period. 1. The full stop that marks the end of a sentence. **2.** A grammatically complete sentence. **3.** A paragraph; a series of sentences that make up a unit of thought.

period-dots. See ELLIPSIS (2).

periodic sentence. *Rhetoric.* A sentence in which a complete thought is not expressed until the main clause and other rhetorical balancing devices are all read. • By using the opening clauses to give context and delay, the speaker slowly builds to a climax.

periphrasis /pə-**rif**-rə-sis/. **1.** *Rhetoric.* The use of a roundabout expression in place of a direct one; circumlocution <an elongated yellow fruit = banana>. **2.** *Grammar.* A phrase used to express what might otherwise be expressed in one inflected word (e.g., *did go* = went; *more tight* = tighter). — **periphrastic** /pair-ə-**fras**-tik/, adj. See p. 684.

periphrastic comparative. See COMPARATIVE.

perissology /per-i-**sahl**-i-jee/, n. The use of more words than necessary; superfluity of expression; PLEONASM.

perlocution /pər-loh-**kyoo**-shən/, n. Speech or writing intended to persuade or convince; language designed to bring about an action not itself constituting that action. Cf. ILLOCUTION.

perlocutionary, adj. *Linguistics.* Of or designating an act of speech or writing intended to produce an effect on the audience, such as persuading, convincing, inspiring, scaring, insulting, or motivating. • This word appears most frequently in the term *perlocutionary act*.

permissive. (Of a modal auxiliary) expressing permission or exhortation (as with *may* or *should*). Cf. OBLIGATIVE.

perorate /**pər**-ə-rayt/, vb. **1.** To sum up; to conclude. **2.** To make a long, elaborate speech in a formal and dignified manner; to harangue grandiloquently. — **peroration,** n.

persiflage /**pər**-si-flahzh/. Banter that is a mixture of frivolity and mockery, sometimes sardonic or contemptuous in tone. Cf. BADINAGE.

person. A characteristic of a noun or pronoun that identifies it as the speaker (first person), the thing spoken to (second person), or the thing spoken of (third person). • In English, *I* (singular) and *we* (plural) are the first-person pronouns; *you* (singular and plural) is the second-person pronoun; and *he*, *she*, and *it* (singular) and *they* (plural) are the third-person pronouns. See also CONCORD.

personal pronoun. See PRONOUN.

personification. *Rhetoric.* The representation of an object, esp. an inanimate one, or an idea as having a personality or human attributes. • Examples:

- Sir Walter Raleigh (1552–1618) referred to flowers as "you pretty daughters of the earth and sun."
- The Pyramids, doting with age, have forgotten the names of their founders. (Thomas Fuller [1608–1661])
- England expects every man to do his duty. (Lord Horatio Nelson [1758–1805])

— Also termed *prosopopoeia*.

perspicuity /pər-spi-**kyoo**-i-tee/. Clarity of expression or style; freedom from obscurity, ambiguity, and undue complexity; lucidity. — **perspicuous** /pər-**spik**-yoo-wəs/, adj.

phatic /**fat**-ik/, adj. Of, relating to, or involving communication used for polite social interaction rather than to elicit or convey information; characterized by small talk.

phatic exchange. A rudimentary, superficial conversation made only for general purposes of social interaction and not for literal meaning (e.g., *Hey. How's it going? Great. And you? Fine, thanks. Nice weather. Yeah. Have a great day.*).

philologaster /fi-**lol**-ə-gas-tər/, n. An inept or blundering philologist.

philology /fi-**lol**-ə-jee/. **1.** The study of literature from many points of view, including metaphor, criticism, grammar, etymology, and the like. **2.** The study of language apart from its literature. **3.** The love of learning and literature.

phoneme /foh-**neem**/. The smallest unit of sound in a language. • Phonemes are represented in writing by single letters for many consonants, such as *p* in *pot* and *rip*. See ALLOPHONE; CONSONANT; MORPHOPHONEMICS.

phonemics /foh-**nee**-miks/. *Linguistics.* The study of a language's sound system, focusing on analyzing and classifying the language's phonemes.

phonetic, adj. Representing speech sounds.

phonetics. *Linguistics.* The study of the properties of speech sounds, how they are made by the human voice, how they are combined with one another, and the acoustic effect that they produce. — **phonetician,** n.

phonocentrism /foh-nə-**sen**-triz-əm/, n. A bias in favor of speech over writing in linguistic analysis; the view that the spoken language is paramount over the written language. • This view had its most prominent origins in the work of Ferdinand de Saussure (1857–1913). — **phonocentric,** adj.

phonology /fə-**nol**-ə-jee/. *Linguistics.* The study of the sound structure of a language; specif., the study of the sounds found in any one language or group of related languages. — **phonological,** adj.

phonotactics, n. **1.** The branch of linguistics that studies the rules for phoneme sequences in a language or in languages generally. **2.** The rules themselves.

phrasal /**fray**-zəl/, adj. Of, relating to, or consisting of a phrase. • The word dates from the mid-19th century. Cf. CLAUSAL.

phrasal adjective. See ADJECTIVE.

phrasal preposition. See PREPOSITION.

phrasal verb. See VERB.

phrase. A combination of words that make sense but do not make a complete sentence; in modern linguistics, a constituent that consists of a single word (the "head") plus all its modifiers. Cf. CLAUSE; WORD.

adjective phrase. **1.** A prepositional phrase that functions as an adjective, qualifying a noun <the ambassador from Brazil>. **2.** A phrase with an adjective as its head <My teddy bear is afraid of the dark> (the adjective phrase being *afraid of the dark*). **3.** Loosely, a phrasal adjective. See *phrasal adjective* under ADJECTIVE. — Also termed *adjectival phrase.*

adverbial phrase. Two or more words in a sentence jointly having the force of an adverb <They do that work *every day*> <*By the way*, he was not found guilty>.

gerundive phrase. See *gerund phrase.*

gerund phrase. A noun phrase with the gerund as its head. — Also termed *gerundive phrase.*

infinitive phrase. A noun phrase with an infinitive as its head. • An infinitive phrase may be either (1) an infinitive and its accompanying complements or adverbs <to strike a bargain> <to think deeply> or (2) a sequence such as *to be tapped, to be tapping, to have been tapped,* or *to have been tapping.*

participial phrase. A phrase consisting of a participle and a modifier or complement and functioning as an adjective. • The phrase may appear before or after the subject. In *The monarch butterflies migrating from Mexico look fragile but are quite hardy,* the participial phrase *migrating from Mexico* modifies the subject, *monarch butterflies.* Likewise, *hiding behind the curtains* modifies the subject *burglar* in *Hiding behind the curtains, the burglar planned his next move.* A participial phrase may also be appositive: *The lecture, delivered as a favor to the president, drew an enthusiastic audience.*

prepositional phrase. A constituent that consists of a preposition followed by a noun phrase.

verb phrase. A phrase composed of the main verb plus the complement, objects, and adverbs. • In *I bought her a new necklace, I* is the subject and the other words make up the verb phrase.

phrasemonger. 1. A person who seeks to impress others by coining or using grandiose phrases, usu. to excess. **2.** Someone who engages in underhanded sloganeering in a way calculated to mislead. Cf. WORDMONGER.

pictogram. A character that represents an idea or object independently of words, as with ancient cave paintings. — Also termed *pictograph.* Cf. LOGOGRAM; IDEOGRAM.

pictograph. See PICTOGRAM.

pidgin /**pij**-ən/, n. A language developed from elements of dissimilar languages (e.g., English and Tagalog) and using a simplified grammatical form so that people without a common language may communicate. • The vocabulary is usually limited. A pidgin language may be local (in the sense that it has elements of the local language), but it is not a native language; it is a product of contact between speakers of different languages. (Cf. CREOLE.) The word *pidgin* is a corruption of the Chinese word for "business." One of the first recorded pidgins was an amalgam of English and Chinese words arranged according to Chinese syntax and used to conduct trade.

pied-piping, n. The habit or convention of avoiding a terminal preposition by putting it right before the relative or interrogative pronoun that it relates to (or, to illustrate the habit itself, *the relative or interrogative pronoun to which it relates*). • The term was first used in J.R. Ross's 1967 Ph.D. dissertation at MIT and since has appeared in many other linguistic contexts. The allusion, of course, is to the way charmed rats follow the piper in the fairy tale.

pilcrow /**pil**-kroh/, n. A paragraph marker (¶).

pitch, n. The high or low tone of a spoken sound produced by the vibrational frequency of the vocal cords; spoken stress. See INTONATION.

pithy, adj. Stylistically concentrated in force and energy.

pivot-pun. A pun that implies one meaning with the words preceding it, another with the words following it. • The term originated to denote a device in classical Japanese poetry.

pivot word. 1. A word central to the meaning or syntax of a sentence or paragraph. **2.** The word on which a pivot-pun turns. See PIVOT-PUN. **3.** One of the core words that a child acquires at an early stage of linguistic development.

placeholder. A word or phrase that is required by syntax but that carries little or no semantic information; esp., the impersonal pronoun in a sentence in which the subject clause occurs after the verb <Do you believe it?>.

place of articulation. The point in the mouth where two organs form an obstruction to form a speech sound.

plain English. Straightforward, simple, easy-to-understand English. • Although few people would seriously wish someone a *Jubilant Natal Anniversary* instead of *Happy Birthday,* many writers seem to fear that they won't appear intelligent unless they routinely use complex language. In their view, the bigger and more obscure the words, the more convoluted the statement, the better the impact. In fact, writers who express their ideas in plain English tend to be more highly regarded than those who don't. There are four reasons for this. First, clear writing reflects clear thinking. And clear thinking means understanding what you intend to write about. If you don't have a clear idea, your prose will be obscure; so will its meaning. Second, plain English is easy to read and understand quickly. It makes the reader feel smart. Third, plain English reflects a greater intellect because using it requires more brainwork. Albert Einstein once said that his goal in stating an idea was to make it as simple as possible but no simpler. He also said: "Most of the fundamental ideas of science are essentially simple, and may, as a rule, be expressed in a language comprehensible to everyone." Yet few achieve that type of expression. Fourth, using plain English marks a writer as a professional whose subject is approachable by all readers, specialists or not. Complication and obscurity often reflect insecurity on the part of the writer or speaker. See pp. 697–98.

plain infinitive. See INFINITIVE.

plain language. 1. A simple, direct style of speech or writing. **2.** The expertise involved in preparing documents in clear, accessible language that accurately embodies the intended sense.

platitude. A vapid truism; a statement that is dully predictable or insipidly commonplace. — **platitudinous,** adj.

pleonasm /plee-ə-naz-əm/. *Rhetoric.* The use of more words than necessary to express an idea; a superfluity of words (e.g., *continues even today to remain obstinate* for *remains obstinate*). • Although pleonasms may be used for effect, they are frequently produced through ignorance. In *would you repeat that again, please?*, *again* is unnecessary. And since your ears are permanently attached, *ears pierced while you wait!* states the obvious. Cf. TAUTOLOGY; PERISSOLOGY. — **pleonastic,** adj.

pleophony /plee-of-ə-nee/, n. Vowel epenthesis in which the inserted vowel sound is the same as that of the preceding syllable (as when *substantive* is pronounced /səb-stə-nə-tiv/, with a superfluous schwa sound in the penultimate syllable). See EPENTHESIS. Cf. ANAPTYXIS.

ploce /ploh-see/. Emphatic repetition of a word, esp. with the sense of conveying some special connotation. Cf. EPIZEUXIS; PALILOGY; SYMPLOCE.

pluperfect tense /ploo-pər-fikt/. See *past-perfect tense* under TENSE.

plural, n. & adj. The inflectional form of a word denoting more than one person or thing. See pp. 702–06.

plurale tantum /pluu-ray-lee tan-təm/, n. A noun that in a particular sense is invariably plural in form <clothes> <riches> <scissors> <thanks>. Cf. SINGULARE TANTUM.

plurisyllable /ploor-ə-sil-ə-bəl/, n. A line or word of more than one syllable. — **plurisyllabic** /ploor-ə-si-lab-ik/, adj.

pointing word. See WORD.

poem /poh-əm/. A particular example of the art of poetry; specif., an

imaginative composition displaying emotional intensity, insight, and imagination, esp. through imagery, evocative language, and measured and rhymical words suggestive of music.

poetaster /poh-it-as-tər/. A bad poet; an inferior writer of rhymes or verses. Cf. GRAMMATICASTER; LOGICASTER.

poetry /poh-ə-tree/. A type of literary composition characterized by metaphorical words, suggestiveness, quickened emotion, beautiful or dramatic language, and imaginative pleasure in the interpretation of life and nature.

polygenesis /pol-ee-jen-ə-sis/, n. The theory that there is more than one independent source of languages. Cf. MONOGENESIS.

polyglot /pol-ee-glot/. A person who speaks and understands more than one language.

polyphone /pahl-i-fohn/, n. A written character that represents more than one sound (as *c* in *Celtic* may be pronounced either as /s/ or as /k/).

polyptote /pahl-ip-toht/. (Of a noun or pronoun) having many cases <I–me–mine–my>.

polyptoton /pahl-ip-toh-tahn/. The repetition of a word in a different case or inflection. • This is a species of paregmenon. English literature provides many examples:

• I will destroy the wisdom of the wise, and the discernment of the discerning I will thwart. (1 Corinthians 1:19)
• With eager feeding food doth choke the feeder. (Shakespeare [1564–1616])
• And dying rise, and rising with him raise. (John Milton [1608–1674])
• Love is an irresistible desire to be irresistibly desired. (Robert Frost [1874–1963])
• A good ad should be like a good sermon: it must not only comfort the afflicted; it also must afflict the comfortable. (Bernice Fitz-Gibbon [1892–1982])

polysemous /pah-lee-seem-əs/ adj. (Of a word) having more than one sense, usu. many senses (e.g., *bank* can mean "a financial institution," "the earth beside a river," or "a billiard shot that bounces off the edge of the table").

polysemy /pə-lis-ə-mee/. A word's quality of having multiple similar meanings. • For instance, *foot* may refer to the base or bottom of two different things <We'll set up camp at the foot of the mountain> <That shoe is too tight for my foot>. — **polysemous,** adj. Cf. MONOSEMY.

polysyllable /pol-i-sil-ə-bəl/, n. A line or word of many syllables, usu. three or more. — **polysyllabic** /po-lee-si-lab-ik/, adj.

polysyndeton /pol-ee-sin-də-ton/. *Rhetoric.* The repetitive use of conjunctions between elements in a

sentence, such as words, phrases, or clauses. • This device can make a speaker or writer sound breathless. Example:

• I said, "Who killed him?" and he said, "I don't know who killed him but he's dead all right," and it was dark and there was water standing in the street and no lights and windows broke and boats all up in the town and trees blown down and everything all blown and I got a skiff and went out and found my boat where I had her inside Mango Bay and she was all right only she was full of water. (Ernest Hemingway [1899–1961])

Cf. ASYNDETON.

polysynthesis /pahl-ee-sin-thə-sis/, n. The combination of several words that often go together into one word <insofar> <inasmuch>.

popularized technicality. A technical term that has come into widespread use outside the field where it originated, usu. having acquired an extended meaning. • When H.W. Fowler (1858–1933) first coined this term in his 1926 book *A Dictionary of Modern English Usage*, the phrase *acid test* was the leading example. In its original scientific context, it referred to using nitric acid to test for gold. It was popularized by President Woodrow Wilson (1856–1924), who used it figuratively to mean "a severe or conclusive test" when he stated, "The treatment accorded Russia by her sister nations in the months to come will be the acid test of their good will." Many specialized subjects have contributed popularized technicalities to English, among them law <leading question>, medicine <cancerous>, logic <dilemma>, chess <gambit>, physics <quantum leap>, and sailing <underway>. Often purists object to a popularized technicality when it is new, but they tend to have little say in its linguistic fate.

portmanteau word /port-man-toh/. See BLEND.

positive, adj. & n. The ordinary condition of a gradable adjective or adverb; the lowest degree of comparison. • The positive degree does not express a comparison to any other thing <strong—not stronger (comparative) or strongest (superlative)>. — Also termed *positive degree; absolute degree.* See ADJECTIVE; ADVERB; DEGREE. Cf. COMPARATIVE; SUPERLATIVE.

possessive /pə-zes-iv/, n. The case used to show possession, ownership, or close relationship. • In English, most nouns form the possessive by adding -'s to the singular and irregular plural forms, and an apostrophe alone to regular plural forms. See pp. 712–15.

second possessive. A personal pronoun commonly used in a nominal position (*mine, yours, his, hers, its, ours,* and *theirs*).

possessive adjective. See ADJECTIVE.

possessive case. See CASE.

possessive pronoun. See PRONOUN.

postclitic /pohst-**klit**-ik/, n. An unemphatic word that is accented as if it were part of the preceding word (as *one* in *good one* or *it* in *Post-it note*). Cf. PROCLITIC.

postmodification. The placement of a modifier after the word it modifies (such as *a man with blue eyes* instead of *a blue-eyed man*).

postmodifier, n. A word that qualifies or limits the sense of a preceding word; a postpositive qualifier. See POSTPOSITIVE. — **postmodification,** n.

postpositive, n. A modifying particle or word that is placed after the word it modifies. • In *he was the man chosen for the job, chosen* is a postpositive because it modifies *man,* clarifies which man is referred to, and comes after the word modified. — Also termed *postmodifier.* Cf. PREPOSITIVE. See p. 716.

postverbal, adj. Following the verb. — **postverbal,** n.

praeteritio /pree-tə-**rit**-ee-oh/. See PARALIPSIS.

pragmatics /prag-**mat**-iks/. *Linguistics.* The study of how language is used in the context of certain communications, such as the beliefs of the speaker and his or her relationship to the audience.

prate, vb. To engage in trivial, empty, or foolish—and often lengthy—talk.

precatory /**prek**-ə-tor-ee/, adj. Expressing a desire that something be done, but in a nonmandatory way <precatory words in a will>.

precisian /pri-**sizh**-ən/. A person who rigidly and precisely observes established rules, forms, or standards. — Also termed *precisionist.*

predicate. A syntactic unit consisting of a finite verb and all the words modifying it or governed by it, such as *are ready to go* in the sentence *We are ready to go.* — Also termed *complete predicate.*

   compound predicate. A predicate consisting of two or more verbs connected by *and.*

   simple predicate. The verb or verb phrase in a sentence without its objects, modifiers, etc.

predicate adjective. See ADJECTIVE.

predicate nominative. A predicate noun in the nominative case, such as *he* <This is he> and *I* <It was I who called their attention to that fact>. — Also termed *predicate noun.*

predicative, adj. Of, relating to, or involving a noun or adjective that follows a linking verb to form a predicate, or is contained within a predicate. • In the sentence *His mentor called him a failure, yet he became a well-respected businessman,* the noun phrase *a failure* is the predicative object of the linking verb *called,* and the noun phrase *a well-respected businessman* is the predicative complement of the linking verb *became.*

predicative adjective. See *predicate adjective* under ADJECTIVE.

prefix. An affix attached to the beginning of a word to modify its meaning. • Prefixes serve many functions. Some, such as *im-, in-,* and *un-,* change a word's meaning to its direct opposition <possible–impossible> <comfortable–uncomfortable>. See AFFIX. Cf. SUFFIX; INFIX.

prelect /pri-**lekt**/, vb. To lecture or discourse publicly. — **prelection** /pri-**lek**-shən/, n.

prelinguistics. The study of biological and physiological aspects of speech. Cf. MICROLINGUISTICS; MACROLINGUISTICS.

premodifier. See PREPOSITIVE.

preoccupation. See PROLEPSIS (2).

preposition. An uninflected word or a phrase that indicates relationships of location, direction, means, agency, etc. between a noun and other words in the sentence. • The preposition's object is usually a noun or pronoun, which is always in the objective case (e.g., in *that sounds good to me,* the pronoun *me* is the object of the preposition *to,* so it is in the objective case). Although the preposition usually appears immediately before its object, it can also follow it (e.g., *we have a serious problem to talk about*). Prepositions frequently serve as particles in phrasal verbs. See PARTICLE & *object of a preposition* under OBJECT. See pp. 723–25.

   complex preposition. See *phrasal preposition.*

   compound preposition. A single-word preposition formed from two or more words <outside> <notwithstanding>.

   deferred preposition. See *terminal preposition.*

   participial preposition. A participial form that functions as a preposition <barring injury, he should win the tournament>.

   phrasal preposition. Two or more separate words that function as a preposition <in front of> <next to>. — Also termed *complex preposition.*

   terminal preposition. A preposition that appears at the end of a clause

because its object has been moved up in the sentence. — Also termed *deferred preposition.* See pp. 723–24.

prepositional complement. See COMPLEMENT.

prepositional phrase. See PHRASE.

prepositive, n. A modifying particle or word that is placed before the word it modifies. • In *the gray squirrel stole the bread, gray* is a prepositive because it comes before *squirrel,* the word it modifies. — Also termed *premodifier.* See ADJECTIVE. Cf. POSTPOSITIVE.

prescriptive grammar. 1. The field of grammar concerned with guiding users to make the most effective use of language through common rules. • Prescriptive grammarians are concerned with preventing heedless departures from Standard English. **2.** A book that lays out such grammar. — Also termed *normative grammar.* See GRAMMAR; STANDARD ENGLISH. Cf. DESCRIPTIVE GRAMMAR.

prescriptive linguistics. See LINGUISTICS.

prescriptivism /pree-**skrip**-ti-viz-əm/. An approach to language study that embraces the role of value judgments in deciding what is linguistically effective or ineffective, better or worse, and therefore guides people toward mastering a standard language. Cf. DESCRIPTIVISM.

present participle. See PARTICIPLE.

present-perfect tense. See TENSE.

present tense. See TENSE.

preterition. See PARALIPSIS.

preterit tense. See *past tense* under TENSE.

preverbal, adj. **1.** (Of a word or phrase) preceding the verb. Cf. POSTVERBAL. — **preverbal,** n. **2.** Preceding the development of speech in an individual or in humankind. **3.** Preceding the moment when a statement is formulated in the mind.

primary verb. See VERB.

principal clause. See *independent clause* under CLAUSE.

principal parts of a verb. The uninflected form of a verb, its past tense, and its past participle. • A verb's complete conjugation can be given if these principal parts are known.

principal verb. See *main verb* under VERB.

priscian /**prish**-ən/ or /-ee-ən/, n. A grammarian or student of grammar. • This term is an eponym derived from the 6th-century grammarian Priscian, whose 18-volume Latin grammar influenced European grammarians for centuries. See BREAK PRISCIAN'S HEAD.

privative /**pri**-və-tiv/, adj. Showing that something has been lost, negated, or removed; esp. (of a particle or affix), expressing negation or privation. • The prefix *a-*, from Greek, is called the *alpha privative*; it is used in such words as *amoral* and *apolitical*. An *-n-* is inserted in the alpha privative for euphony when a vowel sound follows (as in *anaerobic*).

procatalepsis /proh-kat-ə-**lep**-sis/. See PROLEPSIS (2).

prochronism. See PROLEPSIS (1).

proclisis /proh-**klɪ**-sis/, n. The pronunciation of a word or phrase in such a way that an unaccented syllable is combined with an accented word coming after it (as when *to day* evolved into the one-word form: *today*). Cf. ENCLISIS.

proclitic, adj. (Of an unaccented word) leaning forward; esp., dependent in pronunciation on a word that follows. • Among the most prominent examples in English are the articles *a* and *the* and monosyllabic prepositions. — **proclitic,** n. See CLITIC. Cf. ENCLITIC.

proclitic /proh-**klit**-ik/, n. A one-syllable word so closely associated in pronunciation with the word that follows as to have no accent of its own (e.g., *an* in *an inch, for* in *for research purposes, the* in *the nation,* or *to* in *to compose*). Cf. POSTCLITIC.

prodelision /prod-i-**lizh**-ən/. The elision of an initial vowel. Cf. APHESIS.

proem /**proh**-em/ or /-əm/. A preliminary comment or discourse at the beginning of a speech or piece of writing; a prelude, preamble, or preface.

pro-form. A word that substitutes for another, as a pronoun stands in for its noun antecedent. See *pro-verb* under VERB.

progressive aspect, n. See ASPECT.

prolative /proh-**layt**-iv/, adj. Serving to extend or complete predication.

prolegomenon /proh-li-**gom**-i-nən/. An introductory observation or remark; an introduction or preface. Pl. **prolegomena.**

prolepsis /proh-**lep**-səs/. *Rhetoric.* **1.** A figure of speech that expresses something yet to occur as if it has already occurred, as by using a past participle to modify a noun before the action has been done; an anticipatory reference. • Through prolepsis, the speaker may represent something as existing before it actually comes into existence <precolonial United States>, anticipate the circumstance or act that makes a description applicable <the dry lake they drained>, or link a present condition to a consequence <If you don't turn that music down, I'm calling the police>. — Also termed *prochronism.* **2.** Rhetorical anticipation, as by answering a potential objection before

it has been raised, or anticipating and answering a counterargument before it is made; the refutation of possible objections to an argument <"Aha!" you say, "that can't be right!" Here's the proof.>. In sense 2, cf. HYPOPHORA. — Also termed (in sense 2) *procatalepsis; preoccupation.* — **proleptic,** adj.

prolixity /proh-**lik**-sit-ee/. **1.** Undue length of discourse caused by the use of needless words, wearisome repetition of ideas, or too much detail; tedious verbosity. **2.** Indulgence in intolerably long and wordy discussions. — **prolix** /**proh**-liks/, adj.

prologue /**proh**-log/. A prefatory statement or explanation; esp., an evocative introduction spoken by an actor at the beginning of a play or film.

prolusion /proh-**l[y]oo**-zhən/. An essay written in preparation for a more elaborate treatise, esp. as a test of the writer's prowess.

promotion. In transformational grammar, the translation of words from an embedded clause into a main sentence.

pronominal, adj. Of, relating to, or being a pronoun.

pronominal adjective. See ADJECTIVE; *adjective pronoun* under PRONOUN.

pronoun. A word used as a substitute for a noun or, sometimes, another pronoun. • The definition isn't entirely satisfactory, since it does not easily apply to undoubted pronouns such as *I, you,* and the relative *who.* But it is traditional. See DEMONSTRATIVE. Cf. ANTECEDENT. See p. 734.

adjective pronoun. A pronoun that functions as a noun modifier. • Other than *who, none,* and personal pronouns, all pronouns may serve as adjectives <what book> <those apples>. — Also termed *pronominal adjective.*

compound indefinite pronoun. An indefinite pronoun that includes an element such as *-body* (*anybody, everybody, nobody, somebody*), *-thing* (*anything, everything, something*), or *one/-one* (*anyone, everyone, no one, someone*) <Nobody said a word> <The blast was heard by everyone nearby>.

compound personal pronoun. A personal pronoun form with the suffix *-self* (singular) or *-selves* (plural) (e.g., *myself, ourselves, itself*).

compound relative pronoun. A relative pronoun formed with *who, whom, which,* or *what* plus the suffix *-ever* <Whoever committed the crime will be found out> <I will give the award to whomever I please>.

deictic pronoun. See *demonstrative pronoun.*

demonstrative pronoun. A pronoun that points to, instead of defining or describing, the object to which it relates <this> <that> <you>. • The demonstrative pronouns are *this, that* (singular) and *these, those* (plural). Also termed *deictic pronoun.*

distributive pronoun. An indefinite pronoun that separates the objects referred to from others referred to nearby. • The distributive pronouns are *each, either,* and *neither.*

indefinite pronoun. A pronoun that generally or indefinitely represents an object already identified or not needing specific identification. • Indefinite pronouns include *another, any, both, each, either, neither, none, one, other, some,* and *such* <From all the options you can select only one> <Play another from your repertoire>.

intensive pronoun. A pronoun with the suffix *-self* (singular) or *-selves* (plural), used in apposition to its referent, that adds emphasis <I myself made the cake from scratch> <You must take the blame yourselves>.

interrogative pronoun. A pronoun that introduces or asks a question; a pronoun used to elicit the identity of an unknown noun or noun phrase. • The interrogative pronouns are *who* (nominative; objective *whom* and possessive *whose*), *what,* and *which* <Who did the talking?> <To whom am I speaking?> <Which is the right way?>.

personal pronoun. A pronoun that refers to a particular person or thing and changes form to indicate person, number, gender, and case. • This chart lists the personal pronouns and the forms they take in different cases:
Singular
　Subjective: I, you, he, she, it
　Objective: me, you, him, her, it
　Possessive: my, mine, your, yours, his, her, hers, its
Plural
　Subjective: we, you, they
　Objective: us, you, them
　Possessive: our, ours, your, yours, their, theirs

possessive pronoun. A type of pronoun used esp. as a limiting adjective to qualify a noun and denote possession. • The possessive pronouns include *mine, ours, yours, his, hers, its,* and *theirs.* See also ABSOLUTE FORM.

reciprocal pronoun. A singular pronoun that refers to a plural subject <The buildings are close to each other> <The family members are all fond of one another>. • The only reciprocal pronouns in English are *each other* and *one another.*

reflexive pronoun. A pronoun formed with the suffix *-self* (singular) or *-selves* (plural) and used to reflect the action of the verb and refer to the subject <She drove herself to work> <They created trouble for themselves>.

relative pronoun. A pronoun that can link dependent and independent clauses <I will develop whichever idea is the most popular> or join a clause with its antecedent <The boy who delivered our newspaper has moved away>. • The relative pronouns are *who, whom, that,* and *which.* The compounds *whoever, whomever,* and *whichever* are also relative pronouns. *Who* and *whoever* refer to the subject of a clause or sentence; *whom* and *whomever* refer to the objects of a verb, a verbal, or a preposition.

universal pronoun. A pronoun that represents all-inclusive noun phrases (such as *each, all,* and compounds consisting of *every* plus *one, body,* or *thing.* • Grammatically, universal pronouns (apart from *all*) are singular, even though the meaning is plural.

pronunciation /prə-nən-see-**ay**-shən/. The manner or act of articulating words. See pp. 736–38.

proper adjective. See ADJECTIVE.

proper diphthong. See DIPHTHONG.

proper name. See *proper noun* under NOUN.

proper noun. See NOUN.

proposition. 1. A measure or scheme proposed or presented to others for consideration, acceptance, or adoption. **2.** The assertion of a judgment, with subject and predicate, as in *All men are mortal* or *No men are perfect.* **3.** The part of a discourse in which the basic argument or theme is announced.

prop word. See EXPLETIVE.

prosaism /proh-**zay**-iz-əm/. An expression, phrase, or literary style that is dull and unimaginative. — **prosaic** /proh-**zay**-ik/, adj. — **prosaist,** n.

prose /prohz/. Spoken or written language without metrical structure, rhythm, or other characteristics of poetry; language in its ordinary form.

prosify /proh-zi-fɪ/, vb. To turn (poetry) into prose.

prosiopesis /proh-sɪ-ə-**pee**-sis/, n. An ellipsis at the beginning of a grammatical structure <Thank you> (the subject *I* being habitually omitted through ellipsis). • Prosiopesis is especially common in the informal writing found in e-mail, journal entries, and the like <Went to a movie. Liked it. Thought that Meg Ryan was delightful.>.

prosody /**pros**-ə-dee/. **1.** The intonations and rhythms of spoken language. **2.** The study of those intonations and rhythms. **3.** The study of poetic meters and their use. — **prosodic,** adj.

prosopopoeia /prə-soh-pə-**pee**-ə/. See PERSONIFICATION.

prosthesis. See PROTHESIS.

prosy /**proh**-zee/, adj. **1.** Having the nature of prose. **2.** Commonplace and tiresome; dull and wearisome; prosaic. — **prosiness,** n.

prosyllogism /proh-**sil**-ə-jiz-əm/. A syllogism whose conclusion forms the premise of another syllogism. See SYLLOGISM. Cf. EPISYLLOGISM.

protasis /**prah**-tə-sis/. In a conditional sentence, the clause that lays down the condition. • It typically begins with the word *if* or *unless,* but it may also be introduced by *although, though,* or *despite.* — Also termed *conditional clause; condition.* Cf. APODOSIS.

protext. The part of a document or writing that immediately precedes the part under consideration; the preceding context.

prothesis /**prahth**-ə-səs/. The addition of an extra sound or syllable at the beginning of a word <splatter–besplatter>. • By this process, *an ewt* became *a newt.* — Also termed *prosthesis.* Cf. METANALYSIS. — **prothetic** /proh-**thet**-ik/, adj.

protreptic /proh-**tep**-tic/, n. Hortatory writing designed to persuade or to teach. — **protreptic,** adj.

provection /proh-**vek**-shən/. The transfer of a final consonant of one word to the beginning of the next, as when (historically) *an ewt* became *a newt* and *a napron* became *an apron.* See PROTESIS; METANALYSIS.

pro-verb. See VERB.

provincialism. A nonstandard wording peculiar to a region or outlying district; a word or phrase typifying a regional dialect. See DIALECT.

psellism /**sel**-iz-əm/, n. Defective pronunciation, esp. as a result of lisping, stuttering, or stammering.

psittacism /**sit**-ə-siz-əm/. The thoughtless, parrot-like repetition of other people's ideas and words without any personal understanding of or appreciation for what one is saying; PARROTRY.

psychobabble. 1. Language loaded with terms from psychology and psychotherapy, esp. those improperly used by laypeople. **2.** Meaningless psychological jargon, esp. terms from popular rather than mainstream psychology. • In either sense, this term is highly pejorative. It emerged in the popular culture when it appeared in

the title of R.D. Rosen's 1977 book, *Psychobabble: Fast Talk and Quick Cure in the Era of Feeling.*

psycholinguistics. See LINGUISTICS.

pun. See PARONOMASIA.

punctual aspect. See *momentaneous aspect* under ASPECT.

punctuation. 1. The system of marking sentences to help readers understand their structure and the relationship between their parts. **2.** The marks used in that system. See pp. 746–54.

pure infinitive. See INFINITIVE.

purism. 1. The view that linguistic changes should be halted or undone; the attitude that change should not occur in a language. • In its classic form, purism, among other things, promotes strict adherence to the rules of grammar and speech and bars neologisms and borrowed foreign words from the language. In practice, self-described "purists" are often ill informed about what actually constitutes good usage. **2.** The view that a language should be made up only of homegrown words, not words borrowed from other languages. — **purist,** n. — **puristic,** adj.

purple prose. A highly ornate, brilliantly colored passage in a literary composition. • The phrase derives from the Latin phrase *purpureus pannus,* which appears in the *Ars Poetica* of Horace (68–65 B.C.).

quadrisyllable /**kwahd**-ri-sil-ə-bəl/, n. A word of four syllables. — Also termed *tetrasyllable.* — **quadrisyllabic** /kwahd-ri-si-**lab**-ik/, adj.

qualifier. A word that modifies or intensifies an adjective or adverb <rather> <very>. See MODIFIER (1).

qualitative adjective. See ADJECTIVE.

quantitative adjective. See ADJECTIVE.

Queen's English. See KING'S ENGLISH.

question. An interrogative sentence or clause; a sentence that seeks to elicit information. See pp. 759–60.

indirect question. A noun clause that reports a question or asks it indirectly <She asked me where the convenience store is>; esp., a dependent clause or a sentence containing a dependent clause that expresses an implied question. • In the sentence *Tell me who you are,* the question is implied by *who you are.* If asked directly, the sentence would be *Tell me, who are you?*

quibble, n. **1.** A play on words; a pun. **2.** A shifty evasion of a point in argument or discourse; esp., a trivial distinction introduced as a red herring.

quinquesyllable /**kwin**-kwe-sil-ə-bəl/, n. A line or word of five syllables. — **quinquesyllabic** /kwin-kwe-si-**lab**-ik/, adj.

quodlibet /**kwod**-li-bet/. A subtle, debatable point.

quotation. One or more words taken from another person's writing or speech and repeated verbatim (e.g., *a quotation from Shakespeare*).

recipient noun. See NOUN.

reciprocal, adj. Indicating that an action, process, or relationship is mutual (e.g., *Paul and Diane have a reciprocal relationship: Paul likes Diane and Diane likes Paul*).

reciprocal pronoun. See PRONOUN.

red herring. A distracting tangent introduced into an argument in a way that threatens to derail the discussion or sidetrack the debaters. • The metaphor derives from the practice of using a smelly fish (traditionally a red herring) to confuse hunting dogs by dragging it across the trail.

reduced relative clause. See CLAUSE.

redundancy /ri-**dən**-dən-see/. **1.** The use of more words than necessary to impart an idea; the inclusion of superfluous words in an expression. **2.** A word or phrase that adds nothing to the meaning of a passage because its sense has already been expressed (as in *cash money* or *entirely unanimous*).

reduplication. The formation of a double-barreled word or phrase by having the second part repeat some of the first part, as in *flim-flam, helter-skelter, namby-pamby, okey-dokey, shilly-shally,* and *willy-nilly.*

referent. A person or thing referred to; specif., the physical entity or abstract concept represented by a spoken or written symbol. • Exactly what a referent denotes depends on the context in which it appears. For instance, *sun* may refer to the gaseous celestial body that provides heat and light to our planet <orbiting the sun> or just to the heat and light <playing outdoors in the sun>.

reflexive, adj. Indicating that a verb's action reflects back on the subject or agent.

reflexive, n. **1.** A part of speech used for emphasis by repetition. • A reflexive often immediately follows the subject, but it may also follow the verb <I myself believe she lied> <She completed the survey herself>. **2.** Any construction in which two words or noun phrases are understood to have the same referent. See INTENSIFIER; INTENSIVE.

reflexive pronoun. See PRONOUN.

regimen /**rej**-i-mən/, n. One word's governing another; the relation that one word in a sentence has to another one that depends on it.

register, n. **1.** A type of language, esp. in a range of formal–informal,

appropriate to a certain social setting. **2.** *Phonetics.* The range of tones made by a voice.

regular, adj. Conforming to a grammatical norm or standard.

regular verb. See VERB.

relative adjective. See ADJECTIVE.

relative adverb. See *conjunctive adverb* under ADVERB.

relative clause. See CLAUSE.

relative pronoun. See PRONOUN.

remote relative. A relative pronoun that is separated from the noun to which it refers by several intervening words. • A remote relative is typically ambiguous <the doctrine that nations are sovereign entities not to be interfered with by outside forces, which . . . > (where *which* might refer to *doctrine, nations, entities,* or *forces*—but probably either *doctrine* or *forces*). Remote relatives often cause miscues. See pp. 784–86.

remplissage /rahn-pli-**sahzh**/, n. Literary padding; the act or practice of filling out paragraphs and even pages with matter of little value.

reported speech. A person's indirectly quoted words, as in *Sharon told us we had to arrive before 6 PM*, meaning that Sharon said, "You must arrive before 6 PM." — Also termed *indirect speech; oratio obliqua.* See *indirect discourse* under DISCOURSE.

restrictive, adj. (Of the modifier of a noun or phrase) adding information that more positively identifies the referent. • For example, in *The tents that are on aisle 3 are on sale*, the clause *that are on aisle 3* is restrictive because it identifies which tents are on sale—tents on other aisles may not be. Similarly, in *The senator–songwriter Orrin Hatch will perform*, the name *Orrin Hatch* specifically identifies which senator–songwriter is being referred to, so it is a restrictive appositive. Restrictive modifiers are never set off from the rest of the sentence by commas. Cf. NONRESTRICTIVE.

restrictive relative clause. See CLAUSE.

retained object. See OBJECT.

retronym. A word or phrase invented to denote what was originally a genus term but has now become just one species in a larger genus (e.g., *solid-core door* came to describe what all old doors used to be until the advent of the *hollow-core door*). See p. 794.

rigmarole /**rig**-ə-mə-rohl/. A rambling, unintelligible, or unduly elaborate speech or writing, often painfully long; a succession of confused, nonsensical, or disjointed statements. — Also termed *rigamarole* /**rig**-ə-mə-rohl/.

rhematic /ree-**mat**-ik/, adj. **1.** (Of word formation) derived from or based on a verb (as the noun *preparation* is

derived from the verb *prepare*, or the adjective *attributive* is derived from the verb *attribute*). **2.** Of, relating to, or involving word formation.

rhetor /ri-**tor**/, n. **1.** A teacher or professor of rhetoric. **2.** A professional rhetorician.

rhetoric. 1. The art of speaking suitably on any subject. **2.** The art or practice of using sentence construction, figures of speech, etc. for elegant or persuasive effect. **3.** High-flown language intended to stir listeners or readers. — **rhetorical,** adj.

rhetorical question. *Rhetoric.* A question that is asked for effect only, and not for an answer; a question that is intended to remain unanswered because the answer is self-evident. • Usually the speaker is making a point and doesn't want a response, or the answer is obvious and can be left unsaid. The use of an unbroken series of rhetorical questions is called *eperotesis* or *erotesis.* See EROTESIS.

rhotacism /**roh**-tə-siz-əm/. **1.** The overuse of the letter *r* in speaking or writing; a disruption in pronouncing *r*, as in *idea* /idear/ and *wash* /wahrsh/. **2.** The mispronunciation of *r*; esp. the erroneous replacement of an /r/ sound with the sound of some other letter. Cf. LAMBDACISM. **3.** The principle in Indo-European languages by which *s* is often systematically changed to *r.* See p. 738.

rhotic /**roh**-tik/, adj. (Of a word or type of spoken English) retaining the sound of a terminal /r/ in words such as *bigger, father, rather,* and *sir.* • Compared to BrE, AmE is highly rhotic (see, e.g., [among the main entries in this book] **bursar, primer, tartar**).

right-branching sentence. A complicated sentence that has most of its complexity—the conditions, exceptions, etc.—after the principal verb; one that has a majority of its constituents on the right side of the tree diagram. Cf. LEFT-BRANCHING SENTENCE.

rodomontade. /rod-ə-mən-**tayd**/. The rant of a blustering braggart or demagogue.

root. The most basic part of a word, from which another word or words can be formed or derived; the form of a word to which affixes are attached. • The root or inflectional stem of a word constitutes the most meaningful part of an English word. — Also termed *base; theme.* See ETYMON; SYNTHETIC LANGUAGE.

run-on sentence. A sentence in which two or more main clauses are used together without punctuation or a conjunction between them. • For example, *Cyndi spoke highly of her new assistant she hired him last week.* The run-on can be corrected by making two sentences <Cyndi spoke highly of her new assistant. She hired him last week> or by recasting and inserting an appropriate conjunction. — Also termed *comma splice.* See pp. 802–03.

sandhi /**san**-dee/, n. [Sanskrit "a placing together"] The change of the sound of a morpheme in a specific context (e.g., *the* in *the woman* vs. *the elderly woman*).

sans serif. A style of typeface in which the letters do not have any projections. Sans serif type is considered more legible than serif type in headlines and short passages, but not in extended text. Cf. SERIF.

Sapir–Whorf hypothesis. The doctrine that the structure of one's native tongue partly determines how one experiences reality and understands the world. • The hypothesis was first posited by Edward Sapir (1884–1939) in 1929 and was elaborated by his student Benjamin Lee Whorf (1897–1941) in books and articles. The names were coupled as Sapir–Whorf in learned journals beginning in the 1950s.

sarcasm. Sharp, ironic, or humorous language intended to mock a person, thing, or situation by using words to show that the speaker intends the opposite meaning. • Sarcasm is more easily expressed in speech than in writing. In speech, vocal intonations help to convey the speaker's real meaning when making a statement such as, "Well, isn't that special?" when something isn't. Sarcasm is more difficult to express in writing because there are few visual and no aural cues to the speaker's meaning. In informal writing, people sometimes use emphatic fonts or capitalization, emoticons, or special characters to convey sarcasm. But since some of these devices are used for other purposes, such as expressing sincerity or excitement, misinterpretations are common. Cf. HYPERBOLE; IRONY; LITOTES.

scansion /**skan**-shən/. The act of dividing lines of verse to show its metrical parts, according to the rules of quantity and accent.

scesis onomaton. See SYNONYMIA.

schriftsprache /**shrift**-sprahk-ə/. The written form of a standard language; literary language.

schwa. A neutral vowel sound, spelled with various letters, such as the *a* in *alone* and the *e* in *system.* • In pronunciation systems, it is symbolized by an inverted, backward *e*: ə.

screed. 1. A prolonged tirade or harangue. **2.** Any writing that is being referred to dysphemistically.

scurrility /skə-**ril**-i-tee/. **1.** The character or quality of being indecent or vulgar; vileness of language. **2.** That which is foul, obscene, low, and vile.

second person. See PERSON.

second possessive. See POSSESSIVE.

semantic, adj. Of, relating to, or involving the meaning of words.

semantics. The study of the ways in which languages (or a particular language) systematically structure meaning, esp. in words and in sentences; specif., the branch of linguistics dealing with the meaning of words, phrases, and clauses, together with the origins of and shifts of meaning. — Also termed *semasiology.* See LINGUISTICS. Cf. GENERAL SEMANTICS.

semasiology /sə-may-zee-**ahl**-ə-jee/, n. See SEMANTICS.

sememe. The meaning of a morpheme; the smallest possible unit of meaning.

semivowel. A sound that functions as a consonant but has the resonance of a vowel. • The most common are *w* <water> and *y* <yellow>. Cf. CONSONANT; VOWEL.

sentence. A minimum complete utterance; a grammatical and rhetorical device for expressing relationships among the elements of an idea segment, which the writer or speaker wants to separate and present as a unit, and that the reader or listener can accept as capable of standing alone. • The old idea that a sentence is "a group of words expressing a complete thought" has been widely discredited—even though it contains a good deal of truth. But it is true that many single words can be sentences, as C.T. Onions (1873–1965) observed: "Many single words or self-contained groups of words, of any size, may perform the work of a sentence; e.g., *Speaking*; *Thanks*; *Down!*; *Sh!*; *Out with it!*; *Farewell*; *Goodbye*; *What?*; *Murder!*; *Nonsense!*; *Splendid! Yes* and *no* are long-established sentence-words; they are equivalent to sentences; e.g. *Will you come?—Yes. I will come.*"[1] The grammarian James Sledd (1914–2003) wrote aptly that "no useful definition can be framed to include all and only the things [that] are often called sentences."[2]

cleft sentence. In transformational grammar, a two-clause sentence made from a single clause in order

to emphasize a specific element of the clause, so that the resulting sentence begins with *it is* or another *be*-verb <It is peanuts that we want> (resulting from the clauses *We want peanuts* and *It is . . .*). — Also termed *cleft construction.*

complex sentence. A sentence that has an independent clause and one or more dependent clauses joined by a subordinating conjunction <I don't know whether it will rain today>.

compound–complex sentence. A sentence that consists of at least two independent clauses and at least one dependent clause <Either the cat goes or I go, whether you like it or not> <I don't know if he'll be allowed to watch the football game, but he hasn't finished those chores that he was assigned>.

compound sentence. A sentence that has at least two coordinate independent clauses linked by a coordinating conjunction <I told him to go away, so he left> <The cat goes or I go>. See *coordinating conjunction* under CONJUNCTION.

conditional sentence. A sentence that states a condition and the consequence or outcome of that condition's occurring. • Example: *If we lose this game, we'll be excluded from the tournament.* The condition does not have to be stated before the consequence: <We'll be late unless we take a shortcut>.

declarative sentence. A sentence that makes a statement or assertion <The day was long> <It's wise not to fret about what cannot be changed>. — Often shortened to *declarative.*

exclamatory sentence. A sentence that expresses surprise or other strong emotion. — Also termed *exclamative sentence*; *exclamative.*

imperative sentence. A sentence that constitutes a command, order, or firm request <Get your gear and leave> <March down to the bank and tell the manager what you think!>. — Often shortened to *imperative.*

interrogative sentence. A sentence that asks a question <Why did you agree on that price?>. — Often shortened to *interrogative.*

simple sentence. A sentence consisting of only one independent clause and no dependent clauses <I called her> <I saw him only yesterday>.

sentence adverb. See ADVERB.

sententious /sen-**ten**-shəs/, adj. **1.** Giving terse expression to thought. **2.** Habitually using pithy, concise language.

---

[1] C.T. Onions, *Modern English Syntax* 1 (rev. B.D.H. Miller 1971).

[2] James Sledd, *A Short Introduction to English Grammar* 246 (1959).

separative coordinating conjunction. See *disjunctive conjunction* under CONJUNCTION.

sequence of tenses. The fixed pattern by which the tense of one verbal or the form of one verb phrase demands that another verbal or verb phrase be of a particular tense or form <When she arrived, I left> (the past-tense *arrived* demanding the past-tense *left*) <As I peruse books, I mark them> (the present-tense *peruse* demanding the present-tense *mark*). See p. 896.

serif, n. A style of typeface in which the letters have slight finishing strokes, such as "feet." The serifs enhance the readability of significant blocks of text. Cf. SANS SERIF. — **serif, serifed,** adj.

sesquipedality /ses-kwi-pi-**dal**-i-tee/, n. The use of long, arcane words. — **sesquipedalian,** adj. See pp. 818–20.

set phrase. A group of words in an arrangement fixed by long-standing usage. • Proverbs, catchphrases, and idioms are types of set phrases. — Also termed *set expression*. See CLICHÉ; IDIOM. See p. 820.

sexisyllable /**seks**-i-sil-ə-bəl/, n. A line or word of six syllables. — **sexisyllabic** /seks-i-si-**lab**-ik/, adj.

sibilant. A hissing or hushing sound, as in /s/, /z/, or /sh/. — **sibilance,** n.

simile. *Rhetoric.* An explicit comparison of two usu. quite different things, signaled by the use of a word such as *like* or *as* <like a gentle breeze> <as brave as a lion>. • Examples:

- Tall men, like tall houses, are usually ill furnished in the upper story. (Sir Francis Bacon [1561–1626])
- The man who has not any thing to boast of but his illustrious ancestors is like a potato—the only good belonging to him is under ground. (Sir Thomas Overbury [1581–1613])
- She was like an apple pudding tied in the middle. (James Kirk Paulding [1778–1860])

See FIGURE OF SPEECH. Cf. METAPHOR.

simple, adj. **1.** Made up of a single grammatical element. **2.** Having no modifiers, complements, or other elements.

simple adverb. See ADVERB.
simple conjunction. See CONJUNCTION.
simple infinitive. See INFINITIVE.
simple predicate. See PREDICATE.
simple sentence. See SENTENCE.
simple subject. See SUBJECT.
simple tense. See TENSE.
simplex. See KERNEL SENTENCE.
singular, n. The form of a word that denotes or refers to one person or thing. See CONCORD. Cf. PLURAL.

singulare tantum /sing-gyoo-**lair**-ee **tan**-təm/, n. A noun that is invariably singular in form. • This term usually applies to mass nouns. Cf. PLURALE TANTUM.

slang. Nonstandard language that has any two of these four characteristics: (1) it is informal, significantly lower in status than Standard English; (2) it first arises in the language of the street or popular culture; (3) it is more or less unacceptable in formal or polite settings; and (4) it displaces a conventional term with one that is vivid and may even be taboo. • Slang changes very quickly in English and is often used within groups, particularly small or close ones, to help keep the group together and strengthen ties. See DIALECT; IDIOLECT. — **slangy,** adj. See pp. 835–36.

sloganeering. The use of rallying cries or attention-getting phrases in an attempt to convince, persuade, or bias people. — **sloganeer,** vb.

sociolinguistics. See LINGUISTICS.

solecism /**sol**-ə-siz-əm *or* **soh**-lə-siz-əm/. An ungrammatical combination of words, noncompliance with the rules of syntax, or a deviation from standard usage. • The word *solecism* derives from the name of the ancient Greek colony of Soloi, in what is now called Cyprus. The original settlers spoke Attic Greek, but because the colony was far from Greece and infrequently visited, the language gradually drifted and became a local dialect. Greek travelers who stopped in Soloi considered the dialect a corrupt and substandard form of Greek. They coined the word *soloikismos* to describe it. The word was adopted into Latin as *solœcismus*, then passed into French as *solécisme*, and finally appeared in the English form, *solecism*, in the 16th century.

soliloquy /sə-**lil**-ə-kwee/. **1.** A discourse uttered to oneself; a monologue. **2.** In drama (esp. the works of Shakespeare), a monologue representing a character's unspoken thoughts for the audience's benefit. — **soliloquize,** vb.

sonant. See VOICED.

specialization. The narrowing of a word's meaning over time. • For example, *meat* derives from Old English *mete*, meaning "food" (still reflected in the term *nutmeat*), but through specialization it came to refer to the flesh of animals as food. — Also termed *narrowing*. Cf. GENERALIZATION.

speech community. A defined group, esp. regionally or socially, identified by a shared spoken language or dialect. • A community can be as small as a few people or as large as a whole nation or supranational group, such as a Welsh-speaking community in Patagonia.

speechcraft. 1. Skill in public speaking. **2.** A knowledge of or skill in grammatical speech.

spelling pronunciation. The pronunciation of a word according to its spelling, such as *says* with a long-*a* sound, or *often* as /**awf**-tən/. See PRONUNCIATION.

split infinitive. See INFINITIVE.

Spoonerism. A phrase in which the initial consonants of two words are swapped, usu. by accident, to create an amusing expression. • Spoonerisms are named for the Reverend W.A. Spooner (1844–1930), a don of New College, Oxford. He is reputed to have inadvertently uttered statements such as "The Lord is a shoving leopard," and "It is kisstomary to cuss the bride." But one can make Spoonerisms deliberately as a device to belittle or amuse. For instance, W.H. Auden (1907–1973), who had a low opinion of the poets Shelley and Keats, purposefully referred to them as "Kelly and Sheets." And Shel Silverstein (1930–1999) wrote an entire book of poetry, *Runny Babbit: A Billy Sook* (2005 [published posthumously]), filled with Spoonerisms.

sprachbund /**sprahk**-buunt/. **1.** A linguistic community made up of speakers of mutually intelligible dialects and linguistic families having a common set of linguistic features as the result of geographic proximity. **2.** The linguistic evolution that results in this type of community.

sprachgefühl /**sprahk**-gə-fyuul/. **1.** Language-feeling; an intuitive grasp of the genius and idiom of a given language. **2.** The character of a language.

squib. 1. A short satirical speech or writing; a pithy lampoon. **2.** Any brief notice written about some person or thing, as in a newspaper or blog.

stammbaum /**shtam**-bowm/. A family tree of languages, such as Indo-European languages.

standard, adj. (Of usage) speaking and writing that is widely taught and learned as the correct form.

Standard English. The substantially uniform type of English spoken and written by educated people. • It lacks regional and other variations that are considered ungrammatical or nonstandard. It is widely used in the media and by authority figures, and it is sometimes called "the prestige dialect." Cf. ARGOT; DIALECT; JARGON; NONSTANDARD ENGLISH. See pp. 858–59.

stanza /**stan**-zə/. In poetry, a number of lines grouped in a scheme of meter and sequence—a scheme usu. corresponding to other line groups within the same poem. — **stanzaic** /stan-**zay**-ik/, adj.

statement. A sentence that expresses an assertion (as opposed to an exclamation, a question, or a command); a sentence to which the most common response is continuing attention.

stem. 1. The part of a word that remains unchanged when it is inflected. **2.** A word that contains a root and one or more derivational suffixes but no inflectional suffixes <annoyance> <artist> <artistic>.

stigmeology /stig-mee-**ahl**-ə-jee/, n. The art of punctuation.

stichometry /sti-**kom**-ə-tree/. **1.** In paleography, the measurement of books or manuscripts by means of lines (or *stichs*). **2.** An appendix or list stating the number of lines in a book or manuscript. — **stichometric** /stik-ə-**met**-trik/, adj.

stop. 1. A punctuation mark. **2.** A consonant sound made with complete obstruction of the breath stream.

stress. See ACCENT (2).

strong verb. See VERB.

strophe /**stroh**-fee/, n. **1.** In classical poetry, a stanza repeated one or more times in an ode or by a dramatic chorus. **2.** Loosely, any stanza or rhymed group of lines in a poem. — **strophic** /**stroh**-fik/, adj.

structural ambiguity. See AMBIGUITY.

structural linguistics. See LINGUISTICS.

stylistics. *Linguistics.* The study of linguistic variation, often with special attention to the most conscious and complex uses of language in literature.

subclause. See *dependent clause* under CLAUSE.

subject. The noun or noun phrase about which something is said in the predicate of a simple sentence; esp., the doer of the sentence's action or the person or thing that is in the state expressed by the predicate.

complete subject. The simple subject together with all its modifiers.

compound subject. A subject that consists of two or more nouns or noun phrases connected by a conjunction.

simple subject. The particular noun or noun phrase about which something is said in the predicate.

subject complement. See COMPLEMENT.

subjective. See NOMINATIVE.

subjective case. See *nominative case* under CASE.

subject noun clause. See NOUN CLAUSE.

subject–verb agreement. The requirement that the subject and the verb of a clause must match in person and number. See pp. 866–68.

subjunct. In some grammatical systems, an adverb that affects the force of a verb, an adjective, or another adverb, usu. either by softening the statement <fairly> <rather> <relatively> or by strengthening it <extremely> <very> <so>. Cf. ADJUNCT; CONJUNCT; DISJUNCT.

subjunctive /səb-**jən[g]k**-tiv/, adj. (Of a verb) expressing a condition that is uncertain or contrary to fact (e.g., *if I were you*), including doubt, wishfulness, possibility, demand, and the like (e.g., *the crowd demanded that she be heard*). See p. 869.

subjunctive mood. See MOOD.

subordinate, adj. Having an order or rank inferior to something else; lesser in degree or importance <a subordinate clause>. Cf. COORDINATE.

subordinate clause. See *dependent clause* under CLAUSE.

subordinating conjunction. See CONJUNCTION.

subordination. The joining of words or word groups with dependent rank to other elements of the sentence.

subordinator. See *subordinating conjunction* under CONJUNCTION.

subsequent. The word to which an interrogative relative pronoun refers when it follows the pronoun. • Consider *Whose car is that? The mayor's.* The pronoun *Whose* refers to *The mayor's.*

substantive /səb-**stən**-tiv/, n. A word, phrase, or clause that functions as a noun. • Included in the term are nouns <Mammals are a class of vertebrates>, noun-equivalents <To err is human>, and pronouns. — **substantival** /səb-stən-**tɪ**-vəl/, adj.

substitution. A sound change produced by replacing a vowel or consonant with another.

succinct /sək-**sinkt**/. Verbally compact; concise.

suffix. A particle attached to the end of a word to modify its meaning or change it into a different word class. • Some suffixes are widely used, such as *-ly*, which changes an adjective to an adverb <quick–quickly>. But others are rarely seen. For instance, to make *child* plural, the suffix *-ren* is needed. See AFFIX. Cf. INFIX; PREFIX.

suffixoid /**səf**-ik-soyd/, n. A suffix-like ending that is not truly a suffix at all (such as the *-er* in *badger, hammer,* and *shyster*).

superlative, adj. & n. The form of an adjective or adverb used to compare at least three things and show that one has a quality above or below the others. • For example, *best* is the superlative of *good; most refreshingly* is the superlative of *refreshingly.* — Also termed *superlative degree.* See ADJECTIVE; ADVERB; DEGREE. Cf. COMPARATIVE; POSITIVE.

double superlative. A nonstandard construction such as *most best* or *most highest.* Cf. *double comparative* under COMPARATIVE.

periphrastic superlative. A superlative adjective or adverb that changes degree by taking *most* or *least,* esp. when a one-word form ending in *-est* is available.

superlative degree. See SUPERLATIVE.

superordinate clause. See *independent clause* under CLAUSE.

surd /sərd/, n. An unvoiced consonant, such as *f, k, p, s,* or *t.* See UNVOICED.

surface structure. In transformational grammar, the set of semantic and syntactic relationships among the parts of a sentence as actually written or spoken. Cf. DEEP STRUCTURE.

suspensive hyphen. A hyphen used to connect a series of compound modifiers with the same base term <a five- to seven-year term>.

svarabhakti vowel /swahr-ə-**bahk**-tee/, n. [Sanskrit "vowel separation"] A vowel sound inserted through epenthesis. — Often shortened to *svarabhakti.* — Also termed *parasitic vowel.* See EPENTHESIS; ANAPTYXIS.

syllabication. The act or method of forming syllables or dividing words into syllables. — Also termed *syllabification.*

syllable. A phonological unit consisting of one or more sounds, including a vowel sound.

closed syllable. A syllable that ends with a consonant, as both syllables do in *hip-hop.*

open syllable. A syllable that ends with a vowel (such as both syllables in *oboe*).

syllepsis /si-**lep**-sis/. **1.** *Grammar.* The use of a word to modify or syntactically govern two or more other words when it agrees with only one of them in number, voice, or gender, and so on. **2.** ZEUGMA.

syllogism. A logical argument composed of usu. three propositions from which one (the conclusion) is inferred from the others (the major and minor premises). • Each of the premises has a term in common with the conclusion. The major premise is stated first and contains the major term or predicate of the conclusion (usually the principle involved). The minor premise contains the minor term or subject of the conclusion (usually the fact involved). The major premise is general, and the minor is particular. Here are two classic syllogisms:

Major premise
(general):   All men are mortal.
Minor premise
(particular):   Socrates is a man.
Conclusion: Socrates is mortal.

Major premise
(general):   All mortal things die.
Minor premise
(particular):   All humans are mortal.
Conclusion: All humans die.

Cf. ENTHYMEME. — **syllogistic** /sil-ə-**jis**-tik/, adj.

symploce /**sim**-plə-see/. *Rhetoric.* The repetition of one word at the beginning and of another at the end of two successive clauses <Spring clothes with leaves the trees; spring leads back the birds of song to the trees>. • Symploce combines anaphora and epistrophe. See ANAPHORA; EPISTROPHE. Cf. PLOCE.

synaeresis /si-**ner**-ə-sis *or* si-**neer**-ə-sis/. The drawing together or union in one syllable of two vowels that are normally not sounded together; esp., the coalescence of two sounds into a diphthong. • Through synaeresis, the local pronunciation of Louisville, Kentucky, becomes /**loo**-vəl/. And the Arabic *al-Qaeda* /ahl kah-**ee**-də/ becomes, in English, /al **kɪ**-də/ or /al **kay**-də/. — Also spelled *syneresis.* — Also termed *synizesis.* See SYNCOPE; SYNALOEPHA. Cf. DIAERESIS.

synaesthesia /sin-es-**thee**-zhə/, n. The association of a particular sound or group of sounds with a particular meaning (as with the *fl-* in *flame, flare,* and *flicker*). Cf. ONOMATOPOEIA.

synaloepha /sin-ə-**lee**-fə/. The contraction of a syllable by blending of two vowels in adjacent syllables into one syllable, esp. by suppressing a vowel or diphthong at the end of a word when the next word also begins with a vowel or diphthong. • For example, the preferred pronunciation of *extraordinary* is /ek-**stror**-di-ner-ee/ (in five syllables, not six), blending the sounds of the *a* in *extra* and the *o* in *ordinary.* Synaeresis and crasis are types of synaloepha. — Also spelled *synalepha.* See CRASIS; SYNAERESIS.

synchronic /sin-**krah**-nik/, adj. Of, relating to, or involving language as it exists at a specific time. • A synchronic method of linguistic study isolates the present state of a language and tries to study this without the possibility of any preconceived notions suggested by a knowledge of the language's history. Cf. DIACHRONIC.

synchysis /**sing**-kə-sis/. A verbal disruption; the confusion of words in a sentence, so that the meaning is obscure.

syncope /**sing**-kə-pee/. The loss or elision of one or more letters or sounds, esp. a vowel or syllable, from the middle of a word or phrase <ne'er> <Bosox>. • Among everyday examples in Standard English are *chocolate* /**chawk**-lit/, *diaper* /**dɪ**-pər/, *grocery* /**grohs**-ree/, *vacuum* /**vak**-yoom/, and *vegetable* /**vej**-tə-bəl/. The second word in *San Francisco* becomes, in slang (outside the Bay Area of California), *Frisco.* For a more learned example, the Greek word *apophthegm* (= a terse aphorism or maxim) became *apothegm* in medieval Latin—and only when Samuel Johnson expressed a preference for the original Greek spelling did the longer form come into any real currency in English. But the shorter form is standard. — Also termed *syncopation.* See SYNAERESIS; HAPLOLOGY; HYPHAERESIS. — **syncopal**, adj. — **syncopate**, vb.

syncresis. See CRASIS.

syncrisis /**sin**-krɪ-sis/, n. *Rhetoric.* The comparison of opposites.

syndetic /sin-**det**-ik/, adj. **1.** Used to join or connect; copulative; connective. **2.** Joined by a conjunctive word or phrase.

syndeton /**sin**-di-tahn/, n. The use of a conjunction to join elements in a sentence. • This term dates only from the mid-20th century. Cf. ASYNDETON; POLYSYNDETON.

synecdoche /si-**nek**-də-kee/. A metaphor by which a part of something refers to the whole of it, or the whole for a part <thou sacred head> <flesh and blood>. • Hence *wheels* can refer to a *car, threads* to a suit, *blades* to ice skates, and *breaking bread* to having a meal. — Also termed *pars pro toto.*

syneresis. See SYNAERESIS.

synesis /**sin**-ə-sis/. A construction in which the elements are governed not by the rules of syntax but by the sense of the passage; esp., the construction of a collective noun in the singular with a plural verb because the noun denotes a plurality <A number of people were there> (in which the singular noun *number* might mistakenly be thought to require the singular verb *was*). — Also termed *constructio ad sensum.* See pp. 886–87.

synizesis /sin-ə-**zee**-sis/. See SYNAERESIS.

synoeciosis /sɪ-nee-see-**oh**-sis/, n. A figure of speech in which contrary qualities are attributed to the same thing <Studying language can be both tedious and fascinating>.

synonym. A word whose meaning is very similar to that of another word, although the two words may differ in tone, application, formality, etc. •

For example, *wealthy, well-off,* and *loaded* are synonyms of *rich,* but users must choose the appropriate term for a particular context. Synonyms may be (1) words of consistently similar implication <assiduous–sedulous> <improbable–unlikely>; (2) words that only occasionally have a similar implication <unintelligent–slow> <perceptive–sharp>; (3) words that are broadly similar but have quite different applications <doctor–healer–medicine man>; or (4) words with nearly identical denotations but differing connotations <surgeon–sawbones> <crippled–mobility-impaired>. Cf. ANTONYM.

synonymia. *Rhetoric.* The use of several synonymous words or phrases to amplify or explain a term or subject, or to add force and clarity to a statement. • Synonymia can be used for dramatic or comic effect. — Also termed *scesis onomaton* /**skee**-sis ə-**nahm**-ə-tahn/.

- You blocks, you stones, you worse than senseless things! (Shakespeare, *Julius Caesar*)
- His metabolic processes are now history! He's off the twig! He's kicked the bucket, he's shuffled off his mortal coil, rung down the curtain and joined the bleedin' choir invisible!! THIS IS AN EX-PARROT!! (Monty Python, *The Parrot Sketch*)

syntactic /sin-**tak**-tik/, adj. Of, relating to, or involving the construction of clauses and sentences.

syntax. 1. Sentence structure; the orderly arrangement of words, phrases, and clauses into sentences. **2.** The study of the rules governing how words relate to one another and how they are arranged into sentences. • Syntax deals with the meaningful relationships between words within strings, their function, and their modification. — Also termed (in sense 2) *diasynthesis.* See LINGUISTICS. Cf. ACCIDENCE; MORPHOLOGY.

synthetic language. A language in which syntactical relationships are shown by inflections and the use of affixes with roots; a language that relies heavily on affixation to signal meaning. • In synthetic languages, words change form to show their grammatical function, or when expressing new, especially abstract, concepts. Latin and Greek are synthetic languages. See AFFIX; INFLECTING LANGUAGE; ROOT. Cf. ANALYTIC LANGUAGE.

tagmemics /tag-**meem**-iks/, n. The study of language based on tagmemes, which are the syntactic relationships between a given slot or position within an utterance (such as actor/

subject) and the class of units that can fill it. — **tagmemic,** adj. — **tagmeme,** n.

tag question. An interrogative attached to the end of a declarative statement <It's a good book, isn't it?>. — Also termed *confirmatory clause.*

tapinosis /tap-i-**noh**-sis/, n. The debasement of the dignity of something or someone by referring to it as something much less dignified than it is (as by calling the Mississippi River a *streamlet* or the Supreme Court of the United States *a bunch of judges*). • The columnist Molly Ivins (1944–2007) consistently used tapinosis; throughout the two terms of President George W. Bush, she referred to him in her columns as *W.* Cf. DYSPHEMISM.

taradiddle /**ta**-ri-did-əl/, n. **1.** A fib; a minor falsehood. **2.** Pretentious nonsense. — Also spelled **tarradiddle.*

tatpurusha /tat-**puur**-ə-shə/, n. [Sanskrit "his servant"] A compound word in which the first element (usu. an attributive noun) qualifies the second, while the second (the head) determines the part of speech <bookcase> <yearbook>.

tautegorical /taw-tə-**gor**-i-kəl/, adj. Expressing an idea in the same style but in different words.

tautology /taw-**tol**-ə-jee/. **1.** Repetition of something in words that are nearly synonymous and do not add anything <Many people are out of work when unemployment is high> <free gift>. **2.** *Rhetoric.* Repetition of an idea in a different word, phrase, or sentence <with malice toward none, with charity for all (Lincoln, second inaugural address)>. **3.** *Logic.* A statement that must be true for all possibilities or by virtue of its logical form. Cf. PLEONASM. — **tautologize,** vb.

telestich /tə-**les**-tik/ or /**tel**-əs-tik/, n. *Prosody.* A poem in which the last letters of each line, when taken in order, spell a word or words. Cf. ACROSTIC.

tenor. 1. *Linguistics.* The social roles and relationships between the participants in a channel of communication. **2.** *Semiotics.* In a metaphor, the literal, primary subject. • For instance: "*Experience* is a good *school,* but the fees are high" (Heinrich Heine [1797–1856]). In this case, the primary subject of *experience* is expressed in terms of the secondary subject of *school.* Typically, a metaphor expresses an abstraction in terms of a more well-defined model. Cf. VEHICLE.

tense. A verb's quality that shows the time in which an act, state, or condition occurs or occurred; the correspondence between a verb form and the concept of time. Cf. ASPECT; MOOD; VOICE. See pp. 895–97.

complex tense. A tense combined with the perfect or the progressive aspect.

future-perfect tense. The tense denoting an act, state, or condition that will be completed before another specified future time or future action <I will have finished my degree before the end of summer>. • This term is borrowed from Latin grammar to apply to verb phrases such as *will have said, will have been said,* and *will have been saying.*

future tense. The tense denoting an act, state, or condition that will occur <I will go tomorrow>. • Modern grammarians tend to define tense inflectionally—and therefore to limit the description of English to the present and past tenses—but it is conventional to speak of such constructions as *will make, will be made,* and *will be making* as being in the future tense.

historical present tense. The use of present tense when referring to past events (or sometimes absent people) to add immediacy and drama to a narrative or discussion. • This tense is typically used in colloquial or nonstandard English. In writing, it is used only for narration, usually fictional. It is not used for formal writing. Examples:

• So this guy walks in and looks at me like I'm a freak or something.
• I'm just about to leave, when the lights suddenly go out.
• When he has Jack say, "I don't go looking for trouble, trouble comes to me," what is the author trying to tell us?

— Also termed *historic present.*

past-perfect tense. The tense denoting that an act, state, or condition was completed before another specified past time or past action <I had begun to apologize, but she hung up the phone>. • Verb phrases such as *had called, had been called,* and *had been calling* are in past-perfect tense. — Also termed *pluperfect tense.*

past tense. A tense signaling an action or even a state that occurred at some previous time. • The past tense may signal the instantaneous past <Brad broke his leg> or the durational past <Ms. Williams tried for several years to get appointed as an ambassador>. — Also termed *preterit (tense).*

perfect tense. See *present-perfect tense.*

pluperfect tense. See *past-perfect tense.*

present-perfect tense. The tense denoting an act, state, or condition that occurred at an unspecified time before now <We have gone there many times>. — Also termed *perfect tense.*

present tense. A tense signaling that an action, event, or state is timeless or progressive <Life is hard> <The dogs are waiting>.

preterit tense. See *past tense.*

simple tense. A tense with no aspect: present, past, or future.

terminal preposition. See PREPOSITION.

tetrasyllable. See **quadrisyllable.**

theme. See BASE.

thesis. 1. A proposition to be developed, proved, and maintained against attack; the point of a discussion. **2.** A theme for a composition; a statement of the central idea of an argument or writing. **3.** A dissertation of a specified length written to satisfy the requirements of a university degree, esp. a master's degree.

third person. See PERSON.

tilde /**til**-də/. A diacritical mark (~) indicating that an *n* takes a palatized sound, as in *señor.* • Tildes are common in Spanish but are not used in American English. In written British English, the tilde character, typeset in the middle of a line and called a swing-dash, can substitute for words describing activities the reader can imagine. See DIACRITICAL MARK.

time. The indicator of when an action occurred in relation to the occurrence of the utterance itself: past, present, or future.

tittle /**tit**-əl/, n. **1.** The dot over the letter *i.* **2.** A punctuation mark. **3.** DIACRITICAL MARK. • Sense 3 is the earliest, dating from the 14th century. The phrase *jot or tittle* dates from the early 16th century. The phrase is biblical: see Matthew 5:18. See JOT.

tmesis /**tmee**-sis or **mee**-sis/. A separation of the parts of a compound word by one or more inserted words <what condition soever>. • For example, in George Bernard Shaw's *Pygmalion* (1913), Eliza Doolittle says *abso-bloomin'-lutely.* — Also termed *diacope /* dī-**ak**-ə-pee/. See p. 913.

Tom Swifty. A sentence in which a verb or adverb in the clause following a sentence of reported speech produces a pun related to that sentence. • Tom Swift is a fictional character, created by Edward L. Stratemeyer (1862–1930) (using the pseudonym Victor Appleton), who is the hero of a series of adventure books. Almost everything Tom says includes a qualifying adverb, as in *Tom added eagerly* or *Tom said jokingly.* Tom Swifties use a pastiche of this pattern combined with speech. Two examples are the statements "'I only have diamonds, clubs and spades,' said Tom heartlessly" and "'The castle walls are made of granite,' Tom said stonily." Although the name Tom usually appears, it isn't necessary. For example, "'Who discovered radium?' asked Marie curiously." A Tom Swifty is a subtype of Wellerism. See WELLERISM.

toneme, n. The tone or set of tones constituting a morpheme.

toponym /tahp-ə-nim/. A place name, esp. one derived from or describing a topographical feature (e.g., *Death Valley, Palo Duro Canyon*).

transferred epithet. See HYPALLAGE.

transformation. An operation by which one syntactic structure (as a deep structure) is changed into another (as a surface structure) through the application of linguistic rules. See DEEP STRUCTURE; SURFACE STRUCTURE; TRANSFORMATIONAL GRAMMAR.

transformational grammar. A grammar that aims to establish rules for the generation of surface syntactic structures from deep structures; specif., a grammatical theory that seeks to account for the ability of native speakers to generate and understand the sentences of their language.

transitive, adj. (Of a verb) requiring a direct object to complete the idea of showing what action the subject exerts.

transitive verb. See VERB.

transliteration /tranz-lit-ə-ray-shən/. In writing or printing, the use of the closest corresponding letters in a given alphabet or language to express a sound, word, or name in a different language. • For instance, the name of China's leader from 1949 to 1976 was formerly transliterated into English as *Mao Tse Tung* but is now predominantly *Mao Zedong* (considered closer to the Chinese pronunciation).

triglossia /trɪ-**glahs**-ee-ə/, n. The coexistence of three languages within a speech community, usu. standard form, a regional dialect, and an international lingua franca.

trill. Pronunciation, esp. of the consonant *r*, with a rapid vibration of the tongue against the upper teeth, the hard or soft palate, or the uvula. • Trills are more common in BrE than in AmE.

triphthong /**trif**-thahng/. A vowel sound in one syllable that requires the speaker to change the position of the speech organs twice, as in *tire*.

triptote /**trip**-toht/, n. In certain Indo-European languages, a noun having three cases. Cf. APTOTE; DIPTOTE.

trisyllable /trɪ-**sil**-ə-bəl *or* tri-**sil**-ə-bəl/, n. A word of three syllables. — **trisyllabic** /trɪ-si-**lab**-ik/, adj.

trivium /**triv**-ee-əm/, n. In medieval times, three of the seven liberal arts: grammar, rhetoric, and logic.

trope /trohp/, n. *Rhetoric.* **1.** The use of a word in a meaning different from its normal one, as when one thing is called another (metaphor), the name of part of something denotes the whole (synecdoche), or something is called by the name of something else with which it is closely associated (metonymy). • In this strict sense, the two categories of tropes are (1) metaphors, and (2) simple tropes—namely, synecdoche and metonymy. See METAPHOR; METONYMY; SYNECDOCHE. **2.** Loosely, any figure of speech; figurative language generally.

truncated passive. See PASSIVE VOICE; VOICE.

tu quoque /too kwoh-kwee/, n. [Latin "you're another!"] *Rhetoric.* A retort in which one counteraccuses the adversary of the same offense of which one is accused.

turgid /**tər**-jid/, adj. Pompously inflated; bombastically swollen. — **turgidity** /**tər**-ji-də-tee/, n.

tushery /**təsh**-ə-ree/, n. The use of affected archaisms. • The term derives from the archaic interjection *tush*, once used to express rebuke, contempt, or impatience.

twaddle /**twahd**-əl/, n. Pretentious but silly language in which the speaker or writer affects superior knowledge or wisdom; FUSTIAN. — **twaddle,** vb.

typeface. A design of type used in printing. In general, typefaces are either serif or sans serif.

U. The language used by well-educated people in the upper social classes. • This term was coined in 1954 by British linguist Alan Ross (1907–1980), who applied it to the distinctive vocabularies and pronunciations in England. Cf. NON-U.

ultima /**əl**-ti-mə/. A word's last syllable.

umlaut /**uum**-lowt *or* **oom**-lowt/. **1.** A vowel mutation in some languages, such as German, caused by the partial assimilation of the vowel to an adjacent sound (usually the following vowel or semivowel). **2.** A diacritical mark consisting of two dots (¨) placed over a vowel to signal that the marked vowel has a modified sound. • Umlauts are often used in German words and names <*Schäfer*> but omitted in naturalized English equivalents, which may add an *e* after the formerly marked vowel <*Schaefer*>. Only three letters take an umlaut: *a*, *o*, and *u*. The

mark is identical to a diaeresis in German; except for the combination *äu* (pronounced /*oy*/), an umlaut never appears over a vowel that is adjacent to another vowel. See DIACRITICAL MARK; MUTATION. Cf. DIAERESIS.

uncountable noun. See *mass noun* under NOUN.

undeclinable, adj. Having no inflections. — Also termed *indeclinable*. Cf. DECLINABLE.

understatement. The expression of an idea that is deliberately made to seem less important than it actually is. • Typically, the degree, number, or significance involved is purposely diminished, often for the sake of irony or of politeness.

unfinished comparative. See *dangling comparative* under COMPARATIVE.

unit modifier. See *phrasal adjective* under ADJECTIVE.

universal pronoun. See PRONOUN.

unmarked infinitive. See *bare infinitive* under INFINITIVE.

unvoiced, adj. (Of a spoken sound) produced without vibration of the vocal cords. — Also termed *surd*; *voiceless*.

usage. 1. Collectively, the linguistic customs of some group of speakers, such as all native speakers <common usage>, dialectal speakers <nonstandard usage>, literary writers <literary usage>, the best writers and speakers <proper usage>, etc. **2.** A particular linguistic custom of this kind.

variant, n. A different form of a linguistic unit, such as an alternative spelling of a noun.

variorum /va-ree-**or**-əm/. **1.** An edition of a publication containing different readings of the original text. **2.** A text or edition of a publication with notes added by various critics or commentators.

vehicle. *Semiotics.* **1.** In a metaphor, a figurative secondary subject that follows the primary subject. See TENOR. **2.** The form that a sign takes, such as sound or appearance.

verb. A word that shows the performance or occurrence of an action or the existence of a condition or a state of being, such as an emotion.

action verb. A verb that expresses the action of the subject <She moved the chair>.

auxiliary verb. A verb that is joined with another verb to help express voice, mood, tense, person, or some other quality. • For example, *will* is an auxiliary expressing future tense in *She will serve as a Senate intern this summer.* Auxiliaries may be modal (*can, will, may, ought, must,* and *shall* in the present tense; *could, would, might, ought, must,* and *should* in the past tense). Or they may be nonmodal (*do, have, be,* and *get*). — Often shortened to *auxiliary.* — Also termed *helping verb.*

be-*verb*. Any form of the verb *to be*—namely, *am, are, be, been, being, is, was,* and *were*—whether used as an auxiliary verb or as a main verb.

catenative verb /**kat**-ən-ə-tiv/. A transitive verb that can take a verbal as its object <I like to write> <I like writing>.

copular verb; copulative verb. See *linking verb.*

defective verb. A verb that lacks at least one of the typical forms of conjugation; esp., an auxiliary verb.

ditransitive prepositional verb. A verb that takes both a direct and an indirect object, the direct object requiring an introductory preposition <The boss assured her employees of their job security> <My father recommended John Green for the position>.

ditransitive verb. A verb that takes both a direct and an indirect object (e.g., *gave* in the sentence *I gave her a book*). Cf. *monotransitive verb.*

do-*verb*. Any form of the verb *to do*—namely, *did, do, does, doing,* and *done*—whether used as an auxiliary verb or as a main verb.

equational verb. See *linking verb.*

ergative verb. A verb that can be used transitively or intransitively. • With a transitive use, the subject performs the action of the verb; with an intransitive use, the subject receives the action of the verb. For example, *to melt* can be intransitive <The butter melted> or transitive <The sun melted the butter>. See p. 344.

factitive verb. A transitive verb having both a direct object and an object complement, the two of which are closely linked <They called him Joe> <I consider that theory preposterous>. • The most common factitive verbs are *appoint, call, choose, consider, designate, elect, find, imagine, judge, keep, label, make, name, prove,* and *think.*

finite verb. A verb whose form shows that it is limited in number, person, and tense <I go, she goes, they went>. • A finite verb functions as the verb element in a clause and must agree in person and number with the subject of the clause.

helping verb. See *auxiliary verb.*

infinitive verb. See INFINITIVE.

intransitive verb. A verb that does not require an object to complete the thought; a verb that can stand alone in the predicate. • Intransitive verbs

(e.g., *arrive, differ, glow, lie*) do not have a passive form.

irregular verb. A verb whose past tense or past participle isn't formed according to a predictable pattern. • Irregular verbs don't take a simple *-d* or *-ed* ending; they may undergo simple vowel changes <drink–drank–drunk> or change more extensively <go–went–gone> <hide–hid–hidden>. — Also termed *strong verb.* Cf. *regular verb.* See pp. 529–31.

light verb. A verb with relatively little semantic content in a given context (e.g., *take* in the phrasal verb *take up* or *make* in the phrasal verb *make love*).

linking verb. A verb that connects a subject to the complement. • For example, in *dinner smells good, smells* links the subject with the adjective describing it. Among the common linking verbs are *be*-verbs, *appear* <She appeared confident>, *become* <They became incensed>, *feel* <It feels gooey>, *go* <The milk went sour>, *grow* <Some of them grew impatient>, *prove* <It proved impossible>, *remain* <They remained steadfast>, *seem* <He seemed happy>, *smell* <It smells rancid>, *taste* <It tastes bitter>, *wax* <She waxed eloquent>. — Also termed *connecting verb; copula; copular verb; copulative verb; equational verb.*

main verb. The most important verb in a sentence, the one that is necessary to make the sentence complete. • Though sometimes combined with subordinate verbs, the main verb expresses the key idea. It is combined with an auxiliary verb to indicate mood, tense, or voice. — Also termed *principal verb.* See also *progressive aspect* under ASPECT.

modal verb. An auxiliary verb that conveys the mood or mode of the action expressed in the main verb. • Modal verbs are typically used to express possibility, intention, obligation, or necessity <I can do that> <I would have done that, if you had told me to do it>. — Also termed *modal auxiliary.*

monotransitive verb. A verb that takes only one object in a construction, as in *the mountaineers reached the summit.* Cf. *ditransitive verb.*

nonfinite verb. A verb form that has no tense, person, or singular or plural form, and is not limited by inflection. • Nonfinite verbs are never the main verb in a clause. They are infinitives <Do you want to buy a new couch?>, bare infinitives

<Should we run today?>, and present and past participles <The water is running> <The program has ended>. All verbs except auxiliaries have nonfinite forms.

phrasal verb. 1. A verb–adverb or verb–particle combo that functions as a verb <put up with> <stand for>. **2.** An idiomatic transitive verb phrase consisting of a verb and a particle (and distinguished, in this sense, from verb plus a preposition [which may be intransitive], such as *make out* or *show up*). See p. 694.

primary verb. The first verb in a sentence, and the only verb that is affected by the subject. The primary verb can be a main verb (e.g., *drive, run, think*) or an auxiliary verb (e.g., *be, have, do*).

principal verb. See MAIN VERB.

pro-verb. A verb used to stand in for a previously stated predicate; specif., a word or phrase that substitutes for a verb or predicate to avoid repetition when referring to things or details already mentioned. • Verbs that take a bare infinitive, such as *be, have, do,* and most of the auxiliary verbs can function as pro-verbs. The first predicate may be the main verb in a complex sentence (e.g., in *Behave as I do,* the pro-verb *do* in the dependent clause stands in for the main verb *behave*); the first predicate in a compound sentence (e.g., in *He won't tell you, but I will,* the pro-verb *will* stands for the predicate of the first clause, *will tell you*); or the predicate from a previous sentence (e.g., in the exchange *Have you washed the car yet? Yes, I did,* the pro-verb *did* stands in for the predicate of the first sentence, *have washed the car*). Further examples:

- Why can't he do it? — He can [do it], but he won't [do it] for free.
- I've finished my homework, and so have my friends [finished their homework].
- Inga avoided looking at it, and so did we [avoid looking at it].
- Who's been borrowing my clothes without asking? — Mike has [been borrowing them]. (Alternatively, *Mike has been* or *Mike's been doing it* would mean the same thing as *Mike has.*)

regular verb. A verb whose past tense and past participle are formed predictably according to a rule, such as by appending *-ed, -d,* or *-t.* — Also termed *weak verb.* Cf. *irregular verb.*

strong verb. A verb that is inflected (1) by internal vowel change, but not by affixation, (2) by no change at all, or (3) by radically changing in the past-tense and past-participial forms, which are not predictable from the root. • For example, the root verbs *begin* and *drink* might suggest that strong verbs with an *i* take an *a* in the past tense and a *u* in the participle (e.g., *sing–sang–sung, stink–stank–stunk*). But the pattern doesn't apply universally (e.g., *bring–brought–brought*). Some strong verbs do not change at all (e.g., *cast–cast–cast*). And a few verbs, such as *be* and *go*, change radically (i.e., *be–was–been, go–went–gone*). Only about 165 verbs currently used in English are strong verbs.

Some would say that the preceding paragraph is a discourse on *irregular verbs*, and that *strong verbs* are instead a subset of irregular verbs. That distinction goes back to the German philologist and folklorist Jakob Grimm (1785–1863), who coined the terms *stark* ("strong") and *schwach* ("weak"). Following Grimm's definitions to the letter, linguists who favor a third classification restrict the *strong* label to verbs whose vowels change in declension (e.g., *swim–swam–swum*) and exclude the ones that don't change their form (e.g., *quit–quit–quit*) or that take a *-t* rather than an *-ed* ending (e.g., *sleep–slept–slept*). But the distinction is too fine ("inconvenient," the *OED* put it) for most grammarians, who continue to accept the approach of *W2* and use *strong* and *irregular* as synonyms. To them the idea of a "weak irregular verb" is fallacious.

transitive verb. A verb that requires an object to express a complete thought; the verb indicating what action the subject exerts on the object.

weak verb. See *regular verb.*

verbal, n. **1.** A nonfinite verb (e.g., a gerund, infinitive, present participle, or past participle)—so called because it does not carry a tense marker or signal person, number, or mood, and may never appear as the sole item in a verb phrase. • As a nonfinite verb, a verbal makes no assertion. **2.** In some grammatical systems, a word or phrase that occupies a position typically occupied by a verb. — Also termed *verbid.*

verbalist. Someone who coins, criticizes, or otherwise deals with words. — Also termed *verbarian.*

verbality /vər-**bal**-i-tee/. **1.** The state or character of being expressed in words. **2.** A form of words divorced from their proper context or true spirit.

verbal noun. See GERUND.

verbarian /vər-**bair**-ee-ən/. See VERBALIST.

verbatim /vər-**bay**-təm/, adv. In the very same words; word for word. — **verbatim,** adj.

verbiage /**vər**-bee-əj/. Words that have little or no content and are therefore considered unnecessary; superfluous wording. — Often misspelled and mispronounced *verbage.*

verbicide. 1. The killing of a word; esp., the deliberate depreciation or distortion of a word's meaning or sense. **2.** Someone who kills a word, esp. by deliberately distorting its meaning. — **verbicidal,** adj.

verbiculture. The coinage and promotion of new words.

verbid. See VERBAL.

verbify /**vər**-i-fI/, vb. To make (another part of speech) into a verb; to press into service as a verb.

verbigerate /ver-**bij**-ə-rayt/, vb. To repeat words or phrases involuntarily and uncontrollably. See PALILALIA. — **verbigeration,** n.

verbivore /**vər**-bi-vor/, n. Someone who devours words; a relisher of words.

verbomania /vər-boh-**may**-nee-ə/. A passion or mania for or obsession with words, sometimes leading to abnormal talkativeness or a psychotic flow of speech. — **verbomaniac,** n. — **verbomaniacal** /vər-boh-mə-**nI**-i-kəl/, adj.

verbose, adj. Using or containing too many words; wearisomely or intolerably wordy. — **verbosity,** n.

verb phrase. See PHRASE.

vernacular. 1. The language or dialect native to a particular region or country. **2.** An individual's native language. — **vernaculate,** vb.

verse. 1. In poetry, a single metrical line consisting of a number of feet, according to a definite scheme. **2.** A specified type of metrical or nearly metrical composition, as distinguished by type <blank verse> <free verse>. **3.** Any metrical composition, as distinguished from prose. **4.** In prose, a succession of words constituting a short division of text, as in the Bible.

vocable /**voh**-kə-bəl/. **1.** A word or phrase, esp. when regarded merely for its sound. **2.** A vocal sound, as of a musical note.

vocabulary. 1. The aggregate of words used in a work, in the works of a particular author, or in some other collection. **2.** The body of words known to an individual speaker of a language, or used in a language. **3.** A portion of a language's body of words, used for particular purposes <business vocabulary>. **4.** An alphabetical listing of words, as for a dictionary.

vocative, adj. Of, relating to, or involving the act of calling or addressing directly; esp., in some synthetic languages, of, relating to, or involving the form and syntactic relation of a noun, pronoun, or adjective used as, for, or with the name of the person addressed. — **vocative,** n.

voice. The quality by which a transitive verb denotes an action performed either *by* the subject (active voice) or *on* the subject of the clause (passive voice). • The test is whether the subject performs or receives the action of the verb. Cf. ASPECT; MOOD; TENSE.

active voice. The voice that shows that the sentence's subject is the actor. • For example, *Jack drives an old car* is in active voice because *Jack* is both the subject and the actor. Cf. PASSIVE VOICE.

passive voice. See PASSIVE VOICE.

truncated passive voice. Passive voice that does not retain the prepositional phrase of agency <The car was driven (omitting *by* Jack)>.

voiced, adj. (Of a spoken sound) produced with resonance in the vocal cords, such as *b, d, g, v,* or *z.* — Also termed *sonant.*

voiceless. See UNVOICED.

volubility /vol-yə-**bil**-ə-tee/. The state or quality of great fluency of speech; esp., GARRULITY. — **voluble** /**vol**-yə-bəl/, adj.

vowel. 1. A speech sound produced without blocking the breath channel. **2.** A letter that represents such a sound. • Five letters—*a, e, i, o,* and *u*—are normally classified as vowels, but these are used to represent a multitude of sounds. Diphthongs, such as *au, oo,* and *ou,* also represent vowel sounds. The letter *y* behaves as a vowel when it takes on the sound of *i* or *e.* Cf. CONSONANT; SEMIVOWEL.

vowel gradation. See ABLAUT.

vulgarism. A word or phrase suggesting a lack of culture on the part of its user.

vulgarity. 1. Lack of refinement in conduct or speech; coarseness. **2.** Something (usu. an act or expression) that is offensive or obscene; profanity. — **vulgar,** adj.

weak verb. See *regular verb* under VERB.

weasel word. An equivocal word that diminishes the force or meaning of a concept being expressed; esp., an intensive such as *clearly* or *obviously,* which, while intended to strengthen a statement, actually has the effect of weakening it by making its content more questionable. See pp. 955–56.

Wellerism. A punning simile in which words are humorously attributed to someone or something. • The name derives from the fictional character Sam Weller, Mr. Pickwick's witty servant in Charles Dickens's *The Pickwick Papers* (1836–1837). See TOM SWIFTY.

- "We'll have to rehearse that," said the undertaker as the coffin fell out of the car.
- "It all comes back to me now," said the captain as he spat into the wind.
- "That's the spirit," said the medium, as the table began to rise.
- "We are not what we seem," as the needle said to the thread.

whiz deletion. The reduction of a relative clause by omitting a relative pronoun plus a *be*-verb. Example: *My brother, a professional flutist and flute teacher, frequently performs in Asia.* The phrase *who is* (hence "whiz") has been elided after *My brother.*

wh- question. A question that seeks a specific piece of information <why?> <when?> <where?> <who?> <which?>.

word. A minimum free linguistic form, consisting of one or more morphemes; a human vocal habit that has, or may have, the effect of evoking some idea in someone else's mind. • If the definition seems a little opaque, take comfort in the observation of Richard Grant White (1822–1885): "What is a word? Everyone knows. The most ignorant child, if it can speak, needs no definition of *word*."[3] More than a century later, the noted British linguist Randolph Quirk (1920–) expressed a similar idea: "Words come to us so naturally that it takes a serious effort of imagination to realize what miraculous devices they are. Like so many other things that are basic and elemental in our lives, we take them for granted, and we are apt to be surprised to find how hard it is to say exactly what a word is."[4] Cf. CLAUSE; PHRASE.

compound word. A word that is composed of two or more other words <doorknob> or a word plus an affix <biodiversity>. See COMPOUND.

function word. A word whose main role is to assist in the structure of a sentence. • Articles (*a, an,* and *the*) are examples of function words. So are prepositions. See EMPTY WORD.

pointing word. A word that points at something or someone either because it has a demonstrative quality (e.g., *this, that, these,* or *those*) or because it is a pronoun that requires an antecedent. — Also termed *deictic term.* See ANTECEDENT.

portmanteau word. See BLEND.

word-blindness. See ALEXIA.

word class. See PART OF SPEECH.

word formation. See MORPHOLOGY.

word-hoard. See WORD-STOCK.

wordmonger. Someone who deals with words enthusiastically but discreditably, as by showing extreme pedantry or by propagandizing through slick quibbling or dishonest imputations. Cf. PHRASEMONGER.

word-order. The sequence in which words can or typically do appear in a sentence. • Because English is an analytic language, word-order is more important to English grammar than the other basic grammatical devices: inflection and function words.

wordplay. An instance of verbal wit; a jocular use of language.

word-stock. 1. The vocabulary possessed by an individual, whether copious or exiguous. **2.** The vocabulary of a given language, however vast. — Also termed *word-hoard.*

yes–no question. A question that calls for an answer in the simple affirmative or negative.

zero. The absence of an overt change in form where one might be expected or implied.

zero article. See ARTICLE.

zero form. An unchanged form of a word or an unexpressed part of a construction. • Grammarians sometimes use zero forms to account for exceptions to rules. For example, if the rule is that all English nouns have plurals by adding some variety of the plural ending to the proper base, then we must recognize a zero ending for words that don't change their form from the singular when used in a plural sense, such as *trout* <Many trout were in the stream>. If the rule is that all relative clauses are introduced by relative pronouns, then a zero relative appears in a sentence when the pronoun is elided <The putter you used needs a new grip>.

zeugma /z[y]oog-mə/. **1.** *Grammar.* A grammatical construction in which a word applies to two things but matches only one of them in number, gender, or some idiomatic quality <Either you or I am wrong> <waging war and peace>. Cf. ANTANACLASIS. **2.** *Rhetoric.* The use of a word in the same grammatical relation to two nearby words, one having a metaphorical sense and the other a literal sense <I lost my wallet and my temper>. Cf. SYLLEPSIS. — **zeugmatic,** adj. See p. 982.

zombie noun. See NOUN.

---

[3]Richard Grant White, *Words and Their Uses, Past and Present* 199 (1870).

[4]Randolph Quirk, "Thinking of Words," in *The Linguist and the English Language* 128, 128 (1974).

A TIMELINE OF BOOKS ON USAGE

What follows is a chronological list of more than 500 books making up the corpus of literature on English usage. Some are dictionaries of usage; others are discursive treatments of the subject; still others have usage glossaries within them. Even though some of the books have gone through multiple editions, only the date of each one's first appearance is given. (The one exception is H.W. Fowler's *Modern English Usage.*) For those even vaguely familiar with the corpus, it's instructive to see the books arranged chronologically.

Omitted from the list are histories of the English language, pure grammar texts and rhetorics, and the general run of books about writing well—the most helpful of which appear in the Select Bibliography (pp. 1049–51).

1758
Temple, Launcelot. *Sketches: Or Essays on Various Subjects.* London: A. Millar.
Ward, John. *Four Essays upon the English Language.* London: Printed for John Ward in Cornhill.

1762
Girard, Gabriel. *A New Guide to Eloquence; Being a Treatise of the Proper Distinctions to Be Observed Between Words Reckoned Synonymous.* London: James Pritchard.
Lowth. *Short Introduction to English Grammar.* London: A. Millar & R.J. Dodsley.
Priestley, Joseph. *A Course of Lectures on the Theory of Language and Universal Grammar.* Warrington: W. Eyres.

1766
Trusler, John. *The Difference Between Words, Esteemed Synonymous, in the English Language.* London: J. Dodsley.

1770
[Baker, Robert.] *Remarks on the English Language.* London: J. Bell.

1786
Tooke, John Horne. *Epea Ptoerenta, or the Diversions of Purley.* London: J. Johnson.

1787
[Anon.] *Exercises, Instructive and Entertaining, in False English.* Leeds: J. Binns.

1789
Withers, Philip. *Aristarchus, or The Principles of Composition: Containing a Methodical Arrangement of the Improprieties Frequent in Writing and Conversation, with Select Rules for Attaining to Purity and Elegance of Expression.* London: J. Moore.

1794
Piozzi, Hester Lynch. *British Synonymy.* 2 vols. London: G.G. & J. Robinson.

1798
Webster, Noah. *A Letter to the Governors, Instructors and Trustees of the Universities and Other Seminaries of Learning, in the United States, on the Errors of English Grammar.* N.Y.: George F. Hopkins.

1801
Irving, David. *Elements of English Composition.* London: R. Phillips.
Russel, William P. *Multum in Parvo: Or, a Display of More than a Thousand Errors* [etc.]. London.

1804
Ussher, G. Neville. *The Elements of English Grammar.* Exeter: Henry Ranlet.

1805
Perry, William. *The Synonymous, Etymological, and Pronouncing English Dictionary.* London: John Walker, Cuthell & Martin, Longman, et al.

1811
Murdoch, John. *The Dictionary of Distinctions.* London: C. Law.

1813
Taylor, William. *English Synonyms Discriminated.* London: W. Pople.

1816
Dyer, Gilbert. *Vulgar Errors, Ancient and Modern.* London: Longman, Hurst, Rees, Orme & Brown.
Ussher, M.N. *Synonymous Terms in the English Language Explained.* Dublin: R. Coyne.

1817
[Anon.] *The Grammatical Remembrancer.* Huddersfield: Thomas Smart.

1823
Banks, William. *The English Master; or Student's Guide to Reasoning and Composition.* London: Longman, Hurst, Rees, Orme & Brown.

1825
[Anon.] *The English Cratylus; or Essays on Language, Grammar, and Composition.* London: Baldwin, Craddock & Joy.

1826
[Anon.] *The Vulgarities of Speech Corrected, with Elegant Expressions for Provincial and Vulgar English, Scots, and Irish: For the Use of Those Who Are Unacquainted with Grammar.* London: Privately printed.

1832
Emmons, Samuel B. *The Grammatical Instructor.* Boston: Waitt & Dow.

1839
Webster, Noah. *Observations on Language, and on the Errors of Class-Books.* New Haven: S. Babcock.

1841
Vesey, Francis. *Decline of the English Language: The Cause and Probable Consequences.* London: Saunders & Benning.

1842
Hildreth, Ezekiel. *Logopolis, or, City of Words: Containing a Development of the Science, Grammar, Syntax, Logic and Rhetoric of the English Language.* Pittsburgh: A. Jaynes.

1846
Graham, G.F. *English Synonymes Classified and Explained.* London: Longman, Brown, Green & Longmans.

1847
Hurd, Seth T. *A Grammatical Corrector: Or, Vocabulary of the Common Errors of Speech.* Philadelphia: E.H. Butler & Co.

1851
Trench, Richard Chenevix. *On the Study of Words.* London: Macmillan & Co.

1852
Gwynne, Parry. *A Word to the Wise: Or, Hints on the Current Improprieties of Expression in Writing and Speaking.* London: Grant & Griffith.

1855
[Anon.] *Never Too Late to Learn: Mistakes of Daily Occurrence in Speaking,*

Writing, and Pronunciation, Corrected. N.Y.: Daniel Burgess & Co.

[Anon.] *The Schoolmaster at Home: Errors in Speaking and Writing Corrected.* London: James Cornish.

Fallows, Samuel. *Discriminate: A Companion to "Don't": A Manual for Guidance in the Use of Correct Words and Phrases in Proper Speech.* London: Griffith, Farran, Okeden & Welsh.

Trench, Richard Chenevix. *English, Past and Present.* London: Kegan Paul, Trench, Trübner & Co.

1856

[Anon.] *Live and Learn, or 1000 Mistakes Corrected: A Guide for All Who Wish to Speak and Write Correctly.* N.Y.: Dick & Fitzgerald.

Peabody, Andrew. *Conversation: Its Faults and Graces.* Boston: James Munroe & Co.

1858

[Anon.] *The Little Linguist: Or, a Complete Guide to English Philology.* London: W.S. Johnson.

1859

Bailey, Rufus W. *The Scholar's Companion.* Philadelphia: E.H. Butler & Co.

Swinton, William. *Rambles Among Words.* N.Y.: Scribner.

1860

[Anon.] *The Age of Words and Phrases: A Book for Persons Who Undervalue Themselves and Overvalue Others.* Boston: Mudge & Son.

[Anon.] *A Selection of English Synonyms.* Boston: James Munroe & Co.

1864

Alford, Henry. *A Plea for the Queen's English.* London: Alexander Strahan.

Moon, George Washington. *The Dean's English: A Criticism on the Dean of Canterbury's Essays on the Queen's English.* London: Hatchard & Co.

1866

Gould, Edward S. *Good English: Or, Popular Errors in Language.* N.Y.: W.J. Widdleton.

1867

De Vere, Schele. *Studies in English: Glimpses of the Inner Life of Our Language.* N.Y.: Charles Scribner & Co.

Webb, A.C. *The Model Etymology, with Sentences Showing the Correct Use of Words.* Philadelphia: Eldredge & Bro.

1868

Angus, Joseph. *Hand-Book of the English Tongue.* London: Religious Tract Society.

Bache, Richard Meade. *Vulgarisms and Other Errors of Speech.* Philadelphia: Claxton, Remsen & Haffelfinger.

Moon, George Washington. *The Bad English of Lindley Murray and Other Writers on the English Language: A Series of Criticisms.* London: Hatchard & Co.

1869

Blackley, W.L. *Word Gossip.* London: Longmans, Green & Co.

Graham, George Frederick. *A Book About Words.* London: Longmans, Green & Co.

1870

White, Richard Grant. *Words and Their Uses, Past and Present.* N.Y.: Sheldon & Co.

1871

Earle, John. *The Philology of the English Tongue.* Oxford: Clarendon Press.

Smith, C.J. *Synonyms Discriminated: A Complete Catalogue of Synonymous Words in the English Language.* N.Y.: Scribner, Welford & Co.

1872

Drew, Benjamin. *Pens and Types: Or, Hints and Helps for Those Who Write, Print, or Read.* Boston: Lee & Shepard.

Hall, Fitzedward. *Recent Exemplifications of False Philology.* N.Y.: Scribner, Armstrong & Co.

1873

Hall, Fitzedward. *Modern English.* N.Y.: Scribner, Armstrong & Co.

Larrabee, W.H.; and H.A. Buttz. *Helps to Speak and Write Correctly: More than One Thousand Mistakes Corrected and Peculiarities of Language Noted.* N.Y.: N. Tibbals & Son.

1874

Bombaugh, C.C. *Gleanings for the Curious from the Harvest Fields of Literature.* Philadelphia: Lippincott & Co.

Meredith, L.P. *Every-Day Errors of Speech.* Philadelphia: Lippincott & Co.

1875

Shelton, Edward. *The Dictionary of Every-Day Difficulties in Reading, Writing, and Speaking the English Language.* London: Ward, Lock & Tyler.

1876

Mathews, William. *Words: Their Use and Abuse.* Chicago: S.C. Griggs & Co.

Taylor, William. *English Synonyms Discriminated.* London: William Tegg & Co.

1877

[Anon.] *Discriminate, a Companion to "Don't": A Manual for Guidance in the Use of Correct Words and Phrases in Ordinary Speech.* N.Y.: D. Appleton & Co.

Bryant, William Cullen. *Index Expurgatorius.* [Orig. unpublished, but reprinted in Bernstein 1971.]

Hall, Fitzedward. *On English Adjectives in -ABLE, with Special Reference to RELIABLE.* London: Trübner & Co.

Stormonth, James. *The Handy English Word Book.* London & Edinburgh: William P. Nimmo.

1878

Barnes, William. *An Outline of English Speech-Craft.* London: C. Kegan Paul & Co.

1880

Raub, Albert N. *Lessons in English.* Philadelphia: Porter & Coates.

White, Richard Grant. *Every-Day English.* Boston & N.Y.: Houghton, Mifflin & Co.

1881

Ayres, Alfred. *The Verbalist: A Manual Devoted to Brief Discussions of the Right and the Wrong Use of Words.* N.Y.: D. Appleton & Co.

Brewer, Ebenezer C. *Errors of Speech and of Spelling.* London: Tegg & Co.

Hodgson, William B. *Errors in the Use of English.* Edinburgh: David Douglas.

1882

Griswold, William M. *A Manual of Misused Words.* Bangor, Me.: Q.P. Index Publishers.

Palmer, A. Smythe. *Folk-Etymology: A Dictionary of Verbal Corruptions or Words Perverted in Form or Meaning, by False Derivation or Mistaken Analogy.* London: George Bell & Sons.

1883

Bardeen, C.W. *Verbal Pitfalls.* Syracuse: C.W. Bardeen.

1884

[Anon.] *Common Blunders in Writing and Speaking, and How to Avoid Them.* London: Ward, Lock & Co.

Bardeen, C.W. *Outlines of Sentence-Making.* N.Y.: A.S. Barnes & Co.

Bruce, Oliver Bell. *Don't: Or, Directions for Avoiding Improprieties in Conduct and Common Errors of Speech.* Melbourne: E.W. Cole.

1885

[Anon.] *Slipshod English in Polite Society: A Manual for the Educated but Careless.* London: Field & Tuer.

Ballard, Harlan H. *Handbook of Blunders: Designed to Prevent 1,000 Common Blunders in Writing and Speaking*. Boston: Lee & Shepard.

1886

Strong, H.I. *Exercises in False Syntax and Other Forms of Bad English*. 5th ed. Toronto: Copp, Clark & Co. [1st ed. unknown.]

Tibbals, Marion H. *Many Mistakes Mended, Containing Three Thousand Corrections in Speaking, Pronouncing, and Writing the English Language*. N.Y.: Tibbals Book Co.

1887

LeRow, Caroline. *English as She Is Taught*. N.Y.: Cassell & Co.

1888

Duncan, George P. *How to Talk Correctly*. London: William Nicholson & Sons [n.d.; ca. 1888].

Long, J.H. *Slips of Tongue and Pen*. N.Y.: D. Appleton & Co.

1889

[Anon.] *Hints and Helps of English Grammar*. Cleveland: J.R. Holcomb & Co.

1890

Earle, John. *English Prose: Its Elements, History, and Usage*. London: Smith, Elder & Co.

Molee, Elias. *Pure Saxon English: Or, Americans to the Front*. Chicago: Rand, McNally & Co.

Williams, R.O. *Our Dictionaries and Other English Language Topics*. N.Y.: Henry Holt & Co.

1891

Abbott, Edwin A.; and J.R. Seeley. *English Lessons for English People*. Boston: Roberts Bros.

Bradner, George W. *Hints to the Wise and Warnings to the Careless, or a Key to English Vulgarisms*. Oswego, N.Y.: R.J. Oliphant.

Teall, F. Horace. *The Compounding of English Words*. N.Y.: John Ireland.

1892

Johnson, Charles F. *English Words: An Elementary Study of Derivations*. N.Y.: Harper & Bros.

1893

Bechtel, John H. *Practical Synonyms*. Philadelphia: Penn Pub. Co.

Kellogg, Brainerd; and Alonzo Reed. *The English Language*. N.Y.: Maynard, Merrill & Co.

Wheatley, Henry B. *Literary Blunders*. London: Elliot Stock.

1895

Bechtel, John H. *Slips of Speech: A Helpful Book for Every-One Who Aspires to Correct the Everyday Errors of Speaking and Writing*. Philadelphia: Penn Pub. Co.

Bugg, Lelia Hardin. *Correct English*. St. Louis: B. Herder.

Tucker, Gilbert M. *Our Common Speech*. N.Y.: Dodd, Mead & Co.

1896

[Anon.] *Essentials of English*. Battle Creek, Mich.: Ellis Pub. Co.

Fernald, James C. *English Synonyms and Antonyms: With Notes on the Correct Use of Prepositions*. N.Y.: Funk & Wagnalls Co.

1897

Anderson, Jessie Macmillan. *A Study of English Words*. N.Y.: American Book Co.

Palmer, George Herbert. *Self-Cultivation in English*. N.Y.: Thomas Y. Crowell & Co.

Raub, Albert N. *Helps in the Use of Good English*. Philadelphia: Albert N. Raub & Co.

Williams, Ralph Olmstead. *Some Questions of Good English*. N.Y.: Henry Holt & Co.

1898

Clark, C.E. *The Mistakes We Make*. London: C. Arthur Pearson, Ltd.

Compton, Alfred G. *Some Common Errors of Speech*. N.Y.: G.P. Putnam's Sons.

1899

Peck, Harry Thurston. *What Is Good English? and Other Essays*. N.Y.: Dodd, Mead & Co.

1901

Clark, C.E. *More Mistakes We Make*. London: Horace Marshall.

Greenough, James Bradstreet; and George Lyman Kittredge. *Words and Their Ways in English Speech*. N.Y.: Macmillan & Co.

1902

Bell, Ralcy Husted. *The Worth of Words*. N.Y.: Grafton Press.

Gradon, J.T. *Mistakes in English Made by Foreigners Studying the Language*. Strassburg: Karl J. Trübner.

Rine, George W. *The Essentials of Our Language: A Guide to Accuracy in the Use of the English Language*. Oakland: Pacific Press Pub. Co.

1904

Fernald, James C. *Connectives of English Speech: The Correct Usage of Prepositions, Conjunctions, Relative Pronouns and Adverbs Explained and Illustrated*. N.Y.: Funk & Wagnalls Co.

1905

Cody, Sherwin. *Dictionary of Errors*. N.Y.: Funk & Wagnalls Co.

1906

Fowler, H.W.; and F.G. Fowler. *The King's English*. Oxford: Clarendon Press.

Smith, C. Alphonso. *Studies in English Syntax*. Boston: Ginn & Co.

Vizetelly, Frank H. *A Desk-Book of Errors in English*. N.Y.: Funk & Wagnalls Co.

1907

Nesfield, J.C. *Aids to the Study & Composition of English*. London: Macmillan & Co.

1908

Foat, F.W.T. *Grammatical English*. London: Edward Arnold.

Lounsbury, Thomas R. *The Standard of Usage in English*. N.Y.: Harper & Bros.

1909

Baker, Josephine Turck. *Correct English in the Home*. Chicago: Correct English Pub. Co.

Baker, Josephine Turck. *Correct English in the School: Twelve Golden Helps*. Chicago: Correct English Pub. Co.

Bell, Ralcy Husted. *The Changing Values of English Speech*. N.Y.: Hinds, Noble & Eldredge.

Bierce, Ambrose. *Write It Right: A Little Blacklist of Literary Faults*. N.Y.: Walter Neale.

Fernald, James C. *Better Say: A Book of Helpful Suggestions for the Correct Use of English Words and Phrases*. N.Y.: Funk & Wagnalls Co.

1910

Erskine, John; and Helen Erskine. *Written English: A Guide to the Rules of Composition*. N.Y.: Century Co.

1911

Fernald, James C. *Helpful Hints in English*. N.Y.: Funk & Wagnalls Co.

Payne, Gertrude. *Everyday Errors in Pronunciation, Spelling, and Spoken English*. San Francisco: Ricardo J. Orozco.

1912

Orcutt, William Dana. *The Writer's Desk Book*. Norwood, Mass.: Frederick A. Stokes Co.

1913

[Anon.] *Exercises in Practical Grammar*. Chicago: Metropolitan Text Book.

Manly, John Matthews; and John Arthur Powell. *A Manual for Writers.* Chicago: Univ. of Chicago Press.

1914

Utter, Robert Palfrey. *A Guide to Good English.* N.Y.: Harper & Bros.

1915

Baker, Josephine Turck. *The Correct Word: How to Use It.* Evanston, Ill.: Correct English Pub. Co.

O'Neill, H.C., ed. *A Guide to the English Language: Its History, Development, and Use.* London: T.C. & E.C. Jack, Ltd.

1916

Utter, Robert Palfrey. *Everyday Words and Their Uses.* N.Y.: Harper & Bros.

1917

[Anon.] *Faulty Diction as Corrected by the Funk & Wagnalls New Standard Dictionary of the English Language.* N.Y.: Funk & Wagnalls Co.

Hall, J. Lesslie. *English Usage.* Chicago: Scott, Foresman & Co.

Hennesy, James A. *The Dictionary of Grammar.* N.Y.: Funk & Wagnalls Co.

MacCracken, H.N.; and Helen E. Sandison. *Manual of Good English.* N.Y.: Macmillan & Co.

1918

Fernald, James C. *Expressive English.* N.Y.: Funk & Wagnalls Co.

1919

Bradley, Henry. *On the Relations Between Spoken and Written Language.* Oxford: Clarendon Press.

1920

Hartley, Charles. *Everyone's Handbook of Common Blunders: Speaking and Writing Corrected and Explained.* London: Henry Drake [n.d.; ca. 1920].

Vizetelly, Frank H. *Mend Your Speech.* N.Y.: Funk & Wagnalls Co.

1921

Canby, Henry Seidel; and John Baker Opdycke. *Good English.* N.Y.: Macmillan & Co.

Carr, Edwin Hamlin. *Putnam's Minute-a-Day English.* N.Y.: G.P. Putnam's Sons.

Potter, Milton C.; H. Jeschke; and Harry O. Gillet. *Oral and Written English.* Boston: Ginn & Co.

Tucker, Gilbert M. *American English.* N.Y.: Alfred A. Knopf.

1922

Alexander, Henry. *Common Faults in Writing English.* London: T.C. & E.C. Jack, Ltd.

Hanna, O.M.; and Joseph F. Taylor. *1600 Drill Exercises in Corrective English.* N.Y.: Noble & Noble, Inc.

Matthews, Brander. *Essays on English.* N.Y.: Charles Scribner's Sons.

Vizetelly, Frank H. *S.O.S.: Slips of Speech.* N.Y.: Funk & Wagnalls Co.

Weseen, Maurice H. *Everyday Uses of English.* N.Y.: Thomas Y. Crowell Co.

1923

Carew, Paul T. *The Art of Phrasing in Composition.* Boston: Stratford Co.

Lea, John W. *Notes from a Proofreader's Diary.* Philadelphia: By the author.

Manly, John Matthews; and Edith Rickert. *The Writer's Index of Good Form and Good English.* N.Y.: Henry Holt & Co.

1924

Bell, Ralcy Husted. *The Mystery of Words.* N.Y.: Hinds, Hayden & Eldredge.

Mason, W.L. *Troublesome Words and How to Use Them.* N.Y.: A.L. Burt Co.

O'London, John. *Is It Good English?* London: George Newnes Ltd.

1925

Herd, Harold. *Everyday Word Traps.* London: George Allen & Unwin Ltd.

Pearsall Smith, Logan. *Words and Idioms: Studies in the English Language.* London: Constable & Co.

1926

Fowler, H.W. *A Dictionary of Modern English Usage.* Oxford: Clarendon Press.

House, Homer C.; and Susan Emolyn Harman. *Handbook of Correct English for College Classes.* N.Y.: Longmans, Green & Co.

Lurie, Charles N. *How to Say It: Helpful Hints on English.* N.Y.: G.P. Putnam's Sons.

Mawson, C.O. Sylvester. *Style-Book for Writers and Editors.* N.Y.: Thomas Y. Crowell Co.

Orcutt, William Dana. *The Desk Reference Book.* N.Y.: Frederick A. Stokes Co.

1927

Hadida, Sophie C. *Pitfalls in English and How to Avoid Them.* N.Y.: G.P. Putnam's Sons.

Henderson, B.L.K. *Chats About Our Mother Tongue.* London: Macdonald & Evans.

Krapp, George Philip. *A Comprehensive Guide to Good English.* N.Y.: Rand McNally & Co.

1928

Eichler, Lillian. *Well-Bred English.* Garden City, N.Y.: Doubleday, Doran & Co.

Foley, Louis. *Beneath the Crust of Words.* Columbus, Ohio: Ohio State Univ. Press.

I.C.S. Staff. *Composition and Proof-Reading.* Scranton, Pa.: Int'l Textbook Co.

Weseen, Maurice H. *Crowell's Dictionary of English Grammar and Handbook of American Usage.* N.Y.: Thomas Y. Crowell Co.

1929

Leonard, Sterling Andrus. *The Doctrine of Correctness in English Usage: 1700–1800.* Madison: Univ. of Wisconsin Press.

1930

Howell, A.C. *A Handbook of English in Engineering Usage.* N.Y.: John Wiley & Sons.

1931

Anderson, Charles B. *Common Errors in English Corrected.* N.Y.: D. Van Nostrand Co.

Blount, Alma; and Clark S. Northup. *Grammar and Usage.* N.Y.: Prentice-Hall, Inc.

Haberstroh, E.F. *How to Speak Good English.* Racine, Wis.: Whitman Pub. Co.

Weekley, Ernest. *Cruelty to Words; or, First Aid for the Best-Seller.* N.Y.: E.P. Dutton & Co.

1932

Leonard, Sterling Andrus. *Current English Usage.* Chicago: Inland Press.

1933

Cody, Sherwin. *The New Art of Writing & Speaking the English Language.* N.Y.: Sun Dial Press, Inc.

Vizetelly, Frank H. *How to Use English: A Guide to Correct Speech and Writing.* N.Y.: Funk & Wagnalls Co.

1934

Woods, George B. *A Guide to Good English for College Students.* Garden City: Doubleday, Doran & Co.

1935

Herbert, A.P. *What a Word!* Garden City, N.Y.: Doubleday, Doran & Co.

Horwill, H.W. *A Dictionary of Modern American Usage.* London: Clarendon Press.

Kennedy, Arthur G. *Current English: A Study of Present-Day Usages and Tendencies, Including Pronunciation, Spelling, Grammatical Practice, Word Coining, and the Shifting of Meanings.* Boston: Ginn & Co.

Weseen, Maurice H. *Words Confused and Misused.* London: Pitman & Sons.

1936

Davis, C. Rexford. *Toward Correct English*. N.Y.: Appleton-Century-Crofts, Inc.

Pocock, Guy N. *Brush Up Your Own Language*. Philadelphia: David McKay Co.

Treble, H.A.; and G.H. Vallins. *An A.B.C. of English Usage*. Oxford: Clarendon Press.

Weekley, Ernest. *Something About Words*. N.Y.: E.P. Dutton & Co.

1937

Carr, Muriel B.; and John W. Clark. *An ABC of Idiom and Diction*. N.Y.: Farrar Straus & Giroux.

1938

Allen, Edward Frank. *How to Write and Speak Effective English: A Modern Guide to Good Form*. Cleveland: World Syndicate Pub. Co.

Lloyd, Charles Allen. *We Who Speak English, and Our Ignorance of Our Mother Tongue*. N.Y.: Thomas Y. Crowell Co.

Marckwardt, Albert H.; and Fred Walcott. *Facts About Current English Usage*. N.Y.: Appleton-Century-Crofts, Inc.

Palmer, Harold E. *A Grammar of English Words*. London: Longmans, Green & Co.

Thornton, G.H. *Teach Yourself Good English*. London: English Univs. Press.

Weston, W.J. *Using the King's English*. London: Pitman & Sons.

1939

Hixson, Jerome C.; and I. Colodny. *Word Ways: A Study of Our Living Language*. N.Y.: American Book Co.

Walsh, J. Martyn; and Anna Kathleen Walsh. *Plain English Handbook*. Wichita, Kan.: McCormick-Mathers Pub. Co.

Whitten, Wilfred; and Frank Whitaker. *Good and Bad English: A Guide to Speaking and Writing*. London: George Newnes Ltd.

1940

Bryant, Margaret M.; and Janet Rankin Aiken. *Psychology of English*. N.Y.: Columbia Univ. Press.

McElfresh, G.E.; and E.C. Ingalls. *Everyday English*. N.Y.: Thomas Nelson & Sons.

Stratton, Clarence. *Handbook of English*. N.Y.: McGraw-Hill Book Co.

Teall, Edward N. *Putting Words to Work*. N.Y.: D. Appleton-Century Co.

1941

Jordan, Archibald C. *Everyday Grammar: A Guide to Good Usage*. Cleveland & N.Y.: World Pub. Co.

Kilduff, Edward Jones. *Words and Human Nature: How to Choose and Use Effective Words*. N.Y.: Harper & Bros.

Opdycke, John Baker. *Get It Right! A Cyclopedia of Correct English Usage*. N.Y.: Funk & Wagnalls Co.

Thomas, Charles Swain. *Your Mastery of English*. N.Y.: P.F. Collier & Son.

1942

Haber, Tom B. *A Writer's Handbook of American Usage*. N.Y.: Longmans, Green & Co.

Kennedy, Arthur G. *English Usage: A Study in Policy and Procedure*. N.Y.: D. Appleton-Century Co.

Partridge, Eric. *Usage and Abusage: A Guide to Good English*. N.Y.: Harper & Bros.

Perrin, Porter G. *Writer's Guide and Index to English*. Chicago: Scott, Foresman & Co.

Webster's Dictionary of Synonyms: A Dictionary of Discriminated Synonyms. Springfield, Mass.: G. & C. Merriam Co.

1943

Canby, Henry Seidel; and John Baker Opdycke. *Handbook of English Usage*. N.Y.: Macmillan Co.

Witherspoon, Alexander M. *Common Errors in English and How to Avoid Them*. N.Y.: New Home Library.

1944

Colby, Frank. *The Practical Handbook of Better English*. N.Y.: Grosset & Dunlap.

McIntosh, John Ranton. *Learning by Exposure to Wrong Forms in Grammar and Spelling*. N.Y.: Teachers College, Columbia Univ.

Opdycke, John Baker. *Say What You Mean: Everyman's Guide to Diction and Grammar*. N.Y.: Funk & Wagnalls Co.

Pence, Raymond W. *Style Book in English*. N.Y.: Odyssey Press.

Wood, Clement. *More Power to Your Words!* N.Y.: Prentice-Hall, Inc.

1945

Brown, Ivor. *A Word in Your Ear and Just Another Word*. N.Y.: E.P. Dutton & Co.

Jowett, W.P. *Chatting About English*. London & N.Y.: Longmans, Green & Co.

1946

Pooley, Robert C. *Teaching English Usage*. N.Y.: Appleton-Century-Crofts, Inc.

1947

Thompson, Newton. *A Handy Guide for Writers*. St. Louis: B. Herder Book Co.

Whyte, Adam Gowans. *Anthology of Errors with Comments*. London: Chaterson Ltd.

Zeiger, Arthur. *Encyclopedia of English and Dictionary of Grammar, Usage* [etc.]. N.Y.: Caxton House, Inc.

1948

Barnes, Duane Clayton. *Wordlore*. N.Y.: E.P. Dutton & Co.

Brown, Ivor. *I Give You My Word and Say the Word*. N.Y.: E.P. Dutton & Co.

Gowers, Ernest. *Plain Words: A Guide to the Use of English*. London: H.M. Stationery Office.

Lewis, Norman. *Better English*. N.Y.: Thomas Y. Crowell & Co.

Schumaker, Florence. *The Student's Guide*. Cleveland, Tenn.: Church of God Pub. House.

Whitaker-Wilson, C. *Modern English Speech: A Guide to Pronunciation, Construction, and Expression*. London: Sidgwick & Jackson Ltd.

1949

Dorey, J. Milnor. *Good English Made Easy*. N.Y.: Permabooks.

Opdycke, John Baker. *Mark My Words: A Guide to Modern Usage and Expression*. N.Y.: Harper & Bros.

Stratton, Clarence. *Guide to Correct English*. N.Y.: Whittlesey House.

Vallins, G.H. *The Making & Meaning of Words: A Companion to the Dictionary*. London: Adam & Charles Black.

1950

Jacob, Henry. *Printed English: Consistency in Good Style*. London: Sylvan Press.

Opdycke, John Baker. *The Opdycke Lexicon of Word Selection*. N.Y.: Funk & Wagnalls Co.

Van Praag, Arnold; and Paul Elek. *English: How She Is Spoke*. London: Paul Elek.

Weston, William J. *A Manual of Good English*. London: George Newnes Ltd.

1951

Brown, Ivor. *No Idle Words and Having the Last Word*. N.Y.: E.P. Dutton & Co.

Davies, Hugh Sykes. *Grammar Without Tears*. London: Bodley Head.

1952

Collins, V.H. *The Choice of Words: A Book of Synonyms with Explanations*. London: Longmans, Green & Co.

Prins, A.A. *French Influence on English Phrasing*. Leiden: Univ. of Leiden.

Pyles, Thomas. *Words and Ways of American English*. N.Y.: Random House.

Vallins, G.H. *Good English: How to Write It.* N.Y.: British Book Centre.

Vigilans [Partridge, Eric]. *Chamber of Horrors: A Glossary of Official Jargon Both English and American.* N.Y.: British Book Centre.

Warfel, Harry R. *Who Killed Grammar?* Gainesville, Fla.: Univ. of Fla. Press.

1953

The Associated Press Stylebook. N.Y.: Associated Press.

Rossiter, A.P. *Our Living Language: An English-Man Looks at His English.* London: Longmans, Green & Co.

West, Michael. *A General Service List of English Words.* London: Longmans, Green & Co.

1954

Collins, V.H. *One Word and Another: A Book of Synonyms with Explanations and Examples.* London: Longmans, Green & Co.

Gowers, Ernest. *The Complete Plain Words.* London: H.M. Stationery Office.

Hornby, A.S. *A Guide to Patterns and Usage in English.* London: Oxford Univ. Press.

Thomas, Henry. *Better English Made Easy.* N.Y.: Greystone Press.

1955

Whitford, Robert C.; and James R. Foster. *Concise Dictionary of American Usage and Grammar.* N.Y.: Philosophical Library.

1956

Collins, V.H. *Right Word, Wrong Word: A Book of Synonyms with Explanations.* London: Longmans, Green & Co.

Hook, J.N.; and E.G. Mathews. *Modern American Grammar and Usage.* N.Y.: Ronald Press Co.

1957

Evans, Bergen; and Cornelia Evans. *A Dictionary of Contemporary American Usage.* N.Y.: Random House.

Nicholson, Margaret. *A Dictionary of American-English Usage.* N.Y.: Oxford Univ. Press.

Partridge, Eric. *English Gone Wrong.* London: Phoenix House Ltd.

Ward, John Millington. *Peculiarities in English.* London: Longmans, Green & Co.

West, Michael; and P.F. Kimber. *Deskbook of Correct English.* London: Longmans, Green & Co.

1958

Bernstein, Theodore M. *Watch Your Language.* Manhasset, N.Y.: Channel Press.

Levitt, John; and Joan Levitt. *The Spell of Words.* N.Y.: Greenwood Press.

1959

Dean, Leonard F.; and Kenneth G. Wilson. *Essays on Language and Usage.* N.Y.: Oxford Univ. Press.

Strunk, William F., Jr.; and E.B. White. *The Elements of Style.* N.Y.: Macmillan & Co.

1960

Copperud, Roy H. *Words on Paper: A Manual of Prose Style for Professional Writers, Reporters, Authors, Editors, Publishers, and Teachers.* N.Y.: Hawthorn Books, Inc.

Golden, Ruth I. *Improving Patterns of Language Usage.* Detroit: Wayne State Univ. Press.

Thomson, R.D.; and A.H. Irvine. *Collins Everyday English Usage.* London: Collins.

1961

Berry, Thomas Elliott. *The Most Common Mistakes in English Usage.* N.Y.: McGraw-Hill Book Co.

Copley, J. *Shift of Meaning.* London: Oxford Univ. Press.

O'Rourke, L.J. *Self-Aids in English Usage.* Lake Alfred, Fla.: Psychological Institute.

Tucker, Susie I., ed. *English Examined: Two Centuries of Comment on the Mother-Tongue.* Cambridge: Cambridge Univ. Press.

Vallins, G.H. *The Best English.* London: Andre Deutsch.

1962

Anderson, Wallace L.; and Norman C. Stageberg. *Introductory Readings on Language.* N.Y.: Holt, Rinehart & Winston.

Baker, Sheridan. *The Practical Stylist.* N.Y.: Thomas Y. Crowell Co.

Bernstein, Theodore M. *More Language That Needs Watching.* Manhasset, N.Y.: Channel Press.

Brown, Ivor. *Mind Your Language.* London: Bodley Head.

Bryant, Margaret M. *Current American Usage.* N.Y.: Funk & Wagnalls Co.

Evans, Bergen. *Comfortable Words.* N.Y.: Random House.

Flesch, Rudolf. *How to Be Brief: An Index to Simple Writing.* N.Y.: Harper & Row.

Goodman, Roger. *A Concise Handbook of Better English.* N.Y.: Bantam Books.

Hook, J.N. *Hook's Guide to Good Writing.* N.Y.: Ronald Press Co.

Lee, Donald W., ed. *English Language Reader.* N.Y.: Dodd, Mead & Co.

Lieberman, Leo. *Dictionary of Correct English Usage.* Paterson, N.J.: Littlefield Adams & Co.

Shaw, Harry. *Errors in English and Ways to Correct Them.* N.Y.: Barnes & Noble.

Sledd, James; and Wilma R. Ebbitt. *Dictionaries and* That *Dictionary.* Chicago: Scott, Foresman & Co.

Wood, F.T. *Current English Usage: A Concise Dictionary.* London: Macmillan & Co.

1963

Gray, Jack C., ed. *Words, Words, and Words About Dictionaries.* San Francisco: Chandler Pub. Co.

Sanderson, James L.; and Walter K. Gordon, eds. *Exposition and the English Language.* N.Y.: Appleton-Century-Crofts, Inc.

1964

Copperud, Roy H. *Webster's Dictionary of Usage and Style.* N.Y.: E.P. Dutton, Inc.

Flesch, Rudolf. *The ABC of Style: A Guide to Plain English.* N.Y.: Harper & Row.

Foulke, Adrienne. *English for Everyone.* N.Y.: Pocket Books.

Tennant, John. *A Handbook of English Usage.* London: Longmans.

Willis, Hulon. *Structure, Style, and Usage: A Guide to Expository Writing.* N.Y.: Holt, Rinehart & Winston.

1965

Bernstein, Theodore M. *The Careful Writer.* N.Y.: Atheneum.

Fowler, H.W. *A Dictionary of Modern English Usage.* 2d ed. Ernest Gowers, ed. Oxford: Oxford Univ. Press.

1966

Follett, Wilson. *Modern American Usage: A Guide.* N.Y.: Hill & Wang.

Stevens, Leonard A. *The Ill-Spoken Word.* N.Y.: McGraw-Hill Book Co.

Stevens, Martin; and Charles H. Kegel. *A Glossary for College English.* N.Y.: McGraw-Hill Book Co.

1967

Jones, George Arnsby. *English for Adventurers.* N.Y.: Pageant Press, Inc.

Joos, Martin. *The Five Clocks.* N.Y.: Harcourt, Brace & World, Inc.

Lodwig, Richard R.; and Eugene F. Barrett. *The Dictionary and the Language.* N.Y.: Hayden Book Co.

Pei, Mario, ed. *Language Today: A Survey of Current Linguistic Thought.* N.Y.: Funk & Wagnalls.

Pei, Mario. *The Many Hues of English.* N.Y.: Alfred A. Knopf.

Pflug, Raymond J., ed. *The Ways of Language: A Reader*. N.Y.: Odyssey Press.

Vermes, Jean C. *Secretary's Index to English*. West Nyack, N.Y.: Parker Pub. Co.

Watt, William. *A Short Guide to English Usage*. Cleveland: World.

1968

Elsbree, Langdon; and Frederick Bracher. *Brief Handbook of Usage*. Lexington, Mass.: D.C. Heath & Co.

Hayakawa, S.I., ed. *Choose the Right Word: A Modern Guide to Synonyms*. N.Y.: Harper & Row.

Kirtland, Elizabeth. *Write It Right: A Handbook of Homonyms*. N.Y.: Golden Press.

Quirk, Randolph. *Essays on the English Language Medieval and Modern*. Bloomington, Ind.: Indiana Univ. Press.

Shostak, Jerome. *Concise Dictionary of Current American Usage*. N.Y.: Wash. Square Press, Inc.

1969

Greenwood, Joseph A. *Find It in Fowler: An Alphabetical Index*. Princeton, N.J.: Princeton Univ. Press.

Postman, Neil; Charles Weingartner; and Terence P. Moran, eds. *Language in America*. N.Y.: Pegasus.

Potter, Simeon. *Changing English*. London: Andre Deutsch.

1970

Laird, Charlton. *Language in America*. N.Y.: World Pub. Co.

1971

Barzun, Jacques. *On Writing, Editing and Publishing*. Chicago: Univ. of Chicago Press.

Bernstein, Theodore M. *Miss Thistlebottom's Hobgoblins: The Careful Writer's Guide to the Taboos, Bugbears, and Outmoded Rules of English Usage*. N.Y.: Simon & Schuster, Inc.

Crisp, Raymond Dwight. *Changes in Attitudes Toward English Usage*. Dissertation, Univ. of Ill. at Urbana-Champaign.

Laird, Charlton; and Robert M. Gorrell, eds. *Reading About Language*. N.Y.: Harcourt Brace Jovanovich, Inc.

Rothwell, Kenneth S. *Questions of Rhetoric and Usage*. Boston: Little, Brown & Co.

1972

Bell, James Kenton; and Adrian A. Cohn. *Bell & Cohn's Handbook of Grammar, Style, and Usage*. Beverly Hills: Glencoe Press.

Dahlskog, Helen, ed. *A Dictionary of Contemporary and Colloquial Usage*. N.Y.: Avenel Books.

Lamberts, J.J. *A Short Introduction to English Usage*. N.Y.: McGraw-Hill Book Co.

Nurnberg, Maxwell. *Questions You Always Wanted to Ask About English . . . but Were Afraid to Raise Your Hand*. N.Y.: Wash. Square Books.

Scott, Foresman Editorial Staff. *Usage File of American English*. Glenview, Ill.: Scott, Foresman & Co.

1973

Brook, G.L. *Varieties of English*. London: Macmillan & Co.

Brown, Ivor. *Words on the Level*. London: Bodley Head.

Butt, Margot; and Linda Lane. *Collins Gem Dictionary of American Usage*. London: Collins.

Liedlich, Raymond D., ed. *Coming to Terms with Language: An Anthology*. N.Y.: John Wiley & Sons.

Wells, Ronald A. *Dictionaries and the Authoritarian Tradition*. The Hague: Mouton.

1974

Creswell, Thomas James. *Usage in Dictionaries and Dictionaries of Usage*. Dissertation, Univ. of Chicago.

Newman, Edwin. *Strictly Speaking: Will America Be the Death of English?* Indianapolis: Bobbs-Merrill Co.

Nickles, Harry G. *Dictionary of Do's and Don'ts for Writers and Speakers*. N.Y.: Greenwich House.

Quirk, Randolph. *The Linguist and the English Language*. London: Edward Arnold.

Scargill, M.H. *Modern Canadian English Usage*. Toronto: McClelland & Stewart Ltd.

1975

Cottle, Basil. *The Plight of English*. New Rochelle, N.Y.: Arlington House Pub.

Middleton, Thomas H. *Light Refractions*. Essex, Conn.: Verbatim.

Morris, William; and Mary Morris. *Harper Dictionary of Contemporary Usage*. N.Y.: Harper & Row.

Shaw, Harry. *Dictionary of Problem Words and Expressions*. N.Y.: McGraw-Hill Book Co.

Trimble, John. *Writing with Style: Conversations on the Art of Writing*. Englewood Cliffs, N.J.: Prentice-Hall, Inc.

1976

Newman, Edwin. *A Civil Tongue*. Indianapolis: Bobbs-Merrill Co.

1977

Abse, Dannie, et al. *More Words*. London: British Broadcasting Corp.

Bernstein, Theodore M. *Dos, Don'ts and Maybes of English Usage*. N.Y.: Time Books.

Howard, Philip. *New Words for Old*. N.Y.: Oxford Univ. Press.

Hudson, Kenneth. *The Dictionary of Diseased English*. London: Macmillan.

Martin, Phyllis. *Word Watcher's Handbook*. N.Y.: David McKay.

Shaughnessy, Mina P. *Errors and Expectations*. N.Y.: Oxford Univ. Press.

1978

Howard, Philip. *Weasel Words*. N.Y.: Oxford Univ. Press.

MacKillop, James; and Donna Woolfolk Cross. *Speaking of Words: A Language Reader*. N.Y.: Holt, Rinehart & Winston.

Tibbetts, Arn; and Charlene Tibbetts. *What's Happening to American English?* N.Y.: Charles Scribner's Sons.

1979

Bailie, John; and Moyna Kitchin. *The Newnes Guide to English Usage*. Feltham, Middlesex: Newnes Books.

Barnard, Ellsworth. *English for Everybody*. Amherst, Mass.: Dinosaur Press.

Gere, Anne Ruggles; and Eugene Smith. *Attitudes, Language, and Change*. Urbana, Ill.: Nat'l Council of Teachers of English.

The Minster Guide to English Usage. London: Minster Books.

Mitchell, Richard. *Less than Words Can Say*. Boston: Little, Brown & Co.

Phythian, B.A. *A Concise Dictionary of Correct English*. London: Hodder & Stoughton.

Pyles, Thomas. *Selected Essays on English Usage*. John Algeo, ed. Gainesville, Fla.: Univ. Presses of Florida.

Room, Adrian. *Room's Dictionary of Confusibles*. London: Routledge & Kegan Paul Ltd.

1980

Bremner, John B. *Words on Words*. N.Y.: Columbia Univ. Press.

Copperud, Roy H. *American Usage and Style: The Consensus*. N.Y.: Van Nostrand Reinhold.

Finegan, Edward. *Attitudes Toward English Usage: The History of a War on Words*. N.Y.: Teachers College Press.

Howard, Philip. *Words Fail Me*. N.Y.: Oxford Univ. Press.

Michaels, Leonard; and Christopher Ricks, eds. *The State of the Language*. Berkeley: Univ. of California Press.

Quinn, Jim. *American Tongue and Cheek: A Populist Guide to Our Language*. N.Y.: Penguin Books.

Safire, William. *On Language*. N.Y.: Times Books.

Simon, John. *Paradigms Lost: Reflections on Literacy and Its Decline*. N.Y.: Clarkson N. Potter, Inc.

Swan, Michael. *Practical English Usage*. Oxford: Oxford Univ. Press.

Timmons, Christine; and Frank Gibney, eds. *Britannica Book of English Usage*. Garden City, N.Y.: Doubleday/Britannica Books.

1981

Montgomery, Michael; and John Stratton. *The Writer's Hotline Handbook: A Guide to Good Usage and Effective Writing*. N.Y.: Mentor.

Room, Adrian. *Room's Dictionary of Distinguishables*. London: Routledge & Kegan Paul.

Tresidder, Argus John. *Watch-Word! A Glossary of Gobbledygook, Clichés, and Solecisms*. Quantico, Va.: Marine Corps Ass'n.

Williams, Joseph M. *Style: Ten Lessons in Clarity and Grace*. Glenview, Ill.: Scott, Foresman & Co.

1982

Baron, Dennis E. *Grammar and Good Taste*. New Haven, Conn.: Yale Univ. Press.

Boyle, Joe. *The Federal Way with Words*. Wash., D.C.: Twain Pub.

Francis, W. Nelson; and Henry Kucera. *Frequency Analysis of English Usage*. Boston: Houghton Mifflin.

Johnson, Edward D. *The Handbook of Good English*. N.Y.: Facts on File Pub.

Pattison, Robert. *On Literacy: The Politics of the Word from Homer to the Age of Rock*. Oxford: Oxford Univ. Press.

Safire, William. *What's the Good Word?* N.Y.: Times Books.

Venolia, Jan. *Write Right! A Desk Drawer Digest of Punctuation, Grammar and Style*. Berkeley: Ten Speed Press.

1983

Bauer, Laurie. *English Word-Formation*. Cambridge: Cambridge Univ. Press.

Daniels, Harvey A. *Famous Last Words: The American Language Crisis Reconsidered*. Carbondale, Ill.: Southern Illinois Univ. Press.

Enright, D.J. *A Mania for Sentences*. London: Chatto & Windus. [See esp. pp. 143–79.]

Flesch, Rudolf. *Lite English: Popular Words That Are OK to Use*. N.Y.: Crown Pubs., Inc.

Freeman, Morton S. *A Treasury for Word Lovers*. Philadelphia: ISI Press.

Howard, Philip. *A Word in Your Ear*. N.Y.: Oxford Univ. Press.

Hudson, Kenneth. *The Dictionary of Even More Diseased English*. Chicago: Academy Chicago.

Marquez, Ely J.; and J. Donald Bowen. *English Usage*. N.Y.: Harper & Row.

Rattray, David, ed. *Success with Words: A Guide to the American Language*. Pleasantville, N.Y.: Reader's Digest Ass'n.

Weiner, E.S.C. *The Oxford Guide to English Usage*. Oxford: Clarendon Press.

1984

Bryson, Bill. *The Penguin Dictionary of Troublesome Words*. Harmondsworth: Penguin Books.

Crystal, David. *Who Cares About English Usage?* London: Penguin Books.

Howard, Philip. *The State of the Language*. N.Y.: Oxford Univ. Press.

Janis, J. Harold. *Modern Business Language and Usage in Dictionary Form*. Garden City, N.Y.: Doubleday.

Kilpatrick, James J. *The Writer's Art*. Kansas City: Andrews, McMeel & Parker.

Mitchell, Richard. *The Leaning Tower of Babel*. Boston: Little, Brown & Co.

Runkel, Philip; and Margaret Runkel. *A Guide to Usage for Writers and Students in the Social Sciences*. Totawa, N.J.: Rowman & Allanheld.

Safire, William. *I Stand Corrected*. N.Y.: Times Books.

1985

Cook, Claire Kehrwald. *Line by Line: How to Improve Your Own Writing*. Boston: Houghton Mifflin Co.

Einstein, Charles. *How to Communicate: The Manning Selvage & Lee Guide to Clear Writing and Speech*. N.Y.: McGraw-Hill Book Co.

Kilpatrick, James J. *The Ear Is Human: A Handbook of Homophones and Other Confusions*. Kansas City: Andrews, McMeel & Parker.

Milroy, James; and Lesley Milroy. *Authority in Language: Investigating Language Prescription and Standardisation*. London: Routledge & Kegan Paul.

Room, Adrian. *Dictionary of Confusing Words and Meanings*. London: Routledge & Kegan Paul.

Silverlight, John. *Words*. London: Macmillan.

1986

Barzun, Jacques. *A Word or Two Before You Go . . . .* Middletown, Conn.: Wesleyan Univ. Press.

Claiborne, Robert. *Saying What You Mean: A Commonsense Guide to American Usage*. N.Y.: Ballantine Books.

Foley, Stephen Merriam; and Joseph Wayne Gordon. *Conventions and Choices: A Brief Book of Style and Usage*. Lexington, Mass.: D.C. Heath & Co.

Hill, Alette Olin. *Mother Tongue, Father Time: A Decade of Linguistic Revolt*. Bloomington, Ind.: Indiana Univ. Press.

Nash, Walter. *English Usage: A Guide to First Principles*. London: Routledge & Kegan Paul.

Room, Adrian. *Dictionary of Changes in Meaning*. London: Routledge & Kegan Paul.

Safire, William. *Take My Word for It*. N.Y.: Times Books.

Todd, Loreto; and Ian Hancock. *International English Usage*. London: Croom Helm.

Wilson, Kenneth G. *Van Winkle's Return: Change in American English, 1966–1986*. Hanover, N.H.: Univ. Press of New Hampshire.

1987

Bawer, Bruce. *The Contemporary Stylist*. N.Y.: Harcourt Brace Jovanovich.

Boardman, Phillip C., ed. *The Legacy of Language: A Tribute to Charlton Laird*. Reno & Las Vegas: Univ. of Nevada Press.

Cannon, Garland. *Historical Change and English Word-Formation*. N.Y.: Peter Lang.

Clark, John O.E. *Word Perfect: A Dictionary of Current English Usage*. N.Y.: Henry Holt & Co.

Garner, Bryan A. *A Dictionary of Modern Legal Usage*. N.Y.: Oxford Univ. Press.

Harrison, James S. *Confusion Reigns: A Quick and Easy Guide to the Most Easily Mixed-Up Words*. N.Y.: St. Martin's Press.

Lederer, Richard. *Anguished English: An Anthology of Accidental Assaults upon Our Language*. Charleston: Wyrick & Co.

Lewis, Norman. *The New American Dictionary of Good English*. N.Y.: New Am. Lib.

1988

Carter, Bonnie; and Craig Skates. *The Rinehart Guide to Grammar and Usage*. N.Y.: Holt, Rinehart & Winston.

Greenbaum, Sidney. *Good English and the Grammarian*. London: Longman, 1988.

Greenbaum, Sidney; and Janet Whitcut. *Longman Guide to English Usage*. London: Longman.

Manser, Martin. *Bloomsbury Good Word Guide*. London: Bloomsbury.

McNamee, Laurence; and Kent Biffle. *A Few Words: A Cornucopia of Questions and Answers Concerning Language, Literature, and Life*. Dallas: Taylor Pub.

Newman, Edwin. *I Must Say: On English, the News and Other Matters*. N.Y.: Warner Books.

Randall, Bernice. *Webster's New World Guide to Current American Usage.* N.Y.: Simon & Schuster.

Room, Adrian. *A Dictionary of Contrasting Pairs.* London: Routledge.

Urdang, Laurence. *The Dictionary of Confusable Words.* N.Y.: Ballantine Books.

1989

Baron, Dennis. *Declining Grammar and Other Essays on the English Vocabulary.* Urbana, Ill.: Nat'l Council of Teachers of English.

Gilman, E. Ward, ed. *Webster's Dictionary of English Usage.* Springfield, Mass.: Merriam-Webster Inc.

Gummere, John F. *Words &C.* Haverford, Pa.: Words &C.

Honey, John. *Does Accent Matter?* London: Faber & Faber.

Leech, Geoffrey; Benita Cruickshank; and Roz Ivanič. *An A–Z of English Grammar & Usage.* London: Edward Arnold.

Terputac, Thomas J. *A Handbook of English Usage.* Lawrenceville, Va.: Brunswick Pub. Corp.

Trahern, Joseph B., Jr., ed. *Standardizing English: Essays in the History of Language Change.* Knoxville: Univ. of Tennessee Press.

1990

Andersson, Lars-Gunnar; and Peter Trudgill. *Bad Language.* Oxford: Basil Blackwell.

Paxson, William C. *The New American Dictionary of Confusing Words.* N.Y.: Signet.

Phythian, B.A. *A Concise Dictionary of Confusables.* N.Y.: John Wiley & Sons.

Ricks, Christopher; and Leonard Michaels, eds. *The State of the Language.* Berkeley: Univ. of California Press. [This anthology is entirely different from the 1980 book.]

Safire, William. *Fumblerules: A Lighthearted Guide to Grammar and Good Usage.* N.Y.: Doubleday.

Safire, William. *Language Maven Strikes Again.* N.Y.: Doubleday.

Thomas, Lewis. *Et Cetera, Et Cetera: Notes of a Word-Watcher.* Boston: Little, Brown & Co.

1991

Aitchison, Jean. *Language Change: Progress or Decay?* Cambridge: Cambridge Univ. Press.

Crowley, Tony. *Proper English? Readings in Language, History and Cultural Identity.* London: Routledge.

Crystal, David. *Making Sense of English Usage.* Edinburgh: Chambers.

Ehrlich, Eugene; and Daniel Murphy. *The HarperCollins Concise Dictionary of English Usage.* N.Y.: HarperCollins.

Garner, Bryan A. *The Elements of Legal Style.* N.Y. & Oxford: Oxford Univ. Press.

Harris, Muriel. *Prentice Hall Reference Guide to Grammar and Usage.* Upper Saddle River, N.J.: Prentice Hall.

Ivers, Mitchell. *The Random House Guide to Good Writing.* N.Y.: Ballantine Books.

Room, Adrian. *NTC's Dictionary of Changes in Meanings.* Lincolnwood, Ill.: NTC Pub. Group.

Safire, William. *Coming to Terms.* N.Y.: Doubleday.

Schwager, Edith. *Medical English Usage and Abusage.* Phoenix: Oryx Press.

Shipman, Robert Oliver. *A Pun My Word: A Humorously Enlightened Path to English Usage.* N.Y.: Rowman & Littlefield.

Tracz, Richard Francis. *Dr. Grammar's Writes from Wrongs.* N.Y.: Vintage Books.

1992

Andersson, Lars-Gunnar; and Peter Trudgill. *Bad Language.* London: Penguin Books.

Burchfield, Robert. *Points of View: Aspects of Present-Day English.* Oxford: Oxford Univ. Press.

Burgess, Anthony. *A Mouthful of Air: Language, Languages . . . Especially English.* N.Y.: William Morrow.

Collins Cobuild English Usage. London: HarperCollins.

LePan, Don. *The Broadview Book of Common Errors in English.* Peterborough, Ontario: Broadview Press.

McArthur, Tom, ed. *The Oxford Companion to the English Language.* Oxford: Oxford Univ. Press.

Strutt, Peter. *Longman Business English Usage.* London: Longman.

1993

Blackburn, Bob. *Words Fail Us: Good English and Other Lost Causes.* Toronto: McClelland & Stewart Inc.

Howard, Godfrey. *The Good English Guide: English Usage in the 1990s.* London: Macmillan & Co.

Hudson, Nicholas. *Modern Australian Usage.* N.Y.: Oxford Univ. Press.

Kilpatrick, James J. *Fine Print: Reflections on the Writing Art.* Kansas City: Andrews & McMeel.

Linfield, Jordan L.; and Joseph Krevisky. *Word Traps: A Dictionary of the 5,000 Most Confusing Sound-Alike and Look-Alike Words.* N.Y.: Collier Books.

Loberger, Gordon J. *A Concise Guide to Standard English Usage.* Dubuque, Iowa: Kendall/Hunt Pub. Co.

Safire, William. *Quoth the Maven.* N.Y.: Random House.

Wilson, Kenneth G. *The Columbia Guide to Standard American English.* N.Y.: Columbia Univ. Press.

1994

Baron, Dennis. *Guide to Home Language Repair.* Urbana, Ill.: Nat'l Council of Teachers of English.

Blamires, Harry. *The Queen's English.* London: Bloomsbury.

Fiske, Robert Hartwell. *Thesaurus of Alternatives to Worn-Out Words and Phrases.* Cincinnati: Writer's Digest.

Inman, Colin. *The Financial Times Style Guide.* London: Pitman.

Larsen, Karen. *The Miss Grammar Guidebook.* Lake Oswego: Oregon State Bar.

Little, Greta D.; and Michael Montgomery, eds. *Centennial Usage Studies.* American Dialect Society Pub. No. 78. Tuscaloosa: Univ. of Alabama Press.

Lord, Robert. *The Words We Use.* London: Kahn & Averill.

Marshall, Jeremy; and Fred McDonald. *Questions of English.* Oxford: Oxford Univ. Press.

Pinker, Steven. *The Language Instinct.* N.Y.: William Morrow & Co.

Rovin, Jeff. *What's the Difference? A Compendium of Commonly Confused and Misused Words.* N.Y.: Ballantine Books.

Safire, William. *In Love with Norma Loquendi.* N.Y.: Random House.

Sutcliffe, Andrea J., ed. *The New York Public Library Writer's Guide to Style and Usage.* N.Y.: HarperCollins.

1995

Ayto, John. *The Oxford School A–Z of English.* Oxford: Oxford University Press.

Cameron, Deborah. *Verbal Hygiene.* London: Routledge.

Ferguson, Don K. *Grammar Gremlins.* Lakewood, Colo.: Glenbridge Pub. Ltd.

The Hutchinson Concise English Usage. Oxford: Helicon Pub.

McFarlane, J.A.; and Warren Clements. *The Globe and Mail Style Book: A Guide to Language and Usage.* Toronto: Penguin Books.

Williams, Deborah K. *NTC's Dictionary of Easily Confused Words.* Lincolnwood, Ill.: National Textbook Co.

1996

The American Heritage Book of English Usage. Boston: Houghton Mifflin Co.

Blamires, Harry. *Correcting Your English.* London: Bloomsbury.

Buckley, William F. *Buckley: The Right Word.* N.Y.: Random House.

Burchfield, Robert W. *The New Fowler's Modern English Usage.* Oxford: Clarendon Press.

Fisher, James A. *Talking Correctly for Success.* Cincinnati: Avant Pub. Co.

Gooden, Philip. *The Guinness Guide to Better English.* Middlesex: Guinness Pub. Ltd.

Hale, Constance. *Wired Style: Principles of English Usage in the Digital Age.* San Francisco: HardWired.

McGee, Nancy P.; and George E. Kennedy. *Correcting Common Errors in Writing.* Dubuque, Iowa: Kendall/Hunt Pub. Co.

O'Connor, Patricia T. *Woe Is I: The Grammarphobe's Guide to Better English.* N.Y.: G.P. Putnam's Sons.

Sledd, James. *Eloquent Dissent: The Writings of James Sledd.* Richard D. Freed ed. Portsmouth, N.H.: Boynton/Cook Pubs.

1997

Amis, Kingsley. *The King's English: A Guide to Modern Usage.* London: HarperCollins.

Carlin, George. *Brain Droppings.* N.Y.: Hyperion.

Cazort, Douglas. *Under the Grammar Hammer.* Los Angeles: Lowell House.

Eggenschwiler, Jean. *Writing: Grammar, Usage, and Style.* Lincoln, Neb.: Cliffs Notes.

Fee, Margery; and Janice McAlpine. *Guide to Canadian English Usage.* Toronto: Oxford Univ. Press.

Gordon, Ian. *Take My Word for It: The Riddles of English Usage.* New Zealand: Wilson & Horton.

Gordon, Karen Elizabeth. *Torn Wings and Faux Pas.* N.Y.: Pantheon Books.

Grossman, Ellie. *The Grammatically Correct Handbook.* N.Y.: Hyperion.

Lippi-Green, Rosina. *English with an Accent.* London & N.Y.: Routledge, 1997.

Safire, William. *Watching My Language.* N.Y.: Random House.

Stillman, Anne. *Grammatically Correct.* Cincinnati: Writer's Digest Books.

1998

Garner, Bryan A. *A Dictionary of Modern American Usage.* N.Y.: Oxford Univ. Press.

Levin, Samuel R. *Shades of Meaning: Reflections on the Use, Misuse, and Abuse of English.* Boulder, Colo.: Westview Press.

Rozakis, Laurie. *Random House Webster's Pocket Grammar, Usage, and Punctuation.* N.Y.: Random House.

Walker, Janice R.; and Todd Taylor. *The Columbia Guide to Online Style.* N.Y.: Columbia Univ. Press.

1999

Allen, Robert. *Pocket Fowler's Modern English Usage.* Oxford: Oxford Univ. Press.

Burton, Tom. *Words in Your Ear.* Kent Town (Austral.): Wakefield Press.

Cullen, Kay, ed. *Chambers Guide to Common Errors.* Edinburgh: Chambers.

Lederer, Richard; and Richard Dowis. *Sleeping Dogs Don't Lay: Practical Advice for the Grammatically Challenged.* N.Y.: St. Martin's Press.

Lindstrom, Ann-Marie. *Common Embarrassing Mistakes in English and How to Correct Them.* Encinitas, Cal.: United Research Pubs.

Strumpf, Michael; and Auriel Douglas. *The Grammar Bible.* Los Angeles: Knowledgeopolis.

2000

Baron, Naomi S. *Alphabet to Email: How Written English Evolved and Where It's Heading.* London & N.Y.: Routledge.

Bruder, Mary Newton. *The Grammar Lady.* N.Y.: Hyperion.

Harris, Muriel. *The Writer's FAQs.* Upper Saddle River, N.J.: Prentice-Hall.

Hurley, Mike; and Dani Hurley. *Gremlins in Your Ear!* Bridgewater, Mass.: Segregansett Press.

Lovinger, Paul W. *The Penguin Dictionary of American English Usage and Style.* N.Y.: Penguin.

Sherwin, J. Stephen. *Deciding Usage: Evidence and Interpretation.* Lanham, Md.: Univ. Press of America.

Wallraff, Barbara. *Word Court.* N.Y.: Harcourt, Inc.

Walsh, Bill. *Lapsing into a Comma.* Chicago: Contemporary Books.

2001

Coffman, Sue. *That's Just the Way It Is.* N.p.: 1st Books.

Davidson, Mark. *Watchwords: A Dictionary of What's Right, Wrong & Risky in Today's American English Usage.* South Pasadena, Cal.: Harrison Pub. Co.

Smith, Ken. *Junk English.* N.Y.: Blast Books.

Trask, R.L. *Mind the Gaffe.* London: Penguin Books.

2002

Garner, Bryan A. *The Redbook: A Manual on Legal Style.* St. Paul: West Group.

Good, C. Edward. *A Grammar Book for You and I . . . Oops, Me!* Sterling, Va.: Capital Books, Inc.

Lasch, Christopher. *Plain Style.* Stewart Weaver ed. Philadelphia: Univ. of Pennsylvania Press.

Martin, Paul R. *The Wall Street Journal Guide to Business Style and Usage.* N.Y.: Simon & Schuster.

Parrish, Thomas. *The Grouchy Grammarian.* Hoboken, N.J.: John Wiley & Sons.

Reed, Allen Walker. *Milestones in the History of English in America.* Richard W. Bailey ed. American Dialect Society Pub. No. 86. Durham, N.C.: Duke Univ. Press.

Ritter, R.M. *The Oxford Guide to Style.* Oxford: Oxford Univ. Press.

2003

Barber, Katherine. *Canadian A to Z of Grammar, Spelling, and Punctuation.* Toronto: Oxford Univ. Press.

Bender, Elaine. *The Most Common Errors in English Usage and How to Avoid Them.* N.Y.: Barnes & Noble.

Brians, Paul. *Common Errors in English Usage.* Wilsonville, Or.: William, James & Co.

Cochrane, James. *Between You and I: A Little Book of Bad English.* Duxford, Cambridge: Icon Books.

Dunsky, Marda. *Watch Your Words: The Rowman & Littlefield Language-Skills Handbook for Journalists.* Lanham, Md.: Rowman & Littlefield Pub.

Garner, Bryan A. "Grammar and Usage" [new chapter], in *The Chicago Manual of Style.* 15th ed. Chicago: Univ. of Chicago Press.

Glatzer, Jenna. *Words You Thought You Knew . . . 1001 Commonly Misunderstood Words and Phrases.* Avon, Mass.: Adams Media.

Watson, Don. *Death Sentence: The Decay of Public Language.* Sydney: Knopf.

2004

Batko, Ann. *When Bad Grammar Happens to Good People: How to Avoid Common Errors in English.* Franklin Lakes, N.J.: Career Press.

Burridge, Kate. *Weeds in the Garden of Words: Further Observations on the Tangled History of the English Language.* Sydney: Australian Broadcasting Corp.

Fiske, Robert Hartwell, ed. *Vocabula Bound: Outbursts, Insights, Explanations, and Oddities.* Oak Park, Ill.: Marion Street Press.

Gooden, Philip. *Who's Whose: A No-Nonsense Guide to Easily Confused Words.* N.Y.: Walker & Co.

Hicks, Wynford. *Quite Literally: Problem Words and How to Use Them.* London & N.Y.: Routledge.

100 Words Almost Everyone Confuses and Misuses. Boston & N.Y.: Houghton Mifflin.

Peters, Pam. *The Cambridge Guide to English Usage*. Cambridge: Cambridge Univ. Press.

Walsh, Bill. *The Elephants of Style: A Trunkload of Tips on the Big Issues and Gray Areas of Contemporary American English*. N.Y.: McGraw-Hill.

Watson, Don. *Watson's Dictionary of Weasel Words, Contemporary Clichés, Cant & Management Jargon*. Milsons Point, N.S.W.: Knopf.

2005

The American Heritage Guide to Contemporary Usage and Style. Boston: Houghton Mifflin.

Battistella, Edwin L. *Bad Language: Are Some Words Better than Others?* N.Y.: Oxford Univ. Press.

Denman, Terence. *How Not to Write: An Office Primer for the Grammatically Perplexed*. Philadelphia: Quirk Books.

Dowling, Dave. *The Wrong Word Dictionary*. Oak Park, Ill.: Marion Street Press.

La Farge, Thomas S. *Usage: A Workbook for Students of English*. Freeport, Me.: Wayside Pub.

Savan, Leslie. *Slam Dunks and No-Brainers: Language in Your Life, the Media, Business, Politics, and, Like, Whatever*. N.Y.: Alfred A. Knopf.

Wallace, David Foster. "Authority and American Usage," in *Consider the Lobster and Other Essays*. N.Y. & Boston: Little, Brown & Co.

Weiss, Edmond H. *The Elements of International Style*. Armonk, N.Y.: M.E. Sharpe.

2006

Casagrande, June. *Grammar Snobs Are Great Big Meanies*. N.Y.: Penguin.

Halpern, Mark. *Language and Human Nature*. Berkeley: Regent Press.

Liberman, Mark; and Geoffrey K. Pullum. *Far from the Madding Gerund and Other Dispatches from Language Log*. Wilsonville, Or.: William, James & Co.

Nunberg, Geoffrey. *Talking Right*. N.Y.: PublicAffairs.

Yagoda, Ben. *When You Catch an Adjective, Kill It: The Parts of Speech for Better and/or Worse*. N.Y.: Broadway Books.

2007

Butterfield, Jeremy. *Oxford A–Z of English Usage*. Oxford: Oxford Univ. Press.

Marsh, David. *Guardian Style*. London: Guardian Books.

2008

Battista, Edwin L. "Groping for Words: A Guide to Slang and Usage Resources," in *Choice*, Dec. 2008, at 619–31.

Beal, Joan C.; Carmela Nocera; and Massimo Sturiale (eds.). *Perspectives on Prescriptivism*. Bern: Peter Lang.

Brohaugh, Bill. *Everything You Know About English Is Wrong*. Naperville, Ill.: Sourcebooks, Inc.

Casagrande, June. *Mortal Syntax*. N.Y.: Penguin.

Collins, Tim. *Correct Your English Errors: Avoid 99% of the Common Mistakes Made by Learners of English*. N.Y.: McGraw-Hill.

Fogarty, Mignon. *Grammar Girl's Quick and Dirty Tips for Better Writing*. N.Y.: Henry Holt & Co.

Lynch, Jack. *The English Language: A User's Guide*. Newburyport, Mass.: Focus Pub.

Wolman, David. *Righting the Mother Tongue: From Olde English to Email, the Tangled Story of English Spelling*. Wash., D.C.: Smithsonian.

Yeager, Paul. *Literally, the Best Language Book Ever*. N.Y.: Perigee.

2009

Fogarty, Mignon. *The Grammar Devotional: Daily Tips for Successful Writing from Grammar Girl*. N.Y.: Holt Paperbacks.

Fowler, H.W. *A Dictionary of Modern English Usage*. Orig. 1926 ed. with annotations by David Crystal. Oxford: Oxford Univ. Press.

Hicks, Wynford. *The Basics of English Usage*. London & N.Y.: Routledge.

Lynch, Jack. *The Lexicographer's Dilemma: The Evolution of "Proper" English from Shakespeare to South Park*. N.Y.: Walker & Co.

Machan, Tim William. *Language Anxiety: Conflict and Change in the History of English*. Oxford: Oxford Univ. Press.

2010

Clark, Roy Peter. *The Glamour of Grammar: A Guide to the Magic and Mystery of Practical English*. N.Y.: Little Brown & Co.

Elster, Charles Harrington. *The Accidents of Style: Good Advice on How Not to Write Badly*. N.Y.: St. Martin's Griffin.

2011

Fogarty, Mignon. *Grammar Girl's 101 Misused Words You'll Never Confuse Again*. N.Y.: St. Martin's Griffin.

Heffer, Simon. *Strictly English: The Correct Way to Write . . . and Why It Matters*. London: Windmill Books.

2013

Sessions, Keith W. *A Sometimes Snarky Guide to English Usage, Grammar, and Punctuation*. Kansas City: CreateSpace.

Walsh, Bill. *Yes, I Could Care Less: How to Be a Language Snob Without Being a Jerk*. N.Y.: St. Martin's Griffin.

2014

Pinker, Steven. *The Sense of Style: The Thinking Person's Guide to Writing in the 21st Century*. N.Y.: Viking.

Shea, Ammon. *Bad English: A History of Linguistic Aggravation*. N.Y.: Penguin.

2015

Berry, Roger. *From Words to Grammar: Discovering English Usage*. London: Routledge.

Butterfield, Jeremy (ed.). *Fowler's Dictionary of Modern English Usage*. 4th ed. Oxford: Oxford Univ. Press.

Cioffi, Frank L. *One Day in the Life of the English Language: A Microcosmic Usage Handbook*. Princeton: Princeton Univ. Press.

Kamm, Oliver. *Accidence Will Happen: The Non-Pedantic Guide to English Usage*. London: Weidenfeld & Nicolson.

Norris, Mary. *Between You and Me: Confessions of a Comma Queen*. N.Y.: W. W. Norton & Co.

2016

Garner, Bryan A. *The Chicago Guide to Grammar, Usage, and Punctuation*. Chicago: Univ. of Chicago Press.

SELECT BIBLIOGRAPHY

English Dictionaries

The American Heritage Dictionary of the English Language. 5th ed. N.Y.: Dell, 2011.

Chambers 21st Century Dictionary. Edinburgh: Chambers, 1996.

The Concise Oxford Dictionary. 12th ed. Oxford: Clarendon Press, 2011.

Merriam-Webster's Collegiate Dictionary. 11th ed. Springfield, Mass.: Merriam-Webster, 2003.

The New Oxford American Dictionary. 2d ed. N.Y.: Oxford Univ. Press, 2007.

The New Shorter Oxford English Dictionary. 2 vols. Oxford: Clarendon Press, 1993.

The Oxford American Dictionary and Thesaurus. 2d ed. N.Y.: Oxford Univ. Press, 2009.

The Oxford English Dictionary. 2d ed. 20 vols. Oxford: Clarendon Press, 1989. Additions 1993–1997 (John Simpson, Edmund Weiner & Michael Proffitt, eds.). 3d ed. (in progress) Mar. 2000. *OED Online*. Oxford University Press <http://dictionary.oed.com>.

The Random House Dictionary of the English Language. 2d ed. N.Y.: Random House, 1987.

Webster's New International Dictionary of the English Language. 2d ed. Springfield, Mass.: Merriam, 1934.

Webster's New World College Dictionary. 5th ed. N.Y.: Macmillan & Co., 2014.

Webster's Third New International Dictionary of the English Language. Springfield, Mass.: Merriam, 1961.

English Usage

Bernstein, Theodore M. *The Careful Writer*. N.Y.: Atheneum, 1965.

Burchfield, Robert W. *The New Fowler's Modern English Usage*. Oxford: Oxford Univ. Press, 1996.

Copperud, Roy H. *American Usage & Style: The Consensus*. N.Y.: Van Nostrand Reinhold, 1980.

Evans, Bergen; and Cornelia Evans. *A Dictionary of Contemporary American Usage*. N.Y.: Random House, 1957.

Follett, Wilson. *Modern American Usage*. N.Y.: Hill & Wang, 1966.

Fowler, H.W. *A Dictionary of Modern English Usage*. Oxford: Clarendon Press, 1926. 2d ed. Ernest Gowers, ed. Oxford: Oxford Univ. Press, 1965.

Fowler, H.W.; and F.G. Fowler. *The King's English*. Oxford: Clarendon Press, 1906. Repr. Oxford: Oxford Univ. Press, 1973.

Garner, Bryan A. *Garner's Dictionary of Legal Usage*. 3d ed. N.Y.: Oxford Univ. Press, 2011.

Merriam-Webster's Concise Dictionary of English Usage. Springfield, Mass.: Merriam-Webster, 2002.

Norris, Mary. *Between You and Me: Confessions of a Comma Queen*. N.Y.: W.W. Norton, 2015.

O'Conner, Patricia. *Woe Is I: The Grammar-phobe's Guide to Better English in Plain English*. 2d ed. N.Y.: Riverhead, 2003.

Partridge, Eric. *Usage and Abusage*. 1942. 5th ed. Harmondsworth: Penguin Books, 1981; rev. ed. N.Y.: Norton, 1994.

Peters, Pam. *The Cambridge Guide to English Usage*. Cambridge: Cambridge Univ. Press, 2004.

Wallace, David Foster; and Bryan A. Garner. *Quack This Way*. Dallas: RosePen, 2013.

Wallraff, Barbara. *Word Court*. N.Y.: Harcourt, 2000.

Wallraff, Barbara. *Your Own Words*. N.Y.: Counterpoint, 2004.

Walsh, Bill. *The Elephants of Style*. N.Y.: McGraw-Hill, 2004.

Walsh, Bill. *Lapsing into a Comma*. Chicago: Contemporary Books, 2000.

Walsh, Bill. *Yes, I Could Care Less: How to Be a Language Snob Without Being a Jerk*. N.Y.: St. Martin's Griffin, 2013.

English Grammar

Aarts, Bas. *Oxford Modern English Grammar*. Oxford: Oxford Univ. Press, 2011.

Biber, Douglas; Stig Johansson; Geoffrey Leech; Susan Conrad; and Edward Finegan. *Longman Grammar of Spoken and Written English*. Harlow, Essex: Pearson Education Ltd., 1999.

Chalker, Sylvia; and Edmund S.C. Weiner. *The Oxford Dictionary of English Grammar*. Oxford: Clarendon Press, 1994.

Crystal, David. *Making Sense of Grammar*. Harlow, Essex: Pearson Education, 2004.

Curme, George O. *English Grammar*. N.Y.: Barnes & Noble Books, 1947.

Garner, Bryan A. *The Chicago Guide to Grammar, Usage, and Punctuation*. Chicago: Chicago Univ. Press, 2016.

Greenbaum, Sidney. *The Oxford English Grammar*. Oxford: Oxford Univ. Press, 1996.

Jespersen, Otto. *Essentials of English Grammar*. N.Y.: Holt, 1933. Repr. University, Ala.: Univ. of Alabama Press, 1964.

Kittredge, George Lyman; and Frank Edgar Farley. *An Advanced English Grammar*. Boston: Ginn, 1913.

Opdycke, John B. *Harper's English Grammar*. Rev. Stewart Benedict. N.Y.: Harper & Row, 1965.

Quirk, Randolph et al. *A Comprehensive Grammar of Contemporary English*. London: Longmans, 1985.

Sledd, James. *A Short Introduction to English Grammar*. Chicago: Scott, Foresman & Co., 1959.

Zandvoort, R.W. *A Handbook of English Grammar*. 3d ed. Englewood Cliffs, N.J.: Prentice-Hall, 1966.

Writing Style Generally

Baker, Sheridan. *The Practical Stylist*. 8th ed. N.Y.: Harper & Row, 1998.

Barzun, Jacques. *Simple and Direct*. Rev. ed. N.Y.: Harper & Row, 1985.

The Chicago Manual of Style. 16th ed. Chicago: Univ. of Chicago Press, 2010.

Clark, Roy Peter. *Writing Tools: 50 Essential Strategies for Every Writer*. N.Y.: Little Brown, 2008.

Clark, Roy Peter. *The Glamour of Grammar: A Guide to the Magic and Mystery of Practical English*. N.Y.: Little Brown, 2010.

Gowers, Ernest. *Plain Words: A Guide to the Use of English*. Rev. ed. Rebecca Gowers, ed. London: Particular Books, 2014.

Graves, Robert; and Alan Hodge. *The Reader over Your Shoulder: A Handbook for Writers of English Prose*. 2d ed. N.Y.: Vintage Books, 1979.

Kilpatrick, James J. *The Writer's Art*. Kansas City & N.Y.: Andrews, McMeel & Parker, 1984.

Lanham, Richard A. *Revising Prose*. 5th ed. N.Y.: Macmillan & Co., 2006.

Lerner, Betsy. *Forest for the Trees: An Editor's Advice to Writers*. Rev. ed. N.Y.: Riverhead Books, 2010.

Payne, Lucile Vaughan. *The Lively Art of Writing*. 1965. Repr. N.Y.: New American Lib., 1969.

Quiller-Couch, Arthur. *On the Art of Writing*. 1916. Repr. Folcroft, Pa.: Folcroft Library Editions, 1978.

Read, Herbert. *English Prose Style*. 1952. Boston: Beacon Press, 1966.

Strunk, William; and E.B. White. *The Elements of Style*. 4th ed. N.Y.: Macmillan & Co., 1999.

Trimble, John R. *Writing with Style: Conversations on the Art of Writing*. 3d ed. Upper Saddle River, N.J.: Pearson, 2010.

Wilbers, Stephen. *Keys to Great Writing*. Cincinnati: Writer's Digest, 2000.

Yagoda, Ben. *The Sound on the Page: Style and Voice in Writing*. N.Y.: HarperCollins, 2004.

Zinsser, William. *On Writing Well: An Informal Guide to Writing Nonfiction*. 5th ed. N.Y.: Harper & Row, 1994.

Style Manuals

The Associated Press Stylebook and Briefing on Media Law. David Minthorn et al., eds. N.Y.: Basic Books, 2013.

The Chicago Manual of Style. 16th ed. Chicago: Univ. of Chicago Press, 2010.

The Economist Style Guide. Rev. ed. London: Profile Books, 2005.

Garner, Bryan A. *The Redbook: A Manual on Legal Style*. 3d ed. St Paul: West, 2013.

Sabin, William A. *The Gregg Reference Manual: A Manual of Style, Grammar, Usage, and Formatting*. Tribute ed. N.Y.: McGraw-Hill, 2011.

Etymology

Ayto, John. *Dictionary of Word Origins*. N.Y.: Arcade, 1990.

The Barnhart Dictionary of Etymology. Robert K. Barnhart, ed. Bronx: H.W. Wilson, 1988.

The Concise Oxford Dictionary of English Etymology. T.F. Hoad, ed. Oxford: Clarendon Press, 1986.

Hendrickson, Robert. *The Encyclopedia of Word and Phrase Origins*. 4th ed. N.Y.: Facts on File, 2008.

The Merriam-Webster New Book of Word Histories. Springfield, Mass.: Merriam-Webster, 1991.

The Oxford Dictionary of English Etymology. C.T. Onions, ed., with G.W.S. Friedrichsen and R.W. Burchfield. Oxford: Clarendon Press, 1966.

Partridge, Eric. *Origins: A Short Etymological Dictionary of Modern English*. 4th ed. London: Routledge & Kegan Paul, 1966.

Rawson, Hugh. *Devious Derivations*. N.Y.: Crown Trade Paperbacks, 1994.

Room, Adrian. *Dictionary of True Etymologies*. London: Routledge, 1986.

Skeat, Walter W. *An Etymological Dictionary of the English Language*. 4th ed. Oxford: Clarendon Press, 1910.

Weekley, Ernest. *Etymological Dictionary of Modern English*. N.Y.: Dutton, 1921. Repr. (2 vols.) N.Y.: Dover, 1967.

Literary Terms

Abrams, M.H. *A Glossary of Literary Terms*. 9th ed. Boston: Wadsworth, 2005.

Baldick, Chris. *The Concise Oxford Dictionary of Literary Terms*. Oxford & N.Y.: Oxford Univ. Press, 1990.

Barnet, Sylvan; Morton Berman; and William Burto. *A Dictionary of Literary Terms*. Boston: Little, Brown, 1960.

Cuddon, J.A. *The Penguin Dictionary of Literary Terms and Literary Theory*. 4th ed. London: Penguin, 1999.

Farnsworth, Ward. *Farnsworth's Classical English Rhetoric*. Boston: David R. Godine, 2010.

Frye, Northrup; Sheridan Baker; George Perkins; and Barbara M. Perkins. *The Harper Handbook to Literature*. N.Y.: Longman, 1997.

Lanham, Richard A. *A Handlist of Rhetorical Terms: A Guide for Students of English Literature*. 2d ed. Berkeley: Univ. of California Press, 1991.

Liberman, M.M.; and Edward E. Foster. *A Modern Lexicon of Literary Terms*. Glenview: Scott, Foresman & Co., 1968.

The New Princeton Encyclopedia of Poetry and Poetics. Alex Preminger & T.V.F. Brogan, eds. N.Y.: MJF Books, 1993.

Quinn, Edward. *A Dictionary of Literary and Thematic Terms*. N.Y.: Facts on File, 1999.

Ruse, Christina; and Marilyn Hopton. *Cassell Dictionary of Literary and Language Terms*. London: Cassell, 1992.

Pronunciation

Bollard, John K., ed. *Pronouncing Dictionary of Proper Names*. 2d ed. Detroit: Omnigraphics, Inc., 1998.

Ehrlich, Eugene; and Raymond Hand Jr. *NBC Handbook of Pronunciation*. 4th ed. Rev. Thomas Lee Crowell Jr. N.Y.: Crowell, 1984.

Elster, Charles Harrington. *The Big Book of Beastly Mispronunciations*. 2d ed. Boston: Houghton-Mifflin, 2005.

Jones, Daniel. *An English Pronouncing Dictionary*. 14th ed. Rev. A.C. Gimson [as *Everyman's English Pronouncing Dictionary*]. London: J.M. Dent & Sons, 1977. Repr. 1981.

Kenyon, John S.; and Thomas A. Knott. *A Pronouncing Dictionary of American English*. Springfield, Mass.: Merriam, 1953.

Krapp, George Philip. *The Pronunciation of Standard English in America*. N.Y.: Oxford Univ. Press, 1919.

Lewis, Norman. *Dictionary of Modern Pronunciation*. N.Y.: Harper & Row, 1963.

Noory, Samuel. *Dictionary of Pronunciation*. 3d ed. N.Y.: A.S. Barnes, 1979.

Olausson, Lena; and Catherine Sangster. *Oxford BBC Guide to Pronunciation*. Oxford: Oxford Univ. Press, 2006.

Opdycke, John Baker. *Don't Say It: A Cyclopedia of English Use and Abuse*. N.Y.: Funk & Wagnalls Co., 1943.

Phyfe, William Henry P. *20,000 Words Often Mispronounced*. Rev. Fred A. Sweet and Maud D. Williams. N.Y.: Putnam's, 1937.

Princeton Language Institute. *21st Century Guide to Pronunciation*. N.Y.: Dell, 1994.

Ross, Alan S.C. *How to Pronounce It*. London: Hamish Hamilton, 1970.

Vizetelly, Frank H. *Twenty-Five Thousand Words Frequently Mis-*

pronounced. N.Y.: Funk & Wagnalls Co., 1919.

Punctuation

Brittain, Robert. *A Pocket Guide to Correct Punctuation*. 3d ed. Hauppage, N.Y.: Barron's, 1997.

Capon, Rene J. *The Associated Press Guide to Punctuation*. Cambridge, Mass.: Basic Books, 2003.

Carey, G.V. *Mind the Stop: A Brief Guide to Punctuation with a Note on Proof-Correction*. Harmondsworth: Penguin, 1971. Repr. 1977.

Gordon, Karen E. *The New Well-Tempered Sentence: A Punctuation Handbook for the Innocent, the Eager, and the Doomed*. N.Y.: Ticknor & Fields, 1993.

Partridge, Eric. *You Have a Point There: A Guide to Punctuation and Its Allies*. London: Routledge & Kegan Paul, 1953. Repr. 1978.

Paxson, William C. *The Mentor Guide to Punctuation*. N.Y.: New Am. Lib., 1986.

Shaw, Harry. *Punctuate It Right!* N.Y.: Barnes & Noble, 1963.

The English Language

Alexander, Henry. *The Story of Our Language*. Toronto: Thomas Nelson & Sons Ltd., 1940. Rev. ed. Garden City, N.Y.: Dolphin Books, 1962.

Baugh, Albert C.; and Thomas Cable. *A History of the English Language*. 5th ed. Englewood Cliffs, N.J.: Prentice-Hall, Inc., 2001.

Bryant, Margaret M. *Modern English and Its Heritage*. 2d ed. N.Y.: Macmillan & Co., 1962.

Burchfield, Robert W. *The English Language*. Oxford: Oxford Univ. Press, 1985.

Burchfield, Robert W. *Unlocking the English Language*. N.Y.: Hill & Wang, 1991.

Crystal, David. *The Cambridge Encyclopedia of the English Language*. 2d ed. Cambridge: Univ. of Cambridge Press, 2003.

Crystal, David. *The English Language*. London: Penguin Books, 1988.

Flexner, Stuart Berg; and Anne H. Soukhanov. *Speaking Freely: A Guided Tour of American English*. N.Y.: Oxford Univ. Press, 1997.

Garner, Bryan A. *Garner on Language and Writing*. Chicago: Am. Bar Ass'n, 2009.

Jespersen, Otto. *Growth and Structure of the English Language*. 9th ed. 1938. Repr. Chicago: Univ. of Chicago Press, 1982.

Krapp, George Philip. *Modern English: Its Growth and Present Use*. 1909. Repr. N.Y.: Frederick Ungar Pub. Co.,

1966. 2d ed. Albert H. Marckwardt, ed. N.Y.: Charles Scribner's Sons, 1969.

McArthur, Tom, ed. *The Oxford Companion to the English Language.* Oxford: Oxford Univ. Press, 1992.

McKnight, George H. *English Words and Their Background.* N.Y.: D. Appleton & Co., 1925. Repr. N.Y.: Gordian Press, 1969.

McKnight, George H. *Modern English in the Making.* N.Y.: D. Appleton & Co., 1928. Repr. [as *The Evolution of the English Language*] N.Y.: Dover Pubs., Inc., 1968.

Mencken, H.L. *The American Language* [one-volume abridged ed.]. Raven I. McDavid Jr., ed. N.Y.: Alfred A. Knopf, 1963.

Potter, Simeon. *Our Language.* 1950. Rev. ed. Baltimore: Penguin Books, 1966.

Pyles, Thomas. *The Origins and Development of the English Language.* 6th ed. N.Y.: Boston: Wadsworth, 2009.

Smith, Logan Pearsall. *The English Language.* 3d ed. London: Oxford Univ. Press, 1966.

Writing and the Writing Life

Dillard, Annie. *The Writing Life.* N.Y.: Harper & Row, 1989.

Gardner, John. *On Writers and Writing.* Stewart O'Nan, ed. Reading, Mass.: Addison-Wesley Pub. Co., 1994.

King, Larry L. *None but a Blockhead: On Being a Writer.* N.Y.: Viking, 1986.

King, Stephen. *On Writing: A Memoir of the Craft.* 10th anniv. ed. N.Y.: Scribner, 2010.

Lamott, Anne. *Bird by Bird: Some Instructions on Writing and Life.* N.Y.: Pantheon Books, 1994.

Lu Chi. *Wen Fu: The Art of Writing.* Sam Hamill, trans. Rev. ed. Minneapolis: Milkweed Editions, 2000 (written ca. A.D. 303).

Mailer, Norman. *The Spooky Art: Some Thoughts on Writing.* N.Y.: Random House, 2003.

Oates, Joyce Carol. *The Faith of a Writer.* N.Y.: Ecco, 2003.

Rand, Ayn. *The Art of Nonfiction.* Raymond Mayhew, ed. N.Y.: Plume, 2001 (published posthumously from lectures given in 1969).

Woodford, Jack. *Trial and Error: A Key to the Secret of Writing and Selling.* Rev. ed. N.Y.: Carlyle House, 1937.

Woolf, Virginia. *A Writer's Diary: Being Extracts from the Diary of Virginia Woolf.* Leonard Woolf, ed. London: Hogarth Press, 1965.

For More

For an extensive bibliography with more than 125 categories relating to language and writing, see *Garner on Language and Writing* 709–47 (2009).

SELECT INDEX OF WRITERS
QUOTED OR MENTIONED